SAN DIEGO COUNTY

Including Portions of Imperial County

Thomas Bros. Maps®
A RAND MᶜNALLY COMPANY

Call Toll Free:
1-800-899-MAPS
1-800-899-6277

Corporate Office & Showroom
17731 Cowan, Irvine, CA 92614 (949) 863-1984 or 1-888-826-6277

Thomas Bros. Maps & Books
550 Jackson St., San Francisco, CA 94133 (415) 981-7520 or 1-800-969-3072
521 W. 6th St., Los Angeles, CA 90014 (213) 627-4018 or 1-888-277-6277
Customer Service: 1-800-899-6277
World Wide Web: www.thomas.com
e-mail: comments@thomas.com
For more information regarding licensing and copyright permission, please contact us at:
licensing@thomas.com

How To Use this Street Guide & Directory
Modo De Empleo Del Thomas Guide

SAN DIEGO CO.

INTRO

To Find a City or Community:
Manera de Localizar una Ciudad o Comunidad:

Start with the Key Map to Detail Pages, then turn to the Detail Page indicated.

Empiece con el mapa clave de páginas detalladas, luego pase a la página detallada que se indica.

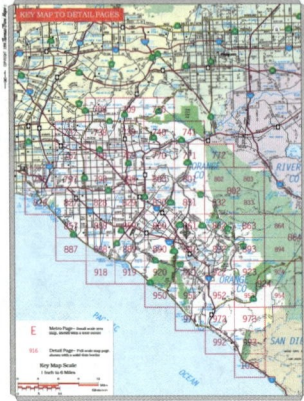

or
o

Community Name	CITY ABBR	ZIP CODE	MILES TO SA	EST. POP	MAP PAGE
ALISO VIEJO		92656	27.00		921
* ANAHEIM	ANA	92801	6.20	293,200	768
ANAHEIM HILLS		92807	7.00		771
ATWOOD		92811	10.60		740
BALBOA		92661	11.50		919
BALBOA ISLAND		92662	10.10		919
* BREA	BREA	92821	12.10	34,800	709
* BUENA PARK	BPK	90620	11.00	72,700	767
CAPISTRANO BEACH		92624	25.30		972
CORONA DEL MAR		92625	10.20		919
COSTA MESA	CMSA	92626	8.20	102,100	859
COTO DE CAZA		92679	39.00		893
COWAN HEIGHTS		92705	6.10		800
* CYPRESS	CYP	90630	12.30	46,400	797
* DANA POINT	DAPT	92629	26.00	36,000	971
DOVE CANYON		92679	39.00		893

Look up the name in the Cities and Communities Index, then turn to the Detail Page indicated.

Busque el nombre en el Indice de Ciudades y Comunidades, luego pase a la página detallada que se indica.

To Find an Address:
Manera de Localizar una Dirección:

① Look up the street name in the Street Index. If there are multiple listings, choose the proper city and/or address. (All city abbreviations are listed in the Cities and Communities Index).

Localice el nombre de la calle en el Indice de Calles. Si aparecen varias listas, seleccione el área apropiada de la ciudad y/o el domicilio. (Todas las abreviaturas de las ciudades figuran en la lista del Indice de Ciudades y Comunidades).

② The street name will include a Thomas Bros. Maps Page and Grid where the address is located.

El nombre de la calle incluye un cuadro de Thomas Bros. Maps Page and Grid con el número de página y de coordenadas que indican la ubicación del domicilio.

COWAN
17600 IRVN 92614 859-G3

③ Turn to the Page indicated.

Pase a la página que se indica.

④ Locate the address by following the indicated Letter column and Number row until the two intersect. The street name is within this Grid area.

Localice el domicilio siguiendo la columna con letras y la hilera con números indicadas hasta que intersecten. El nombre de la calle se encuentra dentro de dicho cuadro.

Thomas Bros. Maps Page and Grid

The pages in this Thomas Guide® are part of our national Page and Grid layout and our new digital mapping system. Each page number is unique, enabling you to have precise page information when looking up a city, community, or street address.

En estas páginas Thomas Guide es parte de nuestra página nacional y arreglo de coordenados y nuestro nuevo mapa de sistema digital. Cada numero de página es única, lo abilidad de tener informacion precisa en una página cuando usted busca una ciudad, comunidad o calle.

Grids are 1/2 Mile Square

The map Grids (shown in magenta on your map) are 1/2 mile square, and go from Grid A1 through Grid J7. This gives you the ability to quickly locate cities, streets, addresses, and points of interest. If you have any questions about the Thomas Bros. Maps Page and Grid, please call us at 1-800-899-6277 (1-800-899-MAPS)

Los coordenados del mapa (indican en color morado de su mapa) son media milla cuadrada e indican del coordenado A1 hasta el coordenado J7. Esto le da la abilidad de poder encontrar ciudades, calles, domicilios y puntos de interés. Si usted tiene alguna pregunta en referencia a Thomas Bros. Maps "Page & Grid", ó página y coordenados, favor de llamar al 1-800-899-6277 (1-800-899-MAPS).

SAN DIEGO CO.

INTRO

Symbol	Description
	Freeway
	Interchange/Ramp
	Highway
	Primary Road
	Secondary Road
	Minor Road
	Restricted Road
	Alley
	Unpaved Road
	Tunnel
	Toll Road
	High Occupancy Veh. Lane
	Stacked Multiple Roadways
	Proposed Road
	Proposed Freeway
	Freeway Under Construction
	One-Way Road
	Two-Way Road
	Trail, Walkway
	Stairs
	Railroad
	Rapid Transit
	Rapid Transit, Underground
	City Boundary
	County Boundary
	State Boundary
	International Boundary
	Military Base, Indian Resv.
	Township, Range, Rancho
	River, Creek, Shoreline
	Ferry
92101	ZIP Code Boundary

Interstate
Interstate (Business)
U.S. Highway
State Highway
County Highway
State Scenic Highway
County Scenic Highway
Carpool Lane
Street List Marker
Street Name Continuation
Street Name Change
Airport
Station (Train, Bus)
Building (see List of Abbreviations page)
Building Footprint
Public Elementary School
Public High School
Private Elementary School
Private High School
Shopping Center
Fire Station
Library
Mission
Winery
Campground
Hospital
Mountain
Section Corner
Boat Launch
Gates, Locks, Barricades
Lighthouse

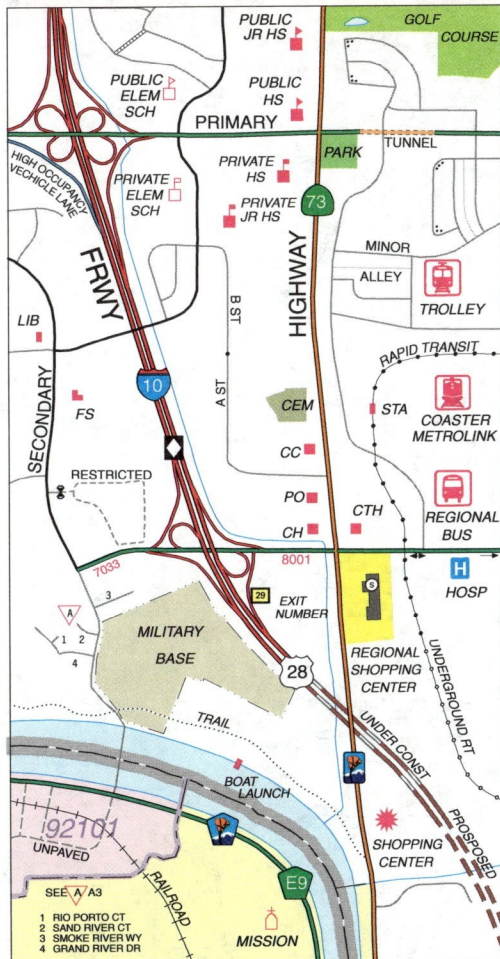

PUBLIC JR HS
GOLF COURSE
PUBLIC ELEM SCH
PUBLIC HS
PRIMARY
PARK
TUNNEL
PRIVATE HS
PRIVATE ELEM SCH
PRIVATE JR HS
73
FRWY
MINOR
ALLEY
TROLLEY
LIB
HIGH OCCUPANCY VEHICLE LANE
HIGHWAY
B ST
RAPID TRANSIT
SECONDARY
10
A ST
FS
CEM
STA
COASTER METROLINK
RESTRICTED
CC
PO
CTH
REGIONAL BUS
CH
HOSP
7033
8001
29 EXIT NUMBER
3
MILITARY BASE
H HOSP
1 2
4
28
REGIONAL SHOPPING CENTER
UNDERGROUND RT
UNDER CONST
TRAIL
BOAT LAUNCH
PROPOSED
SHOPPING CENTER
92101
UNPAVED
SEE A A3
1 RIO PORTO CT
2 SAND RIVER CT
3 SMOKE RIVER WY
4 GRAND RIVER DR
RAILROAD
E9
MISSION

Detail Map Scale
1 Inch to 1900 Feet
0   .25   .5   .75   Miles
0   .5   1.0   Kilometers

Detail Grid Equivalents
1 Grid Equals:
.5 x .5 Miles
2640 x 2640 Feet
1.4 x 1.4 Inches

"Quad-Page" Map Scale
1 Inch to 3800 Feet
0   .25   .5   .75   1.0   Miles
0   .5   1.0   Kilometers

Quad Grid Equivalents
1 Grid Equals:
.5 x .5 Miles
2640 x 2640 Feet

Arterial Map Scale
1 Inch to 4 Miles
0   2   4   6   8   Miles
0   5   10   Kilometers

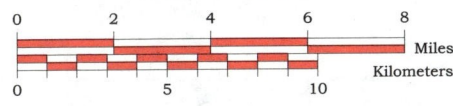

Arterial Grid Equivalents
1 Grid Equals:
1 Detail Page
4.5 x 3.5 Miles
1.125 x .875 inches

Dry Lake, Beach
Dam
Point of Interest
Golf Course, Country Club
Cemetery
Military Base
City, County, State Park
National Forest, Park
Water
Intermittent Lake, Marsh
Airport
Parking Lot
Structure Footprint
Regional Shopping Center
Major Dept. Store
(List of Abbr. page)

Incorporated City
Incorporated City
Incorporated City
Incorporated City
Incorporated City
County
County Seat

Public Land Survey
T2S
T3S
R7W
RANCHO TRABICO
3   2   1
11   12

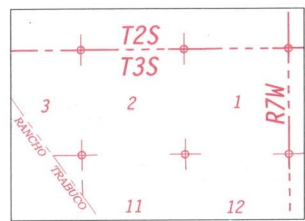

COPYRIGHT 2001 Thomas Bros. Maps ®

NORCO
RIVERSIDE
CORONA
MORENO VALLEY
BANNING
BEAUMONT
SAN JACINTO
PERRIS
HEMET
PALM SPRINGS
CATHEDRAL CITY
RANCHO MIRAGE

ORANGE CO
LAKE ELSINORE
CANYON LAKE
RIVERSIDE CO
San Jacinto Wilderness Area
Mount San Jacinto State Park
San Jacinto Wilderness Area
San Bernardino National Forest
Hemet Reservoir
Lake Henshaw
Cleveland National Forest

MISSION VIEJO
RANCHO SANTA MARGARITA
Ronald W Caspers Wilderness Park
San Mateo Canyon Wilderness
MURRIETA
Santa Rosa Plateau Ecological Reserve
Skinner Reservoir

408
409

SAN JUAN CAPISTRANO
TEMECULA
Vail Lake
Anza–Borrego Desert State Park

SAN CLEMENTE
Agua Tibia Wilderness Area
Cleveland National Observatory
Palomar Mountain State Park
Palomar Observatory
Cleveland National Forest

MARINE CORPS BASE
CAMP JOSEPH H PENDLETON
US NAVAL WEAPONS STATION FALLBROOK

OCEANSIDE
VISTA
SAN MARCOS
Lake Wohlford
Lake Henshaw

PACIFIC
CARLSBAD
ESCONDIDO
SAN DIEGO CO
Cleveland National Forest
Lake Sutherland

ENCINITAS
Lake Hodges
POWAY
Cleveland National Forest
Cuyamaca Reservoir

SOLANA BEACH
DEL MAR
Torrey Pines State Reserve

OCEAN
SAN DIEGO
San Vicente Reservoir
El Capitan Reservoir
429
Cuyamaca Rancho State Park

Mission Bay
USMC Air Station Miramar
SANTEE
USMC Air Station Miramar

LA MESA
EL CAJON
Cleveland National Forest

CORONADO
LEMON GROVE
NATIONAL CITY
Sweetwater Reservoir
Barrett Lake
Morena Reservoir

IMPERIAL BEACH
CHULA VISTA
Otay Reservoir
TIJUANA

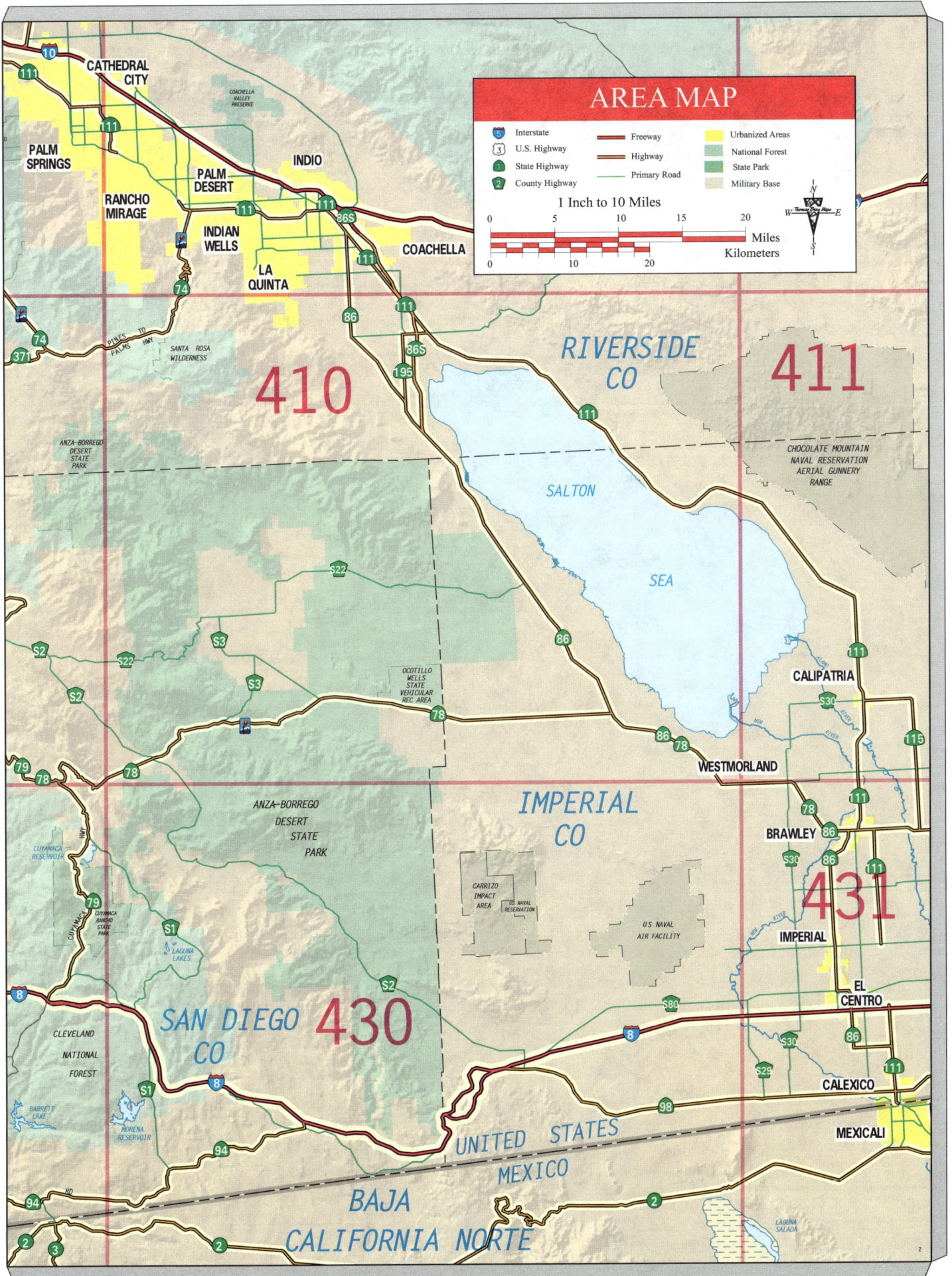

CATHEDRAL CITY

PALM SPRINGS

RANCHO MIRAGE

PALM DESERT

INDIO

INDIAN WELLS

LA QUINTA

COACHELLA

COACHELLA VALLEY PRESERVE

SANTA ROSA WILDERNESS

PINES TO PALMS HWY

ANZA-BORREGO DESERT STATE PARK

AREA MAP

5	Interstate	Freeway	Urbanized Areas
3	U.S. Highway	Highway	National Forest
1	State Highway	Primary Road	State Park
2	County Highway		Military Base

1 Inch to 10 Miles

0   5   10   15   20

Miles

0   10   20

Kilometers

410

411

RIVERSIDE CO

SALTON SEA

CHOCOLATE MOUNTAIN NAVAL RESERVATION AERIAL GUNNERY RANGE

OCOTILLO WELLS STATE VEHICULAR REC AREA

CALIPATRIA

WESTMORLAND

ANZA-BORREGO DESERT STATE PARK

IMPERIAL CO

BRAWLEY

431

CARRIZO IMPACT AREA

US NAVAL RESERVATION

US NAVAL AIR FACILITY

IMPERIAL

EL CENTRO

CUYAMACA RESERVOIR

CUYAMACA RANCHO STATE PARK

LAGUNA LAKES

SAN DIEGO CO

430

CALEXICO

CLEVELAND NATIONAL FOREST

BARRETT LAKE

MORENA RESERVOIR

MEXICALI

UNITED STATES

MEXICO

BAJA CALIFORNIA NORTE

LAGUNA SALADA

SAN DIEGO CO.

INTRO

Key Map
to
Detail Pages

See Page vi for Legend

408
MARINE CORPS BASE
CAMP JOSEPH H PENDLETON

409

429

CLEVELAND NATIONAL FOREST

SAN DIEGO CO.

PACIFIC OCEAN

RIVERSIDE CO.
SAN DIEGO CO.

AGUA TIBIA WILDERNESS AREA

San Bernardino National Forest

ORANGE CO. / RIVERSIDE CO.

EL TORO RD
ONEILL REGIONAL PARK
DOVE CANYON
COTO DE CAZA
SAN JUAN HOT SPRINGS
RANCHO SANTA MARGARITA
RONALD W CASPERS WILDERNESS PARK
ORTEGA HWY
74
SAN JUAN CAPISTRANO
SAN CLEMENTE
TALEGA
SAN ONOFRE STATE BEACH
SAN ONOFRE
CAMP PENDLETON
CLEVELAND NATIONAL FOREST
SAN MATEO CANYON WILDERNESS

LAKE ELSINORE
SEDCO HILLS
215
79
WINCHESTER RD
WILDOMAR
MURRIETA
MURRIETA HOT SPRINGS
TEMECULA VALLEY FRWY
ESCONDIDO FRWY
RANCHO CALIFORNIA
TEMECULA
PALA RD
SKINNER RESERVOIR
SAGE RD
R3
CAHUILLA
CAHUILLA RD
ANZA
371
VAIL LAKE
79
LAKE RIVERSIDE
AGUANGA

DE LUZ
MISSION RD
RAINBOW
FALLBROOK ST
RECHE RD
PALA RD
OAK GROVE
SUNSHINE SUMMIT
CLEVELAND NATIONAL FOREST
PUERTA LA CRUZ
LAKE HENSHAW
79

997 **998** **999** S16
1027 **1028** **1029**
FALLBROOK
LIVE OAK PARK
S15
WINTERWARM
PALA MESA VILLAGE
PALA
76
PAUMA VALLEY
PALOMAR MOUNTAIN
S6
BIRCH HILL
1047 S13 **1048** **1049** **1050** **1051**
SAN LUIS REY HEIGHTS
BONSALL
S GRADE RD
E GRADE RD
RINCON
LA JOLLA AMAGO
S7

1066 **1067** 76 **1068** **1069** **1070** **1071**
OCEANSIDE
SANTA FE
15
VALLEY CENTER
VALLEY CENTER RD
LAKE HENSHAW
MORETTIS
MESA GRANDE

1085 **1086** **1087** **1088** **1089** **1090** **1091**
SAN LUIS REY
VISTA
78
MISSION AV
EL CAMINO
TWIN OAKS
DEER SPRINGS RD
HIDDEN MEADOWS
BEAR VALLEY
S6
SANTA YSABEL
WITCH CREEK

1105 **1106** **1107** **1108** **1109** **1110** **1111**
CARLSBAD
LEISURE VILLAGE
OCEAN HILLS
AIRPORT
BUENA
SAN MARCOS
JESMOND DENE

1126 **1127** **1128** **1129** **1130** **1131**
LA COSTA
PALOMAR
RANCHO SANTA FE RD
HARMONY GROVE
ESCONDIDO
SAN PASQUAL
78
VALLEY RD
JULIAN
BALLENA

1146 **1147** **1148** **1149** **1150** **1151** **1152** **1153** **1154**
LEUCADIA
ENCINITAS
OLIVENHAIN
RANCHO SANTA FE
EL ESCONDIDO HWY
DEL DIOS HWY
BEL DIOS
LAKE HODGES
RANCHO BERNARDO
PINE ST
RAMONA
JULIAN
SAN DIEGO COUNTRY ESTATES

CARDIFF BY THE SEA
S11
1167 **1168** **1169** **1170** **1171** **1172** **1173** **1174**
SOLANA BEACH
LA VALLE
FAIRBANKS RANCH
15
POWAY
ESPOLA RD
ROSEMONT
ROCK HAVEN IRVING'S CREST
SHADY DELL
1192
BARONA MESA
1175

1187 **1188** **1189** **1190** **1191** **1192** **1193** **1194**
DEL MAR
CARMEL VALLEY
LOS PENASQUITOS CANYON PRESERVE
56
POWAY
POWAY RD
FERNBROOK
67
SAN VICENTE RESERVOIR
EL CAPITAN RESERVOIR

1207 **1208** **1209** **1210** **1211** **1212** **1213**
SORRENTO HILLS
SORRENTO VALLEY
MIRA MESA
MIRAMAR
SCRIPPS MIRAMAR RANCH
EUCALYPTUS HILLS
FOSTER
MORENO

1227 **1228** **1229** **1230** **1231** **1232** **1233** **1234**
LA JOLLA
UNIVERSITY CITY
UNITED STATES MARINE CORPS AIR STATION MIRAMAR
MISSION TRAILS REGIONAL PARK
SANTEE
LAKESIDE
LAKEVIEW
FLINN SPRINGS
JOHNSTOWN
GLEN OAKS
VICTORIA
THE WILLOWS
PALO VERDE LAKE

1247 **1248** **1249** **1250** **1251** **1252** **1253** **1254**
PACIFIC BEACH
SOLEDAD
CLAIREMONT
TIERRASANTA
ALLIED GARDENS
DEL CERRO
SAN CARLOS
LA MESA
EL CAJON
BOSTONIA
GLENVIEW
HARBISON CANYON
CREST
DEHESA
HIDDEN GLEN

1267 **1268** **1269** **1270** **1271** **1272** **1273** **1274**
MISSION BEACH
OCEAN BEACH
OLD TOWN
SAN DIEGO
MISSION VALLEY
ROLANDO
LEMON GROVE
LA PRESA
EL CAJON BLVD
COTTONWOOD
NORTH
JAMACHA
JAMUL
HIGHWAY

1287 **1288** **1289** **1290** **1291** **1292** **1293** **1294**
FLEETRIDGE
POINT LOMA
805
PARADISE HILLS
PADISE HILLS
RANCHO SAN DIEGO
JAMACHA
INDIAN SPRINGS
CAMPO

1308 **1309** **1310** **1311**
CORONADO
NATIONAL CITY
CHULA VISTA
SWEETWATER RESERVOIR
SUNNYSIDE
EASTLAKE GREENS
UPPER OTAY RESERVOIR
LOWER OTAY RESERVOIR
94
1312 **1313** **1314**
DULZURA
ENGINEER SPRINGS

1328 **1329** **1330** **1331**
CORONADO CAYS
CASTLE PARK
JACOB DEKEMA FRWY
1332 **1333**
BARRETT JUNCTION

1349 **1350** **1351** **1352** **1353**
IMPERIAL BEACH
OTAY MESA
SAN YSIDRO
TIJUANA
OTAY MESA RD
SAN DIEGO CO.
BAJA CALIFORNIA NORTE
CALIFORNIA

1023

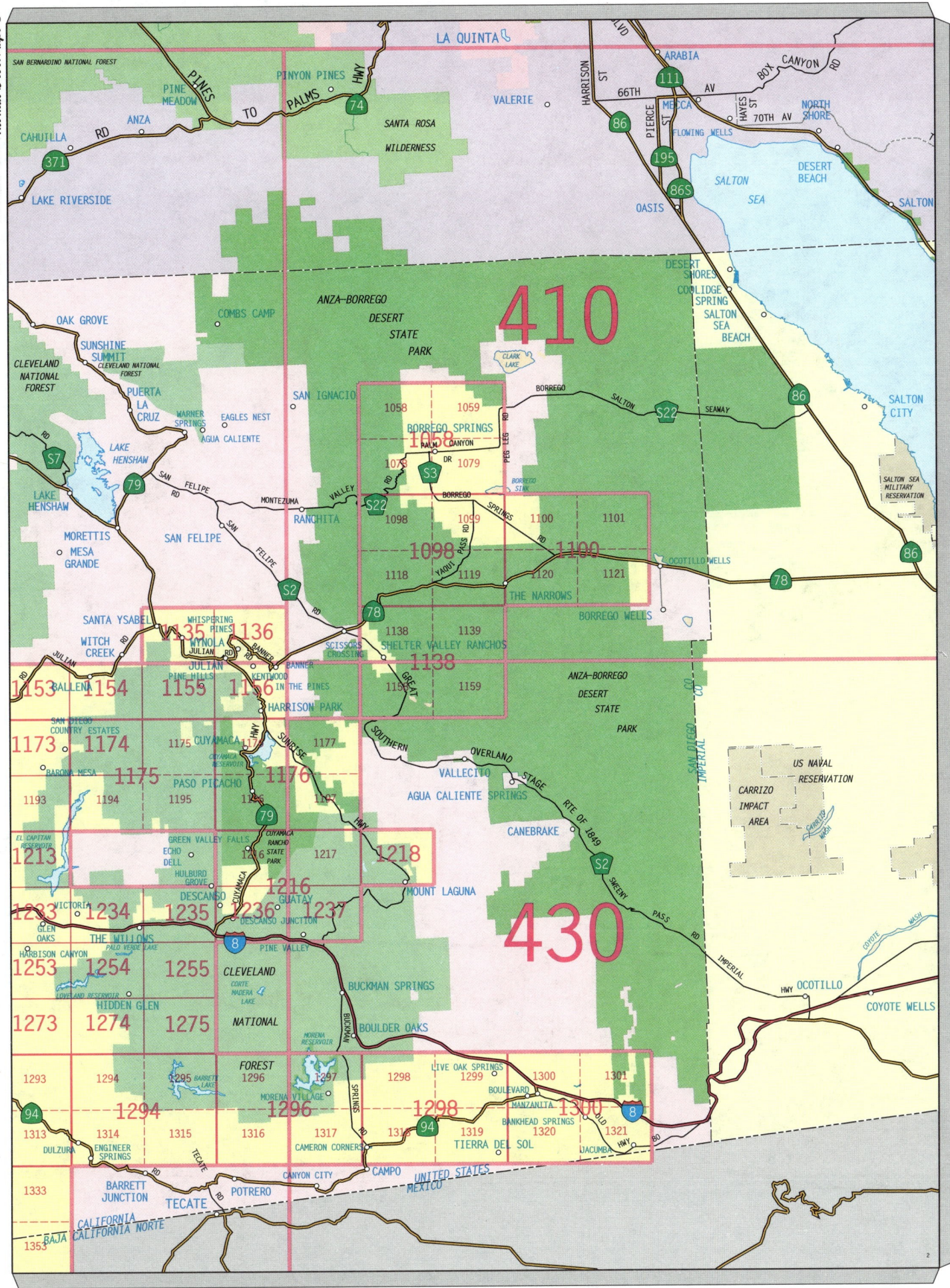

Thomas Bros. Maps®

COPYRIGHT 2001

—N→

LA QUINTA

ARABIA

PINES TO PALMS HWY

PINYON PINES

PINE MEADOW

VALERIE

66TH AV

MECCA

FLOWING WELLS

111

86

195

86S

HARRISON ST
PIERCE ST

HAYES ST
70TH AV

NORTH SHORE

BOX CANYON RD

CAHUILLA RD

ANZA

SUNSHINE SUMMIT

371

LAKE RIVERSIDE

OASIS

SALTON SEA

DESERT BEACH

SALTON

SANTA ROSA WILDERNESS

SAN BERNARDINO NATIONAL FOREST

OAK GROVE

COMBS CAMP

ANZA-BORREGO DESERT STATE PARK

410

DESERT SHORES

COOLIDGE SPRING

SALTON SEA BEACH

CLEVELAND NATIONAL FOREST

CLEVELAND NATIONAL FOREST

PUERTA LA CRUZ

WARNER SPRINGS

EAGLES NEST

AGUA CALIENTE

SAN IGNACIO

CLARK LAKE

BORREGO

SALTON SEAWAY

S22

86

SALTON CITY

1058 1059

BORREGO SPRINGS

1058

SALTON SEA MILITARY RESERVATION

S7

LAKE HENSHAW

79

SAN FELIPE RD

MONTEZUMA

RANCHITA

VALLEY

1078 1079

PALM CANYON DR

S3

BORREGO SINK

86

LAKE HENSHAW

MORETTIS

MESA GRANDE

SAN FELIPE

SAN FELIPE RD

S22

1098

BORREGO

SPRINGS RD

1098 1099

PASS RD

1100 1101

1100

OCOTILLO WELLS

S2

1118 1119

YAQUI

1120 1121

THE NARROWS

78

SANTA YSABEL

WITCH CREEK

135 136

WHISPERING PINES

WYNOLA

JULIAN

JULIAN RD

BANNER

78

1138 1139

SHELTER VALLEY RANCHOS

SCISSORS CROSSING

1138

BORREGO WELLS

ANZA-BORREGO DESERT STATE PARK

1153 1154

BALLENA

1155 1156

PINE HILLS

KENTWOOD IN THE PINES

BANNER

HARRISON PARK

1158 1159

GREAT SOUTHERN

1173 1174

SAN DIEGO COUNTRY ESTATES

1175 CUYAMACA 1176 1177

CUYAMACA RESERVOIR

SUNRISE HWY

OVERLAND

VALLECITO

STAGE

CARRIZO IMPACT AREA

US NAVAL RESERVATION

SAN DIEGO CO. / IMPERIAL CO.

BARONA MESA

1193 1194 1195

PASO PICACHO

1196 1197

AGUA CALIENTE SPRINGS

RTE OF 1849

EL CAPITAN RESERVOIR

1213

GREEN VALLEY FALLS

ECHO DELL

HULBURD GROVE

CUYAMACA RANCHO STATE PARK

1216 1217

1218

CANEBRAKE

S2

SWEENY

1233 1234

VICTORIA

DESCANSO

GUATAY

1235 1236 1237

DESCANSO JUNCTION

MOUNT LAGUNA

430

GLEN OAKS

THE WILLOWS

PALO VERDE LAKE

8

PINE VALLEY

HARBISON CANYON

1253 1254 1255

LOVELAND RESERVOIR

CLEVELAND

PASS RD

IMPERIAL

HIDDEN GLEN

1273 1274 1275

CORTE MADERA LAKE

NATIONAL

BUCKMAN SPRINGS

BOULDER OAKS

COYOTE WELLS

MORENA RESERVOIR

FOREST

LIVE OAK SPRINGS

BUCKMAN

HWY OCOTILLO

1293 1294

BARRETT LAKE

1295 1296 1297

MORENA VILLAGE

1298 1299

BOULEVARD

1300 1301

8

94

1294

SPRINGS

1296

1298

MANZANITA

BANKHEAD SPRINGS

1300

1313 1314 1315 1316

CAMERON CORNERS

1317 1318

94

1319

TIERRA DEL SOL

1320 1321

JACUMBA

OLD HWY 80

DULZURA

ENGINEER SPRINGS

TECATE RD

CANYON CITY

CAMPO

UNITED STATES

1333

BARRETT JUNCTION

TECATE

POTRERO

MEXICO

1353

CALIFORNIA

BAJA CALIFORNIA NORTE

SAN DIEGO CO.

INTRO   SEE   V   MAP

THE BRADSHAW TR

SALTON

410

411

RIVERSIDE CO
IMPERIAL CO

CHOCOLATE

MOUNTAIN

NAVAL

RESERVATION

AERIAL

GUNNERY

RANGE

IMPERIAL GAB

SALTON CITY
SALTON SEA

BOMBAY BEACH

COACHELLA CANAL

WISTER WATERFOWL MANAGEMENT AREA

DAVIS RD

111 NILAND

NOFFSINGER RD

FLOWING WELLS

TED

KIPF

SALTON SEA MILITARY RESERVATION

86

KANE SPRING

ELMORE 86 78

GARST RD

MCDONALD RD

SINCLAIR RD

EDDINS RD

GENTRY RD

S30

CALIPATRIA

DOWDEN RD

115

RAMER LAKE

IMPERIAL WILDLIFE MANAGEMENT AREA

WEIST

RUTHERFORD RD

TED
KIPF

IMPERIAL GAB

WESTMORLAND

GARVEY RD

BOARTS RD

ANDRE RD

S30

KALIN RD

RIVER
SHANK RD

ALAMO RIVER

ALAMORIO

BUTTERS RD

78 GLAMIS

KIPF

VISTA
MINE RD

TED RD

IMPERIAL SAND DUNES RECREATION AREA

DRY LAKE

U S NAVAL AIR FACILITY

IMLER RD

NEW RD

BRAWLEY

KEYSTONE RD

111

HARRIS RD

86 DOGWOOD

115

GREEN RD

S27

S33

RIVER

S32

HIGHLINE

COYOTE WASH

PLASTER CITY

WORTHINGTON RD

FORRESTER RD

IMPERIAL

S31

S28

HOLT RD

HOLTVILLE

KAVANAUGH

DIXIELAND
HUFF

SEELEY HWY

ROSS

EVAN HEWES

MCCABE RD

6499 6500
EL CENTRO

MELOLAND

EVAN HEWES

8 ORCHARD DATE CITY

COYOTE WELLS

430

DREW RD

BROCKMAN RD

6559 6560

HEBER RD

HEBER

8

CONNELLY RD

431

MIDWAY WELL

GORDONS WELL

98

S29

FERRELL RD

DOGWOOD

CALEXICO

BOWKER RD

BARBARA

WORTH RD

BONDS CORNER

MILLER RD

VANDER LINDEN RD

UNITED STATES
MEXICO

98

98

MOUNT SIGNAL

MEXICALI

CALIFORNIA
BAJA CALIFORNIA NORTE

IMPERIAL CO

LAGUNA SALADA

GONZALEZ ORTEGA

PUEBLA

BENITO JUAREZ

QUERETARO

—N—

RIPLEY

WILEY WELLS RD

PALO VERDE

COLORADO

MILPITAS WASH

RD

CIBOLA

CIBOLA
NATIONAL
WILDLIFE
REFUGE

RIVER

78

CIBOLA
LAKE

YUMA

PROVING

GROUND

412

IMPERIAL
GABLES

IMPERIAL GABLES RD

IMPERIAL
NATIONAL
WILDLIFE
REFUGE

IMPERIAL LA PAZ CO

S34

OGILBY

PASS

RD

INDIAN

ISLAND
LAKE

TAYLOR LAKE

ARIZONA
CALIFORNIA

PICACHO

PICACHO STATE
REC AREA

RD

FERGUSON
LAKE

GLAMIS

TED VISTA MINE RD

KIPF

RD

WALKER

RD

WY

OGILBY

SIDEWINDER

IMPERIAL

SAND

DUNES

RECREATION

AREA

PICACHO

SQUAW
LAKE

BARNEY

OLDFIELD

RD

OLDFIELD RD

BARNEY

IMPERIAL

MEHRING
RD

YORK RD

COLBY

RD

OGILBY

S34

432

FORT
YUMA
INDIAN
RESERVATION

ROSS
RD

RD

FELICITY

8

ANDRADE

COLORADO
RIVER

YUMA

FLOOD RD

PICACHO RD

WINTERHAVEN

MIDWAY WELL

GORDONS
WELL

GRAYS WELL

IMPERIAL

CO

VICENTE
GUERRERO

YUMA

CO

CIUDAD MORELOS

PACHUCO

BAJA CALIFORNIA NORTE

SOMERTON

CIUDAD VICTORIA

BENITO JUAREZ

GADSDEN

SAN LUIS

HERMOSILLO

YUMA

CO

SONORA

SAN LUIS
RIO COLORADO

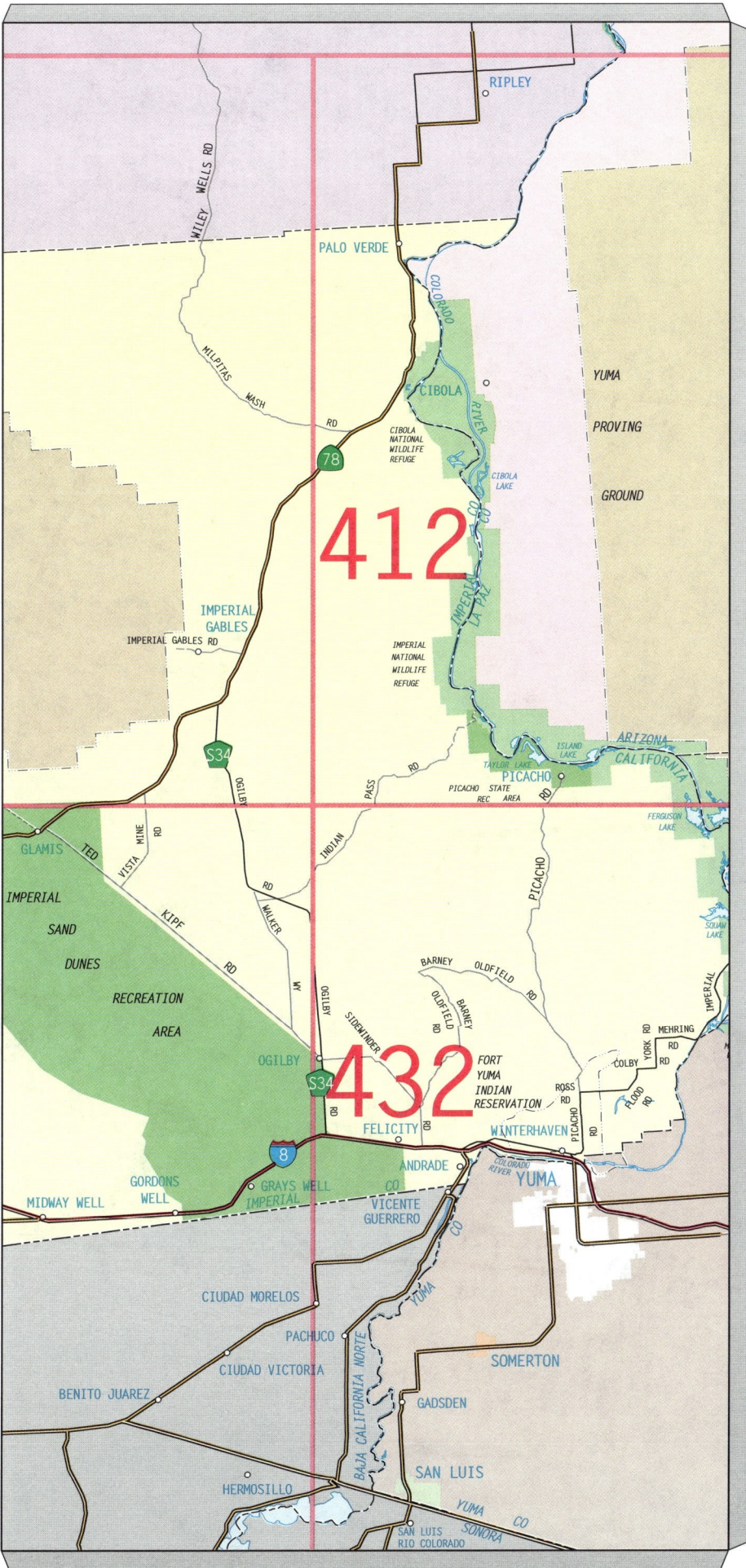

Key Map
to
Detail Pages

The Thomas Guide® contains several
types of map pages:
Arterial, Detail, and Quad

411 Arterial Page- Small scale area
map, shown with a wide border

1218 Detail Page- Full scale map page,
shown with a solid thin border

1058 Quad Page- A single map page
containing four interior pages at half
the detail scale, shown with a bold
border subdivided by thin dashed
lines

1059 Interior pages are shown only inside
Quad pages

Key Legend

○	Community
▬▬▬	Freeway
▬▬▬	Highway
———	Primary
———	Secondary, Minor
———	River, Creek

Key Map Scale
1 Inch to 8 Miles

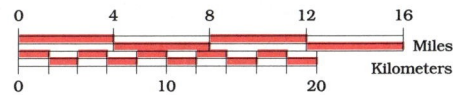

0	4	8	12	16

Miles

0		10		20

Kilometers

SAN DIEGO COUNTY FREEWAY ACCESS MAP

RIVERSIDE COUNTY

ORANGE COUNTY

OCEANSIDE — 5

- CRISTIANITOS RD (1023)
- BASILONE RD (1023)
- LAS PULGAS RD (408)
- HARBOR DR (1085)
- VANDEGRIFT BLVD (1085)
- N COAST HWY (1085)
- MISSION AV (1066)
- OCEANSIDE BLVD (1106)
- CALIFORNIA ST (1106)
- CASSIDY ST (1106)
- VISTA WY (1106)

19.5

CARLSBAD

- JEFFERSON ST (1106)
- EL CAMINO REAL (1106)
- LAS FLORES DR (1106)
- CARLSBAD VILLAGE DR (1106)
- TAMARACK AV (1106)
- CANNON RD (1126)
- PALOMAR AIRPORT RD (1126)
- POINSETTIA LN (1126)
- LA COSTA AV (1147)
- LEUCADIA BLVD (1147)
- ENCINITAS BLVD (1147)
- SANTA FE DR (1167)
- BIRMINGHAM DR (1167)
- MANCHESTER AV (1167)
- LOMAS SANTA FE DR (1167)
- VIA DE LA VALLE (1187)

20.5

DEL MAR

- DEL MAR HEIGHTS RD (1187)
- CARMEL VALLEY RD (1207)
- SORRENTO VALLEY RD (1207)

4.5

VISTA — 78

- SAN LUIS REY MISSION EXWY (1085) — 76
- ESCONDIDO AV (1107)
- SUNSET DR (1107)
- VISTA VILLAGE DR (1087)
- MELROSE DR (1087)
- EMERALD DR (1107)
- PLAZA DR (1107)
- COLLEGE BLVD (1107)
- EL CAMINO REAL (1106)

18.5

SAN MARCOS

- MAR VISTA DR (1107)
- SYCAMORE AV (1108)
- RANCHO SANTA FE RD (1108)
- W SAN MARCOS BLVD (1128)
- TWIN OAKS VALLEY RD (1128)
- BARHAM DR (1109)
- RANCHEROS DR (1109)
- E BARHAM DR (1129)
- NORDAHL RD (1129)

23

ESCONDIDO — 15

- RAINBOW VALLEY BLVD W (998)
- MISSION RD (1028)
- OLD HWY 395 (1028)
- PALA RD (1048)
- OLD HWY 395 (1068)
- CHAMPAGNE BLVD (1068)
- GOPHER CANYON RD (1068)
- OLD CASTLE RD (1068)
- DEER SPRINGS RD (1089)
- MOUNTAIN MEADOW RD (1089)
- CENTRE CITY PKWY (1109)
- EL NORTE PKWY (1109)
- LINCOLN PARKWAY (1129)

1.5

- CENTRE CITY PARKWAY (1129)
- BROADWAY (1129)
- VALLEY PKWY (1129)
- AUTO PARK WY (1129)
- W 9TH AV (1129)
- CITRACADO PKWY (1129)
- FELICITA RD (1129)
- S CENTRE CITY PKWY (1150)
- VIA RANCHO PKWY (1150)
- POMERADO RD (1150)
- W BERNARDO DR (1150)
- RANCHO BERNARDO RD (1170)
- BERNARDO CENTER DR (1170)
- CAMINO DEL NORTE (1169)
- CARMEL MTN RD (1189)

13

POWAY

- TED WILLIAMS PKWY (1189)
- RANCHO PENASQUITOS BLVD (1189)
- POWAY RD (1189)
- MERCY RD (1189)
- SCRIPPS POWAY PKWY (1189)
- MIRA MESA BLVD (1209)
- CARROLL CANYON RD (1209)
- MIRAMAR RD (1209)
- POMERADO RD (1209)
- MIRAMAR WY (1229)

11

MIRA MESA — 56

- CARMEL MTN RD (1189)
- RANCHO PENASQUITOS BLVD (1189)
- BLACK MTN RD (1189)

2.5

- MAST BLVD (1230)
- SANTO RD (1229)

5.5

SANTEE

- KEARNY VILLA RD (1229)
- CONVOY ST (1229)

2.5

- CLAIREMONT MESA BLVD (1229)
- BALBOA BL (1249)
- TIERRASANTA BLVD (1249)
- AERO DR (1249)
- MURPHY CYN RD (1249)
- FRIARS RD (1249)
- MESA COLLEGE (1249)
- VILLA DR (1229)
- KEARNY VILLA RD (1229)

4

2.5

3

ENCINITAS — 56

- CARMEL COUNTRY RD (1188)
- CARMEL CREEK RD (1188)
- EL CAMINO REAL (1208)
- SORRENTO VALLEY RD (1208)
- MIRA MESA BLVD (1228)
- LA JOLLA VILLAGE DR (1228)
- NOBLE DR (1228)
- GOVERNOR DR (1228)

2.5

- RENTO VALLEY RD (1208)
- ROSELLE ST (1208)
- GENESEE AV (1208)
- JOLLA VILLAGE DR (1228)
- NOBEL DR (1228)
- GILMAN DR (1228)
- ARDATH RD (1228)

- GENESEE AV (1228)
- REGENTS RD (1228)
- ARDATH RD (1228)

- MISSION BAY DR (1248)
- BALBOA AV (1248)
- GARNET AV (1248)

6

- CLAIREMONT MESA BLVD (1248)
- BALBOA AV (1248)

3.5

EL CAJON

- LA MESA BLVD (1271)
- GROSSMONT CTR DR (1271)
- JACKSON DR (1270)
- EL CAJON BLVD (1270)
- SPRING ST (1270)
- FLETCHER PARKWAY (1270)
- ALVARADO RD (1270)
- LAKE MURRAY BLVD (1270)
- COLLEGE AV (1270)
- WARING RD (1269)
- MISSION GORGE RD (1269)
- FAIRMOUNT AV (1269)

1.5

- MISSION GORGE RD (1231)
- FANITA DR (1251)
- NAVAJO PKWY
- FLETCHER (1251)

5

- MAGNOLIA AV (1251)
- JOHNSON AV (1251)
- W MAIN ST (1251)
- EL CAJON BLVD (1251)
- SEVERIN DR (1251)
- FUERTE DR (1271)

2.5

- E MAIN ST (1251)
- 2ND ST (1251)
- MOLLISON AV (1251)
- GREENFIELD DR (1252)
- LOS COCHES RD (1252)
- LAKE JENNINGS PARK RD (1232)
- DUNBAR LN (1239)
- ALPINE BLVD (1234)
- TAVERN RD (1234)
- ALPINE BLVD (1233)
- WILLOWS RD (1235)
- JAPATUL VALLEY RD (1235)
- PINE VALLEY RD (1237)
- OLD HWY 80 (430)
- SUNRISE HWY (430)
- OLD BUCKMAN SPRING RD (430)
- SHEEPHEAD MTN RD (430)
- CAMERON INT RD (430)
- CRESTWOOD RD (1298)
- RIBBONWOOD RD (1298)
- CARRIZO GORGE RD (430)

40

21

- ELLIE LN (1171)
- POWAY RD (1191)
- IRON MOUNTAIN DR (1191)
- SCRIPPS POWAY PKWY (1191)
- RIO MARIA RD (1191)
- SYCAMORE PARK DR (1191)
- SLAUGHTERHOUSE CANYON RD (1211)
- VIGILANTE RD (1211)
- JOHNSON LAKE RD (1211)
- SAN VICENTE AV (1211)
- POSTHILL RD (1211)
- SANTA MARIA AV (1212)
- GOLD BAR LN (1212)
- WILLOW RD (1232)
- LAKESIDE AV (1232)
- MAPLEVIEW ST (1232)
- WINTER GARDENS BLVD (1231)
- WOODSIDE AV (1231)
- RIVERFORD RD (1231)
- WOODSIDE AV (1231)
- PROSPECT AV (1231)
- BRADLEY AV (1251)
- FLETCHER PKWY (1251)
- BROADWAY (1251)

SAN DIEGO CO.

INTRO

LEGEND

67	ROUTE 67 FRWY	
78	ROUTE 78 FRWY	
94	MARTIN LUTHER KING JR FRWY	
163	ROUTE 94 FRWY	
905	CABRILLO FRWY	
905	JACOB DEKEMA FRWY	
125	ROUTE 905 FRWY	
	ROUTE 125 FRWY	

5	SAN DIEGO FRWY	
8	ROUTE 8 FRWY / MISSION VALLEY FRWY OCEAN BEACH FRWY	
15	ESCONDIDO FRWY	
15	ROUTE 15 FRWY	
52	ROUTE 52 FRWY	
54	SOUTH BAY PKWY	
56	TED WILLIAMS FRWY	

4.5 ITALICIZED NUMBERS ALONG THE FREEWAY INDICATE THE DISTANCE (IN MILES) BETWEEN FREEWAY INTERCHANGES. (712) THE NUMBER IN PARENTHESES FOLLOWING EACH STREET NAME REFERS TO THE ATLAS PAGE ON WHICH IT APPEARS.

NOT TO SCALE

ON RAMP
OFF RAMP
ON RAMP WITH CARPOOL RAMP
ON RAMP WITH CARPOOL RAMP ONLY
TOLL ROAD
FREEWAY WITH CARPOOL LANE

Thomas Bros. Maps
A RAND MCNALLY COMPANY

N E W S

Thomas Bros. Maps

PACIFIC OCEAN

CORONADO 75

IMPERIAL BEACH

NATIONAL CITY

CHULA VISTA 805

LEMON GROVE

U.S.A.
MÉXICO

94

125

8

8

5

905

75

94

AVOCADO BLVD (1271)
CALAVO DR (1271)
CAMPO RD (1271)
SWEETWATER SPRINGS BLVD (1271)
KENWOOD DR (1271)
BANCROFT DR (1271)

GROSSMONT BLVD (1271)
LEMON AV (1271)
BROADWAY (1271)
SPRING ST (1271)
CAMPO RD (1271)

3
2.5

BROADWAY (1271)
SPRING ST (1270)
GROVE ST (1270)
LEMON GROVE AV (1270)
WAITE DR (1270)
MASSACHUSETTS AV (1270)
COLLEGE AV (1270)
BROADWAY (1270)
COLLEGE GROVE WY (1290)
FEDERAL BLVD (1290)
BAYVIEW HTS WY (1290)
KELTON RD (1290)
EUCLID AV (1290)
49TH ST (1290)
47TH ST (1289)
HOME AV (1289)

ADAMS AV (1269)
EL CAJON BLVD (1269)
UNIVERSITY AV (1269)

6

7

3.5

HOME AV (1289)

1

PARADISE VALLEY RD (1291)
JAMACHA BLVD (1291)
WORTHINGTON ST (1290)
SWEETWATER RD (1290)
MANZANA LN (1290)
BRIARWOOD RD (1290)
WOODMAN ST (1310)
REO DR (1310)
PLAZA BONITA CTR WY (1310)

6.5

MARKET ST (1289)
IMPERIAL AV (1289)
47TH ST (1289)
43RD ST (1289)

5

PALM AV (1289)
PLAZA BLVD (1310)
SWEETWATER RD (1310)

HOME AV (1289)

HOME AV (1289)

MARKET ST (1289)

IMPERIAL AV (1289)

OCEANVIEW BLVD (1289)

2

2

3

BONITA RD (1310)
H ST (1310)
TELEGRAPH CANYON RD (1310)
ORANGE AV (1330)
OTAY VALLEY RD (1330)
PALM AV (1330)

HIGHLAND AV (1310)
4TH AV (1310)
NATIONAL CITY BLVD (1309)
BROADWAY (1309)

7

OTAY MESA RD (1351)

PICADOR BL (1350)
SMYTHE AV (1350)
BEYER BLVD (1350)

2

2

SAN YSIDRO BLVD (1350)

1.5

1

DAIRY MART RD (1350)
SAN YSIDRO BLVD (1350)
VIA DE SAN YSIDRO (1350)
TOCAYO AV (1350)
CORONADO AV (1350)
PALM AV (1330)
MAIN ST (1330)
PALOMAR ST (1330)
J ST (1330)
H ST (1330)
E ST (1309)

905

5

6

INDUSTRIAL BL (1330)

CIVIC CENTER DR (1309)
24TH ST (1309)
MARINA WY (1309)
PLAZA BLVD (1309)
8TH ST (1309)
DIVISION ST (1289)
MAIN ST (1289)

WABASH BLVD (1289)

28TH AV (1289)
BOSTON AV (1289)

CROSBY ST (1289)
LOGAN AV (1289)
IMPERIAL AV (1289)
1ST ST (1289)
17TH ST (1289)
G ST (1289)
F ST (1289)
E ST (1289)
B ST (1289)
C ST (1289)
PERSHING DR (1289)
A ST (1289)
ASH ST (1289)
PARK BLVD (1289)

MISSION BAY DR (1248)
CLAIREMONT DR (1268)
TECOLOTE RD (1268)
SEA WORLD DR (1268)
ROSECRANS ST (1268)

8

2

CM DL RIO W (1268)
MOORE AV (1268)
OLD TOWN AV (1268)
WASHINGTON ST (1268) (AIRPORT)
SASSAFRAS (AIRPORT)
INDIA ST (1268)
PACIFIC HWY (1268)
GRAPE ST (1289)
STATE ST (1289)
HAWTHORN ST (1289)
BRANT ST (1289)
FRONT ST (1289)
1ST AV (1289)
5TH AV (1289)
6TH AV (1289)

MIDWAY DR (1268)
W MISSION BAY DR (1268)
SUNSET CLIFFS BLVD (1268)
NIMITZ BLVD (1268)

Downtown San Diego

Map Scale

```
0      .125     .25      .375     .50
|-------|--------|--------|--------|  Miles
0              .25              .50     Kilometers
```

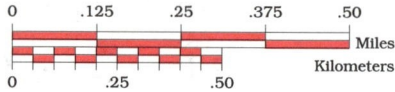

Points of Interest

1. Aerospace Museum & Hall of Fame (Balboa Park) — D3
2. Amtrak Station — B5
3. Best Western Bayside Inn — B5
4. Botanical Building (Balboa Park) — E2
5. Broadway Pier — A5
6. Cabot, Cabot & Forbes Building — B5
7. Carousel (Balboa Park) — E2
8. Casa de Balboa Building (Balboa Park) — E3
9. Casa del Prado (Balboa Park) — E2
10. Childrens Museum of San Diego — C6
11. City Administration Building (City Hall) — C5
12. Civic Center — C5
13. Clarion Hotel Bay View — D6
14. Copley Symphony Hall — D5
15. County Administration Center — B4
16. Courtyard Downtown — D5
17. Dail, Charles C. Community Concourse — C5
18. Embarcadero Marina Park — C7
19. Embassy Suites San Diego Bay — B6
20. Emerald Plaza — C5
21. Fashion Institute of Design & Merchandising — C5
22. Federal Jail — C6
23. Federal Office Building & Courthouse — C5
24. Firehouse Museum — B4
25. First National Bank Building — B5
26. Gaslamp Quarter — D6
27. Greater San Diego Chamber of Commerce — B5
28. Hall of Champions Sports Museum (Balboa Park) — E3
29. Holiday Inn Harbor View — C4
30. Holiday Inn on the Bay — A5
31. Horton Grand Hotel — C6
32. Horton Plaza — C6
33. House of Hospitality (Balboa Park) — E3
34. House of Pacific Relations (Balboa Park) — D3
35. Hyatt Regency Hotel — B6
36. International Visitors Information Center — C6
37. Japanese Friendship Garden (Balboa Park) — E3
38. Maritime Museum (San Diego Bay) — B5
39. Marriott Downtown — D5
40. Marriott San Diego Marina — C7
41. Mingei International Museum (Balboa Park) — E3
42. Museum of Contemporary Art San Diego — B5
43. Museum of Man (Balboa Park) — E3
44. Museum of Photographic Arts (Balboa Park) — E3
45. Museum of San Diego History (Balboa Park) — E3
46. Natural History Museum (Balboa Park) — E2
47. Naval Medical Center — F3
48. Plaza de Panama (Balboa Park) — E2
49. Police Headquarters — E5
50. Radisson Harbor View — C4
51. Reuben H. Fleet Space Theater & Science Center — E3
52. San Diego Automotive Museum (Balboa Park) — D3
53. San Diego Central Library — D5
54. San Diego City College — E5
55. San Diego City Operations Building — C5
56. San Diego Convention Center — C7
57. San Diego Coronado Ferry (Broadway Pier) — A5
58. San Diego County Court House — C5
59. San Diego Cruise Ship Terminal — A5
60. San Diego Fire Department Headquarters — D5
61. San Diego Hotel — C5
62. San Diego Model Railroad Museum (Balboa Park) — E3
63. San Diego Museum of Art (Balboa Park) — E2
64. San Diego Unified Port District — A2
65. San Diego Visitors And Convention Cntr — C5
66. Seaport Village (Shopping Area) — B6
67. Sempra Energy Building — C5
68. Simon Edison Centre for the Performing Arts — E2
69. Spanish Village Art Center (Balboa Park) — E2
70. Starlight Bowl (Balboa Park) — D3
71. State Office Building — C5
72. Timken Museum of Art (Balboa Park) — E2
73. Union Bank of California Building — C5
74. US Grant Hotel — C5
75. Veterans War Memorial (Balboa Park) — E1
76. Westgate Hotel — C5
77. Westin Hotel Horton Plaza — C5
78. Westminster Manor — C4
79. Wyndham Emerald Plaza Hotel — C5

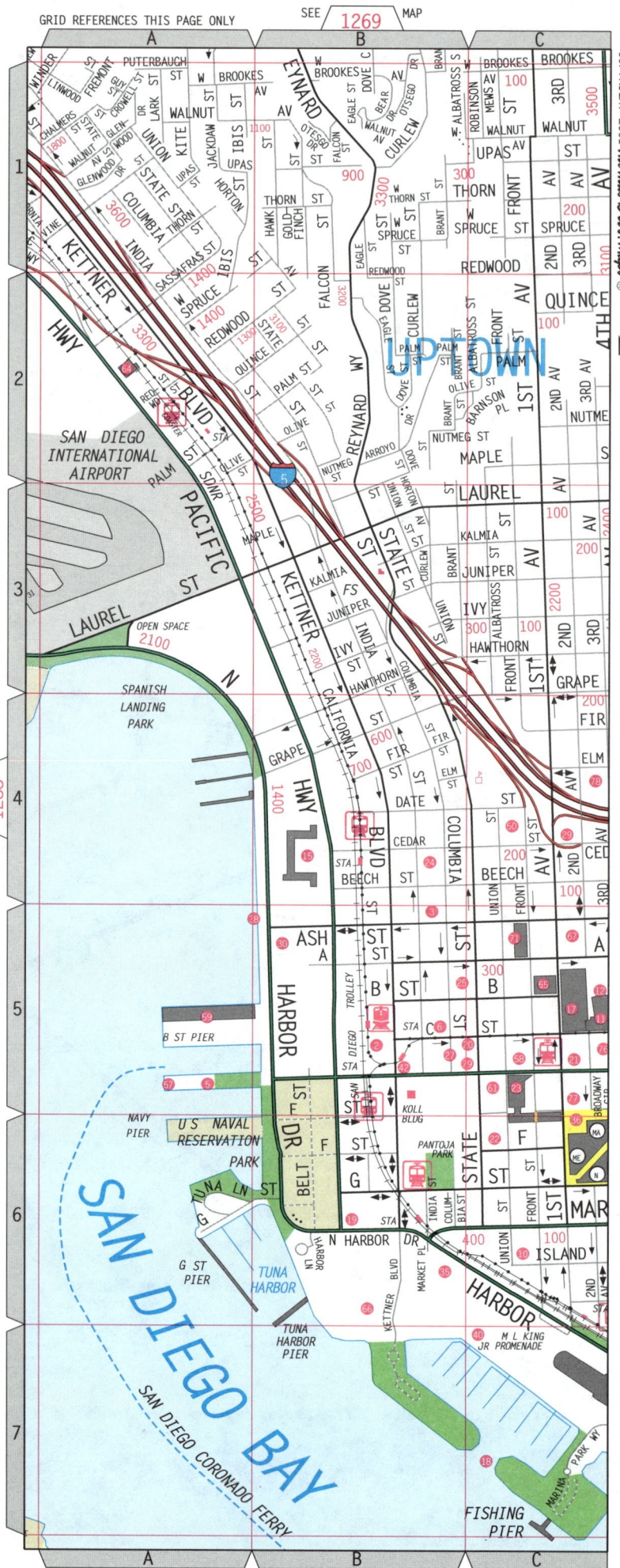

SEE 1269 MAP
SEE 1288 MAP
SEE 1289 MAP

SAN DIEGO CO.

INTRO

COPYRIGHT 2001 Thomas Bros. Maps®

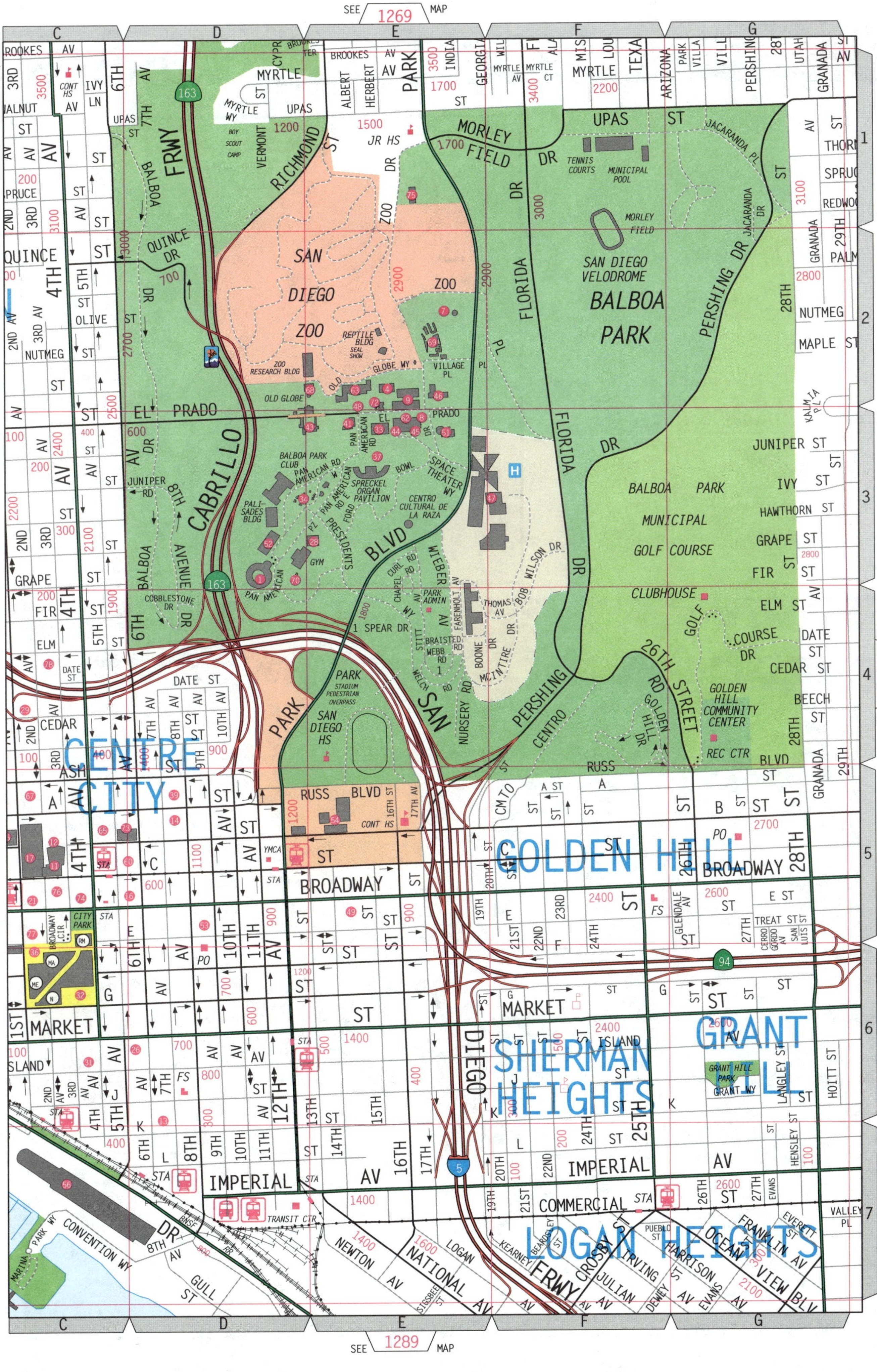

N

CENTRE CITY

GOLDEN HILL

SHERMAN HEIGHTS

GRANT HILL

LOGAN HEIGHTS

SAN DIEGO ZOO

SAN DIEGO VELODROME

BALBOA PARK

MORLEY FIELD

MORLEY FIELD

BALBOA PARK MUNICIPAL GOLF COURSE

CABRILLO

EL PRADO

SPACE THEATER WY

CENTRO CULTURAL DE LA RAZA

SPRECKEL ORGAN PAVILION

BALBOA PARK CLUB

PALISADES BLDG

REPTILE BLDG SEAL SHOW

ZOO RESEARCH BLDG

OLD GLOBE

PAN AMERICAN

SAN DIEGO HS

PARK STADIUM PEDESTRIAN OVERPASS

GOLDEN HILL COMMUNITY CENTER

REC CTR

GRANT HILL PARK

CLUBHOUSE

JR HS

BOY SCOUT CAMP

TENNIS COURTS

MUNICIPAL POOL

CITY PARK

BROADWAY CTR

MARKET

IMPERIAL

COMMERCIAL

CONVENTION WY

MARINA PARK WY

TRANSIT CTR

GYM

PARK ADMIN

SEE 1289 MAP

San Diego International Airport (SAN)

San Diego International Airport (Lindbergh Field) is operated by the Port of San Diego.

Each terminal has been assigned a color which corresponds to all access and driving signs; Terminal 1 is blue, Terminal 2 is purple and the Commuter Terminal is orange.

Check the internet at **www.portofsandiego.org** for current airline terminal locations.

Road signs are color coded to match the terminal colors

Terminal 2

AeroMexico	Continental
Air Canada	Delta
American	Midwest Express
America West	Northwest
British Airways	Reno Air

Terminal 1

Alaska
Southwest
TWA
United
US Airways

Commuter Terminal

Alaska Commuter
American Eagle
Continental Connection
Delta Connection
Northwest AirLink
Skywest
United Express
US Air Express

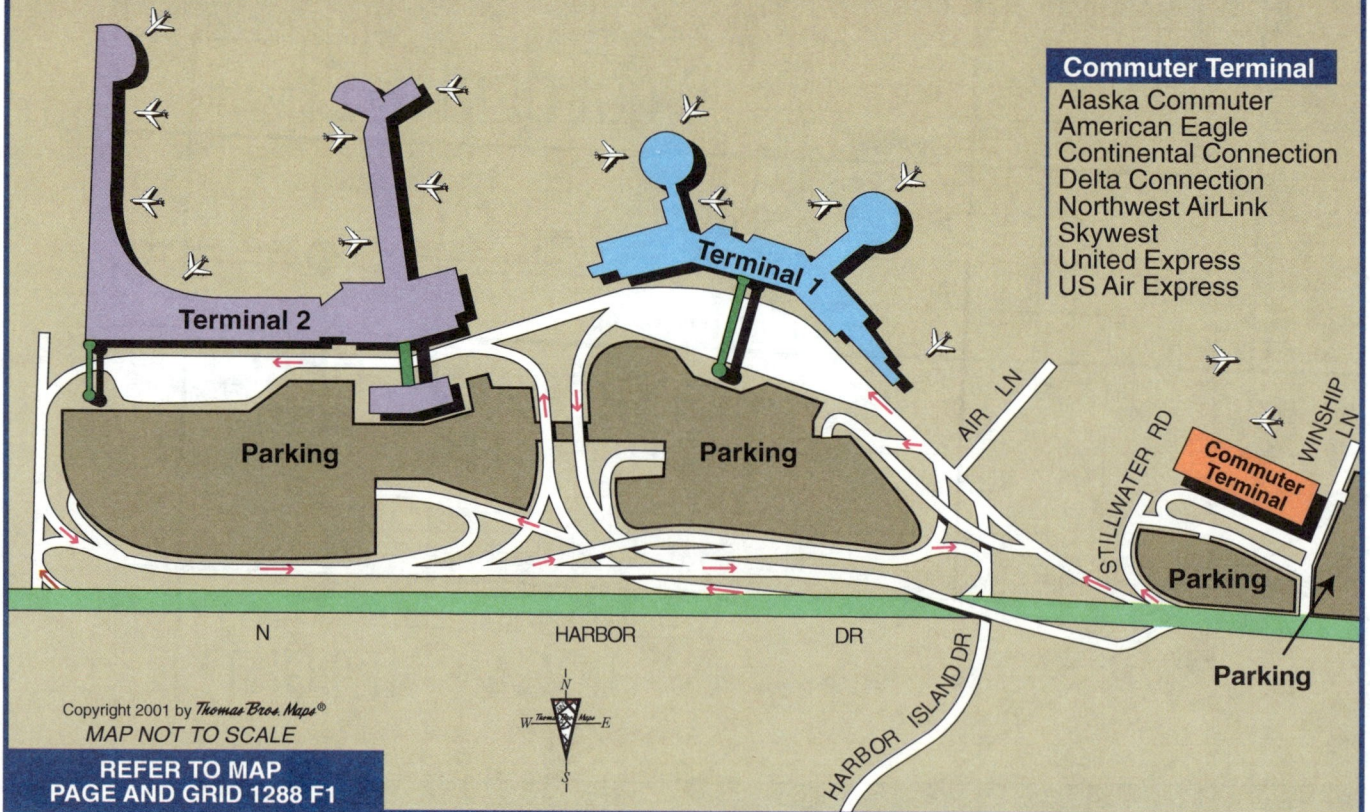

Copyright 2001 by *Thomas Bros. Maps* ®
MAP NOT TO SCALE

**REFER TO MAP
PAGE AND GRID 1288 F1**

SAN DIEGO COUNTY REGIONAL
BUS, TROLLEY, TRAIN, FERRY, AND TAXI INFORMATION

MAJOR BUS AND TROLLEY STATION LOCATIONS
For the location of major bus and trolley stations, see the "Transportation" heading in the Points of Interest Index of this Guide.

MAJOR PARK AND RIDE LOTS
For the location of major park and ride lots, see the "Park and Ride" heading in the Points of Interest Index of this Guide.

ⓘ MORE INFORMATION AND TRIP PLANNING
24-Hour InfoExpress Hotline - If you know your route and need specific schedule information, call (619) 685-4900 from any touch-tone phone.
Regional Transit Map (RTM) - The RTM shows all of San Diego County's public transportation routes. For your copy call 1-800-Commute or send your name, address, and $1.00 to MTDB, 1255 Imperial Av, Suite 1000, San Diego, CA 92101-7490.
The Transit Store: Located in downtown San Diego at 102 Broadway, provides a convenient location to purchase passes, tickets, tokens, and pick up RTM and individual route timetables. Open: Monday-Friday, 8:30 a.m. to 5:30 p.m.; Saturday and Sunday, 12 noon to 4:00 p.m. Closed major holidays.
Regional Telephone Information - Transit information specialists are on duty seven days a week from 5:30 a.m. to 8:30 p.m. to answer questions on public transit routes and schedules and the nearest Pass/Ticket sales outlet. Call (619) 233-3004 (TTY/TDD for persons with hearing impairments: (619) 234-5005). North County communities call 1-800-Commute (TTY/TDD calls in North County 1-888-722-4889). Please have the following information: your departure point; destination point; day and time of travel. Visit **www.sdcommute.com** for current service information.

🚌 🚃 SAN DIEGO BUS AND TROLLEY SYSTEM
San Diego Trolley - Bright red trolleys provide service on Blue and Orange Lines throughout the metropolitan area including: downtown San Diego, Mission Valley, Old Town, South Bay, U.S. Border, and East County. Trolleys operate seven days a week, early morning to late night, with base 15-minute service most of the day.
Metropolitan Transit System (MTS) and North County Transit District (NCTD) Buses - MTS bus routes serve the metropolitan San Diego area including: San Diego Zoo, Balboa Park, the International Airport, Mission Beach, Pacific Beach, La Jolla, and regional shopping, medical, and employment centers. Frequency and hours of operation vary; consult individual route timetables for schedule information. San Diego Transit is the region's largest bus operator, others are Chula Vista Transit, County Transit, National City Transit, and MTS 900 Routes. NCTD routes serve from Del Mar, north to San Clemente and inland to Fallbrook, Pauma Valley, Valley Center, Ramona, and Escondido.

$ FARES AND TRANSFERS
San Diego Trolley - San Diego Trolley cash tickets are priced according to the number of stations traveled. Quick Tripper tickets (good for two hours) are from $1.00-$2.25; Round Tripper tickets (good for a return trip any time on date purchased) are from $2.00-$4.50, both are available from self-service ticket machines at each stop. Exact fare in coins is recommended; some machines accept $1, $5, $10, and $20 bills. Multi-trip ticket books and multi-day and month passes are also available from most Trolley ticket machines.
MTS and NCTD Buses - San Diego Transit urban and express cash fares range from $1.75-$2.25. NCTD bus fare is $1.50. Commuter express fares range from $2.75-$3.25. Community and rural bus fares range from 85¢-$3.35. Senior and Disabled fare (with proper I.D.) is 75¢. Exact change in coins and/or bills is required.
Transfers - Transfers between buses and/or trolleys are free or require an upgrade if the second fare is higher.
Day Tripper Passes - The Day Tripper pass provides unlimited rides on most MTS regional buses and trolleys. Day Trippers are available for one, two, three, or four days ($5, $8, $10, and $12, respectively) and may be purchased from most trolley vendomats, The Transit Store, and many outlets throughout the region.

Monthly Ready Passes and Multi-Ride Tickets - Super Saver QuickTripper packets and tokens are economic alternatives to the cash fare for adult, senior, youth, and disabled riders who ride MTS and NCTD bus and rail systems. Month and Day Passes and Super Saver packets and tokens are available at The Transit Store and at outlets throughout the region, and by mail through MTDB (see address below).

♿ ACCESSIBLE SERVICE
The MTS and NCTD bus and rail operators have 100 percent wheelchair accessible service. Call Regional Transit Information (619) 233-3004 for more information and a copy of "A Wheelchair User's Guide To Getting Around San Diego by Bus and Trolley". In compliance with the Americans with Disabilities Act (ADA), those customers who cannot reach or ride regular bus and rail routes due to a mobility impairment can use MTS ACCESS or CTS Wheels. Eligible customers must be certified through the American Red Cross by calling (619) 542-7513. To schedule a trip call: MTS ACCESS at (619) 266-9000; or CTS Wheels at 1-800-920-9664.

QUALCOMM STADIUM
San Diego Trolley Blue Line and San Diego Transit Route 13 provide regular service to Qualcomm Stadium. San Diego Transit and NCTD also offer special express bus service to and from Qualcomm Stadium for major sporting events. For details, see "Regional Telephone Information" on this page.

🚢 BAY FERRY
The Bay Ferry operates between Coronado and San Diego, seven days a week from 9:00 a.m. to 10:30 p.m. (until 11:30 p.m. on weekends), leaving San Diego on the hour and Coronado on the half-hour. A one-way fare is $2.00; bicycles are 50¢.

🚆 AMTRAK, COASTAL EXPRESS RAIL "COASTER", METROLINK
AMTRAK - Currently, eight AMTRAK trains operate between San Diego, Los Angeles, Santa Barbara, San Luis Obispo, and other Southern California cities in between. These trains stop at three San Diego County Stations: the Santa Fe Depot in Centre City San Diego; Solana Beach; and the Oceanside Transit Center. For AMTRAK information call 1-800-USA-RAIL.
COASTER - Trains operate between Oceanside Transit Center and the Santa Fe Depot, with six intermediate stations including the Old Town Transit Center. Mon-Fri, Coaster provides morning and afternoon rush hour and mid-day service. On Saturday, Coaster runs four trains a day. Cash fares (one-way) range from $3.00 - $3.75 and may be purchased from station ticket machines. Monthly pass discounts for Seniors (60 and older), disabled, and youth (18 and under) riders. For information call 1-800-COASTER.
METROLINK - Weekday morning and afternoon rush-hour, high speed, rail service between Oceanside Transit Center and Union Station in Los Angeles with 13 intermediate stations. For information call 808-371-LINK.

🚕 TAXIS
Taxicab stands are located at most major employment, recreation, and shopping centers. Your fare will be displayed on the meter and will include a flat "flag drop" charge plus a per-mile and/or per-hour charge. All cabs leaving the International Airport charge a uniform rate of fare. Fares for all other cab trips vary from company to company, but cannot exceed a fixed amount set by the Metropolitan Transit Development Board (MTDB). The Taxicab Administration welcomes taxi service comments. Call (619) 557-4518.

This information is provided by the San Diego Metropolitan Transit Development Board (MTDB), North County Transit District (NCTD), and the Metropolitan Transit System (MTS) Operators. Write us at MTDB, 1255 Imperial Avenue Suite 1000, San Diego, CA 92101-7490. 🚆 MTS NCTD

EXISTING HIGH OCCUPANCY VEHICLE (HOV) LANES SUMMARY

ROUTE DESCRIPTION	DIRECTION	LANE MILES	OCCUPANCY	DAYS & HOURS OF OPERATION
I-15 - Ted Williams Pkwy to SR 163	Southbound	8	2 +	(M-F)6:00-9:00AM
I-15 - SR 163 to Ted Williams Pkwy	Northbound	8	2 +	(M-F)3:00-6:30PM
FRWY 54 - Briarwood Rd to 805 Fwy	Westbound	3	2 +	(M-F)6:00-9:00AM
FRWY 54 - 805 Fwy to Briarwood Rd	Eastbound	3	2 +	(M-F)3:00-6:00PM

SAN DIEGO COUNTY
Cities And Communities

Community Name	City Abbr.	ZIP Code	Miles To S.D.	Map Page	Community Name	City Abbr.	ZIP Code	Miles To S.D.	Map Page
AGUA CALIENTE		92086	69.50	409	GLEN OAKS		91901	27.00	1233
AGUA CALIENTE HOT SPRGS		92036	87.50	430	GLENVIEW		92021	21.30	1232
ALLIED GARDENS		92120	7.00	1250	GOLDEN HILL		92102		1289
ALPINE		91901	31.00	1234	GRANT HILL		92102		1289
ALPINE HEIGHTS		91901	29.00	1253	GRANTVILLE		92120	5.80	1249
ALTA VISTA		92114		1290	GREEN VALLEY FALLS		92916	51.00	1216
BALLENA		92065	47.00	1154	GROSSMONT		91942	14.50	1251
BANKHEAD SPRINGS		91934	71.30	1321	GUATAY		91931	43.50	1236
BANNER		92036	66.00	1156	HARBISON CANYON		92019	28.00	1253
BARONA MESA		92065	36.00	1173	HARMONY GROVE		92029	30.20	1129
BARRETT JUNCTION		91917	36.00	429	HARRISON PARK		92036	46.00	1156
BARRIO LOGAN		92113		1289	HIDDEN GLEN		91901	38.50	1254
BAY PARK		92110		1268	HIDDEN MEADOWS		92026	46.00	1089
BEAR VALLEY		92027	40.40	1111	HILLCREST		92103	1.60	1269
BIRCH HILL		92060	68.00	409	HULBURD GROVE		91916	42.00	1236
BLOSSOM VALLEY		92021	23.50	1232	❖ IMPERIAL BEACH	IMPB	91932	14.50	1349
BONITA		91902	10.10	1310	INDIAN SPRINGS		91935	19.50	1292
BONSALL		92003	51.80	1048	IRVING'S CREST		92065	38.10	1172
BORREGO SPRINGS		92004	105.00	1059	JACUMBA		91934	75.50	1321
BORREGO WELLS		92004	94.50	410	JAMACHA (SD)		92114		1290
BOSTONIA		92021	17.60	1252	JAMACHA (SDCO)		91935	18.20	1272
BOULDER OAKS		91962	52.30	430	JAMUL		91935	20.10	1292
BOULEVARD		91905	67.00	1300	JESMOND DENE		92026	44.20	1109
BROADWAY HEIGHTS		92114		1270	JOHNSTOWN		92021	22.10	1232
BUCKMAN SPRINGS		91962	51.50	430	JULIAN		92036	61.00	1136
BUENA		92083	40.50	1108	KEARNY MESA		92111	12.00	1249
CAMERON CORNERS		91906	52.20	1318	KENSINGTON		92116	5.20	1269
CAMPO		91906	51.90	430	KENTWOOD IN THE PINES		92036	48.00	1156
CAMP PENDLETON		92055	38.00	1085	LA COSTA		92009	38.00	1127
CANEBRAKE		92036	108.00	430	LA JOLLA		92037	12.60	1227
CANYON CITY		91906	48.30	430	LA JOLLA AMAGO		92060	64.30	409
CARDIFF-BY-THE-SEA		92007	22.50	1167	LA JOLLA SHORES		92037		1227
❖ CARLSBAD	CRLB	92008	33.00	1106	LAKE HENSHAW		92070	64.80	409
CARMEL MTN RANCH		92128		1190	LAKESIDE		92040	21.40	1232
CARMEL VALLEY		92130		1188	LAKEVIEW		92040	20.20	1232
CASA DE ORO		91977	12.30	1271	❖ LA MESA	LMSA	91941	12.00	1270
CASTLE PARK		91911	8.80	1330	LA PLAYA		92106	6.10	1288
CENTRE CITY		92101		1289	LA PRESA		91977	10.20	1291
CHOLLAS CREEK		92105		1290	❖ LEMON GROVE	LMGR	91945	9.50	1270
CHOLLAS VIEW		92102		1289	LEUCADIA		92024	26.00	1147
❖ CHULA VISTA	CHV	91910	7.00	1310	LINCOLN ACRES		91950	6.50	1310
CITY HEIGHTS		92105	4.00	1269	LINCOLN PARK		92102		1290
CLAIREMONT		92117	11.30	1248	LINDA VISTA		92111	6.00	1249
COMBS CAMP		92004	71.80	409	LIVE OAK PARK		92028	60.60	1028
❖ CORONADO	CORD	92118	3.50	1288	LIVE OAK SPRINGS		91905	64.30	1299
CORONADO CAYS		92118	7.50	1329	LOGAN HEIGHTS		92113	2.30	1289
COTTONWOOD		92019	18.20	1272	LOMA PORTAL		92110	6.70	1268
CREST		92021	27.00	1252	LOMAS SANTA FE		92075	19.00	1167
CROWN POINT		92109	7.50	1268	LOMITA		92114		1290
CUYAMACA		92036	52.40	1176	LYNWOOD HILLS		91910	7.20	1310
DEHESA		92019	25.00	1253	MANZANITA		91905	67.40	1300
DEL CERRO		92120	6.00	1250	MEMORIAL		92113		1289
DEL DIOS		92029	29.10	1149	MESA GRANDE		92070	63.10	409
❖ DEL MAR	DLMR	92014	18.50	1187	MIDDLETOWN		92103	1.00	1268
DE LUZ		92028	70.40	409	MIDWAY		92106		1268
DESCANSO		91916	36.70	1236	MIRAMAR		92126	14.00	1209
DESCANSO JUNCTION		91916	37.70	1236	MIRAMAR RANCH N		92131		1209
DESERT LODGE		92004	80.10	1099	MIRA MESA		92126	12.90	1209
DULZURA		91917	30.00	1314	MISSION BAY PARK		92109		1268
EAGLES NEST		92086	71.00	409	MISSION BEACH		92109	7.40	1267
EAST ELLIOTT		92145		1230	MISSION HILLS		92103	1.50	1268
EASTLAKE		91913	13.50	1311	MISSION VALLEY		92108	4.00	1269
EASTLAKE GREENS		91915	15.00	1311	MISSION VILLAGE		92123	6.50	1249
ECHO DELL		91916	45.50	429	MORENA VILLAGE		91906	56.90	1297
EDEN GARDENS		92075	19.80	1187	MORENO		92040	22.90	1212
❖ EL CAJON	ELCJ	92020	17.00	1251	MORETTIS		92070	61.50	409
EMERALD HILLS		92114		1290	MOUNTAIN VIEW		92113		1289
❖ ENCINITAS	ENCT	92024	24.50	1147	MOUNT HELIX		91941	12.50	1271
ENGINEER SPRINGS		91917	31.30	1314	MOUNT HOPE		92102		1289
❖ ESCONDIDO	ESCN	92025	31.50	1129	MOUNT LAGUNA		91948	57.00	1218
EUCALYPTUS HILLS		92040	22.80	1211	❖ NATIONAL CITY	NATC	91950	5.00	1309
FAIRBANKS CNTRY CLUB		92130		1188	NAVAJO		92120		1250
FAIRBANKS RANCH		92067	19.10	1168	NAVAL AMP BASE		92155	1.00	1309
FALLBROOK		92028	57.10	1027	NESTOR		92154	12.60	1350
FERNBROOK		92065	37.20	1192	NORMAL HEIGHTS		92116	5.20	1269
FLEETRIDGE		92106	6.00	1288	NORTH BAY TERRACES		92114		1290
FLETCHER HILLS		92020	17.80	1251	NORTH ENCANTO		92114	6.50	1290
FLINN SPRINGS		92021	24.50	1232	NORTH ISLAND NAS		92135	1.00	1288
FOSTER		92040	24.50	1211	NORTH JAMUL		91935	21.10	1272

❖ INDICATES INCORPORATED CITY   MILES ARE ESTIMATED FROM DOWNTOWN CIVIC CENTER

SAN DIEGO COUNTY
Cities And Communities

Community Name	City Abbr.	ZIP Code	Miles To S.D.	Map Page	Community Name	City Abbr.	ZIP Code	Miles To S.D.	Map Page
NORTH PARK		92104	4.70	1269	SAN ONOFRE		92672	53.00	1023
OAK GROVE		92086	72.50	409	SAN PASQUAL		92025	41.80	1131
OAK PARK		92105	7.90	1270	SANTA YSABEL		92070	52.50	1135
OCEAN BEACH		92107	7.20	1267	◆ SANTEE	SNTE	92071	18.50	1231
◆ OCEANSIDE	OCN	92054	36.00	1086	SAN YSIDRO		92173	15.50	1350
OCEAN HILLS		92056	45.00	1107	SCISSORS CROSSING		92036	71.00	410
OCOTILLO WELLS		92004	92.00	410	SCRIPPS MIRAMAR RANCH		92131	12.90	1209
OLD TOWN		92110	4.00	1268	SERRA MESA		92123	6.00	1249
OLIVENHAIN		92024	27.50	1148	SHADY DELL		92065	37.60	1192
OTAY		91911	11.60	1330	SHELLTOWN		92113		1289
OTAY MESA		92154	12.60	1350	SHELTER VALLEY RANCHOS		92036	71.00	1138
PACIFIC BEACH		92109	8.50	1247	SHERMAN HEIGHTS		92102		1289
PALA		92059	63.00	1029	SKYLINE		92114		1290
PALA MESA VILLAGE		92028	61.00	1048	◆ SOLANA BEACH	SOLB	92075	21.00	1167
PALM CITY		92154	11.80	1330	SORRENTO HILLS		92130		1208
PALOMAR MOUNTAIN		92060	66.70	409	SORRENTO MESA		92121		1208
PALO VERDE		91901	32.00	1234	SORRENTO VALLEY		92121	13.00	1208
PARADISE HILLS		92139	7.40	1290	SOUTH BAY TERRACES		92139		1290
PASO PICACHO		92036	51.00	1196	SOUTHCREST		92113		1289
PAUMA VALLEY		92061	61.30	1050	SOUTH ENCANTO		92114		1290
PENINSULA		92106		1288	SOUTH OCEANSIDE		92054	34.00	1106
PINE HILLS		92036	62.60	1155	SOUTH PARK		92102		1289
PINE VALLEY		91962	45.50	1237	SPRING VALLEY		91977	11.90	1271
POINT LOMA		92106	3.90	1308	STOCKTON		92102		1289
POTRERO		91963	42.80	429	SUNNYSIDE		91902	11.30	1311
◆ POWAY	PWY	92064	23.00	1190	SUNSHINE SUMMIT		92086	69.00	409
PUERTA LA CRUZ		92086	65.00	409	TALMADGE		92115	6.30	1269
RAINBOW		92028	60.80	998	TECATE		91980	43.50	429
RAMONA		92065	36.00	1152	THE NARROWS		92004	82.50	1120
RANCHITA		92066	94.30	410	THE WILLOWS		91901	33.00	1234
RANCHO BERNARDO		92128	23.50	1170	TIERRA DEL SOL		91905	70.60	1320
RANCHO DEL REY		91910	7.00	1311	TIERRASANTA		92124	9.80	1229
RANCHO PALO VERDE		91901	33.00	1254	TIJUANA RIV VLY		92154		1350
RANCHO PENASQUITOS		92129	23.00	1189	TORREY PINES		92014		1187
RANCHO SAN DIEGO		91978	13.00	1271	TWIN OAKS		92069	41.70	1108
RANCHO SANTA FE		92067	26.60	1168	UNIVERSITY CITY		92122	12.60	1228
RINCON		92082	61.30	1071	UNIVERSITY HEIGHTS		92116	1.70	1269
ROCK HAVEN		92065	31.90	1171	UPTOWN		92103		1269
ROLANDO		92115	8.50	1270	VALENCIA PARK		92114		1290
ROSEMONT		92065	36.40	1172	VALLECITO		92036	84.20	430
ROSEVILLE		92106	6.00	1288	VALLEY CENTER		92082	40.90	1090
SABRE SPRINGS		92128		1189	VIA DE LA VALLE		92014		1187
SAN CARLOS		92119	17.60	1250	VICTORIA		91901	31.00	1234
◆ SAN DIEGO	SD	92101		1289	◆ VISTA	VSTA	92083	45.30	1087
-- SAN DIEGO COUNTY	SDCo				WARNER SPRINGS		92086	68.50	409
SAN DIEGO CNTRY ESTS		92065	37.00	1173	WHISPERING PINES		92036	48.00	1136
SAN FELIPE		92086	92.30	409	WINTER GARDENS		92040	20.30	1232
SAN IGNACIO		92086	94.00	410	WINTERWARM		92028	59.30	1048
SAN LUIS REY		92054	41.40	1086	WITCH CREEK		92065	49.10	409
SAN LUIS REY HEIGHTS		92028	46.50	1048	WYNOLA		92036	62.00	1135
◆ SAN MARCOS	SMCS	92069	38.80	1108					

◆ INDICATES INCORPORATED CITY MILES ARE ESTIMATED FROM DOWNTOWN CIVIC CENTER

IMPERIAL COUNTY

Community Name	City Abbr.	ZIP Code	Map Page	Community Name	City Abbr.	ZIP Code	Map Page
ALAMORIO		92227	431	◆ HOLTVILLE	HOLT	92250	431
ANDRADE			432	◆ IMPERIAL	IMP	92251	6499
BARD		92283	432	-- IMPERIAL COUNTY	ImCo		
BOMBAY BEACH		92257	410	IMPERIAL GABLES			411
BONDS CORNER		92250	431	KANE SPRING		92259	410
◆ BRAWLEY	BRW	92227	431	MELOLAND		92243	431
◆ CALEXICO	CALX	92231	431	MIDWAY WELL			431
◆ CALIPATRIA	CLPT	92233	411	MOUNT SIGNAL		92231	431
COOLIDGE SPRING		92274	410	NILAND		92257	411
COYOTE WELLS		92259	430	OCOTILLO		92259	430
DATE CITY		92250	431	OGILBY			432
DESERT SHORES		92274	410	PALO VERDE			412
DIXIELAND		92251	430	PICACHO			412
◆ EL CENTRO	ELCN	92243	6559	PLASTER CITY		92259	430
ELMORE		92227	410	SALTON CITY		92274	410
FELICITY			432	SALTON SEA BEACH		92274	410
GLAMIS			431	SEELEY		92273	431
GORDONS WELL			431	◆ WESTMORLAND	WEST	92281	431
GRAYS WELL			431	WINTERHAVEN		92283	432
HEBER		92249	6560				

◆ INDICATES INCORPORATED CITY

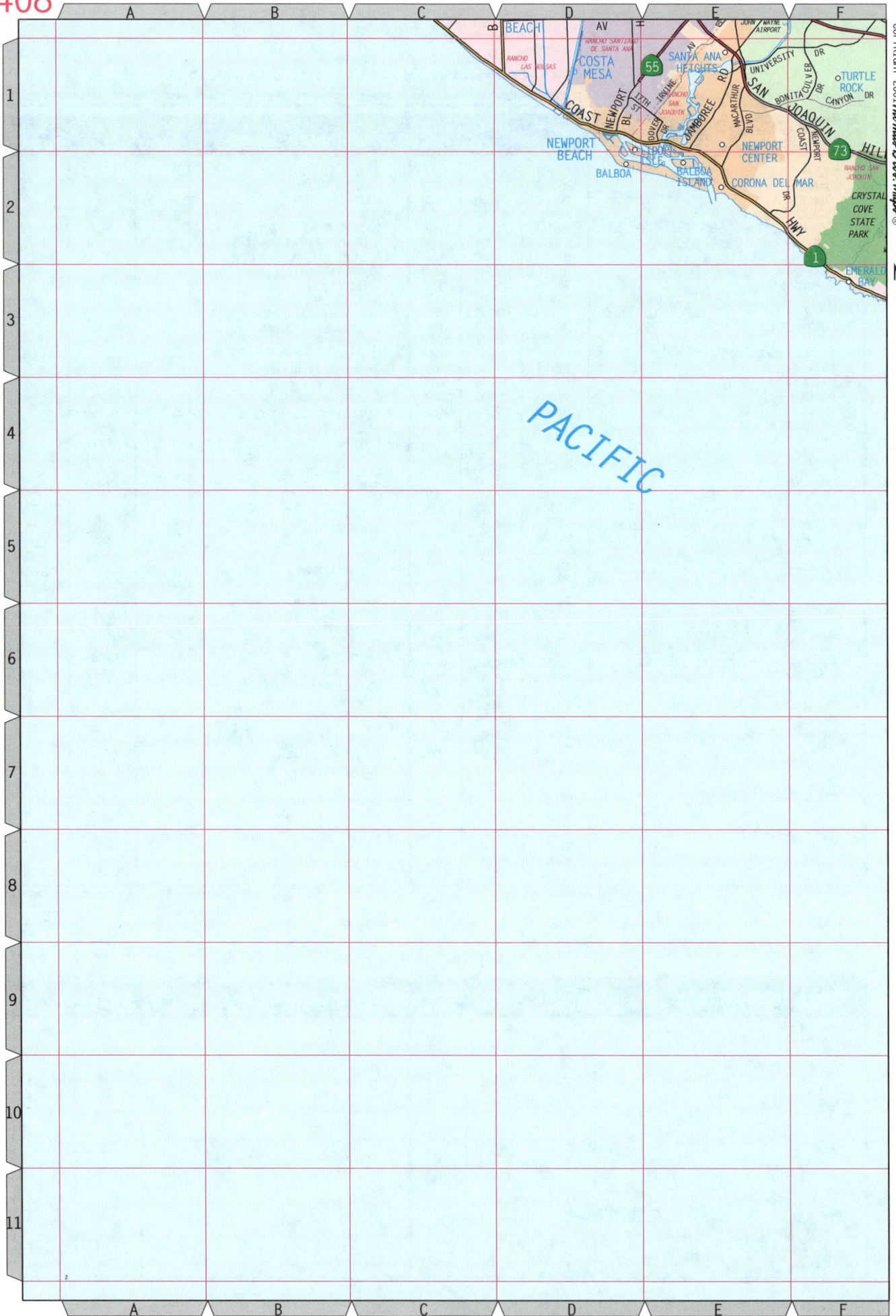

COPYRIGHT 2001 Thomas Bros. Maps ®

—N—

BEACH
AV

RANCHO SANTIAGO
DE SANTA ANA

COSTA
MESA

RANCHO
LAS BOLSAS

55

SANTA ANA
HEIGHTS

JOHN WAYNE
AIRPORT

UNIVERSITY

TURTLE
ROCK

DR

CANYON DR

NEWPORT
BEACH

COAST

NEWPORT BL

DOVER DR

JAMBOREE

IRVINE

RANCHO SAN
JOAQUIN

MACARTHUR BLVD

SAN

BONITA CULVER DR

JOAQUIN

73

HILL

NEWPORT
CENTER

LIDO
ISLE

12TH ST

BALBOA

BALBOA
ISLAND

CORONA DEL MAR

SAN
JOAQUIN
DR

RANCHO SAN
JOAQUIN

COAST

NEWPORT

CRYSTAL
COVE
STATE
PARK

1

EMERALD
BAY

HWY

PACIFIC

A   B   C   D   E   F

0   2.5   5   miles 1 in. = 4 mi.

SAN DIEGO CO.

Thomas Bros. Maps®

—N→

F G H J K L

STURTLE
ROCK
CYON DR

405

RD

133

3 HILLS

RANCHO SAN JOAQUIN

CRYSTAL
COVE
STATE
PARK

EMERALD
BAY

LAGUNA
BEACH

THREE
ARCH BAY

MONARCH
BEACH

SOUTH
LAGUNA

COAST

PACIFIC

DANA
POINT

ALTON
CENTER DR
TRUELINE DR

LEISURE
WORLD

S18

LAGUNA
WOODS

LAGUNA
HILLS

ALISO
VIEJO

LAGUNA
NIGUEL

RANCHO
NIGUEL

CROWN
VALLEY

ISLAND

LANTERN

GOLDEN

CAPISTRANO
BEACH

PKWY
BAKE PKWY

FOREST

LAKE
FOREST
EL TORO

LAKE
TORO

MISSION
VIEJO

MOULTON

OSO

LA PAZ

ALICIA

MARGUERITE

SAN JUAN
CAPISTRANO

SAN
JUAN
CREEK

ST OF THE
AVION

CM DE LAS
MARES

AVO PICO

BAK
RANCHO CANADA
DE LOS OSOS

SANTA
MARGARITA
OLYMPIAD

RANCHO
SANTA
MARGARITA

PKWY

ONEILL
REGIONAL
PARK

LADERA

LAK

TORR FOOTHILL
TRANS CORR

PKWY

ANTONIO

GENERAL
THOMAS F RILEY
WILDERNESS
PARK

WAGON
WHEEL

RONALD
W
CASPERS
WILDERNESS
PARK

CANADA
CHIQUITA

RANCHO MISSION VIEJO
LA PAZ

ORTEGA

LA PATA AV

HAUL

SAN
JUAN CREEK

T7S
T8S

AVD LA
PATA

RD

RANCHO ROCA DE
LA PLAYA

SAN
CLEMENTE

N EL
REAL

SAN
DIEGO
FRWY

SAN
ONOFRE
STATE
BEACH

PACIFIC COAST HWY CAMINO

CRISTIANITOS

SAN

T8S
T9S

S19
DOVE
CANYON

COTO
DE CAZA

COTO DE CAZA

TRABUCO
FLORES

BELL
CANYON

CRISTIANITOS

GABINO CANYON RD

RANGE
RD

SAN MATEO

SAN
ONOFRE

CLEVELAND

NATIONAL

FOREST

SAN JUAN
HOT SPRINGS

74

RD

ORANGE
CO

SAN DIEGO
CO

RIVERSIDE CO
SAN DIEGO
CO

LA PAZ
CANYON RD

TALEGA
SPUR

SAN DIEGO
CO

MATEO

ONOFRE

BASILONE

SAN ONOFRE

OLD

CAMINO

5

101

HWY
REAL

LAS
PULGAS
RD

DE
LUZ

LIMBRE CANYON

EL CARISO

RANCHO POTERO
LOS PINOS

RD

DE CARISO
RD

MAIN DIVIDE RD

MAIN DIVIDE RD

T6S
T7S

RGW

SITTON
PEAK

CARILLO

BELANGES

RIVERSIDE CO
SAN DIEGO CO

SAN MATEO
CANYON

CLEVELAND

NATIONAL
FOREST

WILDERNESS

SPRINGS RD

CASE

CASE

T8S

SAN
MATEO
CANYON
WILDERNESS

TENEJA

CL
DE
VINA

PY

LAK
VIEW

SAN DIEGO CO.

RIVERSIDE
CO

92028

SAN DIEGO
CO

MARINE CORPS BASE

CAMP JOSEPH H PENDLETON

92055

CAMP PENDLETON

RD

CASE SP RINGS

BASILONE

PULGAS
CANYON

ALISO
CANYON

STUART

STAGECOACH
RD

MESA

VANDEGRIFT

1023

1085

1105

VANDE
GRIFT BL

SAN

SOUTH
OCEANS

BUENA
VISTA
LAGOON

OCEAN

1 2 3 4 5 6 7 8 9 10 11

SEE
409
MAP

MAP

F G H J K L

0   2.5   5
miles 1 in. = 4 mi.

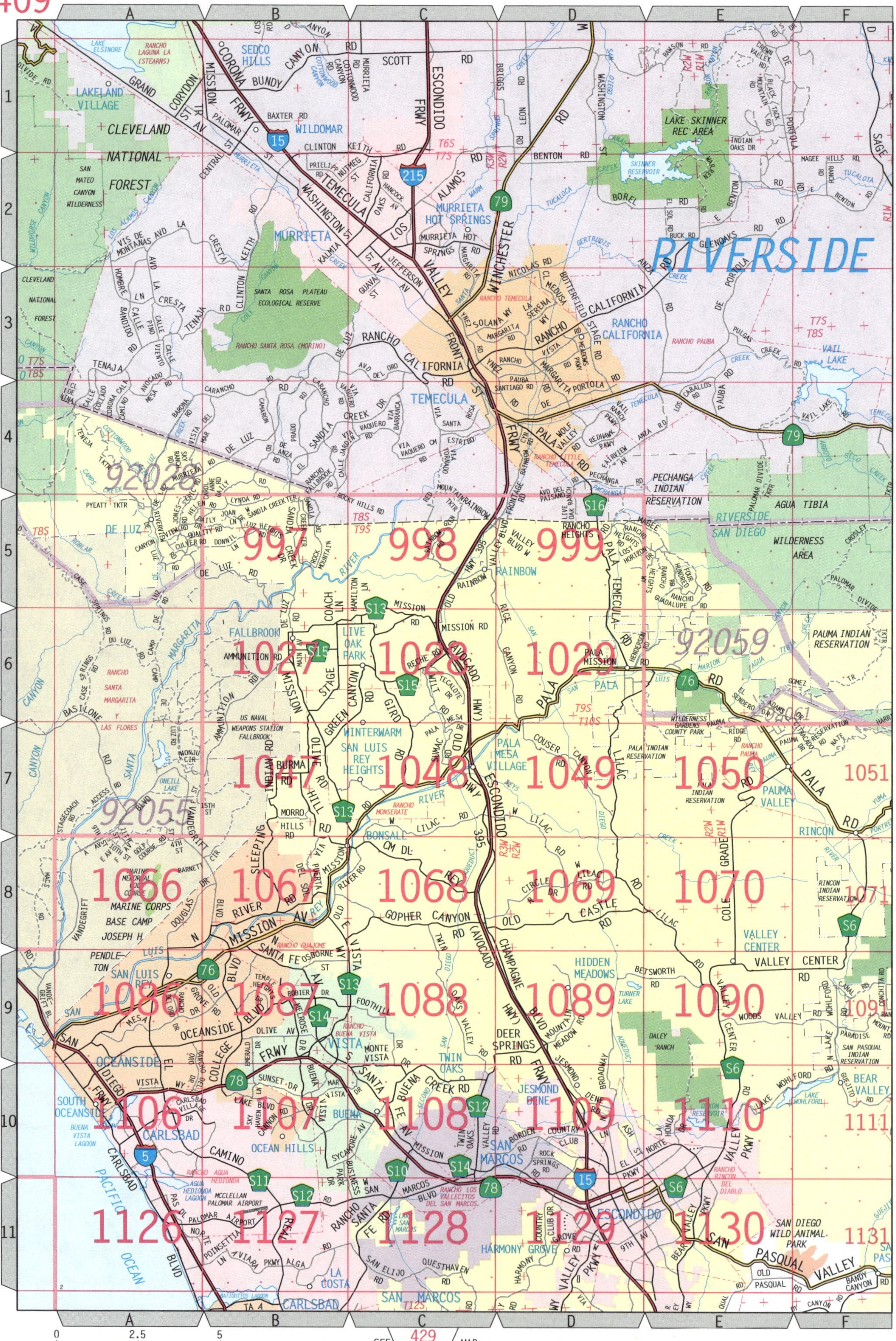

SAN DIEGO CO.

MAP

COPYRIGHT 2001 Thomas Bros. Maps® —N—

RIVERSIDE

SEE 408 MAP

LAKELAND VILLAGE
CLEVELAND NATIONAL FOREST
SAN MATEO CANYON WILDERNESS
MURRIETA
TEMECULA
MURRIETA HOT SPRINGS
WINCHESTER
RANCHO CALIFORNIA
LAKE SKINNER REC AREA
SANTA ROSA PLATEAU ECOLOGICAL RESERVE
RANCHO SANTA ROSA (MORINO)
VAIL LAKE
PECHANGA INDIAN RESERVATION
AGUA TIBIA WILDERNESS AREA
DE LUZ
FALLBROOK
LIVE OAK PARK
RAINBOW
PALA
PAUMA INDIAN RESERVATION
PAUMA VALLEY
RINCON INDIAN RESERVATION
MARINE CORPS BASE CAMP JOSEPH H. PENDLETON
SAN LUIS REY HEIGHTS
BONSALL
VALLEY CENTER
OCEANSIDE
VISTA
SAN MARCOS
ESCONDIDO
DEER SPRINGS
HIDDEN MEADOWS
BEAR VALLEY
SOUTH OCEANSIDE
CARLSBAD
OCEAN HILLS
LA COSTA
SAN MARCOS
SAN DIEGO WILD ANIMAL PARK
PASQUAL VALLEY
PACIFIC OCEAN

92028 92055 92059 92061

997 998 999
1027 1028 1029
1047 1048 1049 1050 1051
1066 1067 1068 1069 1070 1071
1086 1087 1088 1089 1090 1091
1106 1107 1108 1109 1110 1111
1126 1127 1128 1129 1130 1131

0 2.5 5 miles 1 in. = 4 mi.

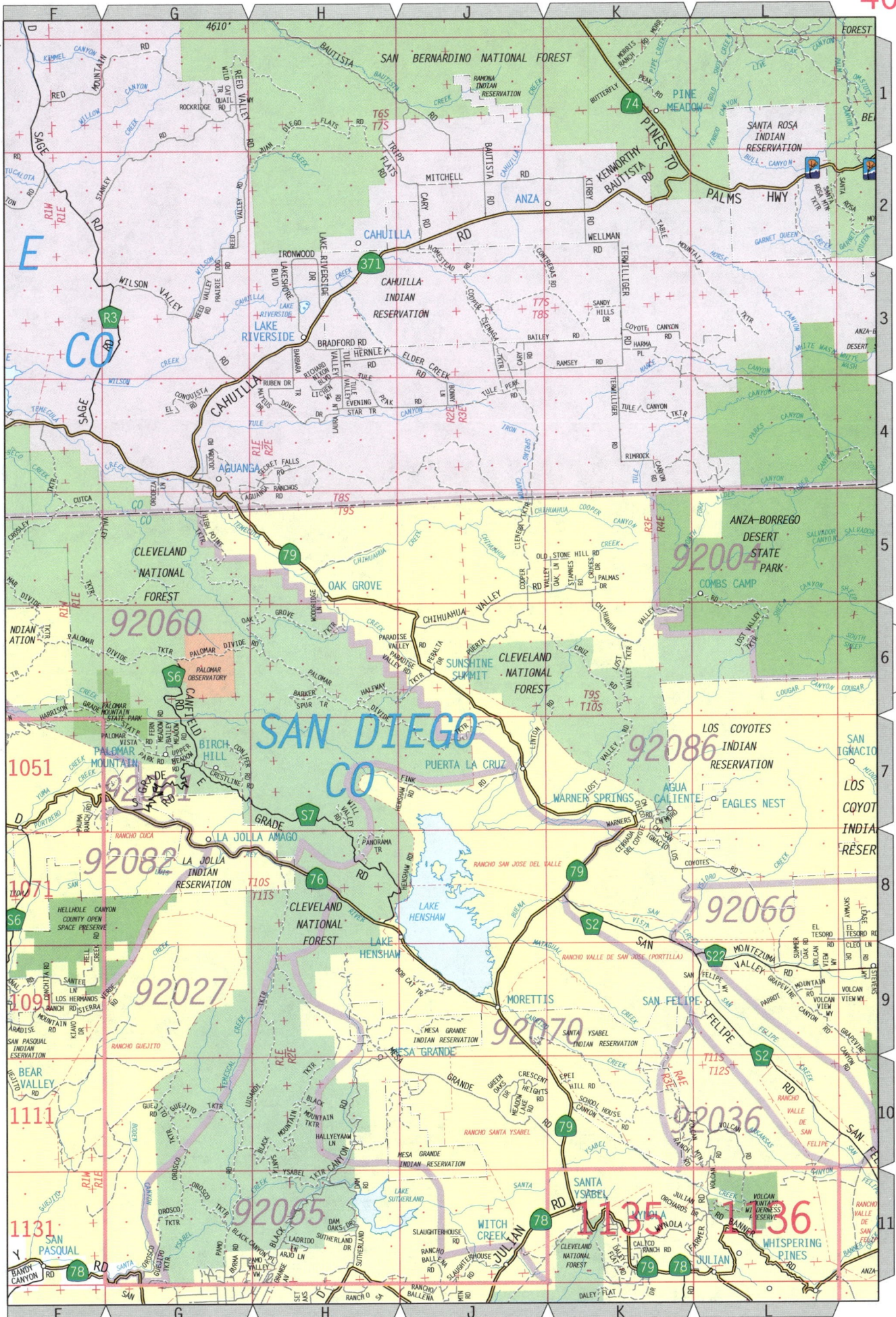

SAN DIEGO CO.

MAP

SAN BERNARDINO NATIONAL FOREST

RIVERSIDE CO

SAN DIEGO CO

CAHUILLA INDIAN RESERVATION

RAMONA INDIAN RESERVATION

SANTA ROSA INDIAN RESERVATION

PINES TO PALMS HWY

KENNWORTHY BAUTISTA RD

ANZA

LAKE RIVERSIDE

IRONWOOD

AGUANGA

ANZA-BORREGO DESERT STATE PARK

92004

CLEVELAND NATIONAL FOREST

92060

OAK GROVE

PALOMAR OBSERVATORY

PALOMAR MOUNTAIN STATE PARK

SAN DIEGO CO

SUNSHINE SUMMIT

PUERTA LA CRUZ

LOS COYOTES INDIAN RESERVATION

92086

SAN IGNACIO

WARNER SPRINGS

AGUA CALIENTE

EAGLES NEST

92082

LA JOLLA INDIAN RESERVATION

LA JOLLA AMAGO

1051

1071

1111

1131

109

92051

92027

LAKE HENSHAW

CLEVELAND NATIONAL FOREST

92066

SAN FELIPE

MONTEZUMA VALLEY RD

92070

MESA GRANDE INDIAN RESERVATION

MORETTIS

SANTA YSABEL INDIAN RESERVATION

92036

92065

SANTA YSABEL

WITCH CREEK

JULIAN

1135

1136

WHISPERING PINES

SAN PASQUAL

BEAR VALLEY

HELLHOLE CANYON COUNTY OPEN SPACE PRESERVE

SEE 410 MAP

SEE 429 MAP

0 2.5 5 miles 1 in. = 4 mi.

—N—

FOREST

SAN BERNARDINO

PINYON PINES

PINES TO PALMS HWY

74

SANTA ROSA

SANTA ROSA WILDERNESS

NATIONAL FOREST

SANTA ROSA INDIAN RESERVATION

Anza-Borrego DESERT STATE PARK

SANTA ROSA MOUNTAINS

LA QUINTA

HARRISON ST

ARABIA

111

TORRES MARTINEZ INDIAN RESERVATION

86S

195

86

PIERCE ST

VALERIE

RIVERSIDE CO

RABBIT PEAK 6623'

TRAVERTINE ROCK

OASIS

RIVERSIDE CO / SAN DIEGO CO

SAN DIEGO CO

ANZA-BORREGO

DESERT

STATE

PARK

CLARK LAKE

SEE 409 MAP

SAN IGNACIO

LOS COYOTES INDIAN RESERVATION

1058   1059

1058

HENDERSON

BORREGO VALLEY

PEG LEG RD

BORREGO

S22   SALTON

SEAWAY

1078   1079

PALM CANYON DR

BORREGO SPRINGS

92004

92066

RANCHITA

MONTEZUMA VALLEY RD

S22   S3

RANGO WY

BORREGO SPRINGS RD

1098   1099   1100   1101

S3

1098

OCOTILLO WELLS STATE VEHICULAR REC AREA

1100

78

1118   1119   1120   1121

YAQUI WELLS RD   THE NARROWS

OCOTILLO WELLS

SPLIT MOUNTAIN

SAN FELIPE RD

S2

SCISSORS CROSSING

78

GREAT SOUTHERN OVERLAND STGE RTE OF 1849

1138   1139

1138

SHELTER VALLEY RANCHOS

ANZA-BORREGO DESERT STATE PARK

BORREGO WELLS

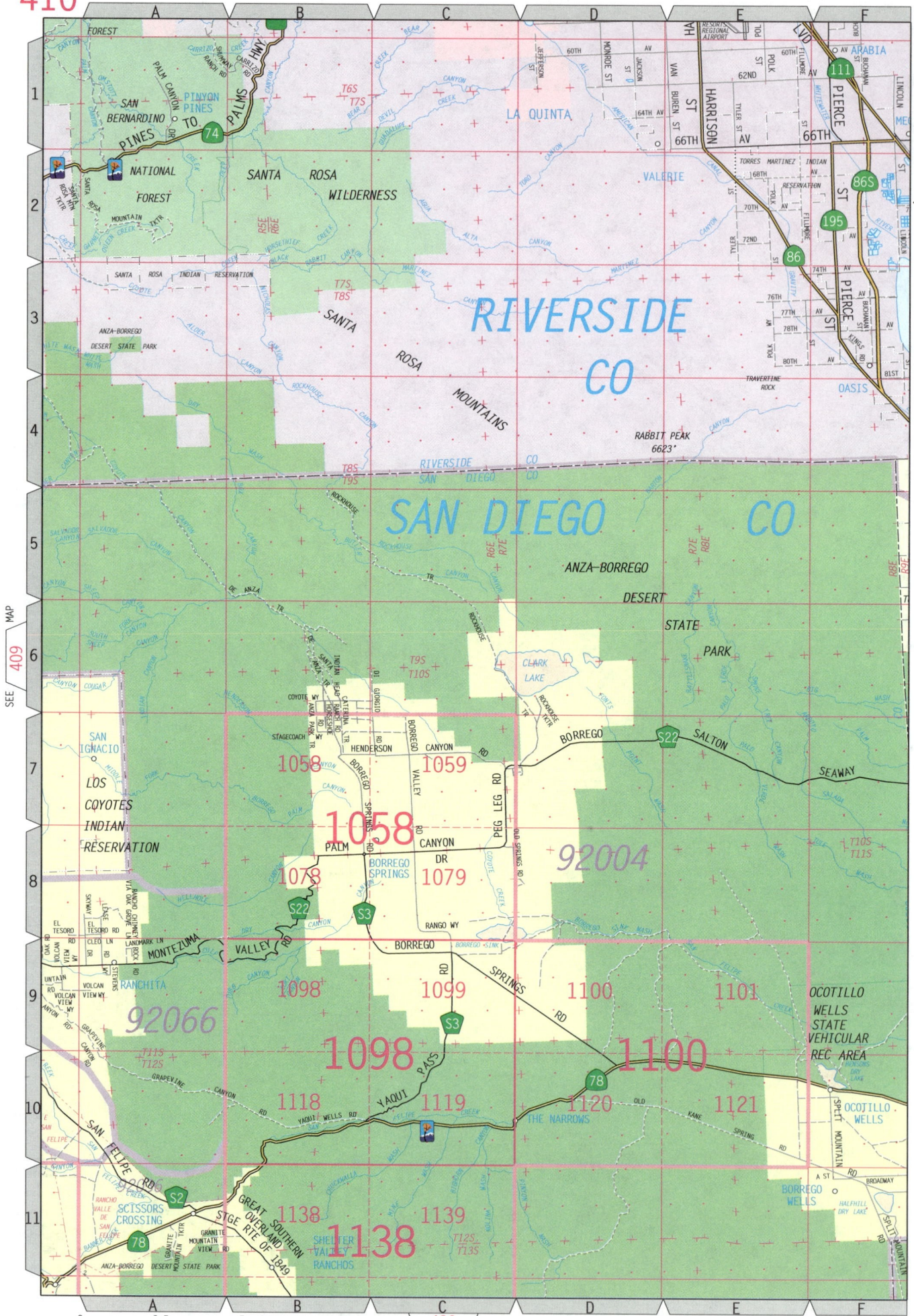

0   2.5   5   miles   1 in. = 4 mi.

SEE 430 MAP

ThomasBros. Maps®

COPYRIGHT 2001

N

SAN DIEGO CO.

MAP

F G H J K L

1
2
3
4
5
6
7
8
9
10
11

ABIA
MECCA
LINCOLN
64TH AV
JOHNSON ST
GRANT ST
HAYES
COACHELLA
PAINTED CYN RD
BOX CANYON RD
PAINTED CANYON
HIDDEN SPRING CANYON

FLOWING WELLS
68TH AV
GARFIELD AV
70TH AV
70TH
72ND AV
R9E R10E
CANAL

NORTH SHORE
DESERT BEACH
CLUB DR VIEW
PARKSIDE DR
SEA BREEZE DR
VIA VERBENA
VIA MIRAGE
DESERT AIRE DR

COACHELLA
THE BRADSHAW
R11E R12E
R12E R13E
SALT CREEK

CHOCOLATE MOUNTAIN
NAVAL RESERVATION
AERIAL GUNNERY
RANGE

SALTON SEA STATE
RECREATION AREA
POWER LINE RD
SALT CREEK RD
111
SALTON
HOT SPRINGS RD

RIVERSIDE CO
IMPERIAL CO

92251

DESERT SHORES
COOLIDGE SPRING
SALTON SEA BEACH
BRAWLEY AV
R8E R9E

SALTON
SEA

SALTON SEA STATE
RECREATION AREA
BOMBAY BEACH
SALTON SEA STATE
RECREATION AREA
ORCHID RD
TRILY RD
SPA RD
HOT MINERAL SPA RD
WAGON RD
HONEY RD
NILAND MARINA RD
FRINK

TORRES MARTINEZ INDIAN RESERVATION
TREADWELL BLVD
NILES AV
ONTARIO
SALTON BAY DR
DOLPHIN DR
MARINA DR
SEA PORT AV
CALIFORNIA MARINA DR
SEA VIEW DR
SAND CREST DR
HARBOR DR
VONKALLI AV
SALTON
KEITH
SALADA DR
SALTON BAY DR
92274

SALTON CITY
SALTON SEA MILITARY RESERVATION

BORREGO SALTON SEAWAY
TRUCKHAVEN TR
SUNRISE DR
SEA
AIRPARK
ARROYO SALADA
SKY VIEW DR
AIR PARK DR
TULE WASH
CAMPBELL
86

SALTON
SEA
MILITARY
RESERVATION

SAN DIEGO CO
IMPERIAL CO

IMPERIAL
CO

T11S T12S
R10E R11E
R9E R10E

QTILLO ELLS
BROADWAY
ILL LAKE
SPLIT MOUNTAIN RD
T12S T13S

KANE SPRING
ELMORE
86
78
ALLEN RD
BARTH RD
R9E RD
92259
3RD
STANDARD
PARALLEL SOUTH
R11E R12E

SALTON SEA NATIONAL
WILDLIFE REFUGE
FOULDS
VENDEL RD
WALKER RD
PELLETT RD
BANNISTER RD
92227

SALT NA WILD

WEST

SEE 411 MAP

SEE 430 MAP

0   2.5   5
miles   1 in. = 4 mi.

SAN DIEGO CO.

MAP

COPYRIGHT 2001 *Thomas Bros. Maps* ®

—N—

A B C D E F

RIVERSIDE

CO

CHUCKAWALLA

MOUNTAINS

SHIP

DUPONT RD

SHIP CREEK

MUD CLOUD CANYON

WASH

T7S

T7S
T8S

SALT CREEK

THE

BRADSHAM

TR

THE

BRADSHAM RD

CHOCOLATE

MOUNTAINS

R13E R14E

R14E R15E

R15E R16E

R16E R17E

AUGUSTINE

RIVERSIDE CO
IMPERIAL CO

T8S
T9S

CHOCOLATE MOUN
NAVAL RESERVA
AERIAL GUNNE

COACHELLA CANAL RD

SPA RD

FRINK RD

AMERICAN COACHELLA CANAL

COACHELLA CANAL

CLIFF

WASH

ARROYO

BEAL RD

T9S
T10S

CHOCOLATE

MOUNTAIN

SEE 410 MAP

111

92257

WISTER

HOWELL

DAVIS

HOBBS

ENGLISH

WATERFOWL

WINSLOW

GILLESPIE RD

MANAGEMENT

AREA

BEACH RD

DAVIS

NILAND EAST MAIN WAY RD

CLIFF

IRIS

BEAL

COACHELLA CANAL

SALVATION

NAVAL

GERMAN PASS

WASH

R16E R17E

WILKINS

NILAND

BEAL

MAIN ST

NOFFSINGER

NOFFSINGER

HIGH LINE

FLOWING WELLS RD

TED

STANLEY RD

KIPF

COACHELLA CANAL

MAMMOTH

SALTON
SEA

ENGLISH

NILAND AV

INTERNATIONAL

WELCH RD

POUND RD

POUND

MCDONALD

MCDONALD RD

NIDER

POUND

DAVIS

SCHRIMPF

IMPERIAL WILDFOWL

RED HILL RD

SIMPSON

SIMPSON RD

R13E R14E

ENGLISH

111

BLAIR

SINCLAIR

R14E R15E

WIEST RD

HALSY

EAST HIGHWAY

R15E R16E

TED

SALTON SEA NATIONAL WILDLIFE REFUGE

SINCLAIR

GAST RD

MCNERNEY RD

COX RD

ALAMO RIVER

PETERSON

MONTGOMERY

LINDSEY

92233

PETERSON RD

MONTGOMERY

LINDSEY

WILKINSON

YOUNG RD

WIRT

IMPERIAL

SAND DUNES

REC

SALTON SEA NATIONAL WILDLIFE REFUGE

NEW RIVER

BOYLE

GENTRY

LINDSEY

HATFIELD RD

WILKINSON

BLAIR

EDDINS

S30

CALIPATRIA

115

SEVERE

KALIN

BRANDT

LYERLY

YOCUM

ALBRIGHT RD

YOCUM

ALBRIGHT RD

KAISER RD

VAIL

RUEGGER

S30

RUEGGER

ALAMO RIVER

DOWDEN RD

DOWDEN

FOULDS

NEW RIVER

IMPERIAL WILDFOWL MANAGEMENT AREA

RAMER LAKE

TITSWORTH

115

TITSWORTH

MESA

WALKER RD

WALKER

92227

FORRESTER RD

KALIN RD

HOVLEY RD

KERSHAW

WILLIAMS

FINNEY LAKE

DIETRICH

PARK AV

JACKSON

PICKETT

WILLIAMS

SANBORN

PICKETT

BUTTERS

RUTHERFORD RD

S32

US NAVAL RESERVATION

PELLETT

LACK RD

BANNISTER

MARTIN ST

7TH ST

H ST

ST

BANNISTER RD

KALIN

S26

111

RUTHERFORD

WEST LAKE

BEST RD

CHAPUL HWY

GIESELMANN

CHAPULNIK

CHAPULNIK RD

DICKERMAN

IRVINE

WESTMORLAND

92281

BOARTS RD

EAST

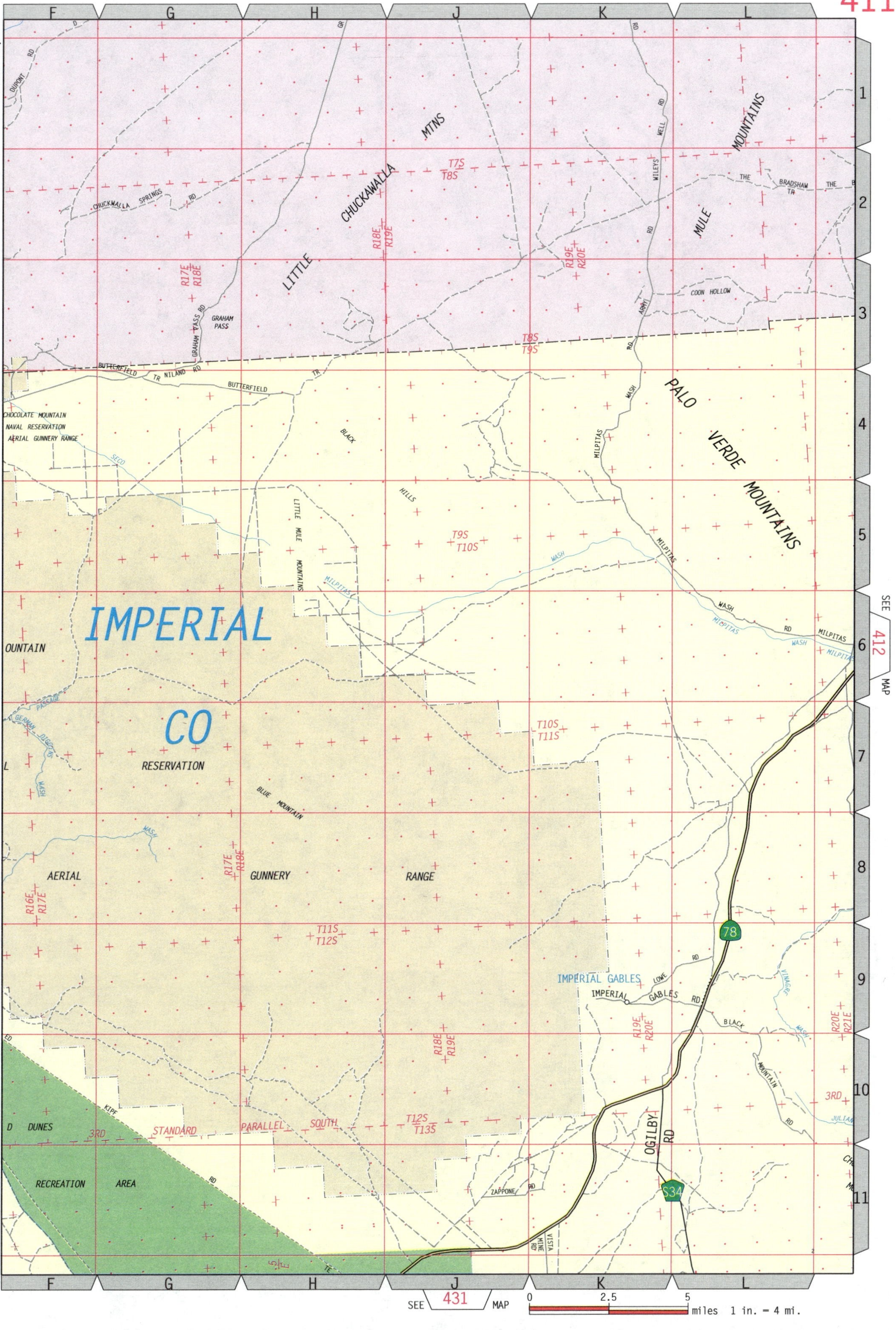

SAN DIEGO CO.

MAP

COPYRIGHT 2001 *Thomas Bros. Maps*®

N

F G H J K L

1
2
3
4
5
6
7
8
9
10
11

DUPONT RD

LITTLE CHUCKWALLA MTNS

CHUCKWALLA SPRINGS RD

GRAHAM PASS RD
GRAHAM PASS

T7S / T8S

R17E R18E
R18E R19E

R19E R20E

MULE MOUNTAINS

THE BRADSHAW TR THE B

COON HOLLOW

WILEYS WELL RD

ARMY RD

T8S / T9S

BUTTERFIELD TR NILAND RD
BUTTERFIELD TR

CHOCOLATE MOUNTAIN
NAVAL RESERVATION
AERIAL GUNNERY RANGE

SECO

BLACK

HILLS

LITTLE MULE MOUNTAINS

MILPITAS

PALO VERDE MOUNTAINS

WASH

T9S / T10S

MILPITAS WASH

MILPITAS WASH RD MILPITAS WASH MILPITAS

IMPERIAL

CO

OUNTAIN

PACUGE

GERMAN GULCH RD

WASH

RESERVATION

BLUE MOUNTAIN

T10S / T11S

SEE 412 MAP

R17E R18E

AERIAL GUNNERY RANGE

R16E R17E

T11S / T12S

IMPERIAL GABLES
IMPERIAL GABLES RD

LONE RD

BLACK MOUNTAIN

R19E R20E

R20E R21E

R18E R19E

78

3RD

JULIAN

DUNES

KIPF

3RD STANDARD PARALLEL SOUTH

T12S / T13S

ZAPPONE RD

OGILBY RD

VISTA RD

MINE RD

S34

RECREATION AREA

0 2.5 5 miles 1 in. = 4 mi.

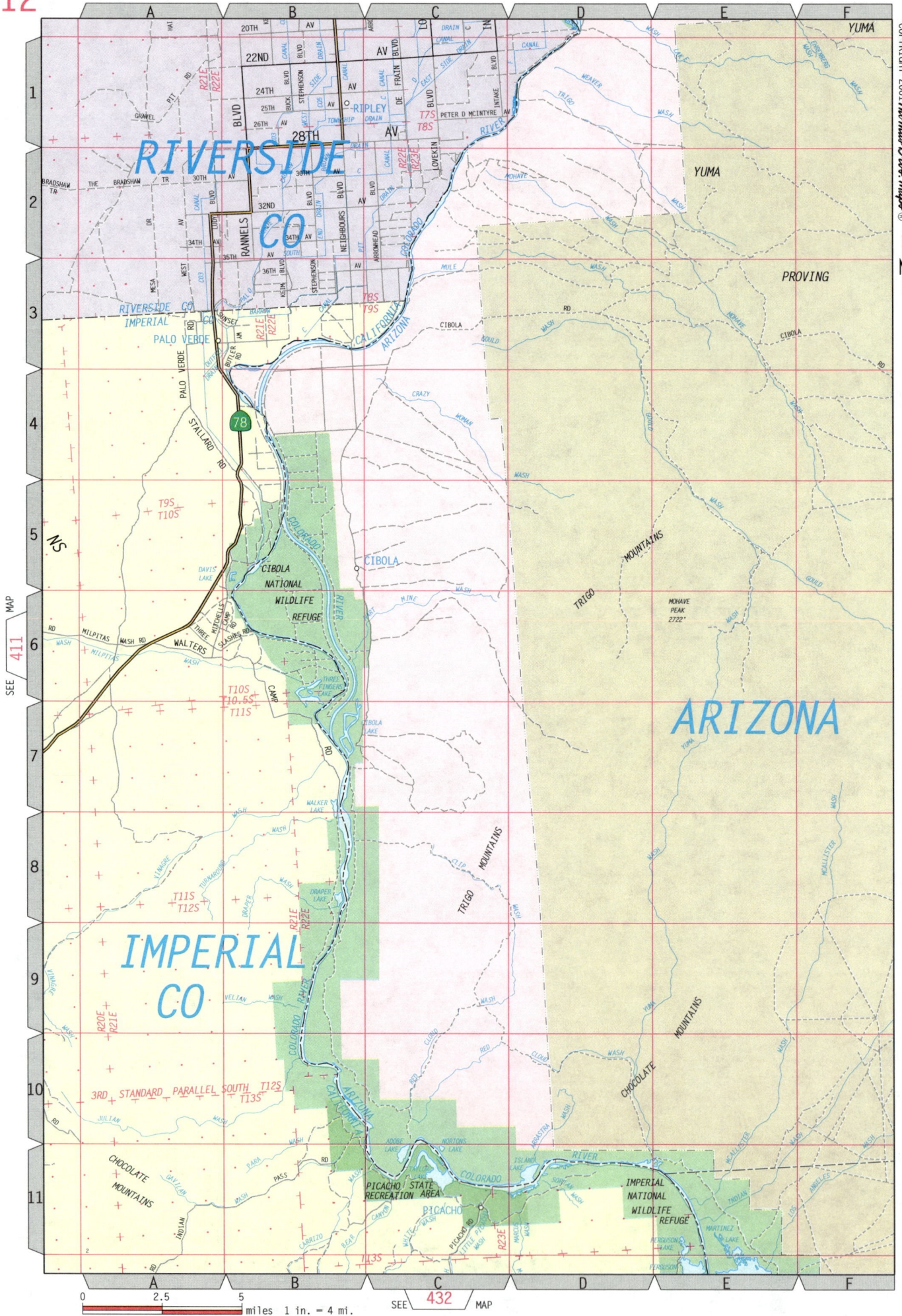

SAN DIEGO CO.

MAP

COPYRIGHT 2001 Thomas Bros. Maps ®

—N—

RIVERSIDE CO

YUMA

YUMA

PROVING

ARIZONA

CALIFORNIA

CIBOLA

CIBOLA

CIBOLA NATIONAL WILDLIFE REFUGE

COLORADO RIVER

TRIGO MOUNTAINS

MOHAVE PEAK 2722'

ARIZONA

IMPERIAL CO

3RD STANDARD PARALLEL SOUTH

CHOCOLATE MOUNTAINS

CHOCOLATE MOUNTAINS

TRIGO MOUNTAINS

CLIP MOUNTAINS

PICACHO STATE RECREATION AREA

PICACHO

COLORADO RIVER

IMPERIAL NATIONAL WILDLIFE REFUGE

RIPLEY

PALO VERDE

WALTERS

RIVERSIDE CO
IMPERIAL

DAVIS LAKE

CIBOLA LAKE

THREE FINGERS LAKE

WALKER LAKE

DRAPER LAKE

ADOBE LAKE

NORTONS LAKE

ISLAND LAKE

MARTINEZ LAKE

FERGUSON LAKE

78

STALLARD RD

PALO VERDE

MILPITAS WASH RD

T9S T10S

T10S T10.5S T11S

T11S T12S

T12S T13S

R20E R21E

R21E R22E

T7S T8S

T8S T9S

R21E R22E

R22E R23E

R23E

SEE 411 MAP

SEE 432 MAP

0   2.5   5   miles   1 in. = 4 mi.

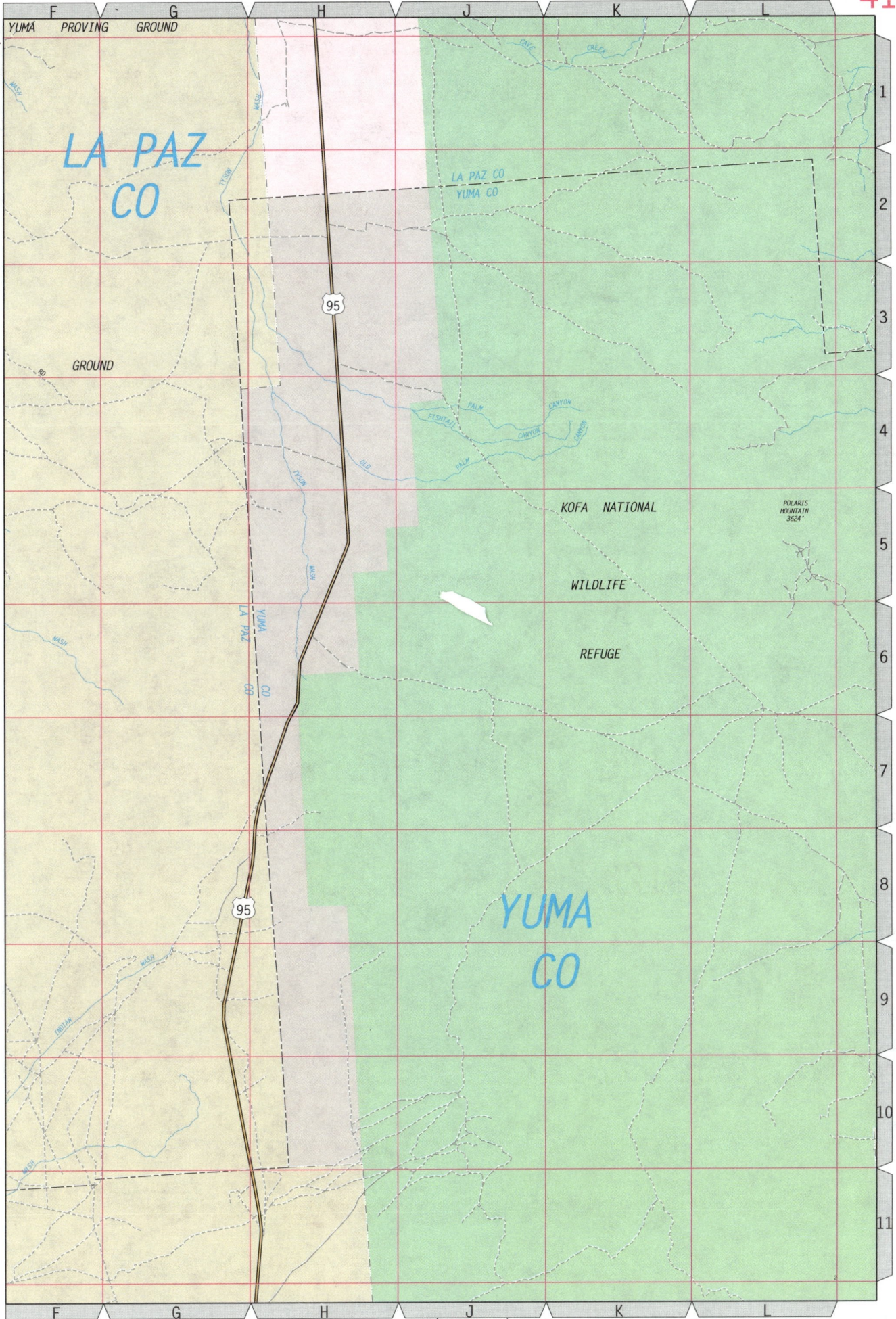

SAN DIEGO CO.

MAP

YUMA PROVING GROUND

LA PAZ CO

GROUND

LA PAZ CO
YUMA CO

95

FISHTAIL PALM CANYON
CANYON
CANYON

KOFA NATIONAL

POLARIS MOUNTAIN 3624'

WILDLIFE

REFUGE

WASH

95

YUMA CO
LA PAZ CO

WASH

WASH

95

WASH

INDIAN

WASH

YUMA

CO

CAVE CREEK

SEE 432 MAP

0   2.5   5   miles   1 in. = 4 mi.

429

SAN DIEGO CO.

MAP

PACIFIC

OCEAN

Grid page numbers:

	A	B	C	D	E	F
1	1146	1147	1148	1149	1150	1151
2	1167	1168	1169	1170	1171	
3	1187	1188	1189	1190	1191	
4	1207	1208	1209	1210	1211	
5	1227	1228	1229	1230	1231	
6	1247	1248	1249	1250	1251	
7	1267	1268	1269	1270	1271	
8	1287	1288	1289	1290	1291	
9		1308	1309	1310	1311	
10			1329	1330	1331	
11			1349	1350	1351	

Place names:

CARLSBAD, SAN MARCOS, ESCONDIDO, LEUCADIA, ENCINITAS, OLIVENHAIN, RANCHO SANTA FE, CARDIFF-BY-THE-SEA, SOLANA BEACH, EDEN GARDENS, LOMAS SANTA FE, FAIRBANKS RANCH, RANCHO PENASQUITOS, RANCHO BERNARDO, LAKE HODGES, RANCHO SAN BERNARDO (SNOOK), TWIN PEAKS, POWAY, LAKE POWAY, DEL MAR, TORREY PINES, CARMEL VALLEY HEIGHTS, TED WILLIAMS FRWY, LOS PENASQUITOS CANYON PRESERVE, BLACK MOUNTAIN, SCRIPPS, GARDEN RD, TORREY PINES STATE RESERVE, SORRENTO VALLEY, MIRA MESA, SORRENTO MESA, MIRAMAR, MIRAMAR RESERVOIR, SCRIPPS MIRAMAR RANCH, UNITED STATES MARINE CORPS AIR STATION MIRAMAR, MISSION RANCHO SAN DIEGO, SANTEE, EAST ELLIOTT, SYCAMORE CANYON COUNTY OPEN SPACE PRESERVE, LA JOLLA, UNIVERSITY CITY, SOLEDAD, KEARNY MESA, TIERRASANTA, MISSION TRAILS REGIONAL PARK, PACIFIC BEACH, CLAIREMONT, LINDA VISTA, SERRA MESA, GRANTVILLE, DEL CERRO, LAKE MURRAY, FLETCHER HILLS, MISSION BAY, MISSION BEACH, BAY PARK, MISSION VALLEY, MISSION HILLS, TALMADGE, ROLANDO, LA MESA, MOUNT HELIX, OCEAN BEACH, MIDDLETOWN, BALBOA PARK, NORTH PARK, OAK PARK, LEMON GROVE, SPRING VALLEY, LA PRESA, GROSSMONT, SAN DIEGO, SAN DIEGO ZOO, SAN DIEGO INTERNATIONAL AIRPORT LINDBERGH FIELD, PT LOMA, NORTH ISLAND NAVAL AIR STATION, CORONADO, NATIONAL CITY, PARADISE HILLS, JAMACHA, SAN DIEGO BAY, CHULA VISTA, BONITA, OTAY LAKES, RANCHO LA NACION, CORONADO CAYS, IMPERIAL BEACH, NESTOR, PALM AV, OTAY MESA, SAN YSIDRO, TIJUANA RIVER NATIONAL ESTUARINE SANCTUARY, TIJUANA, AEROPUERTO DE TIJUANA

Scale:
0 2.5 5 miles 1 in. = 4 mi.

SAN DIEGO CO.

MAP

1151 1152 1153 1154 1155 1156

1171 1172 1173 1174 1175 1176

1191 1192 1192 1193 1194 1195 1196

1211 1212 1213 91901 91916 1216

1231 1232 1233 1234 1235 1236

1251 1252 1253 1254 1255 91901

1271 1272 1273 1274 1275 91906

1291 1292 1293 1294 1295 1296

1293 1294 1296

1311 1312 1313 1314 1315 1316

1331 1332 1333 91917 91980 91963

1351 1352 1353

1332

BAJA CALIFORNIA NORTE

SAN CANYON RD
SAN PASQUAL
VALLEY
RAMONA
JULIAN
SANTA TERESA
RANCHO BALLENA
BALLENA
PINE HILLS
KENTWOOD IN THE PINES
BANNER
ANZA-BORREGO DESERT STATE PARK
HARRISON PARK
MONTECITO RD
HIGHLAND
ROCK HAVEN
ROSEMONT
IRVING'S CREST
SHADY DELL
FERNBROOK
SAN VICENTE RESERVOIR
BARONA MESA
CLEVELAND NATIONAL FOREST
SAN DIEGO COUNTRY ESTATES
INAJA INDIAN RESERVATION
CUYAMACA
PALO PICACHO
CUYAMACA RESERVOIR
CUYAMACA RANCHO STATE PARK
GREEN VALLEY FALLS
BARONA RANCH INDIAN RESERVATION
CAPITAN GRANDE INDIAN RESERVATION
FOSTER
EUCALYPTUS HILLS
EL CAPITAN RESERVOIR
HULBURD GROVE
ECHO DELL
LAKESIDE
BLOSSOM VALLEY
LAKEVIEW
WINTER GARDENS
FLINN SPRINGS
JOHNSTOWN
VICTORIA
ALPINE
PALO VERDE
THE WILLOWS
SWEETWATER
VIEJAS
ESCONDIDO
JAPATUL VALLEY
DESCANSO JUNCTION
PINE VALLEY
GUATAY
OLD HIGHWAY 80
BOSTONIA
EL CAJON
GLENVIEW
HARBISON CANYON
ALPINE HEIGHTS
DEHESA
JAPATUL
LOVELAND RESERVOIR
HIDDEN GLEN
CLEVELAND NATIONAL FOREST
GROSSMONT
MOUNT HELIX
RANCHO SAN DIEGO
JAMACHA
COTTONWOOD
NORTH JAMUL
JAMUL
SKYLINE
BARRETT LAKE
MORENA VILLAGE
SWEETWATER RESERVOIR
INDIAN SPRINGS
RANCHO JAMUL
HONEY SPRINGS
ENGINEER SPRINGS
DULZURA
BARRETT LAKE
EAST LAKE CANYON
EASTLAKE GREENS
OTAY LAKES
UPPER OTAY RESERVOIR
LOWER OTAY RESERVOIR
RANCHO OTAY (ESTUDILLO)
CAMPO
BARRETT JUNCTION
POTRERO
TECATE
USA MEXICO
AEROPUERTO DE TIJUANA
ESA RD

SEE 430 MAP

0   2.5   5   miles   1 in. = 4 mi.

SAN DIEGO CO.

MAP

SEE 410 MAP

SEE 429 MAP

COPYRIGHT 2001 Thomas Bros. Maps ® —N—

ANZA-BORREGO DESERT STATE PARK

BANNER

92036

1158 **1138** 1159

RANCHOS

1177

92004

1176

1197

ZA-BORREGO DESERT STATE PARK

SUNRISE HWY

RANCHO CUYAMACA

GREAT SOUTHERN OVERLAND STAGE ROUTE OF 1849

OVERLAND
VALLECITO COUNTY PARK

AGUA CALIENTE HOT SPRINGS

AGUA CALIENTE COUNTY PARK

ANZA-BORREGO DESERT STATE PARK

PALO VERDE CANYON RD

SAN DIEGO CO

91948

CUYAMACA RANCHO STATE PARK

LAGUNA INDIAN RESERVATION

1217 **1218**

S1

HWY

92036

SWEENEY PASS RD

S2

T15S T16S

1216

1237

UATAY

OLD 80 HIGHWAY

91948

CUYAPAIPE INDIAN RESERVATION

MOUNT LAGUNA

91962

PINE VALLEY

91905

T16S T17S

BUCKMAN SPRINGS

CLEVELAND NATIONAL FOREST

BOULDER OAKS

LA POSTA INDIAN RESERVATION

8

S1

MORENA

1247

1298 1299 1300 1301 91934

LIVE OAK SPRINGS BOULEVARD

TULE LAKE

JACUMBA NATIONAL COOPERATIVE LAND & WILDLIFE MANAGEMENT AREA

MORENA VILLAGE

1296 **1298** CAMPO INDIAN RESERVATION MANZANITA **1300**

94

1317 1313 1319 1320 BANKHEAD SPRINGS 1321 JACUMBA

CAMERON CORNERS

TIERRA DEL SOL

CANYON CITY 91906

CAMPO

UNITED STATES
MEXICO

2

BAJA **CALIFORNIA**

0 2.5 5 miles 1 in. = 4 mi.

SAN DIEGO CO.

MAP

Thomas Bros. Maps®

COPYRIGHT 2001

N

F G H J K L

1 2 3 4 5 6 7 8 9 10 11

FISH

WASH

CARRIZO

DEEP WASH

R9E R10E
R10E R11E
R11E R12E
R12E R13E

T14S T13S

IMLER RD

92259

CARRIZO
IMPACT
AREA

US NAVAL
RESERVATION

(CLOSED TO PUBLIC)

ROCK CANYON
RED
WASH
CARRIZO WASH

WHEELER

DRY LAKE

T14S T15S

U S NAVAL
AIR FACILITY

FILLAREE DRAIN 4

PAYNE

BOLEY

ADAIR RD

HETZEL

HUFF

WORTHINGTON RD
MEALEY

IMLER RD
HUFF RD
JINLER RD
ERSKINE RD
THOMAS
PIERCE
THAREE
WHEELER RD
KUTZ
HOUSE
CANAL
FILLAREE
CANAL

IMPERIAL CO

SAN DIEGO CO
IMPERIAL CO

CREEK

T15S T16S

PLASTER CITY

HEWES

DIXIELAND

92251

S28

HAVENS

HUFF HWY

EL NAV AUX
AIR STA

SPELL
CANYON
PAINTED

COYOTE WASH

DUNAWAY RD

S80

92243

WESTMORELAND
KEY RD
HASKELL RD

IMPERIAL HWY

LAVA
BUTTE
DOS PALM

CABELA

OCOTILLO

S2

COYOTE WELLS

CLARK LN

EVAN

CANYON RD
MYER CREEK

8

R9.5E R9.5E
R9.5E R10E
R10E R11E
R10E R11E

JEFFREY
STEVENS
HARDY RD
CAMPBELL RD
DIEHL RD
WIXOM
LIEBERT
VOGEL RD

MAIN
CANAL

WESTSIDE RD

DIEHL

GRA

R12E
R13E

SEE 431 MAP

DEVILS

BOULDER CREEK

CK RD

PINTO CANYON

T17S T18S

R9E R10E

YUMA

ANZA TRAIL

COYOTE #1 RD

COYOTE #2 RD

T16S T16S
T16S T16.5S
T16.5S T17S

R10E R11E

WASH

98

R11E R12E

SIGNAL RD

UNITED STATES
MEXICO

NORTE

AGUA

GRANDE

2

LAGUNA
SALADA

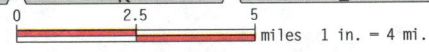

0   2.5   5   miles 1 in. = 4 mi.

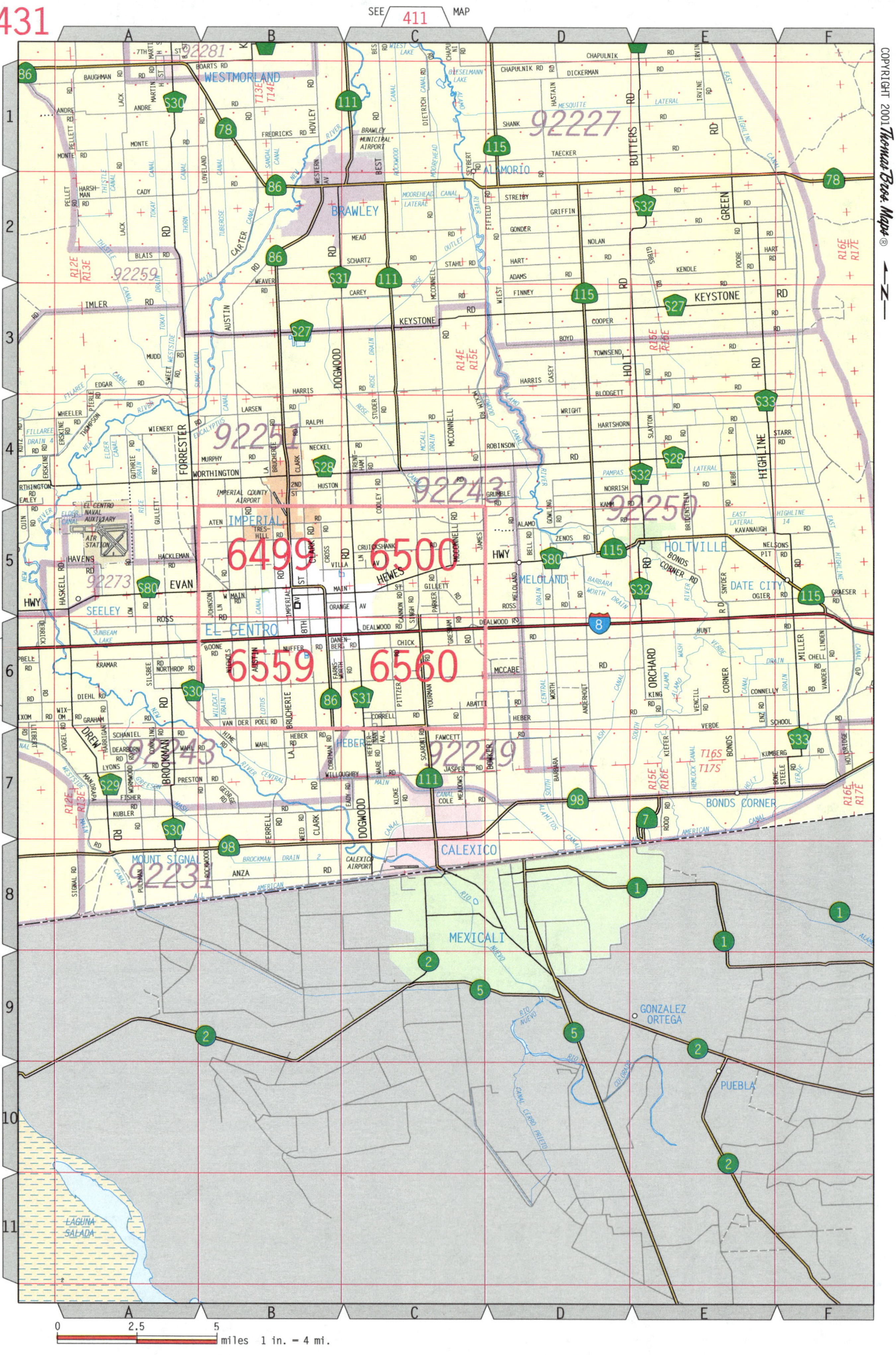

SAN DIEGO CO.

MAP

SEE 430 MAP

WESTMORLAND

BRAWLEY

Brawley Municipal Airport

92227

ALAMORIO

92259

92251

KEYSTONE

IMPERIAL

EL CENTRO NAVAL AUXILIARY AIR STATION

Imperial County Airport

92273

92243

92250

HOLTVILLE

DATE CITY

6499 6500

6559 6560

EL CENTRO

MELOLAND

HEBER

92249

BONDS CORNER

BROCKMAN

92231

Calexico Airport

CALEXICO

MEXICALI

GONZALEZ ORTEGA

PUEBLA

LAGUNA SALADA

miles 1 in. = 4 mi.

0   2.5   5

SAN DIEGO CO.

MAP

Thomas Bros. Maps®

COPYRIGHT 2001

F G H J K L

GLAMIS

TED KIPF RD

OGILBY

R17E R17.5E

R17.5E R18E

T13S T14S

MINE RD

VISTA

WALKER MT

R19E R20E

RD

INDIAN

PASS RD

S34

78

U S NAVAL RESERVATION

R16E R17E

GECKO

CANAL

RD

GECKO RD

R18E R19E

TED

KIPF

RD

GOLD ROCK RANCH RD

GOLD ROCK RD

OGILBY

T14S T15S

U S NAVAL RESERVATION

IMPERIAL

CO

U S NAVAL RESERVATION

IMPERIAL SAND DUNES REC AREA

AMERICAN

RD

TED KIPF

RD

S34

OGILBY RD

T15S T16S

COACHELLA CANAL

MASH

AMERICAN

SUR WASH

GRAESER RD

EAST HIGHLINE CANAL

R19E R20E

8

SEE 432 MAP

R17E R18E

EVAN

RD

HEMES

HWY

R18E R19E

R19E R20E

AMERICAN CANAL

ALL

8

DESERT RD

RD

MIDWAY WELL

EVAN

HEMES

HWY

GORDONS WELL

GRAYS WELL

98

ALL AMERICAN CANAL

IMPERIAL CO CALIFORNIA
BAJA CALIFORNIA NORTE

HOLTRIDGE

R16E R17E

UNITED STATES
MEXICO

15

CIUDAD MORELOS

PACHUCO

1

AIRPORT RODOLFO SANCHEZ T

ALAMO

CIUDAD VICTORIA

6

ALAMO

BENITO JUAREZ

2

2

QUERETARO

3

10

HERMOSILLO

1

CANAL ALIMENTADOR CENTRAL

CANAL

SONORA

BAJA SONORA

2

F G H J K L

0 2.5 5 miles 1 in. = 4 mi.

SEE 412 MAP

SAN DIEGO CO.

MAP

A   B   C   D   E   F

1
2
3
4
5
6
7
8
9
10
11

IMPERIAL CO

92283

FISHERS

Ferguson Lake
Martinez Lake
Imperial National Wildlife Refuge

Senator Wash Res

Imperial Reservoir

Imperial Dam
DAM

Mittry Lake Wildlife Area

COLORADO RIVER
GILA RIVER

T13S T14S
T13.5S T14S
T14S
T14S T15S
T14.5S T15S

R20E R21E
R21E R22E
R22E R23E
R23E R24E

Gold Rock Ranch Rd
Gold Rock Ranch Rd
OGILBY RD
Barney Oldfield Rd
Barney Oldfield Rd
Sidewinder Rd
Sidewinder Rd
OGILBY RD
KIPE RD

FORT YUMA INDIAN RESERVATION

PICACHO RD

MEHRING RD
COLLINS RD
BAILEY
HASBERG RD
LEATHER
NORDAHL
YORK RD
COLBY RD
PARKMAN
FLOOD RD
WHITMORE
BARD
ROSS
MIGUEL
PICACHO RD
BLACKWELL
INDIAN ROCK
WILSON
WILKINS
PEREZ
ARNOLD
QUICK RD
HORNE RD
ARNOLD
PASCUAL
COLEY

BARD

IMPERIAL DAM
S24

R22E

S34
S24

FELICITY

8 (I-8)

IMPERIAL SAND DUNES REC AREA

ANDRADE
186

WINTERHAVEN
8 (I-8)

UNITED STATES
MEXICO

VICENTE GUERRERO

BAJA CALIFORNIA NORTE

8

15

CIUDAD MORELOS
PACHUCO

2

GADSDEN

COLORADO RIVER

2

SAN LUIS

BAJA CALIF NORTE
SONORA

SAN LUIS RIO COLORADO

YUMA CO
SONORA
UNITED STATES
MEXICO

SONORA

40   41

YUMA

COLORADO RIVER

95

YUMA INTERNATIONAL AIRPORT

AVENUE A

SOMERTON
95

ARIZONA

8 (I-8)

0   2.5   5 miles   1 in. = 4 mi.

N

F G H J K L

KOFA NATIONAL WILDLIFE REFUGE

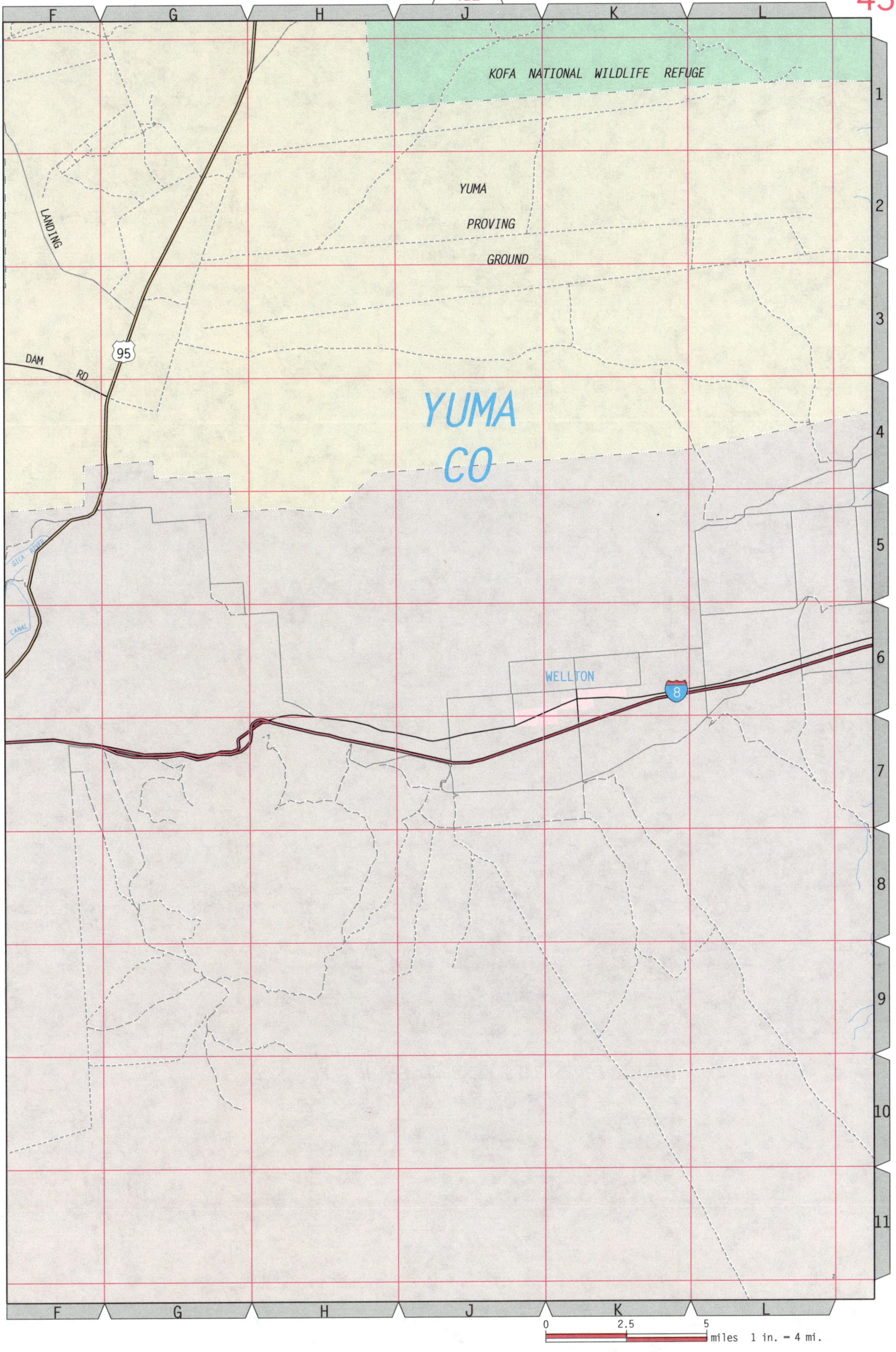

1

SAN DIEGO CO.

LANDING

YUMA

PROVING

2

GROUND

3

95

DAM RD

YUMA

CO

4

GILA RIVER

5

CANAL

WELLTON

8

6

MAP

7

8

9

10

11

F G H J K L

0   2.5   5

miles   1 in. = 4 mi.

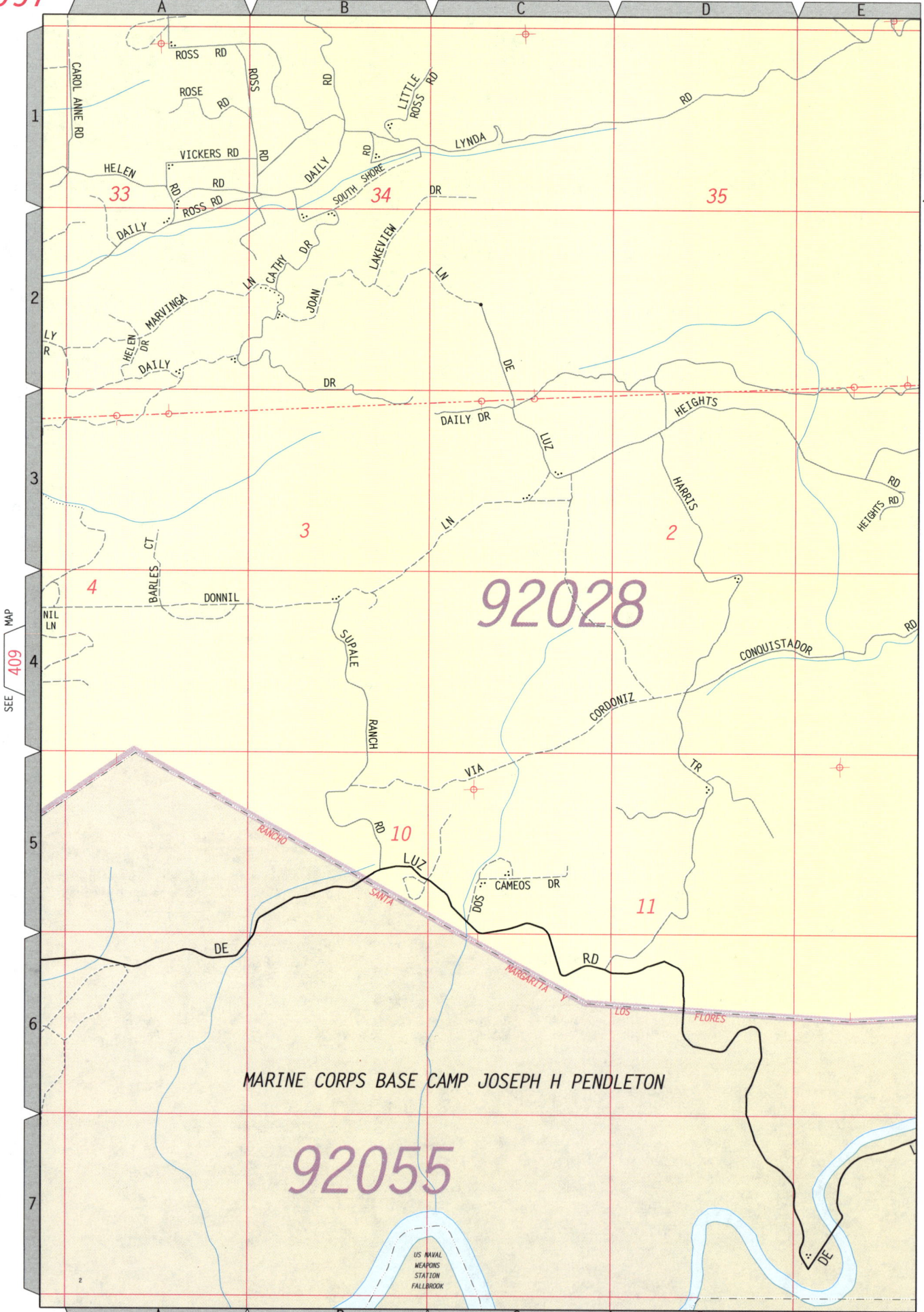

SAN DIEGO CO.

MAP

COPYRIGHT 2001 *Thomas Bros. Maps* ®   ←N—

A   B   C   D   E

ROSS RD

CAROL ANNE RD

ROSE RD

ROSS RD

LITTLE ROSS RD

RD

LYNDA RD

1

VICKERS RD

RD

DAILY

SOUTH SHORE

33   34   35

HELEN RD   ROSS RD

DAILY

CATHY DR

JOAN

LAKEVIEW LN

LN

DR

2

LY R

HELEN DR   MARVINGA

DAILY

DR

DE

DAILY DR

LUZ

HEIGHTS

3

BARLES CT

LN

HARRIS

HEIGHTS RD

RD

3   2

4   DONNIL

SUPALE

92028

CONQUISTADOR

RD

NIL LN

RANCH

CORDONIZ

TR

5

RANCHO

RD   10

LUZ

VIA

DOS

CAMEOS DR

11

SANTA

DE

RD

6

MARGARITA Y   LOS FLORES

MARINE CORPS BASE CAMP JOSEPH H PENDLETON

92055

7

US NAVAL WEAPONS STATION FALLBROOK

DE

A   B   C   D   E

0 .125 .25 .375 .5   miles 1 in. = 1900 ft.

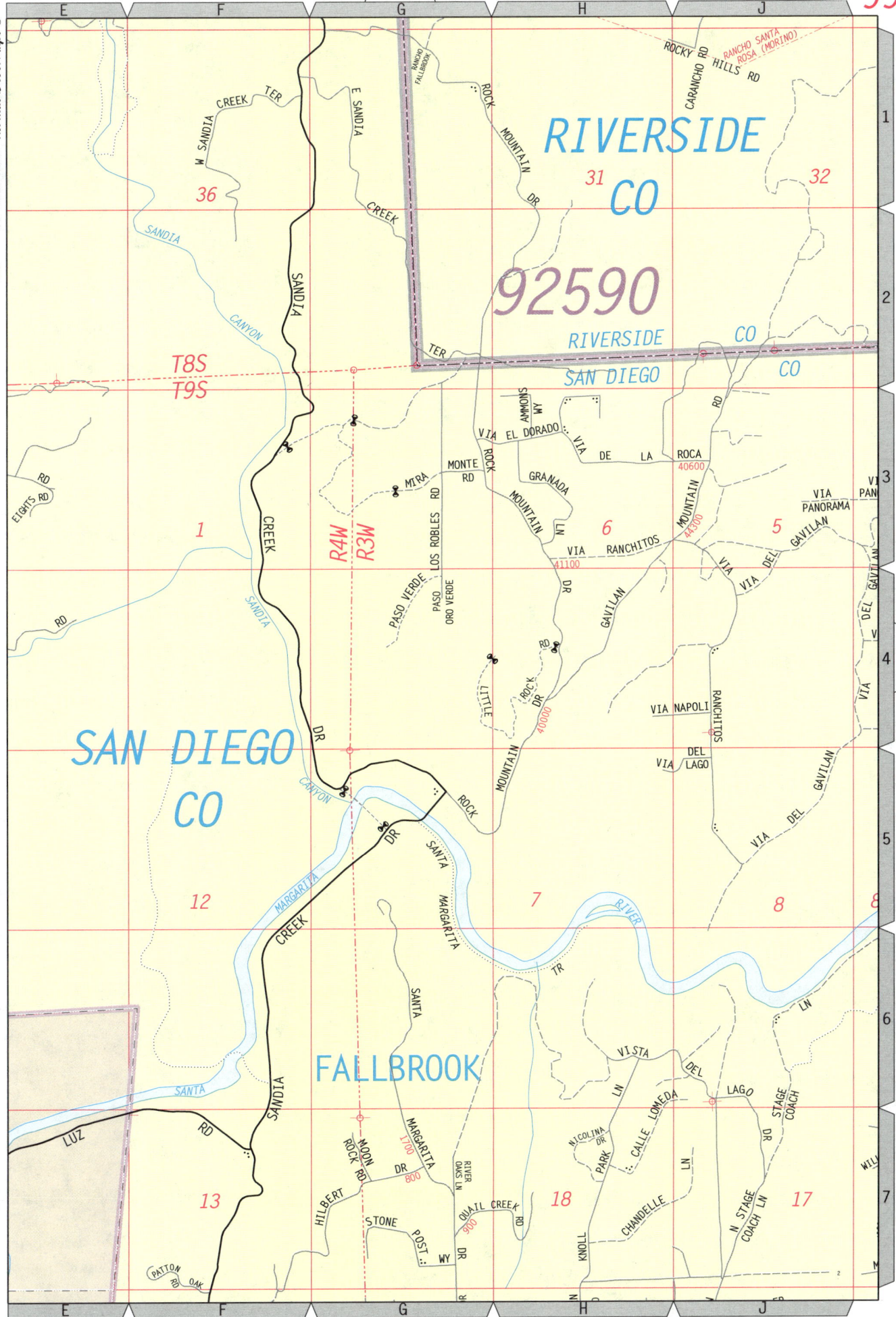

SEE RIV 977 MAP

E F G H J

W SANDIA CREEK TER

E SANDIA CREEK

ROCK MOUNTAIN DR

RIVERSIDE CO
31 32
1

92590

RIVERSIDE CO
SAN DIEGO CO
2

T8S
T9S

SANDIA CANYON

RANCHO FALLBROOK

VIA EL DORADO
AMMONS WY
VIA DE LA ROCA 40600
MONTE RD
MIRA
ROCK MOUNTAIN
GRANADA LN
VIA PANORAMA
VIA PAN

R4W R3W

PASO VERDE
PASO LOS ROBLES RD
ORO VERDE

VIA RANCHITOS 41100
6
MOUNTAIN 44300
5
VIA GAVILAN

1

SANDIA CREEK

GAVILAN DR
VIA DEL GAVILAN
3

LITTLE
ROCK DR 40000
MOUNTAIN
VIA NAPOLI
RANCHITOS
DEL LAGO
VIA DEL GAVILAN
4

SAN DIEGO CO
12

MARGARITA CANYON DR
SANTA MARGARITA

ROCK
7
RIVER
8 8
5

SANDIA CREEK

VISTA LN
DEL LAGO
STAGE COACH
6

FALLBROOK

SANTA

LUZ
SANTA
SANDIA RD
MOON ROCK RD DR
MARGARITA 1700 800
HILBERT
STONE POST WY
RIVER OAKS LN
QUAIL CREEK RD 900
NICOLINA DR
PARK
CALLE LOMEDA
CHANDELLE LN
KNOLL
N STAGE COACH LN
STAGE COACH DR
13 18 17
WIL
7

PATTON RD OAK

E F G H J

SEE 1027 MAP

0 .125 .25 .375 .5 miles 1 in. = 1900 ft.

SEE 998 MAP

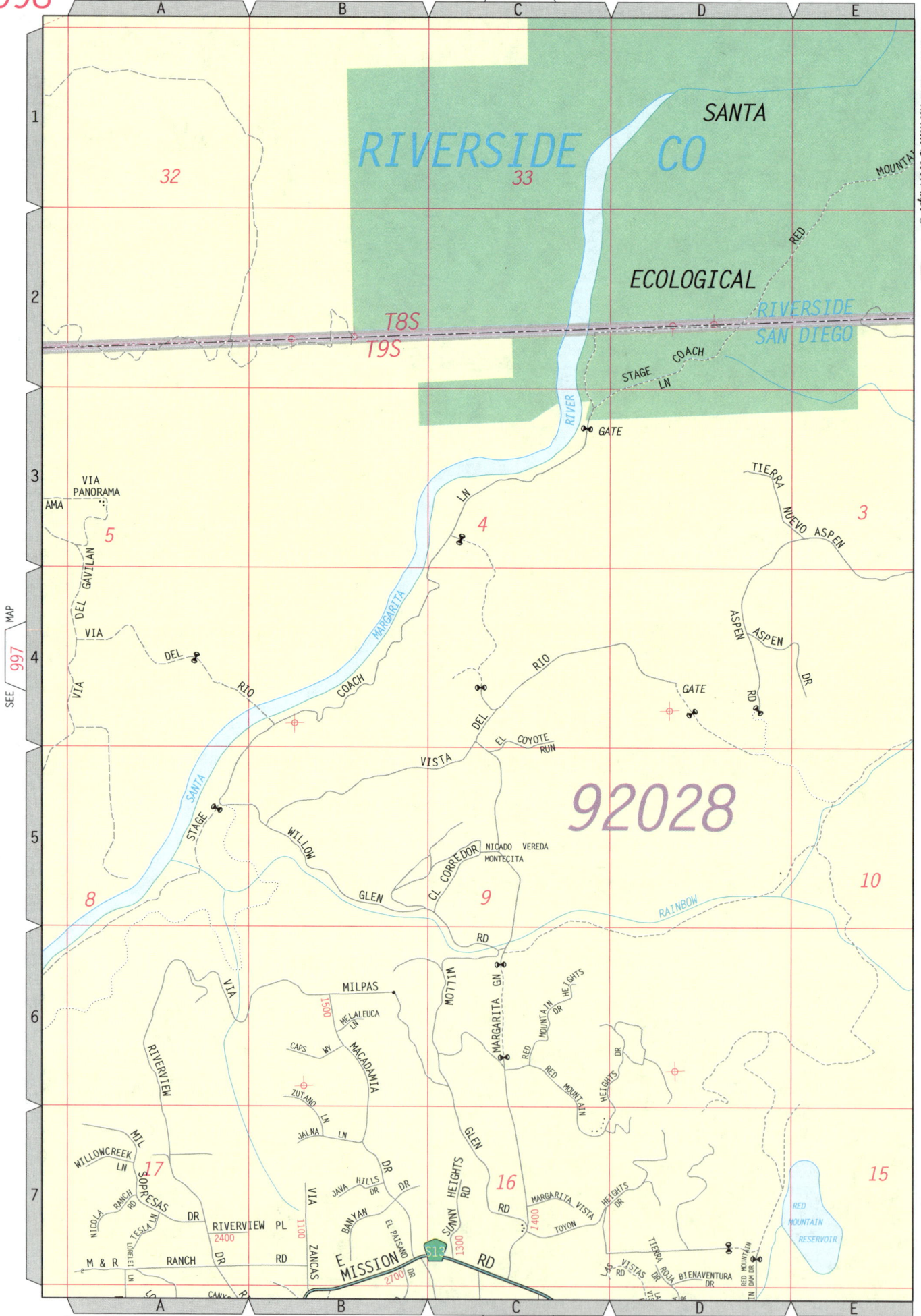

998

SEE RIV 978 MAP

A B C D E

SAN DIEGO CO.

COPYRIGHT 2001 Thomas Bros. Maps ® ←N→

1

RIVERSIDE CO

SANTA

32

33

MOUNTA

RED

2

ECOLOGICAL

T8S
T9S

RIVERSIDE
SAN DIEGO

STAGE COACH LN

VIA PANORAMA

AMA

RIVER

GATE

3

LN

TIERRA NUEVO ASPEN

3

5

DEL GAVILAN

VIA

4

MARGARITA

RIO

COACH

RIO

GATE

ASPEN ASPEN DR

RD

VIA DEL

MAP

SEE 997

VIA

4

DEL

EL COYOTE RUN

VISTA

92028

5

STAGE

SANTA

WILLOW

GLEN

CL CORREDOR NICADO VEREDA
MONTECITA

9

RD

RAINBOW

10

MAP

8

MILPAS

MELALEUCA LN

WILLOW

MARGARITA GN

RED MOUNTAIN HEIGHTS

RED MOUNTAIN

HEIGHTS DR

6

1500

CAPS WY

MACADAMIA

ZUTANO LN

JALNA LN

RIVERVIEW

MIL

WILLOWCREEK LN

SOPRESAS

NICOLA RANCH RD

LOBELEI LN

TESLA

DR

17

RIVERVIEW PL
2400

VIA ZANCAS

BANYAN

JAVA HILLS DR

EL PAISANO DR

DR

SUNNY HEIGHTS RD

GLEN

16

RD

1400

MARGARITA VISTA

TOYON

HEIGHTS DR

TIERRA ROJA RD

LAS VISTAS RD

BIENAVENTURA DR

RED MOUNTAIN DAM RD

RED MOUNTAIN RESERVOIR

15

7

1100

M & R RANCH

RANCH DR

LO CANY R

MISSION RD
2700

1300

SEE 1028 MAP

0 .125 .25 .375 .5
miles 1 in. = 1900 ft.

Thomas Bros. Maps®

COPYRIGHT 2001

—N—

SEE **RIV 978** MAP

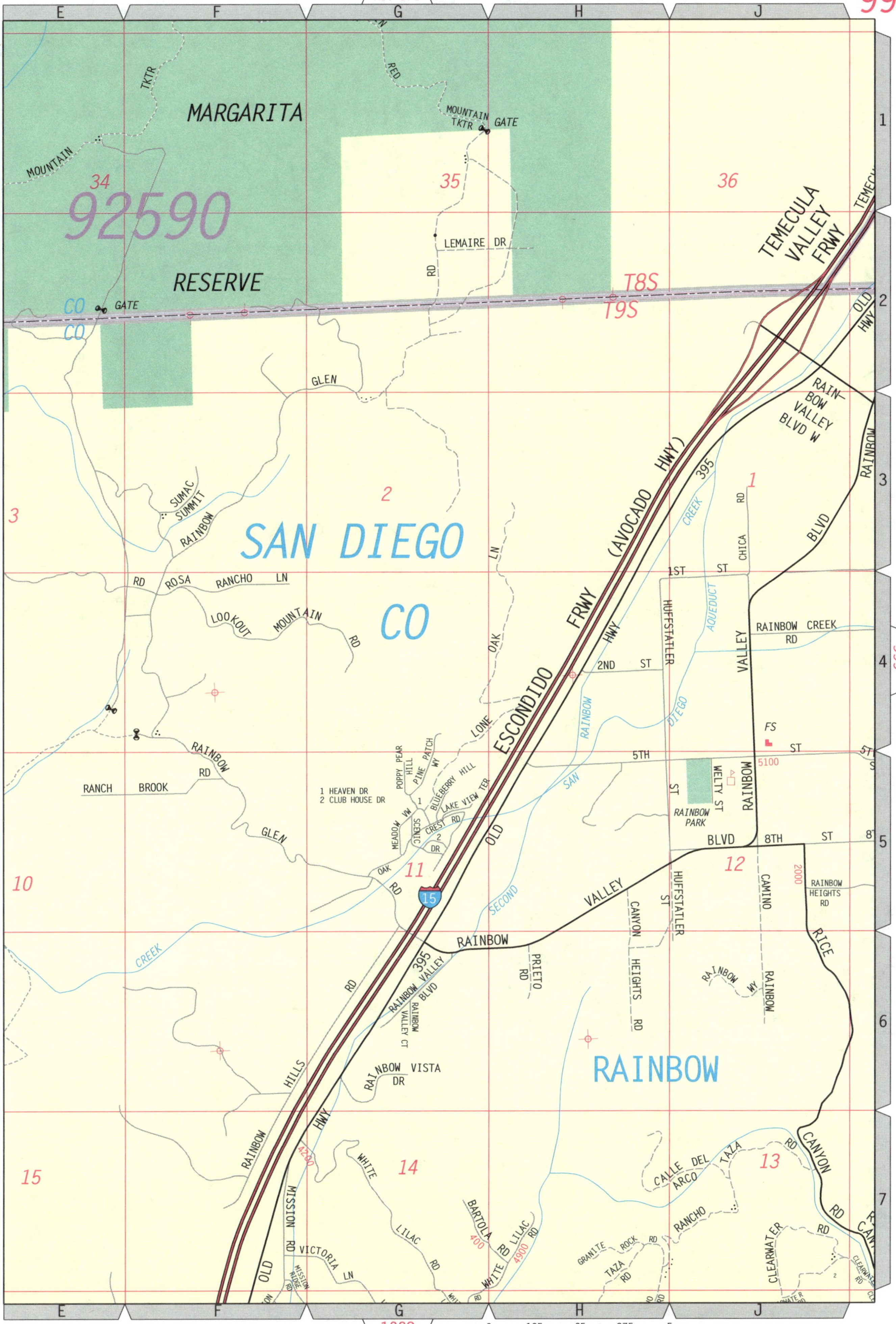

998

SAN DIEGO CO.

E   F   G   H   J

MOUNTAIN TKTR

MARGARITA

MOUNTAIN

34
92590

RED RD

35

MOUNTAIN TKTR GATE

LEMAIRE DR

36

TEMECULA VALLEY FRWY

TEMECH

1

RESERVE

CO GATE
CO
CO

T8S
T9S

RAIN-
BOW
VALLEY
BLVD W

OLD HWY

2

GLEN

SUMAC SUMMIT

RAINBOW

2

SAN DIEGO

CO

LN

OAK LN

ESCONDIDO FRWY (AVOCADO HWY)

395 HWY

CREEK

RD

CHICA

1

BLVD

RAINBOW

3

3

RD ROSA RANCHO LN

LOOKOUT MOUNTAIN RD

1ST ST

HUFFSTATLER

AQUEDUCT

VALLEY

RAINBOW CREEK RD

SEE **999** MAP

4

2ND ST

DIEGO

FS

5100

5TH

RAINBOW

RANCH BROOK RD

GLEN

RAINBOW

POPPY VW
PINE
PEAR HILL
PATCH WY
BLUEBERRY HILL
LAKE VIEW TER
CREST RD
SCENIC DR
MEADOW VW
2
1
1 HEAVEN DR
2 CLUB HOUSE DR

LONE

5TH

RAINBOW

SAN

ST

WELTY ST

ST

RAINBOW PARK

4

5

10

OAK RD

11

15

SECOND

395

RAINBOW VALLEY BLVD

RAINBOW

VALLEY

PRIETO RD

CANYON HEIGHTS ST

HUFFSTATLER

BLVD

12

8TH ST

CAMINO

2000

RAINBOW HEIGHTS RD

RICE

5

6

RAINBOW VALLEY CT

RAINBOW VISTA DR

CANYON HEIGHTS RD

RAINBOW WY

RAINBOW

RAINBOW

6

15

RAINBOW HILLS HWY

MISSION RD

4280

WHITE

14

LILAC RD

BARTOLA RD
400
WHITE LILAC RD
4900

CALLE DEL ARCO
TAZA

RANCHO

GRANITE ROCK
TAZA RD

13

CLEARWATER RD

CANYON RD

CANY

7

OLD
VICTORIA LN
MISSION WILDER RD

LILAC RD

RD

E   F   G   H   J

SEE **1028** MAP

0   .125   .25   .375   .5
miles 1 in. = 1900 ft.

MAP

999

| A | B | C | D | E |

SAN DIEGO CO.

MAP

COPYRIGHT 2001 Thomas Bros. Maps ® —N—

92592
RIVERSIDE CO

31   32

1

36

TEMECULA VALLEY FRWY
(AVOCADO HWY)
RAINBOW CANYON RD
FRONTAGE RD
47200
15
OLD HWY 395
SECOND SAN DIEGO AQUEDUCT

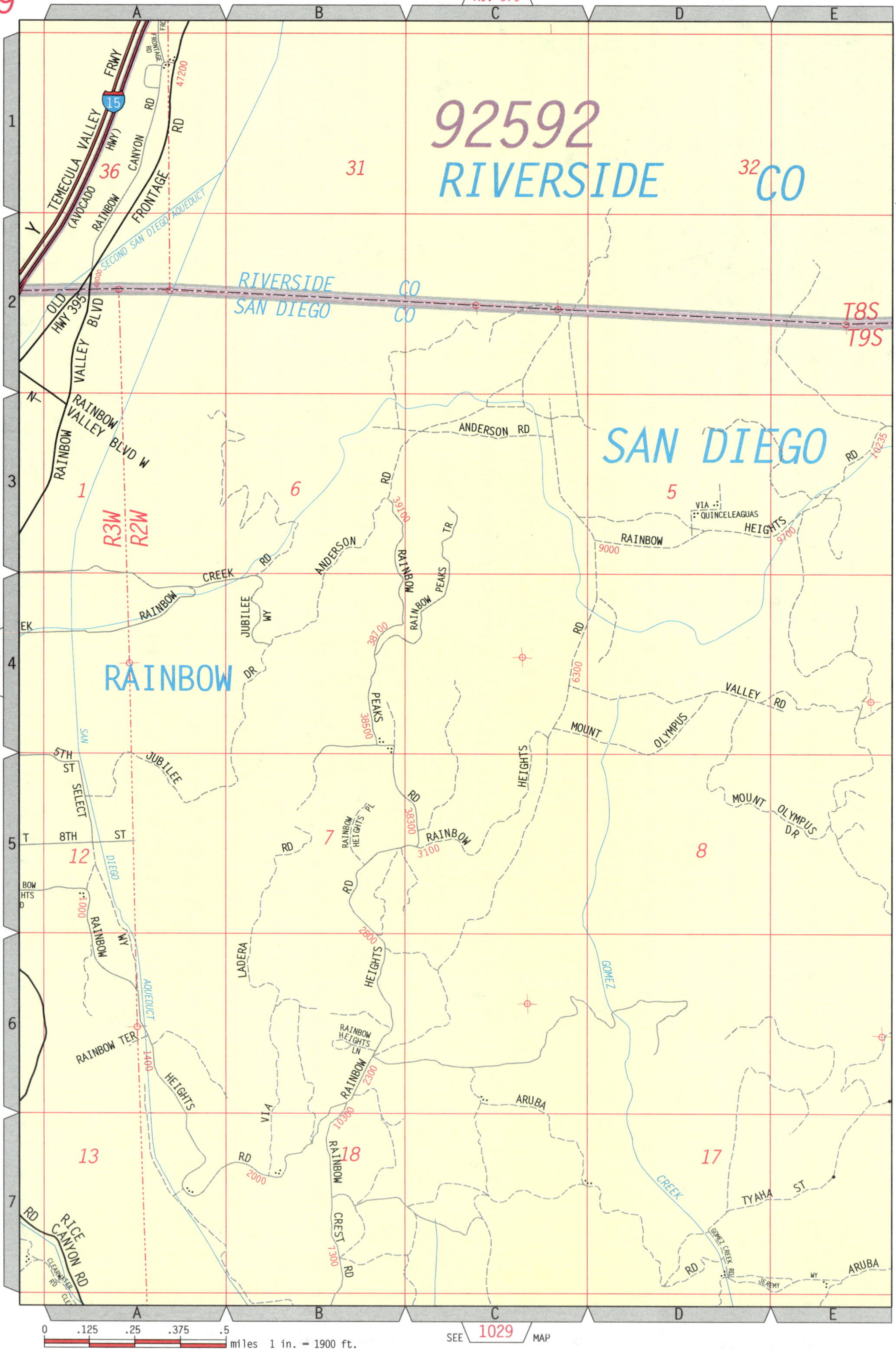

RIVERSIDE CO
SAN DIEGO CO

2

T8S
T9S

RAINBOW VALLEY BLVD
RAINBOW VALLEY BLVD W

ANDERSON RD

SAN DIEGO

3

1   6   5

R3W R2W

VIA QUINCELEAGUAS
RAINBOW HEIGHTS
9000   9200

ANDERSON RD
39100
RAINBOW PEAKS TR
RAINBOW CREEK RD

JUBILEE WY
38100
PEAKS
38600

RD
6300

VALLEY RD
10235

RAINBOW

4

JUBILEE DR

MOUNT OLYMPUS HEIGHTS

MOUNT OLYMPUS DR

5TH ST
SELECT
8TH ST

7   8
RAINBOW HEIGHTS PL
RD
38300
RAINBOW 3100

5

12

SAN DIEGO AQUEDUCT
RAINBOW WY

BOW HTS D
000

RD
LADERA
HEIGHTS RD
2800

6

RAINBOW TER
1400
HEIGHTS

RAINBOW HEIGHTS LN
2300

VIA
RD 2000

RAINBOW 10300

ARUBA
GOMEZ CREEK

17

13   18

RICE CANYON RD
CLEARWATER
RAINBOW CREST RD
7300

TYAHA ST
GOMEZ CREEK RD
RD
JEREMY WY   ARUBA

7

0 .125 .25 .375 .5 miles 1 in. = 1900 ft.

SEE 998 MAP

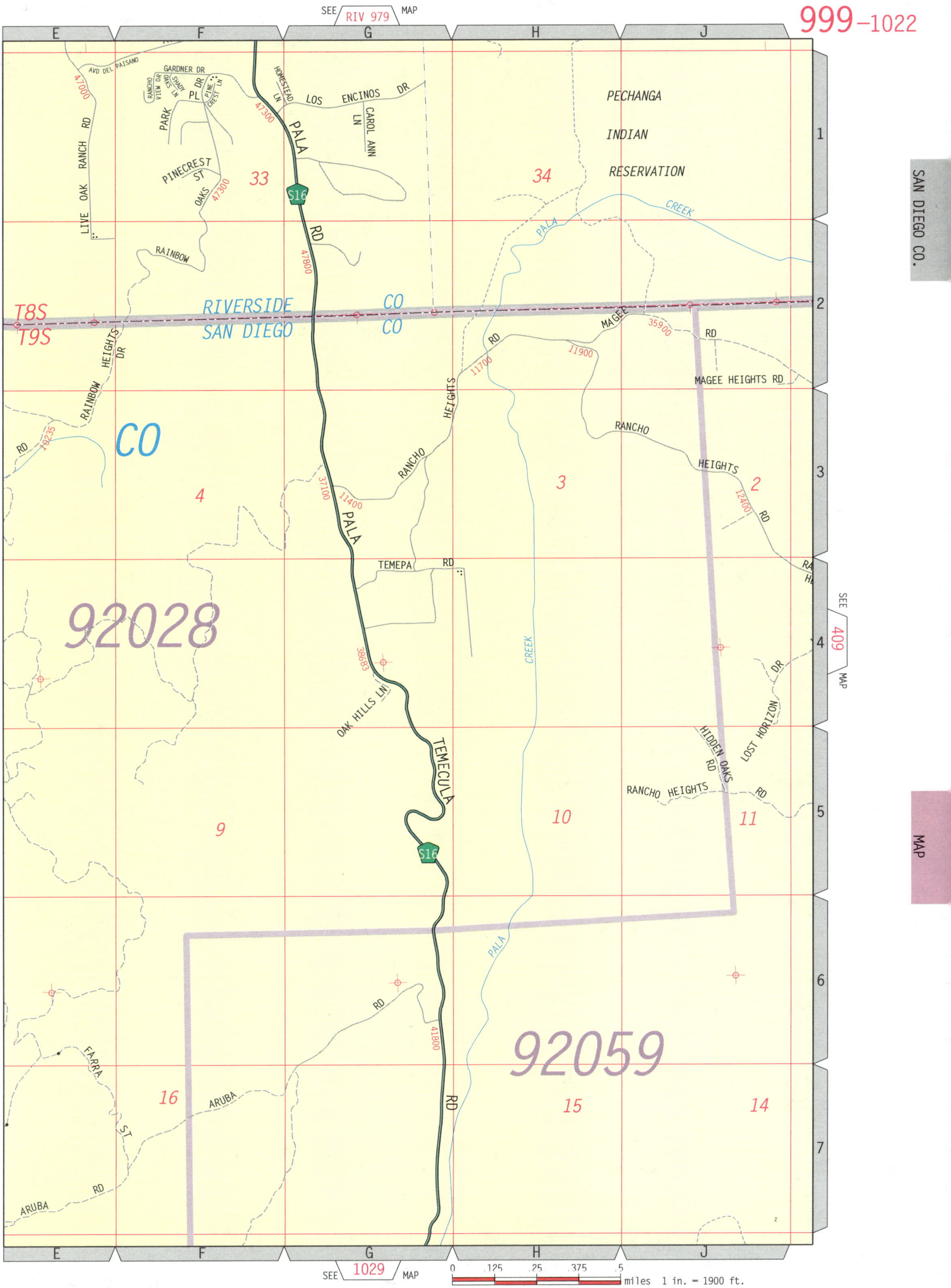

SAN DIEGO CO.

E   F   G   H   J

PECHANGA

INDIAN

RESERVATION

AVD DEL PAISANO

GARDNER DR

RANCHO VIEW DR
SHADY LN
PINE CREST LN

PARK
PL

PINECREST ST

OAKS

47300

33

LIVE OAK RANCH RD

47000

RAINBOW

HOMESTEAD LN
47300

LOS ENCINOS DR

CAROL ANN LN

PALA

S16

47800

RD

34

PALA

CREEK

1

RIVERSIDE CO CO
SAN DIEGO CO CO

T8S
T9S

2

RAINBOW HEIGHTS DR

RD

19235

CO

RAINBOW

HEIGHTS RD

RANCHO HEIGHTS

11700

RD

MAGEE

11900

35900

RD

MAGEE HEIGHTS RD

RANCHO HEIGHTS RD

12400

3

2

92028

4

37100

11400

PALA

TEMEPA RD

3

CREEK

SEE 409 MAP

4

38685

OAK HILLS LN

TEMECULA

HIDDEN OAKS RD

LOST HORIZON DR

RANCHO HEIGHTS RD

RD

9

S16

10

11

5

PALA

CREEK

92059

6

FARRA

ST

16

ARUBA

RD

41800

RD

15

14

7

ARUBA RD

0   .125   .25   .375   .5

miles   1 in. = 1900 ft.

MAP

SAN DIEGO CO.

SEE ORG 993 MAP

SAN CLEMENTE STATE BEACH

SAN CLEMENTE

10

92672

FOOTHILL TRANSPORTATION CORR (EST. COMP. 2003)

SAN ONOFRE STATE BEACH

CRISTIANITOS RD

RANCHO SANTA MARGARITA Y LAS FLORES

EL CAMINO REAL

METROLINK

RR

ORANGE CO
SAN DIEGO CO

15

SAN MATEO POINT

SAN ONOFRE STATE BEACH

SDNR
METROLINK

GATE
GATE

OLD
SAN
HWY

BASILONE

BEACH CLUB RD

BEACH

CHAISSON
SHAPLEY WY
RUPERTUS DR
PATE
PRICE SCHEYER W.
SMITH LN
FEGAN DR
ROCKEY
WIDDECKE LN
RD
PECK
WALKER LN
SELDEN LN
SCHMIDT CT WY
PEPPER LN
SCHMIDT DR
PULLER
DR
HOWARD LN
TORREY LN
PL
ANGLIM CT
EL

PACIFIC

MAP 408 SEE

MAP

SEE 408 MAP

0 .125 .25 .375 .5
miles 1 in. = 1900 ft.

COPYRIGHT 2001 Thomas Bros. Maps®

← N

SAN DIEGO CO.

MAP

SAN ONOFRE

SAN DIEGO CO

HOWARD LN
TORREY LN
PULLER DR
ERSKINE
PL
LN
DR

GARZA
MCKENZIE ST
DE LA
ANDERSON ST
MORGAN ST
ALBATROSS DR
SANDPIPER RD CARDINAL
MEADOWLARK
LONGSPUR DR
ANGLIN CT
LUB

SAN DIEGO RD

WY
AV
DR

CREEK

SAN ONOFRE CREEK

SAN ONOFRE

BASILONE RD

SAN

SAN ONOFRE

MARINE CORPS BASE

CAMP JOSEPH H PENDLETON

92055

EL CAMINO DIEGO 101

BEACH
CLUB
GATE RD
SAN ONOFRE STATE BEACH
GATE

REAL

FRWY

GATE

GATE
SAN ONOFRE NUCLEAR POWER PLANT

OLD
GATE

EL

5

CAMINO

HWY

SAN ONOFRE STATE BEACH
GATE

REAL

101

OCEAN

SEE 408 MAP

0 .125 .25 .375 .5
miles 1 in. = 1900 ft.

2

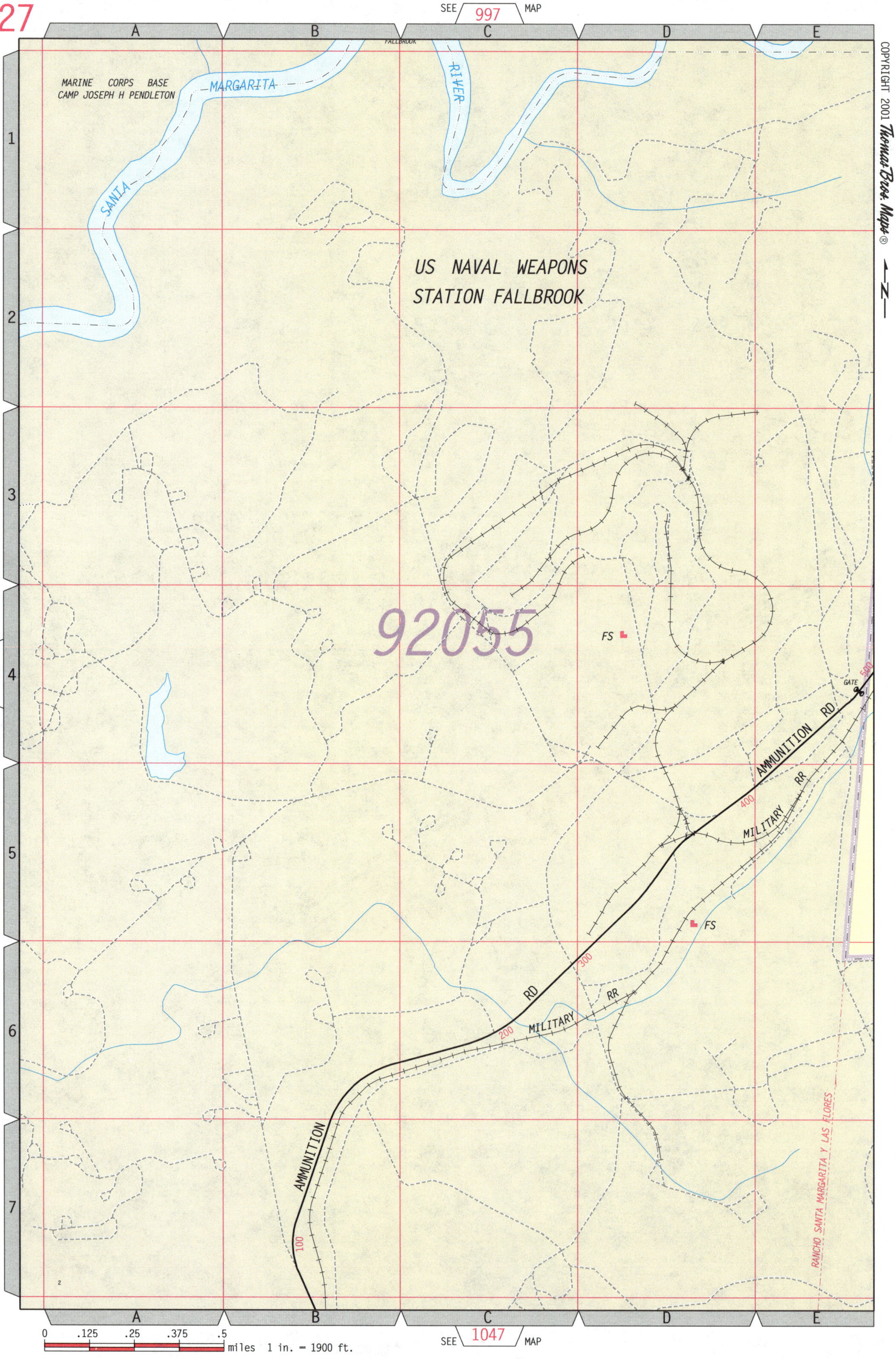

SAN DIEGO CO.

MAP

SEE **997** MAP

A B C D E

MARINE CORPS BASE
CAMP JOSEPH H PENDLETON

SANTA MARGARITA

FALLBROOK

RIVER

1

2

US NAVAL WEAPONS
STATION FALLBROOK

SEE **409** MAP

3

92055

FS

4

GATE

AMMUNITION RD

MILITARY RR

500

5

FS

400

RD

300

200

MILITARY

RR

6

AMMUNITION

100

RANCHO SANTA MARGARITA Y LAS FLORES

7

2

A B C D E

SEE **1047** MAP

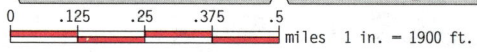

0 .125 .25 .375 .5
miles 1 in. = 1900 ft.

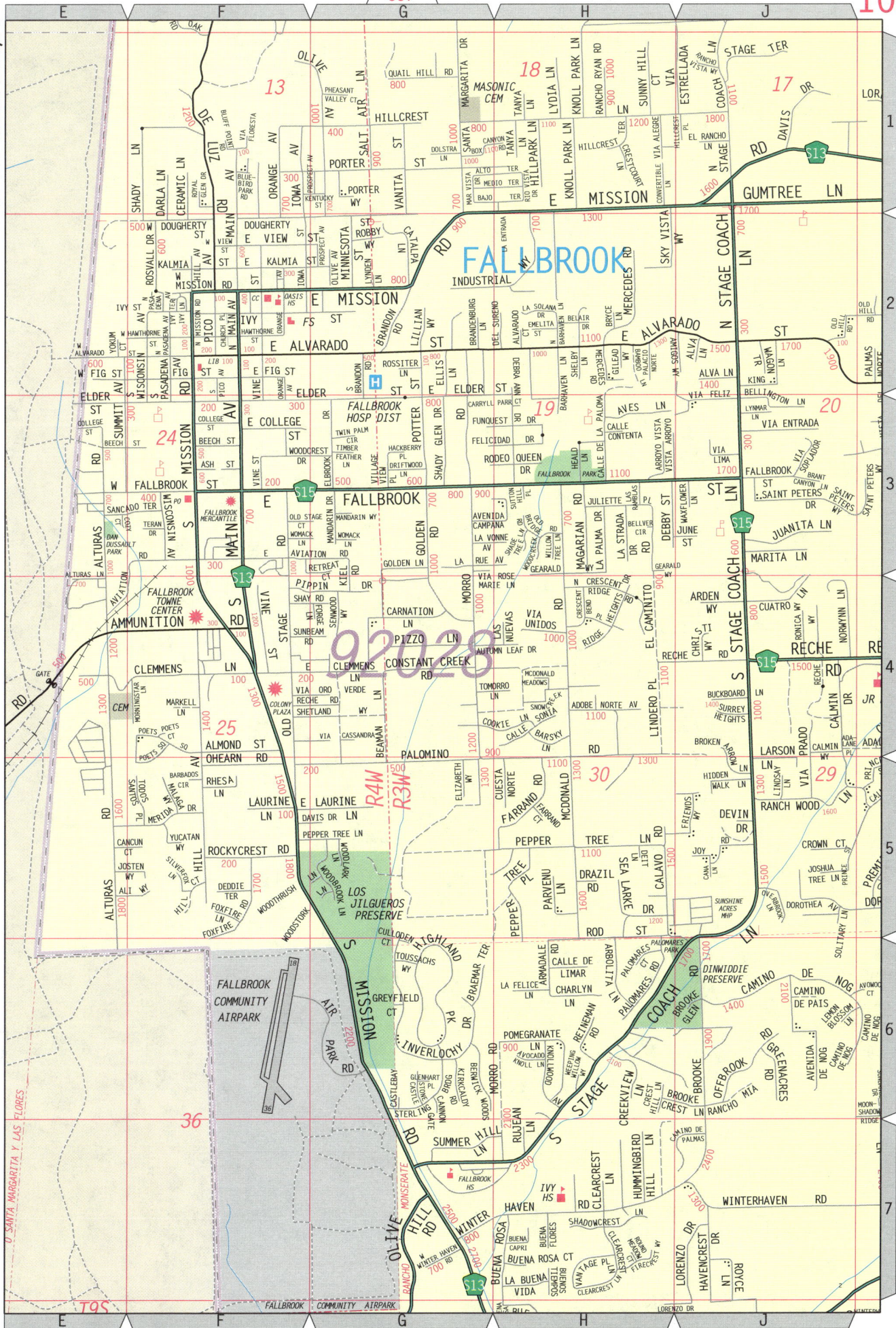

SAN DIEGO CO.

MAP

Thomas Bros. Maps®
COPYRIGHT 2001
—N→

FALLBROOK

92028

FALLBROOK COMMUNITY AIRPARK

LOS JILGUEROS PRESERVE

FALLBROOK TOWNE CENTER

MASONIC CEM

FALLBROOK HOSP DIST

DINWIDDIE PRESERVE

PALOMARES PARK

DAN DUSSAULT PARK

13   18   17

24   19   20

25   30   29

36

MISSION RD
DE LUZ RD
STAGE COACH LN
GUMTREE LN
RECHE RD
OLIVE HILL RD
WINTER HAVEN RD
WINTERHAVEN RD
ALTURAS

0   .125   .25   .375   .5   miles   1 in. = 1900 ft.

SAN DIEGO CO.

MAP

SEE 998 MAP

COPYRIGHT 2001 Thomas Bros. Maps® —N—

FALLBROOK

92028

LIVE OAK PARK

RED MOUNTAIN LN

MISSION RD

A B C D E

1

LORELEI 2000
LORENE LN
FALLEN LEAF LN
E MISSION
HAMILTON LN
JERICHO DR
GUMTREE
RIVERVIEW RD
CANYON VISTA DR 900
EL PALISO DR
EL CERISE
COLINA CREEK TR
YESTERYEAR LN
EL PAISANO DR
CAPRA
VALENTINE 1200 LN
S13
LEON WY
PARK
RED MOUNTAIN DAM DR
TIERRA DR
YERBA BUENA DR
MISSION
ROSA WY 300 3600
YUCCA
RANGER
FS
15

2

FROLIC WY
N FROLIC WY
ORVIL WY
HARRIS DR
PALMAS NORTE
OLD HILL RD
HILL 100
VISTA DEL INDIO
EMILIA
DEL SOL
N CASITAS
VIA D CASA 200
ALVARADO ST 2100
LIVE
OAK
N RIDGE DR
WHITE
FOX RUN
RIDGE CT PL
21
DR
RIDGE DIP WY
DR
SOL 3300
SHEILA LN 400
YUCCA WY
LOS HERMANOS RD
GRAND VISTA LN 600
HAWKS VIEW WY 700
22

3

SAINT PETERS WY
SAINT PETERS
TUDOR LN
BEAVERCREEK LN
TUMBLE CREEK
TUMBLE CREEK TER
TUMBLE CREEK LN 600
CORNER CREEK LN
S LIVE OAK
AUDREY CT
S EMILIA LN
VIA D AMO
LOS 400
HOBBIT LN
CERRITOS LN
VIA
VIA LOS
CUMBRES
VIA CUMBRES LN
HEYNEMAN HOLLOW 900
LOS ALISOS
ARROYO PACIFICA
CAMINO ALISOS
AVENIDA DE LA MADRE
SIERRA BONITA
YUCCA TER
YUCCA RD
VIA ZARA CT
VIA ZARA
DR

4

NORWYNN LN
HILE DALLAS RD
S DALLAS RD
PASEO DEL ARROYO
PASEO DE LOS ARBOLES
JR HS
CHAPULIN LN 1800
ADALANE PL
LOS CONEJOS
LOS AMIGOS
VIA DEL ORO
VIA DE MARANATHA
GREEN CANYON NORTE
SUMMER BLOOM LN
SPRING FLOWER DR
RECHE
S15
PARK RD 2100
RD 2500
LOS 2700
LOS ALISOS S
MARIANNE
VISTA 1500
LIVE OAK COUNTY PARK
BROOKE HOLLOW
KENDI LN
BROOKE HOLLOW RD
TRELAWNEY LN
SCOOTER LN 1700
COLINA VISTA 3300
CAMINO ZARA
CALLE TECOLOTLAN
VIA ZARA
27
28
CHAPARRAL
S15

5

PRINCE ST
CALMIN DR
DICKEY ST
PREMIER ST
FUERTE ST
COYOTE CREST
DOROTHEA AV
CALMIN
CANYON
GREEN BRIAR CIR 1700
GREEN CANYON LN 1600
GREEN BRIAR LN
GREEN BRIAR DR
VIA GIANNITURCO 2700
CARRIAGE LN
LIVE OAK COUNTY PARK VIA 1700
RECHE 2900
RABBIT HILL 1700
CANONITA

6

SOLITARY LN
NOG
AVOWOOD CT
N OSSUM
CAMINO DE NOG
NINO DE NOG
FUERTE
CAROLTON LN
SLOAN DR
TOURMALINE LN
MARDAVIDO PL 2400
MARDAVIDO LN
CAMINO VERDE
BLUEBELL LN
GIRD
DEL
VIA
ROBLES 2800
RD
NUESTRA LN
CANONITA LN
COUNTRY CLUB LN
CIELO DR
COUNTRY RD
GATE
DEL

7

SUNNYCREST LN 2400
WINTERHAVEN RD 1900
GREEN VISTA LN DR
EASTOM WY
QUIET RANCH RD
WESTVIEW RD
WESTVIEW CT
MOON SHADOW RIDGE
ALTA VISTA LN 2200
GREEN
GATE
VIA DEL ROBLES 2500
WINTERHAVEN LN
GRACEY LN
VIA DEL AGUACATE
VIA LA ORILLA RD
WINTER GREEN LN
WELDON WY
PALO VISTA RD
VALERIE
VIA DEL VERDE
KYNAR RIDGE DR
FALLBROOK GOLF CLUB
CANONITA
COUNTRY CLUB LN
LOS SICOMOROS LN 2600
CASABLANCA LN
SUGARPINE LN
SECRET LN
VIA OESTE
RANCHEROS 2300
VIA ARROYO 2100
WINTERHAVEN CT 2600
WINTERWARM
JACKSON DR

0 .125 .25 .375 .5 miles   1 in. = 1900 ft.

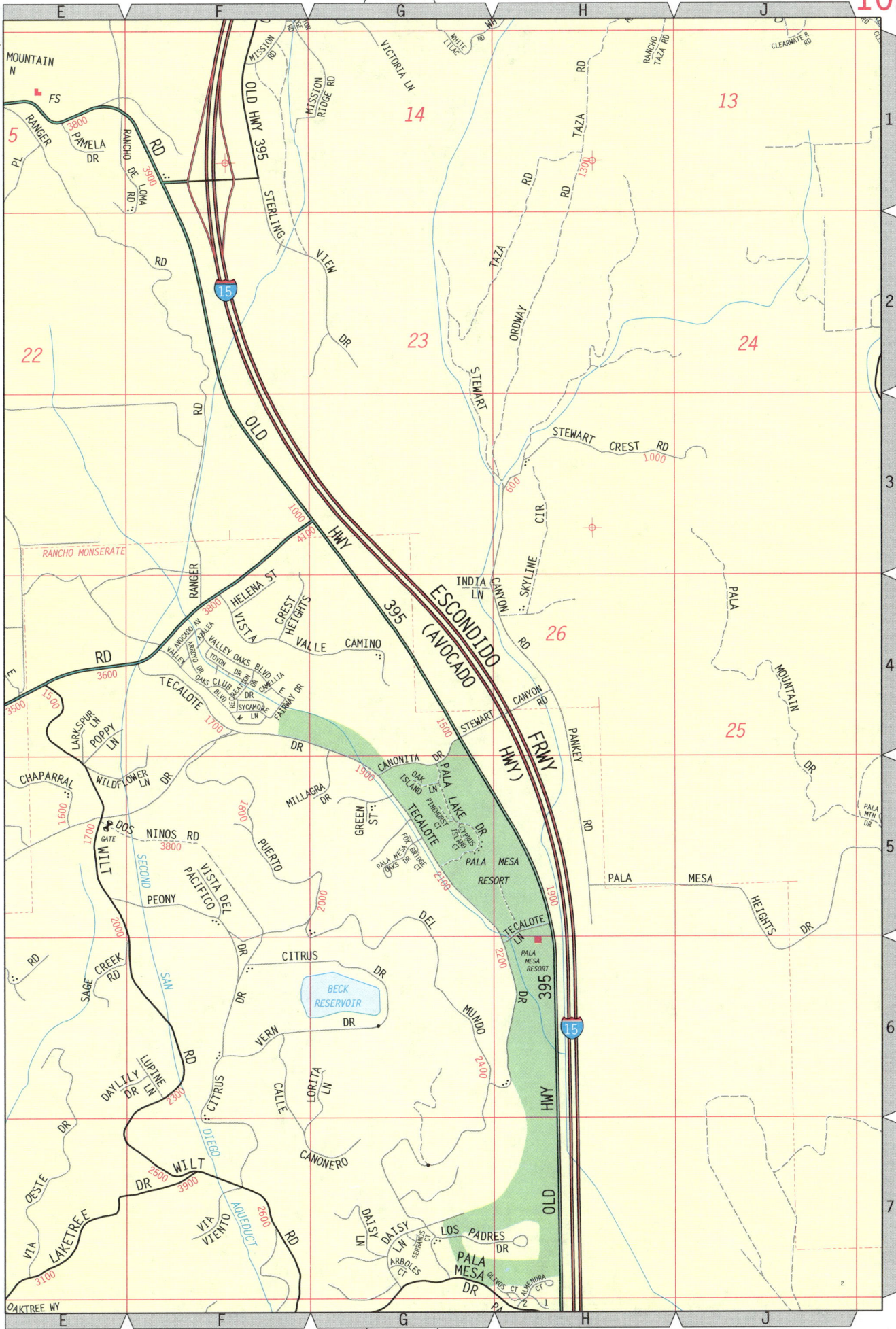

SAN DIEGO CO.

MAP

Thomas Bros. Maps®
COPYRIGHT 2001

N

E F G H J

MOUNTAIN N
FS
RANGER
PAMELA DR
RANCHO DE LOMA RD
3800
3900
5
PL
22

OLD HWY 395
MISSION RD
MISSION RIDGE RD
STERLING
VIEW
DR

WHITE LILAC RD
VICTORIA LN
14
13
TAZA RD
TAZA RD
RANCHO TAZA RD
CLEARWATE R RD
1300

1
2

15

23
STEWART
24

ORDWAY
STEWART

RD
HWY
ESCONDIDO (AVOCADO FRWY HWY)
395

STEWART CREST RD
1000
600
CIR
SKYLINE
CANYON RD
INDIA LN
26
CANYON RD
3

RANCHO MONSERATE
4100
1000
RANGER
3800
HELENA ST
CREST HEIGHTS
VISTA
VALLE
CAMINO
AVOCADO AV
AZALEA
ARROYO DR
VALLEY OAKS BLVD
TOYON DR
CLUB
OAKS BLVD
CAMELLIA
CREATION DR
SYCAMORE LN
FAIRWAY DR

PALA
MOUNTAIN
PANKEY RD
25

RD
3600
E
3500 1500
TECALOTE
1700
DR
LARKSPUR LN
POPPY LN
WILDFLOWER LN
DR
CHAPARRAL
1600
1700
DOS
GATE
NINOS RD
3800
VISTA DEL PACIFICO
PEONY
WILT
SECOND
SAN
CANONITA
MILLAGRA DR
GREEN ST
PUERTO
1900
1800
2000
OAK ISLAND
TECALOTE
PINEHURST
CYPRUS
ISLAND CT
PALA LAKE DR
STEWART
1500
PALA MESA RESORT
1900
2100
PALA MESA HEIGHTS DR
DR
PALA MTN DR
4
5

DEL
CITRUS
BECK RESERVOIR
VERN
DR
DR
SAGE CREEK RD
RD
2000
SAN
2000
DR
MUNDO
2400
TECALOTE LN
PALA MESA RESORT
2200
PALA MESA
6

DAYLILY DR
LUPINE LN
2300
CITRUS RD
CALLE
LORITA LN
DIEGO
HWY 395
15

VIA OESTE
LAKETREE
WILT DR
2500 3900
VIA VIENTO
AQUEDUCT RD
2600
CANONERO
DAISY LN
DAISY LN
ARBOLES CT
SERRANOS CT
LOS PADRES DR
OLIVOS CT
ALMENDRA CT
PALA MESA DR
OLD
HWY
7

3100
OAKTREE WY

0 .125 .25 .375 .5 miles 1 in. = 1900 ft.

SEE 1029 MAP

1029

SAN DIEGO CO.

MAP

SEE 999 MAP

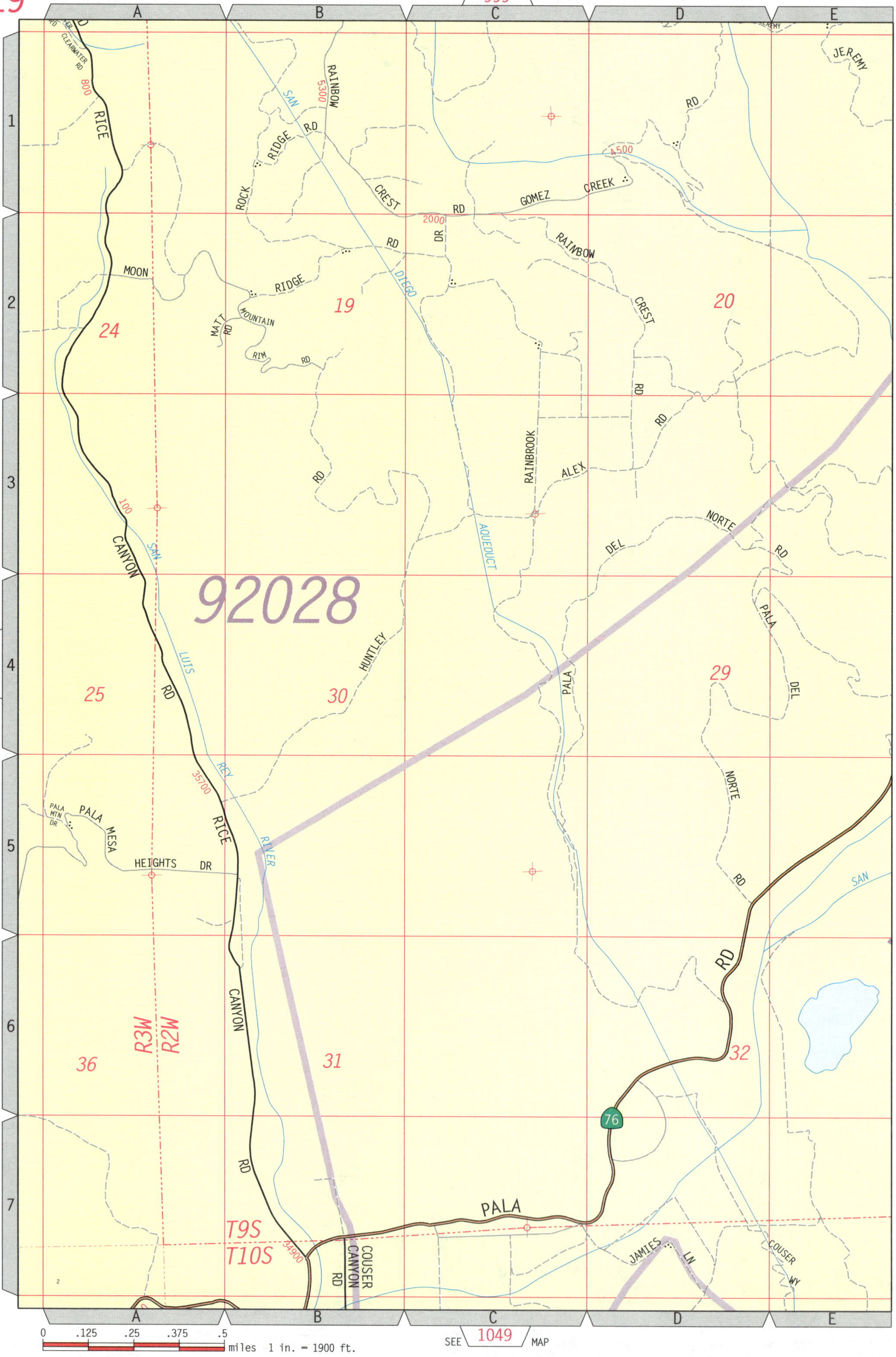

COPYRIGHT 2001 Thomas Bros. Maps ®

A B C D E

JEREMY

RICE
CLEARWATER RD
800
RAINBOW 5300
SAN
RAINBOW
RD
ROCK RIDGE RD
CREST
RD
GOMEZ CREEK
4500
RAINBOW
CREST
RD
JEREMY
RD

MOON
RIDGE
RD
DR
2000
RD

24
19
MATT RD
MOUNTAIN
RIM RD
DIEGO
20

RAINBROOK
ALEX
RD
RD

RD
CANYON
100
SAN
AQUEDUCT
DEL
NORTE
RD
PALA
DEL

92028

LUIS RD
HUNTLEY
25
30
PALA
29

35100
REY
NORTE
PALA MTN DR
PALA MESA
RICE
RIVER
RD

HEIGHTS DR
SAN

R3W R2W
CANYON
RD

36
31
32

76

RD
CANYON
RD
PALA
COUSER
JAMIES LN
WY

T9S
T10S
34900
COUSER CANYON RD

SEE 1028 MAP

SEE 1049 MAP

0 .125 .25 .375 .5 miles 1 in. = 1900 ft.

—N→

E F G H J

JEREMY

WY

JEREMY

WY

GOMEZ

CREEK

21

1

2

PALA

TEMECULA

RD

46100

PALA

S16

22

PALA

INDIAN

RESERVATION

3

47200

RD

HENDERSON RD

TRUJILLO CREEK

SEE 409 MAP

PALA

TEMPALA

CREEK

PALA

CREEK

MISSION
SAN ANTONIO
DE PALA

27

MISSION

A ST   FS

B ST

C ST

D ST

PALA

RD

12200

6TH ST

3RD ST

2ND ST

1ST ST

ST

ST

500 ST

ST

12100

RD

28

PALA

76

4

RIVER

SAN

LUIS

REY

92059

33

34

LILAC

RD

5

6

LILAC

7

92082

SEE 1049 MAP

0   .125   .25   .375   .5

miles   1 in. = 1900 ft.

E F G H J

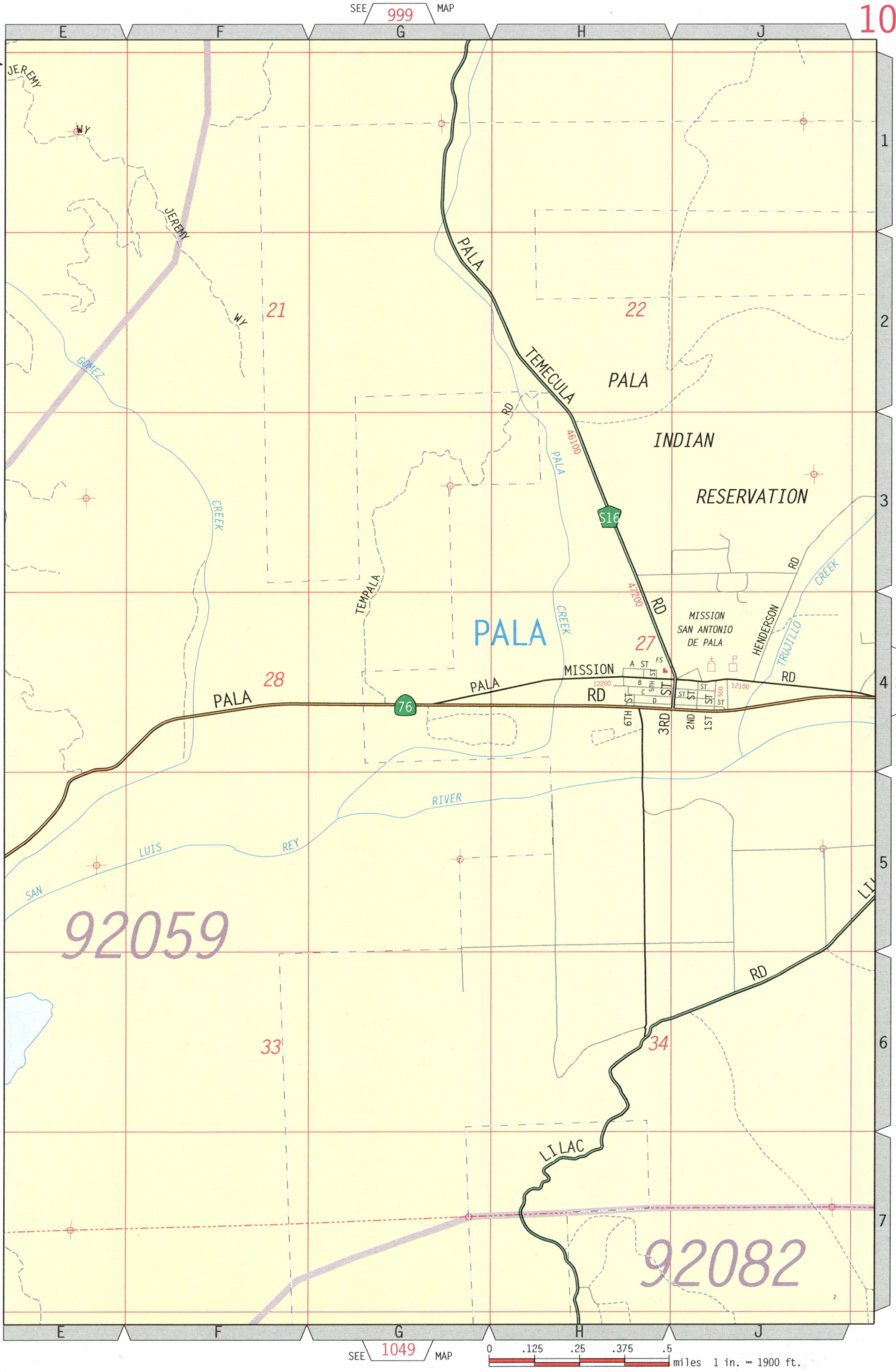

SAN DIEGO CO.

MAP

SEE 1027 MAP

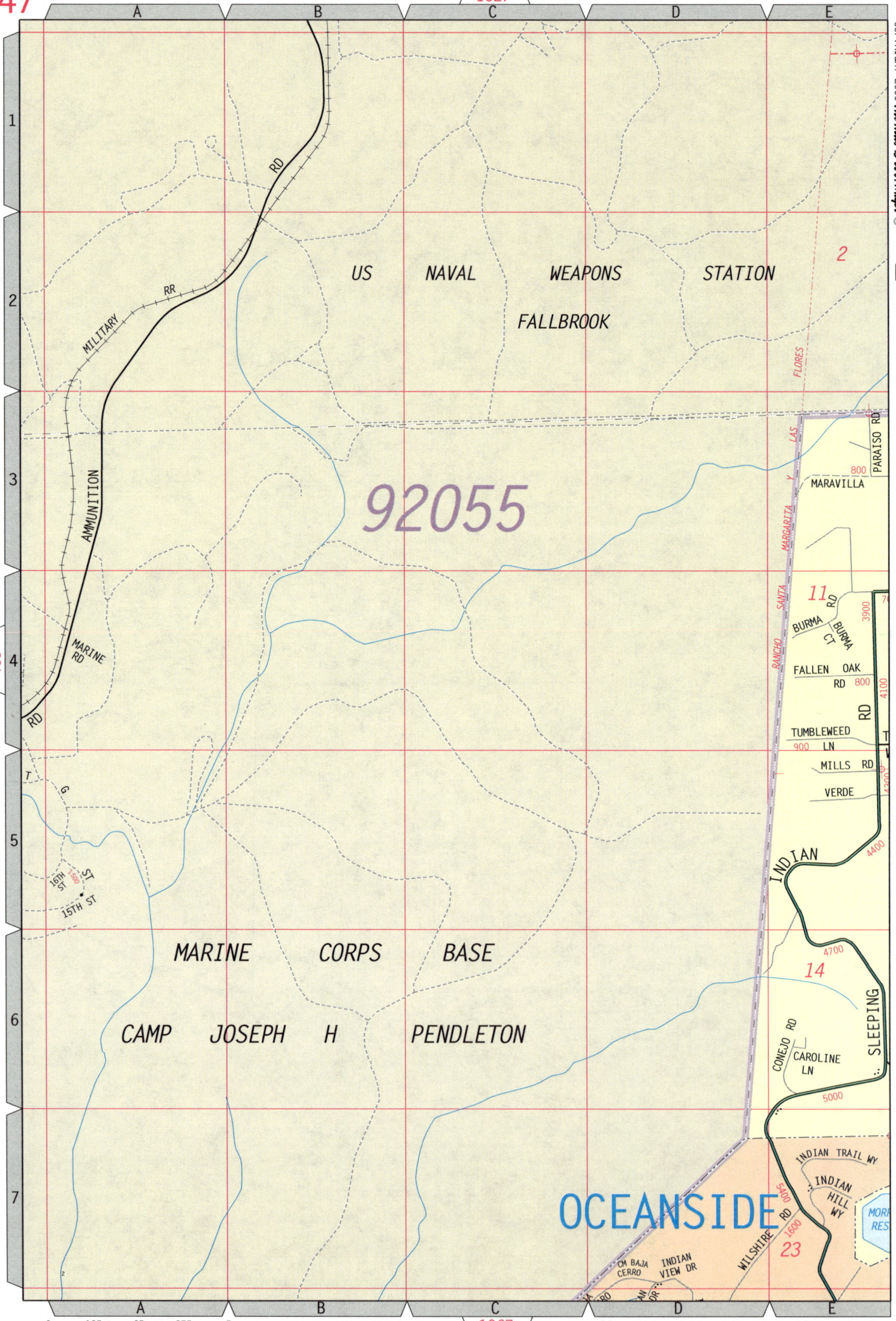

A   B   C   D   E

COPYRIGHT 2001 *Thomas Bros. Maps* ®

—N→

1

2

US   NAVAL   WEAPONS   STATION

FALLBROOK

2

FLORES

LAS

MARGARITA

SANTA

RANCHO

PARAISO RD

800
MARAVILLA

3

92055

11
BURMA   BURMA
CT
3900
FALLEN   OAK
RD   800

4100
RD
SEE 409 MAP

MILITARY

RR

AMMUNITION

MARINE
RD

RD

TUMBLEWEED
LN
900

MILLS   RD

VERDE

4

T
G
16TH
ST   ST
15TH   ST

INDIAN

4400

5

14
4700

CONEJO   RD

CAROLINE
LN

5000

SLEEPING

6

MARINE   CORPS   BASE

CAMP   JOSEPH   H   PENDLETON

INDIAN TRAIL WY

INDIAN
HILL
WY

MORA
RES

5400

23

OCEANSIDE

WILSHIRE   RD

1600

CM BAJA
CERRO   INDIAN
VIEW DR

7

A   B   C   D   E

0   .125   .25   .375   .5
miles   1 in. = 1900 ft.

SAN DIEGO CO.

MAP

Thomas Bros. Maps®

COPYRIGHT 2001

—N—

E F G H J

T9S
T10S

FALLBROOK COMMUNITY AIRPARK

VIDA
CLEARCRE
BUENA SUERTE
LORENZO DR
MONTECITO LN
TIOGA
JACKSON RD
WINTE
RD
WI

2 1

ELM TREE LN
700
MACKEY
MACKEY LN
DR HILL LN

HUGHES LN
1000
QUAIL KNOLL RD

MISSION TR
2800

MONTECITO DR
CRESTA LOMA LN
CRESTA LOMA
2800
WINTERWARM RD
1400
ACACIA LN

OLIVE TR
2400
OVERLAND

HILL RD

OVERLAND TR
TRAILS
END

S13
BIG OAK
SILVER SPRINGS LN
RANCH RD
1100
RAM
JASON RD
3000
SNOWS
3100
3000

WINTER–WARM

AQUA HILL RD
OLIVE HILL WY 500
ARABIAN TR
LA TARA LN
2500

GREEN CANYON RD
3200
CAMINO CIELO
1100

SYCAMORE WY
MORE
SYCAMORE
NORSTAR LN
NOR-STAR LN

SYCAMORE HEIGHTS DR
HILLSIDE
SILVER BIRCH LN
1500
HILLSIDE PL
HILLSIDE DR
3000
DR

HILL
3600

MISSION CREEK RD
1000

MISSION S RD
1100
SUNSET DR
VECINO DR
EL VECINO DR
SUNSET

SECLUDED GROVE RD
3500

HILL
DR

PREAKNESS CT
HORSE LN

WHITE
FUTURITY LN
PASEO

PASEO MONTE
HANCOCK RD
DE
PASEO DEL LAGO

VIA ENCINOS DR
SUNSET DR
1300

NIDO
GRACE CT
1400
PALOMAR DR

PALO DR
BAJA

VERDE ORO
300
AVILLA LN
PARAISO RD LN
LUNETA LN
LN
STEPHENS PORT 400
CAZADOR 3800

LAKE RIDGE
3700
LAKE RIDGE CIR
RD

OLIVE
3800

OLIVOS
7
3700

MISSION
3700

1200
EL LAS FLORES DR
NIDO DR
CIRRO VISTA WY
SAN LUIS REY HEIGHTS
PALOMAR DR
3800
FORBELL PL
EL NIDO DR

800

BURMA RD
BURMA SPUR
700
900
BURMA OAK RD 800
WEED N
ILLS RD
ERDE

CONCORDIA LN
300
FERNDALE LN
4100

RANCHO BONITO RD
12
SPANISH SPUR
100

R4W R3W
3700

VISTA RD
7

SINGLETREE PL
3800
PALOMAR DR
3900
MONSERATE WY
MON-SERATE WY

GEORGINE RD 600
HIGHLAND OAKS CT
HIGHLAND OAKS

FS
BONITA VALLE
CALLE DE SUENO
LEMON GROVE DR
CALLE LINDA 100

OLIVE HILL RD
4200

VIA ACQUAVIVA
4300
LOS VECINOS
RANCHO CAMINO NORTE
200
CAMINO
400

HELLERS
JUNGLE OAKS DR
MONSERATE
BEND

S13
4200

VIA MONSERATE

PALOMAR DR

TUMBLE-WEED LN
DEL VALLE DR
AV 500

92028

HIGHLAND OAKS ST
JACINTO TER
HIGHLAND OAKS LN
4700
13
BRIANA CT
SAN JACINTO CT
SAN JACINTO CIR E
4800

SADDLE CREEK RD
COUNTRY
GOLDEN MEADOW LN

RANCHO RD
400

ROLLINGVIEW
SHADY LN
HILL LN
18

BAJA MISSION RD S
LA CANADA DR
PALO DR

SLEEPING
700
SAN JACINTO CIR W
MORRO HILLS RD
4900
300

GATEVIEW DR
GLEN RD
ROLLINGWOOD LN

MISSION RD S
4500

SAN JACINTO CIR
500
SOLANA REAL 600

MORRO HILLS PL

BONSALL PRESERVE
RIO VALLE

TRAIL WY
IAN ILLI WY
MORRO RES
CAMINO CORTO

24
DE LOMAS
CIRCA DEL CIELO
DE CIRCA DEL CIELO
DE LOMA
PUERTA 500
MILES WY
WILLMAN WY
RANCH RD
OLIVE HILL RD

92003
19
BONSALL
SHAMROCK RD
SHAMROCK
32100
TRIPLE CROWN DR
MISSION S RD
BONSALL PRESE
MIS

0 .125 .25 .375 .5 miles   1 in. = 1900 ft.

SAN DIEGO CO.

MAP

SEE 1028 MAP

COPYRIGHT 2001 Thomas Bros. Maps ® —N—

WINTERWARM

WINTERWARM RD
WINTERWARM RD
WINTERWARM RD
AMBER VISTA LN
ACACIA LN
CORAL TREE LN
GREEN HEATHER LN
SUNRISE 2100
VIEW DR
GREEN HILLS 2900
GREEN HILLS PL 2100
SAFFRON WY
ROSEMARIE LN
VIA ARROYO 2800
VIA ARROYO 2300
SEATAC LN
VIA RANCHEROS 2700
VIA RANCHEROS
TOULOUSE 2500
VISTA DE PALOMAR 2600
OLD POST RD
SKYCREST RD
WESTMONT DR
SUGAR PINE LN
SECRET LAKE LN
CARLTON WY
LAKETREE
OAKTREE WY
GOLFVIEW DR
NORTHCLIFF DR
LAKEMONT DR
FALLBROOK GOLF CLUB
OAK CLIFF
CHERRYPOINT CT
CHERRY BROOK
LAKE
2900
3000
2800

VISTA PALMAS
RANCHO PALMAS
ALTA VERDE DR
NOR-STAR LN
ALTA VERDE
LOS VERDES DR 3100
CAMINO PORTOFINO
VALLE VERDE
CAMINITA CORTINA
VISTA
INTEGRITY WY
HILLSIDE DR
ALTA 3500
DOS LOMAS
DOS LOMAS PL
TRES LOMAS
TRES LOMAS CT
DOS LOMAS
CALLE DOS LOMAS
DOS LOMAS 3300
DOS LOMAS 2500
DOS LOMAS 2400
VIA VONNIE
VIA CORTINA 3100
VIA ALICIA
VIA LOMA
VIA LOMA
CABALLO LN 3500
ROSEWOOD GI GI CT
DOS LOMAS 2900
MONSERATE 3700
MONSERATE 3600
MONSE

VISTA DEL NORTE 1900
PALOMAR DR
ALTA VISTA
BAJA VISTA DR 1500
MONSERATE TER
VISTA
EL NIDO DR
LINDA VISTA TER
ESTERLINA DR 3600
LINDA VISTA WY
CORONA LAGUNA RD
VISTA
KNOTTWOOD WY
BROOKHILLS VISTA
KATE CT
TRACY CT
ADLER
GENISTA PL
LANGEWOOD WY
NETTLE
LARKWOOD CT 3600
CEDAR VALE WY
LOGWOOD PL
KATIE LENDRE DR
MARY LEWIS DR
SARAH
ANN DR
GUMWOOD CT
KNOTTWOOD CT
WORMWOOD CT
PUSSYWILLOW LN
BLUE GUM CT
GENISTA
KNOTTWOOD
WINNEWOOD PL
CREEK
LINDA
TIERRA
RED TOP LN 3600
VIA DULCEA
BRUSHWOOD
STAGHORN CT
JIMSEN CT
PEDRIN PL
GENISTA LN
FLOWERMOOD LN
DEADWOOD CT
LIMBER PINE RD
GIRD RD
MONSERATE 3600
MONSERATE

SAN LUIS REY HEIGHTS

MONSERATE TER
MONSERATE WY
MON-SERATE WY 4700
LYNDY LN
CANDICE
KERI RD 3900
KERI WY
WENDI CT
JENNIFER CT
KRISTI CT
BROOKHILLS RD
LA CANADA RD
VIA CORTO
VIA
ESTATE DR
ORANGE HILL
MONSERATE RD 2200
MONSERATE RD 3100
MENDENARO CT
FLOWERMOOD
LIMBER PINE RD 4300
3400

LA CANADA RD
PALOMAR DR
FALLSBRAE RD
RIO VISTA DR
RAMONA DR 4600
RIO VISTA DR 4300
CALLE DEL VUELTA 4700
RIO VISTA RD
2100
LA CANADA RD
HILLRISE RD 2000
FALLSBRAE RD
LAKE SYCAMORE DR 1900

BONSALL

PALA
MISSION RD
SWEETGRASS CT
SWEETGRASS LN
PARK & RIDE
RANCHO MONSERATE

76
S13 2200
20
RIVER VILLAGE SAN LUIS REY
BONSALL PRESERVE
SAN LUIS REY DOWNS COUNTRY CLUB

W LILAC RD 5900
DEL CIELO ESTE
DEL CIELO OESTE
BARBARY PL
GALLOWAY PL
KENSINGTON PL
JOCKEY CLUB
MISSION VW
AVD JINETE
CIELO REDONDO 5900
MONTE RD
CAMINO CASITAS
VIA LARGA VISTA
DEL CIELO 5400
6300
21
ANNA MARIE LN
JIM DORA WY 5000
TALIESIN WY
VIA VERA 32000
WRIGHTWOOD RD
VIA GIAN-NELLI
22

1 VIA ALTA VISTA

SEE 1047 MAP

SEE 1068 MAP

0 .125 .25 .375 .5 miles 1 in. = 1900 ft.

A B C D E

SAN DIEGO CO.

MAP

SEE 1028 MAP

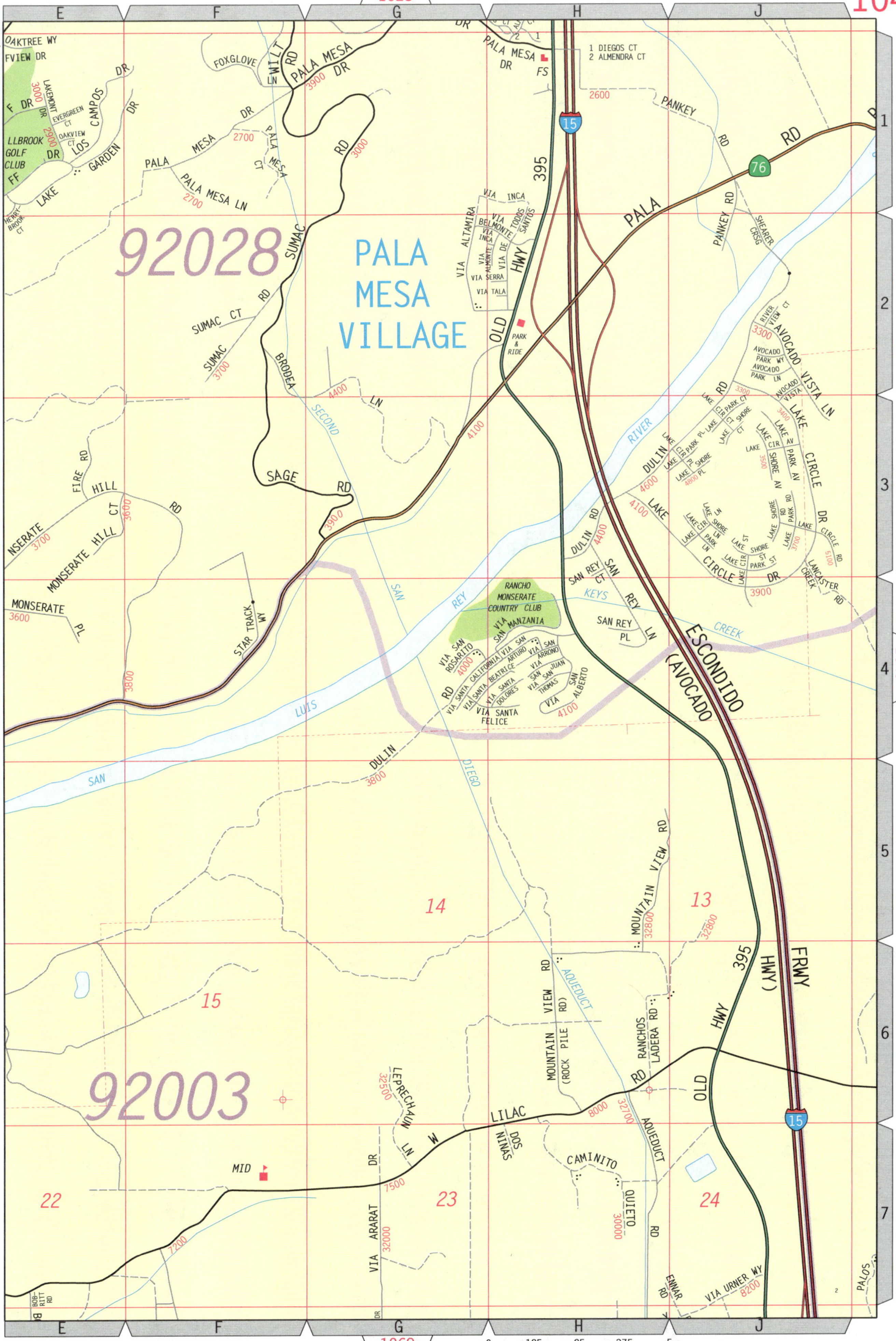

E F G H J

OAKTREE WY
FVIEW DR
F DR 3000
LAKEMONT DR
EVERGREEN CT
OAKVIEW CT
LLBROOK GOLF CLUB
FF
HENK BROOK CT
LAKE
2600
LOS GARDEN
CAMPOS DR
FOXGLOVE
PALA MESA DR
LMILT LN
RD
PALA MESA DR
3900
PALA MESA CT
2700
PALA MESA
2700
PALA MESA LN
2700
SUMAC RD
SUMAC CT
SUMAC 3700
BRODEA LN
4400
SECOND
SAGE RD
3900

PALA MESA DR
FS
PALA MESA DR
2 1
1 DIEGOS CT
2 ALMENDRA CT
2600
PANKEY
PANKEY RD
SHEARER CRSG
PALA RD

15
395
OLD HWY
4100
4100
4400
DULIN RD
4600
SAN REY CT
SAN REY LN
DULIN RD
SAN REY PL
RIVER
RIVER VIEW CT
3300
AVOCADO PARK WY
AVOCADO PARK
AVOCADO PARK
AVOCADO VISTA LN
AVOCADO VISTA
3300
LAKE CIR
LAKE PARK PL
LAKE CIR
PARK CT
LAKE SHORE
4800
LAKE CIR
LAKE PARK RD
3600
LAKE SHORE AV
LAKE PARK AV
LAKE CIRCLE
LAKE SHORE
LAKE SHORE
LAKE CIR
LAKE CT
PARK ST
LAKE CIR
LAKE SHORE ST
LAKE PARK LN
LAKE CIRCLE DR
CIRCLE DR
LANCASTER CREEK RD
5100
3900

92028

PALA MESA VILLAGE

PARK & RIDE

VIA INCA
VIA ALTAMIRA
VIA TODOS SANTOS
VIA BELMONTE
VIA DE
VIA INCA
VIA ALMONTE
VIA SERRA
VIA TALA

RIVER
LAKE
4100
4400

RANCHO MONSERATE COUNTRY CLUB
VIA MANZANIA
SAN MANZANIA
VIA SAN ROSARITO
4000
VIA SAN CALIFORNIA
VIA SANTA BEATRICE
VIA SANTA DOLORES
VIA SAN ARTURO
VIA SAN ARRONO
VIA SAN JUAN
VIA SAN THOMAS
VIA SAN ALBERTO
4100
VIA SANTA FELICE
RD

SAN REY
KEYS
SAN REY PL
ESCONDIDO (AVOCADO
CREEK

FIRE RD
MONSERATE HILL CT
3600
MONSERATE HILL RD
NSERATE 3700
STAR TRACK WY
MONSERATE PL
3600
3600
3800
SAN LUIS
SAN
SAN REY
DULIN
3600
DIEGO

MOUNTAIN VIEW RD
32800
13
32800
AQUEDUCT

14

15

92003

LEPRECHAUN LN
LEPRECHAUN 2500
MID
DR
W
LILAC
DOS NINAS
VIA ARARAT
32000
7500
23
8000
32700
MOUNTAIN VIEW RD
MOUNTAIN VIEW (ROCK PILE) RD
RANCHOS LADERA RD
AQUEDUCT RD
CAMINITO
QUIETO RD
30000
24
OLD HWY
395 HWY
FRWY
15
ESCONDIDO (AVOCADO FRWY)
EINAR RD
VIA URNER WY
8200
PALOS
22
2200
BOB RITT RD
B

SEE 1068 MAP

SEE 1049 MAP

0 .125 .25 .375 .5
miles 1 in. = 1900 ft.

76

1 2 3 4 5 6 7

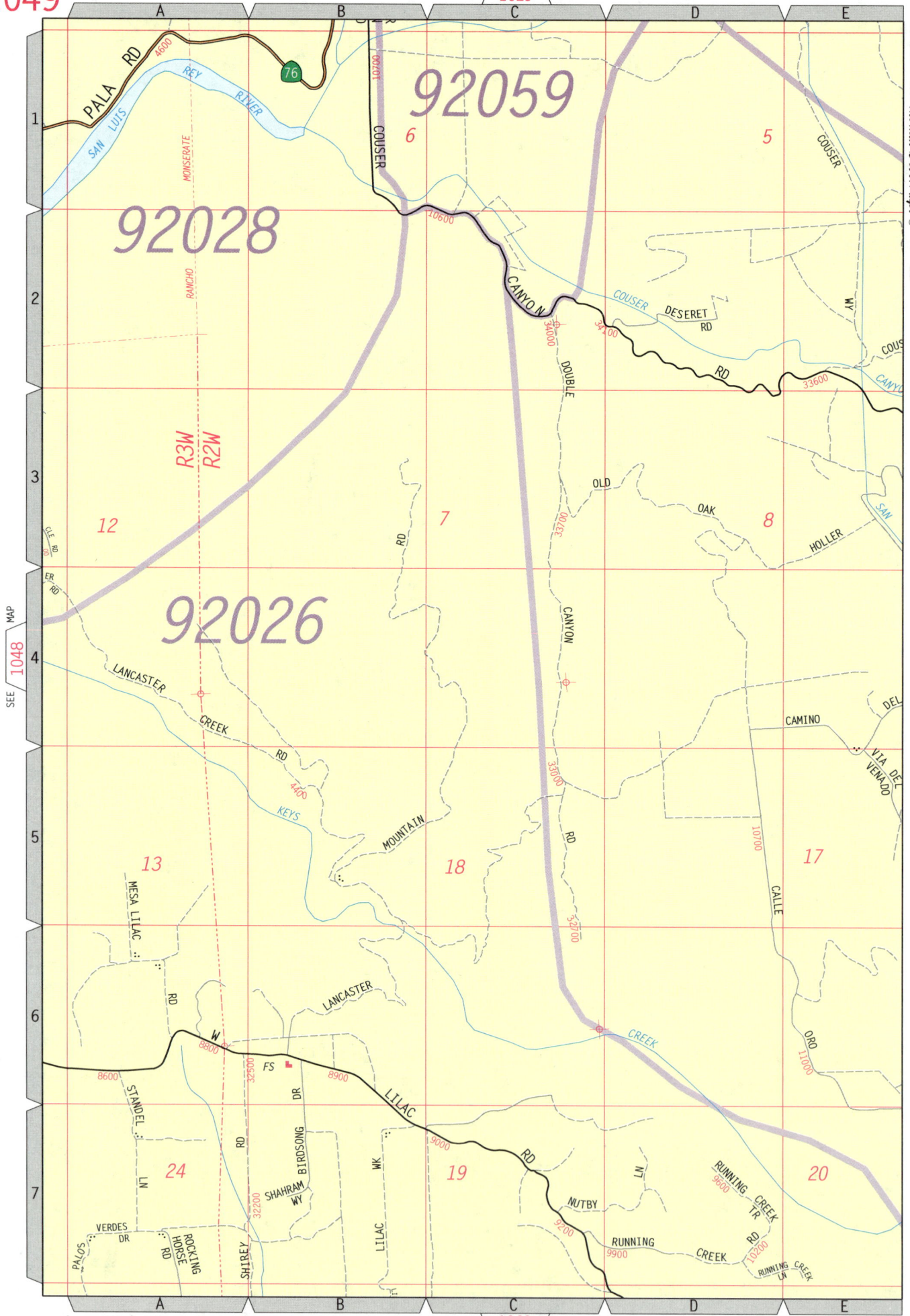

1049

SEE 1029 MAP

A B C D E

COPYRIGHT 2001 Thomas Bros. Maps ® —N—

SAN DIEGO CO.

MAP

92059

92028

92026

PALA RD

SAN LUIS REY RIVER

76

MONSERATE

RANCHO

R3W R2W

CLE RD

ER RD

SEE 1048 MAP

4600

COUSER CANYON

10700

10600

34000

34100

33600

DESERET RD

RD

DOUBLE

OLD OAK

CANYON

33700

HOLLER

COUSER WY

COUSER

SAN

DEL

VIA DEL VENADO

CAMINO

LANCASTER CREEK RD

4400

KEYS

MOUNTAIN

33000

RD

CALLE

10700

LANCASTER

CREEK

MESA LILAC RD

W

8800

8600

FS

32500

8900

LILAC

STANDEL LN

RD

BIRDSONG DR

SHAHRAM WY

32200

9000

WK

LILAC

RD

NUTBY

9200

RUNNING CREEK

9900

ORO

11000

LN

RUNNING CREEK TR

9600

RD

10200

RUNNING CREEK LN

VERDES DR

PALOS

ROCKING HORSE RD

SHIREY

5 6 7 8 5 17 18 19 20 24 13 12

32700

0 .125 .25 .375 .5 miles 1 in. = 1900 ft.

SEE 1069 MAP

E   F   G   H   J

92059

4

3

1

SAN DIEGO CO.

PALA

INDIAN

2

WY

COUSER

WY

SAN ANTONIO WY

33000 LILAC

RESERVATION

CANYON

VIA PATRICIO

33300

LOMA

11200

REY DR

DR

11400

SAN LUIS

PALA

SAN

3

9

10

SEE 1050 MAP

SAN DIEGO

COUSER

32900

10800

GABRIEL WY

PALA INDIAN RESERVATION

SAN

32600 RD

CALLE DE HALCONES

MCNALLY RD

4

DEL

VENADO

AQUEDUCT

RD

MCNALLY

92082

VIA DEL VENADO

CANYON

32200

15

RD

SANTA CATALINA

RD

5

16

32500

SAN GERONIMO DR

SANTA

VIRGINIA DR

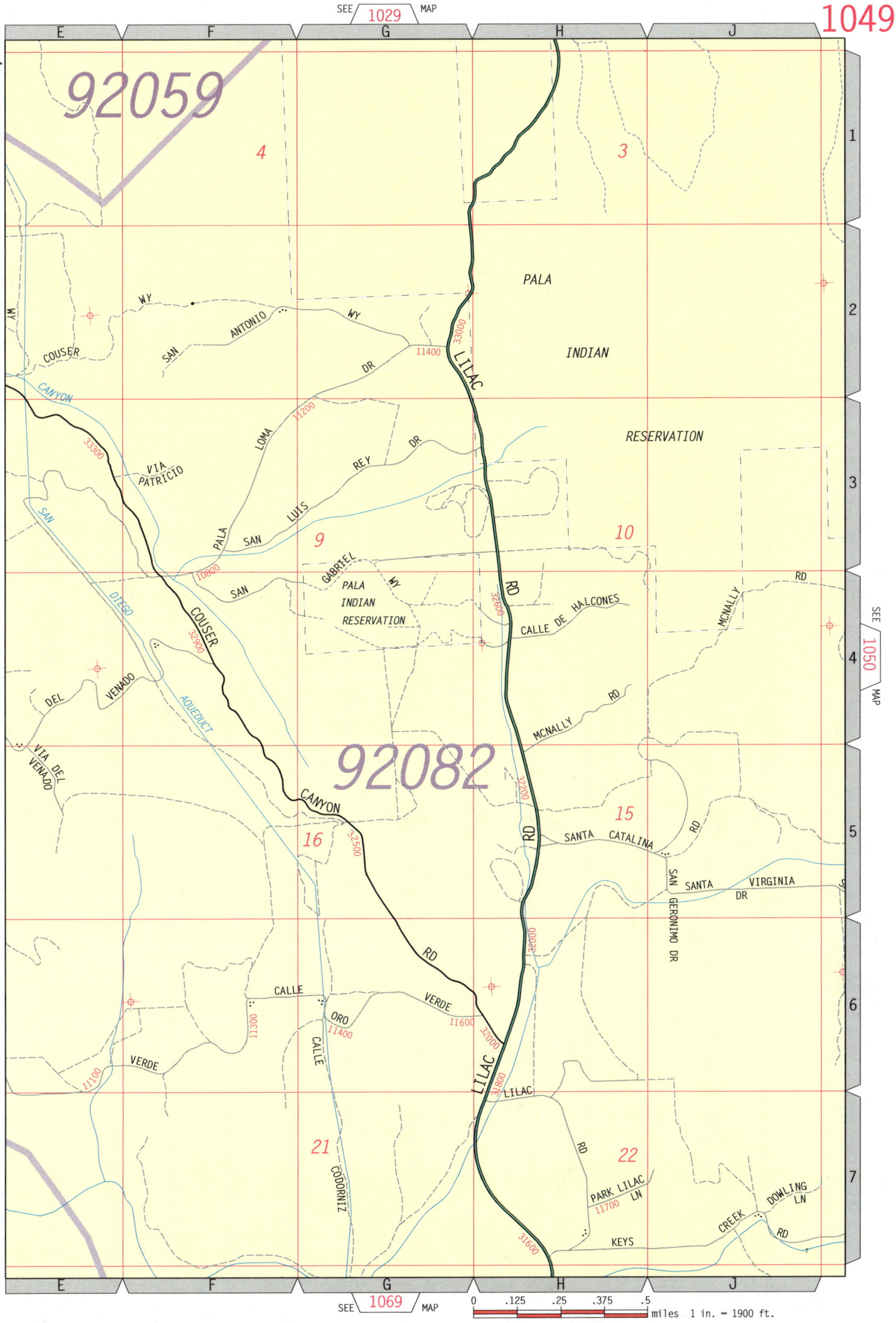

S

RD

CALLE

VERDE

11600

32100

6

ORO

11400

CALLE

11300

VERDE

11100

RD

32000

LILAC

LILAC

21

CODORNIZ

22

PARK LILAC LN

11700

DOWLING LN

7

CREEK

RD

KEYS

31600

E   F   G   H   J

0 .125 .25 .375 .5

miles 1 in. = 1900 ft.

MAP

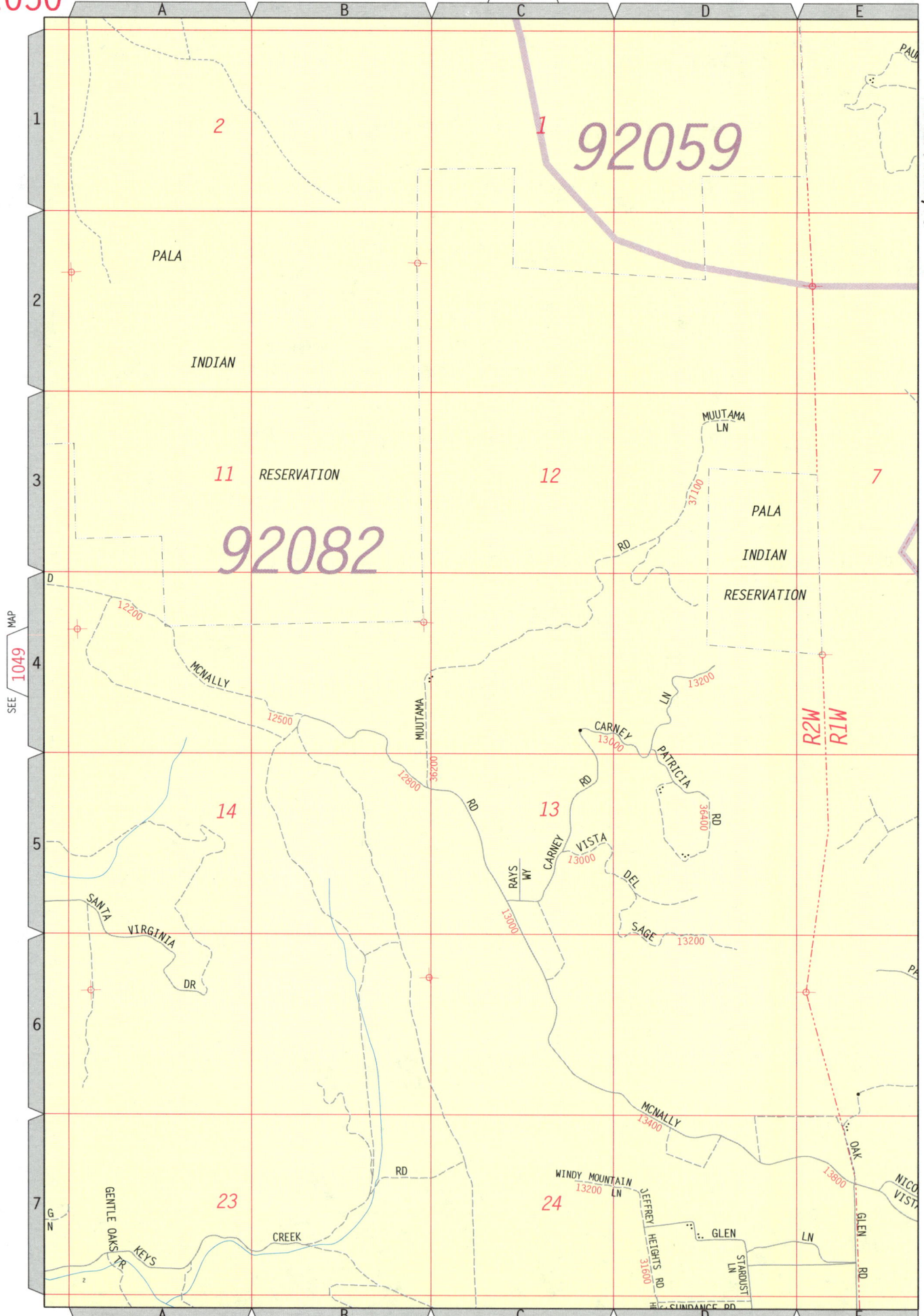

SEE / 409 \ MAP

A   B   C   D   E

2

1

92059

PALA

INDIAN

MUUTAMA LN

92082

11   RESERVATION   12   7

PALA

INDIAN

RESERVATION

SEE / 1049 \ MAP

D

12200

MCNALLY

12500

12800

MUUTAMA

36200

RD

CARNEY
13000

PATRICIA

LN   13200

RD   36400

R2W   R1W

14   13

RAYS WY

CARNEY RD

VISTA
13000

DEL

SANTA

VIRGINIA

DR

13000

SAGE   13200

MCNALLY
13400

OAK

PA

NICO
VISTA

23

CREEK   RD

GENTLE OAKS TR   KEYS

GN
GN

24

WINDY MOUNTAIN LN
13200

JEFFREY HEIGHTS RD
31600

GLEN

STARDUST LN

GLEN   LN

13800

GLEN   RD

SUNDANCE RD

A   B   C   D   E

0 .125 .25 .375 .5
miles 1 in. = 1900 ft.

SEE \ 1070 / MAP

Thomas Bros. Maps®
COPYRIGHT 2001
N

E F G H J

PAUMA RIDGE RD
PAUMA RIDGE CIR
6

EL SENDERO DR
RHONDA LN
34300
34300
HAMPTON RD
34200 34100
PALA
PAUMA
14600
RESERVATION RD
15000
PAUMA
INDIAN
RESERVATION
1

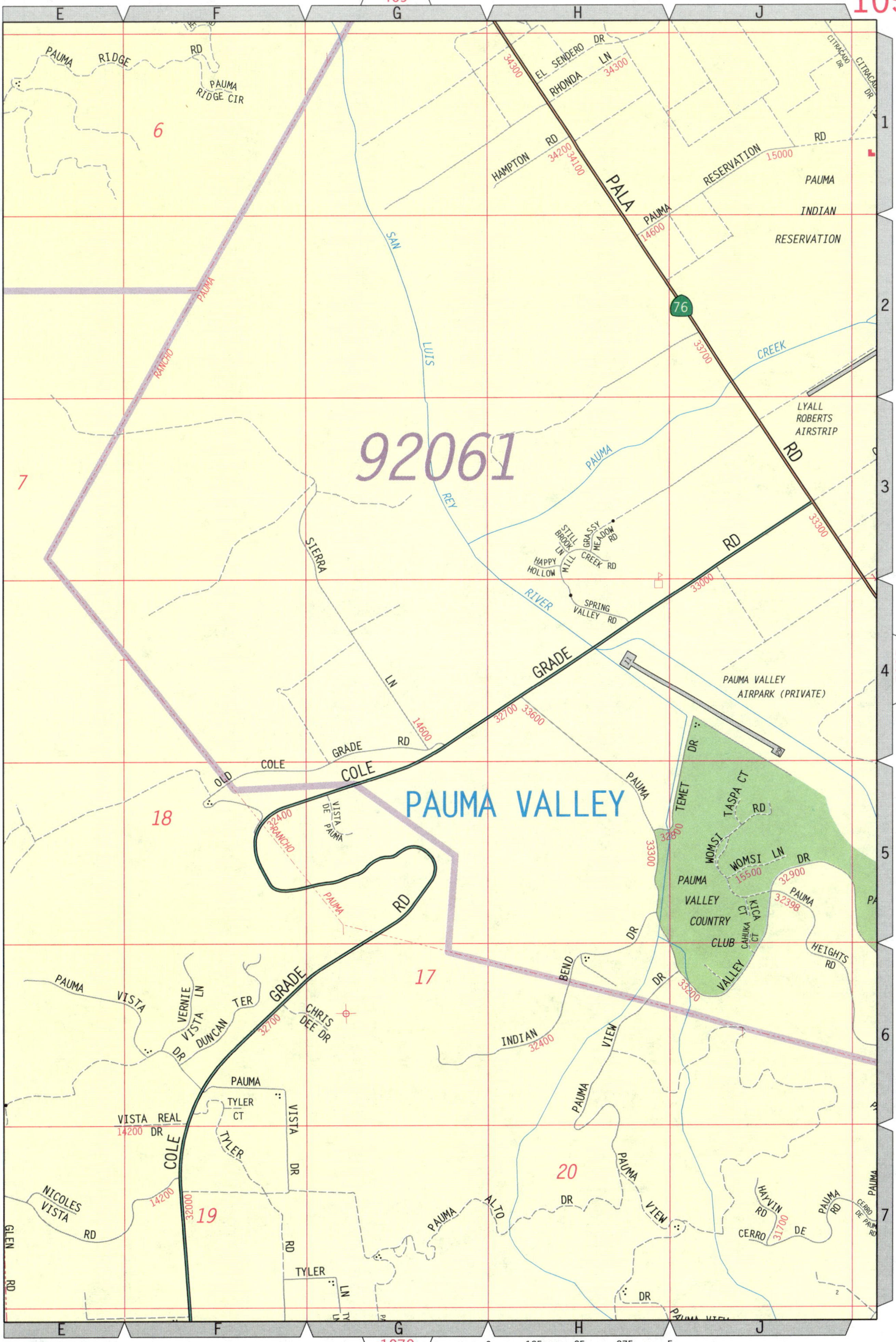

SAN
PAUMA
RANCHO
2
76
33700
CREEK
LYALL ROBERTS AIRSTRIP
RD
33300

7
LUIS
REY
PAUMA
92061
RIVER
STILL BROOK LN
MILL CREEK RD
GRASSY MEADOW RD
HAPPY HOLLOW
SPRING VALLEY RD
RD
33000
3

SIERRA
LN
GRADE
14600
32700 33600
GRADE RD
OLD COLE GRADE RD
COLE
33000
PAUMA VALLEY AIRPARK (PRIVATE)
SEE 1051 MAP
4

18
32400
RANCHO
VISTA DE PAUMA
PAUMA VALLEY
PAUMA
TEMET DR
32800
WOMSI TASPA CT
RD
WOMSI LN
155 00
DR
32900
KICA CT
PAUMA 32398
PAUMA VALLEY COUNTRY CLUB
CAHUILA CT
33300
DR
DR
VALLEY
HEIGHTS RD
5

PAUMA
RD
17
BEND
33200
MAP

PAUMA VISTA
VERNIE LN
VISTA DR
DUNCAN TER
GRADE
CHRIS DEE DR
32700
INDIAN
32400
DR
PAUMA VIEW DR
20
PAUMA VIEW
HAYVIN RD
PAUMA RD DE
CERRO DE PAUMA
6

PAUMA
TYLER CT
VISTA DR
VISTA REAL DR
14200
COLE
TYLER
14200 32000
19
NICOLES VISTA RD
GLEN RD
RD
TYLER LN
ALTO
PAUMA
DR
CERRO
31700
7

0 .125 .25 .375 .5 miles   1 in. = 1900 ft.

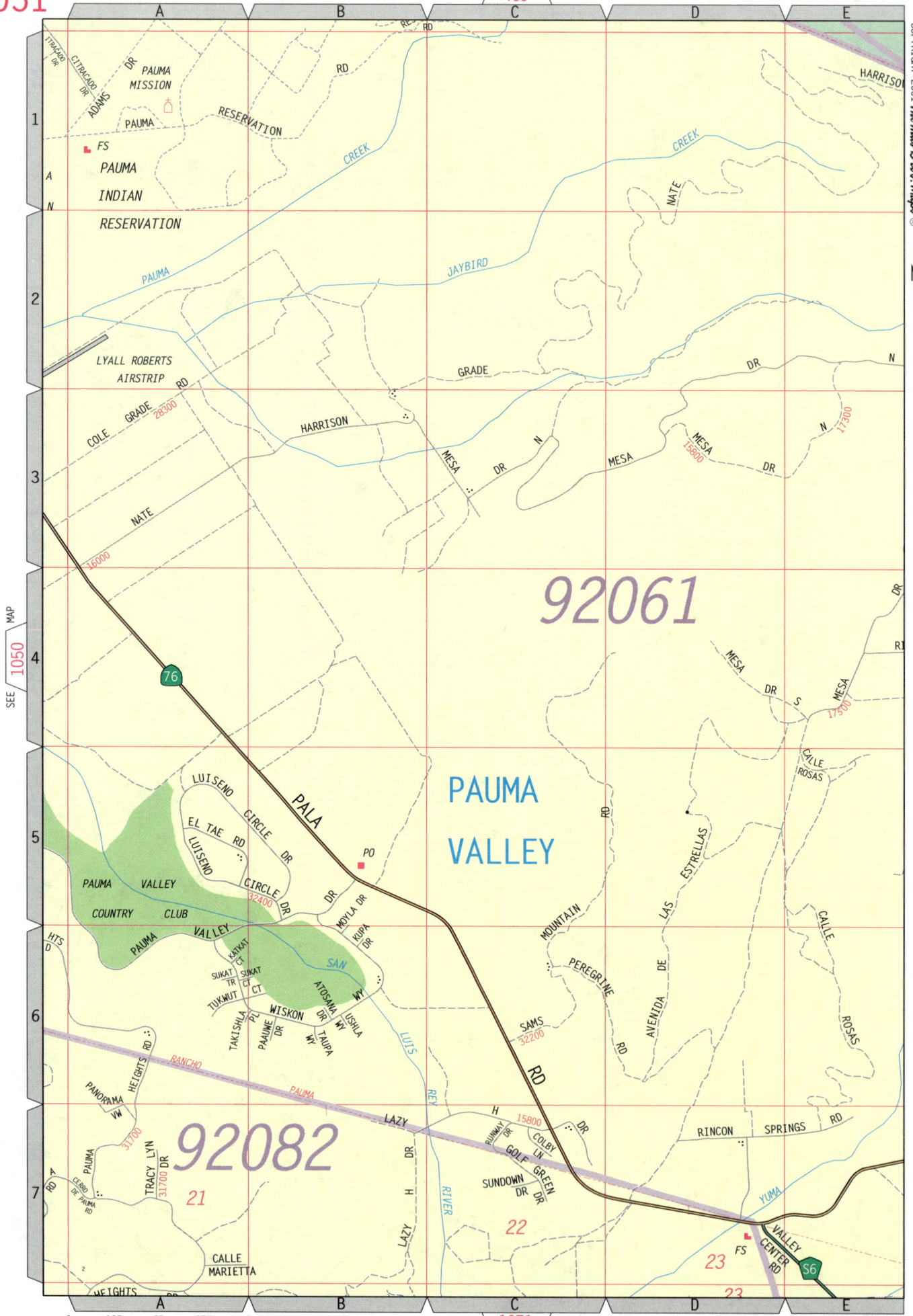

SAN DIEGO CO.

MAP

SEE 409 MAP

COPYRIGHT 2001 *Thomas Bros. Maps®* —N—

A B C D E

ITRACADO DR
CITRACADO DR
ADAMS DR
PAUMA MISSION
PAUMA
FS
PAUMA INDIAN RESERVATION
RESERVATION

REY RD
RD
CREEK

CREEK
NATE

PAUMA
JAYBIRD

1

2

SEE 1050 MAP

LYALL ROBERTS AIRSTRIP
COLE GRADE RD
28300
NATE
16000

HARRISON
GRADE
MESA DR
N
MESA
MESA
15800
DR
N
17300

3

76
PALA
LUISENO CIRCLE DR
EL TAE RD
LUISENO CIRCLE DR
32400
PO

92061

MESA DR S
MESA
17500

CALLE ROSAS
DR

4

PAUMA VALLEY

PAUMA VALLEY COUNTRY CLUB
PAUMA VALLEY
HTS D
DR
MOYLA DR
KUPA DR
KATKAT CT
SUKAT TR
SUKAT CT
SAN
ATOSANA WY
USHLA
WISKON
TUKWUT
TAKISHLA PL
PAUME DR
TAUPA WY
WY
DR

MOUNTAIN RD
LAS ESTRELLAS
AVENIDA DE LAS
PEREGRINE RD

CALLE
CALLE ROSAS

5

6

HEIGHTS RD
PANORAMA VW
RANCHO
PAUMA
31700
PAUMA
CERRO DE PAUMA RD
TRACY LYN DR
31700 DR
RD A

92082
21

LUIS REY
LAZY DR
LAZY
RIVER

SAMS 32200
SAMS RD

RINCON SPRINGS RD

RUNWAY DR
GOLF GREEN DR
15800
COLBY LN
SUNDOWN DR
H DR
22

YUMA
23 FS
VALLEY CENTER RD
S6
23

7

CALLE MARIETTA
HEIGHTS

A B C D E

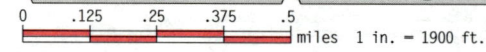

0   .125   .25   .375   .5
miles 1 in. = 1900 ft.

SEE 1071 MAP

—N—

SAN DIEGO CO.

MAP

SEE 409 MAP

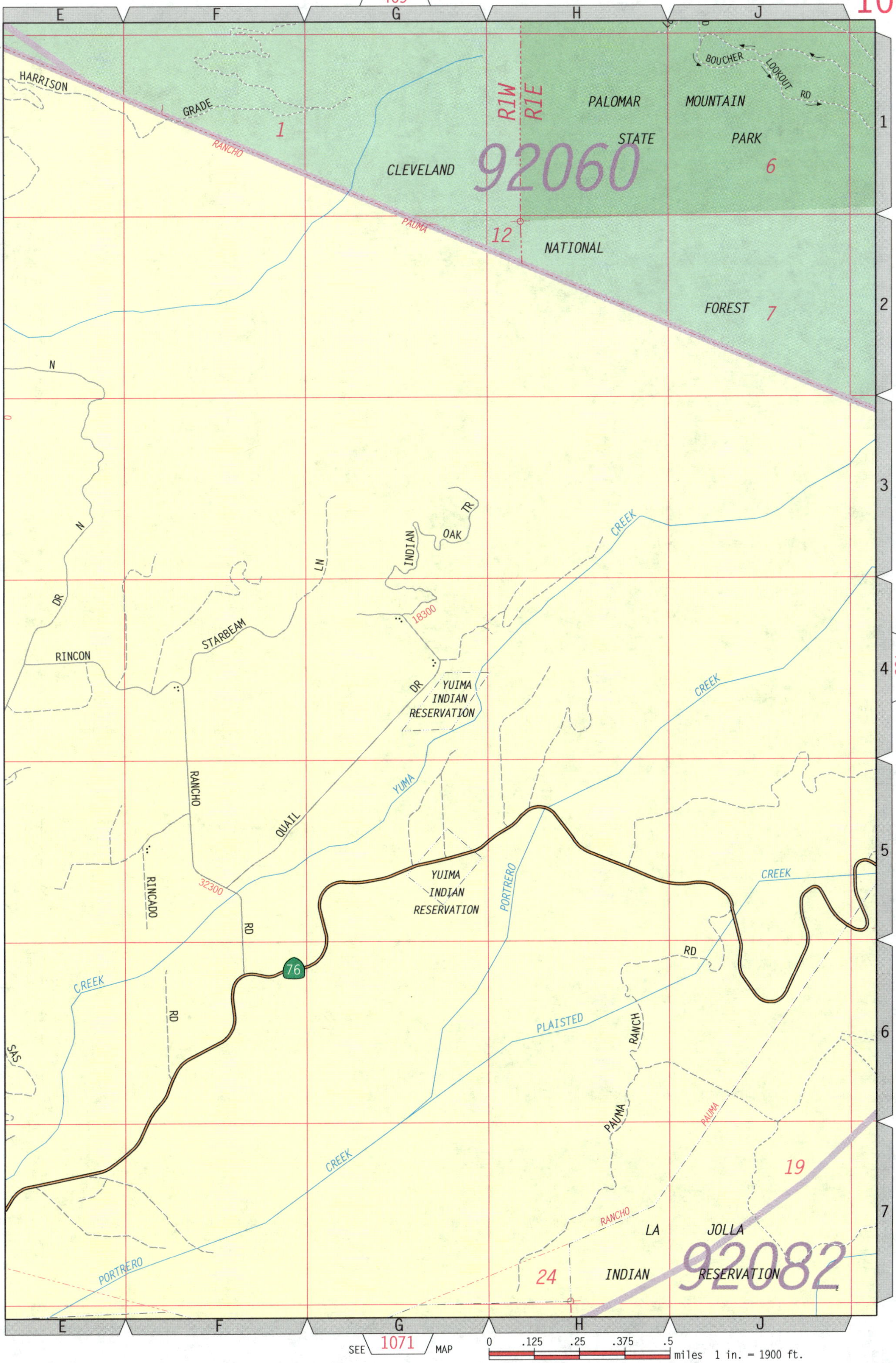

E F G H J

HARRISON

GRADE

RANCHO

1

CLEVELAND

92060

R1W R1E

PALOMAR MOUNTAIN

STATE PARK 6

BOUCHER LOOKOUT RD

PAUMA

12

NATIONAL

FOREST 7

2

N

N N

DR

RINCON

STARBEAM

LN

INDIAN

OAK

TR

3

CREEK

18300

DR YUIMA INDIAN RESERVATION

CREEK

SEE 409 MAP

4

RANCHO

QUAIL

YUMA

CREEK

RINCADO

32300

RD

YUIMA INDIAN RESERVATION

PORTRERO

CREEK

5

CREEK

RD

76

PLAISTED

RANCH

RD

6

SAS

RD

CREEK

PAUMA

PAUMA

19

7

PORTRERO

RANCHO

LA JOLLA

INDIAN RESERVATION

92082

24

E F G H J

0 .125 .25 .375 .5

miles 1 in. = 1900 ft.

SEE 1071 MAP

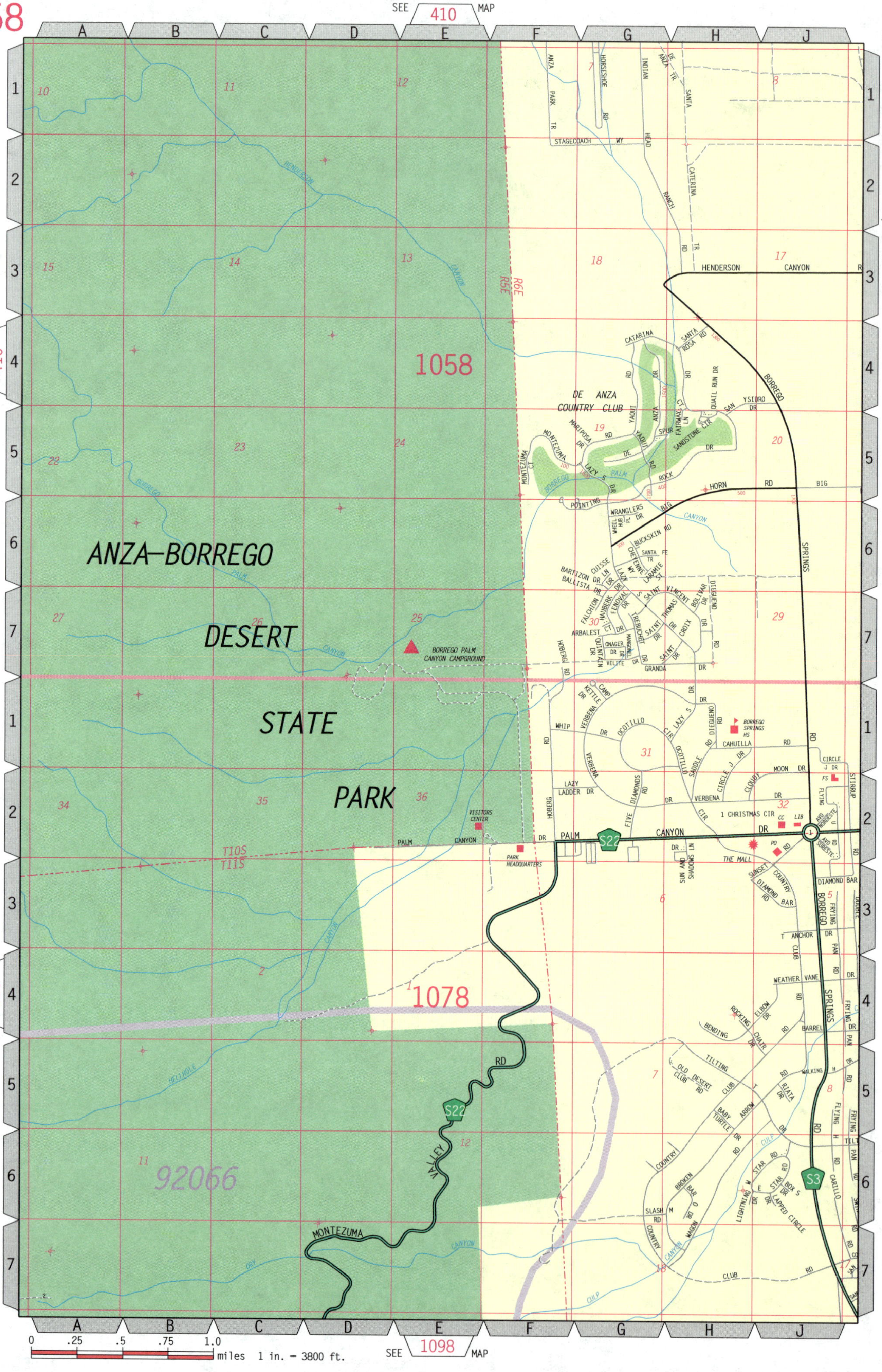

SAN DIEGO CO.

MAP

Thomas Bros. Maps® ←N—

SEE 410 MAP

SEE 410 MAP

SEE 410 MAP

1058

ANZA–BORREGO

DESERT

STATE

PARK

92066

1078

DE ANZA COUNTRY CLUB

BORREGO PALM CANYON CAMPGROUND

VISITORS CENTER

PARK HEADQUARTERS

BORREGO SPRINGS HS

THE MALL

1 CHRISTMAS CIR

MONTEZUMA

Columns (top): A B C D E F G H J

Grid rows: 1 2 3 4 5 6 7

Section numbers: 10 11 12 7 3 15 14 13 18 17 HENDERSON CANYON 22 23 24 19 20 27 26 25 30 29 34 35 36 31 32 2 1 12 11 8 7 6 5

R6E R5E

T10S T11S

HENDERSON CANYON

BORREGO SPRINGS

PALM CANYON DR

S22

S22

S3

0 .25 .5 .75 1.0 miles 1 in. = 3800 ft.

SEE 410 MAP
SEE 1098 MAP

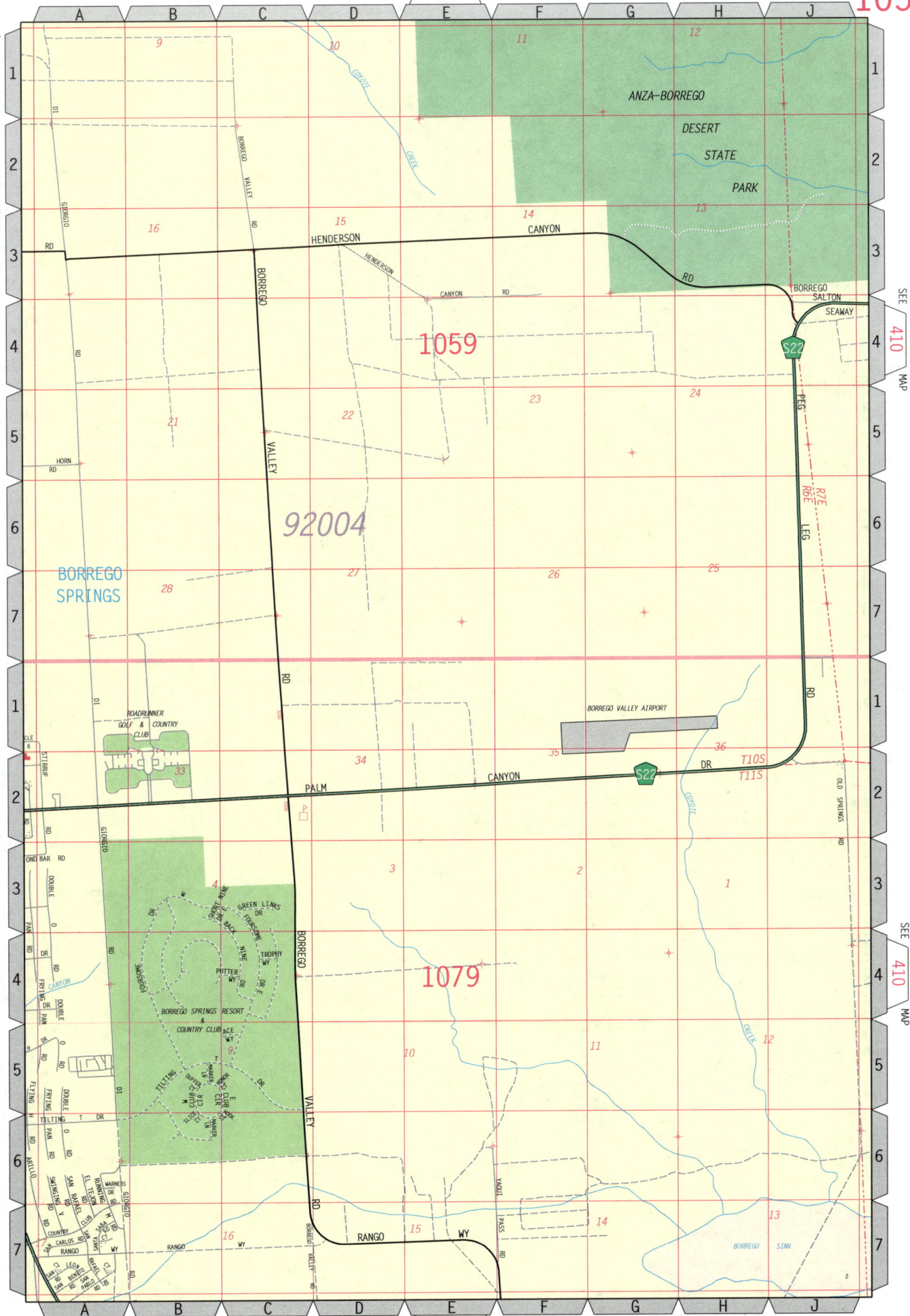

Thomas Bros. Maps ®
COPYRIGHT 2001
—N—

A B C D E F G H J

ANZA–BORREGO
DESERT
STATE
PARK

9 10 11 12

BORREGO VALLEY RD

16 15 HENDERSON 14 CANYON 13 RD

HENDERSON

CANYON RD

BORREGO SALTON
SEAWAY
S22

1059

21 22 23 24

VALLEY

HORN
RD

92004

PEG

R7E
R6E

LEG

BORREGO
SPRINGS

28 27 26 25

RD

ROADRUNNER
GOLF & COUNTRY
CLUB

BORREGO VALLEY AIRPORT

CIRCLE
R
STIRRUP

33 34 35 36
T10S
T11S

GIORGIO

S22 DR

PALM CANYON

RD

OLD SPRINGS RD

COYOTE

OND BAR RD
DOUBLE

4 3 2 1

SHORT NINE DR

GREEN LINKS
DR
FOURSOME

PAN
RD
DR

FRYING DR

PAN
DOUBLE

CANYON

DR

BORREGO

EQUESTRIAN

NINE DR

TROPHY
WY

TROPHY
DR E

PUTTER
WY

1079

BORREGO SPRINGS RESORT
&
COUNTRY CLUB

ACE
WY
9

VALLEY

10 11 12

H
RD
O

FLYING H

FRYING
PAN RD
DOUBLE

TILTING
T

TILTING
PAN DR
RD

DUFFER
CIR

SLICE
CIR

MASHIE
LA

CLUB CIR

E

MASHIE LA

CLUB CIR

DR

ARTILLO

WARNERS
DR

RUNNING
EL TORO

SAN RAFAEL RD

RANGO

SMILING RD

SAN V
SARA LU

COUNTRY
CLUB

SAN CARLOS RD

SAN
KANS

YAQUI

PASS

RD

RD

SAN LEON

SAN BENITO

SAN PABLO
RD

RANGO WY

BORREGO VALLEY RD

16 RANGO WY 15 WY

14 13

YAQUI
PASS
RD

BORREGO SINK

2

SEE 1098 MAP

0 .25 .5 .75 1.0
miles 1 in. = 3800 ft.

SAN DIEGO CO.

MAP

A B C D E

SEE 409 MAP

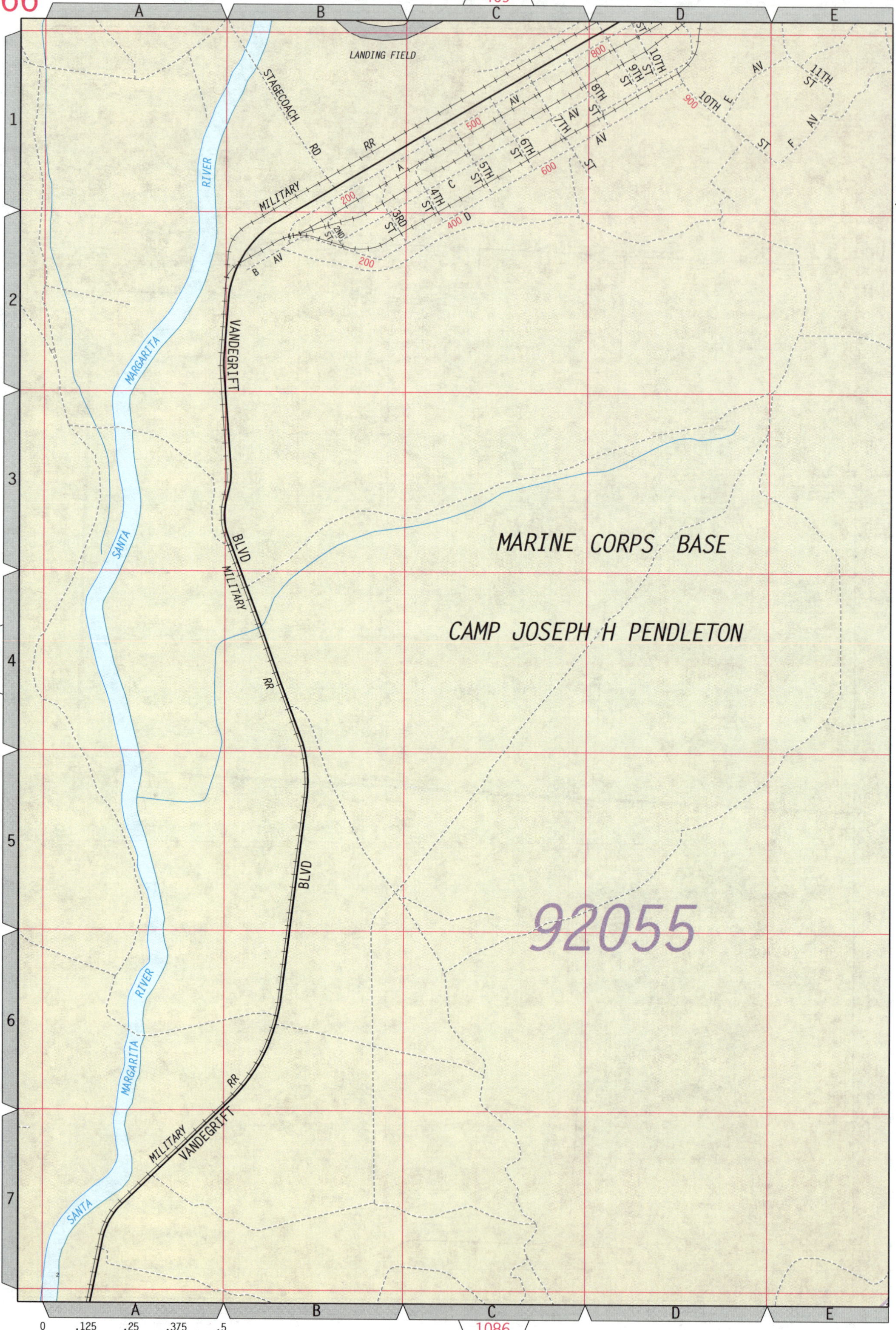

LANDING FIELD

STAGECOACH RD

RR

MILITARY

RIVER

MARGARITA

SANTA

VANDEGRIFT

BLVD

MILITARY

RR

BLVD

MARGARITA RIVER

SANTA

MILITARY

VANDEGRIFT

RR

10TH ST
9TH ST
8TH ST
7TH ST
6TH ST
5TH ST
4TH ST
3RD ST
2ND ST
B AV
A

11TH ST
10TH ST
E
F AV
ST

AV

800
900
500
600
400
200
200

A
B
C
D

MARINE CORPS BASE

CAMP JOSEPH H PENDLETON

92055

1
2
3
4
5
6
7

SEE 408 MAP

—N—

0 .125 .25 .375 .5
miles 1 in. = 1900 ft.

SEE 1086 MAP

A B C D E

SAN DIEGO CO.

MAP

OCEANSIDE

MARINE MEMORIAL GOLF COURSE

CLUBHOUSE

GOLF COURSE RD

OCEANSIDE MUNICIPAL GOLF COURSE

RANCHO SANTA MARGARITA Y LAS FLORES

VANDEGRIFT BLVD

WINDMILL LAKE

WHELAN LAKE

FOSS LAKE

LIBBY LAKE

LIBBY LAKE PARK

WESTWIND MHP

92058

92057

92054

T10S
T11S

N RIVER RD

DOUGLAS DR

POINT DEGADA
POINT VICENTE

28
33
32
5
6
4

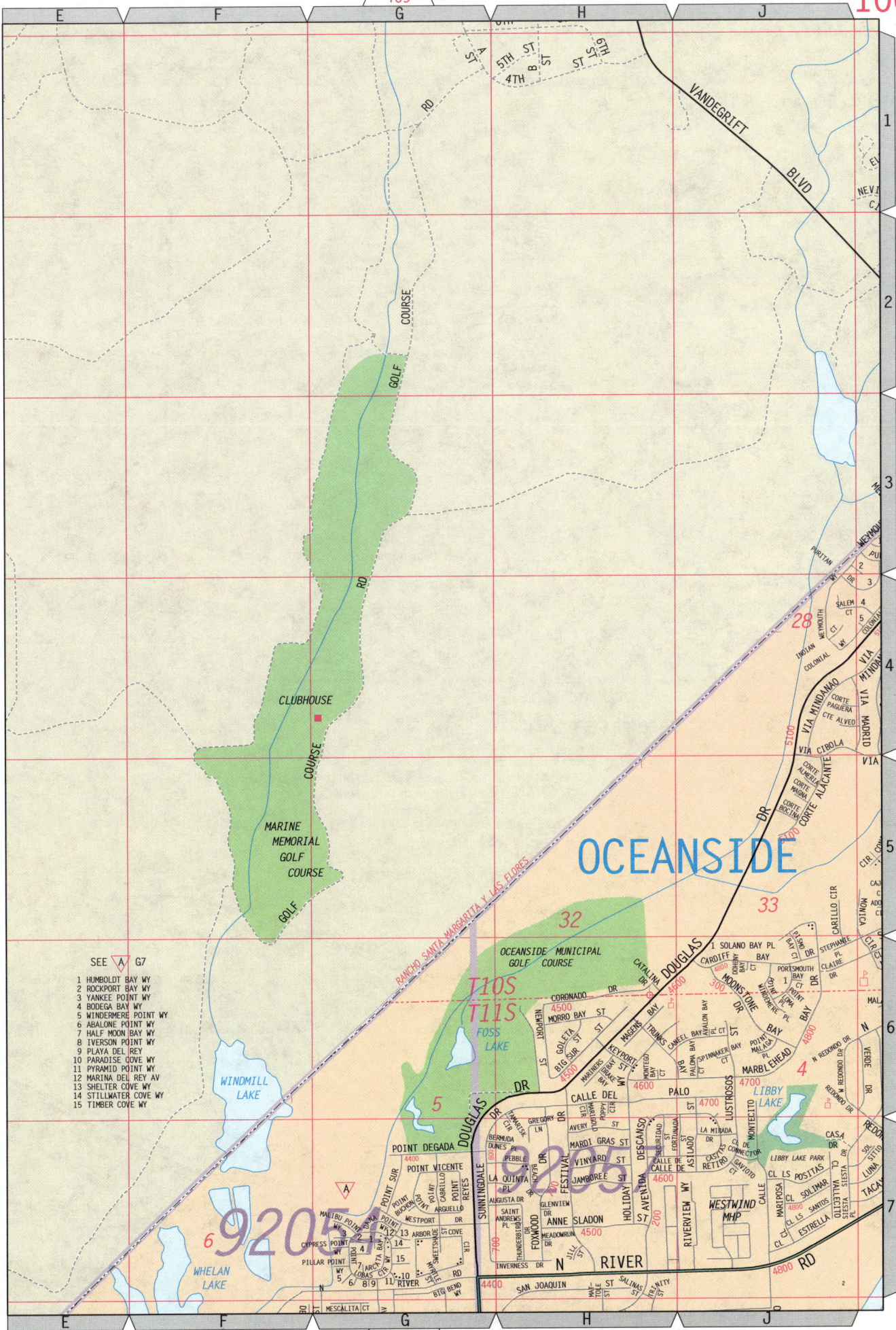

SEE A G7
1 HUMBOLDT BAY WY
2 ROCKPORT BAY WY
3 YANKEE POINT WY
4 BODEGA BAY WY
5 WINDERMERE POINT WY
6 ABALONE POINT WY
7 HALF MOON BAY WY
8 IVERSON POINT WY
9 PLAYA DEL REY
10 PARADISE COVE WY
11 PYRAMID POINT WY
12 MARINA DEL REY AV
13 SHELTER COVE WY
14 STILLWATER COVE WY
15 TIMBER COVE WY

SEE 1067 MAP

0   .125   .25   .375   .5
miles   1 in. = 1900 ft.

SAN DIEGO CO.

MAP

COPYRIGHT 2001 Thomas Bros. Maps ®

—N—

SEE 1047 MAP

92028

92055

MARINE CORPS BASE CAMP
JOSEPH H. PENDLETON

23

22

INDIAN VIEW DR

HIDDEN VALLEY RD

WILSHIRE

SLEEPING INDIAN RD

MORRO HEIGHTS

PALOMA

SLEEPING INDIAN 26

LA DE LA ROSA LN

1500
1400
1200
1100

27

800
600
400
300
200

RD

LAS TUNAS DR 6200

PUERTA

VANDEGRIFT

GATE

PAPAGALLO

TOUCANET CT
TORNET CT

PLYMOUTH
MEDFORD
WEYMOUTH

28
SHELLEY DR
CHILTERN CT
MENDIP ST
EVERETT ST
PURITAN WY
PILGRIM
HARVEST
DOUGLAS BLVD
YEATS DR
SALEM CT
COLONIAL
PINTURA
VIA MINDANAO
VIA MADRID
VIA CASTILLA
VIA MALAGUENA
FROST ST
ELIOT ST
LONGFELLOW DR
SPENCER CT
VIA CIBOLA
ORTEQUERA
ALVEO
LA

SEE A A3
1 DOVER ST
2 PIONEER CIR
3 PURITAN DR
4 SALEM CT
5 FENWAY CIR

1200
1000
5200
900

92057

34

35

WILSHIRE

CALLE ARQUERO
CALLE CABALLO DR
CASTELLANO WY
EL MIRLO
ALBEA DR
PRAIRIE AV
RD
ARTHUR ST
PARKER DR
MICHAEL AV
PARKER
LEON ST
HERBERT ST
HELEN CT
IRENE ST
FRANCIS ST
OMAR CT
BARRY ST
GREENBROOK CIR
GREENERY CT
HOLLOWGLEN RD
LEON ST
STALLION ST
MARE RD
GUAJOME
DE
RIVER
100
200
400
5600
300

CONCHO PL
ROJA DR
PARKER
CAJON CIR
ADOBE CIR
MONICA
STEPHANIE DR
CLAIRE DR
MACARIO DR
ROJA DR
SOL DR
GOLD ST
ELAINE
ARTHUR ST
CHARLES ST
FLORA DR
GOLD
LENDRE

NORTH RIVER ROAD PARK
COMM CTR

MELROSE
CREEKSIDE
EDGEWATER AV
DAYBREAK CT
STARLIGHT AV
EDGEWATER AV
PACESETTER DR
2
1 RAINTREE WY
2 TUMBLEWEED
3 GOLD RUSH

MALAGA DR
REDONDO
N
SIESTA DR
VERDE DR
LUNA DR
N
REDONDO
RIVER RD
MARTIN ST
LOS MORROS
N RIVER DR
RANCHO
100
600
5200
5200

3
JACKSON ST
POLK ST
HARDING ST
MCKINLEY ST
HARRISON ST
MADISON ST
MONROE ST
PIERCE ST
TYLER ST
NIXON CIR
TAFT ST
ANDREW
RIVER RD
RIO RANCHO
RIVER REY
N SAN LUIS RD
SITIO RD
TACAYME DR
TACAYME DR
N VISTAS
SA RD
LUNA

TOLL BRIDGE (WEST BOUND ONLY)
FS

COLLEGE BL
GARDENIA
MANZANITA
CEANOTHUS
SAGINA
SAGUARO
SUMAC PL
PALMETTO
ADAMS
ROMNEYA DR
SCOTTS PL
TARRAGON DR
YUMA ST
GABRIELENO DR
JUANENO ST
LUISENO DR
YUMA ST
VIA CUPENO
METATES
VIA PORTOLA
VIA PAUMA
VIA TIZON
CASPIAN
MISSION MARKETPLACE

MANOS
PICACHO CT
WOLF
GREY HAWK

N SANTA FE AV

MISSION AV
S14
92056
GUAJOME LAKE
GUAJOME REGIONAL PARK

RASPBERRY WY
GOOSEBERRY WY
CRANBERRY WY
LOGANBERRY
SPRINGFIELD AV
GUAJOME LAKE RD
ELDERBERRY
BLACKBERRY
BOYSENBERRY WY
RASPBERRY WY
BLACKBERRY WY

BRIDLE
HITCHING POST RANCH RD
LARIAT PL
ROUNDUP
CHARLIE HORSE
ALBRIGHT
SEATTLE SLEW WY
ROCKING HORSE LN
OLD GUAJOME RD
RD

5500
5400
5600
900
1000
1100
1300

1 CUCHILLO ST
2 SILVER BLUFF DR

SEE 1066 MAP

0 .125 .25 .375 .5 miles 1 in. = 1900 ft.

Thomas Bros. Maps®

COPYRIGHT 2001

—N→

E F G H J

PUERTA CM COR-TO DE LOMAS RANCHO DEL CERRO 600 500
SAINT JOHNS CRSG
CATHERINE RANCHO ADARME LN 24 WILLMAN WY JASMINE PAS LINDO CM OLIVE SHAMROCK RD THOROUGH-BRED LN 76
ERIN GN RD VALLE DEL SOL 400 VALLE DEL SOL PUERTA 19 HILL 5800 TRIPLE CROWN DR PO
  VIA MONTE ALEGRE TIERRA VISTA 4100 92003 BUCKA IBIZA PL TAXCO PL BRASILIA PL 5900 GRENADA MONTEVIDEO
ENTRADA DEL SOL VIA LAGO VIA CALVILLO HEAVENLY PL AVENIDA A BOGOTA VIA GRENADA PL MISSION RD
  VIA RANCHO DEL VALLE DEL SOL VIA SERENA PL ESTORIL PL BUENOS AIRES WY CARACAS PL VIA ASUNCION RD
  BONSALL JANOS HILL CEPILLOS VIA MONTELLANO 5800 5560 7000
DEL LAGOS PASO CAMINITO DE LOS CEPILLOS 4400 6800 76 1 DENTRO DE LOMAS RD
GREEN HILLS RD 6300 25 RD 600 4200 LAGO GRANDE DR VIA DE LOS MISSION 30 RIVER RD 1
HILLS PRECIOUS 500 VIA ROSE LN RD REY RIVER
VIEW RD BIG VIEW RD 6200 6300 PUERTA DEL EMERALD HILL 30500 LITTLE GOPHER CANYON RD 1068
GROVE DR 6200 SOL RD 6100 LITTLE GOPHER CANYON CREEK 4 SEE
INDIAN OCEANSIDE KARI LN LN 31 3800 1100
400 RD LN 4300 LUIS OLD FAIRVIEW CIR 3600
N 6000 RIVER 6200 HOLLY SAN 3600 LAGUNITA EVERGREEN
300 5900 36 6100 R4W R3W AV 3500 RANCH 800 CHUMASH TR HIDDEN HAVEN
T10S T11S 1 RAINTREE WY 2 TUMBLEWEED WY 3 GOLD RUSH WY 5900 MISSION 6000 TUSHAK RANCH LN EVERGREEN LN EVERGREEN LN S13 3100
SAGEBRUSH SADDLE 5700 76 VIEW RD DEL 92084 BLACKWELL PL PENVIEW DR VISTA FRUITLAND GOPHER CANYON CT
SUNDANCE SURREY CT RANCH WAGON VISTA DEL RIO ROCA 6 ST 3000
DR ST BOOT WY CHAPAR- DR SILVERADO JEFFRIES RANCH WHEEL DR TROTTING HORSE RD 1600 HUTCHISON 600 HARRIS DORSEY ST GOPHER CANYON FRUITLAND WY
MELROSE ROANE RANCHERO DR PONY PADDOCK DR BUCKBOARD PL DEL HACKAMORE RD BELMONT PARK RD 2900 HILL FRUITLAND
OLD RANCH 5600 MISSION SPUR 5800 AV AV 5900 CHURCHILL 400 MASON WY 2700 STRAWBERRY HILL LN 900
CHARLIE HORSE WY MUSTANG WY SR RING LN GOLDEN TRAIL ARABIAN WY STETSON SHIRE 1 MEADOWS SHETLAND CT MAR DOWNS RD RD HIGH MEAD CIR GOPHER CANYON RD
BRIGHT ST HORSE SHOE WY APPALOOSA DARTMOOR CT PALOMINO CLYDESDALE POLO CT DERBY CT SERENE RD NEIL TER MASON 2800 RD MASON 1100 MASON CIR S13
LAKE RD SPUR CT 1 THOROUGHBRED AV 92084 BELMONT PARK RD

miles 1 in. = 1900 ft.
0 .125 .25 .375 .5

SEE 1048 MAP

SAN DIEGO CO.

MAP

—N→

92003

20

21

SAN LUIS REY DOWNS

DOWNS COUNTRY CLUB

W LILAC RD

CM DL CIELO

FAIRGREEN WY

VILLAS DR

DEL REY

6200

6100

31500

MISSION RD

MONTEVIDEO PL

OLD RIVER

CM

SAN LUIS REY

D

76

SAN LUIS REY DOWNS COUNTRY CLUB

FS

RD

31300

31500

GOLF CLUB

CLUB VISTA LN

CIRCLE VIEW DR

DR

6500

LAKE VISTA LN

LAKE VISTA CIR

LAKE VISTA DR

6600

LAKE VISTA TER

1 VIA ALTA VISTA

VIA LARGA

VIA CASITAS

VIA VISTA

CAMINO DEL REY

6700

WRIGHTWOOD

RD

BOBRITT RD

VIA GIANNELLI LN

COTTONTAIL LN

BOBRITT LN

EAGLES PERCH LN

VIRGIN LN

31200

VIA MARGARITA

6900

MARIA ELENA

31100

CM D LS CABALLOS

30100   30200

VIA DE LA FLOR

VIA

VIA

MARIA

ELENA

DE

VIA CUESTA ARRIBA

VIA DE PAZ

29

28

DENTRO

CHATEAU

ST

CHATEAU MONTELENA

SAN LOMAS

VISTA DE LA

1

CHARIOT

CT

1600

DE

LOMAS

NORS RANCH

RD

AERIE HEIGHTS RD

RD

CALLE LOMA LN

1800

SAGEWOOD RD

DENTRO DE LOMAS RD

CALLE LA REINA

33

CANYON ESTATES RD

LA PRIMAVERA DR

LITTLE

GOPHER CANYON

1200

FAIRVIEW DR

FAIRVIEW LN

SWEET LIME RD

VIEW TR

3600

ALDORADO DR

DR

CREEK

32

GOPHER

CANYON

RD

VISTA DEL

1600

DEL

MAR

RUNNING STREAM RD

1800

GOPHER

OAK BRIDGE TR

SUMMERLAND

1900

RD

PASEO GRANDE

VIA DEL LOBO

WHISPER TRACE RD

THORN DALE

NORTH FORK DR

ORANGE TREE LN

TRACE

WILLAMAN DR

WHISPER

RD

AUTUMN BREEZE LN

SWEET TREE LN

WIND

RD

PAK

680

T10S

T11S

FAIRVIEW DR

3100

FERN FOREST RD

MOSSY ROCK DR

1600

1700

RUSTIC CANYON RD

1600

CREEK

CROSS CREEK RD

MYSTIC CREEK

OLD BASIN

GOPHER

CANYON CREEK

SOUTH

2400

OAK BRIDGE

WHISPER

POLO CLUB DR

DR

GOPHER

ROBBIE LN

KIRSTEN

29700

DE LOMAS

FELICIA WY

NELLA LN

RD

CANYON

HIDDEN HAVEN CT

VIA DEL CERRO

CARRIO DR

FAIRVIEW

2900

GOPHER CANYON CT

LITTLE GOPHER CANYON

SHEPHERD HILL RD

1300

GOPHER

CANYON

RD

KILBIRNIE LN

FORK

GOPHER

VISTA

VALLEY

COUNTRY CLUB

CLUBHOUSE

TUNRIF CT

HOXIE RANCH RD

2800

29400

VISTA

VALLEY

VIA DEL SANTO

HOLLY VALLEY DR

LAUREL VALLEY DR

OAK VALLEY DR

NELLA LN

CANYON

CREEK

5

4

ORMSBY WY

2900

GOPHER

D

WY

1100

S13

ELEVADO

FLAMETREE RD

2300

RUGER WY

PANORAMIC DR

PANORAMIC WY

PANORAMIC PL

SEE 1067 MAP

SEE 1088 MAP

0   .125   .25   .375   .5
miles 1 in. = 1900 ft.

Thomas Bros. Maps ®

COPYRIGHT 2001

—N—→

SAN DIEGO CO.

MAP

E F G H J

BOBRITT RD

22

23

MOUNT ARARAT WY

MOUNTAIN WY

NIRA LN

VIA ARARAT DR

VIA URNER WY

VIA LENNAR RD

OLD HWY 395

24

PALTIMO DR

VERDES DR

1

VIRGIN ISLANDS RD

VIA MARIPOSA CT

AFTON

FARMES LN

CALLE DE TALAR

31300   31800

RANCHO

AMIGOS

RANCHO AMIGOS RD N 7600

RANCHO AMIGOS RD

31800

RANCHO JOYA

AMIGOS RD

31300

SAN DIEGO AQUEDUCT

PALTIMO DR

2

31200

VIA MARIPOSA

MARIPOSA

NORTE

VIA MARIPOSA

VIA MARIPOSA SUR

27

26

CALLE

SECOND AQUEDUCT

OLD HWY 395

25

NELSON WY

31100

3

CAMINO

7200

REINA

LA

EAGLE

6900

MOUNTAIN 7200 RD

DEL

RANCHO

30800

CALLE

AQUEDUCT RD

8500

REY

7900

92026

ESCONDIDO FRWY

30600

(AVOCADO OLD HWY)

NELSON RD

VIA CANTAMAR

CAPTAINS CT

CAMINO

SEE 1069 MAP

4

VIA DE PAZ

DISNEY LN

KELLYN LN

PICO RD

ARRIBA

LUIS REY HEIGHTS RD

AVENIDA MIL FLORES

36

CM D LS LOMAS

CAMINO DE PINOS

34

CALLE DE LAS PIEDRAS

35

PICO RD

I-15

1 CIRCLE R COURSE LN

EL

5

PAKAMA LN 6800

DISNEY LN

HAWKHILL RD

PICO

LN

PICO RD

AQUEDUCT DR

BRUNS RD

CIRCLE R DR

CIRCLE R CREEK LN

CIRCLE COURSE

CIRCLE R WY

FS

T10S
T11S

SOUTHWIND LN

JENNY LN

MARGALE

DISNEY LN

29700

GOPHER

AVOHILL

WILD RD ACRES

RD

4100

RD

CIRCLE R GREENS DR

29700

CASTLE CREEK COUNTRY CLUB

PARK & RIDE

OLD CASTLE RD

29500

6

NELLA LN

RD

CANYON

3200

29800

CREEK

CANYON

GRAMMER RD

1200

HOLLYHILL RD

LEISURE LN

1

INDIAN HILL RD

8900

TWIN OAKS

VALLEY OF THE KING 29600 RD

3700

TAREK TER

1300

2

1000 4300

SAN DIEGO

EL PASEO

INDIAN

ESCONDIDO FRWY

CHAMPAGNE BLVD

92084

3

PROTEA VISTA

VALLEY

Y VALLEY DR

TWIN OAKS VALLEY RD

SILVERLEAF LN

SECOND SAN DIEGO

11   3900

LAWRENCE WELK LN

12

CHAMPAGNE BLVD

7

E F G H J

0   .125   .25   .375   .5

miles 1 in. = 1900 ft.

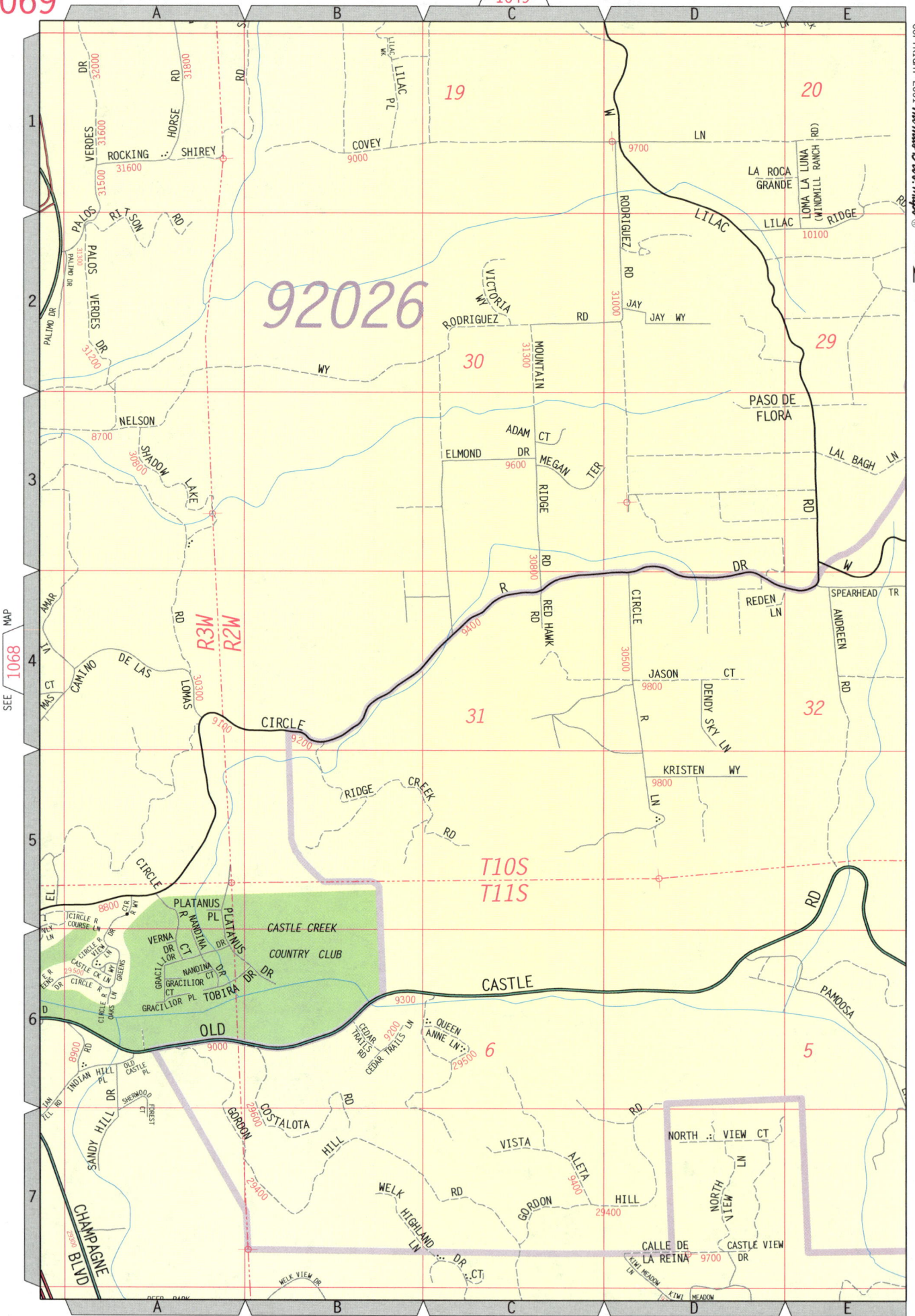

1069

—N—

SAN DIEGO CO.

MAP

SEE 1049 MAP

SEE 1068 MAP

A | B | C | D | E

92026

19 20 30 29 31 32 5 6

VERDES DR 32000
ROCKING SHIREY 31600
HORSE RD 31800
RITSON RD
PALOS VERDES DR 31300
PALMO DR
PALOS VERDES DR 31200
NELSON 8700
SHADOW LAKE 30800
CAMINO DE LAS LOMAS 30300
AMAR VI
MAS CT
CIRCLE 9100
CIRCLE 9200

COVEY 9000
LILAC WK
LILAC PL

VICTORIA WY
RODRIGUEZ WY
RODRIGUEZ RD
MOUNTAIN 31300
ADAM CT
ELMOND DR 9600
MEGAN TER
RIDGE RD 30800
R
RED HAWK RD 9400
CIRCLE 30500
R
JASON CT 9800
DENDY SKY LN
KRISTEN WY 9800
LN

RODRIGUEZ RD 9700
JAY WY
JAY RD 31000
LILAC
LILAC RIDGE RD
LA ROCA GRANDE
LOMA LA LUNA (WINDMILL RANCH RD) 10100
PASO DE FLORA
LAL BAGH LN
RD
DR W
REDEN LN
SPEARHEAD TR
ANDREEN RD

RIDGE CREEK RD

T10S
T11S

CASTLE CREEK COUNTRY CLUB
PLATANUS PL
PLATANUS DR
NANDINA PL
VERNA DR
GRACILIOR CT
NANDINA DR
GRACILIOR CT
GRACILIOR PL
TOBIRA DR
CIRCLE R COURSE LN
CIRCLE R VIEW WY
CASTLE CK LN
GREENS
CIRCLE R OAKS LN
EL 8800
CIRCLE RD
OLD RD 9000
CASTLE 9300
CEDAR TRAILS RD
CEDAR TRAILS LN 9200
QUEEN ANNE LN 29500
INDIAN HILL PL
OLD CASTLE PL
SANDY HILL DR
SHERWOOD CT
FOREST CT
INDIAN HILL RD 8900
GORDON 29600
COSTALOTA HILL
CASTLE RD
PAMOOSA
NORTH VIEW CT
NORTH VIEW LN
VISTA RD
ALETA 9400
GORDON
WELK RD
HIGHLAND LN
WELK VIEW DR
HILL 29400
CALLE DE LA REINA 9700
CASTLE VIEW DR
KIWI MEADOW
CHAMPAGNE BLVD
DEER PARK

R3W R2W

0 .125 .25 .375 .5 miles 1 in. = 1900 ft.

SEE 1089 MAP

SAN DIEGO CO.

MAP

E F G H J

KEYS CREEK

21 22

RD

LILAC

LAUREL RIDGE DR

LARGA

VISTA

27

E RD

BERRY

RD

N LN

OSHIA LN

BERRY RD 11100

CALGARY WY

BERRY RD

SAN

28

LILAC VISTA DR

MESA 11500

FROG HOLLOW

VERDE DR

LILAC HILL

BAGH LN

KING

SANDAY LN

DIAZ RD 10500

LILAC HILLS LN 30900

LILAC

COYOTE TR

OMA RD

ROADRUNNER RIDGE

DIEGO RD

MUNSTER

PLATZ WY 31200

LILAC

LILAC CREST 12000

ARHEAD TR 30500

92082

ROADRUNNER RIDGE S

AQUEDUCT

ROLLING HILLS DR

ROLLING 30500

ALTA

34

RD

LENNIE DR

LENINE DR

BAKTEN WY

PAYMASTER RD

SPEARHEAD

CASTLECREST

33

ROLLING HILLS WY

HILLS

MESA DR

34

LILAC KNOLLS RD

SPEARHEAD TR 29900

CASTLE HEIGHTS DR

AIRFLIGHT DR

BLACKINTON AIRSTRIP

DR

MINNEOLA CIR

GRANDVIEW HEIGHTS

OLD CASTLE WY

LILAC HEIGHTS CT

CASTLE RD

11800

RED MOUNTAIN DR

MAUKA DR

CAMPESTRE VIA

OLD 10800

WILKES 29900

GABLER DR

ALTA

MIRA LN

VIA

RED CANYON DR

CASTLERIDGE RD 29800

COULTER

SAN DIEGO

WILKES RD

4

3

SIERRA ROJO LN

MOUNTAIN 10900

CREEK

WILKES RD

A LN

MYSTERY

SIERRA

DOUBLE K RD

ROJO

EL RETIRO 28700

RD SIE

AQUEDUCT

SEE 1070 MAP

SEE 1089 MAP

0 .125 .25 .375 .5 miles 1 in. = 1900 ft.

1 2 3 4 5 6 7

SAN DIEGO CO.

MAP

—N—

SEE 1050 MAP

SEE 1069 MAP

SEE 1090 MAP

A B C D E

GENTLE OAKS TR

23

24

SUNDANCE RD

RICKS RANCH

JEFFREY HEIGHTS RD

RANCH CT

RICKS RD

OAK

NIKKI LN

REGINA GN

OAK

GLEN

RIVOLI RD

LAUREL RIDGE DR

27

26

STARDUST W 13600

25

HILLTOP TER

31200 DR

WILLOW VIEW

VIA VISTA MEJOR

MESA

VERDE RD

RD

HILLSTAR

LN

HILLTOP

HILLTOP PL LN

CRYSTALLITE

MOONLIGHT PL

31000

LN 13700

30800

OA

MANZANITA CREST DR

DR

HILLCREST

DR

HILLVIEW DR

STARDUST

HILLDALE

31100

13800

CREST

AVENIDA ANNALIE

CREEK

SHADY CREEK

COO 13800

LILAC 13300

CREST

MESA

ARBOLEDA VISTA DR

VIA LA MIRADA

RD

92082

R2W R1W

34

RD

COUNTRY RD

12400

35

ANTHONY HOLLOW

36

COL

KNOLLS

MONTANYA DR

SUPERIOR

MALEK RIDGE LN

RD

MONTANYA

LN

LENNIE DR

LILAC

HOLLOW RD

SUPERIOR

HOLLOW RD

ANTHONY

LN 12800

30000

ANTHONY

REDFERN LN

T10S T11S

MILLER

13800

TORINO CT

QUA

LILAC LIGHTS CT

OLD CASTLE RD

CALLE DE ENSUEÑO

LILAC

VIA SAUCE VEREDA

CUMBRES TER

RD

VIA ANTOINETTE

RD

RD

M

FRY 12100

VIA DEL SAUCE

CUMBRES

DERMID

VIA CAMPESTRE

ROBLES LN

VISTA TERRAZA CT

ROBLE VERDE

2

RD

VALLEY

STREAM RD

1

LITTLE POND RD

SHAD

3

LN

VIA ENCANTADO

SIERRA

INCREDIBLE LN

ANTHONY

VIA PIEDRA

OAKWOOD

ROJO

RD 12500

11

13600

VIA SUENA 13600

12

MISTY

OA

MILLER 13700

WILMINGTON AV

STONEGATE DR

PALOS TIERRA RD

29200

VIA DE LUNA

LITTLE CREEK LN

BLUE SAGE LN

0 .125 .25 .375 .5

miles 1 in. = 1900 ft.

SAN DIEGO CO.

MAP

SEE 1050 MAP
SEE 1090 MAP
SEE 1071 MAP

—N—

E F G H J

19 20

KELOWNA LN
DEBI LN
OAK GLEN RD
GLEN RD
TYLER RD TYLER HEIGHTS
TYLER LN
PAUMA ALTO DR
STANFORD CT
PALOMAR VISTA DR
CRESCENT MOON DR
LA CUESTA DE PALUMA
PAUMA VIEW DR
PAUMA HEIGHTS LN
PAUMA HEIGHTS RD
RIM OF THE VALLEY
RIVOLI RD
GLEN RD 13900
PAUMA HEIGHTS
BLUE MOON WY
JUSTIN PL
(JUANITA)
PALOMAR VW
PALOMAR RD
PAUMA HEIGHTS WY 31000
CURRAN CT
PAUMA HEIGHTS RD

OAK GLEN RD
OAK GLEN RD
VALLEY CENTER HS
30 ALISA PL
KIRA PL
ASHLEY CT
PL
OAK MEADOW RD
WINTER CREEK LN
29 SADDLE CREEK LN 28
AYERS LN
N SADDLEBACK RD
SADDLEBACK RD

OAK GLEN LN
COLE GRADE RD 31200
WHITE STAR LN 14200
MARGARITA LN
REBECCA LN
COOL VALLEY RANCH LN
OAK KNOLL LN
RANCH CREEK RD
RANCH CREEK LN
SADDLE-BACK LN
SADDLEBACK RD

R1W 30800 31100 13800
SHADY CREEK LN
COOL VALLEY RANCH RD
LUCAS LN
KEYS
OAK CREEK
RANCH
CREEK
SADDLEBACK
ROSETTE RUN 15300
QUAIL LN
GAETANO ALTIERI DR
EVA DE LUCA WY
LITTLE QUAIL
ROCK ROSE LN
TORONGA WY
COOL R

COOL VALLEY RD 13800
COOL VALLEY RD 14800
VILLA SIERRA
COOL VALLEY LN

TERRACE VIEW LN
EAGLES NOEL
RUN LN
COYOTE WY
COOL VALLEY HIGHLANDS RD 30400
30100

31 COLE GRADE LN
FARAWAY PL
RABBIT RUN
STURNELLA LN
32 RUN 33
PERSIMMON LN
VILLA SIERRA LN

AVA LN
RESAVA LN 14200
CANE RD
PUMA 14600
30200 TR 14700
30600

LN
NAGORSKI LN
MILLER LN
COLE GRADE RD
MILLER RD 30200
WILHITE RD
RES
SIERRA GRANDE RD
LITTLE SIERRA GR

QUAIL HOLLOW LN 13800 13900 29900
MAUDE RD
PASO ROBLES
SIERRA PL
PASO ROBLES LN 29400

VIA VALENCIA
HAWKSBURY LN 4
VI

MILLER
MILLCO WY
MILLCO LN
6 MILLCO LN
WILHITE LN
5 KENSAL CT
AGUACATE LN
DUFFWOOD
FOX RUN LN
PASO ROBLES CT
PASO ROBLES RD

MILLER RD 14000
SHADY CREEK RD
MISTER B PL
BERNABEO CT
TWAIN WY
STARGAZE ST 29200
VALENCIA WY

OAKWOOD GLEN PL
HORSE CREEK TR
SAINT GEORGES LN
LA MAC LN
HIGH POINT DR
FRUITVALE LN
FRUITVALE 15000
HUSTED
VALENCIA PL 15400

OAK RD 13700
MILLER CREEK
BLUE SAGE LN
VALLEY CENTER CEM
7 COLE GRADE RD 29100 14200
OLIVE LN
PLEASANT KNOLL LN 29000
ROBERT ADAMS COMMUNITY PARK
RANCHO COPA
JANA LN
8 FRUITVALE LN 9
MAC TAN RD

PAUMA

0 .125 .25 .375 .5 miles 1 in. = 1900 ft.

1071

SAN DIEGO CO.

MAP

SEE 1051 MAP

A   B   C   D   E

RINCON

MARIETTA

PAUMA HEIGHTS RD   21   22   23

RIM OF VALLEY

LAZY H DR

GLENAIR WY
15800

SAN

YUMA CREEK

PORTRERO

ROCKY RD

VALLEY CENTER RD

1

RIM OF THE VALLEY   28

LAZY H DR

27

LUIS

GULCH RD   26

2

RODRIGUEZ RD

REY RIVER

MED

S6

ROCK STONE RD

WOOD LN

ARVISO RD   MCC

RD 30500

KEYS CREEK

3

COOL VALLEY RD

CALLEJO FELIZ TER

OZLAND AV

ANGELA CT

COOL STONE VALLEY LN

VISTA

WNTVLVD

CALLEJO FELIZ DR

CALLEJO FELIZ DR

EMERALD CITY DR

34

RINCON INDIAN RESERVATION

35

4

33

ROCK

CALLE LADERA

ALBERTUS LN

30100   30700

30100

VILLA SIERRA

LN

MAC TAN RD
15700   30000

LA RRA LN

LITTLE SIERRA

RD 29900

CAMINO DE ORO

BOUCHER HEIGHTS RD

NDE RD

SIERRA GRANDE RD

BRENDA WY

VILLA SIERRA RD

BRICK

DOROTHY LN

5

SHADY OAKS WY
15700

WIZARD WY
16000

S6

CREEK

MAC TAN

YELLOW

VIKING GROVE LN   SEVERINO LN

VIKING GROVE LN
15800   16000

3

Y

6

MAC   TAN

4

LN
16000

COTTAGE GARDEN RD

THE

CARA LN

LEMON BLOSSOM

EAGLE VIEW LN
15900

PASO ROBLES RD

GRANDFATHERS LN

PLUM FRUITVALE CT

FRUITVALE HTS

RD
16000

MACKINZIE WY

POLVO DR

VALLEY CENTER RD

PARADISE

GATE   FRUITVALE

SO ROBLES RD

7

VIA SALVADOR

GATE

RANCHO VALENCIA ST

TANGELO WY

28900

RD
29000

DIA DEL SOL

10

POLVO DR
28700

9

RANCHO VALENCIA WY

SUNSET WY

ZIGA DR

CAMINO CONEJO

MAC TAN RD

LAJOS LN

JOHN WAYNE LN

SUNSET
28700

VESPER

VESPER RD

SEE 1070 MAP

SEE 1091 MAP

0   .125   .25   .375   .5
miles   1 in. = 1900 ft.

E   F   G   H   J

92061

RANCHO PAUMA

1

EUCALYPTUS RD

26

MAZZETTI LN

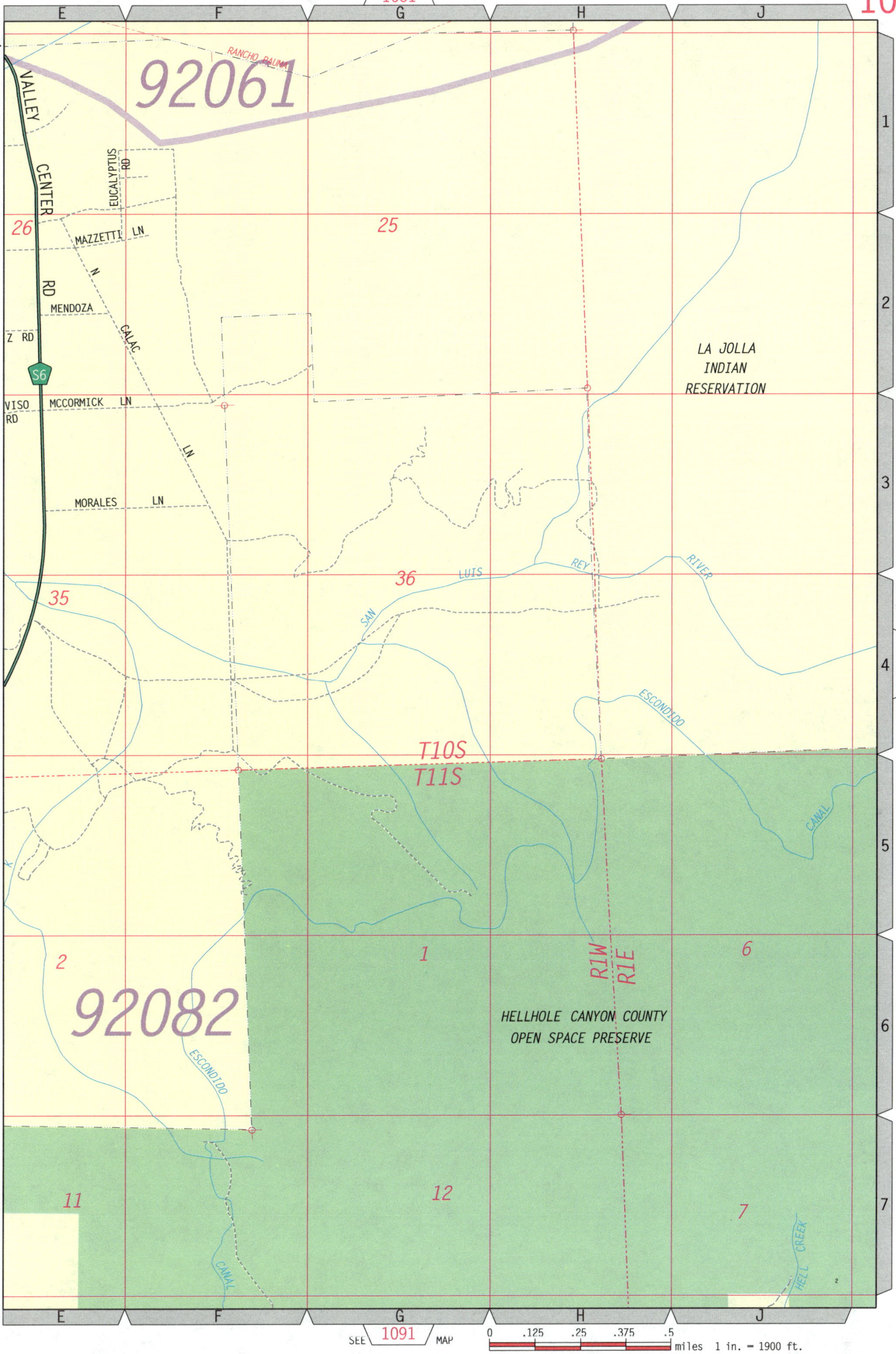

N

CALAC

Z RD

S6

MENDOZA

25

2

VISO RD

MCCORMICK LN

LN

LA JOLLA
INDIAN
RESERVATION

3

MORALES LN

36

LUIS   REY   RIVER

SAN

35

ESCONDIDO

T10S
T11S

CANAL

5

2

1

R1W
R1E

6

92082

ESCONDIDO

HELLHOLE CANYON COUNTY
OPEN SPACE PRESERVE

6

11

12

7

CANAL

HELL CREEK

2

E   F   G   H   J

0   .125   .25   .375   .5
miles   1 in. = 1900 ft.

SAN DIEGO CO.

MAP

SEE 408 MAP

A   B   C   D   E

—N—

1

2

3

SEE 408 MAP

4

PACIFIC

5

6

7

A   B   C   D   E

0 .125 .25 .375 .5

miles 1 in. = 1900 ft.

SEE 1105 MAP

SAN DIEGO CO.

MAP

E F G H J

1

MARINE CORPS BASE
CAMP
JOSEPH H PENDLETON

STUART

MESA

SANTA MARGARITA RIVER

MARGARITA RIVER

92055

SANTA

RR

MILITARY RD

BLVD

ASH

CARNES RD

2

CAMP
PENDLETON

SAN DIEGO FRWY

LEMON

GROVE RD

VANDEGRIFT

RD

PINYON DR

TIERRA BLANCA AV

VOLCAN RD

JACINTO RD

JAMUL

3

14TH ST

13TH ST

12TH ST

A ST

B ST

C ST

100

200

1300

ST

ST

11TH ST

10TH ST

9TH ST

8TH ST

5

I-5

800

VANDEGRIFT

VALLECITO

LN

PAUMA ST

SAN JACINTO

CUYAMACA

PALO VERDE DR

JAMUL

SEE 1086 MAP

4

IMHOFF RD

BOAT ST

BASIN ST

HARBOR RD

9TH ST

9TH ST

FS 7TH ST

A

ST 7TH ST

6TH ST

WIRE ST

5TH ST

1300

MOUNTAIN

GATE

BLVD

5

OCEAN

NORTH
BREAKWATER

B

RANCHO SANTA MARGARITA

HARBOR DR N

NORTH HARBOR

KOELPER ST

SAILFISH LN

SKIP JACK LN

NAUTILUS LN

MARLIN RD

DOLPHIN

LAS FLORES

SANTA FE AV

200

HARBOR DR

SEAHORSE GATE

SAN RAFAEL DR

N COAST

SUNSET DR

CAPISTRANO DR

SAN LUIS REY DR

500

600

6

OCEANSIDE HARBOR

NORTH
JETTY

SEE A J7

1 SEA BREEZE DR
2 BUENA VISTA LN
3 CIRCLE DR
4 WHITE CAP LN

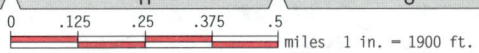

SOUTH HARBOR

HARBOR DR N

RIVERSIDE DR 400

CARMELO DR

MONTEREY DR

WOODLAND DR

HARBOR DR S

SDNR

SAN LUIS REY RIVER

HWY

S21

22

A

BLUFF DR

SANDY CT

CC

SOUTH
JETTY

PACIFIC ST

SAN

7

OCEANSIDE
92054

BREAKWATER WY

METRA WY

METROLINK

PACIFIC

THE STRAND

NEPTUNE

WINDWARD WY

SURFRIDER WY

27

CLEVELAND ST

PARK

800

600

700

400

E F G H J

0 .125 .25 .375 .5 miles   1 in. = 1900 ft.

SAN DIEGO CO.

MAP

SEE 1066 MAP
SEE 1085 MAP
SEE 1106 MAP

92055

92054

MARINE CORPS BASE
CAMP
JOSEPH H
PENDLETON

MILITARY BLVD
VANDEGRIFT
RR
SANTA MARGARITA RIVER

Rancho Santa Margarita y Las Flores

HENSHAW
JONES CT
GAGE DR
ABNER
CABANO
BAILEY CT
DAVIS CT
KING CT
ALONZO CT
EDGER CT
CARNES
FLEISCHMANN CT
RD

DAHLIA ST
DOGHOOD
COTTONWOOD ST
COLUMBINE
BEGONIA
ALDERWOOD
BOXWOOD
AMARYLLIS
ST

SIERRA
ALICIO RD
MADRE DR
CHRISTIANSON CT
JOHNSON
LITTLETON
MOUNTAIN RD
JAMUL
VOLCAN
JACUMBA LN
ASH
WIRE
DAFFODIL ST
BIRCH ST
CHERRY RD
CARNATION
BLUEBELL
ASTER ST
PAUMA
SANTA ROSA DR
MONSERRATE
TEMECULA
CUYAMACA
SAN JACINTO RD
CINTO

PRINCE OF PEACE
ABBEY
BENEDICTINE
MONASTERY

BENET
HILL RD
W AIRPORT RD
AIRPORT RD

SAN SIMEON ST
SANTA ROSA ST
SANTA ANITA
SAN JUAN
LORETTA DR
SAN JUAN PL
SAN PAULA ST
SAN MATEO ST
SAN JOSE ST
CAPISTRANO
SAN LUIS REY DR
MONTEREY DR
LUIS DR

CAPISTRANO PARK

SAN LUIS REY
SAN LUIS REY RIVER

76

HUBBERT LAKE

RICEWOOD

MUIRFIELD DR
DEERFIELD CT
HILLFIELD CT
RIMHURST
RIVERTREE
ASHWOOD CT
NORTHWOOD DR
MARLADO HIGHLANDS PARK
SHADOW TREE
MORNING VIEW
SPINDLEWOOD
MEADOW VIEW DR
NEW BRANCH CT
BRIGHTWOOD CT
REDWING DR
SOUTHWOOD DR
VALLEY CREST
LONG CREST DR
WILLOW TREE CT
TOWNWOOD DR
CRYSTAL WOOD DR
NUMBERS AV
SILVER RIDGE CT
SPRING BROOK CT
SPINDRIFT CT
HOLLOW TREE DR
ROCK LN
RIVERTREE DR
CRESTWOOD DR
SHADOW TREE
RAINWOOD
CHIMNEY

12

13

OCEANSIDE MUNICIPAL AIRPORT

EDDIE JONES WY

CRESTWOOD
RIVER RD
FOUSSAT RD
FOSS
R5W
R4W

EXWY

VIA DE LA VALLE
ROYMAR RD
PRODUCTION AV
EL CENTRO RD
VIA MONTE REY
VIA DEL NORTE
SAN LUIS VIA DEL
AIRPORT
MISSION

BENET
VIA DEL
JONES RD
BENSON PL
BARNWELL
COTTINGHAM
CAROLYN LN
ROBERTA LN
NOREEN LN
NOREEN PL
COTTINGHAM
FOUSSAT
TODD
VISTA MONTANA WY
VALLEY VIEW LN
LADERA WY
BUDDY TODD PARK
PARNASSUS CIR
FOWLES
GUINEVERE
SQUIRE
CAMELOT
LANCELOT

HILLCREST PL
MELODY LN
CARPENTER RD
ECCLESIA DR
AMICK
POPLAR RD
ACACIA AV
WILLOW AV
MID

14

ROSE
ELLERY ST
PAHVANT ST
BUTLER ST
TODD ST
TURNBULL
N BARNWELL
MESA
LOMITA

LUIS REY
IVER
NEVADA ST
MARQUETTE
8TH ST
DUBUQUE
LEMON ST
HIGGINS
MCNEIL
BUSH
BUENA
SHOSHONE ST
HOLLY
SAN DIEGO
SANTA
ARCHER ST
OLIVE ST
BARBARA
LAUREL
NELMS ST
LANGFORD
LANDS END WY
STONEY POINT
CANYONSIDE
EAGLE VISTA
EAGLES NEST
MESA
BREEZE WY
PS
CROSS

WALTON ST
LORETTA ST
PAPIN ST
MARSON ST
ZEISS ST
BREEZE
WYNN ST
LORETTA
KRAFT ST
MISSION
N CANYON DR
N CAREY ST
CANYON DR

SAN DIEGO

5
27
106

CRESTLINE
LIBBY ST
CREGAR ST
CAREY ST
HILLDALE
CRESTLINE DR
DOGWOOD PL
EDGEWOOD DR
LOTUS ST
WALSH ST
LOMA ALTA
PENKEA
PAJAMA
LOMITA ST
KENNEDY LN
MACDONALD
EAST ST
HOOVER
CROUCH
CANYON WY
HIDDEN
CORTO ST
BARNWELL PL
VILLAGE
SQUIRE

OCEANSIDE PLAZA

24

FOSTER ST
DIXIE ST
MAXSON
RAINBOW ST
SARATOGA ST
EL MONTE DR
RAYMOND LN
WINCHESTER
GREENBRIER
CADILLAC CIR
COUNTRY CLUB LN
GRACE ST
DIVISION ST

23

BALDE-RAMA PARK

MISSION AV
PARK & RIDE
BROOKS ST
BARNES ST
1ST ST
PS
PO

RECREATION PARK

SECTION ST

N COAST HWY
NEPTUNE WY
WINDWARD
NEVADA
SUMMIT AV
HORNE ST
WEITZEL ST
CLEMENTINE DR
SURFRIDER
FREEMAN
DITMAR
CIVIC CENTER
TREMONT
CLEVELAND
MISSION
MISSION SQUARE

OCEANSIDE HS

26

CENTER AV
DIVISION
GARFIELD
GRANT
WEITZEL
TOPEKA
MISSOURI AV
PO
BROOKS ST
SEAGAZE
HORNE ST

521

25

CENTER CITY GOLF COURSE

OCEANSIDE
APPLE ST
CHURCH ST
CANYON LODGE
SKYLARK
LOMA
ALTA CR
INDUSTRY
CRESTRIDGE DR
JOE CARRASCO PARK
KEA
AVOCADO
DOWNS

FRWY

OCEANSIDE VLG

SEE 1106 MAP

0 .125 .25 .375 .5
miles 1 in. = 1900 ft.

A   B   C   D   E

E F G H J

SAN DIEGO CO.

MAP

COPYRIGHT 2001

Thomas Bros. Maps®

N

WHELAN LAKE

WHELAN LAKE RD

SAN LUIS REY

SAN LUIS REY RIVER

CALLE JOVEN

CALLE MONTECITO

DESCANSO OLD RIVER ST

BRISAS ST

RAINIER WY

MISSION AV

76

FRAZEE RD

AVENIDA SOLEDAD
AVENIDA LORENZO

ALL SAINTS CEMETERY

MISSION SAN LUIS REY DE FRANCIA

IVEY RANCH PARK

MISSION DOUGLAS PLAZA

MISSION PLAZA REAL

MISSION CENTER

FIRESIDE PARK

PARKSIDE DR

APRICOT TREE WY

EL CAMINO REAL

92057

VISTA BELLA
VISTA REY

VISTA CAMPANA N

VISTA CAMPANA S

MERCADO DE OCEANA

VISTA OCEANA

EMERALD ISLE GOLF COURSE

BUFFUM DR

DEARBORN

EL CAMINO HS

MARTIN LUTHER KING JR PARK

MESA

SEE A J2

1 CAROB WY
2 HAZEL WY
3 JUNIPER WY
4 HYACINTH WY
5 AZALEA WY
6 CHESTNUT WY
7 CURRANT WY
8 CARDINAL WY
9 BLACKBIRD WY
10 LARK WY

SEE 1087 MAP

92056

OCEANSIDE

TROPICANA

FOUSSAT RD

PARK & RIDE

COPPERWOOD CENTER

JIBSAIL ST

STARBOARD CIR

BARTLETT

PEAR BLOSSOM AV
PEAR BLOSSOM ST
PEAR BLOSSOM CIR

BRANDYWINE

OCEANSIDE BLVD

RANCHO DEL ORO

TERRACE GARDENS MHP

OCEAN SHORES HS

OCEANSIDE BLVD

ALTA CREEK

SEE A J7

1 CROWN VIEW TER

AVENIDA DE

CALLE BUENA VENTURA

SAN HELENA

PALISADES PARK

SARBONNE DR

DUNSTAN ST

FIRE MTN PARK

ELDEAN LN

ETERNAL HILLS CEMETERY

EL CAMINO COUNTRY CLUB

HENIE HILLS DR

SKYLINE DR

OCEANVIEW RD

IRONWOOD

GOLFCREST DR

SORRENTO DEL ORO DR

30 29 28

19 21 20

18 17 16

7 8 9

6 5 4

0 .125 .25 .375 .5 miles   1 in. = 1900 ft.

SAN DIEGO CO.

MAP

SEE 1067 MAP

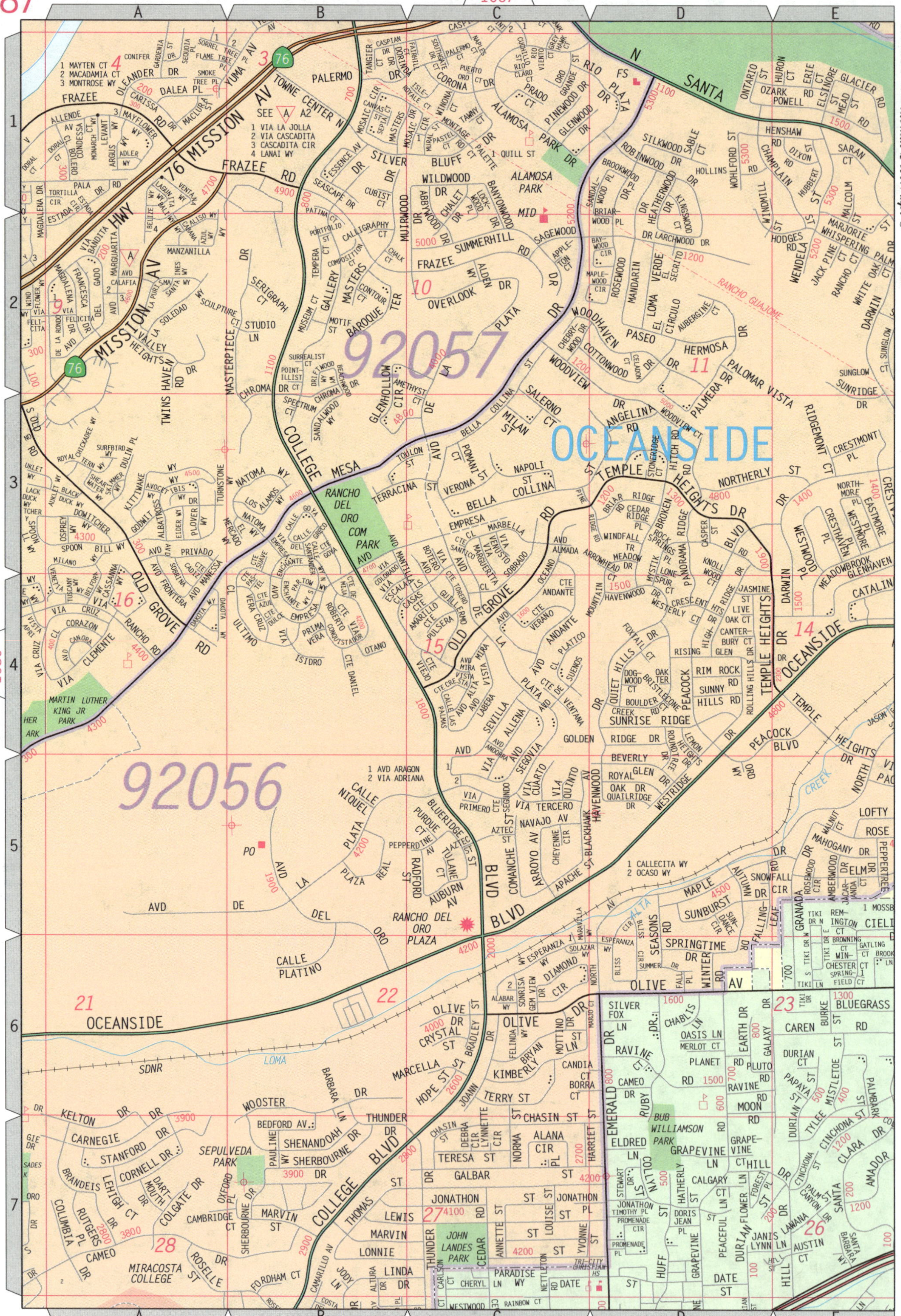

COPYRIGHT 2001 Thomas Bros. Maps® —Z—

92057

92056

OCEANSIDE

SEE 1086 MAP

SEE 1107 MAP

miles 1 in. = 1900 ft.
0 .125 .25 .375 .5

SAN DIEGO CO.

MAP

92084

92083

VISTA

GUAJOME REGIONAL PARK

Rancho Guajome Adobe

ANTIQUE GAS & STEAM ENGINE MUS

MELROSE DR W

BOBIER DR

SANTA FE AV

VISTA FRWY

OSBORNE ST

BANDINI

COPYRIGHT 2001

ThomasBros.Maps®

SAN DIEGO CO.

MAP

—N—

SEE 1068 MAP

SEE 1108 MAP

SEE 1087 MAP

92084

VISTA

VISTA VALLEY COUNTRY CLUB

PANORAMIC WY

MASON RD
OSBORNE ST
VISTA GRANDE DR
WARMLANDS
PRINCE WY
POZZUOLI LN
COUNTRY ESTATES DR
CHARLES LN
CHARLES PL
DOUGLAS DR
EVERETT WY
LARK HILL DR
TAYLOR ST
E TAYLOR ST
W TAYLOR ST
OLD TAYLOR ST
ARCADIA AV
HERMANA CT
MAXWELL LN
AIRBORNE DR
STORMY LN
MONIQUE CT
PALOMAR PL
MADERA LN
MARIPOSA CT
CYPRESS CREEK CT
AMBER CREEK CT
SUMMER CREEK CT
WILLOW CREEK
SHERMAN
CONT HS
MONTE MAR RD
MONTE MAR
BONAIR
INDEPENDENCE
HUMMINGBIRD LN
QUEENS WY
WARMLANDS WY
KINGS WY
KINGS RD
KINGS LN
LAS LOMAS
TIERRA DEL CIELO
CM DEL CIELO
CULEBRA
CERRO DE ORO
CM CANCIONES
VERDE
CAMINO LOMA
GRANDVIEW
ODELL CIR
ALESSANDRO
ALEXSANDRA LN
STONEWALL LN
BARRANCA
VEREDA
CASA DE VEREDA
FRIENDLY DR
SAL LN
SUEMARK TER
TACOMA LN
DRURY LN
BEVERLY
DOLPHIN CIR
ELM
OAK
CHRISTINA DR
VIA PEDRO
CERRO LINDO
ARROW WOOD LN
WOLVERINE WY
CALLE ANTONIO
CALLE TIJERA
ALTA
MESA VERDE
MESA
AVENIDA TAXCO
SINALOA
WARMLANDS
EDGEHILL RD
EDGEHILL GATE
MANGO GLEN
HEIGHTS WY
HARDELL
TROY PL
THOMAS PL
ASHLEY LN
VINE CIR
CATALINA
CATALINA AV
WALINCA WY
LUZEIRO
SAN CLEMENTE AV
DEEB CT
DEEB
FOOTHILL DR
SAPPHIRE PT
LIONS GATE
CALLE HUERTO
LOUISE LN
SAN CLEMENTE WY
CASTLEGATE LN
FOOTHILL RANCH LN
STARHAVEN WY
HUNTALAS LN
PALM HILL DR
VIA DEL MONTE LIBANO
ORA AVO DR
ORA AVO LN
ORA AVO TER
ORA AVO
CAPE BRETON
SHALE ROCK RD
OVERHILL DR
BARREL BLOSSOM LN
LA RUEDA RD
WINTERS HILL RD
WESTBURY RD
TIERRA VERDE RD
LOCH LOMOND HIGHLANDS
GIDDINGS RANCH
KATERRI DR
CUERVO RD
SUNRISE DR
SUNRISE PL
SUNRISE DR E
GIL WY
VALLEY RD
BERKELEY WY
SUNRISE DR
RANCHO BUENA VISTA
EUCALYPTUS AV
EUCALYPTUS LN
ALTA VISTA
CRESCENT
ALTA VISTA DR
CROMWELL WY
FARINA LN
EL PAJODO
CHESTNUT LN
CYPRESS
CHELSEA CT
PATRICIA LN
TRACI LN
TIGER TAIL RD
TIGER TAIL LN
EUCALYPTUS
MARLIN RD
PARKER PL
HILLWAY DR
ALTA VISTA DR
RUDD
PEACH GROVE CT
LEXINGTON
MCGREGORY
COVENTRY
GIRARD WY
BELLERIVE CT
GIRARD PL
ZADA LN
MUDDY CT
BEAUMONT LN N
BEAUMONT LN S
BEAUMONT PL
HEATHER DR
BONNIE BRAE LN
NIE RAE PL
CLEARBROOK LN
MEADOW LAKE DR
DONNAN PL
GLENERN
SAPOTE CT
ROSARIO
CIEGO CT
SHADOW MOUNTAIN
MEMORY TER
OAK KNOLL DR
CAMINO
ALTA VISTA
VALE TERRACE DR
VALE TERRACE
BRENGLE WY
CALLE DEL SOL
LYNMAR
SKYLINE DR
POINTER LN
ROCKHILL RD
UPLAND DR
STEPHANIE LN
CALLE LAS MORAS
FOOTHILL DR
BOBIER DR
FOOTHILL
BRENGLE TERRACE PARK
MOONLIGHT AMPITHEATER
DEERHAVEN DR
DEERHAVEN
PASEO DE ARQUERO
GRANDE ROSS
COLINA TER
EARL ROCK
DONS DR
SUNKIST
JUDIANN
HADDY
HARDELL WY 2898

GREEN HILLS
LITTLE
GOPHER
CANYON
CREEK
BUENA VISTA CK
PLEASANT HEIGHTS DR
WONDER VIEW
ALOHA
GRANDVIEW RD
ELEVADO
GRANDE TER
GRANDE DR
VISTA AV
BELLA ROSA DR
LITTLE RAY LN
CORRE CAMINO WY
QUAIL VIEW DR
OJEDA RD
ELEVADO RD
SUBIDA AL CIELO
VIA DEL PRADO
CAMINO
PANORAMIC DR
MIRADOR
CANTERA
VIA SUBRIA
WESTRIDGE LN
AUTUMN LN
SUMMER CT
LAGUNA LN
PALOMAR WY
E VISTA WY
CORVALLA DR
COLUCCI DR
CORVALLA
BAGSBY CT

VISTA DR

miles 1 in. = 1900 ft.
0 .125 .25 .375 .5

8 9 17 16 19 20 21 28 29

SAN DIEGO CO.

MAP

Thomas Bros. Maps®

COPYRIGHT 2001

N

E F G H J

92026

VIS VALLEY DR
28900
VIS VALLEY LN
2200
SOUTH
SCOTT LN
TWIN OAKS VALLEY
SILVER LEAF LN
28900
PASEO
BUCKSHOT RD
WELK LN
LAWRENCE WELK
LN
28900
1

PAR VALLEY
FORK
28600
DR
28500
GOPHER
TWIN
HUCKLEBERRY
EL
600
RD
AQUEDUCT
LN
500
EL-FARRA
ST
1100
28700
LAWRENCE WELK CT
I-15

10
11
12
1
2

OAKS
28400
CANYON
LN
DOLL
DOLL LN
3300
RAG
3000
SATIN
2700
SECOND SAN DIEGO
VALLEY CREEK
14
CAMINO
MAYOR
13

15
3
4

CREST
DR
3898
GIST
RD
GA
SEE 1089 MAP

TWIN OAKS
EL PASO ALTO
CALLE DE CRISTO
500 600
92069

HARDELL
DEEB
CT
B
2900
DR
LN
EL PASO ALTO
3800
EL PASO ALTO NORTE
3800
EL VALLE PASO
400
PASO ALTO
QUARRY
700
600
RD
500
BRIDLE CREEK LN
CAMINO
TWIN
3300
CALAFIA
OAKS
23
24
22
5

VIA DEL ONTE LIBANO
AVO DR
AVO LN
VISTA PACIFICA
400
CM D LS LOMAS
3500
LN
VALLE
SAN DIEGO AQUEDUCT
VISTA RIM PL
VISTA CANYON CIR
SYLVIE CT
LADYBUG LN
600
VALLEY
3000
BUENA CREEK RD
LADYBUG LN
800
SOLAR LN
SOLAR VIEW DR
TRES ENCINOS
LYNN LN
3000
JONI
HOMESTEAD LN
GIST DR RD
COUNTRY GARDEN LN
SARVER LN
6

SUGARBUSH TER
ER
STBURY D
HOLLYBERRY
SUGARBUSH DR
800
ROYAL
SILVER OAK LN
3400
VALLEY CREST DR
RD
HARDELL RD
900
BERNARDINO LN
SANDOR WY
SALEM ST
EMMA
3500
EMMA LN
27
VIA CONCA DORO
VIA PARADISO
BLUE BIRD CANYON TR
VIA RANCHO PACIFICA
SECOND
PACIFIC VISTA WY
TAMARA LN
26
2900
RD
2800
2700
VISTA MERRIAM
25
DEER SPRINGS RD
S12
7

E F G H J

0 .125 .25 .375 .5
miles 1 in. = 1900 ft.

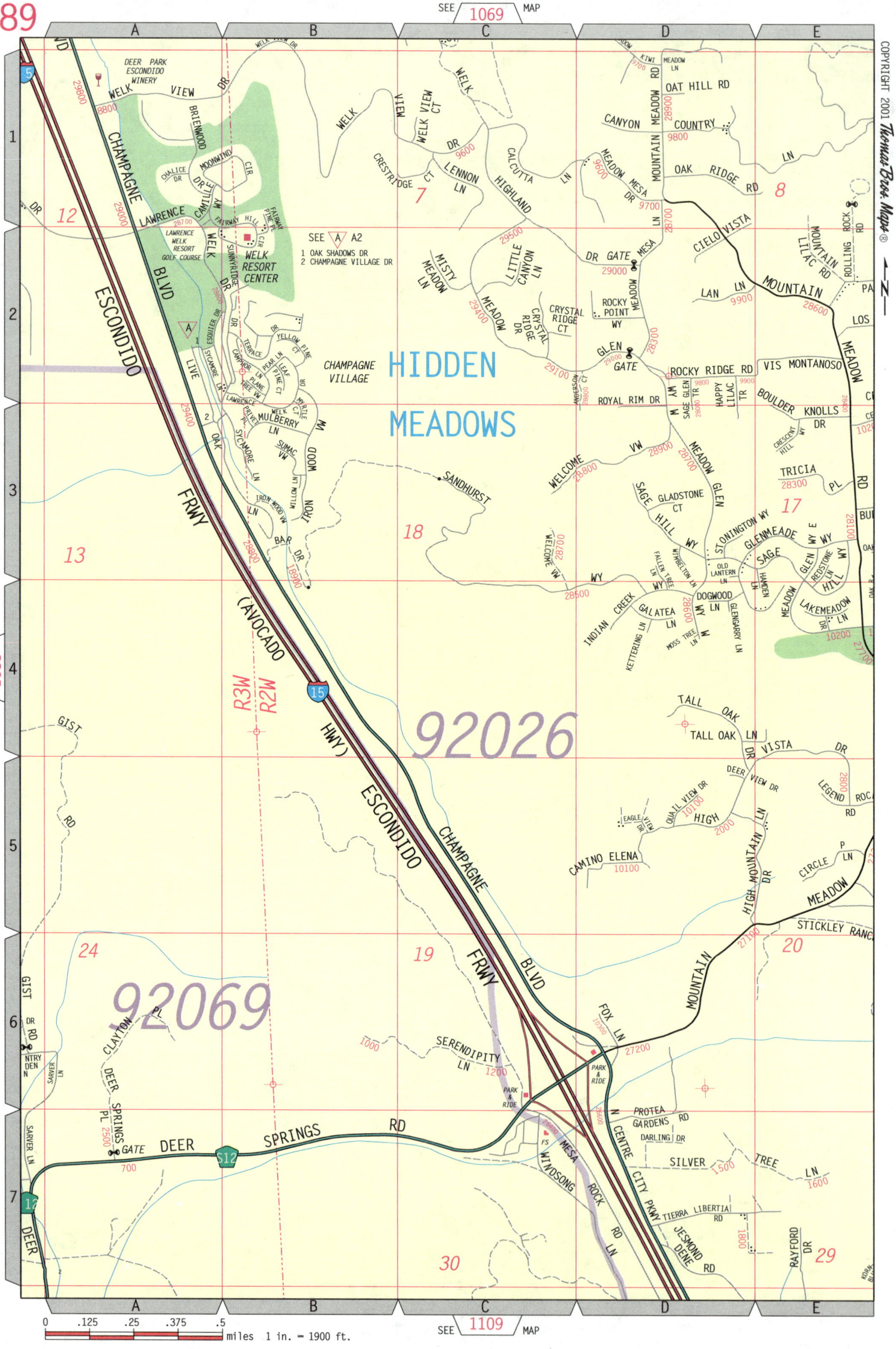

SAN DIEGO CO.

MAP

SEE 1069 MAP

COPYRIGHT 2001 Thomas Bros. Maps®

—N—

HIDDEN

MEADOWS

92026

92069

SEE 1088 MAP

SEE 1109 MAP

DEER PARK ESCONDIDO WINERY

LAWRENCE WELK RESORT GOLF COURSE

WELK RESORT CENTER

CHAMPAGNE VILLAGE

SEE A A2
1 OAK SHADOWS DR
2 CHAMPAGNE VILLAGE DR

ESCONDIDO FRWY (AVOCADO HWY)

CHAMPAGNE BLVD

ESCONDIDO FRWY

DEER SPRINGS RD

CENTRE CITY PKWY

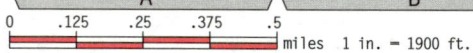

0 .125 .25 .375 .5
miles 1 in. = 1900 ft.

ThomasBros.Maps®

COPYRIGHT 2001

N

92082

ESCONDIDO

DALEY RANCH

TURNER LAKE

TURNER DAM

MEADOW LAKE COUNTRY CLUB

SEE 1090 MAP

9   10

16   15

21   22

9   28   27

HEATHER VIEW LN
ROLLING ROCK RD
TAIN RD
PASEO DE SANTOS
LOS NIDOS LN
NOSO
MEADOW
CERVEZA
OLLS R
CERVEZA
BAJA
CROOKED OAK LN
YUCCA TR
CERVEZA CT
CAVALIER CT
DEEP CANYON CT
FAIRCREST
DEEP CANYON DR
FAIRCREST WY
MEADOW GLEN
TURNER LN
WILKES RD
WILKES RD
WILKES LN
BETSWORTH RD
CEPIN DR
DOUBLE K RD
EL RETIRO
AERIE RD
BURNT MOUNTAIN RD

PL
BURNED
RD
OAK
MEADOW OAK LN
SPARKLING OAKS TR
BURNED OAKS TER
ENGELMANN OAK TER
PAR VIEW CT
GLEN
TREESIDE LN
RIM RD
GLEN
MEADOW GLEN WY E
COUGAR
COUGAR
E
MEADOW GLEN WY E BROADWAY
QUIET HOLLOW LN
BOULDER PASS
COUGAR PASS RD
SAN DIEGO AQUEDUCT
TURNER HEIGHTS LN
TURNER HEIGHTS
ROSECREST DR
ALPS
ALPS LN
ALPS WY
DR

OAK RANCH WY
MOON VIEW WY
GRASSY WY
DSTONE HILL WY
OAK RANCH PL
MEADOW DR
MEADOW LN
OAK RANCH RD
RD
HIDDEN MEADOWS RD
LOTUS POND LN
REIDY CANYON RD
REIDY CANYON
RANCHO ROBLE RD
LEGEND ROCK RD
LOTUS POND LN
GATE
ADOW
CKLEY RANCH
LE P LN
COUGAR PASS RD
SUNNYSIDE LN
BACHELOR LN
CABALLERO CANYON RD
COUGAR
REIDY CANYON PL
REIDY CANYON TR
N BROADWAY (REIDY CANYON RD)
REIDY CANYON
SAN DIEGO
NESMITH PL
CRESCENDO DR
SKY DR
PRICE PL
ARITRANG LN
KAYWOOD LN DR
HARMON PL
LILAC DR
SKY
HILL DR
AQUEDUCT
KORA BLUM DR

0 .125 .25 .375 .5 miles   1 in. = 1900 ft.

SAN DIEGO CO.

MAP

SEE 1070 MAP

COPYRIGHT 2001 Thomas Bros. Maps ®

—N—

A **B** **C** **D** **E**

AERIE RD
WILMINGTON AV
29000
CHOCTAW RIDGE RD
12600
STONEGATE DR

10

11

OAK ST
SPRUCE ST
PINE ST
1500
BEATITUDE DR
12300
SPYGLASS TR
PEPPER DR
SKY PILOT WY
28500
LILAC
VIA PIEDRA
28900
CANDLE WY
29100
13400
28600

12

BLUE SAGE LN
JENNY JAY CT
JAKE RD
V
28700
MILLER

1

VALLEY VIEW RD
12100
SKY VIEW DR
12000
CEPIN DR
AERIE RD
28500
BETSWORTH LN
ALAMAR RD
28200
BIG BEND WY
HIDEAWAY LAKE
12800
28000
LONESOME OAK WY
12800
SOLDIER OAKS LN
GROVE KNOLL LN
OLD RANCH RD
12700
ROCK RIDGE LN
28800
HUNZA
13100
HILL TER
HUNZA CT
HILL
13300
28400
CANYON RD
BALLERINA
CHAPARRAL
13700
28050

2

28300
BETSWORTH
12100
12500
12800
RD
BLUEBERRY HILL LN
SHADY KNOLL RD
13200
RD
13400
28300
R2W R1W

S6

COMM CTR
FS

BURNT MOUNTAIN RD

BURNT MOUNTAIN RD
FRACE LN
VALLEY CENTER

15

BURNT

14

13
OLD RD
CALLE DE
28000
27800
RD

3

MOUNTAIN RD
27700
FRACE LN
27600
RANCHO VISTA CT
MIRAR (CHARLAN)
13300
DE VALLE (RD)
13400
RD
13700
27500
VALLEY

4

SEE 1089 MAP

MIRAR DE VALLE RD
12400
12500
13000
RD
12800
ORCHARD VISTA RD
13300
CYPRESS
RDG
27700
SUGAR BUSH
BANBURY WY
27100
RINEHART LN
DR
TOYON RIDGE TR
27000
FAIRLANE RD
26900
WOODSTOCK DR
13700
SH
BANBURY
26700
PL

22

23

24

5

ESCONDIDO

92026

DALEY

RANCH

6

25

27

26

7

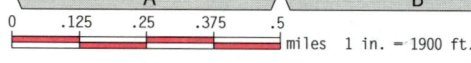

0   .125   .25   .375   .5
miles   1 in. = 1900 ft.

R2W

SEE 1070 MAP

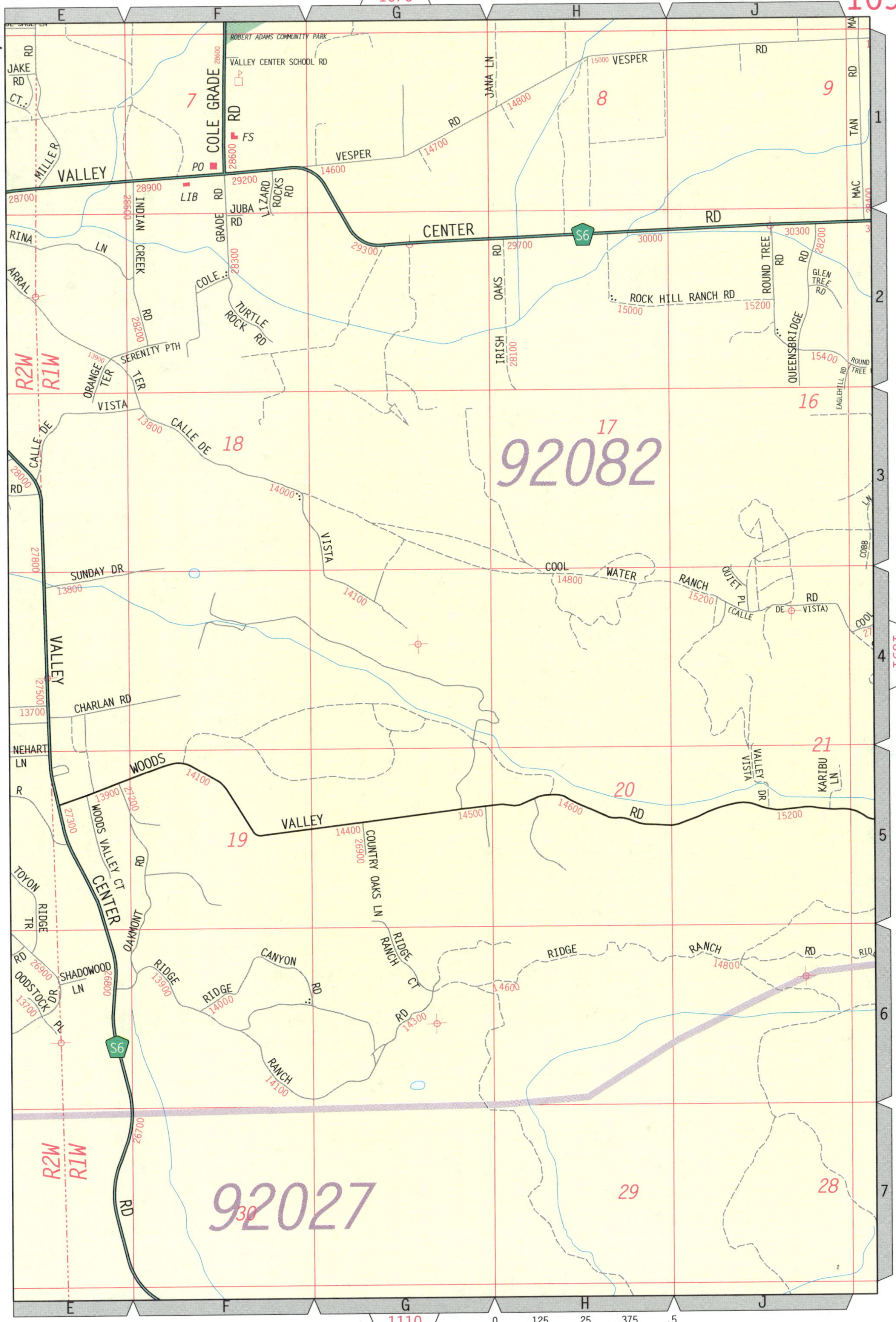

E
F
G
H
J
1
2
3
4
5
6
7
ROBERT ADAMS COMMUNITY PARK
VALLEY CENTER SCHOOL RD
COLE GRADE RD
28600
VESPER RD
15000 VESPER
JANA LN
14800
14700
14600
RD
TAN RD
MAC
JAKE RD
CT.
MILLER
VALLEY
28700
28900
29200
PO
FS
LIB
INDIAN CREEK RD
28500
GRADE RD
JUBA RD
LIZARD ROCKS RD
CENTER RD
S6
29300
29700
30000
30300
28200
RINA LN
ARRAL
COLE
28300
TURTLE ROCK RD
28200
SERENITY PTH
13900
ORANGE TER
TER
VISTA
13800
CALLE DE
IRISH OAKS RD
28100
ROCK HILL RANCH RD
15000
15200
ROUND TREE RD
GLEN TREE RD
QUEENSBRIDGE
15400
ROUND TREE
EAGLEHILL RD
7
8
9
16
17
18
92082
CALLE DE
28000
RD
14000
VISTA
27800
SUNDAY DR
13800
14100
COOL WATER RANCH RD
14800
15200
QUIET PL
(CALLE DE VISTA)
COBB
LN
COOL
VALLEY
27500
13700
CHARLAN RD
NEHART LN
R
WOODS VALLEY RD
14100
13900
27200
27300
WOODS VALLEY CT
19
14400
14500
14600
15200
20
21
26900
COUNTRY OAKS LN
VALLEY VISTA DR
KARIBU LN
TOYON RIDGE TR
CENTER
RD
OAKMONT
RANCH RIDGE CT
RIDGE RANCH RD
14800
RD
RID
RD
26900
OODSTOCK DR
13700
SHADOWOOD LN
26800
PL
RIDGE
13900
RIDGE
14000
CANYON RD
14600
RD
14300
RANCH
14100
S6
R2W
R1W
26700
RD
92027
30
29
28

SEE 1091 MAP

SEE 1110 MAP

0 .125 .25 .375 .5 miles 1 in. = 1900 ft.

SAN DIEGO CO.

MAP

COPYRIGHT 2001 Thomas Bros. Maps ®

—N—

A B C D E

15600 VESPER LN RD VESPER RD
MAC RD LAJOS LN
9 NON RD 10 1
TAN RD SUNSET TER
MAC 28400 SUNSET THUNDERNUT 28600
28300

VALLEY CENTER RD
30400 31100
MID FS
STATION RD
AHERN RANCH RD

NE LN PARADISE CANAL ESCONDIDO
00 ROUND TREE RD CANAL
EAGLEHILL RD COBB 16 VIA VISO 15
LAKE RD
16600 WOHLFORD LN RD
LN GATE WOHLFORD RD CANAL
COBB SUN ENERGY RD
COOL WATER RANCH LN
MATHEW RD WOHLFORD RD ARMSTRONG RANCH RD SAN
27600 4800 PASQUAL
COOL
WATER LAKE INDIAN
RANCH
RESERVATION

LN RD 21 VALLEY 22 23
RD RD
WOODS N RD
15600 SAN PARADISE
PASQUAL MOUNTAIN PAR
INDIAN MAEMAR DR
RESERVATION 16600

RIDGE RANCH RD ESCONDIDO SAN PASQUAL
SAN INDIAN
6 RESERVATION
SAN
PASQUAL N LAKE
INDIAN 28 RESERVATION 27 WOHLFORD
8 RD BEAR VALLEY HEIGHTS RD
2 RD

S6

HELL CREEK

0 .125 .25 .375 .5
miles 1 in. = 1900 ft.

A B C D E

E F G H J

COPYRIGHT 2001

Thomas Bros. Maps®

←N

SAN DIEGO CO.

MAP

11

HELLHOLE   CANYON   COUNTY   12

7

1

OPEN   SPACE   PRESERVE

CREEK

CANAL

CANAL

RD

MERIDIAN

RD

SAN BERNARDINO

CREEK

CREEK

2

92082

14

13

HELL

27700

SAN

HELL

18

LN

SANTEE

VISTA

EL NORTE

VISTA

27600

RD

LN

LN

PRESERVE
ENTRANCE

SANTEE

19600

LN

19800

3

SUNSET

CLEARVIEW
LN

POSSUM
PASS

CARLATA
27400

LN

RICARDO
RANCH

RANCH

RD

DR

MARSHALL
WY

SIESTA
LN

KIAVO

MOUNTAIN

RD

R1W R1E

HELLHOLE CANYON COUNTY

OPEN SPACE PRESERVE

SEE 409 MAP

LOS

HERMANOS

18500

LATIGO RD

BOSAL
CT

CONCHO
CT

27100

ROWEL
CT

CONCHITA

27300

RD

27200

LN

PARADISE

RD

19300

ELIZABETH
DR

DR

MOUNTAIN

VERDE

19

RD

4

RVATION

SKYLINE RANCH
COUNTRY CLUB

CONCHITA

RD

LN

24

DR

SIERRA

27000

19398

23

27000

PARADISE

MEADOW
LN

DELRIDGE
LN

26900

PARADISE

SHILOH

27000

MOUNTAIN

LITTLE   FIELD
LN

KIAVO

5

MOUNTAIN

LN

ENCINAS

26798

RD

LITTLE

FIELD
LN

TRAIL

RANCHO GUEJITO

30

CALLE DE
ENCINAS CT

CALLE DE

OAK

26600

6

SHAUNA

WY

OAK

26000

25

92027

CALLE DE ENCINAS

TRAIL

RD

26

GUEJITO

CREEK

2

7

E F G H J

0 .125 .25 .375 .5
miles 1 in. = 1900 ft.

ESCONDIDO   CREEK

SAN DIEGO CO.

MAP

COPYRIGHT 2001

Thomas Bros. Maps ®

—N—

SEE 1058 MAP

SEE 410 MAP

A B C D E F G H J
1 2 3 4 5 6 7

14

13

S22

MONTEZUMA VALLEY RD

CANYON

CANYON

23

24

TUBB

TUBB CANYON RD

19

1098

25

26

30

29

ANZA–BORREGO

R5E R6E

31

36

35

92066

T11S T12S

1

2

3

3

2

1

6

STATE

GRAPEVINE

10

11

12

7

1118

CANYON

RD

YAQUI

WELLS RD

CREEK

SAN FELIPE

15

14

13

78

18

R5E R6E

92036

22

23

24

19

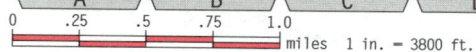

0 .25 .5 .75 1.0 miles   1 in. = 3800 ft.

SEE 1138 MAP

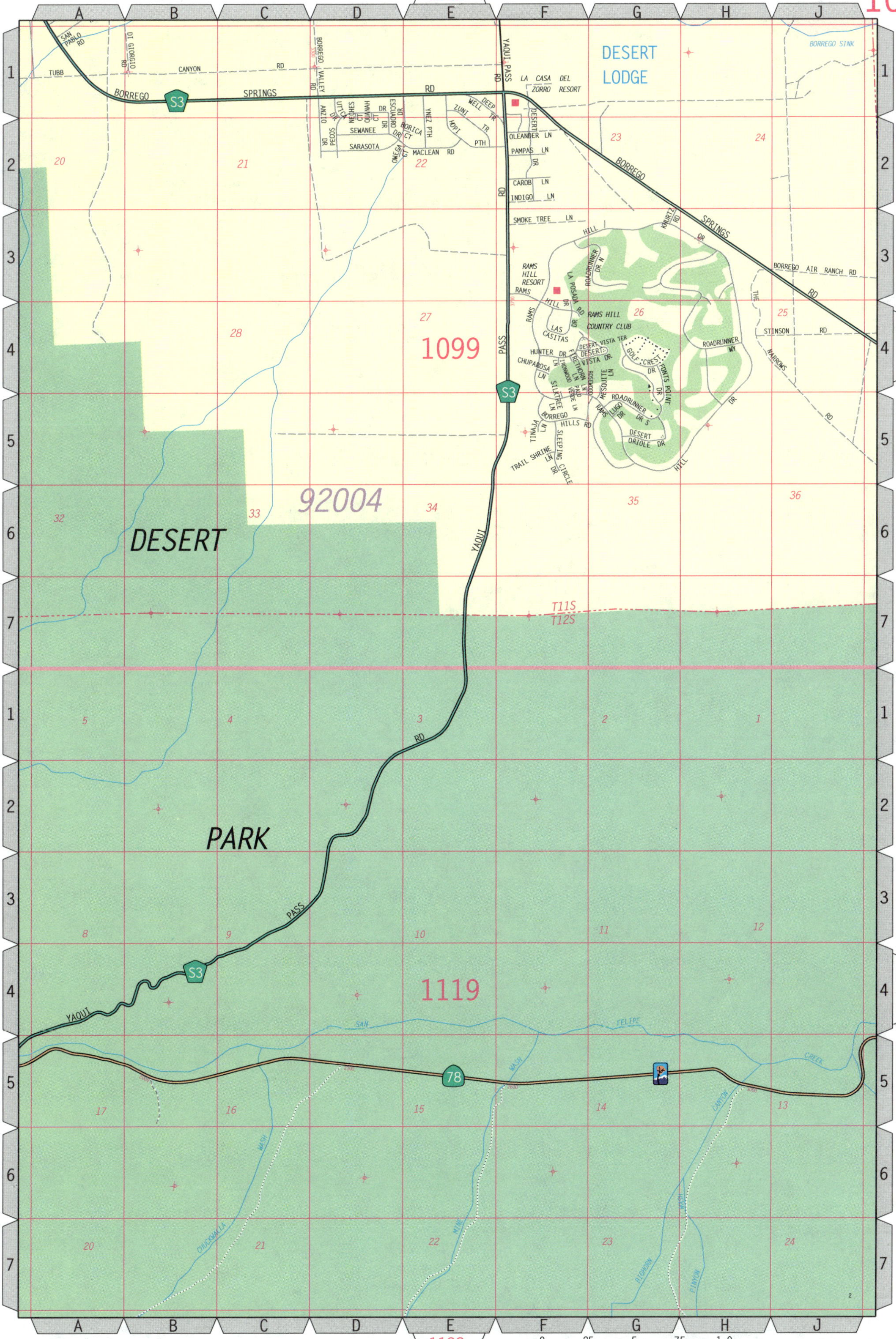

Thomas Bros. Maps®

COPYRIGHT 2001

SAN DIEGO CO.

MAP

DESERT LODGE

SAN PABLO RD
DI GIORGIO RD
TUBB
CANYON RD
BORREGO SPRINGS S3 RD
BORREGO VALLEY RD
YAQUI PASS RD
LA CASA DEL ZORRO RESORT
DEEP WELL TR
DESERT RD
OLEANDER LN
PAMPAS LN
CAROB LN
INDIGO LN
SMOKE TREE LN
BORREGO SPRINGS DR
BORREGO AIR RANCH RD
RAMS HILL RESORT
LA POSADA RD
RAMS HILL DR
RAMS HILL COUNTRY CLUB
ROADRUNNER WY
STINSON RD
NARROWS
DESERT VISTA TER
GOLF CREST DR
ROADRUNNER DR
DESERT ORIOLE DR
HILL DR

92004

DESERT

PARK

YAQUI PASS RD
S3

YAQUI PASS S3

78

SAN FELIPE CREEK

20 21 22 23 24 25 26 27 28 32 33 34 35 36

T11S T12S

1099

1119

SEE 1100 MAP

SEE 1138 MAP

0 .25 .5 .75 1.0 miles 1 in. = 3800 ft.

SAN DIEGO CO.

MAP

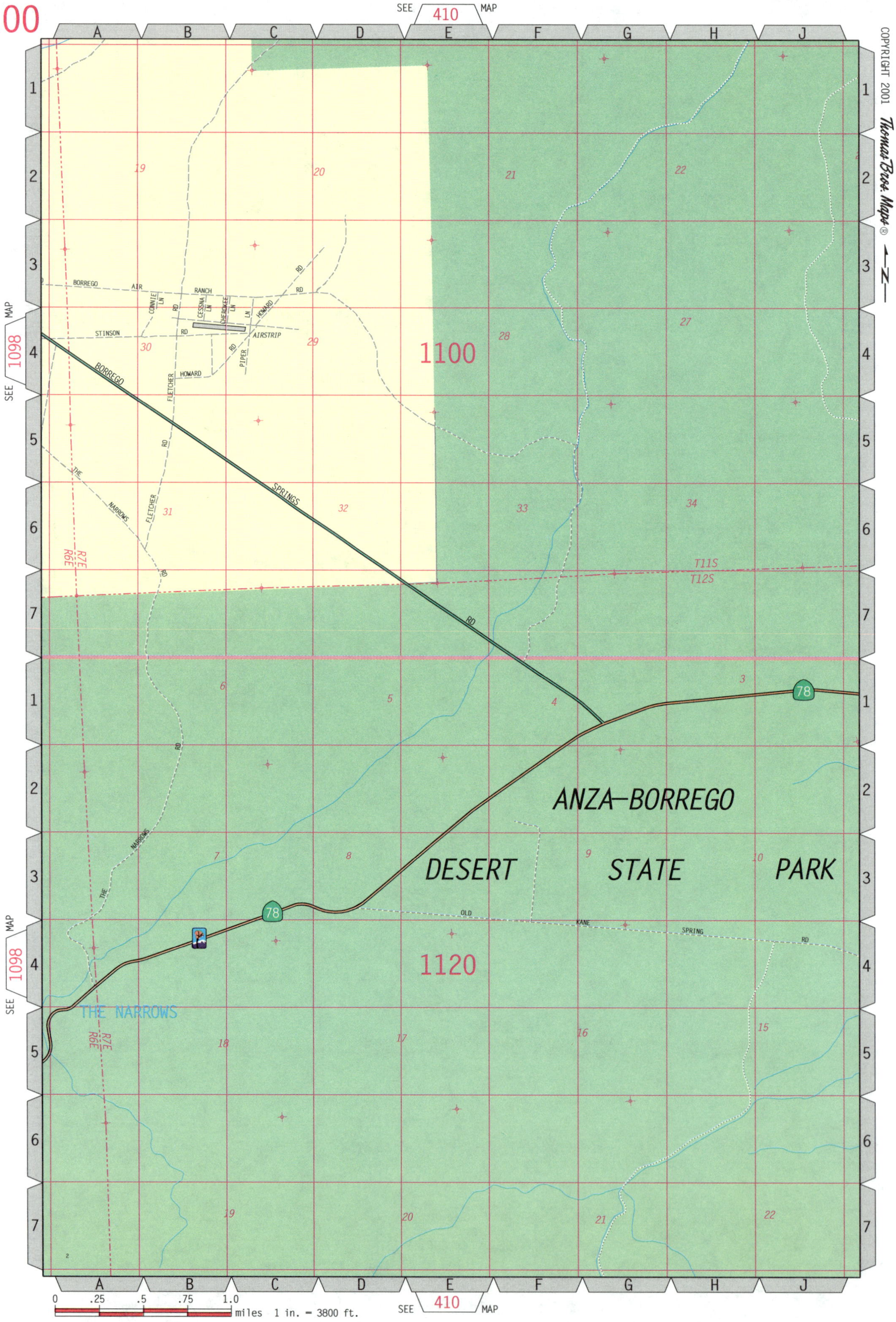

SEE 410 MAP

COPYRIGHT 2001

Thomas Bros. Maps ® —N—

A B C D E F G H J

SEE 1098 MAP

1 2 3 4 5 6 7

19

20

21

22

BORREGO AIR

RANCH

CONNIE LN

CESSNA LN

CHEROKEE LN

HOWARD RD

RD

RD

STINSON RD

AIRSTRIP

PIPER RD

30

29

28

27

1100

FLETCHER

HOWARD

BORREGO

THE

NARROWS

FLETCHER

RD

RD

31

32

33

34

SPRINGS

R7E
R6E

T11S
T12S

RD

6

5

4

3

78

7

8

9

10

ANZA–BORREGO

DESERT STATE PARK

THE

NARROWS

RD

78

OLD

KANE

SPRING

RD

1120

THE NARROWS

R7E
R6E

18

17

16

15

z

19

20

21

22

SEE 1098 MAP

SEE 410 MAP

A B C D E F G H J

0 .25 .5 .75 1.0

miles 1 in. = 3800 ft.

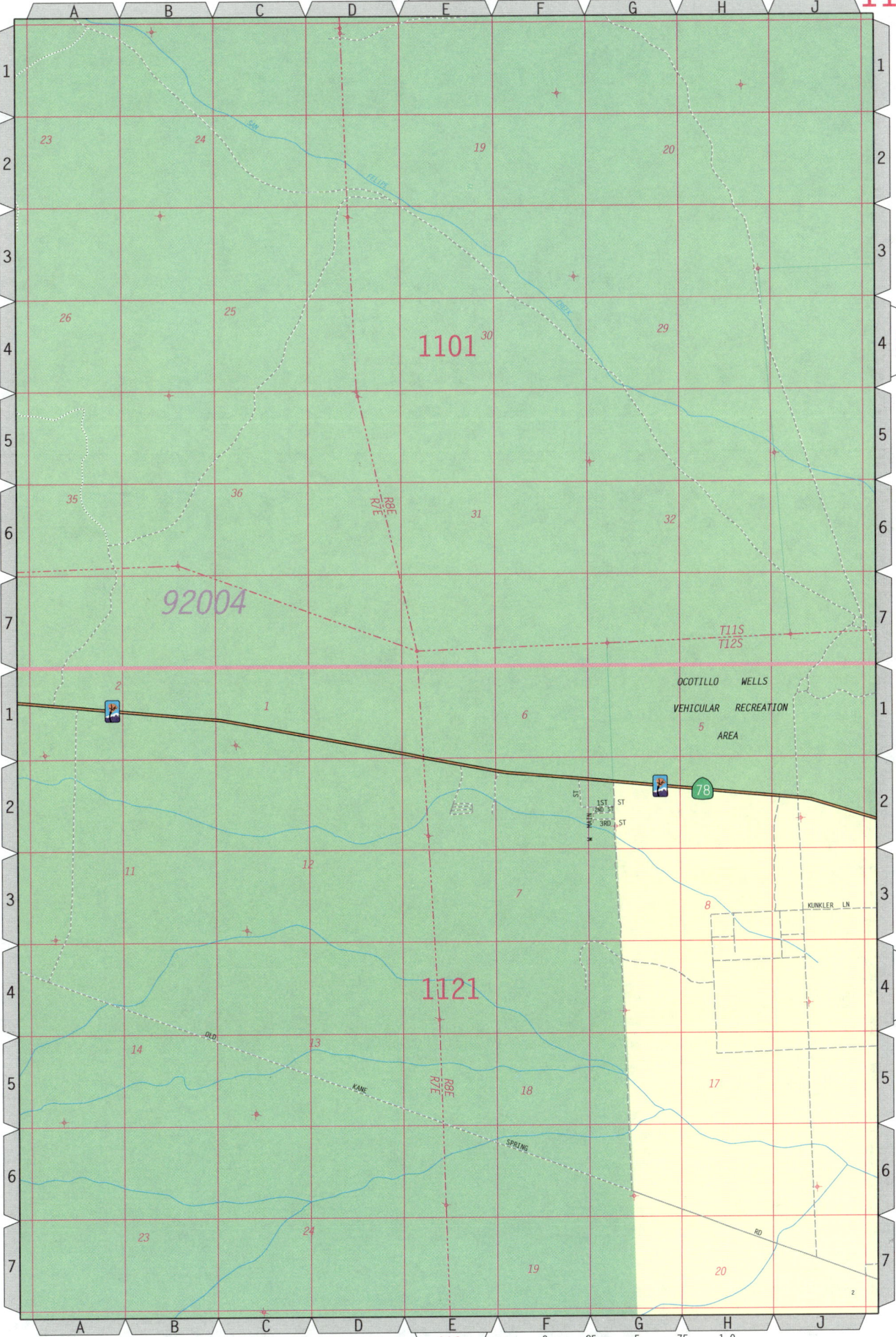

SAN DIEGO CO.

—N—

SEE 410 MAP

MAP

A B C D E F G H J

1

23   24   19   20

2

3

26   25   29

1101 30

4

5

35   36   31   32

6

R8E R7E

92004

7

T11S
T12S

OCOTILLO   WELLS

VEHICULAR RECREATION

AREA

78

1

2   1   6   5

1ST ST
2ND ST
3RD ST
W MAIN

2

11   12   7   8   KUNKLER LN

3

1121

14   13   17

OLD

4

KANE

18

5

SPRING

6

23   24   19   20   RD

7

A B C D E F G H J

0 .25 .5 .75 1.0

miles 1 in. = 3800 ft.

SEE 1085 MAP

A B C D E

1

2

3

PACIFIC

SEE 408 MAP

4

5

6

7

SEE 408 MAP

A B C D E

0 .125 .25 .375 .5
miles 1 in. = 1900 ft.

E F G H J

92054

1 PIER VIEW WY *PIER*

ROTARY PARK

OCEANSIDE

ThomasBros.Maps®

COPYRIGHT 2001

—N→

OCEAN

SAN DIEGO CO.

MAP

SEE 1106 MAP

1

2

3

4

5

6

7

E F G H J

SEE 408 MAP

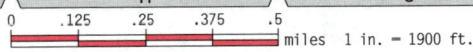

0 .125 .25 .375 .5 miles 1 in. = 1900 ft.

SAN DIEGO CO.

MAP

SEE 1105 MAP

—N—

PACIFIC

OCEAN

OCEANSIDE

92054

OCEANSIDE

SOUTH OCEANSIDE

OCEANSIDE CITY

TYSON STREET PARK

ROTARY PARK

PACIFIC LINEAR PARK

HAYES
MARRON
FORSTER
BEACH GODFREY CROSWAITHE

BUCCANEER BEACH PARK

SAINT MALO BEACH

SEE B J2
1 VISTA WAY VILLAGE DR
2 PAS DE ALICIA
3 PAS DE BRISAS
4 PAS DE COLOMBO
5 RANCHO AGUA HADIONDA DR
6 PAS DE LS AMERICANOS
7 PAS DE COLORES
8 PAS DE ELENITA
9 PAS DE FRANCISCO
10 PAS DE LS CALIFORNIANOS

SEE A H3
1 VIA DIEGO
2 VIA JUDY
3 VIA ROBERTO
4 VIA BOCAS
5 VIA SABINAS
6 VIA VERA
7 VIA CARDEL
8 VIA DENISE
9 VIA MERDE
10 VIA TONALA
11 CL HACIENDA
12 VIA CAJITA

T11S
T12S

R5W R4W

CARLSBAD

ARMY & NAVY ACADEMY HS

MAGEE PARK

CARLSBAD STATE BEACH

(FRAZEE BEACH)

JEFFERSON

CENTER CITY GOLF COURSE

SAN DIEGO FRWY

miles 1 in. = 1900 ft.
0 .125 .25 .375 .5

SEE 1086 MAP

E
F
G
H
J
92056
92008
CARLSBAD
EL CAMINO NORTH CENTER
PLAZA CAMINO REAL
NORTH COUNTY PLAZA
CARLSBAD PLAZA
CARLSBAD PLAZA SOUTH
PACIFIC COAST PLAZA
CAMINO TOWN & COUNTRY
EL CAMINO COUNTRY CLUB
FIRE MOUNTAIN PARK
HOSP GROVE PARK
LARWIN PARK
LAGUNA RIVIERA PARK
CARLSBAD HS
JR HS
VISTA WY
FRWY
78
5
S11
EL CAMINO REAL
CARLSBAD VILLAGE DR
TAMARACK AV
SAN DIEGO FRWY
CARLSBAD BLVD
MARRON RD
HILLSIDE
CHESTNUT
BUENA VISTA CREEK
AGUA HEDIONDA LAGOON
1
2
3
4
5
6
7

SEE 1107 MAP

SEE 1126 MAP

0 .125 .25 .375 .5 miles 1 in. = 1900 ft.

SAN DIEGO CO.

MAP

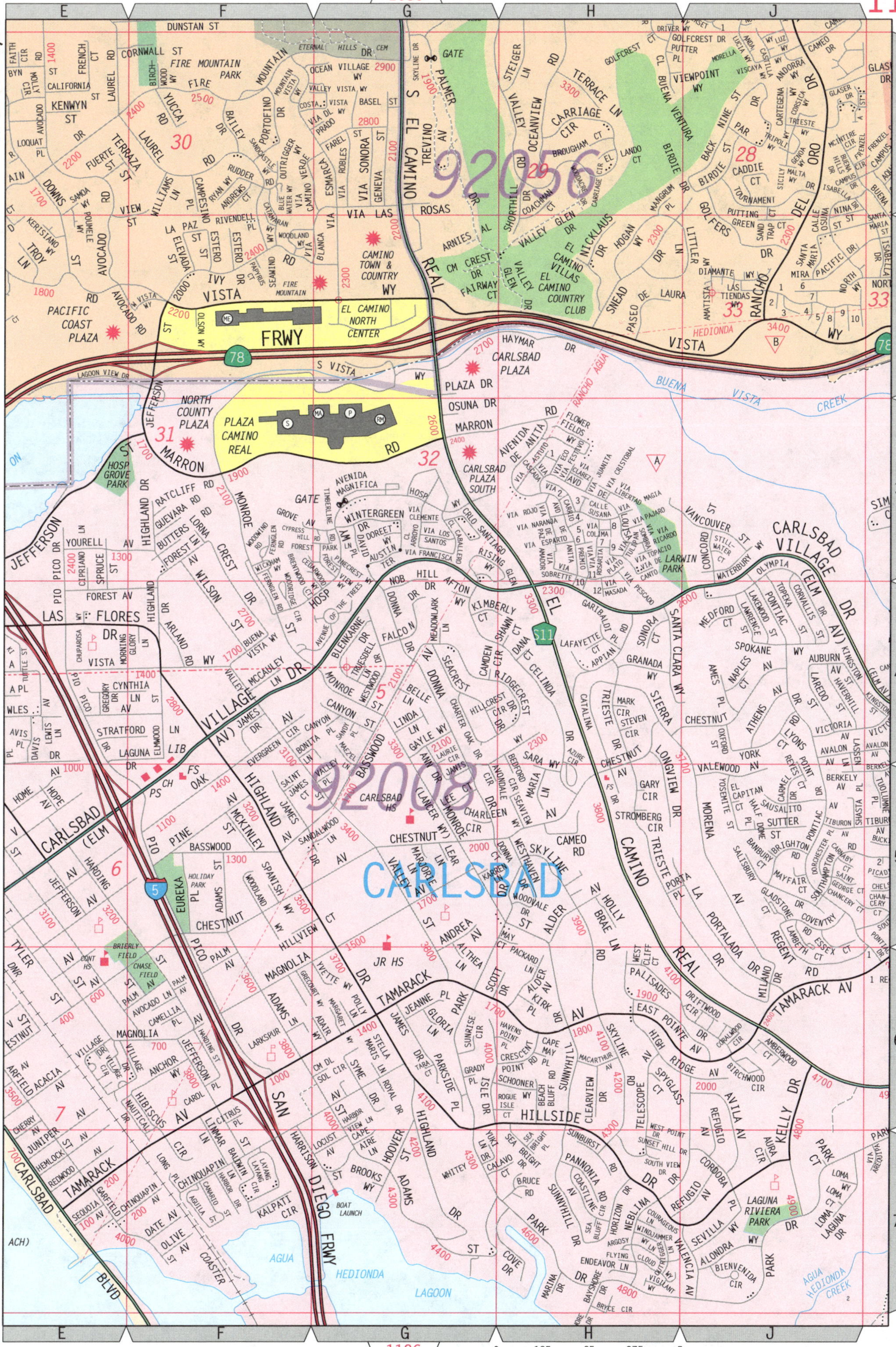

SAN DIEGO CO.

MAP

MIRACOSTA COLLEGE
28

27

26

33

78

92008

CARLSBAD

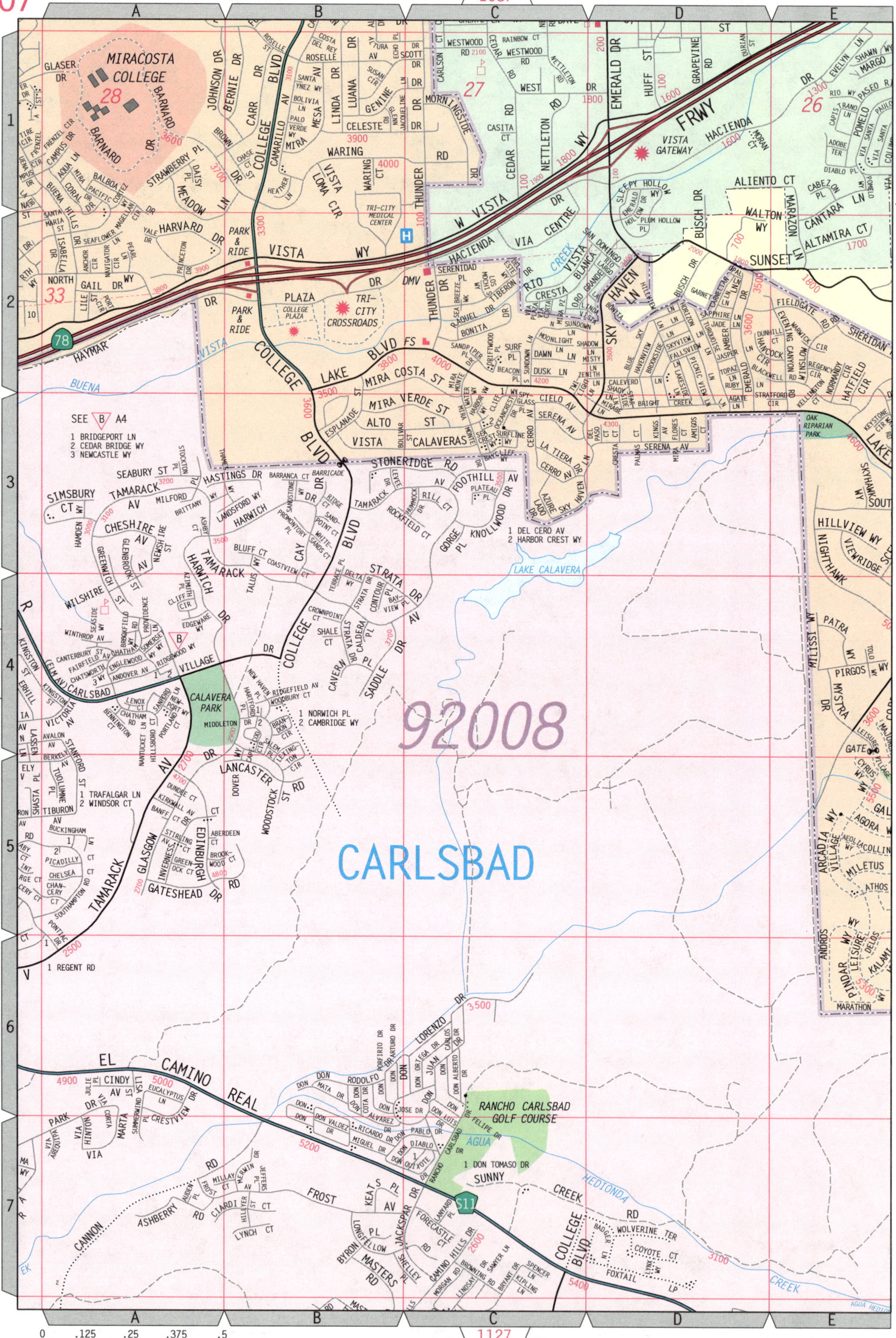

CALAVERA PARK

LAKE CALAVERA

OAK RIPARIAN PARK

RANCHO CARLSBAD GOLF COURSE

TRI-CITY MEDICAL CENTER

VISTA GATEWAY

SEE B A4
1 BRIDGEPORT LN
2 CEDAR BRIDGE WY
3 NEWCASTLE WY

1 DEL CERO AV
2 HARBOR CREST WY

1 NORWICH PL
2 CAMBRIDGE WY

1 TRAFALGAR LN
2 WINDSOR CT

1 REGENT RD

1 DON TOMASO DR

EL CAMINO REAL

COLLEGE BLVD

TAMARACK AV

VISTA WY

W VISTA WY

STONERIDGE RD

FOOTHILL AV

HARWICH DR

EMERALD DR

FRWY

BUENA VISTA CREEK

AGUA HEDIONDA CREEK

0 .125 .25 .375 .5 miles 1 in. = 1900 ft.

—N—

SAN DIEGO CO.

MAP

92083

92056
OCEANSIDE

OCEAN HILLS

VISTA

MELROSE DR

PHILLIPS FRWY

RANCHO BUENA VISTA

78

SHADOWRIDGE COUNTRY CLUB

SHADOWRIDGE COUNTRY CLUB LINKS

Rancho Buena Vista HS

Melrose Village Plaza

LAKE PARK

BREEZE HILL PARK

OCEAN HILLS COUNTRY CLUB

LEISURE VILLAGE

Buena Vista Park

SQUIRES DAM

R4W R3W

711S T12S

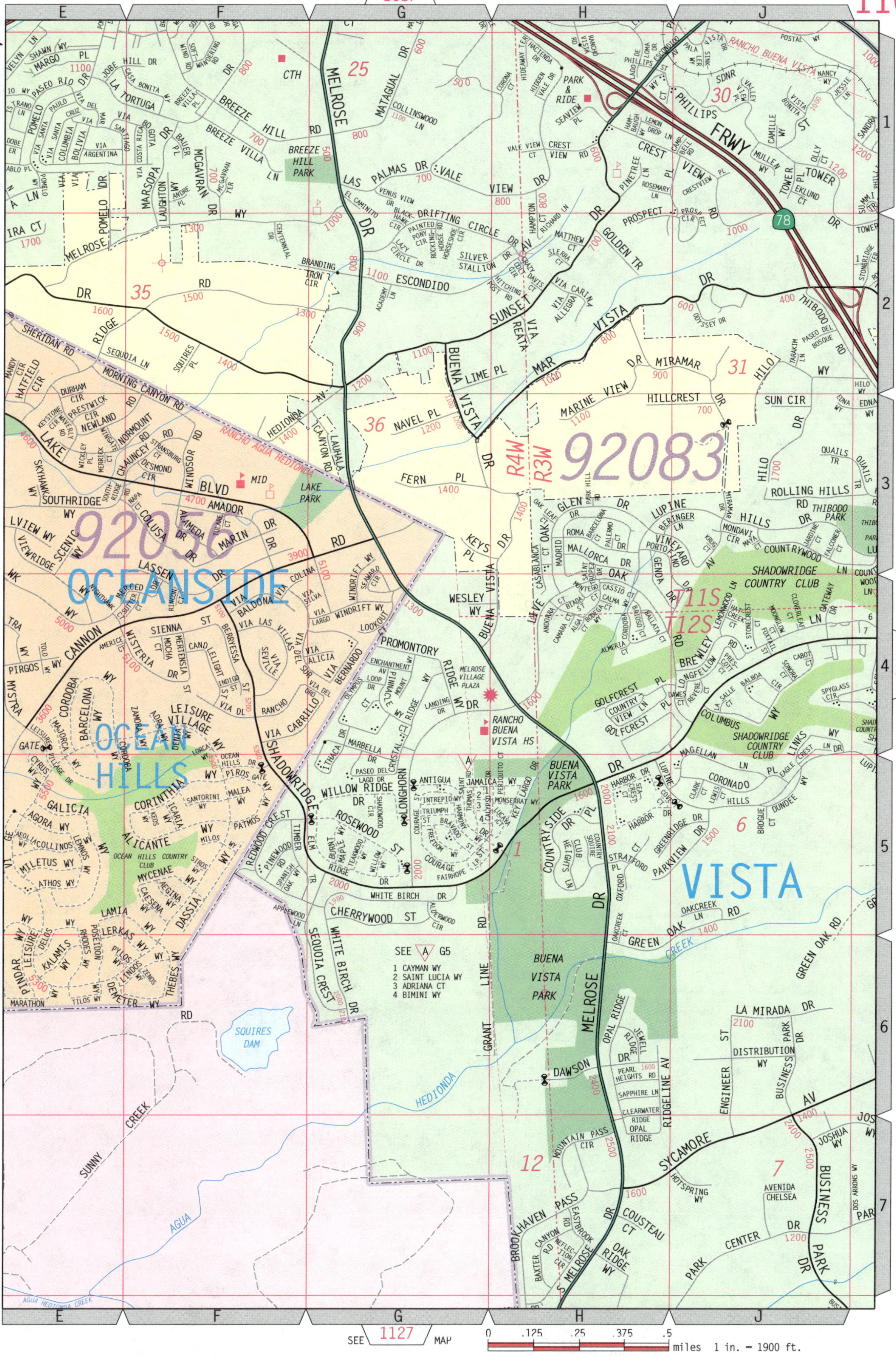

SEE 1108 MAP

SEE 1127 MAP

0 .125 .25 .375 .5 miles 1 in. = 1900 ft.

SEE A G5
1 CAYMAN WY
2 SAINT LUCIA WY
3 ADRIANA CT
4 BIMINI WY

COPYRIGHT 2001 Thomas Bros. Maps®

SEE 1088 MAP

A
B
C
D
E
1
2
3
4
5
6
7
SAN DIEGO CO.
MAP
SEE 1107 MAP
BUENA
VISTA
92083
NATIONAL UNIV NORTH COUNTY CAMPUS
NORTH COUNTY SQUARE
SHADOWRIDGE PLAZA
SHADOWRIDGE COUNTRY CLUB
BRADLEY PARK
SAN MARCOS VILLAGE
MISSION CTR
MONTE VISTA DR
SANTA FE AV
S SANTA FE AV
BUENA CREEK RD
UNIVERSITY DR
SYCAMORE AV
SHADOWRIDGE DR
THIBODO RD
FRWY
78
S14
S10
RANCHO SANTA FE RD
MIRADA DR
POINSETTIA AV
OLEANDER AV
GRAND AV
LA MIRADA DR
LOS VALLECITOS
SAN MARCOS
AGUA HEDIONDA CREEK
SAN MARCOS CREEK
SEE A4
1 FOXHILLS TER
2 GLENEAGLES PL
3 TURNBERRY DR
4 PRESTWICK CT
5 WENTWORTH CIR
6 BREWLEY LN
7 CAMBRIDGE
1 HERITAGE LN
2 COBBLESTONE LN
3 HARVEST LN
4 KITE LN
5 BADGER WY
6 HERON DR
1 VIS MEADOWS WY
2 CLUBHOUSE RD
3 BARRANCA RD
SEE C7
1 VIA DL REY
2 VIA LADERA
3 VIA LIDO
4 VIA PALOMAR
5 VALLECITOS DR
6 VIA ALTA VISTA
7 ALTURA CIR
COPYRIGHT 2001 Thomas Bros. Maps ®

SEE 1128 MAP

0 .125 .25 .375 .5 miles 1 in. = 1900 ft.

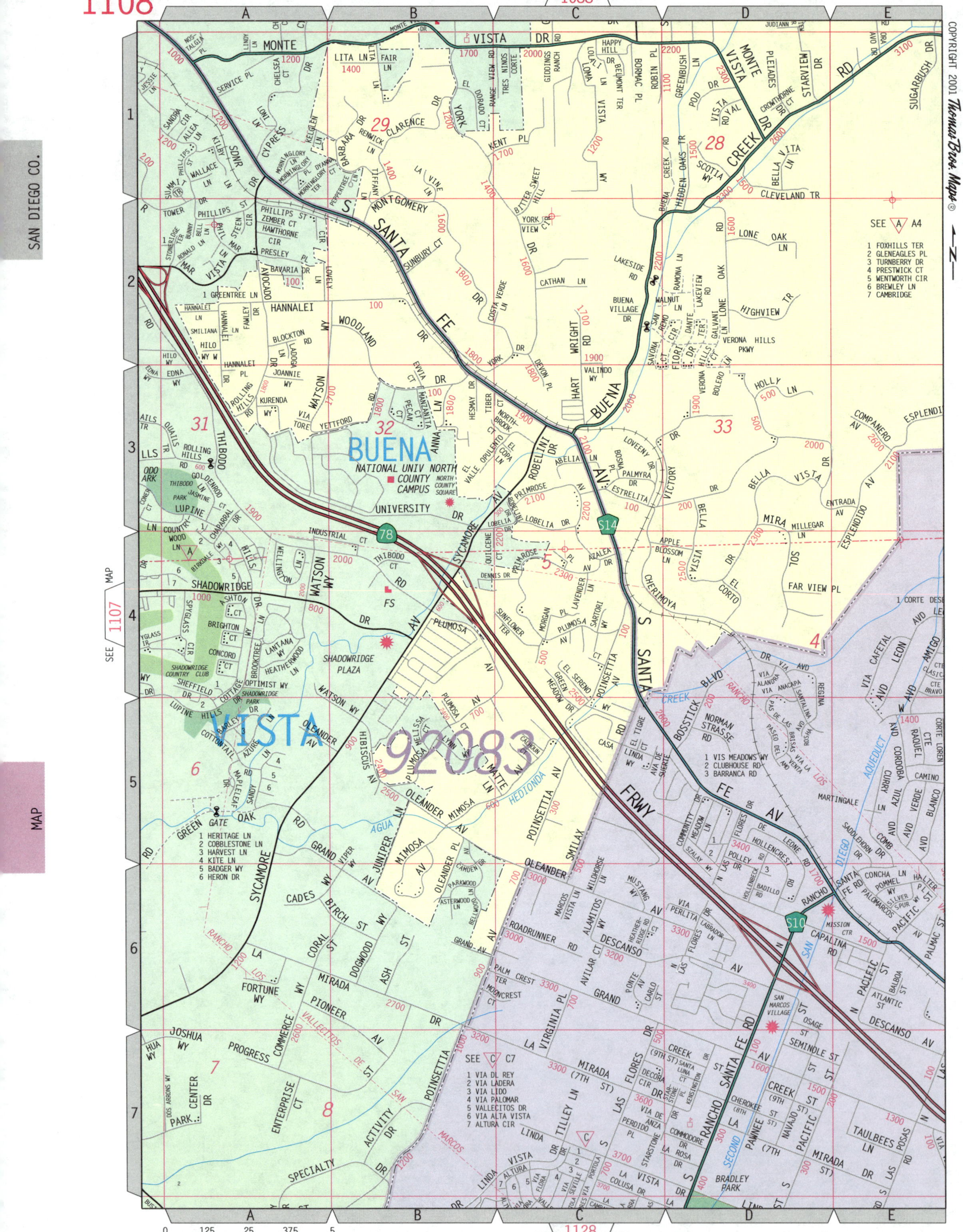

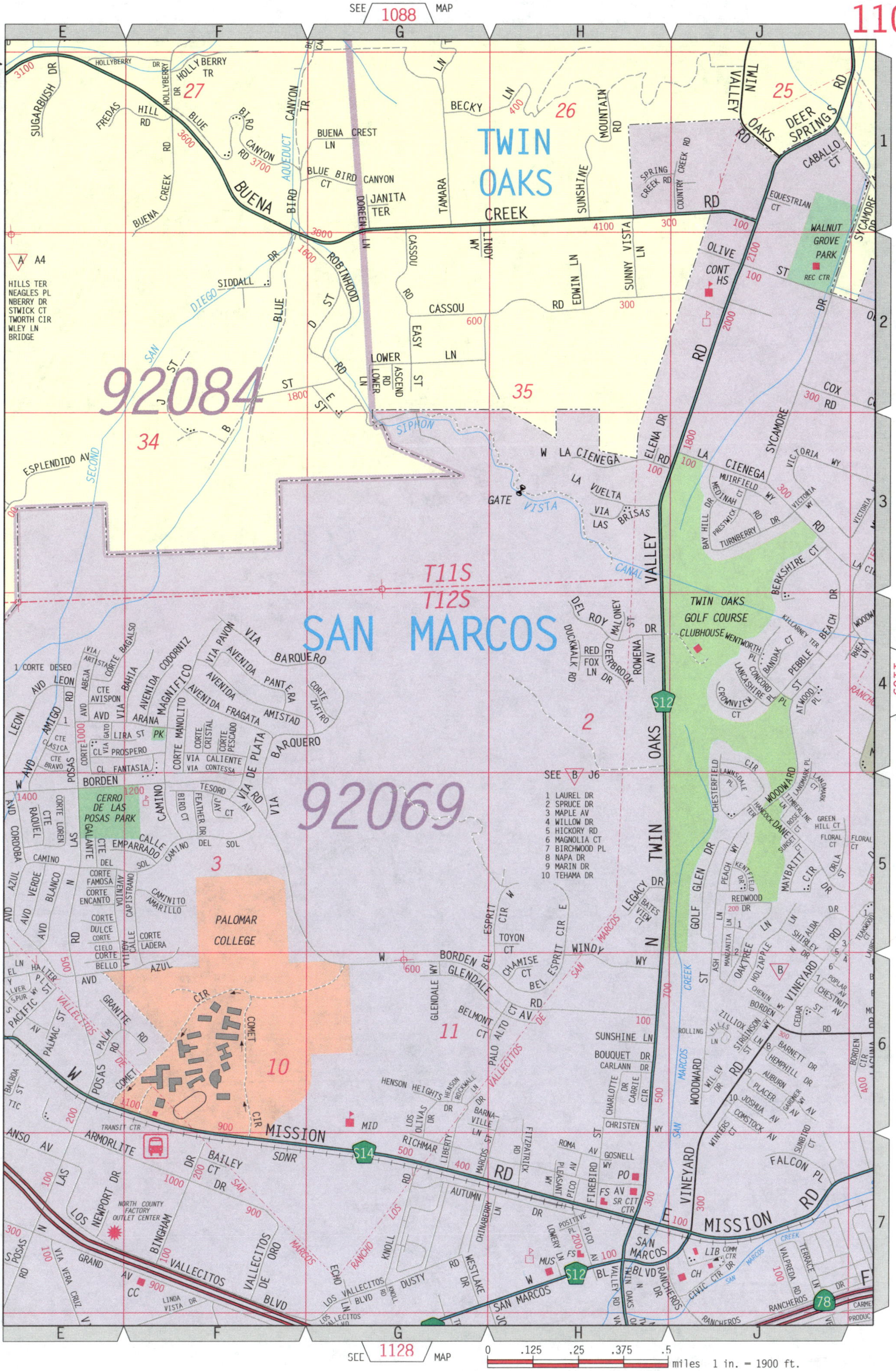

SAN DIEGO CO.

MAP

Thomas Bros. Maps®

COPYRIGHT 2001

92084

92069

TWIN OAKS

SAN MARCOS

TWIN OAKS CREEK

TWIN OAKS GOLF COURSE

CLUBHOUSE

WALNUT GROVE PARK
REC CTR

CERRO DE LAS POSAS PARK

PALOMAR COLLEGE

NORTH COUNTY FACTORY OUTLET CENTER

TRANSIT CTR

SEE B J6
1 LAUREL DR
2 SPRUCE DR
3 MAPLE AV
4 WILLOW DR
5 HICKORY RD
6 MAGNOLIA CT
7 BIRCHWOOD PL
8 NAPA DR
9 MARIN DR
10 TEHAMA DR

HILLS TER
NEAGLES PL
NBERRY DR
STWICK CT
TWORTH CIR
WLEY LN
BRIDGE

A A4

1 CORTE DESEO

T11S
T12S

SEE 1109 MAP

SAN DIEGO CO.

MAP

COPYRIGHT 2001 *Thomas Bros. Maps* ®

92026

ESCONDIDO

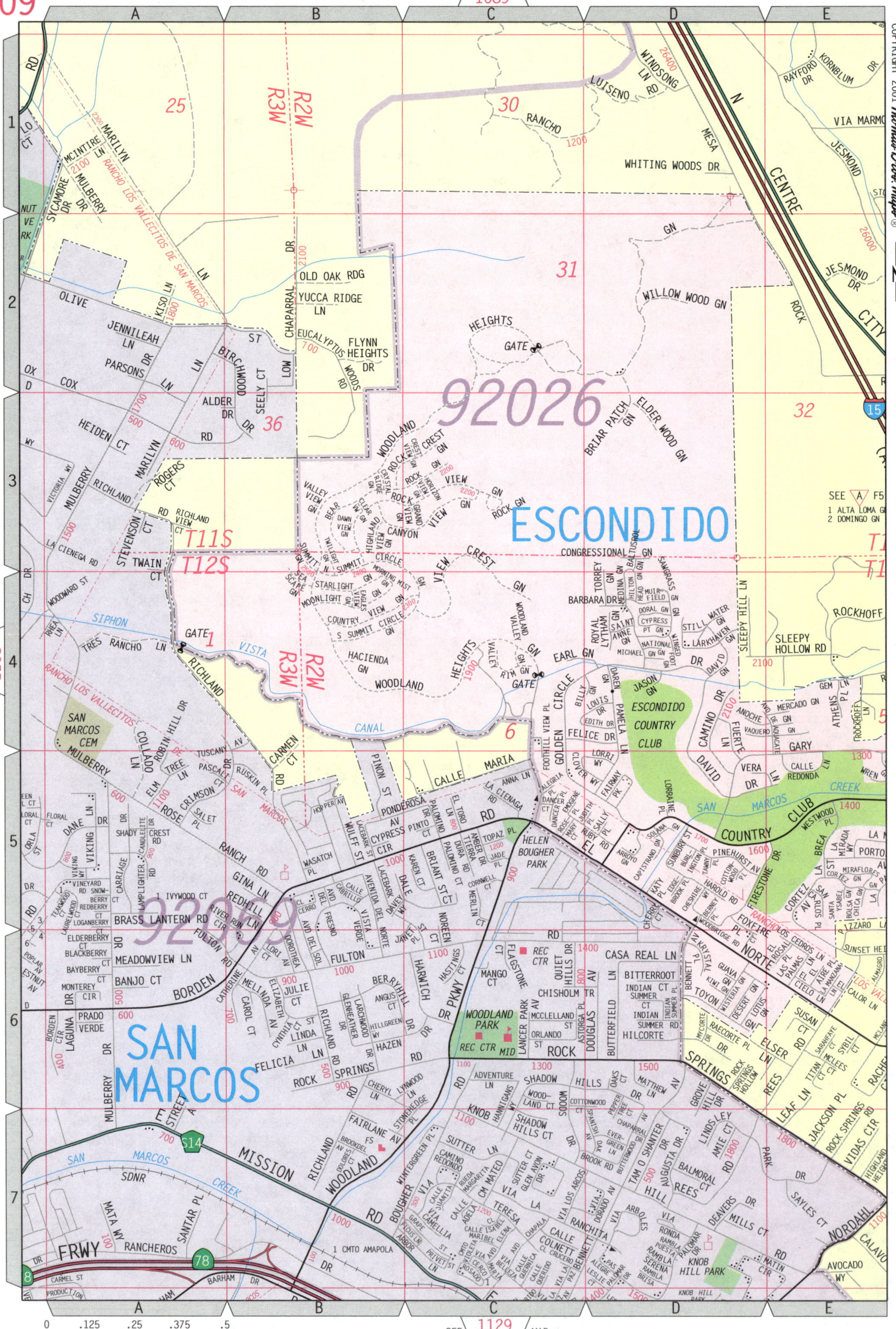

SAN MARCOS

92029

25   30   31   32   36   6

R2W R3W

T11S T12S

WHITING WOODS DR

WILLOW WOOD GN

HEIGHTS GATE

ESCONDIDO COUNTRY CLUB

SAN MARCOS CEM

SAN MARCOS CREEK

COUNTRY CLUB

WOODLAND PARK

HELEN BOUGHER PARK

KNOB HILL PARK

CONGRESSIONAL GN

SLEEPY HOLLOW RD

MISSION

SAN MARCOS CREEK

FRWY

CARMEL ST

PRODUCTION

RANCHEROS

BARHAM DR

S14   78   8

I-15

CITY ... CENTRE ... ROCK

0   .125   .25   .375   .5   miles   1 in. = 1900 ft.

SEE △ F5
1 ALTA LOMA GN
2 DOMINGO GN

SEE 1089 MAP

JESMOND DENE
SAN DIEGO CO.
MAP
SEE 1110 MAP
SEE 1129 MAP
ESCONDIDO FRWY
(AVOCADO HWY)
CENTRE CITY PKWY
COUNTRY CLUB LN
RINCON AV
BROADWAY
(REIDY CANYON RD)
N BROADWAY
EL NORTE PKWY
W EL NORTE PKWY
E EL NORTE PKWY
JESMOND DENE PARK
ROD MCLEOD PARK
DEL NORTE PLAZA
EL NORTE PARKWAY PLAZA
ESCONDIDO HS
CALVIN CHRISTIAN HS
VISTA FLUME
VISTA CANAL
SAN DIEGO AQUEDUCT
REIDY CANYON
RINCON DEL DIABLO
T11S
T12S
92027
miles 1 in. = 1900 ft.
0 .125 .25 .375 .5
SEE A F5
1 ALTA LOMA GN
2 DOMINGO GN

SEE 1090 MAP

SAN DIEGO CO.

MAP

COPYRIGHT 2001 *Thomas Bros. Maps* ® —N—

92026

92027

DALEY RANCH

ESCONDIDO

DIXON LAKE REC AREA

DIXON RESERVOIR

27

26

25

34

35

36

T11S
T12S

RINCON AV

BOULDER LEGEND LN

COLLIER AV

LEHNER CT

SIPHON

3

2

1

11

12

VINTAGE

VISTA

CANAL

HONDA

DUBLIN LN

GLASGOW LA

STEVENS PL
MACNAUGHTON LN

TRIJULLO TER

DIPPONS LN

FIRETHORN GN
BUCKSKIN GN
MAVERICK GN
MADRONE
BULLRUSH

SEE 1109 MAP

EL NORTE PKWY

WASHINGTON AV

EL NORTE PKWY

CITRUS AV

MIDWAY

DAISY ST

GOLDENROD AV

FERN

ERICA

DAISY

CAMELLIA

BEGONIA

ASTER

OLEANDER PL

SUMAC PL

MAGNOLIA

OLINDA ST

WABASH ST

MILLS ST

MISSION

WASHINGTON

VALLEY PKWY

BEAR VALLEY PKWY

CITRUS AV

HAYDEN

ENCANTO DR

MOBILE PARK WEST MHP

EASTWOOD MEADOWS MHP

IMPERIAL ESCONDIDO ESTATES MHP

TOWN & COUNTRY MHP

CAREFREE RANCH MHP

PARK & RIDE

ESCONDIDO HILLS PLZ

FERRARA PLAZA

PALOMAR COMM COLLEGE

ESCONDIDO MISSION VILLAGE

WASHINGTON PARK

JACKS CREEK RD

LAS BRISAS

GEISE CT

S6

LINCOLN AV

ASH ST

92025

SHERIDAN AV
VISTA
SKYVIEW

KINGS WY

EL NORTE

THOMAS WY

DONALD

IRIS

0 .125 .25 .375 .5 miles 1 in. = 1900 ft.

SEE 1130 MAP

1110

N

SAN DIEGO CO.

MAP

E F G H J

30

29

RD

31

CENTER

LAKE WOHLFORD
RESORT AIRSTRIP

32

LAKE
WOHLFORD

LAKE
WOHLFORD

LAKE WOHLFORD

WOHLFORD RD RD

1

2

VISTA CREEK

RD CANAL

S6

ESCONDIDO

LAKE WOHLFORD

DR

FOXLEY

CITRINE DR

SIPHON

BANGERTER CT

3600

3600

LAKE WOHLFORD CT

R2W R1W

VALLEY

3600

LAKE OAKVALE
14900

16

3

LEWIS LN

VALLE LINDO RD
13900

6

5

PKWY

13400

4

JACKS CREEK RD.

ACKS PL

NE

K

L

VALLEY

AV

OAK TREE PL PECAN PL

GATE

LAS BRISAS DR

OSA CT

SOCIN SOLEDAD

AMANECER CT

E

ST

2900

JAMES ST

RICKY PL

RILEY AV

RO SEANN

HYPOINT AV

WALNUT

JANET GN

FARGO

LOKELEY CT

FAST GN

ANTO DR

DEN JED

JODY PL

RD

2800

JONAH DR

WEDGEMERE CT

OAK HILL

AURORA

HALLEY MEADOW

OAK HILL DR

SLIVKOFF

DANIEL

LO CASCIO WY

ALAMITOS CT

FALCONER

MEADOW GROVE CT

3100

WHITE HAWK

HIDDEN VIEW LN

HIDDEN ESTATES LN

RD

18

GUEJITO TO

8

GUEJITO

OLD STONEBRIDGE

GUEJITO RD

RANCHO RINCON DEL DIABLO

OLD

GUEJITO RD

WILLOW TREE LN

MEADOW CREEK LN
15400

BRETTI GROVE PL

WILLOW MEADOW

TRAILS

OAK WOOD LN

DR RIDGELINE PL

SYCAMORE HEIGHTS PL

RIDGEMONT CIR

SYCAMORE CREST PL

7

OAK BLUFF PL

OAK VALLEY LN

OLD OAK FOREST PL

5

6

RD

STONEBR

17

STONEBRIDGE RD

7

E F G H J

MEADOWSIDE PL

HIDDEN

MEADOW CREST PL

MEADOW GRASS LN

MEADOW GRASS PL

0 .125 .25 .375 .5 miles   1 in. = 1900 ft.

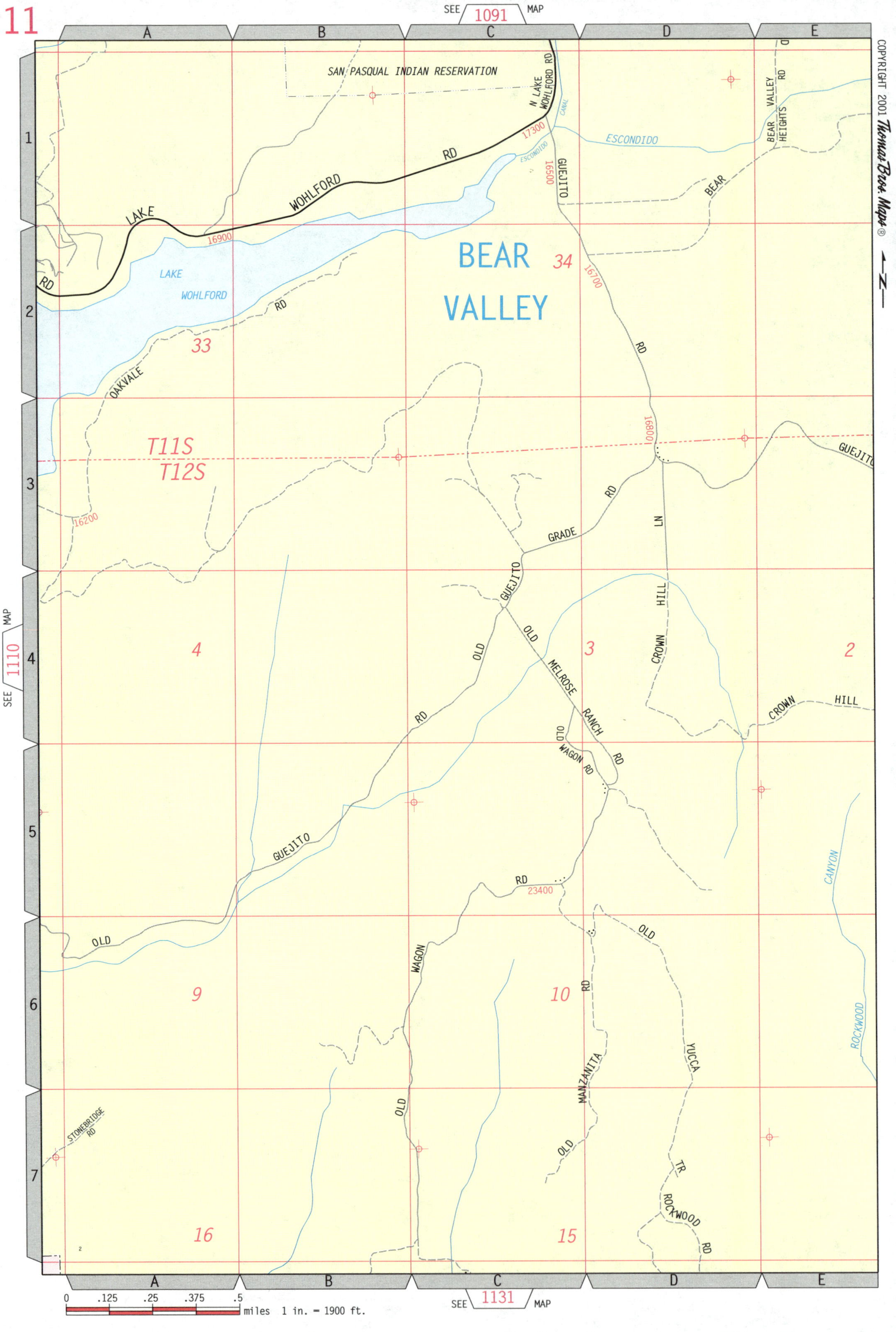

1111

A   B   C   D   E

1

SAN PASQUAL INDIAN RESERVATION

N LAKE WOHLFORD RD

ESCONDIDO CANAL

17300

16500

GUEJITO

ESCONDIDO

BEAR VALLEY HEIGHTS RD

WOHLFORD RD

LAKE

16900

LAKE WOHLFORD

2

BEAR VALLEY

34

16100

BEAR

RD

33

OAKVALE RD

WOHLFORD RD

T11S
T12S

16800

GUEJITO

3

16200

GRADE RD

GUEJITO

LN

CROWN HILL

GUEJITO

SEE 1110 MAP

4

OLD

OLD

MELROSE RANCH RD

3

CROWN HILL

2

OLD WAGON RD

CROWN HILL

5

GUEJITO RD

GUEJITO

RD 23400

OLD

CANYON

6

OLD

9

WAGON

10

RD

MANZANITA

OLD

YUCCA

ROCKWOOD

7

STONEBRIDGE RD

OLD

TR

ROCKWOOD RD

16

15

A   B   C   D   E

0   .125   .25   .375   .5   miles   1 in. = 1900 ft.

SAN DIEGO CO.

MAP

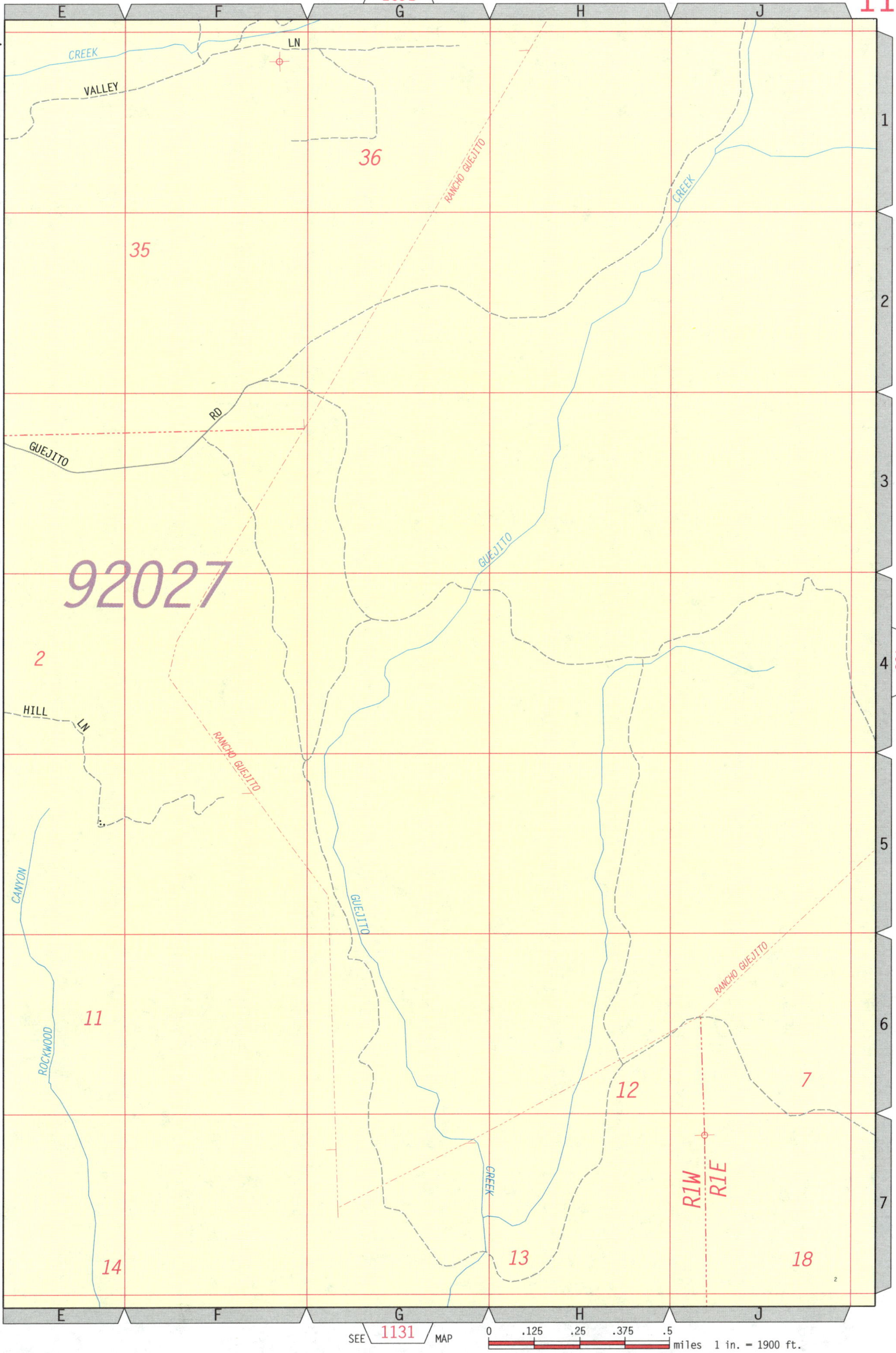

E F G H J

CREEK

LN

VALLEY

36

35

RANCHO GUEJITO

CREEK

1

2

RD

GUEJITO

GUEJITO

3

92027

2

SEE 409 MAP

4

HILL

LN

RANCHO GUEJITO

GUEJITO

CANYON

5

GUEJITO

RANCHO GUEJITO

11

ROCKWOOD

6

12

7

R1W R1E

CREEK

7

14

13

18

E F G H J

0 .125 .25 .375 .5 miles 1 in. = 1900 ft.

1126

SEE 1106 MAP

A B C D E

1

2

3

PACIFIC

SEE 408 MAP

4

5

6

7

A B C D E

SEE 1146 MAP

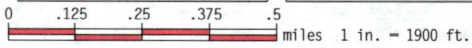

0 .125 .25 .375 .5 miles 1 in. = 1900 ft.

SAN DIEGO CO.

MAP

E F G H J

CARLSBAD
STATE
BEACH

AGUA HEDIONDA LAGOON

AGUA HEDIONDA LAGOON

BRYCE CIR

BANSHORE DR

AGUA HEDIONDA CREEK

AGUA

HIDDEN

VALLE

CANNON

S21

CARLSBAD

CANNON PARK

CANNON

CANNON RD

1000 5100

900

AUTO CENTER CT

CAR COUNTRY DR 5200

CANNON 1100

LEGO DR

LEGOLAND FAMILY PARK

ARMADA DR

FLEET ST

92008

CARLSBAD

SDNR

TIERRA DEL ORO ST

SHORE DR

LOS ROBLES DR

EL ARBOL DR 5200

CEREZO DR 5400

MANZANO DR

SAN

AVENIDA ENCINAS 5400

PASEO DEL NORTE 5500

5600

CC

CARLSBAD COMPANY STORES

5700

ARMADA DR

BLVD

COASTER

5600

HOLIDAY INN

PALOMAR AIRPORT RD

900 6000

S12

1300

92009

5900

SOLAMAR DR

FRIENDLY PL

HAPPINESS WY

OCEAN VIEW

EASY ST

SEA BREEZE DR

AVENIDA

DIEGO

NORTE

RANCHO

AGUA 6400

HEDIONDA

GOLDFINCH

SNIPE CT

GOLD

KITE PL

TURN

SEE 1127 MAP

5

ENCINAS

SURFSIDE LN

ISLAND WY

6600

5

6500

CMTO DEL REPOSO
CMTO DEL MAR
CMTO DEL SOL

LA LOMA

SAN LUIS

CMTO VERDE
CMTO ROSA
CMTO AZUL

CAMINO DEL PARQUE

CMTO MADRIGAL

6500

CMTO ESTRADA

21

POINSETTIA PARK

CM DL PRADO

900

CM DE GATE

LAS ONDAS 1000

POI

WHITESAIL

FUCHSIA LN

OCEAN

26

MARIPOSA

CERRO AZUL

LOMITA

MONTECITO

RAMONA

CALLE COSTA

SKYSAIL AV

SEASHORE

WATERCOURSE DR

SHEARWATER DR

SANDBAR

SOUTH CARLSBAD STATE BEACH

CARLSBAD

BLVD

LAMIKAI DR

LANIKAI LN

STA

1 CLOVER CT
2 FUCHSIA LN
3 WINDWARD LN
4 SEAWATCH LN

AVENIDA ENCINAS

MACADAMIA DR

29

RAINTREE

FRWY

6900

7000

28

LN

800

QUIET COVE DR

DEL NORTE

PASEO

BREAKWATER RD

CATAMARAN DR

CHANNEL

ISTHMUS

TRADEWINDS DR

POINSETTIA

POINSETTIA VILLAGE

400

SDNR

WHITEWATER LN

WINDRANE LN

PONTO

LEEWARD RD

SAN CARLOS

SAN ENCINAS AV

SAN LUIS

SANTA

SANTA ROSA

SAN BARTOLO

LOGANBERRY DR

7200

SAN RAMON

SAN MIGUEL

SAN BENITO

BARBARA

SAN LUCAS

SAN LUIS

SANTA BARBARA

SAN LUIS

COASTER

ANCHORAGE AV

DEW POINT AV

WIND SOCK PL

BUOY

SEAFARER

SPINNAKER

STARBOARD

SPINDRIFT

MARINE

32

7200

3

S21

PONTO DR

ENCINAS

AVD

ESCALONIA

MCLELLAN

7

1 MERIDIAN WY
2 TRIBUL LN
3 HALSING CT
4 RUDDER AV

0 .125 .25 .375 .5 miles   1 in. = 1900 ft.

SEE 1107 MAP

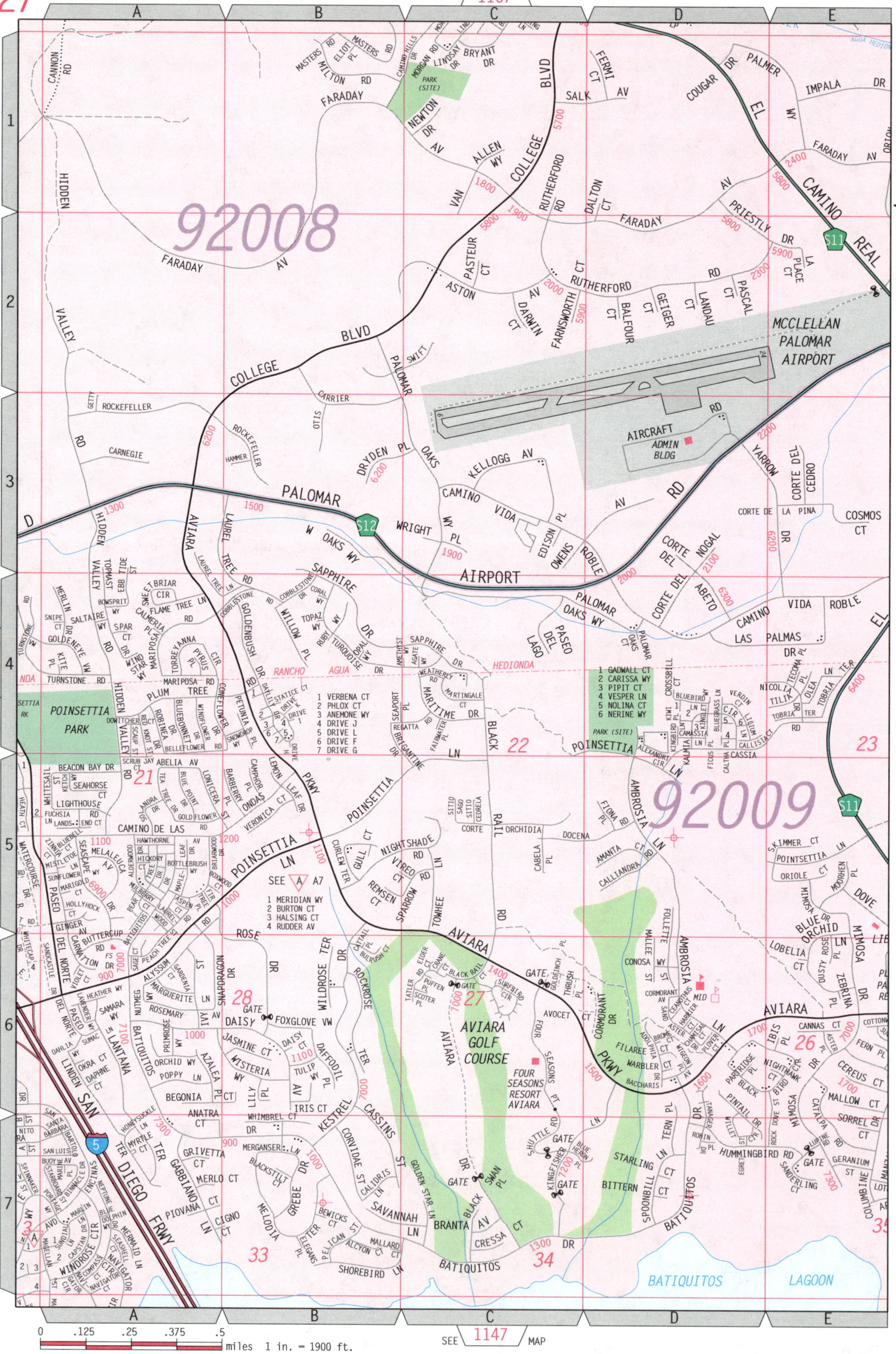

A
B
C
D
E
1
2
3
4
5
6
7
92008
92009
SAN DIEGO CO.
MAP
COPYRIGHT 2001 Thomas Bros. Maps ®
SEE 1126 MAP
MCCLELLAN PALOMAR AIRPORT
AIRCRAFT RD
ADMIN BLDG
COLLEGE BLVD
PALOMAR AIRPORT RD
EL CAMINO REAL
S11
S12
FARADAY AV
HIDDEN VALLEY RD
PALOMAR OAKS WY
CAMINO VIDA ROBLE
POINSETTIA LN
POINSETTIA PARK
AVIARA PKWY
AVIARA GOLF COURSE
FOUR SEASONS RESORT AVIARA
BATIQUITOS DR
BATIQUITOS LAGOON
SAN DIEGO FRWY
5
RANCHO AGUA HEDIONDA
BLACK RAIL RD
AMBROSIA LN
PARK (SITE)
1 GADWALL CT
2 CARISSA WY
3 PIPIT CT
4 VESPER LN
5 NOLINA CT
6 NERINE WY
1 VERBENA CT
2 PHLOX CT
3 ANEMONE WY
4 DRIVE J
5 DRIVE L
6 DRIVE F
7 DRIVE G
SEE A A7
1 MERIDIAN WY
2 BURTON CT
3 HALSING CT
4 RUDDER AV
21
22
23
26
27
28
33
34

0 .125 .25 .375 .5
miles 1 in. = 1900 ft.

SEE 1147 MAP

1127

SAN DIEGO CO.

MAP

Thomas Bros. Maps®
COPYRIGHT 2001

VISTA
92083

7

13

CARLSBAD RACEWAY

EASTBROOK
FARADAY

PARK CENTER DR
OAK RIDGE WY
ASPEN WY
MELROSE DR
LIBERTY WY
SCOTT ST 3100
KEYSTONE WY 1400 1300
BUSINESS PARK

PALOMAR AIRPORT RD S12

18

MELROSE DR

CARLSBAD

SEE B H2
1 PASEO ALMIAR
2 PASEO CAMAS
3 PASEO GRANTO
4 PASEO ENSILLAR
5 PASEO PICADO
6 RANCHO POSTA
7 PASEO VALLE
8 RANCHO BRIDA
9 PASEO SALINERO

COSMOS CT

EL CAMINO REAL

ROBLE

RANCHO RIO CHICO
POINSETTIA

LEO CARRILLO PARK

VIA PANCHO
CONQUISTADOR

RANCHO CARRILLO

R4W R3W

24

19

LA COSTA RESORT & SPA

CARRILLO WY

23

S11

EL FUERTE ST

CORTES

XANA ST

1 ANGUILA PL
2 VIA CALDRON
3 VIA ESTRADA
4 VIA SANTIAGO
5 CTE TRABUCO
6 AVD TOPANGA
7 AVD OLMEDA
8 CAMINO VALENCIA

SWALLOW LN
QUAIL PL
DOVE
MOORHEN
SAND PIPER PL
PLAZA PASEO REAL
WEST BLUFF PLAZA

ALGA RD

UNICORNIO ST

25

30

FUERTE ST

LUCIERNAGA

ARGONAUTA WY
OBELISCO
BABILONIA ST
CORINTIA ST
FUERTE PARK

CAMINO REAL
CALETA
CARACOL CT

LA COSTA

ALICANTE

ALMADEN LN

ARENAL

35

LA COSTA RESORT & SPA

31

36

SAN MARCOS CREEK

miles 1 in. = 1900 ft.
0 .125 .25 .375 .5

SEE 1128 MAP

SAN DIEGO CO.

92083

VISTA

92069

92009

CARLSBAD

92024

SAN

SEE 1108 MAP

SEE 1148 MAP

SEE 1127 MAP

COPYRIGHT 2001 Thomas Bros. Maps ®

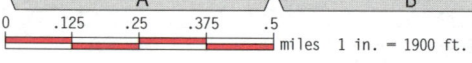

0 .125 .25 .375 .5 miles   1 in. = 1900 ft.

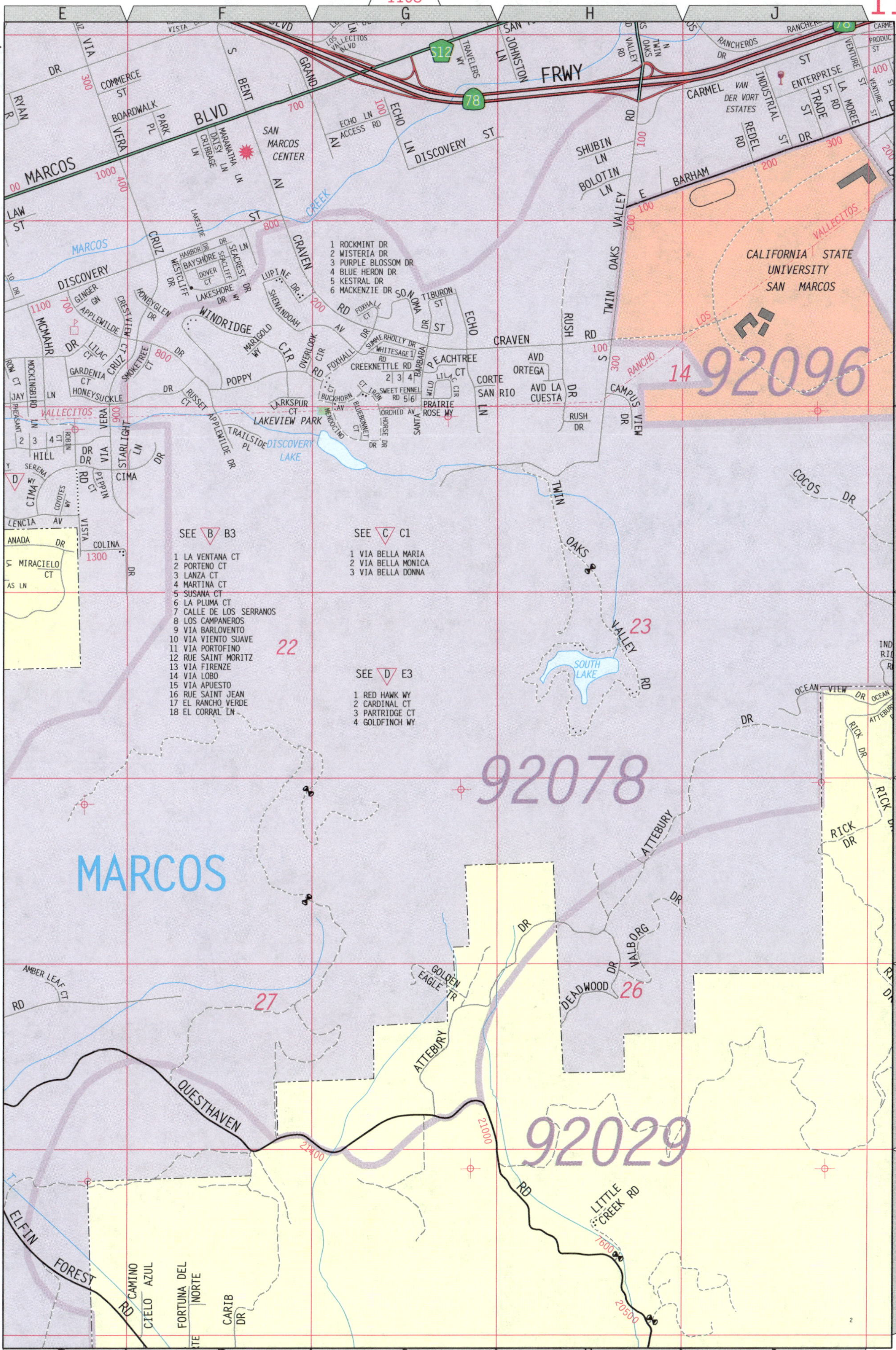

1128

Thomas Bros. Maps®

COPYRIGHT 2001

N

SAN DIEGO CO.

MAP

FRWY

78

Street index - SEE B B3
1 LA VENTANA CT
2 PORTENO CT
3 LANZA CT
4 MARTINA CT
5 SUSANA CT
6 LA PLUMA CT
7 CALLE DE LOS SERRANOS
8 LOS CAMPANEROS
9 VIA BARLOVENTO
10 VIA VIENTO SUAVE
11 VIA PORTOFINO
12 RUE SAINT MORITZ
13 VIA FIRENZE
14 VIA LOBO
15 VIA APUESTO
16 RUE SAINT JEAN
17 EL RANCHO VERDE
18 EL CORRAL LN

SEE C C1
1 VIA BELLA MARIA
2 VIA BELLA MONICA
3 VIA BELLA DONNA

SEE D E3
1 RED HAWK WY
2 CARDINAL CT
3 PARTRIDGE CT
4 GOLDFINCH WY

1 ROCKMINT DR
2 WISTERIA DR
3 PURPLE BLOSSOM DR
4 BLUE HERON DR
5 KESTRAL DR
6 MACKENZIE DR

CALIFORNIA STATE
UNIVERSITY
SAN MARCOS

92096

92078

MARCOS

92029

SAN MARCOS CENTER

LAKEVIEW PARK

DISCOVERY LAKE

SOUTH LAKE

ELFIN FOREST

QUESTHAVEN RD

LITTLE CREEK RD

COMMERCE ST
BOARDWALK
BENT
GRAND AV
BLVD
MARCOS BLVD
LAW ST
DISCOVERY
MCMAHR DR
WINDRIDGE
CRAVEN
CREEK
CRAVEN RD
TWIN OAKS VALLEY RD
CAMPUS VIEW DR
CARMEL ST
ENTERPRISE ST
INDUSTRIAL ST
TRADE ST
VENTURE ST
BARHAM
VALLECITOS
RANCHO
COCOS DR
OCEAN VIEW DR
RICK DR
ATTEBURY
VALBORG
DEADWOOD
GOLDEN EAGLE
AMBER LEAF CT

0 .125 .25 .375 .5 miles   1 in. = 1900 ft.

22   23   14   26   27

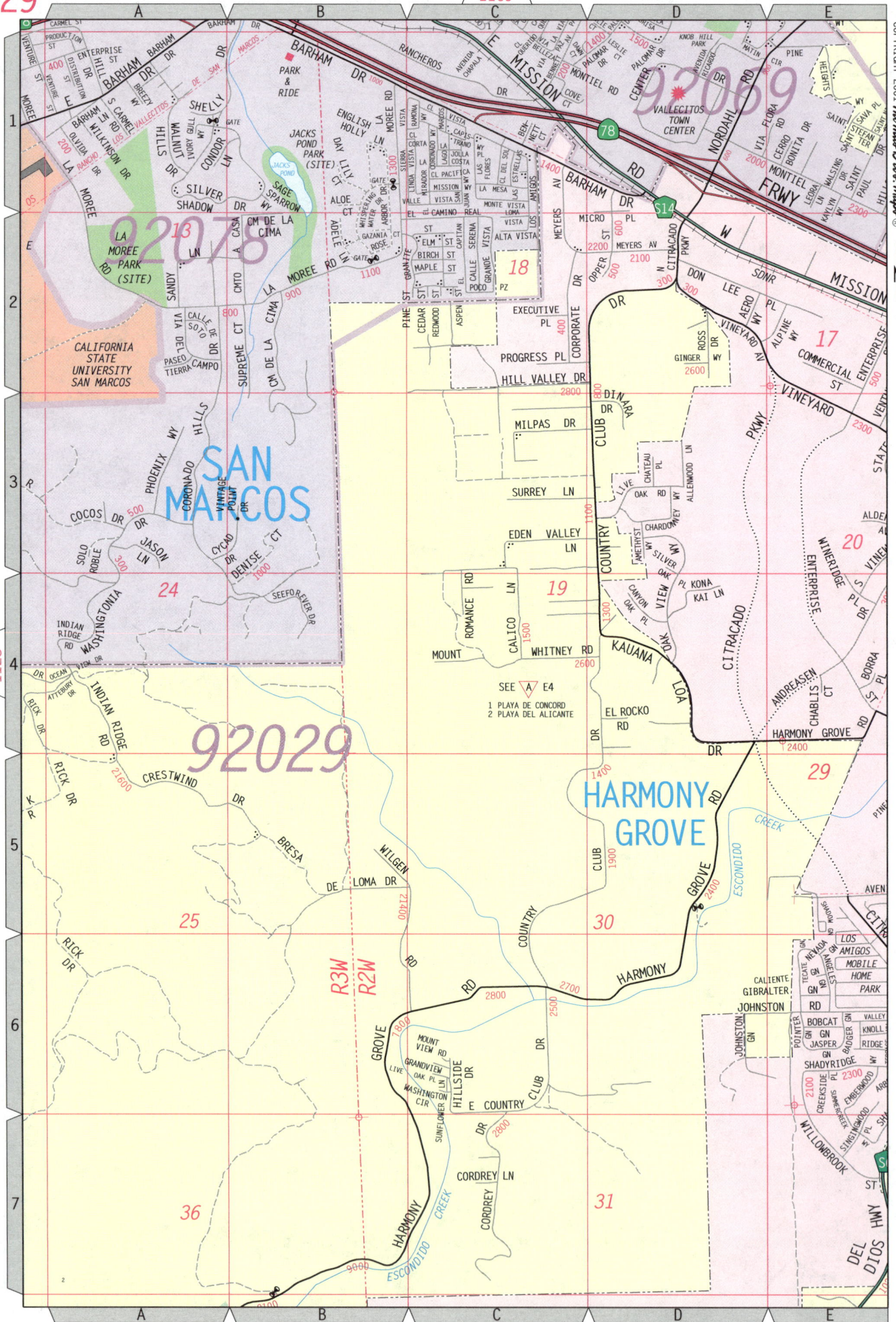

SAN DIEGO CO.

MAP

SEE 1109 MAP

SEE 1128 MAP

SEE 1149 MAP

92069

92078

92029

SAN MARCOS

HARMONY GROVE

CALIFORNIA STATE UNIVERSITY SAN MARCOS

LA MOREE PARK (SITE)

JACKS POND PARK (SITE)

BARHAM Park & Ride

VALLECITOS TOWN CENTER

78

MISSION FRWY

13   18   17   20

24   19   29

25   30

36   31

SEE A E4
1 PLAYA DE CONCORD
2 PLAYA DEL ALICANTE

R3W R2W

0 .125 .25 .375 .5 miles   1 in. = 1900 ft.

-N-

SAN DIEGO CO.

MAP

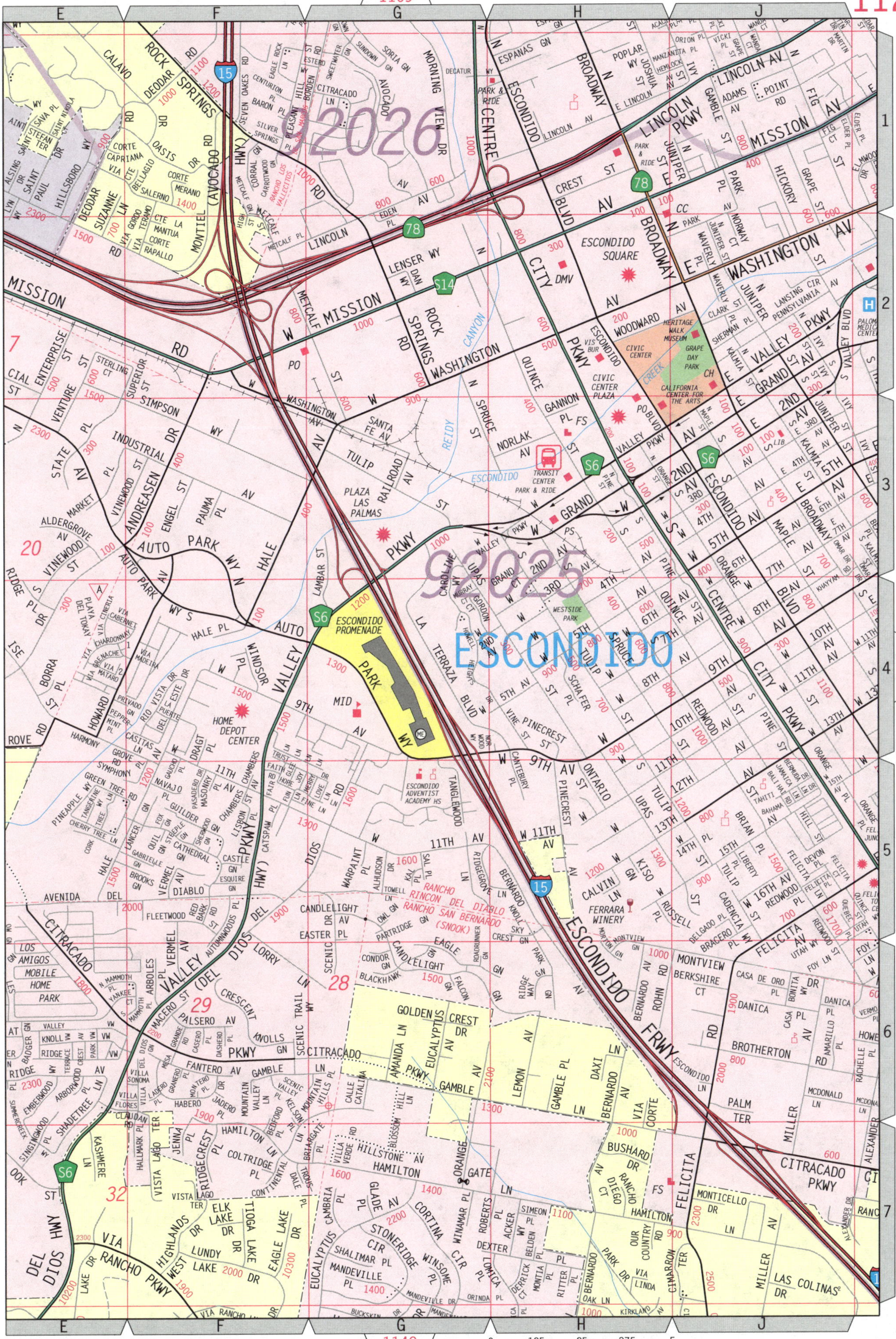

92026

92025

ESCONDIDO

ESCONDIDO FRWY

SEE 1130 MAP

0 .125 .25 .375 .5 miles   1 in. = 1900 ft.

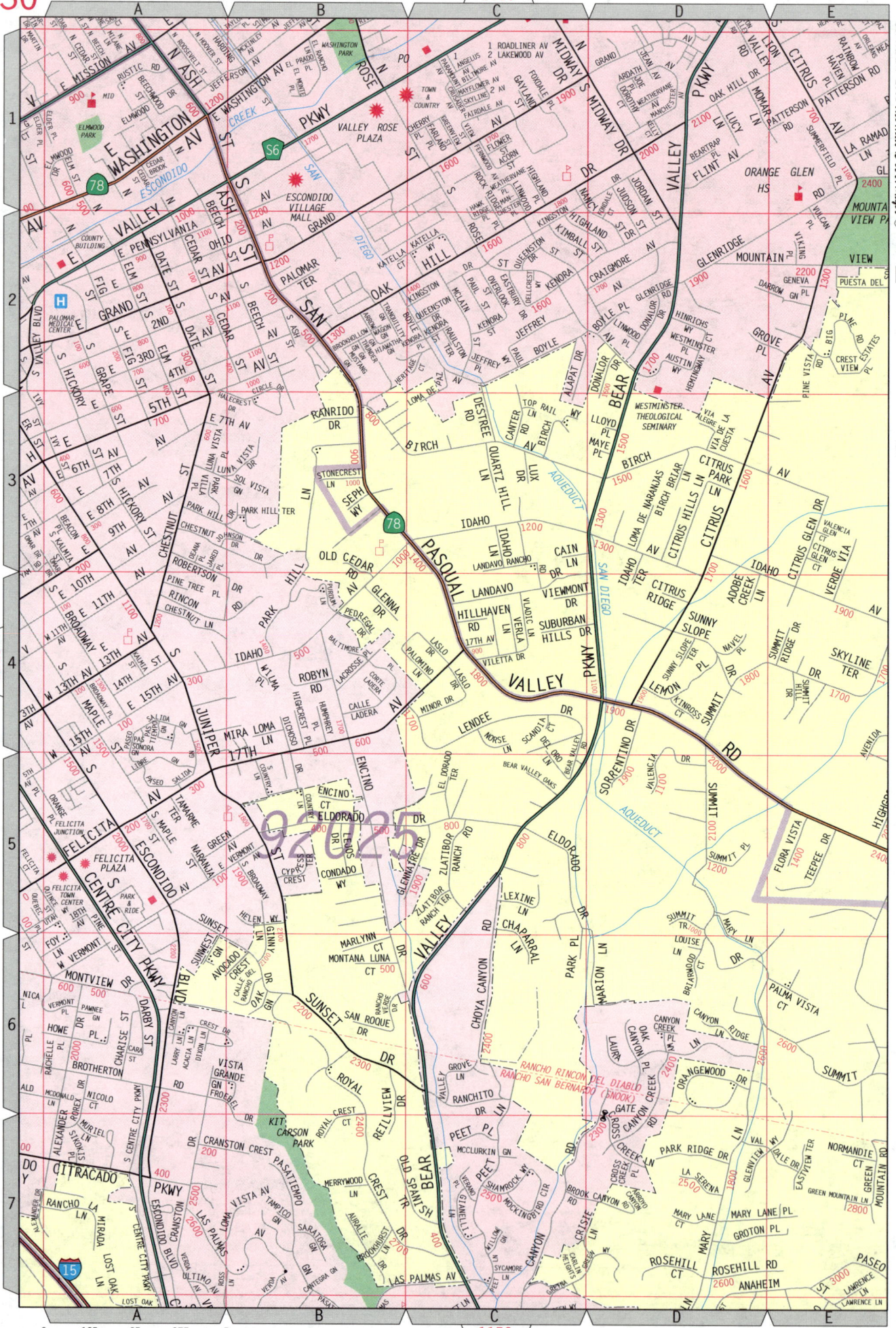

SAN DIEGO CO.

92025

MAP

SEE 1129 MAP

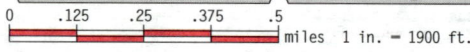

0   .125   .25   .375   .5
miles   1 in. = 1900 ft.

E   F   G   H   J

ESCONDIDO

SAN DIEGO CO.

COPYRIGHT 2001

Thomas Bros. Maps

PATTERSON RD
RATHBUN AV
LA PAZ
ORLEANS
MEADOWBROOK PL
MID
REED
LA RAMADA LN
MOODY
WEDGEWOOD AV
JESSICA
GLENRIDGE
2400
MOUNTAIN VIEW PARK
VIEW
PUESTA DEL SOL

HIDDEN ESTATES RD
HIDDEN ESTATES
BELDING FIELD
FALCONER RD
WHITE
HAWK
LA COLINA DR
CROWNPOINT
COLONY PL
DR
2600
EMERALD PL
WHISPERING HIGHLANDS
MOUNTAIN PARK PL
HIGHLANDS
CANYON CREST
2500
MOUNTAIN CREST LN
2400

OAK HILL MEMORIAL PARK

18

17

1

2

PINE CREST ESTATES RD
CREST VIEW PL
CARROLL LN
ROYAL OAK DR
2600
CARROLL LN

MOUNTAIN
VIEW
DR
2800
RD
2900

92027

SKYLINE DR
2000
SKYLINE AV
1900
2000
SKYLINE TER
1700
1700

ROE VIA
USA
LENCIA LN
ORO VERDE RD
VIA CASCABEL

VIA SINSONTE
1700
1800
CLOVERIDGE
RD

CLOVERDALE
1800
RD
2900

ROCKWOOD

19

20

MESA OAK PL
WILD
GOLDEN OAK PL
OLD
ORANGE GROVE
POMEGRANITE CT
TIMBERWOOD LN
PLUM CT
OAK
HOLLY
OAK
LN
LN
RANCH
ORCHARD VIEW LN
WILLOW CREEK PL
RANCHVIEW PL
ROSEWOOD LN
EAGLE CREST GOLF CLUB
FALLBROOK PL
AMBER OAK LN
HIDDEN PL
KNOLL
OLIVE OAKS LN
CLUBHOUSE
PLUM TREE LN
FERNCREEK LN
TIMBER CT
KNOLL
INKWOOD
CREEK LN
QUAIL CREEK RD
MAPLEWOOD PL
SPRUCEWOOD RD
GATE

GATE

OLD BATTLEFIELD RD
CHARITY WY
BRILLWOOD
HILL RD
11400

3

4

SEE 1131 MAP

AVENIDA LA CIMA DR
HIGHGROVE
COOL RIDGE HEIGHTS
2000
QUAILRIDGE
2400
25
OLD
78
RM28
RM78
RD

30
2500
SAN
2800

SAN DIEGO

PASQUAL

29
ZOO

SAN DIEGO WILD ANIMAL PARK

RD

5

6

MMIT
SUMMIT LN
1600
RANCHO DEL VERDE DR
2900
LEMORA LN
RANCHO DEL VERDE PL
SUMMIT CREST
SAN
14300
SAN PASQUAL RD
SAN PASQUAL TR
SAN PASQUAL WY
VISTA NORTE

SAN PASQUAL RD

OLD
MILKY
WY
14200

SAN PASQUAL

31

32

NORMANDIE CT
GREEN MOUNTAIN RD
RANCHO DEL RAY
RANCHO DEL SOL
MOUNTAIN LN
2800
LOS CIELOS
VIENTO VALLE
CRESTA LOMA
PASEO DEL SOL
3000
LAWRENCE LN
LAWRENCE LN
PASEO
VISTA DEL SOL
SEMBRADO
EL RIO
VIA
SAN RANCHO PKWY

7

0   .125   .25   .375   .5
miles   1 in. = 1900 ft.

SAN DIEGO CO.

MAP

SEE 1111 MAP

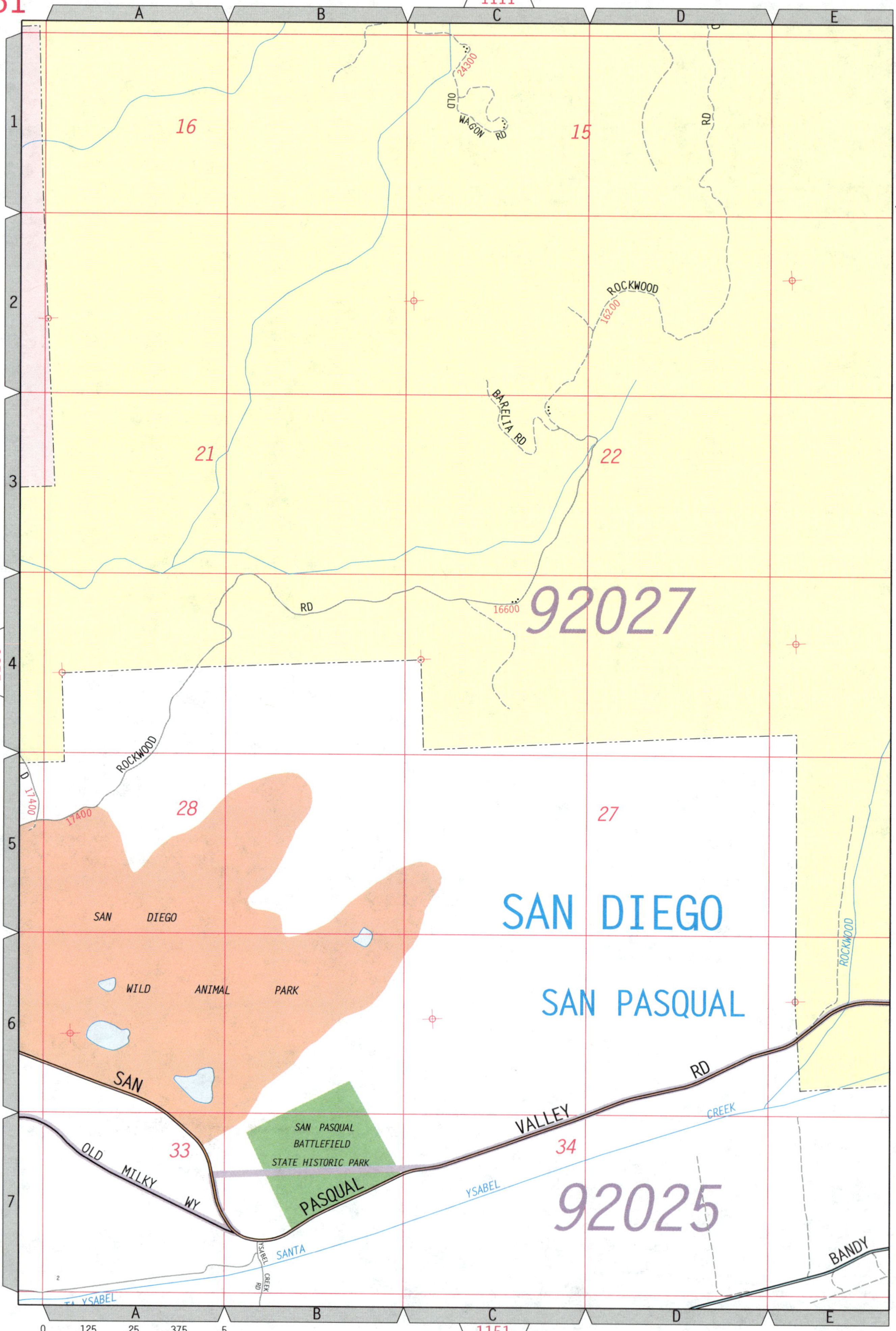

SAN DIEGO CO.

MAP

SEE 1130 MAP

A B C D E

1

16   24300   OLD WAGON RD   15

2   ROCKWOOD   162.00

BARELA RD

3   21   22

RD   16600   92027

4

ROCKWOOD   17400   1/400

5   28   27

SAN DIEGO   SAN DIEGO

WILD ANIMAL PARK   SAN PASQUAL

6   ROCKWOOD

SAN

OLD MILKY WY   33   SAN PASQUAL BATTLEFIELD STATE HISTORIC PARK   VALLEY   RD   CREEK   34

7   PASQUAL   YSABEL   92025

YSABEL CREEK   SANTA   BANDY

STA YSABEL   RD

A B C D E

SEE 1151 MAP

0 .125 .25 .375 .5
miles 1 in. = 1900 ft.

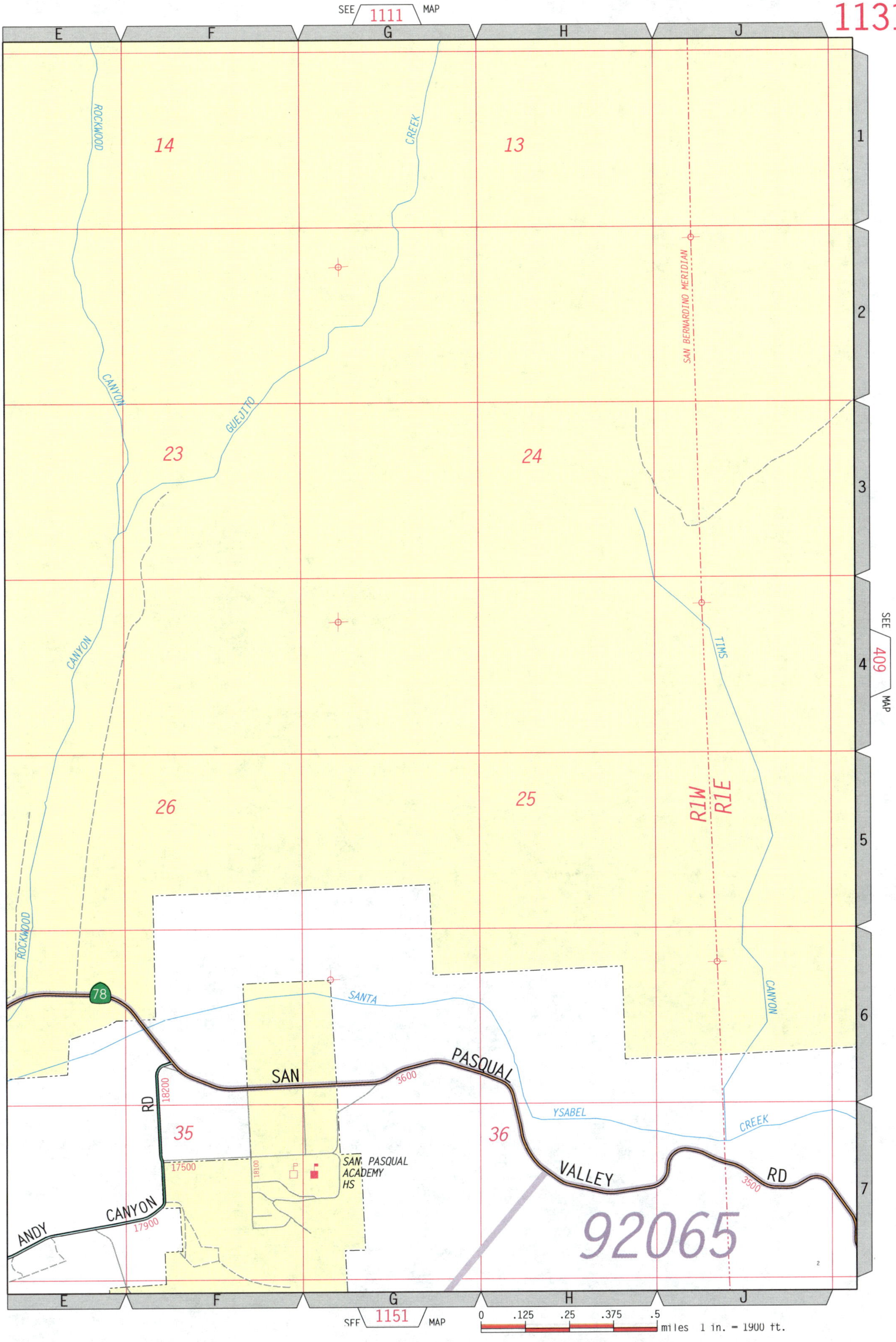

SAN DIEGO CO.

MAP

E F G H J

ROCKWOOD

14

13

CREEK

1

SAN BERNARDINO MERIDIAN

2

CANYON

GUEJITO

23

24

SWIT

3

SEE 409 MAP

CANYON

4

26

25

R1W R1E

5

ROCKWOOD

CANYON

6

78

SANTA

PASQUAL

3600

RD

18200

SAN

YSABEL

CREEK

35

36

17500

18100

SAN PASQUAL
ACADEMY
HS

VALLEY

RD

3500

P

ANDY

CANYON

17900

92065

E F G H J

0 .125 .25 .375 .5
miles 1 in. = 1900 ft.

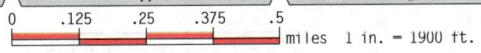

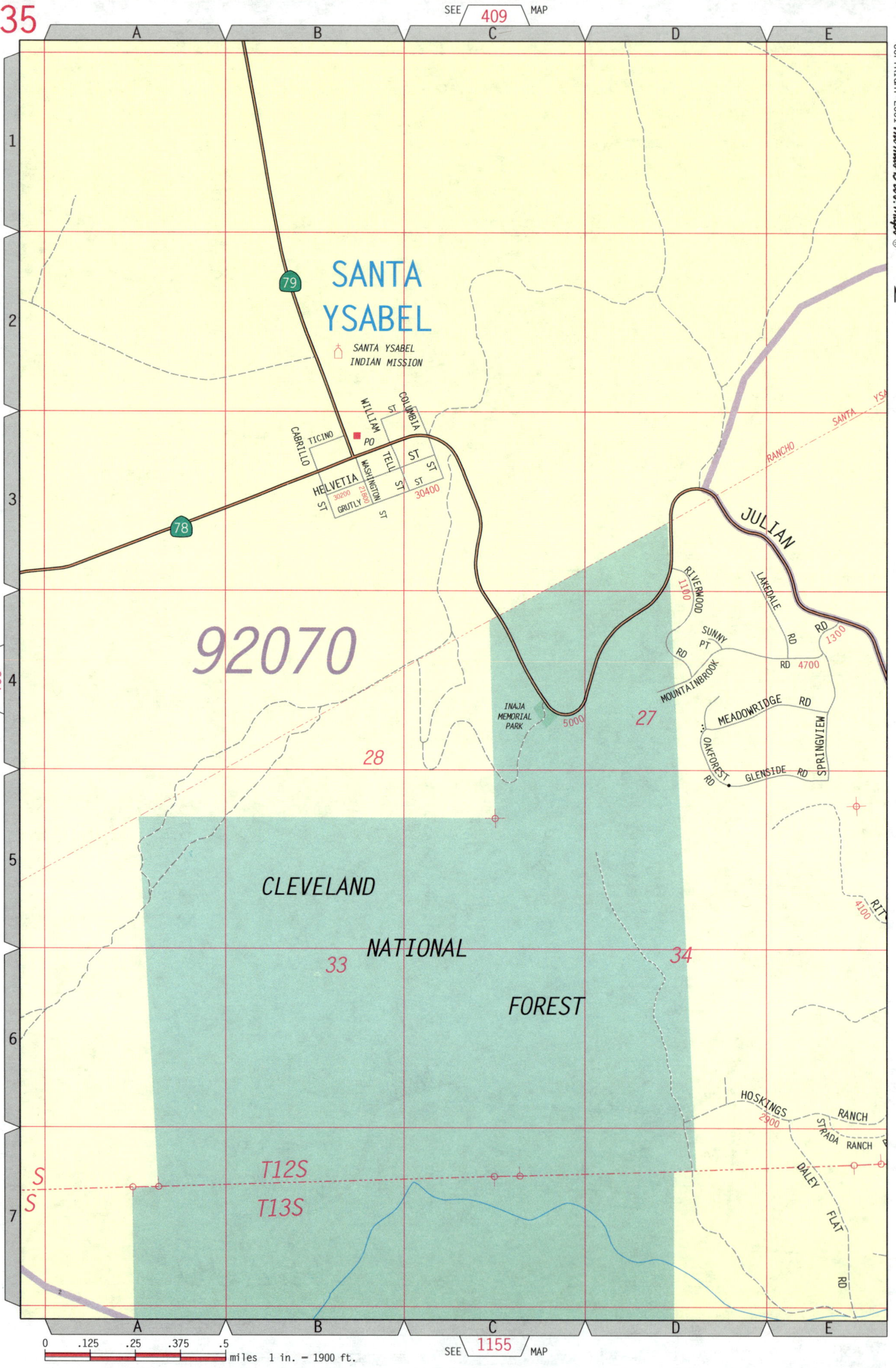

SAN DIEGO CO.

MAP

← N

SEE 409 MAP

A B C D E

1

2

SANTA YSABEL

SANTA YSABEL
INDIAN MISSION

79

COLUMBIA

WILLIAM

CABRILLO

TICINO

PO

ST

ST

HELVETIA
30200

WASHINGTON
21800

TELL

GRUTLY ST

ST

ST

ST
30400

JULIAN

3

78

SEE 409 MAP

92070

RIVERWOOD
1100

LAKEDALE

RD

RD
1300

SUNNY
PT

RD

RD 4700

MOUNTAINBROOK

INAJA
MEMORIAL
PARK

5000

27

MEADOWRIDGE

RD

SPRINGVIEW

OAKFOREST
RD

GLENSIDE RD

4

28

RANCHO

SANTA YSA

RIT
4100

5

CLEVELAND

33

NATIONAL

34

FOREST

6

HOSKINGS
2900

RANCH

STRADA RANCH

S
S

T12S

T13S

DALEY

FLAT

RD

7

A B C D E

0 .125 .25 .375 .5

miles 1 in. = 1900 ft.

SEE 1155 MAP

SAN DIEGO CO.

E   F   G   H   J

1

2

23

92036

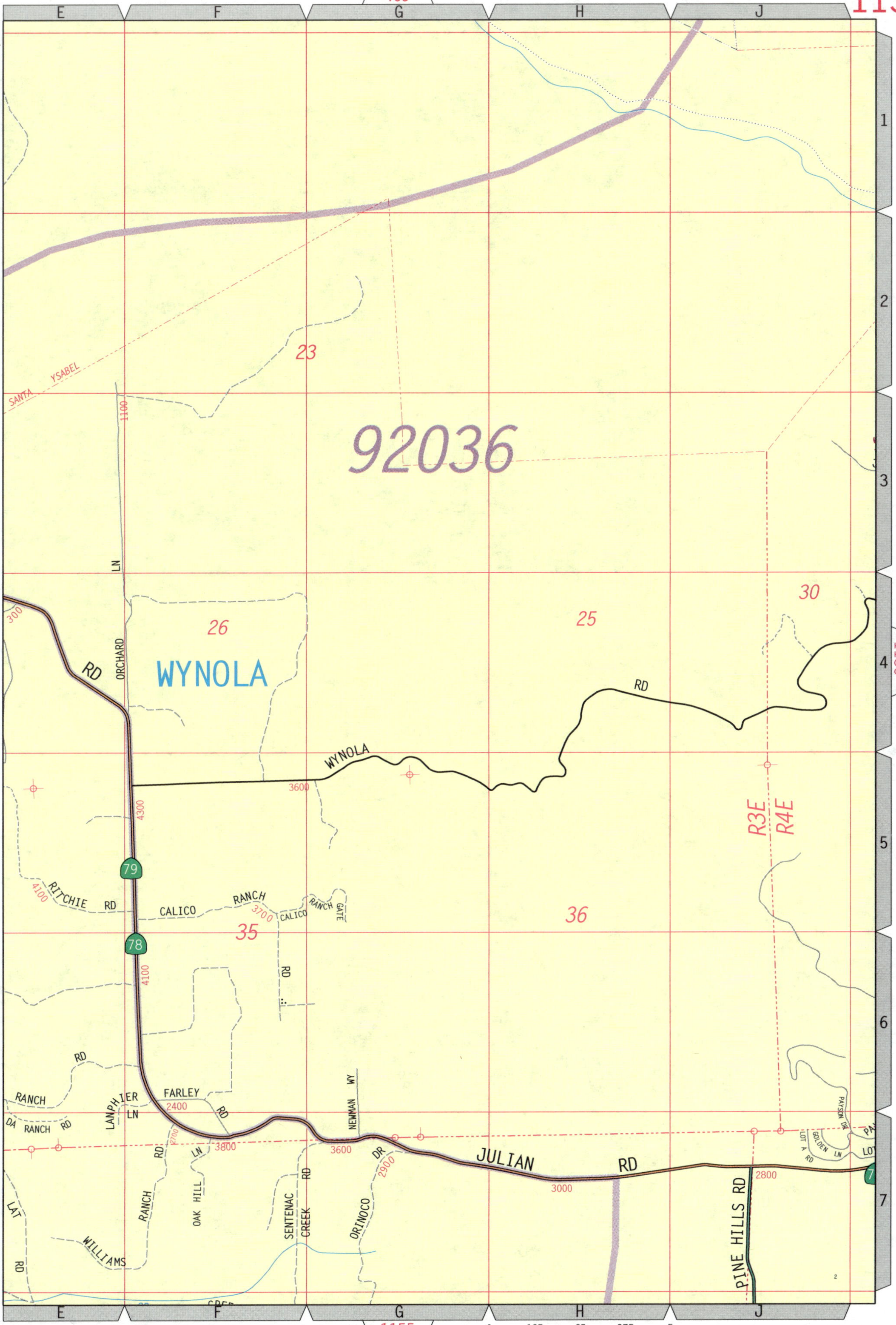

SEE 1136 MAP

30

26   *25*

WYNOLA

RD   ORCHARD

RD

4

WYNOLA

3600

R3E R4E

79

5

RITCHIE   RD   CALICO   RANCH   CALICO   RANCH GATE

4100   3700

35   *36*

RD

78

4100

6

RD

RANCH   LANPHIER   FARLEY   RD   NEWMAN WY

RANCH   LN   2400

DA RANCH RD   RD   LN   3800   NEWMAN   DR   3600   2900

JULIAN   RD

3000   PINE HILLS RD   2800

RANCH   OAK HILL   SENTENAC CREEK RD   ORINOCO   7

LAT

WILLIAMS

RD

E   G   J

0   .125   .25   .375   .5   miles   1 in. = 1900 ft.

MAP

1136

SAN DIEGO CO.

MAP

A   B   C   D   E

1

19

2

20

VOLCAN

JULIAN ORCHARDS
1000

Menghini
Winery

JULIAN

ORCHARDS

MOUNTAIN

3

WILDERNESS

WYNOLA 3600

30   RD   29

PRESERVE

28

SEE 1135 MAP

3800

4

3900

78

5

BANNER

31

32

PINES

WILD LILAC TR

BANNER

WHISPERING

SUNSHINE TR

WHISPERING
PINES

1800

1900

RIDGE TR

CANYON DR

SUNRISE DR

78

6

RD

PROSPECT

CANYON DR

1300

BANNER VIEW DR

VOLCAN VIEW DR

SALTON VIEW

1200

FARMER

FRANK
LANE PARK

EAGLE AND HIGH
PEAK MINES

FS

JULIAN

ETHELWYN
LN

WHISPERING PINES

SLEEPY
HOLLOW
DR

PINES
DR

BANNER RD

GOLD
DUST LN

WOODLAND

KENTWOOD
IN THE
PINES

DAWNCREST CT

PAYSON DR

JULIAN

LN

HENRY SILVERS
PL

OLD MINERS TR

JR HS

AUSTIN WY

MINERS
CT

1200
RD

VISTA
DR

PINE
CREST

HELVETIA DR

PINEZANITA

JULIAN
CEM

1ST ST
2ND ST
3RD ST

BANNER

MANZANITA

SALTON
VISTA

BONITA VISTA
DR

RAMONA DR

SALTON
VISTA

LOT A
DR

SUNSET VIEW

PAYSON
LN

COLEMAN

CIR

WASHINGTON

A ST MAIN ST

4TH ST
5TH ST
LIB ST

CC CH

WITCH
CREEK WINERY

CAPE HORN AV

JULIAN
UNION HS

2300

HOLLOW
GLEN RD

CANYON
RD

LAKEVIEW

LILAC

DR
1100

CHAPIN

VIEW

DR

VISTA
2800

HELIOTROPE

DR

PHEASANT

JULIAN PIONEER MUS

79   78

JULIAN RD

PORTER LN

PO BANNER

APPLE LN

FS

KENISON DR

LAKEVIEW DR

RIDGE

7

79

CUYAMACA HWY

JESS
MARTIN
PARK

JESS

A   B   C   D   E

0   .125   .25   .375   .5
miles   1 in. = 1900 ft.

←N→

E   F   G   H   J

ARKANSAS

CANYON

1

21

22

RANCHO

2

23

VALLE

3

DE

27

28

92036

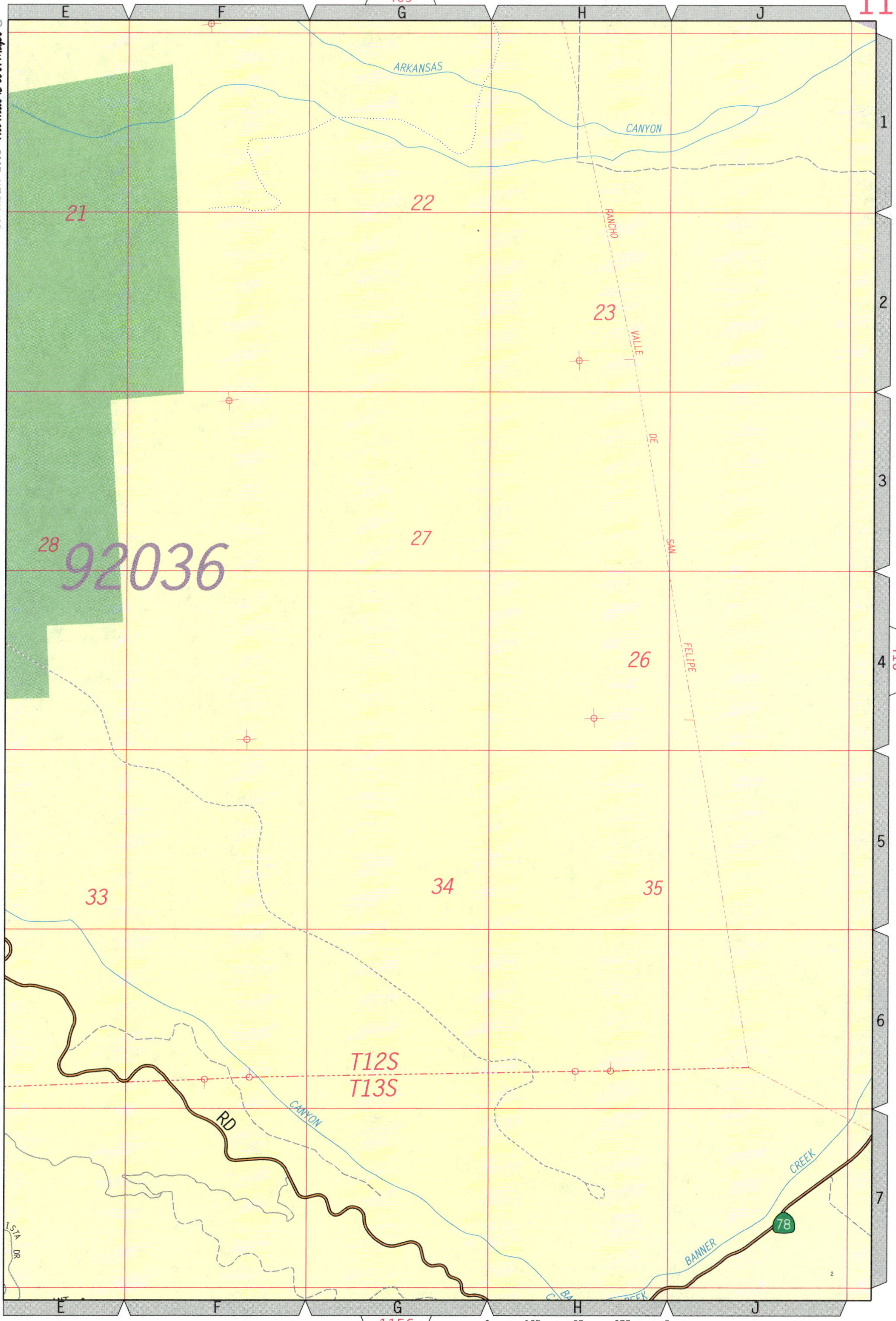

SAN

4

26

FELIPE

SEE / 410 / MAP

5

33

34

35

6

T12S
T13S

RD

CANYON

CREEK

7

78

BANNER

ISTA DR

CREEK

E   F   G   H   J

0 .125 .25 .375 .5

miles 1 in. = 1900 ft.

Thomas Bros. Maps ®

SAN DIEGO CO.

MAP

SEE 1098 MAP

SEE 410 MAP

A B C D E F G H J

1 — 1
2 — 2
3 — 3
4 — 4
5 — 5
6 — 6
7 — 7

22   23   24   19   20

27   26   25   30   29

1138

SHELTER VALLEY
RANCHOS

78

S2

34   35   36   31   32

R5E
R6E

ANZA–BORREGO

T12S
T13S

GRANITE MOUNTAIN
VIEW RD
STAGE COACH TR
WELLS FARGO TR
AIRSTRIP
BUCKBOARD TR

MONTE AZUL
LN
VENTURE VALLEY RD
CACTUS
BRANCH
TR
SHOOTING IRON
TR
MOUNTAIN TR
HARD SCRAMBLE
TR
WINDFALL TR
KICKIN
HORSE
COFFEE POT
TR
HIDDEN
LN
JACKAL
TR
ROCKY
TR
PANHANDLE
TR
SURREY
TR
TANGLEFOOT
TR
JACKASS
TR
FORTY ROD
TR
SANDY TR
LAST
SADDLE
DOLLAR
SORE
TR
GREAT
TR
DEADMANS TR
FIREWATER TR
GUNSLINGER TR
LUCKY
TR
DEVIL
TR
BROKEN
CINCH
TR
LAST CHANCE TR

OVERLAND STAGE ROUTE OF 1849

GREAT SOUTHERN

92036

3   2   6   5

FS

R5E
R6E

10   11   12   7   8

13   18   17

STATE

1158

S2

15   14

1849

22   23   24   19   20

CANYON

OVERLAND

STAGE ROUTE OF

2   27   26   GREAT SOUTHERN   25   30   29

SEE 430 MAP

SEE 430 MAP

0   .25   .5   .75   1.0
miles 1 in. = 3800 ft.

N

Thomas Bros. Maps®

COPYRIGHT 2001

—N→

A B C D E F G H J

21 22 23 24 WASH

PINYON

28 27 26 25

CANYON

410 SEE MAP

92004

33 **1139** 34

35 36

DESERT

T12S
T13S

4 3 2 1 6

R6E R7E

9 10 11 12 7

16 15 14 13 18

PARK

R6E R7E

430 SEE MAP

1159

CANYON

21 22 23 24 19

WASH

28 27 26 25 30

A B C D E F G H J

SEE 430 MAP

0 .25 .5 .75 1.0 miles   1 in. = 3800 ft.

MAP

1146

SAN DIEGO CO.

MAP

SEE 1126 MAP

COPYRIGHT 2001 Thomas Bros. Maps ® —N—

	A	B	C	D	E
1					
2					
3			PACIFIC		
4					
5					
6					
7					

SEE 429 MAP

0 .125 .25 .375 .5 miles 1 in. = 1900 ft.

E F G H J

92011

CRLB

SOUTH

CARLSBAD

4 RUDDER AV

AVD ENCINAS

RUDDER AV

CARLSBAD BLVD

33

STERN WY

MAGELLAN ST

STERN

1

BATIQUITOS LAGOON

S21

CARLSBAD BLVD

92024

STATE

BEACH

PARLIAMENT RD

HAYMARKET RD

WHITEHALL RD

PICCADILLY RD

ENCT

112S 113S

4

SEA

2

1 TATTENHAM RD

1

3

SEE 1147 MAP

4

OCEAN

5

6

7

E F G H J

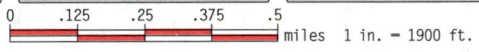

0 .125 .25 .375 .5 miles 1 in. = 1900 ft.

SEE 1127 MAP

SAN DIEGO CO.

MAP

COPYRIGHT 2001 Thomas Bros. Maps ®

—N—

BATIQUITOS LAGOON

LA COSTA AV

LEUCADIA

ENCINITAS

92024

ENCINITAS RANCH GOLF COURSE

PACIFIC OCEAN

LEUCADIA STATE BEACH

BEACONS BEACH

STONE STEPS

MOONLIGHT STATE BEACH

H STREET VIEWPOINT PARK

PAUL ECKE SPORTS PARK

QUAIL BOTANICAL GARDENS

SAN DIEGO FRWY

LEUCADIA BLVD

ENCINITAS BLVD

T12S
T13S

3

4

9

10

15

16

33

34

35

SEE 1146 MAP

SEE 1167 MAP

0 .125 .25 .375 .5 miles 1 in. = 1900 ft.

SAN DIEGO CO.

MAP

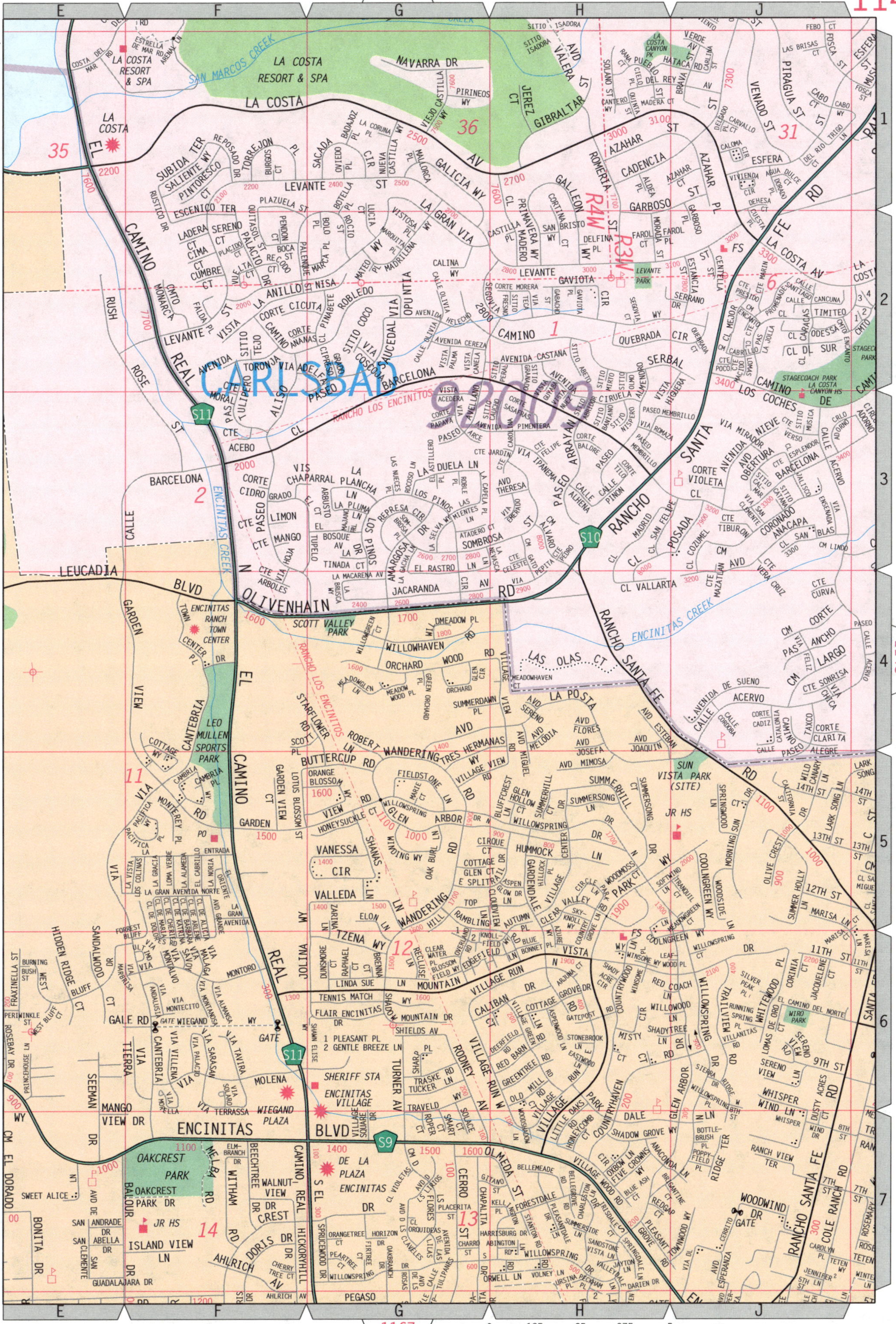

COPYRIGHT 2001 ThomasBros.Maps®

CARLSBAD

ENCINITAS

92009

LA COSTA RESORT & SPA

LA COSTA RESORT & SPA

NAVARRA DR

LA COSTA AV

CAMINO REAL

EL CAMINO REAL

RANCHO SANTA FE RD

OLIVENHAIN RD

LEUCADIA BLVD

ENCINITAS BLVD

ENCINITAS CREEK

SAN MARCOS CREEK

ENCINITAS RANCH TOWN CENTER

SCOTT VALLEY PARK

LEO MULLEN SPORTS PARK

OAKCREST PARK

LEVANTE PARK

STAGECOACH PARK

SUN VISTA PARK (SITE)

WIRO PARK

ENCINITAS VILLAGE

SHERIFF STA

JR HS

JR HS

RANCHO LOS ENCINITOS

0 .125 .25 .375 .5 miles   1 in. = 1900 ft.

N

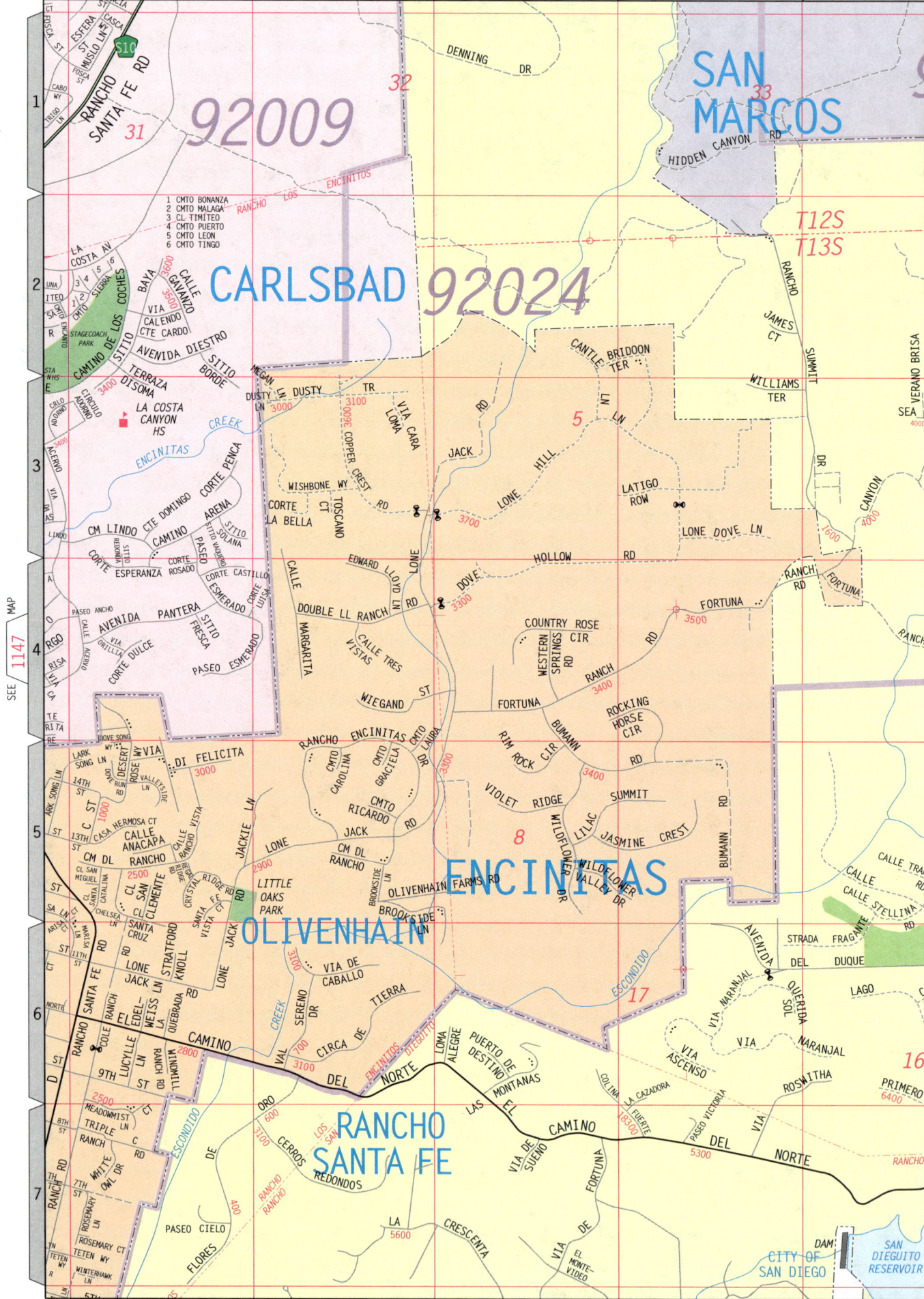

SAN DIEGO CO.

MAP

SEE 1128 MAP

SEE 1147 MAP

COPYRIGHT 2001 Thomas Bros. Maps® —N—

SAN MARCOS

92009

32

31

CARLSBAD 92024

1 CMTO BONANZA
2 CMTO MALAGA
3 CL TIMITEO
4 CMTO PUERTO
5 CMTO LEON
6 CMTO TINGO

T12S
T13S

5

8

17

16

ENCINITAS

OLIVENHAIN

RANCHO SANTA FE

CITY OF SAN DIEGO

SAN DIEGUITO RESERVOIR

SEE 1168 MAP

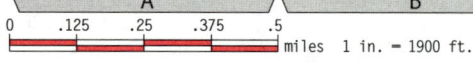

0   .125   .25   .375   .5
miles 1 in. = 1900 ft.

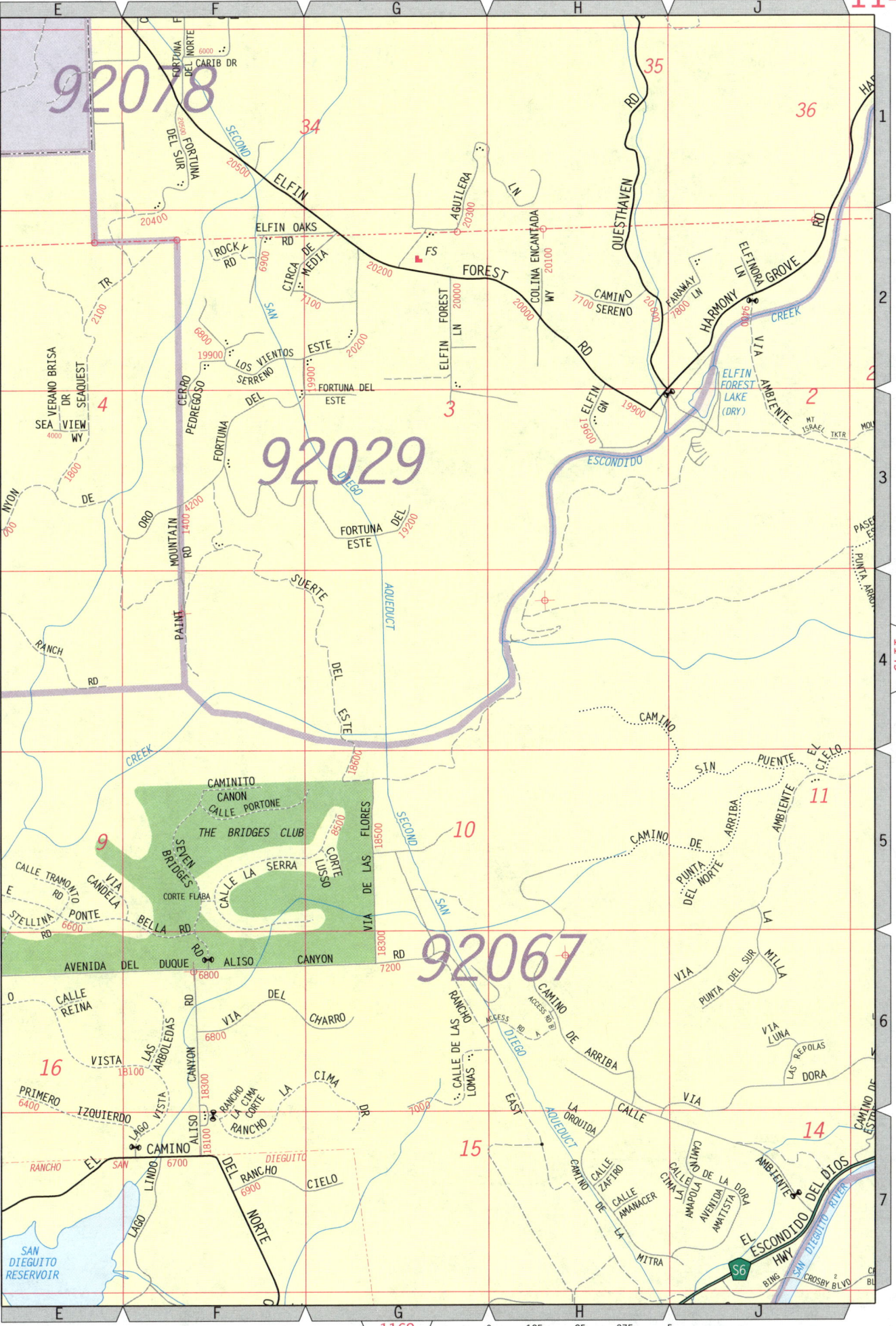

Thomas Bros. Maps®
COPYRIGHT 2001

N

SAN DIEGO CO.

MAP

92078
92029
92067

E F G H J

1
2
3
4
5
6
7

34 35 36
4 3 2
9 10 11
16 15 14

San Dieguito Reservoir

SEE 1149 MAP
SEE 1168 MAP

0 .125 .25 .375 .5 miles 1 in. = 1900 ft.

DEL NORTE
CARIB DR
FORTUNA DEL SUR
SECOND
ELFIN
ELFIN OAKS RD
ROCKY RD
CIRCA DE MEDIA
FS
FOREST
AGUILERA LN
COLINA ENCANTADA WY
CAMINO SERENO
QUESTHAVEN RD
FARAWAY LN
HARMONY LN
ELFINORA GROVE
CREEK
VIA AMBIENTE
ELFIN FOREST LAKE (DRY)
MT ISRAEL TKTR
LOS VIENTOS SERRENO
FORTUNA DEL ESTE
ELFIN FOREST LN
ELFIN GN
ESCONDIDO
SAN DIEGO AQUEDUCT
CERRO PEDREGOSO
FORTUNA DEL ESTE
SUERTE DEL ESTE
MOUNTAIN RD
PAINT
RANCH RD
VERANO BRISA DR
SEAQUEST
SEA VIEW WY
NYON
DE ORO
CREEK
CAMINITO CANON
CALLE PORTONE
THE BRIDGES CLUB
SEVEN BRIDGES
CORTE FLABA
VIA CANDELA
CALLE TRAMONTO RD
STELLINA RD
PONTE
BELLA RD
CALLE LA SERRA
CORTE LUSSO
DE LAS FLORES
SECOND
VIA
CAMINO SIN
PUENTE EL CIELO
CAMINO DE
PUNTA ARRIBA
AMBIENTE
CAMINO DEL NORTE
LA
AVENIDA DEL DUQUE
ALISO CANYON RD
CALLE REINA
VIA DEL CHARRO
RANCHO
CALLE DE LAS LOMAS
CAMINO DE ARRIBA
ACCESS RD
CAMINO DE ARRIBA
PUNTA DEL SUR
VIA MILLA
VIA LUNA
LAS REPOLAS
VIA DORA
VISTA
LAS ARBOLEDAS
PRIMERO
IZQUIERDO
LAGO VISTA
ALISO
CAMINO
DEL RANCHO NORTE
RANCHO LA CIMA CORTE
RANCHO LA CIMA
CIMA DR
CIELO
SAN DIEGO
EAST
AQUEDUCT
LA ORQUIDA
CALLE
CALLE ZAFIRO
CALLE AMANACER
CAMINO DE LA
MITRA
CAMINO DE LA DORA
CALLE CIMA L
AMAPOLA
AVENIDA AMATISTA
AMBIENTE
EL ESCONDIDO HWY
CAMINO DEL DIOS
EL CAMINO REAL
LAGO LINDO
SAN DIEGUITO
RANCHO
CROSBY BLVD
SAN DIEGUITO RIVER
S6

SAN DIEGO CO.

MAP

COPYRIGHT 2001 Thomas Bros. Maps ®

—N—

HARMONY GROVE RD
ESCONDIDO CREEK
9100
9200
THE WAY UP TR
36
R3W R2W

ESCONDIDO

31

92029

T12S
T13S

GATE HWY
10000
ORANGE LN
DATE LN
20000
LOOKOUT LN
BEECH LN
GATE
VALLEY VIEW LEDGE TR
OAK LN
FIR
GRAPE LN
FS
ELM LN
HAZEL LN
IVY LN
JUNIPER PL
20500

DEL DIOS

EQUINE INCLINE TR

ELFIN FOREST RECREATIONAL RESERVE

EQUINE INCLINE TR

KALMIA PL
LAUREL LN
3RD
1ST
MAPLE LN
5TH
2ND DR
20100
NUTMEG LN
OLIVE LN
9800
PALM LN
QUINCE LN
19900
REDWOOD LN
7TH
5TH
4TH
SPRUCE LN
THORN LN
LAKE
19700
VINE LN
UPAS

VALLEY ACCESS TR
OVERLOOK TR
OAK
VALLEY LP

2
1
6

PASEO PIEDRAS
LOS PLATEROS
MOUNT ISRAEL TKTR
8500
TKTR
PASEO ESPLANADA
MOUNT ISRAEL RD
PUNTA ARROYO
LOS SUENOS
CALLE DE SALUD
PASEO DE EL TIEMPO
VIA DE LAS PESETAS

DEL DIOS
5TH
S6

CERCA DEL ARROYO
MOUNT GATE ISRAEL PL
VIA CIELITO
AMBIENTE

WILLOW PL
TAMARACK PL
6TH
4TH
3RD
9100
8TH PL
7TH
BERNARDO LN
SUNNYSLOPE LN
9600
YEW LN
FREMONT
RANCHO
CABRILLO PL
LAGUNA
HERMOSA PL
BALBOA
DE SOTO PL
CARSON PL
9600

11
LO
VIA AMBIENTE
DETWILER RD
8800
MOUNT ISRAEL DR
9100
9400
TOYON CANYON RD
1 DE SOTO PL
2 CARSON PL

12
7
6100

VIA RANCHO
CONNEMARA
SOL
CIELO
CERRO DEL
DR

DEL DIOS HWY
19500
1920

EL BRAZO

92067

CONNEMARA
R3W R2W
DEL DIOS
LAKE

LA CATRINA
VIA DORA
CAMINO DE ESTRELLAS
DAM

14
13
18

LA CATRINA
OS
RIVER
SAN DIEGUITO RIVER
EL ESCONDIDO DEL DIOS HWY
S6

BING CROSBY BLVD
BLUE OF THE
BLVD
HIGH SKIES
NIGHT LN
SAM ANTONIO RDS
BLUE SOCIETY WY
ROSE CT

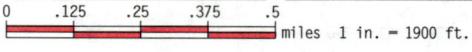

0 .125 .25 .375 .5 miles 1 in. = 1900 ft.

A B C D E

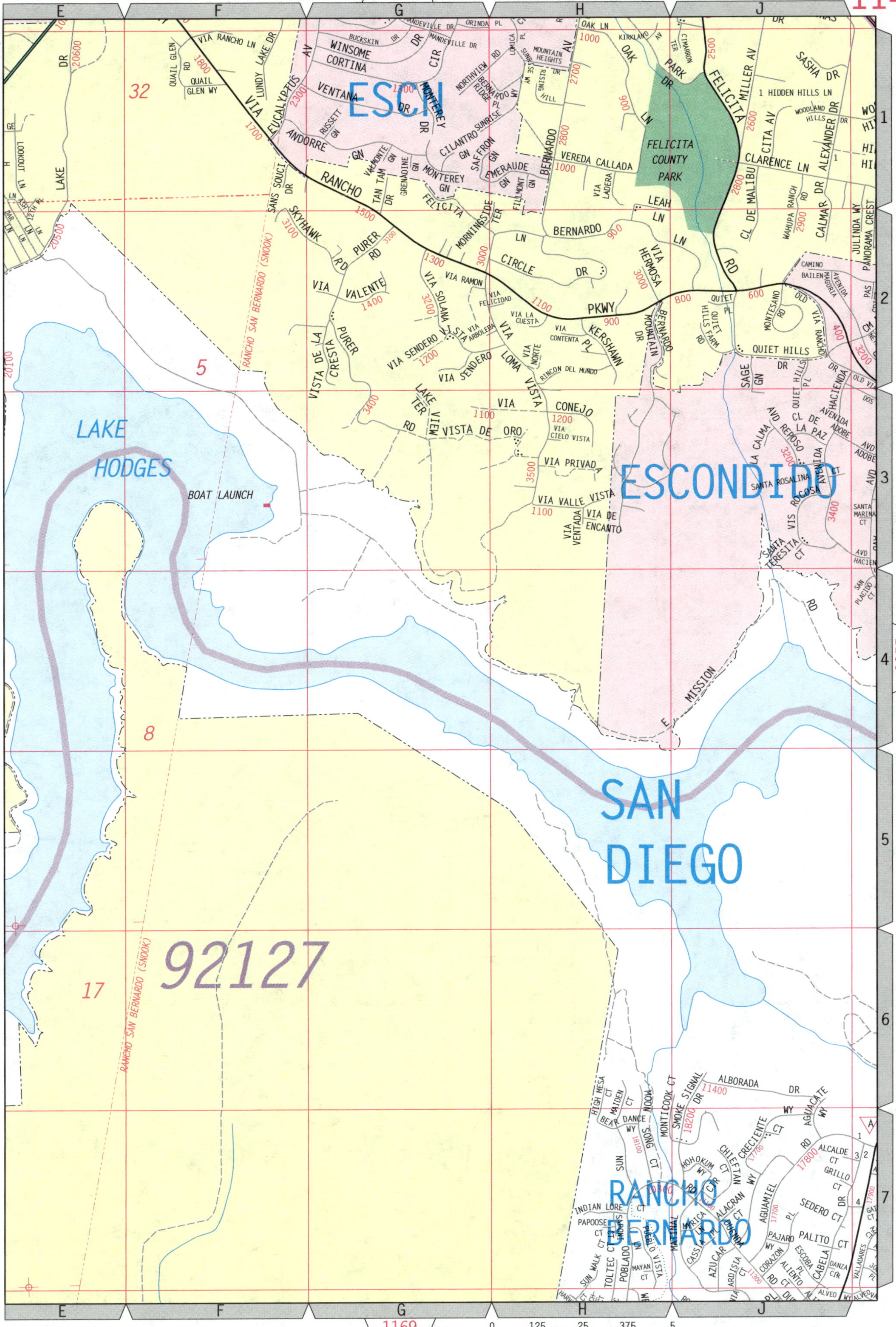

COPYRIGHT 2001

Thomas Bros. Maps®

—N—

ESCN

ESCONDIDO

WINSOME CORTINA

FELICITA COUNTY PARK

VEREDA CALLADA

RANCHO

LAKE HODGES

BOAT LAUNCH

SAN
DIEGO

92127

RANCHO
BERNARDO

QUIET HILLS

VIA RANCHO PKWY

E MISSION RD

0 .125 .25 .375 .5 miles   1 in. = 1900 ft.

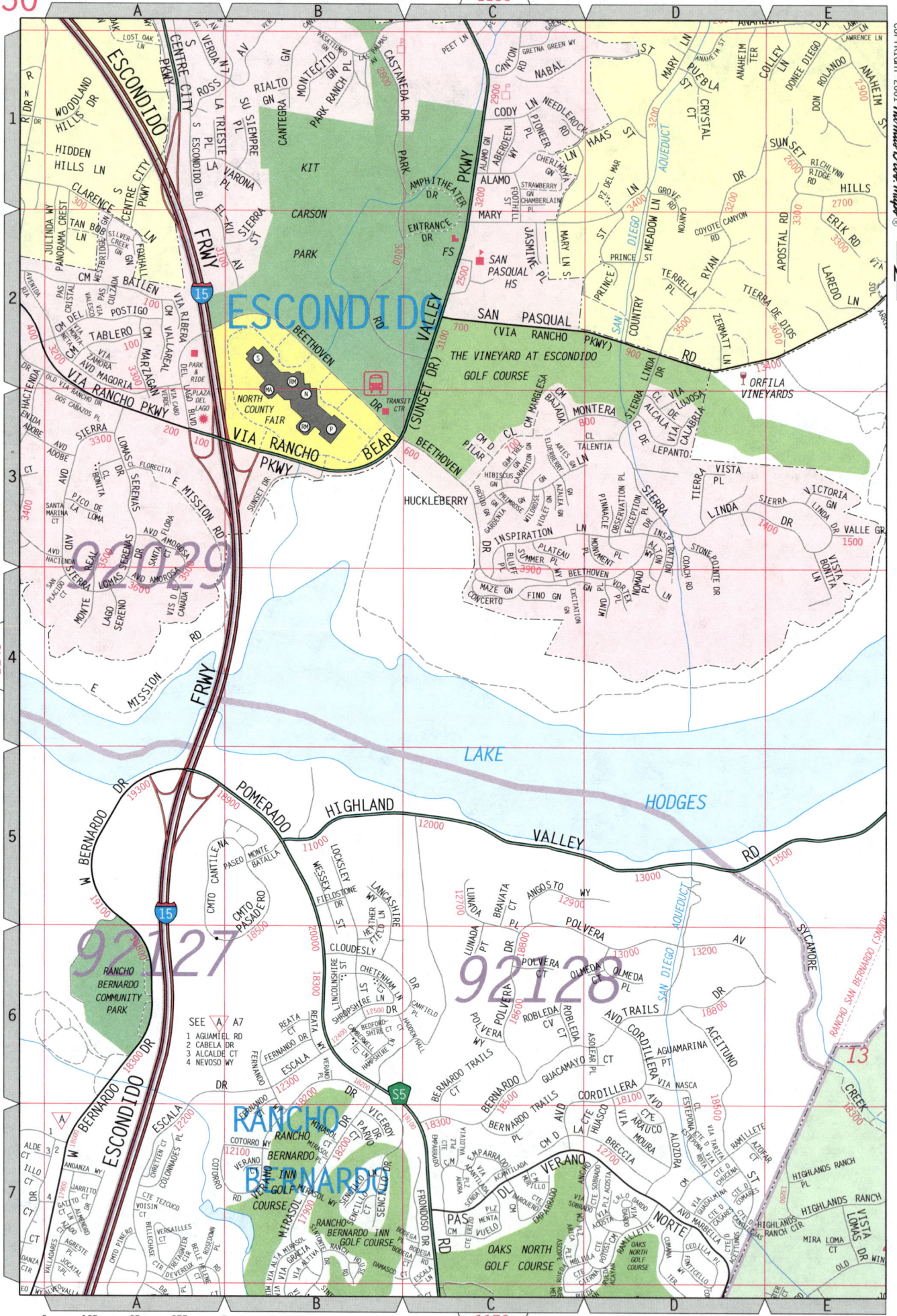

SAN DIEGO CO.

MAP

COPYRIGHT 2001 Thomas Bros. Maps® —N—

A B C D E

ESCONDIDO

ESCONDIDO FRWY

CENTRE CITY PKWY

WOODLAND HILLS DR
HIDDEN HILLS LN
CLARENCE

KIT CARSON PARK

SAN PASQUAL HS

VIA RANCHO PKWY

E MISSION RD

92029

NORTH COUNTY FAIR

PARK & RIDE

VIA RANCHO PKWY

BEAR VALLEY PKWY

BEETHOVEN

HUCKLEBERRY

SAN PASQUAL
(VIA RANCHO PKWY)

THE VINEYARD AT ESCONDIDO GOLF COURSE

ORFILA VINEYARDS

MONTERA

SIERRA LINDA

TIERRA VISTA

VICTORIA
VALLE GR
VISTA BONITA

INSPIRATION

PUEBLA
CRYSTAL
SUN SET HILLS
RICHLYNN RIDGE RD
ERIK RD
LAREDO
TIERRA DE DIOS

E MISSION RD

LAKE HODGES

W BERNARDO DR

POMERADO

HIGHLAND VALLEY RD

AQUEDUCT
SAN DIEGO

SYCAMORE CREEK

92127

RANCHO BERNARDO COMMUNITY PARK

I-15

92128

POLVERA

OLMEDA

AVD TRAILS

CORDILLERA

ACEITUNO

SEE A A7
1 AGUAMIEL RD
2 CABELA DR
3 ALCALDE CT
4 NEVOSO WY

RANCHO BERNARDO

RANCHO BERNARDO INN GOLF COURSE

ESCONDIDO DR

FRONDOSO DR

VERANO NORTE

OAKS NORTH GOLF COURSE

HIGHLANDS RANCH
VISTA LOMAS
MIRA LOMA

0 .125 .25 .375 .5 miles 1 in. = 1900 ft.

A B C D E

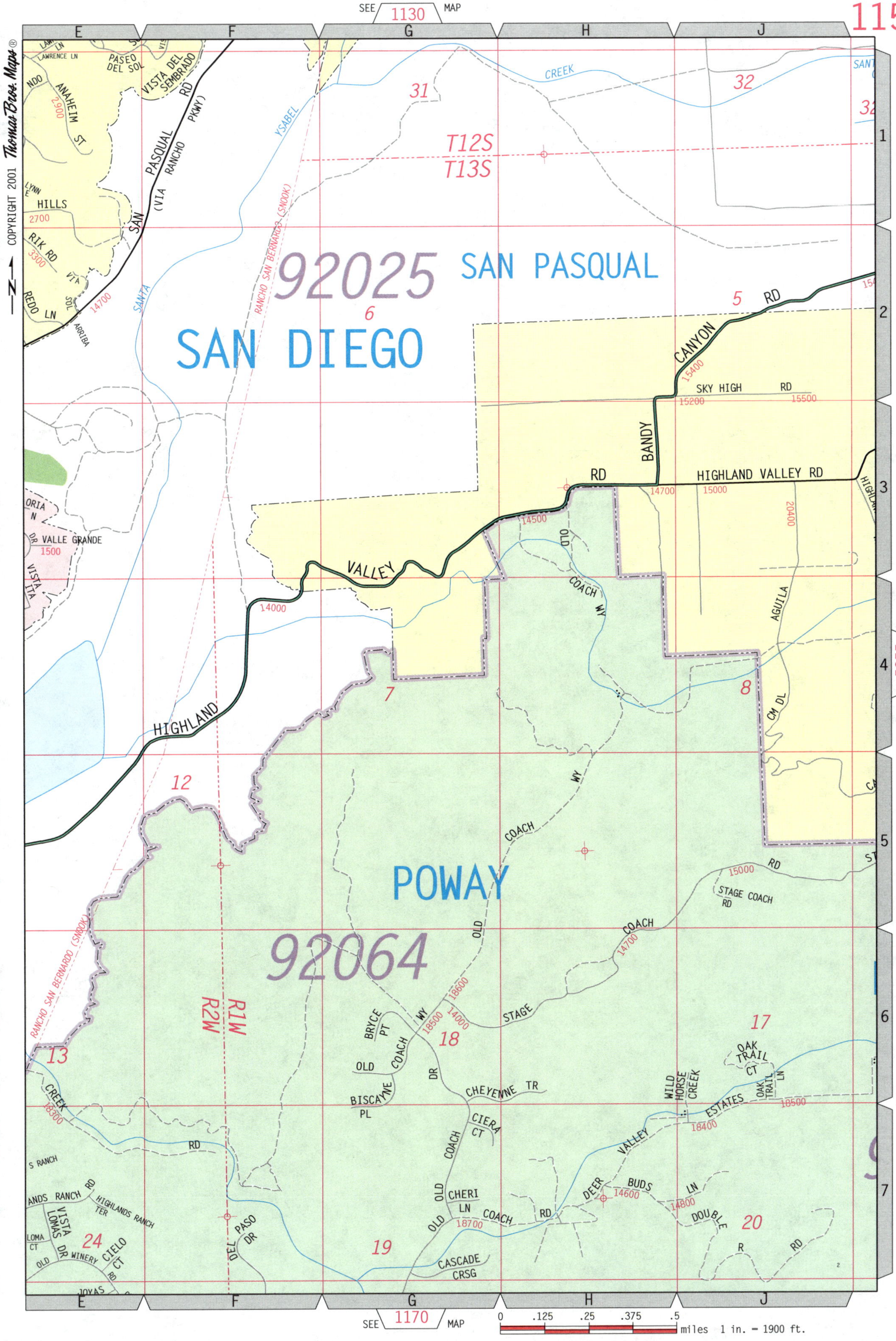

SAN DIEGO CO.

MAP

E F G H J

LAWRENCE LN
PASEO DEL SOL
VISTA DEL SEMBRADO RD
LANI LN
NDO
ANAHEIM ST 2900
HILLS 2700
LYNN 3300
RIK RD
REDO LN
VIA SOL 14700
VISTA DEL
RANCHO (VIA RANCHO PKWY)
SAN PASQUAL
SAN
SANTA
ARRIBA
YSABEL
RANCHO SAN BERNARDO (SMOOK)

CREEK
31
32
SAN PASQUAL
T12S
T13S
SANT

92025
SAN DIEGO
6
5 RD
CANYON
15400
SKY HIGH RD
15200 15500
BANDY
RD
14700
HIGHLAND VALLEY RD
15000
HIGHLAND
20400

ORIA N
DR VALLE GRANDE 1500
VISTA TA

VALLEY
14500
OLD COACH WY
AGUILA
14000
HIGHLAND
7
8
CM DL

12
COACH WY
POWAY
COACH
15000 RD
STAGE COACH RD
14700
ST

RANCHO SAN BERNARDO (SMOOK)
92064
R1W
R2W
BRYCE PT WY
18500 18600 14000
STAGE
18
17
13
CREEK 18300
OLD COACH WY
DR
BISCAYNE PL
CHEYENNE TR
OAK TRAIL CT
WILD HORSE CREEK
ESTATES
OAK TRAIL LN
18500
18400
VALLEY
CIERA CT
COACH CT
DEER 14600
BUDS LN
14800
LN
DOUBLE
20
S RANCH
ANDS RANCH RD
HIGHLANDS RANCH TER
RD
DEL PASO DR
OLD CHERI LN
OLD COACH RD
18700
R RD
VISTA LOMAS DR WINERY
CIELO CT
24
LOMA CT
OLD JOYAS RD
19
CASCADE CRSG

SEE 1170 MAP

SEE 1151 MAP

E F G H J

1
2
3
4
5
6
7

0 .125 .25 .375 .5 miles 1 in. = 1900 ft.

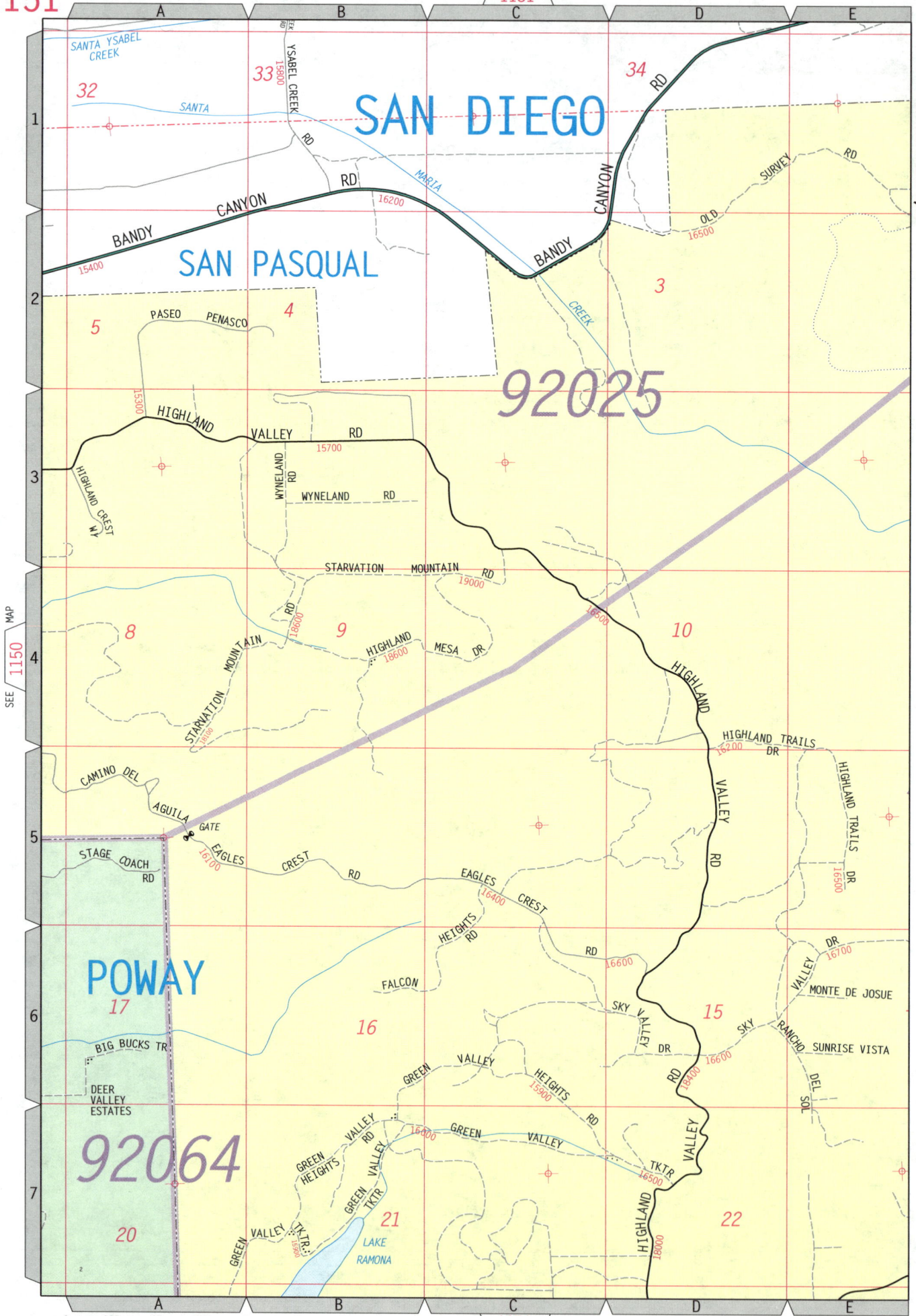

1151

SAN DIEGO CO.

MAP

COPYRIGHT 2001 Thomas Bros. Maps® —N—

SEE 1131 MAP

A B C D E

SANTA YSABEL CREEK

32

33

YSABEL CREEK

SANTA

16600

RD

34

OLD SURVEY RD

SAN DIEGO

BANDY CANYON RD

16200

MARIA

16500

15400

SAN PASQUAL

BANDY CANYON

CREEK

3

5

PASEO PENASCO

4

92025

15300

HIGHLAND VALLEY RD

15700

HIGHLAND CREST WY

WYNELAND RD

WYNELAND RD

STARVATION MOUNTAIN RD

19000

SEE 1150 MAP

8

STARVATION MOUNTAIN RD

18600

9

HIGHLAND MESA DR

18600

16500

10

18100

HIGHLAND VALLEY RD

HIGHLAND TRAILS DR

16200

HIGHLAND TRAILS DR

16500

CAMINO DEL AGUILA

GATE

EAGLES

16100

STAGE COACH RD

EAGLES CREST RD

EAGLES CREST

16400

RD

16600

HEIGHTS RD

FALCON

POWAY

17

SKY VALLEY DR

15

DR

16700

VALLEY

MONTE DE JOSUE

SKY

RANCHO

SUNRISE VISTA

BIG BUCKS TR

16

GREEN VALLEY

GREEN VALLEY HEIGHTS RD

GREEN VALLEY

SKY VALLEY RD

16600

16600

18400

DEL SOL

DEER VALLEY ESTATES

15500

92064

GREEN HEIGHTS

VALLEY RD

16600

GREEN VALLEY

HIGHLAND VALLEY RD

TKTR

16500

20

GREEN VALLEY TKTR

15500

GREEN VALLEY TKTR

21

LAKE RAMONA

22

18000

A B C D E

SEE 1171 MAP

0 .125 .25 .375 .5
miles 1 in. = 1900 ft.

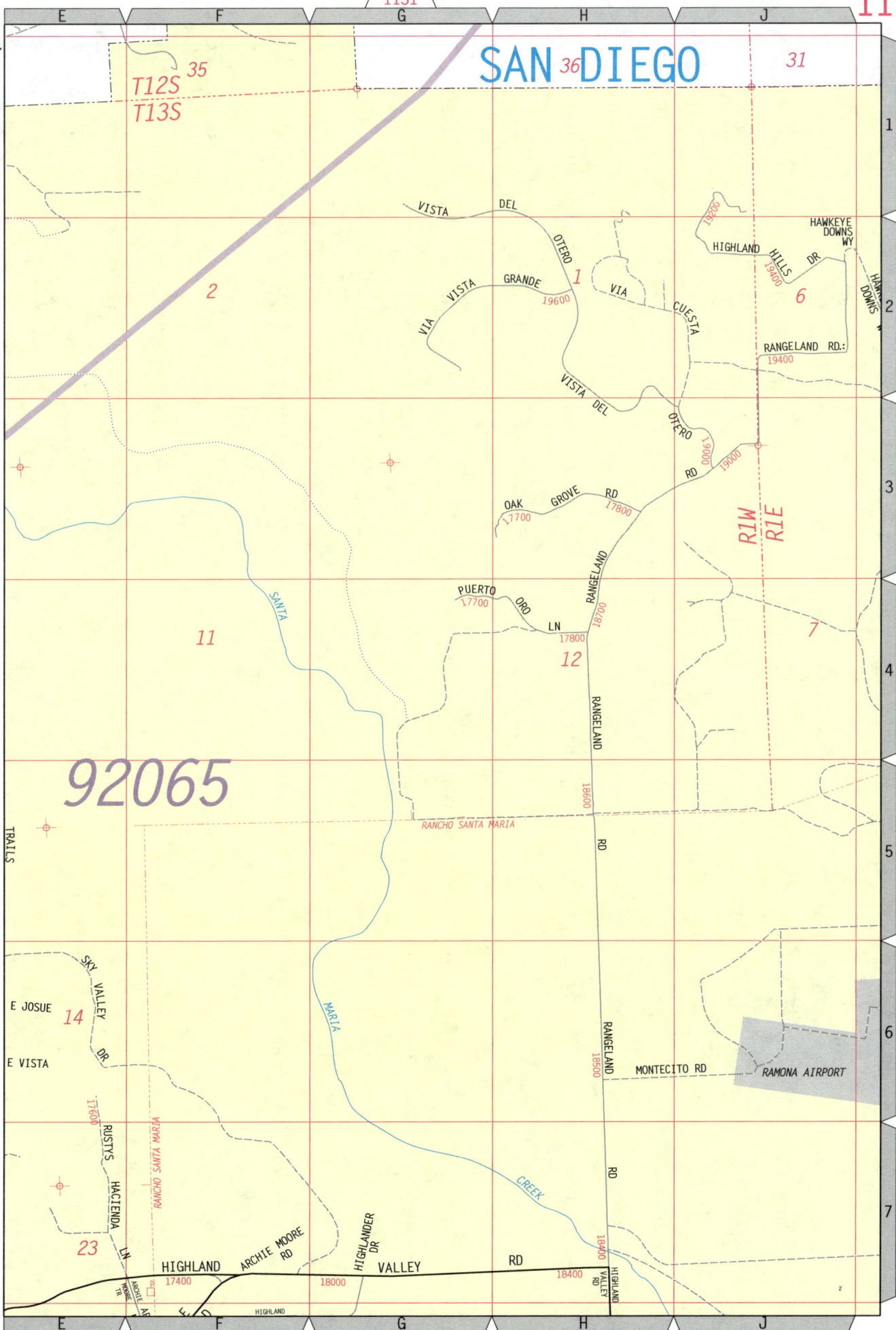

SAN 36 DIEGO 31

—N→

T12S 35
T13S

SAN DIEGO CO.

VISTA DEL

19200
HIGHLAND HILLS DR
HAWKEYE DOWNS WY
19400

VIA VISTA GRANDE 1
19600

OTERO

VIA CUESTA

6

HARR... DOWNS

2

RANGELAND RD.:
19400

VISTA DEL

OTERO RD

19000
19000

R1W | R1E

OAK GROVE RD
17700 17800

PUERTO 17700

ORO LN
17800

RANGELAND

18700

SANTA

11

7

SEE 1152 MAP

12

RANGELAND

92065

RD

18600

RANCHO SANTA MARIA

5

TRAILS

MARIA

RANGELAND RD

18500

MONTECITO RD

RAMONA AIRPORT

6

SKY VALLEY

E JOSUE 14

DR

E VISTA

CREEK

RUSTYS

17600

HACIENDA

RANCHO SANTA MARIA

18400

7

23 LN

HIGHLAND ARCHIE MOORE RD

HIGHLANDER DR

VALLEY RD

17400

18000

18400

HIGHLAND VALLEY RD

MOORE TR

E

HIGHLAND

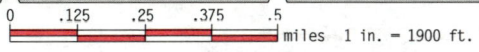
0 .125 .25 .375 .5
miles 1 in. = 1900 ft.

MAP

SD

SAN DIEGO CO.

MAP

T12S
T13S

RANCHO

CLEVELAND

RUSTIC VILLA RD

VILLA EAGLE HILL LN

RUSTIC RANCH RD 20000

PARA SIEMPRE VISTA

QUEST

RAMONA

HIGHLANDS RD 20800

6

RAMONA HIGHLANDS DR

19700

5

SAN

INDIAN OAKS RD

4

DAY STAR WY 20000

PASQUAL HIGHLANDS RD

WASHINGTON ST 1600

RD

HORIZON DR 20000

EYE WNS WY

HAWKEYE DOWNS WY

D.:

VIEW

PASQUAL

CLEVENGER

WEEKEND VILLA

RD 1600

KI 140

MARIA

VALLEY

RD

SANTA

92065

7

8

RANCHO

ASH

ALICE ST 1100

CEDAR SUMMIT DR

DOOMEY DR

CEDAR 1900

SEE 1151 MAP

—N—

MONTECITO WY 900

SONORA WY

SUMMER GLEN RD

OLIVE

2100

ST

DAVIS 900

1600

MONTECITO

LAKY LN

WAYNES WY 1000

SUSAN LN

OLIVE TER 1100

LAMAR 900

ST

JAMES ST

800

WALNUT 1900

700

ST

SUNNY HILLS CT LN

SHADY SPRINGS

5

800

EL

PASO 2100

ST 1900

MONTECITO WY 600

MONTECITO

2100

ASKEW WY

1800

ST

6

FS

RD

2400

MONTECITO

HUGHES ST

TEDS PL

RAMBLING WY

MATTHEW CT

KALBAUGH ST 400

N

HUNTER

MARI

RAMONA AIRPORT

WERNES

LETTON ST

PA

JULIAN ST 200

WOOD ENERGY RD

RAMONA AIRPORT RD

2300

DALEY ST 2600

DURGIN

SANTA

KALBAUGH ST 2300

BEVERLY ST 2300

HALEY ST

300

CARLIN ST

ROBERTSON

S LETTON ST

LA BREA 2100

VERMONT

HUNTER

S JULIAN ST

7

SAWDAY

N HOPE ST

TOUB ST

MITTEN LN

HOWELL ST 2600

TOUB ST 2300

ROTANZI ST 2300

KELLY

67

0   .125   .25   .375   .5
miles 1 in. = 1900 ft.

1152

SAN DIEGO CO.

MAP

E F G H J

CLEVELAND NATIONAL FOREST
LOS ALTOS DE CERRO
KATHERINES VIEW WY
EAGLE HILL LN
PRESTIGE 2100
PINE HEIGHTS 900
PINE RANCHO TRAILS 800 500
LILAC
PAMO
RAMONA REAL
NICOLE STARRS LN
1

QUEST RD
ABBEY RD 900
ELM ST 1960
FS
RD
WASHINGTON ST 1800 800 WASHINGTON
KINGS VILLA RD 1400
PINE WY 800 1700
ST
PILE ST 500
BLACK
PAMO RD
D

N 00 1700
CANYON
RD 78
HAVERFORD RD 1600
CROSSWINDS RD
PINE ST 1400
ELM ST 1300 400
1300
1000
MANDI LN
OLIVE AV 800
PIEDMONT RD 900
MAGNOLIA
B

AVD
REASER LN
MEADOWLARK WY 1300
HARPER RD
ASH ST 900
RAMONA
PENN 100 200
CREEK 700
3

NARANJA ST
NARANJA
ASH 1300 1100
ALICE ST 1100
MAPLE ST 1100
CEDAR 1100
OAK ST
700
ST 500 400 600
MEMORY GARDENS CEM
RAMONA COMMUNITY PARK
SANTA MARIA
HATFIELD CREEK
WY
SEE 1153 MAP
4

DOONEY DR
JOHNSON LN
COUNTRY TER 13NO TO
SAYRS WY 500
POPLAR ST 1100 1000 POPLAR
STOCKALPER LN 400
LOR-LAR LN
ELM ST
DOLORES CT
500
IMOGENE WY
THOMSEN ST
E EARLHAM ST
JULIAN RD 300
LOS BANDITOS
VIA TAQUITA
PASATIEMPO DR 200
AMIGOS
5

ALICE
DAVIS 1600
OLIVE 1100
BRAZOS 700
MAPLE ST
PINE ST 700 900
7TH ST
AQUA 400
5TH ST
6TH ST 600
COMM CTR
2ND ST
B 4TH ST 200
3RD ST
COWBOY CT
E JULIAN RD
VIA ALEGRE
COMANCHERO DR
AMIGOS RD

MOONLIGHT WY
SUNNY HILLS CT LN
SHADY SPRINGS LN
CREEK 1400
8TH ST 800
9TH ST
MAIN ST 500
78
D
5TH ST
F
SUNLIT WY 300
H
1ST ST
HILLCREST ST 900
KRISTI VILLA CT

ST 600
ST 500
RD 0
DELANE ST
CONT HS
HOMESTAR
RAMONA ST
BREA CT
14TH ST
13TH ST
11TH ST
12TH ST
PINE ST
10TH ST
PO
CC
CONT HS
COLLIER COUNTY PARK
SABRINA TER 600
OLD JULIAN HWY
MILLENNIUM WY
TIGER WY
6

MARIA
DAY ST
PALA
PARK & RIDE
CTH PS LIB 1500
16TH ST 1800
E MONTECITO RD 400
LYNDSIE LN
MYRICKS CT
LA MANA ST
TAG LN
HILDDEN LN
FS RD
HEARD LN 800
I ST
9TH ST
TELFORD 600 400
BARBARA ANN LN
DUKES PL
DR
KIRKS WY
TELF
ZI

BREA
LETTON
VERMONT
MAIN
AN ST
RAYMOND
2000 2100
67
RAMOND AV 500
F ST 600
PARKER LN
ARLENE WY
REALTY RD
SOMERSET CT
RANCHO BULLARD PL
ANGEL PL
OAK VILLAGE DR
SAN VICENTE RD 1300
11TH ST
10TH ST
BARGER
BARNETT ST
ASHLEY RD
STEFFY
VIA DWIGHT
BANJO LN
KORY
CAMINO DE AMOR 1500
KEYES 300
7

KELLY ST
GAM LN 1600
GERLAR LN
1 LAWRENCE LN 1 H ST
JAKIRK LN
CAMINO DE AMOR

RAMONA

0 .125 .25 .375 .5 miles 1 in. = 1900 ft.

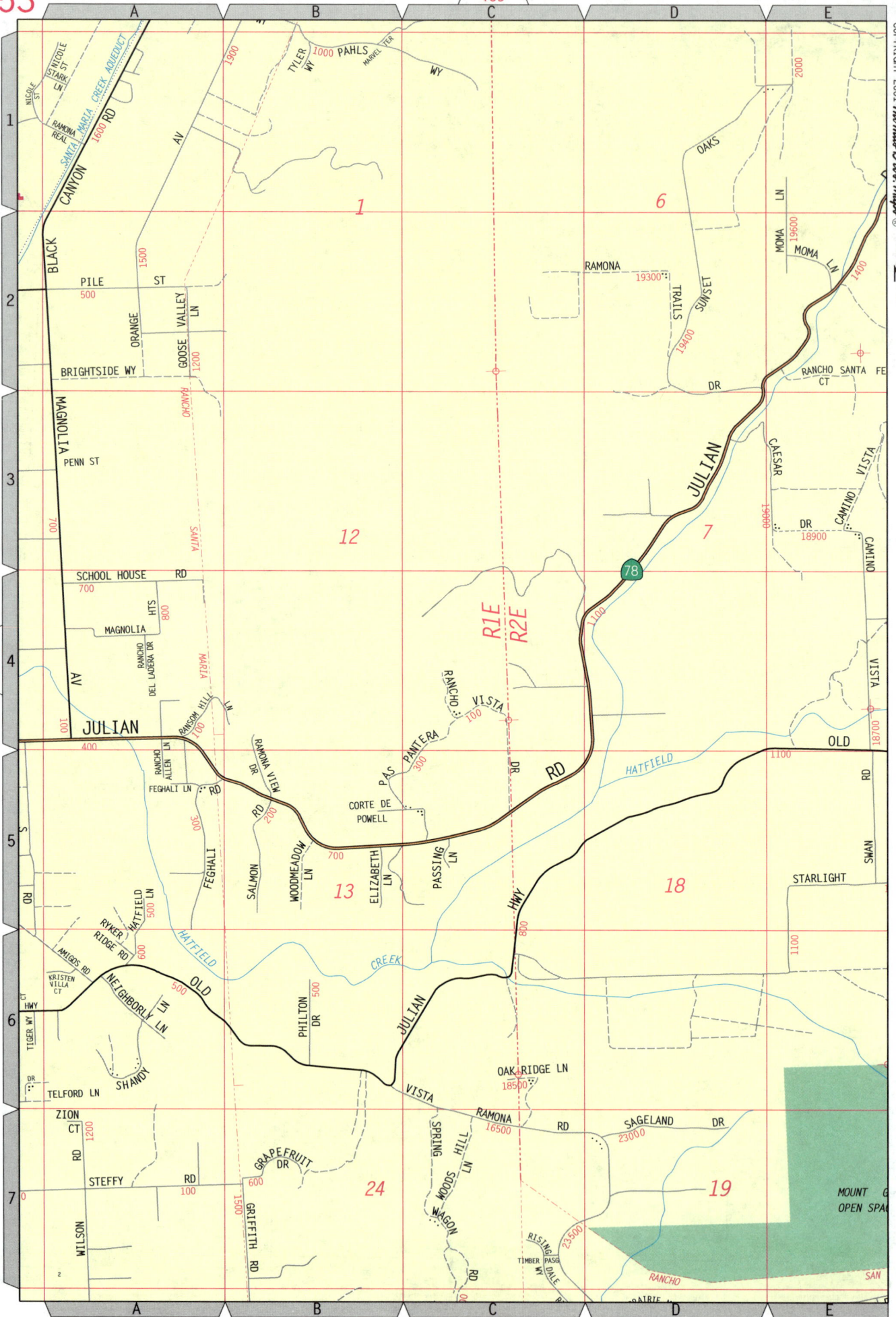

1153

SAN DIEGO CO.

MAP

SEE 1152 MAP

←N→

	A	B	C	D	E

Grid 1:
NICOLE ST
STARK LN
US NICOLE ST
RAMONA REAL
SANTA MARIA CREEK AQUEDUCT
BLACK CANYON RD
1600
1900
TYLER WY
1000 PAHLS
MARVEL VER
WY
WY
AV
OAKS
LN
2000
1
6

Grid 2:
BLACK
PILE ST
500
1500
ORANGE
GOOSE VALLEY LN
1200
RAMONA
19300
TRAILS
19400
SUNSET
MOMA
19600
MOMA LN
1400

Grid 3:
MAGNOLIA
BRIGHTSIDE WY
PENN ST
RANCHO
700
SANTA
12
JULIAN
7
CAESAR
19900
DR
18900
CAMINO VISTA
CAMINO

Grid 4:
SCHOOL HOUSE RD
700
HTS
800
MAGNOLIA
RANCHO DEL LADERA DR
AV
MARIA
100
JULIAN
400
RANSOM HILL
100
RAMONA VIEW
DR
LN
R1E
R2E
RANCHO
100
VISTA
78
1100
VISTA
1800

Grid 5:
S
RD
RANCHO ALLEN LN
FEGHALI LN
RD
300
SALMON
200
RD
WOODMEADOW LN
700
FEGHALI
500 LN
PAS PANTERA
300
CORTE DE POWELL
ELIZABETH LN
PASSING LN
HWY
RD
HATFIELD
1100
OLD
RD
SWAN
STARLIGHT
13
18

Grid 6:
TIGER WY
CT
AMIGOS RD
KRISTEN VILLA CT
RYKER RIDGE RD
HATFIELD
600
NEIGHBORLY LN
500
OLD
HATFIELD
CREEK
PHILTON DR
500
JULIAN
800 HWY
1100

Grid 7:
DR
TELFORD LN
SHANDY
ZION CT
1200
RD
STEFFY RD
100
GRAPEFRUIT DR
600
GRIFFITH RD
1500
24
VISTA
RAMONA
16500
RD
OAK RIDGE LN
18500
SPRING
SPRING HILL LN
WAGON
RISING
23500
TIMBER DALE
PASG
RANCHO
SAGELAND
23000
DR
19
MOUNT G
OPEN SPA
SAN

WILSON
2

0	.125	.25	.375	.5

miles 1 in. = 1900 ft.

A	B	C	D	E

SAN DIEGO CO.

MAP

COPYRIGHT 2001 *Thomas Bros. Maps* ®

N

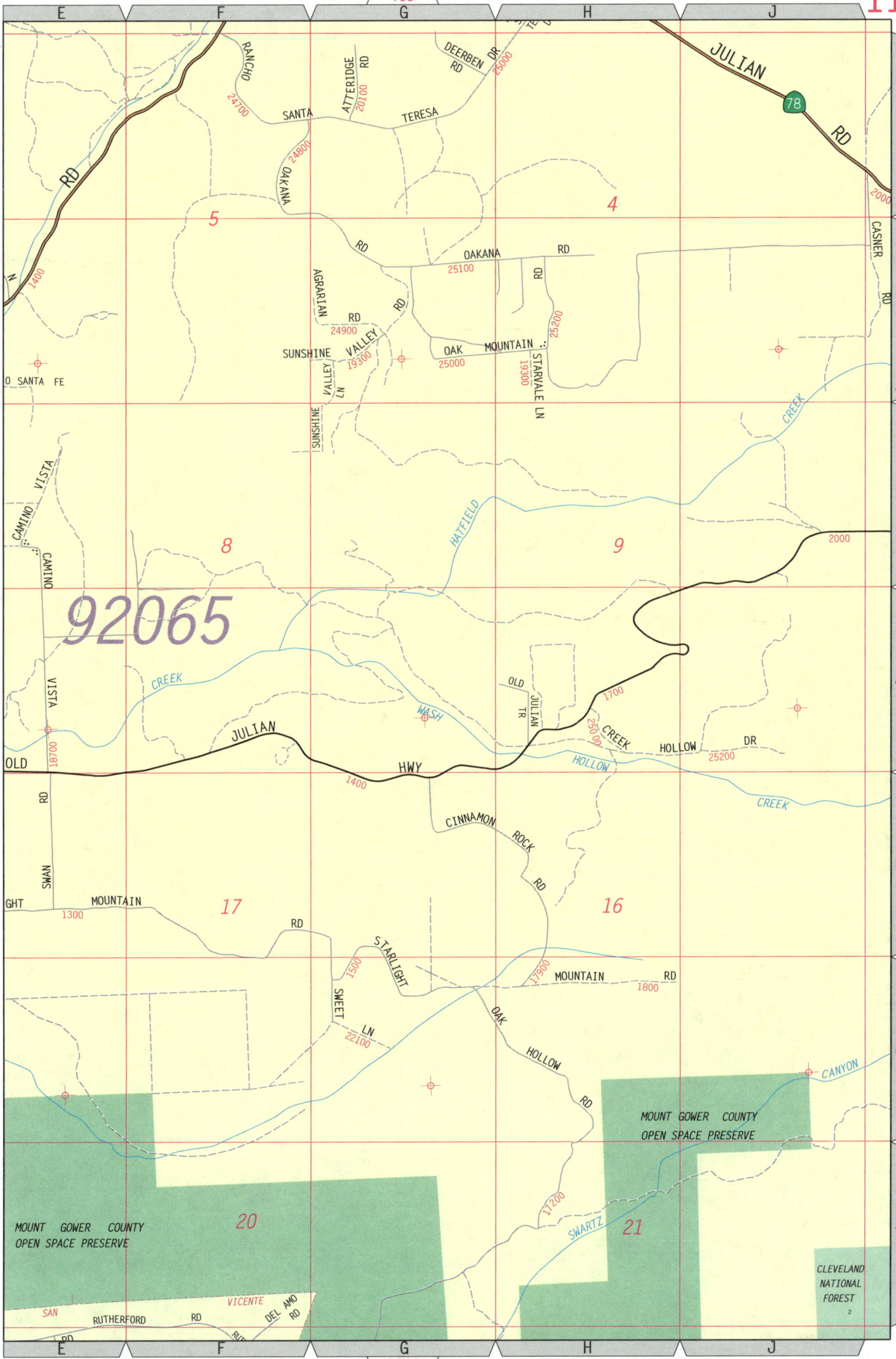

E F G H J

JULIAN RD

78

CASNER RD

RANCHO SANTA RD

24700

ATTERIDGE RD

20100

DEERBEN RD

25000

TERESA

OAKANA

24800

5

4

1

1400

AGRARIAN RD

24900

SUNSHINE VALLEY

19300

OAKANA RD

25100

OAK MOUNTAIN

25000

RD

STARVALE LN

19300

25200

2

SUNSHINE

VALLEY LN

O SANTA FE

CAMINO VISTA

CAMINO

8

HATFIELD

9

CREEK

92065

VISTA

CREEK

WASH

OLD JULIAN TR

2500

CREEK

1700

2000

3

18700

OLD

JULIAN HWY

1400

HOLLOW

HOLLOW DR

25200

CREEK

4

SEE 1154 MAP

RD

SWAN

1300

GHT

MOUNTAIN RD

17

CINNAMON ROCK RD

16

5

STARLIGHT

1500

SWEET LN

22100

MOUNTAIN RD

1800

17900

OAK HOLLOW RD

6

CANYON

MOUNT GOWER COUNTY OPEN SPACE PRESERVE

20

17200

SWARTZ

21

MOUNT GOWER COUNTY OPEN SPACE PRESERVE

7

CLEVELAND NATIONAL FOREST
2

SAN

RUTHERFORD

VICENTE RD

DEL AMO RD

E F G H J

0 .125 .25 .375 .5 miles 1 in. = 1900 ft.

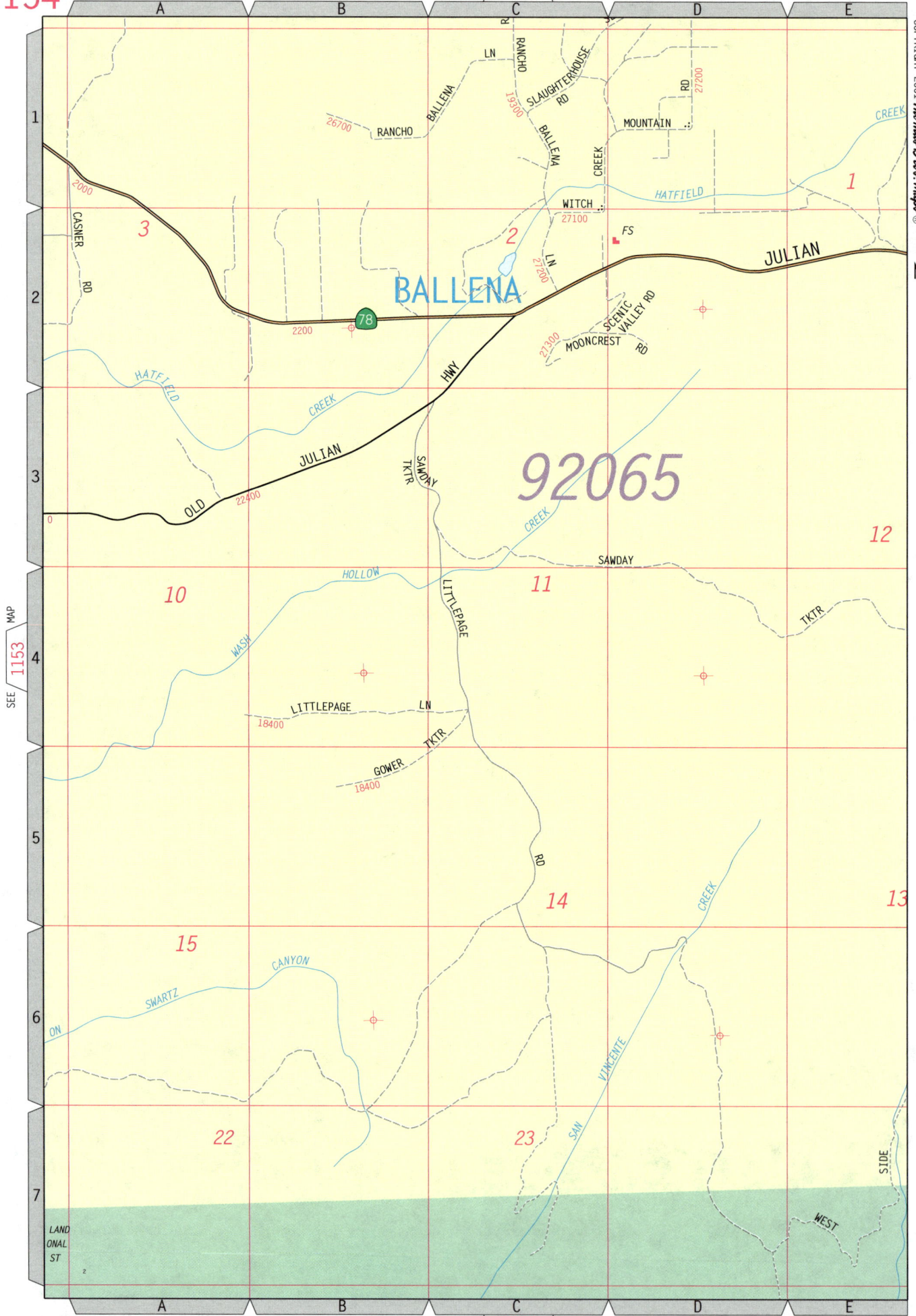

SAN DIEGO CO.

MAP

SEE 409 MAP

—N—

A   B   C   D   E

1

RANCHO LN

SLAUGHTERHOUSE RD

19300

BALLENA

26700

RANCHO

BALLENA

CREEK

MOUNTAIN ..:

RD 27200

CREEK 1

HATFIELD

CASNER

3

2000

WITCH ..:

27100

FS

2

JULIAN

RD

BALLENA

78

2200

MOONCREST

SCENIC VALLEY RD

RD

27300

21300

LN 27200

2

HATFIELD

CREEK

HWY

92065

JULIAN

OLD

22400

SAWDAY TKTR

CREEK

SAWDAY

12

3

0

HOLLOW

10

WASH

11

LITTLEPAGE

TKTR

4

LITTLEPAGE LN

18400

GOWER TKTR

18400

RD

5

14

CREEK

13

15

CANYON

SWARTZ

6

ON

SAN VINCENTE

22

23

SAN

SIDE

7

WEST

LAND ONAL ST

2

SEE 1153 MAP

0   .125   .25   .375   .5   miles   1 in. = 1900 ft.

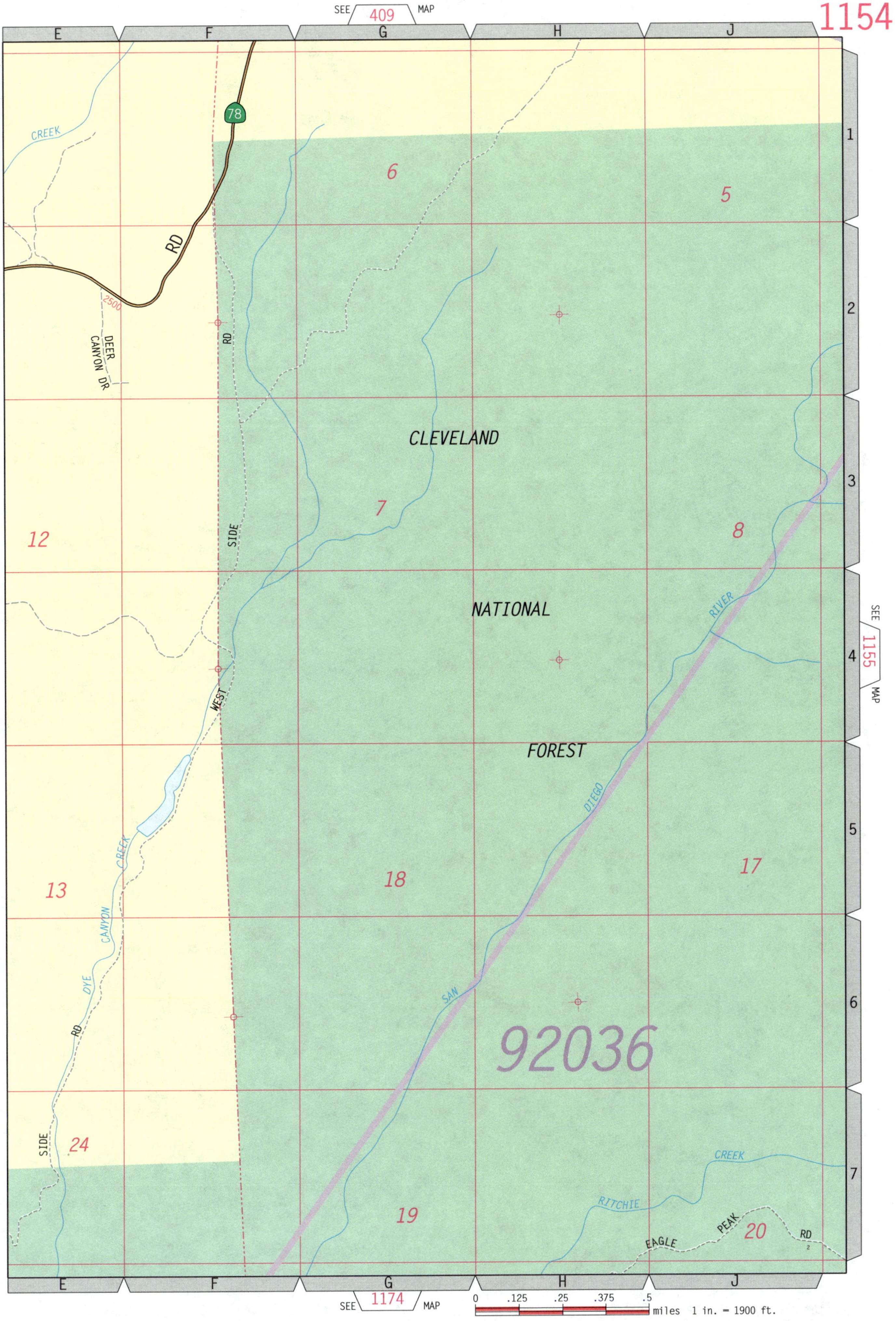

E F G H J

CREEK

78

RD

DEER CANYON DR

2500

RD

SIDE

CLEVELAND

6

5

1

2

3

12

7

8

NATIONAL

RIVER

SEE 1155 MAP

4

WEST

FOREST

DIEGO

CREEK

DYE

CANYON

RD

13

18

17

SAN

5

92036

6

SIDE

24

CREEK

RITCHIE

19

20

EAGLE PEAK RD

7

0   .125   .25   .375   .5
miles 1 in. = 1900 ft.

COPYRIGHT 2001 Thomas Bros. Maps®

N

SAN DIEGO CO.

MAP

—N—

SEE 1135 MAP

A B C D E

SENTENAC

92065

1

4

3

DALEY FLAT
2600

RD

CLEVELAND

2

SAN DIEGO RIVER

SEE 1154 MAP

TEMESCAL CREEK

3

9

10

NATIONAL

4

92036

FOREST

5

16

15

CREEK

6

RITCHIE

RD

7

PEAK

EAGLE

21

22

RD

A B C D E

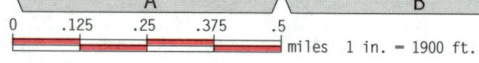

0 .125 .25 .375 .5
miles 1 in. = 1900 ft.

SEE 1175 MAP

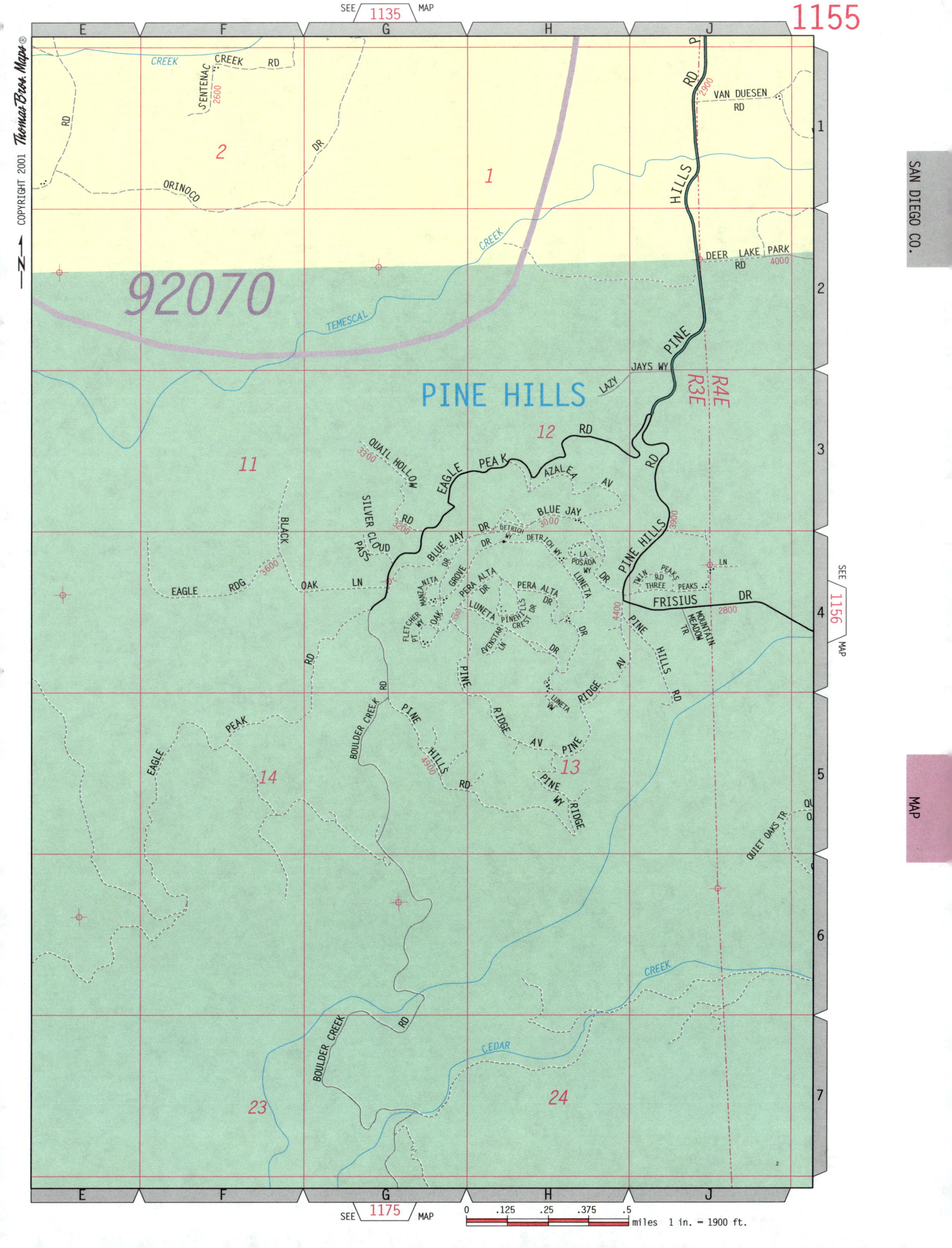

SAN DIEGO CO.

MAP

E F G H J

CREEK
SENTENAC CREEK RD
2600
RD
ORINOCO DR
2
1
VAN DUESEN RD
HILLS
RD
2900

92070

TEMESCAL
CREEK
DEER LAKE PARK RD 4000
2

PINE
LAZY JAYS WY

PINE HILLS

R4E
R3E

11
QUAIL HOLLOW 3300
EAGLE PEAK
AZALEA AV
12 RD
RD
3206
SILVER CLOUD PASS
BLUE JAY 3000
DETRICH WY
DETRICH WY
LA POSADA WY
PINE HILLS 3900
RD
3

BLACK
EAGLE RDG 3600
OAK LN
BLUE JAY DR
GROVE
PERA ALTA DR
MANZANITA
FLETCHER PT WY
OAK
LUNETA
PERA ALTA DR
PINEHILLS CREST DR
AVENSTAR LN
LUNETA
DR
TWIN PEAKS RD
THREE PEAKS
LN
FRISIUS DR 2800
MOUNTAIN MEADOW TR
4400
4

RD
PINE
RIDGE
LUNETA WY
RIDGE AV
PINE HILLS RD
SEE 1156 MAP

14
EAGLE PEAK
BOULDER CREEK RD
PINE HILLS RD 4300
RIDGE
AV
PINE WY
13
PINE RIDGE
QUIET OAKS TR
5

6

CREEK
23
BOULDER CREEK RD
CEDAR
24
7

0 .125 .25 .375 .5 miles 1 in. = 1900 ft.

SEE 1136 MAP

SAN DIEGO CO.

MAP

A B C D E

CUYAMACA

JESS MARTIN PARK

2900

VALLEY VIEW DR

KENISON DR

1 RIDGEWOOD DR

OAKS HEIGHTS RD

HICKMAN PL

HACIENDA

ACACIA DR

ALTA

HILLSIDE DR

WOODLAWN

KENTWOOD WINDWARD

PINE CONE

HIGHLAND DR

KNOB HILL

TERRACE DR

EDGEWOOD DR

ROYAL

LAKEVIEW

PARK DR

CRESCENT DR

CEDAR

IMPERIAL

ECHO

PHEASAN

SALTON

VISTA DR

YUCCA DR

MOUNTAIN

WILDWOOD

SUNSET

COUNTRY

LAKEVIEW

VISTA DR

DR

HAWTHORNE

PLEAS

OLD CUYAMACA RD

1

6

VAN DUESEN RD

5

SLUMBERING

OAKS TR 3200

TEMESCAL

CREEK

LEON LN 1400

OAK LAND RD 1200

OAK LAND RD

79

4

3400

600

800

3600

3600

600

4000

9

ARK 000

3900

DEER LAKE PARK

7

LA TENAJA TR RD 4000

VIA CENOTE 2100

TICANU DR

CLEVELAND

NATIONAL

FOREST

8

PARK RD

2

3

PINEOAK RIDGE RD 700

DEER LAKE DR 4300

4

SEE 1155 MAP

BELVEDERE DR

W INCENSE CEDAR

16

18 FRISIUS DR 1800

BELVEDERE DR

17

WILLIAM HEISE COUNTY PARK

CEDAR RD

W INCENSE

QUIET OAKS TR

FRISIUS DR 1600

HEISE PARK RD

GLENCO LN

WILD ROSE RD

TOYON MOUNTAIN RD

JUL

5

KS TR

QUIET OAKS TR

COULTER LN 4000 2100

QUIET OAKS TR

TOYON MOUNTAIN LN

JULIAN

6

CEDAR

CREEK

HARRISON PARK

JULIAN

21 BIG P

19

STARLIGHT WY

ACORN

PATCH RD

GRANDVIEW RD

CUYAMACA RANCHO STATE PARK

20

BEINN BHREAGH

OAK WY

INDIAN ROCK RD

PARK TR

IRON

HALES PL

SPRINGS

FEN

IRO

BIRDSELL LN

7

0 .125 .25 .375 .5 miles 1 in. = 1900 ft.

—N—

E F G H J

SAN DIEGO CO.

MAP

Thomas Bros. Maps®

COPYRIGHT 2001

N

1

PHEASANT DR PANORAMA DR
SALTON DOLORES DR
VISTA DR MANZANITA DR 3300
OUNTAIN VIEW DR
0 WILDWOOD DR 500
SUNSET DR COUNTRY CLUB DR
COUNTRY 3100
AKEVIEW OPAL DR
A DR CLUB DR
VINEWOOD DR 600 TOPAZ DR
CIRCLE DR EMERALD DR
3700
HAWTHORNE
PLEASANT VIEW
600 DR
CRESCENT 3800 DR
DR ELYSIAN DR
CEDAR ANTLERS DR CHATEAU DR
ECHO DR
IMPERIAL
4000 DR
HWY

KENTWOOD
IN THE PINES 3

BANNER

MAIN ST BANNER RD

BANNER CANYON
BANNER CREEK
78

2

CHARIOT CANYON

11

10

E RD 700

INSPIRATION POINT RD

HIDEWAY RD 700
800

92036

16

E INCENSE CEDAR RD
MOUNTAIN RD
R LN
JULIAN ESTATES RD

15

CUYAMACA

COULTER RIDGE RD

CHARIOT

14

CANYON

SEE 430 MAP

JULIAN ESTATES

JULIAN ESTATES RD

HWY
KQ RANCH RD
TALL
PINE
RD

5

HARRISON PARK RD
16800
TWIN OAK LN QUARTZ WY
MELODY LN
1 BIG PINE LN
LILAC LN
TWIN OAK LN PINE
TREE LN
OAK LAKE LN
PINE CREEK RD
CANYON MILE HIGH RD
FENDER RD
RD
SPRINGS 35100
INDIAN ROCK RD
IRON SPRINGS
ROCK HOUSE RD
IRON SUNSET LN
SPRINGS WY
OAKS RD
LES L
LOTS MILE HIGH RD

RD

RD

6

22
MEADOWS
CUYAMACA

23

79
WINN RANCH RD

RANCHO CUYAMACA

ANZA–BORREGO DESERT
26 STATE PARK

7

0 .125 .25 .375 .5
miles 1 in. = 1900 ft.

SEE 1147 MAP

A   B   C   D   E

SAN DIEGO CO.

MAP

—N—

1
2
3
4
5
6
7

H STREET VIEWPOINT PARK

I STREET VIEWPOINT PARK

J STREET VIEWPOINT PARK

SWAMIS BEACH

SWAMIS PARK

GARDENA CT

BRIGGS AV

MELBA DR

STRATFORD DR

DEVONSHIRE DR

SAN DIEGUITO DR

CORNISH DR

MILDRED ST

MACPHERSON PK PL

MELBA RD

BRACERO RD

TREASURE VIEW LN

REGAL RD

GOLDEN RD

GARDENA RD

ARCADIA RD

NARDO RD

SAN DIEGUITO HS

BLUE SKY DR

BONITA

15

H ST

2ND ST

3RD ST

1ST ST

K ST

W

I

J ST

SCRIPPS MEM HOSP ENCINITAS

H

SANTA

FAITH AV

MACKINNON

MUNEVAR

CATHY RD LN

OCEAN CREST RD

KINGS CROSS DR

GRANGE HALL R

900

76

21

BELLEVIEW AV

SUMMIT PL

RUBENSTEIN PL

SUMMIT COVE LN

SUMMIT

RUBENSTEIN

LOCH LOMOND

ORKNEY

92007

SAN ELIJO AV

AVD DE MONACO

MAY CT

VIVALDI ST

STARLIGHT

BEACH

CARETTA WY

KINGS CROSS CT

KNIGHTS BRIDGE

WINDSOR CREEK

ADA HARRIS PARK

WINDS

WO

SAN

DE

SANDCASTLE

NOLBEY

CARDIFF BY-THE-SEA

WARWICK

SHEFFIELD

BRAHMS AV

VERDI AV

RAVON AV

BRISTOL

WESTMINSTER

SOMERSET

BURKSHIRE

MACKINNON

CARDIFF

FALCON HILL CT

DEBANN RD

ROBL

BRIGHTON

S21

SAN ELIJO STATE BEACH

MONTGOMERY AV

STAFFORD

CARDIFF PARK

BEETHOVEN AV

PARK & RIDE

EMNA

PLAYA RIVIERA DR

LA

BIRMINGHAM

GLASGOW

EDINBURG

CAROL VIEW DR

MOZART AV

ROSSINI AV

PO

TRANS CTR

LIB

LIVERPOOL DR

OXFORD AV

CAMBRIDGE AV

2100

CC

ABER-DEEN

NEWCASTLE

CHESTERFIELD

NORFOLK AV

500

ORINDA DR

GLEN PARK

MANCHESTER AV

MONTGOMERY DR

DUBLIN

NEWPORT AV

KILKENNY

200

300

2500

27

DIEGO

MANCHEST

PACIFIC

OCEAN

COAST

HWY

COASTER

SDNR

CARDIFF STATE BEACH

SAN ELIJO LAGOON

S21

101

COASTER

SDNR

SOLAN POINT C

RIOS CT

CIRCLE DR

OCEAN ST

34

SOLANA VISTA DR

SEABRI

PACIFIC

SEE A H7

1	VILLA HERMOSA CT	20	MANZANILLO CT
2	TAMPICO WY	21	LINARES CT
3	VALLARTA CT	22	GUERRO CT
4	TOLUCA CT	23	JALAPA CT
5	TAMPICO CT	24	IGUALA CT
6	SINALOA CT	25	LAS CANAS CT
7	SALTILLO CT	26	CM D LS VILLAS
8	SALINA CRUZ CT	27	ALLENDE CT
9	SABINAS CT	28	BUENAVENTURA CT
10	SALAMANCA CT	29	CELAYA CT
11	REYNOSA CT	30	CHAPALA CT
12	SABINAS WY	31	COZUMEL CT
13	REMEDIOS CT	32	DELICIAS CT
14	NAVA WY	33	EBANO CT
15	LAS CANAS WY	34	FRESNILLO CT
16	MATAMOROS CT	35	GUANAJUATO CT
17	MORELIA CT	36	CHAPALA WY
18	NAVA CT	37	FRESNILLO WY
19	MEXICALI CT	38	POZA RICA CT

TIDE BEACH PARK

CLIFF ST

ACACIA AV

SIERRA

ESTR

ELL

HELIX

FLETCHER COVE BEACH PARK

COMM CTR PLAZA

PO

3

LINDA

0   .125   .25   .375   .5   miles   1 in. = 1900 ft.

SEE 1147 MAP

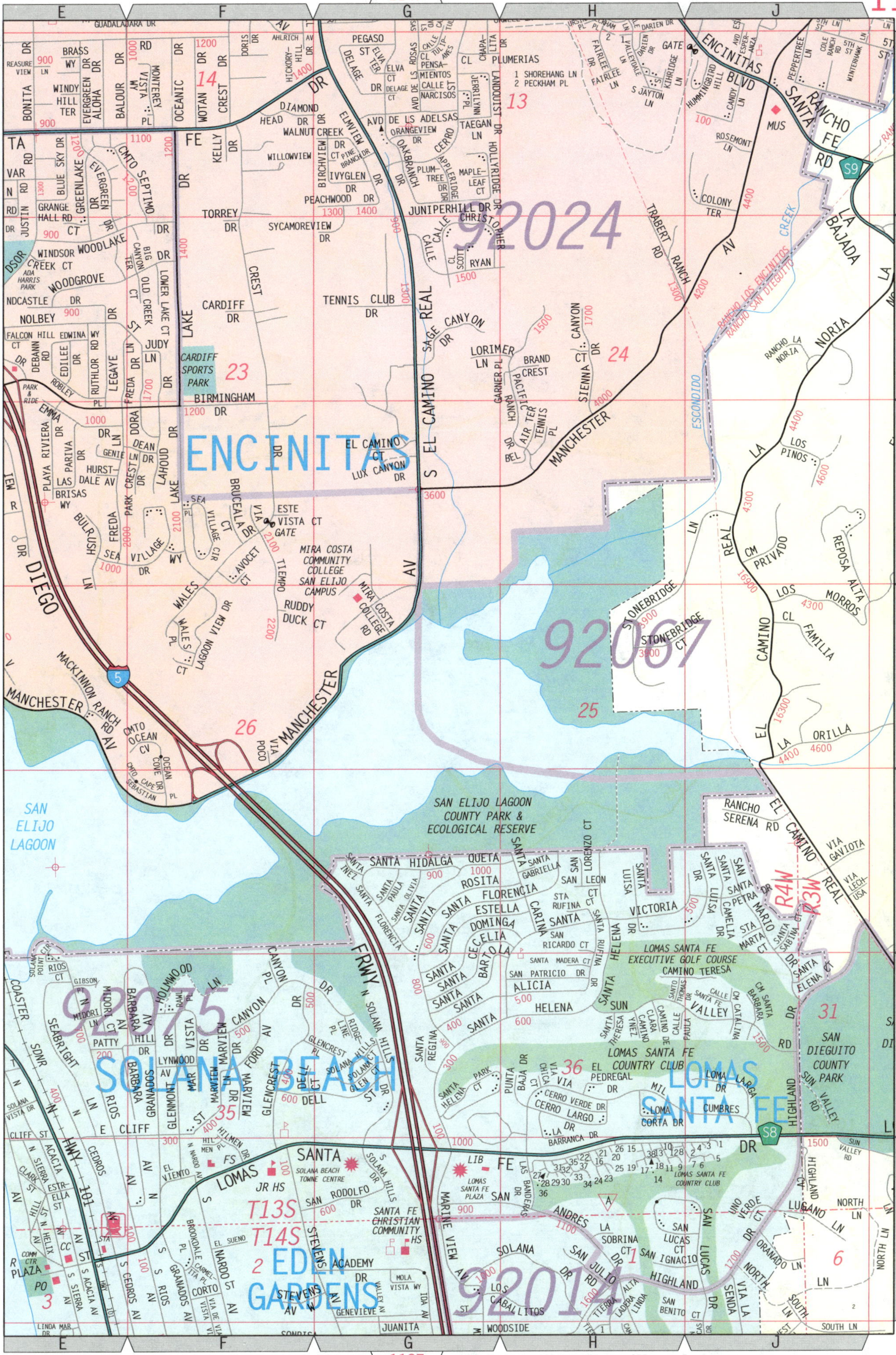
ENCINITAS
SOLANA BEACH
EDEN GARDENS
LOMAS SANTA FE
92024
92067
92075
92014
SAN ELIJO LAGOON
SAN ELIJO LAGOON COUNTY PARK & ECOLOGICAL RESERVE
SAN DIEGUITO COUNTY PARK
CARDIFF SPORTS PARK
MIRA COSTA COMMUNITY COLLEGE SAN ELIJO CAMPUS
LOMAS SANTA FE EXECUTIVE GOLF COURSE
LOMAS SANTA FE COUNTRY CLUB
SOLANA BEACH TOWNE CENTRE
LOMAS SANTA FE PLAZA
SANTA FE CHRISTIAN COMMUNITY HS
JR HS
ACADEMY
COMM CTR PLAZA
MUS
LIB
FS
PO
T13S
T14S
R4W
R3W
ENCINITAS BLVD
RANCHO SANTA FE RD
S EL CAMINO REAL
EL CAMINO REAL
MANCHESTER AV
MANCHESTER DR
SAN DIEGO FRWY
HWY 101
LOMAS SANTA FE DR
LA BAJADA
LA NORIA
CM PRIVADO
LOS MORROS
CL FAMILIA
REPOSA ALTA
LA ORILLA
LOS PINOS
RANCHO LA NORIA
STONEBRIDGE LN
STONEBRIDGE CT
ESCONDIDO CREEK
TRABERT RANCH RD
TENNIS CLUB DR
SAGE CANYON DR
LORIMER LN
BRAND CREST
SIENNA CANYON DR
BIRMINGHAM DR
CARDIFF DR
TORREY CREST DR
SYCAMOREVIEW DR
DIAMOND HEAD DR
WALNUT CREEK DR
LAKE DR
LAGOON VIEW DR
RUDDY DUCK CT
MACKINNON RANCH RD
CEDROS AV
S CEDROS AV
SIERRA AV
ACACIA AV
HIGHLAND DR
SAN ANDRES DR
STEVENS AV
SOLANA HILLS DR
N RIOS AV
GLENCREST DR
MARVIEW DR
CLIFF ST
CANYON DR
SANTA HELENA
SANTA VICTORIA
HELENA
ALICIA
CERRO LARGO
NORTH LN
SOUTH LN
LUGANO LN
SAN DIEGO CO.

SEE 1168 MAP

SEE 1187 MAP

0 .125 .25 .375 .5 miles 1 in. = 1900 ft.

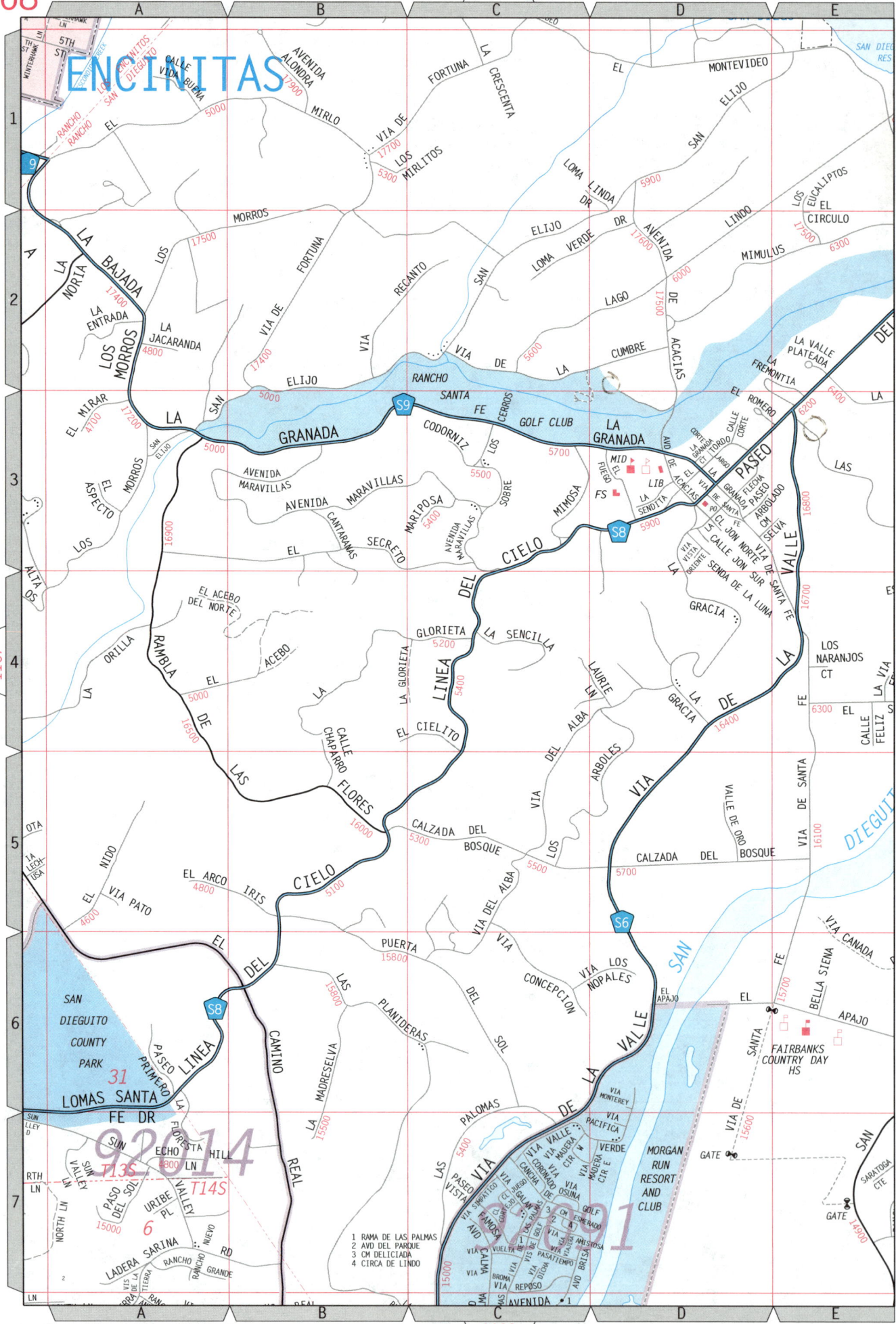

COPYRIGHT 2001 Thomas Bros. Maps®

—N—

SAN DIEGO CO.

MAP

SEE 1167 MAP

SEE 1188 MAP

ENCINITAS

A | B | C | D | E

1
2
3
4
5
6
7

9

S9

S8

S6

LA NORIA
LA BAJADA
LOS MORROS
LA ENTRADA
LA JACARANDA
EL MIRAR
SAN ELIJO
LA GRANADA
EL ASPECTO
LOS MORROS
LA ORILLA
RAMBLA DE LAS
EL ACEBO DEL NORTE
ACEBO
AVENIDA MARAVILLAS
AVENIDA MARAVILLAS
EL SECRETO
CANTARANAS
LA GLORIETA
CALLE CHAPARRO
CIELO IRIS
EL ARCO
VIA PATO
EL NIDO
EL DEL
PASEO PRIMERO
LINEA
CAMINO REAL
MADRESELVA
LA PLANIDERAS
PUERTA
CALZADA DEL BOSQUE
CALZADA DEL BOSQUE
LINEA
GLORIETA
LA SENCILLA
EL CIELITO
DEL CIELO
LAURIE LN
LA GRACIA
VIA DEL ALBA
LOS ARBOLES
VIA DEL ALBA
VIA CONCEPCION
DEL SOL
VIA LOS NOPALES
VALLE DE ORO
VIA DE SANTA FE
LOS NARANJOS CT
CALLE FELIZ
EL
LA VIA
EL APAJO
BELLA SIENA
APAJO
VIA CANADA
VIA DE
GATE
GATE
SARATOGA CTE
SAN

MORGAN RUN RESORT AND CLUB

FAIRBANKS COUNTRY DAY HS

SAN DIEGUITO COUNTY PARK 31

LOMAS SANTA FE DR

92014
T13S
T14S
6

92091

ENCINITAS
AVENIDA ALONDRA
CALLE VIDA BUENA
MIRLO
LA FORTUNA
LA CRESCENTA
EL
MONTEVIDEO
SAN ELIJO
VIA DE LOS MIRLITOS
MORROS
LA FORTUNA
VIA
SAN RECANTO
LOMA LINDA DR
LOMA VERDE DR
AVENIDA DE ACACIAS
LINDO
LOS EUCALIPTOS
EL CIRCULO
MIMULUS
LAGO
LA CUMBRE
LA VALLE PLATEADA
LA FREMONTIA
EL ROMERO
ELIJO
RANCHO SANTA FE GOLF CLUB
LA GRANADA
PASEO VALLE
CODORNIZ
LOS CERROS
MID EL FUEGO
FS
LIB
LA SENDITA
CALLE JON NORTE
VIA DE SANTA FE
SENDA DE LA LUNA
LA GRACIA
MARIPOSA
AVENIDA MARAVILLAS
MIMOSA
VIA DE
LA GRACIA
VIA
PALOMAS
LAS PALMAS
VIA DE LA VALLE
VIA MONTEREY
VIA PACIFICA
VIA VALLE MADERA
MORGAN RUN

1 RAMA DE LAS PALMAS
2 AVD DEL PARQUE
3 CM DELICIADA
4 CIRCA DE LINDO

miles 1 in. = 1900 ft.
0 .125 .25 .375 .5

SAN DIEGO CO.

MAP

Thomas Bros. Maps®
COPYRIGHT 2001

E F G H J

SAN DIEGUITO RES

15

14

LAGO LINDO

EL CAMINO DEL NORTE

ESCONDIDO DEL DIOS HWY

VISTA RANCHO CT

BING CROSBY BLVD

CMTO DE LOS ESCOSES

AVENIDA SECOND

EL PASEO DELICIAS

LA PALMA

VIA DEL SIETE

VIA LEGUAS

AVENIDA PEREGRINA

LUNA DE ORO

LUNA DE MIEL

BRISA

RANCHO DEL RIO

RIO SENDA

SAN DIEGO AQUEDUCT

CLAMBAKE DR

OLD MAN RIVER RD

STAGECOACH PASS

PALE MOON RD

BING CROSBY CT

HIGH LINE RDG

1

EL MONTEVIDEO

VIA DE MAYA

EL VUELO DEL ESTE

CUATRO

BRAVO

LA SOLDADERA

22

NOCHE TAPATIA

EL CAPORAL

CAMINOS

VIA DE LA NOLA

LA

CALLE DOS LAGOS

23

WHITE CHRISTMAS

RIDING HIGH WY

COCONUT GROVE CT

ROSE OF TRALEE

ROAD TO SINGAPORE

ROAD TO ZANZIBAR

2

S6

LA VALLE

PLATEADA

VIA GUADALUPE

VIA MONALEX

VUELO

ROAD TO UTOPIA

TOP OF THE RIO MORNING WY

ROAD TO MOROCCO

TOP OF

DELICIAS

VALLE

PLATEADA

EL

MIRADOR

RANCHO

SAN

DIEGUITO

CAMINITO DE LAS PALMAS

CAMINITO DEL VIENTECITO

3

RANCHO SANTA FE

LA

COLINAS

AVENIDA LUIS

EL ZORRO VISTA

LAS

LOS BARBOS

COLINAS

LAS CUESTAS

ZUNAQUE

7100

ARTESIAN

ARTESIAN RD

RIO VISTA RD

AR

92067

LA ESPADA

ST

27

26

92127

S ANJOS

LA VIA FELIZ

VIA A LA CASA

RIVER

CAMPOSECO

VIA BARRANCA DEL ZORRO

CALLE DEL

POSADA DEL NORTE

AVENIDA PICACHO

AVENIDA CUATRO VIENTOS

AVENIDA ALTERAS MAYOR

LUSARDI CREEK

4

EL SICOMORO

CALLE FELIZ

CALLE DEL

NORTE

PASEO HERMOSA

CALLE

CALLE MAYOR

DIEGUITO

VIA BARRANCA

CIRCA

AVENIDA LOMA DE ORO

VIA DOS

CAMINO ACAMPO

RD

CALLE

ORIENTE

CALLE PIEDRA

SAN DIEGO

35

5

VIA CAMPO VERDE

VIA

FLORESTA

AVENIDA ARROYO PASAJERO

FAIRBANKS LAKE

VALLES

CAMINO LAGO DE CRISTAL

VIA LOS FAROLITOS

CIRCA

CALLE DEL CRUCE

CAMINO DE MONTECILLO

CALLE CORDOBA

AVENIDA

CANADA

DEL OSITO

CAMINO DEL PAJARO

CIRCA

LAGO AZUL

VISTA CANADA

VIA DE LOS ROSALES

CIRCA DEL SUR

CALLE VERDE

CALLE SERENA

34

6

FAIRBANKS RANCH

APAJO

AVENIDA CUESTA LOS OSOS

FS

CALLE DEL CAMPANARIO

DEL NORTE

VIA DE LOS

CAMINO SAUCITO

VIA CUESTA

CIRCA DEL

VIA CUESTA MANSA

ORIENTE

CAMINO

CALLE DEL NIDO

AVENIDA CUESTA DEL SOL

CIRCA DEL

CAMINO SIERRA DEL SUR

SUR

T13S

T14S

SAN

PIMLICO CTE

CHURCHILL DOWNS

AVD DE LOS OLIVOS

VIA CAZADERO

AVENIDA DE LA RONDA

CIRCA DEL

AVENIDA MOLINO VIEJO

SAINT ANDREWS

RD MUIRFIELD WY

TURNBERRY CT

CAMINO DE LA LUNA

CAMINO DE LA ROSA

2

CAMINO RUIZ

7

SARATOGA CTE

VALENCIA

RANCHO DIEGUENO

AVENIDA LAS PERLAS

VALENCIA CIR

CROQUET CT

VILLA GARDINER LN

LA TENISTA

RANCHO

PASEO VALENCIA

4

RANCHO SANTA FE FARMS GOLF CLUB

3

SPYGLASS LN

SAINT ANDREWS RD

LAZANJA DR

ALYDAR CTE

TE

DIEGUITO

SAINT

ANDREWS

RANCHO SANTA FE FARMS GOLF CLUB

E F G H J

0 .125 .25 .375 .5 miles 1 in. = 1900 ft.

SEE 1169 MAP

SEE 1149 MAP

SAN DIEGO CO.

MAP

SEE 1168 MAP

14

13

20

1

BLVD
BLVD
BLVD
LN
LDG
CT
A
B
C
D
E

HIGH SOCIETY WY
COUNTRY GIRL LN
BING CROSBY BLVD
OLD COURSE RD

BAKE DR
STAGECOACH PASS
GOING
PALE MOON RD
LAMOUR LN
MY WY

CAMINO SANTA FE
CAMINO BRISA DEL MAR
17300
PASEO DE PIEDRAS
CAMINO SANTA FE
9500

23
24
19

TOP OF THE MORNING WY
DOWN MEMORY LN
IRISH EYES
HIGH TIME RDG
SA7NT MARY CT
THE MORNING WY
DANNY BOY WY
BING CROSBY BLVD
NATHANIEL CT
SECOND

TALLOW TREE LN
PAGODA TREE LN
TEA TREE LN
SILVER GUM WY
PURPLE LEAF
HOLLY LEAF
LAVENDER DR
STAR
9800
SANGALLO LN
PIENZA PL
MURANO LN
LARIO LN
CASTELLO
CAMPANIA
17000
VITA AV

2

IBAR
AD TO MOROCCO
TOP OF THE
ROAD TO BALI
CALLE HERMOSA
ARTESIAN RD
8900
ARTESIAN RD
8300
10000

COYOTE LN
SAW LEAF
ISLAND PINE WY
BUSH DR
BERNARDO LAKES
WHITE ALDER CT
FOSTORIA CT
FOUR
10100
ARTESIAN RD
8000

BLACK MOUNTAIN RD
BERNARDO
RANCHO

3

ARTESIAN RD
ARTESIAN RD
SAN

92127

ARTESIAN RD
CAMINO DEL NORTE
10000

CAMI

SAN
FALCON VISTA
FALCON BLUFF DR
LIMITS
FALCON BLUFF CT
ST
LONE RIDGE
QUAIL

26
TRAILSIDE RD
9000
ARTESIAN RD

25

DIEGO

30

DEER FOX VALLEY
FOX VALLEY DR
DEER RIDGE PL
FOX MEADOW
CAMINO FOX
DEER RIDGE CT
DEER RIDGE RD
FOX VALLEY CT
DEER RIDGE
WREN BLUFF DR
PINTO RIDGE
TRAIL DR
DEER TRAIL PL
DEER TRAIL CT
PINTO TRAIL
DEER TRAIL WY
RANCHO
BLACK MOUNTAIN RD

R3W
R2W

4

35

36

AQUEDUCT

LUSARDI

31

5

SAN DIEGO

6

CAMINO RUIZ

T13S
T14S

RD

7

RUIZ

2

CANYON

ZANJA

LA

1

6

BLACK
MOUNTAIN

A
B
C
D
E

SEE 1189 MAP

0 .125 .25 .375 .5 miles 1 in. = 1900 ft.

COPYRIGHT 2001

Thomas Bros. Maps®

20

RANCHO BERNARDO

HOLIDAY INN

PARK & RIDE

RADISSON RANCHO BERNARDO

BERNARDO RD

BLACK MOUNTAIN RD

CAMINO DEL NORTE

SAN WILLOW

THORNMINT RD

THORNMINT ST

MESAMINT ST

COASTWOOD RD

GOLDENTOP

RANCHO PATINA

(BLACK) FS

CANBERRA CT STS RD

TUSCANY CT

INDIGO WY

RUSSET LN

BERRYESSA

BLUESTONE ST

ALVA ST

MURANO LN

BERNARDO RD

RANCHO BERNARDO RD

BLACK MOUNTAIN RD

DOVE CANYON RD

DEER RIDGE RD

QUAIL

FOX VALLEY WY

DEER RIDGE PL

FOX MEADOW LN

CAMINO

FOX VALLEY CT

BLUFF DR

PINTO RIDGE CT

LONE BLUFF

DEER TRAIL CT

DEER TRAIL

PINTO RIDGE DR

CIMMARON CANYON DR

BERNARDO

SAN DOVE ST

LONE OAK

LONE BLUFF

NORMANDY

4S RANCH PKWY

PRAIRIE FARM RD

PRAIRIE CREST

LARK VISTA DR

CLASICO CT ST

ABUNDANTE

ARRIBA

LINDA

PASEO ALLEGRIA

EL CABALLO

SANTA TOMASA AV

SANTA CORINA CT

CAMINO NORTE

TECHNOLOGY DR

TECHNOLOGY PL

CENTER DR

VIA FRONTERA

VIA FRONTERA

VIA DEL CAMPO

VIA DEL CAMPO CT

VIA CAMPO

VIA TAZON

W BERNARDO CT

W BERNARDO DR

VIA ESPRILLO

VIA ESPRILLO

BERNARDO DR

CAPILLA RD

BROKEN BOW CT

LIBERTAD

TABLERO PL

CALENDA

FLORINDO

MATINAL RD

AUTILLO

POBLADO

WEAVING LN

CARRANZA

PINZON WY

PICAZA DR

ARMERO CT

LUZ PL

DUENDA RD

CABELA DR

MATINAL

HADA

MATINAL CIR

MASADA

TABLERO

OCULTO RD DR

OCULTO RD

BOTERO DR

POBLADO

10TH ST

10TH ST

BERNARDO CENTER DR

TURTLEBACK

TURTLEBACK LN

CLOUDCREST DR

TRAILSIDE WY

BIG SPRINGS WY

SUN SUMMIT PT

EAGLESVIEW CT

EARTHSTAR

MATURIN DR

MEADOW FLOWER PL

SILVER BUCKLE

REDBUD CT

WINDY SUMMIT PL

GRASSY TRAIL

BOX ELDER

LOFTY TRAIL

GRIMSTONE LN

TRAIL SIDE RD

SUNNYDALE

BLAZEWOOD

WILLOWMORE

WINDROSE

BERNARDO

BERNARDO CENTER DR

NORTE

AVD DE LOS LOBOS

ABEJA

CTE CODORNIZ

TERRAZA FLORACION

CM CRISALIDA

CM CODORNIZ

PASEO MONTANOSO

AVENIDA DE LOS LOBOS

PENANOVA ST

LINARES ST

ALMAZON

NAWA CT

NAWA WY

MEKNES WY

MEKNES ST

PAYMOGO

CTE MONTANGO

ALBACETE

AJANTA

PASEO RADOSO

PASEO JENBITY

MADRIGAL

CALLE JUANITO MARIA

AVD DEL DIABLO

PENASQUITOS DR

ROLLING HILLS PARK

CARLOTA

RAJA

SUSITA ST

SEGOVIA CT

AMALIA

ANDORRA

DEL DIABLO WY

CARMEL HIGHLAND DOUBLETREE GOLF & TENNIS RESORT

SOCORRO RD

SOCORRO WY

SOCORRO CT

AMALIA ST

AMALIA

1 VIA LLANO
2 VIA HONDONADA

1 PRISCILLA ST

ESCONDIDO FRWY

I-15

92129

92128

32

33

34

BLACK MOUNTAIN PARK (OPEN SPACE)

5

4

RANCHO PENASQUITOS

RANCHO SAN BERNARDO (SNOOK)

CREEK

SAN DIEGO CO.

MAP

SEE 1150 MAP

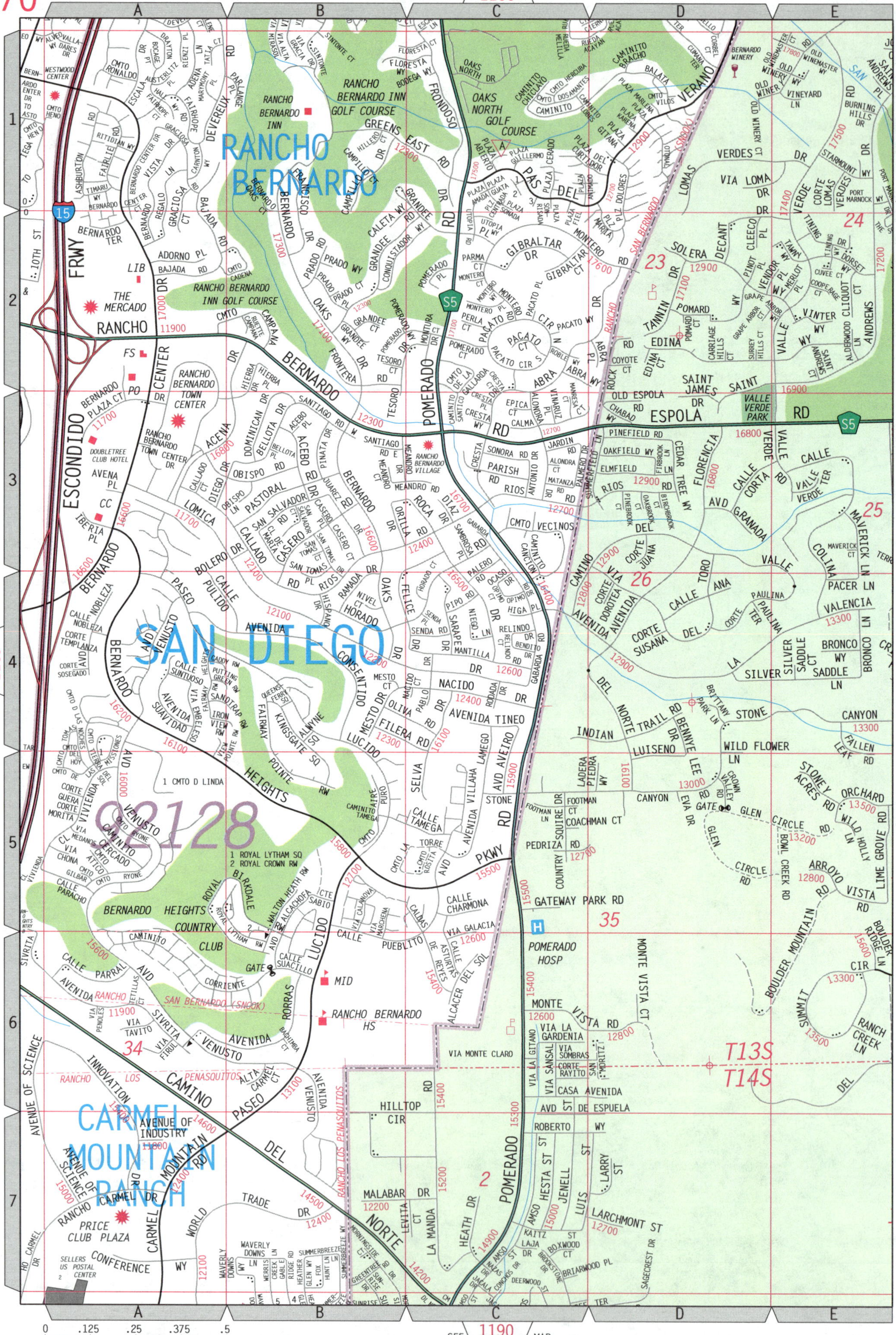

COPYRIGHT 2001 Thomas Bros. Maps ®

—N—

SEE 1169 MAP

RANCHO BERNARDO

SAN DIEGO

92128

CARMEL MOUNTAIN RANCH

Rancho Bernardo Inn Golf Course

Rancho Bernardo Inn

Oaks North Golf Course

THE MERCADO

Bernardo Plaza Ct

Rancho Bernardo Town Center

Doubletree Club Hotel

Bernardo Heights Country Club

Rancho Bernardo HS

Pomerado Hosp

Price Club Plaza

Sellers US Postal Center

Bernardo Winery

Valle Verde Park

Saint James Dr / Saint Andrews

ESCONDIDO FRWY

RANCHO BERNARDO RD

POMERADO RD

ESPOLA RD

CAMINO DEL NORTE

AVENUE OF SCIENCE

I-15

S5

H

23 24 25 26 35 34 2

T13S
T14S

SEE 1190 MAP

0 .125 .25 .375 .5 miles   1 in. = 1900 ft.

SEE 1150 MAP

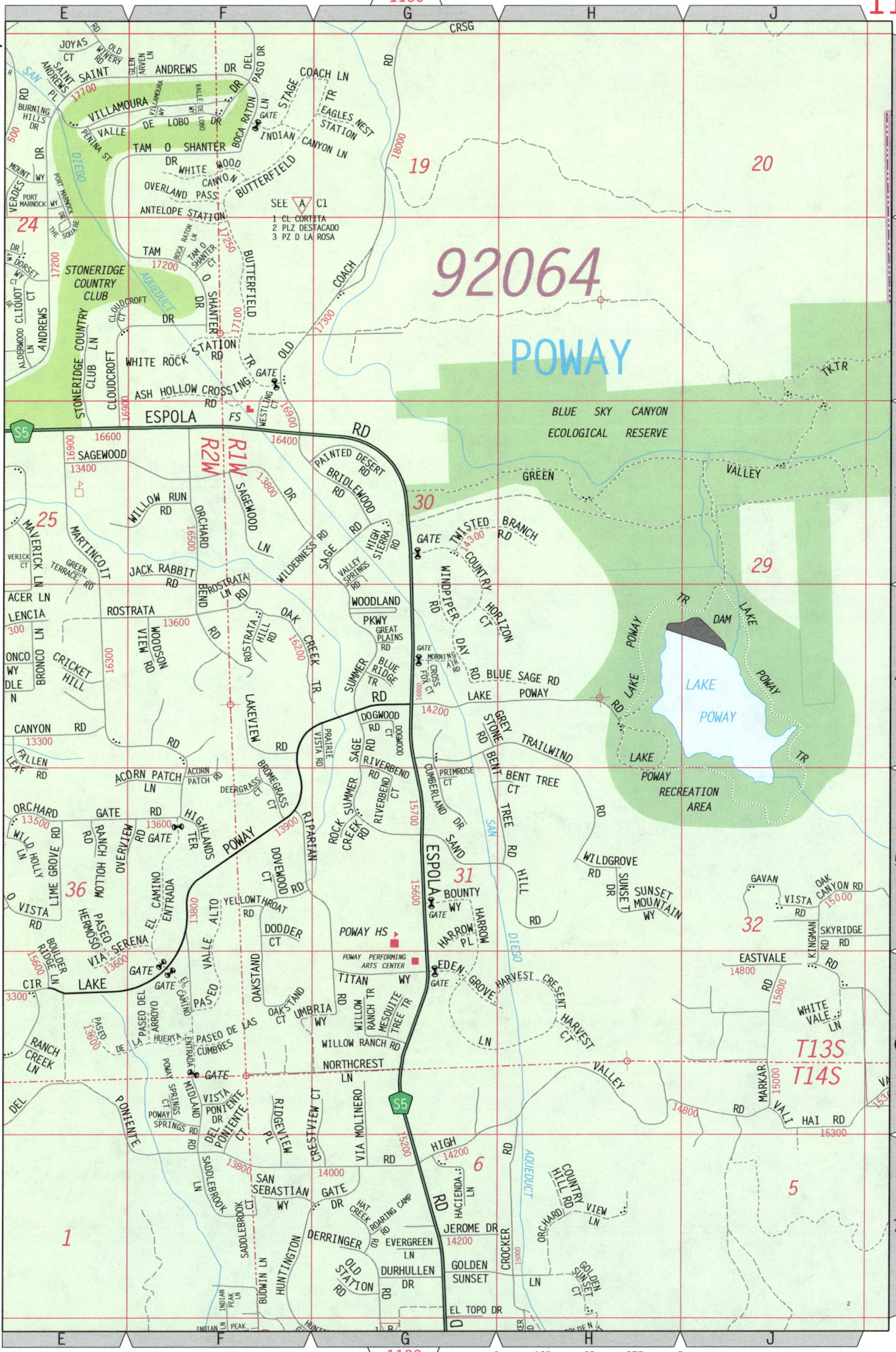

1170

SAN DIEGO CO.

MAP

92064

POWAY

BLUE SKY CANYON ECOLOGICAL RESERVE

LAKE POWAY

POWAY RECREATION AREA

STONERIDGE COUNTRY CLUB

ESPOLA RD

COPYRIGHT 2001 Thomas Bros. Maps®

SEE 1190 MAP

SEE 1171 MAP

0 .125 .25 .375 .5 miles 1 in. = 1900 ft.

T13S
T14S

SAN DIEGO CO.

MAP

SEE 1151 MAP
SEE 1170 MAP
SEE 1191 MAP

A B C D E

1

20

21

22

HIGHLAND VALLEY RD
16300
16500
16400

VERDIGRIS VALLEY RD

QUAIL
16800
17000
CHELAUREN

TKTR

VALLEY

GREEN

LAKE RAMONA

DAM

2

BLUE SKY CANYON ECOLOGICAL RESERVE

PUESTA DEL SOL LN
15400
16100

DEL SOL

SALIDA
16500
16100

SALIDA DEL LUNA RD

VIA DENA
15500

LOMA
15700

SALIDA DEL SOL
15400

WOODSON CREST RD
15400

CREST

GRANITE DR
16900

VISTA SUMMIT DR
BOULDER OAKS DR

OBSIDIAN

HAMLIN CT

IRONSTONE CT
17000

DR

MOUN
WO

16000

3

29

28

27

WOODSON
15400

WOODSON RIDGE RD

4

WOODSON MTN

MOU

5

POWAY

32

33

ROCK HAVEN

34

N RD
00

OAK CANYON RD

15700

IDGE D

SKYRIDGE RD

QUAIL MOUNTAIN RD

COYOTE CREEK TR

RD
16000

6

EASTVALE CANYON PASS

92064

RUNNING DEER TR

67

VALI HAI RD
15500
0

CANYON VIEW WY

WESTVIEW RD

GATE

CHAPARRAL WY

ELLIE LN
15100

CREEK

7

5

WESTVIEW RD

RIDGECREST RD

CLEARVIEW RD

4

MINA DE ORO RD
15300

3

RATTLESNAKE

RIDGECREST RD

2

A B C D E

0 .125 .25 .375 .5 miles 1 in. = 1900 ft.

SAN DIEGO CO.

MAP

COPYRIGHT 2001

Thomas Bros. Maps®

N

E F G H J

ERDIGRISEY RD IL

CRSG

ARCHIE MOORE TR

ARCHIE MOORE RD

HIGHLAND MEADOW CT

DR

TARTAN TER

HIGHLANDER

23

PETROLIA CT

HIGHLAND MEADOW CT

RANCHO VIA SERENIDAD

SUENOS DR

SUNDANCE DR

RANCHO SAN MARTIN DR

17800

AMARILLO RD

ROYAL OAKS LN

17900

TRAYLOR RD

17000

GREENBELT RD

17200

BLUEGRASS RD

17900

18000

HIGHLAND VALLEY RD

17300

17200

17700

VOORHES LN

1

ARCHIE MOORE RING

RANCHO

SANTA

MARIA

GREENBELT RD

ADRIENNE

2

R

RENDON VALLEY RD

SALT MINE RD

17100

PASEO DE LAS BRISAS

SAM LN

CAMINO JESSIE JAMES DEL SABIO

CAMINO DEL ROCA

17700

AVENIDA ROCA GRANDE

LN

WHIRLWIND LN

17100

HANDLEBAR RD

16900

HARBOR

SNUG

MOUNT WOODSON COUNTRY CLUB

16000

S

WOODSON

16700

N FELDSPAR CT

WOODSON CT

N WOODSON

26

SOMBRA DEL MONTE RD

16400

SADDLEBACK MOUNTAIN RD

17400

RANCHO DE CAROLE RD

RANCHO DE KEVIN RD

RANCHO DE LA ANGEL

RIDGEVIEW RD

17700

CAMINO DEL INDIO

HENRY LN

GARJAN LN

16900

GRENACHE ROSE WY

18300

CHABLIS RD

18400

25

RIPPLE WY

OLD CAROUSEL RANCH RD

AIR MAIL LN

16700

3

DR

16400

MOUNTAIN SHADOW LN

MOUNT WOODSON WY

SHADY OAKS

SHADY OAKS LN

OAKS

WHISPERING OAKS DR

WHISPER MG OAKS LN

JOHN

16900

SHADY BEND DR

REESE LN

SHADY BEND

PEACE VALLEY LN

ROCKIN OAKS WY

16600

SCRUB OAKS LN

VIA PENASCO

67

17500

WOODSON VIEW DR

16100

17100 LN

FS

QUAIL ROCK RD

16200

16300

KAY DEE

RANCHO DE ORO RD

SCHWAESDALL WINERY

SEE 1172 MAP

4

MOUNT WOODSON RD

MOUNT WOODSON RD

16000

HEDY DR

JACKIE ST

SADDLE SUMMIT RD

92065

15800

HARDSHIP DR

DOS PICOS MOUNTAIN RD

15800

THOMAS PAINE DR

THOMAS PAINE LN

18500

MARMAC DR

31

17300

TOMMIE LN RD

ROCKHOUSE

17200

35

36

15600

SNUZ

15600

DOS PICOS PARK RD

17900

THOMAS

15500

WFEPORT RD

R1W R1E

5

15700

CLOUDY MOON DR

WEST

17600

DOS PICOS COUNTY PARK

BRANCH

MUSSEY GRADE RD

PAMO WINTERCAMP RD

15500

6

ROSEMONT

MAHOGANY RANCH RD

T13S T14S

15000

6

E F G H J

2

92064

1

6

MUS

7

0 .125 .25 .375 .5 miles   1 in. = 1900 ft.

SAN DIEGO CO.

MAP

—N—

SEE 1152 MAP

A B C D E

1

SANTA MARIA CREEK

WOOD ENERGY RD

N SAWDAY ST
S SAWDAY ST
DURGIN
ROBERTSON
2800
300
S HOPE ST
N HOPE ST
HOWELL ST
ETCHEVERRY
LA VERMONT
2500
WYNOLA ST
BREA ST
KALBAUGH ST
300
KELLY ST
2500
RAYMOND
2600
ROTANZI ST
2380
MAIN ST
2400
HUNTER AV
2200
400
500
KEE
SAN

2

VOORHES LN
EL SOL RD
WOODSON CT
17900
17000
ADRIENNE WY

67

RD
2800
SUSIE WY
RANCHO MARIA LN

SAN DIEGO AV
ETCHEVERRY ST
1100
HUNTER ST
1100
BOUNDARY
2300
2400
2200
MO

3

HIGHLAND VALLEY RD
18500
HIGHLAND VALLEY CT
JULIAN
19000
CHAPEL LN
3000
DYE LN
FS
CECELIA
JO RD
CARNATION AV
LANSDOWN LN
OUTBACK PL
GOLD RUSH CT
EQUESTRIAN TR
VIA RANCHO DOS NINOS
MANDEZ DR

BOORTZ LN
16200

TOCA LN
RD 3000

DYE
2100
RD

4

67
17900
WOOD ROCK LN
BRANTNER LN
CAROL LN
DYE RD
19200
SPLIT ROCK RD
19300
OAK
19200
GRADE
BRAND IRON ST

HILLS DR
2200
AMBER LYNN LN
2400
MORNINGSIDE RD TR
OAK
MESA OAK CT
LAGEWAART

DURAZNITOS
SERENA
VIA MAJELLA
DURAZNITOS PL

RANCHO DE ORO RD
RD

ROSEMONT

32

LUELF CT
LUELF ST
SOUTHERN

1
31

MARMAC DR
MUSSEY
15600
ARBOL LN
MARA LN
LAS MANZANITAS LN
LAS ENCINAS DR
VALLEY DR
19800

OAK SHADE LN
SHADOW OAK CT

5

WIEPORT RD
19200
ROSEMONT LN
19500

DUCK POND LN
WILLOW OAK DR

AQUEDUCT

MAHOGANY RANCH
RD
OAK VALLEY RD
RD
20000
T13S
T14S

6

15000

SAN VICENTE CREEK

SANTA MARIA

7
6
6
WEST
MUSSEY GRADE RD
BRANCH
IRVINGS CREST
5
4
RANCHO
SANTA

A B C D E

SEE 1171 MAP

SEE 1192 MAP

0 .125 .25 .375 .5 miles 1 in. = 1900 ft.

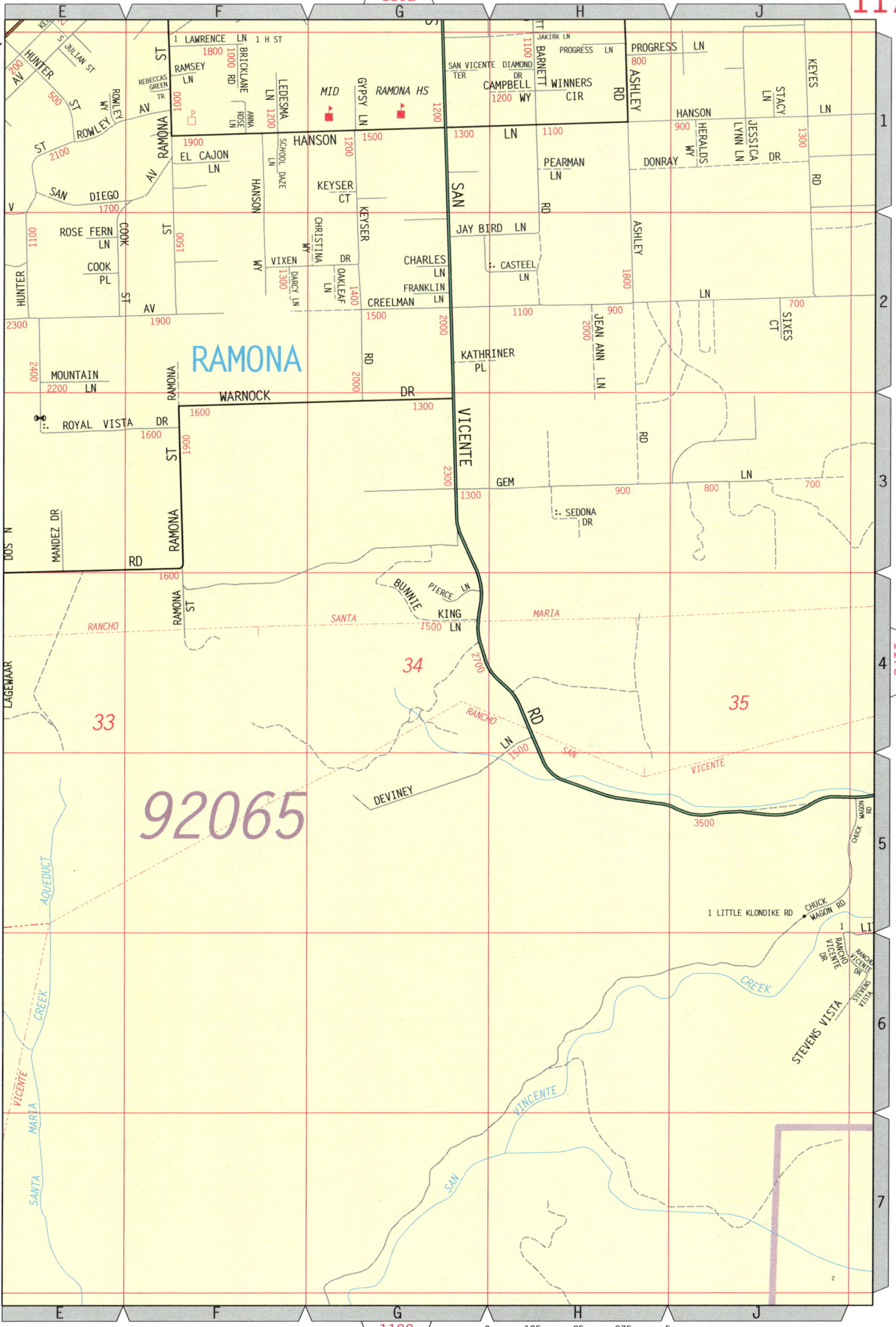

SAN DIEGO CO.

MAP

E | F | G | H | J

1

KEYS
HUNTER AV 200
S. JULIAN ST
ROWLEY WY
S. JULIAN ST 500
ROWLEY ST 2100
RAMONA ST
RAMSEY LN
REBECCAS GREEN TR 1000
1 LAWRENCE LN 1800
1 H ST
BRICKLANE 1000 RD
LEDESMA LN
ANNA ROSE LN
HANSON LN 1200
1900
MID
GYPSY LN
RAMONA HS
SAN VICENTE TER
JAKIRK LN
DIAMOND DR
BARNETT
CAMPBELL WY 1200
PROGRESS LN
WINNERS CIR
ASHLEY RD
PROGRESS LN 800
KEYES
STACY LN
JESSICA DR
HANSON 900
HERALDS WY
LYNN LN
DONRAY
KEYES LN
LN 1300

EL CAJON LN
HANSON ST
SCHOOL DAZE LN
HANSON 1200
1500
SAN
LN 1300
LN 1100
PEARMAN LN

SAN DIEGO AV 1700
COOK ST 1500
KEYSER CT
CHRISTINA WY
KEYSER
VICENTE
JAY BIRD LN
CASTEEL LN
ASHLEY RD 1800

2

HUNTER 1100
ROSE FERN LN
COOK PL
COOK ST
AV 1900
VIXEN WY
DARCY LN 1300
OAKLEAF LN
2000
CHARLES LN
FRANKLIN LN
CREELMAN LN 1100
JEAN ANN LN 2000 900
SIXES CT 700
LN
2300
2400
MOUNTAIN LN 2200
RAMONA ST 1900
WARNOCK
DR 1300
RD 2000
KATHRINER PL

3

ROYAL VISTA DR 1600
1600
RD
DOS N
MANDEZ DR
RAMONA RD 1600
VICENTE 2300
GEM 1300
RD 900
LN 800
700
SEDONA DR

4

LAGEWAAR
RANCHO
RAMONA ST
SANTA
MARIA
PIERCE LN
BUNNIE
KING LN 1500
2700
RANCHO
RD
SAN
VICENTE
SEE 1173 MAP

33

34

35

5

92065
DEVINEY
LN 1500
3500
CHUCK WAGON RD
LI
1 LITTLE KLONDIKE RD
CHUCK WAGON RD

6

AQUEDUCT
CREEK
1 RANCHO VICENTE DR
RANCHO VICENTE DR
STEVENS VISTA
CREEK
STEVENS VISTA

7

VICENTE
SANTA MARIA
SAN VINCENTE
SAN

RAMONA

0 .125 .25 .375 .5 miles 1 in. = 1900 ft.

E | F | G | H | J

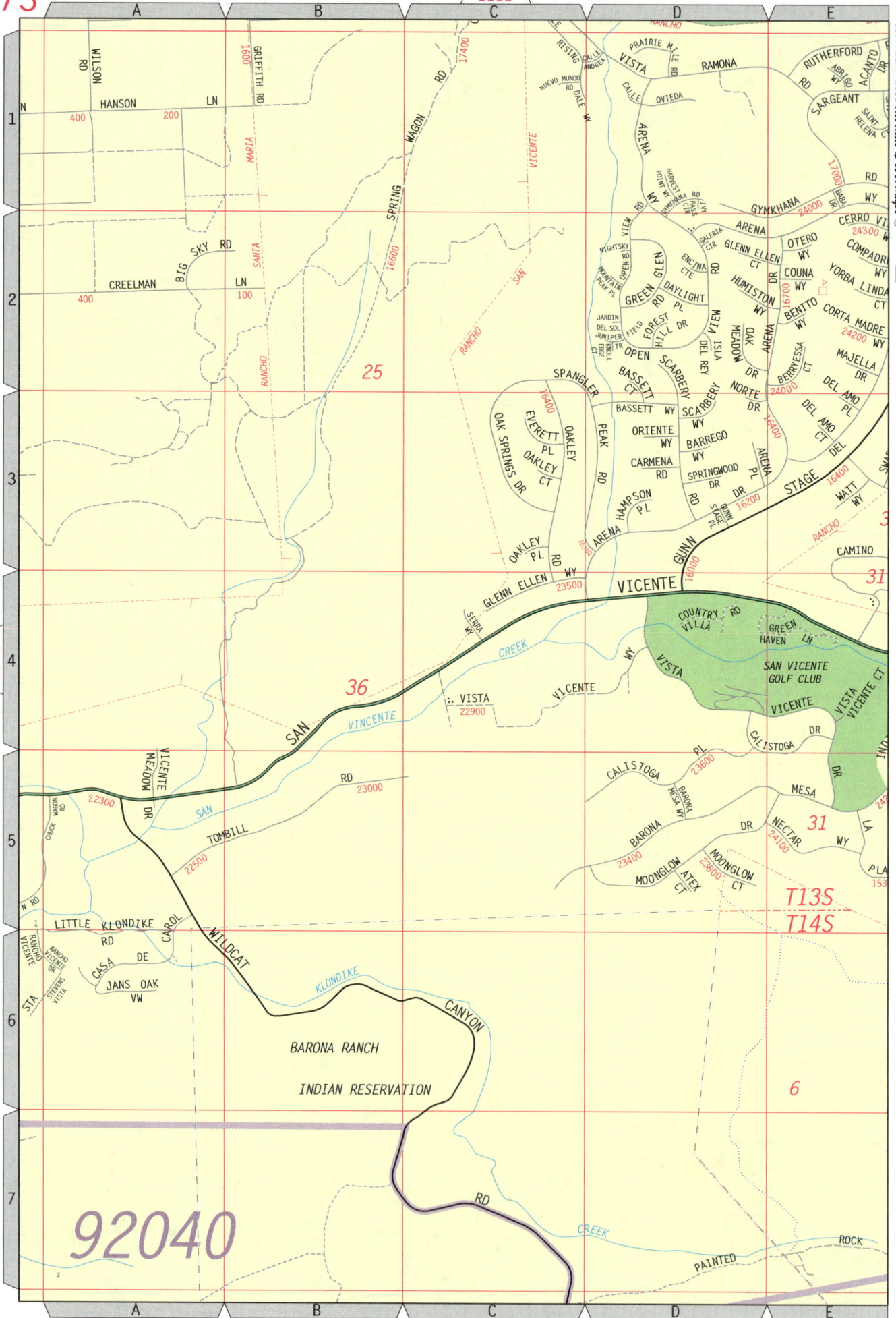

SAN DIEGO CO.

MAP

SEE 1153 MAP

A B C D E

COPYRIGHT 2001 Thomas Bros. Maps®

—N—

WILSON RD

HANSON LN

400 200

GRIFFITH RD

1600

MARIA

SANTA

RANCHO

SPRING WAGON RD

17400

RISING

CALLE ANDREA

NUEVO MUNDO RD

DALE WY

VICENTE

CALLE OVIEDA

VISTA

PRAIRIE MYLE RD

RAMONA

RUTHERFORD RD

ABRIGO RD

ACANTO

SARGEANT WY

SAINT HELENA

ARENA WY

17000

BABA

1

BIG SKY RD

CREELMAN

400

LN

100

16600

SAN

RANCHO

25

HARVEST RD

POINT WY

GYMKHANA CTR

GYMKHANA

24000

CERRO VI

24300

BABA

RD

WY

2

NIGHTSKY

OPEN WY

MOUNTAIN PEAK PL

GREEN GLEN

FIELD

DAYLIGHT PL

JARDIN DEL SOL

JUNIPER CT

KNOLL EDGE

OPEN

FOREST HILL DR

ENCINA CTE

GALERIA CIR

GLENN ELLEN CT

VIEW RD

HUMISTON WY

OTERO WY

COUNA WY

16700

BENITO WY

COMPADRE

YORBA LINDA CT

CORTA MADRE WY

24200

3

SCARBERY

MIA ISLA

DEL REY

OAK MEADOW DR

ARENA

NORTE DR

BERRYESSA CT

MAJELLA DR

DEL AMO PL

DEL

SPANGLER

16400

BASSETT CT

BASSETT WY

SCARBERY WY

ORIENTE WY

BARREGO WY

CARMENA RD

SPRINGWOOD DR

DR

24000

GUNN STAGE PL

ARENA PL

16200

STAGE

16400

DEL AMO CT

WATT WY

RANCHO

EVERETT PL

OAKLEY PL

OAK SPRINGS DR

OAKLEY CT

PEAK

ARENA RD

HAMPSON PL

1800

CAMINO

31

OAKLEY PL

GLENN ELLEN WY

23500

VICENTE

GUNN

16000

COUNTRY VILLA RD

GREEN HAVEN LN

4

SERNA WY

CREEK

VISTA

22900

VICENTE WY

VISTA

SAN VICENTE GOLF CLUB

VICENTE

VISTA VICENTE CT

IND

SEE 1172 MAP

36

SAN VINCENTE

RD

23000

CALISTOGA

PL

23600

CALISTOGA

BARONA MESA WY

MESA

5

VICENTE MEADOW DR

22300

CHUCK WAGON RD

SAN

TOMBILL

22500

BARONA

23400

MOONGLOW ATEX CT

23800

MOONGLOW CT

DR

NECTAR WY

24100

31

24

LA

PLA

153

T13S

T14S

N RD

1

LITTLE KLONDIKE RD

CAROL DE

WILDCAT

KLONDIKE

CANYON

6

RANCHO VICENTE

STEDDIG VISTA

RANCHO VICENTE DR

CASA DE

JANS OAK VW

STA

BARONA RANCH

INDIAN RESERVATION

6

7

92040

RD

CREEK

ROCK

PAINTED

A B C D E

0 .125 .25 .375 .5

miles 1 in. = 1900 ft.

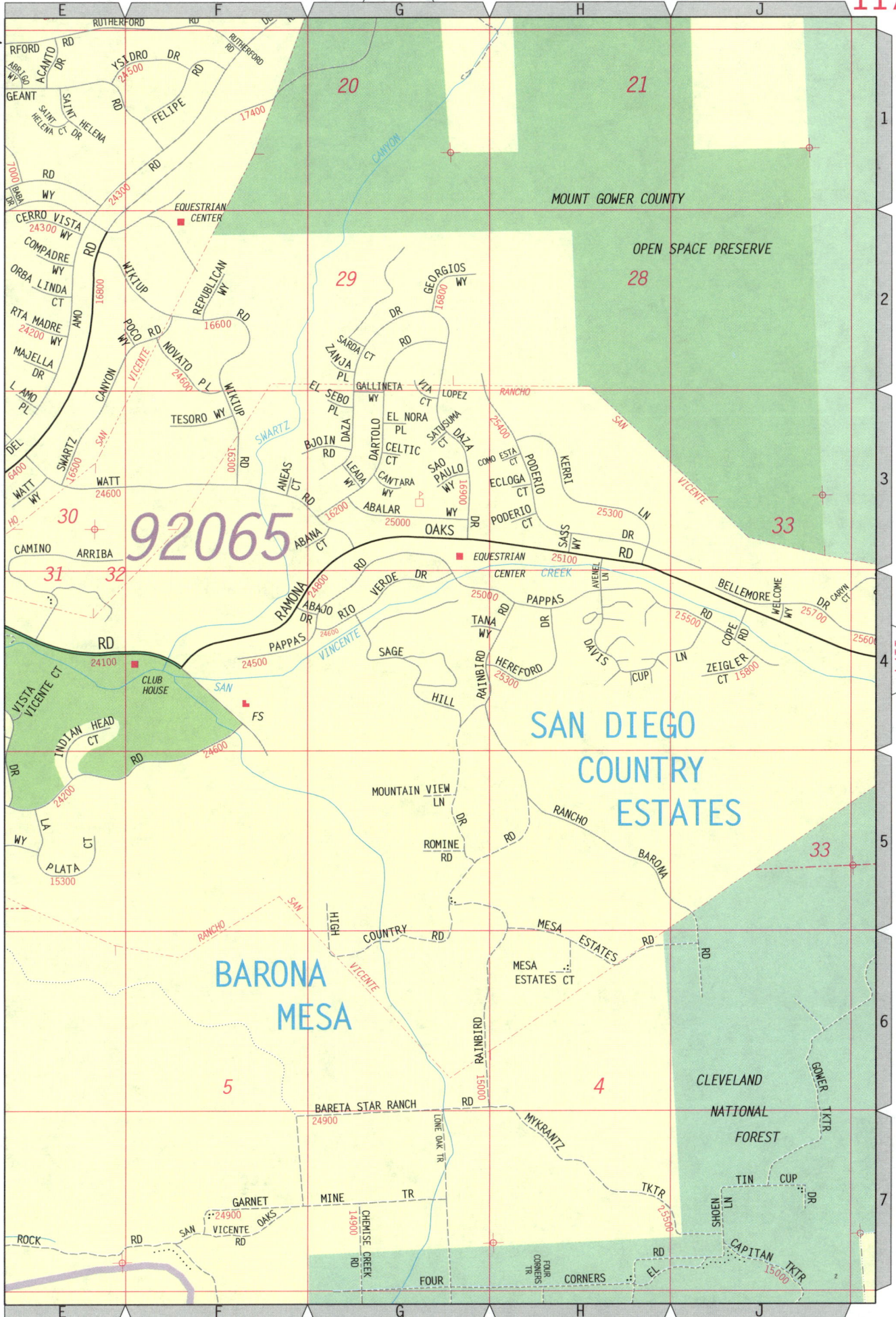

1173

SAN DIEGO CO.

MAP

E F G H J

1
2
3
4
5
6
7

RUTHERFORD RD
RFORD RD
ACANTO DR
YSIDRO DR
GEANT
ABR LGO
SAINT HELENA CT
SAINT HELENA DR
FELIPE RD
24500
RUTHERFORD RD
17400

20
21

MOUNT GOWER COUNTY
OPEN SPACE PRESERVE

28

CANYON

RD WY
7000 BABA
CERRO VISTA WY 24300
COMPADRE WY
ORBA LINDA CT
RTA MADRE WY 24200
MAJELLA DR
L AMO PL
DEL
6400
WATT WY
HO
30
CAMINO ARRIBA
31 32

24300
16800
WIKIUP
POCO RD
VICENTE
SAN CANYON
SWARTZ 16500
WATT 24600

EQUESTRIAN CENTER

REPUBLICAN WY
16600
NOVATO PL 24600
WIKIUP RD
16300
SWARTZ
TESORO WY

29

SARDA CT
ZANJA PL
GALLINETA WY
EL SEBO PL
DAZA
EL NORA PL
DARTOLO CT
CELTIC CT
LEADA WY
CANTARA WY
ABALAR WY 25000
ABANA CT
BJOIN RD
ANEAS CT
16200

GEORGIOS WY
16800
DR
RD
VIA LOPEZ
SATUSUMA CT
SAO PAULO WY 16900
DR

RANCHO
SAN
25400
COMO ESTA CT
ECLOGA CT
PODERIO CT
PODERIO CT
KERRI LN
25300
DR
RD

VICENTE

33

92065

RAMONA
ABAJO DR
24800
PAPPAS 24500
24600

OAKS 25000

ABANA CT
RIO VERDE DR
VINCENTE 24600
SAGE
HILL
EQUESTRIAN CENTER 25100
CREEK
25000
RD
TANA WY
RAINBIRD
HEREFORD 25300
PAPPAS DR
DAVIS
AVENEL LN
SSAS WY
RD
CUP
LN
25500
COPE RD
ZEIGLER CT 15800

BELLEMORE
WELCOME WY 25700
CARYN CT
25600

33

RD 24100
CLUB HOUSE
SAN
FS

VISTA VICENTE CT
INDIAN HEAD CT
DR
24200
RD
24600

SAN DIEGO
COUNTRY
ESTATES

MOUNTAIN VIEW LN
DR
ROMINE RD

RANCHO
BARONA

33

WY
LA PLATA CT 15300

BARONA
MESA

5

RANCHO
SAN
VICENTE
HIGH
COUNTRY RD
BARETA STAR RANCH 24900
LONE OAK TR
RAINBIRD
15000

MESA ESTATES
MESA ESTATES CT
RD
RD

4

CLEVELAND
NATIONAL
FOREST

GOWER TKTR

GARNET 24900
SAN VICENTE RD
OAKS RD
MINE TR
CHEMISE CREEK RD 14900

MYKRANTZ
TKTR 25500

TIN CUP DR
SHOEN LN
CAPITAN TKTR 15000

ROCK
RD
FOUR
FOUR CORNERS TR
EL CORNERS
RD

0 .125 .25 .375 .5 miles   1 in. = 1900 ft.

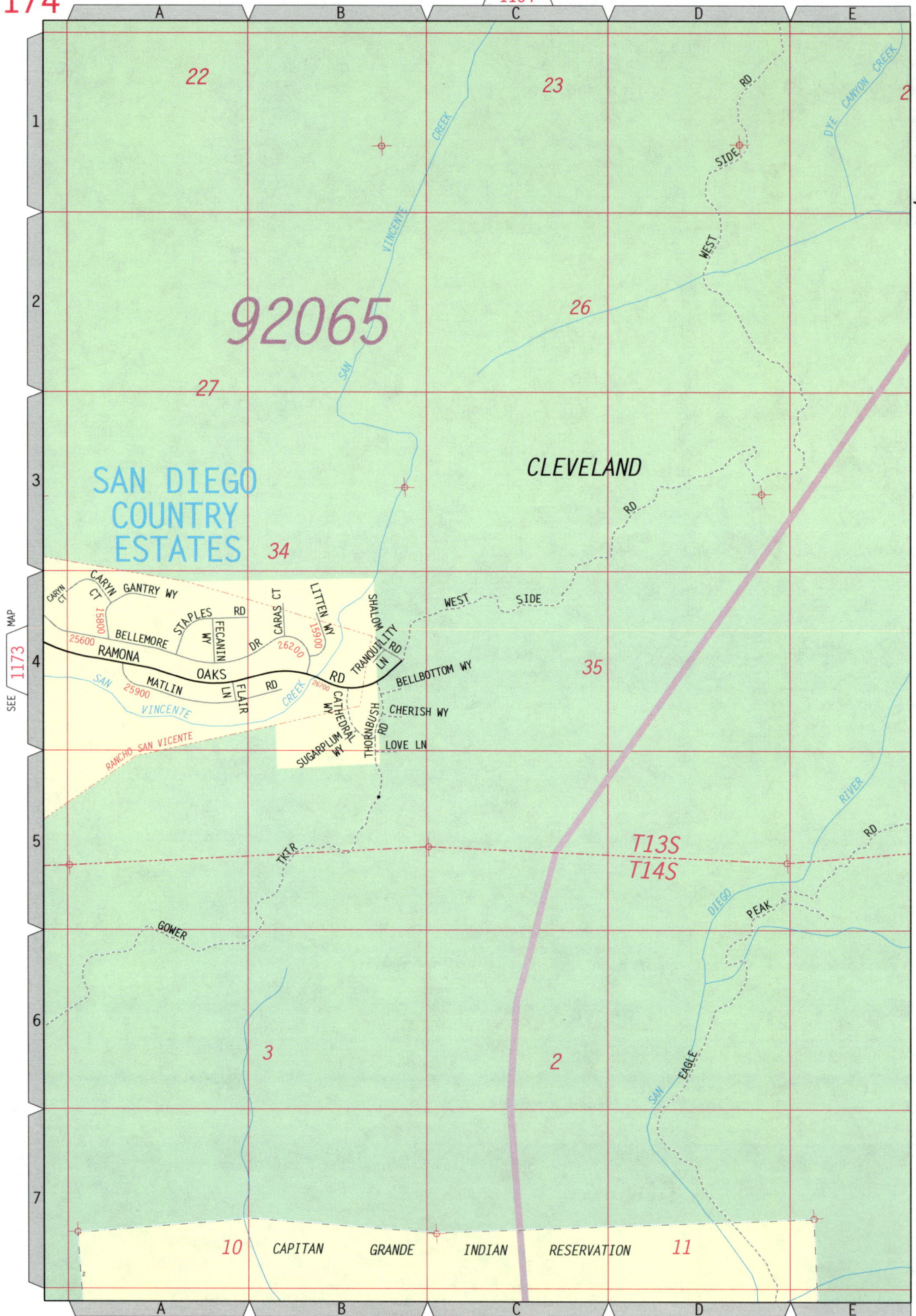

SAN DIEGO CO.

MAP

—N—

SEE 1154 MAP

A B C D E

1

22   23   2

VINCENTE CREEK

DYE CANYON CREEK

RD
SIDE

92065

WEST

26

27

3 CLEVELAND

SAN

RD

SEE 1173 MAP

SAN DIEGO
COUNTRY
ESTATES

34

CARYN CT
CARYN CT   GANTRY WY
15800
STAPLES RD
BELLEMORE   FECANIN WY
25600   CARAS CT
LITTEN WY   15900
2620.0
RAMONA   DR
OAKS   26700
MATLIN LN FLAIR RD
25900   CREEK
SAN VINCENTE
RANCHO SAN VICENTE

SHALOM RD
TRANQUILITY LN
CATHEDRAL WY
THORNBUSH RD
SUGARPLUM WY

WEST   SIDE

BELLBOTTOM WY

CHERISH WY

LOVE LN

35

RIVER

RD

5   TKTR   T13S
T14S

DIEGO   PEAK

GOWER

6

3   2   SAN EAGLE

7

10   CAPITAN   GRANDE   INDIAN   RESERVATION   11

A B C D E

0   .125   .25   .375   .5
miles   1 in. = 1900 ft.

SEE 1175 MAP

—N→

SAN DIEGO CO.

MAP

E   F   G   H   J

24   19   20

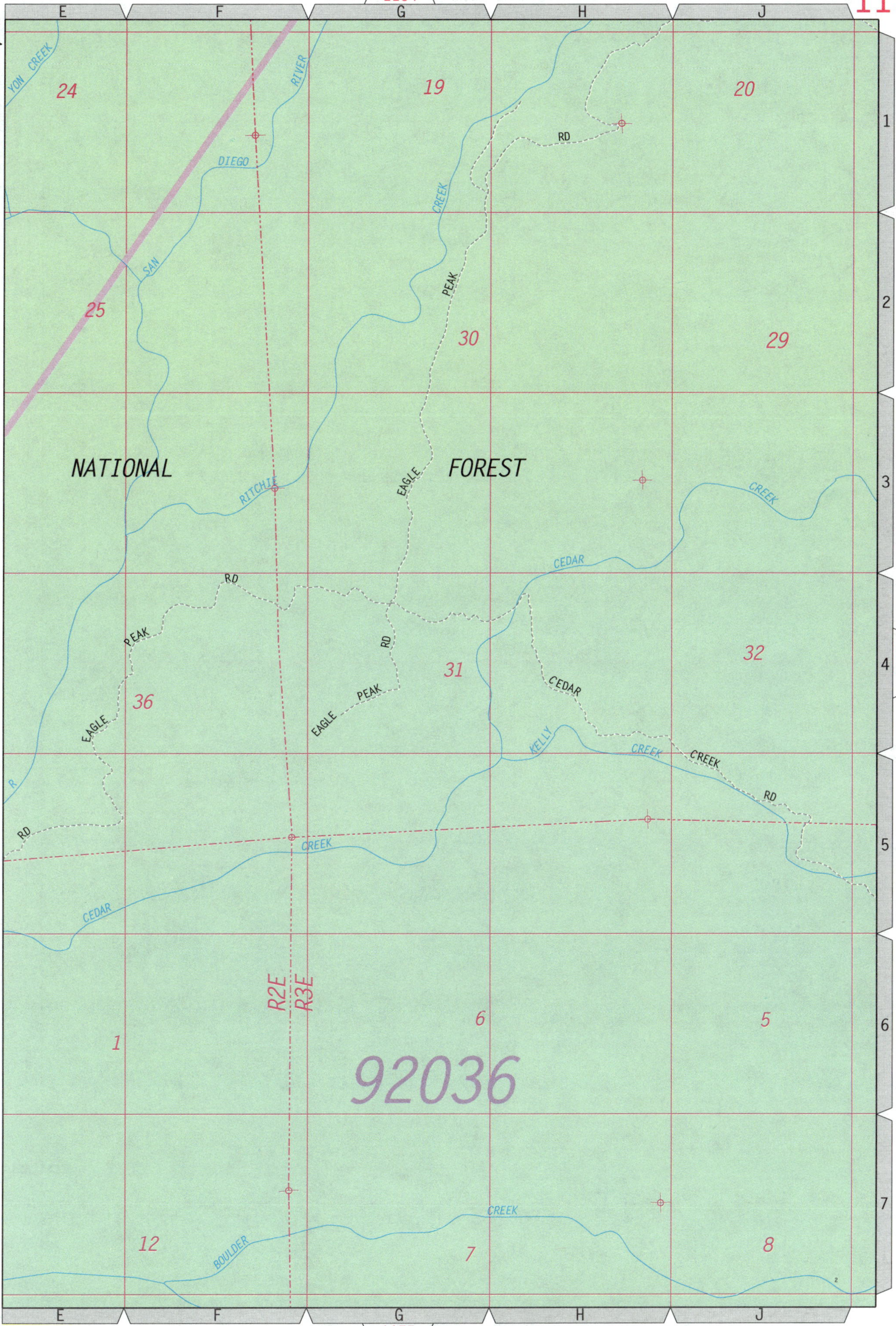

YON CREEK

DIEGO   RIVER

1

25   30   29

SAN

2

NATIONAL   FOREST

RITCHIE

EAGLE

CREEK

CEDAR   CREEK

3

RD

PEAK   RD   CEDAR

36   31   32

EAGLE   PEAK

EAGLE   PEAK

4

R.

RD   KELLY   CREEK   CREEK

CEDAR   CREEK   RD

5

CEDAR

R2E   R3E

1   6   5

6

92036

7

12   BOULDER   CREEK   7   8

E   F   G   H   J

0   .125   .25   .375   .5
miles   1 in. = 1900 ft.

SAN DIEGO CO.

MAP

COPYRIGHT 2001

Thomas Bros. Maps ®

←N—

SEE 1154 MAP

A B C D E F G H J

22 23 24 19 20

92065

26 25 30 29

27

SAN DIEGO
COUNTRY
ESTATES

34

SEE 1192 MAP

GANTRY WY
BELLEMORE
RAMONA
MATLIN
OAKS
STAPLES RD
FERMIN
CASS CT
WEST SIDE
TRANQUILITY
BELLBOTTOM WY
CHERISH WY
LOVE LN
SIGNPLUM
THOMPSON
SAN VICENTE

35 36

SEE MAP
1174

31 CEDAR 32

EAGLE PEAK

T13S
T14S

EAGLE PEAK

R2E
R3E

3 2 1 6 5

92036

10 CAPITAN GRANDE INDIAN RESERVATION 11 12 7 8

CLEVELAND NATIONAL FOREST

1

EL CAPITAN
SAN DIEGO RIVER
PEAK RIVER
EAGLE

2

92040

TKTR

15 14 13 18

TULE

TULE

1194

TULE SPRINGS

SPRINGS

91916

EL CAPITAN
RESERVOIR

22 23 24 CONEJOS VALLEY 19

91901

SAND CREEK

CAPITAN GRANDE INDIAN RESERVATION

EL CAPITAN
TKTR RD

2 27 26 25 29 30

R2E
R3E

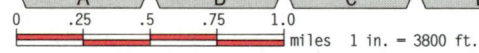

0 .25 .5 .75 1.0
miles 1 in. = 3800 ft.

SEE 429 MAP

SAN DIEGO CO.

MAP

COPYRIGHT 2001

Thomas Bros. Maps®

N

| | A | B | C | D | E | F | G | H | J | |

EAGLE
PEAK
RD
21
22
23
24
19

INAJA INDIAN
RESERVATION

COSMIT INDIAN
RESERVATION

HIGH MEADOW RANCH
HIGH MEADOW RANCH SPUR
FS

28
27
26
25

CEDAR
CREEK
SANDY CREEK

SANDY
CREEK

CEDAR
CREEK

BOULDER
CREEK

CUYAMACA
RANCHO
STATE
PARK

PENSTEMON LN
PENSTEMON
PENSTEMON CT

1175

33
34
35
36

R3E R4E

T13S
T14S

KELLY
CREEK
CREEK

CEDAR
CREEK
RD

CREEK RD

BOULDER

4
3
2
1

BOULDER

BOULDER
CREEK

9
10
11
12

TULE
SPRINGS RD

BOULDER
CREEK
RD

CREEK

1195

17
16
15
14
13

BOULDER
CONEJOS

CONEJOS
CREEK
CREEK

20
21
22
23
24

LOS CONEJOS
CONEJOS TKTR
DUBOIS

CAPITAN
GRANDE
INDIAN
RESERVATION

CAPITAN
GRANDE
INDIAN
RESERVATION

RD

28
27
26
25

TKTR

| | A | B | C | D | E | F | G | H | J | |

SEE 1176 MAP

SEE 1176 MAP

SEE 429 MAP

0 .25 .5 .75 1.0
miles 1 in. = 3800 ft.

SAN DIEGO CO.

MAP

SEE 1156 MAP

—N—

BIRDSELL LN
BIRDSELL RD

MOUNTAIN CIRCLE DR

CLEVELAND NATIONAL FOREST

30

ENGINEERS

HIGH HILL RD

MASON

VALLEY

TKTR

S1

MOUNTAIN CIRCLE DR

PEAK RD

HICKORY DR

UPPER NORTH PEAK WY

LOWER NORTH PEAK WY

CUYAMACA FOREST

NORTH GATE

AZALEA

BOULDER CREEK RD

SEE 1175 MAP

31

CUYAMACA

1176

CUYAMACA RD

BROKEN OAK LN

APACHE TR
PIMA
INCOPA DR
ARRAPAHO
PUEBLO
NAVAJO
TUMA
NATCHEZ TR
PAPAGO TR
FS
PINE
TR

79

T13S
T14S

CREEK

MOHAWK RD

CUYAMACA RESERVOIR

6

CUYAMACA

CUYAMACA RD

MIDDLE PEAK LOOP

FIRE RD

MILK RANCH RD

LITTLE

STONEWALL CREEK

7

7

CLEVELAND

NATIONAL

FOREST

18

PASO PICACHO CAMPGROUND

PASO PICACHO

AZALEA SPRING FIRE TR

LOOKOUT RD

FERN

FLAT FIRE RD

LOOKOUT

FS

CUYAMACA

STATE

RANCHO

PARK

2

HWY

SEE 1175 MAP

19

79

1196

CUYAMACA RD

WEST FORK

R3E R4E

30

2

91916

HARPER

STONEWALL CREEK

SWEETWATER RIVER

FIRE RD

HARPER

STREAM

HWY

PARK HEADQUARTERS

SWEETWATER

0   .25   .5   .75   1.0

miles 1 in. = 3800 ft.

SEE 1216 MAP

Thomas Bros. Maps®
COPYRIGHT 2001
N↑

| | A | B | C | D | E | F | G | H | J | |

ANZA–BORREGO DESERT STATE PARK

ANZA-BORREGO DESERT STATE PARK

1177

92036

1197

CLEVELAND NATIONAL FOREST

91948

S1

SUNRISE HWY

SEE 430 MAP

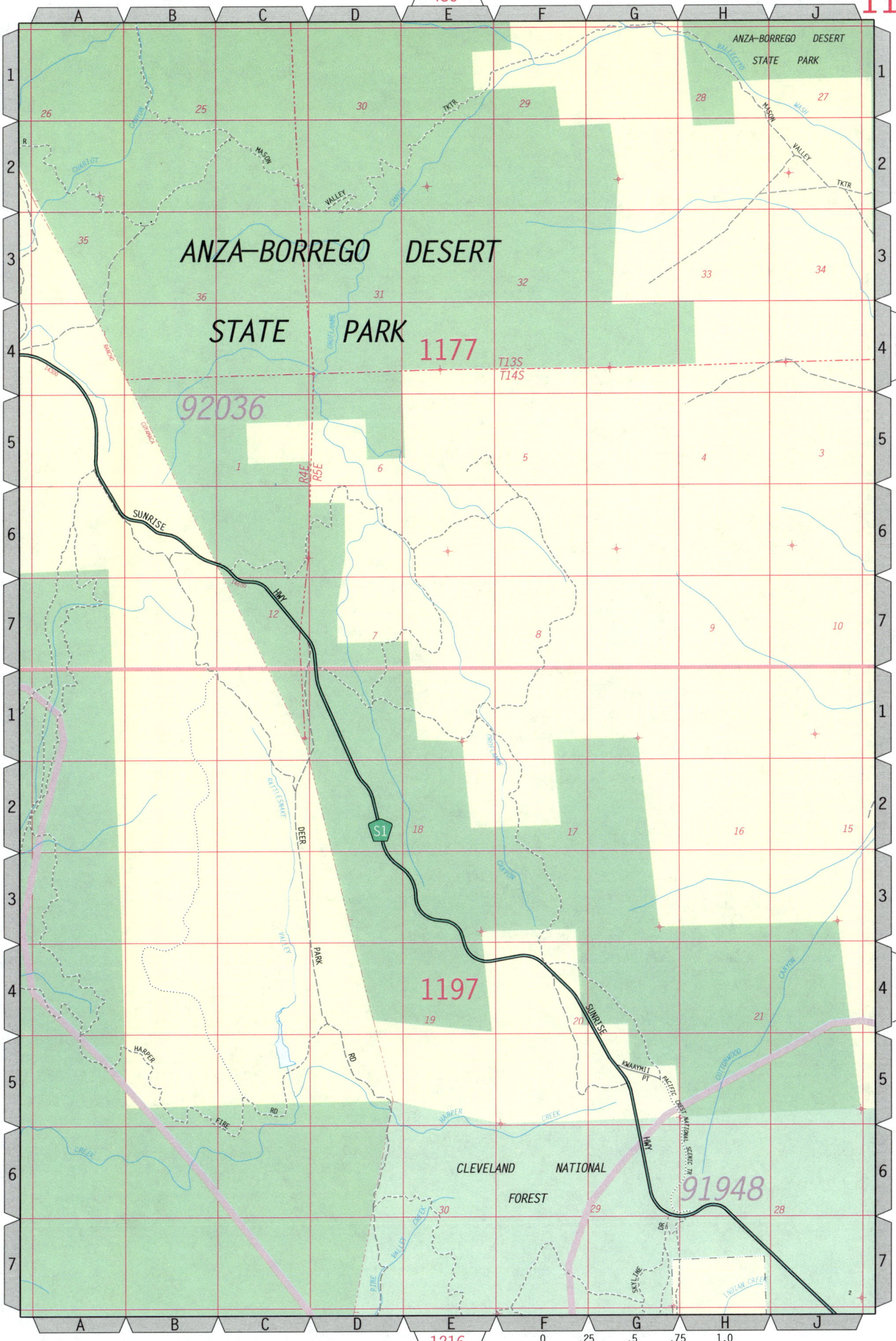

MAP

0 .25 .5 .75 1.0 miles   1 in. = 3800 ft.

1187

SEE 1167 MAP

SAN DIEGO CO.

MAP

	A	B	C	D	E

PACIFIC

OCEAN

LINDA MA
DR
S 13TH AV
3
BEA
WA

NORTH
SEASCAPE
SURF
BEACH
PARK

DEL MAR SHORE
BEACH PARK

1 BEACH FRONT
2 PACIFIC SUR
3 OCEAN SURF

—N—

SEE 429 MAP

SEE 1207 MAP

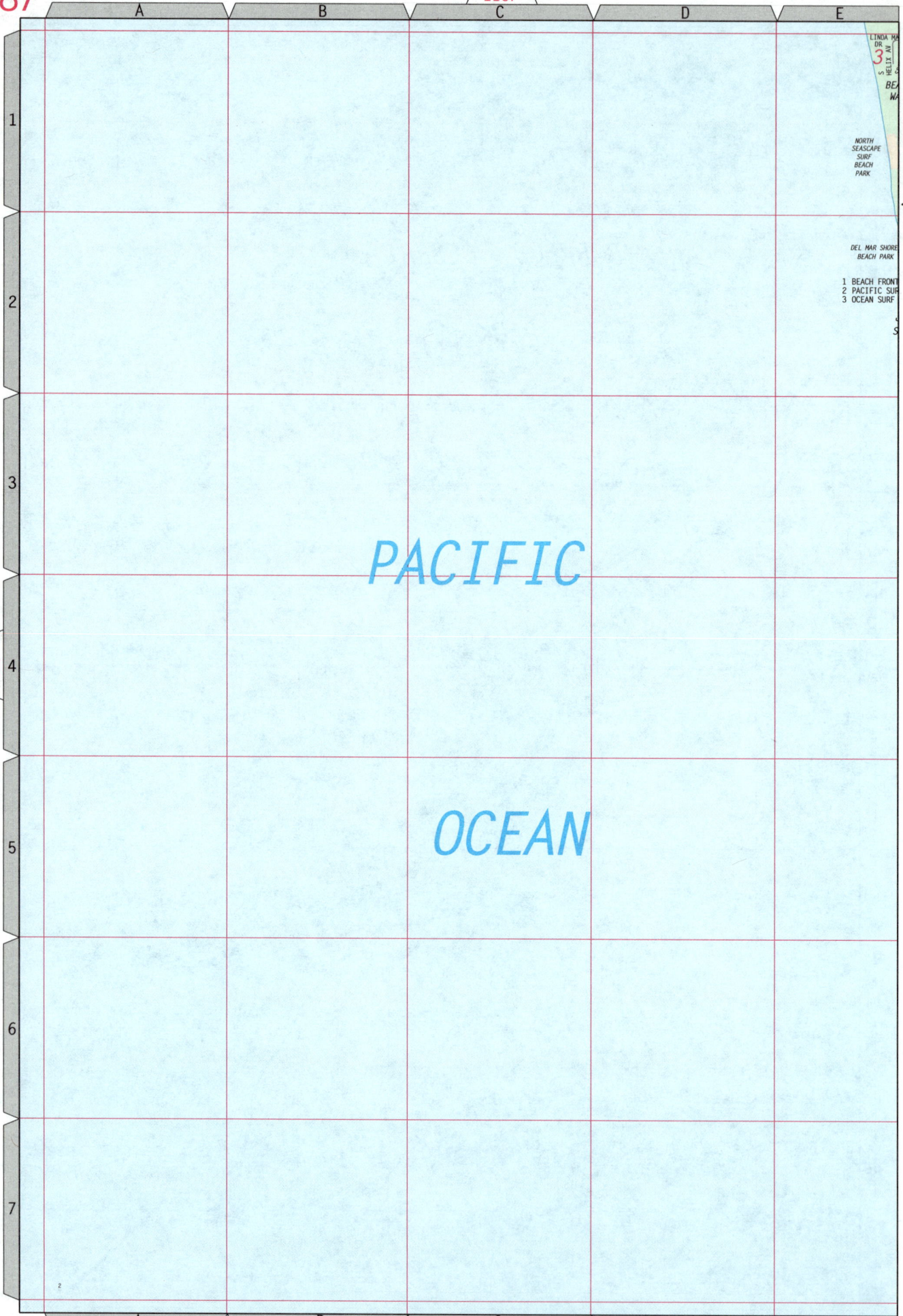

0 .125 .25 .375 .5 miles 1 in. = 1900 ft.

SAN DIEGO CO.

MAP

Thomas Bros. Maps®

COPYRIGHT 2001

—N—

SOLANA BEACH
EDEN GARDENS
92075

BEACH WALK

NORTH SEASCAPE SURF BEACH PARK

JAMES SCRIPPS BLUFF PRESERVE

DEL MAR FAIRGROUNDS
DEL MAR RACE TRACK

VIA DE LA VALLE

HILTON SAN DIEGO/ DEL MAR

SURF AND TURF RECREATION PARK

SAN DIEGUITO RIVER

SAN DIEGO 12
92130

DEL MAR CITY BEACH

92014

DE L MAR

POWERHOUSE PARK

SEAGROVE PARK

CREST CANYON OPEN SPACE PARK

OVERLOOK PARK (OPEN SPACE)

SOLANA HIGHLANDS PARK

DEL MAR HEIGHTS VILLAGE

14

13

TORREY PINES

DEL MAR HEIGHTS RD

SEE C G6
1 PLACE MONACO
2 PLACE SAINT TROPEZ

TORREY PINES STATE BEACH

23

TORREY PINES STATE RESERVE

24

SAN DIEGO LA JOLLA UNDERWATER PARK

SAN DIEGO FRWY

VIA DE LA VALLE

LOMAS SANTA FE COUNTRY CLUB

WOODSIDE WY

VIA DE LA VALLE

1

SEE A H1
1 COLINA LINDA
2 LADERA LINDA
3 LADERA LINDA WY

DEL MAR CENTER

SEE B H1
1 CMTO BADALONA
2 CMTO GIJON
3 CMTO TORREBLANCA
4 CMTO FORTALEZA
5 CMTO CARBONERAS
6 CMTO VISTA ESTRELLADO
7 CMTO CABO VIEJO
8 CMTO VIA CAMPESTRE

EL CAMINO REAL

1 BEACH FRONT DR
2 PACIFIC SURF DR
3 OCEAN SURF DR

SAN DIEGO CO.

MAP

SEE 1168 MAP

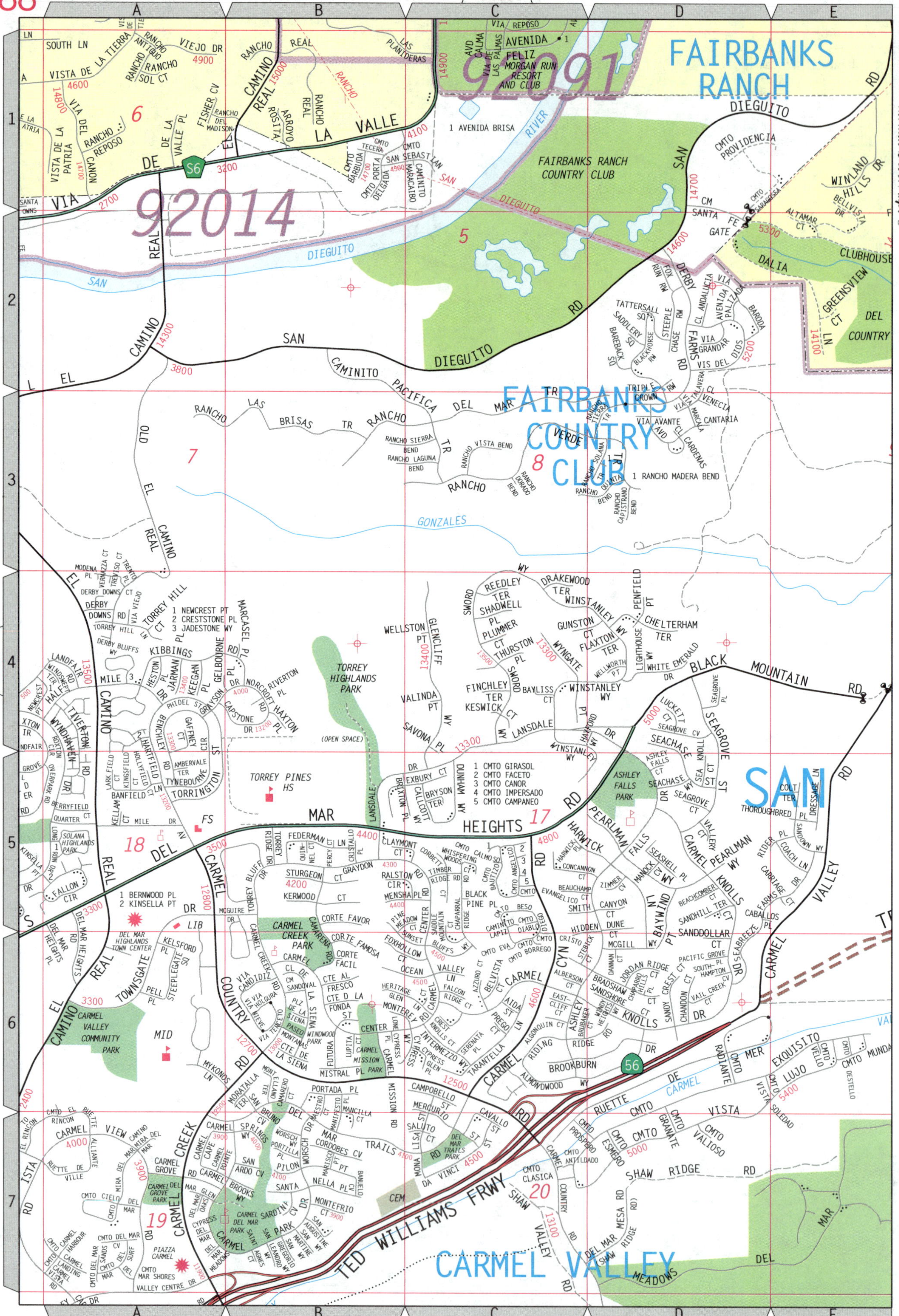

FAIRBANKS RANCH

92091

92014

FAIRBANKS RANCH COUNTRY CLUB

FAIRBANKS COUNTRY CLUB

SAN DIEGUITO

SAN

GONZALES

TORREY HIGHLANDS PARK

(OPEN SPACE)

TORREY PINES HS

ASHLEY FALLS PARK

SAN HEIGHTS

DEL MAR

EL CAMINO REAL

CARMEL VALLEY

TED WILLIAMS FRWY

CARMEL VALLEY

SEE 1187 MAP

SEE 1208 MAP

0 .125 .25 .375 .5 miles 1 in. = 1900 ft.

SOLANA HIGHLANDS PARK

CARMEL VALLEY COMMUNITY PARK

1 Bernwood Pl
2 Kinsella Pt

1 Newcrest Pt
2 Creststone Pl
3 Jadestone Wy

1 Cmto Girasol
2 Cmto Faceto
3 Cmto Canor
4 Cmto Impersado
5 Cmto Campaneo

SAN DIEGO CO.

MAP

92127

92067

92130

92129

DIEGO

RANCHO SANTA FE FARMS GOLF CLUB

SAINT ANDREWS RD

ROYAL BIRKDALE PL

CAMINO DE LA LUNA

CAMINO RUIZ

RANCHO SANTA FE FARMS

RANCHO DIEGUENO

CALLE PRIVADA

CL DIEGUENO RD

CALLE MONTELIBANO

CL TIERRA BLANCA

EL SENTIDO

LAS MANANAS

AVD INSURGENTES

LAS VENTANAS

LADYS SECRET

CALLE DIEGUENO

MARIA

LAS QUINTAS CL

CARLA

EL RODEO CT

LAGO

POCO

ROXBURY TER

WINLAND HILLS DR

BELLVISTA DR

FAIRWAY PL

STRAWBERRY RD

EMERALD LN

CLUBHOUSE DR

ZANJA

LA ZANJA DR

RANCHO SANTA FE

LAGO CTE

CAMINITO SANTO TOMAS

FARMS VIEW CT

MIRA ZANJA

MIRA ZANJA CTE

HONRY COLLINS TER

COLLINS RANCH CT

SNTTIO RANCH PL

CRYSTAL GROVE CT

DEL MAR COUNTRY CLUB

EENSVIEW

CLUBHOUSE

MONTE FUEGO

MIL ARBOLES

NIEMANN

TWIN LAKES CT

LAKES DR

RANCH RD

CLARKVIEW LN

RANCHO LAKES CT

CARMEL VALLEY RD

MONA LN

MONA

VISTA ORION LN

AMBER PL DR

KINDE CT

LN RD

MARKER WAY

KERRY

TORREY

MCGONIGLE TER

HEATHERLY DR

56

MCGONIGLE

CANYON

FARMS RD

BLACK MOUNTAIN WY

BLACK MOUNTAIN

MOUNTAIN

BLACK RD

CAMINITO MENDIOLA

CAMINITO MENDIOLA

FRWY

TED WILLIAMS (EST COMP 2004)

MCGONIGLE

DEER

CANYON

VALLEY

CMTO MUNDANO

CMTO DESTELLO

SHAW RIDGE RD

VINE RD

MEADOWS DEL MAR GOLF CLUB

MEADOWS

DEL MAR

LOS PENASQUITOS CANYON PRESERVE

PENASQUITOS RD

MANNIX CT

KELD

SANTY ARJUAINA WY

JUNCUS CT

ARJUAINA WY

ARUCANA WY

PARK VILLAGE RD

CELATA LN

MANNIX

CELOME

LEAST TERN

RANCHO

LOS PENASQUITOS CANYON PRESERVE

miles 1 in. = 1900 ft.

COPYRIGHT 2001 Thomas Bros. Maps

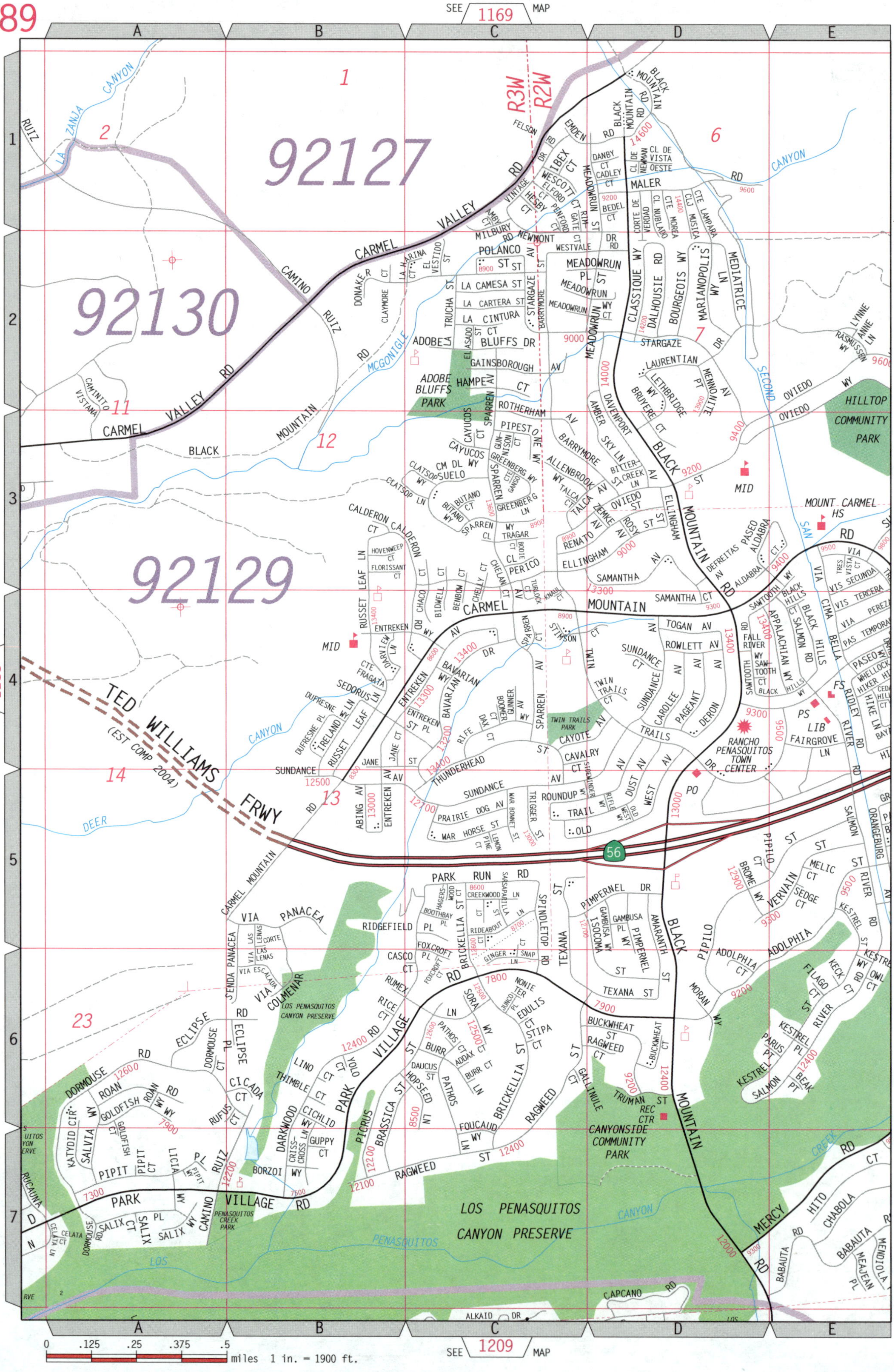

SAN DIEGO CO.

MAP

SEE 1169 MAP

A B C D E

92127

92130

92129

R3W R2W

TED WILLIAMS FRWY (EST COMP 2004)

SEE 1188 MAP

CARMEL VALLEY RD

CAMINO RUIZ RD

CARMEL VALLEY RD

BLACK MOUNTAIN RD

CARMEL MOUNTAIN RD

PARK RUN RD

CARMEL MOUNTAIN RD

BLACK MOUNTAIN RD

LOS PENASQUITOS CANYON PRESERVE

LOS PENASQUITOS CANYON PRESERVE

CANYONSIDE COMMUNITY PARK

HILLTOP COMMUNITY PARK

ADOBE BLUFFS PARK

TWIN TRAILS PARK

MOUNT CARMEL HS

RANCHO PENASQUITOS TOWN CENTER

56

PARK VILLAGE RD

CAMINO RUIZ

PARK VILLAGE RD

MERCY RD

SEE 1209 MAP

0 .125 .25 .375 .5 miles 1 in. = 1900 ft.

1189

SAN DIEGO CO.

MAP

© COPYRIGHT 2001 Thomas Bros. Maps®

—N→

BLACK MOUNTAIN PARK
5
(OPEN SPACE)

RANCHO PENASQUITOS

SAN DIEGO

CARMEL HIGHLAND DOUBLETREE GOLF & TENNIS RESORT

SELLERS US POSTAL CENTER

CARMEL MOUNTAIN PLAZA

MOUNTAIN RD

RESIDENCE INN

DOUBLETREE CARMEL HIGHLANDS RESORT

SEE A H2

1 VIA LOS NARCISOS
2 VIA PEQUINITO
3 VIA LAS POSADAS
4 VIA ALBERTO

4

HILLTOP COMMUNITY PARK

CARMEL MOUNTAIN RANCH COUNTRY CLUB

CARMEL MOUNTAIN RANCH COMMUNITY PARK

1 PORT RUSH RW
2 OLYMPIA FIELDS RW

RANCHO PENASQUITOS PLAZA

PARK & RIDE

WILLIAMS FRWY

56

TED

15

SEE 1190 MAP

15

SABRE SPRINGS
92128

SABRE SPRINGS PARK

VIEWS WEST PARK

RANCHO PENASQUITOS BLVD

PARK & RIDE

POWAY RD

S4

LOS PENASQUITOS PRESERVE CANYON

21

22

TREE HOLLOW LN

92131

20

SCRIPPS POWAY PKWY

28

27

29

SPRING CANYON PARK

0 .125 .25 .375 .5 miles 1 in. = 1900 ft.

SEE 1170 MAP

COPYRIGHT 2001 Thomas Bros. Maps ®

—N—

SAN DIEGO CO.

MAP

92128
CARMEL MOUNTAIN RANCH

SAN DIEGO

SELLERS US POSTAL CENTER

SEE C B1
1 CARROLLTON SQ
2 STANWIX SQ
3 HEWES SQ
4 GABLE RIDGE RD
5 WERRIS CREEK LN

ARBOLITOS SPORT FIELDS

TWIN PEAKS PLAZA

POWAY HILLS

PALISADES

STARRIDGE PARK

POWAY VALLEY CENTER

CARRIAGE CENTER

CIVIC CENTER

POWAY COMMUNITY PARK

POWAY

11

12

13

14

15

22

23

26

27

SAN DIEGO

92128
SABRE SPRINGS

SEE 1189 MAP

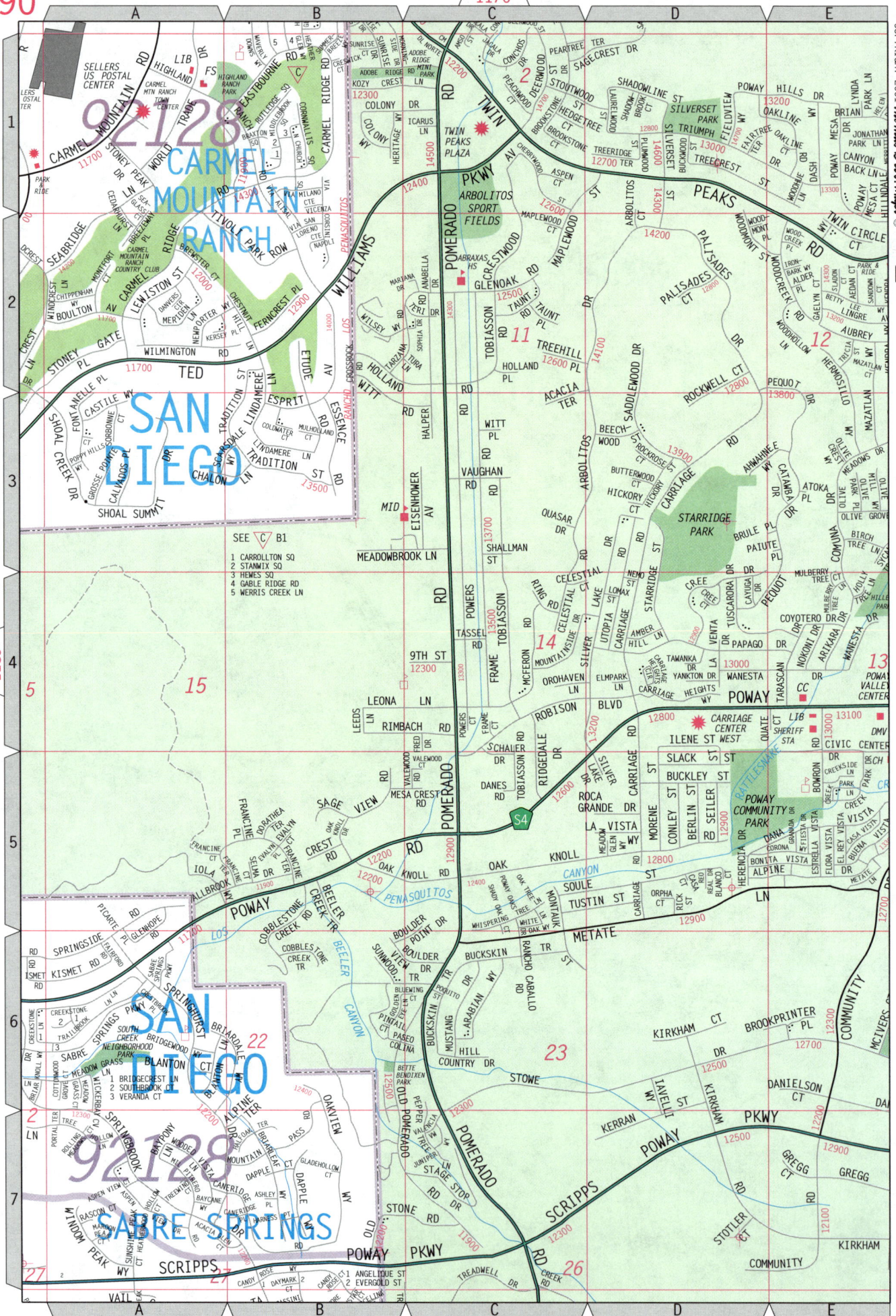

0 .125 .25 .375 .5 miles   1 in. = 1900 ft.

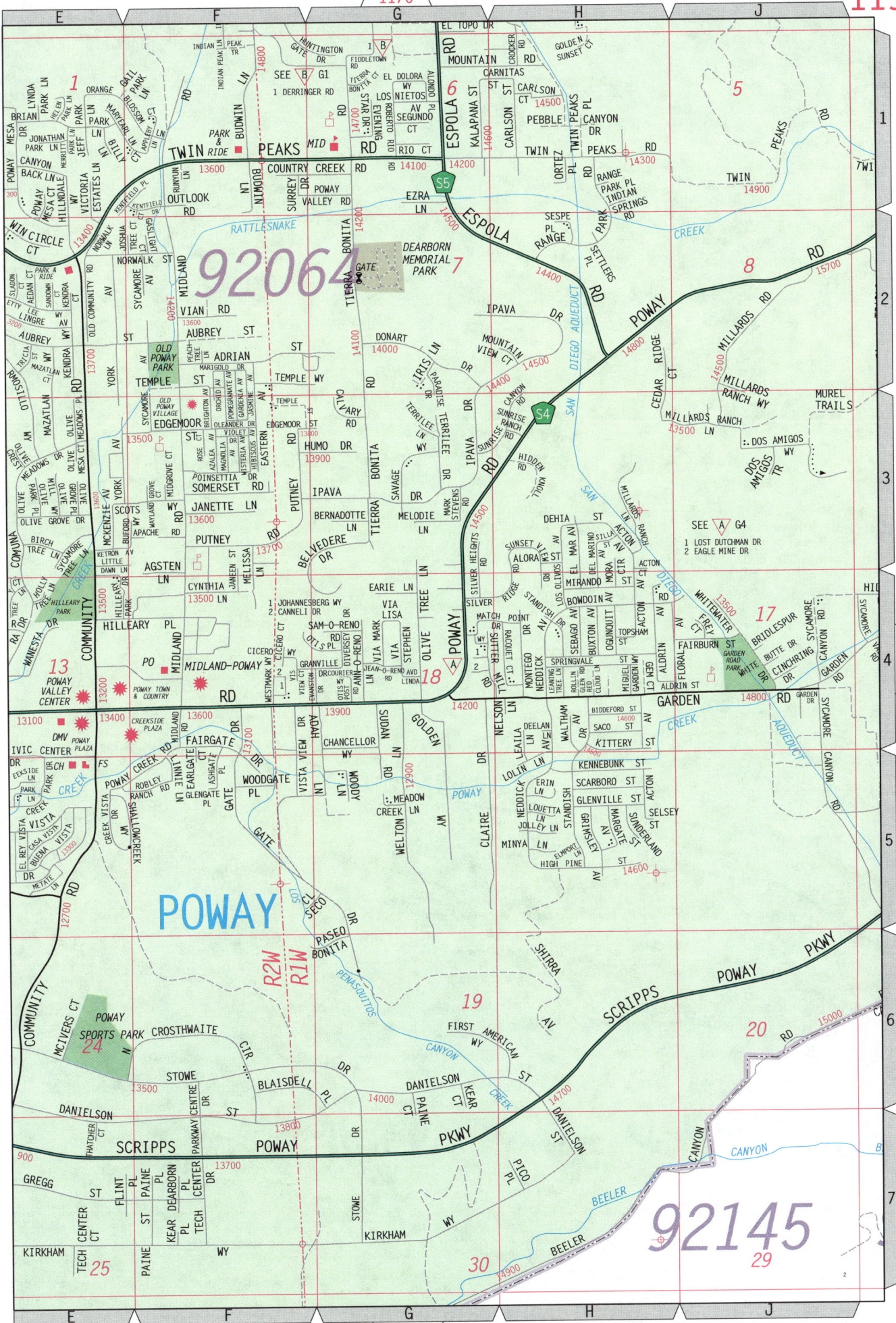

ThomasBros.Maps®
COPYRIGHT 2001

SAN DIEGO CO.

MAP

92064

POWAY

92145

SEE 1191 MAP

SEE 1210 MAP

0 .125 .25 .375 .5 miles 1 in. = 1900 ft.

DEARBORN MEMORIAL PARK

OLD POWAY PARK

POWAY VALLEY CENTER

POWAY SPORTS PARK

HILLEARY PARK

MILLARDS RANCH

SEE B G1 1 DERRINGER RD
SEE A G4 1 LOST DUTCHMAN DR 2 EAGLE MINE DR

TWIN PEAKS

ESPOLA RD

POWAY RD

SCRIPPS POWAY PKWY

DANIELSON

GARDEN RD

—N→

SAN DIEGO CO.

MAP

SEE 1171 MAP

A   B   C   D   E

1

RATTLESNAKE   CREEK

CLEARVIEW RD

EUCALYPTUS HEIGHTS

MINA DE ORO RD 14000

S4   RD

16700

14900

TWIN PEAKS RD

POWAY   15600

00

2

POWAY

DOS HERMANOS RD

BLUE CRYSTAL TRAILS   15700

TRAILS   14200

MUREL

BLUE CRYSTAL TR

CRYSTAL VIEW LN

9

92064

8

10

3

REL ILS

IRON MOUNTAIN   15800

67

CRESTLINE DR   17100

DR

QUIET HILLS DR   DR

SPRUCE LN   VALLEY   16000

13600   15400

QUIET VALLEY LN   15900

PLATINUM PL   16800

CREEK

HIDDEN   BIRCH LN

GARDEN RD

SYCAMORE VALLEY RD

POWAY

SEE 1190 MAP

DEN RD

RIO   MARIA   16800

4

17

16

15

POWAY   PKWY

5

SCRIPPS   15600

D

PENDRAGON RD

VIA LA IZQUIERDA   15400

PARAGON   MESA

RD   16200

ROB

RAPTOR   15400

RD

15400

15000

DE PASEO DE

OCHO MINOS

BEELER CANYON RD   15000

0

SYCAMORE

CANYON

RD   15000

CALLE   12600

CANYON

PARK

6

20

21

CANYON RD

92071

22

SAN DIEGO

DIEGO

GOODAN RANCH COUNTY PARK

SYCAMORE   CANYON   COUNTY

OPEN   SPACE   PRESERVE

7

BEELER CANYON

AQUEDUCT

92145

15000

SYCAMORE   15100

SYCAMORE

SYCAMORE

2

A   B   C   D   E

0   .125   .25   .375   .5
miles   1 in. = 1900 ft.

SEE 1211 MAP

SAN DIEGO CO.

MAP

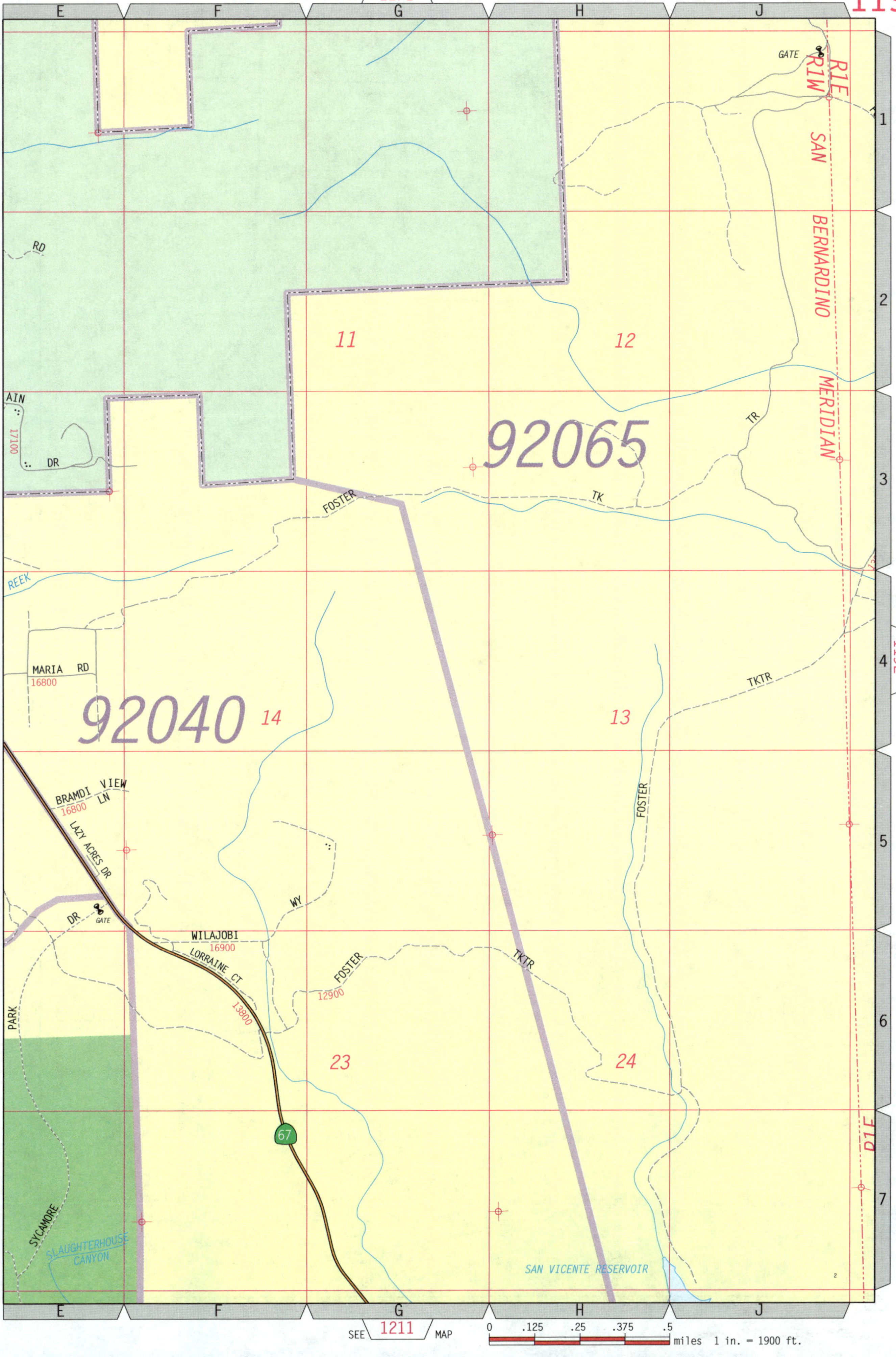

E   F   G   H   J

COPYRIGHT 2001

ThomasBros.Maps®

N

GATE

R1E
R1W

SAN

BERNARDINO

MERIDIAN

1

RD

AIN

17100

DR

11

12

92065

TR

TK

2

FOSTER

REEK

3

MARIA RD
16800

92040   14

13

TKTR

SEE 1192 MAP

4

BRAMDI VIEW LN
16800

LAZY ACRES DR

FOSTER

5

DR   GATE

WILAJOBI
16900

LORRAINE CT

13800

WY

PARK

FOSTER
12900

TKTR

6

23

24

67

R1E

SYCAMORE

SLAUGHTERHOUSE CANYON

SAN VICENTE RESERVOIR

2

7

E   F   G   H   J

0   .125   .25   .375   .5   miles   1 in. = 1900 ft.

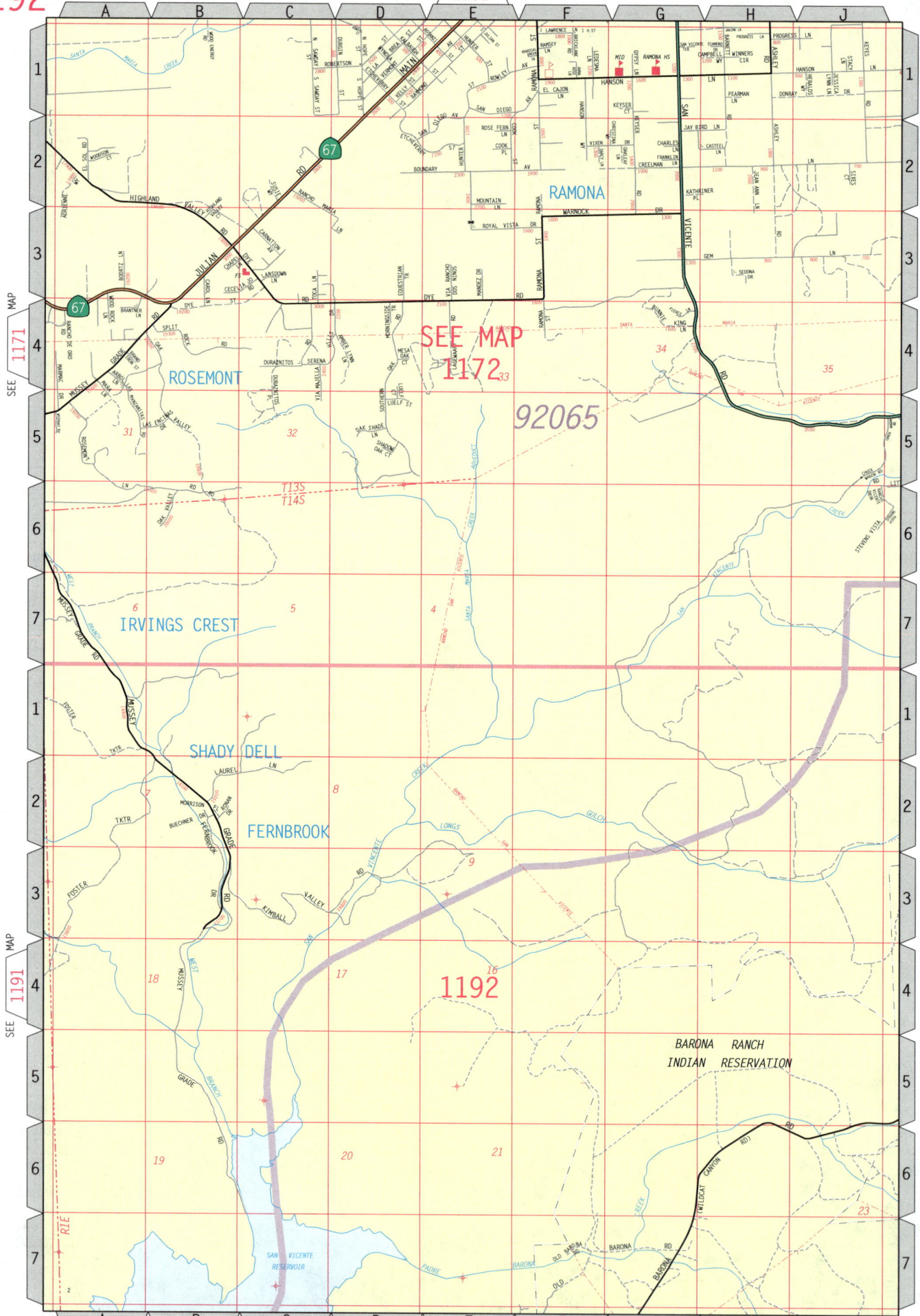

SAN DIEGO CO.

MAP

COPYRIGHT 2001

Thomas Bros. Maps ® — N —

SEE 1152 MAP

A B C D E F G H J

67

RAMONA

SEE MAP 1172

92065

ROSEMONT

IRVINGS CREST

SHADY DELL

FERNBROOK

1192

BARONA RANCH INDIAN RESERVATION

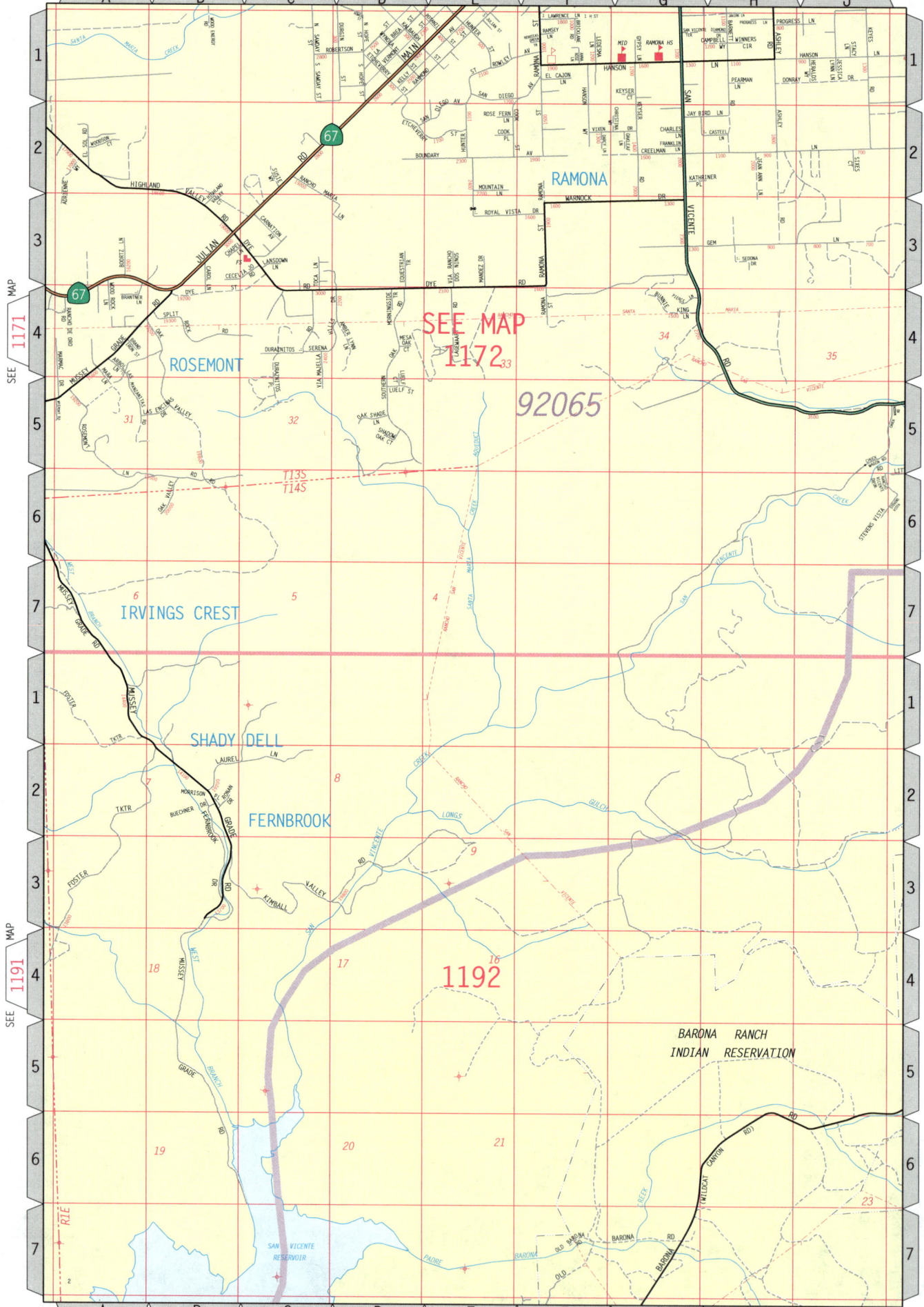

SAN VICENTE RESERVOIR

SEE 1171 MAP

SEE 1191 MAP

SEE 1212 MAP

0 .25 .5 .75 1.0 miles 1 in. = 3800 ft.

31 32 33 34 35

6 5 4

7

1

8

9 16 17

18 19 20 21 23

SAN DIEGO CO.

MAP

1192

SEE 1153 MAP

SEE 1174 MAP

SEE 1175 MAP

SEE 1213 MAP

SAN DIEGO COUNTRY ESTATES

BARONA MESA

BARONA RANCH INDIAN RESERVATION

MOUNT GOWER COUNTY OPEN SPACE PRESERVE

CLEVELAND NATIONAL FOREST

CAPITAN GRANDE INDIAN RESERVATION

EL CAPITAN COUNTY OPEN SPACE PRESERVE

EL CAPITAN RESERVOIR

92040

1193

SAN VICENTE GOLF CLUB

COPYRIGHT 2001 Thomas Bros. Maps®

0 .25 .5 .75 1.0 miles 1 in. = 3800 ft.

SAN DIEGO CO.

MAP

SEE 1187 MAP

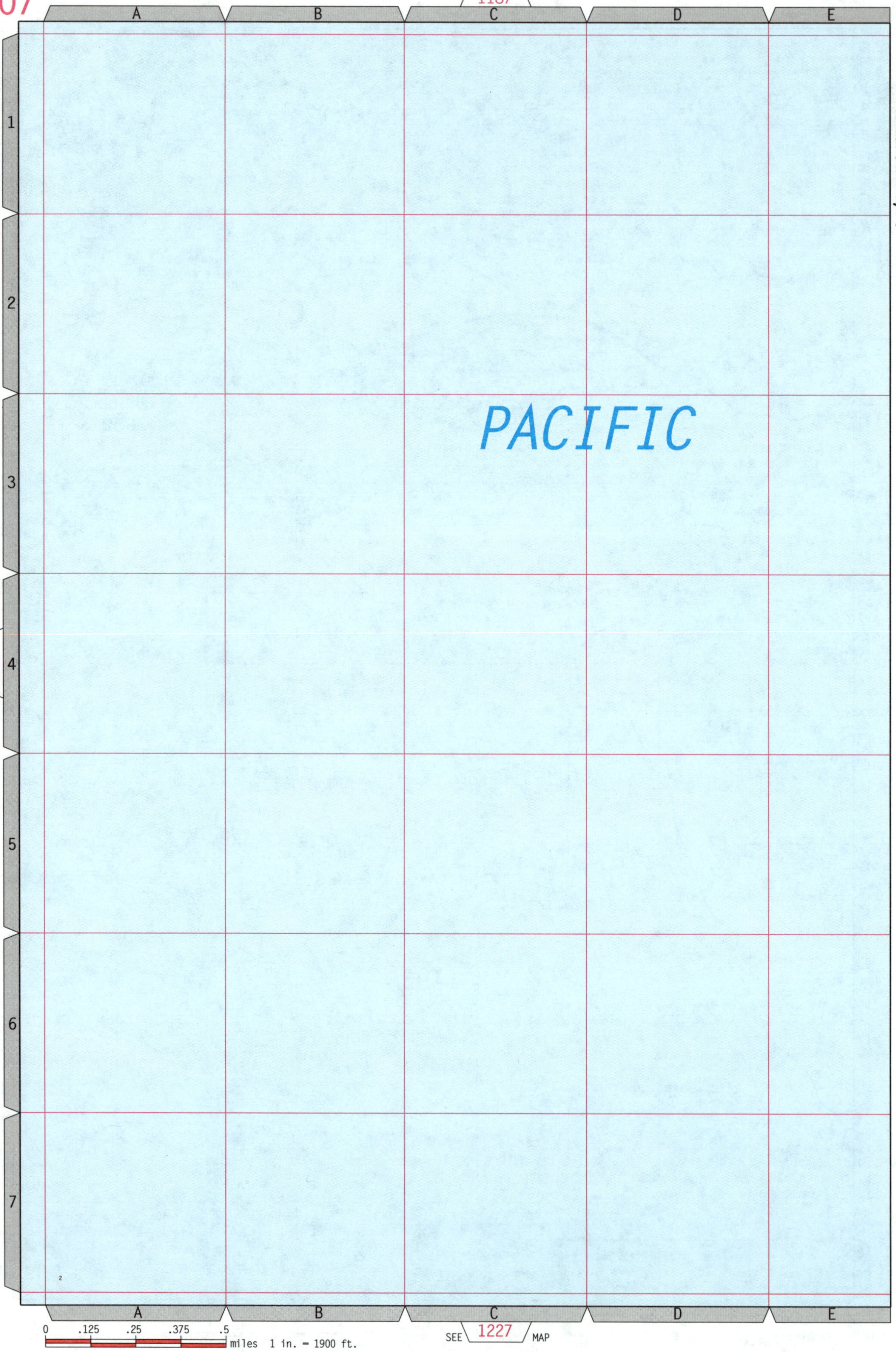

	A	B	C	D	E

1

2

3

PACIFIC

SEE 429 MAP

4

5

6

7

SEE 1227 MAP

0   .125   .25   .375   .5   miles   1 in. = 1900 ft.

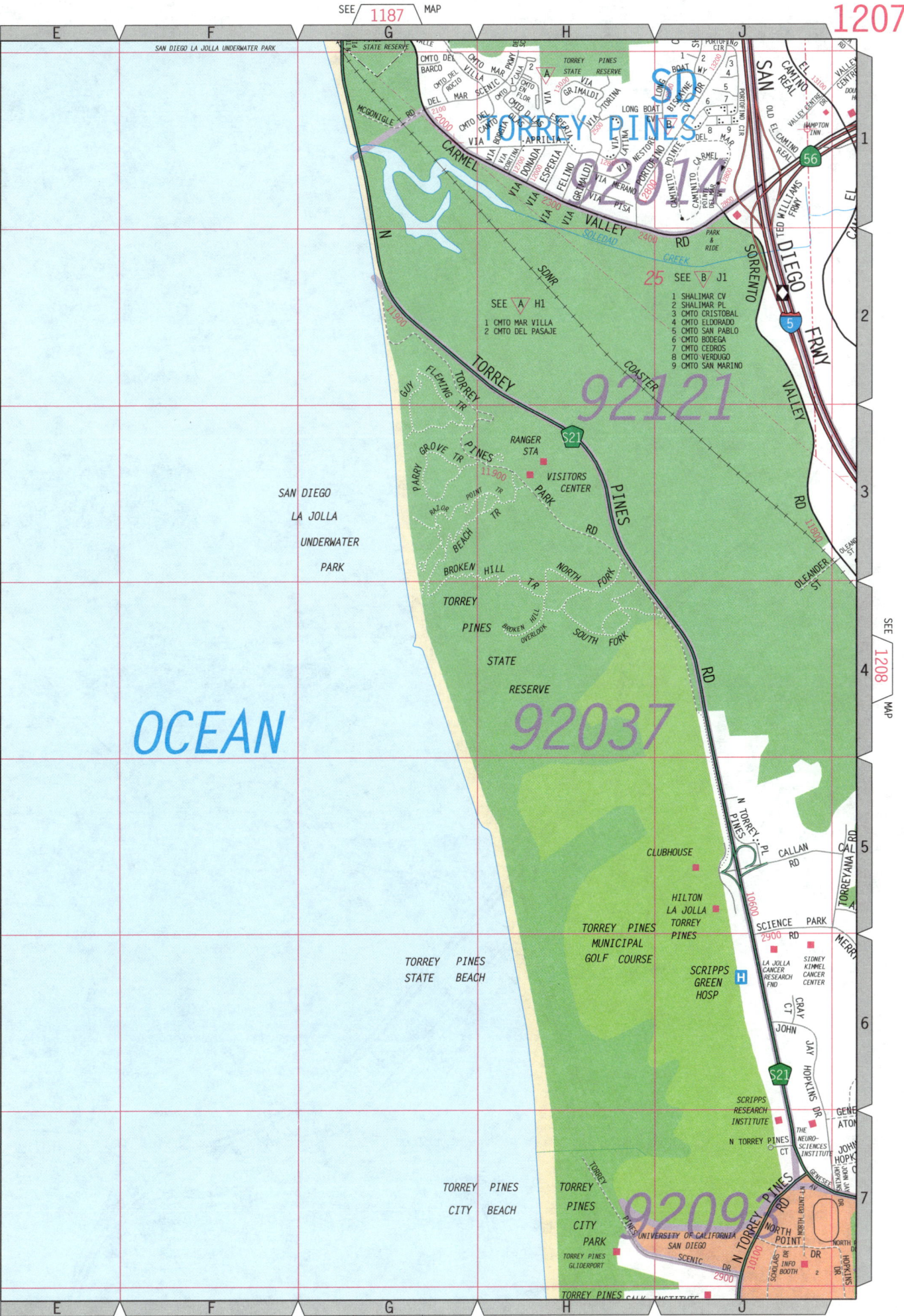

SAN DIEGO CO.

MAP

Thomas Bros. Maps®

COPYRIGHT 2001

N

SAN DIEGO LA JOLLA UNDERWATER PARK

STATE RESERVE

McGONIGLE RD

TORREY PINES STATE RESERVE

A

CMTO DEL BARCO
CMTO DEL VILLA
CMTO DEL ROCIO
CMTO DEL MAR
DEL MAR SCENIC PKWY
VIA BORICA
VIA COLLADA
CALLE EN FLOR
VIA GRIMALDI
VIA TORINA

SD
TORREY PINES
92014

VIA ESPERIA
VIA DONADA
VIA APRILIA
VIA ORTONA
VIA LATINA
VIA NESTORE
VIA FELINO
VIA GRIMALDI
VIA PISA
VIA MERANO

LONG BOAT
BISAYNE

PORTOFINO CIR

SAN

CARMEL

CAMINO CARMEL
CAMINITO PTE DEL MAR

VALLEY RD

SOLEDAD CREEK

PARK & RIDE

SAN DIEGO

SORRENTO VALLEY RD

EL CAMINO REAL
OLD EL CAMINO REAL
HAMPTON INN

WM WILLIAMS FRWY

56

5

SEE A H1
1 CMTO MAR VILLA
2 CMTO DEL PASAJE

25 SEE B J1
1 SHALIMAR CV
2 SHALIMAR PL
3 CMTO CRISTOBAL
4 CMTO ELDORADO
5 CMTO SAN PABLO
6 CMTO BODEGA
7 CMTO CEDROS
8 CMTO VERDUGO
9 CMTO SAN MARINO

92121

COASTER

SDNR

TORREY PINES

GUY FLEMING TR
PARRY GROVE TR
RAZOR POINT TR
BEACH TR
BROKEN HILL TR
TORREY PINES

RANGER STA
11900
VISITORS CENTER

PARK RD

NORTH FORK
SOUTH FORK

PINES

OLEANDER ST

S21

SAN DIEGO
LA JOLLA
UNDERWATER
PARK

BROKEN HILL OVERLOOK

STATE

RESERVE

92037

OCEAN

TORREY PINES STATE BEACH

TORREY PINES MUNICIPAL GOLF COURSE

CLUBHOUSE

HILTON LA JOLLA TORREY PINES

N TORREY PINES RD

SCRIPPS GREEN HOSP H

LA JOLLA CANCER RESEARCH FND
SIDNEY KIMMEL CANCER CENTER

SCIENCE PARK RD

CALLAN RD
TORREYANA RD
CAL RD
MERRY

CRAY CT
JOHN JAY HOPKINS DR

S21

SCRIPPS RESEARCH INSTITUTE
N TORREY PINES CT
THE NEUROSCIENCES INSTITUTE

GENE ATOM
JOHN HOPKI

TORREY PINES CITY BEACH

TORREY PINES CITY PARK

TORREY PINES GLIDERPORT

TORREY PINES SCENIC DR

UNIVERSITY OF CALIFORNIA SAN DIEGO

92093

NORTH POINT DR
INFO BOOTH
N TORREY PINES RD
GENESEE AV
NORTH TORREY PINES

TORREY PINES SALK INSTITUTE

0 .125 .25 .375 .5 miles   1 in. = 1900 ft.

SEE 1208 MAP

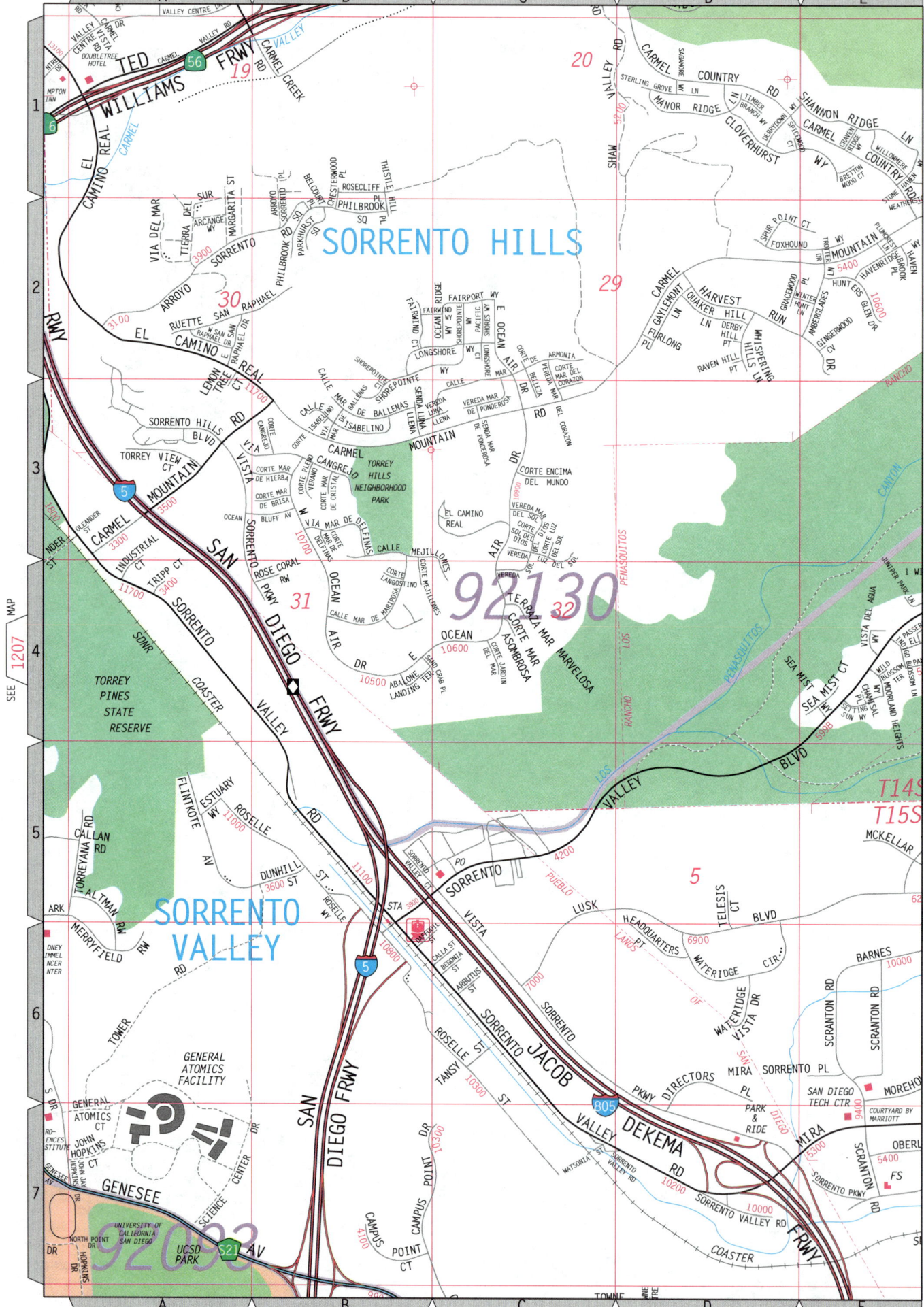

SAN DIEGO CO.

MAP

SEE 1188 MAP
SEE 1207 MAP
SEE 1228 MAP

COPYRIGHT 2001 Thomas Bros. Maps®

SORRENTO HILLS

SORRENTO VALLEY

92130

92093

TED WILLIAMS FRWY

SAN DIEGO FRWY

CARMEL VALLEY

EL CAMINO REAL

TORREY PINES STATE RESERVE

TORREY HILLS NEIGHBORHOOD PARK

GENERAL ATOMICS FACILITY

UNIVERSITY OF CALIFORNIA SAN DIEGO

UCSD PARK

SORRENTO VALLEY RD

SORRENTO VALLEY BLVD

PENASQUITOS

LOS PENASQUITOS CANYON

T14S
T15S

0   .125   .25   .375   .5   miles   1 in. = 1900 ft.

SAN DIEGO CO.

MAP

COPYRIGHT 2001 Thomas Bros. Maps®

N

92129

92126

92121

SAN DIEGO

MEADOWS DEL MAR GOLF CLUB

21
22
27
28

LOS PENASQUITOS CANYON PRESERVE

LOS PENASQUITOS CREEK

COUNTRY RD
GE LN
WILLOWMERE WY
STONE HAVEN CT
WEATHERSTONE LN
LAUREL CHASE
BRITTANY FORREST
BRIARLAKE WOODS DR
MOSSWOOD
CONCORDE DR
WOODS WY
TIMBER BROOK WY
EVANS WY
GABELWOOD
EVANS WOOD WY
PLUMTREE RD
AVENRIDGE BROOK
GLEN DR
10600

WINDWARD RIDGE WY
WHISPERING HEIGHTS LN
SUNNY MESA
PEINADO WY
CEDARCREST CT
HOLLYCREST CT
MAYCREST LN
SORRENTO RD
SUNSET CREST WY
SEACREST VIEW RD
JASMINE CREST LN
PACIFIC HAVEN CT
OCEANVIEW RIDGE
PACIFIC RIDGE
HILLBRAE
LOMBARD
CANYON BLUFF CT
SEACREST WY
PACIFIC CANYON WY
LOPEZ RIDGE WY
SHAW LOPEZ RD
SHAW LOPEZ RW

VALLEY BLVD
6900
CAMINO SANTA FE
LOPEZ RIDGE PARK

27
34

CMTO A/CLARA
CMTO
RODA
QUAD
PROPETIO
7100

CALLE CRISTOBAL SEAN

KEISHA CV
CM MIRANDA
WIETTA TER
RAVEN RIDGE PL
CHERYL RIDGE
FRAMES PORT PL
WINDY RIDGE RD
WINDY RID
7500
KEISHA HEIGHTS
CMTO LA BAR
APRIL LN
ALVAREZ
BIRDS VIEW CT
ALONA
ACAMA ST
AE
750
TAYLOR
MASON LN
PORREGA CT
PAUL BARNICK CT
ROCKSTON DR
RED ROBIN PL
ALONDA ROCK
ANDASOL
26
ROCK CANYON

92126
CANYON HILL CT
CANYON HILL WY
CANYON HILL
CROWS NEST LN
SUNNY MEADOW CT
CANYON BREEZE RD
CANYON BREEZE DR
CANYON PEAK LN
NEW SALEM ST
NEW SALEM ST
HAWKS
CANYON
BARBADOS

WINTERWOOD COMMUNITY PARK
35
PENARA ST CT
BLAKSTAD CT
CALSTON
PENARA PL
CALSTON AV
KENSLEY WY
GRANBY WY
SCHILLING
WORCHESTER ST
GLENDOVER LN
10700
WINC

PENARA
WALLINGFORD
CHINON CIR
TUSCANY
BROOK-HOLLOW
DARNEY CT
LARGATE TER
ADERMAN
1 ADKINS WY
ADK
10500
KEMPERTON
PENRIDGE ST
WESTFIELD PL
LANGFORD LN
BLVD
ALVAREZ
7100
CAMINTO

COBRA WY
TOP
GUN WY
VIPER WY
HEATER CT
MESA
6800
PLAZA SORRENTO

LOPEZ CANYON OPEN SPACE
33

VISTA DEL AGUA
JUNIPER PARK LN
1 WINDY BLUFF LN
GREENSHADE RD
5300
EL ONTORO
PASSERINE
FALLEN WOOD LN
GLENSTONE WY
ARBOR GROVE CT
ARBOR HTS LN
WILD BLOSSOM
MOORLAND HEIGHTS
RIO BLOSSOM LN
PANORAMA CT
CHAMISAL
5400

T14S
T15S

SEQUENCE DR
SEQUENCE DR
SEQUENCE
CENTER DR
GENETIC CENTER DR
MIRA
PACIFIC CENTER CT
PACIFIC CENTER BLVD
5900
PACIFIC HEIGHTS BLVD
10200
CENTER
PACIFIC
MARRIOTT RESIDENCE INN
PACIFIC MESA CT
WAPLES ST
9400
STEADMAN
WAPLES
9500
HUENNEKENS CT
WEATHERS PL
FLANDERS RD
FLANDERS
FLANDERS CT
FLANDERS
6900
10100
MESA RIM RD
MESA RIDGE RD
MESA RIDGE CT
SANTA FE

KEOKI CT
KEOKI PL
KAMWOOD PL
KAMWOOD
DANCY
DANCY PL
7400
DANCY DR
ANGELTON DR
CARRINGTON
BANNISTER
LANGETON
CRAISTOWN
MATSON PL
ADERMAN AV
MATS PV
DARDEN RD
PRESLEY
DARDEN
DARDEN
KAUFMAN
NORTHRUP DR
OSGOOD WY
NOR
OS

9212
McKELLAR CT
PACIFIC
PACIFIC
LUSK BLVD
6200
ARNES
CANYON
10000
6100
MOREHOUSE DR
SCRANTON RD
COURTYARD BY MARRIOTT
OBERLIN
5400
TON RD
FS
CARROLL
9

4 WYNDHAM GARDEN HOTEL
CORNERSTONE
PACIFIC HEIGHTS BLVD
9700
PACIFIC HEIGHTS CT
9200
BLVD
6000
MESA
YOUNGSTOWN WY
CANYON RD
6800
NANCY RIDGE DR

SORRENTO MESA
3
2

EL CAMINO MEMORIAL PARK (CEMETERY)

EL CAMINO DR
6100
CARROLL FENTON RD
6500
RD
6700

FERRIS SQ
BROWN DEER RD
CARROLL
6600
10
CARROLL PARK CT
CARROLL PARK DR
9300
REHCO RD
CAMINO SANTA FE
10116
TRADE ST
7100
8900
11
CRESTMAR PT
WARE CT
PRODUCTION AV
TERMAN
CARROLL RD
DISTRIBUTION AV
CAR
COASTER
SDNR
9700
NANCY

1 in. = 1900 ft.
0 .125 .25 .375 .5 miles

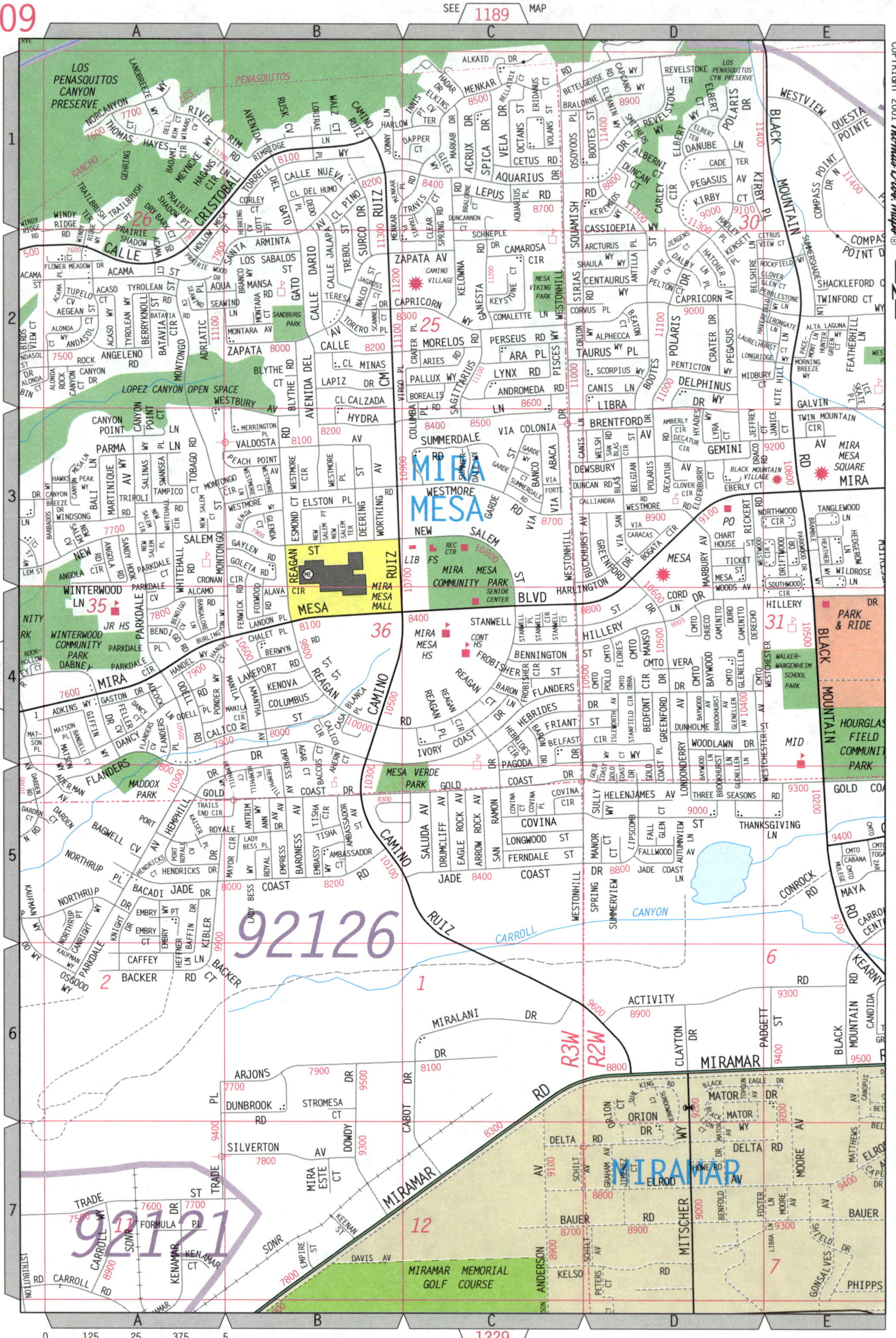

SEE 1189 MAP

SAN DIEGO CO.

COPYRIGHT 2001 Thomas Bros. Maps®

LOS PENASQUITOS CANYON PRESERVE

LOS PENASQUITOS CYN PRESERVE

MAP

SEE 1208 MAP

LOPEZ CANYON OPEN SPACE

MIRA MESA

MIRA MESA COMMUNITY PARK

MIRA MESA MALL

WINTERWOOD COMMUNITY PARK

MESA VIKING PARK

SANDBURG PARK

MESA VERDE PARK

MADDOX PARK

MIRA MESA SQUARE

MIRA MESA

BLACK MOUNTAIN VILLAGE

PARK & RIDE

HOURGLASS FIELD COMMUNITY PARK

WALKER-WANGENHEIM SCHOOL PARK

WESTVIEW

COMPASS POINTE

SHACKLEFORD CT

92126

92121

MIRAMAR

MIRAMAR MEMORIAL GOLF COURSE

CAMINO RUIZ

CAMINO SANTA FE

BLACK MOUNTAIN RD

MIRA MESA BLVD

0 .125 .25 .375 .5
miles 1 in. = 1900 ft.

SEE 1229 MAP

SEE 1189 MAP

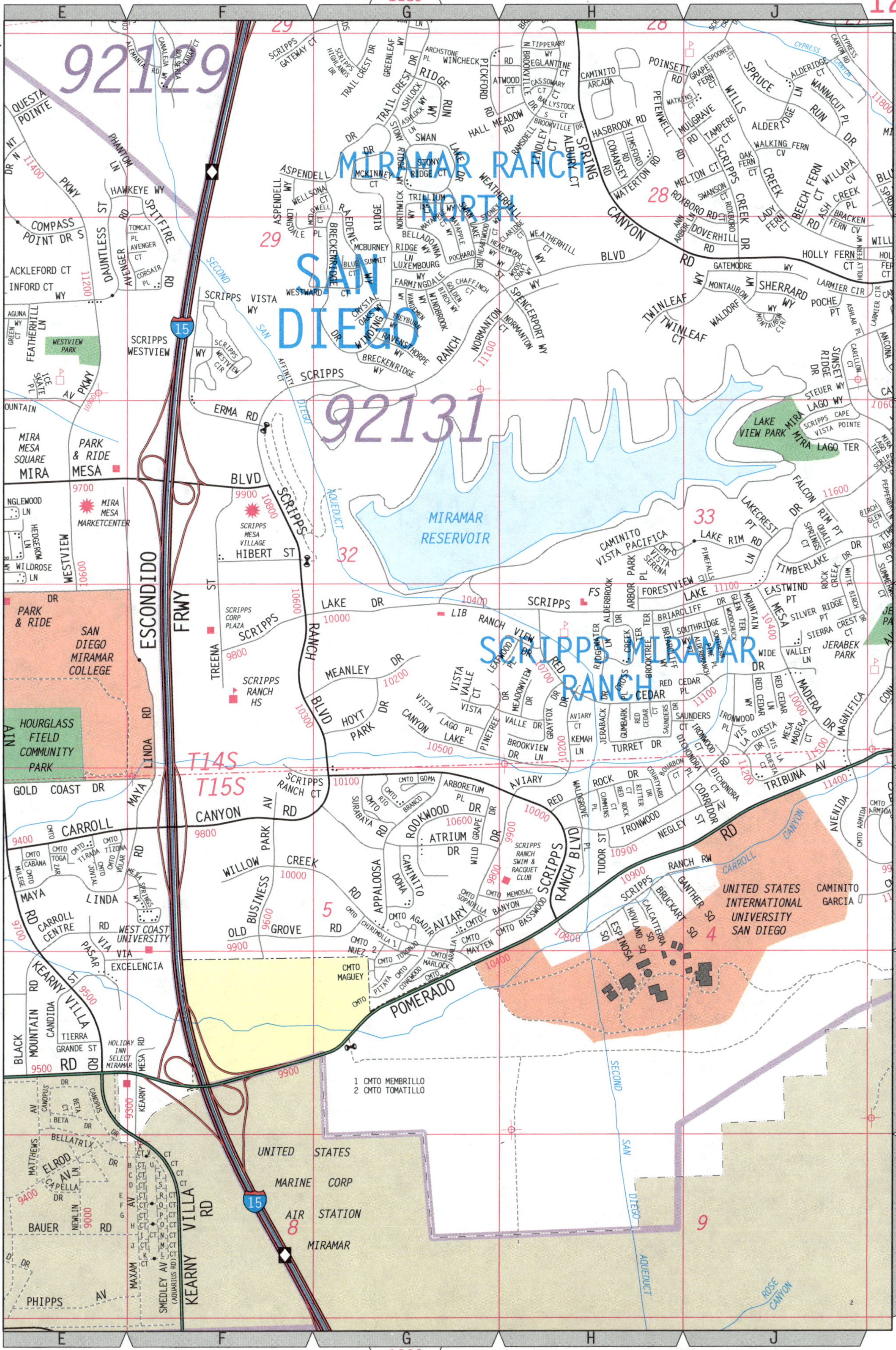

92129
92131
MIRAMAR RANCH NORTH
SAN DIEGO
SCRIPPS MIRAMAR RANCH
MIRAMAR RESERVOIR
LAKE VIEW PARK
JERABEK PARK
WESTVIEW PARK
MIRA MESA SQUARE
MIRA MESA MARKETCENTER
SCRIPPS MESA VILLAGE
SCRIPPS CORP PLAZA
SCRIPPS RANCH HS
SAN DIEGO MIRAMAR COLLEGE
HOURGLASS FIELD COMMUNITY PARK
PARK & RIDE
SCRIPPS RANCH SWIM & RACQUET CLUB
UNITED STATES INTERNATIONAL UNIVERSITY SAN DIEGO
WEST COAST UNIVERSITY
HOLIDAY INN SELECT MIRAMAR
UNITED STATES MARINE CORP AIR STATION MIRAMAR
ESCONDIDO FRWY
MIRA MESA BLVD
SCRIPPS RANCH BLVD
SCRIPPS LAKE DR
SPRING CANYON RD
POMERADO RD
CARROLL CANYON RD
BLACK MOUNTAIN RD
KEARNY VILLA RD
SECOND SAN DIEGO AQUEDUCT
T14S
T15S
1 CMTO MEMBRILLO
2 CMTO TOMATILLO

SEE 1210 MAP

SEE 1229 MAP

0 .125 .25 .375 .5 miles 1 in. = 1900 ft.

SAN DIEGO CO.

MAP

SEE 1190 MAP

A B C D E

POWAY

SAN DIEGO CO.

MAP

—N→

VAIL CT

CANDY CT   DAYMARK CT   CANDY ROSE   2 EVERGOLD ST
MARGINATA CT   CASSINI   FANTASIA CT   GINSTREET
AVONETTE CT   ELEONORE   FIDELIO   EVERGOLD CT   MISTY BLUE   TRAVERTINE CT   DR   ORANGE
ALDERHILL   SARDIS PL   ALDERCREST TER   ENID   BLUE DIAMOND CT   ANGELIQUE CT   FIDELIO WY   CANDY ROSE WY   BEREA CT   CREEK BLUFF DR
ELWELL CT   ENID CT   LITTLE SILVER   CYN   PARK DR   JAGUAR ST   STONEMILL DR   EASTVIEW   EASTRIDGE
CYPRESS   CYPRESS   NIKITA CT   LIBELLE ST   TREADWELL DR   EASTFIELD
MID   CANYON RD   ZIRBEL CT   MUNDIAL ST   CYPRESS WOODS DR   SWAN CANYON   EASTVIEW PL   26
BLUET PT   RINGDOVE CT   11700   CYPRESS VALLEY DR   CYPRESS WOODS   SWAN CANYON DR   LEGACY   12700   BEELER
SCRIPPS RANCH COMMUNITY PARK   SWEETBRIAR   CYPRESS CANYON PARK   CYPRESS TER PL   SWAN CANYON RD   EASTVIEW PL   LEGACY TER   CANYON TER   10700
SPRUCE RUN   MANDRAKE DR   PEPPERVINE LN   ARBORDALE   ELDERWOOD CT   1 CMTO FESTIVO   LEGACY PL   POMERADO   BEELER
WILLS   MANDRAKE   SPRING   CANYON RD   2 CMTO SERENO   CYPRESS CANYON RD   3 CMTO ENCANTO   4 CMTO ALEGRA
HOLLY FERN CT   CANARY WOOD   11600   CLEARWOOD   1 2 3 4   CMTO BRIOSO   17100   POMERADO RD
SUNSET RIDGE   FRANK   ELDERWOOD LN   CHARDONNAY   CMTO VIBRANTE   POMERADO RD
BONJON   SEMILLON TER   WEATHERWOOD   CLOVERFIELD PT   CHARDONNAY DR   MIRADA   CMTO CUESTA
CARILLON   DANIELS WY   WOODSTREAM   CREEKSIDE   CHARBONO PT   PINOT   COLORADO   SEE A B2
ANCONA LN   BRIGHAM RIDGE   DEERFOOT RD   CHARBONO ST   RIESLING   SUTTERNE AV   FRONSAC   1 CMTO ARBOLES
HELMER CT   GLENCREEK CIR   CHARBONO TER   LOIRE   CMTO PERAL   2 CMTO CEREZO
SUNSET RIDGE DR   POYNTELL CIR   ARBORLAKE WY   OAK LN   12000   LOIRE   CAMINITO   3 CMTO TIERRA
RED FERN CIR   POINTED   REDCLIFF CT   LOIRE CT   4 CMTO CANADA
OAKBEND   10600   RIESLING   5 CMTO CANON
TIMBERLAKE   EASTGLEN ST   MEDOC LN   FIGTREE   FIGTREE CT   ST   6 CMTO CANELO
ROCK CREEK   LA VITA SCRIPPS   MEDOC ST   SEMILLON AV   FIGTREE   BIRCH BLUFF PL
PINECLIFFS   MORITZ PIERRE   DES ARBRES   MOSELLE ST   SPRUCE GROVE PL   EDENOAKS   BIRCH BLUFF AV   SAN DIEGO
SUMMERWOOD   RUE DU MIRAGE   RUE DES FLEURS   MAGNIFICA   SPRUCE GROVE AV   CHAPARAL VALLEY CT   SYCAMORE   BIRCH BLUFF CT   35
JERABEK PARK   LAKE GROVE   CLARET   SPRUCE GROVE   LIVEWOOD WY   RIDGE CT   BIRCH
AVD   MAYMIND DR   HANDRICH DR   BARRYWOOD WY   GRAINWOOD WY   BLVD   OAKFORT RD   OAKFORT CT
NEGLEY   HANDRICH   92131   KINGSPINE   THORNBUSH CT   WALNUTDALE ST   WALNUTDALE LN
WILDLIFE   CONNELL RD   HANDRICH RD   POMERADO   FONTENAY   RUE   PINECASTLE   ST   MEADOWDALE LN
COLINA LA   RUE GRENOBLE   RUE FOUNTAINEBLEAU   RUE MARRA-BELLE   FINISTERRE
CARROLL   CAMINITO   PUDREGAL   FAIRBROOK   RUE SIENNE   RUE CHAMONIX   RUE FINISTERRE
CAMINITO MUNOZ   CAMINITO PELON   RUE   RUE   RUE PARC   RUE TOURAINE
CMTO   CMTO MAGNIFICA   CAMINITO LASANE   CAMINITO   CHEAUMONT   RUE SAINT JACQUES   RUE CANNES
ROGELIO   CMTO ARMIDA   CMTO ELADIO   CAMINITO MOJADO   MONTEREAU   RUE SAINT LAZARE   CHAMBERRY   RUE CHANTEMAR   RUE VINCENNES
GARCIA   CMTO GUSTO   CAMINITO SUELTO   RUE BIARRITZ   RUE   RUGEMONT
CMTO CALOR   CAMINITO JOVEN   3   10   11   2

SEE 1209 MAP
SEE 1230 MAP

T14S
T15S

CLEMENTE

SAN   CANYON   OAK

0 .125 .25 .375 .5
miles 1 in. = 1900 ft.

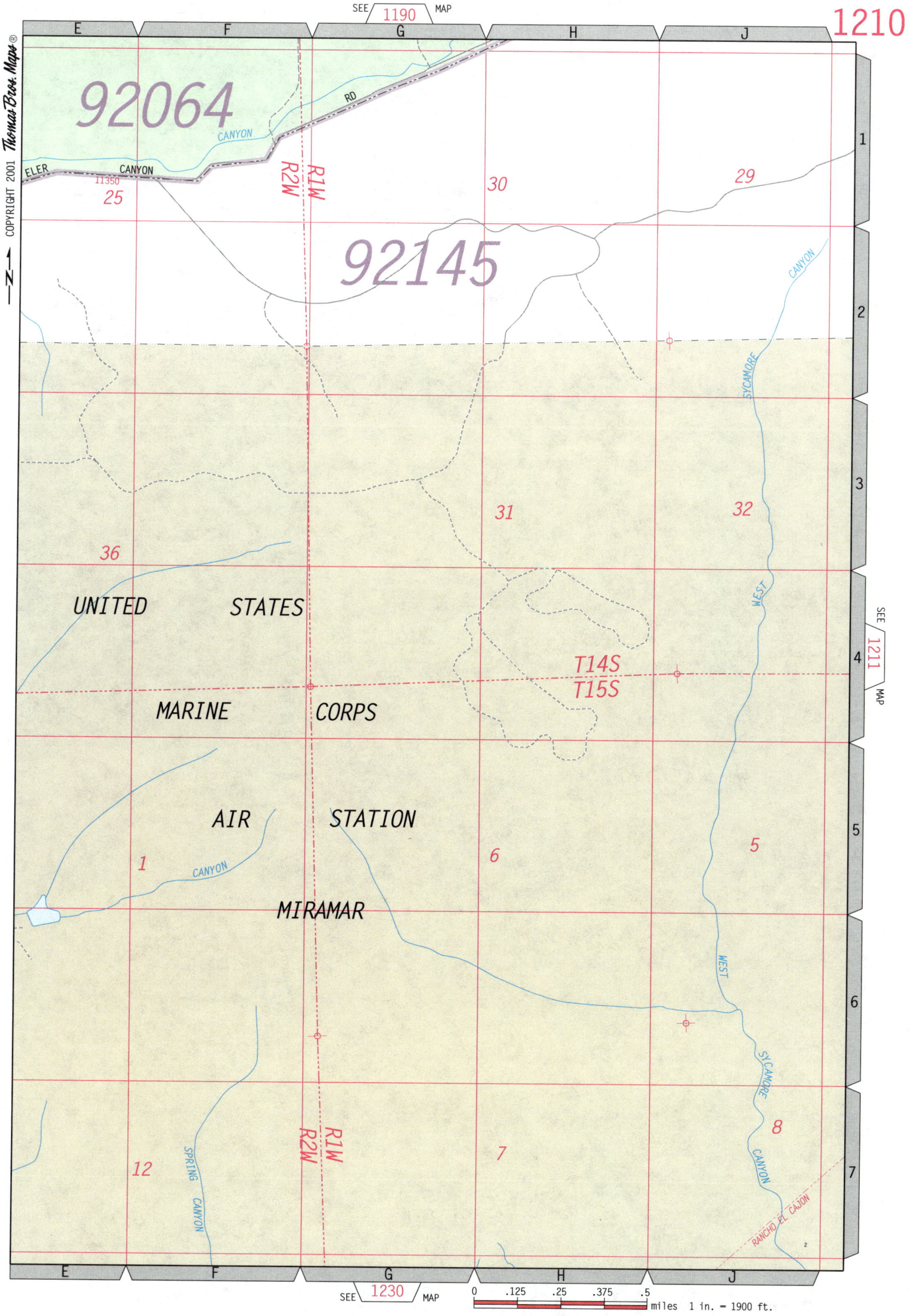

SAN DIEGO CO.

E   F   G   H   J

92064

ELER   CANYON
11350
25

CANYON   RD
CANYON

R2W
R1W

30

29

1

92145

CANYON

2

SYCAMORE

36

31

32

3

UNITED   STATES

WEST

SEE 1211 MAP

MAP

T14S
T15S

4

MARINE   CORPS

AIR   STATION

1

CANYON

6

5

WEST

5

MIRAMAR

WEST

6

SYCAMORE

12

SPRING CANYON

R2W
R1W

7

8

CANYON

RANCHO EL CAJON

7

2

E   F   G   H   J

0   .125   .25   .375   .5
miles 1 in. = 1900 ft.

SAN DIEGO CO.

SEE 1191 MAP

COPYRIGHT 2001 *Thomas Bros. Maps* ®

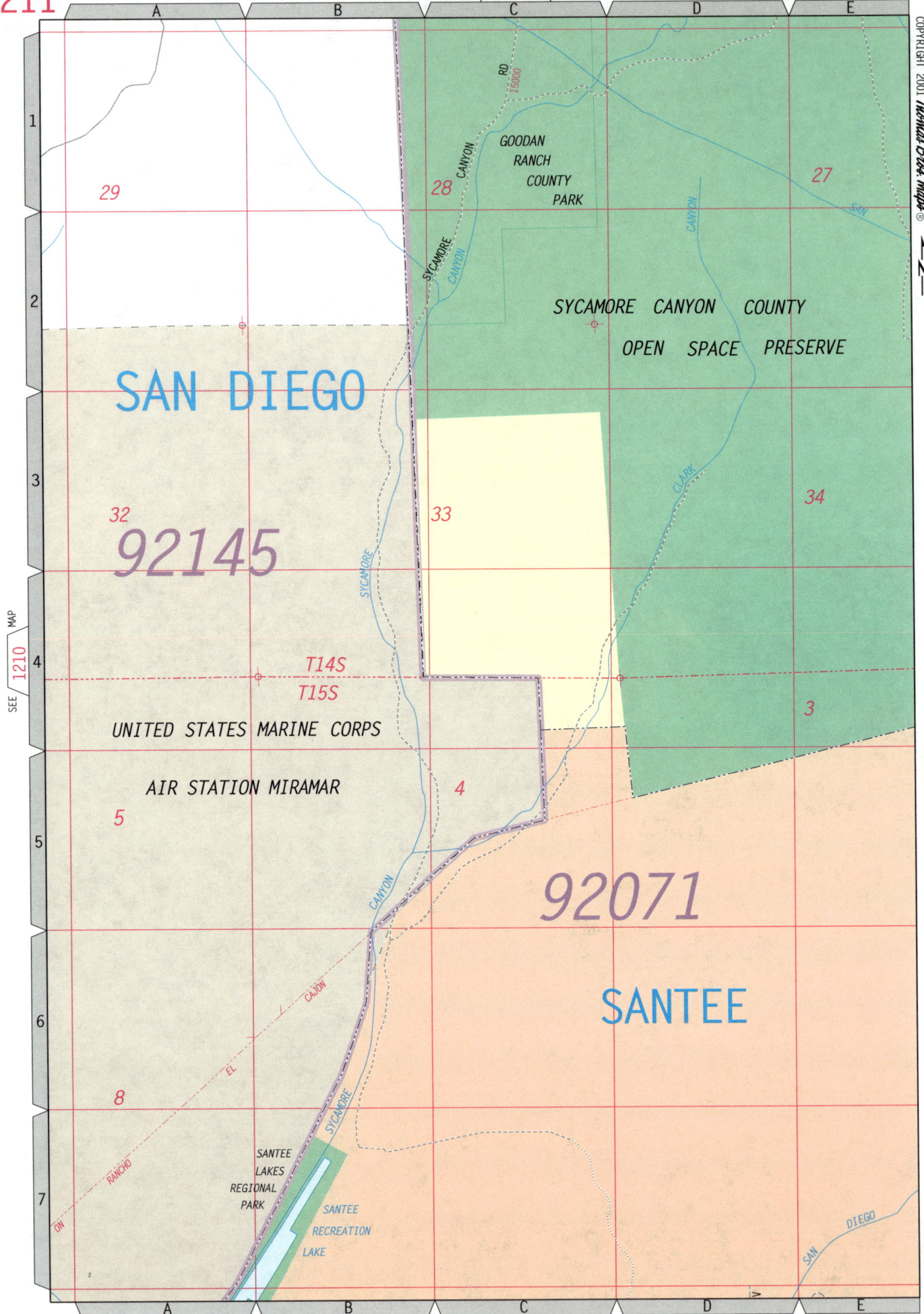

—N—

MAP

A B C D E

1

29

28 27

GOODAN
RANCH
COUNTY
PARK

SYCAMORE CANYON

2

SYCAMORE CANYON COUNTY

OPEN SPACE PRESERVE

SAN DIEGO

SYCAMORE CANYON

CLARK CANYON

SAN

SEE 1210 MAP

3

32

92145

33

34

SYCAMORE

4

T14S
T15S

UNITED STATES MARINE CORPS

AIR STATION MIRAMAR

3

4

5

5

92071

CANYON

6

EL CAJON

SANTEE

8

RANCHO

SYCAMORE

7

SANTEE
LAKES
REGIONAL
PARK

SANTEE
RECREATION
LAKE

SAN DIEGO

SAN

A B C D E

SEE 1231 MAP

0 .125 .25 .375 .5 miles 1 in. = 1900 ft.

SEE 1212 MAP

SAN DIEGO CO.

MAP

E F G H J

92065

25

SAN VICENTE
RESERVOIR

26

SLAUGHTERHOUSE

SAN DIEGO

AQUEDUCT

CANYON

67

92040

BOAT
LAUNCH

R1W

35

36

FOSTER

MORENO

AV

SLAUGHTERHOUSE CANYON RD
(GRIFFITH RD)
EL CAJON

12500

VIGILANTE

2

RANCHO

DR

12300

SAN VICENTE CREEK

MORENO AV

12300

HI HOPES
11800

67

ERICAS WY

12100

ROCOSO

RD

JOHNSON LAKE RD
11800

COSTALOT LN
11900

CERRO DE PAZ
11600

RD

JOHNSON LAKE

RD

OAK

VALLE

11500

RD

VISTA

RD
11500

HI RIDGE

11700

1

2

3

4

5

6

HIGH RANCH
RD 11300

11700

11600

RD

MANZANITA

RD
11600

HI

11500

BRIDLE PATH LN

SAN VICENTE AV
12000

CREEK

GEM HILL LN

LEGENDALE

DR

11200

11500

MANZANITA

RD
11400

ROCOSO

PINEHURST

11500

POSTHILL

POSTHILL
PL

RD

CRAZY HORSE DR

DR

11700

11200

MANZANITA
LN

RD

11800

RD

EUCALYPTUS HILLS

11300

11500

CA

OAK

MORNING DOVE
RD
11000

ALBA

ROSA

DR

EUCALYPTUS HILLS
11500   11600

VALLE

DR VISTA

FS

POSTHILL RD

6

CRAZY
HORSE
DR

GREEN OAKS RD
11100

CREEK DR

CAMINO DEL
TIERRA

DR

POSTHILL

7

JAMES HILL
DR

DR

TOYON HILL DR

TOYON
HILL
DR

SERENA

GOL

2

E F G H J

0 .125 .25 .375 .5
miles 1 in. = 1900 ft.

—N—

SAN DIEGO CO.

MAP

SEE 1192 MAP

A B C D E

92065

30

29

SAN VICENTE RESERVOIR

OAK OASIS COUNTY
OPEN SPACE PRESERVE

SD

AT NCH

R1W R1E

SAN VICENTE CREEK

LAKE VICENTE DR

VICENTE VIEW DR

31

YERBA VALLEY

YERBA VALLEY RD

WY

32

WY

SEE 1211 MAP

AV

MUTH

VALLEY

BUENA VIDA RD

12000

12300

GENESIS

12800

ELK

12300

RANCHO

EAGLE RD

MUTH VALLEY

12400

GOLDEN

12200

WHIPTAIL CT

OPOSSUM CT

RACCOON CT

RD

MOUNTAIN LION RD

12200

RD

12800

RD

12900

RD

ENO AV

HIGH MEADOW

RANCHES

12400

RED TAIL

11500

BADGER

RD

LION RD

11900

CT

12900

SQUIRREL RD

MOUNTAIN

11800

MOUNTAIN QUAIL CT

HORNED OWL

HAWK CT

6

MOUNTAIN RANCHES RD

5

MORENO

EL

SPARROW HAWK CT

11300

RD

MOUNTAIN

MOUNTAIN BLUEBIRD CT

11400

SAN VICENTE

12200

11700

TOPO

ROCKY

CAJON

AV

CANYON

9

TE AV

SAN

MORENO

CAMINO RIO

12300

MIDRANCH AV

LN

12500

11300 LN

CRADLE MOUNTAIN LN

7

8

CAJON

EL

WILDCAT

11200

WILDCAT

SANTA MARIA AV

11500

VICENTE

ACADIA

LN WY

11200

MARY LN

CREEK

RANCHO

LOUIS A STELZER
COUNTY PARK

67

GOLD BAR WY

SEE 1232 MAP

A B C D E

0 .125 .25 .375 .5
miles 1 in. = 1900 ft.

SAN DIEGO CO.

MAP

COPYRIGHT 2001

Thomas Bros. Maps®

N

E F G H J

BARONA RANCH
INDIAN
RESERVATION

27

RANCHO CANADA DE SAN VICENTE
Y MESA DEL PADRE BARONA

28

BARONA (WILDCAT) CANYON RD)

OLD BARONA RD

1000

12900

BARONA

GANDER CIRCUIT

FRANK ROCK SHELL

GEOLOGY TR

QUAIL TR

MCGINNIS

WOODWARD RIDGE TR

BOTANY TR

SUNSET TR

CREEKSIDE

BETTY PEAK TR

FRANK CANYON TR

CYPRESS TR

CHIPMUNK TR

GANDER

CIENAGA TR

SPRING TR

CHAPARRAL

WING ROCK TR

BIG OAK TR

ROUGH TR

CIRCUIT

SILVERWOOD

WILDLIFE

SANCTUARY

SILVERSPRINGS

N DOME TR

TR

SILVERSPRINGS HIGH

SILVERSPRINGS

OLGAS CTO

DOME TR

DOME TR

CANYON RD

BLUE SKY RANCH RD

33

PATA RANCH

13700

RANCH RD

EL CAPITAN COUNTY

34

OPEN SPACE PRESERVE

WILDCAT

12900

T14S
T15S

92040

4

3

CANYON RD

9

RD

RANCHO

EL

CAJON

SEE 1213 MAP

MARGUERITE CANYON RD

PATA VIEW DR

GOLDA

ODESSA LN

WILLOW

RIVER

MOUNTAIN VALLEY PL

15600

MOUNT PL

HAZY MEADOW LN

WILLOW

RD

RD 15500

6

WILLOW

RD

EXT 14400

WILLOW RD

EL MONTE

15100

SAN DIEGO

7

E F G H J

0 .125 .25 .375 .5 miles 1 in. = 1900 ft.

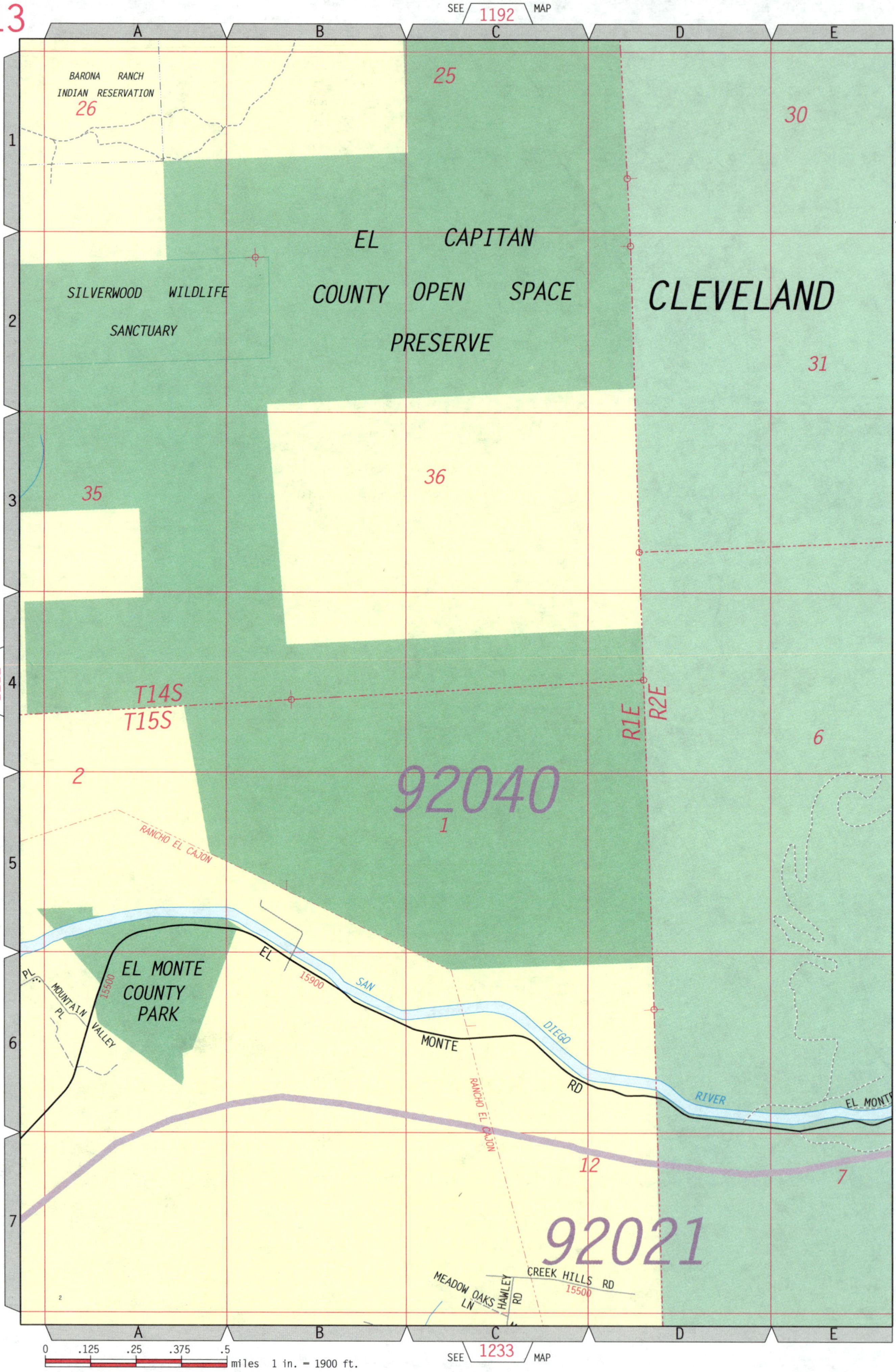

SEE 1192 MAP
A
B
C
D
E
1
2
3
4
5
6
7
BARONA RANCH
INDIAN RESERVATION
26
25
30
EL CAPITAN
COUNTY OPEN SPACE
PRESERVE
SILVERWOOD WILDLIFE
SANCTUARY
CLEVELAND
31
36
35
SEE 1212 MAP
T14S
T15S
R1E
R2E
6
2
92040
1
RANCHO EL CAJON
EL MONTE
COUNTY
PARK
15500
PL
MOUNTAIN
PL
VALLEY
EL
15900
SAN
MONTE
DIEGO
RD
RIVER
EL MONTE
RANCHO EL CAJON
12
7
92021
MEADOW OAKS
LN
HAWLEY
RD
CREEK HILLS RD
15500
SEE 1233 MAP
0 .125 .25 .375 .5
miles 1 in. = 1900 ft.

SAN DIEGO CO.

MAP

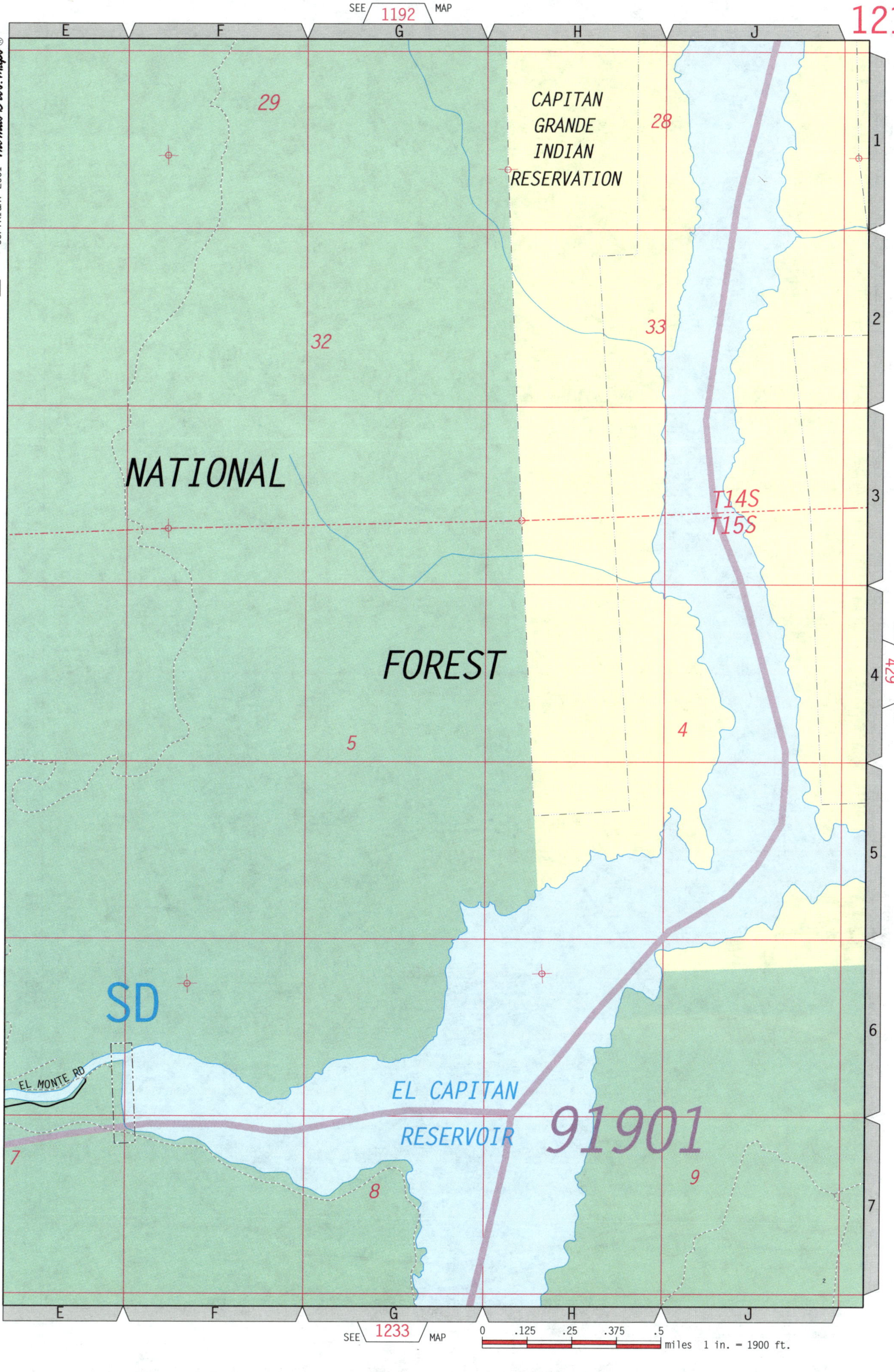

SEE 1192 MAP
E
F
G
H
J
CAPITAN
GRANDE
INDIAN
RESERVATION
29
28
33
32
NATIONAL
FOREST
T14S
T15S
5
4
SD
EL MONTE RD
EL CAPITAN
RESERVOIR
91901
7
8
9
1
2
3
4
5
6
7
SEE 429 MAP
SEE 1233 MAP
0
.125
.25
.375
.5
miles 1 in. = 1900 ft.

SAN DIEGO CO.

MAP

SAN DIEGO CO.

MAP

Thomas Bros. Maps ®

—N—

SEE 1176 MAP

A B C D E F G H J

1

30

SHERILTON VALLEY RD

MESA

CUYAMACA RANCHO

R3E R4E

31

TK TR

GREEN VALLEY CAMPGROUND

SEE 429 MAP

T14S T15S

6

KING CREEK

BOUNDARY

S

FIRE

1216

CUYAMACA

E MESA FIRE

RD

RD

RD

4

HWY

SWEETWATER

Deerhorn Dr

7

79

GREEN VALLEY FALLS

DESCANSO

FARLEY

FLAT

RD

10

DEER VALLEY TR

TANGLEWOOD LN

18

DE TIERRA

CAMINO

RD

15

79

HULBURD GROVE

1 TENNIS CT
2 CYPRESS LN
3 GARDEN LN
4 FLOWERS LN

MIZPAH SPUR
MIZPAH LN

91916

16

FLAT

FS

RIVER OAK GROVE BLVD

MANZANITA

MANZANITA

MIZPAH

MUGGED DR

DESCANSO

CREEK

TEATE CYPRESS TR

TECATE CYPRESS

HIGHWAY

PARLEY

GATE

GUATAY

VIEJAS

VIEJAS BLVD

OLD

2

CUYAMACA

GRADE RD

RIVERSIDE

CUYAMACA

80

GUATAY VIEW LN

22

3

DESCANSO

CUYAMACA

21

RANCHO CUYAMACA

SEE MAP 1236

91931

4

R3E R4E

79

CLEVELAND

30

NATIONAL

28

FOREST

27

DESCANSO JUNCTION

PINE VALLEY LAS BANCAS RD

29

VALLEY

BANCAS

PINE

RD

5

JAPATUL VALLEY

WILLWOOD GLEN

5 LOS TERRECITOS

HORSETHIEF RD

91901

31

32

GABIONI CREEK

91962

33

PINE

VALLEY

34

6

8

FRWY

RD

8

7

2

A B C D E F G H J

0 .25 .5 .75 1.0 miles 1 in. = 3800 ft.

SEE 1235 MAP

SEE 429 MAP

Thomas Bros. Maps®

COPYRIGHT 2001

N

A B C D E F G H J

S1

92036

LAGUNA INDIAN
RESERVATION

1 1

31 32 33

LUCAS CREEK

SKYLINE

2 STATE PARK 2

DEER

VALLEY

MEADOW RD

T14S
T15S

PARK

INDIAN

RMF
R5E

3 2 1 6 5 4 SAGE RD 3

LAGUNA

PINE

RD

1217

LAGUNA MEADOW RD

4 4

5 CLEVELAND NATIONAL FOREST 5

RD

LAGUNA MEADOW

PINE VALLEY

11 12 7 8 9

CREEK

NOBLE

6 LAKE OF THE WOODS 6

PINE CREEK RD

7 PINE 7

CREEK

PINE

NOBLE

14 13 18 CANYON 17 16

1 GATE 1

91948

19 GATE HWY

GATE

SPREAD

CREEK PINE RD

R5E
R4E

2 23 24 GATE S1 20 21 2

SUNRISE

GATE

SPREADHEAD

3 CLEVELAND 3

OLD

HIGHWAY

PINE

NATIONAL SEE MAP

CREEK RD

MOUNTAIN RD

4 FOREST 1237 4

GATE PINE RD PINE VALLEY

28

SUNRISE

5 26 25 30 29 5

PINE VALLEY BLVD

FOOTHILL BLVD

PINE VALLEY

6 6

PINE VALLEY COUNTY PARK

S1 SUNRISE

31 32 33

35 36 91962

7 HIGHWAY 80 7

8 FRWY 1 5 2

T15S
T16S

A B C D E F G H J

0 .25 .5 .75 1.0
miles 1 in. = 3800 ft.

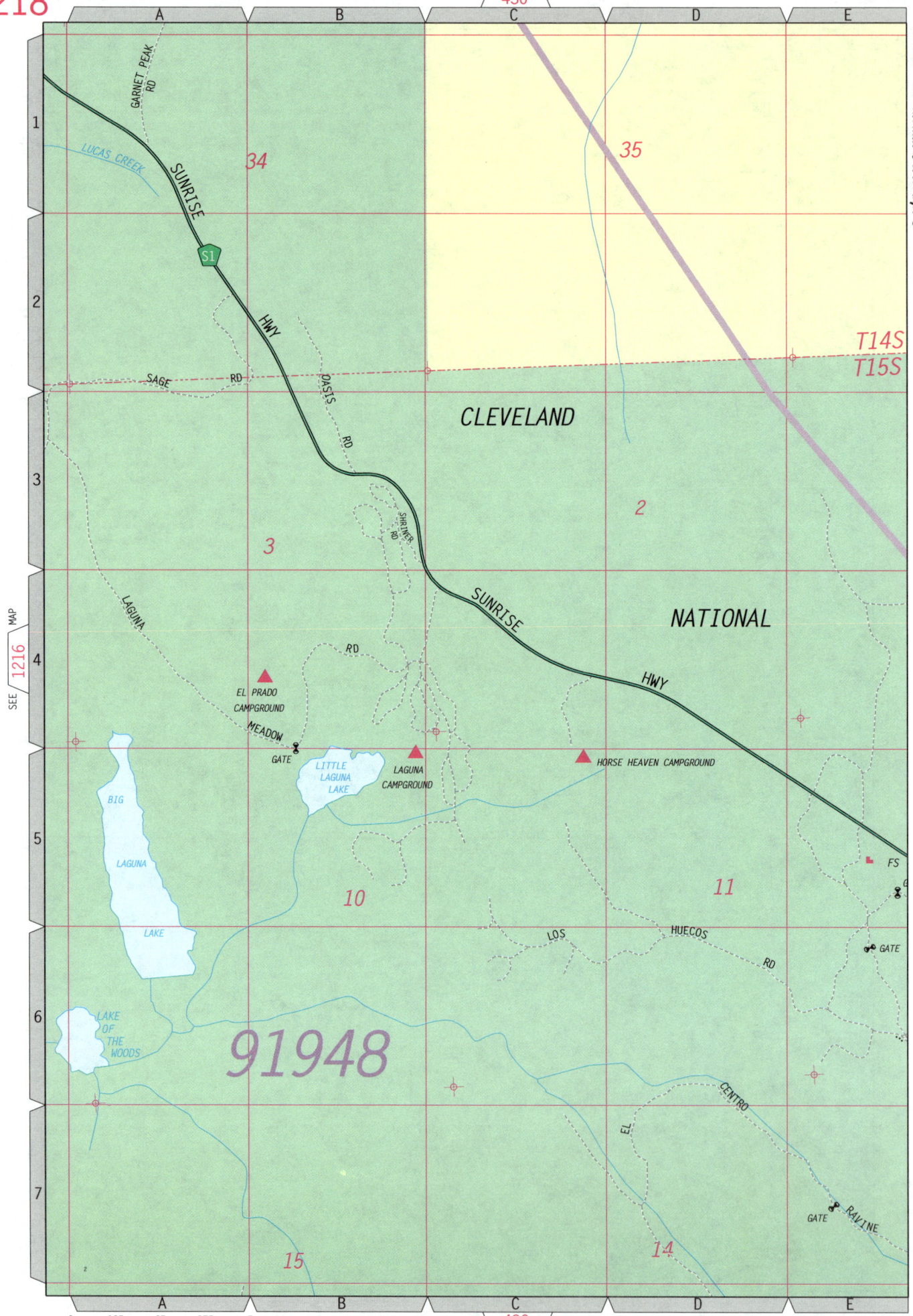

SAN DIEGO CO.

MAP

—N—

A   B   C   D   E

SEE 430 MAP

1

GARNET PEAK RD

LUCAS CREEK

SUNRISE

34

35

S1

2

HWY

OASIS RD

SAGE RD

T14S
T15S

CLEVELAND

3

SHRIVER RD

2

LAGUNA

NATIONAL

SEE 1216 MAP

RD

SUNRISE

4

EL PRADO CAMPGROUND

MEADOW

HWY

GATE

LITTLE LAGUNA LAKE

LAGUNA CAMPGROUND

HORSE HEAVEN CAMPGROUND

BIG

FS

5

LAGUNA

LOS

HUECOS

RD

GATE

LAKE

10

11

6

LAKE OF THE WOODS

91948

EL

CENTRO

7

GATE

RAVINE

15

14

A   B   C   D   E

SEE 430 MAP

0   .125   .25   .375   .5   miles   1 in. = 1900 ft.

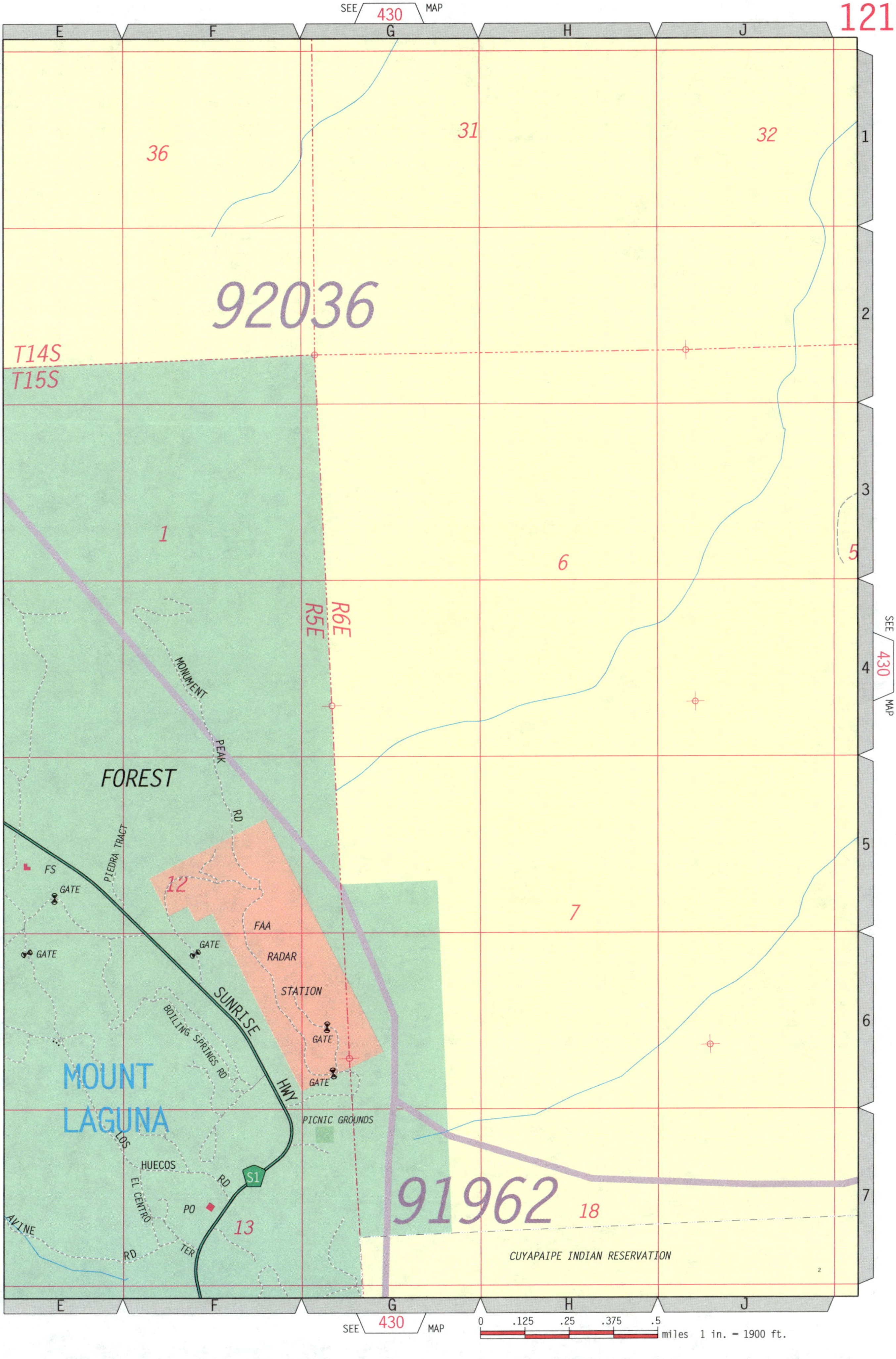

SAN DIEGO CO.

MAP

SEE 430 MAP

E   F   G   H   J

36

31

32

1

92036

T14S
T15S

1

6

5

R6E
R5E

4

SEE 430 MAP

FOREST

MONUMENT PEAK RD.

PIEDRA TRACT

FS
GATE
GATE

12

FAA
RADAR
STATION

GATE

7

5

SUNRISE

BOTLING SPRINGS RD

GATE

HWY

GATE

6

MOUNT
LAGUNA

PICNIC GROUNDS

LOS
HUECOS
RD.

EL CENTRO

PO

S1

91962

18

13

AVINE

RD

TER

CUYAPAIPE INDIAN RESERVATION

7

SEE 430 MAP

E   F   G   H   J

0 .125 .25 .375 .5
miles 1 in. = 1900 ft.

COPYRIGHT 2001 Thomas Bros. Maps® —N—

SEE 1207 MAP

	A	B	C	D	E
1					
2					
3			PACIFIC		
4					
5					
6					
7					

SEE 429 MAP

ELLEN BRO
SCRIPPS

SOUTH   CHILDRENS
CASA   POOL
                BEACH
BEACH

WIPEOUT BEACH

SAN DIEGO MUSEUM
OF CONTEMPORARY
ART
CUVIER PARK

COAST
BLVD
PARK

PROSPECT

COAST
COAST BLVD S
LN BLVD S

COMM

LA JOLLA

SCRIPPS COAST

BISHOPS
EPIS
HS

NICHOLSON
PT
WHISPERING
SANDS
BEACH

RAVINA ST
TORRIAN ST
OLIVETAS
AV

MARINE
ST

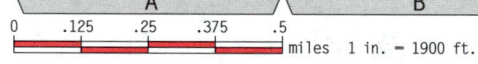

0   .125   .25   .375   .5
miles 1 in. = 1900 ft.

SEE 1247 MAP

	A	B	C	D	E

SAN DIEGO CO.

MAP

E F G H J

OCEAN

SAN DIEGO LA JOLLA UNDERWATER PARK

92037

SCRIPPS INSTITUTION

SUBMERGED LAND AREA

(PRIVATE)

SCRIPPS PIER

SCRIPPS INSTITUTION OF OCEANOGRAPHY

TORREY PINES CITY BEACH

TORREY PINES CITY PARK

SALK INSTITUTE
SALK INSTITUTE RD

BLACK GOLD RD

CROWN CREST LN
HAMBURG SQ
IDLE HOUR LN
BROOKMEAD LN

RIMAC

SCHOLARS DR
PANGEA DR
VOIGT LN

UCSD–THURGOOD MARSHALL COLLEGE

MUIR COLLEGE DR

MUIR LN

UCSD–JOHN MUIR COLLEGE

SCHOLARS LN

UCSD–REVELLE COLLEGE

PINES RD
TORREY PINES RD

LA JOLLA FARMS RD

LA JOLLA FARMS

WHITECLIFF DR

INYAHA LN

SCHOLARS DR

REVELLE COLLEGE DR

WEISS CENTER

LA JOLLA SHORES LN

HORIZON WY

ELLENTOWN LN

AZUL ST

POOLE ST
GILMAN DR
DISCOVERY
REDWOOD

92093

BIOLOGICAL GRADE

LA JOLLA SHORES DR

SHELLBACK

UNIVERSITY OF CALIFORNIA SAN DIEGO

LA JOLLA ATHLETIC AREA

MANDELL WEISS LN

EXPEDITION WY

BIRCH AQUARIUM

GLENWICK

BORDEAUX

CLIFFRIDGE

HOOD DR

NOTTINGHAM PL

GLENBROOK WY

N BROOK

INVERNESS

LA JOLLA SCENIC DR N

RUETTE MONT NICE

RUETTE NICOLE

SUGARMAN CT

SUGARMAN DR

CLIFFRIDGE AV

INVERNESS DR

LA JOLLA SHORES SAN DIEGO

CHIQUITA

COLLADO

AVD DE LS

WESTWAY

WHALE WATCH WY

CLIFFRIDGE

SCENIC

CLIFFRIDGE AV

LINTERNA

CMTO ECHO

SEE 1228 MAP

EL PASEO GRANDE

DISCOVERY DR

CM DL

CL CARLO

CL CORTADA

CL DL ORO

CL DONDAS

CL D LA CIELO

ORO

PRESTWICK

PINES

CLIFFRIDGE PARK

VIA POSADA

CMTO MARITIMO

CMTO LACAYO

CL OPIMA

LA JOLLA SHORES BEACH

VEREDA

PASEO GRANDE

KELLOGG PK

CL DEL ORO

CL D LA GARZA

FRESCOTA

VALLECITOS CT

AVD D LA CLARA PLAYA

CMTO BELLO

AVD D LA PLAYA

SPINDRIFT GOLF COURSE

REPOSO PAS

DORADO

CMTO DEL TORREY RD

CMTO DEL CIELO

LA JOLLA BAY

PT LA JOLLA

SHELL BEACH

LA JOLLA COVE

COAST WALK CTR

LA JOLLA CAVES

ELLEN BROWNING SCRIPPS PARK

SEAL ROCK RESERVE

CHILDRENS POOL BEACH

PAS DORADO

ROSELAND DR

SPINDRIFT DR

VIKING WY

PRINCESS ST

PINES

PROSPECT

COAST BLVD

COAST BLVD S

OCEAN LN

ROSLYN LN

CAVE ST

THE VALENCIA HOTEL

LA JOLLA COVE SUITES

EXCHANGE PL

LUDINGTON LN

TORREY PINES

AMALFI ST

SIERRA MAR DR

HILLSIDE DR

LOOKOUT DR

LOOK OUT

E JUELA

JUELA

ROSELAND

CMTO AVOLA

VIA BARLETTA

VIA AVOLA

HIDDEN VALLEY RD

ARDATH RD

SAINT TROPEZ PL

AZURE COAST DR

SAINT LAURENT PL

COSTEBELLE DR

ROSARIO DR

STARLIGHT DR

JOLLA SCENIC DR N

REVELLE DR

CMTO CORONADEL

LA JOLLA SCENIC DR

SAN DIEGO

92037

SILVERADO ST

JENNER ST

GIRARD AV

HERSCHEL AV

DRURY LN

PROSPECT ST

IVANHOE AV

PARK ROW

VIRGINIA WY

OLIVET ST

PEARL ST

DRAPER AV

KLINE ST

TORREY PINES

EADS AV

CUVIER ST

BISHOPS LN

PEARL ST

LA JOLLA COMMUNITY PARK

BISHOPS EPIS HS

LA JOLLA BLVD

OLIVETAS AV

MARINE ST

GENTER ST

CABRILLO AV

MIRAMAR AV

MASSENA ST

RODA ST

DELLCREST LN

BLUE BIRD LN

HIGH AV

LEIGH AV

MECCA DR

BAHR DR

COUNTRY

REMLEY PL

BRODIAEA WY

UPPER HILLSIDE

ENCELIA DR

ROMERO DR

CARRIZO DR

FAIRWAY RD

MIMULUS WY

MINT CANYON PTH

LA JOLLA COUNTRY CLUB

LA JOLLA NATURAL PARK

KEARSARGE RD

CRESPO DR

VALDES DR

CASTELLANA RD

PUENTE DR

HILLSIDE DR

CMTO MONROVIA

CMTO BRISA

CMTO CAPA

CMTO VELASCO

CMTO MARZELLA

CMTO QUINTERO

CMTO VELEZ

CMTO DONOSO

CMTO OLMO

RUE ANNE

RUE ADRIANE

RUE DENISE

VIA MICHAEL

VIA CAPRI

VIA SIENA

VIA SIENA VIESTA

VIA RIALTO

VIA RUE D ROARK

HIDDEN VALLEY CMTO CARINO

HIDDEN VALLEY PL

CMTO CASA ALTA

SOLEDAD NATURAL PARK

MT SOLEDAD MEMORIAL CROSS

SOLEDAD RD

CMTO MERION

CMTO BLYTHEFIELD

CMTO HERMITAGE

LA JOLLA SCENIC DR S

TOM MORRIS

SAN DIEGO CO.

MAP

SEE 1208 MAP

SEE 1227 MAP

SEE 1248 MAP

92093
92037
92161
92037
92122

UCSD PARK

SCRIPPS MEMORIAL HOSPITAL LA JOLLA

UNIVERSITY OF CALIFORNIA SAN DIEGO
UCSD MED CTR
THORNTON HOSPITAL

SHILEY EYE
PERLMAN AMBULATORY CARE
HEALTH SCIENCES

UCSD-WARREN COLLEGE
UCSD-JOHN MUIR COLLEGE
UCSD-ELEANOR ROOSEVELT COLLEGE
UCSD SCHOOL OF MEDICINE

VETERANS AFFAIRS MED CTR

INFORMATION BOOTH

MANDELL WEISS EASTGATE CITY PARK

LA JOLLA COUNTRY DAY SCHOOL

SAN DIEGO MARRIOTT LA JOLLA

REGENTS MARKETPLACE

EMBASSY SUITES

LA JOLLA GATEWAY

UNIVERSITY TOWNE CENTRE

TRANSIT CTR

LA JOLLA VILLAGE DR

HYATT REGENCY LA JOLLA

RADISSON HOTEL LA JOLLA

MARRIOTT RESIDENCE INN

MORNING WY

LA JOLLA VILLAGE DR

MORMON TEMPLE

LA JOLLA VILLAGE SQUARE

COMMUNITY PARK
DOYLE REC CTR

COLONY PLAZA

PALMILLA

CMTO EASTBLUFF

VILLA LA JOLLA PARK

UNIVERSITY CITY

STANDLEY COMMUNITY PARK

UNIVERSITY CITY HS

UNIVERSITY SQUARE

RADCLIFFE MID

REC CTR

PARK & RIDE

ROSE CANYON OPEN SPACE

MARCY PARK

SOLEDAD NATURAL PARK

BEAR MEMORIAL NATURAL PARK

CLAIREMONT

ARDATH RD

SOLEDAD

miles 1 in. = 1900 ft.

0 .125 .25 .375 .5

COPYRIGHT 2001 Thomas Bros. Maps®

E F G H J

92121

92145

92111

SAN DIEGO

UNITED STATES

MARINE CORPS

AIR STATION

MIRAMAR

9

10

11

JACOB

EASTGATE DR
EASTGATE
OLSON DR
EASTGATE CT
9700
5200

MIRAMAR MALL
AUTOPORT MALL
MIRAMAR
5500
5700
5600
5900
8300

MIRAMAR MALL
MARINDUSTRY DR
6200
6300
8400

NANCY RIDGE DR
LIQUID CT
REHCO RD
CARROLL RD
COASTER
RASHA ST
SANTA FE
SPECTRUM
CONSTRUCTION CT
COMMERCE AV
PRODUCTION AV
DISTRIBUTION AV
8700
8400
9600

TONI RIDGE PL
SANTA FE CTE
MIRACREST PL
FROSTMAR PL
CM
SDNR
CONSOLIDATED WY
6500
6700
WILCH

ROSE CANYON
DE LA GARZA RD
GARZA RD

RD
JOHNSON RD

JOHNSON

JOHNSON

RD

DEKEMA FRWY
RANCHO MISSION SAN DIEGO
PUEBLO LANDS OF SAN DIEGO

NOBEL ATHLETIC AREA
TOSCANA DR
ELINE DR
NA WY
ER

SDNR

HUGGINS ST WY
HUGGINS
CATHER ST
ROUS ST
WELLER ST
PAULING AV
ROCK VALLEY AV
FLOREY AV
WERNER ST
UNIVERSITY VILLAGE PARK
BOVET WY
STEINBECK AV
ENDERS AV
TEASDALE AV
WHIPPLE AV
TULA WHIPPLE CT
ENDERS AV
PARK & RIDE

ROBBINS
HAWORTH AV
RAMSAY AV
FINSEN AV
MURPHY AV
ST
4300
6800
7100
7000

DMONTON
DEER AV
STETTLER DR
LIPMANN
FARLEY DR
FARLEY LN
FARLEY CT
COM BE WY
ROBBINS ST
ROBBINS
BENHURST
CAMROSE AV
BENHURST CT
PANEL CT
4100
4200
4300
4400
4600
00

RNOR
LIB
UNIVERSITY SQUARE
RAYA WY
CHARAE ST
AGEE ST
PAVLOV AV
BROMFIELD
COZZENS ST
JANAN WY
VALOMA PL
DIRAC AV
ZENAKO ST
TAM'LYN CT
SUE AV
KAREN
KANTOR
ERLANGER ST
FERBER ST
KANTOR CT
GULLSTRAND AV
5800
5800
5800

UNIVERSITY GARDENS PARK
VIA LAPTI
VIA CORLITA
DORENA CT
LAKEWOOD ST
REGLA ST
VIA REGLA
MAYNARD
VIA CINTA
VIA CINTA
RUTLEDGE CT
GREENWICH DR
LAKEWOOD PL
SHOREHAM
NANETTE LN
PAPEL LN
WOLF STAR CT
6300
6000
6200
5000
6000
6100

JACOB DEKEMA DR

52

GENESEE AV
COLE CT
LODI CT
LODI ST
COLE ST
COLE WY
POST RD
MAYFLOWER WY
CAYWOOD
DUBOIS ST
PROVIDENCE DR
OTTO
GALT WY
GALT ST
PLETON
5500
5400
5200
5100
5000
0

JAMESTOWN WY
CONSTITUTION RD
MILLWOOD RD
REBEL RD
CHAMPLAIN
VIEW
FIRN
NONDINI
HAVEN RD
COBB PL
COBB CT
COBB
BAXTER DR
FRINK
FIRESTONE ST
BAXTER ST
TOWN
4800
5100
4900

NOAH AV
CLOUD WY
CRISP WY
CRISP WY
DIANE DR
LEHRER ST
ABERDEEN ST
APPLETON ST
ARLENE CT
CORK PL
ARLENE ST
ARLENE ST
BRILLO
ENSIGN RD
CADET ST
DAWNE
ARTESIAN ST
ANNESS ST
BARSTOW ST
DIANE CIR

MARIAN BEAR MEMORIAL NATURAL PARK

DIANE PL
DIANE CT
REGINA AV
LIMERICK CT
PALMYRA AV
NORTHRIDGE AV
SUNGLOW AV
PEYTON PL
ENERA
ARLENE
WINTHROP ST
ARLENE ST
LEHRER DR
LIMERICK ST
ABERDEEN AV
APPLETON
ROSCREA ST
ARVINELS AV
CONRAD ST
NORWICH ST
BERGEN ST
MACDOWELL PARK
5100

KILKEE ST
BARSTOW AV
MID AV
LONGFORD
BARSTOW

MESA BLVD
CLAIREMONT

COPLEY DR
6300
6500

HICKMAN FIELD DR
CONVOY CT
MABLE WY

805

52

SEE 1229 MAP

MAP

1 2 3 4 5 6 7

SEE 1209 MAP

COPYRIGHT 2001 *Thomas Bros. Maps* ®

—N—

SAN DIEGO CO.

MAP

92126

11

12

7

MIRAMAR VILLAGE

MIRAMAR MEMORIAL GOLF COURSE

DISTRIBUTION AV

SDNR RD

KENMAR DR

CARROLL

MIRAMAR RD

MIRAMAR SDNR

MIRAMAR AV

9500

7200

7600

7900

8600

PLESS

ROSE RD

DE LA GARZA RD

RANCHO MISSION SAN DIEGO

7700

SIDEWINDER

JOHNSON RD

7100

ANDERSON AV

BURKE RD

SILVA RD

PETERS RD

SCHILT AV

OBREGON AV

EDSON RD

EDSON RD

CANYON

WILLIAMS WY

7800

PLESS RD

EDSON WY

FLEMING CT

TALBOT AV

SKYROCK LN

BOYINGTON

SMITH RD

MITSCHER WY

ZEPPELIN

WALS

9000

8600

8600

R2W R3W

UNITED STATES MARINE

CORPS AIR STATION

MIRAMAR

SAN DIEGO

JOHNSON RD

JOHNSON

MIRAMAR GUN PLANT

HARRIS

PLANT RD

GATE

HARRIS 8900

SAN CLEMENTE

CANYON

CABRILLO FRWY

163

KEARNY VILLA

KEARNY 6100

MIRAMAR RECYCLING CENTER

5200 ST

FRWY

52

COPLEY 7200

92111

CONVOY TER

COPLEY PARK PL

RICHER LS

CONVOY CT

CONVOY

5000

MERCURY ST 5200

MERCURY PT

GATE

MERCURY CT

RAMADA INN NORTH

HAMPTON INN

MAGNATRON BLVD

RESIDENCE INN

KEARNY MESA RD 8900

KEARNY VILLA RD

WAXIE WY

CHESAPEAKE 5900

KEARNY VILLA CT

KEARNY VILLA WY

TOPAZ

MONEL AV

OVERLAND AV

RUFFIN RD 9400

ROSCOE CT

CHESAPEAKE DR 9300

HAZARD WY

DEPARTMENT OF PUBLIC WORKS

COUNTY OPERATIONS CENTER

CHESAPEAKE 5600

KEARNY MESA 92123

9100 CT

5700

FARNHAM ST

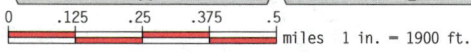

0   .125   .25   .375   .5

miles   1 in. = 1900 ft.

E F G H J

SAN DIEGO CO.

MAP

COPYRIGHT 2001

ThomasBros.Maps®

N

1

8

9

MIRAMAR
GATE
WY
MIRAMAR WY
ROSE
CANYON

BOYINGTON WY
ROBINSON RD
WALSH
ZEPPELIN
KEARNY
GATE
9400
9500
9700

15

RANCHO MISSION SAN DIEGO
CANYON

2

BYRD AV
KEARNY BLVD
AUSTIN
VILLA
8000
SAN CLEMENTE
CLINTON AV
FRWY

JOHNSON
POTTER AV
AV
RD
JOSEPHINE AV

RD
SECOND

3

92145

GREEN
FARM
SAN DIEGO

GATE
GUN CLUB
PLANT RD GATE
GATE
RD
H AV
9700
10100
ESCONDIDO
AV

4

SEE 1230 MAP

AQUEDUCT

FRWY
VILLA
RD

5

15

92124

6

FRWY
52

SEC

IE WY
ROSCOE CT
CHESAPEAKE DR
9400
MURPHY CANYON RD
5500

LA MORADA CT
DESEEJO PL
SALACOT CT
TORCA CT
LA MORADA DR
10400
EL COMAL DR
10500
PORTOBELO CT
PORTOBELO DR
10900
CTE PLAYA CARTAGENA
CTE PLAYA PACIFICA
VILLARICA WY
CORTE PLAYA BARCELONA
ESCORIAL CTE
PLAYA AZUL
CAMINO PLAYA CARMEL
CTE PLAYA MERIDA
Porto DR

7

AVD OROZCO
PEREZ CT RD
CIRCO
10400
LA BUENA WY
GUINCHO RD
5700
SANTO SANCHEZ
8000
RD
MENORCA
MENORCA WY
MARISELDA
ANTIGUA AV
6200
CTE PLAYA MAZATLAN
MALAGA CTE PLAYA JACINTO
CTE PLAYA ENCINO
CTE PLAYA CORONA
PORTOFINO CM PLAYA NORTE
CM PLAYA
CTE PLAYA AZTECA
VILLA NORTE CTE PARK
PLAYA ORO
PLAYA MADERA

TIERRASANTA

VILLA MONTSERATE PARK
MUCHACHA WY
AMARO
ROBUSTO
EL HONGO
EL CABO
TORTUGA
GUINCHO CT
MATADOR CT
BRAVO CT
HERMANOS BLVD
MANOS CT
HER-
AVD
5600
5700
TORTUGA
5900
CTE PLAYA VERACRUZ
CM PLAYA PALMERA
AVD PLAYA CASTILLA
AVD PLAYA ENCINO
PLAYA VERACRUZ
10700
VIA VALERA AVD

CLAIREMONT MESA BLVD
MATADOR CT
UNITED STATES MARINE CORPS
ST

0 .125 .25 .375 .5
miles 1 in. = 1900 ft.

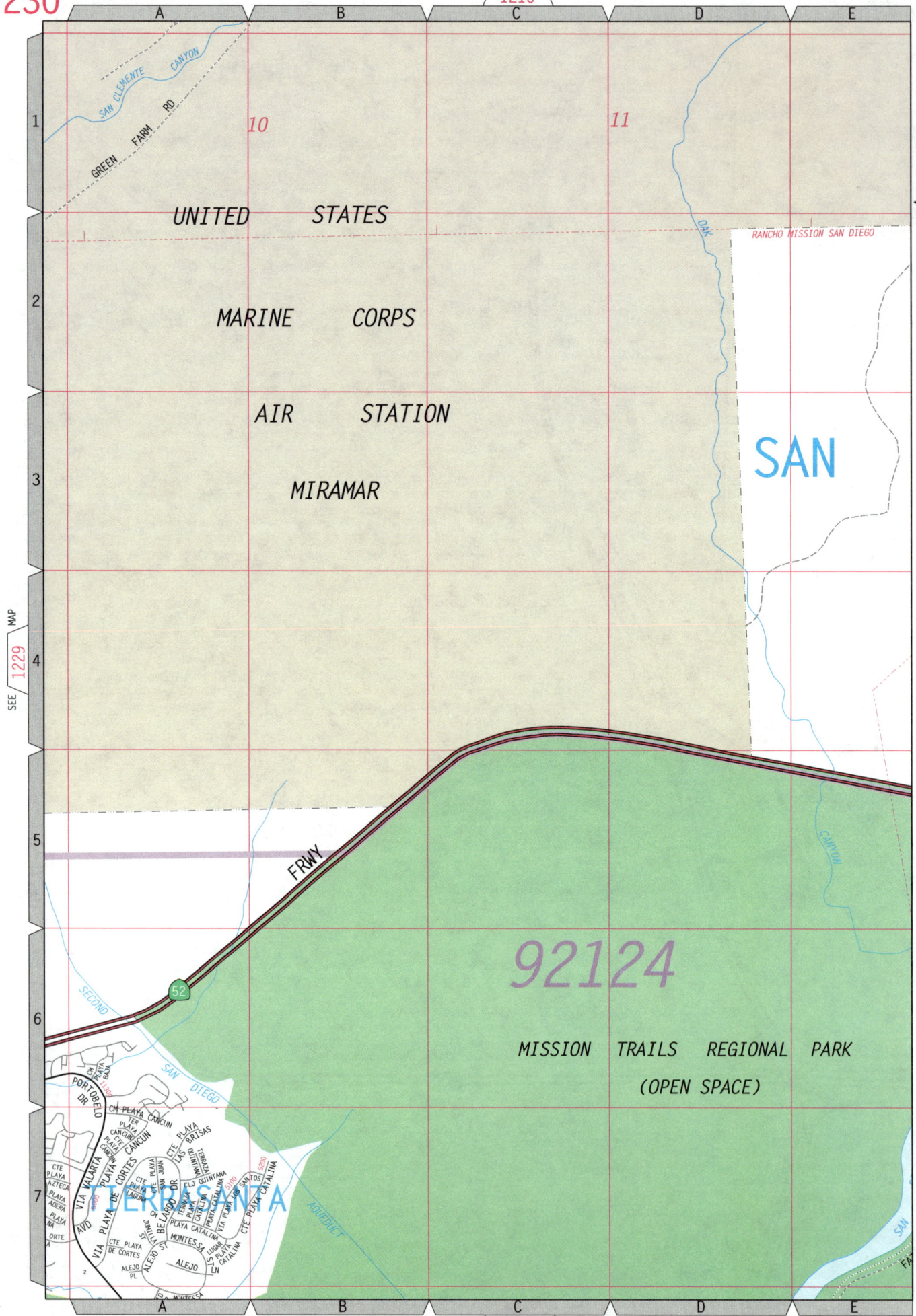

SAN DIEGO CO.

MAP

SEE 1210 MAP

A B C D E

1

10 11

UNITED STATES

MARINE CORPS

AIR STATION

MIRAMAR

2

3

SEE 1229 MAP

4

RANCHO MISSION SAN DIEGO

SAN

OAK

CANYON

FRWY

SECOND

52

SAN DIEGO

AQUEDUCT

5

6

7

92124

MISSION TRAILS REGIONAL PARK

(OPEN SPACE)

TIERRASANTA

PORTOBELO DR

CM PLAYA CANCUN
TER PLAYA CANCUN
PLAYA CANCUN
CTE PLAYA CANCUN
CTE PLAYA BRISAS
VIA VILARTA
VIA PLAYA DE CORTES
CTE PLAYA AZTECA
PLAYA ADERA
PLAYA NA ORTE
ALERO ST
BELARDO DR
MONTES ST
ALEJO
ALEJO PL
ALEJO LN
MONTESA

CTE PLAYA DE CORTES

TIERRAZA
CLJ QUINTANA
PLAYA CATALINA
PLAYA LAGUNA
VIA PLAYA SANTOS
CTE PLAYA CATALINA
VIA PLAYA CATALINA

5100
5200

0 .125 .25 .375 .5
miles 1 in. = 1900 ft.

SEE 1250 MAP

SAN CLEMENTE CANYON
GREEN FARM RD

CANYON

SAN
FA

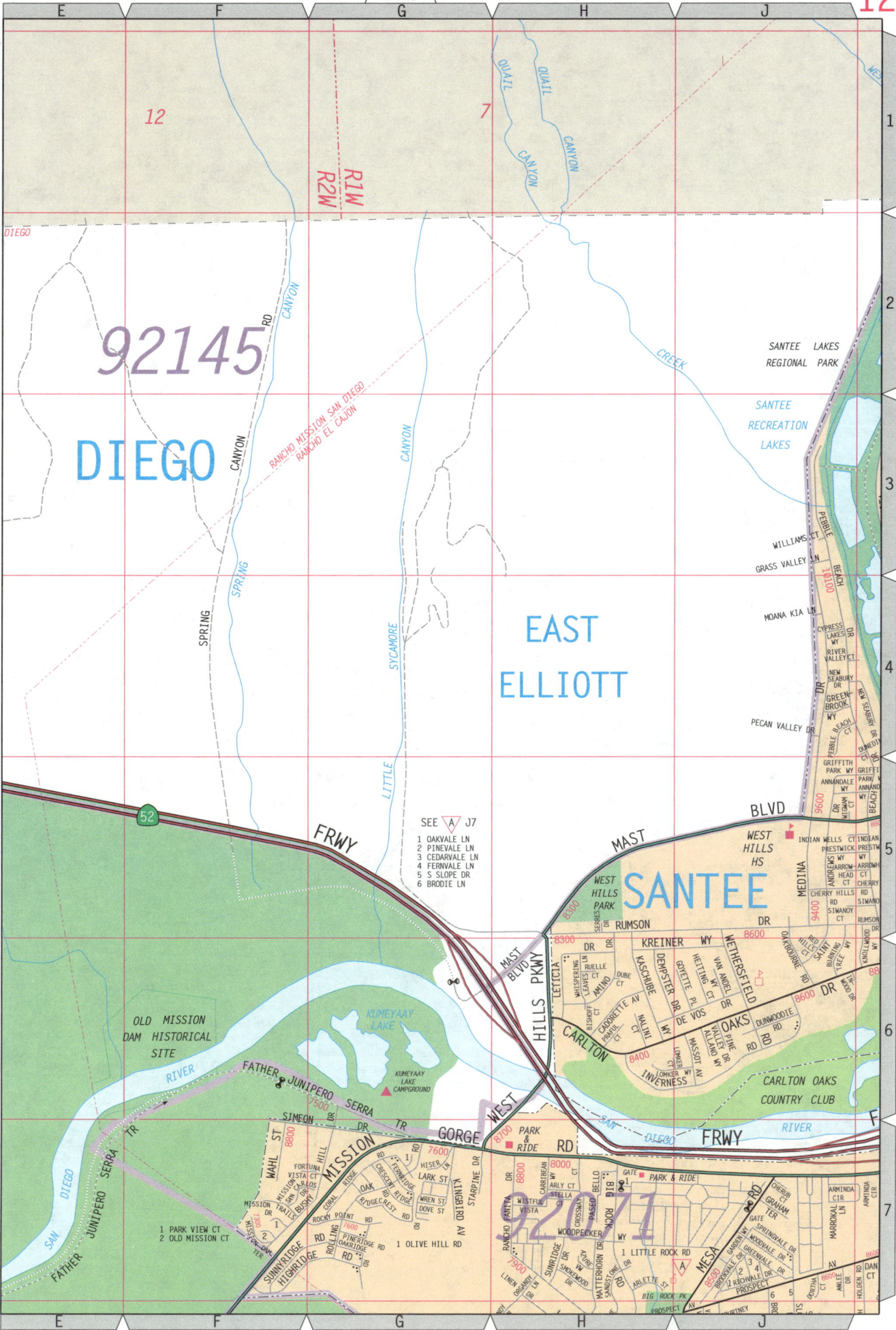

E F G H J

R1W
R2W

DIEGO

1

QUAIL CANYON
QUAIL CANYON

CREEK

SANTEE LAKES
REGIONAL PARK

2

12

7

92145

SANTEE
RECREATION
LAKES

3

DIEGO

RD
CANYON

RANCHO MISSION SAN DIEGO
RANCHO EL CAJON

CANYON

SPRING
SPRING
SPRING

CANYON

SYCAMORE

EAST

ELLIOTT

LITTLE

WILLIAMS CT
GRASS VALLEY LN

MOANA KIA LN

CYPRESS
LAKES
WY
RIVER
VALLEY CT
NEW
SEABURY
DR
GREEN-
BROOK
WY

PEBBLE BEACH
CT

PECAN VALLEY DR

GRIFFITH
PARK WY
ANNANDALE
WY

DINEDIN

PEBBLE
BEACH
DR

BEACH

NEW SEABURY DR

GRIFFITH
PARK W
ANNAN-
DALE

SEE 1231 MAP

4

92
52
FRWY

SEE A J7
1 OAKVALE LN
2 PINEVALE LN
3 CEDARVALE LN
4 FERNVALE LN
5 S SLOPE DR
6 BRODIE LN

MAST BLVD

MAST

BLVD

WEST
HILLS
HS

INDIAN WELLS CT INDIAN
PRESTWICK
WY
ARROW-
HEAD CT
ANDREWS
WY

PRESTW

ARROWH

CHERRY
CT

MEDINA

CHERRY HILLS
RD
SIWANOY
CT

CHERRY

SIWANO

9600
DR
WILLIAM
CT

BEACH

5

WEST
HILLS
PARK

8300

SANTEE

RUMSON

SIWANOY DR

RUMSON

SAINT
BURNING
TREE WY

OAKBOURNE RD

KNOLLWOOD

RED
HILLS
CT

8600

MAST BLVD

HILLS PKWY

MAST BLVD

8300
DR
DR

KREINER WY

8600
WETHERSFIELD

DEMPSTER DR
GOYETTE
PL
HEITING
WY
VAN ANDEL

8600 DR

88

6

LETICIA

WHISPERING
LEAVES LN
RUELLE
CT
BISMOFF
CT
CADORETTE AV
CAROLIN
CT
NALINI
DE VOS
WY
KASCHUBE

PINE
VALLEY DR
ALLANO WY
MASSOT AV

OAKS

DUNWOODIE
RD

OLD MISSION
DAM HISTORICAL
SITE

KUMEYAAY
LAKE

CARLTON

8400
LOWKER WY

INVERNESS

CARLTON OAKS
COUNTRY CLUB

F

KUMEYAAY
LAKE CAMPGROUND

RIVER

FATHER
JUNIPERO SERRA

TR

SAN DIEGO

FRWY

RIVER

WEST
GORGE
RD

7500

FATHER JUNIPERO SERRA TR

SAN DIEGO RIVER

FATHER

JUNIPERO SERRA TR

SIMEON
DR

MISSION

WAHL ST
8800
HILL
FORTUNA
VISTA CT
SAN CARLOS DR
BUSHY

OAK
CORAL
RD
RIDGECREST
ROCKY POINT
7600
PINERIDGE
OAKRIDGE

SUNNYRIDGE
HIGHRIDGE

ROLLING
RD

MISSION
GORGE
RD

RD

7600

MISSION
TRAIL
REGIONAL
PARK

HISER
FERNRIDGE

CREST RIDGE

LARK ST
WREN ST
DOVE ST

1 OLIVE HILL RD

7900

8700
RANCHO
FANITA
DR

KINGBIRD AV
STARPINE DR

8800

8000

PARK &
RIDE

WISTFUL
VISTA

ARLY CT
STELLA

CARRIBEAN
WY
CROSSWAY
PASEO

WOODPECKER
WY

92071

GATE
GATE

LINEN GARTH

SUNRIDGE DR

MATTERHORN DR

SMOKEWOOD

ARLETTE ST

PARK & RIDE

BELLO

BIG
ROCK
WY

1 LITTLE ROCK RD

BIG ROCK PK
AV

PROSPECT

MESA RD

A
1 RICHVALE DR
PROSPECT

8600

CHERIB
GRAHAM
GATE

SPRINGVALE DR

MOODALE CT
GREENVALE DR
GREENVALE AV

RD

ARMINDA
CIR

MARROKAL LN

ARMINDA

DAN CT

HOLDEN RD

DORTHA
CT

COURTNEY

BRO

ANLEE

6 5

1 PARK VIEW CT
2 OLD MISSION CT

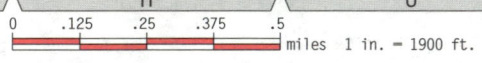

7

0 .125 .25 .375 .5 miles 1 in. = 1900 ft.

COPYRIGHT 2001

Thomas Bros. Maps®

N

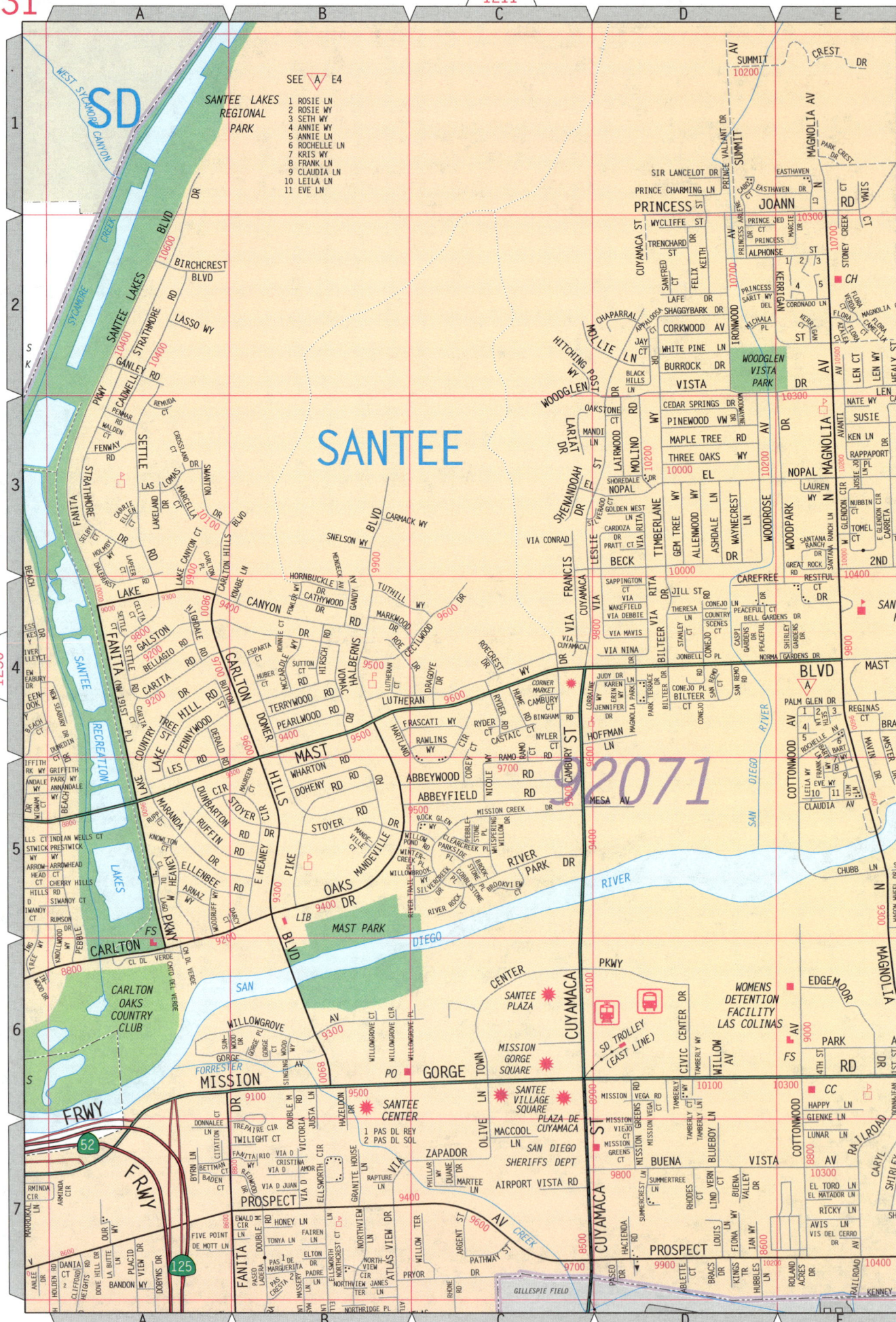

SD

SAN DIEGO CO.

MAP

SANTEE

92071

SANTEE LAKES REGIONAL PARK

SEE △ E4
1 ROSIE LN
2 ROSIE WY
3 SETH WY
4 ANNIE WY
5 ANNIE LN
6 ROCHELLE LN
7 KRIS WY
8 FRANK LN
9 CLAUDIA LN
10 LEILA LN
11 EVE LN

WEST SYCAMORE CANYON

SYCAMORE CREEK

CARLTON OAKS COUNTRY CLUB

WOODGLEN VISTA PARK

WOMENS DETENTION FACILITY LAS COLINAS

SANTEE PLAZA

MISSION GORGE SQUARE

SANTEE VILLAGE SQUARE

SANTEE CENTER

MAST PARK

GILLESPIE FIELD

SD TROLLEY (EAST LINE)

FANITA RECREATION LAKES

SANTEE LAKES BLVD
BIRCHCREST BLVD
STRATHMORE
MAGNOLIA AV
PRINCESS
JOANN
CUYAMACA ST
MISSION GORGE
CUYAMACA ST
CARLTON BLVD
MAST BLVD
WILLOWGROVE
FRWY 52
FRWY 125
PROSPECT

SEE 1211 MAP
SEE 1230 MAP
SEE 1251 MAP

0 .125 .25 .375 .5 miles   1 in. = 1900 ft.

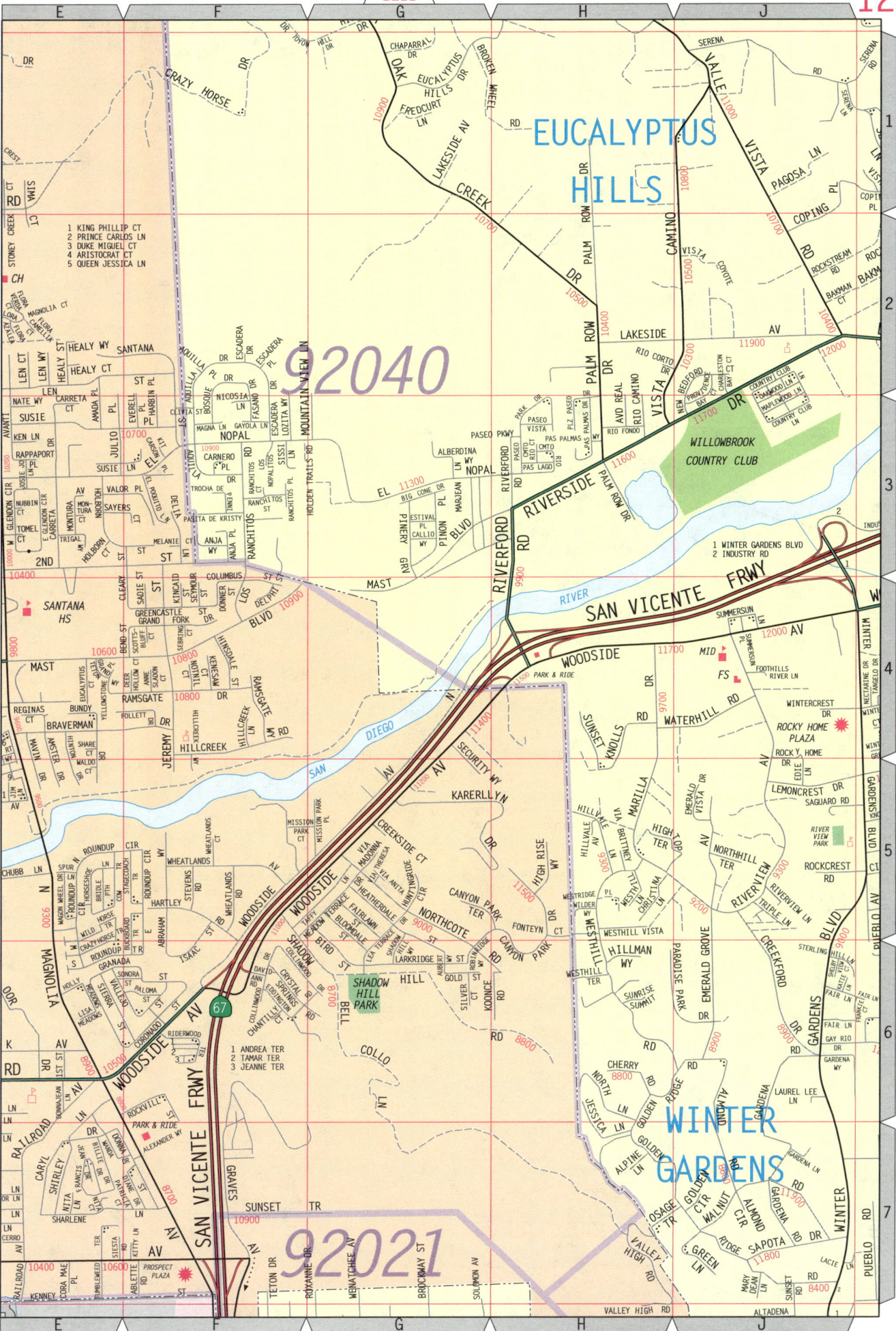

© COPYRIGHT 2001

Thomas Bros. Maps®

SAN DIEGO CO.

MAP

EUCALYPTUS HILLS

92040

92021

WILLOWBROOK COUNTRY CLUB

WINTER GARDENS

SAN VICENTE FRWY

SAN VICENTE FRWY

RIVERFORD RD

RIVERSIDE DR

WOODSIDE AV

MAGNOLIA AV

MOUNTAIN VIEW

SHADOW HILL PARK

RIVER VIEW PARK

Rocky Home Plaza

LAKESIDE AV

PALM ROW DR

VISTA CAMINO

VALLE VISTA

GARDENS BLVD

PUEBLO

SANTANA HS

PARK & RIDE

Prospect Plaza

1 KING PHILLIP CT
2 PRINCE CARLOS LN
3 DUKE MIGUEL CT
4 ARISTOCRAT CT
5 QUEEN JESSICA LN

1 WINTER GARDENS BLVD
2 INDUSTRY RD

1 ANDREA TER
2 TAMAR TER
3 JEANNE TER

67

SAN DIEGO RIVER

0 .125 .25 .375 .5 miles   1 in. = 1900 ft.

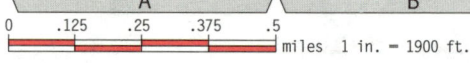

E F G H J

SAN DIEGO CO.

MAP

SEE 1233 MAP

WILLOW RD EXT 14200

EL MONTE RD 14800

MISS ELLIE LN 14500

VER

SILVER CREEK LN

PEBBLE CREEK LN

SLEEPY

CREEK

ROCK CREEK LN

POSSUM CREEK LN

BLOSSOM

CANYON

SPRINGS RD 10000

VALLE VERDE RD 10300 10350

CIRCA

LAZY CREEK 10100

KINGFISHER CREEK RD

FURNACE CREEK RD

10500

QUAIL

KING CRE

BLOS VAL

BLOSSOM VALLEY LN 10100

INDIAN CREEK LN

DRIFTWOOD CREEK RD

QUAIL COWEY 9800

VALLE CABALLO LN

LN

QUAIL VALLEY WY

RD

OAK CREEK RD 14800

SHANTEAU DR 14800

LAKE JENNINGS COUNTY PARK

DR

BLOSSOM VALLEY

QUAIL 9800

TRAIL

RED

DR

PONY LN

VALLEY

FLINN SPRINGS 9700

FS

FLINN SPRING RD

LAKE JENNINGS

BASS

K

RANCH

NEW COLT CT

FRWY

9600

MARINA SPRINGS LN

CRYSTAL VIEW RD

CIRCLE

FLINN SPRINGS RD

SADDLE HILL RD

FLINN LABRADOR LN

9100

SR 9400 RD

PROSPECTORS SQ

ARROWHEAD

BEAR CRATER

HAKONE

TELKAIF

GENEVA EDWARD

COMO

INDIAN

DALAI

VISTA HILLS JENNINGS WY

VISTA JENNINGS

VISTA JENNINGS ST TER

PALOMINO RIDGE DR

VISTA CT

VISTA DR

VISTA PANORAMA

BLOSSOM 9300

9300

ROCK LN

DEBBIE CT

CHIMNEY LN

DEVERILL DR

ERIC PL

BRIAN WY

FLINN CREST ST

9000

MIGUEL LN

80

FLINN SPRINGS COUNTY PARK

FLINN SPRINGS

AMERICAN SETTLERS RD STAGE COACH 13800

FREEDOM WY

HABBITT

BUTTERFIELD

EXPRESS TER

PIONEER

GOLD NUGGET

MINERS

PL

ALBERT RD

B

JENNINGS

SESI LN

ATTISHA WY 9100

HIGHWAY 14500

BOND CT

BOND AV

COSTA LN

COCHES

SPRING VIEW

SOLDIN LN

DEANLY CT

JACK OAK LN

JACK OAK

DEANLY RD

CHERYL LEE CT 14000

RANCHO DEL VILLA

RANCHO DEL CORTE

FS

PARK & RIDE

JENNINGS VISTA CIR

14200

OLDE 14100

SEE B F4
1 DIAMOND
2 FRANKLIN
3 GEORGE
4 FROME
5 TEHNSEN
6 BELOE
7 KLAMATH
8 LEWIS

92021

DEANLY WY

DEANLY

DEL ESTE PL

MILIA ER DR

DULENE PL

LYALL PL

SUMNER GLEN VISTA

DARRYL CT

RAMONA CT

SARAH CT

WYETH RD

PINKARD WY

PINKARD WY

LAKE VALLEY LN

13800 14000

FS

HILL RD

GAUCHO LN

ROUTE

PECAN

ALTA WY

SIERRA

KELLI LN

OLIVE

CALLE DR

ERNESTO

TWIN

PECAN TER

PINE

PARK LN

OAK OAK TER

PECAN TER

PECAN PEAK TER

LOS

LEGACY LN

14100

14290

RIOS

LEGACY CT

JOHNSTOWN

MITZI LN

EL DORADO PKWY 8700

8

13800

VIA CONSUELO

DEL

CHARRO TER

BLANCO

ROSADA WY

ROSADA

CASTANO LN

LANGHOLM RD 8600

RIDGE GORRION

CORDIAL LN

HAWICK DR

HAWICK TER

D

RUIS RD

RIOS CANYON LN 14300

CANYON

RD

RIOS

RIOS

GLENVIEW

PASEO DEL MAR

LAGUNA VISTA

LAGUNA VISTA

SANTA LUCIA

CANADA RD

MARBROOK

EAST COUNTY

STONEYBROOK

BRASKO RD

PIPING ROCK LN

ROCKY CREEK RD

TWELVE OAKS TR

LAKE VIEW LN

LA CRESTA BL

SUNNYBROOK LN

HORSMILL RD

0 .125 .25 .375 .5 miles 1 in. = 1900 ft.

SAN DIEGO CO.

MAP

SEE 1213 MAP

—N—

CLEVELAND

A B C D E

R1E R2E

13

18

19

24

25

26

30

92021

92019

KINGFISHER CREEK RD
QUAIL
HER RD
CANYON RD
TOMBSTONE CREEK RD 15100
CHAD RD 14800
BLOSSOM VALLEY LN
DILLON RD
REAL RD 10400
BROAD
MEADOW OAKS LN
EL CAPITAN PEAK 15400
OAKS RD
CARTA
RANCHO
SILVA
SILVER SPRING
HAWLEY
VACHELL LN 15500
TOYA LN
BON VUE DR
SAINT LUCY LN
EL CAPITAN REAL LN
EL CAPITAN REAL 10400
OAK
CREEK 15200
TOWNE LN
OAK
VIEW DR 9900
OAKMONT TER
SHANTEAU DR 14800
SNOW
ROBLEDO
SNAPDRAGON
WISTERIA
OLEANDER DAFFODIL
DOGWOOD
AZALEA
MAPLE
APPLE
EDELWEISS 15300
ELM
MARIGOLD
SPRUCE
WHITEHORN LN 9600
CARTA
REAL
HAWLEY PL
HAWLEY CT
HAWLEY CREEK
DELL VIEW RD 15600
VALLE DE PAZ RD
LAS LOMAS RD 15600
RD 10100
COCHES
HAWLEY
VIEWSIDE 15700
HIGHWAY 15400
VIEWSIDE
BLACK RIDGE
CEDAR RIDGE
E RIDGE
SILVER SPUR CT
SILVER SPUR RD
OAKS PL
SILVER SPRING
E CREEK RD
S PLAINS CT
DUNBAR PL
SILVER OAKS RD
DUNBAR
BRIDON
CREEK
BRIDON RD 9900
80
24
16000
CHOCOLATE LN
ALPINE
DIVELLOS DR 17000
OLDE
FLINN SPRINGS RD 15000
LOS
SEE 1232 MAP
CAJON
CAJON
EL
RIOS 14900
RANCHO
SERENA 1400
MONTANA
MONTANA SERENA CT
TRACEY LN
GIBSON
CANYON RD 1200
TONER CT
MOUNTAIN TOP DR
RYAN RIDGE RD
MOUNTAIN VIEW 1300
OLD MOUNTAIN VIEW RD
GREENHILL RD
HIGHLANDS PT 1500
PICTURESQUE
FERRELL LN 1400
MOUNTAIN VIEW RD
HARBISON
TH BAR RANCH TR 8000
BULLARD LN
BULLARD LN
BRIDLE RUN TER
BRIDLE RUN VW
BRIDLE RUN LN
BRIDLE RUN CT
BRIDLE RUN PL
BRIDLE RUN
MID
GALLOWAY 300
TAMMADGE HEIGHTS
TAMMADGE
A B C D E

SEE 1253 MAP

0 .125 .25 .375 .5 miles 1 in. = 1900 ft.

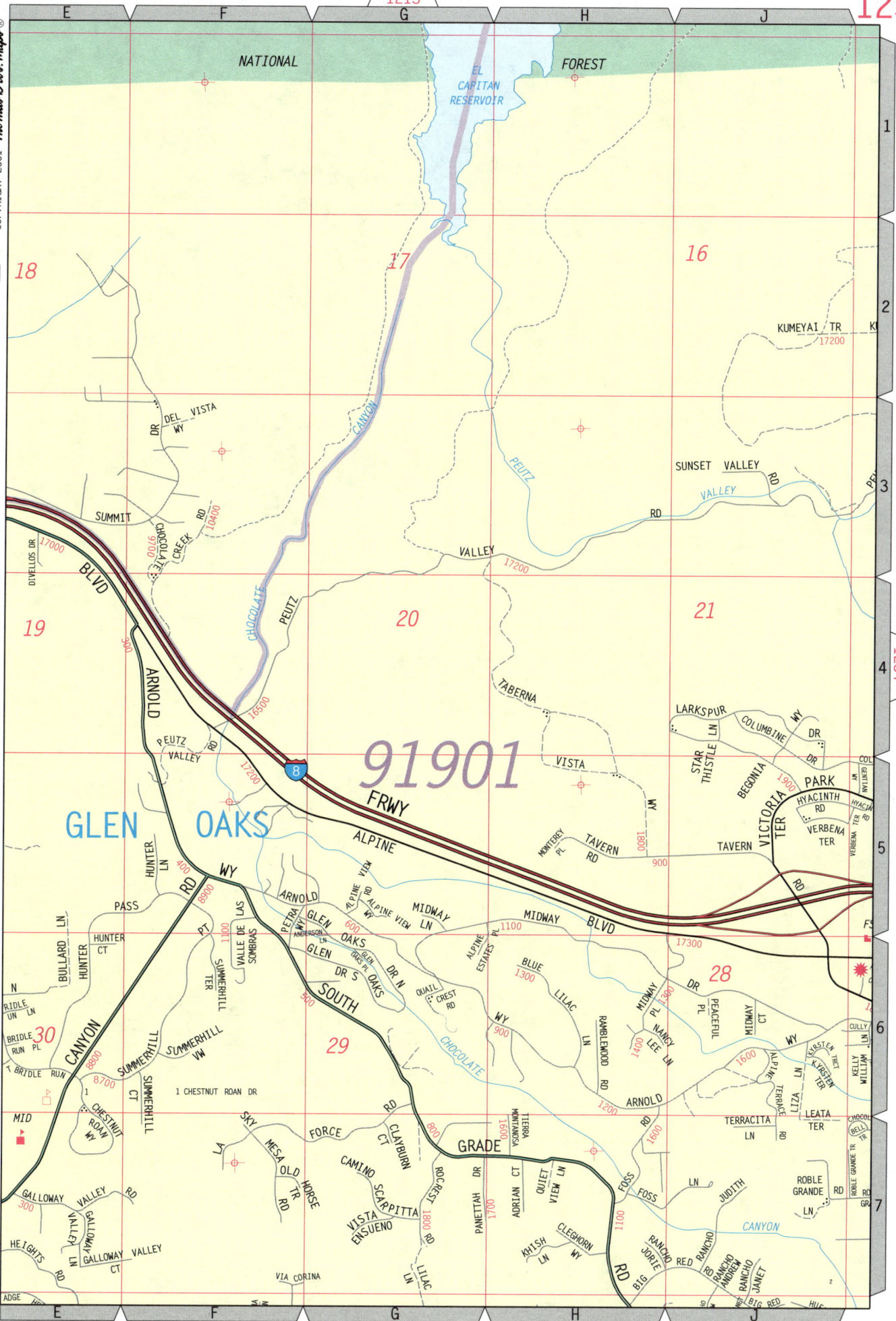

SAN DIEGO CO.

MAP

SEE 1213 MAP
SEE 1234 MAP
SEE 1253 MAP

E F G H J

NATIONAL   FOREST

EL CAPITAN RESERVOIR

18   17   16

KUMEYAI TR   17200

DEL VISTA DR WY

SUMMIT

CHOCOLATE CREEK RD   10400   9700

DIVELLOS DR   17000

BLVD

ARNOLD

PEUTZ   CANYON

CHOCOLATE

PEUTZ VALLEY

SUNSET VALLEY RD

VALLEY   VALLEY RD   17200

19   20   21

TABERNA

LARKSPUR LN   COLUMBINE DR   WY

STAR THISTLE LN   BEGONIA TER   1900   VICTORIA TER   PARK

VISTA   WY   1000

MONTEREY PL   TAVERN RD   900   TAVERN

HYACINTH RD   HYACH RD   VERBENA TER   VERBENA TER

300   16500   17200   8   91901

FRWY

GLEN OAKS

ALPINE   BLVD   17300

HUNTER LN   WY   RD   8900

PASS

BULLARD LN   HUNTER CT   HUNTER   PT   400   1000   LAS SOMBRAS   VALLE DE SEVILLE   SUMMERHILL TER   ARNOLD   PETRA WY   ANDERSON LN   GLEN OAKS PL N   ALPINE VIEW   ALPINE VIEW LN   MIDWAY LN   MIDWAY

ALPINE ESTATES PL   1100   ALPINE PL

GLEN OAKS DR S   GLEN OAKS DR N   QUAIL   CREST RD   BLUE   1300   LILAC   RAMBLEWOOD RD   MIDWAY PL   1300   NANCY LEE LN   1400   DR   PEACEFUL PL   MIDWAY CT   WY   28

N   RIDLE UN LN   BRIDLE RUN PL   30   CANYON   8800   SUMMERHILL CT   SUMMERHILL   SUMMERHILL VW   500   SOUTH   29   CHOCOLATE   WY   900   ARNOLD   1200   RD   1600   ALPINE TERRACE   LIZA   CULLY LN   KIRSTEN TRCT   KIRSTEN TER   KELLY WILLIAM

BRIDLE RUN   8700   1 CHESTNUT ROAN DR   LEATA TER

MID   CHESTNUT ROAN WY   1   TERRACITA LN   ROBLE GRANDE RD   CHOCOL BELL TR

LA   SKY   MESA   OLD   HORSE   RD   FORCE   CT   CLAYBURN   GRADE   ROC REST RD   1800   PANETTAH DR   1700   TIERRA MONTANOSA LN   1600   ADRIAN CT   QUIET VIEW LN   FOSS   1100   FOSS   LN   JUDITH   ROBLE GRANDE RD   ROBLE GRANDE TR

GALLOWAY VALLEY   300   CAMINO SCARPITTA   VISTA ENSUENO   890   KHISH LN   CLEGHORN WY   RD   RANCHO JORIE   RANCHO RED RD   RANCHO ANDREW   RANCHO JANET   CANYON

HEIGHTS   GALLOWAY VALLEY LN   GALLOWAY VALLEY CT   VALLEY   RD   LILAC LN   BIG   RED   HUE

ADGE   VIA CORINA

E F G H J

SAN DIEGO CO.

COPYRIGHT 2001 Thomas Bros. Maps® —N—

SEE 429 MAP

A   B   C   D   E

CAPITAN GRANDE INDIAN RESERVATION

1

15   14

CLEVELAND

WEST VALLEY

2

KUMEYAI TR 200   TR   17300

VIEJAS RD 9600

WHISPERING TR

ANITA WY 9600

VALLEY   RD 2400

VISTA 9600

PEUTZ 2000

PEUTZ

BOUNDRY   TKTR

3

CURTIS LN

SNEATH WY   STARKEY WY

KLUCEWICH

ANDERSON RD

HOLLY 23 RD 3100

BRAUER PT

4

SNEATH

SANDLER CT

VARS WY   ARMEN ROUT LN

22

MCDOUGAL PL

SKY MOUNTAIN LN

OLD STAGECOACH RUN

OLD STAGECOACH

ENGLAND PL   WY   N

STARBRIGHT LN

KNOLLS CT   VICTORIA DR   KLUCEWICH RD

JOSH WY

RD

VICTORIA DR 2800

HOMEWARD WY

COYOTE RD

OAK   LEE LN

700

HOLLY RD 2900

ANDERSON DR 3000

ZUMBROTA RD

ACACIA LN

TORREON 3100 DR 800

PACIFIC SUNSET TR 3000

HEATHER LN

DAWN MARIE LN   RANCHO BRAYDON LN

BRAYDON LN

LINDSAY   MICHELLE TR DR

COLUMBINE RD

LOBELIA RD

QUAIL CREEK PL   VALETTA LN

HALE DR 2300

2400

POLK RD

800

VICTORIA

BIG BOULDER LN

OVERLAND SPUR

VICTORIA DR 1000

5

K TH

ENA TER

VICTORIA PARK TER

HYACINTH RD

WILD IRIS RD

SNAPDRAGON

VERBENA TER

COSGROVE DR

VICTORIA DR 2400 2300

VICTORIA 2100

ALPINE CEMETERY

NIGHT STAR PL   NIGHT STAR CT   SHOOTING STAR PL   CIR

VICTORIA MEADOWS DR

COUNTRY MEADOWS RD

VICTORIA HEIGHTS PL

OVERLAND PASG

OTTO DR 2200   AV

FRWY

FS

BOULDERS RD   BOULDER LN   BOULDERS CT

ALPINE GLEN PL   MARSHALL RD

27   2100

2100

VICTORIA PL   1400

VICTORIA LN

26

OTTO DR

8

FS

6

ALPINE CREEK CTR

ADMINISTRATION WY

ARNOLD   SUNSET PL

CULLY CT

ALPINE GROVE LN

CONEJO LN

VINEYARD VILLAGE WY

CALLE VIEJAS

PLAZA CIR   CTE AMOR

PLAZA

ALPINE VILLAGE

VILLAGE

LIB

PO

CC

WHEELER ST

ALPINE

ALPINE 2300

MARSHALL RD

ELTINGE

MARSHALL WY 2800

RAMSEY KNOLL CT   TERRACE

SMOKEY MEAD LN

HIALEAH DR

CALIENTE CT

TERRACE RD 2700

ROCK TERRACE RD

RIVER SHADOW

SUNWY LN

OLDE SOUTH GRADE RD

HIGHLANDS WY

2900

RIVER DANCE CT

RIVER DANCE WY

SUNCREST VISTA LN

BLVD 3600

FS

GARDIAN

KELLY

WILLIAM CT

TAVERN CT

ALPINE CREEK LN

CHOCOLATE

BELL TR

BALL RANCH RD

OAK   HAVEN RD

ROBLE GRANDE TR

ROBLE GRANDE RD

OLIVEWOOD RD

MARIOLA

CORTE AMOR

MANZANA DR

MARSHALL CT 1700

WEST WINDS RIDGE

PIMLICO PL

MISS ELLE WY 1400

KENDA WY

ELTINGE PL

DR 2600

LOUISE WY

BLUEBERRY HILL

SAGE VIEW DR

MANZANITA VIEW

VIEJAS VIEW

OLIVE VIEW 2900

VIEW PL

PINE VIEW

SCENIC VIEW PL

VIEJAS RD

PALO VERDE

7

RD

2

1900

1800

1500

1061

1800

SOUTH GRADE RD

SCENIC VIEW PL 2200

VERDE VIEW RD

OAK VIEW PL

CALLE CALETA VIEJAS

PASEO DONITO

VIA DONITO

CAMINO DEL VIE

BOULDER OAKS LN

ANGELA LN

ENGELMANN LN   OAK MANN LN

2400

3100

3000

A   B   C   D   E

SEE 1233 MAP

SEE 1254 MAP

MAP

0   .125   .25   .375   .5   miles   1 in. = 1900 ft.

VICTORIA

ALPINE

1234

—N—

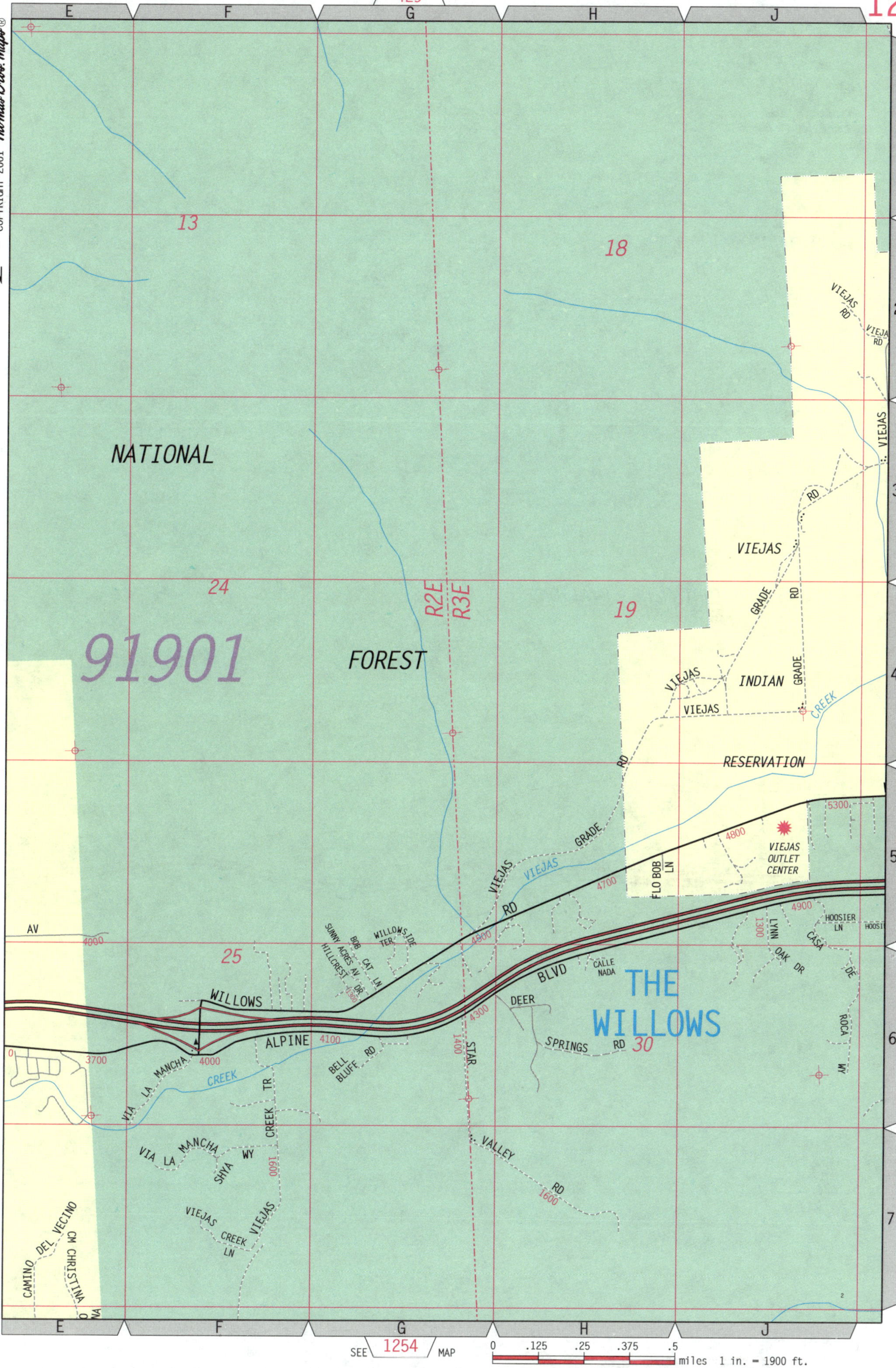

SAN DIEGO CO.

E   F   G   H   J

13

18

VIEJAS RD

VIEJAS RD

1

2

NATIONAL

VIEJAS RD

VIEJAS

3

24

FOREST

R2E R3E

19

VIEJAS

INDIAN

GRADE RD

GRADE RD

GRADE CREEK

4

SEE 1235 MAP

91901

VIEJAS

VIEJAS

RESERVATION

5300

4800

4700

VIEJAS OUTLET CENTER

FLO BOB LN

5

AV

4000

VIEJAS GRADE

VIEJAS

RD

4900

VIEJAS

HOOSIER LN

HOOSI

LYNN OAK DR

CASA DE

1300

4900

25

WILLOWS IDE TER

SUNNY ACRES AV DR

BOB CAT LN

HILLCREST

4500

BLVD

CALLE NADA

THE

WILLOWS

ROCA WY

WILLOWS

DEER

30

ALPINE 4100

4300

SPRINGS RD

6

VIA LA MANCHA

0   3700   4000

BELL BLUFF RD

STAR

1400

CREEK

CREEK TR

VIA LA MANCHA WY

SHVA WY

0091

VALLEY

RD

1600

7

CAMINO DEL VECINO

CM CHRISTINA

NA

VIEJAS CREEK LN

VIEJAS

2

E   F   G   H   J

MAP

0 .125 .25 .375 .5

miles 1 in. = 1900 ft.

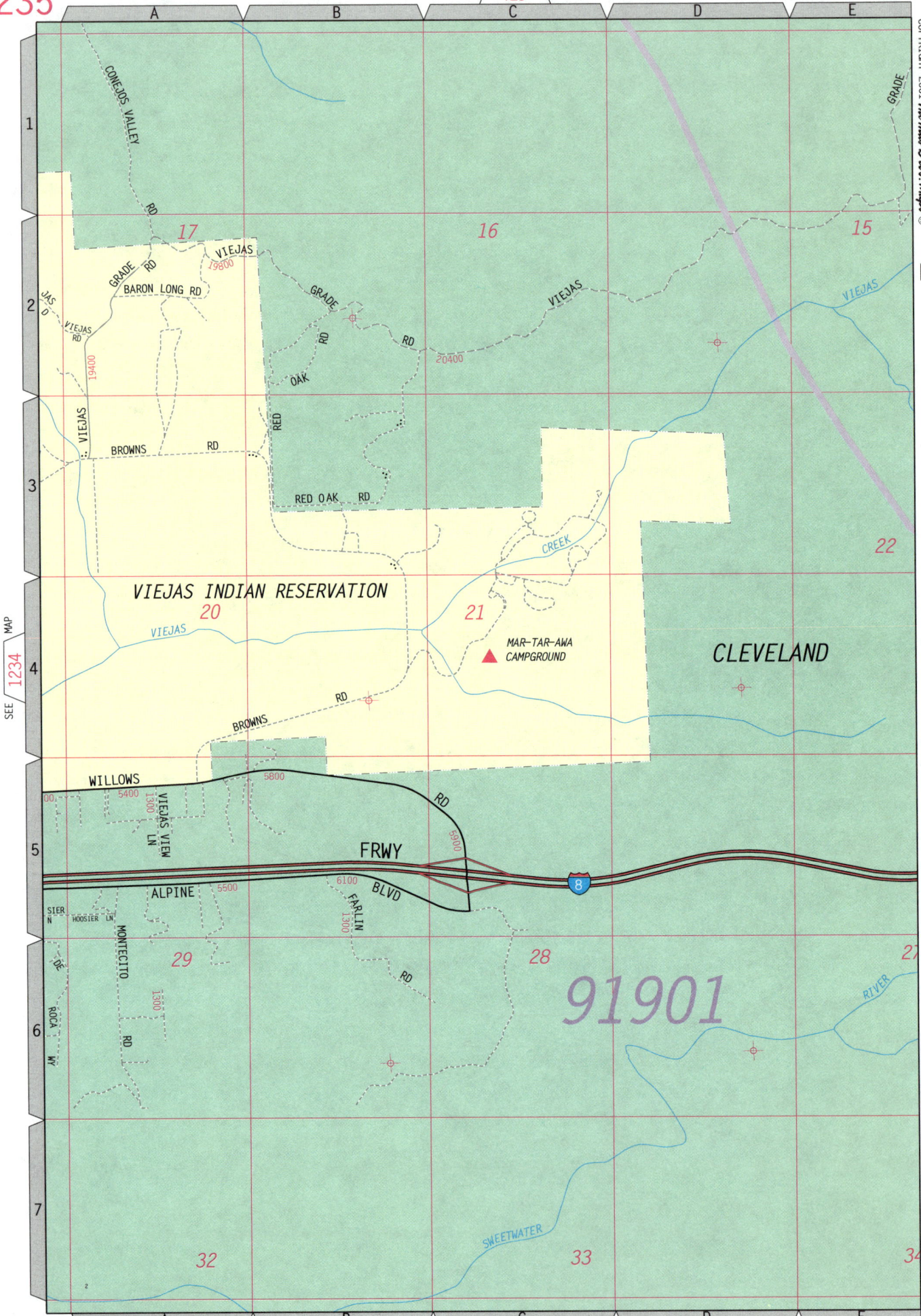

SAN DIEGO CO.

MAP

SEE 1234 MAP

A B C D E

1

17 16 15

CONEJOS VALLEY RD

GRADE

GRADE RD

BARON LONG RD

JAS D

VIEJAS RD 19400

19800

VIEJAS

2

GRADE RD

OAK

RED

RD 20400

VIEJAS

VIEJAS

3

BROWNS RD

RED OAK RD

22

CREEK

VIEJAS INDIAN RESERVATION

20 21

VIEJAS

4

BROWNS RD

MAR-TAR-AWA CAMPGROUND

CLEVELAND

WILLOWS

5800

5400

VIEJAS VIEW LN 1300

RD

5900

5

FRWY

8

ALPINE 5500

6100

BLVD

FARLIN 1300

SIER N

HOOSIER LN

MONTECITO

DE

ROCA

WY

RD 1300

RD

29 28 27

91901

RIVER

6

7

SWEETWATER

32 33 34

A B C D E

0 .125 .25 .375 .5

miles 1 in. = 1900 ft.

—N—

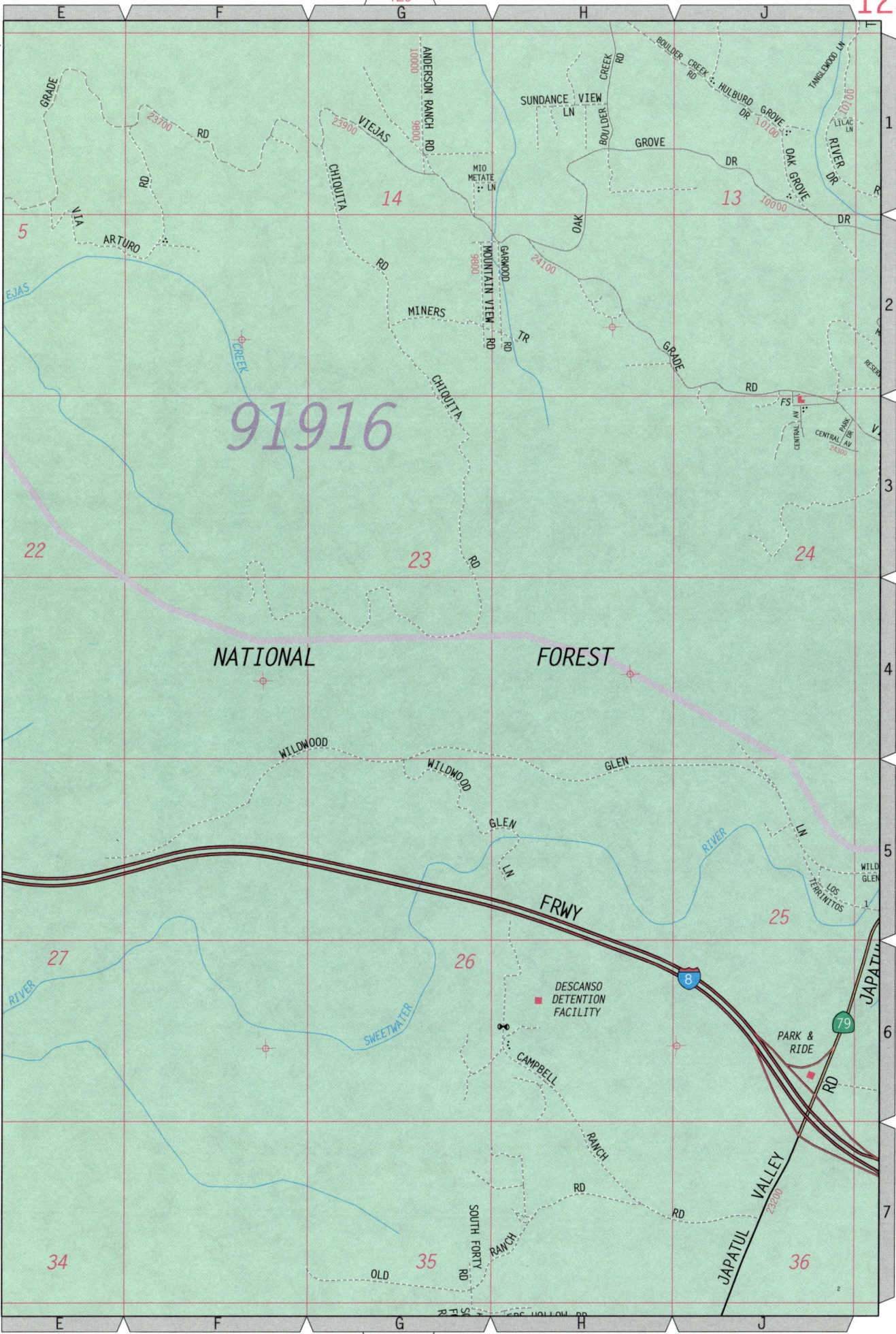

SEE 429 MAP

SAN DIEGO CO.

MAP

COPYRIGHT 2001 Thomas Bros. Maps®

N

| E | F | G | H | J |

GRADE

VIA ARTURO

VIEJAS

CHIQUITA RD

23700 RD

23900

ANDERSON RANCH RD 10000 9800

MIO METATE LN

MOUNTAIN VIEW RD 9800

GARWOOD RD

MINERS RD

CHIQUITA RD

TR

SUNDANCE VIEW LN

BOULDER CREEK RD

OAK GROVE DR

OAK GROVE DR

BOULDER CREEK RD

HULBURD GROVE DR 10100

TANGLEWOOD LN

LILAC LN

RIVER DR

10100

10000

GRADE RD

24100

24300

FS

CENTRAL AV

CENTRAL AV

PARK DR

RESERV

91916

5 14 13

22 23 24

NATIONAL   FOREST

WILDWOOD

WILDWOOD GLEN

GLEN

GLEN LN

LN

RIVER

LOS TERRITOS

WILD GLEN

SEE 1236 MAP

FRWY

27 26 25

RIVER

SWEETWATER

DESCANSO DETENTION FACILITY

CAMPBELL

RANCH

RD

I-8

79

PARK & RIDE

JAPATUL

JAPATUL VALLEY RD 23200

SOUTH FORTY RD

RANCH

OLD

34 35 36

SEE 1255 MAP

| E | F | G | H | J |

0 .125 .25 .375 .5 miles 1 in. = 1900 ft.

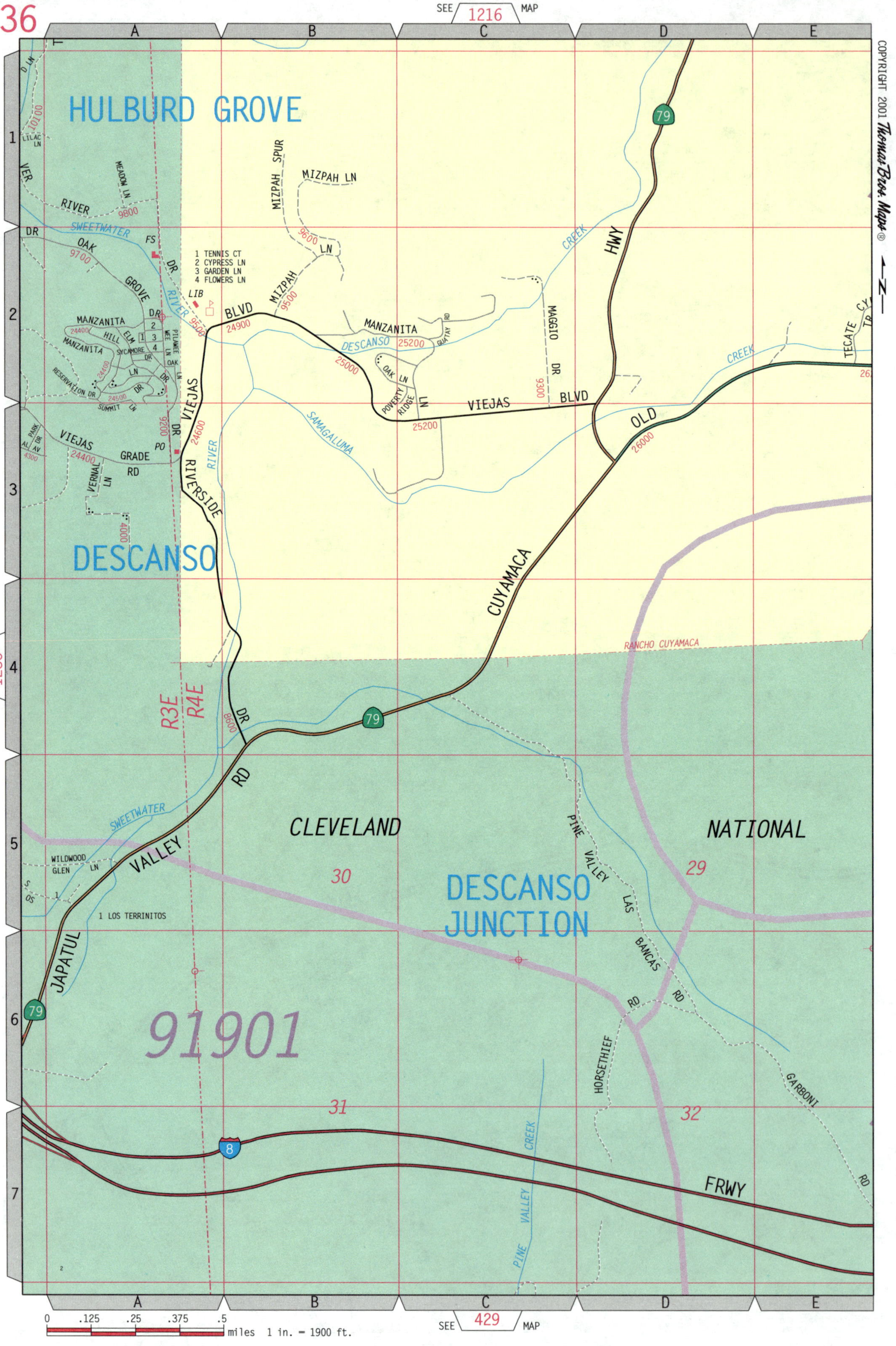

SAN DIEGO CO.

MAP

SEE 1216 MAP

COPYRIGHT 2001 Thomas Bros. Maps ® ←N→

A B C D E

HULBURD GROVE

1

DIM LN
LILAC LN
10100
VER
RIVER
DR
SWEETWATER

MEADOW LN
9800

MIZPAH SPUR
MIZPAH LN
9600
LN

OAK
9700
GROVE
DR
FS
LIB
RIVER DR
9500

1 TENNIS CT
2 CYPRESS LN
3 GARDEN LN
4 FLOWERS LN

MIZPAH
9500

2

MANZANITA HILL
24400
MANZANITA
24400
RESERVATION DR
24400
24500
SUMMIT LN
PILLWEE LN
WEE LN
OAK
SYCAMORE DR
ELM
LN
DR

BLVD
24900

DESCANSO
25000
MANZANITA
25200

GAITAY RD

MAGGIO
DR
9000

VIEJAS BLVD

OLD

VIEJAS GRADE RD
PARK AL AV
4300
VIEJAS
24400
VERNAL LN
PO
24600
RIVERSIDE
RIVER
24600
9000

OAK LN
POVERTY RIDGE LN
25200

26000

3

DESCANSO

SAMAGALUMA
RIVER

CUYAMACA

R3E R4E

8600
DR

RANCHO CUYAMACA

4

SEE 1235 MAP

79

5

SWEETWATER

VALLEY

WILDWOOD GLEN LN
S OS
1

CLEVELAND
30

PINE VALLEY

NATIONAL
29

DESCANSO JUNCTION

1 LOS TERRINITOS

JAPATUL

LAS BANCAS RD

6

79

91901

HORSETHIEF RD

GARBONI

7

31
8
FRWY

PINE VALLEY CREEK

32

A B C D E

0 .125 .25 .375 .5 miles 1 in. = 1900 ft.

SEE 429 MAP

SAN DIEGO CO.

E   F   G   H   J

91916

15

16

CREEK

RD

FLAT

SAMAGALUMA

FARLEY

RANCHO CUYAMACA

TECATE CYPRESS TR

26200

HIGHWAY

SAMAGATUMA VALLEY RD

GATE

GUATAY

21

26600

80

22

GUATAY VIEW LN

HAMILTON LN

CHRIS LN

9200

9000

27600

91931

1

2

3

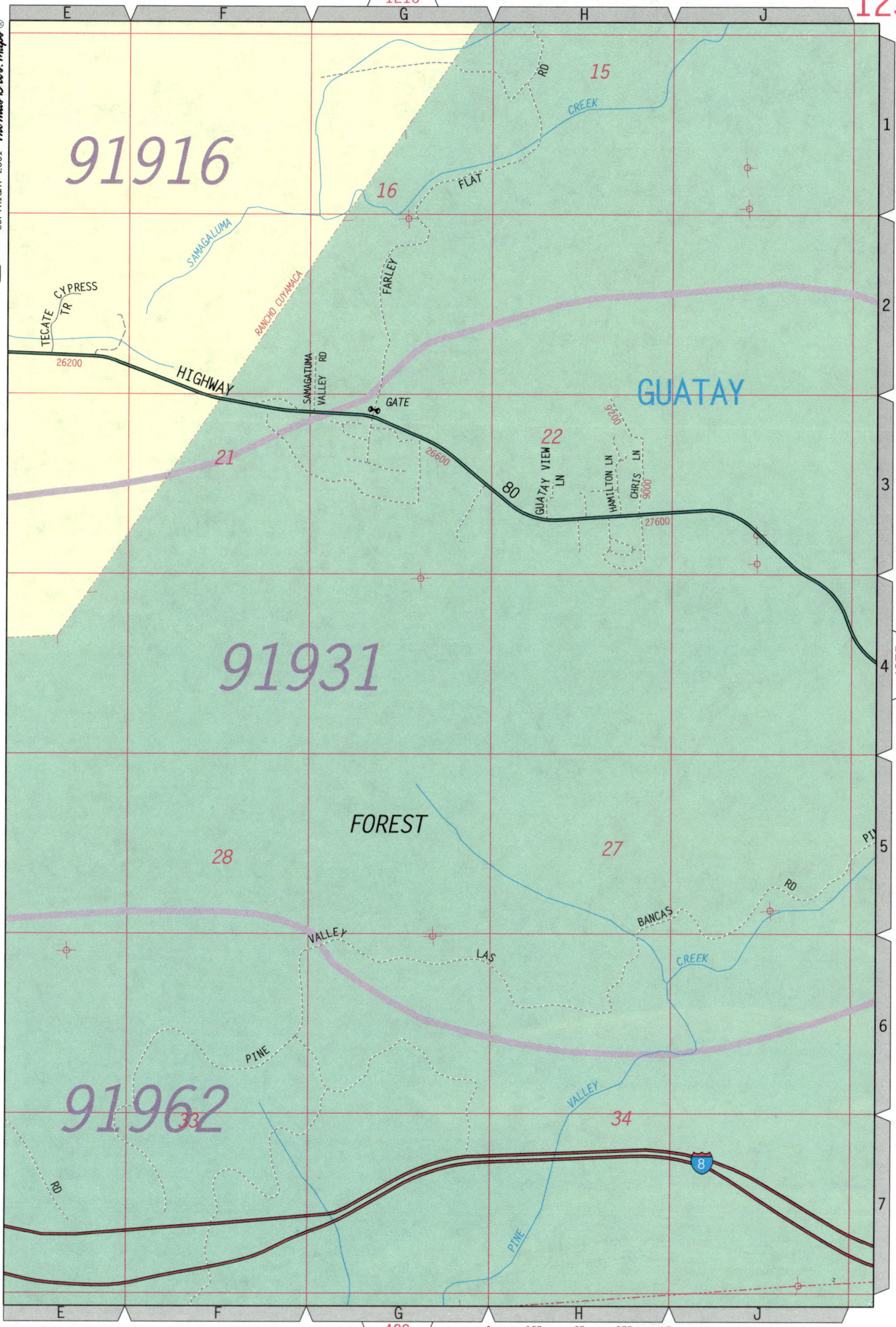

SEE 1237 MAP

4

FOREST

28

27

PI

RD

BANCAS

VALLEY

LAS

CREEK

5

6

91962

33

PINE

RD

VALLEY

34

PINE

8

7

E   F   G   H   J

0   .125   .25   .375   .5

miles   1 in. = 1900 ft.

MAP

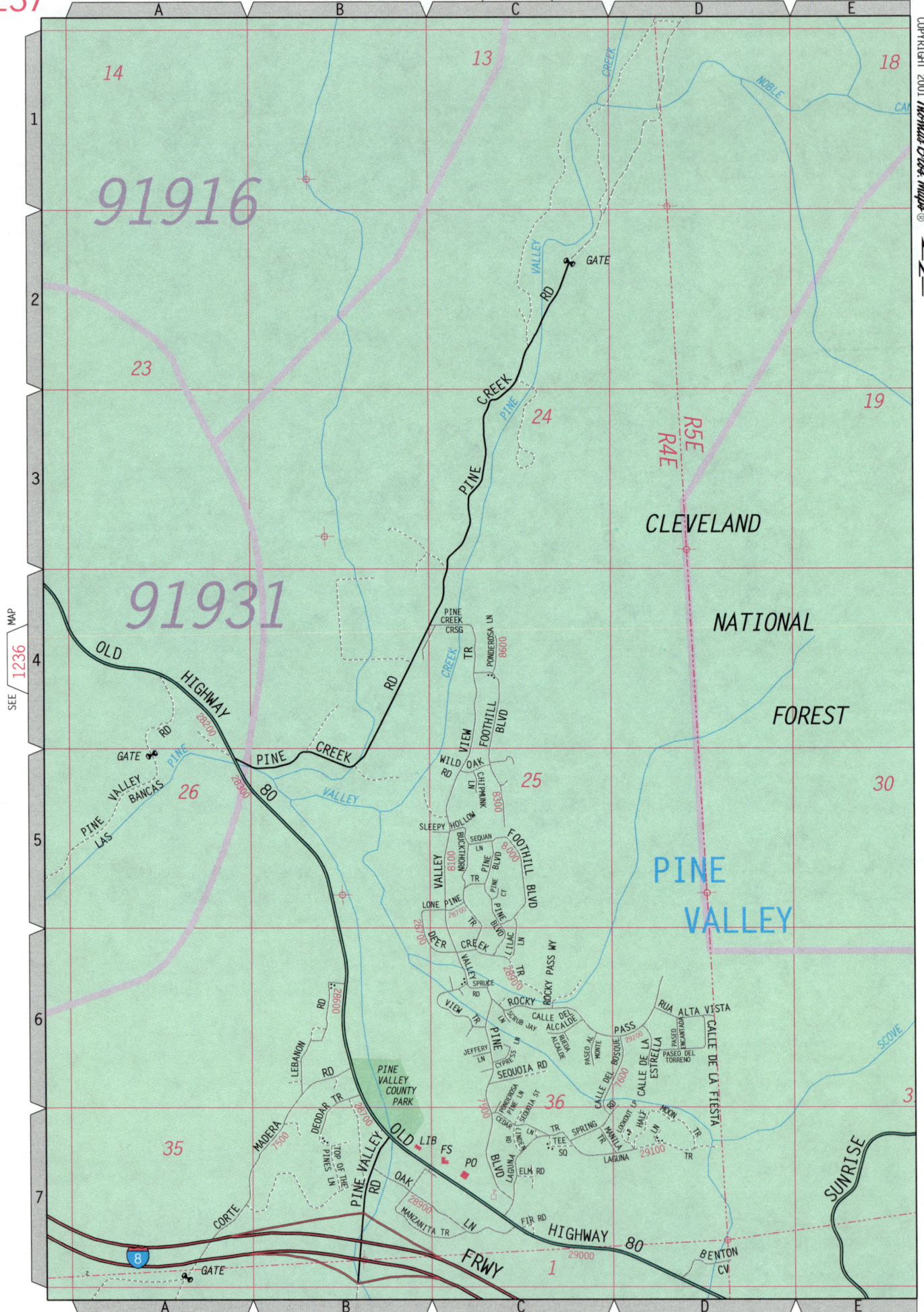

←—N—→

SAN DIEGO CO.

MAP

91916

91931

SEE 1216 MAP

A   B   C   D   E

14   13   18

23   24   R5E   19
                          R4E

CLEVELAND

NATIONAL

91931

SEE 1236 MAP

OLD   HIGHWAY

PINE CREEK CRSG

FOREST

PONDEROSA LN 8600

FOOTHILL BLVD

VIEW

WILD OAK RD   8300

CHIPMUNK

25   30

GATE

PINE VALLEY BANCAS   26   28000

PINE LAS

SLEEPY HOLLOW

BUCKTHORN   8100

SEQUAN LN

FOOTHILL BLVD

PINE BLVD 8100

PINE CT

VALLEY 8100

LONE PINE   28700

DEER   CREEK VALLEY

SPRUCE RD

ROCKY

PINE BLVD   28900

LILAC LN

ROCKY PASS WY

PINE VALLEY

28600

VIEW TR

SCRUB JAY LN

PINE

LN

Calle del ALCALDE

PASEO AL MONTE

PASS

RUA ALTA VISTA

CALLE DE LA FIESTA

SCOVE

JEFFERY LN

CYPRESS LN

SEQUOIA RD

CALLE DEL BOSQUE

Calle de la ESTRELLA

PASEO DEL TORRENO

RRAMNJ IMJNO

LEBANON RD

PINE VALLEY COUNTY PARK

OLD

PONDEROSA PINE LN

SEQUOIA ST

MANILA TR

SPRING TK

HALF MOON TR

MADERA 7500

DEODAR TR   28100

PINE VALLEY RD

LIB

FS

PO

CEDAR RD

PONDEROSA PINE LN

PINE

TR

SQ

LAGUNA

SUNRISE

35

TOP OF THE PINES LN

OAK

28900

BLVD

LAGUNA

ELM RD

TEE

36

7500   7600

LOCKOUT LP

29100

CORTE

GATE

MANZANITA TR

LN

FIR RD

HIGHWAY   80

8

FRWY   29000   1

BENTON CV

SEE 430 MAP

A   B   C   D   E

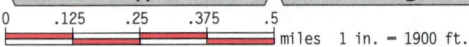

0   .125   .25   .375   .5

miles 1 in. = 1900 ft.

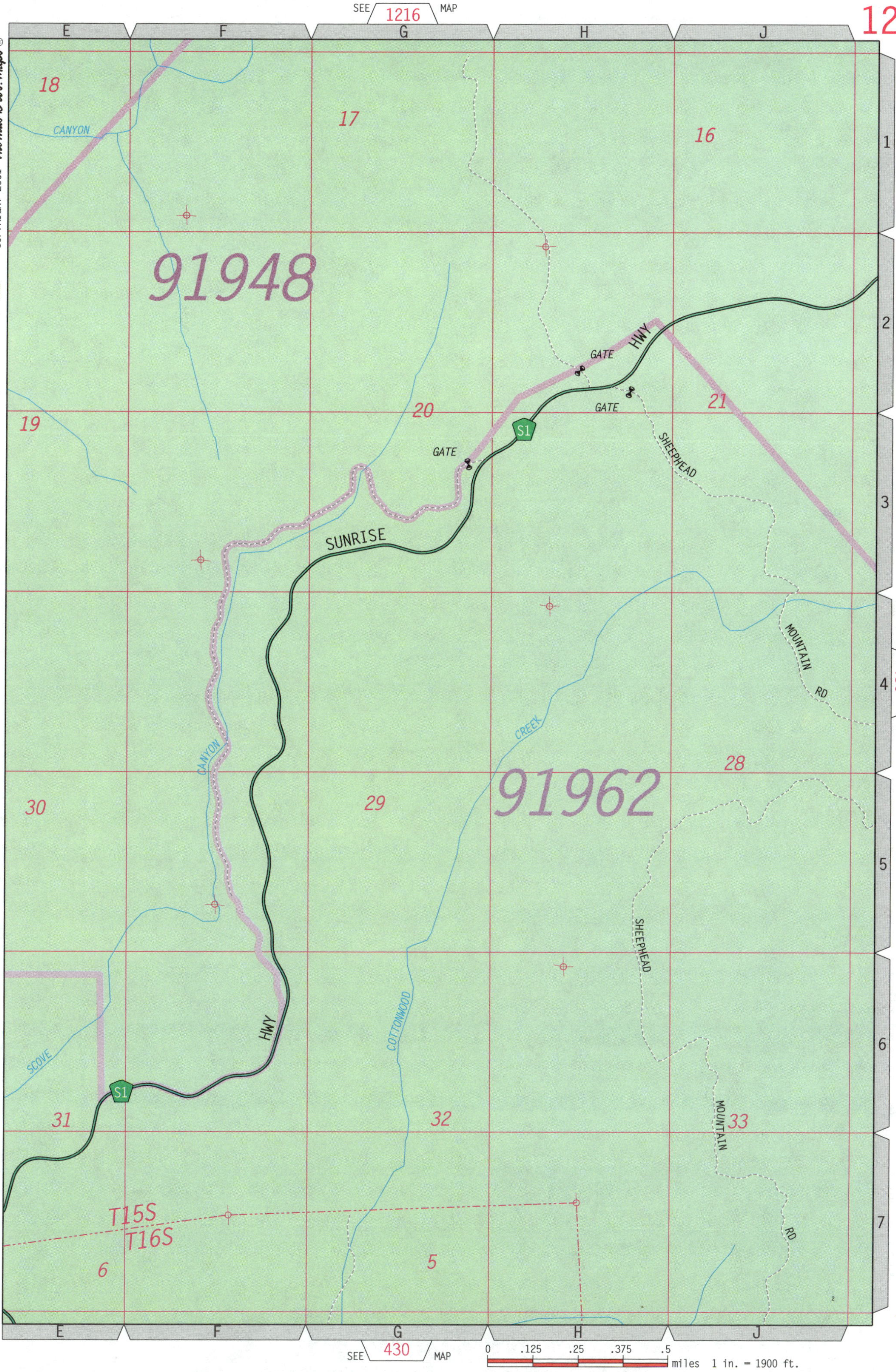

SAN DIEGO CO.

MAP

COPYRIGHT 2001

Thomas Bros. Maps ®

—N—

E   F   G   H   J

18

CANYON

17

16

1

91948

2

HWY

GATE

20

GATE

21

S1

GATE

SHEEPHEAD

19

3

SUNRISE

SEE 430 MAP

MOUNTAIN

RD

4

CREEK

28

91962

30

29

CANYON

5

SHEEPHEAD

6

SCOVE

COTTONWOOD

HWY

S1

MOUNTAIN

31

32

33

7

RD

T15S
T16S

6

5

E   F   G   H   J

0   .125   .25   .375   .5

miles   1 in. = 1900 ft.

SAN DIEGO CO.

MAP

SEE 1227 MAP

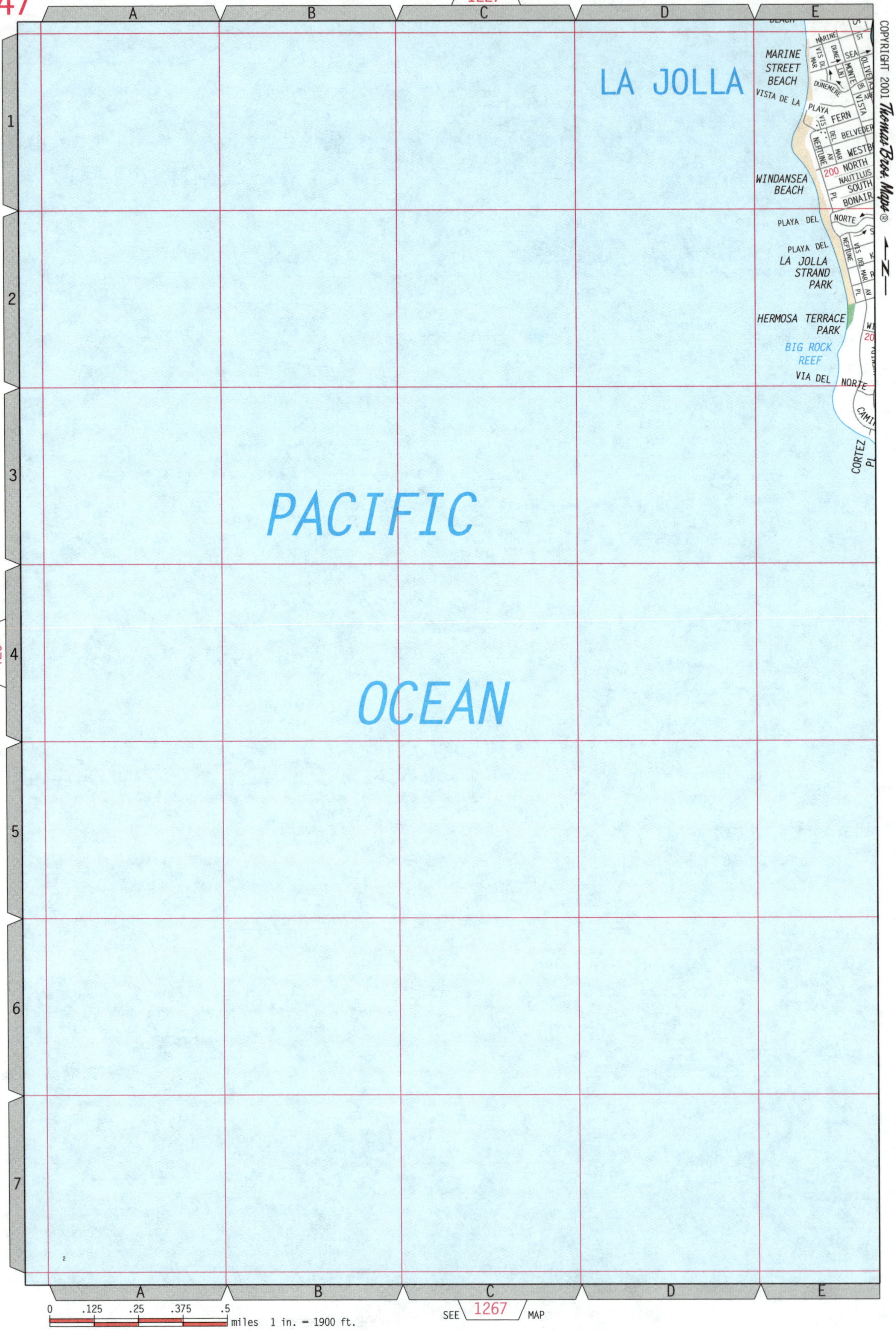

A B C D E

LA JOLLA

MARINE STREET BEACH

VISTA DE LA

WINDANSEA BEACH

PLAYA DEL

PLAYA DEL
LA JOLLA
STRAND
PARK

HERMOSA TERRACE PARK

BIG ROCK REEF

VIA DEL

VIA DEL NORTE

CAMI

CORTEZ PL

MARINE ST
DUNE
SEA LN
OLIVETAS
MONTE
CLARE
VISTA
DUNEMERE
PLAYA
FERN
VIS
DEL
MAR
NEPTUNE
BELVEDER
WESTB
NORTH
NAUTILUS
SOUTH
BONAIR
NORTE
NEPTUNE
VIS DEL MAR
K
PL
200

PACIFIC

OCEAN

SEE 429 MAP

1
2
3
4
5
6
7

2

0 .125 .25 .375 .5

miles 1 in. = 1900 ft.

SEE 1267 MAP

Thomas Bros. Maps®
COPYRIGHT 2001

SAN DIEGO CO.

MAP

—N—

E   F   G   H   J

1

LA JOLLA COUNTRY CLUB

MUIRLANDS DR

MINT CANYON

FAIRWAY

COUNTRY CLUB DR

NAUTILUS ST

SCENIC DR S

CASTEJON DR

SOLEDAD MOUNTAIN RD

SOLEDAD RD

2

92037

SAN DIEGO

LA JOLLA BLVD

MUIRLANDS DR

EL PASO REAL

EL CAMINO DEL TEATRO

LA JOLLA RANCHO RD

CARDENO DR

CALLE TIARA

CAMINITO ASCUA

3

LA JOLLA HERMOSA PARK

BIRD ROCK

SUN GOLD POINT

COSTA

CHELSEA

LA JOLLA BLVD

MESA

CANDLELIGHT DR

BAHIA VISTA WY

CARDENO DR

SOLEDAD RD

4

CALUMET PARK

COLIMA

MIDWAY

BELLEVUE AV

TAFT AV

COLIMA ST

NUYS ST

ARCHER ST

AGATE ST

TURQUOISE ST

FOOTHILL BLVD

FANUEL ST

LORING

5

TOURMALINE SURFING PARK

PACIFIC VIEW DR

OCEAN BLVD

PALISADES PARK (LAW ST PARK)

92109

MISSION BLVD

SAPPHIRE ST
OPAL ST
TOURMALINE ST
LORING ST
WILBUR
BERYL ST
BAYARD
LAW ST
CHALCEDONY ST
MISSOURI ST
DIAMOND ST

CASS ST

EVERTS ST

GRESHAM ST

INGRAHAM ST

HAINES

PACIFIC BEACH

PACIFIC BEACH COMM PARK

6

PACIFIC BEACH PARK

CRYSTAL PIER

OCEAN BLVD

EMERALD ST
GARNET AV
HORNBLEND
GRAND AV
THOMAS
REED
OLIVER

BAYARD
CASS ST
DAWES
EVERTS
FANUEL DR

GRESHAM

BEACH

7

MISSION BEACH

MISSION BEACH PARK

MISSION BLVD

SAIL BAY

MISSION BAY PARK

MISSION BAY

CATAMARAN RESORT HOTEL

FANUEL STREET PARK

PROMENADE AT PACIFIC BEACH

BOAT CENTER

0 .125 .25 .375 .5 miles   1 in. = 1900 ft.

SEE 1248 MAP

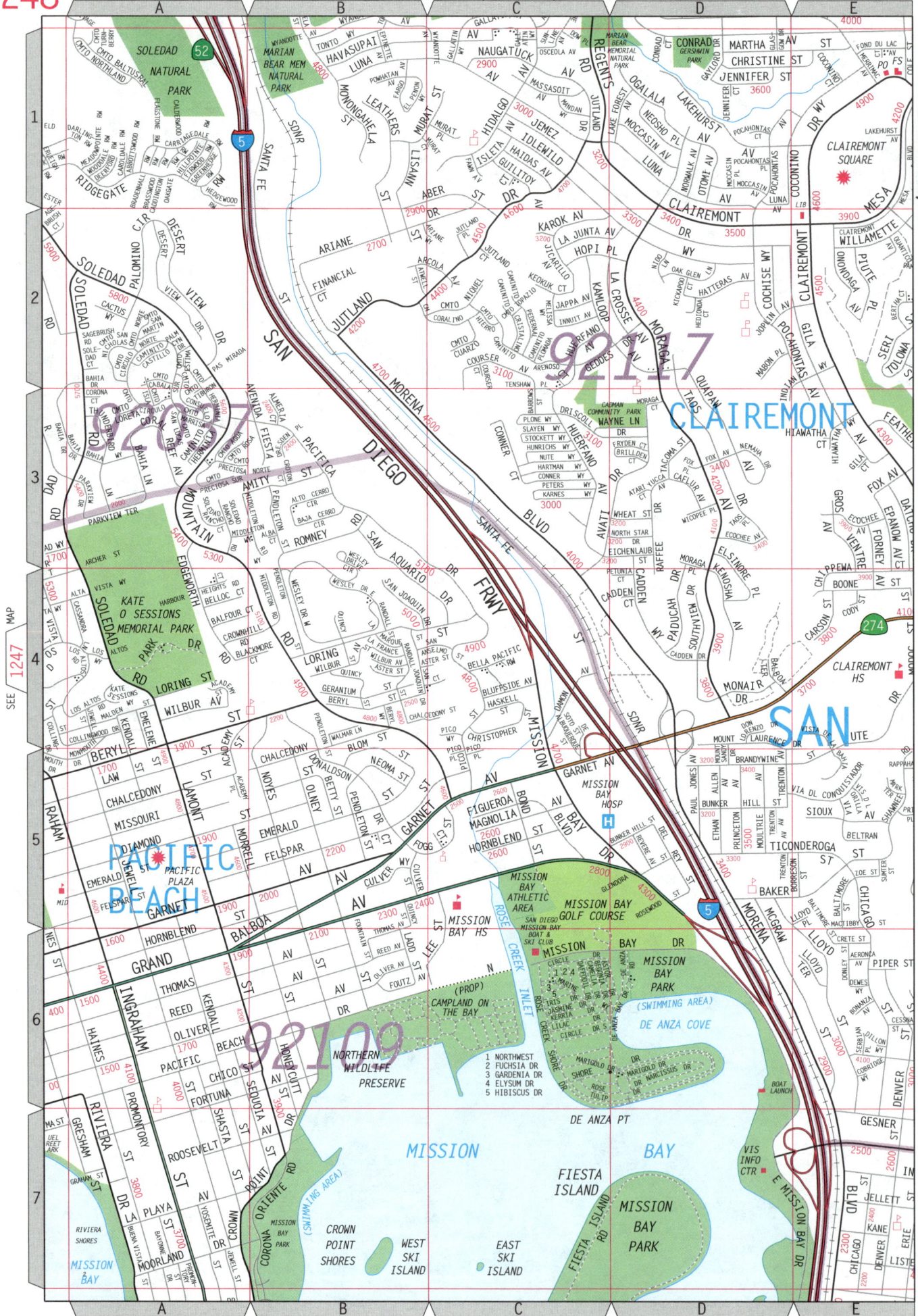

1248

SAN DIEGO CO.

MAP

SEE 1228 MAP

SEE 1247 MAP

SEE 1268 MAP

SOLEDAD NATURAL PARK

MARIAN BEAR MEM NATURAL PARK

MARIAN BEAR MEMORIAL NATURAL PARK

CONRAD GERSHWIN PARK

CLAIREMONT SQUARE

92117

92037

CLAIREMONT

CLAIREMONT HS

SAN

SAN DIEGO FRWY

SANTA FE

KATE O SESSIONS MEMORIAL PARK

BELLA PACIFIC RW

PACIFIC BEACH

92109

MISSION BAY HOSP

MISSION BAY ATHLETIC AREA

MISSION BAY GOLF COURSE

SAN DIEGO MISSION BAY BOAT & SKI CLUB

MISSION BAY PARK

DE ANZA COVE (SWIMMING AREA)

MISSION BAY HS

CAMPLAND ON THE BAY (PROP)

NORTHERN WILDLIFE PRESERVE

ROSE CREEK INLET

1 NORTHWEST
2 FUCHSIA DR
3 GARDENIA DR
4 ELYSUM DR
5 HIBISCUS DR

1 NORTHWEST
2 FUCHSIA DR
3 GARDENIA DR
4 ELYSUM DR
5 HIBISCUS DR

DE ANZA PT

MISSION BAY

FIESTA ISLAND

MISSION BAY PARK

VIS INFO CTR

BOAT LAUNCH

CROWN POINT SHORES

WEST SKI ISLAND

EAST SKI ISLAND

FIESTA ISLAND

RIVIERA SHORES

MISSION BAY

0   .125   .25   .375   .5

miles 1 in. = 1900 ft.

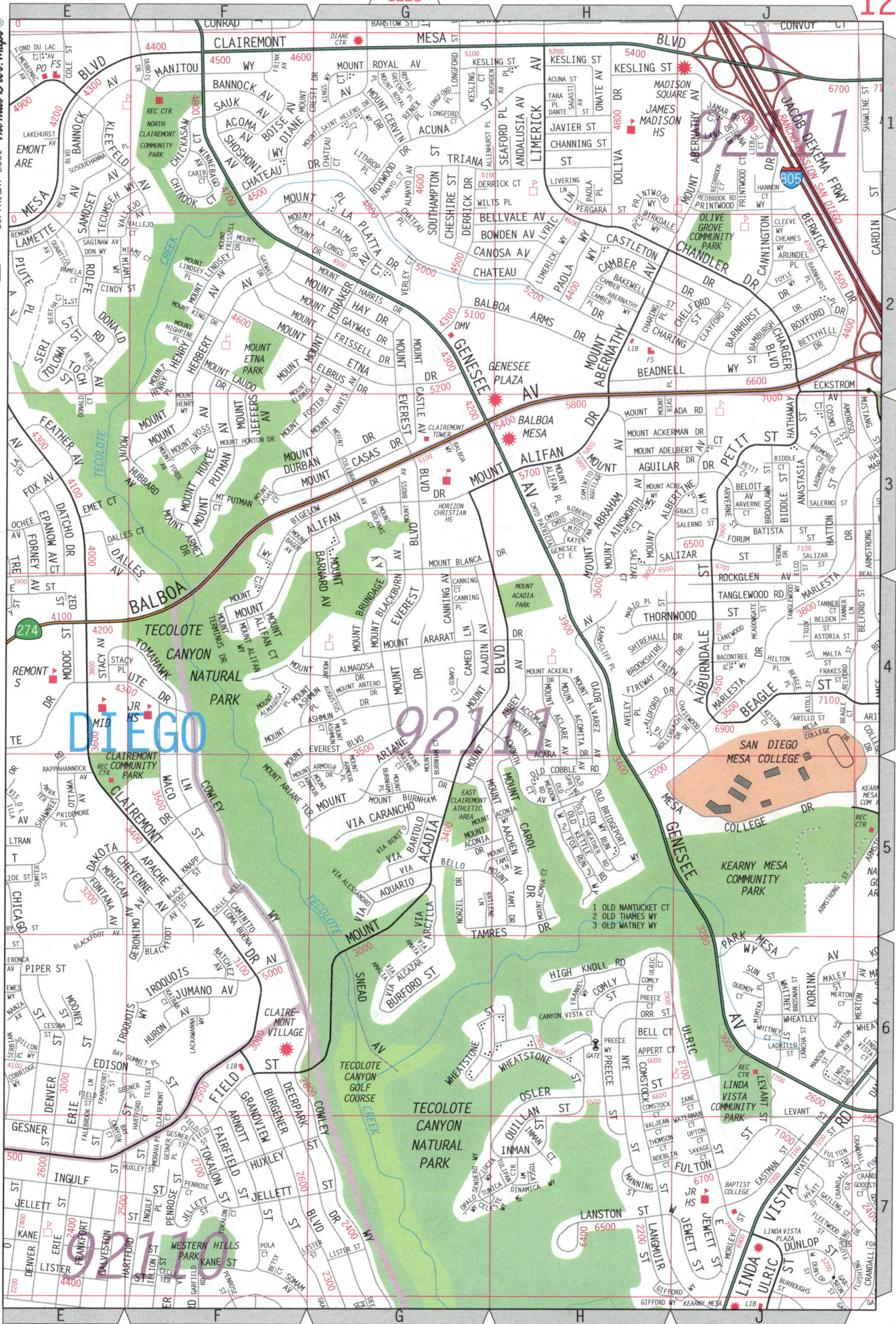

THOMAS BROS. MAPS®

COPYRIGHT 2001

SAN DIEGO CO.

MAP

92111

92110

DIEGO

CLAIREMONT MESA BLVD

JACOB DEKEMA FRWY
RANCHO MISSION SAN DIEGO

GENESEE AV

BALBOA AV

MOUNT ALIFAN AV

CLAIREMONT DR

GENESEE AV

SAN DIEGO MESA COLLEGE

MESA COLLEGE DR

KEARNY MESA COMMUNITY PARK

LINDA VISTA COMMUNITY PARK

TECOLOTE CANYON NATURAL PARK

TECOLOTE CANYON GOLF COURSE

TECOLOTE CANYON NATURAL PARK

NORTH CLAIREMONT COMMUNITY PARK

MOUNT ETNA PARK

CLAIREMONT COMMUNITY PARK

CLAIREMONT VILLAGE

WESTERN HILLS PARK

OLIVE GROVE COMMUNITY PARK

MADISON SQUARE

JAMES MADISON HS

HORIZON CHRISTIAN HS

EAST CLAIREMONT ATHLETIC AREA

LINDA VISTA PLAZA

MOUNT ACADIA PARK

GENESEE PLAZA

BALBOA MESA

CLAIREMONT TOWER

LINDA VISTA RD

I-805

0 .125 .25 .375 .5
miles   1 in. = 1900 ft.

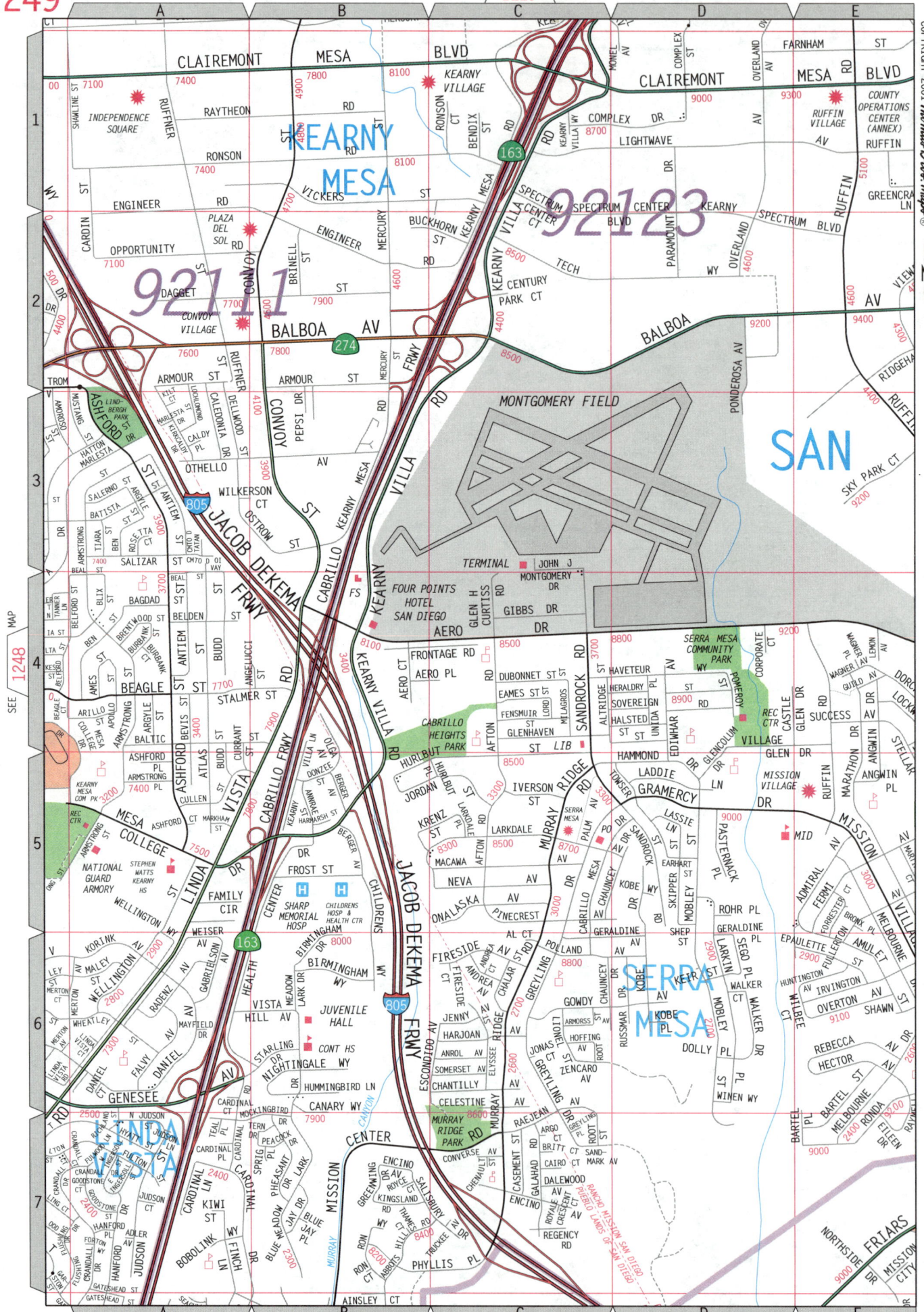

SAN DIEGO CO.

MAP

SEE 1248 MAP

COPYRIGHT 2001 Thomas Bros. Maps ®

CLAIREMONT MESA BLVD

KEARNY MESA

92111

92123

SAN

MONTGOMERY FIELD

BALBOA AV

SERRA MESA

LINDA VISTA

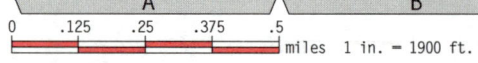

0 .125 .25 .375 .5 miles 1 in. = 1900 ft.

SAN DIEGO CO.

MAP

TIERRASANTA

DIEGO

MISSION VILLAGE

92124

92120

92108

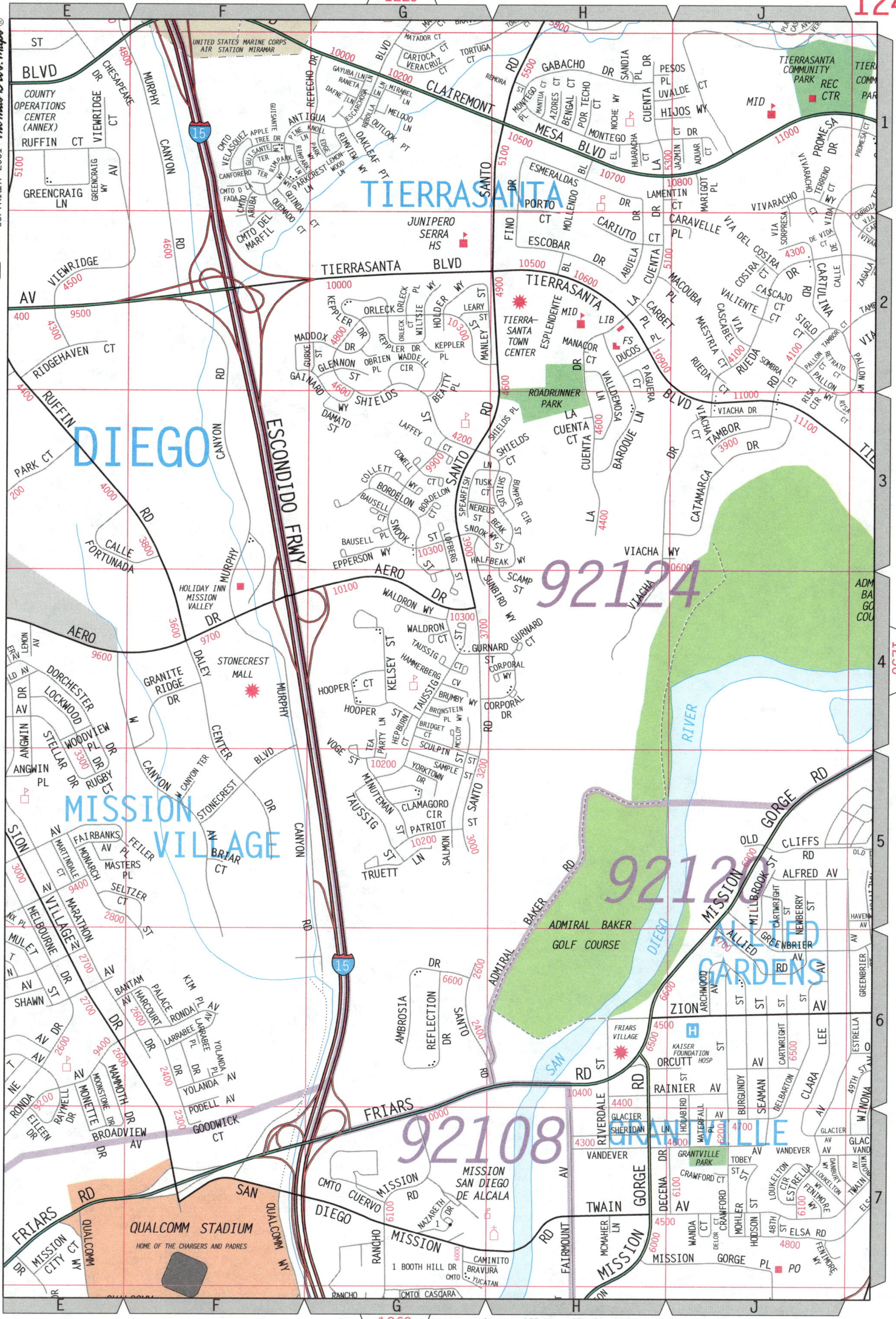

GRANTVILLE

ALLIED GARDENS

UNITED STATES MARINE CORPS AIR STATION MIRAMAR

COUNTY OPERATIONS CENTER (ANNEX)

JUNIPERO SERRA HS

TIERRASANTA TOWN CENTER

ROADRUNNER PARK

TIERRASANTA COMMUNITY PARK

REC CTR

HOLIDAY INN MISSION VALLEY

STONECREST MALL

GRANITE RIDGE

ADMIRAL BAKER GOLF COURSE

FRIARS VILLAGE

KAISER FOUNDATION HOSP

GRANTVILLE PARK

QUALCOMM STADIUM
HOME OF THE CHARGERS AND PADRES

MISSION SAN DIEGO DE ALCALA

ESCONDIDO FRWY

SAN DIEGO RIVER

© COPYRIGHT 2001 Thomas Bros. Maps®

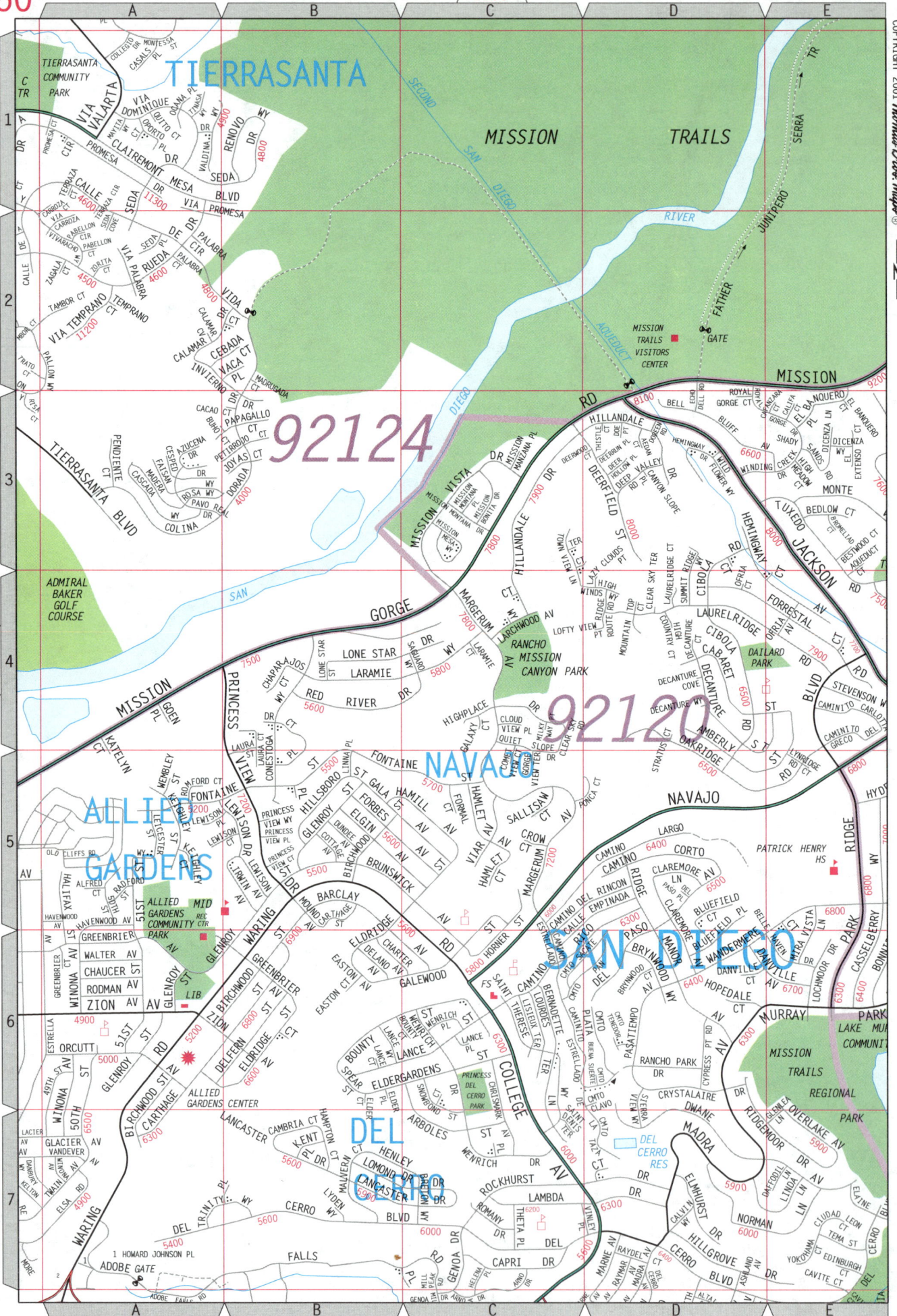

SAN DIEGO CO.

MAP

SEE 1230 MAP
SEE 1249 MAP
SEE 1270 MAP

TIERRASANTA

MISSION TRAILS

92124

92120

NAVAJO

ALLIED GARDENS

SAN DIEGO

DEL CERRO

MISSION TRAILS REGIONAL PARK

TIERRASANTA COMMUNITY PARK

ADMIRAL BAKER GOLF COURSE

MISSION TRAILS VISITORS CENTER

RANCHO MISSION CANYON PARK

DAILARD PARK

ALLIED GARDENS COMMUNITY PARK

PRINCESS DEL CERRO PARK

LAKE MURRAY COMMUNITY

DEL CERRO RES

SAN DIEGO RIVER

PATRICK HENRY HS

—N—

0 .125 .25 .375 .5
miles 1 in. = 1900 ft.

Thomas Bros. Maps®
COPYRIGHT 2001

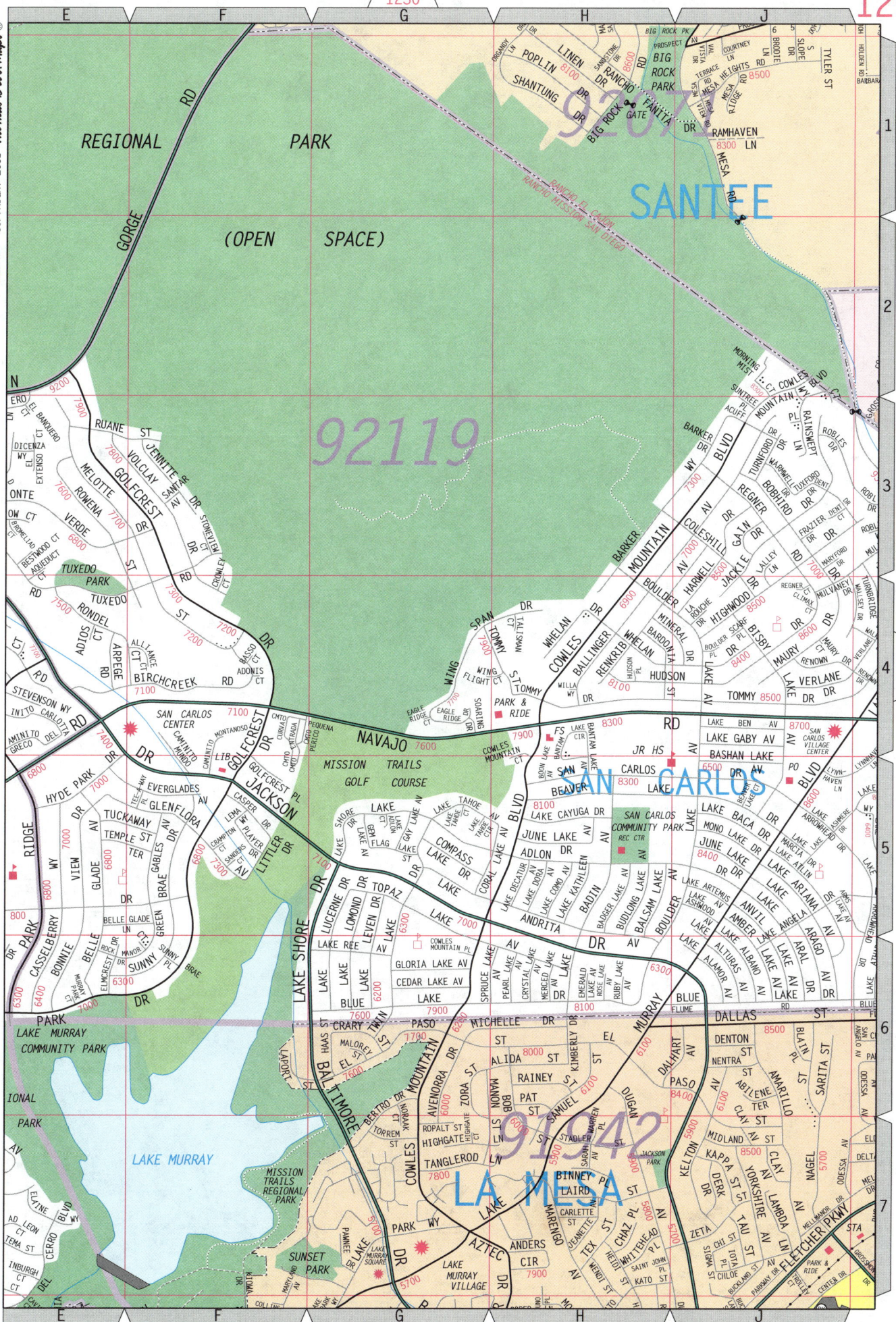

—N→

SEE 1251 MAP

SAN DIEGO CO.

MAP

SANTEE

SAN CARLOS

LA MESA

92071
92119
91942

REGIONAL PARK
(OPEN SPACE)

BIG ROCK PARK

MISSION TRAILS GOLF COURSE

SAN CARLOS COMMUNITY PARK

LAKE MURRAY
LAKE MURRAY COMMUNITY PARK

MISSION TRAILS REGIONAL PARK

MISSION TRAILS REGIONAL PARK

LAKE MURRAY VILLAGE

SUNSET PARK

NAVAJO RD
FLETCHER PKWY
DALLAS ST

0 .125 .25 .375 .5
miles 1 in. = 1900 ft.

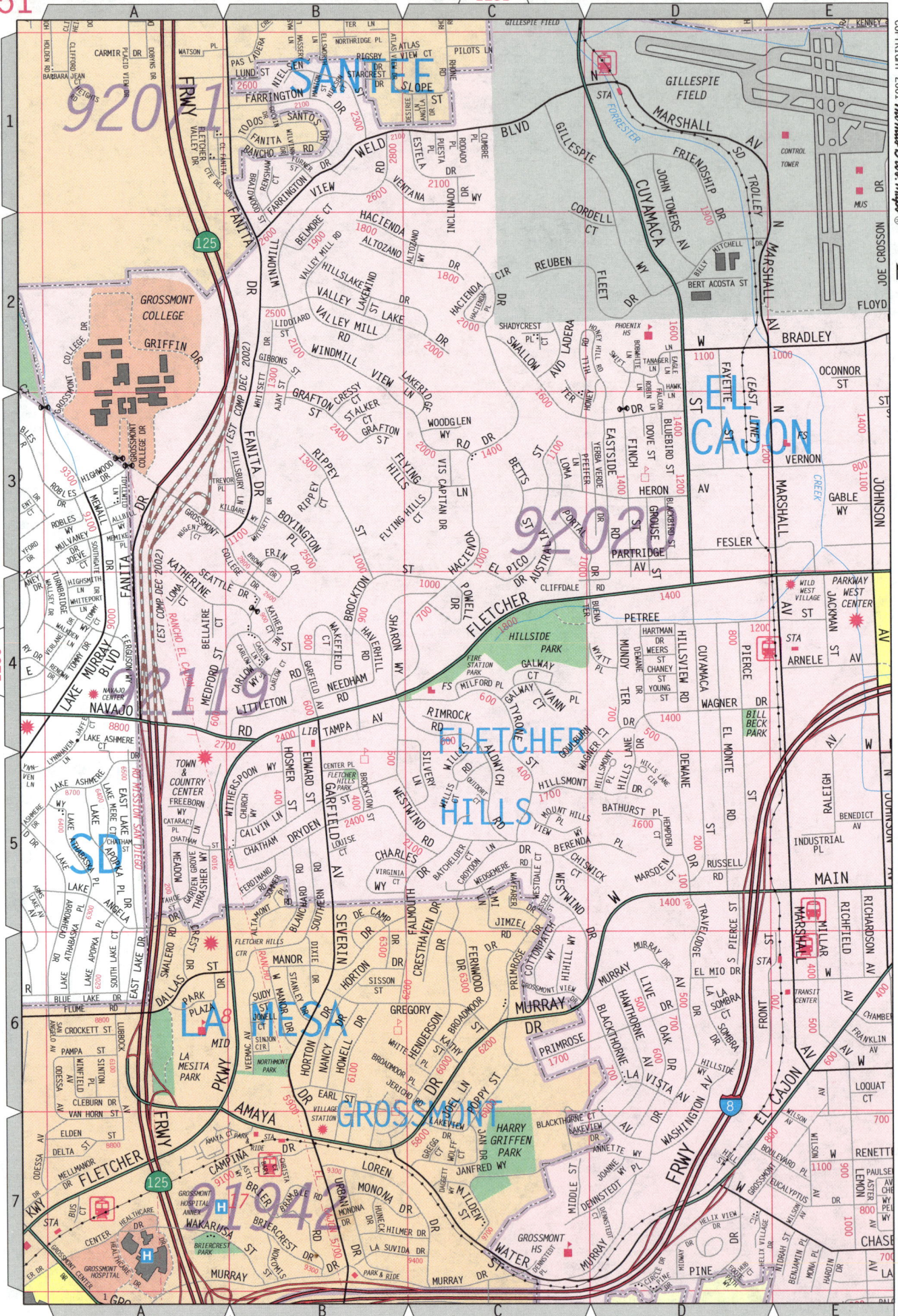

SAN DIEGO CO.

MAP

SEE 1231 MAP

SEE 1250 MAP

SEE 1271 MAP

COPYRIGHT 2001 Thomas Bros. Maps®

92071

SANTEE

GROSSMONT COLLEGE

GILLESPIE FIELD

EL CAJON

92020

92019

92021

FLETCHER HILLS

LA MESA

GROSSMONT

Harry Griffen Park

Hillside Park

Bill Beck Park

Parkway West Center

La Mesita Park

Town & Country Center

Grossmont Hospital

GROSSMONT COLLEGE DR

FANITA DR

LAKE MURRAY BLVD

NAVAJO

FLETCHER PKWY

FLETCHER FRWY

MURRAY DR

EL CAJON BLVD

WATER ST

MAIN

CUYAMACA

MARSHALL AV

0   .125   .25   .375   .5   miles   1 in. = 1900 ft.

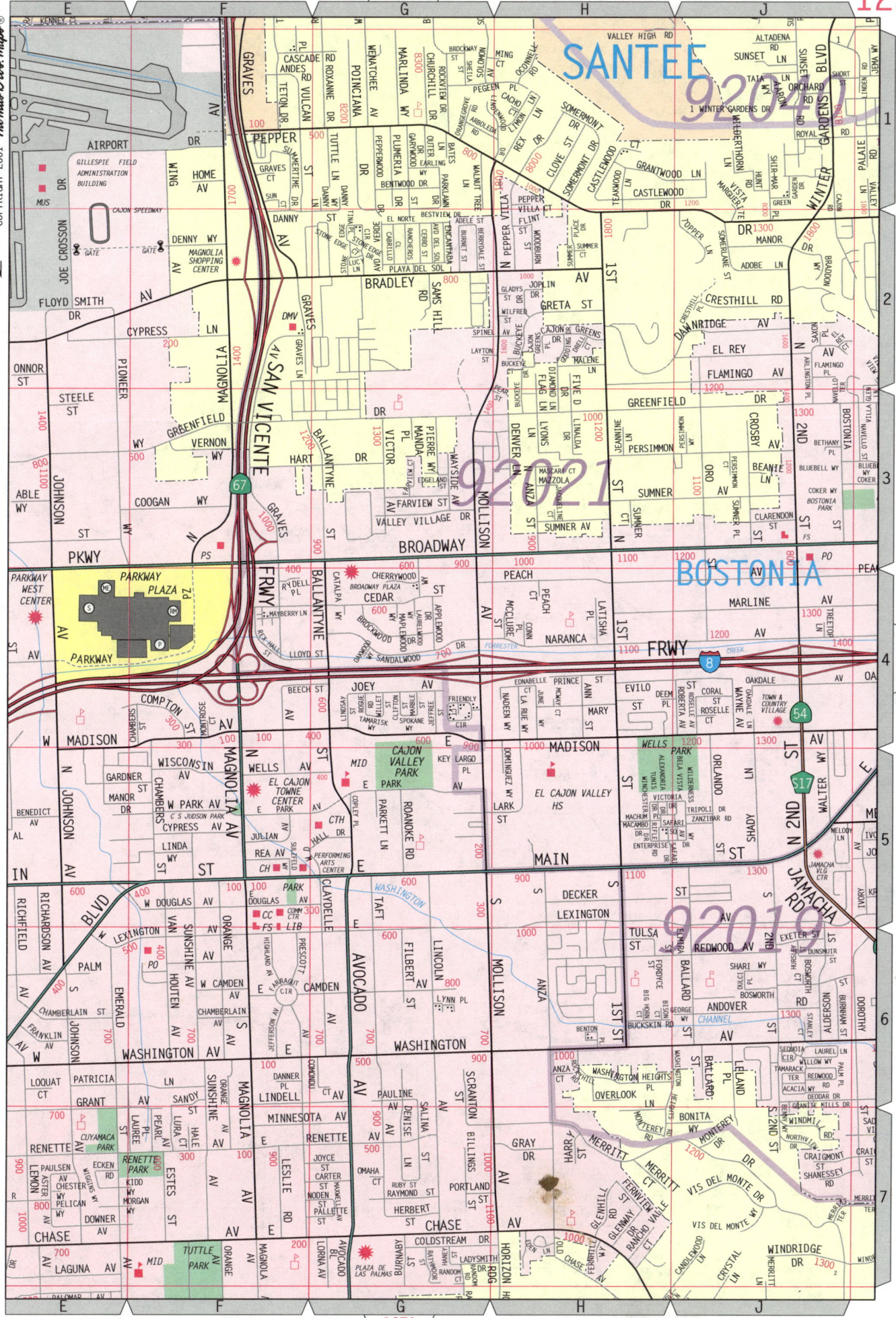

ThomasBros.Maps®

© COPYRIGHT 2001

—N—

SANTEE

92040

92021

92019

BOSTONIA

92019

GILLESPIE FIELD
ADMINISTRATION
BUILDING

AIRPORT

CAJON SPEEDWAY

MAGNOLIA
SHOPPING
CENTER

PARKWAY
WEST
CENTER

PARKWAY
PLAZA

EL CAJON
TOWNE
CENTER
PARK

CAJON
VALLEY
PARK

EL CAJON VALLEY
HS

PERFORMING
ARTS CENTER

CUYAMACA
PARK

RENETTE
PARK

TUTTLE
PARK

67

8

54

S17

0 .125 .25 .375 .5
miles 1 in. = 1900 ft.

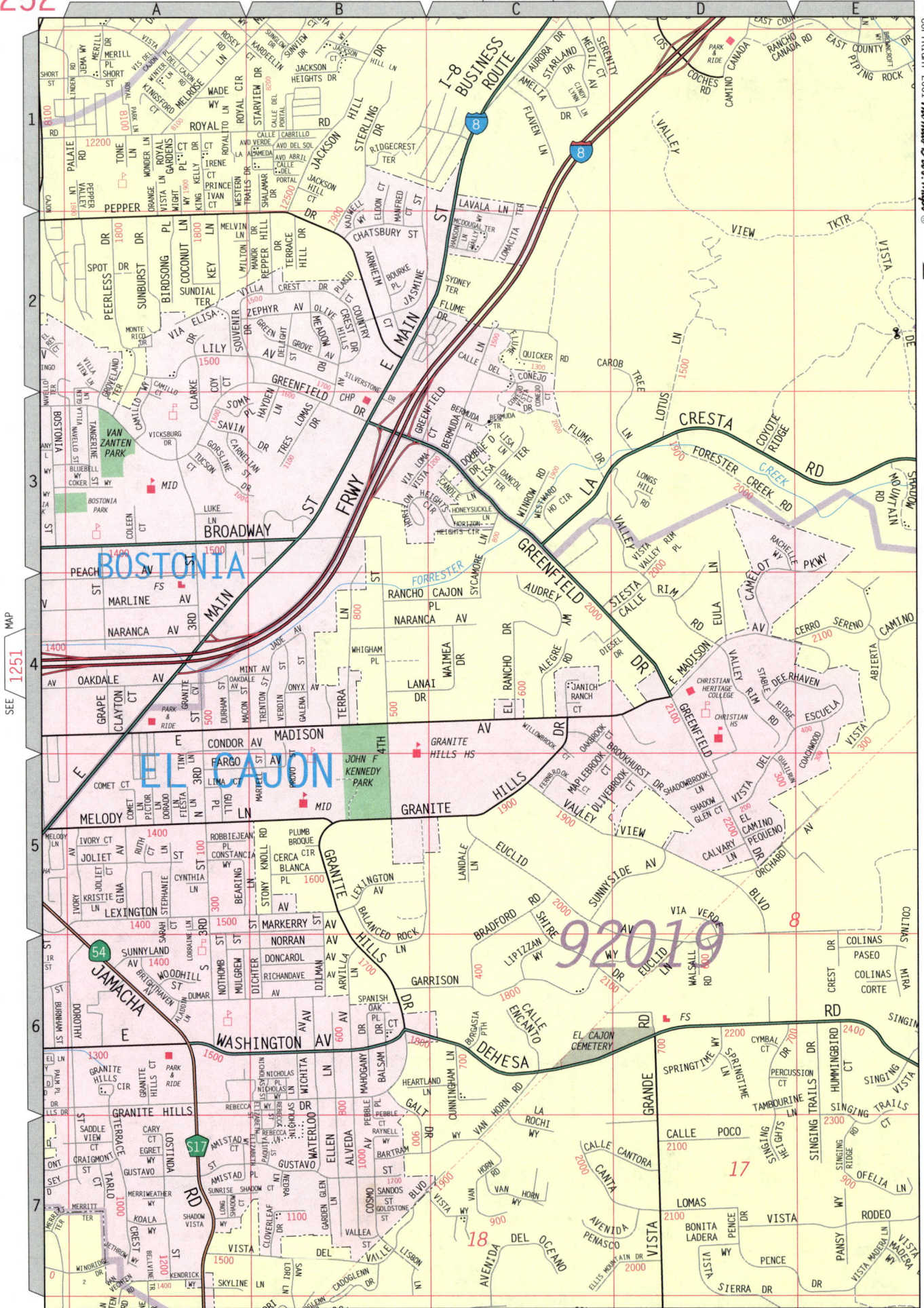

SAN DIEGO CO.

MAP

SEE 1232 MAP

SEE 1251 MAP

COPYRIGHT 2001 Thomas Bros. Maps ®

BOSTONIA

EL CAJON

JAMACHA

92019

I-8 BUSINESS ROUTE

CRESTA

GRANITE HILLS

0 .125 .25 .375 .5
miles 1 in. = 1900 ft.

SAN DIEGO CO.

MAP

COPYRIGHT 2001 Thomas Bros. Maps®

—N—

92021

CREST

DEHESA

T15S
T16S

34

3

4

9

10

15

16

6

SINGING HILLS MEMORIAL PARK

SINGING HILLS COUNTRY CLUB

SINGING HILLS LODGE

1 SHORT WY
2 NORTH PARK DR

1 PROMONTORY DR
2 OCEANVIEW PL
3 EL MONTE PL

CRESTA CREEK

FORRESTER

LA CAJON

OLD BEND RD

SHADOW MOUNTAIN RD

MONTEMAR

VISTA

SIERRA

CALLE DE LA

MONTE SOMBRA

ABIERTA

CAMINO

RANCHO

HEATH CLIFF CT

BRANCROFT DR

COUNTY

ING ROCK

VISTA

DE GATE

GATE

RANCH TWELVE

BRIAR HOLLOW LN

OAKS

KENT DR

LA CRESTA HEIGHTS CT

VIA LA CRESTA LA

CRESTA HEIGHTS

ROCKY

LAKE VIEW

CREEK RD

SUNNYBROOK

CHICORY LN

SCOTTFORD DR

CRESTA BLVD

W TASHA VIEW WY
E TASHA VIEW WY

DORMAE LN

N CREST

MELISSA

PARK TER RD

MOUNTAIN VIEW RD

AL BAHR RD

HAWLEY

CANYON VIEW DR

SAGE RD

PARADOX LN

ALAMO WY

EAST LN

THORNTON DR

LILAC DR

SCENIC

PARK BLVD

WILKIE DR

SIERRA VISTA DR

KENS RD

HIGHLINE TR

LATHROP LN

LA CRESTA DR

WEST LN

HOLLY LN

JARRETT LN

NORTH LN

LENTO LN

ALTA

ALTA PL

ESTORNINO LN

LILA LN

PALOMA LN

LENNY

CODORNIZ LN

RANCHO MEADOWCREST RD

VISTA DEL CORONADOS

TEA MOUNTAIN LN

SUNCREST

ORCHARD AV

GATE

SUNCREST BLVD

LOMA VISTA PL

MADERA VERDE PL

EUCALYPTUS PL

FS

SUNRISE MOUNTAIN RD

JUANITA LN

WALL PL

BEECH PL

BONITA PL

ALBATROSS PL

SOUTH LANE PARK

VISTA

SOUTH LN

ALVA LN

HILLSIDE PL

WOODLAND LN

CREST

EUCALYPTUS

CHEMISAL LN

CORNER

DEHESA WY

SENDA LN

SOUTH PARK PL

DESCANSO LN

DEHESA MOUNTAIN LN

EUCALYPTUS

LINAS

ASEO

OLINAS

CORTE

COLINAS

MIRA

SINGING VISTA

SINGING VISTA WY

SINGING VISTA CT

SINGING VISTA DR

G TRAILS CT

FELIA LN

RODEO

GLEN DR

WILLOW

DEHESA

OAK GLEN CIR

OAK GLEN WY

MATAMO PL

SYCUAN SUMMIT DR

DEHESA MEADOW RD

DEHESA RD

SWEETWATER

RIVER

WEST VILLAGE DR

CORTE DE LAS PIEDRAS

BUTTONWOOD CT

PEARLBUSH LN

SALTBUSH LN

BITTERBUSH

SILVERBERRY CT

SMOKEBUSH

BOXWOOD DR

VISTA MADERA WY

MADERA LN

SAN DIEGO CO.

MAP

SEE 1233 MAP

COPYRIGHT 2001 *Thomas Bros. Maps* ®

A B C D E

1

TAMMADGE HEIGHTS

HORSEMILL RD
100
CHICORY LN
ALONZO DR 700 OLD MOUNTAIN VIEW RD
1300
35 92021
500 STONERIDGE RD
400

W NOAKES ST 200 EDITHA DR
ALMYRA W NOAKES ST
FRANCES DR 100 MILDRED
RIDGE DR E NOAKES ST
HUDSON LN
FS

PATRICK

OLD IRONSIDES COUNTY PARK

KRISHEN HEIGHTS
RD

31

HARBISON CANYON

LA CRESTA TR
36
500

SUMMIT LN
300 PATRICK

MOUNTAIN VIEW RD

DAWN VIEW WY
DAWN EM

KELLY DR
NORMANDY WY
POST TR
ROSALIE DR
DR
GLADIOLA LN
ALBA WY

SAINT GEORGE
LINGEL
SAINT GEORGE
700
600
500 WARFIELD WY

2

HR
AL BAHR RD
CANYON RIM
400
DR
800

PLACER TR
RIDGE TR
EVERELL TR
SAINT GEORGE PL
900
400

COCHRAN TR

TAYLOR WY
SILVERBROOK
1000
COLTER TR
REMFRO WY
900
LOOKOUT TR

R1E R2E

T15S
T16S

—N—

RD

BAHR
900

3

CANYON
1100

2

WILLSON
1100

1

RED GUM RD
1400

RIVER
6300

AL

MOOREFIELD DR
1500

RD

4

1500

SEE 1252 MAP

92019

DEHESA

TRAFALGAR
RD

RD
5900

STALLION

OAKS RD

RIGGS
STALLION OAKS LN

HARBISON

VISTA DE LA MONTANA

5

QUAIL
14600
11

DEHESA
5300
5600
12
SWEETWATER
FS

RD

HAVEN LN

RD
5000

2100
RD

6

FS

SYCUAN

FORK

SYCUAN
NORTH

DEHESA
4500

SLOANE CANYON

7

SWEETWATER
RIVER
RD

14

SYCUAN INDIAN RESERVATION

13

A B C D E

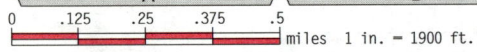

0 .125 .25 .375 .5
miles 1 in. = 1900 ft.

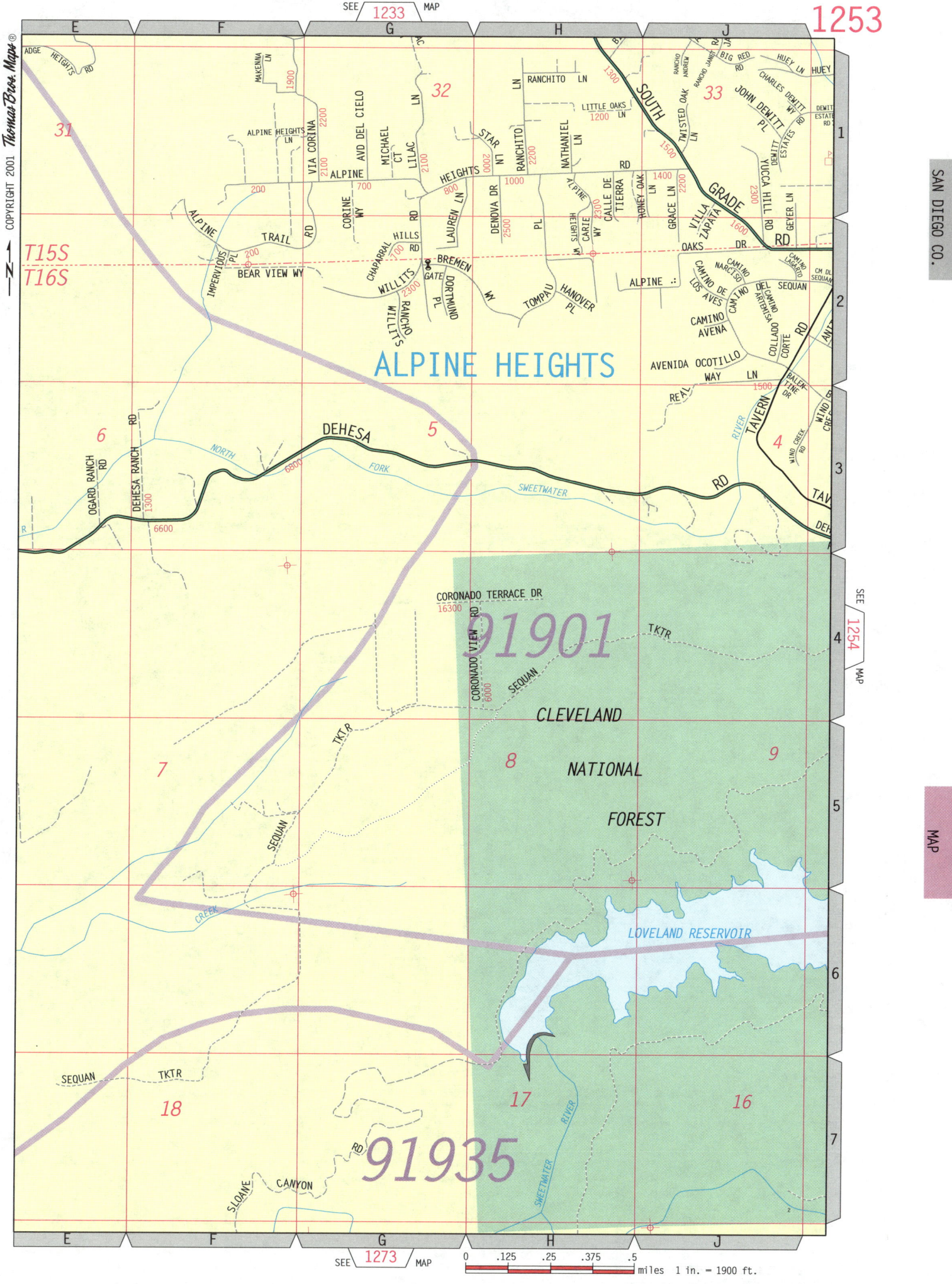

1253

SAN DIEGO CO.

MAP

Thomas Bros. Maps®
COPYRIGHT 2001

N

T15S
T16S

E F G H J

31 32 33

ADGE HEIGHTS RD
MAKENNA LN
1900
ALPINE HEIGHTS LN
VIA CORINA 2200
AVD DEL CIELO
MICHAEL CT
LILAC
ALPINE 2100
2100
CORINE WY 700
200
ALPINE TRAIL RD
IMPERVITOUS PL
BEAR VIEW WY 200
CHAPARRAL HILLS RD
700
WILLITS PL
RANCHO WILLITS 2300
GATE DORTMUND PL
BREMEN WY

HEIGHTS
LAUREN LN 800
STAR LN
RANCHITO LN 2000
DENOVA DR 1000
2500
ALPINE HEIGHTS PL 2300
CARIE WY
TOMPAU
HANOVER PL

RANCHITO LN
LITTLE OAKS LN 1200
LN 1300
NATHANIEL LN
2200
CALLE DE TIERRA RD
HONEY OAK 1400
GRACE LN 2200
VILLA ZAPATA 1600
OAKS DR
ALPINE

SOUTH GRADE RD
TWISTED OAK LN 1500
2300
YUCCA LN
GEYER LN

RANCHO ANDREW
RANCHO JANET
BIG RED
HUEY LN HUEY
CHARLES DEWITT RD
JOHN DEWITT PL
DEWITT ESTATES
DEWITT ESTATE RD

1
CAMINO NARCISO
CAMINO DE LOS AVES
CAMINO ARTEMISA
DEL CAMINO
CORTE
COLLADO
CAMINO AVENA
AVENIDA OCOTILLO WAY
REAL LN
REAL 1500

CM DL SEQUAN
SEQUAN
CAMINO LAGATO
BALEN TINE DR
WIND CREEK RD
WIND B CREEK

TAVERN RD
RIVER

ALPINE HEIGHTS

DEHESA
NORTH FORK
6800
SWEETWATER
6600
DEHESA RANCH RD 1300
OGARD RANCH RD
R

6 5 4

TAVERN RD
TAV
DEH

SEE 1254 MAP

CORONADO TERRACE DR
16300
CORONADO VIEW RD 6000
SEQUAN
TKTR
91901

CLEVELAND
NATIONAL
FOREST

8 9

TKTR
SEQUAN
7
CREEK

LOVELAND RESERVOIR

18 17 16
91935
SEQUAN TKTR
SLOANE CANYON RD
SWEETWATER RIVER

E F G H J

0 .125 .25 .375 .5 miles   1 in. = 1900 ft.

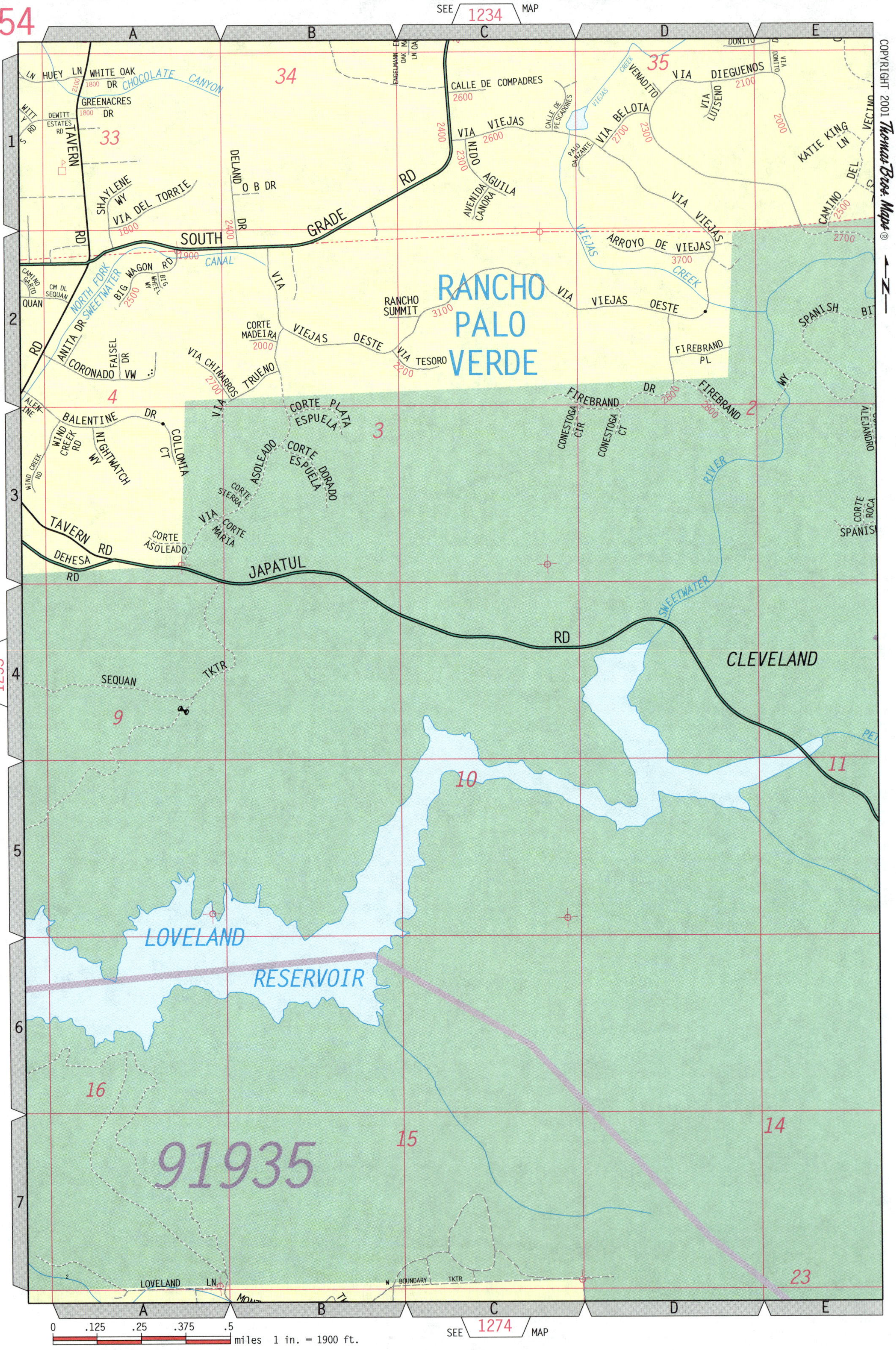

SAN DIEGO CO.

MAP

SEE 1234 MAP

COPYRIGHT 2001 Thomas Bros. Maps ®

—N—

A B C D E

1

HUEY LN   WHITE OAK DR   CHOCOLATE CANYON
WITT RD
GREENACRES DR
DEWITT ESTATES RD
TAVERN
33
34
CALLE DE COMPADRES 2600
VIA VIEJAS 2400
2600
VIA NIDO 2300
AVENIDA CANORA
CALLE DE PESCADORES
PALO MAZANTE
VIA BELOTA 2700
VIA VENADITO
VIA DIEGUENOS 2100
VIA LUISENO
VIA VIEJAS
KATIE KING LN
CAMINO DEL
2500
35
DONITO
2000
VENDOTA

SHAYLENE WY
VIA DEL TORRIE 1800
DELAND O B DR
SOUTH GRADE RD
DR 2400

2

CAMINO SARTO
CM DL SEQUAN
QUAN
RD
NORTH FORK SWEETWATER
BIG WAGON RD 2500
BIG WHEEL
CANAL 1900
VIA VIEJAS OESTE
CORTE MADEIRA 2000
RANCHO SUMMIT 3100
VIA TESORO 2200
RANCHO PALO VERDE
VIA VIEJAS OESTE
ARROYO DE VIEJAS 3700
VIEJAS CREEK
FIREBRAND PL
SPANISH BIT
2700

ANITA DR
CORONADO VW
FAISEL DR
VIA CHINARROS 2700
VIA TRUENO
4
3
CORTE PLATA ESPUELA
CORTE DORADO ESPUELA
FIREBRAND DR 2800
FIREBRAND 2
CONESTOGA CIR
CONESTOGA CT
WY
ALEJANDRO

3

ALEK LNE
BALENTINE
WIND CREEK RD
NIGHTWATCH
WY
DR
COLLOMA CT
ASOLEADO
CORTE SIERRA
VIA CORTE MARIA
RIVER
CORTE ROCA
SPANISH

TAVERN RD
DEHESA RD
CORTE ASOLEADO
JAPATUL
SWEETWATER

SEE 1253 MAP

4

SEQUAN TKTR
9
RD
CLEVELAND
11
PET

5

10

LOVELAND RESERVOIR

6

16

7

91935

15
14

LOVELAND LN
MONT
W BOUNDARY TKTR
23

A B C D E

0 .125 .25 .375 .5 miles   1 in. = 1900 ft.

SEE 1274 MAP

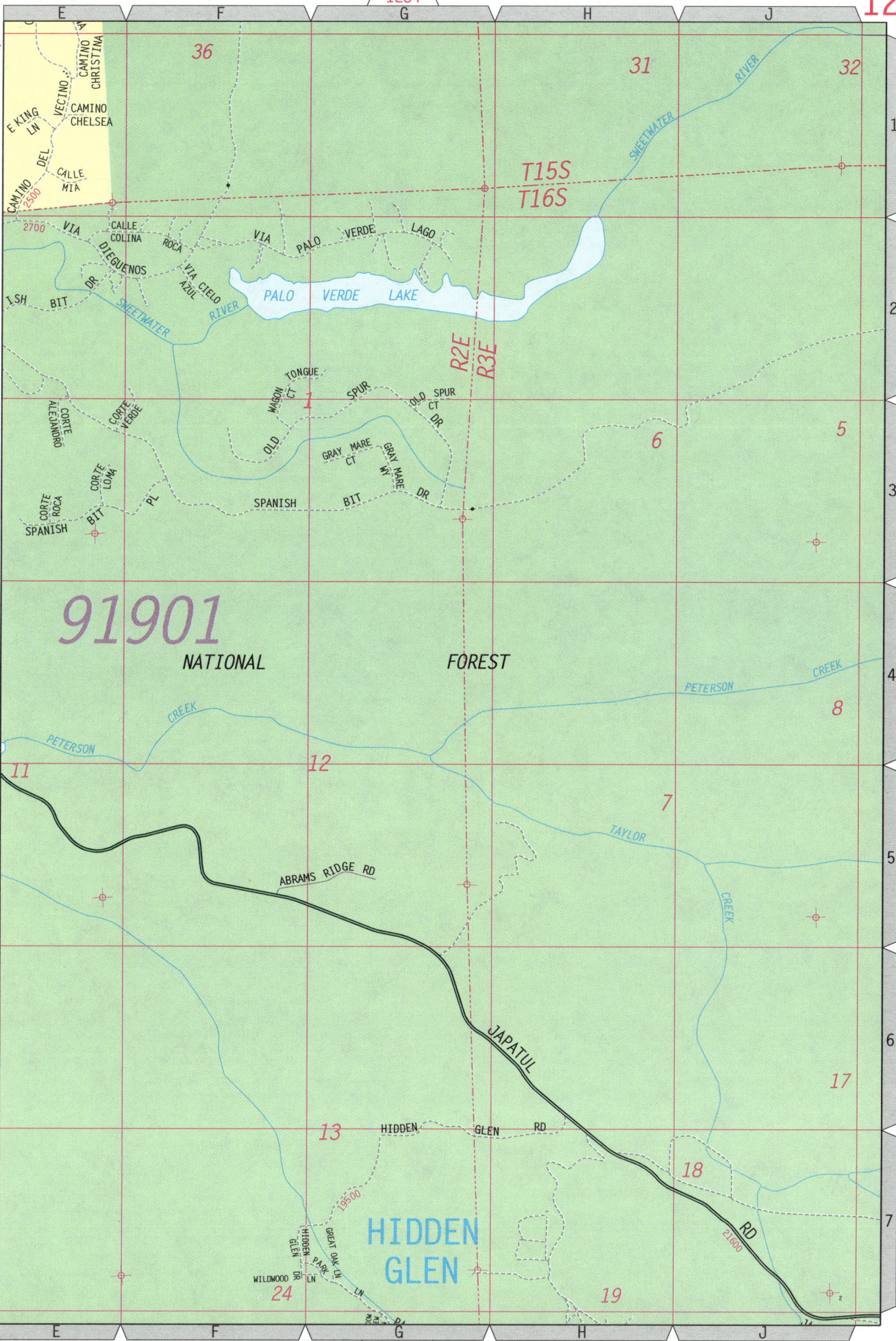

E   F   G   H   J

36

31   32

SAN DIEGO CO.

CAMINO CHRISTINA
CAMINO CHELSEA
CAMINO VECINO
E KING LN
CAMINO DEL
CALLE MIA
2500
2700

T15S
T16S

1

VIA COLINA
VIA
CALLE COLINA
ROCA
PALO   VERDE   LAGO
DIEGUENOS
VIA CIELO AZUL
RIVER
SWEETWATER

SWEETWATER   RIVER

ISH   BIT
DR

PALO   VERDE   LAKE

2

R2E
R3E

CORTE ALEJANDRO
CORTE VERDE

WAGON TONGUE CT
1
OLD   SPUR
OLD   SPUR CT
SPUR DR

6

5

CORTE LOMA
CORTE ROCA
SPANISH   BIT
PL

OLD
GRAY MARE CT
GRAY MARE WY
GRAY MARE DR

SPANISH   BIT

3

91901

NATIONAL   FOREST

PETERSON   CREEK

4

8

CREEK

PETERSON

11   12

7

ABRAMS RIDGE RD

TAYLOR
CREEK

5

SEE 1255 MAP

JAPATUL

6

17

13   HIDDEN   GLEN   RD

18

19500

RD
21600

HIDDEN
GLEN

GREAT OAK LN
HIDDEN GLEN LN
WILDWOOD DR
24

19

7

MAP

E   F   G   H   J

0   .125   .25   .375   .5
miles   1 in. = 1900 ft.

1255

—N—

SAN DIEGO CO.

MAP

	A	B	C	D	E

32

32

33

1

CLEVELAND

2

NATIONAL

5

4

91901

3

FOREST

PETERSON

CREEK

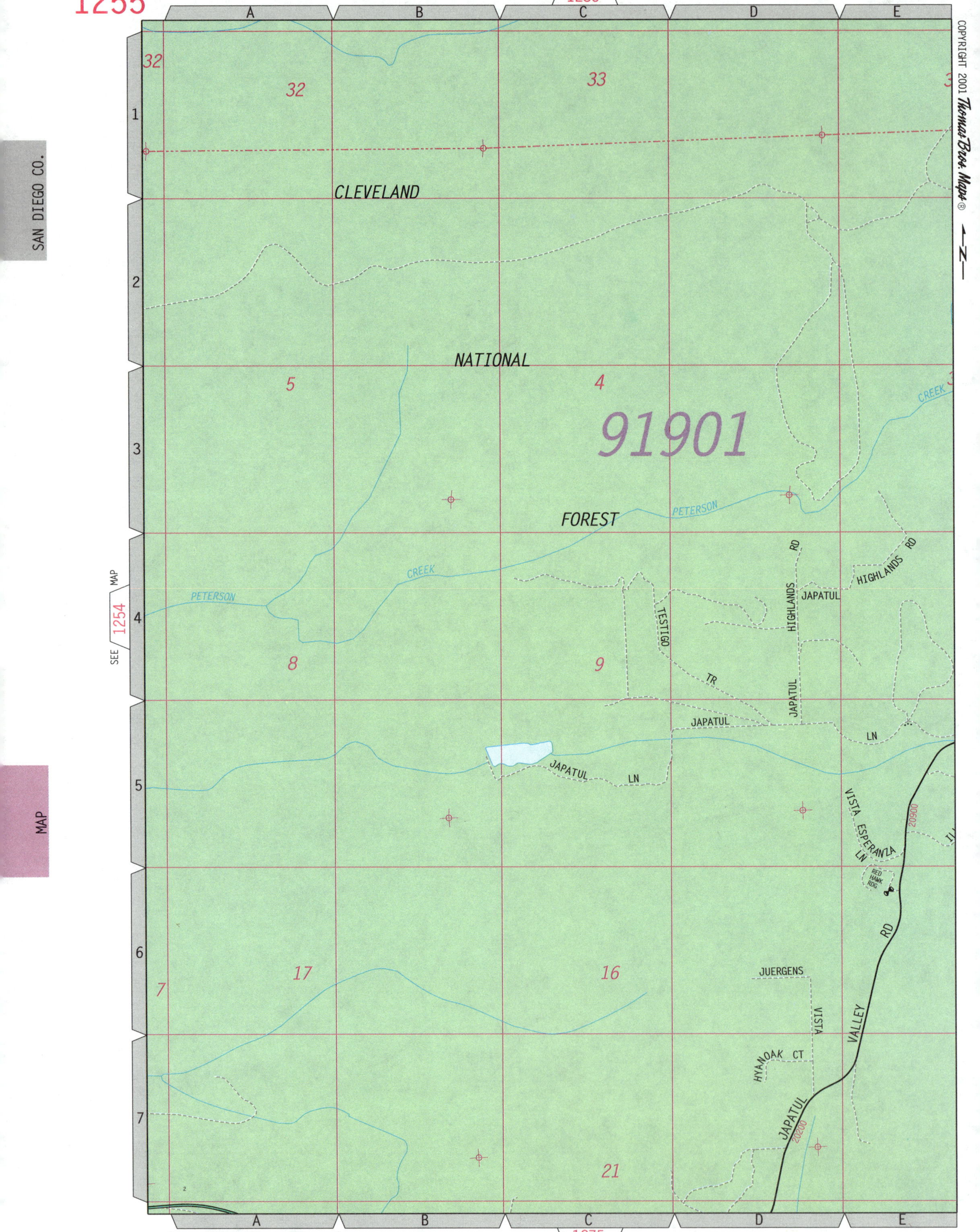

SEE / 1254 / MAP

PETERSON

CREEK

HIGHLANDS RD

HIGHLANDS RD

HIGHLANDS JAPATUL

TESTIGO

4

8

9

TR

JAPATUL

LN

JAPATUL

JAPATUL LN

JAPATUL LN

VISTA ESPERANZA LN

20600

5

RED HAWK RDG

VISTA ESPERANZA LN

6

7

17

16

JUERGENS

VISTA

VALLEY RD

HYANOAK CT

7

JAPATUL

20200

21

	A	B	C	D	E

0 .125 .25 .375 .5 miles   1 in. = 1900 ft.

ThomasBros.Maps®

COPYRIGHT 2001

SAN DIEGO CO.

MAP

—N—→

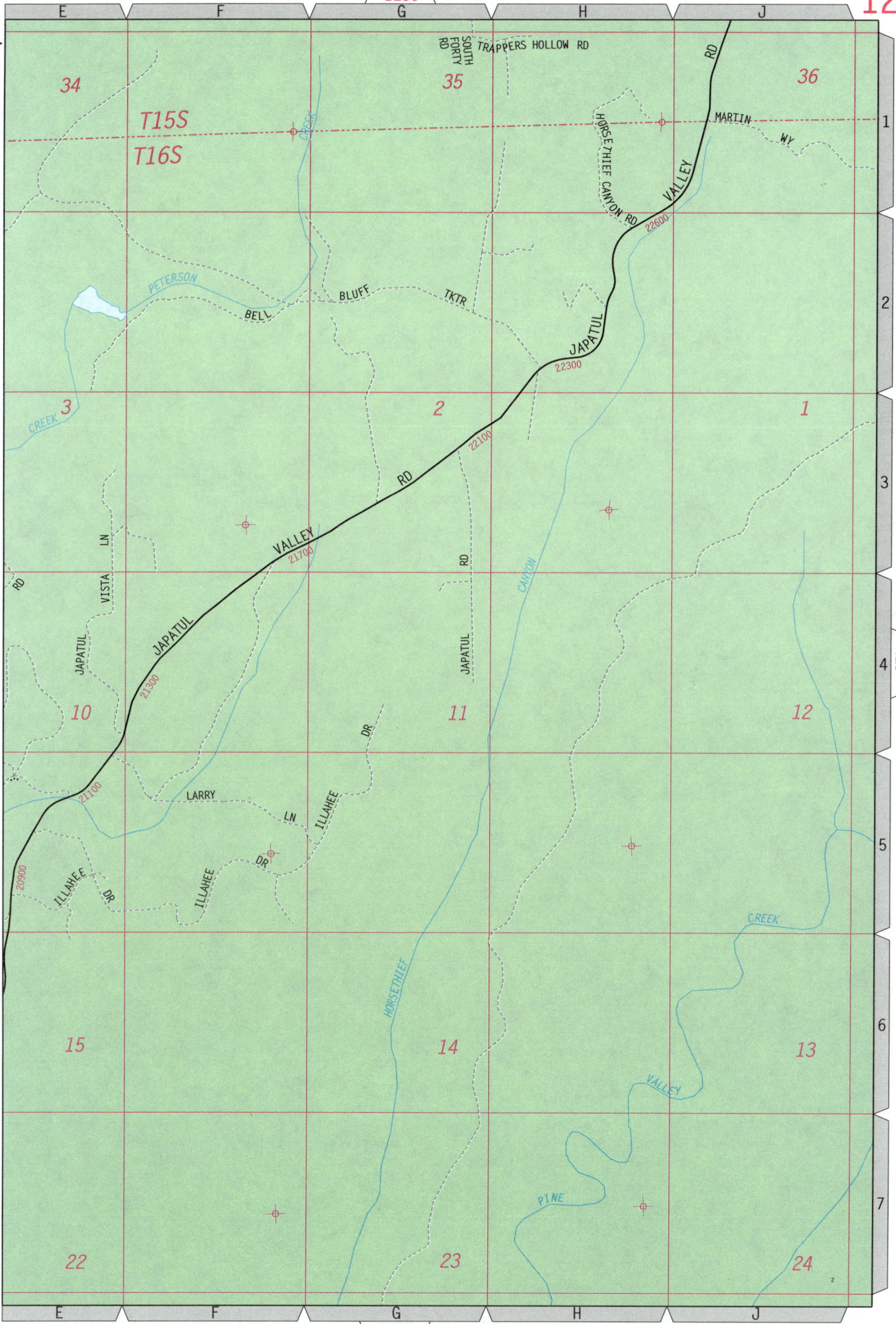

E F G H J

34

SOUTH FORTY RD

TRAPPERS HOLLOW RD

35

36

T15S
T16S

1

MARTIN WY

CREEK

HORSETHIEF CANYON RD

RD

VALLEY

22600

2

PETERSON

BELL BLUFF TKTR

JAPATUL

22300

CREEK 3

2

1

22100

RD

3

VALLEY

21700

RD

LN

VISTA

JAPATUL

JAPATUL

CANYON

SEE 429 MAP

RD

JAPATUL

4

21300

10

11

12

DR

21100

LARRY

LN

ILLAHEE

DR

5

20900

ILLAHEE DR

ILLAHEE

CREEK

HORSETHIEF

6

15

14

VALLEY

13

PINE

7

22

23

24

2

E F G H J

0 .125 .25 .375 .5

miles 1 in. = 1900 ft.

1267

SAN DIEGO CO.

MAP

A   B   C   D   E

1

2

3

PACIFIC

SEE 429 MAP

4

5

6

7

A   B   C   D   E

0 .125 .25 .375 .5 miles 1 in. = 1900 ft.

SAN DIEGO CO.

MAP

E F G H J

92109

MISSION
BEACH

MISSION

BEACH

PARK

MISSION

BEACH

PARK

TOULON CT
TANGIERS CT
SUNSET CT
SEAGIRT
SALEM CT
SAN JOSE
BAYSIDE
ROCKAWAY
REDONDO
QUEENSTOWN
PISMO PL
PORTSMOUTH
SANTA CLARA
OSTEND CT
ORMOND CT
NIANTIC CT
SAN JUAN PL
NANTASKET
NAHANT CT
MONTEREY CT
EL CARMEL CT
MANHATTAN CT
LIVERPOOL CT
SAN LUIS OBISPO PL
KINGSTON WY
KENNEBECK
SANTA BARBARA
JAMAICA CT
ISTHMUS CT
ISLAND CT
VENTURA PL
MISSION BEACH PLUNGE
BEL-MONT PARK
SAN FERNANDO PL
ENSENADA CT
DOVER CT
DEVON
SAN GABRIEL
DEAL CT
CORONADO CT
COHASSET CT
CAPISTRANO
BRIGHTON CT
BALBOA
AVALON CT
SAN LUIS
REY
ASBURY CT

SANTA CLARA COVE
REC CTR
BOAT CENTER
SANTA CLARA POINT COMMUNITY PARK
BOAT LAUNCH
BOAT HOUSE

MISSION

BAY

EL CARMEL POINT
SAN JUAN COVE
MISSION BAY YACHT CLUB
SANTA BARBARA COVE
BAHIA POINT
GLEASON RD
BAHIA RESORT HOTEL
VENTURA COVE
MISSION BAY PL
MISSION BAY
MISSION BAY MARINERS
MISSION BAY PARK
BONITA COVE (SWIMMING AREA)
MARINERS WY
MARINERS BASIN
GUEST ANCHORAGE
MARINERS POINT
MISSION POINT
ALLERTON CT
ANACAPA CT
ASPIN CT
SAN DIEGO PL

MISSION BLVD
BAYSIDE WK
OCEAN FRONT WK

FARAC FOGHORN

OCEAN

MISSION BAY CHANNEL

SAN DIEGO RIVER FLOODWAY

DOG BEACH
OCEAN BEACH ATHLETIC AREA
OCEAN AREA

POINT LOMA
W LOTUS ST
VOLTAIRE ST
MUIR ST
LONG BRANCH
BRIGHTON
SPRAY ST
CAPE MAY ST
SARATOGA AV
SANTA MONICA AV
NEWPORT AV
BACON ST
NARRAGANSETT AV
DEL
SANTA CRUZ
CORONADO
DEL
CABLE
SUNSET CLIFFS
MONTE AV
ORCHARD
PESCADERO
BERMUDA AV
POINT LOMA
PESCADERO AV
GUIZOT
FROUDE

OCEAN BEACH

OCEAN BEACH MUNICIPAL PIER

92107

SAN DIEGO

OCEAN BEACH COMM PARK
LIB
PO

PESCADERO BEACH
SUNSET CLIFFS PARK
ADAIR
LOMA AV

0 .125 .25 .375 .5 miles 1 in. = 1900 ft.

SEE 1248 MAP

SAN DIEGO CO.

MAP

CROWN POINT

CROWN POINT SHORES

MISSION BAY

RIVIERA SHORES

VACATION ISLE

SKI BEACH

FIESTA BAY

MISSION BAY PARK

92109

US GOVERNMENT ISLAND

FIESTA SHORES

FIESTA ISLAND

HILTON SAN DIEGO

LEISURE LAGOON (SWIMMING AREA)

ENCHANTED COVE

ENCHANTED ISLE

PACIFIC PASSAGE

NORTH COVE

SAN DIEGO PARADISE POINT RESORT

VACATION RD

BOAT LAUNCH

MODEL YACHT POND

SOUTH COVE

VENTURA POINT

CHANNEL

STONY POINT (WATER SKI AREA)

PEREZ COVE

HIDDEN ANCHORAGE

(WATER SKI AREA)

SEE A B6
1 CMTO DEHESA
2 CMTO POCO
3 CMTO UMBRAL
4 CMTO MENOR
5 CMTO AFUERA
6 CMTO SEGURO
7 CMTO EXIMIO
8 CMTO ESPEJO
9 CMTO ANDADA
10 CMTO ESTERO

PACIFIC PASSAGE

SOUTH SHORES

FIESTA ISLAND

W MISSION BAY DR

DANA INN & MARINA

BOAT LAUNCH

LANDING

HYATT ISLANDIA

QUIVIRA

SEA WORLD

SOUTH SHORES RD

BOAT LAUNCH

MISSION BAY PARK

WORLD

SEA WORLD WY

SEA WY

QUIVIRA POINT

QUIVIRA BASIN

HOSPITALITY POINT

LIFEGUARD

QUIVIRA WY

MISSION BAY DR

FRIARS RD

FLOODWAY

SAN DIEGO RIVER

W MISSION BAY DR FRWY

OCEAN BEACH

SAN DIEGO SPORTS ARENA

SPORTS ARENA

SPORTS ARENA PLAZA

HANCOCK ST

KURTZ

OCEAN BEACH ATHLETIC AREA (ROBB FIELD)

SUNSET CLIFFS

DUSTY RHODES PARK

W POINT LOMA

MIDWAY

POINT LOMA PLAZA

MEADOW GROVE

LOMA SQUARE

MIDWAY SAN DIEGO

92107

VOLTAIRE

NIMITZ

COLLIER PARK WEST

CLEATOR COMMUNITY PARK

JR HS

YMCA

LONG BRANCH

MUIR

SOTO

CAPE

MAY

FROUDE

SARATOGA

SANTA MONICA

OCEAN BEACH

NARRAGANSETT

DEL MAR

SANTA CRUZ

CORONADO

NEWPORT

NIAGARA

SANTA BARBARA

VENICE

CATALINA

BERNICE DR

CENTRALOMA

POE

WAWONA

POINT LOMA HS

VOLTAIRE

CHATSWORTH

WHITTIER

CLOVE

92106

ELLIOTT

DUMAS

BROWNING

ZOLA

WILLOW

EVERGREEN

LOCUST

ROSECRANS ST

SAIL HO GOLF COURSE

LYTTON

SELLERS

UPSHUR

WHARTON RD

DUNLAP RD

SAN DIEGO BAY

92133

SEE 1267 MAP

SEE 1288 MAP

0 .125 .25 .375 .5 miles 1 in. = 1900 ft.

Thomas Bros. Maps®
COPYRIGHT 2001

N

BAY PARK

92110

92111

LINDA VISTA

TECOLOTE CANYON GOLF COURSE

TECOLOTE CANYON NATURAL PARK

KELLY STREET PARK

UNIVERSITY OF SAN DIEGO

MISSION HEIGHTS PARK

FASHION VALLEY
TRANSIT CENTER

92108

RIVERWALK GOLF COURSE

SAN DIEGO RIVER

VALLEY WEST

CLUBHOUSE

TOWN & COUNTRY HOTEL

MISSION VALLEY FRWY

MISSION HILLS

UCSD MED CTR HILLCREST

HILLCREST

PACIFIC

Presidio Community Park
Serra Cross
OLD TOWN

HERITAGE PARK

MISSION HILLS PARK

UNIVERSITY AV

WASHINGTON

92103

LOMA PORTAL

LOMA SQUARE

SPORTS ARENA BLVD

MIDDLE TOWN

92140

HOCHMUTH
US MARINE CORPS RECRUIT DEPOT

MIDWAY

GUADALCANAL

GUANTANAMO

92101

SAN DIEGO INTERNAT'L AIRPORT
LINDBERGH FIELD

SAN DIEGO UNIFIED PORT DISTRICT

PACIFIC HWY

KETTNER BLVD

TERMINAL 2

0 .125 .25 .375 .5 miles   1 in. = 1900 ft.

SEE 1249 MAP

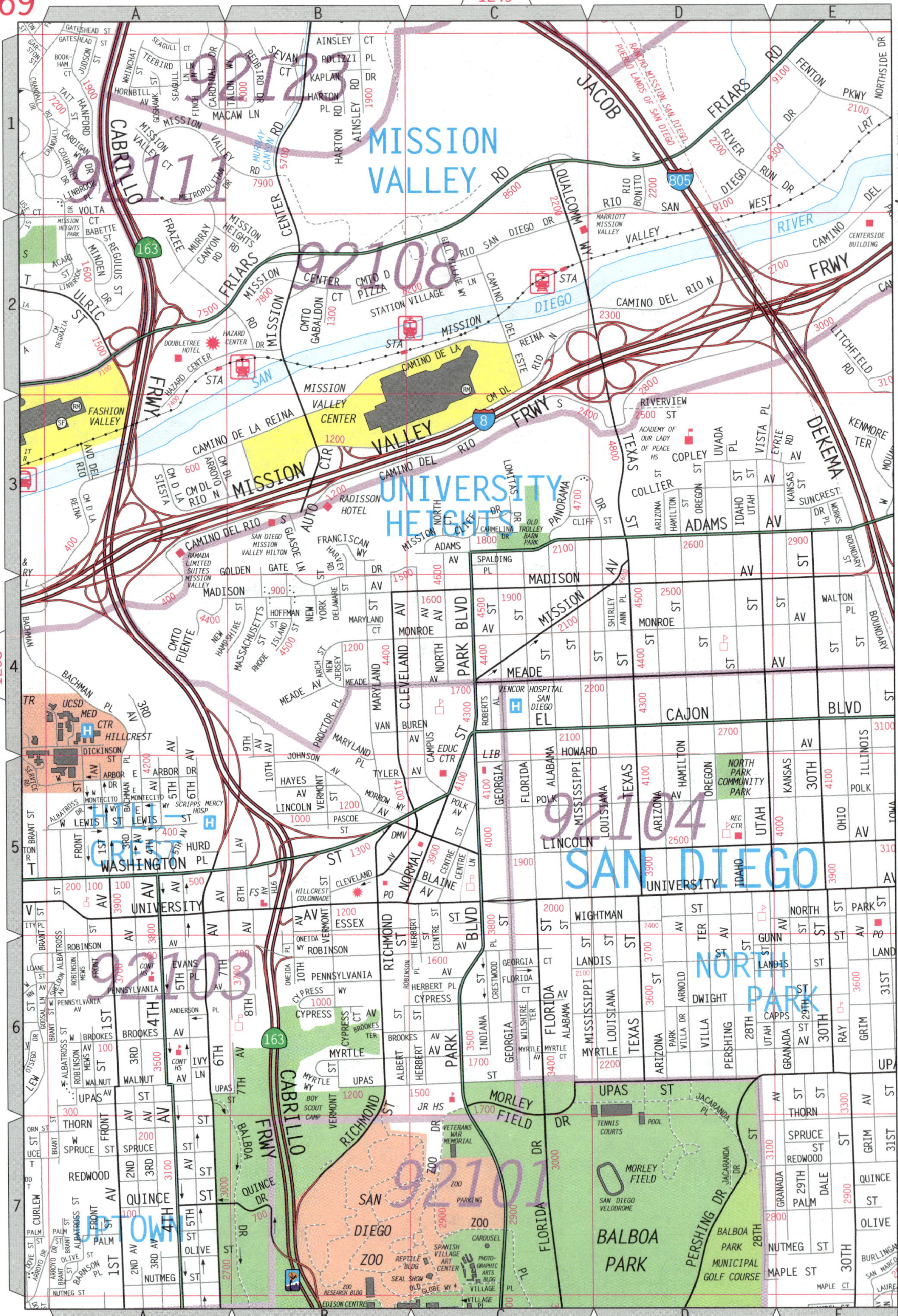

SAN DIEGO CO.

MAP

COPYRIGHT 2001 Thomas Bros Maps®

—N—

92123

92111

92108

MISSION VALLEY

UNIVERSITY HEIGHTS

92104

SAN DIEGO

NORTH PARK

92103

92101

HILLCREST

UPTOWN

SAN DIEGO ZOO

BALBOA PARK

MORLEY FIELD

SEE 1268 MAP

SEE 1289 MAP

0 .125 .25 .375 .5 miles   1 in. = 1900 ft.

COPYRIGHT 2001 Thomas Bros. Maps®

SAN DIEGO CO.

MAP

Major Areas / ZIP Codes

KENSINGTON

NORMAL HEIGHTS

TALMADGE

CITY HEIGHTS

92120

92115

92116

92105

Landmarks

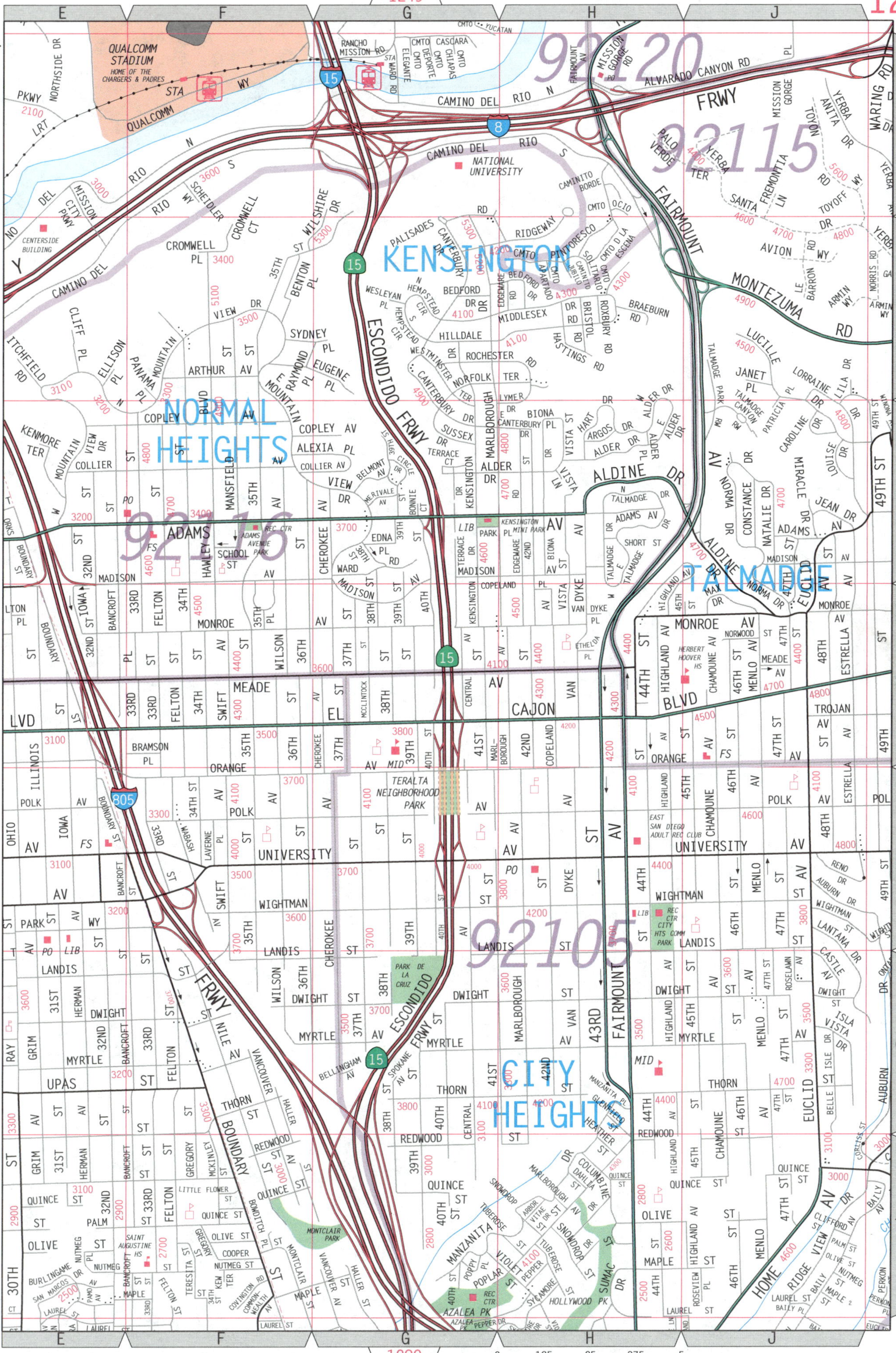

QUALCOMM STADIUM — HOME OF THE CHARGERS & PADRES

NATIONAL UNIVERSITY

CENTERSIDE BUILDING

SAINT AUGUSTINE HS

ADAMS AVENUE SCHOOL

KENSINGTON MINI PARK

TERALTA NEIGHBORHOOD PARK

PARK DE LA CRUZ

MONTCLAIR PARK

AZALEA PARK

HERBERT HOOVER HS

EAST SAN DIEGO ADULT REC CLUB

LITTLE FLOWER

Freeways / Major Roads

I-15 ESCONDIDO FRWY

I-8 / FAIRMOUNT FRWY

I-805

CAMINO DEL RIO N

CAMINO DEL RIO S

ALVARADO CANYON RD

MISSION GORGE RD

MONTEZUMA RD

FAIRMOUNT AV

EL CAJON BLVD

UNIVERSITY AV

ADAMS AV

MEADE AV

MADISON AV

MONROE AV

ALDINE DR

WARING RD

EUCLID AV

43RD ST

49TH ST

BOUNDARY ST

Scale: 0 .125 .25 .375 .5 miles   1 in. = 1900 ft.

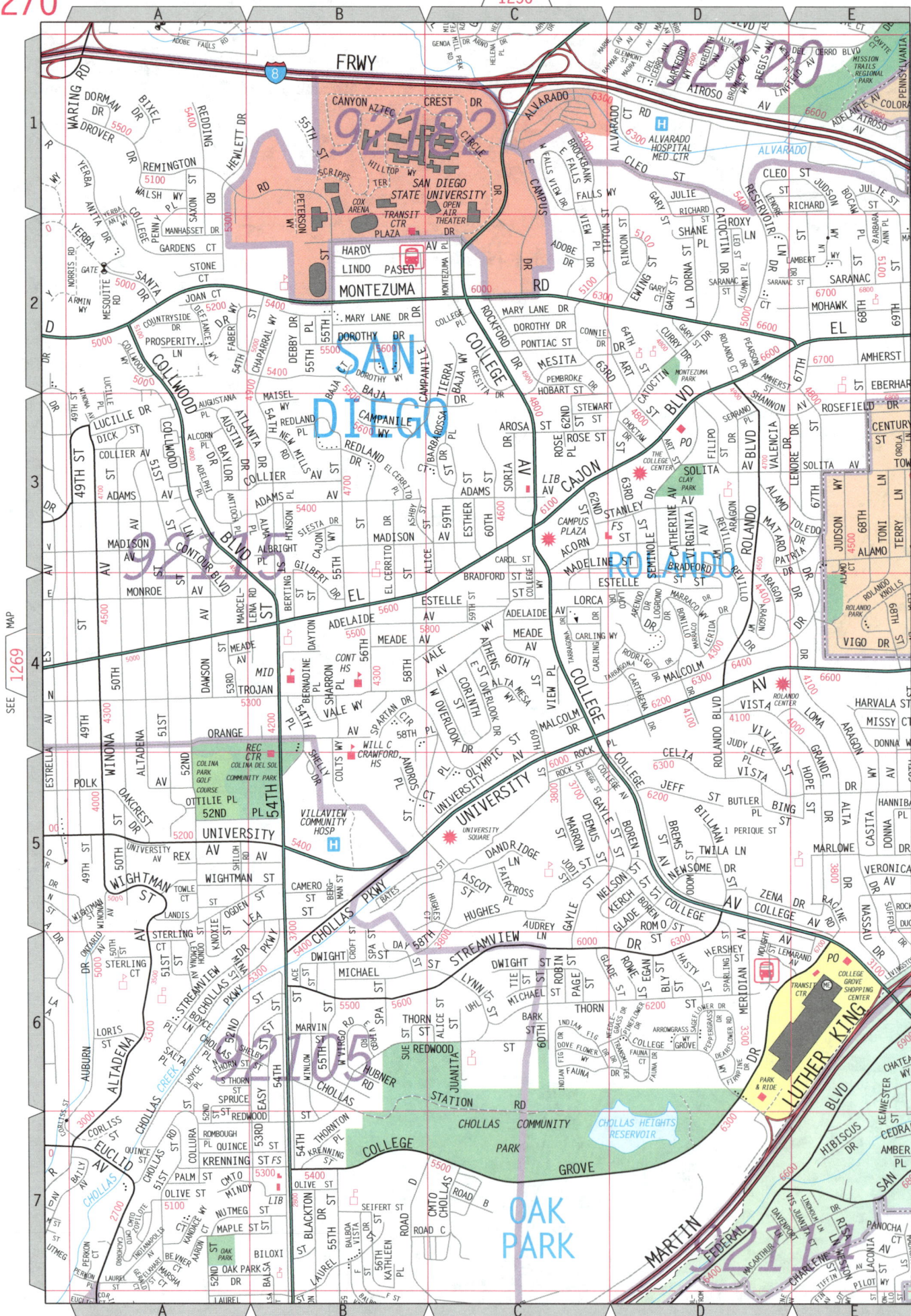

1270

SEE 1250 MAP

SAN DIEGO CO.

MAP

92120

92182

92115

92105

92114

I-8 FRWY

SAN DIEGO STATE UNIVERSITY

COX ARENA
TRANSIT CTR PLAZA
OPEN AIR THEATER

MONTEZUMA RD

SAN DIEGO

ROLANDO

OAK PARK

ALVARADO HOSPITAL MED CTR

COLLEGE BLVD

CAJON AV

UNIVERSITY AV

COLLEGE AV

MARTIN LUTHER KING BLVD

COLLEGE GROVE SHOPPING CENTER

CHOLLAS HEIGHTS RESERVOIR

CHOLLAS COMMUNITY PARK

COLINA PARK GOLF COURSE

COLINA DEL SOL COMMUNITY PARK

VILLAVIEW COMMUNITY HOSP

SEE 1269 MAP

SEE 1290 MAP

0 .125 .25 .375 .5 miles   1 in. = 1900 ft.

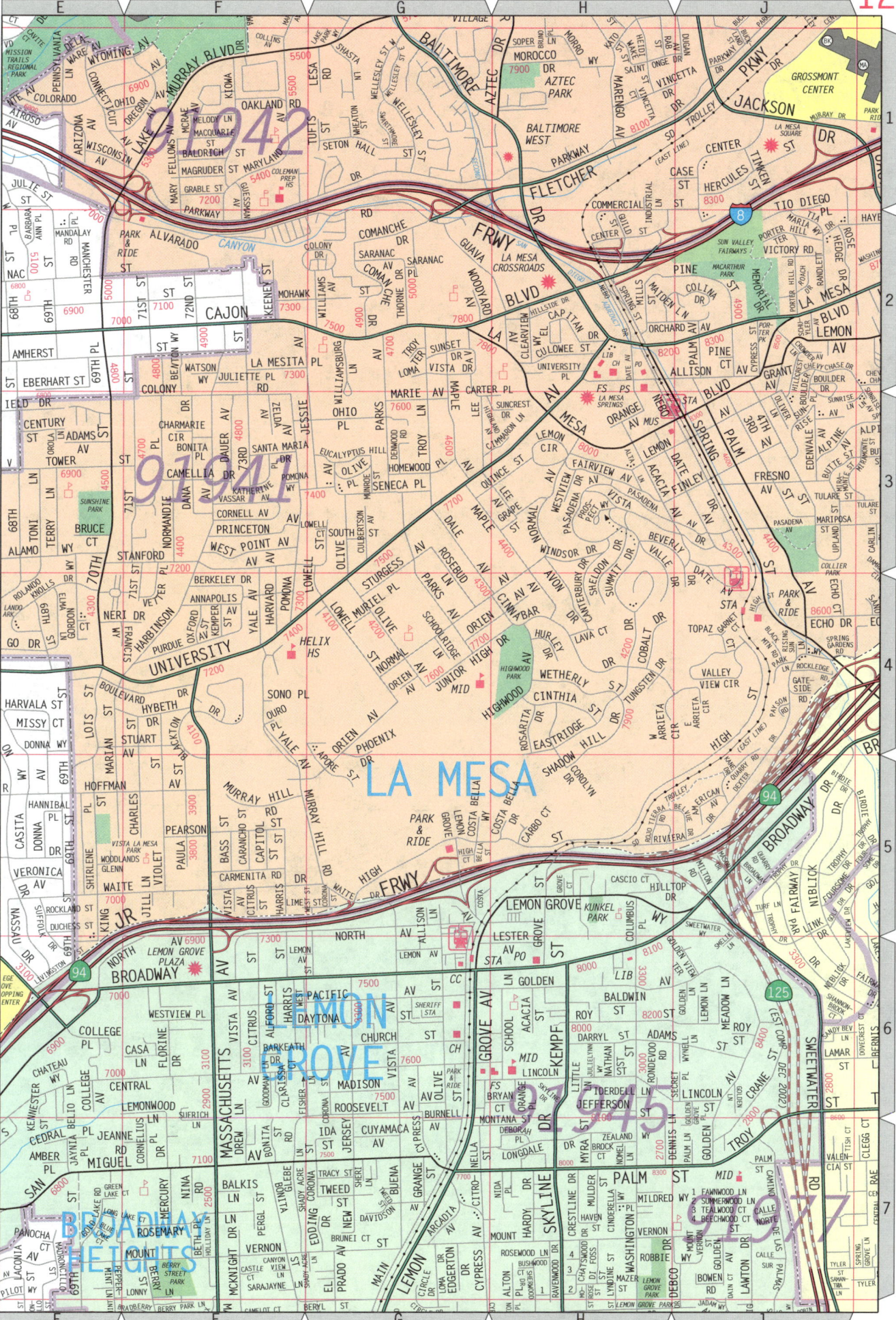

SAN DIEGO CO.

MAP

LA MESA

LEMON GROVE

BROADWAY HEIGHTS

91942

91941

91945

91977

COPYRIGHT 2001

Thomas Bros. Maps®

MISSION TRAILS REGIONAL PARK

GROSSMONT CENTER

BALTIMORE WEST

AZTEC PARK

FLETCHER PKWY

LA MESA CROSSROADS

MACARTHUR PARK

MURRAY BLVD

LAKE MURRAY BLVD

WYOMING AV

CAJON

UNIVERSITY AV

LA MESA BLVD

BROADWAY

MASSACHUSETTS AV

LEMON GROVE PLAZA

PARK & RIDE

HELIX HS

COLEMAN PREP HS

SUNSHINE PARK

BRUCE CT

HIGHWOOD PARK

PACIFIC DAYTONA

KUNKEL PARK

SWEETWATER

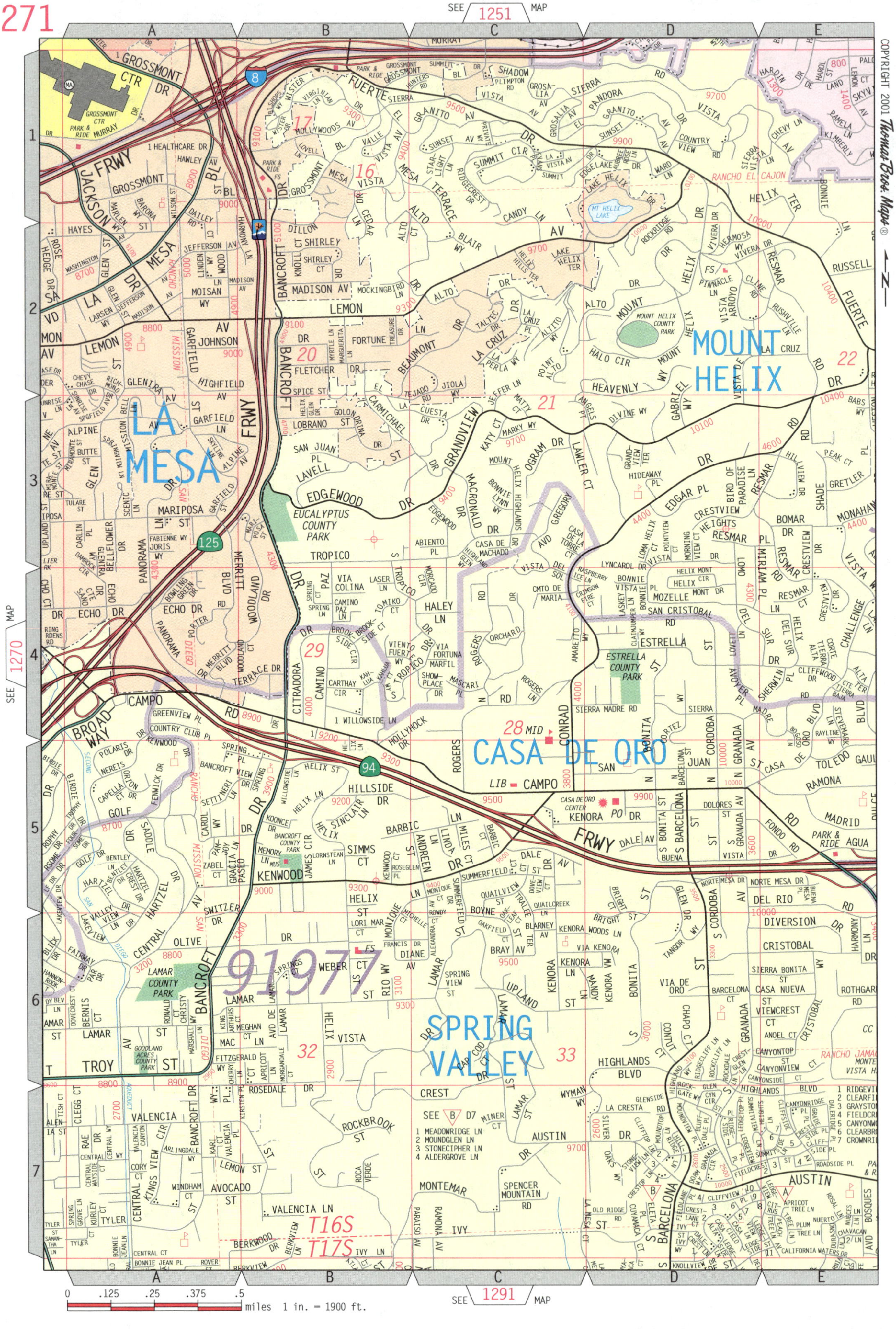

SEE 1251 MAP
SEE 1270 MAP
SEE 1291 MAP
LA MESA
MOUNT HELIX
CASA DE ORO
SPRING VALLEY
91977
GROSSMONT CTR
MT HELIX LAKE
MOUNT HELIX COUNTY PARK
EUCALYPTUS COUNTY PARK
ESTRELLA COUNTY PARK
LAMAR COUNTY PARK
GOODLAND ACRES COUNTY PARK
BANCROFT COUNTY PARK
GROSSMONT FRWY
LA MESA FRWY
CAMPO RD
FUERTE DR
GRANITO DR
SIERRA VISTA AV
RANCHO EL CAJON
BANCROFT DR
LEMON AV
GRANDVIEW DR
EDGEWOOD DR
HELIX ST
CENTRAL AV
JAMACHA BLVD
AUSTIN DR
KENWOOD DR
HELIX VISTA DR
TROY ST
VALENCIA DR
T16S
T17S
SEE B D7
1 MEADOWRIDGE LN
2 MOUNDGLEN LN
3 STONECIPHER LN
4 ALDERGROVE LN
1 RIDGEVIEW
2 CLEARFIELD
3 GRAYSTONE
4 FIELDCREST
5 CANYONWOOD
6 CLEARBROOK
7 CROWNRIDGE
miles 1 in. = 1900 ft.
0 .125 .25 .375 .5

EL CAJON

SAN DIEGO CO.

92020

91941

92019

91978

RANCHO SAN DIEGO

Thomas Bros. Maps ®
COPYRIGHT 2001

TUTTLE PARK

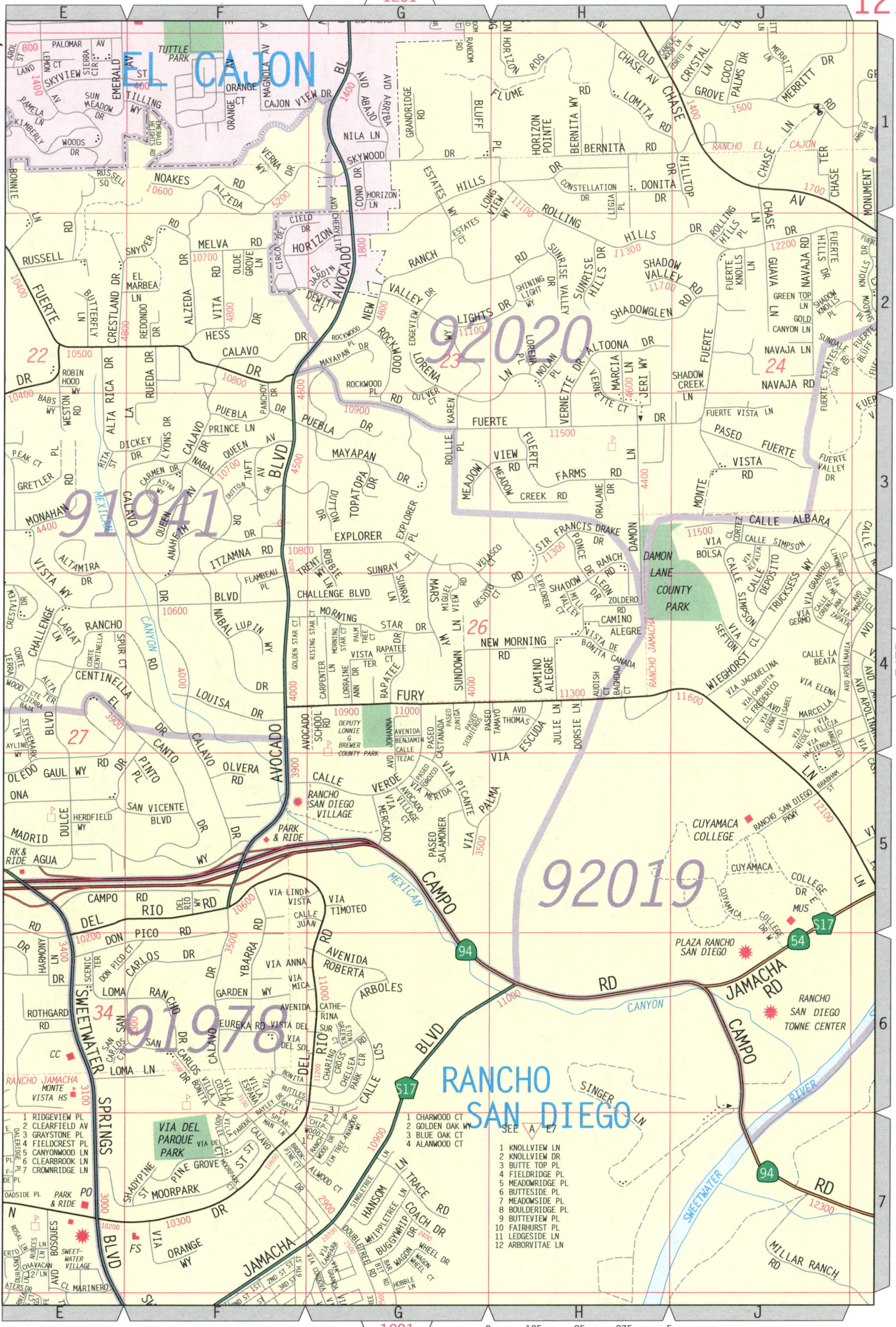

DAMON LANE COUNTY PARK

CUYAMACA COLLEGE

PLAZA RANCHO SAN DIEGO

RANCHO SAN DIEGO TOWNE CENTER

VIA DEL PARQUE PARK

DEPUTY LONNIE G BREWER COUNTY PARK

RANCHO SAN DIEGO VILLAGE

PARK & RIDE

RK & RIDE

PARK & RIDE

22 23 24
27 26
34

SEE 1272 MAP

MAP

0 .125 .25 .375 .5 miles   1 in. = 1900 ft.

1 RIDGEVIEW PL
2 CLEARFIELD AV
3 GRAYSTONE
4 FIELDCREST PL
5 CANYONWOOD LN
6 CLEARBROOK LN
7 CROWNRIDGE PL

1 CHARWOOD CT
2 GOLDEN OAK WY
3 BLUE OAK CT
4 ALANWOOD CT

1 KNOLLVIEW LN
2 KNOLLVIEW DR
3 BUTTE TOP PL
4 FIELDRIDGE PL
5 MEADOWRIDGE PL
6 BUTTESIDE PL
7 MEADOWSIDE PL
8 BOULDERIDGE PL
9 BUTTEVIEW PL
10 FAIRHURST PL
11 LEDGESIDE LN
12 ARBORVITAE LN

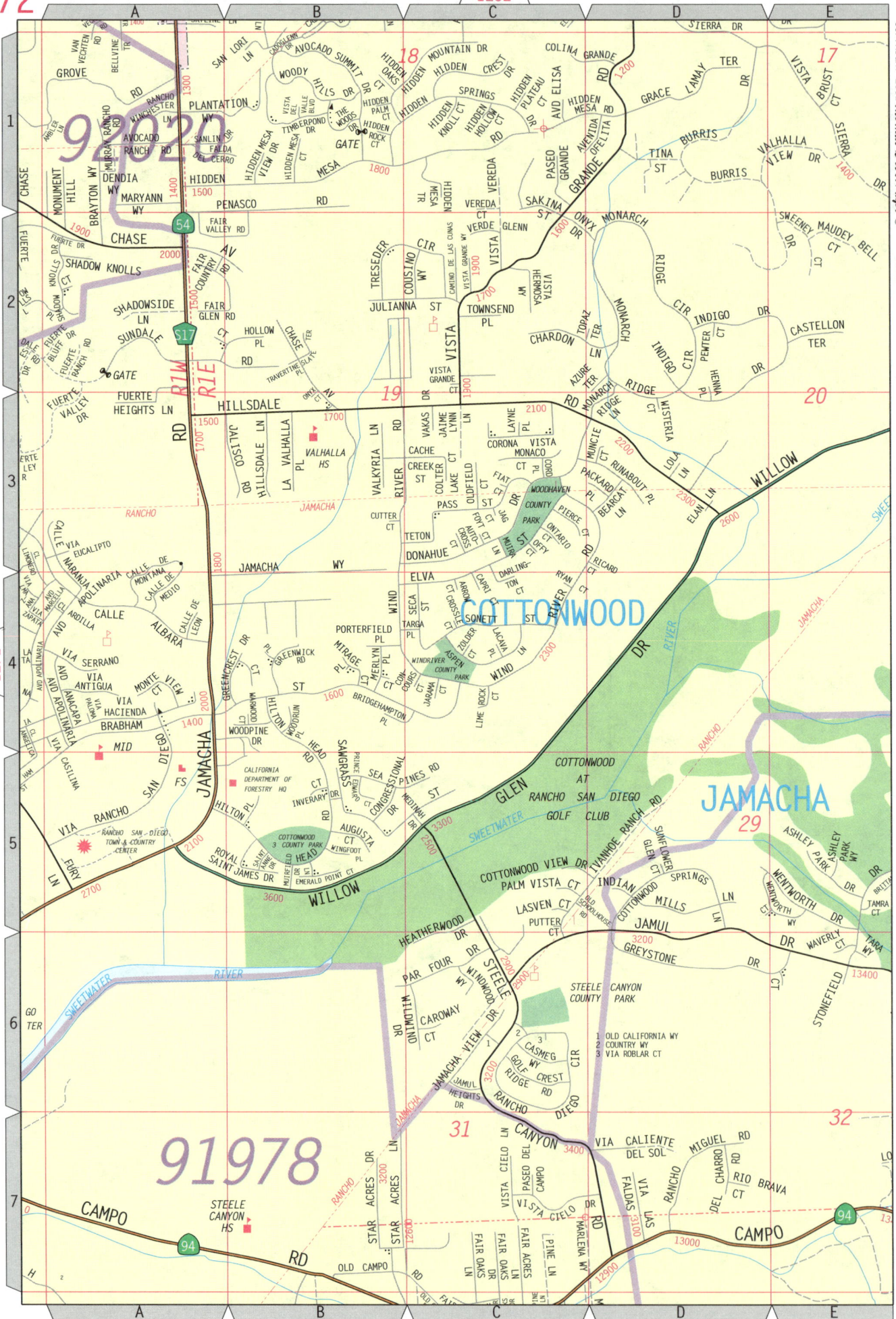

1272

SAN DIEGO CO.

MAP

SEE 1252 MAP

SEE 1271 MAP

SEE 1292 MAP

COPYRIGHT 2001 Thomas Bros. Maps ® —N—

92020

91978

COTTONWOOD

JAMACHA

18   17   19   20   29   31   32

GROVE RD
VAN VECHTEN RD
BELLVINE TR
SKYLINE LN
SAN LORI LN
AVOCADO SUMMIT DR
WOODY HILLS DR
HIDDEN OAKS
HIDDEN MOUNTAIN DR
HIDDEN CREST DR
COLINA GRANDE
SIERRA DR

MONUMENT HILL
BRAYTON WY
DENDIA WY
MARYANN WY
MURRAY RANCHO
RANCHO WINCHESTER LN
RANCHESTER LN
AMBER
PLANTATION WY
AVOCADO RANCH RD
HIDDEN
MESA
PENASCO RD
VISTA DEL CERRO
VALLE VERDE BLVD
THE WOODS
TIMBERPOND DR
HIDDEN MESA
HIDDEN MESA VIEW DR
HIDDEN MESA CT
HIDDEN PALM DR
HIDDEN ROCK CT
GATE
MESA
HIDDEN SPRINGS RD
HIDDEN KNOLL CT
HIDDEN HOLLOW RD
HIDDEN PLATEAU DR
HIDDEN MESA CT
AVD ELISA
AVD HIDDEN MESA
PASEO GRANDE
AVENIDA GRANDE
AVENIDA OFELITA
GRACE
LAMAY DR
TER
TINA ST
BURRIS
BURRIS
VISTA BRUST CT
VALHALLA VIEW DR
SIERRA DR

CHASE
CHASE AV
SHADOW KNOLLS
FUERTE DR
SHADOW KNOLLS
FUERTE
FUERTE BLUFF DR
FUERTE RANCH RD
FAIR VALLEY RD
FAIR COUNTRY RD
FAIR GLEN RD
HOLLOW PL RD
CHASE TER
SLATE
TRAVERTINE
SWEENEY MAUDEY BELL DR
CT

SHADOWSIDE LN
SUNDALE LN
GATE
FUERTE HEIGHTS LN
FUERTE VALLEY DR
FUERTE LN
HILLSDALE
JALISCO RD
HILLSDALE LN
LA VALHALLA PL
VALHALLA HS
ONYX AV
VALKYRIA LN
RIVER
VAKAS LN
JAIME LYNN
LAYNE PL
CORONA VISTA MONACO
VISTA HERMOSA WY
CHARDON
TOPAZ LN
MONARCH TER
MONARCH RIDGE
MONARCH RIDGE CT
INDIGO CIR
PEWTER
WISTERIA
HENNA
AZURE TER
INDIGO DR
CASTELLON TER

TREATEDER CIR
COUSINO WY
JULIANNA ST
CAMINO DE LAS CIMAS
VISTA GRANDE WY
VISTA VERDE GLENN
VISTA
TOWNSEND PL
VISTA GRANDE
ONYX DR

RANCHO
JAMACHA
CACHE CREEK ST
COLTER LAKE CT
OLDFIELD
FIAT ST
JAG CT
FONT CT
AUTO CROSS
CORD CT
MUNCIE LN
RUNABOUT PL
PACKARD
PIERCE
BEARCAT LN
ONTARIO
WOODHAVEN COUNTY PARK
RICARD
LOLA LN
ELAN LN
WILLOW

CUTTER CT
TETON
DONAHUE
ELVA
WIND
SECA ST
TARGA PL
PORTERFIELD PL
MIRAGE PL
MERLYN PL
CON COURS
BRIDGEHAMPTON PL
SONETT
ZOLDER
LACUNA
CAPRI
ARROW
DARLING TON CT
RYAN ST
RIVER DR
ASPEN
WINDRIVER COUNTY PARK
JARAMA
LIME ROCK
WIND
COTTONWOOD

CALLE EUCALIPTO
CALLE NARANJA
CALLE DE MONTANA
CALLE DE MEDIO
CALLE DE LEON
APOLINARIA
CALLE ALBARA
ARDILLA
AVD ZAPATA
VIA SERRANO
VIA ANTIGUA
AVD ANACAPA
VIA APOLINARIA
VIA HACIENDA
BRABHAM
MONTE VIEW CT
LA TA
AVD APOLINARIA
LA PALOMA
LA ANGELITA
VIA CASTILINA
MID
GREENCREST DR
GREENWICK RD
HILTON PL
WOODRUN
WOODPINE DR
SAWGRASS
PRINCE EDWARD DR
SEA PINES RD
INVERARY DR
CONGRESSIONAL
AUGUSTA CT
MEDINAH DR
HILTON HEAD RD
WINGFOOT PL
COTTONWOOD 3 COUNTY PARK HEAD
MUIRFIELD
ST ANDREWS
EMERALD POINT CT
ROYAL SAINT JAMES DR
WILLOW
GLEN
COTTONWOOD AT RANCHO SAN DIEGO GOLF CLUB
SWEETWATER
COTTONWOOD VIEW DR
PALM VISTA CT
IVANHOE RANCH RD
RANCHO
INDIAN SPRINGS
SUNFLOWER
GLEN CT
COTTONWOOD MILLS LN
JAMACHA DR
ASHLEY PARK LN
ASHLEY PARK WY
WENTWORTH DR
TAMRA CT
TARA WY
BRITTA
JAMUL DR
WAVERLY CT
STONEFIELD DR
13400

VIA RANCHO
SAN DIEGO
JAMACHA
FS
CALIFORNIA DEPARTMENT OF FORESTRY HQ
FURY LN
RANCHO SAN DIEGO TOWN & COUNTRY CENTER
HEATHERWOOD DR
PAR FOUR DR
WINDMOOR WY
STEELE
LASVEN CT
PUTTER CT
OLD SCHOOLHOUSE
GREYSTONE DR
JAMUL
STEELE CANYON COUNTY PARK
3200
3300

SWEETWATER RIVER
GO TER
WILDMONT DR
CAROWAY CT
JAMACHA VIEW DR
JAMUL HEIGHTS DR
CASMEG WY
GOLF CREST RD
GOLF RIDGE
RANCHO DIEGO
CANYON
1 OLD CALIFORNIA WY
2 COUNTRY WY
3 VIA ROBLAR CT
VIA CALIENTE DEL SOL
PASEO DEL CAMPO
MIGUEL RD
DEL CHARRO RD
RIO BRAVA
LO

CAMPO RD
STEELE CANYON HS
STAR ACRES DR
STAR ACRES
OLD CAMPO RD
FAIR OAKS LN
FAIR ACRES LN
PINE LN
VISTA CIELO
VISTA CIELO DR
VIA LAS FALDAS
MARLENA WY
CAMPO
94 54 S17
13000 12900

miles 1 in. = 1900 ft.
0 .125 .25 .375 .5

SAN DIEGO CO.

MAP

SEE 1252 MAP

SEE 1273 MAP

SEE 1292 MAP

Thomas Bros. Maps®

COPYRIGHT 2001

E   F   G   H   J

7   16   15

1

2

3

4

5

6

7

SINGING HILLS COUNTRY CLUB

WEST VILLAGE DR
SALTBRUSH LN
BITTERBUSH LN
SILVERBERRY CT
SMOKEBUSH LN
BLACKBRUSH LN
GOLDEN HARVEST
ROCK WOOD
WILLOW BEND DR
PINE
HIGH DR

SIERRA DR
1400
DR

DUDEY BELL CT
ON

GLEN DR
2000
2200
OAK DR
OAK DR
CAMPBELL LN
SWEETWATER

CORTE DE
VISTA DE MATAMO
3200
1600
VISTA DE LAS PIEDRAS
3100
1800
CAMINO DE LAS
1800
RIVER

SWEETWATER

BEAVER

HOLLOW RD

21   22

CANYON

92019

MEXICAN

STEELE CANYON GOLF COURSE

28   27

LOIS CANYON RD
3400
3500
FERN CANYON RD

HILLS RD

VALLEY PARK WY
DR
BRITTANY CT
TAMRA CT
STONEFIELD CT
STONEFIELD
TURNBERRY WY
DEVON
TARA WY
TURNBERRY DR
DEVON CT
FARRADAY RIDGE
DR
R CT
LD
13400
DANERIN WY
FOWLER
2400
RIO IVANHOE WY
13400

CANYON RD
3700
CANYON
3400

TRINAS WY
JANACHA
13800
LOMA
ALTA

COYOTE VISTA WY
4000
ALTA LOMA
ALTA LOMA LN
LOMA CT

GATE

HIDDEN TRAIL DR
WILD WEST PL
HIDDEN RIDGE
HIDDEN RIDGE RD
HIDDEN RIDGE
HIDDEN

91935

JAMUL RD
3300
TUK-A-WILE
3500
3800

NORTH JAMUL

33   34

2
MELORA CT
LORREL PL

13900
DR

PEG LEG MINE
ROCKY SAGE RD
PEG 3300
RIO GRANDE
VALLEY RD
14700
ROCKY SAGE RD

T16S
T17S

94
13400
RD

VISTA DIEGO DR
CALLE DEL
SOL RD
AVD DE LA LUNA
RESERVOIR ST
YUCCA ST

GATE
MEXICAN CANYON RD
14000
MYRTLE ST
ORANGE ST
LYONS
14200
CL DE ORO
BERUMIA ST
RAVEN DR
CAMPO ST
14400
11TH
PEG LEG MINE RD
RIO MADRE LN
3100
LOMA VISTA DR
3200
LN

JAMUL

0   .125   .25   .375   .5
miles   1 in. = 1900 ft.

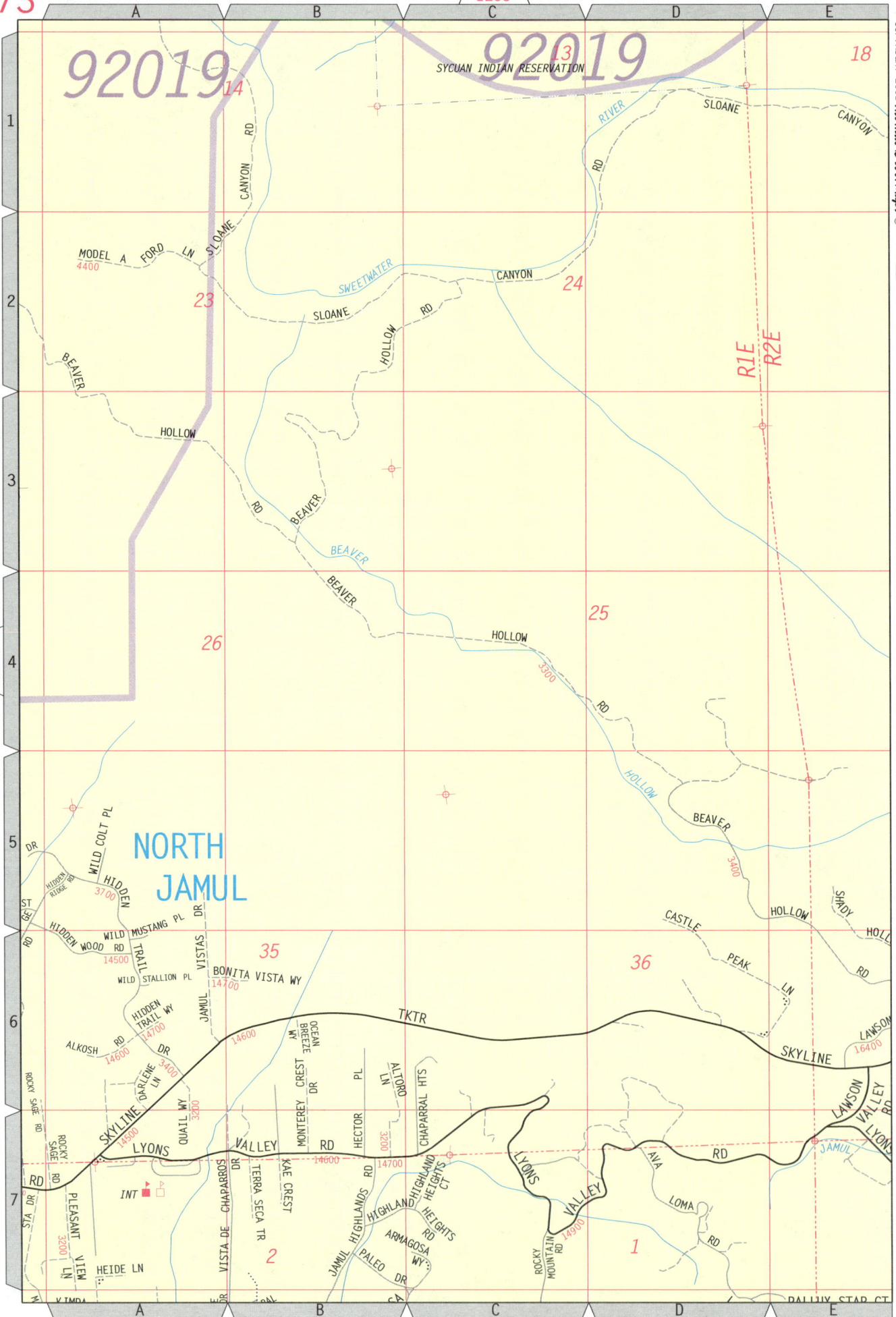

SAN DIEGO CO.

MAP

—N—

SEE 1253 MAP

A B C D E

92019 92019

14 13 18

SYCUAN INDIAN RESERVATION

RIVER

SLOANE

CANYON

1

CANYON

RD

SLOANE

MODEL A FORD LN
4400

23 SLOANE SWEETWATER CANYON 24

2

HOLLOW RD

BEAVER

HOLLOW

R1E R2E

3

RD BEAVER

BEAVER

BEAVER

SEE 1272 MAP

26 HOLLOW 25

3300

4

RD

HOLLOW

WILD COLT PL

BEAVER

3400

DR

NORTH JAMUL

HIDDEN 3700

HIDDEN RIDGE RD

CASTLE HOLLOW SHADY HOLL

5

ST GE RD

HIDDEN WOOD RD WILD MUSTANG PL JAMUL VISTAS DR

14500

WILD TRAIL

35 36

PEAK LN RD

WILD STALLION PL BONITA VISTA WY 14700

HIDDEN TRAIL WY 14700

LAWSON 16400

ALKOSH RD DR 14600 TKTR SKYLINE

6

14600 3400 OCEAN BREEZE WY ALTORO LN LAWSON VALLEY RD

ROCKY SAGE RD DARLENE LN QUAIL WY 3200 MONTEREY CREST DR HECTOR PL 3200 CHAPARRAL HTS LYONS

SKYLINE 14500 VALLEY RD JAMUL

ROCKY SAGE RD LYONS 14600 14700 HIGHLAND HEIGHTS CT LYONS VALLEY

7

STA DR RD VISTA DE CHAPARROS DR TERRA SECA TR KAE CREST JAMUL HIGHLANDS RD HIGHLAND HEIGHTS RD AVA LOMA RD

INT 2 HIGHLAND ARMAGOSA WY ROCKY MOUNTAIN RD 14900 1

PLEASANT VIEW LN 3200 PALEO DR

HEIDE LN KIMDA

SEE 1293 MAP

0 .125 .25 .375 .5 miles 1 in. = 1900 ft.

SAN DIEGO CO.

MAP

Thomas Bros. Maps®

COPYRIGHT 2001

N

CLEVELAND NATIONAL FOREST

E   F   G   H   J

18

19

CANYON

GATE

SWEETWATER RD

RIVER

20

21

LAWSON

CREEK

1

2

91935

30

29

CHOUKAIR

DR

BEAVER

RD

INVERNESS WY

VALLEY

SHADY

HOLLOW

LN
3200

RD

31

SLOANE   CANYON   RD

SLOANE

TKTR

CAMPO   LINDO   RD
12900

VALLEY

28

LAWSON
17200

KRIS   RD

MARK

KRIS RD

TR

HLE

HLE

3

4

5

15900

WOOD   VALLEY   TR

16500

HOLLOW

LILAC WOOD RD

LILAC WOOD
LN

32

33

SEE 1274 MAP

LAWSON
16400

TKTR

SKYLINE

SKYTRAIL RANCH RD

TKTR

6

LAWSON

VALLEY RD

LYONS

MUL

T16S

T17S

15500

VALLEY RD

CREEK

6

DIAMOND GEM LN

DIAMOND JACK
CAMPGROUND

5

4

7

STAR CT

E   F   G   H   J

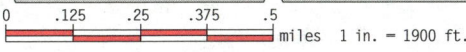

0   .125   .25   .375   .5   miles   1 in. = 1900 ft.

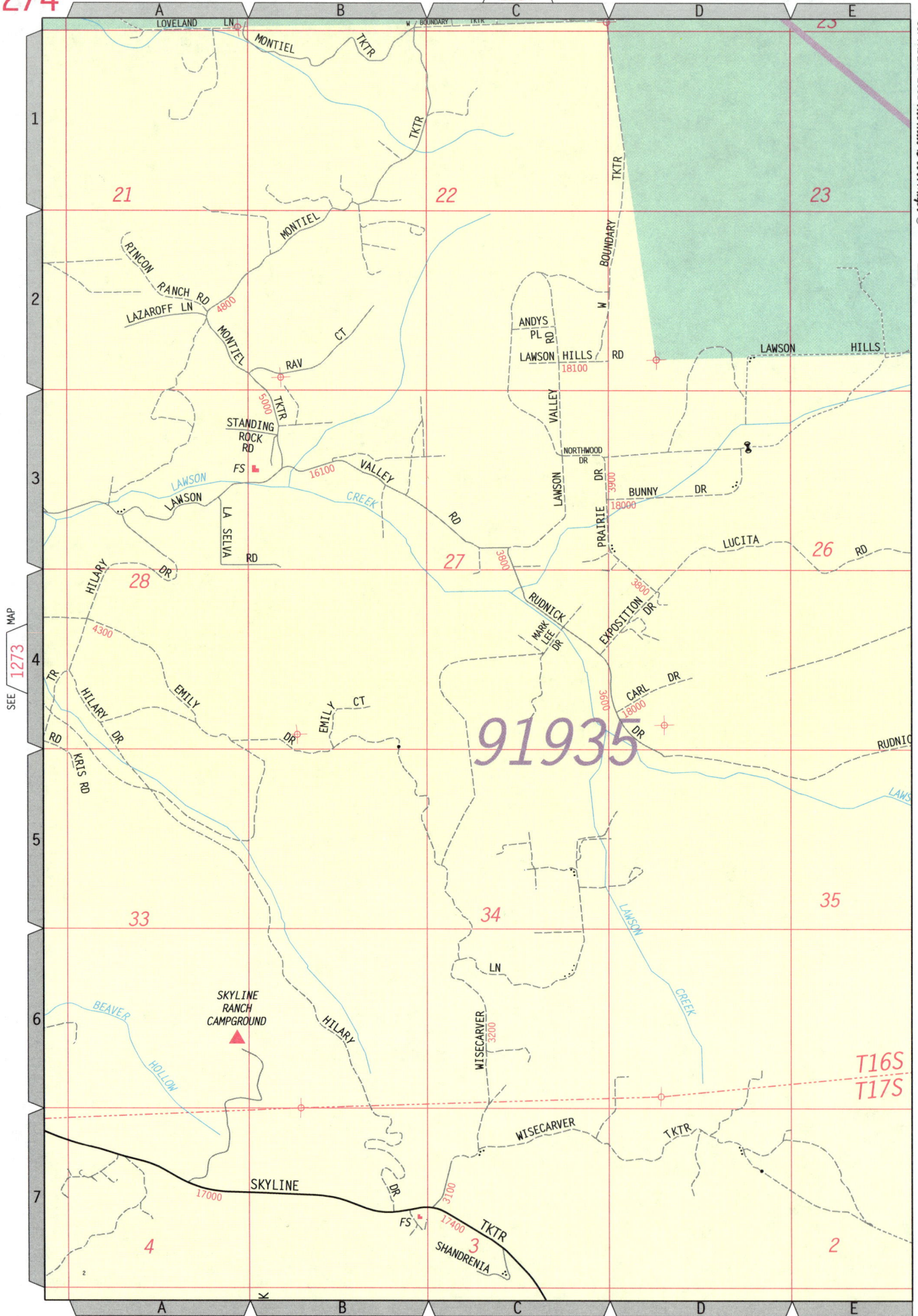

SAN DIEGO CO.

MAP

SEE 1254 MAP

A   B   C   D   E

LOVELAND   LN
MONTIEL
BOUNDARY   TKTR
TKTR
TKTR

23

1

21   22   23

RINCON   RANCH   RD
LAZAROFF   LN
MONTIEL
4800
MONTIEL
CT
RAV
5000
TKTR

BOUNDARY
W
ANDYS
PL   RD
LAWSON HILLS   RD
18100
LAWSON   HILLS
LAWSON   HILLS   RD

2

STANDING
ROCK
RD
FS
LAWSON
LAWSON
LA SELVA
RD
16100
VALLEY
CREEK
RD
VALLEY
LAWSON
NORTHWOOD
DR
PRAIRIE
3900
BUNNY   DR
18000
LUCITA   RD
26

3

HILARY   DR
28
4300
27
3800
RUDNICK
MARK
LEE
DR
EXPOSITION   DR
3800
3600
18000
CARL   DR

4

TR
RD
HILARY   DR
KRIS   RD
EMILY
EMILY
DR
EMILY   CT
DR
RUDNIC
91935
RUDNIC
LAWS

5

33   34   LAWSON   CREEK   35

BEAVER
HOLLOW
SKYLINE
RANCH
CAMPGROUND
HILARY
LN
WISECARVER
3200
T16S
T17S

6

SKYLINE
17000
DR
FS
3100
17400
TKTR
WISECARVER   TKTR

7

4   SHANDRENIA   3   2

A   K   B   C   D   E

0   .125   .25   .375   .5
miles   1 in. = 1900 ft.

SEE 1294 MAP

E F G H J

MEADOW VIEW LN PARK LN

JAPATUL RD

1

HIDDEN
GLEN

24

19

91901

2

HILLS RD

HO

CLEVELAND

LOST TR
30400

3

MAGUAY RD

NATIONAL

25

FOREST

30

RD

R2E R3E

EMMANUEL
3300 WY

SEE 1275 MAP

4

DR 3100

FOREST

RUDNICK

LAWSON

CREEK

PARK

36

5

STEEL RANCH
RD RD

31

VALLEY
RD TR

OAK

6

T16S
T17S

R2E R3E

7

1

6

5

E F G H J

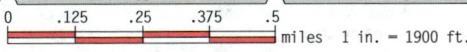

0 .125 .25 .375 .5

miles 1 in. = 1900 ft.

SEE 1255 MAP

A B C D E

UL

JAPATUL

JAPATUL RD

JAPATUL VALLEY RD

CARVEACRE RD

SPUR

FUSCO LN

19300

4800

22100

19700

21000

20

21

CARVEACRE

RD

SPIRIT

TRAIL

LYONS

CARVEACRE

SPIRIT

HONDO LN

2679B

FOG RDG

3900

21000

TR

4500

VALLEY

LOST TR

RD

GASKILL PEAK

RD

EAGLE PASS

91901

EMMANUEL WY

GASKILL PEAK RD

RD

BIG CAT TR

COUGAR SUMMIT

RD

SEE 1274 MAP

29

3500

21200

OLD OAK RD

CARVEACRE

BARRETT VIEW RD

SKY RIDGE RD

SLANT ROCK RD

28

21300

ESP

RD

RD

VALLEY

33

32

LYONS

21900

5

4

3

2

0 .125 .25 .375 .5 miles 1 in. = 1900 ft.

—N→

SEE 1255 MAP

E   F   G   H   J

1

22   23   24

CANYON

HORSETHIEF

VALLEY

CREEK

2

3

CLEVELAND NATIONAL FOREST

27   26

CREEK

2

SEE 429 MAP

ESPINOZA

PINE

CREEK

CREEK

ESPINOZA

4

CREEK

5

34   35   36

MAP

VALLEY

T16S
T17S

6

PINE

3   2   1

7

K

E   F   G   H   J

2

SEE 1294 MAP

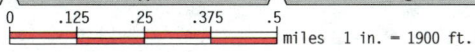

0 .125 .25 .375 .5   miles 1 in. = 1900 ft.

SAN DIEGO CO.

MAP

SEE 1267 MAP

A B C D E

1

2

3

PACIFIC

SEE 429 MAP

4

5

6

7

A B C D E

0 .125 .25 .375 .5

miles   1 in. = 1900 ft.

SEE 429 MAP

1287

SAN DIEGO CO.

MAP

E F G H J

92107

POINT LOMA

OSPREY PT
CLAIBORNES COVE
PAPPY'S PT
ROSS ROCK
SUNSET CLIFFS BLVD
SUNSET CLIFFS PARK

SUNSET CLIFFS BLVD

ORCHARD AV
BERMUDA AV
PESCADERO AV
ADAIR ST
TIVOLI ST
DEVONSHIRE DR
FROUDE ST
GRANGER ST
OSPREY ST
GUIZOT ST
LEON ST
BARBARA ST
SANTA BARBARA ST
LA PALOMA
TRIESTE DR
SORRENTO DR
BARCELONA DR
CALNERAS DR
OSPREY DR
CORNISH DR
PIEDMONT DR
ALEXANDRIA DR
SAVOY ST
SAVOY CIR
BERMUDA CIR

MARSEILLES
MONACO DR
BRINDISI ST
CORDOVA ST
ALGECIRAS ST
CARMELO ST
CASITAS ST
LADERA ST
CORNISH

ROCK PILE

HILL
AMIFORD ST
JOHN
EL MAC PL
ORMA ST
MOANA
TARENTO ST
TALBOT ST
TEMPLE ST
MOANA DR

POINT LOMA NAZARENE UNIVERSITY
LOMALAND
LOMALAND DR

AMALAND DR
STAFFORD PL
PEPPER TREE LN
DUPONT
TARENTO ST
SAVOY ST
TEMPLE ST
CATALINA ST
JENNINGS ST
WILCOX ST
CHARLES ST
DUDLEY ST
WARNER ST
PIO PICO ST
GARDEN LN
ROSECROFT LN

AB'S REEF

SUNSET CLIFFS PARK
RATKAY PT
NEWBREAK BEACH

SAN DIEGO

CATALINA BLVD

GARDEN LN
TRUDY LN
CEDARBRAE LN
AZTEC WY
AZTEC ST
ELECTRON DR
SILVER GATE
MILLS ST
COCHRAN

GATE OPEN 9:00 AM TO 5:30 PM
209

BENNETT

OCEAN

WOODWARD

CABRILLO MEMORIAL DR

92106

CABRILLO MEMORIAL
FLEMING RD
COLE RD
WHISTLER RD
RYNE RD
MCCLELLAN RD
PATTERSON RD

US NAVAL RES

FORT ROSECRANS MILITARY RESERVATION

WOODWARD RD

GATCHELL RD

CABRILLO MEMORIAL DR

FORT ROSECRANS NATIONAL CEMETERY

1 2 3 4 5 6 7

SEE 1288 MAP

0 .125 .25 .375 .5 miles 1 in. = 1900 ft.

92101

BAY

CORONADO

92135

92118

OCEAN

U S MARINE CORPS RECRUIT DEPOT

TERMINAL 2

TERMINAL 1

COMMUTER TERMINAL

AIR FREIGHT BUILDING

GODDARD WY

SAN DIEGO INTERNATIONAL AIRPORT

LINDBERGH FIELD

OPEN SPACE

LAUREL

U S COAST GUARD STATION

SHERATON SAN DIEGO HOTEL & MARINA EAST

HARBOR ISLAND DR

HARBOR ISLAND

SHERATON SAN DIEGO HOTEL & MARINA WEST

HARBOR ISLAND DR PARK

COUNTY ADMINISTRATION CENTER

MARITIME MUS

SAN DIEGO CRUISE SHIP TERMINAL

B ST PIER

BROADWAY

BROADWAY PIER

NAVY PIER

FLEET & INDUSTRIAL SUPPLY CENTER

TUNA HARBOR

SEAPORT VILLAGE

TUNA HARBOR PIER

EMBARCADERO MARINA PARK

EMBASSY SUITES SAN DIEGO BAY

HYATT REGENCY HOTEL

WYNDHAM EMERALD PLAZA HOTEL

HOLIDAY INN ON THE BAY

SAN DIEGO LIMITS

SAUFLEY FS

SAN CORONADO

CURTIS VOUGHT

MURRAY ST

MAXFIELD BLVD

CARSON ST

CECIL ST

SAUFLEY

BARIN RD

ROOSEVELT BLVD

WRIGHT AV

QUENTIN

QUAY RD

NORTH ISLAND NAVAL AIR STATION

MCCAIN BLVD

COLORADO

TOW WAY

GATE 2

SHORELINE PARK

BAYVIEW PARK

SDG&E PARK

CENTENNIAL PARK

FERRY

CORONADO FERRY & FISHING PIER

FERRY LANDING MARKETPLACE

PUBLIC SERVICE BLDG

SHARP CORONADO HOSP

SEA N AIR GOLF COURSE

ALAMEDA

CORONADO HS

SPRECKELS PARK

LIB

PENDLETON

POMONA

GLORIETTA BLVD

BALBOA

CARRILLO

COUNTRY CLUB

SHERMAN RD

SEA N AIR GOLF COURSE

ACACIA

CAROB WY

ALAMEDA BLVD

OLIVE ST

ORANGE

ADELLA

SUNSET PARK

OCEAN DR

CORONADO MUNICIPAL BLVD

NORTH BEACH

CENTRAL BEACH

LIFEGUARD FACILITY

STAR PARK

CORONADO GOLF COURSE

PACIFIC HWY

KETTNER BLVD

STATE ST

INDIA ST

COLUMBIA ST

HARBOR DR

GRAPE ST

ASH ST

BEECH ST

B ST

BROADWAY

SEE 1308 MAP
See Page ix for Detail Airport Map
0 .125 .25 .375 .5 miles 1 in. = 1900 ft.
E F G H J

SAN DIEGO CO.

MAP

SEE 1269 MAP

SEE 1288 MAP

COPYRIGHT 2001 Thomas Bros. Maps®

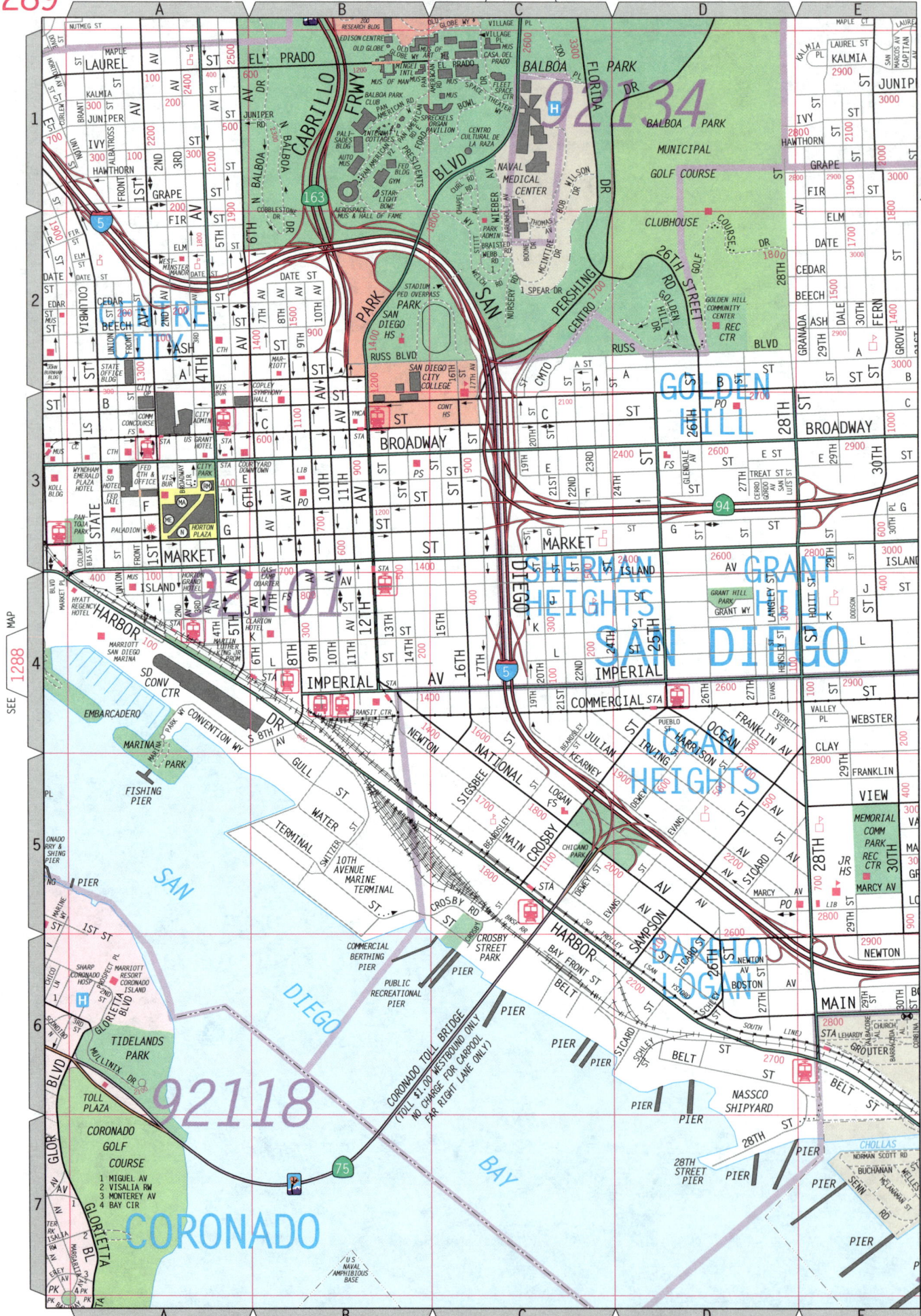

—N—

92134

92101

92118

CENTRE CITY

GOLDEN HILL

SHERMAN HEIGHTS

GRANT HILL

SAN DIEGO

LOGAN HEIGHTS

BARRIO LOGAN

CORONADO

BALBOA PARK

Balboa Park Municipal Golf Course

Naval Medical Center

CABRILLO FRWY

SAN DIEGO FRWY

HARBOR DR

EMBARCADERO

MARINA PARK

FISHING PIER

SD CONV CTR

SAN DIEGO BAY

10TH AVENUE MARINE TERMINAL

COMMERCIAL BERTHING PIER

PUBLIC RECREATIONAL PIER

CROSBY STREET PARK

NASSCO SHIPYARD

28TH STREET PIER

CHOLLAS

TIDELANDS PARK

MILLINIX DR

CORONADO GOLF COURSE

1 MIGUEL AV
2 VISALIA RW
3 MONTEREY AV
4 BAY CIR

TOLL PLAZA

US NAVAL AMPHIBIOUS BASE

CORONADO TOLL BRIDGE
(TOLL $1.00 WESTBOUND ONLY
NO CHARGE FOR CARPOOL
FAR RIGHT LANE ONLY)

SAN DIEGO CITY COLLEGE

SAN DIEGO HS

HORTON PLAZA

BROADWAY

MARKET ST

IMPERIAL AV

COMMERCIAL ST

NATIONAL AV

MEMORIAL COMM PARK REC CTR

GOLDEN HILL COMMUNITY CENTER REC CTR

0 .125 .25 .375 .5 miles 1 in. = 1900 ft.

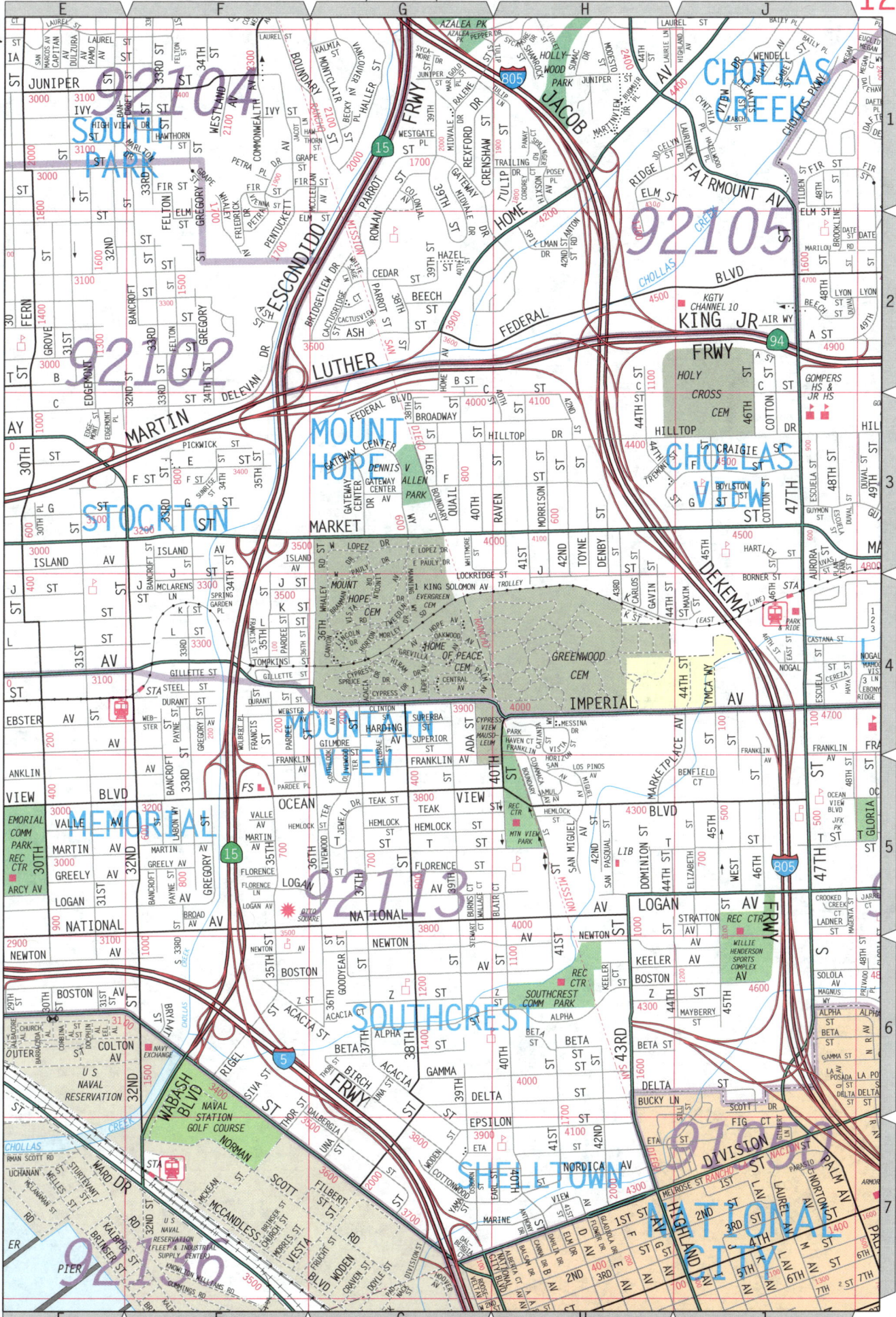

1289

SAN DIEGO CO.

MAP

ThomasBros. Maps®
COPYRIGHT 2001

92104

SOUTH PARK

92105

CHOLLAS CREEK

92102

MOUNT HOPE

STOCKTON

CHOLLAS VIEW

KING JR FRWY

HOLY CROSS CEM

GOMPERS HS & JR HS

KGTV CHANNEL 10

MOUNT HOPE CEM

EVERGREEN CEM

HOME OF PEACE CEM

GREENWOOD CEM

MOUNTAIN VIEW

IMPERIAL AV

DEKEMA

MEMORIAL

EMORIAL COMM PARK REC CTR

92113

SOUTHCREST

SOUTHCREST COMM PARK

WILLIE HENDERSON SPORTS COMPLEX

US NAVAL RESERVATION

COLTON

NAVY EXCHANGE

WABASH BLVD

NAVAL STATION GOLF COURSE

US NAVAL RESERVATION FLEET & INDUSTRIAL SUPPLY CENTER

SHELLTOWN

NATIONAL CITY

92136

PIER

805

94

15

15

5

I-5

805

ESCONDIDO FRWY

0 .125 .25 .375 .5 miles 1 in. = 1900 ft.

SEE 1290 MAP

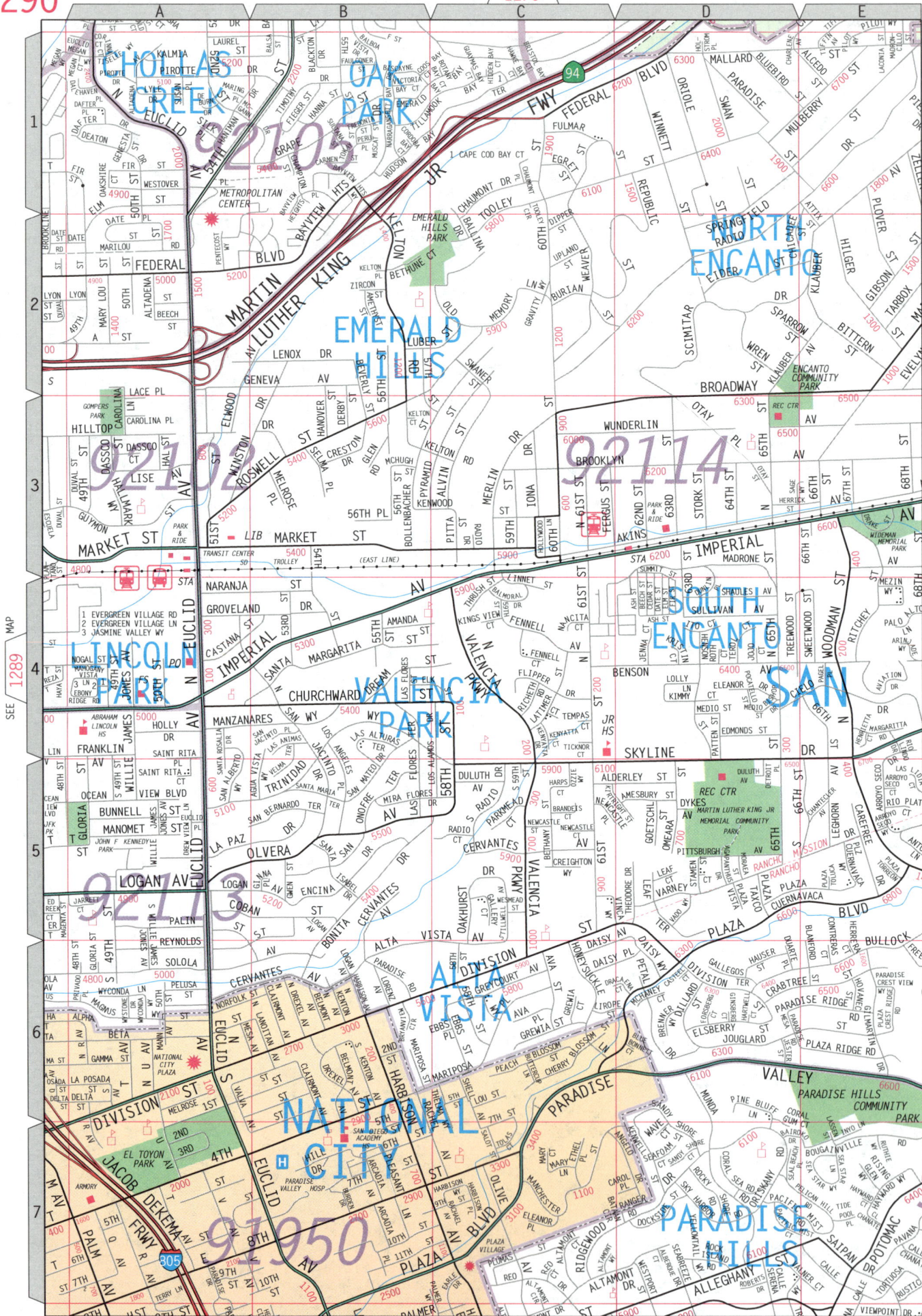

SAN DIEGO CO.

MAP

SEE 1270 MAP

SEE 1289 MAP

COPYRIGHT 2001 Thomas Bros. Maps ®

HOLLAS CREEK

OAK PARK

92105

EMERALD HILLS

NORTH ENCANTO

92102

92114

HILLTOP

SOUTH ENCANTO

SAN

LINCOLN PARK

VALENCIA PARK

ALTA VISTA

92113

NATIONAL CITY

PARADISE HILLS

91950

ENCANTO COMMUNITY PARK

WIDEMAN MEMORIAL PARK

MARTIN LUTHER KING JR MEMORIAL COMMUNITY PARK

PARADISE HILLS COMMUNITY PARK

EL TOYON PARK

METROPOLITAN CENTER

GOMPERS PARK

JOHN F KENNEDY PARK

MARTIN LUTHER KING JR FWY

FEDERAL BLVD

MARKET ST

IMPERIAL AV

BROADWAY

SKYLINE DR

DIVISION ST

PARADISE VALLEY RD

EUCLID AV

VALENCIA PKWY

1 EVERGREEN VILLAGE RD
2 EVERGREEN VILLAGE LN
3 JASMINE VALLEY WY

805

94

SEE 1310 MAP

0 .125 .25 .375 .5 miles 1 in. = 1900 ft.

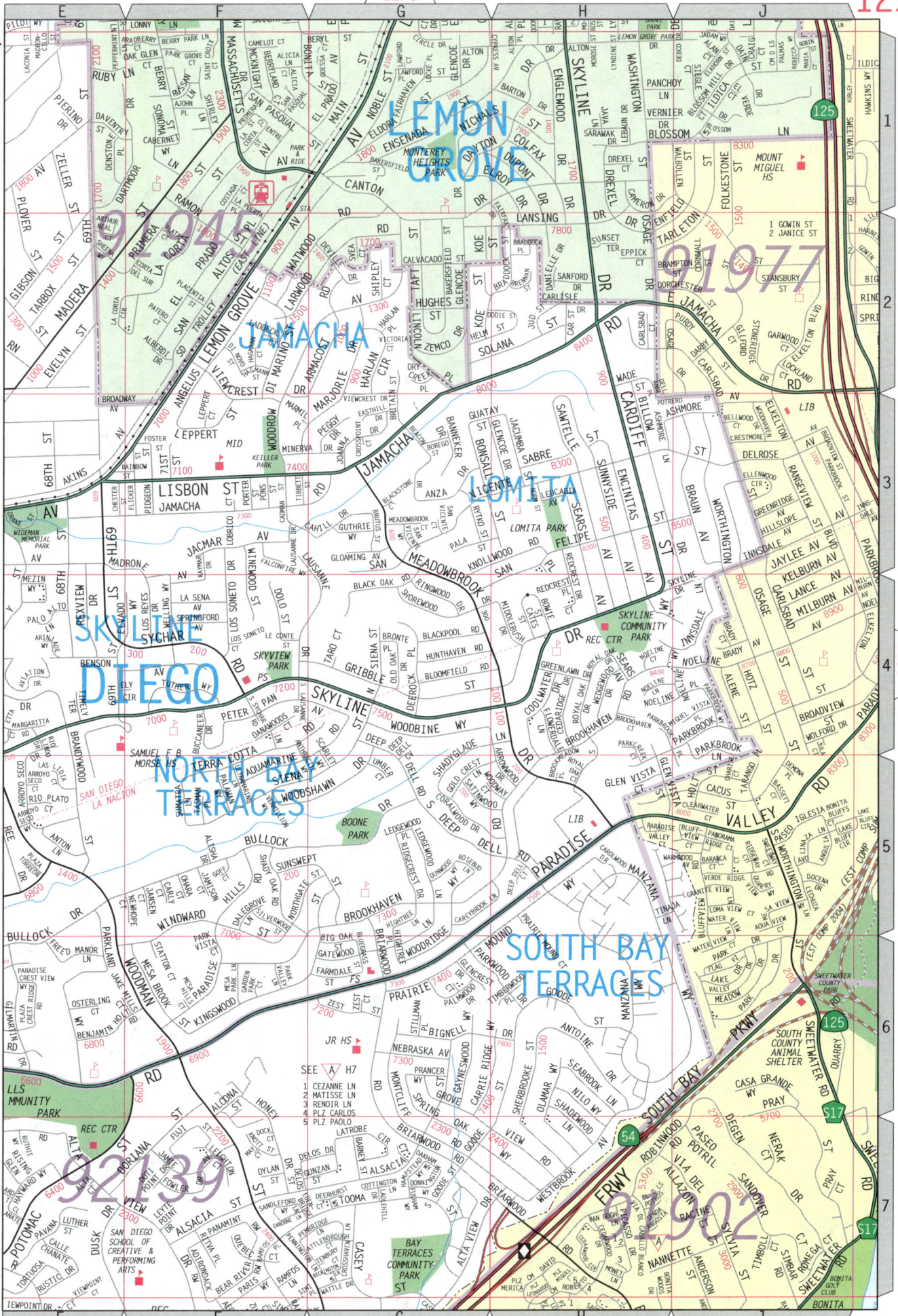

1290

SAN DIEGO CO.

MAP

LEMON GROVE

JAMACHA

92045

91977

LISBON ST

SKYLINE
DIEGO

LOMITA

CARDIFF

NORTH BAY
TERRACES

SOUTH BAY
TERRACES

PARADISE

VALLEY

92139

91902

SEE A H7
1 CEZANNE LN
2 MATISSE LN
3 RENOIR LN
4 PLZ CARLOS
5 PLZ PAOLO

1 GOWIN ST
2 JANICE ST

MOUNT
MIGUEL
HS

SOUTH COUNTY
ANIMAL
SHELTER

SWEETWATER
COUNTY PARK

BAY TERRACES
COMMUNITY PARK

SAN DIEGO
SCHOOL OF
CREATIVE &
PERFORMING
ARTS

0 .125 .25 .375 .5
miles 1 in. = 1900 ft.

SEE 1291 MAP

SAN DIEGO CO.

MAP

91977

SPRING VALLEY

91902

LA PRESA

SWEETWATER

RESERVOIR

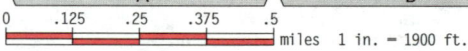

0 .125 .25 .375 .5 miles 1 in. = 1900 ft.

SAN DIEGO CO.

MAP

E   F   G   H   J

Thomas Bros. Maps®

COPYRIGHT 2001

N

ATERS DR
A CL MARINERO
CALIFORNIA
SPRINGS CT
TRES
LAGOS CT
FOOTHILL CT
FABLED WATERS CT

SWEET-
WATER
SPRINGS
BLVD

BLVD

1ST ST
2ND ST
3RD
ST
1ST ST
3RD ST
4TH ST
5TH ST
10TH ST
6TH ST
7TH ST
8TH ST
9TH ST
10TH ST

VIA CORDOVA
VIA GRANDA
VIA TORTOLA
LAMPARA
VIA

DOUBLETREE RD
BAR
BIT
RD

2300

SWEETWATER
SPRINGS
BLVD

10700

S17

PKWY
JAMACHA
BLVD
ISHAM
SPRINGS
CT

RES

E LN SPRING
ALE DR
GLEN LN
SPRING

JAMACHA

POINTE

10500

GOLF POINTE DR LN

0

10600

SER-
VOIR

DR

US
ELEVATOR
RD 10500

VALLEY WATERS CT

MAGICAL WATERS CT

VALLEY
WATERS
CT

FRESH
WATERS
CT

CRYSTAL CLEAR DR
PKWY
CRYSTAL CLEAR
LN

POINTE

CHALLENGER CT
CHALLENGER CIR

PURE WATERS CT

DESTINY
MOUNTAIN
CT

RIVER

SWEETWATER

RANCHO JAMACHA

2

1

12

11

10

91978

15

13

14

91914

22

23

24

CHV

1   2   3   4   5   6   7

SEE 1292 MAP

0   .125   .25   .375   .5   miles   1 in. = 1900 ft.

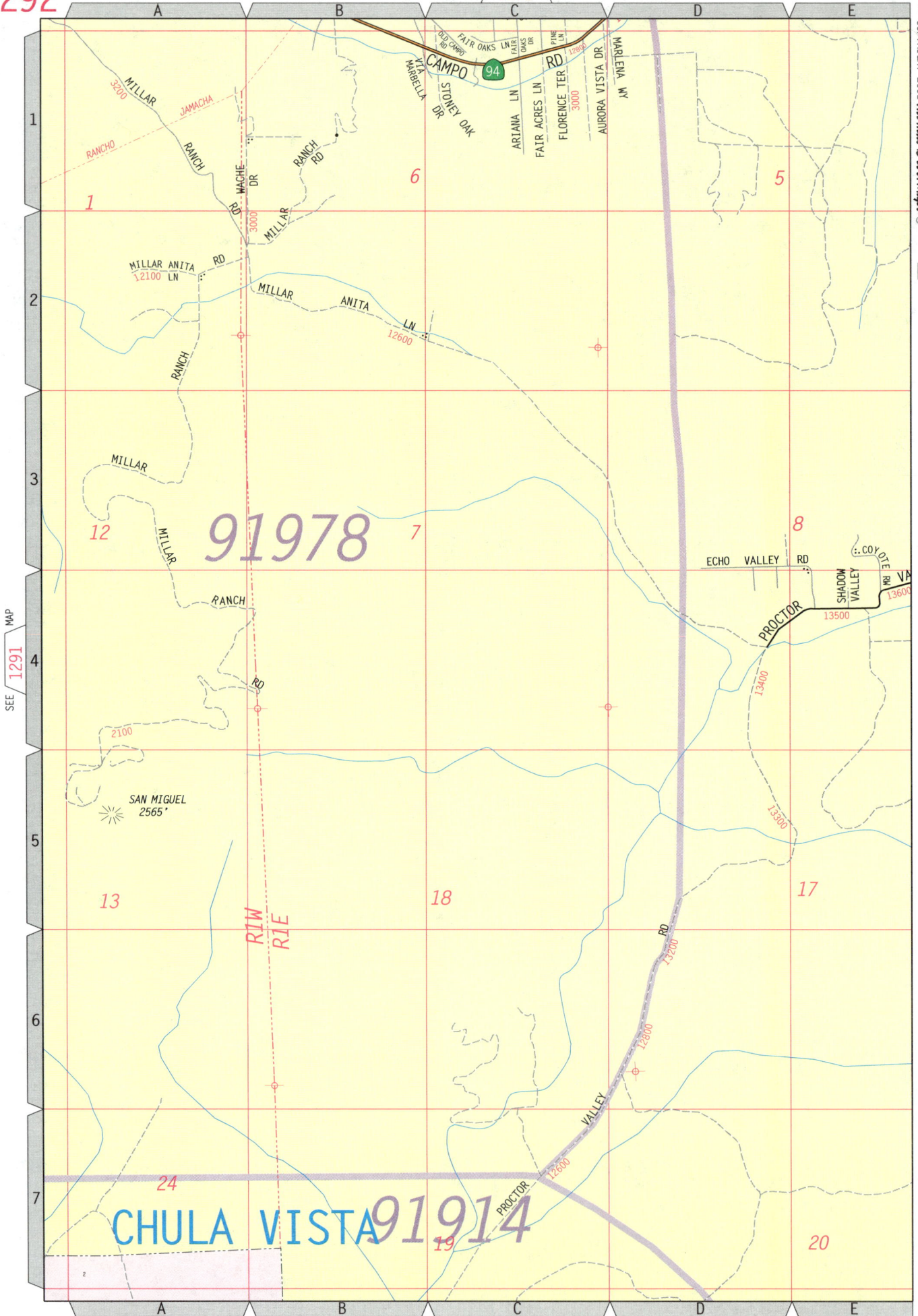

SAN DIEGO CO.

MAP

—N—

COPYRIGHT 2001 *Thomas Bros. Maps* ®

SEE 1272 MAP

SEE 1291 MAP

| A | B | C | D | E |

1

91978

CHULA VISTA **91914**

FAIR OAKS LN
OLD CAMPO RD
CAMPO
94
FAIR OAKS DR
PINE LN
RD
MARLENA WY
VIA MARBELLA
STONEY OAK DR
ARIANA LN
FAIR ACRES LN
FLORENCE TER
AURORA VISTA DR
3000

MILLAR
3200
RANCHO
JAMACHA
RANCH RD
WACHE DR
MILLAR
RANCH RD
3000

1
6
5

MILLAR ANITA LN
12100
MILLAR ANITA LN
12600

RANCH

MILLAR

12
MILLAR
RANCH
RD
7
8

ECHO VALLEY RD
COYOTE RW
PROCTOR
SHADOW VALLEY
13500
VA
13600

2100
13400

SAN MIGUEL
2565'

R1W R1E

13
18
17
13300

RD
13200
VALLEY
12800

24
PROCTOR
VALLEY
12600

19
20

SEE 1293 MAP

0 .125 .25 .375 .5
miles 1 in. = 1900 ft.

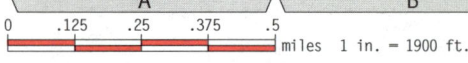

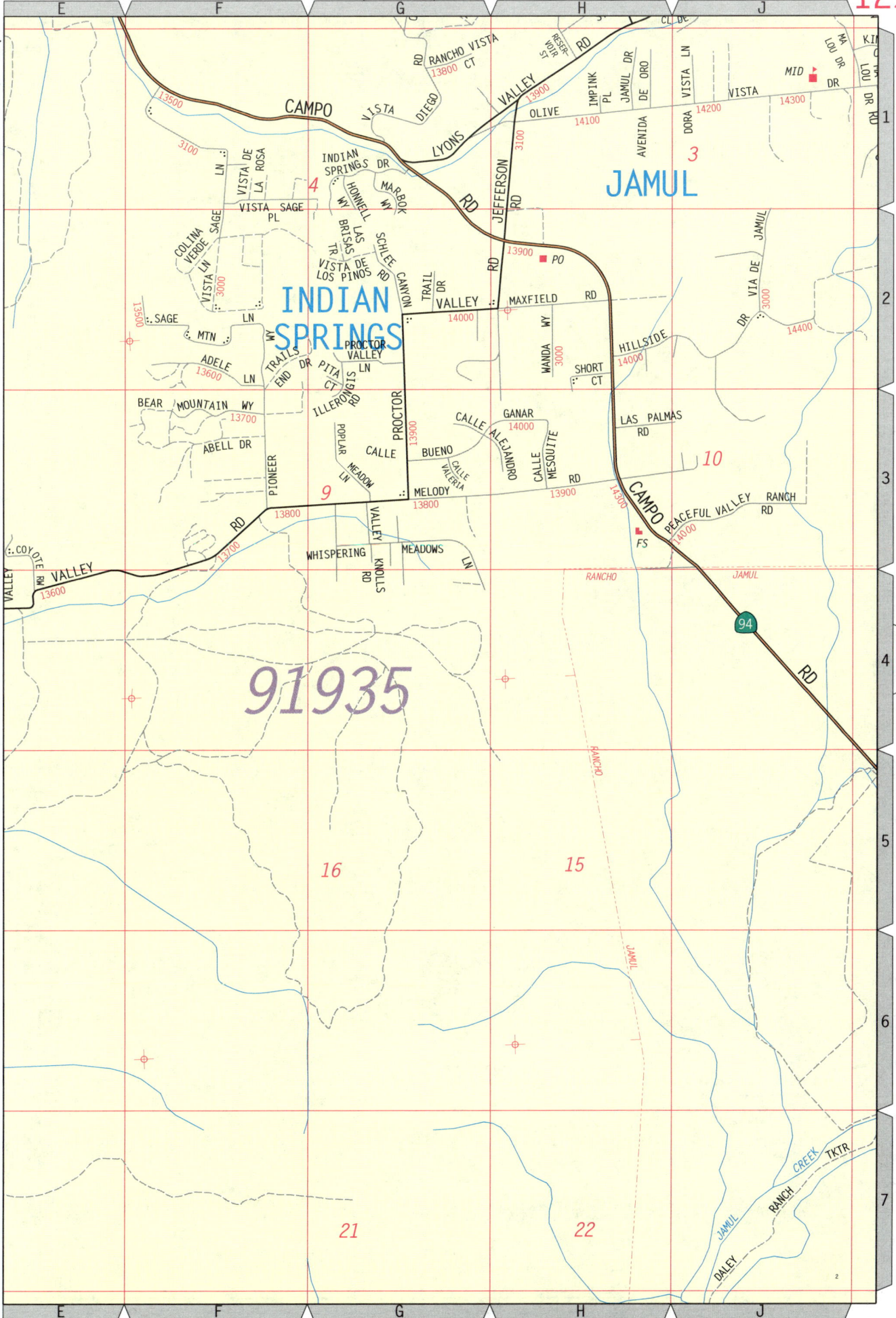

E F G H J

SAN DIEGO CO.

MAP

N

RANCHO VISTA CT
VISTA DIEGO RD
13800
RD
CAMPO
13500
3100

RESERVOIR ST
VALLEY
LYONS
RD

CL DE

MID

KIM

MA LOU DR
LOU DR

JAMUL DR
IMPINK PL
DE ORO
OLIVE
14100
AVENIDA
3100

DORA VISTA LN
VISTA
14200
14300
DR

LOU DR RD

1

JAMUL
3

INDIAN SPRINGS DR
VISTA DE LA ROSA
LN
VISTA SAGE PL
4
HONNELL WY
MAR-BOK WY
COLINA VERDE SAGE LN
LAS BRISAS TR
VISTA DE LOS PINOS
VISTA 3000 LN
SCHLEE RD
CANYON

JEFFERSON RD

13900

PO

2

INDIAN SPRINGS

SAGE MTN LN
13500
ADELE LN
13600
TRAILS END DR
PITA CT
SIGMA LN
ILLEROAD
PROCTOR VALLEY LN

TRAIL DR
VALLEY
14000
MAXFIELD RD
WANDA WY 3000
VIA DE JAMUL
3000
DR
14400

HILLSIDE RD
14000
SHORT CT

BEAR MOUNTAIN WY
13700
ABELL DR
PIONEER RD
13800
13700
CALLE
PROCTOR
13900
POPLAR LN
MEADOW LN
CALLE BUENO
CALLE VALERIA
MELODY
13800

GANAR
14000
CALLE ALEJANDRO
CALLE
MESQUITE RD
13900

LAS PALMAS RD

CAMPO
14300
FS
14000
PEACEFUL VALLEY
RANCH RD

10

3

VALLEY COYOTE RW
VALLEY 13600
13700
WHISPERING KNOLLS RD
MEADOWS LN

RANCHO

JAMUL

SEE 1293 MAP

94

RD

4

91935

16

15

JAMUL

RANCHO

5

6

CREEK TKTR
JAMUL
RANCH
DALEY

21

22

7

2

E F G H J

0 .125 .25 .375 .5
miles 1 in. = 1900 ft.

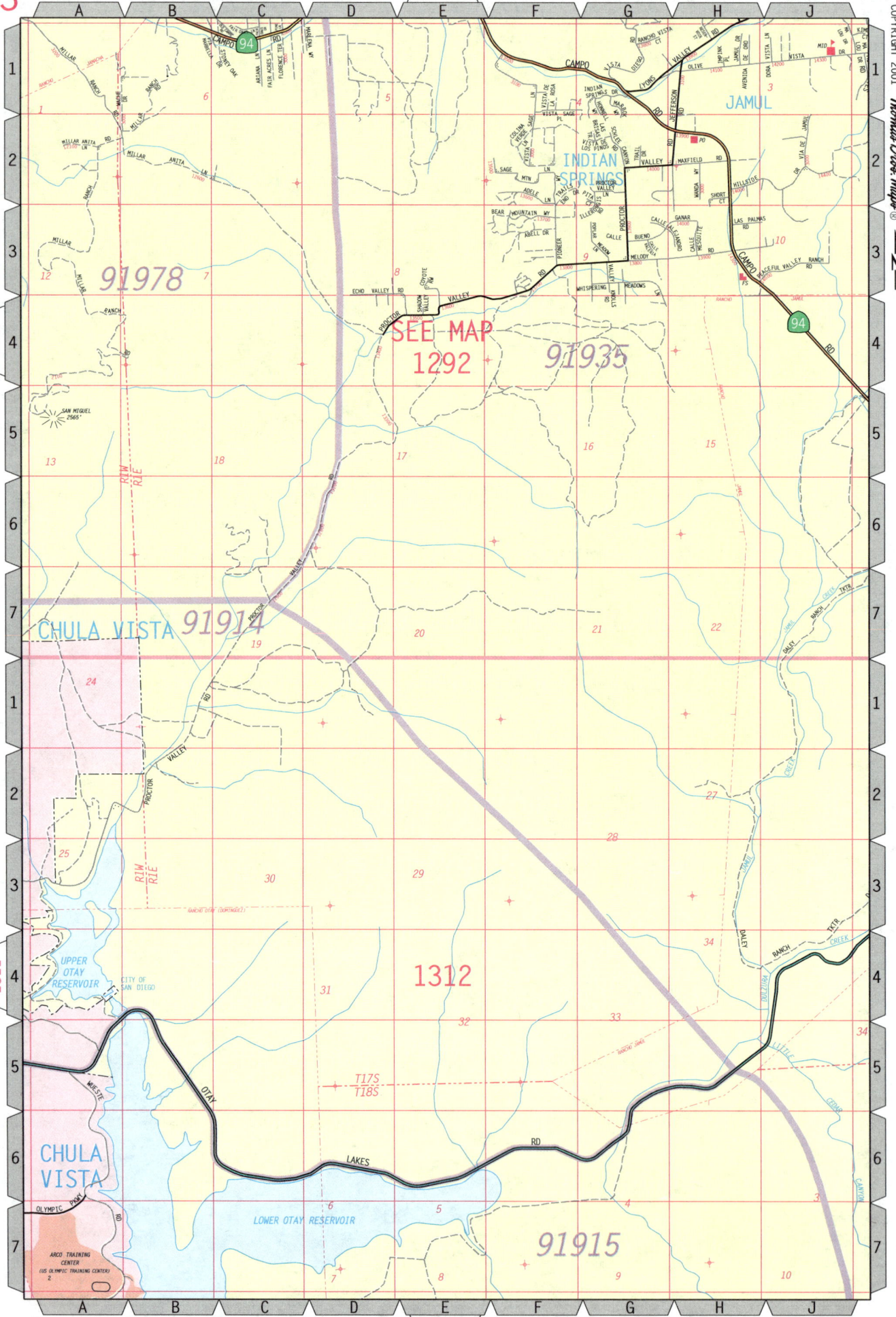

SAN DIEGO CO.

MAP

SEE 1272 MAP

COPYRIGHT 2001

Thomas Bros. Maps ®

←N→

JAMUL

INDIAN SPRINGS

91978

91935

SEE MAP 1292

91914

CHULA VISTA

91915

1312

CHULA VISTA

UPPER OTAY RESERVOIR

CITY OF SAN DIEGO

LOWER OTAY RESERVOIR

ARCO TRAINING CENTER (US OLYMPIC TRAINING CENTER)

SAN MIGUEL 2565'

SEE 1291 MAP

SEE 1311 MAP

SEE 1332 MAP

OLYMPIC PKWY

0 .25 .5 .75 1.0
miles 1 in. = 3800 ft.

T17S
T18S

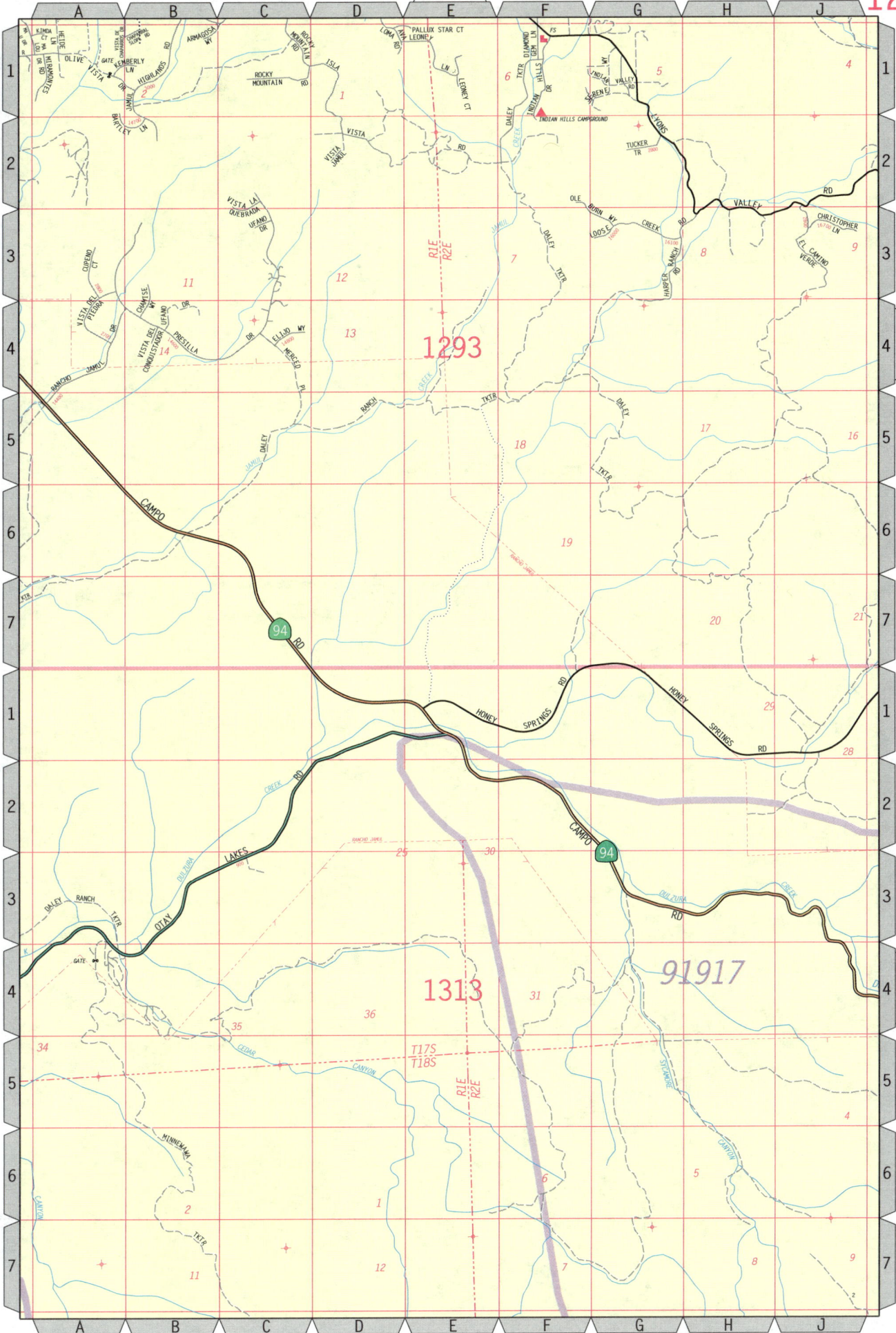

Thomas Bros. Maps®
— COPYRIGHT 2001

N →

SEE 1273 MAP

A B C D E F G H J

KINDA LN
HEIDE LN
OLIVE
VISTA
BARTLEY LN
KEMBERLY LN
GATE
JAMUL HIGHLANDS
ARMAGOSA WY
ROCKY MOUNTAIN RD
ROCKY MOUNTAIN
ISLA
LOMA RD
AYA RD
LEONEY
PALLUX STAR CT
LEONEY LN
LEONEY CT
DIAMOND DEM LN
INDIAN HILLS
FS
IND 14A VALLEY WY
SERENE
LYONS
TUCKER TR
INDIAN HILLS CAMPGROUND
VALLEY RD
CHRISTOPHER LN
EL CAMINO VERDE

VISTA
VISTA JAMUL
VISTA LA QUEBRADA
UFANO DR
CUPENO CT
VISTA DEL PIEDRA
CHAMISE WY
UFANO DR
PRESILLA
CONQUISTADOR
RANCHO JAMUL
ELIJO WY
MERCED PL
DR
RANCH
DALEY
CAMPO RD
HONEY SPRINGS RD
HONEY SPRINGS RD
CAMPO
RD
DULZURA
LAKES
CREEK RD
OTAY
DALEY RANCH TKTR
GATE
MINNEWAWA
CEDAR CANYON
TKTR
RANCHO JAMUL
DULZURA CREEK
SYCAMORE
CANYON

R1E R2E
94 RD
94
T17S T18S
R1E R2E

1293
1313
91917

SEE 1294 MAP
SEE 1294 MAP
SEE 1332 MAP

OLE BURN WY
LOOSE
CREEK
HARPER RANCH RD
DALEY
TKTR
TKTR
DALEY

11 12 1 2 3 4 5 6 7 8 9
13 14 16 17 18 19 20 21 28 29
25 30 31 36 35 34
1 2 11 12 4 5 6 8 9

0 .25 .5 .75 1.0 miles 1 in. = 3800 ft.

SAN DIEGO CO.

MAP

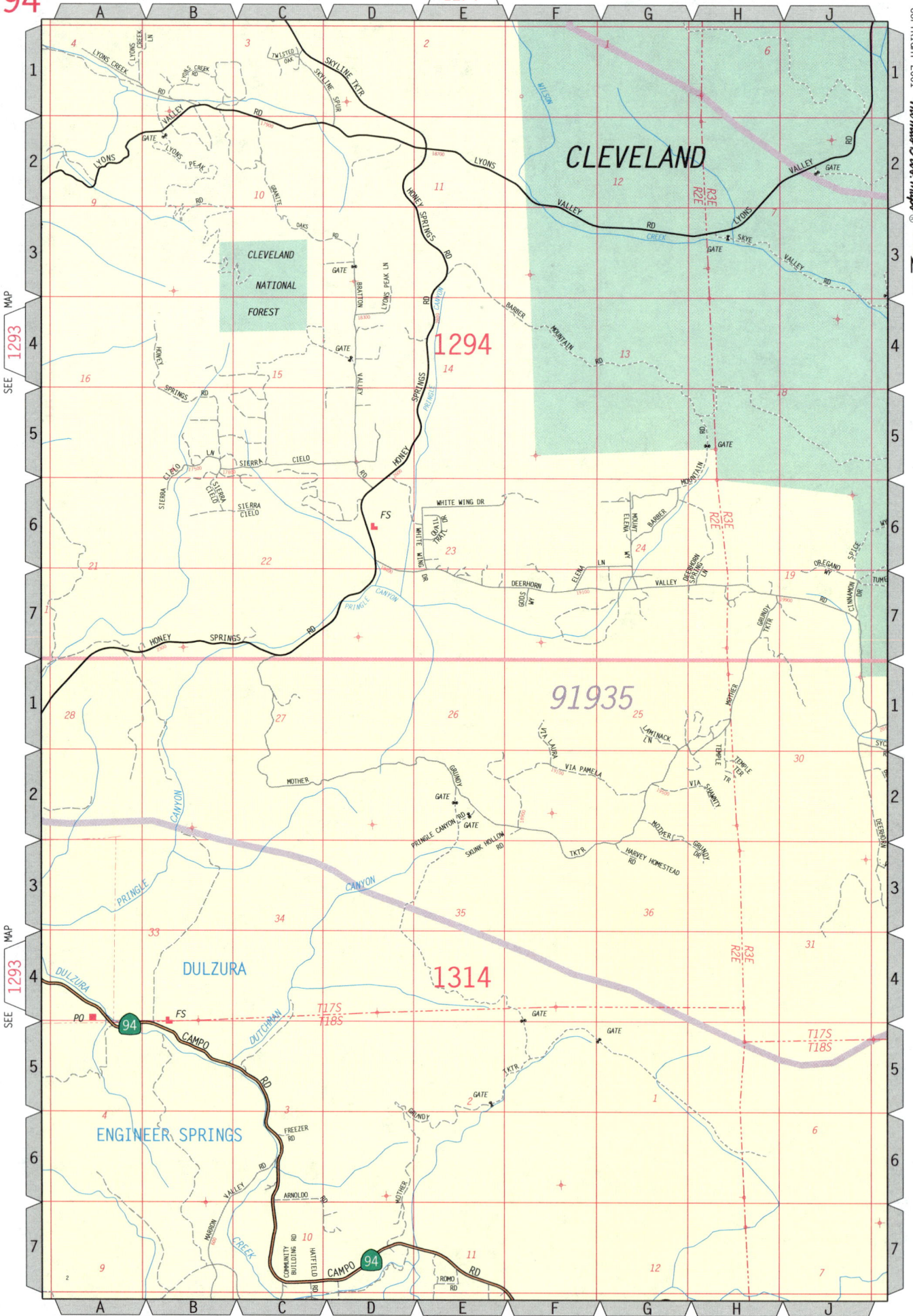

SAN DIEGO CO.

MAP

SEE 1293 MAP

SEE 1293 MAP

COPYRIGHT 2001 Thomas Bros. Maps®

—N—

CLEVELAND

CLEVELAND
NATIONAL
FOREST

1294

91935

1314

DULZURA

ENGINEER SPRINGS

LYONS CREEK RD
LYONS CREEK LN
LYONS VALLEY
LYONS PEAK
TWISTED OAK
SKYLINE TKTR
SKYLINE SPUR
GATE
GRANITE RD
OAKS RD
HONEY SPRINGS RD
LYONS VALLEY RD
WILSON
LYONS VALLEY GATE
SKYE VALLEY RD
CREEK
GATE
R3E R2E
BRATTON
MT SKULLY PEAK LN
VALLEY RD
BARBER MOUNTAIN
RD
HONEY SPRINGS RD
SIERRA CIELO LN
SIERRA CIELO
SIERRA CIELO
HONEY RD
HONEY SPRINGS RD
WHITE WING DR
FS
WHITE WING DR
TRAIL DR
BARBER MOUNTAIN
MOUNT ELENA
ELENA LN
MOUNT ELENA WY
DEERHORN VALLEY
DEERHORN SPRINGS LN
OREGANO WY
SPICE
CINNAMON DR
TUME
PRINGLE CANYON RD
HONEY SPRINGS RD
GODS WY
DEERHORN VALLEY
GRUNDY TKTR
MOTHER
VIA LAURA
VIA PAMELA
AMINACK LN
TEMPLE TR
TEMPLE TIER
PRINGLE CANYON
GATE
PRINGLE CANYON RD
GATE
SKUNK HOLLOW RD
TKTR
VIA SHANTY
HARVEY HOMESTEAD RD
MOTHER DR
GRUNDY DR
DEERHORN
SYC
PRINGLE CANYON
DUTCHMAN RD
DULZURA
PO
FS
CAMPO RD
GATE
GATE
T17S T18S
T17S T18S
R3E R2E
TKTR
GRUNDY
FREEZER RD
VALLEY RD
ARNOLDO RD
MARRON CREEK
COMMUNITY BUILDING RD
HATFIELD RD
CAMPO
ROMO RD
MOTHER
CAMPO RD

94

94

0 .25 .5 .75 1.0 miles 1 in. = 3800 ft.

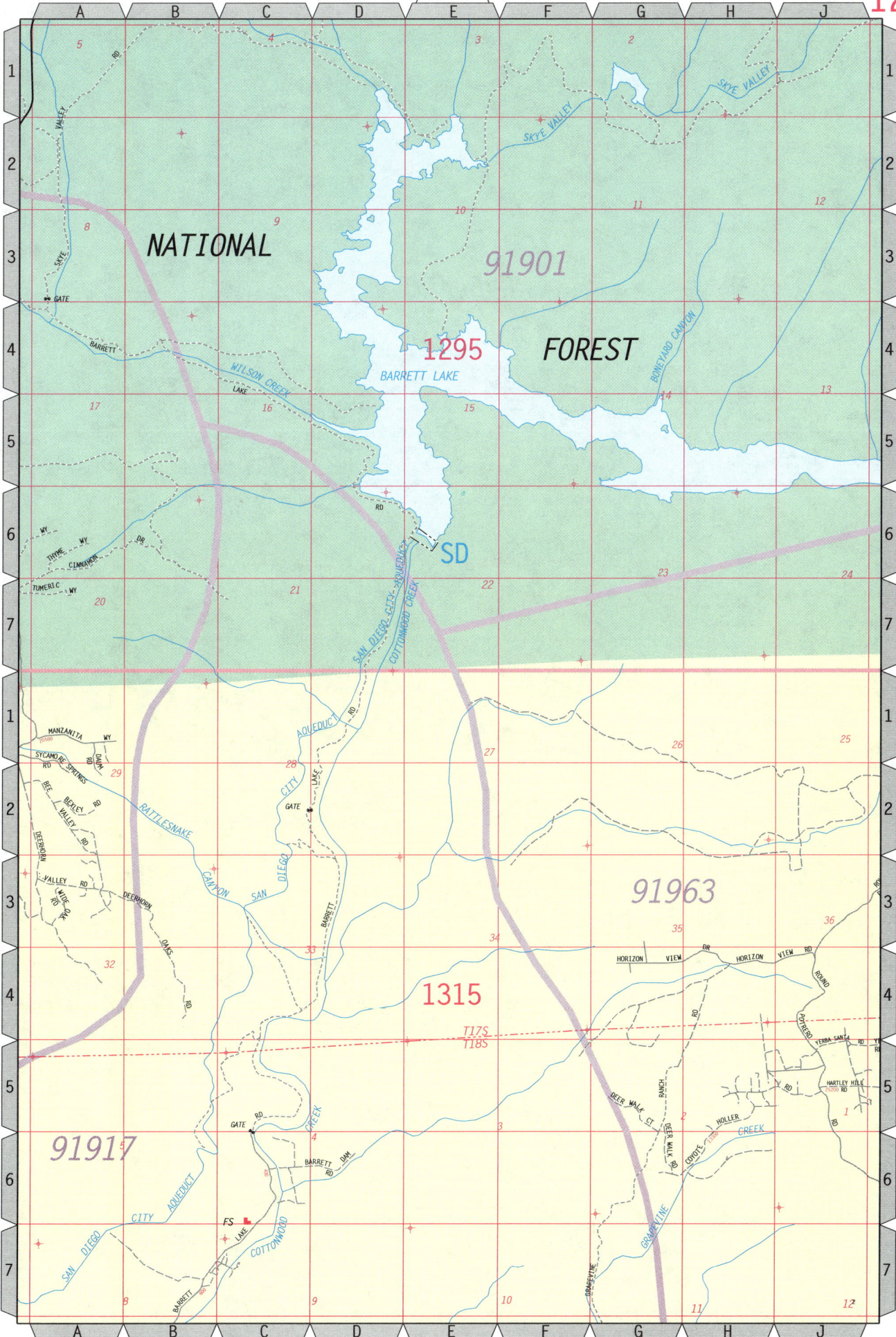

SAN DIEGO CO.

MAP

SEE 1296 MAP

SEE 1296 MAP

ThomasBros. Maps®

COPYRIGHT 2001

N

NATIONAL

FOREST

91901

1295

BARRETT LAKE

SKYE VALLEY

SKYE VALLEY

BONEYARD CANYON

SKYE

VALLEY

GATE

BARRETT

WILSON CREEK

LAKE

THYME WY

CINNAMON

WY

DR

TUMERIC WY

SD

SAN DIEGO CITY AQUEDUCT

COTTONWOOD CREEK

RD

91963

AQUEDUCT

RATTLESNAKE

CANYON

SAN DIEGO

CITY

LAKE

GATE

BARRETT

MANZANITA WY

SYCAMORE SPRINGS RD

DAM RD

BEE

BEXLEY

VALLEY RD

DEERHORN

VALLEY RD

WIDE OAK RD

DEERHORN

OAKS

RD

1315

T17S

T18S

HORIZON VIEW DR

HORIZON VIEW RD

ROUND

DEER WALK CT

RANCH RD

DEER WALK RD

COYOTE HOLLER

CREEK

POTRERO

YERBA SANTA RD

HARTLEY HILL

RD

91917

91917

GATE RD

CREEK

BARRETT RD

BARRETT DAM

SAN DIEGO CITY AQUEDUCT

FS

LAKE

COTTONWOOD

BARRETT

GRAPELINE

GRAPELINE

0 .25 .5 .75 1.0 miles 1 in. = 3800 ft.

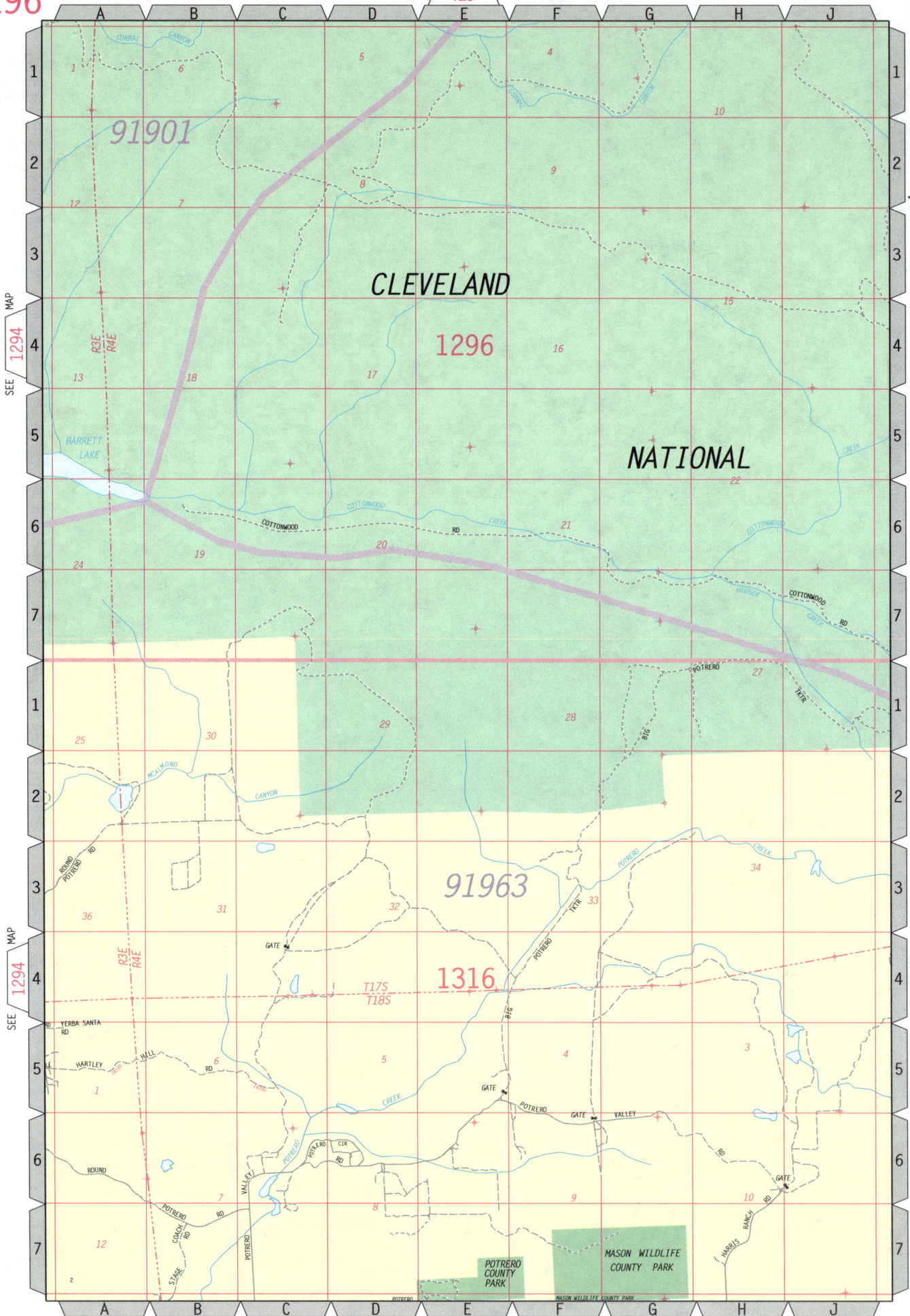

1296

SAN DIEGO CO.

MAP

SEE 429 MAP

A B C D E F G H J

1

91901

CORRAL CANYON

5

4

10

2

9

12 7

8

CLEVELAND

SEE 1294 MAP

R3E R4E

3

15

1296

16

4

13 18 17

BARRETT LAKE

5

22

NATIONAL

CREEK

COTTONWOOD CREEK

COTTONWOOD RD

21

COTTONWOOD

6

24 19 20

HAUSER CREEK

COTTONWOOD RD

7

POTRERO

27

TKTR

1

25 30

29

28

BIG

MCALMOND

CANYON

2

ROUND POTRERO RD

31

POTRERO CREEK

34

3

91963

TKTR

36 32 33

GATE

POTRERO

SEE 1294 MAP

R3E R4E

4

T17S T18S

1316

BIG

YERBA SANTA RD

HARTLEY HILL RD

6

5

4

3

5

1

CREEK

GATE

POTRERO GATE VALLEY

POTRERO CIR RD

VALLEY

GATE

6

ROUND

POTRERO

9

10

HARRIS RANCH RD

GATE

7

POTRERO COACH RD

STAGE

12

POTRERO COUNTY PARK

MASON WILDLIFE COUNTY PARK

2

POTRERO

MASON WILDLIFE COUNTY PARK

A B C D E F G H J

0 .25 .5 .75 1.0

miles 1 in. = 3800 ft.

SEE 429 MAP

MAP

Thomas Bros. Maps®

COPYRIGHT 2001

A B C D E F G H J

1
11
12
GOAT ISLAND
7
8
9

2
MORENA STOKES VALLEY RD
COTTONWOOD CREEK
BUCKMAN LA
BUCKMAN RD
VISTA
CREEK

3
14
13
MORENA RESERVOIR
18
17
16
SPRINGS
CAMERON TKTR

R4E R5E

4
MORENA RESERVOIR RD
1297
PACIFIC CREST WY
EVERGREEN DR
QUARTZ DR
PAPRIKA DR
RD RD
RUNNER WY
OAK DR
BUCKMAN
S1
CAMERON
1298 MAP

5
SAN DIEGO
MORENA RESERVOIR RD
LAKE MORENA COUNTY PARK
BUCKHORN
GLADIOLA
POPPY DR
WIDGEON
LILAC
LAUREL DR
MANZANITA DR
19
PRIMROSE
OAK
MANZANITA DR
TONALITE
HARPER
QUAIL RD
CANVAS BACK DR
20
MORENA VILLAGE
21

6
23
24
91906
LUPINE DR
CLEVELAND FOREST
LAKE MORENA DR
BLUE GILL
WHITE GOOSE
CANADIAN HONKER RD
MORENA DR
CAMERON TKTR
SUNRISE RANCH LN
PARK
28
HYDE

7
FOREST
26
25
30
TKTR
29
SPRINGS RD

1
BIG POTRERO
COTTONWOOD
RATHER TKTR
RD
GATE CREEK
TKTR
LAKE
MORENA DR
AMANDA CT
BUCKMAN SPRINGS

2
35
36
31
BIG POTRERO
32
MORENA DR
BUCKMAN
SPRINGS LN
33

3
T17S T18S
PHELPS RD
PHELPS RD
LAZY LN
RD
P
S1
CAMPO INDIAN RES

R4E R5E

4
1317
1
6
5
1
BUC
1298 MAP

5
2

6
11
12
7
8
9

7
18
17
16
2

A B C D E F G H J

0 .25 .5 .75 1.0 miles   1 in. = 3800 ft.

SAN DIEGO CO.

MAP

SEE 430 MAP

SEE 1296 MAP

SEE 1296 MAP

SEE 430 MAP

A B C D E F G H J

1 9 10 11 12 7

CLEVELAND NATIONAL FOREST

2

3 16 15 14 13 18

1298

CAMERON TKTR

CAMERON TKTR

LA POSTA RD

R5E R6E

CREEK

4 TKTR GATE 24

CAMERON GATE 21

LA POSTA 22 TKTR 23 SD & AE RR 19

5 LA POSTA MILLER

6 TKTR 28 CAMPO TKTR

LA POSTA MICROWAVE STATION

7 27 GATE 26 GATE 25 30

91906

1 TKTR

2 33 34 CAMPO GATE 35 36 SCENIC MOUNTAIN RD 31 GATE

T17S
T18S ROYAL WILLIE RD

3 CAMPO INDIAN RESERVATION TKTR MARC TR SD & AE RR R5E R6E

4 4 3 2 1318 1 KIMBERLY CREEK 6

BUCKMAN SPRINGS RD SHOCKEY WY TKTR

5 S1 FS CAMPO FAR VALLEY RD SHOCKEY

LIB DENNY MCCAINVILLE RANCH RD LAS MONTANAS CALLE LORETO

6 CAMERON CORNERS 9 SD & AE RR BUCKWHEAT TR SAND CASTER CTR LOCKETT RD 10 11 12 7

SHERIDAN RD CAMPO EVENING PRIMROSE TR SMITH CANYON

7 CAMPO MUS DODD 16 DUSTER LN 15 14 13 18

2 PARKER RD

0 .25 .5 .75 1.0
miles 1 in. = 3800 ft.

SEE 430 MAP

SAN DIEGO CO.

Thomas Bros. Maps®

COPYRIGHT 2001

N↑

91905

91962

1299

LIVE OAK SPRINGS

CAMPO

INDIAN

RESERVATION

1319

SEE 430 MAP

SEE 1300 MAP

MAP

94

94

HIGHWAY 80

FRWY

8

miles 1 in. = 3800 ft.

0 .25 .5 .75 1.0

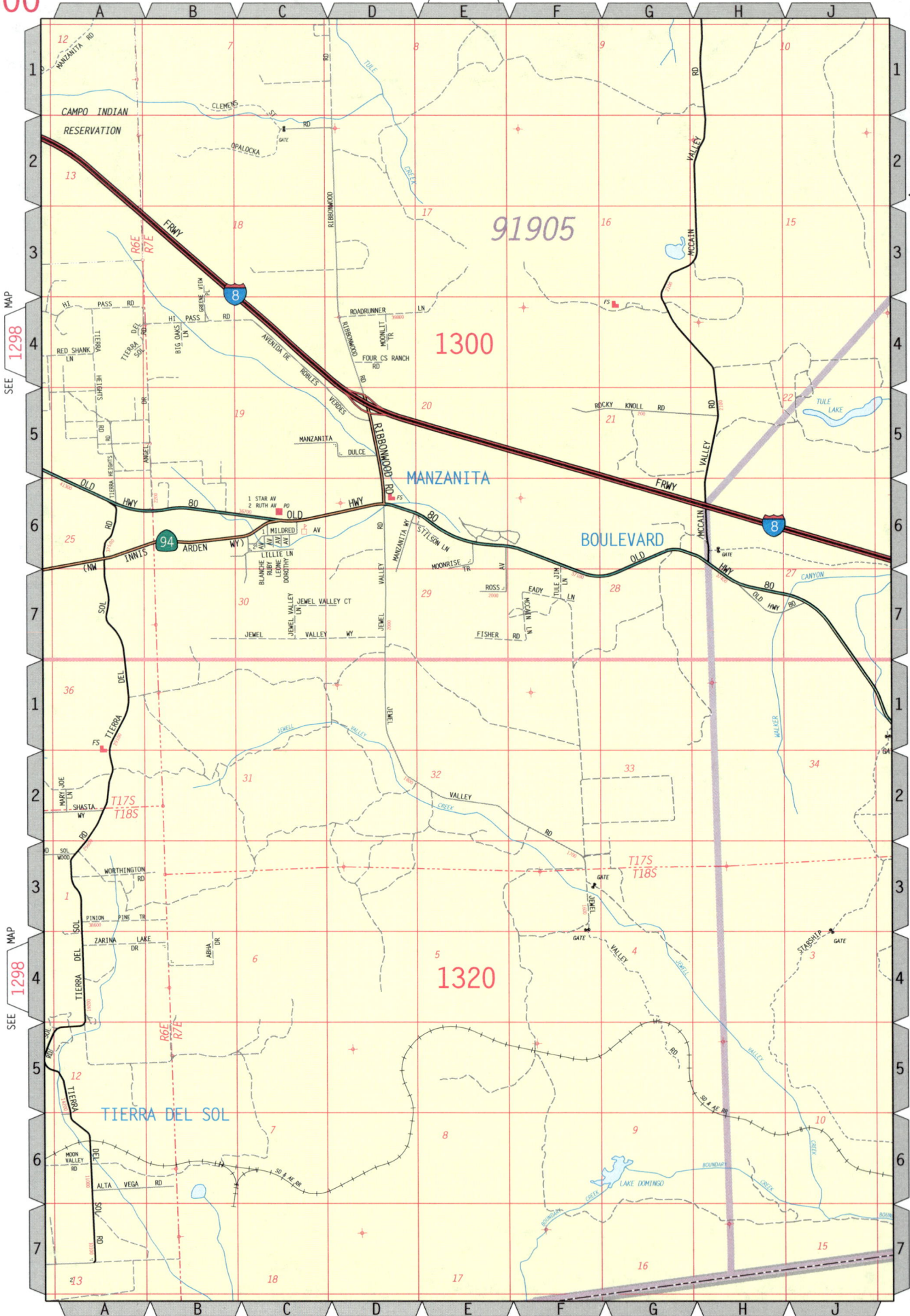

1300

SAN DIEGO CO.

MAP

91905

1300

1320

CAMPO INDIAN RESERVATION

MANZANITA

BOULEVARD

TIERRA DEL SOL

SEE 1298 MAP

miles 1 in. = 3800 ft.

SEE 430 MAP

COPYRIGHT 2001 Thomas Bros. Maps®

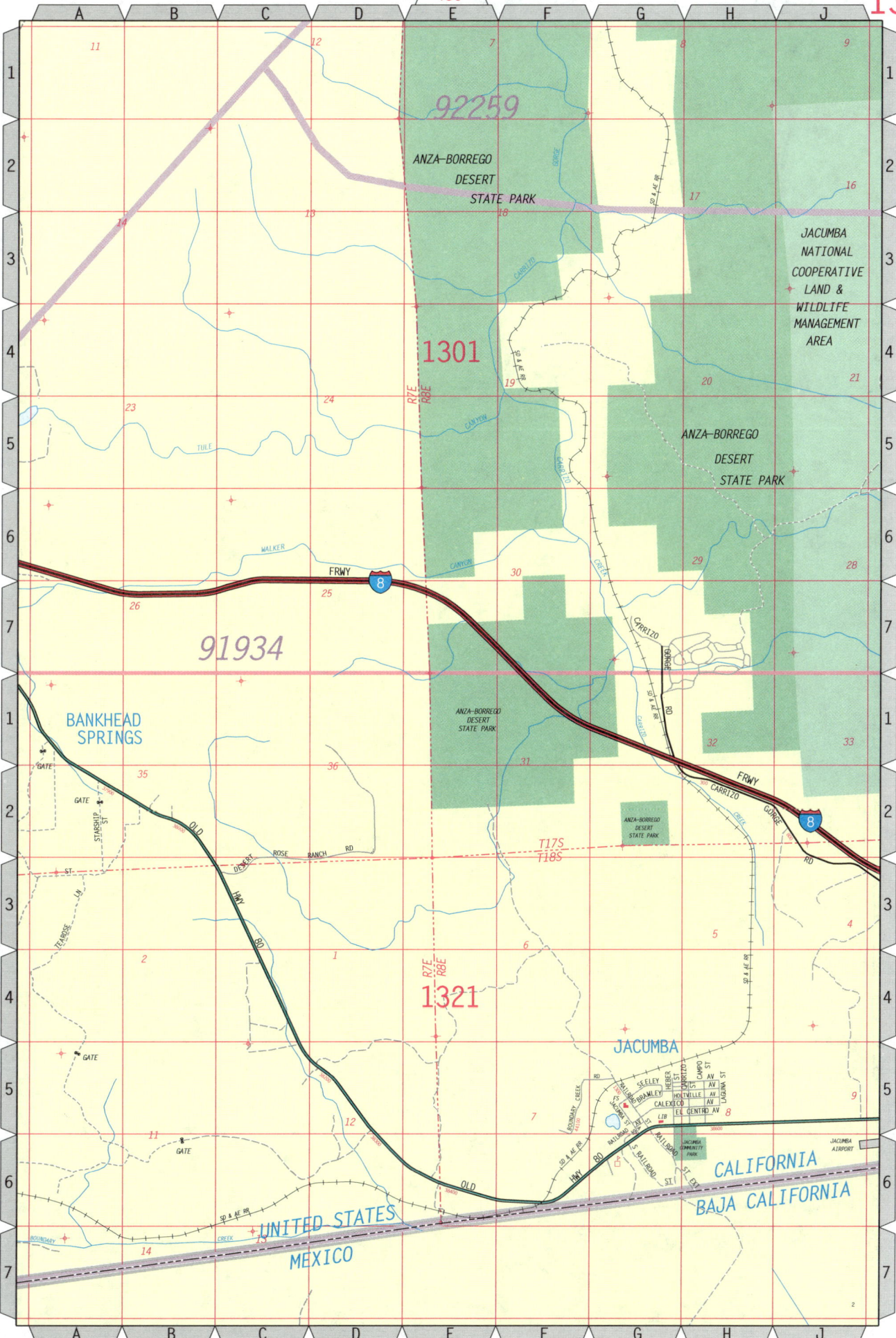

1300

SAN DIEGO CO.

N

	A	B	C	D	E	F	G	H	J	

1 11 12 7 8 9

92259

2 ANZA–BORREGO 16 17

DESERT

STATE PARK 14 13 18

JACUMBA
NATIONAL
COOPERATIVE
LAND &
WILDLIFE
MANAGEMENT
AREA

3

4 1301 19 20 21

R7E
R8E

5 23 24 ANZA–BORREGO

TULE DESERT

STATE PARK

6 WALKER 29 28

FRWY 8 CANYON 30

7 26 25 CARRIZO

91934

1 BANKHEAD
SPRINGS Anza–Borrego
Desert
State Park 32 33

GATE 35 36 31 FRWY 8

2 GATE OLD Anza–Borrego
Desert
State Park CARRIZO

STARSHIP
ST T17S
T18S

3 ST ROSE RANCH RD 5 4

DESERT

TEAROSE LN HWY

4 80 2 1 6

R7E
R8E 1321

JACUMBA

5 GATE SEELEY CAMPO ST

HEBER

CARRIZO ST ST LAGUNA AV

BRAMLEY 9

11 12 7 CALEXICO HOLTVILLE AV 8

EL CENTRO AV

6 GATE LIB JACUMBA
COMMUNITY
PARK JACUMBA
AIRPORT

OLD CALIFORNIA

HWY BAJA CALIFORNIA

7 14 UNITED STATES CREEK

MEXICO 2

	A	B	C	D	E	F	G	H	J	

MAP

SEE 430 MAP

SEE 430 MAP

0 .25 .5 .75 1.0
miles 1 in. = 3800 ft.

SAN DIEGO CO.

MAP

—N—

SEE 1288 MAP

A   B   C   D   E

ZUNIGA PT

NORTH ISLAND
NAVAL AIR STATION

ZUNIGA
POINT

POINT
LOMA

FORT
ROSECRANS
NATIONAL CEM

WHITE

SERVICE RD

SYLVESTER RD

ROSECRANS BLVD

2ND ST

3RD ST

CABRILLO MEMORIAL

209

DR

CABRILLO RD

GATCHELL RD

MONUMENT HQ

FORT
ROSECRANS
MILITARY
RESERVATION

CABRILLO NATIONAL
MONUMENT

HUMPHREYS

SYLVESTER RD

PT
LOMA
TIDE
POOL

HISTORIC
LIGHTHOUSE

92106

SAN
DIEGO

ZUNIGA POINT JETTY

U S
COAST
GUARD
STATION

RD

OPERATIONAL
LIGHTHOUSE

PACIFIC

1

2

3

4

5

6

7

SEE 429 MAP

A   B   C   D   E

0   .125   .25   .375   .5
miles 1 in. = 1900 ft.

SEE 429 MAP

—N→

E   F   G   H   J

BEACH

PARK

OCEAN BLVD

R H DANA PL

CHURCHILL

CORONADO
MUNICIPAL
BEACH

CORONADO

SOUTH
BEACH

ADELLA

FLORA AV

ORANGE AV

HOTEL
DEL
CORONADO

GATE

1800

AVD DEL SOL

AVENIDA DEL

AVENIDA DE LAS ARENAS

AVENIDA LUNAR

75

SILVER STRAND

GATE

9118

POMONA AV

GLORIETTA BLVD

CORONADO
YACHT
CLUB

CORONADO
GOLF
COURSE

GLORIETTA
BAY

STRAND CH

GLORIETTA
BAY
PK

STRAND
BL

VISTA PL

PK BAY

PK BAY CIR

GLORIETTA

1

2

AVENIDA LUNAR

U S
NAVAL
AMPHIBIOUS
BASE

3

SEE 1309 MAP

4

OCEAN

5

6

7

E   F   G   H   J

0 .125 .25 .375 .5 miles   1 in. = 1900 ft.

SAN DIEGO CO.

MAP

COPYRIGHT 2001 *Thomas Bros. Maps* ®

PIER

A B C D E

1

CORONADO GOLF COURSE

PK BAY CIR
PK BAY CIR
PK 4 BAY CIR
TTA D
VISTA PL
GLORIETTA BLVD

GLORIETTA BAY

TTA Y PK

BOAT LAUNCH
GLORIETTA BAY PARK
GLORIETTA BAY PARK

92155

INCHON RD
ENIWETOK RD
KWAJALEIN RD
MAKIN RD
ATTU
GUADALCANAL
BOUGAINVILLE
LAE
MUNDA
TULAGI
ROI WY
ROI WY
TARAWA
VELLA
RENDOVA RD
ADMIRALTY
STRAND
LAVELLA RD
RENDOVA RD
RENDOVA WY
RENDOVA CIR

D

2

U S NAVAL AMPHIBIOUS BASE

SAN DIEGO

SILVER

3

75

DELTA BEACH (US GOVERNMENT)

CORONADO

STRAND

BAY

SEE 1308 MAP

4

U S NAVAL AMPHIBIOUS BASE

PACIFIC

BLVD

NAVY YACHT CLUB

PALAU RD
OKINAWA RD
LEYTE RD
PALAU CIR
SAIPAN RD
WAKE RD
LEYTE
INCHON CT
DA NANG DR
ATTU AV
LEYTE RD

1100
1200
1300
1400

92118

5

OCEAN

6

7

SILVER STRAND STATE BEACH

75

LOEWS CORONADO BAY RESORT

CORONADO BAY RD

CROW ISL

CORONADO

A B C D E

0 .125 .25 .375 .5
miles 1 in. = 1900 ft.

SAN DIEGO CO.

MAP

Thomas Bros. Maps®

COPYRIGHT 2001

N

SAN DIEGO

U S NAVAL RESERVATION

92136

PIER

CITY OF SAN DIEGO

NATIONAL CITY

91950

CIVIC CENTER DR

KIMBALL PARK

BOYS & GIRLS CLUB

SOUTH BAY PLAZA

PLAZA BLVD

HIGHLAND AV

HOOVER AV

NATIONAL AV

TRANSIT CENTER
PARK & RIDE

MILE-OF-CARS

TRANSPORTATION AV

24TH STREET MARINE TERMINAL

TIDELANDS AV

BAY MARINA DR

QUAY AV

PEPPER PARK

BOAT LAUNCH

FISHING PIER

SWEETWATER MARSH NATIONAL WILDLIFE REFUGE

SAN DIEGO FRWY

SWEETWATER RIVER

54

SOUTH BAY MARKET PLACE

BROADWAY

91910

GUNPOWDER POINT

CHULA VISTA NATURE CENTER

GUNPOWDER POINT DR

GATE

SEA VALE ST

CHULA VISTA

TRANSIT CENTER PARK & RIDE

S17

BAY BLVD

CHULA VISTA

BAY BOULEVARD PARK

LAGOON

MARINA PKWY

SWEETWATER MARSH NATIONAL WILDLIFE REFUGE

CROWN ISLE

NADO BAY RD

CITY OF NATIONAL CITY

CITY OF SAN DIEGO

I-5

0 .125 .25 .375 .5 miles 1 in. = 1900 ft.

SEE 1310 MAP

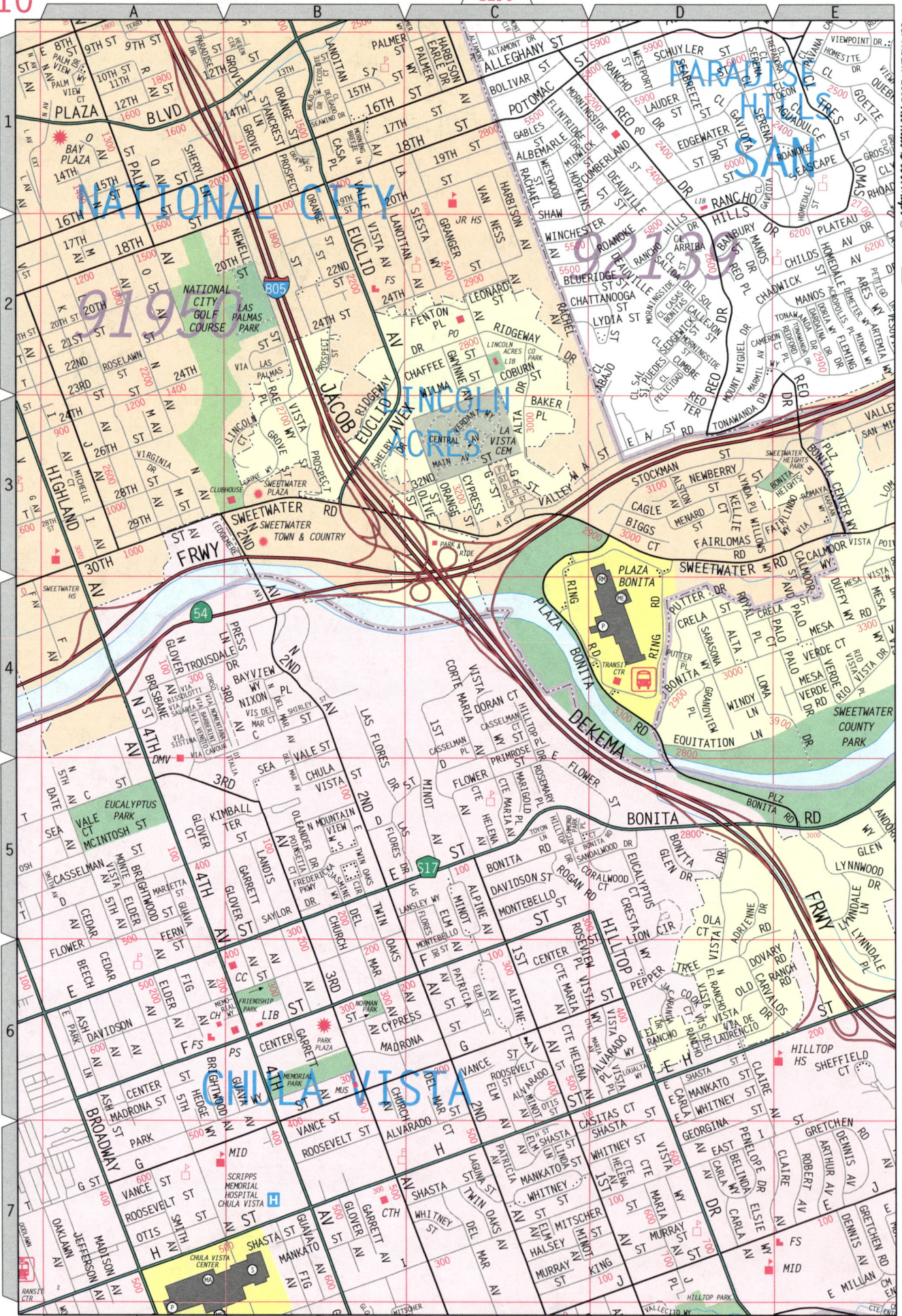

1310

SEE 1290 MAP

SAN DIEGO CO.

MAP

NATIONAL CITY

91950

PARADISE HILLS SAN

92139

LINCOLN ACRES

NATIONAL CITY GOLF COURSE

Las Palmas Park

SWEETWATER RD

FRWY

SWEETWATER TOWN & COUNTRY

PLAZA BONITA

SWEETWATER COUNTY PARK

DEKEMA

BONITA RD

CHULA VISTA

EUCALYPTUS PARK

Eucalyptus Park

FRIENDSHIP PARK

MEMORIAL PARK

SCRIPPS MEMORIAL HOSPITAL CHULA VISTA

CHULA VISTA CENTER

SEE 1309 MAP

SEE 1330 MAP

COPYRIGHT 2001 Thomas Bros. Maps

0 .125 .25 .375 .5 miles 1 in. = 1900 ft.

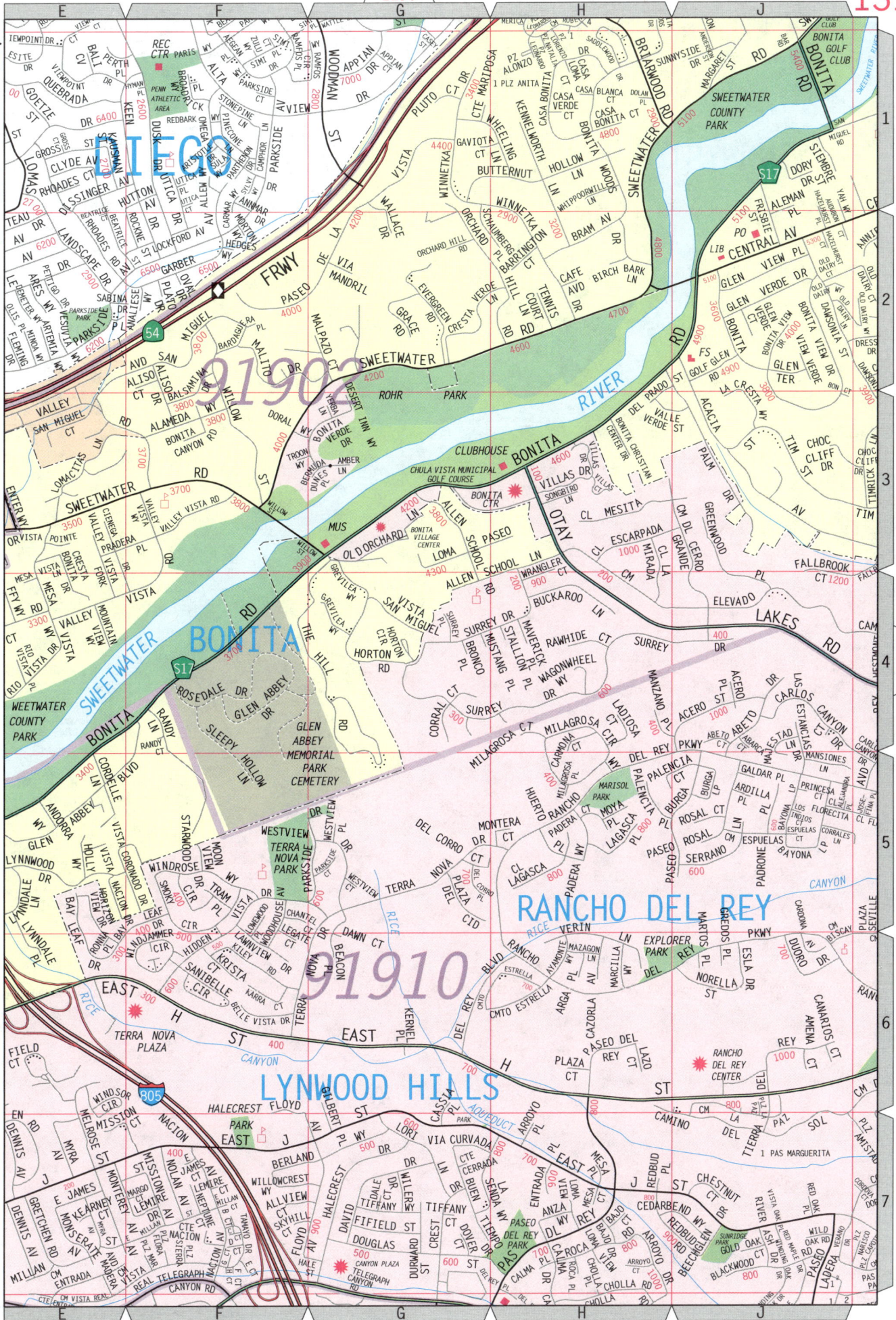

DIEGO

91902

SWEETWATER

BONITA

91910

RANCHO DEL REY

LYNWOOD HILLS

SAN DIEGO CO.

MAP

SEE 1311 MAP

0 .125 .25 .375 .5 miles   1 in. = 1900 ft.

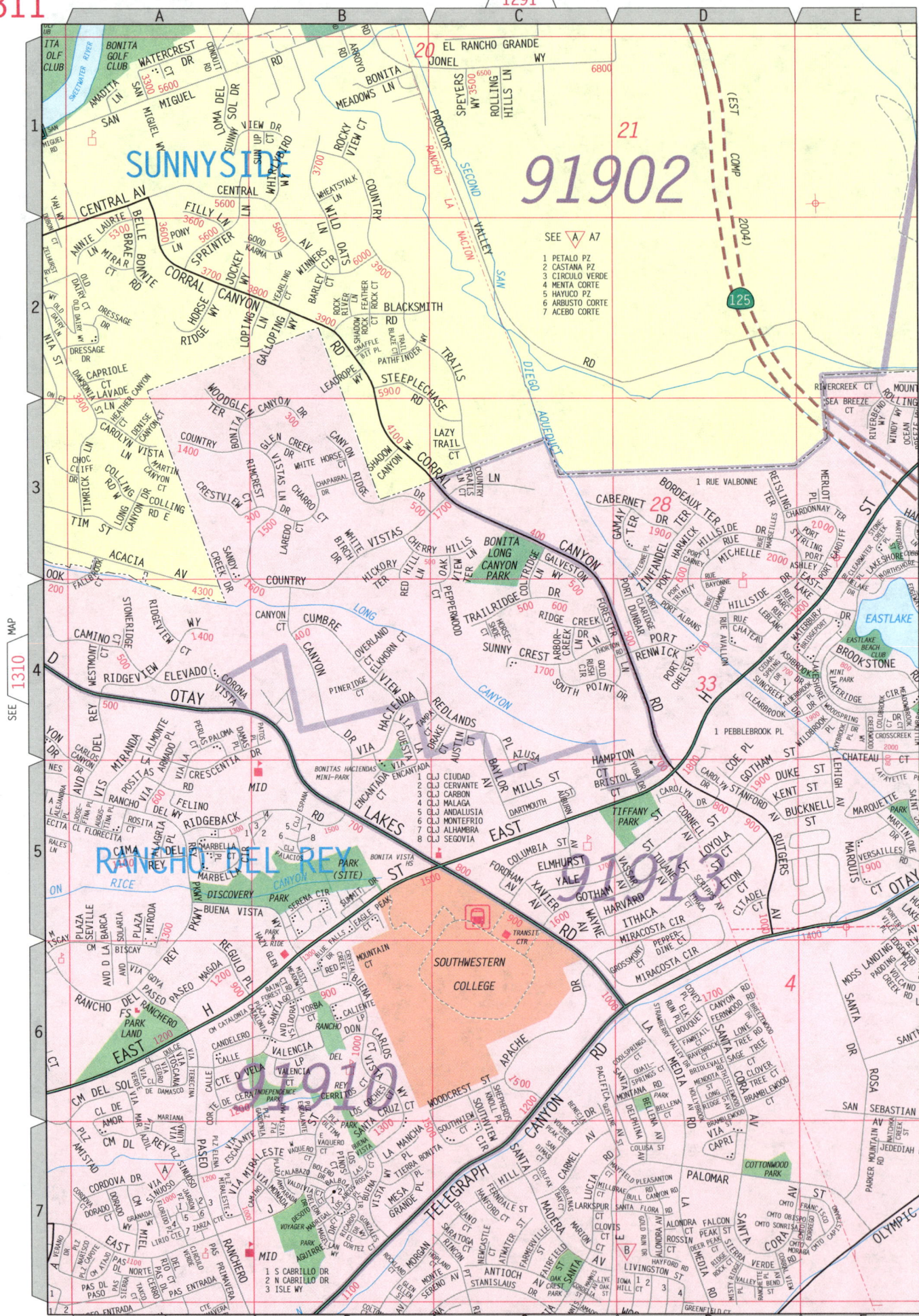

SEE 1291 MAP

SAN DIEGO CO.

MAP

SUNNYSIDE

91902

21

20

RANCHO DEL REY

91913

91910

SOUTHWESTERN COLLEGE

EASTLAKE

BROOKSTONE

BONITA LONG CANYON PARK

COTTONWOOD PARK

SEE A A7

1 PETALO PZ
2 CASTANA PZ
3 CIRCULO VERDE
4 MENTA CORTE
5 HAYUCO PZ
6 ARBUSTO CORTE
7 ACEBO CORTE

COPYRIGHT 2001 Thomas Bros. Maps ®

SEE 1310 MAP

SEE 1331 MAP

0 .125 .25 .375 .5 miles 1 in. = 1900 ft.

Thomas Bros. Maps®

COPYRIGHT 2001

–N–

22   23   24

27   26   25

EASTLAKE

91914

CHULA VISTA

EASTLAKE STONE

EASTLAKE LAKE BEACH CLUB

125

EASTLAKE GREENS

EASTLAKE COUNTRY CLUB

91915

34

OTAY

T17S
T18S

EASTLAKE HS

EASTLAKE VILLAGE CENTER GREENSGATE

CHULA VISTA LAGUNA COMMUNITY PARK

LIB

3

OLYMPIC PKWY

POGGI CANYON (EST)

SEE B D7
1 WESTMORLAND ST
2 GOLD RUN RD
3 PIEDMONT ST
4 APPLEGATE ST

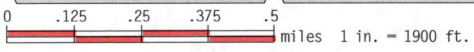

GREENSVIEW SPORTS PARK (SITE)

ARCO TRAINING CENTER (US OLYMPIC TRAINING CENTER)

RANCHO OTAY (ESTU DILLO)

0 .125 .25 .375 .5
miles 1 in. = 1900 ft.

SAN DIEGO CO.

MAP

SEE 1309 MAP

A   B   C   D   E

1

SILVER
STRAND
STATE
BEACH

**CORONADO
CAYS**

92118

CORONADO
CAYS
PARK

PARK
CORONADO BAY RD
MONTEGO CT
JAMAICA VILLAGE HALF MOON RD
GINGER-TREE LN
BEND
THE INLET GREEN
CATSPAW
BAHAMA BEND

THE POINT
ADMIRALTY CROSS
SANDPIPER STRAND
SIXPENCE WY
TURTLE RD

CAPE
ANTIGUA
CARTER
CARTER

CAYS
FS
1.00
GRAND
KINGSTON CT
KINGSTON CT
KINGSLEY W

SILVER STRAND

HALFPENNY
BLVD

1 DELAPORT LN
2 DELAPORT CT
3 MARDI GRAS CT
4 DELAPORT PL
5 SOUTH CAYS CT
6 DELAPORT WY

TRINIDAD BEND LN
PORT-OF-SPAIN RD
BLUE ANCHOR
SAINT CROIX
TOBAGO
SAINT KITT'S LN
SAINT TORRES
PORT BRIDGETOWN
ROYALE
MARDI GRAS BLVD
TOBAGO WY
ROTAY
RD

TUNAPUNA

LN

75

GATE

RONCLIFF BLVD

2

3

N

SEE 429 MAP

4

PACIFIC

OCEAN

5

6

7

2

A   B   C   D   E

0 .125 .25 .375 .5
miles 1 in. = 1900 ft.

SEE 1349 MAP

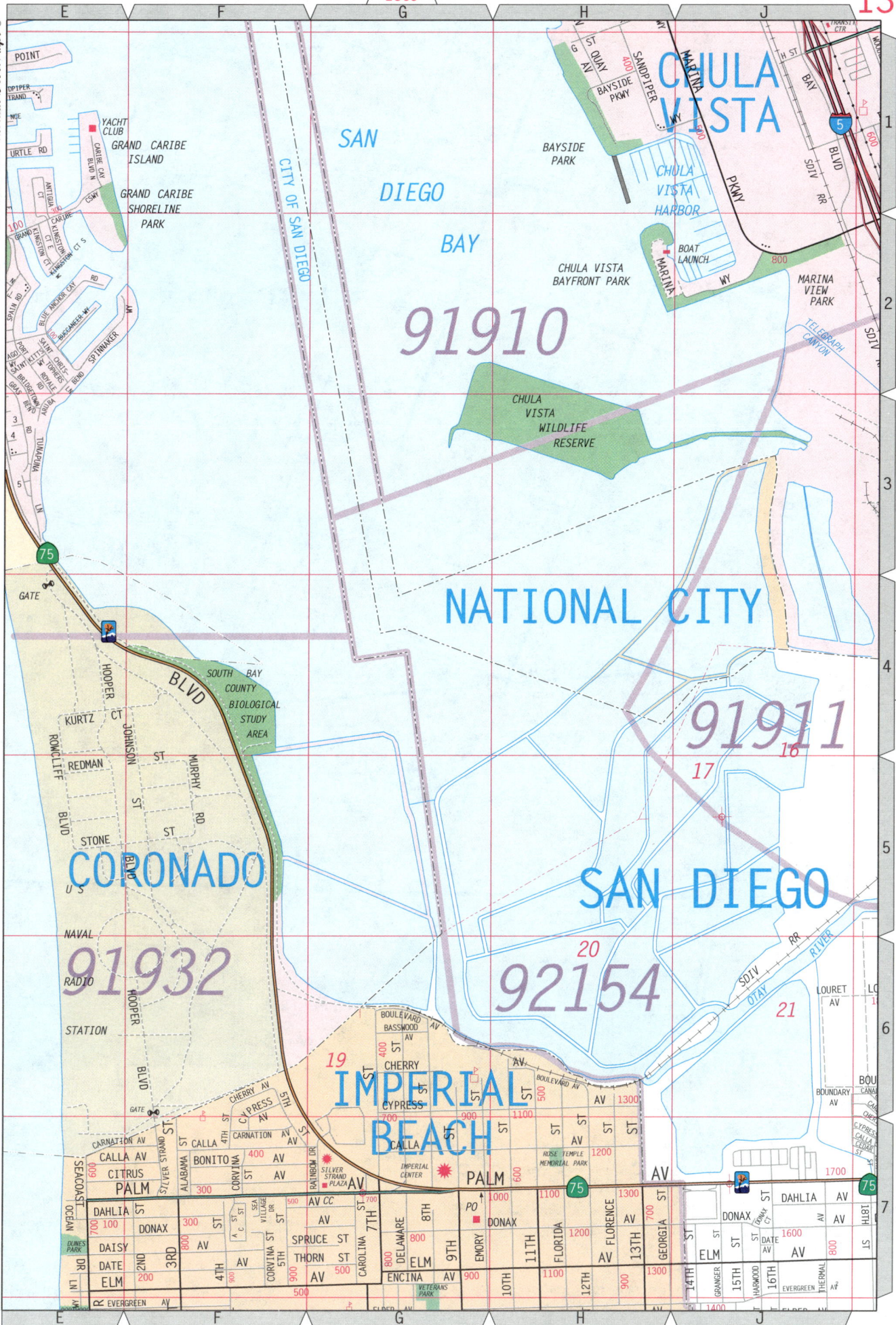

SAN DIEGO CO.

MAP

E   F   G   H   J

POINT

DPIPER TRAND

RANGE

TURTLE RD

URTLE RD

YACHT CLUB

GRAND CARIBE ISLAND

CARIBE CAY BLVD N

GRAND CARIBE SHORELINE PARK

ANTIGUA

KINGSTON CT E

KINGSTON CT S

GRAND CARIBE CSWY

100

SPAIN RD

BLUE ANCHOR CAY RD

SAINT CROIX

PORT ANT KITTY

ROYALE

BELLOUSTOWN

RD

AGO

SPINNAKER

BUCCANEER W

GRAS BIEN

ARUBA

BEND

TUMAPUNA LN

3

4

75

GATE

HOOPER

KURTZ CT

JOHNSON ST

MURPHY RD

BLVD

ROMCLIFF

REDMAN

STONE ST

ST

ST

BLVD

US

CORONADO

91932

NAVAL RADIO STATION

HOOPER BLVD

GATE

SOUTH BAY COUNTY BIOLOGICAL STUDY AREA

BLVD

CITY OF SAN DIEGO

SAN DIEGO BAY

91910

CHULA VISTA WILDLIFE RESERVE

CHULA VISTA

G ST

H ST

400

BAY QUAY

BAYSIDE PKWY

SANDPIPER WY

BAYSIDE PARK

CHULA VISTA HARBOR

MARINA WY

BOAT LAUNCH

CHULA VISTA BAYFRONT PARK

MARINA

MARINA VIEW PARK

TELEGRAPH CANYON

PKWY

SDIV

RR

BAY BLVD

H ST

WOOD

TRANSIT CTR

I-5

600

800

SDIV

NATIONAL CITY

91911

17   16

SAN DIEGO

20

92154

21

SDIV

RR

OTAY RIVER

LOURET AV

LO

BOUNDARY AV

BOU CANA

CYPRESS

CALLA

CEDAR ST

1700

1

2

3

SEE 1330 MAP

4

5

6

IMPERIAL BEACH

19

BOULEVARD DR

BASSWOOD AV

CHERRY AV

400 ST

CYPRESS AV

CHERRY AV

CYPRESS AV

5TH ST

CARNATION AV

CALLA AV

CITRUS AV

PALM

CALLA ST

CORVINA ST

BONITO ST

ALABAMA

700

SILVER STRAND

RAINBOW DR

SILVER STRAND PLAZA

SEA VILLAGE DR

IMPERIAL CENTER

PO

BOULEVARD AV

500 ST

ST

AV

1100

600

AV

1000

PALM

DONAX

ST

1100

1200

AV

ROSE TEMPLE MEMORIAL PARK

FLORIDA ST

FLORENCE AV

13TH ST

1300

GEORGIA ST

1300

AV

700

AV

75

AV

DAHLIA AV

DONAX AV

ELM ST

14TH ST

GRANGER ST

15TH ST

HARWOOD ST

16TH ST

1600

DATE AV

1400

EVERGREEN

THERMAL AV

18TH ST

SEACOAST DR

OCEAN LN

DUNES PARK

DAHLIA 100

DONAX 700

DAISY

DATE 200

ELM

EVERGREEN AV

CALLA AV 600

2ND ST

3RD ST

300

800

PALM

CC AV

A C ST

4TH ST

CORVINA ST

5TH ST

900

CARNATION AV 400

SPRUCE ST

THORN ST

ENCINA AV

500

DELAWARE ST

CAROLINA ST

7TH ST

700

800

8TH ST

EMORY ST

900

9TH ST

ELM AV

VETERANS PARK

DONAX

10TH ST

11TH ST

ELDER AV

900

1100

1200

1300

7

0   .125   .25   .375   .5   miles   1 in. = 1900 ft.

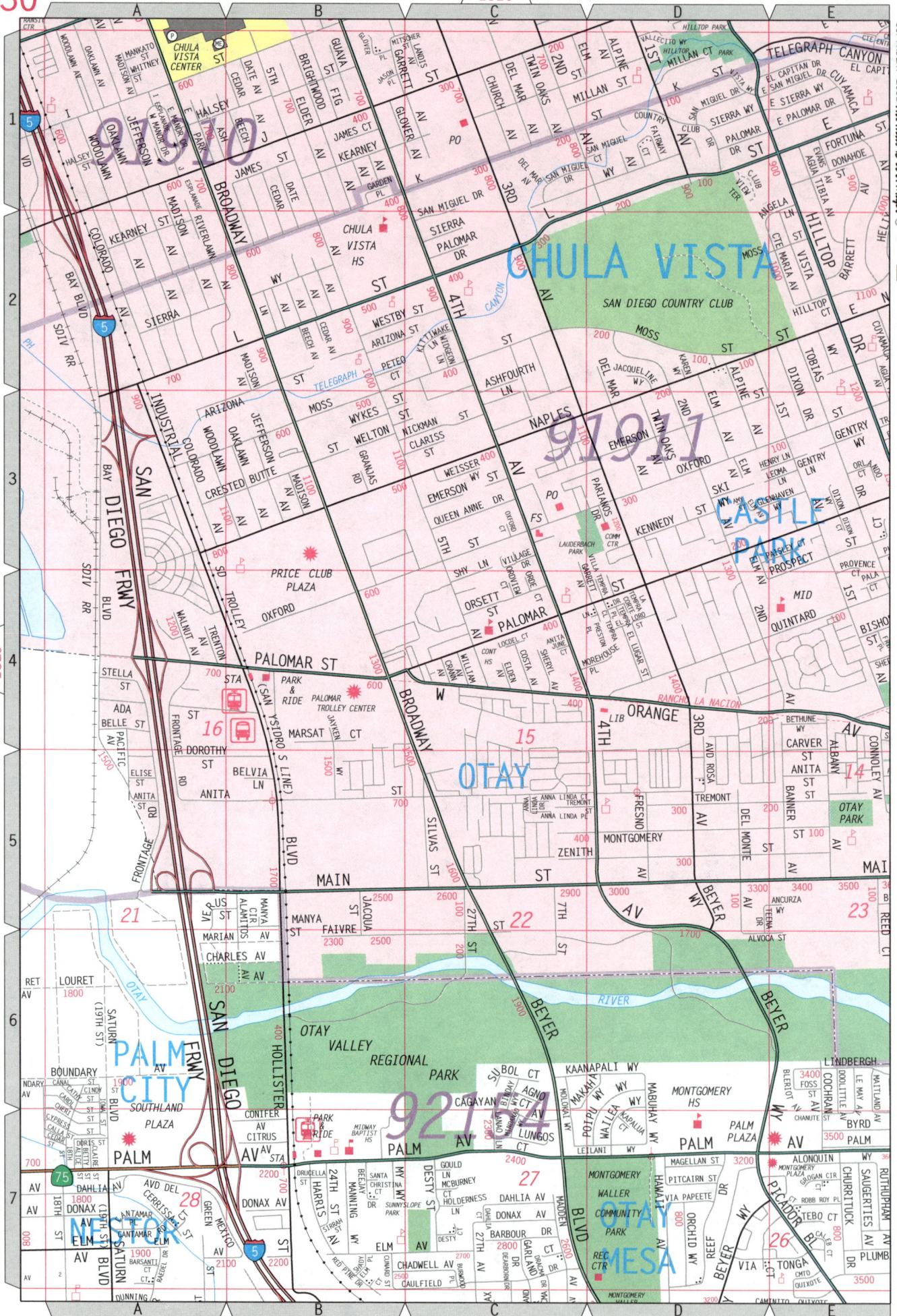

SAN DIEGO CO.

MAP

SEE 1310 MAP

CHULA VISTA

SAN DIEGO COUNTRY CLUB

91910

91911

CASTLE PARK

SEE 1329 MAP

OTAY

PALOMAR ST

BROADWAY

MAIN ST

PALM CITY

OTAY VALLEY REGIONAL PARK

92154

NESTOR

OTAY MESA

MONTGOMERY HS

MONTGOMERY WALLER COMMUNITY PARK

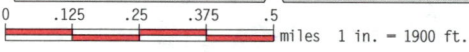

0   .125   .25   .375   .5
miles   1 in. = 1900 ft.

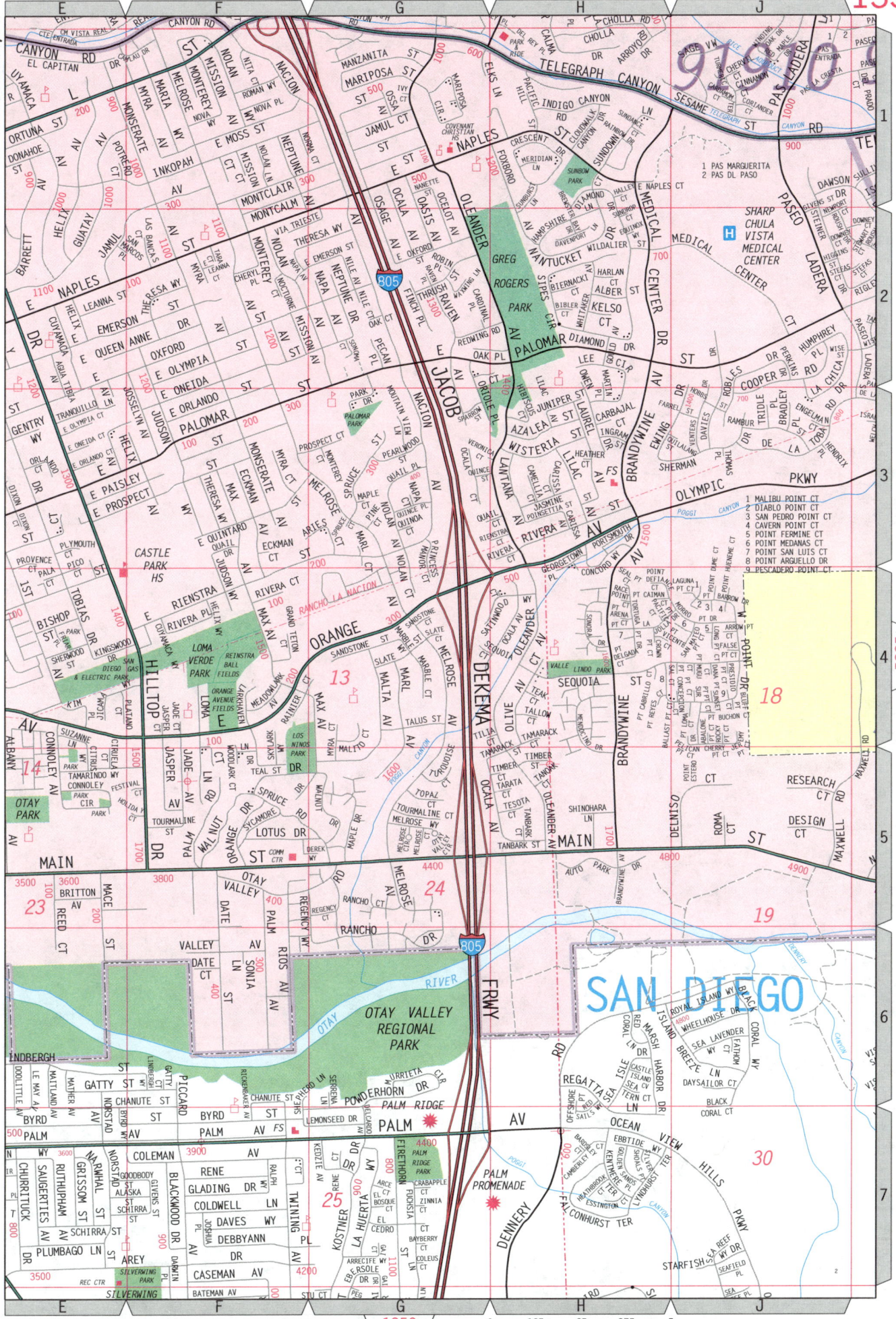

SAN DIEGO CO.

MAP

ThomasBros.Maps®

COPYRIGHT 2001

N

SAN DIEGO

OTAY VALLEY REGIONAL PARK

OTAY RIVER

805 FRWY

SHARP CHULA VISTA MEDICAL CENTER

GREG ROGERS PARK

CASTLE PARK HS

LOMA VERDE PARK

OTAY PARK

SILVERWING PARK

PALM PROMENADE

OCEAN VIEW HILLS PKWY

TELEGRAPH CANYON

OLYMPIC PKWY

MAIN ST

PALM AV

DENNERY RD

1 MALIBU POINT CT
2 DIABLO POINT CT
3 SAN PEDRO POINT CT
4 CAVERN POINT CT
5 POINT FERMINE CT
6 POINT MEDANAS CT
7 POINT SAN LUIS CT
8 POINT ARGUELLO DR
9 PESCADERO POINT CT

1 PAS MARGUERITA
2 PAS DL PASO

SEE 1331 MAP

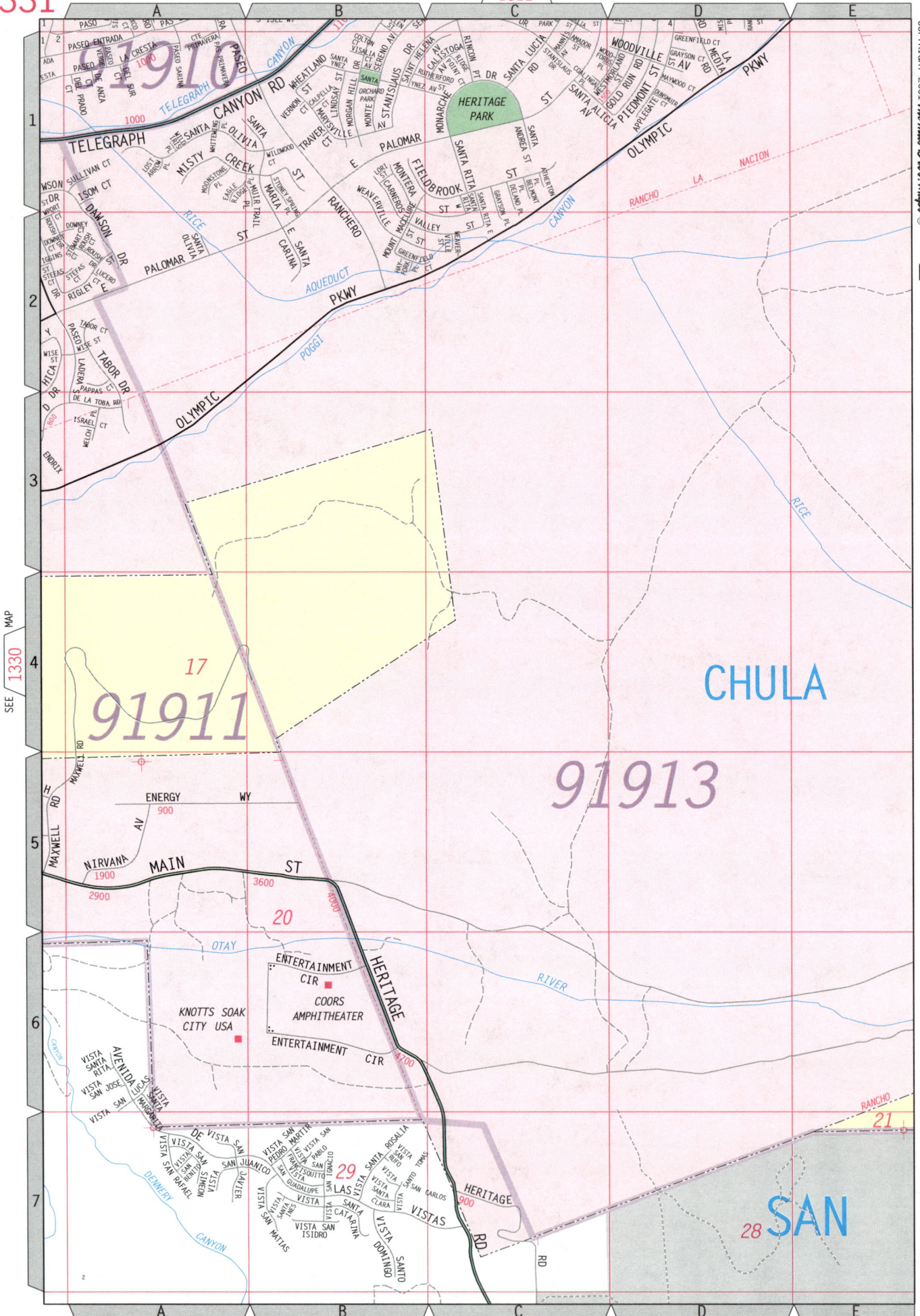

SAN DIEGO CO.

MAP

COPYRIGHT 2001 Thomas Bros. Maps ®

—N→

SEE 1311 MAP

SEE 1330 MAP

SEE 1351 MAP

91910

91911

91913

CHULA

SAN

17

20

29

21

28

TELEGRAPH CANYON RD

PASEO ENTRADA

PASEO RANCHERO

OLYMPIC PKWY

AQUEDUCT

POGGI

OLYMPIC

RANCHO LA NACION

RICE

HERITAGE PARK

WOODVILLE AV

SANTA LUCIA

PIEDMONT ST

GOLD RUN RD

GREENFIELD CT

SANTA RITA

FIELDBROOK

PALOMAR

MISTY CREEK

WHEATLAND ST

VERNON ST

MONARCH

MONTERA

WEAVERVILLE

VALLEY

GREENFIELD

RIGLEY

DAWSON DR

TABOR DR

LADERA

DE LA TOBA RD

ISRAEL PL

WELCH PL

ENDRIX

PAPPAS

MAXWELL RD

ENERGY WY
900

NIRVANA
1900
2900

MAIN ST
3600
4000
4700

HERITAGE RD
900

OTAY

RIVER

CANYON

DENNERY

ENTERTAINMENT CIR

COORS AMPHITHEATER

ENTERTAINMENT CIR

KNOTTS SOAK CITY USA

VISTA SANTA RITA

VISTA SAN JOSE

AVENIDA DE LAS VISTAS

VISTA SAN JUANICO

VISTA SAN JAPIER

VISTA SAN RAFAEL

VISTA SAN GUADALUPE

VISTA SAN PEDRO

VISTA SAN MARTIR

VISTA SAN FRANCISCO

VISTA SAN PABLO

VISTA SANTA ROSALIA

VISTA SANTA INES

VISTA SANTA CLARA

VISTA SANTA CATARINA

VISTA SAN ISIDRO

VISTA SAN MATIAS

VISTA SANTO DOMINGO

VISTA SANTO TOMAS

VISTA SAN CARLOS

miles 1 in. = 1900 ft.

0 .125 .25 .375 .5

1331

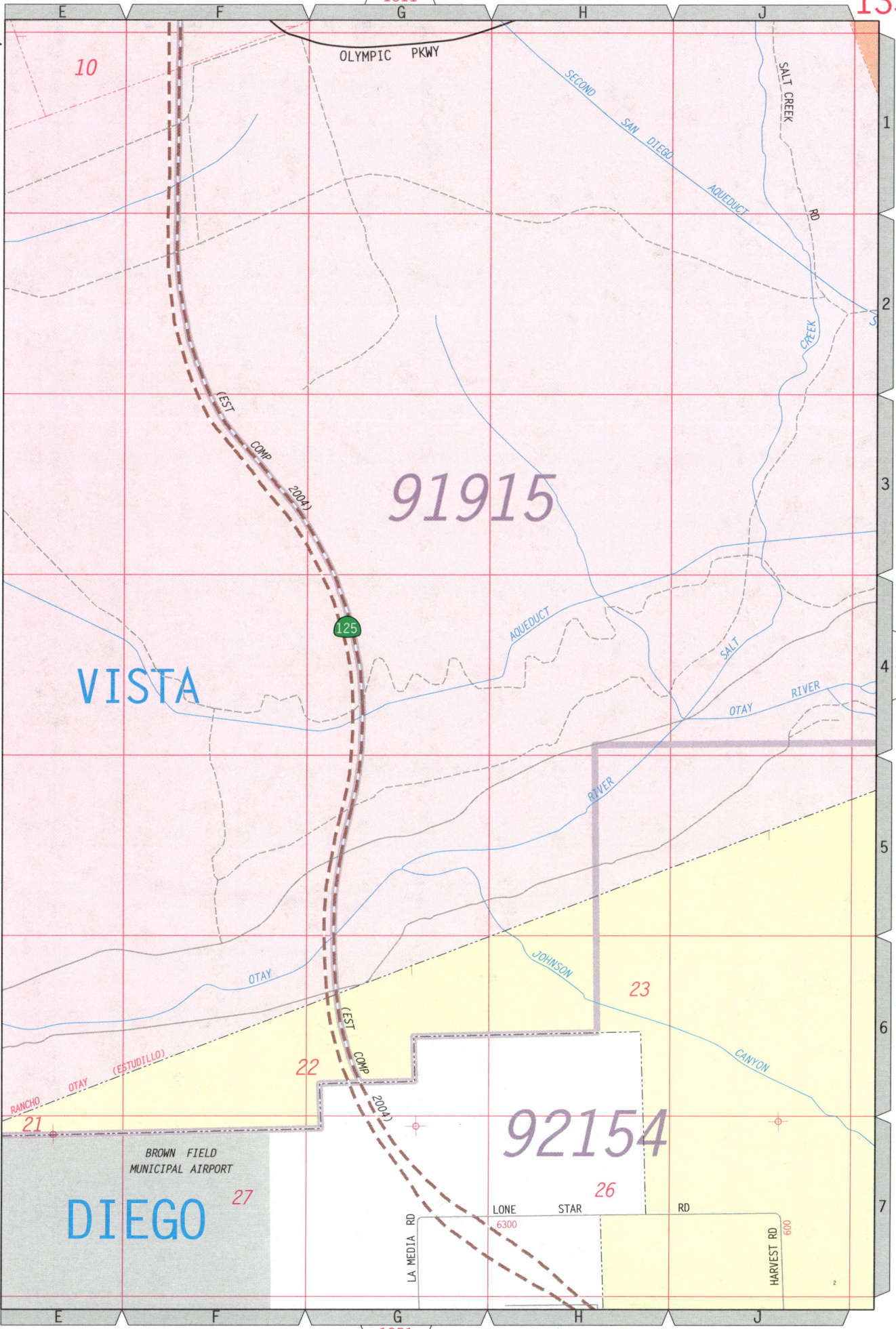

N↑

SAN DIEGO CO.

E   F   G   H   J

10

OLYMPIC   PKWY

SALT CREEK

SECOND   SAN   DIEGO   AQUEDUCT

RD

S

CREEK

1

2

(EST COMP 2004)

91915

3

AQUEDUCT

SALT

SEE 1332 MAP

125

VISTA

OTAY   RIVER

RIVER

4

MAP

OTAY

JOHNSON

23

5

OTAY

CANYON

22

(EST COMP 2004)

92154

6

RANCHO   OTAY   (ESTUDILLO)

21

BROWN FIELD
MUNICIPAL AIRPORT

26

LONE   STAR   RD

DIEGO

27

LA MEDIA RD

6300

HARVEST RD

600

7

2

E   F   G   H   J

0 .125 .25 .375 .5
miles 1 in. = 1900 ft.

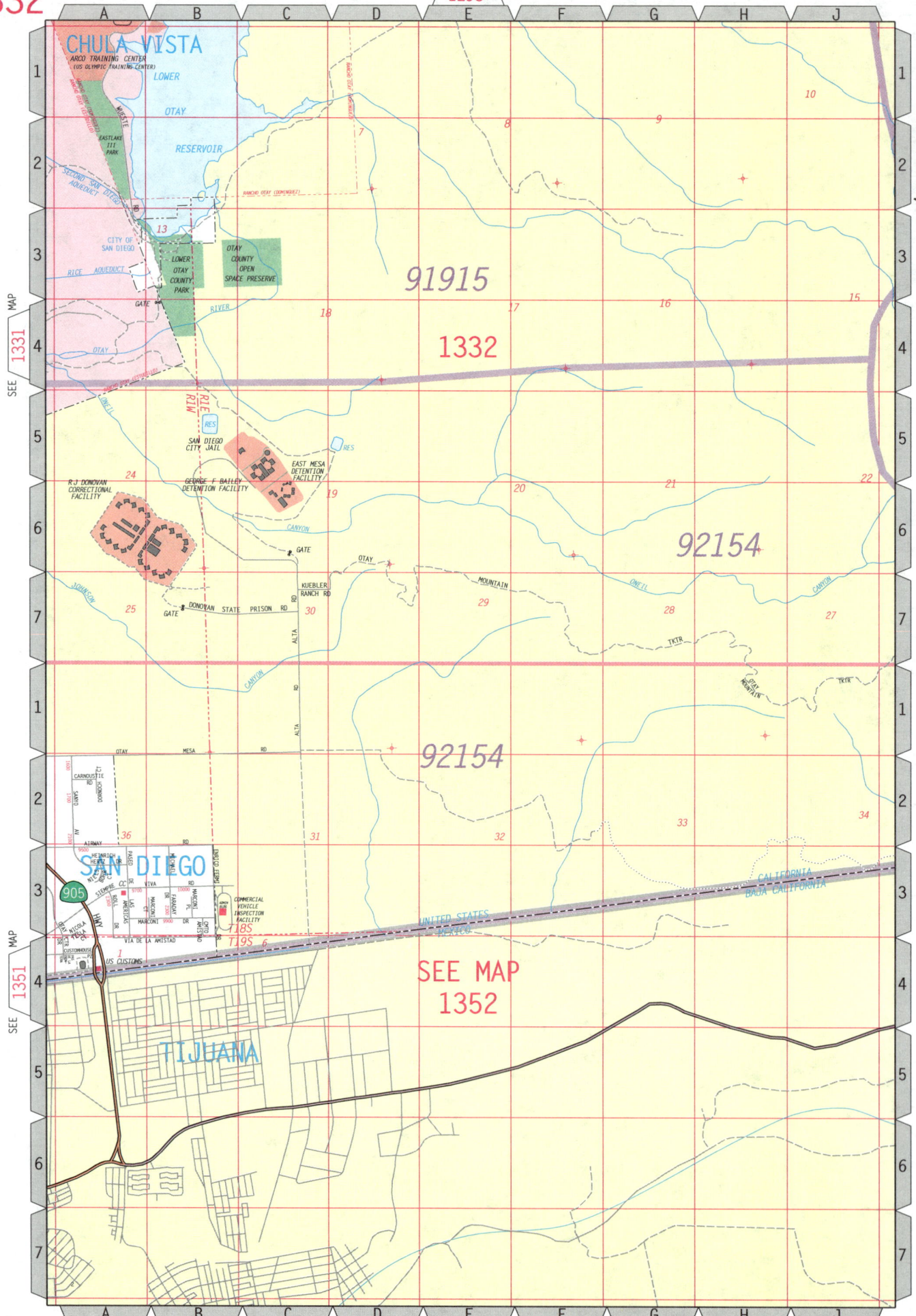

SAN DIEGO CO.

MAP

SEE 1293 MAP

COPYRIGHT 2001 Thomas Bros. Maps® ←N→

A B C D E F G H J

CHULA VISTA
ARCO TRAINING CENTER
(US OLYMPIC TRAINING CENTER)

LOWER

OTAY

RESERVOIR

EASTLAKE III PARK

SECOND SAN DIEGO AQUEDUCT

CITY OF SAN DIEGO

RICE AQUEDUCT

LOWER OTAY COUNTY PARK

OTAY COUNTY OPEN SPACE PRESERVE

GATE

RIVER

OTAY

91915

1332

RANCHO OTAY (DOMINGUEZ)

18   17   16   15

RIE RIM

RES

SAN DIEGO CITY JAIL

RES

EAST MESA DETENTION FACILITY

R J DONOVAN CORRECTIONAL FACILITY

24

GEORGE F BAILEY DETENTION FACILITY

19   20   21   22

CANYON

92154

GATE

JOHNSON

25

GATE

DONOVAN STATE PRISON RD

30

KUEBLER RANCH RD

OTAY

MOUNTAIN

29   28   27

ONEIL

CANYON

TKTR

ALTA   RD

CANYON

OTAY MOUNTAIN

TKTR

OTAY   MESA   RD

92154

36

CARNDUSTIE RD

SANYO

ALTA   RD

31   32   33   34

AIRWAY

SAN DIEGO

905

HEINRICH HERTZ

NICOLE

BELL

SIEMPRE

VIVA

LAS AMERICAS

PASEO

MICHAEL   RD

MARCONI   PL

FARADAY   DR

MARCONI   DR

ENRICO FERMI

COMMERCIAL VEHICLE INSPECTION FACILITY

VIA DE LA AMISTAD

CALIFORNIA
BAJA CALIFORNIA

T18S
T19S

UNITED STATES
MEXICO

US CUSTOMS

CUSTOMHOUSE

DAIRY

SEE MAP 1352

TIJUANA

1   2   3   4   5   6   7

SEE 1331 MAP

SEE 1351 MAP

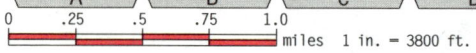

0   .25   .5   .75   1.0
miles   1 in. = 3800 ft.

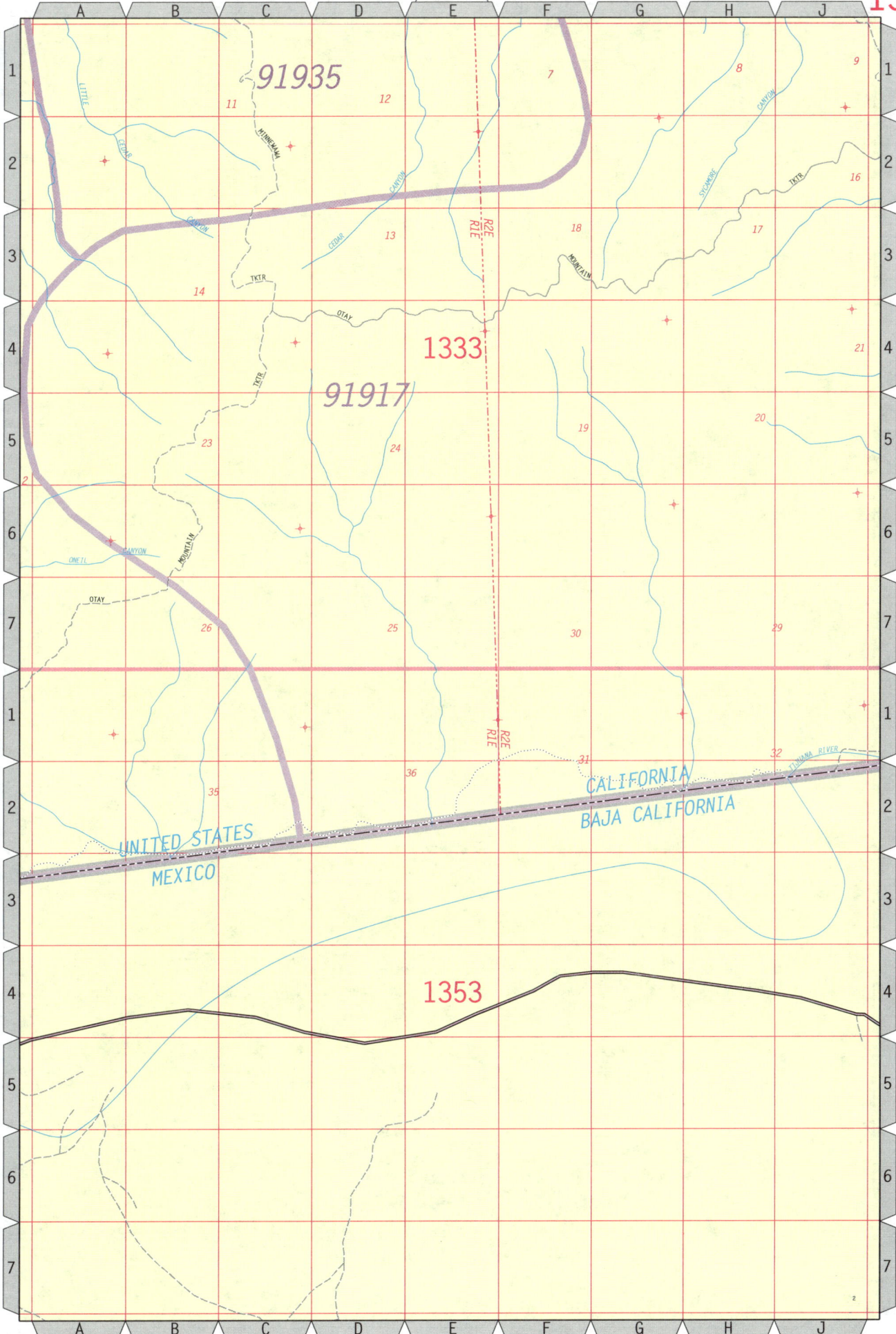

91935

91917

1333

1353

SAN DIEGO CO.

SEE 429 MAP

MAP

SEE 429 MAP

UNITED STATES
MEXICO

CALIFORNIA
BAJA CALIFORNIA

TIJUANA RIVER

0   .25   .5   .75   1.0   miles   1 in. = 3800 ft.

Thomas Bros. Maps®
© COPYRIGHT 2001

N

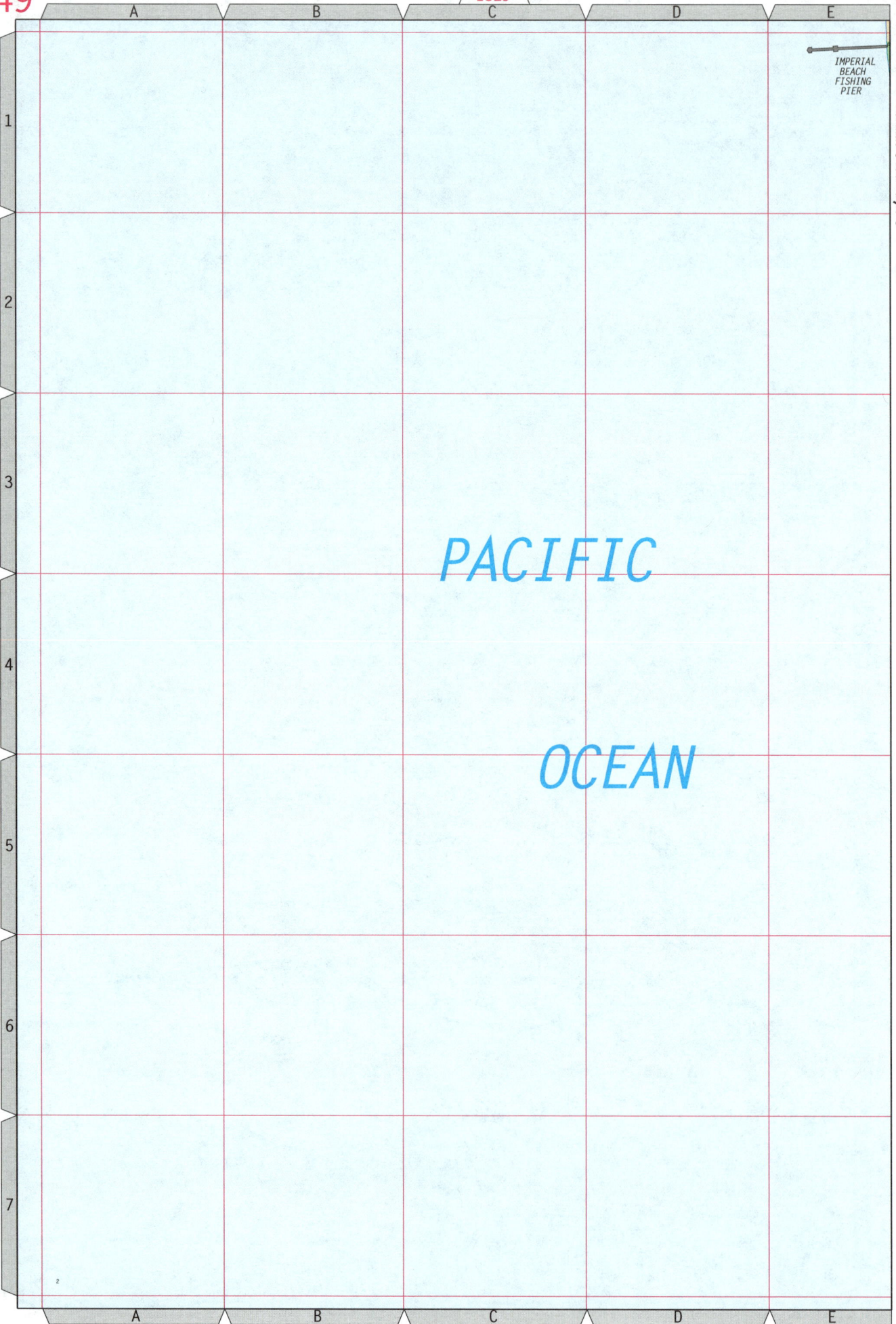

SEE 1329 MAP

A   B   C   D   E

IMPERIAL
BEACH
FISHING
PIER

←N→

1

2

3

PACIFIC

SEE 429 MAP

4

OCEAN

5

6

7

A   B   C   D   E

0 .125 .25 .375 .5 miles 1 in. = 1900 ft.

SEE 429 MAP

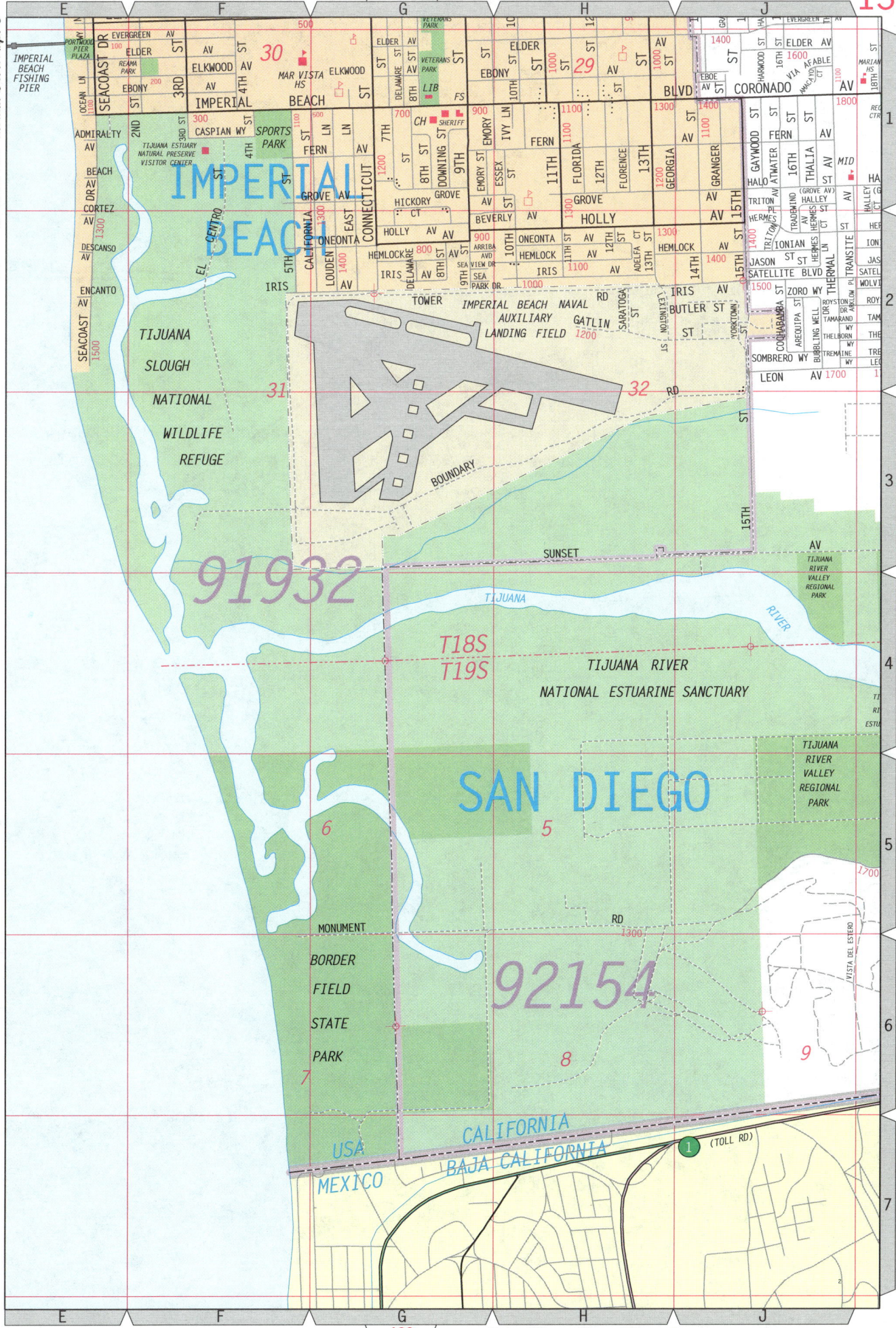

SAN DIEGO CO.

MAP

N

E F G H J

IMPERIAL BEACH FISHING PIER

PORTWOOD PIER PLAZA

EVERGREEN AV
ELDER AV
ELKWOOD AV
EBONY AV
IMPERIAL BEACH BLVD

SEACOAST DR
2ND ST
3RD ST
4TH ST
5TH ST

REAMA PARK

30

MAR VISTA HS

VETERANS PARK
ELDER ST
ELKWOOD ST
EBONY ST
DELAWARE ST
8TH ST
LIB
FS

ELDER AV
EBONY AV

ELDER ST
9TH ST
10TH ST
11TH ST
12TH ST
13TH ST

29

CORONADO AV

VIA AFABLE
MARIAN HS
REC CTR

ADMIRALTY AV
BEACH DR
CORTEZ AV
DESCANSO AV
ENCANTO AV
SEACOAST

CASPIAN WY
SPORTS PARK

TIJUANA ESTUARY NATURAL PRESERVE VISITOR CENTER

CALIFORNIA
CONNECTICUT
EL CENTRO
LOUDEN
EAST
ONEONTA

FERN LN
GROVE AV
HICKORY CT
HOLLY AV
HEMLOCK AV
IRIS AV

7TH ST
8TH ST
DOWNING ST
9TH ST

EMORY ST
IVY LN
FERN ST
ESSEX ST
SEA VIEW DR
SEA PARK DR

CH
SHERIFF

EMORY ST
10TH ST
11TH ST
ADELFA CT
12TH ST
13TH ST

FERN AV
FLORENCE
GEORGIA
GRANGER AV

GROVE AV
HOLLY AV
HEMLOCK AV
IRIS AV

14TH ST
15TH ST

BEVERLY AV

GAYWOOD ST
ATWATER
16TH ST
THALIA ST
HALO ST
TRITON
HERMES ST
HERMES ST
IONIAN ST
JASON ST
SATELLITE BLVD
ZORO WY

HARWOOD ST
16TH ST
FERN ST
HALLEY

MID

TOWER

IRIS

IMPERIAL BEACH

31

TIJUANA SLOUGH

NATIONAL

WILDLIFE

REFUGE

IMPERIAL BEACH NAVAL AUXILIARY LANDING FIELD

SARATOGA ST
LEXINGTON ST
YORKTOWN ST

GATLIN ST

BUTLER ST
IRIS AV

32

LEON AV

RD

15TH ST

SATELLITE BLVD
COCHABAMBA ST
AREQUIPA ST
BUBBLING WELL
ROYSTON DR
ARKLOW PL
TRANSITE
SOMBRERO WY
TAMARAND WY
THELBORN WY
TREMAINE WY

91932

SUNSET

TIJUANA

RIVER

TIJUANA RIVER VALLEY REGIONAL PARK

SEE 1350 MAP

T18S
T19S

TIJUANA RIVER

NATIONAL ESTUARINE SANCTUARY

SAN DIEGO

6

5

TIJUANA RIVER VALLEY REGIONAL PARK

MONUMENT

RD

VISTA DEL ESTERO

92154

BORDER

FIELD

STATE

PARK

7

8

9

USA
MEXICO

CALIFORNIA
BAJA CALIFORNIA

1 (TOLL RD)

0 .125 .25 .375 .5 miles   1 in. = 1900 ft.

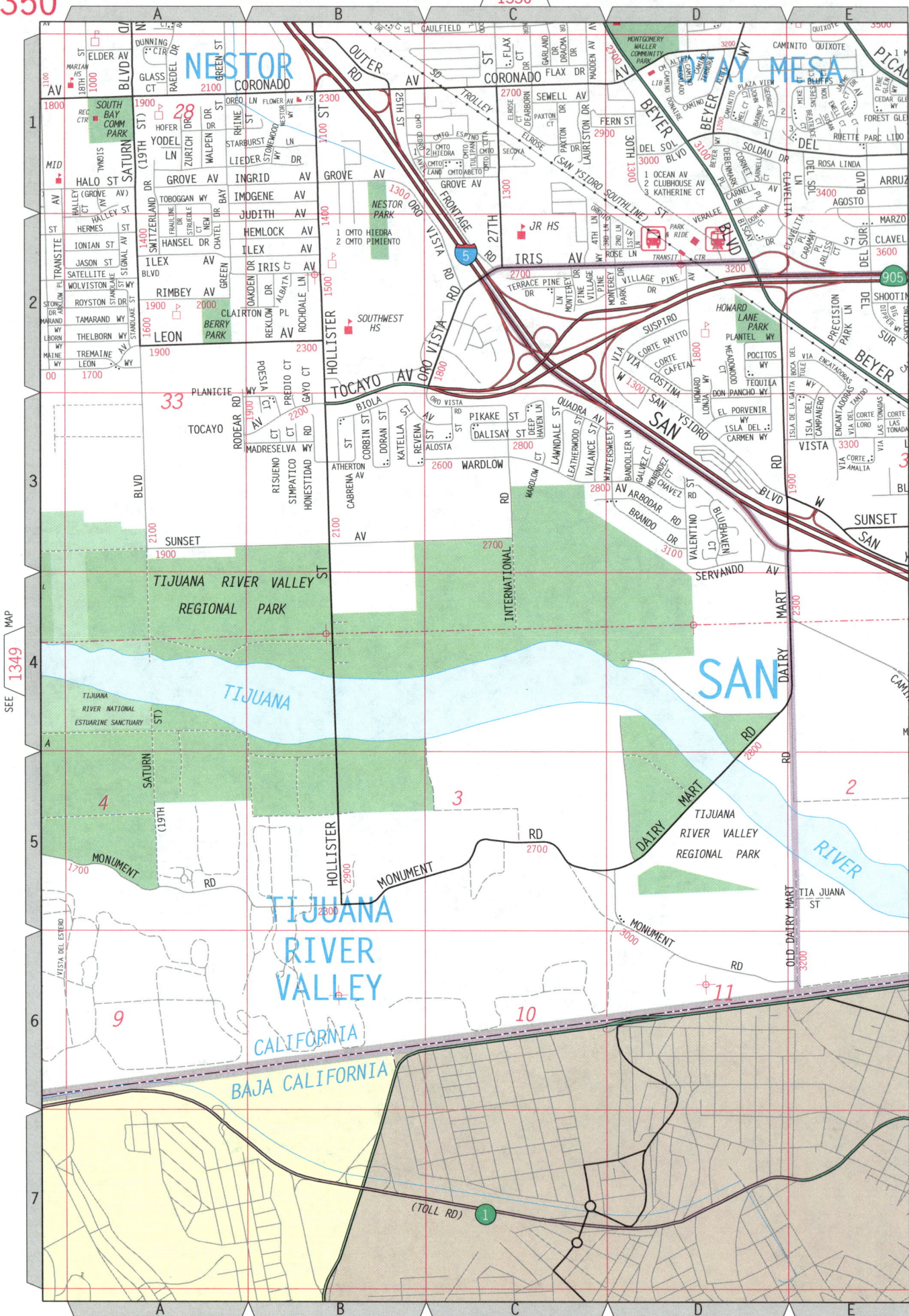

1350

SEE 1330 MAP

COPYRIGHT 2001 Thomas Bros. Maps ®

SAN DIEGO CO.

MAP

NESTOR

OTAY MESA

NESTOR PARK
1 CMTO HIEDRA
2 CMTO PIMIENTO

SOUTH BAY COMM PARK

SOUTHWEST HS

JR HS

IRIS AV

SAN YSIDRO

SAN

TIJUANA RIVER VALLEY REGIONAL PARK

TIJUANA RIVER NATIONAL ESTUARINE SANCTUARY

TIJUANA

TIJUANA RIVER VALLEY REGIONAL PARK

RIVER

SAN

SUNSET

TIJUANA RIVER VALLEY

CALIFORNIA

BAJA CALIFORNIA

(TOLL RD)

SEE 1349 MAP

SEE 429 MAP

0 .125 .25 .375 .5 miles 1 in. = 1900 ft.

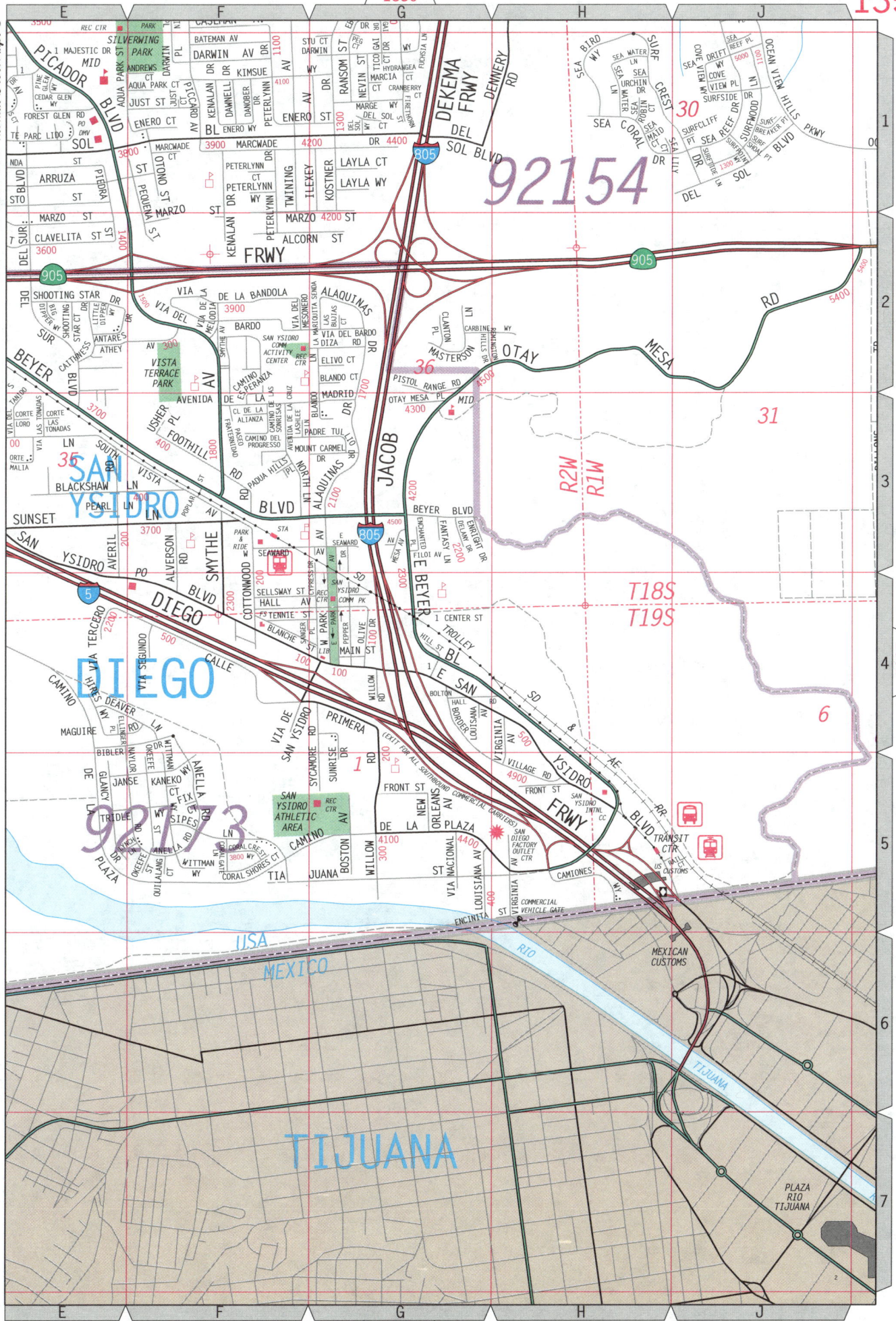

Thomas Bros. Maps®

COPYRIGHT 2001

N

SAN DIEGO CO.

MAP

92154

92173

SAN YSIDRO

DIEGO

TIJUANA

PICADOR BLVD

SILVERWING PARK

MAJESTIC DR

AQUA PARK

DARWIN AV

DARWIN

ANDREWS

BATEMAN AV

KIMSUE

RANSOM ST

NEVIN ST

STU CT DARWIN WY

PEG DR

TICO GAI

HYDRANGEA

MARCIA CT

CRANBERRY CT

FIRETHORN

DEKEMA FRWY

DENNERY RD

SEA BIRD WY

SEA WATER LN

SURF CREST

SEA URCHIN DR

SEA WATER LN

COVE VIEW WY

SEA COVE

VIEW PL

SURFSIDE DR

SEA REEF PL

OCEAN VIEW HILLS PKWY

30

CEDAR GLEN WY

FOREST GLEN RD

ENERO CT

PICCORD WY

PETERLYNN DR

ENERO ST

ENERO WY

MARGE DEL SOL CT

DEL SOL

DEL SOL BLVD

SURFCLIFF PT

SEA REEF DR

SURFWOOD DR

SURF BREAKER PL

DEL SOL

SOL

ARRUZA ST

PIEDRA ST

OTONO ST

PEQUENA ST

MARCWADE

MARCWADE DR

PETERLYNN CT

PETERLYNN WY

TWINING

ILEXEY

KOSTNER

LAYLA CT

LAYLA WY

MARZO ST

CLAVELITA ST

KENALAN DR

MARZO ST

ALCORN ST

MARZO 4200 ST

FRWY

92154

805

905

905

MESA RD

SHOOTING STAR DR

BIG DIPPER WY

LITTLE DIPPER WY

SHOOTING STAR CT

ANTARES

ATHEY

VIA DE LA BANDOLA

VIA DEL MELODIA

BARDO

SMYTHE AV

LAS BUJAS

LA MARTQUITA SENDA

VIA DEL BARDO DR

ALAQUINAS

SAN YSIDRO COMM ACTIVITY CENTER

REC CTR

ALAQUINAS DR

CARBINE WY

CLANTON PL

MASTERSON LN

PRINCETON

OTAY MESA RD

31

R2W R1W

VISTA TERRACE PARK

AVENIDA

USHER PL

FOOTHILL

CAITHNESS WY

CORTE LORO

VIA LAS TONADAS

ELIVO CT

BLANDO CT

MADRID

BLANDO DR

CAMINO ESPERANZA

CAMINO DE LA ALIANZA

PASEO FRATERNIDAD

AVENIDA DE LAS SONRISAS

CAMINO DEL PROGRESO

PADRE TULI

MOUNT CARMEL DR

PISTOL RANGE RD

OTAY MESA PL

MID

36

BEYER BLVD

SOUTH VISTA

BLACKSHAW LN

PEARL LN

SUNSET

SAN YSIDRO

POPLAR AV

PADUA HILLS PL

ALAQUINAS RD

JACOB

BLVD

BEYER BLVD

ENRIGHT DR

DELANY WY

ENCHANTED DR

FANTASY LN

FILOI AV

T18S T19S

6

35

SAN YSIDRO

BEYER BLVD

SAN YSIDRO BLVD

AVERIL

ALVERSON RD

SMYTHE

COTTONWOOD

SELLSWAY ST

HALL AV

TENNIE

BLANCHE

PARK & RIDE

SEAWARD

STA

SEAWARD

CYPRESS DR

SD

SAN YSIDRO COMM PK

REC CTR

W PARK

E PARK

PEPPER

OLIVE

MAIN ST

MESA AV

E BEYER

CENTER ST

TROLLEY BL

HILL ST

DIEGO

SAN DIEGO

5

VIA TERCERO

DIEGO

CALLE

SANGER

WILLOW DR

BOLTON

HALL

LOUISIANA

VIRGINIA AV

VILLAGE RD

FRONT ST

SD

YSIDRO FRWY

SAN YSIDRO INTNL

CC

RR

TRANSIT CTR

CAMINO DE LA PLAZA

HIRES DEAVER LN

ELLINGER RD

NAYLOR RD

WITTMAN

MAGUIRE

BIBLER

JANSE

KANEKO

OKEEFE

ANELLA RD

FIXE CT

SIPES

VIA DE SAN YSIDRO

PRIMERA

SYCAMORE RD

SUNRISE AV

FRONT ST

NEW ORLEANS ST

DE LA PLAZA

VIRGINIA AV

92173

SAN YSIDRO ATHLETIC AREA

REC CTR

SAN DIEGO FACTORY OUTLET CTR

US CUSTOMS

TRIDLE

ANELLA RD

WITTMAN WY

CORAL SHORES CT

BOSTON

WILLOW

TIA JUANA

VIA NACIONAL

LOUISIANA AV

VIRGINIA AV

CAMIONES

COMMERCIAL VEHICLE GATE

ENCINITA

MEXICAN CUSTOMS

U.S.A.

MEXICO

RIO

TIJUANA

TIJUANA

PLAZA RIO TIJUANA

0 .125 .25 .375 .5 miles 1 in. = 1900 ft.

SEE 1351 MAP

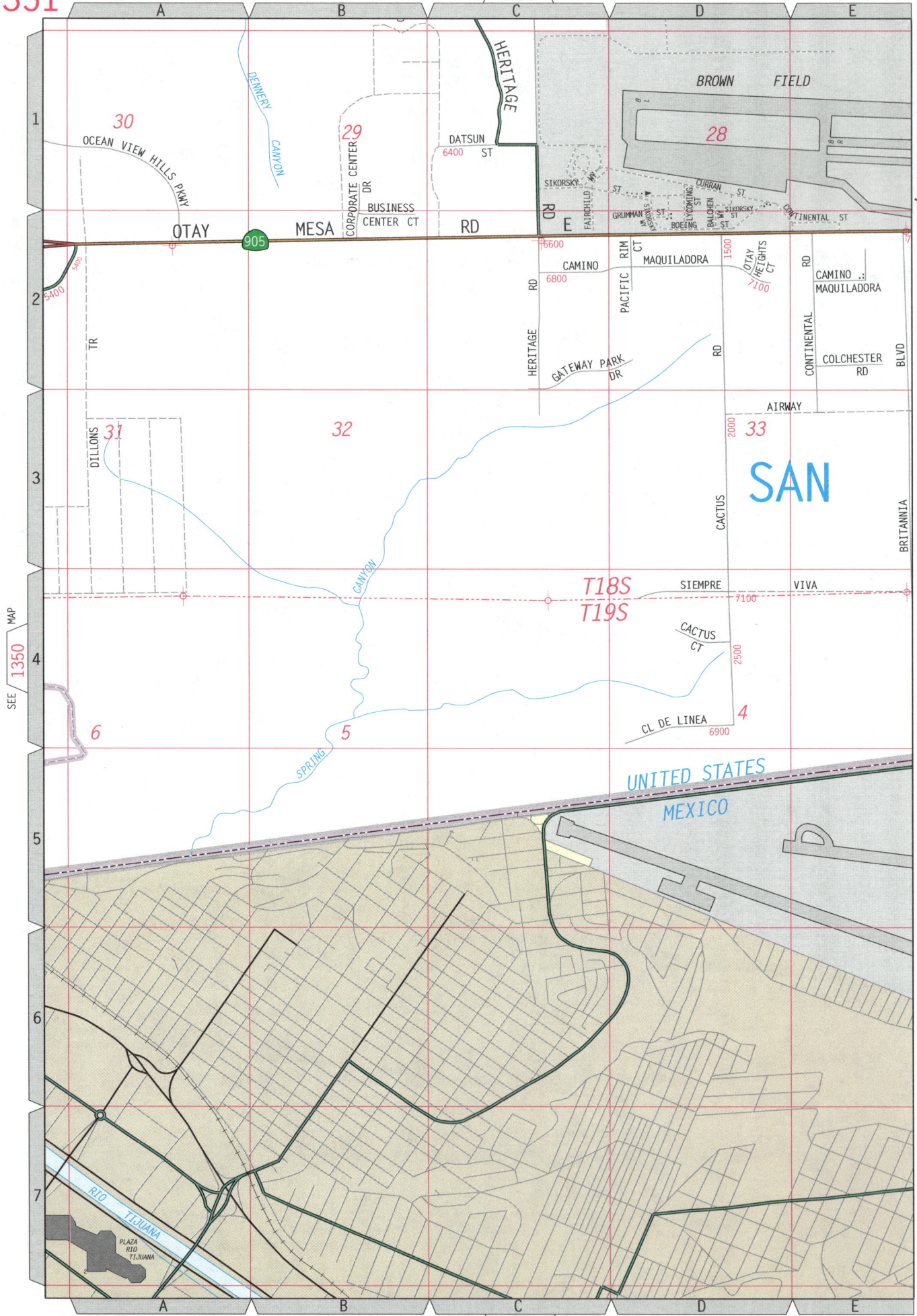

1351

SAN DIEGO CO.

MAP

COPYRIGHT 2001 Thomas Bros. Maps® —N—

A | B | C | D | E

1

OCEAN VIEW HILLS PKWY

DENNERY CANYON

30

29

BROWN FIELD

28

CORPORATE CENTER DR

DATSUN ST
6400

HERITAGE

7
8

8 RC

SIKORSKY ST
FAIRCHILD WY
CURRAN ST
GRUMMAN ST
MOFFETT ST
LYCOMING ST
BALCHEN ST
SIKORSKY WY
BOEING ST
CONTINENTAL ST

2

OTAY   MESA   905   BUSINESS CENTER CT   RD

RD
6600

CAMINO
6800
PACIFIC RIM CT
MAQUILADORA
OTAY HEIGHTS CT
1500
7100

CAMINO MAQUILADORA

CONTINENTAL RD

5400
5400

TR

HERITAGE RD

GATEWAY PARK DR

RD

COLCHESTER RD

BRITANNIA BLVD

3

31
DILLONS

32

AIRWAY

2000

33

SAN

CANYON

CACTUS

4

T18S
T19S

SIEMPRE   VIVA
7100

CACTUS CT
2500

6
5

CL DE LINEA
6900

4

SPRING

5

UNITED STATES
MEXICO

6

7

RIO TIJUANA

PLAZA RIO TIJUANA

A | B | C | D | E

SEE 1350 MAP

0 .125 .25 .375 .5
miles 1 in. = 1900 ft.

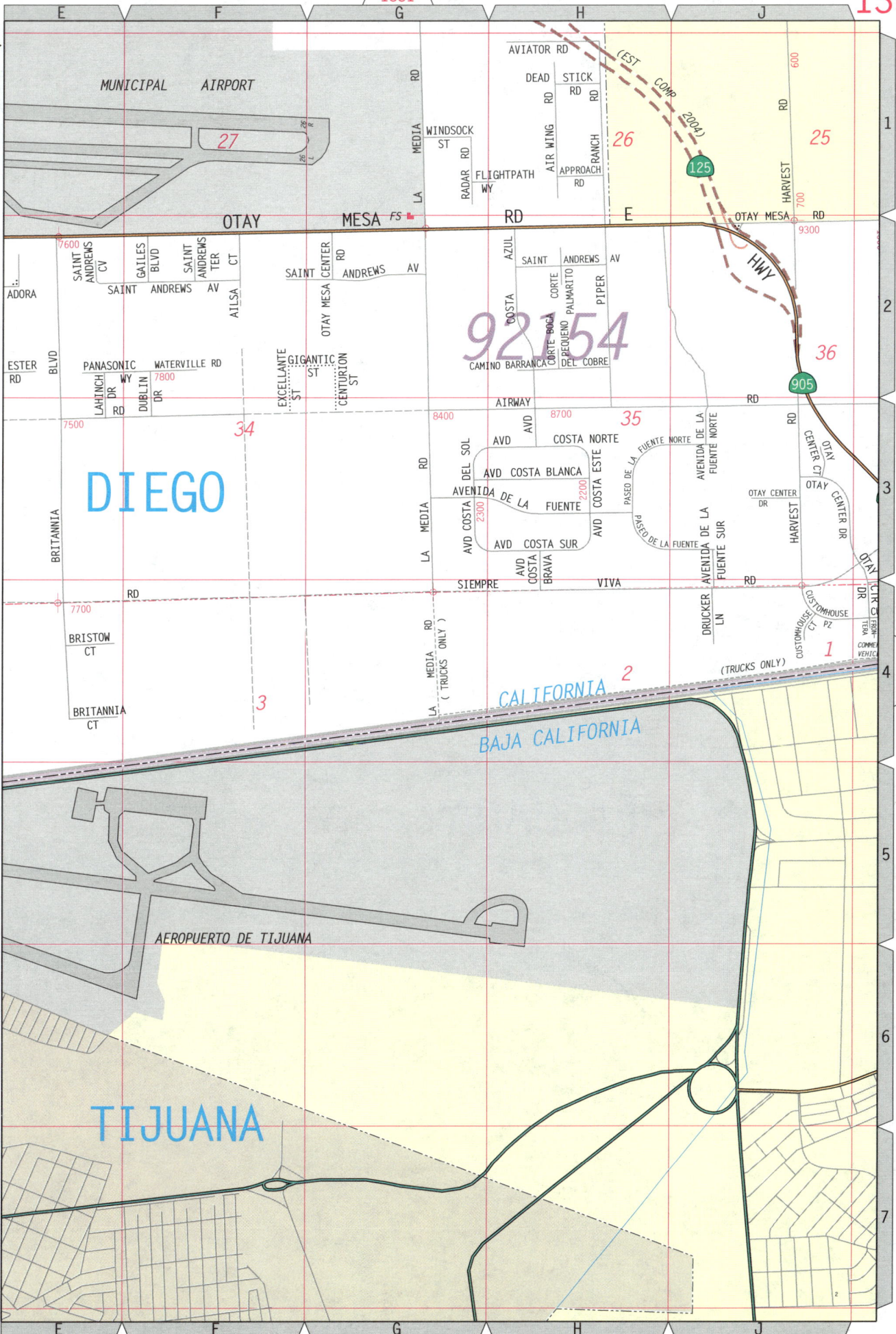

SAN DIEGO CO.

MAP

Thomas Bros. Maps ®

COPYRIGHT 2001

N

SEE 1331 MAP

E F G H J

MUNICIPAL   AIRPORT

27

26 R
26 L

AVIATOR RD
(EST COMP 2004)
DEAD   STICK
RD RD RD
AIR WING
RANCH
APPROACH
RD

WINDSOCK ST
MEDIA RD
RADAR RD
FLIGHTPATH WY

26

25

600
HARVEST RD
700

125

OTAY   MESA   RD   FS

E
OTAY MESA RD
9300

7600

ADORA
SAINT ANDREWS CV
GATLES BLVD
SAINT ANDREWS TER
SAINT ANDREWS CT
AILSA
SAINT ANDREWS AV
OTAY MESA CENTER RD
SAINT   ANDREWS   AV

COSTA AZUL
SAINT   ANDREWS   AV
CORTE BOCA
CORTE PEQUENO
CORTE PALMARITO
DEL COBRE
PIPER

HWY

2

ESTER RD
BRITANNIA BLVD
PANASONIC WY
WATERVILLE RD
LAHINCH DR
DUBLIN DR
RD
7800
EXCELLANTE ST
GIGANTIC ST
CENTURION ST

92154

CAMINO BARRANCA

36

905

7500

34

AIRWAY   RD
8400 8700

35

3

DIEGO

LA MEDIA RD
BRITANNIA

AVD DEL SOL
AVD COSTA BLANCA
AVENIDA DE LA FUENTE
2300
AVD COSTA SUR
AVD COSTA BRAVA
AVD COSTA ESTE
2200
COSTA NORTE
PASEO DE LA FUENTE NORTE
AVENIDA DE LA FUENTE NORTE
PASEO DE LA FUENTE SUR
AVENIDA DE LA FUENTE SUR
RD
OTAY CENTER DR
HARVEST
OTAY CENTER CT
OTAY CENTER DR
OTAY CIR

3

7700
RD
SIEMPRE   VIVA   RD
DRUCKER LN
CUSTOMHOUSE PZ
CUSTOMHOUSE DR
OTAY CIR DR
COMMERCIAL VEHICLE

BRISTOW CT
LA MEDIA RD (TRUCKS ONLY)
(TRUCKS ONLY)
1

BRITANNIA CT

3

2

CALIFORNIA

SEE 1352 MAP

4

BAJA CALIFORNIA

5

AEROPUERTO DE TIJUANA

6

TIJUANA

7

E F G H J

SEE 429 MAP

0 .125 .25 .375 .5 miles   1 in. = 1900 ft.

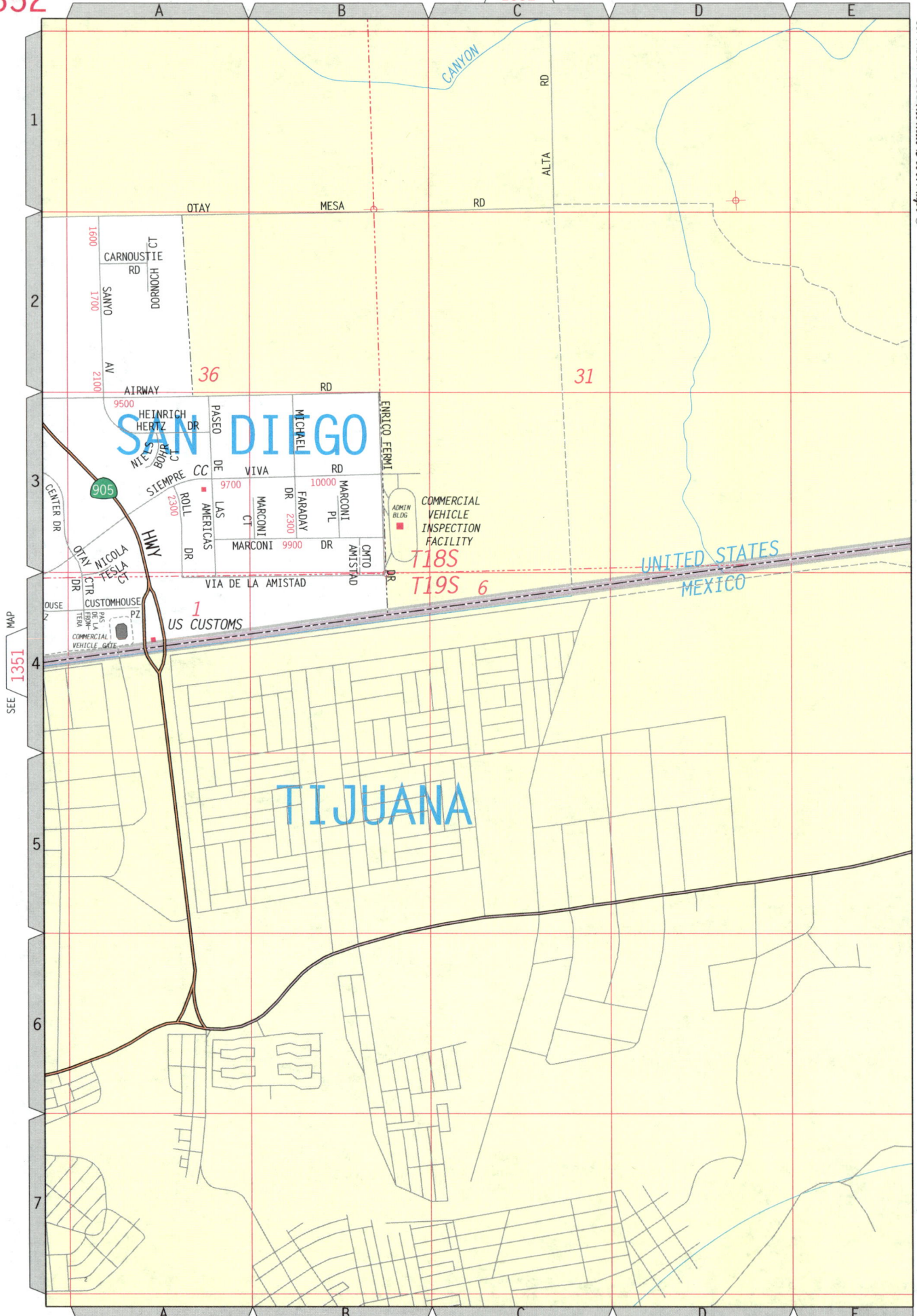

1352

SAN DIEGO CO.

MAP

A B C D E

1

CANYON

OTAY MESA RD

ALTA RD

1600 CARNOUSTIE RD
1700 SANYO
DONNOCH CT
36

2

SANYO AV 2100

31

AIRWAY RD

9500
HEINRICH
HERTZ DR

SAN DIEGO

PASEO DE
MICHAEL

ENRICO FERMI

NIELS BOHR CT
SIEMPRE CC
VIVA RD
905
3

CENTER DR
ROLL 2300
LAS AMERICAS
9700
MARCONI CT
FARADAY DR
10000
MARCONI PL
MARCONI 9900 DR

COMMERCIAL
VEHICLE
INSPECTION
FACILITY

ADMIN
BLDG

T18S

OTAY CTR DR
NICOLA TESLA CT
HWY
DR
VIA DE LA AMISTAD
CMTO AMISTAD

T19S 6

UNITED STATES
MEXICO

4

OUSE
Z
CUSTOMHOUSE
PAS DE LA TERRA
PZ
1
US CUSTOMS

COMMERCIAL
VEHICLE GATE

TIJUANA

5

6

7

A B C D E

0 .125 .25 .375 .5
miles 1 in. = 1900 ft.

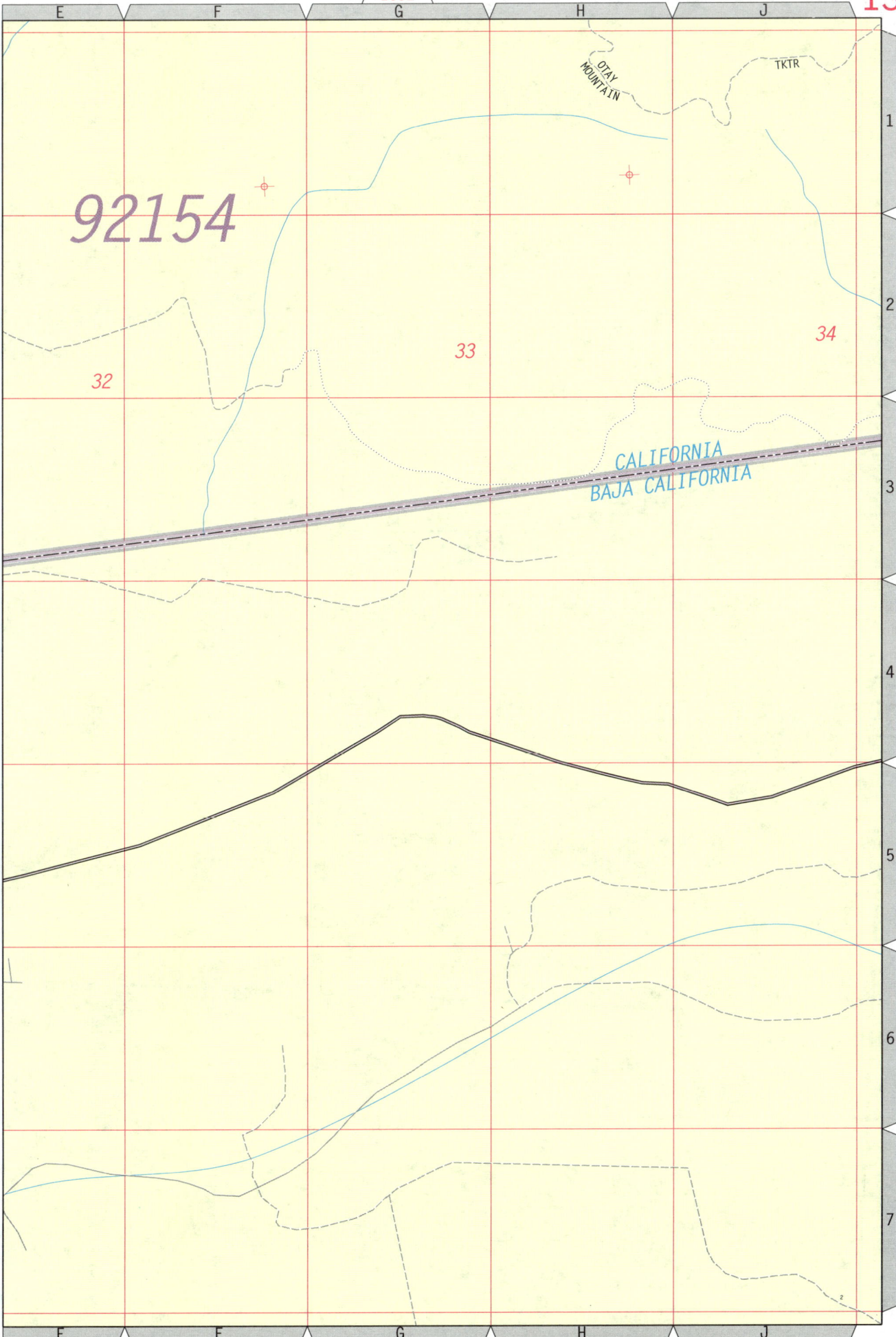

E F G H J

OTAY MOUNTAIN

TKTR

SAN DIEGO CO.

1

92154

2

32   33   34

CALIFORNIA
BAJA CALIFORNIA

3

SEE 1332 MAP

4

MAP

5

6

7

E F G H J

0 .125 .25 .375 .5 miles 1 in. = 1900 ft.

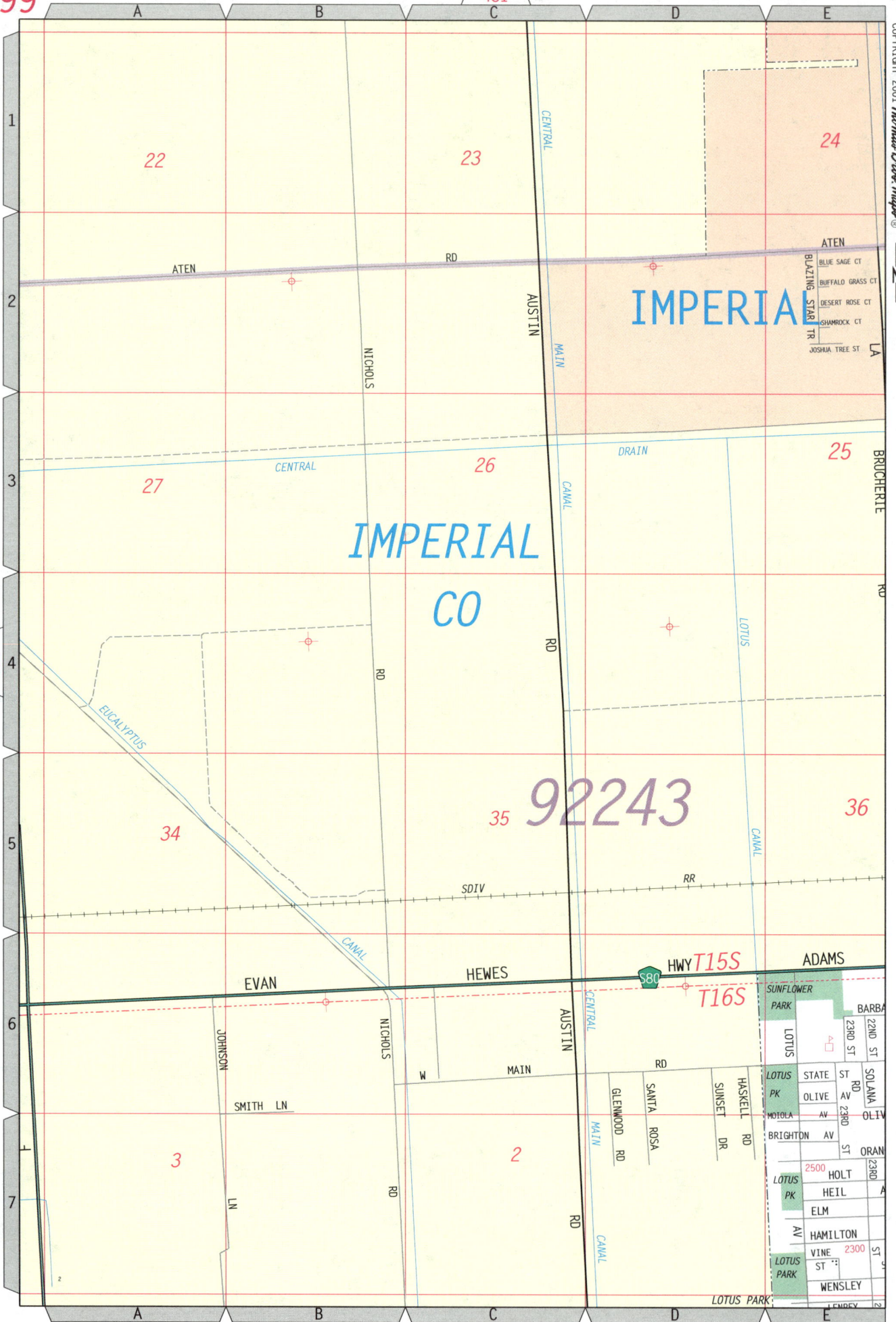

SAN DIEGO CO.

—N—→

SEE 431 MAP

A B C D E

1

22 23 24

ATEN RD ATEN

BLUE SAGE CT

BUFFALO GRASS CT

IMPERIAL

DESERT ROSE CT

SHAMROCK CT

2

AUSTIN

MAIN

JOSHUA TREE ST

NICHOLS

CENTRAL DRAIN 25

CANAL

27 26

BRUCHERIE

3

IMPERIAL

CO

RD

SEE 431 MAP

4

RD

EUCALYPTUS

LOTUS

92243

5

34 35 36

CANAL

CANAL

SDIV RR

MAP

HWY T15S ADAMS

S80

6

EVAN HEWES T16S SUNFLOWER PARK

CENTRAL

BARBA

LOTUS

22ND ST

23RD ST

JOHNSON

NICHOLS

RD

LOTUS PK STATE ST RD SOLANA

W MAIN

RD SANTA ROSA

SUNSET DR

HASKELL RD

OLIVE AV 23RD OLIV

GLENWOOD RD

MOTOLA AV

BRIGHTON AV ST ORAN

SMITH LN

23RD

MAIN

2500 HOLT 23RD A

3 2 LOTUS PK HEIL

7

LN RD CANAL ELM

AV HAMILTON

VINE 2300 ST

LOTUS PARK ST

WENSLEY

2

LOTUS PARK LENREY

A B C D E

0 .125 .25 .375 .5

miles 1 in. = 1900 ft.

SEE 6559 MAP

MAP

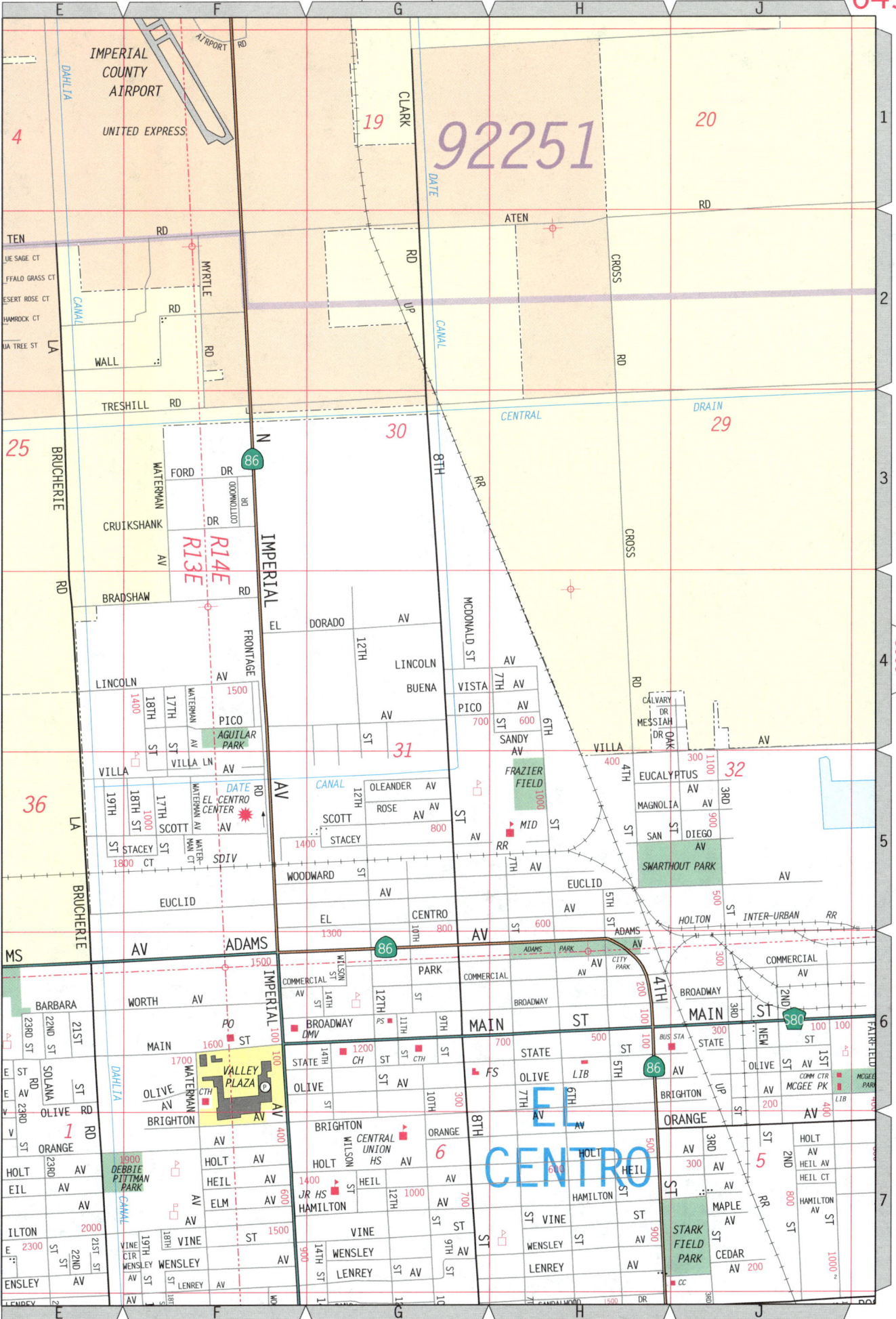

SAN DIEGO CO.

MAP

ThomasBros. Maps ®

COPYRIGHT 2001

N

E F G H J

1

IMPERIAL COUNTY AIRPORT

UNITED EXPRESS

AIRPORT RD

DAHLIA

4

CLARK

19

92251

20

DATE

ATEN RD

CROSS RD

2

TEN RD

UE SAGE CT
FFALO GRASS CT
ESERT ROSE CT
HAMROCK CT
UA TREE ST

CANAL

MYRTLE

RD

WALL

RD

UP CANAL

TRESHILL RD

CENTRAL DRAIN

30 29

25

BRUCHERIE RD

LA

FORD DR

WATERMAN

CRUIKSHANK AV

BRADSHAW

CULLINGTON DR

86

IMPERIAL

N

FRONTAGE

8TH

RR

CROSS RD

3

R14E
R13E

EL DORADO AV

12TH ST

LINCOLN

BUENA VISTA AV

MCDONALD ST

7TH AV

6TH

RD

CALVARY DR
MESSIAH DR OAK

4

SEE 6500 MAP

LINCOLN AV

1400

18TH ST
17TH ST

WATERMAN

1500

PICO

AGUILAR PARK

VILLA

VILLA LN

AV

PICO AV

700 600

SANDY AV

FRAZIER FIELD

1000

VILLA

400

EUCALYPTUS

300 1100

MAGNOLIA AV

3RD

AV

32

36

LA

19TH
18TH ST
17TH ST

1000

WATERMAN AV

SCOTT

DATE RD
EL CENTRO CENTER

WATER MAN CT

CANAL

12TH ST

OLEANDER AV

ROSE AV

SCOTT

800

AV

ST

MID

RR

7TH AV

4TH ST

SAN DIEGO AV

900

SWARTHOUT PARK

5

STACEY CT

SDIV

1800

1400

STACEY

WOODWARD ST

AV

5TH AV

EUCLID

AV

500

HOLTON

INTER-URBAN RR

BRUCHERIE

EUCLID AV

EL CENTRO AV

600

800

ADAMS

6

MS

AV

ADAMS

1500

86

1300

10TH

PARK

COMMERCIAL

ADAMS PARK

CITY PARK

200

4TH ST

COMMERCIAL AV

2ND

S80

100 100

FAIRFIELD

BARBARA

WORTH AV

IMPERIAL 100

WILSON ST

COMMERCIAL AV

12TH ST

BROADWAY

AV

COMMERCIAL

BROADWAY

300

BROADWAY AV

3RD

MAIN ST

NEW

23RD ST
22ND ST
21ST

MAIN AV

PO

ST

1600

14TH

BROADWAY
DMV

PS

11TH ST

9TH ST

MAIN ST

700

500 100

STATE

BUS STA

300

STATE

1ST ST

OLIVE

COMM CTR

MCGEE PK

MCGEE PARK

E ST
SOLANA AV

1700

WATERMAN

CTH

1200

STATE
CH ST

CTH

FS

300

STATE ST

LIB

5TH

6TH

86 AV

OLIVE ST

LIB

V 23RD
E AV

OLIVE RD

VALLEY PLAZA

P

400

OLIVE ST

AV

10TH ST

300

7TH

BRIGHTON

UP

200

400

1

ORANGE AV

BRIGHTON

AV

BRIGHTON AV

WILSON ST

CENTRAL UNION HS

ORANGE AV

6

EL CENTRO

8TH ST

86

ORANGE AV

3RD ST

HOLT AV
HEIL AV
HEIL CT

5

HOLT AV

23RD

DEBBIE PITTMAN PARK

1900

HEIL AV

ELM ST

1400

HAMILTON

HEIL AV

12TH ST

1000

700

HOLT

HEIL

HAMILTON

500

MAPLE ST

900

800

2ND ST

HAMILTON AV

ILTON

2000

21ST ST

JR HS

1500

VINE ST

900

VINE AV

STARK FIELD PARK

RR

CEDAR AV

1000

7

E
ENSLEY

2300

22ND ST

VINE CIR
19TH ST
18TH ST
WENSLEY

WENSLEY AV

14TH ST

WENSLEY

9TH ST

WENSLEY AV

LENREY

LENREY AV

LENREY AV

200

CC

2

0 .125 .25 .375 .5
miles 1 in. = 1900 ft.

SEE 431 MAP

A B C D E

SAN DIEGO CO.

20 21 22

92251

COOLEY

ALDER LATERAL 7

IMPERIAL VALLEY COLLEGE

DOGWOOD

1

ATEN RD

ALDER

DRAIN

2

DOGWOOD

29 28 27

CENTRAL

ALDER

SEE 6499 MAP

S31

CENTRAL RD

3

CRUICKSHANK RD

CANAL

CENTRAL

LATERAL 7

RD

4

VILLA LN

DRAIN 3

CANAL

32 33 34

VILLA AV VILLA AV

DOGWOOD

COOLEY RD

5

HOLTON

RR

MAP

EL CENTRO

HOLTON

INTER-URBAN

1ST

CANNON

NEILL RD

COMMERCIAL AV

EARLS ST

EVAN HEWES HWY

COOLEY

GILLETT RD GILLETT RD GILLETT

FAIRFIELD DR

MAIN ST

E GILLETT

S80

300

600

6

100 200 100

STATE ST

McCULLOM ST

DOGWOOD

OLIVE AV

FAIRFIELD

HOPE ST

OLIVE

400 300

AIRPORT

CENTRAL DRAIN 3

McGEE PARK

BRIGHTON AV

LIB

400

ORANGE ST AV

3

HOLT AV

300 500

4

ALDER LATERAL 7

VT

600 200

HEIL RD

HEIL AV

RD

7

HAMILTON AV

INDUSTRY WY

ON DR

5 300 FS

ALDER

CANAL

SINGH RD

GOMEZ PARK

WENSLEY AV

McCULLOM ST

S31

1000 1000

ROSS RD

2

ROSS AV

A B C D E

0 .125 .25 .375 .5 miles 1 in. = 1900 ft.

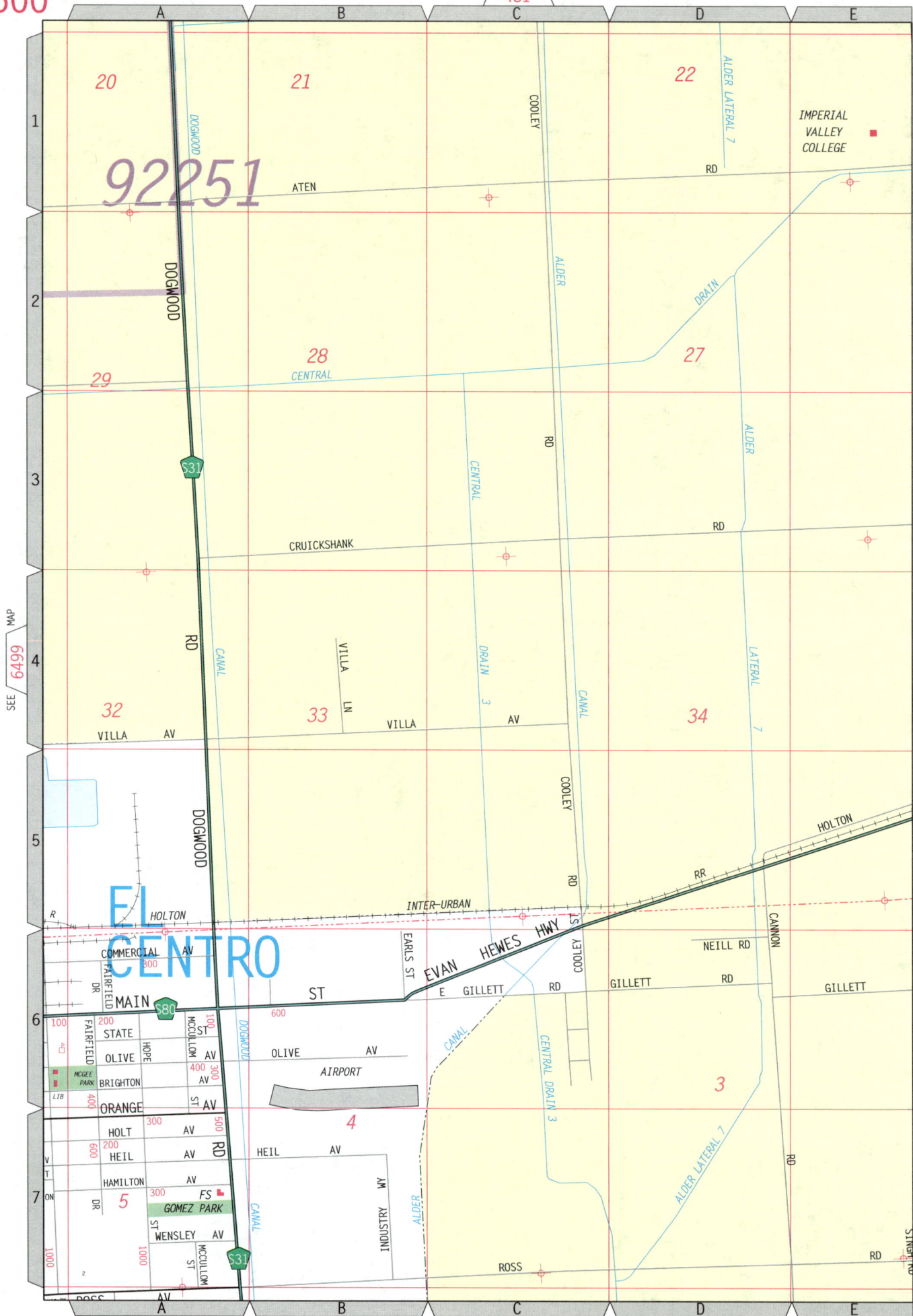

←N→

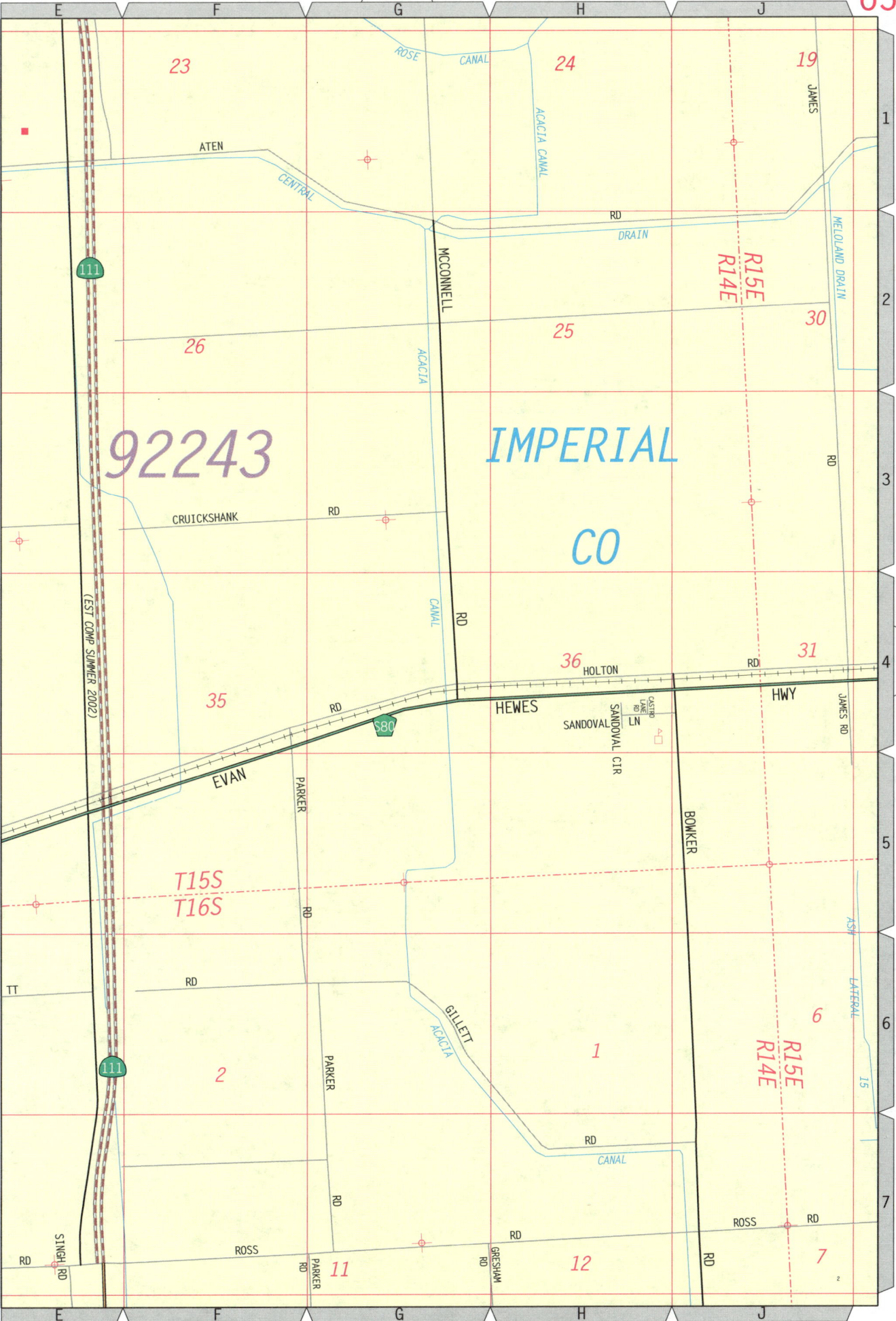

SAN DIEGO CO.

MAP

E F G H J

ROSE CANAL
23 24 19
JAMES
ACACIA CANAL
ATEN 1
CENTRAL
RD
DRAIN
MELOLAND DRAIN
111
MCCONNELL R15E R14E 2
26 25 30
ACACIA
92243 IMPERIAL
CO
RD
CRUICKSHANK RD 3
CANAL RD
SEE 431 MAP
36 HOLTON RD 31 4
35 RD HEWES HWY JAMES RD
S80 SANDOVAL CASTRO LANE RD
EVAN PARKER SANDOVAL CIR LN
T15S BOWKER 5
T16S RD
ASH LATERAL
RD 15
TT RD GILLETT 6 6
2 PARKER ACACIA 1 R15E R14E
PARKER
RD CANAL
RD 7
RD ROSS RD
SINGH RD ROSS RD
RD PARKER 11 GRESHAM 12 RD 7
PARKER
E F G H J

SEE 6560 MAP

0 .125 .25 .375 .5 miles 1 in. = 1900 ft.

(EST COMP SUMMER 2002)

Thomas Bros. Maps® COPYRIGHT 2001 N

SAN DIEGO CO.

MAP

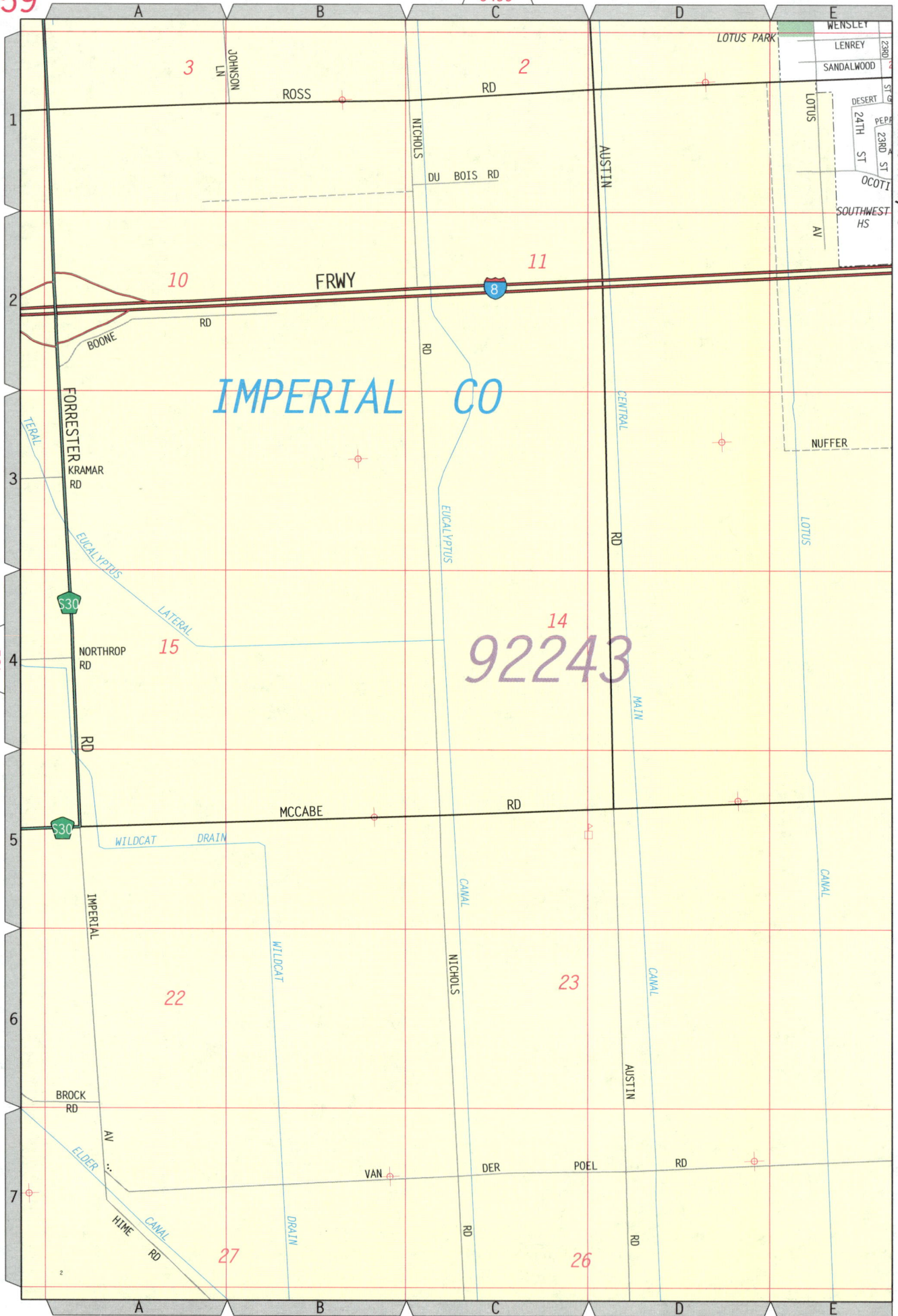

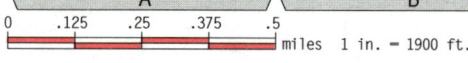

SEE 6499 MAP

A B C D E

WENSLEY

LOTUS PARK

LENREY

SANDALWOOD

JOHNSON LN

ROSS RD

NICHOLS RD

DU BOIS RD

3

2

DESERT

24TH ST

23RD ST

PEPP

ST G

23RD ST

OCOTI

LOTUS

AUSTIN

SOUTHWEST HS

AV

1

FRWY

8

10

11

BOONE RD

RD

IMPERIAL CO

FORRESTER

TERAL

KRAMAR RD

EUCALYPTUS

EUCALYPTUS RD

CENTRAL RD

NUFFER

LOTUS

2

3

S30

EUCALYPTUS

LATERAL

15

14

92243

MAIN

NORTHROP RD

RD

SEE 431 MAP

4

S30

MCCABE RD

WILDCAT DRAIN

IMPERIAL

5

WILDCAT

NICHOLS

CANAL

CANAL

AUSTIN

CANAL

22

23

6

BROCK RD

AV

ELDER

VAN DER POEL RD

HIME RD

CANAL

DRAIN

RD

RD

7

27

26

A B C D E

SEE 431 MAP

0 .125 .25 .375 .5 miles 1 in. = 1900 ft.

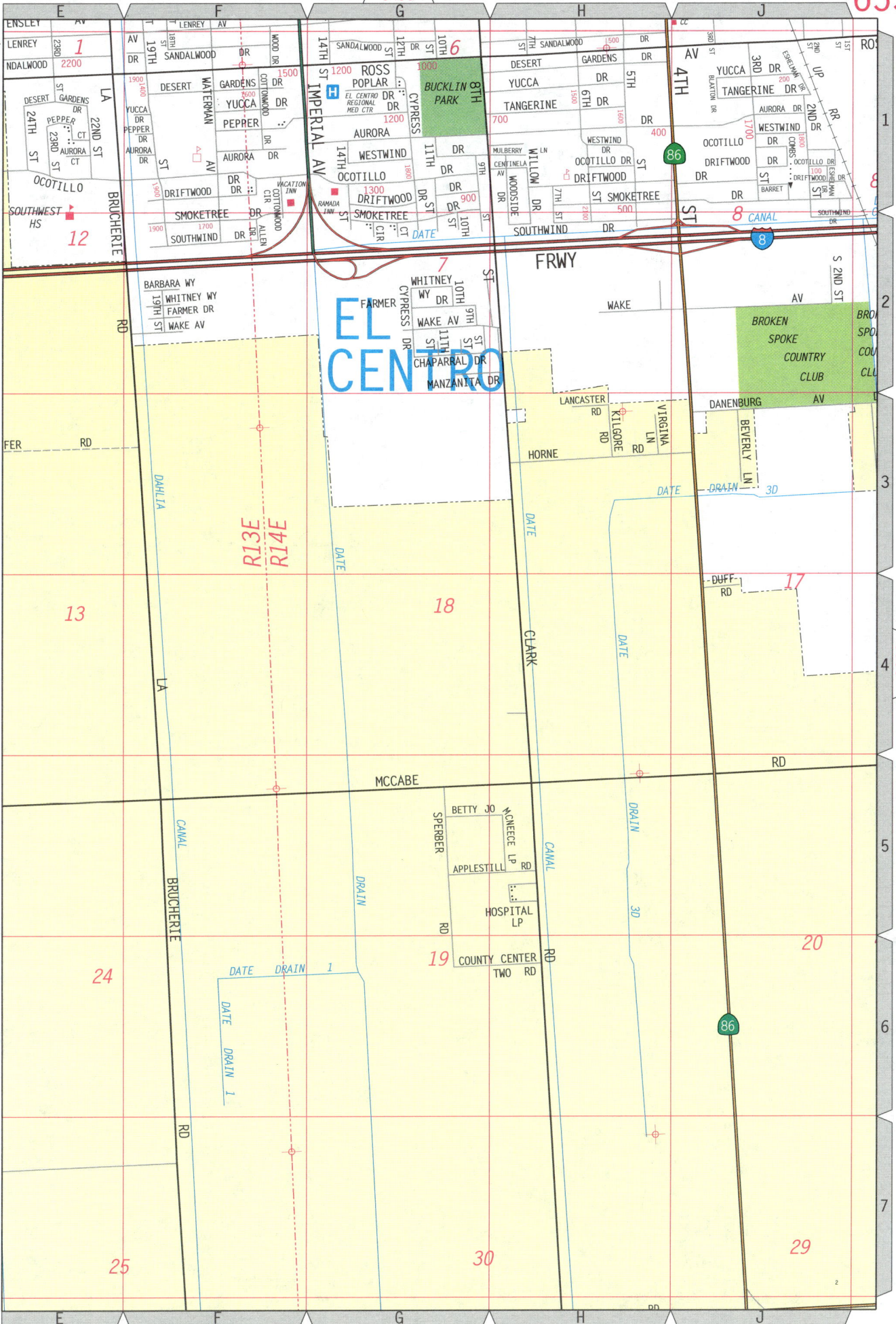
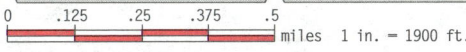

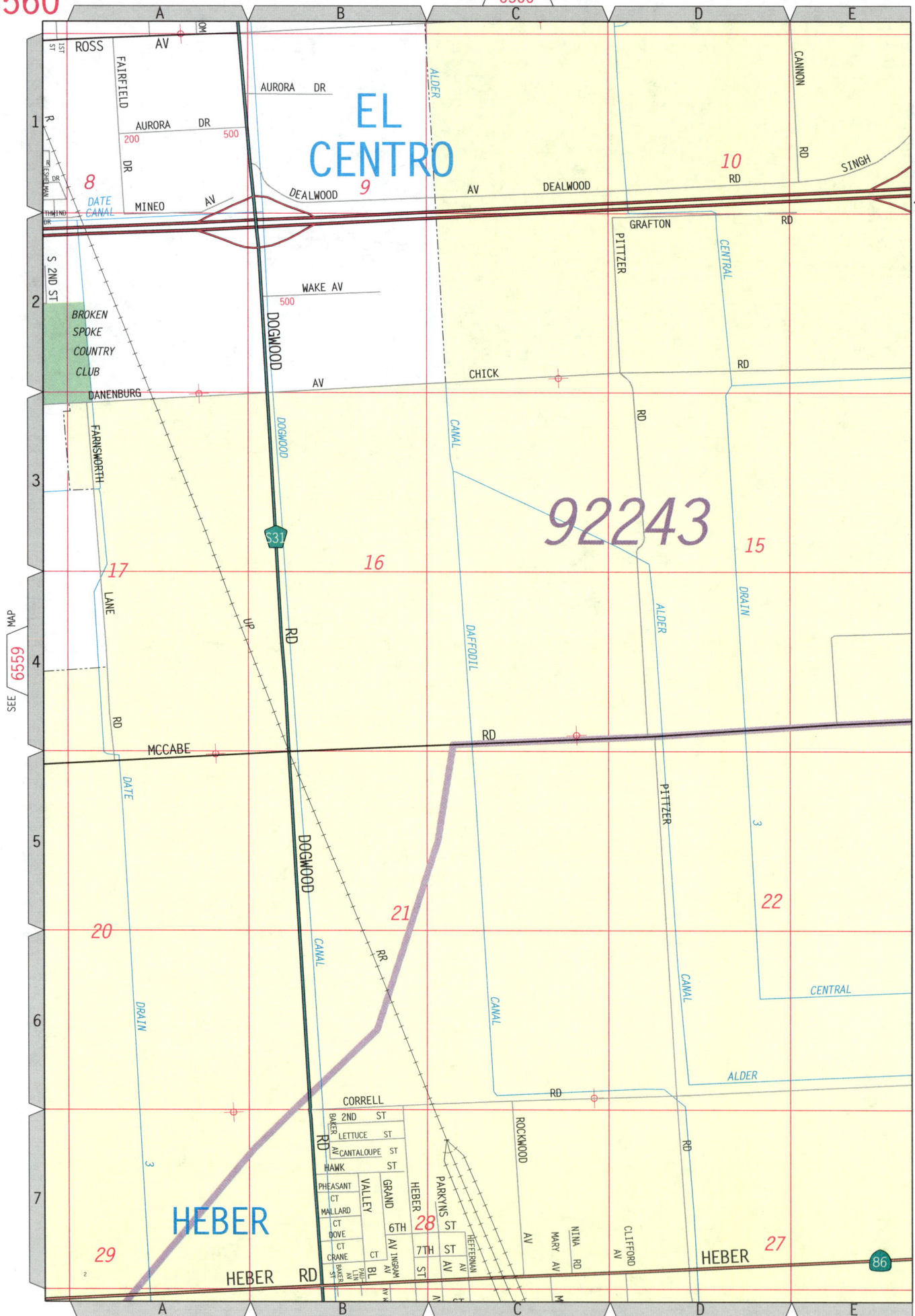

SAN DIEGO CO.

MAP

SEE 6500 MAP

A   B   C   D   E

COPYRIGHT 2001 Thomas Bros. Maps ®

←N→

ROSS AV

FAIRFIELD

1ST ST

OM

AURORA DR

AURORA DR

200   500

DR

MINEO AV

DATE CANAL

8

EL CENTRO

9

DEALWOOD AV   DEALWOOD

10

RD

CANNON

RD

SINGH

GRAFTON RD

PITZER

CENTRAL

1

R

ESHMAN DR

TININD DR

S 2ND ST

DOGWOOD

WAKE AV

500

BROKEN SPOKE COUNTRY CLUB

DANENBURG AV

CHICK

RD

RD

2

FARNSWORTH

DOGWOOD

CANAL

RD

92243

DAFFODIL

ALDER

DRAIN

15

3

S31

17

LANE

16

UP

RD

4

SEE 6559 MAP

RD

MCCABE

RD

DATE

PITZER

3

22

5

DOGWOOD

CANAL

21

RR

CANAL

CANAL

CENTRAL

6

DRAIN

3

ALDER

RD

CORRELL

BAKER   2ND ST

RD   LETTUCE ST

AV   CANTALOUPE ST

HAWK   ST

PHEASANT CT

MALLARD CT

DOVE CT

CRANE CT

VALLEY

GRAND AV

6TH

7TH

BL

BAKER ST

HEBER ST

INGRAM

PARKYNS ST

HEFFERNAN AV

ROCKWOOD AV

MARY AV

NINA RD

CLIFFORD AV

HEBER

27

86

7

HEBER

29

2

HEBER RD

28

0   .125   .25   .375   .5

miles   1 in. = 1900 ft.

SEE 431 MAP

A   B   C   D   E

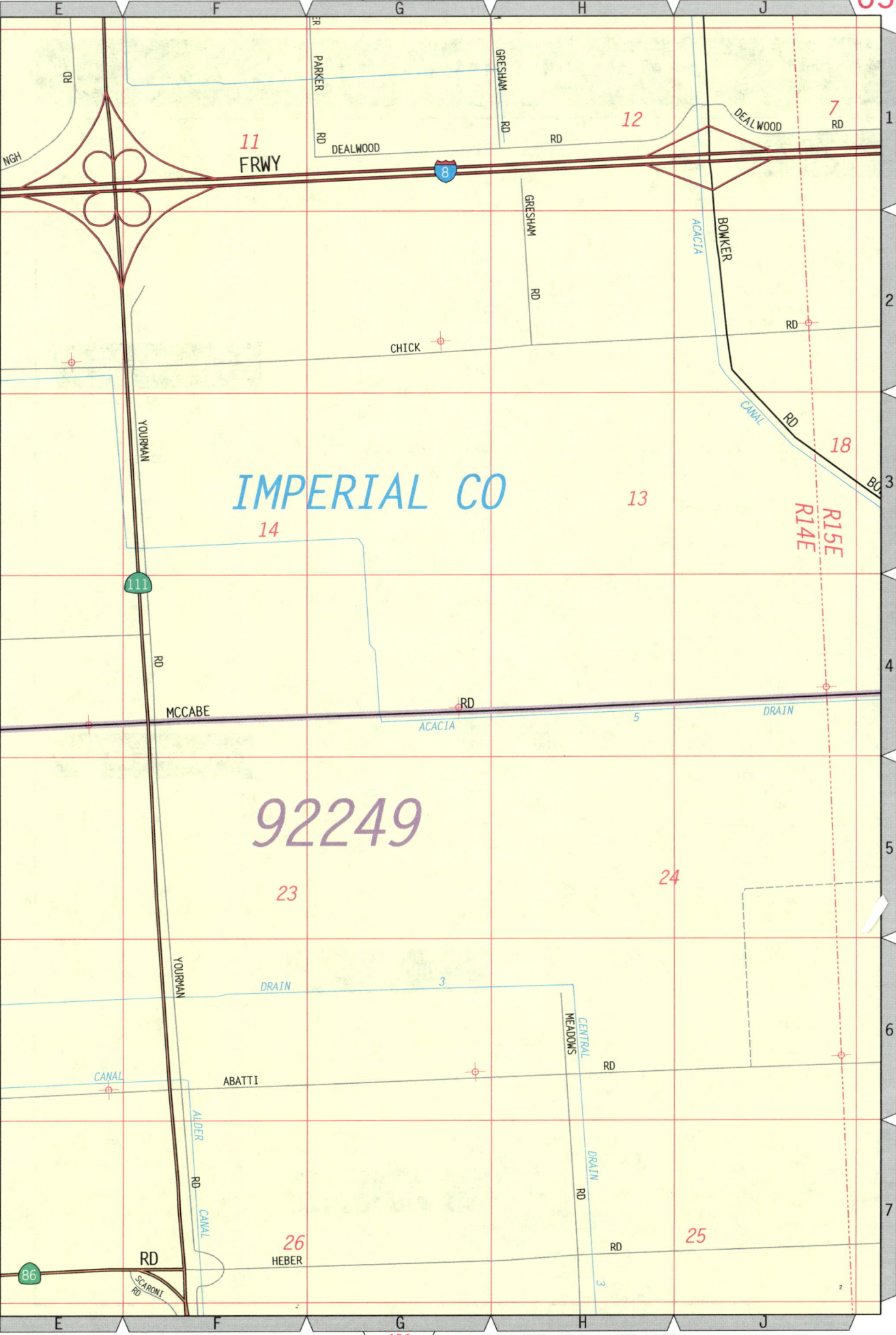

SAN DIEGO CO.

MAP

Thomas Bros. Maps®
COPYRIGHT 2001

N

E F G H J

PARKER
GRESHAM RD
DEALWOOD RD
11 12
RD
DEALWOOD
FRWY
8
7 RD
DEALWOOD
1

NGH

GRESHAM RD

ACACIA
BOWKER
RD
2

CHICK

CANAL
RD
18
BO

YOURMAN

R15E
R14E

IMPERIAL CO
13
14
3

111

SEE 431 MAP
4

MCCABE RD
ACACIA
5 DRAIN

RD

92249

23 24
5

YOURMAN
DRAIN
3
CENTRAL MEADOWS
6

CANAL
ABATTI
RD

ALDER RD
CANAL
DRAIN
RD

7

86
RD
26
HEBER
25
RD
3

SCARONI RD

0 .125 .25 .375 .5 miles 1 in. = 1900 ft.

LIST OF ABBREVIATIONS

PREFIXES AND SUFFIXES

AL	ALLEY
ARC	ARCADE
AV, AVE	AVENUE
AVCT	AVENUE COURT
AVD	AVENIDA
AVD D LA	AVENIDA DE LA
AVD D LOS	AVENIDA DE LOS
AVD DE	AVENIDA DE
AVD DE LAS	AVENIDA DE LAS
AVD DEL	AVENIDA DEL
AVDR	AVENUE DRIVE
AVEX	AVENUE EXTENSION
AV OF	AVENUE OF
AV OF THE	AVENUE OF THE
AVPL	AVENUE PLACE
BAY	BAY
BEND	BEND
BL, BLVD	BOULEVARD
BLCT	BOULEVARD COURT
BLEX	BOULEVARD EXTENSION
BRCH	BRANCH
BRDG	BRIDGE
BYPS	BYPASS
BYWY	BYWAY
CIDR	CIRCLE DRIVE
CIR	CIRCLE
CL	CALLE
CL DE	CALLE DE
CL DL	CALLE DEL
CL D LA	CALLE DE LA
CL D LAS	CALLE DE LAS
CL D LOS	CALLE DE LOS
CL EL	CALLE EL
CLJ	CALLEJON
CL LA	CALLE LA
CL LAS	CALLE LAS
CL LOS	CALLE LOS
CLTR	CLUSTER
CM	CAMINO
CM D	CAMINO DE
CM DL	CAMINO DEL
CM D LA	CAMINO DE LA
CM D LAS	CAMINO DE LAS
CM D LOS	CAMINO DE LOS
CMTO	CAMINITO
CMTO DEL	CAMINITO DEL
CMTO D LA	CAMINITO DE LA
CMTO D LAS	CAMINITO DE LAS
CMTO D LOS	CAMINITO DE LOS
CNDR	CENTER DRIVE
COM	COMMON
COMS	COMMONS
CORR	CORRIDOR
CRES	CRESCENT
CRLO	CIRCULO
CRSG	CROSSING
CST	CIRCLE STREET
CSWY	CAUSEWAY
CT	COURT
CTAV	COURT AVENUE
CTE	CORTE
CTE D	CORTE DE
CTE DEL	CORTE DEL
CTE D LAS	CORTE DE LAS
CTO	CUT OFF
CTR	CENTER
CTST	COURT STREET
CUR	CURVE
CV	COVE
DE	DE

DIAG	DIAGONAL
DR	DRIVE
DRAV	DRIVE AVENUE
DRCT	DRIVE COURT
DRLP	DRIVE LOOP
DVDR	DIVISION DR
EXAV	EXTENSION AVENUE
EXBL	EXTENSION BOULEVARD
EXRD	EXTENSION ROAD
EXST	EXTENSION STREET
EXT	EXTENSION
EXWY	EXPRESSWAY
FOREST RT	FOREST ROUTE
FRWY	FREEWAY
FRY	FERRY
GDNS	GARDENS
GN, GLN	GLEN
GRN	GREEN
GRV	GROVE
HTS	HEIGHTS
HWY	HIGHWAY
ISL	ISLE
JCT	JUNCTION
LN	LANE
LNCR	LANE CIRCLE
LNDG	LANDING
LNDR	LANE DRIVE
LNLP	LANE LOOP
LP	LOOP
MNR	MANOR
MT	MOUNT
MTWY	MOTORWAY
MWCR	MEWS COURT
MWLN	MEWS LANE
NFD	NAT'L FOREST DEV
NK	NOOK
OH	OUTER HIGHWAY
OVL	OVAL
OVLK	OVERLOOK
OVPS	OVERPASS
PAS	PASEO
PAS DE	PASEO DE
PAS DE LA	PASEO DE LA
PAS DE LAS	PASEO DE LAS
PAS DE LOS	PASEO DE LOS
PAS DL	PASEO DEL
PASG	PASSAGE
PAS LA	PASEO LA
PAS LOS	PASEO LOS
PASS	PASS
PIKE	PIKE
PK	PARK
PKDR	PARK DRIVE
PKWY, PKY	PARKWAY
PL	PLACE
PLWY	PLACE WAY
PLZ, PZ	PLAZA
PT	POINT
PTAV	POINT AVENUE
PTH	PATH
PZ DE	PLAZA DE
PZ DEL	PLAZA DEL
PZ D LA	PLAZA DE LA
PZ D LAS	PLAZA DE LAS
PZWY	PLAZA WAY
RAMP	RAMP
RD	ROAD
RDAV	ROAD AVENUE
RDBP	ROAD BYPASS
RDCT	ROAD COURT
RDEX	ROAD EXTENSION
RDG	RIDGE
RDSP	ROAD SPUR
RDWY	ROAD WAY

RR	RAILROAD
RUE	RUE
RUE D	RUE DE
RW	ROW
RY	RAILWAY
SKWY	SKYWAY
SQ	SQUARE
ST	STREET
STAV	STREET AVENUE
STCT	STREET COURT
STDR	STREET DRIVE
STEX	STREET EXTENSION
STLN	STREET LANE
STLP	STREET LOOP
ST OF	STREET OF
ST OF THE	STREET OF THE
STOV	STREET OVERPASS
STPL	STREET PLACE
STPM	STREET PROMENADE
STWY	STREET WAY
STXP	STREET EXPRESSWAY
TER	TERRACE
TFWY	TRAFFICWAY
THWY	THROUGHWAY
TKTR	TRUCK TRAIL
TPKE	TURNPIKE
TRC	TRACE
TRCT	TERRACE COURT
TR, TRL	TRAIL
TRWY	TRAIL WAY
TTSP	TRUCK TRAIL SPUR
TUN	TUNNEL
UNPS	UNDERPASS
VIA D	VIA DE
VIA DL	VIA DEL
VIA D LA	VIA DE LA
VIA D LAS	VIA DE LAS
VIA D LOS	VIA DE LOS
VIA LA	VIA LA
VW	VIEW
VWY	VIEW WAY
VIS	VISTA
VIS D	VISTA DE
VIS D L	VISTA DE LA
VIS D LAS	VISTA DE LAS
VIS DEL	VISTA DEL
WK	WALK
WY	WAY
WYCR	WAY CIRCLE
WYDR	WAY DRIVE
WYLN	WAY LANE
WYPL	WAY PLACE

DIRECTIONS

E	EAST
KPN	KEY PENINSULA NORTH
KPS	KEY PENINSULA SOUTH
N	NORTH
NE	NORTHEAST
NW	NORTHWEST
S	SOUTH
SE	SOUTHEAST
SW	SOUTHWEST
W	WEST

DEPARTMENT STORES

BD	BLOOMINGDALES
BN	THE BON MARCHE
D	DIAMONDS
DL	DILLARDS

G	GOLDWATERS
GT	GOTTSCHALKS
H	HARRIS
IM	I MAGNIN
MA	MACY'S
ME	MERVYN'S
MF	MEIER & FRANK
N	NORDSTROM
NM	NEIMAN-MARCUS
P	J C PENNEY
RM	ROBINSONS MAY
S	SEARS
SF	SAKS FIFTH AVENUE

BUILDINGS

CC	CHAMBER OF COMMERCE
CH	CITY HALL
CHP	CALIFORNIA HIGHWAY PATROL
COMM CTR	COMMUNITY CENTER
CON CTR	CONVENTION CENTER
CONT HS	CONTINUATION HIGH SCHOOL
CTH	COURT HOUSE
DMV	DEPT OF MOTOR VEHICLES
FAA	FEDERAL AVIATION ADMIN
FS	FIRE STATION
HOSP	HOSPITAL
HS	HIGH SCHOOL
INT	INTERMEDIATE SCHOOL
JR HS	JUNIOR HIGH SCHOOL
LIB	LIBRARY
MID	MIDDLE SCHOOL
MUS	MUSEUM
PO	POST OFFICE
PS	POLICE STATION
SR CIT CTR	SENIOR CITIZENS CENTER
STA	STATION
THTR	THEATER
VIS BUR	VISITORS BUREAU

OTHER ABBREVIATIONS

BCH	BEACH
BLDG	BUILDING
CEM	CEMETERY
CK	CREEK
CO	COUNTY
COMM	COMMUNITY
CTR	CENTER
EST	ESTATE
HIST	HISTORIC
HTS	HEIGHTS
LK	LAKE
MDW	MEADOW
MED	MEDICAL
MEM	MEMORIAL
MHP	MOBILE HOME PARK
MT	MOUNT
MTN	MOUNTAIN
NATL	NATIONAL
PKG	PARKING
PLGD	PLAYGROUND
RCH	RANCH
RCHO	RANCHO
REC	RECREATION
RES	RESERVOIR
RIV	RIVER
RR	RAILROAD
SPG	SPRING
STA	SANTA
VLG	VILLAGE
VLY	VALLEY
VW	VIEW

SAN DIEGO CO. STREET INDEX

ALIENTO CT 6562

Thomas Bros. Maps®

COPYRIGHT 2001

STREET
Block City ZIP Pg-Grid

A

A AV
100 CORD 92118 1288-J6
200 SDCo 92055 1066-B1
200 NATC 91950 1289-H7
200 NATC 91950 1309-H1
12200 SDCo 92040 1232-A4
A AVD
5500 SDCo 92003 1067-H2
A CT
- SD 92126 1209-F7
A ST
- NATC 91950 1310-C3
- OCN 92056 1106-J1
- SDCo 92055 409-A7
- SDCo 92055 1066-G1
- SDCo 91934 (1321-G5 See Page 1300)
- CHV 91910 1309-J6
100 ENCT 92024 1147-B6
100 SD 92101 1289-A2
400 SDCo 92055 1085-H3
500 SDCo 92065 1152-G5
600 SD 92101 1288-J2
700 IMPB 91932 1329-F7
1300 SD 92110 1268-E2
2200 SD 92102 1289-C2
2600 SDCo 92036 1136-B7
4900 SD 92102 1290-A2
6200 SDCo 92004 410-F11
7300 CRLB 92009 1126-J7
11800 SDCo 92059 1029-H4
E A ST
3000 SD 92139 1310-D3
W A ST
100 SD 92101 1289-A2
500 SD 92101 1288-J2
2900 NATC 91950 1310-D3
AARON CT
2500 SD 92105 1270-A7
AARON WY
8200 SDCo 92040 1251-J1
ABAJO DR
15900 SDCo 92065 1173-G4
ABALAR WY
24800 SDCo 92065 1173-G3
ABALONE PL
5600 SD 92037 1247-F4
ABALONE LANDING TER
4400 SD 92130 1208-B4
ABALONE POINT CT
1600 CHV 91911 1330-J4
ABALONE POINT WY
700 OCN 92054 1066-E6
ABANA CT
16000 SDCo 92065 1173-F3
ABANTO ST
6700 CRLB 92009 1127-G6
ABARCA CT
1000 CHV 91910 1310-J4
ABATTI RD
- ImCo 92249 431-D6
- ImCo 92249 6560-F6
ABBE ST
1900 SD 92111 1268-J1
ABBEY GDNS
2700 ESCN 92027 1110-E7
ABBEY RD
800 SDCo 92065 1152-F1
ABBEYFIELD RD
9500 SNTE 92071 1231-C5
ABBEYWOOD RD
9600 SNTE 92071 1231-C5
ABBOTS HILL RD
8200 SD 92123 1249-B7
ABBOTT ST
1900 SD 92107 1267-J5
ABBOTTSWOOD RW
6000 SD 92037 1248-A1
ABBYWOOD DR
700 OCN 92057 1087-C1
ABEDUL PL
6700 CRLB 92009 1127-G5
ABEDUL ST
2500 CRLB 92009 1127-G5
ABEJORRO ST
2700 CRLB 92009 1127-H6
ABELIA AV
- CRLB 92009 1127-A5
ABELIA LN
1900 SDCo 92083 1108-C3
2100 SDCo 92084 1108-C3
ABELL DR
13700 SDCo 91935 1292-F3
ABER ST
2900 SD 92117 1248-C1
ABERDEEN CT
4700 CRLB 92008 1107-A5
ABERDEEN DR
100 ENCT 92007 1167-D3
ABERDEEN ST
4700 SD 92117 1228-G7
ABERDEEN WY
3100 ESCN 92025 1150-C1
ABERNATHY WY
5700 SD 92117 1248-H2
ABETO CT
1000 CHV 91910 1310-J4
ABETO DR
400 CHV 91910 1310-J4
ABHA DR
- SDCo 91905 (1320-B4 See Page 1300)
ABIENTO PL
9400 SDCo 91941 1271-C3
ABILENE TER
8400 LMSA 91942 1250-J6
ABING AV
13000 SD 92129 1189-B5
ABINGTON LN
1600 ENCT 92024 1147-H7
ABINGTON RD
300 ENCT 92024 1147-H7
ABLETTE CT
8500 SNTE 92071 1231-D7
ABLETTE RD
8500 ELCJ 92020 1231-F7
8500 SNTE 92071 1231-F7
ABNER CT
- SDCo 92055 1086-A2
ABRA DR
12600 SD 92128 1170-C2
ABRA PL
12800 SD 92128 1170-D2
ABRA WY
17000 SD 92128 1170-C2
ABRAHAM WY
9200 SNTE 92071 1231-F6
ABRAMS RIDGE RD
- SDCo 91901 1254-F5
ABRELL RD
- SDCo 92055 1086-A2
ABRIGO WY
17300 SDCo 92065 1173-E1
ABRIL WY
- ESCN 92026 1109-G7
ABUELA DR
5000 SD 92124 1249-H2
ABUNDANTE ST
- SDCo 92127 1169-F4
ACACIA AV
100 CRLB 92008 1106-E6
800 OCN 92054 1086-C5
3700 SDCo 91902 1310-J3
4000 SDCo 91902 1311-A3
4300 LMSA 91941 1270-H3
N ACACIA AV
200 SOLB 92075 1167-E7
S ACACIA AV
100 SOLB 92075 1167-E7
ACACIA CT
3600 SD 92113 1289-G6
ACACIA DR
- SD 92102 1289-G4
1900 SMCS 92069 1128-A2
3300 SDCo 92036 1156-D1
ACACIA LN
- ESCN 92025 1130-A6
1500 SDCo 92028 1047-J1
1600 SDCo 92028 1048-A1
3100 SDCo 91901 1234-D4
ACACIA PL
300 ESCN 92026 1109-H7
ACACIA ST
3200 LMGR 91945 1270-H6
3400 SD 92113 1289-F6
9600 SDCo 92040 1232-C4
ACACIA TER
12600 PWY 92064 1190-C3
ACACIA WY
- ELCJ 92019 1251-J6
100 CORD 92118 1288-G7
ACACIA GLEN CT
11900 SD 92128 1190-A7
ACADEMY DR
700 SOLB 92075 1167-G7
ACADEMY LN
1100 VSTA 92083 1107-G2
ACADEMY PL
4700 SD 92109 1248-A5
ACADEMY RD
300 OCN 92057 1086-H2
ACADEMY ST
4800 SD 92109 1248-A4
ACADIA WY
12500 SDCo 92040 1212-A7
ACAMA CT
11300 SD 92126 1209-A2
ACAMA PL
7600 SD 92126 1209-A2
ACAMA ST
7400 SD 92126 1208-J2
7400 SD 92126 1209-A2
ACANTO DR
17300 SDCo 92065 1173-E1
ACARI ST
7200 SD 92111 1269-A2
ACASO CT
7600 SD 92126 1209-A2
ACASO WY
11100 SD 92126 1209-A2
ACATENO AV
300 VSTA 92084 1087-H4
ACCENT WY
3800 OCN 92057 1086-H4
ACCESS RD
- SDCo 92055 409-A7
ACCESS RD A
- SDCo 92067 1148-G6
ACCESS RD B
- SDCo 92067 1148-H6
ACCOMAC AV
3400 SD 92111 1248-H4
ACCRA LN
11100 SD 92131 1210-A2
ACE ST
3400 SD 92105 1270-B6
ACE WY
1100 SDCo 92004 (1079-C5 See Page 1058)
ACEBO CTE
1100 CHV 91910 1311-C2
ACEBO DR
16700 SD 92128 1170-B3
ACEBO PL
12100 SD 92128 1170-B3
ACEITUNO ST
18200 SD 92128 1150-D6
ACENA DR
16700 SD 92128 1170-A3
ACERO PL
400 CHV 91910 1310-J4
ACERO ST
1000 CHV 91910 1310-J4
ACHESON ST
1400 SD 92111 1268-J2
ACKER WY
2000 ESCN 92029 1129-H7
ACOMA AV
4500 SD 92117 1248-F1
ACORN GN
1900 ESCN 92027 1110-B5
ACORN RD
1900 SMCS 92069 1128-B2
ACORN ST
1700 ESCN 92027 1130-C1
6100 SD 92115 1270-C3
ACORN TR
- SDCo 91906 (1318-C7 See Page 1298)
ACORN PATCH LN
13600 PWY 92064 1170-E5
ACORN PATCH RD
- SDCo 92036 1156-A7
- SDCo 92036 1176-A1
13700 PWY 92064 1170-F5
ACROPOLIS PL
2900 SD 92139 1310-E2
ACRUX DR
11300 SD 92126 1209-C1
ACTIVITY DR
1200 VSTA 92083 1108-B7
ACTIVITY RD
9000 SD 92126 1209-D6
ACTIVITY WY
400 OCN 92054 1086-B6
ACTON AV
13000 PWY 92064 1190-H3
ACTON CT
14600 PWY 92064 1190-H3
ACUFF DR
8400 SD 92119 1250-J3
ACUNA CT
2600 CRLB 92009 1127-G6
ACUNA ST
4900 SD 92117 1248-G1
ACWORTH AV
3100 SD 92111 1248-H4
ADA ST
200 SD 92113 1289-G4
700 CHV 91911 1330-A4
ADAGIO WY
11200 SDCo 92026 1089-H7
11200 SDCo 92026 1109-H1
ADAH LN
12800 PWY 92064 1190-F4
ADAIR RD
- ImCo 92251 430-L5
ADAIR ST
4400 SD 92107 1287-H1
4700 SD 92107 1267-H7
ADAIR WY
3800 CRLB 92008 1106-G6
ADALANE PL
1600 SDCo 92028 1027-J4
1600 SDCo 92028 1028-A4
ADAM CT
9700 SDCo 92026 1069-C3
ADAMS AV
400 ELCN 92243 6499-H6
400 ESCN 92026 1129-J1
1600 SD 92116 1269-C3
4700 SD 92115 1269-J3
4800 SD 92115 1270-A3
6800 LMSA 91941 1270-E3
ADAMS AV Rt#-S80
600 ELCN 92243 6499-E6
600 ImCo 92243 6499-E6
ADAMS AV Rt#-86
400 ELCN 92243 6499-F6
ADAMS DR
15200 SDCo 92061 409-E6
15300 SDCo 92059 409-E6
15400 SDCo 92061 1051-A1
15600 SDCo 92061 1050-J1
ADAMS RD
- ImCo 92227 431-D2
ADAMS ST
3400 CRLB 92008 1106-F5
4700 OCN 92057 1067-A7
8200 LMGR 91945 1270-H6
ADCOCK LN
10600 SD 92126 1209-A4
ADDAX CT
12400 SD 92129 1189-C6
ADDISON ST
3300 SD 92106 1288-A2
ADELAIDE AV
5500 SD 92115 1270-B4
ADELANTE AV
6700 SD 92120 1270-E1
6700 LMSA 91942 1270-E1
ADELE LN
1100 SMCS 92078 1129-B2
13700 SDCo 91935 1292-F2
ADELE ST
800 ELCJ 92021 1251-G2
ADELFA CT
1400 IMPB 91932 1349-H2
ADELIA WY
100 OCN 92057 1086-H3
ADELLA AV
700 CORD 92118 1288-J7
1100 CORD 92118 1308-J1
ADELLA LN
400 CORD 92118 1288-J7
ADELPHI PL
4700 SD 92115 1270-A3
ADENA LN
17500 SD 92128 1150-A7
17500 SD 92128 1170-A1
ADERMAN AV
10300 SD 92126 1209-A5
10400 SD 92126 1208-J4
ADIOS CT
7300 SD 92119 1250-E4
ADIRONDACK RW
2400 SD 92139 1290-F7
2400 SD 92139 1310-F1
ADKINS WY
7600 SD 92126 1208-J4
7600 SD 92126 1209-A4
ADLAI LN
13500 SDCo 92040 1232-D5
ADLAI RD
9200 SDCo 92040 1232-D5
ADLER AV
7400 SD 92111 1249-A7
ADLER WY
4700 OCN 92057 1087-A1
ADMINISTRATION WY
1300 SDCo 91901 1234-A6
ADMIRAL AV
2900 SD 92123 1249-E5
ADMIRAL BAKER RD
2400 SD 92124 1249-H6
2400 SD 92120 1249-H6
ADMIRALTY AV
- IMPB 91932 1349-E1
ADMIRALTY RD
2200 CORD 92155 1309-A2
ADMIRALTY CROSS
- CORD 92118 1329-E1
ADOBE CIR
600 OCN 92057 1067-A5
ADOBE DR
6200 SD 92115 1270-C2
ADOBE LN
1200 SDCo 92021 1251-J2
ADOBE PL
700 CHV 91914 1311-G3
ADOBE TER
1200 VSTA 92083 1107-E1
ADOBE BLUFFS DR
8700 SD 92129 1189-C2
ADOBE CREEK LN
1900 SDCo 92027 1130-D4
ADOBE FALLS PL
5600 SD 92120 1250-C7
ADOBE FALLS RD
5200 SD 92120 1250-A7
5500 SD 92120 1270-A1
ADOBE NORTE AV
1100 SDCo 92028 1027-H4
ADOBE RIDGE RD
12200 PWY 92064 1190-B1
ADOBE VILLA DR
5900 SDCo 92067 1168-F7
ADOLPHIA CT
12700 SD 92129 1189-D6
ADOLPHIA DR
6800 CRLB 92009 1127-D6
ADOLPHIA ST
9200 SD 92129 1189-E6
ADONIS CT
7300 SD 92119 1250-F4
ADORNO PL
11900 SD 92128 1170-A2
ADRA WY
4700 OCN 92056 1107-F4
ADRIAN CT
1700 SDCo 91901 1233-H7
ADRIAN ST
2800 SD 92110 1268-B5
13600 PWY 92064 1190-F2
ADRIANA CT
1800 VSTA 92083 1107-G6
ADRIANA ST
8700 SDCo 91977 1291-A3
ADRIATIC PL
11100 SD 92126 1209-A2
ADRIENNE DR
4300 SDCo 91910 1310-D5
ADRIENNE WY
16600 SDCo 92065 1172-A3
ADUAR CT
5300 SD 92124 1249-J1
ADVENTURE LN
1200 SMCS 92069 1109-C6
AEDAN CT
8100 SD 92120 1250-D3
14300 PWY 92064 1190-E2
AEGEAN CT
7500 SD 92126 1209-A2
AEGEAN DR
2500 SD 92139 1310-F1
AEGEAN PL
6700 SD 92139 1310-F1
AEGEAN WY
6700 SD 92139 1310-F1
AEGINA WY
5000 OCN 92056 1107-F5
AEOLIA WY
4000 OCN 92056 1107-E5
AERIE RD
28200 SDCo 92082 1090-A1
29100 SDCo 92082 1089-J1
AERIE HEIGHTS RD
1300 SDCo 92003 1068-B4
AERO CT
3500 SD 92123 1249-B4
AERO DR
7900 SD 92111 1249-C4
7900 SD 92123 1249-C4
9900 SD 92124 1249-G4
AERO PL
8200 SD 92123 1249-B4
AERO WY
600 ESCN 92029 1129-D2
AERONCA AV
4100 SD 92117 1248-E6
AFFINITY CT
11100 SD 92131 1209-F2
AFTON RD
3000 SD 92123 1249-C4
AFTON WY
2200 CRLB 92008 1106-G4
AFTON FARMES LN
31200 SDCo 92003 1068-F2
AGAPANTHUS DR
1300 SD 92114 1290-D5
AGAR CT
10300 SD 92126 1209-B4
AGATE GN
- ESCN 92027 1110-D7
AGATE LN
4400 OCN 92056 1107-D3
AGATE ST
700 SD 92109 1247-H4
AGATE WY
- CRLB 92009 1127-C4
AGAVE FLATS LN
2500 CHV 91915 1311-H5
AGEE ST
5800 SD 92122 1228-E5
AGNO CT
2700 SD 92154 1330-C6
AGORA WY
4700 OCN 92056 1107-E5
AGOSTO ST
3400 SD 92154 1350-E1
AGRARIAN RD
25000 SDCo 92065 1153-G2
AGRESTE PL
11600 SD 92127 1150-A7
AGSTEN LN
13600 PWY 92064 1190-F3
AGUACATE LN
15200 SDCo 92082 1070-J6
AGUACATE WY
17800 SD 92127 1149-J7
AGUA DULCE BLVD
3900 SDCo 91941 1271-E5
4700 SDCo 91977 1271-E5
AGUA DULCE CT
7500 CRLB 92009 1147-J1
AGUAMARINA PT
13000 SD 92128 1150-D6
AGUAMIEL RD
17700 SD 92127 1149-J7
17900 SD 92127 1150-A6
AGUA TIBIA AV
900 CHV 91911 1330-E1
AGUA VISTA WY
300 SD 92114 1290-B5
AGUILA ST
4000 CRLB 92008 1106-F7
AGUILERA LN
20300 SDCo 92029 1148-G2
AGUIRRE DR
1200 CHV 91910 1311-B7
AHERN CT
10300 SD 92126 1209-B5
AHERN RANCH RD
28100 SDCo 92082 1091-C2
AHLRICH AV
1200 ENCT 92024 1147-F7
1300 ENCT 92024 1167-F1
AHMU TER
200 VSTA 92084 1087-H2
AHWAHNEE WY
13600 PWY 92064 1190-D3
AIDA ST
12600 SD 92130 1188-C6
AILSA CT
1600 SD 92154 1351-F2
AINSLEY CT
8200 SD 92123 1269-B1
AINSLEY RD
1900 SD 92123 1269-B1
2000 SD 92123 1249-B7
AIR LN
2300 SD 92101 1288-F1
AIR WY
4600 SD 92105 1289-J2
AIRBORNE DR
1200 VSTA 92084 1088-B3
AIRCRAFT RD
2000 CRLB 92008 1127-D3
AIRFLIGHT DR
30000 SDCo 92082 1069-G5
AIR MAIL LN
16600 SDCo 92065 1171-J3
AIROSO AV
6400 SD 92120 1270-D1
6900 LMSA 91942 1270-E1
AIR PARK DR
- ImCo 92259 410-H8
AIR PARK RD
1700 SDCo 92028 1027-G6
AIRPORT DR
10500 ELCJ 92020 1251-E1
10500 SDCo 92020 1251-E1
AIRPORT RD
- IMP 92251 6499-F1
100 OCN 92054 1086-D5
W AIRPORT RD
- OCN 92054 1086-C4
AIRPORT VISTA RD
9700 SNTE 92071 1231-C7
AIRWAY RD
7100 SD 92154 1351-D3
9200 SD 92154 1352-A3
9400 SDCo 92154 1352-A3
AIR WING RD
1200 SD 92154 1351-H1
AJANTA CT
11300 SD 92129 1169-J6
AJAY ST
1500 ELCJ 92020 1251-B3
AJOHN PL
- LMGR 91945 1290-F1
AKARD ST
9000 SDCo 91977 1291-B4
AKINS AV
5900 SD 92114 1290-D3
AKRON ST
1100 SD 92106 1288-B2
AL CT
8600 SD 92123 1249-C6
ALABAMA ST
600 IMPB 91932 1329-F7
2200 SD 92101 1269-C6
2400 SD 92104 1269-C5
4300 SD 92116 1269-C5
ALABAR WY
4100 OCN 92056 1087-C6
ALACENA CT
500 SDCo 91977 1291-D3
ALACRAN CT
17700 SD 92127 1149-J7
ALADDIN LN
600 ELCJ 92019 1252-A6
ALADO PL
8400 SDCo 92021 1232-D7
ALAGRIA PL
600 CHV 91910 1311-A5
ALAMAR RD
28300 SDCo 92082 1090-B2
ALAMEDA BLVD
- CORD 92118 1288-G7
- CORD 92135 1288-G7
ALAMEDA BLVD Rt#-282
300 CORD 92135 1288-G6
300 CORD 92118 1288-G6
ALAMEDA DR
3900 SD 92103 1268-G5
4900 OCN 92056 1107-F3
ALAMEDA GN
1500 ESCN 92027 1110-A5
ALAMEDA PL
3700 SD 92103 1268-G6
ALAMEDA TER
1900 SD 92103 1268-G5
ALAMEDA WY
3700 SDCo 91902 1310-F3
ALAMITOS AV
100 SD 92154 1330-B5
ALAMITOS PL
2900 ESCN 92027 1110-F7
ALAMITOS WY
500 SMCS 92069 1108-C6
ALAMO
- CRLB 92009 1126-H5
ALAMO CT
4500 LMSA 91941 1270-E4
ALAMO DR
4300 SD 92115 1270-D3
ALAMO GN
3200 ESCN 92025 1150-C1
ALAMO LN
700 ESCN 92025 1150-C1
700 SDCo 92025 1150-C1
ALAMO RD
1000 ImCo 92250 431-D5
ALAMO WY
100 SDCo 92021 1252-J2
4400 LMSA 91941 1270-E3
4400 SD 92115 1270-E3
ALAMOSA PARK DR
5100 OCN 92057 1087-C1
ALAN CT
2100 LMGR 91945 1290-J1
ALANA CIR
4100 OCN 92056 1087-C7
ALANA WY
1500 ESCN 92027 1110-A5
ALANWOOD CT
2900 SDCo 91978 1271-G7
ALAPAT DR
1600 ESCN 92027 1130-C2
ALAQUINAS DR
1600 SD 92173 1350-G2
ALASKA ST
3700 SD 92154 1330-E7
ALAVA CIR
8000 SD 92126 1209-B4
ALBA CT
2200 SD 92109 1248-B3
ALBA WY
200 SDCo 92019 1253-D1
ALBACORE AL
- SD 92136 1289-E6
AL BAHR DR
300 SDCo 92021 1253-A4
1400 SD 92037 1227-G7
AL BAHR RD
300 SDCo 92021 1252-J2
300 SDCo 92021 1253-A2
ALBANY AV
1400 CHV 91911 1330-E4
ALBA ROSA DR
11500 SDCo 92040 1211-G7
ALBATA CT
1500 SD 92154 1350-B2
ALBATROSS DR
- SDCo 92055 1023-F3
4100 SD 92103 1269-A5
ALBATROSS PL
100 SDCo 92021 1252-H4
ALBATROSS ST
2000 SD 92101 1289-A1
2900 SD 92103 1269-A6
ALBATROSS WY
1000 OCN 92057 1087-A3
ALBEMARLE ST
5500 SD 92139 1310-C1
ALBER ST
- CHV 91911 1330-H2
ALBERDI DR
7300 LMGR 91945 1290-F2
ALBERDINA WY
11400 SDCo 92040 1231-G3
ALBERNI CT
11300 SD 92126 1209-D1
ALBERQUE CT
2000 SD 92139 1290-D7
ALBERSON CT
4800 SD 92130 1188-C6
ALBERT
9200 SDCo 92040 1232-F4
ALBERT CT
- ESCN 92027 1110-E6
ALBERT ST
3400 SD 92103 1269-B6
ALBERTA AV
800 OCN 92054 1106-B1
ALBERTA CT
- NATC 91950 1289-H7
- SD 92113 1289-H7
ALBERTA PL
1000 SD 92103 1268-J6
ALBERTUS LN
30100 SDCo 92082 1071-A4
ALBION ST
500 SD 92106 1288-A2
ALBORADA DR
11500 SD 92127 1149-J6
ALBRIGHT PL
2600 ESCN 92027 1110-D6
4500 SD 92115 1270-B3
ALBRIGHT RD
- ImCo 92233 411-C10
ALBRIGHT ST
5400 OCN 92057 1067-E7
ALBUQUERQUE ST
4600 SD 92109 1248-C4
ALBURY CT
11600 SD 92131 1209-H1
ALCACER DEL SOL
12500 SD 92128 1170-C6
ALCALA CT
1500 SD 92111 1268-H2
ALCALA DR
3600 OCN 92054 1086-F2
ALCALA PL
1500 SD 92111 1268-H2
ALCALA KNOLLS DR
6500 SD 92111 1268-H2
ALCALDE CT
11400 SD 92127 1149-J7
11400 SD 92127 1150-A6
ALCAMO RD
7700 SD 92126 1209-A4
ALCARAS CT
400 OCN 92057 1086-J4
ALCEDO ST
2100 SD 92114 1290-E1
ALCONA ST
6900 SD 92139 1290-F6
ALCORN PL
5200 SD 92115 1270-A3
ALCORN ST
4000 SD 92154 1350-F2
ALCOTT CT
2400 SD 92106 1268-C6
ALCOTT ST
3000 SD 92106 1268-C6
ALCYON CT
- CRLB 92009 1127-B7
N ALDA DR
600 SMCS 92069 1108-J5
700 SMCS 92069 1109-A5
ALDABRA CT
9300 SD 92129 1189-D3
ALDAMA CT
16500 SDCo 92127 1169-F4
ALDEA DR
700 OCN 92057 1067-B5
ALDEA PL
7600 CRLB 92009 1147-H1
ALDEN WY
800 OCN 92057 1087-C2
ALDER AV
3800 CRLB 92008 1106-H5
ALDER DR
600 SMCS 92069 1109-A3
4000 SD 92116 1269-G3
E ALDER DR
4800 SD 92116 1269-H3
W ALDER DR
4800 SD 92116 1269-H3
ALDER PL
300 ESCN 92026 1109-H7
4800 SD 92116 1269-H3
13200 PWY 92064 1190-E2
ALDER ST
- CORD 92118 1288-G7
ALDERBRANCH PT
10400 SD 92131 1209-J4
ALDERBROOK DR
10400 SD 92131 1209-H4
ALDERBROOK PL
1900 CHV 91913 1311-D4
ALDERCREST PT
11600 SD 92131 1210-A1
ALDERGROVE AV
2000 ESCN 92029 1129-E3
ALDERGROVE LN
9800 SDCo 91977 1271-C7
ALDERHILL TER
11500 SD 92131 1210-A1
ALDERIDGE CT
11300 SD 92131 1209-J1
ALDERIDGE LN
11600 SD 92131 1209-J1
ALDERLEY ST
6100 SD 92114 1290-C5
ALDERNEY CT
1200 OCN 92054 1106-D2
ALDERSGATE RD
1700 ENCT 92024 1147-A2
ALDERSON ST
300 ELCJ 92019 1251-J6
ALDERWOOD CIR
1900 VSTA 92083 1107-G5
ALDERWOOD DR
6800 CRLB 92009 1127-A5
ALDERWOOD LN
17000 PWY 92064 1170-E2
ALDERWOOD ST
- SDCo 92055 1086-B2
ALDFORD DR
3400 SD 92111 1248-H4
ALDFORD PL
6200 SD 92111 1248-H4
ALDINE DR
4300 SD 92115 1269-J3
4300 SD 92116 1269-H3
ALDORADO DR
1400 SDCo 92084 1068-A5
ALDRIN AV
13300 PWY 92064 1190-H4
ALDRIN ST
14600 PWY 92064 1190-H4
ALDWYCH RD
300 ELCJ 92020 1251-C5
ALEGRE RD
700 SDCo 92019 1252-C4
ALEGRIA DR
1800 SDCo 92021 1252-H4
ALEGRIA PL
2000 ESCN 92026 1109-C5
ALEJANDRA PL
600 CHV 91910 1310-J5
ALEJO LN
11200 SD 92124 1230-A7
ALEJO PL
11100 SD 92124 1230-A7
ALEJO ST
4900 SD 92124 1230-A7
4900 SD 92124 1250-A1
ALEMAN PL
5200 SDCo 91902 1310-J1
ALEMANIA RD
11800 SD 92129 1189-E7
11800 SD 92129 1209-F1
ALENE ST
500 SDCo 91977 1290-J4
ALESSANDRO LN
1200 VSTA 92084 1088-C4
ALESSANDRO TR
1800 VSTA 92084 1088-C4
1800 SDCo 92084 1088-C4
ALESTAR ST
200 VSTA 92084 1087-J6
ALEX RD
10100 SDCo 92028 1029-C3
ALEXANDER DR
1900 ESCN 92025 1130-A7
2100 SDCo 92025 1130-A7
2200 SDCo 92025 1129-J7
2400 SDCo 92029 1149-J1
2400 SDCo 92029 1150-A1
ALEXANDER WY
10500 SNTE 92071 1231-F7
ALEXANDRA AV
3300 SDCo 91977 1271-C6
ALEXANDRA LN
900 ENCT 92024 1147-D4
ALEXANDRI CIR
6300 CRLB 92009 1127-D4
ALEXANDRIA DR
- ELCJ 92021 1251-H5
1000 SD 92107 1287-J2
ALEXIA PL
3600 SD 92116 1269-F3
ALFORD ST
3200 LMGR 91945 1270-F6
ALFRED AV
4600 SD 92120 1249-J5
4800 SD 92120 1250-A5
ALFRED CT
4900 SD 92120 1250-A5
ALGA CT
1400 VSTA 92083 1107-H4
ALGA RD
1900 CRLB 92009 1127-F6
3200 CRLB 92009 1128-A4
ALGECIRAS ST
4400 SD 92107 1287-H2
ALGIERS ST
2500 ESCN 92027 1110-E7
ALGONQUIN CT
4800 SD 92130 1188-C6
ALHAMBRA ST
4400 SD 92107 1287-H1
ALHUDSON DR
1700 ESCN 92029 1129-G5
ALI WY
400 SDCo 92028 1027-E5
ALICANTE RD
2500 CRLB 92009 1127-F7
ALICANTE WY
4900 OCN 92056 1107-F5
ALICE ST
400 SDCo 92065 1152-E4
600 SD 92154 1330-A7
3200 SD 92105 1270-C6
4500 SD 92115 1270-C3
ALICIA CT
2000 LMGR 91945 1290-F1
ALICIA DR
3900 SD 92107 1268-B7
ALICIA LN
7300 LMGR 91945 1290-F1
ALICIA WY
100 OCN 92057 1086-H3
ALICIO RD
- SDCo 92055 1086-A3
ALIDA ST
7800 LMSA 91942 1250-H6
ALIENTO CT
600 VSTA 92083 1107-D1
11400 SD 92127 1149-J7

SAN DIEGO CO.

INDEX

SAN DIEGO CO. INDEX

STREET
Block City ZIP Pg-Grid

ALIENTO CT
11400 SD 92127 1169-J1
ALIPAZ CT
3900 OCN 92054 1086-G2
16300 SDCo 92127 1169-F4
ALISA PL
31300 SDCo 92082 1070-F1
ALISAL LN
- CHV 91915 1311-G6
ALISHA DR
1400 SD 92114 1290-F5
ALISO CT
3700 SDCo 91902 1310-F2
ALISO DR
3400 SDCo 91902 1310-F2
ALISO PL
1400 ESCN 92027 1109-J5
1400 ESCN 92027 1110-A6
ALISO WY
- OCN 92057 1087-A2
ALISO CANYON RD
6800 SDCo 92067 1148-F6
N ALISO CANYON RD
18100 SDCo 92067 1148-F7
ALITA LN
1300 ESCN 92027 1110-B5
ALKAID DR
11500 SD 92126 1209-C1
ALKOSH RD
14500 SDCo 91935 1273-A6
ALLANO WY
9200 SNTE 92071 1230-J6
ALLBILL WY
8900 SD 92119 1251-A3
ALLBROOK DR
11800 PWY 92064 1190-A5
ALLEA LN
1200 VSTA 92083 1108-A1
ALLEGHANY ST
5500 SD 92139 1310-C1
5800 SD 92139 1290-D7
ALLEN DR
2100 ELCN 92243 6559-F2
ALLEN RD
- ImCo 92227 410-K10
4300 SD 92103 1268-H4
ALLENBROOK WY
8900 SD 92129 1189-C3
ALLENDE AV
4500 OCN 92057 1086-J1
4500 OCN 92057 1087-A1
ALLENDE CT
100 SOLB 92075 1167-D6
ALLENHURST PL
4700 SD 92117 1248-G1
ALLEN SCHOOL LN
4200 CHV 91902 1310-G4
4200 SDCo 91902 1310-G4
ALLEN SCHOOL RD
3800 CHV 91902 1310-G3
3800 SDCo 91902 1310-G3
ALLENWOOD LN
500 ESCN 92029 1129-D3
ALLENWOOD WY
10000 SNTE 92071 1231-D3
ALLERTON CT
800 SD 92109 1267-J4
ALLEW WY
2800 SD 92139 1310-F1
ALLIANCE CT
7200 SD 92119 1250-F4
ALLIED RD
4700 SD 92120 1249-J6
ALLISON AV
8000 LMSA 91941 1270-J2
ALLISON LN
3600 LMGR 91945 1270-G6
ALLSPICE
500 OCN 92057 1086-H4
ALLSPICE WY
200 OCN 92057 1086-H4
ALLVIEW CT
400 CHV 91910 1310-F7
ALMA PL
4600 SD 92115 1270-B3
ALMADEN LN
7000 CRLB 92009 1127-F7
ALMAGRO LN
- SDCo 92026 1109-E6
ALMAHURST RW
3100 SD 92037 1227-J1
ALMAYO AV
4600 SD 92117 1248-G1
ALMAYO CT
4900 SD 92117 1248-G1
ALMAZON ST
11100 SD 92129 1169-H6
ALMENDRA CT
2700 SDCo 92028 1028-H7
2700 SDCo 92028 1048-H1
ALMENDRO LN
17900 SD 92127 1150-A7
ALMERIA CT
1000 VSTA 92083 1107-H4
2300 SD 92037 1248-B3
ALMOND CIR
8500 SDCo 92040 1231-J7
ALMOND LN
200 OCN 92054 1086-G3
ALMOND RD
8600 SDCo 92040 1231-J6
ALMOND ST
100 SDCo 92028 1027-F4
ALMONDWOOD WY
4800 SD 92130 1188-C6
ALMONTE PL
500 CHV 91910 1311-A4
ALMY ST
- SD 92106 1288-A5
ALMYRA RD
100 SDCo 92019 1253-C1
ALOE CT
1100 SMCS 92078 1129-B1
ALOHA DR
1000 ENCT 92024 1167-E1
ALOHA LN
2000 SDCo 92084 1088-B2
ALOHA PL
4200 SD 92103 1268-G5
ALONDA CT
11000 SD 92126 1208-J2
11000 SD 92126 1209-A2
ALONDA WY
7500 SD 92126 1209-A2
ALONDO PL
14700 PWY 92064 1190-G1
ALONDRA AV
1200 CHV 91913 1311-D7
ALONDRA CT
1600 CHV 91913 1311-D7
12700 SD 92128 1170-C3
ALONDRA DR
16700 SD 92128 1170-C3
ALONDRA WY
4800 CRLB 92008 1106-J7
ALONQUIN WY
3400 SD 92154 1330-E7
ALONZO CT
- SDCo 92055 1086-A2
ALONZO DR
1300 SDCo 92021 1253-A1
ALORA ST
14400 PWY 92064 1190-H3
ALOSTA ST
2400 SD 92154 1350-C3
ALPHA AV
200 SDCo 91977 1291-A4
ALPHA ST
1600 NATC 91950 1289-J6
1600 NATC 91950 1290-A6
1600 SD 92113 1289-G6
ALPHECCA WY
8800 SD 92126 1209-D2
ALPHONSE ST
10200 SNTE 92071 1231-D2
ALPINE AV
200 CHV 91910 1310-C5
700 CHV 91910 1330-D1
1000 CHV 91911 1330-D2
8500 LMSA 91941 1270-J3
8500 LMSA 91941 1271-A3
ALPINE BLVD
800 SDCo 91901 1233-G5
1700 SDCo 91901 1234-B6
5800 SDCo 91901 1235-A5
16000 SDCo 92021 1233-E3
ALPINE DR
13000 PWY 92064 1190-D5
ALPINE LN
300 OCN 92054 1106-C2
11500 SDCo 92040 1231-H7
ALPINE PL
1400 ESCN 92027 1110-A6
1400 SMCS 92069 1128-D1
ALPINE TER
11900 SD 92128 1190-B7
ALPINE WY
600 ESCN 92029 1129-E2
ALPINE CREEK LN
1900 SDCo 91901 1234-A6
ALPINE ESTATES PL
1200 SDCo 91901 1233-G6
ALPINE GLEN PL
2100 SDCo 91901 1234-B6
ALPINE GROVE LN
1400 SDCo 91901 1234-A6
ALPINE HEIGHTS LN
500 SDCo 91901 1253-F1
ALPINE HEIGHTS RD
200 SDCo 91901 1253-G1
ALPINE HEIGHTS WY
2200 SDCo 91901 1253-H1
ALPINE OAKS DR
1000 SDCo 91901 1253-H2
ALPINE TERRACE RD
1500 SDCo 91901 1233-J6
ALPINE TRAIL RD
300 SDCo 91901 1253-F2
ALPINE VIEW RD
600 SDCo 91901 1233-G5
ALPINE VIEW WY
600 SDCo 91901 1233-G5
ALPINE VILLAGE DR
- SDCo 91901 1234-A6
ALPS LN
11500 SDCo 92026 1089-H4
ALPS WY
11400 SDCo 92026 1089-H4
11600 SDCo 92082 1089-H4
ALSACIA CT
2200 SD 92139 1290-G7
ALSACIA ST
6700 SD 92139 1290-F7
ALSTON AV
3600 NATC 91950 1310-D3
ALTA CT
6600 SD 92139 1290-E7
ALTA DR
2800 SDCo 91950 1310-C3
ALTA LN
200 SDCo 92021 1252-G3
4500 LMSA 91941 1270-H3
ALTA PL
1800 SDCo 92021 1252-G3
ALTA RD
500 SDCo 92154 1332-C7
500 SDCo 92154 1352-C1
ALTA TER
10200 SDCo 91941 1271-E4
ALTA WY
- SD 92037 1247-F3
ALTA BAHIA CT
5300 SD 92109 1247-J4
ALTA CALLE
1000 VSTA 92084 1088-A7
1000 VSTA 92084 1087-J7
ALTA CAMINO CT
2300 ESCN 92027 1110-D6
ALTA CARMEL CT
12000 SD 92128 1170-B6
ALTADENA AV
2200 SD 92105 1290-A1
3000 SD 92105 1270-A5
4200 SD 92115 1270-A5
ALTADENA RD
11800 SDCo 92040 1251-J1
ALTADENA ST
1400 SD 92102 1290-A2
ALTAIR CT
6500 SD 92120 1270-D1
ALTA LAGUNA WY
9300 SD 92126 1209-E2
ALTA LA JOLLA DR
1500 SD 92037 1247-J3
1700 SD 92037 1248-A3
ALTA LOMA CT
3800 SDCo 91935 1272-H6
ALTA LOMA DR
3300 SDCo 91935 1272-G6
3600 SDCo 91902 1310-D4
ALTA LOMA GN
800 ESCN 92026 1109-E3
ALTA LOMA LN
3900 SDCo 91935 1272-H6
ALTAMAR CT
14400 SDCo 92067 1188-E2
ALTA MEADOW LN
500 ESCN 92027 1110-D6
ALTA MESA DR
100 VSTA 92084 1088-B5
30400 SDCo 92082 1069-H4
ALTA MESA WY
5900 SD 92115 1270-C4
ALTAMIRA CT
1700 VSTA 92083 1107-E2
ALTAMIRA DR
4200 SDCo 91941 1271-E3
ALTA MIRA LN
30000 SDCo 92082 1069-H5
ALTAMIRA PL
1800 SD 92103 1268-H4
ALTAMIRANO WY
4300 SD 92103 1268-F4
ALTAMONT CIR
1900 SD 92139 1290-C7
1900 SD 92139 1310-C1
ALTAMONT CT
1800 SD 92139 1290-C7
ALTAMONT DR
5700 SD 92139 1310-C1
5700 SD 92139 1290-C7
ALTAMONT PL
1900 SD 92139 1310-C1
ALTAMONT RD
9100 LMSA 91942 1251-B5
ALTAMONT WY
1900 SD 92139 1290-C7
ALTAR
- SDCo 92040 1232-B7
ALTA RICA DR
4600 SDCo 91941 1271-E3
ALTA VEGA RD
- SDCo 91905 (1320-A6 See Page 1300)
ALTA VERDE DR
1600 SDCo 92028 1048-A2
ALTA VIEW DR
1800 SD 92139 1290-E7
2400 SD 92139 1310-F1
ALTA VISTA
- SMCS 92078 1129-C2
7300 CRLB 92009 1127-J7
ALTA VISTA AV
1100 ESCN 92027 1109-J6
1700 ESCN 92027 1110-A6
5600 SD 92114 1290-B6
ALTA VISTA DR
600 VSTA 92084 1087-J6
1000 VSTA 92084 1088-A5
2500 SDCo 92028 1028-A7
2600 SDCo 92028 1048-A2
3300 SDCo 92036 1156-D1
ALTA VISTA ST
5100 SD 92109 1247-J4
ALTA VISTA TER
900 VSTA 92084 1088-A7
ALTA VISTA WY
1700 SD 92109 1247-J4
1700 SD 92109 1248-A4
ALTHEA LN
3800 CRLB 92008 1106-G6
ALTISMA WY
2200 CRLB 92009 1127-G7
ALTITO WY
4800 SDCo 91941 1271-C2
ALTIVA PL
7300 CRLB 92009 1127-G7
ALTMAN RW
10800 SD 92121 1208-A5
ALTO CT
9300 SDCo 91941 1271-B2
ALTO DR
9300 SDCo 91941 1271-C1
9500 LMSA 91941 1271-C2
ALTO ST
4000 OCN 92056 1107-B3
ALTO TER
900 SDCo 92028 1027-G1
ALTO CERRO CIR
2400 SD 92109 1248-B3
ALTON DR
7700 LMGR 91945 1290-G1
ALTON PL
2200 LMGR 91945 1270-H7
2200 LMGR 91945 1290-H1
ALTON WY
4000 ESCN 92025 1150-D3
ALTOONA DR
11600 SDCo 92020 1271-H2
ALTORO LN
3200 SDCo 91935 1273-B6
ALTOZANO DR
1800 ELCJ 92020 1251-B2
ALTOZANO WY
1700 ELCJ 92020 1251-C2
ALTRIDGE ST
3400 SD 92123 1249-C4
ALTURA CIR
1700 SMCS 92069 1108-B7
ALTURA DR
700 SMCS 92069 1108-C7
800 SMCS 92069 1128-C1
2900 OCN 92056 1087-B7
2900 OCN 92056 1107-B1
ALTURA PL
1800 SD 92103 1268-H5
ALTURAS LN
600 SDCo 92028 1027-E4
ALTURAS RD
400 SDCo 92028 1027-E3
ALUMNI PL
5000 SD 92115 1270-D2
ALVA LN
100 SDCo 92028 1027-J2
2300 SDCo 92021 1252-H4
ALVA RD
17100 SDCo 92127 1169-F2
ALVARADO CT
100 SDCo 92028 1027-H2
6300 SD 92120 1270-D1
ALVARADO PL
200 CHV 91910 1310-D6
ALVARADO RD
6100 SD 92120 1270-C1
6700 LMSA 91941 1270-F2
6700 LMSA 92115 1270-F2
6700 SD 92115 1270-F2
ALVARADO ST
100 CHV 91910 1310-C6
1500 OCN 92054 1106-C3
E ALVARADO ST
100 SDCo 92028 1027-F2
1800 SDCo 92028 1028-A2
W ALVARADO ST
100 SDCo 92028 1027-E2
500 SDCo 92055 1027-E2
ALVARADO TER
400 VSTA 92084 1087-H5
ALVARADO CANYON RD
4300 SD 92120 1269-H1
ALVAREZ MEADOW CT
11300 SD 92126 1208-J2
ALVEDA AV
600 ELCJ 92019 1252-B7
600 SDCo 92019 1252-B7
ALVEO WY
11600 SD 92127 1169-J1
11600 SD 92127 1170-A1
ALVERSON RD
100 SD 92173 1350-F4
ALVIN ST
600 SD 92114 1290-C3
ALVISO WY
300 ENCT 92024 1147-C5
ALVOCA ST
3300 CHV 91911 1330-D6
ALWOOD CT
2900 SDCo 91978 1271-G7
ALWYNE SQ
16100 SD 92128 1170-B4
ALYDAR CTE
5800 SDCo 92067 1168-E7
5800 SDCo 92067 1188-E1
ALYSSUM RD
900 CRLB 92009 1127-A6
ALYSSUM WY
400 OCN 92057 1086-J4
ALZEDA DR
5200 ELCJ 92020 1271-F1
5200 SDCo 91941 1271-F1
5200 SDCo 92020 1271-F1
AMACAYO CT
1000 SD 92154 1349-J1
AMADA PL
10300 SNTE 92071 1231-E3
AMADITA LN
5500 SDCo 91902 1311-A1
AMADOR AV
1100 VSTA 92083 1087-E7
AMADOR DR
4900 OCN 92056 1107-F3
AMADOR ST
1500 CHV 91913 1331-C1
AMALFI DR
1800 ENCT 92024 1147-C1
AMALFI PL
1200 ESCN 92027 1110-A6
AMALFI ST
1700 SD 92037 1227-G6
AMALIA CT
11100 SD 92129 1169-J7
AMALIA ST
15100 SD 92129 1169-J7
AMANDA CT
- SDCo 91906 (1317-G2 See Page 1296)
AMANDA LN
2100 SDCo 92029 1129-G6
2100 ESCN 92029 1129-G6
AMANDA ST
5600 SD 92114 1290-B4
AMANECER PL
3000 ESCN 92027 1110-E6
AMANTA CT
1600 CRLB 92009 1127-D5
AMANTE DR
13400 SDCo 92021 1232-D7
AMANTHA AV
10400 SD 92126 1209-B4
AMAPOLA CT
- SDCo 91901 1234-A6
AMARANTH ST
12700 SD 92129 1189-D5
AMARETTO WY
4100 SDCo 91977 1271-C4
AMARGOSA DR
1300 ENCT 92024 1147-G4
7900 CRLB 92009 1147-G4
AMARILLO AV
5700 LMSA 91942 1250-J6
AMARILLO PL
1900 ESCN 92025 1129-J6
AMARILLO RD
17200 SDCo 92065 1171-G1
AMARO CT
10300 SD 92124 1229-G7
AMARO DR
5600 SD 92124 1229-G7
AMARYLLIS DR
3600 SD 92106 1268-C6
AMARYLLIS ST
- SDCo 92055 1086-B3
AMATISTA WY
- OCN 92056 1106-J2
AMATO DR
8500 SDCo 92040 1232-A7
AMAYA CT
5500 LMSA 91942 1251-A7
AMAYA DR
5600 LMSA 91942 1251-B7
AMBASSADOR AV
10100 SD 92126 1209-B5
AMBASSADOR CT
8100 SD 92126 1209-B5
AMBER DR
900 SMCS 92069 1109-C5
AMBER LN
300 VSTA 92084 1087-J6
2200 ESCN 92026 1109-F4
3400 OCN 92056 1107-D2
4000 CHV 91902 1310-G3
AMBER PL
- SD 92130 1188-J3
6800 LMGR 91945 1270-E7
AMBER CREEK CT
- VSTA 92084 1088-B3
AMBER CREST PL
2800 SD 92128 1189-J3
AMBERGLADES LN
10600 SD 92130 1208-E2
AMBER HILL LN
12800 PWY 92064 1190-D4
AMBER LAKE AV
6200 SD 92119 1250-J5
AMBER LEAF CT
- SMCS 92078 1128-E6
AMBERLY CIR
9000 SD 92126 1209-D3
AMBERLY ST
6400 SD 92120 1250-D4
AMBER LYNN LN
2300 SDCo 92065 1172-D4
AMBER OAK LN
- ESCN 92027 1130-H3
AMBER SKY LN
13900 SD 92129 1189-D2
AMBERVALE TER
3900 SD 92130 1188-A5
AMBER VISTA
2800 SDCo 92028 1048-A1
AMBERWOOD CT
4700 CRLB 92008 1106-J6
AMBERWOOD DR
2700 OCN 92056 1087-E5
AMBERWOOD LN
- ESCN 92027 1130-H2
AMBLER LN
1200 SDCo 92020 1271-J1
1200 SDCo 92020 1272-A1
AMBROSIA DR
6400 SD 92124 1249-G6
AMBROSIA LN
6900 CRLB 92009 1127-D5
AMBY CT
14400 SD 92129 1189-C1
AMELIA DR
8100 SDCo 92021 1252-C1
AMELIA PL
- ESCN 92026 1109-J4
AMELIA ISLAND DR
2300 CHV 91915 1311-G5
AMENA CT
800 CHV 91910 1310-J6
AMERICA WY
800 SOLB 92014 1187-G1
AMERICAN AV
3800 LMSA 91941 1270-J5
AMERICAN WY
13800 SDCo 92040 1232-E4
AMERICAN GIRL MINE RD
- ImCo - 432-A4
AMERICE CT
3900 OCN 92056 1107-E4
AMES PL
3500 CRLB 92008 1106-J4
AMES ST
3500 SD 92111 1249-A4
AMESBURY ST
6200 SD 92114 1290-D5
AMETHYST CT
800 OCN 92057 1087-B2
AMETHYST ST
1300 SD 92114 1290-B2
AMETHYST WY
- CRLB 92009 1127-B4
900 ESCN 92029 1129-D3
AMHERST ST
6600 SD 92115 1270-D2
AMICK ST
2300 OCN 92054 1086-C5
AMIE CT
1800 SMCS 92069 1109-D7
AMIFORD DR
700 SD 92107 1287-J2
AMIGOS CT
3600 OCN 92056 1107-D3
AMIGOS LN
500 SDCo 92065 1152-J5
AMIGOS RD
100 SDCo 92065 1152-J5
600 SDCo 92065 1153-A6
AMIGOS WY
100 SDCo 92028 1027-H2
AMINO DR
8300 SNTE 92071 1230-H6
AMISTAD CT
900 ELCJ 92019 1252-A7
AMISTAD PL
900 ELCJ 92019 1252-A7
AMITY ST
2300 SD 92109 1248-B3
AMMONS WY
40700 SDCo 92028 997-H3
AMMUNITION RD
- SDCo 92055 1047-A3
100 SDCo 92028 1027-E4
100 SDCo 92055 1027-E5
AMNEST ST
4900 SD 92117 1228-G7
AMOR PL
1400 ESCN 92027 1110-A6
AMOROSA GN
2100 ESCN 92026 1109-F4
AMOROSO ST
4100 SD 92111 1248-J3
4100 SD 92111 1249-A3
AMPHITHEATER DR
- ESCN 92025 1150-C1
AMPHITHEATRE DR
500 DLMR 92014 1187-G5
AMPUDIA ST
3800 SD 92110 1268-F5
4200 SD 92103 1268-G5
4400 SD 92108 1268-G5
AMSO ST
14900 PWY 92064 1170-C7
14900 PWY 92064 1190-C1
AMSTEL LN
2300 SDCo 92084 1087-J1
AMSTER DR
9500 SNTE 92071 1231-E4
AMULET ST
2700 SD 92123 1249-E6
AMY ST
100 CHV 91911 1330-D3
AMY WY
12500 SDCo 92040 1232-B4
AMYS PL
600 ESCN 92027 1110-D6
AMYS ST
9200 SDCo 91977 1291-B2
ANABELLA DR
14200 PWY 92064 1190-C2
ANACAPA CT
800 SD 92109 1267-J4
ANACONDA LN
2000 ENCT 92024 1147-H7
ANAHEIM DR
10500 SDCo 91941 1271-F3
ANAHEIM ST
2600 SDCo 92025 1130-D7
2600 SDCo 92025 1150-D1
ANAHEIM TER
3000 SDCo 92025 1130-D7
3000 SDCo 92025 1150-D1
ANALIESE WY
3000 SD 92139 1310-F2
ANASTASIA ST
3900 SD 92111 1248-J3
ANATRA CT
900 CRLB 92009 1127-A7
ANAWOOD WY
2900 SDCo 91978 1271-G7
ANCHOR CIR
3200 OCN 92056 1107-A2
ANCHOR WY
500 CRLB 92008 1106-F6
ANCHORAGE AV
- CRLB 92009 1126-J7
ANCHORAGE LN
1000 SD 92106 1288-B3
ANCONA LN
10700 SD 92131 1210-A2
ANCURZA WY
3300 CHV 91911 1330-E5
ANDA LUCIA WY
2100 OCN 92056 1106-J1
2100 OCN 92056 1086-J7
ANDALUSIA AV
4700 SD 92117 1248-H1
ANDANZA WY
11600 SD 92127 1150-A7
ANDASOL ST
7400 SD 92126 1208-J2
7400 SD 92126 1209-A2
ANDERHOLT RD
1100 ImCo 92250 431-D6
ANDERS CIR
7900 LMSA 91942 1250-H7
ANDERSON AV
8800 SD 92126 1209-C7
8800 SD 92126 1229-C1
ANDERSON CT
- SDCo 92026 1089-D2
ANDERSON LN
1700 SDCo 91901 1233-F6
ANDERSON PL
500 SD 92103 1269-A6
ANDERSON RD
500 SDCo 91901 1234-D3
5600 SDCo 92028 999-C3
ANDERSON ST
- SDCo 92055 1023-E2
3000 SDCo 91902 1290-J7
3000 SDCo 91902 1310-J1
ANDERSON RANCH RD
9800 SDCo 91916 1235-G1
ANDES RD
300 SDCo 92021 1251-F1
ANDORRA CT
1400 VSTA 92083 1107-H4
ANDORRA WY
3000 OCN 92056 1106-J1
4200 SDCo 91910 1310-E5
15000 SD 92129 1169-J7
ANDORRE GN
1400 ESCN 92029 1149-F1
ANDOVER AV
2800 CRLB 92008 1107-A4
ANDOVER RD
1200 ELCJ 92019 1251-J6
ANDRE PL
1300 VSTA 92083 1107-F1
ANDRE RD
1200 ImCo 92227 431-A1
ANDREA AV
1700 CRLB 92008 1106-G5
2800 SD 92123 1249-C6
ANDREA CT
8500 SD 92123 1249-C6
ANDREA TER
10700 SNTE 92071 1231-F6
ANDREASEN DR
700 ESCN 92029 1129-F3
ANDREEN RD
30500 SDCo 92082 1069-E4
ANDREEN ST
3700 SDCo 91977 1271-C5
ANDREW AV
100 ENCT 92024 1147-A2
ANDREW JACKSON ST
5000 OCN 92057 1067-A6
ANDREWS CT
1900 OCN 92054 1106-F1
3700 SD 92154 1350-F1
ANDREWS ST
3400 SD 92103 1268-H6
ANDROMEDA RD
8500 SD 92126 1209-C2
ANDROS CT
5800 SD 92115 1270-C5
ANDROS PL
5700 SD 92115 1270-B5
ANDROS WY
4100 OCN 92056 1107-E6
ANDY LN
1800 OCN 92054 1106-D2
ANDYS PL
- SDCo 91935 1274-C2
ANEAS CT
16200 SDCo 92065 1173-F3
ANELLA RD
3200 SD 92173 1350-F5
ANEMONE WY
- CRLB 92009 1127-B4
ANGEL DR
2200 SDCo 91905 1300-B5
ANGEL PL
1500 SDCo 92065 1152-F7
ANGEL ST
- SDCo 92055 1085-G1
ANGELA CT
16000 SDCo 92082 1071-B3
ANGELA LN
- CHV 91911 1330-D2
ANGELA WY
2600 SDCo 91901 1234-C7
ANGELENO RD
7600 SD 92126 1209-A2
ANGELES GN
1800 ESCN 92029 1129-E6
ANGELES VISTA DR
100 VSTA 92084 1087-G3
ANGELINA RD
5200 OCN 92056 1087-D3
ANGELIQUE ST
11500 SD 92131 1210-B1
11800 SD 92131 1190-B7
ANGELL AV
2500 SD 92122 1228-B6
ANGELL PL
6200 SD 92122 1228-B5
ANGELO DR
800 NATC 91950 1290-D7
1000 SD 92139 1290-D7
ANGELS PT
4700 SDCo 91941 1271-C3
ANGELUCCI ST
3500 SD 92111 1249-B4
ANGELUS AV
- ESCN 92027 1130-C1
800 SD 92114 1290-F3
900 LMGR 91945 1290-F3
ANGETON CT
7500 SD 92126 1208-J4
ANGETON DR
7500 SD 92126 1208-J5
ANGILA DR
8400 ELCJ 92020 1251-C1
8400 SNTE 92071 1251-C1
ANGLIM CT
- SDCo 92055 1023-E3
- SDCo 92672 1023-E3
ANGOLA CIR
7500 SD 92126 1209-A3
ANGOLA RD
10800 SD 92126 1209-A3
ANGOSTO WY
12900 SD 92128 1150-C5
ANGUILA PL
- CRLB 92009 1127-J5
ANGUS CT
1000 SMCS 92069 1109-B6
ANGWIN DR
3400 SD 92123 1249-E5
ANGWIN PL
9300 SD 92123 1249-E5
ANILLO WY
7700 CRLB 92009 1147-F2
ANITA DR
2700 SDCo 91901 1254-A2
ANITA ST
100 CHV 91911 1330-A5
ANITA WY
9600 SDCo 91901 1234-B2
ANITA JUNE CT
400 CHV 91911 1330-C4
ANJA PL
10000 SDCo 92040 1231-F3
ANJA WY
10900 SDCo 92040 1231-F3
ANKA LN
1600 SDCo 92026 1109-E7
ANLEE DR
8500 SNTE 92071 1230-J7
ANN DR
3400 CRLB 92008 1106-G4
ANN ST
500 ELCJ 92021 1251-H4
600 OCN 92057 1067-A5
ANNA AV
800 SD 92110 1268-E3
ANNA LN
1100 SMCS 92069 1109-C5
1800 SDCo 92083 1108-B3
ANNADALE WY
- CHV 91915 1311-G7
ANNA LINDA CT
400 CHV 91911 1330-C5
ANNA LINDA DR
1600 CHV 91911 1330-C5
ANNA LINDA PL
400 CHV 91911 1330-C5
ANNA MARIE LN
5200 SDCo 92003 1048-D7
ANNANDALE WY
8800 SNTE 92071 1230-J5
8800 SNTE 92071 1231-A5
ANNAPOLIS AV
7200 LMSA 91941 1270-F4
ANN ARBOR LN
11400 SD 92131 1209-H2
ANNA ROSE LN
1200 SDCo 92065 1172-F1
ANNE SLADON CT
9700 SNTE 92071 1231-F4
ANNE SLADON ST
4400 OCN 92057 1066-H7
ANNETTE ST
2800 OCN 92056 1087-C7
ANNETTE WY
1500 ELCJ 92020 1251-D7
ANNIE LN
10300 SNTE 92071 1231-B1
ANNIE WY
9600 SNTE 92071 1231-B1
ANNIE LAURIE LN
5400 SDCo 91902 1311-A2
ANNMAR DR
6700 SD 92139 1310-F1
ANN-O-RENO LN
13200 PWY 92064 1190-G4
ANNRAE ST
3100 SD 92123 1249-B5
ANNS WY
200 VSTA 92083 1087-E6
ANOCHE GN
1400 ESCN 92026 1109-D4
ANOEL CT
10000 SDCo 91977 1271-E6
ANROL AV
8600 SD 92123 1249-C6
ANTA CT
2700 CRLB 92009 1127-H5
ANTARES DR
1600 SD 92173 1350-E2
ANTELOPE HILLS DR
12600 SDCo 92040 1232-B4
ANTELOPE STATION
13600 PWY 92064 1170-F1
ANTHONY DR
2100 SD 92113 1289-H7
ANTHONY LN
12700 SDCo 92082 1070-B5
ANTHONY RD
29200 SDCo 92082 1070-C4
ANTHONY HEIGHTS DR
1400 SDCo 92026 1109-E7
ANTHONY HOLLOW
30200 SDCo 92082 1070-D4
ANTHONY RIDGE RD
13200 SDCo 92082 1070-C5
ANTHRACITE WY
100 SD 92114 1290-F4
ANTIEM ST
3500 SD 92111 1249-A3
ANTIGUA BLVD
5200 SD 92124 1249-F1
5500 SD 92124 1229-H7
6500 SD 92124 1230-A7
ANTIGUA CT
- CORD 92118 1329-E1
ANTIGUA DR
1800 VSTA 92083 1107-G5
ANTILLA PL
11200 SD 92126 1209-D2

ANTILOPE ST — SAN DIEGO CO. STREET INDEX — AUDREY CT 6564

SAN DIEGO CO.
INDEX

STREET
Block City ZIP Pg-Grid

ANTILOPE ST
6700 CRLB 92009 1127-H5
ANTIOCH AV
1400 CHV 91913 1311-C7
ANTIOCH PL
4600 SD 92115 1270-A3
ANTLERS DR
4000 SDCo 92036 1156-E3
ANTOINE DR
1300 SD 92139 1290-H6
ANTON LN
6700 SD 92114 1290-E5
ANTONIO DR
16700 SD 92128 1170-C3
ANTRIM WY
10200 SD 92126 1209-B5
ANVIL LAKE AV
6200 SD 92119 1250-J5
ANZA AV
900 VSTA 92084 1087-J4
ANZA CT
- ELCJ 92019 1251-H6
ANZA DR
7900 SD 92114 1290-G3
ANZA PL
1700 ESCN 92027 1110-C7
ANZA RD
- ImCo 92231 431-B8
N ANZA ST
900 ELCJ 92021 1251-H3
900 SDCo 92021 1251-H3
S ANZA ST
100 ELCJ 92020 1251-H6
500 ELCJ 92019 1251-H6
ANZA WY
700 CHV 91910 1310-H7
ANZA PARK TR
500 SDCo 92004 410-B6
500 SDCo 92004 1058-F1
ANZA TRAIL RD
- ImCo 92259 430-J8
ANZIO DR
3800 SDCo 92004 (1099-D1 See Page 1098)
APACHE AV
3200 SD 92117 1248-F5
APACHE DR
1500 CHV 91910 1311-C6
34600 SDCo 92036 1176-D4
APACHE GN
1800 ESCN 92027 1110-A5
APACHE RD
13500 PWY 92064 1190-F3
APACHE ST
4200 OCN 92056 1087-C5
APOLLO DR
200 VSTA 92084 1087-H4
APOLLO ST
3400 SD 92111 1249-A4
APORE ST
3900 LMSA 91941 1270-G5
APOSTAL RD
2800 SDCo 92025 1150-E2
APPALACHIAN PL
1400 CHV 91915 1311-H6
APPALACHIAN WY
13400 SD 92129 1189-E4
APPALOOSA CT
- SNTE 92071 1231-D2
APPALOOSA DR
13300 SDCo 92040 1232-D3
APPALOOSA RD
9700 SD 92131 1209-G5
APPALOOSA WY
1700 OCN 92057 1067-F7
APPERT CT
6600 SD 92111 1248-H6
APPIAN CT
- SD 92139 1310-G1
APPIAN DR
2900 SD 92139 1310-G1
APPIAN RD
2300 CRLB 92008 1106-H4
APPLE
9600 SDCo 92021 1233-B3
APPLE ST
1900 OCN 92054 1086-D7
9400 SDCo 91977 1291-C2
APPLE BLOSSOM LN
100 SDCo 92084 1108-D4
APPLE BLOSSOM WY
3500 OCN 92054 1086-F2
APPLEBY CT
14600 PWY 92064 1190-F1
APPLEBY LN
14600 PWY 92064 1190-F1
APPLEGATE ST
- CHV 91913 1311-F7
- CHV 91913 1331-D1
APPLERIDGE DR
700 ENCT 92024 1167-G1
APPLESTILL RD
- ImCo 92243 6559-G5
APPLETON CT
800 OCN 92057 1087-C2
APPLETON ST
4000 SD 92117 1228-E7
APPLE TREE DR
9700 SD 92124 1249-F1
APPLEWILDE DR
700 SMCS 92069 1128-E2
800 SMCS 92069 1128-F3
APPLEWOOD DR
700 ELCJ 92021 1251-G4
APPLEWOOD LN
2000 VSTA 92083 1107-F5
APPROACH RD
8700 SD 92154 1351-H1
APRICOT LN
2900 SDCo 91977 1271-B6
APRICOT TREE LN
2300 SDCo 91977 1271-E7
APRICOT TREE WY
3400 OCN 92054 1086-E3
APRIL CT
3800 SD 92122 1228-E5
APRIL LEIGH TER
11300 SD 92126 1208-J2
AQUA LN
200 SDCo 92065 1152-H5
3600 OCN 92056 1107-A1
AQUA HILL RD
2400 SDCo 92028 1047-G2
AQUA MANSA RD
7900 SD 92126 1209-A2
AQUAMARINE RD
7300 SD 92114 1290-F5
AQUA PARK CT
3700 SD 92154 1350-F1

AQUA PARK ST
1100 SD 92154 1350-E1
AQUARIUS DR
8300 SD 92126 1209-C1
AQUARIUS PL
11200 SD 92126 1209-C1
AQUARIUS RD
8900 SD 92126 1209-F7
AQUA VIEW CT
8300 SDCo 91977 1290-J5
AQUEDUCT CT
6700 SD 92119 1250-E3
AQUEDUCT RD
31700 SDCo 92003 1068-H2
32200 SDCo 92003 1048-H7
AQUILLA DR
10100 SDCo 92040 1231-F3
AQUILLA PL
10300 SDCo 92040 1231-F2
ARA PL
8500 SD 92126 1209-C2
ARABELLA WY
200 OCN 92057 1086-H3
ARABIAN TR
2400 SDCo 92028 1047-G2
ARABIAN WY
1600 OCN 92057 1067-E7
12500 PWY 92064 1190-C6
ARABIAN RANCH LN
2600 SDCo 92084 1087-H1
2600 SDCo 92084 1067-H7
ARABIAN RANCH WY
500 SDCo 92084 1087-H1
ARAGON DR
3600 SD 92115 1270-D3
ARAGON WY
4300 SD 92115 1270-D4
ARANDA AV
6600 SD 92037 1247-F1
ARAPAHO ST
9700 SDCo 91977 1291-D3
ARAWAK CT
17700 SD 92127 1169-H1
ARBALEST DR
300 SDCo 92004 1058-G7
ARBODAR RD
2800 SD 92154 1350-D3
ARBOL LN
15700 SDCo 92065 1172-A4
ARBOLEDA RD
800 SDCo 92021 1251-G1
ARBOLEDA VISTA DR
12500 SDCo 92082 1070-A4
ARBOLES CT
4100 SDCo 92028 1028-G7
ARBOLES PL
2000 ESCN 92029 1129-F6
ARBOLES ST
5800 SD 92120 1250-C7
ARBOLITA LN
- SDCo 92028 1027-H6
ARBOLITOS CT
14200 PWY 92064 1190-D2
ARBOLITOS DR
14000 PWY 92064 1190-D3
ARBOR CT
1400 ENCT 92024 1147-B3
ARBOR DR
300 SD 92103 1268-H5
E ARBOR DR
100 SD 92103 1269-A5
W ARBOR DR
100 SD 92103 1269-A5
ARBOR LN
1000 SMCS 92069 1109-B7
ARBOR COVE CIR
4300 OCN 92054 1066-G7
ARBORCREEK LN
600 CHV 91902 1311-C4
ARBORETUM PL
10600 SD 92131 1209-G5
ARBOR GROVE CT
5600 SD 92121 1208-F4
ARBOR HEIGHTS LN
10600 SD 92121 1208-E4
ARBORLAKE WY
11800 SD 92131 1210-A3
ARBOR PARK PL
10500 SD 92131 1209-H4
ARBORSIDE WY
11200 SD 92131 1210-B2
ARBOR VITAE DR
4100 SD 92105 1269-H7
ARBORVITAE LN
2200 SDCo 91977 1271-H7
ARBORWOOD PL
2000 ESCN 92029 1129-E6
ARBUCKLE PL
700 CRLB 92008 1106-E5
ARBUSTO CT
7900 CRLB 92009 1147-G3
ARBUSTO CTE
1100 CHV 91910 1311-C2
ARBUTUS ST
3800 SD 92121 1208-C6
ARCADIA AV
600 NATC 91950 1290-B7
800 VSTA 92084 1087-J3
1000 VSTA 92084 1088-A3
2400 LMGR 91945 1270-G7
ARCADIA DR
4300 SD 92103 1268-J4
ARCADIA PL
800 NATC 91950 1290-B7
ARCADIA RD
1000 ENCT 92024 1167-D1
ARCADIA WY
5300 OCN 92056 1107-E5
ARCANGE WY
- SD 92130 1208-A2
ARCARO LN
300 SOLB 92075 1187-F2
ARCATA BAY WY
4200 OCN 92054 1066-G7
ARCE CT
4300 SD 92154 1330-G7
ARCH ST
4400 SD 92116 1269-B4
ARCHER RD
- SMCS 92078 1128-D6
ARCHER ST
200 OCN 92054 1086-B6
700 SD 92109 1247-H4
1700 SD 92109 1248-A3
ARCHIE MOORE RD
16400 SDCo 92065 1171-F1
17400 SDCo 92065 1151-F7
ARCHIE MOORE TR
17400 SDCo 92065 1151-F7

ARCHIE MOORE TR
17400 SDCo 92065 1171-F1
ARCHIE MOORE RING
- SDCo 92065 1171-F2
ARCHSTONE PL
- SD 92131 1209-G1
ARCHWOOD AV
6600 SD 92120 1249-J6
ARCHWOOD PL
1400 ESCN 92026 1109-H7
ARCO DR
3600 SDCo 92026 1109-H1
ARCOLA AV
2700 SD 92117 1248-B2
ARCTURUS WY
8700 SD 92126 1209-D2
ARDATH AV
2000 ESCN 92027 1130-D1
ARDATH CT
2500 SD 92037 1227-J6
ARDATH LN
7800 SD 92037 1227-H6
ARDATH RD
2400 SD 92037 1227-H6
2700 SD 92037 1228-A7
ARDEN DR
400 ENCT 92024 1147-C7
600 ENCT 92024 1167-C1
ARDEN WY
1400 SDCo 92028 1027-J4
4100 SD 92103 1268-G5
ARDILLA PL
1000 CHV 91910 1310-J5
ARDISIA CT
17800 SD 92127 1149-J7
17800 SD 92127 1169-J1
ARDMORE CT
7000 SD 92111 1248-J3
ARDMORE DR
3900 SD 92111 1248-J3
ARDYS PL
200 VSTA 92084 1087-H5
ARENA CIR
1000 VSTA 92083 1087-G4
ARENA DR
15900 SDCo 92065 1173-E2
ARENA PL
16200 SDCo 92065 1173-D3
ARENA WY
23700 SDCo 92065 1173-D1
ARENAL LN
7100 CRLB 92009 1127-F7
7200 CRLB 92009 1147-F1
ARENAL RD
1800 CRLB 92009 1127-E7
ARENAS AV
400 SD 92037 1247-E1
ARENAS ST
500 SD 92037 1247-E1
ARENDO DR
4400 SD 92115 1270-D4
AREQUIPA ST
1500 SD 92154 1349-J2
ARES WY
2900 SD 92139 1310-E2
AREY DR
3400 SD 92154 1330-F7
ARGA PL
600 CHV 91910 1310-H6
ARGENT ST
8600 SNTE 92071 1231-C7
ARGO CT
8700 SD 92123 1249-C7
ARGONAUTA ST
2600 CRLB 92009 1127-H6
ARGONAUTA WY
7100 CRLB 92009 1127-H6
ARGONNE CT
5000 SD 92117 1228-D7
ARGONNE ST
- SD 92140 1268-F6
3400 SD 92117 1228-D7
ARGOS DR
4300 SD 92116 1269-H3
ARGOSY LN
4700 CRLB 92008 1106-H7
ARGUELLO ST
4200 SD 92103 1268-G5
ARGUS WY
200 OCN 92057 1087-A1
ARGYLE ST
3400 SD 92111 1249-A3
ARIA AV
500 SDCo 92026 1109-H2
ARIANA LN
3100 SDCo 91978 1292-C1
ARIANE DR
2700 SD 92117 1248-B2
ARIANE WY
4500 SD 92117 1248-C2
ARIEL PL
- ESCN 92027 1130-F1
ARIES CT
1400 CHV 91911 1330-G3
ARIES GN
3700 ESCN 92025 1150-C3
ARIES RD
8300 SD 92126 1209-C2
ARIKARA DR
13300 PWY 92064 1190-E4
ARILLO ST
7000 SD 92111 1248-J4
7200 SD 92111 1249-A4
ARINJADE WY
- SD 92114 1290-E4
ARIRANG LN
11300 SDCo 92026 1089-H7
ARISTA CT
2400 SD 92103 1268-G4
ARISTA DR
4300 SD 92103 1268-G4
ARISTA ST
3800 SD 92110 1268-F5
4100 SD 92103 1268-G4
4400 SD 92108 1268-G4
ARISTA WY
3900 OCN 92054 1086-G1
ARISTOCRAT CT
10600 SNTE 92071 1231-E2
ARISTOTLE DR
2700 SD 92139 1310-F1
ARISTOTLE GN
1200 ESCN 92026 1109-J7
ARIZONA AV
5300 LMSA 91942 1270-E1
ARIZONA ST
400 CHV 91911 1330-B2
3400 SD 92104 1269-D5
4300 SD 92116 1269-D3

ARJO LN
23000 SDCo 92065 409-H11
ARJONS DR
7900 SD 92126 1209-B6
ARJUNA CT
300 ENCT 92024 1147-H6
ARKLOW PL
1500 SD 92154 1349-J2
ARLAND RD
2700 CRLB 92008 1106-F4
ARLENE CT
5100 SD 92117 1228-G7
ARLENE PL
5100 SD 92117 1228-G7
ARLENE ST
4800 SD 92117 1228-G7
ARLENE WY
1500 SDCo 92065 1152-F7
ARLETTE ST
8100 SNTE 92071 1230-H7
ARLINGDALE WY
8900 SDCo 91977 1271-A7
ARLINGTON DR
300 OCN 92057 1086-J4
ARLINGTON PL
- SDCo 92003 1048-B7
1300 ELCJ 92021 1251-J2
ARLINGTON ST
3600 SD 92117 1228-D7
ARLISS CT
1500 SD 92154 1350-E2
ARLY CT
7900 SNTE 92071 1230-H7
ARMACOST RD
900 SD 92114 1290-G2
ARMADA DR
5300 CRLB 92008 1126-H2
ARMADA PL
700 SD 92106 1288-A3
ARMADA TER
700 SD 92106 1288-A3
ARMADALE RD
1700 SDCo 92028 1027-H6
ARMAGOSA WY
3200 SDCo 91935 1293-B1
3300 SDCo 91935 1273-B7
ARMENTROUT LN
2400 SDCo 91901 1234-B4
ARMERO CT
11000 SD 92127 1169-H1
ARMIN WY
4900 SD 92115 1269-J2
4900 SD 92115 1270-A2
ARMINDA CIR
8600 SNTE 92071 1230-J7
8600 SNTE 92071 1231-A7
ARMITAGE ST
3600 SD 92117 1228-D7
ARMORLITE DR
900 SMCS 92069 1108-E7
ARMORSS ST
8800 SD 92123 1249-C6
ARMOUR ST
7600 SD 92111 1249-A2
ARMS LAKE AV
6300 SD 92119 1250-J5
6300 SD 92119 1251-A5
ARMSTRONG CIR
1200 ESCN 92026 1110-A7
1200 ESCN 92027 1110-A7
ARMSTRONG PL
7400 SD 92111 1249-A5
ARMSTRONG ST
2900 SD 92111 1248-J5
2900 SD 92111 1249-A3
ARMSTRONG RANCH RD
- SDCo 92082 1091-C4
ARNAZ WY
9200 SNTE 92071 1231-A5
ARNEL AV
300 VSTA 92083 1087-G5
ARNELE AV
700 ELCJ 92020 1251-E4
ARNHEIM CT
1500 ELCJ 92021 1252-B2
ARNIES AL
3000 OCN 92056 1106-G2
ARNO DR
6100 SD 92120 1270-C1
6100 SD 92120 1250-C7
ARNOLD AV
3300 SD 92101 1269-D6
3400 SD 92104 1269-D6
ARNOLD RD
- ImCo 92283 432-C5
ARNOLD WY
100 SDCo 91901 1233-F4
1700 SDCo 91901 1234-A6
ARNOLDO RD
1400 SDCo 91917 (1314-C6 See Page 1294)
ARNOLDSON AV
2600 SD 92122 1228-B5
ARNOLDSON CT
6100 SD 92122 1228-B6
ARNOLDSON PL
6100 SD 92122 1228-B5
ARNOTT ST
2500 SD 92110 1248-F7
AROSA ST
6000 SD 92115 1270-C3
ARPEGE RD
7200 SD 92119 1250-E4
ARRAN AV
100 SDCo 91977 1291-A5
ARRAPAHOE PL
34600 SDCo 92036 1176-D4
ARRECIFE WY
4300 SD 92154 1330-G7
ARRIBA AVD
900 IMPB 91932 1349-G2
ARRIBA ST
3700 SD 92122 1228-B4
ARRIBA LINDA AV
- SDCo 92127 1169-F3
E ARRIETA CIR
4100 LMSA 91941 1270-J4
W ARRIETA CIR
4100 LMSA 91941 1270-H4
ARROW CT
2000 SDCo 92019 1272-C4
ARROW GN
500 ESCN 92027 1130-B2
ARROWGRASS WY
3200 SD 92115 1270-D6
ARROWHEAD
14100 SDCo 92040 1232-F4
ARROWHEAD CT
2400 CHV 91915 1311-H6

ARROWHEAD CT
4600 OCN 92056 1087-C3
8800 SNTE 92071 1230-J5
8800 SNTE 92071 1231-A5
ARROW PT CT
600 CHV 91911 1330-J4
ARROW ROCK AV
10200 SD 92126 1209-C5
ARROWWOOD DR
100 SD 92114 1290-H4
ARROW WOOD LN
1500 VSTA 92084 1088-B5
ARROYO AV
1900 OCN 92056 1087-C5
ARROYO CT
700 CHV 91910 1310-H7
ARROYO DR
300 ENCT 92024 1147-C6
600 SD 92103 1288-J1
900 CHV 91910 1310-H7
1000 CHV 91910 1330-H1
1600 SDCo 92028 1028-F4
3000 SD 92103 1268-J7
3000 SD 92103 1269-A7
ARROYO GN
1700 ESCN 92026 1109-D5
ARROYO PL
800 CHV 91910 1310-H7
ARROYO RD
3400 SDCo 91902 1291-B7
3400 SDCo 91902 1311-B1
ARROYO CANYON RD
2500 SDCo 92025 1130-D7
ARROYO DE VIEJAS
3800 SDCo 91901 1254-D2
ARROYO LINDO AV
4900 SD 92117 1228-C7
ARROYO PACIFICA
700 SDCo 92028 1028-C3
ARROYO ROSITA
14800 SD 92014 1188-B1
14800 SDCo 92014 1188-B1
ARROYO SECO CT
400 SD 92114 1290-E5
ARROYO SECO DR
400 SD 92114 1290-E5
ARROYO SECO WY
6700 SD 92114 1290-E5
ARROYO SORRENTO PL
3800 SD 92130 1208-B2
ARROYO SORRENTO RD
3100 SD 92130 1208-A2
ARROYO VISTA
500 SDCo 92028 1027-H3
3100 CRLB 92009 1127-J7
ARROYO VISTA RD
13200 PWY 92064 1170-E5
ARROYO VISTA WY
4200 OCN 92057 1086-J3
ARRUZA ST
3400 SD 92154 1350-E1
ART ST
4700 SD 92115 1270-D2
ARTEMIA WY
3000 SD 92139 1310-E2
ARTESIAN RD
6100 SDCo 92067 1168-G3
6100 SDCo 92127 1168-G3
7900 SD 92127 1169-C3
8000 SDCo 92127 1169-A3
ARTESIAN ST
5000 SD 92117 1228-G7
ARTESIAN TR
9000 SD 92127 1169-A4
9000 SDCo 92127 1169-A4
ARTESIAN SPRINGS CT
10400 SDCo 91977 1291-D1
ARTHUR AV
500 OCN 92057 1067-A5
600 CHV 91910 1310-E7
3300 SD 92116 1269-F2
ARTHUR NEAL CT
1400 LMGR 91945 1290-E2
ARUBA BEND
- CORD 92118 1329-E3
ARUBA CV
1200 CHV 91915 1311-F6
ARUBA RD
- SDCo 92059 999-F7
6400 SDCo 92028 999-C6
ARUCAUNA CT
7400 SD 92129 1188-J7
ARUCAUNA WY
12100 SD 92129 1188-J7
12100 SD 92129 1189-A7
ARUNDEL PL
6500 SD 92117 1248-J2
ARVERNE CT
6800 SD 92111 1248-J3
ARVERNE ST
3800 SD 92111 1248-J3
ARVILLA LN
1700 SDCo 92019 1252-B6
1700 ELCJ 92019 1252-B6
ARVIN CT
2100 SDCo 91977 1291-A1
ARVINELS AV
4900 SD 92117 1228-H7
ARVISO RD
- SDCo 92082 1071-E3
ARYANA DR
1700 ENCT 92024 1147-D2
ASBURY CT
700 SD 92109 1267-J4
ASCEND RD
- SDCo 92069 1108-G2
ASCOT DR
600 VSTA 92083 1087-F6
ASCOT ST
5800 SD 92115 1270-C5
ASH AV
200 CHV 91910 1310-A6
600 CHV 91910 1330-A1
800 CHV 91911 1330-A1
ASH LN
800 SMCS 92069 1108-J6
20200 SDCo 92029 1149-E1
ASH RD
- SDCo 92055 1085-J2
- SDCo 92055 1086-A4
ASH ST
100 SDCo 92028 1027-F3
100 SDCo 92065 1152-G3
100 OCN 92054 1106-A1
100 SD 92101 1289-E2
300 CHV 91910 1310-A6
500 SMCS 92069 1128-C1
600 SD 92101 1288-J2
2400 VSTA 92083 1108-B6

ASH ST
2800 SD 92102 1289-E2
3600 SD 92105 1289-G2
6100 SD 92114 1290-D4
N ASH ST
500 ESCN 92027 1130-A1
500 ESCN 92025 1130-A1
800 ESCN 92027 1110-A7
900 ESCN 92026 1110-A7
1100 ESCN 92026 1109-J6
1200 ESCN 92026 1109-H5
1700 SDCo 92026 1109-H5
N ASH ST Rt#-78
400 ESCN 92027 1130-A1
400 ESCN 92025 1130-A1
S ASH ST
300 ESCN 92025 1130-B2
S ASH ST Rt#-78
100 ESCN 92025 1130-A1
100 ESCN 92027 1130-A1
W ASH ST
100 SD 92101 1289-A2
500 SD 92101 1288-J2
ASHBERRY RD
- CRLB 92008 1107-A7
ASHBROOK DR
700 CHV 91913 1311-D4
ASHBURN RD
3000 SD 92106 1308-A1
ASHBURTON RD
17500 SD 92128 1170-A1
ASHBURY ST
100 ENCT 92024 1147-A2
ASHBY CT
3600 CRLB 92008 1107-A3
ASHBY ST
4600 SD 92115 1270-B3
ASH CREEK PL
11400 SD 92131 1209-J1
ASHDALE LN
10000 SNTE 92071 1231-D3
ASHER ST
4100 SD 92110 1268-E1
ASHFORD CT
7500 SD 92111 1249-A5
ASHFORD GN
2400 ESCN 92027 1110-D6
ASHFORD PL
7400 SD 92111 1249-A5
ASHFORD ST
3200 SD 92111 1249-A3
ASHFORD CASTLE DR
1300 CHV 91915 1311-H7
ASHFOURTH LN
300 CHV 91911 1330-C2
ASHGATE PL
13000 PWY 92064 1190-F5
ASH HOLLOW CROSSING RD
13100 PWY 92064 1170-F2
ASHLAND AV
5600 SD 92120 1270-D1
5600 SD 92120 1250-D7
ASHLAR PL
10800 SD 92131 1209-J2
ASHLEY CT
30900 SDCo 92082 1070-G2
ASHLEY LN
- VSTA 92084 1088-C5
ASHLEY PL
11900 SD 92128 1190-B7
ASHLEY RD
1100 SDCo 92065 1152-H7
1300 SDCo 92065 1172-H1
ASHLEY FALLS CT
5000 SD 92130 1188-D5
ASHLEY FALLS DR
12600 SD 92130 1188-C6
ASHLEY PARK DR
3300 SDCo 91935 1272-E5
ASHLEY PARK WY
3100 SDCo 91935 1272-E5
ASHLOCK LN
- SD 92131 1209-G1
ASHLOCK WY
- SD 92131 1209-G1
ASHMORE AV
8600 SD 92114 1290-H3
8800 SDCo 91977 1290-H3
ASHMORE LN
700 SD 92114 1290-H3
ASHTON CT
900 VSTA 92083 1108-A4
ASHTON ST
4100 SD 92110 1268-E1
ASHWOOD CT
3400 OCN 92054 1086-E2
ASHWOOD ST
10100 SDCo 92040 1232-B2
ASILADO ST
200 OCN 92057 1066-J7
ASKEW WY
- SDCo 92065 1152-E6
ASOLEAR PL
18600 SD 92128 1150-D6
ASPEN CT
2000 SMCS 92069 1128-A2
3300 SD 92037 1228-B4
6800 CRLB 92009 1127-A5
12700 PWY 92064 1190-C1
ASPEN DR
- SDCo 92028 998-D4
ASPEN LN
1900 SDCo 92019 1272-C4
ASPEN RD
3400 SDCo 92028 998-E3
ASPEN ST
- SMCS 92078 1129-C2
3400 OCN 92054 1086-E2
ASPEN WY
- SDCo 92040 1232-D6
300 ESCN 92026 1109-H7
1300 VSTA 92083 1127-H1
ASPENDELL DR
- SD 92131 1209-F1
ASPENDELL WY
- SD 92131 1209-F2
ASPEN GLOW DR
1700 ENCT 92024 1147-H5
ASPEN VIEW CT
- SD 92128 1190-A7
ASPEN VIEW DR
- SD 92128 1190-A7
ASPENWOOD LN
- ENCT 92024 1147-H6
ASPERO CT
1500 ESCN 92026 1109-H5
ASPIN CT
800 SD 92109 1267-J4

ASTER AV
800 ELCJ 92020 1251-E7
ASTER DR
2500 SDCo 91906 (1297-E5 See Page 1296)
ASTER PL
7000 CRLB 92009 1127-E6
ASTER ST
- SDCo 92055 1086-A4
2400 SD 92109 1248-B4
N ASTER ST
500 ESCN 92027 1110-B7
ASTERWOOD LN
- SDCo 92083 1108-B6
- VSTA 92083 1108-B6
ASTI WY
5800 LMSA 91942 1251-B7
ASTON AV
1800 CRLB 92008 1127-C2
ASTOR DR
- SD 92109 1248-C6
ASTORGA PL
600 SMCS 92069 1109-C6
ASTORIA ST
7000 SD 92111 1248-J4
7100 SD 92111 1249-A4
ASTRA WY
4400 SDCo 91941 1271-F3
ASTRO CT
200 VSTA 92083 1087-H7
ATADERO CT
2800 CRLB 92009 1147-G3
ATARI CT
3200 SD 92117 1248-D3
ATASCADERO DR
3800 SD 92107 1268-A7
ATEN RD
- ImCo 92243 6500-B1
100 ImCo 92251 6499-A2
100 ImCo 92251 6500-B1
200 IMP 92251 6499-E2
400 IMP 92243 6499-E2
800 ImCo 92251 431-A5
800 ImCo 92243 431-A5
800 ImCo 92243 6499-A2
ATEX CT
23600 SDCo 92065 1173-D5
ATHENA ST
100 ENCT 92024 1147-B5
ATHENS AV
2700 CRLB 92008 1106-J4
ATHENS PL
1300 ESCN 92026 1109-E4
ATHENS ST
4300 SD 92115 1270-C4
ATHERTON AV
1900 SD 92154 1350-B3
ATHERTON PL
1400 CHV 91913 1331-C1
ATHEY AV
300 SD 92173 1350-E2
ATHOS WY
4700 OCN 92056 1107-E5
ATLANTA DR
4700 SD 92115 1270-A3
ATLANTIC ST
1400 SMCS 92069 1108-E6
ATLANTIS ST
9100 SDCo 91977 1271-B7
9100 SDCo 91977 1291-B1
ATLAS ST
3100 SD 92111 1249-A5
ATLAS VIEW CT
9400 SNTE 92071 1251-C1
ATLAS VIEW DR
8500 SNTE 92071 1251-B1
8500 SNTE 92071 1231-B7
ATOKA PL
13600 PWY 92064 1190-E3
ATOLL ST
3400 SD 92111 1248-J4
ATOSANA DR
32100 SDCo 92061 1051-B6
ATRIUM DR
10400 SD 92131 1209-G5
ATTEBURY DR
300 SDCo 92078 1128-G6
400 SMCS 92029 1128-H5
400 SMCS 92078 1128-H5
700 SDCo 92029 1128-H5
700 SDCo 92029 1129-A4
ATTERIDGE RD
20100 SDCo 92065 1153-G1
ATTISHA WY
14200 SDCo 92040 1232-G5
ATTIX ST
1700 SD 92114 1290-E1
ATTLEBOROUGH CT
7000 SD 92139 1290-G7
ATTU AV
- CORD 92118 1309-D6
ATTU RD
3300 CORD 92155 1309-A2
ATWATER ST
1100 SD 92154 1349-J1
1200 CHV 91913 1311-C7
ATWELL ST
4400 SD 92117 1248-B2
ATWOOD CT
10600 SD 92131 1209-G1
ATWOOD PL
- SMCS 92069 1108-J4
AUBERGINE CT
- OCN 92056 1087-D2
AUBERT WY
9000 SNTE 92071 1231-G6
AUBREE ROSE LN
5200 SDCo 91941 1271-D1
AUBREY ST
13200 PWY 92064 1190-E2
AUBURN AV
400 SMCS 92069 1108-J6
700 CHV 91913 1311-C5
2700 CRLB 92008 1106-J4
4100 OCN 92056 1087-C5
AUBURN DR
4700 SD 92105 1269-J5
4700 SD 92105 1270-A6
AUBURN GN
100 ESCN 92027 1110-E7
AUBURNDALE ST
3500 SD 92111 1248-J4
AUDEN PL
- CRLB 92008 1107-A7
AUDISH CT
- SDCo 91941 1271-H4
- SDCo 92019 1271-H4
AUDREY CT
- SDCo 92028 1028-A3

STREET Block City ZIP Pg-Grid

AUDREY LN
3400 SD 92115 1270-C5
AUDREY WY
800 SDCo 92019 1252-C4
AUDUBON CT
3600 SDCo 91902 1310-J1
AUDUBON GN
2000 ESCN 92027 1110-A5
AUDUBON RD
9400 SDCo 92040 1232-E5
AUGUST CT
2200 SD 92110 1268-G1
AUGUST ST
5000 SD 92110 1268-G1
AUGUSTA CT
1700 SDCo 92019 1272-B5
AUGUSTA DR
500 SMCS 92069 1109-D7
4400 OCN 92057 1066-G7
AUGUSTA PL
1000 CHV 91915 1311-G5
AUGUSTANA PL
5200 SD 92115 1270-A3
AUGUSTINA PL
600 CHV 91910 1311-A5
AUKLET WY
4300 OCN 92057 1086-J3
4300 OCN 92057 1087-A3
AURA CIR
2000 CRLB 92008 1106-J7
AURALIE DR
2600 SDCo 92025 1130-B7
AURORA CT
- ELCN 92243 6559-E1
AURORA DR
200 ELCN 92243 6560-A1
200 ELCN 92243 6559-F1
13000 SDCo 92021 1252-C1
13100 SDCo 92021 1232-C7
AURORA GN
2600 ESCN 92027 1110-E7
AURORA ST
400 SD 92102 1289-J3
AURORA VISTA DR
3100 SDCo 91978 1272-C7
3100 SDCo 91978 1292-C1
AUSTERLITZ PL
11900 SD 92128 1170-A1
AUSTIN AV
7500 SD 92145 1229-F2
AUSTIN CT
1300 VSTA 92083 1087-E7
1500 CHV 91902 1311-C4
1500 CHV 91913 1311-C4
AUSTIN DR
4700 SD 92115 1270-A3
9700 SDCo 91977 1271-C7
10200 SDCo 91978 1271-E7
AUSTIN RD
- ImCo 92251 6499-C2
1100 ImCo 92243 6559-D1
1800 ImCo 92243 6499-C2
2300 IMP 92243 6499-C2
3600 ImCo 92227 431-B3
AUSTIN TER
- CRLB 92008 1106-G3
AUSTIN WY
- SDCo 92036 1136-C7
1400 ESCN 92027 1130-D2
AUSTRALIA ST
1100 ELCJ 92020 1251-C4
AUTILLO WY
10800 SD 92127 1169-H1
AUTO CIR
4900 SD 92108 1269-B3
AUTO CENTER CT
1000 CRLB 92008 1126-H2
AUTOCROSS CT
1900 SDCo 92019 1272-C3
AUTO PARK DR
500 CHV 91911 1330-H5
AUTO PARK WY
1100 ESCN 92029 1129-F4
AUTO PARK WY N
1500 ESCN 92029 1129-F3
AUTO PARK WY S
1500 ESCN 92029 1129-E3
AUTOPORT MALL
5700 SD 92121 1228-G2
AUTUMN DR
200 SMCS 92069 1108-G7
2200 OCN 92056 1087-D5
AUTUMN LN
- VSTA 92084 1088-A2
AUTUMN PL
1800 ENCT 92024 1147-H5
AUTUMN BREEZE LN
- SDCo 92084 1068-D5
AUTUMN LEAF DR
900 SDCo 92028 1027-G4
AUTUMNVIEW LN
10100 SDCo 92126 1209-D5
AUTUMNWOODS PL
1400 ESCN 92029 1129-F6
AVA LN
14200 SDCo 92082 1070-F4
AVA PL
5800 SD 92114 1290-C6
AVA ST
1300 SD 92114 1290-C6
AVA LOMA RD
3100 SDCo 91935 1273-D7
3100 SDCo 91935 1293-D1
AVALON AV
2700 CRLB 92008 1106-J4
2700 CRLB 92008 1107-A4
AVALON CT
700 SD 92109 1267-H4
AVALON DR
100 VSTA 92084 1087-J6
4300 SD 92103 1268-J4
AVALON BAY PL
300 OCN 92057 1066-J6
AVANTI AV
10200 SNTE 92071 1231-E2
AVATI DR
4000 SD 92117 1248-C3
AVELEY PL
3400 SD 92111 1248-H4
AVENA PL
11600 SD 92128 1170-A3
AVENEL LN
15900 SDCo 92065 1173-H4
AVENGER CT
9800 SD 92126 1209-F2
AVENGER RD
11300 SD 92126 1209-F2
AVENIDA ABAJO
400 ELCJ 92020 1271-G1

AVENIDA ABEJA
- SD 92127 1169-H5
400 SMCS 92069 1108-E4
AVENIDA ABRIL
- SDCo 92026 1109-G7
12400 SDCo 92021 1252-B1
AVENIDA ACERO
9400 SDCo 91977 1291-C4
AVENIDA ADOBE
400 ESCN 92029 1149-J3
400 ESCN 92029 1150-A3
AVENIDA AGUILA
500 SMCS 92069 1108-E5
AVENIDA ALAMAR
7900 SD 92037 1227-G5
AVENIDA ALCACHOFA
15400 SD 92128 1170-B5
AVENIDA ALCOR
3100 CRLB 92009 1127-J7
AVENIDA ALMADA
1600 OCN 92056 1087-C3
AVENIDA ALONDRA
17900 SDCo 92067 1168-B1
AVENIDA ALOZDRA
17800 SD 92128 1150-D7
AVENIDA ALTA MIRA
1700 OCN 92056 1087-C4
AVENIDA ALTERAS
6000 SDCo 92067 1168-H5
AVENIDA AMANTEA
1000 SD 92037 1247-G3
AVENIDA AMATISTA
17800 SDCo 92067 1148-J7
AVENIDA AMIGO
700 SMCS 92069 1108-E4
AVENIDA AMISTAD
- SMCS 92069 1108-F4
AVENIDA AMOROSA
3500 ESCN 92029 1150-A3
AVENIDA ANACAPA
3200 CRLB 92009 1147-J3
11600 SDCo 92019 1272-A4
AVENIDA ANDANTE
1500 OCN 92056 1087-C4
AVENIDA ANDORRA
1500 OCN 92056 1087-C4
6600 SD 92037 1247-H1
AVENIDA ANGULIA
8400 SDCo 91977 1290-J5
AVENIDA ANNALIE
12600 SDCo 92082 1070-B3
AVENIDA APOLINARIA
11500 SDCo 92019 1272-A4
11500 SDCo 92019 1271-J4
AVENIDA ARAGON
1800 OCN 92056 1087-B5
AVENIDA ARANA
400 SMCS 92069 1108-F4
AVENIDA ARRIBA
1400 ELCJ 92020 1271-G1
AVENIDA ARROYO PASAJERO
16700 SDCo 92067 1168-F5
AVENIDA AVEIRO
16000 SD 92128 1170-C5
AVENIDA AZUL
1300 SMCS 92069 1108-E5
AVENIDA BENJAMIN
10900 SDCo 91941 1271-G4
AVENIDA BIZARRO
6600 SD 92037 1247-F2
AVENIDA BLANCO
500 SMCS 92069 1108-E5
AVENIDA BOSQUES
2100 SDCo 91977 1271-E7
AVENIDA BRISA
3800 SDCo 92091 1168-C7
3800 SDCo 92091 1188-C1
AVENIDA BUENA VENTURA
100 SCLE 92672 1023-B1
AVENIDA CALAFIA
4500 OCN 92057 1087-A2
AVENIDA CALMA
15900 SDCo 92091 1168-C7
15900 SDCo 92091 1188-C1
AVENIDA CAMPANA
900 SDCo 92028 1027-G3
AVENIDA CANORA
400 OCN 92057 1087-A4
2400 SDCo 91901 1254-C1
AVENIDA CANTANTE
6900 SDCo 92067 1188-H1
AVENIDA CANTARIA
5100 SD 92130 1188-D3
AVENIDA CARMELO
100 SCLE 92672 1023-B1
AVENIDA CASTANA
2800 CRLB 92009 1147-H2
AVENIDA CATHERINA
10700 SDCo 91978 1271-G6
AVENIDA CEREZA
2800 CRLB 92009 1147-G2
AVENIDA CHAMNEZ
5900 SD 92037 1247-G2
AVENIDA CHAPALA
100 SMCS 92069 1109-C7
100 SMCS 92069 1129-C1
AVENIDA CHELSEA
2400 VSTA 92083 1107-J7
AVENIDA CHERYLITA
1700 ELCJ 92020 1271-G2
AVENIDA CHRISTINA
3100 CRLB 92009 1127-J4
AVENIDA CIELO
600 SMCS 92069 1128-A2
AVENIDA CIRCO
5700 SD 92124 1229-G7
AVENIDA CIRUELA
2900 CRLB 92009 1147-H3
AVENIDA CODORNIZ
700 SMCS 92069 1108-F4
AVENIDA COLINO
9700 SDCo 91977 1291-D3
AVENIDA CONSENTIDO
11900 SD 92128 1170-B4
AVENIDA CORDILLERA
17800 SD 92128 1150-D6
AVENIDA CORDOBA
700 SMCS 92069 1108-E5
AVENIDA CORTEZ
200 SD 92037 1247-E3
AVENIDA COSTA AZUL
2000 SD 92154 1351-H2
AVENIDA COSTA BLANCA
8600 SD 92154 1351-H3
AVENIDA COSTA BRAVA
2300 SD 92154 1351-H3

AVENIDA COSTA DEL SOL
2200 SD 92154 1351-G3
AVENIDA COSTA ESTE
2200 SD 92154 1351-H3
AVENIDA COSTA NORTE
8500 SD 92154 1351-H3
AVENIDA COSTA SUR
8500 SD 92154 1351-H3
AVENIDA CRESTA
6000 SD 92037 1247-E2
AVENIDA CUATRO VIENTOS
6000 SDCo 92067 1168-H4
AVENIDA CUESTA DEL SOL
16400 SDCo 92067 1168-F6
AVENIDA CUESTA LOS OSOS
6000 SDCo 92067 1168-E6
AVENIDA DE ACACIAS
16900 SDCo 92067 1168-D2
AVENIDA DE ANITA
2700 CRLB 92008 1106-H3
AVENIDA DE AQUACATE
2000 ESCN 92026 1109-E4
AVENIDA DE BENITO JUAREZ
500 VSTA 92083 1087-G5
AVENIDA DE CONTENTA
17500 SDCo 92067 1168-J1
AVENIDA DE ESPUELA
12600 PWY 92064 1170-C6
AVENIDA DE LA BARCA
700 CHV 91910 1311-A5
AVENIDA DE LA CANTINA
10200 SD 92129 1189-G4
AVENIDA DE LA CRUZ
1800 SD 92173 1350-F3
AVENIDA DE LA FUENTE
8400 SD 92154 1351-H3
AVENIDA DE LA FUENTE NORTE
1500 SD 92154 1351-J3
AVENIDA DE LA FUENTE SUR
2300 SD 92154 1351-J3
AVENIDA DE LA LUNA
13800 SDCo 91935 1272-H7
AVENIDA DE LA MADRE
2900 SDCo 92028 1028-C3
AVENIDA DE LA MADRID
100 SD 92173 1350-G3
AVENIDA DE LAMAR
3000 SDCo 91977 1271-B6
AVENIDA DE LA PLATA
4000 OCN 92056 1087-C4
4900 OCN 92057 1087-C2
AVENIDA DE LA PLAYA
- ESCN 92026 1109-G7
2000 SD 92037 1227-H5
AVENIDA DE LA PLAZA
200 VSTA 92083 1087-G5
AVENIDA DE LA RIBERA
2100 SD 92037 1227-H5
AVENIDA DE LA RONDA
6800 SDCo 92067 1168-F7
AVENIDA DE LAS ADELSAS
1400 ENCT 92024 1167-G1
AVENIDA DE LAS ARENAS
1800 CORD 92118 1308-J2
AVENIDA DE LAS ESTRELLAS
32300 SDCo 92061 1051-D5
AVENIDA DE LAS FLORES
3300 SMCS 92069 1128-B1
AVENIDA DE LAS LILAS
200 ENCT 92024 1147-G7
AVENIDA DE LAS ONDAS
8400 SD 92037 1227-H4
AVENIDA DE LAS PALMERAS
200 SCLE 92672 1023-B1
AVENIDA DE LAS PESCAS
6600 SD 92037 1247-G1
AVENIDA DE LAS ROSAS
300 ENCT 92024 1147-G7
300 ENCT 92024 1167-G1
500 SMCS 92069 1128-B1
AVENIDA DE LAS TIENDAS
- SD 92108 1268-J3
AVENIDA DE LAS VISTAS
- SD 92154 1331-B7
AVENIDA DEL CHARRO
13500 SDCo 92021 1232-E6
AVENIDA DEL CIELO
2100 SDCo 91901 1253-G1
AVENIDA DEL DIABLO
1800 ESCN 92029 1129-F5
2300 SDCo 92029 1129-F5
AVENIDA DEL DUQUE
6200 SDCo 92067 1148-E6
AVENIDA DEL FRESNO
800 SMCS 92069 1109-B5
AVENIDA DEL GADO
100 OCN 92057 1087-A2
AVENIDA DEL GATO
8200 SD 92126 1209-B1
AVENIDA DEL GENERAL
12900 SD 92129 1189-G5
AVENIDA DEL MAR
3300 SMCS 92069 1128-B2
AVENIDA DEL MEXICO
1900 SD 92154 1330-A7
AVENIDA DEL MUNDO
1700 CORD 92118 1308-J1
AVENIDA DEL NORTE
700 SMCS 92069 1109-B6
AVENIDA DEL OCEANO
- SDCo 92019 1252-C7
- SDCo 92019 1272-C1
AVENIDA DEL ORO
1800 OCN 92056 1087-B5
AVENIDA DE LOS ARBOLES
3300 SMCS 92069 1128-A2

AVENIDA DE LOS CLAVELES
200 ENCT 92024 1147-G7
AVENIDA DE LOS LIRIOS
100 ENCT 92024 1147-G7
AVENIDA DE LOS LOBOS
10800 SD 92127 1169-H5
AVENIDA DE LOS OLIVOS
16300 SDCo 92067 1168-F6
AVENIDA DE LOUISA
2800 CRLB 92008 1106-H3
AVENIDA DE LOYOLA
3300 OCN 92056 1086-H7
AVENIDA DEL PAISANO
32100 RivC 92592 999-E1
AVENIDA DEL PARAISO ST
6500 CRLB 92009 1127-G5
AVENIDA DEL PARQUE
3800 SDCo 92091 1168-B7
AVENIDA DEL PRESIDENTE
2900 SCLE 92672 1023-B1
3900 SDCo 92672 1023-B1
AVENIDA DEL REY
500 CHV 91910 1311-A4
AVENIDA DEL RIO
- SD 92108 1269-A3
AVENIDA DEL SOL
- ESCN 92026 1109-G7
700 SMCS 92069 1109-B5
1300 CORD 92118 1308-J1
1500 SDCo 92021 1251-G2
12400 SDCo 92021 1252-B1
AVENIDA DE MONACO
100 ENCT 92007 1167-D2
AVENIDA DE NOG
1500 SDCo 92028 1027-J6
AVENIDA DE ORO
3000 SDCo 91935 1292-H1
AVENIDA DE PALAIS
2400 CRLB 92009 1127-G7
AVENIDA DE POMPEII
16600 SDCo 92127 1168-H3
AVENIDA DE PORTUGAL
2800 SD 92106 1288-B2
AVENIDA DE ROBLES VERDES
39500 SDCo 91905 1300-C4
AVENIDA DE SAN CLEMENTE
500 ENCT 92024 1147-E7
AVENIDA DESCANSO
- OCN 92057 1086-H1
- OCN 92057 1066-H7
AVENIDA DE SUENO
- CRLB 92009 1147-J4
AVENIDA DE SUENOS
1700 OCN 92056 1087-C4
AVENIDA DE SUERTE
200 SMCS 92069 1108-D5
AVENIDA DIESTRO
7900 CRLB 92009 1148-A2
AVENIDA DOLORES
100 SCLE 92672 1023-B1
AVENIDA ELENA
100 SMCS 92069 1109-C7
AVENIDA ELISA
1200 SDCo 92019 1272-C1
AVENIDA EMPRESA
4500 OCN 92056 1087-C3
AVENIDA ENCINAS
- CRLB 92009 1146-J1
5000 CRLB 92008 1126-G3
5700 CRLB 92008 1126-H4
7100 CRLB 92009 1127-A7
AVENIDA ESPERANZA
100 ENCT 92024 1147-J7
100 ENCT 92024 1167-J1
AVENIDA ESTEBAN
1100 ENCT 92024 1147-H4
AVENIDA FELIZ
3700 SDCo 92091 1188-C1
AVENIDA FIESTA
5400 SD 92037 1248-B3
AVENIDA FLORENCIA
16200 PWY 92064 1170-D3
AVENIDA FLORES
1800 ENCT 92024 1147-H4
AVENIDA FLORESTA
6200 SDCo 92067 1168-F5
AVENIDA FRAGATA
- SMCS 92069 1108-F4
AVENIDA FRONTERA
1100 OCN 92057 1087-A4
AVENIDA GRANADA
13000 PWY 92064 1170-D3
AVENIDA GRANDE
13000 SD 92129 1189-G5
AVENIDA GREGORY
4200 SDCo 91977 1271-C3
AVENIDA GUILLERMO
1500 OCN 92056 1087-C4
AVENIDA HACIENDA
3100 ESCN 92029 1149-J3
3100 ESCN 92029 1150-A3
AVENIDA HELECHO
2800 CRLB 92009 1147-G2
AVENIDA INSURGENTES
14700 SDCo 92067 1188-H1
AVENIDA JINETE
32000 SDCo 92003 1048-B7
AVENIDA JOAQUIN
1900 ENCT 92024 1147-H5
AVENIDA JOHANNA
3700 SDCo 91941 1271-G4
AVENIDA JOSEFA
1800 ENCT 92024 1147-H5
AVENIDA KIRJAH
7800 SD 92037 1228-A6
AVENIDA LA BAHIA
8600 SD 92122 1228-D3
AVENIDA LA CIMA
2300 SDCo 92027 1130-E4
AVENIDA LA CUESTA
- SMCS 92078 1128-H2
AVENIDA LADERA
1500 ELCJ 92020 1251-C2
AVENIDA LAMEGO
15900 SD 92128 1170-C5
AVENIDA LA POSTA
1400 ENCT 92024 1147-H4
AVENIDA LA REINA
6600 SD 92037 1247-F1

AVENIDA LAS BRISAS
100 OCN 92057 1086-J2
AVENIDA LAS PERLAS
16400 SDCo 92067 1168-F7
AVENIDA LA VALENCIA
12700 PWY 92064 1170-D4
12700 SD 92128 1170-D4
AVENIDA LEON
900 SMCS 92069 1108-E4
AVENIDA LINDA
14000 PWY 92064 1190-G4
AVENIDA LOMA DE ORO
6200 SDCo 92067 1168-F5
AVENIDA LORENZO
4300 OCN 92057 1086-J2
AVENIDA LUCIA
100 SCLE 92672 1023-B1
AVENIDA LUIS
16900 SDCo 92067 1168-F3
AVENIDA LUNAR
1200 CORD 92118 1308-J2
AVENIDA MADERA
800 CHV 91910 1310-E7
800 CHV 91910 1330-E1
AVENIDA MAGNIFICA
2200 CRLB 92008 1106-G3
9900 SD 92131 1209-J4
9900 SD 92131 1210-A4
AVENIDA MAGORIA
3000 ESCN 92029 1149-J2
3000 ESCN 92029 1150-A2
AVENIDA MANANA
6400 SD 92037 1247-F2
AVENIDA MANESSA
4500 OCN 92057 1087-A4
AVENIDA MANTILLA
1500 OCN 92056 1087-B3
AVENIDA MARAVILLAS
4700 SDCo 92067 1168-B3
AVENIDA MARBELLA
12900 SD 92128 1150-D7
AVENIDA MARCELLA
11500 SDCo 92019 1271-J4
11900 SDCo 92019 1272-A4
AVENIDA MARCO
8600 SDCo 92021 1232-E6
AVENIDA MARGUARITA
200 OCN 92057 1087-A2
AVENIDA MARIA
11000 SD 92129 1169-H7
AVENIDA MARIPOSA
600 SMCS 92069 1128-B1
AVENIDA MELODIA
1600 ENCT 92024 1147-H4
AVENIDA MICHELLE
500 SMCS 92069 1128-B1
AVENIDA MIGUEL
1200 ENCT 92024 1147-H5
AVENIDA MIL FLORES
7900 SDCo 92003 1068-H4
AVENIDA MIMOSA
1800 ENCT 92024 1147-H5
AVENIDA MIRA VISTA
1700 OCN 92056 1087-C4
AVENIDA MIROLA
6600 SD 92037 1247-F1
AVENIDA MOLINO VIEJO
16600 SDCo 92067 1168-G7
AVENIDA MONTUOSA
14900 SD 92129 1169-H7
AVENIDA NARANJA
- SDCo 92065 1152-F3
AVENIDA NAVIDAD
7600 SD 92122 1228-D4
AVENIDA NIEVE
3300 CRLB 92009 1147-J3
AVENIDA NOBLEZA
16200 SD 92128 1170-A4
AVENIDA NORDESTE
- SDCo 92004 (1078-J2 See Page 1058)
AVENIDA OBERTURA
3300 CRLB 92009 1147-J3
AVENIDA OCEANO
1500 OCN 92056 1087-C4
AVENIDA OCOTILLO
2500 SDCo 91901 1253-J2
AVENIDA OFELITA
1300 SDCo 92019 1272-D1
AVENIDA OLMEDA
3100 CRLB 92009 1127-J5
3100 CRLB 92009 1128-A4
AVENIDA ORTEGA
- SMCS 92078 1128-H2
AVENIDA PALA
100 SCLE 92672 1023-B1
AVENIDA PALIZADA
14300 SD 92130 1188-D2
AVENIDA PALO VERDE
3700 SDCo 91902 1310-E4
AVENIDA PANTERA
- CRLB 92009 1148-A4
- SMCS 92069 1108-F4
AVENIDA PENASCO
2000 SDCo 92019 1252-C7
AVENIDA PEREGRINA
17300 SDCo 92067 1168-H1
AVENIDA PICACHO
6100 SDCo 92067 1168-G4
AVENIDA PIMENTERA
2900 CRLB 92009 1147-H3
AVENIDA PLAYA CANCUN
5000 SD 92124 1230-A7
AVENIDA PLAYA VERACRUZ
10700 SD 92124 1229-J7
10700 SD 92124 1249-J1
AVENIDA PRIMAVERA
400 DLMR 92014 1187-F4
AVENIDA PRIVADO
4500 OCN 92057 1087-A3
AVENIDA REAL
10200 SDCo 92040 1231-H3
AVENIDA REGINA
3000 SMCS 92069 1108-D4
AVENIDA REPOSO
3200 ESCN 92029 1149-J3
AVENIDA RICARDO
800 SMCS 92069 1129-D1
9700 SDCo 91977 1291-D3
AVENIDA ROBERTA
10700 SDCo 91978 1271-G6
AVENIDA ROCA GRANDE
- SDCo 92065 1171-H2
AVENIDA RONALDO
800 SDCo 91977 1291-D3

AVENIDA RORRAS
15100 SD 92128 1170-B6
AVENIDA ROSA
1400 CHV 91911 1330-D4
AVENIDA ROSHA
3000 SMCS 92069 1108-D5
AVENIDA SANCHEZ
5700 SD 92124 1229-H7
AVENIDA SAN DIEGO
100 SCLE 92672 1023-B1
AVENIDA SAN FERNANDO
100 SCLE 92672 1023-B1
AVENIDA SAN MIGUEL
3700 NATC 91902 1310-F2
3700 SDCo 91902 1310-F2
AVENIDA SANTA MARGARITA
100 SCLE 92672 1023-C1
AVENIDA SEGOVIA
1700 OCN 92056 1087-C5
AVENIDA SERENO
1300 ENCT 92024 1147-H4
AVENIDA SEVILLA
1700 OCN 92056 1087-C4
AVENIDA SIERRA
3300 ESCN 92029 1150-A3
AVENIDA SIVRITA
11500 SD 92128 1169-J6
11500 SD 92128 1170-A6
AVENIDA SOBRINA
1100 OCN 92057 1087-A3
AVENIDA SOLARIA
700 CHV 91910 1311-A5
AVENIDA SOLEDAD
4300 OCN 92057 1086-J2
AVENIDA SUAVIDAD
16200 SD 92128 1170-A4
AVENIDA SURESTE
700 SDCo 92004 (1078-J2 See Page 1058)
AVENIDA TAXCO
800 VSTA 92084 1088-C5
AVENIDA THERESA
2900 CRLB 92009 1147-H3
AVENIDA THOMAS
11200 SDCo 91941 1271-H4
AVENIDA TINEO
12500 SD 92128 1170-C4
AVENIDA TOPANGA
3100 CRLB 92009 1127-J5
3100 CRLB 92009 1128-A4
AVENIDA TORONJA
- CRLB 92009 1147-F2
AVENIDA VALERA
2700 CRLB 92009 1127-H7
2800 CRLB 92009 1147-H1
AVENIDA VENUSTO
15000 SD 92128 1170-A4
AVENIDA VERDE
- SDCo 92021 1252-B1
500 SMCS 92069 1108-E5
1500 SDCo 92021 1251-G2
AVENIDA VERDE N
- ESCN 92026 1109-G7
AVENIDA VERDE S
- ESCN 92026 1109-G7
AVENIDA VILLAHA
15700 SD 92128 1170-C5
AVENIDA VISTA LABERA
1700 OCN 92056 1087-C4
AVENIDA WILFREDO
6400 SD 92037 1247-F2
AVENIDA YSIDORA
800 CHV 91910 1311-B6
AVENORRA DR
6100 LMSA 91942 1250-G6
AVENUE A
10000 SDCo 91977 1291-D3
AVENUE B
9900 SDCo 91977 1291-D3
AVENUE C
9900 SDCo 91977 1291-D3
AVENUE D
9900 SDCo 91977 1291-D3
AVENUE E
9900 SDCo 91977 1291-D3
AVENUE F
9900 SDCo 91977 1291-D3
AVENUE G
9900 SDCo 91977 1291-D3
AVENUE OF INDUSTRY
11800 SD 92128 1170-A7
AVENUE OF SCIENCE
15000 SD 92128 1169-J6
15000 SD 92128 1170-A7
AVENUE OF THE TREES
2000 CRLB 92008 1106-G4
AVERIL RD
100 SD 92173 1350-E3
AVERY ST
4600 OCN 92057 1066-H7
AVES LN
200 SDCo 92028 1027-H3
AVIARA DR
7000 CRLB 92009 1127-C6
AVIARA PKWY
1100 CRLB 92009 1127-A3
AVIARY CT
10800 SD 92131 1209-H4
AVIARY DR
9700 SD 92131 1209-G5
AVIATION DR
6600 SD 92114 1290-E4
AVIATION RD
200 SDCo 92028 1027-E4
E AVIATION RD
100 SDCo 92028 1027-F3
AVIATOR RD
8600 SD 92154 1351-H1
AVILA AV
4900 CRLB 92008 1106-J6
AVILA CT
2000 SD 92037 1247-H2
AVILAR CT
600 SMCS 92069 1108-C6
AVION WY
4700 SD 92115 1269-J2
AVIS LN
10300 SNTE 92071 1231-E7
AVOCADO AV
300 ELCJ 92020 1251-G6
1000 ESCN 92026 1129-G1
3500 SDCo 92028 1028-F4
AVOCADO BLVD
1100 ELCJ 92020 1251-G7
1100 ELCJ 92020 1271-G2
1400 SDCo 92020 1271-G2

AVOCADO BLVD
3500 SDCo 91978 1271-F5
3500 SDCo 91941 1271-G2
3500 SDCo 91977 1271-F5
AVOCADO CT
700 SOLB 92014 1187-H1
AVOCADO DR
1500 SDCo 92083 1108-A2
1500 VSTA 92083 1108-A2
AVOCADO HWY I-15
- ESCN - 1109-E3
- ESCN - 1129-F1
- RivC - 998-H3
- RivC - 999-A2
- SDCo - 998-H3
- SDCo - 1028-G4
- SDCo - 1048-H4
- SDCo - 1068-J4
- SDCo - 1088-J1
- SDCo - 1089-B4
- SDCo - 1109-E3
- SDCo - 1129-F1
AVOCADO LN
700 CRLB 92008 1106-F6
AVOCADO PL
800 SOLB 92014 1187-H1
900 SD 92014 1187-H1
AVOCADO PT
2700 SD 92014 1187-H1
2700 SOLB 92014 1187-H1
AVOCADO RD
1300 OCN 92054 1086-E7
1400 OCN 92054 1106-E1
AVOCADO ST
100 ENCT 92024 1147-A3
9200 SDCo 91977 1271-A7
AVOCADO WY
1500 SDCo 92026 1109-E7
1500 SMCS 92069 1109-E7
AVOCADO CREST
100 SDCo 92025 1130-A6
AVOCADO KNOLL LN
- SDCo 92028 1027-H6
AVOCADO PARK LN
5000 SDCo 92028 1048-J2
AVOCADO PARK WY
5000 SDCo 92028 1048-J2
AVOCADO RANCH RD
1800 SDCo 92019 1272-A1
1800 SDCo 92020 1272-A1
AVOCADO SCHOOL RD
3800 SDCo 91941 1271-G4
AVOCADO SUMMIT DR
1100 SDCo 92019 1272-B1
AVOCADO VILLAGE CT
3600 SDCo 91941 1271-G5
AVOCADO VISTA
5000 SDCo 92028 1048-J2
AVOCADO VISTA LN
3300 SDCo 92028 1048-J2
AVOCET CT
1200 ENCT 92007 1167-F3
1500 CRLB 92009 1127-C6
AVOCET WY
4400 OCN 92057 1087-A3
AVOHILL DR
29700 SDCo 92084 1068-G6
AVON DR
4200 LMSA 91941 1270-H4
AVON LN
1900 SDCo 91977 1291-A1
AVONDALE CIR
3500 CRLB 92008 1106-G5
AVONDALE ST
3600 SD 92117 1228-D7
AVONETTE CT
12000 SD 92131 1210-B1
AVOWOOD CT
- SDCo 92028 1027-J6
- SDCo 92028 1028-A6
AVOYER PL
4100 SDCo 91941 1271-D4
AWANA GN
1000 ESCN 92027 1110-A7
AWARD RW
3000 SD 92122 1228-C6
AYAMONTE WY
600 CHV 91910 1310-H6
AYERS LN
- SDCo 92082 1070-H2
AZADO CT
11600 SD 92127 1150-A7
AZAHAR CT
3000 CRLB 92009 1147-J1
AZAHAR PL
3200 CRLB 92009 1147-J1
AZAHAR ST
3000 CRLB 92009 1147-H1
AZALEA
3500 SDCo 92028 1028-F4
15300 SDCo 92021 1233-B3
AZALEA AV
- SDCo 92036 1155-H3
13900 PWY 92064 1190-F3
AZALEA DR
100 SDCo 92083 1108-C4
100 SDCo 92084 1108-C4
2700 SD 92106 1268-C6
AZALEA GN
3800 ESCN 92025 1150-C3
AZALEA PL
7100 CRLB 92009 1127-A6
AZALEA ST
500 CHV 91911 1330-H3
AZALEA TR
- SDCo 92060 409-G7
AZALEA WY
200 OCN 92057 1086-H5
AZALEA SPRING FIRE TR
- SDCo 92036 (1196-C2 See Page 1176)
AZIMUTH PL
- CRLB 92008 1107-A4
AZOFAR CT
18400 SD 92128 1150-D7
AZORES CT
5400 SD 92124 1249-H1
AZTEC DR
5400 LMSA 91942 1270-H1
5500 LMSA 91942 1250-G7
AZTEC ST
3600 SD 92106 1287-J4
4100 OCN 92056 1087-C5
AZTEC WY
3500 SD 92106 1287-J4
AZTEC CIRCLE DR
- SD 92115 1270-B1
- SD 92182 1270-B1

SAN DIEGO CO. | INDEX

Street	Block	City	ZIP	Pg-Grid
AZUAGA ST	9900	SD	92129	1189-F4
AZUCAR WY	17600	SD	92127	1149-J7
	17600	SD	92127	1169-J1
AZUCENA DR	11400	SD	92124	1250-A3
AZUL ST	2700	SD	92037	1227-J3
	2700	SD	92037	1248-A2
AZUL WY	2700	SD	92093	1227-J3
	-	OCN	92057	1087-A2
AZURE CIR	3600	CRLB	92008	1106-H4
AZURE CV	2000	CHV	91915	1311-F6
AZURE LN	2300	VSTA	92083	1108-A5
AZURE TER	1900	SDCo	92019	1272-C2
AZURE VW	8000	SNTE	92071	1230-H7
AZURE WY	1900	OCN	92024	1147-H5
AZURE COAST DR	2400	SD	92037	1227-J6
AZURE LADO DR	3600	OCN	92056	1107-C3
AZUSA CT	1600	CHV	91902	1311-C4
	1600	CHV	91913	1311-C4
AZUSA ST	1100	SD	92110	1268-F3
AZZURO CT	12700	SD	92130	1188-C6

B

Street	Block	City	ZIP	Pg-Grid
B AV	-	SDCo	92055	1066-B2
	100	CORD	92118	1288-J7
	100	NATC	91950	1289-H7
	200	NATC	91950	1309-H1
B CT	-	SD	92126	1209-F7
	800	CHV	91910	1310-F7
B RD E	-	CORD	92135	1288-F5
B ST	-	SD	92059	1029-H4
	-	CHV	91910	1309-J6
	100	SD	92036	1136-B7
	100	ENCT	92024	1147-B6
	200	SDCo	92065	1152-G5
	300	SD	92101	1289-D2
	400	SDCo	92055	1066-H1
	400	SDCo	92055	1085-H3
	600	SD	92101	1288-J3
	1300	SD	92110	1268-F2
	1400	SD	92102	1289-D2
	1800	SDCo	92084	1108-F3
	2500	NATC	91950	1310-C3
	7200	CRLB	92009	1126-J7
W B ST	500	SD	92101	1288-J3
	500	SD	92101	1289-A3
BABA DR	16900	SDCo	92065	1173-E1
BABAUTA RD	9300	SD	92129	1189-E7
BABETTE ST	7300	SD	92111	1269-A2
BABILONIA ST	7100	CRLB	92009	1127-H6
BABS WY	10400	SDCo	91941	1271-E3
BABY TURTLE DR	500	SDCo		(1078-H6) See Page 1058
BACADI DR	7700	SD	92126	1209-A5
BACCHARIS AV	6800	CRLB	92009	1127-D6
BACCUS CT	10300	SD	92126	1209-B5
BACH ST	-	ENCT	92007	1167-D2
	600	VSTA	92083	1087-F5
BACHELOR LN	11000	SDCo	92026	1089-G6
BACHIMBA CT	12300	SD	92128	1170-B6
BACHMAN PL	4100	SD	92103	1269-A4
	4200	SD	92103	1268-J4
	4200	SD	92108	1268-J4
BACKER CT	9900	SD	92126	1209-A6
BACKER RD	7600	SD	92126	1209-A6
BACK NINE DR	2800	SDCo	92004	(1079-C3) See Page 1058
BACK NINE ST	2300	OCN	92056	1106-J1
BACON ST	1600	SD	92107	1267-J5
BACONTREE PL	3500	SD	92111	1248-J4
BACONTREE WY	6900	SD	92111	1248-J4
BADAJOZ PL	2400	CRLB	92009	1147-G1
BADAMI CIR	7900	SD	92126	1209-A1
BADEN CT	9000	SNTE	92071	1231-A7
BADGER CT	12800	SDCo	92040	1212-D5
BADGER GN	2000	ESCN	92029	1129-E6
BADGER LN	4200	SD	92008	1107-D7
BADGER WY	1000	VSTA	92083	1108-A6
BADGER LAKE AV	6300	SD	92119	1250-H5
BADILLO RD	3500	SMCS	92069	1108-D6
BAFFIN DR	10300	SD	92126	1209-A6
BAGDAD ST	7400	SD	92111	1249-A4
BAGHDAD CT	2800	SDCo	92019	1271-H4
BAGLEY DR	3300	SD	92110	1268-E6
BAGWELL CV	7600	SD	92126	1209-A5
BAHAMA BEND	-	CORD	92118	1329-E1
BAHAMA CV	14100	SD	92014	1187-H5
BAHAMA DR	-	ESCN	92025	1129-J5
BAHIA DR	2300	SD	92037	1247-J3
	2300	SD	92037	1248-A2
BAHIA LN	100	OCN	92054	1086-G3
	100	ESCN	92026	1109-H6
	5400	SD	92037	1248-A3
	5400	SDCo	92109	1248-A3
BAHIA WY	1900	SD	92037	1248-A3
BAHIA VISTA WY	1600	SD	92037	1247-H3
BAILEY CT	-	SDCo	92055	1086-A2
	900	SMCS	92069	1108-F7
BAILEY DR	1800	OCN	92054	1106-F1
BAILEY RD	1600	SD	92110	1268-G6
	1600	SD	92110	1268-H6
	4500	SD	92130	1188-D4
BAILY AV	2200	SD	92105	1289-J1
	2400	SD	92105	1269-J7
	2600	SD	92105	1270-A7
BAILY PL	4700	SD	92105	1269-J7
	4700	SD	92105	1289-J1
BAINBRIDGE CT	2600	SDCo	92133	1288-C1
BAINBRIDGE ST	3100	SD	92139	1309-F1
BAIROKO DR	12300	SD	92139	1290-D7
BAJA CT	4900	SD	92115	1270-B3
BAJA DR	5400	SD	92115	1270-B3
BAJA WY	1100	SMCS	92069	1128-E3
BAJA CERRO CIR	2400	SD	92109	1248-B3
BAJADA RD	12300	SD	92128	1170-A1
BAJA MAR	5720	SD	92037	1247-G3
BAJA MISSION RD	4300	SDCo	92014	1047-J5
BAJA VISTA DR	3700	SDCo	92014	1048-A3
	3900	OCN	92054	1086-G1
BAJER ST	6200	SD	92122	1228-B6
BAJO CT	700	CHV	91910	1310-H7
BAJO DR	3300	CRLB	92009	1128-A7
	900	CHV	91910	1310-H7
BAJO TER	900	SDCo	92028	1027-H5
BAKER AV	-	ImCo	92249	6560-B7
BAKER PL	2900	SDCo	91950	1310-C3
BAKER ST	-	ImCo	92249	6560-B7
	3300	SD	92117	1248-D5
BAKER WY	500	OCN	92054	1086-G1
	500	OCN	92054	1066-G2
BAKERSFIELD ST	1300	LMGR	91945	1290-G1
BAKEWELL ST	5700	SD	92117	1248-H2
BAKMAN CT	12100	SDCo	92040	1231-J2
	12100	SDCo	92040	1232-A2
BAKTEN WY	10200	SDCo	92082	1069-E4
BALANCED ROCK LN	1700	SDCo	91901	1252-B5
BALBOA AV	1900	SD	92109	1248-A6
	1900	DLMR	92014	1187-F4
	6000	CORD	92118	1288-G6
	8300	SD	92123	1249-D2
BALBOA AV Rt#-274	2900	SD	92109	1248-F4
	3000	SD	92117	1248-F4
	4400	SD	92116	1269-E4
BALBOA CIR	1200	CHV	91910	1311-B7
	2000	VSTA	92083	1107-J4
BALBOA CT	700	SD	92109	1267-H4
BALBOA DR	3700	OCN	92056	1107-A1
N BALBOA DR	600	SD	92101	1289-B1
	2500	SD	92103	1269-B7
	2500	SD	92103	1289-B1
BALBOA PL	9700	SDCo	92029	1149-D4
BALBOA ST	100	SMCS	92069	1108-E6
BALBOA TER	3700	SD	92117	1248-D5
BALBOA WY	4100	SD	92111	1248-G3
BALBOA ARMS DR	5100	SD	92117	1248-G2
BALBOA VISTA DR	2300	SD	92105	1270-B7
	2300	SD	92105	1290-B1
BALCHEN WY	1000	SD	92154	1351-D2
BALDRICH ST	7100	LMSA	91942	1270-F1
BALDWIN LN	4000	CRLB	92008	1106-F7
BALDWIN ST	8100	LMGR	91945	1270-H6
BALENTINE DR	-	SDCo	91901	1253-J2
	-	SDCo	91901	1254-A3
BALFOUR CT	2100	SD	92109	1248-A4
	5900	CRLB	92008	1127-D2
BALI CV	2400	SD	92139	1310-E1
BALI LN	10900	SD	92126	1209-A3
BALI WY	100	OCN	92057	1087-A1
BALI HAI RD	-	ESCN	92025	1129-J5
BALKIS LN	7200	LMGR	91945	1270-F7
BALL AV	700	SD	92026	1109-J7
	1000	ESCN	92027	1109-J7
BALLANTYNE ST	100	ELCJ	92020	1251-G4
	600	ELCJ	92021	1251-G3
	900	SDCo	92021	1251-G3
BALLARD ST	100	ELCJ	92019	1251-J6
BALLAST POINT CT	1600	CHV	91911	1330-H4
BALLATA CT	1100	VSTA	92083	1107-H4
BALLENA WY	600	CRLB	92009	1127-J5
BALLENTINE LN	13700	SDCo	92082	1090-E2
BALLINA DR	1800	SD	92114	1290-C2
BALLINGER AV	6600	SD	92119	1250-H4
BALLISTA DR	6500	SD	92004	1058-F6
BALL RANCH RD	1700	SDCo	91901	1234-A7
BALLYBUNION SQ	11400	SD	92128	1189-J2
BALLYSTOCK CT	10700	SD	92131	1209-H1
BALMORAL CT	1400	SMCS	92069	1109-D7
BALMORAL DR	5800	SD	92114	1290-C4
BALOUR DR	500	ENCT	92024	1147-F7
	900	ENCT	92024	1167-E1
BALSA ST	2300	SD	92105	1290-B1
	2400	SD	92105	1290-B7
BALSAM CT	600	ELCJ	92019	1252-B6
BALSAM DR	-	NATC	91950	1289-H7
	300	SD	92113	1289-H7
	600	ELCJ	92019	1252-B6
BALSAMINA DR	3800	SD	91902	1310-F3
BALSAM LAKE AV	6300	SD	92119	1250-H5
BALTIC ST	7400	SD	92111	1249-A4
BALTIMORE DR	4900	LMSA	91941	1270-G1
	5100	LMSA	91942	1270-G1
	5500	LMSA	91942	1250-G6
	5900	SD	91942	1250-G6
	6100	SD	92119	1250-G6
BALTIMORE PL	1500	ESCN	92025	1130-B4
BALTIMORE ST	3300	SD	92117	1248-E5
BALTUSROL GN	2100	ESCN	92026	1109-D3
BAMBOO LN	100	SD	92028	1027-H2
BAMBURGH DR	6500	SD	92117	1248-J2
BAMBURGH PL	4500	SD	92117	1248-J2
BANBURY CT	2600	CRLB	92008	1106-J5
BANBURY DR	26700	SDCo	92082	1090-E6
BANBURY ST	6000	SD	92139	1310-D2
BANCROFT DR	2600	SD	91977	1271-A6
	3900	LMSA	91941	1271-B2
	3900	LMSA	91977	1271-B2
	4900	SDCo	91941	1271-B2
BANCROFT GN	400	ESCN	92027	1110-D6
BANCROFT ST	400	SD	92102	1289-E1
	2100	SD	92104	1289-E1
	2500	SD	92104	1269-E5
	4400	SD	92116	1269-E4
S BANCROFT ST	400	SD	92113	1289-F5
BANCROFT VIEW DR	8900	SDCo	91977	1271-A5
BANDAK CT	-	SMCS	92069	1108-J4
BANDELL CT	800	SD	92126	1209-A4
BANDERA ST	1200	SD	92037	1247-F5
BANDINI PL	300	VSTA	92083	1087-H7
BANDINI ST	3400	SD	92140	1268-G6
	3600	SD	92110	1268-G5
	4700	SD	92110	1268-G5
BANDOLIER LN	1900	SD	92154	1350-D3
BANDON WY	8800	SNTE	92071	1231-A7
BANDY CANYON RD	15200	SDCo	92025	1150-H3
	15300	SDCo	92025	1150-H3
	15300	SDCo	92025	1151-A2
	17000	SDCo	92025	1131-E7
	17000	SDCo	92025	1131-E7
BANFF CT	2600	CRLB	92008	1107-A5
BANFIELD LN	1800	SD	92130	1188-A5
BANGALORE LN	200	SDCo	92029	1109-A4
BANGERTER CT	200	SMCS	92078	1128-A1
BANGOR PL	3400	SD	92106	1288-A2
BANGOR ST	700	SD	92106	1288-A2
BANJO CT	600	SMCS	92069	1109-A6
BANJO LN	-	SMCS	92065	1152-J7
BANKS ST	5300	SD	92110	1268-F3
BANNEKER DR	800	SD	92114	1290-G3
BANNER AV	1200	CHV	91911	1330-E5
BANNER RD	1300	SDCo	92036	1136-C6
BANNER RD Rt#-78	1200	SDCo	92036	1136-B5
	36100	SDCo	92036	1156-H1
BANNER WY	2300	SD	92036	1136-C7
BANNER VIEW DR	1200	SDCo	92036	1136-C6
BANNING ST	4300	SD	92107	1268-B6
BANNISTER LN	10500	SD	92126	1208-J4
BANNISTER RD	10500	SD	92227	410-L11
	-	ImCo	92227	411-A11
	-	SDCo	92281	411-B11
BANNISTER WY	10500	SD	92126	1208-J4
BANNOCK AV	4200	SD	92117	1248-E1
BANOCK ST	800	SD	91977	1291-C3
BANTAM AV	9400	SD	92123	1249-E6
BANTAM LAKE AV	6500	SD	92119	1250-H4
BANTAM LAKE CIR	6500	SD	92119	1250-H4
BANTY CT	12200	SD	92129	1188-J7
BANUELO CV	12300	SD	92130	1188-B7
BANYAN DR	1300	SD	92028	998-B7
BANYAN WY	300	ESCN	92026	1109-H7
BANYONWOOD DR	700	OCN	92057	1087-C1
BAR DR	28500	SDCo	92026	1089-B3
BARANCA CT	300	SDCo	92026	1027-F5
	8300	SD	91977	1290-J5
BARBADOS CIR	300	SDCo	92026	1027-F5
BARBADOS CV	2000	CHV	91915	1311-F6
BARBADOS WY	10800	SD	92126	1209-A3
	13300	SD	92014	1187-J7
BARBARA AV	200	SOLB	92075	1167-E6
BARBARA DR	1100	SDCo	92065	1108-B1
BARBARA LN	2700	SDCo	92056	1087-B6
BARBARA WY	-	ELCJ	92243	6559-F2
	1100	SDCo	92065	1152-J6
BARBARA ANN LN	5100	SD	92115	1270-E2
BARBARA ANN PL	1100	SDCo	92065	1152-J6
BARBARA JEAN CT	-	SNTE	92071	1251-A1
BARBARA WORTH AV	1800	ELCN	92243	6499-E6
BARBARA WORTH RD	-	ImCo	92249	431-D7
BARBARBA LN	1700	ENCT	92024	1147-B2
BARBAROSSA CT	5800	SD	92115	1270-B3
BARBAROSSA DR	4700	SD	92115	1270-C3
BARBAROSSA PL	4800	SD	92115	1270-C3
BARBARY PL	5700	SD	92003	1048-B7
BARBER MOUNTAIN RD	2300	SDCo	91935	1294-F4
BARBERRY AV	-	CRLB	92009	1127-B5
BARBIC CT	3700	SD	91977	1271-C5
BARBIC LN	9300	SD	91977	1271-B5
BAR BIT RD	2300	SD	91978	1271-G7
	2300	SD	91978	1291-G1
BARBOUR DR	2700	SD	92154	1330-C7
BARBY PL	3000	SD	92117	1228-C7
BARCELONA CT	1900	VSTA	92083	1107-H3
	3200	SD	91977	1271-D6
BARCELONA DR	1000	SD	92107	1287-J2
N BARCELONA ST	3900	SD	91977	1271-D5
S BARCELONA ST	2000	SD	91977	1291-D1
	2200	SDCo	91977	1271-D5
BARCELONA WY	4700	OCN	92056	1107-E4
BARCLAY AV	5400	SD	92120	1250-B5
BARD RD Rt#-S24	1100	ImCo	92283	432-D5
BARDAGUERA PL	3900	SDCo	91902	1310-F2
BARDONIA ST	6600	SD	92119	1250-H4
BARDSLEY CT	3200	SD	92154	1330-H7
BAREBACK SQ	5100	SD	92130	1188-D2
BARELIA RD	1600	SDCo	92027	1131-C3
BARETA STAR RANCH RD	24900	SDCo	92065	1173-G7
BARGER PL	900	CHV	91911	1330-E2
BARHAM DR	600	SMCS	92078	1109-A7
	600	SMCS	92078	1129-A1
	700	SMCS	92029	1129-C1
E BARHAM DR	100	SMCS		1128-H1
	100	SMCS	92078	1128-H1
	100	SMCS		1129-A1
BARHAM LN	100	SMCS	92078	1129-A1
BARHAVEN LN	-	SDCo	92028	1027-H3
N BARHAVEN LN	-	SDCo	92028	1027-H2
BARI CT	5800	LMSA	91942	1251-B7
BARIN ST	2300	SD	92135	1288-F4
BARIONI ST Rt#-S28	-	CORD	92135	1288-F5
BARK ST	5900	SD	92115	1270-C6
BARKEATH DR	7300	LMGR	91945	1270-F6
BARKER DR	8400	SD	92119	1250-J3
BARKER WY	6800	SD	92119	1250-H3
BARKER SPUR TR	-	SDCo	92060	409-H6
BARKLA ST	3300	SD	92122	1228-A7
BARLES CT	38800	SDCo	92028	997-A4
BARLEY CT	5700	SDCo	91902	1311-B2
BARLEY DR	2300	VSTA	92083	1108-A5
BARNARD DR	3500	OCN	92056	1107-A1
BARNARD ST	2800	SD	92110	1268-C5
BARNAVILLE LN	9600	SNTE	92071	1231-E7
N BARNES ST	-	SDCo	92054	1086-B6
S BARNES ST	-	SDCo	92054	1086-B7
BARNES CANYON RD	9900	SD	92121	1208-E6
BARNETT AV	3000	SD	92110	1268-E6
	3000	SD	92140	1268-E6
E BARNETT CIR	-	SDCo	92055	1067-A2
W BARNETT CIR	-	SDCo	92055	1067-A1
BARNETT DR	500	SMCS	92069	1108-J6
BARNETT RD	1200	SDCo	92065	998-G7
BARNEVELD ST	9100	SDCo	91977	1291-B4
BARNEY CT	1100	SD	92154	1350-D1
BARNEY ST	2300	ESCN	92027	1290-G2
BARNEY OLDFIELD RD	6500	CRLB	92009	1127-H5
BARNHURST DR	6500	SD	92117	1248-J2
BARNHURST PL	4500	SD	92117	1248-J2
BARNSON PL	2900	SD	92103	1269-A7
BARNWELL PL	500	OCN	92054	1086-E7
E BARNWELL ST	400	OCN	92054	1086-D6
N BARNWELL ST	-	SDCo	92054	1086-D6
S BARNWELL ST	-	SDCo	92054	1086-E6
BAR O DR	-	SDCo	92055	(1078-H6) See Page 1058
BARON DR	10300	SD	92126	1209-C4
BARON LN	10500	SD	92126	1209-C4
BARON PL	900	ESCN	92026	1129-F1
BARONA RD	1000	SDCo	92040	1212-F2
	1100	SDCo	92040	1192-G7
	-	SDCo	92040	(1193-B2) See Page 1192
	15000	SDCo	92065	(1193-B2) See Page 1192
BARON LONG RD	6600	SD	91901	1235-A2
BARONESS AV	10100	SD	92126	1209-B5
BAROQUE LN	3800	SD	92124	1249-H3
BAROQUE PL	500	ESCN	92026	1109-J7
BAROQUE TER	4800	OCN	92057	1087-B2
BARR AV	300	SD	92103	1268-J4
BARRANCA CT	3600	CRLB	92008	1107-B3
BARRANCA RD	7400	SMCS	92069	1108-D5
BARREGO WY	23400	SDCo	92065	1173-D3
BARREL DR	600	SDCo	92004	(1078-J4) See Page 1058
BARREL BLOSSOM LN	2700	SDCo	92084	1088-D7
BARRET	-	ELCN	92243	6559-J1
BARRETT DAM RD	-	SDCo	91917	(1315-C6) See Page 1294
BARRETT LAKE RD	-	SDCo	91901	(1295-A4) See Page 1294
BARRETT LAKE RD	-	SDCo	92019	(1295-A4) See Page 1294
	-	SDCo	91917	(1315-D3) See Page 1294
BARRETT SMITH RD	-	SDCo	91917	429-K10
BARRETT VIEW RD	3400	SDCo	91901	1275-B4
BARRINGTON CT	4600	SD	91902	1310-H2
BARROWS ST	4300	SD	92117	1248-C3
BARRY ST	5000	OCN	92057	1067-A5
BARRYMORE ST	13800	SD	92129	1189-C2
BARRYWOOD WY	10300	SD	92131	1210-A6
BARSANTI CT	1900	SD	92154	1330-A7
BARSBY ST	300	VSTA	92084	1087-H2
	900	VSTA	92084	1087-H2
BARSKY LN	1000	SDCo	92028	1027-H4
BARSTOW ST	4800	SD	92117	1228-G7
BART LN	9600	SNTE	92071	1231-E7
BART WY	10300	SNTE	92071	1231-E4
BARTEL PL	2400	SD	92123	1249-E6
BARTEL ST	2500	SD	92123	1249-E6
BARTH RD	6100	ImCo	92227	410-K10
BARTIZON DR	300	SDCo	92004	1058-F6
BARTLETT AV	3500	OCN	92057	1086-F5
BARTLETT DR	1000	VSTA	92084	1087-H5
BARTLEY LN	14700	SDCo	91935	1293-A2
BARTLEY PL	1200	ESCN	92026	1109-J5
BARTOLA RD	-	SDCo	92028	998-G7
BARTON DR	7800	LMGR	91945	1290-H1
BARTRAM WY	1600	ELCJ	92019	1252-B7
	1600	ELCJ	92019	1252-B7
BASALTO ST	6500	CRLB	92009	1127-H5
BASCOMB PL	3600	SD	92117	1228-D7
BASEL ST	2900	OCN	92054	1106-G1
BASHAN LAKE AV	8400	SD	92119	1250-J5
BASHFUL WY	8500	SD	92021	1232-E7
BASIL ST	100	ENCT	92024	1147-B5
BASILICA ST	100	OCN	92057	1086-H3
BASILICA WY	100	OCN	92057	1086-H3
BASILONE RD	-	SDCo	92055	408-K6
	-	SDCo	92055	409-A6
	-	SDCo	92672	1023-D3
	-	SDCo	92672	1023-H2
BASILONE ST	3800	SD	92126	1268-C5
BASS DR	10100	SDCo	92040	1232-E3
BASS LN	3700	OCN	92054	1086-G2
BASS RD	2400	SDCo	91906	(1297-F5) See Page 1296
BASS ST	3800	LMSA	91941	1270-F5
BASSETT CT	100	SD	91977	1290-J5
BASSETT WY	23500	SDCo	92065	1173-D3
BASSMORE DR	13700	SD	92129	1189-F3
BASSO CT	7300	SD	92119	1250-F4
BASSWOOD AV	700	IMPB	91932	1329-G6
	1200	CRLB	92008	1106-F5
BATAAN CIR	5900	SD	92139	1290-C7
BATAVIA CIR	11100	SD	92126	1209-A2
BATAVIA RD	7700	SD	92126	1209-A2
BATCHELDER CT	2000	ELCJ	92020	1251-C5
BATEMAN AV	4000	SD	92154	1350-F1
BATES LN	300	SDCo	92021	1251-G1
BATES ST	5700	SD	92115	1270-B6
BATES VIEW CT	-	SDCo	92065	1108-H5
BATHURST PL	1300	ELCJ	92020	1251-D5
BATIQUITOS DR	600	CRLB	92011	1127-A6
E BATIQUITOS DR	900	CRLB	92011	1127-C7
BATISTA ST	6900	SD	92111	1248-J3
	7300	SD	92111	1249-A3
BAUER PL	600	VSTA	92083	1107-F1
BAUER RD	8500	SD	92126	1209-C7
BAUGHMAN RD	1300	ImCo	92227	431-A1
BAUSELL CT	10100	SD	92124	1249-G3
BAUSELL PL	10100	SD	92124	1249-G3
BAUTISTA AV	2300	SDCo	92084	1087-G1
	2500	SDCo	92084	1067-F7
BAUTISTA CT	100	SD	92057	1086-H3
BAVARIA DR	100	SDCo	92083	1108-A2
	100	VSTA	92083	1108-A2
BAVARIAN DR	13100	SD	92129	1189-C4
BAVARIAN WY	8400	SD	92129	1189-C4
BAXTER CT	4600	SD	92117	1228-F7
BAXTER ST	5000	SD	92117	1228-F7
BAXTER CANYON RD	2200	VSTA	92083	1107-J3
BAY BLVD	200	CHV	91910	1309-H6
	300	CHV	91910	1329-J1
	600	CHV	91910	1330-A2
	1200	SD	91911	1330-A3
BAY CIR	900	CORD	92118	1288-J1
	900	CORD	92118	1289-A7
	900	CORD	92118	1308-J1
	900	CORD	92118	1309-A1
BAYAMON RD	9500	SD	92129	1189-E4
BAYARD ST	4800	SD	92109	1247-J4
BAYBERRY CT	800	SMCS	92069	1109-A6
	4300	SD	92154	1330-G7
BAYBERRY DR	1800	OCN	92054	1106-E2
BAY BERRY PL	-	ENCT	92024	1147-C5
BAYCANE WY	11800	SD	92128	1190-A7
BAY CANYON CT	2700	SD	92117	1248-E7
BAYCLIFF WY	4100	OCN	92056	1107-C3
BAY FRONT ST	1900	SD	92113	1289-C6
BAY HILL DR	1600	SMCS	92069	1108-J3
BAY HILL RD	2300	CHV	91915	1311-G6
BAY LEAF DR	300	CHV	91910	1310-E5
BAY LEAF WY	3700	OCN	92057	1086-H4
BAYLISS CT	4900	SD	92130	1188-C4
BAYLOR AV	700	SD	91902	1311-C5
	700	CHV	91913	1311-C5
BAYLOR DR	800	SD	92115	1270-A3
BAY MARINA DR	2900	OCN	92054	1106-G1
BAY MEADOWS DR	1400	SDCo	91901	1234-B6
BAY MEADOWS LN	4500	SOLB	92075	1187-F1
BAYONA LP	500	CHV	91910	1310-J5
BAYONET TER	13400	SD	92128	1189-H4
BAYONNE DR	3400	SD	92109	1268-A1
	3600	SD	92109	1248-A7
BAYPONY LN	11800	SD	92128	1190-A7
BAYSHORE DR	4700	CRLB	92008	1106-H7
	4700	CRLB	92008	1126-H1
BAYSHORE LN	800	SMCS	92069	1128-F4
BAYSIDE PKWY	900	SD	91911	1329-H1
BAYSIDE WK	2600	SD	92109	1267-H1
	3800	SD	92109	1247-H7
BAY SUMMIT PL	4000	SD	92117	1248-E6
BAY VIEW CT	4000	SD	92103	1268-J4
BAYVIEW PL	3600	CRLB	92008	1107-B4
BAYVIEW WY	200	CHV	91910	1310-B4
BAYVIEW HEIGHTS DR	1600	SD	92105	1290-B2
BAYVIEW HEIGHTS WY	1800	SD	92105	1290-B1
BAYWIND PT	12800	SD	92130	1188-D6
BAYWOOD AV	10400	SD	92126	1209-D4
BAYWOOD CIR	3300	CHV	91915	1311-G5
	5100	OCN	92056	1087-D2
BAYWOOD WY	10300	SD	92126	1209-D5
BEACH AV	-	IMPB	91932	1349-E1
BEACH RD	-	ImCo	92257	411-B7
BEACH BLUFF RD	4100	CRLB	92008	1106-H6
BEACH CLUB DR	100	SOLB	92075	1187-E2
BEACH CLUB RD	100	SOLB	92075	1187-E2
BEACHCOMBER CT	1800	SD	92154	1350-D5
BEACH CREST CT	4100	CRLB	92008	1126-J4
BEACH FRONT DR	700	SOLB	92075	1187-E2
BEACHWOOD WY	-	OCN	92057	1087-B2
BEACON DR	2900	SD	92114	1290-G3
BEACON PL	700	CHV	91910	1310-G6
	700	ESCN	92025	1130-A3
	700	OCN	92054	1107-C2
BEACON BAY DR	1000	CRLB	92009	1127-A5

6567 BEACON HILL CT SAN DIEGO CO. STREET INDEX BIRCH LN

SAN DIEGO CO.

INDEX

STREET
Block City ZIP Pg-Grid

BEACON HILL CT
1100 SMCS 92069 1128-B3
BEADNELL WY
6500 SD 92117 1248-H2
BEAGLE CT
3400 SD 92111 1248-J4
3400 SD 92111 1249-A4
BEAGLE PL
3400 SD 92111 1248-J4
BEAGLE ST
6900 SD 92111 1248-J4
7200 SD 92111 1249-A4
BEAK PT
9300 SD 92129 1189-E6
BEAK WY
3900 SD 92124 1249-H3
BEAL RD
- ImCo - 411-E6
400 ImCo 92257 411-C7
BEAL ST
7300 SD 92111 1249-A4
BEAMAN LN
1200 SDCo 92028 1027-G4
BEAN ST
3200 SD 92101 1268-H7
BEANIE LN
1200 SDCo 92021 1251-J3
BEAR
14100 SDCo 92040 1232-F4
BEAR DR
3500 SD 92103 1268-J6
BEARCAT LN
1800 SDCo 92019 1272-D3
BEAR CREEK PL
2300 CHV 91915 1311-G7
BEAR DANCE WY
11100 SD 92127 1149-H7
BEARDSLEY ST
600 SD 92113 1289-C4
BEARING LN
100 ELCJ 92019 1252-A5
BEAR MOUNTAIN WY
13600 SDCo 91935 1292-F3
BEAR RIVER RW
6800 SD 92139 1290-F7
6800 SD 92139 1310-F1
BEAR ROCK GN
2200 ESCN 92026 1109-B3
BEARTRAP PL
2100 ESCN 92027 1130-D1
BEAR VALLEY LN
16500 SDCo 92027 1111-D1
BEAR VALLEY PKWY
300 ESCN 92025 1130-C7
300 ESCN 92025 1150-B3
300 SDCo 92025 1130-C7
1100 SDCo 92027 1130-D3
1700 ESCN 92027 1130-D3
2400 ESCN 92027 1110-D7
BEAR VALLEY RD
900 SDCo 92025 1130-C5
BEAR VALLEY HEIGHTS RD
25700 SDCo 92027 1111-E1
26000 SDCo 92027 1091-D7
BEAR VALLEY OAKS
1900 SDCo 92025 1130-C5
BEAR VIEW WY
400 SDCo 91901 1253-F2
BEATITUDE DR
12300 SDCo 92082 1090-B1
BEATON CT
11100 SD 92126 1209-D2
BEATRICE CT
1100 SD 92154 1350-E1
6300 SD 92139 1310-E2
BEATRICE ST
2700 SD 92139 1310-E2
BEATTY PL
4600 SD 92124 1249-G3
BEAUCHAMP CT
4900 SD 92130 1188-C5
BEAUMONT AV
5300 SD 92037 1247-F3
BEAUMONT CIR
1000 VSTA 92084 1088-A6
BEAUMONT CT
300 VSTA 92084 1088-A6
BEAUMONT DR
100 VSTA 92084 1088-A6
4700 SDCo 91941 1271-B2
4700 LMSA 91941 1271-B2
BEAUMONT GN
400 ESCN 92026 1109-G6
BEAUMONT LN N
100 VSTA 92084 1088-A6
BEAUMONT LN S
100 VSTA 92084 1088-A6
BEAVERCREEK LN
200 SDCo 92028 1028-A3
BEAVER HOLLOW RD
3100 SDCo 91935 1273-B3
3400 SDCo 92019 1272-H2
3400 SDCo 92019 1273-A2
BEAVER LAKE CT
6400 SD 92119 1250-J5
BEAVER LAKE DR
7900 SD 92119 1250-H5
BECK DR
9900 SNTE 92071 1231-D3
BECKINGTON LN
7000 SD 92139 1290-G7
BECKINGTON WY
2600 SD 92139 1290-G7
BECKY LN
600 SDCo 92069 1108-G1
BECKY PL
2100 SD 92104 1289-G1
BEDEL CT
9100 SD 92129 1189-D1
BEDFONT CIR
10400 SD 92126 1209-D4
BEDFORD AV
3900 OCN 92056 1087-B7
BEDFORD CIR
3500 CRLB 92008 1106-H4
BEDFORD DR
4100 SD 92116 1269-G2
BEDFORD PL
1900 ESCN 92029 1129-F7
BEDFORDSHIRE CT
12600 SD 92128 1150-B6
BEDLOW CT
6700 SD 92119 1250-E3
BEE CANYON RD
18000 SDCo 91917 429-J10
BEECH AV
100 CRLB 92008 1106-D5
200 CHV 91910 1310-A6

BEECH AV
600 CHV 91910 1330-B1
800 CHV 91911 1330-B2
BEECH LN
20100 SDCo 92029 1149-E1
BEECH PL
100 SDCo 92021 1252-H4
1400 ESCN 92026 1109-J6
BEECH ST
100 SD 92101 1289-E2
100 SDCo 92028 1027-E3
200 ELCJ 92020 1251-F4
300 SD 92114 1290-D4
600 SD 92101 1288-J2
2800 SD 92102 1289-E2
3800 SD 92105 1289-G2
5000 SD 92102 1290-A2
N BEECH ST
100 ESCN 92025 1130-A1
900 ESCN 92026 1110-A7
900 ESCN 92026 1130-A1
S BEECH ST
100 ESCN 92025 1130-B2
W BEECH ST
100 SD 92101 1289-A2
500 SD 92101 1288-J2
BEECH FERN CT
11400 SD 92131 1209-J1
BEECHGLEN DR
1000 CHV 91910 1310-J7
BEECHTREE DR
100 ENCT 92024 1147-F7
BEECHTREE RD
- SMCS 92078 1128-D6
BEECHTREE ST
12800 SDCo 92040 1232-B3
BEECHWOOD CT
8000 LMGR 91945 1270-J7
BEECHWOOD LN
100 OCN 92054 1106-C2
BEECHWOOD ST
600 ESCN 92025 1130-A1
12600 PWY 92064 1190-D3
BEEJAY DR
700 SD 92154 1330-B7
BEELER CANYON RD
11100 PWY 92064 1210-E1
11100 SD 92145 1210-E1
14900 PWY 92064 1190-H7
14900 PWY 92064 1191-A6
14900 SD 92145 1190-H7
BEELER CANYON TER
11400 SD 92145 1210-D1
BEELER CREEK TR
12700 PWY 92064 1190-B5
BEETHOVEN AV
100 ENCT 92007 1167-D3
BEETHOVEN DR
600 ESCN 92025 1150-B2
BEE VALLEY RD
20600 SDCo 91935 (1314-J2 See Page 1294)
20600 SDCo 91935 (1315-A2 See Page 1294)
BEGONIA CT
900 CRLB 92009 1127-A6
BEGONIA DR
- SD 92109 1248-C6
BEGONIA ST
- SDCo 92055 1086-B2
3800 SD 92121 1208-C6
N BEGONIA ST
500 ESCN 92027 1110-B6
BEGONIA WY
2400 SDCo 91901 1233-J5
BEHBERG RD
- SD 92106 1287-J4
- SD 92106 1288-A4
BEINN BHREAGH
- SDCo 92036 1156-D7
- SDCo 92036 1176-D1
BEL AIR DR
700 VSTA 92084 1087-J5
BELAIR DR
1100 SDCo 92028 1027-H2
BEL AIR DR E
900 VSTA 92084 1087-J5
BEL AIR DR W
100 VSTA 92084 1087-J5
BEL AIR TER
1800 ENCT 92024 1167-H3
BELARDO DR
5200 SD 92124 1230-A7
BELA VISTA AV
- ELCJ 92021 1251-J5
BELCOURT PL
- SD 92130 1208-B1
BELDEN PL
2100 ESCN 92029 1129-H7
BELDEN ST
7000 SD 92111 1248-J4
7200 SD 92111 1249-A4
BELDENS FIELD RD
900 ESCN 92027 1130-F1
BEL ESPRIT CIR E
800 SMCS 92069 1108-H6
BEL ESPRIT CIR W
800 SMCS 92069 1108-H6
BELFAST CIR
8600 SD 92126 1209-C4
BELFAST GN
100 ESCN 92027 1110-E7
BELFORA WY
100 OCN 92057 1087-A4
BELFORD ST
3500 SD 92111 1248-J4
3600 SD 92111 1249-A4
BELGIAN ST
10900 SD 92126 1209-D3
BELINDA WY
600 CHV 91910 1310-D7
BELIO LN
2900 LMGR 91945 1270-E7
BELIZE WY
- OCN 92057 1087-A2
BELKNAP WY
2000 ESCN 92027 1110-B6
BELL CT
6600 SD 92111 1248-H6
BELL RD
- ImCo 92250 431-D5
BELLA COLLINA ST
4900 OCN 92056 1087-C3
BELLADONNA WY
- SD 92131 1209-G2
BELLAGIO RD
9200 SNTE 92071 1231-A4
BELLAIRE CT
800 ELCJ 92020 1251-A4

BELLAIRE ST
300 DLMR 92014 1187-F4
BELLAKAREN PL
7800 SD 92037 1228-A6
BELLA LAGUNA CT
- ENCT 92024 1147-D1
BELLA PACIFIC RW
2700 SD 92109 1248-C4
BELLA ROSA DR
1600 SDCo 92084 1088-B2
BELLA SIENA
15800 SDCo 92067 1168-E6
BELLATRIX CT
11400 SD 92126 1209-C1
BELLATRIX DR
1600 SD 92126 1209-E7
BELLA VISTA DR
1500 ENCT 92024 1147-D2
1900 SDCo 92084 1108-D3
BELLA VITA LN
- SDCo 92084 1108-D1
BELL BLUFF AV
6400 SD 92119 1250-D3
BELL BLUFF RD
1400 SDCo 91901 1234-G6
BELL BLUFF TKTR
- SDCo 91901 1255-F2
BELLBOTTOM WY
- SDCo 92065 1174-B4
BELL COLLO LN
8700 SNTE 92071 1231-G6
BELLE LN
3300 CRLB 92008 1106-G4
BELLE ST
- SD 91911 1330-A4
800 CHV 91911 1330-A4
BELLEAIRE ST
1400 OCN 92054 1106-D2
BELLEAU WOOD
- SD 92101 1268-G7
- SD 92140 1268-F6
BELLE BONNIE BRAE RD
3600 SDCo 91902 1311-A2
BELLECHASE CIR
17700 SD 92128 1150-A7
BELLE FLEUR WY
- SD 92128 1189-G6
BELLEFLOWER RD
1300 CRLB 92009 1127-A4
BELLE GLADE AV
6400 SD 92119 1250-E6
BELLE GLADE LN
7000 SD 92119 1250-E5
BELLEGROVE RD
1800 ENCT 92024 1147-H7
BELLE HAVEN DR
6600 SD 92120 1250-D5
BELLE HELENE CT
17600 SD 92128 1150-A7
17600 SD 92128 1170-A1
BELLE ISLE DR
3100 SD 92105 1269-J6
BELLEMEADE RD
1600 ENCT 92024 1147-H7
BELLEMORE DR
25500 SDCo 92065 1173-J4
25700 SDCo 92065 1174-A4
BELLENA AV
1100 CHV 91913 1311-D6
BELLENA CT
1600 CHV 91913 1311-D6
BELLERIVE CT
100 VSTA 92084 1088-A6
BELLERIVE DR
100 VSTA 92084 1088-A6
BELLEVIEW AV
1300 ENCT 92007 1167-C1
BELLE VISTA DR
400 CHV 91910 1310-F6
BELLEVUE AV
5300 SD 92037 1247-F3
BELLEVUE PL
700 SD 92037 1247-G4
700 SD 92109 1247-G4
BELLFLOWER DR
4300 LMSA 91941 1271-A3
BELL GARDENS DR
10200 SNTE 92071 1231-D4
BELLINGHAM AV
3600 SD 92105 1269-G6
BELLINGTON LN
1700 SDCo 92028 1027-J3
BELLIS LN
9000 SDCo 92040 1232-D6
BELLOC CT
2100 SD 92109 1248-A4
BELLO HILLS LN
1800 SDCo 92026 1109-H5
1800 ESCN 92026 1109-H5
BELLO MAR DR
1300 ENCT 92024 1147-D1
BELLOTA DR
16800 SD 92128 1170-B3
BELLOTA PL
12100 SD 92128 1170-B3
BELLVALE AV
5100 SD 92117 1248-G2
BELLVER CIR
1200 SDCo 92028 1027-H3
BELLVINE TR
1100 SDCo 92019 1252-A7
1100 SDCo 92019 1272-A1
1100 SDCo 92020 1272-A1
BELLVISTA DR
14400 SDCo 92067 1188-E1
BELLWOOD CT
8800 SDCo 91977 1290-J3
BELLWOOD LN
- SDCo 92083 1108-B6
- VSTA 92083 1108-B6
BELMONT AV
100 NATC 91950 1290-B6
3800 SD 92116 1269-G3
N BELMONT AV
100 NATC 91950 1290-B6
100 SD 92114 1290-B6
BELMONT CT
300 SMCS 92069 1108-G6
BELMONT PL
1400 CHV 91913 1331-C1
BELMONT TER
1100 SDCo 92084 1108-C1
BELMONT PARK RD
1400 OCN 92057 1067-G7
1400 OCN 92057 1087-G1
BELMORE CT
1900 ELCJ 92020 1251-B2

BELOE
9200 SDCo 92040 1232-H5
BELOIT AV
6800 SD 92111 1248-J3
BELSHIRE LN
11300 SD 92126 1209-D2
BELT ST
600 SD 92101 1288-J3
2000 SD 92113 1289-C6
2700 SD 92136 1289-E6
BELVEDERE DR
4700 SDCo 92036 1156-B5
13900 PWY 92064 1190-F3
BELVEDERE ST
200 SD 92037 1247-E1
BELVIA LN
700 CHV 91911 1330-B5
BELVISTA CT
4600 SD 92130 1188-C6
BELVUE DR
3700 LMSA 91941 1270-J5
BEN ST
3500 SD 92111 1249-A3
BENAVENTE PL
9700 SD 92129 1189-F5
BENAVENTE ST
9600 SD 92129 1189-F6
BENAVENTE WY
12600 SD 92129 1189-F6
BENBOW CT
13400 SD 92129 1189-C4
BENCHLEY RD
13200 SD 92130 1188-A4
BEND ST
9800 SNTE 92071 1231-F4
BENDIGO CV
10700 SD 92126 1209-A4
BENDIGO RD
7700 SD 92126 1209-A4
BENDING ELBOW DR
2800 SDCo 92004 (1078-H4 See Page 1058)
BENDITO DR
12600 SD 92128 1170-C4
BENDIX ST
4800 SD 92111 1249-C1
BENECIA CT
1100 CHV 91913 1311-C6
BENEDICT AV
700 ELCJ 92020 1251-E5
BENET RD
200 OCN 92054 1086-D5
BENET HILL RD
- OCN 92054 1086-C4
BENEVENTE DR
200 OCN 92057 1086-J4
BENFIELD CT
4400 SD 92113 1289-J5
BENFOLD DR
9000 SD 92126 1209-D7
BENGAL CT
5400 SD 92124 1249-H1
BENHURST AV
4200 SD 92122 1228-F5
BENHURST CT
6300 SD 92122 1228-F5
BENICIA ST
1100 SD 92110 1268-F2
BENICIA WY
100 OCN 92057 1086-H3
BENITO WY
23900 SDCo 92065 1173-E2
BENJAMIN PL
9300 SDCo 92127 1169-C2
BENJAMIN HOLT RD
6800 SD 92114 1290-E6
BENNETT AV
100 SMCS 92069 1129-C1
200 SMCS 92069 1109-D6
500 SDCo 92026 1109-D6
800 ESCN 92026 1109-D6
BENNETT CT
100 SMCS 92078 1129-C1
BENNETT ST
- SD 92106 1287-J4
BENNINGTON CT
3700 CRLB 92008 1107-A4
BENNINGTON ST
8600 SD 92126 1209-C4
BENNY WY
800 ELCJ 92019 1251-J7
BENNYE LEE DR
16100 PWY 92064 1170-D4
BENSON AV
6100 SD 92114 1290-D4
BENSON PL
100 OCN 92054 1086-D5
S BENT AV
100 SMCS 92069 1108-F7
100 SMCS 92069 1128-F1
BENTLEY DR
3500 SDCo 91977 1271-A5
BENTLEY LN
3500 SDCo 91977 1271-A5
BENTON CV
6800 SDCo 92066 1237-D7
BENTON PL
600 ELCJ 92020 1251-H6
5100 SD 92116 1269-F2
BENTON WY
4800 LMSA 91941 1270-F2
4800 SD 92115 1270-F2
BENT TREE CT
14300 PWY 92064 1170-H5
BENT TREE PL
2200 ESCN 92026 1109-J4
BENT TREE RD
15200 PWY 92064 1170-G4
BENTWOOD DR
600 SDCo 92021 1251-G1
BEREA CT
- PWY 92064 1210-C1
BERENDA PL
1400 ELCJ 92020 1251-C5
BERGEN ST
5500 SD 92117 1228-H7
BERGER AV
3100 SD 92123 1249-B5
BERGMAN ST
3700 SD 92105 1270-B5
BERINGER LN
1300 VSTA 92083 1107-H3
BERINO CT
3900 SD 92122 1228-C4
BERKELEY DR
7200 LMSA 91941 1270-F4
BERKELEY WY
700 VSTA 92084 1088-B7

BERKELY AV
2700 CRLB 92008 1106-J5
2700 CRLB 92008 1107-A5
BERKSHIRE CT
900 ESCN 92025 1129-J6
1500 SMCS 92069 1108-J3
BERKVIEW LN
9000 SDCo 91977 1271-B7
9000 SDCo 91977 1291-A1
BERKWOOD DR
9000 SDCo 91977 1271-A7
BERLAND WY
400 CHV 91910 1310-F7
BERLIN ST
12900 PWY 92064 1190-D5
BERMUDA AV
4400 SD 92107 1287-J1
4600 SD 92107 1267-H7
BERMUDA CIR
4300 SD 92107 1287-J1
BERMUDA LN
- ESCN 92025 1129-J5
1200 ELCJ 92021 1252-C3
BERMUDA PL
1200 ELCJ 92021 1252-C3
BERMUDA TR
1200 ELCJ 92021 1252-C3
1200 SDCo 92021 1252-C3
BERMUDA DUNES PL
4000 CHV 91902 1310-F3
4400 OCN 92057 1066-G7
BERNABE CT
14200 SD 92129 1189-H2
BERNABE DR
10500 SD 92129 1189-G2
BERNABEO CT
- SDCo 92082 1070-F6
BERNADETTE LN
5900 SD 92120 1250-C6
BERNADINE PL
4200 SD 92115 1270-B4
BERNADOTTE LN
13900 PWY 92064 1190-G3
BERNARDINO LN
3400 SDCo 92084 1088-F7
BERNARDO AV
900 SDCo 92029 1129-H6
900 SDCo 92029 1149-H1
1100 ESCN 92029 1129-H5
1900 ESCN 92025 1129-H6
W BERNARDO CT
11500 SD 92127 1169-J2
W BERNARDO DR
16100 SD 92127 1169-J3
17700 SD 92127 1149-J7
17700 SD 92127 1150-A5
BERNARDO LN
3000 SDCo 92029 1149-H2
BERNARDO TER
11800 SD 92128 1170-A2
BERNARDO CENTER CT
11900 SD 92128 1170-A1
BERNARDO CENTER DR
11600 SD 92127 1169-J1
11600 SD 92127 1170-A1
16400 SD 92128 1170-A1
BERNARDO HEIGHTS PKWY
15700 PWY 92064 1170-A4
15700 SD 92128 1170-A4
BERNARDO LAKES DR
- SD 92127 1169-C2
9300 SDCo 92127 1169-C2
BERNARDO MOUNTAIN DR
3100 ESCN 92029 1149-H2
3100 SDCo 92029 1149-H2
BERNARDO OAKS CT
12100 SD 92128 1170-B1
BERNARDO OAKS DR
16300 SD 92128 1170-B1
BERNARDO PLAZA CT
11700 SD 92128 1170-A3
BERNARDO PLAZA DR
11900 SD 92128 1170-A3
BERNARDO RIDGE PL
- ESCN 92029 1149-G1
BERNARDO TRAILS CT
18300 SD 92128 1150-C6
BERNARDO TRAILS DR
18300 SD 92128 1150-C7
BERNARDO TRAILS PL
17900 SD 92128 1150-C7
BERNARDO VISTA DR
17300 SD 92128 1170-A2
BERNEY PL
1700 ESCN 92026 1109-D5
BERNICE DR
3800 SD 92107 1268-A7
BERNIE DR
3000 OCN 92056 1087-B7
3000 OCN 92056 1107-B1
BERNIS CT
3100 SDCo 91977 1271-A6
BERNITA RD
900 SDCo 92020 1271-H1
BERNITA WY
1400 SDCo 92020 1271-H1
BERNWOOD PL
3600 SD 92130 1188-A5
BERRY RD
11100 SDCo 92082 1069-F2
N BERRY RD
- SDCo 92082 1069-G1
BERRY ST
1900 LMGR 91945 1290-F1
2200 LMGR 91945 1270-F7
BERRYDALE ST
1700 ELCJ 92021 1251-G2
1700 SDCo 92021 1251-G2
BERRYESSA CT
23900 SDCo 92065 1173-E2
BERRYESSA LN
10600 SDCo 92127 1169-F2
BERRYESSA ST
5100 OCN 92056 1107-F4
BERRYFIELD CT
- SD 92130 1188-A5
BERRYHILL DR
500 SMCS 92069 1109-B6
BERRYKNOLL ST
11100 SD 92126 1209-A2
BERRYLAND CT
2000 LMGR 91945 1290-F1
BERRY PARK LN
- LMGR 91945 1270-F7
7000 LMGR 91945 1290-F1
BERT CT
4200 SD 92117 1248-E2

BERT LN
100 OCN 92054 1086-G2
BERT ACOSTA ST
10000 ELCJ 92020 1251-D2
BERTHA CT
4400 SD 92117 1248-E2
BERTHA ST
4400 SD 92117 1248-E2
BERTING ST
4400 SD 92115 1270-B4
BERTRO DR
5800 LMSA 91942 1250-G7
BERVY ST
1500 SD 92110 1268-E2
BERWICK DR
4300 SD 92117 1248-J2
BERWICK WOODS
2100 SDCo 92028 1027-G6
BERWYN RD
7900 SD 92126 1209-B4
BERYL ST
700 SD 92109 1247-H5
1600 SD 92109 1248-B4
7300 LMGR 91945 1290-F1
7400 LMGR 91945 1270-G7
BERYL WY
4800 SD 92109 1248-B4
BESSEMER ST
2800 SD 92106 1288-B3
BEST RD
4600 BRW 92227 431-C1
4600 ImCo 92227 431-C1
5000 ImCo 92227 411-C11
BESTVIEW DR
700 SDCo 92021 1251-G2
BESTWOOD CT
6700 SD 92119 1250-E3
BETA CT
1600 SD 92126 1209-E6
BETA DR
1600 SD 92126 1209-E6
BETA ST
100 NATC 91950 1290-A6
1400 SD 92113 1289-G6
1700 NATC 91950 1289-J6
BETELGEUSE WY
8700 SD 92126 1209-C1
BETH PL
2400 LMGR 91945 1270-F7
BETHANY PL
- ELCJ 92021 1251-J3
BETHANY ST
400 SD 92114 1290-C5
BETHUNE CT
5600 SD 92114 1290-B2
BETHUNE WY
100 CHV 91911 1330-E4
BETSWORTH LN
28300 SDCo 92082 1090-B2
BETSWORTH RD
11200 SDCo 92026 1089-J2
11200 SDCo 92082 1089-J2
11800 SDCo 92082 1090-A2
BETSY CT
2500 SD 92110 1248-F7
BETTMAN CT
9000 SNTE 92071 1231-A7
BETTS ST
1100 ELCJ 92020 1251-C3
BETTY ST
600 SD 92154 1330-A7
4600 SD 92109 1248-B5
BETTYHILL DR
6900 SD 92117 1248-J2
BETTY JO MCNEECE LP
- ImCo 92243 6559-G5
BETTY LEE WY
13200 PWY 92064 1190-E2
BEVERLY AV
900 IMPB 91932 1349-G2
BEVERLY DR
700 VSTA 92084 1088-B4
4300 LMSA 91941 1270-H3
BEVERLY LN
1500 ImCo 92243 6559-J3
BEVERLY PL
500 SMCS 92069 1128-D1
BEVERLY ST
1000 SD 92114 1290-B2
2300 SDCo 92065 1152-D7
BEVERLY WY
1100 ESCN 92026 1110-A7
BEVERLY GLEN DR
4500 OCN 92056 1087-D5
BEVIS ST
3300 SD 92111 1249-A4
BEVNER CT
5100 SD 92105 1270-A7
BEWICKS CT
- CRLB 92009 1127-B7
BEXLEY RD
20500 SDCo 91935 (1315-A2 See Page 1294)
BEYER BLVD
2300 CHV 91911 1330-C6
2300 SD 92154 1330-C6
2700 SD 92154 1350-D1
3200 SD 92173 1350-E2
E BEYER BLVD
2200 SD 92173 1350-G4
BEYER WY
100 CHV 91911 1330-D5
100 SD 92154 1330-D6
700 SD 92154 1350-D1
BIADA ST
1300 VSTA 92083 1107-H4
BIANCA ST
5000 SD 92110 1268-F2
BIA RD #10
- SDCo 91906 (1299-D6 See Page 1298)
- SDCo 91906 (1319-D1 See Page 1298)
BIA RD #11
- SDCo 91905 430-C7
- SDCo 92066 430-C7
- SDCo 92066 (1299-D1 See Page 1298)
BIBLER CT
- CHV 91911 1330-H2
BIBLER DR
- SD 92173 1350-E5
BIDDEFORD ST
14500 PWY 92064 1190-H4
BIDDLE CT
6900 SD 92111 1248-J3
BIDDLE ST
- SDCo 92055 1067-A2
3800 SD 92111 1248-J3

BIDWELL CT
13400 SD 92129 1189-C4
BIENAVENTURA DR
- SDCo 92028 998-D7
BIENVENIDA CIR
1800 CRLB 92008 1106-J7
BIENVENIDO LN
1900 ESCN 92026 1109-H5
BIERNACKI CT
- CHV 91911 1330-H2
BIG BEND WY
500 OCN 92054 1086-G1
500 OCN 92054 1066-G7
12600 SDCo 92082 1090-C2
BIG BOULDER LN
3400 SDCo 91901 1234-C5
BIG BUCKS TR
- PWY 92064 1151-A6
BIG CANYON TER
1400 ENCT 92007 1167-F2
BIG CAT TR
3500 SDCo 91901 1275-B3
BIG CONE DR
- SDCo 92040 1231-G3
BIG DIPPER WY
1600 SD 92173 1350-E2
BIGFORD ST
8600 SDCo 91977 1290-J2
8600 SDCo 91977 1291-A2
BIGGS CT
3000 NATC 91950 1310-D3
BIG HORN CT
600 ELCJ 92019 1251-H6
BIG HORN RD
300 SDCo 92004 1058-J5
700 SDCo 92004 (1059-A5 See Page 1058)
BIGNELL DR
7300 SD 92139 1290-G6
BIG OAK ST
7200 SD 92114 1290-G6
BIG OAK RANCH RD
1000 SDCo 92028 1047-H1
BIG OAKS LN
- SDCo 91905 1300-B4
BIG PINE LN
35000 SDCo 92036 1156-E7
BIG PINE RD
2200 ESCN 92027 1130-E2
2200 SDCo 92027 1130-E2
BIG POTRERO TKTR
- SDCo 91963 1296-H7
- SDCo 91906 (1317-E2 See Page 1296)
- SDCo 91963 (1316-G1 See Page 1296)
- SDCo 91963 (1317-A1 See Page 1296)
2200 SDCo 91906 (1297-F7 See Page 1296)
BIG RED RD
1200 SDCo 91901 1233-H7
1200 SDCo 91901 1253-J1
BIG ROCK RD
8300 SNTE 92071 1250-H1
8500 SNTE 92071 1230-H7
BIG SKY RD
- SDCo 92065 1173-A2
BIG SPRINGS WY
15800 SD 92127 1169-J4
BIG SUR ST
4500 OCN 92057 1066-H6
BIG VIEW RD
500 OCN 92057 1067-F4
BIG WAGON RD
2500 SDCo 91901 1254-A2
BIG WHEEL WY
2600 SDCo 91901 1254-A2
BILLIE DR
8700 SNTE 92071 1231-E7
BILLINGS ST
900 ELCJ 92020 1251-G7
BILLMAN ST
3600 SD 92115 1270-D5
BILLOW DR
300 SD 92114 1290-H3
BILLY GN
2000 ESCN 92026 1109-C4
BILLY LN
14600 PWY 92064 1190-E1
BILLY MITCHELL DR
1100 ELCJ 92020 1251-D2
BILOXI ST
2500 SD 92105 1270-B7
BILTEER CT
10000 SNTE 92071 1231-D4
BILTEER DR
9800 SNTE 92071 1231-D4
BILTMORE AV
- ESCN 92027 1130-C1
BILTMORE ST
5000 SD 92117 1228-E7
BIMINI WY
1800 VSTA 92083 1107-G6
BINDAY WY
2200 SD 92154 1330-C6
BING ST
6500 SD 92115 1270-D5
BING CROSBY BLVD
- SDCo 92067 1148-J7
- SDCo 92067 1168-J2
- SDCo 92127 1148-J7
- SDCo 92127 1149-A7
- SDCo 92127 1168-J2
- SDCo 92127 1169-A1
BINGHAM DR
100 SMCS 92069 1108-F7
BINGHAM RD
9700 SNTE 92071 1231-C4
BINNACLE DR
- CRLB 92009 1127-A7
BINNACLE WY
3500 OCN 92054 1086-E6
BINNEY PL
8000 LMSA 91942 1250-H7
BIOLA AV
2300 SD 92154 1350-B3
BIOLOGICAL GRADE
8700 SD 92093 1227-H3
BIONA DR
4600 SD 92116 1269-H3
BIONA PL
4200 SD 92116 1269-H3
BIRCH AV
800 ESCN 92027 1130-C3
800 SDCo 92027 1130-C3
BIRCH LN
13000 PWY 92064 1191-A4

SAN DIEGO CO.   INDEX

Street	Block	City	ZIP	Pg-Grid
BIRCH RD				
	200	SDCo	92055	1086-A4
BIRCH ST				
	-	SMCS	92078	1129-C2
	500	SMCS	92069	1128-C1
	1000	SD	92101	1291-B2
	2400	VSTA	92083	1108-A6
	3600	SD	92113	1289-G6
BIRCH WY				
	1200	SD	92101	1130-C3
BIRCH BARK LN				
	3400	SDCo	92107	1310-H2
BIRCH BLUFF AV				
	10600	SD	92131	1210-C3
BIRCH BLUFF CT				
	12500	SD	92131	1210-C3
BIRCH BLUFF PL				
	12500	SD	92131	1210-C3
BIRCH BRIAR LN				
	1500	SDCo	92126	1130-D3
BIRCHBROOK CT				
	12600	PWY	92064	1170-D3
BIRCHCREEK RD				
	6900	SD	92119	1250-F4
BIRCHCREST BLVD				
	9100	SNTE	92071	1231-A2
BIRCH GLEN CT				
	11700	SD	92131	1209-J3
	11700	SD	92131	1210-A3
BIRCHLEY				
	700	OCN	92054	1106-C1
BIRCH TREE LN				
	13200	PWY	92064	1190-E3
BIRCHVIEW DR				
	700	ENCT	92024	1167-G1
BIRCHWOOD CIR				
	4700	CRLB	92008	1106-J6
BIRCHWOOD DR				
	1700	SMCS	92069	1109-A2
BIRCHWOOD PL				
	200	SMCS	92069	1108-H5
BIRCHWOOD ST				
	6300	SD	92120	1250-B5
BIRCHWOOD WY				
	2400	OCN	92054	1106-F1
BIRD CT				
	-	SMCS	92069	1108-F5
BIRD ST				
	9200	SNTE	92071	1231-G6
BIRDIE DR				
	2300	OCN	92056	1106-H1
	3500	SDCo	91971	1271-A5
	3500	SDCo	91977	1169-H2
	3600	SDCo	91941	1270-J5
BIRDIE ST				
	2300	OCN	92056	1106-J1
BIRD OF PARADISE LN				
	4500	SDCo	91941	1271-D3
BIRD ROCK AV				
	100	SD	92037	1247-F4
BIRDSELL LN				
	17100	SDCo	92036	1156-E7
	17100	SDCo	92036	1176-E1
BIRDSELL RD				
	17100	SDCo	92036	1176-E1
BIRDSONG DR				
	32400	SDCo	92026	1049-B7
BIRDSONG PL				
	1600	SD	92021	1252-A2
BIRDS VIEW CT				
	11100	SD	92126	1208-J2
BIRKDALE PL				
	5500	SD	92117	1248-H2
BIRKDALE WY				
	1800	VSTA	92083	1108-A4
	5500	SD	92117	1248-H2
BIRMINGHAM DR				
	100	ENCT	92007	1167-J3
	1200	ENCT	92024	1167-F3
	7900	SD	92123	1249-B6
BIRMINGHAM WY				
	7900	SD	92123	1249-B6
BISBY LAKE AV				
	6400	SD	92119	1250-J4
BISCAY DR				
	3200	SD	92154	1350-D2
BISCAYNE BAY				
	5700	SD	92105	1290-B1
BISCAYNE CV				
	12900	SD	92014	1207-J1
BISCAYNE PL				
	18500	PWY	92064	1150-G6
BISHOFF CT				
	8300	SNTE	92071	1230-H6
BISHOP DR				
	6400	SD	92114	1290-D4
BISHOP ST				
	-	CHV	91911	1330-E4
BISHOPS LN				
	7100	SD	92037	1247-F1
	7300	SD	92037	1227-F7
BISHOPS WY				
	5400	LMSA	91941	1271-B1
	5400	SDCo	91941	1271-B1
BISHOPSGATE RD				
	100	ENCT	92024	1147-A2
BISON DR				
	600	ELCJ	92019	1251-H6
BITTERBUSH LN				
	1200	SDCo	92019	1252-F7
	1300	SDCo	92019	1272-F1
BITTERCREEK LN				
	9100	SD	92129	1189-D3
BITTERN CT				
	1800	CRLB	92009	1127-D7
BITTERN ST				
	1200	SD	92114	1290-E2
BITTERROOT CT				
	1500	ESCN	92026	1109-D6
	1500	SMCS	92069	1109-D6
BITTERSWEET ST				
	900	ESCN	92026	1109-F5
BITTER SWEET HILL				
	1700	SDCo	92084	1108-C2
BIXEL DR				
	5100	SD	92115	1270-A1
BJOIN RD				
	24700	SDCo	92065	1173-G3
BLACKBERRY CIR				
	800	SMCS	92069	1109-A6
BLACKBERRY WY				
	5400	OCN	92057	1067-D6
BLACK BIRD CIR				
	1700	CRLB	92009	1127-D6
BLACKBIRD DR				
	500	VSTA	92083	1087-G4
BLACKBIRD ST				
	1000	ELCJ	92020	1251-D3
BLACKBIRD WY				
	200	OCN	92057	-1086-H5
BLACKBUSH LN				
	2700	SDCo	92019	1272-F1
BLACK CANYON PL				
	-	SDCo	92065	409-G11
BLACK CANYON RD				
	1400	SDCo	92065	1153-A2
	21000	SDCo	92065	409-H11
	23500	SDCo	92070	409-H11
BLACK CORAL CT				
	4800	SD	92154	1330-J6
BLACK CORAL WY				
	400	SD	92154	1330-J6
BLACK DUCK WY				
	4200	OCN	92057	1086-J3
BLACK EAGLE PL				
	4200	OCN	92057	1087-A3
BLACKFOOT CT				
	4200	SD	92117	1248-F6
BLACKFOOT ST				
	4700	SD	92117	1248-F5
BLACK GOLD RD				
	9600	SD	92037	1227-H1
BLACKHAWK AV				
	1800	OCN	92056	1087-D5
BLACKHAWK CIR				
	700	VSTA	92083	1107-G1
BLACKHAWK GN				
	1300	ESCN	92029	1129-G6
BLACK HILLS CT				
	9400	SD	92129	1189-E4
BLACK HILLS LN				
	-	SNTE	92071	1231-D2
BLACK HILLS RD				
	13400	SD	92129	1189-E4
BLACK HILLS WY				
	9300	SD	92129	1189-D4
BLACKHORSE RW				
	14000	SD	92130	1188-D2
BLACK LION CT				
	3000	SD	92126	1209-D6
BLACKMORE CT				
	2100	SD	92109	1248-A4
BLACK MOUNTAIN RD				
	-	ImCo		411-L9
	-	SD	92130	1189-A3
	4100	SD	92130	1188-D4
	4100	LMSA	91941	1270-J4
	9400	SD	92126	1209-E1
	10200	SDCo	92127	1169-E2
	10400	SDCo	92127	1169-H2
	11100	SD	92129	1189-D5
	11100	SD	92129	1189-D1
	14800	SD	92129	1169-D1
BLACK MOUNTAIN TKTR				
	19500	SDCo	92065	409-H10
BLACK MOUNTAIN WY				
	6300	SD	92130	1188-G4
BLACK OAK LN				
	-	SDCo	92036	1155-F3
BLACK OAK RD				
	7400	SD	92114	1290-G4
BLACK PINE PL				
	4600	SD	92130	1188-C5
BLACKPOOL RD				
	7800	SD	92114	1290-G4
BLACK RAIL CT				
	-	CRLB	92009	1127-C6
BLACK RAIL RD				
	-	CRLB	92009	1127-C4
BLACK RIDGE RD				
	9700	SDCo	92021	1233-D2
BLACKSHAW LN				
	400	SD	92173	1350-E3
BLACKSMITH RD				
	5800	SDCo	91902	1311-B2
BLACKSTILT CT				
	900	CRLB	92009	1127-B7
BLACKSTONE CT				
	7600	SD	92114	1290-G3
BLACK SWAN PL				
	7300	CRLB	92009	1127-C7
BLACKTHORNE AV				
	400	ELCJ	92020	1251-D6
BLACKTHORNE CT				
	1600	ELCJ	92020	1251-C7
BLACKTON DR				
	2400	SD	92105	1270-B7
	2400	SD	92105	1290-B1
	4100	LMSA	91941	1270-F4
BLACK WALNUT DR				
	-	SMCS	92078	1128-C6
BLACKWELL CT				
	2700	SDCo	92084	1067-H6
BLACKWELL RD				
	4500	OCN	92056	1107-D2
BLACKWOOD DR				
	700	SD	92154	1330-F7
BLACKWOOD RD				
	-	SDCo	91905	430-C7
	800	CHV	91910	1310-J7
BLAIN PL				
	6100	LMSA	91942	1250-J6
BLAINE AV				
	1500	SD	92103	1269-C5
BLAIR CT				
	900	SD	92113	1289-H5
BLAIR RD				
	-	ImCo	92233	411-C9
BLAIR WY				
	9500	SDCo	91941	1271-C2
BLAIS RD				
	-	ImCo	92259	431-A2
BLAISDELL PL				
	13700	PWY	92064	1190-F6
BLAKELY DR				
	3000	SD	92110	1268-E6
BLAKSTAD CT				
	7100	SD	92126	1208-J4
BLANCHARD RD				
	100	ELCJ	92020	1251-B5
BLANCHE AV				
	-	SDCo	91905	1300-C7
BLANCHE ST				
	200	SD	92173	1350-F4
BLANCO CT				
	12800	PWY	92064	1190-D5
BLANCO TER				
	8500	SDCo	92021	1232-E6
BLANDO CT				
	1350	SDCo	91950	1350-G3
BLANDO LN				
	1700	SDCo	91950	1350-G3
BLANFORD ST				
	1500	SD	92114	1290-E5
BLANTON CT				
	11800	SD	92128	1190-A6
BLANTON LN				
	12200	SD	92128	1190-A6
BLARNEY AV				
	9600	SDCo	91977	1271-C6
BLAXTON DR				
	1500	SD	92078	1128-G2
BLAZEWOOD PL				
	16000	SD	92127	1169-J5
BLAZEWOOD WY				
	16000	SD	92127	1169-J5
BLAZING STAR TR				
	-	IMP	92243	6499-E2
BLENKARNE DR				
	3000	CRLB	92008	1106-G4
BLERIOT AV				
	500	SD	92154	1330-E6
BLESSED MOTHER DR				
	3400	SDCo	92028	1047-J2
BLISS CIR				
	-	OCN	92056	1087-D5
BLIX ST				
	7300	SD	92111	1249-A4
BLOCH ST				
	5100	SD	92122	1228-A7
BLOCKTON RD				
	200	SDCo	92083	1108-A2
BLODGETT RD				
	1300	ImCo	92250	431-D4
BLOM ST				
	2300	SD	92109	1248-B5
BLOOMDALE ST				
	9200	SNTE	92071	1231-G5
BLOOMFIELD RD				
	7700	SD	92114	1290-G4
BLOSSOM LN				
	7900	LMGR	91945	1290-H1
	8400	SDCo	91977	1290-H1
BLOSSOM WY				
	200	OCN	92054	1086-F3
	8200	LMGR	91945	1290-J1
BLOSSOM FIELD WY				
	1600	ENCT	92024	1147-G6
BLOSSOM HILL CT				
	8200	LMGR	91945	1290-J1
BLOSSOM HILL DR				
	8300	LMGR	91945	1290-J1
BLOSSOM HILL LN				
	1700	ESCN	92029	1129-G2
BLOSSOM SPRINGS RD				
	9800	SDCo	92021	1232-G2
BLOSSOM VALLEY LN				
	15000	SDCo	92021	1233-A2
	15000	SDCo	92021	1232-J2
BLOSSOM VALLEY RD				
	9000	SDCo	92040	1232-G4
	9000	SDCo	92021	1232-G4
BLUE ANCHOR CAY RD				
	-	CORD	92118	1329-E2
BLUE ASH CT				
	100	ENCT	92024	1147-H7
BLUEBELL CT				
	800	CRLB	92009	1127-A5
BLUEBELL LN				
	1900	SDCo	92004	1106-C2
BLUEBELL ST				
	10100	SDCo	91977	1291-D2
BLUEBELL WY				
	1300	ELCJ	92021	1251-J3
	1300	ELCJ	92021	1252-A3
BLUEBERRY CIR				
	400	SDCo	92054	1086-G2
BLUEBERRY HILL				
	-	SD	92028	998-G5
	1400	SDCo	91901	1234-C6
BLUEBERRY HILL LN				
	13200	SDCo	92082	1090-D2
BLUEBIRD LN				
	-	CRLB	92009	1127-D4
	-	OCN	92057	1086-H2
BLUE BIRD LN				
	1000	SD	92037	1227-F7
BLUEBIRD ST				
	1300	ELCJ	92020	1251-D3
	2100	SD	92114	1290-D1
BLUE BIRD CANYON CT				
	3700	SDCo	92084	1108-G1
BLUE BIRD CANYON RD				
	1800	SDCo	92084	1108-F1
BLUE BIRD CANYON TR				
	900	SDCo	92084	1088-G7
BLUEBIRD PARK RD				
	100	ENCT	92024	1027-F1
BLUEBONNET LN				
	900	SMCS	92078	1128-G3
BLUEBONNET DR				
	6400	CRLB	92009	1127-A4
BLUE BONNET PL				
	400	SDCo	92028	1027-F1
BLUE BONNETT CT				
	500	NATC	91950	1290-D6
BLUEBOY LN				
	8800	SNTE	92071	1231-D7
BLUE CRANE WY				
	8200	SDCo	91977	1169-F4
BLUE CRYSTAL TR				
	15500	PWY	92064	1191-A2
BLUE CRYSTAL TRAILS				
	15300	PWY	92064	1191-J2
	15300	PWY	92064	1191-A2
BLUECUP PL				
	9300	SDCo	92040	1232-D4
BLUE CYPRESS DR				
	11200	SD	92131	1210-A1
BLUE DIAMOND CT				
	12000	SD	92131	1210-B1
BLUE DOLPHIN WY				
	-	CRLB	92009	1127-A7
BLUE FALLS DR				
	1300	CHV	91910	1311-B6
BLUEFIELD CT				
	6600	SD	92120	1250-D5
BLUEFIELD PL				
	6400	SD	92120	1250-D6
BLUE GILL DR				
	2400	SD	91906	(1297-F6 See Page 1296)
BLUEGILL LN				
	600	SDCo	92054	1086-G2
BLUEGRASS LN				
	-	CRLB	92009	1127-D4
BLUEGRASS RD				
	1000	VSTA	92083	1087-E6
	17900	SDCo	92065	1171-G1
BLUEGRASS ST				
	400	SD	92114	1290-G6
BLUE GUM CT				
	2900	SDCo	92028	1048-C3
BLUEHAVEN CT				
	1800	SD	92154	1350-D3
BLUE HERON AV				
	1300	SD	92024	1147-D2
BLUE HERON DR				
	300	SMCS	92078	1128-G2
BLUE HERON PL				
	1500	SD	92127	1127-C7
BLUE JAY DR				
	2400	SD	92123	1249-B7
	3000	SDCo	92036	1155-H3
BLUE JAY LN				
	1000	SMCS	92069	1128-E2
BLUE JAY PL				
	7900	SD	92123	1249-B7
BLUE LAKE CT				
	6900	LMGR	91945	1270-E7
BLUELAKE DR				
	600	CHV	91913	1311-E4
BLUE LAKE DR				
	7500	SD	92119	1250-G6
	8600	SD	92119	1251-A6
BLUE LILAC LN				
	1300	SDCo	91901	1233-H6
BLUE MOON WY				
	3400	SDCo	92083	1070-G1
BLUE OAK CT				
	3000	SDCo	91978	1271-G7
BLUE OF THE NIGHT LN				
	-	SDCo	92127	1149-A7
BLUE ORCHID LN				
	6900	CRLB	92009	1127-E5
BLUE POINT DR				
	-	CRLB	92009	1127-A5
BLUERIDGE PL				
	400	ESCN	92029	1109-G4
BLUERIDGE ST				
	1800	OCN	92056	1087-C5
	5500	SD	92139	1310-C2
BLUE RIDGE TR				
	14000	PWY	92064	1170-G4
BLUE SAGE CT				
	-	IMP	92243	6499-E2
BLUESAGE DR				
	900	SMCS	92069	1128-B2
BLUE SAGE LN				
	13800	SDCo	92082	1070-E7
BLUE SAGE RD				
	14300	PWY	92064	1170-G4
BLUE SAGE WY				
	400	OCN	92057	1086-J4
BLUE SKIES RDG				
	-	SDCo	92127	1149-A7
	9000	SDCo	92127	1169-A1
BLUE SKY DR				
	1200	ENCT	92007	1167-E1
BLUE SKY LN				
	-	SDCo	92127	1107-D2
BLUE SKY RANCH RD				
	-	SDCo	92040	1212-F3
BLUESPRINGS LN				
	200	SDCo	92054	1106-C2
BLUESTONE CT				
	10100	SDCo	91977	1291-D2
BLUESTONE DR				
	13300	SDCo	92040	1232-D5
BLUESTONE ST				
	10500	SDCo	92127	1169-F2
BLUE SUMMIT CT				
	-	SD	92131	1209-G2
BLUET PT				
	-	SD	92131	1210-A1
BLUEWATER LN				
	2100	CHV	91913	1311-E4
BLUEWATER RD				
	800	CRLB	92009	1126-J5
BLUE WATER WY				
	1900	OCN	92054	1106-F1
BLUEWING CT				
	12300	PWY	92064	1190-B6
BLUFF CT				
	3500	CRLB	92008	1107-B3
BLUFF DR				
	2100	SD	92109	1248-A4
BLUFF PL				
	3900	ESCN	92025	1150-C3
	5000	SDCo	92020	1271-G1
BLUFF WY				
	-	SDCo	92054	1086-F6
BLUFFCREST LN				
	800	ENCT	92024	1147-H5
BLUFFDALE PL				
	2700	SDCo	91977	1271-D7
BLUFF POINT RD				
	100	SDCo	92028	1027-F1
BLUFF PT CT				
	1600	CHV	91911	1330-J4
BLUFFS AV				
	1100	SD	92154	1350-E1
BLUFFSIDE AV				
	2600	SD	92109	1248-C4
BLUFFVIEW CT				
	8200	SDCo	91977	1290-J5
BLUFF VIEW PL				
	-	SMCS	92069	1128-A3
BLUFFVIEW RD				
	15400	SDCo	91977	1290-J5
BLY ST				
	3400	SD	92115	1270-D6
BLYTHE CT				
	8100	SD	92126	1209-B2
BLYTHE RD				
	11000	SDCo	92126	1209-B2
BOARDWALK				
	900	SMCS	92069	1128-E1
BOARTS RD Rt#-S26				
	400	ImCo	92281	411-B11
	400	ImCo	92281	431-B1
BOAT BASIN RD				
	400	SD	92055	1085-G4
BOB LN				
	-	OCN	92054	1086-G3
BOB ST				
	3900	SD	92110	1268-E6
	5900	LMSA	91942	1250-H6
BOBBIE LN				
	4200	SDCo	91977	1271-G3
BOBCAT GN				
	2400	ESCN	92029	1129-E6
BOB CAT LN				
	800	SD	91901	1234-G5
BOB CAT TR				
	27100	SDCo	92070	409-H9
BOBHIRD DR				
	6900	SD	92119	1250-J3
E BOBIER DR				
	100	VSTA	92084	1087-H3
	1000	VSTA	92084	1088-A4
W BOBIER DR				
	-	SDCo	92083	1087-F3
	100	SDCo	92056	1087-F3
	1100	VSTA	92083	1087-G4
BOBOLINK DR				
	1100	VSTA	92083	1087-G4
BOBOLINK WY				
	2100	SD	92123	1249-A7
BOBRITT LN				
	31500	SDCo	92003	1068-E1
BOBRITT RD				
	31900	SDCo	92003	1068-E1
	31900	SDCo	92003	1048-E7
BOBWHITE LN				
	100	ELCJ	92020	1251-D2
BOB WILSON DR				
	2100	SD	92101	1289-C1
	2100	SD	92134	1289-C1
BOCA ST				
	2200	CRLB	92009	1147-F2
BOCA DEL TULE				
	8500	SDCo	91977	1290-J5
BOCA RATON DR				
	1200	CHV	91915	1311-G6
BOCA RATON LN				
	17200	PWY	92064	1170-F1
BOCA RATON ST				
	1200	CHV	91915	1311-G6
BOCAW PL				
	5100	SD	92115	1270-E1
BODEGA CT				
	12400	SD	92128	1150-B7
BODEGA PL				
	12400	SD	92128	1150-B7
BODEGA RD				
	12400	SD	92128	1150-B7
BODEGA WY				
	1300	VSTA	92083	1107-H4
	12400	SD	92128	1170-B1
BODEGA BAY DR				
	-	SDCo	92014	1187-H7
BODEGA BAY WY				
	4200	OCN	92054	1066-E6
BODIE CT				
	13600	SD	92129	1189-C3
BOEING ST				
	-	SD	92154	1351-D2
BOGART CIR				
	8900	SD	92126	1209-D3
BOGOSO LN				
	3900	SDCo	91977	1271-E4
BOGOTA				
	-	SDCo	92003	1067-J2
BOILING SPRINGS RD				
	-	SDCo	91948	1218-F6
BOISE AV				
	4700	SD	92117	1248-F1
BOLERO DR				
	-	CHV	91910	1311-B7
BOLERO LN				
	2100	SDCo	92084	1108-D3
BOLERO ST				
	7300	CRLB	92009	1127-H7
BOLERORIDGE PL				
	100	ESCN	92026	1109-G4
BOLEY RD				
	2100	ImCo	92251	430-L4
BOLIN ST				
	10100	SD	92126	1208-J5
BOLINAS ST				
	2200	SD	92107	1268-A6
BOLINAS BAY CT				
	1200	CHV	91913	1311-C7
BOLIVAR DR				
	1900	SDCo	92004	1058-H7
BOLIVAR ST				
	3600	OCN	92056	1107-B3
	5500	SD	92139	1310-C1
BOLIVIA LN				
	3700	OCN	92056	1107-B1
BOLLENBACHER ST				
	600	SD	92114	1290-B3
BOLO PL				
	7700	CRLB	92009	1147-G2
BOLOTIN LN				
	100	SMCS	92078	1128-H1
BOLSA CHICA GN				
	2000	ESCN	92026	1109-E5
BOLSERIA LN				
	9500	SD	92129	1189-F7
	9500	SD	92129	1209-F1
BOLT ST				
	-	SD	92126	1288-A4
BOLTON HALL RD				
	300	OCN	92054	1086-E5
BOMAR DR				
	4400	SDCo	91941	1271-E3
BON CT				
	3800	SD	92110	1310-J2
BONAIR PL				
	8200	SDCo	91977	1290-J5
BONAIR RD				
	1300	VSTA	92084	1088-A4
BONAIR ST				
	300	SD	92037	1247-E1
BONAIR WY				
	500	SD	92037	1247-E1
BONANZA AV				
	9300	SDCo	92021	1232-H5
BOND AV				
	4100	SD	92117	1248-E6
BOND CT				
	14400	SDCo	92021	1232-G4
BOND ST				
	4400	SD	92109	1248-C5
BONDS CORNER RD				
	-	HOLT	92250	431-E5
	-	ImCo	92250	431-E5
BONESTEELE RD Rt#-S33				
	5900	SDCo	92250	431-F7
BONILLO DR				
	300	SD	92115	1270-D4
BONITA DR				
	-	SMCS	92069	1128-E2
	700	ENCT	92024	1147-E6
	700	VSTA	92083	1087-E6
	800	ENCT	92024	1167-E1
	4100	OCN	92056	1107-C2
	4100	SD	92114	1290-B6
BONITA LN				
	1700	CRLB	92008	1106-F4
	6900	SD	92119	1250-J3
BONITA PL				
	100	SDCo	92021	1252-H4
	7200	LMSA	91941	1270-F3
BONITA RD Rt#-S17				
	100	CHV	91910	1310-D5
	2800	SDCo	91910	1310-E4
	3000	SD	91902	1310-J1
	3000	SD	91902	1310-H3
E BONITA RD				
	-	CHV	91910	1310-C5
W BONITA RD				
	-	CHV	91910	1310-C5
N BONITA ST				
	2000	LMGR	91945	1290-F1
	2200	SDCo	91945	1270-F7
S BONITA ST				
	4100	SD	91977	1271-D5
BONITA WY				
	2100	SD	91977	1271-D5
	1100	SDCo	92019	1251-J7
BONITA BLUFFS CT				
	2200	CRLB	92009	1147-F2
BONITA CANYON DR				
	8500	SDCo	91977	1290-J5
BONITA CANYON PT				
	200	CHV	91902	1311-A3
BONITA CANYON RD				
	17500	SD	92127	1170-A1
BONITA CHRISTIAN CENTER DR				
	3500	SDCo	91902	1310-F3
	200	CHV	91902	1311-A3
BONITA GLEN DR				
	200	CHV	91910	1310-D5
BONITA GLEN TER				
	200	CHV	91910	1310-D5
BONITA HEIGHTS LN				
	3600	SDCo	91902	1310-J2
BONITA LADERA WY				
	3300	NATC	91950	1310-E3
	3300	SDCo	91950	1310-E3
BONITA MEADOWS LN				
	2100	SDCo	91902	1252-D7
BONITA MESA RD				
	6000	SDCo	91902	1311-B1
	2900	SDCo	91902	1310-D4
BONITA VALLE				
	400	SDCo	91902	1310-D4
BONITA VERDE DR				
	3600	CHV	91902	1310-G3
BONITA VIEW DR				
	3600	SDCo	91902	1310-J2
BONITA VISTA				
	13000	PWY	92064	1190-D5
BONITA VISTA DR				
	2500	SDCo	91902	1310-J1
BONITA VISTA WY				
	14700	SDCo	91935	1273-A6
BONITA WOODS DR				
	3000	SDCo	91902	1290-H7
	3000	SD	91902	1310-H1
BONITO AV				
	300	IMPB	91932	1329-F7
BONJON LN				
	10800	SD	92131	1210-A2
BONNEYVILLE DR				
	1700	SD	91977	1291-B2
BONNIE CT				
	4700	SD	92116	1269-G3
BONNIE LN				
	10300	SDCo	91941	1271-E1
BONNIE BLUFF CIR				
	1300	ENCT	92024	1147-D2
BONNIE BLUFF CT				
	1500	ENCT	92024	1147-D2
BONNIE BRAE PL				
	1000	VSTA	92084	1087-J6
	1000	VSTA	92084	1088-A6
BONNIE JEAN LN				
	8700	SDCo	91977	1271-A7
	8700	SDCo	91977	1291-A1
BONNIE JEAN PL				
	8800	SDCo	91977	1291-A1
BONNIE LYNN WY				
	9500	SDCo	91941	1271-C3
BONNIE VIEW DR				
	6400	SD	92119	1250-E6
BONNIE VISTA DR				
	9800	SDCo	91941	1271-D4
BONNIE VISTA PL				
	9800	SDCo	91941	1271-D4
BONSALL ST				
	500	SD	92114	1290-G3
BONUS DR				
	1800	SD	92110	1268-F2
BON VUE DR				
	9800	SDCo	92021	1233-B2
BOOKHAM CT				
	7400	SD	92111	1269-A1
BOOMER CT				
	13200	SD	92129	1189-C4
BOOMVANG CT				
	300	OCN	92054	1086-E5
BOONE DR				
	-	SD	92101	1289-C2
BOONE RD				
	-	ImCo	92243	6559-J4
BOONE ST				
	3800	SD	92117	1248-E4
BOON LAKE AV				
	6500	SD	92119	1250-H5
BOORTZ LN				
	16200	SDCo	92065	1172-A3
BOOT WY				
	5600	OCN	92057	1067-E6
BOOTES ST				
	11000	SD	92126	1209-D1
BOOTHBAY PL				
	8500	SD	92129	1189-C5
BOOTH HILL DR				
	14400	SDCo	92021	1232-G4
BOQUITA DR				
	13600	SD	92014	1187-H6
BORANA ST				
	1500	SD	92111	1268-H2
BORDEAUX AV				
	2700	SD	92037	1227-J3
BORDEAUX TER				
	1900	CHV	91913	1311-D7
BORDELON CT				
	3700	SDCo	92124	1249-G6
BORDELON ST				
	10000	SDCo	92124	1249-G6
BORDEN CIR				
	300	SMCS	92069	1108-J6
BORDEN RD				
	400	SMCS	92069	1109-A6
	500	SMCS	92069	1108-J6
	1000	ESCN	92026	1129-G1
	1200	ESCN	92026	1109-F6
W BORDEN RD				
	35	SDCo	92069	1108-E5
BORDER AV				
	-	SD	92014	1187-F2
BORDER VILLAGE RD				
	-	SDCo	92173	1350-G4
BOREALIS RD				
	8300	SD	92126	1209-C2
BOREGO ST				
	7700	SD	92114	1290-G3
BOREN ST				
	3600	SD	92115	1270-D5
BORICA CT				
	1500	SDCo	92004	(1099-E2 See Page 1098)
BORLA PL				
	7300	CRLB	92009	1128-A7
	7300	CRLB	92009	1148-A1
BORMAC PL				
	3200	SDCo	92084	1108-C1
BORNE CT				
	3300	SD	92129	1189-B7
BORNER ST				
	4500	SD	92102	1289-J4
BORRA CT				
	4200	OCN	92056	1087-C6
	4200	VSTA	92083	1087-C6
BORRA PL				
	900	ESCN	92029	1129-E4
BORREGO CT				
	200	SDCo	92057	1086-J4
BORREGO AIR RANCH RD				
	-	SDCo	92004	(1099-J3 See Page 1098)
BORREGO HILLS RD				
	2000	SDCo	92004	(1099-F5 See Page 1098)
BORREGO SALTON SEAWAY				
	-	SDCo	92004	(1059-J3 See Page 1058)
BORREGO SALTON SEAWAY Rt#-S22				
	-	ImCo	92259	410-F7
	-	ImCo	92259	410-F7
	-	ImCo	92274	410-F7
	-	SDCo	92004	410-D7
	-	SDCo	92004	(1059-J4 See Page 1058)
BORREGO SPRINGS RD				
	13000	PWY	92064	1190-D5
	-	SDCo	92004	(1120-F1 See Page 1100)
	1200	SDCo	92004	1058-J4
	1300	CHV	91915	1311-H6
	1900	SDCo	92004	(1078-J1 See Page 1098)
	4500	SDCo	92004	(1099-G2 See Page 1098)
	5500	SDCo	92004	1100-A4
BORREGO SPRINGS RD Rt#-S3				
	2500	SDCo	92004	(1078-J3 See Page 1058)
	3500	SDCo	92004	(1079-A7 See Page 1058)
	3500	SDCo	92004	(1099-A1 See Page 1098)
BORREGO VALLEY RD				
	1200	SDCo	92004	(1059-C2 See Page 1058)
	3200	SDCo	92004	(1079-C4 See Page 1058)
	3300	SDCo	92004	(1099-D1 See Page 1098)
BORRESON ST				
	-	SD	92117	1248-E5
BORROMEO CT				
	-	OCN	92057	1086-H3
BORZOI WY				
	-	SD	92129	1189-B7
BOSAL CT				
	3500	SDCo	92082	1091-E4
BOSCOVICH RD				
	-	ImCo	92283	432-D5
BOSNA PL				
	2200	SD	92108	1108-C3
BOSQUE DR				
	10300	SDCo	92040	1231-F3
BOSSTICK BLVD				
	-	SMCS	92069	1108-D5
BOSTON AV				
	-	SD	92173	1350-G5
	2600	SD	92113	1289-C6
BOSTONIA ST				
	1100	ELCJ	92021	1251-J3
BOSWELL CT				
	2300	CHV	91914	1311-F4
BOSWELL RD				
	2300	CHV	91914	1311-F4
BOSWORTH CT				
	500	ELCJ	92019	1251-J6
BOSWORTH ST				
	1200	ELCJ	92019	1251-J6
	1300	ELCJ	92019	1252-A6
BOTANY BAY CT				
	8100	SD	92105	1290-C1
BOTE CT				
	9600	SDCo	91977	1291-C4
BOTELLA PL				
	2300	CRLB	92009	1147-G1
BOTERO DR				
	17000	SD	92127	1169-J2
BOTHE AV				
	3800	SD	92122	1228-B7
BOTTLEBRUSH CT				
	700	OCN	92056	1086-F1
BOTTLEBRUSH PL				
	10800	ENCT	92024	1147-J7
BOTTLEBRUSH WY				
	200	SDCo	92028	1028-B2
BOTTONWOOD RD				
	1500	SD	92111	1268-H2
BOUCHER HEIGHTS RD				
	2700	SDCo	92037	1227-J3
BOUCHER LOOKOUT RD				
	-	SDCo	92060	409-G7
	-	SDCo	92060	1051-J1
BOUGAINVILLE RD				
	3000	CORD	92155	1309-B2
	3200	SD	92139	1290-E7
BOUGHER RD				
	-	SD	92126	1209-B7
BOULDER DR				
	-	SD	92115	1270-J2
BOULDER PASS				
	11100	SDCo	92026	1089-G4
BOULDER PL				
	4700	LMSA	91941	1270-J3

STREET
Block City ZIP Pg-Grid

BOULDER PL
8400 SD 92119 1250-J4
BOULDER CREEK RD
1500 OCN 92056 1087-D4
3000 SDCo 92036 1155-G5
4700 SDCo 92036 1175-G3
10000 SDCo 91916 429-K4
10000 SDCo 91916 (1195-G4 See Page 1175)
10000 SDCo 91916 1235-H1
10000 SDCo 92036 (1195-C1 See Page 1175)
BOULDER CREEK ST
2200 CHV 91915 1311-G6
BOULDERIDGE PL
2300 SDCo 91977 1271-H7
BOULDER KNOLLS DR
10000 SDCo 92026 1089-E2
BOULDER LAKE AV
6200 SD 92119 1250-H4
BOULDER LEGEND LN
2400 SDCo 92026 1109-J3
BOULDER MOUNTAIN RD
15600 PWY 92064 1170-E6
BOULDER OAKS DR
16900 SDCo 92065 1171-D2
BOULDER OAKS LN
2400 SDCo 91901 1234-B7
BOULDER PT DR
12200 PWY 92064 1190-B6
BOULDER RIDGE LN
15600 PWY 92064 1170-E5
BOULDERS CT
- SDCo 91901 1234-A6
BOULDERS LN
- SDCo 91901 1234-A6
BOULDERS RD
- SDCo 91901 1234-A6
BOULDER VIEW DR
12100 PWY 92064 1190-C6
BOULEVARD AV
700 IMPB 91932 1329-G6
BOULEVARD DR
6900 LMSA 91941 1270-E4
6900 SD 92115 1270-E4
BOULEVARD PL
1100 ELCJ 92020 1251-D7
7800 SD 92037 1227-G6
BOULTON AV
11600 SD 92128 1190-A2
BOUNDARY AV
1700 SD 92154 1329-J6
1700 SD 92154 1330-A6
1900 SDCo 92065 1172-D2
BOUNDARY RD
400 IMPB 91932 1349-G3
BOUNDARY ST
400 SD 92113 1289-H5
1900 SD 92104 1289-F1
2500 SD 92104 1269-E5
4300 SD 92116 1269-E3
N BOUNDARY ST
600 SD 92102 1289-G3
W BOUNDARY TKTR
4800 SDCo 91935 1254-B7
18100 SDCo 91935 1274-D2
BOUNDARY CREEK RD
44100 SDCo 91934 (1321-F5 See Page 1300)
S BOUNDARY FIRE RD
- SDCo 91916 1216-C3
BOUNTY CT
6400 SD 92120 1250-B6
BOUNTY ST
5600 SD 92120 1250-B6
BOUNTY WY
14200 PWY 92064 1170-G5
BOUQUET DR
100 SMCS 92069 1108-H6
BOUQUET CANYON RD
1700 CHV 91913 1311-D6
BOURBON CT
9900 SD 92131 1209-H5
BOURBON RD
1200 ESCN 92026 1109-F6
BOURGEOIS WY
14200 SD 92129 1189-D2
BOURKE PL
1700 ELCJ 92021 1252-B2
BOUSSACK LN
3500 OCN 92057 1086-F5
BOVET WY
7400 SD 92122 1228-G4
BOWDEN AV
5100 SD 92117 1248-G2
BOWDITCH PL
2800 SD 92104 1269-F7
BOWDOIN RD
14400 PWY 92064 1190-H4
BOWEN RD
8300 LMGR 91945 1270-J7
BOWER LN
8900 SDCo 92040 1232-C6
BOWIE ST
300 SD 92114 1290-H4
BOWKER RD
800 ImCo 92249 431-D7
1600 ImCo 92243 6560-J2
1700 ImCo 92243 6500-J5
BOWL CREEK RD
15800 PWY 92064 1170-E5
BOWLING GREEN DR
8800 LMSA 91941 1271-A4
BOWRON RD
12800 PWY 92064 1190-E5
BOWSPRIT DR
3500 OCN 92054 1086-F6
BOWSPRIT WY
- CRLB 92009 1127-A4
BOX CANYON RD
1000 SDCo 92028 1027-G1
5800 SD 92037 1247-G3
BOX ELDER PL
11400 SD 92127 1169-J5
BOX ELDER WY
11500 SD 92127 1169-J5
BOXFORD DR
6800 SD 92117 1248-J2
BOX S DR
3300 SDCo 92004 (1078-J6 See Page 1058)
BOXWOOD CT
- SMCS 92078 1128-D6
900 CRLB 92009 1127-A5
12700 PWY 92064 1170-C7
BOXWOOD DR
2500 SDCo 92019 1252-E7
2600 SDCo 92019 1272-F1
4600 SD 92117 1248-G1
BOXWOOD GN
500 ESCN 92027 1110-C7
BOXWOOD ST
- SDCo 92055 1086-B3
BOYCE LN
3300 SD 92105 1270-A6
BOYD AV
3200 SD 92111 1248-H4
BOYD RD
- ImCo 92227 431-D3
- ImCo 92250 431-D3
BOYINGTON PL
2400 ELCJ 92020 1251-B3
BOYINGTON RD
7900 SD 92145 1229-E1
BOYLE AV
600 ESCN 92027 1130-B2
1100 SDCo 92027 1130-C2
BOYLE PL
1700 ESCN 92027 1130-D2
BOYLE RD
- ImCo 92233 411-A10
BOYLSTON ST
4500 SD 92102 1289-J3
BOYNE ST
3400 SDCo 91977 1271-C6
BOYSEN LN
3700 OCN 92054 1086-G3
BOYSENBERRY WY
500 OCN 92057 1067-D7
BOZANICH CIR
600 VSTA 92084 1087-J7
BRABHAM ST
1700 SDCo 92019 1272-A4
1700 SDCo 92019 1271-J5
BRACERO PL
800 ESCN 92025 1129-J6
BRACERO RD
700 ENCT 92024 1147-E7
800 ENCT 92024 1167-E1
BRACKEN FERN CV
11400 SD 92131 1209-J2
11400 SD 92131 1210-A2
BRACS DR
8500 SNTE 92071 1231-D7
BRADBERRY CT
7000 LMGR 91945 1290-E1
BRADDOCK PL
8100 SD 92114 1290-H2
BRADDOCK ST
1200 SD 92114 1290-H2
1400 LMGR 91945 1290-H2
BRADDON WY
1600 SDCo 92021 1251-J2
BRADENHALL RW
6000 SD 92037 1248-A1
BRADFORD RD
600 SDCo 92019 1252-C6
BRADFORD ST
6000 SD 92115 1270-D3
BRADLEY AV
100 SDCo 92020 1251-G2
100 SDCo 92021 1251-G2
800 ELCJ 92021 1251-G2
W BRADLEY AV
100 SDCo 92020 1251-E2
100 ELCJ 92020 1251-E2
BRADLEY PL
1400 CHV 91911 1330-J3
BRADLEY ST
2400 OCN 92056 1087-C6
BRADMAN DR
3200 SD 92110 1268-E6
BRADSHAW CT
4800 SD 92130 1188-D6
BRADSHAW RD
- ELCN 92243 6499-E4
- ImCo 92243 6499-E4
BRADY AV
8700 SDCo 91977 1290-J4
BRADY CT
600 SDCo 91977 1290-J4
BRAEBURN RD
4400 SD 92116 1269-H2
BRAEMAR LN
900 SD 92109 1247-H7
BRAEMAR TER
- SDCo 92028 1027-G6
BRAESWOOD TER
13600 SDCo 92021 1232-E7
BRAGG ST
5300 SD 92122 1228-B7
BRAHMS RD
1600 ENCT 92007 1167-D2
BRAIDWOOD ST
2000 ELCJ 92020 1251-B1
BRAISTED RD
1700 SD 92101 1289-C2
BRALORNE CT
11200 SD 92126 1209-C1
BRALORNE WY
8700 SD 92126 1209-C1
BRAM AV
4700 SDCo 91902 1310-H2
BRAMBLE RD
9200 LMSA 91942 1251-B7
BRAMBLE WY
10600 SD 92126 1209-E3
BRAMBLEWOOD CT
1700 CHV 91913 1311-D6
BRAMBLEWOOD ST
1700 CHV 91913 1311-D7
BRAMDI VIEW LN
16900 SDCo 92040 1191-E5
16900 SDCo 92064 1191-E5
BRAMPTON ST
8100 SDCo 91977 1290-H2
BRAMSON PL
3200 SD 92104 1269-F4
BRANCH CT
3600 OCN 92054 1086-F1
BRANCO WY
11200 SD 92126 1209-B2
BRAND CREST
3700 ENCT 92024 1167-H2
BRANDEIS CT
6000 SD 92114 1290-C5
BRANDEIS DR
2800 OCN 92056 1087-A7
BRANDENBURG LN
100 SDCo 92028 1027-G2
BRANDING IRON CIR
1200 VSTA 92083 1107-F2
BRAND IRON ST
15700 SDCo 92065 1172-A4
BRANDO DR
2800 SD 92154 1350-D3
BRANDON CIR
2900 CRLB 92008 1107-B4
N BRANDON RD
100 SDCo 92028 1027-G2
S BRANDON RD
100 SDCo 92028 1027-G2
BRANDT RD
- ImCo 92233 411-B10
BRANDYWINE AV
1400 CHV 91911 1330-H3
BRANDYWINE ST
3100 SD 92117 1248-D5
3600 OCN 92057 1086-G5
BRANDYWOOD ST
100 SD 92114 1290-E4
BRANFORD RD
10000 SD 92129 1189-F3
BRANICOLE LN
12100 SD 92129 1189-F7
BRANMAN DR
- SD 92102 1289-G4
BRANNICK PL
2800 SD 92122 1228-B5
BRANT ST
300 SD 92103 1269-A6
2100 SD 92101 1289-A1
3800 SD 92103 1268-J5
BRANTA AV
1400 CRLB 92009 1127-C7
BRANT CANYON LN
1800 SDCo 92028 1027-J3
BRANTING ST
6100 SD 92122 1228-C5
BRANTNER LN
15900 SDCo 92065 1172-A4
BRASILIA PL
- SDCo 92003 1067-J2
BRASS LN
100 VSTA 92083 1087-F7
BRASS WY
900 ENCT 92024 1167-E1
BRASSICA ST
12200 SD 92129 1189-B7
BRASS LANTERN RD
700 SMCS 92069 1109-A5
BRASSWOOD RW
6300 SD 92037 1248-A1
BRATTON VALLEY RD
2600 SDCo 91935 1294-D3
BRAUER PT
500 SDCo 91901 1234-E4
BRAUN AV
300 SD 92114 1290-J3
BRAVA PL
100 ESCN 92026 1109-H5
BRAVA ST
7400 CRLB 92009 1147-J1
BRAVADO ST
2000 VSTA 92083 1107-G5
BRAVATA CT
18800 SD 92128 1150-C5
BRAVERMAN DR
10400 SNTE 92071 1231-E4
BRAVO CT
5500 SD 92124 1229-G7
BRAWLEY AV
- SDCo 91934 (1321-G5 See Page 1300)
- ImCo 92274 410-G5
BRAXTON SQ
12100 SD 92128 1190-B1
BRAY AV
9500 SDCo 91977 1271-C6
BRAYTON WY
1400 SDCo 92020 1272-A2
BRAZOS ST
600 SDCo 92065 1152-F5
BREAKWATER RD
100 CRLB 92009 1126-H6
BREAKWATER WY
100 OCN 92054 1085-J7
BRECKENRIDGE DR
- SD 92131 1209-G2
BRECKENRIDGE WY
- SD 92131 1209-G2
BREEZE ST
1300 OCN 92054 1086-A5
BREEZE HILL RD
700 VSTA 92083 1107-F1
800 VSTA 92083 1087-F7
BREEZE VILLA LN
700 VSTA 92083 1107-F1
BREEZE VILLA PL
1000 VSTA 92083 1107-F1
BREEZEWAY PL
14200 SD 92128 1190-A2
BREEZEWOOD DR
1000 CHV 91913 1311-D6
BREEZY WY
200 SMCS 92078 1129-A1
BREMEN WY
800 SDCo 91901 1253-G2
BREMERTON PL
3100 SD 92037 1228-A4
BREMS ST
3700 SD 92115 1270-D5
BRENDA WY
- SDCo 92082 1071-A5
BRENGLE WY
1500 VSTA 92084 1088-B6
BRENNA CT
400 ENCT 92024 1147-G6
BRENNAN ST
8100 SD 92114 1290-H2
BRENNER WY
1600 SD 92114 1290-D6
BRENNER SPRINGS WY
11300 SD 92126 1208-J2
BRENT LN
100 VSTA 92084 1087-H5
BRENTFORD AV
8700 SD 92126 1209-D3
BRENTWOOD CT
2800 CRLB 92008 1106-F3
BRENTWOOD ST
7400 SD 92111 1249-A4
BRESA DE LOMA DR
21300 SDCo 92029 1129-B5
BRETON WY
5700 SD 92120 1250-C7
BRETT PL
100 ESCN 92027 1110-F6
BRETT HARTE DR
13500 SDCo 92040 1232-D3
BRETTON WOOD CT
5500 SD 92130 1208-E1
BREWLEY LN
1000 VSTA 92083 1107-J4
1000 VSTA 92083 1108-E2
BREWSTER CT
11900 SD 92128 1190-A2
BREWSTER BAY DR
1200 CHV 91911 1330-H1
BRIAN PL
1500 ESCN 92025 1129-J5
BRIAN WY
9400 SDCo 92021 1232-H4
BRIANA CT
4700 SDCo 92028 1047-F6
BRIAND AV
2900 SD 92122 1228-C5
BRIAN PARK LN
13300 PWY 92064 1190-E1
BRIANT ST
900 SMCS 92069 1109-C5
BRIAR CT
- SD 92123 1249-F5
BRIAR GN
8400 SDCo 92021 1232-E7
8400 SDCo 92021 1252-E1
BRIARCLIFF DR
11000 SD 92131 1209-H4
BRIARCLIFF WY
10400 SD 92131 1209-H4
BRIARDALE WY
12200 SD 92128 1190-A6
E BRIARFIELD DR
1000 SD 92109 1247-J7
W BRIARFIELD DR
1000 SD 92109 1247-J7
BRIARGATE PL
1900 ESCN 92029 1129-G7
BRIAR HOLLOW LN
800 SDCo 92021 1252-G1
BRIAR KNOLL WY
- SD 92128 1189-J6
BRIARLAKE WOODS DR
- SD 92130 1208-E2
BRIARLEAF WY
11900 SD 92128 1190-B7
BRIAR PATCH GN
2400 ESCN 92026 1109-D3
BRIAR RIDGE RD
4600 OCN 92056 1087-D3
BRIARWAY CT
1000 VSTA 92083 1087-G5
BRIARWOOD CT
2400 SDCo 92025 1130-D6
BRIARWOOD DR
6800 CRLB 92009 1127-A5
BRIARWOOD PL
900 OCN 92056 1087-D2
2300 ESCN 92026 1109-J3
12700 PWY 92064 1170-C7
BRIARWOOD RD
400 SD 92114 1290-G5
500 SD 92139 1290-G7
600 SDCo 92139 1290-H7
1300 SDCo 91902 1290-J6
2900 SDCo 91902 1310-H1
BRICKELLIA ST
12100 SD 92129 1189-C6
BRICKLANE RD
900 SDCo 92065 1172-F1
BRIDANNELA TR
8700 SDCo 92040 1232-B6
BRIDENSTINE RD
2300 ImCo 92250 431-E4
BRIDGECREST LN
12400 SD 92128 1190-A6
BRIDGEHAMPTON PL
1700 SDCo 92019 1272-B4
BRIDGEHAMPTON ST
1100 SMCS 92069 1128-B3
BRIDGEPORT
2000 CHV 91913 1311-E4
BRIDGEPORT LN
3500 CRLB 92008 1107-A3
N BRIDGEPORT ST
1000 ESCN 92027 1110-A6
BRIDGET CT
10200 SD 92124 1249-G4
BRIDGETOWN BEND
- CORD 92118 1329-E2
BRIDGEVIEW DR
1500 SD 92105 1289-G2
BRIDGEWOOD WY
11700 SD 92128 1190-A6
BRIDLE PTH
9300 SNTE 92071 1231-E5
BRIDLE RUN
8800 SDCo 91901 1233-E6
BRIDLE CREEK LN
3100 SDCo 92069 1088-G5
BRIDLE PATH LN
11400 SDCo 92040 1211-J6
BRIDLE PATH WY
1000 OCN 92057 1067-E7
BRIDLE RUN CT
200 SDCo 91901 1233-E6
BRIDLE RUN LN
300 SDCo 91901 1233-E6
BRIDLE RUN PL
300 SDCo 91901 1233-E6
BRIDLE RUN TER
200 SDCo 91901 1233-E6
BRIDLE RUN VW
200 SDCo 91901 1233-E6
BRIDLESPUR
14900 PWY 92064 1190-J4
BRIDLEVALE RD
1700 CHV 91913 1311-D6
BRIDLEWOOD RD
16400 PWY 92064 1170-G3
BRIDON RD
9800 SDCo 92021 1233-E2
BRIDOON TER
3800 ENCT 92024 1148-C2
BRIENWOOD DR
28800 SDCo 92026 1089-A1
BRIER RD
9100 LMSA 91942 1251-B7
BRIERCREST DR
9200 LMSA 91942 1251-B7
BRIGANTINE CT
2100 ENCT 92024 1147-H7
BRIGANTINE DR
6500 CRLB 92009 1127-B4
BRIGGS AV
- ENCT 92024 1167-C1
BRIGHT CT
3400 SDCo 91977 1271-D5
BRIGHT ST
9800 SDCo 91977 1271-D6
BRIGHT CREEK LN
100 OCN 92056 1107-D3
BRIGHTHAVEN AV
500 ELCJ 92019 1252-A6
BRIGHTON AV
100 ELCN 92243 6499-H6
100 ELCN 92243 6500-A6
300 ENCT 92007 1167-D2
4400 SD 92107 1268-A6
4700 SD 92107 1267-J5
14000 PWY 92064 1190-F3
BRIGHTON CT
700 SD 92109 1267-H4
900 VSTA 92083 1108-A4
BRIGHTON RD
2600 CRLB 92008 1106-J5
BRIGHTON RIDGE CT
10700 SD 92131 1210-A2
BRIGHTSIDE WY
800 SDCo 92065 1153-A2
BRIGHTWOOD AV
100 CHV 91910 1310-A5
600 CHV 91910 1330-B1
BRIGHTWOOD CT
3200 OCN 92054 1086-D2
BRILENE LN
3100 SD 92111 1248-G5
BRILLDEN CT
3100 SD 92117 1248-D3
BRILLO ST
5000 SD 92117 1228-F7
BRILLWOOD HILL RD
15100 SD 92027 1130-J5
15100 SDCo 92027 1130-J5
BRINDISI ST
4400 SD 92107 1287-H2
BRINELL ST
4600 SD 92111 1249-B2
BRINSER ST
2200 SD 92136 1289-E7
3400 SD 92136 1309-F1
BRIOSO CT
1100 VSTA 92083 1107-H4
BRISAS CT
200 OCN 92054 1086-G1
BRISAS ST
100 OCN 92054 1086-G1
BRISBANE ST
- CHV 91910 1310-A4
BRISTLECONE CT
4600 OCN 92056 1087-D4
BRISTOL AV
400 ENCT 92007 1167-D2
BRISTOL CT
1700 CHV 91902 1311-C5
1700 CHV 91913 1311-C5
BRISTOL RD
5000 SD 92116 1269-H2
BRISTOL BAY CT
2000 SD 92105 1290-C1
BRISTOW CT
7500 SD 92154 1351-E4
BRITAIN ST
800 SD 92114 1290-G3
BRITANNIA BLVD
1500 SD 92154 1351-E3
BRITANNIA CT
7500 SD 92154 1351-E4
BRITEM CT
- VSTA 92083 1087-E6
BRITT CT
8700 SD 92123 1249-C7
BRITTANY CT
3500 SDCo 91935 1272-E5
BRITTANY RD
800 ENCT 92024 1147-C4
BRITTANY WY
3500 CRLB 92008 1107-A3
BRITTANY FORREST LN
- SD 92130 1208-E1
BRITTANY PARK LN
16100 PWY 92064 1170-D4
BRITTON AV
3600 CHV 91911 1330-E5
BRIXTON PL
13000 SD 92130 1188-B5
BROAD AV
3300 SD 92113 1289-F5
BROADLAWN ST
3900 SD 92111 1248-J3
BROADMOOR CT
1000 CHV 91915 1311-F5
BROADMOOR DR
5900 LMSA 91942 1251-C6
BROADMOOR PL
9400 LMSA 91942 1251-B6
BROAD OAKS RD
15300 SDCo 92021 1233-C1
BROADRICK PL
6500 SD 92139 1310-F1
BROADRICK WY
2600 SD 92139 1310-F1
BROADVIEW AV
9300 SD 92123 1249-E7
BROADVIEW ST
400 SDCo 91977 1290-J3
400 SDCo 91977 1291-A3
BROADWAY
- SDCo 92004 410-F11
- CHV 91910 1309-J5
- NATC 91950 1309-J5
100 ELCJ 92021 1251-G3
100 SD 92101 1289-B3
100 CHV 91910 1310-A6
400 CHV 91910 1330-A1
600 SD 92101 1288-J3
700 ELCN 92243 6499-G6
800 CHV 91911 1330-B4
1300 ELCJ 92021 1252-A3
1500 ELCJ 92019 1252-A3
1600 OCN 92054 1106-C3
1600 SDCo 92019 1252-A3
1700 SD 92102 1289-E3
6200 SD 92114 1290-D2
7100 LMGR 91945 1270-J5
8300 SDCo 91941 1270-J5
8500 SDCo 91941 1271-A4
E BROADWAY
100 VSTA 92084 1087-H6
N BROADWAY
100 ESCN 92025 1129-H1
800 ESCN 92026 1129-H1
1100 ESCN 92026 1109-H5
2900 SDCo 92026 1109-G1
17900 SDCo 92026 1089-G4
N BROADWAY Rt#-78
600 ESCN 92025 1129-H2
800 ESCN 92026 1129-H2
S BROADWAY
100 ESCN 92025 1129-J3
900 ESCN 92025 1130-A4
W BROADWAY
100 SD 92101 1289-A3
500 SD 92101 1288-J3
BROADWAY AV
6900 LMGR 91945 1290-E3
6900 SD 92114 1290-E3
BROADWAY CIR
900 SD 92101 1289-A3
BROADWAY LN
3600 LMGR 91945 1270-J5
BROADWAY PL
1300 ESCN 92025 1130-A4
BROCK CT
8100 LMGR 91945 1270-H7
BROCK RD
- ImCo 92243 6559-A6
BROCKBANK PL
5100 SD 92115 1270-C1
5200 SD 92120 1270-C1
BROCKMAN RD Rt#-S30
500 ImCo 92231 431-A7
600 ImCo 92243 431-A7
BROCKTON ST
900 ELCJ 92020 1251-B4
BROCKWAY ST
11200 SDCo 92021 1231-G7
11200 SDCo 92021 1251-G1
BROCKWOOD DR
500 ELCJ 92021 1251-G4
BRODEA LN
4000 SDCo 92028 1048-F2
BRODIAEA WY
7300 SD 92037 1227-G7
BRODIE LN
8500 SNTE 92071 1230-G5
8500 SNTE 92071 1250-J1
BROGUE CT
1500 VSTA 92083 1107-J5
BROKEN ARROW LN
1400 SDCo 92028 1027-J4
BROKEN ARROW RD
2800 SDCo 92004 (1078-H6 See Page 1058)
BROKEN BOW CT
17000 SD 92127 1169-H2
BROKEN CINCH TR
7500 SDCo 92036 1138-C7
7500 SDCo 92036 (1158-D1 See Page 1138)
BROKEN HITCH RD
1300 OCN 92056 1087-D3
BROKEN OAK LN
34200 SDCo 92036 1176-D4
BROKEN ROCK RD
1700 SDCo 92069 1128-B2
1700 SMCS 92069 1128-B2
BROKEN WHEEL RD
10800 SDCo 92040 1231-G1
BROME CT
1600 CRLB 92009 1127-D6
BROME WY
12900 SD 92129 1189-D5
BROMEGRASS CT
15800 PWY 92064 1170-F4
BROMELIAD CT
7600 SD 92119 1250-E3
BROMFIELD AV
4300 SD 92122 1228-E5
BROMLEY WY
5600 SD 92120 1270-D1
BRONCO LN
16400 PWY 92064 1170-E4
BRONCO PL
300 CHV 91902 1310-G4
BRONCO WY
1600 OCN 92057 1067-E7
13300 PWY 92064 1170-E4
BRONSTEIN PL
10200 SD 92124 1249-G4
BRONTE PL
7500 SD 92114 1290-G4
BRONX PL
2800 SD 92123 1249-E5
BRONZE WY
600 VSTA 92083 1087-F7
BROOK RD
1400 SMCS 92069 1109-C7
BROOKBURN DR
4800 SD 92130 1188-C6
BROOK CANYON RD
2400 ESCN 92025 1130-C7
2400 SDCo 92025 1130-C7
BROOKDALE PL
100 SOLB 92075 1167-F7
BROOKDEL AV
- SMCS 92069 1109-B7
BROOKE GN
1300 SDCo 92028 1027-J6
BROOKE RD
1800 SDCo 92028 1027-J6
BROOKE CREST LN
1300 SDCo 92028 1027-H6
BROOKE HOLLOW RD
1200 SDCo 92028 1028-C4
BROOKES AV
500 SD 92103 1269-B6
W BROOKES AV
100 SD 92103 1268-J6
200 SD 92103 1269-A6
BROOKES TER
1200 SD 92103 1269-B6
BROOKFIELD WY
3500 CRLB 92008 1107-A4
BROOKHAVEN CT
8100 SD 92114 1290-H4
BROOKHAVEN PASS
2200 VSTA 92083 1107-H7
2200 VSTA 92083 1127-H1
BROOKHAVEN RD
7000 SD 92114 1290-H4
BROOKHILLS RD
3700 SDCo 92028 1048-B3
BROOKHOLLOW CT
10600 SD 92126 1208-J4
BROOKHOLLOW GN
600 ESCN 92027 1130-B2
BROOKHURST AV
10400 SD 92126 1209-D4
BROOKHURST DR
1900 ELCJ 92019 1252-C4
BROOKHURST LN
2600 SDCo 92025 1130-B7
10300 SD 92126 1209-D5
BROOKINS LN
700 VSTA 92083 1087-E6
BROOKLINE ST
1600 SD 92102 1289-J2
BROOKLYN AV
5800 SD 92114 1290-C3
BROOKMEAD LN
2600 SD 92037 1227-J1
BROOKMEADOW PL
7900 SD 92114 1290-H5
BROOKPINE CT
3000 SDCo 91978 1271-F7
BROOKPRINTER PL
12600 PWY 92064 1190-D6
BROOKS GN
1900 ESCN 92029 1129-F5
BROOKS ST
300 OCN 92054 1086-B7
400 OCN 92054 1106-B1
N BROOKS ST
100 OCN 92054 1086-B7
S BROOKS ST
300 OCN 92054 1086-B7
BROOKS WY
4200 CRLB 92008 1106-G7
BROOKSHIRE ST
3500 SD 92111 1248-H4
BROOKSIDE CIR
9200 SDCo 91977 1271-B4
BROOKSIDE CT
- SMCS 92078 1128-C6
9200 SDCo 91977 1271-B4
BROOKSIDE LN
- OCN 92056 1107-D2
3100 ENCT 92024 1148-B5
BROOKSTONE CT
12600 PWY 92064 1190-C1
BROOKSTONE DR
14600 PWY 92064 1190-C1
14900 PWY 92064 1170-C7
BROOKSTONE PL
300 SNTE 92071 1231-C5
BROOKSTONE RD
700 CHV 91913 1311-E4
BROOKS TRAIL CT
2200 CHV 91915 1311-F6
BROOKTREE LN
800 VSTA 92083 1108-A4
BROOKTREE TER
10400 SD 92131 1209-H4
BROOKVALE DR
8500 SNTE 92071 1230-J7
BROOKVIEW CT
200 SNTE 92071 1231-C5
BROOKVIEW LN
10700 SD 92131 1209-H4
N BROOKVILLE DR
10600 SD 92131 1209-H1
11800 SD 92131 1189-H7
S BROOKVILLE DR
10600 SD 92131 1209-H1
BROOKWOOD CT
2200 ESCN 92026 1109-H4
4700 CRLB 92008 1107-A5
BROOKWOOD PL
900 OCN 92056 1087-D1
BROSNAN ST
2800 SD 92111 1248-J6
BROTHERTON RD
300 ESCN 92025 1130-A6
600 ESCN 92025 1129-J6
BROUGHAM CT
3100 OCN 92056 1106-H1
BROWN DR
2500 ELCJ 92020 1251-B3
BROWN ST
3900 OCN 92056 1107-A1
BROWNCROFT WY
8500 SDCo 92021 1252-E1
BROWN DEER RD
9100 SD 92121 1208-G7
BROWNELL ST
5100 SD 92110 1268-F2
BROWNING CT
1200 VSTA 92083 1087-E6
BROWNING RD
5100 CRLB 92008 1107-C7
BROWNING ST
3000 SD 92106 1268-C7
3800 SD 92107 1268-B6
BROWNS RD
- SDCo 91901 1235-A3
BRUBAKER CT
12600 SD 92130 1188-C6
BRUCE CT
6900 LMSA 91941 1270-E3
BRUCE RD
1700 CRLB 92008 1106-H7
BRUCEALA CT
2000 ENCT 92007 1167-F3
BRUCKART SQ
9900 SD 92131 1209-H5
BRUCKER AV
700 SDCo 91977 1291-A3
BRULE PL
13000 PWY 92064 1190-D3
BRUMA CT
500 SDCo 91977 1291-C3
BRUMBY WY
10200 SD 92124 1249-G4
BRUNEI CT
7400 LMGR 91945 1270-G7
BRUNNER ST
1200 SD 92110 1268-G2
BRUNO PL
5600 LMSA 91942 1250-H7
5600 LMSA 91942 1270-H1
BRUNS RD
1700 SDCo 92084 1068-H5
BRUNSWICK AV
5400 SD 92120 1250-B5
BRUSHWOOD LN
3800 SDCo 92028 1048-C4
BRUST CT
2500 SDCo 92019 1272-E1
BRUTUS ST
500 SD 92114 1290-G3
BRUYERE CT
13800 SD 92129 1189-D2
BRYAN CT
7800 LMGR 91945 1270-H6
BRYAN ST
4100 OCN 92056 1087-C6
BRYANT DR
2200 CRLB 92008 1107-C7
2200 CRLB 92008 1127-C1
BRYANT ST
1200 SD 92113 1289-F6
BRYANVIEW CIR
1300 SD 92114 1290-B6
BRYCE CIR
4700 CRLB 92008 1106-H7
BRYCE LN
100 SDCo 92028 1027-H2
BRYCE PT
- PWY 92064 1150-G6

BRYNWOOD CT — SAN DIEGO CO. STREET INDEX — CALLE CORAZON 6570

STREET
Block City ZIP Pg-Grid

BRYNWOOD CT
6200 SD 92120 1250-D6
BRYNWOOD WY
6400 SD 92120 1250-D6
BRYSON TER
4600 SD 92130 1188-C5
BUBBLING LN
13400 SDCo 92040 1232-D6
BUBBLING WELL DR
1500 SD 92154 1349-J2
BUBBLING WELLS RD
9000 SDCo 92040 1232-D6
BUCCANEER DR
100 SD 92114 1290-F4
BUCCANEER WY
- CORD 92118 1329-E2
BUCHANAN ST
600 ESCN 92027 1110-B7
2800 SD 92136 1289-E7
N BUCHANAN ST
800 ESCN 92027 1110-A7
BUCKA PL
- SDCo 92003 1067-H1
BUCKAROO LN
900 CHV 91902 1310-H4
BUCKBOARD DR
1500 OCN 92057 1067-F6
BUCKBOARD LN
1400 SDCo 92028 1027-J4
BUCKBOARD TR
7100 SDCo 92036 1138-C5
9200 SNTE 92071 1231-F6
BUCKEYE CT
900 ELCJ 92021 1251-H2
BUCKEYE DR
1300 SDCo 92021 1251-H3
1300 ELCJ 92021 1251-H2
BUCKHORN AV
700 SMCS 92078 1128-G2
BUCKHORN DR
29300 SDCo 91906 (1297-D5
See Page 1296)
BUCKHORN ST
8300 SD 92111 1249-B2
BUCKHURST AV
10800 SD 92126 1209-D3
BUCKINGHAM DR
1400 SD 92037 1247-G2
BUCKINGHAM LN
4500 CRLB 92008 1107-A5
BUCKLAND ST
8400 LMSA 91942 1250-J7
8400 LMSA 91942 1270-J1
BUCKLEY ST
12800 PWY 92064 1190-D5
BUCKMAN SPRINGS LN
2200 SDCo 91906 (1317-H2
See Page 1296)
BUCKMAN SPRINGS RD Rt#-S1
1300 SDCo 91906 (1318-A4
See Page 1298)
1300 SDCo 91906 (1317-H1
See Page 1296)
2100 SDCo 91906 (1297-G1
See Page 1296)
2600 SDCo 91906 430-A7
2600 SDCo 92066 430-A7
BUCKNELL AV
5800 SD 92037 1247-H3
BUCKNELL ST
1900 CHV 91913 1311-D5
BUCKSHOT RD
29100 SDCo 92026 1088-H1
BUCKSKIN DR
1400 ESCN 92029 1129-G7
1400 ESCN 92029 1149-G1
BUCKSKIN GN
1800 ESCN 92027 1110-A4
BUCKSKIN RD
400 SDCo 92004 1058-G6
1100 ELCJ 92019 1251-H6
BUCKSKIN TR
12200 PWY 92064 1190-C6
BUCKTHORN TR
2400 SDCo 91905 (1299-H3
See Page 1298)
8000 SDCo 92066 1237-C5
BUCKWHEAT CT
12600 SD 92129 1189-D6
BUCKWHEAT ST
9000 SD 92129 1189-D6
BUCKWHEAT TR
1200 SDCo 91906 (1318-B6
See Page 1298)
BUCKWOOD ST
14600 PWY 92064 1190-D1
BUCKY LN
800 NATC 91950 1289-H6
BUDD ST
3300 SD 92111 1249-A4
BUDLONG LAKE AV
6300 SD 92119 1250-H5
BUDMUIR PL
4300 SD 92105 1289-H1
BUDS LN
14600 PWY 92064 1150-H7
BUDWIN LN
14500 PWY 92064 1190-F1
14800 PWY 92064 1170-F7
BUECHNER DR
14100 SDCo 92065 1192-B2
BUENA PL
900 CRLB 92008 1106-E4
BUENA ST
1300 OCN 92054 1086-B7
BUENA TER
800 ELCJ 92020 1251-D4
BUENA CAPRI
900 SDCo 92028 1027-H7
BUENA CREEK RD
100 SMCS 92069 1108-F1
200 SDCo 92069 1108-F1
800 SDCo 92069 1088-G7
1500 SDCo 92084 1108-F1
BUENA CREST LN
3700 SDCo 92069 1108-G1
3700 SDCo 92084 1108-G1
BUENA FLORES
2500 SDCo 92028 1027-H7
BUENA HILLS DR
3000 OCN 92056 1106-J1
3100 OCN 92056 1107-A1
BUENA MESA PL
10100 SDCo 91977 1271-E5
BUENA ROSA
2500 SDCo 92028 1027-H7
2600 SDCo 92028 1047-H1

STREET
Block City ZIP Pg-Grid

BUENA ROSA CT
900 SDCo 92028 1027-H7
BUENA SUERTE
900 SDCo 92028 1047-H1
BUENA TIERRA WY
700 OCN 92057 1086-J3
BUENA VALLEY DR
8700 SNTE 92071 1231-D7
BUENAVENTURA CT
100 SOLB 92075 1167-D7
BUENA VIDA RD
12300 SDCo 92040 1212-C4
BUENA VILLAGE DR
1900 SDCo 92084 1108-C2
BUENA VISTA
- ESCN 92026 1109-G7
13200 PWY 92064 1190-E5
BUENA VISTA AV
600 ELCN 92243 6499-G4
1100 ESCN 92027 1109-J6
1200 SDCo 91977 1291-C2
2400 LMGR 91945 1270-G7
9800 SNTE 92071 1231-D7
BUENA VISTA CIR
2300 CRLB 92008 1106-D4
BUENA VISTA CT
1000 CHV 91910 1311-B7
BUENA VISTA DR
1000 VSTA 92083 1107-G2
1200 SDCo 92083 1107-G2
9900 SDCo 91977 1271-D5
BUENA VISTA LN
1000 OCN 92054 1085-H6
BUENA VISTA ST
3300 SD 92109 1268-A1
3600 SD 92109 1248-A7
BUENA VISTA WY
800 CHV 91910 1311-A5
1000 CRLB 92008 1106-E4
BUENOS AV
1000 SD 92110 1268-E3
BUENOS ST
1100 SD 92110 1268-F3
BUENOS AIRES WY
31200 SDCo 92003 1067-H2
BUENOS TIEMPOS
900 SDCo 92028 1027-H7
BUEN TIEMPO DR
800 CHV 91910 1310-G7
BUFFALO GRASS CT
- IMP 92243 6499-E2
BUFFUM DR
1000 OCN 92057 1086-F5
BUFORD WY
13700 PWY 92064 1190-F3
BUGGYWHIP DR
10800 SDCo 91978 1271-G7
BUHO CT
4000 SD 92124 1250-A3
BUISSON ST
6200 SD 92122 1228-C5
BULLARD LN
100 SDCo 91901 1233-D6
BULL CANYON RD
1600 CHV 91913 1311-D7
BULLOCK DR
6400 SD 92114 1290-F5
BULLRUSH GN
2000 ESCN 92027 1110-A5
BULRUSH CT
- CRLB 92009 1127-B6
BULRUSH LN
2000 ENCT 92007 1167-E3
BUMANN RD
3300 ENCT 92024 1148-C4
BUMPER CIR
4000 SD 92124 1249-H3
BUNA PL
100 VSTA 92084 1087-H5
BUNCHE AV
3100 SD 92122 1228-C5
BUNCHE TER
6300 SD 92122 1228-C5
BUNCHE WY
6300 SD 92122 1228-C5
BUNDY DR
9500 SNTE 92071 1231-E4
BUNKER HILL ST
2900 SD 92109 1248-D5
3200 SD 92117 1248-D5
BUNKER VIEW WY
2100 OCN 92056 1086-J7
BUNNELL ST
4800 SD 92113 1290-A5
BUNNIE KING LN
1300 SDCo 92065 1172-G4
BUNNY DR
18000 SDCo 91935 1274-D3
BUNNY BELL LN
1400 VSTA 92083 1108-A2
BUOY AV
- CRLB 92009 1127-A7
BURBANK CT
3500 SD 92111 1249-A4
BURBANK ST
7400 SD 92111 1249-A4
BURDEN DR
700 NATC 91950 1290-B7
BURDETT WY
100 SDCo 92021 1252-H3
BURFORD ST
5300 SD 92111 1248-G6
BURGA LP
500 CHV 91910 1310-J5
BURGASIA PTH
500 SDCo 92019 1252-C6
BURGENER BLVD
2100 SD 92110 1268-G1
2300 SD 92110 1248-F6
BURGOS CT
2400 CRLB 92009 1147-F1
BURGUNDY RD
1400 ENCT 92024 1147-C2
BURGUNDY ST
6300 SD 92120 1249-J7
BURIAN ST
6000 SD 92114 1290-C2
BURKE RD
8600 SD 92145 1229-D1
BURKE ST
800 VSTA 92083 1087-E6
BURKSHIRE AV
600 ENCT 92007 1167-D2
BURKSHIRE PL
8800 SDCo 92040 1232-C6
BURLINGAME DR
3000 SD 92104 1269-E7
BURLINGTON PL
1800 ESCN 92026 1109-D5

STREET
Block City ZIP Pg-Grid

BURLINGTON WY
7800 SD 92126 1209-A4
BURMA CT
- SDCo 92028 1047-E4
BURMA RD
100 SDCo 92028 1047-E4
400 SDCo 92065 409-G11
BURMA SPUR
3900 SDCo 92028 1047-F4
BURNABY ST
1100 ELCJ 92020 1251-G7
BURNED OAK LN
10200 SDCo 92026 1089-E3
BURNED OAK TER
28200 SDCo 92026 1089-F3
BURNELL AV
7600 LMGR 91945 1270-G6
BURNET ST
1700 ELCJ 92021 1251-G2
BURNHAM ST
600 ELCJ 92019 1251-J6
BURNING BUSH ST
800 ENCT 92024 1147-E6
BURNING HILLS DR
13300 PWY 92064 1170-E1
BURNING TREE WY
9300 SNTE 92071 1230-J6
BURNS CT
900 SD 92113 1289-G5
BURNT MAPLE WY
1800 VSTA 92083 1107-G5
BURNT MOUNTAIN RD
27700 SDCo 92082 1090-A2
27900 SDCo 92082 1089-J3
BURR CT
12400 SD 92129 1189-C6
BURR LN
900 SD 92129 1189-C6
BURRIS DR
1000 SDCo 92019 1272-D1
BURROCK DR
10000 SNTE 92071 1231-D2
BURROUGHS ST
1400 OCN 92054 1106-C2
1900 SD 92111 1268-J1
2100 SD 92111 1248-J7
BURTON CT
- CRLB 92009 1127-B5
BURTON ST
1400 SD 92111 1268-J2
BURWOOD PL
2300 SD 92154 1330-C7
BUS CT
5700 LMSA 91942 1251-A7
BUSCH DR
800 SDCo 92083 1107-D2
800 VSTA 92083 1107-D2
3400 OCN 92056 1107-D2
BUSH ST
400 OCN 92054 1086-B7
600 SD 92103 1268-J6
BUSHARD DR
1000 SDCo 92029 1129-H7
BUSHWOOD CT
7800 LMGR 91945 1270-H7
BUSHY HILL DR
8700 SD 92071 1230-F7
8700 SNTE 92071 1230-F7
BUSINESS CENTER CT
- SD 92154 1351-B2
BUSINESS PARK AV
9600 SD 92131 1209-F5
BUSINESS PARK DR
2000 VSTA 92083 1107-J6
2500 VSTA 92083 1128-A1
2500 VSTA 92083 1127-J1
2800 SMCS 92069 1128-A1
BUSINESS ROUTE I-8 Bus
2000 ELCJ - 1252-C1
9700 SDCo - 1252-C1
13000 SDCo - 1232-E6
BUTANO CT
8700 SD 92129 1189-C3
BUTANO WY
13700 SD 92129 1189-C3
BUTLER PL
6400 SD 92115 1270-D5
BUTLER RD
- ImCo - 412-B3
BUTLER ST
1300 IMPB 91932 1349-J2
2800 OCN 92054 1086-D6
BUTTE ST
8500 LMSA 91941 1270-J3
8500 LMSA 91941 1271-A3
BUTTERCUP LN
600 NATC 91950 1290-C6
BUTTERCUP RD
800 CRLB 92009 1127-A6
1600 ENCT 92024 1147-G5
BUTTERFIELD DR
- SDCo 92040 1232-F4
BUTTERFIELD LN
700 SMCS 92069 1109-D6
BUTTERFIELD RD
700 OCN 92057 1067-B5
BUTTERFIELD TR
- ImCo - 411-G4
17000 PWY 92064 1170-F1
BUTTERFLY LN
4800 SDCo 91941 1271-E2
BUTTERNUT HOLLOW LN
4700 SDCo 91902 1310-G1
BUTTERS RD
1700 CRLB 92008 1106-F3
5500 ImCo 92227 411-E11
BUTTERS RD Rt#-S32
4300 ImCo 92227 431-E1
5300 ImCo 92227 411-E11
BUTTERWOOD AV
500 SMCS 92069 1109-D7
BUTTERWOOD CT
12600 PWY 92064 1190-D3
BUTTESIDE PL
2400 SDCo 91977 1271-H7
BUTTE TOP PL
2400 SDCo 91977 1271-H7
BUTTEVIEW PL
2400 SDCo 91977 1271-H7
BUTTON ST
9700 SNTE 92071 1231-A4
BUTTONBRUSH LN
1200 SDCo 92019 1252-E7
1300 SDCo 92019 1272-E1
BUTTONWOOD CT
1200 SDCo 92019 1252-E7
BUXTON AV
13400 PWY 92064 1190-H4

STREET
Block City ZIP Pg-Grid

BYRD ST
3500 SD 92154 1330-E7
BYRD WY
600 SD 92154 1330-E7
BYRN LN
8700 SNTE 92071 1231-A7
BYRON PL
2300 CRLB 92008 1107-B7
BYRON ST
3000 SD 92106 1288-B2

C

C AV
100 CORD 92118 1288-J7
200 SDCo 92055 1066-C1
500 NATC 91950 1309-H1
C CT
- SD 92126 1209-F7
200 CHV 91910 1310-F7
C ST
- SDCo 92036 1136-B7
- CHV 91910 1310-B4
100 SDCo 92059 1029-H4
100 ENCT 92024 1147-B7
100 SD 92101 1289-B3
200 CHV 91910 1309-J5
600 SD 92101 1288-J3
700 IMPB 91932 1329-F7
700 SDCo 92055 1085-G3
1000 ENCT 92024 1148-A5
1100 SD 92102 1289-H2
1300 SD 92110 1268-F2
1500 NATC 91950 1309-J2
2500 NATC 91950 1310-C3
W C ST
200 SD 92101 1289-A3
500 SD 92101 1288-J3
CABALLERO CANYON RD
26800 SDCo 92026 1089-G6
CABALLO CT
100 SMCS 92069 1108-J1
CABALLO LN
3400 SDCo 92028 1048-D2
CABALLOS PL
2100 SD 92130 1188-D5
CABANA WY
- OCN 92057 1087-A2
CABANO
- SDCo 92055 1086-B2
CABARET ST
6100 SD 92120 1250-D4
CABELA DR
17400 SD 92127 1169-J1
17800 SD 92127 1149-J7
18000 SD 92127 1150-A6
CABELA PL
6500 CRLB 92009 1127-C5
11400 SD 92127 1169-J1
CABERNET DR
1800 CHV 91913 1311-C3
CABERNET WY
7100 LMGR 91945 1290-F1
CABEZAS CV
1200 CHV 91915 1311-F6
CABEZON PL
700 VSTA 92083 1107-E1
12500 SD 92129 1189-F6
CABLE CT
600 OCN 92054 1086-F2
CABLE ST
1500 SD 92107 1267-J6
CABO CT
400 OCN 92054 1086-G2
3300 CRLB 92009 1147-J1
10900 SNTE 92071 1231-D1
CABO WY
3300 CRLB 92009 1147-J1
3300 CRLB 92009 1148-A1
CABO BAHIA
2300 CHV 91914 1311-F3
CABOT CT
1100 VSTA 92083 1107-J4
CABOT DR
9300 SD 92126 1209-C7
CABRENA ST
1800 SD 92154 1350-B3
CABRILLO AV
600 CORD 92118 1288-G6
7300 SD 92037 1227-F7
CABRILLO CIR
1100 VSTA 92084 1087-J4
N CABRILLO DR
1100 CHV 91910 1311-B7
S CABRILLO DR
1100 CHV 91910 1311-B7
CABRILLO FRWY Rt#-163
- SD - 1229-D6
- SD - 1249-B4
- SD - 1269-A1
- SD - 1289-B1
CABRILLO LN
200 VSTA 92084 1087-H4
CABRILLO PL
2600 CRLB 92008 1106-E4
9700 SDCo 92029 1149-D4
CABRILLO RD
- SD 92106 1308-A2
CABRILLO ST
21800 SDCo 92070 1135-B3
CABRILLO MEMORIAL DR Rt#-209
- SD 92106 1288-A6
- SD 92106 1308-A1
1800 SD 92106 1287-J5
CABRILLO MESA DR
2900 SD 92123 1249-C5
CACAO CT
11600 SD 92124 1250-A3
CACATUA ST
2800 CRLB 92009 1127-H5
CACHE CREEK ST
1700 SDCo 92019 1272-C3
CACHO CT
11400 SDCo 92021 1251-H1
CACTI DR
29400 SDCo 91906 (1297-E4
See Page 1296)
CACTUS CT
6900 SD 92154 1351-D4
CACTUS PL
2000 ESCN 92027 1110-C7
CACTUS RD
1500 SD 92154 1351-D3
CACTUS ST
9700 SDCo 92040 1232-A4
CACTUS WY
5800 SD 92037 1248-A2

STREET
Block City ZIP Pg-Grid

CACTUS BRANCH TR
7100 SDCo 92036 1138-B6
CACTUSRIDGE CT
3600 SD 92105 1289-G2
CACTUSRIDGE ST
1400 SD 92105 1289-H2
CACTUSVIEW DR
3600 SD 92105 1289-G2
CACUS ST
8100 SDCo 91977 1290-J5
CADDEN CT
3200 SD 92117 1248-C4
CADDEN DR
3300 SD 92117 1248-D4
CADDEN WY
3800 SD 92117 1248-D4
CADDIE CT
2300 OCN 92056 1106-J1
CADDINGTON RW
6000 SD 92037 1248-A2
CADDY RW
12100 SD 92128 1170-A4
CADE TER
9000 SD 92126 1209-D1
CADENA DR
3900 OCN 92054 1086-G2
CADENCE CT
11000 SDCo 92026 1109-H1
CADENCIA GN
800 ESCN 92026 1109-F5
CADENCIA ST
3000 CRLB 92009 1147-H1
3100 CRLB 92009 1127-J7
3200 CRLB 92009 1128-A7
3300 CRLB 92009 1148-A1
CADENCIA WY
1600 ESCN 92025 1129-J5
CADES WY
2400 VSTA 92083 1108-A6
CADET ST
5000 SD 92117 1228-G7
CADILLAC CIR
300 OCN 92054 1086-C7
CADIZ ST
2700 SD 92110 1268-D6
CADLEY CT
9100 SD 92129 1189-D1
CADMAN ST
500 SD 92114 1290-F3
CADMUS ST
100 ENCT 92024 1147-B5
CADOGLENN DR
1200 SDCo 92019 1252-B7
1300 SDCo 92019 1272-B1
CADORETTE AV
9300 SNTE 92071 1230-H6
CADWELL RD
10300 SNTE 92071 1231-A3
CADY RD
- ImCo 92227 431-A2
CAESAR DR
18900 SDCo 92065 1153-E3
CAESENA WY
5000 OCN 92056 1107-F5
CAFANZARA CT
8200 SD 92119 1250-E3
CAFE AVD
8500 SDCo 91902 1310-H2
CAFFEY LN
7600 SD 92126 1209-A6
CAFLUR AV
4100 SD 92117 1248-D3
CAGAYAN AV
2600 SD 92154 1330-C6
CAGLE ST
3000 NATC 91950 1310-D3
CAHILL DR
7400 SD 92114 1290-G3
CAHUILLA RD
500 SDCo 92004 (1078-H1
See Page 1058)
CAHUKA CT
32300 SDCo 92061 1050-J6
CAIN LN
1200 SDCo 92027 1130-C3
CAIRO CT
8700 SD 92123 1249-C7
CAITHNESS DR
1800 SD 92173 1350-E2
CAJON CIR
600 OCN 92057 1067-A5
1100 VSTA 92083 1087-G4
CAJON PL
1600 CORD 92118 1288-J7
CAJON RD
7900 SDCo 92021 1251-J1
CAJON WY
4600 SD 92115 1270-B3
CAJON GREENS DR
1000 ELCJ 92021 1251-H2
CAJON GREENS PL
1500 ELCJ 92021 1251-H2
CAJON MOUNTAIN TKTR
- SDCo 92040 (1193-G2
See Page 1192)
CAJON VIEW DR
300 ELCJ 92020 1271-F1
300 ELCJ 91941 1271-F1
300 SDCo 91941 1271-F1
300 SDCo 92020 1271-F1
CAJON VISTA CT
12500 SDCo 92021 1232-B7
CALABRIA CT
7100 SD 92122 1228-E3
N CALAC LN
31000 SDCo 92082 1071-E2
CALAIS DR
13400 SD 92014 1187-H7
CALAMAR CT
11600 SD 92124 1250-B2
CALAMAR CV
11600 SD 92124 1250-A2
CALAMAR DR
11600 SD 92124 1250-A2
CALAVERAS DR
300 SD 92107 1287-J2
CALAVO CT
1700 CRLB 92008 1106-G7
CALAVO DR
1000 SDCo 92026 1109-E7
1000 SDCo 92026 1129-E1
2600 SNTE 91978 1271-F6
3600 SDCo 91977 1271-F4
3700 SDCo 91941 1271-F2
6500 SDCo 92020 1271-F2
CALAVO RD
1400 SDCo 92028 1027-H5
CALCATTERRA SQ
9900 SD 92131 1209-H5

STREET
Block City ZIP Pg-Grid

CALCUTTA LN
9800 SDCo 92026 1089-C1
CALDAS DE REYES
15400 SD 92128 1170-C5
CALDERA PL
3700 CRLB 92008 1107-B4
CALDERON CT
8400 SD 92129 1189-B3
CALDERON RD
13400 SD 92129 1189-B3
CALDERWOOD RW
2900 SD 92037 1248-A1
CALDY PL
7600 SD 92111 1249-A3
CALEB CT
900 SD 92154 1330-E7
CALEDONIA DR
4100 SD 92111 1249-A3
CALENDA RD
11200 SD 92127 1169-H2
CALERA ST
1300 VSTA 92084 1087-H4
CALETA CT
2000 CRLB 92009 1127-F6
CALETA WY
12400 SD 92128 1170-B2
CALEVERO LN
100 OCN 92056 1107-D2
CALEXICO AV
- SDCo 91934 (1321-G5
See Page 1300)
CALGARY AV
3900 SD 92122 1228-E4
CALGARY CT
1400 VSTA 92083 1087-D7
6500 SD 92122 1228-E5
CALGARY DR
6500 SD 92122 1228-D4
CALGARY WY
11100 SDCo 92082 1069-G2
CALHOUN CT
2500 SDCo 92083 1108-C5
CALHOUN ST
2600 SD 92110 1268-F4
CALIBAN CT
200 ENCT 92024 1147-G6
CALIBAN DR
200 ENCT 92024 1147-G6
CALICO CIR
10400 SD 92126 1209-B4
CALICO LN
1400 SDCo 92029 1129-C4
CALICO ST
7800 SD 92126 1209-A4
CALICO RANCH RD
3600 SDCo 92066 1135-F5
CALICO RANCH GATE
3600 SDCo 92066 1135-F5
CALIDRIS LN
7200 CRLB 92009 1127-B7
CALIENTE CT
1400 SDCo 91901 1234-C6
CALIENTE GN
2200 ESCN 92029 1129-D6
CALIENTE LP
1300 CHV 91910 1311-B6
CALIFA CT
8100 SD 92119 1250-E3
E CALIFORNIA AV
100 VSTA 92084 1087-H5
W CALIFORNIA AV
100 VSTA 92083 1087-G5
CALIFORNIA DR
- ImCo 92274 410-H7
CALIFORNIA ST
700 SD 92101 1288-J1
700 OCN 92054 1106-D1
1000 ENCT 92024 1147-J5
1100 IMPB 91932 1349-G2
2100 SD 92110 1268-G6
2800 SD 92101 1268-H7
CALIFORNIA SPRINGS CT
- SDCo 91977 1271-E7
- SDCo 91977 1291-E1
CALIFORNIA WATERS DR
- SDCo 91977 1271-E7
- SDCo 91977 1291-E1
CALINA WY
2100 CRLB 92009 1147-G2
CALISTOGA AV
1200 CHV 91913 1331-C1
CALISTOGA DR
15500 SDCo 92065 1173-D4
CALISTOGA PL
23500 SDCo 92065 1173-D5
CALLA AV
100 IMPB 91932 1329-E7
CALLA ST
1700 SD 92154 1329-J7
1700 SD 92154 1330-A7
3800 SD 92121 1208-C6
CALLADO CT
16700 SD 92128 1170-A3
CALLADO RD
11900 SD 92128 1170-B3
CALLAN RD
2800 SD 92121 1207-J5
2800 SD 92037 1207-J5
2900 SD 92121 1208-A5
CALLCOTT WY
13000 SD 92130 1188-C5
CALLE PL
1400 ESCN 92027 1109-J6
CALLE ABAJO
3000 NATC 91950 1310-D2
3000 SD 92139 1310-D2
CALLE ABUELITO
12900 SD 92129 1189-G5
CALLE ACERVO
1500 CRLB 92009 1147-J3
1500 ENCT 92024 1147-J4
7200 CRLB 92009 1148-A4
CALLE ADELA
300 SMCS 92069 1109-C7
CALLE AGUADULCE
2400 SD 92139 1310-E1
CALLE ALBARA
11500 SDCo 92019 1271-J3
11700 SDCo 92019 1272-A4
CALLE ALEGRO
700 VSTA 92084 1087-J3
CALLE ALEJANDRO
3000 SDCo 91935 1292-H3
CALLE ALHENA
3000 CRLB 92009 1147-H3
CALLE ALICIA
400 SCLE 92672 1023-B2

STREET
Block City ZIP Pg-Grid

CALLE ALMA
7300 CRLB 92009 1127-J7
CALLE ALTA
1500 SD 92037 1247-J3
CALLE ALTO
- SDCo 92040 1232-A1
CALLE ALTURA
1400 SD 92037 1247-H4
CALLE AMANACER
7700 SDCo 92067 1148-H7
CALLE AMBIENTE
7600 SDCo 92067 1148-J7
CALLE AMISTAD DR
300 SDCo 92065 1152-J6
300 SDCo 92065 1153-A6
CALLE AMISTAD LN
1200 SDCo 92065 1152-J7
CALLE ANA
16400 PWY 92064 1170-D4
CALLE ANACAPA
1000 ENCT 92024 1148-A5
CALLE ANDALUCIA
14300 SD 92130 1188-D2
CALLE ANDREA
- SDCo 92065 1173-D1
CALLE ANGELICA
11600 SDCo 92019 1271-J4
CALLE ANTONIO
1800 VSTA 92084 1088-B5
CALLE ARDILLA
12000 SDCo 92019 1272-A4
CALLE ARIANA
3800 SCLE 92672 1023-B2
CALLE ARQUERO
4900 OCN 92057 1067-B4
CALLE ARRIBA
5800 SD 92139 1310-D2
CALLE ARROYO
2700 CRLB 92008 1106-G3
CALLE ASTURTAS
15500 SD 92128 1170-C6
CALLE BARCELONA
1200 CRLB 92024 1147-G2
1200 ENCT 92024 1147-G2
2000 CRLB 92009 1147-G2
CALLE BIENVENIDO
1300 VSTA 92084 1087-J3
CALLE BOLERO
200 OCN 92057 1087-A1
CALLE BONITA
300 ESCN 92029 1150-A3
CALLE BUENA VENTURA
1900 OCN 92056 1086-H7
2000 OCN 92056 1106-H1
CALLE BUENO GANAR
13900 SDCo 91935 1292-G3
CALLE CABALLERO
2700 CRLB 92008 1106-G3
CALLE CABALLEROS
13000 SD 92129 1189-G5
CALLE CABRILLO
- ESCN 92026 1109-F6
800 SMCS 92069 1109-B5
1500 SDCo 92021 1251-G2
12500 SDCo 92021 1252-B1
CALLE CAJON
- SDCo 92040 1232-C2
CALLE CALETA VIEJAS
2900 SDCo 91901 1234-D7
CALLE CALZADA
8200 SD 92126 1209-B2
CALLE CAMILLE
1600 SD 92037 1247-J3
CALLE CAMPESINO
200 SCLE 92672 1023-B1
CALLE CAMPOSECO
6100 SDCo 92067 1168-F4
CALLE CANCUNA
3300 CRLB 92009 1147-J2
CALLE CANDELA
1600 SD 92037 1247-J3
CALLE CANDELERO
1200 CHV 91910 1311-A6
CALLE CANONERO
3900 SDCo 92028 1028-F7
CALLE CANTORA
2000 SDCo 92019 1252-D7
CALLE CAPISTRANO
500 SMCS 92069 1108-F5
CALLE CARACAS
3300 CRLB 92009 1147-J2
CALLE CARDENAS
13900 SD 92130 1188-D3
CALLE CARLA
14500 SDCo 92067 1188-G2
CALLE CASAS BONITAS
5700 SD 92139 1310-D2
CALLE CATALINA
1700 ESCN 92029 1129-G6
CALLE CATALONIA
- CRLB 92009 1147-J4
CALLE CERRO
900 SMCS 92069 1109-B5
CALLE CHANATE
2200 SD 92139 1290-E7
CALLE CHAPARRO
5400 SDCo 92067 1168-B4
CALLE CHAPULTEPEC
500 VSTA 92083 1087-G6
CALLE CHARMONA
12600 SD 92128 1170-C5
CALLE CHIQUITA
2300 SD 92037 1227-H4
CALLE CHRISTOPHER
1300 ENCT 92024 1167-G2
CALLE CIMA
7800 SDCo 92067 1148-H7
CALLECITA WY
2300 OCN 92056 1087-D5
CALLE CLARA
2200 SD 92037 1227-H5
CALLE CODORNIZ
11100 SDCo 92082 1049-G7
13300 SDCo 92082 1069-G1
CALLE COLINA
13200 PWY 92064 1170-E3
CALLE COLINA ROCA
- SDCo 91901 1254-E2
CALLE COLNETT
1200 SMCS 92069 1109-C7
CALLE COLORADO
1600 VSTA 92084 1087-J3
CALLE CONEJO
- SDCo 91901 1234-A6
CALLE CONTENTA
200 SDCo 92028 1027-H3
CALLE CORAZON
400 OCN 92057 1087-A4

SAN DIEGO CO.
INDEX

6571 CALLE CORDOBA
SAN DIEGO CO. STREET INDEX
CAMINITO AMARILLO

STREET
Block City ZIP Pg-Grid

CALLE CORDOBA
- CRLB 92009 1147-J4
CALLE CORREDOR
2100 SDCo 92028 998-C5
CALLE CORTA
- SMCS 92078 1129-C1
2300 SD 92139 1227-H4
16700 PWY 92064 1170-D3
CALLE CORTE
17100 SDCo 92067 1168-D3
CALLE CORTEJO
16000 SDCo 92091 1168-C7
CALLE CORTEZ
4300 SD 92019 1271-J3
CALLE CORTITA
12500 SD 92128 1170-F2
CALLE COZUMEL
7900 CRLB 92009 1147-J3
CALLE CRISTOBAL
7200 SD 92126 1209-A1
7300 SD 92126 1208-J3
CALLE CRUCERO
1300 SMCS 92069 1109-C7
CALLE CUMBRE
2900 SD 92139 1310-D2
CALLE DARIO
11100 SD 92126 1209-B2
CALLE DE ADELE
300 ENCT 92024 1147-C6
CALLE DE ALCALA
900 ESCN 92025 1150-D3
CALLE DE ALICIA
500 ENCT 92024 1147-F5
CALLE DE AMOR
- CHV 91910 1311-A7
CALLE DE ANDLUCA
1600 SD 92037 1247-J3
CALLE DE ARLENE
500 ENCT 92024 1147-F5
CALLE DE BARBARA
500 ENCT 92024 1147-F5
CALLE DE BUENA FE
8500 SDCo 92021 1232-D7
CALLE DE CASITAS
4600 OCN 92057 1066-J7
CALLE DE CHERIE
500 ENCT 92024 1147-F5
CALLE DE CINCO
1600 SD 92037 1247-J3
CALLE DE COMPADRES
2600 SDCo 91901 1254-C1
CALLE DE CONNECTOR
4600 OCN 92057 1066-J7
CALLE DE CRISTO
3000 SDCo 92069 1088-G4
CALLE DE DAMASCO
- CHV 91910 1311-A6
CALLE DE DOLORES RD
500 ENCT 92024 1147-F5
CALLE DE ENCINAS
26000 SDCo 92082 1091-G5
CALLE DE ENCINAS CT
27000 SDCo 92082 1091-F6
CALLE DE ENSUENO
12300 SDCo 92082 1070-A5
CALLE DE ERNESTO
14100 SDCo 92021 1232-G6
CALLE DE FUENTES
7300 CRLB 92009 1127-H7
CALLE DE HALCONES
12300 SDCo 92082 1049-H4
CALLE DE KATRINA
500 ENCT 92024 1147-F5
CALLE DE LA ALIANZA
200 SD 92173 1350-F3
CALLE DE LA ESTRELLA
7700 SDCo 92066 1237-D6
CALLE DE LA FIESTA
7700 SDCo 92066 1237-D6
CALLE DE LA GARZA
2300 SD 92037 1227-H5
CALLE DEL ALCALDE
7700 SDCo 92066 1237-C6
CALLE DEL ALCAZAR
7700 SDCo 92067 1168-G5
CALLE DE LA PALOMA
300 SDCo 92028 1027-H3
CALLE DE LA PAZ
500 ESCN 92029 1149-J3
CALLE DE LA PLATA
7900 SD 92037 1227-H5
CALLE DEL ARCO
1400 SDCo 92028 998-J7
CALLE DE LA REINA
9700 SDCo 92026 1069-D7
9700 SDCo 92082 1069-D7
CALLE DEL ARROYO
1500 SDCo 92069 1128-C3
CALLE DE LAS FOCAS
3800 SCLE 92672 1023-B1
CALLE DE LA SIENA
12600 SD 92130 1188-B6
CALLE DE LA SIERRA
500 SDCo 92019 1252-F4
CALLE DE LAS LOMAS
7000 SDCo 92067 1148-G6
CALLE DE LAS PIEDRAS
3300 SDCo 92084 1068-F5
CALLE DE LAS ROSAS
12700 SD 92129 1189-F5
CALLE DE LA TIERRA BAJA
- SDCo 92040 1232-C2
CALLE DEL BASTON
1000 SDCo 92069 1128-C3
CALLE DEL BOSQUE
7600 SDCo 92066 1237-D6
CALLE DEL CAMPANARIO
16200 SDCo 92067 1168-F6
CALLE DEL CIELO
- SDCo 92040 1232-A1
8000 SD 92037 1227-H5
CALLE DEL CONEJO
1800 ELCJ 92021 1252-C2
CALLE DEL CRUCE
6600 SDCo 92067 1168-H5
CALLE DE LEON
12000 SDCo 92019 1272-A4
CALLE DE LEPANTO
900 ESCN 92025 1150-D3
CALLE DEL ESTABLO
3800 SCLE 92672 1023-B1
CALLE DELGADO
1400 NATC 91950 1310-B1
CALLE DEL GRECO
4600 OCN 92056 1087-B3

CALLE DEL HUMO
8100 SD 92126 1209-B1
CALLE DELICADA
1600 SD 92037 1247-J3
CALLE DE LIMAR
1000 SDCo 92028 1027-H6
CALLE DE LINEA
6900 SD 92154 1351-D4
CALLE DEL LAGO
9400 SNTE 92071 1231-A5
CALLE DEL NIDO
16200 SDCo 92067 1168-E6
CALLE DEL ORO
2300 SD 92037 1227-H5
CALLE DE LOS NINOS
13100 SD 92129 1189-G5
CALLE DE LOS POTROS
5100 SDCo 91902 1290-H7
CALLE DE LOS SERRANOS
1100 SDCo 92069 1128-F4
CALLE DEL PALO
4500 OCN 92057 1066-H6
CALLE DEL PORTAL
- ESCN 92026 1109-G7
7900 SDCo 92021 1252-B1
CALLE DEL RANCHO
100 SDCo 92025 1130-B6
CALLE DEL RIO
12000 SDCo 92040 1232-A6
CALLE DEL SOL
- SMCS 92078 1129-C1
1400 VSTA 92084 1088-B6
13700 SDCo 91935 1272-G7
13700 SDCo 91935 1292-G1
CALLE DEL SUR
3300 CRLB 92009 1147-J2
CALLE DEL VERDE
8900 SNTE 92071 1231-A6
CALLE DEL VUELTA
4700 SDCo 92028 1048-B5
CALLE DE MADERA
200 ENCT 92024 1147-B4
CALLE DE MALIBU
2800 SDCo 92029 1149-J2
CALLE DE MARIA
500 ENCT 92024 1147-F5
12000 SD 92128 1170-B3
CALLE DE MEDIO
12000 SDCo 92019 1272-A4
CALLE DE MONTANA
12000 SDCo 92019 1272-A4
CALLE DE NEWMAN
14500 SD 92129 1189-D1
CALLE DE ORO
3100 SDCo 91935 1272-J7
3100 SDCo 91935 1292-J1
CALLE DE PESCADORES
2400 SDCo 91901 1254-C1
CALLE DEPOSITO
11800 SDCo 92019 1271-J4
CALLE DE PRIMRA
1600 SD 92037 1247-J3
CALLE DE RETIRO
4600 OCN 92057 1066-J7
CALLE DE ROB
12600 SDCo 92064 1191-D5
12600 SDCo 92071 1191-D5
CALLE DE SALUD
- SDCo 92067 1149-B3
CALLE DE SERENO
200 ENCT 92024 1147-B5
CALLE DE SOTO
- SMCS 92078 1129-A2
CALLE DE SUENO
4100 SDCo 92028 1047-F4
CALLE DE TALAR
31300 SDCo 92003 1068-H2
CALLE DE TIERRA
2200 SDCo 91901 1253-H1
CALLE DEVANAR
1500 SDCo 92069 1128-C4
CALLE DE VIDA
4200 SD 92124 1249-J2
4400 SD 92124 1250-B2
CALLE DE VISTA
13800 SDCo 92082 1090-E3
27300 SDCo 92082 1091-A4
CALLE DE VISTA OESTE
9200 SD 92129 1189-D1
CALLE DIEGUENO
15100 SDCo 92067 1188-F2
CALLE DIEGUENO RD
6700 SDCo 92067 1188-G1
CALLE DOS LAGOS
7600 SDCo 92067 1168-J2
CALLE DOS LOMAS
2200 SDCo 92028 1048-B2
CALLE DULCE
- CHV 91910 1311-A6
1600 VSTA 92084 1087-J3
CALLE EMPARRADO
500 SMCS 92069 1108-E5
CALLE EMPINADA
6100 SD 92120 1250-D5
CALLE ENCANTO
500 SDCo 92019 1252-C6
CALLE ENTRE
1900 LMGR 91945 1290-F1
CALLE ESCARPADA
1000 CHV 91902 1310-H3
CALLE ESTEPONA
18000 SD 92128 1150-D6
CALLE ESTRELLA
4700 OCN 92057 1066-J7
CALLE FAMILIA
4300 SDCo 92067 1167-J4
CALLE FANITA
8000 SNTE 92071 1251-A1
CALLE FANTASIA
1100 SMCS 92069 1108-E4
CALLE FELICIDAD
5700 SD 92139 1310-D3
CALLE FELIZ
16400 SDCo 92067 1168-E4
CALLE FLORECITA
200 ESCN 92029 1150-A3
1100 CHV 91910 1310-J5
1100 CHV 91910 1311-A5
CALLE FORTUNADA
3800 SD 92123 1249-E3
CALLE FRANCESCA
3800 SCLE 92672 1023-B1
CALLE FREDERICO
11600 SDCo 92019 1271-J4
CALLE FRESCOTA
2100 SD 92037 1227-H5

CALLE FUEGO
3100 CRLB 92009 1127-J7
CALLE GAVANZO
3500 CRLB 92009 1148-A2
CALLE GAVIOTA
2400 SD 92139 1310-D1
CALLE GOYA
1300 OCN 92056 1087-B3
CALLE GUAYMAS
2100 SD 92037 1247-J2
CALLE GUERNICA
100 SMCS 92069 1109-C7
CALLE HACIENDA
2700 CRLB 92008 1106-C6
CALLE HERMOSA
16700 SDCo 92127 1169-A3
CALLE HIDALGO
- CRLB 92009 1128-A5
CALLE HUERTO
100 VSTA 92084 1088-D6
CALLE INDEPENDENCIA
500 VSTA 92083 1087-G5
CALLE ISABEL
100 SMCS 92069 1109-C7
CALLE ISABELINO
- SD 92130 1208-B3
CALLE ISABELLA
4000 SCLE 92672 1023-B2
CALLE JALAPA
11200 SD 92126 1209-B2
CALLE JALISCO
7800 CRLB 92009 1147-J3
CALLEJA RISA
8400 SDCo 92021 1232-D7
CALLEJO FELIZ DR
15900 SDCo 92082 1071-A4
CALLEJO FELIZ TER
30400 SDCo 92082 1071-A3
CALLEJON ST
2800 SD 92139 1310-D2
CALLEJON ALHAMBRA
1300 CHV 91910 1311-B5
CALLEJON ANDALUSIA
1300 CHV 91910 1311-B5
CALLEJON CARBON
1300 CHV 91910 1311-C5
CALLEJON CERVANTE
1300 CHV 91910 1311-B5
CALLEJON CIUDAD
700 CHV 91910 1311-B5
CALLEJON ESPANA
600 CHV 91910 1311-B5
CALLEJON MALAGA
600 CHV 91910 1311-B5
CALLEJON MONTEFRIO
1300 CHV 91910 1311-C5
CALLEJON MUSICA
14400 SD 92129 1189-D1
CALLE JON NORTE
16900 SDCo 92067 1168-D3
CALLEJON PALACIOS
1300 CHV 91910 1311-B5
CALLEJON QUINTANA
11500 SD 92124 1230-A7
CALLEJON SEGOVIA
1300 CHV 91910 1311-B5
CALLE JON SUR
16900 SDCo 92067 1168-D3
CALLE JOVEN
4600 OCN 92057 1086-J1
CALLE JOYA
31200 SDCo 92003 1068-H2
CALLE JUAN
10700 SDCo 91978 1271-F5
CALLE JUANITA
300 SMCS 92069 1109-C7
CALLE JUANITO
15000 SD 92129 1169-H7
CALLE JUEGO
16000 SDCo 92091 1168-C7
CALLE JUELA
7800 SD 92037 1227-H6
CALLE JULES
1200 VSTA 92084 1087-J4
CALLE LA BEATA
11600 SDCo 92019 1271-J4
CALLE LADERA
600 ESCN 92025 1130-B4
30100 SDCo 92082 1071-A4
CALLE LAGASCA
800 CHV 91910 1310-H5
CALLE LA MIRADA
200 CHV 91902 1310-H3
CALLE LA PREZA
- SDCo 92040 1232-C2
CALLE LA REINA
30300 SDCo 92003 1068-D4
CALLE LAS CASAS
1600 OCN 92056 1087-C4
CALLE LA SERRA
8500 SDCo 92067 1148-F5
CALLE LAS MORAS
1500 VSTA 92084 1088-B4
CALLE LAS PALMAS
1800 OCN 92056 1087-C4
CALLE LAS POSITAS
4700 OCN 92057 1066-J7
CALLE LETICIA
1600 SD 92037 1247-J3
CALLE LIMONERO
11900 SDCo 92019 1271-J3
11900 SDCo 92019 1272-A4
CALLE LINDA
100 SDCo 92028 1047-G4
CALLE LISA
4000 SCLE 92672 1023-B2
CALLE LOMA LN
30400 SDCo 92003 1068-B4
CALLE LOMAS
- CRLB 92009 1147-J2
CALLE LOMEDA
1400 SDCo 92028 997-H7
CALLE LORENZANA
11900 SDCo 92019 1271-J4
11900 SDCo 92019 1272-A4
CALLE LORETO
- SDCo 91906 (1318-H6 See Page 1298)
CALLE LOS ARBOLES
3000 SDCo 91978 1271-G6
CALLE LOS SANTOS
4700 OCN 92057 1066-J7
CALLE LOUISA
4000 SCLE 92672 1023-B2
CALLE LUCIA
9000 SDCo 92040 1232-B6
CALLE LUCIA CT
9000 SDCo 92040 1232-B6

CALLE LUCIA LN
9000 SDCo 92040 1232-B6
CALLE LUCIA TER
12400 SDCo 92040 1232-B6
CALLE LUNA
7300 CRLB 92009 1127-J7
CALLE MADERO
7600 CRLB 92009 1147-H2
CALLE MADRID
7900 CRLB 92009 1147-H3
CALLE MADRIGAL
1900 SD 92037 1247-H1
CALLE MAGDALENA
100 ENCT 92024 1147-D7
CALLE MAJORCA
6200 SD 92037 1247-G2
CALLE MARBELLA
1400 OCN 92056 1087-C3
CALLE MAR DE ARMONIA
4400 SD 92130 1208-C2
CALLE MAR DE BALLENAS
2400 SD 92130 1208-B3
CALLE MAR DE MARIPOSA
- SD 92130 1208-B4
CALLE MARGARITA
3300 ENCT 92024 1148-B4
CALLE MARIA
1100 SDCo 92069 1109-C5
1200 SMCS 92069 1109-C5
CALLE MARIBEL
100 SMCS 92069 1109-C7
CALLE MARIETTA
- SDCo 92082 1051-A7
CALLE MARINERO
10100 SDCo 91977 1271-E7
10100 SDCo 91977 1291-E1
CALLE MARIPOSA
300 OCN 92057 1066-J7
CALLE MARISELDA
6100 SD 92124 1229-H7
CALLE MARLENA
4000 SCLE 92672 1023-B2
CALLE MAYOR
17200 SDCo 92067 1168-H5
CALLE MEJILLONES
4200 SD 92130 1208-B3
CALLE MEJOR
- CRLB 92009 1147-J2
CALLE MESITA
1000 CHV 91902 1310-H3
CALLE MESQUITE
3000 SDCo 91935 1292-H3
CALLE MIA
3400 SDCo 91901 1254-E1
CALLE MINAS
8200 SD 92126 1209-B2
CALLE MIRADOR
8600 SDCo 92021 1232-E7
CALLE MIRAMAR
5500 SD 92037 1247-J3
CALLE MONTECITO
200 OCN 92057 1066-J7
200 OCN 92057 1086-J1
CALLE MONTELIBANO
14800 SDCo 92067 1188-G1
CALLE MONTERA
700 ESCN 92025 1150-C3
CALLE MORELOS
8100 SD 92126 1209-C2
CALLE NADA
1400 SDCo 91901 1234-H6
CALLE NARANJA
11900 SDCo 92019 1272-A3
CALLE NARCISOS
1500 ENCT 92024 1167-G1
CALLE NEIL
4800 SD 92117 1248-F5
4800 SD 92111 1248-F5
CALLE NIQUEL
1800 OCN 92056 1087-B5
CALLE NOBLEZA
11700 SD 92128 1170-A4
CALLE NORTE
8500 LMGR 91945 1270-J7
CALLE NUBLADO
14400 SD 92129 1189-D1
CALLE NUEVA
8200 SD 92126 1209-B1
CALLE ODESSA
3300 CRLB 92009 1147-J2
CALLE OLIVIA
7800 CRLB 92009 1147-G2
CALLE OPIMA
1900 SD 92037 1227-H4
CALLE ORO VERDE
10700 SDCo 92082 1049-E6
CALLE ORQUIDEAS
1500 ENCT 92024 1147-G7
CALLE OSUNA
3100 OCN 92056 1106-J2
3100 OCN 92056 1107-A1
CALLE OVIEDA
- SDCo 92065 1173-D1
CALLE PACIFICA
- SMCS 92078 1129-C1
CALLE PARACHO
11500 SD 92128 1170-A5
11500 SD 92128 1169-J5
CALLE PARRAL
11800 SD 92128 1170-A6
CALLE PAULA
600 SOLB 92075 1167-J6
CALLE PAVANA
6200 SD 92139 1290-E7
6200 SD 92139 1310-E1
CALLE PENSAMIENTOS
1500 ENCT 92024 1167-G1
CALLE PEQUENA
6600 SDCo 92067 1168-H5
CALLE PERICO
8800 SD 92129 1189-C3
CALLE PINABETE
- CRLB 92009 1147-G2
CALLE PINO
8200 SD 92126 1209-B1
CALLE PINON
8000 CRLB 92009 1147-H3
CALLE PLATICO
1700 OCN 92056 1087-C4
CALLE PLATINO
4000 OCN 92056 1087-B6
CALLE PLUMERIAS
1600 ENCT 92024 1167-G1
CALLE POCO
2100 SDCo 92019 1252-D7

CALLE PONTE BELLA RD
6500 SDCo 92067 1148-E5
CALLE PORTONE
6800 SDCo 92067 1148-F5
CALLE POSADA
7900 CRLB 92009 1147-J3
CALLE POTRANCA
200 SCLE 92672 1023-B1
CALLE POTRO
200 SCLE 92672 1023-B1
CALLE PRIMERA
200 SD 92173 1350-G4
CALLE PRIVADA
14800 SDCo 92067 1188-F1
CALLE PROSPERO
1100 SMCS 92069 1108-E4
CALLE PUEBLITO
15300 SD 92128 1170-B6
CALLE PULIDO
16400 SD 92128 1170-A4
CALLE QUEBRADA
2400 SD 92139 1310-E1
CALLE QUERIDO
100 SMCS 92069 1109-C7
100 SMCS 92069 1129-C1
CALLE RANCHO VISTA
2600 ENCT 92024 1148-A5
CALLE REDONDA LN
1400 ESCN 92026 1109-E5
CALLE REGAL
700 ENCT 92024 1147-D7
CALLE REINA
6500 SDCo 92067 1148-E6
CALLE RICARDO
400 SDCo 92026 1109-G1
CALLE ROSADO
8700 SDCo 92021 1232-E6
CALLE ROSAS
32000 SDCo 92061 1051-E5
CALLE RYAN
1400 ENCT 92024 1167-G2
CALLE SALIDA DEL SOL
2800 SD 92139 1310-D2
CALLE SAL SI PUEDES
5600 SD 92139 1310-D2
CALLE SAN BLAS
3300 CRLB 92009 1147-J3
CALLE SAN CLEMENTE
2400 ENCT 92024 1148-A5
CALLE SAN FELIPE
7900 CRLB 92009 1147-H3
CALLE SAN MIGUEL
2400 ENCT 92024 1148-A5
CALLE SANTA CATALINA
2600 ENCT 92024 1148-A5
CALLE SANTA CRUZ
800 ENCT 92024 1148-A6
CALLE SANTA FE
600 SOLB 92075 1167-J6
CALLE SANTANDER
4000 OCN 92056 1087-B3
CALLE SANTIAGO
900 CHV 91910 1311-B6
7700 CRLB 92009 1147-J2
CALLE SCOTT
1300 ENCT 92024 1167-G2
CALLE SECO
13700 PWY 92064 1190-G5
CALLE SERENA
- SMCS 92078 1129-C2
2100 SD 92139 1290-D7
2100 SD 92139 1310-D1
17200 SDCo 92067 1168-H6
CALLE SIERRA
8700 SDCo 91977 1291-A2
CALLE SIMPSON
11500 SDCo 92019 1271-J3
CALLE SINALOA
1800 VSTA 92084 1088-C5
CALLE SOBRADO
4900 OCN 92056 1087-C3
CALLE SOLIMAR
4700 OCN 92057 1066-J7
CALLE SONIA
1200 SDCo 92028 1027-H4
CALLE STELLINA RD
18300 SDCo 92067 1148-E5
CALLE SUACILLO
12100 SD 92128 1170-B6
CALLE SUNTUOSO
11900 SD 92128 1170-A4
CALLE SUR
8500 LMGR 91945 1270-J7
CALLE SUSANA
2600 CRLB 92008 1106-H3
CALLE TALENTIA
800 ESCN 92025 1150-C3
CALLE TAMEGA
12500 SD 92128 1170-C5
CALLE TECOLOTLAN
1300 SDCo 92028 1028-E4
CALLE TEMPRA
1300 CHV 91911 1330-D4
CALLE TESORO
1000 CHV 91915 1311-H5
CALLE TEZAC
10900 SDCo 91941 1271-G5
CALLE TIARA
2200 SD 92037 1247-J2
3800 SCLE 92672 1023-B1
CALLE TIBURON
3800 SCLE 92672 1023-B1
CALLE TIERRA BLANCA
6500 SDCo 92067 1188-G1
CALLE TIJERA
1800 VSTA 92084 1088-B5
CALLE TIMITEO
3300 CRLB 92009 1147-J2
3400 CRLB 92009 1148-A2
CALLE TOCON
6100 SD 92139 1310-E1
CALLE TORTUOSA
2100 SD 92139 1290-E7
CALLE TRAGAR
8800 SD 92129 1189-C3
CALLE TRAMONTO RD
18300 SDCo 92067 1148-E5
CALLE TREPADORA
5800 SD 92139 1290-D7
5800 SD 92139 1310-D1
CALLE TRES LOMAS
2200 SD 92139 1310-E1
CALLE TRES VISTAS
- ENCT 92024 1148-B4
CALLE TRUCKSESS
11700 SDCo 92019 1271-J4

CALLE TULIPANES
1500 ENCT 92024 1147-G7
1500 ENCT 92024 1167-G1
CALLE ULTIMO
1100 OCN 92056 1087-B4
CALLE VALERIA
3000 SDCo 91935 1292-G3
CALLE VALLARTA
3200 CRLB 92009 1147-H4
CALLE VALLECITO
300 OCN 92057 1066-J7
CALLE VALPERIZO
3000 CRLB 92009 1127-J4
CALLE VAQUERO
1400 SD 92037 1247-J3
CALLE VENADO
1600 SDCo 92069 1128-B3
1600 SMCS 92069 1128-B3
CALLE VENECIA
14000 SD 92130 1188-D3
CALLE VERA CRUZ
6200 SD 92037 1247-J2
CALLE VERANO
7300 CRLB 92009 1127-J7
CALLE VERDE
- SDCo 92040 1232-A1
10800 SDCo 91941 1271-G5
CALLE VIDA BUENA
17900 SDCo 92067 1168-A1
CALLE VIENTO
3100 CRLB 92009 1127-J7
CALLE VIOLETAS
1500 ENCT 92024 1147-G7
CALLE VISTA
1100 SMCS 92078 1129-C1
5300 SD 92037 1247-J4
5300 SD 92109 1247-J4
CALLE VISTA AV
1100 ESCN 92027 1109-J6
CALLE VIVIANO
8600 SDCo 92021 1232-D6
CALLE VIVIENDA
11700 SD 92128 1169-J5
11700 SD 92128 1170-A5
CALLE ZAFIRO
7700 SDCo 92067 1148-H7
CALLIANDRA RD
- CRLB 92009 1127-D5
8800 SD 92126 1209-D3
CALLIGRAPHY CT
4700 OCN 92057 1087-B2
CALLIO WY
- SDCo 92040 1231-G3
CALLISIA CT
- CRLB 92009 1127-D4
CALMA CT
1200 VSTA 92083 1107-H4
12600 SD 92128 1170-C3
CALMA DR
900 CHV 91910 1310-H7
900 CHV 91910 1330-H1
CALMA PL
600 CHV 91910 1310-H7
CALMAR DR
2800 SDCo 92029 1149-J2
CALMERIA PL
6400 CRLB 92009 1127-A4
CALMIN DR
1100 SDCo 92028 1027-J4
1700 SDCo 92028 1028-A5
CALMIN WY
1600 SDCo 92028 1027-J4
CALMOOR ST
4000 NATC 91950 1310-E3
CALMOOR WY
3700 NATC 91950 1310-E3
CALOMA CIR
7500 CRLB 92009 1147-J1
CALPELLA CT
- CHV 91913 1331-B1
CALSTON PL
7100 SD 92126 1208-J4
CALSTON WY
10600 SD 92126 1208-J4
CALTHA PL
- CRLB 92009 1127-D5
CALUMET AV
5300 SD 92037 1247-F4
CALVACADO ST
7500 LMGR 91945 1290-G2
CALVADOS PL
- SD 92128 1190-A3
CALVARY DR
300 ELCN 92243 6499-H4
CALVARY LN
100 ELCJ 92019 1252-D5
CALVARY RD
13900 PWY 92064 1190-G3
CALVIN LN
1200 ESCN 92025 1129-H5
2500 ELCJ 92020 1251-B5
CALVIN WY
5700 SD 92120 1250-D7
CALYPSO DR
1800 VSTA 92083 1107-H5
CALYPSO PL
3000 SD 92106 1268-C5
CALZADA DEL BOSQUE
5300 SDCo 92067 1168-C5
CAMARA CT
1400 VSTA 92083 1107-H4
CAMARENA RD
12700 SD 92130 1188-B5
CAMARERO CT
12500 SD 92130 1188-B6
CAMARGO CT
14300 SD 92129 1189-H2
CAMARILLO AV
3000 OCN 92056 1087-B7
3000 OCN 92056 1107-B1
CAMAROSA CIR
11200 SD 92126 1209-C2
CAMASSIA LN
- CRLB 92009 1127-D4
CAMBER CT
5600 SD 92117 1248-H2
CAMBER DR
5500 SD 92117 1248-H2
CAMBER PL
5700 SD 92117 1248-H2
CAMBERLEY CT
- SD 92154 1330-H7
CAMBERWELL CT
12600 SD 92128 1150-B6
CAMBERWELL LN
18300 SD 92128 1150-B6
CAMBON CT
9100 SDCo 91977 1291-B4

CAMBON ST
9100 SDCo 91977 1291-B4
CAMBRIA CT
5500 SD 92120 1250-B7
CAMBRIA PL
- ENCT 92024 1147-F5
1600 ESCN 92029 1129-G7
CAMBRIA WY
- ENCT 92024 1147-F5
CAMBRIDGE
1900 VSTA 92083 1108-E2
CAMBRIDGE AV
1900 ENCT 92007 1167-D3
CAMBRIDGE CT
1100 SMCS 92069 1128-B3
3800 OCN 92056 1087-A7
8800 SDCo 92040 1232-C6
CAMBRIDGE WY
4500 CRLB 92008 1107-B4
CAMBURY CT
9700 SNTE 92071 1231-C4
CAMBURY DR
9400 SNTE 92071 1231-C5
E CAMDEN AV
100 ELCJ 92020 1251-G6
W CAMDEN AV
100 ELCJ 92020 1251-F6
CAMDEN CIR
3400 CRLB 92008 1106-G4
CAMDEN DR
- VSTA 92083 1108-B6
CAMELIA DR
- SD 92109 1248-C6
CAMELIA ST
1100 OCN 92054 1106-C2
CAMELLIA
3500 SDCo 92028 1028-F4
CAMELLIA CT
1400 CHV 91911 1330-H3
CAMELLIA DR
7100 LMSA 91941 1270-F3
CAMELLIA PL
700 CRLB 92008 1106-F6
N CAMELLIA ST
600 ESCN 92027 1110-B6
CAMELOT CT
7200 LMGR 91945 1290-F1
CAMELOT DR
300 OCN 92054 1086-E6
CAMELOT PKWY
- ELCJ 92019 1252-D4
CAMEO CT
3700 SD 92111 1248-G4
CAMEO DR
500 ESCN 92026 1109-H6
1700 VSTA 92083 1087-D6
3400 OCN 92056 1086-J7
3400 OCN 92056 1106-J1
3500 OCN 92056 1087-A7
CAMEO LN
3600 SD 92111 1248-G4
CAMEO RD
2200 CRLB 92008 1106-H5
CAMERO ST
5400 SD 92105 1270-B5
CAMERON CT
6000 SD 92139 1310-D2
CAMERON DR
1600 LMGR 91945 1290-H1
8100 SDCo 91977 1290-H1
CAMERON PL
2700 ESCN 92027 1110-D6
CAMERON TKTR
2200 SDCo 91906 (1297-J3 See Page 1296)
2300 SDCo 91906 1298-A2
2400 SDCo 91906 430-B7
CAMILLE WY
200 VSTA 92083 1107-J1
8900 SDCo 92026 1089-A1
CAMILLO CT
1400 ELCJ 92021 1252-A2
CAMILLO WY
1200 ELCJ 92021 1252-A3
CAMINATA BREVE
13900 SD 92129 1189-H3
CAMINATA DELUZ
10700 SD 92129 1189-H3
CAMINATA DOURO
11000 SD 92129 1189-H2
CAMINATA EBRO
10700 SD 92129 1189-H2
CAMINATA SOLEADO
14300 SD 92129 1189-H2
CAMINATA TAUGUS
14300 SD 92129 1189-H2
CAMINITA AMADOR
14000 SD 92129 1189-H2
CAMINITA CORTINA
3100 SDCo 92028 1048-A2
CAMINITO ABETO
2600 SD 92154 1350-C1
CAMINITO ABRAZO
8700 SD 92037 1228-A3
CAMINITO A CASA
400 SMCS 92078 1129-B2
CAMINITO ACENTO
1300 SD 92037 1247-H3
CAMINITO ACLARA
11200 SD 92126 1208-H2
CAMINITO AFUERA
2300 SD 92107 1268-C2
CAMINITO AGADIR
10200 SD 92131 1209-G5
CAMINITO AGRADO
2300 SD 92107 1268-B6
CAMINITO AGUA
5400 SD 92037 1248-A3
CAMINITO AGUAR
1500 SDCo 92069 1128-C3
CAMINITO AGUILAR
3800 SD 92111 1248-H3
CAMINITO AIRE PURO
15800 SD 92128 1170-B5
CAMINITO ALEGRA
11000 SD 92131 1210-B2
CAMINITO ALIVIADO
1600 SD 92037 1247-J3
CAMINITO ALMONTE
14000 SD 92129 1189-H3
CAMINITO ALTO
10800 SD 92131 1210-C2
CAMINITO ALVAREZ
11100 SD 92126 1208-J4
CAMINITO AMAPOLA
100 SMCS 92069 1109-B7
CAMINITO AMARILLO
1100 SMCS 92069 1108-F5

SAN DIEGO CO.
INDEX

CAMINITO AMECA — SAN DIEGO CO. STREET INDEX — CAMINITO VELASCO 6572

STREET	Block	City	ZIP	Pg-Grid
CAMINITO AMECA	3100	SD	92037	1228-A5
CAMINITO AMERGON	1800	SD	92037	1247-J2
CAMINITO AMISTAD	2400	SD	92154	1352-B3
CAMINITO AMPARO	3900	SD	92122	1228-B4
CAMINITO ANDADA	2300	SD	92107	1268-C3
CAMINITO ANDRETA	6200	SD	92111	1268-H2
CAMINITO ANGELICO	12900	SD	92130	1188-C5
CAMINITO ANTILDADO	4800	SD	92130	1188-C7
CAMINITO ANZIO	13700	SD	92129	1189-H3
CAMINITO APARTADO	5200	SD	92108	1269-H2
CAMINITO ARALIA	10300	SD	92131	1209-G6
CAMINITO ARAYA	6200	SD	92122	1228-E5
CAMINITO ARBOLES	10900	SD	92131	1210-C2
CAMINITO ARCADA	10800	SD	92131	1209-H1
CAMINITO ARDIENTE	1700	SD	92037	1247-J2
CAMINITO ARENOSO	3000	SD	92117	1248-C2
CAMINITO ARMIDA	11400	SD	92131	1209-J5
	11400	SD	92131	1210-A5
CAMINITO ARONIMINK	2500	SD	92037	1247-J1
CAMINITO ARRIATA	1300	SD	92037	1247-J4
CAMINITO ARUBA	5200	SD	92124	1249-F2
CAMINITO ASCUA	1800	SD	92037	1247-J2
CAMINITO ASTERISCO	1600	SD	92037	1247-J2
CAMINITO ATICO	15700	SD	92128	1170-A5
CAMINITO AVELLANO	2500	SD	92154	1350-B1
CAMINITO AVOLA	7600	SD	92037	1227-H6
CAMINITO AZUL	800	CRLB	92009	1126-J5
CAMINITO BADALONA	3000	SD	92014	1187-H3
CAMINITO BAEZA	6100	SD	92122	1228-E6
CAMINITO BALADA	1300	SD	92037	1247-H3
CAMINITO BALATA	17500	SD	92128	1170-D1
CAMINITO BALTUSRAL	6400	SD	92037	1248-A1
CAMINITO BANYON	10300	SD	92131	1209-H5
CAMINITO BARBUDA	14700	SD	92014	1188-B1
CAMINITO BARLOVENTO	1600	SD	92037	1247-J3
CAMINITO BASILIO	6200	SD	92111	1268-G3
CAMINITO BASSANO E	7300	SD	92037	1227-H7
CAMINITO BASSANO W	7300	SD	92037	1227-H7
CAMINITO BASSWOOD	10500	SD	92131	1209-H5
CAMINITO BATEA	1300	SD	92037	1247-J3
CAMINITO BAUTIZO	12900	SD	92130	1188-C5
CAMINITO BAYA	17400	SD	92127	1169-J1
CAMINITO BAYO	5400	SD	92037	1247-H4
CAMINITO BAYWOOD	10500	SD	92126	1209-D4
CAMINITO BELLO	2900	SD	92037	1227-J5
	2900	SD	92037	1228-A5
CAMINITO BESO	12800	SD	92130	1188-C5
CAMINITO BLYTHEFIELD	6400	SD	92037	1247-J1
	6600	SD	92037	1227-J7
CAMINITO BODEGA	12900	SD	92014	1207-J2
CAMINITO BOLSA	9700	SD	92129	1189-F4
CAMINITO BONANZA	7700	CRLB	92009	1148-A2
CAMINITO BORDE	5400	SD	92108	1269-H1
CAMINITO BORREGO	-	CHV	91913	1311-E7
	4700	SD	92130	1188-C6
CAMINITO BRACHO	13000	SD	92128	1170-D1
CAMINITO BRAGA	7000	SD	92122	1228-B4
CAMINITO BRAVURA	10700	SD	92108	1249-G7
CAMINITO BRIOSO	12400	SD	92131	1210-C2
CAMINITO BRISA	1800	SD	92037	1227-H7
CAMINITO BUENA SUERTE	6200	SD	92120	1250-D6
CAMINITO CABALA	2200	SD	92037	1248-A2
CAMINITO CABANA	9400	SD	92126	1209-E5
CAMINITO CABO VIEJO	3300	SD	92014	1187-H3
CAMINITO CACHORRO	5000	SD	92105	1270-A7
CAMINITO CADENA	12000	SD	92128	1170-B2
CAMINITO CALA	2300	SD	92014	1207-H1
CAMINITO CALDO	17500	SD	92127	1169-J1
CAMINITO CALMOSO	4700	SD	92130	1188-C5
CAMINITO CALOR	9700	SD	92131	1210-A5
CAMINITO CAMPANA	11900	SD	92128	1170-B2
CAMINITO CAMPANEO	4700	SD	92130	1188-C5
CAMINITO CANADA	10900	SD	92131	1210-C3
CAMINITO CANASTO	17200	SD	92127	1169-J1
CAMINITO CANCION	12700	SD	92128	1170-C3
CAMINITO CANELO	12400	SD	92131	1210-C3
CAMINITO CANON	6800	SDCo	92067	1148-F5
	12400	SD	92131	1210-C3
CAMINITO CANOR	4700	SD	92130	1188-C5
CAMINITO CANTARAS	15800	SD	92014	1187-H1
CAMINITO CANTILENA	18600	SD	92128	1150-A5
CAMINITO CAPA	2000	SD	92037	1227-H7
CAMINITO CAPE SEBASTIAN	2900	ENCT	92007	1167-F5
CAMINITO CAPISTRANO	-	CHV	91913	1311-E7
CAMINITO CARBONERAS	3000	SD	92014	1187-H3
CAMINITO CARDELINA	5800	SD	92037	1247-J2
CAMINITO CARINO	2600	SD	92037	1227-J6
CAMINITO CARLOTTA	7200	SD	92120	1250-E4
CAMINITO CARMEL	13300	SD	92014	1207-J1
CAMINITO CARMEL LNDG	3500	SD	92130	1188-A7
CAMINITO CARMEL HARBOUR	12100	SD	92130	1188-A7
CAMINITO CAROLINA	1200	ENCT	92024	1148-B5
CAMINITO CARRENA	6200	SD	92122	1228-E5
CAMINITO CARTGATE	2400	SD	92037	1247-J1
CAMINITO CASCARA	10500	SD	92108	1269-G1
CAMINITO CASSIS	3900	SD	92122	1228-B5
CAMINITO CASTILLO	2200	SD	92037	1248-A2
CAMINITO CATALAN	6400	SD	92037	1247-J1
CAMINITO CEDRO	1200	SD	92154	1350-B1
CAMINITO CEDROS	2700	SD	92014	1207-J2
CAMINITO CENTRO	1300	SD	92102	1289-C2
	1400	SD	92101	1289-C2
CAMINITO CERCADO	15700	SD	92128	1170-A5
CAMINITO CEREZO	10900	SD	92131	1210-C3
CAMINITO CHIAPAS	5900	SD	92108	1269-G1
CAMINITO CHICLAYO	17600	SD	92128	1170-C1
CAMINITO CHIRIMOLLA	9900	SD	92131	1209-G5
CAMINITO CHOLLAS	2700	SD	92105	1270-C7
CAMINITO CHUECO	10600	SD	92126	1209-D4
CAMINITO CIELO DEL MAR	3600	SD	92130	1188-A7
CAMINITO CIERA	13300	SD	92129	1189-G4
CAMINITO CIRCULO NORTE	2000	SD	92037	1248-A2
CAMINITO CIRCULO SUR	2000	SD	92037	1248-A3
CAMINITO CITA	1200	SD	92154	1350-C1
CAMINITO CLARO	8800	SD	92037	1228-A3
CAMINITO CLASICA	4800	SD	92130	1188-C7
CAMINITO CLAVO	6100	SD	92120	1250-D7
CAMINITO COLORADO	10800	SD	92131	1210-B2
CAMINITO CONSUELO	5500	SD	92037	1248-A3
CAMINITO COROMANDEL	7500	SD	92037	1227-J6
CAMINITO CORRIENTE	11800	SD	92128	1170-A6
CAMINITO COVEWOOD	10200	SD	92131	1209-G6
CAMINITO CRISTALINO	4400	SD	92117	1248-C2
CAMINITO CRISTO	4700	SD	92130	1188-C6
CAMINITO CRISTOBAL	13000	SD	92014	1207-J2
CAMINITO CRUZADA	7100	SD	92037	1227-H7
CAMINITO CUADRO	9800	SD	92129	1189-F4
CAMINITO CUARZO	4400	SD	92117	1248-C2
CAMINITO CUERVO	10200	SD	92108	1249-G7
CAMINITO CUESTA	10800	SD	92131	1210-C2
CAMINITO CURVA	6900	SD	92119	1250-F4
CAMINITO DANIELLA	3400	SD	92014	1187-J1
	3400	SOLB	92014	1187-J1
CAMINITO DANZARIN	5600	SD	92037	1247-H3
CAMINITO DAVILA	3900	SD	92122	1228-B5
CAMINITO DEHESA	3900	SD	92107	1268-C2
CAMINITO DE LA ESCENA	4300	SD	92108	1269-H2
CAMINITO DE LA FADA	9700	SD	92124	1249-F1
CAMINITO DE LA GALLARDA	12500	SD	92128	1170-C3
CAMINITO DE LAS MISSIONES	11700	SD	92128	1170-A5
CAMINITO DE LAS NOCHES	16000	SD	92128	1170-A4
CAMINITO DE LAS OLAS	12800	SD	92014	1207-H1
CAMINITO DE LAS PALMAS	16700	SDCo	92127	1168-J3
CAMINITO DE LA TAZA	5900	SD	92120	1250-D7
CAMINITO DEL BARCO	2100	SD	92014	1207-G1
CAMINITO DEL CANTO	12900	SD	92014	1207-H1
CAMINITO DEL CERVATO	6300	SD	92111	1268-H1
CAMINITO DEL CID	7900	SD	92037	1227-H6
CAMINITO DEL DIAMANTE	4300	SD	92121	1228-D1
CAMINITO DEL ESTIO	5800	SD	92037	1247-H3
CAMINITO DEL FELIZ	9500	SD	92121	1228-D1
CAMINITO DEL GRECO	6700	SD	92120	1250-E4
CAMINITO DEL HOY	11700	SD	92128	1170-A5
CAMINITO DE LINDA	16000	SD	92128	1170-A5
CAMINITO DEL MAR	800	CRLB	92009	1126-J4
CAMINITO DEL MAR CV	3900	SD	92130	1188-A7
CAMINITO DEL MARFIL	9700	SD	92124	1249-F2
CAMINITO DEL MAR SANDS	12200	SD	92130	1188-A7
CAMINITO DEL MAR SHORES	12100	SD	92130	1188-A7
CAMINITO DEL MAR SURF	3900	SD	92130	1188-A7
CAMINITO DEL OESTE	6100	SD	92111	1268-H1
CAMINITO DE LOS CEPILLOS	-	SDCo	92003	1067-H3
CAMINITO DE LOS ESCOSES	17500	SDCo	92067	1168-J1
CAMINITO DEL PASAJE	12900	SD	92014	1207-H2
CAMINITO DEL PASTEL	6300	SD	92111	1268-H1
CAMINITO DEL REPOSO	800	CRLB	92009	1126-J4
CAMINITO DEL ROCIO	13000	SD	92014	1207-G1
CAMINITO DEL SOL	800	CRLB	92009	1126-J5
CAMINITO DEL VERDE	9200	SNTE	92071	1231-A6
CAMINITO DEL VIDA	9600	SD	92121	1228-D1
CAMINITO DEL VIENTECITO	16700	SDCo	92127	1168-J3
CAMINITO DEL ZAFIRO	4300	SD	92121	1228-D1
CAMINITO DE MARIA	4200	SDCo	91977	1271-C4
CAMINITO DE OI VAY	7500	SD	92111	1249-A3
CAMINITO DE PIZZA	8000	SD	92108	1269-B2
CAMINITO DEPORTE	5900	SD	92108	1269-G1
CAMINITO DERECHO	10600	SD	92126	1209-D4
CAMINITO DESEO	2900	SD	92037	1228-A3
CAMINITO DESTELLO	12600	SD	92130	1188-E6
CAMINITO DE TATAN	3800	SD	92111	1249-A3
CAMINITO DIA	7900	SD	92122	1228-C4
CAMINITO DIABLO	4700	SD	92130	1188-C5
CAMINITO DIADEMA	1300	SD	92037	1247-J3
CAMINITO DIEGO	12700	SD	92130	1188-C5
CAMINITO DOHA	9700	SD	92131	1209-G5
CAMINITO DONOSO	7000	SD	92037	1227-H7
CAMINITO DOSAMANTES	12900	SD	92128	1170-C1
CAMINITO DULCE	11000	SD	92131	1210-B2
CAMINITO DURO	10600	SD	92126	1209-D4
CAMINITO EASTBLUFF	3300	SD	92037	1228-A4
CAMINITO ELADO	11400	SD	92131	1210-A5
CAMINITO EL CANARIO	2000	SD	92037	1227-H7
	2000	SD	92037	1247-H1
CAMINITO ELDORADO	2700	SD	92014	1207-J2
CAMINITO ELEGANTE	5900	SD	92108	1269-G1
CAMINITO EL RINCON	3500	SD	92130	1187-J7
	3500	SD	92130	1188-A6
CAMINITO EL ROSARIO	7800	SD	92037	1227-J6
CAMINITO EMPRESA	5700	SD	92037	1247-J3
CAMINITO ENCANTO	7700	CRLB	92009	1147-J2
	11000	SD	92131	1210-B2
CAMINITO EN FLOR	12800	SD	92014	1207-H1
CAMINITO ENTRADA	6900	SD	92119	1250-F4
CAMINITO ESMERO	12300	SD	92130	1188-D7
CAMINITO ESPEJO	4000	SD	92107	1268-C3
CAMINITO ESPINO	2500	SD	92154	1350-C1
CAMINITO ESTERO	2300	SD	92107	1268-C3
CAMINITO ESTIMA	5600	SD	92037	1248-A2
CAMINITO ESTRADA	900	CRLB	92009	1126-J5
	7000	SD	92037	1227-H7
	7000	SD	92037	1247-H1
CAMINITO ESTRELLA	700	CHV	91910	1310-H6
CAMINITO ESTRELLADO	6100	SD	92120	1250-C6
CAMINITO EVA	4700	SD	92130	1188-C6
CAMINITO EVANGELICO	4700	SD	92130	1188-C5
CAMINITO EXIMIO	2300	SD	92107	1268-C2
CAMINITO EXQUISITO	4800	SD	92130	1188-E6
CAMINITO FACETO	4700	SD	92130	1188-C5
CAMINITO FARO	1300	SD	92037	1247-H3
CAMINITO FESTIVO	12300	SD	92131	1210-B2
CAMINITO FLECHA	6300	SD	92111	1268-H3
CAMINITO FLOREO	1300	SD	92037	1247-H4
CAMINITO FLORES	10500	SD	92126	1209-D4
CAMINITO FORMBY	6400	SD	92037	1247-J1
CAMINITO FORTALEZA	3000	SD	92014	1187-H3
CAMINITO FRANCHE	7000	SD	92122	1228-B5
CAMINITO FRANCISCO	-	CHV	91913	1311-E7
CAMINITO FRESCO	8900	SD	92037	1228-A3
CAMINITO FUENTE	4400	SD	92116	1269-A4
CAMINITO GABALDON	1300	SD	92108	1269-B2
CAMINITO GANDARA	3200	SD	92037	1228-A5
CAMINITO GANTON	2800	SD	92037	1227-J7
	2800	SD	92037	1228-A7
CAMINITO GARCIA	11400	SD	92131	1209-J5
	11400	SD	92131	1210-A5
CAMINITO GENIO	5500	SD	92037	1247-H3
CAMINITO GIANNA	8000	SD	92037	1228-A5
CAMINITO GIJON	3000	SD	92014	1187-H3
CAMINITO GILBAR	15700	SD	92128	1170-A5
CAMINITO GIRASOL	4700	SD	92130	1188-C5
CAMINITO GLENELLEN	10500	SD	92126	1209-D4
CAMINITO GOMA	10300	SD	92131	1209-G5
CAMINITO GRACIELA	1200	ENCT	92024	1148-B5
CAMINITO GRANATE	12300	SD	92130	1188-D7
CAMINITO GRIMALDI	7000	SD	92122	1228-B4
CAMINITO GUSTO	11500	SD	92131	1210-A5
CAMINITO HALAGO	1300	SD	92037	1247-J3
CAMINITO HELECHO	8300	SD	92037	1227-J5
CAMINITO HENO	17500	SD	92127	1169-J1
	17500	SD	92127	1170-A1
CAMINITO HERALDO	5400	SD	92037	1247-H4
CAMINITO HERCUBA	17600	SD	92128	1170-C1
CAMINITO HERMINIA	5400	SD	92037	1248-A3
CAMINITO HERMITAGE	6600	SD	92037	1227-J7
	6600	SD	92037	1228-A7
CAMINITO HIEDRA	2500	SD	92154	1350-C1
CAMINITO HIERRO	4400	SD	92117	1248-C2
CAMINITO IMPERSADO	10100	SD	92126	1209-E5
CAMINITO INOCENTA	11100	SD	92126	1208-H2
CAMINITO ISLA	5600	SD	92037	1248-A3
CAMINITO JOSE	5500	SD	92111	1248-H3
CAMINITO JOVEN	9700	SD	92131	1210-A5
CAMINITO JOVIAL	10100	SD	92126	1209-E5
CAMINITO JUANICO	6200	SD	92111	1268-G3
CAMINITO JUBILO	5200	SD	92108	1269-H2
CAMINITO KATERINA	5500	SD	92111	1248-H3
CAMINITO KITTANSETT	6500	SD	92037	1247-J1
CAMINITO LA BAR	11500	SD	92126	1208-J2
CAMINITO LA BENERA	7000	SD	92037	1227-H7
CAMINITO LACAYO	8200	SD	92037	1227-J5
CAMINITO LADERA	14900	SOLB	92014	1187-H1
CAMINITO LA PAZ	2500	SD	92037	1227-J6
CAMINITO LAPIZ	4700	SD	92130	1188-C6
CAMINITO LASWANE	9700	SD	92131	1210-A5
CAMINITO LA TORRE	15600	SD	92128	1170-C5
CAMINITO LAURA	1300	ENCT	92024	1148-B5
CAMINITO LAZARO	6300	SD	92111	1268-H3
CAMINITO LEON	7700	CRLB	92009	1148-A2
CAMINITO LINDRICK	6600	SD	92037	1228-A7
CAMINITO LINTERNA	8300	SD	92037	1227-J5
CAMINITO LISTO	6400	SD	92111	1268-H1
CAMINITO LITORAL	3800	SD	92107	1268-B7
CAMINITO LOBES	13000	SD	92128	1170-C1
CAMINITO LOMA BUENA	3100	SD	92117	1248-F5
CAMINITO LORETA	1900	SD	92037	1248-A3
CAMINITO LORREN	14700	SD	92014	1187-J1
CAMINITO LUISITO	6200	SD	92111	1268-H2
CAMINITO LUNA NUEVA	3300	SD	92014	1187-J1
CAMINITO MADRIGAL	900	CRLB	92009	1126-J4
CAMINITO MAGNIFICA	11400	SD	92131	1210-A5
CAMINITO MAGUEY	10200	SD	92131	1209-G6
CAMINITO MALAGA	7700	CRLB	92009	1148-A2
CAMINITO MALLORCA	8000	SD	92037	1228-A5
CAMINITO MANRESA	7000	SD	92037	1227-H7
	7000	SD	92037	1247-H1
CAMINITO MANSO	10600	SD	92126	1209-D4
CAMINITO MARACAIBO	14700	SD	92014	1188-C1
CAMINITO MARCIAL	6200	SD	92111	1268-H2
CAMINITO MAR DE PLATA	14700	SD	92014	1187-H1
CAMINITO MARIA	15100	SDCo	92067	1188-F1
CAMINITO MARITIMO	8200	SD	92037	1227-J5
CAMINITO MARLOCK	9800	SD	92131	1209-G6
CAMINITO MARRISA	2100	SD	92037	1248-A3
CAMINITO MAR VILLA	2200	SD	92014	1207-H1
	13100	SD	92014	1187-G7
CAMINITO MARZELLA	1800	SD	92037	1227-H7
CAMINITO MASADA	17300	SD	92127	1169-J1
CAMINITO MAYTEN	10400	SD	92131	1209-G6
CAMINITO MELIADO	4000	SD	92122	1228-B4
CAMINITO MEMBRILLO	9900	SD	92131	1209-G6
CAMINITO MEMOSAC	10500	SD	92131	1209-H5
CAMINITO MENDIOLA	12800	SD	92130	1188-G4
CAMINITO MENOR	4000	SD	92107	1268-C2
CAMINITO MERION	2700	SD	92037	1227-J7
	2700	SD	92037	1228-A7
CAMINITO MINDY	5200	SD	92105	1270-A7
CAMINITO MIRA	2300	SD	92107	1268-B6
CAMINITO MIRADA	12300	SD	92131	1210-B2
CAMINITO MIRA DEL MAR	12100	SD	92130	1188-A7
CAMINITO MODENA	8200	SD	92037	1228-A5
CAMINITO MOJADO	9700	SD	92131	1210-B5
CAMINITO MONARCA	7700	CRLB	92009	1147-F2
CAMINITO MONROVIA	1800	SD	92037	1227-H7
CAMINITO MONTANOSO	6800	SD	92119	1250-F4
CAMINITO MORAGA	-	CHV	91913	1311-D7
CAMINITO MUIRFIELD	2400	SD	92037	1247-J1
CAMINITO MULEGE	10100	SD	92126	1209-E5
CAMINITO MUNDANO	5500	SD	92130	1188-E6
CAMINITO MUNDO	6800	SD	92119	1250-F4
CAMINITO MUNOZ	9700	SD	92131	1210-A5
CAMINITO NIQUEL	2900	SD	92117	1248-C2
CAMINITO NORTE	5700	SD	92037	1248-A2
CAMINITO NORTHLAND	6400	SD	92037	1248-A1
	6400	SD	92037	1228-A7
CAMINITO NUEZ	10100	SD	92131	1209-G6
CAMINITO OBISPO	-	CHV	91913	1311-D7
CAMINITO OBRA	10500	SD	92126	1209-D4
CAMINITO OCEAN CV	2400	ENCT	92007	1167-F4
CAMINITO OCIO	4400	SD	92108	1269-H1
CAMINITO OLMO	7100	SD	92037	1227-H7
CAMINITO ORENSE ESTE	14600	SD	92129	1189-J1
CAMINITO ORENSE OESTE	14700	SD	92129	1189-J1
CAMINITO PACIFICA TR	-	SD	92130	1188-B2
CAMINITO PAJARITO	2200	SD	92107	1268-B6
CAMINITO PAN	6000	SD	92120	1250-D6
CAMINITO PANTOJA	7100	SD	92122	1228-B4
CAMINITO PARTIDA	6300	SD	92111	1268-H3
CAMINITO PASADA	2200	SD	92107	1268-B6
CAMINITO PASADERO	18500	SD	92128	1150-B6
CAMINITO PATRICIA	3900	SD	92111	1248-H3
CAMINITO PEDERNAL	4400	SD	92117	1248-C2
CAMINITO PELON	9800	SD	92131	1210-A5
CAMINITO PEPINO	7100	SD	92037	1227-H7
CAMINITO PEQUENA	7300	SD	92119	1250-G4
CAMINITO PERAL	12300	SD	92131	1210-C2
CAMINITO PERICO	6900	SD	92119	1250-G4
CAMINITO PESCADO	2200	SD	92107	1268-B6
CAMINITO PIMIENTO	1200	SD	92154	1350-B2
CAMINITO PINERO	17800	SD	92128	1150-A7
CAMINITO PINTORESCO	4200	SD	92108	1269-H2
CAMINITO PITAYA	10200	SD	92131	1209-G6
CAMINITO PLATA	6100	SD	92120	1250-C6
CAMINITO PLAZA VW	1100	SD	92154	1350-D1
CAMINITO PLAZA CENTRO	8800	SD	92122	1228-B3
CAMINITO PLOMADA	4400	SD	92117	1248-C2
CAMINITO POCO	2400	SD	92107	1268-C2
CAMINITO POINTE DEL MAR	12800	SD	92014	1207-J1
CAMINITO POLLO	10500	SD	92126	1209-D4
CAMINITO PORTA DELGADA	14700	SD	92014	1188-B1
	14700	SDCo	92014	1188-B1
CAMINITO PORTHCAWL	2500	SD	92037	1247-J1
CAMINITO PORTO ALEGRE	14700	SD	92014	1187-J1
CAMINITO PRADO	2700	SD	92037	1227-J6
CAMINITO PRECIOSA NORTE	2200	SD	92037	1248-A3
CAMINITO PRECIOSA SUR	2200	SD	92037	1248-A3
	2200	SD	92109	1248-A3
CAMINITO PRENTICIA	11700	SD	92131	1210-B5
CAMINITO PRIMAVERA	8800	SD	92037	1228-A3
CAMINITO PROPICO	6900	SD	92126	1208-H2
CAMINITO PROSPERO	12400	SD	92130	1188-C7
CAMINITO PROVIDENCIA	5300	SD	92067	1188-D1
CAMINITO PUDREGAL	9700	SD	92131	1210-B4
CAMINITO PUERTO	7700	CRLB	92009	1148-A2
CAMINITO PULSERA	5700	SD	92037	1247-H3
CAMINITO PUNTA ARENAS	14700	SD	92014	1187-J1
CAMINITO QUEVEDO	14100	SD	92129	1189-H3
CAMINITO QUIETO	32000	SDCo	92003	1048-H7
CAMINITO QUINTANA	7100	SD	92122	1228-B4
CAMINITO QUINTERO	1800	SD	92037	1227-H7
CAMINITO QUIXOTE	3100	SD	92154	1330-E7
	3100	SD	92154	1350-E1
CAMINITO RADIANTE	12500	SD	92130	1188-D6
CAMINITO RECODO	2300	SD	92107	1268-B6
CAMINITO RIALTO	7400	SD	92037	1227-H6
CAMINITO RICARDO	3100	ENCT	92024	1148-B5
CAMINITO RIMINI	10400	SD	92129	1189-G3
CAMINITO RIO	11500	SDCo	92040	1231-H3
CAMINITO RIO CT	10200	SDCo	92040	1231-H3
CAMINITO RIO ALTA	2900	SD	92014	1187-H1
CAMINITO RIO BRANCO	10200	SD	92131	1209-G5
CAMINITO ROBERTO	5600	SD	92111	1248-H3
CAMINITO RODAR	11100	SD	92126	1208-H2
CAMINITO ROGELIO	9800	SD	92131	1210-A5
CAMINITO RONALDO	11800	SD	92128	1170-A1
CAMINITO ROSA	800	CRLB	92009	1126-J5
	5400	SD	92037	1248-A3
CAMINITO ROSITA	12500	SD	92128	1170-C5
CAMINITO RYONE	11800	SD	92128	1170-A5
CAMINITO SACATE	6100	SD	92120	1250-C6
CAMINITO SAGUNTO	3000	SD	92014	1187-H1
CAMINITO SALADO	6200	SD	92111	1268-H2
CAMINITO SANA	4400	SD	92122	1228-D4
CAMINITO SAN LUCAS	5400	SD	92037	1248-A3
CAMINITO SAN MARINO	2700	SD	92014	1207-J2
CAMINITO SAN MARTIN	2100	SD	92037	1248-A2
CAMINITO SAN NICHOLAS	2000	SD	92037	1248-A2
CAMINITO SAN PABLO	2700	SD	92014	1207-J2
CAMINITO SAN SEBASTIAN	4500	SD	92014	1188-B1
CAMINITO SANTA FE DOWNS	2600	SD	92014	1187-J1
CAMINITO SANTICO	16900	SD	92128	1170-C3
CAMINITO SANTO TOMAS	14500	SDCo	92067	1188-H2
CAMINITO SANUDO	11800	SD	92131	1210-B5
CAMINITO SARAGOSSA	14400	SD	92067	1188-D1
CAMINITO SCIOTO	6500	SD	92037	1247-J1
CAMINITO SECOYA	2600	SD	92154	1350-C1
CAMINITO SEGURO	2300	SD	92107	1268-C2
CAMINITO SEPTIMO	1200	ENCT	92007	1167-F1
CAMINITO SERENO	12300	SD	92131	1210-B2
CAMINITO SIEGA	17300	SD	92127	1169-J1
CAMINITO SIERRA	3400	CRLB	92009	1147-J2
	3500	CRLB	92009	1148-A2
CAMINITO SILVELA	3900	SD	92122	1228-B4
CAMINITO SINNECOCK	6400	SD	92037	1247-J1
CAMINITO SOLIDAGO	1400	SD	92037	1247-H3
CAMINITO SOLITARIO	5200	SD	92108	1269-H2
CAMINITO SONOMA	7900	SD	92037	1228-A5
CAMINITO SONRISA	-	CHV	91913	1311-D7
CAMINITO SOPADILLA	10500	SD	92131	1209-G5
CAMINITO SUELTO	9700	SD	92131	1210-A5
CAMINITO SUENO	6800	CRLB	92009	1128-A5
	8700	SD	92037	1228-A3
CAMINITO SUERO	4000	SD	92122	1228-B4
CAMINITO SULMONA	10400	SD	92129	1189-G3
CAMINITO SURABAYA	10200	SD	92131	1209-G5
CAMINITO TAMBORREL	11700	SD	92131	1210-B5
CAMINITO TAMEGA	12500	SD	92128	1170-B5
CAMINITO TECERA	4400	SD	92014	1188-B1
CAMINITO TELMO	6200	SD	92111	1268-H2
CAMINITO TENEDOR	6200	SD	92120	1250-D6
CAMINITO TERCER VERDE	3000	SD	92014	1187-H1
CAMINITO TERVISO	3900	SD	92122	1228-B5
CAMINITO TIBURON	2100	SD	92037	1248-A3
CAMINITO TIERRA	10900	SD	92131	1210-C3
CAMINITO TIERRA DEL SOL	16100	SD	92128	1170-A5
CAMINITO TINGO	7700	CRLB	92009	1148-A2
CAMINITO TIRADA	9500	SD	92126	1209-E5
CAMINITO TIZONA	9600	SD	92126	1209-E5
CAMINITO TOGA	9500	SD	92126	1209-E5
CAMINITO TOMAS	16000	SD	92128	1170-A4
CAMINITO TOMATILLO	9900	SD	92131	1209-G6
CAMINITO TOM MORRIS	2600	SD	92037	1247-J1
CAMINITO TOPAZIO	3000	SD	92117	1248-C2
CAMINITO TORONJO	10200	SD	92131	1209-G6
CAMINITO TORREBLANCA	3000	SD	92014	1187-H3
CAMINITO TULIPAN	1200	SD	92154	1350-C1
CAMINITO TURIA	1600	SD	92037	1247-H3
CAMINITO TURNBERRY	6400	SD	92037	1248-A1
CAMINITO UMBRAL	4000	SD	92107	1268-C2
CAMINITO VALERIANO	3800	SD	92122	1228-B5
CAMINITO VALIOSO	12400	SD	92130	1188-D7
CAMINITO VALVERDE	7000	SD	92037	1227-H7
	7000	SD	92037	1247-H1
CAMINITO VANTANA	11700	SD	92131	1210-A4
CAMINITO VASTO	3200	SD	92037	1228-A5
CAMINITO VECINOS	16400	SD	92128	1170-C3
CAMINITO VELASCO	1800	SD	92037	1227-H7

SAN DIEGO CO.
INDEX

Each entry lists: Block — City — ZIP — Pg-Grid

CAMINITO VELASQUEZ
5300 SD 92124 1249-F1
CAMINITO VELEZ
1800 SD 92037 1227-H7
CAMINITO VELLO
5500 SD 92130 1188-E6
CAMINITO VENIDO
2400 SD 92107 1268-B6
2400 SD 92110 1268-B6
CAMINITO VERA
8900 SD 92126 1209-D4
CAMINITO VERANO
8900 SD 92037 1228-A3
8900 SD 92037 1227-J3
CAMINITO VERDE
- CRLB 92009 1126-J5
CAMINITO VERDUGO
2700 SD 92014 1207-J2
CAMINITO VIA CAMPESTRE
3100 SD 92014 1187-H3
CAMINITO VIBRANTE
12300 SD 92131 1210-C2
CAMINITO VIEJO
2500 SD 92037 1227-J6
CAMINITO VILOS
13000 SD 92128 1170-D1
CAMINITO VIOLETA
100 SMCS 92069 1109-C7
CAMINITO VISTA ESTRELLADO
14700 SD 92014 1187-H3
CAMINITO VISTA LUJO
4900 SD 92130 1188-D7
CAMINITO VISTANA
- SD 92130 1189-A2
CAMINITO VISTA PACIFICA
11000 SD 92131 1209-H3
CAMINITO VISTA SERENA
11100 SD 92131 1209-H3
CAMINITO VISTA SOLEDAD
12500 SD 92130 1188-D6
CAMINITO VIVA
8800 SD 92037 1228-A3
CAMINITO VIZZINI
13700 SD 92129 1189-G3
CAMINITO VOLAR
10100 SD 92126 1209-E5
CAMINITO WESTCHESTER
10500 SD 92126 1209-E4
CAMINITO YUCATAN
5900 SD 92108 1249-G1
5900 SD 92108 1269-G1
CAMINITO ZABALA
7100 SD 92122 1228-B4
CAMINITO ZAR
10100 SD 92126 1209-E5
CAMINITO ZOCALO
2400 SD 92107 1268-B6
2400 SD 92110 1268-B6
CAMINITO ZOPILOTE
2600 SD 92105 1270-A7
CAMINO DR
- ImCo 92274 410-G6
2000 ESCN 92026 1109-D4
CAMINO ABROJO
10900 SD 92127 1169-H5
CAMINO ACAMPO
17100 SDCo 92067 1168-G5
CAMINO AGUILA
7800 SD 92122 1228-C4
CAMINO ALEGRE
3400 CRLB 92009 1147-J5
4000 SD 92154 1271-H4
CAMINO ALETA
3000 SD 92154 1350-D1
CAMINO ALISOS
3100 SDCo 92028 1028-C3
CAMINO ALTEZA
3000 SD 92127 1168-J7
3000 SD 92127 1188-J1
CAMINO ALVARO
1200 CRLB 92009 1147-H3
CAMINO AMERO
6900 SD 92111 1268-J2
CAMINO ANCHO
17500 SD 92128 1150-D7
CAMINO ARENA
3500 CRLB 92009 1148-A3
CAMINO ARMILLA
15800 SD 92127 1169-H5
CAMINO ARRIBA
15900 SDCo 92065 1173-E3
CAMINO ARROYO
3100 CRLB 92009 1127-J7
CAMINO ARTEMISA
2600 SDCo 91901 1253-J2
CAMINO ATAJO
900 CHV 91910 1310-J7
900 CHV 91910 1311-A7
CAMINO AVENA
2500 SDCo 91901 1253-J2
CAMINO BAILEN
100 ESCN 92029 1150-A2
300 ESCN 92029 1149-J2
CAMINO BAJA CERRO
1200 SD 92028 1047-D7
1200 SD 92028 1067-C1
CAMINO BAJADA
3600 SDCo 92003 1150-C3
CAMINO BARRANCA DEL COBRE
- SD 92154 1351-H2
CAMINO BERDECIO
6800 SD 92111 1268-J2
CAMINO BISCAY
1100 CHV 91910 1310-J6
1100 CHV 91910 1311-A6
CAMINO BRISA DEL MAR
17300 SDCo 92127 1169-D1
CAMINO CABRILLO
- CRLB 92009 1147-J2
CAMINO CALABAZO
1000 CHV 91910 1311-B7
CAMINO CALAFIA
200 SDCo 92069 1088-H5
CAMINO CALMA
3900 SD 92122 1228-C4
CAMINO CANADA
13200 SDCo 92021 1252-D1
13500 SDCo 92021 1232-E7
CAMINO CANCIONES DEL CIELO
- VSTA 92084 1088-C3

CAMINO CANTERA
2000 SDCo 92091 1088-C1
CAMINO CAPISTRANO
6500 CRLB 92009 1127-J5
CAMINO CATALINA
700 SOLB 92075 1167-J6
CAMINO CATALONIA
1200 CHV 91910 1311-A6
CAMINO CHELSEA
- SDCo 91901 1254-E1
CAMINO CHICO
31300 SDCo 92086 409-K7
CAMINO CHRISTINA
- SDCo 91901 1234-E7
- SDCo 91901 1254-E1
CAMINO CIEGO CT
1000 VSTA 92084 1088-A4
CAMINO CIELO
800 SD 92028 1047-H1
CAMINO CIELO AZUL
20700 SDCo 92029 1128-F7
20700 SDCo 92029 1148-F1
CAMINO CODORNIZ
10800 SD 92127 1169-H5
CAMINO CONEJO
15800 SDCo 92086 1071-A7
CAMINO COPETE
1100 SD 92127 1268-H2
CAMINO CORALINO
2900 SD 92117 1248-G2
CAMINO CORONADO
3200 CRLB 92009 1147-J3
CAMINO CORTE
3400 CRLB 92009 1147-J4
CAMINO CORTO
100 VSTA 92084 1087-G6
1500 OCN 92028 1047-E7
1500 OCN 92028 1067-E1
6200 SD 92120 1250-D5
CAMINO CORTO DR
- SMCS 92069 1128-D2
CAMINO COSTANERO
6300 SD 92111 1268-H3
CAMINO CREST DR
3000 SD 92056 1106-G2
CAMINO CRISALIDA
15700 SD 92127 1169-G5
CAMINO CULEBRA
1900 VSTA 92084 1088-C3
1900 VSTA 92084 1088-C3
CAMINO DAVID
4800 SDCo 91902 1290-H7
4900 SDCo 91902 1310-H1
CAMINO DE AGUAS
3100 CRLB 92009 1127-J7
CAMINO DE AMIGOS
1800 SD 92128 1128-A5
CAMINO DE AMOR
500 SD 92065 1152-H7
CAMINO DE ARRIBA
7400 SDCo 92067 1148-J5
CAMINO DE CLARA
600 SOLB 92075 1167-H6
CAMINO DE ESTRELLAS
18000 SDCo 92067 1149-A7
CAMINO DEGRAZIA
6900 SD 92111 1268-J2
6900 SD 92111 1269-A2
CAMINO DE LA BRECCIA
12700 SD 92128 1150-D7
CAMINO DE LA CIMA
300 SMCS 92078 1129-B2
CAMINO DE LA COSTA
700 SD 92037 1247-F3
CAMINO DE LA DORA
7700 SDCo 92067 1148-J7
CAMINO DEL AGUILA
19300 SDCo 92025 1150-J4
20200 SDCo 92025 1151-A5
20300 SDCo 92065 1151-A5
CAMINO DE LA LUNA
11600 SDCo 92040 1211-H7
CAMINO DE LA MITRA
7700 SDCo 92067 1148-H7
CAMINO DE LA PLAZA
2200 SD 92173 1350-E5
CAMINO DEL ARCO
3100 CRLB 92009 1127-H7
CAMINO DE LA REINA
100 SD 92108 1268-J4
100 SD 92108 1269-C2
CAMINO DE LA ROSA
- SD 92127 1168-J7
CAMINO DEL ARROYO
5000 SD 92108 1269-A3
5000 SD 92028 1028-A6
CAMINO DEL ARROYO DR
1400 SDCo 92069 1128-B3
1500 SMCS 92069 1128-B3
CAMINO DE LAS CUNAS
1900 SDCo 92029 1272-C2
CAMINO DE LAS FLORES
100 ENCT 92024 1147-G7
CAMINO DE LA SIESTA
5000 SD 92108 1269-A3
CAMINO DE LAS LOMAS
3500 SDCo 92084 1088-F6
30400 SDCo 92026 1069-A4
30500 SDCo 92026 1068-J4
CAMINO DE LAS ONDAS
900 CRLB 92009 1126-J5
1000 CRLB 92009 1127-B5
CAMINO DE LAS PALMAS
2200 LMGR 91945 1270-J7
2200 LMGR 91945 1290-J1
CAMINO DE LAS PIEDRAS
2900 SDCo 92019 1272-G1
CAMINO DE LAS SONRISAS
1800 SD 92173 1350-F2
CAMINO DE LAS VILLAS
1100 SOLB 92075 1167-D6
CAMINO DEL CERRO GRANDE
100 CHV 91910 1310-J3
CAMINO DEL CIELO
5500 SDCo 92003 1068-B1
5600 SDCo 92003 1048-C7
CAMINO DEL COLLADO
2100 SD 92037 1227-H4
CAMINO DEL ESTE
5000 SD 92108 1269-C2

CAMINO DELICIADA
16000 SDCo 92091 1168-B7
CAMINO DEL INDIO
16700 SDCo 92065 1171-G2
CAMINO DEL LAGO
1200 SDCo 92069 1128-C3
CAMINO DEL MAR Rt#-S21
400 DLMR 92014 1187-F4
S CAMINO DEL MAR Rt#-S21
- DLMR 92014 1187-G7
CAMINO DEL MONTE
- SDCo 91905 (1319-H2)
See Page 1298)
CAMINO DEL NORTE
14200 PWY 92064 1170-B7
14200 PWY 92064 1190-C1
14200 SD 92128 1170-B7
14600 SD 92128 1169-H5
15100 SD 92127 1169-D3
16200 SDCo 92127 1169-F3
CAMINO DEL ORO
8100 SD 92127 1227-H5
CAMINO DE LOS AVES
2500 SDCo 91901 1253-J2
CAMINO DE LOS CABALLOS
30100 SDCo 92003 1068-D3
CAMINO DE LOS COCHES
3400 CRLB 92009 1147-J3
3400 CRLB 92009 1148-A2
CAMINO DEL PAJARO
6200 SD 92009 1168-F6
CAMINO DEL PARQUE
6400 CRLB 92009 1126-J4
CAMINO DEL POSTIGO
100 ESCN 92025 1150-A2
400 ESCN 92029 1149-J2
CAMINO DEL PRADO
- CRLB 92009 1126-J5
CAMINO DEL PROGRESSO
200 SD 92173 1350-F3
CAMINO DEL RANCHO
2300 ENCT 92024 1148-A5
CAMINO DEL REPOSO
2100 SD 92037 1227-H5
CAMINO DEL REY
- CHV 91910 1311-A7
5400 SDCo 92003 1068-A1
5900 SDCo 92003 1067-J1
8500 SDCo 92003 1068-G4
CAMINO DEL RINCON
6000 SD 92120 1250-D5
CAMINO DEL RIO N
1800 SD 92108 1269-F1
3800 SD 92108 1269-H1
CAMINO DEL RIO S
300 SMCS 92069 1109-C7
400 SD 92108 1269-F1
CAMINO DEL RIO W Rt#-209
3600 SD 92108 1268-E5
CAMINO DEL ROCA
17800 SDCo 92065 1171-H2
CAMINO DEL SABIO
17100 SDCo 92065 1171-G2
CAMINO DEL SEQUAN
1200 SDCo 91901 1253-J2
1300 SDCo 91901 1254-A2
CAMINO DEL SOL
100 SD 92037 1227-H5
500 SMCS 92069 1108-F5
100 CHV 91910 1310-J7
100 CHV 91910 1311-A6
CAMINO DEL SOL CIR
1100 SD 92008 1106-G6
CAMINO DEL SUELO
13700 SD 92129 1189-C3
CAMINO DEL TIERRA
11600 SDCo 92040 1211-H7
CAMINO DEL VALLE
12800 PWY 92064 1170-D3
CAMINO DEL VECINO
- SDCo 91901 1234-E1
2500 SDCo 91901 1254-E1
CAMINO DEL VENADO
10400 SDCo 92127 1049-E4
CAMINO DEL VERDE
9200 SNTE 92071 1231-A6
CAMINO DE MONTECILLO
17100 SDCo 92067 1168-H6
CAMINO DE NOG
1500 SDCo 92028 1027-J6
1500 SDCo 92028 1028-A6
CAMINO DE ORCHIDIA
500 ENCT 92024 1147-E7
CAMINO DE ORO
15900 SDCo 92082 1071-B5
CAMINO DE PAIS
1900 SDCo 92029 1272-C2
CAMINO DE PALMAS
1300 SDCo 92028 1027-J7
CAMINO DE PILAR
3600 ESCN 92025 1150-C3
CAMINO DE TIERRA
- SD 91916 1216-D7
CAMINO DE VELA
1400 SDCo 92084 1088-C3
CAMINO DONAIRE
- SD 92154 1350-D1
CAMINO EL DORADO
- ENCT 92024 1147-E7
CAMINO ELENA
10100 SDCo 92026 1089-D5
CAMINO ELEVADO
200 CHV 91902 1310-J4
200 CHV 91902 1310-J4
400 CHV 91902 1311-A4
CAMINO EMPARRADO
12500 SD 92130 1150-C7
CAMINO ENCANTO
- CRLB 92009 1127-B5
CAMINO ENTRADA
100 CHV 91910 1330-E1
100 CHV 91910 1310-E7
CAMINO ESMERADO
3800 SDCo 92091 1168-C7
CAMINO ESPERANZA
1800 SD 92173 1350-F3
CAMINO ESPUELAS
100 CHV 91910 1310-J5
CAMINO ESTRELLADO
6700 SDCo 92120 1250-C5
CAMINO GATO
7900 SD 92009 1147-H3

CAMINO GLORITA
7700 SDCo 92122 1228-C4
CAMINO HILLS DR
2300 CRLB 92008 1107-C7
2300 SDCo 92008 1127-C1
CAMINO HUERTA
7800 SD 92122 1228-C4
CAMINO ISLAY
4100 SD 92122 1228-C4
CAMINO JASMINE
5300 SDCo 92003 1067-G1
CAMINO JONATA
7800 SD 92122 1228-D4
CAMINO KIOSCO
7900 SD 92122 1228-D4
CAMINO LAGARTO
2500 SDCo 91901 1253-J2
CAMINO LAGO DE CRISTAL
16800 SDCo 92067 1168-G6
CAMINO LAGO VISTA
8900 SDCo 91977 1291-B5
CAMINO LA PAZ
- SD 92124 1310-J7
CAMINO LA PUENTE
6600 CRLB 92009 1128-A5
CAMINO LARGO
100 SDCo 92067 1168-G2
100 VSTA 92084 1087-G2
3400 CRLB 92009 1147-J4
6000 SD 92120 1250-D5
CAMINO LIMERO
6500 CRLB 92009 1127-J5
CAMINO LINDA DR
1300 SDCo 92069 1128-B3
CAMINO LINDO
- CRLB 92009 1147-J3
- CRLB 92009 1148-A3
3800 SD 92122 1228-C4
CAMINO LITA
4200 SD 92122 1228-C4
CAMINO LOMA VERDE
1900 SDCo 92084 1088-C4
2000 SDCo 92084 1088-C4
CAMINO LORADO
1600 SDCo 92084 1088-B3
CAMINO LUJAN
6700 SD 92111 1268-J2
CAMINO MAGNIFICO
800 SMCS 92069 1108-F4
CAMINO MANGANA
1400 SD 92111 1268-J2
CAMINO MAQUILADORA
100 SDCo 92154 1350-A2
6800 SD 92154 1351-D2
CAMINO MARGLESA
3600 ESCN 92025 1150-C3
CAMINO MARZAGAN
3200 ESCN 92029 1150-A2
CAMINO MATEO
300 SMCS 92069 1109-C7
CAMINO MAYOR
3700 SDCo 92064 1088-H3
CAMINO MICHELLE
3400 CRLB 92009 1127-J5
3400 CRLB 92009 1128-A5
CAMINO MIEL
1000 CHV 91910 1311-A7
CAMINO MILITA
4100 SD 92122 1228-C4
CAMINO MIRA DEL MAR
12600 SD 92130 1188-A7
CAMINO MIRANDA
11100 SD 92126 1208-J7
CAMINO MONTE SOMBRA
2400 SDCo 92019 1252-E4
CAMINO MORO
- SDCo 92086 409-K7
CAMINO MURILLO
17700 SD 92128 1150-C7
CAMINO NARCISO
13700 SD 92128 1189-C3
CAMINO NOGUERA
7700 SDCo 92122 1228-C4
CAMINO PACHECO
1400 SD 92111 1268-J2
CAMINO PALOMAR ALTO
6500 SDCo 92037 1247-F2
CAMINO PALOMAR BAJO
700 SDCo 92037 1247-F2
CAMINO PARQUE
300 OCN 92057 1086-H3
CAMINO PATRICIA
100 VSTA 92084 1087-G6
CAMINO PAZ
4000 SDCo 91977 1271-B4
4200 SDCo 91941 1271-B4
CAMINO PAZ LN
9600 SDCo 91977 1271-B4
9200 SDCo 91941 1271-B4
CAMINO PLAYA ACAPULCO
5000 SD 92124 1229-J7
CAMINO PLAYA AZUL
5200 SD 92124 1229-J7
CAMINO PLAYA BAJA
5200 SD 92124 1229-J7
CAMINO PLAYA CANCUN
11300 SD 92124 1230-A7
CAMINO PLAYA CARMEL
10900 SD 92124 1230-A7
CAMINO PLAYA CATALINA
11500 SD 92124 1230-A7
CAMINO PLAYA DE ORO
5000 SD 92124 1229-J7
CAMINO PLAYA MALAGA
5000 SD 92124 1229-J7
CAMINO PLAYA NORTE
5300 SD 92124 1229-J7
5300 SD 92124 1230-A7
CAMINO PLAYA PORTOFINO
- SD 92124 1229-H7
CAMINO PORTOFINO
3000 SDCo 92028 1048-A2
CAMINO PRIVADO
4300 SDCo 92067 1167-J3
CAMINO RAINBOW
1900 SDCo 92028 998-J6
CAMINO RAMILLETTE
12800 SDCo 92130 1150-D7
CAMINO RAPOSA
7800 SD 92122 1228-C4
CAMINO REDONDO
300 SMCS 92069 1109-C7
CAMINO REGALADO
1100 SDCo 92154 1350-D1
CAMINO REVUELTOS
6900 SD 92111 1268-J2

CAMINO RICO
6000 SD 92120 1250-C6
CAMINO RIO
12100 SDCo 92040 1212-A7
CAMINO ROBERTO
4800 SDCo 91902 1310-H1
4800 SDCo 91902 1290-H7
CAMINO ROBLEDO
- CRLB 92009 1147-G2
CAMINO ROCIAR
1600 SDCo 92069 1128-C4
CAMINO RUIZ
- SD 92127 1168-J7
- SD 92127 1169-A7
- SD 92127 1188-J1
- SD 92127 1189-A7
9400 SD 92126 1209-B1
12100 SD 92129 1189-A7
CAMINO SAN BERNARDO
- SD 92127 1169-F4
16900 SDCo 92127 1169-G3
CAMINO SANDOVAL
4200 SD 92130 1188-B6
CAMINO SAN IGNACIO
32200 SDCo 92086 409-K8
CAMINO SANTA BARBARA
700 SOLB 92075 1167-J6
CAMINO SANTA FE
5200 SD 92067 1188-D2
8100 SD 92121 1228-H1
8800 SD 92121 1208-H4
9400 SDCo 92127 1169-C1
CAMINO SAUCITO
6600 SDCo 92067 1168-G6
CAMINO SCARPITTA
3500 OCN 92056 1106-J1
3500 OCN 92056 1107-A1
CAMINO SELVA
6100 SDCo 92067 1168-E3
CAMINO SERBAL
2800 CRLB 92009 1147-H2
CAMINO SERENO
7700 SDCo 92069 1148-H2
CAMINO SIERRA DEL SUR
16900 SDCo 92067 1168-G6
CAMINO SIN PUENTE
- SDCo 92067 1148-J5
CAMINO SUSANA
13700 SDCo 92021 1232-E6
CAMINO TABLERO
100 SDCo 92154 1350-A2
CAMINO TERESA
1300 SOLB 92075 1167-J6
CAMINO TERNURA
1100 SDCo 92154 1350-D1
CAMINO TICINO
4100 SD 92122 1228-C4
CAMINO TRANQUILO
7800 SD 92122 1228-C4
CAMINO TRES AVES
35300 SDCo 92066 (1299-A1)
See Page 1298)
CAMINO VALENCIA
3400 CRLB 92009 1127-J5
3400 CRLB 92009 1128-A5
CAMINO VALLAREAL
3200 SDCo 92154 1350-A2
CAMINO VERDE
2300 SDCo 92028 1028-B5
CAMINO VIDA ROBLE
1900 CRLB 92008 1127-C3
2000 CRLB 92009 1127-E4
CAMINO VINCENTE
- SD 92037 1247-F2
CAMINO VISTA
18700 SDCo 92065 1153-E3
CAMINO VISTA REAL
100 CHV 91910 1330-E1
100 CHV 91910 1310-F7
CAMINO VUELO
12500 SD 92128 1150-C7
CAMINO YNEZ
600 SD 92075 1167-H6
CAMINO ZALCE
1400 SD 92111 1268-J2
CAMINO ZARA
1300 SDCo 92028 1028-D4
CAMIONES WY
5500 SD 92173 1350-H5
CAMLAU DR
200 CHV 91911 1330-E1
CAMP CT
4000 SDCo 91977 1291-A2
CAMPANIA AV
9600 SDCo 92127 1169-E2
CAMPANILE DR
4700 SD 92115 1270-C3
CAMPANILE WY
5600 SD 92115 1270-B3
CAMPBELL LN
- SDCo 92019 1272-F2
CAMPBELL RD
400 VSTA 92083 1107-J1
2000 ImCo 92243 430-L6
CAMPBELL WY
1100 SDCo 92065 1172-H1
CAMPBELL RANCH RD
1300 SDCo 91901 1235-H6
CAMP DE LUZ RD
- SD 92028 409-A6
- SD 92055 409-A6
CAMPESINO PL
1800 SDCo 92026 1106-F1
CAMPHOR LN
6800 SD 92139 1310-F1
CAMPHOR PL
- CRLB 92009 1127-B5
CAMPILLO CT
12300 SD 92128 1170-B1
CAMPILLO DR
17200 SD 92128 1170-B1
CAMPINA DR
9000 LMSA 91942 1251-A7
CAMPINA PL
6400 SD 92037 1247-H1
CAMP KETTLE DR
- SDCo 92028 1058-G7
(See Page 1058)
CAMP LOCKETT RD
- SDCo 91906 (1318-B7)
(See Page 1298)
CAMPO PL
2100 ESCN 92027 1110-B5
CAMPO RD
8700 SDCo 91941 1271-A4

CAMPO RD
8700 SDCo 91977 1271-C5
10400 SDCo 91978 1271-E5
CAMPO RD Rt#-94
11100 SDCo 91978 1272-A7
11100 SDCo 91978 1271-G5
11100 SDCo 91941 1271-G5
11100 SDCo 92019 1271-J6
12100 SDCo 91978 1292-C1
12700 SDCo 91935 1292-D7
13100 SDCo 91935 1292-F1
14100 SDCo 91935 1293-B6
14700 SDCo 91935 (1313-F2)
See Page 1293)
16000 SDCo 91917 (1313-F2)
See Page 1293)
21100 SDCo 91917 (1314-B8)
(See Page 1293)
22000 SDCo 91917 429-J10
22600 SDCo 91980 429-K10
CAMPO ST
- SDCo 91934 (1321-H4)
(See Page 1300)
CAMPO TKTR
3200 OCN 92056 1106-J1
CAMPOBELLO ST
4500 SD 92130 1188-C6
CAMPO LINDO RD
12900 SDCo 91935 1273-H4
CAMPUS AV
4100 SD 92103 1269-C5
4300 SD 92116 1269-C5
CAMPUS DR
3500 OCN 92056 1106-J1
E CAMPUS DR
6000 SD 92120 1270-C1
6000 SD 92182 1270-C1
CAMPUS POINT CT
4100 SD 92121 1208-B7
CAMPUS POINT DR
9400 SD 92037 1228-B1
9700 SD 92121 1208-B7
9700 SD 92121 1228-C1
CAMPUS VIEW DR
- SMCS 92078 1128-H2
CAMROSE AV
4400 SD 92122 1228-F5
CAMULOS ST
2500 SD 92107 1268-B6
3200 SD 92110 1268-C5
CANA LN
1300 SDCo 92154 1330-A7
CANADIAN HONKER RD
29800 SDCo 91906 (1297-F6)
See Page 1296)
CANAL RD
16600 SDCo 92082 1091-C2
CANAL ST
1700 SD 92154 1329-J6
1700 SD 92154 1330-A6
CANALEJA WY
9700 SD 92129 1209-F1
CANANEA ST
200 VSTA 92084 1087-H4
CANARIO ST
4000 CRLB 92008 1106-F7
CANARIOS CT
800 CHV 91910 1310-J6
CANARY CT
1100 SMCS 92069 1128-E3
CANARY WY
7900 SD 92037 1249-B6
CANARYWOOD CT
10800 SD 92131 1210-A2
CANBERRA CT
- SDCo 92127 1169-F2
CANCHA DE GOLF
3700 SDCo 92091 1168-C7
CANCUN CT
400 SDCo 92028 1027-E5
CANDELA PL
12900 SD 92130 1187-J5
CANDIA CT
4200 OCN 92056 1087-C6
4200 VSTA 92083 1087-C6
CANDICE CT
1900 SDCo 92028 1048-A4
CANDICE PL
100 VSTA 92083 1087-G3
CANDIDA ST
3200 SD 92126 1209-E6
CANDIL PL
2900 CRLB 92009 1127-H7
CANDLE LN
1800 ELCJ 92019 1252-C3
1800 ELCJ 92019 1252-C3
CANDLE WY
13400 SD 92082 1090-D1
CANDLEBERRY CT
11200 SD 92128 1189-J2
CANDLELIGHT DR
5300 SD 92109 1247-H4
5300 SD 92037 1247-H3
CANDLELIGHT GN
1300 ESCN 92029 1129-G6
CANDLELIGHT PL
800 SD 92037 1247-G4
800 SD 92109 1247-G4
CANDLELIGHT ST
5200 OCN 92056 1107-F4
CANDLELITE DR
900 SMCS 92069 1109-A5
CANDLEWOOD LN
1100 SDCo 92026 1251-J2
1100 SDCo 92026 1271-J1
CANDLEWOOD PL
2700 OCN 92056 1087-E5
CANDY LN
100 ENCT 92024 1167-J1
9600 SDCo 91941 1271-C1
CANDY ROSE CT
12200 SD 92131 1190-B7
12200 SD 92131 1210-B1
CANDY ROSE WY
11700 PWY 92131 1210-B1
11700 SD 92131 1210-B1
11700 SD 92131 1190-B7
CANE RD
14200 SDCo 92082 1070-F4
CANEBRAKE RD
300 SDCo 92083 430-D3
2200 SDCo 91905 430-L5
CANEEL BAY CT
4600 OCN 92057 1066-H6

CANERIDGE PL
11900 SD 92128 1190-B7
CANERIDGE RD
11900 SD 92128 1190-A7
CANFIELD PL
18200 SD 92128 1150-C6
CANFIELD RD Rt#-S6
3400 SDCo 92060 409-G6
CANFORERO TER
5300 SD 92124 1249-F1
CANIS LN
- CRLB 92008 1127-A1
CANNA DR
- NATC 91950 1289-H7
3800 SD 92113 1289-H7
CANNAS CT
1700 CRLB 92009 1127-E6
CANNELI DR
13700 PWY 92064 1190-H4
CANNING AV
3800 SD 92111 1248-G4
CANNING CT
5200 SD 92111 1248-G4
CANNING PL
5200 SD 92111 1248-G4
CANNINGTON DR
4200 SD 92117 1248-J2
CANNON RD
- CRLB 92008 1127-A1
100 CRLB 92008 1126-G2
1700 ImCo 92243 6500-D5
1700 ImCo 92243 6560-E1
3500 OCN 92056 1107-E4
4000 SDCo 92083 1107-E4
4600 CRLB 92008 1107-A7
CANNON GATE
- SD 92028 1027-G6
CANON ST
2600 SD 92106 1288-B2
CANON ST Rt#-209
900 SD 92106 1287-J3
3000 SD 92106 1288-A1
CANONITA DR
1900 SDCo 92028 1028-E5
CANOPUS DR
- SD 92126 1209-E6
CANOSA AV
5000 SD 92117 1248-G2
CANRIGHT WY
9900 SD 92126 1209-A6
CANTA LOMAS
1900 SDCo 92019 1252-C7
CANTALOUPE ST
- ImCo 92249 6560-B7
CANTAMAR PL
1300 SDCo 92154 1330-A7
CANTAMAR RD
1300 SDCo 92154 1330-A7
CANTARA LN
1700 SDCo 92083 1107-E2
CANTARA WY
24800 SDCo 92065 1173-G2
CANTARANAS
16900 SDCo 92067 1168-B3
CANTEBURY PL
- ESCN 92025 1129-H4
CANTEGRA GN
2800 ESCN 92025 1130-B7
2800 ESCN 92025 1150-B1
CANTER RD
1200 SDCo 92027 1130-C3
CANTERBURY CT
4700 OCN 92056 1087-D4
CANTERBURY DR
4300 LMSA 91941 1270-H4
4800 SD 92116 1269-G2
E CANTERBURY DR
4100 SD 92116 1269-H3
CANTERBURY ST
2800 CRLB 92008 1107-A4
CANTERO WY
3000 CRLB 92009 1147-H1
CANTIL ST
6700 CRLB 92009 1127-H5
CANTLE LN
3800 ENCT 92024 1148-C2
CANTON DR
7300 LMGR 91945 1290-G1
8000 SDCo 91977 1290-G1
CANVAS ST
4700 OCN 92057 1087-B1
CANVAS BACK DR
29900 SDCo 91906 (1297-G5)
See Page 1296)
W CANYON AV
3000 SD 92123 1249-F5
CANYON CT
1400 CHV 91902 1311-B4
CANYON DR
400 SOLB 92075 1167-F6
500 CHV 91902 1311-B4
500 CHV 91913 1311-B4
1200 SDCo 92036 1136-C6
1500 SDCo 92036 1156-D1
10100 SDCo 92040 1109-E2
N CANYON DR
100 OCN 92054 1086-B5
S CANYON DR
100 OCN 92054 1086-C6
CANYON LN
- ESCN 92025 1130-A6
1700 PWY 92064 1171-A6
CANYON PASS
1700 PWY 92064 1171-A6
CANYON PL
600 SOLB 92075 1167-F6
1800 CRLB 92008 1106-F4
CANYON RD
3100 SD 92102 1289-G4
- SDCo 92036 430-D4
100 SDCo 92036 1156-F7
1500 SDCo 92036 1291-B2
CANYON ST
3100 CRLB 92008 1106-G4
W CANYON TER
3000 SD 92123 1249-F5
CANYON BACK LN
13300 PWY 92064 1190-E1
CANYON BLUFF CT
6200 SD 92121 1208-G3
CANYON BREEZE DR
7400 SDCo 92021 1208-J3
7400 SDCo 92021 1209-A3
CANYON BREEZE RD
7200 SDCo 92021 1209-A3
CANYON COUNTRY LN
9700 SDCo 92026 1089-D1

CANYON COUNTRY LN — SAN DIEGO CO. STREET INDEX — CASTILLA WY 6574

STREET Block City ZIP Pg-Grid

CANYON COUNTRY LN
10100 SDCo 92026 1069-E7
CANYON CREEK AV
2000 CHV 91913 1311-E5
CANYON CREEK PL
1000 ESCN 92025 1130-D6
CANYON CREEK RD
1000 ESCN 92025 1130-D7
CANYON CREEK WY
2400 ESCN 92025 1130-D6
CANYON CREST DR
2500 ESCN 92027 1130-F2
2500 SDCo 92027 1130-F2
5600 SD 92182 1270-B1
CANYON DE ORO
3900 ENCT 92024 1148-E3
3900 SDCo 92024 1148-E3
4200 SDCo 92029 1148-E3
CANYON ESTATES RD
30300 SDCo 92084 1068-A4
CANYON HEIGHTS RD
1500 SDCo 92028 998-H5
CANYON HILL CT
7200 SD 92126 1208-J3
CANYON HILL LN
10800 SD 92126 1208-J3
CANYON HILL PL
7100 SD 92126 1208-J3
CANYON HILL WY
7100 SD 92126 1208-J3
CANYON LAKE DR
10500 SD 92131 1209-G4
CANYON LODGE PL
500 OCN 92054 1086-D7
CANYON MESA LN
10900 SD 92126 1209-A3
CANYON OAK PL
2700 ESCN 92029 1129-D4
CANYON PARK DR
11200 SNTE 92071 1231-H6
CANYON PARK TER
9100 SNTE 92071 1231-G5
CANYON PEAK LN
7300 SD 92126 1208-J3
CANYON POINT CT
11000 SD 92126 1209-A3
CANYON POINT LN
7600 SD 92126 1209-A3
CANYON RIDGE DR
300 CHV 91902 1311-B3
CANYON RIDGE LN
1200 SDCo 92025 1130-D6
CANYONRIDGE PL
10100 SDCo 91977 1271-E7
CANYON RIM DR
300 SDCo 92021 1253-A2
CANYON RIM RW
6600 SD 92111 1268-H3
CANYONSIDE CT
10000 SDCo 91977 1271-D6
CANYONSIDE WY
300 OCN 92054 1086-B6
CANYON SLOPE PL
7900 SD 92120 1250-D3
CANYONTOP ST
10000 SDCo 91977 1271-D6
CANYONVIEW CT
10000 SDCo 91977 1271-E6
CANYON VIEW DR
100 SDCo 92021 1252-H2
CANYON VIEW GN
2300 ESCN 92026 1109-B3
CANYON VIEW LN
7300 LMGR 91945 1270-F7
CANYON VIEW WY
- PWY 92064 1171-A6
CANYON VISTA CT
6400 SD 92111 1248-H6
CANYON VISTA DR
2300 SDCo 92028 1028-A1
CANYONWOOD LN
10000 SDCo 91977 1271-E7
CAPALINA RD
3400 SMCS 92069 1108-D6
CAPAZO CT
2900 CRLB 92009 1127-H4
CAPCANO RD
8900 SD 92126 1189-D7
8900 SD 92126 1209-D1
CAP COD CT
- SDCo 91977 1271-C6
CAPE AIRE LN
1100 CRLB 92008 1106-G7
CAPE BRETON
500 SDCo 92084 1088-D7
CAPE COD CIR
2900 CRLB 92008 1107-B5
CAPE COD BAY CT
2000 SD 92105 1290-C1
CAPEHART ST
5000 SD 92117 1228-E7
CAPE HORN AV
2300 SDCo 92036 1136-B7
CAPELLA CT
3700 SDCo 91941 1271-A5
CAPELLA DR
9500 SD 92126 1209-E7
CAPE MAY AV
4300 SD 92107 1268-A6
4700 SD 92107 1267-J5
CAPE MAY PL
1700 CRLB 92008 1106-H6
2000 SD 92107 1267-J5
CAPE SEBASTIAN PL
2900 ENCT 92007 1167-F5
CAPEWOOD LN
13900 SD 92128 1189-J2
CAPILLA CT
17000 SD 92127 1169-J2
CAPILLA PL
17000 SD 92127 1169-H2
CAPILLA RD
11100 SD 92127 1169-H2
CAPISTRANO
- CRLB 92009 1126-H4
CAPISTRANO AV
1000 SDCo 91977 1291-C2
CAPISTRANO DR
500 OCN 92054 1085-J6
500 OCN 92054 1086-A5
CAPISTRANO GN
1700 ESCN 92026 1109-D5
CAPISTRANO LN
1200 VSTA 92083 1107-E1
CAPISTRANO PL
700 SD 92109 1267-H4
CAPISTRANO ST
1800 SD 92106 1288-B1
1900 SD 92106 1268-B7
CAPISTRANO WY
- SMCS 92078 1129-C1
CAPITAN AV
2400 SD 92104 1269-E7
2400 SD 92104 1289-E1
CAPITOL ST
3800 LMSA 91941 1270-F5
CAPPS ST
2800 SD 92104 1269-D6
CAPRA WY
1000 SDCo 92028 1028-C1
CAPRI CT
2000 SDCo 92019 1272-C4
CAPRI DR
1000 VSTA 92084 1087-J5
6100 SD 92120 1250-C7
CAPRI RD
800 ENCT 92024 1147-C3
CAPRICE PL
11300 SDCo 92026 1089-H7
CAPRICORN WY
8400 SD 92126 1209-B2
CAPRIOLE CT
5300 SDCo 91902 1311-A2
CAPS WY
2500 SDCo 92028 998-B6
CAPSTAN DR
- CRLB 92009 1127-A7
CAPSTONE DR
13100 SD 92130 1188-B4
CAPTAINS CT
8600 SDCo 92026 1068-J4
CAR ST
1100 SD 92114 1290-H2
CARA CT
8800 SDCo 91977 1291-A5
CARA LN
16000 SDCo 92082 1071-B6
CARA ST
400 ESCN 92025 1130-A6
CARA WY
11700 SD 92128 1189-F7
11700 SD 92131 1189-F7
CARACAS PL
31300 SDCo 92003 1067-J2
CARACOL CT
2000 CRLB 92009 1127-F6
CARAMAY PL
1500 SD 92154 1350-E2
CARANCHO RD
27300 RivC 92590 997-J1
CARANCHO ST
3800 LMSA 91941 1270-F5
CARAS CT
15900 SDCo 92065 1174-B4
CARAVELLE PL
10800 SD 92124 1249-J2
CARAWAY CT
12700 SDCo 92040 1232-B4
CARAWAY ST
2000 ESCN 92026 1109-F5
9600 SDCo 92040 1232-B4
CARBAJAL CT
600 CHV 91911 1330-H3
CARBET PL
10800 SD 92124 1249-H2
CARBINE WY
- SD 92154 1350-G2
CARBO CT
3800 LMSA 91941 1270-H5
CAR COUNTRY DR
5200 CRLB 92008 1126-H2
CARDAMOM CT
800 CHV 91910 1330-J1
CARDENO DR
5200 SD 92109 1247-J4
5400 SD 92037 1247-J2
CARDIFF DR
1100 ENCT 92024 1167-F2
CARDIFF ST
300 SD 92114 1290-H3
CARDIFF BAY DR
4800 OCN 92057 1066-J6
CARDIGAN WY
1900 SD 92111 1269-A1
CARDIN ST
4600 SD 92111 1249-A2
CARDINAL CT
1000 SMCS 92069 1128-G4
7600 SD 92123 1249-A6
CARDINAL DR
2000 SD 92123 1269-A1
2100 SD 92123 1249-A7
CARDINAL LN
2400 SD 92123 1249-A7
CARDINAL PL
1200 CHV 91911 1330-G2
7600 SD 92123 1249-A7
CARDINAL RD
2600 SD 92123 1249-A7
CARDINAL WY
- SDCo 92055 1023-E3
200 OCN 92057 1086-H5
CARDONA AV
700 CHV 91910 1310-J5
CARDOZA DR
9900 SNTE 92071 1231-D3
CAREFREE DR
700 SD 92114 1290-E5
10100 SNTE 92071 1231-D4
CAREN RD
1100 VSTA 92083 1087-E6
CARETTA WY
400 ENCT 92007 1167-D2
CAREY RD
- ImCo 92227 431-C3
N CAREY RD
300 OCN 92054 1086-C6
S CAREY RD
100 OCN 92054 1086-C6
CAREYBROOK LN
7500 SD 92114 1290-G5
CARGILL AV
7700 SD 92122 1228-C4
CARIB CT
4400 SD 92117 1248-F1
CARIB DR
6900 SDCo 92029 1128-F7
6900 SDCo 92029 1148-F1
CARIBE CAY BLVD N
- CORD 92118 1329-E1
CARIE WY
2300 SDCo 91901 1253-H2
CARILLO CIR
600 OCN 92057 1066-J5
CARILLO RD
3300 SDCo 92004 (1078-J6 See Page 1058)
CARILLO RD
3300 SDCo 92004 (1079-A7 See Page 1058)
CARILLO WY
- CRLB 92009 1127-J3
CARILLON CT
10600 SD 92131 1209-J2
10600 SD 92131 1210-A2
CARINGA WY
2300 CRLB 92009 1127-G7
CARIOCA CT
10200 SD 92124 1249-G1
CARISSA AV
1400 CHV 91911 1330-H3
CARISSA CT
1400 CHV 91911 1330-H3
CARISSA DR
200 OCN 92057 1087-A1
CARISSA LN
10000 SDCo 91977 1291-D2
CARISSA WY
- CRLB 92009 1127-D4
CARITA CT
9700 SNTE 92071 1231-A4
CARITA RD
9200 SNTE 92071 1231-A4
CARIUTO CT
10700 SD 92124 1249-H2
CARL DR
18000 SDCo 91935 1274-D4
CARLA AV
500 CHV 91910 1310-D6
CARLA WY
400 SD 92037 1247-G4
CARLANN DR
100 SMCS 92069 1108-H6
CARLANN LN
600 ESCN 92027 1110-C6
CARLATA LN
27300 SDCo 92082 1091-G4
CARLETON SQ
1400 SD 92106 1288-A1
CARLETON ST
2700 SD 92106 1288-B1
CARLETTE ST
8000 LMSA 91942 1250-H7
CARLEY CIR
8900 SD 92126 1209-D1
CARLIN HTS
2500 SDCo 92025 1130-C7
CARLIN PL
4400 LMSA 91941 1271-A3
CARLIN ST
100 SDCo 92065 1152-D7
CARLINA ST
7400 CRLB 92009 1147-J1
CARLING DR
4400 SD 92115 1270-C4
CARLING WY
6100 SD 92115 1270-C4
CARLISLE DR
7800 LMGR 91945 1290-H2
7800 SD 92114 1290-H2
CARLO ST
400 SMCS 92069 1108-C6
CARLOS ST
300 SD 92102 1289-H4
CARLOS CANYON CT
500 CHV 91910 1310-J4
CARLOS CANYON DR
1100 CHV 91910 1310-J4
1100 CHV 91910 1311-A4
CARLOTA ST
11000 SD 92129 1169-H7
CARLOTTA WY
200 OCN 92057 1086-H3
CARLOW CT
600 ELCJ 92020 1251-B4
CARLOW LN
- ELCJ 92020 1251-B4
CARLOW ST
2500 ELCJ 92020 1251-B4
CARLOW WY
700 ELCJ 92020 1251-B4
CARLSBAD BLVD Rt#-S21
200 CRLB 92009 1126-H6
2200 CRLB 92008 1106-D4
3900 CRLB 92008 1126-F1
7100 CRLB 92009 1146-J1
7300 CRLB 92024 1147-A2
7300 ENCT 92024 1147-A2
7400 CRLB 92024 1146-J1
CARLSBAD CT
1000 SD 92114 1290-H2
CARLSBAD ST
500 SDCo 91977 1290-J2
800 SD 92114 1290-J2
CARLSBAD VILLAGE DR
100 CRLB 92008 1106-J3
2700 CRLB 92008 1107-A4
CARLSON CT
300 VSTA 92083 1087-C7
300 VSTA 92083 1107-C1
14400 PWY 92064 1190-H1
CARLSON ST
14600 PWY 92064 1190-H1
CARLTON PL
9900 SNTE 92071 1231-A3
CARLTON WY
2800 SDCo 92028 1048-E1
CARLTON HILLS BLVD
8900 SNTE 92071 1231-A4
CARLTON OAKS DR
8200 SD 92071 1230-H6
8200 SNTE 92071 1230-H6
9300 SNTE 92071 1231-A6
CARLY CT
1400 SD 92114 1290-F5
CARMACK WY
9500 SNTE 92071 1231-B3
CARMAR WY
2800 SD 92139 1310-F2
CARMEL AV
1500 CHV 91913 1311-C7
CARMEL CIR
700 VSTA 92084 1087-J3
CARMEL DR
2600 CRLB 92008 1106-J5
S CARMEL RD
200 SMCS 92078 1129-A1
CARMEL ST
100 SMCS 92078 1128-J1
400 SMCS 92078 1108-J7
400 SMCS 92078 1109-A7
CARMEL BROOKS WY
3900 SD 92130 1188-A7
CARMEL CANYON RD
4400 SD 92130 1188-C6
CARMEL CAPE
12400 SD 92130 1188-A7
CARMEL CENTER RD
4200 SD 92130 1188-B6
CARMEL COUNTRY RD
- SD 92130 1208-D1
4000 SD 92130 1188-A5
CARMEL CREEK RD
11900 SD 92130 1208-B1
12700 SD 92130 1188-B5
CARMEL CREEPER PL
- ENCT 92024 1147-C5
CARMEL GROVE RD
3800 SD 92130 1188-A7
CARMELINA DR
1800 SD 92116 1269-C3
CARMELITA PL
200 SOLB 92075 1167-F7
CARMEL KNOLLS DR
5000 SD 92130 1188-D5
CARMEL MISSION RD
12600 SD 92130 1188-B6
CARMEL MOUNTAIN RD
3300 SD 92121 1208-A3
3500 SD 92130 1208-D2
8200 SD 92129 1189-J1
11200 SD 92128 1189-J1
11600 SD 92128 1190-A1
12000 SD 92128 1170-A7
CARMELO DR
1300 OCN 92054 1085-J6
1500 SDCo 92055 1085-J6
CARMELO ST
4400 SD 92107 1287-H2
CARMEL PARK DR
11900 SD 92130 1188-A7
CARMEL POINTE
12400 SD 92130 1188-A7
CARMEL RIDGE RD
14500 SD 92128 1190-B1
CARMEL SPRINGS WY
3900 SD 92130 1188-A7
CARMEL VALLEY RD
- SD 92130 1189-A3
100 DLMR 92014 1187-G7
100 SD 92014 1187-G7
1800 SD 92014 1207-G1
2100 SD 92121 1207-G1
3000 SD 92130 1207-G1
3800 SD 92130 1208-A1
4100 SD 92130 1188-H3
14400 SD 92127 1189-B2
14400 SD 92129 1189-B2
CARMEL VIEW RD
3600 SD 92130 1188-A7
4000 SD 92130 1187-J7
CARMEL VISTA RD
12200 SD 92130 1187-J7
12200 SD 92130 1188-A7
12200 SD 92130 1208-A1
CARMEN CT
900 SDCo 92069 1109-B5
CARMEN DR
4400 SDCo 91941 1271-F3
CARMEN ST
5500 SD 92105 1290-B1
CARMENA RD
23500 SDCo 92065 1173-D3
CARMENITA RD
7200 LMSA 91941 1270-F5
CARMICHAEL DR
9300 SDCo 91941 1271-B3
9300 LMSA 91941 1271-B3
CARMIR DR
8800 SNTE 92071 1251-A1
CARMONA CT
800 CHV 91910 1310-H5
CARNABY CT
4500 CRLB 92008 1106-J5
CARNATION AV
100 CORD 91932 1329-E7
100 IMPB 91932 1329-F7
3300 SDCo 92065 1172-C3
CARNATION DR
6600 CRLB 92009 1127-A6
CARNATION GN
3700 ESCN 92025 1150-C3
CARNATION LN
600 SDCo 92028 1027-G4
CARNATION ST
- SDCo 92055 1086-A4
CARNEGIE
1700 CRLB 92008 1127-A3
CARNEGIE CT
3100 SD 92122 1228-C6
CARNEGIE DR
3700 OCN 92056 1086-J7
3700 OCN 92056 1087-A7
CARNEGIE PL
3100 SD 92122 1228-C6
CARNEGIE ST
5600 SD 92122 1228-C6
CARNEGIE WY
3200 SD 92122 1228-C6
CARNELIAN LN
3400 OCN 92056 1107-D2
CARNELIAN ST
10500 SD 92126 1208-J4
CARNELL AV
3200 SD 92154 1350-D1
CARNELL CT
1300 SD 92154 1350-D1
CARNERO PL
10200 SDCo 92040 1231-J3
CARNEROS VALLEY ST
1300 CHV 91913 1331-B1
CARNES RD
- SDCo 92055 1085-J2
- SDCo 92055 1086-A3
CARNEY LN
13000 SDCo 92082 1050-C4
CARNEY RD
36300 SDCo 92082 1050-C5
CARNITAS ST
14300 PWY 92064 1190-H1
CARNOUSTIE RD
6900 SDCo 92154 1352-A2
CARNTON WY
17400 SD 92128 1170-A1
CARNY ST
- SD 92106 1288-A5
CAROB LN
1700 SDCo 92004 (1099-F2 See Page 1098)
CAROB WY
100 CORD 92118 1288-G7
200 OCN 92057 1086-H5
CAROB TREE LN
1800 SDCo 92021 1252-C2
CAROL CT
700 SMCS 92069 1109-B6
CAROL LN
3700 SDCo 92065 1172-B3
CAROL PL
800 CRLB 92008 1106-F6
1300 NATC 91950 1290-C7
CAROL ST
1800 SD 92154 1329-J6
1800 SD 92154 1330-A6
6000 SD 92115 1270-C3
CAROL WY
3700 SDCo 91977 1271-A5
CAROL ANN LN
47400 RivC 92592 999-G1
CAROL ANNE RD
40000 SDCo 92028 997-A1
40000 SDCo 92028 409-A4
CAROLDALE RW
6000 SD 92037 1248-A1
CAROLEE AV
13200 SD 92129 1189-D4
CAROLINA LN
900 SD 92102 1290-A3
CAROLINA PL
4900 SD 92102 1290-A3
CAROLINA RD
400 DLMR 92014 1187-F5
CAROLINA ST
700 IMPB 91932 1329-G7
CAROLINE DR
4700 SD 92115 1269-J3
CAROLINE LN
4900 SDCo 92028 1047-E6
CAROLINE WY
100 ESCN 92025 1129-G4
CAROLITA
- SDCo 92040 1232-B7
CAROLTON LN
1900 SDCo 92028 1028-A6
CAROL VIEW DR
2200 ENCT 92007 1167-E3
CAROLWOOD DR
500 SD 92139 1290-H5
CAROLYN CIR
3200 OCN 92054 1086-E5
CAROLYN DR
1800 CHV 91913 1311-D5
CAROLYN PL
2300 ENCT 92024 1147-J7
CAROLYN VISTA LN
5300 SDCo 91902 1311-A3
CAROUSEL LN
13100 SD 92014 1187-J7
CAROWAY CT
3500 SDCo 92019 1272-C6
CARPA
7200 CRLB 92009 1128-A7
CARPENTER LN
4000 SDCo 91941 1271-G4
CARPENTER RD
2300 OCN 92054 1086-C5
CARR DR
3200 OCN 92056 1107-B1
CARRANZA DR
17000 SD 92127 1169-H1
CARRARA PL
5100 SD 92122 1228-D3
CARRERA CT
2400 SDCo 91977 1291-B1
CARRETA CT
10300 SNTE 92071 1231-E3
CARRETA DR
10000 SNTE 92071 1231-E3
CARRIAGE CIR
2300 OCN 92056 1106-H1
CARRIAGE CT
- SD 92130 1188-D5
CARRIAGE DR
800 SMCS 92069 1109-A5
CARRIAGE LN
1700 SDCo 92028 1028-B5
CARRIAGE RD
12800 PWY 92064 1190-D3
CARRIAGEDALE RW
2500 SD 92037 1248-A1
CARRIAGE HEIGHTS CIR
13300 PWY 92064 1190-D4
CARRIAGE HEIGHTS WY
12700 PWY 92064 1190-D4
CARRIAGE HILLS CT
17000 PWY 92064 1170-D2
CARRIBEAN WY
8700 SNTE 92071 1230-H7
CARRIE CIR
500 SMCS 92069 1108-H6
CARRIE ELLEN CT
10100 SNTE 92071 1231-A3
CARRIER
- CRLB 92008 1127-B3
CARRIE RIDGE WY
7400 SD 92139 1290-G6
CARRILLO WY
2800 CRLB 92009 1127-F4
CARRINGTON DR
10500 SD 92126 1208-J4
CARRIO DR
1300 SDCo 92084 1068-A6
CARRIZO DR
7200 SD 92037 1227-G7
CARRIZO PL
1500 ESCN 92027 1110-A5
CARRIZO ST
- SDCo 91934 (1321-H5 See Page 1300)
CARRIZO CREEK RD
- SDCo 91934 430-F9
CARRIZO GORGE RD
- SDCo 91934 (1301-G7 See Page 1300)
- SDCo 91934 (1321-H2 See Page 1300)
1100 SDCo 91934 430-F9
CARROLL LN
2300 SDCo 92027 1130-E2
CARROLL RD
6000 SD 92121 1208-G7
6700 SD 92121 1228-H1
7400 SD 92121 1209-A7
7500 SD 92121 1229-A1
7500 SD 92126 1229-A1
CARROLL WY
9000 SD 92121 1209-A7
CARROLL CANYON RD
4900 SD 92121 1208-E7
9400 SD 92126 1209-E5
9800 SD 92131 1209-E5
CARROLL CENTRE RD
9600 SD 92126 1209-E5
CARROLL PARK CT
9200 SD 92121 1208-H7
CARROLL PARK DR
9300 SD 92121 1208-H7
CARROLLTON SQ
12100 SD 92128 1190-B3
CARROTWOOD GN
1100 ESCN 92026 1129-F1
CARROZA CT
11200 SD 92124 1249-J2
11200 SD 92124 1250-A2
CARRYLL PARR CT
1000 SDCo 92028 1027-G3
CARSON PL
9800 SDCo 92029 1149-E4
CARSON ST
- CORD 92135 1288-F4
3800 SD 92117 1248-E4
CARSTENZ
500 SMCS 92069 1128-C1
CARTA LN
9700 SDCo 92021 1233-C1
CARTAGENA DR
4100 SD 92115 1270-D4
CARTEGENA WY
2300 OCN 92056 1106-J1
CARTER PL
7800 LMSA 91941 1270-G3
CARTER RD
600 ImCo 92227 431-B2
CARTER ST
200 ELCJ 92020 1251-G7
CARTHAGE ST
6300 SD 92120 1250-B5
CARTHAY CIR
9200 SDCo 91977 1271-B4
CARTULINA RD
4200 SD 92124 1249-J2
CARTWRIGHT ST
6500 SD 92120 1249-J5
CARVALLO CT
3200 CRLB 92009 1147-J1
CARVALOS DR
400 SDCo 91910 1310-D6
CARVEACRE RD
3300 SDCo 91901 1275-A1
CARVER ST
100 CHV 91911 1330-E4
CARY CT
1400 ELCJ 92019 1252-A7
CARY WY
1300 SD 92109 1247-J4
CARYL DR
10500 SNTE 92071 1231-E7
CARYN CT
25700 SDCo 92065 1173-J4
25700 SDCo 92065 1174-A4
CASA AVD
12700 PWY 92064 1170-C6
CASA CT
12800 PWY 92064 1190-D5
CASA DR
- OCN 92057 1066-J7
CASA LN
7000 LMGR 91945 1270-F6
CASA PL
1600 NATC 91950 1310-B1
CASA ALTA
2200 SDCo 91977 1271-D7
CASABA LN
3700 SDCo 92054 1086-G3
CASABLANCA CT
1900 VSTA 92083 1107-H4
CASA BLANCA CT
3100 SDCo 91902 1310-H1
CASA BLANCA PL
8100 SD 92126 1209-B4
CASABLANCA WY
2900 SDCo 92028 1028-D7
CASA BONITA CT
4800 SDCo 91902 1310-H1
CASA BONITA DR
3100 SDCo 91902 1310-H1
CASA BONITA WY
1100 VSTA 92083 1107-E1
1900 ESCN 92025 1129-J6
CASA BUENA WY
4200 OCN 92057 1086-J3
CASA CIELO
2200 SDCo 91977 1271-D7
CASA DE CAROL
22300 SDCo 92065 1173-A6
CASA DE LA TORRE CT
9600 SDCo 91977 1271-C3
CASA DE MACHADO
4200 SDCo 91941 1271-C3
CASA DE ORO BLVD
10000 SDCo 91977 1271-E5
CASA DE ORO PL
800 ESCN 92025 1129-J6
CASA DE ROCA WY
1400 SDCo 91901 1234-J5
CASA DE VEREDA
2000 SDCo 92084 1088-D4
CASA GRANDE AV
13100 SDCo 92040 1232-C2
CASA GRANDE WY
5700 SDCo 91902 1290-J6
CASA HERMOSA CT
- ENCT 92024 1148-A5
CASA LINDA WY
2700 SMCS 92069 1108-C5
CASA LOMA CT
3100 SDCo 91902 1310-H1
CASALS PL
4800 SD 92124 1250-A1
CASA NUEVA ST
10000 SDCo 91977 1271-E6
CASA REAL CT
700 VSTA 92083 1087-F5
CASA REAL LN
1500 ESCN 92026 1109-D6
1500 SMCS 92069 1109-D6
CASA VERDE CT
3200 SDCo 91902 1310-H1
CASA VISTA
13200 PWY 92064 1190-E5
CASA VISTA RD
12600 SDCo 92040 1232-B4
CASCA WY
3300 CRLB 92009 1148-A1
CASCADA WY
11200 SD 92124 1250-A3
CASCADE
500 SMCS 92069 1128-B1
CASCADE CRSG
- PWY 92064 1150-G7
CASCADE CT
3700 SD 92122 1228-D5
CASCADE PL
1400 SDCo 92021 1231-F7
1400 SDCo 92021 1251-F1
CASCADE RD
300 SDCo 92021 1251-F1
CASCADE ST
6300 SD 92122 1228-D5
CASCADITA CIR
4500 OCN 92057 1087-B1
CASCAJO CT
10800 SD 92124 1249-J2
CASCIO CT
8100 LMGR 91945 1270-H5
CASCO CT
8400 SD 92129 1189-B6
CASE ST
8300 LMSA 91942 1270-J1
CASEMAN AV
3900 SD 92154 1330-F7
CASEMENT ST
2300 SD 92123 1249-C7
CASERAS DR
3400 OCN 92056 1086-J7
CASERO CT
12200 SD 92128 1170-B3
CASERO PL
1700 ESCN 92029 1129-F6
12200 SD 92128 1170-B3
CASERO RD
16500 SD 92128 1170-B3
CASE SPRINGS RD
- SDCo 92055 408-L4
- SDCo 92055 409-A5
CASEY RD
3200 ImCo 92250 431-D3
CASEY ST
2500 SD 92139 1290-G7
2700 SD 92139 1310-G1
CASITA CT
100 VSTA 92083 1107-C1
CASITA WY
3900 SD 92115 1270-E5
CASITAS CT
- CHV 91910 1310-C7
CASITAS LN
- ESCN 92029 1129-F4
CASITAS ST
700 SD 92107 1287-H3
CASITAS DEL SOL
2200 SDCo 92028 1028-A2
CASMEG WY
3000 SDCo 92019 1272-C6
CASNER RD
19500 SDCo 92065 1154-A2
CASPER DR
7200 SD 92119 1250-F5
CASPER LN
200 VSTA 92084 1087-J6
CASPER ST
1300 OCN 92056 1087-D3
CASPIAN DR
5000 OCN 92057 1087-B1
5000 OCN 92057 1067-C7
CASPIAN WY
300 IMPB 91932 1349-F1
CASPI GARDENS DR
9800 SNTE 92071 1231-D4
CASS ST
4100 SD 92109 1247-H4
CASSANDRA LN
5100 SD 92109 1248-A4
CASSANNA WY
4300 OCN 92057 1087-A4
CASSELBERRY WY
6300 SD 92119 1250-E6
CASSELMAN CT
- CHV 91910 1310-C4
CASSELMAN PL
500 CHV 91910 1310-C4
CASSELMAN ST
400 CHV 91910 1310-A5
500 CHV 91910 1309-J5
CASSIA PL
700 CHV 91910 1310-G7
17900 SD 92127 1149-J7
CASSIA RD
4000 CRLB 92009 1127-D5
CASSIDY ST
100 OCN 92054 1106-D2
CASSINI CT
12000 SD 92131 1210-B1
CASSINS ST
1300 CRLB 92009 1127-B6
CASSIO CT
1200 VSTA 92083 1107-H4
CASSIOEPIA WY
8800 SD 92126 1209-D2
CASSOU RD
100 SDCo 92069 1108-G2
100 SMCS 92069 1108-G2
CASSOWARY CT
10600 SD 92131 1209-H1
CASTAIC CT
9600 SNTE 92071 1231-C4
CASTANA PZ
1000 CHV 91910 1311-C2
CASTANA ST
4700 SD 92102 1289-J4
5100 SD 92114 1290-A4
CASTANEDA DR
2800 ESCN 92025 1150-B1
CASTANO LN
8600 SDCo 92021 1232-F6
CASTEEL CT
1500 SD 92114 1290-D6
CASTEEL LN
1600 SDCo 92065 1172-H2
CASTEJON DR
6100 SD 92037 1247-J1
CASTELAR ST
4400 SD 92107 1268-A5
CASTELLANA RD
1700 SD 92037 1227-G6
CASTELLANO WY
4900 OCN 92057 1067-A5
CASTELLO CIR
17000 SDCo 92127 1169-E2
CASTELLON TER
2500 SDCo 92019 1272-E2
CASTILE WY
- SD 92128 1190-A3
CASTILLA PL
2800 CRLB 92009 1147-H2
CASTILLA WY
2100 OCN 92056 1086-J7
2100 OCN 92056 1106-J1

SAN DIEGO CO.
INDEX

STREET
Block City ZIP Pg-Grid

CASTLE AV
4700 SD 92105 1269-J6
CASTLE CT
7200 LMGR 91945 1270-F7
CASTLE GN
1800 ESCN 92029 1129-F5
CASTLE HTS
- SDCo 92082 1069-F5
CASTLEBAY
- SDCo 92028 1027-G6
CASTLE BROOK CT
8800 SDCo 92040 1232-C6
CASTLE COURT DR
12500 SDCo 92040 1232-B4
CASTLE CREEK LN
29500 SDCo 92026 1069-A6
CASTLE CREEK WY
- SDCo 92026 1069-A6
CASTLECREST DR
30100 SDCo 92082 1069-F4
CASTLEGATE LN
2200 VSTA 92084 1088-C6
CASTLE GLEN DR
3400 SD 92123 1249-D4
CASTLE HILLS DR
5100 SD 92109 1247-J4
5400 SD 92037 1247-J4
CASTLE ISLAND CV
4700 SD 92154 1330-H6
CASTLE PEAK LN
15600 SDCo 91935 1273-D5
CASTLERIDGE RD
29600 SDCo 92082 1069-F6
CASTLETON DR
5400 SD 92117 1248-H2
CASTLETON WY
4500 SD 92117 1248-H2
CASTLE VIEW DR
29100 SDCo 92026 1069-D7
CASTLEWOOD CT
1800 SDCo 92021 1251-H1
CASTLEWOOD DR
1100 SDCo 92021 1251-H1
CASTRO ST
700 SOLB 92075 1187-G1
CASTRO LANE RD
2000 ImCo 92243 6500-H4
CATALINA AV
2000 SDCo 92084 1088-C5
2000 VSTA 92084 1088-C5
CATALINA BLVD
500 SD 92106 1287-J3
1000 SD 92106 1288-A1
1000 SD 92107 1287-J3
1000 SD 92107 1288-A1
1600 SD 92107 1268-A7
CATALINA BLVD Rt#-209
200 SD 92106 1287-J4
CATALINA CIR
2300 OCN 92056 1087-E4
CATALINA CT
4200 SD 92107 1268-A6
CATALINA DR
3400 CRLB 92008 1106-H4
4500 OCN 92057 1066-H6
CATALINA PL
2500 SDCo 92084 1088-D5
2500 VSTA 92084 1088-D5
4100 SD 92107 1268-A7
CATALINA HEIGHTS WY
2400 SDCo 92084 1088-D5
2400 VSTA 92084 1088-D5
CATALPA LN
400 SDCo 92028 1027-G2
CATALPA RD
1700 CRLB 92009 1127-E6
CATALPA WY
700 ELCJ 92021 1251-G4
CATAMARAN DR
6800 CRLB 92009 1126-H6
CATAMARAN WY
1900 OCN 92054 1106-F1
CATAMARCA DR
3700 SD 92124 1249-J3
CATANIA ST
200 SD 92113 1289-H4
CATARACT PL
2800 ELCJ 92020 1251-A5
CATARINA DR
200 SDCo 92004 1058-G4
CATAWBA DR
13600 PWY 92064 1190-E3
CATES ST
- SDCo 92055 1067-A1
300 SD 92114 1290-H4
CATFISH LN
3800 OCN 92054 1086-G2
CATHAN LN
1800 SDCo 92084 1108-C2
CATHEDRAL GN
1800 ESCN 92029 1129-F5
CATHEDRAL WY
- SDCo 92065 1174-B4
CATHER AV
4400 SD 92122 1228-E4
CATHER CT
7100 SD 92122 1228-E4
CATHERINE AV
700 SMCS 92069 1109-A6
4500 SD 92115 1270-D3
CATHERINE RD
- SDCo 92003 1067-E1
CATHY CT
600 ESCN 92026 1109-J7
CATHY DR
39700 SDCo 92028 997-B2
CATHY LN
700 ENCT 92007 1167-E1
CATHY ST
1800 SD 92154 1330-A6
CATHYWOOD DR
9400 SNTE 92071 1231-B4
CATOCTIN DR
4800 SD 92115 1270-D2
CATSPAW PL
1100 ESCN 92029 1129-F5
CATSPAW CAPE
- CORD 92118 1329-E1
CATTAIL PL
- CRLB 92009 1127-B6
CATTAIL RD
15700 SD 92127 1169-J5
CAUBY ST
3000 SD 92110 1268-E5
CAUDOR ST
1400 ENCT 92024 1147-B2
CAULFIELD DR
2500 SD 92154 1330-C7

CAVALIER CT
28300 SDCo 92026 1089-F3
CAVALLO ST
12400 SD 92130 1188-C7
CAVALRY CT
13000 SD 92129 1189-C4
CAVE ST
1200 SD 92037 1227-F6
CAVERN PL
3700 CRLB 92008 1107-B4
CAVERN POINT CT
1500 CHV 91911 1330-J3
CAVIT ST
- SD 92140 1268-F6
CAVITE CT
6700 SD 92120 1250-E7
6700 SD 92120 1270-E1
CAY DR
3500 CRLB 92008 1107-B3
CAYENNE LN
6400 CRLB 92009 1127-G5
CAYMAN WY
1800 VSTA 92083 1107-G6
CAYOTE AV
13000 SD 92129 1189-C4
CAYUCOS CT
13900 SD 92129 1189-C3
CAYUCOS WY
8700 SD 92129 1189-C3
CAYUGA DR
13400 PWY 92064 1190-D4
CAYWOOD ST
5000 SD 92117 1228-E7
CAZADERO DR
2600 CRLB 92009 1127-H5
CAZADOR LN
3600 SDCo 92028 1047-F3
3600 SDCo 92055 1047-F3
CAZORLA AV
600 CHV 91910 1310-H6
CEANOTHUS CT
1600 CRLB 92009 1127-D6
CEANOTHUS PL
4800 OCN 92057 1067-A7
CEBADA CT
11600 SD 92124 1250-A2
CEBU CT
2800 CRLB 92009 1127-H5
CEBU PL
2800 CRLB 92009 1127-H5
CECELIA TER
2000 SD 92110 1268-F1
2200 SD 92110 1248-F7
CECELIA JO RD
3400 SDCo 92065 1172-B3
CECIL RD
- CORD 92135 1288-F4
CECILIA WY
200 OCN 92057 1086-H3
CECILWOOD DR
9500 SNTE 92071 1231-C4
CEDAR AV
100 CHV 91910 1310-A5
200 ELCN 92243 6499-J7
600 CHV 91910 1330-B1
800 CHV 91911 1330-B2
CEDAR CT
- SDCo 92040 1232-D6
CEDAR DR
2400 SDCo 91906 (1297-E5 See Page 1296)
3900 SDCo 92036 1156-E2
CEDAR LN
5000 LMSA 91941 1271-B1
5000 SDCo 91941 1271-B1
7600 SDCo 92066 1237-C7
20200 SDCo 92029 1149-E1
CEDAR RD
100 VSTA 92083 1107-C1
900 VSTA 92083 1087-C7
1900 OCN 92056 1087-C7
CEDAR ST
- SMCS 92078 1129-C2
100 ELCJ 92021 1251-G4
100 SD 92101 1289-E2
300 SD 92114 1290-D4
400 SDCo 92065 1152-D4
500 SMCS 92069 1108-J6
500 SMCS 92069 1128-C1
600 SD 92101 1288-J2
1800 SD 92154 1329-J6
1800 SD 92154 1330-A7
2800 SD 92102 1289-E2
3700 SD 92105 1289-G2
N CEDAR ST
100 ESCN 92025 1130-A1
900 ESCN 92026 1110-A7
900 ESCN 92026 1130-A1
S CEDAR ST
100 ESCN 92025 1130-A2
W CEDAR ST
100 SD 92101 1289-A2
500 SD 92101 1288-J2
CEDAR WY
900 ESCN 92026 1110-A7
CEDARBEND WY
800 CHV 91910 1310-H7
CEDARBRAE LN
3600 SD 92106 1287-J4
CEDAR BRIDGE WY
3500 CRLB 92008 1107-A3
CEDAR BROOK
1000 ESCN 92025 1130-A1
CEDAR CREEK RD
- SDCo 92036 1174-H4
- SDCo 92036 1175-A5
CEDARCREST WY
11000 SD 92121 1208-G3
CEDAR GLEN WY
3600 SD 92154 1350-E1
CEDAR GROVE CT
2500 CHV 91915 1311-J6
CEDAR HILL CT
9500 SD 92129 1189-E4
CEDARHURST LN
11700 SD 92128 1190-A1
CEDARIDGE DR
200 SD 92114 1290-H4
CEDAR LAKE AV
7800 SD 92119 1250-G6
CEDAR RIDGE CT
14500 PWY 92064 1190-H3
CEDAR RIDGE PL
4600 OCN 92056 1087-D3
CEDAR RIDGE RD
9700 SDCo 92021 1233-C2
CEDARSPRING DR
1900 CHV 91913 1311-D4

CEDAR SPRINGS DR
10000 SNTE 92071 1231-D3
CEDAR SUMMIT DR
1100 SDCo 92065 1152-D4
CEDAR TRAILS LN
9200 SDCo 92082 1069-B6
CEDAR TRAILS RD
29500 SDCo 92082 1069-B6
CEDAR TREE WY
12600 PWY 92064 1170-D3
CEDARVALE LN
- SNTE 92071 1230-G5
CEDAR VALE WY
3700 SDCo 92028 1048-D3
CEDARWOOD CIR
2900 SDCo 91902 1290-H7
CEDARWOOD DR
3000 SDCo 91902 1290-H7
CEDARWOOD WY
2800 CRLB 92008 1106-F3
CEDILLA PL
12900 SD 92128 1150-D7
12900 SD 92128 1170-D1
CEDRAL PL
6800 LMGR 91945 1270-E7
N CEDROS AV
100 SOLB 92075 1167-E7
S CEDROS AV
100 SOLB 92075 1167-E7
100 SOLB 92075 1187-F2
800 DLMR 92014 1187-F2
CEDROS DESIGN DISTRICT
300 SOLB 92075 1187-F1
CELADON CT
1300 OCN 92056 1087-D2
CELATA CT
7500 SD 92129 1189-A7
CELATA LN
7300 SD 92129 1189-A7
7900 SD 92129 1188-J7
CELAYA CT
100 SOLB 92075 1167-D7
CELESTE DR
3800 OCN 92056 1107-B1
CELESTE WY
6200 SD 92111 1248-G7
CELESTIAL CT
12600 PWY 92064 1190-C4
CELESTIAL RD
13500 PWY 92064 1190-C4
CELESTINE AV
8600 SD 92123 1249-C6
CELIA VISTA DR
6300 SD 92115 1270-D5
CELINDA DR
3200 CRLB 92008 1106-H4
CELITA CT
9800 SNTE 92071 1231-A4
CELOME CT
7100 SD 92129 1188-J7
CELOME LN
12000 SD 92129 1188-J7
CELOME WY
7100 SD 92129 1188-J7
CELTIC CT
24800 SDCo 92065 1173-G3
CENTAURUS WY
8800 SD 92126 1209-D2
CENTELLA ST
7800 CRLB 92009 1147-J2
CENTENNIAL DR
800 VSTA 92083 1107-F2
CENTENNIAL WY
1800 ESCN 92026 1110-A5
1800 ESCN 92026 1109-J5
CENTER AV
1000 OCN 92054 1086-B7
CENTER DR
700 SMCS 92069 1129-D1
8200 LMSA 91942 1270-J1
8800 LMSA 91942 1250-J7
8800 LMSA 91942 1251-A7
CENTER PL
2300 ELCJ 92020 1251-B5
CENTER ST
- CHV 91910 1310-A6
100 SD 92173 1350-G4
8100 LMSA 91942 1270-H2
CENTER WY
1700 SD 92110 1268-F2
CENTINELA AV
700 ELCN 92243 6559-H1
CENTINELLA DR
10200 SDCo 91941 1271-E4
CENTRAL AV
- SD 92102 1289-G4
- SDCo 91950 1310-C3
2100 SDCo 91977 1291-A1
2100 SDCo 91977 1271-A6
3000 SD 92105 1269-G4
4300 SD 92116 1269-G4
5000 CHV 91902 1310-J2
5000 SDCo 91902 1310-J2
5300 SDCo 91902 1311-A1
6700 LMGR 91945 1270-E6
24200 SDCo 91916 1235-J3
24300 SDCo 91916 1236-A3
CENTRAL CT
8700 SDCo 91977 1271-A7
8700 SDCo 91977 1291-A1
CENTRAL WY
2400 SDCo 91977 1271-A7
CENTRALOMA DR
3700 SD 92107 1268-B7
CENTRAL WAYSIDE CT
2400 SDCo 91977 1271-A7
CENTRE LN
3900 SD 92103 1269-C5
CENTRE ST
3700 SD 92103 1269-C5
CENTRE CITY PKWY
- ESCN 92025 1129-G1
1800 ESCN 92025 1129-G1
2100 SDCo 92026 1109-F4
25700 SDCo 92026 1109-F4
N CENTRE CITY PKWY
1800 ESCN 92026 1109-E1
1800 SDCo 92026 1109-E1
25500 SDCo 92026 1089-D7
S CENTRE CITY PKWY
1800 ESCN 92025 1129-J4
2300 ESCN 92025 1130-A5
2600 ESCN 92025 1150-A1
2700 SDCo 92025 1150-A1
2900 ESCN 92029 1150-A2
2900 SDCo 92029 1150-A2
CENTURION PL
900 ESCN 92026 1129-F1

CENTURION ST
2000 SD 92154 1351-G3
CENTURY ST
6800 LMSA 91941 1270-E3
6800 SD 92115 1270-E3
CENTURY WY
1800 ESCN 92026 1110-A5
1900 ESCN 92026 1109-J4
CENTURY PARK CT
8300 SD 92123 1249-C2
CEPIN DR
28400 SDCo 92082 1089-J2
28400 SDCo 92082 1090-A2
CERAMIC LN
700 SDCo 92028 1027-F1
CERCA BLANCA PL
1600 SDCo 92019 1252-B5
CERCA DEL ARROYO
6800 SDCo 92067 1149-A4
CERCO ROSADO
100 SMCS 92069 1109-C7
CEREUS CT
1700 CRLB 92009 1127-E6
CEREUS ST
200 ENCT 92024 1147-B5
CEREZA ST
4700 SD 92102 1289-J4
CEREZO DR
100 CRLB 92008 1126-G2
CERRADA DEL COYOTE
32100 SDCo 92086 409-K8
CERRISSA CT
2000 SD 92154 1330-A7
CERRISSA ST
700 SD 92154 1330-A7
CERRITOS CT
1300 CHV 91910 1311-B6
CERRO AV
3600 OCN 92056 1107-C3
CERRO ST
100 ENCT 92024 1147-G7
300 ENCT 92024 1167-G1
1500 SDCo 92021 1251-G2
CERRO BONITA DR
700 SMCS 92069 1129-E1
CERRO DEL SOL
17900 SDCo 92067 1149-B6
CERRO DE ORO
2100 SDCo 92084 1088-C3
2100 VSTA 92084 1088-C3
CERRO DE PAUMA RD
31600 SDCo 92082 1050-J7
31600 SDCo 92082 1051-A7
CERRO DE PAZ
11500 SDCo 92040 1211-G5
CERRO GORDO AV
700 SD 92102 1289-D3
CERRO LARGO DR
1000 SOLB 92075 1167-H6
CERRO LINDO
800 VSTA 92084 1088-B5
CERRO PEDREGOSO
19900 SDCo 92029 1148-F3
CERRO SERENO
2100 ELCJ 92019 1252-E4
2100 SDCo 92019 1252-E4
CERROS REDONDOS
3100 SDCo 92067 1148-B7
CERRO VERDE DR
1000 SOLB 92075 1167-H6
CERRO VISTA WY
24200 SDCo 92065 1173-E2
CERVANTES AV
5000 SD 92113 1290-A6
5100 SD 92114 1290-B5
CERVEZA CT
28400 SDCo 92026 1089-F2
CERVEZA DR
10300 SDCo 92026 1089-E2
CERVEZA BAJA
10200 SDCo 92026 1089-E3
CESPED DR
11400 SD 92124 1250-A3
CESSNA LN
4200 SDCo 92004 1100-B4
CESSNA ST
4200 SD 92117 1248-E6
CETUS RD
8600 SD 92126 1209-C1
CEZANNE LN
5200 SDCo 91902 1290-G6
CHABAD WY
17000 PWY 92064 1170-D3
CHABLIS CT
900 ESCN 92029 1129-E4
CHABLIS LN
800 VSTA 92083 1087-D6
CHABLIS RD
18200 SDCo 92065 1171-H3
CHABOLA RD
9400 SD 92129 1189-E7
CHACO CT
13400 SD 92129 1189-C4
CHAD CT
400 VSTA 92083 1087-G4
CHAD RD
15100 SDCo 92021 1233-A2
CHADWELL AV
2500 SD 92154 1330-B7
CHADWICK AV
6000 SD 92139 1310-D2
CHAFFEE ST
2700 SDCo 91950 1310-C2
CHAFFIN PL
9000 SDCo 91977 1291-B4
CHAFFINCH CT
- SD 92131 1209-G2
CHAISSON DR
- SDCo 92672 1023-D2
CHALAR ST
2700 SD 92123 1249-C6
CHALCEDONY ST
700 SD 92109 1247-H5
1500 SD 92109 1248-B4
CHALET DR
4900 OCN 92057 1087-C1
CHALET PL
8000 SD 92126 1209-B4
CHALICE DR
8800 SDCo 92026 1089-A1
CHALK CT
4800 OCN 92057 1087-B2
CHALLENGE BLVD
10200 SDCo 91941 1271-E4
CHALLENGER CIR
- SDCo 91977 1291-F2
CHALLENGER CT
- SDCo 91977 1291-E2

CHALMERS ST
1500 SD 92103 1268-H6
1900 SD 92101 1268-H6
CHALON LN
11900 SD 92128 1190-A3
CHALUPNIK RD
- ImCo 92227 411-E11
1100 ImCo 92227 431-D1
CHAMBERLAIN AV
100 ELCJ 92020 1251-F6
CHAMBERLAIN PL
800 ESCN 92025 1150-C1
CHAMBERLAIN ST
600 ELCJ 92020 1251-E6
CHAMBERS AV
1800 ESCN 92029 1129-F5
CHAMBERS ST
100 ELCJ 92020 1251-F4
1900 ESCN 92029 1129-F5
CHAMBORD CT
1200 OCN 92054 1106-D3
CHAMISAL CT
- CRLB 92009 1127-D6
CHAMISAL PL
9500 SD 92121 1208-E4
CHAMISE CT
800 SMCS 92069 1108-H6
CHAMISE WY
2700 SDCo 91935 1293-B4
CHAMOUNE AV
2900 SD 92105 1269-J5
4200 SD 92115 1269-J4
CHAMPA ST
100 VSTA 92083 1087-G3
CHAMPAGNE BLVD
26900 SDCo 92026 1089-A1
27800 SDCo 92026 1069-A7
28800 SDCo 92026 1068-J6
CHAMPAGNE VILLAGE DR
- SDCo 92026 1089-B2
CHAMPION ST
1900 SD 92105 1290-B1
CHAMPLAIN ST
2700 OCN 92056 1087-D1
CHAMPLAIN WY
4400 SD 92117 1228-E7
CHANCELLOR WY
13900 PWY 92064 1190-G4
CHANCERY CT
4500 CRLB 92008 1106-J5
4500 CRLB 92008 1107-A5
CHANDELLE LN
1500 SDCo 92028 997-H7
CHANDLER DR
5500 SD 92117 1248-J2
CHANDON CT
12700 SD 92130 1188-D6
CHANEY ST
1300 ELCJ 92020 1251-D4
CHANNEL LN
300 OCN 92054 1106-C3
CHANNEL RD
100 CRLB 92009 1126-H6
9700 SDCo 92040 1232-A3
CHANNEL WY
3300 SD 92110 1268-D4
CHANNING ST
5200 SD 92117 1248-H1
CHANTECLER AV
6500 SD 92114 1290-E5
CHANTEL CT
500 CHV 91910 1310-F5
CHANTILLY AV
8600 SD 92123 1249-C6
CHANTILLY CT
10900 SNTE 92071 1231-F6
CHANUTE ST
3500 SD 92154 1330-E6
CHAPALA CT
100 SOLB 92075 1167-D7
CHAPALA WY
100 SOLB 92075 1167-D7
CHAPALITA DR
100 ENCT 92024 1147-G7
300 ENCT 92024 1167-G1
CHAPARAJOS CT
5400 SD 92120 1250-B4
CHAPARAL VALLEY CT
- SD 92131 1210-C3
CHAPARRAL DR
- ELCN 92243 6559-G2
- SNTE 92071 1231-D2
1500 CHV 91902 1311-B3
1500 SMCS 92069 1109-D7
1800 VSTA 92083 1108-A4
11400 SDCo 92040 1211-G7
11400 SDCo 92040 1231-G1
CHAPARRAL HTS
3200 SDCo 91935 1273-C7
CHAPARRAL LN
700 ESCN 92025 1130-C5
700 SDCo 92025 1130-C5
CHAPARRAL TER
13700 SDCo 92082 1090-E2
CHAPARRAL WY
1400 OCN 92057 1067-F6
4900 SD 92115 1270-B2
16600 PWY 92064 1171-D6
CHAPARRAL HILLS RD
700 SDCo 91901 1253-G2
CHAPARRAL RIDGE RD
4600 SD 92130 1188-C5
CHAPARRAL SLOPE RD
3100 SDCo 91935 1293-B1
CHAPARRO WY
10800 SD 92121 1208-F3
CHAPARRO HILLS PL
12700 SD 92130 1188-D6
CHAPEL LN
3300 SDCo 92065 1172-B3
CHAPEL RD
- SD 92101 1289-C1
CHAPIN DR
900 SDCo 92036 1136-D7
CHAPMAN ST
3900 SD 92110 1268-C5
CHAPO CT
3000 SDCo 91977 1271-D6
CHAPULIN LN
1800 SDCo 92028 1028-A4
CHARAE ST
6000 SD 92122 1228-E5
CHARBONO PT
10800 SD 92131 1210-B2
CHARBONO ST
12100 SD 92131 1210-B3
CHARBONO TER
10700 SD 92131 1210-B3

CHARDON LN
2000 SDCo 92019 1272-C2
CHARDONNAY PL
10900 SD 92131 1210-B2
CHARDONNAY ST
12100 SD 92131 1210-B2
CHARDONNAY TER
2000 CHV 91913 1311-D3
CHARDONNEY WY
800 ESCN 92029 1129-D3
CHARGER BLVD
4200 SD 92117 1248-J2
CHARING PL
4300 SD 92117 1248-H2
CHARING ST
5900 SD 92117 1248-H2
CHARING CROSS RD
10800 SDCo 91978 1271-G6
CHARIOT CT
1300 SDCo 92003 1068-A4
1300 SDCo 92084 1068-A4
CHARISE CT
200 SDCo 91977 1290-J5
CHARISE ST
2100 ESCN 92025 1130-A6
CHARITY WY
15000 SDCo 92027 1130-J5
CHARLAN RD
13000 SDCo 92082 1090-D4
CHARLEEN CIR
2000 CRLB 92008 1106-G5
CHARLENE AV
6600 SD 92114 1270-E7
6600 SD 92114 1290-D1
CHARLES AV
2100 SD 92154 1330-A6
2200 CHV 91911 1330-A6
CHARLES DR
500 OCN 92057 1067-A6
CHARLES LN
1200 VSTA 92084 1088-A2
1300 SDCo 92065 1172-G2
CHARLES ST
3400 SD 92106 1288-A3
3500 SD 92106 1287-J3
3900 LMSA 91941 1270-F5
CHARLES WY
2200 ELCJ 92020 1251-B5
CHARLES DEWITT WY
2100 SDCo 91901 1253-J1
CHARLESTON LN
1700 ENCT 92024 1147-H7
CHARLESTON BAY CT
10200 SDCo 92040 1231-J2
CHARLIE HORSE WY
1600 OCN 92057 1067-E7
CHARLOTTA WY
1300 ESCN 92026 1110-A5
CHARLOTTE DR
500 SMCS 92069 1108-H6
CHARLYN LN
1000 SDCo 92028 1027-H6
CHARMANT DR
7300 SD 92122 1228-B3
CHARMARIE CIR
7100 LMSA 91941 1270-F3
CHARRO CT
1500 CHV 91902 1311-B3
CHARRO ST
1600 ENCT 92024 1147-G7
CHARTER AV
5600 SD 92120 1250-B6
CHARTER OAK DR
3400 CRLB 92008 1106-G4
CHART HOUSE ST
9000 SD 92126 1209-D3
CHARWOOD CT
3000 SDCo 91978 1271-G7
CHASE AV
1100 SDCo 92020 1251-H7
1100 SDCo 92020 1271-H1
1700 SDCo 92020 1272-A2
1900 SDCo 92019 1272-B2
E CHASE AV
100 ELCJ 92020 1251-G7
700 SDCo 92020 1251-G7
W CHASE AV
100 ELCJ 92020 1251-E7
CHASE CT
3200 OCN 92056 1107-B1
CHASE LN
1400 SDCo 92020 1271-J1
CHASE TER
1400 SDCo 92020 1271-J1
CHASEWOOD DR
3400 SD 92111 1248-J4
CHASIN ST
4100 OCN 92056 1087-C7
4200 VSTA 92083 1087-C7
CHATEAU CT
2000 CHV 91913 1311-E5
4600 SD 92117 1248-G1
CHATEAU DR
3800 SDCo 92036 1156-E2
4500 SD 92117 1248-F1
CHATEAU PL
600 ESCN 92029 1129-D3
4800 SD 92117 1248-G2
CHATEAU WY
3100 LMGR 91945 1270-E6
CHATEAU MONTELENA
- SDCo 92003 1068-B3
CHATEAU ST JEAN
- SDCo 92003 1068-A3
CHATHAM RD
3500 CRLB 92008 1107-A4
CHATHAM ST
2200 SD 92119 1251-A5
2200 ELCJ 92020 1251-A5
CHATSBURY ST
1600 ELCJ 92021 1252-B2
CHATSWOOD DR
2200 LMGR 91945 1270-H7
CHATSWORTH BLVD
1500 SD 92107 1288-A1
1500 SD 92106 1288-A1
1800 SD 92106 1268-C7
1800 SD 92107 1268-C7
CHATSWORTH WY
2800 CRLB 92008 1107-A4
CHATTANOOGA ST
5500 SD 92139 1310-C2
CHAUCER AV
4900 SD 92120 1250-A6
CHAUMONT DR
5800 SD 92114 1290-C1
CHAUMONT PL
1900 SD 92114 1290-C1

CHAUNCEY DR
2600 SD 92123 1249-C5
CHAUNCEY RD
1900 SD 92133 1288-D1
2100 SD 92133 1268-D7
3500 OCN 92056 1107-E3
CHAVACAN LN
10100 SDCo 91977 1271-E7
CHAVEZ RD
2900 SD 92154 1350-D3
CHAZ PL
8100 LMSA 91942 1250-H7
CHEAMES WY
6500 SD 92117 1248-J2
CHELAN CT
13400 SD 92129 1189-C3
CHELAUREN
17000 SDCo 92065 1171-E2
CHELFORD ST
- SD 92117 1248-J2
CHELLY CT
13400 SD 92129 1189-C4
CHELSEA AV
5500 SD 92037 1247-F3
CHELSEA CT
1000 VSTA 92084 1088-A7
1000 VSTA 92084 1108-A1
4500 CRLB 92008 1107-A5
CHELSEA LN
800 ENCT 92024 1148-A5
CHELSEA PL
300 SD 92037 1247-F4
CHELSEA ST
5100 SD 92037 1247-G4
CHELSEA PARK CIR
3200 SDCo 91978 1271-G6
CHELTERHAM TER
5000 SD 92130 1188-D4
CHEMISAL LN
2200 SDCo 92021 1252-J4
CHEMISE CREEK RD
14700 SDCo 92065 1173-G7
14700 SDCo 92065 (1193-G1 See Page 1192)
CHENAULT ST
2300 SD 92123 1249-C7
CHENIN WY
200 SMCS 92069 1108-J6
CHERI LN
17500 PWY 92064 1150-G7
CHERI ST
1700 SD 92154 1329-J6
1700 SD 92154 1330-A6
CHERIMOYA DR
2200 SDCo 92084 1108-C4
2500 SMCS 92069 1108-C4
CHERIMOYA GN
3200 ESCN 92025 1150-C1
CHERIMOYA ST
3100 SDCo 91935 1272-H7
CHERISH WY
- SDCo 92065 1174-B4
CHEROKEE AV
3300 SD 92104 1269-G4
3300 SD 92105 1269-G4
4400 SD 92116 1269-G3
CHEROKEE LN
2000 ESCN 92026 1109-F5
4200 SDCo 92004 1100-B4
CHEROKEE ST
1500 SMCS 92069 1108-D7
CHERRY AV
100 CRLB 92008 1106-E7
400 IMPB 91932 1329-F6
CHERRY CT
800 ESCN 92026 1109-D5
800 SMCS 92069 1109-D5
CHERRY LN
2900 SDCo 91977 1271-A6
CHERRY PL
1600 ESCN 92027 1130-C1
CHERRY RD
- SDCo 92055 1086-A4
8800 SDCo 92040 1231-H6
CHERRY BLOSSOM ST
3600 NATC 91950 1290-C6
CHERRYBROOK CT
3500 SDCo 92028 1048-E2
CHERRY HILLS LN
400 CHV 91902 1311-B3
CHERRY HILLS RD
8700 SNTE 92071 1230-J5
8800 SNTE 92071 1231-A5
CHERRYPOINT CT
3100 SDCo 92028 1048-E1
CHERRY POINT DR
600 CHV 91911 1330-J5
CHERRYSTONE ST
3700 OCN 92054 1086-G2
CHERRY TREE CT
1300 ENCT 92024 1147-F7
CHERRY TREE LN
- ESCN 92029 1129-E5
CHERRYWOOD DR
5000 OCN 92056 1087-C2
CHERRYWOOD ST
1900 VSTA 92083 1107-G5
12600 PWY 92064 1190-C1
CHERRYWOOD WY
800 ELCJ 92021 1251-G4
CHERUB CT
8500 SNTE 92071 1230-J7
CHERVIL CT
800 CHV 91910 1330-J1
CHERYL LN
1000 SMCS 92069 1109-B6
2000 VSTA 92083 1087-C7
CHERYL PL
- CHV 91911 1330-F2
CHERYL LEE CT
14000 SDCo 92021 1232-F5
CHERYL RIDGE CT
11600 SD 92126 1208-J1
CHESAPEAKE CT
5700 SD 92123 1229-D7
CHESAPEAKE DR
9100 SD 92123 1229-D7
9400 SD 92123 1249-E1
CHESHIRE AV
3600 CRLB 92008 1107-A3
CHESHIRE ST
4600 SD 92117 1248-G2
CHESHIRE WY
1700 ESCN 92026 1109-D5
CHESTER ST
500 SD 92114 1290-E3
CHESTER WY
700 ELCJ 92020 1251-E7

COPYRIGHT 2001 Thomas Bros. Maps ®

SAN DIEGO CO.
INDEX

STREET
Block City ZIP Pg-Grid

CHESTERFIELD CIR
- SMCS 92069 1108-J5
CHESTERFIELD DR
- ENCT 92007 1167-D3
CHESTERWOOD PL
- SD 92130 1208-B2
CHESTNUT AV
300 CRLB 92008 1106-J4
400 SMCS 92069 1108-J6
CHESTNUT CT
900 CHV 91910 1310-J7
CHESTNUT DR
900 ESCN 92025 1130-A3
CHESTNUT LN
300 ESCN 92025 1130-A4
1400 VSTA 92084 1088-A7
CHESTNUT ST
500 ESCN 92025 1130-A3
9400 SDCo 91977 1291-C2
9700 SDCo 92040 1232-B3
CHESTNUT WY
200 OCN 92057 1086-H5
CHESTNUT HILL LN
14000 SD 92128 1190-B2
CHESTNUT ROAN DR
400 SDCo 91901 1233-F6
CHESTNUT ROAN WY
8800 SDCo 91901 1233-E6
CHETENHAM CT
18300 SD 92128 1150-B6
CHETENHAM LN
12500 SD 92128 1150-B6
CHEVIOT CT
10300 SD 92126 1208-J5
CHEVY LN
10400 SDCo 91941 1271-E1
CHEVY CHASE DR
8500 LMSA 91941 1270-J2
8500 LMSA 91941 1271-A2
CHEYENNE AV
3200 SD 92117 1248-E5
CHEYENNE CIR
1900 OCN 92056 1087-C5
CHEYENNE LN
200 ESCN 92026 1109-G5
CHEYENNE TR
- PWY 92064 1150-G6
CHEYENNE WY
1700 SDCo 92004 1058-G6
CHEYNE RD
- SDCo 92026 1109-F3
CHI ST
8400 LMSA 91942 1250-J7
CHICA RD
2500 SDCo 92028 998-J3
CHICADEE ST
1500 SD 92114 1290-D2
CHICAGO ST
1800 SD 92110 1268-E1
2200 SD 92110 1248-E7
2800 SD 92117 1248-E5
CHICARITA CREEK RD
13900 SD 92128 1189-J2
CHICK RD
400 ImCo 92243 6560-C2
CHICKADEE WY
4400 OCN 92057 1087-A3
CHICKASAW CT
4600 SD 92117 1248-F1
CHICO LN
- OCN 92054 1086-G3
CHICO ST
1700 SD 92109 1248-A6
CHICORY LN
200 SD 92021 1253-A1
CHIEFTAN CT
18000 SD 92127 1149-J7
CHIHUAHUA VALLEY RD
- SDCo 92004 409-K6
27500 SDCo 92086 409-J6
CHILDRENS WY
3000 SD 92123 1249-B5
CHILDS AV
6100 SD 92139 1310-E2
CHILTERN CT
- OCN 92057 1067-A3
CHIMNEY FLATS LN
1100 CHV 91915 1311-H5
CHIMNEY ROCK DR
600 OCN 92054 1086-D3
CHIMNEY ROCK LN
9300 SDCo 92021 1232-H5
CHINA ST
- SD 92140 1268-F6
CHINABERRY LN
200 SMCS 92069 1108-G7
CHINON CIR
10600 SD 92126 1208-J4
CHINOOK CT
4500 SD 92117 1248-F1
CHINQUAPIN AV
200 CRLB 92008 1106-F7
CHIPMUNK LN
8300 SDCo 92066 1237-C5
CHIPPENHAM WY
11600 SD 92128 1190-A2
CHIPPEWA CT
3800 SD 92117 1248-E4
CHIPWOOD CT
3000 SDCo 91978 1271-G7
CHIQUITA RD
- SDCo 91916 1235-G1
CHIRIQUI LN
6400 CRLB 92009 1127-H5
CHISHOLM TR
1300 SMCS 92069 1109-C6
CHISWICK CT
1600 ELCJ 92020 1251-C5
CHLOE AV
8400 LMSA 91942 1250-J7
CHOC CLIFF DR
5100 SDCo 91902 1310-J3
5100 SDCo 91902 1311-A3
CHOCOLATE BELL TR
1600 SDCo 91901 1234-A7
CHOCOLATE CREEK RD
9700 SDCo 92021 1233-F3
CHOCOLATE SUMMIT DR
9600 SDCo 92021 1233-E3
CHOCTAW DR
4700 SD 92115 1270-D3
CHOCTAW RIDGE RD
12300 SDCo 92082 1090-B1
CHOISSER LN
13600 SDCo 92040 1232-D3
CHOLLA PL
1000 CHV 91910 1310-H7
1000 CHV 91910 1330-H1

CHOLLA RD
700 CHV 91910 1310-H7
700 CHV 91910 1330-H1
CHOLLAS PKWY
4600 SD 92105 1289-J1
4600 SD 92102 1289-J1
5000 SD 92105 1270-A6
5400 SD 92115 1270-B6
CHOLLAS PL
3200 SD 92105 1270-A6
CHOLLAS RD
2800 SD 92105 1270-A7
CHOLLAS STATION RD
5400 SD 92105 1270-B6
5500 SD 92115 1270-B6
CHORLITO ST
6300 CRLB 92009 1127-H4
CHOUKAIR DR
- SDCo 91935 1273-F4
CHOURREE ST
- CORD 92135 1288-G3
CHOYA CANYON RD
2100 ESCN 92025 1130-C6
CHRETIEN CT
18100 SD 92128 1150-A7
CHRIS LN
9000 SDCo 91931 1236-H3
CHRIS DEE DR
14200 SDCo 92082 1050-G6
CHRISMARK AV
6000 SD 92120 1250-C6
CHRISSY WY
13000 SDCo 92040 1232-C3
CHRISTA CT
5800 LMSA 91942 1251-B7
CHRISTATA WY
9000 SDCo 92040 1232-C6
CHRISTEN WY
100 SMCS 92069 1108-H6
CHRISTI DR
1800 VSTA 92084 1087-H3
CHRISTI WY
1000 SDCo 92028 1027-J4
CHRISTIANA ST
9000 SDCo 91977 1291-B3
CHRISTIANSEN WY
100 CRLB 92008 1106-D5
CHRISTIANSON CT
- SDCo 92055 1086-A3
CHRISTINA LN
9300 SDCo 92040 1231-H5
CHRISTINA WY
1400 SDCo 92065 1172-G2
CHRISTINE ST
3600 SD 92117 1248-D1
CHRISTMAS CIR
Rt#-S22
600 SDCo 92004 (1078-H2
See Page 1058)
CHRISTMAS TREE LN
9600 SDCo 92040 1232-C4
CHRISTOPHER LN
16300 SDCo 91935 1293-J3
CHRISTOPHER ST
2600 SD 92109 1248-C4
CHRISTY LN
1900 DLMR 92014 1187-F3
CHRISTY WY
3100 SDCo 91977 1271-A6
CHROMA DR
4700 OCN 92057 1087-B3
CHUBB LN
10400 SNTE 92071 1231-E5
CHUCK WAGON RD
15400 SDCo 92065 1172-J5
15400 SDCo 92065 1173-A5
CHU LAI AV
- SD 92140 1268-F7
CHULA VISTA ST
200 CHV 91910 1310-B5
600 CHV 91910 1309-J5
CHUMASH TR
900 SDCo 92084 1067-J6
CHUPAROSA LN
1800 SDCo 92004 (1099-F4
See Page 1098)
CHUPAROSA WY
1300 CRLB 92008 1106-E4
CHURCH AV
200 CHV 91910 1310-B5
700 CHV 91910 1330-C1
CHURCH PL
100 SDCo 92028 1027-F2
N CHURCH SQ
14100 SD 92128 1190-B1
CHURCH ST
2200 SD 92136 1289-E6
7500 LMGR 91945 1270-G6
CHURCH WY
400 ELCJ 92020 1251-B5
CHURCHILL DR
8200 SDCo 92021 1251-G1
CHURCHILL PL
1200 CORD 92118 1288-H7
1200 CORD 92118 1308-H1
CHURCHILL DOWNS
15400 SDCo 92067 1168-E7
CHURCHILL DOWNS RD
5800 OCN 92057 1067-G7
CHURCHWARD ST
5100 SD 92114 1290-B4
CHURRITUCK DR
700 SD 92154 1330-E7
CIARDI CT
- CRLB 92008 1107-A7
CIBOLA CT
8000 SD 92120 1250-D4
CIBOLA RD
6200 SD 92120 1250-D4
CICADA CT
7900 SD 92129 1189-B6
CICERO CT
13200 PWY 92064 1190-F4
CICERO WY
13800 PWY 92064 1190-F4
CICHLID WY
8100 SD 92129 1189-B6
CIELITA LINDA DR
900 VSTA 92083 1087-E5
CIELO AV
4200 OCN 92056 1107-C3
CIELO CT
17900 PWY 92064 1150-E7
CIELO DR
6500 SD 92114 1290-D4
CIELO PL
3000 CRLB 92009 1147-H1
CIELO VISTA
9800 SDCo 92026 1089-D2

CIENEGA DR
3600 SDCo 91902 1310-E3
CIERA CT
- PWY 92064 1150-G7
CIGNO CT
- CRLB 92009 1127-B7
CIJON ST
12600 SD 92129 1189-F5
CILANTRO GN
2400 ESCN 92029 1149-G1
CIMA CT
2000 CRLB 92009 1147-F2
CIMA DR
1000 SMCS 92069 1128-E3
CIMA DEL REY
1200 CHV 91910 1311-A5
CIMARRON TER
900 SDCo 92029 1129-J7
2500 SDCo 92029 1149-J1
CIMBRIA WY
- SDCo 92040 1232-A5
CIMMARON LN
7800 LMSA 91941 1270-G3
CIMMARON CANYON DR
- SDCo 92127 1169-E4
CIMMARON CREST DR
- SDCo 92127 1169-E4
CINCHONA ST
1200 VSTA 92083 1087-E7
CINCHRING DR
14900 PWY 92064 1190-J4
CINDERELLA PL
8100 LMGR 91945 1270-H7
CINDERELLA WY
2500 LMGR 91945 1270-H7
CINDY AV
4900 CRLB 92008 1107-A6
CINDY LN
400 VSTA 92083 1087-G5
CINDY ST
1800 SD 92154 1330-A6
4200 SD 92117 1248-E2
CINDY JO LN
- SDCo 92026 1109-J3
CINDY LYNN LN
8000 SDCo 92021 1252-C1
CINNABAR DR
7800 LMSA 91941 1270-H4
CINNAMON CT
800 CHV 91910 1330-J1
CINNAMON DR
20400 SDCo 91935 (1295-A6
See Page 1294)
20500 SDCo 91935 1294-J7
CINNAMON WY
3800 OCN 92057 1086-H5
CINNAMON ROCK RD
17900 SDCo 92065 1153-G5
CINTA CT
4800 SD 92122 1228-F6
CINTHIA ST
7900 LMSA 91941 1270-H4
CIPRIANO LN
2300 CRLB 92008 1106-E4
CIRCA DEL CIELO
- SDCo 92028 1047-G7
CIRCA DE LINDO
3800 SDCo 92091 1168-B7
CIRCA DEL LAGO
1500 SDCo 92069 1128-C3
CIRCA DEL NORTE
16300 SDCo 92067 1168-F5
CIRCA DE LOMA
- SDCo 92028 1047-G7
CIRCA DEL SUR
6600 SDCo 92067 1168-F6
CIRCA DE MEDIA
7100 SDCo 92029 1148-F2
CIRCA DE TIERRA
3100 ENCT 92024 1148-B6
CIRCA ORIENTE
17100 SDCo 92067 1168-G5
CIRCA VALLE VERDE
9800 SDCo 92021 1232-H2
CIRCLE DR
- SD 92109 1248-C6
200 OCN 92054 1085-H6
600 SOLB 92075 1167-E6
1000 ESCN 92025 1130-B3
1400 ELCJ 92020 1251-D7
2500 SDCo 92029 1149-H2
3600 SDCo 92036 1156-E2
4800 SD 92116 1269-G3
7600 LMGR 91945 1270-G7
7600 LMGR 91945 1290-G1
CIRCLE DR S
- SD 92109 1248-C6
CIRCLE HILL RD
9400 SDCo 92021 1232-J4
CIRCLE J DR
300 SDCo 92004 (1078-J1
See Page 1058)
700 SDCo 92004 (1079-A1
See Page 1058)
CIRCLE P LN
10100 SDCo 92026 1089-E5
CIRCLE PARK LN
1900 ENCT 92024 1147-H5
CIRCLE R CT
29600 SDCo 92026 1069-A5
CIRCLE R DR
8600 SDCo 92026 1068-J5
8600 SDCo 92026 1069-B4
9100 SDCo 92082 1069-B4
CIRCLE R LN
30000 SDCo 92082 1069-D4
CIRCLE R WY
29800 SDCo 92026 1069-A5
CIRCLE R COURSE LN
8500 SDCo 92026 1068-J5
8500 SDCo 92026 1069-A5
CIRCLE R CREEK LN
29800 SDCo 92026 1068-J6
CIRCLE R GREENS DR
29500 SDCo 92026 1068-J6
29500 SDCo 92026 1069-A6
CIRCLE R OAKS LN
9000 SDCo 92026 1069-A6
CIRCLE R VALLEY LN
8700 SDCo 92026 1068-J6
8700 SDCo 92026 1069-A5
CIRCLE R VIEW LN
8900 SDCo 92026 1069-A6
CIRCLE VIEW DR
5600 SDCo 92003 1068-B1
CIRCO DEL CIELO DR
1700 ELCJ 92020 1271-F2
CIRCO DIEGUENO
6300 SDCo 92067 1168-F7

CIRCO DIEGUENO
10000 SDCo 92067 1188-F1
CIRCO DIEGUENO CT
6500 SDCo 92067 1188-F1
CIRCULO ADORNO
3400 CRLB 92009 1147-J3
3400 CRLB 92009 1148-A3
CIRCULO DARDO
12800 SD 92128 1150-D7
CIRCULO MARGEN
9100 SDCo 91977 1291-B5
CIRCULO SANTIAGO
2300 CRLB 92008 1106-G3
CIRCULO VERDE
1000 CHV 91910 1311-A7
CIRQUE CT
1600 ENCT 92024 1147-G5
CIRRO VISTA WY
3900 SDCo 92028 1047-J4
CIRRUS ST
5900 SD 92110 1268-G3
6000 SD 92111 1268-G3
CIRUELA CT
1500 CHV 91911 1330-E4
CITA AV
2700 SDCo 92029 1149-J1
CITADEL CIR
5900 SD 92037 1247-H2
CITADEL CT
1800 CHV 91913 1311-D5
CITATION CT
8800 SNTE 92071 1231-A7
CITRACADO CIR
6000 CRLB 92009 1127-H2
CITRACADO DR
34400 SDCo 92061 409-E6
34400 SDCo 92061 1050-J1
34500 SDCo 92061 1051-A1
CITRACADO LN
- ESCN 92026 1129-G1
CITRACADO PKWY
300 ESCN 92025 1130-A7
500 ESCN 92025 1129-J7
800 ESCN 92029 1129-D4
1300 SDCo 92029 1129-D4
N CITRACADO PKWY
300 ESCN 92029 1129-D2
CITRADORA DR
4000 SDCo 91977 1271-B4
CITRINE DR
- ESCN 92027 1110-F4
CITRONELLA ST
2400 LMGR 91945 1270-G7
CITRUS AV
100 IMPB 91932 1329-E7
400 ESCN 92027 1110-D7
400 ESCN 92027 1130-E1
1000 SDCo 92027 1130-D3
2200 SD 92154 1330-B7
N CITRUS AV
100 ESCN 92027 1110-C6
100 VSTA 92084 1087-H4
S CITRUS AV
100 VSTA 92084 1087-H6
CITRUS DR
4000 SDCo 92028 1028-F6
CITRUS PL
800 CRLB 92008 1106-F6
CITRUS RDG
1400 SDCo 92027 1130-D4
CITRUS ST
3100 LMGR 91945 1270-F6
3600 LMSA 91941 1270-F5
CITRUS WY
500 OCN 92054 1086-F3
1500 CHV 91911 1330-E5
CITRUS GLEN CT
1800 SDCo 92027 1130-E3
CITRUS GLEN DR
1700 SDCo 92027 1130-E3
CITRUS HILLS LN
1600 SDCo 92027 1130-D3
CITRUS PARK LN
1400 SDCo 92027 1130-D3
CITRUS TREE LN
2100 SDCo 91977 1271-E7
CITRUS VIEW CT
9200 SD 92126 1209-D2
CITY VIEW LN
- SDCo 92026 1109-G4
CIUDAD LEON CT
5800 SD 92120 1250-E7
CIVIC CENTER DR
- NATC 91950 1309-G2
- SMCS 92069 1108-J7
100 OCN 92054 1085-J7
100 OCN 92054 1086-A7
8900 SNTE 92071 1231-D6
13200 PWY 92064 1190-E4
CLAIBORNE SQ
9600 SD 92037 1227-J1
CLAIMJUMPER WY
4100 SDCo 91977 1271-D4
CLAIRE AV
400 CHV 91910 1310-D6
CLAIRE DR
4700 OCN 92057 1066-J6
4700 OCN 92057 1067-A6
CLAIRE ST
600 SD 92154 1330-A7
CLAIREMONT CT
2800 SD 92117 1248-F7
CLAIREMONT DR
2300 SD 92109 1248-E5
2300 SD 92110 1248-E5
2500 SD 92117 1248-E2
CLAIREMONT MESA BLVD
3200 SD 92117 1248-F1
4800 SD 92111 1248-F1
4800 SD 92111 1249-A1
8500 SD 92123 1249-D1
9700 SD 92123 1229-F7
9800 SD 92124 1229-F7
10000 SD 92124 1249-G1
10900 SD 92124 1250-A1
CLAIRMONT AV
100 NATC 91950 1290-B6
N CLAIRMONT AV
- NATC 91950 1290-B6
200 SD 92114 1290-B6
CLAIRTON PL
2100 SD 92154 1350-A2
CLAMAGORO CIR
10200 SD 92124 1249-G5
CLAMATH ST
600 SDCo 91977 1291-C3

CLAMBAKE DR
- SDCo 92127 1168-J1
CLANTON PL
- SD 92154 1350-G2
CLARA LEE AV
6300 SD 92120 1249-J6
CLAREMORE AV
6500 SD 92120 1250-D5
CLAREMORE LN
6300 SD 92120 1250-D5
CLARENCE DR
1200 SDCo 92084 1108-B1
1200 VSTA 92084 1108-B1
CLARENCE LN
100 ESCN 92029 1150-A1
100 SDCo 92029 1150-A1
300 SDCo 92029 1149-J1
CLARENDON ST
1200 ELCJ 92021 1251-J3
CLARET CT
11900 SD 92131 1210-B4
CLARIDGE CT
10600 SD 92131 1209-H2
CLARISS ST
400 CHV 91911 1330-C3
CLARISSA CT
3000 LMGR 91945 1270-F6
CLARK AV
700 ENCT 92024 1147-C5
CLARK CT
1400 VSTA 92083 1107-J5
CLARK LN
- ImCo 92259 430-H7
CLARK RD
- ImCo 92231 431-B7
- ImCo 92251 431-B4
- IMP 92243 6499-G1
- IMP 92251 431-B4
1100 ImCo 92243 6559-H4
1400 ELCN 92243 6499-G1
1400 ELCN 92243 6559-H4
2300 ImCo 92243 6499-G1
2300 ImCo 92251 6499-G1
2500 IMP 92251 6499-G1
CLARK ST
100 ESCN 92025 1129-J2
300 SOLB 92075 1167-E7
1800 SD 92110 1268-H6
3000 SD 92103 1268-H6
CLARKE DR
1200 ELCJ 92021 1252-A3
CLARKVIEW LN
14200 SD 92130 1188-H3
14200 SDCo 92067 1188-H3
CLASICO CT
- SDCo 92127 1169-F3
CLASSIQUE WY
14100 SD 92129 1189-D2
CLATSOP LN
8500 SD 92129 1189-B3
CLAUDAN RD
2000 ESCN 92029 1129-E6
2000 SDCo 92029 1129-E6
CLAUDIA AV
10300 SNTE 92071 1231-E5
CLAUDIA LN
10300 SNTE 92071 1231-B1
CLAUDIA WY
100 OCN 92057 1086-H3
CLAUSER ST
10100 SD 92126 1208-J5
CLAVELITA PL
1500 SD 92154 1350-E2
CLAVELITA ST
3200 SD 92154 1350-D1
CLAY AV
2700 SD 92113 1289-E4
5800 LMSA 91942 1250-J7
CLAYBURN CT
- SDCo 91901 1233-G7
CLAYDELLE AV
100 ELCJ 92020 1251-G5
CLAYFORD ST
4300 SD 92117 1248-J2
CLAYMONT CT
12900 SD 92130 1188-B5
CLAYMORE CT
- SD 92129 1189-B2
CLAYTON CT
500 ELCJ 92021 1252-A4
CLAYTON DR
9400 SD 92126 1209-D6
CLAYTON PL
2700 SDCo 92069 1089-A6
CLEARBROOK DR
1900 CHV 91913 1311-D4
CLEARBROOK LN
1000 VSTA 92084 1087-J5
1000 VSTA 92084 1088-A5
10000 SDCo 91977 1271-E7
CLEARCREEK PL
200 SNTE 92071 1231-C5
CLEAR CREST CIR
600 VSTA 92084 1087-H4
CLEARCREST LN
1100 SDCo 92028 1027-H7
CLEARFIELD AV
2500 SDCo 91977 1271-E7
CLEARLAKE WY
9100 SDCo 92040 1232-C5
CLEAR SKY RD
7500 SD 92120 1250-C5
CLEAR SKY TER
6700 SD 92120 1250-D4
CLEAR SPRING RD
11300 SD 92126 1209-C2
CLEAR VALLEY RD
1900 ENCT 92024 1147-H5
CLEARVIEW DR
4200 CRLB 92008 1106-H6
CLEAR VIEW GN
2100 ESCN 92026 1109-B3
CLEARVIEW LN
18700 SDCo 92082 1091-F3
CLEARVIEW RD
14900 PWY 92064 1171-B7
14900 PWY 92064 1191-B1
CLEARVIEW WY
4800 LMSA 91941 1270-H2
CLEARWATER CT
8300 SDCo 91977 1290-J5
CLEAR WATER PL
1600 ENCT 92024 1147-G6
CLEARWATER PL
2000 CHV 91913 1311-E3
CLEARWATER RD
8800 SDCo 92028 998-J7
8800 SDCo 92028 999-A7
8800 SDCo 92028 1028-J1

CLEARWATER RD
8800 SDCo 92028 1029-A1
CLEARWATER RDG
1500 VSTA 92083 1107-H6
CLEARWOOD CT
11700 SD 92131 1210-A2
CLEARY ST
9900 SNTE 92071 1231-F4
CLEBURN DR
8700 LMSA 91942 1251-A6
CLEECO PL
17300 PWY 92064 1170-D2
CLEEVE WY
6400 SD 92117 1248-J2
CLEGG CT
2700 SDCo 91977 1271-A7
CLEGHORN WY
1100 SDCo 91901 1233-H7
CLEMATIS ST
2100 SD 92105 1289-J1
CLEMENS ST
- SDCo 91905 1300-B1
CLEMENTE PL
5300 SD 92117 1228-D7
CLEMENTINE ST
300 OCN 92054 1106-B1
N CLEMENTINE ST
100 OCN 92054 1086-A7
S CLEMENTINE ST
100 OCN 92054 1086-A7
100 OCN 92054 1106-B1
CLEMMENS LN
200 SDCo 92028 1027-F4
E CLEMMENS LN
100 SDCo 92028 1027-G4
CLEMSON CIR
1600 SD 92037 1247-H3
CLEO CT
1000 ESCN 92027 1110-B6
CLEO ST
6300 SD 92115 1270-D1
6300 SD 92120 1270-D1
CLEVELAND AV
100 ESCN 92026 1109-H3
500 SDCo 92026 1109-H3
1200 SD 92103 1269-B5
1500 SD 92116 1269-C4
N CLEVELAND ST
100 OCN 92054 1106-A1
200 OCN 92054 1086-A7
500 OCN 92054 1085-J7
S CLEVELAND ST
100 OCN 92054 1106-A1
CLEVELAND TR
1500 SDCo 92084 1108-D1
CLEVELAND FOREST DR
29400 SDCo 91906 (1297-E6
See Page 1296)
CLIFF CIR
- CRLB 92008 1107-A4
N CLIFF DR
900 OCN 92054 1085-J6
CLIFF PL
5000 SD 92116 1269-E2
CLIFF ST
2200 SD 92116 1269-C3
E CLIFF ST
100 SOLB 92075 1167-E6
W CLIFF ST
100 SOLB 92075 1167-E6
CLIFF WY
3600 OCN 92056 1107-C3
CLIFFDALE RD
1500 ELCJ 92020 1251-C4
CLIFFORD AV
1000 ImCo 92249 6560-D7
CLIFFORD ST
4700 SD 92105 1269-J7
CLIFFORD HEIGHTS RD
8500 SNTE 92071 1251-A1
8600 SNTE 92071 1231-A7
CLIFFRIDGE AV
8300 SD 92037 1227-J3
CLIFFRIDGE CT
2800 SD 92037 1227-J4
CLIFFRIDGE LN
8300 SD 92037 1227-J4
CLIFFRIDGE WY
2800 SD 92037 1227-J4
CLIFFSIDE AV
2500 SDCo 91977 1271-E7
CLIFFSIDE PL
10100 SDCo 91977 1271-E7
CLIFFTOP LN
2600 SDCo 91977 1271-D7
CLIFFVIEW PL
9900 SDCo 91977 1271-D7
CLIFFWOOD DR
10100 SDCo 91941 1271-E4
CLIFTON ST
500 ELCJ 92020 1251-G4
CLIMAX CT
8600 SD 92119 1250-J4
CLINE RD
4900 SDCo 91941 1271-D2
CLINTON AV
- SD 92145 1229-G3
CLINTON ST
3700 SD 92113 1289-G4
CLIPPER CT
1000 SOLB 92014 1187-H1
CLIQUOT CT
17100 PWY 92064 1170-E2
CLIVIA ST
10900 SDCo 92040 1231-F3
10900 SNTE 92071 1231-F3
CLOUD WY
5300 SD 92117 1228-G6
CLOUDCREST DR
11200 SD 92127 1169-J4
CLOUDCROFT CT
13500 PWY 92064 1170-E2
CLOUDCROFT DR
16900 PWY 92064 1170-E3
CLOUDESLY DR
12400 SD 92128 1150-B6
CLOUDVIEW LN
500 ENCT 92024 1147-G5
CLOUD VIEW PL
5900 SD 92120 1250-C4
CLOUDWALK CANYON DR
1100 CHV 91911 1330-H1
CLOUDY MOON DR
600 SDCo 92004 (1078-H2
See Page 1058)
15900 SDCo 92065 1171-F5
CLOVE ST
1200 SD 92106 1288-B1

CLOVE ST
1300 SDCo 92021 1251-H1
2100 SD 92106 1268-C7
CLOVE WY
3700 OCN 92057 1086-H5
CLOVER CIR
9000 SD 92126 1209-D3
CLOVER CT
6700 CRLB 92009 1126-J5
CLOVER TR
37800 SDCo 91905 (1299-H3
See Page 1298)
CLOVER WY
1900 ESCN 92026 1109-C5
CLOVERDALE RD
1400 ESCN 92027 1130-G4
1400 SDCo 92027 1130-G4
1900 SD 92027 1130-G5
CLOVERFIELD PT
10800 SD 92131 1210-B2
CLOVER GLEN CT
9200 SD 92126 1209-E2
CLOVERHURST WY
10800 SD 92130 1208-D1
CLOVERIDGE RD
2300 SDCo 92027 1130-F4
CLOVERLEAF CT
1900 VSTA 92083 1107-J4
CLOVERLEAF DR
1100 ELCJ 92019 1252-B7
CLOVER TREE CT
1700 CHV 91913 1311-D6
CLOVIS CT
1500 CHV 91913 1311-C7
CLOVIS ST
2500 SD 92107 1268-B5
E CLUB CIR
3100 SDCo 92004 (1079-C5
See Page 1058)
W CLUB CIR
3100 SDCo 92004 (1079-B5
See Page 1058)
CLUB DR
1500 SDCo 92028 1028-F4
CLUB LN
200 OCN 92054 1106-C2
CLUB HEIGHTS LN
1700 VSTA 92083 1107-H5
CLUBHOUSE AV
3300 SD 92154 1350-D1
CLUB HOUSE DR
- SDCo 92028 998-G5
CLUBHOUSE DR
2300 CHV 91915 1311-G6
5300 SD 92067 1188-E2
5300 SDCo 92067 1188-E2
CLUBHOUSE RD
200 SMCS 92069 1108-D5
CLUB VIEW TER
900 CHV 91911 1330-D1
CLUB VISTA LN
31300 SDCo 92003 1068-B2
CLYDE AV
6300 SD 92139 1310-E1
CLYDESDALE CT
1700 OCN 92057 1067-F7
CLYTIE LN
2100 SDCo 91977 1291-A1
COACH DR
2400 SDCo 91978 1271-G7
COACH LN
- SD 92130 1188-E5
COACH RD
- ESCN 92025 1150-D3
COACHELLA CANAL RD
- ImCo - 411-C7
12200 ImCo 92257 411-A5
18800 ImCo 92257 410-L4
COACHMAN CT
3100 OCN 92056 1106-H1
12700 PWY 92064 1170-C5
COACHWOOD
300 ELCJ 92019 1252-E5
COALINGA PL
1300 CHV 91913 1331-C1
COAST AV
- SMCS 92069 1128-A3
COAST BLVD
100 SD 92037 1227-E6
1500 DLMR 92014 1187-F4
COAST BLVD S
300 SD 92037 1227-E6
N COAST HWY
1400 SDCo 92055 1085-J6
N COAST HWY Rt#-S21
1000 OCN 92054 1086-A7
1200 OCN 92054 1085-J6
1400 SDCo 92055 1085-J6
S COAST HWY Rt#-S21
100 OCN 92054 1086-A7
100 OCN 92054 1106-B2
2000 CRLB 92008 1106-B2
COAST WK
1500 SD 92037 1227-F6
N COAST HWY 101
Rt#-S21
100 ENCT 92024 1147-A2
S COAST HWY 101
Rt#-S21
300 ENCT 92024 1147-C7
800 ENCT 92024 1167-D3
900 ENCT 92007 1167-D3
COASTLINE AV
4400 CRLB 92008 1106-H7
COAST OAK TR
- SDCo 91906 (1318-B7
See Page 1298)
COASTVIEW CT
3500 CRLB 92008 1107-B3
COASTWOOD RD
10700 SDCo 92127 1169-G3
COBALT DR
4200 LMSA 91941 1270-H4
COBAN ST
5200 SD 92114 1290-A5
COBB CT
5200 SD 92117 1228-F7
COBB DR
4600 SD 92117 1228-F7
COBB LN
27600 SDCo 92082 1091-A2
COBB PL
5200 SD 92117 1228-F7
COBBLESTONE DR
- CRLB 92009 1127-B4
800 SD 92101 1289-B2
COBBLESTONE LN
2300 VSTA 92083 1108-A5

SAN DIEGO CO.

INDEX

6577 COBBLESTONE PL
SAN DIEGO CO. STREET INDEX
CORPORATE CT

STREET
Block City ZIP Pg-Grid

COBBLESTONE PL
300 SNTE 92071 1231-C5
COBBLESTONE RD
1400 CRLB 92009 1127-B4
COBBLESTONE CREEK RD
12600 PWY 92064 1190-B6
COBBLESTONE CREEK TR
11900 PWY 92064 1190-B6
COBB MEADOW PL
2200 CHV 91915 1311-G5
COBRA WY
6600 SD 92121 1208-H4
COBRIDGE WY
4100 SD 92117 1248-E6
COBURN ST
2800 SDCo 91950 1310-C2
COCAPAH ST
500 VSTA 92083 1087-F5
COCHABAMBA ST
1500 SD 92154 1349-J2
COCHERA RD
12800 SDCo 92040 1232-B5
COCHISE CT
- VSTA 92084 1087-H4
COCHISE WY
4500 SD 92117 1248-D2
COCHRAN AV
400 SD 92154 1330-E6
COCHRAN ST
3600 SD 92106 1287-J4
COCHRAN TR
800 SDCo 92019 1253-C2
COCKATOO CIR
500 VSTA 92083 1087-F4
COCONINO CT
3700 SD 92117 1248-E1
COCONINO WY
4600 SD 92117 1248-E1
COCONUT LN
1600 SDCo 92021 1252-A2
COCONUT WY
3500 OCN 92054 1086-F2
COCONUT GROVE CT
- SDCo 92127 1168-J2
COCO PALMS DR
300 OCN 92054 1086-F2
1100 SDCo 92020 1271-J1
COCOS DR
800 SMCS 92078 1128-J3
800 SMCS 92078 1129-A3
CODORNIZ
5400 SDCo 92067 1168-C3
CODORNIZ LN
300 SDCo 92021 1252-H4
CODY LN
700 ESCN 92025 1150-C1
CODY ST
3800 SD 92117 1248-E4
COE PL
1900 CHV 91913 1311-D5
COFAIR AV
100 SOLB 92075 1187-F1
COFAIR CT
800 SOLB 92075 1187-F2
COFFEE POT TR
700 SDCo 92036 1138-B6
COHANSEY RD
11500 SD 92131 1209-H1
COHASSET CT
700 SD 92109 1267-H4
COKELEY CT
2800 ESCN 92027 1110-E7
COKER WY
1300 ELCJ 92021 1251-J3
1300 ELCJ 92021 1252-A3
COLBERT DR
100 SDCo 91977 1291-A5
COLBY LN
31800 SDCo 92061 1051-C7
COLBY RD Rt#-S24
- ImCo 92283 432-D4
COLCHESTER RD
- SD 92154 1351-E2
COLDBROOK CT
800 CHV 91913 1311-E4
COLD SPRINGS CT
10900 SD 92128 1189-H4
COLDSTREAM DR
600 ELCJ 92020 1251-G7
700 SDCo 92020 1251-G7
COLDWATER CT
12100 SD 92128 1190-B3
COLDWELL LN
3900 SD 92154 1330-F7
COLE CT
4100 SD 92117 1228-E6
COLE DR
2800 SD 92110 1268-E6
COLE RD
- SD 92106 1287-J5
100 CALX 92231 431-C7
100 ImCo 92231 431-C7
COLE ST
4800 SD 92117 1248-E1
4900 SD 92117 1228-E6
COLE WY
4100 SD 92117 1228-E7
COLEEN CT
900 ELCJ 92021 1252-A3
COLE GRADE LN
13800 SDCo 92082 1070-E4
COLE GRADE RD
28200 SDCo 92082 1090-F1
28900 SDCo 92082 1070-F3
31800 SDCo 92082 1050-F7
32600 SDCo 92061 1050-G5
33200 SDCo 92061 1051-A3
COLEMAN AV
3700 SD 92154 1330-F7
COLEMAN CIR
2900 SDCo 92036 1136-A7
COLEMAN CT
700 SD 92154 1330-F7
COLE RANCH RD
100 ENCT 92024 1147-J7
100 ENCT 92024 1167-J1
400 ENCT 92024 1148-A6
COLESHILL DR
6900 SD 92119 1250-J3
COLEUS CT
4300 SD 92154 1330-G7
COLFAX CT
1100 CHV 91913 1311-C7
COLFAX DR
1600 LMGR 91945 1290-H1
COLGATE CIR
1700 SD 92037 1247-H2

COLGATE DR
2800 OCN 92056 1087-A7
COLIBRI LN
2600 CRLB 92009 1127-G5
COLIMA CT
300 SD 92037 1247-F4
COLIMA ST
300 SD 92037 1247-G4
COLIN CT
2200 SDCo 92027 1109-J4
2200 SDCo 92027 1110-A4
COLINA CT
3900 OCN 92054 1086-G1
COLINA DR
4900 LMSA 91941 1270-J2
COLINA TER
200 VSTA 92084 1088-A5
COLINA CREEK TR
800 SDCo 92028 1028-B1
COLINA DE LA COSTA
- CRLB 92009 1127-F7
COLINA DORADA DR
3800 SD 92124 1250-A3
COLINA ENCANTADA WY
20100 SDCo 92029 1148-H2
COLINA FUERTE
18300 SDCo 92067 1148-C6
COLINA GRANDE
- SDCo 92019 1272-C1
COLINA LINDA
1100 SOLB 92014 1187-J2
COLINAS CTE
2400 SDCo 92019 1252-E6
COLINAS MIRA
600 SDCo 92019 1252-E5
COLINAS PASEO
2400 SDCo 92019 1252-E6
COLINA VERDE LN
3000 SDCo 91935 1292-F2
COLINA VISTA
1600 SDCo 92028 1028-D5
COLLADO CTE
2600 SDCo 91901 1253-J2
COLLADO LN
1000 SMCS 92069 1109-A4
COLLEGE AV
2900 LMGR 91945 1270-E6
3000 LMGR 92115 1270-E6
3100 SD 92115 1270-C2
5100 SD 92182 1270-C2
5300 SD 92120 1270-C2
5500 SD 92120 1250-C6
COLLEGE BLVD
3600 OCN 92056 1107-B1
3700 CRLB 92008 1107-B4
3800 OCN 92056 1087-B7
4400 OCN 92057 1087-B3
4700 OCN 92057 1067-B7
5600 CRLB 92008 1127-C1
COLLEGE PL
3200 LMGR 91945 1270-E6
5000 SD 92115 1270-C2
COLLEGE ST
100 SDCo 92028 1027-E3
700 SDCo 92055 1027-E3
E COLLEGE ST
100 SDCo 92028 1027-F3
COLLEGE WY
4500 SD 92115 1270-C4
COLLEGE GARDENS CT
4900 SD 92115 1270-A2
COLLEGE GROVE DR
5400 SD 92105 1270-B7
5900 SD 92115 1270-B7
COLLEGE GROVE WY
2500 SD 92115 1270-D6
COLLEGIO DR
11100 SD 92124 1250-A1
COLLETT WY
10100 SD 92124 1249-G3
COLLEY LN
3000 SDCo 92025 1130-E7
3000 SDCo 92025 1150-E1
COLLIER AV
2500 SD 92116 1269-D3
4900 SD 92115 1270-A3
COLLIER WY
700 SDCo 92019 1253-C2
COLLING RD E
4300 SDCo 91902 1311-A3
COLLING RD W
4200 SDCo 91902 1311-A3
COLLINGWOOD DR
1700 SD 92109 1248-A4
2700 SD 92109 1247-J4
COLLINOS WY
4700 OCN 92056 1107-E5
COLLINS AV
5400 LMSA 91942 1270-F1
COLLINS RD
1200 ImCo 92283 432-D4
COLLINS TER
600 SDCo 92026 1109-H5
COLLINS RANCH CT
- SD 92130 1188-J3
COLLINS RANCH PL
- SD 92130 1188-J3
COLLINS RANCH TER
- SD 92130 1188-J2
COLLINSWOOD LN
1100 VSTA 92083 1107-G1
COLLINWOOD DR
10900 SNTE 92071 1231-F6
COLLOMIA CT
- SDCo 91901 1254-A3
COLLURA ST
2900 SD 92105 1270-A7
COLLWOOD BLVD
4400 SD 92115 1270-A2
COLLWOOD LN
4100 SD 92115 1270-A3
COLLWOOD WY
5000 SD 92115 1270-A2
COLLYN ST
500 VSTA 92083 1087-D7
COLO CT
11800 SD 92129 1189-F7
COLONEL CT
500 SDCo 92065 1152-G4
COLONIAL AV
1800 SD 92105 1289-G1
COLONIAL WY
5100 OCN 92057 1066-J4
5100 OCN 92057 1067-A4
COLONNADES PL
18000 SD 92128 1150-A7
COLONY DR
7300 LMSA 91941 1270-G2
12200 PWY 92064 1190-B1

COLONY PL
2700 ESCN 92027 1130-F1
COLONY RD
7000 LMSA 91941 1270-F3
COLONY TER
4200 ENCT 92024 1167-J1
COLONY WY
14600 PWY 92064 1190-B1
COLORADO AV
400 CHV 91910 1309-J7
600 CHV 91910 1330-A2
700 CHV 91911 1330-A3
6800 LMSA 91942 1270-E1
COLORADO ST
- CORD 92135 1288-G5
COLORAMA WY
9200 SDCo 92040 1232-D5
COLT LN
9800 SDCo 92040 1232-D3
COLT TER
- SD 92130 1188-E5
COLTER LAKE CT
1700 SDCo 92019 1272-C3
COLTON AV
3100 SD 92136 1289-E6
COLTON CT
1200 CHV 91913 1331-B1
COLTRIDGE LN
1700 CHV 91902 1311-C4
COLTRIDGE PL
1800 ESCN 92029 1129-F7
COLTS WY
4100 SD 92115 1270-B5
COLUCCI DR
2000 VSTA 92084 1087-J2
COLUMBA PL
11000 SD 92126 1209-C3
COLUMBIA DR
2800 OCN 92056 1087-A7
COLUMBIA ST
600 SD 92101 1289-A2
1600 CHV 91913 1311-C5
1800 SD 92101 1288-J1
2500 SD 92103 1288-J1
2700 SD 92103 1268-H7
21800 SDCo 92070 1135-B2
COLUMBINE DR
2300 SDCo 91901 1233-J4
2500 SDCo 91901 1234-A5
7000 CRLB 92009 1127-E7
COLUMBINE RD
2500 SDCo 91901 1234-A5
COLUMBINE ST
- SDCo 92055 1086-B2
2600 SD 92105 1269-H7
COLUMBUS PL
3500 LMGR 91945 1270-H5
COLUMBUS ST
8000 SD 92126 1209-B4
10900 SNTE 92071 1231-F4
COLUMBUS WY
1100 VSTA 92083 1107-J4
COLUSA DR
4900 OCN 92056 1107-F3
COLUSA ST
800 SD 92110 1268-G3
1600 CHV 91913 1311-D7
COLUSA WY
200 VSTA 92083 1087-E7
COLVER AV
25800 SDCo 92026 1109-E1
COLVIN DR
8300 SNTE 92071 1251-B1
COMALETTE LN
8500 SD 92126 1209-C2
COMANCHE DR
4900 LMSA 91941 1270-G2
COMANCHE ST
1800 OCN 92056 1087-C5
COMANCHERO DR
300 SDCo 92065 1152-J5
COMBE WY
4100 SD 92122 1228-E5
COMBS
1900 ELCN 92243 6559-J1
COMET CIR
- SMCS 92069 1108-E6
COMET CT
1400 ELCJ 92019 1252-A5
COMET LN
200 ELCJ 92019 1252-A5
COMET VIEW CT
7400 SD 92120 1250-C5
COMLY CT
6600 SD 92111 1248-H6
COMLY ST
6500 SD 92111 1248-H6
COMMERCE AV
8400 SD 92121 1228-J1
COMMERCE ST
900 SMCS 92069 1128-E1
1100 OCN 92054 1106-C1
COMMERCE WY
2500 VSTA 92083 1108-A7
COMMERCIAL AV
- ELCN 92243 6500-A6
400 ELCN 92243 6499-F6
COMMERCIAL ST
1300 SD 92101 1289-C4
1300 SD 92113 1289-C4
1900 ESCN 92029 1129-E2
8100 LMSA 91942 1270-H1
COMMODORE DR
3800 SMCS 92069 1108-D7
COMMONWEALTH AV
2100 SD 92104 1289-F1
2400 SD 92104 1269-F7
COMMUNITY DR
100 SMCS 92069 1108-D5
COMMUNITY RD
12100 PWY 92064 1190-E4
COMMUNITY BUILDING RD
1200 SDCo 91917 (1314-C7 See Page 1294)
COMO
9400 SDCo 92040 1232-F4
COMO ESTA CT
25100 SDCo 92065 1173-G3
COMONDU CT
700 ELCJ 92020 1251-F6
COMPADRE WY
24200 SDCo 92065 1173-E2
COMPANERO AV
2600 SDCo 92084 1108-E3
COMPASS CT
600 CRLB 92009 1127-A7
COMPASS RD
300 OCN 92054 1086-F6

COMPASS LAKE DR
7700 SD 92119 1250-G5
COMPASS POINT DR N
9400 SD 92126 1209-E1
COMPLEX DR
8700 SD 92123 1249-C1
COMPLEX ST
5300 SD 92123 1229-D7
5300 SD 92123 1249-D1
COMPOSITION CT
4900 OCN 92057 1087-B2
COMPTON ST
300 ELCJ 92020 1251-F4
COMSTOCK AV
300 SMCS 92069 1108-J6
COMSTOCK CT
6600 SD 92111 1248-H6
COMSTOCK ST
2100 SD 92111 1268-J1
2200 SD 92111 1248-H6
COMUNA DR
13500 PWY 92064 1190-E3
CONCANNON CT
1700 SDCo 92019 1272-C3
CONCEPCION AV
400 SDCo 91977 1291-B4
CONCERTO GN
600 ESCN 92025 1150-C4
CONCHA LN
400 SMCS 92069 1108-E6
CONCHITA RD
18800 SDCo 92082 1091-F4
CONCHO CIR
4800 OCN 92057 1067-A5
CONCHO CT
18200 SDCo 92082 1091-E4
CONCHO PL
4900 OCN 92057 1067-A5
CONCHOS DR
14900 PWY 92064 1170-C7
14900 PWY 92064 1190-C1
CONCORD CT
900 VSTA 92083 1108-A4
CONCORD PL
200 SMCS 92069 1108-J4
CONCORD ST
1000 SD 92106 1288-A2
3300 CRLB 92008 1106-J3
CONCORD WY
1500 CHV 91911 1330-H4
CONCORDIA LN
4000 SDCo 92028 1047-F4
CONCORD WOODS WY
- SD 92130 1208-F2
CONCOURS CT
2100 SDCo 92019 1272-B4
CONDADO WY
2000 SDCo 92025 1130-B5
CONDE PL
4400 SD 92103 1268-G4
CONDE ST
3800 SD 92110 1268-F5
4400 SD 92103 1268-G4
CONDESA DR
13700 SD 92014 1187-G6
CONDESSA CT
200 OCN 92057 1087-A1
CONDON DR
6800 SD 92122 1228-D4
CONDOR AV
1400 ELCJ 92019 1252-A4
CONDOR CT
1300 ENCT 92024 1147-D4
CONDOR GN
1300 ESCN 92029 1129-G6
CONDOR LN
500 SMCS 92078 1129-A1
CONDUIT RD
3200 SDCo 91902 1291-A7
3200 SDCo 91902 1311-A1
CONEFLOWER DR
6300 CRLB 92009 1127-A4
CONEFLOWER ST
200 ENCT 92024 1147-E6
CONEJO CT
1300 ELCJ 92021 1252-C3
CONEJO LN
10100 SNTE 92071 1231-D4
CONEJO PL
10000 SNTE 92071 1231-D4
CONEJO RD
4900 SDCo 92028 1047-E6
9700 SNTE 92071 1231-D4
CONEJOS VALLEY RD
- SDCo 91901 429-J4
- SDCo 91901 1235-A1
- SDCo 91916 429-J4
- SDCo 91916 (1194-H5 See Page 1175)
CONEJO VISTA CT
1300 ELCJ 92021 1252-C3
CONESTOGA CIR
2800 SDCo 91901 1254-C3
CONESTOGA CT
2800 SDCo 91901 1254-D3
7300 SD 92120 1250-B4
CONESTOGA DR
5300 SD 92120 1250-B4
CONESTOGA PL
7200 SD 92120 1250-B5
CONESTOGA WY
7100 SD 92120 1250-B5
CONFERENCE WY
11700 SD 92128 1170-A7
CONGRESS ST
2200 SD 92110 1268-F5
CONGRESSIONAL DR
2300 SDCo 92019 1272-B5
CONGRESSIONAL GN
1700 ESCN 92026 1109-C3
CONIFER AV
300 SD 92154 1330-B7
CONIFER DR
200 OCN 92057 1087-A1
CONIFER GN
300 ESCN 92026 1109-G6
CONIFER RD
- SDCo 92060 409-G7
CONKLING RD
- ImCo 92243 431-A7
CONLEY ST
12900 PWY 92064 1190-D5
CONN PL
700 ELCJ 92021 1251-H4
CONNECTICUT AV
5400 LMSA 91942 1270-E1
E CONNECTICUT AV
100 VSTA 92084 1087-H5

W CONNECTICUT AV
100 VSTA 92083 1087-G6
CONNECTICUT ST
900 IMPB 91932 1329-G7
900 IMPB 91932 1349-G2
CONNELL RD
10000 SD 92131 1210-A4
CONNELLY RD
- ImCo 92250 431-E6
CONNEMARA DR
- SDCo 92029 1149-C5
- SDCo 92067 1149-C5
CONNER CT
4100 SD 92117 1248-C3
CONNER WY
3000 SD 92117 1248-C3
CONNIE DR
6300 SD 92115 1270-C2
CONNIE LN
4200 SDCo 92004 1100-B4
CONNOLEY AV
1500 CHV 91911 1330-E4
CONNOLEY CIR
- CHV 91911 1330-E5
CONO DR
1700 ELCJ 92020 1271-G1
CONOSA WY
- CRLB 92009 1127-D6
CONQUISTADOR
4100 OCN 92056 1087-B4
CONQUISTADOR RD
3100 SDCo 92028 997-D4
CONQUISTADOR WY
12400 SD 92128 1170-B2
CONRAD AV
3400 SD 92117 1228-F7
3400 SD 92117 1248-D1
CONRAD CT
4800 SD 92117 1248-D1
CONRAD DR
3800 SDCo 91977 1271-C4
4100 SDCo 91941 1271-C4
CONROCK RD
9000 SD 92126 1209-E5
CONSOLIDATED WY
6700 SD 92121 1228-J2
CONSTANCE DR
4600 SD 92115 1269-J3
CONSTANCIA WY
1500 ELCJ 92019 1252-A5
CONSTANT CREEK RD
700 SDCo 92028 1027-G4
CONSTELLATION DR
11200 SDCo 92020 1271-H1
CONSTITUTION RD
5100 SD 92117 1228-F6
CONSTRUCTION CT
7100 SD 92121 1228-J1
CONTINENTAL LN
1700 ESCN 92029 1129-F7
CONTINENTAL RD
1400 SD 92154 1351-E2
CONTINENTAL ST
- SD 92154 1351-D1
CONTOUR BLVD
4500 SD 92115 1270-A3
CONTOUR CT
4800 OCN 92057 1087-B2
CONTOUR PL
3600 CRLB 92008 1107-B4
CONTRERAS CT
1500 SD 92114 1290-E5
CONTUT CT
3000 SDCo 91977 1271-D6
CONVENTION WY
300 SD 92101 1289-A4
CONVERSE AV
8600 SD 92123 1249-C7
CONVERTIBLE LN
700 SDCo 92028 1027-H1
CONVOY CT
6600 SD 92111 1228-J7
6600 SD 92117 1228-J7
7000 SD 92111 1229-A7
CONVOY ST
3800 SD 92111 1249-B2
4900 SD 92111 1229-B7
5200 SD 92145 1229-B7
CONVOY TER
7300 SD 92111 1229-A7
CONWAY DR
1000 ESCN 92027 1110-A5
1400 ESCN 92027 1109-J6
1700 ESCN 92026 1109-H3
N CONWAY DR
1600 ESCN 92027 1109-J5
1600 ESCN 92027 1110-A5
CONWAY WY
1600 ESCN 92026 1109-J5
1600 ESCN 92027 1109-J5
COOGAN WY
100 ELCJ 92020 1251-F3
COOK CT
- CHV 91910 1310-D6
COOK PL
2100 SDCo 92065 1172-E2
COOK ST
1100 SDCo 92065 1172-E2
COOKIE LN
800 SDCo 92028 1027-G4
COOLEY RD
- ELCN 92243 6500-C5
- ImCo 92243 431-C4
- ImCo 92243 6500-C1
COOLEY ST
400 ELCN 92243 6500-C6
1900 ImCo 92243 6500-C6
COOLIDGE AV
900 NATC 91950 1309-H2
COOLIDGE ST
1500 SD 92111 1268-J2
COOL LAKE TER
10900 SD 92128 1189-H4
COOL LAKE WY
13300 SD 92128 1189-H4
COOLNGREEN LN
2000 ENCT 92024 1147-H5
COOLNGREEN WY
2000 ENCT 92024 1147-J5
COOL RIDGE HTS
1500 SDCo 92027 1130-E5
COOLSPRINGS CT
1600 CHV 91913 1311-D6
COOL VALLEY LN
15500 SDCo 92082 1071-A3
COOL VALLEY RD
13900 SDCo 92082 1070-E3
15500 SDCo 92082 1071-A3

COOL VALLEY HIGHLANDS RD
30400 SDCo 92082 1070-H4
COOL VALLEY RANCH LN
14700 SDCo 92082 1070-G2
COOL VALLEY RANCH RD
14600 SDCo 92082 1070-F3
COOLWATER DR
100 SD 92114 1290-H4
COOL WATER RANCH LN
27400 SDCo 92082 1091-A4
COOL WATER RANCH RD
27000 SDCo 92082 1091-A4
27300 SDCo 92082 1090-H4
COOP CT
100 ENCT 92024 1147-A3
COOP ST
1400 ENCT 92024 1147-A3
COOPER RD
- ImCo 92227 431-D3
700 CHV 91911 1330-J3
COOPER ST
3400 SD 92104 1269-F7
COOPERAGE CT
13200 PWY 92064 1170-E2
COOPER CIENEGA TKTR
38100 SDCo 92086 409-J5
COOS BAY CT
5700 SD 92105 1290-B1
COPA DE ORO DR
1500 SD 92037 1247-H3
COPE RD
15800 SDCo 92065 1173-J4
COPELAND AV
4200 SD 92105 1269-H4
4400 SD 92116 1269-H4
COPELAND PL
4200 SD 92116 1269-G4
COPING PL
12000 SDCo 92040 1231-J2
12000 SDCo 92040 1232-A1
COPLEY AV
2700 SD 92116 1269-D3
COPLEY DR
6400 SD 92111 1228-J7
6400 SD 92111 1229-A7
COPLEY PL
200 ELCJ 92020 1251-G5
COPLEY PARK PL
7400 SD 92111 1229-A7
COPPER AV
100 VSTA 92083 1087-F7
COPPER CT
- SMCS 92078 1128-C6
COPPER DR
500 VSTA 92083 1087-F7
COPPER CREST RD
3500 ENCT 92024 1148-B3
COPPERWOOD WY
100 OCN 92054 1086-E4
CORAL DR
3100 OCN 92056 1107-A1
CORAL ST
1100 ELCJ 92021 1251-J4
2400 VSTA 92083 1108-A6
CORAL WY
- CRLB 92009 1127-B4
- SMCS 92078 1128-D6
CORAL CREST WY
3800 SD 92173 1350-F5
CORAL GATE LN
1300 SD 92173 1350-F5
CORAL GUM CT
- SD 92139 1290-D6
CORAL LAKE AV
6300 SD 92119 1250-G5
CORAL REEF AV
5400 SD 92037 1248-A3
CORAL RIDGE RD
8700 SNTE 92071 1230-G7
CORAL SEA RD
1900 SD 92139 1290-D7
CORAL SHORES CT
3700 SD 92173 1350-F5
CORAL TREE LN
3000 SDCo 92028 1048-A1
CORALWOOD CIR
4600 CRLB 92008 1106-J6
CORALWOOD CT
200 CHV 91910 1310-C5
CORALWOOD DR
100 SD 92114 1290-G5
CORA MAE PL
8500 SNTE 92071 1231-E7
CORAZON PL
17600 SD 92127 1149-J7
CORBEL CT
17500 SD 92128 1170-D1
CORBETT CT
12800 SD 92130 1188-C5
CORBIE CIR
1300 VSTA 92083 1087-G4
CORBIN ST
1800 SD 92154 1350-B3
CORBINA AL
- SD 92136 1289-E6
CORD LN
8900 SD 92126 1209-D4
CORD PL
1800 SDCo 92019 1272-C3
CORDELIA ST
1500 CHV 91913 1311-C7
1500 CHV 91913 1331-C1
CORDELL CT
1500 ELCJ 92020 1251-C1
CORDELLE LN
4200 SDCo 91910 1310-E5
CORDERO RD
2000 DLMR 92014 1187-G6
2000 SD 92014 1187-G6
CORDIAL RD
8400 SDCo 92021 1232-F7
CORDOBA CV
2700 SD 92014 1187-J6
CORDOBA PL
2000 CRLB 92008 1106-J7
N CORDOBA ST
3900 SDCo 91977 1271-D5
S CORDOBA ST
3400 SDCo 91977 1271-D6
CORDOBA WY
1000 VSTA 92083 1107-H4
4500 OCN 92056 1107-E4
CORDOBA BAY CT
- SD 92105 1290-B1
CORDOBES CV
4200 SD 92130 1188-B7

CORDOVA CT
1000 CHV 91910 1311-A7
CORDOVA DR
900 CHV 91910 1310-J7
900 CHV 91910 1311-A7
CORDOVA ST
700 SD 92107 1287-H2
CORDREY CT
1800 SD 92105 1289-H1
CORDREY DR
2800 SDCo 92029 1129-C7
CORDREY LN
3100 SDCo 92029 1129-C7
COREY CT
9500 SNTE 92071 1231-C5
CORFMAN RD
1000 ImCo 92249 431-B7
CORIANDER CT
800 CHV 91910 1330-J1
CORINE WY
2200 SDCo 91901 1253-G2
CORINIA CT
700 ENCT 92024 1147-J6
CORINNA CT
2400 SD 92105 1290-A1
CORINTH ST
4200 SD 92115 1270-C4
CORINTHIA WY
4900 OCN 92056 1107-F5
CORINTIA ST
3100 CRLB 92009 1128-A5
6500 CRLB 92009 1127-H5
CORK PL
4800 SD 92117 1228-G7
CORK TREE LN
1200 ESCN 92029 1129-E5
CORKWOOD AV
10000 SNTE 92071 1231-D2
CORLEY CT
11400 SD 92126 1209-B1
CORLISS ST
4800 SD 92105 1269-J7
4800 SD 92105 1270-A7
CORLITA CT
4900 SD 92122 1228-G5
CORMORANT AV
- CRLB 92009 1127-D6
CORMORANT DR
- CRLB 92009 1127-D6
CORNELIUS PL
2700 LMGR 91945 1270-F7
CORNELL AV
800 CHV 91913 1311-D5
7100 LMSA 91941 1270-F3
CORNELL DR
3800 OCN 92056 1087-A7
CORNER PL
500 SDCo 92021 1252-J4
CORNER CREEK LN
- SDCo 92028 1028-A3
CORNERSTONE CT
6000 SD 92121 1208-F6
CORNET PL
1300 SD 92154 1350-D1
CORNISH DR
400 SD 92106 1287-H3
500 ENCT 92024 1147-C7
500 SD 92107 1287-J2
900 ENCT 92024 1167-C1
1300 OCN 92054 1086-F7
1300 ENCT 92007 1167-C1
CORNWALL ST
1300 SDCo 91977 1290-J2
2500 OCN 92054 1106-E1
CORNWALLIS SQ
12200 SD 92128 1190-B1
CORNWELL CT
900 SMCS 92069 1109-C5
COROLYN DR
3900 LMSA 91941 1270-H5
CORONA CT
600 VSTA 92083 1107-H1
2400 SD 92037 1248-A3
CORONA DR
700 OCN 92057 1087-C1
CORONA ST
2500 LMGR 91945 1270-G7
3700 LMSA 91941 1270-G5
CORONA WY
13000 PWY 92064 1190-E5
CORONADO AV
600 CORD 92118 1288-G6
1000 SDCo 91977 1291-C2
1400 SD 91932 1349-J1
1400 SD 92154 1349-J1
1700 SD 92154 1350-A1
3700 SD 92107 1288-A1
4200 SD 92107 1268-A7
4400 SD 92107 1267-H7
CORONADO CIR
600 VSTA 92084 1087-J4
CORONADO CT
700 SD 92109 1267-H3
CORONADO DR
4500 OCN 92057 1066-H6
CORONADO PL
2500 VSTA 92083 1107-J5
CORONADO ST
10500 SNTE 92071 1231-F6
CORONADO VW
1800 SDCo 91901 1253-J2
1800 SDCo 91901 1254-A2
CORONADO WY
- SMCS 92078 1129-C1
CORONADO BAY RD
5000 CORD 92118 1309-E7
5000 CORD 92118 1329-D1
CORONADO CAYS BLVD
5000 CORD 92118 1329-D1
CORONADO HILLS DR
400 SMCS 92078 1129-A3
CORONADO TERRACE DR
16300 SDCo 91901 1253-G4
CORONADO VIEW RD
6000 SDCo 91901 1253-H4
CORONA ORIENTE RD
3500 SD 92109 1268-B1
3600 SD 92109 1248-B7
CORONA VISTA
1300 CHV 91902 1311-A4
1300 CHV 91913 1311-A4
1900 SDCo 92019 1272-C3
CORPORAL DR
3200 SD 92124 1249-H4
CORPORAL WY
10400 SD 92124 1249-H4
CORPORATE CT
3500 SD 92123 1249-D4

SAN DIEGO CO.
INDEX

CORPORATE DR — SAN DIEGO CO. STREET INDEX — COYOTE #1 RD 6578

STREET
Block City ZIP Pg-Grid

CORPORATE DR
400 ESCN 92029 1129-C2
CORPORATE VW
3200 VSTA 92083 1128-A1
CORPORATE CENTER DR
- SD 92154 1351-B2
CORRAL CT
300 CHV 91902 1310-G4
CORRAL GN
1100 ESCN 92026 1129-F1
CORRAL WY
5800 SD 92037 1247-G3
CORRAL CANYON RD
700 CHV 91902 1311-B3
700 CHV 91913 1311-B3
3600 SDCo 91902 1311-A2
CORRALES LN
1100 CHV 91910 1310-J5
1100 CHV 91910 1311-A5
CORRAL VIEW AV
- CHV 91913 1311-D7
CORREA LN
900 SDCo 91977 1291-D3
CORRE CAMINO
1900 SDCo 92084 1088-C1
CORRE CAMINO WY
1800 SDCo 92084 1088-B1
CORRELL RD
- ImCo 92249 6560-B6
CORRIDOR ST
9900 SD 92131 1209-J5
CORRIGAN ST
14200 SD 92129 1189-G2
CORSAIR PL
9800 SD 92126 1209-F2
CORSICA ST
1500 SD 92111 1268-H2
CORSICA WY
3300 OCN 92056 1106-J1
6400 SD 92111 1268-H2
CORSO DI ITALIA
- CHV 91910 1310-A4
CORTA ST
100 OCN 92054 1086-G1
CORTA DEL SUR
1500 LMGR 91945 1290-F2
CORTA MADRE WY
24100 SDCo 92065 1173-E2
CORTE ACEBO
- CRLB 92009 1147-F3
CORTE ADALINA
- CRLB 92009 1128-A5
CORTE ALACANTE
5000 OCN 92057 1066-J5
CORTE ALEJANDRO
- SDCo 91901 1254-E3
CORTE AL FRESCO
4300 SD 92130 1188-B6
CORTE ALMERIA
1300 OCN 92057 1066-J5
CORTE ALVEO
1300 OCN 92057 1066-J4
1300 OCN 92057 1067-A4
CORTE AMALIA
- SD 92173 1350-E3
CORTE AMARILLO
1800 OCN 92056 1087-C4
CORTE AMOR
- SDCo 91901 1234-A6
CORTE ANANAS
- CRLB 92009 1147-F2
CORTE ANDANTE
1600 OCN 92056 1087-C4
CORTE ARAUCO
12800 SD 92128 1150-D7
CORTE ARBOLES
1000 CRLB 92009 1147-F4
CORTE ASOLEADO
- SDCo 91901 1254-A3
CORTE AVISPON
1300 SMCS 92069 1108-E4
CORTE AZUL
4500 OCN 92056 1087-B4
CORTE BAGALSO
- SMCS 92069 1108-E4
CORTE BALDRE
3000 CRLB 92009 1147-H3
CORTE BARQUERO
17700 SD 92128 1150-C7
CORTE BELLAGIO
800 SDCo 92026 1129-F1
CORTE BELLEZA
- SD 92130 1208-C2
CORTE BELLO
1200 SMCS 92069 1108-E6
CORTE BOCA PEQUENO
- SD 92154 1351-H2
CORTE BOCINA
1300 OCN 92057 1066-J5
CORTE BRAVO
1400 SMCS 92069 1108-E4
CORTE CADIZ
- CRLB 92009 1147-J4
1100 OCN 92057 1087-A3
CORTE CAFETAL
2800 SD 92173 1350-D2
CORTE CALANDRIA
10900 SD 92127 1169-H5
CORTE CANGREJO
- SD 92130 1208-B3
CORTE CAPRIANA
1500 SDCo 92026 1129-E1
CORTE CARDO
7900 CRLB 92009 1148-A2
CORTE CAROLINA
7900 CRLB 92009 1147-H3
CORTE CASITAS
2500 CRLB 92009 1127-G6
CORTE CASTILLO
- CRLB 92009 1148-A4
CORTE CELESTE
2900 CRLB 92009 1147-H4
CORTE CENTINELLA
4100 SDCo 91941 1271-E4
CORTE CERRADA
600 CHV 91910 1310-G7
CORTE CICUTA
- CRLB 92009 1147-F2
CORTE CIDRO
- CRLB 92009 1147-F3
CORTE CIELO
1200 SMCS 92069 1108-E5
CORTE CIERNA
12700 SD 92128 1150-D7
CORTE CISCO
6500 CRLB 92009 1127-J5
CORTE CLARITA
3400 CRLB 92009 1147-J4
CORTE CLASICA
1400 SMCS 92069 1108-E4
CORTE CODORNIZ
10900 SD 92127 1169-H5
CORTE CRESTA
1700 OCN 92056 1087-C4
CORTE CRISALIDA
10700 SD 92127 1169-G5
CORTE CRISTAL
- SMCS 92069 1108-F4
CORTE CURVA
3400 CRLB 92009 1147-J4
CORTE DANIEL
1500 OCN 92056 1087-B4
CORTE DE ACEITUNOS
18100 SD 92128 1150-D7
CORTE DE CANDILEJAS
13100 SD 92128 1150-D7
CORTE DE CASARES
18200 SD 92128 1150-D7
CORTE DE CERA
1100 CHV 91910 1311-A6
CORTE DE CHUCENA
13300 SD 92128 1150-D7
CORTE DE COMARES
13300 SD 92128 1150-D7
CORTE DE ESTEPONA
13300 SD 92128 1150-D7
CORTE DEL ABETO
6200 CRLB 92009 1127-D4
CORTE DE LA FONDA
4300 SD 92130 1188-B6
CORTE DE LA PINA
2200 CRLB 92009 1127-E3
CORTE DE LA SIENA
4100 SD 92130 1188-B6
CORTE DE LAS PIEDRAS
1300 SDCo 92019 1252-F7
1300 SDCo 92019 1272-G1
CORTE DE LA VISTA
2800 CRLB 92009 1127-H7
CORTE DEL CEDRO
6100 CRLB 92009 1127-E3
CORTE DEL NOGAL
2000 CRLB 92009 1127-D3
CORTE DEL SOL
8000 SNTE 92071 1251-A1
CORTE DE MIJA
1500 OCN 92056 1087-B4
CORTE DE POWELL
1500 SDCo 92065 1153-B5
CORTE DESEO
1400 SMCS 92069 1108-E4
CORTE DE VELA
1200 CHV 91910 1311-A6
CORTE DE VERDAD
14400 SD 92129 1189-D1
CORTE DIANA
6600 CRLB 92009 1127-H5
CORTE DIEGO
- CRLB 92009 1128-A5
CORTE DOMINGO
- CRLB 92009 1148-A3
CORTE DORADO ESPUELA
- SDCo 91901 1254-B3
CORTE DOROTEA
12800 PWY 92064 1170-D4
CORTE DULCE
- CRLB 92009 1148-A4
1200 SMCS 92069 1108-E5
4500 OCN 92056 1087-B4
CORTE EDUARDO
- CRLB 92009 1128-A4
CORTE EMPARRADO
17800 SD 92128 1150-C7
CORTE ENCANTO
1200 SMCS 92069 1108-E5
CORTE ENCIMA DEL MUNDO
4600 SD 92130 1208-C3
CORTE ENTRADA
100 CHV 91910 1310-E7
100 CHV 91910 1330-E1
CORTE ERIZO
17700 SD 92128 1150-C7
CORTE ESPERANZA
3500 CRLB 92009 1148-A4
CORTE ESPLENDOR
3300 CRLB 92009 1147-J3
CORTE FACIL
4200 SD 92130 1188-B6
CORTE FAMOSA
1200 SMCS 92069 1108-E5
4200 SD 92130 1188-B6
CORTE FAVOR
4200 SD 92130 1188-B5
CORTE FELIPE
7900 CRLB 92009 1147-H3
CORTE FLABA
- SDCo 92067 1148-F5
CORTE FRAGATA
8400 SD 92129 1189-B4
CORTE GACELA
9400 SDCo 91977 1291-B4
CORTE GALANTE
600 SMCS 92069 1108-E5
CORTE GANSO
13800 SD 92129 1189-C3
CORTE GANZO
9300 SDCo 91977 1291-B4
CORTE GOYA
1400 OCN 92056 1087-B3
CORTE GUERA
11600 SD 92128 1170-A5
CORTE HELENA AV
100 CHV 91910 1310-C5
CORTE HUASCO
17800 SD 92128 1150-D7
CORTE ISABELINO
- SD 92130 1208-B3
CORTE JARDIN
2900 CRLB 92009 1147-H3
CORTE JARDIN DEL MAR
4400 SD 92130 1208-C4
CORTE JUANA
12900 PWY 92064 1170-D3
CORTE LA BELLA
- ENCT 92024 1148-B3
CORTE LADERA
1100 SMCS 92069 1108-F5
1600 ESCN 92025 1130-B4
CORTE LAGARTO
15800 SD 92127 1169-H5
CORTE LA LUZ
- CRLB 92009 1127-J4
CORTE LA MANTUA
1400 SDCo 92026 1129-F2
CORTE LAMPARA
14400 SD 92129 1189-D1
CORTE LANGOSTINO
4200 SD 92130 1208-B4
CORTE LA PAZ
6500 CRLB 92009 1127-J5
CORTE LARGO
6000 SDCo 92067 1168-D3
CORTE LAS LENAS
- SD 92129 1189-B6
CORTE LAS TONADAS
3400 SD 92173 1350-E3
CORTE LIMON
- CRLB 92009 1147-F3
CORTE LIRA ST
1300 SMCS 92069 1108-E4
CORTE LOMA
2700 SDCo 91901 1254-E3
6600 CRLB 92009 1127-J5
CORTE LOMAS VERDES
17500 PWY 92064 1170-E1
CORTE LOREN
600 SMCS 92069 1108-E5
CORTE LORO
3400 SD 92173 1350-E3
CORTE LUISA
3600 CRLB 92009 1148-B4
CORTE LUPE
- CRLB 92009 1128-A4
CORTE LUSSO
6900 SDCo 92067 1148-G5
CORTE LUZ DEL SOL
10900 SD 92130 1208-C3
CORTE MACIDO
- CRLB 92009 1147-J2
CORTE MADEIRA
2000 SDCo 91901 1254-B2
CORTE MADERA RD
5700 SDCo 92066 429-L6
7300 SDCo 92066 1237-B7
CORTE MAGNA
1300 OCN 92057 1066-J5
CORTE MANGO
- CRLB 92009 1147-F3
CORTE MANOLITO
700 SMCS 92069 1108-F4
CORTE MAR ASOMBROSA
- SD 92130 1208-C4
CORTE MAR DE BRISA
- SD 92130 1208-B3
CORTE MAR DE CRISTAL
- SD 92130 1208-B3
CORTE MAR DE DELFINAS
- SD 92130 1208-B3
CORTE MAR DE HIERBA
- SD 92130 1208-B3
CORTE MAR DEL CORAZON
- SD 92130 1208-C2
CORTE MARIA
- SDCo 91901 1254-A3
6600 CRLB 92009 1127-J5
CORTE MARIA AV
- CHV 91910 1310-C4
900 CHV 91911 1330-E2
CORTE MARIN
- CRLB 92009 1147-J2
CORTE MARIPOSA
4700 SDCo 91902 1310-G1
CORTE MAZATLAN
3200 CRLB 92009 1147-J4
CORTE MEJILLONES
10900 SD 92130 1208-B4
CORTE MERANO
800 SDCo 92026 1129-F1
CORTE MONTANOSO
15500 SD 92127 1169-H6
CORTE MONTECITO
3000 CRLB 92009 1127-J4
CORTE MORA
- CRLB 92009 1128-A5
CORTE MORAL
- CRLB 92009 1147-F3
CORTE MOREA
14400 SD 92129 1189-D1
CORTE MORERA
2800 CRLB 92009 1147-H2
CORTE MORITA
11600 SD 92128 1170-A5
CORTE NACION
300 CHV 91910 1310-F7
CORTE NAPOLI
12100 SD 92128 1190-B2
CORTE NINA
- CRLB 92009 1127-H7
CORTE ORCHIDIA
- CRLB 92009 1127-C5
CORTE PAGUERA
1300 OCN 92057 1066-J4
1300 OCN 92057 1067-A4
CORTE PALMARITO
- SD 92154 1351-H2
CORTE PAPAYA
2800 CRLB 92009 1147-G3
CORTE PASTEL
4500 OCN 92056 1087-B4
CORTE PATO
9300 SDCo 91977 1291-B4
CORTE PAULINA
16500 PWY 92064 1170-D4
CORTE PEDRO
2900 CRLB 92009 1147-H3
CORTE PELLEJO
8900 SDCo 91977 1291-A5
CORTE PENCA
- CRLB 92009 1148-A3
CORTE PESCADO
- SMCS 92069 1108-F4
CORTE PINTURA
5200 OCN 92057 1067-A4
CORTE PLATA ESPUELA
- SDCo 91901 1254-B3
CORTE PLAYA AZTECA
11200 SD 92124 1229-J7
11200 SD 92124 1230-A7
CORTE PLAYA BARCELONA
10900 SD 92124 1229-J7
CORTE PLAYA CANCUN
13300 SD 92124 1230-A7
CORTE PLAYA CARTAGENA
5900 SD 92124 1229-J6
CORTE PLAYA CATALINA
5000 SD 92124 1230-A7
CORTE PLAYA CORONA
11200 SD 92124 1229-J7
CORTE PLAYA DE CASTILLA
4900 SD 92124 1229-J7
CORTE PLAYA DE CORTES
11300 SD 92124 1230-A7
CORTE PLAYA ENCINO
4900 SD 92124 1229-J7
CORTE PLAYA JACINTO
5300 SD 92124 1229-J7
CORTE PLAYA LAGUNA
11400 SD 92124 1230-A7
CORTE PLAYA LAS BRISAS
11500 SD 92124 1230-A7
CORTE PLAYA MADERA
11200 SD 92124 1229-J7
CORTE PLAYA MAJORCA
10800 SD 92124 1229-J7
CORTE PLAYA MAZATLAN
10900 SD 92124 1229-J7
CORTE PLAYA MERIDA
11000 SD 92124 1229-J7
CORTE PLAYA PACIFICA
5900 SD 92124 1229-J6
CORTE PLAYA PALMERA
4900 SD 92124 1229-H7
CORTE PLAYA SAN JUAN
5100 SD 92124 1230-A7
CORTE PLAYA SOLANA
10800 SD 92124 1229-J7
CORTE PLAYA TAMPICO
11000 SD 92124 1229-J7
CORTE PLAYA TOLUCA
10800 SD 92124 1229-J7
CORTE PLENO VERANO
- SD 92130 1208-B3
CORTE POCO
- CRLB 92009 1147-J2
CORTE POTOSI
12800 SD 92128 1150-D7
CORTE POZOS
8900 SDCo 91977 1291-B5
CORTE PRESIDO
- CRLB 92009 1147-J2
CORTE PRIMAVERA
1100 CHV 91910 1311-A7
1100 CHV 91910 1331-A1
CORTE PROMENADE
- CRLB 92009 1147-J2
CORTE PULSERA
1800 OCN 92056 1087-C4
CORTE QUEZADA
8900 SDCo 91977 1291-B5
CORTE QUINTA MAR
7300 CRLB 92009 1127-F7
CORTE RAMON
6800 CRLB 92009 1128-A5
CORTE RAPALLO
1400 SDCo 92026 1129-F2
CORTE RAPOSO
15500 SD 92127 1169-J6
CORTE RAQUEL
600 SMCS 92069 1108-E5
CORTE RAYITO
2800 SD 92173 1350-D2
12700 PWY 92064 1170-C6
CORTE REAL
6600 CRLB 92009 1128-A5
CORTE ROBERTO
1500 OCN 92056 1087-B4
CORTE ROCA
2700 SDCo 91901 1254-E3
CORTE ROSADO
- CRLB 92009 1148-A4
CORTE SABIO
12200 SD 92128 1170-B5
CORTE SANO
4300 LMSA 91941 1271-A4
CORTE SAN RIO
- SMCS 92078 1128-G2
CORTE SANTA FE
6900 SD 92121 1228-H1
CORTE SANTICO
4900 OCN 92056 1087-C3
CORTE SASAFRAS
8000 CRLB 92009 1147-H3
CORTE SEGUNDO
1800 OCN 92056 1087-C5
CORTE SIERRA
- SDCo 91901 1254-A3
CORTE SOBRADO
17600 SD 92128 1150-D7
CORTE SOL DEL DIOS
4600 SD 92130 1208-C3
CORTE SONRISA
3400 CRLB 92009 1147-J4
CORTE SOSEGADO
11700 SD 92128 1170-A4
CORTE SUAVE
4500 OCN 92056 1087-B3
CORTE SUSANA
13000 PWY 92064 1170-D4
CORTE TEMPLANZA
11700 SD 92128 1170-A4
CORTE TERRAL
3300 CRLB 92009 1128-A5
CORTE TEZCUCO
11900 SD 92128 1150-A7
CORTE TIBURON
3300 CRLB 92009 1147-J3
CORTE TIERRA ALTA
4000 SDCo 91941 1271-E4
CORTE TIERRA BAJA
10200 SDCo 91941 1271-E4
CORTE TILO
3000 CRLB 92009 1147-H3
CORTE TORERO
1800 OCN 92056 1087-C4
CORTE TRABUCO
3000 CRLB 92009 1127-J5
CORTE VALDEZ
3000 CRLB 92009 1127-J4
CORTE VENTANA
1700 OCN 92056 1087-C4
CORTE VERA CRUZ
3200 CRLB 92009 1147-J4
CORTE VERANO
1600 OCN 92056 1087-C4
CORTE VERDE
2900 SDCo 91901 1254-F3
CORTE VERSO
3300 CRLB 92009 1147-J3
CORTE VICENZA
12100 SD 92128 1190-B2
CORTE VIEJO
1700 OCN 92056 1087-C4
3400 CRLB 92009 1127-J5
CORTE VIOLETA
7700 CRLB 92009 1147-J3
CORTE YOLANDA
- CRLB 92009 1128-A4
CORTEZ
19200 SDCo 92029 1149-E4
CORTEZ AV
- SDCo 92026 1109-E5
- IMPB 91932 1349-E2
600 VSTA 92084 1087-H4
1800 ESCN 92026 1109-E5
CORTEZ GN
1800 ESCN 92026 1109-E5
CORTEZ PL
200 SD 92037 1247-E3
CORTEZ WY
3700 OCN 92056 1107-A1
4000 SDCo 91977 1271-D4
CORTE ZAFIRO
- SMCS 92069 1108-G4
CORTINA CIR
1400 ESCN 92029 1149-G1
1900 ESCN 92029 1129-G7
CORTINA CT
7600 CRLB 92009 1147-H1
CORTO LN
1300 SDCo 92020 1271-J1
CORTO ST
300 SOLB 92075 1167-F7
2800 OCN 92054 1086-E6
CORVALLA DR
1700 VSTA 92084 1087-J2
1700 VSTA 92084 1088-A2
CORVALLIS ST
3400 CRLB 92008 1106-J4
CORVIDAE ST
1300 CRLB 92009 1127-B7
CORVINA ST
600 IMPB 91932 1329-F7
CORVUS PL
8700 SD 92126 1209-C2
CORY CT
8800 SDCo 91977 1271-A7
COSALA ST
200 VSTA 92084 1087-H4
COSGROVE DR
2200 SDCo 91901 1234-A5
COSIRA CT
4200 SD 92124 1249-J2
COSMIT LN
- SDCo 92036 1175-J3
- SDCo 92036 1176-A2
COSMIT WY
- SDCo 92036 1175-J3
- SDCo 92036 1176-A2
COSMO AV
800 ELCJ 92019 1252-B7
1500 SDCo 92019 1252-B7
COSMO CT
7000 SD 92111 1248-J3
COSMO ST
4000 SD 92111 1248-J3
COSMOS CT
2200 CRLB 92009 1127-E3
COSOY WY
4200 SD 92103 1268-F4
COSTA AV
1300 CHV 91911 1330-C4
COSTA LN
14400 SDCo 92021 1232-H5
COSTA PL
300 SD 92037 1247-F3
COSTA ALTA DR
3000 CRLB 92009 1127-J5
COSTA BELLA DR
3800 LMSA 91941 1270-H5
COSTA BELLA ST
3600 LMGR 91945 1270-G5
3800 LMSA 91941 1270-G5
COSTA BELLA WY
3800 LMSA 91941 1270-G5
COSTADA CT
1700 LMGR 91945 1290-F1
COSTA DEL MAR RD
2000 CRLB 92009 1147-E1
2100 CRLB 92009 1127-E7
COSTA DEL REY
3700 OCN 92056 1107-B1
COSTA LAGO ST
9800 SDCo 91977 1291-D3
COSTALOT LN
11800 SDCo 92040 1211-J5
COSTALOTA RD
29300 SDCo 92082 1069-B7
COSTA VERDE BLVD
8500 SD 92122 1228-C3
COSTA VERDE LN
1700 SDCo 92084 1108-C2
COSTA VISTA WY
2000 OCN 92054 1106-F1
COSTEBELLE DR
2600 SD 92037 1227-J6
COSTEBELLE WY
7900 SD 92037 1227-J5
COTORRO RD
18000 SD 92128 1150-A7
COTORRO WY
12000 SD 92128 1150-B7
COTTAGE AV
5400 SD 92120 1250-B5
COTTAGE WY
- ENCT 92024 1147-F4
2000 VSTA 92083 1108-A5
COTTAGE GARDEN RD
- SDCo 92082 1071-A6
COTTAGE GLEN CT
1600 ENCT 92024 1147-G5
COTTAGE GROVE DR
1700 ENCT 92024 1147-H6
COTTAGE GROVE LN
200 ENCT 92024 1147-H6
COTTINGHAM CT
200 OCN 92054 1086-E5
COTTINGHAM ST
2900 OCN 92054 1086-D5
COTTINGTON LN
7100 SD 92139 1290-G7
COTTON ST
600 SD 92102 1289-J3
COTTONPATCH WY
100 ELCJ 92020 1251-C6
COTTONTAIL LN
1300 SD 92037 1247-G2
31300 SDCo 92003 1068-D2
COTTONTAIL RD
1000 VSTA 92083 1108-A5
COTTONWOOD AV
1700 CRLB 92009 1127-E6
8600 SNTE 92071 1231-E5
COTTONWOOD CIR
2000 ELCN 92243 6559-F1
COTTONWOOD CT
1400 SMCS 92069 1109-C6
3300 SD 92037 1228-B4
COTTONWOOD DR
1100 ELCN 92243 6499-F3
1100 ELCN 92243 6559-F1
1200 OCN 92056 1087-C2
COTTONWOOD PL
1800 ESCN 92026 1109-D5
COTTONWOOD RD
- SDCo 91906 1296-C6
- SDCo 91906 (1297-A7 See Page 1296)
- SDCo 91906 (1317-C1 See Page 1296)
100 SD 92173 1350-F4
COTTONWOOD ST
- SDCo 92055 1086-B2
3700 SD 92113 1289-G7
COTTONWOOD GROVE CT
- SD 92128 1190-A6
COTTONWOOD SPRINGS LN
3000 SDCo 91935 1272-D5
3000 SDCo 92019 1272-D5
COTTONWOOD VIEW DR
3000 SDCo 92019 1272-C5
COUGAR DR
2400 CRLB 92008 1127-D1
COUGAR PASS RD
26800 SDCo 92026 1089-G3
27200 ESCN 92026 1089-H4
COUGAR SUMMIT
3500 SDCo 91901 1275-B4
COULTER LN
2100 SDCo 92036 1156-A5
COULTER CREEK
29400 SDCo 92082 1069-G6
COULTER RIDGE RD
- SDCo 92036 1156-F5
COUNA WY
23900 SDCo 92065 1173-E2
COUNTRY LN
300 ESCN 92025 1130-B5
300 SDCo 92025 1130-B5
2300 SDCo 92028 1028-D6
S COUNTRY LN
1700 ESCN 92025 1130-B5
COUNTRY PL
2100 ESCN 92026 1109-G5
COUNTRY RD
2200 SDCo 92028 1028-E6
12500 SDCo 92082 1070-B4
COUNTRY TER
500 SDCo 92065 1152-G4
COUNTRY WY
2900 SDCo 92019 1272-D6
COUNTRY CLUB DR
- CHV 91911 1330-D1
400 ESCN 92029 1129-D3
400 SDCo 92029 1129-D3
3100 SDCo 92036 1156-E1
6800 SD 92037 1247-G1
6800 SD 92037 1227-G7
E COUNTRY CLUB DR
2500 SDCo 92029 1129-C6
COUNTRY CLUB LN
200 OCN 92054 1086-C7
300 ESCN 92026 1109-D5
400 CORD 92118 1288-G6
2900 SDCo 92028 1028-D7
12000 SDCo 92040 1231-J2
COUNTRY CLUB PL
8800 SDCo 91977 1271-A4
COUNTRY CLUB RD
2500 SDCo 92004 (1078-J3 See Page 1058)
4000 SDCo 92004 (1079-A7 See Page 1058)
COUNTRY CREEK RD
2200 SMCS 92069 1108-J1
13800 PWY 92064 1190-F1
COUNTRY CREST DR
1300 ELCJ 92021 1252-B2
COUNTRY DAY LN
- SD 92037 1228-C2
COUNTRY DAY RD
16000 PWY 92064 1170-G3
COUNTRY ESTATES DR
1200 VSTA 92084 1088-A2
COUNTRY GARDEN LN
500 SDCo 92069 1088-J6
600 SDCo 92069 1089-A6
COUNTRY GIRL LN
- SD 92127 1169-A1
COUNTRY GLEN RD
- SDCo 92028 1047-G6
COUNTRY GROVE LN
1900 ENCT 92024 1147-H6
COUNTRYHAVEN CT
2000 ENCT 92024 1147-H6
COUNTRYHAVEN RD
100 ENCT 92024 1147-H7
COUNTRY HILL RD
15100 PWY 92064 1170-H7
COUNTRY MEADOW LN
3200 SDCo 92025 1150-D2
3400 ESCN 92025 1150-D2
COUNTRY MEADOWS RD
2600 SDCo 91901 1234-C5
COUNTRY OAKS LN
26900 SDCo 92082 1090-G5
COUNTRY ROSE CIR
3200 ENCT 92024 1148-C4
COUNTRY SCENES CT
10100 SNTE 92071 1231-D4
COUNTRYSIDE DR
1600 VSTA 92083 1107-H5
5100 SD 92115 1270-A2
COUNTRYSIDE PL
1700 VSTA 92083 1107-H5
COUNTRY SQUIRE
1700 VSTA 92083 1107-H5
COUNTRY SQUIRE DR
15800 PWY 92064 1170-C5
COUNTRY TRAILS
3600 SDCo 91902 1311-B1
4300 CHV 91913 1311-B1
COUNTRY TRAILS LN
4300 CHV 91913 1311-C3
COUNTRY VIEW GN
2300 ESCN 92026 1109-B4
COUNTRYVIEW LN
1400 VSTA 92083 1107-H4
COUNTRY VIEW RD
10000 SDCo 91941 1271-D1
COUNTRY VILLA RD
15800 SDCo 92065 1173-D4
COUNTRY VISTAS LN
1500 CHV 91902 1311-A3
1600 CHV 91913 1311-B4
COUNTRYWOOD CT
2000 ENCT 92024 1147-H6
COUNTRYWOOD LN
100 ENCT 92024 1147-H6
1100 VSTA 92083 1107-J3
1100 VSTA 92083 1108-A4
COUNTRYWOOD WY
2000 ENCT 92024 1147-H6
COUNTY CENTER TWO RD
- ImCo 92243 6559-G6
COURAGE ST
- VSTA 92083 1107-G5
COURAGEOUS LN
4800 CRLB 92008 1106-H7
COURIER WY
13900 PWY 92064 1190-G4
COURSER AV
2900 SD 92117 1248-C2
COURSER CT
4300 SD 92117 1248-C2
COURT ST
2100 DLMR 92014 1187-F3
COURT WY
900 SD 92103 1268-J4
COURTLAND TER
13200 SD 92130 1187-J5
COURTNEY DR
7200 SD 92111 1268-J1
7200 SD 92111 1269-A1
COURTNEY LN
8300 SNTE 92071 1250-J1
COURTYARD DR
9900 SD 92131 1209-H5
COUSER WY
10400 SDCo 92059 1029-E7
10400 SDCo 92059 1049-E1
10400 SDCo 92082 1049-E1
COUSER CANYON RD
10600 SDCo 92026 1049-B1
10600 SDCo 92028 1049-B1
10600 SDCo 92059 1049-B1
10600 SDCo 92028 1029-B7
14600 SDCo 92082 1049-F4
COUSHATTA LN
1100 SDCo 91977 1291-A2
COUSINO WY
1700 SDCo 92019 1272-C2
COUSTEAU CT
2300 VSTA 92083 1107-H7
COUTS ST
3400 SD 92140 1268-G6
3500 SD 92110 1268-G6
4100 SD 92103 1268-G5
COVE CT
1500 SMCS 92069 1129-C1
2600 VSTA 92083 1107-H5
COVE DR
4500 CRLB 92008 1106-H7
COVENTRY RD
1200 VSTA 92084 1088-A6
2600 CRLB 92008 1106-J5
COVE VIEW PL
5000 SD 92154 1350-J1
COVE VIEW WY
1100 SD 92154 1350-J1
COVEY LN
8900 SDCo 92026 1069-B1
COVEY PL
1000 CHV 91913 1311-D6
COVINA CIR
8700 SD 92126 1209-C5
COVINA CT
10200 SD 92126 1209-C5
COVINA PL
10200 SD 92126 1209-C5
COVINA ST
8500 SD 92126 1209-C5
COVINGTON RD
2600 SD 92104 1269-F7
COW TR
9300 SNTE 92071 1231-E5
COWBOY CT
100 SDCo 92065 1152-J5
COWELL CT
10100 SD 92124 1249-G3
COWLES MOUNTAIN BLVD
5600 LMSA 91942 1250-G7
6100 SD 92119 1250-J2
7600 SNTE 92071 1250-J2
COWLES MOUNTAIN CT
7800 SD 92119 1250-G4
COWLES MOUNTAIN PL
7800 SD 92119 1250-G6
COWLEY WY
2100 SD 92110 1268-G1
2300 SD 92110 1248-G6
2800 SD 92111 1248-F5
2800 SD 92117 1248-F5
COWRIE AV
- SD 92037 1227-G6
COX RD
- ImCo 92233 411-A9
300 SMCS 92069 1108-J2
300 SMCS 92069 1109-A2
COY CT
1300 ELCJ 92021 1252-A2
COYOTE CT
- CRLB 92008 1107-D7
1700 VSTA 92084 1087-J3
17000 PWY 92064 1170-D2
COYOTE RD
700 SDCo 91901 1234-C4
COYOTE RDG
1800 SDCo 92021 1252-D3
COYOTE RUN
30200 SDCo 92082 1070-G4
COYOTE RW
- SDCo 91935 1292-E3
COYOTE TR
- SDCo 92082 1069-F3
COYOTE WY
- SDCo 92004 410-B6
COYOTE #1 RD
- ImCo 92259 430-H8

SAN DIEGO CO.
INDEX

STREET
Block City ZIP Pg-Grid
COYOTE #2 RD
- ImCo 92259 430-J8
COYOTE BUSH DR
9200 SD 92127 1169-D2
9200 SDCo 92127 1169-D2
COYOTE CANYON RD
2500 SDCo 92025 1150-D2
COYOTE CREEK TR
15900 PWY 92064 1171-C6
COYOTE CREST
1700 SDCo 92028 1028-A5
COYOTE HILL GN
10500 ESCN 92026 1109-F3
10500 SDCo 92026 1109-F3
COYOTE HOLLER RD
23200 SDCo 91963 (1315-H6
See Page 1294)
COYOTE RIDGE LN
- CHV 91915 1311-H5
COYOTE RIDGE TER
- CHV 91915 1311-H5
COYOTERO DR
13100 PWY 92064 1190-E4
COYOTES WY
1100 SMCS 92069 1128-E3
COYOTE VISTA WY
13000 SDCo 91935 1272-H6
COZUMEL CT
100 SOLB 92075 1167-D7
COZY CT
800 SDCo 92028 1027-E3
COZZENS CT
4300 SD 92122 1228-E6
COZZENS ST
5800 SD 92122 1228-E6
CRABAPPLE CT
4300 SD 92154 1330-G7
CRABTREE ST
6400 SD 92114 1290-D6
CRADLE MOUNTAIN LN
12700 SDCo 92040 1212-B7
CRAIG CT
2100 LMGR 91945 1290-J1
CRAIG RD
- SD 92106 1288-A5
CRAIGIE ST
4400 SD 92102 1289-J3
CRAIGMONT ST
1300 ELCJ 92019 1251-J7
1300 ELCJ 92019 1252-A7
CRAIGMORE AV
1700 ESCN 92027 1130-D2
CRAMPTON CT
6600 SD 92119 1250-F5
CRANBERRY CT
4300 SD 92154 1350-G1
CRANBERRY ST
5300 OCN 92057 1067-D6
CRANBROOK CT
3000 SD 92037 1228-A4
CRANDALL CT
2500 SD 92111 1248-J7
2500 SD 92111 1249-A7
CRANDALL DR
1800 SD 92111 1268-J1
1800 SD 92111 1269-A1
2100 SD 92111 1249-A7
2500 SD 92111 1248-J7
CRANE CT
- CRLB 92009 1127-C6
- ImCo 92249 6560-B7
CRANE PL
3700 SD 92103 1268-J6
CRANE ST
2800 LMGR 91945 1270-J6
CRANN AV
1300 CHV 91911 1330-C4
CRANSTON DR
2200 ESCN 92025 1130-A7
CRANSTON CREST
200 ESCN 92025 1130-A7
CRARY ST
7500 LMSA 91942 1250-G6
CRATER
14100 SDCo 92040 1232-F4
CRATER DR
11100 SD 92126 1209-D2
CRATER PL
11100 SD 92126 1209-C2
CRATER LAKE WY
4300 OCN 92054 1086-G1
CRAVEN RD
100 SMCS 92069 1128-F2
100 SMCS 92078 1128-F2
4100 OCN 92057 1086-H3
CRAVEN ST
2300 NATC 92136 1309-G1
2300 SD 92136 1289-G7
2300 SD 92136 1309-G1
CRAVEN RIDGE WY
10800 SD 92130 1208-E1
CRAWFORD CT
- SD 92120 1249-J7
CRAWFORD ST
6000 SD 92120 1249-J7
CRAY CT
10600 SD 92121 1207-J6
CRAZY COLT CIR
800 VSTA 92083 1107-H2
CRAZY HORSE DR
11200 SDCo 92040 1211-F6
11300 SDCo 92040 1231-F1
11300 SNTE 92071 1231-F1
CRAZY HORSE TR
10500 SNTE 92071 1231-E6
CRECIENTE CT
11300 SD 92127 1149-J7
CRECIENTE WY
17700 SD 92127 1149-J7
CREE CT
12900 PWY 92064 1190-D4
CREE DR
13000 PWY 92064 1190-D4
CREEK RD
- SDCo 92036 1156-E7
400 OCN 92054 1086-G2
11800 PWY 92064 1210-D1
11800 SD 92145 1210-D1
11800 PWY 92064 1190-C7
E CREEK RD
15800 SDCo 92021 1233-C3
CREEK ST
1500 SMCS 92069 1108-D7
CREEK BLUFF DR
11700 PWY 92064 1210-C1
CREEKBRIDGE PL
10800 SD 92128 1189-H6
CREEKFORD DR
8900 SDCo 92040 1231-J6
CREEK HILLS RD
15500 SDCo 92021 1213-C7
CREEK HOLLOW DR
25000 SDCo 92065 1153-H4
CREEK HOLLOW PL
2200 ESCN 92026 1109-J3
CREEKNETTLE RD
600 SMCS 92078 1128-G2
CREEK PARK DR
12900 PWY 92064 1190-E5
CREEK PARK LN
13200 PWY 92064 1190-E5
CREEKSIDE AV
600 OCN 92057 1067-D6
CREEKSIDE CT
9300 SNTE 92071 1231-G5
12100 SD 92131 1210-A2
N CREEKSIDE DR
- CHV 91915 1311-H5
S CREEKSIDE DR
1300 CHV 91915 1311-J7
CREEKSIDE LN
13200 PWY 92064 1190-E5
CREEKSIDE PL
700 CHV 91914 1311-G3
2100 ESCN 92029 1129-E6
CREEKSTONE LN
11300 SD 92128 1189-J6
11300 SD 92128 1190-A6
CREEKVIEW DR
12300 SD 92128 1189-H6
CREEKVIEW LN
2100 SDCo 92028 1027-H7
CREEK VISTA DR
13000 PWY 92064 1190-E5
CREEKWOOD CT
12600 SD 92129 1189-C5
CREEKWOOD LN
8600 SD 92129 1189-C5
CREEKWOOD WY
800 CHV 91913 1311-E4
CREELMAN LN
100 SDCo 92065 1173-A2
300 SDCo 92065 1172-G2
CREENCIA PL
1400 ESCN 92027 1110-A6
CREGAR ST
100 OCN 92054 1086-C6
CREIGHTON WY
5900 SD 92114 1290-C5
CRELA ST
3000 SDCo 91902 1310-D4
CRENSHAW ST
1800 SD 92105 1289-G1
CRESCENDO DR
26300 SDCo 92026 1109-H1
26400 SDCo 92026 1089-H7
CRESCENT BEND
900 SDCo 92028 1027-H4
CRESCENT CT
900 VSTA 92084 1088-A7
N CRESCENT CT
600 SD 92103 1268-J6
S CRESCENT CT
600 SD 92103 1268-J6
CRESCENT DR
500 VSTA 92084 1087-J7
600 CHV 91911 1330-H1
900 VSTA 92084 1088-A7
2300 SD 92103 1268-G5
3800 SDCo 92036 1156-E2
CRESCENT LN
600 VSTA 92084 1088-A7
CRESCENT PL
- SMCS 92078 1128-C6
CRESCENT BEND PL
1100 SDCo 92028 1027-H4
CRESCENT HEIGHTS DR
4700 OCN 92056 1087-D4
CRESCENT HEIGHTS RD
22800 SDCo 92070 409-J10
CRESCENT HILL WY
28300 SDCo 92026 1089-E3
CRESCENT KNOLLS GN
1600 ESCN 92029 1129-F6
CRESCENT MOON DR
30300 SDCo 92082 1070-G1
CRESCENT POINT RD
4000 CRLB 92008 1106-H6
CRESCENT RIDGE RD
7500 SNTE 92071 1230-G7
N CRESCENT RIDGE RD
1100 SDCo 92028 1027-H4
CRESITA DR
5000 SD 92115 1270-C2
CRESPO DR
1500 SD 92037 1227-G6
CRESSA CT
1400 CRLB 92009 1127-C7
CRESSY CT
1500 ELCJ 92020 1251-B3
CREST DR
- ESCN 92025 1130-A6
400 VSTA 92084 1087-J7
500 ENCT 92024 1147-F7
500 CHV 91910 1310-G7
500 CHV 91910 1330-G1
600 SDCo 92019 1252-E6
900 ENCT 92024 1167-F1
1700 ENCT 92007 1167-F2
2000 SDCo 92021 1252-H4
2500 CRLB 92008 1106-F3
9300 SDCo 91977 1271-C7
CREST HTS
4000 SDCo 92028 1028-F4
CREST RD
700 DLMR 92014 1187-G4
700 SD 92014 1187-G5
12000 PWY 92064 1190-B5
N CREST RD
100 SDCo 92021 1252-J2
CREST ST
100 ESCN 92025 1129-H1
2000 ESCN 92029 1129-E6
CREST WY
13800 SD 92014 1187-G6
CRESTA CT
3600 OCN 92056 1107-D3
12500 SD 92128 1170-C2
CRESTA DR
16600 SD 92128 1170-C3
CRESTA PL
12500 SD 92128 1170-C3
CRESTA WY
- CHV 91910 1310-D5
12500 SD 92128 1170-C3
CRESTA BLANCA
- VSTA 92083 1107-C2
CRESTA BONITA DR
3700 SDCo 91902 1310-E3
CRESTA LOMA
2800 SDCo 92025 1130-E7
CRESTA LOMA DR
2700 SDCo 92028 1047-J1
CRESTA LOMA LN
2700 SDCo 92028 1047-J1
CRESTA VERDE LN
4400 SDCo 91902 1310-G2
CRESTBROOK PL
- SD 92128 1190-A6
CRESTCOURT LN
- SDCo 92028 1027-H1
CRESTED BUTTE ST
500 CHV 91911 1330-A3
CRESTGLEN LN
9900 SDCo 91977 1271-D6
CRESTHAVEN DR
1900 VSTA 92084 1087-H2
6200 LMSA 91942 1251-C6
CRESTHAVEN PL
1400 OCN 92056 1087-E3
CREST HILL LN
2200 SDCo 92028 1027-H6
CRESTHILL PL
1100 SDCo 92021 1251-J2
CRESTHILL RD
1200 SDCo 92021 1251-J2
CREST KNOLLS CT
12600 SD 92130 1188-C6
CRESTLAND DR
4800 SDCo 91941 1271-E2
CRESTLANE CT
9900 SDCo 91977 1271-D7
CRESTLINE DR
2100 OCN 92054 1086-C6
2400 LMGR 91945 1270-H7
14500 PWY 92064 1191-E3
CRESTLINE RD
32600 SDCo 92060 409-G7
CRESTMAR PT
8900 SD 92121 1208-J7
8900 SD 92121 1228-J1
CRESTMONT PL
4700 OCN 92056 1087-E3
CRESTMORE AV
8800 SDCo 91977 1290-J3
CRESTON DR
5500 SD 92114 1290-B3
CRESTOP LN
2500 SDCo 91977 1271-D7
CRESTRIDGE CT
- SDCo 92026 1089-B1
CRESTRIDGE DR
1400 OCN 92054 1086-E7
CRESTSIDE PL
10100 SDCo 91977 1271-E7
CRESTSTONE PL
3800 SD 92130 1188-A4
CRESTVIEW CT
700 SMCS 92069 1128-E2
15200 PWY 92064 1170-G7
CRESTVIEW DR
300 CHV 91902 1311-A3
1300 OCN 92056 1087-E3
4200 SDCo 91941 1271-E4
4700 CRLB 92008 1107-A7
CRESTVIEW GN
200 ESCN 92026 1109-G4
CREST VIEW GN
2300 ESCN 92026 1109-C3
CRESTVIEW HTS
10100 SDCo 91941 1271-D3
CRESTVIEW PL
300 VSTA 92083 1107-J1
CREST VIEW RD
700 VSTA 92083 1107-H1
CREST VIEW ESTATES PL
2300 SDCo 92027 1130-E2
CRESTWIND DR
21600 SDCo 92029 1129-A5
CRESTWOOD AV
12700 PWY 92064 1190-C2
CRESTWOOD DR
500 OCN 92054 1086-D3
CRESTWOOD PL
600 ESCN 92026 1109-H4
3600 SD 92103 1269-C6
CRESTWOOD RD
- SDCo 91906 (1299-E1
See Page 1298)
- SDCo 92066 (1299-E1
See Page 1298)
CRESWICK CT
12200 SD 92128 1190-B1
CRETE ST
3300 SD 92117 1248-E6
CRIBBAGE LN
400 SMCS 92069 1128-F1
CRICKET HILL
13400 PWY 92064 1170-E4
CRIMSON DR
800 SMCS 92069 1109-A5
CRIMSON FIRE CT
9700 SDCo 91941 1271-C4
CRISIE LN
2600 SDCo 92025 1130-C7
2600 ESCN 92025 1130-C7
CRISP CT
5300 SD 92117 1228-G6
CRISP WY
4700 SD 92117 1228-G7
CRISSCROSS LN
12200 SD 92129 1189-B7
CRISTALLO PL
12900 SD 92130 1188-B5
CRISTIANITOS RD
- SDCo 92055 408-J5
- SDCo 92672 1023-C1
CRISTOBAL DR
9900 SDCo 91977 1271-E6
CRISTOBAL WY
3200 SDCo 91977 1271-E6
CROCKER RD
14800 PWY 92064 1190-H1
14800 PWY 92064 1170-H7
CROCKETT ST
8700 LMSA 91942 1251-A6
CROCUS CT
300 ENCT 92024 1147-B4
CROFT ST
3600 SD 92105 1270-B6
E CROFTON LN
1700 ESCN 92027 1110-C7
CROFTON ST
2000 SDCo 91977 1291-A1
CROMWELL CT
5200 SD 92116 1269-F2
CROMWELL PL
3400 SD 92116 1269-F2
CROMWELL WY
700 VSTA 92084 1088-A7
CRONAN CIR
7900 SD 92126 1209-A3
CROOKED CREEK CT
4700 SD 92113 1289-J5
CROOKED OAK LN
28300 SDCo 92026 1089-E3
CROQUET CT
- SDCo 92067 1168-F7
CROSBY RD
400 SD 92113 1289-C5
400 SD 92101 1289-C5
CROSBY ST
400 SD 92113 1289-C5
900 ELCJ 92021 1251-J3
1000 SDCo 92021 1251-J3
CROSLEY TKTR
- SDCo 92060 409-F5
CROSS RD
- ImCo 92251 6499-H2
- IMP 92243 6499-H2
- IMP 92251 6499-H2
- SDCo 91905 430-C7
2100 ELCN 92243 6499-H3
2100 ImCo 92243 6499-H3
CROSS ST
1800 SD 92110 1268-G2
CROSSBILL CT
- CRLB 92009 1127-D4
CROSS CREEK LN
2400 ESCN 92025 1130-D6
CROSS CREEK PL
2500 ESCN 92025 1130-D7
CROSS CREEK RD
1600 SDCo 92084 1068-B6
CROSSCREEK RD
2000 CHV 91913 1311-E4
CROSS CREEK TER
10300 SD 92131 1209-H4
CROSS FOX CT
16000 PWY 92064 1170-G4
CROSSHAVEN LN
2500 SD 92139 1290-G7
CROSSLAND CT
10100 SNTE 92071 1231-A3
CROSSLE CT
2000 SDCo 92019 1272-C4
CROSSPOINT CT
800 SD 92114 1290-G3
CROSSROCK RD
14000 PWY 92064 1190-B2
CROSSWAY CT
8700 SNTE 92071 1230-H7
CROSSWINDS RD
1400 SDCo 92065 1152-F3
N CROSTHWAITE CIR
12200 PWY 92064 1190-F6
CROSWAITHE ST
100 OCN 92054 1106-B3
CROTON CT
5300 SD 92109 1248-B3
CROUCH ST
100 OCN 92054 1086-D7
800 OCN 92054 1106-D1
CROW CT
5900 SD 92120 1250-C5
CROWDER LN
4700 LMSA 91941 1270-J2
CROWELL ST
1500 SD 92103 1268-H6
CROWLEY CT
7100 SD 92119 1250-F4
CROWN CT
1600 SDCo 92028 1027-J5
CROWN ST
5100 SD 92110 1268-F2
CROWN CREST LN
2600 SD 92037 1227-J1
CROWN HILL LN
23600 SDCo 92027 1111-D4
CROWNHILL RD
2100 SD 92109 1248-A4
CROWN POINT CT
1500 CHV 91911 1330-H4
CROWNPOINT CT
3800 CRLB 92008 1107-B4
CROWN POINT DR
3300 SD 92109 1268-A1
3600 SD 92109 1248-A7
CROWNPOINT PL
2700 ESCN 92027 1130-F1
CROWNRIDGE LN
2700 SDCo 91977 1271-E7
CROWN VALLEY RD
15900 PWY 92064 1170-D5
CROWNVIEW CT
- SMCS 92069 1108-J4
CROWN VIEW TER
3400 OCN 92056 1086-H7
CROWN VIEW WY
2100 OCN 92056 1086-J7
CROWS NEST LN
7200 SD 92126 1208-J3
CROWTHORNE CT
- SDCo 92084 1108-D1
CROYDON LN
100 ELCJ 92020 1251-C5
CRUCES DR
37500 SDCo 92086 409-K5
CRUICKSHANK RD
- ImCo 92243 6500-B3
CRUIKSHANK DR
- ELCN 92243 6499-E3
CRUSADER AV
- ESCN 92027 1130-C1
CRYSTAL CT
- SMCS 92078 1128-D6
3100 SDCo 92025 1150-D1
CRYSTAL DR
4900 SD 92109 1247-G5
5100 SD 92037 1247-G5
CRYSTAL LN
1100 SDCo 92020 1251-J7
1100 SDCo 92020 1271-J1
CRYSTAL ST
4100 OCN 92056 1087-C6
CRYSTALAIRE DR
6400 SD 92120 1250-D6
CRYSTAL CLEAR DR
- SDCo 91977 1291-F2
CRYSTAL CLEAR LN
- SDCo 91977 1291-F2
CRYSTAL COVE WY
- SMCS 92069 1128-A3
CRYSTAL CREEK CT
800 CHV 91910 1311-B6
CRYSTAL DAWN LN
4000 SD 92122 1228-C3
CRYSTAL DOWNS DR
1100 CHV 91915 1311-G6
CRYSTAL GROVE CT
- SD 92130 1188-J3
CRYSTAL LAKE AV
6200 SD 92119 1250-H6
CRYSTALLITE LN
13600 SDCo 92082 1070-D2
CRYSTAL OAKS WY
- SD 92131 1209-G2
CRYSTAL RIDGE CT
1600 VSTA 92083 1107-G4
9700 SDCo 92026 1089-C2
CRYSTAL RIDGE DR
9700 SDCo 92026 1089-C2
CRYSTAL RIDGE GN
2200 ESCN 92026 1109-B3
CRYSTAL RIDGE RD
2800 ENCT 92024 1148-A5
CRYSTAL RIDGE WY
1700 VSTA 92083 1107-G5
CRYSTAL SPRINGS DR
1200 CHV 91915 1311-G6
CRYSTAL SPRINGS RD
10900 SNTE 92071 1231-F6
CRYSTAL VIEW LN
15500 PWY 92064 1191-B2
CRYSTAL VIEW RD
14800 SDCo 92021 1232-J4
CRYSTAL WOOD DR
3400 OCN 92054 1086-E3
CUATRO LN
1700 SDCo 92028 1027-J4
CUBA AV
- SD 92140 1268-F6
CUBIST CT
4700 OCN 92057 1087-B1
CUCA ST
14100 SD 92129 1189-H2
CUCHARA DR
1100 DLMR 92014 1187-G5
CUCHILLO ST
700 OCN 92057 1067-C7
700 OCN 92057 1087-C1
CUDAHY PL
1000 SD 92110 1268-E3
CUERVO RD
1900 SDCo 92084 1088-C7
CUESTA PL
3300 CRLB 92009 1147-J2
CUESTA DEL SOL
11400 SDCo 92040 1232-E5
CUESTA NORTE
1300 SDCo 92028 1027-H5
CUFF RD
- ImCo - 411-C5
- ImCo 92257 411-C7
CUIN RD
- ImCo 92251 430-L5
CUISSE LN
1800 SDCo 92004 1058-G6
CULBERTSON AV
4400 LMSA 91941 1270-G3
CULEBRA AV
- SD 92140 1268-F6
CULEBRA ST
400 DLMR 92014 1187-F4
CULLEN ST
7500 SD 92111 1249-A5
CULLODEN CT
- SDCo 92028 1027-G5
CULLY CT
1700 SDCo 91901 1233-J6
1700 SDCo 91901 1234-A6
CULOWEE ST
7900 LMSA 91941 1270-H2
CULVER CT
11200 SDCo 92020 1271-G3
CULVER RD
2300 SDCo 92028 409-A5
CULVER ST
4400 SD 92109 1248-B5
CULVER WY
2300 SD 92109 1248-B5
CUMANA TER
17600 SD 92128 1150-D7
17600 SD 92128 1170-D1
CUMBERLAND DR
15800 PWY 92064 1170-G5
CUMBERLAND ST
5500 SD 92139 1310-D1
CUMBRE CT
2000 CRLB 92009 1147-F2
CUMBRE PL
2100 ELCJ 92020 1251-C1
CUMBRE VW
600 CHV 91902 1311-B4
600 CHV 91913 1311-B4
CUMBRES RD
12400 SDCo 92082 1070-B5
CUMBRES TER
12400 SDCo 92082 1070-B5
CUMMINGS RD
100 NATC 92136 1309-F1
100 SD 92136 1309-F1
3400 SD 92136 1289-F7
CUMMINS PL
9900 SD 92131 1209-H5
CUMULUS LN
6000 SD 92110 1268-G3
CUNARD ST
900 SD 92154 1330-B7
CUNNING LN
13600 SDCo 92040 1232-D3
CUNNINGHAM LN
600 SDCo 92019 1252-C6
CUPENO CT
2800 SDCo 91935 1293-A3
CURIE PL
2500 SD 92122 1228-B7
CURIE ST
2900 SD 92122 1228-C7
CURIE WY
5400 SD 92122 1228-C7
CURL RD
1700 SD 92101 1289-C1
CURLEW ST
2200 SD 92101 1288-J1
2200 SD 92101 1289-A1
2500 SD 92103 1268-J6
2500 SD 92103 1288-J1
CURLEW TER
6600 CRLB 92009 1127-B5
CURRAN CT
30900 SDCo 92082 1070-J1
CURRAN ST
- SD 92154 1351-D1
CURRANT CT
13000 SDCo 92040 1232-C4
CURRANT ST
3300 SD 92111 1249-A5
CURRANT WY
200 OCN 92057 1086-H5
CURRY DR
4800 SD 92115 1270-D2
CURRY WY
3700 OCN 92057 1086-H4
CURRY COMB DR
1600 SMCS 92069 1108-E5
CURTIS DR
1900 SDCo 92084 1087-H2
CURTIS LN
1400 SDCo 91901 1234-B3
CURTIS ST
- CORD 92135 1288-E4
3000 SD 92106 1268-C7
3700 SD 92110 1268-C6
CUSHING RD
1700 SD 92133 1288-D1
2100 SD 92133 1268-D7
CUSHMAN AV
1100 SD 92110 1268-F2
CUSHMAN PL
5200 SD 92110 1268-F3
CUSTER RD
- SDCo 91906 (1318-B7
See Page 1298)
300 SDCo 91906 430-B10
CUSTER ST
5300 SD 92110 1268-F3
CUSTOMHOUSE CT
2600 SD 92154 1351-J4
CUSTOMHOUSE PZ
9200 SD 92154 1351-J4
9300 SD 92154 1352-A4
CUTTER CT
1800 SDCo 92019 1272-B3
CUVEE CT
17200 PWY 92064 1170-E2
CUVIER ST
7300 SD 92037 1247-E1
7300 SD 92037 1227-E7
CUYAMACA AV
400 SD 92113 1289-H5
800 CHV 91911 1330-E1
1100 SDCo 91977 1291-D2
7500 LMGR 91945 1270-G7
CUYAMACA CT
2100 SDCo 91977 1271-D7
2100 SDCo 91977 1291-D1
CUYAMACA HWY Rt#-79
3400 SDCo 92036 1136-B7
3700 SDCo 92036 1156-D1
8200 SDCo 91916 1236-C4
8500 SDCo 92036 1176-F4
9600 SDCo 91916 1216-E3
12500 SDCo 91916 (1196-F4
See Page 1176)
13900 SDCo 92036 (1196-F4
See Page 1176)
CUYAMACA ST
- SDCo 92055 1085-J4
- SDCo 92055 1086-A4
700 ELCJ 92020 1251-D1
1900 ELCJ 92020 1231-C6
8500 SNTE 92071 1231-D2
CUYAMACA WY
1400 CHV 91911 1330-F4
CUYAMACA COLLEGE DR E
- SDCo 92019 1271-J5
CUYAMACA COLLEGE DR W
- SDCo 92019 1271-J5
CUYAMACA FOREST RD
- SDCo 92036 1176-E3
CUYAMACA MEADOWS RD
- SDCo 92036 1156-G7
CYCAD DR
900 SMCS 92078 1129-A3
CYMBAL CT
2200 SDCo 92019 1252-D6
CYNTHIA CT
600 SMCS 92069 1109-B6
CYNTHIA LN
1200 CRLB 92008 1106-E4
1400 ELCJ 92019 1252-A5
13600 PWY 92064 1190-F4
CYNTHIA PL
4400 SD 92105 1289-J1
CYPRESS AV
- SD 92102 1289-G4
100 CRLB 92008 1106-E5
100 ELCJ 92020 1251-F5
400 IMPB 91932 1329-G6
1000 SD 92103 1269-B6
1800 SD 92104 1269-C6
2200 LMGR 91945 1270-G7
2200 LMGR 91945 1290-H1
CYPRESS CIR
1000 SMCS 92069 1109-B5
CYPRESS CT
1200 SD 92103 1269-B6
CYPRESS DR
- SD 92102 1289-G4
200 SD 92173 1350-G4
800 VSTA 92084 1088-A7
1100 VSTA 92084 1108-A1
1400 ELCN 92243 6559-G1
2400 SDCo 91906 (1297-E5
See Page 1296)
CYPRESS LN
100 ELCJ 92020 1251-F2
1700 ELCJ 92020 1251-F2
24700 SDCo 91916 1236-A2
28900 SDCo 92066 1237-C6
CYPRESS RD
3600 OCN 92054 1086-F1
CYPRESS RDG
27000 SDCo 92082 1090-D5
CYPRESS ST
100 CHV 91910 1310-B6
1700 SD 92154 1329-J7
1700 SD 92154 1330-A7
3200 NATC 91950 1310-C3
3200 SDCo 91950 1310-C3
4800 LMSA 91941 1270-J2
9500 SDCo 92040 1232-C4
CYPRESS WY
1000 SD 92103 1269-B6
CYPRESS CANYON RD
11400 SD 92131 1210-A1
11800 SD 92131 1189-J7
11800 SD 92131 1209-J1
CYPRESS CANYON PARK DR
11000 SD 92131 1210-B1
11500 PWY 92064 1210-B1
CYPRESS CREEK CT
- VSTA 92084 1088-B3
CYPRESS CREST TER
300 ESCN 92025 1130-B5
CYPRESS DEL MAR
3900 SD 92130 1188-A7
CYPRESS GLEN PL
4600 SD 92130 1188-C6
CYPRESS HILL RD
2700 CRLB 92008 1106-F3
CYPRESS HILLS DR
- ENCT 92024 1147-E5
CYPRESS LAKES WY
8800 SNTE 92071 1230-J4
CYPRESS POINT CT
1300 CHV 91915 1311-H6
CYPRESS POINT GN
1700 ESCN 92026 1109-D4
CYPRESS POINT RD
6100 SD 92120 1250-D6
CYPRESS POINT WY
800 OCN 92054 1066-F7
CYPRESS TERRACE PL
11400 SD 92131 1210-C1
CYPRESS VALLEY DR
11800 SD 92131 1210-A1
CYPRESS WOODS CT
12500 SD 92131 1210-C1
CYPRESS WOODS DR
11300 SD 92131 1210-C1
CYPRUS ISLAND CT
- SDCo 92028 1028-G5
CYRUS WY
4600 OCN 92056 1107-E5

D

D AV
- NATC 91950 1289-H7
100 CORD 92118 1288-H7
200 SDCo 92055 1066-C2
300 NATC 91950 1309-H1
3100 CHV 91950 1309-J3
D CT
- SD 92126 1209-F7
200 CHV 91910 1310-F7
D ST
- CHV 91910 1310-A5
- SDCo 92059 1029-H4
200 SDCo 92036 1136-B7
200 SDCo 92065 1152-H5
500 CHV 91910 1309-J5
1300 SD 92110 1268-F2
1600 SDCo 92084 1108-G2
2500 NATC 91950 1310-C3
E D ST
- ENCT 92024 1147-C7
W D ST
400 ENCT 92024 1147-B7
DABNEY DR
10400 SD 92126 1209-A4
10700 SD 92126 1208-J4
DAFFODIL
15300 SDCo 92021 1233-B3
DAFFODIL DR
- SD 92109 1248-C6
DAFFODIL LN
5700 SD 92120 1250-E7
DAFFODIL PL
7100 CRLB 92009 1127-B6
DAFFODIL ST
- SDCo 92055 1086-A4
3800 SD 92121 1208-B6
DAFNE LN
10100 SD 92124 1249-G1
DAFTER DR
4900 SD 92102 1290-A1
DAFTER PL
4900 SD 92102 1290-A1
DA GAMA CT
- SDCo 92026 1109-E6
DAGGET ST
7600 SD 92111 1249-A2
DAGGETT WY
5800 LMSA 91942 1251-C7
DAHLIA AV
- IMPB 91932 1329-E7
1600 SD 92154 1329-J7
1700 SD 92154 1330-A7
DAHLIA CT
800 SD 92154 1330-C7
DAHLIA DR
- NATC 91950 1289-H7
100 SOLB 92075 1187-E1
DAHLIA ST
- SDCo 92055 1086-B2
2900 SD 92105 1269-H7
DAHLIA WY
800 CRLB 92009 1127-A6
DAILEY CT
5100 LMSA 91941 1271-A2
DAILEY RD
8900 LMSA 91941 1271-A1
DAILY DR
2300 SDCo 92028 997-A2
DAILY RD
2500 SDCo 92028 997-B1
48400 SDCo 92028 409-B4
DAIN CT
2200 LMGR 91945 1270-J7
2200 LMGR 91945 1290-J1
DAIN DR
1900 LMGR 91945 1290-J1
DAIRY RD
3100 SDCo 91902 1291-B7
DAIRY MART RD
1600 SD 92173 1350-E4
2100 SD 92154 1350-E4
DAISY AV
- IMPB 91932 1329-E7
900 CRLB 92009 1127-B6
6000 SD 92114 1290-C6
DAISY CT
1000 CRLB 92009 1127-B6
DAISY LN
400 SMCS 92069 1128-F1
2500 SDCo 92028 1028-G7
DAISY PL
3900 OCN 92056 1107-A1
6000 SD 92114 1290-C6
DAISY ST
1100 ESCN 92027 1110-B6
N DAISY ST
700 ESCN 92027 1110-A6

DAISY WY — SAN DIEGO CO. STREET INDEX — DELOS DR 6580

STREET
Block City ZIP Pg-Grid

DAISY WY
1400 SD 92114 1290-D6
DAKOTA DR
4200 SD 92117 1248-E5
DAKOTA WY
400 OCN 92056 1087-A4
DALAI
9200 SDCo 92040 1232-F4
DALBERGIA CT
3800 SD 92113 1289-G7
DALBERGIA ST
3500 SD 92113 1289-G6
DALBY CV
8900 SD 92126 1209-D2
DALBY PL
11200 SD 92126 1209-D2
DALE AV
400 ESCN 92026 1109-H7
4300 LMSA 91941 1270-G3
9600 SDCo 91977 1271-C5
DALE CT
800 CHV 91910 1310-G7
900 SMCS 92069 1109-B5
DALE ST
1300 SD 92102 1289-E2
2000 SD 92104 1289-E2
2700 SD 92104 1269-E7
DALEA PL
4700 OCN 92057 1087-A1
DALECREST LN
2200 SDCo 91977 1271-D7
DALEGROVE LN
300 SD 92114 1290-F5
DALEHAVEN PL
4900 SD 92102 1290-A1
DALEHURST RD
9200 SNTE 92071 1231-A3
DALEN AV
5400 SD 92122 1228-C6
DALEN PL
3000 SD 92122 1228-C6
DALERIDGE PL
2600 SDCo 91977 1271-E7
DALEWOOD AV
8700 SD 92123 1249-C7
DALEY ST
2400 SDCo 92065 1152-C7
DALEY TKTR
15700 SDCo 91935 1293-F2
DALEY CENTER DR
3300 SD 92123 1249-F4
DALEY FLAT RD
2500 SDCo 92070 1155-D1
3100 SDCo 92070 1135-E7
DALEY RANCH TKTR
15700 SDCo 91935 (1312-H4 See Page 1293)
15700 SDCo 91935 (1313-A3 See Page 1293)
15700 SDCo 91935 1292-J7
15700 SDCo 91935 1293-C5
DALHART AV
6100 LMSA 91942 1250-H6
DALHOUSIE RD
14200 SD 92129 1189-D2
DALIA LN
14100 SDCo 92067 1188-D2
14200 SD 92067 1188-D2
DALISAY ST
2600 SD 92154 1350-C3
DALLAS RD
1100 SDCo 92028 1028-A4
S DALLAS RD
1100 SDCo 92028 1028-A4
DALLAS ST
8300 LMSA 91942 1250-J6
8600 LMSA 91942 1251-A6
DALLES AV
3900 SD 92117 1248-E3
DALLES CT
4300 SD 92117 1248-E3
DALTON CT
2100 CRLB 92008 1127-D1
DAMAS PL
500 CHV 91910 1311-A4
DAMASCO CT
12400 SD 92128 1150-B7
DAMATO ST
4500 SD 92124 1249-G3
DAM OAKS DR
24800 SDCo 92065 409-H11
DAMON AV
2900 SD 92109 1248-C4
DAMON LN
4400 SDCo 92020 1271-H3
DAMROCK CIR
8600 LMSA 91941 1271-A3
DAN WY
800 ESCN 92025 1129-G2
DANA CT
2300 CRLB 92008 1106-H4
DANA DR
700 VSTA 92083 1087-F5
4500 LMSA 91941 1270-F3
DANA PL
3700 SD 92103 1268-J6
DANA LANDING RD
1300 SD 92109 1268-A3
DANANCY CT
9500 SDCo 91977 1291-C4
DA NANG DR
\- CORD 92118 1309-D6
DANA POINT CT
1600 CHV 91911 1330-J4
DANA POINT WY
800 OCN 92054 1066-G7
DANA VISTA
13000 PWY 92064 1190-E5
DANAWOODS CT
7100 SD 92114 1290-F4
DANAWOODS LN
\- SD 92114 1290-F4
DANBURY WY
6200 SD 92120 1249-J7
6200 SD 92120 1250-A7
DANBY CT
9100 SD 92129 1189-D1
DANCER CT
\- ESCN 92026 1109-C5
DANCER PL
\- ESCN 92026 1109-C5
DANCOL TER
1800 SDCo 92021 1252-C3
DANCY CT
10500 SD 92126 1209-A4
DANCY PL
10400 SD 92126 1208-J5
DANCY RD
7200 SD 92126 1208-J5
7600 SD 92126 1209-A4
DANDRIDGE LN
5800 SD 92115 1270-C5
DANE DR
600 SMCS 92069 1108-J5
700 SMCS 92069 1109-A5
DANENBURG AV
100 ELCN 92243 6559-J3
100 ImCo 92243 6559-J3
100 ELCN 92243 6560-A3
100 ImCo 92243 6560-A3
DANERIN WY
2900 SDCo 91935 1272-E6
DANES RD
12400 PWY 92064 1190-C5
DANIA CT
8700 SNTE 92071 1231-A7
DANICA PL
600 ESCN 92025 1129-J6
DANICA MAE DR
8800 SD 92122 1228-C3
DANIEL AV
2600 SD 92111 1249-A6
DANIEL CT
7300 SD 92111 1249-A6
DANIEL GN
2600 ESCN 92027 1110-E7
DANIELLE DR
7700 LMGR 91945 1290-H2
DANIELSON CT
12600 PWY 92064 1190-E6
DANIELSON ST
13000 PWY 92064 1190-E6
DANNAN CT
12700 SD 92130 1188-D6
DANNER PL
100 ELCJ 92020 1251-F6
DANNY LN
1600 SDCo 92021 1251-G1
DANNY ST
300 SDCo 92021 1251-F2
DANNY WY
1600 SDCo 92021 1251-G1
DANNY BOY WY
\- SDCo 92127 1169-A2
DANOBER DR
1100 SD 92154 1350-F1
DANTE ST
5200 SD 92117 1248-H1
DANTE TER
2200 SDCo 92084 1108-D2
DANUBE LN
9000 SD 92126 1209-D1
DANVERS CIR
11900 SD 92128 1190-A2
DANVILLE AV
6600 SD 92120 1250-D6
DANVILLE CT
6500 SD 92120 1250-D6
DANZA CIR
11500 SD 92127 1149-J7
DAPHNE CT
800 CRLB 92009 1127-A6
DAPHNE ST
100 ENCT 92024 1147-A5
DAPPER CT
8400 SD 92126 1209-C1
DAPPLE CT
11900 SD 92128 1190-B7
DAPPLE WY
11900 SD 92128 1190-B7
DARBY ST
1100 SDCo 91977 1290-J2
2100 ESCN 92025 1130-A6
DARCY CT
9300 SNTE 92071 1231-B5
DARCY LN
1300 SDCo 92065 1172-F2
DARDAINA DR
3000 SD 92139 1310-E2
DARDANELLE GN
2400 ESCN 92027 1110-D7
DARDEN CT
7500 SD 92126 1208-J5
7500 SD 92126 1209-A5
DARDEN RD
10300 SD 92126 1208-J5
DAREN GN
2000 ESCN 92026 1109-D4
DARIEN DR
100 ENCT 92024 1147-H7
100 ENCT 92024 1167-H1
DARKWOOD RD
12100 SD 92129 1189-B7
DARLA LN
700 SDCo 92028 1027-F1
DARLENE LN
3300 SDCo 91935 1273-A6
DARLING DR
1500 SDCo 92026 1089-D7
DARLINGTON CT
2000 SDCo 92019 1272-C4
DARLINGTON RW
2300 SD 92037 1247-J1
2400 SD 92037 1248-A1
DARROW GN
2100 ESCN 92027 1130-D2
DARRYL CT
13600 SDCo 92021 1232-E5
DARRYL ST
8000 LMGR 91945 1270-H6
DARTFORD WY
5600 SD 92120 1270-D1
DARTMOOR CIR
1500 OCN 92057 1067-F7
DARTMOOR DR
1600 LMGR 91945 1290-E1
DARTMOUTH DR
2800 OCN 92056 1087-A7
DARTMOUTH ST
1600 CHV 91913 1311-C5
DARTOLO RD
16100 SDCo 92065 1173-G3
DARVIEW LN
13300 SD 92129 1189-B4
DARWELL CT
10500 SD 92126 1208-J4
DARWIN AV
3800 SD 92154 1350-F1
DARWIN CT
5900 CRLB 92008 1127-C2
DARWIN DR
1400 OCN 92056 1087-E2
DARWIN PL
1000 SD 92154 1330-F7
1000 SD 92154 1350-F1
DARWIN WY
4200 SD 92154 1350-F1
DASH WY
14600 PWY 92064 1190-E1
DASHERO PL
1700 ESCN 92029 1129-F6
DASSCO CT
4900 SD 92102 1290-A3
DASSCO ST
700 SD 92102 1290-A3
DASSIA WY
5000 OCN 92056 1107-F5
DATCHO DR
4000 SD 92117 1248-E3
DATE AV
\- CHV 91910 1310-A5
\- IMPB 91932 1329-E7
200 CRLB 92008 1106-F7
600 CHV 91910 1330-B1
800 CHV 91911 1330-B1
1500 SD 92154 1329-J7
4300 LMSA 91941 1270-H2
DATE CT
400 CHV 91911 1330-F6
DATE LN
3800 OCN 92054 1086-G3
20000 SDCo 92029 1149-E1
DATE PL
4900 SD 92102 1290-A2
DATE ST
100 CHV 91911 1330-F5
300 SD 92101 1289-A2
300 SD 92114 1290-D4
600 SD 92101 1288-J2
1300 ESCN 92026 1109-J6
1500 VSTA 92083 1087-C7
2800 SD 92102 1289-E2
4800 SD 92102 1290-A2
9400 SDCo 91977 1291-C2
N DATE ST
100 ESCN 92025 1130-A2
S DATE ST
100 ESCN 92025 1130-A2
W DATE ST
200 SD 92101 1289-A2
500 SD 92101 1288-J2
DATHE ST
200 SDCo 91977 1291-B4
DATSUN ST
6400 SD 92154 1351-C1
DAUCUS ST
8400 SD 92129 1189-C6
DAUER AV
4500 LMSA 91941 1270-F3
DAUM RD
20800 SDCo 91935 (1315-A1 See Page 1294)
DAUNTLESS ST
9800 SD 92126 1209-E2
DAVENPORT AV
13800 SD 92129 1189-D2
DAVENPORT LN
500 CHV 91911 1330-H2
2600 LMGR 91945 1270-D7
DAVENRICH ST
9000 SDCo 91977 1291-A3
DAVENTRY ST
6900 LMGR 91945 1290-E1
DAVES WY
3900 SD 92154 1330-F7
DAVEY WY
900 SMCS 92069 1109-B5
DAVID DR
800 CHV 91910 1310-G7
1500 ESCN 92026 1109-D5
DAVID GN
1900 ESCN 92026 1109-D4
DAVID PL
\- CRLB 92008 1106-G3
DAVID ST
1800 SD 92111 1268-J1
DAVID WY
2100 DLMR 92014 1187-F3
DAVIDANN RD
10800 SNTE 92071 1231-F6
DAVIDSON AV
7500 LMGR 91945 1270-G7
DAVIDSON ST
200 CHV 91910 1310-C5
DAVIES DR
\- CHV 91911 1330-J3
DA VINCI ST
4500 SD 92130 1188-C7
DAVIS AV
\- SD 92126 1209-B7
2500 CRLB 92008 1106-E4
DAVIS CT
\- SDCo 92055 1086-B2
900 VSTA 92083 1107-H2
DAVIS DR
200 SDCo 92028 1027-J1
DAVIS PL
2600 CRLB 92008 1106-E4
DAVIS RD
\- ImCo 92233 411-B8
\- ImCo 92257 411-B6
DAVIS ST
500 SDCo 92065 1152-E5
DAVIS CUP LN
15600 SDCo 92065 1173-H4
DAWES CT
1900 VSTA 92083 1107-J4
DAWES ST
4000 SD 92109 1247-H4
DAWN CT
500 CHV 91910 1310-G6
1400 SMCS 92069 1129-C1
DAWN LN
4200 OCN 92056 1107-C2
DAWN PL
1700 ESCN 92027 1110-C7
DAWNCREST CT
2500 SDCo 92036 1136-D7
DAWNE ST
4900 SD 92117 1228-G7
DAWNELL DR
1100 SD 92154 1350-F1
DAWN MARIE DR
3300 SDCo 91901 1234-D5
DAWNRIDGE AV
1100 SDCo 92021 1251-J2
1100 ELCJ 92021 1251-J2
DAWN VIEW GN
2000 ESCN 92026 1109-B3
DAWN VIEW WY
100 SDCo 92021 1252-J2
100 SDCo 92021 1253-A2
DAWSON AV
4300 SD 92115 1270-A4
DAWSON DR
1200 CHV 91911 1330-J1
1200 CHV 91911 1331-A1
1200 CHV 91913 1331-A1
1500 VSTA 92083 1107-H6
DAWSONIA ST
3600 SDCo 91902 1310-J2
3700 SDCo 91902 1311-A2
DAX CT
13200 SD 92129 1189-C4
DAXI LN
1100 SDCo 92029 1129-H6
DAY ST
100 SDCo 92065 1152-E7
3400 SD 92105 1270-B6
DAYBREAK CT
5500 OCN 92057 1067-D6
DAYBREAK PL
1600 ESCN 92027 1109-J5
1600 ESCN 92027 1110-A5
DAYLIGHT PL
\- SDCo 92065 1173-D2
DAY LILY CT
800 SMCS 92078 1129-B1
DAYLILY DR
\- CRLB 92009 1127-B4
2300 SDCo 92028 1028-E6
DAYMARK CT
12000 SD 92131 1190-B7
DAYSAILOR CT
4800 SD 92154 1330-J6
DAY STAR WY
20000 SDCo 92065 1152-D2
DAYTON DR
1700 LMGR 91945 1290-G1
DAYTON ST
4400 SD 92115 1270-B4
DAYTONA ST
7300 LMGR 91945 1270-F6
DAZA DR
16200 SDCo 92065 1173-G3
DEAD STICK RD
8700 SD 92154 1351-H1
DEADWOOD CT
4100 SDCo 92028 1048-D4
DEADWOOD DR
500 SMCS 92029 1128-H6
DEAL CT
700 SD 92109 1267-J3
DEALWOOD AV
500 ELCN 92243 6560-B1
500 ImCo 92243 6560-C1
DEALWOOD RD
700 ImCo 92243 431-D6
700 ImCo 92243 6560-G1
DEAN DR
1100 ENCT 92007 1167-F3
DEANA PL
1000 ESCN 92025 1130-A3
DEANLY CT
13800 SDCo 92040 1232-E4
DEANLY ST
9400 SDCo 92040 1232-E5
DEANLY WY
9300 SDCo 92040 1232-E5
DE ANZA CT
400 OCN 92057 1086-J4
1100 CHV 91910 1331-A1
DE ANZA DR
1400 SDCo 92004 1058-G5
DE ANZA RD
2700 SD 92109 1248-D6
DE ANZA SPUR
400 SDCo 92004 1058-G5
DE ANZA TR
\- SDCo 92004 410-B5
\- SDCo 92004 1058-H1
DE ANZA BAY DR
\- SD 92109 1248-D6
DEARBORN DR
1000 SD 92154 1330-C7
1000 SD 92154 1350-C1
DEARBORN PL
12100 PWY 92064 1190-F7
DEARBORN RD
\- ImCo 92243 431-A7
DEARBORN ST
3600 OCN 92057 1086-G5
DEARFLOWER RD
3100 SD 92115 1270-D6
DEATON DR
4800 SD 92102 1290-A1
DEAUVILLE ST
2400 SD 92139 1310-D1
DEAVER LN
\- SD 92173 1350-E4
DEAVERS DR
500 SMCS 92069 1109-D7
DEBANN RD
1600 ENCT 92007 1167-E2
DEBBIE CT
9400 SDCo 92021 1232-H4
DEBBY DR
5000 SD 92115 1270-B2
DEBBY PL
600 ESCN 92026 1109-J7
DEBBY ST
400 SDCo 92028 1027-H3
DEBBYANN PL
3900 SD 92154 1330-F7
DEBCO DR
2200 LMGR 91945 1270-J7
2200 LMGR 91945 1290-J1
DEBENMARK PL
1200 SD 92154 1350-D1
DEBI LN
14200 SDCo 92082 1070-E1
DEBORAH PL
7800 LMGR 91945 1270-H7
DEBRA CIR
4100 OCN 92056 1087-C7
DEBRA LN
1800 VSTA 92084 1087-H2
DEBRA PL
500 SMCS 92069 1128-D1
DEBRA ANN DR
400 SDCo 92028 1027-H2
DE BURN DR
5100 SD 92105 1290-A1
DE CAMP DR
6200 LMSA 91942 1251-B5
DECANT DR
12900 PWY 92064 1170-D2
DECANTURE CT
6100 SD 92120 1250-D4
DECANTURE CV
7200 SD 92120 1250-D4
DECANTURE ST
6200 SD 92120 1250-D4
DECANTURE WY
7200 SD 92120 1250-D4
DECATUR CIR
9000 SD 92126 1209-D3
DECATUR RD
1700 SD 92133 1288-C1
2000 SD 92133 1268-D7
10900 SD 92126 1209-D3
DECATUR WY
300 ESCN 92026 1129-G1
DECENA DR
6100 SD 92120 1249-J7
DECISION ST
500 VSTA 92083 1128-A1
DECKER ST
1000 ELCJ 92020 1251-H5
1000 ELCJ 92019 1251-H5
DECORA CIR
3500 SMCS 92069 1108-C7
DECORO ST
4100 SD 92122 1228-C4
DEDDIE TER
200 SDCo 92028 1027-F5
DEDO PL
11400 SD 92126 1209-B1
DEEB CT
100 SDCo 92084 1088-E5
DEEB DR
2800 SDCo 92084 1088-E6
DEELAN LN
13100 PWY 92064 1190-H4
DEEM PL
1100 ELCJ 92021 1251-H4
DEEP CANYON CT
10600 SDCo 92026 1089-F3
DEEP CANYON DR
10800 SDCo 92026 1089-G3
DEEP DELL CT
7600 SD 92114 1290-H5
DEEP DELL CV
7400 SD 92114 1290-G4
DEEP DELL RD
\- SD 92114 1290-G4
500 SD 92139 1290-G4
S DEEP DELL RD
300 SD 92114 1290-G5
DEEP HAVEN LN
1800 SD 92154 1350-C3
DEEP VALLEY RD
6800 SD 92120 1250-D3
DEEP WELL TR
\- SDCo 92004 (1099-E1 See Page 1098)
DEER PTH
400 ENCT 92024 1147-A2
DEERBEN RD
20100 SDCo 92065 1153-G1
DEERBROOK DR
\- SMCS 92069 1108-H4
DEER CANYON DR
26900 SDCo 92065 1154-E2
DEER CREEK TR
28700 SDCo 92066 1237-C6
DEERFIELD CT
800 OCN 92054 1086-E2
DEERFIELD RD
1700 ENCT 92024 1147-H6
DEERFIELD ST
7800 SD 92120 1250-D3
DEERFOOT RD
11900 SD 92131 1210-B3
DEERFORD RW
6000 SD 92037 1248-A1
DEERGRASS CT
13800 PWY 92064 1170-F5
DEERHAVEN
500 ELCJ 92019 1252-D4
DEERHAVEN DR
1000 VSTA 92084 1087-J5
1000 VSTA 92084 1088-A5
DEER HILL CT
1400 SD 92037 1247-G3
DEER HOLLOW CT
9700 SNTE 92071 1231-F4
DEER HOLLOW PL
6800 SD 92120 1250-D3
DEERHORN OAKS RD
\- SDCo 91917 (1315-B3 See Page 1294)
\- SDCo 91935 (1315-B3 See Page 1294)
DEERHORN SPRING LN
2300 SDCo 91935 1294-H7
DEERHORN VALLEY RD
18400 SDCo 91935 1294-F7
20500 SDCo 91935 (1314-J1 See Page 1294)
20500 SDCo 91935 (1315-A2 See Page 1294)
DEERHURST CT
7000 SD 92139 1290-G7
DEERHURST WY
2400 SD 92139 1290-G7
DEERING ST
10800 SD 92126 1209-B3
DEER LAKE PARK RD
3900 SDCo 92036 1155-J2
3900 SDCo 92036 1156-A2
DEEROCK PL
100 SD 92114 1290-G4
DEERPARK DR
2100 SD 92110 1268-G1
2300 SD 92110 1248-F6
DEER PARK RD
\- SDCo 92036 (1177-C7 See Page 1176)
\- SDCo 92036 (1197-C2 See Page 1176)
\- SDCo 92036 (1217-D2 See Page 1216)
\- SDCo 92066 (1217-D2 See Page 1216)
DEER PEAK CT
1600 CHV 91913 1311-D7
DEER RIDGE CT
\- SDCo 92127 1169-E4
DEER RIDGE PL
\- SDCo 92127 1169-E4
DEER RIDGE RD
\- SDCo 92127 1169-E4
DEERRUN PL
6800 SD 92120 1250-D3
DEER SPRINGS PL
2500 SDCo 92069 1089-A6
DEER SPRINGS RD
1400 SDCo 91901 1234-H6
DEER SPRINGS RD Rt#-S12
100 SMCS 92069 1108-J1
500 SDCo 92069 1088-J7
500 SDCo 92069 1089-A7
500 SDCo 92069 1108-J1
500 SDCo 92069 1109-A1
1000 SDCo 92026 1089-A7
DEER TRAIL CT
\- SDCo 92127 1169-E5
DEER TRAIL DR
\- SD 92127 1169-E5
\- SDCo 92127 1169-E5
DEER TRAIL PL
\- SDCo 92127 1169-E5
DEER TRAIL WY
\- SDCo 92127 1169-E5
DEER VALLEY TR
\- SDCo 91916 429-K4
\- SDCo 91916 1216-A7
DEER VALLEY ESTATES
18300 PWY 92064 1150-H7
18500 PWY 92064 1151-A6
DEER VIEW DR
10100 SDCo 92026 1089-D5
DEER WALK CT
\- SDCo 91917 (1315-G5 See Page 1294)
\- SDCo 91963 (1315-G5 See Page 1294)
DEER WALK RD
\- SDCo 91963 (1315-G5 See Page 1294)
DEERWOOD CT
6700 SD 92120 1250-C3
DEERWOOD ST
14600 PWY 92064 1190-C1
14800 PWY 92064 1170-C7
DEFENDER CT
1000 SOLB 92014 1187-H1
DEFIANCE WY
4900 SD 92115 1270-A2
DEFREITAS AV
9200 SD 92129 1189-D3
DEGEN DR
3000 SDCo 91902 1290-J7
DEHESA CT
7500 CRLB 92009 1147-J1
DEHESA RD
1700 ELCJ 92019 1252-C6
1700 SDCo 92019 1252-C6
3700 SDCo 92019 1253-G3
7000 SDCo 91901 1253-G3
7600 SDCo 91901 1254-A3
DEHESA WY
300 SDCo 92021 1252-J4
DEHESA MEADOW RD
3500 SDCo 92019 1252-H7
DEHESA MOUNTAIN LN
500 SDCo 92021 1252-J5
DEHESA RANCH RD
1200 SDCo 92019 1253-F3
DEHIA ST
14500 PWY 92064 1190-H3
DEIT LN
1200 SDCo 92028 1027-H5
DE LA GARZA RD
\- SD 92145 1228-J2
\- SD 92145 1229-A2
DE LA GARZA ST
\- SDCo 92055 1023-E2
DELAGE CT
400 ENCT 92024 1167-G1
DELAGE DR
300 ENCT 92024 1167-G1
DEL AMO CT
16300 SDCo 92065 1173-E3
DEL AMO PL
24000 SDCo 92065 1173-E2
DEL AMO RD
23900 SDCo 92065 1173-E3
24500 SDCo 92065 1153-F7
DE LAND CT
700 ELCJ 92020 1271-E1
DELAND DR
2400 SDCo 91901 1254-B1
DELANE ST
1700 SDCo 92065 1152-E6
DELANO AV
5600 SD 92120 1250-B6
DELANO CT
\- CHV 91913 1311-C7
DELANO PL
1400 CHV 91913 1331-C1
DELANY DR
2200 SD 92173 1350-G3
DELAPORT CT
\- CORD 92118 1329-D3
DELAPORT LN
\- CORD 92118 1329-D3
DELAPORT PL
\- CORD 92118 1329-D3
DELAPORT WY
\- CORD 92118 1329-D3
DE LA RONDO
100 OCN 92057 1087-A2
DE LA ROSA LN
6000 OCN 92057 1067-D3
DE LA TOBA RD
700 CHV 91911 1330-J3
700 CHV 91911 1331-A3
DE LA VALLE PL
14800 SD 92014 1188-A1
14800 SDCo 92014 1188-A1
DELAWARE AV
6800 LMSA 91942 1270-E1
DELAWARE ST
300 IMPB 91932 1329-G7
900 IMPB 91932 1349-G1
4500 SD 92116 1269-B4
DELBARTON ST
6300 SD 92120 1249-J6
DELCARDO AV
600 SD 92154 1330-G7
DEL CERO AV
3600 OCN 92056 1107-C3
DEL CERRO AV
5600 SD 92120 1270-D1
5600 SD 92120 1250-D7
DEL CERRO BLVD
5400 SD 92120 1250-A7
6500 SD 92120 1270-E1
DEL CERRO CT
6300 SD 92120 1270-D1
DEL CHARRO RD
3300 SDCo 91935 1272-D7
DEL CIELO ESTE
5300 SDCo 92003 1048-B7
DEL CIELO OESTE
5000 SDCo 92003 1048-B7
DEL CORONADO LN
10300 SNTE 92071 1231-D2
DEL CORRO CT
500 CHV 91910 1310-G5
DEL CORRO PL
700 CHV 91910 1310-G5
DEL DIABLO LN
14900 SD 92129 1169-H7
14900 SD 92129 1189-H1
DEL DIABLO ST
11000 SD 92129 1189-H1
11200 SD 92129 1169-J7
DEL DIABLO WY
11100 SD 92129 1169-J7
DEL DIOS HWY Rt#-S6
500 SDCo 92029 1149-D2
500 SDCo 92067 1149-D6
1100 ESCN 92029 1129-F6
9800 ESCN 92029 1149-D2
9900 SDCo 92029 1129-F6
DEL DIOS RD
900 ESCN 92029 1129-F5
DELEON DR
1100 CHV 91910 1311-B7
DE LEONE RD
3500 SMCS 92069 1108-D5
DEL ESTE DR
\- ESCN 92029 1129-F4
DEL ESTE WY
3400 OCN 92056 1107-C2
DELEVAN DR
1100 SD 92102 1289-F3
DELFERN ST
6500 SD 92120 1250-B6
DELFINA PL
3000 CRLB 92009 1147-H2
DEL FLORA ST
300 OCN 92054 1086-F1
DELGADO PL
800 ESCN 92025 1129-J5
7500 CRLB 92009 1147-J1
DELIA LN
9900 SNTE 92071 1231-F3
DELICIAS CT
100 SOLB 92075 1167-D7
DELIGHT ST
1400 ELCJ 92021 1252-B2
DELIGHT WY
1100 ESCN 92026 1109-J7
DELL CT
400 SOLB 92075 1167-F6
DELL ST
600 SOLB 92075 1167-F6
DELLA LN
1600 OCN 92054 1106-D1
DELLA PL
4900 SD 92117 1228-C7
DEL LAGO BLVD
\- ESCN 92025 1150-A2
3200 ESCN 92029 1150-A2
DELL ANNE PL
800 SD 92114 1290-H2
DELLCREST LN
1300 SD 92037 1227-F7
DELLCREST WY
700 ESCN 92027 1130-C2
DELL RIM CT
7900 SD 92126 1209-A1
DELLTOP LN
2100 SDCo 91977 1271-D7
2100 SDCo 91977 1291-D1
DELL VIEW RD
15600 SDCo 92021 1233-C3
DELLWOOD ST
4100 SD 92111 1249-A3
DEL MAR AV
\- CHV 91910 1310-B4
600 CHV 91910 1330-C1
800 CHV 91911 1330-C1
3700 SD 92106 1288-A1
3900 SD 92107 1288-A1
4300 SD 92107 1267-J7
4300 SD 92107 1268-A7
N DEL MAR AV
\- CHV 91910 1310-B4
DEL MAR CT
400 CHV 91910 1310-C6
DEL MAR GN
3900 SD 92130 1188-A7
DEL MAR RD
1500 OCN 92057 1067-G6
DEL MAR DOWNS RD
800 DLMR 92014 1187-F2
800 SOLB 92075 1187-F2
DEL MAR HEIGHTS PL
12900 SD 92130 1188-A5
DEL MAR HEIGHTS RD
300 DLMR 92014 1187-H6
300 SD 92014 1187-H6
2800 SD 92130 1187-H6
3000 SD 92130 1188-A5
DEL MAR HILLS DR
13800 SD 92130 1187-J6
DEL MARINO AV
13500 PWY 92064 1190-H3
DEL MAR MEADOWS
3900 SD 92130 1188-A7
DEL MAR MESA RD
\- SD 92130 1188-D7
DEL MAR OAKS
12300 SD 92130 1188-A7
DEL MAR SCENIC PKWY
2100 SD 92014 1207-G1
2300 SD 92014 1187-H7
DEL MAR SHORES TER
100 SOLB 92075 1187-E1
DEL MAR TRAILS RD
3900 SD 92130 1188-B7
DEL MESA CT
200 OCN 92054 1086-G1
DEL MESA ST
200 OCN 92054 1086-G1
DEL MONTE AV
100 CHV 91911 1330-D5
4200 SD 92107 1268-A7
4500 SD 92107 1267-J6
DELNISO CT
1700 CHV 91911 1330-J5
DEL NORTE
16000 PWY 92064 1170-D4
DELOR CT
6000 SD 92120 1249-J7
DEL ORO CT
8300 SD 92037 1227-H4
DEL ORO LN
1900 SDCo 92025 1130-C4
DELOS DR
7000 SD 92139 1290-F7

SAN DIEGO CO.
INDEX

6581 DELOS ST
SAN DIEGO CO. STREET INDEX
DOUBLE R RD

STREET
Block City ZIP Pg-Grid

DELOS ST
2200 SD 92139 1290-F7
DELOS WY
4700 OCN 92056 1107-E6
DEL PASO AV
6100 SD 92120 1250-D6
DEL PASO CT
3600 OCN 92056 1107-D3
DEL PASO DR
17700 PWY 92064 1150-F7
17700 PWY 92064 1170-F1
DEL PASO PL
6800 SD 92120 1250-D5
DEL PENA CT
11100 SD 92128 1189-J4
DELPHI ST
9900 SNTE 92071 1231-F4
DELPHINIUM ST
100 ENCT 92024 1147-E6
DELPHINUS WY
11000 SD 92126 1209-D2
DEL PONIENTE CT
15200 PWY 92064 1170-F7
DEL PONIENTE RD
13500 PWY 92064 1170-E6
DEL PRADO CT
1100 CHV 91910 1331-A1
DEL PRADO ST
4800 SDCo 91902 1310-H3
DEL RAY PL
600 CHV 91910 1310-G7
600 CHV 91910 1330-H1
DEL REY AV
3000 CRLB 92009 1147-H1
DEL REY BLVD
700 CHV 91910 1310-G6
DEL REY ST
3400 SD 92109 1248-D5
DELRIDGE LN
26900 SDCo 92082 1091-F5
DEL RIEGO AV
700 ENCT 92024 1147-C4
DEL RIO AV
700 ENCT 92024 1147-C4
DEL RIO CT
1100 CHV 91910 1311-A7
3300 CRLB 92009 1147-J1
DEL RIO RD
10000 SDCo 91977 1271-D5
10200 SDCo 91978 1271-E5
DEL RIO WY
300 VSTA 92083 1087-G5
3500 SDCo 91978 1271-F5
DEL ROSA LN
1300 SDCo 92069 1128-B3
DELROSE AV
8800 SDCo 91977 1290-J3
DEL ROY DR
100 SMCS 92069 1108-H4
DEL SOL BLVD
3000 SD 92154 1350-D1
DEL SOL CT
4200 SD 92154 1350-G1
DEL SOL LN
1200 SD 92154 1350-E1
DEL SOL RD
12500 SDCo 92040 1232-B5
DEL SOL WY
1200 SD 92154 1350-G1
DEL SUR BLVD
1200 SD 92154 1350-E2
1500 SD 92173 1350-E2
DEL SUR CT
1100 CHV 91910 1331-A1
DEL SURENO
100 SDCo 92028 1027-H2
DELTA LN
300 VSTA 92083 1087-F7
DELTA RD
8700 SD 92126 1209-C7
DELTA ST
1700 NATC 91950 1289-J6
1700 NATC 91950 1290-A6
3800 SD 92113 1289-G6
4600 SD 91950 1289-J6
8700 LMSA 91942 1250-J7
8700 LMSA 91942 1251-A7
DELTA WY
- CRLB 92008 1107-B3
DE LUZ RD
700 SDCo 92028 1027-F1
800 SDCo 92028 997-A6
800 SDCo 92055 997-A6
38800 SDCo 92028 409-A5
38800 SDCo 92055 409-A5
DE LUZ HEIGHTS RD
2500 SDCo 92028 997-C2
DE LUZ MURRIETA RD
35900 SDCo 92028 409-A5
DEL VALLE DR
200 SDCo 92028 1047-F5
DEL VISTA WY
16300 SDCo 92021 1233-F3
DE MAYO RD
2000 DLMR 92014 1187-G6
2000 SD 92014 1187-G6
DEMETER WY
2900 SD 92139 1310-E2
4800 OCN 92056 1107-E6
DEMONA PL
100 SDCo 91977 1290-J5
DE MOTT LN
9000 SNTE 92071 1231-A7
DEMPSTER DR
9300 SNTE 92071 1230-H6
DEMUS ST
3800 SD 92115 1270-C5
DENARA RD
13200 SD 92130 1187-J5
DENBY ST
400 SD 92102 1289-H3
DENDIA WY
1300 SDCo 92020 1272-A1
DENDY SKY LN
- SDCo 92082 1069-D4
DENIA WY
4700 OCN 92056 1107-F4
DENISE CIR
1400 OCN 92054 1106-E1
DENISE CT
1000 SMCS 92078 1129-B4
DENISE LN
700 ELCJ 92020 1251-G7
DENISE CANYON CT
3800 SDCo 91902 1311-A3
DENISON WY
300 SDCo 92084 1087-G1
DENNERY RD
600 SD 92154 1330-H7
600 SD 92154 1350-H1
DENNING PL
11300 SD 92126 1208-J2
DENNING DR
- CRLB 92009 1128-B7
- CRLB 92009 1148-C1
- SDCo 92024 1128-C7
- SDCo 92024 1148-C1
- SMCS 92024 1128-C7
DENNIS AV
600 CHV 91910 1310-E7
DENNIS DR
2200 SDCo 92083 1108-B4
2200 VSTA 92083 1108-B4
DENNIS LN
2700 LMGR 91945 1270-J7
DENNISON PL
7100 SD 92122 1228-D4
DENNISON ST
6300 SD 92122 1228-D4
DENNSTEDT CT
1000 ELCJ 92020 1251-D7
DENNSTEDT PL
900 ELCJ 92020 1251-C7
DENNY WY
100 SDCo 92020 1251-F2
DENOVA DR
2300 SDCo 91901 1253-H2
DENSTONE PL
1700 LMGR 91945 1290-E1
DENT CT
8600 SD 92119 1250-J3
DENT DR
8600 SD 92119 1250-J3
8600 SD 92119 1251-A3
DENTON ST
8400 LMSA 91942 1250-J6
DENTRO DE LOMAS
2700 SDCo 92084 1068-E5
DENTRO DE LOMAS RD
1500 SDCo 92003 1067-J3
1500 SDCo 92003 1068-A3
DENVER LN
1100 ELCJ 92021 1251-H3
DENVER ST
1800 SD 92110 1268-E1
2200 SD 92110 1248-E7
2700 SD 92117 1248-E6
DENWOOD RD
4600 LMSA 91941 1270-G3
DEODAR DR
- ELCJ 92019 1251-J6
DEODAR RD
700 SDCo 92026 1129-E1
900 SMCS 92026 1129-E1
1100 ESCN 92026 1109-F7
1100 ESCN 92026 1129-F1
DEODAR TR
7600 SDCo 92066 1237-B7
DERALD RD
9600 SNTE 92071 1231-A4
DERBY CT
5700 OCN 92057 1067-G7
DERBY ST
900 SD 92114 1290-B3
DERBY BLUFFS WY
3700 SD 92130 1188-A4
DERBY DOWNS CT
- SD 92130 1188-A4
DERBY DOWNS RD
3700 SD 92130 1188-A4
DERBY FARMS RD
4300 SD 92130 1188-D2
4500 SD 92067 1188-D2
DERBY HILL PT
- SD 92130 1208-D2
DEREK WY
1600 CHV 91911 1330-G5
DERK DR
5700 LMSA 91942 1250-J7
DERMID RD
29800 SDCo 92082 1070-C5
DERON AV
13100 SD 92129 1189-D4
DERRICK CT
2200 ESCN 92029 1129-H7
5100 SD 92117 1248-G1
DERRICK DR
4300 SD 92117 1248-G2
DERRICK RD
1800 ImCo 92243 430-L6
DERRINGER PL
2700 ESCN 92027 1110-D6
DERRINGER RD
14800 PWY 92064 1170-G7
14800 PWY 92064 1190-F1
DERRYDOWN WY
10900 SD 92130 1208-D1
DESCANSO AV
- IMPB 91932 1349-E2
1300 SMCS 92069 1108-E6
DESCANSO LN
2400 SDCo 92021 1252-H4
DESCANSO TR
- SDCo 91916 429-K4
DESCANSO CREEK PL
1200 CHV 91915 1311-H6
DESERET RD
10200 SDCo 92082 1049-D2
DESERT DR
3800 SDCo 92004 (1099-F1 See Page 1098)
DESERT GN
1600 ESCN 92026 1109-D6
DESERT RD
- ImCo - 431-F6
- ImCo 92250 431-F6
DESERT GARDENS DR
400 ELCN 92243 6559-E1
DESERT INN WY
3500 CHV 91902 1310-G2
DESERT ORIOLE DR
4600 SDCo 92004 (1099-G5 See Page 1098)
DESERT ROSE CT
- IMP 92243 6499-E2
DESERT ROSE WY
1000 CRLB 92009 1148-A5
1000 ENCT 92024 1148-A5
DESERT ROSE RANCH RD
- SDCo 91934 (1321-C3 See Page 1300)
DESERT VIEW DR
5600 SD 92037 1248-A2
DESERT VISTA DR
4400 SDCo 92004 (1099-F4 See Page 1098)
DESERT VISTA TER
- SDCo 92004 (1099-F4 See Page 1098)
DESIGN CT
700 CHV 91911 1330-J5
DESIREE LN
8400 ELCJ 92020 1251-C1
8400 SNTE 92071 1251-C1
DESMOND CIR
4600 OCN 92056 1107-F3
DE SOLA ST
- SDCo 92127 1169-F4
DESOTO CT
1100 CHV 91910 1311-B7
4200 SDCo 91941 1271-G4
DE SOTO PL
19200 SDCo 92029 1149-E4
DE SOTO ST
4600 SD 92109 1248-C4
DESPEJO PL
5800 SD 92124 1229-H7
DESTINY MOUNTAIN CT
- SDCo 91977 1291-F2
DESTREE RD
1100 ESCN 92027 1130-C3
1100 SDCo 92027 1130-C3
DESTY CT
2600 SD 92154 1330-C7
DESTY ST
700 SD 92154 1330-C7
DETRICH WY
- SDCo 92036 1155-H3
DETROIT PL
400 SD 92114 1290-D5
DETWILER RD
8800 SDCo 92029 1149-B4
DEVELBISS ST
400 NATC 92136 1309-F1
DEVEREUX RD
17500 SD 92128 1170-A1
17600 SD 92128 1150-A7
DEVERILL DR
14500 SDCo 92021 1232-H4
DE VIDA CT
10900 SD 92124 1249-J2
DEVILLE DR
7400 LMGR 91945 1290-G2
7500 SD 92114 1290-G2
DEVIN DR
- SDCo 92028 1027-J5
DEVINEY LN
1500 SDCo 92065 1172-G5
DEVON CT
- SDCo 91935 1272-F5
700 SD 92109 1267-H3
DEVON DR
- SDCo 91935 1272-E5
DEVON PL
- ESCN 92025 1129-J5
1600 SDCo 92084 1108-C3
DEVONSHIRE DR
900 ENCT 92024 1147-C7
900 ENCT 92024 1167-C1
900 SD 92107 1287-H1
DEVONSHIRE GN
400 ESCN 92027 1110-D6
DEVONSHIRE RD
1000 ENCT 92024 1167-C1
DE VOS DR
8400 SNTE 92071 1230-J6
DEWANE DR
200 ELCJ 92020 1251-D4
DEWES WY
4100 SD 92117 1248-E6
DEWEY PL
1300 SDCo 91906 (1318-A5 See Page 1298)
DEWEY RD
- SD 92133 1268-D7
DEWEY ST
300 SD 92113 1289-C5
1200 NATC 91950 1309-F3
DEWITT AV
700 ENCT 92024 1147-C7
700 ENCT 92024 1167-C1
DEWITT CT
100 ELCJ 92020 1271-G2
100 SDCo 91941 1271-G2
DEWITT ESTATES RD
1600 SDCo 91901 1253-J1
1700 SDCo 91901 1254-A1
DEW POINT AV
- CRLB 92009 1126-J7
DEWSBURY AV
8700 SD 92126 1209-C3
DEXTER DR
3800 LMSA 91941 1270-J5
DEXTER PL
1100 ESCN 92029 1129-G7
1100 SDCo 92029 1129-G7
DIABLO PL
1200 VSTA 92083 1107-E1
DIABLO POINT CT
1500 CHV 91911 1330-J3
DIA DEL SOL
16200 SDCo 92082 1071-B7
DIAMANTE WY
- OCN 92056 1106-J2
DIAMOND
14100 SDCo 92040 1232-H5
DIAMOND CIR
4100 OCN 92056 1087-C6
DIAMOND CT
1100 CHV 91911 1330-H1
DIAMOND DR
600 CHV 91911 1330-H1
1100 SDCo 92065 1172-H1
DIAMOND GN
- ESCN 92027 1110-D7
DIAMOND LN
1300 SDCo 92021 1251-H2
1400 ELCJ 92021 1251-H2
DIAMOND ST
600 SD 92109 1247-H6
1500 SD 92109 1248-A5
1800 SMCS 92069 1128-B6
DIAMOND WY
600 VSTA 92083 1087-F7
DIAMOND BAR RD
600 SDCo 92004 (1078-J3 See Page 1058)
700 SDCo 92004 (1079-A3 See Page 1058)
DIAMOND GEM LN
3200 SDCo 91935 1273-F7
3200 SDCo 91935 1293-F1
DIAMOND HEAD CT
10100 SDCo 91977 1291-D2
DIAMOND HEAD DR
1300 ENCT 92024 1167-F1
DIAMOND TRAIL RD
1700 SDCo 92069 1128-A3
DIANA ST
700 CHV 91911 1330-J5
DIANE
100 ENCT 92024 1147-A4
DIANE AV
4600 SD 92117 1248-F1
4900 SD 92117 1228-G7
9400 SDCo 91977 1271-B6
DIANE CT
4900 SD 92117 1228-G7
DIANE DR
8700 SNTE 92071 1231-F7
DIANE PL
600 ESCN 92026 1109-J7
4900 SD 92117 1228-G6
DIANE WY
4500 SD 92117 1248-F1
DIAZ DR
16600 SD 92128 1170-C3
DIAZ GN
2700 ESCN 92027 1110-E7
DIAZ RD
30500 SDCo 92082 1069-E3
30600 SDCo 92026 1069-E3
DICENZA LN
8000 SD 92119 1250-E3
DICENZA WY
6700 SD 92119 1250-E3
DICHONDRA CT
9900 SD 92131 1209-J5
DICHONDRA PL
9900 SD 92131 1209-H4
DICHOSO DR
1600 ESCN 92025 1130-B4
DICHTER ST
300 ELCJ 92019 1252-B6
DICK ST
4900 SD 92115 1270-A3
DICKENS ST
2800 SD 92106 1288-B2
DICKERMAN RD
- ImCo 92227 431-D1
DICKEY DR
4500 SDCo 91941 1271-E3
DICKEY ST
1600 SDCo 92028 1028-A5
DICKINSON ST
100 SD 92103 1269-A4
2600 SD 92103 1268-J4
DIEGO DR
16700 SD 92128 1170-A3
DIEGOS CT
4300 SDCo 92028 1028-H7
4300 SDCo 92028 1048-H1
DIEGUENO RD
- SDCo 92004 1058-H6
2000 SDCo 92004 (1078-H1 See Page 1058)
DIEHL RD
- ImCo 92243 431-A6
2100 ImCo 92243 430-L6
DIESEL DR
1800 SDCo 92019 1252-C4
DIETRICH RD
- ImCo 92227 431-C1
5300 ImCo 92227 411-C11
DI FOSS ST
2300 LMGR 91945 1270-H7
DI GIORGIO RD
- SDCo 92004 410-C6
- SDCo 92004 (1099-B1 See Page 1098)
800 SDCo 92004 (1059-A1 See Page 1058)
2300 SDCo 92004 (1079-A1 See Page 1058)
DILLARD ST
1500 SD 92114 1290-D6
DILLON DR
9100 LMSA 91941 1271-B2
9100 SDCo 91941 1271-B2
DILLON RD
15200 SDCo 92021 1233-B2
DILLON WY
400 SD 92117 1248-E6
DILLONS TR
1100 SD 92154 1351-A3
DILMAN ST
300 SDCo 92019 1252-B6
400 ELCJ 92019 1252-B6
DI MARINO ST
900 SD 92114 1290-F2
DINAMICA WY
6300 SD 92111 1248-H7
DINARA DR
2300 SDCo 92029 1129-D3
DI NOVO ST
7100 SD 92114 1290-F2
DIP DR
3000 SDCo 92028 1028-C2
DIPPER ST
6000 SD 92114 1290-C2
DIPPONS LN
2200 ESCN 92027 1110-C5
DIRAC ST
5800 SD 92122 1228-E6
DIRECTORS PL
- SD 92121 1208-D6
DISCOVERY ST
300 SMCS 92069 1128-G1
DISCOVERY WY
8600 SD 92093 1227-J3
DISCOVERY BAY DR
1200 CHV 91915 1311-G6
DISNEY LN
29800 SDCo 92084 1068-E4
30300 SDCo 92003 1068-E4
DISSINGER AV
6300 SD 92139 1310-E1
DISTRIBUTION AV
9500 SD 92121 1228-J1
9700 SD 92121 1208-J7
DISTRIBUTION ST
200 SMCS 92078 1129-A1
DISTRIBUTION WY
1400 VSTA 92083 1107-J6
N DITMAR ST
100 OCN 92054 1086-A7
S DITMAR ST
100 OCN 92054 1086-A7
200 OCN 92054 1106-B1
DIVELLOS DR
- SDCo 91901 1233-E4
DIVERSEY DR
13300 PWY 92064 1190-G4
DIVERSION DR
3400 SDCo 91977 1271-E6
DIVINE WY
4700 SDCo 91941 1271-D3
DIVISION ST
- SD 92113 1289-G7
- NATC 91950 1289-J7
200 OCN 92054 1086-B7
1700 NATC 91950 1290-A7
3700 NATC 92136 1289-G7
3700 SD 92136 1289-G7
5400 SD 92114 1290-C6
DIXIE DR
4800 SD 92109 1247-H5
6100 LMSA 91942 1251-B6
DIXIE ST
1700 OCN 92054 1086-C7
DIXON CT
1300 CHV 91911 1330-E3
DIXON DR
1100 CHV 91911 1330-E2
DIXON LN
- ESCN 92025 1130-A6
DIXON PL
3700 SD 92107 1288-A1
DIXON RD
5200 OCN 92056 1087-E1
DIXON WY
1200 CHV 91911 1330-E3
DIZA RD
100 SD 92173 1350-G2
DOBYNS DR
8500 SNTE 92071 1231-A7
8500 SNTE 92071 1251-A1
DOCENA DR
8400 SDCo 91977 1290-J5
DOCENA RD
- CRLB 92009 1127-C5
DOCK CT
6900 SD 92139 1290-F7
DOCK ST
- SD 92106 1288-A5
DOCKSIDE ST
5900 SD 92139 1290-D7
DODD LN
- SDCo 91906 (1318-B7 See Page 1298)
DODDER CT
13800 PWY 92064 1170-F5
DODGE DR
700 SD 92037 1247-F3
DODIE ST
8100 SD 92114 1290-G2
DODSON ST
300 SD 92102 1289-E4
DOE PT
8100 SD 92120 1250-D3
DOGWOOD
9800 SDCo 92021 1233-B3
DOGWOOD CT
4500 OCN 92056 1087-D4
15800 PWY 92064 1170-G4
DOGWOOD LN
9800 SDCo 92026 1089-D4
DOGWOOD PL
2100 ESCN 92026 1109-G4
DOGWOOD RD
15800 PWY 92064 1170-G4
DOGWOOD RD Rt#-S31
- ImCo 92243 431-B3
- ImCo 92249 431-C7
- ImCo 92251 6500-A2
200 BRW 92227 431-B3
400 ImCo 92231 431-C7
1300 ImCo 92243 6560-B5
1300 ImCo 92249 6560-B5
1600 ELCN 92243 6560-B2
1700 ELCN 92243 6500-A5
2100 ImCo 92243 6500-A2
2800 ImCo 92251 431-B3
3600 ImCo 92227 431-B3
DOGWOOD ST
- SDCo 92055 1086-B2
DOGWOOD WY
2400 VSTA 92083 1108-B6
DOHENY RD
9400 SNTE 92071 1231-B5
DOHENY BAY CT
4800 OCN 92057 1066-J6
DOLAN PL
3200 SDCo 91902 1310-H1
DOLIVA DR
4600 SD 92117 1248-H1
DOLLAR CT
10800 SDCo 92040 1232-B1
DOLLIMORE RD
300 ENCT 92024 1147-C6
DOLLY PL
9000 SD 92123 1249-D6
DOLO ST
200 SD 92114 1290-F4
DOLORE PL
1400 ESCN 92027 1110-A6
DOLORES CT
- SMCS 92069 1109-B7
500 SDCo 92065 1152-G5
DOLORES DR
3200 SDCo 92036 1156-E1
DOLORES ST
9900 SDCo 91977 1271-D5
DOLPHIN AL
- SD 92136 1289-E6
DOLPHIN CIR
1200 VSTA 92084 1088-B4
DOLPHIN CT
- SMCS 92078 1128-D6
DOLPHIN CV
200 DLMR 92014 1187-G7
DOLPHIN DR
- ImCo 92274 410-H6
DOLPHIN PL
5600 SD 92037 1247-F4
DOLPHIN RD
- SDCo 92055 1085-H6
DOLSTRA LN
900 SDCo 92028 1027-G1
DOMER RD
9400 SNTE 92071 1231-B4
DOMINGO GN
2100 ESCN 92026 1109-E3
DOMINGUEZ WY
300 ELCJ 92021 1251-H5
DOMINICAN DR
16800 SD 92128 1170-B3
DOMINION ST
800 SD 92113 1289-H5
DOMINO DR
9600 SDCo 92040 1232-D4
DON CT
1100 SD 92154 1350-E1
DON WY
4200 SD 92117 1248-E2
DONAHOE ST
- CHV 91911 1330-E1
DONAHUE DR
1800 SDCo 92019 1272-C3
DONAHUE ST
1000 SD 92110 1268-G3
DONAKER ST
8600 SD 92129 1189-B2
DON ALBERTO DR
3400 CRLB 92008 1107-C6
DONALD AV
4300 SD 92117 1248-E2
DONALD CT
4100 SD 92117 1248-E3
N DONALD WY
1200 ESCN 92027 1110-B6
DONALDSON DR
4500 SD 92109 1248-B5
DONALOR DR
1600 SDCo 92027 1130-D2
1700 ESCN 92027 1130-D2
DON ALVAREZ DR
3200 CRLB 92008 1107-B6
DONART DR
14000 PWY 92064 1190-G2
DON ARTURO DR
3400 CRLB 92008 1107-B6
DONAX AV
100 IMPB 91932 1329-F7
1300 IMPB 92154 1329-J7
1300 SD 92154 1329-J7
1700 SD 92154 1330-A7
DONAX CT
1500 SD 92154 1329-J7
DON CARLOS CT
1300 CHV 91910 1311-B6
DON CARLOS DR
3400 CRLB 92008 1107-C6
DONCAROL AV
1500 ELCJ 92019 1252-B6
DON COTA DR
3400 CRLB 92008 1107-B6
DON DIABLO DR
3300 CRLB 92008 1107-C7
DONEE DIEGO
3100 SDCo 92025 1150-E1
DON FELIPE DR
5400 CRLB 92008 1107-C6
DONITA DR
1500 SDCo 92020 1271-H1
DON JOSE DR
3400 CRLB 92008 1107-B6
DON JUAN DR
2900 CRLB 92008 1107-C6
DON LEE PL
1800 ESCN 92029 1129-D2
DONLEY ST
3200 SD 92117 1248-E6
DON LORENZO DR
3400 CRLB 92008 1107-C6
3500 SD 92117 1248-D4
DON LUIS DR
5400 CRLB 92008 1107-C6
DON MATA DR
5100 CRLB 92008 1107-B6
DON MIGUEL DR
5100 CRLB 92008 1107-B7
DONNA AV
3900 SD 92115 1270-E5
DONNA CT
3700 CRLB 92008 1106-G5
DONNA DR
3200 CRLB 92008 1106-G4
DONNA ST
8700 SNTE 92071 1231-E7
DONNA WY
6800 SD 92115 1270-E4
DONNAJEAN LN
8800 SNTE 92071 1231-E6
DONNALEE LN
9000 SNTE 92071 1231-A7
DONNAN PL
900 VSTA 92084 1088-A5
DONNER ST
9900 SNTE 92071 1231-F4
DONNIL LN
2300 SDCo 92028 997-A4
DONNINGTON WY
2300 SD 92139 1290-G7
DON ORTEGA DR
3400 CRLB 92008 1107-C6
DONOVAN STATE PRISON RD
- SDCo 92154 1332-B7
DON PABLO DR
3300 CRLB 92008 1107-B7
DON PANCHO WY
3000 SD 92173 1350-D3
DON PICO CT
10300 SDCo 91978 1271-E6
DON PICO RD
10200 SDCo 91978 1271-E6
DON PORFIRIO DR
5100 CRLB 92008 1107-B6
DON QUIXOTE DR
3300 CRLB 92008 1107-B7
DONRAY DR
700 SDCo 92065 1172-H1
DON RICARDO DR
5200 CRLB 92008 1107-B6
DON RODOLFO DR
5100 CRLB 92008 1107-B6
DON ROLANDO
3000 SDCo 92025 1150-E1
DONS WY
2100 SDCo 92084 1088-C7
DON TOMASO DR
3300 CRLB 92008 1107-C7
DON VALDEZ DR
5200 CRLB 92008 1107-B7
DONZEE ST
3400 SD 92123 1249-B5
DOOLITTLE AV
500 SD 92154 1330-E6
DOOMEY DR
1100 SDCo 92065 1152-E4
DORA DR
1700 ENCT 92007 1167-F3
DORADO CT
1000 CHV 91910 1311-A7
7900 SD 92037 1227-H5
DORADO LN
200 ELCJ 92019 1252-A5
DORADO PL
3300 CRLB 92009 1147-J1
DORADO WY
1000 CHV 91910 1311-A7
DORAL CT
4600 OCN 92057 1086-J1
4600 OCN 92057 1087-A1
DORAL GN
1700 ESCN 92026 1109-D4
DORAL WY
4000 CHV 91902 1310-F3
DORAN CT
- CHV 91910 1310-C4
DORAN ST
1800 SD 92154 1350-B3
DORATHEA TER
12900 PWY 92064 1190-B5
DORA VISTA LN
3000 SDCo 91935 1292-J1
DORCAS ST
1100 SD 92110 1268-F2
DORCHESTER DR
3300 SD 92123 1249-E4
DORCHESTER PL
4400 CRLB 92008 1106-J5
DORCHESTER ST
8100 SDCo 91977 1290-H2
DOREEN LN
2100 SDCo 92069 1108-G1
DOREEN RD
8200 SD 92120 1250-D3
DOREET WY
2900 CRLB 92008 1106-G3
DORENA CT
4900 SD 92122 1228-G5
DORIA WY
2900 SD 92139 1310-E2
DORIANA ST
6700 SD 92139 1290-F7
DORINDA CT
1500 SD 92154 1350-D2
DORINDA DR
600 OCN 92057 1087-B1
DORIS DR
700 ENCT 92024 1147-F7
900 ENCT 92024 1167-F1
DORIS ST
1800 SD 92154 1330-A7
DORIS JEAN PL
1600 VSTA 92083 1087-D7
DORM WY
2500 SDCo 91977 1271-D7
DORMAE LN
100 SDCo 92021 1252-J2
DORMAN DR
5100 SD 92115 1270-A1
DORMOUSE CT
7900 SD 92129 1189-A6
DORMOUSE RD
12100 SD 92129 1189-A6
DORNOCH CT
1700 SD 92154 1352-A2
DOROTHEA AV
700 SMCS 92069 1109-B6
1500 SDCo 92028 1027-J5
1600 SDCo 92028 1028-A5
DOROTHY AV
- SDCo 91905 1300-C7
DOROTHY CT
200 ESCN 92027 1130-D1
DOROTHY DR
5400 SD 92115 1270-B2
DOROTHY LN
16000 SDCo 92082 1071-B5
DOROTHY ST
400 ELCJ 92019 1252-A6
700 CHV 91911 1330-A5
DOROTHY WY
5600 SD 92115 1270-B2
DORSAL DR
9600 SDCo 92040 1232-D3
DORSET WY
13000 PWY 92064 1170-E2
DORSEY WY
200 VSTA 92083 1087-G4
DORSIE LN
3900 SDCo 91941 1271-H4
DORTHA CT
8500 SNTE 92071 1230-J7
DORTMUND PL
2500 SDCo 91901 1253-G2
DORY DR
3500 SDCo 91902 1310-J1
DORY LN
- CRLB 92009 1126-J7
DOS AMIGOS TR
13800 PWY 92064 1190-J3
DOS AMIGOS WY
17000 PWY 92064 1190-J3
DOS ARRONS WY
2700 VSTA 92083 1108-A7
DOS CABAZOS PL
- ESCN 92029 1149-J2
- ESCN 92029 1150-A3
DOS CABEZA RD
- ImCo 92259 430-F7
- SDCo 92259 430-F7
DOS CAMEOS DR
38400 SDCo 92028 997-C5
DOS HERMANOS GN
1200 ESCN 92027 1110-B5
DOS HERMANOS RD
17100 PWY 92064 1191-D2
DOS LOMAS
2500 SDCo 92028 1048-C1
DOS LOMAS PL
2900 SDCo 92028 1048-C2
DOS NINAS
32100 SDCo 92003 1048-H7
DOS NINOS RD
3700 SDCo 92028 1028-E5
DOS PICOS PARK RD
17500 SDCo 92065 1171-H5
DOTI POINT DR
6700 SD 92139 1290-F7
DOUBLE CANYON RD
32700 SDCo 92082 1049-C2
33300 SDCo 92059 1049-C2
DOUBLE D DR
1800 ELCJ 92021 1252-C3
1800 SDCo 92021 1252-C3
DOUBLE K RD
28400 SDCo 92082 1089-J1
28800 SDCo 92082 1069-J7
DOUBLE LL RANCH RD
2300 ENCT 92024 1148-B4
DOUBLE M RD
8600 SNTE 92071 1231-B7
DOUBLE O RD
2600 SDCo 92004 (1079-A3 See Page 1058)
DOUBLE R RD
14600 PWY 92064 1150-J7

SAN DIEGO CO.

INDEX

COPYRIGHT 2001 Thomas Bros. Maps ®

STREET
Block City ZIP Pg-Grid

DOUBLE R RD
14600 PWY 92064 1170-J1
DOUBLETREE RD
2200 SDCo 91978 1291-G1
2300 SDCo 91978 1271-G7
DOUGHERTY ST
100 SDCo 92028 1027-F2
W DOUGHERTY ST
200 SDCo 92028 1027-F2
DOUGLAS AV
600 SMCS 92069 1109-D6
E DOUGLAS AV
100 ELCJ 92020 1251-F5
W DOUGLAS AV
100 ELCJ 92020 1251-F5
DOUGLAS DR
100 OCN 92057 1086-G3
300 OCN 92054 1066-G7
800 OCN 92057 1066-H6
1300 VSTA 92084 1088-A2
5000 OCN 92057 1067-A4
N DOUGLAS DR
100 OCN 92054 1086-G2
200 OCN 92057 1086-G2
600 OCN 92054 1066-G7
600 OCN 92057 1066-G7
DOUGLAS ST
500 CHV 91910 1310-G7
DOVARY RD
200 SDCo 91910 1310-D6
DOVE AV
29900 SDCo 91906 (1297-F6
See Page 1296)
DOVE CIR
500 VSTA 92083 1087-F5
DOVE CT
- ImCo 92249 6560-B7
3500 SD 92103 1268-J6
DOVE LN
1700 CRLB 92009 1127-E5
DOVE ST
1300 ELCJ 92020 1251-D3
2600 SD 92103 1288-J1
2700 SD 92103 1268-J6
7700 SNTE 92071 1230-G7
DOVE CANYON RD
- SDCo 92127 1169-F4
DOVECREST CT
3100 SDCo 91977 1271-A6
DOVE FLOWER WY
6000 SD 92115 1270-C6
DOVE HILL DR
8600 SNTE 92071 1231-A7
DOVE HOLLOW RD
3200 ENCT 92024 1148-C4
DOVER CT
700 SD 92109 1267-J3
800 CHV 91910 1310-G7
800 SMCS 92069 1128-F2
DOVER ST
1400 OCN 92057 1067-B4
DOVER WY
4500 CRLB 92008 1107-B5
DOVERHILL RD
11000 SD 92131 1209-J2
DOVE RUN RD
1100 ENCT 92024 1148-A5
DOVE SONG WY
- ENCT 92024 1148-A5
DOVE TAIL TER
11000 SD 92128 1189-H4
DOVEVIEW CT
3500 SDCo 91977 1271-C5
DOVEWOOD CT
15700 PWY 92064 1170-F5
DOW PL
3000 SD 92117 1248-C1
DOW ST
- SD 92106 1287-J4
DOWDEN RD
600 ImCo 92233 411-C10
DOWDY DR
9300 SD 92126 1209-B7
DOWITCHER CT
1100 CRLB 92009 1127-A4
DOWITCHER WY
4200 OCN 92057 1087-A3
4200 OCN 92057 1086-J3
DOWLING DR
6300 SD 92037 1247-F2
DOWLING LN
32100 SDCo 92082 1049-J7
32100 SDCo 92082 1050-A7
DOWNER AV
500 ELCJ 92020 1251-E7
DOWNEY CT
900 CHV 91911 1330-J2
900 CHV 91911 1331-A2
DOWNING ST
1100 IMPB 91932 1349-G1
DOWN MEMORY LN
- SDCo 92127 1169-A2
DOWNS ST
1200 OCN 92054 1086-D7
1300 OCN 92054 1106-E1
DOWNWIND WY
2300 SD 92093 1227-H3
DOYLE ST
400 NATC 92136 1289-G7
400 NATC 92136 1309-G1
400 SD 92136 1289-G7
DRACAENA CT
6100 SD 92114 1290-C6
DRACMA DR
1000 SD 92154 1330-C7
1000 SD 92154 1350-C1
DRACO RD
10900 SD 92126 1209-D3
DRAGOYE DR
9700 SNTE 92071 1231-C4
DRAGT PL
1000 ESCN 92029 1129-F4
DRAKE BAY
300 OCN 92057 1066-H6
DRAKE CT
1500 CHV 91902 1311-C4
DRAKE ST
6700 SD 92114 1290-E3
DRAKEWOOD TER
4800 SD 92130 1188-C4
DRAPER AV
6600 SD 92037 1247-F1
7300 SD 92037 1227-E7
DRAYTON HALL WY
17400 SD 92128 1170-A1
17500 SD 92128 1150-A7
DRAZIL RD
1100 SDCo 92028 1027-H5

DREAM ST
5500 SD 92114 1290-B4
DRELL CT
1500 ELCJ 92021 1251-H2
DRESCHER ST
1800 SD 92111 1268-J1
W DRESCHER ST
1700 SD 92111 1268-H1
DRESDEN PL
2400 SD 92037 1248-B3
DRESSAGE DR
5300 SDCo 91902 1311-A2
5300 SDCo 91902 1310-J2
DRESSAGE LN
- SD 92130 1188-E5
DREW LN
2700 LMGR 91945 1270-F7
DREW RD Rt#-S29
- ImCo 92273 431-A7
400 ImCo 92231 431-A7
400 ImCo 92243 431-A7
DREW VIEW LN
- SD 92113 1290-A5
DREXEL AV
- NATC 91950 1290-B6
N DREXEL AV
- NATC 91950 1290-B6
- SD 92114 1290-B6
DREXEL CT
8000 LMGR 91945 1290-H1
DREXEL DR
1500 LMGR 91945 1290-H1
1500 SDCo 91977 1290-H2
DRIFTING CIRCLE DR
1000 VSTA 92083 1107-G2
DRIFTWOOD CIR
1800 CRLB 92008 1106-J6
DRIFTWOOD CT
3200 SD 92037 1228-B4
DRIFTWOOD DR
100 ELCN 92243 6559-F1
10600 SD 92126 1209-E3
DRIFTWOOD LN
700 SDCo 92028 1027-G3
DRIFTWOOD PL
3500 OCN 92056 1107-C2
DRIFTWOOD WY
4700 OCN 92057 1087-B2
DRIFTWOOD CREEK RD
14900 SDCo 92021 1232-H3
DRISCOLL DR
3000 SD 92117 1248-C3
DRIVE F
- CRLB 92009 1127-B4
DRIVE G
- CRLB 92009 1127-B4
DRIVE H
- CRLB 92009 1127-B4
DRIVE I
- CRLB 92009 1127-B4
DRIVE J
- CRLB 92009 1127-B4
DRIVE K
- CRLB 92009 1127-B4
DRIVE L
- CRLB 92009 1127-B4
DRIVER WY
3300 OCN 92056 1086-H7
DROVER DR
5300 SD 92115 1270-A1
DRUCELLA ST
2300 SD 92154 1330-B7
DRUCKER LN
2500 SD 92154 1351-J4
DRUMCLIFF AV
10200 SD 92126 1209-C5
DRURY LN
1600 VSTA 92084 1088-B4
7400 SD 92037 1227-F6
DRY BARK CT
11500 SD 92126 1209-A1
DRY CREEK DR
700 CHV 91914 1311-G3
DRY CREEK PL
7700 LMGR 91945 1290-G2
7700 SD 92114 1290-G2
DRYDEN PL
5800 CRLB 92008 1127-B3
DRYDEN RD
2200 ELCJ 92020 1251-B5
DRY FLATS RD
- SDCo 92066 430-B6
DUANE DR
8700 SNTE 92071 1231-C7
DUARTE PL
1500 SD 92114 1290-D6
DUBE CT
8300 SNTE 92071 1230-H6
DUBLIN DR
100 ENCT 92007 1167-D4
2000 SD 92154 1351-F3
DUBLIN LN
1500 ESCN 92027 1110-B4
DUBOIS DR
4800 SD 92117 1248-F1
4900 SD 92117 1228-E7
DU BOIS RD
- ImCo 92243 6559-C1
DUBOIS TKTR
- SDCo 91901 429-J4
- SDCo 91916 429-J4
- SDCo 91916 (1195-C7
See Page 1175)
DUBONNET ST
8500 SD 92123 1249-C4
DUBUQUE ST
1300 OCN 92054 1086-B6
DUCHESS ST
6800 SD 92115 1270-E5
DUCK POND LN
- SDCo 92065 1172-D5
DUCKWALK RD
- SMCS 92069 1108-H4
DUCKWEED TR
- SDCo 91906 (1318-C6
See Page 1298)
DUCOMMUN AV
2900 SD 92122 1228-C5
DUCOS PL
4900 SD 92124 1249-H2
DUDLEY ST
700 SD 92106 1288-A3
3600 SD 92106 1287-J3
DUENDA RD
11100 SD 92127 1149-J7
11400 SD 92127 1169-J1
DUFF RD
100 ImCo 92243 6559-J4

DUFFER CT
3100 SDCo 92004 (1079-B5
See Page 1058)
DUFFWOOD LN
29100 SDCo 92082 1070-J6
DUFFY WY
3700 SDCo 91902 1310-E4
DUFRESNE PL
8300 SD 92129 1189-B4
DUGAN AV
5500 LMSA 91942 1270-J1
5500 LMSA 91942 1250-H6
DUKE ST
1900 CHV 91913 1311-D5
3200 SD 92110 1268-C5
DUKE MIGUEL CT
10600 SNTE 92071 1231-E2
DUKES PL
1200 SDCo 92065 1152-J6
DULCI PL
500 ELCJ 92019 1251-J6
DULENE DR
9100 SDCo 92040 1232-E6
DULIN PL
4400 OCN 92057 1087-A3
DULIN RD
3800 SDCo 92003 1048-G5
3800 SDCo 92028 1048-H3
DULUTH AV
5800 SD 92114 1290-C5
DU LUZ RD
- SDCo 92055 409-A6
DULZURA AV
2400 SD 92104 1289-E1
DUMAR AV
1400 ELCJ 92019 1252-A6
DUMAS ST
3000 SD 92106 1268-C6
DUNANT ST
6000 SD 92122 1228-C5
DUNAWAY DR
8600 SD 92037 1227-J4
DUNAWAY RD
- ImCo 92259 430-K6
DUNBAR LN
9600 SDCo 92021 1233-D2
DUNBAR PL
16000 SDCo 92021 1233-D3
DUNBARTON RD
9200 SNTE 92071 1231-A5
DUNBROOK RD
7800 SD 92126 1209-B6
DUNCAN CT
11300 SD 92126 1209-D1
DUNCAN DR
10100 SDCo 92040 1232-C2
DUNCAN RD
8800 SD 92126 1209-C3
DUNCAN TER
32200 SDCo 92082 1050-F6
DUNCANNON CT
8500 SD 92126 1209-C1
DUNDEE AV
5400 SD 92120 1250-B5
DUNDEE CT
2700 CRLB 92008 1107-A5
DUNDEE WY
2500 VSTA 92083 1107-J5
DUNE LN
7200 SD 92037 1247-E1
DUNEDIN CT
9700 SNTE 92071 1231-A4
DUNEMERE DR
300 SD 92037 1247-E1
DUNES PL
3400 OCN 92054 1086-F4
DUNHAM WY
4600 SD 92130 1188-C5
DUNHAVEN ST
2100 SD 92110 1268-F1
DUNHILL CT
4500 OCN 92056 1107-D2
DUNHILL ST
3500 SD 92121 1208-B5
DUNHOLME ST
8900 SD 92126 1209-D4
DUNLAP RD
- SD 92140 1268-E7
DUNLIN PL
300 SD 92114 1290-D4
DUNLOP ST
2200 SD 92111 1248-J7
W DUNLOP ST
2200 SD 92111 1248-J7
DUNNING CIR
1900 SD 92154 1350-A1
DUNSMORE CT
400 ENCT 92024 1147-G6
DUNSMUIR CT
- CHV 91913 1331-D1
DUNSMUIR ST
1300 ELCJ 92019 1251-J6
DUNSTAN ST
2200 OCN 92054 1086-E7
DUNWOOD WY
7500 SD 92114 1290-G5
DUNWOODIE RD
8500 SNTE 92071 1230-J6
DUO CT
800 VSTA 92084 1087-H5
DUORO DR
700 CHV 91910 1310-J6
DUPONT DR
1500 LMGR 91945 1290-H1
DU PONT ST
3500 SD 92106 1288-A3
DUPONT ST
3500 SD 92106 1288-A3
3600 SD 92106 1287-J3
DURANGO CIR
7200 CRLB 92009 1127-E7
DURANGO DR
13600 SD 92014 1187-H6
DURANT ST
3200 SD 92113 1289-F4
DURASNO LN
1300 SDCo 91977 1271-E7
DURAZNITOS PL
2400 SDCo 92065 1172-C4
DURAZNITOS RD
2300 SDCo 92065 1172-C4
DURGIN ST
100 SDCo 92065 1172-D1
200 SDCo 92065 1152-D7
DURHAM CIR
3500 OCN 92056 1107-E3
DURHAM ST
- SD 92106 1288-A4
500 ELCJ 92019 1252-A4

DURHULLEN DR
14100 PWY 92064 1170-G7
DURIAN CT
1300 VSTA 92083 1087-E6
DURIAN ST
100 VSTA 92083 1087-D7
100 VSTA 92083 1107-D1
DURWARD ST
800 CHV 91910 1310-G7
DUSK DR
2100 SD 92139 1290-E7
2100 SD 92139 1310-F1
DUSK LN
4200 OCN 92056 1107-C2
DUSTY LN
3000 ENCT 92024 1148-A3
DUSTY RD
200 SMCS 92069 1108-G7
DUSTY TR
3000 ENCT 92024 1148-B3
DUSTY ACRES CT
500 ENCT 92024 1147-J7
DUSTY ROSE PL
6900 CRLB 92009 1127-E6
DUTTON DR
10700 SDCo 91941 1271-F3
DUVAL ST
600 SD 92102 1289-J2
700 SD 92102 1290-A3
DWANE AV
6300 SD 92120 1250-D7
DWIGHT ST
2100 SD 92104 1269-D6
3600 SD 92105 1269-G6
5400 SD 92105 1270-B6
5900 SD 92115 1270-C6
DYANNA CT
1200 SDCo 92084 1108-A1
1200 VSTA 92084 1108-A1
DYE RD
2000 SDCo 92065 1172-C3
DYE ST
200 SDCo 92065 1172-B4
DYER DR
2600 SD 92110 1268-E6
DYKES AV
6300 SD 92114 1290-D5
DYLAN ST
6900 SD 92139 1290-F7
DYLAN WY
- ENCT 92024 1147-D2

E

E AV
- SDCo 92055 1066-D1
100 CORD 92118 1288-H7
200 NATC 91950 1289-H7
300 NATC 91950 1309-H1
E CT
- SD 92126 1209-E7
E ST
- NATC 91950 1310-C3
200 CHV 91910 1310-F7
300 SDCo 92065 1152-F6
300 SD 92101 1289-A3
700 SD 92101 1288-J3
1300 SD 92110 1268-F2
1800 SDCo 92084 1108-G2
1900 SD 92102 1289-C3
E ST Rt#-S17
- CHV 91910 1310-B5
200 CHV 91910 1309-J6
E E ST
- ENCT 92024 1147-C7
W E ST
100 ENCT 92024 1147-B7
EADS AV
7100 SD 92037 1247-F1
7200 SD 92037 1227-E6
EADY LN
40500 SDCo 91905 1300-F7
EADY RD
- ImCo 92231 431-C7
EAGLE CRSG
400 OCN 92054 1086-B6
EAGLE GN
1300 ESCN 92029 1129-G6
EAGLE LN
1500 ELCJ 92020 1251-D2
EAGLE PASS
3600 SDCo 91901 1275-B3
EAGLE RDG
3600 SDCo 92036 1155-F4
EAGLE ST
600 SD 92103 1268-J5
EAGLE CREST LN
2400 VSTA 92083 1107-J5
EAGLE HILL LN
20200 SDCo 92065 1152-E1
EAGLEHILL RD
28000 SDCo 92082 1090-J3
28000 SDCo 92082 1091-A2
EAGLE LAKE DR
10300 SDCo 92029 1129-F7
EAGLE MINE DR
14200 PWY 92064 1190-J3
EAGLE MOUNTAIN RD
6900 SDCo 92003 1068-E4
EAGLE PEAK CT
1400 CHV 91910 1311-B5
EAGLE PEAK RD
- SDCo 92036 1154-H7
- SDCo 92036 1174-G3
- SDCo 92036 1175-A1
- SDCo 92036 (1194-C2
See Page 1175)
4000 SDCo 92036 1155-G3
EAGLE RIDGE CT
7600 SD 92119 1250-G4
EAGLE RIDGE DR
7700 SD 92119 1250-G4
EAGLE RIDGE PL
1000 CHV 91913 1331-A1
EAGLE ROCK AV
10200 SD 92126 1209-C5
EAGLE ROCK LN
1300 ESCN 92026 1129-F1
EAGLE ROCK WY
- OCN 92054 1086-B6
EAGLES CREEK CT
11200 SD 92128 1189-J4
EAGLES CREST RD
16400 SDCo 92065 1151-A5
EAGLES NEST WY
1700 OCN 92054 1086-B6
EAGLES NEST STATION
- PWY 92064 1170-G1

EAGLES NOEL
30300 SDCo 92082 1070-G4
EAGLES PERCH LN
31200 SDCo 92003 1068-E2
EAGLE SUMMIT PL
1800 ESCN 92026 1109-F6
EAGLESVIEW CT
11500 SD 92127 1169-J5
EAGLES VIEW GN
1800 ESCN 92026 1109-B4
EAGLE VALLEY DR
2400 CHV 91914 1311-F3
EAGLE VIEW DR
9600 SDCo 92026 1089-D5
EAGLE VIEW LN
15800 SDCo 92082 1071-A6
EAMES ST
8500 SD 92123 1249-C4
EARHART ST
8900 SD 92123 1249-D5
EARIE LN
14000 PWY 92064 1190-G4
EARL GN
2000 ESCN 92026 1109-C4
EARL ST
2000 SD 92113 1289-H7
9200 LMSA 91942 1251-B6
EARLE DR
1200 NATC 91950 1290-C7
1200 NATC 91950 1310-C1
EARLGATE CT
13000 PWY 92064 1190-F5
EARLHAM ST
100 SDCo 92065 1152-H5
E EARLHAM ST
200 SDCo 92065 1152-J4
EARLING WY
700 SDCo 92021 1251-G1
EARLS ST
100 ELCN 92243 6500-B6
EARNSCLIFF PL
3600 SD 92111 1248-H4
EARTH DR
700 VSTA 92083 1087-D6
EARTHSTAR CT
11500 SD 92127 1169-J4
EAST DR
300 VSTA 92083 1087-G4
3400 SD 92110 1268-E5
E EAST DR
100 VSTA 92084 1087-H4
EAST LN
100 SDCo 92021 1252-J3
1100 IMPB 91932 1349-G2
EAST ST
- SD 92102 1289-J4
2700 OCN 92054 1086-D7
EASTBOURNE RD
11900 SD 92128 1190-B1
EASTBROOK RD
2200 VSTA 92083 1127-G1
2200 VSTA 92083 1107-H7
EASTBURY DR
700 ESCN 92027 1130-C2
EASTCLIFF CT
4800 SD 92130 1188-C6
EAST COUNTY DR
8500 SDCo 92021 1232-D7
8500 SDCo 92021 1252-E1
EASTER PL
1600 ESCN 92029 1129-F5
EASTER WY
9400 SD 92121 1228-D1
EASTERLEIGH RW
6300 SD 92037 1247-J1
EASTERN AV
13900 PWY 92064 1190-F3
EASTFIELD RD
11600 PWY 92064 1210-C1
EASTGATE CT
8400 SD 92121 1228-F1
EASTGATE DR
5700 SD 92121 1228-E1
EASTGATE MALL
4100 SD 92037 1228-D2
4300 SD 92121 1228-E1
EASTGLEN ST
11900 SD 92131 1210-A3
EASTHAVEN CT
10800 SNTE 92071 1231-E1
EASTHAVEN DR
10200 SNTE 92071 1231-D1
EASTHILL DR
7500 SD 92114 1290-G3
EASTLAKE DR
600 CHV 91913 1311-E4
EAST LAKE DR
6200 LMSA 91942 1251-A6
6200 SD 92119 1251-A5
EASTLAKE PKWY
700 CHV 91913 1311-F4
700 CHV 91914 1311-F4
1000 CHV 91915 1311-F6
EASTMAN ST
6900 SD 92111 1248-J7
EASTMONT PL
900 SDCo 92026 1109-H2
EASTMORE PL
1400 OCN 92056 1087-E3
EASTOM WY
2100 SDCo 92028 1028-A6
EASTON AV
5600 SD 92120 1250-B6
EASTON CT
6800 SD 92120 1250-B6
EAST POINTE AV
1700 CRLB 92008 1106-H6
EASTRIDGE CT
12700 SD 92131 1210-C1
EASTRIDGE DR
4100 LMSA 91941 1270-H4
EASTRIDGE LN
200 ESCN 92026 1109-G4
EASTRIDGE LP
2300 CHV 91915 1311-G5
EASTRIDGE PL
11400 SD 92131 1210-C1
EASTSHORE TER
700 CHV 91913 1311-E4
EASTSIDE RD
900 ELCJ 92020 1251-D3
EASTVALE RD
14800 PWY 92064 1170-J6
15300 PWY 92064 1171-A6
EASTVIEW CT
1400 OCN 92056 1087-E3
11400 SD 92131 1210-C1
EASTVIEW PT
11400 SD 92131 1210-C2

EASTVIEW TER
- SDCo 92025 1130-E7
EASTWIND PT
11400 SD 92131 1209-J4
EASTWOOD LN
1800 ENCT 92024 1147-H6
EASY PL
200 CRLB 92009 1126-H4
EASY ST
1700 SDCo 92069 1108-G2
3200 SD 92105 1270-B6
6400 CRLB 92009 1126-H4
EATON ST
100 OCN 92054 1106-C4
EATON WY
100 VSTA 92084 1087-H5
EBANO CT
100 SOLB 92075 1167-D7
EBBS PL
5600 SD 92114 1290-C6
EBBS ST
1400 SD 92114 1290-C6
EBB TIDE ST
- CRLB 92009 1127-A4
EBBTIDE WY
- SD 92154 1330-H7
EBERHART ST
6800 SD 92115 1270-E2
EBERLY CT
10800 SD 92126 1209-D3
EBERS ST
1300 SD 92107 1287-H1
1300 SD 92107 1267-J7
2000 SD 92107 1268-A6
EBERSOLE DR
4300 SD 92154 1330-G7
EBOE AV
1400 SD 92154 1349-J1
EBONY AV
- IMPB 91932 1349-E1
EBONY RIDGE RD
- SD 92102 1290-A4
ECCLESIA DR
100 OCN 92054 1086-C5
ECHO CT
8600 LMSA 91941 1270-J4
ECHO DR
4000 SDCo 92036 1156-E3
4200 LMSA 91941 1271-A4
8500 LMSA 91941 1270-J4
ECHO LN
- SD 92101 1288-C2
- SD 92133 1288-C2
- SMCS 92078 1128-G2
100 SMCS 92069 1128-G1
100 SMCS 92069 1108-G7
ECHO PL
4000 OCN 92056 1107-B1
ECHO DELL RD
8200 SD 92119 1250-D3
ECHO HILL LN
4800 SDCo 92014 1168-A7
ECHO LN ACCESS RD
- SMCS 92069 1128-G1
ECHO VALLEY LN
1700 ESCN 92026 1109-F4
1700 SDCo 92026 1109-F4
ECHO VALLEY RD
2800 SDCo 91935 1292-D3
ECKEN RD
600 ELCJ 92020 1251-E7
ECKE RANCH RD
- ENCT 92024 1147-D5
ECKMAN AV
1300 CHV 91911 1330-F3
ECKMAN CT
100 CHV 91911 1330-F3
ECKSTROM AV
7000 SD 92111 1248-J2
7300 SD 92111 1249-A2
ECLIPSE PL
12500 SD 92129 1189-B6
ECLIPSE RD
7900 SD 92129 1189-A6
ECLOGA CT
25100 SDCo 92065 1173-H3
ECOCHEE AV
3300 SD 92117 1248-D3
3800 SD 92117 1248-E3
EDDIE DR
300 VSTA 92083 1087-H7
EDDIE JONES WY
- OCN 92054 1086-D4
EDDING DR
2400 LMGR 91945 1270-G7
EDDINGTON RD
10900 SNTE 92071 1231-F6
EDDINS RD Rt#-S30
- ImCo 92233 411-A10
EDELL PL
2900 SD 92117 1228-C7
EDELWEISS
15200 SDCo 92021 1233-B3
EDELWEISS LN
700 ENCT 92024 1148-A6
EDEN CT
- SMCS 92078 1128-C6
EDEN DR
1700 SD 92109 1268-A1
EDEN GRV
14200 PWY 92064 1170-G6
EDEN LN
900 ELCJ 92020 1251-H7
900 SDCo 92020 1251-H7
EDEN PL
800 ESCN 92026 1129-G2
EDENBRIDGE LN
2300 SD 92139 1290-F7
EDENOAKS ST
10600 SD 92131 1210-C3
EDENVALE AV
4600 LMSA 91941 1270-J3
EDEN VALLEY LN
2600 SDCo 92029 1129-C3
EDGAR PL
9800 SDCo 91941 1271-D3
EDGAR RD
- ImCo 92251 431-A3
EDGEBROOK PL
1700 ESCN 92026 1109-D5
EDGEBURT DR
100 ENCT 92024 1147-A3
EDGE CLIFF DR
1400 SD 92109 1268-A1
EDGEFIELD LN
1700 ENCT 92024 1147-G6
EDGEHILL LN
300 OCN 92054 1086-E6

EDGEHILL RD
2000 SDCo 92084 1088-D4
2000 VSTA 92084 1088-D4
EDGELAKE DR
9800 SDCo 91941 1271-D1
EDGELAND ST
700 ELCJ 92021 1251-G3
EDGEMERE AV
- CHV 91910 1310-A3
3000 NATC 91950 1310-A3
3200 CHV 91950 1310-A3
EDGEMONT PL
1000 SD 92102 1289-E3
EDGEMONT ST
1000 SD 92102 1289-E3
EDGEMOOR DR
8900 SNTE 92071 1231-E6
EDGEMOOR ST
13500 PWY 92064 1190-F3
EDGE PARK WY
4800 SD 92124 1249-G1
EDGER CT
- SDCo 92055 1086-A2
EDGERTON DR
2300 LMGR 91945 1270-G7
EDGERTON WY
800 NATC 91950 1309-J1
EDGEVIEW DR
4800 SDCo 92020 1271-G2
EDGEVIEW ST
3300 SMCS 92069 1128-B1
EDGEWARE RD
4500 SD 92116 1269-H2
EDGEWARE WY
2900 CRLB 92008 1107-A4
EDGEWATER AV
500 OCN 92057 1067-D6
EDGEWATER DR
700 CHV 91913 1311-E4
EDGEWATER ST
5900 SD 92139 1310-D1
EDGEWOOD CT
4300 SDCo 91941 1271-C3
EDGEWOOD DR
100 OCN 92054 1086-D6
3600 SDCo 92036 1156-E2
9100 LMSA 91941 1271-B3
9100 SDCo 91941 1271-B3
EDGEWOOD PL
1000 CHV 91913 1311-E6
2200 OCN 92054 1086-C6
EDGEWORTH RD
5000 SD 92109 1248-A3
EDIE LN
9500 SDCo 92040 1231-J5
EDILEE DR
1600 ENCT 92007 1167-E2
EDINA CT
13100 PWY 92064 1170-D2
EDINA WY
13000 PWY 92064 1170-D2
EDINBURG AV
1800 ENCT 92007 1167-D3
EDINBURGH CT
6700 SD 92120 1250-E7
EDINBURGH DR
4700 CRLB 92008 1107-A5
EDISON PL
5800 CRLB 92008 1127-C3
EDISON ST
4100 SD 92117 1248-E6
EDITH DR
1900 ESCN 92026 1109-D4
EDITH LN
3100 SD 92106 1268-C7
EDITHA DR
200 SDCo 92019 1253-D1
EDIWHAR AV
3400 SD 92123 1249-D4
EDMONDS ST
6300 SD 92114 1290-D4
EDMONTON AV
6400 SD 92122 1228-E4
EDNA PL
3800 SD 92116 1269-G3
EDNA WY
500 VSTA 92083 1107-J3
500 VSTA 92083 1108-A3
EDNABELLE CT
900 ELCJ 92021 1251-H4
EDSON RD
8600 SD 92145 1229-C1
EDULIS CT
8700 SD 92129 1189-C6
EDWARD
9400 SDCo 92040 1232-F4
EDWARD ST
400 ELCJ 92020 1251-B5
EDWARD LLOYD LN
- ENCT 92024 1148-B4
EDWIN LN
1900 SDCo 92069 1108-H2
EDWIN PL
4900 SD 92117 1228-C7
EDWINA WY
900 ENCT 92007 1167-E2
EDWORDS ACCESS RD
10200 SDCo 92026 1109-G3
EEL AL
- SD 92136 1289-E6
EGAN ST
3400 SD 92115 1270-D6
EGLANTINE CT
10600 SD 92131 1209-H1
EGRET ST
- CRLB 92009 1127-D7
6000 SD 92114 1290-C1
EGRET WY
1400 ELCJ 92019 1252-A7
EICHENLAUB ST
- SD 92117 1248-D3
EIDER CT
- CRLB 92009 1127-C6
EIDER ST
6400 SD 92114 1290-D2
EIDER WY
1000 OCN 92057 1087-A3
EILEEN DR
2400 SD 92123 1249-E7
EILEEN ST
8600 SDCo 91977 1291-A2
EISENHOWER AV
13800 PWY 92064 1190-C3
EKLUND CT
1100 VSTA 92083 1107-J1
EL ACEBO
5000 SDCo 92067 1168-A4
EL ACEBO DEL NORTE
- SDCo 92067 1168-A4

STREET Block City ZIP Pg-Grid

EL AGUILA LN
2500 CRLB 92009 1127-G5
ELAINE AV
500 OCN 92057 1067-A6
ELAINE WY
6800 SD 92120 1250-E7
EL AIRE PL
1700 ESCN 92026 1109-E6
EL AMIGO RD
300 DLMR 92014 1187-G6
2100 SD 92014 1187-H6
EL AMO
400 OCN 92054 1086-F2
ELAN LN
1800 SDCo 92019 1272-D3
EL APAJO
5700 SDCo 92067 1168-D6
5700 SDCo 92091 1168-D6
EL ARBOL DR
5300 CRLB 92008 1126-G2
EL ARCO IRIS
4800 SDCo 92067 1168-A5
EL ASADO ST
14200 SD 92129 1189-C2
EL ASPECTO
4700 SDCo 92067 1168-A3
EL ASTILLERO PL
7900 CRLB 92009 1147-G3
EL BANQUERO CT
8100 SD 92119 1250-E3
EL BANQUERO PL
6700 SD 92119 1250-E3
EL BERRO
400 OCN 92054 1086-F2
ELBERT CT
11500 SD 92126 1209-D1
ELBERT TER
9000 SD 92126 1209-D1
ELBERT WY
11400 SD 92126 1209-D1
EL BOSQUE AV
2400 CRLB 92009 1147-G3
EL BOSQUE CT
4300 SD 92154 1330-G7
EL BRAZO
17900 SDCo 92067 1149-A5
ELBROOK DR
300 SDCo 92028 1027-G3
EL CABALLO AV
10600 SDCo 92127 1169-F4
EL CABALLO DR
700 OCN 92057 1067-A5
EL CABO CT
5700 SD 92124 1229-H7
EL CABRILLO
600 ENCT 92024 1147-F5
EL CAJON BLVD
- LMSA 91942 1270-E2
100 ELCJ 92020 1251-D7
1800 SD 92103 1269-C4
1900 SD 92104 1269-C4
3700 SD 92105 1269-G4
4300 SD 92115 1269-G4
4400 SD 92115 1270-E2
7300 LMSA 91941 1270-E2
EL CAJON LN
1800 SDCo 92065 1172-F1
EL CALOR LN
1400 ESCN 92026 1109-E6
EL CAMINITO
1000 VSTA 92083 1107-G1
EL CAMINITO RD
700 SDCo 92028 1027-H4
EL CAMINO CT
1400 ENCT 92024 1167-G3
EL CAMINO DR
1200 SMCS 92069 1128-D2
5600 SD 92121 1208-F6
EL CAMINO DEL LA FLORES
- ESCN 92026 1109-F7
EL CAMINO DEL NORTE
2200 ENCT 92024 1147-J6
2300 ENCT 92024 1148-A6
2700 SDCo 92024 1148-A6
2800 SDCo 92067 1148-C7
6800 SDCo 92067 1168-F1
EL CAMINO DEL TEATRO
1500 SD 92037 1247-G1
EL CAMINO DE PINOS
8700 SDCo 92026 1068-J5
EL CAMINO ENTRADA
15400 PWY 92064 1170-F5
EL CAMINO PEQUENO
100 ELCJ 92019 1252-D5
EL CAMINO REAL
- SDCo 92055 408-K7
- SDCo 92055 1023-E3
- SDCo 92672 1023-E3
- SMCS 92078 1129-C2
11300 SD 92130 1207-J1
11300 SD 92130 1208-A1
12000 SD 92130 1187-J3
12400 SD 92130 1188-A2
14300 SD 92014 1188-B1
14800 SDCo 92014 1188-B1
14900 SDCo 92067 1188-B1
15100 SDCo 92014 1168-A6
15100 SDCo 92067 1168-A6
16000 SDCo 92014 1167-J5
16000 SDCo 92067 1167-J4
EL CAMINO REAL Rt#-S11
1000 CRLB 92024 1147-E1
1000 ENCT 92024 1147-E1
1000 CRLB 92009 1147-E1
1200 CRLB 92009 1127-E4
1600 CRLB 92008 1127-D1
1800 CRLB 92008 1107-A6
2100 CRLB 92008 1106-H4
2300 OCN 92054 1106-H4
2300 OCN 92056 1106-H4
2400 CRLB 92054 1106-H4
N EL CAMINO REAL
- OCN 92054 1086-G2
100 OCN 92057 1086-G2
N EL CAMINO REAL Rt#-S11
100 ENCT 92024 1147-F4
1000 CRLB 92009 1147-F4
1000 CRLB 92024 1147-F4
1000 ENCT 92009 1147-F4
S EL CAMINO REAL
100 ENCT 92024 1147-G7
100 OCN 92057 1086-F5
100 OCN 92054 1086-F5
400 ENCT 92024 1167-G3
1200 OCN 92056 1086-G7

S EL CAMINO REAL
1400 OCN 92054 1106-G1
1400 OCN 92056 1106-G1
3100 SCLE 92672 1023-B1
3900 SDCo 92672 1023-B1
EL CAMINO VERDE
2800 SDCo 91935 1293-J3
EL CAMINO VILLAS
2300 OCN 92056 1106-H2
EL CANTO DR
3600 SDCo 91977 1271-E4
3800 SDCo 91941 1271-E4
EL CAPITAN
- SMCS 92078 1129-C2
EL CAPITAN CT
4300 CRLB 92008 1106-J5
EL CAPITAN DR
- CHV 91911 1330-E1
7900 LMSA 91941 1270-H2
EL CAPITAN TKTR
- SDCo 91901 429-J4
- SDCo 91916 429-J4
- SDCo 91916 (1194-G7 See Page 1175)
14700 SDCo 92040 (1193-G1 See Page 1192)
14700 SDCo 92065 1173-H7
14700 SDCo 92065 (1193-G1 See Page 1192)
14900 SDCo 92036 (1194-A1 See Page 1175)
14900 SDCo 92040 (1194-A1 See Page 1175)
14900 SDCo 92065 (1194-A1 See Page 1175)
EL CAPITAN PEAK
15500 SDCo 92021 1233-C1
EL CAPITAN REAL LN
15400 SDCo 92021 1233-B2
EL CAPITAN REAL RD
10200 SDCo 92021 1233-B2
EL CAPORAL
17200 SDCo 92067 1168-H2
EL CARMEL PL
700 SD 92109 1267-H2
EL CEDRO CT
4300 SD 92154 1330-G7
EL CENTRO AV
- SDCo 91934 (1321-G5 See Page 1300)
400 ELCN 92243 6499-G5
EL CENTRO ST
1100 IMPB 91932 1349-F2
EL CENTRO TER
- SDCo 91948 1218-F7
EL CENTRO RAVINE RD
- SDCo 91948 1218-D7
EL CERISE
900 SDCo 92028 1028-B1
EL CERRITO DR
4500 SD 92115 1270-B4
EL CERRITO PL
4700 SD 92115 1270-B3
EL CERRO
400 OCN 92054 1086-F2
EL CERRO DR
9100 SDCo 92040 1232-D6
EL CHICO
1400 SDCo 92069 1128-C3
EL CHICO LN
200 CORD 92118 1288-J6
EL CIELITO
5400 SDCo 92067 1168-B4
EL CIELO
- SDCo 92067 1148-J5
- SDCo 92067 1149-A5
EL CIELO LN
1400 ESCN 92026 1109-E6
EL CIRCULO
5100 OCN 92056 1087-D2
6300 SDCo 92067 1168-E1
ELCO ST
3700 SD 92111 1248-J3
EL COMAL DR
10400 SD 92124 1229-H7
EL COPA LN
100 SDCo 92083 1108-C3
EL CORRAL LN
1300 SDCo 92069 1128-F4
EL CORTEZ CT
1200 CHV 91910 1311-B7
EL CORTO
2400 SDCo 92084 1108-D4
EL COYOTE RUN
2800 SDCo 92028 998-C4
ELDEAN LN
1300 OCN 92054 1086-F7
ELDEN AV
1300 CHV 91911 1330-C4
ELDEN ST
8700 LMSA 91942 1250-J7
8700 LMSA 91942 1251-A7
ELDER AV
- IMPB 91932 1349-E1
100 CHV 91910 1310-A5
600 CHV 91910 1330-B1
1300 SD 92154 1349-J1
1800 SD 92154 1350-A1
ELDER CT
800 CRLB 92009 1126-J5
6300 SD 92120 1250-B6
ELDER PL
700 ESCN 92025 1129-J1
700 ESCN 92025 1130-A1
6200 SD 92120 1250-B6
ELDER ST
200 SDCo 92028 1027-E3
500 SDCo 92055 1027-E3
E ELDER ST
100 SDCo 92028 1027-G2
ELDERBERRY CT
800 SMCS 92069 1109-A6
ELDERBERRY GN
3700 ESCN 92025 1150-C3
ELDERBERRY WY
5400 OCN 92057 1067-D7
ELDERBURRY CT
10800 SD 92126 1209-D3
ELDERGARDENS ST
5800 SD 92120 1250-B6
ELDERWOOD CT
10900 SD 92131 1210-B2
ELDER WOOD GN
1700 ESCN 92026 1109-D3
ELDERWOOD LN
10700 SD 92131 1210-B2
ELDERWOOD RD
10900 SD 92131 1210-B2

EL DIABLO CT
400 ESCN 92026 1109-H5
EL DOLORA WY
14100 PWY 92064 1190-G1
ELDON CT
1700 ELCJ 92021 1252-B2
ELDORA ST
1700 LMGR 91945 1290-G1
EL DORADO AV
800 ELCN 92243 6499-F4
EL DORADO CT
1700 VSTA 92084 1108-B1
ELDORADO DR
300 ESCN 92025 1130-B5
300 SDCo 92025 1130-B5
EL DORADO PKWY
8900 SDCo 92021 1232-E6
EL DORADO TER
1700 SDCo 92025 1130-C5
ELDRED LN
1700 VSTA 92083 1087-D7
ELDRIDGE CT
5400 SD 92120 1250-B6
ELDRIDGE ST
6500 SD 92120 1250-B6
ELEANOR DR
6400 SD 92114 1290-D4
ELEANOR PL
3400 NATC 91950 1290-C7
ELEANOR ROOSEVELT LN
- SD 92093 1228-A2
ELECTRIC AV
6200 SD 92037 1247-E2
ELECTRON DR
3700 SD 92106 1287-J4
ELEGANS PL
- CRLB 92009 1127-B7
ELENA DR
1700 SMCS 92069 1108-H3
ELENA LN
19300 SDCo 91935 1294-F7
ELENA WY
100 OCN 92057 1086-H3
ELEONORE CT
12100 SD 92131 1210-B1
EL ESCNDDO DEL DIOS HWY Rt#-S6
6900 SDCo 92067 1168-F1
7600 SDCo 92067 1149-A7
7800 SDCo 92067 1148-J7
EL ESCORIAL WY
5900 SD 92124 1229-J6
ELETA PL
2200 SDCo 91977 1271-D7
ELEVADA ST
2000 OCN 92054 1106-F2
ELEVADO RD
1600 SDCo 92084 1088-C1
1600 VSTA 92084 1088-B2
2200 SDCo 92084 1068-B7
ELEVADO HILLS DR
2000 SDCo 92084 1088-B2
ELEVATION RD
1300 SD 92110 1268-F2
EL EXTENSO CT
8000 SD 92119 1250-E3
EL-FARRA ST
500 SDCo 92069 1088-G2
ELFIN GN
19600 SDCo 92029 1148-H3
ELFIN FOREST LN
19900 SDCo 92029 1148-G2
ELFIN FOREST RD
19900 SDCo 92029 1148-F1
20500 SMCS 92029 1128-E7
20500 SMCS 92078 1128-D6
20500 SDCo 92029 1128-E7
ELFIN OAKS RD
6900 SDCo 92029 1148-F2
ELFINORA LN
9500 SDCo 92029 1148-J2
ELFORD CT
8700 SD 92129 1189-C1
EL FUEGO
16900 SDCo 92067 1168-D3
EL FUERTE ST
5900 CRLB 92008 1127-G2
6200 CRLB 92009 1127-H4
EL GAVILAN CT
2500 CRLB 92009 1127-G4
ELGIN AV
5400 SD 92120 1250-B5
EL GRANADA RD
2600 CHV 91914 1311-G2
EL GRANDE PL
9600 SDCo 92040 1232-C4
EL GRANITO AV
9400 SDCo 91941 1271-B1
EL HONCHO PL
10300 SD 92124 1229-G7
ELIASON DR
- SDCo 92055 1085-G1
ELIJO WY
14800 SDCo 91935 1293-C4
ELIOT PL
5200 CRLB 92008 1127-B1
ELIOT ST
- OCN 92057 1067-A4
ELISE ST
800 CHV 91911 1330-A5
800 SD 91911 1330-A5
ELISE WY
100 OCN 92057 1086-H3
ELIVO CT
100 SD 92173 1350-G2
ELIZABETH DR
19300 SDCo 92082 1091-H4
ELIZABETH LN
300 SDCo 92065 1153-B5
ELIZABETH ST
- ELCJ 92019 1252-A7
500 SD 92113 1289-J5
600 SMCS 92069 1109-B6
ELIZABETH WY
- ELCJ 92019 1252-B6
1300 SDCo 92028 1027-G5
EL JARDIN CT
1800 ELCJ 92020 1271-G2
ELK ST
5600 SD 92114 1290-B4
ELKELTON BLVD
400 SDCo 91977 1291-A4
600 SDCo 91977 1290-J2
ELKELTON PL
300 SDCo 91977 1291-A4
ELKHART ST
5000 SD 92105 1270-A7

ELKHORN CT
500 CHV 91902 1311-B4
ELKHORN LN
400 ESCN 92026 1109-G5
ELKHORN ST
8300 LMGR 91945 1290-J1
ELKINS CV
11800 SD 92126 1209-C1
ELK LAKE DR
2000 SDCo 92029 1129-F7
ELK RUN PL
1000 CHV 91913 1311-D6
ELKS LN
900 CHV 91911 1330-G1
EL-KU AV
3000 ESCN 92025 1150-A2
ELKWOOD AV
- IMPB 91932 1349-F1
EL LANDO CT
3100 OCN 92056 1106-H1
ELLEN LN
- OCN 92054 1086-G3
600 ELCJ 92019 1252-B7
ELLENBEE RD
9200 SNTE 92071 1231-A5
ELLENTOWN RD
2400 SD 92037 1227-J3
ELLENWOOD CIR
8800 SDCo 91977 1290-J3
ELLERY ST
100 OCN 92054 1086-D6
ELLIE LN
16300 PWY 92064 1171-D7
ELLINGER PL
- SD 92173 1350-E4
ELLINGHAM ST
8800 SD 92129 1189-C3
ELLIOTT CIR
- SDCo 92055 1067-A2
ELLIOTT ST
- SDCo 92055 1067-A1
3000 SD 92106 1268-C6
ELLIS LN
100 SDCo 92028 1027-G2
ELLIS MOUNTAIN DR
2000 SDCo 92019 1252-C7
ELLISON PL
5000 SD 92116 1269-E2
EL LORO ST
300 CHV 91911 1330-D4
ELLSWORTH CIR
8700 SNTE 92071 1231-B7
ELLSWORTH LN
8500 SNTE 92071 1231-B7
8500 SNTE 92071 1251-B1
ELLSWORTH ST
5100 SD 92110 1268-F2
EL LUGAR ST
1300 CHV 91911 1330-D4
ELM
9700 SDCo 92021 1233-B3
ELM AV
- IMPB 91932 1329-E7
100 CRLB 92008 1106-J3
200 CHV 91910 1310-C5
700 CHV 91910 1330-C1
800 CHV 91911 1330-D2
1300 IMPB 92154 1329-J7
1300 SD 92154 1329-J7
1500 ELCN 92243 6499-E7
1700 SD 92154 1330-A7
2700 CRLB 92008 1107-A4
ELM CT
- SDCo 92040 1232-D6
ELM DR
- NATC 91950 1289-H7
1500 VSTA 92084 1088-B4
9400 SDCo 91916 1236-A2
ELM LN
20100 SDCo 92029 1149-E2
ELM RD
28900 SDCo 92066 1237-C7
ELM ST
- SMCS 92078 1129-C2
100 OCN 92054 1106-A1
100 SD 92101 1289-A2
300 CHV 91910 1310-C6
300 SD 92114 1290-D4
300 SDCo 92065 1152-H1
400 SDCo 92028 998-B7
500 VSTA 92083 1087-F6
600 ESCN 92025 1130-A1
1300 ESCN 92026 1109-J6
2800 SD 92102 1289-E2
3600 SMCS 92069 1128-C1
3600 SD 92104 1289-F2
4300 SD 92105 1289-H1
6700 SD 92102 1290-A1
N ELM ST
100 ESCN 92025 1130-A2
S ELM ST
100 ESCN 92025 1130-A2
W ELM ST
400 SD 92101 1289-A2
ELMA LN
4300 LMSA 91941 1270-E4
EL MAC PL
900 SD 92106 1287-J2
N ELMAN ST
6700 SD 92111 1268-H1
S ELMAN ST
6700 SD 92111 1268-J1
EL MAR AV
13500 PWY 92064 1190-H3
EL MARBEA LN
10700 SDCo 91941 1271-F2
EL MATADOR LN
10300 SNTE 92071 1231-E7
ELMBRANCH DR
1100 ENCT 92024 1147-F7
ELMCREST DR
6300 SD 92119 1250-E6
ELMDALE DR
10300 SDCo 91977 1291-E2
EL MERCADO WY
1200 OCN 92057 1087-B3
ELMFIELD LN
12800 PWY 92064 1170-D3
ELMHURST DR
6300 SD 92120 1250-D7
ELMHURST ST
1600 CHV 91913 1311-C5
EL MIO DR
1200 ELCJ 92020 1251-D6
ELMIRA ST
300 ELCJ 92019 1251-J6
EL MIRADOR
- SMCS 92078 1129-C1
16800 SDCo 92067 1168-F2

EL MIRAR
4700 SDCo 92067 1168-A3
EL MIRASO
500 VSTA 92083 1087-H7
EL MIRLO
4500 SDCo 92067 1168-A1
EL MIRLO DR
4900 OCN 92057 1067-A5
ELMOND DR
9500 SDCo 92026 1069-C3
EL MONTE DR
2100 OCN 92054 1086-C6
EL MONTE PL
300 SDCo 92021 1252-H4
400 ESCN 92027 1130-B1
EL MONTE RD
100 ELCJ 92020 1251-D4
13900 SDCo 92040 1232-G1
15400 SDCo 92040 1212-J7
15500 SDCo 92040 1213-B6
EL MONTEVIDEO
5500 SDCo 92067 1148-C7
5500 SDCo 92067 1168-D1
ELMORE ST
6700 SD 92111 1268-J2
EL MORRO LN
- OCN 92054 1086-G3
ELMPARK LN
12700 PWY 92064 1190-D4
ELMPORT LN
14400 PWY 92064 1190-H5
ELM RIDGE DR
1900 VSTA 92083 1107-G5
ELMSTONE CT
11400 SD 92131 1210-A2
ELM TREE CT
2900 SDCo 91978 1271-G7
ELM TREE DR
4700 OCN 92056 1087-E5
ELM TREE LN
500 SDCo 92028 1047-G1
1100 SMCS 92069 1109-A5
ELMVIEW DR
800 ENCT 92024 1167-G1
ELMWOOD CT
1400 CHV 91915 1311-G7
ELMWOOD DR
600 ESCN 92025 1130-A1
ELMWOOD LN
- OCN 92054 1106-C1
ELMWOOD ST
2800 CRLB 92008 1106-F4
ELMWOOD WY
3300 SMCS 92069 1128-B1
EL NIDO
4600 SDCo 92067 1168-A5
EL NIDO DR
1200 SDCo 92028 1047-J3
1600 SDCo 92028 1048-A4
EL NOCHE WY
5300 SD 92124 1249-H1
EL NOPAL
9900 SNTE 92071 1231-C3
10800 SDCo 92040 1231-F3
EL NORA PL
24800 SDCo 92065 1173-G3
EL NORTE
600 SDCo 92021 1251-G2
3600 OCN 92054 1086-F2
E EL NORTE PKWY
100 ESCN 92026 1109-H7
800 ESCN 92027 1109-H7
900 ESCN 92027 1110-A6
W EL NORTE PKWY
100 ESCN 92026 1109-C5
1800 SDCo 92026 1109-F6
EL NORTE HILLS PL
500 ESCN 92027 1110-D5
EL NORTE VISTA
27600 SDCo 92082 1091-F3
ELON LN
1500 ENCT 92024 1147-G5
EL ONTONO WY
5400 SD 92121 1208-E4
EL ORIENTE
600 ENCT 92024 1147-F5
EL PAISANO DR
600 SDCo 92028 1028-B1
1000 SDCo 92028 998-B7
EL PAJODO PL
900 VSTA 92084 1088-A7
EL PASEO
500 SDCo 92084 1088-G1
700 SDCo 92084 1068-H7
EL PASEO DR
1500 SDCo 92069 1128-B3
EL PASEO GRANDE
7800 SD 92037 1227-H4
8500 SD 92093 1227-H4
EL PASILLO
2100 SDCo 91977 1291-A1
EL PASO ST
1700 SDCo 92065 1152-C5
7500 LMSA 91942 1250-G6
EL PASO ALTO
400 SDCo 92084 1088-F5
600 SDCo 92069 1088-G4
EL PASO ALTO NORTE
3700 SDCo 92084 1088-F5
EL PASO REAL
1500 SD 92037 1247-G1
EL PATO CT
6400 CRLB 92009 1127-G4
EL PEDREGAL DR
300 SOLB 92075 1167-H6
EL PENON WY
4600 SD 92117 1248-B1
EL PERICO LN
6400 CRLB 92009 1127-H5
EL PICO CT
900 VSTA 92083 1087-G5
EL PICO DR
1700 ELCJ 92020 1251-C4
EL POQUITO LN
10100 SNTE 92071 1231-F3
EL PORTAL DR
600 CHV 91914 1311-G2
EL PORTAL ST
100 ENCT 92024 1147-B5
N EL PORTAL ST
200 ENCT 92024 1147-B5
S EL PORTAL ST
100 ENCT 92024 1147-B6
EL PORVENIR WY
3000 SD 92173 1350-D3
EL PRADO
1200 SD 92101 1289-B1
EL PRADO AV
1400 LMGR 91945 1290-G1

EL PRADO AV
2200 LMGR 91945 1270-G7
EL PRADO LN
- OCN 92054 1086-G3
EL PRADO PL
1400 ESCN 92027 1130-B1
EL PRADO ST
1500 SD 92101 1289-C1
EL RANCHO DR
600 ELCJ 92019 1252-C4
600 SDCo 92019 1252-C4
EL RANCHO LN
400 ESCN 92027 1130-B1
1600 SDCo 92028 1027-J1
EL RANCHO GRANDE
3300 SDCo 91902 1291-C7
3300 SDCo 91902 1311-C1
EL RANCHO VERDE
1600 SDCo 92069 1128-F4
EL RANCHO VISTA
- CHV 91910 1310-D6
- SDCo 91910 1310-D6
N EL RANCHO VISTA
400 SDCo 91910 1310-D6
EL RASTRO LN
2800 CRLB 92009 1147-G4
EL RETIRO
28600 SDCo 92082 1089-J1
28700 SDCo 92082 1069-J7
EL REY AV
1100 ELCJ 92021 1251-J2
1100 SDCo 92021 1251-J2
EL REY CT
1300 ELCJ 92021 1251-J2
EL REY VISTA
12800 PWY 92064 1190-E5
EL ROCKO RD
2700 SDCo 92029 1129-D4
ELROD AV
8700 SD 92126 1209-D7
ELROD RD
9400 SD 92126 1209-E7
EL RODEO CT
6500 SDCo 92067 1188-H2
EL ROMERO
6100 SDCo 92067 1168-D3
EL ROSAL PL
1700 ESCN 92026 1109-E6
ELROSE CT
1100 SD 92154 1350-C1
ELROSE DR
2700 SD 92154 1350-C1
ELROY DR
1600 LMGR 91945 1290-G1
ELSA RD
4700 SD 92120 1249-J7
4800 SD 92120 1250-A7
ELSBERRY ST
6300 SD 92114 1290-D6
EL SEBO PL
24700 SDCo 92065 1173-G2
EL SECRETO
4700 SDCo 92067 1168-B3
EL SECRITO
5100 OCN 92056 1087-D2
EL SENDERO DR
34300 SDCo 92061 1050-H1
EL SENTIDO
14800 SDCo 92067 1188-H1
ELSER LN
1700 SDCo 92026 1109-D6
EL SERENO WY
2500 SDCo 92083 1108-C4
2600 SDCo 92069 1108-C4
2600 SMCS 92069 1108-C4
EL SICOMORO
6300 SDCo 92067 1168-E4
ELSIE WY
600 CHV 91910 1310-D7
ELSINORE PL
3400 SD 92117 1248-D3
ELSINORE ST
5300 OCN 92056 1087-E1
EL SOL RD
16900 SDCo 92065 1172-A2
ELSTON PL
8100 SD 92126 1209-B3
EL SUENO
- SOLB 92075 1167-F7
EL SUR
300 OCN 92054 1086-F3
EL TAE RD
32400 SDCo 92061 1051-A5
ELTANIN WY
11400 SD 92126 1209-D1
EL TEJADO RD
9300 SDCo 91941 1271-B2
9400 LMSA 91941 1271-B2
EL TEJON RD
3300 SDCo 92004 (1079-A6 See Page 1058)
EL TESORO RD
27100 SDCo 92066 410-A8
37000 SDCo 92066 409-L8
EL TIEMPO
- SDCo 92067 1149-B3
EL TIGRE CT
200 SMCS 92069 1108-C5
ELTINGE DR
2300 SDCo 91901 1234-B6
ELTINGE PL
2800 SDCo 91901 1234-B7
ELTON DR
9200 SNTE 92071 1231-B7
EL TOPO DR
14200 PWY 92064 1170-G7
EL TORDO
5900 SDCo 92067 1168-D3
EL TORO LN
800 SMCS 92069 1109-C5
10300 SNTE 92071 1231-E7
ELVA CT
1400 ENCT 92024 1167-G1
ELVA ST
1800 SDCo 92019 1272-C4
ELVA TER
1400 ENCT 92024 1167-G1
ELVADO WY
200 SD 92114 1290-E4
EL VALLE
- SDCo 92040 1232-D6
EL VALLECITO
1000 VSTA 92083 1087-G4
EL VALLE OPULENTO
100 SDCo 92083 1108-B3
EL VECINO DR
3300 SDCo 92028 1047-J2
EL VERDE CT
1900 LMGR 91945 1290-J1

EL VESTIDO ST
14300 SD 92129 1189-C2
EL VIENTO
300 SOLB 92075 1167-F7
ELVIS CT
1100 SD 92154 1350-E1
EL VUELO
17100 SDCo 92067 1168-F2
EL VUELO DEL ESTE
7000 SDCo 92067 1168-G2
ELWELL CT
11600 SD 92131 1210-A1
ELWOOD AV
900 SD 92114 1290-A3
ELY CIR
6900 SD 92114 1290-F4
ELY ST
100 OCN 92054 1086-F5
ELYSIAN DR
3800 SDCo 92036 1156-E2
ELYSSEE ST
2500 SD 92123 1249-C6
ELYSUM DR
- SD 92109 1248-C6
EL ZORRO VISTA
16500 SDCo 92067 1168-E3
EMBARCADERO LN
- CRLB 92009 1126-J5
EMBASSY WY
10100 SD 92126 1209-B5
EMBERWOOD WY
2100 ESCN 92029 1129-E6
EMBRY CT
7700 SD 92126 1209-A5
EMBRY PT
7700 SD 92126 1209-A5
EMBRY WY
10000 SD 92126 1209-A6
EMDEN RD
9100 SD 92129 1189-C1
EMELENE ST
4900 SD 92109 1248-A4
EMELITA ST
1000 SDCo 92028 1027-H2
EMERALD AV
300 ELCJ 92020 1251-E6
1200 ELCJ 92020 1271-E1
EMERALD BAY
5700 SD 92105 1290-B1
EMERALD CT
700 SD 92109 1247-H6
EMERALD DR
100 OCN 92056 1107-D2
100 VSTA 92083 1107-D1
400 OCN 92056 1087-D7
400 VSTA 92083 1087-D7
3500 SDCo 92083 1107-D2
3600 SDCo 92036 1156-E2
EMERALD LN
14400 SDCo 92067 1188-F2
EMERALD PL
- CRLB 92009 1127-H5
2600 ESCN 92027 1130-F1
EMERALD ST
600 SD 92109 1247-H6
1500 SD 92109 1248-A5
EMERALD CITY DR
16000 SDCo 92082 1071-B4
EMERALD GROVE AV
8900 SDCo 92040 1231-J6
EMERALD HEIGHTS RD
1200 ELCJ 92020 1271-F1
1200 SDCo 91941 1271-F1
EMERALD HILL LN
9700 SDCo 92040 1232-A4
EMERALD HILL RD
30500 OCN 92003 1067-H4
30500 SDCo 92003 1067-H4
EMERALD HOLLOW DR
- VSTA 92083 1107-D1
EMERALD LAKE AV
6200 SD 92119 1250-H6
EMERALD POINT CT
- SDCo 92019 1272-B5
EMERALD POINT LN
- SDCo 92019 1272-B5
EMERALD SEA WY
- SMCS 92069 1128-A2
EMERALD VISTA DR
9400 SDCo 92040 1231-J5
EMERAUDE GN
1300 ESCN 92029 1149-G1
1300 SDCo 92029 1149-G1
EMERSON ST
- CHV 91911 1330-C3
2800 SD 92106 1288-A1
E EMERSON ST
- CHV 91911 1330-E2
EMERY RD
600 SDCo 91980 429-L10
EMET CT
4200 SD 92117 1248-E3
N EMILIA LN
100 SDCo 92028 1028-A2
S EMILIA LN
100 SDCo 92028 1028-A2
EMILY CT
4300 SDCo 91935 1274-B4
EMILY DR
4300 SDCo 91935 1274-A4
EMMA DR
900 ENCT 92007 1167-E3
EMMA LN
700 SDCo 92084 1088-F7
EMMA RD
3600 SDCo 92084 1088-F7
3800 SDCo 92069 1088-F7
EMMANUEL WY
3300 SDCo 91901 1274-J4
3300 SDCo 91901 1275-A3
EMMAUS RD
11900 SDCo 92040 1232-A7
EMOGENE PL
1700 ESCN 92026 1109-C5
EMORY ST
500 IMPB 91932 1329-G7
900 IMPB 91932 1349-G1
3200 SD 92101 1268-H6
EMPIRE ST
8900 SD 92126 1209-B7
EMPORER LN
100 OCN 92054 1086-G3
EMPRESS AV
10100 SD 92126 1209-B5
ENBORNE LN
6900 SD 92139 1290-F7
ENCANTADA
1500 SDCo 92021 1251-G2

ENCANTADA CT
SAN DIEGO CO. STREET INDEX
FALCON RIM PT 6584

Thomas Bros. Maps ®
COPYRIGHT 2001

STREET
Block City ZIP Pg-Grid

ENCANTADA CT
1400 CHV 91913 1311-B5
ENCANTO AV
- IMPB 91932 1349-E2
ENCANTO DR
100 ESCN 92027 1110-E7
ENCELA LN
1000 SDCo 91977 1291-D3
ENCELIA DR
7100 SD 92037 1227-G7
ENCHANTE WY N
1300 OCN 92056 1087-B4
ENCHANTE WY S
1400 OCN 92056 1087-B4
ENCHANTED PL
2200 SD 92173 1350-G3
ENCHANTMENT AV
1500 VSTA 92083 1107-G4
ENCINA AV
800 IMPB 91932 1329-G7
ENCINA CTE
- SDCo 92065 1173-D2
ENCINA DR
5300 SD 92114 1290-B5
ENCINA VERDE
- SDCo 91905 (1319-H3
See Page 1298)
ENCINITA ST
4500 SD 92173 1350-G5
ENCINITAS AV
200 SD 92114 1290-H3
ENCINITAS BLVD
Rt#-S9
- ENCT 92024 1147-C6
1900 ENCT 92024 1167-J1
ENCINITAS WY
8500 SD 92114 1290-H4
ENCINO AV
8400 SD 92123 1249-B7
ENCINO CT
400 ESCN 92025 1130-B5
400 SDCo 92025 1130-B5
ENCINO DR
300 VSTA 92083 1087-G3
500 ESCN 92025 1130-B5
1800 SDCo 92025 1130-B5
ENCINO LN
800 CORD 92118 1288-H7
ENCINO RW
1000 CORD 92118 1288-H7
ENDEAVOR LN
4700 CRLB 92008 1106-H7
ENDERS AV
6900 SD 92122 1228-G4
ENELRA PL
5100 SD 92117 1228-G7
ENERGY WY
700 CHV 91911 1331-A5
ENERO CT
3700 SD 92154 1350-F1
ENERO ST
4100 SD 92154 1350-F1
ENERO WY
3900 SD 92154 1350-F1
ENFIELD ST
1500 SDCo 91977 1290-H2
ENGEL ST
100 ESCN 92029 1129-F3
ENGELMAN CT
1500 CHV 91911 1330-J3
ENGELMANN OAK LN
2500 SDCo 91901 1234-C7
2500 SDCo 91901 1254-C1
ENGELMANN OAK TR
28200 SDCo 92026 1089-F3
ENGINEER RD
7100 SD 92111 1249-A1
ENGINEER ST
2000 VSTA 92083 1107-J6
ENGINEERING LN
- SD 92093 1228-A1
ENGINEERS RD
6000 SDCo 92036 1175-H2
6900 SDCo 92036 1176-A2
ENGLAND PL
700 SDCo 91901 1234-B4
ENGLEWOOD DR
1700 LMGR 91945 1290-H1
ENGLEWOOD WY
2800 CRLB 92008 1107-A4
ENGLISH RD
- ImCo 92233 411-B9
- ImCo 92257 411-B6
ENGLISH HOLLY LN
700 SMCS 92078 1129-B1
ENID CT
11600 SD 92131 1210-A1
ENIWETOK RD
2300 CORD 92155 1309-B1
ENNAR RD
31000 SDCo 92003 1048-H7
31000 SDCo 92003 1068-J1
ENRICO FERMI DR
2000 SD 92154 1352-B3
2000 SDCo 92154 1352-B3
ENRIGHT DR
2200 SD 92173 1350-G3
ENSENADA CT
700 SD 92109 1267-H3
ENSENADA ST
1700 LMGR 91945 1290-G1
ENSIGN ST
5000 SD 92117 1228-F7
ENTERPRISE CT
1300 VSTA 92083 1108-A7
ENTERPRISE DR
- ELCJ 92021 1251-H5
ENTERPRISE ST
100 ESCN 92029 1129-E2
300 SMCS 92078 1128-J1
400 SMCS 92078 1129-A1
3500 SD 92110 1268-F6
ENTERTAINMENT CIR
- CHV 91911 1331-B6
- CHV 91913 1331-B6
ENTRADA AV
2200 SDCo 92084 1108-D3
ENTRADA GN
1200 ESCN 92027 1110-B5
ENTRADA PL
800 CHV 91910 1310-H7
ENTRADA DEL SOL
3900 SDCo 92003 1067-F2
ENTRANCE DR
3700 ESCN 92025 1150-C2
ENTREKEN AV
13000 SD 92129 1189-C4
ENTREKEN PL
8400 SD 92129 1189-C4

ENTREKEN WY
8300 SD 92129 1189-B4
ENTRY ST
300 OCN 92057 1086-H2
ENZ RD
1000 ImCo 92250 431-E6
EOLUS AV
800 ENCT 92024 1147-B2
EPANOW AV
4000 SD 92117 1248-E3
EPAULETTE ST
2800 SD 92123 1249-D6
EPEI HILL RD
- SDCo 92070 409-K10
EPICA CT
12600 SD 92128 1170-C3
EPINETTE AV
4700 SD 92117 1248-B1
EPPERSON WY
10000 SD 92124 1249-G3
EPPICK CT
8000 LMGR 91945 1290-H2
8000 SDCo 91977 1290-H2
EPSILON ST
3800 SD 92113 1289-G7
EQUALITY LN
- SD 92093 1228-A1
EQUESTRIAN CT
100 SMCS 92069 1108-J1
EQUESTRIAN TR
2000 SDCo 92065 1172-D3
EQUINOX WY
1200 CHV 91911 1330-H2
EQUITATION LN
3000 SDCo 91902 1310-D4
ERIC LN
- SDCo 91977 1291-B2
ERIC PL
9400 SDCo 92021 1232-H4
ERIC RD
2400 SDCo 92028 409-A4
N ERICA ST
600 ESCN 92027 1110-B6
ERICAS WY
11900 SDCo 92040 1211-H5
ERIDANUS CT
11400 SD 92126 1209-C1
ERIE CT
5300 OCN 92056 1087-E1
ERIE ST
1800 SD 92110 1268-E1
2200 SD 92110 1248-E7
2700 SD 92117 1248-E7
ERIK RD
3400 SDCo 92025 1150-E2
ERIN DR
900 ELCJ 92020 1251-B3
ERIN GN
- SDCo 92003 1067-E1
ERIN LN
14300 PWY 92064 1190-H5
ERIN WY
9700 SNTE 92071 1231-D4
ERINS PL
2000 ESCN 92027 1110-B5
ERITH ST
6700 SD 92111 1248-H4
ERLANGER ST
5700 SD 92122 1228-F6
ERMA RD
9700 SD 92131 1209-F3
ERSKINE DR
- SDCo 92672 1023-E2
ERSKINE RD
- ImCo 92251 430-L4
- ImCo 92251 431-A4
ERWIN LN
9700 SDCo 92040 1232-A4
ESCADERA DR
10200 SDCo 92040 1231-F2
ESCADERA PL
11000 SDCo 92040 1231-F2
ESCALA CV
3900 OCN 92054 1086-G1
ESCALA DR
11800 SD 92128 1170-A1
11900 SD 92128 1150-B6
ESCALA LN
12400 SD 92128 1150-C7
12400 SD 92128 1170-C1
ESCALLONIA CT
7300 CRLB 92009 1126-J7
ESCARCHOSA LN
5400 SD 92124 1249-G1
ESCENICO TER
2000 CRLB 92009 1147-F2
ESCHELMAN DR
- ELCN 92243 6559-J1
ESCOBA PL
11400 SD 92127 1149-J7
11500 SD 92127 1169-J1
ESCOBAR DR
10600 SD 92124 1249-H2
ESCONDIDO AV
100 VSTA 92084 1087-J6
900 VSTA 92083 1087-J6
2500 SD 92123 1249-B6
ESCONDIDO BLVD
100 ESCN 92025 1129-H2
N ESCONDIDO BLVD
600 ESCN 92025 1129-H1
900 ESCN 92026 1129-H1
1200 ESCN 92026 1109-G7
S ESCONDIDO BLVD
100 ESCN 92025 1129-J3
1300 ESCN 92025 1130-A5
2400 ESCN 92025 1150-A1
ESCONDIDO FRWY I-15
- ESCN - 1109-E3
- ESCN - 1129-H5
- ESCN - 1150-A1
- RivC - 998-H5
- SD - 1150-A1
- SD - 1169-J6
- SD - 1170-A3
- SD - 1189-F6
- SD - 1209-F4
- SD - 1229-F5
- SD - 1249-F3
- SD - 1269-G2
- SDCo - 998-H5
- SDCo - 1028-G4
- SDCo - 1048-J4
- SDCo - 1068-J3
- SDCo - 1088-J1
- SDCo - 1089-A2
- SDCo - 1109-E3
- SDCo - 1129-H5
- SDCo - 1130-A7

ESCONDIDO FRWY I-15
- SDCo - 1150-A1
- SDCo - 1209-F4
ESCONDIDO FRWY
Rt#-15
- SD - 1269-G6
- SD - 1289-F2
ESCONDIDO LN
300 CORD 92118 1288-J6
300 CORD 92118 1289-A6
900 ESCN 92025 1129-J6
ESCUADRO DR
3800 SDCo 92004 (1099-D1
See Page 1098)
ESCUELA GN
100 ESCN 92026 1109-H6
ESCUELA ST
100 SD 92102 1289-J3
ESFERA ST
7200 CRLB 92009 1128-A7
7300 CRLB 92009 1148-A1
7300 CRLB 92009 1147-J1
ESHELMAN DR
- ELCN 92243 6559-J1
ESLA DR
700 CHV 91910 1310-J6
ESMERALDAS DR
10600 SD 92124 1249-H1
ESMOND CT
10800 SD 92126 1209-B3
ESPANA DR
3600 OCN 92054 1086-F3
ESPANAS GN
100 ESCN 92026 1109-H7
100 ESCN 92026 1129-H1
ESPARTA CT
9700 SNTE 92071 1231-B4
ESPERANZA PL
700 CHV 91914 1311-H3
ESPERANZA WY
4100 OCN 92056 1087-C6
E ESPERANZA WY
1400 ESCN 92027 1110-A6
ESPERAR DR
13400 SDCo 92021 1232-D7
ESPINOSA SQ
9900 SD 92131 1209-H5
ESPLANADE CT
4200 SD 92122 1228-C3
ESPLANADE ST
3600 OCN 92056 1107-B3
ESPLENDENTE BLVD
5100 SD 92124 1249-H2
ESPLENDIDO AV
1900 SDCo 92084 1108-E3
ESPOLA RD Rt#-S5
14100 PWY 92064 1190-G1
14800 PWY 92064 1170-D3
16900 SD 92128 1170-D3
ESPRIT AV
13500 SD 92128 1190-B3
ESPUELA LN
400 SDCo 92026 1109-G3
ESPUELAS CT
1000 CHV 91910 1310-J5
ESQUIER DR
- SDCo 92026 1089-A2
ESQUIRE GN
1800 ESCN 92029 1129-F5
ESSENCE AV
800 OCN 92057 1087-B1
ESSENCE RD
13500 SD 92128 1190-B3
ESSEX CT
4500 CRLB 92008 1106-J5
ESSEX ST
1000 SD 92103 1269-B5
1200 IMPB 91932 1349-H1
6300 ELCJ 92020 1251-C5
6300 LMSA 91942 1251-C5
ESSINGTON CT
- SD 92154 1330-H7
ESTADA CIR
300 OCN 92057 1087-A1
ESTADA DR
4400 OCN 92057 1087-A2
ESTANCIA DR
3900 OCN 92054 1086-G2
ESTANCIA ST
7800 CRLB 92009 1147-J2
ESTATE DR
4300 SDCo 92028 1048-B5
ESTATES CT
4900 SDCo 92020 1271-G2
ESTATES WY
4900 SDCo 92020 1271-G1
ESTELA DR
1900 ELCJ 92020 1251-C1
ESTELLE ST
5800 SD 92115 1270-C4
ESTEREL DR
7700 SD 92037 1227-J5
ESTERLINA DR
3500 SDCo 92028 1048-B3
ESTERO DR
2000 OCN 92054 1106-F2
ESTERO ST
2000 OCN 92054 1106-F2
ESTERO WY
2000 ESCN 92026 1129-G1
ESTES ST
800 ELCJ 92020 1251-F7
ESTE VISTA CT
1300 ENCT 92007 1167-F3
ESTHER ST
4500 SD 92115 1270-C3
ESTIVAL PL
- SDCo 92040 1231-G3
ESTORIL PL
- SDCo 92003 1067-H2
ESTORNINO LN
300 SDCo 92021 1252-H3
ESTRADA CT
14300 SD 92129 1189-H2
ESTRADA ST
- SDCo 92055 1085-G1
ESTRADA WY
1900 SD 92037 1247-H1
ESTRELITA DR
100 SDCo 92084 1108-C3
ESTRELLA AV
3800 SD 92105 1269-J5
4600 SD 92115 1269-J4
6100 SD 92120 1249-J7
6400 SD 92120 1250-A6
ESTRELLA DR
9800 SDCo 91977 1271-D4
9900 SDCo 91941 1271-D4

ESTRELLA LN
- OCN 92054 1086-G3
ESTRELLA ST
100 SOLB 92075 1167-E7
ESTRELLA DE MAR CT
1900 CRLB 92009 1127-F6
ESTRELLA DE MAR RD
- CRLB 92009 1147-F1
7000 CRLB 92009 1127-E7
ESTRELLA VISTA
12800 PWY 92064 1190-E5
ESTREMOZ CT
500 OCN 92057 1086-H4
ESTUARY WY
3500 SD 92121 1208-A5
ESTUDILLO ST
3500 SD 92110 1268-G6
ESTURION CT
2800 CRLB 92009 1127-H4
ESTURION PL
2800 CRLB 92009 1127-H4
ESTURION ST
2800 CRLB 92009 1127-H4
ETA ST
800 NATC 91950 1289-H7
800 SD 92113 1289-G7
ETCHEVERRY ST
100 SDCo 92065 1172-D1
ETCHINGS WY
9100 SDCo 92040 1232-D5
ETHAN ALLEN AV
3500 SD 92117 1248-D5
ETHEL PL
800 NATC 91950 1290-C7
ETHEL TR
800 SDCo 92019 1253-C2
ETHELDA PL
4200 SD 92116 1269-H4
ETHELWYN LN
- SDCo 92036 1136-C6
ETIWANDA ST
2200 SD 92107 1268-A6
ETON AV
3300 SD 92122 1228-D6
ETON CT
900 CHV 91913 1311-D5
5900 SD 92122 1228-D6
ETON GREENS CT
3300 SDCo 91978 1271-G6
ETUDE RD
13600 SD 92128 1190-B2
EUBANK LN
9900 SDCo 91977 1291-D2
EUCALYPTUS AV
100 VSTA 92084 1087-H6
300 ELCN 92243 6499-H5
800 VSTA 92084 1088-A6
1700 ENCT 92024 1147-A2
2100 SDCo 92029 1129-G6
2100 ESCN 92029 1129-G6
2300 ESCN 92029 1149-F1
EUCALYPTUS CT
200 CHV 91910 1310-D5
9700 SNTE 92071 1231-E4
EUCALYPTUS DR
800 ELCJ 92020 1251-E7
1400 SDCo 92021 1252-H3
EUCALYPTUS LN
1200 VSTA 92084 1088-A7
3200 SD 92037 1228-A4
4900 CRLB 92008 1107-A6
EUCALYPTUS RD
- SDCo 92082 1071-E1
EUCALYPTUS ST
200 OCN 92054 1106-B2
9400 SDCo 91977 1291-C1
EUCALYPTUS GROVE LN
- SD 92093 1227-J2
- SD 92093 1228-A2
EUCALYPTUS HEIGHTS
RD
16000 PWY 92064 1191-B1
EUCALYPTUS HILL
7400 LMSA 91941 1270-G3
EUCALYPTUS HILLS DR
11300 SDCo 92040 1231-G1
11400 SDCo 92040 1211-H7
EUCALYPTUS WOODS RD
700 SDCo 92069 1109-B2
EUCLID AV
100 SD 92114 1290-A5
100 SD 92113 1290-A5
400 ELCN 92243 6499-F5
1300 SD 91950 1290-A5
1500 NATC 91950 1310-B2
1700 ImCo 92243 6499-F5
1800 ELCJ 92019 1252-C5
1800 SDCo 92019 1252-C5
2100 SDCo 91950 1310-B2
2500 SD 92105 1270-A7
2800 SD 92105 1269-J6
4100 SD 92115 1269-J4
N EUCLID AV
- NATC 91950 1290-A6
1000 SD 92114 1290-A1
1100 SD 92102 1290-A6
1300 SD 92113 1290-A6
1300 SD 91950 1290-A6
1700 SD 92105 1290-A1
2300 SD 92105 1270-A7
2300 SD 92102 1270-A7
S EUCLID AV
- NATC 91950 1290-B7
700 NATC 91950 1310-B1
EUCLID AVEX
2800 SDCo 91950 1310-B3
2900 NATC 91950 1310-B3
EUCLID CT
4900 SD 92102 1290-A1
4900 SD 92105 1290-A1
EUCLID LN
600 SDCo 92019 1252-D6
EUCLID PL
- SD 92113 1290-A5
EUGENE PL
3500 SD 92116 1269-G2
EUGENIE AV
700 ENCT 92024 1147-D4
EULA LN
2000 ELCJ 92019 1252-D4
2000 SDCo 92019 1252-D4
EUREKA PL
3200 CRLB 92008 1106-F5
EUREKA RD
10600 SDCo 91978 1271-F6
EUREKA ST
1000 SD 92110 1268-G3
EUROPA ST
100 ENCT 92024 1147-A4

EVA DR
15900 PWY 92064 1170-D5
EVA DE LUCA WY
15400 SDCo 92082 1070-J3
EVALYN CT
12900 PWY 92064 1190-B5
EVALYN PL
12900 PWY 92064 1190-B5
EVAN HEWES HWY
- ImCo - 431-F6
900 ImCo 92250 431-F6
EVAN HEWES HWY
Rt#-S80
- ImCo 92250 431-A5
200 ImCo 92243 6500-F5
600 ImCo 92243 6499-B6
900 ELCN 92243 6500-C6
900 ImCo 92243 431-A5
1700 ImCo 92273 431-A5
1800 ImCo 92273 430-J6
1900 ImCo 92251 430-J6
2800 ImCo 92259 430-J6
EVAN HEWES HWY
Rt#-115
400 HOLT 92250 431-E5
1500 ImCo 92250 431-D5
EVANS AV
900 CHV 91911 1330-E1
EVANS PL
500 SD 92103 1269-A6
9600 SDCo 91941 1271-C1
EVANS RD
1800 SD 92133 1288-D1
EVANS ST
- SD 92113 1289-C5
N EVANS ST
100 SD 92102 1289-D4
200 SD 92113 1289-D4
EVANSTON DR
13200 PWY 92064 1190-G4
EVANS WOOD WY
- SD 92130 1208-F2
EVE LN
9500 SNTE 92071 1231-B1
EVE WY
10300 SNTE 92071 1231-E5
EVELYN LN
1200 VSTA 92083 1087-E7
1200 VSTA 92083 1107-E1
EVELYN ST
1000 SD 92114 1290-E2
EVENING WY
3100 SD 92037 1228-A3
EVENING CANYON RD
3500 OCN 92056 1107-E2
EVENING CREEK DR E
10900 SD 92128 1189-H4
EVENING CREEK DR N
13100 SD 92128 1189-H4
EVENING CREEK DR S
13100 SD 92128 1189-H5
EVENING PRIMROSE TR
32000 SDCo 91906 (1318-B6
See Page 1298)
EVENINGSIDE GN
200 ESCN 92026 1109-G4
EVENING STAR DR
14600 PWY 92064 1190-G1
EVENSTAR LN
- SDCo 92036 1155-H4
EVERELL PL
10300 SNTE 92071 1231-F3
EVERETT PL
23400 SDCo 92065 1173-C3
EVERETT ST
2100 SD 92113 1289-D4
5200 OCN 92057 1067-A3
EVERETT WY
- VSTA 92084 1088-A2
EVERGLADES AV
6900 SD 92119 1250-F5
EVERGOLD ST
11500 SD 92131 1210-B1
11800 SD 92131 1190-B7
EVERGREEN AV
100 IMPB 91932 1349-E1
1500 SD 92154 1349-E1
1500 SD 92154 1329-J7
EVERGREEN CIR
1700 CRLB 92008 1106-F5
EVERGREEN CT
3700 SDCo 92028 1048-E1
EVERGREEN DR
900 ENCT 92024 1167-E1
1200 ENCT 92007 1167-E1
3400 SDCo 92084 1067-J6
29400 SDCo 91906 (1297-E4
See Page 1296)
EVERGREEN LN
800 SDCo 92084 1067-H6
1400 SMCS 92069 1109-D7
14100 PWY 92064 1170-G7
EVERGREEN PKWY
100 OCN 92054 1106-C2
EVERGREEN RD
3300 SDCo 91902 1310-G2
EVERGREEN ST
1000 SD 92106 1288-B2
2000 SD 92106 1268-C7
2900 SD 92110 1268-D6
N EVERGREEN ST
2900 SD 92110 1268-D6
EVERGREEN VILLAGE
LN
- SD 92102 1290-A4
EVERGREEN VILLAGE
RD
- SD 92102 1290-A4
EVERSTON RD
12600 SD 92128 1189-J6
EVERTS ST
4000 SD 92109 1247-J5
EVERVIEW RD
1400 SD 92110 1268-F2
EVILO ST
1100 ELCJ 92021 1251-H4
EVLOUISE DR
25200 SDCo 92026 1109-H2
EVVIA CT
100 SDCo 92083 1108-B3
100 VSTA 92083 1108-B3
EWALD CIR
9100 SNTE 92071 1231-B7
EWELL CT
1100 SD 92154 1350-E1
EWING DR
1400 CHV 91911 1330-H3
EWING ST
5100 SD 92115 1270-D2

EXBURY CT
4400 SD 92130 1188-C5
EXCALIBUR WY
4500 SD 92122 1228-D3
EXCELLANTE ST
2000 SD 92154 1351-F3
EXCEPTION PL
3800 ESCN 92025 1150-D3
EXCHANGE PL
7600 SD 92037 1227-F6
EXCITATION GN
4000 ESCN 92025 1150-C4
EXECUTIVE DR
4100 SD 92037 1228-D2
4300 SD 92121 1228-D2
EXECUTIVE PL
2800 ESCN 92029 1129-C2
EXECUTIVE RDG
3200 VSTA 92083 1128-A1
EXECUTIVE SQ
4200 SD 92037 1228-C2
EXECUTIVE WY
9000 SD 92121 1228-D2
EXETER ST
1200 ELCJ 92019 1251-J6
EXPEDITION WY
8700 SD 92093 1227-H3
EXPLORER CT
4200 SDCo 91941 1271-H4
EXPLORER PL
10900 SDCo 91941 1271-G3
EXPLORER RD
10800 SDCo 91941 1271-G3
EXPOSITION DR
18000 SDCo 91935 1274-D4
EYRIE RD
4900 SD 92116 1269-E3
EZEE ST
600 ENCT 92024 1147-C5
EZRA LN
14100 PWY 92064 1190-G1

F

F AV
- SDCo 92055 1066-E1
100 NATC 91950 1289-H7
100 CORD 92118 1288-H7
400 NATC 91950 1309-H1
3000 NATC 91950 1310-A4
F CT
- SD 92126 1209-E7
800 CHV 91910 1310-F7
F ST
- CHV 91910 1310-A6
200 SDCo 92065 1152-H5
500 CHV 91910 1309-J7
700 SD 92101 1288-J3
1600 SDCo 92055 409-A7
2400 SD 92105 1270-B7
2400 SD 92105 1290-B1
2500 NATC 91950 1310-C3
4500 SD 92102 1289-J3
E F ST
- ENCT 92024 1147-C7
W F ST
100 ENCT 92024 1147-B7
FABER WY
5000 SD 92115 1270-A2
FABIENNE WY
8800 LMSA 91941 1271-A3
FABLED WATERS CT
- SDCo 91977 1291-E1
FABLED WATERS DR
- SDCo 91977 1271-E7
- SDCo 91977 1291-E1
FAIR LN
1500 VSTA 92084 1108-B1
1600 ESCN 92029 1129-F5
8900 SDCo 92040 1231-J6
9000 SDCo 92040 1232-A6
FAIR ACRES LN
3100 SDCo 91978 1292-C1
3100 SDCo 91978 1272-C7
FAIRBANKS AV
9400 SD 92123 1249-E5
FAIRBROOK RD
12500 SD 92131 1210-B4
FAIRBURN ST
14600 PWY 92064 1190-J4
FAIRCHILD WY
- SD 92154 1351-C2
FAIR COUNTRY RD
1500 SDCo 92019 1272-A2
FAIRCREST WY
28200 SDCo 92026 1089-G2
FAIRCROSS PL
3900 SD 92115 1270-C5
FAIRDALE AV
1700 ESCN 92027 1130-C1
FAIREN LN
9200 SNTE 92071 1231-B7
FAIRFAX DR
1600 LMGR 91945 1290-H1
FAIRFIELD AV
2800 CRLB 92008 1107-A4
FAIRFIELD DR
100 ELCN 92243 6500-A6
1500 ELCN 92243 6560-A1
FAIRFIELD ST
1200 CHV 91913 1311-C7
2100 SD 92110 1268-F1
2600 SD 92110 1248-F7
FAIRFORD RD
12600 SD 92128 1190-A6
FAIRGATE DR
13600 PWY 92064 1190-F4
FAIR GLEN RD
1500 SDCo 92019 1272-A2
FAIRGREEN WY
5400 SDCo 92003 1068-B1
FAIRGROVE LN
9400 SD 92129 1189-E4
FAIRHAVEN ST
1900 LMGR 91945 1290-G1
FAIRHILL CT
600 OCN 92057 1087-C1
FAIRHILL DR
10100 SDCo 91977 1291-E2
FAIRHILL TER
1000 SDCo 91977 1291-E2
FAIRHOPE CT
17400 SD 92128 1170-A1
FAIRHOPE LP
2100 VSTA 92083 1107-G5
FAIRHOPE RD
11900 SD 92128 1170-A1
FAIRHURST PL
2400 SDCo 91977 1271-H7

FAIRLANE AV
900 SMCS 92069 1109-B7
FAIRLANE RD
26800 SDCo 92082 1090-E6
FAIRLAWN ST
9200 SNTE 92071 1231-G5
FAIRLEE DR
1900 ENCT 92024 1147-H7
1900 ENCT 92024 1167-H1
FAIRLEE LN
200 ENCT 92024 1167-H1
FAIRLIE RD
17400 SD 92128 1170-A1
FAIRLINDO WY
3600 NATC 91950 1310-D3
FAIRLOMAS RD
3200 NATC 91950 1310-D3
FAIRMONT PL
1500 ESCN 92027 1110-A5
FAIRMOUNT AV
1800 SD 92105 1289-J1
2400 SD 92105 1269-H6
4200 SD 92115 1269-H1
4300 SD 92116 1269-H1
4600 SD 92108 1269-H1
4700 SD 92120 1269-H1
5800 SD 92108 1249-H7
5800 SD 92120 1249-H7
FAIR OAK CT
2200 ESCN 92026 1109-H3
FAIR OAKS DR
3100 SDCo 91978 1292-C1
3100 SDCo 91978 1272-C7
FAIR OAKS LN
3100 SDCo 91978 1292-C1
3200 SDCo 91978 1272-C7
FAIRPORT WY
- SD 92130 1208-C2
FAIRTREE TER
14700 PWY 92064 1190-D1
FAIR VALLEY RD
1500 SDCo 92019 1272-A2
FAIRVIEW AV
8000 LMSA 91941 1270-H3
9000 SDCo 91977 1291-A5
FAIRVIEW CIR
3600 SDCo 92084 1067-J5
3600 SDCo 92084 1068-A5
FAIRVIEW DR
2900 SDCo 92084 1068-A5
FAIRVIEW LN
3300 SDCo 92084 1068-A5
FAIRWATER PL
6400 CRLB 92009 1127-C4
FAIRWAY CT
- SDCo 92004 1058-H4
800 CHV 91911 1330-D1
3000 OCN 92056 1106-G2
FAIRWAY DR
3200 SDCo 91941 1270-J5
3200 SDCo 91941 1271-A6
3200 SDCo 91977 1271-A6
3500 SDCo 92028 1028-F4
FAIRWAY LN
1500 SDCo 92004 1058-H5
FAIRWAY PK
1800 ESCN 92026 1109-D5
FAIRWAY PL
5900 SDCo 92067 1188-E2
FAIRWAY RD
6800 SD 92037 1247-G1
6900 SD 92037 1227-G7
FAIRWAY CIRCLE DR
1800 SDCo 92069 1128-D2
FAIRWAY HEIGHTS RW
16200 SD 92128 1170-A4
FAIRWAY HILL CIR
- SDCo 92026 1089-A1
FAIRWAY OAKS DR
2300 CHV 91915 1311-G5
FAIRWAY PINE PL
- SDCo 92026 1089-B1
FAIRWAY POINTE RW
12200 SD 92128 1170-B4
FAIRWAY VISTA
- ENCT 92024 1147-D3
FAIRWIND CT
- SD 92130 1208-B2
FAIRWIND WY
- SD 92130 1208-B2
FAISAN WY
11400 SD 92124 1250-A3
FAISEL DR
2700 SDCo 91901 1254-A2
FAITH AV
500 ENCT 92007 1167-D1
FAITH CIR
1400 OCN 92054 1106-E1
FAITH RD
1800 ESCN 92029 1129-F5
FAIVRE ST
2300 CHV 91911 1330-B6
FALCHION DR
1800 SDCo 92004 1058-G7
FALCON DR
3100 CRLB 92008 1106-G4
FALCON GN
1300 ESCN 92029 1129-G6
FALCON LN
1400 ELCJ 92020 1251-D2
FALCON PL
400 SMCS 92069 1108-J7
700 SD 92103 1268-J6
FALCON ST
3000 SD 92103 1268-J4
FALCON BLUFF CT
- SDCo 92127 1169-E3
FALCON BLUFF ST
- SDCo 92127 1169-E3
FALCONER CT
1800 VSTA 92083 1107-J3
FALCONER RD
100 ESCN 92027 1110-E6
900 ESCN 92027 1130-F1
FALCONFIRE WY
300 SD 92114 1290-F3
FALCON HEIGHTS RD
16200 SDCo 92065 1151-B6
FALCON HILL CT
1600 ENCT 92007 1167-E2
FALCONHURST TER
4700 SD 92154 1330-H7
FALCON PEAK ST
1600 CHV 91913 1311-D7
FALCON RIDGE CT
4500 SD 92130 1188-C6
FALCON RIM PT
10600 SD 92131 1209-J3

SAN DIEGO CO.
INDEX

STREET
Block City ZIP Pg-Grid

FALCON VALLEY DR
2400 CHV 91914 1311-F3
FALDA PL
7700 CRLB 92009 1147-F2
FALDA DEL CERRO
- SDCo 92019 1272-A1
FALKIRK RW
2300 SD 92037 1247-J1
FALL PL
2400 OCN 92056 1087-D6
2400 VSTA 92083 1087-D6
FALLBROOK CT
1200 CHV 91902 1310-J3
1200 CHV 91902 1311-A4
1200 SDCo 91902 1311-A4
FALLBROOK LN
2800 SD 92117 1248-E7
FALLBROOK PL
- ESCN 92027 1130-H3
- SD 92027 1130-H3
E FALLBROOK ST
1700 SDCo 92028 1027-J3
E FALLBROOK ST Rt#-S15
100 SDCo 92028 1027-G3
W FALLBROOK ST
100 SDCo 92028 1027-F3
600 SDCo 92055 1027-F3
FALLEN LEAF LN
2100 SDCo 92028 1028-A1
FALLEN LEAF RD
13300 PWY 92064 1170-E4
FALLEN OAK RD
800 SDCo 92028 1047-E4
FALLEN TREE LN
28400 SDCo 92026 1089-D3
FALLEN WOOD LN
5700 SD 92121 1208-F4
FALL GLEN CT
10200 SD 92126 1209-D5
FALLING LEAF CT
1900 SMCS 92069 1128-B2
FALLINGLEAF RD
2200 OCN 92056 1087-D6
FALLON CIR
3700 SD 92130 1188-A5
FALLRIVER WY
1200 SMCS 92069 1128-B4
FALL RIVER WY
9200 SD 92129 1189-D4
FALLS WY
6300 SD 92115 1270-C1
FALLSBRAE RD
4100 SDCo 92028 1048-A5
E FALLS VIEW DR
5100 SD 92115 1270-C1
W FALLS VIEW DR
5300 SD 92115 1270-C1
FALLSVIEW LN
100 OCN 92056 1107-D2
FALLSVIEW PL
1400 ESCN 92027 1109-J6
FALLWOOD AV
8900 SD 92126 1209-D5
FALMOUTH DR
1900 ELCJ 92020 1251-C5
2100 LMSA 91942 1251-C5
FALSE PT CT
600 CHV 91911 1330-J4
FALVY AV
2700 SD 92111 1249-A6
FAMILY CIR
7600 SD 92111 1249-A5
FAMOSA BLVD
2200 SD 92107 1268-B6
2400 SD 92110 1268-B5
FANITA DR
600 ELCJ 92020 1251-B3
6900 SNTE 92071 1251-B1
8400 SNTE 92071 1231-B7
FANITA PKWY
9300 SNTE 92071 1231-A3
FANITA RANCHO RD
9000 SNTE 92071 1251-B1
9200 ELCJ 92020 1251-B1
FANITA RIO WY
8700 SNTE 92071 1231-B7
FANTASIA CT
11700 SD 92131 1210-B1
FANTASIA WY
11700 SD 92131 1210-B1
FANTASY LN
2200 SD 92173 1350-G3
FANTERO AV
1900 ESCN 92029 1129-F6
FANUEL ST
4000 SD 92109 1247-J4
FANWOOD CT
1900 OCN 92054 1106-E2
FARADAY AV
- CRLB 92008 1126-J1
1600 CRLB 92008 1127-B1
FARADAY ST
1400 VSTA 92083 1127-H1
1400 CRLB 92008 1127-H1
FARAWAY LN
7900 SDCo 92029 1148-J2
FARAWAY PL
14200 SDCo 92082 1070-F4
FAREL ST
2600 OCN 92054 1106-G1
FARENHOLT AV
1800 SD 92101 1289-C2
1800 SD 92134 1289-C2
FARGATE TER
7200 SD 92126 1208-J4
FARGO AV
1500 ELCJ 92019 1252-A5
4600 SD 92117 1248-B1
FARGO GN
100 ESCN 92027 1110-E7
FARINA PL
600 VSTA 92084 1088-A7
FARLAND PL
100 ESCN 92027 1130-C1
FARLEY CT
4200 SD 92122 1228-E5
FARLEY DR
6300 SD 92122 1228-E5
FARLEY LN
4200 SD 92122 1228-E5
FARLEY RD
2400 SDCo 92066 1135-F6
FARLEY FLAT RD
- SDCo 91916 1216-F6
- SDCo 91916 1236-G2
- SDCo 91931 1236-G2
FARLIN RD
1600 SDCo 91901 1235-B5

STREET
Block City ZIP Pg-Grid

FARMDALE ST
7200 SD 92114 1290-G6
FARMER DR
- ELCN 92243 6559-F2
FARMER RD
700 SDCo 92036 1136-B3
FARMERVILLE ST
1200 CHV 91913 1311-C7
FARMINGDALE ST
- SD 92131 1209-G2
FARMINGTON DR
9500 SDCo 92040 1232-A4
FARMINGTON PL
2000 SMCS 92069 1128-B3
FARMS VIEW CT
6800 SDCo 92067 1188-H2
FARNHAM ST
9300 SD 92123 1249-D1
FARNSWORTH CT
5900 CRLB 92008 1127-C2
FARNSWORTH LANE RD
1400 ImCo 92243 6560-A3
1400 ELCN 92243 6560-A3
FAROL CT
7700 CRLB 92009 1147-H2
FAROL PL
7700 CRLB 92009 1147-H2
FARR AV
900 ESCN 92026 1109-J7
1000 ESCN 92026 1110-A7
FARRA ST
- SDCo 92028 999-E6
FARRADAY RIDGE DR
3400 SDCo 91935 1272-F5
FARRAGUT CIR
400 ELCJ 92020 1251-F6
FARRAGUT RD
2500 SD 92133 1288-D1
2900 SD 92133 1268-C7
FARRAND CT
1000 SDCo 92028 1027-H5
FARRAND RD
1300 SDCo 92028 1027-H5
FARREL ST
600 CHV 91911 1330-H3
FARRINGTON DR
2000 ELCJ 92020 1251-B1
6800 SNTE 92071 1251-B1
FAR VALLEY RD
1200 SDCo 91906 (1318-F5 See Page 1298)
FARVIEW CT
- ELCJ 92021 1251-G3
FAR VIEW PL
2400 SDCo 92084 1108-D4
FARVIEW ST
600 ELCJ 92021 1251-G3
FASANO DR
10300 SDCo 92040 1231-F3
FASHION HILLS BLVD
6800 SD 92111 1268-J2
FASHION VALLEY RD
1100 SD 92108 1268-J3
FATHER JUNIPERO SERRA TR
- SD 92124 1250-D2
7300 SD 92071 1230-F6
7300 SD 92124 1230-E7
7500 SNTE 92071 1230-F6
FATHOM CT
500 SD 92154 1330-J6
FAULCONER ST
5400 SD 92105 1290-B1
FAUNA CT
6100 SD 92115 1270-D6
FAUNA DR
6000 SD 92115 1270-C6
FAWCETT RD
- ImCo 92249 431-C7
FAWLEY DR
1600 SDCo 92083 1108-A2
FAWN AV
3000 SD 92117 1248-C1
FAWN CREEK LN
2400 SDCo 92026 1109-J3
FAWNTAIL CT
1700 CHV 91913 1311-D6
FAWNWOOD LN
7900 LMGR 91945 1270-J7
FAXON ST
100 SDCo 91977 1291-B4
FAY AV
6300 SD 92037 1247-F1
7300 SD 92037 1227-F7
FAYETTE ST
1300 ELCJ 92020 1251-D2
FEATHER AV
4200 SD 92117 1248-E3
FEATHER DR
- SMCS 92069 1108-F5
FEATHER BLUFF DR
- SDCo 92127 1169-E3
FEATHERHILL LN
11200 SD 92126 1209-E2
FEATHER RIVER PL
1400 CHV 91915 1311-H7
FEATHER RIVER RD
2300 CHV 91915 1311-H7
FEATHER ROCK CT
3900 SDCo 91902 1311-B2
FEATHERSTONE CANYON RD
22100 SDCo 92040 (1193-C4 See Page 1192)
FEBO CT
3300 CRLB 92009 1127-J7
FEBRUARY CT
2100 SD 92110 1268-G1
FEBRUARY ST
4900 SD 92110 1268-G1
FECANIN WY
15800 SDCo 92065 1174-A4
FEDERAL BLVD
3900 SD 92105 1289-H2
4700 SD 92102 1289-H2
4800 SD 92102 1290-A2
5100 SD 92105 1290-A2
6000 SD 92114 1290-C1
6300 SD 92114 1270-D7
6400 LMGR 91945 1270-D7
FEDERAL BLVD W
3700 SD 92102 1289-G3
FEDERMAN LN
4100 SD 92130 1188-B5
FEGAN DR
- SDCo 92672 1023-E2
FEGHALI LN
500 SDCo 92065 1153-A5

STREET
Block City ZIP Pg-Grid

FEGHALI RD
200 SDCo 92065 1153-A5
FEILER PL
3000 SD 92123 1249-F5
FELDSPAR CT
16600 SDCo 92065 1171-F2
FELICE DR
1900 ESCN 92026 1109-C4
16300 SD 92128 1170-B4
FELICIA LN
500 SMCS 92069 1109-B6
9900 SDCo 91977 1291-D3
FELICIA WY
2800 SDCo 92084 1068-E5
FELICIDAD DR
900 SDCo 92028 1027-G3
FELICITA AV
400 SDCo 91977 1291-B4
500 ESCN 92025 1129-J6
W FELICITA AV
500 ESCN 92025 1129-J5
500 ESCN 92025 1130-A5
FELICITA CT
1600 ESCN 92025 1129-J5
FELICITA LN
1200 SDCo 92029 1149-G1
1600 ESCN 92025 1129-J5
1700 VSTA 92083 1087-G3
FELICITA PL
600 ESCN 92025 1129-J5
FELICITA RD
1900 ESCN 92025 1129-J7
2100 ESCN 92029 1129-J7
2200 SDCo 92029 1129-J7
2500 SDCo 92029 1149-J1
FELINDA WY
2500 OCN 92056 1087-C6
FELINO WY
600 CHV 91910 1311-A5
FELIPE RD
17200 SDCo 92065 1173-F1
FELIX DR
10600 SNTE 92071 1231-D2
FELLER CV
10500 SD 92126 1209-A4
FELSON RD
9000 SD 92129 1189-C1
FELSPAR CT
4500 SD 92109 1248-B5
FELSPAR ST
700 SD 92109 1247-H6
1500 SD 92109 1248-A5
FELTON ST
1300 SD 92102 1289-F2
1800 SD 92104 1289-F1
2500 SD 92104 1269-F4
4400 SD 92116 1269-F4
FENDER RD
- SDCo 92036 1156-E7
FENELON ST
2900 SD 92106 1288-B1
FENIMORE WY
6000 SD 92120 1249-J7
FENNELL AV
5900 SD 92114 1290-C4
FENNELL CT
200 SD 92114 1290-C4
FENOVAL DR
1800 SDCo 92004 1058-G7
FENSMUIR ST
8500 SD 92123 1249-C4
FENTON PKWY
2100 SD 92108 1269-E1
FENTON PL
2500 SDCo 91950 1310-C2
FENTON RD
5700 SD 92121 1208-G7
FENTON ST
2300 CHV 91914 1311-G4
FENWAY CIR
1400 OCN 92057 1067-B4
FENWAY RD
9200 SNTE 92071 1231-A3
FENWICK DR
3700 SDCo 91941 1271-A5
3700 SDCo 91977 1271-A5
FENWICK RD
10700 SD 92126 1209-B4
FERBER ST
5700 SD 92122 1228-F6
FERDINAND RD
2500 ELCJ 92020 1251-B5
FERGUS ST
700 SD 92114 1290-C3
FERGUSON RD
- ImCo - 432-E1
- ImCo 92283 432-E1
FERGUSON WY
8900 SD 92119 1251-A4
FERMI AV
9100 SD 92123 1249-E5
FERMI CT
5600 CRLB 92008 1127-D1
FERN AV
400 IMPB 91932 1349-F1
1500 SD 92154 1349-J1
FERN GN
200 SD 92037 1247-E1
FERN PL
1300 SDCo 92083 1107-G3
7000 CRLB 92009 1127-E6
FERN ST
400 CHV 91910 1310-A5
1300 SD 92102 1289-E2
2000 SD 92104 1289-E2
2900 SD 92154 1350-C1
N FERN ST
600 ESCN 92027 1110-B6
FERNANDO CT
12200 SD 92128 1150-B7
FERNANDO DR
12300 SD 92128 1150-B6
FERNANDO WY
18200 SD 92128 1150-B6
FERNBROOK CT
- ELCJ 92019 1252-C5
FERNBROOK DR
14000 SDCo 92065 1192-B2
FERN CANYON RD
3400 SDCo 91935 1272-H5
FERNCREEK LN
- ESCN 92027 1130-J3
FERNCREST PL
12000 SD 92128 1190-B2
FERNDALE LN
4100 SDCo 92028 1047-E4
FERNDALE ST
- CHV 91913 1311-C7
8600 SD 92126 1209-C5

STREET
Block City ZIP Pg-Grid

FERN FLAT FIRE RD
- SDCo 91916 (1196-C3 See Page 1176)
- SDCo 92036 (1196-C3 See Page 1176)
FERN FOREST RD
1600 SDCo 92084 1068-B6
FERNGLEN RD
2700 CRLB 92008 1106-F3
FERNHILL WY
1100 ELCJ 92020 1251-H7
FERN MEADOW RD
- SDCo 92060 409-G7
FERN RIDGE CT
500 OCN 92054 1086-D3
FERNRIDGE RD
7500 SNTE 92071 1230-G7
FERNTREE LN
2100 SDCo 91977 1291-D1
FERNVALE LN
- SNTE 92071 1230-G5
FERN VALLEY RD
2500 CHV 91915 1311-J6
FERNVIEW ST
1000 ELCJ 92020 1251-H7
FERNWOOD AV
100 ESCN 92027 1130-C1
FERNWOOD DR
6200 LMSA 91942 1251-C6
FERNWOOD RD
1700 CHV 91913 1311-D6
FERRARA WY
300 VSTA 92083 1087-G6
FERRELL LN
15000 SDCo 92021 1233-B7
FERRELL RD
400 ImCo 92231 431-B7
FERRIS SQ
6200 SD 92121 1208-G7
FESLER ST
500 ELCJ 92020 1251-D3
FESTIVAL CT
3700 CHV 91911 1330-E5
FESTIVAL DR
100 OCN 92057 1066-H7
FEZ ST
4300 SD 92121 1228-C2
FIAT CT
2000 SDCo 92019 1272-C3
FICUS LN
1000 SMCS 92069 1109-B7
FICUS PL
- CRLB 92009 1127-D5
FIDDLETOWN RD
14000 PWY 92064 1190-G1
FIDELIO CT
11700 SD 92131 1210-B1
FIDELIO WY
12100 SD 92131 1210-B1
FIEGER ST
2100 SD 92105 1290-B1
FIELD CT
2900 SD 92110 1248-F7
FIELD ST
4400 SD 92117 1248-E6
4800 SD 92110 1248-F6
FIELDBROOK ST
1300 CHV 91913 1331-B1
FIELDBROOK WY
500 ESCN 92027 1110-D5
FIELDCREST PL
2500 ESCN 92027 1110-E7
2500 SDCo 91977 1271-E7
FIELDCREST ST
10000 SDCo 91977 1271-D7
FIELDGATE RD
4500 OCN 92056 1107-E2
FIELDLANE PL
2400 SDCo 91977 1271-D7
FIELDRIDGE PL
2400 SDCo 91977 1271-H7
FIELDSTONE DR
12400 SD 92128 1150-B5
FIELDSTONE LN
700 ENCT 92024 1147-G5
FIELDVIEW WY
14700 PWY 92064 1190-D1
FIESTA DR
12800 PWY 92064 1190-E5
FIESTA GN
2000 ESCN 92027 1110-B5
FIESTA LN
200 ELCJ 92019 1252-A5
FIESTA WY
4200 OCN 92057 1086-J3
FIESTA ISLAND RD
- SD 92109 1248-C7
1700 SD 92109 1268-C1
FIFIELD RD
4300 ImCo 92227 431-D2
FIFIELD ST
500 CHV 91910 1310-G7
FIG AV
200 CHV 91910 1310-A6
500 CHV 91910 1330-B1
FIG CT
600 ESCN 92025 1129-J1
1200 NATC 91950 1289-J7
FIG ST
100 SDCo 92028 1027-F2
3900 SMCS 92069 1128-C1
E FIG ST
100 SDCo 92028 1027-F2
N FIG ST
100 ESCN 92025 1130-A2
700 ESCN 92025 1129-J1
800 ESCN 92026 1109-J7
800 ESCN 92026 1129-J1
S FIG ST
100 ESCN 92025 1130-A2
W FIG ST
- SDCo 92028 1027-E2
FIGTREE CT
- SD 92131 1210-C3
FIGTREE ST
12400 SD 92131 1210-B3
FIGUEROA BLVD
2600 SD 92109 1248-C5
FILAGO CT
9400 SD 92129 1189-E6
FILAREE CT
1600 CRLB 92009 1127-D6
FILBERT ST
300 ELCJ 92020 1251-G6
3600 SD 92136 1289-G7
FILERA RD
12300 SD 92128 1170-B4
FILIPO ST
4700 SD 92115 1270-D3

STREET
Block City ZIP Pg-Grid

FILLBROOK DR
10900 SDCo 92040 1232-B1
FILLMONT GN
2600 ESCN 92029 1149-H1
FILLY LN
3600 SDCo 91902 1311-A1
FILOI AV
4500 SD 92173 1350-G3
FINANCIAL CT
2600 SD 92117 1248-B2
FINCH LN
2000 SD 92123 1269-A1
2000 SD 92123 1249-A7
FINCH PL
1200 CHV 91911 1330-G2
FINCH ST
900 ELCJ 92020 1251-D3
FINCHLEY TER
4700 SD 92130 1188-C4
FINE LN
1800 ESCN 92029 1129-F5
FINK RD
- SDCo 92070 409-J7
FINLEY AV
8200 LMSA 91941 1270-J3
FINNEY RD
- ImCo 92227 431-D3
FINO DR
5100 SD 92124 1249-H2
FINO GN
700 ESCN 92025 1150-C4
FINSEN AV
4600 SD 92122 1228-F4
FIONA PL
6600 CRLB 92009 1127-D5
FIONA WY
8600 SNTE 92071 1231-D7
FIORE TER
5200 SD 92122 1228-E3
FIORI DR
2200 SDCo 92084 1108-D2
FIR LN
9700 SDCo 92029 1149-E2
FIR RD
- SDCo 92066 1237-C7
FIR ST
100 OCN 92054 1106-A1
100 SD 92101 1289-A2
300 SD 92114 1290-D4
600 VSTA 92083 1087-F6
600 SD 92101 1288-J2
2800 SD 92102 1289-E1
3400 SD 92104 1289-F1
3800 SMCS 92069 1128-C1
4800 SD 92102 1290-A1
W FIR ST
100 SD 92101 1289-A2
500 SD 92101 1288-J2
FIRBROOK LN
12800 PWY 92064 1170-D3
FIRE RD
3700 SDCo 92028 1048-E3
FIREBIRD ST
300 SMCS 92069 1108-H7
FIREBRAND DR
2800 SDCo 91901 1254-C2
FIREBRAND PL
2600 SDCo 91901 1254-D2
FIREBRAND WY
2800 SDCo 91901 1254-D2
FIRECREST WY
- SDCo 92028 1027-H7
FIRE MOUNTAIN DR
1700 OCN 92054 1106-F1
FIRE MOUNTAIN PL
300 ESCN 92026 1109-H5
FIRESIDE AV
8400 SD 92123 1249-C6
FIRESIDE CT
2800 SD 92123 1249-C6
FIRESIDE LN
700 VSTA 92084 1088-B7
FIRESIDE ST
100 OCN 92054 1086-F3
FIRESTONE DR
1700 ESCN 92026 1109-D5
FIRESTONE ST
4600 SD 92117 1228-F7
FIRETHORN GN
1900 ESCN 92027 1110-A4
FIRETHORN LN
4500 SDCo 92004 (1099-F4 See Page 1098)
FIRETHORN ST
700 SD 92154 1330-G7
900 SD 92154 1350-G1
FIREWATER TR
7500 SDCo 92036 1138-C7
7500 SDCo 92036 (1158-C1 See Page 1138)
FIREWAY DR
3400 SD 92111 1248-H4
FIRNPINE DR
3100 SD 92115 1270-D6
FIRST AMERICAN WY
- PWY 92064 1190-G6
FIRTREE CT
300 ENCT 92024 1147-G7
FIR TREE PL
900 CRLB 92009 1127-A5
FIRWOOD RW
6000 SD 92037 1248-A1
FISHER CV
14800 SDCo 92014 1188-A1
FISHER LN
2900 LMGR 91945 1270-F6
FISHER RD
- SDCo 91905 1300-E7
1200 ImCo 92283 432-D4
1300 ImCo 92231 431-A7
1300 ImCo 92243 431-A7
FISK AV
6600 SD 92122 1228-D4
FITCH CT
6900 SD 92111 1268-J2
FITCH LP
- SD 92106 1288-A6
FITZGERALD WY
9000 SDCo 91977 1271-A6
FITZPATRICK RD
300 SMCS 92069 1108-H6
FIVE CROWNS WY
100 ENCT 92024 1147-H7
FIVE D DR
1300 SDCo 92021 1251-H2
FIVE DIAMONDS RD
2300 SDCo 92004 (1078-G2 See Page 1058)

STREET
Block City ZIP Pg-Grid

FIVE POINT LN
9100 SNTE 92071 1231-A7
FIX CT
- SD 92173 1350-F5
FLAG LN
1300 SDCo 92021 1251-H2
FLAG PZ
8300 SDCo 91977 1290-J6
FLAG LAKE ST
7600 SD 92119 1250-G5
FLAGSHIP CT
- SMCS 92078 1128-D5
FLAGSTAFF CT
2500 CHV 91914 1311-G3
FLAGSTONE CT
700 SMCS 92069 1109-C6
FLAGSTONE RW
6100 SD 92037 1248-A1
FLAIR LN
15700 SDCo 92065 1174-A4
FLAIR ENCINITAS DR
1400 ENCT 92024 1147-G6
FLAMBEAU PL
10700 SDCo 91941 1271-F4
FLAMENCO ST
6400 CRLB 92009 1127-H5
FLAME TREE LN
1400 CRLB 92009 1127-A4
FLAME TREE PL
200 OCN 92057 1087-A1
FLAMETREE RD
2300 SDCo 92084 1068-C7
FLAMINGO AV
1100 ELCJ 92021 1251-J2
1100 SDCo 92021 1251-J2
FLAMINGO DR
100 OCN 92054 1086-F4
FLAMINGO PL
1300 ELCJ 92021 1251-J2
FLANDERS CT
10200 SD 92121 1208-H5
FLANDERS CV
10400 SD 92126 1209-A4
FLANDERS DR
6400 SD 92121 1208-H5
7500 SD 92126 1208-H5
7600 SD 92126 1209-C4
FLANDERS PL
10400 SD 92126 1209-A4
FLAVEN LN
8100 SDCo 92021 1252-C1
FLAX CT
1000 SD 92154 1350-C1
FLAX DR
2800 SD 92154 1350-C1
FLAXTON TER
4900 SD 92130 1188-C4
FLEET ST
- CRLB 92008 1126-H2
FLEETRIDGE DR
1100 SD 92106 1288-A2
FLEETWOOD ST
1800 ESCN 92029 1129-F5
2300 SD 92111 1248-J7
FLEISCHMANN CT
- SDCo 92055 1086-A2
FLEMING CT
8400 SD 92145 1229-C2
FLEMING DR
3000 SD 92139 1310-E2
FLEMING RD
- SD 92106 1287-J5
FLEMISH PL
800 OCN 92057 1086-G5
FLETCHER DR
9100 LMSA 91941 1271-B2
FLETCHER PKWY
1000 ELCJ 92020 1251-C4
1000 ELCJ 92021 1251-C4
2900 LMSA 91942 1251-A7
7700 LMSA 91941 1270-H1
7700 LMSA 91942 1270-H1
8500 LMSA 91942 1250-J7
FLETCHER RD
4200 SDCo 92004 1100-B5
FLETCHER PT WY
- SDCo 92036 1155-G4
FLETCHER VALLEY DR
8900 SNTE 92071 1251-A1
FLICKER LN
100 OCN 92057 1086-H2
FLICKER ST
600 SD 92114 1290-F3
FLIGHTPATH WY
8500 SD 92154 1351-G1
FLINN CREST ST
9300 SDCo 92021 1232-H4
FLINN SPRINGS LN
9400 SDCo 92021 1232-J4
FLINN SPRINGS RD
- CHV 91915 1311-H6
9500 SDCo 92021 1232-J3
9500 SDCo 92021 1233-A4
FLINT AV
2100 ESCN 92027 1130-D1
FLINT PL
12100 PWY 92064 1190-E7
FLINT ST
900 ELCJ 92021 1251-H2
FLINTKOTE AV
11000 SD 92121 1208-A5
FLINTRIDGE DR
2100 SD 92139 1310-C1
FLINTRIDGE PL
600 ESCN 92026 1109-F4
FLIPPER DR
5900 SD 92114 1290-C4
FLO DR
1400 SDCo 91901 1234-A6
FLO BOB LN
- SDCo 91901 1234-H5
FLOOD RD
1300 ImCo 92283 432-D4
FLORA AV
1000 CORD 92118 1288-H7
1100 CORD 92118 1308-H1
FLORA DR
600 OCN 92057 1067-A6
FLORA AZALEA CT
10500 SNTE 92071 1231-E2
FLORA CAMELLIA CT
10500 SNTE 92071 1231-E2
FLORAL AV
13300 PWY 92064 1190-J4
FLORAL CT
800 SMCS 92069 1108-J5
800 SMCS 92069 1109-A5
FLORA MAGNOLIA CT
10400 SNTE 92071 1231-E2

STREET
Block City ZIP Pg-Grid

FLORA VERDA CT
10500 SNTE 92071 1231-E2
FLORA VISTA
1400 SDCo 92027 1130-E5
12800 PWY 92064 1190-E5
FLORENCE LN
3400 SD 92113 1289-F5
FLORENCE ST
500 IMPB 91932 1329-H7
900 IMPB 91932 1349-H1
3400 SD 92113 1289-F5
FLORENCE TER
3100 SDCo 91978 1292-C1
FLORENCIA LN
400 VSTA 92083 1087-G6
FLORES DE ORO
300 SDCo 92067 1148-A7
500 SDCo 92024 1148-A7
FLORESTA CT
12400 SD 92128 1170-B1
FLORESTA WY
12400 SD 92128 1170-B1
FLOREY CT
7300 SD 92122 1228-F4
FLOREY ST
6800 SD 92122 1228-F4
FLORIDA CT
1900 SD 92104 1269-C6
FLORIDA DR
1700 SD 92101 1289-C1
2600 SD 92101 1269-C7
FLORIDA ST
400 IMPB 91932 1329-H7
900 IMPB 91932 1349-H1
3400 SD 92104 1269-C5
4300 SD 92116 1269-C5
FLORIDO PZ
1000 CHV 91910 1311-A7
FLORINDO RD
11100 SD 92127 1169-H2
FLORINE DR
3100 LMGR 91945 1270-F6
FLORISSANT CT
8400 SD 92129 1189-B3
FLORITA ST
100 ENCT 92024 1147-B6
FLOWER AV
- CORD 92135 1288-F4
2200 SD 92154 1350-B1
FLOWER DR
- NATC 91950 1289-H7
FLOWER LN
300 VSTA 92083 1087-D7
FLOWER ST
- CHV 91910 1310-C5
500 CHV 91910 1309-J6
1700 ESCN 92027 1130-C1
E FLOWER ST
- CHV 91910 1310-C5
FLOWERDALE LN
200 SD 92114 1290-H4
FLOWER FIELDS WY
2600 CRLB 92008 1106-H3
FLOWER HILL DR
2500 SD 92014 1187-H1
FLOWER MEADOW CT
11500 SD 92126 1209-A2
FLOWER MEADOW DR
7500 SD 92126 1209-A2
FLOWERS LN
24700 SDCo 91916 1236-A2
FLOWERWOOD LN
4000 SDCo 92028 1048-D4
FLOWING WELLS
- ImCo - 411-C8
FLOYD AV
600 CHV 91910 1310-F6
FLOYD SMITH DR
300 ELCJ 92020 1251-E2
FLUME DR
1700 SDCo 92021 1252-C2
1700 ELCJ 92021 1252-C2
FLUME RD
- SDCo 92020 1271-G1
8300 LMSA 91942 1250-J6
8300 SD 92119 1250-J6
8700 SD 92119 1251-A6
FLUSHING DR
2200 SD 92111 1248-J7
2200 SD 92111 1249-A7
2200 SD 92111 1268-J1
FLYING CLOUD WY
4700 CRLB 92008 1106-H7
FLYING H RD
3100 SDCo 92004 (1078-J5 See Page 1058)
FLYING HILLS CT
2000 ELCJ 92020 1251-B3
FLYING HILLS LN
1900 ELCJ 92020 1251-B3
FLYING LC
- CRLB 92009 1127-J3
FLYING U RD
2400 SDCo 92004 (1078-J2 See Page 1058)
2400 SDCo 92004 (1079-A2 See Page 1058)
FLYNN HEIGHTS DR
700 SDCo 92069 1109-B2
FOG RDG
21000 SDCo 91901 1275-A3
FOGG CT
4400 SD 92109 1248-C5
FOGG ST
2400 SD 92109 1248-B5
FOLKESTONE ST
1500 LMGR 91945 1290-J1
1500 SDCo 91977 1290-J1
FOLLETT DR
9600 SNTE 92071 1231-F4
FOLLETTE ST
- CRLB 92009 1127-D5
FOLSOM DR
5800 SD 92037 1247-F3
FONDALE CT
600 ESCN 92027 1130-D2
FOND DU LAC AV
4000 SD 92117 1248-E1
FOND DU LAC CT
4800 SD 92117 1248-E1
FONDO RD
10000 SDCo 91977 1271-E5
FONTAINE PL
7100 SD 92120 1250-B5
FONTAINE ST
5100 SD 92120 1250-A5
FONTANA AV
3200 SD 92117 1248-E5

FONTANELLE CT — SAN DIEGO CO. STREET INDEX — GAMBLE ST 6586

STREET
Block City ZIP Pg-Grid

FONTANELLE CT
- SD 92128 1190-A3
FONTANELLE PL
- SD 92128 1190-A3
FONTEYN CT
9100 SNTE 92071 1231-H5
FONTICELLO WY
17600 SD 92128 1150-D7
17600 SD 92128 1170-D1
FONTS POINT DR
2800 SDCo 92004 (1099-G4 See Page 1098)
FOOTBRIDGE WY
600 ESCN 92027 1110-D6
FOOTE PATH WY
1200 SDCo 91941 1251-D7
1200 ELCJ 92020 1251-D7
FOOTHILL AV
3900 CRLB 92008 1107-C3
FOOTHILL BLVD
4900 SD 92109 1247-J4
8000 SDCo 92066 1237-C4
FOOTHILL CT
- SDCo 91977 1291-E1
FOOTHILL DR
1100 VSTA 92084 1088-A4
2000 SDCo 92084 1088-C6
2800 SDCo 92084 1108-C1
FOOTHILL RD
200 SD 92173 1350-F3
FOOTHILL ST
3200 ESCN 92025 1150-C1
FOOTHILL RANCH LN
2200 SDCo 92084 1088-C6
2200 VSTA 92084 1088-C6
FOOTHILLS RIVER LN
9700 SDCo 92040 1231-J4
FOOTHILL TRANS CORR Rt#-241
- SDCo 92672 1023-C2
FOOTHILL VIEW PL
2000 ESCN 92026 1109-C5
2000 SDCo 92069 1109-C5
FOOTMAN CT
12700 PWY 92064 1170-C5
FOOTMAN LN
12600 PWY 92064 1170-C5
FORBELL PL
3800 SDCo 92028 1047-J4
FORBES AV
5400 SD 92120 1250-B5
FORD AV
500 SOLB 92075 1167-F6
FORD DR
- ELCN 92243 6499-F3
- ImCo 92243 6499-F3
FORD BOWL DR
- SD 92101 1289-B1
FORDHAM AV
800 CHV 91913 1311-C5
FORDHAM CT
3600 OCN 92056 1087-B7
FORDHAM ST
3200 SD 92110 1268-D5
FORDYCE ST
300 ELCJ 92019 1251-H6
FORECASTLE CT
5300 CRLB 92008 1107-C7
FOREST AV
1200 CRLB 92008 1106-F3
FOREST DR
11400 SDCo 92026 1109-J1
FOREST GN
1500 ESCN 92026 1109-G6
FOREST PL
300 VSTA 92083 1087-D7
FOREST RD
3600 OCN 92054 1086-F2
FOREST WY
500 DLMR 92014 1187-G4
FORESTDALE DR
1600 ENCT 92024 1147-H7
FORESTER LN
600 CHV 91902 1311-C4
FORESTER CREEK RD
1900 SDCo 92021 1252-D3
FOREST GLEN RD
3600 SD 92154 1350-E1
FOREST HILL DR
- SDCo 92065 1173-D2
FOREST HILL PL
1000 CHV 91913 1311-F5
FOREST LAKE DR
1000 CHV 91915 1311-G5
FOREST MEADOW CT
2300 CHV 91915 1311-H7
FOREST MEADOW RD
- SDCo 92036 1175-J2
FOREST OAKS DR
2300 CHV 91915 1311-G5
FOREST PARK LN
2000 CRLB 92008 1106-F3
FOREST PARK RD
2500 SDCo 91935 1274-F4
FORESTVIEW LN
11000 SD 92131 1209-H4
FOREST VIEW WY
2700 CRLB 92008 1106-G3
FORGE LN
1100 SDCo 92028 1027-G4
FORMAL CT
7300 SD 92120 1250-C5
FORMULA PL
7600 SD 92121 1209-A7
FORNEY AV
3900 SD 92117 1248-E3
FORRESTAL CT
6900 SD 92120 1250-E4
FORRESTAL RD
7600 SD 92120 1250-E4
FORREST BLUFF
500 ENCT 92024 1147-E6
FORRESTER CT
3000 SD 92123 1249-E5
FORRESTER RD
1100 ImCo 92243 6559-A6
FORRESTER RD Rt#-S30
- ImCo 92227 411-A11
- WEST 92281 411-A11
1100 ImCo 92243 6559-A3
1800 ImCo 92243 431-A4
2200 ImCo 92251 431-A4
3900 ImCo 92227 431-A4
3900 ImCo 92259 431-A4
5000 ImCo 92281 431-A4
5200 WEST 92281 431-A4
5300 ImCo 92281 411-A11
FORREST GATE RD
400 SDCo 91906 430-B10
FORSBERG CT
1600 SD 92114 1290-D6
FORSTER ST
100 OCN 92054 1106-A2
FORTON WY
7400 SD 92111 1249-A7
FORT STOCKTON DR
400 SD 92103 1268-G5
FORTUNA AV
1400 SD 92109 1248-A6
FORTUNA ST
- CHV 91911 1330-E1
FORTUNADA ST
200 OCN 92057 1066-J7
FORTUNA DEL ESTE
19400 SDCo 92029 1148-F3
FORTUNA DEL NORTE
20700 SDCo 92029 1148-F1
20700 SDCo 92029 1128-F7
FORTUNA DEL SUR
20300 SDCo 92029 1148-F1
20300 SDCo 92024 1148-F1
FORTUNA RANCH RD
3200 ENCT 92024 1148-C4
3500 SDCo 92024 1148-D4
FORTUNA VISTA CT
7400 SNTE 92071 1230-F7
FORTUNE LN
9300 LMSA 91941 1271-B2
FORTUNE WY
2400 VSTA 92083 1108-A6
FORTY ROD TR
7400 SDCo 92036 1138-C7
FORUM ST
6500 SD 92111 1248-J3
FORWARD ST
300 SD 92037 1247-F4
FOSCA ST
3200 CRLB 92009 1127-J7
3300 CRLB 92009 1147-J1
3300 CRLB 92009 1148-A1
FOSS LN
1300 SDCo 91901 1233-H7
FOSS RD
1300 SDCo 91901 1233-H7
FOSS ST
3400 SD 92154 1330-E6
FOSTER LN
9000 SD 92126 1209-D7
FOSTER ST
2100 OCN 92054 1086-C7
7000 SD 92114 1290-F3
FOSTER TKTR
12900 SDCo 92040 1191-G3
12900 SDCo 92065 1191-H5
13800 SDCo 92065 1192-A1
FOSTORIA CT
9200 SDCo 92127 1169-D2
FOUCAUD WY
8500 SD 92129 1189-C7
FOULDS RD
- ImCo 92227 411-A10
FOUNTAIN PL
1000 ESCN 92026 1109-F5
FOUNTAIN ST
4200 SD 92109 1248-B5
FOUNTAIN GROVE PL
1400 CHV 91915 1311-H7
FOUR CORNERS RD
24900 SDCo 92065 1173-G7
24900 SDCo 92065 (1193-F1 See Page 1192)
FOUR CORNERS TR
- SDCo 92065 1173-H7
- SDCo 92065 (1193-H1 See Page 1192)
FOUR CS RANCH RD
39800 SDCo 91905 1300-D4
FOUR GEE RD
- SD 92127 1169-E2
9800 SDCo 92127 1169-E2
FOUR HUNDRED RD
- SDCo 92059 409-E5
FOUR SEASONS PT
7100 CRLB 92009 1127-C6
FOURSOME DR
3500 SDCo 91941 1270-J5
3500 SDCo 91977 1270-J5
3500 SDCo 91977 1271-A5
FOURSOME DR E
2700 SDCo 92004 (1079-C3 See Page 1058)
FOURSOME DR W
- SDCo 92004 (1079-B4 See Page 1058)
FOUSSAT RD
100 OCN 92054 1086-E4
N FOUSSAT RD
100 OCN 92054 1086-E4
FOUTZ AV
2200 SD 92109 1248-B6
FOWLER DR
2100 SD 92139 1290-F7
FOWLER WY
9800 SNTE 92071 1231-B4
FOWLER CANYON RD
3400 SDCo 91935 1272-F6
FOWLES ST
200 OCN 92054 1086-E6
FOX AV
3400 SD 92117 1248-D3
FOX GN
1200 ESCN 92029 1129-F5
FOX LN
10300 SDCo 92026 1089-D6
FOX PL
3300 SD 92117 1248-D3
FOXBORO AV
1100 CHV 91911 1330-H1
FOXBOROUGH CT
8700 SDCo 92040 1232-C6
FOXBOROUGH LN
8800 SDCo 92040 1232-C7
FOX BRIDGE CT
1800 SDCo 92028 1028-G5
FOXCROFT CT
12500 SD 92129 1189-C6
FOXCROFT PL
8500 SD 92129 1189-C5
FOXDALE PL
100 ESCN 92027 1130-C1
FOXFIRE CT
- ESCN 92026 1109-D6
FOXFIRE LN
200 SDCo 92028 1027-F5
FOXFIRE PL
1600 ESCN 92026 1109-D5
FOXFIRE RD
1700 SDCo 92028 1027-F5
FOXGLOVE LN
3800 SDCo 92028 1048-F1
FOXGLOVE ST
700 ENCT 92024 1147-E6
FOXGLOVE VW
1000 CRLB 92009 1127-B6
FOXGROVE PL
3600 SD 92130 1187-J5
3600 SD 92130 1188-A5
FOXHALL CT
- SMCS 92078 1128-G2
FOXHALL DR
700 SMCS 92078 1128-G2
FOXHALL GN
3000 ESCN 92029 1150-A2
FOXHILLS TER
1800 VSTA 92083 1108-E2
FOXHOLLOW CT
4400 SD 92130 1188-B6
FOXHOUND WY
- SD 92130 1208-D2
FOX HUNT LN
14800 SD 92128 1170-B7
FOXLEY DR
3600 ESCN 92027 1110-F4
FOX MEADOW RD
- SDCo 92127 1169-E4
FOX RUN LN
29100 SDCo 92082 1070-J7
FOX RUN RW
14200 SD 92130 1188-D2
E FOX RUN WY
3000 SD 92111 1248-H5
W FOX RUN WY
3000 SD 92111 1248-H5
FOXTAIL CT
4500 OCN 92056 1087-D4
FOXTAIL LP
- CRLB 92008 1107-D7
FOXTAIL ST
1900 VSTA 92083 1107-J4
FOX VALLEY CT
- SDCo 92127 1169-E4
FOX VALLEY DR
- SDCo 92127 1169-E4
FOX VALLEY LN
- SDCo 92127 1169-E4
FOX VALLEY WY
- SDCo 92127 1169-E4
FOXWOOD DR
600 OCN 92057 1066-H7
FOXWOOD RD
10700 SD 92126 1209-B4
FOY LN
600 ESCN 92025 1129-J6
600 ESCN 92025 1130-A6
FOYLE WY
6500 SD 92117 1248-J2
FOYT CT
1900 SDCo 92019 1272-C3
FRACE LN
27500 SDCo 92082 1090-B3
FRAKES ST
7100 SD 92111 1248-J4
FRAME CT
13200 PWY 92064 1190-C4
FRAME RD
13300 PWY 92064 1190-C4
FRAMES PORT PL
11600 SD 92126 1208-J1
FRANCES DR
100 SDCo 92019 1253-C1
800 VSTA 92084 1087-J5
FRANCESCA DR
100 OCN 92057 1087-A2
FRANCINE CT
12800 PWY 92064 1190-A5
FRANCINE PL
12800 PWY 92064 1190-B5
FRANCINE TER
12800 PWY 92064 1190-A5
FRANCIS DR
8700 SNTE 92071 1231-E7
9400 SDCo 91977 1271-B6
FRANCIS ST
200 SD 92102 1289-F4
5100 OCN 92057 1067-B5
S FRANCIS ST
- SD 92113 1289-F4
FRANCIS WY
4200 LMSA 91941 1270-F4
FRANCISCAN RD
- CRLB 92009 1126-H5
FRANCISCAN WY
1100 SD 92116 1269-B3
FRANCISCO DR
17300 SD 92128 1170-B1
FRANK LN
10300 SNTE 92071 1231-B1
FRANK WY
9500 SNTE 92071 1231-E5
FRANK DANIELS WY
10600 SD 92131 1210-A2
FRANKEL WY
2900 SD 92111 1248-H6
FRANKFORT ST
1300 SD 92110 1268-E1
2200 SD 92110 1248-E7
2700 SD 92117 1248-E6
FRANKIE CT
9000 SDCo 92040 1231-J6
9000 SDCo 92040 1232-A6
FRANKLIN
14100 SDCo 92040 1232-H5
FRANKLIN AV
800 ELCJ 92020 1251-E6
2000 SD 92113 1289-D4
4800 SD 92113 1290-A4
FRANKLIN LN
500 VSTA 92084 1087-H5
1300 SDCo 92065 1172-G2
FRASCATI WY
9500 SNTE 92071 1231-B4
FRAULINE DR
1300 SD 92154 1350-A2
FRAXINELLA ST
200 ENCT 92024 1147-E6
FRAZEE RD
1300 SD 92108 1269-A2
5000 OCN 92057 1086-J2
5000 OCN 92057 1087-A1
FRAZIER DR
8600 SD 92119 1250-J3
FRED DR
13200 PWY 92064 1190-C4
FREDA LN
1600 ENCT 92007 1167-F2
FREDAS HILL RD
3300 SDCo 92084 1108-E1
FRED CANYON RD
- SDCo 92066 430-B6
FREDCURT LN
11300 SDCo 92040 1231-G1
FREDERICK ST
8900 SDCo 91977 1291-A3
FREDERICKA PKWY
200 CHV 91910 1310-B5
FREDONIA ST
5500 SD 92105 1290-B1
FREDRICKS AV
200 OCN 92054 1086-F3
FREDRICKS RD
500 ImCo 92227 431-B1
FREEBORN WY
2800 ELCJ 92020 1251-A5
FREED MANOR LN
6800 SD 92114 1290-E6
FREEDOM CT
1000 SOLB 92014 1187-H1
FREEDOM WY
- VSTA 92083 1107-G5
FREEDOM HILL
- SDCo 92040 1232-F4
FREEMAN ST
100 OCN 92054 1086-A7
100 OCN 92054 1106-A1
3000 SD 92106 1268-C6
N FREEMAN ST
100 OCN 92054 1086-A7
FREEPORT CT
10100 SD 92129 1189-F4
FREEPORT RD
13500 SD 92129 1189-F3
FRWY I-8
- ELCJ - 1251-J4
- ELCJ - 1252-B3
- ELCJ - 1271-C1
- ELCN - 6559-J2
- ELCN - 6560-C1
- ImCo - 430-K6
- ImCo - 431-D6
- ImCo - 432-A5
- ImCo - 6559-F2
- ImCo - 6560-J1
- LMSA - 1251-B7
- LMSA - 1270-E1
- LMSA - 1271-C1
- SD - 1269-H1
- SD - 1270-B1
- SDCo - 430-B7
- SDCo - 1232-J4
- SDCo - 1233-E3
- SDCo - 1234-A5
- SDCo - 1235-F5
- SDCo - 1236-D7
- SDCo - 1237-A7
- SDCo - 1252-B3
- SDCo - (1299-F1 See Page 1298)
- SDCo - 1300-H6
- SDCo - (1301-A6 See Page 1300)
- SDCo - (1321-F1 See Page 1300)
FRWY Rt#-52
- SD - 1228-H6
- SD - 1229-C7
- SD - 1230-G6
- SD - 1231-A7
- SNTE - 1230-H6
- SNTE - 1231-A7
FRWY Rt#-54
- CHV - 1309-J4
- CHV - 1310-A3
- NATC - 1309-J4
- NATC - 1310-B4
- SDCo - 1290-H7
- SDCo - 1291-A4
- SDCo - 1310-C3
- NATC - 1310-E3
FRWY Rt#-78
- ESCN - 1129-E2
- OCN - 1106-H2
- OCN - 1107-A2
- SDCo - 1108-C5
- SDCo - 1129-F2
- SMCS - 1108-C5
- SMCS - 1109-A7
- SMCS - 1128-H1
- SMCS - 1129-D1
- VSTA - 1087-G7
- VSTA - 1107-E1
- VSTA - 1108-A2
FRWY Rt#-94
- LMGR - 1270-J5
- LMSA - 1271-A4
- SDCo - 1270-J4
- SDCo - 1271-C5
FRWY Rt#-111
- ImCo - 6500-E1
FRWY Rt#-125
- CHV - 1311-F5
- CHV - 1331-F1
- ELCJ - 1251-A2
- LMGR - 1270-J6
- LMGR - 1290-J1
- LMSA - 1251-A5
- LMSA - 1270-J5
- LMSA - 1271-A1
- SD - 1251-A6
- SD - 1331-G6
- SD - 1351-H1
- SDCo - 1270-J4
- SDCo - 1271-A4
- SDCo - 1290-J1
- SDCo - 1291-A3
- SDCo - 1311-D1
- SDCo - 1331-G6
- SDCo - 1351-H1
- SNTE - 1231-A7
- SNTE - 1251-A1
FRWY Rt#-163
- SD - 1249-A6
FRWY Rt#-905
- SD - 1350-H2
- SD - 1351-A2
FREEWAY LN
- OCN 92054 1106-C1
FREEZER RD
- SDCo 91917 (1314-C6 See Page 1294)
FREMONT PL
19200 SDCo 92029 1149-E4
FREMONT ST
1400 VSTA 92084 1087-J4
3500 SD 92103 1268-H6
FREMONTIA LN
5400 SD 92115 1269-J1
FRENCH CT
1400 OCN 92054 1106-E1
FRENZEL CIR
3600 OCN 92056 1106-J1
3600 OCN 92056 1107-A1
FRESCA CT
700 SOLB 92075 1187-F1
FRESCA ST
600 SOLB 92075 1187-F1
FRESH WATERS CT
- SDCo 91977 1291-E2
FRESHWIND CT
11500 SD 92127 1169-J5
FRESNILLO CT
100 SOLB 92075 1167-D7
FRESNILLO WY
100 SOLB 92075 1167-D7
FRESNO AV
1600 CHV 91911 1330-D5
8300 LMSA 91941 1270-J3
FRESNO ST
- SD 92110 1268-G3
FREY CT
13400 PWY 92064 1190-J4
FRIANT ST
8600 SD 92126 1209-C4
FRIAR PL
1400 CHV 91911 1330-E4
FRIARS RD
4500 SD 92109 1268-E3
4700 SD 92110 1268-F3
5500 SD 92108 1269-D1
5900 SD 92111 1268-F3
5900 SD 92108 1268-F3
7100 SD 92111 1269-B2
9200 SD 92108 1249-E7
9900 SD 92124 1249-G7
10100 SD 92120 1249-G7
FRIED AV
2900 SD 92122 1228-C6
FRIEDELL DR
2600 SD 92110 1268-E6
FRIEDRICK DR
1700 SD 92104 1289-F2
FRIENDLY CIR
800 ELCJ 92021 1251-G4
FRIENDLY CT
500 ELCJ 92021 1251-G4
FRIENDLY DR
1900 SDCo 92084 1088-C4
1900 VSTA 92084 1088-C4
FRIENDLY PL
6500 CRLB 92009 1126-H4
FRIENDS WY
1300 SDCo 92028 1027-J5
FRIENDSHIP DR
1900 ELCJ 92020 1251-D1
FRIENDSHIP LN
1600 SDCo 92026 1109-E6
FRINK AV
4800 SD 92117 1248-F1
4900 SD 92117 1228-F7
FRINK RD
- ImCo 92257 411-A5
FRISBIE ST
3500 SDCo 91902 1310-J1
FRISIUS DR
1600 SDCo 92036 1156-A5
2300 SDCo 92036 1155-J4
FROBISHER CIR
10500 SD 92126 1209-C4
FROBISHER ST
8600 SD 92126 1209-C4
FROEBEL DR
200 ESCN 92025 1130-A6
FROG HOLLOW
11500 SDCo 92082 1069-H2
FROLIC WY
1800 SDCo 92028 1028-A2
N FROLIC WY
100 SDCo 92028 1028-A2
FROME
9300 SDCo 92040 1232-H5
FRONDOSO DR
17300 SD 92128 1170-C1
17600 SD 92128 1150-C7
FRONSAC ST
12300 SD 92131 1210-B2
FRONT ST
- SD 92106 1288-A5
100 ELCJ 92020 1251-D6
200 SD 92101 1289-A1
500 SD 92173 1350-G5
FRONTAGE RD
1200 ELCN 92243 6499-F4
1200 SD 92154 1350-C1
1200 CHV 91911 1330-A4
1600 SD 91911 1330-A5
8100 SD 92123 1249-B4
8100 SD 92037 1228-A6
47000 RivC 92592 999-A1
FRONTERA RD
12200 SD 92128 1170-B2
FRONTIER DR
100 OCN 92054 1086-F4
FROST AV
- CRLB 92008 1107-A7
FROST ST
5000 OCN 92057 1067-A4
7900 SD 92123 1249-B5
FROSTMAR PL
8300 SD 92121 1228-H2
FROUDE ST
1000 SD 92107 1287-H1
1400 SD 92107 1267-J7
1800 SD 92107 1268-A6
FRUCHT ST
2200 SD 92136 1289-G7
FRUITLAND DR
2900 SDCo 92084 1068-A7
2900 SDCo 92084 1067-J6
FRUIT TREE WY
500 OCN 92054 1086-F2
FRUITVALE HTS
29100 SDCo 92082 1071-A7
FRUITVALE LN
29000 SDCo 92082 1070-H7
FRUITVALE RD
14200 SDCo 92082 1070-H7
15600 SDCo 92082 1071-A7
FRY LN
12100 SDCo 92082 1070-A5
FRYDEN CT
3100 SD 92117 1248-D3
FRYING PAN RD
2600 SDCo 92004 (1078-J3 See Page 1058)
FRYING PAN RD
2900 SDCo 92004 (1079-A4 See Page 1058)
FUCHSIA CT
1800 OCN 92054 1106-E2
FUCHSIA DR
- SD 92109 1248-C6
FUCHSIA LN
800 SD 92154 1330-G7
900 CRLB 92009 1126-J5
900 CRLB 92009 1127-A5
1000 SD 92154 1350-G1
FUERTE DR
1800 SDCo 92020 1272-A2
3400 SDCo 92020 1271-J2
9100 LMSA 91941 1271-B1
9300 SDCo 91941 1271-B1
FUERTE LN
2000 ESCN 92026 1109-D4
FUERTE ST
1700 SDCo 92028 1028-A5
2200 OCN 92054 1106-E1
FUERTE BLUFF DR
1600 SDCo 92019 1272-A2
FUERTE ESTATES DR
1700 SDCo 92019 1271-J3
FUERTE FARMS RD
11300 SDCo 92020 1271-H3
FUERTE HEIGHTS LN
1400 SDCo 92019 1272-A3
FUERTE HILLS DR
1600 SDCo 92020 1271-J2
FUERTE KNOLLS LN
1600 SDCo 92020 1271-J2
FUERTE RANCH RD
1600 SDCo 92019 1272-A2
FUERTE VALLEY DR
1700 SDCo 92019 1271-J3
1700 SDCo 92019 1272-A3
FUERTE VISTA LN
1700 SDCo 92020 1271-J3
FUJI ST
6800 SD 92139 1290-F7
FULHAM WY
2300 SD 92139 1290-G7
FULLER ST
- SDCo 92055 1067-A2
FULLERTON AV
9200 SD 92123 1249-E6
FULMAR ST
6000 SD 92114 1290-C1
FULTON RD
800 SMCS 92069 1109-A6
1400 ESCN 92026 1109-B6
FULTON ST
6700 SD 92111 1248-J7
7200 SD 92111 1249-A7
FULVIA ST
300 ENCT 92024 1147-B4
FULWOOD LN
7300 SD 92111 1249-A7
FUN LN
1600 ESCN 92029 1129-F5
FUNQUEST DR
900 SDCo 92028 1027-G3
FURLONG PL
- SD 92130 1208-D2
FURNACE CREEK RD
15200 SDCo 92021 1232-J1
FURNER ST
2100 ELCJ 92020 1251-B1
FURY LN
10800 SDCo 91941 1271-G4
11300 SDCo 92019 1271-G4
11900 SDCo 92019 1272-A5
FUSCO LN
22100 SDCo 91901 1275-C1
FUTURA ST
12600 SD 92130 1188-B6
FUTURITY LN
200 SDCo 92028 1047-G3

G

G AV
100 CORD 92118 1288-H6
200 NATC 91950 1289-H7
400 NATC 91950 1309-J1
G CT
- SD 92126 1209-E7
800 CHV 91910 1310-F7
G RD E
- CORD 92135 1288-F6
G ST
- NATC 91950 1310-C3
- CHV 91910 1310-C6
300 SDCo 92065 1152-H6
600 SD 92101 1288-J3
700 CHV 91910 1309-H7
900 CHV 91910 1329-H1
1000 SD 92101 1289-A3
1500 SDCo 92055 1047-A5
1900 SD 92102 1289-C3
E G ST
- ENCT 92024 1147-C7
W G ST
100 ENCT 92024 1147-B7
200 SD 92101 1289-A3
500 SD 92101 1288-J3
GABACHO DR
10600 SD 92124 1249-H1
GABACHO ST
7800 CRLB 92009 1147-H2
GABARDA RD
16200 SD 92128 1170-C3
GABBIANO LN
1600 CRLB 92009 1127-A7
GABELWOOD WY
- SD 92130 1208-F2
GABILAN RD
13200 SD 92128 1189-J4
GABLE WY
700 ELCJ 92020 1251-E3
GABLER DR
29900 SDCo 92082 1069-H6
GABLE RIDGE RD
14800 SD 92128 1170-B7
14800 SD 92128 1190-B4
GABLES ST
5500 SD 92139 1310-C1
GABRIEL WY
4700 SDCo 91941 1271-D3
GABRIELIENO AV
4900 OCN 92057 1067-B7
GABRIELLE GN
2000 ESCN 92029 1129-F5
GABRIELSON AV
2800 SD 92111 1249-A6
GADWALL CT
- CRLB 92009 1127-D4
GAELYN CT
14200 PWY 92064 1190-E2
GAETANO ALTIERI DR
30600 SDCo 92082 1070-J3
GAFFNEY CT
3900 SD 92130 1188-A4
GAGE DR
- SDCo 92055 1086-A2
500 SD 92106 1288-A3
GAGE LN
3400 SD 92106 1288-A3
GAGE PL
3400 SD 92106 1288-A3
GAI CT
900 SD 92154 1330-G7
GAI DR
1000 SD 92154 1330-G7
1000 SD 92154 1350-G1
GAIL DR
200 VSTA 92084 1087-H3
3700 OCN 92056 1107-A2
GAIL PL
13200 SDCo 92040 1232-C5
GAILES BLVD
1600 SD 92154 1351-F2
GAIL PARK LN
14700 PWY 92064 1190-F1
GAIN DR
7000 SD 92119 1250-J3
GAINARD WY
4500 SD 92124 1249-F2
GAINES ST
3200 SD 92110 1268-F3
5400 SD 92110 1268-F3
GAINSBOROUGH AV
8800 SD 92129 1189-C2
GALA AV
5400 SD 92120 1250-B5
GALAHAD RD
2200 SD 92123 1249-C7
GALATEA LN
9600 SDCo 92026 1089-D4
GALAXY CT
7500 SD 92120 1250-C4
GALAXY DR
500 VSTA 92083 1087-D6
800 SDCo 92083 1087-D6
GALBAR PL
4100 OCN 92056 1087-C7
GALBAR ST
4000 OCN 92056 1087-C7
GALDAR PL
1000 CHV 91910 1310-J5
GALE ST
1000 ESCN 92027 1110-B6
GALENA AV
4900 SD 92110 1268-F1
GALENA ST
500 ELCJ 92019 1252-B4
GALEON CT
500 SDCo 91977 1291-C3
GALERIA CIR
- SDCo 92065 1173-D2
GALEWOOD ST
6900 SD 92120 1250-C6
GALICIA WY
2600 CRLB 92009 1147-G1
4700 OCN 92056 1107-E5
GALLATIN WY
4700 SD 92117 1248-C1
4800 SD 92117 1228-C7
GALLEGOS TER
6300 SD 92114 1290-D6
GALLEON WY
7600 CRLB 92009 1147-H1
GALLERY CT
900 SD 92114 1290-C5
GALLERY DR
800 OCN 92057 1087-B2
GALLINETA WY
24700 SDCo 92065 1173-G2
GALLINULE CT
8800 SD 92129 1189-C6
GALLOP PL
13200 SDCo 92040 1232-C5
GALLOPING WY
5600 SDCo 91902 1311-B2
GALLOWAY DR
3100 SD 92122 1228-C5
GALLOWAY PL
5700 SDCo 92003 1048-B7
GALLOWAY VALLEY CT
300 SDCo 91901 1233-E7
GALLOWAY VALLEY LN
400 SDCo 91901 1233-E7
GALLOWAY VALLEY RD
300 SDCo 91901 1233-E7
GALOPAGO ST
600 SDCo 91977 1291-C3
GALSTON DR
9200 SNTE 92071 1231-A4
GALT DR
800 ELCJ 92019 1252-B6
800 SDCo 92019 1252-B6
GALT ST
200 SD 92117 1228-E7
GALT WY
5100 SD 92117 1228-E7
GALVANI LN
2200 SDCo 92084 1108-D2
GALVESTON ST
1400 SD 92110 1268-E1
2200 SD 92110 1248-E7
GALVESTON WY
500 CHV 91902 1311-C3
GALVEZ CT
1900 SD 92154 1350-D3
GALVIN AV
9300 SD 92126 1209-E2
GALWAY CT
1600 ELCJ 92020 1251-C4
GALWAY PL
1600 ELCJ 92020 1251-C4
GAM LN
1600 SDCo 92065 1152-F7
GAMAN ST
9100 SDCo 92040 1232-D6
GAMAY TER
1800 CHV 91913 1311-D3
GAMBLE LN
- ESCN 92029 1129-F6
900 SDCo 92029 1129-G6
GAMBLE PL
- SDCo 92029 1129-H6
GAMBLE ST
800 ESCN 92025 1129-J1
800 ESCN 92026 1129-J1

SAN DIEGO CO.
INDEX

STREET Block City ZIP Pg-Grid

GAMBLE ST
1000 ESCN 92026 1109-H7
GAMBUSA PL
9100 SD 92129 1189-D5
GAMBUSA WY
12800 SD 92129 1189-D5
GAMMA ST
1700 NATC 91950 1289-J6
1700 NATC 91950 1290-A6
3800 SD 92113 1289-G6
GANDY AV
9800 SNTE 92071 1231-B4
GANESTA RD
11100 SD 92126 1209-C2
GANLEY RD
9000 SNTE 92071 1231-A2
GANNET DR
200 VSTA 92083 1087-G4
GANNON DR
2500 SD 92110 1268-E6
GANNON PL
500 ESCN 92025 1129-H3
GANTHER SQ
9900 SD 92131 1209-H5
GANTRY WY
15900 SDCo 92065 1174-A4
GARBER AV
6400 SD 92139 1310-F2
GARBONI RD
- SDCo 92066 1236-E6
GARBOSO PL
7700 CRLB 92009 1147-J2
GARBOSO ST
3000 CRLB 92009 1147-H2
GARDE CT
8600 SD 92126 1209-C3
GARDE ST
10900 SD 92126 1209-C3
GARDE WY
8600 SD 92126 1209-C3
GARDEN DR
14900 PWY 92064 1190-J4
GARDEN LN
3700 SD 92106 1287-J3
24700 SDCo 91916 1236-A2
GARDEN PL
400 CHV 91911 1330-B1
GARDEN RD
14200 PWY 92064 1190-H4
14900 PWY 92064 1191-A4
GARDEN WY
8200 SNTE 92071 1230-J7
10600 SDCo 91978 1271-F6
GARDENA AV
4500 SD 92110 1268-E1
GARDENA CT
500 ENCT 92024 1147-D7
GARDENA LN
11800 SDCo 92040 1231-J7
GARDENA PL
1800 SD 92110 1268-F2
GARDENA RD
700 ENCT 92024 1147-D7
700 ENCT 92024 1167-D1
8500 SDCo 92040 1231-J6
GARDENA WY
8800 SDCo 92040 1231-J6
GARDENDALE RD
200 ENCT 92024 1147-H5
GARDEN GLEN LN
1000 ELCJ 92019 1252-B7
GARDEN GROVE LN
200 ELCJ 92020 1251-A5
GARDENIA AV
14000 PWY 92064 1190-F3
GARDENIA CT
1000 SMCS 92069 1128-E2
7000 CRLB 92009 1127-A6
GARDENIA DR
- SD 92109 1248-C6
GARDENIA GN
600 ESCN 92025 1150-C3
GARDENIA ST
4700 OCN 92057 1087-A1
4700 OCN 92057 1067-A7
GARDEN KNOLL WY
9400 SDCo 92040 1232-A5
GARDEN PARK CT
1900 SD 92114 1290-F6
GARDEN VIEW CT
700 ENCT 92024 1147-F5
GARDEN VIEW RD
1200 ENCT 92024 1147-E4
GARDINER LN
6100 SDCo 92067 1168-F7
GARDNER DR
32100 RivC 92592 999-F1
GARDNER ST
400 ELCJ 92020 1251-E5
GARDNER WY
500 SMCS 92069 1108-J6
GAREY DR
400 VSTA 92084 1087-H3
GARFIELD AV
800 ELCJ 92020 1251-B4
GARFIELD LN
4700 LMSA 91941 1271-A3
GARFIELD RD
2000 SD 92110 1268-F1
2200 SD 92110 1248-F7
GARFIELD ST
300 OCN 92054 1086-B7
400 OCN 92054 1106-B1
2400 CRLB 92008 1106-D5
4500 LMSA 91941 1271-A2
GARIBALDI PL
3300 CRLB 92008 1106-H4
GARJAN LN
16900 SDCo 92065 1171-H2
GARLAND DR
900 SD 92154 1330-C7
1000 SD 92154 1350-C1
GARNER PL
3600 ENCT 92024 1167-H2
GARNET AV
700 SD 92109 1247-H6
1500 SD 92109 1248-A5
GARNET AV Rt#-274
2800 SD 92109 1248-C5
GARNET CT
8300 LMSA 91941 1270-J4
GARNET LN
4400 OCN 92056 1107-D2
GARNET PL
- CRLB 92009 1127-H5
GARNET MINE TR
24400 SDCo 92065 1173-F7
GARNET PEAK RD
- SDCo 91948 430-B3
- SDCo 91948 1218-A1
2500 CHV 91915 1311-H6
GARRETT AV
100 CHV 91910 1310-B5
600 CHV 91910 1330-B1
1200 CHV 91911 1330-C3
GARRISON PL
1500 SD 92106 1288-A1
GARRISON ST
400 OCN 92054 1086-F6
2900 SD 92106 1288-B1
GARRISON WY
1700 SDCo 92019 1252-B6
GARST RD
7500 ImCo 92233 411-B9
GARSTON ST
2100 SD 92111 1248-J7
2100 SD 92111 1268-J1
2100 SD 92111 1269-A1
GARWOOD CT
8400 SDCo 91977 1290-J2
GARWOOD RD
9500 SDCo 91916 1235-H2
GARY CIR
2400 CRLB 92008 1106-H5
GARY CT
6400 SD 92115 1270-D2
GARY LN
1100 ESCN 92026 1109-E4
GARY ST
4900 SD 92115 1270-D1
GARYWOOD ST
1600 SDCo 92021 1251-G1
GASCONADE AV
5000 SD 92110 1268-F2
GASCONY RD
1500 ENCT 92024 1147-C2
GASKILL PEAK RD
3700 SDCo 91901 1275-A3
GASLIGHT CT
14400 PWY 92064 1190-F2
GASTON DR
7700 SD 92126 1209-A4
GATCHELL RD
- SD 92106 1287-J7
- SD 92106 1308-A2
GATE DR
12900 PWY 92064 1190-F5
GATE RD
- SD 92106 1288-A5
GATEMOORE WY
11100 SD 92131 1209-J2
GATEPOST RD
1800 ENCT 92024 1147-H6
GATESHEAD RD
4700 CRLB 92008 1107-A5
GATESHEAD ST
7400 SD 92111 1249-A7
7500 SD 92111 1269-A1
GATESIDE RD
3800 LMSA 91941 1270-J4
GATESIDE WY
8500 LMSA 91941 1270-J4
8500 SDCo 91941 1270-J4
GATEVIEW DR
- SDCo 92028 1047-H6
GATEWAY DR
1700 SD 92105 1289-G1
1800 VSTA 92083 1107-J4
GATEWAY CENTER AV
3600 SD 92102 1289-G3
GATEWAY CENTER DR
600 SD 92102 1289-G3
GATEWAY CENTER WY
600 SD 92102 1289-G3
GATEWAY PARK DR
6500 SD 92154 1351-C2
GATEWAY PARK RD
12600 PWY 92064 1170-C5
GATEWOOD AV
10100 SDCo 92040 1232-B3
GATEWOOD LN
7200 SD 92114 1290-G6
GATITO CT
11600 SD 92127 1150-A7
GATLIN ST
1100 IMPB 91932 1349-H2
GATLING CT
1200 VSTA 92083 1087-E6
2300 SD 92111 1248-J7
2300 SD 92111 1249-A7
GATTY CT
500 SD 92154 1330-F6
GATTY ST
3600 SD 92154 1330-E6
GATUN ST
2000 DLMR 92014 1187-G4
GAUCHO LN
9000 SDCo 92021 1232-F6
GAUCHO PL
1100 ESCN 92029 1129-F5
GAUL WY
10200 SDCo 91977 1271-E5
GAVAN VISTA RD
14800 PWY 92064 1170-J5
GAVILAN MOUNTAIN RD
40300 SDCo 92028 997-H4
GAVIN ST
300 SD 92102 1289-H4
GAVIOTA CIR
2900 CRLB 92009 1147-H2
GAVIOTA CT
4600 SDCo 91902 1310-G1
GAVIOTA PL
7800 CRLB 92009 1147-H2
GAVIOTO CT
4600 OCN 92057 1066-J7
GAYLA CT
3000 SDCo 91978 1271-F6
GAY LAKE AV
6400 SD 92119 1250-G5
GAYLAND ST
100 ESCN 92027 1130-C1
GAYLE ST
3500 SD 92115 1270-C5
GAYLE WY
2000 CRLB 92008 1106-G4
GAYLEMONT LN
- SD 92130 1208-D2
GAYLEN RD
7900 SD 92126 1209-B3
GAYLORD CT
3500 SD 92117 1228-D7
GAYLORD DR
4900 SD 92117 1248-D1
5000 SD 92117 1228-D7
GAYLORD PL
5200 SD 92117 1228-D7
GAYNESWOOD WY
7400 SD 92139 1290-G6
GAYO CT
1600 SD 92154 1350-B3
GAYOLA LN
10900 SDCo 92040 1231-F3
GAY RIO DR
12000 SDCo 92040 1231-J6
12000 SDCo 92040 1232-A6
12400 SDCo 92021 1232-A6
GAY RIO LN
- SDCo 92040 1232-A6
GAY RIO TER
12100 SDCo 92040 1232-A6
GAY RIO WY
12000 SDCo 92040 1232-A7
GAYUBA LN
10100 SD 92124 1249-G1
GAYWOOD ST
1100 SD 92154 1349-J1
GAZANIA CT
1100 SMCS 92078 1129-B2
GEARALD WY
1000 SDCo 92028 1027-H3
GEARING DR
2600 SD 92110 1268-E6
4700 SD 92133 1288-D1
GEDDES DR
3200 SD 92117 1248-C2
GEHRING CT
11800 SD 92126 1209-A1
GEIGER CT
5900 CRLB 92008 1127-D2
GEISE CT
2800 ESCN 92027 1110-E6
GELBOURNE PL
13300 SD 92130 1188-A4
GEM CT
13300 PWY 92064 1190-H4
GEM LN
500 SDCo 92065 1172-H3
2000 ESCN 92026 1109-E4
GEM HILL LN
11200 SDCo 92040 1211-G6
GEMINI AV
9000 SD 92126 1209-D3
GEM LAKE AV
6400 SD 92119 1250-G5
GEM TREE WY
10000 SNTE 92071 1231-D3
GEM VIEW DR
2300 OCN 92056 1087-C6
GENERAL ATOMICS CT
3300 SD 92121 1207-J7
3300 SD 92121 1208-A7
GENESEE AV
2400 SD 92123 1249-A6
2400 SD 92111 1249-A6
2700 SD 92111 1248-H5
4200 SD 92117 1248-G2
5200 SD 92117 1228-E6
5800 SD 92122 1228-D4
8300 SD 92121 1228-B1
8300 SD 92037 1228-B1
9900 SD 92121 1208-B7
10300 SD 92037 1208-B7
GENESEE AV Rt#-S21
10400 SD 92037 1208-A7
10400 SD 92121 1208-A7
10400 SD 92093 1208-A7
10700 SD 92121 1207-J7
GENESEE CT E
5500 SD 92111 1248-H3
GENESEE CV
5200 SD 92122 1228-E5
GENESIS WY
12900 SDCo 92040 1212-D4
GENESTA ST
1900 SD 92102 1290-A1
GENETIC CENTER DR
10200 SD 92121 1208-G5
GENEVA
9400 SDCo 92040 1232-F4
GENEVA AV
5000 SD 92114 1290-B2
GENEVA CIR
1800 SMCS 92069 1128-B2
GENEVA PL
2100 ESCN 92027 1130-E2
GENEVA ST
2000 OCN 92054 1106-G1
GENEVIEVE AV
800 CHV 91913 1311-E5
GENEVIEVE ST
700 SOLB 92075 1167-G7
900 SOLB 92014 1167-G7
GENIE LN
1000 ENCT 92007 1167-E3
GENINE DR
3900 OCN 92056 1107-B1
GENISTA PL
3600 SDCo 92028 1048-C3
GENOA DR
1400 VSTA 92083 1107-H3
5600 SD 92120 1270-C1
5600 SD 92120 1250-C7
GENOA WY
3300 OCN 92056 1106-J1
GENTER ST
500 SD 92037 1247-E1
900 SD 92037 1227-F7
GENTIAN WY
2000 SDCo 91901 1234-A5
GENTLE BREEZE LN
400 ENCT 92024 1147-G6
GENTLE OAKS TR
- SDCo 92082 1050-A7
- SDCo 92082 1069-J1
- SDCo 92082 1070-A1
GENTRY LN
- CHV 91911 1330-E3
GENTRY RD
6500 ImCo 92233 411-A10
GENTRY RD Rt#-S30
5800 ImCo 92227 411-A11
5800 ImCo 92233 411-A11
GENTRY WY
- CHV 91911 1330-E3
GEORGE
14100 SDCo 92040 1232-H5
GEORGE CT
1100 SD 92154 1350-D1
GEORGE RD
600 ImCo 92231 431-B7
600 ImCo 92243 431-B7
GEORGE WY
1100 ELCJ 92019 1251-J6
GEORGETOWN AV
5000 SD 92110 1268-F2
GEORGETOWN PL
500 CHV 91911 1330-H4
GEORGIA CT
1900 SD 92104 1269-C6
GEORGIA LN
1000 VSTA 92083 1087-G5
GEORGIA ST
700 IMPB 91932 1329-H7
900 IMPB 91932 1349-H1
3500 SD 92104 1269-C5
3500 SD 92103 1269-C5
4300 SD 92116 1269-C5
GEORGINA ST
- CHV 91910 1310-D7
GEORGINE RD
500 SDCo 92028 1047-E5
GEORGIOS WY
16700 SDCo 92065 1173-G2
GERALD CT
2600 SD 92105 1270-A7
GERALDINE AV
8800 SD 92123 1249-C6
GERALDINE PL
9000 SD 92123 1249-D5
GERANA ST
10800 SD 92129 1189-H2
GERANIUM ST
1700 CRLB 92009 1127-E7
2300 SD 92109 1248-B4
GERLAR LN
1400 SDCo 92065 1152-G7
GERMAINE LN
5900 SD 92037 1247-G3
GERONA CT
14200 SD 92129 1189-H2
GERONIMO AV
3100 SD 92117 1248-F6
GERONIMO PL
- VSTA 92084 1087-H4
GERSHWIN ST
- ENCT 92007 1167-D2
GERTRUDE ST
1200 SD 92110 1268-E2
GESNER PL
2600 SD 92110 1248-F7
4600 SD 92117 1248-E6
GESNER ST
4000 SD 92117 1248-E7
4800 SD 92110 1248-F7
GETTY
- CRLB 92008 1127-A3
GEYER LN
2400 SDCo 91901 1253-J2
GIANELLI LN
2600 ESCN 92025 1130-C7
GIBBONS ST
2400 ELCJ 92020 1251-B2
GIBBS DR
8500 SD 92123 1249-C4
GIBBS RD
- ImCo 92227 431-E2
GIBRALTAR CT
17400 SD 92128 1170-C2
GIBRALTAR DR
12600 SD 92128 1170-C2
GIBRALTAR ST
7500 CRLB 92009 1147-H1
GIBRALTER GN
2100 ESCN 92029 1129-D6
GIBSON PT
- SOLB 92075 1167-E6
GIBSON ST
1400 SD 92114 1290-E2
1600 LMGR 91945 1290-E2
GIBSON HIGHLANDS
1300 SDCo 92021 1233-A7
GIDDINGS RANCH RD
1000 SDCo 92084 1088-C7
1000 SDCo 92084 1108-C1
GIDEON CIR N
9100 SDCo 92040 1232-D6
GIDEON CIR S
9100 SDCo 92040 1232-D6
GIDEON CT
13300 SDCo 92040 1232-D6
GIENKE LN
10300 SNTE 92071 1231-E7
GIFFIN WY
10500 SD 92126 1209-A4
GIFFORD WY
6700 SD 92111 1248-H7
6700 SD 92111 1268-H1
GIGANTIC ST
8100 SD 92154 1351-F2
GI GI CT
3300 SDCo 92028 1048-D2
GIL WY
1600 SDCo 92084 1088-B7
GILA AV
4200 SD 92117 1248-E2
GILA CT
3800 SD 92117 1248-E3
GILBERT DR
5400 SD 92115 1270-B3
GILBERT LN
- NATC 91950 1289-J7
GILBERT PL
600 CHV 91910 1310-G6
GILDRED SQ
9200 SD 92037 1228-C2
GILEAD WY
100 SDCo 92028 1027-H2
GILES WY
11700 SD 92126 1209-C1
GILFORD CT
1200 SDCo 91977 1290-J2
GILLESPIE RD
- ImCo 92257 411-B7
GILLESPIE WY
1700 ELCJ 92020 1251-C1
GILLETT RD
200 ImCo 92243 6500-E6
E GILLETT RD
900 ELCN 92243 6500-C6
1200 ImCo 92243 6500-D6
GILLETTE ST
3200 SD 92102 1289-F4
GILLISPIE DR
600 SDCo 91977 1291-A3
GILL VILLAGE WY
2200 SD 92108 1269-C2
GILMAN CT
- SD 92037 1228-A5
GILMAN DR
4200 SD 92093 1228-A2
8100 SD 92037 1228-A4
8100 SD 92122 1228-A4
9400 SD 92161 1228-A2
GILMARTIN DR
1500 SD 92114 1290-E6
GILMORE PL
1300 ESCN 92026 1110-A5
GILMORE ST
3600 SD 92113 1289-G4
GINA AV
100 ELCJ 92019 1252-A5
GINA LN
800 SMCS 92069 1109-B5
GINA WY
200 VSTA 92083 1087-G5
GINGER AV
800 CRLB 92009 1127-A5
GINGER GN
1000 SMCS 92069 1128-E2
GINGER WY
2600 SDCo 92029 1129-D2
3700 OCN 92057 1086-H5
GINGER SNAP CT
12500 SD 92129 1189-C5
GINGER SNAP LN
8700 SD 92129 1189-C6
GINGERTREE LN
- CORD 92118 1329-D1
GINGERWOOD CV
- SD 92130 1208-E2
GINNA PL
800 SD 92114 1290-B5
GINNY LN
2000 ESCN 92025 1130-B5
2000 SDCo 92025 1130-B5
GINSBERG CT
1600 SD 92114 1290-D6
GINSTAR CT
12200 SD 92131 1190-B7
12200 SD 92131 1210-B1
GIRARD AV
7400 SD 92037 1227-F6
GIRARD CT
1200 VSTA 92084 1088-A6
GIRARD WY
300 VSTA 92084 1088-A6
GIRD RD
1700 SDCo 92028 1028-C6
2700 SDCo 92028 1048-D3
GIST RD
2600 SDCo 92069 1088-J4
2900 SDCo 92069 1089-A4
GITANO ST
1600 ENCT 92024 1147-G7
GIVENS ST
800 SD 92154 1330-F7
900 CHV 91911 1330-J2
GLACIER AV
4400 SD 92120 1249-H7
4800 SD 92120 1250-A7
GLACIER RD
1500 OCN 92056 1087-E1
GLADE PL
1600 ESCN 92029 1129-G7
GLADE ST
3300 SD 92115 1270-D5
GLADEHOLLOW CT
12200 SD 92128 1190-B7
GLADING DR
4000 SD 92154 1330-F7
GLADIOLA DR
- NATC 91950 1289-H7
2400 SDCo 91906 (1297-E5
See Page 1296)
GLADIOLA LN
100 SDCo 92019 1253-C1
GLADSTONE CT
4400 CRLB 92008 1106-J5
28500 SDCo 92026 1089-D3
GLADYS ST
900 ELCJ 92021 1251-H2
GLANCY DR
3100 SD 92173 1350-E5
GLASER DR
3400 OCN 92056 1106-J1
3400 OCN 92056 1107-A1
GLASGOW AV
1700 ENCT 92007 1167-D2
GLASGOW DR
2600 CRLB 92008 1107-A5
4800 SD 92117 1248-D1
4900 SD 92117 1228-D7
GLASGOW LN
1500 ESCN 92027 1110-C5
GLASOE LN
4800 SD 92108 1269-B3
4800 SD 92116 1269-B3
GLASS CT
1900 SD 92154 1350-A1
E GLAUCUS ST
100 ENCT 92024 1147-B3
W GLAUCUS ST
100 ENCT 92024 1147-A4
GLEASON RD
900 SD 92109 1267-J2
GLEBE RD
2400 LMGR 91945 1270-F7
GLEE LN
1600 ESCN 92029 1129-F5
GLEN DR
3400 SDCo 91977 1271-D5
GLEN LN
13500 SDCo 92082 1050-D7
GLEN RD
900 SD 92114 1290-B3
GLEN ST
4400 LMSA 91941 1271-A2
GLEN ABBEY BLVD
3100 SDCo 91910 1310-E5
GLEN ABBEY DR
3600 SDCo 91902 1310-F4
GLENAIR WY
15800 SDCo 92082 1071-C1
GLEN ARBOR DR
100 ENCT 92024 1147-G5
GLEN ARVEN LN
17000 PWY 92064 1170-F1
GLEN AVON DR
1400 SMCS 92069 1109-C7
GLENBROOK ST
2900 CRLB 92008 1107-A3
GLENBROOK WY
2800 SD 92037 1227-J3
GLEN CANYON CIR
2800 SDCo 91977 1271-D7
GLEN CIRCLE RD
12800 PWY 92064 1170-D5
GLENCLIFF WY
13200 SD 92130 1188-C4
GLENCO LN
- SDCo 92036 1156-C5
GLENCOE DR
800 SD 92114 1290-H3
900 LMGR 91945 1290-G1
GLENCOLUM DR
3300 SD 92123 1249-D5
GLENCREEK CIR
10900 SD 92131 1210-A3
GLEN CREEK DR
300 CHV 91902 1311-B3
GLENCREST DR
- SMCS 92078 1128-D5
300 SOLB 92075 1167-F6
500 SD 92139 1290-G6
GLENCREST PL
600 SOLB 92075 1167-F6
GLENDA CT
10900 SD 92126 1209-B3
GLENDA WY
7900 SD 92126 1209-B3
GLENDALE AV
200 SMCS 92069 1108-G6
800 SD 92102 1289-D3
GLENDALE WY
- SMCS 92069 1108-G6
E GLENDON CIR
10000 SNTE 92071 1231-E3
W GLENDON CIR
10000 SNTE 92071 1231-E3
GLENDORA ST
2900 SD 92109 1248-C5
GLENDOVER LN
10600 SD 92126 1208-H4
GLEN DREW RD
1900 ESCN 92027 1110-B5
GLENEAGLES PL
1000 VSTA 92083 1108-E2
GLENELLEN AV
10400 SD 92126 1209-D4
GLENELLEN LN
10300 SD 92126 1209-D5
GLEN ELLEN ST
- CHV 91913 1311-B7
- CHV 91913 1331-B1
GLENFIELD ST
3100 SD 92105 1269-H6
GLENFLORA AV
6900 SD 92119 1250-F5
GLENGARRY LN
28100 SDCo 92026 1089-D4
GLENGATE PL
13600 PWY 92064 1190-F5
GLENHART PL
- SDCo 92028 1027-G6
GLENHAVEN DR
4800 OCN 92056 1087-E4
GLENHAVEN ST
8600 SD 92123 1249-C4
GLENHAVEN WY
100 CHV 91911 1330-D3
GLEN H CURTISS RD
3600 SD 92123 1249-C4
GLENHEATHER DR
500 SMCS 92069 1109-B6
GLENHILL RD
1000 ELCJ 92020 1251-H7
GLENHOLLOW CIR
4800 OCN 92057 1087-B3
GLEN HOLLOW CT
1600 ENCT 92024 1147-H5
GLENHOPE RD
11800 SD 92128 1190-A6
GLENHURST WY
11300 SD 92128 1189-J2
GLENIRA AV
8700 LMSA 91941 1271-A2
GLENIRA WY
4300 LMSA 91941 1271-A3
GLENLEA LN
5900 SD 92120 1250-E7
GLENMEADE WY
9800 SDCo 92026 1089-D3
GLEN MEADOW LN
2300 ESCN 92027 1110-D6
GLENMERE RD
1000 VSTA 92084 1088-A5
1000 VSTA 92084 1087-J5
GLENMONT DR
300 SOLB 92075 1167-F6
GLENMONT ST
6300 SD 92120 1270-D1
GLENN RD
3100 OCN 92056 1107-B1
GLENNA DR
1500 SDCo 92025 1130-B4
GLENNAIRE DR
1900 ESCN 92025 1130-B5
1900 SDCo 92025 1130-B5
GLENNCHESTER RW
6100 SD 92037 1247-J1
GLENN ELLEN CT
23800 SDCo 92065 1173-D2
GLENN ELLEN WY
23300 SDCo 92065 1173-C4
GLENNON ST
10000 SD 92124 1249-G2
GLENOAK RD
12300 PWY 92064 1190-C2
GLEN OAKS DR N
500 SDCo 91901 1233-G5
GLEN OAKS DR S
500 SDCo 91901 1233-G6
GLEN OAKS PL
600 SDCo 91901 1233-G6
GLENRIDGE RD
1800 ESCN 92027 1130-E1
GLENROY ST
6400 SD 92120 1250-B5
GLENSIDE PL
10000 SDCo 91977 1271-D7
GLENSIDE RD
4800 SDCo 92070 1135-D5
GLENSIDE ST
300 SDCo 91977 1271-D7
GLENSTONE WY
5600 SD 92121 1208-E4
GLEN TREE RD
15400 SDCo 92082 1090-J2
GLEN VERDE CT
3700 SDCo 91902 1310-J2
GLEN VERDE DR
5000 SDCo 91902 1310-J2
GLENVIEW DR
4500 OCN 92057 1066-H7
GLENVIEW LN
500 SD 92037 1247-E1
2200 SDCo 92084 1087-F1
GLEN VIEW PL
5100 SDCo 91902 1310-J2
GLENVIEW WY
- SDCo 92025 1130-D7
GLENVILLE ST
14500 PWY 92064 1190-H5
GLEN VISTA CT
8300 SD 92114 1290-H5
GLEN VISTA ST
200 SD 92114 1290-H5
300 SDCo 91977 1290-H5
GLENWAY DR
1000 ELCJ 92020 1251-H7
GLENWICK LN
8600 SD 92037 1227-J4
GLENWICK PL
2700 SD 92037 1227-J4
GLENWOOD DR
800 OCN 92057 1087-C1
1400 SD 92103 1268-H6
GLENWOOD RD
1800 ImCo 92243 6499-D6
GLENWOOD WY
800 ESCN 92026 1109-H3
GLIDDEN CT
1700 SD 92111 1268-H1
GLIDDEN LN
6500 SD 92111 1268-H1
GLIDDEN ST
6300 SD 92111 1268-H2
GLOAMING AV
7400 SD 92114 1290-G3
GLORIA LN
3900 CRLB 92008 1106-G6
GLORIA ST
300 SD 92113 1290-A5
GLORIA LAKE AV
7700 SD 92119 1250-G6
GLORIETTA BLVD
200 CORD 92118 1289-A6
400 CORD 92118 1288-J7
900 CORD 92118 1308-J1
900 CORD 92118 1309-A1
GLORIETTA PL
300 CORD 92118 1288-J5
300 CORD 92118 1289-A6
GLOVER AV
100 CHV 91910 1310-B5
700 CHV 91910 1330-B1
N GLOVER AV
- CHV 91910 1310-A4
GLOVER CT
- CHV 91910 1310-A5
GLOVER PL
600 CHV 91910 1330-B1
GLOXINA ST
200 ENCT 92024 1147-E6
GOBAT AV
2600 SD 92122 1228-B6
GODDARD WY
2400 SD 92101 1288-G1
GODFREY ST
100 OCN 92054 1106-B2
GODS WY
- SDCo 91935 1294-F7
GODSAL LN
300 SD 92103 1268-J6
GODWIT DR
4400 OCN 92057 1087-A3
GOEN PL
- SD 92120 1250-A4
GOESNO PL
3200 NATC 91950 1309-G5
GOETSCHL ST
600 SD 92114 1290-D5
GOETTING WY
200 VSTA 92083 1087-G6
GOETZE ST
2500 SD 92139 1310-E1
GOFF CT
1400 SD 92114 1290-F5
GOING MY WY
- SDCo 92127 1169-A2
GOLD DR
500 OCN 92057 1067-A6
GOLD ST
11100 SNTE 92071 1231-G6
GOLDA ODESSA LN
15200 SDCo 92040 1212-H6
GOLD BAR LN
- SDCo 92040 1212-A7
GOLD BAR WY
- SDCo 92040 1212-A7
- SDCo 92040 1232-A1
GOLDBORO ST
1800 SD 92110 1268-F2
GOLD CANYON LN
- SDCo 92020 1271-J2
GOLD COAST CT
10300 SD 92126 1209-D5
GOLD COAST DR
7900 SD 92126 1209-A5
GOLD COAST PL
10300 SD 92126 1209-D5
GOLD COAST WY
10300 SD 92126 1209-D5
GOLD CREST LN
7600 SD 92114 1290-G5
GOLD DUST LN
- SDCo 92036 1136-D7
- SDCo 92036 1175-J3
GOLDEN AV
2200 LMGR 91945 1270-H6
GOLDEN CIR
11700 SDCo 92040 1231-J7
GOLDEN LN
- SDCo 92036 1136-A7
- SDCo 92066 1135-J7
700 SDCo 92028 1027-G3
3200 LMGR 91945 1270-J6
GOLDEN RD
400 SDCo 92028 1027-G3
1000 ENCT 92024 1167-D1
GOLDEN TR
1000 VSTA 92083 1107-H2
GOLDEN WY
13200 PWY 92064 1190-G4
GOLDEN BIRCH WY
12400 SD 92131 1209-G2
GOLDENBUSH DR
6400 CRLB 92009 1127-B4
GOLDEN CIRCLE DR
1800 ESCN 92026 1109-C5
GOLDEN CREST DR
1400 SDCo 92029 1129-G6
GOLDEN EAGLE RD
12100 SDCo 92040 1212-C4
GOLDEN EAGLE TR
- SDCo 92078 1128-G6
- SMCS 92078 1128-G6

SAN DIEGO CO.
INDEX

COPYRIGHT 2001 Thomas Bros. Maps ®

GOLDEN EYE LN SAN DIEGO CO. STREET INDEX GROSS ST 6588

Thomas Bros. Maps ®
COPYRIGHT 2001

STREET
Block City ZIP Pg-Grid

GOLDEN EYE LN
12400 PWY 92064 1190-B6
GOLDENEYE VW
- CRLB 92009 1126-J4
- CRLB 92009 1127-A4
GOLDEN GATE DR
900 SD 92116 1269-A4
GOLDEN GROVE PL
2800 LMGR 91945 1270-J7
GOLDEN HARVEST LN
1400 SDCo 92019 1272-F1
GOLDEN HAVEN DR
4600 SD 92122 1228-D3
GOLDEN HILL DR
- SD 92101 1289-D2
1900 VSTA 92084 1087-H2
GOLDEN MEADOW LN
- SDCo 92028 1047-H5
GOLDEN OAK PL
- ESCN 92027 1130-H2
GOLDEN OAK WY
3000 SDCo 91978 1271-G7
GOLDEN PARK AV
700 SD 92106 1288-A3
GOLDEN RIDGE DR
4500 OCN 92056 1087-C4
GOLDEN RIDGE RD
8400 SDCo 92040 1231-H7
GOLDENROD LN
1800 VSTA 92083 1108-A3
N GOLDENROD ST
600 ESCN 92027 1110-B6
GOLDENROD WY
7000 CRLB 92009 1127-E6
GOLDEN SANDS PL
- SD 92154 1330-H7
GOLDEN STAR CT
4100 SDCo 91941 1271-F4
GOLDEN STAR LN
7300 CRLB 92009 1127-C7
GOLDEN SUNSET CT
14800 PWY 92064 1170-H7
14800 PWY 92064 1190-H1
GOLDEN SUNSET DR
- SMCS 92078 1128-D6
GOLDEN SUNSET LN
14300 PWY 92064 1170-G7
GOLDENTOP DR
- SDCo 92040 1232-C5
GOLDENTOP RD
16900 SDCo 92127 1169-F3
GOLDEN TRAIL WY
5600 OCN 92057 1067-F7
GOLDEN VIEW TER
3400 LMGR 91945 1270-H6
GOLDEN WEST LN
9900 SNTE 92071 1231-D3
GOLDFIELD ST
1500 SD 92110 1268-E1
GOLDFINCH PL
700 SD 92103 1268-J6
7100 CRLB 92009 1127-C6
GOLDFINCH ST
3100 SD 92103 1268-J5
GOLDFINCH WY
900 SMCS 92069 1128-G4
4400 OCN 92057 1086-J1
GOLDFISH CT
12300 SD 92129 1189-A6
GOLDFISH WY
7700 SD 92129 1189-A6
GOLD FLOWER RD
- CRLB 92009 1127-A5
GOLD LAKE RD
2300 LMGR 91945 1270-E7
GOLD NUGGET LP
- SDCo 92040 1232-F4
GOLD OAK CT
800 CHV 91910 1310-J7
GOLD PAN AL
- SDCo 92040 1212-A7
- SDCo 92040 1232-A1
GOLD ROCK RANCH RD
- ImCo - 431-L3
GOLD RUN DR
1200 CHV 91913 1311-D7
GOLD RUN RD
1500 CHV 91913 1331-D1
1500 CHV 91913 1311-F7
GOLD RUSH CIR
600 CHV 91902 1311-C4
GOLD RUSH CT
- SDCo 92065 1172-D3
GOLD RUSH WY
1400 OCN 92057 1067-E6
GOLDSMITH ST
3000 SD 92106 1268-D6
GOLDSTONE ST
1600 ELCJ 92019 1252-B7
GOLETA RD
7900 SD 92126 1209-B3
GOLETA ST
900 OCN 92057 1066-H6
GOLF DR
3300 SDCo 91941 1270-J5
5200 SDCo 91977 1270-J5
5200 SDCo 91977 1271-A5
8700 SDCo 91941 1271-A5
GOLF CLUB DR
31300 SDCo 92003 1068-B2
GOLF COURSE DR
1400 SD 92101 1289-D2
1400 SD 92102 1289-D2
GOLF COURSE RD
- SDCo 92055 1066-G2
GOLFCREST CT
2100 OCN 92056 1106-H1
GOLFCREST DR
3300 OCN 92056 1086-H7
3300 OCN 92056 1106-H1
GOLF CREST DR
4600 SDCo 92004 (1099-G4
See Page 1098)
GOLFCREST DR
6400 SD 92119 1250-E3
GOLFCREST LP
2400 CHV 91915 1311-G5
GOLFCREST PL
1400 VSTA 92083 1107-H4
7300 SD 92119 1250-F5
GOLF CREST RIDGE RD
3000 SDCo 92019 1272-C6
GOLFERS DR
3300 OCN 92056 1106-J1
GOLF GLEN DR
- SMCS 92069 1108-J5
GOLF GLEN RD
4900 SDCo 91902 1310-J2

GOLF GREEN DR
31700 SDCo 92061 1051-C7
31700 SDCo 92082 1051-C7
GOLF POINTE DR
10400 SDCo 91977 1291-E2
GOLFVIEW DR
2800 SDCo 92028 1048-E1
GOLONDRINA DR
9100 LMSA 91941 1271-B3
9200 SDCo 91941 1271-B3
GOMEZ TR
- SDCo 92059 409-E6
- SDCo 92061 409-E6
GOMEZ CREEK RD
400 SDCo 92028 999-D7
1300 SDCo 92028 1029-C1
GONDER RD
1100 ImCo 92227 431-D2
GONDER RD Rt#-S32
- ImCo 92227 431-E2
GONDER RD Rt#-S33
- ImCo 92227 431-E2
GONSALVES AV
- SD 92126 1209-E7
- SD 92126 1229-E1
- SD 92145 1229-E1
GONZALES ST
800 SOLB 92075 1187-G1
GONZALES WY
1200 CHV 91910 1311-B7
GOODBODY ST
3700 SD 92154 1330-E7
GOODE ST
7300 SD 92139 1290-H6
S GOODE ST
2300 SD 92139 1290-G7
GOODING DR
1500 ELCJ 92021 1251-H2
1500 SDCo 92021 1251-H2
GOOD KARMA LN
5700 SDCo 91902 1311-B2
GOODLAND DR
400 OCN 92054 1085-J6
GOODMAN LN
7300 LMGR 91945 1270-F6
GOODSTONE CT
7200 SD 92111 1249-A7
GOODSTONE ST
2400 SD 92111 1249-A7
GOODWICK CT
9400 SD 92123 1249-F7
GOODWIN DR
1500 VSTA 92084 1087-H3
GOODWIN ST
6500 SD 92111 1268-H1
GOODYEAR ST
1000 SD 92113 1289-G6
GOOSEBERRY WY
5300 OCN 92057 1067-D6
GOOSE VALLEY LN
1200 SDCo 92065 1153-A2
GOPHER CANYON CT
2600 SDCo 92084 1068-A7
GOPHER CANYON RD
600 SDCo 92084 1067-J7
600 SDCo 92084 1068-A6
6700 SDCo 92026 1068-F6
GORDON CT
100 ESCN 92025 1129-G4
6900 LMSA 91941 1270-E4
GORDON WY
4200 LMSA 91941 1270-E4
GORDON HILL RD
28400 SDCo 92082 1069-A7
GORGE AV
9000 SNTE 92071 1231-A6
GORGE CT
8900 SNTE 92071 1231-B6
GORGE PL
3500 CRLB 92008 1107-C3
8900 SNTE 92071 1231-B6
GORGE VIEW TER
7400 SD 92120 1250-C5
GORRION CT
13800 SDCo 92021 1232-F6
GORSLINE DR
1000 ELCJ 92021 1252-A3
GOSHAWK ST
2000 SD 92123 1269-A1
GOSHEN ST
1000 SD 92110 1268-G3
GOSNELL WY
100 SMCS 92069 1108-H7
GOTHAM ST
1600 CHV 91913 1311-C5
GOTTA PL
9100 SDCo 92040 1232-D6
GOUDIE TKTR
- SDCo 91901 429-K4
- SDCo 91916 429-K4
GOULBURN CT
400 ELCJ 92020 1251-C5
GOULD AV
- CHV 91911 1330-H2
GOULD LN
2600 SD 92154 1330-C7
GOVERNOR DR
2800 SD 92122 1228-E5
5200 SD 92145 1228-E5
GOWAN ST
- CORD 92135 1288-F4
GOWDY AV
8800 SD 92123 1249-C6
GOWER TKTR
- SDCo 92065 1173-J6
- SDCo 92065 1174-A6
18400 SDCo 92065 1154-B5
GOWIN ST
1400 SDCo 91977 1291-A2
1500 SDCo 91977 1290-J2
GOWLING RD
2300 ImCo 92250 431-D5
GOYETTE PL
9300 SNTE 92071 1230-J6
GRABLE ST
7100 LMSA 91942 1270-F1
GRACE CT
3800 SDCo 92028 1047-J3
6400 SD 92111 1248-J3
GRACE LN
2200 SDCo 91901 1253-J2
GRACE RD
4300 SDCo 91902 1310-G2
GRACE ST
100 OCN 92054 1086-C7
GRACE WY
1200 SDCo 92026 1109-E7
GRACE LAMAY TER
- SDCo 92019 1272-D1

GRACELAND WY
9600 SD 92129 1189-E5
GRACEWOOD PL
10600 SD 92130 1208-D2
GRACEY LN
2100 SDCo 92028 1028-B7
GRACIA PASEO
3500 SDCo 91977 1271-A5
GRACILIOR CT
9000 SDCo 92026 1069-A6
GRACILIOR DR
8900 SDCo 92026 1069-A6
GRACILIOR PL
8900 SDCo 92026 1069-A6
GRACIOSA CT
17300 SD 92128 1170-A2
GRACIOSA RD
17300 SD 92128 1170-A1
GRADE PL
2700 SDCo 91977 1271-E7
E GRADE RD Rt#-S7
21500 SDCo 92060 409-H7
23500 SDCo 92070 409-H7
S GRADE RD Rt#-S6
31600 SDCo 92060 409-G7
31600 SDCo 92082 409-G7
31600 SDCo 92061 409-G7
GRADO CIPRESO
- CRLB 92009 1147-G2
GRADO EL TUPELO
- CRLB 92009 1147-F3
GRADO MARBELLA
7000 CRLB 92009 1127-G6
GRADY PL
1500 CRLB 92008 1106-G6
GRAESER RD
- ImCo 92250 431-F5
GRAFTON RD
200 ImCo 92243 6560-D2
GRAFTON ST
2100 ELCJ 92020 1251-B3
GRAHAM AV
9100 SD 92126 1209-D7
GRAHAM PL
1300 ESCN 92026 1109-J5
GRAHAM RD
1700 ImCo 92243 431-A6
GRAHAM ST
1300 SD 92109 1248-A7
GRAHAM TER
8500 SNTE 92071 1230-J7
GRAIN LN
13500 SD 92129 1189-E4
GRAINWOOD WY
12400 SD 92131 1210-B4
GRAMERCY DR
8800 SD 92123 1249-D5
GRAMMER RD
3600 SDCo 92084 1068-G6
GRANADA AV
1300 SD 92102 1289-E2
2000 SD 92104 1289-E2
2700 SD 92104 1269-E6
N GRANADA AV
3900 SDCo 91977 1271-D5
S GRANADA AV
2500 SDCo 91977 1271-D5
GRANADA CIR
2500 SDCo 91977 1271-D7
GRANADA DR
700 OCN 92056 1087-E5
700 VSTA 92083 1087-E5
12800 PWY 92064 1190-E5
GRANADA LN
- SDCo 92028 997-H3
GRANADA ST
10500 SNTE 92071 1231-E6
GRANADA WY
1000 CHV 91910 1311-A7
1200 SMCS 92069 1128-E2
2400 CRLB 92008 1106-H4
N GRANADOS AV
100 SOLB 92075 1167-F6
S GRANADOS AV
100 SOLB 92075 1167-F7
300 SOLB 92075 1187-F1
GRANBY WY
10600 SD 92126 1208-H4
GRAND AV
300 SDCo 91977 1291-B2
600 SMCS 92069 1128-F1
600 SMCS 92069 1108-C6
700 SD 92109 1247-H6
1000 CRLB 92008 1106-D5
1100 ImCo 92249 6560-B7
1300 ESCN 92027 1130-D1
1500 SD 92109 1248-A6
1700 DLMR 92014 1187-F4
2400 VSTA 92083 1108-A5
2400 SDCo 91977 1271-B7
E GRAND AV
100 ESCN 92025 1129-J2
400 ESCN 92025 1130-A2
1200 ESCN 92027 1130-A2
W GRAND AV
100 ESCN 92025 1129-H3
W GRAND AV Rt#-S6
800 ESCN 92025 1129-G3
GRAND CT
900 ESCN 92025 1129-H4
GRANDA DR
400 SDCo 92004 1058-G7
GRAND CARIBE CSWY
500 CORD 92118 1329-E2
GRANDEE CT
12300 SD 92128 1170-B2
GRANDEE PL
17200 SD 92128 1170-C1
GRANDEE RD
12300 SD 92128 1170-B2
GRANDEE WY
17000 SD 92128 1170-B2
GRANDE VISTA
- SMCS 92078 1129-C2
GRANDFATHERS LN
29200 SDCo 92082 1071-A6
GRAND FORK DR
10700 SNTE 92071 1231-F4
GRAND FORKS RD
2300 CHV 91915 1311-H7
GRANDON AV
1600 SMCS 92069 1128-C1
GRANDRIDGE RD
5200 SDCo 92020 1271-G1
GRAND TETON CT
1500 CHV 91911 1330-F4
GRAND TETON WY
10600 SNTE 92071 1231-E4

GRANDVIA PT
13300 SD 92130 1187-J5
GRANDVIEW
2900 SDCo 92029 1129-C6
GRANDVIEW DR
9500 SDCo 91941 1271-C3
GRAND VIEW GN
2000 ESCN 92026 1109-C3
GRANDVIEW HTS
30100 SDCo 92082 1069-J5
GRANDVIEW PL
3800 SDCo 91902 1310-D4
GRANDVIEW RD
- SDCo 92036 1156-A7
- SDCo 92036 1176-A1
1300 VSTA 92084 1088-C4
1700 SDCo 92084 1088-B2
GRANDVIEW ST
100 ENCT 92024 1147-A3
1500 OCN 92054 1106-D1
2300 SD 92110 1248-F6
2300 SD 92110 1268-G1
GRANDVIEW TER
4600 SDCo 91941 1271-D3
GRANDVIEW WY
- SDCo 92036 1176-A1
GRAND VISTA LN
- SDCo 92028 1028-D2
GRANERO PL
1800 ESCN 92029 1129-F6
GRANGE PL
- PWY 92064 1210-C1
GRANGE ST
2500 LMGR 91945 1270-G7
GRANGE HALL RD
900 ENCT 92007 1167-E1
GRANGER AV
1400 ESCN 92027 1110-A7
1800 NATC 91950 1310-C2
2400 SDCo 91950 1310-C2
GRANGER ST
700 SD 92154 1329-J7
900 SD 92154 1349-J1
1200 IMPB 91932 1349-J1
1400 IMPB 92154 1349-J1
4400 SD 92107 1287-J1
GRANITE CV
500 ELCJ 92021 1252-A4
GRANITE DR
16600 SDCo 92065 1171-D2
GRANITE RD
300 SMCS 92069 1108-E6
GRANITE ST
800 SMCS 92078 1129-C2
GRANITE CREEK RD
13300 SD 92128 1189-J4
GRANITE HILLS CIR
700 ELCJ 92019 1252-A6
GRANITE HILLS CT
1400 ELCJ 92019 1252-A6
GRANITE HILLS DR
1200 ELCJ 92019 1251-J7
1200 ELCJ 92019 1252-B5
1200 SDCo 92019 1251-J7
1500 SDCo 92019 1252-B5
GRANITE HOUSE LN
8700 SNTE 92071 1231-B7
GRANITE MOUNTAIN TKTR
1100 SDCo 92036 410-A11
GRANITE MOUNTAIN VIEW RD
1200 SDCo 92036 410-A11
1200 SDCo 92036 1138-A5
GRANITE OAKS RD
- SDCo 91935 1294-C2
GRANITE RIDGE DR
9600 SD 92123 1249-F4
GRANITE ROCK RD
1700 SDCo 92028 998-H7
GRANITE SPRINGS DR
1300 CHV 91915 1311-H6
GRANITE VIEW LN
500 SDCo 91977 1290-J5
GRANJAS RD
1000 CHV 91911 1330-B3
GRANT AV
400 ELCJ 92020 1251-E6
8400 LMSA 91941 1270-J2
GRANT ST
300 OCN 92054 1086-B7
400 OCN 92054 1106-B1
5300 SD 92110 1268-F3
GRANT WY
2600 SD 92102 1289-D4
GRANT LINE RD
1900 VSTA 92083 1107-H6
GRANTO CT
8000 SD 92122 1228-C4
GRANTWOOD LN
1100 SDCo 92021 1251-H1
GRANVILLE DR
13800 PWY 92064 1190-F4
GRAPE LN
9700 SDCo 92029 1149-E2
GRAPE ST
100 SD 92101 1289-A1
200 ESCN 92025 1130-A2
300 ESCN 92025 1129-J1
400 OCN 92054 1086-G2
500 ELCJ 92021 1252-A4
500 SD 92101 1288-J2
1000 ESCN 92026 1129-J1
1000 SMCS 92069 1109-C7
1000 ESCN 92026 1109-J7
1300 SD 92102 1289-E1
1300 SD 92104 1289-F1
5400 SD 92105 1290-B1
7800 LMSA 91941 1270-H3
S GRAPE ST
100 ESCN 92025 1130-A2
W GRAPE ST
100 SD 92101 1289-A1
GRAPE ARBOR CT
17100 PWY 92064 1170-D2
GRAPE ARBOR WY
13100 PWY 92064 1170-D2
GRAPE FERN CT
11100 SD 92131 1209-J1
GRAPEFRUIT DR
500 SDCo 92065 1153-B7
GRAPEVINE CT
1400 VSTA 92083 1087-D7
GRAPEVINE LN
1500 VSTA 92083 1087-D7
GRAPEVINE RD
100 VSTA 92083 1107-D1
100 VSTA 92083 1087-D7
800 OCN 92056 1087-D7

GRAPEVINE CANYON RD
- SDCo 92036 (1118-A3
See Page 1098)
- SDCo 92066 410-A10
- SDCo 92066 (1118-A3
See Page 1098)
29200 SDCo 92066 409-L9
GRAPEVINE RANCH RD
- SDCo 91917 429-K10
- SDCo 91917 (1315-G7
See Page 1294)
- SDCo 91963 (1315-G7
See Page 1294)
GRASS VALLEY LN
8700 SNTE 92071 1230-J3
GRASS VALLEY RD
1000 CHV 91913 1311-E5
GRASSY WY
28000 SDCo 92026 1089-F3
GRASSY MEADOW RD
- SDCo 92061 1050-H3
GRASSY TRAIL DR
11200 SD 92127 1169-J5
GRAVES AV
400 ELCJ 92020 1251-F3
600 ELCJ 92021 1251-F3
1200 SDCo 92021 1251-F2
2700 SNTE 92021 1251-F1
3200 SNTE 92021 1231-F7
8600 SNTE 92071 1231-F7
GRAVES CT
300 SDCo 92021 1251-F1
GRAVES LN
1200 SDCo 92021 1251-F2
GRAVILLA PL
500 SD 92037 1247-E2
GRAVILLA ST
200 SD 92037 1247-E2
GRAVITY WY
1400 SD 92114 1290-C2
GRAY DR
900 ELCJ 92020 1251-H7
GRAYBAR CT
3300 OCN 92056 1086-J7
GRAYDON RD
4100 SD 92130 1188-B5
GRAYFISH LN
500 OCN 92054 1086-G2
GRAYFOX DR
10200 SD 92131 1209-H4
GRAY MARE CT
- SDCo 91901 1254-G3
GRAY MARE WY
- SDCo 91901 1254-G3
GRAYSON CT
- CHV 91913 1331-D1
GRAYSON DR
4000 SD 92130 1188-A4
GRAYSON PL
1400 CHV 91913 1331-C1
GRAYSTONE PL
2500 SDCo 91977 1271-E7
GREAT BLUE HERON WY
- SDCo 92066 (1299-B1
See Page 1298)
GREAT EAGLE WY
- SDCo 92066 (1299-B2
See Page 1298)
GREAT OAK LN
- SDCo 91901 1254-G7
GREAT PLAINS RD
14000 PWY 92064 1170-G4
GREAT ROCK RD
10300 SNTE 92071 1231-E3
GREAT SANDY TR
600 SDCo 92036 1138-B7
GREAT STHN OVLD STG RT OF 1849
- SDCo 92036 410-A11
- SDCo 92036 430-B2
- SDCo 92036 1138-A5
- SDCo 92036 (1158-C7
See Page 1138)
14900 SDCo 92036 430-B2
GREBE DR
7300 CRLB 92009 1127-B7
GRECOURT WY
3700 CRLB 92008 1106-F6
GREDOS PL
700 CHV 91910 1310-J5
GREELY AV
3000 SD 92113 1289-E5
GREEN AV
100 ESCN 92025 1130-A5
GREEN LN
11500 SDCo 92040 1231-J7
GREEN RD Rt#-S33
4200 ImCo 92227 431-E2
GREEN ST
- SDCo 92028 1028-G5
700 SD 92154 1330-A7
800 SD 92154 1350-A1
GREENACRES DR
1800 SDCo 91901 1254-A1
GREENACRES RD
2100 SDCo 92028 1027-J6
GREEN BAY ST
1100 SD 92154 1350-A2
GREENBELT RD
17200 SDCo 92065 1171-H1
GREENBERG LN
8800 SD 92129 1189-C3
GREENBERG WY
8800 SD 92129 1189-C3
GREEN BRIAR CIR
1600 SDCo 92028 1028-A5
GREEN BRIAR DR
1600 SDCo 92028 1028-B5
GREENBRIAR DR
2300 CHV 91915 1311-G5
GREEN BRIAR LN
1600 SDCo 92028 1028-B5
GREENBRIER AV
4700 SD 92120 1249-J6
4900 SD 92120 1250-A6
GREENBRIER CT
6700 SD 92120 1250-A6
GREENBRIER DR
500 OCN 92054 1086-C7
500 OCN 92054 1106-D1
GREENBROOK ST
5100 OCN 92057 1067-B5
GREENBROOK WY
8800 SNTE 92071 1230-J4
GREENBUSH LN
1100 SDCo 92084 1108-D1
GREEN CANYON LN
2100 SDCo 92028 1028-A5

GREEN CANYON RD
1300 SDCo 92028 1028-A7
1400 SDCo 92028 1047-H2
2300 SDCo 92028 1027-J7
GREENCASTLE ST
10700 SNTE 92071 1231-F4
GREENCRAIG LN
4800 SD 92123 1249-E1
GREENCRAIG WY
5000 SD 92123 1249-E1
GREENCREST CT
1500 SDCo 92019 1272-B4
GREENCREST DR
2100 SDCo 92019 1272-B4
GREENE ST
4300 SD 92107 1268-A5
GREENERY CIR
700 OCN 92057 1067-B5
GREENE VIEW PL
2600 SDCo 91905 1300-B4
GREEN FARM RD
- SD 92145 1230-A1
10000 SD 92145 1229-G4
GREENFIELD CT
1300 CHV 91913 1331-D1
1700 ELCJ 92021 1252-B3
GREENFIELD DR
200 SDCo 92020 1251-F3
200 SDCo 92021 1251-H3
500 ELCJ 92021 1251-H3
1300 ELCJ 92021 1252-B2
1700 ELCJ 92019 1252-D4
1800 SDCo 92019 1252-C3
1800 SDCo 92021 1252-C3
GREENFORD DR
10300 SD 92126 1209-D3
GREEN GABLES AV
6500 SD 92119 1250-F5
GREEN GABLES CT
6500 SD 92119 1250-F6
GREEN GARDEN DR
1200 SDCo 92021 1251-J1
GREEN GLEN RD
- SDCo 92065 1173-D2
GREEN GROVE AV
1500 ELCJ 92021 1252-B2
GREEN HAVEN LN
15800 SDCo 92065 1173-E4
GREEN HEATHER LN
3000 SDCo 92028 1048-A1
GREENHEDGE RW
6000 SD 92037 1248-A1
GREEN HILL CT
800 SMCS 92069 1108-J5
GREEN HILLS DR
2800 SDCo 92028 1048-A1
GREEN HILLS PL
2100 SDCo 92028 1048-B1
GREEN HILLS RD
6200 OCN 92057 1067-F3
GREEN HILLS WY
2200 SDCo 92084 1088-B1
GREEN HOUSE LN
- SD 92093 1228-B1
GREENLAKE CT
900 ENCT 92007 1167-E2
GREEN LAKE CT
6900 LMGR 91945 1270-E7
GREENLAKE DR
1200 ENCT 92007 1167-E1
GREENLAWN DR
8100 SD 92114 1290-H4
GREENLEAF RD
10100 SDCo 91977 1291-E2
GREENLEAF WY
- SD 92131 1189-G7
- SD 92131 1209-G1
GREEN LINKS DR
- SDCo 92004 (1079-C3
See Page 1058)
GREEN MEADOW DR
2400 SDCo 92083 1108-C4
GREEN MOUNTAIN LN
2800 SDCo 92025 1130-E7
GREEN MOUNTAIN RD
2800 SDCo 92025 1130-E7
GREEN OAK RD
700 VSTA 92083 1108-A5
1100 VSTA 92083 1107-H6
GREEN OAKS DR
26700 SDCo 92070 409-J10
GREEN OAKS RD
11100 SDCo 92040 1211-F7
GREENOCK CT
2700 CRLB 92008 1107-A5
GREEN ORCHARD PL
1200 ENCT 92024 1147-G4
GREENRIDGE AV
8800 SDCo 91977 1290-J3
GREENRIDGE DR
1500 VSTA 92083 1107-H5
GREEN RIVER DR
2200 CHV 91915 1311-G6
GREENS EAST RD
12200 SD 92128 1170-B1
GREENSGATE DR
2200 CHV 91915 1311-F5
GREENSHADE RD
5600 SD 92121 1208-E4
GREENSVIEW CT
5900 SDCo 92067 1188-E2
N GREENSVIEW DR
1100 CHV 91915 1311-G5
S GREENSVIEW DR
1200 CHV 91915 1311-G7
GREEN TERRACE RD
13400 PWY 92064 1170-E3
GREEN TOP LN
1600 SDCo 92020 1271-J2
GREENTREE LN
1300 VSTA 92083 1108-A2
2600 SD 92037 1227-J2
GREEN TREE RD
- ESCN 92029 1129-E5
GREENTREE RD
1700 ENCT 92024 1147-H6
12200 PWY 92064 1170-B7
GREEN TURTLE RD
- CORD 92118 1329-E1
GREENVALE DR
8400 SNTE 92071 1230-J7
GREEN VALLEY RD
2500 CHV 91915 1311-H6
GREEN VALLEY TKTR
14200 PWY 92064 1170-H3
14200 PWY 92064 1171-A2
15900 SDCo 92065 1151-A7
15900 SDCo 92065 1171-A2

GREEN VALLEY HEIGHTS RD
15800 SDCo 92065 1151-B6
GREENVIEW DR
- CRLB 92009 1127-F7
GREEN VIEW LN
200 SDCo 92028 1028-A1
GREENVIEW PL
8800 SDCo 91977 1271-A4
GREENVIEW RD
800 ESCN 92026 1109-F6
GREENVIEW ST
1900 ESCN 92027 1130-C1
GREEN VISTA LN
1900 SDCo 92028 1028-A7
GREENWAY RISE
1300 ESCN 92027 1110-B5
GREENWICH DR
6200 SD 92122 1228-G5
GREENWICH ST
2900 CRLB 92008 1107-A3
GREENWICK PL
1600 SDCo 92019 1272-B4
GREENWICK RD
2100 SDCo 92019 1272-B4
GREENWING DR
2300 SD 92123 1249-B7
GREENWOOD LN
100 OCN 92054 1106-C1
GREENWOOD PL
300 CHV 91902 1310-J3
GREENWOOD ST
3700 SD 92110 1268-E5
GREGG CT
5800 LMSA 91942 1251-C7
12900 PWY 92064 1190-E7
GREGG ST
13000 PWY 92064 1190-E7
GREGORY DR
2500 CRLB 92008 1106-E4
GREGORY LN
700 OCN 92057 1066-H7
GREGORY ST
100 SD 92113 1289-F4
1300 SD 92102 1289-F2
2000 SD 92104 1289-F2
2700 SD 92104 1269-F7
9300 LMSA 91942 1251-B6
GREMLIN WY
1600 SDCo 91977 1291-D2
GRENACHE ROSE WY
18300 SDCo 92065 1171-H2
GRENADINE GN
2500 ESCN 92029 1149-G1
GRESHAM RD
- ImCo 92243 6500-H7
- ImCo 92243 6560-H1
GRESHAM ST
3900 SD 92109 1248-A7
4000 SD 92109 1247-J5
GRETA ST
1000 ELCJ 92021 1251-H2
1000 SDCo 92021 1251-H2
GRETCHEN RD
600 CHV 91910 1310-E7
GRETLER PL
10400 SDCo 91941 1271-E3
GRETNA GREEN WY
700 ESCN 92025 1130-C7
700 ESCN 92025 1150-C1
700 SDCo 92025 1130-C7
GREVILEA WY
700 SDCo 91902 1310-G3
GREVILLA AV
- SD 92102 1289-G4
GREWIA CT
1500 SD 92114 1290-C6
GREWIA ST
5800 SD 92114 1290-C6
GREYCOURT AV
5700 SD 92114 1290-C6
GREYCOURT WY
1400 SD 92114 1290-C6
GREYFIELD CT
- SDCo 92028 1027-G6
GREY HAWK CT
700 OCN 92057 1067-C7
700 OCN 92057 1087-C1
GREYLING DR
2400 SD 92123 1249-C6
GREYLING PL
8800 SD 92123 1249-C7
GREY OAKS CT
1400 OCN 92056 1087-E3
GREYSTONE AV
10300 SDCo 92026 1109-F1
GREYSTONE CT
2900 SDCo 91935 1272-E6
GREYSTONE DR
3400 SDCo 91935 1272-D6
3400 SDCo 92019 1272-D6
GREY STONE RD
15900 PWY 92064 1170-G4
GRIBBLE ST
7300 SD 92114 1290-G4
GRIFFIN DR
- ELCJ 92020 1251-A2
GRIFFIN RD
- ImCo 92227 431-D2
GRIFFIN ST
1600 OCN 92054 1106-D2
GRIFFITH RD
- SDCo 92040 1211-G4
1400 SDCo 92065 1153-B7
1600 SDCo 92065 1173-B1
GRIFFITH PARK WY
8800 SNTE 92071 1230-J5
8800 SNTE 92071 1231-A5
GRILLO CT
11400 SD 92127 1149-J7
GRIM AV
3100 SD 92104 1269-E6
GRIMSLEY AV
12700 PWY 92064 1190-H5
GRISSOM ST
700 SD 92154 1330-E7
GRIVETTA CT
900 CRLB 92009 1127-A7
GROGAN CIR
3400 SD 92154 1330-E7
GROGAN CT
700 SD 92154 1330-E7
GROSALIA AV
9800 SDCo 91941 1271-C1
GROSS CT
2600 SD 92139 1310-E1
GROSS ST
6300 SD 92139 1310-E1

SAN DIEGO CO.
INDEX

6589 GROSSE POINTE SAN DIEGO CO. STREET INDEX HAWKHILL RD

STREET
Block City ZIP Pg-Grid
GROSSE POINTE
- SD 92128 1190-A3
GROSSMONT AV
700 ELCJ 92020 1251-D7
GROSSMONT BLVD
8700 LMSA 91941 1271-A1
9000 SDCo 91941 1271-B1
9500 LMSA 91942 1251-C7
9500 LMSA 91942 1271-B1
GROSSMONT CT
900 CHV 91913 1311-D6
GROSSMONT CENTER DR
5400 LMSA 91942 1271-A1
5500 LMSA 91942 1251-A7
5600 LMSA 91942 1250-J7
GROSSMONT COLLEGE DR
2400 ELCJ 92020 1251-A3
GROSSMONT SUMMIT DR
9400 LMSA 91941 1271-B1
GROSSMONT VIEW DR
1600 ELCJ 92020 1251-C6
GROS VENTRE AV
4000 SD 92117 1248-E3
GROTON PL
2500 SDCo 92025 1130-D7
GROTON ST
3800 SD 92110 1268-C5
GROTON WY
3100 SD 92110 1268-C5
GROUSE ST
900 ELCJ 92020 1251-D3
GROUTER ST
- SD 92136 1289-E6
GROVE AV
400 IMPB 91932 1349-F1
1500 SD 92154 1349-J1
1700 SD 92154 1350-A1
2700 CRLB 92008 1106-F3
GROVE CT
3600 LMGR 91945 1270-H5
GROVE PL
1900 ESCN 92027 1130-D2
GROVE RD
1200 SDCo 92020 1271-J1
1700 SDCo 92020 1272-A1
GROVE ST
1200 NATC 91950 1310-B1
1300 SD 92102 1289-E2
2200 SDCo 91950 1310-B3
3400 LMGR 91945 1270-H6
3700 LMGR 91941 1270-H6
3700 LMSA 91941 1270-H6
GROVE WY
2700 NATC 91950 1310-B3
2700 SDCo 91950 1310-B3
GROVE CANYON RD
3500 SDCo 92025 1150-D1
GROVE HILL DR
600 SDCo 92026 1109-D6
600 SMCS 92069 1109-D6
GROVE KNOLL LN
12800 SDCo 92082 1090-C2
GROVELAND DR
5100 SD 92114 1290-A4
GROVELAND TER
1300 ELCJ 92021 1252-A3
GROVE PARK PL
- CHV 91915 1311-G7
GROVE VIEW RD
700 OCN 92057 1067-E4
2200 SD 92139 1290-G6
GRUBSTAKE TR
7500 SDCo 92036 1138-C7
7500 SDCo 92036 (1158-C1 See Page 1138)
GRULLA ST
6600 CRLB 92009 1127-G5
GRUMBLE RD
800 ImCo 92243 431-D4
GRUMMAN ST
- SD 92154 1351-D2
GRUTLY ST
30200 SDCo 92070 1135-B3
GUACAMAYO CT
12900 SD 92128 1150-C6
GUADALAJARA DR
1000 ENCT 92024 1147-E7
GUADALCANAL AV
- SD 92140 1268-E7
GUADALCANAL RD
2900 CORD 92155 1309-A2
GUADALIMAR WY
10900 SD 92129 1189-H1
GUADALUPE AV
600 CORD 92118 1288-J7
GUADALUPE DR
3600 OCN 92054 1086-F2
GUAJOME ST
100 VSTA 92083 1087-H7
GUAJOME LAKE RD
500 OCN 92057 1067-D6
1700 OCN 92056 1067-D7
2200 SDCo 92084 1087-F1
2200 VSTA 92084 1087-F1
2800 OCN 92056 1087-F1
2800 OCN 92057 1087-F1
GUANAJUATO CT
100 SOLB 92075 1167-D7
GUANTANAMO ST
- SD 92101 1268-F7
- SD 92140 1268-F7
GUATAY AV
900 CHV 91911 1330-E2
GUATAY RD
24800 SDCo 91916 1236-C2
GUATAY ST
8100 SD 92114 1290-G3
GUATAY VIEW LN
9000 SDCo 91931 1236-H3
GUAVA AV
100 CHV 91910 1310-A5
600 CHV 91910 1330-B1
4900 LMSA 91941 1270-G2
GUAVA GN
1700 ESCN 92026 1109-D6
GUAVA LN
1600 SDCo 92020 1271-J2
GUAVA WY
3500 OCN 92054 1086-F2
GUAYMAS BAY CT
2100 SD 92105 1290-C1
GUEJITO RD
15700 SDCo 92027 1111-C1
GUEJITO TKTR
- SDCo 92027 409-G10
GUERRO CT
100 SOLB 92075 1167-D6

STREET
Block City ZIP Pg-Grid
GUESSMAN AV
5200 LMSA 91942 1270-F1
GUEVARA RD
1700 CRLB 92008 1106-F3
GUIDERO WY
500 ENCT 92024 1147-C5
GUIJAROS RD
- SD 92106 1288-B7
- SD 92106 1308-B1
GUILD AV
9200 SD 92123 1249-E4
GUILD ST
5100 LMSA 91942 1270-H2
GUILDER GN
1800 ESCN 92029 1129-F5
GUILDFORD CT
1000 ENCT 92024 1147-D4
GUILITOY AV
3000 SD 92117 1248-C1
GUILITOY CT
4600 SD 92117 1248-C1
GUINCHO CT
5600 SD 92124 1229-G7
GUINCHO PL
10400 SD 92124 1229-H7
GUINCHO RD
5600 SD 92124 1229-G7
GUINDA CT
5200 SD 92124 1249-F1
GUINEVERE ST
2600 OCN 92054 1086-E6
GUISANTE LN
5200 SD 92124 1249-F1
GUISANTE TER
9700 SD 92124 1249-F1
GUIZOT ST
1000 SD 92107 1287-J1
1500 SD 92107 1267-J7
1700 SD 92107 1268-A7
GULCH RD
- SDCo 92082 1071-D2
GULL CT
1300 CRLB 92009 1127-B5
GULL PL
200 ELCJ 92019 1252-A5
GULL ST
800 SD 92101 1289-B5
GULLETT RD
2500 ImCo 92251 431-A5
GULLSTRAND ST
5800 SD 92122 1228-F6
GUMBARK PL
10200 SD 92131 1209-H4
GUM TREE GN
3700 ESCN 92025 1150-C3
GUMTREE LN
1600 SDCo 92028 1027-J1
1900 SDCo 92028 1028-B1
GUMWOOD CT
2900 SDCo 92028 1048-C3
GUNN ST
2800 SD 92104 1269-D6
GUNNER AV
13200 SD 92129 1189-C4
GUNNISON CT
13900 SD 92129 1189-C3
GUNN STAGE PL
16900 SDCo 92065 1173-D3
GUNN STAGE RD
15900 SDCo 92065 1173-D3
GUNPOWDER POINT DR
1000 CHV 91910 1309-H6
GUNSLINGER TR
7500 SDCo 92036 1138-C7
7500 SDCo 92036 (1158-C1 See Page 1138)
GUNSTON CT
4900 SD 92130 1188-C4
GUNZAN ST
7000 SD 92139 1290-G7
GUPPY CT
8200 SD 92129 1189-B7
GURKE ST
4700 SD 92124 1249-G2
GURNARD CT
3400 SD 92124 1249-H4
GURNARD ST
10100 SD 92124 1249-G4
GURUJAN WY
1400 SDCo 91901 1234-A6
GUSTAVO ST
1400 ELCJ 92019 1252-A7
GUSTINE ST
1100 CHV 91913 1311-C6
GUTHRIE RD
- ImCo 92251 431-A4
GUTHRIE WY
7400 SD 92114 1290-G3
GUY ST
1500 SD 92103 1268-G5
1700 SD 92110 1268-H6
GUYMON ST
4700 SD 92102 1289-J3
4800 SD 92102 1290-A3
GWEN ST
6100 SD 92114 1290-B5
GWYNNE AV
2600 SDCo 91950 1310-C2
GYMKHANA RD
23800 SDCo 92065 1173-D1
GYPSY LN
1200 SDCo 92065 1172-G1

H

H AV
100 CORD 92118 1288-H6
9700 SD 92145 1229-F5
H CT
- CHV 91910 1310-F7
- SD 92126 1209-F7
H RD E
- CORD 92135 1288-F6
H ST
- ImCo 92281 431-A1
- CHV 91910 1310-A7
200 SDCo 92065 1152-J5
700 CHV 91910 1329-J1
700 CHV 91910 1330-A1
1800 SDCo 92065 1172-F1
E H ST
- ENCT 92024 1147-C7
100 CHV 91910 1310-D6
300 SDCo 91910 1310-F6
1000 CHV 91910 1311-A6
1300 CHV 91913 1311-D4
1500 CHV 91914 1311-D4
W H ST
100 ENCT 92024 1147-C7

STREET
Block City ZIP Pg-Grid
W H ST
100 ENCT 92024 1167-B1
HAAS ST
2400 SDCo 92025 1150-D1
6100 LMSA 91942 1250-G6
HABER ST
5800 SD 92122 1228-B6
HABERO DR
2000 ESCN 92029 1129-F6
HACIENDA CIR
1900 ELCJ 92020 1251-C2
HACIENDA CT
200 VSTA 92083 1087-G7
HACIENDA DR
100 VSTA 92083 1087-E7
200 VSTA 92083 1107-D1
600 ELCJ 92020 1251-B2
800 SDCo 92036 1156-D1
3400 OCN 92054 1086-F4
HACIENDA GN
2400 ESCN 92026 1109-B4
HACIENDA LN
14200 PWY 92064 1170-G7
HACIENDA PL
1700 ELCJ 92020 1251-C2
HACIENDA RD
8500 SNTE 92071 1231-D7
HACKAMORE RD
1000 VSTA 92083 1087-E7
1600 OCN 92057 1067-G6
HACKBERRY PL
700 SDCo 92028 1027-G3
HACKLEMAN RD
1000 ImCo 92243 431-A5
1000 ImCo 92251 431-A5
HADA DR
17400 SD 92127 1169-J1
HADAR DR
11400 SD 92126 1209-C1
HADDEN HALL CT
18200 SD 92128 1150-C6
HADLEY PL
9000 SD 92126 1209-D1
HAFFLY AV
1900 NATC 91950 1309-G3
HAGANS CIR
8000 SD 92126 1209-A1
HAGBERG RD
1400 ImCo 92283 432-D4
HAGERSWOOD CT
12700 SD 92129 1189-C5
HAGMANN CT
900 SD 92114 1290-F2
HAGMANN ST
7200 SD 92114 1290-F2
HA-HANA RD
12900 SDCo 92040 1232-C6
HAIDAS AV
3000 SD 92117 1248-C1
HAINES ST
3700 SD 92109 1248-A6
4400 SD 92109 1247-J5
HAITI AV
- SD 92140 1268-F6
HAKONE
9300 SDCo 92040 1232-F4
HAL ST
200 SD 92102 1290-A3
HALBERNS BLVD
9400 SNTE 92071 1231-B4
HALCYON RD
100 ENCT 92024 1147-B5
HALE AV
100 ESCN 92025 1129-F3
100 ESCN 92029 1129-F3
HALE CT
800 ELCJ 92020 1251-F7
HALE DR
700 SDCo 91901 1234-B4
HALE PL
100 ESCN 92029 1129-F4
900 CHV 91914 1311-G4
HALE ST
400 CHV 91910 1310-F7
HALECREST DR
800 CHV 91910 1310-G7
900 ESCN 92025 1130-A3
HALES PL
- SDCo 92036 1156-E7
HALEY LN
9400 SDCo 91941 1271-C4
HALEY RD
- ImCo - 411-D9
HALEY ST
200 SDCo 92065 1152-D7
HALFBEAK WY
3700 SD 92124 1249-G3
HALF DOME PL
2600 CRLB 92008 1106-J5
HALF MILE DR
3700 SD 92130 1187-J4
3700 SD 92130 1188-A4
HALF MOON BEND
- CORD 92118 1329-D1
HALF MOON TR
- SDCo 92066 1237-D7
HALF MOON BAY DR
1200 CHV 91915 1311-G6
14100 SD 92014 1187-H5
HALF MOON BAY WY
4200 OCN 92054 1066-E6
HALFOAK TER
11900 SD 92128 1190-B7
HALFPENNY LN
- CORD 92118 1329-E2
HALFWAY TKTR
- SDCo 92060 409-H6
- SDCo 92086 409-H6
HALIFAX ST
6800 SD 92120 1250-A5
HALL AV
100 SD 92173 1350-F4
HALLER ST
2400 SD 92104 1269-F6
2400 SD 92104 1289-G1
HALLEY CT
1200 CHV 91911 1330-H1
1300 SD 92154 1350-A1
HALLEY ST
1600 SD 92154 1349-J1
1700 SD 92154 1350-A2
HALLMARK PL
- ESCN 92029 1129-F7
HALLMARK WY
600 SD 92102 1290-A3
HALL MEADOW RD
10600 SD 92131 1209-G1
HALLYEYAAW LN
100 SDCo 92070 409-H10

STREET
Block City ZIP Pg-Grid
HALO CIR
9900 SDCo 91941 1271-D2
HALO ST
1500 IMPB 91932 1349-J1
1500 SD 92154 1349-J1
1700 SD 92154 1350-A1
HALPER RD
14000 PWY 92064 1190-C3
HALSEY RD
4400 SD 92133 1288-D1
HALSEY ST
100 CHV 91910 1310-C7
400 CHV 91910 1330-A1
HALSING CT
- CRLB 92009 1126-J7
- CRLB 92009 1127-B5
HALSTED ST
8800 SD 92123 1249-D4
HALTER PL
1500 SMCS 92069 1108-E6
HAMBAUGH WY
400 VSTA 92083 1107-H1
HAMBURG SQ
3100 SD 92037 1227-J1
HAMDEN DR
2100 CHV 91913 1311-E3
HAMDEN LN
28100 SDCo 92026 1089-E3
HAMDEN WY
3100 CRLB 92008 1107-A3
HAMILL AV
5500 SD 92120 1250-C5
HAMILTON AV
100 ELCN 92243 6499-E7
100 ELCN 92243 6500-A7
HAMILTON LN
- SDCo 91931 1236-H3
700 SDCo 92028 1028-A1
700 SDCo 92029 1129-H7
800 ESCN 92029 1129-F7
HAMILTON ST
3900 SD 92104 1269-D5
4300 SD 92116 1269-D3
HAMLET AV
7200 SD 92120 1250-C5
HAMLET CT
7200 SD 92120 1250-C5
HAMLET DR
1100 SDCo 92021 1252-J2
HAMLIN CT
- SDCo 92065 1171-D3
HAMMER
1800 CRLB 92008 1127-B3
HAMMERBERG CV
10300 SD 92124 1249-G4
HAMMOND DR
8800 SD 92123 1249-D5
HAMPE CT
8800 SD 92129 1189-C2
HAMPSHIRE LN
600 CHV 91911 1330-H2
18300 SD 92128 1150-B6
HAMPSON PL
16100 SDCo 92065 1173-D3
HAMPSTEAD WY
2300 SD 92139 1290-G7
HAMPTON CT
- ENCT 92024 1147-D4
800 VSTA 92083 1107-H2
1700 CHV 91902 1311-C5
1700 CHV 91913 1311-C5
5800 SD 92120 1250-B7
HAMPTON RD
1100 SMCS 92069 1128-B3
34100 SDCo 92061 1050-H1
HANCOCK CIR
4500 OCN 92056 1107-D2
HANCOCK RD
3500 SDCo 92028 1047-H3
HANCOCK ST
1600 SD 92110 1268-G6
1600 SD 92110 1268-H6
2000 SD 92110 1268-D4
HANCOCK TER
- SMCS 92069 1108-J5
HANDEL CT
7900 SD 92126 1209-A4
HANDEL WY
7800 SD 92126 1209-A4
HANDLEBAR RD
16900 SDCo 92065 1171-J2
HANDRICH CT
11900 SD 92131 1210-A4
HANDRICH DR
11700 SD 92131 1210-A4
HANES PL
100 VSTA 92084 1087-H6
HANEY ST
1100 ELCJ 92020 1251-G7
HANFORD CT
- CHV 91913 1311-C7
HANFORD DR
1800 SD 92111 1269-A1
2100 SD 92111 1249-A7
HANFORD GN
400 ESCN 92027 1110-D7
HANFORD PL
2000 SD 92111 1249-A7
HANIMAN DR
8600 SD 92105 1290-A1
HANNA ST
5400 SD 92105 1290-B1
HANNALEI DR
100 SDCo 92083 1108-A2
HANNALEI LN
400 SDCo 92083 1108-A2
HANNALEI PL
300 SDCo 92083 1108-A3
HANNIBAL PL
3900 SD 92115 1270-E5
HANNIGANS WY
500 SMCS 92069 1109-C7
HANNON CT
6200 SD 92117 1248-J1
HANOVER PL
1100 SDCo 91901 1253-H2
HANOVER ST
700 SD 92114 1290-B3
HANSEL DR
900 SD 92154 1350-A2
HANSOM LN
10800 SDCo 91978 1271-G7
HANSON LN
- ELCJ 92021 1252-C2
100 SDCo 92065 1173-A1
400 SDCo 92065 1172-F1
HANSON WY
1200 SDCo 92065 1172-F1

STREET
Block City ZIP Pg-Grid
HAPPINESS WY
800 CRLB 92009 1126-H4
HAPPY LN
10300 SNTE 92071 1231-E6
HAPPY WY N
8500 SDCo 92021 1232-D7
HAPPY WY S
8400 SDCo 92021 1232-D7
HAPPY HILL DR
1100 SDCo 92084 1108-C1
HAPPY HOLLOW
- SDCo 92061 1050-H3
HAPPY LILAC TR
28400 SDCo 92026 1089-D2
HARBIN PL
10300 SNTE 92071 1231-F3
HARBINSON AV
4200 LMSA 91941 1270-F4
4800 SD 92115 1270-F4
HARBISON AV
- NATC 91950 1290-B6
- SD 92114 1290-B6
1200 NATC 91950 1310-C1
HARBISON PL
800 NATC 91950 1290-C7
HARBISON WY
3100 NATC 91950 1290-C7
HARBISON CANYON RD
100 SDCo 91901 1233-D7
100 SDCo 92019 1233-D7
100 SDCo 92019 1253-B5
HARBOR DR
- ImCo 92274 410-H7
300 SD 92101 1289-A4
800 SMCS 92069 1128-F2
1100 SD 92113 1289-C6
1200 OCN 92054 1085-J6
1200 SDCo 92055 1085-J6
1500 VSTA 92083 1107-H5
1600 NATC 91950 1309-G1
2200 NATC 92136 1309-G1
2700 SD 92136 1289-C6
3500 SD 92136 1309-G1
4000 CRLB 92008 1106-F7
N HARBOR DR
500 SD 92101 1288-J3
3700 SD 92133 1288-E1
3700 SD 92140 1288-E1
4700 SD 92106 1288-E1
W HARBOR DR
500 SD 92101 1289-A4
500 SD 92101 1288-J4
HARBOR DR N
400 OCN 92054 1085-H5
HARBOR DR S
1200 OCN 92054 1085-J6
HARBOR LN
500 SD 92101 1288-J4
HARBOR RD
- SDCo 92055 1085-H4
HARBOR CREST WY
3600 OCN 92056 1107-C3
HARBOR ISLAND DR
800 SD 92101 1288-E2
HARBOR POINT RD
800 CRLB 92009 1126-J5
800 CRLB 92009 1127-A5
HARBOR VIEW DR
900 SD 92106 1288-A3
HARBOR VIEW LN
1100 CRLB 92008 1106-G6
HARBOR VIEW PL
800 SD 92106 1288-A3
HARBOR VIEW WY
3600 OCN 92056 1107-C3
HARBOUR HEIGHTS CT
5200 SD 92109 1248-A4
HARBOUR HEIGHTS RD
2100 SD 92109 1248-A4
HARBOUR TOWN PL
- CHV 91915 1311-G7
HARCOURT DR
2300 SD 92123 1249-F6
HARDELL LN
400 SDCo 92084 1088-E5
HARDIN DR
1100 ELCJ 92020 1251-E7
1200 ELCJ 92020 1271-E1
HARDING AV
1100 NATC 91950 1309-H2
3700 SD 92113 1289-G4
HARDING ST
100 OCN 92057 1067-B6
600 ESCN 92027 1130-A1
700 ESCN 92027 1110-A7
800 CRLB 92008 1106-E5
HARDING WY
2800 NATC 91950 1309-H4
HARD SCRAMBLE TR
7200 SDCo 92036 1138-B6
HARDSHIP DR
15700 SDCo 92065 1171-H4
HARDY AV
5500 SD 92115 1270-B2
HARDY DR
2400 LMGR 91945 1270-H7
HARDY RD
2500 ImCo 92243 430-L6
HARJOAN AV
8600 SD 92123 1249-C6
HARLAN CIR
900 SD 92114 1290-G2
HARLAN CT
- CHV 91911 1330-H2
HARLAN PL
7500 SD 92114 1290-G2
HARLINGTON DR
8700 SD 92126 1209-C4
HARLOW TER
8400 SD 92126 1209-B1
HARMARSH ST
7900 SD 92123 1249-B5
HARMONY LN
3400 SDCo 91977 1271-E6
5000 LMSA 91941 1271-B1
HARMONY PL
11300 SDCo 92026 1089-H7
HARMONY WY
- VSTA 92083 1107-G5
HARMONY GROVE RD
1800 ESCN 92029 1129-E4
2300 SDCo 92029 1129-D6
7800 SDCo 92029 1149-A1
9200 SDCo 92029 1148-J2
HARNESS PT
11800 SD 92128 1190-B7
HARNESS ST
8500 SDCo 91977 1290-J2
8600 SDCo 91977 1291-A2

STREET
Block City ZIP Pg-Grid
HARNEY ST
3800 SD 92110 1268-F5
4100 SD 92103 1268-G4
HAROL ST
1300 ELCJ 92020 1271-E1
HAROLD PL
- CHV 91914 1311-G4
HAROLD RD
1700 ESCN 92026 1109-D5
HARPER RD
- ImCo 92283 432-D5
1200 SDCo 92065 1152-G3
HARPER FIRE RD
- SDCo 91916 (1196-H6 See Page 1176)
- SDCo 91916 (1197-B5 See Page 1176)
- SDCo 92036 (1196-H6 See Page 1176)
- SDCo 92036 (1197-B5 See Page 1176)
HARPER RANCH RD
2800 SDCo 91935 1293-G3
HARPS CT
6000 SD 92114 1290-C5
HARRIER CT
1600 CRLB 92009 1127-D6
HARRIET ST
2700 OCN 92056 1087-D7
HARRIGAN RD
1000 ImCo 92243 431-A7
HARRIS AV
700 SD 92154 1330-B7
HARRIS DR
- SDCo 92055 1067-A1
100 SDCo 92028 1028-A2
2900 SDCo 92084 1067-H7
HARRIS RD
600 ImCo 92251 431-B3
1000 ImCo 92250 431-D3
HARRIS ST
3200 LMGR 91945 1270-F6
3600 LMSA 91941 1270-F5
HARRIS TR
38300 SDCo 92028 997-D3
HARRISBURG DR
300 ENCT 92024 1147-G7
HARRISON AV
1700 NATC 91950 1309-G3
1800 SD 92113 1289-D4
HARRISON ST
100 OCN 92057 1067-B6
4000 CRLB 92008 1106-F7
HARRISON PARK RD
16800 SDCo 92036 1156-F6
HARRIS PLANT RD
8900 SD 92145 1229-E4
HARRIS RANCH RD
600 SDCo 91963 429-L10
600 SDCo 91963 (1316-H7 See Page 1296)
HARRITT RD
9300 SDCo 92040 1232-F4
HARROW LN
15300 PWY 92064 1170-G5
HARROW PL
14200 PWY 92064 1170-G5
HARRY ST
900 ELCJ 92020 1251-H7
HART DR
100 ELCJ 92021 1251-F3
100 SDCo 92021 1251-F3
4800 SD 92116 1269-H3
HART RD
- ImCo 92227 431-D2
HARTFELL RD
30000 SDCo 91906 (1297-G5 See Page 1296)
HARTFIELD AV
13000 SD 92130 1188-A4
HARTFORD CT
2800 SD 92117 1248-F7
HARTFORD PL
4500 CRLB 92008 1107-B4
HARTFORD ST
600 CHV 91913 1311-E3
2100 SD 92110 1268-E1
2200 SD 92110 1248-F7
HARTLAND CIR
9600 SNTE 92071 1231-B4
HARTLEY DR
6300 SD 92037 1247-G2
HARTLEY RD
10800 SNTE 92071 1231-F5
HARTLEY ST
4500 SD 92102 1289-J3
HARTLEY HILL RD
24100 SDCo 91963 (1315-J5 See Page 1294)
25200 SDCo 91963 (1316-A5 See Page 1296)
HARTMAN DR
1300 ELCJ 92020 1251-D4
HARTMAN WY
3000 SD 92117 1248-C3
HARTON PL
8200 SD 92123 1269-B1
HARTON RD
1900 SD 92123 1269-B1
HARTSHORN RD
- ImCo 92250 431-D4
HARTWELL CT
1600 SD 92114 1290-D6
HART WRIGHT RD
1700 SDCo 92084 1108-C3
HARTZEL DR
3400 SDCo 91977 1271-A5
8700 SDCo 91941 1271-A5
HARTZEL CREST DR
3500 SDCo 91977 1271-A5
HARVALA ST
6800 SD 92115 1270-E4
HARVARD AV
4300 LMSA 91941 1270-F4
HARVARD DR
3600 OCN 92056 1107-A2
HARVARD ST
1600 CHV 91913 1311-C5
HARVEST CRES
14200 PWY 92064 1170-H6
HARVEST CT
5200 OCN 92057 1067-A3
14300 PWY 92064 1170-H6
HARVEST LN
1100 VSTA 92083 1108-A5
HARVEST RD
600 SDCo 92154 1331-J7
600 SD 92154 1351-J1
1600 SD 92154 1351-J3

STREET
Block City ZIP Pg-Grid
HARVEST DANCE WY
11000 SD 92127 1169-H1
HARVEST POINT WY
- SDCo 92065 1173-D1
HARVEST RUN DR
- SD 92130 1208-D2
HARVEST VIEW WY
- SD 92128 1189-G6
HARVEY RD
4600 SD 92116 1269-B3
HARVEY HOMESTEAD RD
- SDCo 91935 (1314-G3 See Page 1294)
HARWELL DR
8400 SD 92119 1250-J4
HARWICH DR
1000 SMCS 92069 1109-C6
3400 CRLB 92008 1107-A3
HARWICK LN
12800 SD 92130 1188-C5
HARWICK PL
4900 SD 92130 1188-C5
HARWOOD ST
800 SD 92154 1329-J7
900 SD 92154 1349-J1
HASBROOK RD
10800 SD 92131 1209-H1
HASKELL RD
1800 ImCo 92243 6499-D6
1900 ImCo 92273 431-A5
HASKELL ST
2600 SD 92109 1248-C4
HASTAIN RD
- ImCo 92227 411-D11
HASTINGS CT
700 SMCS 92069 1109-C6
HASTINGS DR
3500 CRLB 92008 1107-A3
HASTINGS RD
5000 SD 92116 1269-H2
HASTY ST
3300 SD 92115 1270-D6
HATACA RD
3100 CRLB 92009 1147-H1
HATCHER LN
9000 SD 92126 1209-D2
HATCREEK CT
1200 VSTA 92083 1107-J4
HAT CREEK RD
15000 PWY 92064 1170-G7
HATFIELD CIR
3500 OCN 92056 1107-E2
HATFIELD LN
500 SDCo 92065 1153-A5
HATFIELD RD
- ImCo 92233 411-B10
- SDCo 91917 (1314-C7 See Page 1294)
HATHAWAY ST
4000 SD 92111 1248-J3
HATHERLY ST
500 VSTA 92083 1087-D7
HATTERAS AV
3500 SD 92117 1248-D2
HATTON ST
3700 SD 92111 1248-J3
3900 SD 92111 1249-A3
HAUBERK CT
300 SDCo 92004 1058-G7
HAUBERK DR
1800 SDCo 92004 1058-G7
HAUSER ST
6400 SD 92114 1290-D6
HAVASUPAI AV
2600 SD 92117 1248-B1
2900 SD 92117 1228-C7
HAVEN PL
600 ESCN 92027 1130-E1
HAVEN ST
8000 LMGR 91945 1270-H7
HAVEN BROOK PL
10600 SD 92130 1208-E2
HAVENCREST DR
2500 SDCo 92028 1027-J7
2600 SDCo 92028 1047-J1
HAVENHURST DR
900 SD 92037 1247-F2
HAVENHURST PL
6100 SD 92037 1247-F3
HAVENHURST PT
800 SD 92037 1247-F2
HAVENRIDGE WY
5500 SD 92130 1208-E2
HAVENS RD
- ImCo 92243 431-A5
- ImCo 92273 431-A5
HAVENS POINT PL
1700 CRLB 92008 1106-H6
HAVENVIEW LN
- OCN 92056 1107-D2
HAVENWOOD AV
4800 SD 92120 1250-A5
HAVENWOOD DR
1500 OCN 92056 1087-D4
HAVERFIELD WY
11200 SD 92126 1209-D2
HAVERFORD RD
300 SDCo 92065 1152-F3
HAVERFORD RD Rt#-78
1200 SDCo 92065 1152-F3
HAVERHILL RD
700 ELCJ 92020 1251-B4
HAVERHILL ST
3600 CRLB 92008 1106-J4
HAVETEUR WY
8700 SD 92123 1249-D4
HAWAII AV
700 SD 92154 1330-D7
1000 SD 92154 1350-D1
HAWAII PL
900 ESCN 92026 1109-F4
HAWICK DR
13900 SDCo 92021 1232-E7
HAWICK TER
13900 SDCo 92021 1232-F7
HAWK LN
1300 ELCJ 92020 1251-D2
HAWK ST
- ImCo 92249 6560-B7
3100 SD 92103 1268-J4
HAWKE BAY CT
2000 SD 92105 1290-C1
HAWKEYE WY
11500 SD 92126 1209-E1
HAWKEYE DOWNS WY
19600 SDCo 92065 1151-J2
19600 SDCo 92065 1152-A2
HAWKHILL RD
29900 SDCo 92084 1068-F5

SAN DIEGO CO.
INDEX

HAWKINS WY SAN DIEGO CO. STREET INDEX HIGHWAY Rt#-78 6590

STREET
Block City ZIP Pg-Grid

HAWKINS WY
2000 SDCo 91977 1291-A1
HAWK RIDGE PL
1600 ESCN 92027 1130-C1
HAWKSBURY LN
15400 SDCo 92082 1070-J6
HAWKS PEAK WY
7500 SD 92126 1209-A3
HAWKS VIEW WY
- SDCo 92028 1028-D3
HAWK VIEW DR
1600 ENCT 92024 1147-D2
HAWLEY AV
9000 LMSA 91941 1271-A1
HAWLEY BLVD
4500 SD 92116 1269-F3
HAWLEY CT
15600 SDCo 92021 1233-C3
HAWLEY DR
2000 VSTA 92084 1087-J2
HAWLEY PL
15500 SDCo 92021 1233-B3
HAWLEY RD
9700 SDCo 92021 1233-C1
10500 SDCo 92021 1213-C7
HAWLEY CREEK
- SDCo 92021 1233-C3
HAWORTH ST
6900 SD 92122 1228-F5
HAWTHORN GN
2400 ESCN 92027 1110-D7
HAWTHORN ST
100 SD 92101 1288-J1
500 SD 92101 1289-A1
2800 SD 92104 1289-D1
HAWTHORNE AV
400 ELCJ 92020 1251-D6
900 CRLB 92009 1127-A5
HAWTHORNE CIR
200 VSTA 92083 1108-A2
HAWTHORNE CT
900 SMCS 92069 1128-B2
HAWTHORNE DR
500 SDCo 92036 1156-E2
HAWTHORNE ST
100 SDCo 92028 1027-F2
W HAWTHORNE ST
100 SDCo 92028 1027-F2
HAXTON PL
13200 SD 92130 1188-B4
HAY CT
12500 SDCo 92021 1232-B7
HAYA ST
100 SD 92102 1289-J4
HAYDEN DR
100 ESCN 92027 1110-E7
HAYDEN LN
1200 ELCJ 92021 1252-B3
HAYDEN WY
2100 SD 92110 1268-G5
HAYDN DR
1600 ENCT 92007 1167-C2
HAYES AV
900 SD 92103 1269-B5
HAYES ST
100 OCN 92054 1106-A2
8600 LMSA 91941 1270-J2
8600 LMSA 91941 1271-A2
HAYFORD RD
1500 CHV 91913 1311-D7
HAYFORD WY
- SD 92130 1188-C4
HAYFORK PL
1400 CHV 91913 1331-B2
HAYMAR DR
2700 CRLB 92008 1106-H2
3500 OCN 92008 1106-H2
3500 OCN 92008 1107-A2
3500 OCN 92056 1107-A2
HAYMARKET RD
1800 ENCT 92024 1147-A2
HAYUCO PZ
1000 CHV 91910 1311-C2
HAYVIN RD
31700 SDCo 92082 1050-J7
HAYWARD CT
2100 SD 92139 1290-E7
HAYWARD PL
500 ESCN 92027 1110-D6
HAYWARD WY
6400 SD 92139 1290-E7
HAZARD WY
9300 SD 92123 1229-E7
HAZARD CENTER DR
7600 SD 92108 1269-A2
HAZEL LN
9700 SDCo 92029 1149-E2
HAZEL ST
3900 SD 92105 1289-G2
HAZEL WY
200 OCN 92057 1086-H5
HAZELDON DR
8800 SNTE 92071 1231-B7
HAZELHURST CT
3600 SDCo 91902 1310-J2
HAZELHURST PL
3600 SDCo 91902 1310-J1
HAZELNUT CT
1900 SMCS 92069 1128-B2
HAZELWOOD PL
1900 SD 92105 1289-J1
HAZEN DR
900 SMCS 92069 1109-B6
HAZY GLEN CT
800 CHV 91910 1311-B5
HAZY MEADOW LN
15600 SDCo 92040 1212-J6
HEADQUARTERS PT
5100 SD 92121 1208-D5
HEALD LN
300 SDCo 92028 1027-H3
HEALTHCARE DR
8800 LMSA 91942 1251-A7
8900 LMSA 91942 1271-A1
HEALTH CTR DR
2700 SD 92123 1249-B6
HEALTH SCIENCES DR
- SD 92037 1228-C2
HEALY CT
10600 SNTE 92071 1231-E2
HEALY ST
10400 SNTE 92071 1231-E2
HEALY WY
10600 SNTE 92071 1231-E2
E HEANEY CIR
9300 SNTE 92071 1231-B5
W HEANEY CIR
9300 SNTE 92071 1231-A5

HEARD LN
700 SDCo 92065 1152-H6
HEARTLAND LN
1700 SDCo 92019 1252-B6
HEARTWOOD CT
- SD 92131 1209-G2
HEARTWOOD WY
- SD 92131 1209-G2
HEATER CT
10500 SD 92121 1208-H4
HEATH CT
6700 CRLB 92009 1126-J5
HEATH DR
14900 PWY 92064 1170-C7
HEATHBROOK CT
- SD 92154 1330-H7
HEATH CLIFF CT
8500 SDCo 92021 1252-E1
HEATHER CT
500 CHV 91911 1330-H3
HEATHER DR
1000 VSTA 92084 1087-J5
1000 VSTA 92084 1088-A5
HEATHER LN
2100 DLMR 92014 1187-F3
3100 SDCo 91901 1234-D4
3300 OCN 92056 1107-B1
HEATHER PL
2500 ESCN 92027 1110-E7
HEATHER ST
3000 SD 92105 1269-H6
HEATHER WY
800 CRLB 92009 1127-A6
10600 SD 92126 1209-E3
HEATHER CANYON CT
3800 SDCo 91902 1311-A3
HEATHERDALE ST
9100 SNTE 92071 1231-G5
HEATHER FIELD LN
12500 SD 92128 1150-B6
HEATHER GLEN WY
14800 SD 92128 1170-B7
14800 SD 92128 1190-B1
HEATHERLY DR
- SD 92129 1188-J3
HEATHERRIDGE CT
3300 SMCS 92069 1108-C6
HEATHERRIDGE RD
500 SMCS 92069 1108-C6
HEATHERS COUNTRY LN
- SDCo 92066 (1299-C2 See Page 1298)
HEATHERTON CT
12500 SD 92128 1189-J6
HEATHER VIEW LN
28600 SDCo 92026 1089-E2
HEATHERWOOD CT
2400 ESCN 92026 1109-H3
HEATHERWOOD DR
3400 SDCo 92019 1272-C6
5200 OCN 92056 1087-D2
HEATHERWOOD LN
800 VSTA 92083 1108-A4
HEATHERWOOD HOLLOW CT
- SD 92128 1190-A7
HEAVEN DR
- SDCo 92028 998-G5
HEAVENLY PL
31600 SDCo 92003 1067-H2
HEAVENLY WY
9900 SDCo 91941 1271-D2
HEBER RD
200 ImCo 92243 431-B7
300 ImCo 92249 6560-F7
900 ImCo 92249 431-D6
900 ImCo 92250 431-D6
HEBER RD Rt#-86
- ImCo 92243 431-C7
- ImCo 92249 431-C7
- ImCo 92249 6560-D7
HEBER ST
- SDCo 91934 (1321-G5 See Page 1300)
1000 ImCo 92249 6560-B7
HEBRIDES CIR
10400 SD 92126 1209-C4
HEBRIDES DR
8500 SD 92126 1209-C4
HECTOR AV
9100 SD 92123 1249-E6
HECTOR PL
3200 SDCo 91935 1273-B7
HEDGE WY
300 CHV 91910 1310-A6
HEDGEROW LN
- SD 92126 1209-E3
HEDGES WY
6600 SD 92139 1310-F2
HEDGETREE CT
12600 PWY 92064 1190-C1
HEDGEWOOD RW
5900 SD 92037 1248-A1
HEDIONDA AV
1300 VSTA 92083 1107-F3
1400 SDCo 92083 1107-F3
HEDIONDA CT
4400 SD 92117 1248-D2
HEDY DR
16100 SDCo 92065 1171-F4
HEFFERNAN AV
1000 ImCo 92249 431-C7
1100 ImCo 92249 6560-C7
HEFFNER LN
9900 SD 92126 1209-A6
HEGG ST
4000 SD 92115 1270-C5
HEIDE LN
3200 SDCo 91935 1273-A7
3200 SDCo 91935 1293-A1
HEIDEN CT
500 SMCS 92069 1109-A3
HEIDI CIR
1400 VSTA 92084 1087-H4
HEIDI ST
5400 LMSA 91942 1270-H1
5500 LMSA 91942 1250-H7
HEIGHTS LN
2600 SDCo 91977 1271-E7
HEIGHTS RD
- SDCo 92028 997-E3
HEIL AV
100 ELCN 92243 6499-E7
100 ELCN 92243 6500-A7
HEIL CT
100 ELCN 92243 6499-J7
HEINRICH HERTZ DR
9400 SD 92154 1352-A3

HEISE PARK RD
- SDCo 92036 1156-C5
HEITING CT
9300 SNTE 92071 1230-J6
HELEN CIR
1000 NATC 91950 1310-B1
HELEN DR
600 OCN 92057 1067-B5
39700 SDCo 92028 997-A2
HELEN RD
2300 SDCo 92028 997-A1
HELEN WY
100 ESCN 92025 1130-B5
100 SDCo 92025 1130-B5
HELENA PL
5600 SD 92120 1250-C7
5600 SD 92120 1270-C1
HELENA ST
4000 SDCo 92028 1028-F4
HELENJAMES AV
8800 SD 92126 1209-D5
HELEN PARK LN
14700 PWY 92064 1190-E1
HELIOTROPE DR
- SDCo 92036 1136-E7
- SDCo 92036 1156-E1
HELIX AV
800 CHV 91911 1330-E2
N HELIX AV
100 SOLB 92075 1167-E7
S HELIX AV
200 SOLB 92075 1187-E1
HELIX CT
8700 SDCo 91977 1291-A2
HELIX LN
3900 SDCo 91977 1271-B5
HELIX PL
1800 SDCo 91977 1291-A1
HELIX ST
1200 SDCo 91977 1291-B1
2500 SDCo 91977 1271-B5
HELIX TER
5000 SDCo 91941 1271-D1
HELIX WY
400 OCN 92057 1086-J4
1400 CHV 91911 1330-F4
HELIX DEL SUR
4200 SDCo 91941 1271-E4
HELIX GLEN DR
4700 LMSA 91941 1271-B3
HELIX HILLS TER
4900 LMSA 91941 1271-C2
HELIX MONT CIR
9900 SDCo 91941 1271-D4
HELIX MONT DR
9900 SDCo 91941 1271-D4
HELIX VIEW DR
1200 ELCJ 92020 1251-D7
HELIX VILLAGE CT
1200 ELCJ 92020 1251-D7
HELIX VILLAGE DR
1000 ELCJ 92020 1251-D7
HELIX VISTA DR
8700 SDCo 91977 1291-A2
HELL CREEK RD
27800 SDCo 92082 1091-H3
HELLERS BEND
3800 SDCo 92028 1047-H4
HELM ST
8000 SD 92114 1290-G2
HELMER LN
11800 SD 92131 1210-A3
HELVETIA DR
2600 SDCo 92036 1136-D7
HELVETIA ST
30200 SDCo 92070 1135-B3
HEMINGWAY AV
7800 SD 92120 1250-D3
HEMINGWAY CT
1800 ESCN 92027 1130-D2
6900 SD 92120 1250-E4
HEMINGWAY DR
6600 SD 92120 1250-D3
HEMLOCK AV
100 CRLB 92008 1106-E7
300 ESCN 92026 1129-H1
700 IMPB 91932 1349-G2
2100 SD 92154 1350-B2
HEMLOCK ST
3600 SD 92113 1289-G5
HEMLOCK WY
200 OCN 92057 1086-J2
HEMPDEN CT
1300 ELCJ 92020 1251-D5
HEMPHILL CT
10300 SD 92126 1209-B5
HEMPHILL DR
7700 SD 92126 1209-A5
HEMPHILL PL
10300 SD 92126 1209-B5
HEMPHILL WY
10300 SD 92126 1209-A5
N HEMPSTEAD CIR
4000 SD 92116 1269-G2
S HEMPSTEAD CIR
4000 SD 92116 1269-G2
HENDERSON AV
1200 SD 92140 1268-E7
HENDERSON CT
1700 VSTA 92083 1087-G3
HENDERSON DR
- SDCo 92055 1067-A1
6000 LMSA 91942 1251-C6
6300 ELCJ 92020 1251-C6
HENDERSON RD
- SDCo 92059 1029-J4
HENDERSON CANYON RD
400 SDCo 92004 1058-H3
400 SDCo 92004 (1059-D3 See Page 1058)
HENDRICKS CT
10100 SD 92126 1209-A5
HENDRICKS DR
7800 SD 92126 1209-A5
HENDRIX PL
1500 CHV 91911 1330-J3
HENIE HILLS DR
1900 OCN 92056 1086-G7
HENLEY DR
5800 SD 92120 1250-B7
HENNA PL
1800 SDCo 92019 1272-D2
HENRIETTA CT
200 SD 92114 1290-E4
HENRY LN
100 CHV 91911 1330-D3
HENRY ST
3900 SD 92103 1268-G6

HENRY ST
3900 SD 92110 1268-G6
HENRY SILVERS PL
2400 SDCo 92036 1136-B6
HENSHAW CT
- SDCo 92055 1086-A2
HENSHAW RD
- SDCo 92070 409-J7
1300 OCN 92056 1087-D1
HENSLEY ST
100 SD 92102 1289-D4
200 SD 92113 1289-D4
S HENSLEY ST
100 SD 92113 1289-D4
HENSON
500 SMCS 92069 1108-G6
HENSON ST
100 SD 92114 1290-D4
HENSON HEIGHTS DR
500 SMCS 92069 1108-G6
HEPBURN CT
3200 SD 92124 1249-G4
HERALDRY ST
8800 SD 92123 1249-D4
HERALDS WY
1500 SDCo 92065 1172-J1
HERBERT PL
1600 SD 92103 1269-C6
HERBERT ST
500 ELCJ 92020 1251-G7
700 OCN 92057 1067-B5
3400 SD 92103 1269-C6
HERBERT YORK LN
- SD 92093 1228-A3
HERBY WY
1200 OCN 92054 1106-C2
HERCULES ST
8300 LMSA 91942 1270-J1
HERDER LN
700 ENCT 92024 1147-E7
HERDFIELD WY
10200 SDCo 91977 1271-E5
HEREFORD DR
25100 SDCo 92065 1173-H4
HERENCIA DR
12800 PWY 92064 1190-D5
HERITAGE CT
1300 ESCN 92027 1130-B2
HERITAGE LN
- ENCT 92024 1147-E5
900 VSTA 92083 1108-A5
HERITAGE RD
900 CHV 91913 1331-B6
900 CHV 92154 1331-C7
900 SD 92154 1331-C7
900 SD 92154 1351-C1
5100 CHV 91911 1331-B6
HERITAGE ST
100 OCN 92054 1086-F3
HERITAGE WY
14600 PWY 92064 1190-B1
HERITAGE GLEN CT
12700 SD 92130 1188-C6
HERITAGE GLEN LN
4400 SD 92130 1188-B6
HERITAGE PARK RW
2400 SD 92103 1268-F5
HERMAN AV
3100 SD 92104 1269-E6
HERMANA CT
1300 VSTA 92084 1088-A3
HERMANOS CT
10500 SD 92124 1229-H7
HERMANOS RD
10400 SD 92124 1229-H7
HERMES AV
500 ENCT 92024 1147-A3
HERMES CT
1300 SD 92154 1349-J2
HERMES LN
1400 SD 92154 1349-J2
HERMES ST
1500 SD 92154 1349-J2
1700 SD 92154 1350-A2
HERMOSA PL
20600 SDCo 92029 1149-E4
HERMOSA WY
4100 SD 92103 1268-H4
10100 SDCo 91941 1271-D2
HERMOSILLO GN
1100 ESCN 92026 1109-E5
HERMOSILLO WY
14000 PWY 92064 1190-E2
HERMOSITA DR
1200 SDCo 92069 1128-B4
HERNANDEZ ST
800 SOLB 92075 1187-G1
HERON AV
1300 ELCJ 92020 1251-D3
HERON DR
1000 VSTA 92083 1108-A6
HERRERA CT
1500 SD 92114 1290-E5
HERRICK ST
6500 SD 92114 1290-D3
HERRING CV
11300 SD 92126 1209-B2
HERSCHEL AV
7400 SD 92037 1227-F6
HERSHEY ST
3400 SD 92115 1270-D6
HESBY CT
8700 SD 92129 1189-C1
HESMAY DR
100 SDCo 92083 1108-B3
HESS DR
10700 SDCo 91941 1271-F2
HESTA ST
15000 PWY 92064 1170-C7
HESTIA WY
- ENCT 92024 1147-B5
HESTON PL
13300 SD 92130 1188-A4
HETZEL RD
2200 ImCo 92251 430-L5
HEWES SQ
12100 SD 92128 1190-B4
HEWLETT DR
5200 SD 92115 1270-A1
HEYNEMAN HOLLOW
2400 SDCo 92028 1028-B3
HEYWOOD CIR
- SDCo 92055 1067-A1
HIALEAH LN
2400 SDCo 91901 1234-C6
HIAWATHA CT
3800 SD 92117 1248-D3
HIAWATHA GN
1300 ESCN 92027 1130-B2

HIAWATHA WY
3800 SD 92117 1248-E3
HIBBERT ST
9900 SD 92131 1209-F3
HIBISCUS AV
2300 VSTA 92083 1108-B5
2400 SDCo 92083 1108-B5
13900 PWY 92064 1190-F3
HIBISCUS CIR
3700 CRLB 92008 1106-F6
HIBISCUS CT
500 CHV 91911 1330-H3
HIBISCUS DR
- SD 92109 1248-C6
6700 LMGR 91945 1270-E7
HIBISCUS GN
600 ESCN 92025 1150-C3
HICKMAN PL
3200 SDCo 92036 1156-D1
HICKMAN FIELD DR
5100 SD 92111 1228-J7
HICKORY CT
700 IMPB 91932 1349-G1
900 CRLB 92009 1127-A5
12600 PWY 92064 1190-D3
HICKORY RD
200 SMCS 92069 1108-H5
HICKORY ST
100 ESCN 92025 1129-J1
1900 SD 92103 1268-G4
13900 PWY 92064 1190-D3
S HICKORY ST
100 ESCN 92025 1130-A2
HICKORY TER
400 CHV 91902 1311-B4
HICKORY WY
3700 OCN 92057 1086-H4
HICKORYHILL DR
200 ENCT 92024 1147-F7
300 ENCT 92024 1167-F1
HICKS ST
1600 OCN 92054 1106-D2
HICOCK ST
3900 SD 92110 1268-E4
HIDALGO AV
4500 SD 92117 1248-C1
HIDDEN LN
800 SDCo 92036 1138-B6
HIDDEN BAY CT
2100 SD 92105 1290-C1
HIDDEN CANYON RD
- SDCo 92024 1128-D7
- SDCo 92024 1148-D1
- SDCo 92078 1148-D1
- SMCS 92024 1128-D7
- SMCS 92024 1148-D1
- SMCS 92078 1148-D1
HIDDEN CANYON WY
500 OCN 92054 1086-D7
HIDDEN CREEK LN
3000 SDCo 92026 1109-J2
HIDDEN CREST DR
1900 SDCo 92019 1272-C1
HIDDEN DUNE CT
4900 SD 92130 1188-C5
HIDDEN ESTATES LN
- ESCN 92027 1110-F7
- ESCN 92027 1130-F1
HIDDEN GLEN DR
- SDCo 91901 1254-F7
HIDDEN GLEN RD
19500 SDCo 91901 1254-G7
HIDDEN HAVEN
3100 SDCo 92084 1068-A6
HIDDEN HILLS LN
400 SDCo 92029 1149-J1
400 SDCo 92029 1150-A1
HIDDEN HOLLOW CT
1300 SDCo 92019 1272-C1
HIDDEN KNOLL CT
1300 SDCo 92019 1272-C1
HIDDEN KNOLL RD
14600 PWY 92064 1190-H3
HIDDEN LAKE LN
300 SDCo 92084 1087-H1
HIDDEN MEADOWS RD
10100 SDCo 92026 1089-E4
HIDDEN MESA CT
1400 SDCo 92019 1272-B1
HIDDEN MESA RD
1500 SDCo 92019 1272-A1
HIDDEN MESA TR
1400 SDCo 92019 1272-C1
HIDDEN MESA VIEW DR
1400 SDCo 92019 1272-B1
HIDDEN MOUNTAIN DR
1200 SDCo 92019 1272-C1
HIDDEN OAKS CT
1800 SDCo 92019 1272-B1
HIDDEN OAKS LN
- ESCN 92027 1130-H3
HIDDEN OAKS RD
- SDCo 92028 999-J5
- SDCo 92059 999-J5
HIDDEN OAKS TR
1200 SDCo 92084 1108-D2
HIDDEN PALM CT
1800 SDCo 92019 1272-B1
HIDDEN PINES LN
400 DLMR 92014 1187-G7
HIDDEN PINES RD
300 DLMR 92014 1187-G7
HIDDEN PLATEAU CT
1300 SDCo 92019 1272-C1
HIDDEN RIDGE CT
- ENCT 92024 1147-E6
HIDDEN RIDGE RD
3600 SDCo 91935 1272-J6
3700 SDCo 91935 1273-A5
HIDDEN ROCK CT
1800 SDCo 92019 1272-B1
HIDDEN SPRINGS DR
1800 SDCo 92019 1272-C1
HIDDEN SPRINGS PL
1300 CHV 91915 1311-H6
HIDDEN SPRINGS TR
1100 SDCo 92026 1109-J2
HIDDEN TRAIL DR
3400 SDCo 91935 1273-A5
3800 SDCo 91935 1272-J5
HIDDEN TRAIL WY
14700 SDCo 91935 1273-A6
HIDDEN TRAILS RD
- ESCN 92027 1110-F6
HIDDEN VALE DR
1000 VSTA 92083 1107-H1
HIDDEN VALLEY AV
1400 CHV 91915 1311-H7

HIDDEN VALLEY CT
7700 SD 92037 1227-J6
HIDDEN VALLEY DR
15300 PWY 92064 1191-A4
HIDDEN VALLEY PL
2500 SD 92037 1227-J6
HIDDEN VALLEY RD
- CRLB 92009 1127-A3
2500 SD 92037 1227-H6
5700 CRLB 92008 1107-A7
5800 CRLB 92008 1126-J1
5800 CRLB 92008 1127-A1
6100 OCN 92028 1067-D1
HIDDEN VIEW LN
- ESCN 92027 1110-F7
- ESCN 92027 1130-F1
800 SDCo 92065 1152-G6
HIDDEN VISTA DR
400 CHV 91910 1310-F6
HIDDEN WALK LN
1400 SDCo 92028 1027-J5
HIDDEN WOOD RD
14500 SDCo 91935 1272-J5
14500 SDCo 91935 1273-A5
HIDEAWAY LN
28800 SDCo 92082 1090-C1
HIDEAWAY PL
4400 SDCo 91941 1271-D3
HIDEAWAY TER
700 VSTA 92083 1107-H1
HIDEAWAY LAKE RD
12600 SDCo 92082 1090-C1
HIDEWAY RD
- SDCo 92036 1156-E4
HIEL ST
8700 SDCo 91977 1291-A3
HIERBA DR
16900 SD 92128 1170-B2
HIERBA PL
12000 SD 92128 1170-B2
HIGA PL
12600 SD 92128 1170-C4
HIGGINS ST
900 CHV 91911 1330-J2
1300 OCN 92054 1086-B6
HIGGINS TER
12200 SDCo 92040 1232-A6
HIGH AV
7300 SD 92037 1227-F7
HIGH CT
7700 LMSA 91941 1270-G5
HIGH ST
1100 SDCo 92026 1129-F2
7500 LMGR 91945 1270-G5
7500 LMSA 91941 1270-J4
HIGH BLUFF DR
12300 SD 92130 1187-J5
HIGH COUNTRY CT
6700 SD 92120 1250-D4
HIGH COUNTRY RD
- SDCo 92065 1173-G5
HIGHCREST PL
1600 ESCN 92025 1130-B4
HIGHDALE RD
9700 SNTE 92071 1231-A4
HIGHFIELD AV
8900 LMSA 91941 1271-A2
HIGHGATE CT
5900 LMSA 91942 1250-G7
HIGHGATE LN
7700 LMSA 91942 1250-G7
HIGHGROVE DR
1500 SDCo 92027 1130-E5
HIGH HILL RD
- SDCo 92036 1176-A2
HIGH KNOLL RD
6400 SD 92111 1248-H6
HIGHLAND AV
- NATC 91950 1289-H7
300 ELCJ 92020 1251-F6
500 NATC 91950 1309-J1
800 DLMR 92014 1187-G5
2400 SD 92105 1269-H5
2400 SD 92105 1289-J1
2400 NATC 91950 1310-A3
3200 NATC 91910 1310-A3
4100 SD 92115 1269-H4
7800 LMSA 91941 1270-G3
HIGHLAND CT
900 SOLB 92075 1187-G1
3500 SD 92075 1187-G1
HIGHLAND CV
1600 SDCo 92014 1167-J7
1600 SOLB 92014 1167-J7
HIGHLAND DR
700 VSTA 92083 1087-F5
900 SOLB 92075 1187-G1
1000 SOLB 92014 1187-H1
1100 SOLB 92014 1167-J6
1200 SOLB 92075 1167-J6
1700 SDCo 92014 1167-J6
1800 SDCo 92067 1167-J6
1800 SDCo 92075 1167-J6
2200 CRLB 92008 1106-F3
3600 SDCo 92036 1156-D2
HIGHLAND PK
- SDCo 92028 1027-G6
HIGHLAND PL
300 ESCN 92027 1130-C1
HIGHLAND ST
600 ESCN 92027 1130-C2
HIGHLAND WY
2900 SDCo 91977 1271-D7
HIGHLAND CREST WY
- SDCo 92025 1151-A3
HIGHLANDER DR
- SDCo 92065 1151-G7
- SDCo 92065 1171-F1
HIGHLAND GLEN WY
4200 SDCo 91941 1271-C3
HIGHLAND HEIGHTS CT
3400 SDCo 91935 1273-C7
HIGHLAND HEIGHTS LN
1100 SDCo 92026 1109-E7
HIGHLAND HEIGHTS RD
14800 SDCo 91935 1273-B7
HIGHLAND HILLS DR
19300 SDCo 92065 1151-J2
HIGHLAND MEADOW CT
17100 SDCo 92065 1171-F1
HIGHLAND MESA DR
16000 SDCo 92025 1151-B4
16000 SDCo 92065 1151-B4
HIGHLAND OAKS CT
300 SDCo 92028 1047-F5
HIGHLAND OAKS LN
- SDCo 92028 1047-F5
HIGHLAND OAKS ST
200 SDCo 92028 1047-F5

HIGHLAND RANCH RD
14100 SD 92128 1190-A1
HIGHLANDS BLVD
2600 SDCo 91977 1271-D6
HIGHLANDS TER
13700 PWY 92064 1170-F5
HIGHLANDS RANCH CIR
17800 PWY 92064 1150-D7
HIGHLANDS RANCH PL
17900 PWY 92064 1150-E7
HIGHLANDS RANCH RD
13200 PWY 92064 1150-E7
HIGHLANDS RANCH TER
17900 PWY 92064 1150-E7
HIGHLANDS VIEW RD
1600 SDCo 91901 1234-D6
HIGHLANDS WEST DR
2000 SDCo 92029 1129-F7
HIGHLAND TRAILS DR
16500 SDCo 92065 1151-D4
HIGHLAND VALLEY CT
- SDCo 92065 1172-B3
HIGHLAND VALLEY RD
3300 SDCo 92065 1151-D4
11000 SD 92128 1150-B5
13000 SD 92025 1150-F4
13400 SDCo 92025 1150-J3
15300 SDCo 92025 1151-A3
16300 SDCo 92065 1171-D1
18500 SDCo 92065 1172-A2
HIGHLAND VIEW GN
2000 ESCN 92026 1109-B3
HIGHLINE RD Rt#-S33
- ImCo 92227 431-E4
2200 ImCo 92250 431-E4
HIGHLINE TR
100 SDCo 92021 1252-J3
HIGH MEAD CIR
2700 SDCo 92084 1067-J7
HIGH MEADOW CT
8000 SD 92119 1250-E3
HIGH MEADOW RD
12400 SDCo 92040 1212-C5
HIGH MEADOW RANCH LN
5800 SDCo 92036 1175-G1
HIGH MEADOW RANCH SPUR
6000 SDCo 92036 1175-H1
HIGH MESA CT
18200 SD 92127 1149-H7
HIGH MOUNTAIN DR
10200 SDCo 92026 1089-E5
HIGH MOUNTAIN LN
27800 SDCo 92026 1089-D5
HIGH PARK LN
9500 SD 92129 1189-E4
HIGH PINE ST
14300 PWY 92064 1190-H5
HIGHPLACE DR
5800 SD 92120 1250-C4
HIGH POINT DR
29300 SDCo 92082 1070-G7
HIGH POINT TKTR
- SDCo 92060 409-G5
- SDCo 92086 409-G5
HIGH RANCH RD
11300 SDCo 92040 1211-G6
HIGH RIDGE AV
1800 CRLB 92008 1106-H6
HIGHRIDGE DR
1400 OCN 92056 1087-D4
HIGHRIDGE RD
1500 SDCo 91977 1291-D1
7400 SNTE 92071 1230-F7
HIGH RISE WY
9200 SNTE 92071 1231-H5
HIGH SIERRA RD
14000 PWY 92064 1170-G3
HIGHSMITH LN
8800 SD 92119 1251-A4
HIGH SOCIETY WY
- SDCo 92127 1149-A7
- SDCo 92127 1169-A1
HIGH TIME RDG
- SDCo 92127 1169-A2
HIGHTOP TER
9200 SDCo 92040 1231-H5
HIGHTREE LN
7300 SD 92114 1290-G5
HIGHTREE PL
400 SD 92114 1290-G5
HIGH VALLEY RD
14200 PWY 92064 1170-G7
HIGH VIEW DR
3200 SD 92104 1289-E1
HIGHVIEW LN
2300 SDCo 91977 1291-B1
HIGH VIEW PT
2500 SDCo 91905 (1299-H4 See Page 1298)
HIGHVIEW TR
2200 SDCo 92084 1108-D2
HIGH VISTA DR
27500 SDCo 92026 1089-D5
HIGHWAY Rt#-7
- ImCo 92231 431-E7
HIGHWAY Rt#-67
10200 SDCo 92040 1232-A1
11200 SDCo 92040 1212-A7
11300 SDCo 92040 1211-G1
13000 SDCo 92040 1191-D3
13800 SDCo 92071 1191-E5
13900 SDCo 92064 1191-D3
14400 PWY 92064 1191-D1
15000 PWY 92064 1171-E5
15400 SDCo 92065 1171-F3
17600 SDCo 92065 1172-A3
HIGHWAY Rt#-75
- CORD 92113 1289-B7
1500 CORD 92118 1288-J6
1500 CORD 92118 1289-A6
1900 SD 92113 1289-C5
HIGHWAY Rt#-76
300 OCN 92057 1086-J2
300 OCN 92054 1086-J2
4700 OCN 92057 1087-A1
14800 SDCo 92061 1051-H5
19900 SDCo 92061 409-G7
20400 SDCo 92060 409-G7
20400 SDCo 92082 409-G7
23500 SDCo 92070 409-H8
23500 SDCo 92027 409-G8
HIGHWAY Rt#-78
- ImCo - 411-L7
- ImCo - 412-A3
- ImCo - 431-J1
- ImCo 92227 410-K10
- ImCo 92227 430-L1

SAN DIEGO CO.
INDEX

STREET
Block City ZIP Pg-Grid

HIGHWAY Rt#-78
- ImCo 92227 431-A1
- ImCo 92259 410-J10
- ImCo 92259 430-L1
- ImCo 92281 431-A1
- SDCo 92004 410-F10
- SDCo 92036 1138-C1
- WEST 92281 431-A1
1700 SDCo 92004 (1118-J5
See Page 1098)
1700 SDCo 92004 (1119-D5
See Page 1098)
1700 SDCo 92036 (1118-J5
See Page 1098)
3000 SDCo 92004 (1120-J1
See Page 1100)
4400 SDCo 92004 (1121-A1
See Page 1100)
35600 SDCo 92036 410-A11
35800 SDCo 92036 1136-J7
35800 SDCo 92036 1156-H1
HIGHWAY Rt#-79
21900 SDCo 92070 409-K8
21900 SDCo 92070 1135-B1
23400 SDCo 92086 409-G5
HIGHWAY Rt#-86
- BRW 92227 431-B2
- ImCo 92227 431-B2
- ImCo 92243 431-B7
- ImCo 92249 6560-F7
- ImCo 92251 431-B3
- ImCo 92259 410-H7
- ImCo 92274 410-F4
- IMP 92243 6499-F2
- IMP 92251 431-B4
- IMP 92251 6499-F1
1300 ImCo 92243 6559-J3
1500 ELCN 92243 6559-J2
HIGHWAY Rt#-94
- SDCo 91906 430-B10
- SDCo 91963 429-L10
- SDCo 91963 430-A10
- SDCo 91980 429-K10
28500 SDCo 91906 (1318-J2
See Page 1298)
32100 SDCo 91906 (1319-G1
See Page 1298)
36700 SDCo 91906 (1299-H7
See Page 1298)
37100 SDCo 91905 (1299-J6
See Page 1298)
37700 SDCo 91905 1300-C6
HIGHWAY Rt#-98
- CALX 92231 431-C7
- ImCo - 431-H6
- ImCo 92249 431-D7
- ImCo 92250 431-F7
- ImCo 92259 430-G7
- ImCo 92259 431-A8
900 ImCo 92231 431-E7
HIGHWAY Rt#-111
- BRW 92227 431-C1
- CALX 92231 431-C7
- CLPT 92233 411-C10
- ImCo - 410-J4
- ImCo 92227 411-C11
- ImCo 92227 431-C1
- ImCo 92231 431-E7
- ImCo 92233 411-B8
- ImCo 92243 6500-E7
- ImCo 92243 6560-E1
- ImCo 92249 431-C7
- ImCo 92249 6560-F4
- ImCo 92251 431-C3
- ImCo 92257 410-L5
- ImCo 92257 411-A5
- ImCo 92259 410-K5
HIGHWAY Rt#-115
- HOLT 92250 431-E5
- ImCo 92227 411-D11
- ImCo 92227 431-D1
- ImCo 92233 411-C10
2900 ImCo 92250 431-D3
HIGHWAY Rt#-186
- ImCo - 432-B6
HIGHWAY Rt#-905
1400 SD 92154 1351-J2
2100 SD 92154 1352-A3
N HWY 101 Rt#-S21
100 SOLB 92075 1167-E7
S HWY 101 Rt#-S21
100 SOLB 92075 1167-E7
100 SOLB 92075 1187-F1
200 DLMR 92014 1187-F1
200 DLMR 92075 1187-F1
1700 ENCT 92024 1167-E7
HIGHWAY TO THE STARS Rt#-S6
3400 SDCo 92060 409-G6
HIGH WINDS WY
8300 SD 92120 1250-D4
HIGHWOOD AV
7800 LMSA 91941 1270-H4
HIGHWOOD DR
8400 SD 92119 1250-J4
8600 SD 92119 1251-A3
8900 ELCJ 92020 1251-A3
HIHILL WY
300 ELCJ 92020 1251-C6
HI HOPES DR
11800 SDCo 92040 1211-H5
HIJOS WY
10900 SD 92124 1249-H1
HIKE LN
13500 SD 92129 1189-E4
HIKER HILL RD
9400 SD 92129 1189-E4
HILARY DR
4100 SDCo 91935 1274-A4
HILBERT DR
500 SDCo 92028 997-G7
600 SDCo 92028 1027-F1
HILCORTE DR
1500 SDCo 92026 1109-D6
1500 SMCS 92069 1109-D6
HILDA RD
5000 SD 92110 1268-F2
HILDALE CIR
- VSTA 92083 1087-H7
HILE LN
1900 SDCo 92028 1028-A4
HILGER ST
1200 SD 92114 1290-E2
HILL AV
400 SDCo 92028 1027-F2
HILL CT
300 SDCo 92028 1027-F5
HILL DR
100 VSTA 92083 1087-D7

HILL DR
100 VSTA 92083 1107-E1
500 SMCS 92078 1109-A7
500 SMCS 92078 1129-A1
2500 NATC 91950 1290-B7
HILL LN
9400 SDCo 91916 1236-A2
HILL ST
200 SOLB 92075 1167-E7
300 SD 92173 1350-G4
1300 ELCJ 92020 1251-D7
1400 VSTA 92083 1087-D7
1500 ESCN 92025 1129-J5
3200 SD 92106 1288-A2
4100 SD 92107 1287-J2
4100 SD 92106 1287-J2
HILLANDALE CT
6000 SD 92120 1250-C4
HILLANDALE DR
7700 SD 92120 1250-C3
HILLBRAE CT
10800 SD 92121 1208-F3
HILL COUNTRY DR
12300 PWY 92064 1190-C6
HILLCREEK LN
9600 SNTE 92071 1231-F4
HILLCREEK RD
10800 SNTE 92071 1231-F4
HILLCREEK WY
9500 SNTE 92071 1231-F4
HILLCREST
600 SDCo 92083 1107-H3
HILLCREST AV
4700 LMSA 91941 1270-J2
25700 SDCo 92026 1109-F2
HILLCREST CIR
3400 CRLB 92008 1106-G4
HILLCREST DR
100 ENCT 92024 1147-A3
1200 SDCo 91901 1234-G6
13300 SDCo 92082 1070-D2
HILLCREST LN
100 SDCo 92065 1152-J6
200 SDCo 92028 1027-G1
HILLCREST PL
800 SDCo 92028 1027-J1
900 OCN 92054 1086-C5
HILLCREST TER
- SDCo 92028 1027-H1
HILLCREST SCENIC LN
1700 ENCT 92024 1147-A2
HILLDALE RD
4000 SD 92116 1269-G2
13500 SDCo 92082 1070-E3
HILLDALE ST
2100 OCN 92054 1086-C6
HILLEARY PL
13500 PWY 92064 1190-E4
HILLEARY PARK DR
13400 PWY 92064 1190-E4
HILLERO CT
17300 SD 92128 1170-B1
HILLERY DR
8600 SD 92126 1209-D4
HILLFIELD CT
900 OCN 92054 1086-E2
HILLGREEN WY
1000 SMCS 92069 1109-B6
HILLGROVE DR
6400 SD 92120 1250-D7
HILLHAVEN DR
600 SMCS 92069 1128-B1
HILLHAVEN RD
900 SDCo 92027 1130-C4
HILLMAN WY
9100 SDCo 92040 1231-H6
HILLNDALE WY
14400 PWY 92064 1190-E1
HILLOCK PL
500 ENCT 92024 1147-H5
HILLPARK LN
800 SDCo 92028 1027-H1
HILLPOINTE RW
6000 SD 92037 1248-A1
HILLRIDGE LN
2500 SDCo 91977 1271-D7
HILLRISE RD
1900 SDCo 92028 1048-A5
S HILLS DR
- CHV 91915 1311-G7
HILLSBORO CT
2800 CRLB 92008 1107-A5
HILLSBORO ST
7000 SD 92120 1250-B5
HILLSBORO WY
- SMCS 92026 1129-E1
- SMCS 92069 1129-E1
HILLSDALE LN
1700 SDCo 92019 1272-B3
HILLSDALE RD
1500 SDCo 92019 1272-A3
HILLSIDE CT
300 VSTA 92084 1087-H5
HILLSIDE DR
800 SDCo 92036 1156-D1
1200 SDCo 92028 1047-J2
1600 SDCo 92028 1048-A2
1900 CHV 91913 1311-D3
4100 CRLB 92008 1106-H6
7000 SD 92037 1227-G6
7800 LMSA 91941 1270-H2
9200 SDCo 91977 1271-B5
9400 SDCo 92029 1129-C6
14000 SDCo 91935 1292-H2
HILLSIDE LN
1000 OCN 92054 1106-C2
3300 SDCo 92028 1047-J2
HILLSIDE PL
200 SDCo 92021 1252-H4
HILLSIDE TER
100 VSTA 92084 1087-H5
HILLSIDE WY
1300 ELCJ 92020 1251-D6
HILLSLAKE DR
2000 ELCJ 92020 1251-B2
HILLS LANE CIR
400 ELCJ 92020 1251-D5
HILLS LANE DR
400 ELCJ 92020 1251-D5
HILLSLOPE AV
8800 SDCo 91977 1290-J3
HILLSMONT DR
1400 ELCJ 92020 1251-C5
HILLSMONT PL
400 ELCJ 92020 1251-D5
HILLSTAR LN
13200 SDCo 92082 1070-C2
HILLSTONE AV
1500 ESCN 92029 1129-G7

HILLSVIEW RD
600 ELCJ 92020 1251-D4
HILLTOP CIR
15200 PWY 92064 1170-B6
HILLTOP CT
- CHV 91911 1330-E2
HILLTOP DR
- CHV 91910 1310-C4
600 CHV 91910 1330-E2
700 CHV 91911 1330-E2
800 SD 92102 1289-H3
800 SD 92102 1290-A3
1500 SDCo 92020 1271-J1
3700 LMGR 91945 1270-H5
5000 SD 92114 1290-A3
31000 SDCo 92082 1070-D2
HILL TOP LN
1600 ENCT 92024 1147-G5
HILLTOP PL
13400 SDCo 92082 1070-D2
HILLTOP TER
13400 SDCo 92082 1070-D2
HILLTOP WY
5600 SD 92182 1270-B1
HILLVALE AV
9300 SDCo 92040 1231-H5
HILLVALE LN
9300 SDCo 92040 1231-H5
HILL VALLEY DR
2900 ESCN 92029 1129-C2
2900 SDCo 92029 1129-C2
HILLVIEW CT
1300 CRLB 92008 1106-F6
HILLVIEW DR
4400 SDCo 91941 1271-E3
30800 SDCo 92082 1070-D3
HILLVIEW LN
- OCN 92056 1107-D2
HILLVIEW WY
3700 OCN 92056 1107-E3
HILLWARD ST
600 ESCN 92027 1110-C6
HILLWAY DR
400 VSTA 92084 1088-A6
HILLYER ST
- CRLB 92008 1107-B7
HILMEN DR
300 SOLB 92075 1167-F6
HILMEN PL
400 SOLB 92075 1167-F7
HILMER DR
9300 LMSA 91942 1251-B7
HILO DR
1700 VSTA 92083 1107-J3
HILO GN
1100 ESCN 92026 1109-E6
HILO WY
500 VSTA 92083 1107-J2
500 VSTA 92083 1108-A2
600 SDCo 92083 1107-J2
HILO WY W
400 SDCo 92083 1108-A2
HILTON PL
7000 SD 92111 1248-J4
HILTON HEAD CT
1600 SDCo 92019 1272-B5
HILTON HEAD GN
2200 ESCN 92026 1109-D4
HILTON HEAD PL
2400 SDCo 92019 1272-B5
HILTON HEAD RD
1800 SDCo 92019 1272-B4
2200 CHV 91915 1311-G5
HIMALAYA DR
3500 SMCS 92069 1128-B1
HIME RD
1100 ImCo 92243 431-B7
1100 ImCo 92243 6559-A7
HIMMER ST
- SDCo 92055 1085-G1
HINES ST
- SD 92106 1288-A4
HINRICHS WY
1300 ESCN 92027 1130-D2
HINSDALE ST
9700 SNTE 92071 1231-F4
HINSON PL
4600 SD 92115 1270-B3
HINTON DR
9500 SNTE 92071 1231-E4
HI PASS RD
37900 SDCo 91905 (1299-J4
See Page 1298)
37900 SDCo 91905 1300-A4
HIRAM DR
- SD 92102 1289-G4
HIRAM WY
10000 SDCo 92040 1232-C3
HIRES WY
2200 SD 92173 1350-E4
HI RIDGE RD
11500 SDCo 92040 1211-H6
HIRSCH RD
9700 SNTE 92071 1231-B4
HISER LN
8700 SNTE 92071 1230-G7
HISPANO DR
16400 SD 92128 1170-B4
HITCHING POST DR
1000 OCN 92057 1067-D7
HITCHING POST LN
1100 CHV 91915 1311-H5
HITCHING POST RD
800 VSTA 92083 1107-H2
HITCHING POST WY
- SNTE 92071 1231-C2
HITO CT
9300 SD 92129 1189-E7
HIXSON AV
1800 SD 92105 1289-H1
HOBART ST
6200 SD 92115 1270-C3
HOBBIT LN
2400 SDCo 92028 1028-B2
HOBBLE LN
10800 SDCo 91978 1271-G7
HOBBS RD
300 ImCo 92257 411-B6
HOBBS ST
- CHV 91911 1330-J3
HOBERG RD
2100 SDCo 92004 1058-F7
2100 SDCo 92004 (1078-F2
See Page 1058)
HOCHMUTH AV
- SD 92140 1268-F6
HODGES RD
1300 OCN 92056 1087-E2

HODSON ST
6000 SD 92120 1249-J7
HOFER DR
2000 SD 92154 1350-A1
HOFFING AV
8800 SD 92123 1249-C6
HOFFMAN AV
6900 LMSA 91941 1270-E5
6900 SD 92115 1270-E5
HOFFMAN LN
9800 SNTE 92071 1231-D4
HOFFMAN ST
900 SD 92116 1269-B4
HOGAN WY
2300 OCN 92056 1106-H2
HOHOKUM WY
11300 SD 92127 1149-J7
HOITT ST
300 SD 92102 1289-E4
HOLABIRD ST
6200 SD 92120 1249-J7
HOLBORN CT
10600 SNTE 92071 1231-E3
HOLBORN ST
10000 SNTE 92071 1231-E3
HOLCOMBE RD
- SD 92106 1288-A5
HOLDEN RD
8500 SNTE 92071 1231-A7
8500 SNTE 92071 1251-A1
HOLDEN TRAILS RD
10200 SDCo 92040 1231-G3
HOLDER WY
10200 SD 92124 1249-G2
HOLDERNESS LN
2600 SD 92154 1330-C7
HOLDRIDGE RD
- ImCo - 431-F7
HOLIDAY CT
3200 SD 92037 1228-A3
3700 CHV 91911 1330-E5
HOLIDAY WY
200 OCN 92057 1066-H7
HOLLAND PL
12500 PWY 92064 1190-C2
HOLLAND RD
12100 PWY 92064 1190-B2
HOLLENBECK RD
200 SMCS 92069 1108-D6
HOLLENCREST RD
3400 SMCS 92069 1108-D5
HOLLIDAY LN
- LMGR 91945 1270-F7
HOLLINS RD
1300 OCN 92056 1087-D1
HOLLISTER ST
100 CHV 91911 1330-B6
100 SD 92154 1330-B6
800 SD 92154 1350-B2
HOLLOW CT
1500 SDCo 92019 1272-A2
HOLLOW PL
1600 SDCo 92019 1272-B2
HOLLOWGLEN CT
600 OCN 92057 1067-B5
HOLLOWGLEN RD
600 OCN 92057 1067-B5
HOLLOW GLEN RD
1300 SDCo 92036 1136-C7
HOLLOW MESA CT
7900 SD 92126 1209-A2
HOLLOW TREE DR
3300 OCN 92054 1086-D3
HOLLY AV
700 IMPB 91932 1349-G2
2100 ESCN 92027 1110-C6
25800 SDCo 92026 1109-F1
HOLLY DR
4900 SD 92113 1290-A4
HOLLY LN
500 SDCo 92084 1108-D3
4100 OCN 92057 1067-G5
4100 SDCo 92003 1067-G5
HOLLY RD
100 SDCo 92021 1252-H3
2800 SDCo 91901 1234-D4
HOLLY ST
200 OCN 92054 1086-B6
HOLLY WY
3200 SDCo 91910 1310-E5
HOLLYBERRY DR
1200 SDCo 92084 1108-E1
HOLLYBERRY TR
3700 SDCo 92084 1088-F7
3700 SDCo 92084 1108-F1
HOLLY BRAE LN
3900 CRLB 92008 1106-H5
HOLLYBROOK AV
1100 CHV 91913 1311-D6
HOLLYCREST CT
6600 SD 92121 1208-G3
HOLLY FERN CT
11400 SD 92131 1209-J2
11400 SD 92131 1210-A2
HOLLY FERN WY
11300 SD 92131 1209-J2
HOLLYFIELD CT
- SD 92130 1188-A5
HOLLYHILL RD
4300 SDCo 92084 1068-H6
HOLLYHOCK AV
1300 ESCN 92027 1110-A6
HOLLYHOCK CT
800 CRLB 92009 1127-A5
HOLLYHOCK DR
9300 SDCo 91977 1271-B5
HOLLY LEAF CT
17200 SDCo 92127 1169-D2
HOLLY MEADOWS
10700 SNTE 92071 1231-E6
HOLLY OAK LN
- ESCN 92027 1130-H2
HOLLYRIDGE DR
600 ENCT 92024 1167-G1
HOLLY TREE LN
13200 PWY 92064 1190-E4
HOLLY VALLEY DR
2300 SDCo 92084 1068-E7
HOLLYWOOD DR
2500 SDCo 91906 (1297-E5
See Page 1296)
HOLLYWOOD LN
400 SD 92114 1290-C3
HOLMBY WY
9200 SNTE 92071 1231-A3
HOLMWOOD LN
300 SOLB 92075 1167-F6
HOLSOFAR RD
8400 SDCo 92021 1232-D7

HOLSTROM PL
2300 SD 92114 1290-D1
HOLT AV
100 ELCN 92243 6499-E7
100 ELCN 92243 6500-A7
HOLT AV Rt#-S32
400 HOLT 92250 431-E5
1500 ImCo 92250 431-E5
HOLT RD Rt#-S32
2300 ImCo 92250 431-E3
3900 ImCo 92227 431-E3
HOLT ST
8200 SDCo 91977 1290-J5
HOLTON RD
300 ImCo 92243 6500-H4
HOLTVILLE ST
- SDCo 91934 (1321-G5
See Page 1300)
HOLZAPPLE LN
600 SMCS 92069 1108-J6
HOME AV
800 CRLB 92008 1106-E5
3600 SD 92102 1289-G2
3700 SD 92105 1289-H2
4500 SD 92105 1269-J7
10700 SDCo 92020 1251-F1
HOMEDALE ST
2600 SD 92139 1310-E2
HOMER ST
3000 SD 92106 1268-D6
HOMESITE DR
2400 SD 92139 1310-E1
HOMESTEAD DR
2700 SDCo 92069 1088-J6
HOMESTEAD LN
47300 RivC 92592 999-F1
HOMESTEAD PL
900 ESCN 92026 1109-F7
HOMEWARD WY
700 SDCo 91901 1234-C4
HOMEWOOD PL
7600 LMSA 91941 1270-G3
HONDO LN
20700 SDCo 91901 1275-A2
HONDO ST
3600 SD 92105 1270-A6
HONESTIDAD RD
1700 SD 92154 1350-B3
HONEY DR
2100 SD 92139 1290-F6
HONEY LN
9100 SNTE 92071 1231-B7
HONEY BEE LN
- SDCo 92066 (1299-B2
See Page 1298)
HONEYCOMB CT
100 ENCT 92024 1147-H7
HONEYCUTT ST
3900 SD 92109 1248-B6
HONEYDEW LN
700 VSTA 92084 1087-J3
HONEYGLEN DR
1100 SMCS 92069 1128-F2
HONEY HILL RD
1400 ELCJ 92020 1251-D2
HONEY HILL TER
1500 ELCJ 92020 1251-C3
HONEY LAKE RD
- CHV 91913 1311-E5
HONEY OAK LN
2200 SDCo 91901 1253-J1
HONEY SPRINGS RD
1800 SDCo 91935 (1313-E1
See Page 1293)
1900 SDCo 91935 1293-F7
2000 SDCo 91935 1294-D2
2000 SDCo 91935 (1314-A1
See Page 1294)
HONEYSUCKLE CT
1600 ENCT 92024 1147-G5
HONEYSUCKLE DR
900 SMCS 92078 1128-E2
900 SMCS 92069 1128-E2
HONEYSUCKLE LN
500 NATC 91950 1290-C6
900 CRLB 92009 1127-A7
1100 SD 92114 1290-C6
1800 SDCo 92019 1252-C3
HONEYSUCKLE WY
1000 ESCN 92026 1109-J4
HONEY WAGON RD
- ImCo 92259 410-L5
HONNELL WY
3000 SDCo 91935 1292-G1
HONOR CT
3100 SDCo 92004 (1079-C5
See Page 1058)
HONORS CT
2900 SD 92122 1228-C6
HONORS DR
5400 SD 92122 1228-B6
HOOK CT
3100 SDCo 92004 (1079-C6
See Page 1058)
HOOP ST
- SD 92106 1288-A5
HOOPER BLVD
- CORD 91932 1329-E4
HOOPER CT
10100 SD 92124 1249-G4
HOOPER ST
10100 SD 92124 1249-G4
HOOSIER LN
5000 SDCo 91901 1234-J5
5000 SDCo 91901 1235-A5
HOOVER AV
100 NATC 92136 1289-G7
100 NATC 92136 1309-G1
100 SD 92136 1289-G7
800 NATC 91950 1309-H2
HOOVER ST
200 OCN 92054 1086-D7
1000 CRLB 92008 1106-G7
N HOOVER ST
600 ESCN 92027 1110-A6
600 ESCN 92027 1130-A1
HOPE AV
- SD 92102 1289-G4
2700 CRLB 92008 1106-E5
HOPE LN
1800 ESCN 92029 1129-F5
HOPE ST
100 ELCN 92243 6500-A6
800 ELCN 92243 6560-A1
2600 OCN 92056 1087-C6
3900 SD 92115 1270-E5
N HOPE ST
100 SDCo 92065 1172-D1
200 SDCo 92065 1152-D7

S HOPE ST
- SDCo 92065 1172-D1
HOPEDALE CT
6500 SD 92120 1250-D6
HOPI PL
3300 SD 92117 1248-C2
HOPI PTH
3800 SDCo 92004 (1099-E2
See Page 1098)
HOPKINS DR
- SD 92093 1208-A7
9700 SD 92093 1228-A1
HOPKINS ST
2300 SD 92139 1310-C1
HOPLAND CT
1200 CHV 91913 1311-B7
HOPPER AV
900 SMCS 92069 1109-B5
HOPSEED LN
8400 SD 92129 1189-C6
HORADO CT
16400 SD 92128 1170-C4
HORADO RD
12200 SD 92128 1170-B4
HORIZON CT
14300 PWY 92064 1170-G4
HORIZON DR
200 ENCT 92024 1147-G7
4200 CRLB 92008 1106-H7
HORIZON LN
100 OCN 92056 1107-D2
400 ELCJ 92020 1271-G1
HORIZON RDG
1100 ELCJ 92020 1251-H7
1100 SDCo 92020 1251-H7
1200 SDCo 92020 1271-H1
HORIZON WY
2400 SD 92037 1227-H2
2400 SD 92093 1227-H2
HORIZON HEIGHTS CIR
- ELCJ 92019 1252-C3
HORIZON HILLS DR
200 ELCJ 92020 1271-F2
400 SDCo 92020 1271-F2
HORIZON POINTE
1400 SDCo 92020 1271-H1
HORIZON VIEW DR
400 CHV 91910 1310-E5
19100 SDCo 92065 1152-B2
23100 SDCo 91963 (1315-G4
See Page 1294)
HORIZON VIEW GN
2100 ESCN 92026 1109-C3
HORIZON VIEW RD
22900 SDCo 91963 (1315-H4
See Page 1294)
HORNBILL AV
7600 SD 92123 1269-A1
HORNBLEND ST
700 SD 92109 1247-H6
1500 SD 92109 1248-C5
HORNBUCKLE DR
9400 SNTE 92071 1231-B4
HORNE PL
900 OCN 92054 1106-C2
HORNE RD
- ImCo 92283 432-C5
200 ImCo 92243 6559-H3
N HORNE ST
100 OCN 92054 1086-A7
S HORNE ST
100 OCN 92054 1086-B7
200 OCN 92054 1106-B1
HORNED OWL RD
11600 SDCo 92040 1212-C5
HORNER ST
7100 SD 92120 1250-C6
HORSEBACK LN
9300 SDCo 92040 1232-C5
HORSE CREEK TR
13900 SDCo 92082 1070-F7
HORSEMILL RD
200 SDCo 92021 1232-J7
200 SDCo 92021 1233-A7
200 SDCo 92021 1253-A1
HORSE RIDGE WY
5400 SDCo 91902 1311-A2
HORSESHOE CIR
700 VSTA 92083 1107-G2
HORSESHOE CT
1700 CHV 91902 1311-C4
HORSESHOE LN
9300 SNTE 92071 1231-E5
HORSESHOE RD
- SDCo 92004 410-B6
- SDCo 92004 1058-G1
HORSE SHOE WY
1600 OCN 92057 1067-E7
HORSETHIEF RD
- SDCo 91901 1236-D6
- SDCo 91916 1236-D6
- SDCo 92066 1236-D6
HORSETHIEF CANYON RD
- SDCo 91901 1255-H1
HORTENSIA ST
3800 SD 92110 1268-G6
4200 SD 92103 1268-G4
HORTON AV
- SD 92102 1289-G4
2400 SD 92101 1288-J1
3100 SD 92103 1268-J7
HORTON CIR
700 SDCo 91902 1310-G4
HORTON DR
6000 LMSA 91942 1251-B6
HORTON RD
4100 SDCo 91902 1310-G4
4100 CHV 91902 1310-G4
HOSKA DR
600 DLMR 92014 1187-G5
HOSKA LN
- DLMR 92014 1187-G5
HOSKINGS RANCH RD
2700 SDCo 92070 1135-D6
HOSMER ST
300 ELCJ 92020 1251-B5
HOSP WY
2000 CRLB 92008 1106-G3
HOSPITAL LP
- ImCo 92243 6559-H5
HOTEL CIR N
500 SD 92108 1268-H4
HOTEL CIR S
- SD 92108 1268-G4
200 SD 92108 1269-A4
HOTEL CIRCLE CT
4400 SD 92108 1268-J4

HOTEL CIRCLE PL
2400 SD 92108 1268-G4
HOT MINERAL SPA RD
1700 ImCo 92257 410-L5
HOTSPRING WY
- VSTA 92083 1107-J7
HOTZ ST
400 SDCo 91977 1290-J4
HOUSE RD
2900 ImCo 92259 430-L4
HOUSTON ST
3800 SD 92110 1268-D4
HOVANEC ST
1600 SD 92114 1290-E6
HOVENWEEP CT
8400 SD 92129 1189-B3
HOVLAND SQ
9900 SD 92131 1209-H5
HOVLEY RD
- BRW 92227 431-B1
4800 ImCo 92227 431-B1
HOWARD AV
300 ESCN 92029 1129-E4
1500 SD 92173 1350-D3
1800 SD 92103 1269-C5
1900 SD 92104 1269-C5
HOWARD LN
- SDCo 92672 1023-E1
HOWARD RD
4300 SDCo 92004 1100-B4
HOWARD JOHNSON PL
5200 SD 92120 1250-A7
HOWE CT
6900 SD 92111 1268-J2
HOWE PL
400 ESCN 92025 1129-J6
400 ESCN 92025 1130-A6
HOWE RD
9100 SD 92126 1209-D7
HOWELL DR
5900 LMSA 91942 1251-B6
HOWELL RD
- ImCo 92257 411-A6
HOWELL ST
2500 SDCo 92065 1152-C7
2500 SDCo 92065 1172-D1
HOWELL HEIGHTS DR
- ESCN 92025 1129-G4
HOXIE RANCH PL
2700 SDCo 92084 1068-D6
HOXIE RANCH RD
29600 SDCo 92084 1068-D6
HOYDALE RW
11300 SD 92128 1189-J3
HOYT PARK DR
10000 SD 92131 1209-G4
HUARACHA CT
5300 SD 92124 1249-H1
HUB CT
1100 ELCJ 92020 1251-D7
1100 SDCo 91941 1251-D7
HUBBARD AV
700 ESCN 92026 1109-H6
700 SDCo 92026 1109-H6
1000 ESCN 92027 1109-H6
HUBBARD PL
- ESCN 92027 1109-J5
HUBBARD RD
600 SDCo 91905 (1319-J1
See Page 1298)
HUBBERT ST
5200 OCN 92056 1087-E1
HUBBLES LN
8500 ELCJ 92020 1231-D7
8500 ELCJ 92020 1251-D1
8500 SNTE 92071 1231-D7
HUBER CT
9700 SNTE 92071 1231-B4
HUBNER RD
5500 SD 92105 1270-B6
HUCKLEBERRY LN
800 ESCN 92025 1150-C3
3700 SDCo 92069 1088-F2
21000 SDCo 92084 1088-F2
HUDSON DR
8000 SD 92119 1250-H4
HUDSON LN
100 SDCo 92019 1253-C1
HUDSON PL
6600 SD 92119 1250-H4
HUDSON BAY TER
5600 SD 92105 1290-B1
5900 SD 92115 1290-B1
HUE CITY AV
- SD 92140 1268-F7
HUELVA CT
300 OCN 92057 1086-J4
HUENEME ST
1200 SD 92110 1268-G3
HUENNEKENS ST
9900 SD 92121 1208-G5
HUERFANO AV
4000 SD 92117 1248-C2
HUERFANO CT
3200 SD 92117 1248-C2
HUERTO PL
500 CHV 91910 1310-H5
HUEY LN
1500 SDCo 91901 1253-J1
1500 SDCo 91901 1254-A1
HUFF RD
2000 ImCo 92251 430-L4
HUFF ST
100 VSTA 92083 1087-D7
100 VSTA 92083 1107-D1
HUFFSTATLER ST
1900 SDCo 92028 998-H4
HUGGINS ST
4300 SD 92122 1228-E4
HUGGINS WY
4600 SD 92122 1228-F4
HUGHES CT
- SD 92115 1270-C5
HUGHES LN
800 SDCo 92028 1047-H1
HUGHES ST
500 SDCo 92065 1152-C6
5700 SD 92115 1270-C5
7500 LMGR 91945 1290-G2
7500 SD 92114 1290-G2
HUGO ST
3000 SD 92106 1288-B1
HULBURD GROVE DR
9900 SDCo 91916 1235-J1
HULL ST
200 SD 92106 1287-J4
HUMBOLDT BAY WY
4200 OCN 92054 1066-E6

SAN DIEGO CO.

INDEX

STREET Block City ZIP Pg-Grid

HUME RD
9600 SNTE 92071 1231-C4
HUMISTON WY
23800 SDCo 92065 1173-D2
HUMMINGBIRD CT
700 SDCo 92019 1252-E6
HUMMINGBIRD LN
- OCN 92057 1086-H2
1700 VSTA 92084 1088-B3
7800 SD 92123 1249-B6
HUMMINGBIRD RD
1900 CRLB 92009 1127-D7
HUMMINGBIRD HILL
100 ENCT 92024 1167-J1
HUMMINGBIRD HILL LN
2400 SDCo 92028 1027-H7
HUMMOCK DR
3500 CRLB 92008 1107-C3
HUMMOCK LN
1800 ENCT 92024 1147-H5
HUMO DR
13900 PWY 92064 1190-G3
HUMPHREY PL
800 CHV 91911 1330-J2
1600 ESCN 92025 1130-B4
HUMPHREYS RD
- SD 92106 1308-A2
HUMPHRIES RD
24100 SDCo 91980 429-L10
HUNECK DR
5700 LMSA 91942 1251-B7
HUNRICHS WY
3000 SD 92117 1248-C3
HUNSAKER ST
1400 OCN 92054 1106-D2
HUNT RD
1600 SDCo 92021 1251-J1
2100 ImCo 92250 431-E6
HUNTALAS LN
2400 SDCo 92084 1088-D6
HUNTE PKWY
- CHV 91914 1311-H2
- SDCo 91914 1311-H2
1100 CHV 91915 1311-H5
HUNTER CT
300 SDCo 91901 1233-E6
HUNTER DR
1800 SDCo 92004 (1099-F4 See Page 1098)
HUNTER LN
300 SDCo 91901 1233-F5
HUNTER PASS
8800 SDCo 91901 1233-E6
HUNTER ST
400 SDCo 92065 1172-E1
600 OCN 92054 1086-F2
1000 SD 92103 1268-H5
N HUNTER ST
100 SDCo 92065 1152-D6
S HUNTER ST
100 SDCo 92065 1152-E7
400 SDCo 92065 1172-E1
HUNTER GREEN CT
11200 SD 92126 1209-E2
HUNTERS RD
9200 SDCo 91941 1271-C1
HUNTERS GLEN DR
10600 SD 92130 1208-E2
HUNTHAVEN RD
7700 SD 92114 1290-G4
HUNTINGRIDE CIR
11200 SNTE 92071 1231-G5
HUNTINGTON AV
9100 SD 92123 1249-D6
HUNTINGTON RD
1100 SMCS 92069 1128-B3
HUNTINGTON GATE DR
15000 PWY 92064 1170-F7
15000 PWY 92064 1190-F1
HUNTINGTON POINT RD
- CHV 91914 1311-F3
HUNTLEY RD
9100 SDCo 92028 1029-B4
HUNZA HILL CT
13100 SDCo 92082 1090-D2
HUNZA HILL TER
13000 SDCo 92082 1090-D2
HURD CT
6200 SD 92122 1228-D5
HURD PL
4100 SD 92103 1269-A5
HURLBUT PL
3300 SD 92123 1249-C5
HURLBUT ST
8200 SD 92123 1249-B5
HURLEY DR
4100 LMSA 91941 1270-H4
HURON AV
4600 SD 92117 1248-F6
HURON CT
5300 OCN 92056 1087-E1
HURON ST
9700 SDCo 91977 1291-D3
HURSLEY ST
400 ELCJ 92019 1251-J6
HURSTDALE AV
1000 ENCT 92007 1167-E3
HUSTED PL
28700 SDCo 92082 1070-H7
HUSTON RD
100 ImCo 92251 431-B4
HUTCHISON ST
2000 SDCo 92084 1087-H1
2600 SDCo 92084 1067-H7
HUTTON AV
6400 SD 92139 1310-F1
HUXLEY ST
4600 SD 92110 1248-F7
HYACINTH CIR
6700 CRLB 92009 1126-J5
HYACINTH DR
3600 SD 92106 1268-C6
HYACINTH RD
2300 SDCo 91901 1233-J5
2300 SDCo 91901 1234-A5
HYACINTH WY
200 OCN 92057 1086-H5
HYADES WY
10900 SD 92126 1209-D3
HYANOAK CT
- SDCo 91901 1255-D7
HYATT AV
3500 OCN 92054 1086-F3
HYATT ST
7100 SD 92111 1248-J7
7200 SD 92111 1249-A7
E HYATT ST
7100 SD 92111 1248-J7

STREET Block City ZIP Pg-Grid

HYBETH DR
7000 LMSA 91941 1270-F4
HYDE RD
1300 ImCo 92243 430-L6
HYDE PARK DR
6800 SD 92119 1250-E5
HYDE PARK LN
2200 SDCo 91906 (1297-J7 See Page 1296)
2200 SDCo 91906 (1317-H1 See Page 1296)
HYDRA LN
8100 SD 92126 1209-B3
HYDRANGEA CT
4300 SD 92154 1350-G1
HYGEIA AV
500 ENCT 92024 1147-A2
HYGEIA CT
200 ENCT 92024 1147-B4
HYMAN PL
6500 SD 92139 1310-F1
HYMETTUS AV
700 ENCT 92024 1147-B3
HYPATIA WY
1900 SD 92037 1227-G6
HYPOINT AV
2800 ESCN 92027 1110-E6
HYPOINT PL
200 ESCN 92027 1110-F6

I

I AV
100 CORD 92118 1288-H6
400 NATC 91950 1289-J7
500 NATC 91950 1309-J1
2200 NATC 91950 1310-A3
I CT
- SD 92126 1209-F7
I RD E
- CORD 92135 1288-F6
I ST
- CHV 91910 1310-C7
400 CHV 91910 1330-A1
600 SDCo 92065 1152-H6
700 CHV 91910 1329-J1
E I ST
- CHV 91910 1310-D7
- ENCT 92024 1167-C1
W I ST
100 ENCT 92024 1167-B1
I 3RD ST N
- CORD 92135 1288-F4
I 4TH ST N
- CORD 92135 1288-F3
- SD 92135 1288-F3
I 5TH ST N
- CORD 92135 1288-F4
IAN WY
8600 SNTE 92071 1231-D7
IAVELLI WY
12200 PWY 92064 1190-D6
IBERIA PL
11600 SD 92128 1170-A3
IBEX CT
14600 SD 92129 1189-C1
IBIS CT
3900 SD 92103 1268-J5
IBIS PL
7000 CRLB 92009 1127-E6
IBIS ST
1100 SD 92103 1268-J5
IBIS WY
4400 OCN 92057 1087-A3
IBIZA PL
- SDCo 92003 1067-H1
IBSEN ST
3000 SD 92106 1268-D6
ICARIA WY
4900 OCN 92056 1107-F5
ICARUS LN
12300 PWY 92064 1190-C1
ICE SKATE PL
11000 SD 92126 1209-E2
IDA AV
500 SOLB 92075 1167-G7
600 SOLB 92075 1187-G1
IDA ST
7400 LMGR 91945 1270-G7
IDAHO AV
300 ESCN 92025 1130-B4
600 SDCo 92025 1130-C3
800 SDCo 92027 1130-C3
IDAHO LN
1500 SDCo 92027 1130-C3
IDAHO ST
3900 SD 92104 1269-D5
4400 SD 92116 1269-D3
IDAHO TER
1700 SDCo 92027 1130-D4
IDERDELL LN
8200 LMGR 91945 1270-H6
IDLE HOUR LN
2600 SD 92037 1227-J1
IDLEWILD LN
300 OCN 92054 1106-C2
IDLEWILD WY
3000 SD 92117 1248-C1
IDYL DR
13200 SDCo 92040 1232-C5
IDYL PL
9200 SDCo 92040 1232-C5
IDYLLWILD LN
8900 SD 92119 1251-A3
I ESPLANADE
600 CHV 91910 1330-A1
IGUALA CT
100 SOLB 92075 1167-D6
ILDICA CT
2100 SDCo 91977 1291-A1
ILDICA ST
8100 LMGR 91945 1290-J1
8600 SDCo 91977 1290-J1
8700 SDCo 91977 1291-A1
9000 SDCo 91977 1271-A7
ILDICA WY
2000 SDCo 91977 1291-A1
ILENE ST
12900 PWY 92064 1190-D4
ILEX AV
1900 SD 92154 1350-A2
ILEXEY AV
1100 SD 92154 1350-G1
ILLAHEE DR
- SDCo 91901 1255-E5
ILLERONGIS RD
3000 SDCo 91935 1292-G3
ILLINOIS ST
3900 SD 92104 1269-E5

STREET Block City ZIP Pg-Grid

ILLINOIS ST
4400 SD 92116 1269-E5
ILLION ST
1800 SD 92110 1268-F1
2200 SD 92110 1248-F7
IMHOFF RD
- SDCo 92055 1085-G4
IMLER RD
- ImCo 92251 430-L3
- ImCo 92251 431-A3
- ImCo 92259 430-L3
IMOGENE AV
2100 SD 92154 1350-A1
IMOGENE WY
- SDCo 92065 1152-J4
IMPALA DR
2400 CRLB 92008 1127-E1
IMPERIAL AV
200 ELCN 92243 6499-F6
800 SD 92101 1289-B4
1100 ELCN 92243 6559-G1
1200 SD 92113 1289-B4
1500 LMGR 91945 1290-D3
1700 SD 92102 1289-C4
3900 SDCo 92102 1289-H4
4800 SD 92113 1290-A4
4800 SD 92102 1290-A4
5000 SD 92114 1290-D3
N IMPERIAL AV Rt#-86
600 ELCN 92243 6499-F3
1800 ImCo 92243 6499-F3
1800 IMP 92243 6499-F3
IMPERIAL DR
500 ESCN 92026 1109-F5
3800 SDCo 92036 1156-E3
IMPERIAL HWY Rt#-S2
- ImCo 92259 430-G6
IMPERIAL RD Rt#-S24
- ImCo 92283 432-E4
IMPERIAL BEACH BLVD
1000 IMPB 91932 1349-F1
IMPERIAL DAM RD
- ImCo 92283 432-F3
IMPERIAL DAM RD Rt#-S24
1900 ImCo 92283 432-E4
IMPERIAL GABLES RD
- ImCo - 411-K9
IMPERVIOUS PL
2300 SDCo 91901 1253-F2
IMPINK PL
3100 SDCo 91935 1292-H1
INCAPA RD
15400 SDCo 92036 1176-D4
W INCENSE CEDAR LN
4200 SDCo 92036 1156-E4
E INCENSE CEDAR RD
700 SDCo 92036 1156-E5
W INCENSE CEDAR RD
900 SDCo 92036 1156-D5
INCHON CT
- CORD 92118 1309-D6
INCHON RD
2300 CORD 92155 1309-B1
INCLINADO DR
1800 ELCJ 92020 1251-C2
INCREDIBLE LN
12100 SDCo 92082 1070-A7
INDEPENDENCE WY
1200 VSTA 92084 1088-B4
INDIA LN
500 SDCo 92028 1028-G4
INDIA ST
500 SD 92101 1288-J1
1000 SD 92103 1288-J1
1700 SD 92103 1268-H6
INDIAN
14100 SDCo 92040 1232-F4
INDIAN CT
5100 OCN 92057 1066-J4
INDIAN PL
2000 ESCN 92027 1110-C7
INDIAN WY
3600 SD 92117 1248-D3
INDIANA AV
100 VSTA 92084 1087-H6
S INDIANA AV
100 VSTA 92084 1087-H6
INDIANA ST
3500 SD 92103 1269-C6
INDIANAPOLIS AV
2500 SD 92105 1270-A7
INDIAN BEND DR
32400 SDCo 92061 1050-H6
32400 SDCo 92082 1050-H6
INDIAN CANYON LN
13900 PWY 92064 1170-F1
INDIAN CREEK DR
1200 CHV 91915 1311-H6
INDIAN CREEK LN
9900 SDCo 92021 1232-G3
INDIAN CREEK PL
1300 CHV 91915 1311-H6
INDIAN CREEK RD
28200 SDCo 92082 1090-F1
INDIAN CREEK WY
9600 SDCo 92026 1089-D4
INDIAN FIG DR
3100 SD 92115 1270-C6
INDIAN FLATS TKTR
- SDCo 92086 409-J6
INDIAN HEAD CT
15500 SDCo 92065 1173-E5
INDIAN HEAD RANCH RD
500 SDCo 92004 410-B6
500 SDCo 92004 1058-G1
INDIAN HILL PL
- SDCo 92026 1069-A6
INDIAN HILL RD
8700 SDCo 92026 1068-J7
8700 SDCo 92026 1069-A6
INDIAN HILL WY
6500 OCN 92028 1047-E7
INDIAN HILLS DR
3100 SDCo 91935 1293-F1
INDIAN LORE CT
11000 SD 92127 1149-H7
INDIAN MILLS LN
3100 SDCo 91935 1272-D5
INDIAN OAK TR
- SDCo 92061 1051-G3
INDIAN OAKS RD
19800 SDCo 92065 1152-C2
INDIAN PALMS CT
900 CHV 91915 1311-G4
INDIAN PASS RD
- ImCo - 412-A11

STREET Block City ZIP Pg-Grid

INDIAN PASS RD
- ImCo - 431-L2
- ImCo - 432-A1
INDIAN PEAK LN
14800 PWY 92064 1170-F7
14800 PWY 92064 1190-F1
INDIAN PEAK TR
13700 PWY 92064 1190-F1
INDIAN RIDGE RD
- SDCo 92029 1128-J4
8400 SDCo 92029 1129-A4
8400 SMCS 92078 1129-A4
INDIAN ROCK RD
- ImCo 92283 432-C5
- SDCo 92036 1156-E7
E INDIAN ROCK RD
100 VSTA 92084 1087-H4
W INDIAN ROCK RD
100 VSTA 92083 1087-G4
INDIAN SPRINGS DR
13600 SDCo 91935 1292-G1
INDIAN SPRINGS RD
14500 PWY 92064 1190-H1
INDIAN SUMMER CT
1500 SMCS 92069 1109-D6
INDIAN SUMMER PL
700 SMCS 92069 1109-D6
INDIAN SUMMER RD
1500 SDCo 92026 1109-D6
1500 SMCS 92069 1109-D6
INDIAN TRAIL RD
12800 PWY 92064 1170-C4
INDIAN TRAIL WY
6500 OCN 92028 1047-E7
INDIAN VALLEY RD
- SDCo 91935 1293-G1
INDIAN VIEW DR
1500 OCN 92028 1047-D7
1500 OCN 92028 1067-D1
INDIAN WELLS CT
8800 SNTE 92071 1230-J5
8800 SNTE 92071 1231-A5
INDIGO DR
2200 SDCo 92019 1272-D2
INDIGO LN
1700 SDCo 92004 (1099-F2 See Page 1098)
INDIGO ST
3800 OCN 92056 1107-F4
INDIGO WY
10600 SDCo 92127 1169-F2
INDIGO BLOSSOM LN
10600 SD 92121 1208-E4
INDIGO CANYON RD
600 CHV 91911 1330-H1
INDIO
- SDCo 92040 1232-D7
INDUSTRIAL AV
1100 ESCN 92029 1129-E3
INDUSTRIAL BLVD
900 CHV 91911 1330-A3
1600 SD 92154 1330-A3
INDUSTRIAL CT
2100 VSTA 92083 1108-A4
3300 SD 92121 1208-A4
INDUSTRIAL LN
8300 LMSA 91942 1270-H2
INDUSTRIAL PL
1000 ELCJ 92020 1251-E5
INDUSTRIAL ST
100 SMCS 92078 1128-J1
INDUSTRIAL WY
500 SDCo 92028 1027-G2
INDUSTRY RD
12100 SDCo 92040 1231-J3
12100 SDCo 92040 1232-A3
INDUSTRY ST
2300 OCN 92054 1086-E7
INDUSTRY WY
- ELCN 92243 6500-B7
INEZ LN
3500 SD 92106 1288-A2
INEZ ST
3500 SD 92106 1288-A2
INEZ WY
200 OCN 92057 1086-H3
INGALLS ST
4000 SD 92103 1268-J5
INGELOW ST
2900 SD 92106 1288-B1
E INGERSOLL ST
2400 SD 92111 1249-A7
W INGERSOLL ST
2400 SD 92111 1249-A7
INGLESIDE AV
4200 SD 92103 1268-G5
INGLESIDE PL
600 ESCN 92026 1109-H6
INGLEWOOD CT
800 VSTA 92084 1087-H5
INGRAHAM ST
3400 SD 92109 1268-A2
3600 SD 92109 1248-A6
4700 SD 92109 1247-J5
INGRAM AV
- ImCo 92249 6560-B7
INGRAM ST
- CHV 91911 1330-H3
INGRID AV
2100 SD 92154 1350-A1
INGULF ST
2500 SD 92110 1248-E7
INKOPAH ST
100 CHV 91911 1330-F1
INMAN CT
2500 SD 92111 1248-H7
INMAN ST
6200 SD 92111 1248-H7
INNIS PT
11800 SD 92126 1209-C1
NW INNIS ARDEN WY Rt#-94
36700 SDCo 91906 (1299-G7 See Page 1298)
36700 SDCo 91906 (1319-G1 See Page 1298)
37100 SDCo 91905 (1299-G7 See Page 1298)
37700 SDCo 91905 1300-A6
INNOVATION DR
15000 SD 92128 1170-A6
INNSDALE AV
8700 SD 92114 1290-J3
8700 SDCo 91977 1290-J3
8900 SDCo 91977 1291-A3
INNSDALE LN
8400 SD 92114 1290-J4
INNUIT AV
3200 SD 92117 1248-C2

STREET Block City ZIP Pg-Grid

INSPIRATION DR
1100 SD 92037 1247-G2
INSPIRATION LN
600 ESCN 92025 1150-C3
INSPIRATION WY
6100 SD 92037 1247-G2
INSPIRATION POINT RD
400 SDCo 92036 1156-F3
INTEGRITY WY
3200 SDCo 92028 1048-B2
INTERMEZZO WY
12600 SD 92130 1188-C6
INTERNATIONAL AV
- ImCo 92233 411-C8
INTERNATIONAL RD
1800 SD 92154 1350-C4
INTREPID CT
900 SOLB 92014 1187-H1
INTREPID WY
- VSTA 92083 1107-G5
INVERARY DR
1700 SDCo 92019 1272-B5
INVERLOCHY DR
- SDCo 92028 1027-G6
INVERNESS AV
- CHV 91915 1311-H6
INVERNESS CT
2700 SD 92037 1227-J4
4700 CRLB 92008 1107-A5
INVERNESS DR
2700 CRLB 92008 1107-A5
2700 SD 92037 1227-J4
4400 OCN 92057 1066-H7
INVERNESS RD
9000 SNTE 92071 1230-H6
INVERNESS WY
3200 SDCo 91935 1273-E5
INVIERNO DR
11600 SD 92124 1250-A2
INWOOD DR
9200 SNTE 92071 1230-J6
9200 SNTE 92071 1231-A6
INYAHA LN
2600 SD 92037 1227-J2
INYO LN
6400 SD 92139 1290-E7
IOLA WY
12800 PWY 92064 1190-A5
IONA CT
500 ESCN 92027 1110-D6
IONA DR
400 SD 92114 1290-C3
IONIAN ST
1500 IMPB 91932 1349-J2
1500 IMPB 92154 1349-J2
1500 SD 92154 1349-J2
1700 SD 92154 1350-A2
IOTA PL
5600 LMSA 91942 1250-J7
IOWA AV
700 SDCo 92028 1027-F1
IOWA ST
300 SDCo 92028 1027-F2
600 SD 92154 1330-A6
3900 SD 92104 1269-E5
4400 SD 92116 1269-E4
IOWA HILL CT
1300 CHV 91913 1311-D7
IPAI CT
11000 SD 92127 1169-H1
IPAVA DR
13900 PWY 92064 1190-G2
IRELAND LN
13100 SD 92129 1189-B4
IRENE CT
8000 SDCo 92021 1252-A1
IRENE ST
600 OCN 92057 1067-B5
IRIS AV
600 IMPB 91932 1349-F2
2100 SD 92154 1350-B2
2400 SD 92173 1350-C2
IRIS CT
1000 CRLB 92009 1127-B6
IRIS DR
- SD 92109 1248-C6
IRIS LN
14000 PWY 92064 1190-G2
N IRIS LN
1800 ESCN 92026 1109-G4
1900 SDCo 92026 1109-G5
S IRIS LN
1600 ESCN 92026 1109-G6
IRIS WY
1700 ESCN 92027 1110-B6
IRISDALE CT
1900 ENCT 92024 1147-H7
IRISH EYES
- SDCo 92127 1169-A2
IRISH OAKS RD
28100 SDCo 92082 1090-H2
IRON DR
200 VSTA 92083 1087-F6
IRONBARK WY
13200 PWY 92064 1190-E2
IRONGATE LN
9200 SD 92126 1209-E2
IRON HORSE CT
800 SMCS 92078 1128-G2
IRON HORSE DR
800 SMCS 92078 1128-G2
IRON MOUNTAIN DR
16800 PWY 92064 1191-D3
17300 SDCo 92040 1191-D3
IRON SPRINGS PL
35100 SDCo 92036 1156-E7
IRON SPRINGS RD
16900 SDCo 92036 1156-E7
35200 SDCo 92036 1176-D1
IRON SPRINGS WY
35100 SDCo 92036 1156-E7
IRONSTONE CT
16600 SDCo 92065 1171-D3
IRON VIEW RW
12100 SD 92128 1170-A4
IRONWOOD AV
10400 SNTE 92071 1231-D2
IRONWOOD CT
9900 SD 92131 1209-J4
IRONWOOD LN
4500 SDCo 92004 (1099-F4 See Page 1098)
IRONWOOD PL
3300 OCN 92056 1086-H7
9900 SD 92131 1209-J4
IRONWOOD RD
10800 SD 92131 1209-H5

STREET Block City ZIP Pg-Grid

IRON WOOD VW
- SDCo 92026 1089-B3
IROQUOIS AV
4600 SD 92117 1248-F6
IROQUOIS WY
3000 SD 92117 1248-E6
IRVINE RD
- ImCo 92227 411-E11
- ImCo 92227 431-E1
IRVING AV
1800 SD 92113 1289-D4
IRVINGTON AV
9100 SD 92123 1249-E6
IRWIN AV
5200 SD 92120 1250-B5
ISAAC ST
9200 SNTE 92071 1231-F6
ISABEL ST
2200 SD 92105 1289-J1
ISABELLA AV
1000 CORD 92118 1288-H7
ISABELLA DR
3100 OCN 92056 1106-J1
3100 OCN 92056 1107-A2
ISHAM SPRINGS CT
2700 SDCo 91977 1291-E1
ISHIHARA
700 VSTA 92084 1087-J3
ISIDORE ST
700 OCN 92057 1067-B5
ISLA DE LA GAITA
1800 SD 92173 1350-E3
ISLA DEL CAMPANERO
1700 SD 92173 1350-E3
ISLA DEL CARMEN WY
1700 SD 92173 1350-D3
ISLA DEL REY
- SDCo 92065 1173-D2
ISLAND AV
100 SD 92101 1289-D4
400 SD 92102 1289-E3
W ISLAND AV
100 SD 92101 1289-A4
ISLAND CT
700 SD 92109 1267-H2
ISLAND DR
- SDCo 92069 1128-B3
- SMCS 92069 1128-B3
ISLAND WY
1800 CRLB 92009 1126-H5
ISLAND BREEZE LN
400 SD 92154 1330-H6
ISLANDER ST
300 OCN 92054 1086-E6
ISLAND PINE WY
- SDCo 92127 1169-D2
ISLAND SHORE WY
- SMCS 92069 1128-A2
ISLAND VIEW LN
1100 ENCT 92024 1147-F7
ISLAND VIEW WY
3100 VSTA 92083 1128-A1
ISLA VISTA DR
3200 SD 92105 1269-J6
ISLA VISTA RD
15200 SDCo 91935 1293-D1
ISLE DR
4000 CRLB 92008 1106-G6
ISLE WY
1100 CHV 91910 1311-B7
ISLE ROYALE CT
5000 OCN 92057 1087-C1
ISLETA AV
4600 SD 92117 1248-C1
ISLEWORTH AV
10400 SD 92126 1209-D4
ISOCOMA ST
12900 SD 92129 1189-D5
ISOM CT
900 CHV 91911 1331-A1
900 CHV 91913 1331-A1
ISRAEL CT
- CHV 91911 1331-A3
ISTHMUS CT
700 SD 92109 1267-H2
ISTHMUS DR
- CRLB 92009 1126-H6
ISTHMUS WY
300 OCN 92054 1086-B6
ITHACA CT
900 CHV 91913 1311-D5
ITHACA DR
1700 VSTA 92083 1107-G5
ITHACA PL
5800 SD 92122 1228-D6
ITHACA ST
1600 CHV 91913 1311-D5
3400 SD 92122 1228-D6
ITO CT
6300 SD 92114 1290-D4
ITZAMNA RD
10600 SDCo 91941 1271-F3
IVANHO ST
9700 SDCo 91977 1291-D3
IVANHOE AV
7600 SD 92037 1227-F6
IVANHOE AV E
7600 SD 92037 1227-F6
IVANHOE RANCH RD
3000 SDCo 92019 1272-D5
IVERSON ST
8500 SD 92123 1249-C5
IVERSON POINT WY
700 OCN 92054 1066-E6
IVES CT
6800 SD 92111 1268-J2
IVEY RANCH RD
1200 OCN 92057 1086-J4
IVEY VISTA WY
4000 OCN 92057 1086-J4
IVORY AV
100 ELCJ 92019 1252-A5
IVORY CT
1300 ELCJ 92019 1252-A5
IVORY COAST DR
8300 SD 92126 1209-C4
IVORY GULL WY
200 SMCS 92078 1129-A1
IVY CT
500 CHV 91911 1330-G1
IVY LN
100 VSTA 92084 1087-H6
300 SDCo 92028 1027-F2
500 SD 92103 1269-A6
1100 IMPB 91932 1349-H1
2300 ESCN 92027 1110-D6
9200 SDCo 91977 1271-B7
9700 SDCo 92029 1149-E2

STREET Block City ZIP Pg-Grid

IVY RD
1700 OCN 92054 1106-E2
IVY ST
100 SDCo 92028 1027-F2
200 ESCN 92025 1129-J3
300 ESCN 92025 1130-A3
500 SD 92101 1289-E1
700 SD 92101 1288-J1
1000 ESCN 92026 1129-J1
1000 ESCN 92026 1109-H7
2800 SD 92104 1289-E1
7000 CRLB 92009 1127-A6
9300 SDCo 91977 1271-C7
N IVY ST
100 ESCN 92025 1129-J2
S IVY ST
100 ESCN 92025 1129-J2
W IVY ST
100 SDCo 92028 1027-E2
100 SD 92101 1289-A1
500 SD 92101 1288-J1
IVY TER
300 SDCo 92028 1027-F2
IVY WY
2200 SDCo 91977 1271-D7
IVY DELL LN
2700 SDCo 92026 1109-F3
IVYGLEN DR
1400 ENCT 92024 1167-G1
IVY HILL DR
10800 SD 92131 1189-H7
IVY PASS CIR
- SDCo 92065 1173-D1
IVYWOOD CT
700 SMCS 92069 1109-A5
IWO AV
- SD 92140 1268-F7

J

J AV
- NATC 91950 1289-J7
100 CORD 92118 1288-H6
500 NATC 91950 1309-J1
2000 NATC 91950 1310-A3
J CT
- SD 92126 1209-F7
J PL
700 CHV 91910 1310-D7
J RD E
- CORD 92135 1288-F6
J ST
- CHV 91910 1310-D7
100 CHV 91910 1330-B1
1000 SD 92101 1289-B4
1700 SDCo 92084 1108-F2
1900 SD 92102 1289-C4
E J ST
- CHV 91910 1310-E7
- ENCT 92024 1167-C1
900 CHV 91910 1311-B7
W J ST
100 ENCT 92024 1167-C1
JACALA DR
12400 PWY 92064 1170-C7
12400 PWY 92064 1190-C1
JACARANDA AV
2500 CRLB 92009 1147-G4
JACARANDA CT
2700 OCN 92056 1087-E5
JACARANDA DR
400 CHV 91910 1310-D6
400 SDCo 91910 1310-D6
3000 SD 92101 1269-D7
JACARANDA PL
800 ESCN 92026 1109-J6
2500 SD 92101 1269-D6
JACARTE CT
13200 SD 92130 1187-J5
JACINTO PL
700 CORD 92118 1288-J7
JACINTO RD
- SDCo 92055 1085-J3
JACKAL TR
7500 SDCo 92036 1138-B7
JACKASS TR
800 SDCo 92036 1138-B7
JACKDAW ST
3400 SD 92103 1268-J5
JACKIE DR
8400 SD 92119 1250-J4
JACKIE LN
2900 ENCT 92024 1148-A5
JACKIE ST
17300 SDCo 92065 1171-F4
JACKMAN ST
700 ELCJ 92020 1251-E4
JACK OAK LN
13800 SDCo 92040 1232-E5
JACK OAK RD
9400 SDCo 92040 1232-E5
JACK PINE CT
5200 OCN 92056 1087-E2
JACK RABBIT RD
13600 PWY 92064 1170-F3
JACK RABBIT ACRES
25000 SDCo 92026 1109-G4
25000 ESCN 92026 1109-G4
JACKS CREEK PL
- ESCN 92027 1110-E5
JACKS CREEK RD
- ESCN 92027 1110-E5
JACKSON DR
4900 LMSA 91941 1271-A1
5200 LMSA 91942 1270-J1
5200 LMSA 91942 1271-A1
5600 LMSA 91942 1250-F5
6100 SD 92119 1250-E3
7400 SD 92120 1250-E3
JACKSON PL
1100 SDCo 92026 1109-E7
JACKSON RD
- ImCo 92227 411-C11
- ImCo 92233 411-C11
1500 SDCo 92028 1047-J1
JACKSON ST
2500 SD 92103 1268-F4
2500 SD 92110 1268-F4
JACKSON HEIGHTS CT
8300 SDCo 92021 1252-B1
JACKSON HEIGHTS DR
12500 SDCo 92021 1252-B1
JACKSON HILL CT
1600 SDCo 92021 1252-B1
JACKSON HILL DR
12500 SDCo 92021 1252-B1
12700 SDCo 92021 1232-B7
JACKSON HILL LN
12500 SDCo 92021 1252-B1

STREET / Block City ZIP Pg-Grid

JACKSON HILL LN
12500 SDCo 92021 1232-B7
JACKSON HILL WY
12700 SDCo 92021 1232-B7
12700 SDCo 92021 1252-B1
JACKSPAR DR
- CRLB 92008 1107-B7
JACMAR AV
7100 SD 92114 1290-F3
JACOB LN
800 ENCT 92024 1147-B4
JACOB DEKEMA FRWY I-805
- CHV - 1310-B3
- CHV - 1330-G2
- NATC - 1289-H1
- NATC - 1290-A7
- NATC - 1310-B3
- SD - 1208-C6
- SD - 1228-E1
- SD - 1248-J1
- SD - 1249-A3
- SD - 1269-C1
- SD - 1289-H1
- SD - 1330-G2
- SD - 1350-G3
- SDCo - 1310-B3
JACOBY RD
9900 SDCo 91977 1291-D2
JACOT LN
2100 SD 92104 1289-F1
JACQUA ST
100 CHV 91911 1330-B5
JACQUELENE CT
700 ENCT 92024 1147-J6
JACQUELINE CT
900 SDCo 92021 1251-H3
JACQUELINE LN
3000 OCN 92056 1107-C1
JACQUELINE WY
1000 CHV 91911 1330-D2
JACUMBA LN
- SDCo 92055 1086-A3
JACUMBA ST
- SDCo 91934 (1321-G5 See Page 1300)
700 SD 92114 1290-H3
JADAM WY
8300 LMGR 91945 1270-J7
8300 LMGR 91945 1290-J1
JADE AV
1500 ELCJ 92019 1252-B4
1500 CHV 91911 1330-F5
JADE CT
1400 CHV 91911 1330-F4
JADE LN
4400 OCN 92056 1107-D2
JADE PL
1200 SMCS 92069 1109-C5
JADE COAST DR
8300 SD 92126 1209-C5
JADE COAST LN
8900 SD 92126 1209-D5
JADE COAST RD
7600 SD 92126 1209-A5
JADERO PL
1900 ESCN 92029 1129-F6
JADESTONE WY
13500 SD 92130 1188-A4
JAEGER RD
900 SDCo 91977 1291-D2
JAFFE CT
6500 SD 92119 1251-A4
JAG CT
1900 SDCo 92019 1272-C3
JAGROSS CT
8300 SD 92126 1209-B2
JAGUAR CT
11500 SD 92131 1210-B1
JAIME CT
1000 SD 92154 1350-E1
JAIME LYNN LN
1700 SDCo 92019 1272-C3
JAKE RD
13800 SDCo 92082 1090-E1
JAKE MILLS CT
1800 SD 92114 1290-E6
JAKIRK LN
1000 SDCo 92065 1172-H1
JALAL ST
8400 SDCo 92040 1232-A7
JALAPA CT
100 SOLB 92075 1167-D6
JALISCO RD
1800 SDCo 92019 1272-B3
JALNA LN
2600 SDCo 92028 998-B7
JAMACHA BLVD
9300 SDCo 91977 1291-E1
JAMACHA BLVD Rt#-S17
8700 SDCo 91977 1291-E2
10600 SDCo 91978 1271-F7
10600 SDCo 91978 1291-E2
JAMACHA LN
1100 SDCo 91977 1291-A2
JAMACHA RD
6800 SD 92114 1290-F3
8500 LMGR 91945 1290-G3
8500 SDCo 91977 1290-G3
8600 SDCo 91977 1291-B2
JAMACHA RD Rt#-54
100 ELCJ 92019 1251-J5
100 ELCJ 92019 1252-A6
1000 SDCo 92019 1252-A6
1100 ELCJ 92019 1272-A5
1100 SDCo 92019 1272-A5
1100 SDCo 92020 1272-A5
2700 SDCo 92019 1271-J6
E JAMACHA RD
8000 SDCo 91977 1290-J2
8500 SDCo 91977 1291-A2
JAMACHA WY
1500 SDCo 92019 1272-B3
JAMACHA HILLS RD
14000 SDCo 91935 1272-G6
JAMACHA VIEW DR
3000 SDCo 92019 1272-C6
3100 SDCo 91978 1272-C6
JAMAICA CT
700 SD 92109 1267-H2
JAMAICA LN
- ESCN 92025 1129-J5
JAMAICA WY
1800 VSTA 92083 1107-G5
JAMAICA VILLAGE RD
- CORD 92118 1329-D1
JAMAR CT
4700 SD 92117 1248-J1
JAMAR DR
5900 SD 92117 1248-J1
JAMBOREE ST
4500 OCN 92057 1066-H7
JAMES CIR
3500 SDCo 91977 1271-B5
JAMES CT
- SDCo 92024 1148-D2
400 CHV 91910 1330-B1
E JAMES CT
300 CHV 91910 1310-F7
JAMES DR
1600 CRLB 92008 1106-F4
JAMES RD
2000 ImCo 92243 6500-J1
JAMES ST
200 ESCN 92027 1110-E6
500 CHV 91910 1330-B1
800 SDCo 92065 1152-D5
3000 SD 92106 1268-C6
E JAMES ST
200 CHV 91910 1310-E7
JAMES HILL DR
10900 SDCo 92040 1211-F7
JAMESTOWN CT
4500 SD 92117 1228-F7
JAMESTOWN RD
5100 SD 92117 1228-F6
JAMESTOWN WY
4500 SD 92117 1228-F7
JAMIE AV
2100 SD 92139 1290-F7
JAMIE CT
8900 SDCo 91977 1291-A5
JAMIES LN
- SDCo 92059 1029-D7
- SDCo 92082 1029-D7
JAMISON CT
1400 SD 92114 1290-F5
JAMUL AV
100 CHV 91911 1330-E2
4100 SD 92113 1289-H5
JAMUL CT
400 CHV 91911 1330-G1
JAMUL DR
3200 SDCo 91935 1272-D5
14200 SDCo 91935 1292-H1
JAMUL LN
- SDCo 92055 1085-J4
- SDCo 92055 1086-A3
JAMUL HEIGHTS DR
2800 SDCo 92019 1272-C6
JAMUL HIGHLANDS RD
2800 SDCo 91935 1293-B1
3100 SDCo 91935 1273-B7
JAMUL VISTAS DR
3500 SDCo 91935 1273-A6
JAN DR
5800 LMSA 91942 1251-C7
JANA CT
8900 SDCo 91977 1291-B5
JANA LN
28800 SDCo 92082 1070-G7
28800 SDCo 92082 1090-H1
JANA PL
900 ESCN 92026 1109-F5
JANAL WY
14300 SD 92129 1189-H2
JANAN WY
4300 SD 92122 1228-E5
JANE CT
13100 SD 92129 1189-B4
JANE ST
8300 SD 92129 1189-B4
JANEEN ST
13600 PWY 92064 1190-F4
JANES LN
9300 SNTE 92071 1231-B7
JANET CIR
2000 OCN 92054 1106-E1
JANET LN
9400 SDCo 92040 1232-A5
JANET PL
1000 SMCS 92069 1109-B6
400 SD 92115 1269-J2
JANET KAY WY
12400 SDCo 92021 1232-A7
12400 SDCo 92021 1252-A1
JANETTA PL
13100 SD 92130 1187-J5
JANETTE LN
13700 PWY 92064 1190-F3
JANFRED WY
9400 LMSA 91942 1251-C7
JANICE CT
10900 SD 92126 1209-E3
JANICE ST
1400 SDCo 91977 1290-J2
1400 SDCo 91977 1291-A2
JANICH RANCH CT
1900 ELCJ 92019 1252-C4
JANIS WY
2000 CRLB 92008 1106-G5
JANIS LYNN LN
1400 VSTA 92083 1087-D7
JANITA TER
3900 SDCo 92069 1108-G1
JANNEY CT
6800 SD 92111 1268-J2
JANOS HILL
4400 SDCo 92003 1067-H2
JANSE WY
- SD 92173 1350-E5
JANSEN CT
1400 SD 92114 1290-F5
JANS OAK VW
22300 SDCo 92065 1173-A6
JANUARY PL
8900 SD 92122 1228-D3
JAPATUL LN
- SDCo 91901 1255-C5
JAPATUL RD
- SDCo 91901 1255-G4
6200 SDCo 91901 1254-B3
18900 SDCo 91901 1274-J1
18900 SDCo 91901 1275-A1
JAPATUL SPUR
- SDCo 91901 1275-B1
JAPATUL HIGHLANDS RD
- SDCo 91901 1255-D4
JAPATUL VALLEY RD
19900 SDCo 91901 1275-D1
21800 SDCo 91901 1255-H2
23200 SDCo 91901 1235-J7
JAPATUL VALLEY RD Rt#-79
8100 SDCo 91901 1236-A6
8100 SDCo 91916 1236-A6
JAPATUL VALLEY RD Rt#-79
23400 SDCo 91901 1235-J6
JAPATUL VISTA LN
- SDCo 91901 1255-E4
JAPPA AV
3200 SD 92117 1248-C2
JARAMA CT
2100 SDCo 92019 1272-C4
JARDIN CT
8200 SD 92122 1228-C3
JARDIN RD
12700 SD 92128 1170-C3
JARDIN DEL SOL
- SDCo 92065 1173-D2
JARDINE CT
1800 VSTA 92083 1107-J3
JARED PL
1000 ESCN 92025 1130-A3
JARMAN PL
13300 SD 92130 1188-A4
JARRETT CT
4800 SD 92113 1290-A5
JARRETT LN
100 SDCo 92021 1252-H3
JARRITO CT
11600 SD 92127 1150-A7
JARRON PZ
1000 CHV 91910 1311-A7
JARVIS ST
2800 SD 92106 1288-B1
JASMINE AV
14000 PWY 92064 1190-F3
JASMINE CT
900 CRLB 92009 1127-B6
1000 VSTA 92083 1108-A3
JASMINE DR
- SD 92109 1248-C6
JASMINE PL
3300 ESCN 92025 1150-C2
JASMINE ST
500 CHV 91911 1330-H3
1600 ELCJ 92021 1252-B2
4700 OCN 92056 1087-D4
JASMINE WY
100 CHV 91910 1310-B5
JASMINE CREST
3300 ENCT 92024 1148-C5
JASMINE CREST LN
10900 SD 92121 1208-F3
JASMINE VALLEY WY
- SD 92102 1290-A4
JASON CT
2500 OCN 92056 1087-E4
9800 SDCo 92082 1069-D4
JASON GN
2000 ESCN 92026 1109-D4
JASON LN
400 SMCS 92078 1129-A3
JASON PL
300 CHV 91910 1330-B1
JASON RD
3000 SDCo 92028 1047-J1
JASON ST
1500 IMPB 91932 1349-J2
1500 IMPB 92154 1349-J2
1500 SD 92154 1349-J2
1700 SD 92154 1350-A2
2500 OCN 92056 1087-E4
E JASON ST
100 ENCT 92024 1147-A3
W JASON ST
100 ENCT 92024 1147-A3
JASPER AV
1500 CHV 91911 1330-F5
JASPER CT
1400 CHV 91911 1330-F4
JASPER GN
2400 ESCN 92029 1129-E6
JASPER LN
4400 OCN 92056 1107-D2
JASPER RD
500 ImCo 92249 431-C7
JASPER ST
100 ENCT 92024 1147-A4
JAVA LN
1800 LMGR 91945 1290-H1
JAVA HILLS DR
1400 SDCo 92028 998-B7
JAVELIN WY
9900 SDCo 91977 1291-D2
JAVIER ST
5200 SD 92117 1248-H1
JAY CT
- SMCS 92069 1108-F5
- SNTE 92071 1231-D2
JAY BIRD LN
1100 SDCo 92065 1172-G2
JAY JAY WY
- SDCo 92026 1069-D2
JAYKEN WY
1400 CHV 91911 1330-B4
JAYLEE AV
8800 SDCo 91977 1290-J3
JAYNIA PL
2700 LMGR 91945 1270-E7
JAYTON LN
1900 ENCT 92024 1147-H7
S JAYTON LN
2100 ENCT 92024 1167-H1
JAZMIN CT
5300 SD 92124 1249-J1
JEAN AV
100 ESCN 92027 1130-D1
JEAN DR
4700 SD 92115 1269-J3
8700 SNTE 92071 1231-E7
JEAN ANN LN
2000 SDCo 92065 1172-H2
JEANETTE AV
5700 LMSA 91942 1250-H7
JEANNE PL
1500 CRLB 92008 1106-G6
JEANNE RD
7000 LMGR 91945 1270-E7
JEANNE TER
10700 SNTE 92071 1231-F6
JEANNINE LN
1200 SDCo 92021 1251-H3
JEAN-O-RENO RD
14000 PWY 92064 1190-G4
JED RD
2700 ESCN 92027 1110-E7
JEDEDIAH RD
- CHV 91913 1311-E7
JEFF ST
6300 SD 92115 1270-D5
JEFFER LN
4700 SDCo 91941 1271-C3
JEFFERS PL
- CRLB 92008 1107-B7
JEFFERSON AV
100 CHV 91910 1309-J6
500 CHV 91910 1310-A7
500 CHV 91910 1330-A1
500 ELCJ 92020 1251-F6
800 CHV 91911 1330-B3
1200 ESCN 92027 1130-A1
1400 ESCN 92027 1110-C6
8700 LMSA 91941 1271-A2
JEFFERSON RD
3000 SDCo 91935 1292-H2
JEFFERSON ST
2300 SD 92110 1268-E4
3800 CRLB 92008 1106-F3
8100 LMGR 91945 1270-H6
JEFFERY LN
28800 SDCo 92066 1237-C6
JEFF PARK LN
14600 PWY 92064 1190-E1
JEFFREE ST
500 ELCJ 92020 1251-G4
JEFFERY AV
1500 ESCN 92027 1130-C2
JEFFREY CT
10900 SD 92126 1209-D3
JEFFREY PL
1400 ESCN 92027 1130-C2
JEFFREY RD
900 SOLB 92014 1187-H1
1800 ImCo 92243 430-L6
JEFFREY HEIGHTS RD
31800 SDCo 92082 1070-D1
31800 SDCo 92082 1050-D7
JEFFRIES RANCH RD
5700 OCN 92057 1067-F6
JELLETT ST
4100 SD 92110 1248-E7
JEMA WY
8200 SDCo 92040 1252-A1
JEMEZ DR
3000 SD 92117 1248-C1
JENELL ST
15000 PWY 92064 1170-C7
JENKINS ST
3100 SD 92106 1288-A4
JENNA CT
200 SD 92114 1290-D4
JENNA PL
2000 ESCN 92029 1129-F7
JENNER ST
7900 SD 92037 1227-E6
JENNIFER CIR
1000 VSTA 92083 1087-G4
JENNIFER CT
1100 ESCN 92026 1109-J7
1900 SDCo 92028 1048-B4
4800 SD 92117 1248-D1
JENNIFER DR
9900 SNTE 92071 1231-D4
JENNIFER LN
2300 ENCT 92024 1147-J7
JENNIFER ST
3600 SD 92117 1248-D1
JENNILEAH LN
400 SMCS 92069 1109-A2
JENNINGS PL
800 SD 92106 1288-A3
JENNINGS ST
800 SD 92106 1287-J3
3400 SD 92106 1288-A3
JENNINGS VISTA CIR
9100 SDCo 92040 1232-F5
JENNINGS VISTA CT
14200 SDCo 92040 1232-F4
JENNINGS VISTA DR
14100 SDCo 92040 1232-F5
JENNINGS VISTA TR
14200 SDCo 92040 1232-F4
JENNINGS VISTA WY
14200 SDCo 92040 1232-F4
JENNITE DR
7500 SD 92119 1250-F3
JENNY AV
8600 SD 92123 1249-C6
JENNY LN
29700 SDCo 92084 1068-E6
JENNY JAY CT
28600 SDCo 92082 1090-E1
JENSEN CT
- ENCT 92024 1147-E4
JEPSON LN
- SD 92131 1189-G7
JERABACK DR
10200 SD 92131 1209-H4
JEREMY LN
2000 ESCN 92027 1110-B5
JEREMY PL
2100 ESCN 92027 1110-B5
JEREMY ST
9500 SNTE 92071 1231-F5
JEREMY WY
36000 SDCo 92028 999-D7
36100 SDCo 92028 1029-E1
36600 SDCo 92059 1029-F1
JEREMY POINT CT
1600 CHV 91911 1330-J5
JEREZ CT
7500 CRLB 92009 1147-H1
JERGENS CT
9000 SD 92126 1209-D2
JERI WY
4600 SDCo 92020 1271-H2
JERICHO DR
700 SDCo 92028 1028-A1
JERICHO RD
9400 LMSA 91942 1251-B6
JERICHO CIRCLE GN
200 ESCN 92027 1110-E7
JEROME DR
14200 PWY 92064 1170-G7
JERRILYNN PL
1600 ENCT 92024 1167-G1
JERSEY CT
700 SD 92109 1267-H2
JESMOND DR
10100 SDCo 92026 1109-E2
JESMOND DENE RD
2800 ESCN 92026 1109-E1
2800 SDCo 92026 1109-E1
2900 SDCo 92026 1089-D7
JESMOND DENE HEIGHTS RD
2900 SDCo 92026 1109-F2
JESMOND DENE HEIGHTS RD
2800 SDCo 92026 1109-F3
J ESPLANADE
600 CHV 91910 1330-A1
JESSICA LN
- ESCN 92027 1130-E1
11500 SDCo 92040 1231-H6
JESSICA LYNN LN
1500 SDCo 92065 1172-J1
JESSIE AV
4600 LMSA 91941 1270-G3
JESSIE LN
200 VSTA 92083 1107-J1
JESSIE JAMES LN
- SDCo 92065 1171-G2
JESSOP LN
2300 SD 92110 1268-F6
JESTER ST
1700 SD 92114 1290-D6
JETHROW WY
1400 ELCJ 92019 1252-A7
JEWELL DR
500 SD 92113 1289-G5
JEWELL RDG
2000 VSTA 92083 1107-H6
JEWELL ST
3300 SD 92109 1268-A1
3600 SD 92109 1248-A4
JEWEL VALLEY CT
39500 SDCo 91905 1300-C7
JEWEL VALLEY LN
2000 SDCo 91905 1300-C7
JEWEL VALLEY RD
1400 SDCo 91905 (1320-D1 See Page 1300)
1500 SDCo 91905 1300-D7
JEWEL VALLEY WY
39500 SDCo 91905 1300-C7
E JEWETT ST
2200 SD 92111 1248-J7
W JEWETT ST
2300 SD 92111 1248-J7
JIBSAIL ST
3300 OCN 92054 1086-F5
JICAMA WY
- CHV 91911 1330-E4
JICARILLO AV
4500 SD 92117 1248-C2
JILL LN
3700 LMSA 91941 1270-F5
JILL ST
4400 OCN 92057 1066-H7
9900 SNTE 92071 1231-D4
JIM LN
9500 SNTE 92071 1231-E5
JIMDORA WY
2300 SDCo 92003 1048-D7
JIMENEZ CT
- SD 92126 1209-D7
JIMMY DURANTE BLVD
1900 DLMR 92014 1187-F3
JIMMY DURANTE WY
2200 DLMR 92014 1187-G3
JIMSEN CT
3300 SDCo 92028 1048-C4
JIMZEL RD
9600 LMSA 91942 1251-C5
JIOLA WY
9500 LMSA 91941 1271-C2
JOAN CT
5200 SD 92115 1270-A2
JOAN LN
2700 SDCo 92028 997-B2
JOAN ST
9000 SDCo 91977 1291-A4
JOANN CIR
400 VSTA 92084 1087-H4
JOANN DR
2500 OCN 92056 1087-C6
JOANNA DR
700 SD 92114 1290-G3
JOANNE WY
800 ELCJ 92020 1251-D7
JOANNIE WY
200 SDCo 92083 1108-A3
JOBE HILL DR
500 VSTA 92083 1107-E1
JOCATAL PL
11600 SD 92127 1150-A7
JOCELYN ST
4400 SD 92105 1289-H1
JOCKEY WY
5600 SDCo 91902 1311-A2
JOCKEY CLUB
2300 SDCo 92003 1048-B7
JODI ST
3800 SD 92115 1270-C5
JODY LN
2900 OCN 92056 1087-B7
JODY PL
2700 ESCN 92027 1110-E7
JOE PL
200 ESCN 92027 1130-D1
JOE CROSSON DR
1600 ELCJ 92020 1251-E2
JOEL LN
6000 LMSA 91942 1251-C7
JOEVE CT
8700 SD 92119 1251-A3
JOEY AV
400 ELCJ 92020 1251-G4
JOEY PL
400 ESCN 92026 1109-J7
JOHANNESBERG WY
13200 PWY 92064 1190-F4
JOHN CT
1100 SD 92154 1350-D1
JOHN ST
3400 SD 92106 1287-J2
3400 SD 92106 1288-A3
JOHN DEWITT PL
2100 SDCo 91901 1253-J1
JOHN HENRY LN
16600 SDCo 92065 1171-H3
JOHN HOPKINS CT
3300 SD 92121 1207-J7
3300 SD 92121 1208-A7
JOHN JAY HOPKINS DR
3500 SD 92121 1207-J6
10900 SD 92121 1208-A7
JOHN J MONTGOMERY DR
3700 SD 92123 1249-C3
JOHNSON AV
800 SD 92103 1269-B5
N JOHNSON AV
1000 ELCJ 92020 1251-E3
S JOHNSON AV
200 ELCJ 92020 1251-E6
JOHNSON CT
- SDCo 92055 1086-A3
JOHNSON DR
1100 ESCN 92025 1130-A3
3000 OCN 92056 1087-A7
3000 OCN 92056 1107-A1
8900 LMSA 91941 1271-A2
JOHNSON LN
900 SDCo 92065 1152-G4
1900 ImCo 92243 6499-A6
1900 ImCo 92243 6559-B1
JOHNSON RD
- SD 92145 1228-H3
- SD 92145 1229-A3
JOHNSON ST
- CORD 91932 1329-E4
JOHNSON LAKE RD
11500 SDCo 92040 1211-H5
JOHNSTON GN
- ESCN 92029 1129-D6
- SDCo 92029 1129-D6
JOHNSTON LN
100 SMCS 92069 1108-H7
100 SMCS 92069 1128-H1
JOHNSTON RD
2100 ESCN 92029 1129-D6
2100 SDCo 92029 1129-D6
JOHNS VIEW WY
2200 SDCo 91977 1291-A1
JOHN TOWERS AV
1800 ELCJ 92020 1251-D1
JOHN WAYNE LN
18600 SDCo 92082 1071-B7
18600 SDCo 92082 1091-B1
JOJO CT
200 SD 92114 1290-D4
JOLIET CT
100 ELCJ 92019 1252-A5
JOLIET ST
1300 ELCJ 92019 1252-A5
JOLINA WY
400 ENCT 92024 1147-G6
JOLLEY LN
14300 PWY 92064 1190-H5
JON LN
- OCN 92054 1086-G2
JONAH RD
300 ESCN 92027 1110-F7
JONAS CT
8800 SD 92123 1249-C6
JONATHAN PARK LN
13300 PWY 92064 1190-E1
JONATHON PL
600 ESCN 92027 1110-C6
4200 OCN 92056 1087-C7
4200 VSTA 92083 1087-C7
JONATHON ST
1500 VSTA 92083 1087-D7
4000 OCN 92056 1087-C7
JONBELL PL
10000 SNTE 92071 1231-D4
JONEL WY
6400 SDCo 91902 1311-C1
JONELL CT
9100 LMSA 91942 1251-B6
JONES CT
- SDCo 92055 1086-A2
JONES RD
500 OCN 92054 1086-D5
39500 SDCo 92028 409-A5
JONI LN
3000 SDCo 92069 1088-J6
JONNY LN
11700 SD 92126 1209-B1
JONQUIL DR
2600 SD 92106 1268-C6
JOPLIN AV
3600 SD 92117 1248-D2
JOPLIN DR
900 ELCJ 92021 1251-H2
JORDAN ST
600 ESCN 92027 1130-D1
8200 SD 92123 1249-B5
JORDAN RIDGE CT
12700 SD 92130 1188-D6
JORIS WY
8800 LMSA 91941 1271-A3
JOSE LN
1600 ESCN 92026 1109-H6
JOSEFINA PL
600 CHV 91910 1311-A5
JOSEPHINE AV
9700 SD 92145 1229-E3
JOSEPHINE ST
1300 SD 92110 1268-G3
JOSH WY
500 SDCo 91901 1234-C4
JOSHUA AV
300 SMCS 92069 1108-J6
JOSHUA PL
800 SD 92154 1330-F7
JOSHUA ST
1000 ESCN 92026 1129-H1
1100 ESCN 92026 1109-H7
JOSHUA WY
1100 VSTA 92083 1107-J7
1100 VSTA 92083 1108-A7
JOSHUA TREE CT
14400 PWY 92064 1190-F2
JOSHUA TREE LN
1600 SDCo 92028 1027-J5
JOSHUA TREE ST
- IMP 92243 6499-E2
JOSIE JO LN
10100 SNTE 92071 1231-E3
JOSSELYN AV
1200 CHV 91911 1330-E3
JOSTEN WY
400 SDCo 92028 1027-E5
JOUGLARD ST
6300 SD 92114 1290-D6
JOVIC RD
9200 SDCo 92040 1232-A5
JOY LN
2000 ESCN 92029 1129-F5
JOY RD
1200 SDCo 92028 1027-J5
JOYAS CT
11600 SD 92124 1250-B3
17800 PWY 92064 1170-E1
JOYCE PL
5100 SD 92105 1270-A6
JOYCE ST
200 ELCJ 92020 1251-G7
JUAN ST
2200 SD 92103 1268-G5
2300 SD 92110 1268-F4
JUANENO AV
200 OCN 92057 1067-B7
JUANITA LN
100 SDCo 92021 1252-J4
1800 SDCo 92028 1027-J3
JUANITA ST
800 SOLB 92075 1187-G1
3200 SD 92105 1270-C6
JUANITA WY
30500 SDCo 92082 1070-G1
JUAREZ DR
16600 SD 92128 1170-B3
JUBA RD
29200 SDCo 92082 1090-F1
JUBILEE DR
5600 SDCo 92028 999-A5
JUBILEE WY
38900 SDCo 92028 999-B4
JUD ST
1100 SD 92114 1290-H2
JUDIANN LN
2800 SDCo 92084 1088-D7
JUDICIAL DR
9200 SD 92121 1228-D1
JUDILYN DR
900 VSTA 92083 1087-F5
JUDITH AV
2000 SD 92154 1350-B2
JUDITH PL
1700 ESCN 92026 1109-C5
JUDSON CT
7500 SD 92111 1249-A7
JUDSON ST
600 ESCN 92027 1130-D1
2000 SD 92111 1269-A1
2200 SD 92111 1249-A7
N JUDSON ST
7400 SD 92111 1249-A7
JUDSON WY
1100 CHV 91911 1330-F3
4500 LMSA 91941 1270-E3
4500 SD 92115 1270-E1
JUDY DR
9900 SNTE 92071 1231-D4
JUDY LN
1100 ENCT 92007 1167-F2
JUDY LEE PL
6500 SD 92115 1270-D4
JUERGENS VISTA
- SDCo 91901 1255-D6
JUGADOR CT
1100 SDCo 92069 1128-E3
1100 SMCS 92069 1128-E3
JULA CT
300 SDCo 91977 1290-J4
JULIAN AV
100 ELCJ 92020 1251-F5
1700 SD 92113 1289-C4
12300 SDCo 92040 1232-B4
JULIAN LN
- SDCo 92036 1136-A7
JULIAN RD Rt#-67
2500 SDCo 92065 1172-B3
JULIAN RD Rt#-78
100 SDCo 92065 1152-J4
300 SDCo 92065 1153-J1
1700 SDCo 92065 409-J11
2000 SDCo 92065 1154-D2
18600 SDCo 92070 409-J11
18600 SDCo 92070 1135-B3
JULIAN RD Rt#-79
2200 SDCo 92036 1136-A7
2800 SDCo 92066 1135-D3
2800 SDCo 92070 1135-D3
E JULIAN RD
100 SDCo 92065 1152-J5
JULIAN ST
100 SDCo 92065 1152-E7
S JULIAN ST
100 SDCo 92065 1152-E7
400 SDCo 92065 1172-E1
JULIAN ESTATES RD
700 SDCo 92036 1156-E5
JULIANNA ST
1800 SDCo 92019 1272-B2
JULIAN ORCHARDS DR
1000 SDCo 92036 1136-A3
1000 SDCo 92066 1135-J3
JULIE CT
800 SMCS 92069 1109-B6
JULIE LN
3900 SDCo 91941 1271-H4
JULIE PL
2200 CRLB 92008 1107-A6
JULIE ST
6400 SD 92115 1270-D1
JULIELYNN WY
- LMGR 91945 1270-H6
JULIETTE PL
1100 SDCo 92028 1027-H3
7200 LMSA 91941 1270-F2
JULINDA WY
2800 SDCo 92029 1150-A2
JULIO PL
10200 SNTE 92071 1231-E3
JULY ST
5000 SD 92110 1268-G1
JUMANO AV
4700 SD 92117 1248-F6
JUMILLA ST
5100 SD 92124 1230-A7
JUNCO PL
8700 SD 92129 1189-C6
JUNCUS CT
7300 SD 92129 1188-J7
JUNE ST
1300 SDCo 92028 1027-J3
JUNE WY
500 ELCJ 92021 1251-H4
JUNE LAKE DR
7900 SD 92119 1250-H5
JUNGLE OAKS DR
3600 SDCo 92028 1047-H4
JUNIOR HIGH DR
7600 LMSA 91941 1270-G4
JUNIPER AV
100 CRLB 92008 1106-E7
JUNIPER LN
900 SDCo 92083 1108-B6
9700 SDCo 92029 1149-E2
JUNIPER ST
100 SD 92101 1289-E1
500 SD 92101 1288-J1
500 CHV 91911 1330-H3
2800 SD 92104 1289-E1
3800 SD 92105 1289-G1
N JUNIPER ST
200 ESCN 92025 1129-J2
S JUNIPER ST
100 ESCN 92025 1129-J3
500 ESCN 92025 1130-A4
2000 ESCN 92025 1130-A4

W JUNIPER ST — SAN DIEGO CO. STREET INDEX — KITE HILL LN 6594

Thomas Bros. Maps ® COPYRIGHT 2001

STREET Block City ZIP Pg-Grid

W JUNIPER ST
100 SD 92101 1289-A1
JUNIPER WY
200 OCN 92057 1086-H5
12200 PWY 92064 1190-C7
JUNIPER FIELD TR
- SDCo 92065 1173-D2
JUNIPERHILL DR
1500 ENCT 92024 1167-G1
JUNIPER PARK LN
10700 SD 92121 1208-E3
JUNO AV
100 ENCT 92024 1147-A3
JUPITER ST
100 ENCT 92024 1147-A3
3900 SD 92110 1268-C4
JUST CT
1100 SD 92154 1350-F1
JUST ST
3700 SD 92154 1350-F1
JUSTA LN
8800 SNTE 92071 1231-B7
JUSTICE LN
- SD 92093 1228-A1
JUSTIN PL
31300 SDCo 92082 1070-G1
JUSTIN RD
1300 ENCT 92007 1167-E2
JUSTIN WY
500 ESCN 92027 1110-D6
JUSTINA DR
300 OCN 92057 1086-J4
JUSTO CT
11800 SD 92129 1189-F7
JUTLAND CT
3000 SD 92117 1248-C2
JUTLAND DR
4200 SD 92117 1248-C1
JUTLAND PL
4500 SD 92117 1248-C2

K

K AV
400 NATC 91950 1289-J7
700 NATC 91950 1309-J1
1800 NATC 91950 1310-A2
K CT
- SD 92126 1209-F7
K ST
- CHV 91910 1330-C1
- CHV 91911 1330-C1
300 SD 92101 1289-B4
1900 SD 92102 1289-C4
W K ST
100 ENCT 92024 1167-C1
KAANAPALI WY
2900 SD 92154 1330-C6
KACHINA CT
17800 SD 92127 1169-H1
KADWELL WY
1700 ELCJ 92021 1252-B2
KAE CREST
3100 SDCo 91935 1273-B7
KAHLUA CT
9300 SDCo 91941 1271-B4
9300 SDCo 91977 1271-B4
KAHLUA WY
4000 SDCo 91941 1271-B4
4000 SDCo 91977 1271-B4
KAIBAB CT
3000 SD 92117 1248-F6
KAILE LN
500 ESCN 92027 1110-E6
KAIMALINO LN
1300 SD 92109 1247-H4
KAISER PL
10200 SD 92126 1209-A5
KAISER RD
6000 ImCo 92233 411-D10
KAITZ ST
12600 PWY 92064 1170-C7
KAL PL
1700 ESCN 92029 1129-G5
KALAMATH DR
700 DLMR 92014 1187-G5
KALAMIS WY
4700 OCN 92056 1107-E6
KALAPANA ST
14600 PWY 92064 1190-G1
KALBAUGH ST
100 SDCo 92065 1152-D6
200 SDCo 92065 1172-D1
KALBFUS ST
3100 SD 92136 1289-E7
3400 SD 92136 1309-F1
KALIN RD
- ImCo 92233 411-B10
- ImCo 92281 411-B11
KALIN RD Rt#-S26
- ImCo 92281 411-B11
KALMIA CIR
- CRLB 92009 1127-D5
KALMIA LN
9700 SDCo 92029 1149-E2
KALMIA PL
2800 SD 92104 1289-E1
KALMIA ST
100 SD 92101 1289-E1
900 SD 92101 1288-J1
1300 ESCN 92025 1130-A4
2300 SD 92104 1289-E1
5000 SD 92105 1290-A1
E KALMIA ST
100 SDCo 92028 1027-F2
N KALMIA ST
100 ESCN 92025 1129-J2
S KALMIA ST
100 ESCN 92025 1129-J3
800 ESCN 92025 1130-A3
W KALMIA ST
100 SDCo 92028 1027-F2
100 SD 92101 1289-A1
400 SD 92101 1288-J1
KALPATI CIR
800 CRLB 92008 1106-F7
KAMLOOP AV
4300 SD 92117 1248-C2
KAMM RD
1500 ImCo 92250 431-D4
KAMWOOD CT
10200 SD 92126 1208-J5
KAMWOOD PL
10200 SD 92126 1208-J5
KAMWOOD ST
7200 SD 92126 1208-J5
KANDACE CT
5100 SD 92105 1270-A7
KANDACE WY
2700 SD 92105 1270-A7
KANE DR
8200 LMSA 91941 1270-J5
KANE ST
4100 SD 92110 1248-E7
KANEKO CT
- SD 92173 1350-F5
KANSAS ST
3900 SD 92104 1269-E5
4300 SD 92116 1269-E3
KANTOR CT
5800 SD 92122 1228-F6
KANTOR ST
5800 SD 92122 1228-F6
KAPALUA CT
3000 SD 92154 1330-D7
KAPLAN DR
8200 SD 92123 1269-B1
KAPLAN WY
3900 NATC 91950 1310-E3
KAPPA ST
5800 LMSA 91942 1250-J7
KARDEELIN CT
12500 SDCo 92021 1252-B1
KAREN CT
900 SMCS 92069 1109-C5
KAREN LN
9900 SNTE 92071 1231-D4
KAREN WY
1000 CHV 91911 1330-D2
4600 SDCo 92020 1271-G3
KARENA CT
700 VSTA 92083 1087-F4
KAREN SUE AV
4200 SD 92122 1228-E6
KAREN SUE LN
5900 SD 92122 1228-E6
KARERLLYN DR
9200 SNTE 92071 1231-G5
KARI CT
2600 SDCo 91977 1271-A7
KARI LN
4100 OCN 92057 1067-G4
4100 SDCo 92003 1067-G4
KARIBU LN
27000 SDCo 92082 1090-J5
KARNES WY
3000 SD 92117 1248-C3
KAROK AV
3200 SD 92117 1248-C2
KARRA CT
400 CHV 91910 1310-F6
KARREN LN
2000 CRLB 92008 1106-G5
KARWARREN CT
500 SDCo 92026 1109-H5
KASCHUBE WY
9300 SNTE 92071 1230-H6
KASHMERE LN
10300 SDCo 92029 1129-E7
KATE CT
1900 SDCo 92028 1048-B3
KATELLA CT
1400 ESCN 92027 1130-B2
KATELLA ST
1800 SD 92154 1350-B3
KATELLA WY
1400 ESCN 92027 1130-C2
KATELYN CT
- SD 92120 1250-A4
KATERRI DR
2000 SDCo 92084 1088-C7
KATE SESSIONS WY
5000 SD 92109 1248-A4
KATHERINE CT
1200 SD 92154 1350-D1
2500 ELCJ 92020 1251-B4
KATHERINE PL
4600 LMSA 91941 1270-F3
KATHERINE ST
2300 ELCJ 92020 1251-A3
KATHERINES VIEW WY
900 SDCo 92065 1152-F1
KATHLEEN PL
2400 SD 92105 1270-B7
KATHRINER PL
1200 SDCo 92065 1172-G2
KATHY ST
9500 LMSA 91942 1251-C6
KATIE LN
- SDCo 92040 1231-J6
KATIE KING LN
- SDCo 91901 1254-E1
KATIE LENDRE DR
3600 SDCo 92028 1048-D3
KATKAT CT
32300 SDCo 92061 1051-A6
KATO ST
8100 LMSA 91942 1270-H1
8100 LMSA 91942 1250-H7
KATY CT
4600 SDCo 91941 1271-C3
KATY PL
1700 ESCN 92026 1109-D5
KATYDID CIR
12200 SD 92129 1189-A7
KAUANA LOA DR
2600 ESCN 92029 1129-D4
2600 SDCo 92029 1129-D4
KAUFMAN WY
9900 SD 92126 1208-J5
9900 SD 92126 1209-A6
KAUSMAN ST
2700 SD 92139 1310-E1
KAVANAUGH RD
- ImCo 92250 431-E5
KAVANAUGH RD Rt#-S33
- ImCo 92250 431-E5
KAY DEE LN
16000 SDCo 92065 1171-H4
KAY JAY CT
13600 SDCo 92040 1232-E6
KAY JAY LN
9000 SDCo 92040 1232-E6
KAYLYN WY
600 SMCS 92069 1129-E2
KAYMAR DR
300 SD 92114 1290-F3
KAYWOOD CIR
11400 SDCo 92026 1109-H1
KAYWOOD CT
25900 SDCo 92026 1109-J1
KAYWOOD DR
3000 SDCo 92026 1109-H1
25900 SDCo 92026 1089-H7
KAYWOOD LN
11500 SDCo 92026 1109-J2
KAYWOOD PL
11500 SDCo 92026 1109-J1
KAYWOOD TER
26000 SDCo 92026 1109-H1
KAYWOOD WY
25900 SDCo 92026 1109-J1
KEA ST
1300 OCN 92054 1086-E7
KEAR CT
- PWY 92064 1190-G6
KEAR PL
12100 PWY 92064 1190-F7
KEARNEY AV
1700 SD 92113 1289-C5
KEARNEY CT
200 CHV 91910 1310-E7
KEARNEY ST
100 CHV 91910 1330-B1
KEARNY MESA RD
4100 SD 92111 1249-C2
5400 SD 92111 1229-C7
9100 SD 92126 1209-F6
KEARNY SPECTRUM BLVD
9000 SD 92123 1249-D1
KEARNY VILLA CT
9100 SD 92123 1229-D7
KEARNY VILLA LN
3200 SD 92123 1249-B5
KEARNY VILLA RD
3300 SD 92123 1249-D2
5400 SD 92123 1229-E6
6100 SD 92124 1229-E6
6100 SD 92145 1229-F1
8400 SD 92126 1229-F1
9100 SD 92126 1209-E6
KEARNY VILLA WY
5200 SD 92123 1249-C1
KEARSARGE RD
1600 SD 92037 1227-G6
KEATING ST
1600 SD 92103 1268-H6
3500 SD 92110 1268-H6
KEATS PL
- CRLB 92008 1107-B7
KEATS ST
2800 SD 92106 1288-B1
KECK CT
9400 SD 92129 1189-E6
KEDZIE AV
700 SD 92154 1330-G7
KEEGAN PL
13300 SD 92130 1188-A4
KEELER AV
4200 SD 92113 1289-H6
KEELER CT
1200 SD 92113 1289-H6
KEEMO CT
8800 SDCo 92040 1232-B6
KEEMO TER
12400 SDCo 92040 1232-B6
KEEN DR
2500 SD 92139 1310-E1
KEENAN ST
9000 SD 92126 1209-B7
KEENELAND RW
9700 SD 92037 1227-J1
KEENEY ST
4900 LMSA 91941 1270-F2
4900 SD 92115 1270-F2
KEIGHLEY CT
7000 SD 92120 1250-A5
KEIGHLEY ST
7000 SD 92120 1250-A5
KEIR ST
9000 SD 92123 1249-D6
KEISHA CV
11400 SD 92126 1208-J2
KEISHA TER
7400 SD 92126 1208-J2
KEITH ST
10600 SNTE 92071 1231-D2
KELBURN AV
8800 SDCo 91977 1290-J4
KELD CT
12200 SD 92129 1188-J7
KELGLEN LN
1300 SDCo 92084 1108-A1
1300 VSTA 92084 1108-A1
KELLAM CT
13100 SD 92130 1188-A5
KELLBARA CT
14100 SD 92129 1189-E2
KELLEEN DR
100 VSTA 92083 1087-G4
KELLI LN
14100 SDCo 92021 1232-G5
KELLIE CT
3700 NATC 91950 1310-D3
KELLINGTON CT
3500 OCN 92056 1107-E3
KELLINGTON PL
1700 ENCT 92024 1147-H7
KELLOGG AV
1900 CRLB 92008 1127-C3
KELLOGG DR
3300 SD 92106 1287-J4
3300 SD 92106 1288-A4
KELLOGG ST
2800 SD 92106 1288-A4
KELLOGG WY
3300 SD 92106 1288-A4
KELLRAE LN
400 ESCN 92026 1109-G2
KELLY AV
1900 SDCo 92065 1152-E7
2100 SDCo 92065 1172-D1
KELLY CT
400 ESCN 92027 1130-D1
KELLY DR
900 SDCo 92019 1253-B1
1200 ENCT 92024 1167-F1
4800 CRLB 92008 1106-J7
KELLY PL
6500 SD 92111 1268-H1
KELLY ST
100 OCN 92054 1106-C3
6500 SD 92111 1268-H1
KELLYN LN
4200 SDCo 92084 1068-E4
KELLY WILLIAM LN
1400 SDCo 91901 1234-A6
1400 SDCo 91901 1233-J6
KELOWNA LN
14000 SDCo 92082 1070-E1
KELOWNA RD
11100 SD 92126 1209-C2
KELSEY ST
3300 SD 92124 1249-G4
KELSFORD PL
3300 SD 92130 1188-A6
KELSO CT
- CHV 91911 1330-H2
KELSO RD
8700 SD 92126 1209-C7
KELSO ST
8700 SDCo 91977 1291-A3
KELSON PL
1800 ESCN 92029 1129-F6
KELTON AV
5700 LMSA 91942 1250-J7
KELTON CT
5600 SD 92114 1290-B3
KELTON DR
3700 OCN 92056 1086-J6
3700 OCN 92056 1087-A7
KELTON PL
5600 SD 92114 1290-B2
KELTON RD
800 SD 92114 1290-B2
KEMAH LN
10800 SD 92131 1209-H4
KEMBERLY LN
3100 SDCo 91935 1293-A1
KEMERTON RD
10500 SD 92126 1208-J4
KEMPER CT
3600 SD 92110 1268-D5
KEMPER ST
3100 SD 92110 1268-D5
4300 LMSA 91941 1270-F4
KEMPF ST
3000 LMGR 91945 1270-H6
KEMPTON ST
100 SDCo 91977 1291-B3
KEN LN
10400 SNTE 92071 1231-E3
KENALAN DR
1100 SD 92154 1350-F1
KENAMAR CT
7700 SD 92121 1209-A7
KENAMAR DR
8900 SD 92121 1229-A1
9000 SD 92121 1209-A7
KENDA WY
2400 SDCo 91901 1234-C6
KENDALL ST
3700 SD 92109 1248-A4
KENDI LN
1200 SDCo 92028 1028-D4
KENDLE RD
- ImCo 92227 431-E2
KENDRA CT
14300 PWY 92064 1190-E2
KENDRA WY
14100 PWY 92064 1190-E2
KENDRICK WY
1400 ELCJ 92019 1252-A7
KENESAW CT
9700 SNTE 92071 1231-F4
KENISON DR
900 SDCo 92036 1136-D7
900 SDCo 92036 1156-D1
KENMORE TER
4700 SD 92116 1269-E3
KENNEBECK CT
700 SD 92109 1267-H2
KENNEBUNK ST
14400 PWY 92064 1190-H5
KENNEDY LN
300 OCN 92054 1086-D6
KENNEDY ST
200 CHV 91911 1330-D3
KENNELWORTH LN
3200 SDCo 91902 1310-H1
KENNESTER ST
3000 LMGR 91945 1270-E7
KENNEY ST
10300 ELCJ 92020 1231-E7
KENNINGTON RD
1700 ENCT 92024 1147-A2
KENORA DR
1600 ESCN 92027 1130-C2
3200 SDCo 91977 1271-C5
KENORA LN
9600 SDCo 91977 1271-C6
KENORA PL
1300 ESCN 92027 1130-B2
KENORA ST
1400 ESCN 92027 1130-C2
KENORA VW
9600 SDCo 91977 1271-D6
KENORA WOODS LN
9700 SDCo 91977 1271-C6
KENOSHA AV
3900 SD 92117 1248-D4
KENOVA ST
8000 SD 92126 1209-B4
KENS RD
100 SDCo 92021 1252-J3
KENSAL CT
15000 SDCo 92082 1070-H6
KENSETT PL
9100 SD 92126 1209-D2
KENSINGTON DR
100 SMCS 92069 1108-D7
4500 SD 92116 1269-G3
KENSINGTON PL
5700 SDCo 92003 1048-B7
KENSLEY WY
6900 SD 92126 1208-H4
KENT AV
1200 ESCN 92026 1110-A7
1200 ESCN 92027 1110-A7
KENT DR
700 SDCo 92021 1252-H1
KENT PL
1700 SDCo 92024 1108-C1
5800 SD 92120 1250-B7
KENT ST
1900 CHV 91913 1311-D5
KENTFIELD CT
- PWY 92064 1190-F2
KENTFIELD DR
- PWY 92064 1190-F1
- SMCS 92069 1108-J5
KENTFIELD PL
- PWY 92064 1190-E1
KENTMERE TER
700 SD 92154 1330-H7
N KENTON AV
- NATC 91950 1290-B6
- SD 92114 1290-B6
S KENTON AV
- NATC 91950 1290-B6
KENTUCKY ST
400 SDCo 92028 1027-F1
KENTWOOD DR
700 SDCo 92036 1156-D1
KENWELL ST
5900 SD 92139 1290-D7
KENWOOD CT
3700 SDCo 91977 1271-B5
KENWOOD DR
4000 SDCo 91977 1271-B5
4000 SDCo 91941 1271-A5
KENWOOD ST
5600 SD 92114 1290-B3
KENWYN ST
2300 OCN 92054 1106-E1
KENYATTA CT
100 SD 92114 1290-C4
KENYATTA DR
100 SD 92114 1290-C4
KENYON CT
3100 SD 92110 1268-D5
KENYON ST
3400 SD 92110 1268-D5
KEOKI CT
7200 SD 92126 1208-J5
KEOKI ST
10200 SD 92126 1208-J5
KEOKUK CT
3200 SD 92117 1248-C2
KEOS WY
4900 OCN 92056 1107-F5
KEPHART RD
- SD 92106 1288-A7
KEPPLER DR
10000 SD 92124 1249-G2
KEPPLER PL
10200 SD 92124 1249-G2
KERCH ST
6100 SD 92115 1270-D5
KEREMEOS WY
8800 SD 92126 1209-D1
KERI WY
3700 SDCo 92028 1048-A4
KERISIANO WY
1700 OCN 92054 1106-E2
KERN CT
- OCN 92057 1086-H1
KERN PL
1100 ESCN 92027 1109-J6
KERNEL PL
900 CHV 91910 1310-G6
KERR WY
1300 OCN 92054 1106-D2
KERRAN ST
12300 PWY 92064 1190-D7
KERRI LN
25100 SDCo 92065 1173-H3
KERRIA DR
- SD 92109 1248-C6
KERRICK RD
- SD 92106 1288-B7
KERRIGAN CT
10500 SNTE 92071 1231-E2
KERRIGAN ST
10100 SNTE 92071 1231-E2
KERRY LN
- SD 92129 1188-J3
- SD 92130 1188-J3
KERSEY PL
11900 SD 92128 1190-A2
KERSHAW RD
- ImCo 92227 411-C11
- ImCo 92233 411-C11
KERSHAWN PL
1000 SDCo 92029 1149-H2
KERWOOD CT
4100 SD 92130 1188-B5
KESLING CT
4800 SD 92117 1248-G1
KESLING PL
4800 SD 92117 1248-H1
KESLING ST
5000 SD 92117 1248-G1
KESTON CT
3400 SD 92111 1248-J4
KESTRAL DR
300 SMCS 92078 1128-G2
KESTREL DR
7000 CRLB 92009 1127-B7
KESTREL PL
9300 SD 92129 1189-E6
KESTREL ST
12400 SD 92129 1189-E5
KESTREL WY
9400 SD 92129 1189-E6
KESWICK CT
4700 SD 92130 1188-C4
KETCH WY
6700 CRLB 92009 1127-A5
KETRON AV
13400 PWY 92064 1190-E3
KETTERING LN
28300 SDCo 92026 1089-D4
KETTNER BLVD
500 SD 92101 1288-J4
2700 SD 92103 1288-J1
2700 SD 92101 1268-H7
2700 SD 92103 1268-H7
3600 SD 92110 1268-H6
KEVIN DR
1800 VSTA 92084 1087-H3
KEW ST
10200 SDCo 92026 1109-E1
KEW TER
2600 SD 92104 1269-F7
KEY LN
1700 ELCJ 92021 1252-A2
1700 SDCo 92021 1252-A2
KEYES RD
1100 SDCo 92065 1152-J7
1500 SDCo 92065 1172-J1
KEY LARGO DR
1800 VSTA 92083 1107-H5
KEY LARGO PL
300 ELCJ 92021 1251-G5
KEYPORT ST
300 OCN 92057 1066-H6
KEYS PL
1400 SDCo 92083 1107-G3
KEYS CREEK RD
11900 SDCo 92082 1049-H7
12100 SDCo 92082 1050-A7
KEYSER CT
1500 SDCo 92065 1172-G1
KEYSER RD
1300 SDCo 92065 1172-G2
KEYSTONE CIR
3500 OCN 92056 1107-E3
KEYSTONE CT
8600 SD 92126 1209-C2
KEYSTONE RD Rt#-S27
- ImCo 92227 431-C3
- ImCo 92251 431-C3
KEYSTONE WY
1200 VSTA 92083 1127-J1
1200 VSTA 92083 1128-A1
KHAYYAM RD
100 ESCN 92025 1129-J4
100 ESCN 92025 1130-A3
KHE SANH ST
- SD 92140 1268-F7
KHISH LN
1000 SDCo 91901 1233-H7
KHURAM ST
13400 SDCo 92040 1232-D4
KHURTZ RD
4800 SDCo 92004 (1099-G3 See Page 1098)
KIAVO DR
19300 SDCo 92027 1091-H5
19300 SDCo 92082 1091-H4
KIBBINGS RD
13200 SD 92130 1188-A4
KIBLER DR
10000 SD 92126 1209-A5
KICA CT
32300 SDCo 92061 1050-J5
KICKAPOO CT
4500 SD 92117 1248-D2
KICKIN HORSE TR
7300 SDCo 92036 1138-C6
KIDD ST
900 NATC 91950 1309-G2
900 NATC 92136 1309-G2
KIDD WY
500 ELCJ 92020 1251-F7
KIEFER RD
900 ImCo 92250 431-E7
KIEFFER LN
3600 OCN 92057 1086-G5
KIEL RD
1000 SDCo 92028 1027-G4
S KIHRIDGE LN
100 ENCT 92024 1167-H1
KIKA CT
9700 SD 92129 1189-F7
KILBIRNIE LN
- SDCo 92084 1068-C6
KILBOURN DR
8600 SD 92037 1228-A4
KILBY LN
1300 VSTA 92083 1108-A1
KILDARE WY
1100 ELCJ 92020 1251-A3
KILDEER CT
1100 ENCT 92024 1147-D3
KILEY RD
500 CHV 91910 1310-F6
KILGORE RD
1600 ImCo 92243 6559-H3
KILKEE ST
5000 SD 92117 1228-H7
KILKENNY DR
100 ENCT 92007 1167-D4
KILLARNEY TER
400 SMCS 92069 1108-J4
KILLDEER LN
- OCN 92057 1086-H2
KILT CT
7600 SD 92111 1249-A3
KIM PL
1400 CHV 91911 1330-E4
2600 SD 92123 1249-F6
KIMBALL ST
600 ESCN 92027 1130-C2
KIMBALL TER
300 CHV 91910 1310-A5
KIMBALL WY
400 NATC 91950 1309-J2
KIMBALL VALLEY RD
19300 SDCo 92065 1192-C3
KIMBER LN
9000 SDCo 92040 1232-D6
KIMBERLY CT
2300 CRLB 92008 1106-G4
KIMBERLY DR
6100 LMSA 91942 1250-H6
KIMBERLY LN
4100 OCN 92056 1087-C6
KIMBERLY PL
2400 ESCN 92027 1110-D6
KIMBERLY WY
1400 SDCo 91906 (1318-G4 See Page 1298)
KIMBERLY WOODS DR
1500 ELCJ 92020 1271-E1
KIMDA CT
14400 SDCo 91935 1292-J1
14400 SDCo 91935 1293-A1
KIMI LN
6300 ELCJ 92020 1251-C5
6300 LMSA 91942 1251-C5
KIMMY CT
6300 SD 92114 1290-D4
KIMSUE WY
3800 SD 92154 1350-F1
KINCAID RD
1900 SD 92133 1288-E1
2100 SD 92133 1268-E7
KINCAID ST
9900 SNTE 92071 1231-F4
KING CT
- SDCo 92055 1086-A2
KING LN
100 SDCo 92028 1027-J2
KING RD
- ImCo 92250 431-E6
KING ST
- CHV 91910 1310-D7
3600 LMSA 91941 1270-E5
3600 LMSA 92115 1270-E5
3600 SD 92115 1270-E5
KING ARTHUR CT
2300 SD 92037 1247-H1
KING ARTHURS CT
3100 SDCo 91977 1271-A6
KINGBIRD AV
8600 SNTE 92071 1230-G7
KINGBIRD LN
- CRLB 92009 1127-D4
KING CREEK CIR
- CHV 91915 1311-H5
KING CREEK DR
- CHV 91915 1311-H5
KING CREEK WY
- CHV 91915 1311-H5
KINGFISHER LN
7100 CRLB 92009 1127-C7
KINGFISHER CREEK RD
10700 SDCo 92021 1232-J1
10700 SDCo 92021 1233-A1
KING KELLY CT
8000 SDCo 92021 1252-A1
KING KELLY DR
7900 SDCo 92021 1252-A1
KINGLET RD
1700 SDCo 92069 1128-A4
KINGLET WY
- CRLB 92009 1127-D4
KINGMAN RD
15600 PWY 92064 1170-J6
KING PHILLIP CT
10600 SNTE 92071 1231-E2
KINGRIDGE DR
2400 SDCo 92028 1028-C7
KINGS AV
3600 OCN 92056 1107-D3
KINGS RD
1000 ESCN 92027 1110-B6
1700 VSTA 92084 1088-B3
KINGS TR
8500 SNTE 92071 1231-D7
KINGS WY
1500 ESCN 92027 1110-A5
1700 VSTA 92084 1088-B3
4800 SD 92117 1248-G1
KING SANDAY LN
10400 SDCo 92082 1069-E3
KINGS CROSS CT
700 ENCT 92007 1167-E2
KINGS CROSS DR
1400 ENCT 92007 1167-E2
KINGSFIELD CT
- SD 92130 1188-A5
KINGSFORD CT
12200 SDCo 92021 1252-A1
KINGSGATE SQ
12200 SD 92128 1170-B4
KINGSLAND RD
8400 SD 92123 1249-B7
KINGSLEY ST
3000 SD 92106 1268-C5
KING SOLOMON AV
- SD 92102 1289-G4
KINGSPINE AV
12300 SD 92131 1210-B4
KINGSTON CT
700 SD 92109 1267-H2
KINGSTON CT E
- CORD 92118 1329-E2
KINGSTON CT S
- CORD 92118 1329-E2
KINGSTON CT W
- CORD 92118 1329-E2
KINGSTON DR
1400 ESCN 92027 1130-C2
KINGSTON ST
3600 CRLB 92008 1106-J4
3600 CRLB 92008 1107-A4
KINGS VIEW CIR
2100 SDCo 91977 1271-A7
KINGS VIEW CT
5800 SD 92114 1290-C4
KINGS VILLA RD
1400 SDCo 92065 1152-E2
KINGSWOOD CT
5200 OCN 92056 1087-D1
KINGSWOOD DR
- CHV 91911 1330-E4
KINGSWOOD ST
300 SD 92114 1290-F6
KINROSS CT
1900 SDCo 92027 1130-D4
KINSELLA PT
13000 SD 92130 1187-J5
13000 SD 92130 1188-A5
KIOWA DR
5300 LMSA 91942 1270-F1
5500 SD 91942 1270-F1
5500 SD 91942 1250-F7
KIPLING LN
5400 CRLB 92008 1107-C7
KIRA PL
31300 SDCo 92082 1070-F2
KIRBY CT
9000 SD 92126 1209-D1
KIRBY PL
11500 SD 92126 1209-D1
KIRK PL
1700 CRLB 92008 1106-H6
KIRKCALDY DR
4100 SD 92111 1249-A3
KIRKCALDY RD
900 SDCo 92028 1027-G6
KIRKHAM CT
12400 PWY 92064 1190-D6
KIRKHAM RD
12100 PWY 92064 1190-D6
KIRKHAM WY
13000 PWY 92064 1190-E7
KIRKLAND AV
2500 SDCo 92029 1129-H7
2500 SDCo 92029 1149-H1
KIRKS WY
500 SDCo 92065 1152-J7
KIRKWALL AV
2700 CRLB 92008 1107-A5
KIRKWOOD PL
600 SD 92037 1247-G4
KIRMAR PL
1200 OCN 92054 1106-D3
KIRSTEN LN
29800 SDCo 92084 1068-D6
KIRSTEN PL
2800 SDCo 91977 1271-B7
KIRTRIGHT ST
500 SD 92114 1290-C5
KISMET RD
11700 SD 92128 1189-J6
11700 SD 92128 1190-A6
KISO GN
1300 ESCN 92025 1129-H5
KISO LN
1800 SDCo 92069 1109-A2
1800 SMCS 92069 1109-A2
KIT CARSON PL
10200 SNTE 92071 1231-F3
KITCHEN CREEK RD
3100 SDCo 92066 430-B7
KITE LN
1000 VSTA 92083 1108-A5
KITE PL
- CRLB 92009 1127-A4
KITE ST
3400 SD 92103 1268-J6
KITE HILL LN
11000 SD 92126 1209-E2

SAN DIEGO CO. INDEX

6595 KITTERY ST — SAN DIEGO CO. STREET INDEX — LAKESHORE DR

STREET
Block City ZIP Pg-Grid

KITTERY ST
14500 PWY 92064 1190-H4
KITTIWAKE LN
900 CHV 91911 1330-C2
KITTIWAKE WY
4400 OCN 92057 1087-A3
KITTY LN
8600 SNTE 92071 1231-F7
KIVA LN
1500 VSTA 92084 1087-H3
KIWI GN
1700 ESCN 92026 1109-D6
KIWI PL
- CRLB 92009 1127-D4
KIWI ST
7600 SD 92123 1249-A7
KIWI MEADOW LN
9600 SDCo 92026 1069-D7
9600 SDCo 92026 1089-D1
KLAMATH
14100 SDCo 92040 1232-H5
KLAMATH ST
- OCN 92057 1086-H1
KLAUBER AV
1000 SD 92114 1290-D2
1900 LMGR 91945 1290-E2
KLEAVELAND PL
500 VSTA 92084 1087-H4
KLEEFELD AV
4500 SD 92117 1248-E1
KLINE ST
700 SD 92037 1227-E7
KLISH WY
800 DLMR 92014 1187-G5
KLOKE RD
600 ImCo 92231 431-C7
KLUCEWICH RD
2900 SDCo 91901 1234-B4
KNABE LN
9900 SNTE 92071 1231-B4
KNAPP DR
1700 VSTA 92084 1087-G3
W KNAPP DR
300 VSTA 92083 1087-G3
KNAPP ST
4600 SD 92117 1248-F5
KNAUL CT
8900 SD 92129 1189-C4
KNIGHT DR
10000 SD 92126 1209-A5
KNIGHTSBRIDGE CT
700 ENCT 92007 1167-E2
KNIGHTS REALM
1500 SMCS 92069 1128-D2
KNOB HILL DR
800 SDCo 92036 1156-D2
1900 SDCo 91977 1291-A1
KNOB HILL RD
1100 SMCS 92069 1109-C7
KNOLL CT
5000 LMSA 91941 1271-B2
KNOLL DR
1300 OCN 92054 1086-F7
KNOLL RD
- VSTA 92083 1087-G6
500 SMCS 92069 1108-G7
KNOLL VW
2200 ESCN 92029 1129-E6
KNOLL CREST PL
12100 SDCo 92040 1232-A5
KNOLL EDGE CT
- SDCo 92065 1173-D2
KNOLLFIELD WY
1700 ENCT 92024 1147-G6
KNOLL PARK GN
- ESCN 92029 1129-H5
KNOLL PARK LN
800 SDCo 92028 997-H7
800 SDCo 92028 1027-H1
KNOLLVIEW DR
9900 SDCo 91977 1291-D1
9900 SDCo 91977 1271-H7
KNOLLVIEW LN
2200 SDCo 91977 1271-H7
2200 SDCo 91977 1291-D1
KNOLL VISTA DR
900 SDCo 92069 1128-D2
KNOLLWOOD AV
2100 SDCo 92028 1027-H6
KNOLL WOOD CT
4700 OCN 92056 1087-D3
KNOLLWOOD DR
3500 CRLB 92008 1107-C3
KNOLLWOOD PL
1400 CHV 91915 1311-G7
KNOLLWOOD RD
7900 SD 92114 1290-G3
KNOLLWOOD WY
9300 SNTE 92071 1231-A6
KNOTS LN
- CRLB 92009 1146-J1
KNOTT ST
2100 SD 92139 1290-F7
KNOTTWOOD WY
2600 SDCo 92028 1048-B3
KNOWLES AV
900 CRLB 92008 1106-E4
KNOWLTON CT
9400 SNTE 92071 1231-A5
KNOWLTON WILLIAMS RD
100 NATC 92136 1309-F1
100 SD 92136 1309-F1
3600 SD 92136 1289-F7
KNOX ST
4900 SD 92110 1268-F2
KNOXIE ST
3600 SD 92105 1270-A6
KNOXVILLE ST
1200 SD 92110 1268-E2
KOALA WY
1400 ELCJ 92019 1252-A7
KOBE DR
2600 SD 92123 1249-D6
KOBE PL
8900 SD 92123 1249-D6
KOBE WY
8900 SD 92123 1249-D5
KOE ST
1100 SD 92114 1290-G2
1500 LMGR 91945 1290-G2
KOELPER ST
- SDCo 92055 1085-H5
KOLMAR ST
200 SD 92037 1247-E2
KONA WY
3000 SD 92106 1288-A3
KONA KAI LN
1400 ESCN 92029 1129-D4

KOONCE DR
9000 SDCo 91977 1271-B5
KOONCE RD
8900 SNTE 92071 1231-H6
KOREA ST
- SD 92140 1268-E6
KORINK AV
2600 SD 92111 1249-A6
2600 SD 92111 1248-J6
KORNBLUM DR
26000 SDCo 92026 1089-E7
26000 SDCo 92026 1109-E1
KORREY DR
14100 SD 92129 1189-G2
KORY LN
1400 SDCo 92065 1152-J7
KOSTNER DR
700 SD 92154 1330-G7
900 SD 92154 1350-G1
KOZY CREST LN
12200 PWY 92064 1190-B1
KQ RANCH RD
- SDCo 92036 1156-G6
KRAFT ST
1600 OCN 92054 1086-B5
KRAMAR RD
- ImCo 92243 431-A6
1000 ImCo 92243 6559-A3
KRAMER ST
6700 SD 92111 1268-J1
KREINER WY
8400 SNTE 92071 1230-H6
KREMEYER CIR
2600 CRLB 92008 1106-E4
KRENNING ST
5100 SD 92105 1270-A7
KRENZ ST
8300 SD 92123 1249-B5
KRIM PL
1500 OCN 92054 1106-D2
KRIS RD
4100 SDCo 91935 1273-J4
4100 SDCo 91935 1274-A5
KRIS WY
9500 SNTE 92071 1231-B1
KRISHEN HEIGHTS RD
300 SDCo 92019 1253-D1
KRISTA CT
400 CHV 91910 1310-F6
KRISTEN CT
200 ENCT 92024 1147-D6
KRISTEN WY
9800 SDCo 92082 1069-D5
KRISTEN VILLA CT
100 SDCo 92065 1153-A6
KRISTI CT
2000 SDCo 92028 1048-B4
KRISTIE LN
1300 ELCJ 92019 1252-A5
KRISTIN CT
200 SD 92114 1290-D4
KRISTY LN
200 OCN 92054 1106-C3
KRUG CT
1300 VSTA 92083 1107-J3
KRYSTAL PL
- ESCN 92026 1109-D6
KUBLER RD
- ImCo 92231 431-A7
KUEBLER RANCH RD
- SDCo 92154 1332-C7
KUHN DR
800 CHV 91914 1311-F4
KUHNER WY
12100 SDCo 92040 1232-A1
KUMBERG MESA RD
- ImCo 92250 431-E7
KUMBERG MESA RD Rt#-S33
- ImCo 92250 431-F7
KUMEYAI TR
17300 SDCo 91901 1233-J2
17300 SDCo 91901 1234-A2
KUMQUAT DR
9600 SDCo 92040 1232-A4
KUMQUAT WY
600 OCN 92054 1086-F2
KUNDE CT
- SD 92130 1188-J3
KUNKLER LN
- SDCo 92004 (1121-J3 See Page 1100)
KUPA DR
16200 SDCo 92061 1051-B6
KURDSON WY
400 SDCo 91977 1291-B4
KURENDA WY
1800 SDCo 92083 1108-A3
KURLEY CT
2000 SDCo 91977 1290-J1
2300 SDCo 91977 1271-A7
KURTZ CT
- CORD 91932 1329-E4
KURTZ ST
1400 OCN 92054 1106-D1
1600 SD 92101 1268-G6
1700 SD 92110 1268-D4
KUTZ RD
- ImCo 92251 430-L4
KWAAYMII PT
- SDCo 92036 (1197-G5 See Page 1176)
KWAJALEIN RD
2300 CORD 92155 1309-B1
KYLE LN
1100 VSTA 92084 1087-J4
KYRSTEN TER
1400 SDCo 91901 1233-J6
KYRSTEN TRCT
1400 SDCo 91901 1233-J6

L

L AV
100 NATC 91950 1289-J7
800 NATC 91950 1309-J1
1400 NATC 91950 1310-A2
L AVEX
1200 NATC 91950 1309-J1
1200 NATC 91950 1310-A1
L CT
- SD 92126 1209-F7
L ST
- CHV 91911 1330-B2
500 SD 92101 1289-B4
1900 SD 92102 1289-C4
E L ST
- CHV 91911 1330-E1

LA ALAMEDA
- ESCN 92026 1109-G7
600 ENCT 92024 1147-F5
12400 SDCo 92021 1252-A1
LA ALBERCA AV
- SDCo 92127 1169-F4
LA AMAPOLA
17800 SDCo 92067 1148-J7
LA AMATISTA RD
300 DLMR 92014 1187-G6
300 SD 92014 1187-G6
LA BAJADA Rt#-S9
17400 SDCo 92067 1168-A2
17600 SDCo 92067 1167-J2
LA BARCA ST
500 SDCo 91977 1291-C3
LA BARRANCA DR
200 SOLB 92075 1167-H6
LA BELLA CIR
1800 OCN 92054 1106-D1
LABON WY
500 SD 92113 1289-F5
LA BONITA
- VSTA 92083 1107-D2
LA BONITA CT
1600 SDCo 92069 1128-C2
1600 SMCS 92069 1128-C2
LA BONITA DR
800 SDCo 92069 1128-C3
800 SMCS 92069 1128-C3
LA BONITA WY
1600 SDCo 92069 1128-C2
1600 SMCS 92069 1128-C2
LABRADOR LN
3500 SMCS 92069 1108-D6
9500 SDCo 92021 1232-J4
LA BREA CT
100 SDCo 92065 1152-F6
LA BREA ST
1600 SDCo 92065 1152-E7
1900 ESCN 92026 1109-E5
2200 SDCo 92065 1172-D1
LA BRISA
17200 SDCo 92067 1168-H2
LA BRUCHERIE RD
- IMP 92251 6499-E2
800 ImCo 92243 431-B7
1300 ImCo 92243 6559-F4
1600 ELCN 92243 6559-E1
1800 ELCN 92243 6499-E5
2000 ImCo 92243 6499-E5
2300 IMP 92243 6499-E2
2700 IMP 92251 431-B4
LA BRUSCA WY
7900 CRLB 92009 1147-G4
LA BUENA VIDA
900 SDCo 92028 1027-H7
LA BUTTE LN
8600 SNTE 92071 1231-A7
LA CALLECITA
2200 SD 92103 1268-G5
LA CALMA
500 ESCN 92029 1149-J3
LA CAMESA ST
8800 SD 92129 1189-C2
LA CAMPANA CT
3800 SMCS 92069 1128-C1
LA CANADA RD
3600 SDCo 92028 1048-A4
4600 SDCo 92028 1047-J5
LA CANADA ST
300 SD 92037 1247-F3
LA CAPELA PL
7900 CRLB 92009 1147-G3
LA CARTERA ST
8800 SD 92129 1189-C2
LA CASA DR
1000 SDCo 92069 1128-B3
LA CASA LN
1100 SDCo 92069 1128-C3
LA CASITA DR
1500 SDCo 92069 1128-C2
LA CASITA WY
4200 OCN 92057 1086-J3
LA CATRINA
17600 SDCo 92067 1149-A6
LACAVA PL
2000 SDCo 92019 1272-C4
LA CAZADORA
18300 SDCo 92067 1148-D7
LACE PL
4900 SD 92102 1290-A2
LACEBARK ST
800 SMCS 92069 1109-B5
LA CHICA DR
1400 CHV 91911 1330-J3
LACIE LN
12000 SDCo 92040 1231-J7
12000 SDCo 92040 1232-A7
LA CIENAGA RD
1200 SMCS 92069 1109-C5
LA CIENEGA RD
100 SMCS 92069 1108-J3
100 SMCS 92069 1109-A3
W LA CIENEGA RD
- SMCS 92069 1108-H3
LA CIMA DR
1500 SD 92109 1268-A1
LA CINTURA CT
8800 SD 92129 1189-C2
LACK RD
- ImCo 92227 431-A1
- ImCo 92259 431-A2
5600 ImCo 92227 411-A11
LACKAWANNA WY
3000 SD 92117 1248-F6
LACO DR
4500 SD 92115 1270-D4
LA COLINA DR
900 ESCN 92027 1130-F1
LA COLINA RD
11600 SD 92131 1210-A4
LA COLUSA DR
3700 SMCS 92069 1108-C7
3700 SMCS 92069 1128-D1
LACONIA ST
2200 SD 92114 1270-E7
2200 SD 92114 1290-E1
LA CORTA CIR
1400 LMGR 91945 1290-E2
LA CORTA ST
1400 LMGR 91945 1290-F1
LA CORUNA PL
7600 CRLB 92009 1147-G1
LA COSTA
- CRLB 92009 1126-H5
- SMCS 92078 1129-C1
LA COSTA AV
100 ENCT 92024 1147-D1

LA COSTA AV
100 CRLB 92024 1147-A2
2200 CRLB 92009 1147-F1
2500 CHV 91915 1311-G4
3400 CRLB 92009 1148-A2
LA COSTA MEADOWS DR
1600 SMCS 92069 1128-A5
1700 CRLB 92069 1128-A5
LA CRESCENTA
5500 SDCo 92067 1148-B7
5500 SDCo 92067 1168-C1
LA CRESCENTIA DR
400 SD 92106 1288-A4
1200 CHV 91910 1311-A5
LA CRESTA BLVD
100 SDCo 92021 1232-J7
100 SDCo 92021 1252-J1
LA CRESTA DR
400 OCN 92054 1086-F6
3600 SD 92107 1268-B7
3700 SD 92107 1288-B1
LA CRESTA RD
9800 SDCo 91977 1271-D7
E LA CRESTA RD
1900 SDCo 92021 1252-C3
W LA CRESTA RD
100 SDCo 92021 1252-F3
LA CRESTA TR
100 SDCo 92019 1253-C1
LA CRESTA WY
3900 SDCo 91902 1310-J3
LA CRESTA HEIGHTS CT
800 SDCo 92021 1252-H2
LA CRESTA HEIGHTS RD
100 SDCo 92021 1252-H2
LA CROSSE AV
4400 SD 92117 1248-D2
LACROSSE PL
600 ESCN 92025 1130-B4
LA CRUZ DR
4700 LMSA 91941 1271-C2
4700 SDCo 91941 1271-C2
LA CRUZ PL
4800 SDCo 91941 1271-C2
LA CUENTA CT
10700 SD 92124 1249-H3
LA CUENTA DR
4400 SD 92124 1249-H1
LA CUESTA DR
9300 SDCo 91941 1271-B3
LA CUESTA DE PAUMA
- SDCo 92082 1070-G1
LA CUMBRE DR
1500 SD 92037 1247-G2
LADD ST
4100 SD 92109 1248-B6
LADDECK CT
7200 SD 92114 1290-F2
LADDIE LN
8800 SD 92123 1249-D5
LADERA CT
2000 CRLB 92009 1147-F2
LADERA ST
4400 SD 92107 1287-H3
LADERA WY
200 OCN 92054 1086-E6
LADERA LINDA
1200 SOLB 92014 1167-H7
1200 SOLB 92014 1187-J2
LADERA LINDA WY
1200 SOLB 92014 1187-J2
LADERA PIEDRA WY
16100 PWY 92064 1170-C5
LADERA SARINA
4800 SDCo 92014 1168-A7
LADERA VISTA RD
3800 SDCo 92028 1047-G4
LADERO PL
1900 ESCN 92029 1129-F6
LADIOSA CT
900 CHV 91910 1310-H4
LADLEHILL DR
2300 SD 92139 1290-G7
LADNER ST
4700 SD 92113 1289-J5
LADO DE LOMA DR
100 VSTA 92083 1087-G7
600 VSTA 92083 1107-H1
LADOGA LN
1700 SDCo 92083 1108-A2
LA DONNA LN
12200 SDCo 92040 1232-A7
LA DORNA ST
5000 SD 92115 1270-D2
LADRIDO LN
23600 SDCo 92065 409-H11
LADRILLO ST
7000 SD 92111 1248-J6
LA DUELA LN
2600 CRLB 92009 1147-G3
LA DUENA WY
10300 SD 92124 1229-G7
LADY LN
10800 SDCo 92040 1232-B1
LADY BESS PL
8000 SD 92126 1209-B5
LADY BESS WY
10100 SD 92126 1209-B5
LADYBIRD LN
5500 SD 92037 1247-G4
LADYBUG LN
600 SDCo 92069 1088-G6
LADY FERN CT
11200 SD 92131 1209-J2
LADY HILL RD
3400 SD 92130 1187-J5
LADYSMITH DR
700 ELCJ 92020 1251-G7
700 SDCo 92020 1251-G7
LADYS SECRET CT
5900 SDCo 92067 1188-E1
LADYS SECRET DR
15200 SDCo 92067 1188-F1
LAE RD
2200 CORD 92155 1309-A2
LA ENTRADA
400 ENCT 92024 1147-F5
1100 SDCo 92028 1027-H2
3000 SDCo 92026 1109-G2
17400 SDCo 92067 1168-A2
LA ENTRADITA
3200 SDCo 92026 1109-G2
LA ESPADA
6500 SDCo 92067 1168-E4
LA FAMILIA CT
13600 SDCo 92040 1232-E5

LAFAYETTE CT
2300 CRLB 92008 1106-H4
LAFAYETTE PL
800 CHV 91913 1311-E5
LAFE DR
10000 SNTE 92071 1231-D2
LA FELICE LN
900 SDCo 92028 1027-H6
LAFFEY CT
10100 SD 92124 1249-G3
LA FIESTA CT
1500 SDCo 92069 1128-C2
LA FIESTA DR
1500 SDCo 92069 1128-C2
LA FIESTA LN
900 SDCo 92069 1128-C2
LA FIESTA PL
900 SDCo 92069 1128-C2
LA FIESTA WY
900 SDCo 92069 1128-C2
LA FLECHA
5900 SDCo 92067 1168-D3
LA FLORA DR
1600 SDCo 92069 1128-C2
LA FLORESTA
4800 SDCo 92014 1168-A6
LA FORCE RD
400 SDCo 91901 1233-F7
LA FRANCE ST
2400 SD 92109 1248-B4
LA FREMONTIA
6100 SDCo 92067 1168-D2
LA GACHA LN
7900 CRLB 92009 1147-G4
LAGAN AV
1200 VSTA 92083 1087-G4
LA GARZA CT
6400 CRLB 92009 1127-G5
LAGASCA PL
800 CHV 91910 1310-H5
LAGEWAART RD
2200 SDCo 92065 1172-E4
LA GLORIETA
5200 SDCo 92067 1168-B4
LAGO CTE
6600 SDCo 92067 1188-G2
LAGO GRANDE DR
6400 SDCo 92003 1067-G3
LAGO LINDO
5600 SDCo 92067 1168-E1
6400 SDCo 92067 1148-F7
LA GOLONDRINA ST
2500 CRLB 92009 1127-G4
LAGO MADERO
2200 CHV 91914 1311-F3
LAGO MARCOS
- SMCS 92078 1129-C1
LAGOON DR
700 CHV 91910 1309-H7
LAGOON VIEW CT
1100 ENCT 92007 1167-F4
LAGOON VIEW DR
1800 CRLB 92008 1106-E2
1800 OCN 92054 1106-E2
2200 ENCT 92007 1167-F4
LAGO SERENO
3600 ESCN 92029 1150-A4
LAGO VENTANA
2200 CHV 91914 1311-E3
LAGO VISTA
18000 SDCo 92067 1148-E6
LA GRACIA
600 ENCT 92024 1147-F5
15800 SDCo 92067 1168-D3
LA GRAN AVD
1200 ENCT 92024 1147-F5
LA GRAN VIA
2500 CRLB 92009 1147-G1
LA GRANADA
6000 SDCo 92067 1168-D3
LA GRANADA Rt#-S9
4800 SDCo 92067 1168-A3
LA GRANADA CT
- SDCo 92067 1168-D3
LA GRANADA DR
1100 SDCo 92069 1128-E3
LA GRAN AVENIDA NORTE
1100 ENCT 92024 1147-F5
LAGUNA AV
600 ELCJ 92020 1251-E7
LAGUNA DR
500 CRLB 92008 1106-E4
500 SMCS 92069 1109-A6
LAGUNA LN
- SDCo 92066 1237-D7
1700 VSTA 92084 1088-A3
LAGUNA PL
19200 SDCo 92029 1149-D4
LAGUNA ST
200 SDCo 91934 (1321-H5 See Page 1300)
500 CHV 91910 1310-C7
1100 OCN 92054 1106-C2
LAGUNA TR
7400 SDCo 92066 1237-C7
LAGUNA MEADOW RD
- SDCo 91948 (1217-F4 See Page 1216)
- SDCo 91948 1218-A4
- SDCo 92066 (1217-F4 See Page 1216)
LAGUNA POINT CT
600 CHV 91911 1330-J4
LAGUNA SECA LP
1000 CHV 91915 1311-F5
LAGUNA VISTA
13500 SDCo 92021 1232-E7
LAGUNA VISTA CT
13500 SDCo 92021 1232-E7
LAGUNITA LN
900 SDCo 92084 1067-J6
S LAGUNITA LN
1000 SDCo 92084 1067-J6
LAGUNITA WY
- OCN 92057 1087-A1
LA HABRA DR
1400 SDCo 92069 1128-C3
LA HABRA GN
2000 ESCN 92026 1109-E5
LA HABRA ST
2000 ESCN 92026 1109-E5
LA HAINA PL
500 SDCo 92065 1152-F7
LA HAINA ST
1300 SDCo 92065 1152-F7
LA HARINA CT
14300 SD 92129 1189-C2

LAHINCH DR
1900 SD 92154 1351-E3
LAHITTE CT
3200 SD 92122 1228-C5
LA HONDA DR
1100 ESCN 92027 1110-B4
1300 SDCo 92027 1110-B4
LAHOUD DR
1700 ENCT 92007 1167-F3
LA HUERTA WY
700 SD 92154 1330-G7
LAIRD ST
8000 LMSA 91942 1250-H7
LAIRWOOD DR
10200 SNTE 92071 1231-D3
LAJA DR
12400 PWY 92064 1170-C7
LA JACARANDA
4800 SDCo 92067 1168-A2
LA JOLLA
- CRLB 92009 1126-J5
LA JOLLA BLVD
5000 SD 92109 1247-F4
5100 SD 92037 1247-E1
7300 SD 92037 1227-E7
LA JOLLA PL
- SMCS 92078 1129-C1
LA JOLLA COLONY DR
6000 SD 92122 1228-A5
LA JOLLA CORONA CT
800 SD 92037 1247-G3
LA JOLLA CORONA DR
5700 SD 92037 1247-G3
LA JOLLA FARMS RD
9300 SD 92037 1227-H1
LA JOLLA HERMOSA AV
5200 SD 92037 1247-F3
LA JOLLA KNOLL
1400 SD 92037 1227-G7
LA JOLLA MESA DR
5200 SD 92109 1247-G2
5300 SD 92037 1247-G2
LA JOLLA RANCHO RD
800 SD 92037 1247-H2
LA JOLLA SCENIC DR N
7600 SD 92037 1227-J3
7800 SD 92037 1228-A4
LA JOLLA SCENIC DR S
5900 SD 92037 1247-H2
6600 SD 92037 1227-J6
LA JOLLA SHORES DR
7900 SD 92037 1227-H5
8500 SD 92093 1227-H3
LA JOLLA SHORES LN
9000 SD 92037 1227-H3
9000 SD 92093 1227-H3
LA JOLLA VILLAGE DR
2800 SD 92093 1227-J3
2800 SD 92037 1227-J3
2900 SD 92037 1228-D2
2900 SD 92093 1228-A3
3200 SD 92161 1228-A3
3400 SD 92122 1228-D2
4300 SD 92121 1228-D2
LA JOLLA VISTA DR
7700 SD 92037 1227-J6
7700 SD 92037 1228-A6
LAJOS LN
15800 SDCo 92082 1071-A7
15800 SDCo 92082 1091-A1
LA JOTA WY
7900 SD 92037 1227-G6
LA JUNTA AV
3300 SD 92117 1248-C2
LAKE BLVD
3500 OCN 92056 1107-B2
LAKE CT
6800 SD 92111 1268-J1
LAKE DR
1200 ENCT 92007 1167-F3
1200 ENCT 92024 1167-F2
8300 SDCo 91977 1290-J6
19000 SD 92029 1149-D6
19000 SD 92067 1149-D6
19000 SDCo 92067 1149-D6
19500 SDCo 92029 1149-E1
20100 SDCo 92029 1129-E7
LAKE ADLON CT
6400 SD 92119 1250-G5
LAKE ADLON DR
7600 SD 92119 1250-G5
LAKE ALAMOR AV
6200 SD 92119 1250-J6
LAKE ALBANO AV
6200 SD 92119 1250-J5
LAKE ALTURAS AV
6200 SD 92119 1250-J5
LAKE ANDRITA AV
7700 SD 92119 1250-G5
LAKE ANGELA DR
8600 SD 92119 1250-J6
8600 SD 92119 1251-A5
8800 LMSA 91942 1251-A5
8900 ELCJ 92020 1251-A5
LAKE APOPKA PL
6200 SD 92119 1251-A5
LAKE ARAGO AV
6200 SD 92119 1250-J5
LAKE ARAL DR
6200 SD 92119 1250-J5
LAKE ARIANA AV
6200 SD 92119 1250-J5
LAKE ARROWHEAD DR
6200 SD 92119 1251-A5
6400 SD 92119 1250-J5
LAKE ARTEMUS AV
8300 SD 92119 1250-J5
LAKE ASHMERE CT
6500 SD 92119 1251-A4
LAKE ASHMERE DR
8600 SD 92119 1250-J5
8700 SD 92119 1251-A5
LAKE ASHWOOD AV
8300 SD 92119 1250-J5
LAKE ATHABASKA PL
6200 SD 92119 1251-A5
LAKE ATHABASKA WY
8700 SD 92119 1251-A5
LAKE ATLIN AV
6200 SD 92119 1250-J5
LAKE BACA DR
8300 SD 92119 1250-J5
LAKE BADIN AV
6200 LMSA 91942 1250-H6
6200 SD 92119 1250-H6
LAKE BEN AV
8300 SD 92119 1250-J4

LAKE BLUFF CIR
8500 SDCo 91977 1290-J5
8500 SDCo 91977 1291-A5
LAKE CANYON CT
9900 SNTE 92071 1231-A4
LAKE CANYON RD
9200 SNTE 92071 1231-A4
LAKE CAYUGA DR
7900 SD 92119 1250-H5
LAKE CIRCLE AV
4900 SDCo 92028 1048-J3
LAKE CIRCLE CT
3300 SDCo 92028 1048-J3
LAKE CIRCLE DR
3300 SDCo 92028 1048-H3
LAKE CIRCLE LN
4800 SDCo 92028 1048-J3
LAKE CIRCLE PL
3300 SDCo 92028 1048-H3
LAKE CIRCLE RD
4900 SDCo 92028 1048-J3
LAKE CIRCLE ST
4200 SDCo 92028 1048-J4
LAKE COMO AV
6300 SD 92119 1250-H5
LAKE COUNTRY DR
9200 SNTE 92071 1231-A5
LAKECREST PT
10600 SD 92131 1209-J3
LAKEDALE RD
1300 SDCo 92070 1135-D3
LAKE DECATUR AV
6300 SD 92119 1250-H5
LAKE DORA AV
6300 SD 92119 1250-H5
LAKE DRIVE CIR
- SDCo 92082 1090-B1
LAKE FOREST AV
4700 SD 92117 1248-D1
LAKE FOREST ST
2300 ESCN 92026 1109-J4
LAKE GABY AV
8300 SD 92119 1250-J4
LAKE GARDEN DR
3100 SDCo 92028 1048-E1
LAKE GROVE CT
11700 SD 92131 1210-A4
LAKE HELIX DR
- LMSA 91941 1271-D1
LAKE HELIX TER
9700 LMSA 91941 1271-C2
LAKE HILL RD
9200 SNTE 92071 1231-A5
LAKEHURST AV
3200 SD 92117 1248-D1
LAKE JENNINGS PARK RD
9200 SDCo 92021 1232-D3
9200 SDCo 92040 1232-D3
LAKE KATHLEEN AV
6300 SD 92119 1250-H5
LAKELAND DR
10100 SNTE 92071 1231-A3
LAKE LEVEN DR
6200 SD 92119 1250-G6
LAKE LOMOND DR
6200 SD 92119 1250-G6
LAKE LUCERNE DR
6200 SD 92119 1250-G6
LAKE MADERA CT
9200 SDCo 92040 1232-C5
LAKE MARCIA DR
6300 SD 92119 1250-J5
LAKEMEADOW DR
27900 SDCo 92026 1089-E4
LAKEMEADOW LN
10100 SDCo 92026 1089-E4
LAKE MERE CT
6400 SD 92119 1251-A5
LAKEMONT DR
2800 SDCo 92028 1048-E1
LAKE MORENA DR
1700 SDCo 91906 (1297-F6 See Page 1296)
1700 SDCo 91906 (1317-G1 See Page 1296)
LAKE MURRAY BLVD
5200 LMSA 91941 1270-F1
5200 LMSA 91942 1270-F1
5500 LMSA 91942 1250-G7
8300 SD 92119 1250-G7
8800 SD 92119 1251-A4
LAKE PARK AV
3500 SDCo 92028 1048-J3
LAKE PARK CT
4900 SDCo 92028 1048-J3
LAKE PARK LN
3900 SDCo 92028 1048-J3
LAKE PARK PL
4800 SDCo 92028 1048-J3
LAKE PARK RD
3500 SDCo 92028 1048-J3
LAKE PARK ST
3800 SDCo 92028 1048-J3
LAKE PARK WY
5500 LMSA 91942 1250-G7
5500 LMSA 91942 1270-G1
LAKEPORT RD
7900 SD 92126 1209-B4
LAKE POWAY RD
13400 PWY 92064 1170-G4
LAKE REE AV
7500 SD 92119 1250-G6
LAKE RIDGE CIR
100 SDCo 92028 1047-F3
LAKERIDGE CIR
2000 CHV 91913 1311-E4
LAKE RIDGE CT
10300 SDCo 91977 1291-E2
LAKE RIDGE DR
900 SMCS 92069 1128-B2
LAKERIDGE LN
1400 ELCJ 92020 1251-C2
LAKE RIDGE RD
3600 SDCo 92028 1047-G3
LAKE RIM RD
11200 SD 92131 1209-J3
LAKE SAN MARCOS DR
1500 SDCo 92069 1128-C2
1600 SMCS 92069 1128-C2
LAKE SHORE AV
3500 SDCo 92028 1048-J3
LAKE SHORE CT
4900 SDCo 92028 1048-J3
LAKESHORE DR
800 SMCS 92069 1128-F2
2000 CHV 91913 1311-E3

LAKE SHORE DR
SAN DIEGO CO. STREET INDEX
LAUREN LN 6596

SAN DIEGO CO.
INDEX

STREET
Block City ZIP Pg-Grid

LAKE SHORE DR
2400 SDCo 91906 (1297-E5 See Page 1296)
6100 SD 92119 1250-G5
LAKESHORE DR
12200 SDCo 92040 1232-A3
LAKE SHORE LN
3900 SDCo 92028 1048-J3
LAKE SHORE PL
4800 SDCo 92028 1048-J3
LAKE SHORE RD
3500 SDCo 92028 1048-J3
LAKE SHORE ST
3800 SDCo 92028 1048-J3
LAKESIDE AV
11300 SDCo 92040 1231-G1
12000 SDCo 92040 1232-A2
LAKESIDE DR
700 SMCS 92069 1128-F1
LAKESIDE LN
100 OCN 92056 1107-D2
LAKESIDE RD
2000 SDCo 92084 1108-C2
LAKE SYCAMORE DR
4500 SDCo 92028 1048-A6
LAKE TAHOE AV
7700 SD 92119 1250-G5
LAKE TAHOE CIR
6400 SD 92119 1250-G5
LAKE TAHOE CT
6400 SD 92119 1250-G5
LAKETREE DR
2900 SDCo 92028 1048-D1
3500 SDCo 92028 1028-E7
LAKE VALLEY RD
9100 SDCo 92021 1232-E6
LAKE VICENTE DR
11400 SDCo 92040 1212-C3
LAKEVIEW AV
100 SDCo 91977 1291-A5
LAKEVIEW CT
13700 SDCo 92040 1232-E5
LAKEVIEW DR
1600 ELCJ 92020 1251-C7
1600 LMSA 91942 1251-C7
2700 SDCo 92036 1136-D7
3000 SDCo 92036 1156-D1
3300 SDCo 91977 1270-J6
3300 SDCo 91977 1271-A6
9400 LMSA 91942 1251-C7
LAKE VIEW DR
29800 SDCo 91906 (1297-F5 See Page 1296)
LAKEVIEW DR
40000 SDCo 92028 997-B2
LAKE VIEW LN
100 SDCo 92021 1232-J7
100 SDCo 92021 1252-J1
LAKEVIEW RD
2100 SDCo 92084 1108-D2
8800 SDCo 92040 1232-D3
16100 PWY 92064 1170-F4
E LAKEVIEW RD
13300 SDCo 92040 1232-D5
W LAKEVIEW RD
13200 SDCo 92040 1232-D5
LAKEVIEW ST
25700 SDCo 92026 1109-E2
LAKE VIEW TER
- SDCo 92028 998-G5
3300 SDCo 92029 1149-G3
LAKEVIEW TER
9200 SDCo 92040 1232-E5
LAKEVIEW WY
13300 SDCo 92040 1232-C3
LAKEVIEW GRANADA DR
13000 SDCo 92040 1232-C5
LAKE VISTA CIR
5600 SDCo 92003 1068-B2
LAKE VISTA DR
5600 SDCo 92003 1068-B2
LAKE VISTA TER
30900 SDCo 92003 1068-B3
LAKEWIND ST
1600 ELCJ 92020 1251-B2
LAKE WOHLFORD CT
24800 ESCN 92027 1110-F4
LAKE WOHLFORD LN
16600 SDCo 92082 1091-C3
LAKE WOHLFORD RD
3600 ESCN 92027 1110-F3
24800 SDCo 92027 1110-J2
25500 SDCo 92027 1111-A1
N LAKE WOHLFORD RD
25900 SDCo 92027 1091-C6
25900 SDCo 92027 1111-C1
25900 SDCo 92082 1091-C4
LAKEWOOD AV
- ESCN 92027 1130-C1
LAKEWOOD CT
4900 SD 92122 1228-G5
LAKEWOOD LN
200 OCN 92054 1106-C2
LAKEWOOD ST
3400 CRLB 92008 1106-J4
6100 SD 92122 1228-G5
LAKY LN
900 SDCo 92065 1152-C5
LA LARGA VISTA
9100 SDCo 91977 1291-B1
LAL BAGH LN
10300 SDCo 92026 1069-E3
LA LINDA DR
1400 SDCo 92069 1128-C3
LALLEY LN
6900 SD 92119 1250-J3
LA LOMA
- CRLB 92009 1126-H4
LA LOMA DR
1400 SDCo 92069 1128-C3
LA LOMA SERENA
2100 SDCo 92084 1088-C1
LA LOMITA DR
100 ESCN 92026 1109-H6
LA MAC LN
29100 SDCo 92082 1070-F7
LA MACARENA AV
2400 CRLB 92009 1147-G4
LA MADERA
1600 SDCo 92069 1128-C2
LA MADRESELVA
15500 SDCo 92067 1168-B7
LA MANCHA DR
1400 SD 92109 1268-A1
LA MANCHA PL
1300 CHV 91910 1311-B7
LA MANDA RD
15000 PWY 92064 1170-C7

STREET
Block City ZIP Pg-Grid

LA MANZANA LN
1700 ESCN 92026 1109-E6
LAMAR ST
900 SDCo 92065 1152-D5
8600 SDCo 91977 1270-J6
8600 SDCo 91977 1271-A6
LA MARIQUITA SENDA
1600 SD 92173 1350-G2
LA MARQUE ST
2400 SD 92109 1248-B4
LAMAR SPRINGS CT
3100 SDCo 91977 1271-B6
LAMAS ST
5600 SD 92122 1228-B6
LAMBAR ST
1200 ESCN 92029 1129-G4
LAMBDA DR
6100 SD 92120 1250-C7
LAMBDA LN
5600 LMSA 91942 1250-J7
LAMBERT LN
5000 SD 92115 1270-E2
LAMBERT WY
6700 SD 92115 1270-E2
LAMBETH CT
2600 CRLB 92008 1106-J5
LA MEDIA RD
- CHV 91913 1311-D6
- CHV 91913 1331-D1
1200 SD 92154 1331-G7
1200 SD 92154 1351-G1
LAMENTIN CT
10800 SD 92124 1249-H1
LA MESA
- SMCS 92078 1129-C1
LA MESA AV
100 ENCT 92024 1147-B5
1000 SDCo 91977 1291-D2
LA MESA BLVD
7800 LMSA 91941 1270-H2
8600 LMSA 91941 1271-A2
8900 LMSA 91942 1271-A2
LA MESA CT
2100 SDCo 91977 1271-C7
2100 SDCo 91977 1291-D1
LA MESA CV
1400 SDCo 91977 1291-C2
LA MESITA PL
7300 LMSA 91941 1270-F2
LAMIA WY
4900 OCN 92056 1107-E5
LA MILLA
8000 SDCo 92067 1148-J5
LAMINACK LN
18900 SDCo 91935 (1314-G1 See Page 1294)
LA MIRADA AV
700 ENCT 92024 1147-C4
1100 ESCN 92026 1109-E5
LA MIRADA DR
1400 SMCS 92069 1108-C7
2100 VSTA 92083 1107-J6
2400 VSTA 92083 1108-A6
4600 OCN 92057 1066-J7
LA MIRADA WY
1300 ESCN 92026 1109-E5
LAMONT ST
3800 SD 92109 1248-A5
LA MORADA CT
5800 SD 92124 1229-G7
LA MORADA DR
10300 SD 92124 1229-G7
LA MOREE RD
100 SMCS 92078 1128-J1
100 SMCS - 1128-J1
100 SMCS - 1129-A1
100 SMCS 92078 1129-A1
LAMOUR LN
- SDCo 92127 1169-A1
LAMPASAS WY
3900 SMCS 92069 1128-C1
LAMPLIGHT DR
800 SD 92037 1247-G4
LAMPLIGHTER RD
700 SMCS 92069 1109-A5
LAMPLITE LN
13200 SDCo 92040 1232-C7
LAN LN
9900 SDCo 92026 1089-D2
LANA DR
5900 SD 92117 1248-J1
LANA LN
4700 SD 92117 1248-J1
LANAI DR
1700 SDCo 92019 1252-B4
LANAI WY
- OCN 92057 1087-B1
LANAKAI LN
- CRLB 92009 1126-H5
LANAO LN
2300 SD 92154 1330-C7
LANCASHIRE PL
- SMCS 92069 1108-J4
LANCASHIRE WY
18500 SD 92128 1150-B5
LANCASTER DR
5500 SD 92120 1250-B7
LANCASTER RD
200 ImCo 92243 6559-H3
2800 CRLB 92008 1107-B5
LANCASTER CREEK RD
4300 SDCo 92026 1049-A4
4300 SDCo 92028 1048-J3
4300 SDCo 92028 1049-A4
LANCASTER MOUNTAIN RD
31800 SDCo 92026 1049-B6
LANCE AV
8800 SDCo 91977 1290-J4
LANCE CT
6400 SD 92120 1250-B6
LANCE DR
9900 SDCo 92040 1232-C3
LANCE PL
6200 SD 92120 1250-C6
LANCE ST
5700 SD 92120 1250-C6
LANCE WY
6400 SD 92120 1250-B6
LANCELOT DR
2600 OCN 92054 1086-E6
LANCER AV
100 OCN 92054 1086-F3
LANCER GN
1200 ESCN 92029 1129-F5
LANCER WY
3300 CRLB 92008 1106-G5
LANCER PARK AV
600 SMCS 92069 1109-C6

STREET
Block City ZIP Pg-Grid

LANCEWOOD WY
2800 SDCo 92028 1048-C3
LANCHA ST
2700 SD 92111 1248-J6
LANDALE LN
100 SDCo 92019 1252-C5
LANDAU CT
5900 CRLB 92008 1127-D2
LANDAVO DR
900 SDCo 92027 1130-C4
LANDAVO RANCHO RD
1000 SDCo 92027 1130-C3
LANDBREEZE WY
11800 SD 92126 1209-A1
LANDFAIR CT
3600 SD 92130 1187-J4
LANDFAIR RD
13300 SD 92130 1187-J5
13500 SD 92130 1188-A4
LANDING DR
1700 VSTA 92083 1107-G4
LANDIS AV
100 CHV 91910 1310-B5
600 CHV 91910 1330-C1
LANDIS ST
2100 SD 92104 1269-C6
3600 SD 92105 1269-J5
5100 SD 92105 1270-A5
LANDMARK CT
- SMCS 92069 1108-J5
LANDMARK LN
37500 SDCo 92066 410-A9
LANDMARK PL
400 SMCS 92069 1108-J5
LANDON PL
7900 SD 92126 1209-B4
LANDQUIST DR
1600 ENCT 92024 1167-G1
LANDSCAPE DR
2700 SD 92139 1310-E2
LANDS END CT
1000 CRLB 92009 1127-A5
LANDS END WY
- OCN 92054 1086-B6
LANDSFORD WY
3500 CRLB 92008 1107-A3
LANE AV
900 CHV 91914 1311-G4
LA NEVASCA LN
2800 CRLB 92009 1147-H3
LANEWOOD CT
6800 SD 92111 1248-J4
LANEWOOD PL
800 ESCN 92026 1109-H4
LANG AV
2100 SDCo 91977 1291-A1
LANGDON LN
9000 SDCo 91977 1291-A1
LANGE AV
2600 SD 92122 1228-B6
LANGFORD
2600 SDCo 92084 1087-G1
LANGFORD ST
800 OCN 92054 1086-B6
LANGHOLM RD
8600 SDCo 92021 1232-F6
LANGLEY CT
10100 SDCo 92026 1109-E1
LANGLEY ST
300 SD 92102 1289-D4
LANGMUIR ST
2200 SD 92111 1248-H7
LANING RD
2600 SD 92133 1288-C1
LA NOCHE DR
900 SMCS 92069 1128-D2
1100 SDCo 92069 1128-D2
LANOITAN AV
1300 NATC 91950 1310-B1
N LANOITAN AV
- NATC 91950 1290-B6
LA NORIA
600 ENCT 92024 1147-F5
4300 SDCo 92067 1167-J3
4600 SDCo 92067 1168-A2
LA NORIA DR
3600 OCN 92054 1086-F2
LANPHIER LN
2700 SDCo 92070 1135-E7
LANSDALE DR
4600 SD 92130 1188-C4
LANSDOWN LN
3200 SDCo 92065 1172-C3
LANSFORD LN
10500 SD 92126 1208-H4
LANSING CIR
300 ESCN 92025 1129-J2
LANSING DR
7600 LMGR 91945 1290-H2
LANSLEY WY
100 CHV 91910 1310-B5
LANSTON ST
6400 SD 92111 1248-H7
LANTANA AV
1400 CHV 91911 1330-H3
LANTANA DR
- NATC 91950 1309-H1
4700 SD 92105 1269-J5
4900 SD 92105 1270-A6
LANTANA TER
7000 CRLB 92009 1127-A6
LANTANA WY
800 VSTA 92083 1108-A4
LANYARD PL
2300 CRLB 92008 1107-C7
LANZA CT
1000 SDCo 92069 1128-F3
LA ORILLA
4400 SDCo 92067 1167-J4
4400 SDCo 92067 1168-A4
LA ORQUIDA
7600 SDCo 92067 1148-H6
LA PALMA
7000 SDCo 92067 1168-F1
LA PALMA DR
700 SDCo 92028 1027-H3
LA PALMA ST
1300 SD 92109 1247-J7
1300 SD 92109 1248-A7
LA PALOMA
6300 OCN 92057 1067-E3
LA PALOMA AV
1200 ESCN 92026 1109-E5
LA PALOMA GN
1200 ESCN 92026 1109-E5
LA PALOMA ST
4100 SD 92107 1288-A1
4100 SD 92107 1287-J1
6400 CRLB 92009 1127-G5

STREET
Block City ZIP Pg-Grid

LA PAZ DR
5000 SD 92113 1290-A5
5000 SD 92114 1290-A5
LA PAZ ST
2300 OCN 92054 1106-F2
LAPEER CT
9200 SNTE 92071 1231-A3
LA PERLA WY
4800 SDCo 91941 1271-C2
LA PINATA WY N
4200 OCN 92057 1086-J3
LA PINATA WY S
4200 OCN 92057 1086-J3
LA PINTURA DR
6100 SD 92037 1247-H1
LAPIZ DR
8200 SD 92126 1209-B2
LA PLACE CT
5900 CRLB 92008 1127-E2
LA PLANCHA LN
2400 CRLB 92009 1147-G3
LA PLATA CT
15200 SDCo 92065 1173-E5
LA PLAYA AV
1400 SD 92109 1248-A7
LA PLAZA DR
1400 SDCo 92069 1128-C3
LA PLUMA CT
1000 SDCo 92069 1128-F4
LA PLUMA LN
2400 CRLB 92009 1147-G3
LAPORT ST
6100 LMSA 91942 1250-F6
LA PORTALADA DR
4100 CRLB 92008 1106-J5
LA POSADA DR
- SDCo 92004 (1099-F3 See Page 1098)
LA POSADA ST
1800 NATC 91950 1289-J6
1800 NATC 91950 1290-A6
LA POSADA WY
- SDCo 92036 1155-H4
LA POSTA CIR
2900 SDCo 91906 430-B7
2900 SDCo 92066 430-B7
LA POSTA RD
1800 SDCo 91906 1298-E3
1800 SDCo 91906 (1318-F1 See Page 1298)
2400 SDCo 91906 430-B7
LA POSTA TKTR
- SDCo 91906 1298-A5
3400 SDCo 92066 430-B7
LAPPED CIRCLE DR
3300 SDCo 92004 (1078-J6 See Page 1058)
LA PRADERA LN
500 ESCN 92026 1109-G2
500 SDCo 92026 1109-G2
LA PRESA AV
1000 SDCo 91977 1291-C2
LA PRESA ST
400 SDCo 91977 1291-C4
LA PRIMAVERA DR
30400 SDCo 92084 1068-A4
LA PUERTA PL
1800 LMGR 91945 1290-F1
LA PUERTE
- ESCN 92029 1129-F4
LA PURISMA WY
300 OCN 92057 1087-A2
LA QUEBRADA
700 ENCT 92024 1148-A6
LA QUINTA PL
4400 OCN 92057 1066-G7
LA RAMADA LN
2400 ESCN 92027 1130-E1
LARAMIE CT
7700 SD 92120 1250-C4
LARAMIE ST
300 SDCo 92004 1058-G6
LARAMIE WY
5500 SD 92120 1250-B4
LARCH ST
4500 SD 92105 1289-J1
LARCHMONT ST
12700 PWY 92064 1170-D7
LARCHWOOD AV
5900 SD 92120 1250-C4
LARCHWOOD DR
500 SMCS 92069 1109-B6
1200 OCN 92056 1087-D2
LARCHWOOD WY
7700 SD 92120 1250-C4
LAREDO CT
1400 CHV 91902 1311-B3
LAREDO LN
3400 SDCo 92025 1150-E2
LAREDO ST
3600 CRLB 92008 1106-J4
LA REINA DR
1000 SDCo 92069 1128-D3
LARGA CIR
3400 SD 92110 1268-D5
LARGA CT
3100 SD 92110 1268-D6
LARGA VISTA
31400 SDCo 92082 1069-J2
LARGA VISTA CT
9100 SDCo 91977 1291-B1
LARGO LN
3100 SDCo 92026 1109-H2
LARIAT DR
- SNTE 92071 1231-C3
LARIAT LN
10300 SDCo 91941 1271-E4
LARIAT WY
5400 OCN 92057 1067-D7
LARIO LN
9600 SDCo 92127 1169-E2
LARK GN
2100 ESCN 92026 1109-E5
LARK ST
900 ELCJ 92021 1251-H5
3400 SD 92103 1268-H5
7700 SNTE 92071 1230-G7
LARK WY
200 OCN 92057 1086-H5
LARKDALE AV
8200 SD 92123 1249-C5
LARKDALE PL
3200 SD 92123 1249-C5
LARK FIELD CT
- SD 92130 1188-A5
LARKHAVEN DR
1500 CHV 91911 1330-F4
LARKHAVEN GN
1700 ESCN 92026 1109-D4

STREET
Block City ZIP Pg-Grid

LARK HILL DR
1100 VSTA 92084 1088-A2
LARKIN PL
2600 SD 92123 1249-D6
LARKRIDGE ST
9000 SNTE 92071 1231-G6
LARK SONG LN
1000 ENCT 92024 1147-J5
1100 ENCT 92024 1148-A5
LARKSPUR CT
800 SMCS 92078 1128-F3
1500 CHV 91913 1311-C7
LARKSPUR DR
1900 SDCo 91901 1233-J4
LARKSPUR LN
1100 CRLB 92008 1106-F6
1500 SDCo 92028 1028-E4
LARKSPUR ST
4600 SD 92107 1268-A5
LARK VISTA DR
- SDCo 92127 1169-E3
LARKWOOD CT
3100 SDCo 92028 1048-D3
LARMIER CIR
11400 SD 92131 1209-J2
11400 SD 92131 1210-A2
LA ROCA GRANDE
10100 SDCo 92026 1069-D1
LA ROCHI WY
700 SDCo 92019 1252-C6
LA ROSA DR
3800 SMCS 92069 1108-D7
LA ROUCHE DR
8400 SD 92119 1250-J4
LARRABEE AV
9400 SD 92123 1249-F6
LARRABEE PL
2400 SD 92123 1249-F6
LARRY LN
- SDCo 91901 1255-F5
- ESCN 92025 1130-A6
LARRY ST
15100 PWY 92064 1170-D7
LARSEN RD
500 ImCo 92251 431-B4
LARSEN WY
8600 LMSA 91941 1271-A2
LARSON LN
1500 SDCo 92028 1027-J4
LA RUE AV
900 SDCo 92028 1027-G3
LA RUE WY
500 ELCJ 92021 1251-H4
LA RUEDA DR
4600 SDCo 91941 1271-F3
LA RUEDA RD
900 SDCo 92084 1088-D7
1000 SDCo 92084 1108-D1
LARWOOD RD
1000 SD 92114 1290-F2
1100 LMGR 91945 1290-F2
LA SALINA PL
1400 OCN 92054 1106-C2
LA SALINA ST
300 OCN 92054 1106-C2
LA SALLE CT
1300 VSTA 92083 1107-J4
2000 CHV 91913 1311-E5
LA SALLE ST
3900 SD 92110 1268-C4
LAS ALTURAS TER
5500 SD 92114 1290-B4
LAS ANIMAS
5200 SD 92114 1290-B4
LAS ARBOLEDAS
6600 SDCo 92067 1148-F6
LAS ARDILLAS
- SDCo 92026 1109-G4
LAS BANCAS CT
1000 CHV 91911 1330-F2
LAS BANDERAS DR
100 SOLB 92075 1167-H7
LAS BRISAS CT
7300 CRLB 92009 1147-J1
LAS BRISAS DR
400 ESCN 92027 1110-E6
LAS BRISAS TR
3000 SDCo 91935 1292-G2
LAS BRISAS WY
900 ENCT 92007 1167-E3
LAS BUJIAS CT
1600 SD 92173 1350-G2
LAS CANAS CT
100 SOLB 92075 1167-D6
LAS CANAS WY
100 SOLB 92075 1167-D7
LAS CASITAS DR
- SDCo 92004 (1099-F4 See Page 1098)
LAS COLINAS
6300 SDCo 92067 1168-E3
LAS COLINAS DR
- SDCo 92029 1129-J7
LAS CONICAS
9900 SD 92129 1189-F5
LAS CRUCES AV
3900 SMCS 92069 1128-C1
LAS CUESTAS
16500 SDCo 92067 1168-F4
LA SELVA RD
4700 SDCo 91935 1274-A3
LA SELVA WY
7900 CRLB 92009 1147-G3
LA SENA AV
7000 SD 92114 1290-F4
LA SENCILLA
5300 SDCo 92067 1168-C4
LAS ENCINAS DR
19100 SDCo 92065 1172-A5
LA SENDA WY
800 CHV 91910 1310-H7
LA SENDITA
5900 SDCo 92067 1168-D3
LASER LN
9300 SDCo 91941 1271-B4
LA SERENA
2500 SDCo 92025 1130-D7
LAS ESTANCIAS DR
500 CHV 91910 1310-J4
LAS ESTRELLAS
- SMCS 92078 1129-C1
LAS FLORES
- SMCS 92078 1129-C1
LAS FLORES DR
- CHV 91910 1310-B4
1000 CRLB 92008 1106-E4
3800 SDCo 92028 1047-J3
N LAS FLORES DR
- SMCS 92069 1108-D6

STREET
Block City ZIP Pg-Grid

S LAS FLORES DR
300 SMCS 92069 1108-C7
700 SMCS 92069 1128-C1
LAS FLORES ST
100 SD 92114 1290-B4
LAS FLORES TER
100 SD 92114 1290-B5
LASHLEE LN
1800 SD 92173 1350-F3
LA SIERRA DR
600 SMCS 92069 1108-C7
600 SMCS 92069 1128-C1
LA SIESTA WY
1800 NATC 91950 1310-B1
LASKEY LN
9700 SDCo 91941 1271-D4
LAS LIDIA CT
6700 SD 92114 1290-E5
LASLO DR
1600 SDCo 92025 1130-C4
LAS LOMAS
2000 VSTA 92084 1088-C3
LAS LOMAS DR
9300 SNTE 92071 1231-A3
LAS LOMAS RD
15600 SDCo 92021 1233-C2
LAS LOMAS ST
2100 SD 92107 1268-B7
LAS MANANAS
14800 SDCo 92067 1188-H1
LAS MANZANITAS RD
15400 SDCo 92065 1172-A4
LAS MIENTES LN
7900 CRLB 92009 1147-G3
LAS MILPAS
- SDCo 92040 1232-D7
LAS MONTANAS
- SDCo 91906 (1318-G6 See Page 1298)
18200 SDCo 92067 1148-C7
LAS NUBES CT
1200 SDCo 92069 1128-E3
LAS NUECES PL
7900 CRLB 92009 1147-G3
LAS NUEVAS
1000 SDCo 92028 1027-H4
LA SOBRINA CT
1300 SOLB 92014 1167-H7
1300 SOLB 92075 1167-H7
LA SOLANA DR
1000 SDCo 92028 1027-H2
LAS OLAS CT
1600 CRLB 92009 1147-H4
LA SOLDADERA
7200 SDCo 92067 1168-G2
LA SOLEDAD
- SDCo 92040 1232-B7
LA SOLEDAD WY
300 OCN 92057 1087-A2
LA SOMBRA CT
1200 ELCJ 92020 1251-D6
LA SOMBRA DR
400 ELCJ 92020 1251-D6
900 SMCS 92069 1128-E2
1100 SDCo 92069 1128-E2
LAS PALMAS AV
2600 ESCN 92025 1130-A7
3000 ESCN 92025 1150-B1
3100 SDCo 92025 1130-B7
LAS PALMAS CV
2700 SD 92014 1187-J7
LAS PALMAS DR
700 VSTA 92083 1107-G1
2000 CRLB 92009 1127-D4
LAS PALMAS LN
1400 ESCN 92026 1109-E6
LAS PALMAS RD
14000 SDCo 91935 1292-H3
LAS PALMAS SQ
4100 SD 92122 1228-C3
LAS PALOMAS
5400 SDCo 92067 1168-C7
LAS PESETAS
- SDCo 92067 1149-A3
LAS PLANIDERAS
15100 SDCo 92067 1168-B6
15100 SDCo 92067 1188-B1
N LAS POSAS RD
100 SMCS 92069 1108-E5
S LAS POSAS RD
200 SMCS 92069 1108-E7
300 SMCS 92069 1128-E1
LAS POTRAS WY
13500 SDCo 92040 1232-D5
LAS PULGAS RD
- SDCo 92055 408-L7
LAS QUINTAS
14700 SDCo 92067 1188-F2
LAS RAMBLAS
700 SDCo 92028 1027-H3
LAS REPOLAS
17600 SDCo 92067 1148-J6
LAS ROSAS CT
1000 CHV 91910 1311-B7
LASSEN DR
4900 OCN 92056 1107-F3
LASSEN LN
4300 CRLB 92008 1106-J4
LASSEN ST
1800 SD 92139 1290-E6
LASSEN PEAK PL
1100 CHV 91913 1311-E6
LASSIE LN
8800 SD 92123 1249-D5
LASSIN RD
- SD 92106 1288-A5
LASSO WY
9200 SNTE 92071 1231-A2
LAST CHANCE TR
7500 SDCo 92036 (1158-C1 See Page 1138)
LAST DOLLAR TR
7400 SDCo 92036 1138-C7
LAS TIENDAS WY
- OCN 92056 1106-J2
LA STRADA DR
700 SDCo 92028 1027-H3
LAS TUNAS DR
5900 OCN 92057 1067-D4
LA SUBIDA WY
1900 SDCo 92069 1128-E3
LA SUVIDA DR
9300 LMSA 91942 1251-B7
LAS VEGAS DR
3300 OCN 92054 1086-E5
LASVEN CT
2400 SDCo 92019 1272-C5
LAS VENTANAS
6700 SDCo 92067 1188-H1

STREET
Block City ZIP Pg-Grid

LAS VERAS PL
500 ESCN 92026 1109-G2
500 SDCo 92026 1109-G2
LAS VILLAS WY
1300 ESCN 92026 1109-G7
LAS VISTAS RD
900 SDCo 92028 998-C7
900 SDCo 92028 1028-D1
LAS VISTILLAS LN
1200 SDCo 92069 1128-E3
LA TARA LN
2300 SDCo 92028 1047-G2
LA TEMPRA CTE
1300 CHV 91911 1330-D4
LA TENAJA TR
4000 SDCo 92036 1156-B3
LA TENISTA
6100 SDCo 92067 1168-F7
LA TERRAZA BLVD
- ESCN 92025 1129-G4
LATHROP LN
100 SDCo 92021 1252-J3
LA TIERA DR
4200 OCN 92056 1107-C3
LA TIERRA CT
1700 SDCo 92069 1128-C2
LA TIERRA DR
800 SDCo 92069 1128-C2
800 SMCS 92069 1128-C2
LA TIERRA LN
1600 SDCo 92069 1128-C2
LATIGO CV
1100 CHV 91915 1311-F6
LATIGO RD
27100 SDCo 92082 1091-F4
LATIGO RW
3400 ENCT 92024 1148-D3
LATIMER CT
5900 SD 92114 1290-C4
LATIMER ST
100 SD 92114 1290-C4
LA TINADA CT
2400 CRLB 92009 1147-G3
LATISHA PL
700 ELCJ 92021 1251-H4
LA TORTOLA
12500 SD 92129 1189-F6
LA TORTOLA CT
9800 SD 92129 1189-F5
LA TORTOLA PL
9800 SD 92129 1189-F6
LA TORTUGA DR
800 VSTA 92083 1087-F7
800 VSTA 92083 1107-E1
LA TRIESTE PL
2900 ESCN 92025 1150-A1
LATROBE CIR
7100 SD 92139 1290-G7
LA TRUCHA ST
14200 SD 92129 1189-C2
LAUDER ST
5900 SD 92139 1310-D1
LAUGHTON WY
700 VSTA 92083 1107-F2
LAUHALA CANYON RD
1000 SDCo 92083 1107-G3
1000 VSTA 92083 1107-G3
LAURA CT
7200 SD 92120 1250-B5
LAURA DR
2000 ESCN 92027 1110-B5
LAURA LN
1000 ESCN 92025 1130-D6
LAURA ST
5300 SD 92120 1250-B5
LAURALYNN PL
1500 OCN 92054 1106-D2
LAURASHAWN LN
2900 SDCo 92026 1109-H1
LAUREE ST
700 ELCJ 92020 1251-F7
LAUREL AV
- NATC 91950 1289-J7
1300 CHV 91911 1330-H3
LAUREL DR
100 SMCS 92069 1108-H5
29400 SDCo 91906 (1297-E5 See Page 1296)
LAUREL LN
- ELCJ 92019 1251-J6
9700 SDCo 92029 1149-E2
19200 SDCo 92065 1192-B2
LAUREL RD
1500 OCN 92054 1086-E7
1500 OCN 92054 1106-E1
LAUREL ST
100 SD 92101 1289-A1
200 SD 92101 1288-H1
800 SD 92103 1288-H1
1400 OCN 92054 1086-B6
2900 SD 92104 1289-E1
3000 SD 92104 1269-E7
4300 SD 92105 1269-H7
5000 SD 92105 1270-A7
5200 SD 92105 1290-A1
12200 SDCo 92040 1232-B3
W LAUREL ST
200 SD 92101 1289-A1
400 SD 92101 1288-J1
LAUREL CHASE DR
- SD 92130 1208-E1
LAURELHURST CT
9200 SD 92126 1209-D2
LAUREL LEE LN
11900 SDCo 92040 1231-J6
LAURELRIDGE CT
6700 SD 92120 1250-D4
LAUREL RIDGE DR
31500 SDCo 92082 1069-J1
31500 SDCo 92082 1070-A1
LAURELRIDGE RD
7700 SD 92120 1250-D4
LAUREL TREE LN
- CRLB 92009 1127-A3
LAUREL TREE RD
6100 CRLB 92009 1127-B3
LAUREL VALLEY DR
2200 SDCo 92084 1068-E7
LAURELWOOD CT
800 SMCS 92069 1109-A6
LAURELWOOD ST
900 CRLB 92009 1127-A5
14700 PWY 92064 1190-D1
LAURELWOOD WY
700 ELCJ 92021 1251-G4
LAUREN CT
- ENCT 92024 1147-D3
LAUREN LN
- SDCo 91901 1253-G2

STREET
Block City ZIP Pg-Grid

LAUREN WY
- SNTE 92071 1231-E3
LAURENTIAN DR
9300 SD 92129 1189-D2
LAURETTA ST
5400 SD 92110 1268-F3
LAURIE CIR
2000 CRLB 92008 1106-G4
LAURIE LN
2400 SD 92105 1269-H7
2400 SD 92105 1289-H1
5400 SDCo 92067 1168-D4
LAURINDA PL
2000 SD 92105 1289-J1
LAURINE LN
100 SDCo 92028 1027-F5
E LAURINE LN
100 SDCo 92028 1027-G5
LAURISTON DR
1100 SD 92154 1350-C1
LAUSANNE DR
100 SD 92114 1290-F3
S LAUSANNE DR
100 SD 92114 1290-F4
LAVA CT
7900 LMSA 91941 1270-H4
LAVADE LN
5300 SDCo 91902 1311-A2
LAVALA LN
1700 ELCJ 92021 1252-C1
LA VALHALLA PL
1700 SDCo 92019 1272-B3
LA VALLE PLATEADA
6300 SDCo 92067 1168-E2
LA VANCO CT
6400 CRLB 92009 1127-G5
LA VARONA PL
100 ESCN 92025 1150-A1
LAVELL ST
9100 SDCo 91941 1271-B3
9200 LMSA 91941 1271-B3
LAVENDER LN
200 SDCo 92083 1108-C4
LAVENDER WY
7000 CRLB 92009 1127-A6
LAVENDER STAR DR
9500 SDCo 92127 1169-D2
LA VENTA DR
13200 PWY 92064 1190-D4
LA VENTANA CT
1000 SDCo 92069 1128-F3
LA VERDE DR
1600 SDCo 92069 1128-B3
LA VERDE LN
1200 SDCo 92069 1128-B3
LA VEREDA
8100 SD 92037 1227-G5
LAVERNE PL
4000 SD 92104 1269-F5
LA VETA AV
100 ENCT 92024 1147-B5
LA VIA FELIZ
16400 SDCo 92067 1168-E4
LA VIDA CIR
700 VSTA 92083 1087-G5
LA VIDA CT
1100 CHV 91915 1311-H5
LA VINE LN
1500 SDCo 92084 1108-B1
LA VISTA
- ESCN 92026 1109-F7
600 ENCT 92024 1147-F5
LA VISTA AV
1400 ELCJ 92020 1251-D6
9700 SDCo 91941 1271-C1
LA VISTA WY
12700 PWY 92064 1190-D5
LA VITA CT
10400 SD 92131 1210-A3
LA VONNE AV
900 SDCo 92028 1027-G3
LA VUELTA
100 SMCS 92069 1108-H3
LAW ST
600 SD 92109 1247-H5
1100 SMCS 92069 1128-E1
1600 SD 92109 1248-A5
LAWANA ST
1300 VSTA 92083 1087-E7
LAWFORD CT
7600 LMGR 91945 1290-G1
LAWFORD PL
7600 LMGR 91945 1290-G1
LAWLER CT
4600 SDCo 91941 1271-C3
LAWNDALE ST
1900 SD 92154 1350-C3
LAWNSDALE PL
- SMCS 92069 1108-J5
LAWNVIEW DR
400 CHV 91910 1310-F6
LAWRENCE LN
1800 SDCo 92065 1172-F1
2900 SDCo 92025 1130-E7
2900 SDCo 92025 1150-E1
LAWRENCE ST
2800 SD 92106 1288-A4
3400 CRLB 92008 1106-J4
LAWRENCE WELK CT
28300 SDCo 92026 1088-J2
LAWRENCE WELK DR
8800 SDCo 92026 1089-A1
28800 SDCo 92026 1088-J1
LAWRENCE WELK LN
29100 SDCo 92026 1088-J1
29200 SDCo 92026 1068-H7
29200 SDCo 92084 1068-H7
LAWSON HILLS RD
18100 SDCo 91935 1274-C2
LAWSON VALLEY RD
15200 SDCo 91935 1273-H4
15200 SDCo 91935 1274-A3
LAWTON DR
2200 LMGR 91945 1270-J7
2200 LMGR 91945 1290-J1
LAYANG LAYANG CIR
4000 CRLB 92008 1106-F7
LAYLA CT
4200 SD 92154 1350-G1
LAYLA WY
4200 SD 92154 1350-G1
LAYNE PL
1700 SDCo 92019 1272-C3
LAYTON ST
900 ELCJ 92021 1251-G2
LAZANJA DR
- SD 92127 1168-J7
LAZAROFF LN
- SDCo 91935 1274-A2

LAZO CT
800 CHV 91910 1310-H6
LAZY ACRES DR
- SDCo 92040 1191-E5
- SDCo 92064 1191-E5
LAZY CIRCLE DR
700 VSTA 92083 1107-G2
LAZY CLOUDS PT
6800 SD 92120 1250-D4
LAZY CREEK RD
15100 SDCo 92021 1232-H2
LAZY H DR
- SDCo 92082 1071-B1
15600 SDCo 92061 1051-B7
15600 SDCo 92082 1051-B7
LAZY JAYS WY
3800 SDCo 92036 1155-H3
LAZY LADDER DR
200 SDCo 92004 (1078-F2 See Page 1058)
LAZY M LN
- SDCo 91906 (1317-G3 See Page 1296)
LAZY S DR
1600 SDCo 92004 1058-G5
2100 SDCo 92004 (1078-H1 See Page 1058)
LAZY TRAIL CT
5900 SDCo 91902 1311-C3
LEA ST
5200 SD 92105 1270-B5
LEADA WY
24700 SDCo 92065 1173-G3
LEADROPE WY
5800 SDCo 91902 1311-B2
LEAF CT
6200 SD 92114 1290-D5
LEAF LN
1100 SDCo 92026 1109-E7
LEAF TER
1200 SD 92114 1290-D5
LEAF PINE CT
- SDCo 92026 1089-B2
LEAFWOOD PL
2000 ENCT 92024 1147-H6
10300 SD 92131 1209-G4
LEAH LN
800 SDCo 92029 1149-H1
LEAILA LN
13100 PWY 92064 1190-H5
LEANING TREE LN
13300 PWY 92064 1190-H4
E LEANNA CT
200 CHV 91911 1330-F2
LEANNA ST
- CHV 91911 1330-E2
LEAR LN
3500 CRLB 92008 1106-G5
LEARY ST
10300 SD 92124 1249-G2
LEASE RD
- SDCo 92066 410-A8
LEAST TERN CT
12000 SD 92129 1188-J7
LEATA TER
1500 SDCo 91901 1233-J7
LEA TERRACE DR
11000 SNTE 92071 1231-G6
LEATHERS RD
1100 ImCo 92283 432-D4
LEATHERS ST
4500 SD 92117 1248-B1
LEATHERWOOD ST
1900 SD 92154 1350-C3
LEBANON RD
28600 SDCo 92066 1237-B6
LE BARRON RD
5200 SD 92115 1269-J2
LEBAUN DR
1800 LMGR 91945 1290-H1
LEBON DR
3300 SD 92122 1228-B3
LECHUZA LN
100 SDCo 91977 1290-J5
LE CLAIR LN
400 SDCo 92026 1109-G3
LE CONTE ST
700 OCN 92057 1086-G5
7300 SD 92114 1290-F4
LEDESMA LN
1200 SDCo 92065 1172-F1
LEDGE AV
2100 SDCo 91977 1291-D1
LEDGESIDE LN
2100 SDCo 91977 1271-D7
2100 SDCo 91977 1291-D1
LEDGESIDE ST
9900 SDCo 91977 1291-D1
9900 SDCo 91977 1271-D7
LEDGETOP PL
2600 SDCo 91977 1271-D7
LEDGEVIEW AV
2100 SDCo 91977 1271-E7
LEDGEVIEW LN
2500 SDCo 91977 1271-D7
LEDGEVIEW PL
2500 SDCo 91977 1271-D7
LEDGEWOOD LN
200 SD 92114 1290-G5
LEDGEWOOD PL
7400 SD 92114 1290-G5
LEE AV
2100 ESCN 92027 1110-C6
4400 LMSA 91941 1270-G3
LEE CIR
500 CHV 91911 1330-H2
LEE CT
2000 CRLB 92008 1106-G5
LEE DR
1300 OCN 92056 1087-E4
2000 ESCN 92027 1110-C6
LEE RD
1900 SD 92133 1288-D1
LEE ST
4300 SD 92109 1248-C6
LEEANN LN
300 ENCT 92024 1147-B4
LEEDS LN
- PWY 92064 1190-B4
LEEDS ST
4000 SD 92121 1228-C1
LEEWARD CT
300 OCN 92054 1086-F6
LEEWARD ST
100 CRLB 92009 1126-J6
LEGACY CT
14200 SDCo 92021 1232-G6
LEGACY DR
1400 SMCS 92069 1108-H5

LEGACY LN
14200 SDCo 92021 1232-G6
LEGACY PL
12700 SD 92131 1210-C2
LEGACY RD
12600 SD 92131 1210-C1
LEGACY TER
11300 SD 92131 1210-C2
LEGACY CANYON PL
11300 SD 92131 1210-C2
LEGACY CANYON WY
12700 SD 92131 1210-C2
LEGATE CT
500 CHV 91910 1310-F5
LEGAYE DR
1500 ENCT 92007 1167-E2
LEGEND WY
- SDCo 92026 1109-G1
LEGENDALE DR
11500 SDCo 92040 1211-G6
LEGEND ROCK RD
10200 SDCo 92026 1089-E5
LEGHORN AV
400 SD 92114 1290-E5
LEGO DR
- CRLB 92008 1126-H2
LEHARDY ST
2800 SD 92136 1289-E6
LEHIGH AV
700 CHV 91913 1311-E5
LEHIGH CT
2800 OCN 92056 1087-A7
LEHIGH ST
1300 SD 92110 1268-E2
LEHNER AV
500 SDCo 92026 1109-H5
800 ESCN 92026 1109-H5
1100 SDCo 92027 1109-H5
1100 SDCo 92027 1110-A4
LEHRER DR
4500 SD 92117 1228-G7
LEICESTER ST
7000 SD 92120 1250-A5
LEICESTER WY
5100 SD 92120 1250-A5
LEIGH AV
8700 SDCo 91977 1291-A5
LEIGHTON CT
2100 SD 92139 1290-F7
LEILA LN
10300 SNTE 92071 1231-B1
LEILA WY
9500 SNTE 92071 1231-E5
LEILANI WY
2900 SD 92154 1330-C7
LEISURE LN
8600 SDCo 92026 1068-J6
LEISURE VILLAGE DR
4600 OCN 92056 1107-E4
LEISURE VILLAGE WY
4600 OCN 92056 1107-F4
LE JEUNE ST
- SDCo 92055 1067-A2
LEJOS DR
1900 SDCo 92025 1130-B5
LELAND PL
700 ELCJ 92019 1251-J6
700 SDCo 92019 1251-J6
LELAND ST
800 SDCo 91977 1291-A3
3600 SD 92106 1268-C5
3600 SD 92110 1268-C5
LELAND WY
1300 SDCo 92026 1109-E6
LEMA WY
6700 SD 92119 1250-F5
LEMAIRE DR
- RivC 92590 998-G2
LEMARAND AV
6500 SD 92115 1270-D6
LE MAY AV
500 SD 92154 1330-E6
LEMIRE CT
300 CHV 91910 1310-F7
LEMIRE DR
300 CHV 91910 1310-F7
LEMNOS WY
4000 OCN 92056 1107-E5
LEMON AV
600 VSTA 92084 1087-H5
600 ELCJ 92020 1251-E7
1200 ELCJ 92020 1271-E1
2000 ESCN 92029 1129-H6
2000 SDCo 92029 1129-H6
3400 SD 92123 1249-E4
7400 LMGR 91945 1270-F6
8000 LMSA 91941 1270-J2
8600 LMSA 91941 1271-A2
9100 SDCo 91941 1271-B2
LEMON CIR
7900 LMSA 91941 1270-H3
LEMON LN
3200 LMGR 91945 1270-J6
LEMON PL
1200 SDCo 92027 1130-D4
LEMON ST
1300 OCN 92054 1086-B6
9000 SDCo 91977 1271-A7
LEMONA AV
3500 SD 92105 1270-A6
LEMON BLOSSOM LN
- SDCo 92028 1027-J6
- SDCo 92028 1028-A6
LEMON BLOSSOM RD
- SDCo 92082 1071-A6
LEMONCREST DR
9500 SDCo 92040 1231-J5
9500 SDCo 92040 1232-A4
LEMON DROP LN
400 VSTA 92083 1107-H1
LEMON GROVE AV
900 LMGR 91945 1290-F2
900 SD 92114 1290-F2
2200 LMGR 91945 1270-G7
3700 LMGR 91941 1270-G5
3700 LMSA 91941 1270-G5
LEMON GROVE DR
100 SDCo 92028 1047-F4
LEMON GROVE RD
- SDCo 92055 1085-H3
LEMON GROVE WY
7800 LMGR 91945 1270-H5
LEMON HEIGHTS DR
1700 OCN 92056 1087-D4
LEMON LEAF DR
- CRLB 92009 1127-B5
LEMON PINE CT
13000 SD 92129 1189-C5

LEMONSEED DR
4100 SD 92154 1330-G7
LEMON TREE CT
3900 SD 92130 1208-A3
LEMONWOOD CT
500 OCN 92054 1086-F2
LEMONWOOD LN
1900 VSTA 92083 1107-J4
7000 LMGR 91945 1270-F6
9900 SD 92124 1249-G1
LEMORA LN
3200 SDCo 92025 1130-F6
LEN CT
10400 SNTE 92071 1231-E2
LEN ST
10400 SNTE 92071 1231-E2
LEN WY
10400 SNTE 92071 1231-E2
LENDEE DR
1700 ESCN 92025 1130-C4
1700 SDCo 92025 1130-C4
LENINE DR
30300 SDCo 92082 1070-A4
LENNIE DR
30300 SDCo 92082 1069-J4
LENNON LN
29000 SDCo 92026 1089-C1
LENNY LN
300 SDCo 92021 1252-H4
LENORE DR
4600 SD 92115 1270-D1
LENORE ST
5100 OCN 92057 1067-A5
LENOX CT
3700 CRLB 92008 1107-A4
LENOX DR
5100 SD 92114 1290-B2
LENREY AV
400 ELCN 92243 6499-F7
1800 ELCN 92243 6559-E1
LENSER WY
700 ESCN 92025 1129-G2
LENTEJA LN
13600 SDCo 92040 1232-D3
LENTO LN
300 SDCo 92021 1252-H3
LEO CT
2000 ESCN 92026 1109-F5
LEO ST
5000 SD 92115 1270-D2
LEOMA LN
100 CHV 91911 1330-E3
LEON AV
1500 SD 92154 1349-J2
1700 SD 92154 1350-A2
LEON LN
1400 SDCo 92036 1156-D2
LEON ST
4400 SD 92107 1287-H1
5100 OCN 92057 1067-B5
LEON WY
3400 SDCo 92028 1028-D1
LEONA LN
12200 PWY 92064 1190-B4
LEONARD AV
300 OCN 92054 1106-B1
LEONARD ST
2800 NATC 91950 1310-C2
LEONE AV
- SDCo 91905 1300-C7
LEONEY CT
15500 SDCo 91935 1293-E1
LEONEY LN
15500 SDCo 91935 1293-E1
LEORA LN
600 SMCS 92069 1129-E1
1600 ENCT 92024 1147-B2
LEPPERT CT
800 SD 92114 1290-F3
LEPPERT ST
800 SD 92114 1290-F3
LEPRECHAUN LN
32200 SDCo 92003 1048-G6
LEPUS RD
8500 SD 92126 1209-C1
LERIDA DR
4200 SD 92115 1270-D4
LERKAS WY
4900 OCN 92056 1107-E5
LEROY ST
1000 SD 92106 1288-B2
LES RD
9000 SNTE 92071 1231-A5
LESA RD
5400 LMSA 91942 1270-G1
LES ARBRES PL
10400 SD 92131 1210-A3
LES FLEURS TER
10400 SD 92131 1210-A3
LESLIE CT
1400 SMCS 92069 1109-D7
1400 SMCS 92069 1129-D1
LESLIE LN
100 ESCN 92026 1109-H6
400 SDCo 92026 1109-H6
LESLIE RD
900 ELCJ 92020 1251-F7
LESTER AV
7800 LMGR 91945 1270-H6
LETHBRIDGE WY
9200 SD 92129 1189-D2
LETICIA DR
9300 SNTE 92071 1230-H6
LETTON ST
100 SDCo 92065 1152-E7
S LETTON ST
100 SDCo 92065 1152-E7
LETTUCE ST
- ImCo 92249 6560-B7
LEUCADIA AV
8200 SD 92114 1290-H3
LEUCADIA BLVD
100 ENCT 92024 1147-B4
W LEUCADIA BLVD
100 ENCT 92024 1147-A4
LEUCADIA SCENIC CT
1900 ENCT 92024 1147-B2
LEUCADIA VILLAGE CT
1600 ENCT 92024 1147-B2
LEVANT ST
6900 SD 92111 1248-J6
LEVANT WY
200 OCN 92057 1087-A1
LEVANTE ST
- CRLB 92024 1147-F2
2100 CRLB 92009 1147-F1
LEVEE DR
3500 CRLB 92008 1107-B3

LEVEE RD
1500 ImCo 92283 432-E5
LEVITA CT
15000 PWY 92064 1170-C7
LEWIS
14100 SDCo 92040 1232-H5
LEWIS CT
1400 VSTA 92083 1107-J5
LEWIS LN
2600 CRLB 92008 1106-E4
13900 ESCN 92027 1110-F4
LEWIS ST
600 SD 92103 1268-H5
4000 OCN 92056 1087-B7
4200 VSTA 92083 1087-B7
E LEWIS ST
100 SD 92103 1269-A5
W LEWIS ST
200 SD 92103 1269-A5
300 SD 92103 1268-J5
LEWISON AV
5200 SD 92120 1250-B5
LEWISON CT
5200 SD 92120 1250-A5
LEWISON DR
7000 SD 92120 1250-B5
LEWISON PL
5200 SD 92120 1250-A5
LEWISTON ST
13800 SD 92128 1190-A2
LEXINE LN
700 ESCN 92025 1130-C5
700 SDCo 92025 1130-C5
LEXINGTON AV
1300 ELCJ 92019 1252-A5
1600 SDCo 92019 1252-B5
E LEXINGTON AV
1000 ELCJ 92020 1251-H5
1200 ELCJ 92019 1251-H5
1200 ELCJ 92019 1252-A5
W LEXINGTON AV
600 ELCJ 92020 1251-E6
LEXINGTON CIR
400 OCN 92057 1086-J3
2900 CRLB 92008 1107-B5
LEXINGTON CT
- OCN 92057 1086-J4
LEXINGTON DR
1200 VSTA 92084 1088-A6
LEXINGTON ST
1500 IMPB 91932 1349-H2
LEYENDEKKER CT
9500 SDCo 92040 1232-B4
LEYENDEKKER RD
12500 SDCo 92040 1232-B4
LEYTE DR
- CORD 92118 1309-C6
LEYTE RD
1100 CORD 92118 1309-C5
LEYTE POINT DR
6700 SD 92139 1290-F7
LIBBY ST
100 OCN 92054 1086-C6
LIBELLE CT
12100 SD 92131 1210-B1
LIBERTAD DR
17100 SD 92127 1169-H2
LIBERTY DR
300 SMCS 92069 1108-G7
LIBERTY PL
1500 ESCN 92025 1129-J5
LIBERTY WY
1200 VSTA 92083 1127-J1
1200 VSTA 92083 1128-A1
LIBRA DR
8700 SD 92126 1209-D2
LIBRA LN
8900 SD 92126 1209-E7
LIBRE GN
100 ESCN 92025 1130-A5
LICIA WY
12100 SD 92129 1189-A7
LIDDIARD ST
2500 ELCJ 92020 1251-B2
LIDO CT
700 SD 92109 1267-H2
LIEBEL CT
4800 SD 92117 1248-J1
LIEBERT RD
1100 ImCo 92243 430-L7
LIEDER DR
1900 SD 92154 1350-A1
LIETA ST
1400 SD 92110 1268-E2
LIGGETT DR
3500 SD 92106 1288-A1
LIGGETT WY
1400 SD 92106 1288-A1
LIGHTHOUSE RD
- SMCS 92078 1128-D5
1000 CRLB 92009 1127-A5
LIGHTHOUSE WY
13400 SD 92130 1188-D4
LIGHTNING DR
3300 SDCo 92004 (1078-H6 See Page 1058)
LIGHTWAVE AV
9000 SD 92123 1249-D1
LIGIA PL
5000 SDCo 92020 1271-H1
LILA DR
4700 SD 92115 1269-J2
4700 SD 92115 1270-A3
LILA LN
300 SDCo 92021 1252-H4
LILAC AV
1300 CHV 91911 1330-H3
LILAC CT
800 SMCS 92069 1128-E2
1800 CRLB 92009 1127-E6
LILAC DR
- SD 92109 1248-C6
200 SDCo 92021 1252-H3
2700 SDCo 92036 1136-D7
29400 SDCo 91906 (1297-E5 See Page 1296)
LILAC LN
- SDCo 91916 1235-J1
- SDCo 91916 1236-A1
- SDCo 92036 1156-F7
1800 SDCo 91901 1233-G7
1800 SDCo 91901 1253-G1
8000 SDCo 92066 1237-C6
38400 SDCo 91905 (1299-J5 See Page 1298)
LILAC PL
- SDCo 92026 1069-B1
LILAC RD
- SDCo 92059 409-E6

LILAC RD
1300 SDCo 92065 1152-G1
28200 SDCo 92082 1090-C1
28900 SDCo 92082 1070-A5
29900 SDCo 92082 1069-H2
31500 SDCo 92082 1049-G2
33200 SDCo 92082 1029-H7
33600 SDCo 92059 1029-H7
W LILAC RD
5500 SDCo 92003 1048-H6
5500 SDCo 92003 1068-B1
8500 SDCo 92026 1048-H6
8500 SDCo 92026 1049-B6
9300 SDCo 92026 1069-D2
10200 SDCo 92082 1069-F3
LILAC TR
2500 SDCo 91905 (1299-H3 See Page 1298)
LILAC WK
9500 SDCo 92026 1049-B7
9500 SDCo 92026 1069-B1
LILAC CREST
12200 SDCo 92082 1070-A4
12200 SDCo 92082 1069-J4
LILAC HEIGHTS CT
- SDCo 92082 1070-A5
30000 SDCo 92082 1069-J5
LILAC HILL
12000 SDCo 92082 1069-H3
LILAC HILL DR
26500 SDCo 92026 1089-H7
26500 ESCN 92026 1089-H7
LILAC HILLS LN
12100 SDCo 92082 1069-E3
LILAC KNOLLS RD
12000 SDCo 92082 1069-J4
12000 SDCo 92082 1070-A4
LILAC RIDGE RD
10100 SDCo 92026 1069-D2
LILAC SUMMIT
3400 ENCT 92024 1148-C5
LILAC VISTA DR
11200 SDCo 92082 1069-G2
LILAC WOOD LN
16000 SDCo 91935 1273-G5
LILAC WOOD RD
3200 SDCo 91935 1273-G6
LILA HILL LN
11900 SDCo 92040 1232-A7
LILAS
14200 SD 92129 1189-H2
LILE ST
3300 OCN 92056 1107-A2
LILIUM LN
- CRLB 92009 1127-D4
LILLIAN ST
4900 SD 92110 1268-E2
LILLIAN WY
100 SDCo 92028 1027-G2
LILLIE LN
- SDCo 91905 1300-C6
LILY AV
1400 ELCJ 92021 1252-A2
1400 SDCo 92021 1252-A2
LILY PL
7300 CRLB 92009 1127-B6
LIMA CT
1500 ELCJ 92019 1252-A5
LIMAR WY
9600 SD 92129 1189-E5
LIMBER PINE RD
4100 SDCo 92028 1048-D4
LIME PL
1000 VSTA 92083 1107-G2
LIME ST
7300 LMSA 91941 1270-F5
LIME GROVE RD
15800 PWY 92064 1170-E5
LIMERICK AV
4500 SD 92117 1248-H1
4900 SD 92117 1228-H7
LIMERICK CT
5400 SD 92117 1228-G6
LIMERICK WY
4400 SD 92117 1248-H2
LIME ROCK CT
2100 SDCo 92019 1272-C4
LIMETREE LN
10300 SDCo 91977 1291-E2
LIME TREE WY
500 OCN 92054 1086-E2
LIMON LN
8200 SDCo 92021 1251-H1
LINALDA DR
1200 SDCo 92021 1251-H3
LINARES CT
100 SOLB 92075 1167-D6
LINARES ST
11100 SD 92129 1169-H6
LINAZA LN
100 SDCo 91977 1290-J5
LINBROOK DR
1500 SD 92111 1268-J1
1500 SD 92111 1269-A2
LINBROOK PL
7300 SD 92111 1269-A1
LINCOLN AV
200 ELCJ 92020 1251-G6
300 ESCN 92026 1129-H1
600 ELCN 92243 6499-E4
700 ESCN 92026 1109-J7
900 ESCN 92026 1110-A7
1000 SD 92103 1269-B5
1000 ESCN 92027 1110-A7
1800 ELCN 92243 6499-E4
1900 SD 92104 1269-C5
E LINCOLN AV
100 ESCN 92026 1129-H1
LINCOLN CT
2700 NATC 91950 1310-B3
2700 SDCo 91950 1310-B3
LINCOLN DR
- SD 92102 1289-G4
LINCOLN PKWY
100 ESCN 92026 1129-H1
LINCOLN PL
900 LMGR 91945 1290-G2
900 SD 92114 1290-G2
LINCOLN ST
1900 OCN 92054 1106-D3
3000 CRLB 92008 1106-E6
7800 LMGR 91945 1270-H6
LINCOLNSHIRE ST
12400 SD 92128 1150-B6
LINDA CT
- ESCN 92027 1110-D6
LINDA DR
2900 OCN 92056 1087-B7
3000 OCN 92056 1107-B1

LINDA LN
500 CHV 91910 1310-C7
800 SMCS 92069 1109-B6
2000 CRLB 92008 1106-G4
3700 SDCo 91977 1271-C5
6500 SD 92120 1250-E7
LINDA ST
1500 SDCo 92028 1028-A4
LINDA WY
300 ELCJ 92020 1251-F5
5300 SD 92037 1247-G4
LINDA MAR DR
200 SOLB 92075 1187-E1
LINDAMERE LN
13500 SD 92128 1190-B3
LINDA ROSA AV
5400 SD 92037 1247-G3
LINDA SUE LN
1400 ENCT 92024 1147-G6
LINDA VISTA
- SMCS 92078 1129-C1
- VSTA 92083 1107-C2
LINDA VISTA CT
2700 SD 92111 1249-A6
LINDA VISTA DR
900 SMCS 92069 1108-B7
900 SMCS 92069 1128-D1
3200 SDCo 92083 1128-B1
3200 VSTA 92083 1128-B1
3300 SDCo 92069 1128-B1
3600 SDCo 92028 1048-B3
LINDA VISTA RD
5100 SD 92110 1268-G2
6000 SD 92111 1268-G2
6900 SD 92111 1248-J6
7300 SD 92111 1249-A5
LINDA VISTA TER
3400 SDCo 92028 1048-A3
LINDBERGH ST
3400 SD 92154 1330-E6
LINDBERGH WY
500 SD 92154 1330-F6
LINDELL AV
100 ELCJ 92020 1251-F6
LINDEN DR
900 VSTA 92083 1087-F6
LINDEN LN
8900 LMSA 91941 1271-A2
LINDEN RD
7500 SDCo 92066 1237-C7
8200 SDCo 92040 1252-A1
8200 SDCo 92040 1251-J1
LINDEN TER
7100 CRLB 92009 1127-A6
LINDEN WY
4900 LMSA 91941 1271-A2
LINDENWOOD DR
1300 SDCo 92021 1251-G1
LINDERO PL
100 SDCo 92028 1027-H4
LINDHOLM LN
2600 LMGR 91945 1270-E7
LINDLEY CT
11600 SD 92131 1209-H1
LINDO LN
12700 SDCo 92040 1232-C3
LINDO LAKE PL
9900 SDCo 92040 1232-B3
LINDO PASEO
5500 SD 92115 1270-B2
LINDOS WY
4200 OCN 92056 1107-F6
LINDSAY DR
2200 CRLB 92008 1127-C1
2200 CRLB 92008 1107-C7
LINDSAY LN
1100 SDCo 92028 1027-J5
LINDSAY ST
- CHV 91913 1331-B1
500 ELCJ 92020 1251-G4
LINDSAY MICHELLE DR
2100 SDCo 91901 1234-A4
LINDSEY LN
- ENCT 92024 1147-D6
LINDSEY RD
- CLPT 92233 411-B9
- ImCo 92233 411-A9
LINDSLEY PARK DR
1100 SMCS 92069 1109-D7
1900 SDCo 92026 1109-D7
LIND VERN CT
8700 SNTE 92071 1231-D7
LINDY LN
1000 VSTA 92084 1108-A1
LINDY WY
2000 SDCo 92069 1108-G2
LINEA DEL CIELO
Rt#-S8
4800 SDCo 92014 1168-A6
4900 SDCo 92067 1168-C4
LINEN DR
7900 SNTE 92071 1230-H7
7900 SNTE 92071 1250-H1
LINFIELD AV
5600 SD 92120 1270-D1
LINGEL DR
600 SDCo 92019 1253-C2
LINGRE AV
13200 PWY 92064 1190-E2
LINK DR
3300 SDCo 91941 1270-J5
LINKS WY
2400 VSTA 92083 1107-J4
LINMAR LN
3900 CRLB 92008 1106-F6
LINNA PL
7300 SD 92120 1250-B5
LINNET ST
5900 SD 92114 1290-C4
LINNIE LN
13000 PWY 92064 1190-F5
LINO CT
8200 SD 92129 1189-B6
LINROE DR
12200 SDCo 92040 1232-A7
LINSAY PL
1300 ESCN 92026 1109-J5
1800 ESCN 92026 1109-J5
LINTHICUM DR
1500 SDCo 92026 1109-H6
LINTON RD
27200 SDCo 92086 409-J7
LINVIEW AV
900 ESCN 92026 1109-J6
900 ESCN 92027 1109-J6
LINWOOD PL
1100 SDCo 92027 1130-D2
LINWOOD ST
300 ESCN 92027 1130-C1

SAN DIEGO CO.
INDEX

STREET
Block City ZIP Pg-Grid

LINWOOD ST
1500 SD 92103 1268-H6
1700 SD 92110 1268-F5
LION CIR
- CHV 91910 1310-D6
LIONEL ST
2600 SD 92123 1249-C6
LIONS GATE
- VSTA 92084 1088-C6
LION VALLEY RD
100 ESCN 92027 1110-D7
100 ESCN 92027 1130-D1
LIPIZZAN WY
600 SDCo 92019 1252-C6
LIPMANN ST
6200 SD 92122 1228-E5
LIPSCOMB DR
10100 SD 92126 1209-D5
LIQUID CT
8800 SD 92121 1228-H1
LIRIO CTE
1100 CHV 91910 1311-A7
LIRIO ST
300 SOLB 92075 1187-F1
LIRIOS
10800 SD 92129 1189-H2
LIROPE ST
6000 SD 92114 1290-C6
LISA AV
1600 VSTA 92084 1087-H3
LISA LN
1800 SDCo 92021 1252-C3
LISA ST
2200 CRLB 92008 1107-A6
LISA TER
1800 SDCo 92021 1252-C3
LISA WY
1400 ESCN 92027 1110-B5
LISA MEADOWS
10700 SNTE 92071 1231-E6
LISANN ST
4500 SD 92117 1248-B1
LISBON LN
1600 SDCo 92019 1252-B7
LISBON PL
1600 ESCN 92029 1129-F5
LISBON ST
6900 SD 92114 1290-F3
LISE AV
4900 SD 92102 1290-A3
LISIEUX TER
6100 SD 92120 1250-C6
LISTER ST
4100 SD 92110 1248-E7
LISZT AV
100 ENCT 92007 1167-D2
LITA LN
1100 SDCo 92084 1108-B1
1100 VSTA 92084 1108-B1
LITCHFIELD RD
5000 SD 92116 1269-E2
LITHROP PL
4700 SD 92117 1248-G1
LITTEN WY
15900 SDCo 92065 1174-B4
LITTLE DR
- SD 92140 1268-E6
LITTLE LN
2900 LMGR 91945 1270-H6
9300 SDCo 92040 1232-B5
LITTLE ST
1900 SD 92037 1227-G6
LITTLE BROOK LN
13400 SDCo 92040 1232-D5
LITTLE CANYON LN
9700 SDCo 92026 1089-C2
LITTLE CREEK LN
13800 SDCo 92082 1070-E7
LITTLE CREEK RD
7600 SDCo 92029 1128-H7
LITTLE DAWN LN
13400 PWY 92064 1190-E3
LITTLE DIPPER WY
1600 SD 92173 1350-E2
LITTLE FIELD LN
18900 SDCo 92082 1091-G5
19300 SDCo 92027 1091-H5
LITTLEFIELD ST
4100 SD 92110 1268-E1
LITTLE FLOWER ST
3400 SD 92104 1269-F7
LITTLE GOPHER CANYON RD
1000 SDCo 92084 1067-J4
1000 SDCo 92084 1068-A5
LITTLE KLONDIKE RD
22200 SDCo 92065 1172-J5
22200 SDCo 92065 1173-A5
LITTLE OAKS LN
1100 SDCo 91901 1253-H1
LITTLE OAKS RD
100 ENCT 92024 1147-H7
LITTLE ORPHAN AL
100 DLMR 92014 1187-F6
LITTLEPAGE LN
18400 SDCo 92065 1154-B4
LITTLEPAGE RD
18400 SDCo 92065 1154-C4
LITTLE POND RD
13600 SDCo 92082 1070-D6
LITTLE QUAIL RUN
15300 SDCo 92082 1070-J3
LITTLER DR
6600 SD 92119 1250-F5
LITTLER LN
2300 OCN 92056 1106-J2
LITTLE ROCK RD
4000 SDCo 92028 997-G4
8100 SNTE 92071 1230-H7
LITTLE ROSS RD
40300 SDCo 92028 997-B1
LITTLE SIERRA
15500 SDCo 92082 1071-A5
LITTLE SILVER CT
12000 SD 92131 1210-B1
LITTLETON CT
- SDCo 92055 1086-A3
LITTLETON RD
2400 ELCJ 92020 1251-B4
LIVE OAK CT
4700 OCN 92056 1087-D4
LIVE OAK DR
400 ELCJ 92020 1251-D6
LIVE OAK LN
- SDCo 92026 1089-A2
LIVE OAK PL
2900 SDCo 92029 1129-B6
LIVE OAK RD
900 VSTA 92083 1107-H4

LIVE OAK RD
2300 ESCN 92029 1129-D3
LIVE OAK ST
1500 CHV 91913 1311-C7
LIVE OAK TR
2400 SDCo 91905 (1299-H2 See Page 1298)
LIVE OAK PARK RD
2500 SDCo 92028 1028-B2
S LIVE OAK PARK RD
100 SDCo 92028 1028-B3
LIVE OAK RANCH RD
46900 RivC 92592 999-E2
LIVE OAK SPRINGS RD
- SDCo 91906 (1299-G6 See Page 1298)
- SDCo 91905 (1299-G6 See Page 1298)
LIVERING LN
5200 SD 92117 1248-H1
LIVERPOOL CT
700 SD 92109 1267-H2
LIVERPOOL DR
100 ENCT 92007 1167-D3
LIVEWOOD WY
10400 SD 92131 1210-B4
LIVINGSTON ST
1300 CHV 91913 1311-D7
6800 SD 92115 1270-E6
6800 LMGR 92115 1270-E6
LIZA LN
1400 SDCo 91901 1233-J6
LIZARD ROCKS RD
28400 SDCo 92082 1090-F1
LLAMA CT
2700 CRLB 92009 1127-H6
LLAMA ST
2700 CRLB 92009 1127-H6
LLOYD PL
1400 SDCo 92027 1130-D3
3600 SD 92117 1248-E5
LLOYD ST
200 ELCJ 92021 1251-F4
2800 SD 92117 1248-E6
LLOYD TER
3600 SD 92117 1248-E6
LOBELIA CT
1700 CRLB 92009 1127-E6
LOBELIA DR
200 VSTA 92083 1108-B3
200 SDCo 92083 1108-C3
LOBELIA PTH
6700 SD 92037 1247-G1
LOBELIA RD
2600 SDCo 91901 1234-A5
LOBO LN
8700 SDCo 91977 1291-A2
LOBRANO ST
9100 LMSA 91941 1271-B3
LOBRICO CT
600 SD 92114 1290-F3
LO CASCIO WY
2700 ESCN 92027 1110-E7
LOCDEL CT
400 CHV 91911 1330-C4
LOCH LOMOND DR
1300 ENCT 92007 1167-D1
LOCHLOMOND ST
4200 SD 92111 1249-A2
LOCH LOMOND HIGHLANDS
2000 SDCo 92084 1088-C7
LOCHMOOR DR
6300 SD 92120 1250-E6
LOCHWOOD PL
700 ESCN 92026 1109-H3
LOCKE PL
2100 LMGR 91945 1290-G1
LOCKFORD AV
6400 SD 92139 1310-F2
LOCKLAND CT
8400 SDCo 91977 1290-J2
LOCKRIDGE PL
2300 ESCN 92026 1109-G4
LOCKRIDGE ST
3900 SD 92102 1289-G4
LOCKSLEY ST
18300 SD 92128 1150-B5
LOCKWOOD DR
3300 SD 92123 1249-E4
LOCKWOOD PL
700 OCN 92057 1087-C1
LOCUST AV
1000 CRLB 92008 1106-G7
LOCUST ST
1100 SD 92106 1288-B2
2100 SD 92106 1268-C7
3000 SD 92110 1268-C7
LODGEPOLE RD
1700 SDCo 92069 1128-B2
1700 SMCS 92069 1128-B2
LODI CT
4300 SD 92117 1228-E6
LODI GN
1800 ESCN 92026 1109-F6
LODI PL
5400 SD 92117 1228-E6
LODI ST
5200 SD 92117 1228-D6
LODI WY
4100 SD 92117 1228-E7
LOFBERG ST
3500 SD 92124 1249-G3
LOFTY GROVE DR
4600 OCN 92056 1087-E5
LOFTY TRAIL CT
15500 SD 92127 1169-J5
LOFTY TRAIL DR
15700 SD 92127 1169-J5
LOFTY VIEW PT
6700 SD 92120 1250-C4
LOGAN AV
1600 SD 92113 1289-C5
4700 SD 92113 1290-A5
5000 SD 92114 1290-A5
LOGANBERRY CT
800 SMCS 92069 1109-A5
LOGANBERRY DR
7100 CRLB 92009 1126-J6
LOGANBERRY WY
5400 OCN 92057 1067-D6
LOGRONO DR
4300 SD 92115 1270-D4
LOGWOOD PL
3600 SDCo 92028 1048-D2
LOIRE AV
10600 SD 92131 1210-B3
LOIRE CIR
12100 SD 92131 1210-B3

LOIRE CT
12100 SD 92131 1210-B3
LOIS LN
- SDCo 92036 1156-E7
100 DLMR 92014 1187-F5
LOIS ST
4000 LMSA 91941 1270-E4
4000 SD 92115 1270-E4
LOIS CANYON RD
3500 SDCo 91935 1272-H5
LOKER AV E
2800 CRLB 92008 1127-G2
LOKER AV W
2700 CRLB 92008 1127-F2
LOLA LN
1800 SDCo 92019 1272-D3
LOLALI LN
1100 SDCo 92084 1108-C1
LOLIN LN
14200 PWY 92064 1190-H5
LOLITA ST
200 ENCT 92024 1147-B6
LOLLY LN
6200 SD 92114 1290-D4
LOMA AV
1000 CORD 92118 1288-H7
LOMA CT
900 ELCJ 92020 1251-A4
1500 CHV 91911 1330-F5
4900 CRLB 92008 1106-J7
LOMA DR
2300 LMGR 91945 1270-G7
2300 LMGR 91945 1290-G1
LOMA LN
100 ESCN 92026 1109-F6
1100 CORD 92118 1288-H7
1100 CORD 92118 1308-H1
1400 CHV 91911 1330-F4
10300 SDCo 91978 1271-E6
LOMA PASS
4100 SD 92103 1268-G5
LOMA VW
900 CHV 91910 1310-H7
LOMA WY
3600 SD 92106 1288-A2
4900 CRLB 92008 1106-J7
LOMA ALEGRE
- SDCo 92067 1148-C6
LOMA ALTA DR
100 OCN 92054 1086-D6
3800 SD 92115 1270-E4
LOMA ALTA TER
700 VSTA 92083 1087-F5
LOMACITA TER
1600 ELCJ 92021 1252-C2
LOMACITAS LN
3500 SDCo 91902 1310-E3
3500 NATC 91902 1310-E3
LOMA CORTA DR
200 SOLB 92075 1167-H6
LOMA DEL SOL DR
3200 SDCo 91902 1311-A1
LOMA DE NARANJAS
1300 SDCo 92027 1130-D3
LOMA DE PAZ
1300 ESCN 92027 1130-C3
1300 SDCo 92027 1130-C3
LOMA HELIX CT
4300 SDCo 91941 1271-D3
LOMA LAGUNA DR
4900 CRLB 92008 1106-J7
LOMA LA LUNA
31400 SDCo 92026 1069-E1
LOMALAND DR
3800 SD 92106 1287-J3
3900 SD 92107 1287-J3
LOMA LARGA DR
300 SOLB 92075 1167-J6
LOMA LINDA DR
17600 SDCo 92067 1168-C1
LOMA PASEO
4300 SDCo 91902 1310-G3
LOMA PORTAL DR
900 ELCJ 92020 1251-C3
LOMA RANCHO DR
10200 SDCo 91978 1271-E6
LOMA RIVIERA CIR
4000 SD 92110 1268-C5
LOMA RIVIERA CT
4300 SD 92110 1268-B5
LOMA RIVIERA DR
3000 SD 92110 1268-C5
LOMA RIVIERA LN
4100 SD 92110 1268-C5
LOMAS DE ORO CT
600 ENCT 92024 1147-J6
LOMAS SANTA FE DR Rt#-S8
100 SOLB 92075 1167-F7
1500 SDCo 92014 1167-F7
1500 SOLB 92014 1167-F7
1600 SDCo 92014 1168-A6
LOMAS SERENAS DR
3300 ESCN 92029 1150-A3
LOMAS VERDES DR
13000 PWY 92064 1170-D1
LOMA VALLEY PL
800 SD 92106 1288-A3
LOMA VALLEY RD
700 SD 92106 1288-A3
LOMA VERDE
- ESCN 92026 1109-F7
600 ENCT 92024 1147-F5
5100 OCN 92056 1087-D2
LOMA VERDE DR
5500 SDCo 92067 1168-C2
LOMA VIEW CT
8200 SDCo 91977 1290-J5
LOMA VISTA
- SMCS 92078 1129-C2
LOMA VISTA AV
2600 ESCN 92025 1130-B7
LOMA VISTA DR
3200 SDCo 91935 1272-J7
7600 LMSA 91941 1270-G2
LOMA VISTA PL
200 SDCo 92021 1252-H3
LOMA VISTA WY
1100 SDCo 92084 1108-C1
LOMAX ST
12700 PWY 92064 1190-D4
LOMBARD PL
8900 SD 92122 1228-D3
LOMBARD ST
1400 VSTA 92084 1087-J4
LOMICA DR
11800 SD 92128 1170-A3
LOMICA PL
2200 ESCN 92029 1129-G7

LOMICA PL
2300 ESCN 92029 1149-H1
LOMITA
- CRLB 92009 1126-J5
LOMITA RD
1100 SDCo 92020 1271-H1
LOMITA ST
2600 OCN 92054 1086-D6
LOMITA WY
3900 SMCS 92069 1128-C1
LOMITA DEL SOL
800 VSTA 92083 1087-G5
LOMITAS DR
4700 SD 92116 1269-C3
LOMKER CT
9200 SNTE 92071 1230-J6
LOMKER WY
8400 SNTE 92071 1230-H6
LOMO DEL SUR
4200 SDCo 91941 1271-D3
LOMOND DR
5800 SD 92120 1250-B7
LONDONDERRY AV
10300 SD 92126 1209-D5
LONE BLUFF CT
- SDCo 92127 1169-E4
LONE BLUFF DR
- SDCo 92127 1169-E4
LONE BLUFF WY
- SDCo 92127 1169-F4
LONE CYPRESS PL
12600 SD 92130 1188-B6
LONE DOVE LN
3600 ENCT 92024 1148-D3
LONE DOVE ST
- SDCo 92127 1169-E4
LONE HAWK DR
- SDCo 92127 1169-F4
LONE HILL LN
3200 ENCT 92024 1148-C3
LONE JACK RD
2400 ENCT 92024 1148-B4
LONE OAK LN
- SDCo 92028 998-G4
2200 SDCo 92084 1108-D2
LONE OAK RD
1500 SDCo 92084 1108-D2
LONE OAK TR
14900 SDCo 92065 1173-G7
LONE PINE CT
2500 CHV 91915 1311-H6
LONE PINE TR
28700 SDCo 92066 1237-B5
LONE QUAIL RD
- SD 92127 1169-E3
- SDCo 92127 1169-E3
LONE RAY LN
1900 SDCo 92084 1088-B2
1900 VSTA 92084 1088-B2
LONESOME OAK WY
12600 SDCo 92082 1090-C1
LONESPUR CT
4600 OCN 92056 1087-D3
LONE STAR DR
5500 SD 92120 1250-B4
LONE STAR RD
6300 SD 92154 1331-H7
6300 SDCo 92154 1331-H7
LONE STAR ST
7600 SD 92120 1250-B4
LONE TREE RD
1700 CHV 91913 1311-D6
LONE VALLEY RD
- CHV 91913 1311-E6
LONG PL
3900 CRLB 92008 1106-F7
LONG BOAT CV
2600 SD 92014 1207-H1
LONG BOAT WY
12900 SD 92014 1207-J1
LONG BRANCH AV
4300 SD 92107 1268-A6
4700 SD 92107 1267-J5
LONG CANYON DR
3900 SDCo 91902 1311-A3
LONG CREST DR
500 OCN 92054 1086-D3
LONGDALE DR
7800 LMGR 91945 1270-H7
LONGDALE PL
- SD 92131 1209-F1
LONGDEN LN
300 SOLB 92075 1187-F2
LONGFELLOW CT
- OCN 92057 1067-A4
LONGFELLOW LN
13500 SD 92129 1189-E4
LONGFELLOW RD
- CRLB 92008 1107-B7
1300 VSTA 92083 1107-J4
LONGFORD CT
4900 SD 92117 1248-G1
LONGFORD PL
4900 SD 92117 1248-G1
LONGFORD ST
4800 SD 92117 1248-G1
4900 SD 92117 1228-G7
LONGHORN DR
1600 VSTA 92083 1107-G5
LONG LAKE CT
6900 LMGR 91945 1270-E7
LONG PALM ST
300 OCN 92054 1106-C2
LONG POINT CT
1500 CHV 91911 1330-J4
LONG RIDGE ST
1700 CHV 91913 1311-D6
LONGRIDGE WY
9200 SD 92126 1209-D2
LONG RUN DR
3500 SD 92130 1187-J5
3500 SD 92130 1188-A5
LONG SHADOW CT
1000 ELCJ 92019 1252-A7
LONGS HILL RD
3400 SDCo 92021 1252-D3
LONGSHORE CT
- SD 92130 1208-C2
LONGSHORE WY
- SD 92130 1208-B2
LONGSPUR DR
- SDCo 92055 1023-E3
LONGVIEW DR
3700 CRLB 92008 1106-H4
LONG VIEW WY
4900 SDCo 92020 1271-G1
LONGWOOD ST
8600 SD 92126 1209-C5

LONI LN
1200 VSTA 92084 1108-A1
LONICERA ST
- CRLB 92009 1127-A5
LONJA WY
1700 SD 92173 1350-D3
LONNIE ST
4000 OCN 92056 1087-B7
LONNY LN
7000 LMGR 91945 1270-F7
LONSDALE DR
1000 VSTA 92084 1087-J5
LONSDALE LN
700 VSTA 92084 1087-J4
LOOKOUT CT
3500 OCN 92056 1107-G4
LOOKOUT DR
7700 SD 92037 1227-G6
LOOKOUT LN
20200 SDCo 92029 1149-E1
LOOKOUT LP
7500 SDCo 92066 1237-D7
LOOKOUT PL
3300 SMCS 92069 1128-B1
LOOKOUT RD
- SDCo 92036 (1196-B3 See Page 1176)
LOOKOUT TR
800 SDCo 92019 1253-C2
LOOKOUT MOUNTAIN RD
2400 SDCo 92028 998-F4
LOOKOUT POINT PL
1800 ESCN 92026 1109-F5
LOOSE CREEK RD
2800 SDCo 91935 1293-G3
E LOPEZ DR
- SD 92102 1289-G3
W LOPEZ DR
- SD 92102 1289-G3
LOPEZ ST
1600 OCN 92054 1106-D2
LOPEZ RIDGE WY
11000 SD 92121 1208-G3
LOPING LN
5600 SDCo 91902 1311-A2
LOQUAT CT
800 ELCJ 92020 1251-E6
LOQUAT PL
2100 OCN 92054 1106-E1
LORCA DR
6100 SD 92115 1270-C4
LORCA WY
4700 OCN 92056 1107-F4
LORD ST
3500 SD 92123 1249-C4
LORD CECIL ST
5600 SD 92122 1228-B6
LORELEI LN
2000 SDCo 92028 998-A7
2000 SDCo 92028 1028-A1
LOREN DR
9200 LMSA 91942 1251-B7
LORENA LN
11200 SDCo 92020 1271-G2
LORENA PL
4700 SDCo 92020 1271-H2
LORENE LN
800 SDCo 92028 1028-A1
LORENZ AV
1400 SD 92114 1290-B6
LORENZO DR
1300 SDCo 92028 1027-J7
1300 SDCo 92028 1047-H1
LORETO GN
1800 ESCN 92027 1110-A5
1800 ESCN 92026 1110-A5
2000 ESCN 92026 1109-J4
2000 SDCo 92026 1109-J4
LORETTA ST
700 OCN 92054 1086-A5
LORI CT
800 SMCS 92069 1109-B6
LORI LN
700 CHV 91910 1310-G7
LORI ST
1200 CHV 91913 1331-B1
LORIKEET ST
- OCN 92057 1067-B3
LORI MAR CT
9300 SDCo 91977 1271-B6
LORIMER LN
3600 ENCT 92024 1167-G2
LORING ST
600 SD 92109 1247-J4
1900 SD 92109 1248-A4
LORIRAE PL
11500 SD 92126 1209-B1
LORIS ST
4900 SD 92105 1270-A6
LORITA LN
3900 SDCo 92028 1028-G6
LOR-LAR LN
400 SDCo 92065 1152-G5
LORNA AV
1100 ELCJ 92020 1251-G7
1100 ELCJ 92020 1271-G1
LORNA LN
2400 CRLB 92008 1106-F3
LORNSTEAN LN
- SDCo 91977 1271-B5
LORRAINE CT
13700 SDCo 92040 1191-F6
LORRAINE DR
1500 ENCT 92024 1147-A3
4700 SD 92115 1269-J2
4700 SD 92115 1270-A3
LORRAINE LN
- ELCJ 92019 1252-A6
LORRAINE PL
1700 ESCN 92026 1109-D5
LORRAINE WY
9700 SNTE 92071 1231-C4
LORRAINE ANN DR
4000 SDCo 91941 1271-G4
LORREL PL
3400 SDCo 91935 1272-E7
LORRI WY
1900 ESCN 92026 1109-D5
LORRY LN
1700 ESCN 92029 1129-F6
LOS ALAMOS DR
100 SD 92114 1290-C5
LOS ALAMOS WY
4600 OCN 92057 1087-B3
LOS ALISOS N
700 SDCo 92028 1028-B4
LOS ALISOS S
2500 SDCo 92028 1028-C4

LOS ALISOS DR
2400 SDCo 92028 1028-B4
LOS ALISOS N LN
2700 SDCo 92028 1028-B3
LOS ALTOS CT
5100 SD 92109 1247-J4
LOS ALTOS DR
500 CHV 91914 1311-G2
LOS ALTOS RD
1600 SD 92109 1248-A4
1600 SD 92109 1247-J4
LOS ALTOS WY
1700 SD 92109 1248-A4
LOS ALTOS DE CERRO
2200 SDCo 92065 1152-F1
LOS AMIGOS
- SMCS 92078 1129-C2
1300 SDCo 92028 1028-A4
LOS AMIGOS WY
12000 SDCo 92040 1232-A6
W LOS ANGELES DR
100 VSTA 92083 1087-G5
LOS ANGELES PL
300 SD 92114 1290-B4
LOS ARBOLES
16100 SDCo 92067 1168-C5
LOS ARBOLES RANCH RD
26000 SDCo 92026 1109-G1
LOS ARBOLITOS BLVD
700 OCN 92054 1086-F2
LOS ARCHOS
- SDCo 92040 1232-D6
LOS ARCOS PL
1200 CHV 91910 1311-B7
LOS BANDITOS DR
100 SDCo 92065 1152-J5
LOS BARBOS
16500 SDCo 92067 1168-F4
LOS CABALLITOS
1000 SOLB 92014 1167-G7
LOS CAMPANEROS
1100 SDCo 92069 1128-F4
LOS CAMPOS DR
2900 SDCo 92028 1048-E1
LOS CEDROS LN
1400 ESCN 92026 1109-E6
LOS CERRITOS LN
2500 SDCo 92028 1028-B3
LOS CIELOS
14000 SDCo 92025 1130-F7
LOS COCHES CT
1300 CHV 91910 1311-B6
12700 SDCo 92040 1232-B6
LOS COCHES RD
8300 SDCo 92021 1252-D1
9400 SDCo 92021 1232-D7
9600 SDCo 92040 1232-B4
LOS COCHES RD E
13300 SDCo 92021 1232-D7
LOS COLINAS
400 OCN 92054 1086-F3
600 ENCT 92024 1147-F5
LOS CONEJOS
- SDCo 91916 (1195-D6 See Page 1175)
1300 SDCo 92028 1028-A4
LOS CORDEROS
1100 SDCo 92069 1128-C3
LOS COYOTES RD
- SDCo 92086 409-K8
LOS ENCINOS DR
32600 RivC 92592 999-G1
LOS EUCALIPTOS
17500 SDCo 92067 1168-E1
LOS HERMANOS RD
3500 SDCo 92028 1028-E2
LOS HERMANOS RANCH RD
18500 SDCo 92082 1091-F4
LOS HUECOS RD
- SDCo 91948 1218-C6
LOS INDIOS CT
1100 CHV 91910 1310-J5
LOS MIRLITOS
5300 SDCo 92067 1168-B1
LOS MOCHIS WY
3400 OCN 92056 1107-C2
LOS MORROS
10800 SDCo 92067 1167-J4
10800 SDCo 92067 1168-A2
LOS MORROS Rt#-S9
17200 SDCo 92067 1168-A2
LOS MORROS WY
100 OCN 92057 1067-A6
LOS NARANJOS CT
6200 SDCo 92067 1168-E4
LOS NIDOS LN
10000 SDCo 92026 1089-E2
LOS NIETOS AV
14100 PWY 92064 1190-G1
LOS NOPALITOS
10200 SDCo 92040 1231-F3
LOS OLIVAS DR
400 SMCS 92069 1108-G6
LOS OLIVOS AV
13400 PWY 92064 1190-H4
LOS PADRES DR
4100 SDCo 92028 1028-G7
LOS PINOS
4500 SDCo 92067 1167-J3
LOS PINOS AV
4200 SD 92113 1289-H5
LOS PINOS CIR
7800 CRLB 92009 1147-G3
7800 ENCT 92024 1147-G3
LOS PINOS CT
1000 CHV 91910 1311-B7
LOS PINOS DR
7900 CRLB 92009 1147-G3
LOS PINOS RD
- SDCo 92066 429-L7
LOS PLATEROS
8300 SDCo 92067 1149-A3
LOS RANCHITOS RD
9900 SNTE 92071 1231-F4
9900 SDCo 92040 1231-F4
LOS REYES DR
300 SD 92114 1290-F4
LOS ROBLES DR
5100 CRLB 92008 1126-G2
LOS ROBLES RD
40500 SDCo 92028 997-G3
LOS ROSALES ST
16300 SDCo 92127 1169-F4
LOS SABALOS ST
8100 SD 92126 1209-B2
LOS SANTOS
- SDCo 92040 1232-B7

LOS SICOMOROS LN
3400 SDCo 92028 1028-D7
LOS SONETO CT
7100 SD 92114 1290-F4
LOS SONETO DR
200 SD 92114 1290-F4
LOST TR
20400 SDCo 91901 1274-J3
20400 SDCo 91901 1275-A3
LOST ARROW PL
1200 CHV 91913 1331-A1
LOST DUTCHMAN DR
14200 PWY 92064 1190-J3
LOS TERRINITOS
- SDCo 91901 1235-J5
- SDCo 91901 1236-A5
LOST HORIZON DR
- SDCo 92059 409-E5
- SDCo 92059 999-J5
LOSTINDA ST
1100 ELCJ 92019 1252-A7
LOST OAK LN
400 ESCN 92025 1150-A1
400 SDCo 92025 1130-A7
400 SDCo 92025 1150-A1
LOST VALLEY CT
- CHV 91913 1311-E6
LOST VALLEY RD
- SDCo 92086 409-K7
LOST VALLEY TKTR
- SDCo 92004 409-K6
- SDCo 92086 409-K6
LOS VALLECITOS BLVD
500 SMCS 92069 1108-E7
500 SMCS 92069 1128-G1
LOS VECINOS
4200 SDCo 92028 1047-G5
LOS VERDES DR
3100 SDCo 92028 1048-A2
LOS VIENTOS SERRENO
6900 SDCo 92029 1148-F2
LOT A RD
2600 SDCo 92036 1136-A7
2600 SDCo 92066 1135-J7
LOTT PT
11300 SD 92126 1209-B1
LOTUS AV
100 ELCN 92243 6499-E6
1700 ImCo 92243 6559-E1
1700 ELCN 92243 6559-E1
LOTUS CT
1800 CRLB 92009 1127-E7
LOTUS DR
100 CHV 91911 1330-F5
3600 SD 92106 1268-C6
LOTUS GN
1600 ESCN 92026 1109-D6
LOTUS LN
1200 SDCo 92021 1252-D3
LOTUS ST
100 OCN 92054 1086-D6
4600 SD 92107 1268-A5
4800 SD 92107 1267-J5
LOTUS BLOSSOM ST
700 ENCT 92024 1147-F5
LOTUS POND LN
10500 SDCo 92026 1089-F4
LOU ST
3300 NATC 91950 1290-C6
LOUALTA WY
- CHV 91910 1310-D6
LOUDEN LN
1100 IMPB 91932 1349-G2
LOUETTA LN
14300 PWY 92064 1190-H5
LOUIE PL
1000 VSTA 92084 1087-H4
LOUIS DR
1900 ESCN 92026 1109-D4
LOUIS LN
8600 SNTE 92071 1231-D7
LOUISA DR
10500 SDCo 91941 1271-F4
LOUISANA AV
100 SD 92173 1350-G4
LOUISE CT
2300 ELCJ 92020 1251-C5
LOUISE DR
1400 SDCo 91901 1234-C6
4800 SD 92115 1269-J3
LOUISE LN
- VSTA 92084 1088-D6
1000 SDCo 92025 1130-D6
LOUISE ST
2800 OCN 92056 1087-C7
LOUISIANA AV
300 SD 92173 1350-G5
LOUISIANA ST
3400 SD 92104 1269-D5
4300 SD 92116 1269-D5
LOUKELTON CIR
6100 SD 92120 1249-J7
LOUKELTON WY
4800 SD 92120 1249-J7
LOURDES TER
6100 SD 92120 1250-C6
LOURET AV
1700 SD 92154 1329-J6
1700 SD 92154 1330-A6
LOVAJO RD
1600 SD 92109 1247-J4
LOVE LN
- SDCo 92065 1174-B4
1600 ESCN 92029 1129-G5
LOVEENY DR
2000 SDCo 92084 1108-C3
LOVELAND LN
17400 SDCo 91935 1254-A7
17400 SDCo 91935 1274-A1
LOVELAND RD
4500 ImCo 92227 431-B2
LOVELL LN
9200 LMSA 91941 1271-B1
9200 SDCo 91941 1271-B1
LOVELOCK ST
5200 SD 92110 1268-E3
LOVELY LN
1500 SDCo 92083 1108-A2
LOVETT LN
4200 SDCo 91941 1271-D4
LOW RD
- ImCo 92243 431-A5
LOW CHAPARRAL DR
1800 SMCS 92069 1109-B2
1900 SDCo 92069 1109-B2
LOWE RD
- ImCo - 411-K9
LOWELL CT
7400 LMSA 91941 1270-F3

STREET
Block City ZIP Pg-Grid

LOWELL ST
3100 SD 92106 1288-B1
4000 LMSA 91941 1270-G4
LOWELL WY
3500 SD 92106 1288-B1
LOWER LN
900 SDCo 92069 1108-G2
900 SDCo 92084 1108-G2
LOWER LAKE CT
1500 ENCT 92007 1167-F2
LOWER NORTH PEAK WY
- SDCo 92036 1176-C3
LOWER RIDGE RD
3100 SD 92130 1187-J5
LOWERY LN
- SMCS 92069 1108-H7
LOWEWOOD PL
500 CHV 91910 1310-F5
LOWRY PL
2000 SD 92037 1227-H6
LOWRY TER
7900 SD 92037 1227-H5
LOYOLA CT
1800 CHV 91913 1311-D5
LOZANA RD
2300 SD 92014 1187-H5
LOZITA WY
10300 SDCo 92040 1231-F3
LUANA DR
2900 OCN 92056 1107-B1
LUBBOCK AV
5900 LMSA 91942 1251-A6
LUBER ST
5600 SD 92114 1290-B2
LUCAS LN
- SDCo 92082 1070-G3
LUCAYA CT
- VSTA 92083 1107-H5
LUCERA CT
17000 SD 92127 1169-J2
LUCERA PL
11400 SD 92127 1169-J2
LUCERNE CIR
1800 SMCS 92069 1128-B2
LUCERNE DR
2200 SD 92106 1268-B7
LUCERO CT
1300 CHV 91911 1331-A2
LUCIA CT
7700 CRLB 92009 1147-G1
LUCIA WY
200 OCN 92057 1086-H3
6200 SD 92111 1248-G7
LUCIERNAGA CT
6800 CRLB 92009 1127-G6
LUCIERNAGA PL
6700 CRLB 92009 1127-G5
LUCIERNAGA ST
2500 CRLB 92009 1127-H5
LUCILLA ST
3700 SMCS 92069 1128-C1
LUCILLE DR
4500 SD 92115 1269-J2
4800 SD 92115 1270-A3
LUCILLE PL
4800 SD 92115 1270-A2
LUCINDA ST
3200 SD 92106 1288-A3
LUCITA RD
- SDCo 91935 1274-D3
LUCKETT CT
13200 SD 92130 1188-D4
LUCKY ST
1400 OCN 92054 1106-C2
LUCKY DEVIL TR
600 SDCo 92036 (1158-C1
See Page 1138)
LUCY LN
300 SDCo 92021 1251-G2
500 ESCN 92027 1130-D1
LUCYLLE LN
600 ENCT 92024 1148-A6
LUDINGTON LN
1600 SD 92037 1227-G6
LUDINGTON PL
7700 SD 92037 1227-G6
LUELF CT
2400 SDCo 92065 1172-D4
LUELF ST
2700 SDCo 92065 1172-D5
LUGANO LN
1600 SDCo 92014 1167-J7
1600 SOLB 92014 1167-J7
LUGAR PLAYA CATALINA
11600 SD 92124 1230-A7
LUGO DR
- SDCo 92004 (1099-G5
See Page 1098)
LUIGI TER
5100 SD 92122 1228-D4
LUIS ST
15000 PWY 92064 1170-C7
LUISENO
12800 PWY 92064 1170-D5
LUISENO AV
200 OCN 92057 1067-B7
LUISENO CIRCLE DR
32400 SDCo 92061 1051-A5
LUIS REY HEIGHTS RD
7500 SDCo 92003 1068-G4
LUKE LN
1500 ELCJ 92020 1252-A3
LUNA AV
2600 SD 92117 1248-B1
LUNA CT
1000 VSTA 92083 1087-G4
LUNA DR
500 OCN 92057 1067-A6
3700 OCN 92057 1066-J7
LUNADA PL
12700 SD 92128 1150-C5
LUNADA PT
18700 SD 92128 1150-C6
LUNA DE MIEL
17400 SDCo 92067 1168-H1
LUNA DE ORO
7400 SDCo 92067 1168-H1
LUNAR LN
10300 SNTE 92071 1231-E7
LUNA VISTA DR
700 ESCN 92025 1130-A3
LUNA VISTA PL
700 ESCN 92025 1130-A3
LUND ST
2500 ELCJ 92020 1251-B1
2500 SNTE 92071 1251-B1
LUNDY LAKE DR
2000 SDCo 92029 1129-F7
2200 SDCo 92029 1149-F1
LUNETA DR
- SDCo 92036 1155-H4
1100 DLMR 92014 1187-F4
LUNETA LN
3500 SDCo 92028 1047-E3
3500 SDCo 92055 1047-E3
LUNETA VW
- SDCo 92036 1155-H5
LUNGOS CT
2700 SD 92154 1330-C7
LUPIN WY
10700 SDCo 91941 1271-F4
LUPINE DR
700 SMCS 92078 1128-F2
2400 SDCo 91906 (1297-E6
See Page 1296)
LUPINE LN
3600 SDCo 92028 1028-F6
LUPINE RD
1600 CRLB 92009 1127-E7
LUPINE WY
400 OCN 92057 1086-J4
LUPINE HILLS DR
900 VSTA 92083 1108-A3
1200 VSTA 92083 1107-H3
LUPITA CT
12600 SD 92130 1188-B6
LURA AV
800 ELCJ 92020 1251-F7
LUSARDI TKTR
19500 SDCo 92065 409-G10
LUSK BLVD
6000 SD 92121 1208-C5
LUSTROSOS ST
200 OCN 92057 1066-J6
LUTHER DR
700 SDCo 91977 1291-C3
LUTHER ST
2400 SD 92139 1290-E7
LUTHERAN CT
9700 SNTE 92071 1231-B4
LUTHERAN WY
9500 SNTE 92071 1231-B4
LUX DR
1300 SDCo 92027 1130-C3
LUX CANYON DR
1300 ENCT 92024 1167-G3
LUXEMBOURG WY
- SD 92131 1209-G2
LUZ PL
11400 SD 92127 1169-J1
LUZ RD
11400 SD 92127 1169-J1
LUZ WY
2100 OCN 92056 1086-J7
2100 OCN 92056 1106-J1
LUZEIRO DR
100 SDCo 92084 1088-D5
100 VSTA 92084 1088-D5
LUZON AV
300 DLMR 92014 1187-F4
LYALL PL
13700 SDCo 92021 1232-E5
13700 SDCo 92040 1232-E5
LYCOMING ST
- SD 92154 1351-D2
LYDEN WY
5700 SD 92120 1250-B7
LYDIA LN
1100 SDCo 92028 1027-H1
LYDIA ST
5500 SD 92139 1310-D2
LYERLY RD
- ImCo 92233 411-B10
LYLE DR
5000 SD 92105 1290-A1
LYMAN LN
3100 SD 92093 1228-A2
LYMER DR
4100 SD 92116 1269-H3
LYNCAROL DR
9800 SDCo 91941 1271-D3
LYNCH CT
- CRLB 92008 1107-B7
LYNCH LN
3500 SD 92173 1350-E5
LYNDA PL
3700 NATC 91950 1310-D3
LYNDA RD
2500 SDCo 92028 997-C1
LYNDA PARK LN
14700 PWY 92064 1190-E1
LYNDEN LN
500 SDCo 92028 1027-G2
LYNDHURST TER
- SD 92154 1330-H7
LYNDINE ST
2200 LMGR 91945 1270-H7
2200 LMGR 91945 1290-H1
LYNDON RD
1800 SD 92103 1268-H5
LYNDSIE LN
1000 SDCo 92065 1152-G6
LYNDY LN
1800 SDCo 92028 1048-A4
LYNMAR LN
100 VSTA 92084 1088-B6
1600 SDCo 92028 1027-J3
LYNN CT
3100 OCN 92056 1086-G7
LYNN LN
- OCN 92054 1086-G2
3000 SDCo 92069 1088-J6
LYNN PL
- ELCJ 92020 1251-G6
LYNN ST
5800 SD 92105 1270-C6
LYNN WY
2500 VSTA 92083 1108-B5
LYNNDALE LN
4300 SDCo 91910 1310-E5
LYNNDALE PL
3100 SDCo 91910 1310-E5
LYNNE ANNE LN
9600 SD 92129 1189-E2
LYNNETTE CIR
500 VSTA 92084 1087-H4
4100 OCN 92056 1087-C7
LYNNHAVEN LN
6500 SD 92119 1250-J5
6500 SD 92119 1251-A5
LYNN OAK DR
1400 SDCo 91901 1234-J5
LYNNWOOD DR
3300 SDCo 91910 1310-E5
3300 CHV 91910 1310-E5
LYNRIDGE CT
7100 SD 92120 1250-E5
LYNRIDGE RD
7200 SD 92120 1250-E5
LYNWOOD AV
300 SOLB 92075 1167-F6
LYNWOOD LN
400 SMCS 92069 1109-B6
LYNX GN
1800 ESCN 92026 1109-F6
LYNX RD
8600 SD 92126 1209-C2
LYNX WY
- CRLB 92008 1107-D7
LYON CIR
200 VSTA 92083 1087-H7
LYON ST
4800 SD 92102 1289-J2
4800 SD 92102 1290-A2
LYONS CT
2700 CRLB 92008 1106-J4
LYONS DR
4500 SDCo 91941 1271-F3
LYONS LN
1200 SDCo 92021 1251-H3
LYONS RD
- ImCo 92243 431-A7
LYONS CREEK LN
2900 SDCo 91935 1294-A1
LYONS CREEK RD
17200 SDCo 91935 1294-A1
LYONS PEAK LN
18300 SDCo 91935 1294-D4
LYONS PEAK RD
- SDCo 91935 1294-B2
LYONS VALLEY RD
13800 SDCo 91935 1292-G1
14000 SDCo 91935 1272-J7
14300 SDCo 91935 1273-A7
15700 SDCo 91935 1293-G2
16500 SDCo 91935 1294-A2
19200 SDCo 91901 1294-H3
21000 SDCo 91901 1274-J7
21000 SDCo 91901 1275-D2
21000 SDCo 91901 (1295-A1
See Page 1294)
LYRA CT
10900 SD 92126 1209-D3
LYRIC LN
4500 SD 92117 1248-H2
LYTTON ST
2900 SD 92110 1268-D6
3000 SD 92133 1268-D6
3000 SD 92140 1268-D6
3100 SD 92106 1268-D6

M

M AV
400 NATC 91950 1289-J7
600 NATC 91950 1309-J1
1700 NATC 91950 1310-A2
2800 CHV 91950 1310-A3
N M AV
300 CORD 92135 1288-H5
S M AV
400 CORD 92135 1288-G5
M CT
- SD 92126 1209-F7
M ST
100 ENCT 92007 1167-C1
M & R RANCH RD
2200 SDCo 92028 998-A7
M 1ST ST W
- CORD 92135 1288-C7
- SD 92135 1288-C7
M 2ND ST W
- SD 92135 1288-C7
M 3RD ST S
- CORD 92135 1288-C7
- SD 92135 1288-C7
MABLE WY
4900 SD 92117 1228-H7
MABON PL
3600 SD 92117 1248-D2
MABUHAY WY
2200 SD 92154 1330-D6
MAC LN
9000 SDCo 91977 1271-A6
MACADAMIA CT
4700 OCN 92057 1067-B7
4700 OCN 92057 1087-A1
MACADAMIA DR
700 CRLB 92009 1126-J6
1300 SDCo 92028 998-B6
MACAMBO DR
- ELCJ 92021 1251-H5
MACARIO DR
4900 OCN 92057 1067-A6
MACARTHUR AV
2000 CRLB 92008 1106-H6
MACARTHUR RD
6400 LMGR 91945 1270-D7
6400 SD 92114 1270-D7
MACAULAY ST
3000 SD 92106 1288-B1
MACAW LN
7600 SD 92123 1269-A1
MACAWA AV
8300 SD 92123 1249-C5
MACCOOL LN
9600 SNTE 92071 1231-C7
MACDONALD ST
2700 OCN 92054 1086-D6
MACE ST
100 CHV 91911 1330-E5
MACERO ST
1700 ESCN 92029 1129-F6
MACHADO ST
1400 OCN 92054 1106-C2
MACHUM PL
- ELCJ 92021 1251-H5
MACKENZIE DR
300 SMCS 92078 1128-G2
MACKENZIE CREEK RD
2300 CHV 91914 1311-F3
MACKEY DR
2900 SDCo 92028 1047-G1
MACKEY LN
800 SDCo 92028 1047-G1
MACKINNON AV
600 ENCT 92007 1167-E2
MACKINNON CT
700 ENCT 92007 1167-E1
MACKINNON RANCH RD
- ENCT 92007 1167-E4
MACKINZIE WY
16200 SDCo 92082 1071-B7
MACLAY ST
600 SDCo 91977 1291-B3
MACLEAN RD
1500 SDCo 92004 (1099-E2
See Page 1098)
MACLURA ST
4700 OCN 92057 1087-A1
MACNAUGHTON LN
2100 ESCN 92027 1110-C4
MACON ST
500 ELCJ 92019 1252-A4
MACOUBA PL
10800 SD 92124 1249-J2
MACQUARIE ST
7100 LMSA 91942 1270-F1
MACRONALD DR
4300 SDCo 91941 1271-C3
MACS RD
- SDCo 92055 408-L8
MAC TAN LN
15600 SDCo 92082 1071-A6
MAC TAN RD
28400 SDCo 92082 1091-A1
28700 SDCo 92082 1071-A4
28900 SDCo 92082 1070-J7
MACTIBBY ST
3700 SD 92117 1248-E5
MADDEN AV
800 SD 92154 1330-C7
900 SD 92154 1350-C1
MADDEN CT
2800 SD 92154 1330-C7
MADDOX DR
10000 SD 92124 1249-F2
MADELINE ST
6100 SD 92115 1270-C3
MADERA CT
3100 CRLB 92009 1147-H1
MADERA LN
1100 VSTA 92084 1088-A3
MADERA ST
800 SD 92114 1290-E2
1300 LMGR 91945 1290-E2
MADERA ROSA WY
- SDCo 91935 1274-E3
MADERA VERDE PL
1800 SDCo 92021 1252-H3
MADIERA DR
2100 OCN 92056 1086-J7
MADISON AV
- CHV 91910 1309-J5
500 CHV 91910 1330-A1
500 CHV 91910 1310-A7
600 SD 92116 1269-E3
800 ESCN 92026 1109-J6
800 CHV 91911 1330-B2
900 ESCN 92027 1109-J6
4500 SD 92115 1269-J3
4800 SD 92115 1270-A3
7400 LMGR 91945 1270-G6
8700 LMSA 91941 1271-A2
9200 SDCo 91941 1271-B2
E MADISON AV
100 ELCJ 92020 1251-H5
400 ELCJ 92021 1251-H5
1000 ELCJ 92021 1252-B4
1100 ELCJ 92019 1252-B4
1200 SDCo 92019 1252-D4
W MADISON AV
100 ELCJ 92020 1251-E4
MADISON ST
100 OCN 92057 1067-B7
2600 CRLB 92008 1106-E5
MADRA AV
5700 SD 92120 1250-D7
5700 SD 92120 1270-D1
MADRA LN
- OCN 92054 1086-G3
MADRESELVA WY
2100 SD 92154 1350-B3
MADRID DR
1500 VSTA 92083 1107-H3
MADRID ST
3100 SD 92110 1268-D6
MADRID WY
10100 SDCo 91977 1271-E5
MADRIGAL CT
1200 CHV 91910 1311-B7
MADRIGAL ST
10900 SD 92129 1169-H6
MADRILENA WY
7600 CRLB 92009 1147-G2
MADRONA ST
100 CHV 91910 1310-A6
MADRONCILLO ST
2300 SD 92114 1270-E7
2300 SD 92114 1290-E1
MADRONE AV
6300 SD 92114 1290-D3
MADRONE GN
1600 ESCN 92027 1110-A5
MADRUGADA CT
11700 SD 92124 1250-B2
MAELEE DR
2200 SDCo 92084 1087-H1
MAEMAR DR
16600 SDCo 92082 1091-C5
MAESTRIA CT
10800 SD 92124 1249-J2
MAESTRO CT
12500 SD 92130 1188-B7
MAEZEL LN
3200 CRLB 92008 1106-G4
MAGARIAN RD
700 SDCo 92028 1027-H3
MAGDALENA DR
100 OCN 92057 1087-A2
300 OCN 92057 1086-J1
MAGDALENE WY
1900 SD 92110 1268-E1
MAGEE RD
35900 SDCo 92028 999-H2
35900 SDCo 92059 999-H2
MAGEE HEIGHTS RD
- SDCo 92059 999-J2
MAGELLAN CIR
3700 OCN 92056 1107-A2
MAGELLAN LN
2500 VSTA 92083 1107-J4
MAGELLAN ST
- CRLB 92009 1127-A7
- CRLB 92009 1147-A1
3100 SD 92154 1330-D7
MAGELLAN WY
1100 CHV 91910 1311-B7
MAGENS BAY
4600 OCN 92057 1066-H6
MAGENTA ST
900 SD 92113 1289-J5
MAGGIO DR
9300 SDCo 91916 1236-C2
MAGICAL WATERS CT
- SDCo 91977 1291-F1
MAGNA LN
10900 SDCo 92040 1231-F3
MAGNATRON BLVD
5500 SD 92111 1229-C7
MAGNOLIA AV
100 SDCo 92065 1153-A3
300 ELCN 92243 6499-H5
600 CRLB 92008 1106-E6
1100 ELCJ 92020 1251-F7
1100 ELCJ 92020 1271-F1
1200 ESCN 92027 1110-A7
2600 SD 92109 1248-C5
13900 PWY 92064 1190-F3
N MAGNOLIA AV
- ELCJ 92021 1251-F3
100 ELCJ 92020 1251-F5
1000 SDCo 92020 1251-F3
1700 ELCJ 92020 1231-E6
8500 SNTE 92071 1231-E1
S MAGNOLIA AV
100 ELCJ 92020 1251-F6
MAGNOLIA CT
400 SMCS 92069 1108-H5
1800 OCN 92054 1106-E2
MAGNOLIA HTS
800 SDCo 92065 1153-A4
MAGNOLIA PL
1500 ESCN 92027 1110-B7
MAGNOLIA RD
3800 OCN 92054 1086-F2
MAGNOLIA PARK DR
9700 SNTE 92071 1231-D4
MAGNUS WY
4700 SD 92113 1289-J6
4700 SD 92113 1290-A6
4900 NATC 91950 1290-A6
MAGRUDER ST
7100 LMSA 91942 1270-F1
MAGUAY RD
- SDCo 91935 1274-E3
MAGUIRE RD
- SD 92173 1350-E4
MAHAILA AV
3900 SD 92122 1228-C3
MAHOGANY DR
600 ELCJ 92019 1252-B6
4700 OCN 92056 1087-E5
MAHOGANY GN
300 ESCN 92026 1109-G6
MAHOGANY RANCH RD
- SDCo 92065 1171-J6
- SDCo 92065 1172-A6
MAHOGANY VISTA LN
- SD 92102 1290-A4
MAIDEN LN
1200 DLMR 92014 1187-F5
4900 LMSA 91941 1270-H2
MAIN AV
- SDCo 91950 1310-C3
400 SDCo 92028 1027-F2
N MAIN AV Rt#-S13
100 SDCo 92028 1027-F2
S MAIN AV Rt#-S13
100 SDCo 92028 1027-F3
W MAIN RD
2500 ELCN 92243 6499-C6
2500 ImCo 92243 6499-C6
MAIN ST
- SDCo 92036 1156-H1
100 SD 92173 1350-G4
100 VSTA 92083 1087-H6
100 VSTA 92084 1087-H6
400 CHV 91911 1330-B5
400 ELCN 92243 6499-F6
700 CHV 91911 1331-A5
1500 LMGR 91945 1290-G1
1600 SD 92113 1289-C5
2000 SD 91911 1330-B5
2000 SD 92154 1330-B5
2200 SDCo 92036 1136-B7
2200 LMGR 91945 1270-G7
2700 SD 92136 1289-E6
3800 NATC 91950 1289-E6
MAIN ST Rt#-S30
300 CLPT 92233 411-C10
MAIN ST Rt#-67
900 SDCo 92065 1152-E7
1900 SDCo 92065 1172-D1
MAIN ST Rt#-78
100 BRW 92227 431-C2
200 ImCo 92227 431-C2
200 SDCo 92065 1152-G6
MAIN ST Rt#-79
1800 SDCo 92036 1136-B7
MAIN ST Rt#-S80
100 ELCN 92243 6499-J6
100 ELCN 92243 6500-A6
MAIN ST Rt#-115
- ImCo 92233 411-C10
500 CLPT 92233 411-C10
E MAIN ST
100 ELCJ 92020 1251-H5
500 ELCJ 92021 1251-H5
500 ELCJ 92019 1251-H5
1200 ELCJ 92019 1252-A4
1200 ELCJ 92021 1252-B2
1900 SDCo 92021 1252-B2
W MAIN ST
- SDCo 92004 (1121-G2
See Page 1100)
1000 ELCJ 92020 1251-E5
MAINE AV
9700 SDCo 92040 1232-B3
MAINSAIL RD
300 OCN 92054 1086-F6
MAISEL WY
5400 SD 92115 1270-B3
MAITLAND AV
500 SD 92154 1330-E6
MAJANO PL
2400 CRLB 92009 1147-G3
MAJELLA DR
24100 SDCo 92065 1173-E2
MAJELLA RD
2500 SDCo 92084 1087-F1
2500 SDCo 92084 1067-F7
MAJESTAD LN
1100 CHV 91910 1310-J5
MAJESTIC DR
3500 SD 92154 1350-E1
MAJORCA WY
4600 OCN 92056 1107-E4
MAKAHA WY
2900 SD 92154 1330-C6
MAKENNA LN
- SDCo 91901 1253-F1
MAKIN RD
2300 CORD 92155 1309-A1
MALABAR DR
12200 PWY 92064 1170-B7
MALAGA DR
4900 OCN 92057 1067-A6
MALAGA ST
3000 SD 92110 1268-D6
MALAGA WY
1500 SDCo 92028 1027-F5
MALCOLM DR
6000 SD 92115 1270-C4
MALCOLM ST
5300 OCN 92056 1087-E1
MALDEN ST
1600 SD 92109 1247-J4
1600 SD 92109 1248-A4
MALEA WY
6000 OCN 92056 1107-F5
MALEK LN
12100 SDCo 92082 1070-C4
MALENE LN
1000 SDCo 92021 1251-H2
MALER RD
9100 SD 92129 1189-D1
MALEY ST
7100 SD 92111 1248-J6
7100 SD 92111 1249-A6
MALIBU PL
2700 ESCN 92027 1110-D6
MALIBU WY
2400 SD 92014 1187-H5
MALIBU POINT CT
1500 CHV 91911 1330-J3
MALIBU POINT WY
800 OCN 92054 1066-G7
MALITO CT
200 CHV 91911 1330-G5
MALITO DR
3400 SDCo 91902 1310-F2
MALLARD CT
- CRLB 92009 1127-B7
- ImCo 92249 6560-B7
MALLARD DR
29800 SDCo 91906 (1297-F5
See Page 1296)
MALLARD ST
6300 SD 92114 1290-D1
6800 LMGR 91945 1290-D1
MALLEE ST
- CRLB 92009 1127-D5
MALLORCA DR
1500 VSTA 92083 1107-H3
MALLORCA PL
2600 CRLB 92009 1147-G1
MALLOW CT
1700 CRLB 92009 1127-E6
MALONEY ST
1300 SMCS 92069 1108-H4
MALOREY ST
7500 LMSA 91942 1250-G6
MA LOU DR
3000 SDCo 91935 1292-J1
3000 SDCo 91935 1293-A1
3100 SDCo 91935 1272-J7
MALPAZO CT
3400 SDCo 91902 1310-G2
MALTA AV
1500 CHV 91911 1330-G4
MALTA ST
7100 SD 92111 1248-J4
MALTA WY
3300 OCN 92056 1106-J1
MALVERN CT
5700 SD 92120 1250-B7
MAMMOTH DR
2500 SD 92123 1249-E6
N MAMMOTH PL
2100 ESCN 92029 1129-E6
S MAMMOTH PL
1700 ESCN 92029 1129-F6
MANACOR CT
10800 SD 92124 1249-H2
MANAGUA PL
2900 CRLB 92009 1127-H7
MANAJO RD
9100 SDCo 92040 1232-C6
MANAJO WY
13000 SDCo 92040 1232-C5
MANANA PL
6500 SD 92037 1247-F2
MANCHESTER AV
1900 ENCT 92007 1167-D3
2000 ESCN 92027 1130-D1
3400 ENCT 92067 1167-F4
3500 ENCT 92024 1167-H3
MANCHESTER PL
1700 ESCN 92027 1130-C1
MANCHESTER RD
5100 SD 92115 1270-E2
MANCHESTER ST
900 NATC 91950 1290-C7
MANCILLA CT
4200 SD 92130 1188-B6
MANDA PL
1200 ELCJ 92021 1251-G3
1200 SDCo 92021 1251-G3
MANDALAY PL
5200 SD 92115 1270-E2
MANDALAY RD
6900 SD 92115 1270-E2
MANDAN WY
3100 SD 92117 1248-C1
MANDARIN DR
800 SDCo 92028 1027-G3
5100 OCN 92056 1087-D2
MANDARIN WY
500 SDCo 92028 1027-G3
MANDELL WEISS LN
- SD 92093 1227-J3
MANDEVILLE CT
9400 SNTE 92071 1231-B5
MANDEVILLE DR
1400 ESCN 92029 1149-G1
1400 ESCN 92029 1129-G7
MANDEVILLE PL
1400 ESCN 92029 1129-G7
MANDEVILLE RD
9400 SD 92093 1228-A2
9400 SNTE 92071 1231-B5
MANDEZ DR
2000 SDCo 92065 1172-E3
MANDI LN
- SNTE 92071 1231-C3
100 SDCo 92065 1152-J3
MANDRAKE CT
11700 SD 92131 1210-A2
MANDRAKE PT
11300 SD 92131 1210-A2
MANDY LN
3300 SDCo 91977 1271-D6
MANFRED CT
1700 ELCJ 92021 1252-B2
MANGANO CIR
100 ENCT 92024 1147-C6
MANGO CT
700 SMCS 92069 1109-C6
MANGO CV
14300 SD 92014 1187-H5
MANGO DR
13200 SD 92014 1187-H5
MANGO GN
900 SDCo 92084 1088-D5
MANGO WY
2400 SD 92014 1187-H5
MANGONEL DR
2000 SDCo 92004 1058-G7
MANGO VIEW DR
200 ENCT 92024 1147-E7
MANGRUM PL
2300 OCN 92056 1106-H1
MANHASSET DR
5100 SD 92115 1270-A2
MANHATTAN CT
700 SD 92109 1267-H2
MANIFESTO PL
12500 SD 92130 1188-B7
MANILA AV
10400 SD 92126 1209-B4
MANILA CIR
7900 SD 92126 1209-B4
MANILA TR
7500 SDCo 92066 1237-C7
MANION ST
2300 ELCJ 92020 1251-B1
MANITOU WY
4400 SD 92117 1248-F1
MANKATO ST
100 CHV 91910 1310-B7
600 CHV 91910 1330-A1
E MANKATO ST
- CHV 91910 1310-D6
MANLEY ST
4700 SD 92124 1249-G2
MANN AV
100 NATC 91950 1290-A6
MANNEN WY
13200 SDCo 92040 1232-C7
MANNING ST
6600 SD 92111 1248-H7
MANNING WY
- SD 92102 1289-G3
800 SD 92154 1330-B7
MANNIS AV
- CHV 91913 1311-C7
- CHV 91913 1331-C1
MANNIX CT
7300 SD 92129 1188-J7
MANNIX RD
12000 SD 92129 1188-J7
MANOCK CV
13000 SD 92130 1188-D5
MANOMET ST
4900 SD 92113 1290-A5
MANON ST
5800 LMSA 91942 1250-G6
MANOR DR
500 ELCJ 92020 1251-E5
1200 SDCo 92021 1251-J2
1600 VSTA 92084 1087-G3
9100 LMSA 91942 1251-B6
E MANOR DR
600 CHV 91910 1330-A1
W MANOR DR
600 CHV 91910 1330-A1
6100 LMSA 91942 1251-B6
MANOR WY
900 SD 92106 1288-A2
MANOR RIDGE LN
4900 SD 92130 1208-D1
MANOS DR
2700 SD 92139 1310-D2
MANRESA CT
16900 SD 92128 1170-C2
MANSFIELD ST
4600 SD 92116 1269-F3
MANSIONES LN
1100 CHV 91910 1310-J5
MANSON ST
7200 SD 92111 1248-J6
MANTILLA RD
12300 SD 92128 1170-C4
MANTON WY
100 VSTA 92084 1087-G2
MANTUA CT
5400 SD 92124 1249-H1
MANYA CIR
7000 SD 92154 1330-B5
MANYA ST
2200 SD 92154 1330-B5
MANZANA WY
2300 SD 92139 1290-H5
MANZANARES WY
5100 SD 92114 1290-A4
MANZANILLA WY
- OCN 92057 1087-A2
MANZANILLO CT
100 SOLB 92075 1167-D6
MANZANITA AV
1400 ESCN 92027 1110-A7
MANZANITA CT
1800 VSTA 92083 1108-B3
MANZANITA DR
- ELCN 92243 6559-G2
- ImCo 92243 6559-G2
- SDCo 92036 1155-G4
200 OCN 92057 1067-A7
600 SDCo 92036 1156-E1
800 SDCo 92036 1136-C7
3800 SD 92105 1269-G7
24300 SDCo 91916 1236-A2
29400 SDCo 91906 (1297-E5
See Page 1296)
MANZANITA LN
800 SMCS 92069 1108-J6
11500 SDCo 92040 1211-F7
25000 SDCo 91916 1236-B2
MANZANITA PL
300 ESCN 92026 1129-H1
3200 SD 92105 1269-H6
MANZANITA RD
- SDCo 91905 430-D7
- SDCo 91905 (1299-J1
See Page 1298)
- SDCo 91905 1300-A1
11200 SDCo 92040 1211-H6

MANZANITA ST   SAN DIEGO CO. STREET INDEX   MCBURNEY CT 6600

Thomas Bros. Maps ®
COPYRIGHT 2001

STREET
Block City ZIP Pg-Grid

MANZANITA ST
500 CHV 91911 1330-G1
7000 CRLB 92009 1127-E7
MANZANITA TR
2400 SDCo 91905 (1299-H4 See Page 1298)
28900 SDCo 92066 1237-B7
MANZANITA WY
- SDCo 91905 1300-D6
4300 OCN 92057 1086-J2
20500 SDCo 91935 (1315-A1 See Page 1294)
MANZANITA CREST RD
31100 SDCo 92082 1070-A3
MANZANITA DULCE
39500 SDCo 91905 1300-C5
MANZANITA VIEW RD
2800 SDCo 91901 1234-C7
MANZANO DR
100 CRLB 92008 1126-G3
MANZANO PL
400 CHV 91910 1310-H4
MANZELLA DR
14200 SD 92129 1189-G2
MAPLE
9700 SDCo 92021 1233-B3
MAPLE AV
100 CRLB 92008 1106-E6
200 ELCN 92243 6499-J7
500 SMCS 92069 1108-H5
500 SMCS 92069 1109-A5
4200 LMSA 91941 1270-G2
MAPLE CT
300 CHV 91911 1330-G3
2900 SD 92104 1269-E7
MAPLE DR
1600 CHV 91911 1330-G5
4400 OCN 92056 1087-D5
MAPLE LN
9700 SDCo 92029 1149-E2
MAPLE ST
- SMCS 92078 1129-C2
100 SD 92103 1289-A1
100 SDCo 92065 1152-F4
400 SD 92101 1289-A1
500 SD 92103 1288-J1
500 SD 92101 1288-J1
2500 SD 92104 1269-D7
4300 SD 92105 1269-H7
5200 SD 92105 1270-A7
N MAPLE ST
100 ESCN 92025 1129-J3
S MAPLE ST
100 ESCN 92025 1129-J3
1000 ESCN 92025 1130-A4
W MAPLE ST
100 SD 92103 1289-A1
MAPLEBROOK CT
1900 ELCJ 92019 1252-C5
MAPLELEAF CT
1600 ENCT 92024 1167-G1
MAPLELEAF DR
2300 VSTA 92083 1108-A5
6800 CRLB 92009 1127-A5
MAPLE TREE RD
10100 SNTE 92071 1231-D3
MAPLEVIEW ST
12300 SDCo 92040 1232-C2
MAPLEWOOD CIR
5100 OCN 92056 1087-D2
MAPLEWOOD CT
12700 PWY 92064 1190-C2
MAPLEWOOD LN
11900 SDCo 92040 1231-J3
MAPLEWOOD PL
- ESCN 92027 1130-J3
MAPLEWOOD ST
14300 PWY 92064 1190-C2
MAPLEWOOD WY
700 ELCJ 92021 1251-G4
MAR AV
7300 SD 92037 1227-F7
MARA LN
15800 SDCo 92065 1172-A4
MARABOU LN
1300 VSTA 92083 1087-F4
MARANATHA LN
400 SMCS 92069 1128-F1
MARANDA DR
9100 SNTE 92071 1231-A5
MARATHON DR
2500 SD 92123 1249-E5
MARATHON WY
4800 OCN 92056 1107-E6
MARAVILLA LN
600 SDCo 92028 1047-E3
MARAVILLA WY
2400 OCN 92056 1087-C5
MARAZON LN
700 VSTA 92083 1107-E1
MAR AZUL WY
2000 CRLB 92009 1127-F7
MARBELLA CIR
700 CHV 91910 1311-A5
MARBELLA CT
1200 CHV 91910 1311-A5
MARBELLA DR
1600 VSTA 92083 1107-G4
MARBELLA PL
1200 CHV 91910 1311-A5
MARBLE CT
1500 CHV 91911 1330-G4
MARBLE ST
500 ELCJ 92020 1251-G4
MARBLE WY
1500 CHV 91911 1330-G4
MARBLEHEAD BAY DR
4600 OCN 92057 1066-J6
MARBO TER
1000 VSTA 92084 1087-J4
MARBOK WY
3000 SDCo 91935 1292-G1
MARBROOK WY
13700 SDCo 92021 1232-E7
MARBURY AV
10600 SD 92126 1209-D3
MARC TR
1700 SDCo 91906 (1318-E3 See Page 1298)
MARCA PL
2300 CRLB 92009 1147-G2
MARCASEL PL
13400 SD 92130 1188-B4
MARCELLA CT
10100 SNTE 92071 1231-A3
MARCELLA ST
4100 OCN 92056 1087-B6
MARCELLENA RD
4400 SD 92115 1270-A4
MARCH PL
2100 SD 92110 1268-F1
MARCHETA ST
100 ENCT 92024 1147-B6
MARCIA CT
4300 SD 92154 1350-G1
MARCIA LN
4600 SDCo 92020 1271-H2
MARCILLA WY
600 CHV 91910 1310-H6
MARCONI CT
2300 SD 92154 1352-B3
MARCONI DR
9700 SD 92154 1352-A3
MARCONI PL
2300 SD 92154 1352-B3
MARCOS ST
300 SMCS 92069 1108-G7
MARCOS VISTA LN
700 SMCS 92069 1108-C6
MARCWADE CT
3800 SD 92154 1350-F1
MARCWADE DR
3900 SD 92154 1350-F1
MARCY AV
2600 SD 92113 1289-D5
MARCYN LN
1600 ESCN 92026 1109-H6
MARDAVIDO LN
2100 SDCo 92028 1028-B6
MARDAVIDO PL
2100 SDCo 92028 1028-B6
MARDI GRAS CT
- CORD 92118 1329-D3
MARDI GRAS RD
- CORD 92118 1329-E2
MARDI GRAS ST
4600 OCN 92057 1066-H7
MARE RD
5300 OCN 92057 1067-B5
MARENGO AV
5200 LMSA 91942 1270-H1
5500 LMSA 91942 1250-H7
MARGALE LN
29800 SDCo 92084 1068-F6
MARGARET CT
9000 SDCo 91977 1291-A2
MARGARET ST
5200 SDCo 91902 1310-J1
MARGARET WY
3800 CRLB 92008 1106-G6
MARGARITA AV
500 CORD 92118 1288-J7
800 CORD 92118 1289-A7
MARGARITA GN
1300 SDCo 92028 998-C6
MARGARITA LN
14100 SDCo 92082 1070-F2
MARGARITA ST
12600 SD 92130 1208-A2
MARGARITA VISTA
3000 SDCo 92028 998-C7
MARGARITTA RD
6600 SD 92114 1290-E4
MARGATE AV
12800 PWY 92064 1190-H5
MARGE WY
4200 SD 92154 1350-G1
MARGERUM AV
7200 SD 92120 1250-C4
MARGIE PL
500 SMCS 92069 1128-D1
MARGINATA CT
11900 SD 92131 1210-A1
MARGO CT
300 CHV 91910 1310-F7
MARGO PL
1100 VSTA 92083 1107-E1
MARGUERITA LN
4800 LMSA 91941 1271-B2
4800 SDCo 91941 1271-B2
MARGUERITE LN
900 CRLB 92009 1127-A6
MARGUERITE WY
200 OCN 92057 1086-H3
MARGUERITE CANYON RD
11100 SDCo 92040 1212-H6
MARIA AV
400 SDCo 91977 1291-C2
MARIA CT
2100 LMGR 91945 1290-J1
MARIA LN
3600 CRLB 92008 1106-H5
MARIA PL
1500 CORD 92118 1288-J7
MARIA WY
800 CHV 91911 1330-F1
MARIAN AV
2100 SD 92154 1330-A6
MARIAN ST
3900 LMSA 91941 1270-E5
MARIAN WY
5400 SD 92110 1268-F3
MARIANA DR
14200 PWY 92064 1190-B2
MARIANA WY
- OCN 92057 1086-H3
MARIANNE LN
2600 SDCo 92028 1028-B4
MARIANOPOLIS WY
14200 SD 92129 1189-D2
MARICOPA
- CRLB 92009 1126-H5
MARICOTTE PL
13200 SD 92130 1187-J5
MARIE AV
7600 LMSA 91941 1270-G3
MARIE CT
700 ENCT 92024 1147-G5
MARIE LN
1600 SDCo 91977 1291-A2
MARIETTA ST
400 CHV 91910 1310-A5
MARIGOLD
9600 SDCo 92021 1233-B3
MARIGOLD CIR
300 OCN 92057 1066-H6
MARIGOLD CT
800 CRLB 92009 1127-A5
MARIGOLD DR
- SD 92109 1248-C6
600 VSTA 92083 1087-F5
13600 PWY 92064 1190-F2
MARIGOLD PL
100 CHV 91910 1310-C5
2200 SD 92105 1289-G1
MARIGOLD ST
2300 SD 92105 1289-G1
MARIGOLD WY
800 SMCS 92078 1128-F2
MARIGOT PL
5200 SD 92124 1249-J1
MARILLA DR
9200 SDCo 92040 1231-H5
MARILOU RD
4800 SD 92102 1289-J2
4800 SD 92102 1290-A2
MARILOUISE WY
2400 SD 92103 1268-G4
MARILYN LN
1600 SMCS 92069 1109-A1
1900 SDCo 92069 1109-A1
MARIN DR
- SMCS 92069 1108-H5
4900 OCN 92056 1107-F3
MARINA AV
500 CORD 92118 1288-G7
MARINA DR
- ImCo 92274 410-H6
4700 CRLB 92008 1106-H7
MARINA PKWY
300 CHV 91910 1309-H7
400 CHV 91910 1329-J1
700 CHV 91910 1330-A2
MARINA WY
900 CHV 91910 1329-H2
MARINA DEL REY AV
100 OCN 92054 1066-E6
MARINA PARK WY
200 SD 92101 1289-A5
MARINA SPRINGS LN
9300 SDCo 92021 1232-J4
MARINDUSTRY DR
6200 SD 92121 1228-G1
MARINE PL
- CRLB 92009 1127-A7
MARINE RD
- SDCo 92055 1047-A4
MARINE ST
200 SD 92037 1247-E1
400 SD 92037 1227-E7
MARINE WY
- SD 92109 1248-C6
1400 CORD 92118 1288-J5
MARINER ST
900 CRLB 92009 1126-J4
MARINERS BAY
4500 OCN 92057 1066-H6
MARINERS WY
1000 SD 92109 1267-J3
MARINE VIEW AV
100 SOLB 92075 1167-G7
400 SOLB 92014 1167-G7
600 SOLB 92014 1187-G1
3900 SD 92113 1289-G7
MARINE VIEW DR
1000 SDCo 92083 1107-H3
MARING PL
5200 SD 92105 1290-A1
MARIO PL
3700 SD 92111 1248-H4
MARION CT
1500 CHV 91913 1311-C7
MARION LN
2200 SDCo 92025 1130-D6
MARIPOSA
5400 SDCo 92067 1168-C3
MARIPOSA CIR
600 CHV 91911 1330-G1
MARIPOSA CT
1200 VSTA 92084 1088-A3
MARIPOSA DR
1500 SDCo 92004 1058-F5
MARIPOSA LN
8500 LMSA 91941 1271-A3
MARIPOSA PL
900 ESCN 92026 1109-F5
5600 SD 92114 1290-C6
MARIPOSA RD
1100 CRLB 92009 1127-A4
MARIPOSA ST
500 CHV 91911 1330-G1
1400 SD 92114 1290-B6
8600 LMSA 91941 1270-J3
8600 LMSA 91941 1271-A3
MARISA CT
2300 ENCT 92024 1147-J6
2300 ENCT 92024 1148-A5
MARISA LN
800 ENCT 92024 1147-J5
800 ENCT 92024 1148-A6
MARISCO PT
12300 SD 92130 1188-B7
MARISMA WY
1600 SD 92037 1247-G1
MARITA LN
1700 SDCo 92028 1027-J3
MARITIME DR
1500 CRLB 92009 1127-C4
MARITIME PL
12900 SD 92130 1187-J5
MARJAY DR
13300 SDCo 92040 1232-D6
MARJEAN LN
10200 SDCo 92040 1231-G3
MARJO CT
2500 OCN 92056 1087-D6
MARJORIE AV
1400 ESCN 92027 1110-A6
MARJORIE DR
700 SD 92114 1290-G3
MARJORIE LN
3600 CRLB 92008 1106-G5
MARJORIE PL
1200 ESCN 92027 1110-A7
MARJORIE ST
1500 OCN 92056 1087-E2
MARK AV
2000 ESCN 92027 1110-B6
MARK CIR
2400 CRLB 92008 1106-H4
MARK PL
2200 ESCN 92027 1110-C6
MARK TER
4000 SD 92117 1248-E5
MARK TR
- SDCo 91935 1274-A4
16700 SDCo 91935 1273-J5
MARKAB DR
11300 SD 92126 1209-C1
MARKAR RD
15000 PWY 92064 1170-J6
MARKELL LN
300 SDCo 92028 1027-F4
MARKER LN
3100 SDCo 92004 (1079-B5 See Page 1058)
MARKER RD
- SD 92130 1188-J3
- SD 92130 1189-A3
MARKERRY AV
1500 ELCJ 92019 1252-B5
MARKET PL
- SD 92101 1288-J4
- ESCN 92029 1129-E3
MARKET ST
100 SD 92101 1289-A3
500 SD 92101 1288-J4
1400 VSTA 92084 1087-J4
1700 SD 92102 1289-C3
4700 SD 92102 1290-A3
5000 SD 92114 1290-B3
W MARKET ST
100 SD 92101 1289-A3
MARKETPLACE AV
- SD 92113 1289-H5
MARKHAM ST
7600 SD 92111 1249-A5
MARK LEE DR
17900 SDCo 91935 1274-C4
MARK STEVENS RD
13700 PWY 92064 1190-G3
MARKWOOD DR
9500 SNTE 92071 1231-B4
MARKY WY
9700 SDCo 91941 1271-C3
MARL AV
1500 CHV 91911 1330-G4
MARL CT
1400 CHV 91911 1330-G3
MARLBOROUGH AV
2900 SD 92105 1269-H6
4400 SD 92116 1269-G4
MARLBOROUGH DR
4700 SD 92116 1269-G3
MARLEN WY
5100 LMSA 91941 1271-A1
MARLENA WY
3100 SDCo 91978 1292-D1
3100 SDCo 91978 1272-C7
MARLESTA DR
3200 SD 92111 1248-J4
3900 SD 92111 1249-A3
MARLIN DR
900 VSTA 92084 1087-J6
900 VSTA 92084 1088-A6
MARLIN LN
- CRLB 92009 1127-A6
MARLIN RD
- SDCo 92055 1085-H6
MARLINDA WY
1800 SDCo 92021 1251-G1
MARLINE AV
1100 ELCJ 92021 1251-J4
1300 ELCJ 92021 1252-A4
MARLOWE DR
6600 SD 92115 1270-E5
MARLTON DR
3200 SD 92102 1289-F1
3200 SD 92104 1289-F1
MARLYNN CT
400 SDCo 92025 1130-B6
MARMAC DR
15600 SDCo 92065 1172-A4
MARMIL AV
3000 SD 92139 1310-D2
MARMIL PL
7300 SD 92114 1290-F3
MARMIL WY
5900 SD 92139 1310-D2
MARMOL CT
2600 CRLB 92009 1127-G6
MARNE AV
5600 SD 92120 1250-D7
5600 SD 92120 1270-C1
MAROON PEAK CT
11600 SD 92131 1190-A7
MARQUETTE PL
3800 SD 92106 1268-C5
MARQUETTE RD
2000 CHV 91913 1311-E5
MARQUETTE ST
1200 OCN 92054 1086-A6
2900 SD 92106 1268-C5
MARQUEZ CT
2300 SDCo 92084 1087-H1
MARQUIS CT
1900 CHV 91913 1311-E5
MARQUITA PL
2600 CRLB 92009 1147-G2
MARRACO DR
4300 SD 92115 1270-D4
MARRACO WY
4400 SD 92115 1270-D4
MARROKAL LN
8600 SNTE 92071 1230-J7
MARRON RD
1700 CRLB 92008 1106-F3
MARRON ST
100 OCN 92054 1106-A2
3800 SD 92115 1270-C5
MARRON VALLEY RD
500 SDCo 91917 429-J10
500 SDCo 91917 (1314-B7 See Page 1294)
MARS WY
4000 SDCo 91941 1271-G4
MARSAT CT
600 CHV 91911 1330-B4
MAR SCENIC DR
13600 SD 92014 1187-H7
MARSDEN CT
100 ELCJ 92020 1251-D5
MARSEILLES ST
4400 SD 92107 1287-H2
MARSHA CT
2600 SD 92105 1270-A7
MARSHALL AV
100 ELCJ 92020 1251-E5
N MARSHALL AV
400 ELCJ 92020 1251-D1
MARSHALL CT
2300 SDCo 91901 1234-B6
MARSHALL LN
3000 SDCo 91977 1271-A6
MARSHALL RD
1400 SDCo 91901 1234-B6
N MARSHALL RD
1300 SDCo 91901 1234-B6
MARSHALL ST
1400 OCN 92054 1106-C2
MARSHALL WY
2300 SDCo 91901 1234-B6
19400 SDCo 92082 1091-H3
MARSH HARBOR DR
400 SD 92154 1330-H6
MARSOLAN AV
600 SOLB 92075 1187-F1
MARSON ST
1700 OCN 92054 1086-B5
MARSOPA
3000 CRLB 92009 1127-J5
MARSOPA DR
700 VSTA 92083 1107-F1
MARTA PL
- VSTA 92084 1087-H6
MARTEE LN
9400 SNTE 92071 1231-C7
MARTELL ST
300 ELCJ 92019 1252-B5
MARTHA ST
3600 SD 92117 1248-D1
MARTIN AV
3000 SD 92113 1289-E5
MARTIN DR
900 ESCN 92026 1109-J7
900 ESCN 92026 1129-J1
MARTIN PL
1300 CHV 91911 1330-H2
MARTIN ST
5000 OCN 92057 1067-A6
MARTIN WY
- SDCo 91901 1255-J1
MARTINA CT
1000 SDCo 92069 1128-F3
MARTIN CANYON CT
4000 SDCo 91902 1311-A3
MARTINCOIT RD
16000 PWY 92064 1170-E3
MARTINDALE CT
3000 SD 92123 1249-E5
MARTINEZ ST
900 SD 92106 1288-A2
MARTINGALE CT
1500 CRLB 92009 1127-C4
MARTINGALE LN
500 SMCS 92069 1108-D5
MARTINIQUE DR
900 CHV 91913 1311-E5
MARTINIQUE WY
10900 SD 92126 1209-A3
MARTIN L KING JR FRWY Rt#-94
- LMGR - 1270-D7
- SD - 1270-D7
- SD - 1289-F3
- SD - 1290-A2
MARTINVIEW DR
2000 SD 92105 1289-H1
MARTOS PL
700 CHV 91910 1310-J5
MARVEJO
- SDCo 92040 1232-D6
MARVEL TER
1100 SDCo 92065 1153-B1
MARVIEW DR
400 SOLB 92075 1167-F6
MARVIEW LN
500 SOLB 92075 1167-F6
MARVIN ST
3800 OCN 92056 1087-B7
5400 SD 92105 1270-B6
MARVINGA LN
2700 SDCo 92028 997-A2
MAR VISTA DR
100 VSTA 92083 1108-A2
400 VSTA 92083 1107-H2
500 SOLB 92075 1167-F6
700 SDCo 92028 1027-G1
MARWOOD LN
100 OCN 92054 1106-C2
MARY AV
1000 ImCo 92249 6560-C7
MARY CT
800 NATC 91950 1290-C7
MARY LN
1000 SDCo 92025 1130-D5
1100 NATC 91950 1290-C7
2600 ESCN 92025 1130-D5
2600 SDCo 92025 1150-D1
3500 ESCN 92025 1150-C2
11300 SDCo 92040 1212-B7
11300 SDCo 92040 1232-B1
MARY LN S
3300 SDCo 92025 1150-C2
MARY ST
1000 ELCJ 92021 1251-H4
MARY ANN ST
1500 SDCo 91977 1291-B2
MARYANN WY
1900 SDCo 92019 1272-A1
MARY DEAN LN
- SDCo 92040 1231-J7
MARYEARL CT
13500 PWY 92064 1190-F1
MARYEARL LN
13400 PWY 92064 1190-E1
MARY FELLOWS AV
5200 LMSA 91942 1270-F1
MARYFORD DR
8600 SD 92119 1250-J3
MARYGOLD DR
2500 SDCo 91906 (1297-E5 See Page 1296)
MARY JOE LN
1600 SDCo 91905 (1320-A2 See Page 1300)
MARYLAND AV
5200 LMSA 91942 1270-F1
5500 LMSA 91942 1250-F7
MARYLAND CT
700 VSTA 92083 1087-F6
4500 SD 92116 1269-B4
MARYLAND DR
700 VSTA 92083 1087-F6
MARYLAND PL
1200 SD 92103 1269-B4
MARYLAND ST
4100 SD 92103 1269-B4
4400 SD 92116 1269-B4
MARY LANE CT
1100 SDCo 92025 1130-D7
MARY LANE DR
5400 SD 92115 1270-B2
MARY LANE PL
2600 SDCo 92025 1130-D7
MARY LEWIS DR
2900 SDCo 92028 1048-D3
MARY LOU ST
1400 SD 92102 1290-A2
MARYMAC PL
1800 SDCo 92028 1028-A6
MARYMONT PL
17600 SD 92128 1170-A1
MARYSVILLE AV
- CHV 91913 1331-B1
MARZO ST
3500 SD 92154 1350-E2
MASCARI CT
1100 SDCo 92021 1251-H3
MASCARI PL
3900 SDCo 91941 1271-C4
3900 SDCo 91977 1271-C4
MASON CIR
600 SDCo 92084 1067-J7
600 SDCo 92084 1087-J1
MASON DR
3700 LMGR 91945 1270-J5
MASON RD
100 SDCo 92084 1067-H7
100 SDCo 92084 1087-H1
900 SDCo 92084 1088-A1
MASON ST
3900 SD 92110 1268-F4
MASON WY
2700 SDCo 92084 1067-H7
MASON HEIGHTS LN
7400 SD 92126 1208-J2
MASONRY PL
1100 ESCN 92029 1129-F5
MASON VALLEY TKTR
- SDCo 92036 1176-G1
- SDCo 92036 (1177-H1 See Page 1176)
MASSACHUSETTS AV
400 VSTA 92084 1087-H6
1800 LMGR 91945 1290-F1
2200 LMGR 91945 1270-F7
3700 LMGR 91941 1270-F7
3700 LMSA 91941 1270-F7
MASSACHUSETTS ST
4500 SD 92116 1269-B4
MASSASOIT AV
2900 SD 92117 1248-C1
MASSENA ST
1300 SD 92037 1227-F7
MASSERY LN
8500 SNTE 92071 1231-B7
8500 SNTE 92071 1251-B1
MASSOT AV
9200 SNTE 92071 1230-J6
MAST BLVD
- SD 92124 1230-H6
- SDCo 92040 1231-G4
8200 SD 92145 1230-H5
8200 SD 92071 1230-H5
8200 SNTE 92071 1230-H5
8900 SNTE 92071 1231-E4
MASTERPIECE DR
1100 OCN 92057 1087-B2
MASTERS DR
700 OCN 92057 1087-B1
MASTERS PL
3000 SD 92123 1249-E5
MASTERS RD
- CRLB 92008 1107-B7
- CRLB 92008 1127-B1
MASTERSON LN
- SD 92154 1350-G2
MASTERS RIDGE RD
1000 CHV 91915 1311-G4
MATA WY
100 SMCS 92069 1109-A7
MATADOR CT
10200 SD 92124 1229-G7
10200 SD 92124 1249-G1
MATAGUAL DR
500 VSTA 92083 1087-G7
500 VSTA 92083 1107-G1
MATAMO PL
1000 SDCo 92019 1252-G6
MATAMOROS CT
100 SOLB 92075 1167-D7
MATANZA RD
12700 SD 92128 1170-C3
MATARO DR
4400 SD 92115 1270-D3
MATCH POINT DR
14200 PWY 92064 1190-G4
MATEO PL
2700 CRLB 92009 1147-G2
MATHER AV
500 SD 92154 1330-E6
MATHEW RD
15600 SDCo 92082 1091-A4
MATHEWS DR
2700 SD 92110 1268-E6
MATHIESON ST
10500 SD 92129 1189-G2
MATIN CIR
200 SMCS 92069 1109-E7
1800 SMCS 92069 1129-D1
MATINAL CIR
10500 SD 92127 1149-J7
10700 SD 92127 1169-J1
MATINAL DR
17400 SD 92127 1169-J1
MATINAL RD
17000 SD 92127 1169-H1
MATISSE LN
5200 SDCo 91902 1290-G6
MATLIN RD
25900 SDCo 92065 1174-A4
MATOR AV
9200 SD 92126 1209-D7
MATOR DR
9100 SD 92126 1209-D6
MATOR WY
9100 SD 92126 1209-D6
MATSON PL
7600 SD 92126 1208-J4
7600 SD 92126 1209-A4
MATSON WY
10500 SD 92126 1209-A4
MATT RD
- SDCo 92028 1029-A2
MATTE LN
- SDCo 92083 1108-B5
MATTERHORN DR
8500 SNTE 92071 1230-H7
8500 SNTE 92071 1250-H1
MATTHEW CT
500 SDCo 92065 1152-D6
900 VSTA 92083 1107-H2
MATTHEW LN
600 SMCS 92069 1109-D6
MATTHEW PL
2000 ESCN 92027 1110-C6
MATTHEWS AV
- SD 92126 1209-E7
MATTHEWS LN
- SD 92093 1228-A1
MATTOLE ST
- OCN 92057 1066-H7
- OCN 92057 1086-H1
MATTY CT
4700 SDCo 91941 1271-C3
MATURIN DR
15200 SD 92127 1169-J5
MAUDE RD
13800 SDCo 92082 1070-E5
MAUDEY BELL CT
2500 SDCo 92019 1272-E2
MAUKA DR
11700 SDCo 92082 1069-J5
MAUREEN CT
9500 SNTE 92071 1231-B5
MAURY CT
8600 SD 92119 1250-J4
MAURY DR
6600 SD 92119 1250-J4
MAVERICK CT
16600 PWY 92064 1170-E3
MAVERICK GN
1900 ESCN 92027 1110-A4
MAVERICK LN
16600 PWY 92064 1170-E3
MAVERICK PL
300 CHV 91902 1310-H4
MAVIN DR
9500 SNTE 92071 1231-E4
MAX AV
1300 CHV 91911 1330-F3
MAX DR
4500 SD 92115 1269-J4
MAXAM AV
8800 SD 92126 1209-F7
8800 SD 92126 1229-F1
MAXFIELD BLVD
- CORD 92135 1288-F4
MAXFIELD RD
13900 SDCo 91935 1292-H2
MAXIE PL
- ESCN 92027 1130-E1
MAXIM ST
300 SD 92102 1289-J4
MAXSON ST
1600 OCN 92054 1086-C7
MAXWELL AV
1000 ELCJ 92020 1251-G7
MAXWELL LN
1500 VSTA 92084 1088-B3
MAXWELL RD
1700 CHV 91911 1330-J5
1800 CHV 91911 1331-A5
MAY CT
200 ENCT 92007 1167-D2
3900 CRLB 92008 1106-H5
6900 SD 92139 1290-F7
MAYA CT
1800 VSTA 92083 1107-J3
MAYA ST
900 SDCo 91977 1291-C2
MAYA LINDA RD
9900 SD 92126 1209-E5
MAYAN CT
11200 SD 92127 1149-H7
MAYAPAN DR
4300 SDCo 91941 1271-G3
4700 SDCo 92020 1271-G2
MAYAPPLE CT
- SD 92131 1209-G2
MAYAPPLE WY
- SD 92131 1209-G2
MAYBERRY LN
- ELCJ 92021 1251-F4
1100 VSTA 92083 1087-G4
MAYBERRY ST
4300 SD 92113 1289-J6
MAYBRITT CIR
600 SMCS 92069 1108-J5
MAYCREST LN
6600 SD 92121 1208-G3
MAYE PL
1400 SDCo 92027 1130-D3
MAYFAIR CT
4400 CRLB 92008 1106-J5
MAYFAIR ST
100 OCN 92054 1086-F4
MAYFIELD CT
1500 CHV 91913 1311-C7
MAYFIELD DR
- OCN 92057 1086-J4
7600 SD 92111 1249-A6
MAYFLOWER AV
- ESCN 92027 1130-C1
MAYFLOWER WY
4300 SD 92117 1228-E7
4600 OCN 92057 1087-A1
MAYITA WY
4700 SD 92124 1250-A1
MAYNARD ST
4900 SD 92122 1228-G6
9100 SDCo 91977 1291-B3
MAYO RD
2800 SD 92133 1288-D1
2800 SD 92133 1268-C7
MAYO ST
4200 SD 92110 1268-E1
MAYOR CIR
10200 SD 92126 1209-B5
MAYS HOLLOW LN
700 ENCT 92024 1147-D6
MAYTEN CT
4700 OCN 92057 1067-A7
4700 OCN 92057 1087-A1
MAYWIND CT
11700 SD 92131 1210-A4
MAYWOOD CT
- CHV 91913 1331-D1
MAYWOOD LN
- OCN 92054 1106-C1
MAYWOOD ST
600 ESCN 92027 1110-C6
MAZAGON LN
800 CHV 91910 1310-H6
MAZATLAN CT
14100 PWY 92064 1190-E2
MAZATLAN WY
14000 PWY 92064 1190-E3
MAZE GN
600 ESCN 92025 1150-C4
MAZER ST
8000 LMGR 91945 1270-H7
MAZZETTI LN
- SDCo 92082 1071-E2
MAZZOLA
1000 SDCo 92021 1251-H3
MCBURNEY CT
2600 SD 92154 1330-C7

SAN DIEGO CO.
INDEX

6601 MCBURNEY RIDGE LN SAN DIEGO CO. STREET INDEX MIDWICK ST
SAN DIEGO CO.
INDEX

STREET Block City ZIP Pg-Grid
MCBURNEY RIDGE LN
- SD 92131 1209-G2
MCCABE RD
- ImCo 92243 6560-F4
100 ImCo 92243 6559-B5
100 ImCo 92249 6560-F4
MCCABE RD Rt#-S30
- ImCo 92243 6559-A5
1100 ImCo 92243 431-A6
MCCAIN BLVD
100 CORD 92135 1288-G5
MCCAIN LN
- SDCo 91905 1300-F7
MCCAIN RD
1900 SD 92133 1288-E1
2100 SD 92133 1268-E7
MCCAIN VALLEY RD
2100 SDCo 91934 1300-H6
2100 SDCo 91905 1300-H3
2300 SDCo 91905 430-C5
MCCALL ST
2800 SD 92106 1288-A4
MCCANDLESS BLVD
100 NATC 92136 1309-G1
3300 SD 92136 1289-F7
3700 SD 92136 1309-G1
MCCARDLE WY
9700 SNTE 92071 1231-B4
MCCAULEY LN
1800 CRLB 92008 1106-F4
MCCAWLEY DR
- SDCo 92055 1067-A1
MCCLELLAN AV
- SD 92104 1289-G2
MCCLELLAN RD
- SD 92106 1287-J5
- SD 92106 1288-A6
MCCLELLAND ST
1200 SMCS 92069 1109-C6
MCCLINTOCK ST
4300 SD 92105 1269-G4
4400 SD 92116 1269-G4
MCCLOUD RIVER RD
1900 CHV 91913 1311-E6
MCCLOY WY
3200 SD 92124 1249-G4
MCCLURE ST
700 ELCJ 92021 1251-H4
MCCLURKIN GN
- ESCN 92025 1130-C7
MCCONNELL RD
- ImCo 92227 431-C3
- ImCo 92251 431-C4
1700 SD 92133 1288-D2
2100 ImCo 92243 6500-G2
MCCONNELL RD Rt#-S27
- ImCo 92227 431-C3
- ImCo 92251 431-C3
MCCORMICK LN
- SDCo 92082 1071-E3
MCCULLOM ST
- ELCN 92243 6560-A1
300 ELCN 92243 6500-A6
MCCUNE RD
- SD 92106 1288-A7
MCDANIEL RD
1100 ImCo 92283 432-D5
MCDONALD LN
600 ESCN 92025 1129-J6
600 ESCN 92025 1130-A6
MCDONALD RD
200 ImCo 92233 411-B8
700 SDCo 92028 1027-H5
MCDONALD ST
2100 ELCN 92243 6499-G4
MCDONALD MEADOWS
- SDCo 92028 1027-H4
MCDONOUGH RD
2400 SD 92101 1288-C1
2400 SD 92133 1288-C1
MCDOUGAL PL
2400 SDCo 91901 1234-B4
MCDOUGAL TER
- ELCJ 92021 1252-C2
MCDOWELL CT
- SD 92131 1209-G2
MCENTEE ST
9700 SD 92129 1189-E2
MCFERON RD
12400 PWY 92064 1190-C4
MCGANN DR
5300 SD 92105 1290-A1
MCGAVRAN DR
700 VSTA 92083 1107-F1
MCGAVRAN TER
1200 VSTA 92083 1107-F1
MCGILL WY
4900 SD 92130 1188-D6
MCGONIGLE RD
1900 SD 92014 1207-G1
1900 SD 92121 1207-G1
MCGONIGLE TER
- SD 92129 1188-J3
MCGRAW ST
2900 SD 92117 1248-D5
MCGREGORY LN
1700 VSTA 92084 1088-B6
MCGUIRE DR
4000 SD 92130 1188-A5
MCHANEY CT
6100 SD 92114 1290-D6
MCHUGH ST
5600 SD 92114 1290-B3
MCINNEY RD
- SD 92106 1288-A5
MCINTIRE CIR
3500 OCN 92056 1106-J1
MCINTIRE DR
1900 SD 92101 1289-C2
MCINTIRE LN
2100 SDCo 92069 1109-A1
MCINTOSH ST
500 CHV 91910 1309-J5
500 CHV 91910 1310-A5
MCIVERS CT
12300 PWY 92064 1190-E6
MCKEAN ST
2200 SD 92136 1289-F7
MCKEE ST
1900 SD 92110 1268-H6
MCKELLAR CT
10100 SD 92121 1208-E5
MCKENZIE AV
13700 PWY 92064 1190-E3
MCKENZIE ST
- SDCo 92055 1023-F2
MCKIM RD
- ImCo 92251 431-C4
MCKINLEY AV
800 NATC 92136 1309-G2
1200 NATC 91950 1309-G2
1200 ESCN 92027 1130-B1
1300 ESCN 92027 1110-B7
MCKINLEY ST
100 OCN 92054 1067-B6
3000 SD 92104 1269-F7
3200 CRLB 92008 1106-F5
MCKINNEY CT
- SD 92131 1209-G1
MCKNIGHT DR
2200 LMGR 91945 1290-F1
2200 LMGR 91945 1270-F7
MCLAIN ST
500 ESCN 92027 1130-C2
MCLANAMAN ST
3100 SD 92136 1289-E7
MCLANE LN
1300 SDCo 92026 1109-E6
MCLARENS LN
3200 SD 92102 1289-F4
MCLEES CT
1900 SDCo 92026 1109-E6
MCMAHER LN
5800 SD 92120 1249-H7
MCMAHR RD
900 SMCS 92069 1128-E2
MCNALLY RD
11500 SDCo 92082 1049-H4
12100 SDCo 92082 1050-A4
MCNEIL ST
500 OCN 92054 1086-B6
MCNEILL AV
- ENCT 92024 1147-C7
MCNERNEY RD
- ImCo 92233 411-A9
MCRAE AV
5400 LMSA 91942 1270-F1
MCWAY CT
500 ELCJ 92021 1251-H4
MCWEST LN
12000 SDCo 92040 1232-A7
MEAD RD
100 ImCo 92227 431-C2
MEAD ST
5300 OCN 92056 1087-E1
MEADE AV
1000 SD 92116 1269-B4
1200 SD 92103 1269-B4
1900 SD 92104 1269-F4
3600 SD 92105 1269-F4
4300 SD 92115 1269-J4
4400 SD 92115 1270-A4
MEADOW DR
1400 NATC 91950 1310-B1
8300 SDCo 91977 1290-J6
MEADOW LN
200 SMCS 92069 1108-D5
2500 ESCN 92027 1130-E1
2600 ESCN 92027 1110-E7
3200 LMGR 91945 1270-J6
3600 OCN 92056 1107-A1
9800 SDCo 91916 1236-A1
MEADOW RD
1400 ELCJ 92021 1252-B2
MEADOW VW
- SDCo 92028 998-G5
MEADOWBROOK CT
800 CHV 91913 1311-E4
7600 SD 92114 1290-G3
MEADOWBROOK DR
200 SD 92114 1290-G3
4700 OCN 92056 1087-E4
MEADOWBROOK LN
12100 PWY 92064 1190-B3
MEADOWBROOK PL
2500 ESCN 92027 1130-E1
MEADOW CREEK LN
- ESCN 92027 1110-F6
12900 PWY 92064 1190-G5
MEADOW CREEK RD
11400 SDCo 92020 1271-H3
MEADOW CREST DR
100 ELCJ 92020 1251-A5
6200 LMSA 91942 1251-A5
MEADOW CREST PL
- ESCN 92027 1110-F6
MEADOWDALE LN
12800 SD 92131 1210-C4
MEADOW FLOWER PL
11300 SD 92127 1169-J5
MEADOWGATE ST
3700 SD 92111 1248-J4
MEADOWGLEN LN
1600 ENCT 92024 1147-G4
MEADOW GLEN WY
12900 PWY 92064 1190-D5
MEADOW GLEN WY E
9900 SDCo 92026 1089-G3
MEADOW GLEN WY W
28300 SDCo 92026 1089-C2
MEADOW GRASS CT
- SD 92128 1190-A6
MEADOW GRASS LN
- ESCN 92027 1110-F6
- SD 92128 1189-J6
- SD 92128 1190-A6
MEADOW GRASS PL
- ESCN 92027 1110-G6
MEADOWGREEN CT
2100 ENCT 92024 1147-J5
MEADOW GROVE DR
3000 SD 92110 1268-D5
MEADOW GROVE PL
500 ESCN 92027 1110-E7
MEADOWHAVEN CT
1800 ENCT 92024 1147-H4
MEADOW LAKE DR
900 VSTA 92084 1087-J5
900 VSTA 92084 1088-A5
MEADOW LAKE RD
- SDCo 92127 1169-F3
26500 SDCo 92070 409-J10
MEADOWLARK AV
100 CHV 91911 1330-F4
MEADOWLARK DR
- SDCo 92055 1023-E3
MEADOW LARK DR
2200 SD 92123 1249-B6
MEADOWLARK LN
2500 ESCN 92027 1110-E7
3200 CRLB 92008 1106-G4
MEADOWLARK WY
1100 SDCo 92065 1152-F3
MEADOWLARK RANCH CIR
2000 SDCo 92069 1128-A5
MEADOWLARK RANCH LN
2000 SDCo 92069 1128-A5
2000 CRLB 92009 1128-A5
2100 SDCo 92009 1128-A5
MEADOWLARK RANCH RD
1800 CRLB 92009 1128-A5
1800 SDCo 92069 1128-A5
1800 SMCS 92069 1128-A5
MEADOW MESA DR
9600 SDCo 92026 1089-D1
MEADOW MESA LN
28300 SDCo 92026 1089-D2
MEADOWMIST CT
500 ENCT 92024 1148-A7
MEADOWMIST LN
2500 ENCT 92024 1148-A7
MEADOW OAK LN
28200 SDCo 92026 1089-E3
MEADOW OAKS LN
15500 SDCo 92021 1213-C7
15500 SDCo 92021 1233-C1
MEADOWOOD CT
1700 SD 92173 1350-D2
MEADOWPOINTE RW
6000 SD 92037 1248-A1
MEADOWRIDGE LN
9800 SDCo 91977 1271-C7
MEADOWRIDGE PL
2300 SDCo 91977 1271-H7
MEADOWRIDGE RD
4700 SDCo 92070 1135-D4
MEADOWRUN CT
9000 SD 92129 1189-C2
MEADOWRUN DR
4500 OCN 92057 1066-H7
MEADOWRUN PL
9000 SD 92129 1189-C2
MEADOWRUN ST
14200 SD 92129 1189-D2
MEADOWRUN WY
9000 SD 92129 1189-C2
MEADOWS RD
- ImCo 92231 431-C7
1000 ImCo 92249 6560-H6
MEADOWS DEL MAR
- SD 92130 1188-D7
- SD 92130 1208-F1
MEADOWSIDE PL
- ESCN 92027 1110-F6
2300 SDCo 91977 1271-H7
MEADOW TERRACE DR
13400 SDCo 91935 1272-E7
11000 SNTE 92071 1231-G5
MEADOW VIEW DR
3400 OCN 92054 1086-D2
MEADOWVIEW DR
10200 SD 92131 1209-H4
MEADOW VIEW LN
- SDCo 91901 1274-G1
MEADOWVIEW LN
600 SMCS 92069 1109-A6
MEADOW VIEW RD
11300 SDCo 92020 1271-G3
MEADOW WOOD PL
1200 ENCT 92024 1147-G4
MEAJEAN PL
11800 SD 92129 1189-E7
MEALEY RD
- ImCo 92251 430-L4
MEANDRO CT
16700 SD 92128 1170-B3
MEANDRO DR
16700 SD 92128 1170-B3
MEANDRO RD
12300 SD 92128 1170-B3
MEANLEY DR
10000 SD 92131 1209-G4
MEANWHILE RANCH RD
1000 SDCo 91906 (1318-E6 See Page 1298)
MECCA DR
1600 SD 92037 1227-G7
MEDALLION LN
13200 SDCo 92040 1232-C6
MEDFORD AV
2100 ESCN 92027 1110-C6
MEDFORD CT
2600 CRLB 92008 1106-J4
MEDFORD PL
2200 ESCN 92027 1110-C6
MEDFORD ST
300 ELCJ 92021 1251-A4
1400 OCN 92057 1067-A3
MEDIATRICE LN
14200 SD 92129 1189-D2
MEDICAL CENTER CT
700 CHV 91911 1330-J2
MEDICAL CENTER DR
- SD 92037 1228-B2
900 CHV 91911 1330-H1
MEDILL AV
8100 SDCo 92021 1252-C1
8200 SDCo 92021 1232-C7
MEDINA DR
9400 SNTE 92071 1230-J5
MEDINA GN
2200 ESCN 92026 1109-D4
MEDINAH DR
2400 SDCo 92019 1272-B5
MEDINAH RD
1600 SMCS 92069 1108-J3
MEDIO ST
6300 SD 92114 1290-D4
MEDIO TER
900 SDCo 92028 1027-G1
MEDOC CT
10500 SD 92131 1210-B3
MEDOC LN
12000 SD 92131 1210-B3
MEGAN CT
2400 SD 92102 1290-A1
MEGAN LN
3800 ENCT 92024 1148-B2
MEGAN TER
9700 SDCo 92026 1069-C3
MEGAN WY
4900 SD 92102 1290-A1
4900 SD 92105 1289-J1
4900 SD 92105 1290-A1
MEGHAN CT
9000 SDCo 91977 1271-B6
MEKNES ST
15400 SD 92129 1169-J6
MEKNES WY
11400 SD 92129 1169-H6
MEL CT
1100 SD 92154 1350-D1
MELALEUCA AV
6800 CRLB 92009 1127-A5
MELALEUCA LN
2700 SDCo 92028 998-B6
MELANIE CT
10800 SNTE 92071 1231-F3
MELANIE WY
- DLMR 92014 1187-F5
MELBA RD
100 ENCT 92024 1147-F5
200 ENCT 92024 1167-C1
MELBOURNE DR
2400 SD 92123 1249-E5
MELIC CT
12900 SD 92129 1189-E5
MELINDA AV
800 SMCS 92069 1109-B6
MELINDA WY
200 OCN 92057 1086-H3
MELINDA DE ORO
- SDCo 91905 (1319-H7 See Page 1298)
MELISSA CT
2400 VSTA 92083 1108-B5
MELISSA LN
13500 PWY 92064 1190-F4
MELISSA WY
4400 SD 92117 1248-C2
MELISSA PARK TER
900 SDCo 92021 1252-J2
MELLMANOR DR
8500 LMSA 91942 1250-J7
8600 LMSA 91942 1251-A7
MELODIA TER
- CRLB 92009 1127-B7
MELODIE LN
14100 PWY 92064 1190-G3
MELODY LN
- OCN 92054 1086-C5
1300 ELCJ 92019 1251-J5
1300 ELCJ 92019 1252-A5
1400 SDCo 92019 1252-A5
7000 LMSA 91942 1270-F1
35000 SDCo 92036 1156-E7
MELODY RD
13800 SDCo 91935 1292-G3
MELOJO LN
10200 SD 92124 1249-G1
MELOLAND RD
1900 ImCo 92243 431-D5
1900 ImCo 92250 431-D5
MELORA CT
13400 SDCo 91935 1272-E7
MELOTTE ST
7300 SD 92119 1250-E3
MELROSE AV
100 ENCT 92024 1147-B6
200 CHV 91911 1310-E7
200 CHV 91911 1330-F1
600 CHV 91910 1310-E7
MELROSE CIR
1600 CHV 91911 1330-G5
MELROSE CT
1600 CHV 91911 1330-G5
MELROSE DR
- CRLB 92008 1127-H2
- CRLB 92009 1127-H2
100 VSTA 92083 1087-F3
300 VSTA 92083 1107-G1
500 OCN 92057 1067-D6
1200 OCN 92056 1107-G1
1500 OCN 92056 1087-F3
1500 SDCo 92083 1107-G1
6600 CRLB 92009 1128-A5
N MELROSE DR
100 VSTA 92083 1087-F4
S MELROSE DR
1700 VSTA 92083 1107-H7
1800 VSTA 92083 1127-H1
MELROSE LN
8100 SDCo 92021 1252-A1
8200 SDCo 92021 1232-B7
8400 SDCo 92040 1232-B7
MELROSE PL
600 VSTA 92083 1087-F5
700 SD 92114 1290-B3
12500 SDCo 92021 1232-B7
MELROSE ST
800 NATC 91950 1289-H7
2200 NATC 91950 1290-A6
MELROSE WY
300 CHV 91911 1330-G5
1000 VSTA 92083 1107-E2
1500 SDCo 92083 1107-E2
MELRU LN
2400 SDCo 92026 1109-J2
MELTON CT
11100 SD 92131 1209-H1
MELVA RD
10700 SDCo 91941 1271-F2
MELVIN LN
1500 SDCo 92021 1252-A2
MELWIER WY
12900 SDCo 92040 1232-C4
MEMIKE PL
8900 SD 92119 1251-A3
MEMORIAL DR
4800 LMSA 91941 1270-J2
MEMORIAL WY
400 CHV 91910 1310-A6
MEMORY LN
1000 ESCN 92026 1109-F5
1200 VSTA 92084 1088-A4
9000 SDCo 91977 1271-B5
MENARD ST
3200 NATC 91950 1310-D3
MENDE CT
2200 SD 92103 1268-G5
MENDECK AV
9900 SNTE 92071 1231-B3
MENDEL RIVERS RD
- SDCo 92055 1067-A1
MENDENARO CT
3200 SDCo 92028 1048-C5
MENDIOLA PT
11800 SD 92129 1189-E7
MENDIP ST
5300 OCN 92057 1067-A3
MENDOCINO BLVD
1900 SD 92107 1268-A7
MENDOCINO CT
800 SMCS 92078 1128-G2
MENDOCINO DR
900 SMCS 92078 1128-G3
1500 CHV 91911 1330-H4
MENDOTA ST
1700 CHV 91913 1311-D6
1800 SD 92106 1268-B7
1800 SD 92106 1288-B1
MENDOZA
- SDCo 92082 1071-E2
MENENDEZ CT
1900 SD 92154 1350-D3
MENGIBAR AV
12700 SD 92129 1189-F6
MENKAR PL
11400 SD 92126 1209-B1
MENKAR RD
8300 SD 92126 1209-C1
MENLO AV
2700 SD 92105 1269-J5
4100 SD 92115 1269-J4
MENNONITE PT
13900 SD 92129 1189-D2
MENORCA DR
5600 SD 92124 1229-H7
MENORCA WY
10500 SD 92124 1229-H7
MENSHA PL
4400 SD 92130 1188-B5
MENTA CTE
1100 CHV 91910 1311-C2
MENTONE ST
4200 SD 92107 1268-B5
MERCADO DR
13600 SD 92014 1187-H6
MERCADO GN
1400 ESCN 92026 1109-E4
MERCANTILE ST
500 VSTA 92083 1087-H7
MERCED DR
3600 OCN 92056 1107-E4
MERCED PL
2600 SDCo 91935 1293-C4
MERCEDES RD
100 SDCo 92028 1027-H2
MERCED LAKE AV
6200 SD 92119 1250-H6
MERCER CT
3500 SD 92122 1228-D5
MERCER LN
3000 SD 92122 1228-C5
MERCER ST
6100 SD 92122 1228-D5
MERCURIO ST
4500 SD 92130 1188-C6
MERCURY CT
8100 SD 92111 1229-B7
MERCURY DR
2500 LMGR 91945 1270-F7
MERCURY PT
5100 SD 92111 1229-B7
MERCURY ST
4400 SD 92111 1249-B2
5000 SD 92111 1229-B7
MERCY RD
9300 SD 92129 1189-F6
MEREDITH AV
5600 SD 92120 1250-D7
5600 SD 92120 1270-D1
MERGANSER LN
7400 CRLB 92009 1127-B7
MERGHO IMPASSE
2100 SD 92110 1268-G6
MERIDA CT
2100 SD 92037 1247-H1
MERIDA DR
300 SDCo 92028 1027-F5
MERIDEN LN
11800 SD 92128 1190-A2
MERIDIAN AV
3400 SD 92115 1270-D6
MERIDIAN LN
1100 CHV 91911 1330-H1
MERIDIAN WY
- CRLB 92009 1126-J7
- CRLB 92009 1127-B5
MERIDIAN RIDGE TR
- SDCo 92066 (1299-C2 See Page 1298)
MERILL DR
8200 SDCo 92040 1252-A1
8300 SDCo 92040 1232-A7
MERILL PL
12000 SDCo 92040 1252-A1
MERIVALE AV
3800 SD 92116 1269-G3
MERL RD Rt#-78
- ImCo 92281 431-A1
- WEST 92281 431-A1
MERLIN CT
900 SMCS 92069 1109-C5
MERLIN DR
- CRLB 92009 1127-A4
400 SD 92114 1290-C3
MERLIN PL
2700 OCN 92054 1086-E6
MERLO CT
900 CRLB 92009 1127-A7
MERLOT CT
1500 VSTA 92083 1087-D6
MERLOT PL
500 CHV 91913 1311-E3
17200 PWY 92064 1170-E2
MERLYN CT
1700 SDCo 92019 1272-B4
MERLYN PL
2100 SDCo 92019 1272-B4
MERMAID LN
7400 CRLB 92009 1127-A7
MERRIAM RD
1700 SDCo 92069 1128-B2
MERRICK CT
4600 OCN 92056 1107-E3
MERRIMAC AV
3400 SD 92117 1228-D7
3700 SD 92117 1248-E1
MERRIMAC CT
5000 SD 92117 1228-D7
MERRING RD Rt#-S24
800 ImCo 92283 432-E4
MERRINGTON PL
7900 SD 92126 1209-B3
MERRITT BLVD
4100 LMSA 91977 1271-A4
4100 SDCo 91977 1271-A4
4100 LMSA 91941 1271-A3
MERRITT CT
1000 SDCo 92020 1251-H7
MERRITT DR
800 ELCJ 92020 1251-H7
900 ELCJ 92019 1251-H7
1400 SDCo 92020 1271-J1
MERRITT LN
1000 SDCo 92020 1251-J7
1000 SDCo 92020 1271-J1
MERRITT TER
1300 SDCo 92020 1251-J7
1300 SDCo 92020 1252-A7
MERRITT PARK LN
14600 PWY 92064 1190-E1
MERRIWEATHER WY
1400 ELCJ 92019 1252-A7
MERRY LN
1600 ESCN 92029 1129-G5
MERRYFIELD RW
3100 SD 92121 1207-J5
3100 SD 92121 1208-A6
MERRYMOUNT CT
5700 OCN 92057 1067-F7
MERRYWOOD LN
300 SDCo 92025 1130-B7
MERTENSIA ST
5100 OCN 92056 1107-F4
MERTON AV
2700 SD 92111 1248-J6
2700 SD 92111 1249-A6
MERTON CT
7100 SD 92111 1248-J6
MERWELL ST
6600 SD 92122 1228-D5
MERWIN DR
- CRLB 92008 1107-B7
C MESA
- SD 92037 1228-C2
N MESA
- SD 92037 1228-C2
MESA AV
- NATC 91950 1290-A6
200 SD 92173 1350-G3
9800 SNTE 92071 1231-D5
MESA CT
900 CHV 91910 1310-H7
MESA DR
2200 OCN 92054 1086-F5
3100 OCN 92056 1086-F5
3100 OCN 92057 1086-H5
4000 OCN 92057 1087-B3
4000 OCN 92056 1087-B3
MESA DR N
16300 SDCo 92061 1051-C3
MESA DR S
17600 SDCo 92061 1051-D4
MESA PL
800 CHV 91910 1310-H7
MESA RD
8100 SNTE 92071 1250-J1
8200 SNTE 92071 1230-J7
MESA TER
5000 SDCo 91941 1271-B1
8400 SNTE 92071 1250-J1
W MESA TKTR
- SDCo 91916 1216-A1
MESA WY
300 SD 92037 1247-E2
MESA BREEZE WY
500 OCN 92054 1086-B6
MESA BROOK ST
800 SD 92114 1290-F6
MESA COLLEGE DR
3200 SD 92111 1249-A4
7300 SD 92111 1248-J4
7700 SD 92123 1249-A5
MESA CREST RD
- SDCo 92082 1070-B4
12300 PWY 92064 1190-B5
MESA ESTATES CT
15200 SDCo 92065 1173-H6
MESA ESTATES RD
25000 SDCo 92065 1173-H5
E MESA FIRE RD
- SDCo 91916 1216-F4
MESA GRANDE PL
1300 CHV 91910 1311-B7
MESA GRANDE RD
1700 ESCN 92029 1129-F6
24000 SDCo 92070 409-H9
MESA HEIGHTS RD
8400 SNTE 92071 1250-J1
MESA HILLS CT
1900 SD 92114 1290-F6
MESA LILAC RD
32500 SDCo 92026 1049-A5
MESA MADERA CT
11500 SD 92131 1209-J4
MESA MADERA DR
9900 SD 92131 1209-J4
MESAMINT ST
16900 SDCo 92127 1169-G3
MESA OAK CT
2700 SDCo 92065 1172-D4
MESA OAK PL
- ESCN 92027 1130-H2
MESA PARK LN
1900 SD 92114 1290-F6
MESA RIDGE CT
10000 SD 92121 1208-H5
MESA RIDGE RD
6600 SD 92121 1208-H5
8400 SNTE 92071 1250-J1
MESA RIM RD
9900 SD 92121 1208-H5
MESA ROCK RD
1200 SDCo 92026 1089-C7
25900 SDCo 92026 1109-D1
MESA SPRINGS WY
9700 SD 92126 1209-F5
MESA TOP PL
11000 SD 92121 1208-G3
MESA VERDE DR
1500 VSTA 92084 1088-B5
11500 SDCo 92082 1069-H2
12000 SDCo 92082 1070-A2
MESA VERDE RD
3200 SDCo 91902 1310-E4
MESA VIEW RD
8400 SNTE 92071 1250-J1
MESA VIEW WY
8300 SDCo 91977 1290-J5
MESA VISTA AV
9200 LMSA 91941 1271-B1
9200 SDCo 91941 1271-B1
MESA VISTA LN
3300 SDCo 91902 1310-E4
MESA VISTA WY
3600 SDCo 91902 1310-E4
4200 OCN 92057 1086-J3
MESA WOODS AV
9000 SD 92126 1209-D3
MESCALITA CT
200 OCN 92054 1086-G1
MESETA LN
12800 SDCo 92040 1232-B5
MESITA DR
6000 SD 92115 1270-C2
MESQUITE LN
4600 SDCo 92004 (1099-G5 See Page 1098)
MESQUITE RD
5000 SD 92115 1270-A2
MESQUITE TREE TR
15400 PWY 92064 1170-G6
MESSIAH DR
300 ELCN 92243 6499-H4
MESSINA DR
4000 SD 92113 1289-H4
MESSINA WY
100 SD 92113 1289-H4
MESTO CT
16200 SD 92128 1170-B4
MESTO DR
16100 SD 92128 1170-B4
METATE LN
12400 PWY 92064 1190-E5
METCALF GN
1000 ESCN 92026 1129-F1
1000 SDCo 92026 1129-F1
METCALF PL
1000 ESCN 92026 1129-F2
METCALF ST
600 ESCN 92025 1129-F2
900 ESCN 92026 1129-F1
1000 SDCo 92026 1129-F1
METRO ST
5300 SD 92110 1268-F3
METROPOLITAN DR
7500 SD 92108 1269-A1
MEWALL DR
6700 SD 92119 1251-A3
MEXICALI CT
100 SOLB 92075 1167-D7
MEXICAN CANYON RD
14100 SDCo 91935 1272-H7
MEYERS AV
2100 ESCN 92029 1129-C2
MEYERS RD
- SD 92106 1288-A6
MEYNCKE WY
7900 SD 92126 1209-A1
MEZIN WY
6700 SD 92114 1290-E4
MIAMI CT
4300 SD 92117 1248-E2
MIAMI WY
4500 SD 92117 1248-E2
MICAELA CT
- SDCo 92040 1232-E5
MICHAEL CT
2100 SDCo 91901 1253-G1
MICHAEL GN
1700 ESCN 92026 1109-D4
MICHAEL ST
600 OCN 92057 1067-A5
5500 SD 92105 1270-B6
5900 SD 92115 1270-C6
MICHAEL FARADAY DR
2100 SD 92154 1352-B3
MICHAEL JOHN DR
6600 SD 92037 1247-F1
MICHAELMAS TER
2100 SD 92110 1268-E6
MICHALA PL
10200 SNTE 92071 1231-D2
MICHELE DR
300 VSTA 92084 1087-H3
MICHELLE CT
2600 NATC 91950 1310-A3
9400 SDCo 91977 1271-B6
MICHELLE DR
7800 LMSA 91942 1250-G6
MICHIGAN AV
100 VSTA 92084 1087-H6
300 OCN 92054 1106-A1
900 OCN 92054 1086-B7
MICRO PL
2200 ESCN 92029 1129-C2
MIDBLUFF AV
13100 SD 92128 1189-H4
MIDBURY CT
9200 SD 92126 1209-D2
MIDDLE ST
900 ELCJ 92020 1251-C7
MIDDLEBROOK SQ
12100 SD 92128 1190-B1
MIDDLEBUSH DR
200 SD 92114 1290-H4
MIDDLE PEAK LOOP FIRE RD
- SDCo 92036 1176-C6
MIDDLE RIDGE TER
11300 SD 92128 1189-J4
MIDDLESEX DR
4100 SD 92116 1269-H2
MIDDLETON DR
4500 CRLB 92008 1107-A4
MIDDLETON RD
5100 SD 92109 1248-A3
MIDDLETON WY
2200 SD 92109 1248-A3
MIDGROVE CT
13800 PWY 92064 1190-F3
MIDLAND RD
13300 PWY 92064 1190-F2
15200 PWY 92064 1170-F6
MIDLAND ST
8400 LMSA 91942 1250-J7
MIDORI CT
- SOLB 92075 1167-E6
MIDORI LN
700 SOLB 92075 1167-E6
MIDRANCH LN
12300 SDCo 92040 1212-A7
MIDVALE DR
1700 SD 92105 1289-G1
MIDWAY AV
- SD 92101 1268-F7
- SD 92140 1268-F7
MIDWAY CT
1300 SDCo 91901 1233-J6
MIDWAY DR
800 SDCo 91901 1233-H5
1100 ELCJ 92020 1251-D7
2300 SD 92110 1268-D5
N MIDWAY DR
100 ESCN 92027 1130-C1
200 ESCN 92027 1110-B6
S MIDWAY DR
100 ESCN 92027 1130-C1
MIDWAY LN
800 SDCo 91901 1233-G5
MIDWAY PL
1300 SDCo 91901 1233-H6
MIDWAY ST
300 SD 92037 1247-F4
MIDWICK ST
5700 SD 92139 1310-C1

STREET
Block City ZIP Pg-Grid

MIGUEL AV
1600 CORD 92118 1288-J7
1700 CORD 92118 1289-A7
MIGUEL LN
14500 SDCo 92021 1232-H4
MIGUEL RD
- ImCo 92283 432-D5
MIGUEL GARDEN WY
13300 PWY 92064 1190-H4
MIGUEL VIEW RD
4200 SDCo 91941 1271-G4
MIGUEL VISTA PL
8400 SD 92114 1290-J4
MIJO LN
13500 SDCo 92040 1232-D5
MIKE CT
1100 SD 92154 1350-E1
MILAGROS ST
3400 SD 92123 1249-C4
MILAGROSA CIR
400 CHV 91910 1310-H4
MILAGROSA CT
800 CHV 91910 1310-G5
MILAGROSA PL
800 CHV 91910 1310-H5
MILAGROSA WY
500 CHV 91910 1310-H5
MILAN GN
1400 ESCN 92026 1110-A5
1400 ESCN 92027 1110-A5
MILAN ST
1200 OCN 92056 1087-C3
3700 SD 92107 1288-B1
3800 SD 92107 1268-A7
N MILANE LN
800 ESCN 92026 1110-A7
800 ESCN 92026 1130-A1
MILANO DR
4200 CRLB 92008 1106-J6
MILANO WY
4200 OCN 92057 1087-A3
MIL ARBOLES
14400 SDCo 92067 1188-G2
MILBANK RD
1700 ENCT 92024 1147-A2
MILBRAE ST
300 SD 92113 1289-G5
MILBURN AV
8800 SDCo 91977 1290-J4
8800 SDCo 91977 1291-A4
MILBURY RD
8500 SD 92129 1189-C2
MILCH RD
9400 SD 92121 1228-J2
MILDEN ST
9500 LMSA 91942 1251-C7
MILDRED AV
100 SDCo 91905 1300-C6
MILDRED ST
5400 SD 92110 1268-F3
MILDRED WY
100 SDCo 92019 1253-C1
8200 LMGR 91945 1270-H7
MILE HIGH RD
- SDCo 92036 1156-F7
MILE-OF-CARS WY
- NATC 91950 1309-H3
MILES CT
3700 SDCo 91977 1271-C5
MILES RANCH RD
100 SDCo 92028 1047-G7
200 SDCo 92028 1067-G1
MILETUS WY
4700 OCN 92056 1107-E5
MILFORD PL
1900 ELCJ 92020 1251-C4
3600 CRLB 92008 1107-A3
MILISSI WY
5000 OCN 92056 1107-E4
MILK RANCH RD
- SDCo 92036 1176-D7
- SDCo 92036 (1196-D1
See Page 1176)
MILKY WAY PT
7500 SD 92120 1250-C4
MILLAGRA DR
1400 SDCo 92028 1028-F5
MILLAN CT
- CHV 91910 1330-D1
E MILLAN CT
300 CHV 91910 1310-F7
MILLAN ST
100 CHV 91910 1330-C1
E MILLAN ST
100 CHV 91910 1310-E7
MILLAR AV
100 ELCJ 92020 1251-E5
MILLAR ANITA LN
2900 SDCo 91978 1292-A2
MILLARDS RD
13700 PWY 92064 1190-J2
MILLARDS RANCH LN
13500 PWY 92064 1190-H3
MILLARDS RANCH WY
13600 PWY 92064 1190-J2
MILLAR RANCH RD
2100 SDCo 91978 1292-A1
3100 SDCo 91978 1271-J7
3100 SDCo 91978 1272-A7
MILLAY CT
- CRLB 92008 1107-A7
MILLBRAE CT
1500 CHV 91913 1311-C7
MILLBROOK PL
800 ESCN 92026 1109-J7
MILLBROOK ST
6800 SD 92120 1249-J5
MILLCO LN
14000 SDCo 92082 1070-E6
MILLCO WY
29500 SDCo 92082 1070-F6
MILL CREEK RD
- SDCo 92061 1050-H3
MILLCROFT CT
13100 SD 92130 1187-J5
MILLEGAR LN
2400 SDCo 92084 1108-D3
MILLENNIUM CT
1000 SDCo 92065 1152-J6
MILLER AV
1000 ESCN 92025 1129-J7
2300 SDCo 92029 1129-J7
2300 SDCo 92029 1149-J1
MILLER AV Rt#-S26
- ImCo 92281 431-A1
- WEST 92281 431-A1
MILLER DR
800 CHV 91914 1311-F4

MILLER LN
29800 SDCo 92082 1070-F5
MILLER RD
28600 SDCo 92082 1090-E1
28900 SDCo 92082 1070-F5
MILLER RD Rt#-S33
1000 ImCo 92250 431-F6
MILLER ST
4000 SD 92103 1268-G5
MILLER WY
13600 SDCo 92082 1070-E5
MILLER VALLEY RD
2900 SDCo 92066 (1299-A1
See Page 1298)
MILLIKIN AV
3200 SD 92122 1228-D5
MILL PEAK RD
5500 SD 92120 1270-C1
5500 SD 92120 1250-C7
MILLPOND WY
13500 SD 92129 1189-G3
MILLS CT
1400 SMCS 92069 1109-D7
MILLS RD
700 SDCo 92028 1047-E5
MILLS ST
600 ESCN 92027 1110-A7
600 ESCN 92027 1130-B1
1600 CHV 91913 1311-C5
3600 SD 92106 1287-J4
4900 LMSA 91941 1270-H2
MILL VALLEY CT
4100 SDCo 91941 1271-H4
MILLWOOD RD
- SDCo 92036 1175-J2
- SDCo 92036 1176-A2
4900 SD 92117 1228-F7
MILOS WY
5000 OCN 92056 1107-F5
MILPAS DR
2700 SDCo 92029 1129-C3
MILPITAS WASH RD
- ImCo - 411-K4
- ImCo - 412-A6
MIL PITRERO RD
11900 SD 92128 1190-A7
MIL SORPRESAS DR
1900 SDCo 92028 998-A7
MILTON CT
2200 SD 92110 1268-F1
MILTON RD
- CRLB 92008 1127-B1
3700 LMGR 91945 1270-J5
MILTON ST
2200 SD 92110 1268-F1
MILTON MANOR DR
1700 SDCo 92021 1252-A2
MIMIKA PL
2700 SD 92111 1248-J6
MIMOSA
16900 SDCo 92067 1168-C3
MIMOSA AV
100 SDCo 92083 1108-B5
MIMOSA CT
1300 ESCN 92027 1110-B5
4800 OCN 92057 1067-A7
MIMOSA DR
6800 CRLB 92009 1127-E5
MIMOSA CREEK LN
- SDCo 92065 1152-G7
MIMULUS
5700 SDCo 92067 1168-D2
MIMULUS WY
1600 SD 92037 1227-G7
MINA ST
3400 SD 92105 1270-A6
MINA DE ORO RD
14800 PWY 92064 1191-B1
14900 PWY 92064 1171-C7
MINDANAO WY
2300 SD 92154 1330-C7
MINDEN DR
1300 SD 92111 1269-A2
MINEO AV
200 ELCN 92243 6560-A1
MINER CT
9400 SDCo 91977 1271-C7
MINERAL DR
6700 SD 92119 1250-H4
MINERS CT
- SDCo 92036 1136-D7
MINERS PL
- SDCo 92040 1232-F5
MINERS TR
- SDCo 91916 1235-G2
MINERVA DR
7300 SD 92114 1290-F3
MINESHAFT DR
- SDCo 92040 1212-A7
- SDCo 92040 1232-C2
MING CT
11400 SDCo 92021 1251-H1
MINNEOLA CIR
11500 SDCo 92082 1069-H5
MINNESOTA AV
100 ELCJ 92020 1251-F7
200 OCN 92054 1106-A1
MINNESOTA ST
400 SDCo 92028 1027-G2
MINNEWAWA TKTR
- SDCo 91935 (1313-B6
See Page 1293)
- SDCo 91917 (1333-C2
See Page 1332)
- SDCo 91935 (1333-C2
See Page 1332)
MINOA WY
3000 SD 92139 1310-E2
MINOR DR
800 SDCo 92025 1130-C4
MINORCA CV
14200 SD 92014 1187-H5
MINORCA WY
2600 SD 92014 1187-H5
MINOT AV
- CHV 91910 1310-C5
MINT AV
1500 ELCJ 92019 1252-A4
MINT PL
3500 OCN 92054 1086-F4
MINT CANYON PTH
1400 SD 92037 1227-G7
1400 SD 92037 1247-G1
MINUTEMAN ST
3000 SD 92124 1249-G5
MINYA LN
14300 PWY 92064 1190-H5
MIO METATE LN
9800 SDCo 91916 1235-G1

MIRA PZ
- VSTA 92083 1107-C2
MIRABEL LN
10200 SD 92124 1249-G1
MIRACIELO CT
1300 SDCo 92069 1128-E3
MIRACLE DR
4700 SD 92115 1269-J3
MIRACLE WATERS CT
10400 SDCo 91977 1291-D1
MIRACOSTA CIR
1600 CHV 91913 1311-D6
MIRA COSTA ST
4000 OCN 92056 1107-B2
MIRA COSTA COLLEGE RD
2300 ENCT 92007 1167-G4
MIRACREST PL
8400 SD 92121 1228-J1
MIRADOR
2300 SDCo 92084 1088-C1
MIRA ESTE CT
9200 SD 92126 1209-B7
MIRA FLORES CT
1300 OCN 92056 1107-D3
MIRA FLORES DR
5500 SD 92114 1290-B5
MIRAFLORES GN
3600 ESCN 92026 1109-E5
MIRAGE CT
1600 SDCo 92019 1272-B4
MIRAGE LN
4200 OCN 92056 1107-D3
MIRAGE PL
2100 SDCo 92019 1272-B4
MIRA LAGO TER
10600 SD 92131 1209-J3
10600 SD 92131 1210-A3
MIRA LAGO WY
11700 SD 92131 1209-J3
MIRALANI DR
8100 SD 92126 1209-C6
MIRA LOMA CT
13300 PWY 92064 1150-E7
MIRA LOMA LN
300 ESCN 92025 1130-B4
MIRAMAR AV
7500 SD 92037 1227-F7
MIRAMAR CT
9400 SD 92126 1229-F1
MIRAMAR DR
800 SDCo 92083 1107-H2
2000 VSTA 92083 1107-J3
MIRAMAR MALL
8200 SD 92121 1228-G1
MIRA MAR PL
900 OCN 92054 1085-J7
MIRAMAR PL
8300 SD 92121 1228-G1
MIRAMAR RD
5000 SD 92121 1228-F2
5000 SD 92122 1228-F2
5000 SD 92145 1228-F2
7000 SD 92121 1229-A1
7000 SD 92126 1229-A1
7100 SD 92126 1209-D6
9900 SDCo 92126 1209-D6
9900 SD 92145 1209-D6
9900 SD 92131 1209-D6
10100 SD 92145 1229-A1
MIRAMAR ST
- SD 92037 1228-B2
MIRAMAR WY
7200 SD 92126 1229-B1
9400 SD 92145 1229-E1
MIRAMAR GUN CLUB RD
9300 SD 92145 1229-E4
MIRA MESA AV
3100 OCN 92056 1107-B1
MIRA MESA BLVD
5300 SD 92121 1208-G5
7000 SD 92126 1208-G5
7600 SD 92126 1209-E3
9800 SD 92131 1209-E3
MIRA MONTANA DR
13500 SD 92014 1187-H6
MIRA MONTANA PL
2600 SD 92014 1187-H7
MIRA MONTE
300 SD 92037 1247-F3
MIRA MONTE DR
- CRLB 92008 1107-C3
3500 OCN 92056 1107-C2
MIRA MONTE GN
1100 ESCN 92026 1109-E5
MIRA MONTE PZ
6000 SD 92037 1247-F3
MIRA MONTE RD
4100 SDCo 92028 997-G3
MIRAMONTE ST
4600 LMSA 91941 1270-J3
4600 LMSA 91941 1271-A3
MIRAMONTES RD
3000 SDCo 91935 1293-A1
MIRANDO ST
14400 PWY 92064 1190-H4
MIRA PACIFIC DR
3500 OCN 92056 1106-J2
3500 OCN 92056 1107-A1
MIRAR CT
5400 SDCo 91902 1311-A2
MIRAR DE VALLE RD
12200 SDCo 92082 1090-A4
MIRA SOL
2200 SDCo 92084 1108-D3
MIRASOL CT
12200 SD 92128 1150-B7
MIRASOL DR
17800 SD 92128 1150-B7
MIRASOL PL
12200 SD 92128 1150-B7
MIRASOL WY
12100 SD 92128 1150-B7
MIRA SORRENTO PL
5300 SD 92121 1208-D6
MIRA VERDE ST
4000 OCN 92056 1107-B3
MIRA VISTA LN
6400 SD 92120 1250-E6
MIRA ZANJA
7100 SD 92130 1188-H2
MIRA ZANJA CTE
14100 SD 92130 1188-H2
MIRIAM PL
4300 SDCo 91941 1271-D3
MIRROR LAKE PL
2000 CHV 91913 1311-E5
MISS ELLE WY
1400 SDCo 91901 1234-C6

MISS ELLIE LN
15700 SDCo 92040 1232-G1
MISSION AV
- OCN 92054 1106-A1
300 OCN 92054 1086-C6
700 CHV 91910 1310-F7
900 CHV 91911 1330-F1
4300 SD 92116 1269-C4
MISSION AV Rt#-76
3400 OCN 92054 1086-H2
3700 OCN 92057 1086-H2
4500 OCN 92057 1087-A1
4900 OCN 92057 1067-F6
5300 OCN 92056 1067-D7
5600 SDCo 92084 1067-H5
5600 SDCo 92003 1067-H6
E MISSION AV
100 ESCN 92025 1129-J1
800 ESCN 92026 1129-J1
800 ESCN 92026 1130-A1
800 ESCN 92025 1130-A1
1100 ESCN 92027 1130-A1
1200 ESCN 92027 1110-A7
W MISSION AV Rt#-S14
300 ESCN 92025 1129-G2
1200 ESCN 92029 1129-G2
MISSION BLVD
2600 SD 92109 1267-J3
3800 SD 92109 1247-H5
MISSION CT
- SDCo 91905 (1299-H3
See Page 1298)
600 CHV 91910 1310-E7
1000 CHV 91911 1330-F1
MISSION RD
- SDCo 92028 998-F7
- SDCo 92028 1028-F1
MISSION RD Rt#-76
5900 SDCo 92003 1067-H3
5900 SDCo 92084 1067-H3
31200 SDCo 92003 1068-A1
31800 SDCo 92003 1048-A7
E MISSION RD
2100 ESCN 92029 1149-J4
2100 ESCN 92029 1150-A3
2100 SD 92029 1149-J4
2100 SD 92029 1150-A4
2100 SDCo 92029 1149-J4
2100 SDCo 92029 1150-A4
3800 SDCo 92028 1028-E1
E MISSION RD Rt#-S13
200 SDCo 92028 1027-H1
2000 SDCo 92028 1028-A1
2500 SDCo 92028 998-B7
E MISSION RD Rt#-S14
100 SMCS 92069 1108-J7
500 SMCS 92069 1109-B7
1000 SMCS 92069 1129-C1
1400 SMCS 92078 1129-C1
N MISSION RD
100 SDCo 92028 1027-F2
S MISSION RD
100 SDCo 92028 1027-F3
S MISSION RD Rt#-S13
1100 SDCo 92028 1027-G6
2600 SDCo 92028 1047-H1
4900 SDCo 92028 1048-A7
5000 SDCo 92003 1048-A7
W MISSION RD
100 SDCo 92028 1027-F2
W MISSION RD Rt#-S14
1000 SMCS 92069 1108-F7
1300 ESCN 92029 1129-E2
2000 SMCS 92078 1129-E2
MISSION VW
2300 SDCo 92003 1048-B7
MISSION WY
- SMCS 92078 1129-C1
MISSION BAY DR
4200 SD 92109 1248-C4
E MISSION BAY DR
1700 SD 92109 1268-D2
2300 SD 92109 1248-D7
N MISSION BAY DR
2200 SD 92109 1248-C6
W MISSION BAY DR
800 SD 92109 1267-J2
1200 SD 92109 1268-A3
3900 SD 92110 1268-C4
MISSION BAY PKWY
- SD 92109 1268-C3
MISSION BAY PL
800 SD 92109 1267-J2
MISSION BELL LN
4600 LMSA 91941 1271-A3
MISSION BONITA DR
7900 SD 92120 1250-C3
MISSION CARMEL CV
2400 SD 92014 1187-H5
MISSION CENTER CT
7800 SD 92108 1269-B2
MISSION CENTER RD
5100 SD 92108 1269-B2
5400 SD 92123 1269-B2
5500 SD 92123 1249-B7
MISSION CITY CT
9000 SD 92108 1249-E7
MISSION CITY PKWY
5000 SD 92108 1269-E1
MISSION CLIFF DR
1600 SD 92116 1269-C3
MISSION CREEK DR
9500 SNTE 92071 1231-C5
MISSION CREEK RD
1000 SDCo 92028 1047-H2
MISSION DAM TER
7300 SNTE 92071 1230-F7
MISSION GATE DR
4200 OCN 92057 1086-J3
MISSION GORGE PL
4500 SD 92120 1249-H7
4500 SD 92120 1269-J1
MISSION GORGE RD
5900 SD 92120 1249-J5
5900 SD 92120 1269-H1
7100 SD 92120 1250-E2
7100 SD 92124 1249-J5
7100 SD 92124 1250-E2
7300 SNTE 92071 1230-G7
8100 SD 92119 1250-E2
8600 SNTE 92071 1231-A6
9000 SD 92119 1230-G7
MISSION GREENS CT
8800 SNTE 92071 1231-D7

MISSION GREENS RD
8800 SNTE 92071 1231-D7
MISSION HEIGHTS RD
7700 SD 92108 1269-B2
MISSION HILLS BLVD
- SD 92103 1268-H6
- SD 92110 1268-H6
MISSION MANZANA PL
7900 SD 92120 1250-C3
MISSION MEADOWS DR
1500 OCN 92057 1067-F7
MISSION MESA WY
3400 SD 92120 1250-C3
MISSION MONTANA DR
3600 SD 92120 1250-C3
MISSION MONTANA PL
7800 SD 92120 1250-C3
MISSION PARK CT
11000 SNTE 92071 1231-F5
MISSION PARK PL
9400 SNTE 92071 1231-G5
MISSION RIDGE RD
200 SDCo 92028 998-F7
200 SDCo 92028 1028-G1
MISSION SAN CARLOS DR
8600 SNTE 92071 1230-F7
MISSION TRAILS DR
7300 SNTE 92071 1230-F7
MISSION VALLEY CT
7600 SD 92108 1269-A1
MISSION VALLEY FRWY I-8
- SD - 1268-F4
- SD - 1269-B3
MISSION VALLEY RD
7500 SD 92108 1269-A1
MISSION VEGA CT
8800 SNTE 92071 1231-D7
MISSION VEGA RD
8800 SNTE 92071 1231-D6
MISSION VIEJO CT
9800 SNTE 92071 1231-D7
MISSION VILLAGE DR
2100 SD 92108 1249-E5
2100 SD 92123 1249-E5
MISSION VISTA DR
7800 SD 92120 1250-C3
MISSISSIPPI ST
3400 SD 92104 1269-C5
4400 SD 92116 1269-C5
MISSOURI AV
200 OCN 92054 1106-A1
MISSOURI ST
600 SD 92109 1247-H5
1600 SD 92109 1248-A5
MISSY CT
6800 SD 92115 1270-E4
MISTER B PL
- SDCo 92082 1070-F6
MISTLETOE LN
800 CRLB 92009 1127-A5
MISTLETOE ST
400 VSTA 92083 1087-E6
MISTRAL PL
4300 SD 92130 1188-B6
MISTY CIR
1900 ENCT 92024 1147-H6
MISTY LN
4200 OCN 92056 1107-C2
MISTY BLUE CT
12200 SD 92131 1210-B1
MISTY CREEK ST
1000 CHV 91913 1331-A1
MISTY MEADOW CT
800 CHV 91910 1311-B6
MISTY MEADOW LN
9600 SDCo 92026 1089-C2
MISTY OAK RD
13700 SDCo 92082 1070-E7
MISTY RIDGE PL
1300 CHV 91913 1311-D7
1300 CHV 91913 1331-D1
MITCHELL ST
1200 OCN 92054 1106-B2
MITCHELLS CAMP RD
- ImCo - 412-A6
MITRA CT
500 SDCo 91977 1291-D3
MITSCHER RD
1900 SD 92133 1288-D1
MITSCHER ST
- CHV 91910 1310-C7
- CHV 91910 1330-B1
MITSCHER WY
300 CHV 91910 1330-B1
8500 SD 92145 1229-D1
8700 SD 92126 1229-D1
8800 SD 92126 1209-D7
MITTEN LN
2500 SDCo 92065 1152-D7
MITZI LN
9100 SDCo 92021 1232-E6
MIZPAH LN
9500 SDCo 91916 1236-B1
MIZPAH SPUR
9700 SDCo 91916 1236-B1
MOA DR
400 VSTA 92083 1087-F4
MOANA DR
800 SD 92106 1287-J2
1000 SD 92107 1287-J2
MOANA KIA LN
8700 SNTE 92071 1230-J4
MOBLEY ST
2500 SD 92123 1249-D5
MOCCASIN AV
3200 SD 92117 1248-D1
MOCCASIN PL
4700 SD 92117 1248-D1
MOCHA CT
5100 OCN 92056 1107-F4
MOCKINGBIRD CIR
700 ESCN 92025 1130-C7
MOCKINGBIRD DR
7600 SD 92123 1249-A7
MOCKINGBIRD LN
100 OCN 92057 1086-H2
1000 SMCS 92069 1128-E2
9400 SDCo 91941 1271-B2
MODE DR
3100 SDCo 92026 1109-H2
MODEL A FORD LN
4400 SDCo 92019 1273-A2
MODENA PL
- SD 92130 1188-A3
MODESTO ST
2300 SD 92105 1269-H7
2300 SD 92105 1289-H1

MODOC ST
3800 SD 92117 1248-E4
MOFFETT RD
- CORD 92135 1288-C5
- SD 92135 1288-C5
MOHAWK ST
6600 SD 92115 1270-E2
7300 LMSA 91941 1270-F2
MOHICAN AV
3200 SD 92117 1248-E5
MOHLER ST
6100 SD 92120 1249-J7
MOIOLA AV
2300 ELCN 92243 6499-E7
MOISAN WY
8900 LMSA 91941 1271-A2
MOLA VISTA WY
800 SOLB 92075 1167-G7
MOLCHAN RD
2300 SDCo 91906 (1297-F6
See Page 1296)
MOLE RD
1100 NATC 92136 1309-F2
MOLINO RD
10200 SNTE 92071 1231-D3
MOLLENDO BLVD
5200 SD 92124 1249-H2
MOLLIE LN
- SNTE 92071 1231-C2
MOLLIE ST
1200 SD 92110 1268-F3
N MOLLISON AV
300 ELCJ 92020 1251-G3
300 ELCJ 92021 1251-G3
1700 SDCo 92021 1251-G3
S MOLLISON AV
100 ELCJ 92020 1251-H6
100 ELCJ 92021 1251-H6
MOLLY CIR
1500 OCN 92054 1106-E1
MOLLYWOODS AV
9100 LMSA 91941 1271-B1
9300 SDCo 91941 1271-B1
MOLOKAI WY
2200 SD 92154 1330-C6
MOMA LN
19500 SDCo 92065 1153-E2
MOMAR LN
500 ESCN 92027 1130-D1
MONA LN
- SD 92129 1188-J3
- SD 92130 1188-J3
MONA PL
1100 ELCJ 92020 1251-E7
1100 ELCJ 92020 1271-E1
MONACO CT
2000 SDCo 92019 1272-C3
MONACO ST
4300 SD 92107 1287-H2
MONAGHAN CT
2200 SDCo 91977 1291-B1
MONAHAN RD
4400 SDCo 91941 1271-E3
MONAIR DR
3300 SD 92117 1248-D4
MONA LISA ST
12300 SD 92130 1188-C7
MONARCH ST
2700 SD 92123 1249-E5
MONARCH WY
200 OCN 92057 1087-A1
MONARCHE DR
- CHV 91913 1331-C1
MONARCH RIDGE CIR
1700 SDCo 92019 1272-D2
MONARCH RIDGE LN
1900 SDCo 92019 1272-D3
MONDAVI CIR
1200 VSTA 92083 1107-J3
MONEL AV
8900 SD 92123 1229-D7
8900 SD 92123 1249-D1
MONET LN
5200 SDCo 91902 1290-H7
MONETTE DR
2400 SD 92123 1249-E6
MONICA CIR
500 OCN 92057 1067-A5
600 OCN 92057 1066-J5
MONIQUE CT
1200 VSTA 92084 1088-A3
9400 SDCo 91977 1271-C5
MONIQUE LN
3300 SDCo 91977 1271-B6
MONIQUE WY
400 SDCo 92026 1109-G3
MONITOR RD
1300 SD 92110 1268-F2
MONMOUTH DR
1600 SD 92109 1247-J5
1600 SD 92109 1248-A5
MONO LAKE DR
8300 SD 92119 1250-J5
MONONA DR
9200 LMSA 91942 1251-B7
MONONGAHELA ST
4600 SD 92117 1248-B1
4900 SD 92117 1228-B7
MONROE AV
1200 SD 92116 1269-B4
4400 SD 92115 1269-J4
4800 SD 92115 1270-A4
MONROE ST
100 OCN 92057 1067-A7
2100 CRLB 92008 1106-F3
MONSANTO CT
10800 SD 92129 1189-H2
MONSERATE AV
700 CHV 91910 1310-E7
800 CHV 91911 1330-E1
MONSERATE PL
3600 SDCo 92028 1048-E4
MONSERATE TER
3000 SDCo 92028 1048-A3
MONSERATE WY
1600 SDCo 92028 1047-J4
1600 SDCo 92028 1048-A4
MONSERATE HILL CT
3600 SDCo 92028 1048-E4
MONSERATE HILL RD
3400 SDCo 92028 1048-E3
MONSERRAT WY
1800 VSTA 92083 1107-H5
MONSERRATE ST
- SDCo 92055 1086-A4
MONTAGE RD
600 OCN 92057 1087-C1
MONTALVO ST
4200 SD 92107 1268-B5

MONTANA RD
1600 CHV 91913 1311-D6
MONTANA ST
7800 LMGR 91945 1270-G7
MONTANA LUNA CT
400 SDCo 92025 1130-B6
MONTANA SERENA
1400 SDCo 92021 1233-B6
MONTANA SERENA CT
1400 SDCo 92021 1233-B6
MONTANES LN
7000 CRLB 92009 1127-G7
MONTANYA DR
12300 SDCo 92082 1070-A4
MONTANYA LN
13400 SDCo 92082 1070-D4
MONTARA AV
7900 SD 92126 1209-B2
MONTARA CT
11100 SD 92126 1209-B2
MONTAUBON CIR
11000 SD 92131 1209-J2
MONTAUBON WY
11000 SD 92131 1209-J2
MONTAUK ST
12700 PWY 92064 1190-C5
MONTCALM ST
300 CHV 91911 1330-F2
MONTCLAIR ST
200 CHV 91911 1330-F1
2000 SD 92104 1289-G1
2400 SD 92104 1269-F7
MONTCLIFF RD
2000 SD 92139 1290-G6
MONTE RD
1100 ImCo 92227 431-A1
5900 SDCo 92003 1048-C7
MONTE AZUL LN
1000 SDCo 92036 1138-A6
MONTEBELLO ST
- CHV 91910 1310-C5
MONTECITO
- CRLB 92009 1126-J5
MONTECITO DR
- SDCo 92028 1047-J1
MONTECITO GN
300 ESCN 92025 1150-B1
MONTECITO LN
- SDCo 92028 1047-J1
MONTECITO RD
- CHV 91914 1311-G2
- SDCo 91901 1235-A5
- SDCo 92065 1151-H6
1400 SDCo 92065 1152-A6
E MONTECITO RD
100 SDCo 92065 1152-F6
MONTECITO WY
600 SD 92103 1268-H5
800 SDCo 92065 1152-B5
E MONTECITO WY
200 SD 92103 1269-A5
W MONTECITO WY
1000 SD 92103 1269-A5
MONTE DE JOSUE
16900 SDCo 92065 1151-E6
MONTEFRIO CT
3900 SD 92130 1188-B7
MONTE FUEGO
6500 SDCo 92067 1188-G2
MONTEGO AV
700 ESCN 92026 1109-F5
MONTEGO CT
- CORD 92118 1329-D1
1300 VSTA 92083 1107-H4
MONTEGO CV
2700 SD 92014 1187-J6
MONTEGO DR
10500 SD 92124 1249-H1
13300 PWY 92064 1190-H4
MONTEGO PL
5300 SD 92124 1249-H1
MONTEGO BAY CT
300 OCN 92057 1066-H6
MONTELLANO TER
12500 SD 92130 1188-B6
MONTEMAR AV
2100 ESCN 92027 1110-C6
MONTEMAR DR
9300 SDCo 91977 1271-C7
MONTE MAR RD
1100 VSTA 92084 1088-A4
MONTE MIRA DR
1800 ENCT 92024 1147-C1
MONTE MIRA LN
800 ENCT 92024 1147-C1
MONTERA CT
500 CHV 91910 1310-G5
MONTERA ST
1300 CHV 91913 1331-B1
MONTE REAL
3500 ESCN 92029 1150-A4
MONTEREY AV
700 CHV 91910 1310-E7
1000 CHV 91911 1330-F1
1700 CORD 92118 1288-J7
1700 CORD 92118 1308-J1
1800 CORD 92118 1289-A7
MONTEREY CIR
500 SMCS 92069 1109-A6
MONTEREY CT
700 SD 92109 1267-H1
800 CHV 91911 1330-F1
MONTEREY DR
400 OCN 92054 1085-J6
600 OCN 92054 1086-A5
1300 SDCo 92020 1251-J7
2400 ESCN 92029 1149-G1
MONTEREY GN
2400 ESCN 92029 1149-G1
MONTEREY LN
600 VSTA 92084 1087-J3
MONTEREY PL
- ENCT 92024 1147-F5
1300 SDCo 91901 1233-H5
MONTEREY RD
1100 SDCo 92019 1251-H7
MONTEREY CREST DR
3200 SDCo 91935 1273-B7
MONTEREY CYPRESS WY
12600 SD 92130 1188-B6
MONTEREY PARK DR
1500 SD 92173 1350-D2
MONTEREY PINE DR
1500 SD 92173 1350-C2
MONTEREY VISTA PL
1100 ENCT 92024 1167-F1
MONTEREY VISTA WY
1000 ENCT 92024 1167-F1

STREET
Block City ZIP Pg-Grid

MONTE RICO DR
1400 ELCJ 92021 1252-A2
1400 SDCo 92021 1252-A2
MONTERO CT
12500 SD 92128 1170-C2
MONTERO PL
1900 ESCN 92029 1129-F6
12500 SD 92128 1170-C2
MONTERO RD
17200 SD 92128 1170-C2
17700 PWY 92064 1170-C2
MONTERO WY
12500 SD 92128 1170-C2
MONTESANO RD
3100 SDCo 92029 1149-J2
MONTE SERENO AV
1200 CHV 91913 1311-B7
1200 CHV 91913 1331-B1
MONTESSA ST
4900 SD 92124 1250-A1
5000 SD 92124 1230-A7
MONTE VERDE DR
6800 SD 92119 1250-E3
MONTEVIDEO PL
31400 SDCo 92003 1067-J1
MONTE VIEW CT
11700 SDCo 92019 1272-A4
MONTE VISTA
- SMCS 92078 1129-C1
MONTE VISTA AV
- CHV 91910 1310-A5
7000 SD 92037 1247-E1
7400 SD 92037 1227-E7
MONTE VISTA CT
12700 PWY 92064 1170-D6
MONTE VISTA DR
1100 VSTA 92084 1108-A1
1500 VSTA 92084 1088-B7
1700 SDCo 92084 1108-D1
MONTE VISTA RD
1700 SDCo 92020 1271-J3
12600 PWY 92064 1170-C6
MONTEZUMA
- SD 92140 1268-F6
MONTEZUMA CT
1600 SDCo 92004 1058-F5
MONTEZUMA PL
5000 SD 92115 1270-C2
MONTEZUMA RD
- SD 92116 1269-J2
100 SDCo 92004 1058-F5
4500 SD 92115 1269-J2
4900 SD 92115 1270-B2
5400 SD 92182 1270-B2
MONTEZUMA VALLEY RD Rt#-S22
31300 SDCo 92066 410-A9
33400 SDCo 92066 409-L9
33900 SDCo 92066 1098-A2
34400 SDCo 92004 (1078-D7 See Page 1058)
34400 SDCo 92066 (1078-D7 See Page 1058)
35500 SDCo 92086 409-L9
MONTFORT CT
14000 SD 92128 1190-A2
MONTGOMERY AV
1800 ENCT 92007 1167-D2
MONTGOMERY DR
1400 SDCo 92084 1108-B2
MONTGOMERY RD
- ImCo 92233 411-B9
MONTGOMERY ST
100 CHV 91911 1330-D5
MONTIA CT
6700 CRLB 92009 1126-J5
MONTIA PL
2200 ESCN 92029 1129-H7
MONTICELLO DR
800 SDCo 92029 1129-J7
MONTICOOK CT
11200 SD 92127 1149-H7
MONTIEL RD
1100 ESCN 92026 1129-E1
1100 SDCo 92026 1129-F2
1400 SMCS 92069 1129-C1
2300 SMCS 92026 1129-E1
MONTIEL TKTR
3800 SDCo 91935 1254-A7
3800 SDCo 91935 1274-B1
MONTONGO CIR
7900 SD 92126 1209-A3
MONTONGO ST
10700 SD 92126 1209-A2
MONTROS PL
1200 ESCN 92027 1110-A7
MONTROSE CT
500 ELCJ 92020 1251-F4
MONTROSE WY
100 OCN 92057 1087-A1
8900 SD 92122 1228-D3
MONTURA AV
10100 SNTE 92071 1231-E3
MONTURA CT
10600 SNTE 92071 1231-E3
MONTURA DR
17000 SD 92128 1170-C2
MONTURA RD
1100 SDCo 92069 1128-B2
MONTVIEW DR
500 ESCN 92025 1130-A6
600 ESCN 92025 1129-J6
MONTVIEW GN
1100 ESCN 92025 1129-H6
MONUMENT PL
3900 ESCN 92025 1150-D3
MONUMENT RD
400 IMPB 91932 1349-G5
400 SD 91932 1349-G5
400 SD 92154 1349-G5
1800 SD 92154 1350-A5
MONUMENT HILL
1300 SDCo 92020 1272-A1
MONUMENT PEAK RD
- SDCo 91948 1218-F4
- SDCo 92036 1218-F4
MONUMENT TRAIL DR
1300 CHV 91915 1311-H6
MOODY DR
900 ESCN 92027 1130-E1
MOON RD
1400 VSTA 92083 1087-D6
MOONCREST CT
3100 SMCS 92069 1108-B6
3100 VSTA 92083 1108-B6
MOONCREST RD
27300 SDCo 92065 1154-C2
MOONEY ST
3100 SD 92117 1248-E6

MOONGLOW CT
1900 VSTA 92083 1107-J4
23700 SDCo 92065 1173-D5
MOONGLOW DR
15000 SDCo 92065 1173-D5
MOONLIGHT GN
2300 ESCN 92026 1109-B4
MOONLIGHT LN
400 ENCT 92024 1147-B7
4200 OCN 92056 1107-C2
5400 SD 92037 1247-H3
MOONLIGHT PL
31000 SDCo 92082 1070-E2
MOONLIGHT WY
600 SDCo 92065 1152-E5
MOONLIT TR
- SDCo 91905 1300-D4
MOONRIDGE DR
2800 SD 92037 1227-J6
MOONRIDGE PL
7700 SD 92037 1227-J6
MOON RIDGE RD
9100 SDCo 92028 1029-A2
MOONRISE TR
2000 SDCo 91905 1300-E7
MOON ROCK RD
1600 SDCo 92028 997-G7
MOONSHADOW RDG
1700 SDCo 92028 1027-J6
1700 SDCo 92028 1028-A6
MOON SONG CT
18100 SD 92127 1149-H6
MOONSTONE DR
2400 SD 92123 1249-E6
MOONSTONE PL
- CRLB 92009 1127-H5
1000 CHV 91913 1331-A1
MOONSTONE BAY DR
300 OCN 92057 1066-J6
MOON VALLEY RD
37500 SDCo 91905 (1319-G6 See Page 1298)
38000 SDCo 91905 (1320-A6 See Page 1300)
MOON VIEW DR
300 CHV 91910 1310-F5
MOON VIEW WY
10300 SDCo 92026 1089-F3
MOONWIND CIR
- SDCo 92026 1089-A1
MOORE AV
9000 SD 92126 1209-E7
MOORE ST
2200 SD 92110 1268-E5
MOOREFIELD DR
5700 SDCo 92019 1253-D3
MOORGATE RD
100 ENCT 92024 1147-A2
100 ENCT 92024 1146-J2
MOORHEN PL
6800 CRLB 92009 1127-E5
MOORLAND DR
1400 SD 92109 1248-A7
MOORLAND HEIGHTS WY
10500 SD 92121 1208-E4
MOORPARK CT
2900 SDCo 91978 1271-F7
MOORPARK ST
10200 SDCo 91978 1271-F7
MORA CIR
13500 PWY 92064 1190-H4
MORADA ST
7700 CRLB 92009 1147-H2
MORAEA ST
1300 SD 92114 1290-D5
MORAGA AV
3700 SD 92117 1248-D2
MORAGA CT
3300 SD 92117 1248-D3
MORAGA PL
3300 SD 92117 1248-D3
MORAGA WY
400 OCN 92054 1086-G2
MORALES LN
- SDCo 92082 1071-E3
MORAN CT
100 VSTA 92083 1107-D1
MORAN WY
12700 SD 92129 1189-D6
MORANDA CT
11200 SD 92128 1189-J4
MORATALLA TER
4000 SD 92130 1188-B6
MORAVA PL
2700 SD 92110 1248-F7
MORCADO CIR
9400 SDCo 91941 1271-C4
MOREHOUSE DR
5400 SD 92121 1208-E6
MOREHOUSE PL
300 CHV 91911 1330-D4
MORELIA CT
100 SOLB 92075 1167-D7
MORELLA WY
2100 OCN 92056 1086-J7
2100 OCN 92056 1106-J1
MORENA BLVD
400 SD 92110 1268-E1
2200 SD 92110 1248-D5
2700 SD 92117 1248-B3
W MORENA BLVD
1100 SD 92110 1268-E3
MORENA PL
5100 SD 92110 1268-F3
MORENA RESERVOIR RD
- SD 91906 (1297-A5 See Page 1296)
2500 SDCo 91906 (1297-A5 See Page 1296)
MORENA STOKES VALLEY RD
- SDCo 91906 430-A7
- SDCo 91906 (1297-D1 See Page 1296)
MORENA VIEW DR
29800 SDCo 91906 (1297-F5 See Page 1296)
MORENCI ST
1400 SD 92110 1268-E2
MORENE ST
12900 PWY 92064 1190-D5
MORENO AV
11000 SDCo 92040 1232-B1
11100 SDCo 92040 1212-A5
11900 SDCo 92040 1211-J3
MORENO ST
1400 OCN 92054 1106-C2
MORENO WY
1300 OCN 92054 1106-C2

MORGAN PL
300 SDCo 92083 1108-C4
MORGAN RD
2200 CRLB 92008 1107-C7
2200 CRLB 92008 1127-C1
MORGAN ST
- SDCo 92055 1023-F2
MORGAN WY
500 ELCJ 92020 1251-F7
MORGANDALE CT
2900 SDCo 91977 1271-B6
MORGAN HILL DR
1000 CHV 91913 1311-B7
1200 CHV 91913 1331-B1
MORLAN ST
3600 SD 92117 1228-D7
MORLEY DR
- SD 92102 1289-G4
MORLEY ST
2200 SD 92111 1248-J7
2200 SD 92111 1268-J1
MORLEY FIELD DR
1700 SD 92101 1269-C6
1700 SD 92103 1269-C6
MORNING WY
3100 SD 92037 1228-A3
MORNING AIR RD
14200 PWY 92064 1170-G4
MORNING BREEZE LN
1600 NATC 91950 1310-B1
MORNING BREEZE WY
9300 SD 92126 1209-E2
MORNING CANYON RD
4700 OCN 92056 1107-E2
MORNING CREEK DR
10900 SD 92128 1189-H5
MORNING CREEK DR N
10900 SD 92128 1189-H4
MORNING DOVE RD
11000 SDCo 92040 1211-F7
MORNING DOVE WY
4400 OCN 92057 1086-J1
MORNING GLORY DR
9300 SDCo 92040 1232-C5
MORNING GLORY LN
2700 CRLB 92008 1106-E4
MORNINGLORY LN
1400 VSTA 92084 1108-A1
MORNINGLORY PL
1300 VSTA 92084 1108-A1
MORNINGLORY TER
1400 VSTA 92084 1108-A1
MORNING MIST CT
8300 SD 92119 1250-J2
MORNING MIST GN
1900 ESCN 92026 1109-B3
MORNINGSIDE CT
12200 PWY 92064 1170-B7
MORNINGSIDE DR
500 VSTA 92084 1087-H6
3100 OCN 92056 1107-C1
14800 PWY 92064 1170-B7
14800 PWY 92064 1190-B1
MORNINGSIDE PL
500 VSTA 92084 1087-J7
MORNINGSIDE ST
2200 SD 92139 1310-C1
MORNINGSIDE TER
2800 SDCo 92029 1149-G2
MORNINGSIDE TR
200 VSTA 92084 1087-J6
2200 SDCo 92065 1172-D4
MORNING STAR CT
4100 SDCo 91941 1271-G4
MORNING STAR DR
10800 SDCo 91941 1271-G4
MORNINGSTAR LN
1300 SDCo 92028 1027-F4
MORNING SUN CT
2200 ENCT 92024 1147-J5
MORNING SUN DR
800 ENCT 92024 1147-J5
MORNING VIEW CT
4300 SDCo 91941 1271-D3
MORNING VIEW DR
1000 ESCN 92026 1109-G7
1000 ESCN 92026 1129-G1
3300 OCN 92054 1086-D2
MOROCCO DR
8000 LMSA 91942 1270-H1
MOROSE ST
2200 LMGR 91945 1270-H7
2200 LMGR 91945 1290-H1
MORRELL ST
3900 SD 92109 1248-A5
MORRIS ST
2200 SD 92136 1289-F7
MORRISON PL
19300 SDCo 92065 1192-B2
MORRISON ST
400 SD 92102 1289-H3
MORRIS RANCH RD
- SDCo 91948 430-B5
- SDCo 92066 430-B5
MORRO RD
100 SDCo 92028 1027-G4
MORRO WY
5600 LMSA 91942 1270-H1
MORRO BAY ST
4500 OCN 92057 1066-H6
MORRO HEIGHTS RD
6600 OCN 92057 1067-D2
MORRO HILLS PL
5100 SDCo 92028 1047-G7
MORRO HILLS RD
100 SDCo 92028 1047-F6
MORRO POINT DR
600 CHV 91911 1330-J4
MORROW WY
1400 SD 92103 1269-B5
MORSA WY
3200 CRLB 92009 1127-J5
MORSE CT
6900 SD 92111 1268-J1
MORSE ST
100 OCN 92054 1106-D2
1400 OCN 92054 1106-D2
MORTON GN
1900 ESCN 92025 1129-H5
MORTON WY
2900 SD 92139 1310-F2
MOSAIC CIR
600 OCN 92057 1087-B1
MOSELLE ST
10300 SD 92131 1210-A3
MOSELLE WY
12000 SD 92131 1210-B3
MOSS ST
- CHV 91911 1330-D2

E MOSS ST
300 CHV 91911 1330-F1
MOSSBERG CT
1200 VSTA 92083 1087-E5
MOSS LANDING AV
1900 CHV 91913 1311-E6
MOSS TREE LN
9700 SDCo 92026 1089-D4
MOSSWOOD CV
- SD 92130 1208-E2
MOSSY ROCK DR
1700 SDCo 92084 1068-B6
MOTHER GRUNDY DR
1800 SDCo 91935 (1314-G2 See Page 1294)
MOTHER GRUNDY TKTR
- SDCo 91917 (1314-D6 See Page 1294)
300 SDCo 91935 (1314-H1 See Page 1294)
1500 SDCo 91935 1294-H7
MOTIF ST
4800 OCN 92057 1087-B2
MOTT ST
5700 SD 92122 1228-B6
MOTTINO DR
2500 OCN 92056 1087-C6
MOULTRIE AV
3500 SD 92117 1248-D5
MOUND AV
5400 SD 92120 1250-B5
MOUNDGLEN LN
2600 SDCo 91977 1271-C7
MOUNDTOP LN
2600 SDCo 91977 1271-D7
MOUNDVIEW PL
2600 SDCo 91977 1271-D7
MOUNT WY
1700 VSTA 92083 1107-G4
MOUNT AACHEN AV
3200 SD 92111 1248-H5
MOUNT ABBEY AV
3500 SD 92111 1248-H4
MOUNT ABERNATHY AV
4200 SD 92117 1248-J1
MOUNT ABRAHAM AV
3600 SD 92111 1248-H3
MOUNT ACADIA BLVD
2800 SD 92110 1248-G5
2800 SD 92111 1248-G5
MOUNT ACARA DR
5500 SD 92111 1248-H5
MOUNT ACKERLY DR
5600 SD 92111 1248-H4
MOUNT ACKERMAN DR
6200 SD 92111 1248-H3
MOUNT ACLARE AV
3400 SD 92111 1248-H4
MOUNT ACMAR CT
3100 SD 92111 1248-H5
MOUNT ACOMITA AV
3400 SD 92111 1248-H4
MOUNT ACONIA DR
5500 SD 92111 1248-G5
MOUNT ACONIA WY
5500 SD 92111 1248-H5
MOUNT ACRE WY
6300 SD 92111 1248-H3
MOUNT ADA RD
6300 SD 92111 1248-J3
MOUNT ADELBERT DR
6300 SD 92111 1248-H3
MOUNT AGUILAR DR
5900 SD 92111 1248-H3
S MOUNTAIN DR
13000 SDCo 92040 1232-C3
MOUNTAIN LN
2200 SDCo 92065 1172-E2
MOUNTAIN RD
14200 PWY 92064 1190-G1
E MOUNTAIN VW
100 CHV 91910 1310-B5
N MOUNTAIN VW
100 CHV 91910 1310-B5
S MOUNTAIN VW
200 CHV 91910 1310-B5
MOUNTAIN WY
31500 SDCo 92003 1068-G1
MOUNTAIN BLUEBIRD CT
11300 SDCo 92040 1212-C6
MOUNTAINBROOK RD
4700 SDCo 92070 1135-D4
MOUNTAIN CIRCLE DR
35700 SDCo 92036 1176-D1
MOUNTAIN CREST LN
- ESCN 92027 1130-F2
MOUNTAIN GLEN TER
10400 SD 92131 1209-J4
MOUNTAIN HEIGHTS DR
1000 ESCN 92029 1149-H1
1000 SDCo 92029 1149-H1
MOUNTAIN HILLS PL
1700 ESCN 92029 1129-F6
MOUNTAIN LILAC RD
28600 SDCo 92026 1089-E2
MOUNTAIN LION RD
11400 SDCo 92040 1212-D4
MOUNTAIN MEADOW DR
1400 OCN 92056 1087-D4
MOUNTAIN MEADOW RD
- SDCo 92036 1175-J2
15700 SDCo 92026 1089-D1
28800 SDCo 92026 1069-D7
MOUNTAIN MEADOW TR
4400 SDCo 92036 1155-J4
MOUNTAIN PARK PL
1200 ESCN 92027 1130-E2
MOUNTAIN PASS CIR
1600 VSTA 92083 1107-H7
MOUNTAIN PASS RD
11900 SD 92128 1190-B7
MOUNTAIN PEAK PL
- SDCo 92065 1173-D2
MOUNTAIN QUAIL CT
11400 SDCo 92040 1212-C5
MOUNTAIN RANCHES RD
11800 SDCo 92040 1212-C5
MOUNTAIN RIDGE RD
2200 CHV 91914 1311-E2
31000 SDCo 92026 1069-C2
31000 SDCo 92082 1069-C2
MOUNTAIN RIM RD
- SDCo 92028 1029-B2
MOUNTAIN SHADOW DR
9200 SDCo 92040 1232-D5
MOUNTAIN SHADOW LN
16400 SDCo 92065 1171-F3

MOUNTAINSIDE DR
13400 PWY 92064 1190-C4
MOUNT AINSWORTH AV
3700 SD 92111 1248-H3
MOUNT AINSWORTH CT
6300 SD 92111 1248-H3
MOUNT AINSWORTH WY
6300 SD 92111 1248-H3
MOUNTAIN TOP CT
6700 SD 92120 1250-D4
MOUNTAIN TOP DR
1100 SDCo 92021 1233-A7
MOUNTAIN VALLEY LN
1900 ESCN 92029 1129-F6
MOUNTAIN VALLEY PL
15600 SDCo 92040 1212-J6
15600 SDCo 92040 1213-A6
MOUNTAIN VIEW AV
1600 OCN 92054 1106-C1
MOUNTAIN VIEW CT
600 VSTA 92083 1087-F4
14100 PWY 92064 1190-G2
MOUNTAIN VIEW DR
500 SDCo 92036 1156-E1
2000 ESCN 92027 1130-D2
2400 CRLB 92008 1106-D4
2400 SDCo 92027 1130-F2
E MOUNTAIN VIEW DR
4600 SD 92116 1269-F2
N MOUNTAIN VIEW DR
3100 SD 92116 1269-F2
W MOUNTAIN VIEW DR
3200 SD 92116 1269-E3
MOUNTAIN VIEW LN
1300 CHV 91911 1330-G3
10300 SDCo 92040 1231-G3
24800 SDCo 92065 1173-G5
MOUNTAIN VIEW RD
100 SDCo 92021 1252-J2
400 SDCo 92021 1253-A2
1100 SDCo 92021 1233-B7
1300 SDCo 92019 1233-B7
1300 SDCo 92019 1253-A2
9500 SDCo 91916 1235-G2
32200 SDCo 92003 1048-H5
MOUNTAIN VIEW WY
3800 SDCo 91902 1310-E4
MOUNTAIN VISTA DR
400 ENCT 92024 1147-G6
MOUNTAIN VISTA WY
2000 OCN 92054 1106-F1
MOUNT ALADIN AV
3700 SD 92111 1248-G4
MOUNT ALBERTINE AV
3800 SD 92111 1248-H3
MOUNT ALBERTINE CT
6500 SD 92111 1248-J3
MOUNT ALBERTINE WY
3900 SD 92111 1248-J3
MOUNT ALIFAN CT
4000 SD 92111 1248-F4
MOUNT ALIFAN DR
4400 SD 92111 1248-G3
MOUNT ALIFAN PL
4100 SD 92111 1248-H3
MOUNT ALIFAN WY
4000 SD 92111 1248-F4
MOUNT ALMAGOSA DR
4700 SD 92111 1248-G4
MOUNT ALMAGOSA PL
3700 SD 92111 1248-F4
MOUNT ALVAREZ AV
3400 SD 92111 1248-H4
MOUNT ANTERO DR
4900 SD 92111 1248-G4
MOUNT ARARAT DR
4800 SD 92111 1248-G4
MOUNT ARARAT WY
7700 SDCo 92003 1068-G1
MOUNT ARIANE CT
5200 SD 92111 1248-G5
MOUNT ARIANE DR
3300 SD 92111 1248-G5
MOUNT ARIANE TER
5200 SD 92111 1248-F5
MOUNT ARMET DR
4600 SD 92117 1248-F3
MOUNT ARMOUR CT
3400 SD 92111 1248-F5
MOUNT ARMOUR DR
4800 SD 92111 1248-G5
MOUNT ARMOUR PL
3400 SD 92111 1248-G5
MOUNT ASHMUN CT
3600 SD 92111 1248-G4
MOUNT ASHMUN DR
4700 SD 92111 1248-G4
MOUNT ASHMUN PL
3700 SD 92111 1248-F4
MOUNT AUGUSTUS AV
3700 SD 92111 1248-G4
MOUNT BAGOT AV
4100 SD 92111 1248-F3
MOUNT BARNARD AV
4000 SD 92111 1248-G3
MOUNT BIGELOW CT
4100 SD 92111 1248-F4
MOUNT BIGELOW DR
4400 SD 92111 1248-F3
MOUNT BIGELOW WY
4100 SD 92111 1248-F3
MOUNT BLACKBURN AV
3600 SD 92111 1248-G4
MOUNT BLANCA DR
5000 SD 92111 1248-G3
MOUNT BOLANAS CT
4000 SD 92111 1248-G3
MOUNT BROSS AV
4000 SD 92111 1248-G3
MOUNT BRUNDAGE AV
3800 SD 92111 1248-G4
MOUNT BURNHAM CT
3400 SD 92111 1248-G5
MOUNT BURNHAM DR
5200 SD 92111 1248-G5
MOUNT BURNHAM PL
3500 SD 92111 1248-G5
MOUNT CARMEL DR
100 SD 92173 1350-G3
MOUNT CAROL DR
3000 SD 92111 1248-H5
MOUNT CASAS CT
4200 SD 92117 1248-F3
MOUNT CASAS DR
4700 SD 92117 1248-G3
MOUNT CASTLE AV
4300 SD 92117 1248-G2
MOUNT CERVIN DR
4700 SD 92117 1248-G1

MOUNT CRESTI DR
4700 SD 92117 1248-G1
MOUNT CULEBRA AV
4100 SD 92111 1248-G3
4200 SD 92117 1248-G3
MOUNT DAVIS AV
4200 SD 92117 1248-G3
MOUNT DURBAN DR
4700 SD 92117 1248-F3
MOUNT ELBRUS CT
4300 SD 92117 1248-F3
MOUNT ELBRUS DR
4800 SD 92117 1248-G2
MOUNT ELENA WY
2300 SDCo 91935 1294-G6
MOUNT ETNA DR
4600 SD 92117 1248-G2
MOUNT EVEREST BLVD
3400 SD 92111 1248-G4
4200 SD 92117 1248-G3
MOUNT FORAKER AV
4300 SD 92117 1248-G2
MOUNT FORDE AV
4600 SD 92117 1248-F3
MOUNT FOSTER AV
4200 SD 92117 1248-F3
MOUNT FRISSELL DR
4500 SD 92117 1248-F2
MOUNT GAYWAS DR
4500 SD 92117 1248-F2
MOUNT HARRIS DR
4700 SD 92117 1248-G2
MOUNT HAY DR
4700 SD 92117 1248-G2
MOUNT HELIX DR
4700 SDCo 91941 1271-D2
MOUNT HELIX HIGHLANDS DR
4200 SDCo 91941 1271-C3
MOUNT HENRY AV
4200 SD 92117 1248-F2
MOUNT HENRY PL
4500 SD 92117 1248-F3
MOUNT HENRY WY
4500 SD 92117 1248-F3
MOUNT HERBERT AV
4100 SD 92117 1248-F2
MOUNT HIGHPINE PL
4500 SD 92117 1248-F2
MOUNT HILLS PL
300 ELCJ 92020 1251-C5
MOUNT HORTON DR
4600 SD 92117 1248-F3
MOUNT HUBBARD AV
4500 SD 92117 1248-F3
MOUNT HUKEE AV
4100 SD 92117 1248-F3
MOUNT ISRAEL PL
8900 SDCo 92029 1149-C4
MOUNT ISRAEL RD
8700 SDCo 92029 1149-C4
MOUNT ISRAEL TKTR
8500 SDCo 92067 1148-J3
8500 SDCo 92067 1149-A3
MOUNT JEFFERS AV
4300 SD 92117 1248-F3
MOUNT KING DR
4500 SD 92117 1248-F2
MOUNT LANGLEY DR
- CHV 91913 1311-F6
MOUNT LA PALMA DR
4700 SD 92117 1248-G2
MOUNT LA PLATTA CT
4500 SD 92117 1248-G2
MOUNT LA PLATTA DR
4600 SD 92117 1248-G2
MOUNT LA PLATTA PL
4500 SD 92117 1248-G1
MOUNT LAUDO DR
4600 SD 92117 1248-F2
MOUNT LAURENCE DR
3300 SD 92117 1248-D4
MOUNT LINDSEY AV
4400 SD 92117 1248-F2
MOUNT LINDSEY PL
4500 SD 92117 1248-F2
MOUNT LONGS DR
4600 SD 92117 1248-G2
MOUNT MACCLURE ST
1400 CHV 91913 1331-B2
MOUNT MIGUEL DR
3000 SD 92139 1310-D3
MOUNT MIGUEL RD
2100 CHV 91914 1311-F3
2100 SDCo 91914 1311-F3
MOUNT MIGUENO
2200 CHV 91914 1311-F3
MOUNT OLYMPUS DR
6900 SDCo 92028 999-E5
MOUNT OLYMPUS VALLEY RD
9900 SDCo 92028 999-D4
MOUNT PUTMAN AV
4100 SD 92117 1248-F3
MOUNT PUTMAN CT
4600 SD 92117 1248-F3
MOUNT RIAS PL
4100 SD 92111 1248-H3
MOUNT ROYAL AV
4700 SD 92117 1248-G1
MOUNT ROYAL CT
4800 SD 92117 1248-G1
MOUNT ROYAL PL
4800 SD 92117 1248-G1
MOUNT SAINT HELENS CT
4700 SD 92117 1248-G1
MOUNT SAINT HELENS DR
4700 SD 92117 1248-G1
MOUNT SAINT HELENS WY
4700 SD 92117 1248-G1
MOUNT SANDY DR
3700 SD 92117 1248-D5
MOUNT SHASTA
3500 SMCS 92069 1128-B1
MOUNT TAMI DR
3100 SD 92111 1248-H5
MOUNT TAMI LN
3300 SD 92111 1248-H5
MOUNT TERMINUS DR
4000 SD 92111 1248-F4
MOUNT VERNON AV
800 OCN 92057 1086-G5
MOUNT VERNON ST
6900 LMGR 91945 1270-F7
MOUNT VIEW RD
- SDCo 92029 1129-C6

MOUNT VOSS DR
4200 SD 92117 1248-F3
MOUNT WHITNEY RD
2800 SDCo 92029 1129-C4
MOUNT WOODSON RD
17100 SDCo 92065 1171-E4
MOUNT WOODSON WY
17300 SDCo 92065 1171-F3
MOYA PL
500 CHV 91910 1310-H5
MOYLA DR
16200 SDCo 92061 1051-B5
MOZART AV
100 ENCT 92007 1167-D3
MOZELLE LN
9800 SDCo 91941 1271-D4
MUCHACHA WY
10300 SD 92124 1229-G7
MUDDY LN
300 VSTA 92084 1088-A6
MUDGE LN
1700 ESCN 92026 1109-F5
MUFFIN CT
9900 SD 92129 1189-F3
MUIR AV
4300 SD 92107 1268-A6
4800 SD 92107 1267-J5
MUIR LN
9500 SD 92093 1227-J2
MUIRA LN
2000 SDCo 92019 1272-C3
MUIR COLLEGE DR
2700 SD 92093 1227-J1
MUIRFIELD DR
800 OCN 92054 1086-D2
2500 SDCo 92019 1272-B5
MUIRFIELD GN
1700 ESCN 92026 1109-D4
MUIRFIELD WY
200 SMCS 92069 1108-J3
17000 SDCo 92067 1168-G7
MUIRLANDS DR
800 SD 92037 1247-G1
W MUIRLANDS DR
900 SD 92037 1247-F1
MUIRLANDS LN
6300 SD 92037 1247-G2
MUIRLANDS VISTA WY
700 SD 92037 1247-F2
MUIR TRAIL PL
1300 CHV 91913 1331-B1
MUIRWOOD DR
700 OCN 92057 1087-C2
MULBERRY CT
1100 CRLB 92009 1127-A5
MULBERRY DR
300 SMCS 92069 1109-A3
1800 SDCo 92069 1109-A1
MULBERRY LN
- SDCo 92026 1089-B3
700 ELCN 92243 6559-H1
MULBERRY ST
3700 OCN 92054 1086-F2
6500 SD 92114 1290-D1
MULBERRY TREE CT
13600 PWY 92064 1190-E4
MULBERRY TREE LN
13100 PWY 92064 1190-E4
MULDER ST
2400 LMGR 91945 1270-H7
MULGRAVE RD
11000 SD 92131 1209-H1
MULGREW ST
400 ELCJ 92019 1252-A6
MULHOLLAND CT
12200 SD 92128 1190-B3
MULLEN WY
1000 VSTA 92083 1107-J1
MULLINIX DR
1700 CORD 92118 1289-A6
MULVANEY DR
8600 SD 92119 1250-J4
8600 SD 92119 1251-A3
MUNCIE CT
1800 SDCo 92019 1272-D3
MUNDA RD
1500 SD 92139 1290-D6
2300 CORD 92155 1309-A2
MUNDIAL ST
11500 SD 92131 1210-B1
MUNDY TER
600 ELCJ 92020 1251-D4
MUNEVAR CT
700 ENCT 92007 1167-E1
MUNEVAR RD
700 ENCT 92007 1167-E1
MUNROE ST
4600 LMSA 91941 1270-G3
MUNSTER PLATZ WY
31100 SDCo 92082 1069-G3
MURAL ST
600 OCN 92057 1087-C1
MURANO LN
9500 SDCo 92127 1169-E2
MURAT CT
4600 SD 92117 1248-C1
MURAT PL
4700 SD 92117 1248-C1
MURAT ST
2800 SD 92117 1248-B1
MURCIA CT
2100 SD 92037 1247-H1
MUREL TRAILS
14000 PWY 92064 1190-J3
14000 PWY 92064 1191-A2
MURIEL LN
500 ESCN 92025 1130-A7
MURIEL PL
7400 LMSA 91941 1270-G4
MURILLO LN
7000 CRLB 92009 1127-G7
MURPHY AV
4500 SD 92122 1228-F5
MURPHY RD
- CORD 91932 1329-F5
- ImCo 92251 431-B4
MURPHY CANYON RD
2400 SD 92123 1249-F1
5500 SD 92123 1229-E7
MURRAY AV
400 ELCJ 92020 1251-D6
MURRAY CT
100 ESCN 92025 1129-G4
MURRAY DR
200 ELCJ 92020 1251-D6
200 LMSA 91942 1271-A1
5200 LMSA 91942 1270-J1
8900 LMSA 91942 1251-C6

MURRAY ST — SAN DIEGO CO. STREET INDEX — NORTHCREST CT 6604

STREET
Block City ZIP Pg-Grid

MURRAY ST
- CORD 92135 1288-F3
- CHV 91910 1310-C7
MURRAY CANYON RD
1600 SD 92108 1269-A2
MURRAY HILL RD
3800 LMSA 91941 1270-F5
MURRAY PARK CT
6300 SD 92119 1250-E6
MURRAY PARK DR
6600 SD 92120 1250-E6
6700 SD 92119 1250-E6
MURRAY RANCHO RD
1900 SDCo 92020 1272-A1
MURRAY RIDGE RD
3300 SD 92123 1249-C5
MURRIETA CIR
4400 SD 92154 1330-G6
MUSCAT ST
2000 SD 92105 1290-B1
MUSEUM CT
1000 OCN 92057 1087-B2
MUSIC LN
500 SDCo 92026 1109-H2
MUSLO LN
7300 CRLB 92009 1148-A1
MUSSEY GRADE RD
13700 SDCo 92065 1192-A1
15000 SDCo 92065 1172-A5
15200 SDCo 92065 1171-J5
MUSTANG DR
12500 PWY 92064 1190-C6
MUSTANG GN
600 ESCN 92027 1130-B2
MUSTANG PL
300 CHV 91902 1310-G4
MUSTANG ST
4100 SD 92111 1249-A3
MUSTANG WY
1600 OCN 92057 1067-E7
3200 SMCS 92069 1108-C6
MUTH VALLEY RD
11800 SDCo 92040 1212-B3
MUUTAMA LN
13500 SDCo 92082 1050-D3
MUUTAMA RD
36200 SDCo 92082 1050-B4
MY WY
700 SD 92154 1330-B7
MYCENAE WY
5000 OCN 92056 1107-F5
MYCORTE DR
700 SDCo 92026 1109-D6
MYERS DR
9400 SD 92093 1228-A2
MYERS ST
100 OCN 92054 1106-A1
300 OCN 92054 1086-A7
400 OCN 92054 1085-J7
S MYERS ST
100 OCN 92054 1106-A1
MYKONOS LN
3800 SD 92130 1188-A6
MYKRANTZ TKTR
25100 SDCo 92065 1173-H7
MYNAH PL
500 VSTA 92083 1087-F4
MYRA AV
600 CHV 91910 1310-E7
800 CHV 91911 1330-F1
1100 CHV 91911 1330-F2
MYRA CT
1300 CHV 91911 1330-F3
1600 CHV 91911 1330-G4
1600 CHV 91911 1330-G5
MYRA ST
2700 LMGR 91945 1270-H7
MYRICA LN
17900 SD 92127 1149-J7
MYRICKS CT
1000 SDCo 92065 1152-G6
MYRTLE AV
1200 SD 92103 1269-B6
1900 SD 92104 1269-C6
3300 SD 92105 1269-G6
MYRTLE CT
- SDCo 92026 1089-B2
900 CRLB 92009 1127-A7
MYRTLE LN
4800 LMSA 91941 1271-B2
MYRTLE RD
2300 ImCo 92243 6499-F2
2300 IMP 92243 6499-F2
MYRTLE ST
- OCN 92054 1066-G7
14100 SDCo 91935 1272-H7
MYRTLE WY
1000 SD 92103 1269-B6
MYRTLE BEACH WY
2400 CHV 91915 1311-H7
MYRTLEWOOD CT
500 ESCN 92027 1110-D6
600 OCN 92054 1086-F2
MYSTERY MOUNTAIN RD
11000 SDCo 92082 1069-F7
MYSTIC HILL RD
1500 SDCo 92084 1068-B6
MYSTIK RD
4600 OCN 92056 1087-D4
MYSTRA DR
4000 OCN 92056 1107-E4

N

N AV
800 NATC 91950 1309-J1
800 NATC 91950 1310-A1
2800 CHV 91950 1310-A3
N CT
- SD 92126 1209-F7
N ST
100 ENCT 92007 1167-C1
NABAL DR
4000 SDCo 91941 1271-F3
NABAL ST
700 ESCN 92025 1150-C1
700 SDCo 92025 1150-C1
NACIDO CT
16200 SD 92128 1170-C4
NACIDO DR
12300 SD 92128 1170-C4
NACION AV
700 CHV 91910 1310-F7
900 CHV 91911 1330-F1
NADEEN WY
500 ELCJ 92021 1251-H4
NAGA WY
8700 SD 92093 1227-H3
NAGEL ST
5600 LMSA 91942 1250-J7
NAGORSKI LN
29900 SDCo 92082 1070-E5
NAHANT CT
700 SD 92109 1267-H1
NAIAD ST
400 ENCT 92024 1147-B4
NALCO ST
11100 SD 92126 1209-B2
NALINI CT
9300 SNTE 92071 1230-H6
NANCITA CT
6000 SD 92114 1290-C4
NANCY DR
6000 LMSA 91942 1251-B6
NANCY ST
500 ESCN 92027 1130-C1
NANCY WY
1100 VSTA 92083 1107-J1
NANCY LEE LN
1300 SDCo 91901 1233-H6
NANCY RIDGE DR
6300 SD 92121 1208-F7
6300 SD 92121 1228-H1
NANDINA CT
9000 SDCo 92026 1069-A6
NANDINA DR
29700 SDCo 92026 1069-A5
NANETTE LN
6100 SD 92122 1228-G5
NANETTE ST
400 CHV 91911 1330-G1
NANNETTE ST
5100 SDCo 91902 1290-H7
NANSEN AV
2600 SD 92122 1228-B6
NANTASKET CT
700 SD 92109 1267-H1
NANTUCKET CT
500 ENCT 92024 1147-B2
NANTUCKET DR
500 CHV 91911 1330-H2
NANTUCKET GN
400 ESCN 92027 1110-D6
NANTUCKET LN
2800 CRLB 92008 1107-A5
NAOMI DR
1000 VSTA 92083 1087-G4
NAPA AV
1100 CHV 91911 1330-F2
NAPA CT
1400 CHV 91911 1330-G3
3600 OCN 92056 1107-F3
NAPA DR
200 SMCS 92069 1108-H5
NAPA ST
5300 SD 92110 1268-F3
NAPIER ST
4100 SD 92110 1268-E1
NAPLES CT
600 OCN 92057 1067-C7
600 OCN 92057 1087-C1
2700 CRLB 92008 1106-J4
E NAPLES CT
200 CHV 91911 1330-H1
NAPLES PL
4900 SD 92110 1268-E3
NAPLES ST
- CHV 91911 1330-C3
1100 SD 92110 1268-E2
E NAPLES ST
- CHV 91911 1330-G1
NAPOLI ST
1300 OCN 92056 1087-C3
NARANCA AV
700 ELCJ 92021 1251-H4
1300 ELCJ 92021 1252-A4
1600 SDCo 92019 1252-B4
NARANJA ST
1800 ESCN 92025 1130-A5
5100 SD 92114 1290-A4
NARCISSUS DR
- SD 92109 1248-D6
2600 SD 92106 1268-C6
NARDITO LN
600 SOLB 92075 1187-F1
N NARDO AV
100 SOLB 92075 1167-F7
S NARDO AV
100 SOLB 92075 1167-F7
300 SOLB 92075 1187-F1
NARDO RD
600 ENCT 92024 1147-D7
900 ENCT 92024 1167-D1
NARRAGANSETT AV
3600 SD 92106 1288-B1
3700 SD 92107 1268-A7
3700 SD 92107 1288-B1
4500 SD 92107 1267-H6
NARRAGANSETT CT
1800 SD 92107 1268-A7
NARRAGANSETT BAY DR
1900 SD 92105 1290-B1
NARWHAL ST
800 SD 92154 1330-E7
NASH LN
1100 VSTA 92083 1087-E7
NASHVILLE ST
1300 SD 92110 1268-E2
NASSAU DR
3600 SD 92115 1270-E5
NATAL WY
100 VSTA 92083 1087-J7
NATALIE DR
4500 SD 92115 1269-J3
NATCHEZ AV
3100 SD 92117 1248-F6
NATCHEZ TR
34500 SDCo 92036 1176-E4
NATCHKA CREEK ST
- CHV 91913 1311-E7
NATE WY
10400 SNTE 92071 1231-E3
NATE HARRISON GRADE
- SDCo 92060 409-F6
- SDCo 92060 1051-D1
16000 SDCo 92061 1051-D1
NATHAN ST
3000 LMGR 91945 1270-H6
NATHANIEL CT
- SDCo 92127 1169-A3
NATHANIEL LN
- SDCo 91901 1253-H1
NATIONAL AV
- SD 92113 1289-C5
1200 SD 92101 1289-C5
NATIONAL GN
1700 ESCN 92026 1109-D4
NATIONAL CITY BLVD
- NATC 91950 1289-H7
200 NATC 91950 1309-H1
NATOMA WY
1200 OCN 92057 1087-B3
NATURES WY
- SDCo 92066 (1299-C2 See Page 1298)
NAUGATUCK AV
2900 SD 92117 1248-C1
NAUTICAL DR
3700 CRLB 92008 1106-F6
NAUTILUS ST
- SDCo 92055 1085-H5
200 SD 92037 1247-E1
NAVA CT
100 SOLB 92075 1167-D7
NAVA WY
100 SOLB 92075 1167-D7
NAVAJA LN
11900 SDCo 92020 1271-J2
NAVAJA RD
1600 SDCo 92020 1271-J2
NAVAJO AV
4300 OCN 92056 1087-C5
NAVAJO PL
1800 ESCN 92029 1129-F5
NAVAJO RD
2600 ELCJ 92020 1251-A4
5800 SD 92120 1250-D5
6800 SD 92119 1250-G4
8600 SD 92119 1251-A4
34600 SDCo 92036 1176-D4
NAVAJO ST
100 SMCS 92069 1108-D7
NAVARRA DR
2500 CRLB 92009 1147-G1
NAVARRO ST
4400 OCN 92057 1086-H1
NAVEL PL
1200 SDCo 92083 1107-G3
1200 VSTA 92083 1107-G3
1400 SDCo 92027 1130-D4
NAVELLO ST
1100 ELCJ 92021 1252-A3
NAVELLO TER
1300 ELCJ 92021 1251-J3
1300 ELCJ 92021 1252-A2
NAVIGATOR CIR
3200 OCN 92056 1107-A2
7500 CRLB 92009 1127-A7
7500 CRLB 92009 1147-A1
NAVIGATOR CT
600 CRLB 92009 1127-A7
NAWA CT
15400 SD 92129 1169-H6
NAWA WY
11300 SD 92129 1169-H6
NAYLOR RD
2700 SD 92173 1350-F4
NAZARETH DR
- SD 92108 1249-G7
NAZAS DR
12400 PWY 92064 1170-C7
NEALE ST
1600 SD 92103 1268-H6
NEBLINA DR
4900 CRLB 92008 1106-H7
NEBO DR
4400 LMSA 91941 1270-H2
NEBRASKA AV
7200 SD 92139 1290-G6
NECHES CT
3800 SDCo 92004 (1099-D2 See Page 1098)
NECKEL RD
100 ImCo 92251 431-B4
NECTAR WY
23900 SDCo 92065 1173-E5
NECTARINE CIR
3700 OCN 92054 1086-G2
NECTARINE DR
9600 SDCo 92040 1232-A4
NEDDICK AV
1700 PWY 92064 1190-H4
NEDRA LN
800 ELCJ 92019 1252-B7
NEEDHAM RD
2300 ELCJ 92020 1251-B4
NEEDLEGRASS DR
3300 SD 92115 1270-D6
NEEDLEROCK RD
800 ESCN 92025 1150-C1
800 SDCo 92025 1150-C1
NEGLEY AV
4900 SD 92117 1228-F7
NEGLEY DR
11600 SD 92131 1210-A4
NEIGHBORLY LN
900 SDCo 92065 1153-A6
NEIL TER
200 SDCo 92084 1067-H7
NEILL RD
200 ImCo 92243 6500-D6
NEILSON LN
1700 SDCo 92026 1109-F4
NELLA LN
29700 SDCo 92084 1068-E6
NELMS ST
1200 OCN 92054 1086-B6
NELSON LN
13100 PWY 92064 1190-H4
NELSON RD
8600 SDCo 92026 1068-J4
NELSON ST
6100 SD 92115 1270-C5
NELSON WY
8600 SDCo 92026 1068-J3
8600 SDCo 92026 1069-A3
NELSON PIT RD
2500 ImCo 92250 431-F5
NEMAHA DR
- SD 92117 1248-D3
NEMO ST
12700 PWY 92064 1190-D4
NENTRA ST
8400 LMSA 91942 1250-J6
NEOMA ST
2400 SD 92109 1248-B5
NEOSHO PL
3200 SD 92117 1248-D1
NEPETA WY
6700 CRLB 92009 1126-J5
NEPTUNE AV
1000 CHV 91911 1330-F1
1000 ENCT 92024 1147-A3
NEPTUNE CT
700 CHV 91910 1310-F7
NEPTUNE DR
1000 CHV 91911 1330-G2
7400 CRLB 92009 1127-A7
NEPTUNE PL
100 ESCN 92026 1109-H6
200 SD 92037 1247-E1
NEPTUNE WY
200 OCN 92054 1085-J7
500 OCN 92054 1086-A7
NERAK CT
5500 SDCo 91902 1290-J7
NEREIS DR
3600 SDCo 91941 1271-A5
3600 SDCo 91977 1271-A5
NEREUS ST
10400 SD 92124 1249-G3
NERI DR
7000 LMSA 91941 1270-E4
NERINE WY
- CRLB 92009 1127-D4
NESMITH DR
11000 SDCo 92026 1089-G7
NESMITH PL
26500 SDCo 92026 1089-H7
NESTOR WY
1100 SD 92154 1350-B1
NETTLE PL
3500 SDCo 92028 1048-C3
NETTLETON RD
100 VSTA 92083 1107-C1
200 VSTA 92083 1087-C7
NEVA AV
8300 SD 92123 1249-C5
NEVADA AV
100 VSTA 92084 1087-H5
NEVADA GN
2200 ESCN 92029 1129-E6
NEVADA ST
100 OCN 92054 1086-A6
100 OCN 92054 1106-B1
N NEVADA ST
100 OCN 92054 1086-A7
NEVILLE CIR
- SDCo 92055 1066-J1
- SDCo 92055 1067-A1
NEVILLE RD
- SD 92140 1268-E7
NEVIN ST
1100 SD 92154 1350-G1
NEVOSO WY
11500 SD 92127 1149-J7
11500 SD 92127 1150-A6
NEW ST
100 ELCN 92243 6499-J6
NEW BEDFORD CT
10200 SDCo 92040 1231-J3
NEWBERRY ST
3200 NATC 91950 1310-D3
6800 SD 92120 1249-J5
NEWBOLD CT
6800 SD 92111 1268-J1
NEW BRANCH CT
3300 OCN 92054 1086-D2
NEWCASTLE AV
2000 ENCT 92007 1167-D3
NEWCASTLE CT
1200 CHV 91913 1311-C7
6000 SD 92114 1290-C5
NEWCASTLE PL
6100 SD 92114 1290-C5
NEWCASTLE ST
5900 SD 92114 1290-C5
NEWCASTLE WY
2800 CRLB 92008 1107-A3
NEW CHATEL DR
1300 SD 92154 1350-A2
NEW COLT CT
9400 SDCo 92021 1232-G4
NEWCREST PT
3600 SD 92130 1187-J4
3600 SD 92130 1188-A4
NEWELL ST
1800 NATC 91950 1310-B2
2500 SDCo 91950 1310-B2
3000 SD 92106 1288-B1
NEW HAMPSHIRE ST
4400 SD 92116 1269-A4
NEW HAVEN DR
2100 CHV 91913 1311-E3
NEW HAVEN PL
4400 SD 92117 1228-F7
4500 CRLB 92008 1107-B4
NEW HAVEN RD
1900 SMCS 92069 1128-B4
4900 SD 92117 1228-F7
NEWHOPE CT
1400 SD 92114 1290-F5
NEW JERSEY AV
2400 LMGR 91945 1270-G7
NEW JERSEY ST
4300 SD 92103 1269-B4
4300 SD 92116 1269-B4
NEWKIRK DR
900 SD 92037 1247-F2
NEWLAND RD
3500 OCN 92056 1107-E3
NEWLIN LN
9000 SD 92126 1209-E7
NEWMAN WY
- SDCo 92066 1135-G7
NEW MILLS RD
5400 SD 92115 1270-B3
NEWMONT DR
8900 SD 92129 1189-C2
NEW MORNING RD
11200 SDCo 91941 1271-G4
NEW ORLEANS AV
200 SD 92173 1350-G5
NEWPORT AV
2200 ENCT 92007 1167-D4
4200 SD 92107 1268-A7
4600 SD 92107 1267-J6
NEWPORT CT
900 CHV 91911 1330-J2
NEWPORT DR
100 SMCS 92069 1108-E7
600 VSTA 92084 1087-J5
NEWPORT ST
900 OCN 92057 1066-H6
NEWPORT TER
700 VSTA 92084 1087-J5
NEWPORT WY
3700 CRLB 92008 1107-A4
NEWPORTER WY
14000 SD 92128 1190-A2
NEW RANCH RD
4800 SDCo 92020 1271-H2
NEW SALEM CIR
10900 SD 92126 1209-A3
NEW SALEM CT
10900 SD 92126 1209-A3
NEW SALEM CV
10800 SD 92126 1209-A3
NEW SALEM PL
10800 SD 92126 1209-A3
NEW SALEM PT
10800 SD 92126 1209-B3
NEW SALEM ST
7300 SD 92126 1208-J3
7500 SD 92126 1209-A3
NEW SALEM TER
10800 SD 92126 1209-B3
NEW SALEM WY
10800 SD 92126 1208-J3
NEW SEABURY DR
8900 SNTE 92071 1230-J4
8900 SNTE 92071 1231-A4
NEW SEABURY WY
2400 CHV 91915 1311-H7
NEWSHIRE ST
3000 CRLB 92008 1107-A3
NEWSOME DR
6300 SD 92115 1270-D5
NEWTON AV
3700 SD 92113 1289-G6
NEWTON DR
5800 CRLB 92008 1127-C1
NEW YORK ST
4500 SD 92116 1269-B4
NEXUS CENTRE DR
4700 SD 92121 1228-E2
NIAGARA AV
4200 SD 92107 1268-A7
4500 SD 92107 1267-J6
NIANTIC CT
700 SD 92109 1267-H1
NIBLICK DR
3300 SDCo 91941 1270-J5
NIBLICK TER
2100 OCN 92056 1086-H7
NICADO VEREDA
MONTECITA
2100 SDCo 92028 998-C5
NICARAGUA CIR
- SD 92140 1268-F6
NICHALS ST
7800 LMGR 91945 1290-G1
NICHOLAS LN
700 ELCJ 92019 1252-B7
NICHOLAS PL
1500 ELCJ 92019 1252-B6
NICHOLAS ST
- SDCo 92055 1067-A1
700 ELCJ 92019 1252-B6
NICHOLAS WY
1600 ELCJ 92019 1252-B6
NICHOLS RD
- ImCo 92251 6499-B2
900 ImCo 92243 6559-C1
1900 ImCo 92243 6499-B2
NICHOLS ST
2900 SD 92106 1288-A4
NICKLAUS DR
2300 OCN 92056 1106-H2
NICKMAN ST
400 CHV 91911 1330-C3
NICOLA RANCH RD
2100 SDCo 92028 998-A7
NICOLA TESLA CT
9400 SD 92154 1352-A3
NICOLE DR
300 VSTA 92084 1087-H4
NICOLE ST
1900 SDCo 92065 1153-A1
1900 SDCo 92065 1152-J1
NICOLE WY
9500 SNTE 92071 1231-C5
NICOLES VISTA
- SDCo 92082 1050-E7
NICOLIA DR
1800 CRLB 92009 1127-D4
NICOLINA DR
8300 SDCo 92028 997-H7
NICOLO CT
500 ESCN 92025 1130-A6
NICOSIA LN
10900 SDCo 92040 1231-F3
NIDA PL
2600 LMGR 91945 1270-H7
NIDER RD
- ImCo - 411-D8
NIDO LN
4500 SD 92117 1248-D2
NIDO AGUILA
2300 SDCo 91901 1254-C1
NIDRAH ST
1000 ELCJ 92020 1251-E7
NIEGO LN
12500 SD 92128 1170-C4
NIELS BOHR CT
2200 SD 92154 1352-A3
NIELSEN CT
2300 ELCJ 92020 1251-B1
NIELSEN ST
2200 ELCJ 92020 1251-B1
NIEMANN RANCH RD
6600 SDCo 92067 1188-G2
NIGHTFALL TER
13000 SD 92128 1189-H5
NIGHTHAWK CT
5000 OCN 92056 1107-E4
7000 CRLB 92009 1127-E6
NIGHTHAWK WY
4900 OCN 92056 1107-E3
NIGHTINGALE PL
1000 ESCN 92027 1110-C5
NIGHTINGALE WY
4700 SD 92123 1249-B6
NIGHTSHADE RD
1300 CRLB 92009 1127-B5
NIGHTSKY RD
- SDCo 92065 1173-D2
NIGHT STAR CT
2400 SDCo 91901 1234-B5
NIGHT STAR PL
2400 SDCo 91901 1234-B5
NIGHTWATCH WY
- SDCo 91901 1254-A3
NIKI LYNN PL
1100 CRLB 92008 1106-E4
NIKITA CT
12100 SD 92131 1210-B1
NIKKI LN
13400 SDCo 92082 1070-D1
NILA LN
400 ELCJ 92020 1271-G1
NILAND AV
- ImCo 92233 411-B8
NILAND AV
- ImCo 92257 411-B8
NILAND MARINA RD
- ImCo 92257 411-A6
NILE AV
1100 CHV 91911 1330-G2
NILE CT
1200 CHV 91911 1330-G2
NILE ST
2700 SD 92104 1269-F6
NILES AV
- ImCo 92274 410-H6
NILO WY
1700 SD 92139 1290-H6
NIMBUS LN
1100 SD 92110 1268-G3
NIMITZ BLVD
2700 SD 92133 1288-C1
2700 SD 92106 1288-C1
3500 SD 92106 1268-B6
3700 SD 92107 1268-B6
NINA CT
1900 SDCo 91977 1291-A1
NINA PL
1900 ESCN 92026 1109-H5
NINA RD
- ImCo 92249 6560-C7
2600 LMGR 91945 1270-F7
NINA ST
3500 OCN 92056 1106-J1
NIPOMA PL
3800 SD 92106 1268-C5
NIPOMA ST
2700 SD 92106 1268-C6
NIRA LN
31700 SDCo 92003 1068-G1
NIRVANA AV
1800 CHV 91911 1331-A5
NITA CT
900 CHV 91911 1330-F1
8700 SNTE 92071 1231-E7
NITA LN
1000 VSTA 92083 1087-G4
8700 SNTE 92071 1231-E7
NIVEL CT
12000 SD 92128 1170-B4
NIXON CIR
100 OCN 92057 1067-B6
NIXON PL
5900 SD 92120 1250-D7
NOAH WY
5200 SD 92117 1228-F6
NOAKES RD
10500 SDCo 91941 1271-F1
E NOAKES ST
100 SDCo 92019 1253-D1
W NOAKES ST
100 SDCo 92019 1253-C1
NOB AV
100 DLMR 92014 1187-G6
100 SD 92014 1187-G6
NOB CIR
700 VSTA 92084 1087-J4
NOBEL DR
- SD 92145 1228-D4
3300 SD 92037 1228-A3
3400 SD 92122 1228-D4
NOB HILL DR
1500 ESCN 92026 1109-H6
1500 SDCo 92026 1109-H6
2200 CRLB 92008 1106-G4
NOBLE ST
1800 LMGR 91945 1290-G1
NOBLE CANYON RD
2500 CHV 91915 1311-H5
NOCHE TAPATIA
7300 SDCo 92067 1168-G2
NOCTURNE CT
300 CHV 91911 1330-F2
NODEN ST
200 ELCJ 92020 1251-G7
NOELINE AV
8300 SD 92114 1290-J4
8500 SDCo 91977 1290-J4
8800 SDCo 91977 1291-A4
NOELINE CT
100 SD 92114 1290-H4
NOELINE LN
8300 SD 92114 1290-H4
NOELINE PL
8400 SD 92114 1290-H4
NOELINE WY
100 SD 92114 1290-J4
NOELL ST
3400 SD 92110 1268-G6
NOFFSINGER RD
- ImCo - 411-C8
- ImCo 92233 411-C8
- ImCo 92257 411-B8
NOGAL ST
200 SD 92102 1289-J4
4800 SD 92102 1290-A4
NOGALES DR
13600 SD 92014 1187-G6
NOKOMIS ST
5500 LMSA 91942 1251-B7
NOKONI DR
13300 PWY 92064 1190-E4
NOLAN AV
700 CHV 91910 1310-F7
1100 CHV 91911 1330-F2
NOLAN CT
1400 CHV 91911 1330-G3
NOLAN LN
1000 CHV 91911 1330-F1
NOLAN PL
4700 SDCo 92020 1271-H2
NOLAN RD
- ImCo 92227 431-D2
NOLAN WY
300 CHV 91911 1330-F1
NOLBEY ST
800 ENCT 92007 1167-E2
NOLINA CT
- CRLB 92009 1127-D4
NOMA LN
1600 ENCT 92024 1147-B2
NOMAD PL
4000 ESCN 92025 1150-D4
NOMEL LN
2700 LMGR 91945 1270-H7
NON RD
16300 SDCo 92082 1091-B1
NONIE TER
12400 SD 92129 1189-C6
NORAAK CT
5900 LMSA 91942 1250-G6
NORCANYON WY
7600 SD 92126 1209-A1
NORCROFT RD
13200 SD 92130 1188-B4
NORDAHL RD
500 ESCN 92029 1129-D1
500 SMCS 92029 1129-D1
600 SMCS 92069 1129-D1
900 SMCS 92069 1109-E7
900 ImCo 92283 432-D4
1000 SDCo 92026 1109-E7
1300 ESCN 92026 1109-E7
NORDICA AV
4000 SD 92113 1289-H7
NOREEN CT
900 SMCS 92069 1109-C5
NOREEN PL
100 OCN 92054 1086-E5
NOREEN WY
3100 OCN 92054 1086-E5
N NOREEN WY
1100 ESCN 92027 1110-A6
1100 ESCN 92027 1109-J6
NORELLA ST
900 CHV 91910 1310-J6
NOREN PL
2800 SD 92106 1288-B3
NORFOLK DR
100 ENCT 92007 1167-E3
NORFOLK ST
2400 NATC 91950 1290-A6
NORFOLK TER
4000 SD 92116 1269-G2
NORLAK AV
700 ESCN 92025 1129-H3
NORM ST
600 SD 92114 1290-H3
NORMA CT
1000 CHV 91911 1330-F1
NORMA DR
4500 SD 92115 1269-J3
NORMA ST
2600 OCN 92056 1087-C7
NORMA GARDENS DR
10200 SNTE 92071 1231-D4
NORMAL AV
7500 LMSA 91941 1270-H3
NORMAL ST
3900 SD 92103 1269-C5
NORMAN LN
5900 SD 92120 1250-D7
NORMANDIE CT
2700 SDCo 92025 1130-E7
NORMANDIE PL
4500 LMSA 91941 1270-F3
4800 SD 92115 1270-F3
NORMANDY CIR
3500 OCN 92056 1107-E2
NORMANDY GN
1800 ESCN 92027 1110-A5
NORMANDY LN
200 CRLB 92008 1106-D5
NORMANDY RD
600 ENCT 92024 1147-C4
NORMANDY WY
700 SDCo 92019 1253-C2
NORMANDY HILL LN
1000 ENCT 92024 1147-C4
NORMAN SCOTT RD
2800 SD 92136 1289-E7
3700 NATC 92136 1289-F7
NORMAN SMITH ST
2700 SD 92110 1268-E6
NORMAN STRASSE RD
2900 SMCS 92069 1108-D5
NORMANTON CT
11200 SD 92131 1209-H2
NORMANTON WY
11100 SD 92131 1209-G2
NORMARK TER
800 VSTA 92084 1087-J6
NORMOUNT RD
3500 OCN 92056 1107-F3
NORRAN AV
1500 ELCJ 92019 1252-B6
NORRIS RD
5100 SD 92115 1270-A2
NORRISH RD
1700 ImCo 92250 431-D4
NORSE LN
800 SDCo 92025 1130-C4
NORS RANCH RD
1400 SDCo 92003 1068-B4
NORSTAD AV
500 SD 92154 1330-E6
NORSTAD ST
600 SD 92154 1330-E7
NORSTAR LN
1500 SDCo 92028 1047-J2
1600 SDCo 92028 1048-A2
NORTE DR
23800 SDCo 92065 1173-D2
NORTE MESA DR
9900 SDCo 91977 1271-D5
NORTE VILLA WY
2700 ESCN 92027 1110-D5
NORTH AV
500 SDCo 92026 1109-H2
600 ESCN 92026 1109-H2
700 OCN 92056 1087-E5
700 VSTA 92083 1087-E5
1700 SD 92116 1269-C4
6800 LMGR 91945 1270-E6
NORTH CT
100 ENCT 92024 1147-B5
4700 SD 92116 1269-C3
NORTH DR
1000 VSTA 92083 1087-G4
NORTH LN
100 SDCo 92021 1252-H3
200 SD 92037 1247-E1
400 SD 92173 1350-F3
4200 SDCo 92014 1167-J7
4200 SOLB 92014 1167-J7
4400 SDCo 92014 1168-A7
11400 SDCo 92040 1231-H6
NORTH WY
3500 OCN 92056 1106-J2
3600 OCN 92056 1107-A2
NORTHAVEN AV
4900 SD 92110 1248-F7
4900 SD 92110 1268-F1
NORTHBROOK CT
1900 SDCo 92083 1108-C3
NORTHCLIFF DR
3500 SDCo 92028 1048-E1
NORTHCOTE RD
9000 SNTE 92071 1231-G5
NORTHCREST CT
8500 SNTE 92071 1231-B7

SAN DIEGO CO.
INDEX

STREET
Block City ZIP Pg-Grid

NORTHCREST LN
1500 VSTA 92083 1087-G3
13800 PWY 92064 1170-G6
NORTHERLY ST
4800 OCN 92056 1087-D3
NORTH FORK DR
- SDCo 92084 1068-D5
NORTHGATE ST
300 SD 92114 1290-F5
NORTHHILL TER
11800 SDCo 92040 1231-J5
NORTHMORE PL
4700 OCN 92056 1087-E3
NORTH PARK DR
100 SDCo 92021 1252-H3
NORTH PARK WY
2800 SD 92104 1269-E5
NORTH PEAK RD
15400 SDCo 92036 1176-C3
NORTH POINT DR
- SD 92093 1207-J7
- SD 92093 1208-A7
NORTH POINT LN
10000 SD 92093 1207-J7
NORTHRIDGE AV
5200 SD 92117 1228-H7
NORTHRIDGE CT
5400 SD 92117 1228-H6
NORTHRIDGE PL
9300 SNTE 92071 1251-B1
NORTHRIM CT
1400 SD 92111 1268-H2
NORTHROP RD
- ImCo 92243 431-A6
- ImCo 92243 6559-A4
NORTHRUP DR
7400 SD 92126 1208-J5
7400 SD 92126 1209-A5
NORTHRUP PL
7600 SD 92126 1209-A5
NORTHRUP PT
10000 SD 92126 1209-A5
NORTH SHORE DR
100 SOLB 92075 1187-E2
NORTHSHORE DR
2000 CHV 91913 1311-E3
NORTHSIDE DR
2300 SD 92108 1249-E7
2300 SD 92108 1269-E1
NORTH SLOPE TER
8900 SDCo 91977 1291-A1
NORTH STAR DR
3200 SD 92117 1248-D3
NORTHVIEW CIR
9300 SNTE 92071 1231-B7
NORTH VIEW CT
9800 SDCo 92026 1069-D7
NORTHVIEW DR
1300 SDCo 92019 1251-J7
NORTHVIEW LN
8500 SNTE 92071 1231-B7
8500 SNTE 92071 1251-B1
NORTH VIEW LN
29100 SDCo 92026 1069-D7
NORTHVIEW RD
- ESCN 92029 1149-G1
NORTHVIEW TER
9300 SNTE 92071 1231-B7
NORTHWEST
- SD 92109 1248-C6
NORTHWICK WY
- SD 92131 1209-G2
NORTHWOOD CIR
9100 SD 92126 1209-D3
NORTHWOOD DR
3300 OCN 92054 1086-E2
18000 SDCo 91935 1274-C3
NORTON AV
100 NATC 91950 1289-J7
NORWALK AV
4700 SD 92117 1248-D1
NORWALK LN
14400 PWY 92064 1190-E2
NORWALK ST
13400 PWY 92064 1190-E2
NORWAY CT
600 ESCN 92025 1129-J2
NORWICH PL
4500 CRLB 92008 1107-B4
NORWICH ST
5500 SD 92117 1228-H7
NORWOOD ST
4500 SD 92115 1269-J4
NORWOOD WY
800 ESCN 92025 1129-G4
NORWYNN LN
600 SDCo 92028 1027-J4
NORZEL DR
3100 SD 92111 1248-G5
NOSTALGIA PL
1000 VSTA 92084 1108-A1
NOTHOMB ST
300 ELCJ 92019 1252-A6
NOTNIL CT
9700 SNTE 92071 1231-F4
NOTRE DAME AV
3700 SD 92122 1228-D6
NOTTINGHAM GN
2400 ESCN 92027 1110-D7
NOTTINGHAM PL
8500 SD 92037 1227-J3
NOUGHT ST
3500 SD 92115 1270-D6
NOVA GN
1800 ESCN 92026 1109-F6
NOVA PL
300 CHV 91911 1330-F1
NOVA WY
300 CHV 91911 1330-F1
NOVARA ST
1000 SD 92107 1287-H2
NOVATO PL
24400 SDCo 92065 1173-F2
NOVELETA ST
- SD 92140 1268-F7
NOYA WY
3200 OCN 92056 1086-J7
NOYES ST
4100 SD 92109 1248-B5
NUBBIN CT
10400 SNTE 92071 1231-E3
NUECES LN
2300 SDCo 91977 1271-E7
NUERTO LN
10000 SDCo 91977 1271-E7
NUESTRA LN
2800 SDCo 92028 1028-D6
NUEVA CASTILLA WY
7600 CRLB 92009 1147-G1

NUEVO MUNDO RD
- SDCo 92065 1173-C1
NUFFER RD
600 ImCo 92243 6559-E3
NUGENT CT
1000 ELCJ 92020 1251-A3
NUGGET CT
- SDCo 92040 1232-A1
NUMBERS AV
3400 OCN 92054 1086-E3
NURSERY RD
1500 SD 92101 1289-C2
NUTBY LN
9700 SDCo 92026 1049-C7
NUTE WY
3000 SD 92117 1248-C3
NUTMEG CIR
1800 ESCN 92026 1109-F6
NUTMEG LN
9700 SDCo 92029 1149-E2
NUTMEG PL
2700 SD 92104 1269-E7
NUTMEG ST
100 SD 92103 1269-A7
800 SD 92103 1288-J1
1800 ESCN 92026 1109-F3
1800 SDCo 92026 1109-F3
2800 SD 92104 1269-D7
4700 SD 92105 1269-J7
5200 SD 92105 1270-A7
W NUTMEG ST
400 SD 92103 1268-J7
400 SD 92103 1269-A7
NUTMEG WY
3800 OCN 92057 1086-H4
7000 CRLB 92009 1127-A6
NYE ST
2500 SD 92111 1248-H6
NYLER CT
9500 SNTE 92071 1231-C4

O

O AV
1200 NATC 91950 1310-A1
O CT
- SD 92126 1209-F7
OAK
- SDCo 92040 1232-D6
9800 SDCo 92021 1233-B3
OAK AV
300 CRLB 92008 1106-F5
OAK CT
300 CHV 91911 1330-G2
OAK DR
- SDCo 92019 1272-E3
1000 VSTA 92084 1087-J4
1000 VSTA 92084 1088-A4
29400 SDCo 91906 (1297-E5 See Page 1296)
OAK GN
100 SDCo 92025 1130-B6
OAK LN
- SDCo 92036 1156-F6
900 SDCo 92029 1149-E1
900 SDCo 92029 1129-H7
25100 SDCo 91916 1236-A2
28800 SDCo 92066 1237-B7
OAK PL
400 CHV 91911 1330-G2
37700 SDCo 91905 (1299-H3 See Page 1298)
OAK ST
- SDCo 92082 1090-B1
100 OCN 92054 1106-A2
300 SDCo 92065 1152-G4
600 VSTA 92083 1087-F6
900 ELCN 92243 6499-H4
3800 SMCS 92069 1128-C1
OAK TER
4600 OCN 92056 1087-D4
OAK WY
35000 SDCo 92036 1156-D7
OAKANA RD
24800 SDCo 92065 1153-F1
OAKBEND DR
10500 SD 92131 1210-A3
OAK BLUFF PL
- ESCN 92027 1110-G6
OAKBOURNE RD
9300 SNTE 92071 1230-J5
OAKBRANCH DR
300 ENCT 92024 1147-G7
300 ENCT 92024 1167-G1
OAK BRIDGE DR
- SDCo 92084 1068-C6
OAK BRIDGE TR
- SDCo 92003 1068-C4
OAKBROOK CT
1900 ELCJ 92019 1252-C4
12600 PWY 92064 1170-D3
OAK BURL LN
700 ENCT 92024 1147-G5
OAK CANYON PL
2400 ESCN 92025 1130-D6
OAK CANYON RD
15300 PWY 92064 1170-J5
15300 PWY 92064 1171-A5
OAK CLIFF DR
3100 SDCo 92028 1048-E1
OAK CREEK
14200 SDCo 92021 1232-G5
14800 SDCo 92082 1070-H3
OAKCREEK CT
2000 VSTA 92083 1107-H6
OAK CREEK DR
10600 SDCo 92040 1231-G1
11000 SDCo 92040 1211-F6
OAKCREEK LN
1400 VSTA 92083 1107-J5
OAK CREEK RD
14800 SDCo 92021 1232-J3
14800 SDCo 92021 1233-A2
OAK CREEK TR
16200 PWY 92064 1170-F4
OAKCREST DR
4000 SD 92105 1270-A5
OAK CREST RD
- SDCo 92028 998-G5
OAKCREST PARK DR
1100 ENCT 92024 1147-F7
OAKDALE AV
1200 ELCJ 92021 1251-J4
1300 ELCJ 92021 1252-A4
1500 ELCJ 92019 1252-A4
OAKDALE LN
500 ELCJ 92021 1251-J4
OAKDEN DR
1500 SD 92154 1350-B2

OAK FERN CT
11100 SD 92131 1209-J1
OAKFIELD CT
9500 SDCo 91977 1271-C6
OAKFIELD WY
12800 PWY 92064 1170-D3
OAK FOREST PL
- ESCN 92027 1110-G6
OAKFOREST RD
1500 SDCo 92070 1135-D4
OAKFORT CT
12400 SD 92131 1210-C4
OAKFORT PL
12400 SD 92131 1210-C4
OAKGATE RW
6000 SD 92037 1248-A1
OAK GLEN CIR
1000 SDCo 92019 1252-G6
OAK GLEN CT
7000 LMGR 91945 1290-F1
OAK GLEN DR
2000 VSTA 92083 1107-H3
OAK GLEN LN
3400 SD 92117 1248-D2
31000 SDCo 92082 1070-E1
OAK GLEN RD
13800 SDCo 92082 1070-E1
23400 SDCo 92082 1050-E7
W OAK GLEN RD
13600 SDCo 92082 1070-E1
OAK GLEN WY
3300 SDCo 92019 1252-G6
OAK GROVE DR
- SDCo 92036 1155-G4
9400 SDCo 91916 1236-A2
9700 SDCo 91916 1235-J1
OAK GROVE RD
17000 SDCo 92065 1151-H3
OAK GROVE TKTR
23400 SDCo 92060 409-G6
27000 SDCo 92086 409-G6
OAKHAM WY
7200 SD 92139 1290-G7
OAK HAVEN RD
1800 SDCo 91901 1234-A7
OAK HILL DR
1000 CHV 91915 1311-G5
1200 ESCN 92025 1130-B2
1300 ESCN 92027 1130-D1
2700 ESCN 92027 1110-E7
OAK HILL LN
2700 SDCo 92070 1135-F7
OAK HILLS LN
- SDCo 92028 999-G5
OAK HOLLOW RD
17200 SDCo 92065 1153-G6
OAKHURST DR
700 SD 92114 1290-C5
OAK ISLAND LN
4200 SDCo 92028 1028-G5
OAK KNOLL CT
2500 CHV 91914 1311-G3
OAK KNOLL DR
1200 VSTA 92084 1088-A4
13000 PWY 92064 1190-B5
OAK KNOLL LN
14600 SDCo 92082 1070-G3
OAK KNOLL RD
12200 PWY 92064 1190-B5
OAK LAKE LN
17800 SDCo 92036 1156-F7
OAK LAND RD
1600 SDCo 92036 1156-D2
OAKLAND RD
5300 LMSA 91942 1270-F1
OAKLAWN AV
- CHV 91910 1309-J5
400 CHV 91910 1310-A7
500 CHV 91910 1330-A1
800 CHV 91911 1330-B3
OAK LEAF CT
2000 VSTA 92083 1107-H3
OAKLEAF CT
3500 SDCo 91977 1271-C6
OAKLEAF DR
600 OCN 92054 1086-F2
OAKLEAF LN
1300 SDCo 92065 1172-G2
OAKLEAF PT
5300 SD 92124 1249-G1
OAK LEE LN
700 SDCo 91901 1234-C4
OAKLEY CT
23400 SDCo 92065 1173-C3
OAKLEY PL
23400 SDCo 92065 1173-C3
OAKLEY RD
16000 SDCo 92065 1173-C3
OAKLINE CT
13100 PWY 92064 1190-E1
OAKLINE RD
14700 PWY 92064 1190-E1
OAK MEADOW DR
23800 SDCo 92065 1173-D2
OAK MEADOW RD
14200 SDCo 92082 1070-F2
OAKMONT RD
26800 SDCo 92082 1090-F6
OAKMONT TER
9800 SDCo 92021 1233-A3
OAK MOUNTAIN RD
19400 SDCo 92065 1153-G2
OAK PARK DR
5200 SD 92105 1270-A7
OAK RANCH LN
10300 SDCo 92026 1089-E4
OAK RANCH PL
28000 SDCo 92026 1089-E3
OAK RANCH RD
27700 SDCo 92026 1089-E4
OAK RANCH WY
10300 SDCo 92026 1089-E3
OAKRIDGE CV
2400 SD 92014 1187-H5
OAK RIDGE LN
18500 SDCo 92065 1153-C6
OAKRIDGE PL
2300 ESCN 92026 1109-G4
OAKRIDGE RD
6200 SD 92120 1250-D4
7500 SNTE 92071 1230-G7
OAK RIDGE RD
9800 SDCo 92026 1089-D1
OAK RIDGE WY
2500 VSTA 92083 1107-H7
2500 VSTA 92083 1127-H1
OAKS CT
1400 SMCS 92069 1109-D6

OAKS CT
37700 SDCo 91905 (1299-H3 See Page 1298)
W OAKS WY
1700 CRLB 92009 1127-B3
OAK SHADE LN
- SDCo 92065 1172-D5
OAK SHADOWS DR
- SDCo 92026 1089-B2
OAKS HEIGHTS RD
900 SDCo 92036 1156-D1
OAKSHIRE CT
1800 SD 92102 1290-A1
OAKS NORTH DR
12500 SD 92128 1170-C1
OAK SPRINGS DR
2500 CHV 91915 1311-H6
16100 SDCo 92065 1173-C3
OAKSTAND CT
15500 PWY 92064 1170-F6
OAKSTAND RD
13800 PWY 92064 1170-F6
OAKSTONE CT
9900 SNTE 92071 1231-C3
OAKSTONE CREEK PL
- ESCN 92027 1110-E5
OAK TRAIL CT
14800 PWY 92064 1150-J6
OAK TRAIL RD
- SDCo 92027 1091-G6
26000 SDCo 92082 1091-G6
OAKTREE LN
700 SMCS 92069 1108-J6
OAK TREE LN
12800 PWY 92064 1190-C5
OAK TREE PL
500 ESCN 92027 1110-E6
OAKTREE WY
2800 SDCo 92028 1048-E1
OAKVALE LN
- SNTE 92071 1230-G5
OAKVALE RD
14900 SDCo 92027 1110-H3
14900 SDCo 92027 1111-A2
OAK VALLEY LN
- ESCN 92027 1110-G6
2800 SDCo 92084 1068-E7
OAK VALLEY RD
2000 SDCo 92065 1172-B4
OAK VALLEY TR
2400 SDCo 91935 1274-G6
OAKVIEW CT
3700 SDCo 92028 1048-E1
OAK VIEW PL
1900 SDCo 91901 1234-C7
OAK VIEW TER
1600 CHV 91902 1311-C3
OAK VIEW WY
1100 ESCN 92029 1129-D4
OAKVIEW WY
11900 SD 92128 1190-B6
OAK VILLAGE DR
- SDCo 92065 1152-G7
OAK VILLAGE PL
- SDCo 92065 1152-G7
OAKWOOD AV
- SD 92102 1289-G4
- SDCo 92102 1289-G4
OAKWOOD DR
3200 SDCo 92036 1156-E1
OAK WOOD LN
- ESCN 92027 1110-G7
OAKWOOD LN
- OCN 92054 1106-C1
11800 SDCo 92040 1231-J3
OAKWOOD WY
600 ELCJ 92021 1251-G4
OAKWOOD CREEK WY
- ESCN 92027 1110-E5
OAKWOOD GLEN PL
13800 SDCo 92082 1070-E7
OASIS AV
1100 CHV 91911 1330-G1
OASIS DR
1200 ESCN 92026 1129-F1
1200 SDCo 92026 1129-F1
OASIS LN
1500 VSTA 92083 1087-D6
OASIS RD
- SDCo 91948 1218-B2
OAT HILL RD
9800 SDCo 92026 1089-D1
O B DR
2100 SDCo 91901 1254-B1
OBELISCO CIR
7100 CRLB 92009 1127-H6
OBELISCO CT
2700 CRLB 92009 1127-H6
OBELISCO PL
2600 CRLB 92009 1127-H6
OBERLIN DR
5500 SD 92121 1208-E7
OBISPO LN
16700 SD 92128 1170-B3
OBISPO RD
11900 SD 92128 1170-B3
OBREGON AV
8500 SD 92145 1229-C1
8600 SD 92126 1229-C1
OBRIEN PL
2600 ESCN 92027 1110-D6
10100 SD 92124 1249-G2
OBSERVATION PL
3800 ESCN 92025 1150-D3
OBSIDIAN DR
16800 SDCo 92065 1171-D3
OBSIDIAN GN
- ESCN 92027 1110-C7
OCALA AV
1100 CHV 91911 1330-G1
OCALA CT
1400 CHV 91911 1330-G3
OCANA PL
4700 SD 92124 1250-A1
OCASO DR
12600 SD 92128 1170-C4
OCASO WY
4100 OCN 92056 1087-D5
OCCIDENTAL ST
3100 SD 92122 1228-C6
OCEAN AV
900 DLMR 92014 1187-F5
1200 SD 92154 1350-D1
OCEAN BLVD
200 CORD 92118 1288-G7
1000 CORD 92118 1308-H1
4100 SD 92109 1247-G5
OCEAN CT
- CORD 92118 1288-G7

OCEAN DR
- CORD 92118 1288-G7
OCEAN LN
700 IMPB 91932 1329-E7
900 IMPB 91932 1349-E1
8000 SD 92037 1227-E6
OCEAN ST
100 SOLB 92075 1167-E6
2300 CRLB 92008 1106-D5
OCEAN WY
900 IMPB 91932 1349-E1
E OCEAN AIR DR
10600 SD 92130 1208-C4
W OCEAN AIR DR
10500 SD 92130 1208-B4
OCEAN BEACH FRWY I-8
- SD - 1268-B5
OCEAN BLUFF AV
- SD 92130 1208-A3
OCEAN BLUFF WY
- ENCT 92024 1147-E7
OCEAN BREEZE CT
5200 SD 92109 1247-J4
OCEAN BREEZE ST
2000 SMCS 92069 1128-B3
OCEAN BREEZE WY
500 CHV 91914 1311-E3
3300 SDCo 91935 1273-B6
OCEAN COVE DR
2500 ENCT 92007 1167-F4
OCEANCREST DR
4200 OCN 92056 1107-C3
OCEAN CREST RD
700 ENCT 92007 1167-E1
OCEAN FRONT
1700 DLMR 92014 1187-F3
OCEAN FRONT ST
1400 SD 92107 1267-H6
OCEAN FRONT WK
2500 SD 92109 1267-H1
3800 SD 92109 1247-H7
OCEAN HEIGHTS WY
10700 SD 92121 1208-E4
OCEAN HILLS DR
4800 OCN 92056 1107-F5
OCEANIC DR
1000 ENCT 92024 1167-F1
OCEAN RIDGE WY
- SD 92130 1208-C2
OCEANSIDE BLVD
100 OCN 92054 1106-C1
1800 OCN 92054 1086-D7
3000 OCN 92056 1086-H6
3600 OCN 92056 1087-E4
OCEANSIDE BLVD S
1700 OCN 92054 1106-C1
OCEAN SURF DR
700 SOLB 92075 1187-E2
OCEAN VALLEY LN
4400 SD 92130 1188-C6
OCEAN VIEW AV
100 DLMR 92014 1187-G7
200 ENCT 92024 1147-C4
OCEAN VIEW BLVD
300 SD 92113 1289-D4
4800 SD 92113 1290-A5
OCEAN VIEW CT
100 VSTA 92084 1087-H7
300 ENCT 92024 1147-C6
OCEAN VIEW DR
- SDCo 92029 1128-J4
- SDCo 92029 1129-A4
- SMCS 92078 1128-J4
100 VSTA 92084 1087-H6
6400 CRLB 92009 1126-H4
OCEAN VIEW LN
500 CHV 91914 1311-E3
OCEAN VIEW PL
100 VSTA 92084 1087-J7
OCEANVIEW PL
2400 SDCo 92021 1252-H4
OCEANVIEW RD
2000 OCN 92056 1086-H7
2000 OCN 92056 1106-H1
OCEAN VIEW TER
- ENCT 92024 1147-C6
OCEAN VIEW HILLS PKWY
- SD 92154 1351-A1
4900 SD 92154 1330-H7
5000 SD 92154 1350-J1
OCEANVIEW RIDGE LN
5800 SD 92121 1208-F4
OCEAN VILLAGE WY
2800 OCN 92054 1106-G1
OCEAN VISTA RD
13200 SD 92130 1187-J5
OCELOT AV
1100 CHV 91911 1330-G1
OCHRE CT
11000 SD 92128 1189-H4
OCONNELL RD
8300 SDCo 92021 1251-H1
OCONNOR ST
700 ELCJ 92020 1251-E2
OCOTILLO CIR
200 SDCo 92004 (1078-G1 See Page 1058)
OCOTILLO DR
- ImCo 92243 6559-E1
200 ELCN 92243 6559-E1
600 VSTA 92083 1087-G5
OCOTILLO PL
200 OCN 92057 1067-B7
OCTANS ST
8600 SD 92126 1209-C1
OCULTO CT
17000 SD 92127 1169-J2
OCULTO PL
17000 SD 92127 1169-J2
OCULTO RD
11400 SD 92127 1169-J2
OCULTO WY
17000 SD 92127 1169-J2
ODELL CIR
1800 VSTA 92084 1088-C4
ODELL PL
7900 SD 92126 1209-A4
ODELL RD
10400 SD 92126 1209-A4
ODESSA AV
5800 LMSA 91942 1250-J7
5800 LMSA 91942 1251-A6
ODESSA CT
2100 LMGR 91945 1290-G1
ODOM ST
3700 SD 92115 1270-D5

ODYSSEY DR
2000 VSTA 92083 1107-J2
OFELIA LN
900 SDCo 92019 1252-E7
OFFBROOK RD
2100 SDCo 92028 1027-J6
OFFSHORE PT
500 SD 92154 1330-H7
OFFY CT
2000 SDCo 92019 1272-C3
OFRIA AV
6800 SD 92120 1250-E4
OFRIA CT
6900 SD 92120 1250-D4
OFTEDAHL WY
13500 SD 92129 1189-E4
OGALALA AV
3100 SD 92117 1248-D1
OGARD RANCH RD
1200 SDCo 92019 1253-E3
OGDEN ST
5200 SD 92105 1270-A5
OGIER RD
- ImCo 92250 431-E5
OGILBY RD Rt#-S34
- ImCo - 411-K11
- ImCo - 431-L1
- ImCo - 432-A3
OGRAM DR
9800 SDCo 91941 1271-C3
OGUNQUIT AV
13400 PWY 92064 1190-H4
OHARA CT
1400 SD 92114 1290-F5
OHEARN RD
100 SDCo 92028 1027-F5
OHIO AV
6900 LMSA 91942 1270-E1
E OHIO AV
700 ESCN 92025 1130-A2
1100 ESCN 92027 1130-A2
OHIO PL
7400 LMSA 91941 1270-G3
OHIO ST
3900 SD 92104 1269-E5
4300 SD 92116 1269-E5
OHM CT
6200 SD 92122 1228-D5
OJEDA RD
1600 SDCo 92084 1088-B1
OKEEFE ST
3100 SD 92173 1350-F5
OKINAWA RD
- CORD 92118 1309-C5
OKRA CT
800 CRLB 92009 1127-A6
OLA CT
4300 SDCo 91910 1310-D5
OLAMAR WY
1600 SD 92139 1290-H6
OLD RD
13400 SDCo 92082 1090-D3
OLD BARN RD
3300 SDCo 92084 1068-B5
OLD BARONA RD
12900 SDCo 92040 1212-F2
12900 SDCo 92040 1192-F7
OLD BATTLEFIELD RD
15400 SDCo 92027 1130-J4
17400 SD 92027 1130-J4
OLD BEND RD
2000 SDCo 92021 1252-F3
OLD BRIDGE RD
700 SDCo 92028 1027-H3
OLD BRIDGEPORT WY
3000 SD 92111 1248-H5
OLD BUCKMAN SPRINGS RD
4000 SDCo 92066 430-A6
OLD CALIFORNIA WY
2800 SDCo 92019 1272-D6
OLD CAMPO RD
12500 SDCo 91978 1272-B7
12600 SDCo 91978 1292-C1
OLD CAROUSEL RANCH RD
18300 SDCo 92065 1171-J3
OLD CASTLE PL
- SDCo 92026 1069-A6
OLD CASTLE RD
8700 SDCo 92026 1068-J6
8700 SDCo 92026 1069-A6
8700 SDCo 92082 1069-F6
11900 SDCo 92082 1070-A5
OLD CASTLE WY
- SDCo 92082 1069-H5
OLD CEDAR RD
1400 SDCo 92025 1130-B3
OLD CHASE AV
1000 ELCJ 92020 1251-H7
1000 SDCo 92020 1251-H7
1000 SDCo 92020 1271-H1
OLD CLIFFS RD
4700 SD 92120 1249-J5
4700 SD 92120 1250-A5
OLD COACH DR
18200 PWY 92064 1150-G7
OLD COACH RD
16900 PWY 92064 1170-F2
17600 PWY 92064 1150-G7
OLD COACH WY
18500 PWY 92064 1150-H3
19900 SDCo 92025 1150-H3
OLD COBBLE CT
3400 SD 92111 1248-H5
OLD COBBLE RD
3500 SD 92111 1248-H5
OLD COLE GRADE RD
- SDCo 92061 1050-F5
- SDCo 92082 1050-F5
OLD COLONY RD
2300 OCN 92056 1087-E1
2300 SDCo 92084 1087-E1
OLD COMMUNITY RD
14200 PWY 92064 1190-E2
OLD COURSE RD
- SDCo 92127 1169-A1
OLD CREEK CT
1500 ENCT 92007 1167-F2
OLD CUYAMACA RD
3200 SDCo 92036 1156-C1
OLD DAIRY CT
5300 SDCo 91902 1310-J2
5300 SDCo 91902 1311-A2
OLD DAIRY LN
3800 SDCo 91902 1310-J2
3800 SDCo 91902 1311-A2
OLD DAIRY WY
5300 SDCo 91902 1310-J2

OLD DAIRY WY
8500 SDCo 91902 1311-A2
OLD DAIRY MART RD
2500 SD 92154 1350-E6
2900 SD 92173 1350-E6
OLD DESERT CLUB RD
3100 SDCo 92004 (1078-H5 See Page 1058)
OLDE GROVE LN
4900 SDCo 91941 1271-F2
OLDE HIGHWAY 80
14100 SDCo 92021 1232-G5
14900 SDCo 92021 1233-A4
OLD EL CAMINO REAL
12600 SD 92130 1207-J1
13600 SD 92130 1188-A3
OLDE SOUTH GRADE RD
- SDCo 91901 1234-D6
OLD ESPOLA RD
16900 PWY 92064 1170-D3
OLDFIELD CT
1800 SDCo 92019 1272-C3
OLD GLOBE WY
1200 SD 92101 1269-C7
1200 SD 92101 1289-B1
OLD GROVE RD
200 OCN 92057 1087-A4
4000 OCN 92056 1087-C4
9900 SD 92131 1209-F5
N OLD GROVE RD
100 OCN 92057 1086-J1
S OLD GROVE RD
100 OCN 92057 1086-J3
100 OCN 92057 1087-A3
OLD GUEJITO RD
15500 ESCN 92027 1110-E6
15600 SDCo 92027 1110-H7
16200 SDCo 92027 1111-A6
OLD GUEJITO GRADE RD
16600 SDCo 92027 1111-C4
OLDHAM CT
900 ENCT 92024 1147-D4
OLDHAM WY
1000 ENCT 92024 1147-C4
OLD HEATHER RD
3100 SD 92111 1248-H5
OLD HIGHWAY 80
26000 SDCo 91916 1236-D3
26400 SDCo 91931 1236-D3
28600 SDCo 91931 1237-A4
29500 SDCo 92066 1237-B7
29700 SDCo 92066 430-A7
34000 SDCo 91906 430-A7
34400 SDCo 92066 (1299-B1 See Page 1298)
36100 SDCo 91906 (1299-G3 See Page 1298)
36700 SDCo 91905 1300-G6
36700 SDCo 91905 (1299-G3 See Page 1298)
37300 SDCo 91934 1300-H7
37600 SDCo 91934 (1320-J1 See Page 1300)
37600 SDCo 91934 (1321-B2 See Page 1300)
38500 SDCo 91905 1300-A6
38700 SDCo 91934 430-F9
OLD HIGHWAY 80 Rt#-S1
29800 SDCo 92066 430-A6
OLD HIGHWAY 80 Rt#-94
36800 SDCo 91905 1300-C6
OLD HWY 101
- SDCo 92055 408-K6
- SDCo 92055 1023-H5
- SDCo 92672 1023-D3
OLD HWY 395
- SDCo 92028 998-H5
700 SDCo 92028 1028-F1
1900 SDCo 92028 1048-H2
29700 SDCo 92026 1068-J3
31700 SDCo 92003 1068-J1
31800 SDCo 92003 1048-J6
47900 RivC 92592 999-A2
47900 SDCo 92028 999-A2
OLD HILL RD
200 SDCo 92028 1027-J2
200 SDCo 92028 1028-A2
OLD HORSE TR
- SDCo 91901 1233-F7
OLD JULIAN HWY
200 SDCo 92065 1152-J6
300 SDCo 92065 1153-E4
19400 SDCo 92065 1154-A3
OLD JULIAN TR
23000 SDCo 92065 1153-H4
OLD KANE SPRING RD
5900 SDCo 92004 (1120-E3 See Page 1100)
5900 SDCo 92004 (1121-B5 See Page 1100)
OLD KETTLE RD
3000 SD 92111 1248-H5
OLD LANTERN LN
9800 SDCo 92026 1089-D3
OLD MAN RIVER RD
- SDCo 92127 1168-J1
OLD MANZANITA RD
23500 SDCo 92027 1111-C7
OLD MEADOW RD
3300 SD 92111 1248-H5
OLD MELROSE RANCH RD
24200 SDCo 92027 1111-C4
OLD MEMORY LN
1300 SD 92114 1290-C2
OLD MILKY WY
3200 SD 92025 1130-H7
3200 SD 92025 1131-A7
3200 SD 92027 1131-A7
14200 SD 92027 1130-H7
OLD MILL CT
1700 ENCT 92024 1147-H6
OLD MILL RD
1700 ENCT 92024 1147-H6
OLD MINE RD
- SDCo 91905 430-C7
OLD MINERS TR
2300 SDCo 92036 1136-B6
OLD MISSION CT
7300 SNTE 92071 1230-F7
OLD MOUNTAIN VIEW RD
1000 SDCo 92021 1233-A7
1000 SDCo 92021 1253-A1
OLD NANTUCKET CT
5600 SD 92111 1248-H5

OLD OAK DR SAN DIEGO CO. STREET INDEX PAAUWE DR 6606

STREET
Block City ZIP Pg-Grid

OLD OAK DR
100 SD 92114 1290-G4
OLD OAK RDG
700 SDCo 92069 1109-B2
OLD OAK TR
21200 SDCo 91901 1275-B4
OLD OAK HOLLER
10900 SDCo 92082 1049-C3
OLD OAK TREE LN
1100 SDCo 92026 1109-H2
OLD ORCHARD LN
100 CHV 91902 1310-G3
200 SDCo 91902 1310-G3
OLD POMERADO RD
11800 PWY 92064 1190-B6
OLD POST RD
3000 SDCo 92028 1048-D1
OLD RANCH DR
12600 SDCo 92082 1090-C2
OLD RANCH RD
- ESCN 92027 1130-H2
- SDCo 91901 1235-G7
100 SDCo 91910 1310-D6
5400 OCN 92057 1067-E7
OLD RIDGE RD
- SDCo 91977 1271-D7
OLD RIVER RD
3500 SDCo 92003 1067-J5
3500 SDCo 92084 1067-J5
6000 SDCo 92003 1068-A2
OLD RIVER ST
600 OCN 92057 1086-H1
OLD SAN PASQUAL RD
2500 SDCo 92027 1130-F5
4100 SDCo 92025 1130-F5
OLD SAYBROOK DR
10700 SD 92129 1189-H2
OLD SCHOOLHOUSE RD
3100 SDCo 92019 1272-C5
OLD SPANISH TR
2400 SDCo 92025 1130-B7
OLD SPRING CT
3400 SD 92111 1248-H5
OLD SPRINGS RD
- SDCo 92004 (1079-J2
See Page 1058)
OLD SPUR CT
- SDCo 91901 1254-G3
OLD SPUR DR
- SDCo 91901 1254-F3
OLD STAGE CT
300 SDCo 92028 1027-F3
OLD STAGE RD
100 SDCo 92028 1027-F4
OLD STAGECOACH RUN
300 SDCo 91901 1234-B4
OLD STAGECOACH TR
- SDCo 91901 1234-A4
OLD STATION RD
14000 PWY 92064 1170-G7
OLD STONE RD
12300 PWY 92064 1190-B7
12300 PWY 92128 1190-B7
12300 SD 92128 1190-B7
OLD STONE HILL RD
30600 SDCo 92086 409-J5
OLD SURVEY RD
16500 SD 92025 1151-D2
16500 SDCo 92025 1151-D2
OLD SYCAMORE DR
13000 SD 92128 1189-H5
OLD TAYLOR ST
900 VSTA 92084 1087-J2
900 VSTA 92084 1088-A2
OLD THAMES WY
5500 SD 92111 1248-H5
OLD TOWN AV
3800 SD 92110 1268-F5
OLD TRAIL DR
2000 CHV 91914 1311-G2
OLD VIA RANCHO DR
300 ESCN 92029 1149-J2
300 ESCN 92029 1150-A2
OLD WAGON RD
23200 SDCo 92027 1111-C4
23800 SDCo 92027 1131-C1
OLD WATNEY WY
5500 SD 92111 1248-H5
OLD WEST AV
13000 SD 92129 1189-C5
OLD WEST WY
13000 SD 92129 1189-D5
OLD WINEMASTER CT
13300 PWY 92064 1170-D1
OLD WINEMASTER WY
17800 PWY 92064 1170-E1
OLD WINERY CT
13100 PWY 92064 1170-D1
OLD WINERY RD
13100 PWY 92064 1170-D1
13300 PWY 92064 1150-E7
OLD WINERY WY
17700 PWY 92064 1170-E1
OLD YUCCA TR
16400 SDCo 92027 1111-D6
OLEA LN
6400 CRLB 92009 1127-E4
OLEANDER
15300 SDCo 92021 1233-B3
OLEANDER AV
700 VSTA 92083 1108-A5
700 SDCo 92083 1108-B5
900 CHV 91911 1330-G1
1000 ELCN 92243 6499-G5
2900 SMCS 92069 1108-C6
OLEANDER DR
100 CHV 91910 1310-B5
200 OCN 92057 1087-A1
3600 SD 92106 1268-C6
13600 PWY 92064 1190-F3
OLEANDER LN
1700 SDCo 92004 (1099-F2
See Page 1098)
OLEANDER PL
700 SDCo 92083 1108-B6
700 VSTA 92083 1108-B6
800 ESCN 92027 1110-B7
3700 SD 92106 1268-C6
OLEANDER ST
3300 SD 92121 1207-J4
3300 SD 92121 1208-A3
OLEANDER WY
6700 CRLB 92009 1126-J5
OLE BURN WY
16000 SDCo 91935 1293-F2
OLGA AV
3400 SD 92123 1249-B4
OLINDA ST
600 ESCN 92027 1110-B7

OLIPHANT ST
3000 SD 92106 1288-B1
3600 SD 92106 1268-B7
OLITE CT
2000 SD 92037 1247-H1
OLIVA RD
12300 SD 92128 1170-B4
OLIVE AV
100 ELCN 92243 6499-E6
100 VSTA 92083 1087-E6
200 CRLB 92008 1106-F7
200 ELCN 92243 6500-A6
400 SDCo 92028 1027-F1
700 CORD 92118 1288-H7
800 SDCo 92065 1152-J3
800 NATC 91950 1290-C7
1000 SD 92139 1290-C7
1200 SDCo 92083 1087-D6
1400 OCN 92056 1087-D6
1500 CHV 91911 1330-H4
1900 SD 92139 1310-C1
4100 LMSA 91941 1270-G3
7300 SDCo 91902 1291-D7
OLIVE CT
1500 CHV 91911 1330-H4
OLIVE DR
1000 SD 92173 1350-G4
4000 OCN 92056 1087-C6
5000 SDCo 91977 1271-A6
OLIVE LN
100 CORD 92118 1288-G7
8800 SNTE 92071 1231-C7
9700 SDCo 92029 1149-D3
28900 SDCo 92082 1070-G7
OLIVE PL
4600 LMSA 91941 1270-G3
OLIVE RD
500 ELCN 92243 6499-E7
OLIVE ST
100 SDCo 92069 1108-J2
100 SMCS 92069 1108-J2
200 SMCS 92069 1109-A2
300 SD 92103 1269-A7
700 SDCo 92065 1152-D5
1000 SD 92103 1268-J7
1000 SD 92103 1288-J1
1200 SD 92101 1288-J1
1400 OCN 92054 1086-B7
2700 LMGR 91945 1270-G6
3000 SD 92104 1269-E7
3200 SDCo 91950 1310-C3
4300 SD 92105 1269-H7
5100 SD 92105 1270-A7
12500 SDCo 92040 1232-B4
W OLIVE ST
300 SD 92103 1269-A7
OLIVE TER
1000 SDCo 92065 1152-D5
14100 SDCo 92021 1232-G5
OLIVEBROOK CT
1900 ELCJ 92019 1252-C5
OLIVE CREST DR
900 ENCT 92024 1147-J5
OLIVE CREST WY
13900 PWY 92064 1190-E3
OLIVE GROVE DR
13200 PWY 92064 1190-E3
OLIVE GROVE PL
13800 PWY 92064 1190-E3
OLIVE HILL LN
2400 SDCo 92028 1047-G1
OLIVE HILL RD
- SNTE 92071 1230-G7
2500 SDCo 92028 1027-G7
2500 SDCo 92028 1047-G3
5100 SDCo 92003 1047-G7
5300 SDCo 92003 1067-H1
OLIVE HILL WY
200 SDCo 92028 1047-G2
OLIVE HILLS AV
1300 ELCJ 92021 1252-B2
OLIVE KNOLL PL
- ESCN 92027 1130-H3
OLIVE MEADOWS DR
13200 PWY 92064 1190-E3
OLIVE MEADOWS PL
14000 PWY 92064 1190-E3
OLIVE MESA CT
13900 PWY 92064 1190-E3
OLIVE MILL WY
13800 PWY 92064 1190-E3
OLIVENHAIN RD
Rt#-S10
1600 ENCT 92024 1147-F4
1600 CRLB 92009 1147-F4
OLIVENHAIN FARMS RD
1600 ENCT 92024 1148-B5
OLIVE PARK PL
13800 PWY 92064 1190-E3
OLIVER AV
700 SD 92109 1247-H7
1400 SD 92109 1248-A6
OLIVER CT
4200 SD 92109 1247-H7
OLIVER LN
4700 LMSA 91941 1270-J3
OLIVER PL
700 SD 92109 1247-H7
OLIVERA AV
- SDCo 92127 1169-F4
OLIVET LN
1400 SD 92037 1227-F6
OLIVET ST
1300 SD 92037 1227-F7
OLIVETAS AV
7100 SD 92037 1247-E1
7300 SD 92037 1227-E7
OLIVE TREE LN
13200 PWY 92064 1190-G4
OLIVE VIEW RD
2800 SDCo 91901 1234-C7
OLIVE VISTA DR
13900 SDCo 91935 1292-H1
14400 SDCo 91935 1293-A1
OLIVEWOOD LN
1400 SDCo 91901 1234-B7
OLIVEWOOD TER
3000 SD 92113 1289-G5
OLIVOS CT
4200 SDCo 92028 1028-G7
4200 SDCo 92028 1048-H1
OLLIE ST
3200 SD 92110 1268-C5
OLLY CT
1000 VSTA 92083 1107-J1
OLMEDA CT
- SD 92128 1150-C6
OLMEDA PL
18700 SD 92128 1150-D6

OLMEDA ST
1600 ENCT 92024 1147-H7
OLMEDA WY
17000 SD 92127 1169-H2
OLNEY ST
4100 SD 92109 1248-B5
OLSON DR
9700 SD 92121 1228-F1
OLSON WY
- OCN 92054 1106-F2
OLVERA AV
5100 SD 92114 1290-B5
OLVERA RD
10600 SDCo 91977 1271-F5
OLVIDA DR
200 SMCS 92078 1129-A1
E OLYMPIA CT
- CHV 91911 1330-E3
OLYMPIA DR
2600 CRLB 92008 1106-J3
E OLYMPIA ST
100 CHV 91911 1330-F2
OLYMPIA FIELDS RW
11300 SD 92128 1189-J3
OLYMPIC PKWY
- CHV 91913 1311-H7
- CHV 91913 1331-A3
- CHV 91915 1311-H7
- CHV 91915 (1312-A7
See Page 1293)
- CHV 91915 1331-G1
700 CHV 91911 1330-J3
700 CHV 91911 1331-A3
OLYMPIC PL
5700 SD 92115 1270-C5
OLYMPIC ST
4000 SD 92115 1270-C5
OLYMPIC WY
500 OCN 92054 1086-G1
OLYMPUS ST
600 ENCT 92024 1147-B3
OLYMPUS LOOP DR
1600 VSTA 92083 1107-G4
OMA RD
30700 SDCo 92082 1069-F3
OMAHA CT
400 ELCJ 92020 1251-G7
OMAR CT
5100 OCN 92057 1067-B5
OMAR DR
800 ESCN 92025 1129-J3
800 ESCN 92025 1130-A3
OMEARA ST
400 SD 92114 1290-D5
OMEGA DR
6500 SD 92139 1310-F1
OMEGA ST
600 SDCo 91977 1291-D3
ONAGER DR
300 SDCo 92004 1058-G7
ONALASKA AV
8300 SD 92123 1249-C5
ONATE AV
4800 SD 92117 1248-H1
ONDA PL
6500 CRLB 92009 1127-G5
E ONEIDA CT
- CHV 91911 1330-E3
ONEIDA PL
3700 SD 92103 1269-B6
E ONEIDA ST
- CHV 91911 1330-F3
ONEIDA WY
900 SD 92103 1269-B6
ONEONTA AV
400 IMPB 91932 1349-G2
ONLEY DR
600 VSTA 92083 1087-F5
ONLEY WY
600 VSTA 92083 1087-F5
ONONDAGA AV
4300 SD 92117 1248-E2
ONSTAD ST
5000 SD 92110 1268-F2
ONTARIO AV
3600 SD 92105 1270-A6
ONTARIO CT
2000 SDCo 92019 1272-C3
ONTARIO ST
900 ESCN 92025 1129-H5
5300 OCN 92056 1087-D1
ONYX AV
1600 ELCJ 92019 1252-B4
ONYX CT
- SDCo 92019 1272-B3
ONYX DR
2200 SDCo 92019 1272-C2
ONYX GN
- ESCN 92027 1110-D7
OPAL DR
500 SDCo 92036 1156-E1
OPAL GN
- ESCN 92027 1110-D7
OPAL LN
4400 OCN 92056 1107-D2
OPAL RDG
2100 VSTA 92083 1107-H6
OPAL ST
700 SD 92109 1247-H5
1600 SMCS 92069 1128-B5
OPAL WY
- CRLB 92009 1127-B4
OPALO WY
2300 SD 92111 1248-G7
OPALOCKA RD
39200 SDCo 91905 1300-C2
OPEN VIEW RD
- SDCo 92065 1173-D2
OPIMO CT
16400 SD 92128 1170-C4
OPIMO DR
12600 SD 92128 1170-C4
OPORTO CT
4700 SD 92124 1250-A1
OPORTO PL
4700 SD 92124 1250-A1
OPOSSUM CT
12100 SDCo 92040 1212-C5
OPPER ST
500 ESCN 92029 1129-D2
OPPORTUNITY RD
7100 SD 92111 1249-A2
OPTIMIST WY
2200 VSTA 92083 1108-A4
ORA AVO DR
600 SDCo 92084 1088-E7
1000 SDCo 92084 1108-E1
ORA AVO LN
3100 SDCo 92084 1088-E7

ORA AVO TER
1100 SDCo 92084 1088-E7
ORA BELLE LN
8300 SDCo 92021 1232-D7
ORALANE DR
11400 SDCo 92020 1271-H3
ORANADO LN
- SDCo 92014 1167-J7
- SOLB 92014 1167-J7
ORANGE AV
100 ELCJ 92020 1251-F5
100 ELCN 92243 6499-E7
200 SDCo 92028 1027-F1
200 ELCN 92243 6500-A7
1300 ELCJ 92020 1271-F1
1500 SDCo 92065 1153-A2
2100 SDCo 92029 1129-G7
2100 SDCo 92065 409-H11
2200 ESCN 92029 1129-G7
3200 SD 92104 1269-F5
3600 SD 92105 1269-H4
4300 SD 92115 1269-H4
4800 SD 92105 1270-A4
4800 SD 92115 1270-A4
8000 LMSA 91941 1270-H3
ORANGE AV Rt#-75
1000 CORD 92118 1288-H7
1300 CORD 92118 1308-J1
E ORANGE AV
- CHV 91911 1330-G4
S ORANGE AV
200 SDCo 92028 1027-F3
W ORANGE AV
- CHV 91911 1330-D4
ORANGE CT
1400 ELCJ 92020 1271-F1
ORANGE DR
100 CHV 91911 1330-F5
ORANGE LN
9800 SDCo 92029 1149-E1
ORANGE PL
1500 ESCN 92025 1129-J4
1500 ESCN 92025 1130-A5
2800 LMGR 91945 1270-H6
ORANGE ST
1300 NATC 91950 1310-B1
3100 SDCo 91935 1272-H7
3200 SDCo 91950 1310-C3
E ORANGE ST
100 VSTA 92084 1087-H6
N ORANGE ST
- ESCN 92025 1129-H3
S ORANGE ST
100 ESCN 92025 1129-J3
W ORANGE ST
100 VSTA 92083 1087-G6
ORANGE TER
28100 SDCo 92082 1090-E2
ORANGE WY
3800 OCN 92057 1086-H4
ORANGE BLOSSOM LN
13400 PWY 92064 1190-E1
ORANGE BLOSSOM WY
1000 ESCN 92026 1109-J4
1700 ENCT 92024 1147-G5
ORANGEBURG AV
12800 SD 92129 1189-E5
ORANGEBURG CT
9600 SD 92129 1189-E5
ORANGECREST CT
12100 SDCo 92040 1232-A4
ORANGECREST DR
9500 SDCo 92040 1232-A4
ORANGE GROVE AV
400 VSTA 92084 1087-J6
ORANGE GROVE PL
- ESCN 92027 1130-H2
ORANGEGROVE RD
1300 SDCo 92021 1251-G1
ORANGE HILL
4300 SDCo 92028 1048-B5
ORANGETREE CT
1400 ENCT 92024 1147-G7
ORANGE TREE LN
- SDCo 92003 1068-D5
- SDCo 92084 1068-D5
ORANGEVIEW DR
1500 ENCT 92024 1167-G1
ORANGE VISTA LN
1800 SDCo 92021 1252-A1
ORANGEWOOD DR
1000 SDCo 92025 1130-D6
ORCAS WY
10000 SDCo 92040 1232-C3
ORCHARD AV
- SDCo 92021 1252-D5
2200 ELCJ 92019 1252-D5
2200 SDCo 92019 1252-D5
3800 SD 92107 1288-A1
4300 SD 92107 1287-J1
4400 SD 92107 1267-J7
8200 LMSA 91941 1270-H2
ORCHARD DR
4200 SDCo 91977 1271-C4
ORCHARD LN
900 SDCo 92066 1135-E4
ORCHARD RD
1400 ImCo 92250 431-E6
11900 SDCo 92040 1251-J1
ORCHARD RD Rt#-S32
- HOLT 92250 431-E5
1600 ImCo 92250 431-E5
ORCHARD WY
3400 OCN 92054 1086-F2
ORCHARD BEND RD
16200 PWY 92064 1170-F3
ORCHARD GATE RD
13400 PWY 92064 1170-E5
ORCHARD GLEN CIR
1200 ENCT 92024 1147-G4
ORCHARD HILL RD
3200 SDCo 91902 1310-G2
ORCHARD VIEW LN
- ESCN 92027 1130-H2
14900 PWY 92064 1170-H7
ORCHARD VISTA RD
13000 SDCo 92082 1090-B5
ORCHARD WOOD RD
1600 ENCT 92024 1147-G4
ORCHID AV
700 SMCS 92078 1128-G3
14100 PWY 92064 1190-F3
ORCHID GN
3700 ESCN 92025 1150-C3
ORCHID LN
500 DLMR 92014 1187-G5
2800 SD 92154 1350-C1
ORCHID WY
800 SD 92154 1330-D7

ORCHID WY
900 CRLB 92009 1127-A6
ORCUTT AV
4500 SD 92120 1249-H6
4800 SD 92120 1250-A6
ORD WY
1800 OCN 92056 1087-D5
ORDE CT
1200 CHV 91911 1330-C4
ORDVIEW CT
1200 CHV 91911 1330-C4
ORDWAY RD
600 SDCo 92028 1028-H2
OREGANO WY
3800 OCN 92057 1086-H4
20400 SDCo 91935 1294-J6
OREGON AV
6900 LMSA 91942 1270-F1
OREGON ST
3900 SD 92104 1269-D5
4300 SD 92116 1269-D3
OREO LN
2100 SD 92154 1350-A1
ORGANDY LN
8500 SNTE 92071 1230-H7
8500 SNTE 92071 1250-H1
ORIBIA RD
1200 DLMR 92014 1187-G4
ORIEN AV
7300 LMSA 91941 1270-G4
ORIENTE DR
700 SDCo 92084 1067-H6
ORIENTE PL
700 SDCo 92084 1067-H6
ORIENTE WY
23500 SDCo 92065 1173-D3
ORILLA DR
16600 SD 92128 1170-B3
ORINDA DR
2100 ENCT 92007 1167-D3
ORINDA PL
1300 ESCN 92029 1129-G7
ORINOCO DR
2800 SDCo 92070 1135-G7
2800 SDCo 92070 1155-F1
ORIOLE CT
400 CHV 91911 1330-H2
1700 CRLB 92009 1127-E5
ORIOLE LN
- OCN 92057 1086-H2
ORIOLE PL
1300 CHV 91911 1330-G3
ORIOLE ST
1700 SD 92114 1290-D1
ORIOLE WY
1000 SMCS 92069 1128-E2
ORION CT
9200 SD 92126 1209-D6
ORION DR
3600 SDCo 91941 1271-A5
8900 SD 92126 1209-D6
ORION PL
400 ESCN 92026 1109-J7
400 ESCN 92026 1129-J1
ORION ST
5700 CRLB 92008 1127-E1
ORION WY
2500 CRLB 92008 1127-E1
11100 SD 92126 1209-C2
ORISKANY RD
1800 SD 92139 1290-D7
ORIZABA ST
2000 SD 92103 1268-G5
ORKNEY LN
1200 ENCT 92007 1167-D1
ORLA ST
800 SMCS 92069 1108-J5
ORLANDO CT
- CHV 91911 1330-E3
E ORLANDO CT
- CHV 91911 1330-E3
ORLANDO ST
400 ELCJ 92021 1251-J5
1200 SMCS 92069 1109-C6
E ORLANDO ST
100 CHV 91911 1330-F3
ORLEANS E
3000 SD 92110 1268-C5
ORLEANS AV
100 ESCN 92027 1110-E7
400 ESCN 92027 1130-E1
ORLEAVO DR
900 VSTA 92084 1087-J7
ORLECK CT
4800 SD 92124 1249-G2
ORLECK PL
4900 SD 92124 1249-G2
ORLECK ST
10100 SD 92124 1249-G2
ORMA DR
900 SD 92106 1287-J2
ORMOND CT
700 SD 92109 1267-H1
ORMSBY ST
800 SDCo 92084 1067-J7
ORMSBY WY
2700 SDCo 92084 1068-A7
OR NO WY
10800 SDCo 92040 1232-A1
ORO CT
- CHV 91915 1311-H6
ORO GN
1500 ESCN 92026 1109-H6
ORO ST
700 ELCJ 92021 1251-J3
900 SDCo 92021 1251-J3
ORO GRANDE
3400 VSTA 92083 1107-C2
ORO GRANDE ST
800 OCN 92057 1087-C1
OROHAVEN LN
12600 PWY 92064 1190-C4
OROLA LN
6800 LMSA 91941 1270-E3
OROSCO TKTR
- SDCo 92065 409-G11
OROSCO GUEJITO TKTR
- SD 92027 409-G11
- SDCo 92027 409-G11
- SDCo 92065 409-G11
ORO VERDE RD
2000 SDCo 92027 1130-E4
ORO VISTA RD
1300 SD 92154 1350-B1
OROZCO RD
10300 SD 92124 1229-G7
ORPHA CT
12800 PWY 92064 1190-D5

ORPHEUS AV
300 ENCT 92024 1147-B3
ORR ST
3500 OCN 92054 1086-E2
6600 SD 92111 1248-H6
ORRELL DR
400 NATC 91950 1309-J3
ORSETT ST
400 CHV 91911 1330-C4
ORTEN ST
4500 SD 92110 1268-E1
ORTEZ PL
14400 PWY 92064 1190-H1
ORVIL WY
100 SDCo 92028 1028-A2
ORVILLE ST
8600 SDCo 91977 1291-A3
ORWELL LN
300 ENCT 92024 1147-G7
ORWELL RD
300 ENCT 92024 1147-H7
OSAGE AV
1000 CHV 91911 1330-G1
OSAGE DR
1000 SDCo 91977 1290-H2
1600 LMGR 91945 1290-H2
OSAGE ST
300 SDCo 91977 1290-J4
900 SD 92114 1290-J4
1500 SMCS 92069 1108-D6
9600 SDCo 91977 1291-C3
OSAGE TR
11500 SDCo 92040 1231-H7
OSBORN ST
2000 SD 92113 1289-G7
OSBORNE ST
100 SDCo 92084 1087-G1
100 VSTA 92084 1087-G1
1000 SDCo 92084 1088-A1
OSBORNE TER
2400 SDCo 92084 1087-J1
OSCEOLA AV
3000 SD 92117 1248-C1
OSGOOD WY
10000 SD 92126 1208-J5
10000 SD 92126 1209-A6
OSHIA LN
11200 SDCo 92082 1069-G2
OSLER LN
3000 SD 92093 1228-A2
OSLER ST
6200 SD 92111 1248-H6
OSO RD
9100 SDCo 91977 1291-B1
OSOYOOS PL
11400 SD 92126 1209-C1
OSPREY ST
4200 SD 92107 1287-H1
OSPREY WY
300 OCN 92057 1087-A3
OSSA AV
1000 CHV 91911 1330-G1
OSTEND CT
700 SD 92109 1267-H1
OSTERLING CT
6800 SD 92114 1290-E6
OSTROW ST
7700 SD 92111 1249-A3
OSUNA DR
2400 CRLB 92008 1106-G3
OTAY PL
700 SD 92114 1290-D3
OTAY ST
700 SD 92114 1290-D3
OTAY CENTER CT
2200 SD 92154 1351-J3
OTAY CENTER DR
2400 SD 92154 1351-J3
2400 SD 92154 1352-A3
OTAY HEIGHTS CT
1600 SD 92154 1351-D2
OTAY LAKES RD
2600 CHV 91915 1311-E5
2600 CHV 91914 1311-E5
2600 CHV 91915 (1312-B5
See Page 1293)
2600 CHV 91914 (1312-B5
See Page 1293)
2600 SDCo 91915 (1312-B5
See Page 1293)
2600 SDCo 91914 (1312-B5
See Page 1293)
2800 CHV 91913 1311-E5
3200 CHV 91910 1311-A4
3500 CHV 91902 1311-A4
3700 CHV 91902 1310-H3
3700 CHV 91910 1310-H3
3800 SDCo 91902 1310-H3
13500 SDCo 91935 (1312-B5
See Page 1293)
13500 SDCo 91935 (1313-B3
See Page 1293)
14600 SDCo 91917 (1313-B3
See Page 1293)
OTAY MESA PL
4300 SD 92173 1350-G3
OTAY MESA RD
4200 SD 92173 1350-H2
4500 SD 92154 1350-H2
5100 SD 92154 1351-J2
9000 SDCo 92154 1351-J2
9300 SDCo 92154 1352-A2
OTAY MESA RD E
Rt#-905
5100 SD 92154 1351-A2
8800 SDCo 92154 1351-F2
OTAY MESA CENTER RD
1600 SD 92154 1351-G2
OTAY MOUNTAIN TKTR
200 SDCo 91917 429-J10
400 SDCo 91917 (1333-D4
See Page 1332)
1300 SDCo 92154 1332-D6
1300 SDCo 92154 (1333-A7
See Page 1332)
1300 SDCo 92154 1352-H1
1300 SDCo 92154 (1353-A1
See Page 1332)
OTAY VALLEY CIR
300 CHV 91911 1330-G5
OTAY VALLEY RD
200 CHV 91911 1330-F5
OTERO WY
23900 SDCo 92065 1173-E2
OTESGO DR
800 SD 92103 1268-J6
OTHELLO AV
7500 SD 92111 1249-A3

OTIS
6200 CRLB 92008 1127-B3
OTIS CT
6900 SD 92111 1268-J1
OTIS PL
13800 PWY 92064 1190-F4
OTIS ST
100 CHV 91910 1310-C6
OTIS POST RD
13200 PWY 92064 1190-G4
OTOMI AV
4600 SD 92117 1248-D1
OTONO ST
1200 SD 92154 1350-F1
OTSEGO DR
500 SD 92103 1268-J6
OTTAWA AV
3400 SD 92117 1248-E5
OTTILIE PL
5100 SD 92105 1270-A5
OTTO AV
3200 SDCo 91901 1234-D5
OTTO DR
3000 SDCo 91901 1234-D6
OUR WY
8700 SNTE 92071 1231-A7
OUR COUNTRY RD
2400 SDCo 92029 1129-H7
OURO PL
7300 LMSA 91941 1270-F4
OUTBACK PL
2900 SDCo 92065 1172-C3
OUTER DR
1700 SDCo 92021 1251-G1
OUTER RD
1000 SD 92154 1350-B1
OUTINDA ST
9000 SDCo 91977 1291-B4
OUTLOOK PT
5300 SD 92124 1249-G1
OUTLOOK RD
13600 PWY 92064 1190-F1
OUTRIGGER LN
1800 CRLB 92008 1106-H7
OUTRIGGER WY
1900 OCN 92054 1106-F1
OVAL DR
3000 SD 92139 1310-F2
OVERBROOK LN
1000 SDCo 92028 1027-J5
OVERHILL DR
2900 SDCo 92084 1088-D7
OVERLAKE AV
5800 SD 92120 1250-E7
OVERLAND AV
4600 SD 92123 1249-D1
5000 SD 92123 1229-D7
OVERLAND CT
500 CHV 91902 1311-B4
OVERLAND PASG
2800 SDCo 91901 1234-D5
OVERLAND PASS
13600 PWY 92064 1170-F1
OVERLAND RD
400 ENCT 92024 1147-G6
OVERLAND SPUR
3400 SDCo 91901 1234-D5
OVERLAND TR
2800 SDCo 92028 1047-G1
OVERLOOK CIR
800 SMCS 92078 1128-F2
OVERLOOK DR
4900 OCN 92057 1087-C2
E OVERLOOK DR
4200 SD 92115 1270-C4
W OVERLOOK DR
4200 SD 92115 1270-C4
OVERLOOK LN
800 SDCo 92019 1251-H6
OVERLOOK ST
600 ESCN 92027 1130-C2
OVERPARK RD
3400 SD 92130 1187-J5
11600 SD 92130 1188-A5
OVERTON AV
9200 SD 92123 1249-E6
OVERVIEW RD
15900 PWY 92064 1170-E5
OVID PL
5000 SD 92117 1228-E7
OVIEDO PL
2400 CRLB 92009 1147-G1
OVIEDO ST
8900 SD 92129 1189-E2
OVIEDO WY
9300 SD 92129 1189-E3
OWEGA CT
3900 SDCo 92004 (1099-D2
See Page 1098)
OWEN DR
1300 CHV 91911 1330-H2
OWEN ST
2800 SD 92106 1288-A4
OWENS AV
1900 CRLB 92008 1127-C3
OWL CT
9400 SD 92129 1189-E6
OWL GN
1300 ESCN 92029 1129-G5
OXBOW CIR
100 ENCT 92024 1147-H7
OXBOW LN
100 ENCT 92024 1147-H7
OXFORD AV
1700 ENCT 92007 1167-D2
OXFORD CT
- VSTA 92083 1107-H5
1100 CHV 91911 1330-C3
OXFORD PL
3800 OCN 92056 1087-A7
OXFORD ST
- CHV 91911 1330-D3
3600 CRLB 92008 1106-J4
4300 LMSA 91941 1270-F4
E OXFORD ST
- CHV 91911 1330-F2
OZARK RD
100 OCN 92056 1087-D1
OZLAND AV
15900 SDCo 92082 1071-A3
OZZIE WY
400 SD 92114 1290-C5

P

P CT
- SD 92126 1209-F7
PAAUWE DR
32200 SDCo 92061 1051-B6

SAN DIEGO CO.
INDEX

STREET
Block City ZIP Pg-Grid

PABELLON CIR
11200 SD 92124 1250-A2
PABELLON CT
11200 SD 92124 1250-A2
PABLO DR
16200 SD 92128 1170-C4
PABLO PL
1200 ESCN 92027 1109-J7
PACATO CIR N
12500 SD 92128 1170-C2
PACATO CIR S
12500 SD 92128 1170-C2
PACATO CT
17100 SD 92128 1170-C2
PACATO PL
17200 SD 92128 1170-C2
PACATO WY
17100 SD 92128 1170-C2
PACEMONT LN
11100 SD 92126 1209-E2
PACER LN
13300 PWY 92064 1170-E4
PACESETTER ST
500 OCN 92057 1067-E6
PACIFIC AV
100 CRLB 92008 1106-D5
100 SOLB 92075 1167-E6
1500 CHV 91911 1330-A4
1500 SD 91911 1330-A4
7200 LMGR 91945 1270-G6
PACIFIC HWY
600 SD 92101 1288-J1
1700 SD 92109 1268-E3
1900 SD 92110 1268-E3
3000 SD 92101 1268-H7
4800 SD 92140 1268-F6
PACIFIC LN
1200 DLMR 92014 1187-F5
PACIFIC ST
300 ENCT 92024 1147-B2
300 SMCS 92069 1108-E6
300 OCN 92054 1085-J6
300 OCN 92054 1105-J1
300 OCN 92054 1106-A1
N PACIFIC ST
100 SMCS 92069 1108-E6
S PACIFIC ST
100 SMCS 92069 1108-D7
200 OCN 92054 1106-A1
200 SMCS 92069 1128-D1
PACIFICA AV
1100 CHV 91913 1311-C6
PACIFICA DR
4800 SD 92109 1248-B3
5300 SD 92037 1248-B3
PACIFICA PL
- ENCT 92024 1147-F5
PACIFICA WY
- ENCT 92024 1147-F5
PACIFIC BEACH DR
700 SD 92109 1247-H7
1700 SD 92109 1248-A6
PACIFIC CANYON WY
10700 SD 92121 1208-F4
PACIFIC CENTER BLVD
5700 SD 92121 1208-E5
PACIFIC CENTER CT
10400 SD 92121 1208-F5
PACIFIC CREST WY
29400 SDCo 91906 (1297-E4
See Page 1296)
PACIFIC GROVE LP
1100 CHV 91915 1311-F6
PACIFIC GROVE PL
5200 SD 92130 1188-D6
PACIFIC HAVEN CT
5800 SD 92121 1208-F3
PACIFIC HEIGHTS BLVD
9500 SD 92121 1208-F5
PACIFIC HILL ST
1000 CHV 91911 1330-H1
PACIFIC MESA BLVD
10000 SD 92121 1208-F6
PACIFIC MESA CT
5900 SD 92121 1208-F5
PACIFIC MIST CT
1900 SD 92139 1290-D7
PACIFIC MIST RD
1900 SD 92139 1290-D7
PACIFICO RD
7100 CRLB 92009 1127-F6
PACIFIC RANCH DR
1500 ENCT 92024 1167-H2
PACIFIC RIM CT
800 SD 92154 1351-D2
PACIFIC SHORES WY
- SD 92130 1208-C2
PACIFIC SUNSET TR
3000 SDCo 91901 1234-D4
PACIFIC SURF DR
700 SOLB 92075 1187-E2
PACIFIC VIEW DR
600 SD 92109 1247-G5
PACIFIC VIEW LN
- ENCT 92024 1147-D6
PACIFIC VISTA WY
800 SDCo 92069 1088-G7
PACKARD LN
3900 CRLB 92008 1106-H6
PACKARD PL
2100 SDCo 92019 1272-C3
PADDING RIVER RD
1900 CHV 91913 1311-E6
PADDOCK RD
5600 OCN 92057 1067-F7
PADDY PL
2000 ESCN 92027 1110-B6
PADEN DR
200 SDCo 91977 1291-B4
PADERA CT
800 CHV 91910 1310-H5
PADERA WY
500 CHV 91910 1310-H5
PADGETT ST
9500 SD 92126 1209-E6
PADRE LN
9200 SNTE 92071 1231-B7
PADRE TULLIO DR
100 SD 92173 1350-G3
PADRONE PL
500 CHV 91910 1310-J5
PADUA HILLS PL
200 SD 92173 1350-F3
PADUCAH DR
3900 SD 92117 1248-D4
PAGE RD
- SD 92106 1288-A7

PAGE ST
3400 SD 92115 1270-C6
PAGEANT AV
13200 SD 92129 1189-D4
PAGEL PL
100 SD 92114 1290-E4
PAGODA WY
8500 SD 92126 1209-C5
PAGODA TREE LN
- SDCo 92127 1169-D2
PAGOSA LN
12100 SDCo 92040 1231-J1
PAGUERA CT
4900 SD 92124 1249-H2
PAHLS WY
900 SDCo 92065 1153-B1
PAHVANT ST
2500 OCN 92054 1086-D6
PAINE CT
- PWY 92064 1190-G6
PAINE PL
12100 PWY 92064 1190-F7
PAINE ST
12100 PWY 92064 1190-F7
PAINT BRUSH CIR
- SDCo 91906 (1318-B7
See Page 1298)
PAINTED DESERT RD
14000 PWY 92064 1170-G3
PAINTED GORGE RD
- ImCo 92259 430-H5
PAINTED PONY CIR
1000 VSTA 92083 1107-G2
PAINTED ROCK RD
23400 SDCo 92065 1173-D7
23400 SDCo 92065 (1193-F1
See Page 1192)
PAINT MOUNTAIN RD
1400 SDCo 92024 1148-F4
1400 SDCo 92029 1148-F4
PAISLEY CT
100 CHV 91911 1330-E3
E PAISLEY ST
- CHV 91911 1330-E3
PAIUTE PL
13000 PWY 92064 1190-D3
PAJAMA DR
100 OCN 92054 1086-D6
PAJARO WY
11300 SD 92127 1149-J7
PAKAMA LN
6800 SDCo 92084 1068-E5
PALA CT
- CHV 91911 1330-E4
PALA RD
3400 OCN 92054 1086-G1
3900 OCN 92057 1086-G1
4400 OCN 92057 1087-A1
PALA RD Rt#-S16
47000 RivC 92592 999-G1
47800 SDCo 92028 999-G1
PALA RD Rt#-76
2200 SDCo 92028 1048-H2
2200 SDCo 92028 1048-H2
5600 SDCo 92059 409-E6
5600 SDCo 92061 409-E6
7500 SDCo 92059 1029-F4
8500 SDCo 92028 1029-C7
8600 SDCo 92028 1049-A1
16800 SDCo 92061 1051-B5
16800 SDCo 92082 1051-B5
33100 SDCo 92061 1050-H1
PALA ST
100 SDCo 92065 1152-E7
7900 SD 92114 1290-G3
PALABRA CIR
11400 SD 92124 1250-A2
PALABRA CT
11400 SD 92124 1250-A2
PALACE DR
2400 SD 92123 1249-F6
PALACIO CT
17000 SD 92127 1169-H2
PALACIO DR
7700 CRLB 92009 1147-F2
PALACIO PL
17000 SD 92127 1169-H2
PALACIO NORTE
100 SDCo 92028 1027-H2
PALA DEL NORTE RD
36300 SDCo 92059 1029-C4
36300 SDCo 92028 1029-C4
PALAIE RD
7900 SDCo 92021 1252-A1
PALA LAKE DR
- SDCo 92028 1028-G5
PALA LOMA DR
10800 SDCo 92082 1049-F3
PALA MESA CT
2700 SDCo 92028 1048-F1
PALA MESA DR
3600 SDCo 92028 1048-F1
4000 SDCo 92028 1028-G7
PALA MESA LN
3100 SDCo 92028 1048-F1
PALA MESA HEIGHTS DR
1200 SDCo 92028 1028-H5
1200 SDCo 92028 1029-A5
PALA MESA OAKS DR
4000 SDCo 92028 1028-G5
PALA MISSION RD
12100 SDCo 92059 1029-G4
PALA MOUNTAIN DR
900 SDCo 92028 1028-J4
900 SDCo 92028 1029-A5
PALARO DR
800 ENCT 92024 1147-C2
PALA TEMECULA RD Rt#-S16
37100 SDCo 92028 999-G3
38600 SDCo 92059 999-G3
41800 SDCo 92059 1029-G2
PALAU CIR
1200 CORD 92118 1309-C5
PALAU RD
1100 CORD 92118 1309-C5
PALA VISTA DR
100 VSTA 92083 1087-J7
100 VSTA 92083 1107-J1
PALAWAN WY
100 SD 92114 1290-F5
PALE MOON RD
- SDCo 92127 1169-A1
PALENCIA CT
900 CHV 91910 1310-H5
PALENCIA PL
900 CHV 91910 1310-H5

PALENQUE ST
7700 CRLB 92009 1147-F2
PALEO DR
- SDCo 91935 1293-C1
14800 SDCo 91935 1273-B7
PALERMO CT
1900 VSTA 92083 1107-H3
5000 OCN 92057 1087-C1
PALERMO DR
2200 SD 92106 1268-B7
2400 SD 92107 1268-B7
5000 OCN 92057 1087-B1
PALERO RD
12500 SD 92128 1170-C4
PALETTE CT
700 OCN 92057 1087-C1
PALIMO DR
31200 SDCo 92026 1068-J2
31200 SDCo 92026 1069-A2
PALIN ST
4900 SD 92113 1290-A5
5100 SD 92114 1290-A5
PALISADES CT
12800 PWY 92064 1190-D2
PALISADES DR
1800 CRLB 92008 1106-H6
13900 PWY 92064 1190-D2
PALISADES RD
4100 SD 92116 1269-G2
PALITO CT
11400 SD 92127 1149-J7
PALLETTE ST
200 ELCJ 92020 1251-G7
PALLON CT
4100 SD 92124 1249-J2
PALLON WY
10900 SD 92124 1249-J2
10900 SD 92124 1250-A2
PALLUX WY
8400 SD 92126 1209-C2
PALLUX STAR CT
15500 SDCo 91935 1293-E1
PALM AV
- SD 92102 1289-G4
- SD 92123 1249-C5
- IMPB 91932 1329-F7
100 CHV 91911 1330-F5
100 CORD 92118 1288-H5
200 NATC 91950 1289-J7
300 NATC 91950 1290-A7
700 CRLB 92008 1106-F6
900 NATC 91950 1310-A1
2200 SD 92154 1330-B7
4200 LMSA 91941 1270-J2
PALM AV Rt#-75
900 IMPB 91932 1329-G7
1300 SD 92154 1329-G7
1300 IMPB 92154 1329-G7
1700 SD 92154 1330-A7
W PALM AV
100 ELCJ 92020 1251-E6
PALM DR
- DLMR 92014 1187-G3
200 VSTA 92084 1087-H5
3700 SDCo 91902 1310-J3
3800 CHV 91902 1310-J3
PALM LN
- SDCo 92040 1232-D6
2700 LMGR 91945 1270-J7
9700 SDCo 92029 1149-E3
PALM PL
- ELCJ 92019 1251-J6
PALM RD
400 SMCS 92069 1108-E6
1600 CHV 91911 1330-F5
PALM ST
100 SD 92103 1269-A7
400 SD 92103 1268-J7
700 VSTA 92083 1087-F6
1300 SD 92101 1268-J7
1300 SD 92101 1288-J1
2600 LMGR 91945 1270-H7
2800 SD 92104 1269-E7
3700 SMCS 92069 1128-C1
4700 SD 92105 1269-J7
5100 SD 92105 1270-A7
8500 LMGR 91977 1270-J7
8500 SDCo 91977 1270-J7
PALM TER
800 ESCN 92025 1129-J6
PALMAC ST
300 SMCS 92069 1108-E6
PALMAS CT
3600 OCN 92056 1107-D3
PALMAS DR
31500 SDCo 92086 409-K5
PALMAS NORTE
100 SDCo 92028 1028-A2
PALMA VISTA CT
1200 SDCo 92025 1130-E6
PALMBARK ST
300 VSTA 92083 1087-E6
PALM BEACH LN
9600 SD 92129 1189-E5
PALM BEACH ST
1400 CHV 91915 1311-H7
PALM CANYON DR
- SDCo 92004 (1078-E2
See Page 1058)
200 VSTA 92083 1087-E7
2600 SD 92037 1248-A2
PALM CANYON DR Rt#-S22
200 SDCo 92004 (1078-F2
See Page 1058)
700 SDCo 92004 (1079-D2
See Page 1058)
PALM CREST TER
3100 SMCS 92069 1108-C6
3100 VSTA 92083 1108-C6
PALMER DR
1900 OCN 92056 1106-G1
PALMER ST
2900 NATC 91950 1310-B1
PALMER WY
1200 NATC 91950 1290-B7
1200 NATC 91950 1310-C1
5600 CRLB 92008 1127-D1
PALMERA DR
5000 OCN 92056 1087-D3
PALMERO DR
16700 SD 92128 1170-C3
PALMETTO DR
4800 SD 92057 1067-B7
PALMETTO WY
4000 SD 92103 1268-H5
PALM GLEN DR
10100 SNTE 92071 1231-E4

PALM HILL DR
3000 SDCo 92084 1088-E6
PALMILLA DR
7100 SD 92122 1228-B4
PALMITAS ST
400 SOLB 92075 1187-F1
PALM ROW DR
10100 SDCo 92040 1231-H2
PALM TREE CT
4100 SDCo 91941 1271-G4
PALM VALLEY CIR
900 CHV 91915 1311-G5
PALM VIEW CT
1500 NATC 91950 1310-A1
PALM VIEW DR
1400 NATC 91950 1310-A1
PALM VIEW WY
900 NATC 91950 1310-A1
PALM VISTA CT
3000 SDCo 92019 1272-C5
PALMWOOD CT
500 SD 92139 1290-G6
PALMWOOD DR
500 SD 92139 1290-G6
PALMYRA AV
5200 SD 92117 1228-H7
PALMYRA DR
100 SDCo 92083 1108-C3
100 SDCo 92084 1108-C3
PALO CT
3700 SDCo 91902 1310-E4
PALO DR
3800 SDCo 91902 1310-E4
PALO GN
1800 ESCN 92026 1109-F6
PALO ALTO CT
800 SMCS 92069 1108-H6
PALO ALTO LN
6700 SD 92114 1290-E4
PALO DANZANTE
3000 SDCo 91901 1254-C1
PALOMA LN
300 SDCo 92021 1252-H4
PALOMA ST
10700 SNTE 92071 1231-F6
PALOMA WY
1600 SDCo 91905 (1319-J2
See Page 1298)
PALOMA BAY CT
300 OCN 92057 1066-J6
PALOMAR AV
200 SD 92037 1247-E2
600 ELCJ 92020 1271-E1
PALOMAR DR
- CHV 91911 1330-D1
300 SMCS 92069 1109-D7
300 SMCS 92069 1129-D1
1500 SDCo 92028 1047-J3
3700 SDCo 92028 1048-A3
E PALOMAR DR
- CHV 91911 1330-E1
PALOMAR PL
1100 VSTA 92084 1088-A3
PALOMAR ST
- CHV 91911 1330-B4
E PALOMAR ST
- CHV 91911 1331-A2
- CHV 91913 1311-D7
- CHV 91913 1331-A2
- CHV 91911 1330-H2
PALOMAR TER
1200 ESCN 92027 1130-B2
PALOMAR VW
- SDCo 92082 1070-G1
PALOMAR AIRPORT RD Rt#-S12
- CRLB 92008 1126-H3
- CRLB 92009 1126-H3
1200 CRLB 92009 1127-F2
1200 CRLB 92009 1127-F2
3100 CRLB 92008 1128-A2
3100 SMCS 92069 1128-A2
3100 CRLB 92009 1128-A2
PALOMARCOS AV
1400 SMCS 92069 1108-E6
PALOMAR DIVIDE RD
- SDCo 92060 409-G6
PALOMAR DIVIDE TKTR
- SDCo 92060 409-F5
PALOMARES CT
1200 SDCo 92028 1027-H6
PALOMARES RD
1800 SDCo 92028 1027-H6
PALOMAR OAKS CT
6300 CRLB 92009 1127-D4
PALOMAR OAKS WY
1700 CRLB 92009 1127-C4
1800 CRLB 92008 1127-B2
PALOMAR VISTA DR
1500 OCN 92056 1087-D2
30300 SDCo 92082 1070-F1
PALOMAR VISTA RD
3400 SDCo 92060 409-G7
PALOMINO CIR
2600 SD 92037 1248-A2
PALOMINO CT
900 SMCS 92069 1109-C5
1700 OCN 92057 1067-F7
PALOMINO DR
800 SMCS 92069 1109-C5
PALOMINO LN
1600 SDCo 92025 1130-C4
PALOMINO RD
200 SDCo 92028 1027-G5
PALOMINO RIDGE DR
9000 SDCo 92040 1232-G4
9400 SDCo 92021 1232-G4
PALOMIRA CT
2200 CHV 91915 1311-G6
PALOS TIERRA RD
12400 SDCo 92082 1070-B7
PALOS VERDES DR
31400 SDCo 92026 1069-A2
31700 SDCo 92026 1049-A7
31900 SDCo 92026 1068-J2
PALO VERDE DR
- SDCo 92055 1085-J4
PALO VERDE LN
- SDCo 92036 430-D3
4600 SDCo 92004 (1099-F4
See Page 1098)
PALO VERDE RD
- ImCo - 412-A4
PALO VERDE TER
4300 SD 92120 1269-H1
4400 SD 92115 1269-H1
PALO VERDE WY
3700 OCN 92056 1107-B1

PALO VISTA RD
2300 SDCo 92028 1028-C7
PALSERO AV
1900 ESCN 92029 1129-F6
PAM LN
13100 SDCo 92040 1232-C3
PAMBARA CIR
1400 OCN 92054 1106-E1
PAMELA CT
4100 SD 92117 1248-E2
PAMELA DR
100 SDCo 92028 1028-E1
PAMELA LN
800 ELCJ 92020 1271-E1
1800 ESCN 92026 1109-D4
PAMJOY LN
3400 SDCo 91977 1271-A5
PAMO AV
2400 SD 92104 1289-E1
2500 SD 92104 1269-E7
PAMO RD
1300 SDCo 92065 1152-H1
6500 SDCo 92065 409-G11
PAMOOSA LN
29300 SDCo 92082 1069-E6
PAMO VALLEY VW
22400 SDCo 92065 409-H11
PAMO WINTERCAMP RD
18700 SDCo 92065 1171-J5
PAMPA ST
8700 LMSA 91942 1251-A6
PAMPAS LN
1700 SDCo 92004 (1099-F2
See Page 1098)
PAMPLONA WY
2200 CRLB 92009 1127-F7
PANA DR
- SDCo 92040 1232-D6
PANAMA PL
4900 SD 92116 1269-F2
PAN AMERICAN PZ
1900 SD 92101 1289-B1
PAN AMERICAN RD
2200 SD 92101 1289-B1
PAN AMERICAN RD E
2100 SD 92101 1289-B1
PAN AMERICAN RD W
2300 SD 92101 1289-B1
PANAMINT RW
2400 SD 92139 1290-F7
PANASONIC WY
7500 SD 92154 1351-E2
PANAY CT
1900 SD 92105 1289-H1
PANCHOY DR
4600 SDCo 91941 1271-F3
PANCHOY LN
8200 LMGR 91945 1290-H1
PANDORA DR
9900 SDCo 91941 1271-D1
PANEL CT
6400 SD 92122 1228-F5
PANETTAH DR
1700 SDCo 91901 1233-G7
PANGEA DR
2700 SD 92093 1227-J1
PANHANDLE TR
7300 SDCo 92036 1138-B7
PANKEY RD
- SDCo 92028 1028-H4
2600 SDCo 92028 1048-H1
PANNONIA RD
4600 CRLB 92008 1106-H7
PANOCHA CT
6800 SD 92114 1270-E7
PANORAMA DR
1400 SDCo 92069 1128-C4
3200 SDCo 92036 1156-E1
4200 LMSA 91941 1271-A4
4200 LMSA 91977 1271-A4
4700 SD 92116 1269-C3
PANORAMA RD
1700 VSTA 92083 1087-G3
PANORAMA TR
- SDCo 92060 409-H8
- SDCo 92070 409-H8
PANORAMA VW
- SDCo 92082 1051-A6
PANORAMA CREST
2800 SDCo 92029 1150-A2
PANORAMA RIDGE CT
8300 SDCo 91977 1290-J5
PANORAMA RIDGE RD
1300 OCN 92056 1087-D4
PANORAMIC DR
- SDCo 92084 1068-C7
- SDCo 92084 1088-C1
PANORAMIC LN
5400 SD 92121 1208-E4
PANORAMIC PL
- SDCo 92084 1068-D7
PANORAMIC WY
- SDCo 92084 1068-D7
- SDCo 92084 1088-D1
PANSY WY
1000 SDCo 92019 1252-F7
PANTERA RD
13200 SD 92130 1187-J5
PANTERA WY
3500 SD 92130 1187-J5
PANTHER WY
- VSTA 92084 1087-H3
PAOLA PL
4600 SD 92117 1248-H1
PAOLA WY
4400 SD 92117 1248-H2
PAPAGALLO CT
11600 SD 92124 1250-B3
PAPAGALLO DR
- OCN 92057 1067-A3
PAPAGO DR
12700 PWY 92064 1190-D4
PAPAGO TR
15300 SDCo 92036 1176-E4
PAPAYA ST
400 VSTA 92083 1087-E6
PAPAYA WY
3500 OCN 92054 1086-F2
PAPIN ST
1400 OCN 92054 1086-B5
PAPOOSE CT
11100 SD 92127 1149-H7
PAPPAS CT
- CHV 91911 1331-A2
PAPPAS RD
24500 SDCo 92065 1173-F4
PAPRIKA RD
30100 SDCo 91906 (1297-F4
See Page 1296)

PAPRIKA WY
3800 OCN 92057 1086-H4
PAPYRUS CT
- OCN 92054 1106-F2
PAQUITA ST
900 ELCJ 92019 1252-B7
PAR DR
3200 SDCo 91941 1270-J5
3200 SDCo 91941 1271-A6
3200 SDCo 91977 1271-A6
3300 OCN 92056 1106-J1
PARADISE DR
800 NATC 91950 1290-A7
900 NATC 91950 1310-A1
14000 PWY 92064 1190-G2
PARADISE RD
1400 SD 92114 1290-B6
PARADISE ST
400 NATC 92136 1309-F1
1700 ESCN 92026 1109-H5
1800 SD 92114 1290-D1
PARADISE WY
2000 VSTA 92083 1087-C7
PARADISE COVE WY
700 OCN 92054 1066-E6
PARADISE CREST VIEW WY
6600 SD 92114 1290-E6
PARADISE GLEN WY
1700 SDCo 92069 1128-A4
1700 SMCS 92069 1128-A4
PARADISE HILLS RD
1400 SD 92114 1290-F6
PARADISE MEADOW LN
26900 SDCo 92082 1091-E4
PARADISE MESA RD
1700 SD 92114 1290-D6
PARADISE MOUNTAIN LN
17400 SDCo 92082 1091-E5
PARADISE MOUNTAIN RD
17200 SDCo 92082 1091-H4
PARADISE PARK DR
9000 SDCo 92040 1231-J6
PARADISE RIDGE RD
6400 SD 92114 1290-D6
PARADISE VALLEY CT
8100 SDCo 91977 1290-H5
PARADISE VALLEY RD
3400 NATC 91950 1290-C6
6400 SD 92139 1290-H5
6400 SD 92114 1290-H5
8000 SDCo 91977 1290-H5
8300 SDCo 91977 1291-A4
26400 SDCo 92086 409-H6
PARADOX LN
200 SDCo 92021 1252-J2
PARAGON MESA RD
16000 SDCo 92064 1191-C5
PARAISO AV
300 SDCo 91977 1291-C2
2100 SDCo 91977 1271-C7
PARAISO RD
3500 SDCo 92028 1047-E3
PARAKEET PL
1100 VSTA 92083 1087-G4
PARAMOUNT AV
- ESCN 92027 1130-C1
PARAMOUNT DR
4600 SD 92123 1249-D2
PARA SIEMPRE VISTA
20100 SDCo 92065 1152-E1
PARASIO CT
1400 NATC 91950 1289-J7
PARDEE PL
3500 SD 92113 1289-F5
PARDEE ST
- SD 92102 1289-F4
S PARDEE ST
- SD 92113 1289-F4
PAR FOUR DR
3400 SDCo 92019 1272-C6
PARIANOS DR
- CHV 91911 1330-D3
PARIS WY
6700 SD 92139 1310-F1
6800 SD 92139 1290-F7
PARISH RD
12500 SD 92128 1170-C3
PARIVA DR
1800 ENCT 92007 1167-E3
PARK AV
- ImCo 92233 411-C11
100 VSTA 92084 1087-H6
200 ESCN 92025 1129-J2
400 ELCN 92243 6499-G6
10300 SNTE 92071 1231-E6
E PARK AV
100 ELCJ 92020 1251-F5
200 SD 92173 1350-G4
1000 ELCJ 92021 1251-G5
W PARK AV
100 ELCJ 92020 1251-F5
100 SD 92173 1350-G4
PARK BLVD
200 SDCo 92021 1252-H3
1400 SD 92101 1289-B2
1700 SD 92134 1289-B2
2800 SD 92101 1269-C6
2900 SD 92103 1269-C6
4400 SD 92116 1269-C4
PARK CT
4900 CRLB 92008 1106-J7
PARK DR
300 VSTA 92084 1087-H6
800 SDCo 92029 1149-H1
900 SDCo 92029 1129-H7
1300 CHV 91911 1330-G3
1800 SD 92109 1248-A4
3700 CRLB 92008 1106-G6
3800 SDCo 92036 1156-E2
4900 CRLB 92008 1107-A7
5400 SDCo 91977 1290-J6
9300 SDCo 91916 1235-J3
PARK LN
- ENCT 92024 1147-D7
- SDCo 91901 1254-G7
- SDCo 91901 1274-G1
200 OCN 92054 1085-J7
7900 LMSA 91941 1270-J4
E PARK LN
200 CHV 91910 1310-A6
600 CHV 91910 1330-A1
800 CHV 91911 1330-A1
PARK PL
300 SMCS 92069 1128-F1
500 ESCN 92025 1129-J1
800 SDCo 92025 1130-C6

PARK PL
1000 CORD 92118 1288-H7
4100 SD 92116 1269-G3
32200 RivC 92592 999-F1
PARK RD
2900 ESCN 92025 1150-B1
PARK RW
1200 SD 92037 1227-F6
PARK ST
25800 SDCo 92026 1109-F2
PARK TR
- SDCo 92036 1156-D7
PARK VW
2000 ESCN 92029 1129-E6
PARK WY
300 CHV 91910 1310-A7
PARKBROOK LN
8400 SD 92114 1290-J4
PARKBROOK PL
200 SD 92114 1290-H4
PARKBROOK ST
200 SDCo 91977 1290-J3
400 SDCo 91977 1291-A3
8300 SD 92114 1290-J4
PARKBROOK WY
100 SD 92114 1290-J4
PARK CENTER DR
900 VSTA 92083 1108-A7
900 VSTA 92083 1107-J7
1000 VSTA 92083 1127-H1
PARKCREEK CT
100 SD 92114 1290-H4
PARK CREST DR
1900 ENCT 92007 1167-F3
10400 SNTE 92071 1231-E1
PARKCREST LN
9800 SD 92124 1249-F1
PARKCREST WY
5200 SD 92124 1249-F1
PARKDALE AV
9800 SD 92126 1209-A4
PARKDALE CIR
7600 SD 92126 1209-A4
PARKDALE CT
7700 SD 92126 1209-A3
PARKDALE CV
7700 SD 92126 1209-A4
PARK DALE LN
1800 ENCT 92024 1147-H6
PARKDALE PL
7700 SD 92126 1209-A4
PARKER LN
1600 SDCo 92065 1152-F7
PARKER PL
1000 VSTA 92084 1087-J6
1000 VSTA 92084 1088-A6
1200 SD 92109 1247-J7
PARKER RD
- ImCo 92243 6560-G1
- SDCo 92055 1085-G1
200 SDCo 91906 430-B10
200 SDCo 91906 (1318-A7
See Page 1298)
1800 ImCo 92243 6500-F5
PARKER ST
600 OCN 92057 1067-A5
E PARKER ST
5100 OCN 92057 1067-A5
PARKER MOUNTAIN RD
- CHV 91911 1311-E7
PARKETT LN
300 ELCJ 92020 1251-G5
PARK GROVE CT
7000 LMGR 91945 1290-F1
PARK HAVEN CT
4000 SD 92113 1289-H4
PARK HILL DR
900 ESCN 92025 1130-A3
PARK HILL LN
1000 ESCN 92025 1130-B4
1000 SDCo 92025 1130-B4
PARK HILL RD
2000 VSTA 92083 1107-H3
PARK HILL TER
1000 ESCN 92025 1130-B3
PARKHURST SQ
- SD 92130 1208-B2
PARKLAND WY
1500 SD 92114 1290-E5
PARKLAWN DR
1600 SDCo 92021 1251-G1
PARK LILAC LN
11600 SDCo 92082 1049-H7
PARKMEAD CT
5800 SD 92114 1290-C5
PARK MEADOWS RD
1000 CHV 91915 1311-H5
PARK MESA WY
6900 SD 92111 1248-J6
PARK PLAZA DR
9000 LMSA 91942 1251-A6
PARK RANCH PL
300 ESCN 92025 1150-B1
PARK RIDGE BLVD
6300 SD 91942 1250-E6
6300 SD 92120 1250-E6
6400 SD 92119 1250-E6
PARK RIDGE DR
- SDCo 92025 1130-D7
PARK RIM CT
3300 SD 92117 1228-D7
PARK RIM DR
4900 SD 92117 1228-D7
PARK RUN RD
8500 SD 92129 1189-C5
PARKS AV
4200 LMSA 91941 1270-G3
PARKSIDE AV
6000 SD 92139 1310-F1
PARKSIDE CT
400 CHV 91910 1310-G5
7000 SD 92139 1310-F1
PARKSIDE DR
400 OCN 92054 1086-E3
500 CHV 91910 1310-G5
PARKSIDE GN
200 ESCN 92026 1109-G5
PARKSIDE PL
200 SNTE 92071 1231-C5
3000 SD 92139 1310-E2
4100 CRLB 92008 1106-G6
PARKSIDE ST
12300 SDCo 92040 1232-A3
PARK TERRACE DR
9700 SNTE 92071 1231-D4
PARKTREE LN
2100 ESCN 92026 1109-H4
PARK VALLEY LN
1900 SD 92114 1290-F6

SAN DIEGO CO.

INDEX

PARK VIEW CT
SAN DIEGO CO. STREET INDEX
PENARA CT 6608

STREET
Block City ZIP Pg-Grid

PARK VIEW CT
7300 SNTE 92071 1230-F7
PARKVIEW DR
1500 VSTA 92083 1107-H5
5400 SD 92037 1248-A3
5400 SD 92109 1248-A3
PARK VIEW PL
1500 CORD 92118 1288-J7
PARKVIEW TER
1900 SD 92109 1248-A3
PARK VILLA DR
3500 SD 92104 1269-D6
PARK VILLA PL
900 ESCN 92025 1130-A3
PARK VILLAGE RD
7100 SD 92129 1188-J7
7200 SD 92129 1189-B6
PARK VISTA CT
6900 SD 92114 1290-F6
PARKWAY DR
6800 LMSA 91942 1250-J7
7000 LMSA 91942 1270-H1
PARKWAY PZ
600 ELCJ 92020 1251-E4
PARKWAY CENTRE DR
12200 PWY 92064 1190-F7
PARK WEST AV
5000 SD 92117 1228-D7
PARK WEST LN
3400 SD 92117 1228-D7
PARKWOOD AV
- SDCo 92083 1108-B6
- VSTA 92083 1108-B6
PARKWOOD DR
500 SD 92139 1290-G6
10600 SD 92126 1209-E3
PARKWOOD LN
- OCN 92054 1106-C1
400 ENCT 92024 1147-B2
PARKYNS AV
1000 ImCo 92249 6560-C7
PARLANGE PL
17600 SD 92128 1170-B1
PARLIAMENT RD
1800 ENCT 92024 1146-J2
PARMA CT
12500 SD 92128 1170-C2
PARMA LN
7600 SD 92126 1209-A3
PARNASSUS CIR
100 OCN 92054 1086-E6
PARRISH LN
300 DLMR 92014 1187-F5
PARROT ST
1500 SD 92105 1289-G1
PARROT MOUNTAIN RD
36700 SDCo 92066 409-L9
PARSLEY WY
800 OCN 92057 1086-H5
PARSONS LN
400 SMCS 92069 1109-A2
PARTHENON DR
2600 SD 92139 1310-F1
PARTOW WY
4600 OCN 92056 1087-B4
PARTRIDGE AV
1300 ELCJ 92020 1251-D3
PARTRIDGE CIR
400 VSTA 92083 1087-G5
PARTRIDGE CT
1000 SMCS 92069 1128-G4
PARTRIDGE GN
1300 ESCN 92029 1129-G5
PARTRIDGE LN
1300 OCN 92054 1086-E7
PARTRIDGE PL
7000 CRLB 92009 1127-D6
PARUS PT
9300 SD 92129 1189-D6
PAR VALLEY DR
28500 SDCo 92069 1088-E1
28500 SDCo 92084 1088-E1
PARVENU LN
1500 SDCo 92028 1027-H5
PAR VIEW CT
28100 SDCo 92026 1089-F3
PARVO CT
18100 SD 92128 1150-B7
PASADENA AV
4200 LMSA 91941 1270-H3
N PASADENA AV
100 SDCo 92028 1027-F2
S PASADENA AV
100 SDCo 92028 1027-F2
PASADERO DR
1100 ESCN 92029 1129-F5
PASATIEMPO AV
6100 SD 92120 1250-D6
PASATIEMPO DR
100 SDCo 92065 1152-J5
PASATIEMPO GN
2500 ESCN 92025 1130-B7
2700 ESCN 92025 1150-B1
PASCAL CT
5900 CRLB 92008 1127-D2
PASCALI CT
- SMCS 92069 1109-A5
PASCOE ST
1000 SD 92103 1269-B5
PASEO DR
8500 ELCJ 92020 1231-D7
8500 SNTE 92071 1231-D7
PASEO PKWY
11500 SDCo 92040 1231-G3
PASEO ACAMPO
2900 CRLB 92009 1127-H2
PASEO ADELANTE
6500 CRLB 92009 1127-J4
PASEO AIROSO
- CRLB 92009 1127-J2
PASEO AJANTA
15300 SD 92129 1169-J6
PASEO ALAMEDA
6000 CRLB 92009 1127-J2
PASEO ALBACETE
11300 SD 92129 1169-J6
PASEO ALDABRA
13800 SD 92129 1189-D3
PASEO ALEGRE
400 SMCS 92069 1109-D7
PASEO ALISO
- CRLB 92009 1147-F3
- ENCT 92024 1147-F3
PASEO ALLEGRIA AV
10600 SDCo 92127 1169-F4
PASEO ALMENDRO
7800 CRLB 92009 1147-H3
PASEO ALMIAR
6100 CRLB 92009 1127-G3

PASEO AL MONTE
7700 SDCo 92066 1237-C6
PASEO ALTA RICO
- CRLB 92009 1127-H3
PASEO ANCHO
3400 CRLB 92009 1147-J4
3400 CRLB 92009 1148-A4
PASEO ARBOLADO
6100 SDCo 92067 1168-D3
PASEO ARRAYAN
8000 CRLB 92009 1147-H3
PASEO ASPADA
6300 CRLB 92009 1127-J4
PASEO AVELLANO
8000 CRLB 92009 1147-G3
PASEO BELLO
8700 SNTE 92071 1230-H7
PASEO BONITA
1600 SD 92037 1247-H3
13700 PWY 92064 1190-G6
PASEO BURGA
500 CHV 91910 1310-J5
PASEO CALLADO
6200 CRLB 92009 1127-J3
PASEO CAMAS
6100 CRLB 92009 1127-G3
PASEO CANDELERO
2300 CRLB 92009 1127-G6
PASEO CARDIEL
13500 SD 92129 1189-F4
PASEO CARRETA
6000 CRLB 92009 1127-J2
PASEO CASTANADA
11000 SDCo 91941 1271-G5
PASEO CAZADOR
2900 CRLB 92009 1127-J4
PASEO CERRO
6300 CRLB 92009 1127-J4
6300 CRLB 92009 1128-A4
PASEO CEVERA
13700 SD 92129 1189-E3
PASEO CIELO
3000 SDCo 92067 1148-A7
PASEO COLINA
- CRLB 92009 1127-H3
12300 PWY 92064 1190-B6
PASEO CORONO
6300 CRLB 92009 1127-J4
PASEO CORTO
- CRLB 92009 1127-J3
PASEO CRESTA
2000 VSTA 92084 1087-G2
9100 SNTE 92071 1231-B7
PASEO CRISTAL
3000 ESCN 92029 1150-A2
PASEO CULZADA
3100 ESCN 92029 1150-A2
PASEO DE ALICIA
3400 OCN 92056 1106-B4
PASEO DE ANZA
2000 VSTA 92084 1087-G2
PASEO DE BRISAS
3400 OCN 92056 1106-B4
PASEO DE COLOMBO
3500 OCN 92056 1106-B4
PASEO DE COLORES
3400 OCN 92056 1106-B4
PASEO DE ELENITA
3500 OCN 92056 1106-B4
PASEO DE FRANCISCO
3500 OCN 92056 1106-B4
PASEO DE LA FRONTERA
- SD 92154 1352-A4
PASEO DE LA FUENTE
- SD 92154 1351-J3
PASEO DE LA FUENTE NORTE
- SD 92154 1351-H3
PASEO DE LA HUERTA
13600 PWY 92064 1170-F6
PASEO DEL AMO
3200 SMCS 92069 1108-D5
PASEO DEL ARQUERO
200 VSTA 92084 1088-A5
PASEO DEL ARROYO
1800 SDCo 92028 1028-A4
15500 PWY 92064 1170-F6
PASEO DE LAS AMERICAS
2100 SD 92154 1352-A3
PASEO DE LAS BRISAS
3000 SMCS 92069 1108-D5
16600 SDCo 92065 1171-F2
PASEO DE LAS CUMBRES
13700 PWY 92064 1170-F6
PASEO DE LAS FLORES
- ENCT 92024 1147-E4
PASEO DE LAS VERDES
- ENCT 92024 1147-E6
PASEO DE LAURA
2300 OCN 92056 1106-H2
PASEO DE LA VISTA
4000 SDCo 91902 1310-G1
PASEO DEL BOSQUE
500 VSTA 92083 1107-J2
PASEO DEL CAMPO
3200 SDCo 91978 1272-C7
PASEO DEL CERRO
1100 CHV 91910 1311-A7
PASEO DELICIAS
7000 SDCo 92067 1168-F1
PASEO DELICIAS Rt#-S6
6200 SDCo 92067 1168-F2
PASEO DELICIAS Rt#-S8
6100 SDCo 92067 1168-E2
PASEO DEL LAGO
1100 SDCo 92028 1047-H3
6300 CRLB 92009 1127-C4
PASEO DEL LAGO DR
1800 VSTA 92083 1107-G5
PASEO DEL MAR
13500 SDCo 92021 1232-E7
PASEO DEL NORTE
1000 CHV 91910 1311-A7
5400 CRLB 92008 1126-H4
6000 CRLB 92008 1126-H4
6600 CRLB 92009 1127-A6
PASEO DEL OCASO
7900 SD 92037 1227-H5
PASEO DE LOS AMERICANOS
3500 OCN 92056 1106-B4
PASEO DE LOS ARBOLES
1800 SDCo 92028 1028-A4

PASEO DE LOS CALIFORNIANOS
3500 OCN 92056 1106-B4
PASEO DE LOS SUENOS
- SDCo 92067 1149-B3
PASEO DEL PASO
900 CHV 91910 1311-A7
900 CHV 91910 1330-J1
900 CHV 91910 1331-A1
PASEO DEL REY
600 CHV 91910 1310-H6
600 CHV 91910 1330-H1
1900 VSTA 92084 1087-G2
8600 SNTE 92071 1231-B7
PASEO DEL SOL
1900 VSTA 92084 1087-G2
2900 SDCo 92025 1130-E7
2900 SDCo 92025 1150-E1
8500 SNTE 92071 1231-B7
PASEO DEL TORRENO
29300 SDCo 92066 1237-D6
PASEO DEL VERANO
12500 SD 92128 1170-D1
PASEO DEL VERANO NORTE
12000 SD 92128 1150-C7
13000 SD 92128 1170-D1
PASEO DEL VISTA
6700 CRLB 92009 1128-A5
PASEO DE MARGUERITA
9100 SNTE 92071 1231-B7
PASEO DE OCHO MINOS
12600 SDCo 92064 1191-D6
12600 SDCo 92071 1191-D6
PASEO DE OLIVOS
3600 SDCo 92028 1047-H4
PASEO DE PIEDRAS
17300 SDCo 92127 1169-D1
PASEO DE SANTOS
9900 SDCo 92026 1089-E2
PASEO DESCANSO
6300 CRLB 92009 1127-J3
6300 CRLB 92009 1128-A4
PASEO DOMINGUEZ
6500 CRLB 92009 1127-J5
PASEO DONITO
2100 SDCo 91901 1234-D7
PASEO DORADO
1900 SD 92037 1227-G5
PASEO ELEGANCIA
- CRLB 92009 1127-H3
PASEO ENCANTADA
7700 SDCo 92066 1237-D6
PASEO ENSILLAR
6100 CRLB 92009 1127-G3
PASEO ENTRADA
900 CHV 91910 1330-J1
900 CHV 91910 1331-A1
1000 CHV 91910 1311-A7
PASEO ESCUELA
- CRLB 92009 1127-H3
PASEO ESMERADO
- CRLB 92009 1148-A4
PASEO ESPLANADA
- SDCo 92067 1149-A3
PASEO ESTABLO
6300 CRLB 92009 1127-H4
PASEO ESTRIBO
- CRLB 92009 1127-H3
PASEO FRATERNIDAD
1800 SD 92173 1350-F3
PASEO FRONTERA
6500 CRLB 92009 1127-J5
PASEO FUERTE
11900 SDCo 92020 1271-J3
PASEO GRANDE
2100 SDCo 92019 1272-C1
PASEO GRANDE RD
- SDCo 92003 1068-C5
- SDCo 92084 1068-C5
PASEO GRANTO
6100 CRLB 92009 1127-G3
PASEO HERMOS
- CRLB 92009 1127-H2
PASEO HERMOSA
1200 OCN 92056 1087-D2
17100 SDCo 92067 1168-G5
PASEO HERMOSO
15700 PWY 92064 1170-E5
PASEO IGLESIA
8400 SDCo 91977 1290-J5
PASEO JAQUITA
- CRLB 92009 1127-H3
PASEO JENGHIZ
15500 SD 92129 1169-J6
PASEO LA CRESTA
900 CHV 91910 1330-J1
900 CHV 91910 1331-A1
PASEO LADERA
900 CHV 91910 1310-J7
900 CHV 91910 1330-J1
1200 CHV 91911 1330-J1
2000 VSTA 92084 1087-G2
8600 SNTE 92071 1231-B7
8600 SNTE 92071 1251-B1
PASEO LADERA S
- CHV 91911 1330-J2
- CHV 91911 1331-A2
PASEO LAGO
11500 SDCo 92040 1231-H3
PASEO LA JOLLA
- CRLB 92009 1147-J2
PASEO LAREDO
6800 SD 92037 1247-H1
PASEO LAZO
6400 CRLB 92009 1127-H4
PASEO LINDO
31800 SDCo 92003 1067-G1
PASEO LUCIDO
11800 SD 92128 1170-B4
PASEO LUNADA
- CRLB 92009 1127-H4
PASEO MAGDA
1200 CHV 91910 1311-A6
PASEO MARGUERITA
- VSTA 92084 1087-G2
1100 CHV 91910 1310-J7
1100 CHV 91910 1330-J1
PASEO MEMBRILLO
7900 CRLB 92009 1147-H3
PASEO MIRADA
2600 SD 92037 1248-A2
PASEO MONONA
6000 CRLB 92009 1127-J2
PASEO MONTALBAN
9300 SD 92129 1189-E4
PASEO MONTANAS
4100 SD 92130 1188-B6

PASEO MONTANOSO
11200 SD 92127 1169-H6
PASEO MONTE
2400 SDCo 92028 1047-H3
PASEO MONTE BATALLA
12200 SD 92128 1150-B5
PASEO MONTRIL
9500 SD 92129 1189-F5
PASEO OROZCO
3700 SDCo 91941 1271-G5
PASEO PACIFICA
300 ENCT 92024 1147-C7
PASEO PALERO
6100 CRLB 92009 1127-J3
PASEO PALMAS DR
10100 SDCo 92040 1231-H3
PASEO PALMAS WY
10300 SDCo 92040 1231-H3
PASEO PANTERA
200 SDCo 92065 1153-C5
PASEO PARK DR
10200 SDCo 92040 1231-H3
PASEO PENASCO
15300 SDCo 92025 1151-A2
PASEO PICADO
6100 CRLB 92009 1127-G3
PASEO PIEDRAS
19200 SDCo 92067 1149-A3
PASEO PORTRERO
6300 CRLB 92009 1127-J4
PASEO POTRIL
2700 SDCo 91902 1290-J7
PASEO PRADERA
6000 CRLB 92009 1127-J2
PASEO PRIMAVERA
1100 CHV 91910 1311-A7
1100 CHV 91910 1331-A1
PASEO PRIMERO
- SDCo 92014 1168-A6
PASEO PRIVADO
6100 CRLB 92009 1127-J3
6100 CRLB 92009 1128-A3
PASEO RANCHERO
- CHV 91913 1331-B1
800 CHV 91910 1311-A6
1100 CHV 91910 1331-B1
PASEO RIO
600 VSTA 92083 1107-E1
PASEO ROBLES RD
29400 SDCo 92082 1070-J5
PASEO ROSAL
500 CHV 91910 1310-J5
PASEO SALAMONER
3500 SDCo 91941 1271-G5
PASEO SALIDA GN
1500 ESCN 92025 1130-A4
PASEO SALINERO
6000 CRLB 92009 1127-G3
PASEO SARINA
1100 CHV 91910 1311-A7
1100 CHV 91910 1331-A1
PASEO SAUCEDAL
- CRLB 92009 1147-G2
PASEO SEQUIEROS
3900 SDCo 91941 1271-G4
PASEO SIERRA
1100 CHV 91910 1311-A7
PASEO SONORA GN
1500 ESCN 92025 1130-A4
PASEO TAMAYO
3900 SDCo 91941 1271-H4
PASEO TAPAJOS
- CRLB 92009 1127-J3
PASEO TAXCO
8100 CRLB 92009 1147-J4
PASEO TEMPORADA
9500 SD 92129 1189-E4
PASEO TENIS
16100 SDCo 92067 1168-G7
PASEO TESORO
6100 CRLB 92009 1127-J2
PASEO TIEMPO GN
1500 ESCN 92025 1130-A4
PASEO TIENDA
6100 CRLB 92009 1127-J3
PASEO TIERRA
- SMCS 92078 1129-A2
PASEO TULIPERO
- CRLB 92009 1147-F3
PASEO VALENCIA
16000 SDCo 92067 1168-F7
PASEO VALIENTE
6100 CRLB 92009 1127-J2
PASEO VALINO
- CRLB 92009 1127-J2
PASEO VALLE
6100 CRLB 92009 1127-G3
PASEO VALLE ALTO
15500 PWY 92064 1170-F6
PASEO VERDE
1100 CHV 91910 1331-A1
7300 CRLB 92009 1127-J7
PASEO VICTORIA
18200 SDCo 92067 1148-D7
PASEO VISTA
11500 SDCo 92040 1231-H3
PASEO VISTA FAMOSA
3700 SDCo 92091 1168-C7
PASEO VOLANTE
- CRLB 92009 1127-J2
PASEO VUELO
6400 CRLB 92009 1147-J4
PASEO ZALDIVAR
13800 SD 92129 1189-E3
PASEO ZUNIGA
3900 SDCo 91941 1271-G4
PASITA DE KRISTY
10900 SDCo 92040 1231-F3
PASO ALTO CT
2600 SDCo 91905 (1299-J3 See Page 1298)
PASO DE FLORA
- SDCo 92026 1069-D3
PASO DEL LAGOS
4000 SDCo 92003 1067-F2
PASO DEL NORTE
300 SDCo 92026 1109-G2
PASO DEL SOL
15000 SDCo 92014 1168-A7
PASO ORO VERDE
3900 SDCo 92028 997-G4
PASO ROBLES CT
2400 CHV 91914 1311-F3
29300 SDCo 92082 1070-J6
PASO ROBLES LN
- SDCo 92082 1070-J5
PASO ROBLES PL
15400 SDCo 92082 1070-J5

PASO ROBLES RD
29100 SDCo 92082 1070-J5
29100 SDCo 92082 1071-A6
PASO VERDE
3900 SDCo 92028 997-G4
PASQUAL HIGHLANDS RD
19900 SDCo 92065 1152-D2
PASSERINE WY
10600 SD 92121 1208-E4
PASSIFLORA AV
700 ENCT 92024 1147-D4
PASSIFLORA PL
800 ENCT 92024 1147-D4
PASSING LN
200 SDCo 92065 1153-C5
PASSY AV
2800 SD 92122 1228-B6
PASTEL CT
4800 OCN 92057 1087-C1
PASTERNACK PL
3200 SD 92123 1249-D5
PASTEUR CT
2000 CRLB 92008 1127-C2
PASTORAL RD
12000 SD 92128 1170-B3
PASTORAL WY
1700 SDCo 92069 1128-B2
PAT ST
7900 LMSA 91942 1250-H6
PATA RANCH RD
13700 SDCo 92040 1212-F3
PATA VIEW DR
15300 SDCo 92040 1212-H6
PATE RD
- SDCo 92672 1023-D2
PATERO CT
1400 LMGR 91945 1290-F2
PATHFINDER WY
5900 SDCo 91902 1311-B2
PATHOS CT
8400 SD 92129 1189-C6
PATHOS LN
12300 SD 92129 1189-C6
PATHWAY ST
9500 SNTE 92071 1231-C7
PATIENCES PL
3200 OCN 92056 1067-D7
PATINA CT
4800 OCN 92057 1087-B1
10900 SD 92131 1210-A2
PATINA ST
- SDCo 92127 1169-F3
PATMOS WY
6000 OCN 92056 1107-F5
PATOS PL
500 CHV 91910 1311-B4
PATRA WY
5000 OCN 92056 1107-E4
PATRIA DR
4500 SD 92115 1270-D3
PATRICIA AV
300 CHV 91910 1310-C6
PATRICIA CIR
1100 VSTA 92084 1088-A7
PATRICIA CT
8700 SNTE 92071 1231-E7
PATRICIA LN
300 ELCJ 92020 1251-E6
600 VSTA 92084 1088-A7
PATRICIA PL
4600 SD 92115 1269-J3
PATRICIA RD
36400 SDCo 92082 1050-D5
PATRICK DR
200 SDCo 92019 1253-D1
PATRIOT ST
10200 SD 92124 1249-G5
PATTEN ST
300 SD 92114 1290-D4
PATTERSON RD
- SD 92106 1287-J5
2300 ESCN 92027 1130-E1
PATTI DR
300 VSTA 92084 1087-H3
PATTON ST
1800 SMCS 92069 1128-B5
PATTON OAK RD
200 SDCo 92028 997-F7
200 SDCo 92028 1027-F1
PATTY LN
300 ENCT 92024 1147-B3
PATTY HILL DR
200 SOLB 92075 1167-E6
PATTY LOU DR
10100 SDCo 92040 1232-B3
PAUL ST
600 ESCN 92027 1130-C2
PAUL WY
1000 ESCN 92027 1130-C2
PAULA DR
- ESCN 92026 1109-G6
PAULA ST
800 ESCN 92027 1110-C6
3800 LMSA 91941 1270-F5
PAULA WY
1000 ESCN 92027 1110-B5
PAUL BARWICK CT
11200 SD 92126 1208-J2
PAULIN AV
- ImCo 92249 6560-B7
PAULINA TER
16500 PWY 92064 1170-D4
PAULINE AV
400 ELCJ 92020 1251-G6
PAULINE WY
2700 OCN 92056 1087-B7
PAULING AV
4500 SD 92122 1228-F4
PAUL JONES AV
3500 SD 92117 1248-D5
PAULSEN AV
700 ELCJ 92020 1251-E7
E PAULY DR
- SD 92102 1289-G3
W PAULY DR
- SD 92102 1289-G3
PAUMA PL
300 ESCN 92029 1129-F3
PAUMA ST
- SDCo 92055 1085-J4
- SDCo 92055 1086-A4
PAUMA ALTO DR
14200 SDCo 92082 1050-G7
14200 SDCo 92082 1070-G1
PAUMA HEIGHTS LN
31600 SDCo 92082 1070-J1
PAUMA HEIGHTS RD
30200 SDCo 92082 1070-F1

PAUMA HEIGHTS RD
31100 SDCo 92082 1071-A1
31300 SDCo 92082 1051-A7
32100 SDCo 92061 1050-J5
32100 SDCo 92061 1051-A7
PAUMA RANCH RD
31600 SDCo 92061 1051-H7
PAUMA RESERVATION RD
14600 SDCo 92061 1050-H2
15000 SDCo 92061 1051-A1
15500 SDCo 92061 409-F6
PAUMA RIDGE CIR
- SDCo 92059 1050-F1
PAUMA RIDGE RD
- SDCo 92059 1050-E1
PAUMA VALLEY DR
32300 SDCo 92061 1051-A6
32500 SDCo 92061 1050-H5
PAUMA VIEW DR
- SDCo 92082 1070-J1
14400 SDCo 92061 1050-H6
31100 SDCo 92061 1050-H6
PAUMA VISTA DR
13700 SDCo 92082 1050-E6
PAUNACK ST
300 NATC 92136 1289-G7
300 NATC 92136 1309-G1
PAVLOV AV
4200 SD 92122 1228-E5
PAVO REAL DR
3900 SD 92124 1250-A3
PAWNEE DR
5800 LMSA 91942 1250-G7
PAWNEE GN
500 ESCN 92025 1130-A6
PAWNEE ST
100 SMCS 92069 1108-D7
PAXTON CT
2800 SD 92154 1350-C1
PAXTON DR
1100 SD 92154 1350-C1
PAYMASTER RD
10200 SDCo 92026 1069-E4
PAYMOGO CT
11300 SD 92129 1169-H6
PAYMOGO ST
15500 SD 92129 1169-H6
PAYNE RD
- ImCo 92251 430-L4
- ImCo 92259 430-L4
PAYNE ST
100 SD 92113 1289-F4
PAYSON DR
2700 SDCo 92036 1136-A7
2800 SDCo 92066 1135-J6
PAYSON RD
4000 LMSA 91941 1270-J4
PEACEFUL CT
10100 SNTE 92071 1231-D4
PEACEFUL DR
9800 SNTE 92071 1231-D4
PEACEFUL LN
400 VSTA 92083 1087-D7
700 ESCN 92026 1109-J7
PEACEFUL PL
1300 SDCo 91901 1233-J6
PEACEFUL VALLEY RANCH RD
14000 SDCo 91935 1292-J3
PEACE VALLEY LN
16600 SDCo 92065 1171-H3
PEACH AV
900 ELCJ 92021 1251-H4
1300 ELCJ 92021 1252-A4
PEACH CT
900 ELCJ 92021 1251-H4
PEACH WY
500 SMCS 92069 1108-J5
900 ESCN 92026 1109-H6
PEACH BLOSSOM ST
3600 NATC 91950 1290-C6
PEACH GROVE LN
1200 VSTA 92084 1088-A6
PEACH POINT AV
7900 SD 92126 1209-B3
PEACHTREE CIR
2200 CHV 91915 1311-F5
PEACHTREE CT
- SMCS 92078 1128-G2
PEACH TREE LN
2200 SDCo 91977 1271-E7
PEACHTREE LN
14100 PWY 92064 1190-F2
PEACH TREE RD
6900 CRLB 92009 1127-A6
PEACH TREE WY
3400 OCN 92054 1086-F2
PEACHWOOD CT
12600 PWY 92064 1190-C1
PEACHWOOD DR
1300 ENCT 92024 1167-F1
PEACOCK BLVD
1300 OCN 92056 1087-D4
PEACOCK DR
7700 SD 92123 1249-B7
PEACOCK VALLEY RD
2300 CHV 91915 1311-H7
PEAK CT
4500 SDCo 91941 1271-E3
PEAR LN
- SDCo 92026 1089-B2
PEAR ST
900 ELCJ 92021 1251-H2
PEAR BLOSSOM AV
800 OCN 92057 1086-F5
PEAR BLOSSOM CIR
600 OCN 92057 1086-F5
PEAR BLOSSOM DR
600 OCN 92057 1086-F5
PEAR BLOSSOM PL
400 ESCN 92026 1109-H7
PEARCE GROVE DR
300 ENCT 92024 1147-B3
PEARL AV
1200 ESCN 92027 1110-A7
PEARL LN
500 SD 92173 1350-E3
3200 OCN 92056 1107-A2
PEARL PL
800 ELCJ 92020 1251-F7
1400 ESCN 92027 1110-A7
2900 CRLB 92009 1127-H5
PEARL ST
400 SD 92037 1227-E7
PEARLBUSH CT
1200 SDCo 92019 1252-E7
PEARL HEIGHTS RD
1500 VSTA 92083 1107-H6

PEARL LAKE AV
6200 SD 92119 1250-H6
PEARLMAN WY
4900 SD 92130 1188-D5
PEARLWOOD RD
9400 SNTE 92071 1231-B4
PEARLWOOD ST
300 CHV 91911 1330-G3
PEARMAN LN
1000 SDCo 92065 1172-H1
PEARSON DR
4900 SD 92115 1270-D2
PEARSON ST
7100 LMSA 91941 1270-F5
PEARTREE CT
400 ENCT 92024 1147-G7
PEAR TREE DR
6800 CRLB 92009 1127-A5
PEAR TREE LN
700 OCN 92057 1086-G5
PEAR TREE PL
400 ESCN 92026 1109-J7
PEARTREE TER
12700 PWY 92064 1190-C1
PEARWOOD DR
700 OCN 92057 1086-G5
800 OCN 92056 1086-G5
PEBBLE CT
800 ELCJ 92019 1252-B7
PEBBLE PL
800 ELCJ 92019 1252-B7
PEBBLE BEACH CT
8900 SNTE 92071 1230-J4
PEBBLE BEACH DR
700 SMCS 92069 1108-J4
4400 OCN 92057 1066-H7
9300 SNTE 92071 1231-A6
9700 SNTE 92071 1230-J3
PEBBLEBROOK LN
14000 SD 92128 1189-J2
PEBBLEBROOK PL
1900 CHV 91913 1311-D4
PEBBLEBROOK WY
14100 SD 92128 1189-J2
PEBBLE CANYON DR
14400 PWY 92064 1190-H1
PEBBLE CREEK LN
10000 SDCo 92021 1232-G1
PEBBLE SPRINGS LN
1100 SDCo 92026 1109-E7
PEBBLESTONE LN
9200 SD 92126 1209-D2
PEBBLESTONE PL
400 SNTE 92071 1231-C5
PECAN CT
1800 VSTA 92083 1108-B3
PECAN PL
1200 CHV 91911 1330-G2
3000 ESCN 92027 1110-E6
PECAN TER
14100 SDCo 92021 1232-G6
PECAN PARK LN
13900 SDCo 92021 1232-G5
PECAN PEAK
14200 SDCo 92021 1232-G5
PECAN VALLEY DR
8700 SNTE 92071 1230-J4
PECK
- SDCo 92672 1023-E2
PECKHAM PL
1200 ENCT 92024 1147-H7
1200 ENCT 92024 1167-H1
PECOS DR
3800 SDCo 92004 (1099-D2 See Page 1098)
PECOS ST
600 SDCo 91977 1291-C3
PEDRAGAL DR
500 OCN 92054 1086-G1
PEDREGAL DR
1500 ESCN 92025 1130-B4
1500 SDCo 92025 1130-B4
PEDRIN PL
3200 SDCo 92028 1048-C4
PEDRIZA RD
12600 PWY 92064 1170-C5
PEERLESS DR
1200 ELCJ 92021 1252-A2
1200 SDCo 92021 1252-A2
PEET LN
2300 ESCN 92025 1130-C7
2300 SDCo 92025 1130-C7
2700 ESCN 92025 1150-C1
PEET PL
- ESCN 92025 1130-C7
PEG CT
4200 SD 92154 1350-G1
PEGASO ST
1400 ENCT 92024 1167-G1
PEGASUS AV
10900 SD 92126 1209-D1
PEGEEN PL
11300 SDCo 92021 1251-G1
PEGGY DR
700 SD 92114 1290-G3
PEG LEG RD Rt#-S22
1300 SDCo 92004 (1059-J5 See Page 1058)
1300 SDCo 92004 (1079-J1 See Page 1058)
PEG LEG MINE RD
3100 SDCo 91935 1272-J7
PEINADO WY
6400 SD 92121 1208-G3
PELICAN ST
- CRLB 92009 1127-B7
PELICAN WY
700 ELCJ 92020 1251-E7
PELICAN HILL RD
1900 SD 92139 1290-D7
PELICAN POINT CT
1600 CHV 91911 1330-J4
PELL PL
3300 SD 92130 1188-A6
PELLET RD
- ImCo 92227 411-A11
- ImCo 92227 431-A1
PELTON CT
8900 SD 92126 1209-D2
PELUSA ST
5000 SD 92113 1290-A6
PEMBRIDGE LN
7000 SD 92139 1290-F7
PEMBROKE DR
6100 SD 92115 1270-C2
PENANOVA ST
11300 SD 92129 1169-H6
PENARA CT
7100 SD 92126 1208-J4

SAN DIEGO CO.
INDEX

6609 PENARA PL — SAN DIEGO CO. STREET INDEX — PLAZA AMPARADA

STREET
Block City ZIP Pg-Grid

PENARA PL
7300 SD 92126 1208-J4
PENARA ST
10600 SD 92126 1208-J4
PENASCO RD
1500 SDCo 92019 1272-A1
PENASQUITOS CT
14700 SD 92129 1189-H1
PENASQUITOS DR
14300 SD 92129 1189-H1
14800 SD 92129 1169-H7
PENCE DR
2200 SDCo 92019 1252-D7
PENDIENTE CT
3800 SD 92124 1250-A3
PENDLETON DR
- SD 92140 1268-E6
PENDLETON RD
1500 CORD 92118 1288-J6
PENDLETON ST
4500 SD 92109 1248-B3
PENDON CT
7700 CRLB 92009 1147-F2
PENDRAGON RD
15400 SDCo 92064 1191-C5
PENELOPE DR
600 CHV 91910 1310-D7
PENFIELD PT
13500 SD 92130 1188-D4
PENFORD CT
14400 SD 92129 1189-C1
PENGUIN CIR
900 VSTA 92083 1087-G5
PENINA ST
13600 PWY 92064 1170-E1
PENKEA DR
2700 OCN 92054 1086-D6
PENMAR RD
9200 SNTE 92071 1231-A3
PENN ST
100 SDCo 92065 1152-J3
400 SDCo 92065 1153-A3
PENNACOOK CT
17700 SD 92127 1169-H1
PENNANT WY
2900 SD 92122 1228-C6
PENNINGTON LN
2500 SD 92139 1290-F7
PENNSYLVANIA AV
100 ESCN 92025 1129-J2
100 SD 92103 1269-B6
E PENNSYLVANIA AV
500 ESCN 92025 1130-A2
1200 ESCN 92027 1130-A2
W PENNSYLVANIA AV
- SDCo 92061 1051-C6
100 SD 92103 1269-A6
300 SD 92103 1268-J6
PENNSYLVANIA LN
5300 LMSA 91942 1270-E1
5300 LMSA 92120 1270-E1
PENNY PL
5300 SD 92115 1270-A2
PENNYROYAL WY
2500 LMGR 91945 1270-F7
PENNYWOOD RD
9200 SNTE 92071 1231-A4
PENRIDGE ST
10500 SD 92126 1208-J4
PENROD CT
300 VSTA 92083 1087-G4
PENROD LN
10300 SD 92126 1208-J5
PENROSE CT
4800 SD 92110 1248-F7
PENROSE ST
2100 SD 92110 1268-F1
2300 SD 92110 1248-F7
PENSTEMON CT
- SDCo 92036 1175-H4
PENSTEMON LN
- SDCo 92036 1175-H3
PENSTEMON RD
- SDCo 92036 1175-H4
PENTAS CT
1800 CRLB 92009 1127-E6
PENTECOST WY
1600 SD 92105 1290-A2
PENTICTON WY
9000 SD 92126 1209-D2
PENTUCKETT AV
1700 SD 92104 1289-F2
PENVIEW DR
3100 SDCo 92084 1067-J6
PEONY DR
3800 SDCo 92028 1028-F5
PEPITA WY
7500 SD 92037 1227-F7
PEPPER CT
- ELCN 92243 6559-E1
PEPPER DR
100 SD 92173 1350-G4
300 SDCo 92021 1251-F1
300 SNTE 92021 1251-F1
900 ELCJ 92021 1251-F1
1200 ELCN 92243 6559-F1
1300 SDCo 92021 1252-A2
1400 SDCo 92082 1090-B1
1600 ELCJ 92021 1252-A2
4000 SD 92105 1289-G1
4000 SD 92105 1269-H7
PEPPER LN
- SDCo 92672 1023-E2
PEPPERBROOK LN
10500 SD 92131 1210-A3
PEPPERDINE AV
4100 OCN 92056 1087-B5
PEPPERDINE CT
900 CHV 91913 1311-D6
PEPPER GLEN WY
700 CHV 91914 1311-G3
PEPPERGRASS DR
3200 SD 92115 1270-D6
PEPPER HILL DR
1600 ELCJ 92021 1252-B2
1600 SDCo 92021 1252-B2
PEPPERMINT LN
2300 LMGR 91945 1270-E7
2300 LMGR 91945 1290-E1
PEPPERMINT PL
1900 ESCN 92029 1129-E4
PEPPER TREE CT
500 SMCS 92069 1109-D7
PEPPERTREE DR
2700 OCN 92056 1087-E5
PEPPERTREE LN
- ENCT 92024 1147-J7
PEPPER TREE LN
- SD 92106 1287-J3
PEPPERTREE LN
100 ENCT 92024 1167-J1
PEPPER TREE LN
100 SDCo 92028 1027-F5
PEPPERTREE LN
500 SOLB 92075 1187-F1
1100 SDCo 92084 1108-B2
1100 VSTA 92084 1108-B2
PEPPER TREE LN
12100 PWY 92064 1190-C6
PEPPER TREE PL
1500 SDCo 92028 1027-H5
2100 ESCN 92026 1109-G5
PEPPER TREE RD
- CHV 91910 1310-D6
- SDCo 91910 1310-D6
PEPPER VALLEY LN
1800 SDCo 92021 1252-A1
PEPPERVIEW TER
11200 SD 92131 1210-A2
PEPPER VILLA CT
900 ELCJ 92021 1251-H1
PEPPER VILLA DR
1300 SDCo 92021 1251-H2
1700 ELCJ 92021 1251-H2
PEPPERWOOD CT
500 CHV 91902 1311-C4
PEPPERWOOD DR
1600 SDCo 92021 1251-G1
PEPSI DR
4200 SD 92111 1249-B3
PEQUENA ST
1300 SD 92154 1350-F1
PEQUENITO CT
9300 SDCo 92040 1232-B5
PEQUENO PL
1200 ESCN 92027 1110-A6
PEQUOT DR
13400 PWY 92064 1190-E2
PERA ALTA DR
3000 SDCo 92036 1155-G4
PERALTA DR
35300 SDCo 92086 409-J6
PERCH LN
500 OCN 92054 1086-G2
PERCUSSION CT
2300 SDCo 92019 1252-D6
PERCY CT
12900 SD 92130 1188-B5
PERDIDO PL
3600 SMCS 92069 1108-C7
PERDIZ ST
7300 CRLB 92009 1127-J7
PEREGRINE RD
- SDCo 92061 1051-C6
PEREZ CT
10200 SD 92124 1229-G7
PEREZ RD
- ImCo 92283 432-D5
PEREZ COVE WY
2200 SD 92109 1268-B3
PERGL ST
2500 LMGR 91945 1270-F7
PERIQUE ST
6200 SD 92115 1270-D5
PERIQUITO CT
1800 VSTA 92083 1107-H5
PERIWINKLE ST
700 ENCT 92024 1147-E6
PERIWINKLE WY
4000 OCN 92057 1086-J4
PERKINS DR
1400 CHV 91911 1330-J2
PERKON CT
2500 SD 92105 1270-A7
PERKON PL
4900 SD 92105 1270-A7
PERLA CT
12500 SD 92128 1170-C2
PERLAS CT
1300 CHV 91910 1311-A4
PERRY ST
2800 SD 92106 1288-A3
PERSA ST
6500 CRLB 92009 1127-G5
PERSEUS RD
8600 SD 92126 1209-C2
PERSHING AV
3400 SD 92104 1269-D6
PERSHING DR
1200 SD 92101 1289-C2
1600 SD 92102 1289-C2
1900 SD 92101 1269-D7
PERSIMMON AV
1100 SDCo 92021 1251-H3
1200 ELCJ 92021 1251-H3
PERSIMMON CT
1100 SDCo 92021 1251-J3
PERSIMMON LN
30600 SDCo 92082 1070-H4
PERSIMMON WY
600 OCN 92054 1086-F2
1200 SDCo 92021 1251-J3
PERTH PL
6500 SD 92139 1310-E1
PERU PL
5500 SD 92105 1290-B1
PESCA CT
400 SDCo 91977 1291-C4
PESCADERO AV
4300 SD 92107 1287-J1
4500 SD 92107 1267-J7
PESCADERO DR
1400 SD 92107 1267-H7
PESCADERO POINT CT
1600 CHV 91911 1330-J4
PESCADO PL
400 ENCT 92024 1147-C7
PESOS PL
10800 SD 92124 1249-H1
PETAL DR
1500 SD 92114 1290-D6
PETALO PZ
1000 CHV 91910 1311-C2
PETENWELL RD
11500 SD 92131 1209-H1
PETEO CT
400 CHV 91911 1330-B2
PETERLYNN CT
4000 SD 92154 1350-F1
PETERLYNN DR
1000 SD 92154 1330-F7
1000 SD 92154 1350-F1
PETERLYNN WY
4000 SD 92154 1350-F1
PETER PAN AV
7100 SD 92114 1290-F4
PETERS CT
8800 SD 92126 1209-D7
8800 SD 92126 1229-D1
PETERS DR
300 VSTA 92083 1087-H7
PETERS WY
3000 SD 92117 1248-C3
PETERSON RD
- ImCo 92233 411-B9
PETERSON WY
5300 SD 92182 1270-B1
PETIRROJO CT
11600 SD 92124 1250-A3
PETIT CT
6900 SD 92111 1248-J3
PETIT ST
6800 SD 92111 1248-J3
PETITE LN
9500 SDCo 92040 1232-C3
PETRA DR
1700 SD 92104 1289-F2
PETRA PL
3400 SD 92104 1289-F1
PETRA WY
1100 SDCo 91901 1233-F5
PETREE ST
1000 ELCJ 92020 1251-D4
PETROLIA CT
- SDCo 92065 1171-F1
PETTIGO DR
2900 SD 92139 1310-E2
PETUNIA CT
3200 SD 92117 1248-D4
PETUNIA PL
6400 CRLB 92009 1127-B4
PEUTZ VALLEY RD
200 SDCo 91901 1233-F4
900 SDCo 91901 1234-A3
PEWTER CT
1700 SDCo 92019 1272-D2
PEYRI DR
100 OCN 92057 1086-G2
PEYTON PL
5200 SD 92117 1228-H7
PFEIFER LN
1200 ELCJ 92020 1251-C3
PHANTOM LN
11500 SD 92126 1209-E1
PHEASANT CT
- ImCo 92249 6560-B7
1000 SMCS 92069 1128-E3
PHEASANT DR
2500 SD 92123 1249-B7
2900 SDCo 92036 1136-E7
2900 SDCo 92036 1156-E1
PHEASANT LN
- OCN 92057 1086-H2
PHEASANT PL
1900 ESCN 92026 1109-H5
PHEASANT RUN
2000 SDCo 92028 1028-A4
PHEASANT HILL
- SDCo 92026 1109-E6
PHEASANT VALLEY CT
500 SDCo 92028 1027-G1
PHELPS RD
2000 SDCo 91906 (1317-H3 See Page 1296)
PHIDEL ST
3900 SD 92130 1188-A4
PHILBROOK SQ
- SD 92130 1208-B2
PHILLAR WY
8700 SNTE 92071 1231-C7
PHILLIPS CIR
1400 VSTA 92083 1108-A2
PHILLIPS CT
400 VSTA 92083 1107-H1
6800 SD 92111 1268-J1
PHILLIPS ST
600 VSTA 92083 1107-H1
1000 VSTA 92083 1108-A1
PHILLIPS WY
400 VSTA 92083 1107-J1
PHIL MAR LN
200 VSTA 92083 1108-A2
PHILTON DR
600 SDCo 92065 1153-B6
PHIPPS AV
- SD 92126 1209-E7
PHIRE PL
400 SDCo 91977 1291-B4
PHLOX CT
- CRLB 92009 1127-B4
PHOEBE ST
100 ENCT 92024 1147-A4
PHOENIX DR
7500 LMSA 91941 1270-G4
PHOENIX WY
700 SMCS 92078 1129-A3
PHYLLIS PL
8200 SD 92123 1249-B7
PICACHO CT
600 OCN 92057 1067-C7
PICACHO RD
- ImCo - 412-C11
- ImCo - 432-C2
1100 ImCo 92283 432-C2
PICACHO RD Rt#-S24
300 ImCo 92283 432-D5
PICADILLY CT
4500 CRLB 92008 1107-A5
PICADOR BLVD
700 SD 92154 1330-E7
900 SD 92154 1350-E1
1600 SD 92173 1350-E1
PICARTE PL
12600 SD 92128 1190-A5
PICASSO DR
2900 SDCo 91902 1290-H7
PICAZA PL
11000 SD 92127 1169-H1
PICCADILLY RD
1700 ENCT 92024 1147-A2
PICCARD AV
500 SD 92154 1330-F6
1000 SD 92154 1350-F1
PICKETT GN
500 ESCN 92027 1110-D6
PICKETT RD
- ImCo 92233 411-C11
1700 ImCo 92227 411-D11
PICKETT ST
3400 SD 92110 1268-E4
PICKFORD RD
11700 SD 92131 1209-G1
PICKWICK ST
3300 SD 92102 1289-F3
PICNIC VIEW LN
200 OCN 92056 1107-D2
PICO AV
100 SDCo 92028 1027-F2
100 SMCS 92069 1108-H7
600 ELCN 92243 6499-F4
S PICO AV
200 SDCo 92028 1027-F2
PICO CT
- CHV 91911 1330-E3
PICO PL
- PWY 92064 1190-H7
800 ESCN 92026 1109-J6
2500 SD 92109 1248-C5
PICO RD
3500 SDCo 92084 1068-F4
3500 SDCo 92003 1068-F4
PICO ST
4600 SD 92109 1248-C5
PICO WY
200 ESCN 92026 1109-H7
2500 SD 92109 1248-C4
PICO DE LA LOMA
300 ESCN 92029 1150-A3
PICRUS ST
12200 SD 92129 1189-B7
PICTOR LN
200 ELCJ 92019 1252-A5
PICTURESQUE PT
15100 SDCo 92021 1233-B7
PIDGEON ST
500 SD 92114 1290-F3
PIEDMONT DR
4300 SD 92107 1287-J2
PIEDMONT RD
900 SDCo 92065 1152-J3
PIEDMONT ST
1500 CHV 91913 1331-D1
1600 CHV 91913 1311-F7
9200 SDCo 91977 1291-B3
PIEDRA ST
1300 SD 92154 1350-E1
PIEDRAS ORO CALLE
700 ENCT 92024 1147-D7
PIEDRA TRACT
- SDCo 91948 1218-E5
PIEL PL
9100 SDCo 91977 1291-B4
PIENZA PL
9500 SDCo 92127 1169-E2
PIERCE CT
2000 SDCo 92019 1272-C3
PIERCE LN
1300 SDCo 92065 1172-G4
PIERCE PL
4900 OCN 92057 1067-A7
PIERCE ST
700 ELCJ 92020 1251-D4
S PIERCE ST
300 ELCJ 92020 1251-D6
PIERINO DR
2000 SD 92114 1290-E1
PIERLE RD
- ImCo 92251 431-A4
PIERRE WY
1100 ELCJ 92021 1251-G3
1100 SDCo 92021 1251-G3
PIER VIEW WY
- OCN 92054 1105-J1
- OCN 92054 1106-A1
100 OCN 92054 1086-A7
PIKAKE ST
2600 SD 92154 1350-C3
PIKE LN
500 OCN 92054 1086-G2
PIKE RD
9300 SNTE 92071 1231-B5
PILAWEE WEE LN
9500 SDCo 91916 1236-A2
PILE ST
100 SDCo 92065 1152-H2
700 SDCo 92065 1153-A2
PILGRIM WY
1400 OCN 92057 1067-A3
PILLAR POINT WY
800 OCN 92054 1066-F7
PILLSBURY LN
1200 ELCJ 92020 1251-B3
PILON PT
4100 SD 92130 1188-B7
PILOT WY
6700 SD 92114 1270-E7
6700 SD 92114 1290-E1
PILOTS LN
9500 SNTE 92071 1251-C1
PIMA TR
34600 SDCo 92036 1176-D4
PIMLICO CTE
15400 SDCo 92067 1168-E7
PIMLICO PL
2400 SDCo 91901 1234-C6
PIMPERNEL DR
9000 SD 92129 1189-D5
PIMPERNEL WY
12800 SD 92129 1189-D5
PINA LN
300 VSTA 92083 1087-H7
PINAR PL
2100 SD 92014 1187-G6
PINATA DR
16700 SD 92128 1170-B3
PINDAR WY
4100 OCN 92056 1107-E6
PINE AV
200 CRLB 92008 1106-F5
PINE BLVD
7400 SDCo 92066 1237-C5
PINE CT
- CORD 92118 1288-G7
- SDCo 92066 1237-C5
300 CHV 91911 1330-G3
8300 LMSA 91941 1270-J2
PINE DR
1000 ELCJ 92020 1251-D7
1100 SDCo 91941 1251-D7
2400 SDCo 91906 (1297-E5 See Page 1296)
PINE HTS
800 SDCo 92065 1152-F1
PINE LN
3100 SDCo 91978 1272-C7
3100 SDCo 91978 1292-C1
PINE ST
- SMCS 92078 1129-C2
100 OCN 92054 1106-A1
1000 CORD 92118 1288-G7
1400 VSTA 92083 1087-F6
1400 SDCo 92082 1090-B1
1500 SDCo 92065 1152-F1
1700 ESCN 92025 1130-A5
2100 SD 92103 1268-G4
3700 SMCS 92069 1128-C1
4800 LMSA 91941 1270-J2
PINE ST Rt#-78
100 SDCo 92065 1152-G3
N PINE ST
100 ESCN 92025 1129-H3
S PINE ST
100 ESCN 92025 1129-H3
S PINE ST Rt#-78
2900 SDCo 92065 1152-G6
PINE TER
14100 SDCo 92021 1232-G6
PINE WY
700 SDCo 92065 1152-F2
PINEAPPLE PL
9600 SDCo 92040 1232-A4
PINEAPPLE WY
1200 ESCN 92029 1129-E5
PINE BLUFF LN
6100 SD 92139 1290-D6
PINE BRANCH DR
800 ENCT 92024 1167-G1
PINEBROOK CT
12600 PWY 92064 1170-D3
PINECASTLE ST
10100 SD 92131 1210-C4
PINECLIFFS CT
10400 SD 92131 1210-A3
PINE CONE DR
700 SDCo 92036 1156-D1
PINECONE LN
6500 SD 92139 1310-F1
PINE CREEK CRSG
8400 SDCo 92066 1237-C4
PINE CREEK RD
8300 SDCo 91931 1237-B5
8300 SDCo 92066 1237-C3
8400 SDCo 92066 (1217-D7 See Page 1216)
PINECREST AV
900 ESCN 92025 1129-H5
1100 SDCo 92025 1129-H5
8500 SD 92123 1249-C5
PINE CREST DR
2500 SDCo 92036 1136-D7
PINE CREST LN
47200 RivC 92592 999-F1
PINECREST ST
800 ESCN 92025 1129-H4
32200 RivC 92592 999-F1
PINECREST WY
2100 CRLB 92008 1106-G3
PINEFALLS CT
10500 SD 92131 1209-J3
PINEFIELD RD
12800 PWY 92064 1170-D3
PINEFLOWER DR
3300 SD 92115 1270-D6
PINE GLEN WY
1100 SD 92154 1350-E1
PINE GROVE CT
2900 SDCo 91978 1271-F7
PINE GROVE ST
10300 SDCo 91978 1271-F7
PINE HEIGHTS WY
1400 SDCo 92069 1129-E1
1400 SMCS 92069 1129-E1
PINE HILLS RD
3000 SDCo 92036 1155-J2
3200 SDCo 92066 1135-J7
PINEHILLS CREST DR
- SDCo 92036 1155-H4
PINEHURST AV
1600 ESCN 92026 1109-D5
PINEHURST CT
1700 SDCo 92028 1028-G5
PINEHURST DR
11100 SDCo 92040 1211-H6
11100 SDCo 92040 1231-H1
PINEHURST RD
1200 CHV 91915 1311-G6
PINE ISLAND DR
1000 CHV 91915 1311-G5
PINE KNOLL LN
9900 SD 92124 1249-F1
PINE MANOR CT
12900 SD 92129 1189-F5
PINE MEADOW CT
12800 SD 92130 1188-B5
PINE NEEDLES DR
300 DLMR 92014 1187-G7
13600 SD 92014 1187-G7
PINEOAK RIDGE RD
700 SDCo 92036 1156-D3
PINE OAKS RD
17100 SDCo 92036 1156-F7
PINE PATCH WY
- SDCo 92028 998-G5
PINE RIDGE AV
4700 SDCo 92036 1155-G4
PINERIDGE CT
500 CHV 91902 1311-B4
PINE RIDGE RD
1400 OCN 92056 1087-C3
PINERIDGE RD
7500 SNTE 92071 1230-G7
PINE RIDGE WY
- SDCo 92036 1155-H5
PINERY GRV
- SDCo 92040 1231-G3
PINESTONE CT
11200 SD 92128 1189-J2
PINETREE DR
10100 SD 92131 1209-G4
PINETREE LN
600 VSTA 92083 1107-H1
PINE TREE LN
17400 SDCo 92036 1156-F7
PINE TREE PL
400 ESCN 92025 1130-A4
PINEVALE LN
- SNTE 92071 1230-G5
PINE VALLEY DR
9200 SNTE 92071 1230-J6
PINE VALLEY RD
7400 SDCo 92066 1237-B7
PINE VALLEY LAS
BANCAS RD
- SDCo 91916 1236-C5
- SDCo 91931 1236-F6
- SDCo 91931 1237-A5
- SDCo 92066 1236-F6
PINE VIEW RD
1700 SDCo 91901 1234-D7
PINE VISTA RD
1400 SDCo 92027 1130-E2
PINEWOOD CT
3200 SD 92037 1228-B4
PINEWOOD DR
800 OCN 92057 1087-C1
14200 SD 92014 1187-H5
PINEWOOD RD
1900 VSTA 92083 1107-F5
PINEWOOD ST
2500 SD 92014 1187-H5
PINEWOOD VW
10000 SNTE 92071 1231-D3
PINEZANITA LN
2900 SDCo 92036 1136-A7
PINION PINE TR
38600 SDCo 91905 (1320-A3 See Page 1300)
PINKARD LN
9100 SDCo 92021 1232-F5
PINKARD WY
13800 SDCo 92021 1232-F5
PINNACLE CT
1700 VSTA 92083 1107-G4
PINNACLE LN
10100 SDCo 91941 1271-D2
PINNACLE PL
3800 ESCN 92025 1150-D3
PINNACLE WY
1600 VSTA 92083 1107-G4
PINNACLE PEAK DR
1200 CHV 91915 1311-H6
PINO CT
13100 SDCo 92040 1232-C2
PINO DR
10200 SDCo 92040 1232-C3
PINON PL
- SDCo 92040 1231-G3
PINON ST
900 SMCS 92069 1109-B5
PINON HILLS RD
1900 CHV 91913 1311-E6
PINOT PL
17200 PWY 92064 1170-D2
PINOT NOIR CIR
10800 SD 92131 1210-B2
PINTAIL CT
12400 PWY 92064 1190-B6
PINTAIL DR
6800 CRLB 92009 1127-D6
PINTO CT
1000 SMCS 92069 1109-C5
PINTO PL
3800 SDCo 91977 1271-F5
PINTORESCO CT
2000 CRLB 92009 1147-F1
PINTO RIDGE CT
- SDCo 92127 1169-E4
PINTO RIDGE DR
- SDCo 92127 1169-E5
PINYON DR
- SDCo 92055 1085-J3
PINYON RIDGE DR
- CHV 91915 1311-H6
PINZON WY
10900 SD 92127 1169-H1
PIONEER AV
2500 VSTA 92083 1108-A6
PIONEER CIR
1400 OCN 92057 1066-J3
1400 OCN 92057 1067-B4
PIONEER PL
3100 ESCN 92025 1150-C1
3700 SD 92103 1268-J6
PIONEER TER
- SDCo 92040 1232-F4
PIONEER WY
1000 ELCJ 92020 1251-E2
2800 SDCo 91935 1292-F3
PIO PICO DR
2300 CRLB 92008 1106-E4
PIO PICO ST
3600 SD 92106 1287-J3
3600 SD 92106 1288-A3
PIOVANA CT
800 CRLB 92009 1127-A7
PIPER LN
4200 SDCo 92004 1100-C4
PIPER ST
4200 SD 92117 1248-E6
PIPER RANCH RD
1200 SD 92154 1351-H2
PIPESTONE WY
8800 SD 92129 1189-C3
PIPILO CT
12900 SD 92129 1189-D5
PIPILO ST
9200 SD 92129 1189-D6
PIPING ROCK LN
13500 SDCo 92021 1252-E1
13500 SDCo 92021 1232-E7
PIPIT CT
- CRLB 92009 1127-D4
12200 SD 92129 1189-A7
PIPIT PL
7600 SD 92129 1189-A7
PIPIT WY
12200 SD 92129 1189-A7
PIPO RD
12400 SD 92128 1170-C4
PIPPIN CT
- SMCS 92069 1128-E3
PIPPIN DR
200 SDCo 92028 1027-F4
PIRAEUS ST
900 ENCT 92024 1147-B3
1800 CRLB 92024 1147-B3
PIRAGUA ST
3300 CRLB 92009 1147-J1
5100 CRLB 92009 1127-J7
PIRE AV
5400 SD 92122 1228-C7
PIRGOS WY
3400 OCN 92056 1107-E4
PIRINEOS WY
2600 CRLB 92009 1147-G1
PIROS WY
6000 OCN 92056 1107-F5
PIROTTE DR
5000 SD 92105 1290-A1
PISCES WY
11000 SD 92126 1209-C2
PISMO CT
700 SD 92109 1267-H1
PISMO BAY CT
300 OCN 92057 1066-J5
PISTOL RANGE RD
4300 SD 92173 1350-G2
PITA CT
13700 SDCo 91935 1292-G2
PITCAIRN ST
3100 SD 92154 1330-D7
PITMAN PL
900 ESCN 92027 1110-C6
PITMAN ST
600 ESCN 92027 1110-C6
PITTA ST
400 SD 92114 1290-C3
PITTSBURGH AV
6300 SD 92114 1290-D5
PITTZER RD
1000 ImCo 92249 6560-D5
1500 ImCo 92243 6560-D2
PIUTE PL
4400 SD 92117 1248-E2
PIUTE TR
34800 SDCo 92036 1176-E5
PIZZARO LN
- SDCo 92026 1109-E6
PIZZO LN
700 SDCo 92028 1027-G4
PLACE MONACO
2200 SD 92014 1187-F6
PLACENTIA ST
7300 LMGR 91945 1290-F2
PLACER AV
400 SMCS 92069 1108-J6
PLACER TR
800 SDCo 92019 1253-B2
PLACERITA ST
1500 ENCT 92024 1147-G7
PLACE SAINT TROPEZ
2200 SD 92014 1187-F6
PLACID CT
1600 ELCJ 92021 1252-B2
PLACIDO CT
2100 CRLB 92009 1147-F2
PLACID VIEW DR
8500 SNTE 92071 1231-A7
8500 SNTE 92071 1251-A1
S PLAINS CT
15800 SDCo 92021 1233-D3
PLAINVIEW RD
5000 SD 92110 1268-F2
PLANET RD
1400 VSTA 92083 1087-D6
PLANE TREE VW
- SDCo 92026 1089-B2
PLANICIE WY
1600 SD 92154 1350-A3
PLANTANO ST
400 SD 92102 1289-J3
PLANTATION WY
1500 SDCo 92019 1272-A1
PLANTEL WY
3100 SD 92173 1350-D2
PLATA CT
1600 LMGR 91945 1290-F2
PLATANO CT
1400 CHV 91911 1330-E4
PLATANUS DR
29600 SDCo 92026 1069-A5
PLATANUS PL
9100 SDCo 92026 1069-A5
PLATEAU DR
6200 SD 92139 1310-E2
PLATEAU PL
3900 CRLB 92008 1107-C3
3900 ESCN 92025 1150-C3
PLATINUM PL
- CRLB 92009 1127-H5
16900 SDCo 92040 1191-D3
16900 SDCo 92064 1191-D3
PLATO DR
3000 SD 92139 1310-F2
PLATO PL
700 ENCT 92024 1147-B2
PLAYA RD
2000 CRLB 92009 1127-F7
PLAYA BLANCA
300 ENCT 92024 1147-C6
PLAYA CATALINA
5000 SD 92124 1230-A7
PLAYA DE CONCORD
- ESCN 92029 1129-C4
PLAYA DEL ALICANTE
- ESCN 92029 1129-C4
PLAYA DEL NORTE
200 SD 92037 1247-E2
PLAYA DEL REY
- OCN 92054 1066-E6
PLAYA DEL REY AV
100 OCN 92054 1086-G1
100 OCN 92054 1066-G7
PLAYA DEL SOL
- ESCN 92026 1109-F7
600 SDCo 92021 1251-G2
PLAYA DEL SUR
200 SD 92037 1247-E2
PLAYA DEL TOKAY
- ESCN 92029 1129-E4
PLAYA RIVIERA DR
1800 ENCT 92007 1167-E3
PLAYER DR
7300 SD 92119 1250-F5
PLAYMOR TER
7900 SD 92122 1228-C4
PLAZA BLVD
1200 NATC 91950 1310-A1
2400 NATC 91950 1290-B7
4000 SD 92114 1290-D5
E PLAZA BLVD
- NATC 91950 1309-J1
1200 NATC 91950 1310-A1
W PLAZA BLVD
- NATC 91950 1309-H1
PLAZA CT
700 CHV 91910 1310-H6
PLAZA DR
2300 CRLB 92008 1106-G2
3300 OCN 92056 1107-B2
3700 VSTA 92083 1107-B2
5400 SD 92182 1270-B2
5500 SD 92115 1270-B2
PLAZA ST
100 SOLB 92075 1167-E7
PLAZA ABIERTO
17400 SD 92128 1170-C1
PLAZA ACOSTA
17600 SD 92128 1150-D7
PLAZA AHORA
17800 SD 92128 1150-C7
PLAZA ALONZO
3000 SDCo 91902 1310-H1
PLAZA AMADA
12500 SD 92128 1170-C1
PLAZA AMISTAD
900 CHV 91910 1310-J7
900 CHV 91910 1311-A7
PLAZA AMPARADA
1100 CHV 91910 1311-B7

SAN DIEGO CO.
INDEX

PLAZA ANIMADO — SAN DIEGO CO. STREET INDEX — PRIMA VERA 6610

STREET	Block	City	ZIP	Pg-Grid
PLAZA ANIMADO	17400	SD	92128	1170-D1
PLAZA ANITA	3000	SDCo	91902	1290-H7
	3000	SDCo	91902	1310-H1
PLAZA ARICA	17600	SD	92128	1150-C7
PLAZA ASCOPE	17600	SD	92128	1150-C7
PLAZA BONITA	2300	CRLB	92009	1127-F7
PLAZA BONITA RD	2900	SDCo	91902	1310-C4
	2900	SDCo	91910	1310-D5
	2900	CHV	91902	1310-D5
	2900	CHV	91910	1310-D5
	3000	NATC	91950	1310-C4
PLAZA BONITA CENTER WY	3000	NATC	91950	1310-E3
PLAZA CAPOTE	1000	CHV	91910	1311-A7
PLAZA CARLOS	2900	SDCo	91902	1290-G6
PLAZA CATALONIA	800	CHV	91910	1311-A6
PLAZA CENTRADA	12500	SD	92128	1170-C2
PLAZA CERADO	17400	SD	92128	1170-C1
PLAZA CREST RIDGE RD	1600	SD	92114	1290-E6
PLAZA CUERNAVACA	6300	SD	92114	1290-D5
PLAZA CUERNAVACA WY	800	SD	92114	1290-E5
PLAZA DE BENITO JUAREZ	300	VSTA	92083	1087-G5
PLAZA DE LA COSTA	7200	CRLB	92009	1127-F7
PLAZA DE LA ROSA	17400	SD	92128	1170-F2
PLAZA DE LAS FLORES	2300	CRLB	92009	1127-F7
PLAZA DE LA SIENA	12600	SD	92130	1188-B6
PLAZA DEL CID	500	CHV	91910	1310-G5
PLAZA DEL CURTIDOR	17400	SD	92128	1170-C1
PLAZA DEL MAR	2400	SDCo	92025	1150-D1
PLAZA DE PALMAS	4000	SD	92122	1228-C3
PLAZA DESTACADO	17400	SD	92128	1170-F2
PLAZA DOLORES	17400	SD	92128	1170-D1
PLAZA ELENA	1000	CHV	91910	1311-A7
PLAZA ESCALANTE	1000	CHV	91910	1311-B6
PLAZA FIEL	17400	SD	92128	1170-C2
PLAZA FLORA	800	CHV	91910	1310-F7
PLAZA GARDENIA	1000	CHV	91910	1311-B6
PLAZA GITANA	17500	SD	92128	1170-D1
PLAZA GUATA	12500	SD	92128	1170-C1
PLAZA GUILLERMO	17400	SD	92128	1170-C1
PLAZA KARENA	17500	SD	92128	1170-D1
PLAZA LA PAZ	-	CHV	91910	1310-J7
PLAZA LEONARDO	3000	SDCo	91902	1310-H1
	3000	SDCo	91902	1290-H7
PLAZA LORENZO	4600	SDCo	91902	1290-H7
	4600	SDCo	91902	1310-H1
PLAZA MANZANA	-	SDCo	91901	1234-A6
PLAZA MAR	800	CHV	91910	1310-F7
PLAZA MARIA	17300	SD	92128	1170-D2
PLAZA MARLENA	17500	SD	92128	1170-D1
PLAZA MENTA	12600	SD	92128	1150-C7
PLAZA MERICA	3000	SDCo	91902	1290-H7
PLAZA MIGUEL	2900	SDCo	91902	1290-H7
PLAZA MIRALESTE	1100	CHV	91910	1311-A7
PLAZA MIRODA	700	CHV	91910	1311-A5
PLAZA NARISCO	1000	CHV	91910	1310-J7
	1000	CHV	91910	1311-A7
PLAZA NATALIA	3000	SDCo	91902	1310-H1
PLAZA OTONAL	17200	SD	92128	1170-D1
PLAZA PAOLO	3000	SDCo	91902	1290-G7
PLAZA PASEO DR	10300	SDCo	92040	1231-H3
PLAZA REAL	1900	OCN	92056	1087-B5
PLAZA RIDGE RD	6400	SD	92114	1290-E6
PLAZA SEVILLE	700	CHV	91910	1311-A5
PLAZA SIERRA	800	CHV	91910	1310-F7
PLAZA SINUOSO	1000	CHV	91910	1311-A7
PLAZA SONADA	17400	SD	92128	1170-C2
PLAZA SONRISADA	17400	SD	92128	1170-C1
PLAZA TAXCO	800	SD	92114	1290-D5
PLAZA TOLUCA	800	SD	92114	1290-E5
PLAZA TORREON	800	SD	92114	1290-E5
PLAZA ULTIMA	1000	CHV	91910	1311-B7
PLAZA VALDIVIA	17800	SD	92128	1150-C7
PLAZA VIEJAS	-	SDCo	91901	1234-A6
PLAZA VISTA	1300	SD	92114	1290-D5
PLAZA VISTA MAR	1000	CHV	91910	1311-B7
PLAZUELA ST	2200	CRLB	92009	1147-F1
PLEASANT LN	700	NATC	91950	1290-B7
PLEASANT PL	1600	ENCT	92024	1147-G6
PLEASANT WY	300	SMCS	92069	1108-H7
PLEASANTDALE DR	1700	ENCT	92024	1147-H7
PLEASANTDALE LN	200	ENCT	92024	1147-H7
PLEASANT GROVE RD	2100	ENCT	92024	1147-H7
PLEASANT HEIGHTS DR	1700	SDCo	92084	1088-B2
PLEASANT HILL ST	1100	ESCN	92026	1129-F1
	1200	ESCN	92026	1109-F7
PLEASANT KNOLL LN	28700	SDCo	92082	1070-G7
	28700	SDCo	92082	1090-G1
PLEASANTON RD	1500	CHV	91913	1311-D7
PLEASANT VALLEY PL	-	CHV	91915	1311-G7
PLEASANT VIEW DR	500	SDCo	92036	1156-E2
PLEASANT VIEW LN	3200	SDCo	91935	1273-A7
	3200	SDCo	91935	1293-A1
PLEASANTWOOD LN	2100	ESCN	92026	1109-H4
PLEIADES DR	1200	SDCo	92084	1108-D1
PLESS RD	7300	SD	92126	1229-A1
	7300	SD	92145	1229-A1
PLIMPTON RD	9600	LMSA	91941	1271-C1
	9600	SDCo	91941	1271-C1
PLONE WY	3000	SD	92117	1248-C3
PLOVER CT	-	CRLB	92009	1127-D6
PLOVER ST	1500	SD	92114	1290-E1
PLOVER WY	1000	OCN	92057	1087-A3
PLUM CT	-	ESCN	92027	1130-H2
	29100	SDCo	92082	1071-A6
PLUM ST	-	SD	92133	1268-D7
	1200	SD	92106	1288-B2
	1900	SD	92106	1268-C7
PLUMAS ST	5600	SD	92139	1290-C7
PLUMAS PINES PL	1400	CHV	91915	1311-H7
PLUMBAGO LN	3500	SD	92154	1330-E7
PLUMB BROQUE CIR	1700	SDCo	92019	1252-B5
PLUMCREST LN	-	SD	92130	1208-E2
PLUMERIA DR	1600	SDCo	92021	1251-G1
PLUM HOLLOW PL	1700	VSTA	92083	1107-D2
PLUMMER CT	4700	SD	92130	1188-C4
PLUMOSA AV	200	SDCo	92083	1108-B4
	500	VSTA	92083	1108-B4
PLUMOSA CT	2400	SDCo	92083	1108-B5
PLUMOSA DR	3600	SD	92106	1268-C6
PLUMOSA ST	100	OCN	92054	1086-F1
	100	OCN	92054	1066-G7
PLUMOSA WY	1400	SD	92103	1268-H5
PLUMTREE DR	1500	ENCT	92024	1167-G1
PLUM TREE LN	-	ESCN	92027	1130-J3
	11000	SDCo	91977	1271-E7
PLUM TREE RD	1300	CRLB	92009	1127-A4
PLUM TREE WY	500	OCN	92054	1086-F2
PLUMWOOD ST	14600	PWY	92064	1190-D1
PLUTO CT	3400	SDCo	91902	1310-G1
PLUTO RD	1400	VSTA	92083	1087-D6
PLYMOUTH CT	-	CHV	91911	1330-E3
PLYMOUTH DR	100	VSTA	92083	1087-G6
PLYMOUTH ST	5200	OCN	92057	1067-A3
POBLADO CT	17100	SD	92127	1169-J2
POBLADO RD	10000	SD	92127	1149-H7
	10500	SD	92127	1169-H1
POBLADO WY	17100	SD	92127	1169-J2
POCAHONTAS AV	4300	SD	92117	1248-D1
POCAHONTAS CT	3600	SD	92117	1248-D1
POCAHONTAS PL	3600	SD	92117	1248-D1
POCANO WY	13300	SD	92128	1189-J4
POCATELLO ST	100	SD	92114	1290-D4
POCHARD WY	-	SD	92131	1209-G2
POCHE PT	11200	SD	92131	1209-J2
POCITOS WY	3100	SD	92173	1350-D2
POCO PZ	-	SMCS	92078	1129-C2
POCO WY	24300	SDCo	92065	1173-F2
POCO LAGO	6500	SDCo	92067	1188-G2
POCO MONTANA	-	SDCo	92036	1175-H1
POD DR	2300	SDCo	92084	1108-D1
PODELL AV	9400	SD	92123	1249-F7
PODERIO CT	16100	SDCo	92065	1173-H3
PODERIO DR	25000	SDCo	92065	1173-H3
POE RD	5900	ImCo	92227	410-L11
	5900	ImCo	92259	410-L11
POE ST	3000	SD	92106	1288-B1
	3400	SD	92106	1268-B7
	3600	SD	92107	1268-B7
	10300	SDCo	92026	1109-F2
POESIA CT	1600	SD	92154	1350-B2
POETS CT	1400	SDCo	92028	1027-F4
POETS SQ	300	SDCo	92028	1027-F4
POHL PL	800	VSTA	92083	1087-F5
POINCIANA DR	1600	SDCo	92021	1251-G1
POINSETIA CT	100	CHV	91910	1310-B5
POINSETT RD	11000	SD	92131	1209-H1
POINSETTIA AV	100	SDCo	92083	1108-C4
	100	SDCo	92084	1108-C4
	800	VSTA	92083	1108-B7
	2100	VSTA	92083	1128-A1
POINSETTIA CT	200	SDCo	92083	1108-C4
POINSETTIA DR	2100	SD	92107	1268-B7
	2200	SD	92106	1268-C6
	13600	PWY	92064	1190-F3
POINSETTIA LN	-	CRLB	92009	1126-J6
	800	CRLB	92009	1127-H4
POINSETTIA PK	700	ENCT	92024	1147-C5
POINSETTIA PK N	600	ENCT	92024	1147-C5
POINSETTIA PK S	600	ENCT	92024	1147-C5
POINSETTIA ST	500	CHV	91911	1330-H3
POINSETTIA PARK CT	600	ENCT	92024	1147-C5
W POINT DR	1500	CHV	91911	1330-J4
POINT RD	900	ESCN	92026	1129-J1
POINT ST	900	SD	92106	1288-A2
POINT ALTO	4800	SDCo	91941	1271-C2
POINT ARENA CT	500	CHV	91911	1330-H4
POINT ARGUELLO	700	OCN	92054	1066-G7
POINT ARGUELLO DR	1600	CHV	91911	1330-J3
POINT BARROW DR	600	CHV	91911	1330-J4
POINT BUCHON	800	OCN	92054	1066-G7
POINT BUCHON CT	600	CHV	91911	1330-J4
POINT CABRILLO	700	OCN	92054	1066-G7
POINT CABRILLO CT	1600	CHV	91911	1330-H4
POINT CAIMAN CT	600	CHV	91911	1330-H4
POINT CONCEPCION CT	1600	CHV	91911	1330-J4
POINT DEFIANCE CT	600	CHV	91911	1330-H4
POINT DEGADA	4400	OCN	92054	1066-G7
	4400	OCN	92057	1066-G7
POINT DELGADA CT	1500	CHV	91911	1330-H4
POINT DUME CT	1500	CHV	91911	1330-J4
POINTE PKWY	2700	SDCo	91977	1291-E1
POINTE DEL MAR WY	12800	SD	92014	1207-J1
POINTED OAK LN	10700	SD	92131	1210-A3
POINTER GN	2000	ESCN	92029	1129-E6
POINTER LN	100	VSTA	92084	1088-B5
POINT ESTERO DR	1600	CHV	91911	1330-J5
POINT FERMINE CT	600	CHV	91911	1330-J3
POINT HUENEME CT	1500	CHV	91911	1330-J4
POINTILLIST CT	4800	OCN	92057	1087-B2
POINTING ROCK DR	200	SDCo	92004	1058-F6
POINT LA JOLLA DR	1500	CHV	91911	1330-H4
POINT LOBAS CIR	700	OCN	92054	1066-G7
POINT LOMA AV	3800	SD	92106	1288-A1
	4000	SD	92107	1288-A1
	4100	SD	92107	1287-J1
	4700	SD	92107	1267-H7
W POINT LOMA BLVD	3900	SD	92110	1268-A5
	4300	SD	92107	1268-A5
	4800	SD	92107	1267-J5
POINT LOMA CT	1600	CHV	91911	1330-J4
POINT LOMA PL	4800	OCN	92057	1066-J6
POINT LOMA WY	1400	SD	92106	1288-A1
POINT MALAGA PL	4700	OCN	92057	1066-J6
POINT MEDANAS CT	600	CHV	91911	1330-J3
POINT MUGU CT	1600	CHV	91911	1330-J4
POINT PACIFIC CT	1500	CHV	91911	1330-H4
POINT REYES	700	OCN	92054	1066-G7
POINT REYES CT	1600	CHV	91911	1330-H4
	4300	CRLB	92008	1106-J4
POINT SAL CT	1600	CHV	91911	1330-H4
POINT SAN LUIS CT	500	CHV	91911	1330-J3
POINTSETTIA LN	-	CRLB	92009	1127-E5
POINT SUR	700	OCN	92054	1066-G7
POINT SUR CT	1600	CHV	91911	1330-J4
POINT VICENTE	4400	OCN	92054	1066-G7
POINT VICENTE CT	600	CHV	91911	1330-H4
POINTVIEW CT	4300	SDCo	91941	1271-D3
POINT WINDEMERE PL	300	OCN	92057	1066-J6
POIPU WY	2200	SD	92154	1330-D7
POLA CT	4900	SD	92110	1248-F7
POLACK ST	3900	SD	92110	1268-C6
POLANCO ST	8800	SD	92129	1189-C2
POLARIS DR	3800	SDCo	91941	1271-A5
	10900	SD	92126	1209-D1
POLIZZI PL	8200	SD	92123	1269-B1
POLK AV	1600	SD	92103	1269-C5
	1900	SD	92104	1269-C5
	3600	SD	92105	1269-J5
	4000	SD	92105	1270-A5
POLK RD	2800	SDCo	91901	1234-C4
POLK ST	100	OCN	92057	1067-B6
POLLAND AV	8700	SD	92123	1249-C6
POLLEY DR	3400	SMCS	92069	1108-D5
POLLY LN	3800	CRLB	92008	1106-G6
POLLYANNA TER	400	VSTA	92083	1087-G5
POLO CT	1700	OCN	92057	1067-F7
POLO CLUB DR	-	SDCo	92084	1068-D6
POLVERA AV	12900	SD	92128	1150-C5
POLVERA CT	12900	SD	92128	1150-C6
POLVERA DR	18500	SD	92128	1150-C6
POLVERA WY	18000	SD	92128	1150-C6
POLVO DR	28700	SDCo	92082	1071-C7
	28700	SDCo	92082	1091-C1
POMANI CT	1200	OCN	92056	1087-C3
POMARD CT	17100	PWY	92064	1170-D2
POMARD WY	12900	PWY	92064	1170-D2
POMEGRANATE AV	14000	PWY	92064	1190-F3
POMEGRANATE LN	1900	SDCo	92028	1027-H6
POMEGRANITE CT	-	ESCN	92027	1130-H2
POMELO DR	300	VSTA	92083	1087-E7
	300	VSTA	92083	1107-E1
	700	SDCo	92083	1107-E2
POMELO WY	600	VSTA	92083	1107-E1
POMERADO CT	12400	SD	92128	1170-B2
POMERADO PL	12400	SD	92128	1170-C2
POMERADO RD	9900	SD	92131	1209-G6
	9900	SD	92145	1209-G6
	9900	SDCo	92131	1209-G6
	9900	SDCo	92145	1209-G6
	11200	SD	92131	1210-C2
	11400	SD	92145	1210-C2
	11800	PWY	92064	1190-C2
	12600	PWY	92064	1210-C2
	14800	PWY	92064	1170-C7
	15800	PWY	92064	1170-C7
POMERADO RD Rt#-S5	-	SD	92127	1150-B5
	16900	SD	92128	1170-C3
	17700	SD	92128	1150-B5
POMERADO WY	17100	SD	92128	1170-B2
POMEROY ST	3400	SD	92123	1249-D4
POMMEL WY	400	SMCS	92069	1108-E6
POMONA AV	900	CORD	92118	1288-J7
	1500	CORD	92118	1308-J1
	4300	LMSA	91941	1270-F4
POMONA AV Rt#-282	1200	CORD	92118	1288-J6
POMONA WY	7300	LMSA	91941	1270-F3
PONCA CT	6000	SD	92120	1250-D5
PONCE DE LEON DR	4100	SDCo	91941	1271-H3
POND PL	100	VSTA	92083	1087-G3
PONDER WY	10500	SD	92126	1209-A4
PONDEROSA AV	1000	SMCS	92069	1109-B5
	4100	SD	92123	1249-D3
PONDEROSA DR	900	VSTA	92084	1088-A5
	3500	OCN	92054	1086-F2
PONDEROSA LN	8600	SDCo	92066	1237-C4
PONDEROSA PINE LN	7600	SDCo	92066	1237-C7
PONS ST	600	SD	92114	1290-F3
PONTE AV	400	SMCS	92069	1108-C6
PONTE VEDRA WY	2400	CHV	91915	1311-H6
PONTIAC DR	3400	CRLB	92008	1106-J4
	4500	CRLB	92008	1107-A5
PONTIAC ST	6000	SD	92115	1270-C2
PONTO DR	1800	CRLB	92009	1126-H5
	6200	CRLB	92009	1146-J1
PONTO RD	7100	CRLB	92009	1126-J7
PONY CT	5600	OCN	92057	1067-F7
PONY LN	5500	SDCo	91902	1311-A2
PONY EXPRESS CIR	-	SDCo	92040	1232-F4
POOLE ST	9400	SD	92037	1227-J2
POORE RD	-	ImCo	92227	431-E2
POPLAR AV	400	SMCS	92069	1108-J6
POPLAR DR	1200	ELCN	92243	6559-G1
POPLAR RD	2000	OCN	92054	1086-C5
POPLAR ST	300	SD	92173	1350-F3
	500	SDCo	92065	1152-F5
	4000	SD	92105	1269-G7
POPLAR WY	300	ESCN	92026	1129-H1
POPLAR MEADOW LN	2800	SDCo	91935	1292-G3
POPLAR SPRING RD	-	CHV	91915	1311-H5
POPLIN DR	7900	SNTE	92071	1250-H1
POPPY CIR	300	OCN	92057	1066-H6
POPPY DR	29500	SDCo	91906	(1297-E5 See Page 1296)
POPPY LN	900	CRLB	92009	1127-A6
	3700	SDCo	92028	1028-E4
POPPY PL	4000	SD	92105	1269-G7
POPPY RD	800	SMCS	92078	1128-F2
POPPY ST	5900	LMSA	91942	1251-C6
POPPYFIELD GN	300	ESCN	92026	1109-H5
POPPYFIELD PL	2100	ENCT	92024	1147-J7
POPPY HILLS DR	2200	CHV	91915	1311-H7
POPPY HILLS WY	-	SD	92128	1190-A3
POPPY PEAR HILL	-	SDCo	92028	998-G5
POQUITO ST	12400	PWY	92064	1190-C6
POQUITO WY	4200	OCN	92057	1086-H3
PORCELINA CT	12200	SD	92131	1210-B1
PORRECA PT	11300	SD	92126	1208-J2
PORT CIR	3300	OCN	92056	1107-A2
PORTA PL	2400	CRLB	92008	1106-H5
PORTADA PL	12500	SD	92130	1188-B6
PORTAGE WY	-	CRLB	92009	1126-J7
	-	CRLB	92009	1127-A7
PORTAL TER	11500	SD	92128	1190-A7
PORT ALBANS	1800	CHV	91913	1311-D4
PORT ASHLEY	600	CHV	91913	1311-E3
PORT CARDIFF	2000	CHV	91913	1311-E3
PORT CARNEY	1900	CHV	91913	1311-D3
PORT CHELSEA	600	CHV	91913	1311-D4
PORT CLARIDGE	600	CHV	91913	1311-D4
PORT DUNBAR	600	CHV	91913	1311-D4
POR TECHO CT	5400	SD	92124	1249-H1
PORTE DE MERANO	4100	SD	92122	1228-B4
PORTE DE PALMAS	4000	SD	92122	1228-B4
PORTE LA PAZ	4000	SD	92122	1228-B5
PORTENO CT	1000	SDCo	92069	1128-F3
PORTER LN	1800	SDCo	92036	1136-B7
PORTER RD	1700	SD	92133	1288-C1
	1800	SD	92133	1268-D7
	4200	LMSA	91941	1271-A4
PORTER ST	300	SDCo	92028	1027-G1
	600	SD	92114	1290-F3
PORTER WY	800	SDCo	92028	1027-G1
PORTERFIELD PL	1700	SDCo	92019	1272-B4
PORTER HILL RD	4900	LMSA	91941	1270-J2
PORTER HILL TER	8400	LMSA	91941	1270-J2
PORTERVILLE PL	1000	CHV	91913	1311-E5
PORTFOLIO ST	4800	OCN	92057	1087-B2
PORT HARWICK	500	CHV	91913	1311-D4
PORTIA AV	200	VSTA	92084	1087-H3
PORTICO DR	500	OCN	92054	1086-G1
PORTILLA PL	4100	SD	92130	1188-B7
PORTLAND CT	3700	CRLB	92008	1107-A4
PORTLAND ST	800	ELCJ	92020	1251-G7
PORT MARNOCK DR	17400	PWY	92064	1170-E1
PORT MARNOCK WY	13400	PWY	92064	1170-E1
PORTO CT	10500	SD	92124	1249-H1
PORTOBELO CT	5800	SD	92124	1229-H6
PORTOBELO DR	10500	SD	92124	1229-H7
	10900	SD	92124	1230-A6
PORTOFINO CIR	12900	SD	92014	1207-J1
	13100	SD	92014	1187-J7
PORTOFINO DR	1400	VSTA	92083	1107-H3
	1800	OCN	92054	1106-F1
	12700	SD	92014	1207-H1
	13100	SD	92014	1187-J6
PORT-OF-SPAIN RD	-	CORD	92118	1329-E2
PORTOLA AV	1000	SDCo	91977	1291-C2
	1100	ESCN	92026	1109-E5
PORTOLA PL	3900	SD	92103	1268-H5
PORTOLA ST	1000	VSTA	92084	1087-J4
PORT RENWICK	1800	CHV	91902	1311-D4
	1800	CHV	91913	1311-D4
PORT ROYALE CV	10200	SD	92126	1209-A5
PORT ROYALE DR	7800	SD	92126	1209-A5
PORT ROYALE RD	-	CORD	92118	1329-E2
PORT RUSH RW	11400	SD	92128	1189-J3
PORTSIDE PL	-	SMCS	92078	1128-D6
PORTSMOUTH CT	700	SD	92109	1267-H1
PORTSMOUTH DR	500	CHV	91911	1330-H3
PORTSMOUTH BAY CT	4800	OCN	92057	1066-J6
PORT STIRLING	600	CHV	91913	1311-E3
PORT TRINITY	600	CHV	91913	1311-D4
POSADA CT	3900	OCN	92054	1086-G1
POSEIDON WY	4800	OCN	92056	1107-E5
POSEY PL	4200	SD	92105	1289-H1
POSITAS RD	1200	CHV	91910	1311-A5
POSITIVE PL	-	SMCS	92069	1108-H7
POSSUM PASS	18800	SDCo	92082	1091-F3
POSSUM CREEK LN	9900	SDCo	92021	1232-G2
POST RD	4300	SD	92117	1228-E7
POST TR	700	SDCo	92019	1253-C2
POSTAL WY	900	VSTA	92083	1087-J7
	1000	VSTA	92083	1107-J1
POSTHILL PL	11400	SDCo	92040	1211-J7
POSTHILL RD	11100	SDCo	92040	1211-J7
POTOMAC ST	5500	SD	92139	1310-C1
	6000	SD	92139	1290-E7
POTRERO CIR	1400	SDCo	91963	(1316-C6 See Page 1296)
POTRERO CT	900	CHV	91911	1330-E1
POTRERO ST	8600	SD	92114	1290-H3
	8600	SDCo	91977	1290-H3
POTRERO PARK DR	25600	SDCo	91963	429-L10
POTRERO VALLEY RD	600	SDCo	91963	(1316-F5 See Page 1296)
POTTER AV	9700	SD	92145	1229-F3
POTTER ST	100	SDCo	92028	1027-G3
POUMELE WY	1800	OCN	92054	1106-E2
POUND RD	300	ImCo	92233	411-B8
	300	ImCo	92257	411-B8
POVERTY RDG	25100	SDCo	91916	1236-B3
POWAY RD Rt#-S4	11600	PWY	92064	1190-H2
	11600	SD	92128	1190-B5
	12000	SD	92128	1189-G6
	15500	PWY	92064	1191-A1
POWAY CREEK RD	13000	PWY	92064	1190-E5
POWAY HILLS DR	13100	PWY	92064	1190-D1
POWAY MESA CT	14500	PWY	92064	1190-E1
POWAY MESA DR	14500	PWY	92064	1190-E1
POWAY OAKS DR	12800	PWY	92064	1190-C5
POWAY SPRINGS CT	15300	PWY	92064	1170-F6
POWAY SPRINGS RD	13600	PWY	92064	1170-F6
POWAY VALLEY RD	13800	PWY	92064	1190-G1
POWDERHORN DR	4100	SD	92154	1330-G6
POWELL DR	1900	ELCJ	92020	1251-C4
POWELL RD	1500	OCN	92056	1087-E1
POWERS CT	13200	PWY	92064	1190-C4
POWERS RD	13300	PWY	92064	1190-C4
POWHATAN AV	2700	SD	92117	1248-B1
POYNTELL CIR	10800	SD	92131	1210-A3
POZA RICA CT	100	SOLB	92075	1167-D7
POZZUOLI LN	-	VSTA	92084	1088-A1
PRADERA PL	3500	SDCo	91902	1310-E3
PRADO CT	5100	OCN	92057	1087-C1
	12300	SD	92128	1170-B2
PRADO PL	17100	SD	92128	1170-B2
PRADO RD	17200	SD	92128	1170-B2
PRADO WY	12200	SD	92128	1170-B2
PRADO VERDE	500	SMCS	92069	1109-A6
PRAFUL CT	9300	SNTE	92071	1230-H6
PRAIRIE DR	-	CHV	91914	1311-G3
	3800	SDCo	91935	1274-C3
PRAIRIE RD	700	OCN	92057	1067-B5
PRAIRIE DOG AV	12700	SD	92129	1189-C5
PRAIRIE FAWN CT	-	SDCo	92127	1169-F3
PRAIRIE FAWN DR	-	SDCo	92127	1169-E3
PRAIRIE MILE RD	-	SDCo	92065	1173-D1
PRAIRIE MOUND CT	500	SD	92139	1290-H5
PRAIRIE MOUND WY	7300	SD	92139	1290-G6
PRAIRIE ROSE WY	-	SMCS	92078	1128-G3
PRAIRIE SHADOW PT	11500	SD	92126	1209-A1
PRAIRIE SHADOW RD	7700	SD	92126	1209-A2
PRAIRIE SPRINGS RD	-	SDCo	92127	1169-E3
PRAIRIESTONE WY	2700	ESCN	92027	1110-D5
PRAIRIE VISTA RD	15800	PWY	92064	1170-G4
PRAIRIE WOOD DR	11400	SD	92126	1209-A2
PRANCER WY	7300	SD	92139	1290-G6
PRATHER PL	400	SDCo	91977	1291-B4
PRATT CT	9900	SNTE	92071	1231-D3
PRAY CT	5600	SDCo	91902	1290-J7
PRAY ST	5500	SDCo	91902	1290-J6
PREAKNESS CT	3400	SDCo	92028	1047-G3
PRECIOUS HILLS RD	500	OCN	92057	1067-F4
PRECISION PARK LN	1600	SD	92173	1350-E2
PREDIO CT	1600	SD	92154	1350-B3
PREECE CT	6600	SD	92111	1248-H6
PREECE ST	2600	SD	92111	1248-H6
PREECE WY	6500	SD	92111	1248-H6
PREGO CT	12600	SD	92130	1188-C6
PREMIER ST	1700	SDCo	92028	1028-A5
PRESCOTT AV	400	ELCJ	92020	1251-F6
PRESCOTT CT	1900	VSTA	92083	1107-J4
PRESCOTT GN	2400	ESCN	92027	1110-D7
PRESIDENTS WY	1900	SD	92101	1289-B1
PRESIDIO DR	2200	SD	92103	1268-F4
	2600	SD	92110	1268-F4
PRESIDIO POINT CT	1600	CHV	91911	1330-J4
PRESILLA DR	14900	SDCo	91935	1293-B4
PRESIOCA ST	1200	SDCo	91977	1291-B2
PRESLEY PL	200	VSTA	92083	1108-A2
PRESLEY ST	10100	SD	92126	1208-J5
PRESS LN	100	CHV	91910	1310-B4
PRESTIGE RD	1900	SDCo	92065	1152-E1
PRESTON LN	1300	CHV	91911	1330-D4
PRESTON PL	1300	CHV	91911	1330-D4
PRESTON RD	-	ImCo	92243	431-A7
PRESTWICK CIR	3500	OCN	92056	1107-E3
PRESTWICK CT	900	VSTA	92083	1108-E2
	1600	SMCS	92069	1108-J3
	2600	SD	92037	1227-J4
PRESTWICK DR	8100	SD	92037	1227-J5
PRESTWICK WY	8800	SNTE	92071	1230-J5
	8800	SNTE	92071	1231-A5
PRICE WY	-	SDCo	92672	1023-D2
PRIDEMORE PL	4100	SD	92117	1248-E5
PRIESTLY DR	5800	CRLB	92008	1127-D1
PRIETO RD	1000	SDCo	92028	998-H6
PRIMA VERA	1500	OCN	92056	1087-B4

SAN DIEGO CO. INDEX

STREET Block City ZIP Pg-Grid

PRIMAVERA LN
1500 DLMR 92014 1187-G4
PRIMAVERA WY
7600 CRLB 92009 1147-H1
PRIMENTEL LN
7000 CRLB 92009 1127-G7
PRIMERA ST
1500 LMGR 91945 1290-F1
PRIMERO IZQUIERDO
6400 SDCo 92067 1148-E6
PRIMROSE AV
2100 SDCo 92083 1108-C3
2100 VSTA 92083 1108-C3
PRIMROSE CT
14200 PWY 92064 1170-G5
PRIMROSE DR
1400 ELCJ 92020 1251-C6
1600 LMSA 91942 1251-C6
29400 SDCo 91906 (1297-E5 See Page 1296)
N PRIMROSE DR
6100 LMSA 91942 1251-C6
PRIMROSE GN
3800 ESCN 92025 1150-C3
PRIMROSE PL
- CHV 91910 1310-C5
300 SDCo 92083 1108-C4
PRIMROSE WY
400 OCN 92057 1086-J4
7100 CRLB 92009 1127-A6
PRINCE LN
10700 SDCo 91941 1271-F3
PRINCE ST
1000 ELCJ 92021 1251-H4
1500 SDCo 92028 1028-A5
1600 SDCo 92028 1027-J5
3500 SDCo 92025 1150-D2
PRINCE WY
1200 VSTA 92084 1088-A2
PRINCE CARLOS LN
10600 SNTE 92071 1231-E2
PRINCE CHARMING LN
10100 SNTE 92071 1231-D1
PRINCE EDWARD CT
2300 SDCo 92019 1272-B5
PRINCEHOUSE LN
100 ENCT 92024 1147-E6
PRINCE IVAN CT
7900 SDCo 92021 1252-A1
PRINCE JED CT
10200 SNTE 92071 1231-D2
PRINCESA CT
1100 CHV 91910 1310-J5
PRINCESS ST
7900 SD 92037 1227-G6
PRINCESS ARLENE DR
10700 SNTE 92071 1231-D2
PRINCESS JOANN RD
9900 SNTE 92071 1231-D1
PRINCESS MANOR CT
1400 CHV 91911 1330-G3
PRINCESS MARCIE DR
10200 SNTE 92071 1231-D2
PRINCESS SARIT WY
10200 SNTE 92071 1231-D2
PRINCESS VIEW CT
5400 SD 92120 1250-B5
PRINCESS VIEW DR
6800 SD 92120 1250-B4
PRINCESS VIEW PL
5400 SD 92120 1250-B5
PRINCESS VIEW WY
5400 SD 92120 1250-B5
PRINCETON AV
3500 SD 92117 1248-D5
7200 LMSA 91941 1270-F3
PRINCETON DR
3300 OCN 92056 1107-A2
PRINCE VALIANT DR
10800 SNTE 92071 1231-D1
PRINGLE ST
3400 SD 92110 1268-H6
3600 SD 92103 1268-H6
PRINGLE CANYON RD
- SDCo 91935 (1314-E3 See Page 1294)
PRINTWOOD CT
4700 SD 92117 1248-J1
PRINTWOOD WY
5700 SD 92117 1248-H1
PRISCILLA ST
14800 SD 92129 1169-J7
14800 SD 92129 1189-J1
PRIVADO GN
1900 ESCN 92029 1129-E4
PRIVADO PL
1300 SD 92113 1290-A6
PRIVATE WY
5200 SDCo 91941 1271-C1
PRIVET PL
- SDCo 92026 1089-B3
PRIVET ST
1100 SMCS 92069 1109-C7
PROCTOR PL
4200 SD 92116 1269-B4
4200 SD 92103 1269-B4
PROCTOR VALLEY LN
13700 SDCo 91935 1292-G2
PROCTOR VALLEY RD
2200 CHV 91914 1311-G3
2200 SDCo 91902 1311-C1
2200 SDCo 91914 1311-C1
3400 SDCo 91902 1291-B7
5600 CHV 91914 (1312-B2 See Page 1293)
7300 SDCo 91914 (1312-B2 See Page 1293)
11200 SDCo 91914 1292-C7
11200 SDCo 91935 1292-G3
12600 SDCo 91978 1292-D4
PRODUCTION AV
3200 OCN 92054 1086-D5
8400 SD 92121 1228-J1
8400 SD 92121 1208-J7
PRODUCTION ST
400 SMCS 92078 1128-J1
400 SMCS 92078 1129-A1
PROGRESS LN
700 SDCo 92065 1172-H1
PROGRESS PL
2800 ESCN 92029 1129-C2
PROGRESS ST
2500 VSTA 92083 1108-A7
PROMENADE CIR
1700 OCN 92056 1087-D7
1700 VSTA 92083 1087-D7
PROMENADE PL
1700 VSTA 92083 1087-D7
1700 OCN 92056 1087-D7

PROMESA CIR
4400 SD 92124 1250-A1
PROMESA CT
4400 SD 92124 1250-A1
PROMESA DR
11000 SD 92124 1249-J1
11000 SD 92124 1250-A1
PROMONTORY DR
100 SDCo 92021 1252-H4
PROMONTORY PL
3600 CRLB 92008 1107-B3
PROMONTORY ST
3500 SD 92109 1268-A1
3600 SD 92109 1248-A6
PROMONTORY RIDGE WY
1500 VSTA 92083 1107-G4
PROSPECT AV
500 SDCo 92028 1027-G1
8200 SNTE 92071 1250-H1
8300 SNTE 92071 1230-J7
8600 SNTE 92071 1231-B7
9500 SDCo 92040 1232-A4
10800 SNTE 92021 1231-D7
PROSPECT CIR
1100 VSTA 92083 1107-J1
PROSPECT CT
- CHV 91911 1330-F3
PROSPECT PL
200 CORD 92118 1289-A6
1000 VSTA 92083 1107-H2
2000 SDCo 92036 1136-C6
7700 SD 92037 1227-F6
PROSPECT ST
- CHV 91911 1330-E4
200 SD 92037 1227-E7
1600 NATC 91950 1310-B1
2300 SDCo 91950 1310-B2
E PROSPECT ST
- CHV 91911 1330-E3
PROSPECT WY
8000 LMSA 91941 1270-H3
PROSPECTORS SQ
9400 SDCo 92040 1232-E4
PROSPERITY DR
5300 SD 92115 1270-A2
PROSPERITY LN
5200 SD 92115 1270-A2
PROTEA DR
8400 SDCo 92040 1232-A7
8400 SDCo 92040 1252-A1
PROTEA GARDENS RD
1500 SDCo 92026 1089-D7
PROTEA VISTA RD
3000 SDCo 92084 1068-E6
PROVENCAL PL
11100 SD 92128 1189-J3
PROVENCE CT
- CHV 91911 1330-E3
PROVIDENCE LN
3500 CRLB 92008 1107-A4
PROVIDENCE RD
4900 SD 92117 1228-E7
PROVIDENCE BAY CT
11800 SDCo 92040 1231-J3
PROVO ST
300 ELCJ 92019 1252-B5
PRUETT DR
2400 SDCo 92084 1087-H1
PRYOR DR
9400 SNTE 92071 1231-B7
PUEBLA DR
3600 OCN 92054 1086-F2
10700 SDCo 91941 1271-F3
PUEBLA ST
400 ENCT 92024 1147-C5
2600 SDCo 92025 1150-D1
PUEBLO AV
9100 SDCo 92040 1232-A6
PUEBLO DR
34700 SDCo 92036 1176-E4
PUEBLO GN
2100 ESCN 92027 1110-B5
PUEBLO PL
700 CHV 91914 1311-G3
PUEBLO RD
8400 SDCo 92040 1232-A7
PUEBLO ST
1900 SD 92113 1289-D4
3000 CRLB 92009 1147-H1
PUEBLO VISTA LN
17800 SD 92127 1149-H7
PUENTE DR
1800 SD 92037 1227-G6
PUERTA DE LOMAS
100 SDCo 92028 1047-F7
300 SDCo 92028 1067-E1
500 OCN 92028 1067-E1
PUERTA DEL SOL
15600 SDCo 92067 1168-B6
PUERTA LA CRUZ RD
- SDCo 92086 409-J6
PUERTO DE DESTINO
3200 SDCo 92067 1148-C6
PUERTO DEL MUNDO
1700 SDCo 92028 1028-F5
PUERTO ORO CT
700 OCN 92057 1087-C1
PUERTO ORO LN
19600 SDCo 92065 1151-G4
PUESTA PL
2100 ELCJ 92020 1251-C1
PUESTA DEL SOL
2200 ESCN 92027 1130-E2
2200 SDCo 92027 1130-E2
PUESTA DEL SOL LN
15800 SDCo 92065 1171-C1
PUFFEN PL
- CRLB 92009 1127-C6
PUFFIN DR
200 VSTA 92083 1087-G4
PULITZER PL
4000 SD 92122 1228-C3
PULLER PL
- SDCo 92672 1023-E2
PULLMAN RD
- ImCo 92231 431-A8
PULS ST
1300 OCN 92054 1086-B6
PUMA TR
14600 SDCo 92082 1070-G4
PUNTA ARROYO
- SDCo 92067 1149-A3
PUNTA BAJA DR
300 SOLB 92075 1167-H6
PUNTA DEL NORTE
- SDCo 92067 1148-J5
PUNTA DEL SUR
17800 SDCo 92067 1148-J6

PURDUE AV
7100 LMSA 91941 1270-F4
PURDUE CT
1800 OCN 92056 1087-C5
PURDUM LN
1400 ESCN 92025 1130-B4
PURDY ST
1100 SDCo 91977 1290-J2
PURER RD
400 SDCo 92029 1149-G2
PURE WATERS CT
- SDCo 91977 1291-F2
PURITAN DR
1400 OCN 92057 1066-J3
1400 OCN 92057 1067-B4
PURITAN WY
1400 OCN 92057 1067-A3
PURPLE BLOSSOM DR
300 SMCS 92078 1128-G2
PURPLE LEAF WY
- SDCo 92127 1169-D2
PUSSY WILLOW LN
2900 SDCo 92028 1048-C3
PUTERBAUGH ST
1300 SD 92103 1268-H6
PUTNEY RD
13600 PWY 92064 1190-F3
PUTTER CT
3000 SDCo 92019 1272-C5
PUTTER DR
3500 SDCo 91902 1310-D4
PUTTER PL
3400 OCN 92056 1106-H1
3700 SDCo 91902 1310-D4
PUTTER WY
1100 SDCo 92004 (1079-B4 See Page 1058)
PUTTING GREEN CT
3300 OCN 92056 1106-J2
PUTTING GREEN RW
12100 SD 92128 1170-A4
PYEATT TKTR
- SDCo 92028 409-A5
PYLOS WY
4900 OCN 92056 1107-E6
PYRAMID ST
600 SD 92114 1290-B3
PYRAMID POINT WY
500 OCN 92054 1066-E6
PYRENEES DR
500 SMCS 92069 1128-C1
PYRUS PL
6400 CRLB 92009 1127-A4

Q

Q AV
100 NATC 91950 1289-J6
400 NATC 91950 1290-A7
1400 NATC 91950 1310-A1
Q CT
- SD 92126 1209-F7
QUADRA AV
2800 SD 92154 1350-C3
QUAIL CRSG
16800 SDCo 92065 1171-E1
QUAIL CT
400 CHV 91911 1330-G3
QUAIL DR
100 CHV 91911 1330-F3
18000 SDCo 92061 1051-F5
QUAIL LN
200 OCN 92057 1086-H2
QUAIL PL
300 CHV 91911 1330-G3
6900 CRLB 92009 1127-E5
QUAIL RD
100 ENCT 92024 1147-D6
2700 ESCN 92026 1109-G2
2700 SDCo 92026 1109-G2
29900 SDCo 91906 (1297-G5 See Page 1296)
QUAIL ST
600 SD 92102 1289-G3
QUAIL TER
8500 SDCo 92021 1232-B7
8500 SDCo 92040 1232-B7
QUAIL WY
3200 SDCo 91935 1273-A7
QUAIL CANYON RD
9300 SDCo 92021 1232-G3
10600 SDCo 92021 1233-A2
QUAIL COVEY LN
9800 SDCo 92021 1232-H3
QUAILCREEK LN
9600 SDCo 91977 1271-C5
QUAIL CREEK PL
- ESCN 92027 1130-J3
2500 SDCo 91901 1234-A5
QUAIL CREEK RD
1000 SDCo 92028 997-G7
QUAIL CREST RD
600 SDCo 91901 1233-G6
QUAIL GARDENS CT
500 ENCT 92024 1147-D6
QUAIL GARDENS DR
100 ENCT 92024 1147-D2
QUAIL GARDENS RD
500 ENCT 92024 1147-D5
QUAIL GLEN RD
1900 SDCo 92029 1149-F1
QUAIL GLEN WY
1900 SDCo 92029 1149-F1
QUAIL HAVEN LN
14600 SDCo 92019 1253-A5
QUAIL HILL DR
800 SMCS 92069 1128-E3
QUAIL HILL RD
500 SDCo 92028 1027-G1
QUAIL HOLLOW DR
1700 ENCT 92024 1147-C3
QUAIL HOLLOW LN
29700 SDCo 92082 1070-E5
QUAIL HOLLOW RD
- SDCo 92036 1155-G3
QUAIL KNOLL RD
900 SDCo 92026 1047-H1
QUAIL MOUNTAIN RD
15600 PWY 92064 1171-B5
QUAILRIDGE DR
4500 OCN 92056 1087-D5
QUAILRIDGE RD
1500 SDCo 92027 1130-E5
QUAIL ROCK
16200 SDCo 92065 1171-G4
QUAILRUN
300 ELCJ 92019 1252-D5

QUAIL RUN CT
2500 SDCo 91905 (1299-J4 See Page 1298)
QUAIL RUN DR
500 SDCo 92004 1058-H4
QUAILS TR
900 VSTA 92083 1107-J3
900 VSTA 92083 1108-A3
QUAILSPRINGS CT
1600 CHV 91913 1311-D6
QUAIL SPRINGS CT
10500 SD 92131 1209-J3
QUAIL TRAIL DR
18600 SDCo 91935 1294-E6
QUAIL VALLEY WY
14800 SDCo 92021 1232-J2
QUAILVIEW CT
3600 SDCo 91977 1271-C5
QUAIL VIEW DR
1900 SDCo 92084 1088-B2
10100 SDCo 92026 1089-D5
QUAILVIEW ST
3500 SDCo 91977 1271-C5
QUAKER HILL LN
- SD 92130 1208-D2
QUALCOMM WY
1900 SD 92108 1269-C1
2000 SD 92108 1249-E7
QUALTROUGH ST
2700 SD 92106 1288-A3
QUANAH CT
3800 SDCo 92004 (1099-D2 See Page 1098)
QUANTICO AV
4500 SD 92117 1248-E2
QUAPAW AV
4100 SD 92117 1248-D2
QUARRY GN
2100 ESCN 92027 1110-D7
QUARRY RD
500 SDCo 92069 1088-G5
500 SDCo 92084 1088-G5
3700 LMGR 91945 1270-J5
3800 LMSA 91941 1270-J5
5700 SDCo 91902 1290-J6
5700 SDCo 91902 1291-A5
5700 SDCo 91977 1291-A5
QUARRY VIEW WY
500 SDCo 91977 1290-J5
QUARTER MILE DR
3700 SD 92130 1188-A5
QUARTZ DR
- SDCo 91906 (1297-F4 See Page 1296)
QUARTZ WY
- SDCo 92036 1156-F7
QUARTZ HILL LN
1300 SDCo 92027 1130-C3
QUASAR DR
12500 PWY 92064 1190-C3
QUATE CT
13100 PWY 92064 1190-E4
QUAY AV
300 CHV 91910 1309-H7
300 CHV 91910 1329-H1
2400 NATC 91950 1309-G4
QUAY RD
- CORD 92135 1288-G4
QUEBEC CT
6800 SD 92139 1290-F7
QUEBEC PL
1700 ESCN 92025 1129-J5
QUEBRADA CIR
3000 CRLB 92009 1147-H2
QUEBRADA CT
3100 CRLB 92009 1147-J2
QUEEN AV
4300 SDCo 91941 1271-F3
QUEEN ANNE DR
400 CHV 91911 1330-C3
E QUEEN ANNE DR
- CHV 91911 1330-E2
QUEEN ANNE LN
29500 SDCo 92082 1069-C6
QUEEN JESSICA LN
10600 SNTE 92071 1231-E2
QUEENS WY
1400 VSTA 92084 1088-B3
QUEENSBRIDGE RD
28000 SDCo 92082 1090-J2
QUEENSFERRY SQ
16100 SD 92128 1170-B4
QUEENSTON DR
1400 ESCN 92027 1130-C2
QUEENSTOWN CT
700 SD 92109 1267-H1
QUEMADO CT
5200 SD 92124 1249-F1
QUEMOY CT
6900 SD 92111 1248-J6
QUENTIN ROOSEVELT BLVD
- CORD 92135 1288-G4
QUERIDA SOL
18100 SDCo 92067 1148-D6
QUEST RD
1400 SDCo 92065 1152-E1
QUESTA POINTE
9400 SD 92126 1209-E1
QUESTHAVEN RD
14600 SMCS 92078 1128-F6
14700 SMCS 92029 1128-F6
19900 SDCo 92029 1148-H2
19900 SDCo 92029 1128-F6
21000 SDCo 92078 1128-F6
QUICK RD
- ImCo 92283 432-C5
QUICKER RD
1800 SDCo 92021 1252-C2
QUIDDE AV
2500 SD 92122 1228-B6
QUIDDE CT
5600 SD 92122 1228-B6
QUIDORT CT
1900 ELCJ 92020 1251-C5
QUIET PL
700 SDCo 92029 1149-J2
QUIET COVE DR
6700 CRLB 92009 1126-J6
QUIET CREEK WY
- CHV 91914 1311-G3
QUIET HILLS DR
800 SMCS 92069 1109-C6
1500 OCN 92056 1087-D4
3100 SDCo 92029 1149-J2
3100 ESCN 92029 1149-J2
13500 PWY 92064 1191-A4

QUIET HILLS PL
3100 ESCN 92029 1149-J3
3100 SDCo 92029 1149-J3
QUIET HILLS FARM RD
700 SDCo 92029 1149-J2
QUIET HOLLOW LN
27700 SDCo 92026 1089-G4
QUIET OAKS TR
- SDCo 92036 1155-J5
4600 SDCo 92036 1156-A5
QUIET RANCH RD
1800 SDCo 92028 1028-A6
QUIET SLOPE DR
5900 SD 92120 1250-C4
QUIET VALLEY LN
15600 PWY 92064 1191-A3
QUIET VIEW LN
1700 SDCo 91901 1233-H7
QUIGG PL
1000 VSTA 92084 1088-A7
QUIL GN
1200 ESCN 92029 1129-F5
QUILALANG CT
3300 SD 92173 1350-F5
QUILALANG ST
600 CHV 91911 1330-H3
QUILCENE CT
2200 VSTA 92083 1108-B4
QUILL ST
4800 OCN 92057 1087-C1
QUILLAN ST
6300 SD 92111 1248-H7
QUIMBY ST
3000 SD 92106 1288-C1
3400 SD 92106 1268-B7
QUINALT PT
11500 SD 92131 1210-A2
N QUINCE DR
600 SD 92103 1269-B7
700 SD 92101 1269-B7
QUINCE LN
9700 SDCo 92029 1149-E3
QUINCE PL
300 CHV 91911 1330-G3
QUINCE ST
100 SD 92103 1269-A7
400 CHV 91911 1330-G3
900 SD 92103 1268-J7
1700 ESCN 92025 1129-J5
1700 ESCN 92025 1130-A5
2800 SD 92105 1269-G7
3000 SD 92104 1269-E7
5000 SD 92105 1270-A7
7800 LMSA 91941 1270-G3
N QUINCE ST
100 ESCN 92025 1129-H2
S QUINCE ST
100 ESCN 92025 1129-H4
QUINCY ST
4300 SD 92109 1248-B4
4300 SD 92109 1248-B5
QUINN CT
6900 SD 92111 1268-J1
QUINNEL CT
12900 SD 92130 1188-B5
QUINOA CT
300 CHV 91911 1330-G3
QUINTA ST
7500 CRLB 92009 1147-H1
QUINTAIN DR
2000 SDCo 92004 1058-G7
QUINTARD ST
- CHV 91911 1330-E4
E QUINTARD ST
100 CHV 91911 1330-F3
QUINTO CREEK PL
- CHV 91913 1311-E6
QUINTON RD
13600 SD 92129 1189-F3
QUITASOL ST
7700 CRLB 92009 1147-F1
QUITO CT
4700 SD 92124 1250-A1
QUIVIRA CT
2500 SD 92109 1268-A4
QUIVIRA RD
1400 SD 92109 1268-A3
QUIVIRA WY
1400 SD 92109 1268-A4

R

R AV
- NATC 91950 1290-A7
900 NATC 91950 1310-A1
N R AV
- NATC 91950 1290-A6
S R AV
400 CORD 92135 1288-G5
R CT
- SD 92126 1209-F7
RAB ST
5500 LMSA 91942 1250-H7
5500 LMSA 91942 1270-H1
RABBIT RUN
30400 SDCo 92082 1070-G4
RABBIT HILL
1700 SDCo 92028 1028-C5
RACCOON CT
12200 SDCo 92040 1212-C4
RACE POINT CT
500 CHV 91911 1330-H4
RACETRACK VIEW CT
13400 SD 92014 1187-H4
RACETRACK VIEW DR
2900 DLMR 92014 1187-G4
2900 SD 92014 1187-G4
RACHAEL AV
400 NATC 91950 1290-C7
1600 SD 92139 1310-C1
RACHEL CIR
1200 SDCo 92026 1109-E6
RACHELLE PL
2000 ESCN 92025 1129-J6
2000 ESCN 92025 1130-A6
RACHELLE WY
- ELCJ 92019 1252-D3
RACINE CT
5200 SDCo 91902 1290-J7
RACINE RD
3400 SD 92115 1270-E5
RACQUET CT
13300 PWY 92064 1190-H4
RADAR RD
1400 SD 92154 1351-G1
RADCLIFFE CT
6700 SD 92122 1228-D5
RADCLIFFE DR
6200 SD 92122 1228-D4

RADCLIFFE LN
- SD 92122 1228-D5
RADENZ AV
7400 SD 92111 1249-A6
RADFORD ST
1900 OCN 92056 1087-C5
5000 SD 92120 1250-A5
RADIO CT
5800 SD 92114 1290-C5
RADIO DR
500 SD 92114 1290-D2
S RADIO DR
300 SD 92114 1290-C5
RAE DR
2600 SDCo 91977 1271-A7
RAE LN
- OCN 92054 1086-G3
RAE PL
2500 SDCo 91950 1310-B2
RAECORTE PL
700 SDCo 92026 1109-D6
RAEDEL CT
1900 SD 92154 1330-A7
RAEDEL DR
900 SD 92154 1330-A7
900 SD 92154 1350-A1
RAEDENE WY
- SD 92131 1209-G1
RAEJEAN AV
8700 SD 92123 1249-C7
RAFFEE DR
4000 SD 92117 1248-D3
RAG DOLL LN
3000 SDCo 92069 1088-E3
RAGWEED CT
8800 SD 92129 1189-D6
RAGWEED ST
12100 SD 92129 1189-C6
RAIL CT
5900 SD 92173 1350-J5
RAILROAD AV
- SDCo 91934 (1321-G6 See Page 1300)
500 ESCN 92025 1129-G3
8500 ELCJ 92020 1231-E7
8500 SNTE 92071 1231-E7
RAILROAD ST
1100 SDCo 91934 (1321-G5 See Page 1300)
S RAILROAD ST
- SDCo 91934 (1321-G6 See Page 1300)
RAILROAD STEX
- SDCo 91934 (1321-G6 See Page 1300)
RAINBIRD RD
15000 SDCo 92065 1173-G4
RAINBOW CT
2000 VSTA 92083 1087-C7
RAINBOW DR
500 IMPB 91932 1329-G7
600 CHV 91911 1330-H1
RAINBOW LN
200 OCN 92054 1086-C7
RAINBOW PL
600 ESCN 92027 1130-E1
RAINBOW ST
6900 SD 92114 1290-F3
RAINBOW TER
- SDCo 92028 999-A6
RAINBOW WY
- SDCo 92028 998-J6
RAINBOW CANYON RD
47500 RivC 92592 999-A2
RAINBOW CREEK RD
5400 SDCo 92028 998-J4
5400 SDCo 92028 999-A4
RAINBOW CREST RD
300 SDCo 92028 1029-B1
6900 SDCo 92028 999-B7
RAINBOW GLEN RD
1200 SDCo 92028 998-F3
47600 RivC 92590 998-F3
RAINBOW HEIGHTS DR
8000 SDCo 92028 999-E3
RAINBOW HEIGHTS LN
- SDCo 92028 999-B6
RAINBOW HEIGHTS PL
38300 SDCo 92028 999-B5
RAINBOW HEIGHTS RD
5600 SDCo 92028 999-B6
5600 SDCo 92028 999-D3
RAINBOW HILLS RD
1000 SDCo 92028 998-F7
RAINBOW OAKS DR
8300 RivC 92592 999-F2
RAINBOW PEAKS RD
38300 SDCo 92028 999-B3
RAINBOW PEAKS TR
38700 SDCo 92028 999-C4
RAINBOW RIDGE LN
1200 ENCT 92024 1147-C3
RAINBOW VALLEY BLVD
900 SDCo 92028 998-J5
3000 SDCo 92028 999-A3
3100 RivC 92592 999-A3
RAINBOW VALLEY BLVD W
1500 SDCo 92028 998-J2
1500 SDCo 92028 999-A3
RAINBOW VALLEY CT
1000 SDCo 92028 998-G6
RAINBOW VISTA DR
4300 SDCo 92028 998-G6
RAINBROOK DR
100 SDCo 92028 1029-C3
RAINEY CT
- ENCT 92024 1147-D3
RAINEY ST
7900 LMSA 91942 1250-H6
RAIN FOREST RD
1300 CHV 91910 1311-B6
RAINIER AV
4400 SD 92120 1249-H6
RAINIER CT
100 CHV 91911 1330-F4
RAINIER WY
4300 OCN 92054 1086-G1
4300 OCN 92057 1086-G1
RAINSWEPT CT
8500 SD 92119 1250-J2
8500 SNTE 92071 1250-J2
RAINSWEPT LN
7400 SD 92119 1250-J3
7600 SNTE 92071 1250-J3
RAINSWEPT PL
8500 SD 92119 1250-J3
RAINSWEPT WY
8400 SD 92119 1250-J2

RAINTREE DR
500 VSTA 92084 1087-H5
700 CRLB 92009 1126-J6
RAINTREE PL
800 VSTA 92084 1087-H5
2200 ESCN 92026 1109-F4
RAINTREE WY
5600 OCN 92057 1067-E6
RAINWOOD CT
600 OCN 92054 1086-D4
RAJU ST
11100 SD 92129 1169-H7
RALEIGH AV
300 ELCJ 92020 1251-E5
RALENE ST
2200 SD 92105 1289-G1
RALPH RD
- ImCo 92251 431-B4
RALPH WY
700 SD 92154 1330-F7
RALSTON CIR
12800 SD 92130 1188-B5
RAM LN
1300 SDCo 92028 1047-H1
RAMADA DR
2100 OCN 92056 1086-J7
16400 SD 92128 1170-B4
RAMA DE LAS PALMAS
3700 SDCo 92091 1168-B7
RAMBLA BRISA
1400 SMCS 92069 1109-D7
RAMBLA DE LAS FLORES
16000 SDCo 92067 1168-A4
RAMBLA PUESTA
1400 SMCS 92069 1109-D7
RAMBLA SERENA
1400 SMCS 92069 1109-D7
RAMBLEWOOD RD
1500 SDCo 91901 1233-H6
RAMBLING RD
400 ENCT 92024 1147-G5
RAMBLING WY
500 SDCo 92065 1152-D6
RAMBUR ST
700 CHV 91911 1330-J3
RAMFOS CIR
6800 SD 92139 1310-G1
RAMFOS LN
6900 SD 92139 1290-F7
RAMFOS PL
2500 SD 92139 1290-F7
2600 SD 92139 1310-F1
RAMHAVEN LN
8200 SNTE 92071 1250-J1
RAMO CT
9700 SNTE 92071 1231-C4
RAMO RD
9700 SNTE 92071 1231-C5
RAMON ST
1700 LMGR 91945 1290-F1
RAMONA
- CRLB 92009 1126-H5
RAMONA AV
400 SDCo 91977 1291-C1
2000 SDCo 91977 1271-C7
RAMONA CT
9200 SDCo 92021 1232-E5
RAMONA DR
700 SDCo 92036 1136-D7
2400 SDCo 92084 1087-F1
4300 SDCo 92028 1048-B6
10100 SDCo 91977 1271-E5
RAMONA LN
2100 SDCo 92084 1108-D2
RAMONA PL
700 SOLB 92014 1187-G1
RAMONA ST
100 SDCo 92065 1152-F6
500 SDCo 92065 1172-F1
N RAMONA ST
- SDCo 92065 1152-F6
RAMONA WY
- SMCS 92078 1129-C1
100 OCN 92057 1086-H3
RAMONA AIRPORT RD
2300 SDCo 92065 1152-B7
RAMONA HIGHLANDS DR
19700 SDCo 92065 1152-B1
RAMONA HIGHLANDS RD
19500 SDCo 92065 1152-B1
RAMONA OAKS RD
24500 SDCo 92065 1173-F4
26000 SDCo 92065 1174-A4
RAMONA REAL
100 SDCo 92065 1152-J1
1600 SDCo 92065 1153-A1
RAMONA TRAILS DR
19300 SDCo 92065 1153-D2
RAMONA VIEW DR
18400 SDCo 92065 1153-B4
RAMSAY AV
4600 SD 92122 1228-F4
RAMSDELL CT
11600 SD 92131 1209-H1
11800 SD 92131 1189-H7
RAMSEY LN
1800 SDCo 92065 1172-F1
RAMSEY RD
1400 SDCo 91901 1234-B6
RAMSGATE DR
10700 SNTE 92071 1231-F4
RAMSGATE WY
9600 SNTE 92071 1231-F4
RAMS HILL DR
1900 SDCo 92004 (1099-F4 See Page 1098)
RAMS HILL RD
1700 SDCo 92004 (1099-F3 See Page 1098)
RANA CT
3000 CRLB 92009 1147-H1
RANCH RD
- ENCT 92024 1147-D3
W RANCH RD
900 SDCo 92069 1128-C2
RANCH BROOK RD
4000 SDCo 92028 998-E5
RANCH CREEK LN
13500 PWY 92064 1170-E6
14900 SDCo 92082 1070-H2
RANCH CREEK RD
30600 SDCo 92082 1070-G3
RANCHERO DR
1500 OCN 92057 1067-F6
RANCHEROS
1500 SDCo 92021 1251-G2
RANCHEROS DR
100 SMCS 92069 1108-H7

STREET
Block City ZIP Pg-Grid

RANCHEROS DR
300 SMCS 92069 1128-J1
400 SMCS 92069 1109-A7
1100 SMCS 92069 1129-B1
RANCHETTE PL
1300 CHV 91913 1311-D7
RANCH GATE RD
700 SDCo 92021 1252-G1
RANCH HOLLOW RD
15900 PWY 92064 1170-E5
RANCH HOUSE RD
12200 SD 92128 1150-B7
RANCHITO DR
500 ESCN 92025 1130-C6
RANCHITO LN
1900 SDCo 91901 1253-H1
RANCHITOS CT
10100 SDCo 92040 1231-F3
RANCHITOS PL
10100 SDCo 92040 1231-F3
RANCHITOS ST
11000 SDCo 92040 1231-F3
RANCHO CT
200 CHV 91911 1330-G5
5200 OCN 92056 1087-E2
RANCHO CTE
2000 VSTA 92084 1087-H2
RANCHO DR
200 CHV 91911 1330-G6
2100 SD 92139 1310-D1
9600 SDCo 92029 1149-D4
RANCHO RD
10300 SDCo 91941 1271-E4
RANCHO TER
500 SDCo 92026 1109-G3
RANCHO ADARME LN
- SDCo 92003 1067-F1
- SDCo 92028 1067-F1
RANCHO AGUA HADIONDA DR
3500 OCN 92056 1106-B4
RANCHO ALLEN LN
100 SDCo 92065 1153-A5
RANCHO AMIGOS RD
31200 SDCo 92003 1068-H2
RANCHO AMIGOS RD N
7600 SDCo 92003 1068-G2
RANCHO ANDREW
1900 SDCo 91901 1233-J7
1900 SDCo 91901 1253-J1
RANCHO ANTIGUO
14900 SDCo 92014 1188-A1
RANCHO ARROBA
3200 CRLB 92009 1127-J3
RANCHO BALLENA LN
19300 SDCo 92065 1154-B1
RANCHO BALLENA RD
19500 SDCo 92065 409-J11
RANCHO BARONA RD
25400 SDCo 92065 1173-H5
RANCHO BERNARDO RD
10200 SDCo 92127 1169-E3
10400 SD 92127 1169-E3
11700 SD 92127 1170-A2
11700 SD 92128 1170-A2
RANCHO BERNARDO RD Rt#-S5
12500 SD 92128 1170-D3
RANCHO BERNARDO TOWN CENTER DR
11900 SD 92128 1170-A3
RANCHO BONITO RD
3800 SDCo 92028 1047-F4
RANCHO BRASADO
2900 CRLB 92009 1127-J4
RANCHO BRAVADO
6000 CRLB 92009 1127-H2
RANCHO BRAYDON LN
800 SDCo 91901 1234-D5
RANCHO BRIDA
6100 CRLB 92009 1127-G3
RANCHO BULLARD LN
800 SDCo 92065 1152-G7
RANCHO CABALLO
- CRLB 92009 1127-J4
RANCHO CABALLO RD
12600 PWY 92064 1190-C6
RANCHO CAJON PL
1700 SDCo 92019 1252-B4
RANCHO CAMINO
100 SDCo 92028 1047-G5
RANCHO CAMINO NORTE
4300 SDCo 92028 1047-H5
RANCHO CANADA RD
- SDCo 92021 1232-E7
- SDCo 92021 1252-D1
RANCHO CAPISTRANO BEND
- SD 92130 1188-D3
RANCHO CAPITAN
10000 SDCo 92040 1232-C2
RANCHO CARLSBAD DR
3300 CRLB 92008 1107-C7
RANCHO CARMEL DR
10100 SD 92128 1189-J1
11300 SD 92128 1169-J7
11300 SD 92128 1170-A7
RANCHO CARRIZO
3200 CRLB 92009 1127-J2
RANCHO CHARRO
- CRLB 92009 1127-H2
RANCHO CHIMNEY ROCK RD
28200 SDCo 92066 410-A8
RANCHO CIELO
6900 SDCo 92067 1148-F7
RANCHO COMPANERO
3200 CRLB 92009 1127-J3
RANCHO COPA
14500 SDCo 92082 1070-G7
RANCHO CORTES
2800 CRLB 92009 1127-J4
RANCHO COSTERO
- CRLB 92009 1127-H3
RANCHO DE CAROLE RD
17500 SDCo 92065 1171-G2
RANCHO DE KEVIN RD
16400 SDCo 92065 1171-G3
RANCHO DEL CTE
9300 SDCo 92021 1232-F5
RANCHO DE LA ANGEL RD
17400 SDCo 92065 1171-G3
RANCHO DEL CANON
- CRLB 92009 1127-H2
RANCHO DEL CERRO
500 SDCo 92003 1067-F1
500 SDCo 92028 1067-F1

RANCHO DEL LADERA DR
200 SDCo 92065 1153-A4
RANCHO DEL MADISON
5000 SDCo 92014 1188-A1
RANCHO DEL MAR TR
- SD 92130 1188-B3
RANCHO DE LOMA RD
100 SDCo 92028 1028-E1
RANCHO DEL ORO DR
- OCN 92057 1086-H3
600 OCN 92056 1086-J6
2000 OCN 92056 1106-J2
RANCHO DEL RAY
100 SDCo 92025 1130-E7
RANCHO DEL REY PKWY
- CHV 91910 1310-H5
- CHV 91910 1311-A5
RANCHO DEL RIO
17400 SDCo 92067 1168-H1
RANCHO DEL SOL
2800 SDCo 92025 1130-E7
17800 SDCo 92065 1151-D6
RANCHO DEL VERDE
400 SDCo 92025 1130-E7
RANCHO DEL VERDE PL
3000 SDCo 92025 1130-F7
RANCHO DEL VILLA
14000 SDCo 92021 1232-F5
RANCHO DE ORO RD
500 ESCN 92026 1109-G6
17400 SDCo 92065 1171-J4
17400 SDCo 92065 1172-A4
RANCHO DIAMONTE
- CRLB 92009 1127-H3
RANCHO DIEGO CIR
3400 SDCo 92019 1272-C6
RANCHO DIEGO CT
2300 SDCo 92029 1129-H7
RANCHO DIEGUENO RD
5700 SDCo 92067 1168-E7
5800 SDCo 92067 1188-F1
RANCHO DORADO BEND
- SD 92130 1188-C3
RANCHO DULZURA
- CRLB 92009 1127-H3
RANCHO EAST
7300 SDCo 92067 1148-G6
RANCHO ENCINITAS DR
1100 ENCT 92024 1148-B5
RANCHO FALLBROOK
47200 RivC 92590 997-G1
RANCHO FAMOSA
3200 CRLB 92009 1127-J2
RANCHO FANITA DR
7800 SNTE 92071 1230-H7
7900 SNTE 92071 1250-H1
RANCHO GANADERO
2800 CRLB 92009 1127-H4
RANCHO GRANDE
4800 SDCo 92014 1168-A7
RANCHO GUADALUPE RD
13200 SDCo 92059 409-E5
RANCHO HEIGHTS RD
11400 SDCo 92028 999-G3
11900 SDCo 92059 999-J3
13000 SDCo 92059 409-E5
RANCHO HEIGHTS WY
- SDCo 92059 409-E5
RANCHO HILLS DR
5700 SD 92139 1310-D1
RANCHO JAMUL DR
14400 SDCo 91935 1293-A4
RANCHO JANET
1800 SDCo 91901 1233-J7
1800 SDCo 91901 1253-J1
RANCHO JORIE
1800 SDCo 91901 1233-H7
RANCHO JUDITH
1800 SDCo 91901 1233-J7
RANCHO LA CIMA CTE
18000 SDCo 92067 1148-F6
RANCHO LA CIMA DR
6800 SDCo 92067 1148-F7
RANCHO LAGUNA BEND
- SD 92130 1188-B3
RANCHO LAKES CT
6700 SDCo 92067 1188-G3
RANCHO LA MIRADA LN
400 SDCo 92025 1129-J7
400 SDCo 92025 1130-A7
RANCHO LA NORIA
- SDCo 92067 1167-J2
RANCHO LA PRESA
- CRLB 92009 1127-H2
RANCHO LAS BRISAS TR
- SD 92130 1188-A3
RANCHO LAS PALMAS DR
2000 SDCo 92028 1048-A1
RANCHO LATIGO
- CRLB 92009 1127-H3
RANCHO LUISENO RD
1200 SDCo 92026 1109-C1
RANCHO MADERA BEND
- SD 92130 1188-D3
RANCHO MANZANITA DR
700 SDCo 91905 (1299-H7 See Page 1298)
RANCHO MARIA LN
2900 SDCo 92065 1172-C2
RANCHO MEADOWCREST RD
2100 SDCo 92021 1252-G4
RANCHO MIA
1400 SDCo 92028 1027-J6
RANCHO MIEL
- CRLB 92009 1127-J4
RANCHO MIGUEL RD
3200 SDCo 91935 1272-D7
RANCHO MILAGRO
3200 CRLB 92009 1127-J3
RANCHO MIRAGE LN
9600 SDCo 92040 1232-C4
RANCHO MISSION RD
5800 SD 92108 1269-G1
5900 SD 92108 1249-G7
RANCHO MONTANA
3100 CRLB 92009 1128-A4
3100 SDCo 92069 1128-A4
RANCHO NUEVO
14900 SDCo 92014 1168-A7
RANCHO PACIFICA PL
900 VSTA 92084 1087-J7
900 VSTA 92084 1088-A7
RANCHO PANCHO
2800 CRLB 92009 1127-H4

RANCHO PARK DR
6400 SD 92120 1250-D6
RANCHO PENASQUITOS BLVD
12600 SD 92128 1189-F4
12600 SD 92129 1189-F4
RANCHO POSTA
2900 CRLB 92009 1127-G3
RANCHO QUARTILLO
3200 CRLB 92009 1127-J3
RANCHO QUINTA BEND
- SD 92130 1188-C3
RANCHO REAL
15100 SDCo 92014 1188-B1
15100 SDCo 92067 1188-B1
RANCHO REATA
3200 CRLB 92009 1127-J2
RANCHO REPOSO
4600 SDCo 92014 1188-A1
RANCHO RIO CHICO
- CRLB 92009 1127-H3
RANCHO ROBLE RD
10100 SDCo 92026 1089-E5
RANCHO RYAN RD
1100 SDCo 92028 1027-H1
RANCHO SAN DIEGO PKWY
900 SDCo 92019 1271-J5
RANCHO SAN MARTIN DR
17800 SDCo 92065 1171-G1
RANCHO SANTA FE CT
1100 SDCo 92065 1153-E2
RANCHO SANTA FE RD
100 ENCT 92024 1147-J7
100 ENCT 92024 1167-J1
600 ENCT 92024 1148-A6
7000 CRLB 92009 1147-H4
RANCHO SANTA FE RD Rt#-S9
100 ENCT 92024 1167-J1
100 SDCo 92067 1167-J1
2600 SDCo 92067 1168-A1
RANCHO SANTA FE RD Rt#-S10
2300 CRLB 92009 1128-A7
2300 CRLB 92069 1128-A7
2300 CRLB 92078 1128-A7
2900 CRLB 92009 1147-H3
7200 CRLB 92009 1148-A1
N RANCHO SANTA FE RD Rt#-S10
100 SMCS 92069 1108-D6
S RANCHO SANTA FE RD Rt#-S10
100 SMCS 92069 1108-D7
400 SMCS 92069 1128-A3
2100 CRLB 92009 1128-A3
2100 CRLB 92069 1128-A3
RANCHO SANTA FE FARMS DR
6400 SDCo 92067 1188-G1
6900 SD 92127 1188-G1
RANCHO SANTA FE FARMS RD
13400 SD 92130 1188-G2
14100 SDCo 92067 1188-G2
RANCHO SANTA FE LAKES DR
14200 SDCo 92067 1188-G3
14200 SD 92130 1188-G3
RANCHO SANTA TERESA DR
24600 SDCo 92065 1153-F1
RANCHO SERENA RD
1400 SDCo 92067 1167-J5
RANCHO SIERRA BEND
- SD 92130 1188-B3
RANCHOS LADERA RD
32500 SDCo 92003 1048-H6
RANCHO SOL CT
4800 SDCo 92014 1188-A1
RANCHO SOLANA TR
- SD 92130 1188-D3
RANCHO SUENOS DR
17100 SDCo 92065 1171-F2
RANCHO SUMMIT
- SDCo 91901 1254-B2
RANCHO SUMMIT DR
1600 ENCT 92024 1148-D2
1600 SDCo 92024 1148-D2
1600 SMCS 92024 1148-D2
RANCHO TAZA RD
8300 SDCo 92028 998-J7
8300 SDCo 92028 1028-H1
RANCHO TIERRA TR
- SD 92130 1188-D3
RANCHO TRAILS
500 SDCo 92065 1152-G1
RANCHO VACADA
- CRLB 92009 1127-J3
RANCHO VALENCIA DR
16000 SDCo 92067 1168-F7
RANCHO VALENCIA RD
5800 SDCo 92067 1168-E7
RANCHO VALENCIA ST
- SDCo 92082 1071-A7
RANCHO VALENCIA WY
- SDCo 92082 1071-A7
RANCHO VALLE CT
1000 ELCJ 92020 1251-H7
RANCHO VERDE DR
2100 ESCN 92025 1130-B6
2100 SDCo 92025 1130-B6
RANCHO VERDE TR
- SD 92130 1188-C3
RANCHO VICENTE DR
15000 SDCo 92065 1172-J6
15000 SDCo 92065 1173-A6
RANCHO VIEJO DR
4800 SDCo 92014 1188-A1
RANCHO VIEW DR
47100 RivC 92592 999-F1
RANCHO VILLA RD
1700 SDCo 92065 1152-D1
RANCHO VISTA BEND
- SD 92130 1188-C3
RANCHO VISTA CT
12900 SDCo 92082 1090-C4
13800 SDCo 91935 1292-G1
RANCHO VISTA DR
18500 SDCo 92065 1153-C4
RANCHO VISTA PL
300 VSTA 92083 1087-H7
RANCHO VISTA RD
400 VSTA 92083 1087-H7
600 VSTA 92083 1107-H1
RANCHO VISTA WY
1600 SDCo 92028 1027-J1

RANCHO WILLITS
- SDCo 91901 1253-G2
RANCHO WINCHESTER LN
1900 SDCo 92019 1272-A1
RANCH TRAIL DR
14400 SDCo 92021 1232-G4
RANCH VIEW DR
10600 SD 92131 1209-G4
RANCHVIEW PL
- ESCN 92027 1130-J2
RANCH VIEW RD
5800 OCN 92057 1067-G6
RANCH VIEW TER
2100 ENCT 92024 1147-J7
RANCHWOOD DR
10600 SDCo 91978 1271-G7
RANCHWOOD GN
300 ESCN 92026 1109-G4
RANCH WOOD LN
1500 SDCo 92028 1027-J5
RANDALL ST
4800 SD 92109 1248-B4
RANDLETT DR
4900 LMSA 91941 1270-J2
RANDOLPH ST
4000 SD 92103 1268-H5
RANDOM CT
1200 ELCJ 92020 1251-G7
RANDOM RD
1000 ELCJ 92020 1251-G7
1000 SDCo 92020 1251-G7
1100 ELCJ 92020 1271-G1
1100 SDCo 92020 1271-G1
RANDY CT
3300 SDCo 91910 1310-F4
RANDY LN
3400 SDCo 91910 1310-F4
RANETA LN
5400 SD 92124 1249-G1
N RANGE RD
- SDCo 92055 408-J5
RANGE ST
100 ENCT 92024 1147-A3
RANGELAND RD
18400 SDCo 92065 1151-J2
RANGE PARK PL
14500 PWY 92064 1190-H1
RANGE PARK RD
14300 PWY 92064 1190-H2
RANGER RD
200 SDCo 92028 1028-E1
5900 SD 92139 1290-D7
RANGE VIEW RD
1100 VSTA 92084 1108-C1
RANGEVIEW ST
800 SDCo 91977 1290-J3
RANGO WY
700 SDCo 92004 (1078-J7 See Page 1058)
700 SDCo 92004 (1079-A7 See Page 1058)
RANLEIGH CT
3100 SD 92110 1268-D6
RANRIDO DR
800 SDCo 92025 1130-B3
RANRIDOS CT
1200 ESCN 92027 1110-C5
RANSOM ST
900 SD 92154 1330-G7
900 SD 92154 1350-G1
RANSOM HILL LN
100 SDCo 92065 1153-A4
RANZA RD
8700 SDCo 91977 1291-A5
RAPATEE CT
10900 SDCo 91941 1271-G4
RAPATEE DR
4000 SDCo 91941 1271-G4
RAPHAEL CT
400 ENCT 92024 1147-G6
RAPPAHANNOCK AV
4100 SD 92117 1248-E5
RAPPAPORT PL
10400 SNTE 92071 1231-E3
RAPTOR RD
15400 SDCo 92064 1191-B6
RAPTURE LN
9300 SNTE 92071 1231-B7
RAQUEL DR
4200 OCN 92056 1107-C2
RASCON CT
11600 SD 92131 1190-A7
RASHA ST
8600 SD 92121 1228-H1
RASMUSSEN WY
14100 SD 92129 1189-E2
RASPBERRY WY
500 OCN 92057 1067-D7
RASPBERRY ICE LN
9700 SDCo 91941 1271-C4
RATCLIFF RD
1700 CRLB 92008 1106-F3
RATHMOOR ST
1200 ELCJ 92020 1251-G7
RAULSTON TER
800 ESCN 92027 1130-C2
RAV CT
- SDCo 91935 1274-B2
RAVEAN CT
- ENCT 92024 1147-D2
RAVEN AV
1200 CHV 91911 1330-G2
RAVEN PL
1200 CHV 91911 1330-G2
RAVEN ST
500 SD 92102 1289-H3
RAVEN HILL PT
- SD 92130 1208-D2
RAVEN HILL RD
- SDCo 91935 1272-J7
RAVEN RIDGE PT
7500 SD 92126 1208-J2
RAVENROCK CT
1700 CHV 91913 1311-D6
RAVENSCROFT ST
100 NATC 92136 1309-G1
RAVENSTHORPE WY
- SD 92131 1209-G2
RAVENSWOOD RD
5800 SD 92037 1247-G3
RAVENWOOD DR
2200 LMGR 91945 1270-H7
2300 LMGR 91945 1290-H1
RAVINA ST
100 SD 92037 1227-E7
RAVINE CT
700 VSTA 92083 1087-D6

RAVINE RD
1400 VSTA 92083 1087-D6
RAWHIDE CT
900 CHV 91902 1310-H4
RAWL PL
700 SOLB 92075 1167-F6
RAWLINS WY
9500 SNTE 92071 1231-C4
RAY ST
600 ESCN 92026 1109-J7
3400 SD 92104 1269-E6
RAYA WY
4100 SD 92122 1228-E5
RAYDEL CT
6300 SD 92120 1250-D7
RAYFORD DR
10000 SDCo 92026 1109-E1
10100 SDCo 92026 1089-E7
RAYLEY DR
10600 SDCo 91978 1271-F7
RAYLINE WY
10100 SDCo 91977 1271-E4
RAYMAR AV
5600 SD 92120 1250-D7
5600 SD 92120 1270-D1
RAYMELL DR
2500 SD 92123 1249-E7
RAYMOND AV
1800 SDCo 92065 1152-E7
2000 SDCo 92065 1172-D1
RAYMOND LN
1900 OCN 92054 1086-C7
RAYMOND PL
5000 SD 92116 1269-F2
RAYMOND ST
400 ELCJ 92020 1251-G7
RAYNELL WY
1600 ELCJ 92019 1252-B7
RAYS WY
13000 SDCo 92082 1050-C5
RAYTHEON RD
7400 SD 92111 1249-A1
REA AV
100 ELCJ 92020 1251-F5
READ RD
- CORD 92135 1288-F4
REAGAN CIR
8600 SD 92126 1209-C4
REAGAN CT
8600 SD 92126 1209-C4
REAGAN PL
8600 SD 92126 1209-C4
REAGAN RD
9100 SD 92126 1209-B3
REALTY RD
1400 SDCo 92065 1152-F7
REAL WAY LN
1500 SDCo 91901 1253-J3
REASER LN
1000 SDCo 92065 1152-F3
REATA CT
12300 SD 92128 1150-B6
REATA WY
18200 SD 92128 1150-B6
REBECCA AV
200 VSTA 92084 1087-H3
9200 SD 92123 1249-E6
REBECCA LN
- ELCJ 92019 1252-B7
30900 SDCo 92082 1070-F3
REBECCA ST
- ELCJ 92019 1252-B6
REBECCA WY
- ELCJ 92019 1252-A6
2100 LMGR 91945 1290-J1
2100 LMGR 91945 1270-J7
REBECCAS GREEN TR
1900 SDCo 92065 1172-F1
REBEL RD
4900 SD 92117 1228-F7
REBEL WIND DR
- SDCo 91916 1216-A2
REBOLLA LN
5300 SD 92124 1249-G1
RECHE RD
200 SDCo 92028 1027-F4
RECHE RD Rt#-S15
1500 SDCo 92028 1027-J4
1700 SDCo 92028 1028-A4
RECHE WY
700 SDCo 92028 1027-J4
RECLUSE LN
400 ENCT 92024 1147-G6
RECODO CT
2200 CRLB 92009 1147-F2
RECREATION DR
100 VSTA 92083 1087-G6
1500 SDCo 92028 1028-F4
RECUERDO CV
2300 SD 92014 1187-H5
RECUERDO DR
13600 SD 92014 1187-H6
RED ALDER PL
700 ESCN 92027 1110-D5
RED BARK RD
1400 ESCN 92029 1129-F5
REDBARK WY
600 SD 92139 1310-F1
RED BARN RD
1700 ENCT 92024 1147-H6
REDBERRY CT
800 SMCS 92069 1109-A5
REDBIRD DR
2000 SD 92123 1269-B1
2100 SD 92123 1249-A7
REDBROOK CT
4700 SD 92117 1248-J1
REDBROOK RD
5900 SD 92117 1248-J1
REDBUD CT
11200 SD 92127 1169-J5
REDBUD PL
800 CHV 91910 1310-H7
REDBUD RD
900 CHV 91910 1310-H7
RED CANYON DR
29800 SDCo 92082 1069-J6
RED CEDAR CT
10200 SD 92131 1209-H4
RED CEDAR DR
10600 SD 92131 1209-H4
RED CEDAR LN
11300 SD 92131 1209-J4
RED CEDAR PL
10300 SD 92131 1209-H4
RED CEDAR WY
11300 SD 92131 1209-J4
REDCLIFF CT
12000 SD 92131 1210-B3

RED CLOUD LN
13300 PWY 92064 1190-H4
RED COACH LN
2000 ENCT 92024 1147-H6
RED CORAL LN
400 SD 92154 1330-H6
REDCREST CT
8200 SD 92114 1290-H4
REDCREST DR
200 SD 92114 1290-H3
REDCREST PL
8200 SD 92114 1290-H4
RED DEER ST
6600 SD 92122 1228-E4
RED DIAMOND DR
9500 SDCo 92040 1232-C4
REDDING RD
5300 SD 92115 1270-A1
REDEL RD
100 SMCS 92078 1128-J1
REDEN LN
30600 SDCo 92082 1069-D4
RED FERN CIR
10800 SD 92131 1210-A3
REDFERN LN
12900 SDCo 92082 1070-C5
REDFIELD ST
9000 SDCo 91977 1291-A3
REDFORD PL
3000 SD 92139 1310-E2
RED FOX LN
- SMCS 92069 1108-H4
REDGAP CT
2100 ENCT 92024 1147-H7
RED GUM RD
1200 SDCo 92019 1253-E3
RED HAWK RD
30600 SDCo 92082 1069-C4
RED HAWK RDG
- SDCo 91901 1255-E6
RED HAWK WY
1100 SMCS 92069 1128-G4
REDHILL LN
800 SMCS 92069 1109-B5
RED HILL LN
1600 CHV 91902 1311-B4
RED HILL RD
- ImCo 92233 411-A8
- ImCo 92259 411-A8
RED HILLS CT
9300 SNTE 92071 1230-J6
RED KNOT ST
6500 CRLB 92009 1127-A4
REDLAND DR
5400 SD 92115 1270-B3
REDLAND PL
5400 SD 92115 1270-B3
REDLANDER WY
10800 SDCo 92040 1232-B1
REDLANDS PL
600 CHV 91902 1311-C4
700 CHV 91913 1311-C4
REDLANDS ST
400 VSTA 92083 1087-G5
REDMAN ST
- CORD 91932 1329-E5
RED MAPLE DR
1000 CHV 91910 1310-J7
1000 CHV 91910 1330-J1
RED MAPLE WY
4400 OCN 92057 1086-J2
RED MOUNTAIN CT
1300 CHV 91910 1311-B6
RED MOUNTAIN DR
29700 SDCo 92082 1069-J5
RED MOUNTAIN LN
100 SDCo 92028 1028-E1
RED MOUNTAIN TKTR
- RivC 92590 998-G1
- SDCo 92028 998-E2
RED MOUNTAIN DAM DR
3300 SDCo 92028 998-D7
3300 SDCo 92028 1028-D1
RED MOUNTAIN HEIGHTS DR
2800 SDCo 92028 998-C6
RED OAK CT
- SMCS 92078 1128-D6
RED OAK PL
1000 CHV 91910 1310-J7
RED OAK RD
- SDCo 91901 1235-B3
REDONDO CT
700 SD 92109 1267-H1
REDONDO DR
- OCN 92057 1066-J6
300 OCN 92057 1067-A7
4800 SDCo 91941 1271-F2
5700 SDCo 92003 1048-C7
N REDONDO DR
500 OCN 92057 1066-J6
500 OCN 92057 1067-A6
W REDONDO DR
400 OCN 92057 1066-J6
REDONDO ST
1700 SD 92107 1268-A7
1700 SD 92107 1288-A1
RED PINE CT
900 SD 92154 1330-B7
RED PINE DR
2400 SD 92154 1330-B7
2400 SD 92154 1350-B1
RED PONY LN
9600 SDCo 92021 1232-H3
RED RIVER DR
5500 SD 92120 1250-B4
RED ROBIN PL
11000 SD 92126 1208-J2
RED ROCK CT
9900 SD 92131 1209-H5
RED ROCK DR
10800 SD 92131 1209-H5
RED SAILS WY
4700 SD 92154 1330-H7
RED SHANK LN
2200 SDCo 91905 (1299-J4 See Page 1298)
2300 SDCo 91905 1300-A4
RED STONE LN
28200 SDCo 92026 1089-E3
RED TAIL HAWK CT
11500 SDCo 92040 1212-C5
RED TOP LN
3500 SDCo 92028 1048-B4
REDWING DR
3300 OCN 92054 1086-D2
REDWING RD
400 CHV 91911 1330-G2

REDWING ST
1700 SDCo 92069 1128-A4
1800 SMCS 92069 1128-A4
REDWING WY
1700 SDCo 92069 1128-A4
REDWOOD AV
100 CRLB 92008 1106-E7
1000 ELCJ 92020 1251-J6
1100 ELCJ 92019 1251-J6
REDWOOD DR
100 SMCS 92069 1108-J5
8700 SNTE 92071 1231-B7
9100 SD 92093 1227-J3
REDWOOD LN
9700 SDCo 92029 1149-E3
REDWOOD PL
700 ESCN 92025 1129-J5
REDWOOD RD
- ELCJ 92019 1251-J6
REDWOOD ST
- SMCS 92078 1129-C2
100 SD 92103 1269-A7
600 SD 92103 1268-J7
1500 SD 92101 1268-H7
1700 ESCN 92025 1129-J5
1800 ESCN 92025 1130-A6
2700 SD 92101 1269-E7
2800 SD 92104 1269-E7
3000 SD 92105 1269-G7
3500 OCN 92054 1086-F1
5200 SD 92105 1270-B6
5800 SD 92115 1270-B6
S REDWOOD ST
400 ESCN 92025 1129-J4
REDWOOD CREST
2000 VSTA 92083 1107-F5
REED AV
700 SD 92109 1247-H7
1400 SD 92109 1248-A6
REED CT
100 CHV 91911 1330-E5
REED RD
2500 ESCN 92027 1130-E1
REED TER
900 ESCN 92027 1130-F1
REEDLEY TER
4700 SD 92130 1188-C4
REEF DR
700 SD 92154 1330-D7
REES RD
1000 SMCS 92069 1109-D7
1000 SDCo 92026 1109-E6
1200 ESCN 92026 1109-E6
REESE LN
17000 SDCo 92065 1171-H3
REESE ST
800 OCN 92054 1106-B2
REEVE RD
- CRLB 92009 1146-J1
REEVES ST
400 NATC 92136 1309-F1
REFLECTION CIR
2200 VSTA 92083 1107-H7
REFLECTION DR
6500 SD 92124 1249-G6
REFUGIO AV
4800 CRLB 92008 1106-J6
REGAL RD
700 ENCT 92024 1147-D7
900 ENCT 92024 1167-D1
REGALO LN
17200 SD 92128 1170-A2
REGAL RIDGE RD
1000 ENCT 92024 1148-A5
REGATTA LN
4700 SD 92154 1330-H6
REGATTA RD
1500 CRLB 92009 1127-B4
REGENCY CIR
4500 OCN 92056 1107-E2
REGENCY CT
200 CHV 91911 1330-G5
REGENCY RD
8700 SD 92123 1249-C7
REGENCY WY
1700 CHV 91911 1330-F5
REGENT RD
2600 CRLB 92008 1106-J5
2600 CRLB 92008 1107-A6
REGENTS RD
4200 SD 92037 1228-B2
4900 SD 92117 1228-C6
4900 SD 92117 1248-C1
5300 SD 92122 1228-C3
REGENTS PARK RW
4100 SD 92037 1228-C2
REGINA AV
5600 SD 92117 1228-H6
REGINA GN
31300 SDCo 92082 1070-E1
REGINA LN
1100 VSTA 92083 1087-G4
REGINAS CT
10400 SNTE 92071 1231-E4
REGIS AV
5600 SD 92120 1270-D1
REGIS CT
900 VSTA 92084 1087-J5
REGLA CT
4900 SD 92122 1228-G5
REGNER CT
8600 SD 92119 1250-J4
REGNER RD
6900 SD 92119 1250-J3
REGULO PL
700 CHV 91910 1311-A6
REGULUS ST
1500 SD 92111 1269-A2
REHCO RD
8800 SD 92121 1228-H1
8800 SD 92121 1208-H7
REIDY CANYON PL
11200 SDCo 92026 1089-H6
REIDY CANYON RD
7800 SDCo 92026 1109-G1
10400 SDCo 92026 1089-F5
REIDY CANYON TR
10800 SDCo 92026 1089-G7
REILLVIEW DR
2400 SDCo 92025 1130-B7
REINEMAN RD
2100 SDCo 92028 1027-H6
REISLING TER
500 CHV 91913 1311-D3
REKLOW DR
1500 SD 92154 1350-B2
RELIANCE WY
1000 SOLB 92014 1187-G1

STREET
Block City ZIP Pg-Grid

RELINDO CT
16300 SD 92128 1170-C4
RELINDO DR
12600 SD 92128 1170-C4
REMBRANDT GN
1200 ESCN 92026 1109-J7
REMEDIOS CT
100 SOLB 92075 1167-D7
REMINGTON CT
1200 VSTA 92083 1087-E5
REMINGTON RD
5100 SD 92115 1270-A1
5300 SD 92182 1270-A1
REMINGTON HILLS DR
- SD 92154 1350-G2
REMLEY PL
7300 SD 92037 1227-G7
REMORA ST
10500 SD 92124 1249-G1
REMSEN CT
6600 CRLB 92009 1127-B5
REMUDA CT
9300 SNTE 92071 1231-A3
RENA DR
700 OCN 92057 1067-B5
RENAISSANCE AV
5100 SD 92122 1228-D3
RENATO ST
8900 SD 92129 1189-C3
RENAULT PL
2900 SD 92122 1228-C6
RENAULT ST
2900 SD 92122 1228-C6
RENAULT WY
5800 SD 92122 1228-C6
RENDON VALLEY RD
16700 SDCo 92065 1171-E2
RENDOVA CIR
2300 CORD 92155 1309-A2
RENDOVA RD
2000 CORD 92155 1309-A2
RENE CT
700 SD 92154 1330-G7
RENE DR
3900 SD 92154 1330-F7
E RENETTE AV
600 ELCJ 92020 1251-G7
W RENETTE AV
1000 ELCJ 92020 1251-E7
RENEX PL
4700 SD 92117 1248-G1
RENFRO WY
800 SDCo 92019 1253-C2
RENKRIB AV
6600 SD 92119 1250-H4
RENO DR
4700 SD 92105 1269-J5
RENOIR LN
5200 SDCo 91902 1290-G6
RENOVO WY
4800 SD 92124 1250-B1
RENOWN DR
8500 SD 92119 1250-J4
8500 SD 92119 1251-A4
RENSHAW CT
2000 ELCJ 92020 1251-B1
RENWICK LN
1500 SDCo 92084 1108-B1
REO CT
1800 SD 92139 1290-C7
REO DR
- SD 91950 1310-E2
1800 SD 92139 1290-C7
2000 SD 92139 1310-D1
3300 NATC 91950 1310-E2
REO PL
6000 SD 92139 1310-D2
REO TER
5800 SD 92139 1310-D3
REOLA DR
10000 SDCo 92040 1232-C3
REO REAL DR
12800 PWY 92064 1190-D5
REPECHO DR
5300 SD 92124 1249-G1
REPOSA ALTA
16900 SDCo 92067 1167-J3
16900 SDCo 92067 1168-A4
REPOSADO DR
7600 CRLB 92009 1147-F1
REPRESA CIR
7900 CRLB 92009 1147-G3
REPUBLIC ST
1500 SD 92114 1290-D1
REPUBLICAN WY
16700 SDCo 92065 1173-F2
REQUEZA ST
100 ENCT 92024 1147-C7
RESAVA LN
14200 SDCo 92082 1070-F4
RESEARCH CT
- CHV 91911 1330-J5
RESERVATION DR
24500 SDCo 91916 1236-A2
RESERVOIR CT
6600 SD 92115 1270-D2
RESERVOIR DR
5000 SDCo 91977 1291-E2
5200 SD 92115 1270-D1
5200 SD 92120 1270-D1
RESERVOIR LN
6600 SD 92115 1270-D2
RESERVOIR ST
3100 SDCo 91935 1292-H1
3100 SDCo 91935 1272-H7
RESMAR CT
10000 SDCo 91941 1271-E4
RESMAR PL
10000 SDCo 91941 1271-D3
RESMAR RD
4300 SDCo 91941 1271-E2
RESTFUL CT
10300 SNTE 92071 1231-E4
RETAHEIM WY
400 SD 92037 1247-F2
RETRATO CT
11000 SD 92124 1249-J2
11000 SD 92124 1250-A2
RETREAT CT
300 SDCo 92028 1027-G3
REUBEN FLEET DR
1300 ELCJ 92020 1251-C2
REVELLE DR
7700 SD 92037 1227-J6
7800 SD 92037 1228-A6
REVELLE COLLEGE DR
9200 SD 92093 1227-J3
REVELSTOKE TER
8900 SD 92126 1209-D1
REVELSTOKE WY
8800 SD 92126 1209-D1
REVENA ST
1800 SD 92154 1350-B3
REVERE AV
3500 SD 92109 1248-D5
REVERE CT
1900 VSTA 92083 1107-J4
REVILLO DR
4300 SD 92115 1270-D4
REVILLO WY
4500 SD 92115 1270-D3
REX AV
5100 SD 92105 1270-A5
REX LN
1300 SDCo 92021 1251-H1
REXFORD DR
1900 SD 92105 1289-G1
REX HALL ST
700 ELCJ 92021 1251-F4
REXVIEW DR
300 SD 92114 1290-E4
REYNARD WY
2600 SD 92103 1288-J1
2700 SD 92103 1268-J6
REYNOLDS ST
4900 SD 92113 1290-A6
5100 SD 92114 1290-A6
REYNOSA CT
100 SOLB 92075 1167-D7
R H DANA PL
1200 CORD 92118 1308-H1
RHEA GN
1000 ESCN 92026 1109-F6
RHEA LN
400 SMCS 92069 1108-J4
400 SMCS 92069 1109-A4
RHEA PL
1000 VSTA 92084 1087-H4
RHESA LN
200 SDCo 92028 1027-F5
RHINE ST
1100 SD 92154 1350-A1
RHOADES CT
6300 SD 92139 1310-E1
RHOADES RD
2600 SD 92139 1310-E2
RHODA DR
1200 SD 92037 1227-F7
RHODA LN
500 VSTA 92083 1087-H7
RHODE ISLAND ST
4500 SD 92116 1269-B4
RHODES CT
8700 SNTE 92071 1231-D7
RHODES WY
4100 OCN 92056 1107-E5
RHONDA LN
34200 SDCo 92061 1050-H1
RHONE RD
8500 SNTE 92071 1251-C1
8500 ELCJ 92020 1251-C1
8500 SNTE 92071 1231-C7
RIALTO GN
200 ESCN 92025 1150-B1
RIALTO ST
4300 SD 92107 1268-B5
RIATA DR
600 SDCo 92004 (1078-J5 See Page 1058)
RIBBON BEACH WY
400 OCN 92054 1086-B6
RIBBONWOOD RD
2400 SDCo 91905 1300-D3
3500 SDCo 91905 430-D7
RIBBONWOOD RD Rt#-94
2400 SDCo 91905 1300-D5
RICARD CT
2100 SDCo 92019 1272-D3
RICARDO DR
1100 CHV 91910 1311-B7
RICARDO PL
300 SD 92037 1247-F4
RICARDO RANCH RD
19100 SDCo 92082 1091-G4
RICE CT
8400 SD 92129 1189-B6
RICEBIRD DR
500 VSTA 92083 1087-F4
RICE CANYON RD
100 SDCo 92028 1029-A1
1200 SDCo 92028 998-J6
1200 SDCo 92028 999-A7
RICEWOOD DR
3200 OCN 92054 1086-D3
RICHANDAVE AV
1500 ELCJ 92019 1252-B6
1500 SDCo 92019 1252-B6
RICHARD LN
- VSTA 92083 1107-H2
RICHARD ST
6400 SD 92115 1270-E1
RICHARDSON AV
100 ELCJ 92020 1251-E5
RICHETH RD
100 SD 92114 1290-C4
RICHFIELD AV
100 ELCJ 92020 1251-E5
RICHLAND RD
200 SMCS 92069 1109-A3
800 SDCo 92069 1109-A4
RICHLAND ST
2600 SD 92111 1249-A7
RICHLAND VIEW CT
600 SDCo 92069 1109-A3
RICHLYNN RIDGE RD
2700 SDCo 92025 1150-E1
RICHMAR AV
100 SMCS 92069 1108-G7
RICHMOND DR
8700 LMSA 91941 1271-A2
RICHMOND ST
1300 SD 92103 1269-B6
2900 SD 92103 1269-B7
RICHMOND PARK CT
- CHV 91910 1310-D5
RICHMOND PARK PL
200 CHV 91910 1310-C5
RICHVALE DR
8300 SNTE 92071 1230-J7
RICK DR
- SDCo 92029 1128-J4
- SDCo 92029 1129-A5
- SMCS 92029 1128-J5
RICK ST
12800 PWY 92064 1190-D5
RICKENBAKER AV
600 SD 92154 1330-F6
RICKERT RD
10600 SD 92126 1209-D3
RICKS RANCH CT
31600 SDCo 92082 1070-E1
RICKS RANCH RD
13400 SDCo 92082 1070-D1
RICKY LN
10300 SNTE 92071 1231-E7
RICKY PL
200 ESCN 92027 1110-E6
RICO CT
6800 SD 92111 1268-J1
RIDEABOUT CT
12500 SD 92129 1189-C5
RIDEABOUT LN
8600 SD 92129 1189-C5
RIDER PL
- SD 92130 1188-D5
RIDERWOOD TER
8900 SNTE 92071 1231-F6
RIDGE CT
2800 SDCo 92028 1028-C2
3700 CRLB 92008 1107-B3
RIDGE DR
200 SDCo 92028 1028-C2
N RIDGE DR
100 SDCo 92028 1028-C2
RIDGE LN
100 SDCo 92019 1253-C1
RIDGE PL
400 SDCo 92028 1028-C2
RIDGE RD
1200 SDCo 92083 1107-E2
1200 VSTA 92083 1107-E2
1600 OCN 92056 1107-E2
E RIDGE RD
9700 SDCo 92021 1233-C2
RIDGE TER
200 ENCT 92024 1147-J7
RIDGE TR
900 SDCo 92019 1253-C2
1200 SDCo 92036 1136-C6
RIDGE VW
2200 ESCN 92029 1129-E6
RIDGE WY
500 SDCo 92028 1028-C3
RIDGEBACK RD
1400 CHV 91910 1311-A5
RIDGE CANYON RD
14100 SDCo 92082 1090-F6
RIDGECLIFF LN
3000 SDCo 91977 1271-D6
RIDGE CREEK DR
1700 CHV 91902 1311-C4
RIDGE CREEK RD
30000 SDCo 92082 1069-B5
RIDGECREST DR
200 SD 92114 1290-G5
3200 CRLB 92008 1106-H4
9700 SDCo 91941 1271-C1
RIDGECREST PL
2000 ESCN 92029 1129-F7
RIDGECREST RD
7500 SNTE 92071 1230-G7
15300 PWY 92064 1171-A7
RIDGECREST TER
1800 SDCo 92021 1252-B1
RIDGEDALE DR
13100 PWY 92064 1190-C5
RIDGEFIELD AV
2900 CRLB 92008 1107-B4
RIDGEFIELD PL
8500 SD 92129 1189-B5
RIDGEGATE RW
2300 SD 92037 1247-J1
2600 SD 92037 1248-A1
RIDGEGROVE LN
1700 ESCN 92029 1129-G5
RIDGEHAVEN CT
9400 SD 92123 1249-E2
RIDGE HEIGHTS DR
900 SDCo 92028 1027-H4
RIDGE HILL RD
13700 SDCo 92021 1232-F6
RIDGELINE AV
1900 VSTA 92083 1107-J7
RIDGELINE PL
- ESCN 92027 1110-F7
600 SOLB 92075 1167-G6
RIDGE MANOR AV
6300 SD 92120 1250-D5
RIDGEMONT CIR
- ESCN 92027 1110-F7
RIDGEMONT CT
1300 OCN 92056 1087-E3
RIDGEMOOR DR
5800 SD 92120 1250-D7
RIDGEMOORE PL
1000 VSTA 92083 1087-G4
RIDGE POINT CT
1200 CHV 91913 1331-C1
RIDGE RANCH CT
14000 SDCo 92082 1090-G6
RIDGE RANCH RD
13900 SDCo 92082 1090-F6
14700 SDCo 92027 1091-A6
14700 SDCo 92082 1091-A6
RIDGE ROCK CT
1600 CHV 91913 1311-D7
RIDGE ROUTE RD
8300 SD 92120 1250-D4
RIDGE RUN WY
- SD 92131 1209-G1
RIDGESIDE PL
2500 SDCo 91977 1271-D7
RIDGETON CT
8800 SDCo 92040 1232-C6
RIDGETON DR
12400 SDCo 92040 1232-C6
RIDGETON LN
8900 SDCo 92040 1232-C6
RIDGEVIEW CT
400 CHV 91902 1311-A4
RIDGE VIEW DR
1700 SD 92105 1289-H1
2400 SD 92105 1269-J7
2900 SD 92105 1270-A7
RIDGEVIEW LN
17700 SDCo 92065 1171-G3
RIDGEVIEW PL
2100 ESCN 92026 1109-G5
2500 SDCo 91977 1271-E7
15200 PWY 92064 1170-F6
RIDGEVIEW RD
16400 SDCo 92065 1171-G3
RIDGEVIEW WY
1200 CHV 91902 1311-A4
RIDGEWATER DR
800 CHV 91913 1311-E4
RIDGEWATER LN
10300 SD 92131 1209-H4
RIDGEWAY
4100 SD 92116 1269-H2
RIDGEWAY CT
400 SDCo 91977 1290-J5
RIDGEWAY DR
2300 SDCo 91950 1310-C2
2900 NATC 91950 1310-B3
RIDGE WAY GN
- ESCN 92029 1129-H6
RIDGEWAY ST
1400 OCN 92054 1106-D1
RIDGEWOOD DR
700 SDCo 92036 1156-E1
1800 SD 92139 1290-C7
RIDGEWOOD WY
3500 CRLB 92008 1107-A4
RIDING HIGH WY
- SDCo 92127 1168-J2
RIDING RIDGE RD
4800 SD 92130 1188-C6
RIDLEY RD
13500 SD 92129 1189-E4
RIENSTRA CT
400 CHV 91911 1330-G3
E RIENSTRA ST
- CHV 91911 1330-F4
RIENZI PL
17600 SD 92128 1150-A7
17600 SD 92128 1170-A1
RIESLING CT
12200 SD 92131 1210-B3
RIESLING DR
10600 SD 92131 1210-B3
RIFE WY
12700 SD 92129 1189-C4
RIFLE RD
- ELCJ 92021 1251-H5
RIFLE WY
13000 SD 92129 1189-D5
RIGEL ST
1300 SD 92113 1289-F6
RIGGS RD
5400 SDCo 92019 1253-D5
RIGLEY ST
900 CHV 91911 1330-J2
900 CHV 91911 1331-A2
900 CHV 91913 1331-A2
RIGSBY DR
9300 ELCJ 92020 1251-B1
9300 SNTE 92071 1251-B1
RILEY PL
200 ESCN 92027 1110-E6
RILEY ST
3200 SD 92110 1268-F3
3700 SD 92110 1268-E5
3800 SD 92110 1268-E4
3800 SD 92110 1268-E5
3900 SD 92110 1268-E4
5500 SD 92110 1268-F3
5500 SD 92110 1268-G3
RILL CT
3900 CRLB 92008 1107-C3
W RIM CT
9400 SDCo 92040 1232-B4
RIM RD
10900 SDCo 92026 1089-F3
W RIM RD
12600 SDCo 92040 1232-B4
RIMBACH RD
12200 PWY 92064 1190-B4
RIMBEY AV
2000 SD 92154 1350-A2
RIMCREST CT
1400 CHV 91902 1311-A3
RIMGATE CT
14400 SD 92129 1189-C1
RIMHURST CT
300 OCN 92054 1086-D2
RIMINI RD
500 DLMR 92014 1187-G5
RIM OF THE VALLEY
- SDCo 92082 1070-J1
- SDCo 92082 1071-A1
RIMPARK LN
5200 SD 92124 1249-F1
RIMPARK WY
9700 SD 92124 1249-F1
RIMRIDGE LN
8100 SD 92126 1209-B1
RIM ROCK CIR
3200 ENCT 92024 1148-C4
RIMROCK DR
1300 ESCN 92027 1110-A6
RIMROCK RD
500 ELCJ 92020 1251-C4
RIM ROCK RD
4700 OCN 92056 1087-D4
RIMSTONE LN
16100 SD 92127 1169-J4
RIMVIEW WY
5300 SD 92124 1249-G1
RINCADO RD
32000 SDCo 92061 1051-F5
RINCON AV
100 ESCN 92026 1109-J3
1600 SDCo 92026 1109-J3
1700 SDCo 92026 1110-A3
1700 SDCo 92027 1110-A3
RINCON CT
3600 OCN 92056 1107-F4
RINCON PT
- CHV 91913 1331-C1
1200 CHV 91913 1311-C7
RINCON RD
300 ESCN 92025 1130-A4
RINCON ST
700 VSTA 92083 1087-H7
5100 SD 92115 1270-D2
RINCON DEL MUNDO
1100 SDCo 92029 1149-H2
RINCON RANCH RD
17400 SDCo 91935 1274-A2
RINCON RANCHO RD
32200 SDCo 92061 1051-E4
RINCON SPRINGS RD
16800 SDCo 92061 1051-D7
16800 SDCo 92082 1051-D7
RINCON VILLA DR
1300 ESCN 92027 1109-J6
RINCON VILLA PL
1000 ESCN 92027 1109-J6
RINDA LN
8600 SDCo 91977 1290-J2
8600 SDCo 91977 1291-A2
RINEHART LN
13800 SDCo 92082 1090-E5
RING RD
- NATC 91950 1310-C4
13500 PWY 92064 1190-C4
RINGDOVE CT
11400 SD 92131 1210-A1
RINGNECK CT
13200 SDCo 92040 1232-C4
RINGWOOD DR
300 SD 92114 1290-G4
RIO CT
14100 PWY 92064 1190-G1
RIO DR
- SMCS 92069 1128-E2
RIO WY
1200 VSTA 92083 1107-E1
3100 SDCo 91977 1271-B6
RIO BONITO WY
2200 SD 92108 1269-D1
RIO BRAVA CT
13100 SDCo 91935 1272-D7
RIO CAMINO
10200 SDCo 92040 1231-H3
RIO CLARO CT
800 OCN 92057 1087-C1
RIO CORTO DR
11700 SDCo 92040 1231-H2
RIO FONDO
11600 SDCo 92040 1231-H3
RIO GRANDE
3200 SDCo 91935 1272-J7
RIO IVANHOE WY
13400 SDCo 91935 1272-F6
RIO LARGO
- VSTA 92083 1107-D2
RIO LINDO DR
200 SD 92114 1290-E4
RIO MADRE LN
3100 SDCo 91935 1272-J7
RIO MARIA RD
16800 SDCo 92040 1191-E4
RIO PLATA DR
5200 OCN 92057 1087-C1
RIO PLATO CT
6700 SD 92114 1290-E5
RIOS AV
1700 CHV 91911 1330-F6
1700 SD 92154 1330-F6
N RIOS AV
100 SOLB 92075 1167-E6
S RIOS AV
100 SOLB 92075 1167-F7
100 SOLB 92075 1187-F1
RIOS CT
100 SOLB 92075 1167-E6
RIOS RD
12200 SD 92128 1170-C3
12700 PWY 92064 1170-D3
RIO SAN DIEGO DR
8300 SD 92108 1269-D1
RIOS CANYON LN
14300 SDCo 92021 1232-G6
RIOS CANYON RD
14100 SDCo 92021 1232-G6
15000 SDCo 92021 1233-A6
RIO SECO CT
2600 CHV 91915 1311-J6
RIO SENDA
7800 SDCo 92067 1168-J1
RIO VALLE DR
5900 SDCo 92003 1047-J7
5900 SDCo 92003 1067-J1
RIO VERDE DR
24700 SDCo 92065 1173-G4
RIO VIENTO CT
800 OCN 92057 1087-C1
RIO VISTA
- VSTA 92083 1107-C2
RIO VISTA DR
- ESCN 92029 1129-F4
400 OCN 92054 1086-G2
700 SDCo 92028 1027-H1
2000 SDCo 92028 1048-B5
3200 SDCo 91902 1310-E4
RIO VISTA PL
3800 SDCo 91902 1310-E4
RIO VISTA RD
4500 SDCo 92028 1048-B5
16500 SDCo 92127 1168-J4
RIPARIAN RD
15500 PWY 92064 1170-F5
RIPPEY CT
2300 ELCJ 92020 1251-B3
RIPPEY ST
1100 ELCJ 92020 1251-B3
RIPPLE LN
13400 SDCo 92040 1232-D6
RIPPLE WY
16800 SDCo 92065 1171-J3
RISA CIR
4000 SD 92124 1249-J3
RISA CT
4000 SD 92124 1249-J3
RISA LN
6600 LMGR 91945 1270-E7
RISING DALE WY
23000 SDCo 92065 1153-C7
23000 SDCo 92065 1173-C1
RISING GLEN DR
4700 OCN 92056 1087-D4
RISING GLEN WY
2100 SD 92139 1290-E7
2300 CRLB 92008 1106-G3
RISING HILL
1100 SDCo 92029 1149-H1
RISING STAR CT
4100 SDCo 91941 1271-G4
RISING SUN LN
- LMSA 91941 1270-J4
RISUENO CT
1700 SD 92154 1350-B3
RITA ST
4500 SDCo 91941 1271-E3
RITCHEY ST
200 SD 92114 1290-E4
RITCHIE RD
3000 SDCo 92070 1135-E5
RITIDIAN WY
11800 SD 92128 1170-A1
RITSON RD
31600 SDCo 92026 1069-A2
RITTER CT
9900 SD 92131 1209-H5
RITTER PL
2200 ESCN 92029 1129-H7
RITVA PL
2300 SD 92139 1290-F7
RIVA LN
1500 ESCN 92027 1110-B7
RIVENDELL PL
- OCN 92054 1106-F2
N RIVER CIR
400 OCN 92057 1067-A6
RIVER DR
9700 SDCo 91916 1236-A1
9800 SDCo 91916 1235-J1
N RIVER RD
600 OCN 92057 1067-G5
1300 OCN 92003 1067-G5
1300 SDCo 92003 1067-G5
2400 OCN 92057 1066-H7
3000 OCN 92054 1086-D4
3400 OCN 92054 1066-G7
RIVER ST
9800 SDCo 92040 1232-A3
RIVERA CT
100 CHV 91911 1330-F4
400 CHV 91911 1330-H3
RIVERA PL
- CHV 91911 1330-F4
RIVERA ST
500 CHV 91911 1330-H3
RIVER ASH DR
1000 CHV 91910 1310-J7
RIVERBEND CT
15700 PWY 92064 1170-G5
RIVERBEND RD
14000 PWY 92064 1170-G4
RIVERBEND WY
500 CHV 91914 1311-E3
RIVERCREEK CT
400 CHV 91914 1311-E2
RIVER CREST RD
- SMCS 92078 1128-C6
RIVERDALE ST
6200 SD 92120 1249-H7
RIVER DANCE CT
- SDCo 91901 1234-C6
RIVER DANCE WY
- SDCo 91901 1234-C6
RIVERFORD RD
9800 SDCo 92040 1231-H3
RIVER GLEN RW
1200 SD 92111 1268-H2
RIVERHEAD CT
13800 SD 92129 1189-F3
RIVERHEAD DR
9900 SD 92129 1189-F3
RIVERLAWN AV
700 CHV 91910 1330-A2
800 CHV 91911 1330-A2
RIVER OAKS CT
900 CHV 91915 1311-G4
RIVER OAKS LN
- SDCo 92028 997-G7
RIVER PARK DR
100 SNTE 92071 1231-C5
RIVER RIM RD
11600 SD 92126 1209-A1
RIVER ROCK CT
100 SNTE 92071 1231-C5
RIVER ROCK RD
700 CHV 91914 1311-G3
RIVER RUN CIR
- SMCS 92069 1109-A5
RIVER RUN DR
2100 SD 92108 1269-D1
RIVER SHADOW CT
- SDCo 91901 1234-C6
RIVERSIDE DR
400 OCN 92054 1085-J6
8600 SDCo 91916 1236-A3
11400 SDCo 92040 1231-H3
RIVERTON PL
13200 SD 92130 1188-B4
RIVER TRAIL PL
300 SNTE 92071 1231-C5
RIVERTREE DR
600 OCN 92054 1086-D2
RIVER VALLEY CT
8900 SNTE 92071 1230-J4
8900 SNTE 92071 1231-A4
RIVERVIEW AV
9200 SDCo 92040 1231-J5
RIVER VIEW CT
5100 SDCo 92028 1048-J2
RIVERVIEW DR
900 SDCo 92028 1028-A1
1000 SDCo 92028 998-A6
RIVERVIEW LN
11900 SDCo 92040 1231-J5
RIVERVIEW PL
2400 SDCo 92028 998-A7
RIVERVIEW ST
2300 SD 92108 1269-D3
2300 SD 92116 1269-D3
RIVERVIEW WY
200 OCN 92057 1066-J7
RIVER VISTA RW
1200 SD 92111 1268-H3
RIVERWOOD RD
1100 SDCo 92070 1135-D3
RIVIERA CT
600 SDCo 92084 1087-H2
RIVIERA DR
100 OCN 92054 1086-F4
1900 SDCo 92084 1087-J2
1900 VSTA 92084 1087-J2
2400 CHV 91915 1311-H6
3300 SD 92109 1268-A1
3600 SD 92109 1248-A7
3700 LMSA 91941 1270-H5
RIVIERA WY
1300 CHV 91915 1311-H6
RIVOLI RD
- SDCo 92082 1070-E2
ROACH DR
8400 LMSA 91941 1270-J2
ROAD B
2700 SD 92105 1270-C7
ROAD C
5600 SD 92105 1270-C7
ROAD D
2500 SD 92105 1270-B7
ROADLINER AV
- ESCN 92027 1130-C1
ROADRUNNER DR N
- SDCo 92004 (1099-G3 See Page 1098)
ROADRUNNER DR S
3200 SDCo 92004 (1099-G5 See Page 1098)
ROADRUNNER GN
1300 ESCN 92029 1129-G6
ROADRUNNER LN
100 OCN 92057 1086-H2
39900 SDCo 91905 1300-D4
ROADRUNNER RD
3000 SDCo 92083 1108-C6
3000 SMCS 92069 1108-C6
ROADRUNNER RDG
30400 SDCo 92082 1069-F3
ROADRUNNER RDG S
30400 SDCo 92082 1069-F4
ROADRUNNER WY
- SDCo 92004 (1099-H4 See Page 1098)
ROADSIDE PL
10100 SDCo 91977 1271-E7
ROAD TO BALI
- SDCo 92127 1169-A2
ROAD TO MOROCCO
- SDCo 92127 1168-J3
- SDCo 92127 1169-A2
ROAD TO RIO
- SDCo 92127 1168-J2
ROAD TO SINGAPORE
- SDCo 92127 1168-J2
ROAD TO UTOPIA
- SDCo 92127 1168-H2
ROAD TO ZANZIBAR
- SDCo 92127 1168-J2
ROAN RD
7700 SD 92129 1189-A6
ROAN WY
12200 SD 92129 1189-A6
ROANE DR
5600 OCN 92057 1067-F6
ROANOKE RD
100 ELCJ 92020 1251-G5
ROANOKE ST
5500 SD 92139 1310-E1
ROARING CAMP RD
14100 PWY 92064 1170-G7
ROBBIE LN
29700 SDCo 92084 1068-D6
ROBBIE WY
2300 LMGR 91945 1270-H7
ROBBIEJEAN PL
1500 ELCJ 92019 1252-A5
ROBBINS CT
6800 SD 92122 1228-F5
ROBBINS ST
4300 SD 92122 1228-E4
ROBBINS WY
6700 SD 92122 1228-F5
ROBB ROY CT
3300 SD 92154 1330-E7
ROBB ROY PL
3400 SD 92154 1330-E7
ROBBY LN
100 OCN 92054 1086-G2
ROBBY WY
600 SDCo 92028 1027-G2
ROBELINI DR
100 SDCo 92083 1108-C3
100 VSTA 92083 1108-C3
ROBERT AV
600 CHV 91910 1310-E7
ROBERT LN
800 ENCT 92024 1147-G4
ROBERT ST
500 VSTA 92083 1087-F6
ROBERTA AV
500 ELCJ 92021 1251-J4
ROBERTA LN
3200 OCN 92054 1086-E5
ROBERTO WY
12600 PWY 92064 1170-C7
ROBERTO RIO RD
14600 PWY 92064 1190-G1
ROBERTS AL
4300 SD 92103 1269-C4
ROBERTS DR
6100 SD 92139 1290-D7
ROBERTS PL
2000 ESCN 92029 1129-G7
ROBERTS ST
- SD 92106 1288-A5
ROBERTS WY
12200 SDCo 92040 1232-A3
ROBERTSON DR
1000 ESCN 92025 1130-A3
ROBERTSON ST
1900 SDCo 92065 1152-E7
2300 SDCo 92065 1172-C1
ROBIN CT
900 SMCS 92069 1128-E3
ROBIN LN
200 OCN 92057 1086-H2
1400 ELCJ 92020 1251-D2
ROBIN PL
1100 SDCo 92084 1108-C1
1200 CHV 91911 1330-G2
1600 CRLB 92009 1127-D7
ROBIN ST
3400 SD 92115 1270-C6
8500 LMGR 91945 1290-J1
ROBINEA DR
6400 CRLB 92009 1127-A4
ROBIN HILL DR
1100 SMCS 92069 1109-A5
ROBIN HILL LN
400 ESCN 92025 1109-G5
400 SDCo 92026 1109-G5
ROBIN HOOD LN
8700 SD 92037 1227-J4
ROBINHOOD RD
1600 SDCo 92084 1108-G2
ROBIN HOOD WY
10600 SDCo 91941 1271-E2
ROBINIA CT
17700 SD 92127 1169-J1
ROBINRIDGE WY
9000 SNTE 92071 1231-G6
ROBINS NEST WY
- SDCo 92127 1169-F4
ROBINSON AV
100 SD 92103 1269-B6
1900 SD 92104 1269-B6
W ROBINSON AV
100 SD 92103 1269-A6
300 SD 92103 1268-J6
ROBINSON MEWS
3400 SD 92103 1269-A6
ROBINSON PL
3600 SD 92103 1269-B6
ROBINSON RD
- ImCo 92251 431-D4
ROBINSON WY
- SD 92145 1229-E1
ROBINWOOD DR
900 OCN 92056 1087-D1
5200 OCN 92057 1087-D1
ROBINWOOD RD
5100 SDCo 91902 1290-H7

SAN DIEGO CO.

INDEX

ROBISON BLVD SAN DIEGO CO. STREET INDEX RUDDY DR 6614

STREET
Block City ZIP Pg-Grid

ROBISON BLVD
12400 PWY 92064 1190-C4
ROBLE PL
7900 CRLB 92009 1147-G3
ROBLE WY
17000 SD 92128 1170-C2
ROBLEDA CT
18600 SD 92128 1150-C6
ROBLEDA CV
12900 SD 92128 1150-C6
ROBLEDO REAL RD
15000 SDCo 92021 1233-B3
ROBLE GRANDE LN
1500 SDCo 91901 1233-J7
ROBLE GRANDE RD
1600 SDCo 91901 1233-J7
1700 SDCo 91901 1234-A7
ROBLE GRANDE TR
1700 SDCo 91901 1234-A7
ROBLES DR
1400 CHV 91911 1330-J3
8600 SD 92119 1251-A3
8700 SD 92119 1250-J3
ROBLES LN
29700 SDCo 92082 1070-A6
ROBLES WY
8700 SD 92119 1251-A3
ROBLE VERDE
29600 SDCo 92082 1070-B6
ROBLEY PL
900 ENCT 92007 1167-E2
ROBLEY RANCH RD
13400 PWY 92064 1190-F5
ROBUSTO RD
5600 SD 92124 1229-G7
ROBYN RD
1500 ESCN 92025 1130-B4
ROCA DR
16300 SD 92128 1170-C3
ROCA PL
600 SDCo 92084 1067-H6
900 CHV 91910 1310-H7
ROCA RD
700 CHV 91910 1310-H7
ROCA GRANDE DR
12700 PWY 92064 1190-C5
ROCA VERDE
2600 SDCo 91977 1271-B7
ROCHDALE LN
1500 SD 92154 1350-B2
ROCHELLE AV
10300 SNTE 92071 1231-E4
ROCHELLE LN
10300 SNTE 92071 1231-B1
ROCHESTER RD
4000 SD 92116 1269-G2
ROCIO ST
7700 CRLB 92009 1147-G2
ROCK GN
2100 ESCN 92026 1109-C3
ROCK PL
6000 SD 92115 1270-C5
ROCK RD
17000 PWY 92064 1170-D2
ROCK ST
6000 SD 92115 1270-C5
ROCK ACRE DR
9200 SDCo 92040 1232-D5
ROCKAWAY CT
700 SD 92109 1267-H1
ROCKBROOK ST
9200 SDCo 91977 1271-B7
ROCK CANYON CT
11000 SD 92126 1209-A2
ROCK CANYON DR
7200 SD 92126 1208-J3
7400 SD 92126 1209-A2
ROCKCLIFF LN
3000 SDCo 91977 1271-D6
ROCK CREEK DR
10400 SD 92131 1209-J4
10500 SD 92131 1210-A3
ROCK CREEK LN
15300 SDCo 92021 1232-G2
ROCK CREEK PL
1200 CHV 91915 1311-H6
ROCK CREEK RD
13900 PWY 92064 1170-G5
ROCK CREST GN
2200 ESCN 92026 1109-B3
ROCKCREST LN
9400 SDCo 92040 1232-A5
ROCKCREST RD
11900 SDCo 92040 1231-J5
11900 SDCo 92040 1232-A5
ROCKDALE LN
3000 SDCo 91977 1271-D6
ROCK DOVE ST
7000 CRLB 92009 1127-E7
ROCKEFELLER
1700 CRLB 92008 1127-A3
ROCKET RIDGE RD
8900 SDCo 92040 1232-A6
ROCKEY
- SDCo 92672 1023-E2
ROCKFIELD CT
3800 CRLB 92008 1107-B3
ROCKFIELD WY
9200 SD 92126 1209-E2
ROCKFORD DR
4900 SD 92115 1270-C2
ROCKGATE WY
9900 SDCo 91977 1271-D7
ROCKGLEN AV
6600 SD 92111 1248-J4
ROCK GLEN WY
100 SNTE 92071 1231-C5
ROCK HILL PL
1300 ESCN 92026 1109-F7
ROCKHILL RD
100 SDCo 92084 1088-B6
100 VSTA 92084 1088-B6
ROCK HILL RANCH RD
15100 SDCo 92082 1090-H2
ROCKHOFF LN
1900 SDCo 92026 1109-E4
ROCKHOFF RD
1800 SDCo 92026 1109-E4
1900 ESCN 92026 1109-E4
ROCK HOUSE RD
17100 SDCo 92036 1156-F7
ROCKHOUSE RD
17200 SDCo 92065 1171-F5
ROCKHOUSE TKTR
- SDCo 92004 410-D6
ROCKHOUSE TR
- SDCo 92004 410-B5
ROCKHURST CT
5800 SD 92120 1250-D7
ROCKHURST DR
6100 SD 92120 1250-C7
ROCKING CHAIR DR
400 SDCo 92004 (1078-H4
See Page 1058)
ROCKING HORSE CIR
3300 ENCT 92024 1148-C4
ROCKING HORSE DR
600 CHV 91914 1311-F3
ROCKING HORSE LN
5400 OCN 92057 1067-E7
ROCKINGHORSE RD
700 VSTA 92083 1107-G2
ROCKING HORSE RD
31600 SDCo 92026 1049-A7
31600 SDCo 92026 1069-A1
ROCKIN OAKS WY
16600 SDCo 92065 1171-H3
ROCK ISLAND RD
- SD 92139 1290-D7
ROCKLAND CT
1200 CHV 91913 1311-B7
ROCKLAND ST
6800 SD 92115 1270-E5
ROCKLEDGE RD
8500 LMSA 91941 1270-J4
ROCKLEDGE ST
500 OCN 92054 1106-B1
ROCK MANOR DR
6900 SD 92119 1250-E6
ROCKMINT DR
800 SMCS 92078 1128-G2
ROCK MOUNTAIN DR
40000 SDCo 92028 997-G5
ROCK MOUNTAIN RD
- RivC 92590 997-G1
40300 SDCo 92028 997-G3
ROCKNE ST
2800 SD 92139 1310-F2
ROCK PILE RD
32200 SDCo 92003 1048-H6
ROCK POINT WY
10200 SDCo 91977 1291-D2
ROCKPORT CT
500 ENCT 92024 1147-B2
ROCKPORT BAY WY
4200 OCN 92054 1066-E6
ROCK RIDGE LN
12800 SDCo 92082 1090-C2
ROCK RIDGE PL
300 ESCN 92027 1130-C1
ROCK RIDGE RD
- SDCo 92028 1029-B1
ROCKRIDGE RD
5100 SDCo 91941 1271-D2
ROCK RIVER LN
3900 SDCo 91902 1311-B2
ROCKROSE CT
12600 PWY 92064 1190-D3
ROCK ROSE LN
30500 SDCo 92082 1070-J3
ROCKROSE TER
7000 CRLB 92009 1127-B6
ROCKSIDE CT
11000 SD 92126 1208-J2
ROCK SPRINGS PL
4600 OCN 92056 1087-D3
ROCK SPRINGS RD
600 ESCN 92025 1129-G2
800 SMCS 92069 1109-B6
800 ESCN 92026 1129-F1
1000 SDCo 92026 1109-E7
1100 SDCo 92026 1129-F1
ROCK SPRINGS HOLLOW
1100 SDCo 92026 1109-D6
ROCK STONE RD
30100 SDCo 92082 1071-A3
ROCKSTREAM RD
12200 SDCo 92040 1231-J2
12200 SDCo 92040 1232-A2
ROCK TERRACE PL
- CHV 91914 1311-F3
ROCK TERRACE RD
1400 SDCo 91901 1234-C6
ROCK VALLEY CT
7100 SD 92122 1228-F4
ROCKVIEW DR
8200 SDCo 92021 1251-G1
ROCK VIEW GN
2100 ESCN 92026 1109-B3
ROCKVILL ST
10700 SNTE 92071 1231-F6
ROCKWALL LN
500 SMCS 92069 1108-G6
ROCKWELL CT
12800 PWY 92064 1190-D3
ROCKWOOD AV
- ImCo 92249 6560-C7
ROCKWOOD PL
10900 SDCo 92020 1271-G2
ROCKWOOD RD
- ImCo 92231 431-B8
10900 SDCo 92020 1271-G2
16300 SDCo 92027 1131-D2
16400 SDCo 92027 1111-D7
17100 SDCo 92027 1131-A5
17100 SD 92027 1130-G3
17500 ESCN 92027 1130-G3
17500 SDCo 92027 1130-G3
ROCKY LN
11300 SDCo 92040 1212-B6
ROCKY PASS
28900 SDCo 92066 1237-C6
ROCKY RD
- SDCo 92082 1071-D1
19900 SDCo 92029 1148-F2
ROCKY CREEK RD
1600 SDCo 92021 1232-H7
1600 SDCo 92021 1252-H1
ROCKYCREST RD
700 SDCo 92028 1027-F5
ROCKYHILL RD
700 ELCJ 92019 1251-H6
700 SDCo 92019 1251-H6
ROCKY HILLS RD
25700 RivC 92590 997-H1
ROCKY HOME DR
11900 SDCo 92040 1231-J4
ROCKY KNOLL RD
- SDCo 91905 1300-F5
ROCKY MOUNTAIN RD
15300 SDCo 91935 1273-C7
15300 SDCo 91935 1293-C1
ROCKY MOUNTAIN TR
7200 SDCo 92036 1138-B7
ROCKY PASS WY
7800 SDCo 92066 1237-C6
ROCKY POINT CT
1600 CHV 91911 1330-J4
ROCKY POINT RD
7500 SNTE 92071 1230-G7
ROCKY POINT WY
- SMCS 92069 1128-A3
1100 ESCN 92026 1109-J4
29000 SDCo 92026 1089-D2
ROCKY RIDGE RD
9800 SDCo 92026 1089-D2
ROCKY SAGE RD
3200 SDCo 91935 1272-J6
3200 SDCo 91935 1273-A7
ROCKY SHORE RD
1700 SD 92139 1290-D7
ROCKY VIEW CT
5900 SDCo 91902 1311-B1
ROCOSO LN
7900 CRLB 92009 1147-G3
ROCOSO RD
11300 SDCo 92040 1211-G5
ROCREST RD
1700 SDCo 91901 1233-G7
ROD ST
900 SDCo 92028 1027-H5
RODADA DR
16200 SD 92128 1170-C4
RODADO PL
2100 ELCJ 92020 1251-C1
RODEAL WY
12000 SDCo 92040 1232-A6
RODEAR RD
1600 SD 92154 1350-A3
RODELANE ST
2000 SD 92103 1268-G6
RODEO DR
1300 SD 92037 1247-G2
12600 SDCo 92040 1232-B5
RODEO QUEEN DR
900 SDCo 92028 1027-G3
RODERO
- CRLB 92009 1126-H5
RODMAN AV
4900 SD 92120 1250-A6
RODNEY AV
100 ENCT 92024 1147-G6
RODRIGO DR
4300 SD 92115 1270-D4
RODRIGUEZ RD
- SDCo 92082 1071-E2
8900 SDCo 92026 1069-D1
ROE DR
9700 SNTE 92071 1231-B4
ROE ST
- CORD 92135 1288-F3
ROEBLIN CT
6700 SD 92111 1248-H7
ROECREST DR
9700 SNTE 92071 1231-C4
ROGAN RD
200 CHV 91910 1310-C5
ROGERS CT
- SDCo 92069 1109-A3
- SMCS 92069 1109-A3
ROGERS LN
- SDCo 91977 1271-C4
ROGERS RD
- CORD 92135 1288-C7
- SD 92135 1288-E7
3800 SDCo 91977 1271-C5
N ROGERS RD
3900 SDCo 91977 1271-C4
ROGERS ST
2900 SD 92106 1288-A3
ROGUE RD
500 ELCJ 92020 1251-G4
ROGUE ISLE CT
1700 CRLB 92008 1106-H6
ROHN RD
1900 ESCN 92025 1129-H6
ROHR PL
9000 SD 92123 1249-D5
ROI RD
2300 CORD 92155 1309-B1
ROI WY
2300 CORD 92155 1309-B1
ROJA DR
500 OCN 92057 1067-A6
ROJA ST
500 OCN 92057 1067-A5
ROJO TIERRA RD
3700 LMSA 91941 1270-H5
ROLAND ACRES DR
8500 SNTE 92071 1231-E7
ROLANDO BLVD
4100 SD 92115 1270-D3
ROLANDO CT
4800 SD 92115 1270-D2
ROLANDO KNOLLS DR
6700 LMSA 91941 1270-E4
ROLFE RD
4300 SD 92117 1248-E2
ROLL DR
2200 SD 92154 1352-A3
ROLLIE PL
4500 SDCo 91941 1271-G3
4500 SDCo 92020 1271-G3
ROLLING HILLS DR
1400 OCN 92056 1087-D4
11000 SDCo 92020 1271-H2
30100 SDCo 92082 1069-G4
ROLLING HILLS LN
300 SMCS 92069 1108-J6
3500 SDCo 91902 1311-C1
ROLLING HILLS PL
5000 SDCo 92020 1271-J2
ROLLING HILLS RD
400 SDCo 92083 1108-A3
400 VSTA 92083 1108-A3
600 VSTA 92083 1107-J3
ROLLING HILLS WY
11200 SDCo 92082 1069-G4
ROLLIN GLEN RD
13300 PWY 92064 1190-H4
ROLLING MEADOWS CT
12100 SD 92128 1190-A7
ROLLING OAK RD
7500 SNTE 92071 1230-G7
ROLLING RIDGE RD
2200 CHV 91914 1311-E2
2200 SDCo 91902 1311-E2
ROLLING ROCK RD
28600 SDCo 92026 1089-E2
ROLLINGVIEW LN
- SDCo 92028 1047-H5
ROLLINGWOOD LN
- SDCo 92028 1047-H6
ROLLINS WY
100 VSTA 92083 1087-G7
ROLLSREACH DR
3300 SD 92111 1248-H4
ROMA AV
200 SMCS 92069 1108-H7
ROMA CT
1700 CHV 91911 1330-J5
ROMA DR
1500 VSTA 92083 1107-H3
ROMAN WY
300 CHV 91911 1330-F1
ROMANCE RD
1400 SDCo 92029 1129-C4
ROMANY DR
6000 SD 92120 1250-C7
ROMBOUGH PL
5200 SD 92105 1270-A7
ROMEGA CT
5400 SDCo 91902 1290-J7
ROMERIA ST
7500 CRLB 92009 1147-H1
ROMERO CT
7300 SD 92037 1227-G7
ROMERO DR
7200 SD 92037 1227-G7
ROMFORD CT
7100 SD 92120 1250-A5
ROMINE RD
24800 SDCo 92065 1173-G5
ROMNEY RD
2300 SD 92109 1248-B3
ROMNEYA DR
200 OCN 92057 1067-B7
ROMO RD
- SDCo 91917 (1314-E7
See Page 1294)
- SDCo 91917 429-J10
ROMO ST
6200 SD 92115 1270-D5
RON
10700 SD 92129 1189-H2
RON CT
8200 SD 92123 1249-B7
RON WY
2200 SD 92123 1249-B7
RONALD CT
3100 SDCo 91977 1271-A6
RONALD LN
1400 VSTA 92083 1108-A2
RONAN DR
19300 SDCo 92065 1192-B2
RONDA AV
1200 ESCN 92027 1110-A7
9000 SD 92123 1249-F6
RONDA PL
1400 ESCN 92027 1110-B7
RONDEL CT
7200 SD 92119 1250-E4
RONDEVOO RD
3000 LMGR 91945 1270-H6
RONICA WY
700 SDCo 92028 1027-J4
RONNA PL
300 CHV 91910 1310-E6
RONNIE CT
9400 SNTE 92071 1231-B4
RONSON CT
4800 SD 92111 1249-C1
RONSON RD
7100 SD 92111 1249-A1
ROOD RD
- ImCo 92231 431-E7
ROOKWOOD DR
10200 SD 92131 1209-G5
ROOSEVELT AV
100 NATC 91950 1309-H1
100 NATC 91950 1289-G7
1400 SD 92109 1248-A7
2900 LMGR 91945 1270-G6
ROOSEVELT LN
- SDCo 92040 (1193-B5
See Page 1192)
ROOSEVELT RD
- SD 92133 1268-D7
ROOSEVELT ST
100 CHV 91910 1310-C6
500 CRLB 92008 1106-D5
1100 ESCN 92027 1110-A7
1200 ESCN 92027 1109-J6
N ROOSEVELT ST
600 ESCN 92027 1130-A1
ROOT ST
2400 SD 92123 1249-C6
ROPALT ST
7700 LMSA 91942 1250-G7
ROPER CT
100 ENCT 92024 1147-G7
ROREX DR
2000 ESCN 92025 1130-A7
ROSA CT
- ESCN 92027 1110-E6
ROSA ST
400 SOLB 92075 1187-F1
ROSA WY
3500 SDCo 92028 1028-D1
ROSADA CT
8600 SDCo 92021 1232-E6
ROSADA GN
1400 ESCN 92027 1110-A5
ROSADA WY
8500 SDCo 92021 1232-E6
ROSAL CT
900 CHV 91910 1310-J5
ROSAL LN
2300 SDCo 91977 1271-E7
ROSALIE WY
400 SDCo 92019 1253-C1
ROSA LINDA ST
3400 SD 92154 1350-E1
ROSA RANCHO LN
4200 SDCo 92028 998-F4
ROSARIO LN
1000 VSTA 92084 1088-A5
ROSARITA DR
4000 LMSA 91941 1270-H4
ROSAS
10900 SD 92129 1189-H2
ROSCOE CT
5700 SD 92123 1229-E7
ROSCREA AV
- SD 92117 1228-H7
ROSE AV
1000 ELCN 92243 6499-G5
ROSE CT
600 SMCS 92069 1108-J5
13900 PWY 92064 1190-F3
ROSE DR
- SD 92109 1248-C6
400 NATC 91950 1309-J3
800 VSTA 92083 1087-E5
4600 OCN 92056 1087-E5
7000 CRLB 92009 1127-B6
ROSE LN
2900 SD 92154 1350-D2
4200 OCN 92057 1067-G3
4200 SDCo 92003 1067-G3
ROSE PL
100 OCN 92054 1086-D6
4700 SD 92115 1270-C3
ROSE RD
2300 SDCo 92028 997-A1
ROSE ST
6100 SD 92115 1270-C3
N ROSE ST
700 ESCN 92027 1110-A6
800 ESCN 92027 1130-B1
S ROSE ST
100 ESCN 92027 1130-C2
ROSE WY
1500 ESCN 92027 1110-B7
ROSEANN AV
2800 ESCN 92027 1110-E6
ROSE ARBOR DR
900 SMCS 92078 1129-B2
ROSEBAY DR
100 ENCT 92024 1147-E6
ROSEBUD LN
300 SD 92114 1290-G5
4300 LMSA 91941 1270-G3
ROSECLIFF PL
- SD 92130 1208-B1
ROSE CORAL RW
3900 SD 92130 1208-B4
ROSECRANS BLVD
- SD 92106 1288-A7
- SD 92106 1308-B1
ROSECRANS PL
3000 SD 92110 1268-D6
ROSECRANS ST
200 SD 92106 1288-A4
3600 SD 92110 1268-F4
ROSECRANS ST
Rt#-209
1200 SD 92106 1288-B2
1700 SD 92133 1288-B2
2100 SD 92133 1268-D7
2100 SD 92106 1268-D7
3000 SD 92110 1268-D7
ROSE CREEK SHORE DR
- SD 92109 1248-C6
ROSECREST DR
27700 SDCo 92026 1089-H4
ROSECROFT LN
3600 SD 92106 1287-J4
3600 SD 92106 1288-A4
ROSEDALE CT
2900 SDCo 91977 1271-B6
ROSEDALE DR
3600 SDCo 91902 1310-F4
9000 SDCo 91977 1271-B7
ROSEDALE PL
2800 SDCo 91977 1271-A7
ROSEDALE WY
2800 SDCo 91977 1271-A7
ROSEDOWN PL
17700 SD 92128 1150-A7
ROSE FERN LN
2100 SDCo 92065 1172-E2
ROSEFIELD DR
6700 SD 92115 1270-E3
6800 LMSA 91941 1270-E3
ROSEGLEN PL
9400 SDCo 91977 1271-B5
ROSE HEDGE DR
4900 LMSA 91941 1270-J2
ROSEHILL CT
1100 SDCo 92025 1130-D7
ROSEHILL RD
2600 SDCo 92025 1130-D7
ROSE LAKE AV
6200 SD 92119 1250-H6
ROSELAND DR
7900 SD 92037 1227-G5
E ROSELAND DR
- SD 92037 1227-H6
ROSELAND PL
7900 SD 92037 1227-H6
ROSELAWN AV
3600 SD 92105 1269-J6
ROSELAWN ST
1200 NATC 91950 1310-A2
ROSELLE AV
500 ELCJ 92021 1251-J4
3700 OCN 92056 1107-B1
ROSELLE CT
1100 ELCJ 92021 1251-J4
ROSELLE ST
3500 OCN 92056 1087-A7
3600 OCN 92056 1107-B1
10300 SD 92121 1208-A5
ROSELLE WY
11000 SD 92121 1208-B5
ROSEMARIE LN
3000 SDCo 92028 1048-B1
ROSEMARY AV
900 CRLB 92009 1127-A6
ROSEMARY CT
300 ENCT 92024 1148-A7
1700 ESCN 92026 1109-C5
ROSEMARY LN
300 ENCT 92024 1148-A7
1000 VSTA 92083 1107-H1
7000 LMGR 91945 1270-F7
ROSEMARY PL
100 CHV 91910 1310-C5
ROSEMARY WY
3700 OCN 92057 1086-H4
ROSEMONT LN
2200 ENCT 92024 1167-J1
15700 SDCo 92065 1172-A5
ROSEMONT ST
200 SD 92037 1247-E2
ROSENDA CT
4000 SD 92122 1228-B5
ROSE OF TRALEE
- SDCo 92127 1168-J2
ROSE RANCH RD
2600 SMCS 92069 1109-A5
ROSETA ST
200 ENCT 92024 1147-B6
ROSETTA CT
200 SD 92111 1249-A3
ROSETTE RUN
15300 SDCo 92082 1070-J3
ROSEVIEW PL
300 CHV 91910 1310-C5
2500 SD 92105 1269-J7
ROSEWOOD CIR
2700 OCN 92056 1087-E5
ROSEWOOD DR
5100 OCN 92056 1087-D2
ROSEWOOD LN
- ESCN 92027 1130-J2
4600 SDCo 92004 (1099-G4
See Page 1098)
7900 LMGR 91945 1270-H7
ROSEWOOD PL
3600 SDCo 92028 1048-D2
ROSEWOOD ST
1900 VSTA 92083 1107-G5
3000 SD 92109 1248-D5
ROSEY RD
12400 SDCo 92021 1252-A1
ROSIE LN
10300 SNTE 92071 1231-B1
ROSIE WY
9600 SNTE 92071 1231-B1
ROSITA CT
600 CHV 91910 1311-A5
ROSLYN LN
1200 SD 92037 1227-F6
ROSS AV
- ELCN 92243 6500-A7
- ELCN 92243 6560-A1
200 ELCN 92243 6559-G1
2000 SDCo 91905 1300-E7
ROSS DR
500 ESCN 92029 1129-D2
500 SDCo 92029 1129-D2
ROSS LN
2700 ESCN 92025 1130-A7
2700 ESCN 92025 1150-A1
ROSS RD
200 ImCo 92243 6500-C7
500 ELCN 92243 6500-C7
700 ImCo 92243 6559-B1
1000 ImCo 92243 431-D5
1500 ImCo 92283 432-E5
2000 ELCN 92243 6559-B1
2600 SDCo 92028 997-A1
ROSS RD Rt#-S24
1400 ImCo 92283 432-D5
ROSSIN CT
1600 CHV 91913 1311-D7
ROSSINI DR
1800 ENCT 92007 1167-D2
ROSSITER LN
700 SDCo 92028 1027-G2
ROSSO CT
9400 SDCo 92021 1232-H4
ROSTRATA LN
13700 PWY 92064 1170-F4
ROSTRATA RD
13500 PWY 92064 1170-E4
ROSTRATA HILL RD
16200 PWY 92064 1170-F4
ROSVALL DR
600 SDCo 92028 1027-F2
ROSWELL ST
5100 SD 92114 1290-A3
ROSY AV
13600 SD 92129 1189-D3
ROTANZI ST
100 SDCo 92065 1152-D7
100 SDCo 92065 1172-E1
ROTELLA CT
11100 SD 92128 1189-J4
ROTH CT
200 SD 92114 1290-D4
ROTHERHAM AV
8900 SD 92129 1189-C2
ROTHGARD RD
10100 SDCo 91977 1271-E6
ROUGEMONT PL
12500 SD 92131 1210-C5
ROUND MEADOW CT
- SDCo 92028 1027-H7
ROUND POTRERO RD
1300 SDCo 91963 (1316-A3
See Page 1296)
1300 SDCo 91963 (1315-J4
See Page 1294)
ROUNDTREE DR
1700 OCN 92056 1087-D4
ROUNDTREE GN
300 ESCN 92026 1109-G5
ROUND TREE RD
15300 SDCo 92082 1090-J2
15300 SDCo 92082 1091-A2
ROUNDUP AV
13000 SD 92129 1189-C5
E ROUNDUP CIR
9200 SNTE 92071 1231-F5
N ROUNDUP CIR
10500 SNTE 92071 1231-E5
W ROUNDUP CIR
9200 SNTE 92071 1231-E5
S ROUNDUP TR
10500 SNTE 92071 1231-E6
ROUNDUP WY
1100 OCN 92057 1067-E7
ROUS ST
4200 SD 92122 1228-E4
ROUSH CT
900 CHV 91911 1331-A2
ROUSH DR
1200 CHV 91911 1330-J2
1200 CHV 91911 1331-A2
ROVER ST
8900 SDCo 91977 1291-A1
ROWAN ST
1600 SD 92105 1289-G2
ROWCLIFF BLVD
- CORD 91932 1329-E4
ROWDY CT
9400 SDCo 91977 1271-C6
ROWE ST
3400 SD 92115 1270-D6
ROWEL CT
27300 SDCo 92082 1091-F4
ROWENA AV
1200 SMCS 92069 1108-H4
ROWENA ST
7300 SD 92119 1250-E3
ROWLETT AV
9000 SD 92129 1189-D4
ROWLEY AV
1700 SDCo 92065 1172-E1
ROWLEY WY
- SDCo 92065 1172-E1
ROXANNE DR
1300 SDCo 92021 1251-G1
1400 SDCo 92021 1231-G7
ROXBORO CT
11400 SD 92131 1209-J1
ROXBORO RD
11000 SD 92131 1209-H1
ROXBURY RD
5100 SD 92116 1269-H2
ROXBURY TER
6500 SDCo 92067 1188-H1
ROXTON CIR
13300 SD 92130 1187-J4
13300 SD 92130 1188-A4
ROXY LN
6500 SD 92115 1270-D2
ROY ST
8000 LMGR 91945 1270-H6
ROYAL CIR
8100 SDCo 92021 1252-A1
ROYAL DR
3500 SDCo 92036 1156-E2
4000 CRLB 92008 1106-G6
37700 SDCo 91905 (1299-H3
See Page 1298)
ROYAL PL
3700 SDCo 91902 1310-D4
37700 SDCo 91905 (1299-G3
See Page 1298)
ROYAL RD
3300 SDCo 92084 1088-E7
11800 SDCo 92021 1251-J1
11900 SDCo 92021 1252-A1
ROYAL ANN AV
10100 SD 92126 1209-B5
ROYAL BIRKDALE PL
6900 SDCo 92067 1188-H1
ROYAL BIRKDALE RW
12000 SD 92128 1170-A5
ROYAL CREST CT
200 SDCo 92025 1130-B7
ROYAL CREST DR
2300 SDCo 92025 1130-B6
ROYAL CROWN RW
15600 SD 92128 1170-B5
ROYAL DORNOCH SQ
13800 SD 92128 1189-J3
ROYALE CRESCENT CT
2200 SD 92123 1249-C7
ROYAL GARDENS CT
8000 SDCo 92021 1252-A1
ROYAL GARDENS PL
8000 SDCo 92021 1252-A1
ROYAL GLEN DR
200 SDCo 92028 1027-F1
ROYAL GORGE CT
6500 SD 92119 1250-D3
ROYAL GORGE DR
6700 SD 92119 1250-D3
ROYAL GREENS PL
4800 SD 92117 1248-G1
ROYAL ISLAND WY
4800 SD 92154 1330-J6
ROYALITO LN
8000 SDCo 92021 1252-A1
ROYAL LYTHAM GN
2100 ESCN 92026 1109-D4
ROYAL LYTHAM RW
12100 SD 92128 1170-A5
ROYAL LYTHAM SQ
15600 SD 92128 1170-B5
ROYAL MELBOURNE SQ
13700 SD 92128 1189-J3
ROYAL OAK CT
7900 SD 92114 1290-H5
ROYAL OAK DR
100 SD 92114 1290-H4
2300 SDCo 92027 1130-F2
2400 ESCN 92027 1130-F2
4500 OCN 92056 1087-D5
S ROYAL OAK DR
100 SD 92114 1290-H4
ROYAL OAKS LN
17200 SDCo 92065 1171-G1
ROYAL PARK LN
8100 SDCo 92021 1252-A1
8100 SDCo 92040 1252-A1
ROYAL RIM DR
9600 SDCo 92026 1089-D2
ROYAL SAINT JAMES DR
2400 SDCo 92019 1272-A5
ROYAL TERN WY
900 OCN 92057 1087-A3
ROYAL VISTA DR
1300 SDCo 92065 1172-E3
ROYAL WILLIE RD
33400 SDCo 91906 (1318-F3
See Page 1298)
ROYCE CT
8400 SD 92123 1249-B7
ROYCE LN
1400 SDCo 92028 1027-J7
1400 SDCo 92028 1047-J1
ROYMAR RD
100 OCN 92054 1086-D4
ROYSTON DR
1700 SD 92154 1349-J2
1700 SD 92154 1350-A2
RUA ALTA VISTA
29300 SDCo 92066 1237-D6
RUA MICHELLE
25500 SDCo 92026 1109-F2
RUANE ST
7000 SD 92119 1250-E3
RUBENSTEIN AV
1200 ENCT 92007 1167-D1
RUBENSTEIN DR
1600 ENCT 92007 1167-D2
RUBENSTEIN PL
200 ENCT 92007 1167-C1
RUBY AV
- SDCo 91905 1300-C7
RUBY DR
600 VSTA 92083 1087-D6
RUBY LN
4400 OCN 92056 1107-D2
6900 LMGR 91945 1290-E1
RUBY RD
1900 ESCN 92026 1109-D5
RUBY ST
600 ELCJ 92020 1251-G7
5600 SD 92110 1268-F3
RUBY WY
- CRLB 92009 1127-B4
RUBY LAKE AV
6200 SD 92119 1250-H6
RUDD RD
400 VSTA 92084 1088-B6
RUDDER AV
- CRLB 92009 1126-J7
- CRLB 92009 1127-B5
- CRLB 92009 1146-J1
RUDDER RD
2400 OCN 92054 1106-F1
RUDDY DR
29800 SDCo 91906 (1297-F5
See Page 1296)

SAN DIEGO CO.
INDEX

SAN DIEGO CO.
INDEX

STREET
Block City ZIP Pg-Grid

RUDDY DUCK CT
2200 ENCT 92007 1167-F4
RUDNICK DR
3100 SDCo 91935 1274-C4
RUDY RD
1400 SDCo 91977 1291-A2
RUE ADRIANE
2300 SD 92037 1227-H7
RUE AVALLON
600 CHV 91913 1311-D4
RUE BAYONNE
600 CHV 91913 1311-D4
RUE BIARRITZ
9900 SD 92131 1210-B5
RUE CANNES
10200 SD 92131 1210-C5
RUE CAP FERRAT
1200 SDCo 92069 1128-B3
RUE CHAMBERRY
10200 SD 92131 1210-B5
RUE CHAMOND
600 CHV 91913 1311-D4
RUE CHAMONIX
10200 SD 92131 1210-C5
RUE CHANTEMAR
9900 SD 92131 1210-B5
RUE CHATEAU
1900 CHV 91913 1311-D4
RUE CHEAUMONT
12200 SD 92131 1210-B5
RUEDA CT
10800 SD 92124 1249-J2
RUEDA DR
3900 SD 92124 1249-J2
4300 SD 92124 1250-A2
RUEDA ACAYAN
12700 SD 92128 1150-D7
12700 SD 92128 1170-C1
RUEDA ALCALDE
7700 SDCo 92066 1237-C6
RUEDA MARGARITA
300 SMCS 92069 1109-C7
RUEDA MELILLA
12800 SD 92128 1150-C7
12800 SD 92128 1170-C1
RUE DE ANNE
2300 SD 92037 1227-H7
RUE DE ANTIBES
14000 SD 92014 1187-G6
RUE DE AZUR
14000 SD 92014 1187-G6
RUE DE LA MER
1700 OCN 92054 1106-D2
RUE DE LA MONTAGNE
2000 OCN 92054 1106-D1
RUE DENISE
2400 SD 92037 1227-H7
RUE DE ROARK
7200 SD 92037 1227-J7
RUE DES AMIS
11900 SD 92131 1210-A3
RUE DES CHATEAUX
2300 CRLB 92008 1106-D5
RUE DE VALLE
1600 SMCS 92069 1128-D1
RUE DORLEANS
3000 SD 92110 1268-B5
RUE DU NUAGE
10400 SD 92131 1210-A3
RUE FINISTERRE
10200 SD 92131 1210-C5
RUE FONTENAY
10300 SD 92131 1210-B4
RUE FOUNTAINEBLEAU
12300 SD 92131 1210-B4
RUEGGER RD
- ImCo 92233 411-A10
RUE LEBLANC
600 CHV 91913 1311-D4
RUELLE CT
8300 SNTE 92071 1230-H6
RUE MARRABELLE
12600 SD 92131 1210-C4
RUE MARSEILLES
600 CHV 91913 1311-D3
RUE MICHAEL
7200 SD 92037 1227-H7
RUE MICHELLE
1900 CHV 91913 1311-D3
RUE MONACO
14000 SD 92014 1187-G6
RUE MONTEREAU
12000 SD 92131 1210-B5
RUE MONT GRENOBLE
10300 SD 92131 1210-B4
RUE PARC
600 CHV 91913 1311-D4
12600 SD 92131 1210-C5
RUE RIVIERE VERTE
10300 SD 92131 1210-C4
RUE SAINT JACQUES
10200 SD 92131 1210-B5
RUE SAINT JEAN
1200 SDCo 92069 1128-F4
RUE SAINT LAZARE
12400 SD 92131 1210-B5
RUE SAINT MARTIN
1200 SDCo 92069 1128-C3
RUE SAINT MORITZ
1200 SDCo 92069 1128-F4
RUE SAINT RAPHAEL
14000 SD 92014 1187-G6
RUE SAINT TROPEZ
14000 SD 92014 1187-G6
RUE SAN REMO
14000 SD 92014 1187-G6
RUE SIENNE NORD
12600 SD 92131 1210-C4
RUE TOURAINE
10200 SD 92131 1210-C5
RUETTE ABETO
17300 SD 92127 1169-J1
RUETTE ALLIANTE
12400 SD 92130 1188-A7
RUETTE CAMPANA
17100 SD 92128 1170-B2
RUETTE DE MER
4800 SD 92130 1188-D6
RUETTE DE VILLE
3900 SD 92130 1187-J7
3900 SD 92130 1188-A7
RUETTE LE PARC
13600 SD 92014 1187-J6
RUETTE MONTE CARLO
8500 SD 92037 1227-H4
RUETTE NICE
2500 SD 92037 1227-H4
RUETTE NICOLE
2500 SD 92037 1227-H4

RUETTE PARC LIDO
3400 SD 92154 1350-E1
RUETTE SAN RAPHAEL
- SD 92130 1208-A2
RUE VALBONNE
600 CHV 91913 1311-D3
RUE VINCENNES
12600 SD 92131 1210-C5
RUFFIN CT
9300 SD 92123 1249-E1
RUFFIN RD
3100 SD 92123 1249-E1
3100 SD 92123 1249-E5
5400 SD 92123 1229-E7
9200 SNTE 92071 1231-A5
RUFFNER ST
4300 SD 92111 1249-A1
5100 SD 92111 1229-A7
RUFUS CT
7900 SD 92129 1189-A6
RUGBY CT
9300 SD 92123 1249-E5
RUGER WY
- SDCo 92084 1068-C7
RUIS RD
14300 SDCo 92021 1232-G6
RUJEAN LN
2300 SDCo 92028 1027-H7
RUMEX LN
8400 SD 92129 1189-B6
RUMSON DR
8300 SD 92071 1230-H5
8300 SNTE 92071 1230-H5
8800 SNTE 92071 1231-A5
RUNABOUT PL
2100 SDCo 92019 1272-D3
RUNNER RD
2500 SDCo 91906 (1297-G4 See Page 1296)
RUNNING CREEK LN
9700 SDCo 92026 1049-D7
RUNNING CREEK RD
9700 SDCo 92026 1049-D7
RUNNING CREEK TR
9600 SDCo 92026 1049-D7
RUNNING DEER TR
15300 PWY 92064 1171-C6
RUNNING M RD
3300 SDCo 92004 (1079-A6 See Page 1058)
RUNNING SPRING PL
2200 ENCT 92024 1147-J6
RUNNING STREAM RD
1800 SDCo 92084 1068-B5
RUNNYMEAD LN
900 SD 92106 1288-A2
RUNWAY DR
31900 SDCo 92061 1051-C7
RUNYUN LN
14500 PWY 92064 1190-F1
RUPERTUS DR
- SDCo 92672 1023-D2
RUPP CT
9000 SNTE 92071 1231-A5
RUSH AV
1600 VSTA 92084 1087-H3
E RUSH AV
1600 VSTA 92084 1087-H3
RUSH DR
- SMCS 92078 1128-H2
RUSHDEN AV
4800 SD 92117 1248-G1
RUSH ROSE ST
- CRLB 92024 1147-E2
RUSHVILLE LN
4800 SDCo 91941 1271-E2
RUSHVILLE ST
500 SD 92037 1247-E1
RUSK CV
11500 SD 92126 1209-B1
RUSKIN PL
- SMCS 92069 1109-B5
RUSS BLVD
1100 SD 92101 1289-B2
2300 SD 92102 1289-D2
RUSSAN LN
7000 LMGR 91945 1290-F1
RUSSELIA CT
6700 CRLB 92009 1126-J5
RUSSELL AV
- SD 92140 1268-E7
RUSSELL DR
9400 SD 92093 1228-A2
RUSSELL PL
1500 ESCN 92025 1129-H5
RUSSELL RD
1200 ELCJ 92020 1251-D5
10300 SDCo 91941 1271-E2
RUSSELL SQ
5100 SDCo 91941 1271-E1
RUSSELL ST
- SDCo 92055 1067-A2
3000 SD 92106 1288-C1
3400 SD 92106 1268-C7
RUSSET CT
900 SMCS 92078 1128-F2
RUSSET ST
17200 SDCo 92127 1169-F2
RUSSET LEAF LN
13200 SD 92129 1189-B4
RUSSETT GN
2400 ESCN 92029 1149-G1
RUSSMAR DR
2600 SD 92123 1249-D6
RUSTIC DR
6300 SD 92139 1290-E7
RUSTIC RD
1000 ESCN 92025 1130-A1
RUSTIC CANYON RD
1600 SDCo 92084 1068-B6
RUSTICO DR
7600 CRLB 92009 1147-F1
RUSTIC RANCH RD
20000 SDCo 92065 1152-D1
RUSTIC VILLA RD
20200 SDCo 92065 1152-D1
RUSTYS HACIENDA LN
18400 SDCo 92065 1151-E7
RUTGERS AV
800 CHV 91913 1311-D5
RUTGERS PL
2800 OCN 92056 1087-A7
RUTGERS RD
5400 SD 92037 1247-H3
RUTH AV
- SDCo 91905 1300-C6
RUTH CT
100 ELCJ 92019 1252-A5

RUTHERFORD RD
2200 CRLB 92008 1127-C1
24200 SDCo 92065 1173-E1
24200 SDCo 92065 1153-E7
RUTHERFORD RD Rt#-S26
- ImCo 92227 411-D11
- ImCo 92281 411-C11
900 ImCo 92233 411-C11
RUTHERFORD ST
1300 CHV 91913 1331-B1
RUTHIE WY
1900 SD 92139 1290-E7
RUTHLOR RD
1600 ENCT 92007 1167-E2
RUTHUPHAM AV
700 SD 92154 1330-E7
RUTLEDGE CT
5200 SD 92122 1228-G5
RUTLEDGE SQ
14400 SD 92128 1190-B1
RUTTLES CT
3000 SDCo 91978 1271-F6
RUXTON AV
400 SDCo 91977 1291-A4
RYAN CT
2000 SDCo 92019 1272-C4
RYAN DR
300 SMCS 92069 1128-E1
3100 SDCo 92025 1150-D2
3600 ESCN 92025 1150-D2
RYAN RD
- SD 92106 1288-A6
RYAN WY
- OCN 92054 1106-F1
- SDCo 92026 1109-H2
RYAN RIDGE RD
1300 SDCo 92021 1233-A7
RYANS WY
13200 SDCo 92040 1232-C6
RYDELL PL
- ELCJ 92021 1251-F4
RYDER CT
9600 SNTE 92071 1231-C4
RYDER RD
9600 SNTE 92071 1231-C4
RYDER ST
- SD 92106 1288-A5
RYKER RIDGE RD
500 SDCo 92065 1153-A5
RYNE RD
- SD 92106 1287-J5
RYTKO ST
600 SD 92114 1290-G3

S

S AV
- NATC 91950 1290-A6
S CT
- SD 92126 1209-F7
SABADELL DR
400 OCN 92057 1086-H4
SABINA DR
3000 SD 92139 1310-E2
SABINAS CT
100 SOLB 92075 1167-D7
SABINAS WY
100 SOLB 92075 1167-D7
SABLE CT
5200 OCN 92056 1087-D1
SABRE ST
700 SD 92114 1290-H3
SABRE HILL DR
10700 SD 92128 1189-G5
SABRE SPRINGS PKWY
10100 SD 92128 1189-H5
11400 SD 92128 1190-A6
SABRE VIEW CV
- SD 92128 1189-G5
SABRINA TER
600 SDCo 92065 1152-H6
SABRINA WY
600 VSTA 92084 1087-J7
SACADA CIR
2400 CRLB 92009 1147-G1
SACO ST
14500 PWY 92064 1190-H4
SACRAMENTO AV
200 SDCo 91977 1291-B4
SADDLE DR
3400 SDCo 91977 1271-A5
3700 CRLB 92008 1107-B4
SADDLE RD
500 SDCo 92004 (1078-H2 See Page 1058)
SADDLE WY
1400 OCN 92057 1067-E6
SADDLEBACK DR
9900 SDCo 92040 1232-D3
SADDLEBACK LN
30800 SDCo 92082 1070-J2
SADDLEBACK RD
30400 SDCo 92082 1070-J2
N SADDLEBACK RD
31000 SDCo 92082 1070-J2
SADDLEBACK ST
2500 CHV 91914 1311-G3
SADDLEBACK MOUNTAIN RD
17400 SDCo 92065 1171-F2
SADDLEBROOK CT
15000 PWY 92064 1170-F7
SADDLEBROOK LN
15000 PWY 92064 1170-F7
SADDLE CREEK DR
15000 SDCo 92082 1070-H2
SADDLE CREEK RD
- SDCo 92028 1047-G5
SADDLE HILL RD
9400 SDCo 92021 1232-J4
SADDLEHORN DR
- CHV 91914 1311-G3
1600 SMCS 92069 1108-E5
SADDLE MOUNTAIN CT
4500 SD 92130 1188-C5
SADDLE RIDGE CT
13200 SDCo 92040 1232-C5
SADDLE RIDGE RD
13200 SDCo 92040 1232-C5
SADDLE ROCK RD
9100 SDCo 92040 1232-A6
SADDLERY SQ
5100 SD 92130 1188-D2
SADDLE SORE TR
600 SDCo 92036 1138-C7
SADDLE SUMMIT RD
16000 SDCo 92065 1171-G4

SADDLE VIEW CT
1300 ELCJ 92019 1251-J7
1300 SDCo 92019 1252-A7
SADDLEWOOD DR
2900 SDCo 91902 1310-H1
3000 SDCo 91902 1290-H7
13900 PWY 92064 1190-D3
SADIE ST
9900 SNTE 92071 1231-F4
SAFARI DR
100 ELCJ 92021 1251-H5
SAFARI SQ
- ELCJ 92021 1251-H5
SAFFORD AV
700 SDCo 91977 1291-A3
SAFFRON GN
2400 ESCN 92029 1149-G1
SAFFRON RD
2900 SDCo 92028 1048-B1
SAFFRON WY
2100 SDCo 92028 1048-B1
SAGAMORE WY
- SD 92130 1208-D1
SAGASTI AV
4800 SD 92117 1248-H1
SAGE CT
6900 CRLB 92009 1127-A6
SAGE DR
2400 SDCo 91906 (1297-E5 See Page 1296)
SAGE GN
3100 ESCN 92029 1149-J2
3100 SDCo 92029 1149-J2
SAGE RD
- SDCo 91948 (1217-J3 See Page 1216)
- SDCo 91948 1218-A2
100 SDCo 92021 1252-J2
3200 SDCo 92028 1048-F3
SAGE VW
2800 CHV 91910 1330-J1
SAGE WY
600 SD 92114 1290-D3
3700 OCN 92057 1086-H4
SAGEBRUSH CT
2400 SD 92037 1247-J2
9400 SDCo 92040 1232-C5
SAGEBRUSH RD
5800 SD 92037 1247-J2
5800 SD 92037 1248-A2
SAGEBRUSH WY
1400 OCN 92057 1067-E6
SAGE CANYON DR
- ENCT 92024 1167-G2
SAGE CREEK RD
3600 SDCo 92028 1028-E6
SAGECREST DR
12700 PWY 92064 1170-D7
12700 PWY 92064 1190-C1
SAGEFLOWER DR
3200 SD 92115 1270-D6
SAGE GLEN TR
28400 SDCo 92026 1089-D3
SAGE HILL DR
25300 SDCo 92065 1173-G4
SAGE HILL WY
9500 SDCo 92026 1089-D3
SAGELAND DR
23200 SDCo 92065 1153-D7
SAGE MOUNTAIN LN
13600 SDCo 91935 1292-F2
SAGE SPARROW WY
400 SMCS 92078 1129-B1
SAGE TREE CT
1700 CHV 91913 1311-D6
SAGE VIEW DR
2800 SDCo 91901 1234-C6
SAGE VIEW RD
12100 PWY 92064 1190-B5
SAGEWOOD DR
800 OCN 92057 1087-C2
900 OCN 92056 1087-E2
13400 PWY 92064 1170-E3
SAGEWOOD LN
13700 PWY 92064 1170-F3
SAGEWOOD RD
1900 SDCo 92003 1068-B4
1900 SDCo 92084 1068-B4
SAGEWOOD WY
- SMCS 92078 1128-C6
SAGINA CT
4800 OCN 92057 1067-A7
SAGINAW AV
4200 SD 92117 1248-E2
SAGITTARIUS RD
11000 SD 92126 1209-C2
SAGUARO PL
200 OCN 92057 1067-A7
SAGUARO RD
9400 SDCo 92040 1231-J5
9400 SDCo 92040 1232-A5
SAGUARO WY
7600 SD 92120 1250-C4
SAHARA PL
3400 OCN 92054 1086-F4
SAILFISH LN
- SDCo 92055 1085-H5
SAILFISH PL
900 CRLB 92009 1126-J4
SAINT AGNES CT
12100 SD 92130 1188-B7
SAINT ALBANS DR
900 ENCT 92024 1147-D4
SAINT ALBANS PL
1000 ENCT 92024 1147-D4
SAINT ANDREWS AV
7700 SD 92154 1351-E2
SAINT ANDREWS CT
16900 PWY 92064 1170-E2
SAINT ANDREWS CV
1600 SD 92154 1351-E2
SAINT ANDREWS DR
9300 SNTE 92071 1230-J6
16800 PWY 92064 1170-E1
SAINT ANDREWS PL
4400 OCN 92057 1066-H7
13400 PWY 92064 1170-E1
SAINT ANDREWS RD
6600 SDCo 92067 1168-G7
6600 SDCo 92067 1188-G1
SAINT ANDREWS TER
1600 SD 92154 1351-F2
SAINT ANNE DR
2400 SDCo 92019 1272-B5
SAINT ANNE GN
1800 ESCN 92026 1109-D4
SAINT CHARLES ST
3000 SD 92110 1268-D6

SAINT CHRISTOPHERS LN
- CORD 92118 1329-E2
SAINT CLAIRE DR
1900 CHV 91913 1311-E5
SAINT CROIX CT
2100 LMGR 91945 1270-F7
2100 LMGR 91945 1290-F1
SAINT CROIX DR
2000 SDCo 92004 1058-H7
SAINT DENIS TER
5900 SD 92120 1250-C7
SAINT GEORGE CT
900 SDCo 91977 1291-A3
4200 CRLB 92008 1106-J5
SAINT GEORGE DR
500 SDCo 92019 1253-B2
SAINT GEORGE PL
800 SDCo 91977 1291-A3
SAINT GEORGE ST
8600 SDCo 91977 1291-A3
SAINT GEORGES LN
14200 SDCo 92082 1070-F7
SAINT GERMAIN RD
900 CHV 91913 1311-E5
SAINT HELENA AV
1200 CHV 91913 1331-B1
SAINT HELENA CT
17200 SDCo 92065 1173-E1
SAINT HELENA DR
17200 SDCo 92065 1173-E1
SAINT HELENE CT
1100 OCN 92054 1106-D2
SAINT JAMES CT
1600 CRLB 92008 1106-F5
SAINT JAMES DR
16800 PWY 92064 1170-D2
SAINT JAMES PL
3900 SD 92103 1268-H5
SAINT JOHN PL
8100 LMSA 91942 1250-H7
SAINT JOHNS CRSG
1500 OCN 92028 1067-E1
1500 SDCo 92003 1067-E1
1500 SDCo 92028 1067-E1
SAINT KITTS WY
- CORD 92118 1329-E2
SAINT LAURENT PL
2700 SD 92037 1227-J6
SAINT LOUIS TER
7900 SD 92037 1227-G6
SAINT LUCIA WY
1800 VSTA 92083 1107-G6
SAINT LUCY LN
15400 SDCo 92021 1233-B2
SAINT MALO BEACH
2100 OCN 92054 1106-C4
SAINT MARY CT
- SDCo 92127 1169-A2
SAINT MORITZ TER
11800 SD 92131 1210-A3
SAINT NIKOLA CT
- SDCo 92069 1129-E1
SAINT ONGE DR
8100 LMSA 91942 1270-H1
SAINT PAUL DR
700 SDCo 92069 1129-E1
700 SMCS 92069 1129-E1
SAINT PETERS DR
1700 SDCo 92028 1027-J3
SAINT PETERS WY
1700 SDCo 92028 1027-J3
1700 SDCo 92028 1028-A3
SAINT PIERRE WY
11900 SD 92131 1210-A3
SAINT RITA CT
300 SD 92113 1290-A5
SAINT RITA PL
5000 SD 92113 1290-A4
SAINT SAVA PL
- SDCo 92069 1129-E1
SAINT STEFAN TER
- SDCo 92069 1129-E1
SAINT THERESE WY
5900 SD 92120 1250-C6
SAINT THOMAS DR
2000 SDCo 92004 1058-G7
SAINT THOMAS RD
1800 VSTA 92083 1107-G5
SAINT TROPEZ DR
2000 VSTA 92083 1107-H4
SAINT TROPEZ PL
2600 SD 92037 1227-J6
SAINT VINCENT DR
1900 SDCo 92004 1058-G7
SAIPAN DR
2100 SD 92139 1290-E7
2400 SD 92139 1310-E1
SAIPAN RD
1300 CORD 92118 1309-D5
SAKINA ST
1900 SDCo 92019 1272-C1
SAL LN
1100 VSTA 92084 1088-C4
SAL PL
1700 ESCN 92029 1129-G5
SALACOT CT
5800 SD 92124 1229-H7
SALAMANCA CT
100 SOLB 92075 1167-D7
SALEM CT
700 SD 92109 1267-H1
1400 OCN 92057 1066-J4
1400 OCN 92057 1067-B4
SALEM PL
4500 CRLB 92008 1107-B4
SALEM ST
800 SDCo 92084 1088-F7
800 SDCo 92084 1108-F1
SALERNO CT
1200 OCN 92056 1087-C3
SALERNO ST
6600 SD 92111 1248-J3
7400 SD 92111 1249-A3
SALET PL
- SMCS 92069 1109-A5
SALIDA DEL LUNA
16400 SDCo 92065 1171-C2
SALIDA DEL SOL
15800 SDCo 92065 1171-B2
SALIENTE WY
2100 CRLB 92009 1147-F1
SALINA CT
300 VSTA 92083 1087-E7
SALINA ST
800 ELCJ 92020 1251-G7
SALINA CRUZ CT
100 SOLB 92075 1167-D6

SALINAS ST
- OCN 92057 1066-H7
- OCN 92057 1086-H1
SALINAS WY
10900 SD 92126 1209-A3
SALISBURY DR
2200 SD 92123 1249-B7
2600 CRLB 92008 1106-J5
SALIX CT
12100 SD 92129 1189-A7
SALIX PL
7600 SD 92129 1189-A7
SALIX WY
12100 SD 92129 1189-A7
SALIZAR CT
6400 SD 92111 1248-H3
SALIZAR ST
6500 SD 92111 1248-H3
7400 SD 92111 1249-A3
SALK AV
1900 CRLB 92008 1127-C1
SALK INSTITUTE RD
2700 SD 92037 1227-J1
SALLISAW CT
5900 SD 92120 1250-C5
SALLY PL
1700 ESCN 92026 1109-D5
SALMON LN
400 OCN 92054 1086-G2
SALMON RD
200 SDCo 92065 1153-B5
SALMON ST
3000 SD 92124 1249-G5
SALMON RIVER RD
12400 SD 92129 1189-E4
SALOT ST
700 NATC 91950 1290-C7
SALTA PL
3300 SD 92105 1270-A6
SALT AIR LN
900 SDCo 92028 1027-G1
SALTAIRE WY
- CRLB 92009 1127-A4
SALTBUSH LN
1200 SDCo 92019 1252-F7
1300 SDCo 92019 1272-F1
SALT CREEK RD
1500 CHV 91915 1311-J6
1800 CHV 91915 1331-J1
SALTILLO CT
100 SOLB 92075 1167-D6
SALT MINE RD
17100 SDCo 92065 1171-F2
SALTON DR
- ImCo 92274 410-H7
SALTON BAY DR
- ImCo 92259 410-H6
- ImCo 92274 410-H6
SALTON VIEW DR
2100 SDCo 92036 1136-C6
SALTON VISTA DR
700 SDCo 92036 1156-E1
2500 SDCo 92036 1136-D7
SALUDA AV
10200 SD 92126 1209-C5
SALUTO CT
4500 SD 92130 1188-C7
SALVIA WY
12200 SD 92129 1189-A7
SAM LN
17100 SDCo 92065 1171-G2
SAMAGATUMA VALLEY RD
- SDCo 91916 1236-G3
SAMANTHA AV
13300 SD 92129 1189-D3
SAMANTHA CT
9200 SD 92129 1189-D4
SAMANTHA LN
8600 SDCo 91977 1270-J7
SAMAR ST
- SD 92140 1268-E6
SAMARA WY
800 CRLB 92009 1127-A6
SAMBROSA PL
16500 SD 92128 1170-C3
SAMOA ST
- SD 92140 1268-F6
SAMOA WY
1800 OCN 92054 1106-E1
SAM-O-RENO RD
13900 PWY 92064 1190-G4
SAMOSET AV
4200 SD 92117 1248-E2
SAMPLE ST
10200 SD 92124 1249-G5
SAMPSON RD
1700 SD 92133 1288-D1
SAMPSON ST
200 SD 92113 1289-D6
SAMS HILL RD
1300 SDCo 92021 1251-G2
SAMS MOUNTAIN RD
32200 SDCo 92061 1051-C6
SAMUEL ST
5800 LMSA 91942 1250-H7
SAN ABELLA DR
1000 ENCT 92024 1147-E7
SAN ALBERTO WY
300 SD 92114 1290-A5
SAN ALTOS PL
1300 LMGR 91945 1290-F2
1300 SD 92114 1290-F2
SAN ANDRADE DR
1000 ENCT 92024 1147-E7
SAN ANDRES DR
500 SOLB 92075 1167-G7
6100 SOLB 92014 1167-G7
13100 SOLB 92014 1187-H1
15700 SD 92014 1187-H1
SAN ANDRES ST
9100 SDCo 91977 1291-B4
SAN ANGELO AV
6100 LMSA 91942 1251-A6
6100 SD 92119 1251-A6
SAN ANGELO PL
700 CHV 91914 1311-G3
SAN ANSELMO ST
2500 SD 92109 1248-C4
SAN ANTONIO AV
300 SD 92106 1288-A4
SAN ANTONIO PL
800 SD 92106 1288-B3
SAN ANTONIO WY
10900 SDCo 92082 1049-F2
SAN ANTONIO ROSE CT
- SDCo 92127 1149-A7
- SDCo 92127 1169-A1

SAN AQUARIO DR
5000 SD 92109 1248-B3
SAN ARDO CV
4000 SD 92130 1188-B7
SAN AUGUSTINE WY
3900 SD 92130 1188-B7
SAN BARTOLO
7000 CRLB 92009 1126-J6
7300 CRLB 92009 1127-A6
SAN BENITO
7200 CRLB 92009 1126-J7
7300 CRLB 92009 1127-A7
SAN BENITO CT
1400 SOLB 92014 1167-H7
SAN BENITO RD
700 SDCo 92004 (1079-A7 See Page 1058)
SAN BERNARDINO AV
1000 SDCo 91977 1291-D2
SAN BERNARDO TER
5200 SD 92114 1290-B5
SAN BLAS CIR
10900 SD 92126 1209-D3
SANBORN RD
- ImCo 92227 411-D11
SAN BRILLO DR
500 OCN 92054 1086-F2
SAN BRISTO WY
2900 CRLB 92009 1147-H2
SAN BRUNO CV
4000 SD 92130 1188-B6
SAN BRUNO PL
- CHV 91914 1311-G3
SANCADO TER
500 SDCo 92028 1027-E3
SAN CARLOS
7000 CRLB 92009 1126-J6
SAN CARLOS CT
10300 SDCo 91978 1271-E6
SAN CARLOS DR
500 OCN 92054 1086-F2
3200 SDCo 91978 1271-F6
7900 SD 92119 1250-H5
SAN CARLOS PL
1400 ESCN 92026 1109-E5
SAN CARLOS RD
700 SDCo 92004 (1079-A7 See Page 1058)
SAN CARLOS ST
9200 SDCo 91977 1291-B4
SAN CLEMENTE AV
2200 VSTA 92084 1088-D6
SAN CLEMENTE ST
2100 SD 92107 1268-B7
SAN CLEMENTE TER
2500 SD 92122 1228-B7
SAN CLEMENTE WY
200 VSTA 92084 1088-D6
300 SDCo 92084 1088-D6
SAN COLLA ST
300 SD 92037 1247-F4
SAN CRISTOBAL RD
9800 SDCo 91941 1271-D4
9800 SDCo 91977 1271-D4
SANDAL LN
1400 SD 92037 1247-J3
SANDALWOOD CT
- ENCT 92024 1147-E5
SANDALWOOD DR
- CHV 91910 1310-C5
400 ELCJ 92021 1251-G4
1200 ELCN 92243 6559-E1
SANDALWOOD LN
1500 CRLB 92008 1106-F5
SANDAL WOOD PL
500 ESCN 92027 1110-D6
SANDALWOOD PL
5200 OCN 92056 1087-D1
SANDALWOOD WY
4700 OCN 92057 1087-B3
SAND ASTER CIR
32000 SDCo 91906 (1318-B6 See Page 1298)
SAND ASTER DR
- CRLB 92009 1127-D6
SANDBAR DR
- SMCS 92078 1128-C5
SANDBAR WY
800 CRLB 92009 1126-J5
SANDBURG AV
5400 SD 92122 1228-C6
SANDBURG CT
3000 SD 92122 1228-C6
SANDBURG WY
3000 SD 92122 1228-C6
SANDCASTLE DR
800 ENCT 92007 1167-E2
6700 CRLB 92009 1126-J6
6700 CRLB 92009 1127-A6
SANDCASTLE WY
1900 OCN 92054 1106-F1
SAND CRAB PL
- SD 92130 1208-B4
SAND CREST DR
- ImCo 92274 410-H7
SAND CREST WY
- SMCS 92069 1128-A2
SANDDOLLAR CT
5200 SD 92130 1188-D6
SAND DOLLAR WY
- SMCS 92069 1128-A3
SAND DUNE WY
- SMCS 92078 1128-D5
SANDEL DR
300 VSTA 92083 1087-G5
SANDER CT
1100 ESCN 92026 1110-A7
SANDERLING CT
1600 CRLB 92009 1127-E7
SANDERS CT
6600 SD 92119 1250-F5
SANDHILL CT
5200 SD 92130 1188-D5
SAND HILL RD
14200 PWY 92064 1170-G5
SANDHILL TER
5200 SD 92130 1188-D5
SANDHURST WY
28400 SDCo 92026 1089-D4
SANDIA PL
5500 SD 92124 1249-H1
SANDIA CREEK DR
38200 SDCo 92028 997-F2
40300 SDCo 92028 409-B4
E SANDIA CREEK TER
4000 RivC 92590 997-G1
4000 SDCo 92028 997-G1
W SANDIA CREEK TER
3600 SDCo 92028 997-F1

SAN DIEGO AV | SAN DIEGO CO. STREET INDEX | SATANAS ST 6616

STREET Block City ZIP Pg-Grid

SAN DIEGO AV
300 ELCN 92243 6499-H5
1700 SD 92103 1268-G6
1700 SD 92110 1268-F5
1900 SDCo 92065 1172-E1
SAN DIEGO FRWY I-5
- CHV - 1309-H4
- CHV - 1329-J1
- CHV - 1330-A3
- CRLB - 1106-F6
- CRLB - 1126-G2
- CRLB - 1127-A6
- CRLB - 1147-A1
- ENCT - 1147-C5
- ENCT - 1167-D2
- NATC - 1289-C2
- NATC - 1309-G1
- OCN - 1085-G2
- OCN - 1086-A6
- OCN - 1106-C1
- SCLE - 1023-E3
- SD - 1187-H2
- SD - 1207-J1
- SD - 1208-A3
- SD - 1228-B4
- SD - 1248-B2
- SD - 1268-E3
- SD - 1288-J1
- SD - 1289-C2
- SD - 1330-A6
- SD - 1350-D3
- SDCo - 408-H5
- SDCo - 1023-E3
- SDCo - 1085-G2
- SOLB - 1167-D2
- SOLB - 1187-H2
SAN DIEGO PL
1000 SD 92109 1267-J4
SAN DIEGO ST
100 OCN 92054 1086-B6
9200 SDCo 91977 1291-B4
SAN DIEGO CORONADO FERRY
- SD 92101 1288-H4
SAN DIEGO MISSION RD
9400 SD 92108 1249-F7
SAN DIEGUITO DR
500 ENCT 92024 1147-C7
600 ENCT 92024 1167-C1
1400 DLMR 92014 1187-G3
SAN DIEGUITO RD
3700 SD 92130 1188-B2
3900 SD 92067 1188-D1
7200 SDCo 92067 1168-E7
10100 SDCo 92067 1188-D1
SAN DIMAS AV
200 OCN 92057 1086-G3
6000 SD 92111 1268-G2
SAN DIMAS CT
1100 CHV 91913 1311-C7
SAN DIONICIO ST
600 SD 92106 1288-A3
SANDLEFORD WY
6900 SD 92139 1290-F7
SANDLER CT
- SDCo 91901 1234-B3
SANDLEWOOD CT
3300 SD 92037 1228-B4
SANDLEWOOD DR
400 ELCN 92243 6559-H1
SANDMARK AV
8800 SD 92123 1249-C7
SAN DOMINGO
- VSTA 92083 1107-C2
SANDOR WY
3500 SDCo 92084 1088-F7
SANDOS ST
1600 ELCJ 92019 1252-B7
SANDOVAL CIR
2000 ImCo 92243 6500-H4
SANDOVAL LN
600 ImCo 92243 6500-H4
SANDOVER CT
2800 SDCo 91902 1290-J7
SANDOWN CT
14300 PWY 92064 1190-E2
SANDOWN WY
- SD 92130 1188-E5
SANDPIPER AV
- SDCo 92055 1023-E3
SANDPIPER PL
900 SD 92037 1247-G3
3500 OCN 92056 1107-C2
SAND PIPER PL
6900 CRLB 92009 1127-E5
SANDPIPER WY
400 CHV 91910 1309-H7
400 CHV 91910 1329-H1
SANDPIPER STRAND
- CORD 92118 1329-E1
SANDPOINT CT
3700 CRLB 92008 1107-B3
SANDRA CIR
1200 VSTA 92083 1108-A1
SANDROCK RD
3100 SD 92123 1249-C4
SANDS PL
100 OCN 92054 1086-F5
SANDSHORE CT
4900 SD 92130 1188-D6
SANDSTONE CIR
1500 SDCo 92004 1058-H5
SANDSTONE CT
300 CHV 91911 1330-G4
SANDSTONE DR
8500 SNTE 92071 1230-H7
8500 SNTE 92071 1250-H1
SANDSTONE ST
200 CHV 91910 1330-G4
SANDSTONE WY
- CRLB 92008 1107-B3
SANDSTONE VISTA LN
1900 ENCT 92024 1147-H7
SAND TRAP CT
2300 OCN 92056 1106-J2
SANDTRAP RW
12100 SD 92128 1170-A4
SANDY AV
600 ELCN 92243 6499-H4
SANDY CT
200 OCN 92054 1085-J6
SANDY LN
600 SMCS 92078 1129-A2
1100 VSTA 92083 1108-A5
2900 DLMR 92014 1187-F2
SANDY PL
3100 CRLB 92008 1106-G4

SANDY ST
300 ELCJ 92020 1251-F6
SANDY BEV LN
8600 SDCo 91945 1270-J6
8600 SDCo 91977 1270-J6
8600 SDCo 91977 1271-A6
SANDY CREEK
- SDCo 92036 1175-J2
SANDY CREEK DR
400 CHV 91902 1311-A3
SANDY CREST CT
12600 SD 92130 1188-D6
SANDY HILL DR
29300 SDCo 92026 1069-A7
SANDY HOOK RD
10800 SDCo 92126 1209-A3
SANDY POINTE
2900 DLMR 92014 1187-F3
SANDY SHORE CT
- SD 92139 1290-D7
SANDY SHORE ST
1700 SD 92139 1290-D6
SAN ELIJO
4800 SDCo 92067 1168-D1
SAN ELIJO AV
1300 ENCT 92007 1167-C2
SAN ELIJO RD
1500 CRLB 92078 1128-B6
1500 SMCS 92024 1128-B6
1500 SMCS 92078 1128-B6
SAN ELIJO ST
300 SD 92106 1288-A4
SAN FELIPE PL
300 SD 92114 1290-H3
SAN FELIPE RD Rt#-S2
21300 SDCo 92036 410-A10
22300 SDCo 92086 410-A10
25600 SDCo 92086 409-K9
29000 SDCo 92070 409-K9
SAN FELIPE ST
8000 SD 92114 1290-H4
SAN FELIPE WY
27500 SDCo 92086 409-K9
SAN FERNANDO PL
700 SD 92109 1267-H3
SAN FERNANDO ST
200 SD 92106 1288-A4
SANFORD DR
7800 LMGR 91945 1290-H2
SANFORD LN
200 ENCT 92024 1147-B3
2800 CRLB 92008 1107-A4
SANFORD ST
100 ENCT 92024 1147-A3
SAN FRANCISCO ST
8800 SDCo 91977 1291-A3
SANFRED CT
10600 SNTE 92071 1231-D2
SAN GABRIEL DR
3600 OCN 92054 1086-F2
SAN GABRIEL PL
700 CHV 91914 1311-F3
700 SD 92109 1267-H3
SAN GABRIEL WY
10800 SDCo 92082 1049-F4
SANGALLO LN
9500 SDCo 92127 1169-E2
SANGAMON AV
1000 SDCo 91977 1291-D2
SANGER PL
- SD 92173 1350-F4
SAN GERONIMO DR
32700 SDCo 92082 1049-J5
SAN GORGONIO ST
300 SD 92106 1288-A4
SAN GREGORIO WY
3900 SD 92130 1188-B7
SAN HELENA DR
3100 OCN 92056 1086-J7
SANIBELLE CIR
400 CHV 91910 1310-F6
SAN IGNACIO
1400 SOLB 92075 1167-H7
SAN JACINTO CIR
5200 SDCo 92028 1047-E6
SAN JACINTO CIR E
4900 SDCo 92028 1047-F6
SAN JACINTO CIR W
4900 SDCo 92028 1047-E6
N SAN JACINTO DR
100 SD 92114 1290-B4
SAN JACINTO GN
1100 ESCN 92026 1109-E5
SAN JACINTO PL
600 CHV 91914 1311-F3
5200 SD 92114 1290-B4
SAN JACINTO RD
- SDCo 92055 1085-J4
- SDCo 92055 1086-A5
SAN JACINTO TER
4700 SDCo 92028 1047-F6
SAN JOAQUIN CT
2500 SD 92109 1248-C4
SAN JOAQUIN DR
4800 SD 92109 1248-B4
SAN JOAQUIN ST
600 OCN 92057 1086-G1
4400 OCN 92057 1066-H7
SAN JOSE CT
600 CHV 91914 1311-G3
SAN JOSE PL
700 SD 92109 1267-H1
SAN JOSE ST
1500 OCN 92054 1086-A5
SAN JUAN DR
- SMCS 92069 1128-E2
SAN JUAN PL
700 CHV 91914 1311-G3
700 SD 92109 1267-H1
900 OCN 92054 1086-A5
9100 LMSA 91941 1271-B3
9100 SDCo 91941 1271-B3
SAN JUAN RD
- SDCo 92055 408-K6
2200 SD 92103 1268-G5
2200 SD 92110 1268-G5
SAN JUAN ST
1000 OCN 92054 1086-B5
9700 SDCo 91977 1271-D5
SAN JUAN WY
- SMCS 92078 1129-C1
SAN JUHN ST
600 SDCo 91977 1291-C3
SAN JULIAN DR
1000 SDCo 92069 1128-D3
SAN JULIAN LN
1300 SDCo 92069 1128-D3

SAN JULIAN PL
1200 SDCo 92069 1128-D3
SAN JULIO RD
600 SOLB 92014 1167-H7
600 SOLB 92075 1167-H7
SAN LEANDRO WY
3900 SD 92130 1188-B7
SAN LEON CT
1100 SOLB 92075 1167-H5
3500 SDCo 92004 (1079-A7 See Page 1058)
SAN LEON RD
700 SDCo 92004 (1079-A7 See Page 1058)
SANLIN DR
1500 SDCo 92019 1272-A1
SAN LORENZO CT
900 SOLB 92075 1167-H5
3900 OCN 92057 1086-H4
SAN LORI LN
1100 SDCo 92019 1252-B7
1100 SDCo 92019 1272-A1
SAN LUCAS
7200 CRLB 92009 1126-J7
SAN LUCAS CT
1300 SOLB 92075 1167-H7
SAN LUCAS DR
300 SOLB 92075 1167-J7
500 SOLB 92014 1167-J7
500 SOLB 92014 1187-J1
SAN LUCAS PL
500 CHV 91914 1311-F3
SAN LUIS
7200 CRLB 92009 1126-H5
7300 CRLB 92009 1127-A7
SAN LUIS AV
100 OCN 92057 1086-G2
SAN LUIS ST
700 SD 92102 1289-D3
SAN LUIS OBISPO DR
3600 OCN 92054 1086-F3
SAN LUIS OBISPO PL
700 SD 92109 1267-H2
SAN LUIS REY AV
800 CORD 92118 1288-J7
1500 VSTA 92084 1087-H3
SAN LUIS REY DR
500 OCN 92054 1085-J6
700 OCN 92054 1086-A5
11100 SDCo 92082 1049-F3
SAN LUIS REY PL
700 SD 92109 1267-H4
SAN LUIS REY RD
2900 OCN 92054 1086-D5
SAN LUIS REY MSSN EXWY Rt#-76
800 OCN 92054 1085-J6
800 OCN 92054 1086-A5
SAN MARCOS AV
2400 SD 92104 1289-E1
2500 SD 92104 1269-E7
E SAN MARCOS BLVD
100 SMCS 92069 1108-H7
W SAN MARCOS BLVD Rt#-S12
200 SMCS 92069 1108-H7
300 SMCS 92069 1128-A2
SAN MARCOS PL
100 CHV 91911 1330-F2
SAN MARINO DR
900 SDCo 92069 1128-C3
SAN MARINO PL
- CHV 91914 1311-G3
SAN MARIO DR
500 SOLB 92075 1167-J5
SAN MARTIN
- SDCo 92040 1232-B7
SAN MARTINE WY
3900 SD 92130 1188-B7
SAN MATEO DR
5400 SD 92114 1290-B5
SAN MATEO RD
- SDCo 92055 408-J5
SAN MATEO ST
1500 OCN 92054 1086-A5
SAN MATEO POINT CT
1500 CHV 91911 1330-J4
SAN MIGUEL
7200 CRLB 92009 1126-J7
SAN MIGUEL AV
1000 SDCo 91977 1291-C2
4100 SD 92113 1289-H5
6600 LMGR 91945 1270-E7
6800 SDCo 91902 1291-D7
S SAN MIGUEL AV
500 SD 92113 1289-H5
SAN MIGUEL CT
100 CHV 91911 1330-D1
3500 NATC 91902 1310-E3
3900 OCN 92057 1086-H3
SAN MIGUEL DR
- CHV 91911 1330-C1
1100 SMCS 92069 1128-E2
E SAN MIGUEL DR
- CHV 91911 1330-D1
SAN MIGUEL RD
5400 SDCo 91902 1310-J1
5400 SDCo 91902 1311-A1
5900 SDCo 91902 1291-B7
SAN MIGUEL ST
600 SDCo 91977 1291-C3
SAN MIGUEL WY
3300 SDCo 91902 1311-A1
SAN MORITZ
15300 PWY 92064 1170-D6
SAN ONOFRE TER
5300 SD 92114 1290-B5
SAN PABLO AV
3800 OCN 92057 1086-G4
SAN PABLO CT
1300 SDCo 92004 (1079-A7 See Page 1058)
1300 SDCo 92069 1128-D3
SAN PABLO DR
800 SDCo 92069 1128-D2
800 SMCS 92069 1128-D2
SAN PABLO PL
- CHV 91914 1311-F3
SAN PABLO RD
700 SDCo 92004 (1079-A7 See Page 1058)
700 SDCo 92004 (1099-A1 See Page 1098)
SAN PABLO WY
900 SDCo 92069 1128-D2
SAN PASCUAL SCHOOL RD
- ImCo 92283 432-C5

SAN PASQUAL CT
2000 LMGR 91945 1290-F1
SAN PASQUAL RD
- SD 92027 1130-G7
700 ESCN 92025 1150-C2
2900 SD 92025 1130-G7
2900 SD 92025 1150-E2
2900 SDCo 92025 1130-G7
5500 SDCo 92025 1150-E2
14400 SDCo 92027 1130-G7
SAN PASQUAL ST
500 SD 92113 1289-H5
7200 LMGR 91945 1290-F1
SAN PASQUAL TR
14200 SDCo 92025 1130-F6
SAN PASQUAL WY
14300 SDCo 92025 1130-F6
SAN PASQUAL VALLEY RD Rt#-78
100 ESCN 92027 1130-B2
100 ESCN 92025 1130-B2
800 SDCo 92025 1130-B2
800 SDCo 92027 1130-B2
1400 SDCo 92065 1152-C1
2100 SD 92065 409-G11
2100 SDCo 92027 409-G11
2100 SDCo 92065 409-G11
2100 SD 92027 409-G11
2400 SD 92027 1130-G6
3500 SD 92025 1131-A6
3500 SD 92065 1131-F6
3500 SD 92027 1131-A6
16100 SDCo 92027 1131-F6
16100 SDCo 92025 1131-F6
SAN PATRICIO DR
1000 SOLB 92075 1167-H6
SAN PEDRO ST
6000 SD 92111 1268-G2
SAN PEDRO POINT CT
1500 CHV 91911 1330-J3
SAN PLACIDO CT
400 ESCN 92029 1150-A4
SAN RAFAEL DR
1300 OCN 92054 1085-J5
1600 SDCo 92055 1085-J5
SAN RAFAEL PL
700 CHV 91914 1311-G3
700 SD 92109 1247-H7
SAN RAFAEL RD
3300 SDCo 92004 (1079-A6 See Page 1058)
SAN RAMON
7200 CRLB 92009 1126-J7
SAN RAMON DR
3700 OCN 92057 1086-G3
10100 SD 92126 1209-C5
E SAN RAPHAEL DR
- SD 92130 1208-A2
W SAN RAPHAEL DR
- SD 92130 1208-A2
SAN REMO CIR
2200 SDCo 92084 1108-C2
SAN REMO CT
9700 SNTE 92071 1231-D4
SAN REMO DR
2000 OCN 92056 1086-J7
SAN REMO RD
9700 SNTE 92071 1231-D4
SAN REMO WY
400 SD 92106 1288-A4
SAN REY CT
4700 SDCo 92028 1048-H4
SAN REY LN
3300 SDCo 92028 1048-H3
SAN REY PL
4700 SDCo 92028 1048-H4
SAN RICARDO CT
1100 SOLB 92075 1167-H5
SAN RODOLFO DR
600 SOLB 92075 1167-F7
SAN ROQUE DR
300 SDCo 92025 1130-B6
SAN RUFO CT
- SDCo 92127 1169-F4
SAN SALVADOR CT
16600 SD 92128 1170-B3
SAN SALVADOR RD
16500 SD 92128 1170-B3
SAN SEBASTIAN AV
- CHV 91913 1311-E6
SAN SEBASTIAN WY
13900 PWY 92064 1170-F7
SAN SIMEON ST
1400 OCN 92054 1086-B4
SANS SOUCI DR
3100 ESCN 92029 1149-F1
3100 SDCo 92029 1149-F1
SANTA ALICIA
400 SOLB 92075 1167-G6
SANTA ALICIA AV
- CHV 91913 1331-C1
SANTA ANA DR
1500 SD 92110 1268-G2
1500 SD 92111 1268-G2
SANTA ANDREA ST
- CHV 91913 1331-C1
SANTA ANGELA CT
2600 CHV 91914 1311-G2
SANTA ANITA CT
600 CHV 91914 1311-G2
SANTA ANITA DR
100 VSTA 92084 1087-J7
1600 SD 92111 1268-G2
SANTA ANITA ST
1000 OCN 92054 1086-A5
SANTA ANTONIO DR
3600 OCN 92054 1086-F2
SANTA ARMINTA AV
7900 SD 92126 1209-B2
SANTA ASIS DR
3600 OCN 92054 1086-F3
SANTA BARBARA
7100 CRLB 92009 1126-J6
7300 CRLB 92009 1127-A7
SANTA BARBARA CT
2600 CHV 91914 1311-G2
SANTA BARBARA DR
- SMCS 92078 1128-G3
SANTA BARBARA PL
700 SD 92109 1267-H2
SANTA BARBARA ST
200 OCN 92054 1086-B6
1000 SD 92107 1287-J1
1500 SD 92107 1267-J7
1600 SD 92107 1268-A7
SANTA BARBARA WY
100 VSTA 92083 1087-E7
SANTA BARTOLA
400 SOLB 92075 1167-G6

SANTA CAMELIA DR
600 SOLB 92075 1167-J5
SANTA CARINA
500 SOLB 92075 1167-H5
700 ENCT 92007 1167-H5
E SANTA CARINA
- CHV 91913 1331-B2
SANTA CATALINA RD
12300 SDCo 92082 1049-H5
SANTA CATERINA TR
- SDCo 92004 410-B6
- SDCo 92004 1058-H1
SANTA CECELIA
400 SOLB 92075 1167-G6
SANTA CHRISTINA CT
2400 SD 92154 1330-B7
SANTA CLARA
400 OCN 92054 1086-F2
SANTA CLARA CT
600 CHV 91914 1311-G2
SANTA CLARA DR
100 VSTA 92083 1087-E7
SANTA CLARA PL
700 SD 92109 1267-H1
SANTA CLARA WY
3400 CRLB 92008 1106-H4
SANTA CORA AV
1200 CHV 91913 1311-D6
SANTA CORINA CT
- SDCo 92127 1169-F4
SANTA CRISTOBAL ST
16400 SDCo 92127 1169-F4
SANTA CRUZ
7100 CRLB 92009 1126-J6
SANTA CRUZ AV
3800 SD 92107 1288-A1
4000 SD 92107 1268-A7
4400 SD 92107 1267-H6
SANTA CRUZ CT
1300 CHV 91910 1311-B7
SANTA CRUZ DR
3600 OCN 92054 1086-F2
SANTA DELORES DR
3600 OCN 92054 1086-F3
SANTA DELPHINA AV
1100 CHV 91913 1311-D6
SANTA DOMINGA
400 SOLB 92075 1167-G6
SANTA ELENA CT
1500 SOLB 92075 1167-J6
SANTA ESTELLA
900 SOLB 92075 1167-G5
SANTA FE AV
100 SDCo 92055 1085-H5
1000 ESCN 92025 1129-G3
1800 DLMR 92014 1187-F4
N SANTA FE AV
800 OCN 92057 1067-C7
N SANTA FE AV Rt#-S14
300 VSTA 92083 1087-G2
300 VSTA 92084 1087-G2
800 OCN 92057 1067-C7
800 OCN 92056 1087-D1
800 OCN 92057 1087-D1
2200 SDCo 92083 1087-G2
2200 SDCo 92084 1087-G2
2200 OCN 92084 1087-G2
2200 VSTA 92056 1087-G2
S SANTA FE AV Rt#-S14
100 VSTA 92083 1087-H7
100 VSTA 92084 1087-H7
1000 VSTA 92084 1088-A7
1000 VSTA 92084 1108-B2
1000 VSTA 92083 1088-A7
1000 VSTA 92083 1108-B2
1400 SDCo 92084 1108-B2
1400 SDCo 92083 1108-B2
2600 SMCS 92069 1108-C4
SANTA FE DR
- ENCT 92007 1167-E1
100 ENCT 92024 1167-E1
SANTA FE PL
100 VSTA 92083 1087-J7
SANTA FE ST
4700 SD 92109 1248-C3
4700 SD 92117 1248-B1
SANTA FE TR
300 SDCo 92004 1058-G6
SANTA FE DOWNS SQ
2600 SD 92014 1187-J2
SANTA FE VISTA CT
2800 ENCT 92024 1148-A6
SANTA FLORA CT
3500 ESCN 92029 1150-A3
SANTA FLORA RD
1600 CHV 91913 1311-C7
SANTA FLORENCIA
700 SOLB 92075 1167-G5
1000 ENCT 92007 1167-G5
SANTA GABRIELLA
1000 SOLB 92075 1167-H5
SANTA HELENA
200 SOLB 92075 1167-G6
SANTA HELENA PARK CT
900 SOLB 92075 1167-G6
SANTA HIDALGA
800 SOLB 92075 1167-G5
SANTA INES WY
300 OCN 92057 1087-A2
SANTA INEZ
800 SOLB 92075 1167-G5
SANTA ISABEL DR
700 SD 92114 1290-B5
SANTA ISABEL ST
6600 CRLB 92009 1127-H5
SANTA LUCIA
13500 SDCo 92021 1232-E7
SANTA LUCIA RD
- CHV 91913 1331-B1
1200 CHV 91913 1311-C7
SANTA LUISA DR
1100 SOLB 92075 1167-H5
SANTA LUNA CT
3600 SMCS 92069 1108-D7
SANTA MADERA AV
1100 CHV 91913 1311-C7
SANTA MADERA CT
1100 SOLB 92075 1167-H6
SANTA MARGARITA DR
900 SDCo 92028 1027-G1
1100 SDCo 92028 997-G6
SANTA MARGARITA ST
5200 SD 92114 1290-B4
SANTA MARIA
1200 CHV 91913 1331-B1

SANTA MARIA AV
11300 SDCo 92040 1212-A7
SANTA MARIA CT
100 VSTA 92083 1087-G6
2600 CHV 91914 1311-G2
SANTA MARIA DR
- SMCS 92069 1128-E2
7300 LMSA 91941 1270-F3
SANTA MARIA ST
3500 OCN 92056 1106-J2
3500 OCN 92056 1107-A2
SANTA MARIA TER
5200 SD 92114 1290-B5
SANTA MARIANA CT
- SDCo 92127 1169-F4
SANTA MARINA CT
400 ESCN 92029 1150-A3
SANTA MARTA CT
1400 SOLB 92075 1167-J5
SANTA MONICA AV
4300 SD 92107 1268-A6
4600 SD 92107 1267-J6
SANTANA ST
10200 SNTE 92071 1231-E2
SANTANA RANCH DR
10300 SNTE 92071 1231-E3
SANTANA RANCH LN
10000 SNTE 92071 1231-E3
SANTA NELLA PL
3900 SD 92130 1188-B7
SANTANELLA ST
- SDCo 92127 1169-F4
SANTA OLIVIA
700 SOLB 92075 1167-G5
1100 CHV 91913 1331-A1
SANTA PAULA
700 SOLB 92075 1167-G5
SANTA PAULA DR
- CHV 91913 1311-E6
1600 SD 92111 1268-G2
SANTA PAULA ST
800 OCN 92054 1086-A5
SANTA PETRA DR
1400 SOLB 92075 1167-J5
SANTA QUETA
900 SOLB 92075 1167-G5
SANTAR AV
7100 SD 92119 1250-F3
SANTAR PL
100 SMCS 92069 1109-A7
SANTA REGINA
800 SOLB 92075 1167-G6
SANTA RITA
1300 CHV 91913 1331-C1
SANTA RITA E
1400 CHV 91913 1331-C1
SANTA RITA W
1400 CHV 91913 1331-C1
SANTA RITA PL
700 SD 92109 1247-H7
SANTA ROSA
1800 ImCo 92243 6499-D6
7200 CRLB 92009 1126-J6
SANTA ROSA DR
- CHV 91913 1311-E6
- SDCo 92055 1086-A4
SANTA ROSA RD
1300 SDCo 92004 1058-H4
SANTA ROSA ST
1400 OCN 92054 1086-B4
SANTA ROSALIA DR
200 SD 92114 1290-A5
SANTA ROSALINA CT
400 ESCN 92029 1149-J3
SANTA ROSITA
600 SOLB 92075 1167-G5
SANTA RUFINA CT
1100 SOLB 92075 1167-H5
SANTA RUFINA DR
700 SOLB 92075 1167-H5
SANTA SABA CT
800 SDCo 92004 (1079-A7 See Page 1058)
SANTA SABA RD
3400 SDCo 92004 (1079-A7 See Page 1058)
SANTA SABINA CT
1500 SOLB 92075 1167-J5
SANTA TERESITA CT
500 ESCN 92029 1149-J3
SANTA THERESA
600 SOLB 92075 1167-H6
SANTA THERESA PL
500 CHV 91914 1311-G2
SANTA TOMASA AV
- SDCo 92127 1169-F4
SANTA VALERA CT
- SDCo 92127 1169-F4
SANTA VELA DR
400 OCN 92054 1086-F3
SANTA VICTORIA
400 SOLB 92075 1167-H5
SANTA VIRGINIA DR
13000 SDCo 92082 1049-J5
13000 SDCo 92082 1050-A5
SANTA YNEZ AV
- CHV 91913 1331-B1
SANTA YNEZ WY
3700 OCN 92056 1107-B1
SANTA YSABEL GN
2000 ESCN 92026 1109-E5
SANTA YSABEL TKTR
- SDCo 92065 409-H10
SANTEE LN
18600 SDCo 92082 1091-F3
SANTEE LAKES BLVD
10400 SNTE 92071 1231-A2
SANTIAGO AV
- SD 92140 1268-G7
SANTIAGO RD E
12300 SD 92128 1170-B3
SANTIAGO RD W
12100 SD 92128 1170-B3
SANTO RD
2300 SD 92124 1249-G3
2300 SD 92120 1249-G6
5400 SD 92124 1229-H7
SANTO DOMINGO AV
- SD 92140 1268-F6
SAN TOMAS CT
12200 SD 92128 1170-B3
SAN TOMAS DR
3200 OCN 92056 1086-J7
16500 SD 92128 1170-B3
SAN TOMAS PL
12100 SD 92128 1170-B3
SANTORINI WY
5000 OCN 92056 1107-F5

SANTORO WY
13400 SD 92130 1187-J5
SANTO THOMAS DR
1300 SOLB 92075 1167-H6
SAN VICENTE AV
12200 SDCo 92040 1211-J6
12200 SDCo 92040 1212-A6
SAN VICENTE BLVD
10300 SDCo 91977 1271-F5
SAN VICENTE CT
600 SD 92114 1290-G3
SAN VICENTE FRWY Rt#-67
- ELCJ - 1251-F2
- SDCo - 1231-H4
- SDCo - 1232-A3
- SDCo - 1251-F2
- SNTE - 1231-F7
- SNTE - 1251-F2
SAN VICENTE RD
800 SDCo 92065 1152-G7
1100 SDCo 92065 1172-G1
22300 SDCo 92065 1173-B4
SAN VICENTE ST
7400 SD 92114 1290-G3
SAN VICENTE TER
1200 SDCo 92065 1172-G1
SAN VICENTE WY
600 SD 92114 1290-G3
SAN VICENTE OAKS RD
24300 SDCo 92065 1173-F7
SANYO AV
1900 SD 92154 1352-A2
1900 SDCo 92154 1352-A2
E SAN YSIDRO BLVD
700 SD 92173 1350-G4
W SAN YSIDRO BLVD
- SD 92173 1350-D3
SAN YSIDRO DR
600 SDCo 92004 1058-H4
SAO PAULO WY
24900 SDCo 92065 1173-G3
SAPONI CT
17900 SD 92127 1149-H7
SAPOTA DR
11800 SDCo 92040 1231-J7
SAPOTE CT
1000 VSTA 92084 1088-A5
SAPPHIRE DR
- CRLB 92009 1127-B3
SAPPHIRE GN
- ESCN 92027 1110-D7
SAPPHIRE LN
1500 VSTA 92083 1107-H6
4400 OCN 92056 1107-D2
SAPPHIRE PT
2000 VSTA 92084 1088-C5
SAPPHIRE ST
700 SD 92109 1247-H4
SAPPINGTON CT
9900 SNTE 92071 1231-D4
SARA WY
2200 CRLB 92008 1106-H4
SARAH AV
5800 LMSA 91942 1250-H7
SARAH CT
300 ELCJ 92019 1252-A6
SARAH DR
13700 SDCo 92021 1232-E5
SARAH ANN DR
3500 SDCo 92028 1048-D3
SARAHFAYE CT
1200 SDCo 92026 1109-E6
SARAJAYNE LN
7300 LMGR 91945 1270-F7
SARAN CT
1500 OCN 92056 1087-E1
SARANAC AV
7700 LMSA 91941 1270-G2
SARANAC PL
7700 LMSA 91941 1270-G2
SARANAC ST
6500 SD 92115 1270-D2
6900 LMSA 92115 1270-E2
7000 LMSA 91941 1270-E2
SARAPE DR
16300 SD 92128 1170-C4
SARASONA WY
3700 SDCo 91902 1310-D4
SARASOTA DR
1400 SDCo 92004 (1099-D2 See Page 1098)
SARATOGA AV
4300 SD 92107 1268-A6
4600 SD 92107 1267-J6
SARATOGA CT
- CHV 91913 1311-C7
SARATOGA CTE
5800 SDCo 92067 1168-E7
SARATOGA GN
300 ESCN 92025 1130-B7
SARATOGA ST
600 OCN 92054 1086-C7
600 OCN 92054 1106-D1
1500 IMPB 91932 1349-H2
SARAWAK DR
8000 LMGR 91945 1290-H1
SARBONNE DR
2400 OCN 92054 1086-E7
SARDA CT
24700 SDCo 92065 1173-G2
SARDINA CV
12300 SD 92130 1188-B7
SARDIS PL
11600 SD 92131 1210-A1
SARGEANT RD
24000 SDCo 92065 1173-E1
SARITA ST
5900 LMSA 91942 1250-J6
SARNO PL
400 ESCN 92026 1109-G2
SARSAPARILLA ST
12600 SD 92129 1189-C5
SARTORI WY
200 SDCo 92083 1108-C4
SARVER LN
2600 SDCo 92069 1088-J7
2600 SDCo 92069 1089-A6
SASHA DR
500 SDCo 92029 1149-J1
SASKATCHEWAN AV
9600 SD 92129 1189-E5
SASS WY
16000 SDCo 92065 1173-H3
SASSAFRAS ST
1200 SD 92103 1268-J7
1500 SD 92101 1268-J7
SATANAS ST
14800 SD 92129 1169-J7

SAN DIEGO CO.

INDEX

STREET
Block City ZIP Pg-Grid

SATANAS ST
14800 SD 92129 1189-H1
SATELLITE BLVD
1500 IMPB 91932 1349-J2
1500 SD 92154 1349-J2
1700 SD 92154 1350-A2
SATIN DOLL LN
2700 SDCo 92069 1088-F3
SATINWOOD CT
1500 CHV 91911 1330-H4
SATINWOOD WY
200 SD 92114 1290-G5
400 CHV 91911 1330-G4
SATURN BLVD
200 SD 92154 1330-A6
900 SD 92154 1350-A1
SATUSUMA CT
24900 SDCo 92065 1173-G3
SAUFLEY ST
- CORD 92135 1288-F4
- SD 92135 1288-E3
SAUGERTIES AV
700 SD 92154 1330-E7
SAUK AV
4500 SD 92117 1248-F1
SAUNDERS CT
11100 SD 92131 1209-H4
SAUNDERS DR
10200 SD 92131 1209-H4
SAUSALITO AV
2600 CRLB 92008 1106-J5
SAUTERNE PL
500 CHV 91913 1311-D3
10600 SD 92131 1210-B3
SAVAGE CT
6800 SD 92111 1248-J7
SAVAGE WY
13800 PWY 92064 1190-G3
SAVANNAH LN
1300 CRLB 92009 1127-B7
SAVANNAH PL
5000 SD 92110 1268-E3
SAVANNAH ST
4800 SD 92110 1268-E2
SAVIN DR
1500 ELCJ 92021 1252-A3
SAVONA CT
2100 SDCo 92084 1108-C2
SAVONA PL
4600 SD 92130 1188-C4
SAVORY WY
3700 OCN 92057 1086-H4
SAVOY CIR
1400 SD 92107 1287-J1
1400 SD 92107 1288-A1
SAVOY ST
500 SD 92106 1287-J3
1000 SD 92107 1287-J2
1000 SD 92107 1288-A1
SAWDAY ST
300 SDCo 92065 1152-C7
N SAWDAY ST
100 SDCo 92065 1152-C7
100 SDCo 92065 1172-C1
S SAWDAY ST
300 SDCo 92065 1172-C1
SAWDAY TKTR
27100 SDCo 92065 1154-B3
SAWGRASS GN
1700 ESCN 92026 1109-D3
SAWGRASS PL
1400 CHV 91915 1311-H7
SAWGRASS ST
2300 SDCo 92019 1272-B4
SAW LEAF LN
- SDCo 92127 1169-D2
SAWTELLE AV
300 SD 92114 1290-H3
SAWTOOTH CT
9300 SD 92129 1189-D4
SAWTOOTH RD
13400 SD 92129 1189-D4
SAWTOOTH WY
9300 SD 92129 1189-D4
SAWYER LN
2200 CRLB 92008 1107-C7
SAXON PL
1500 ELCJ 92021 1251-J2
SAXON RD
- SDCo 91963 429-L10
SAXON ST
5300 SD 92115 1270-A2
SAXONY LN
300 ENCT 92024 1147-C6
SAXONY PL
- ENCT 92024 1147-C6
SAXONY RD
700 ENCT 92024 1147-C1
1400 CRLB 92024 1147-C1
SAYERS CT
10700 SNTE 92071 1231-E3
SAYLES CT
1100 SMCS 92069 1109-E7
SAYLOR DR
200 CHV 91910 1310-B5
SCABARD PL
13100 SD 92128 1189-H5
SCAMP ST
3500 SD 92124 1249-H4
SCANDIA CT
900 SDCo 92025 1130-C4
SCANNELL CT
11100 SD 92126 1209-B2
SCARBERY RD
16100 SDCo 92065 1173-D2
SCARBERY WY
23600 SDCo 92065 1173-D3
SCARBORO ST
14500 PWY 92064 1190-H5
SCARF PL
8400 SD 92119 1250-J4
SCARLATI PL
1000 SD 92037 1247-F1
SCARLET WY
100 SD 92114 1290-G4
SCARLET OAK WY
4400 OCN 92057 1086-J2
SCARONI RD
- ImCo 92249 6560-F7
SCARSDALE WY
13500 SD 92128 1190-A3
SCAUP ST
6500 CRLB 92009 1127-A4
SCENIC DR
- SDCo 92028 998-G5
100 SDCo 92021 1252-H3
1300 ESCN 92029 1129-G6
SCENIC LN
4400 LMSA 91941 1271-A3
SCENIC PL
2800 SD 92037 1227-J4
2800 SD 92037 1228-A4
SCENIC TER
3400 SDCo 91978 1271-E6
SCENIC WY
3700 OCN 92056 1107-E3
SCENIC MOUNTAIN RD
- SDCo 91906 (1318-G2
See Page 1298)
SCENICO DR
500 OCN 92054 1086-F2
SCENIC TRAIL WY
1700 ESCN 92029 1129-F6
SCENIC VALLEY PL
1800 ESCN 92029 1129-F6
SCENIC VALLEY RD
26800 SDCo 92065 1154-D2
SCENIC VIEW PL
1800 SDCo 91901 1234-D7
SCENIC VIEW RD
2800 SDCo 91901 1234-C7
SCHAFER PL
500 ESCN 92025 1129-H4
SCHALER DR
12400 PWY 92064 1190-C4
SCHANIEL RD
- ImCo 92243 431-A7
SCHARTZ RD
- ImCo 92227 431-C2
SCHAUMBERG PL
4600 SDCo 91902 1310-G2
SCHEIDLER WY
5300 SD 92108 1269-F1
SCHENLEY TER
2700 SD 92122 1228-B7
SCHEYER LN
- SDCo 92672 1023-D2
SCHILLING AV
6900 SD 92126 1208-H4
SCHILT AV
8400 SD 92145 1229-D1
8700 SD 92126 1229-D1
8900 SD 92126 1209-C7
SCHIRRA ST
3500 SD 92154 1330-E7
SCHLEE CANYON RD
3000 SDCo 91935 1292-G2
SCHLEY ST
1200 SD 92113 1289-D6
SCHMIDT CT
- SDCo 92672 1023-E1
SCHMIDT DR
- SDCo 92672 1023-E2
SCHNEPLE DR
8500 SD 92126 1209-C2
SCHOLARS DR
- SD 92093 1207-J7
2800 SD 92093 1227-J1
2900 SD 92093 1228-A2
SCHOLARS LN
- SD 92093 1227-J2
SCHOOL LN
3100 LMGR 91945 1270-H6
SCHOOL ST
3400 SD 92116 1269-F3
SCHOOL DAZE LN
1200 SDCo 92065 1172-F1
SCHOOL HOUSE RD
- CHV 91915 1311-H6
900 SDCo 92065 1153-A4
SCHOOLHOUSE WY
- SMCS 92078 1128-D5
SCHOOL HOUSE CANYON RD
- SDCo 92070 409-K10
SCHOOLRIDGE LN
4200 LMSA 91941 1270-G4
SCHOONER WY
1700 CRLB 92008 1106-H6
SCHRIMPF RD
- ImCo 92233 411-B8
SCHUBERT PTH
100 ENCT 92007 1167-D2
SCHULLER LN
1000 SDCo 92028 1028-C3
SCHUYLER AV
4800 LMSA 91941 1270-J2
SCHUYLER ST
5800 SD 92139 1310-D1
SCIENCE CENTER DR
10300 SD 92121 1208-A7
SCIENCE PARK RD
3000 SD 92121 1207-J5
SCIMITAR DR
6300 SD 92114 1290-D2
SCOOTER LN
1600 SDCo 92028 1028-D5
SCORPIUS WY
8900 SD 92126 1209-D2
SCOTER PL
- CRLB 92009 1127-C6
SCOTIA WY
1500 SDCo 92084 1108-D1
SCOTS WY
13400 PWY 92064 1190-E3
SCOTSMAN RD
13300 SDCo 92040 1232-D5
SCOTT AV
- ImCo 92243 6499-F5
800 ELCN 92243 6499-F5
SCOTT DR
1200 NATC 91950 1289-J6
3900 CRLB 92008 1106-G6
3900 OCN 92056 1107-C1
SCOTT LN
- SDCo 92084 1088-F1
SCOTT PL
1600 ENCT 92024 1147-F4
SCOTT ST
900 SD 92106 1288-B2
3100 VSTA 92083 1127-J1
3100 VSTA 92083 1128-A1
SCOTT WY
2300 ESCN 92027 1110-C6
SCOTTFORD DR
200 SDCo 92021 1252-J1
SCOTTSBLUFF CT
9800 SNTE 92071 1231-F4
SCRANTON RD
9200 SD 92121 1208-E6
SCRANTON ST
700 ELCJ 92020 1251-G6
SCRIPPS AV
900 CHV 91913 1311-D5
SCRIPPS LN
- SD 92037 1227-E7
SCRIPPS ST
5600 SD 92122 1228-C6
SCRIPPS TER
5500 SD 92182 1270-B1
SCRIPPS TR
10200 SD 92131 1210-A4
SCRIPPS WY
3200 SD 92122 1228-C6
SCRIPPS CAPE VISTA POINTE
11700 SD 92131 1209-J3
SCRIPPS CREEK DR
11400 SD 92131 1209-J1
11800 SD 92131 1189-J7
SCRIPPS GATEWAY CT
- SD 92131 1189-G7
- SD 92131 1209-F1
SCRIPPS HIGHLANDS DR
- SD 92131 1189-G7
- SD 92131 1209-G1
SCRIPPS LAKE DR
9800 SD 92131 1209-F4
11600 SD 92131 1210-A3
SCRIPPS POWAY PKWY
9900 SD 92131 1189-G7
11300 SD 92131 1190-A7
11900 PWY 92064 1190-H6
15600 PWY 92064 1191-B5
15600 SDCo 92064 1191-B5
16700 SDCo 92040 1191-B5
SCRIPPS RANCH BLVD
9900 SD 92131 1209-F2
SCRIPPS RANCH CT
10200 SD 92131 1209-F5
SCRIPPS RANCH RW
10700 SD 92131 1209-H5
SCRIPPS SUMMIT CT
10300 SD 92131 1189-G7
SCRIPPS SUMMIT DR
11200 SD 92131 1189-G7
SCRIPPS VISTA WY
9900 SD 92131 1209-F2
SCRIPPS WESTVIEW CIR
9900 SD 92131 1209-F2
SCRIPPS WESTVIEW WY
9900 SD 92131 1209-F2
SCRUB JAY CT
1100 CRLB 92009 1127-A5
SCRUB JAY LN
7800 SDCo 92066 1237-C6
SCRUB OAKS LN
16700 SDCo 92065 1171-H3
SCULPIN ST
10200 SD 92124 1249-G4
SCULPTURE CT
4500 OCN 92057 1087-A2
SEA LN
300 SD 92037 1247-E1
SEA BIRD WY
- SD 92154 1350-H1
SEA BLUFF CIR
4500 CRLB 92008 1106-H7
SEA BLUFFE
100 ENCT 92024 1147-A2
SEA BREEZE CT
1900 ENCT 92024 1147-B2
2100 CHV 91914 1311-E3
SEA BREEZE DR
200 CRLB 92009 1126-H4
1000 OCN 92054 1085-H6
SEABREEZE DR
2000 SD 92139 1290-D7
2100 SD 92139 1310-D1
SEA BREEZE WK
3400 OCN 92056 1107-C2
SEABREEZE FARMS DR
- SD 92130 1188-D6
SEABRIDGE LN
14200 SD 92128 1190-A2
SEA BRIGHT DR
4300 CRLB 92008 1106-H7
SEABRIGHT LN
400 SOLB 92075 1167-E6
SEA BRIGHT PL
4300 CRLB 92008 1106-H7
SEABROOK LN
1500 SD 92139 1290-H6
SEABURY ST
3100 CRLB 92008 1107-A3
SEACHASE ST
5000 SD 92130 1188-D4
SEACHASE WY
5000 SD 92130 1188-D5
SEA CLIFF DR
900 CRLB 92009 1126-J4
SEACLIFF LN
200 SOLB 92075 1187-E1
SEA CLIFF WY
100 OCN 92056 1086-J7
SEACLIFF WY
800 SMCS 92069 1128-F2
SEACOAST DR
600 CORD 91932 1329-E7
600 IMPB 91932 1329-E7
900 IMPB 91932 1349-E1
SEA COLONY CT
2200 SD 92107 1268-B6
SEA CORAL DR
- SD 92154 1350-H1
SEACREST CT
2600 VSTA 92083 1107-H5
SEACREST DR
700 SMCS 92069 1128-F2
3300 CRLB 92008 1106-G4
SEACREST WY
300 ENCT 92024 1147-C6
SEA CREST WY
3600 OCN 92056 1107-C3
SEACREST VIEW RD
5900 SD 92121 1208-F3
SEA DRIFT WY
5000 SD 92154 1350-J1
SEAFARER DR
3500 OCN 92054 1086-E5
SEAFARER PL
- CRLB 92009 1126-J7
SEAFIELD PL
5000 SD 92154 1330-J7
SEAFLOWER LN
3600 OCN 92056 1107-A2
SEAFOAM CT
1600 SD 92139 1290-D7
SEAFORD PL
4700 SD 92117 1248-H1
SEA FOREST CT
200 DLMR 92014 1187-G6
SEA GATE RD
900 CRLB 92009 1126-J4
SEAGAZE DR
- OCN 92054 1106-A1
400 OCN 92054 1086-A7
SEAGIRT CT
700 SD 92109 1267-H1
SEAGLASS CT
11800 SD 92128 1190-A1
SEAGROVE CT
5100 SD 92130 1188-D5
SEAGROVE CV
5000 SD 92130 1188-D4
SEAGROVE PL
5100 SD 92130 1188-D4
SEAGROVE ST
13000 SD 92130 1188-D4
SEAGULL CT
7600 SD 92123 1269-A1
SEAGULL LN
- OCN 92057 1086-H2
2000 SD 92123 1269-A1
SEAHORN CIR
3500 SD 92130 1187-J5
SEAHORSE CT
1000 CRLB 92009 1127-A5
SEAHORSE LN
- SDCo 92055 1085-H6
SEA ISLAND PL
- SMCS 92069 1128-A3
2300 CHV 91915 1311-G5
SEA ISLE DR
500 SD 92154 1330-H6
SEA KNOLL CT
13100 SD 92130 1188-D5
SEALANE DR
900 ENCT 92024 1167-B1
SEA LARKE DR
1100 SDCo 92028 1027-H5
SEA LAVENDER WY
4800 SD 92154 1330-J6
SEAL BEACH PL
- SD 92139 1290-D7
SEA LILY CT
- SD 92154 1350-H1
SEA LION PL
5900 CRLB 92008 1127-G2
SEAL POINT CT
1500 CHV 91911 1330-H4
SEA MAID CT
- SD 92154 1350-H1
SEAMAN ST
6200 SD 92120 1249-J6
SEA MIST CT
5000 SD 92121 1208-E4
SEA MIST WY
10500 SD 92121 1208-D4
SEAN TAYLOR LN
7300 SD 92126 1208-J2
SEA ORBIT LN
100 DLMR 92014 1187-F5
SEA OTTER PL
5900 CRLB 92008 1127-G1
SEA PARK DR
900 IMPB 91932 1349-G2
SEA PINES RD
1700 SDCo 92019 1272-B5
SEAPOINT WY
10800 SD 92121 1208-F3
SEAPORT PL
6400 CRLB 92009 1127-B4
SEAQUEST TR
1800 SDCo 92024 1148-E3
SEA REEF DR
1000 SD 92154 1330-J7
1000 SD 92154 1350-J1
SEA REEF PL
5000 SD 92154 1350-J1
SEA RIDGE DR
300 SD 92037 1247-F5
SEA RIDGE RD
3500 OCN 92054 1086-F5
SEA ROBIN CT
- SD 92154 1350-H1
SEA ROSE PL
5700 SD 92037 1247-F3
SEARS AV
100 SD 92114 1290-H3
SEASCAPE DR
4800 OCN 92057 1087-B1
6100 SD 92139 1310-E1
6900 CRLB 92009 1127-A5
SEA SCAPE GN
2500 ESCN 92026 1109-B4
SEASHELL CT
7400 CRLB 92009 1127-A7
SEASHELL PL
5000 SD 92130 1188-D5
SEASIDE ST
2200 SD 92107 1268-A6
SEASIDE WY
2800 CRLB 92008 1107-A4
SEASONS RD
2300 OCN 92056 1087-D6
SEASPRAY LN
6800 CRLB 92009 1126-J5
SEA STAR LN
1900 SD 92139 1290-E7
SEA STAR WY
1900 SD 92139 1290-E7
SEATAC LN
2300 SDCo 92028 1048-B1
SEA TERN CT
4700 SD 92154 1330-H6
SEATTLE DR
2500 ELCJ 92020 1251-A4
SEATTLE SLEW WY
1600 OCN 92057 1067-E7
SEA TURF CIR
800 SOLB 92075 1187-F2
SEA URCHIN DR
- SD 92154 1350-H1
SEA VALE CT
500 CHV 91910 1309-J5
500 CHV 91910 1310-A5
SEA VALE ST
- CHV 91910 1310-B5
600 CHV 91910 1309-J5
SEAVIEW AV
1300 OCN 92054 1106-D1
1700 DLMR 92014 1187-F4
SEA VIEW CT
- ENCT 92024 1147-D6
SEA VIEW DR
- ImCo 92274 410-H6
900 IMPB 91932 1349-G2
SEAVIEW PL
500 VSTA 92083 1107-H1
SEAVIEW WY
3600 CRLB 92008 1106-H5
SEA VIEW WY
3900 SDCo 92024 1148-E3
SEA VILLAGE CIR
2000 ENCT 92007 1167-F3
SEA VILLAGE DR
700 IMPB 91932 1329-F7
1000 ENCT 92007 1167-E3
SEA VILLAGE PL
1900 ENCT 92007 1167-F3
SEA VILLAGE WY
2000 ENCT 92007 1167-F3
SEA VISTA PL
2000 SMCS 92069 1128-B2
E SEAWARD AV
100 SD 92173 1350-G3
W SEAWARD AV
- SD 92173 1350-F3
SEAWARD CIR
3500 OCN 92056 1107-G4
SEAWATCH LN
800 CRLB 92009 1126-J5
800 CRLB 92009 1127-A6
SEA WATER LN
- SD 92154 1350-H1
SEA WIND CT
900 CRLB 92009 1126-J4
SEAWIND CV
11200 SD 92126 1209-A2
SEAWIND DR
2400 NATC 91950 1310-B1
SEAWIND LN
7900 SD 92126 1209-A2
SEAWIND WY
1900 OCN 92054 1106-F2
SEA WORLD DR
100 SD 92109 1268-C4
SEA WORLD WY
- SD 92109 1268-C3
SEBAGO AV
13400 PWY 92064 1190-H4
SEBRING CT
9800 SNTE 92071 1231-F4
SECA ST
2000 SDCo 92019 1272-C4
SECKEL PEAR
700 OCN 92057 1086-G5
SECLUDED LN
3500 SDCo 92028 1047-J2
SECO GN
1800 ESCN 92026 1109-F6
SECRET PL
3000 LMGR 91945 1270-J6
SECRET LAKE LN
2600 SDCo 92028 1028-E7
2600 SDCo 92028 1048-E1
SECTION ST
300 OCN 92054 1086-B7
SECURIDAD ST
200 OCN 92057 1066-H7
SECURITY PL
1500 SMCS 92069 1128-C1
SECURITY WY
9200 SNTE 92071 1231-G4
SEDA CV
4600 SD 92124 1250-A2
SEDA DR
4600 SD 92124 1250-A1
SEDA PL
11300 SD 92124 1250-A2
SEDERO CT
11500 SD 92127 1149-J7
SEDGE CT
12900 SD 92129 1189-E5
SEDGEWICK ST
5700 SD 92139 1310-D2
SEDONA DR
2400 SDCo 92065 1172-H3
SEDONA GN
1500 ESCN 92027 1110-A5
SEDORUS ST
8300 SD 92129 1189-B4
SEEFOREVER DR
500 SMCS 92078 1129-B4
SEELEY AV
- SDCo 91934 (1321-G5
See Page 1300)
SEELY CT
1700 SMCS 92069 1109-B3
SEEMAN DR
100 ENCT 92024 1147-E6
SEFTON PL
1800 SD 92107 1268-A7
SEGO PL
2900 SD 92123 1249-D6
SEGOVIA CT
3000 CRLB 92009 1147-H2
15100 SD 92129 1169-J7
SEGOVIA WY
2800 CRLB 92009 1147-G2
SEGUNDO CT
14100 PWY 92064 1190-G1
SEIFERT DR
- SD 92106 1288-A5
SEIFERT ST
5500 SD 92105 1270-B7
SEILER ST
12900 PWY 92064 1190-D5
SELBY CT
10100 SNTE 92071 1231-A3
SELDEN WY
- SDCo 92672 1023-E2
SELECT WY
- SDCo 92028 999-A5
SELKIRK RW
2600 SD 92037 1247-J1
2600 SD 92037 1248-A1
SELLERS DR
2900 SD 92110 1268-E6
SELLERS PZ
- SD 92133 1268-D6
SELLO LN
3100 CRLB 92009 1127-J5
SELLSWAY ST
100 SD 92173 1350-F4
SELMA CT
12800 PWY 92064 1190-B5
SELMA DR
1300 OCN 92054 1106-C1
SELMA PL
700 SD 92114 1290-B3
SELMALITA TER
300 VSTA 92083 1087-G5
SELSEY ST
14600 PWY 92064 1190-H5
SELTZER CT
9400 SD 92123 1249-E5
SELVA DR
16100 SD 92128 1170-C5
SEMILLON BLVD
11700 SD 92131 1210-A2
SEMINOLE DR
4500 SD 92115 1270-D3
SEMINOLE ST
- SD 92140 1268-E6
1500 SMCS 92069 1108-D7
SENATOR WASH RD
- ImCo 92283 432-E2
SENCILLO CT
17900 SD 92128 1150-B7
SENCILLO DR
17900 SD 92128 1150-B7
SENCILLO LN
17900 SD 92128 1150-B7
SENDA LN
2300 SDCo 92021 1252-J4
SENDA PL
16400 SD 92128 1170-C4
SENDA RD
12400 SD 92128 1170-C4
SENDA ACANTILADA
12600 SD 92128 1150-C7
SENDA ANGOSTA
5100 SDCo 91902 1290-H7
SENDA DE LA LUNA
16900 SDCo 92067 1168-D3
SENDA LUNA LLENA
11200 SD 92130 1208-B3
SENDA MAR DE PONDEROSA
11200 SD 92130 1208-C3
SENDA PANACEA
- SD 92129 1189-B6
SENDERO AV
800 ESCN 92026 1109-J7
1000 ESCN 92027 1109-J7
SENDERO WY
2400 SD 92111 1248-G7
SENECA PL
7400 LMSA 91941 1270-G3
SENN RD
2200 SD 92136 1289-E7
SENN WY
7700 SD 92037 1227-J7
SENTENAC CREEK RD
2600 SDCo 92070 1135-F7
2600 SDCo 92070 1155-F1
SENWOOD WY
1100 SDCo 92028 1027-G4
SEPH WY
900 SDCo 92027 1130-B3
SEPIA CT
700 OCN 92057 1087-B1
12000 SD 92128 1189-H5
SEPTEMBER ST
4900 SD 92110 1268-G1
SEQUAN LN
28800 SDCo 92066 1237-C5
SEQUAN TKTR
- SDCo 91901 1253-H4
- SDCo 91901 1254-A4
- SDCo 91935 1253-F5
- SDCo 92019 1253-E7
SEQUENCE DR
6100 SD 92121 1208-G4
SEQUOIA AV
100 CRLB 92008 1106-E7
SEQUOIA CIR
- ELCJ 92019 1251-J6
SEQUOIA CT
400 CHV 91911 1330-G4
SEQUOIA LN
1500 SDCo 92083 1107-E2
SEQUOIA PL
4700 OCN 92057 1067-A7
4700 OCN 92057 1087-A1
SEQUOIA RD
28900 SDCo 92066 1237-C6
SEQUOIA ST
- SDCo 92066 1237-C7
500 CHV 91911 1330-H4
2000 SMCS 92069 1128-A2
3800 SD 92109 1248-A6
SEQUOIA CREST
2000 VSTA 92083 1107-G6
SERBIAN PL
3000 SD 92117 1248-E6
SERENA AV
4200 OCN 92056 1107-C3
SERENA CIR
1300 CHV 91910 1311-B5
SERENA LN
12100 SDCo 92040 1231-J1
12100 SDCo 92040 1232-A1
SERENA PL
10900 SDCo 92040 1232-A1
SERENA RD
12000 SDCo 92040 1231-J1
12100 SDCo 92040 1232-A1
SERENA WY
1000 SMCS 92069 1128-E3
SERENA HILLS DR
2200 SDCo 92065 1172-C4
SERENATA PL
4600 SD 92130 1188-C6
SERENDIPITY LN
1000 SDCo 92026 1089-C6
1000 SDCo 92069 1089-C6
SERENE RD
1400 OCN 92057 1067-G7
SERENE WY
- SDCo 91935 1293-G1
SERENIDAD PL
4000 OCN 92056 1107-C2
SERENITY CT
8200 SDCo 92021 1232-C7
8200 SDCo 92021 1252-C1
SERENITY PTH
28300 SDCo 92082 1090-F2
SERENO CT
2100 CRLB 92009 1147-F2
SERENO VIEW LN
2200 ENCT 92024 1147-J6
SERENO VIEW RD
600 ENCT 92024 1147-J6
SERI ST
4100 SD 92117 1248-E2
SERIGRAPH CT
4600 OCN 92057 1087-B2
SERPENTINE DR
300 DLMR 92014 1187-F4
SERRA WY
15900 SDCo 92065 1173-C4
SERRANO DR
3100 CRLB 92009 1147-J2
SERRANO LN
500 CHV 91910 1310-J5
SERRANO PL
6500 SD 92115 1270-D3
SERRANO ST
1700 OCN 92054 1106-C3
SERRANOS CT
4000 SDCo 92028 1028-G7
SERRENA LN
600 SD 92154 1330-G6
SERRES DR
9500 SNTE 92071 1230-H5
SERVANDO AV
2300 SD 92154 1350-D4
SERVICE PL
1000 VSTA 92084 1108-A1
SERVICE RD
- SD 92103 1268-J5
- SD 92103 1269-A5
- SD 92106 1288-A7
- SD 92106 1308-A1
SESAME ST
700 CHV 91910 1330-J1
SESAME WY
3700 OCN 92057 1086-H5
SESI LN
14200 SDCo 92040 1232-G5
SESPE PL
14400 PWY 92064 1190-H2
SETH LN
9600 SNTE 92071 1231-E4
SETH WY
10300 SNTE 92071 1231-B1
SETON HALL ST
7500 LMSA 91942 1270-G1
SETTINERI LN
3800 SDCo 91977 1271-A5
SETTING SUN WY
5200 SD 92121 1208-E4
SETTLE CT
9800 SNTE 92071 1231-A4
SETTLE RD
9700 SNTE 92071 1231-A3
SETTLERS PL
14400 PWY 92064 1190-H2
SETTLERS RD
13800 SDCo 92040 1232-E4
SEVAN CT
7900 SD 92123 1249-B7
7900 SD 92123 1269-B1
SEVEN BRIDGES RD
18300 SDCo 92067 1148-F5
SEVEN OAKES RD
1200 ESCN 92026 1109-F7
1200 ESCN 92026 1129-F1
1200 SDCo 92026 1129-F1
SEVERE RD
- ImCo 92233 411-A10
SEVERIN DR
5300 LMSA 91941 1271-B1
5500 LMSA 91942 1251-B5
5500 LMSA 91942 1271-B1
6300 ELCJ 92020 1251-B5
SEVERINO LN
15800 SDCo 92082 1071-A6
SEVILLA WY
4800 CRLB 92008 1106-J7
SEVILLE ST
3000 SD 92110 1268-D6
SEWANEE DR
1400 SDCo 92004 (1099-D2
See Page 1098)
SEWELL AV
2800 SD 92154 1350-C1
SEYBERT RD
4400 ImCo 92227 431-C1
SEYMOUR ST
9900 SNTE 92071 1231-F4
SHACKLEFORD CT
9300 SD 92126 1209-E2
SHADE RD
4400 SDCo 91941 1271-E3
SHADE TREE LN
700 SDCo 92028 1027-H3
SHADETREE LN
2000 ESCN 92029 1129-E7
SHADEWOOD LN
1700 SD 92139 1290-H6
SHADOW GN
1700 ESCN 92029 1129-E5
SHADOW LN
400 VSTA 92084 1087-J6
4200 OCN 92056 1107-C2
SHADOW RD
9400 LMSA 91941 1271-C1
9400 SDCo 91941 1271-C1
9700 ELCJ 92020 1271-C1
SHADOWBROOK CT
14700 PWY 92064 1190-D1
SHADOWBROOK LN
100 ELCJ 92019 1252-D5
SHADOW CANYON WY
5800 SDCo 91902 1311-B3
SHADOW CREEK LN
11800 SDCo 92020 1271-J2
SHADOWCREST LN
1100 SDCo 92028 1027-H7
SHADOW GLEN CT
100 ELCJ 92019 1252-D5
SHADOWGLEN RD
11600 SDCo 92020 1271-H2
SHADOW GROVE WY
2000 ENCT 92024 1147-H7
SHADOW HILL DR
7900 LMSA 91941 1270-H5
SHADOW HILL RD
9200 SNTE 92071 1231-F6
SHADOW HILL WY
11000 SNTE 92071 1231-G6
SHADOW HILLS CT
1300 SMCS 92069 1109-C7
SHADOW HILLS DR
500 SMCS 92069 1109-C6
SHADOW KNOLLS
1500 SDCo 92020 1272-A2
SHADOW KNOLLS CT
1500 SDCo 92020 1272-A2
SHADOW KNOLLS DR
1500 SDCo 92020 1272-A2
SHADOW KNOLLS PL
1800 SDCo 92020 1271-J2
1800 SDCo 92020 1272-A2
SHADOW LAKE RD
- SDCo 92026 1069-A3
SHADOWLAWN ST
3100 SD 92110 1268-D6
SHADOWLINE ST
12700 PWY 92064 1190-D1
SHADOW MOUNTAIN DR
1400 ENCT 92024 1147-G6

SHADOW MOUNTAIN RD — SAN DIEGO CO. STREET INDEX — SIXPENCE WY 6618

COPYRIGHT 2001 Thomas Bros. Maps ®

STREET
Block City ZIP Pg-Grid

SHADOW MOUNTAIN RD
1900 SDCo 92021 1252-E3
SHADOW MOUNTAIN TER
1100 VSTA 92084 1088-A4
SHADOW OAK CT
- SDCo 92065 1172-D5
SHADOWOOD CIR
1800 VSTA 92083 1107-G5
SHADOWOOD LN
13700 SDCo 92082 1090-E6
SHADOW RANCH RD
11300 SDCo 91941 1271-H4
SHADOWRIDGE DR
700 VSTA 92083 1108-A4
1000 VSTA 92083 1107-F4
1900 OCN 92056 1107-F4
SHADOW ROCK CT
4000 SDCo 91902 1311-B2
SHADOWSIDE LN
1300 SDCo 92019 1272-A2
SHADOW TREE DR
300 OCN 92054 1086-D2
SHADOW VALLEY
2800 SDCo 91935 1292-E4
SHADOW VALLEY RD
11700 SDCo 92020 1271-H2
SHADOW VISTA WY
1500 ELCJ 92019 1252-A7
1500 SDCo 92019 1252-A7
SHADWELL PL
4700 SD 92130 1188-C4
SHADY BEND
16300 SDCo 92065 1171-G3
SHADY LN
400 ELCJ 92021 1251-J5
700 SDCo 92028 1027-F1
4300 OCN 92056 1107-D2
SHADY ACRE CIR
1900 ENCT 92024 1147-H6
SHADY ACRE LN
2300 LMGR 91945 1270-F7
SHADY ACRES LN
- SDCo 92036 1175-J1
- SDCo 92036 1176-A1
SHADYBROOK PL
400 ESCN 92026 1109-G5
SHADY CREEK LN
30500 SDCo 92082 1070-E3
SHADY CREEK RD
13800 SDCo 92082 1070-E6
SHADYCREST CT
1700 ELCJ 92020 1251-C2
SHADYCREST PL
1600 ELCJ 92020 1251-C2
SHADY CREST RD
700 SMCS 92069 1109-A5
SHADY ELM PL
900 SD 92154 1330-B7
SHADYGLADE LN
7600 SD 92114 1290-G5
SHADY GLEN DR
300 SDCo 92028 1027-G3
SHADY HILL LN
- SDCo 92028 1047-H6
SHADY HOLLOW LN
3200 SDCo 91935 1273-E5
SHADY KNOLL RD
28300 SDCo 92082 1090-D3
SHADY OAK CT
12800 PWY 92064 1190-C5
SHADY OAK RD
100 SD 92114 1290-F5
SHADY OAKS DR
16300 SDCo 92065 1171-G3
SHADY OAKS LN
16300 SDCo 92065 1171-G3
47200 RivC 92592 999-F1
SHADY OAKS WY
15700 SDCo 92082 1071-A5
SHADYPINE ST
2900 SDCo 91978 1271-F7
SHADYRIDGE AV
2200 ESCN 92029 1129-E6
SHADY SANDS RD
8000 SD 92119 1250-E3
SHADY SPRINGS LN
600 SDCo 92065 1152-E6
SHADYTREE LN
2000 ENCT 92024 1147-H6
SHADYWOOD DR
500 ESCN 92026 1109-H4
SHAFER ST
1000 OCN 92054 1106-B1
SHAFTER ST
1000 SD 92106 1288-B2
SHAGGYBARK DR
10000 SNTE 92071 1231-D2
SHAHRAM WY
9100 SDCo 92026 1049-B7
SHALAMAR DR
7900 SDCo 92021 1252-B1
SHALE CT
3800 CRLB 92008 1107-B4
SHALE ROCK RD
3000 SDCo 92084 1088-D7
SHALIMAR CV
2600 SD 92014 1207-J2
SHALIMAR PL
1500 ESCN 92029 1129-G7
13000 SD 92014 1207-J2
13100 SD 92014 1187-J7
SHALLMAN ST
12400 PWY 92064 1190-C3
SHALLOWCREEK WY
13000 PWY 92064 1190-E5
SHALOM RD
15900 SDCo 92065 1174-B4
SHAMROCK CT
- IMP 92243 6499-E2
- SDCo 92003 1047-H7
SHAMROCK LN
9700 SDCo 92040 1232-A4
SHAMROCK RD
32000 SDCo 92003 1047-J7
32000 SDCo 92003 1067-J1
SHAMROCK ST
2200 SD 92105 1289-H1
SHAMROCK WY
2500 ESCN 92025 1130-C7
SHANAS LN
500 ENCT 92024 1147-G5
SHANDRENIA
- SDCo 91935 1274-C7
SHANDY LN
100 SDCo 92065 1153-A6
SHANE PL
6400 SD 92115 1270-D2
SHANESSEY RD
1300 ELCJ 92019 1251-J7
1300 ELCJ 92019 1252-A7
SHANK RD
- ImCo 92227 431-D1
SHANNON AV
6600 SD 92115 1270-D3
SHANNONBROOK CT
8600 LMGR 91977 1270-J6
8600 SDCo 91941 1270-J6
8600 SDCo 91977 1270-J6
SHANNON RIDGE LN
5300 SD 92130 1208-E1
SHANTEAU DR
14900 SDCo 92021 1232-J3
14900 SDCo 92021 1233-A3
SHANTUNG DR
7900 SNTE 92071 1250-H1
SHAPLEY WY
- SDCo 92672 1023-D2
SHARE CT
10500 SNTE 92071 1231-E4
SHARI WY
400 OCN 92054 1086-G2
1200 ELCJ 92019 1251-J6
SHARLENE LN
10500 SNTE 92071 1231-E7
SHARON WY
500 ELCJ 92020 1251-B4
SHARP PL
200 ENCT 92024 1147-G6
SHARRON PL
4200 SD 92115 1270-B4
SHASTA CT
- OCN 92057 1086-H1
SHASTA DR
- ENCT 92024 1147-E5
SHASTA LN
5500 LMSA 91942 1270-G1
SHASTA PL
2700 CRLB 92008 1106-J5
SHASTA ST
100 CHV 91910 1310-B7
3700 SD 92109 1248-A7
E SHASTA ST
200 CHV 91910 1310-D6
SHASTA TR
1600 SDCo 91905 (1319-J2 See Page 1298)
SHASTA WY
700 SDCo 91905 (1319-G2 See Page 1298)
700 SDCo 91906 (1319-G2 See Page 1298)
700 SDCo 91905 (1320-A2 See Page 1300)
SHAULA WY
8800 SD 92126 1209-C2
SHAULES AV
6300 SD 92114 1290-D4
SHAUNA WY
26200 SDCo 92082 1091-F6
SHAW ST
5500 SD 92139 1310-C2
SHAWLINE ST
4800 SD 92111 1249-A1
5000 SD 92111 1229-A7
SHAW LOPEZ RD
10700 SD 92121 1208-F4
SHAW LOPEZ RW
10700 SD 92121 1208-F4
SHAWN AV
9200 SD 92123 1249-E6
SHAWN CT
2300 CRLB 92008 1106-H4
SHAWN WY
1100 VSTA 92083 1107-E1
SHAWNEE RD
3400 SD 92117 1248-E5
SHAWN ELISE WY
300 ENCT 92024 1147-G6
SHAW RIDGE RD
5100 SD 92130 1188-D7
SHAW VALLEY RD
11900 SD 92130 1188-C7
11900 SD 92130 1208-C1
SHAY PL
1100 ESCN 92026 1109-J4
SHAY RD
200 SDCo 92028 1027-F4
SHAYANN LN
12600 SDCo 92040 1232-B5
SHAYLENE WY
2300 SDCo 91901 1254-A1
SHAYS WY
500 SDCo 92065 1152-G4
SHEARER CRSG
3000 SDCo 92028 1048-J2
SHEARWATER DR
6700 CRLB 92009 1126-J5
SHEAR WATER WY
4400 OCN 92057 1087-A3
SHEBA WY
10000 SD 92129 1189-F3
SHEENA WY
1500 LMGR 91945 1290-E2
SHEEPHEAD MOUNTAIN RD
- SDCo 92066 430-A6
- SDCo 92066 1237-H3
SHEFFIELD AV
400 ENCT 92007 1167-D2
SHEFFIELD CT
600 CHV 91910 1310-E6
SHEFFIELD DR
900 VSTA 92083 1108-A4
SHEILA LN
300 SDCo 92028 1028-D2
SHEILA ST
8300 SDCo 92021 1251-G1
SHELBY DR
2900 NATC 91950 1310-B3
2900 SDCo 91950 1310-B3
SHELBY LN
100 SDCo 92028 1027-H2
SHELBY ST
5200 SD 92105 1270-A6
SHELBY VIEW CT
- SDCo 92040 1231-J6
SHELDON AV
300 SD 92103 1268-J6
300 SD 92103 1269-A6
SHELDON DR
4300 LMSA 91941 1270-H4
SHELL AV
400 NATC 91950 1290-C6
400 SD 92114 1290-C6
SHELLBACK WY
8800 SD 92093 1227-H3
SHELL CANYON RD
- ImCo 92259 430-G6
SHELLEY DR
- OCN 92057 1067-A3
SHELLEY PL
- CRLB 92008 1107-B7
SHELLY DR
100 SMCS 92078 1109-B7
100 SMCS 92078 1129-A1
4100 SD 92105 1270-B5
SHELSTEVE TER
800 VSTA 92084 1087-J6
SHELTER COVE WY
800 OCN 92054 1066-E6
SHELTER ISLAND DR
1400 SD 92106 1288-B2
SHENANDOAH AV
600 SMCS 92078 1128-F2
SHENANDOAH DR
3800 OCN 92056 1087-B7
10000 SNTE 92071 1231-C3
13000 SDCo 92040 1232-C3
SHEP ST
8900 SD 92123 1249-D6
SHEPHERD LN
600 SD 92154 1330-F7
SHEPHERD HILL RD
1300 SDCo 92084 1068-A6
SHEPHERDS KNOLL PL
1000 CHV 91910 1311-C6
SHERANN DR
12300 SDCo 92040 1232-A6
SHERBOURNE DR
3800 OCN 92056 1087-B7
SHERBROOKE ST
1500 SD 92139 1290-H6
SHERI LN
2600 LMGR 91945 1270-G7
SHERIDAN AV
100 ESCN 92026 1109-J6
800 ESCN 92027 1109-J6
1400 ESCN 92027 1110-A6
1800 SD 92103 1268-G5
SHERIDAN LN
4300 SD 92120 1249-H7
SHERIDAN PL
1500 ESCN 92027 1110-A5
SHERIDAN RD
1100 SDCo 91906 (1318-B7 See Page 1298)
1800 ENCT 92024 1147-A1
4500 OCN 92056 1107-E2
SHERILTON VALLEY RD
- SDCo 91916 1216-A1
SHERLOCK CT
4500 SD 92122 1228-D3
SHERM CIR
9700 SDCo 92040 1232-D3
SHERMAN DR
1500 CHV 91911 1330-H3
SHERMAN PL
100 ESCN 92025 1129-J2
SHERMAN RD
- CORD 92135 1288-F6
SHERMAN ST
800 SD 92110 1268-F3
SHERMAN WY
1500 VSTA 92084 1088-B3
SHERRARD WY
11200 SD 92131 1209-J2
SHERRI LN
300 OCN 92054 1106-C3
SHERRY LN
100 DLMR 92014 1187-F6
SHERWIN PL
4100 SDCo 91941 1271-E4
SHERWOOD DR
700 OCN 92054 1086-F2
2200 LMGR 91945 1270-H7
2200 LMGR 91945 1290-H1
SHERWOOD GN
1200 ESCN 92029 1129-F5
SHERWOOD ST
- CHV 91911 1330-E4
SHERWOOD WY
3300 SMCS 92069 1128-A2
SHERWOOD FOREST CT
8700 SDCo 92026 1069-A6
SHERYL AV
1300 CHV 91911 1330-C4
SHERYL LN
1400 NATC 91950 1310-A1
SHETLAND CT
5700 OCN 92057 1067-F7
SHETLAND WY
200 SDCo 92028 1027-F4
SHIELD DR
- SD 92126 1209-E7
SHIELDS AV
1400 ENCT 92024 1147-G6
SHIELDS CT
10400 SD 92124 1249-H3
SHIELDS PL
4200 SD 92124 1249-H3
SHIELDS ST
3900 SD 92124 1249-G3
SHILOH LN
18800 SDCo 92082 1091-G5
SHILOH RD
3700 SD 92105 1270-A5
SHINING LIGHT WY
11100 SDCo 92020 1271-H2
SHINLEY PL
1300 ESCN 92026 1110-A5
SHINOHARA LN
500 CHV 91911 1330-H5
SHIPLEY CT
1400 SD 92114 1290-G2
SHIPPEY LN
100 DLMR 92014 1187-F6
SHIRE AV
1600 OCN 92057 1067-F7
SHIRE DR
1900 SDCo 92019 1252-C5
SHIREHALL DR
6400 SD 92111 1248-H4
SHIREY RD
32200 SDCo 92026 1049-B7
32200 SDCo 92026 1069-A1
SHIRLE LN
- OCN 92054 1086-G3
SHIRLENE PL
3800 LMSA 91941 1270-E5
SHIRLEY CT
9200 LMSA 91941 1271-B2
SHIRLEY DR
300 SMCS 92069 1108-J5
9100 LMSA 91941 1271-B2
SHIRLEY LN
1900 LMGR 91945 1290-F1
8700 SNTE 92071 1231-E7
SHIRLEY ST
200 CHV 91910 1310-B4
SHIRLEY ANN PL
4500 SD 92116 1269-D4
SHIRLEY GARDENS DR
9800 SNTE 92071 1231-E4
SHIR-MAR PL
7900 SDCo 92021 1251-J1
SHIRRA AV
12600 PWY 92064 1190-H6
SHOAL CREEK DR
11300 SD 92128 1189-J2
11600 SD 92128 1190-A3
SHOAL SUMMIT DR
- SD 92128 1190-A3
SHOCKEY TKTR
33300 SDCo 91906 (1318-F5 See Page 1298)
33500 SDCo 91906 430-C10
33500 SDCo 91906 (1319-A7 See Page 1298)
SHOEMAKER CT
300 SOLB 92075 1187-F2
SHOEMAKER LN
300 SOLB 92075 1187-F1
SHOEN LN
14800 SDCo 92065 1173-J7
SHOOTING IRON TR
700 SDCo 92036 1138-B6
SHOOTING STAR CT
1600 SD 92173 1350-E2
SHOOTING STAR DR
3600 SD 92173 1350-E2
SHOOTING STAR PL
2400 SDCo 91901 1234-B5
SHORE DR
- SD 92109 1248-C6
5200 CRLB 92008 1126-F2
SHOREACRES DR
1400 CHV 91915 1311-H7
SHOREBIRD LN
- CRLB 92009 1127-B7
SHORE CREST RD
900 CRLB 92009 1126-J4
SHOREDALE DR
9900 SNTE 92071 1231-D3
SHOREHAM PL
5000 SD 92122 1228-G5
SHOREHANG LN
200 ENCT 92024 1167-H1
SHORELINE DR
7100 SD 92122 1228-E3
SHOREPOINTE CT
- SD 92130 1208-B2
SHOREPOINTE WY
- SD 92130 1208-B3
SHORE VIEW LN
300 ENCT 92024 1147-B3
SHOREVIEW PL
2100 CHV 91913 1311-E4
SHOREWOOD DR
7600 SD 92114 1290-G4
SHORT CT
3900 SDCo 91935 1292-H2
SHORT ST
4300 SD 92116 1269-H3
8100 SDCo 92040 1252-A1
12000 SDCo 92040 1251-J1
SHORT WY
100 SDCo 92021 1252-H3
SHORTHILL DR
2300 OCN 92056 1106-H2
SHORT NINE DR E
- SDCo 92004 (1079-B3 See Page 1058)
SHOSHONE ST
1400 OCN 92054 1086-A6
SHOSHONI AV
4600 SD 92117 1248-F1
SHOWPLACE DR
9400 SDCo 91941 1271-C4
SHRINER RD
- SDCo 91948 1218-B3
SHROPSHIRE LN
12400 SD 92128 1150-B6
SHUBIN LN
100 SMCS 92078 1128-H1
SHUBORO ST
600 VSTA 92083 1087-F5
SHUTTLE RD
7200 CRLB 92009 1127-C7
SHY LN
400 CHV 91911 1330-C4
SHYA WY
4000 SDCo 91901 1234-F7
SHY BIRD LN
10900 SD 92128 1189-H4
SICARD ST
400 SD 92113 1289-D5
SICILY WY
3300 OCN 92056 1106-J1
SIDDALL DR
1500 SDCo 92084 1108-F2
SIDEWINDER RD
- ImCo 432-A4
7100 SD 92145 1229-A3
SIDEWINDER WY
13000 SD 92129 1189-C4
SIDONIA CT
1100 ENCT 92024 1147-D4
SIDONIA ST
800 ENCT 92024 1147-D4
SIEFORT PL
400 NATC 92136 1309-F1
SIEGLE CT
2100 LMGR 91945 1290-J1
SIEGLE DR
1900 LMGR 91945 1290-J1
SIEMBRE ST
3500 SDCo 91902 1310-J1
SIEMPRE VIVA RD
6900 SD 92154 1351-D4
9200 SD 92154 1352-A3
SIENA ST
100 SD 92114 1290-F5
N SIENA ST
100 SD 92114 1290-G4
SIENNA ST
3600 OCN 92056 1107-F4
SIENNA CANYON CT
3800 ENCT 92024 1167-H2
SIENNA CANYON DR
1700 ENCT 92024 1167-H2
N SIERRA AV
100 SOLB 92075 1167-E7
S SIERRA AV
100 SOLB 92075 1167-E7
100 SOLB 92075 1187-E1
800 DLMR 92014 1187-E1
800 DLMR 92075 1187-E1
SIERRA CIR
1300 ELCJ 92020 1271-E1
SIERRA CT
900 VSTA 92083 1107-H2
SIERRA DR
- ESCN 92026 1109-F7
SIERRA LN
14000 SDCo 92061 1050-G3
SIERRA ST
100 SDCo 92025 1150-B2
8900 SNTE 92071 1231-E6
SIERRA WY
- CHV 91911 1330-D1
E SIERRA WY
- CHV 91911 1330-E1
SIERRA ALTA WY
9000 SDCo 92021 1232-F6
SIERRA BONITA
2900 SDCo 92028 1028-D3
SIERRA BONITA ST
10000 SDCo 91977 1271-D6
SIERRA CIELO
17600 SDCo 91935 1294-C5
SIERRA CIELO LN
17600 SDCo 91935 1294-B6
SIERRA CREST CT
11600 SD 92131 1209-J4
SIERRA GRANDE RD
15500 SDCo 92082 1070-J5
15500 SDCo 92082 1071-A5
SIERRA LINDA DR
1100 ESCN 92025 1150-D3
SIERRA MADRE DR
- SDCo 92055 1086-A3
SIERRA MADRE RD
9800 SDCo 91977 1271-C4
10100 SDCo 91941 1271-D4
SIERRA MAR DR
7700 SD 92037 1227-G6
SIERRA MORENA AV
2400 CRLB 92008 1106-H4
SIERRA RIDGE DR
200 ENCT 92024 1147-J6
SIERRA ROJO LN
29300 SDCo 92082 1069-J6
SIERRA ROJO RD
11400 SDCo 92082 1069-H7
12000 SDCo 92082 1070-A7
SIERRA VERDE
700 VSTA 92084 1087-J7
SIERRA VERDE RD
1600 CHV 91913 1311-D7
19200 SDCo 92082 1091-H5
19300 SDCo 92027 1091-H5
SIERRA VIEW WY
6000 SD 92120 1250-D6
SIERRA VISTA
1300 SMCS 92078 1129-B1
SIERRA VISTA AV
9300 SDCo 91941 1271-B1
9500 LMSA 91941 1271-C1
SIERRA VISTA DR
100 SDCo 92021 1252-J3
SIERRA VISTA LN
10400 SDCo 91941 1271-D1
SIERRA VISTA ST
4200 SD 92103 1268-H5
SIESTA DR
4800 OCN 92057 1066-J7
4800 OCN 92057 1067-A6
5400 SD 92115 1270-B3
SIESTA LN
19300 SDCo 92082 1091-H4
SIESTA PL
4800 OCN 92057 1066-J7
SIESTA RD
8600 SNTE 92071 1231-E7
SIESTA CALLE
1900 SDCo 92019 1252-D4
SIETE LEGUAS
7200 SDCo 92067 1168-G1
SIGGSON AV
1200 ESCN 92027 1109-J6
1200 ESCN 92027 1110-A6
SIGGSON CT
600 ESCN 92026 1109-J7
SIGLO CT
10900 SD 92124 1249-J2
SIGMA ST
5600 LMSA 91942 1250-J7
SIGNAL AV
1300 SD 92154 1350-A1
SIGNAL RD
- ImCo 92259 431-A8
SIGSBEE ST
800 SD 92113 1289-C5
SIKOKIS PL
2000 ESCN 92025 1130-A7
SIKORSKY ST
- SD 92154 1351-C1
SIKORSKY WY
- SD 92154 1351-D1
SILK PL
5100 SD 92105 1290-A1
SILKTREE LN
4600 SDCo 92004 (1099-F4 See Page 1098)
SILKWOOD DR
5200 OCN 92056 1087-D1
SILL ST
1700 NATC 91950 1289-J6
SILLA ST
14500 PWY 92064 1190-H3
SILSBEE RD
1200 ImCo 92243 431-A6
SILVA RD
8600 SD 92145 1229-D1
9700 SDCo 92021 1233-D2
SILVANA WY
500 VSTA 92084 1087-H3
SILVAS ST
1500 CHV 91911 1330-C5
SILVER CT
8900 SNTE 92071 1231-G6
SILVER DR
300 VSTA 92083 1087-F6
SILVER ST
700 SD 92037 1227-E7
SILVERADO CT
10000 SNTE 92071 1231-C3
SILVERADO DR
1200 CHV 91915 1311-G6
1400 OCN 92057 1067-F6
SILVERADO ST
- SD 92037 1227-E6
SILVERBERRY CT
1200 SDCo 92019 1252-F7
1300 SDCo 92019 1272-F1
SILVER BERRY PL
- ENCT 92024 1147-C5
SILVER BIRCH LN
1500 SDCo 92028 1047-J2
SILVER BIRCH WY
200 OCN 92057 1086-J2
SILVER BLUFF DR
4700 OCN 92057 1087-B1
5200 OCN 92057 1067-C7
SILVERBROOK DR
300 SDCo 92019 1253-B2
SILVER BUCKLE WY
11200 SD 92127 1169-J5
SILVER CLOUD PASS
- SDCo 92036 1155-G3
SILVERCREEK DR
100 SNTE 92071 1231-C5
SILVERCREEK GN
200 ESCN 92029 1150-A2
SILVER CREEK LN
10000 SDCo 92021 1232-G2
SILVERFOX LN
1700 SDCo 92028 1027-F5
SILVER FOX LN
1700 VSTA 92083 1087-D6
SILVER GATE AV
- SD 92106 1287-J4
400 SD 92106 1288-A3
SILVER GATE CT
300 SD 92106 1287-J4
SILVERGATE PL
3500 SD 92106 1287-J4
3500 SD 92106 1288-A4
SILVER GUM WY
17100 SD 92127 1169-D2
SILVER HEIGHTS RD
14400 PWY 92064 1190-G4
SILVER LAKE DR
13100 PWY 92064 1190-D4
SILVERLEAF LN
3500 SDCo 92084 1068-G7
3500 SDCo 92084 1088-F1
SILVER OAK LN
3300 SDCo 92084 1088-E7
SILVER OAK PL
2700 ESCN 92029 1129-D3
SILVER OAKS WY
2600 SDCo 91977 1271-D7
SILVER PEAK PL
2200 ENCT 92024 1147-J6
SILVER RIDGE CT
3200 OCN 92054 1086-D3
SILVER RIDGE PT
11600 SD 92131 1209-J4
SILVER RIDGE RD
14200 PWY 92064 1190-G4
SILVER SADDLE CT
16400 PWY 92064 1170-E4
SILVER SADDLE LN
13100 PWY 92064 1170-D4
SILVER SAGE RD
- CHV 91915 1311-H5
SILVERSET ST
14300 PWY 92064 1190-D1
SILVER SHADOW DR
400 SMCS 92078 1129-A1
SILVER SHOALS PT
- SD 92154 1330-H7
SILVER SPRINGS DR
1300 CHV 91915 1311-H6
SILVER SPRINGS LN
1000 SDCo 92028 1047-H1
SILVER SPRINGS PL
1000 ESCN 92026 1129-F1
SILVER SPUR CT
15900 SDCo 92021 1233-D2
SILVER SPUR RD
9700 SDCo 92021 1233-D2
SILVER SPUR WY
400 SMCS 92069 1108-E6
SILVER STALLION DR
1000 VSTA 92083 1107-G2
SILVERSTONE DR
1700 ELCJ 92021 1252-B2
SILVER STRAND
- CORD 91932 1329-F7
500 IMPB 91932 1329-F7
SILVER STRAND BLVD
Rt#-75
500 CORD 91932 1329-D2
500 IMPB 91932 1329-D2
1700 CORD 92118 1308-J1
1900 CORD 92118 1309-A3
1900 CORD 92155 1309-A3
2100 CORD 92118 1329-D2
SILVERTON AV
7800 SD 92126 1209-B7
SILVER TREE LN
1500 SDCo 92026 1089-D7
SILVERWOOD ST
600 OCN 92054 1086-F2
7000 SD 92114 1290-F5
SILVERY LN
400 ELCJ 92020 1251-C5
SIMA CT
10700 SNTE 92071 1231-E1
SIMBAR RD
3100 SDCo 91902 1290-J7
3100 SDCo 91902 1310-J1
SIMEON DR
7400 SNTE 92071 1230-F7
SIMEON PL
1200 ESCN 92029 1129-H7
SIMI CT
2600 SD 92139 1310-F1
SIMI PL
6700 SD 92139 1310-F1
6900 SD 92139 1290-F7
SIMI WY
6900 SD 92139 1310-G1
SIMMS CT
9300 SDCo 91977 1271-B5
SIMPATICO CT
1700 SD 92154 1350-B3
SIMPSON RD
- ImCo 92233 411-B8
SIMPSON WY
1300 ESCN 92029 1129-F3
SIMS RD
- SD 92133 1268-D7
SIMSBURY CT
3500 CRLB 92008 1107-A3
SINALOA CT
100 SOLB 92075 1167-D6
SINCLAIR LN
3700 SDCo 91977 1271-B5
SINCLAIR RD
- CLPT 92233 411-C9
- ImCo 92233 411-A9
SINGER LN
11900 SDCo 91978 1271-H6
SINGH RD
- ImCo 92243 6500-E7
200 ImCo 92243 6560-E1
SINGING HEIGHTS DR
700 SDCo 92019 1252-D7
SINGING RIDGE RD
900 SDCo 92019 1252-E7
SINGING TRAILS CT
700 SDCo 92019 1252-E6
SINGING TRAILS DR
700 SDCo 92019 1252-E7
SINGING VISTA CT
600 SDCo 92019 1252-E6
SINGING VISTA DR
600 SDCo 92019 1252-E6
SINGING VISTA WY
2500 SDCo 92019 1252-E6
SINGINGWOOD PL
2100 ESCN 92029 1129-E7
SINGING WOOD WY
8900 SNTE 92071 1231-B6
SINGLE OAK DR
9100 SDCo 92040 1232-A4
SINGLE OAK PL
12300 SDCo 92040 1232-A5
SINGLETREE LN
10800 SDCo 91978 1271-G7
SINGLETREE PL
1300 SDCo 92028 1047-J4
SINJON CIR
6000 LMSA 91942 1251-B6
SINKLER WY
800 VSTA 92083 1107-J1
SINSONTE LN
9100 SDCo 92040 1232-B5
SINTON PL
6000 LMSA 91942 1251-A6
SINTONTE CT
12200 SD 92128 1170-B1
SINTONTE DR
17700 SD 92128 1170-B1
17800 SD 92128 1150-B7
SIOUX AV
3700 SD 92117 1248-E5
SIPES CIR
- CHV 91911 1330-H2
SIPES LN
3600 SD 92173 1350-F5
SIRENA VISTA
3000 CRLB 92009 1127-J5
SIR FRANCIS DRAKE DR
11300 SDCo 91941 1271-H3
SIRGINSON ST
500 SMCS 92069 1108-J6
SIRGINSON WY
600 SMCS 92069 1108-J6
SIRIAS RD
11200 SD 92126 1209-C2
SIR LANCELOT DR
10100 SNTE 92071 1231-D1
SIROS WY
5000 OCN 92056 1107-F5
SIRRAH ST
800 SD 92154 1330-B7
SISSI LN
10200 SDCo 92040 1231-F3
SISSON ST
9300 LMSA 91942 1251-B6
SITIO ABETO
7800 CRLB 92009 1147-H2
SITIO ABRIDOR
7900 CRLB 92009 1147-H3
SITIO BANIANO
7900 CRLB 92009 1147-H3
SITIO BAYA
3400 CRLB 92009 1148-A2
SITIO BORDE
3400 CRLB 92009 1148-A2
SITIO CALMAR
7800 CRLB 92009 1147-J3
SITIO CATANA
7900 CRLB 92009 1147-J3
SITIO CAUCHO
8000 CRLB 92009 1147-G3
SITIO CEDRELA
- CRLB 92009 1127-C5
SITIO COCO
- CRLB 92009 1147-G2
SITIO FRESCA
7900 CRLB 92009 1148-A4
SITIO FRESNO
7800 CRLB 92009 1147-H2
SITIO GRANADO
7900 CRLB 92009 1147-H2
SITIO ISADORA
- CRLB 92009 1127-H7
- CRLB 92009 1147-H1
SITIO MIRTO
7800 CRLB 92009 1147-H2
SITIO MUSICA
7700 CRLB 92009 1147-J3
SITIO NISPERO
7900 CRLB 92009 1147-H3
SITIO OLMO
7800 CRLB 92009 1147-H2
SITIO PALMAS
6700 CRLB 92009 1127-H5
SITIO PERAL
7900 CRLB 92009 1147-H2
SITIO REDONDA
7700 CRLB 92009 1148-A3
SITIO ROSALIA
7300 CRLB 92009 1127-G7
SITIO SAGO
- CRLB 92009 1127-C5
SITIO SOLANA
- CRLB 92009 1148-A3
SITIO TEJO
- CRLB 92009 1147-F2
SITIO VAQUERO
- CRLB 92009 1148-A3
SIVA ST
1600 SD 92113 1289-F6
SIWANOY CT
8800 SNTE 92071 1230-J5
8800 SNTE 92071 1231-A5
SIXES CT
1800 SDCo 92065 1172-J2
SIXPENCE WY
- CORD 92118 1329-E1

SAN DIEGO CO.
INDEX

6619 SKI WY — SAN DIEGO CO. STREET INDEX — SPRING VALLEY RD

STREET
Block City ZIP Pg-Grid

SKI WY
100 CHV 91911 1330-D3
SKIMMER CT
1700 CRLB 92009 1127-E5
SKIMMER WY
4400 OCN 92057 1087-A3
SKIPJACK LN
- SDCo 92055 1085-H5
SKIPPER ST
3000 SD 92123 1249-D5
SKUNK HOLLOW RD
- SDCo 91935 (1314-E3 See Page 1294)
SKY DR
26200 SDCo 92026 1089-H7
26200 SDCo 92026 1109-H1
SKY ST
4900 SD 92110 1268-F1
SKYBROOK PL
1900 CHV 91913 1311-E4
SKYCREST DR
3100 SDCo 92028 1048-D1
SKY CREST GN
- ESCN 92029 1129-H5
SKYE VALLEY RD
- SDCo 91901 1275-B7
- SDCo 91901 (1295-A3 See Page 1294)
- SDCo 91935 1294-H3
- SDCo 91935 (1295-A3 See Page 1294)
SKY HARBOR RD
1700 SD 92139 1290-D7
SKY HAVEN LN
3400 OCN 92056 1107-D2
SKYHAWK RD
1600 SDCo 92029 1149-F2
SKYHAWK WY
4900 OCN 92056 1107-E3
SKYHIGH CT
12400 SDCo 92021 1232-B7
SKY HIGH RD
15300 SDCo 92025 1150-J2
SKYHILL CT
400 CHV 91910 1310-F7
SKYHILL PL
1800 ESCN 92026 1109-E6
SKYKNOLL WY
1900 ENCT 92024 1147-H5
SKYLARK DR
900 SD 92037 1247-G3
2200 OCN 92054 1086-E7
SKYLARK PL
5600 SD 92037 1247-G3
SKYLARK WY
1500 CHV 91911 1330-F5
SKYLINE AV
- ESCN 92027 1130-C1
SKYLINE CIR
300 SDCo 92028 1028-H4
SKYLINE DR
- SDCo 91948 (1197-G7 See Page 1176)
- SDCo 91948 (1217-F3 See Page 1216)
- SDCo 91977 1290-H1
- SDCo 92066 (1217-F3 See Page 1216)
300 SDCo 92084 1088-B6
300 VSTA 92084 1088-B6
1300 LMGR 91945 1290-H1
1300 SD 92114 1290-D4
1700 SDCo 92027 1130-E4
2000 LMGR 91945 1270-H6
3000 OCN 92056 1086-G7
3000 OCN 92056 1106-G1
SKYLINE LN
1500 ELCJ 92019 1252-A7
1500 SDCo 92019 1252-A7
4600 LMSA 91941 1271-A3
SKYLINE RD
3700 CRLB 92008 1106-H5
SKYLINE SPUR
14500 SDCo 91935 1294-C1
SKYLINE TER
1900 SDCo 92027 1130-E4
SKYLINE TKTR
14500 SDCo 91935 1273-E6
16900 SDCo 91935 1274-B7
18000 SDCo 91935 1294-D1
SKY LOFT LN
1700 ENCT 92024 1147-C2
SKY LOFT RD
600 ENCT 92024 1147-B2
SKY MESA RD
- SDCo 91901 1233-F7
SKY MOUNTAIN LN
700 SDCo 91901 1234-B4
SKY PARK CT
9200 SD 92123 1249-E3
SKY PILOT WY
28500 SDCo 92082 1090-B1
SKY RANCH RD
40000 SDCo 92028 409-A4
SKYRIDGE LN
200 ESCN 92026 1109-G4
SKY RIDGE RD
3400 SDCo 91901 1275-B4
SKYRIDGE RD
15200 PWY 92064 1170-J5
15200 PWY 92064 1171-A6
SKY RIM DR
8500 SDCo 92021 1232-B7
8500 SDCo 92040 1232-B7
SKYROCK LN
8400 SD 92145 1229-C2
SKYSAIL AV
800 CRLB 92009 1126-J5
SKYTRAIL RANCH RD
3100 SDCo 91935 1273-J6
SKY VALLEY DR
16500 SDCo 92065 1151-D6
SKY VIEW DR
- ImCo 92259 410-H7
11900 SDCo 92082 1090-A2
SKYVIEW GN
1900 ESCN 92027 1110-A5
SKYVIEW LN
100 OCN 92056 1107-D2
SKYVIEW ST
500 ELCJ 92020 1271-E1
SKY VISTA WY
300 SDCo 92028 1027-H2
SKYWAY DR
28600 SDCo 92066 410-A8
SKYWOOD DR
10900 ELCJ 92020 1271-G1
10900 SDCo 92020 1271-G1

SLACK ST
12900 PWY 92064 1190-D5
SLADON CT
14300 PWY 92064 1190-E2
SLANT ROCK RD
3400 SDCo 91901 1275-B4
SLASH M RD
300 SDCo 92004 (1078-G6 See Page 1058)
SLATE CT
300 CHV 91911 1330-G4
SLATE ST
200 CHV 91911 1330-G4
SLATE TER
- SDCo 92019 1272-B2
SLAUGHTERHOUSE RD
- SDCo 92070 409-J11
27400 SDCo 92065 409-J11
27400 SDCo 92065 1154-C1
SLAUGHTERHOUSE CANYON RD
- SDCo 92040 1211-G4
SLAYEN WY
3000 SD 92117 1248-C3
SLAYTON RD
- ImCo 92250 431-E4
SLEEPING CIRCLE DR
2100 SDCo 92004 (1099-F5 See Page 1098)
SLEEPING INDIAN RD
500 OCN 92057 1067-D2
1400 OCN 92028 1067-D2
1500 OCN 92028 1047-E6
1500 SDCo 92028 1047-E6
SLEEPY WY
8400 SDCo 92021 1232-D7
SLEEPY CREEK RD
10100 SDCo 92021 1232-F2
SLEEPY HILL LN
2300 SDCo 92026 1109-D4
SLEEPY HOLLOW
2200 SDCo 92036 1136-C6
28700 SDCo 92066 1237-B5
SLEEPY HOLLOW LN
4200 SDCo 91902 1310-F4
SLEEPY HOLLOW RD
2000 SDCo 92026 1109-E4
SLEEPY HOLLOW WY
- VSTA 92083 1107-D1
SLICE CT
3100 SDCo 92004 (1079-B6 See Page 1058)
SLIVKOFF DR
2900 ESCN 92027 1110-F7
SLOAN DR
1900 SDCo 92028 1028-A6
SLOANE ST
400 SD 92103 1268-J6
400 SD 92103 1269-A6
SLOANE TKTR
- SDCo 91935 1273-J3
SLOANE CANYON RD
1100 SDCo 91935 1273-D1
1100 SDCo 91935 1253-F7
1200 SDCo 92019 1273-A2
4500 SDCo 92019 1253-A7
S SLOPE DR
8500 SNTE 92071 1230-G5
8500 SNTE 92071 1250-J1
SLOPE ST
8500 SNTE 92071 1251-C1
SLUMBERING OAKS TR
3200 SDCo 92036 1156-C2
SMALLINS ST
400 NATC 92136 1309-G1
SMART CT
100 ENCT 92024 1147-G7
SMEDLEY AV
8900 SD 92126 1209-F7
SMELIK LN
8400 LMGR 91945 1270-J6
SMILAX RD
100 SDCo 92069 1108-C5
100 SDCo 92084 1108-C5
100 SDCo 92083 1108-C5
200 SMCS 92069 1108-C5
SMILIANA LN
400 SDCo 92083 1108-A2
SMITH AV
- CHV 91910 1309-J5
- CHV 91910 1310-A5
SMITH DR
700 VSTA 92084 1087-J5
1100 VSTA 92083 1087-G4
SMITH LN
- SDCo 92672 1023-D2
800 ImCo 92243 6499-B6
SMITH RD
8000 SD 92145 1229-C2
SMITH ST
3700 SD 92110 1268-F5
SMITH CANYON CT
4900 SD 92130 1188-C5
SMITHERS CT
11400 SD 92126 1209-D1
SMOKEBUSH CT
1200 SDCo 92019 1252-F7
1200 SDCo 92019 1272-F1
SMOKE SIGNAL DR
18100 SD 92127 1149-J7
SMOKETREE CIR
2100 ELCN 92243 6559-G2
SMOKETREE CT
800 SMCS 92078 1128-F2
2100 ELCN 92243 6559-G2
SMOKETREE DR
100 ELCN 92243 6559-H1
SMOKETREE GN
500 ESCN 92026 1109-G5
SMOKE TREE LN
1700 SDCo 92004 (1099-F3 See Page 1098)
SMOKE TREE PL
200 OCN 92057 1087-A1
SMOKEWOOD DR
8000 SNTE 92071 1230-H7
SMOKEWOOD PL
2400 ESCN 92026 1109-J3
SMOKEY LN
- SDCo 92036 1175-J2
1700 SDCo 91977 1291-B1
SMOKY CIR
400 CHV 91910 1310-F5
SMYTHE AV
1600 SD 92173 1350-F2
SNAFFLE BIT PL
5900 SDCo 91902 1311-B2
SNAPDRAGON
15200 SDCo 92021 1233-B3

SNAPDRAGON DR
7000 CRLB 92009 1127-B6
SNAPDRAGON LN
2000 SDCo 91901 1234-A5
SNAPDRAGON ST
700 ENCT 92024 1147-E6
SNEAD AV
2700 SD 92111 1248-G6
SNEAD DR
2300 OCN 92056 1106-H2
SNEATH WY
300 SDCo 91901 1234-B3
SNEEZY CT
13300 SDCo 92021 1232-E7
SNELSON WY
9400 SNTE 92071 1231-B3
SNIPE CT
- CRLB 92009 1127-A4
SNIPES CT
1100 SD 92154 1350-E1
SNOOK ST
9800 SD 92124 1249-G3
SNOWBERRY CT
800 SMCS 92069 1109-A5
SNOWBOND CT
5800 SD 92120 1250-C6
SNOWBOND ST
6200 SD 92120 1250-C6
SNOWCREEK
1000 SDCo 92028 1027-H4
SNOWDEN PL
400 SDCo 92019 1253-C2
SNOWDROP ST
2500 SD 92105 1269-H7
SNOWDROP WY
- CRLB 92009 1127-B4
SNOWFALL CIR
4500 OCN 92056 1087-D5
SNOWS RD
3000 SDCo 92028 1047-J1
SNOW VIEW DR
9600 SDCo 92021 1233-A3
SNOW WHITE DR
8400 SDCo 92021 1232-D7
SNUG HARBOR
- SDCo 92065 1171-J2
SNUZ MOUNTAIN RD
15800 SDCo 92065 1171-H5
SNYDER RD
1900 ImCo 92250 431-E5
10600 SDCo 91941 1271-F2
SOARING DR
6600 SD 92119 1250-G4
SOARING BIRD PT
13000 SD 92128 1189-H5
SOBRE LOS CERROS
16900 SDCo 92067 1168-C3
SOCIN CT
- ESCN 92027 1110-E6
SOCORRO CT
11100 SD 92129 1169-J6
SOCORRO LN
2700 CRLB 92009 1127-H5
SOCORRO PL
15200 SD 92129 1169-J6
SOCORRO ST
11100 SD 92129 1169-J6
SOCORRO WY
15200 SD 92129 1169-J7
SODERBLOM AV
2400 SD 92122 1228-B6
SODERBLOM CT
5500 SD 92122 1228-A6
SOFTWIND LN
2100 ENCT 92024 1147-H5
SOFTWIND RD
800 VSTA 92083 1087-F7
800 VSTA 92083 1107-F1
SOHAIL ST
13400 SDCo 92040 1232-D4
SOL DR
500 OCN 92057 1067-A6
SOLACE CT
100 ENCT 92024 1147-G7
SOLAMAR DR
6000 CRLB 92009 1126-G3
SOLANA CIR E
600 SOLB 92075 1187-F1
SOLANA CIR W
600 SOLB 92075 1187-F1
800 DLMR 92014 1187-F1
SOLANA DR
1000 SOLB 92014 1167-H7
SOLANA GN
1700 ESCN 92026 1109-D5
SOLANA RD
1800 ELCN 92243 6499-E6
SOLANA ST
8000 SD 92114 1290-G2
SOLANA GLEN CT
600 SOLB 92075 1167-G6
SOLANA HILLS CT
600 SOLB 92075 1167-G6
N SOLANA HILLS DR
300 SOLB 92075 1167-G6
S SOLANA HILLS DR
100 SOLB 92075 1167-G7
SOLANA POINT CIR
100 SOLB 92075 1167-E6
SOLANA REAL
400 SDCo 92028 1047-E7
SOLANA VISTA DR
100 SOLB 92075 1167-E6
SOLANDRA DR
- CRLB 92009 1127-A5
SOLANDRA LN
900 SDCo 91977 1291-D3
SOLANO ST
7400 CRLB 92009 1147-H1
SOLANO BAY PL
300 OCN 92057 1066-J6
SOLANO ESTE DR
3600 OCN 92054 1086-F2
SOLAR LN
2700 SDCo 92069 1088-H6
SOLAR ST
5100 SD 92110 1268-F2
SOLAR CIR DR
3300 DLMR 92014 1187-F2
SOLAR VIEW DR
200 SDCo 92069 1088-G6
SOLAZAR WY
2400 OCN 92056 1087-C6
SOLDAU DR
3300 SD 92154 1350-D1
SOLDIER OAKS LN
12800 SDCo 92082 1090-C2
SOLDIN LN
9200 SDCo 92021 1232-H5

SOLEDAD AV
2000 SD 92037 1227-G6
SOLEDAD CT
2400 SD 92037 1248-A2
SOLEDAD FRWY Rt#-52
- SD - 1228-B7
- SD - 1248-A1
SOLEDAD PL
200 CORD 92118 1288-J5
200 CORD 92118 1289-A6
3000 ESCN 92027 1110-E6
SOLEDAD RD
4900 SD 92109 1248-A4
5300 SD 92037 1247-J3
5300 SD 92037 1248-A2
5300 SD 92109 1247-J3
7000 SD 92037 1227-J7
SOLEDAD WY
1700 SD 92109 1247-J3
1700 SD 92109 1248-A3
SOLEDAD MOUNTAIN RD
4600 SD 92109 1248-A2
5300 SD 92037 1248-A2
5900 SD 92037 1247-J1
SOLEDAD RANCHO CT
5200 SD 92109 1248-A3
SOLEDAD RANCHO RD
2200 SD 92109 1248-A3
SOLERA WY
12900 PWY 92064 1170-D2
SOLITA AV
6400 SD 92115 1270-D3
SOLITARY LN
1000 SDCo 92028 1027-J6
SOLOLA AV
4700 SD 92113 1289-J6
4700 SD 92113 1290-A6
5000 SD 92114 1290-A6
SOLOMON AV
8300 SDCo 92021 1231-G7
8300 SDCo 92021 1251-G1
SOLO ROBLE
100 SMCS 92078 1129-A3
SOL SITIO
4800 OCN 92057 1066-J7
4800 OCN 92057 1067-A7
SOL VISTA
3300 SDCo 92028 1028-D1
SOL VISTA GN
800 ESCN 92025 1130-B3
SOL WOOD
1600 SDCo 91905 (1319-J3 See Page 1298)
1600 SDCo 91905 (1320-A3 See Page 1300)
SOLYMAR DR
900 SD 92037 1247-G2
SOMA PL
1500 ELCJ 92021 1252-A3
SOMAM AV
2200 SD 92110 1268-G1
4900 SD 92110 1248-F7
SOMBRA CT
10900 SD 92124 1249-J2
SOMBRA DEL MONTE
16400 SDCo 92065 1171-F3
SOMBRERO WY
1600 SD 92154 1349-J2
SOMBRIA RD
9200 SDCo 92040 1232-B5
SOMBROSA PL
2500 CRLB 92009 1147-G3
SOMBROSA ST
2600 CRLB 92009 1147-G3
SOMERLANE ST
1700 SDCo 92021 1251-J2
SOMERMONT DR
1300 SDCo 92021 1251-H1
SOMERSET AV
1400 ENCT 92007 1167-D2
8600 SD 92123 1249-C6
SOMERSET CT
- SDCo 92065 1152-G7
900 CHV 91915 1311-G4
SOMERSET RD
13600 PWY 92064 1190-F3
SOMERSET WY
3500 CRLB 92008 1107-A4
SOMMER PL
6400 LMSA 91942 1251-B5
SONATA
1600 SDCo 92069 1128-C2
SONDRA CT
2900 CRLB 92009 1127-H7
SONETT ST
1800 SDCo 92019 1272-C4
SONGBIRD LN
900 CHV 91902 1310-H3
SONG SPARROW CIR
- SDCo 91902 1291-B7
SONIA CT
1300 VSTA 92084 1088-C4
SONIA LN
300 CHV 91911 1330-F6
SONIA PL
900 ESCN 92026 1109-F5
SONJA CT
3000 OCN 92056 1086-G7
3000 OCN 92056 1106-G1
SONO PL
7300 LMSA 91941 1270-F4
SONOMA CT
1200 CHV 91911 1330-G2
SONOMA DR
3600 OCN 92054 1086-F2
SONOMA LN
1800 LMGR 91945 1290-F1
SONOMA ST
- SMCS 92078 1128-G2
SONORA CT
2000 VSTA 92083 1107-J4
2400 CRLB 92008 1106-H4
SONORA DR
1500 CHV 91911 1330-H4
SONORA RD
12600 SD 92128 1170-C3
SONORA ST
10600 SNTE 92071 1231-E6
SONORA WY
2200 SDCo 92065 1152-C5
SONRISA ST
600 SOLB 92075 1187-F1
SONRISA WY
2400 OCN 92056 1087-C6
SOPER LN
7900 LMSA 91942 1270-H1
SOPHIA DR
12300 PWY 92064 1190-C2

SOPHIA WY
200 OCN 92057 1086-H3
SORA WY
12500 SD 92129 1189-C6
SORBONNE CT
- SD 92128 1190-A3
SORIA DR
4600 SD 92115 1270-C3
SORIA GN
1200 ESCN 92026 1109-G7
1200 ESCN 92026 1129-G1
SORREL AV
9900 SDCo 92040 1232-C3
SORREL CT
1700 CRLB 92009 1127-E7
SORREL TREE PL
200 OCN 92057 1087-A1
SORRENTINO DR
1900 SDCo 92025 1130-D5
SORRENTO DR
1000 SD 92107 1287-J2
2100 OCN 92056 1086-J7
SORRENTO PKWY
- SD 92121 1208-E7
SORRENTO PL
1200 ESCN 92027 1110-A6
SORRENTO HILLS BLVD
- SD 92130 1208-A3
SORRENTO VALLEY BLVD
3700 SD 92121 1208-F3
6800 SD 92126 1208-F3
SORRENTO VALLEY CT
11000 SD 92121 1208-B5
SORRENTO VALLEY RD
9900 SD 92121 1208-A4
11800 SD 92121 1207-J2
SOTO ST
1500 OCN 92054 1106-D2
2200 SD 92107 1268-A6
SOULE ST
12600 PWY 92064 1190-C5
SOUTH LN
100 SDCo 92021 1252-H4
200 SD 92037 1247-E1
4400 SDCo 92014 1167-J7
4400 SDCo 92014 1187-J1
4400 SDCo 92014 1188-A1
SOUTH ST
7500 LMSA 91941 1270-G3
SOUTHALL ST
800 NATC 92136 1309-F2
SOUTHAMPTON RD
2700 CRLB 92008 1106-J5
2900 CRLB 92008 1107-A5
SOUTHAMPTON ST
1200 SMCS 92069 1128-B3
4500 SD 92117 1248-G2
SOUTH BAY PKWY
5700 SDCo 91902 1290-H7
SOUTH BAY PKWY Rt#-54
5600 SDCo 91902 1290-J6
5600 SDCo 91977 1290-J5
5600 SDCo 91977 1291-A4
SOUTHBRIDGE CT
500 ENCT 92024 1147-B2
SOUTHBROOK CT
11400 SD 92128 1190-A6
SOUTH CAYS CT
- CORD 92118 1329-D3
SOUTHCREST AV
2100 SD 92110 1268-F1
SOUTHERN RD
6300 ELCJ 92020 1251-B5
6300 LMSA 91942 1251-B5
SOUTHERN OAK RD
2300 SDCo 92065 1172-D5
SOUTHERN PINE PL
10400 SD 92131 1209-J4
SOUTHERNWOOD WY
3700 SD 92106 1288-A2
3700 SD 92106 1287-J2
SOUTH FORTY RD
- SDCo 91901 1235-G7
- SDCo 91901 1255-G1
SOUTHGATE CT
700 OCN 92057 1087-C1
SOUTHGATE DR
600 OCN 92057 1087-C1
6900 SD 92119 1251-A3
SOUTH GRADE RD
400 SDCo 91901 1233-G6
1100 SDCo 91901 1253-H1
1800 SDCo 91901 1254-A2
2700 SDCo 91901 1234-C7
SOUTHHAMPTON CV
5200 SD 92130 1188-D6
SOUTH LAKE CT
6200 SD 92119 1251-A6
SOUTHLOOK AV
200 SD 92113 1289-G5
SOUTH PARK PL
600 SDCo 92021 1252-J4
SOUTH POINT DR
1700 CHV 91902 1311-C4
SOUTHPORT WY
2600 NATC 91950 1309-H4
SOUTHRIDGE RD
3700 OCN 92056 1107-E3
SOUTHRIDGE WY
3700 OCN 92056 1107-E3
11100 SD 92131 1209-H4
SOUTH SHORE DR
100 SOLB 92075 1187-E2
SOUTHSHORE DR
800 CHV 91913 1311-E4
SOUTH SHORE RD
40000 SDCo 92028 997-B1
SOUTH SHORES RD
- SD 92109 1268-B3
SOUTHVIEW CIR
1000 CHV 91910 1311-C6
SOUTHVIEW CT
1400 CHV 91910 1311-C7
SOUTH VIEW DR
1800 CRLB 92008 1106-H7
SOUTHVIEW DR
3700 SD 92117 1248-D4
SOUTH VISTA AV
200 SD 92173 1350-E3
SOUTHWIND DR
100 ELCN 92243 6559-F2
100 ELCN 92243 6560-A2
SOUTHWIND LN
3100 SDCo 92084 1068-E6
SOUTHWOOD CIR
9200 SD 92126 1209-E3

SOUTHWOOD DR
3300 OCN 92054 1086-E2
SOUVENIR DR
1400 ELCJ 92021 1252-A2
SOVEREIGN RD
8800 SD 92123 1249-D4
SPA RD
- ImCo 92257 410-L4
- ImCo 92257 411-A5
SPA ST
3300 SD 92105 1270-B6
SPACE THEATER WY
- SD 92101 1289-C1
- SD 92134 1289-C1
SPALDING PL
1800 SD 92116 1269-C3
SPANGLER PEAK RD
16000 SDCo 92065 1173-C2
SPANISH SPUR
100 SDCo 92028 1047-G4
SPANISH WY
3400 CRLB 92008 1106-F5
SPANISH BAY RD
2300 CHV 91915 1311-G6
SPANISH BIT DR
- SDCo 91901 1254-E2
SPANISH BIT PL
3900 SDCo 91901 1254-E3
SPANISH OAK AV
500 SMCS 92069 1109-D7
SPANISH OAK CT
3800 OCN 92054 1086-F2
SPANISH OAK PL
1600 ELCJ 92019 1252-B6
SPANISH OAK WY
1900 VSTA 92083 1107-F5
SPAR CT
- CRLB 92009 1127-A4
SPARKLING OAKS TR
28200 SDCo 92026 1089-F3
SPARKS AV
4800 SD 92110 1268-F1
SPARKS CT
1800 SD 92110 1268-F2
SPARKS PL
1800 SD 92110 1268-F1
SPARLING ST
3400 SD 92115 1270-D6
SPARREN AV
13200 SD 92129 1189-C3
SPARREN CT
13400 SD 92129 1189-C4
SPARREN WY
8700 SD 92129 1189-C3
SPARROW CT
1000 SMCS 92069 1128-E2
SPARROW RD
1300 CRLB 92009 1127-C5
SPARROW ST
400 CHV 91911 1330-G3
1200 SD 92114 1290-D2
SPARROW WY
200 OCN 92057 1086-J1
SPARROW HAWK CT
11300 SDCo 92040 1212-B6
SPARRS RD
- SD 92106 1288-A5
SPARTA DR
600 ENCT 92024 1147-C3
SPARTAN CIR
4200 SD 92115 1270-B4
SPARTAN DR
5600 SD 92115 1270-B4
SPEAR DR
1800 SD 92101 1289-C2
SPEAR ST
6400 SD 92120 1250-B6
SPEARFISH LN
3900 SD 92124 1249-G3
SPEARHEAD TR
30000 SDCo 92082 1069-E4
SPEARMAN LN
3000 SDCo 91978 1271-F7
SPECIALTY DR
1300 VSTA 92083 1108-A7
1300 VSTA 92083 1128-A1
SPECTRUM CT
4800 OCN 92057 1087-B3
SPECTRUM LN
8500 SD 92121 1228-J1
SPECTRUM CENTER BLVD
- SD 92123 1249-C2
SPECTRUM CENTER CT
- SD 92123 1249-C1
SPENCER CT
- OCN 92057 1067-A4
9300 SDCo 92040 1232-B5
SPENCER LN
5400 CRLB 92008 1107-C7
SPENCER MOUNTAIN RD
9600 SDCo 91977 1271-C7
SPENCERPORT WY
11200 SD 92131 1209-H2
SPERBER RD
- ImCo 92243 6559-G5
SPERRY CT
6900 SD 92111 1268-J1
SPEYERS WY
3500 SDCo 91902 1311-C1
SPICA DR
11200 SD 92126 1209-C1
SPICE ST
9100 LMSA 91941 1271-B2
SPICE WY
- SDCo 91935 1294-J6
- SDCo 91935 (1295-A6 See Page 1294)
SPICEWOOD CT
10900 SD 92130 1208-D1
SPILLMAN DR
4100 SD 92105 1289-H2
SPINDLETOP RD
12500 SD 92129 1189-C5
SPINDLEWOOD CT
500 OCN 92054 1086-D2
SPINDRIFT CT
3400 OCN 92054 1086-E3
SPINDRIFT DR
700 SOLB 92014 1187-H1
700 SD 92014 1187-H1
800 SD 92037 1227-G6
SPINDRIFT LN
800 CRLB 92009 1126-J5
SPINEL AV
900 ELCJ 92021 1251-G2
SPINNAKER CT
100 DLMR 92014 1187-F6

SPINNAKER ST
- CRLB 92009 1126-J7
SPINNAKER WY
- CORD 92118 1329-E2
SPINNAKER BAY CT
4600 OCN 92057 1066-J6
SPIRES ST
500 VSTA 92083 1087-F5
SPIRIT TR
4500 SDCo 91901 1275-A2
SPITFIRE RD
11200 SD 92126 1209-F1
SPLENDORWOOD PL
2100 ESCN 92026 1109-H4
SPLIT MOUNTAIN RD
5600 SDCo 92004 410-F10
E SPLITRAIL DR
500 ENCT 92024 1147-G5
SPLIT ROCK RD
19200 SDCo 92065 1172-B4
SPOKANE AV
3200 SD 92105 1269-G6
SPOKANE WY
600 ELCJ 92020 1251-G4
2700 CRLB 92008 1106-J4
SPOONBILL LN
7200 CRLB 92009 1127-D7
SPOON BILL WY
4200 OCN 92057 1086-J3
4200 OCN 92057 1087-A3
SPOONER CT
11100 SD 92131 1209-J1
SPORTFISHER WY
100 OCN 92054 1085-J7
200 OCN 92054 1086-A7
SPORTS ARENA BLVD
2300 SD 92110 1268-D5
SPOT DR
1500 SDCo 92021 1252-A2
SPRAY ST
2100 SD 92107 1267-J5
SPRIG PL
2400 SDCo 91906 (1297-F5 See Page 1296)
2600 SD 92123 1249-B7
SPRING AV
100 OCN 92057 1086-H2
SPRING CT
4200 SDCo 91941 1271-B4
SPRING DR
3800 SDCo 91977 1271-B5
SPRING LN
9100 SDCo 91941 1271-B4
SPRING PL
3900 SDCo 91977 1271-A5
SPRING RD
29000 SDCo 92066 1237-C7
SPRING ST
4200 LMSA 91941 1270-H2
4200 SDCo 91941 1270-J3
5000 LMSA 91942 1270-H2
5700 SDCo 91941 1271-A4
SPRING BROOK CT
3200 OCN 92054 1086-D3
SPRINGBROOK DR
12200 SD 92128 1190-A7
12200 SD 92131 1190-A7
12400 SD 92128 1189-J6
SPRING CANYON DR
8700 SDCo 91977 1291-A5
SPRING CANYON RD
9400 SD 92124 1230-F4
9400 SD 92145 1230-F4
10300 SD 92131 1189-H7
10500 SD 92131 1209-H1
11100 SD 92145 1210-A2
11100 SD 92131 1210-A2
SPRING CREEK LN
1500 OCN 92057 1067-E7
SPRING CREEK RD
300 SMCS 92069 1108-H1
SPRINGDALE LN
1900 ENCT 92024 1147-H7
SPRINGER RD
1900 SD 92105 1289-H1
SPRINGFIELD AV
500 OCN 92057 1067-D6
8600 LMSA 91941 1271-A3
SPRINGFIELD CT
1200 VSTA 92083 1087-E6
SPRINGFIELD ST
6300 SD 92114 1290-D2
SPRING FLOWER DR
- SDCo 92028 1028-A4
SPRINGFORD AV
7000 SD 92114 1290-F4
SPRING GARDEN PL
3300 SD 92102 1289-F4
SPRING GARDENS RD
4200 LMSA 91941 1270-J4
4200 LMSA 91941 1271-A4
SPRING GLEN LN
1300 SDCo 91977 1291-E1
SPRING GROVE LN
2300 SDCo 91977 1271-A7
SPRINGHURST DR
11900 SD 92128 1190-A6
SPRINGLAKE PL
700 ESCN 92027 1110-D5
SPRING MANOR CT
10100 SD 92126 1209-D5
SPRING MEADOW LN
11300 SD 92128 1189-J6
SPRING OAK WY
2200 SD 92139 1290-G6
SPRING OAKS PL
9700 SDCo 92021 1233-D3
SPRING OAKS RD
15900 SDCo 92021 1233-D2
SPRINGSIDE RD
11600 SD 92128 1189-J6
11600 SD 92128 1190-A6
SPRINGS OF LIFE CT
- SDCo 91977 1291-E1
SPRINGTIME DR
4400 OCN 92056 1087-D6
SPRINGTIME LN
2200 SDCo 92019 1252-D6
SPRINGTIME WY
700 SDCo 92019 1252-D6
SPRINGTREE PL
300 ESCN 92026 1109-H4
SPRINGVALE DR
8400 SNTE 92071 1230-J7
SPRINGVALE ST
14400 PWY 92064 1190-H4
SPRING VALLEY RD
- SDCo 92061 1050-H4

SAN DIEGO CO.
INDEX

SPRING VIEW CT SAN DIEGO CO. STREET INDEX SUMMERVIEW CT 6620

SAN DIEGO CO. INDEX

STREET
Block City ZIP Pg-Grid

SPRING VIEW CT
- SDCo 92021 1232-H5
SPRINGVIEW LN
8700 LMSA 91941 1271-A3
SPRINGVIEW RD
1400 SDCo 92070 1135-E5
SPRING VIEW ST
9400 SDCo 91977 1271-C6
SPRING VISTA WY
8600 SDCo 91977 1290-J2
8600 SDCo 91977 1291-A2
SPRING WAGON RD
18300 SDCo 92065 1173-B2
18400 SDCo 92065 1153-C7
SPRINGWATER PT
12300 SD 92128 1189-H6
SPRINGWOOD DR
23600 SDCo 92065 1173-D3
SPRINGWOOD LN
900 ENCT 92024 1147-J5
SPRINTER LN
5600 SDCo 91902 1311-A2
SPRUANCE RD
4400 SD 92133 1288-D1
SPRUCE
9700 SDCo 92021 1233-B3
SPRUCE CT
200 CHV 91911 1330-G3
3500 OCN 92054 1086-F2
SPRUCE DR
- SD 92102 1289-G4
100 SMCS 92069 1108-H5
SPRUCE LN
9700 SDCo 92029 1149-D3
13500 PWY 92064 1191-A3
SPRUCE RD
100 CHV 91911 1330-F5
28800 SDCo 92066 1237-C6
SPRUCE ST
300 CHV 91911 1330-G3
500 IMPB 91932 1329-F7
500 SD 92103 1269-A7
1400 SDCo 92082 1090-B1
2200 CRLB 92008 1106-E3
2800 SD 92104 1269-E7
5200 SD 92105 1270-A6
N SPRUCE ST
400 ESCN 92025 1129-G3
S SPRUCE ST
100 ESCN 92025 1129-H3
W SPRUCE ST
100 SD 92103 1269-A7
500 SD 92103 1268-J7
SPRUCE GROVE AV
10300 SD 92131 1210-B4
SPRUCE GROVE PL
12200 SD 92131 1210-B3
SPRUCE LAKE AV
6200 SD 92119 1250-G6
SPRUCE RUN DR
11300 SD 92131 1210-A1
11600 SD 92131 1209-J1
SPRUCEWOOD DR
200 ENCT 92024 1147-G7
SPRUCEWOOD LN
- ESCN 92027 1130-H4
SPUR AV
5600 OCN 92057 1067-F7
29700 SDCo 92084 1067-G7
SPUR CT
10300 SDCo 91941 1271-E4
SPUR LN
10500 SNTE 92071 1231-E5
SPUR POINT CT
- SD 92130 1208-D2
SPYGLASS CIR
1700 VSTA 92083 1108-A4
1700 VSTA 92083 1107-J4
SPYGLASS CT
1800 CRLB 92008 1106-H6
SPYGLASS LN
17200 SDCo 92067 1168-H7
SPYGLASS PL
3600 OCN 92056 1107-C3
SPYGLASS TR
28600 SDCo 92082 1090-B1
SQUAMISH RD
11200 SD 92126 1209-C2
SQUIRE PL
300 OCN 92054 1086-E6
SQUIRES PL
800 SDCo 92083 1107-F2
SQUIRREL RD
11300 SDCo 92040 1212-B5
STABLE RDG
400 ELCJ 92019 1252-D4
STACEY AV
700 ELCN 92243 6499-G5
STACEY CT
1700 ELCN 92243 6499-F5
STACY AV
3800 SD 92117 1248-E4
STACY LN
1600 SDCo 92065 1172-J1
STACY PL
4300 SD 92117 1248-E4
STADIUM CT
3300 SD 92122 1228-D5
STADIUM PL
3400 SD 92122 1228-D6
STADIUM ST
5700 SD 92122 1228-D5
STADLER ST
8000 LMSA 91942 1250-H7
STAFFORD AV
300 ENCT 92007 1167-D3
STAFFORD PL
700 SD 92107 1287-J3
STAGE TER
800 SDCo 92028 1027-J1
STAGE COACH LN
- PWY 92064 1170-F1
1600 SDCo 92028 997-J6
2000 SDCo 92028 998-D2
N STAGE COACH LN
100 SDCo 92028 1027-J1
1100 SDCo 92028 997-J7
S STAGE COACH LN
100 SDCo 92028 1027-H6
S STAGE COACH LN
Rt#-S15
400 SDCo 92028 1027-J4
STAGECOACH PASS
- SDCo 92127 1168-J1
- SDCo 92127 1169-A1
STAGECOACH RD
- SDCo 92055 409-A7
- SDCo 92055 1066-B1

STAGE COACH RD
300 OCN 92057 1086-G3
14000 PWY 92064 1150-J5
15000 PWY 92064 1151-A5
24400 SDCo 91963 429-L10
24400 SDCo 91963 (1316-B7
See Page 1296)
STAGE COACH TR
900 SDCo 92036 1138-A5
STAGECOACH TR
9300 SNTE 92071 1231-F5
STAGE COACH TR
13800 SDCo 92040 1232-E4
STAGECOACH WY
500 SDCo 92004 1058-F2
STAGECOACH SPRINGS RD
- SDCo 92066 (1299-B2
See Page 1298)
STAGE STOP DR
12300 PWY 92064 1190-C7
STAGHORN CT
3200 SDCo 92028 1048-C4
STAHL RD
- ImCo 92227 431-C2
STALKER CT
1500 ELCJ 92020 1251-B3
STALLARD RD
- ImCo - 412-A4
STALLION DR
200 OCN 92057 1067-B6
STALLION PL
300 CHV 91902 1310-H4
STALLION OAKS LN
- SDCo 92019 1253-E5
STALLION OAKS RD
5800 SDCo 92019 1253-D5
STALMER ST
7700 SD 92111 1249-A4
STAMEN CT
6300 SD 92114 1290-D5
STAMEN ST
1200 SD 92114 1290-D5
STAMNES RD
37600 SDCo 92086 409-K5
STANCREST LN
1400 NATC 91950 1310-B1
STANDEL LN
32400 SDCo 92026 1049-A6
STANDING ROCK RD
17400 SDCo 91935 1274-A3
STANDISH DR
12900 PWY 92064 1190-H4
STANDLAKE ST
1500 SD 92154 1350-A2
STANFIELD CIR
10400 SD 92126 1209-D4
STANFORD AV
800 CHV 91913 1311-D5
7000 LMSA 91941 1270-F3
STANFORD CT
31500 SDCo 92082 1070-F1
STANFORD DR
3700 OCN 92056 1087-A7
STANFORD ST
4300 CRLB 92008 1107-A4
STANISLAUS DR
1300 CHV 91913 1311-C7
1300 CHV 91913 1331-B1
STANLEY AV
200 ESCN 92026 1109-H4
500 SDCo 92026 1109-H4
6200 SD 92115 1270-D3
STANLEY CT
600 ELCJ 92019 1251-J6
600 ESCN 92026 1109-J7
10000 SNTE 92071 1231-D4
STANLEY DR
6100 LMSA 91942 1251-B6
STANLEY RD
- ImCo - 411-D8
STANLEY ST
500 OCN 92054 1106-B1
E STANLEY WY
1200 ESCN 92027 1110-A6
STANSBURY ST
8400 SDCo 91977 1290-J2
STANTON RD
1800 ENCT 92024 1147-H7
4200 SD 92105 1289-H2
STANWELL CIR
10600 SD 92126 1209-C4
STANWELL CT
10600 SD 92126 1209-C4
STANWELL PL
10600 SD 92126 1209-C4
STANWELL ST
8600 SD 92126 1209-C4
STANWIX SQ
12100 SD 92128 1190-B3
STAPLES RD
15800 SDCo 92065 1174-A4
STAR AV
- SDCo 91905 1300-C6
STAR LN
2000 SDCo 91901 1253-H1
E STAR RD
3200 SDCo 92004 (1078-J6
See Page 1058)
W STAR RD
3200 SDCo 92004 (1078-J6
See Page 1058)
STAR ACRES DR
3200 SDCo 91978 1272-B7
STAR ACRES LN
3200 SDCo 91978 1272-B7
3200 SDCo 92019 1272-B7
STARBEAM LN
17900 SDCo 92061 1051-F4
STARBOARD CIR
3500 OCN 92054 1086-F5
STARBOARD ST
- CRLB 92009 1127-A7
STARBRIGHT LN
600 SDCo 91901 1234-B4
STARBURST LN
2100 SD 92154 1350-A1
STARCREST DR
9300 SNTE 92071 1251-B1
STARDUST LN
13400 SDCo 92082 1070-D2
31500 SDCo 92082 1050-D7
STARFISH WY
5000 SD 92154 1330-H7
STARFLOWER RD
800 ENCT 92024 1147-F4
STARGAZE AV
8800 SD 92129 1189-C2

STARGAZE CT
- SMCS 92069 1128-C5
- SMCS 92078 1128-C5
STARGAZE LN
29100 SDCo 92082 1070-H7
STARHAVEN LN
2500 SDCo 92084 1088-C6
STARK LN
600 SDCo 92065 1153-A1
STARKEY WY
2500 SDCo 91901 1234-B3
STARLAND DR
8200 SDCo 92021 1252-C1
STARLIGHT AV
5500 OCN 92057 1067-D6
STARLIGHT DR
1300 ENCT 92007 1167-D2
7700 SD 92037 1227-J5
STARLIGHT GN
2400 ESCN 92026 1109-B4
STARLIGHT LN
- SMCS 92069 1128-E3
9500 SDCo 91941 1271-C1
STARLIGHT WY
- SDCo 92036 1156-A7
- SDCo 92036 1175-J1
- SDCo 92036 1176-A1
STARLIGHT MOUNTAIN RD
1100 SDCo 92065 1153-E5
STARLING CT
1800 CRLB 92009 1127-D7
STARLING DR
500 VSTA 92083 1087-F4
7600 SD 92123 1249-B6
STARLING LN
200 OCN 92057 1086-H2
STARLING SIGHT RD
- SDCo 92127 1169-G4
STARMOUNT WY
13300 PWY 92064 1170-E1
STAR PARK CIR
1100 CORD 92118 1288-H7
STARPINE DR
8700 SNTE 92071 1230-G7
STARR RD
- ImCo 92250 431-F4
STARRIDGE ST
13400 PWY 92064 1190-D3
STARSHIP ST
- SDCo 91934 (1320-J4
See Page 1300)
- SDCo 91934 (1321-A2
See Page 1300)
STARSIDE LN
200 OCN 92056 1107-D3
STARSTONE DR
400 SMCS 92069 1108-C7
STARSTONE PL
600 SMCS 92069 1108-D7
STAR THISTLE LN
2400 SDCo 91901 1233-J5
STAR TRACK WY
3900 SDCo 92028 1048-F4
STARVALE LN
19300 SDCo 92065 1153-H2
STAR VALLEY RD
1400 SDCo 91901 1234-G6
STARVATION MOUNTAIN RD
18600 SDCo 92025 1151-A4
STARVIEW DR
1100 SDCo 92084 1088-D7
1100 SDCo 92084 1108-D1
8100 SDCo 92021 1252-B1
STARWOOD CIR
400 CHV 91910 1310-F5
STATE PL
100 ESCN 92029 1129-E3
STATE ST
- SD 92103 1268-H6
100 ELCN 92243 6499-E6
200 ELCN 92243 6500-A6
600 SD 92101 1289-A2
2000 SD 92101 1288-J1
2400 CRLB 92008 1106-D5
2600 SD 92103 1288-J1
STATE PARK RD
- SDCo 92060 409-G7
STATE TREE DR
600 OCN 92054 1106-C1
STATICE CT
- CRLB 92009 1127-B4
STATION RD
- SDCo 92082 1091-C2
STATION VILLAGE LN
8200 SD 92108 1269-B2
STATTON CT
1500 SD 92114 1290-F6
STEADMAN ST
10100 SD 92121 1208-G5
STEAMBOAT SPRINGS CT
2400 CHV 91915 1311-H7
STEBICK CT
12800 SD 92130 1188-C6
STEEL ST
3200 SD 92113 1289-F4
STEELE ST
600 ELCJ 92020 1251-E3
STEELE CANYON RD
2500 SDCo 92019 1272-C6
3200 SDCo 91978 1272-C6
STEELFISH LN
3700 OCN 92054 1086-G2
STEEL RANCH RD
- SDCo 91935 1274-F5
STEEN CIR
1400 VSTA 92083 1108-A2
STEEPLE GN
1200 ESCN 92029 1129-F5
STEEPLECHASE RD
5900 SDCo 91902 1311-B2
STEEPLE CHASE RW
14200 SD 92130 1188-D2
STEEPLEGATE SQ
12700 SD 92130 1188-A6
STEFAS CT
900 CHV 91911 1330-J2
900 CHV 91911 1331-A2
STEFFY RD
200 SDCo 92065 1153-A7
300 SDCo 92065 1152-J7
STEIGER LN
2100 OCN 92056 1086-H7
2100 OCN 92056 1106-H1
STEINBECK AV
7200 SD 92122 1228-G4

STEINER DR
1200 CHV 91911 1330-J2
STELLA CT
8000 SNTE 92071 1230-H7
STELLA ST
800 CHV 91911 1330-A4
800 SD 91911 1330-A4
STELLA MARIS LN
3900 CRLB 92008 1106-G6
STELLAR DR
3300 SD 92123 1249-E4
STEPHANIE LN
100 ELCJ 92019 1252-A5
100 VSTA 92084 1088-B5
STEPHANIE PL
4700 OCN 92057 1066-J6
4700 OCN 92057 1067-A6
STEPHENS ST
4000 SD 92103 1268-H5
STEPHENS PORT
400 SDCo 92028 1047-F3
STERLING BRDG
700 SDCo 92028 1027-G6
STERLING CT
1500 ESCN 92029 1129-E2
4900 SD 92105 1270-A6
STERLING DR
7900 ELCJ 92021 1252-B1
7900 SDCo 92021 1252-B1
STERLING GROVE LN
4900 SD 92130 1208-D1
STERLING HILL LN
- SDCo 92040 1231-J6
STERLING VIEW DR
900 SDCo 92028 1028-F1
STERN WY
- CRLB 92009 1146-J1
- CRLB 92009 1147-A1
STERNE ST
3000 SD 92106 1288-C1
3300 SD 92106 1268-C7
STETSON AV
3400 SD 92122 1228-D5
STETSON PL
1500 OCN 92057 1067-F7
6100 SD 92122 1228-D5
STETTLER WY
4100 SD 92122 1228-E5
STEUER WY
11700 SD 92131 1209-J2
STEVEMARK LN
3800 SDCo 91977 1271-E4
STEVEN CIR
2400 CRLB 92008 1106-H4
STEVEN LN
- OCN 92054 1086-G2
STEVENS AV
100 SOLB 92075 1167-F7
500 SOLB 92075 1187-G1
STEVENS AV W
600 SOLB 92075 1167-F7
STEVENS PL
2100 ESCN 92027 1110-C4
STEVENS RD
- ImCo 92243 430-L6
9300 SNTE 92071 1231-F5
STEVENS WY
- SDCo 92066 410-A9
STEVENSON CT
1500 SDCo 92069 1109-A3
1500 SMCS 92069 1109-A3
STEVENSON WY
7600 SD 92120 1250-E4
STEVENS VISTA
15000 SDCo 92065 1172-J6
15000 SDCo 92065 1173-A6
STEWART CT
900 CHV 91911 1331-A2
1000 SD 92113 1289-G6
STEWART DR
500 VSTA 92083 1087-D7
STEWART PL
2300 ESCN 92027 1110-C6
STEWART ST
1300 OCN 92054 1106-C2
6200 SD 92115 1270-C3
STEWART CANYON RD
100 SDCo 92028 1028-G2
STEWART CREST RD
600 SDCo 92028 1028-H3
STICKLEY RANCH
10100 SDCo 92026 1089-E5
STILES CT
900 VSTA 92083 1087-F5
STILL BROOK LN
15400 SDCo 92061 1050-H3
STILLMAN PL
2000 SD 92139 1290-G6
STILLWATER CT
3300 CRLB 92008 1106-J3
STILL WATER GN
1700 ESCN 92026 1109-D4
STILLWATER RD
2300 SD 92101 1288-G1
STILLWATER COVE WY
800 OCN 92054 1066-E6
STILLWELL AV
900 SD 92114 1290-C5
STILSON LN
39900 SDCo 91905 1300-E6
STIMSON CT
8900 SD 92129 1189-C4
STINSON RD
2600 SDCo 92004 1100-A4
2700 SDCo 92004 (1099-H4
See Page 1098)
STIPA CT
8700 SD 92129 1189-C6
STIRLING AV
2700 CRLB 92008 1107-A5
STIRLING CT
2700 CRLB 92008 1107-A5
STIRRUP RD
2300 SDCo 92004 (1079-A2
See Page 1058)
STIRRUP WY
5400 OCN 92057 1067-D7
STITT AV
1800 SD 92101 1289-C2
STOCKALPER LN
400 SDCo 92065 1152-G5
STOCKETT WY
3000 SD 92117 1248-C3
STOCKMAN ST
3000 NATC 91950 1310-D3
STOCKTON LN
2400 SDCo 92084 1087-J1
STOCKTON PL
3500 CRLB 92008 1107-A3

STOCKTON RD
2600 SD 92133 1288-D1
STONE CT
5200 SD 92115 1270-A2
STONE DR
1200 SMCS 92069 1128-E1
STONE ST
- CORD 91932 1329-E5
STONEBRIDGE CT
3900 SDCo 92067 1167-H4
STONEBRIDGE LN
3900 SDCo 92067 1167-H4
STONEBRIDGE RD
14800 SDCo 92027 1110-H7
15200 ESCN 92027 1110-H7
15200 ESCN 92027 1130-H1
15300 SDCo 92027 1111-A7
STONEBROOK LN
1800 ENCT 92024 1147-H6
STONE CANYON RD
700 CHV 91914 1311-G3
12500 SD 92128 1170-C5
12600 PWY 92064 1170-D4
STONE CASTLE
1900 SDCo 92028 1027-G6
STONECIPHER LN
2500 SDCo 91977 1271-C7
STONECREEK PL
2100 CHV 91913 1311-E3
STONECREST BLVD
9800 SD 92123 1249-F5
STONECREST CT
1900 VSTA 92083 1107-J4
STONECREST LN
1000 SDCo 92027 1130-B3
STONEDALE CT
11800 SD 92131 1210-A2
STONE EDGE CIR
1500 SDCo 92021 1251-G2
STONE EDGE CT
300 SDCo 92021 1251-G2
STONE EDGE DR
300 SDCo 92021 1251-G2
STONEFIELD CT
3500 SDCo 91935 1272-E5
STONEFIELD DR
3000 SDCo 91935 1272-E5
STONEGATE DR
28700 SDCo 92082 1090-B1
29000 SDCo 92082 1070-B7
STONEGATE PL
3500 SDCo 92028 1028-E2
STONE HAVEN WY
10800 SD 92130 1208-E2
STONEHEDGE PL
1000 SMCS 92069 1109-B7
STONEHURST DR
10100 SDCo 92026 1109-E1
STONEMILL DR
- PWY 92064 1210-C1
STONEPINE LN
6600 SD 92139 1310-F1
STONE POINT LN
10200 SDCo 91977 1291-E2
STONEPOINTE DR
- ESCN 92025 1150-D3
STONE POST WY
700 SDCo 92028 997-G7
STONERIDGE CIR
1300 ESCN 92029 1129-G7
STONERIDGE CT
400 CHV 91902 1311-A4
1300 OCN 92056 1087-D3
STONERIDGE DR
1100 SDCo 91977 1290-J2
STONERIDGE RD
500 SDCo 92021 1253-A1
3800 CRLB 92008 1107-B3
STONERIDGE TER
200 VSTA 92083 1108-A2
STONERIDGE COUNTRY CLUB LN
17100 PWY 92064 1170-E3
STONE VALLEY PL
2200 ESCN 92026 1109-J4
STONEVIEW CT
7400 SD 92119 1250-F3
STONEVIEW LN
2500 SDCo 91977 1271-D7
STONEWALL LN
1900 SDCo 92084 1088-C4
STONEWOOD WY
1200 SD 92154 1350-B1
STONEY LN
- SDCo 92036 1175-J2
STONEY WY
10600 SD 92131 1209-G2
STONEY ACRES RD
16000 PWY 92064 1170-E5
STONEYBRAE PL
500 ESCN 92027 1110-D5
STONEYBROOK LN
13200 SDCo 92021 1232-E7
STONEY CREEK CT
10700 SNTE 92071 1231-E2
STONEY CREEK RD
13500 SD 92129 1189-G3
STONEY GATE PL
13900 SD 92128 1189-J3
13900 SD 92128 1190-A2
STONEY OAK DR
3100 SDCo 91978 1292-C1
3100 SDCo 91978 1272-C7
STONEY PEAK DR
11700 SD 92128 1190-A1
STONEY POINT WY
400 OCN 92054 1086-B6
STONEY SPRING PL
1300 CHV 91913 1331-B1
STONINGTON WY
28200 SDCo 92026 1089-D3
STONYHURST CT
100 VSTA 92084 1087-H5
STONY KNOLL RD
100 SDCo 92019 1252-B5
100 ELCJ 92019 1252-B5
STONY RIDGE CT
- SD 92131 1209-G1
STONY RIDGE WY
- SD 92131 1209-G1
STORK ST
600 SD 92114 1290-D3
STORMY LN
1700 VSTA 92084 1088-B3
STOTLER CT
12500 PWY 92064 1190-D7
STOUTWOOD ST
12500 PWY 92064 1190-C1

STOWE DR
12300 PWY 92064 1190-C6
STOYER DR
9200 SNTE 92071 1231-B5
STRADA FRAGANTE
- SDCo 92067 1148-D6
STRADA RANCH RD
3900 SDCo 92070 1135-E6
STRAND WY
1600 CORD 92118 1308-J1
1700 CORD 92118 1309-A2
1700 CORD 92155 1309-A2
2600 SD 92109 1267-H1
3800 SD 92109 1247-H7
STRANSBURG CT
4600 OCN 92056 1107-F3
STRATA DR
3600 CRLB 92008 1107-B3
STRATFORD CIR
4500 OCN 92056 1107-D3
STRATFORD CT
100 DLMR 92014 1187-F5
1200 SMCS 92069 1128-B3
STRATFORD DR
500 ENCT 92024 1147-C7
600 ENCT 92024 1167-C1
STRATFORD LN
1100 CRLB 92008 1106-E4
STRATFORD PL
- VSTA 92083 1107-H5
STRATFORD WY
300 DLMR 92014 1187-F4
STRATFORD KNOLL
800 ENCT 92024 1148-A6
STRATFORD PARK CIR
200 DLMR 92014 1187-G7
STRATHMORE DR
10100 SNTE 92071 1231-A2
STRATTON AV
1000 SD 92113 1289-J5
STRATUS CT
7200 SD 92120 1250-D5
STRAWBERRY GN
800 ESCN 92025 1150-C1
STRAWBERRY LN
10300 SDCo 91977 1291-E2
STRAWBERRY PL
3500 OCN 92056 1107-A1
STRAWBERRY RD
14400 SDCo 92067 1188-E2
STRAWBERRY HILL LN
900 SDCo 92084 1067-J7
STRAWBERRY VALLEY DR
1000 CHV 91913 1311-D6
STREAMVIEW DR
5000 SD 92105 1270-A6
5900 SD 92115 1270-C6
STREAMVIEW PL
3400 SD 92105 1270-A6
STREET A
- SMCS 92069 1109-A7
100 VSTA 92083 1087-H7
STREIBY RD
1000 ImCo 92227 431-D2
STRESEMANN ST
5500 SD 92122 1228-B6
STROMBERG CIR
2400 CRLB 92008 1106-H5
STROMESA CT
7900 SD 92126 1209-B6
STRONG DR
3800 SD 92111 1248-J3
STROTHE RD
- SD 92106 1288-A4
STRUEDLE CT
1300 SD 92154 1350-A2
STU CT
4200 SD 92154 1350-F1
STUART AV
6900 LMSA 91941 1270-F4
STUART MESA RD
- SDCo 92055 408-L8
- SDCo 92055 1085-H1
STUDER RD
- ImCo 92251 431-C4
STUDIO LN
4600 OCN 92057 1087-B2
STURGEON CT
4100 SD 92130 1188-B5
STURGESS AV
7500 LMSA 91941 1270-G4
STURNELLA WY
14600 SDCo 92082 1070-G4
STURTEVANT ST
3100 SD 92136 1289-E7
SUBIDA TER
2100 CRLB 92009 1147-F1
SUBIDA AL CIELO
2100 SDCo 92084 1088-C1
SUBOL CT
2600 SD 92154 1330-C6
SUBURBAN HILLS DR
1100 SDCo 92027 1130-C4
SUCCESS AV
9300 SD 92123 1249-E4
SUDAN RD
12900 PWY 92064 1190-G4
SUDY ST
9100 LMSA 91942 1251-B6
SUE ST
3300 SD 92105 1270-B6
SUEMARK TER
1800 SDCo 92084 1088-C4
1800 VSTA 92084 1088-C4
SUERICH LN
1000 LMGR 91945 1270-F7
SUERTE DEL ESTE
18600 SDCo 92029 1148-F4
18600 SDCo 92067 1148-F4
SUFFOLK DR
3600 SD 92115 1270-E5
SUGARBUSH DR
900 SDCo 92084 1088-E7
1000 SDCo 92084 1108-E1
SUGARBUSH TER
3200 SDCo 92084 1088-E7
SUGAR BUSH WY
- SDCo 92082 1090-E4
SUGARLOAF DR
900 ESCN 92026 1109-F7
SUGARMAN CT
2800 SD 92037 1227-J4
SUGARMAN DR
8200 SD 92037 1228-A4
8500 SD 92037 1227-J4
SUGARMAN WY
2800 SD 92037 1227-J4

SUGARPINE LN
2500 SDCo 92028 1028-D7
2500 SDCo 92028 1048-D1
SUGAR PINE PL
1400 CHV 91915 1311-J6
SUGAR PINE RD
1700 CRLB 92009 1127-E6
SUGAR PINE ST
700 OCN 92054 1086-F1
SUGARPLUM WY
- SDCo 92065 1174-B5
SUKAT CT
32300 SDCo 92061 1051-A6
SUKAT TR
32300 SDCo 92061 1051-A6
SULA WY
2700 SD 92139 1310-F1
SULLIVAN AV
6300 SD 92114 1290-D4
SULLIVAN CT
900 CHV 91911 1331-A1
1000 CHV 91913 1331-A1
SULLY WY
10200 SD 92126 1209-D5
SULTANA ST
2000 SD 92105 1290-B1
SULZFELD WY
- ELCJ 92020 1251-F5
SUMAC CT
3200 SDCo 92028 1048-F2
SUMAC DR
2300 SD 92105 1289-H1
2400 SD 92105 1269-H7
SUMAC LN
800 CRLB 92009 1127-A6
SUMAC PL
800 ESCN 92027 1110-B7
4800 OCN 92057 1067-A7
SUMAC RD
3100 SDCo 92028 1048-F2
SUMAC VW
- SDCo 92026 1089-B3
SUMAC SUMMIT
3800 SDCo 92028 998-F3
SUMATRA LN
100 SD 92114 1290-F5
SUMMER CT
- VSTA 92084 1088-A2
1000 ELCJ 92021 1251-H2
1000 SDCo 92021 1251-H2
SUMMER DR
2300 OCN 92056 1087-D6
SUMMER WY
3900 ESCN 92025 1150-C3
SUMMER BLOOM LN
- SDCo 92028 1028-A4
SUMMERBREEZE LN
12200 SD 92128 1170-B7
SUMMERBREEZE WY
14800 SD 92128 1170-B7
14800 SD 92128 1190-B1
SUMMER CREEK CT
- VSTA 92084 1088-B4
SUMMERCREEK WY
2300 ESCN 92029 1129-E6
SUMMERCREST LN
8700 SNTE 92071 1231-D7
SUMMERDALE RD
8400 SD 92126 1209-C3
SUMMERDALE WY
10900 SD 92126 1209-C3
SUMMERDAWN PL
1500 ENCT 92024 1147-G4
SUMMERFIELD CT
3600 SDCo 91977 1271-C5
SUMMERFIELD DR
3300 SDCo 91977 1271-C5
SUMMERFIELD LN
12600 PWY 92064 1170-D3
SUMMERFIELD PL
800 ESCN 92027 1130-E1
SUMMERFIELD ST
9500 SDCo 91977 1271-C5
SUMMER GLEN RD
1000 SDCo 92065 1152-C4
SUMMER GLEN VISTA
- SDCo 92021 1232-E5
- SDCo 92040 1232-E5
SUMMERHILL AV
1100 CHV 91915 1311-G5
SUMMERHILL CT
400 SDCo 91901 1233-F6
800 ENCT 92024 1147-H5
SUMMERHILL DR
2100 ENCT 92024 1147-H5
5000 OCN 92057 1087-C2
SUMMER HILL LN
2400 SDCo 92028 1027-G7
SUMMERHILL PT
8800 SDCo 91901 1233-F6
SUMMERHILL TER
400 SDCo 91901 1233-F6
SUMMERHILL VW
400 SDCo 91901 1233-F6
SUMMERHOLLY DR
500 SMCS 92078 1128-G2
SUMMER HOLLY LN
900 ENCT 92024 1147-J5
SUMMER LAND RD
- SDCo 92003 1068-C4
SUMMER OAK RD
- SDCo 92066 409-L9
SUMMER PLACE DR
1700 SDCo 92021 1251-H2
SUMMER SAGE RD
15600 PWY 92064 1170-G4
SUMMERSET WY
3400 OCN 92056 1086-H7
SUMMERSHADE LN
11300 SD 92126 1209-E2
SUMMERSIDE LN
200 ENCT 92024 1147-H7
SUMMERSONG CT
800 ENCT 92024 1147-H5
SUMMERSONG LN
700 ENCT 92024 1147-H5
SUMMERSUN LN
9800 SDCo 92040 1231-J4
SUMMERSUN PL
9800 SDCo 92040 1231-J4
SUMMERTIME DR
1600 SDCo 92021 1251-F1
SUMMERTREE LN
9900 SNTE 92071 1231-D7
SUMMER VIEW CIR
400 ENCT 92024 1147-D7
SUMMERVIEW CT
10100 SD 92126 1209-D5

STREET
Block City ZIP Pg-Grid

SUMMERWIND PL
2300 CRLB 92008 1107-A7
SUMMERWOOD CT
10400 SD 92131 1210-A3
SUMMERWOOD LN
8000 LMGR 91945 1270-J7
SUMMIT AV
100 SDCo 92028 1027-E3
1200 ENCT 92007 1167-C2
10900 SNTE 92071 1211-D7
10900 SNTE 92071 1231-D1
SUMMIT CIR
9600 SDCo 91941 1271-C1
13500 PWY 92064 1170-E6
SUMMIT DR
1400 CHV 91910 1311-B5
1700 SDCo 92027 1130-D4
2000 SDCo 92025 1130-D5
4200 LMSA 91941 1270-H4
9800 SDCo 91941 1271-C1
SUMMIT GN
2500 ESCN 92026 1109-B3
SUMMIT LN
100 SDCo 92019 1253-D1
1600 SDCo 92025 1130-F6
24500 SDCo 91916 1236-A3
SUMMIT PL
1200 ENCT 92007 1167-C1
1600 SDCo 92025 1130-D5
4300 SD 92103 1268-J4
SUMMIT RD
100 SDCo 91917 429-J10
SUMMIT ST
400 OCN 92054 1086-A7
6200 SD 92114 1290-D3
SUMMIT TR
1000 SDCo 92025 1130-D5
1000 VSTA 92083 1108-A1
N SUMMIT CIRCLE GN
2200 ESCN 92026 1109-B4
S SUMMIT CIRCLE GN
2200 ESCN 92026 1109-B4
SUMMIT COVE LN
200 ENCT 92007 1167-C1
SUMMIT CREST
14000 SDCo 92025 1130-F6
SUMMIT CREST DR
10200 SNTE 92071 1231-D1
SUMMIT HILL DR
1800 SDCo 92027 1130-E4
SUMMIT MEADOW RD
1300 SDCo 91902 1291-B7
SUMMIT POINT WY
- SMCS 92069 1128-A3
SUMMIT RIDGE DR
1900 SDCo 92027 1130-E4
SUMMIT RIDGE WY
6800 SD 92120 1250-D4
SUMMITSIDE LN
10000 SDCo 91977 1271-D7
SUMMITVIEW LN
2600 SDCo 91977 1271-D7
SUMMIT VISTA DR
- SDCo 92127 1169-E3
SUMNER AV
1000 SDCo 92021 1251-H3
1000 ELCJ 92021 1251-H3
SUMNER PL
1000 SDCo 92021 1251-J3
SUMTER ST
3300 SD 92117 1248-E5
SUN CIR
- VSTA 92083 1107-J3
SUN CT
300 SDCo 92021 1251-F1
SUN ST
6900 SD 92111 1248-J6
SUN AND SHADOWS DR
400 SDCo 92004 (1078-H2 See Page 1058)
SUN AND SHADOWS LN
2500 SDCo 92004 (1078-H3 See Page 1058)
SUNBEAM RD
300 SDCo 92028 1027-F4
SUNBIRD CT
300 SMCS 92069 1108-J7
SUNBIRD WY
3500 SD 92124 1249-G4
SUNBRIGHT CT
5000 OCN 92056 1087-E2
SUNBRIGHT DR
1100 OCN 92056 1087-E2
SUNBRITE LN
9500 SDCo 92040 1232-A4
SUNBURST DR
1600 SDCo 92021 1252-A2
4400 OCN 92056 1087-D5
SUNBURST LN
500 CHV 91911 1330-H1
SUNBURST RD
4600 CRLB 92008 1106-H7
SUNBURY CT
1500 SDCo 92084 1108-B2
SUNBURY ST
1800 ESCN 92026 1109-D5
SUNCREEK DR
700 CHV 91913 1311-D4
SUNCREST AV
1900 OCN 92056 1087-E2
SUNCREST BLVD
1900 SDCo 92021 1252-G4
SUNCREST CT
5000 OCN 92056 1087-E2
SUNCREST DR
2900 SD 92116 1269-E3
7800 LMSA 91941 1270-H3
SUNCREST VISTA LN
- SDCo 91901 1234-D6
SUNDALE RD
1100 SDCo 92019 1271-J2
1100 SDCo 92019 1272-A2
SUNDANCE AV
- SMCS 92078 1128-D6
12500 SD 92129 1189-D4
SUNDANCE CIR
2300 OCN 92056 1087-D5
SUNDANCE CT
700 CHV 91911 1330-H1
9000 SD 92129 1189-D4
SUNDANCE DR
200 SDCo 92028 1028-A6
17200 SDCo 92065 1171-G2
SUNDANCE RD
13400 SDCo 92082 1070-D1
SUNDANCE WY
1400 OCN 92057 1067-E6
SUNDANCE VIEW LN
- SDCo 91916 1235-H1

SUNDAY DR
13800 SDCo 92082 1090-E4
SUNDERLAND ST
12900 PWY 92064 1190-H5
SUNDEVIL WY
9500 SD 92129 1189-E3
SUNDIAL LN
- CRLB 92009 1127-A7
SUNDIAL TER
1400 SDCo 92021 1252-A2
SUNDOWN DR
16600 SDCo 92082 1051-C7
SUNDOWN GN
1200 ESCN 92026 1129-G1
1200 ESCN 92026 1109-G7
SUNDOWN LN
1100 CHV 91911 1330-H1
3000 SDCo 91941 1271-G4
N SUNDOWN LN
3400 OCN 92056 1107-C2
S SUNDOWN LN
3400 OCN 92056 1107-C2
SUNDOWNER CT
- SD 92126 1209-D6
SUNDRIFT CT
5000 OCN 92056 1087-E2
SUNDROP CT
1200 CHV 91911 1330-H2
SUN ENERGY RD
16700 SDCo 92082 1091-C3
SUNFISH LN
- OCN 92054 1086-G2
SUNFLOWER GN
300 ESCN 92026 1109-H5
SUNFLOWER LN
9400 SDCo 92029 1129-C7
SUNFLOWER ST
700 ENCT 92024 1147-E6
SUNFLOWER TER
2400 SDCo 92083 1108-C4
SUNFLOWER WY
800 CRLB 92009 1127-A5
SUNFLOWER GLEN CT
3100 SDCo 91935 1272-D5
SUNGLOW CT
1200 OCN 92056 1087-E2
5300 SD 92117 1228-H7
SUNGLOW DR
1100 OCN 92056 1087-E2
8200 SDCo 92021 1232-B7
8200 SDCo 92021 1252-B1
SUNHAVEN CT
- SDCo 91901 1234-C6
SUNHAVEN RD
- SDCo 91901 1234-C6
SUN KING RD
- SD 92126 1209-D6
SUNKIST DR
2700 SDCo 92084 1088-D7
2700 SDCo 92084 1108-D1
SUNLIGHT CT
1900 OCN 92056 1087-F2
SUNLINE AV
4700 SD 92117 1248-C1
4900 SD 92117 1228-C7
SUNLIT WY
200 SDCo 92065 1152-J5
SUN MAIDEN CT
18200 SD 92127 1149-H7
SUN MEADOW DR
600 ELCJ 92020 1271-E1
SUNMEADOW RD
5000 OCN 92056 1087-F3
SUNNINGDALE DR
600 OCN 92057 1066-G7
SUNNY DR
- ENCT 92024 1147-C6
SUNNY LN
13400 SDCo 92040 1232-D4
SUNNY PT
1300 SDCo 92070 1135-D4
SUNNY ACRES AV
1300 SDCo 91901 1234-G5
SUNNY BRAE DR
6300 SD 92119 1250-F6
SUNNY BRAE PL
7100 SD 92119 1250-F6
SUNNYBROOK LN
700 SDCo 92021 1232-J7
700 SDCo 92021 1252-J1
SUNNY CREEK RD
2700 CRLB 92008 1107-C7
SUNNY CREST CIR
1200 VSTA 92084 1087-J4
SUNNY CREST LN
1700 CHV 91902 1311-C4
SUNNYCREST LN
2000 SDCo 92028 1028-A7
SUNNYDALE CT
11200 SD 92127 1169-J4
SUNNYFIELD PL
15800 SD 92127 1169-H5
SUNNY HEIGHTS RD
1300 SDCo 92028 998-C7
SUNNY HILL CT
900 SDCo 92028 1027-H1
SUNNYHILL DR
4000 CRLB 92008 1106-H6
SUNNY HILLS CT
700 SDCo 92065 1152-E5
SUNNY HILLS RD
4700 OCN 92056 1087-D4
SUNNYLAND AV
1400 ELCJ 92019 1252-A6
SUNNY MEADOW CT
10900 SD 92126 1208-J3
SUNNY MEADOW ST
10800 SD 92126 1208-J3
SUNNY MESA RD
10900 SD 92121 1208-G3
SUNNYRIDGE DR
- SDCo 92026 1089-B2
SUNNYRIDGE RD
7400 SNTE 92071 1230-F7
SUNNYSIDE AV
300 SD 92114 1290-H3
1900 SDCo 92019 1252-C5
SUNNYSIDE DR
5100 SDCo 91902 1310-H1
SUNNYSIDE LN
11300 SDCo 92026 1089-H6
SUNNY SLOPE DR
1900 SDCo 92027 1130-D4
SUNNYSLOPE LN
9700 SDCo 92029 1149-D4
SUNNY SLOPE TER
1800 SDCo 92027 1130-D4
SUNNY VIEW DR
5700 SDCo 91902 1311-A1

SUNNY VISTA LN
1900 SDCo 92069 1108-H2
1900 SMCS 92069 1108-H2
SUN RAY CT
11500 SD 92131 1210-B1
SUNRAY LN
4200 SDCo 91941 1271-G4
SUNRAY PL
10900 SDCo 91941 1271-G4
SUNRICH LN
800 ENCT 92024 1147-C3
SUNRIDGE DR
400 OCN 92056 1087-E2
8500 SNTE 92071 1230-H7
SUNRIDGE PL
400 ESCN 92026 1109-G4
SUNRISE AV
8400 LMSA 91941 1271-A3
8400 LMSA 91941 1270-J3
SUNRISE CIR
200 SDCo 92084 1088-C6
1500 CRLB 92008 1106-G6
SUNRISE CT
12200 PWY 92064 1190-B1
SUNRISE DR
- ImCo 92274 410-H7
300 SD 92173 1350-G5
400 SDCo 92084 1088-C6
400 VSTA 92084 1088-B7
1200 SDCo 92036 1136-D6
14800 PWY 92064 1170-B7
14800 PWY 92064 1190-B1
SUNRISE DR E
400 SDCo 92084 1088-C7
SUNRISE HWY Rt#-S1
6800 SDCo 92066 430-A6
6800 SDCo 92066 1237-G3
6800 SDCo 91948 1237-G3
9500 SDCo 91948 430-B5
10500 SDCo 91948 1218-A1
12200 SDCo 91948 (1217-J1 See Page 1216)
12300 SDCo 91948 (1197-F4 See Page 1176)
14100 SDCo 92036 1176-G2
14300 SDCo 92036 (1177-B6 See Page 1176)
14700 SDCo 92036 (1197-F4 See Page 1176)
SUNRISE LN
8700 LMSA 91941 1270-J3
8700 LMSA 91941 1271-A3
SUNRISE PL
300 SDCo 92084 1088-B6
SUNRISE RDG
4500 OCN 92056 1087-D4
SUNRISE ST
3300 SD 92102 1289-F3
SUNRISE WY
- ESCN 92029 1149-G1
- SDCo 92029 1149-H1
1100 SMCS 92069 1128-E3
SUNRISE CANYON RD
14600 PWY 92064 1190-G3
SUNRISE HILLS DR
4800 SDCo 92020 1271-H2
SUNRISE MOUNTAIN DR
1200 SDCo 92026 1109-J3
SUNRISE MOUNTAIN RD
1200 SDCo 92021 1252-J3
SUNRISE RANCH LN
- SDCo 91906 (1297-H6 See Page 1296)
SUNRISE RANCH RD
14100 PWY 92064 1190-H3
SUNRISE SHADOW CT
1500 ELCJ 92019 1252-A7
SUNRISE SUMMIT
11600 SDCo 92040 1231-H6
SUNRISE VALLEY DR
4800 SDCo 92020 1271-H2
SUNRISE VIEW DR
2100 SDCo 92028 1048-B1
SUNRISE VISTA
16900 SDCo 92065 1151-E6
SUNROSE CT
5000 OCN 92056 1087-E2
SUNSET AV
900 IMPB 91932 1349-H3
900 SD 92154 1349-H3
1600 SD 92154 1350-A3
9400 SDCo 91941 1271-C1
SUNSET BLVD
1700 SD 92103 1268-H5
SUNSET CT
600 SMCS 92069 1108-J5
700 SD 92109 1267-H1
SUNSET DR
100 ENCT 92024 1147-B6
500 OCN 92054 1085-J5
500 VSTA 92083 1107-H2
600 OCN 92054 1086-A5
1300 SDCo 92083 1107-D2
1800 ImCo 92243 6499-D6
1900 OCN 92056 1107-D2
2000 SDCo 92025 1130-B6
2200 SDCo 92036 1136-C6
2300 ESCN 92025 1130-A5
3100 ESCN 92025 1150-B3
3200 SDCo 92028 1047-H2
3400 SDCo 92036 1156-E1
7700 LMSA 91941 1270-G2
15700 PWY 92064 1170-H5
SUNSET LN
2200 SDCo 92036 1156-F7
3500 SD 92173 1350-E3
11800 SDCo 92040 1251-J1
SUNSET PT
- SDCo 91901 1234-A6
SUNSET RD
500 SDCo 92004 (1078-J3 See Page 1058)
4000 SD 92103 1268-G5
8100 SDCo 92021 1251-J1
8100 SDCo 92040 1251-J1
8300 SDCo 92040 1231-J7
28300 SDCo 92082 1091-B1
28600 SDCo 92082 1071-B7
SUNSET ST
2600 SD 92110 1268-F4
SUNSET TER
7900 LMGR 91945 1290-H2
16200 SDCo 92082 1091-B1
SUNSET TR
10900 SNTE 92071 1231-F7
SUNSET WY
- ImCo - 412-A3
16100 SDCo 92082 1071-B7

SUNSET BLUFFS WY
4400 SD 92130 1188-C6
SUNSET CLIFFS BLVD
- SD 92109 1268-A5
700 SD 92107 1287-H1
1400 SD 92107 1267-H7
2100 SD 92107 1268-A5
SUNSET CREST WY
- SD 92121 1208-F3
SUNSET GROVE RD
1200 SDCo 92028 1047-J3
1300 SDCo 92028 1048-A2
SUNSET HEIGHTS RD
- SDCo 92026 1109-E6
1000 ESCN 92026 1109-E6
SUNSET HILL DR
1800 CRLB 92008 1106-H7
SUNSET HILLS
2600 SDCo 92025 1150-E1
21200 SD 92025 1150-E1
SUNSET KNOLLS RD
11600 SDCo 92040 1231-H4
SUNSET MOUNTAIN WY
15700 PWY 92064 1170-H5
SUNSET OAKS
19400 SDCo 92065 1153-D2
SUNSET POINT CT
1600 CHV 91911 1330-J4
SUNSET RIDGE DR
10500 SD 92131 1210-A2
10600 SD 92131 1209-J2
SUNSET VALLEY RD
- SDCo 91901 1233-J3
SUNSET VIEW DR
- SDCo 92036 1136-A7
SUNSET VIEW RD
13500 PWY 92064 1190-H3
SUNSET VISTA LN
27500 SDCo 92082 1091-E3
SUNSHINE AV
100 ELCJ 92020 1251-F6
SUNSHINE LN
100 SMCS 92069 1108-H6
SUNSHINE TR
1200 SDCo 92036 1136-C5
SUNSHINE MOUNTAIN RD
2100 SDCo 92069 1108-H1
SUNSHINE PEAK CT
11800 SD 92131 1190-A7
11800 SD 92131 1210-A1
SUNSHINE VALLEY LN
19300 SDCo 92065 1153-G3
SUNSHINE VALLEY RD
19000 SDCo 92065 1153-F2
SUN SUMMIT PT
16000 SD 92127 1169-J5
SUNSWEPT ST
200 SD 92114 1290-F5
SUNTREE PL
8400 SD 92119 1250-J2
SUN UP CT
3100 SDCo 91902 1311-B1
SUN VALLEY LN
15100 SDCo 92014 1168-A7
SUN VALLEY RD
- CHV 91915 1311-G6
- SMCS 92069 1128-A2
1200 SOLB 92075 1167-H6
4500 SDCo 92014 1167-J6
4500 SOLB 92014 1167-J6
4700 SDCo 92014 1168-A7
SUNVIEW DR
8300 SDCo 92021 1252-B1
8300 SDCo 92021 1232-B7
SUN WALK CT
17800 SD 92127 1149-H7
17800 SD 92127 1169-H1
SUNWEST GN
- ESCN 92025 1130-A6
- SDCo 92025 1130-A6
SUNWOOD DR
8900 SNTE 92071 1231-A6
SUNWOOD TR
12200 PWY 92064 1190-B6
SUPALE RANCH RD
38600 SDCo 92028 997-B4
SUPERBA ST
3800 SD 92113 1289-G4
SUPERIOR ST
600 ESCN 92029 1129-F2
3800 SD 92113 1289-G4
SUPERIOR HOLLOW RD
29900 SDCo 92082 1070-B4
SUPREME CT
300 SMCS 92078 1129-B2
SURCO DR
11300 SD 92126 1209-B2
SURF PL
3500 OCN 92056 1107-C2
SURF RD
200 ENCT 92024 1147-A3
SURFBIRD CIR
- CRLB 92009 1127-C6
SURFBIRD WY
900 OCN 92057 1087-A3
SURFBREAKER PT
5000 SD 92154 1350-J1
SURFCLIFF PT
4900 SD 92154 1350-J1
SURF CREST DR
1200 SD 92154 1350-H1
SURFLINE WY
3600 OCN 92056 1107-C3
SURFPOINT WY
- SD 92154 1350-J1
SURFRIDER WY
100 OCN 92054 1085-J7
300 OCN 92054 1086-A7
SURF SHOAL PT
5000 SD 92154 1350-J1
SURFSIDE DR
5000 SD 92154 1350-J1
SURFSIDE LN
6400 CRLB 92009 1126-H5
SURFTIDE LN
1300 SD 92154 1350-J1
SURFVIEW CT
300 DLMR 92014 1187-F6
SURFWOOD LN
1100 SD 92154 1350-J1
SURREALIST CT
4800 OCN 92057 1087-B2
SURREY CT
5700 OCN 92057 1067-F6
SURREY DR
200 CHV 91902 1310-G4
14500 PWY 92064 1190-F1

SURREY HTS
1400 SDCo 92028 1027-J4
SURREY LN
2700 SDCo 92029 1129-C3
SURREY PL
200 CHV 91902 1310-G4
SURREY TR
700 SDCo 92036 1138-B7
SURREY HILLS CT
17000 PWY 92064 1170-D2
SURVEY PT
13000 SD 92130 1187-J5
SUSAN CIR
3000 OCN 92056 1107-B1
SUSAN CT
1100 SD 92154 1350-E1
2000 SDCo 92026 1109-E6
SUSAN LN
1000 SDCo 92065 1152-D5
SUSAN PL
2200 SD 92105 1290-A1
SUSANA CT
1000 SDCo 92069 1128-F4
SUSIE LN
10800 SNTE 92071 1231-E3
SUSIE PL
10400 SNTE 92071 1231-E3
SUSIE WY
19300 SDCo 92065 1172-C2
SU SIEMPRE PL
2900 ESCN 92025 1150-B1
SUSITA CT
11100 SD 92129 1169-J7
SUSITA ST
15100 SD 92129 1169-J7
SUSITA TER
11100 SD 92129 1169-J7
SUSQUEHANNA PL
4300 SD 92117 1248-E1
SUSSEX DR
4800 SD 92116 1269-G3
SUTHERLAND DR
20600 SDCo 92065 409-H11
SUTHERLAND ST
3400 SD 92110 1268-G6
SUTHERLAND DAM RD
20600 SDCo 92065 409-H11
SUTTER CT
400 SMCS 92069 1109-C7
3600 OCN 92056 1107-F4
SUTTER LN
1200 SMCS 92069 1109-C7
SUTTER ST
600 SD 92103 1268-H6
2600 CRLB 92008 1106-J5
SUTTER MILL RD
13200 PWY 92064 1190-G4
SUTTER MILL WY
14200 PWY 92064 1190-G4
SUTTON CT
9700 SNTE 92071 1231-B4
SUTTON HILL PL
700 SDCo 92028 1027-H3
SUZANNE LN
- CHV 91911 1330-E4
700 SDCo 92026 1129-E2
SVEA CT
1600 LMGR 91945 1290-G2
SWALERO RD
6200 LMSA 91942 1251-A6
SWALLOW DR
900 VSTA 92083 1087-F4
1300 ELCJ 92020 1251-C2
SWALLOW LN
100 OCN 92057 1086-H2
1900 CRLB 92009 1127-E5
SWALLOWTAIL CT
1200 ENCT 92024 1147-D2
SWALLOWTAIL RD
1700 ENCT 92024 1147-D2
SWAN DR
30000 SDCo 91906 (1297-G5 See Page 1296)
SWAN RD
18600 SDCo 92065 1153-E5
SWAN ST
1800 SD 92114 1290-D1
SWAN CANYON CT
12500 SD 92131 1210-C2
SWAN CANYON PL
12500 SD 92131 1211-C2
SWAN CANYON RD
11300 SD 92131 1210-C2
SWANER ST
1000 SD 92114 1290-C2
SWAN LAKE DR
- SD 92131 1209-G1
SWANSEA PL
10900 SD 92126 1209-A3
SWANSON CT
11100 SD 92131 1209-J1
SWANTON DR
10100 SNTE 92071 1231-A3
SWARTHMORE ST
5300 LMSA 91942 1270-G1
SWARTZ CANYON RD
16200 SDCo 92065 1173-E3
SWATH CT
9900 SD 92129 1189-F5
SWATH PL
12900 SD 92129 1189-F5
SWEENEY CT
1500 SDCo 92019 1272-E2
SWEENEY PASS RD Rt#-S2
- SDCo 92036 430-E4
- SDCo 92259 430-E4
SWEET LN
22000 SDCo 92065 1153-G6
SWEET RD
- ImCo 92251 431-A3
SWEET ALICE LN
100 ENCT 92024 1147-E7
SWEETBRIAR CIR
1400 CRLB 92009 1127-A4
SWEETBRIAR LN
11800 SD 92131 1210-A2
SWEET FENNEL RD
600 SMCS 92078 1128-G2
SWEETGRASS CT
2500 SDCo 92003 1048-A6
SWEETGRASS LN
4800 SDCo 92003 1048-A6
SWEET LIME RD
1100 SDCo 92084 1068-A5
SWEET PEA PL
- ENCT 92024 1147-C5
SWEETSHADE ST
100 OCN 92054 1066-G7

SWEET TREE LN
- SDCo 92084 1068-D5
SWEETWATER GN
1300 ESCN 92026 1129-G1
1300 ESCN 92026 1109-G7
SWEETWATER LN
1100 SDCo 91977 1291-B2
SWEETWATER RD
500 SDCo 91977 1291-A3
1100 SDCo 91977 1290-J1
1400 CHV 91950 1310-B3
1400 NATC 91950 1310-B3
2100 SDCo 91950 1310-B3
2100 SDCo 91977 1270-J6
2800 LMGR 91945 1270-J6
2800 LMGR 91977 1270-J6
2800 SDCo 91945 1270-J6
3400 SDCo 91902 1310-G2
3900 CHV 91902 1310-G2
SWEETWATER RD Rt#-S17
5300 SDCo 91902 1290-J6
5300 SDCo 91902 1310-H1
5600 SDCo 91902 1291-A7
SWEETWATER WY
3100 LMGR 91945 1270-J5
SWEETWATER SPRINGS BLVD
2500 SDCo 91978 1291-F1
2500 SDCo 91977 1291-F1
2800 SDCo 91977 1271-E6
2800 SDCo 91978 1271-E6
SWEETWAY CT
8300 SDCo 91977 1290-J5
SWEETWOOD ST
200 SD 92114 1290-E4
SWIFT
6100 CRLB 92008 1127-C2
SWIFT AV
3600 SD 92104 1269-F4
4400 SD 92116 1269-F4
SWIFT LN
1400 ELCJ 92020 1251-D2
SWINGING V RD
3300 SDCo 92004 (1079-A6 See Page 1058)
SWITZER DR
8900 SDCo 91977 1271-A6
SWITZER ST
400 SD 92101 1289-B5
SWITZERLAND DR
1400 SD 92154 1350-A2
SWORD WY
13300 SD 92130 1188-C4
SYBIL CT
1200 SDCo 92026 1109-E6
SYCAMORE AV
100 CRLB 92008 1106-E6
300 VSTA 92083 1108-B4
500 SDCo 92083 1108-B4
1300 VSTA 92083 1107-H7
14000 PWY 92064 1190-F2
SYCAMORE CT
3300 SD 92037 1228-B4
SYCAMORE DR
1100 SDCo 92028 1047-J2
1600 CHV 91911 1330-F5
1700 SMCS 92069 1108-J3
1800 SDCo 92069 1109-A2
1800 SMCS 92069 1109-A2
2000 SDCo 92069 1108-J3
2600 OCN 92056 1087-F5
3900 SD 92105 1289-G1
4100 SD 92105 1269-H7
24600 SDCo 91916 1236-A2
SYCAMORE HTS
1300 SDCo 92028 1047-J2
SYCAMORE LN
- SDCo 92026 1089-A2
800 ELCJ 92019 1252-C4
800 SDCo 92019 1252-C4
3000 ESCN 92025 1130-C7
3500 SDCo 92028 1028-F4
SYCAMORE PL
1500 SDCo 92028 1047-J2
SYCAMORE RD
200 SD 92173 1350-G5
SYCAMORE WY
1600 SDCo 92028 1047-J2
SYCAMORE CANYON RD
- SD 92145 1211-C2
- SDCo 92145 1211-C2
13200 PWY 92064 1190-J4
13400 PWY 92064 1191-A6
15000 SD 92145 1191-A6
15000 SDCo 92071 1191-C7
15200 SDCo 92064 1191-A6
15400 SD 92071 1191-C7
15400 SDCo 92145 1191-C7
16300 SDCo 92071 1211-C2
SYCAMORE CREEK RD
17900 PWY 92064 1150-E6
18300 SD 92025 1150-E6
18300 SD 92128 1150-E6
SYCAMORE CREST PL
- ESCN 92027 1110-G7
SYCAMORE HEIGHTS RD
- ESCN 92027 1110-F7
SYCAMORE PARK DR
- SDCo 92071 1191-E7
SYCAMORE RIDGE CT
- SD 92131 1210-C3
SYCAMORE SPRINGS RD
20500 SDCo 91935 (1314-J1 See Page 1294)
20500 SDCo 91935 (1315-A1 See Page 1294)
SYCAMORE TREE LN
13600 PWY 92064 1190-E3
SYCAMORE VALLEY RD
13300 PWY 92064 1191-A4
SYCAMOREVIEW DR
1100 ENCT 92024 1167-F2
SYCHAR RD
100 SD 92114 1290-F4
S SYCHAR RD
100 SD 92114 1290-F4
SYCUAN RD
2000 SDCo 92019 1253-C6
SYCUAN SUMMIT DR
1000 SDCo 92019 1252-H6
SYDNEY PL
3500 SD 92116 1269-F2
SYDNEY TER
1700 ELCJ 92021 1252-C2
1700 SDCo 92021 1252-C2
SYLVAN LN
3000 SDCo 92026 1109-H2

SYLVESTER RD
- SD 92106 1288-A7
- SD 92106 1308-A1
SYLVIA ST
300 ENCT 92024 1147-B6
2800 SDCo 91902 1290-J7
3000 SDCo 91902 1310-J1
SYLVIE CT
3600 SDCo 92084 1088-F7
SYLVY WY
2700 SD 92139 1310-F1
SYME DR
3900 CRLB 92008 1106-G6
SYMPHONY PL
1100 ESCN 92029 1129-E5
SYRACUSE AV
3400 SD 92122 1228-D6
SYRACUSE CT
3600 SD 92122 1228-D6
SYRACUSE LN
6100 SD 92122 1228-D6
SYRACUSE WY
6100 SD 92122 1228-D6
SZALAY WY
3300 SMCS 92069 1108-D5

T

T AV
- NATC 91950 1290-A6
T CT
- SD 92126 1209-F7
T ST
3600 SD 92113 1289-G5
4700 SD 92113 1290-A5
TABBY LN
1100 ESCN 92026 1109-J7
1100 ESCN 92026 1110-A7
TABERNA VISTA WY
1800 SDCo 91901 1233-H4
TABLERO CT
17300 SD 92127 1169-J1
TABLERO PL
17300 SD 92127 1169-H1
TABOR CT
900 CHV 91911 1331-A2
TABOR DR
900 CHV 91911 1331-A2
TACAYME DR
4800 OCN 92057 1066-J7
4800 OCN 92057 1067-A7
TACAYME PL
4900 OCN 92057 1067-A7
TACOMA LN
1700 VSTA 92084 1088-B4
TACOMA ST
4200 SD 92117 1248-D3
TAECKER RD
- ImCo 92227 431-D1
TAEGAN LN
1600 ENCT 92024 1167-G1
TAFFY LN
11000 SNTE 92071 1231-G5
TAFT AV
200 ELCJ 92020 1251-G5
800 NATC 92136 1309-G2
900 NATC 91950 1309-G2
4500 SDCo 91941 1271-F3
5400 SD 92037 1247-G3
TAFT CIR
100 OCN 92057 1067-B6
TAFT ST
1300 LMGR 91945 1290-G2
1300 ESCN 92026 1109-H7
TAG LN
500 SDCo 92065 1152-G6
TAGOTA CT
9100 SDCo 92040 1232-E6
TAHITI DR
- ESCN 92025 1129-J5
TAHOE ST
2900 ELCJ 92020 1251-A5
TAIA LN
11800 SDCo 92040 1251-J1
TAIT ST
800 OCN 92054 1106-B2
6500 SD 92111 1268-H1
7200 SD 92111 1269-A1
TAKISHLA PL
32200 SDCo 92061 1051-A6
TALBOT AV
8400 SD 92145 1229-C2
TALBOT ST
2800 SD 92106 1288-A2
3700 SD 92106 1287-J2
TALCA AV
13800 SD 92129 1189-C3
TALCA CT
8900 SD 92129 1189-C3
TALIESIN WY
5200 SDCo 92003 1048-D7
TALISMAN CT
6900 SD 92119 1250-H4
TALL OAK DR
- SDCo 92026 1089-D4
TALL OAK LN
- SDCo 92026 1089-D4
TALLOW CT
500 CHV 91911 1330-H4
TALLOW TREE LN
- SDCo 92127 1169-D2
TALL PINE RD
- SDCo 92036 1156-G6
E TALMADGE DR
4500 SD 92116 1269-H3
W TALMADGE DR
4300 SD 92116 1269-H3
TALMADGE CANYON RW
4600 SD 92115 1269-J2
TALMADGE PARK RW
4700 SD 92115 1269-J2
TALON WY
2000 SD 92123 1269-B1
TALON RIDGE WY
300 OCN 92054 1086-B6
TALTEC DR
4800 LMSA 91941 1271-C2
4800 SDCo 91941 1271-C2
TALUS ST
200 CHV 91911 1330-G4
TALUS WY
- CRLB 92008 1107-B4
TAMAR TER
10700 SNTE 92071 1231-F6
TAMARA DR
600 SDCo 92026 1109-H2
TAMARA LN
2400 SDCo 92069 1088-G7
2400 SDCo 92069 1108-G1

STREET
Block City ZIP Pg-Grid

TAMARACK AV
1000 CRLB 92008 1106-G6
2200 CRLB 92008 1107-A3
TAMARACK CT
500 CHV 91911 1330-H4
TAMARACK LN
9700 SDCo 92029 1149-D4
TAMARACK ST
400 CHV 91911 1330-G5
TAMARACK TER
700 ELCJ 92019 1251-J6
TAMARAK AV
200 ESCN 92026 1109-H7
TAMARAND WY
1700 SD 92154 1349-J2
1700 SD 92154 1350-A2
TAMARINDO WY
- CHV 91911 1330-E5
TAMARISK CIR
4400 OCN 92057 1066-H6
TAMARISK LN
500 SMCS 92069 1128-E2
TAMARISK WY
500 ELCJ 92020 1251-G4
TAMARISK GROVE DR
1300 CHV 91915 1311-H6
TAMARME TER
1700 ESCN 92025 1130-A5
TAMAYO DR
800 CHV 91910 1310-F7
TAMBERLY CT
8800 SNTE 92071 1231-D7
TAMBERLY LN
8800 SNTE 92071 1231-D7
TAMBERLY WY
8800 SNTE 92071 1231-D6
TAMBOR CT
4200 SD 92124 1249-J2
4200 SD 92124 1250-A2
TAMBOR RD
3900 SD 92124 1249-J3
TAMBOURINE LN
2300 SDCo 92019 1252-D6
TAMIL RD
10000 SDCo 92040 1232-B3
TAMILYNN CT
4100 SD 92122 1228-E6
TAMILYNN ST
6000 SD 92122 1228-E6
TAMMADGE HEIGHTS RD
200 SDCo 91901 1233-E7
200 SDCo 91901 1253-E1
200 SDCo 92019 1253-E1
TAM O SHANTER CT
13800 PWY 92064 1170-F2
TAM O SHANTER DR
500 SMCS 92069 1109-D7
17000 PWY 92064 1170-F1
TAMPA AV
2200 ELCJ 92020 1251-B4
TAMPA CT
1500 CHV 91902 1311-B4
TAMPERE CT
11100 SD 92131 1209-J1
TAMPICO CT
100 SOLB 92075 1167-D6
7800 SD 92126 1209-A3
TAMPICO GN
200 ESCN 92025 1130-B7
TAMPICO WY
100 SOLB 92075 1167-D6
TAMRA CT
3500 SDCo 91935 1272-E5
TAMRES DR
5500 SD 92111 1248-G6
TANA WY
25000 SDCo 92065 1173-G4
TANAGER DR
7100 CRLB 92009 1127-D6
TANAGER LN
1300 ELCJ 92020 1251-D2
TANBARK CT
1600 CHV 91911 1330-H5
TANBARK ST
400 CHV 91911 1330-H5
TAN BOB LN
300 ESCN 92029 1150-A2
300 SDCo 92029 1150-A2
T ANCHOR DR
600 SDCo 92004 (1078-J3 See Page 1058)
700 SDCo 92004 (1079-A3 See Page 1058)
TANGELO DR
12100 SDCo 92040 1232-A4
TANGELO WY
- SDCo 92082 1071-A7
TANGERINE DR
200 ELCN 92243 6559-H1
TANGERINE ST
1100 ELCJ 92021 1252-A3
TANGERINE WY
1200 ESCN 92029 1129-E5
TANGERINE COVE DR
500 VSTA 92083 1087-G7
TANGIER CT
600 OCN 92057 1087-B1
TANGIERS CT
700 SD 92109 1247-H7
700 SD 92109 1267-H1
TANGLEFOOT TR
7400 SDCo 92036 1138-B7
TANGLEROD LN
7700 LMSA 91942 1250-G7
TANGLEWOOD LN
1500 ESCN 92029 1129-G5
9300 SD 92126 1209-E3
10400 SDCo 91916 1216-A7
10400 SDCo 91916 1235-J1
10400 SDCo 91916 1236-A1
TANGLEWOOD RD
6500 SD 92111 1248-J4
TANGLEWOOD WY
3700 SD 92111 1248-J4
TANGOR WY
9900 SDCo 91977 1271-D6
TANNER CT
7100 SD 92111 1248-J4
TANNER LN
3700 SD 92111 1248-J4
3700 SD 92111 1249-A4
TANNIN DR
17200 PWY 92064 1170-D2
TANOAK CT
500 CHV 91911 1330-H5
TANSY ST
3700 SD 92121 1208-C6
TAN TAM DR
2800 SDCo 92029 1149-G1
TANYA LN
1000 SDCo 92028 1027-H1
TAOS DR
4000 SD 92117 1248-D3
TAOS PL
3400 SD 92117 1248-D3
TARA CT
- CRLB 92008 1106-G6
1100 CHV 91911 1330-F2
TARA PL
5200 SD 92117 1248-H1
TARA WY
3500 SDCo 91935 1272-E6
TARAKIM LN
1600 VSTA 92083 1107-J2
TARANGO PL
200 SDCo 91977 1290-J5
TARANTELLA LN
4500 SD 92130 1188-C6
TARASCAN DR
13200 PWY 92064 1190-E4
TARATA CT
400 CHV 91911 1330-H5
TARAWA RD
2900 CORD 92155 1309-A2
TARAY CT
9800 SD 92129 1209-F1
TARBOX ST
1300 LMGR 91945 1290-E2
1300 SD 92114 1290-E2
TAREK TER
1000 SDCo 92084 1068-G7
TARENTO DR
500 SD 92106 1287-J3
1000 SD 92107 1287-J2
TARGA PL
1800 SDCo 92019 1272-C4
TARLETON ST
1500 SDCo 91977 1290-H2
1600 LMGR 91945 1290-H2
TARLO CT
1000 ELCJ 92019 1252-A7
TARO CT
100 SD 92114 1290-G4
TARRAGON DR
4800 OCN 92057 1067-B7
TARRAGONA DR
4200 SD 92115 1270-C4
TARTAN TER
- SDCo 92065 1171-G1
TARZANA RD
14100 PWY 92064 1190-B2
E TASHA VIEW WY
100 SDCo 92021 1252-J1
W TASHA VIEW WY
100 SDCo 92021 1252-J1
TASMAN PL
100 SD 92114 1290-F5
TASPA CT
- SDCo 92061 1050-J5
TASSEL RD
12400 PWY 92064 1190-C4
TATAS PL
10400 SDCo 92026 1109-F1
TATIA CT
17600 SD 92128 1170-A1
TATLER RD
- CRLB 92009 1127-C6
TATTENHAM RD
1700 ENCT 92024 1147-A2
1700 ENCT 92024 1146-J2
TATTERSALL SQ
5100 SD 92130 1188-C6
TATUM ST
500 VSTA 92083 1087-F5
TAU ST
5600 LMSA 91942 1250-J7
TAULBEES LN
1300 SMCS 92069 1108-E7
TAUNT PL
12500 PWY 92064 1190-C2
TAUNT RD
12500 PWY 92064 1190-C2
TAUPA WY
- SDCo 92061 1051-B6
TAURUS PL
8700 SD 92126 1209-C2
TAUSSIG CT
10200 SD 92124 1249-G4
TAUSSIG ST
3000 SD 92124 1249-G4
TAVARA PL
400 SD 92106 1288-A4
TAVERN CT
1800 SDCo 91901 1234-A6
TAVERN RD
800 SDCo 91901 1233-H5
1300 SDCo 91901 1234-A6
1900 SDCo 91901 1254-A1
2600 SDCo 91901 1253-J3
TAWANKA DR
13300 PWY 92064 1190-D4
TAWNY CT
700 OCN 92057 1087-C1
TAWNY PL
1800 ESCN 92026 1109-D5
TAWNY WY
13100 PWY 92064 1170-E2
TAXCO CT
1100 CHV 91910 1311-A7
1100 CHV 91910 1331-A1
TAXCO PL
- SDCo 92003 1067-H1
TAYLOR AV
1400 ESCN 92027 1110-B7
TAYLOR PL
1300 ESCN 92027 1110-C6
1300 ESCN 92027 1130-B1
TAYLOR RD
- SD 92106 1288-B7
TAYLOR ST
100 VSTA 92084 1087-H2
4000 SD 92110 1268-F4
4300 SD 92103 1268-F4
4400 SD 92108 1268-F4
E TAYLOR ST
1100 VSTA 92084 1088-A2
W TAYLOR ST
900 VSTA 92084 1087-J3
900 VSTA 92084 1088-A3
TAYLOR WY
1000 SDCo 92019 1253-B2
TAZA RD
1300 SDCo 92028 1028-H1
1500 SDCo 92028 998-H7
TEABERRY GN
2400 ESCN 92027 1110-D7
TEABERRY ST
700 ENCT 92024 1147-E6
TEAK CT
500 CHV 91911 1330-H4
TEAK ST
3700 SD 92113 1289-G5
TEAKWOOD CT
700 SMCS 92069 1109-A5
TEAKWOOD GN
400 ESCN 92026 1109-G6
TEAKWOOD LN
1800 SDCo 92021 1251-H1
TEAKWOOD WY
1800 VSTA 92083 1107-G5
TEAL GN
2100 ESCN 92026 1109-H5
TEAL PL
2600 SD 92123 1249-A7
TEAL RD
29800 SDCo 91906 (1297-F5 See Page 1296)
TEAL ST
100 CHV 91911 1330-F5
TEALWOOD CT
8000 LMGR 91945 1270-J7
TEA MOUNTAIN LN
1900 SDCo 92021 1252-G4
TEA PARTY LN
3100 SD 92124 1249-G4
TEAROSE LN
- SDCo 91934 (1321-A3 See Page 1300)
TEASDALE AV
7000 SD 92122 1228-G4
TEA TREE DR
- CRLB 92009 1127-A5
TEA TREE LN
- SDCo 92127 1169-D2
TEBO CT
3400 SD 92154 1330-E7
TECALOTE DR
1600 SDCo 92028 1028-F4
TECALOTE LN
4000 SDCo 92028 1028-H5
TECATE GN
1900 ESCN 92029 1129-E6
TECATE RD Rt#-188
400 SDCo 91980 429-K10
TECATE CYPRESS TR
- SDCo 91916 1236-E2
TECATE DIVIDE RD
2500 SDCo 91905 (1299-J4 See Page 1298)
TECATE MISSION RD
300 SDCo 91980 429-K10
TECH WY
8500 SD 92123 1249-C2
TECH CENTER CT
- PWY 92064 1190-E7
TECH CENTER DR
12100 PWY 92064 1190-F7
TECHNOLOGY DR
16200 SD 92127 1169-H4
TECHNOLOGY PL
10900 SD 92127 1169-H4
TECOLOTE CT
1300 NATC 91950 1310-B1
TECOLOTE RD
1200 SD 92109 1268-F2
1300 SD 92110 1268-F2
TECOMA PL
6400 CRLB 92009 1127-E4
TECUMSEH WY
4300 SD 92117 1248-E2
TED KIPF RD
- ImCo - 411-D8
- ImCo - 431-H1
- ImCo - 432-A4
TEDS PL
500 SDCo 92065 1152-D7
TED WILLIAMS FRWY Rt#-56
- SD - 1188-E5
- SD - 1189-A4
- SD - 1207-J2
- SD - 1208-A1
TED WILLIAMS PKWY
- SD 92128 1189-H3
- SD 92129 1189-H3
11600 SD 92128 1190-A2
12100 PWY 92064 1190-A2
TEE SQ
29000 SDCo 92066 1237-C7
TEE-A-WAY PL
6800 SD 92119 1250-F5
TEEBIRD LN
7600 SD 92123 1269-A1
TEELIN AV
1200 VSTA 92083 1087-G4
TEENA DR
100 CHV 91911 1330-D5
TEEPEE DR
1300 SDCo 92027 1130-E5
TEHACHAPI DR
500 SMCS 92069 1128-C1
TEHAMA DR
300 SMCS 92069 1108-H5
TEHNSEN
14100 SDCo 92040 1232-H5
TELEGRAPH CANYON RD
- CHV 91910 1330-E1
- CHV 91911 1330-E1
200 CHV 91910 1310-F7
200 CHV 91911 1310-F7
800 CHV 91913 1330-H1
800 CHV 91913 1331-B1
800 CHV 91910 1331-B1
1000 CHV 91910 1311-B7
1000 CHV 91913 1311-B7
TELESCOPE AV
4600 CRLB 92008 1106-H6
TELESIS CT
10100 SD 92121 1208-D5
TELFORD LN
300 SDCo 92065 1152-H6
300 SDCo 92065 1153-A6
TELKAIF ST
9300 SDCo 92040 1232-F4
TEMA ST
6700 SD 92120 1250-E7
TEMECULA ST
- SDCo 92055 1086-A4
4200 SD 92107 1268-B5
TEMECULA VALLEY FRWY I-15
- RivC - 998-J2
- RivC - 999-A1
TEMEPA RD
11500 SDCo 92028 999-G4
TEMET DR
32800 SDCo 92061 1050-J5
TEMPALA RD
- SDCo 92059 1029-G4
TEMPAS CT
6000 SD 92114 1290-C4
TEMPERA CT
900 OCN 92057 1087-B2
TEMPLE ST
700 SD 92106 1287-J2
13500 PWY 92064 1190-F2
TEMPLE TER
2000 SDCo 91935 (1314-H2 See Page 1294)
6900 SD 92119 1250-E5
TEMPLE TR
19600 SDCo 91935 (1314-H1 See Page 1294)
TEMPLE WY
13800 PWY 92064 1190-F2
TEMPLE HEIGHTS DR
1200 OCN 92056 1087-D3
TEMPRA PL
1300 CHV 91911 1330-D4
TEMPRANO CT
4500 SD 92124 1250-A2
TENAJA TKTR
- SDCo 92028 409-A4
TENBURY CT
7000 SD 92139 1290-G7
TENDERFOOT LN
1100 OCN 92057 1067-E7
TENNIE ST
100 SD 92173 1350-F4
TENNIS CT
- SDCo 91916 1236-A2
TENNIS PL
1800 ENCT 92024 1167-H3
TENNIS CLUB DR
1200 ENCT 92024 1167-G2
TENNIS COURT LN
3500 SDCo 91910 1310-H2
TENNIS MATCH WY
1500 ENCT 92024 1147-G6
TENNYSON ST
3000 SD 92106 1288-C1
3100 SD 92106 1268-B7
3700 SD 92107 1268-B7
TENSHAW PL
3200 SD 92117 1248-C2
TEQUILA WY
3000 SD 92173 1350-D2
TERALTA PL
4400 SD 92103 1268-H4
TERAN DR
500 SDCo 92028 1027-F3
TERCER VERDE
3000 SD 92014 1187-H1
3000 SOLB 92014 1187-H1
TERCER VERDE WY
15800 SD 92014 1187-H1
TERESA DR
8200 SD 92126 1209-B2
TERESA ST
4100 OCN 92056 1087-C7
TERESITA ST
2600 SD 92104 1269-F7
TERI DR
12300 PWY 92064 1190-C2
TERMAN CT
8900 SD 92121 1208-J7
TERMINAL AV
2400 NATC 91950 1309-G4
TERMINAL ST
800 SD 92101 1289-B5
TERN DR
2600 SD 92123 1249-B7
TERN PL
7100 CRLB 92009 1127-D7
TEROL CT
200 SD 92114 1290-D4
TERRA LN
500 ELCJ 92019 1252-B4
500 SDCo 92019 1252-B4
TERRACE AV
400 ESCN 92026 1109-H7
TERRACE CT
4000 SD 92116 1269-G3
TERRACE DR
- SDCo 92026 1089-B2
100 VSTA 92084 1087-H7
3300 SDCo 92036 1156-D2
4000 SD 92116 1269-G3
8900 LMSA 91941 1271-B4
8900 LMSA 91977 1271-B4
TERRACE LN
100 SMCS 92069 1108-J7
3300 OCN 92056 1106-H1
TERRACE PL
3600 CRLB 92008 1107-B4
TERRACE VW
2000 ESCN 92029 1129-E6
TERRACE CREST
800 ELCJ 92019 1252-A7
TERRACE HILL DR
1700 SDCo 92021 1252-B2
TERRACE KNOLL
1400 SDCo 91901 1234-B6
TERRACE PINE DR
2700 SD 92173 1350-C2
TERRACE PINE LN
1500 SD 92173 1350-C2
TERRACE VIEW LN
30400 SDCo 92082 1070-G4
TERRACEVIEW PL
2100 ESCN 92026 1109-G5
TERRACEWOOD LN
2100 ESCN 92026 1109-H4
TERRACINA CIR
1900 SDCo 91977 1291-A1
TERRACINA ST
4800 OCN 92056 1087-B3
TERRACINA WY
100 VSTA 92083 1087-G6
TERRACITA LN
1400 SDCo 91901 1233-J7
TERRA COTTA RD
6900 SD 92114 1290-F5
TERRAKAPPA AV
1900 SDCo 91977 1291-A1
TERRA NOVA DR
400 CHV 91910 1310-G5
TERRARAMA AV
8800 SDCo 91977 1291-A1
TERRA SECA TR
3100 SDCo 91935 1273-B7
TERRASPIRO AV
2000 SDCo 91977 1291-A1
TERRAZA CIR
4600 SD 92124 1250-A2
TERRAZA CT
4500 SD 92124 1250-A1
TERRAZA ST
1700 OCN 92054 1106-E1
TERRAZA DISOMA
7900 CRLB 92009 1148-A2
TERRAZA FLORACION
10800 SD 92127 1169-H5
TERRAZA GOYA
2300 CRLB 92009 1127-G7
TERRAZA GUITARA
2300 CRLB 92009 1127-G6
TERRAZA MAR MARVELOSA
- SD 92130 1208-C4
TERRAZA PANGA
2300 CRLB 92009 1127-G6
TERRAZA PLAYA CANCUN
13300 SD 92124 1230-A7
TERRAZA PLAYA CATALINA
5000 SD 92124 1230-A7
TERRAZA PORTICO
- CRLB 92009 1127-J4
- CRLB 92009 1128-A4
TERRAZA QUINTANA
5100 SD 92124 1230-A7
TERRAZA RIBERA
2300 CRLB 92009 1127-G6
TERRAZA SALVO
2300 CRLB 92009 1127-G6
TERRELLA PL
2500 SDCo 92025 1150-D2
TERRENO CT
4400 SD 92124 1249-J1
TERRILEE DR
13800 PWY 92064 1190-G3
TERRILEE LN
14100 PWY 92064 1190-G3
TERRY LN
1900 NATC 91950 1290-A7
1900 NATC 91950 1310-A1
4500 LMSA 91941 1270-E3
TERRY ST
4100 OCN 92056 1087-C6
TERRYHILL DR
6100 SD 92037 1247-F2
TERRYWOOD RD
9400 SNTE 92071 1231-B4
TESLA LN
1100 SDCo 92028 998-A7
TESLA ST
3000 SD 92117 1248-F6
TESORO AV
- SMCS 92069 1108-F5
TESORO CT
12300 SD 92128 1170-B2
TESORO DR
16900 SD 92128 1170-B3
TESORO WY
24500 SDCo 92065 1173-F3
TESOTA CT
400 CHV 91911 1330-H5
TESTIGO TR
- SDCo 91901 1255-C4
TETEN WY
2400 ENCT 92024 1147-J7
2400 ENCT 92024 1148-A7
TETILLAS CT
15300 SD 92128 1170-A6
TETON DR
1300 SDCo 92021 1251-F1
1300 SNTE 92021 1251-F1
1400 SDCo 92021 1231-F7
1400 SNTE 92021 1231-F7
TETON PASS ST
1800 SDCo 92019 1272-C3
TEWA ST
500 DLMR 92014 1187-G5
TEX ST
5700 LMSA 91942 1250-H7
TEXANA ST
12700 SD 92129 1189-C6
TEXAS ST
2000 SD 92108 1269-D3
3300 SD 92101 1269-D6
3400 SD 92104 1269-D5
4300 SD 92116 1269-D3
THALIA ST
1100 SD 92154 1349-J1
THAMES CT
2300 SD 92123 1249-B7
THAMES WY
3600 CRLB 92008 1107-A3
THANKSGIVING LN
10200 SD 92126 1209-D5
THATCHER CT
12200 PWY 92064 1190-E7
THAYER DR
500 SDCo 91977 1291-B3
TH BAR RANCH TR
8000 SDCo 91901 1233-E7
THE CIR
100 VSTA 92084 1087-H6
THE PT
- CORD 92118 1329-E1
THE SQ
13400 PWY 92064 1170-E2
THEBES ST
14600 SD 92129 1189-H1
THEBES WY
4800 OCN 92056 1107-F6
THE HILL RD
3800 SDCo 91902 1310-F4
THE INLET
- CORD 92118 1329-D1
THELBORN WY
1700 SD 92154 1349-J2
1700 SD 92154 1350-A2
THELMA WY
400 NATC 91950 1290-C6
400 SD 92114 1290-C6
THE NARROWS RD
- SDCo 92004 (1099-H3 See Page 1098)
- SDCo 92004 1100-A5
- SDCo 92004 (1120-A3 See Page 1100)
THEODORE DR
1200 SD 92114 1290-D5
THERESA LN
9900 SNTE 92071 1231-D4
THERESA WY
100 CHV 91911 1330-F2
THERMAL AV
600 SD 92154 1349-J2
700 SD 92154 1329-J7
THE STRAND
200 OCN 92054 1105-J1
200 OCN 92054 1106-A1
300 OCN 92054 1085-J7
S THE STRAND
100 OCN 92054 1106-A1
THETA PL
5700 SD 92120 1250-C7
THE WOODS DR
1700 SDCo 92019 1272-B1
THE YELLOW BRICK RD
28900 SDCo 92082 1071-B6
THIBODO CT
2000 VSTA 92083 1108-B4
THIBODO RD
1500 VSTA 92083 1107-J2
1500 VSTA 92083 1108-A3
THIMBLE CT
8200 SD 92129 1189-B6
THING RD
- SDCo 91980 429-L10
THING VALLEY RD
- SDCo 91948 430-B5
- SDCo 92066 430-C6
THISTLE CT
8100 SD 92120 1250-D3
THISTLE BRAES TER
12000 SDCo 92040 1232-A6
THISTLE HILL PL
- SD 92130 1208-B1
THISTLEWOOD AV
1100 CHV 91913 1311-D6
THOMAS AV
- SD 92140 1268-G6
700 SD 92109 1247-H6
1400 SD 92109 1248-A6
1900 SD 92101 1289-C2
1900 SD 92134 1289-C2
THOMAS PL
- VSTA 92084 1088-C5
1500 CHV 91911 1330-J3
THOMAS ST
4000 OCN 92056 1087-B7
N THOMAS WY
1000 ESCN 92027 1110-B6
THOMAS HAYES LN
11600 SD 92126 1209-A1
THOMAS PAINE DR
15600 SDCo 92065 1171-J5
THOMAS PAINE LN
18500 SDCo 92065 1171-J4
THOMPSON RD
- ImCo 92251 431-A4
THOMSEN WY
400 SDCo 92065 1152-H4
THOMSON CT
6700 SD 92111 1248-H7
THOR ST
1600 SD 92113 1289-G6
THORN LN
9700 SDCo 92029 1149-E3
THORN ST
200 SD 92103 1269-E7
600 IMPB 91932 1329-F7
800 SD 92103 1268-J7
2800 SD 92104 1269-F6
3300 SD 92105 1269-G6
5700 SD 92115 1270-B6
5800 SD 92115 1270-C6
N THORN ST
5200 SD 92105 1270-A6
S THORN ST
5200 SD 92105 1270-A6
W THORN ST
300 SD 92103 1269-A7
400 SD 92103 1268-J7
THORNBUSH CT
12400 SD 92131 1210-C4
THORNBUSH RD
- SDCo 92065 1174-B5
THORN DALE RD
- SDCo 92003 1068-D5
- SDCo 92084 1068-D5
THORNE DR
5000 LMSA 91941 1270-G2
THORNMINT CT
17000 SDCo 92127 1169-G3
THORNMINT RD
10700 SDCo 92127 1169-F3
THORNTON DR
200 SDCo 92021 1252-H2
THORNTON PL
3000 SD 92105 1270-B7
THORNWOOD ST
6300 SD 92111 1248-H4
THOROUGHBRED AV
1700 OCN 92057 1067-F7
THOROUGHBRED LN
5900 SDCo 92003 1067-J1
THOROUGHBRED PL
- SD 92130 1188-D5
THORTON RD
1700 CHV 91902 1311-C4
THRASHER WY
100 ELCJ 92020 1251-A5
THREE OAKS WY
10000 SNTE 92071 1231-D3
THREE PEAKS LN
- SDCo 92036 1155-J4
THREE SEASONS RD
9000 SD 92126 1209-D5
THREE SLASHES RD
- ImCo - 412-A6
THRUSH PL
7100 CRLB 92009 1127-C6
THRUSH ST
300 SD 92114 1290-C4
400 CHV 91911 1330-G2
THUMBKIN LN
2200 SDCo 92084 1087-H2
THUNDER DR
100 OCN 92056 1107-C1
2700 OCN 92056 1087-B7
3400 VSTA 92083 1107-C2
THUNDER GN
600 ESCN 92027 1130-B2
THUNDERBIRD DR
600 OCN 92057 1066-H7
THUNDERBIRD LN
5400 SD 92037 1248-A3
5400 SD 92109 1248-A3
THUNDERBIRD PL
1300 CHV 91915 1311-H6
THUNDERHEAD ST
13100 SD 92129 1189-C5
THUNDER MOUNTAIN RD
24900 SDCo 92065 (1193-F1 See Page 1192)
THUNDERNUT LN
28300 SDCo 92082 1091-C1
THUNDER SPRING DR
1300 CHV 91915 1311-H6
THURSTON PL
4700 SD 92130 1188-C4
THYME WY
- SDCo 91935 (1295-A6 See Page 1294)
TIA JUANA ST
3300 SD 92173 1350-E5
TIA MARIA WY
8400 LMSA 91941 1270-J2
TIARA ST
3800 SD 92111 1249-A3
TIBBETT ST
600 SD 92114 1290-F3
TIBER CT
100 SDCo 92083 1108-B3
TIBERON DR
4000 OCN 92056 1107-C2
TIBIDABO DR
1500 ESCN 92027 1110-A6
TIBURON AV
2700 CRLB 92008 1106-J5
2700 CRLB 92008 1107-A5
TIBURON ST
- SMCS 92078 1128-G2
TICANU DR
2100 SDCo 92036 1156-B3
TICINO ST
- SDCo 92070 1135-B3
TICKET ST
9000 SD 92126 1209-D3
TICKNOR CT
6000 SD 92114 1290-C4
TICO CT
1100 SD 92154 1350-G1
TICONDEROGA ST
3200 SD 92117 1248-D5
TIDE CT
900 CRLB 92009 1126-J4
TIDELANDS AV
1300 NATC 91950 1309-G3
TIDE POOL PL
1900 SD 92139 1290-E7
TIE ST
3400 SD 92105 1270-C6
TIENTSE
- SD 92140 1268-F6
TIERRA ALTA
15000 SOLB 92014 1187-H1
15000 SOLB 92014 1167-H7
TIERRA BAJA WY
4900 SD 92115 1270-C2
TIERRA BLANCA AV
- SDCo 92055 1085-J3
TIERRA BONITA CT
14000 PWY 92064 1190-G1
TIERRA BONITA PL
1300 CHV 91910 1311-B7
TIERRA BONITA RD
13500 PWY 92064 1190-G2
TIERRA DE DIOS
3600 SDCo 92025 1150-D2
TIERRA DEL CIELO
1500 SDCo 92084 1088-C3
1500 VSTA 92084 1088-C3
TIERRA DEL ORO ST
5000 CRLB 92008 1126-F2
TIERRA DEL REY
1000 CHV 91910 1310-J7
TIERRA DEL SOL RD
500 SDCo 91905 430-C10
500 SDCo 91906 430-C10
600 SDCo 91905 (1319-J5 See Page 1298)
800 SDCo 91905 (1320-A1 See Page 1300)
1600 SDCo 91905 1300-A4
TIERRA DEL SUR
11500 SD 92130 1208-A2
TIERRA DE LUNA RD
900 SDCo 91905 (1319-H7 See Page 1298)
TIERRA DE MELANIE
37600 SDCo 91905 (1319-G7 See Page 1298)
TIERRA DURA RD
900 SMCS 92069 1109-C5
TIERRA ESTRELLA RD
900 SDCo 91905 (1319-G7 See Page 1298)
TIERRA GRANDE ST
9600 SD 92126 1209-E6
TIERRA HEIGHTS RD
2200 SDCo 91905 1300-A4
TIERRA LIBERTIA RD
1500 SDCo 92026 1089-D7
TIERRA LINDA LN
3500 SDCo 92028 1048-B4
TIERRA MONTANOSA
1600 SDCo 91901 1233-H7
TIERRA NUEVO
2400 SDCo 92028 998-D3
TIERRA REAL LN
1100 SDCo 91905 (1319-H6 See Page 1298)
TIERRA REAL RD
38100 SDCo 91905 (1319-F5 See Page 1298)
38100 SDCo 91906 (1319-F5 See Page 1298)
TIERRA ROJA DR
900 SDCo 92028 1028-D1
900 SDCo 92028 998-D7
TIERRASANTA BLVD
9800 SD 92124 1249-G2
11200 SD 92124 1250-A3
TIERRA VERDE RD
2000 SDCo 92084 1088-C7
TIERRA VISTA
4100 SDCo 92003 1067-G1
TIERRA VISTA PL
3900 ESCN 92025 1150-D3
TIFFANY CT
600 CHV 91910 1310-G7
TIFFANY DR
2000 OCN 92056 1086-J7
TIFFANY LN
1400 SDCo 92084 1108-B1
TIFFANY WY
500 CHV 91910 1310-G7
TIFFIN AV
6600 SD 92114 1270-E7
6600 SD 92114 1290-E1
TIGER WY
1100 SDCo 92065 1152-J6

6623 TIGER TAIL LN
SAN DIEGO CO. STREET INDEX
TULANE WY

STREET
Block City ZIP Pg-Grid

TIGER TAIL LN
900 VSTA 92084 1088-A6
TIGER TAIL RD
800 VSTA 92084 1087-J6
800 VSTA 92084 1088-A6
TIKI DR E
700 VSTA 92083 1087-E6
TIKI DR N
- VSTA 92083 1087-E5
TIKI DR S
700 VSTA 92083 1087-E6
TIKI DR W
700 VSTA 92083 1087-E6
TIKI LN
1200 VSTA 92083 1087-E6
TILDEN ST
1800 SD 92102 1289-J1
TILIA CT
400 CHV 91911 1330-G4
TILIA PL
6400 CRLB 92009 1127-E4
TILLAMOOK BAY
5700 SD 92105 1290-B1
TILLEY LN
600 SMCS 92069 1108-C7
TILLING WY
500 ELCJ 92020 1271-F1
TILOS WY
4900 OCN 92056 1107-E6
TILTING T DR
400 SDCo 92004 (1078-H5 See Page 1058)
700 SDCo 92004 (1079-B5 See Page 1058)
TILTON ST
10100 SD 92126 1208-J5
TIM ST
3900 SDCo 91902 1310-J3
3900 SDCo 91902 1311-A3
TIMARU WY
11800 SD 92128 1170-A1
TIMBER CT
400 CHV 91911 1330-H5
TIMBER GN
1300 ESCN 92027 1110-A5
TIMBER PASG
- SDCo 92065 1153-C7
TIMBER ST
500 CHV 91911 1330-H5
TIMBER TR
1800 VSTA 92083 1107-F5
TIMBER BRANCH WY
5200 SD 92130 1208-D1
TIMBER BROOK LN
- SD 92130 1208-F2
TIMBER COVE WY
700 OCN 92054 1066-E6
TIMBER CREEK LN
- ESCN 92027 1130-J3
TIMBER FEATHER LN
500 SDCo 92028 1027-G3
TIMBERGATE CIR
11200 SD 92128 1189-J2
TIMBERLAKE DR
11500 SD 92131 1209-J3
11600 SD 92131 1210-A3
TIMBERLANE WY
10000 SNTE 92071 1231-D3
TIMBERLINE CT
10000 SD 92131 1210-A4
TIMBERLINE LN
600 SMCS 92069 1108-J5
TIMBERLINE RD
2100 CRLB 92008 1106-G3
TIMBERPOND DR
1100 SDCo 92019 1272-B1
TIMBER RIDGE RD
4500 SD 92130 1188-C5
TIMBERWOOD PL
800 ESCN 92026 1109-H4
7400 SD 92139 1290-H6
TIMBOLL CT
5400 SDCo 91902 1290-J7
TIMELY TER
100 SD 92114 1290-E4
TIMINCO GATE WY
- OCN 92054 1106-E2
TIMKEN ST
5200 LMSA 91942 1270-J1
TIMOTHY DR
5400 SD 92105 1290-B1
TIMOTHY PL
1700 VSTA 92083 1087-D7
TIMRICK LN
3900 SDCo 91902 1311-A3
TIMSFORD RD
11500 SD 92131 1209-H1
TINA PL
1600 SDCo 92021 1251-G2
TINA ST
2200 SDCo 92019 1272-D1
TINAJA LN
4700 SDCo 92004 (1099-F5 See Page 1098)
7900 SD 91977 1290-H5
7900 SD 92139 1290-H5
TINAMOU PL
1100 VSTA 92083 1087-G4
TINASA WY
4800 SD 92124 1250-A1
TIN CUP DR
25500 SDCo 92065 1173-J7
TINGLEY LN
900 SD 92106 1288-A2
TINING DR
13200 PWY 92064 1170-E2
TINING WY
13200 PWY 92064 1170-E2
TINY LN
300 ELCJ 92019 1252-A5
TIO DIEGO PL
8400 LMSA 91941 1270-J1
TIOGA TR
1500 SDCo 92028 1047-J1
TIOGA LAKE DR
10300 SDCo 92029 1129-F7
TIPPERARY WY
10600 SD 92131 1209-H1
TIPTON ST
5100 SD 92115 1270-D2
TISELLE WY
5000 SD 92105 1290-A1
TISH CT
2700 SDCo 91977 1270-J7
TISHA CIR
10200 SD 92126 1209-B5
TISHA ST
8100 SD 92126 1209-B5

TITAN CT
1200 SDCo 92026 1109-E6
TITAN WY
13900 PWY 92064 1170-G6
TITSWORTH RD
- ImCo 92233 411-C11
TITUS ST
1700 SD 92110 1268-H6
1900 SD 92103 1268-H6
TIVERTON RD
3600 SD 92130 1188-A4
TIVOLI ST
4400 SD 92107 1287-J1
TIVOLI PARK RW
11900 SD 92128 1190-A2
TOBACCO RD
1700 ESCN 92026 1109-F6
1700 SDCo 92026 1109-F6
TOBAGO RD
10900 SD 92126 1209-A3
TOBAGO WY
- CORD 92118 1329-E2
TOBEY ST
4700 SD 92120 1249-J7
TOBIAS DR
1100 CHV 91911 1330-E2
TOBIASSON RD
13100 PWY 92064 1190-C2
TOBIRA DR
9000 SDCo 92026 1069-A6
TOBOGGAN WY
1900 SD 92154 1350-A1
TOBRIA TER
6400 CRLB 92009 1127-E4
TOCA LN
2100 SDCo 92065 1172-C3
TOCAYO AV
2100 SD 92154 1350-A3
TOCH ST
4200 SD 92117 1248-E2
TODD CT
200 OCN 92054 1086-E5
TODD ST
2800 OCN 92054 1086-D6
TODOS SANTOS DR
9100 SNTE 92071 1251-B1
TODOS SANTOS PL
1500 SDCo 92028 1027-F5
TOGAN AV
9000 SD 92129 1189-D4
TOKAJ CT
9100 SDCo 91977 1291-B1
TOKAJ LN
9100 SDCo 91977 1291-B1
TOKAJ RD
2200 SDCo 91977 1291-B1
TOKAJ WY
9100 SDCo 91977 1291-B1
TOKALON CT
2500 SD 92110 1248-F7
TOKALON ST
2100 SD 92110 1268-F1
2200 SD 92110 1248-F7
TOKAY ST
2000 SD 92105 1290-B1
TOLAS CT
3400 NATC 91950 1290-C7
TOLEDO DR
4500 SD 92115 1270-E3
TOLEDO RD
10100 SDCo 91977 1271-E5
TOLITA AV
700 CORD 92118 1288-H7
TOLO WY
4900 OCN 92056 1107-E4
TOLOWA ST
4100 SD 92117 1248-E2
TOLTEC CT
17900 SD 92127 1149-H7
17900 SD 92127 1169-H1
TOLUCA CT
100 SOLB 92075 1167-D6
TOMAHAWK LN
3500 SD 92117 1248-F4
TOMBILL RD
22500 SDCo 92065 1173-A5
TOMBSTONE CREEK RD
15100 SDCo 92021 1233-A1
TOMCAT PL
9800 SD 92126 1209-F2
TOMEL CT
10400 SNTE 92071 1231-E3
TOMIKO CT
9300 SDCo 91941 1271-B4
TOMMIE LN
17300 SDCo 92065 1171-F4
TOMMY CT
8800 SD 92119 1251-A4
TOMMY DR
7800 SD 92119 1250-H4
8600 SD 92119 1251-A4
TOMMY ST
7700 SD 92119 1250-G4
TOMORRO LN
900 SDCo 92028 1027-G4
TOMPAU PL
2200 SDCo 91901 1253-H2
TOMPKINS ST
3400 SD 92102 1289-F4
TONALITE WY
30100 SDCo 91906 (1297-F5 See Page 1296)
TONAPAH ST
3300 OCN 92054 1086-E5
TONAWANDA DR
3000 SD 92139 1310-E2
TONDINO CT
11700 SD 92131 1210-A2
TONDINO RD
11000 SD 92131 1210-A2
TONE LN
8000 SDCo 92021 1252-A1
TONER CT
1300 SDCo 92021 1233-A7
TONI LN
4400 LMSA 91941 1270-E3
TONI RIDGE PL
6600 SD 92121 1228-H1
TONOPAH ST
4200 SD 92110 1268-E2
TONTO WY
2600 SD 92117 1248-B1
2700 SD 92117 1228-B7
TONY DR
3400 SD 92122 1228-D4
TONYA LN
9100 SNTE 92071 1231-B7
TOOLEY CIR
1700 SD 92114 1290-C1

TOOLEY ST
5700 SD 92114 1290-C2
TOOMA ST
6900 SD 92139 1290-G7
TOPA HILL CIR
12300 SDCo 92040 1232-A4
TOPATOPA DR
4400 SDCo 91941 1271-G3
TOPAZ CT
300 CHV 91911 1330-G5
500 ESCN 92027 1110-E7
4300 LMSA 91941 1270-J4
TOPAZ DR
500 SDCo 92036 1156-E2
TOPAZ LN
4400 OCN 92056 1107-D2
TOPAZ PL
1200 SMCS 92069 1109-C5
TOPAZ TER
1700 SDCo 92019 1272-C2
TOPAZ WY
- CRLB 92009 1127-B4
9100 SD 92123 1229-D7
TOPAZ LAKE AV
7500 SD 92119 1250-G5
TOPEKA ST
200 OCN 92054 1106-A1
600 OCN 92054 1086-B7
3400 CRLB 92008 1106-J4
TOPGUN AV
- SD 92126 1209-D6
TOP GUN ST
6600 SD 92121 1208-H4
TOPMAST DR
- CRLB 92009 1127-A3
TOPO LN
11000 SDCo 92040 1212-A6
TOP OF THE MORNING WY
- SDCo 92127 1168-J3
- SDCo 92127 1169-A2
TOP OF THE PINES LN
- SDCo 92066 1237-B7
TOPPER LN
1200 SDCo 92021 1251-J2
TOP RAIL LN
1300 SDCo 92027 1130-C3
TOPSHAM ST
14500 PWY 92064 1190-H4
TORANO DR
200 VSTA 92084 1087-H3
TORCA CT
5800 SD 92124 1229-H7
TORERO PL
8200 SD 92126 1209-B2
TORINO CT
29800 SDCo 92082 1070-E5
TOROLE CIR
1000 VSTA 92084 1087-J7
TORONGA WY
30400 SDCo 92082 1070-J3
TORRANCE ST
400 SD 92103 1268-H6
TORREJON PL
2400 CRLB 92009 1147-F1
TORRELL WY
8100 SD 92126 1209-B1
TORREM ST
7600 LMSA 91942 1250-G7
TORREON DR
3100 SDCo 91901 1234-D4
TORREY DR
1200 ENCT 92024 1167-F2
TORREY GN
2100 ESCN 92026 1109-D4
TORREY LN
- SDCo 92672 1023-E1
7800 SD 92037 1227-G6
TORREYANA RD
10900 SD 92121 1207-J5
10900 SD 92121 1208-A5
TORREYANNA CIR
6300 CRLB 92009 1127-A4
TORREY BLUFF DR
13500 SD 92130 1188-B5
TORREY DEL MAR DR
- SD 92129 1188-J3
- SD 92130 1188-J3
TORREY HILL CT
13600 SD 92130 1188-A4
TORREY HILL LN
3700 SD 92130 1188-A4
N TORREY PINES CT
3300 SD 92037 1207-J7
TORREY PINES PL
700 OCN 92054 1086-F1
N TORREY PINES PL
11100 SD 92121 1207-J5
TORREY PINES RD
1000 SD 92037 1227-F7
1000 CHV 91915 1311-H5
7900 SD 92093 1227-H5
N TORREY PINES RD
9000 SD 92093 1227-J2
9200 SD 92037 1227-J2
10000 SD 92037 1207-J7
10000 SD 92093 1207-J7
10200 SD 92121 1207-J7
N TORREY PINES RD Rt#-S21
10300 SD 92121 1207-G2
10500 SD 92037 1207-G2
12100 SD 92014 1207-G2
12600 SD 92014 1187-G7
12800 DLMR 92014 1187-G7
TORREY PINES TER
200 DLMR 92014 1187-G7
TORREY PINES PARK RD
10700 SD 92037 1207-G2
12000 SD 92121 1207-G2
TORREY PINES SCENIC DR
2800 SD 92037 1207-H7
2800 SD 92093 1207-H7
TORREY POINT RD
400 DLMR 92014 1187-G7
TORREY RIDGE DR
12900 SD 92130 1188-B5
TORREY VIEW CT
3700 SD 92130 1208-A3
TORRINGTON ST
3900 SD 92130 1188-A5
TORRY CT
2900 CRLB 92009 1127-G7
TORTILLA CIR
4400 OCN 92057 1087-A1
TORTUGA CT
10300 SD 92124 1229-H7

TORTUGA CT
10300 SD 92124 1249-G1
TORTUGA CV
3900 OCN 92054 1086-G2
TORTUGA RD
5700 SD 92124 1229-H7
TORTUGA POINT DR
500 CHV 91911 1330-H4
TOSCA WY
2400 SD 92111 1248-H7
TOSCANA DR
7500 SD 92122 1228-E3
TOSCANA WY
5200 SD 92122 1228-E3
TOSCANO CT
- ENCT 92024 1148-B3
TOUB ST
2200 SDCo 92065 1152-D7
TOUCAN DR
500 VSTA 92083 1087-F4
TOUCANET CT
- OCN 92057 1067-A3
TOULON CT
700 SD 92109 1247-H7
TOULON ST
1300 OCN 92056 1087-B3
TOULOUSE LN
2700 SDCo 92028 1048-C1
TOURMALINE CT
300 CHV 91911 1330-G5
TOURMALINE LN
2100 SDCo 92028 1028-A6
TOURMALINE ST
- CHV 91911 1330-F5
600 SD 92109 1247-H5
TOURNAMENT DR
3300 OCN 92056 1106-J1
TOUSSACHS WY
- SDCo 92028 1027-G6
TOWELL LN
1600 ESCN 92029 1129-G5
TOWER DR
1100 VSTA 92083 1107-J1
1200 VSTA 92083 1108-A2
TOWER LN
1200 ESCN 92026 1109-J7
TOWER PL
700 ESCN 92026 1109-J7
1100 VSTA 92083 1107-J1
TOWER RD
- SD 92121 1208-A6
400 IMPB 91932 1349-G2
TOWER ST
6800 LMSA 91941 1270-E3
6800 SD 92115 1270-E3
TOWHEE LN
6600 CRLB 92009 1127-C5
TOWHEE ST
1800 SDCo 92069 1128-A4
TOWLE CT
5100 SD 92105 1270-A5
TOWN CENTER DR
1000 ENCT 92024 1147-F4
TOWN CENTER PKWY
200 SNTE 92071 1231-C6
TOWN CENTER PL
- ENCT 92024 1147-F4
TOWNE CTR N
- OCN 92057 1087-B1
TOWNE LN
9700 SDCo 92021 1233-A3
TOWNE CENTRE CT
4500 SD 92121 1228-C1
TOWNE CENTRE DR
8800 SD 92122 1228-D3
9100 SD 92121 1228-C1
TOWNE CENTRE PL
4500 SD 92121 1228-D1
TOWNSEND PL
1900 SDCo 92019 1272-C2
TOWNSEND RD
1500 ImCo 92250 431-D3
TOWNSGATE DR
3300 SD 92130 1188-A6
TOWNSITE DR
100 VSTA 92084 1087-H5
TOWN VIEW CT
6700 SD 92120 1250-C3
TOWN VIEW LN
6800 SD 92120 1250-C3
TOWN VIEW TER
6700 SD 92120 1250-C3
TOWNWOOD CT
3400 OCN 92054 1086-E3
TOWNWOOD WY
100 ENCT 92024 1147-J7
TOWSER ST
3200 SD 92123 1249-D5
TOW WAY RD
- CORD 92135 1288-G5
TOYA LN
15100 SDCo 92021 1233-A2
TOYNE ST
400 SD 92102 1289-H3
TOYOFF WY
4900 SD 92115 1269-J1
TOYON CT
300 SMCS 92069 1108-H5
TOYON DR
1600 SDCo 92028 1028-F4
TOYON GN
1600 ESCN 92026 1109-D6
TOYON LN
- CHV 91910 1310-C5
TOYON RD
5400 SD 92115 1269-J1
TOYON CANYON RD
9500 SDCo 92029 1149-D4
TOYON HEIGHTS DR
3100 SDCo 92028 998-C7
TOYON HILL DR
11000 SDCo 92040 1211-F7
11000 SDCo 92040 1231-F1
TOYON MOUNTAIN LN
900 SDCo 92036 1156-D5
TOYON MOUNTAIN RD
4300 SDCo 92036 1156-E5
TOYON RIDGE TR
- SDCo 92082 1090-E5
TRABERT RANCH RD
1400 ENCT 92024 1167-H1
TRACE RD
2400 SDCo 91978 1271-G7
TRACEY LN
1300 SDCo 92021 1233-A7
TRACI LN
600 VSTA 92084 1088-A7
TRACY CT
1900 SDCo 92028 1048-B4

TRACY ST
7400 LMGR 91945 1270-G7
TRACY LYN DR
31700 SDCo 92082 1051-A7
TRADE PL
9100 SD 92121 1209-A7
9100 SD 92126 1209-A7
TRADE ST
100 SMCS 92078 1128-J1
7500 SD 92121 1208-J7
7500 SD 92121 1209-A7
TRADEWIND AV
1300 SD 92154 1349-J2
TRADEWINDS DR
6800 CRLB 92009 1126-H6
TRADITION ST
13500 SD 92128 1190-B3
TRAFALGAR LN
2700 CRLB 92008 1107-A5
TRAFALGAR RD
5600 SDCo 92019 1253-C4
TRAIL DR
3000 SDCo 91935 1292-G2
TRAIL BLAZE CT
4000 SDCo 91902 1311-B2
TRAILBROOK LN
11400 SD 92128 1190-A6
11400 SD 92128 1189-J6
TRAILBRUSH PT
11500 SD 92126 1209-A1
TRAILBRUSH TER
7600 SD 92126 1209-A1
TRAIL CREST CT
- SD 92131 1189-G7
TRAIL CREST DR
- SD 92131 1189-G7
- SD 92131 1209-G1
TRAIL CREST PL
- SD 92131 1189-G7
TRAIL DUST AV
13000 SD 92129 1189-C5
TRAILING DR
4100 SD 92105 1289-H1
TRAILRIDGE DR
500 CHV 91902 1311-C4
TRAILS END
2300 SDCo 92028 1047-G2
TRAILS END CIR
10200 SD 92126 1209-A5
TRAILS END DR
13900 SDCo 91935 1292-F2
TRAIL SHRINE LN
2100 SDCo 92004 (1099-F5 See Page 1098)
TRAILSIDE CT
11200 SD 92127 1169-J4
TRAILSIDE PL
- SMCS 92078 1128-F3
TRAILSIDE RD
8900 SD 92127 1169-A4
8900 SDCo 92127 1169-A4
TRAILSIDE WY
11300 SD 92127 1169-J4
TRAILVIEW RD
300 ENCT 92024 1147-J6
TRAILWIND RD
14200 PWY 92064 1170-H4
TRALEE TER
3400 SDCo 91977 1271-C5
TRAM PL
400 CHV 91910 1310-F5
TRANQUIL CT
500 ENCT 92024 1147-J5
TRANQUILITY GN
600 ESCN 92027 1130-B2
TRANQUILITY LN
26500 SDCo 92065 1174-B4
TRANQUILLO LN
- CHV 91911 1330-E3
TRANSIT ST
100 OCN 92054 1106-A1
TRANSITE AV
1300 SD 92154 1349-J2
1400 SD 92154 1350-A2
TRANSMITTER DR
3200 SD 92115 1270-D6
TRANSPORTATION AV
2400 NATC 91950 1309-H3
TRAPANI CV
1200 CHV 91915 1311-F6
TRAPPERS HOLLOW RD
- SDCo 91901 1255-G1
TRASKE RD
1500 ENCT 92024 1147-G6
TRAVELD WY
1500 ENCT 92024 1147-G6
TRAVELERS WY
- SMCS 92069 1128-G1
TRAVELODGE DR
200 ELCJ 92020 1251-D5
TRAVER CT
- CHV 91913 1331-B1
TRAVERS WY
6100 SD 92122 1228-B5
TRAVERTINE CT
12100 PWY 92064 1190-C7
12100 PWY 92064 1210-B1
TRAVERTINE PL
- SDCo 92019 1272-B2
TRAVIS CT
8400 SD 92126 1209-C1
TRAVIS PL
11300 SD 92126 1209-C1
TRAYLOR RD
17900 SDCo 92065 1171-H1
TREADWELL BLVD
200 ImCo 92274 410-G6
TREADWELL DR
11700 PWY 92064 1210-C1
11700 PWY 92064 1190-C7
TREASURE DR
4900 LMSA 91941 1271-B2
TREASURE VIEW LN
1000 ENCT 92024 1167-E1
TREAT ST
2700 SD 92102 1289-D3
TREBOL ST
11300 SD 92126 1209-B2
TREBUCHET DR
1900 SDCo 92004 1058-G7
TREE ST
9100 SNTE 92071 1231-A4
TREECREST ST
13100 PWY 92064 1190-D1
TREEHAVEN CT
10000 SD 92131 1210-A4
TREEHILL PL
12600 PWY 92064 1190-C2

TREE HOLLOW LN
11400 SD 92128 1189-J7
11400 SD 92128 1190-A7
TREENA ST
10400 SD 92131 1209-F4
TREERIDGE TER
12700 PWY 92064 1190-D1
TREESIDE LN
10900 SDCo 92026 1089-G3
TREETOP LN
700 ELCJ 92021 1251-J4
TREEVIEW PL
11700 SD 92131 1210-A4
TREEWIND CT
11800 SD 92128 1190-A7
TREEWOOD ST
100 SD 92114 1290-D4
TRELAWNEY LN
1300 SDCo 92028 1028-C4
TRELLIS LN
100 ESCN 92026 1109-H6
TREMAINE WY
1700 SD 92154 1349-J2
1700 SD 92154 1350-A2
TREMONT ST
100 CHV 91911 1330-C5
1600 OCN 92054 1106-C3
4300 SD 92102 1289-H3
N TREMONT ST
200 OCN 92054 1086-A7
600 OCN 92054 1085-J7
S TREMONT ST
100 OCN 92054 1106-A1
TRENCHARD ST
10000 SNTE 92071 1231-D2
TRENT WY
10800 SDCo 91941 1271-F4
TRENTHAM RD
2700 ImCo 92251 431-C4
TRENTO PL
14500 SD 92130 1188-A3
TRENTON AV
1100 CHV 91911 1330-A4
3400 SD 92117 1248-D5
TRENTON ST
500 ELCJ 92019 1252-B4
TREPAIRE CIR
8800 SNTE 92071 1231-B7
TRESEDER CIR
1700 SDCo 92019 1272-B2
TRES ENCINOS
2600 SDCo 92069 1088-H6
TRES HERMANAS WY
1400 ENCT 92024 1147-G5
TRESHILL RD
- ImCo 92243 6499-E3
- IMP 92243 6499-E3
TRES LAGOS CT
10100 SDCo 91977 1271-E7
10100 SDCo 91977 1291-E1
TRES LOMAS
2900 SDCo 92028 1048-C1
TRES LOMAS CT
2900 SDCo 92028 1048-C1
TRES LOMAS DR
1000 ELCJ 92021 1252-B3
TRES NINOS CTE
1100 VSTA 92084 1108-C1
TRES RANCHO LN
500 SDCo 92069 1109-A4
500 SMCS 92069 1109-A4
TRES VISTA CT
13700 SD 92129 1189-E3
TRETAGNIER CIR
12000 SD 92128 1150-A7
TREVINO AV
2100 OCN 92056 1106-G1
TREVISO CT
- SD 92130 1188-A4
TREVOR PL
2600 ELCJ 92020 1251-A3
TREVORS CT
9500 SDCo 92040 1232-D4
TREYBURN WY
- SD 92131 1209-G2
TRIANA ST
4900 SD 92117 1248-G1
TRIAS ST
4100 SD 92103 1268-G5
TRIBUL LN
- CRLB 92009 1126-J7
TRIBUNA AV
11200 SD 92131 1209-J5
TRICIA PL
28300 SDCo 92026 1089-E3
TRICIA ST
14100 PWY 92064 1190-E2
TRIDLE PL
1400 CHV 91911 1330-J3
TRIDLE WY
3500 SD 92173 1350-E5
TRIESTE DR
1200 SD 92107 1287-J1
3400 CRLB 92008 1106-H4
TRIESTE WY
3000 OCN 92056 1106-J1
TRIGAL WY
10600 SNTE 92071 1231-E3
TRIGGER ST
13000 SD 92129 1189-C5
TRIGO LN
7400 CRLB 92009 1147-J1
7400 CRLB 92009 1148-A1
TRIJULLO TER
2100 ESCN 92027 1110-B5
TRILLIUM CT
- SD 92131 1209-G1
TRILLIUM WY
- SD 92131 1209-G1
TRILY RD
- ImCo 92257 410-L4
TRINAS WY
3500 SDCo 91935 1272-G5
TRINIDAD BEND
- CORD 92118 1329-E2
TRINIDAD CV
1200 CHV 91915 1311-F6
TRINIDAD WY
5100 SD 92114 1290-B5
TRINITY PL
5700 SD 92120 1250-B7
TRINITY ST
- OCN 92057 1086-H1
- OCN 92057 1066-H7
TRINITY WY
5500 SD 92120 1250-A7
TRIPLE LN
11900 SDCo 92040 1231-J5

TRIPLE C RANCH RD
2400 ENCT 92024 1148-A7
TRIPLE CROWN DR
5200 SDCo 92003 1047-J7
5200 SDCo 92003 1067-J1
TRIPLE CROWN RW
4900 SD 92130 1188-D2
TRIPOLI
- SD 92140 1268-F6
TRIPOLI DR
- ELCJ 92021 1251-J5
TRIPOLI RD
7700 SD 92126 1209-A3
TRIPOLI WY
3300 OCN 92056 1106-J1
TRIPP CT
3400 SD 92121 1208-A4
TRISTANIA PL
17700 SD 92127 1169-J1
TRITON AV
1300 SD 92154 1349-J2
TRITON CIR
100 ENCT 92024 1147-C7
TRITON PL
1500 SD 92154 1349-J1
TRIUMPH DR
12700 PWY 92064 1190-D1
TRIUMPH ST
- VSTA 92083 1107-G5
TROCHA DE PENNI
10100 SDCo 92040 1231-F3
TROJAN AV
4700 SD 92115 1269-J4
4800 SD 92115 1270-A4
TROLLEY CT
5400 LMSA 91942 1250-J7
TROON WY
4000 CHV 91902 1310-F3
TROPHY DR
3400 SDCo 91941 1270-J5
3500 SDCo 91941 1271-A5
TROPHY WY
- SDCo 92004 (1079-C4 See Page 1058)
TROPICANA DR
100 OCN 92054 1086-E5
TROPICO DR
9100 LMSA 91941 1271-B3
9100 SDCo 91941 1271-B3
9600 SDCo 91977 1271-B3
S TROPICO DR
4000 SDCo 91941 1271-B4
TROTTER DR
- SD 92130 1208-E2
TROTTING HORSE RD
1600 OCN 92057 1067-G6
TROUSDALE DR
200 CHV 91910 1310-A4
TROUSDALE PL
1900 ESCN 92029 1129-F7
TROUT LN
- OCN 92054 1086-G2
TROUTMAN RD
- SD 92106 1288-A5
TROY LN
1700 OCN 92054 1106-E2
4500 LMSA 91941 1270-G3
TROY PL
2000 VSTA 92084 1088-C5
TROY ST
8400 LMGR 91945 1270-J7
8600 LMGR 91977 1270-J7
8600 SDCo 91977 1270-J7
8600 SDCo 91977 1271-A6
TROY TER
7600 LMSA 91941 1270-G2
TRUCKEE AV
2200 SD 92123 1249-C7
TRUCKHAVEN TR
- ImCo 92004 410-G7
- ImCo 92274 410-G7
TRUDY LN
3700 SD 92106 1287-J4
TRUESDELL LN
2000 CRLB 92008 1106-G4
TRUETT LN
10100 SD 92124 1249-G5
TRULY TER
600 VSTA 92084 1087-J5
TRUMAN ST
9000 SD 92129 1189-D6
TRUMBULL ST
3000 SD 92106 1288-A2
TRUNKS BAY
300 OCN 92057 1066-H6
TRUST DR
1800 ESCN 92029 1129-F4
TRUXTUN RD
1600 SD 92133 1288-C1
2000 SD 92133 1268-D7
TUBB CANYON RD
- SDCo 92004 1098-F1
- SDCo 92004 (1099-A1 See Page 1098)
- SDCo 92066 1098-F1
TUBEROSE ST
2400 SD 92105 1269-H7
TUCKAWAY ST
6900 SD 92119 1250-E5
TUCKER LN
1500 ENCT 92024 1147-G6
TUCKER TR
2800 SDCo 91935 1293-G2
TUCSON CT
1100 ELCJ 92021 1252-A3
TUDOR LN
1700 SDCo 92028 1028-A3
TUDOR ST
9900 SD 92131 1209-H5
TUFTS ST
5200 LMSA 91942 1270-G1
TUK-A-WILE
3300 SDCo 91935 1272-G6
TUKWUT CT
100 SDCo 92061 1051-A6
TULA CT
4800 SD 92122 1228-F5
TULAGI RD
- CORD 92155 1309-B2
TULANE AV
900 CHV 91913 1311-D5
TULANE CT
1900 OCN 92056 1087-C5
3300 SD 92122 1228-C6
TULANE ST
5600 SD 92122 1228-C6
TULANE WY
3300 SD 92122 1228-C6

SAN DIEGO CO.
INDEX

STREET
Block City ZIP Pg-Grid

TULARE CT
3600 OCN 92056 1107-F3
TULARE ST
8600 LMSA 91941 1270-J3
8600 LMSA 91941 1271-A3
TULE CT
1800 CRLB 92009 1127-E6
TULE JIM LN
2100 SDCo 91905 1300-F7
TULE SPRINGS RD
- SDCo 91916 (1194-H4 See Page 1175)
- SDCo 91916 (1195-A2 See Page 1175)
- SDCo 92036 (1195-A2 See Page 1175)
TULE SPRINGS TKTR
- SDCo 91901 (1194-B4 See Page 1175)
- SDCo 91916 (1194-D4 See Page 1175)
- SDCo 92036 (1194-B4 See Page 1175)
TULIP DR
- SD 92109 1248-C6
TULIP LN
4000 SD 92105 1289-H1
TULIP ST
500 ESCN 92025 1129-G3
1800 SD 92105 1289-H1
S TULIP ST
100 ESCN 92025 1129-H4
TULIP WY
1000 CRLB 92009 1127-B6
TULIPAN WY
2400 SD 92111 1248-H7
TULSA ST
1100 ELCJ 92019 1251-H6
TUMBLE CREEK LN
400 SDCo 92028 1028-A3
TUMBLE CREEK TER
700 SDCo 92028 1028-A3
TUMBLEWEED LN
500 SDCo 92028 1047-E4
TUMBLEWEED TER
8500 ELCJ 92020 1231-E7
8500 SNTE 92071 1231-E7
TUMBLEWEED WY
5600 OCN 92057 1067-E6
TUMERIC WY
- SDCo 91935 1294-J7
- SDCo 91935 (1295-A7 See Page 1294)
TUNA LN
- SD 92101 1288-J3
TUNAPUNA LN
- CORD 92118 1329-E3
TUNGSTEN DR
4100 LMSA 91941 1270-H4
TUNICA CIR
2400 SD 92111 1248-G7
TUNIS DR
- ELCJ 92021 1251-H5
TUNRIF CT
2500 SDCo 92084 1068-D6
TUOLUMNE PL
4300 CRLB 92008 1107-A5
TUPELO CV
7500 SD 92126 1209-A2
TUPPER ST
1600 SD 92103 1268-H5
TURA LN
12300 PWY 92064 1190-C2
TURF LN
3400 SDCo 91941 1270-J5
TURF RD
15500 DLMR 92014 1187-G2
15500 SD 92014 1187-G2
TURF VIEW DR
200 SOLB 92075 1187-F2
TURLOCK CT
13400 SD 92129 1189-C3
TURMERIC TER
800 CHV 91910 1330-J1
TURNBERRY CT
17100 SDCo 92067 1168-G7
TURNBERRY DR
1600 SMCS 92069 1108-J3
1800 VSTA 92083 1108-E2
3500 SDCo 91935 1272-E6
TURNBERRY WY
3100 SDCo 91935 1272-E5
TURNBRIDGE GN
2400 ESCN 92027 1110-D6
TURNBRIDGE WY
6700 SD 92119 1251-A4
TURNBULL ST
2800 OCN 92054 1086-D6
TURNER AV
100 ENCT 92024 1147-G6
TURNER LN
11100 SDCo 92026 1089-G1
11100 SDCo 92082 1089-G1
TURNER HEIGHTS DR
11500 SDCo 92026 1089-H3
TURNER HEIGHTS LN
27900 SDCo 92026 1089-H3
TURNFORD DR
7300 SD 92119 1250-J3
TURNSTONE RD
- CRLB 92009 1126-J4
- CRLB 92009 1127-A4
TURNSTONE WY
1000 OCN 92057 1087-A3
TURQUOISE CT
300 CHV 91911 1330-G5
TURQUOISE DR
- CRLB 92009 1127-B4
TURQUOISE LN
3400 OCN 92056 1107-D2
TURQUOISE ST
1100 SD 92109 1247-H4
4400 SD 92037 1247-H4
TURRET DR
11000 SD 92131 1209-H4
TURTLEBACK CT
11200 SD 92127 1169-J4
TURTLEBACK LN
11300 SD 92127 1169-J4
TURTLEBACK RD
15800 SD 92127 1169-J5
TURTLE CAY PL
1200 CHV 91915 1311-G6
TURTLE CAY WY
1200 CHV 91915 1311-G6
TURTLE DOVE LN
1000 ESCN 92026 1109-F5
TURTLE ROCK RD
28200 SDCo 92082 1090-F2

TUSCANY AV
1200 SDCo 92069 1109-A5
1200 SMCS 92069 1109-A5
TUSCANY CT
10600 SDCo 92127 1169-F2
TUSCANY LN
7500 SD 92126 1208-J4
TUSCANY WY
300 OCN 92057 1087-A4
TUSCARORA DR
13000 PWY 92064 1190-D4
TUSHAK RANCH RD
800 SDCo 92084 1067-H6
TUSK CT
10400 SD 92124 1249-G3
TUSTIN ST
1800 SD 92106 1288-B1
12600 PWY 92064 1190-C5
TUTELA HTS
1500 ESCN 92026 1109-H6
TUTHER WY
7000 SD 92114 1290-F4
TUTHILL WY
9500 SNTE 92071 1231-B4
TUTTLE LN
1200 SDCo 92021 1251-G1
TUTTLE ST
2400 CRLB 92008 1106-E4
TUXEDO RD
6600 SD 92119 1250-E3
TUXFORD DR
7700 SD 92119 1250-J3
TWAIN AV
4300 SD 92120 1249-H7
4900 SD 92120 1250-A7
TWAIN CT
1300 SDCo 92069 1109-A3
1300 SMCS 92069 1109-A3
TWAIN WY
29300 SDCo 92082 1070-H6
TWEED LN
- SD 92102 1289-G4
TWEED ST
7400 LMGR 91945 1270-G7
TWELVE OAKS TR
- SDCo 92021 1232-H7
5100 SDCo 92021 1252-G2
TWIGGS ST
3900 SD 92110 1268-F5
TWILA LN
6300 SD 92115 1270-D5
TWILIGHT CT
9100 SNTE 92071 1231-B7
TWILIGHT GN
1900 ESCN 92026 1109-B3
TWILIGHT LN
3500 OCN 92056 1107-C2
TWIN CIRCLE CT
13200 PWY 92064 1190-E2
TWIN CIRCLE WY
14400 PWY 92064 1190-E2
TWINFORD CT
9300 SD 92126 1209-E2
TWINING AV
600 SD 92154 1330-F7
1000 SD 92154 1350-F1
TWIN LAKE DR
6200 LMSA 91942 1250-G6
6200 SD 92119 1250-G6
TWIN LAKES CT
14300 SDCo 92067 1188-G2
TWINLEAF CT
10900 SD 92131 1209-H2
TWINLEAF WY
11000 SD 92131 1209-H2
TWIN MOUNTAIN CIR
9300 SD 92126 1209-E3
TWIN OAK
14100 SDCo 92021 1232-G5
TWIN OAK LN
35100 SDCo 92036 1156-E7
TWIN OAKS AV
200 CHV 91910 1310-B5
700 CHV 91910 1330-C1
1100 CHV 91911 1330-D3
TWIN OAKS CIR
100 CHV 91910 1310-B5
TWIN OAKS CREST DR
3700 SDCo 92069 1088-G4
TWIN OAKS VALLEY RD
1400 SMCS 92078 1128-H3
2400 SDCo 92069 1088-F2
2400 SDCo 92069 1108-J1
2400 SMCS 92069 1108-J1
28500 SDCo 92084 1068-F6
28800 SDCo 92084 1088-F1
N TWIN OAKS VALLEY RD
100 SMCS 92069 1128-H1
900 SMCS 92069 1108-H7
N TWIN OAKS VALLEY RD Rt#-S12
11000 SMCS 92069 1108-H5
S TWIN OAKS VALLEY RD
100 SMCS 92069 1128-H2
100 SMCS 92078 1128-H2
200 SMCS - 1128-H2
TWIN PALM CIR
500 SDCo 92028 1027-G3
TWIN PEAKS PL
14600 PWY 92064 1190-H1
TWIN PEAKS RD
- SDCo 92036 1155-J4
12200 PWY 92064 1190-C1
14500 PWY 92064 1191-A1
TWIN POND TER
11000 SD 92128 1189-H4
TWINS HAVEN RD
4600 OCN 92057 1087-A3
TWIN TRAILS CT
9000 SD 92129 1189-D4
TWIN TRAILS DR
8700 SD 92129 1189-C4
TWISTED BRANCH RD
14300 PWY 92064 1170-G3
TWISTED OAK
- SDCo 91935 1294-C1
TWISTED OAK LN
2100 SDCo 91901 1253-J1
TYAHA ST
- SDCo 92028 999-D7
TYLEE ST
1000 VSTA 92083 1087-E7
TYLER AV
1400 SD 92103 1269-B5
TYLER CT
- SDCo 92082 1050-F6
2200 SDCo 91977 1270-J7

TYLER CT
2200 SDCo 91977 1271-A7
TYLER HTS
30400 SDCo 92082 1070-F1
TYLER LN
14500 SDCo 92082 1050-F7
14500 SDCo 92082 1070-G1
TYLER RD
14200 SDCo 92082 1070-F1
14400 SDCo 92082 1050-F7
TYLER ST
2300 SDCo 91977 1271-A7
2800 CRLB 92008 1106-E5
4900 OCN 92057 1067-B7
8500 SNTE 92071 1250-J1
8600 SDCo 91977 1270-J7
TYLER WY
2200 SDCo 92065 1153-B1
TYNEBOURNE CIR
3900 SD 92130 1188-A5
TYRIAN ST
6500 SD 92037 1247-F2
7400 SD 92037 1227-E7
TYROLEAN RD
7700 SD 92126 1209-A2
TYROLEAN WY
11200 SD 92126 1209-A2
TYRONE ST
300 ELCJ 92020 1251-C4
TYSON ST
100 OCN 92054 1106-A1
TZENA WY
1400 ENCT 92024 1147-G6

U

U AV
- NATC 91950 1290-A7
N U AV
- NATC 91950 1290-A6
U CT
- SD 92126 1209-F7
UDALL ST
3000 SD 92106 1268-C7
3000 SD 92106 1288-C1
3700 SD 92107 1268-B6
UFANO DR
2700 SDCo 91935 1293-C3
UHL ST
5800 SD 92105 1270-C6
ULLMAN ST
3300 SD 92106 1288-A2
ULRIC CT
3000 SD 92111 1248-H6
ULRIC ST
1400 SD 92111 1269-A2
1400 SD 92111 1268-J1
2100 SD 92111 1248-J6
ULTIMO AV
200 ESCN 92025 1130-A7
ULTRAMARINE LN
1700 SD 92114 1290-F5
UMATILLA DR
1200 DLMR 92014 1187-G5
UMBER CT
200 SD 92114 1290-G5
UMBRIA WY
13900 PWY 92064 1170-F6
UNA ST
1600 SD 92113 1289-G6
UNICORNIO ST
2400 CRLB 92009 1127-H5
UNIDA PL
3400 SD 92123 1249-D4
UNION PL
1200 SD 92037 1227-F6
UNION ST
100 ENCT 92024 1147-B5
500 SD 92101 1289-A1
2300 SD 92101 1288-J1
2900 SD 92103 1268-H6
UNION PLAZA CT
1300 OCN 92054 1106-D1
UNIONTOWN RD
5100 SD 92117 1228-F7
UNITY WY
100 VSTA 92083 1087-H7
UNIVERSITY AV
700 SD 92103 1268-J5
1000 SD 92103 1269-A5
2100 SD 92104 1269-D5
3600 SD 92105 1269-J5
4800 SD 92105 1270-A5
5400 SD 92115 1270-C5
6900 LMSA 91941 1270-F4
UNIVERSITY DR
1800 VSTA 92083 1108-B3
UNIVERSITY PL
300 SD 92103 1268-J5
8000 LMSA 91941 1270-H2
UNIVERSITY CENTER LN
8900 SD 92122 1228-B3
UNO CT
800 VSTA 92084 1087-H5
UNO VERDE CT
1500 SOLB 92075 1167-J7
UPAS LN
9700 SDCo 92029 1149-D3
UPAS ST
- ESCN 92025 1129-G3
500 SD 92103 1269-A6
700 SD 92103 1268-J6
1700 SD 92104 1269-E6
1700 SD 92101 1269-D6
W UPAS ST
300 SD 92103 1269-A6
UPLAND DR
1700 VSTA 92084 1088-B5
UPLAND ST
4400 LMSA 91941 1270-J3
6000 SD 92114 1290-C2
9500 SDCo 91977 1271-C6
UPPER HILLSIDE DR
1900 SD 92037 1227-H7
UPPER MEADOW RD
33300 SDCo 92060 409-G7
UPPER NORTH PEAK WY
- SDCo 92036 1176-C3
UPS CIR
2000 OCN 92054 1106-E1
UPSHUR DR
2600 SD 92110 1268-E6
UPSHUR ST
2800 SD 92106 1288-B2
UPTON CT
6800 SD 92111 1248-J7
URANIA AV
900 ENCT 92024 1147-C3

URBAN DR
5600 LMSA 91942 1251-B7
URIBE PL
- SDCo 92014 1168-A7
URSINA PL
1900 ENCT 92024 1147-H7
URUBU ST
6800 CRLB 92009 1127-H5
US ELEVATOR RD
10700 SDCo 91977 1291-F1
10700 SDCo 91978 1291-F1
USHER PL
- SD 92173 1350-F3
USHLA WY
32100 SDCo 92061 1051-B6
UTAH ST
3400 SD 92104 1269-D5
4400 SD 92116 1269-D3
UTAH WY
600 ESCN 92025 1129-J6
600 ESCN 92025 1130-A5
UTE DR
4100 SD 92117 1248-E4
UTGOFF AV
- CORD 92135 1288-F4
UTICA CT
6500 SD 92139 1310-F1
UTICA DR
2700 SD 92139 1310-F1
3800 SDCo 92004 (1099-D1 See Page 1098)
UTICA PL
6500 SD 92139 1310-F1
UTOPIA RD
13400 PWY 92064 1190-D4
17300 SD 92128 1170-C2
UTOPIA WY
12500 SD 92128 1170-C2
UVADA PL
4900 SD 92116 1269-D3
UVALDE CT
10800 SD 92124 1249-H1
UVAS ST
4700 SD 92102 1289-J3

V

V AV
400 NATC 91950 1290-A7
V CT
- SD 92126 1209-F7
VACA PL
11600 SD 92124 1250-B2
VACATION RD
1400 SD 92109 1268-A2
VACHELL LN
15500 SDCo 92021 1233-B1
VADO WY
1300 SD 92114 1290-D5
VAIL CT
11600 SD 92131 1210-A1
VAIL RD
900 ImCo 92233 411-A10
VAIL CREEK CT
5100 SD 92130 1188-D6
VAKAS DR
1700 SDCo 92019 1272-C3
VALANCE ST
1900 SD 92154 1350-C3
VALBORG DR
- SMCS 92029 1128-H5
VAL DALE DR
- SDCo 92025 1130-D7
VALDES DR
1700 SD 92037 1227-G6
VALDINA DR
11400 SD 92124 1250-A1
VALDINA WY
4700 SD 92124 1250-A1
VALDIVIA CT
1100 CHV 91910 1311-B7
VALDOSTA AV
7900 SD 92126 1209-B3
VALE WY
5400 SD 92115 1270-B4
VALECREST LN
2100 SDCo 91977 1291-D1
VALEMONT ST
3400 SD 92106 1288-A2
VALENCIA AV
900 SMCS 92069 1128-E3
1800 CRLB 92008 1106-H7
VALENCIA CIR
5900 SDCo 92067 1168-F7
VALENCIA CT
900 CHV 91910 1311-B6
1600 OCN 92054 1106-D2
VALENCIA DR
100 VSTA 92083 1087-G6
1100 SDCo 92025 1130-D5
4500 SD 92115 1270-D3
VALENCIA LN
9200 SDCo 91977 1271-B7
VALENCIA LP
1300 CHV 91910 1311-B6
VALENCIA PKWY
100 SD 92114 1290-C5
N VALENCIA PKWY
100 SD 92114 1290-C4
VALENCIA PL
2600 SDCo 91977 1271-A7
VALENCIA ST
1500 OCN 92054 1106-D2
8600 SDCo 91977 1270-J7
8600 SDCo 91977 1271-A7
VALENCIA VW
- PWY 92064 1190-C7
VALENCIA WY
29000 SDCo 92082 1070-J7
VALENCIA CANYON
2600 SDCo 91977 1271-A7
VALENCIA GLEN CT
1800 SDCo 92027 1130-E3
VALENTINE LN
1200 SDCo 92028 1028-C1
VALENTINO ST
1900 SD 92154 1350-D3
VALERA WY
100 OCN 92057 1086-H3
VALERIE DR
400 VSTA 92084 1087-H4
2400 SDCo 92028 1028-C7
VALETA ST
3900 SD 92110 1268-B5
4000 SD 92107 1268-B5
VALE TERRACE DR
900 VSTA 92084 1087-J5
1000 VSTA 92084 1088-A5

VALE TERRACE PL
1400 VSTA 92084 1088-B6
VALETTA LN
2500 SDCo 91901 1234-A5
VALE VIEW CT
600 VSTA 92083 1107-H1
VALE VIEW DR
400 VSTA 92083 1087-G7
400 VSTA 92083 1107-G1
VALEWOOD AV
2600 CRLB 92008 1106-J5
VALEWOOD CT
12300 PWY 92064 1190-C5
VALEWOOD RD
13100 PWY 92064 1190-C5
VALHALLA DR
12100 SDCo 92040 1232-A5
VALHALLA VIEW DR
2400 SDCo 92019 1272-D1
VALIENTE CT
10800 SD 92124 1249-J2
VALI HAI RD
15000 PWY 92064 1170-J6
15100 PWY 92064 1171-A6
VALINDA PT
4600 SD 92130 1188-C4
VALINDO WY
1900 SDCo 92084 1108-C3
VALJEAN CT
6600 SD 92111 1248-H7
VALKYRIA LN
1700 SDCo 92019 1272-B3
VALLADARES DR
17600 SD 92127 1170-A1
17600 SD 92127 1150-A7
VALLARTA CT
100 SOLB 92075 1167-D6
VALLATA CT
10000 SDCo 91977 1291-D3
VALLATA LN
900 SDCo 91977 1291-D3
VALLDEMOSA LN
10900 SD 92124 1249-H2
VALLE AV
3000 SD 92113 1289-E5
VALLE DR
4300 LMSA 91941 1270-H3
VALLEA ST
1600 ELCJ 92019 1252-B7
VALLE CABALLO LN
9900 SDCo 92021 1232-J2
VALLECITO DR
- SMCS 92069 1128-E2
VALLECITO LN
- SDCo 92055 1085-J4
VALLECITO WY
- CHV 91910 1310-D7
- CHV 91910 1330-D1
VALLECITOS
2100 SD 92037 1227-G5
VALLECITOS CT
2400 SD 92037 1227-H5
VALLECITOS DR
3600 SMCS 92069 1108-B7
3600 SMCS 92069 1128-C1
VALLECITOS DE ORO
100 SMCS 92069 1108-F7
VALLEDA LN
1400 ENCT 92024 1147-G5
VALLE DE LAS SOMBRAS
1100 SDCo 91901 1233-F6
VALLE DE LOBO DR
17700 PWY 92064 1170-E1
VALLE DE LOBO WY
13600 PWY 92064 1170-F1
VALLE DEL SOL
3700 SDCo 92003 1067-F1
4500 OCN 92003 1067-G2
VALLE DE ORO
16100 SDCo 92067 1168-D5
VALLE DE PAZ RD
10000 SDCo 92021 1233-C2
VALLE GRANDE
1400 ESCN 92025 1150-E3
VALLEJO AV
4300 SD 92117 1248-E2
VALLEJO CT
4300 SD 92117 1248-F2
VALLEJO ST
10500 SNTE 92071 1231-E6
VALLE LINDO RD
13900 ESCN 92027 1110-F5
VALLE PASO
100 SDCo 92084 1088-F5
VALLERY CT
5200 SD 92130 1188-D5
VALLE VERDE RD
13200 PWY 92064 1170-E2
VALLE VERDE ST
3800 SDCo 91902 1310-H3
VALLE VERDE TER
13200 PWY 92064 1170-E3
VALLE VISTA
- SMCS 92078 1129-C1
5300 SDCo 91941 1271-B1
VALLE VISTA AV
1900 NATC 91950 1310-B1
VALLE VISTA RD
10400 SDCo 92040 1231-J1
11100 SDCo 92040 1211-G6
VALLE VISTA ST
300 SD 92103 1268-H5
VALLEY AV
600 SOLB 92075 1167-G7
600 SOLB 92075 1187-G1
600 DLMR 92014 1187-G1
3800 CHV 91911 1330-F6
VALLEY BLVD
1100 ImCo 92249 6560-B7
N VALLEY BLVD Rt#-S6
100 ESCN 92025 1129-J2
S VALLEY BLVD Rt#-S6
100 ESCN 92025 1129-J2
VALLEY DR
400 SDCo 92084 1088-B7
700 VSTA 92084 1088-B7
900 VSTA 92084 1088-B6
8300 SDCo 91977 1290-J6
VALLEY PKWY Rt#-S6
900 ESCN 92025 1129-F4
1100 ESCN 92029 1129-F4
E VALLEY PKWY
500 ESCN 92025 1129-J2
E VALLEY PKWY Rt#-S6
100 ESCN 92025 1129-J2

E VALLEY PKWY Rt#-S6
500 ESCN 92025 1130-A2
1100 ESCN 92027 1130-A2
1800 ESCN 92027 1110-E5
W VALLEY PKWY
800 ESCN 92025 1129-G3
W VALLEY PKWY Rt#-S6
200 ESCN 92025 1129-H3
VALLEY PL
1700 CRLB 92008 1106-G5
2800 SD 92113 1289-E4
VALLEY RD
- SD 92139 1310-E3
1900 OCN 92056 1086-H7
2000 OCN 92056 1106-H1
2500 NATC 91950 1310-C3
3500 NATC 91902 1310-E3
3600 SDCo 91902 1310-E3
VALLEY ST
2900 CRLB 92008 1106-F4
VALLEY VW
2200 ESCN 92029 1129-E6
VALLEY BEND ST
1700 CHV 91913 1311-D7
VALLEY CENTER RD Rt#-S6
24700 ESCN 92027 1110-F4
24800 SDCo 92027 1090-E4
24800 SDCo 92027 1110-F4
24800 SDCo 92082 1090-E1
30300 SDCo 92082 1091-A2
31700 SDCo 92082 1071-E1
33600 SDCo 92061 1051-D7
33600 SDCo 92061 1071-E1
VALLEY CENTER SCHOOL RD
14200 SDCo 92082 1090-F1
VALLEY CENTRE DR
3500 SD 92130 1207-J1
3500 SD 92130 1208-A1
3700 SD 92130 1188-A7
VALLEY CREST DR
700 OCN 92054 1086-D3
800 SDCo 92084 1088-E7
1000 SDCo 92084 1108-F1
VALLEYDALE LN
100 ENCT 92024 1147-H7
100 ENCT 92024 1167-H1
VALLEY GARDENS DR
2300 CHV 91915 1311-H7
VALLEY GLEN DR
3100 OCN 92056 1106-H2
VALLEY GROVE LN
500 ESCN 92025 1130-C6
VALLEY HEIGHTS DR
400 OCN 92057 1087-A2
VALLEY HIGH RD
4800 SDCo 92040 1231-H7
4800 SNTE 92040 1231-H7
5700 SNTE 92040 1251-H1
VALLEY KNOLLS RD
2700 SDCo 91935 1292-G3
VALLEY LAKE DR
2000 ELCJ 92020 1251-B2
VALLEY LIGHTS DR
10900 SDCo 92020 1271-G2
VALLEY MEADOW PL
500 ESCN 92027 1110-E7
VALLEY MILL RD
2300 ELCJ 92020 1251-B2
VALLEY OAK LN
38100 SDCo 92086 409-K5
VALLEY OAKS BLVD E
1600 SDCo 92028 1028-F4
VALLEY OAKS BLVD W
1500 SDCo 92028 1028-F4
VALLEY OF THE KING RD
29600 SDCo 92084 1068-F6
VALLEY RIDGE ST
2100 CHV 91914 1311-E2
2100 SDCo 91914 1311-E2
VALLEY RIM GN
2100 ESCN 92026 1109-C4
VALLEY RIM RD
1900 SDCo 92021 1252-D3
2000 SDCo 92019 1252-D3
2000 ELCJ 92019 1252-D4
VALLEYSIDE LN
- ENCT 92024 1148-A5
VALLEY SPRINGS RD
14000 PWY 92064 1170-G3
VALLEY STREAM RD
- SDCo 92082 1070-C6
VALLEYTREE PL
300 ESCN 92026 1109-H4
VALLEY VIEW BLVD
1900 SDCo 92019 1252-C5
1900 ELCJ 92019 1252-C5
VALLEY VIEW CIR
7900 LMSA 91941 1270-J4
VALLEY VIEW DR
900 SDCo 92036 1156-C1
1000 SDCo 92036 1136-C7
N VALLEY VIEW DR
700 CHV 91914 1311-G3
S VALLEY VIEW DR
800 CHV 91914 1311-G3
VALLEY VIEW GN
2500 ESCN 92026 1109-B3
VALLEY VIEW LN
100 OCN 92054 1086-E6
3400 SDCo 91977 1271-A6
VALLEY VIEW PL
200 VSTA 92083 1107-J1
2300 ESCN 92026 1109-G4
VALLEY VIEW RD
12100 SDCo 92082 1090-A2
VALLEY VIEW TKTR
- SDCo 92021 1252-D1
VALLEY VIEW TR
7800 SDCo 92066 1237-C5
VALLEY VILLAGE DR
600 ELCJ 92021 1251-G3
VALLEY VISTA DR
27000 SDCo 92082 1090-J5
VALLEY VISTA RD
3300 SDCo 91902 1310-F3
VALLEY VISTA WY
2800 OCN 92054 1106-F1
3600 SDCo 91902 1310-F3
VALLEY VISTA FORK
3700 SDCo 91902 1310-E3
VALLEY WATERS CT
- SDCo 91977 1291-E2
VALLEY WATERS DR
- SDCo 91977 1291-F2

VALMONTE GN
2500 ESCN 92029 1149-G1
VALNER CT
2100 SD 92139 1290-D7
VALNER WY
6200 SD 92139 1290-D7
VALOMA PL
4300 SD 92122 1228-E6
VALOR PL
10700 SNTE 92071 1231-E3
VALPREDA RD
100 SMCS 92069 1108-J7
VAL SERENO DR
700 ENCT 92024 1148-B6
VALVA AV
- NATC 91950 1290-A6
VAL VERDE CT
14400 SD 92129 1189-H2
VAL VISTA DR
8500 SNTE 92071 1250-J1
VAN ALLEN WY
5800 CRLB 92008 1127-C1
VAN ANDEL WY
9300 SNTE 92071 1230-J6
VAN BUREN AV
1400 SD 92103 1269-B4
VANCE ST
100 CHV 91910 1310-C6
VANCOUVER AV
2200 SD 92104 1289-G1
2400 SD 92104 1269-F6
VANCOUVER ST
2600 CRLB 92008 1106-J3
VANDEGRIFT BLVD
- SDCo 92055 409-A7
- SDCo 92055 1085-H3
- SDCo 92055 1086-A2
400 OCN 92057 1067-A2
900 SDCo 92055 1067-A2
1200 SDCo 92055 1066-J1
VANDEMEN WY
- SD 92131 1209-G2
VANDERBILT PL
700 SD 92103 1268-J6
VAN DER LINDEN RD
- ImCo 92250 431-F6
VAN DER POEL RD
500 ImCo 92243 6559-B7
VANDEVER AV
4300 SD 92120 1249-H7
4800 SD 92120 1250-A7
VAN DUESEN RD
- SDCo 92036 1155-J1
- SDCo 92036 1156-A1
VAN DYKE AV
400 DLMR 92014 1187-G5
3100 SD 92105 1269-H4
4400 SD 92116 1269-H4
VAN DYKE PL
4200 SD 92116 1269-H4
VANESSA CIR
1400 ENCT 92024 1147-G5
VAN GOGH LN
5200 SDCo 91902 1290-H7
VANGUARD PL
8700 SDCo 92021 1232-C7
8700 SDCo 92040 1232-C7
VANGUARD WY
13200 SDCo 92040 1232-C7
VAN HORN RD
600 SDCo 92019 1252-C7
VAN HORN ST
8700 LMSA 91942 1251-A7
VAN HORN WY
800 SDCo 92019 1252-C7
VAN HOUTEN AV
100 ELCJ 92020 1251-F5
VANILLA WY
600 OCN 92057 1086-H5
VANITA ST
800 SDCo 92028 1027-G1
VANITIE CT
700 SD 92109 1247-H7
VANN CT
1600 ELCJ 92020 1251-C4
VAN NESS AV
2000 NATC 91950 1310-C1
2400 SDCo 91950 1310-C1
VAN NUYS CT
5300 SD 92109 1247-H4
VAN NUYS PL
5300 SD 92109 1247-H4
VAN NUYS ST
700 SD 92037 1247-G4
700 SD 92109 1247-G4
VAN NUYS WY
5300 SD 92109 1247-H4
VANTAGE CT
1300 VSTA 92083 1128-A1
VANTAGE PL
- SDCo 92028 1027-H7
VANTAGE WY
2400 SD 92014 1187-H5
VAN VECHTEN RD
1300 ELCJ 92019 1252-A7
1300 SDCo 92019 1252-A7
1300 SDCo 92020 1252-A7
1300 SDCo 92020 1272-A1
E VAQUERO CT
1300 CHV 91910 1311-B7
W VAQUERO CT
1200 CHV 91910 1311-B7
VAQUERO GN
1400 ESCN 92026 1109-D4
VARNEY DR
6100 SD 92114 1290-D5
VARONA ST
4000 SD 92106 1288-A2
4100 SD 92107 1287-J2
4100 SD 92107 1288-A2
VARS WY
- SDCo 91901 1234-B4
VASSAR AV
800 CHV 91913 1311-D5
7200 LMSA 91941 1270-F3
VAUGHAN RD
12400 PWY 92064 1190-C3
VECINIO DEL ESTE PL
13600 SDCo 92040 1232-E5
VECINO CT
300 SDCo 91977 1291-A4
VEEMAC AV
6000 LMSA 91942 1251-B6
VEGA ST
1100 SD 92110 1268-E2
VELA DR
11300 SD 92126 1209-C1
VELASCO CT
4300 SDCo 91941 1271-G3

STREET
Block City ZIP Pg-Grid

VELITE DR
300 SDCo 92004 1058-G7
VELLA LAVELLA RD
2300 CORD 92155 1309-A2
VELMA TER
5200 SD 92114 1290-B5
VENADITO
3000 SDCo 91901 1254-D1
VENADO ST
3100 CRLB 92009 1127-H7
3200 CRLB 92009 1147-J1
VENCILL RD
- ImCo 92250 431-E6
VENDOR PL
17200 PWY 92064 1170-D2
VENETIA WY
100 OCN 92057 1087-A3
VENICE CT
700 SD 92109 1247-H7
VENICE GN
800 ESCN 92026 1109-J7
VENICE ST
1500 SD 92107 1288-A1
1600 SD 92107 1268-A7
VENTANA DR
1500 ESCN 92029 1149-G1
VENTANA WY
- OCN 92057 1087-A1
1900 ELCJ 92020 1251-B1
VENTERS DR
1400 CHV 91911 1330-J3
VENTURA PL
700 SD 92109 1267-H2
VENTURE ST
100 SMCS 92078 1128-J1
100 SMCS 92078 1129-A1
400 ESCN 92029 1129-E3
VENTURE VALLEY RD
1000 SDCo 92036 1138-A6
VENUS ST
4100 SD 92110 1268-C5
VENUS VIEW DR
700 VSTA 92083 1107-G1
VERA CIR
100 VSTA 92084 1087-J5
VERA LN
2000 ESCN 92026 1109-D5
VERA ST
800 SOLB 92075 1187-G1
VERA CRUZ
1200 OCN 92056 1087-B4
VERA CRUZ AV
- SD 92140 1268-G7
VERACRUZ CT
10300 SD 92124 1249-G1
VERALEE DR
3200 SD 92154 1350-D2
VERANDA CT
12400 SD 92128 1190-A6
VERANO CT
12000 SD 92128 1150-B7
VERANO DR
900 CHV 91910 1310-J7
18000 SD 92128 1150-B7
VERANO PL
2500 ESCN 92025 1130-C7
18300 SD 92128 1150-B6
VERANO BRISA DR
4300 SDCo 92024 1148-E3
VERBENA CT
- CRLB 92009 1127-B4
VERBENA DR
100 SDCo 92004 (1078-G1
See Page 1058)
VERBENA LN
10000 SDCo 91977 1291-D2
VERBENA TER
1900 SDCo 91901 1233-J5
1900 SDCo 91901 1234-A5
VERDA AV
2700 ESCN 92025 1130-A7
2700 ESCN 92025 1150-A1
VERDANT PL
600 VSTA 92084 1087-J5
VERDANT WY
2600 SDCo 91950 1310-C3
VERDE AV
500 SDCo 92028 1047-E5
3100 CRLB 92009 1147-J1
VERDE CT
3200 SDCo 91902 1310-E4
VERDE DR
4900 OCN 92057 1067-A6
VERDE VIA
1900 SDCo 92027 1130-E4
VERDE GLENN
1900 SDCo 92019 1272-C2
VERDE ORO
300 SDCo 92028 1047-F3
VERDE RIDGE CT
400 SDCo 91977 1290-J5
VERDE RIDGE RD
8300 SDCo 91977 1290-J5
VERDE SCHOOL RD
- ImCo 92250 431-E6
VERDE VIEW RD
2800 SDCo 91901 1234-C7
VERDI AV
100 ENCT 92007 1167-C2
VERDIGRIS VALLEY RD
17100 SDCo 92065 1171-E1
VERDIN CT
- CRLB 92009 1127-D4
VERDIN ST
500 ELCJ 92019 1252-B4
VEREDA CT
1900 SDCo 92019 1272-C1
VEREDA BARRANCA
1200 SDCo 92084 1088-C4
VEREDA CALLADA
900 SDCo 92029 1149-H1
VEREDA LUNA LLENA
4400 SD 92130 1208-B3
VEREDA LUZ DEL SOL
1700 SD 92130 1208-C3
VEREDA MAR DEL CORAZON
- SD 92130 1208-C2
VEREDA MAR DEL SOL
- SD 92130 1208-C3
VEREDA MAR DE PONDEROSA
4400 SD 92130 1208-C3
VEREDA SOL DEL DIOS
10800 SD 92130 1208-C4
VERGARA ST
5300 SD 92117 1248-H1
VERIN LN
800 CHV 91910 1310-H6

VERLA LN
1600 SDCo 92027 1130-C4
VERLANE DR
8600 SD 92119 1250-J4
8600 SD 92119 1251-A4
VERLEY CT
4400 SD 92117 1248-G2
VERMEL AV
1900 ESCN 92029 1129-F5
VERMILLION WY
100 SD 92114 1290-F5
E VERMONT AV
100 ESCN 92025 1130-B5
W VERMONT AV
200 ESCN 92025 1130-A6
VERMONT PL
600 ESCN 92025 1129-J6
600 ESCN 92025 1130-A6
VERMONT ST
1700 SDCo 92065 1152-E7
2200 SDCo 92065 1172-D1
3400 SD 92103 1269-B5
VERN DR
3800 SDCo 92028 1028-F6
VERNA DR
9000 SDCo 92026 1069-A6
VERNA WY
5100 SDCo 91941 1271-F1
VERNAL LN
4000 SDCo 91916 1236-A3
VERNAZZA CT
- SD 92130 1188-A4
VERNER WY
100 VSTA 92083 1087-F7
VERNETTE CT
11500 SDCo 92020 1271-H2
VERNETTE DR
4600 SDCo 92020 1271-H3
VERNIER DR
8200 LMGR 91945 1290-H1
VERNIE VISTA LN
32400 SDCo 92082 1050-F6
VERNON CT
- CHV 91913 1331-B1
VERNON WY
300 ELCJ 92020 1251-E3
300 SDCo 92020 1251-F3
VERONA CT
700 SD 92109 1247-H7
VERONA ST
4900 OCN 92056 1087-C3
VERONA HILLS CT
2100 SDCo 92084 1108-D3
VERONA HILLS PKWY
2000 SDCo 92084 1108-D2
VERONICA AV
6800 SD 92115 1270-E5
VERONICA CT
- CRLB 92009 1127-B5
400 CHV 91911 1330-G3
VERONICA PL
500 ESCN 92027 1110-D6
VERSAILLES CT
12000 SD 92128 1150-A7
VERSAILLES RD
1900 CHV 91913 1311-E5
VERUS ST
2200 SD 92154 1330-A5
VERVAIN ST
9300 SD 92129 1189-E5
VESPER LN
- CRLB 92009 1127-D4
VESPER RD
14400 SDCo 92082 1090-G1
15400 SDCo 92082 1091-A1
VESTA ST
900 NATC 92136 1309-F1
900 SD 92136 1309-F1
1700 SD 92113 1289-F7
2100 SD 92136 1289-F7
VESUVIA WY
3000 SD 92139 1310-E2
VETTER PL
4300 LMSA 91941 1270-F4
VIA ABACA
10900 SD 92126 1209-C3
VIA ABAJO
11100 SD 92129 1169-H7
VIA ABERTURA
- SDCo 92067 1188-H2
13800 SD 92130 1188-H3
14300 SD 92127 1188-H2
VIA ACANTILADA
17800 SD 92128 1150-C7
VIA ACAPULCO
7900 SD 92122 1228-E4
VIA ACOSTA
12800 SD 92128 1150-D7
VIA ACQUAVIVA
4300 SDCo 92028 1047-G5
VIA ADELFA
- CRLB 92009 1147-F2
VIA ADELIA
- SCLE 92672 1023-B2
VIA ADRIANA
1800 OCN 92056 1087-B5
VIA AFABLE
1600 SD 92154 1349-J1
VIA A LA CASA
16400 SDCo 92067 1168-E4
VIA ALANDRA
3000 SMCS 92069 1108-D4
VIA ALBERTO
10700 SD 92129 1189-G2
VIA ALCAZAR
5300 SD 92111 1248-G6
6500 CRLB 92009 1127-J4
VIA ALDEA
4000 OCN 92057 1086-H2
VIA ALEGRE
800 SDCo 92028 1027-H1
1700 SDCo 92027 1130-D3
VIA ALEGRE DR
1000 SDCo 92065 1152-J6
VIA ALESSANDRO
3200 SD 92111 1248-G5
VIA ALEXANDRA
900 ESCN 92026 1109-F5
900 SDCo 92026 1109-F5
VIA ALFALFA
11900 SDCo 92019 1271-J3
VIA ALICANTE
3100 SD 92037 1228-A4
VIA ALICIA
2400 SDCo 92028 1048-C2
3600 OCN 92056 1107-G4
VIA ALISAL
14100 SD 92128 1190-B1

VIA ALLEGRA
- VSTA 92083 1107-H2
VIA ALLENA
1700 OCN 92056 1087-C4
VIA ALLONDRA
1500 SDCo 92069 1128-B4
1500 SMCS 92069 1128-B4
VIA ALMANSA
300 ENCT 92024 1147-F6
VIA ALMONTE
3200 SDCo 92028 1048-H2
VIA ALTA
1300 DLMR 92014 1187-G5
VIA ALTAMIRA
3200 SDCo 92028 1048-G2
VIA ALTA MIRASOL
17800 SD 92128 1150-B7
17800 SD 92128 1170-B1
VIA ALTA VISTA
3600 SMCS 92069 1108-B7
3600 SMCS 92069 1128-C1
32000 SDCo 92003 1048-C7
32000 SDCo 92003 1068-C1
VIA ALTIVA
17800 SD 92128 1150-B7
VIA AMABLE
4400 SD 92122 1228-D3
VIA AMADOR
3000 CRLB 92008 1106-H3
VIA AMALIA
3100 SD 92111 1248-G6
VIA AMATA
3100 SD 92111 1248-G6
VIA AMBIENTE
8000 SDCo 92067 1148-J2
8000 SDCo 92067 1149-A5
9000 SDCo 92029 1148-J2
VIA AMISTOSA
3800 SDCo 92091 1168-C7
VIA ANACAPA
- SMCS 92069 1108-D4
VIA ANDALUSIA
300 ENCT 92024 1147-F6
VIA ANDAR
8800 SD 92122 1228-D3
VIA ANGELINA
1100 SD 92037 1247-F2
VIA ANITA
2200 SD 92037 1247-J2
9100 SNTE 92071 1231-G5
VIA ANNA
10700 SDCo 91978 1271-F6
VIA ANTIGUA
12100 SDCo 92019 1272-A4
VIA ANTOINETTE
12900 SDCo 92082 1070-C5
VIA APRILIA
2200 SD 92014 1207-H1
VIA APUESTO
1200 SDCo 92069 1128-F4
VIA AQUARIO
5300 SD 92111 1248-G5
VIA ARANGO
10700 SD 92129 1189-H3
VIA ARARAT DR
31700 SDCo 92003 1048-G7
31700 SDCo 92003 1068-G1
VIA ARBOLEDA
1200 SDCo 92029 1149-G2
VIA ARBOLES
400 SMCS 92069 1109-D7
VIA ARCE
8000 CRLB 92009 1147-G3
VIA ARCILLA
3100 SD 92111 1248-G5
VIA AREQUIPA
4900 CRLB 92008 1107-A7
VIA ARGENTINA
1100 VSTA 92083 1107-E1
VIA ARMADO
600 CHV 91910 1311-A5
VIA ARROYO
2700 SDCo 92028 1028-B7
2800 SDCo 92028 1048-B1
VIA ARTISTA
- SMCS 92069 1108-E4
VIA ARTURO RD
- SDCo 91916 1235-E2
VIA ASCENSO
18100 SDCo 92067 1148-D6
VIA ASOLEADO
2700 SDCo 91901 1254-B3
VIA ASTI
11000 SD 92129 1189-H3
VIA ASTUTO
2500 CRLB 92008 1106-H3
VIA ASUNCION
5700 SDCo 92003 1067-J2
VIA AVANTE
4900 SD 92130 1188-D3
VIA AVOLA
7500 SD 92037 1227-H6
VIA BAHIA
700 SMCS 92069 1108-F4
VIA BALDONA
3600 OCN 92056 1107-F4
VIA BANCO
10900 SD 92126 1209-C3
VIA BANDITA
200 OCN 92057 1087-A2
VIA BARBERINI
- CHV 91910 1310-A4
VIA BARLETTA
2500 SD 92037 1227-H6
VIA BARLOVENTO
1600 SDCo 92069 1128-F4
VIA BARODA
14200 SD 92130 1188-D2
VIA BARONA
3000 CRLB 92009 1127-J4
VIA BARQUERO
- SMCS 92069 1108-F4
VIA BARRANCA
1200 SD 92037 1247-G1
VIA BARRANCA DEL ZORRO
6100 SDCo 92067 1168-F4
VIA BARTOLO
3200 SD 92111 1248-G5
VIA BEATRAIZ
10700 SD 92129 1189-H2
VIA BELLA DONNA
800 SMCS 92069 1128-G3
VIA BELLA MARIA
800 SMCS 92069 1128-G3
VIA BELLA MONICA
800 SMCS 92069 1128-G3
VIA BELLEZA
1200 SMCS 92069 1109-C7

VIA BELLEZA
1200 SMCS 92069 1129-C1
VIA BELLO
5300 SD 92111 1248-G5
VIA BELMONTE
4700 SDCo 92028 1048-G2
VIA BELOTA
2900 SDCo 91901 1254-D1
VIA BELTRAN
3400 SD 92117 1248-E5
VIA BENITO
3300 SD 92111 1248-G5
VIA BERNARDO
3600 OCN 92056 1107-G4
VIA BISSOLOTTI
300 CHV 91910 1310-A4
VIA BLANCA
2100 OCN 92054 1106-G2
VIA BOCAS
2600 CRLB 92008 1106-C6
VIA BOGOTA
600 VSTA 92083 1107-F1
VIA BOLIVIA
600 VSTA 92083 1107-E1
VIA BOLSA
11600 SDCo 92019 1271-J3
VIA BOLTANA
13800 SD 92129 1189-E3
VIA BORGIA
12700 SD 92014 1207-H1
VIA BORREGOS
6800 CRLB 92009 1128-A6
VIA BOTERO
1500 OCN 92056 1087-C3
VIA BRILLANTE
4400 SD 92122 1228-D3
VIA BRISA DEL LAGO
1500 SDCo 92069 1128-C3
VIA BRITTNEY
- SDCo 92040 1231-H5
VIA BROMA
15900 SDCo 92091 1168-C7
VIA BUENA VISTA
1500 SDCo 92069 1128-B4
VIA CABALLO ROJO
12800 SD 92129 1189-F5
VIA CABANA
7000 CRLB 92009 1127-G6
VIA CABERNET
- ESCN 92029 1129-E4
VIA CABEZON
12400 SD 92129 1189-F6
VIA CABO VERDE
3300 ESCN 92029 1150-A3
VIA CABRERA
6300 SD 92037 1247-J1
VIA CABRILLO
3700 OCN 92056 1107-F4
VIA CACERES
9800 SD 92129 1189-E3
VIA CAFETAL
900 SMCS 92069 1108-E4
VIA CAJITA
3200 CRLB 92008 1106-C6
VIA CALABRIA
3600 ESCN 92025 1150-D3
VIA CALAFIA
7000 CRLB 92009 1127-G6
VIA CALANDRIA
- SCLE 92672 1023-B2
VIA CALANOVA
15700 SD 92128 1170-B5
VIA CALDRON
6500 CRLB 92009 1127-J5
VIA CALENDO
7900 CRLB 92009 1148-A2
VIA CALIENTE
- SMCS 92069 1108-F4
VIA CALIENTE DEL SOL
3100 SDCo 91935 1272-D7
VIA CALLADO
5500 SD 92037 1247-H3
VIA CALVILLO
5400 SDCo 92003 1067-G2
VIA CAMELLIA
1100 SMCS 92069 1109-C7
VIA CAMINAR
1600 SDCo 92069 1128-C3
VIA CAMINO VERDE
2100 OCN 92054 1106-F1
VIA CAMPESTRE
- SDCo 92082 1070-A6
3000 SD 92014 1187-J1
11800 SDCo 92082 1069-J6
VIA CAMPO VERDE
6200 SDCo 92067 1168-F5
VIA CANADA DEL OSITO
5800 SDCo 92067 1168-E6
VIA CANCION
1600 SDCo 92069 1128-A3
1600 SMCS 92069 1128-A3
VIA CANDELA
18400 SDCo 92067 1148-E5
VIA CANDIDIZ
4100 SD 92130 1188-B6
VIA CANDREJO
7000 CRLB 92009 1127-G6
VIA CANGREJO
3900 SD 92130 1208-B3
VIA CANTAMAR
30500 SDCo 92026 1068-J4
30500 SDCo 92026 1069-A4
VIA CANTEBRIA
100 ENCT 92024 1147-F4
VIA CAPRA DORADO
- SD 92122 1228-E4
VIA CAPRI
1700 CHV 91913 1311-D7
7000 SD 92037 1227-H6
VIA CAPRI CT
2300 SD 92037 1227-H6
VIA CARACAS
8900 SD 92126 1209-D3
VIA CARA LOMA
3700 ENCT 92024 1148-B3
VIA CARANCHO
5300 SD 92111 1248-G5
VIA CARDEL
2700 CRLB 92008 1106-C6
VIA CARINA
- VSTA 92083 1107-H2
VIA CARLOTTA
11600 SDCo 92019 1271-J4
VIA CAROLINA
1100 SD 92037 1247-F2
VIA CARRILLO
1300 SDCo 92069 1128-B4

VIA CARRIO
2800 CRLB 92008 1106-H3
VIA CARROZA
11200 SD 92124 1250-A2
VIA CASA ALTA
2100 SD 92037 1227-H7
VIA CASA DEL SOL
- CRLB 92009 1127-J5
VIA CASCABEL
2100 SDCo 92027 1130-F4
10800 SD 92124 1249-J2
VIA CASCADA
2800 CRLB 92008 1106-H3
VIA CASCADITA
4500 OCN 92057 1087-B1
VIA CASILINA
11600 SDCo 92019 1272-A5
VIA CASITAS
- SDCo 92003 1048-B7
- SDCo 92003 1068-C1
VIA CASSANDRA
200 SDCo 92028 1027-G4
VIA CASTANET
1200 SDCo 92069 1128-B4
VIA CASTILLA
5100 OCN 92057 1067-A4
VIA CAVOUR
300 CHV 91910 1310-A4
VIA CAZADERO
16200 SDCo 92067 1168-F7
VIA CEDRO
- CHV 91910 1311-A6
VIA CENOTE
- SDCo 92036 1156-B3
VIA CENTRE
1900 VSTA 92083 1107-C2
VIACHA CT
10900 SD 92124 1249-J3
VIACHA DR
10300 SD 92124 1249-J3
VIACHA WY
10500 SD 92124 1249-H3
VIA CHAPARRAL
1500 SDCo 92028 1028-E5
VIA CHARDONNAY
- ESCN 92029 1129-E4
VIA CHICA
- CRLB 92009 1147-J4
VIA CHICA CT
300 SOLB 92075 1167-H6
VIA CHINARROS
2700 SDCo 91901 1254-A2
VIA CHONA
11700 SD 92128 1170-A5
VIA CHRISTINA
1200 VSTA 92084 1088-A4
VIA CIBOLA
1300 OCN 92057 1067-A5
1300 OCN 92057 1066-J4
VIA CIELITO
- SDCo 92067 1149-A4
VIA CIELO AZUL
3700 SDCo 91901 1254-F2
VIA CIELO VISTA
1100 SDCo 92029 1149-H3
VIA CIMA BELLA
13500 SD 92129 1189-E4
VIA CIMBORIO CIR
10700 SD 92131 1210-A2
VIA CINERIA
- ESCN 92029 1129-E4
VIA CINTA
5100 SD 92122 1228-G6
VIA CLAREZ
2800 CRLB 92008 1106-H3
VIA CLEMENTE
400 OCN 92057 1087-A4
2300 CRLB 92008 1106-G3
VIA COELLO
7000 CRLB 92009 1127-G6
VIA COLIMA
2700 CRLB 92008 1106-H3
VIA COLINA
3600 OCN 92056 1107-F4
9200 SDCo 91941 1271-B4
VIA COLMENAR
- SD 92129 1189-B6
VIA COLONIA
8600 SD 92126 1209-C3
VIA COLORADO
4700 OCN 92056 1087-B4
VIA COLORSO
- SCLE 92672 1023-B2
VIA COLUMBIA
600 VSTA 92083 1107-E1
VIA CONCA DORO
700 SDCo 92084 1088-F7
VIA CONCEPCION
- SDCo 92067 1168-C6
VIA CONEJO
1100 SDCo 92029 1149-H3
VIA CONQUISTADOR
2800 CRLB 92009 1127-H4
VIA CONRAD
9800 SNTE 92071 1231-C3
VIA CONSUELO
8500 SDCo 92021 1232-E6
VIA CONTENTA
1000 SDCo 92029 1149-H2
VIA CONTESSA
- SMCS 92069 1108-F4
VIA CORDOBA
6700 SDCo 92067 1168-H6
VIA CORDONIZ
2500 SDCo 92028 997-C4
VIA CORDOVA
2200 SDCo 91978 1271-G7
2200 SDCo 91978 1291-G1
VIA CORINA
1800 SDCo 91901 1233-F7
1800 SDCo 91901 1253-G1
VIA CORONA
1500 SD 92037 1247-H3
VIA CORONADO
3700 SDCo 92091 1168-C7
VIA CORSINI
14000 SD 92128 1190-B2
VIA CORTA
- VSTA 92083 1107-C2
4900 CRLB 92008 1107-A6
VIA CORTE
2100 SDCo 92029 1129-H6
VIA CORTINA
12700 SD 92014 1207-H1
VIA CORTO
2200 SDCo 92028 1048-B4
VIA COSCOJA
- CRLB 92009 1147-G2

VIA COSTA RICA
600 VSTA 92083 1107-F1
VIA COSTINA
1600 SD 92173 1350-D2
VIA CRISTOBAL
2800 CRLB 92008 1106-H3
VIA CRUZ
400 OCN 92057 1087-A4
400 OCN 92057 1086-J4
VIA CUARTO
1800 OCN 92056 1087-C5
VIA CUATRO CAMINOS
17200 SDCo 92067 1168-G1
VIA CUENCA
9900 SD 92129 1189-F3
VIA CUESTA
19300 SDCo 92065 1151-H2
VIA CUESTA ARRIBA
30300 SDCo 92003 1068-E4
VIA CUESTA MANSA
6800 SDCo 92067 1168-G7
VIA CUESTA VERDE
17000 SDCo 92067 1168-G6
VIA CUMBRES
2700 SDCo 92028 1028-C3
VIA CUMBRES LN
2800 SDCo 92028 1028-C3
VIA CUPENO
5100 OCN 92057 1067-B7
VIA CURVADA
600 CHV 91910 1310-G7
VIA CUYAMACA
9800 SNTE 92071 1231-C4
VIA DARDO
17600 SD 92128 1150-D7
VIA DAROCA
9900 SD 92129 1189-F3
VIA DE AGUACATE
2300 SDCo 92028 1028-B7
VIA DE AMO
200 SDCo 92028 1028-B3
VIA DE AMOR
9100 SNTE 92071 1231-B7
VIA DE ANZA
3700 SMCS 92069 1108-C7
VIA DEBBIE
9900 SNTE 92071 1231-D4
VIA DE CABALLO
3000 ENCT 92024 1148-B6
VIA DE CANTO
3100 CRLB 92008 1106-H3
VIA DE CASA
100 SDCo 92028 1028-B2
VIA DE CRISTINA
9100 SNTE 92071 1231-B7
VIA DE ENCANTO
1200 SDCo 92029 1149-H3
VIA DE FORTUNA
2300 CRLB 92009 1127-G7
17400 SDCo 92067 1168-C1
17800 SDCo 92067 1148-C7
VIA DE JAMUL
13800 SDCo 91935 1292-J2
VIA DE JUAN
9100 SNTE 92071 1231-B7
VIA DE LA AMISTAD
9700 SD 92154 1352-B4
VIA DE LA BANDOLA
3700 SD 92173 1350-F2
VIA DE LA CUESTA
1700 SDCo 92027 1130-D3
VIA DE LA CUMBRE
5500 SDCo 92067 1168-D2
VIA DE LA FLOR
6200 SDCo 92003 1068-D3
VIA DEL ALBA
15800 SDCo 92067 1168-C4
VIA DEL ALLAZON
2800 SDCo 91902 1290-H7
VIA DE LA MELODIA
1600 SD 92173 1350-F2
VIA DE LA NOLA
7300 SDCo 92067 1168-H2
VIA DE LA PAZ
4000 OCN 92057 1086-H4
VIA DE LA REINA
6700 SDCo 92003 1068-E3
VIA DE LA ROCA
40600 SDCo 92028 997-J3
VIA DE LAS FLORES
18300 SDCo 92067 1148-G5
VIA DE LAS PALMAS
15900 SDCo 92091 1168-C7
15900 SDCo 92091 1188-C1
VIA DEL ASTRO
300 OCN 92057 1086-H4
VIA DE LAURENCIO
- CHV 91910 1310-D6
- SDCo 91910 1310-D6
VIA DE LA VALLE
3300 OCN 92054 1086-E4
VIA DE LA VALLE Rt#-S6
100 DLMR 92014 1187-G2
600 SD 92014 1187-J2
3200 SD 92014 1188-B1
4000 SDCo 92014 1188-B1
14900 SDCo 92067 1188-B1
14900 SDCo 92091 1188-B1
15000 SDCo 92067 1168-E3
15000 SDCo 92091 1168-D6
15100 SD 92075 1187-G2
VIA DEL BARDO
3900 SD 92173 1350-F2
VIA DEL BRAVO
17300 SDCo 92067 1168-G2
VIA DEL CABALLO BLANCO
2800 SDCo 91902 1290-H7
VIA DEL CAMPO
600 SMCS 92078 1129-A2
16500 SD 92127 1169-H2
VIA DEL CAMPO CT
16800 SD 92127 1169-H3
VIA DEL CANON
14700 SD 92014 1188-A1
14700 SDCo 92014 1188-A1
VIA DEL CERRITO
100 ENCT 92024 1147-J7
100 ENCT 92024 1167-J1
VIA DEL CERRO
1200 SDCo 92084 1068-A6
VIA DEL CHARRO
6800 SDCo 92067 1148-G6
VIA DEL CIELO
2900 SDCo 92028 1028-E6
VIA DEL CONQUISTADOR
3600 SD 92117 1248-E5

VIA DEL CORVO
1400 SDCo 92069 1128-B4
VIA DEL COSIRA
10800 SD 92124 1249-J2
VIA DEL GAVILAN
41700 SDCo 92028 997-J3
41900 SDCo 92028 998-A4
VIA DEL LAGO
1700 SDCo 92028 997-J5
VIA DEL LOBO
- SDCo 92003 1068-D4
VIA DEL LUZ
8600 SDCo 92021 1232-D7
VIA DEL MAR
- SD 92130 1208-A2
600 VSTA 92083 1107-E1
VIA DEL MESONERO
1600 SD 92173 1350-F2
VIA DEL MONTE
200 OCN 92054 1086-D5
VIA DEL MONTE LIBANO
3100 SDCo 92084 1088-E6
VIA DEL NORTE
200 SD 92037 1247-F2
200 OCN 92054 1086-D5
VIA DEL ORO
1300 SDCo 92028 1028-A4
5200 OCN 92056 1107-F4
VIA DE LOS CEPILLOS
4400 SDCo 92003 1067-H2
VIA DE LOS ROSALES
16600 SDCo 92067 1168-F6
VIA DEL PARQUE
10500 SDCo 91978 1271-F7
VIA DEL PRADO
2100 SDCo 92084 1088-C1
2600 OCN 92054 1106-G1
VIA DEL RANCHO
3700 OCN 92056 1107-F4
VIA DEL REY
1700 SMCS 92069 1108-B7
VIA DEL RIO
43200 SDCo 92028 998-A4
VIA DEL ROBLES
2300 SDCo 92028 1028-B6
VIA DEL SANTO
29600 SDCo 92084 1068-E6
VIA DEL SAUCE
30000 SDCo 92082 1070-A5
VIA DEL SOL
1400 VSTA 92084 1088-A4
10700 SDCo 91978 1271-F6
VIA DEL SUD
10100 SD 92129 1189-G5
VIA DEL SUR
5200 OCN 92056 1107-F4
VIA DEL TANIDO
1700 SD 92173 1350-E3
VIA DEL TORO
12800 PWY 92064 1170-D4
VIA DEL TORRIE
1800 SDCo 91901 1254-A1
VIA DE LUNA
13200 SDCo 92082 1070-C7
VIA DEL VALEDOR
12900 SD 92129 1189-F5
VIA DEL VENADO
32700 SDCo 92082 1049-E5
VIA DEL VERDE
2500 SDCo 92028 1028-C7
VIA DE MARANATHA
1100 SDCo 92028 1028-A4
VIA DE MAYA
7000 SDCo 92067 1168-F1
VIA DENA LOMA
15800 SDCo 92065 1171-B2
VIA DENISE
3000 CRLB 92008 1106-C6
VIA DE ORO
9900 SDCo 91977 1271-D6
VIA DE PAZ
2900 CRLB 92008 1106-H3
30500 SDCo 92084 1068-E4
VIA DE PLATA
- SMCS 92069 1108-F4
VIA DE SANTA FE
15500 SDCo 92067 1168-D3
VIA DE SAN YSIDRO
100 SD 92173 1350-F5
VIA DE SUENO
17900 SDCo 92067 1148-C7
VIA DE TODOS SANTOS
3200 SDCo 92028 1048-H2
VIA DE VICTORIA
8700 SNTE 92071 1231-B7
VIA DE VISTA
300 SOLB 92075 1167-F7
300 SOLB 92075 1187-F1
VIA DIANA
11600 SDCo 92019 1271-J4
VIA DIANZA
3000 CRLB 92009 1127-J5
VIA DICHA
16300 SDCo 92091 1168-C7
VIA DIEGO
2800 CRLB 92008 1106-C6
12400 SDCo 92040 1232-C6
VIA DIEGO CT
8700 SDCo 92040 1232-B7
VIA DIEGO LN
8800 SDCo 92040 1232-B6
VIA DIEGO TER
8700 SDCo 92040 1232-B6
VIA DIEGUENOS
2000 SDCo 91901 1254-D1
VIA DI FELICITA
1000 ENCT 92024 1148-A5
VIA DOMINIQUE
11100 SD 92124 1250-A1
VIA DONADA
12700 SD 92014 1207-H1
VIA DON BENITO
2000 SD 92037 1247-H1
VIA DONITO
3000 SDCo 91901 1234-E7
3000 SDCo 91901 1254-E1
VIA DORA
8200 SDCo 92067 1148-J6
8200 SDCo 92067 1149-A6
VIA DORADO AV
1200 SMCS 92069 1109-D7
VIA DOS VALLES
6200 SDCo 92067 1168-F5
VIA DULCEA
2200 SDCo 92028 1048-B4
VIA DWIGHT
1300 SDCo 92065 1152-H7

STREET
Block City ZIP Pg-Grid

VIA ECO
2600 CRLB 92008 1106-H3
VIA EL CENTRO
400 OCN 92054 1086-D5
VIA EL DORADO
4200 SDCo 92028 997-H3
VIA ELENA
12100 SDCo 92019 1271-J4
VIA ELISA
1500 ELCJ 92021 1252-A2
1600 SDCo 92021 1252-A2
VIA EMBELESO
16200 SD 92128 1170-A4
VIA EMERADO
2900 CRLB 92009 1147-H3
VIA EMILY
400 OCN 92057 1086-H1
VIA EMPRESA
1200 OCN 92056 1087-B3
VIA ENCANTADA
600 CHV 91913 1311-B5
VIA ENCANTADO
13700 SDCo 92082 1070-E6
VIA ENCANTADORAS
1700 SD 92173 1350-E3
VIA ENCATADORAS
1700 SD 92173 1350-E2
VIA ENCINOS DR
1200 SDCo 92028 1047-H3
VIA ENSENADA
7900 CRLB 92009 1147-J3
VIA ENTRADA
1700 SDCo 92028 1027-J3
VIA ENTRADA DEL LAGO
1500 SDCo 92069 1128-C3
VIA ESCALA
4700 OCN 92056 1087-B4
VIA ESCALADA
- SD 92129 1189-B6
VIA ESCALANTE
1100 CHV 91910 1311-A7
VIA ESCUDA
3800 SDCo 91941 1271-H4
VIA ESMARCA
1800 OCN 92054 1106-G1
VIA ESPANA
1100 SD 92037 1247-G3
VIA ESPARTO
2500 CRLB 92008 1106-H3
VIA ESPERIA
12700 SD 92014 1207-H1
VIA ESPRILLO
16400 SD 92127 1169-H3
VIA ESTRADA
3000 CRLB 92009 1127-J5
6600 SD 92037 1247-H1
VIA ESTRELLADA
1000 SDCo 92028 997-H7
1000 SDCo 92028 1027-J1
VIA EUCALIPTO
12000 SDCo 92019 1272-A3
VIA EXCELENCIA
9600 SD 92126 1209-E6
VIA FELICIA
11900 SDCo 92019 1271-J4
12000 SDCo 92019 1272-A4
VIA FELICIDAD
800 VSTA 92084 1087-J3
1100 SDCo 92029 1149-G2
VIA FELICITA
4400 OCN 92057 1086-J2
4400 OCN 92057 1087-A2
VIA FELINO
12700 SD 92014 1207-H1
VIA FELIZ
1300 SDCo 92028 1027-J3
3400 CRLB 92009 1147-J4
VIA FESTIVO
2700 CRLB 92008 1106-H3
VIA FIRENZE
1200 SDCo 92069 1128-F4
VIA FIRUL
11600 SD 92128 1170-A6
VIA FLORA
700 SMCS 92069 1108-C7
700 SMCS 92069 1128-C1
VIA FLORA RD
700 SMCS 92069 1129-E1
VIA FLORES
3500 SD 92106 1288-A4
VIA FLORESTA
900 SDCo 92028 1027-F1
VIA FORTE
8600 SD 92126 1209-C3
VIA FORTUNA MARFIL
9400 SDCo 91941 1271-C4
VIA FRANCIS
9800 SNTE 92071 1231-C4
VIA FRANCISCA
2300 CRLB 92008 1106-G3
VIA FRESA
2200 SD 92037 1247-J2
VIA FRONTERA
10900 SD 92127 1169-H4
VIA GALACIA
12600 SD 92128 1170-C6
VIA GALAN
15900 SDCo 92091 1168-C7
VIA GATO
900 SMCS 92069 1108-E4
VIA GAVILAN
1800 SDCo 92069 1128-B3
1800 SMCS 92069 1128-B3
VIA GAVIOTA
4500 SDCo 92067 1167-J5
VIA GERMO
11800 SDCo 92019 1271-J4
VIA GIANNELLI
4300 SDCo 92003 1048-E7
4300 SDCo 92003 1068-E1
VIA GIANNITURCO
1700 SDCo 92028 1028-B5
VIA GOLD PAN
- SDCo 92040 1212-A7
VIA GORDO
- SDCo 92026 1129-F2
VIA GOYA
1100 CHV 91910 1311-A6
VIA GRACIA
17800 SD 92128 1150-B7
17800 SD 92128 1170-B1
VIA GRANDA
2200 SDCo 91978 1291-G1
2300 SDCo 91978 1271-G7
VIA GRANDAR
14200 SD 92130 1188-D2
VIA GRANERO
11800 SDCo 92019 1271-J4
VIA GREEN CANYON NORTE
- SDCo 92028 1028-A4
VIA GRENACHE
- ESCN 92029 1129-E4
VIA GRENADA
31400 SDCo 92003 1067-J1
VIA GRIMALDI
12700 SD 92014 1207-H1
VIA GUADALMINA
18200 SD 92128 1150-D7
VIA GUADALUPE
7000 SDCo 92067 1168-G2
VIA GUSTAVO
10700 SD 92129 1189-H2
VIA HACIENDA
1400 CHV 91913 1311-B4
1500 CHV 91902 1311-B4
11800 SDCo 92019 1271-J5
12000 SDCo 92019 1272-A4
VIA HELENA
8600 SDCo 92021 1232-E6
VIA HERMOSA
3000 SDCo 92029 1149-H2
VIA HINTON
4900 CRLB 92008 1107-A7
VIA HOJA
- CRLB 92009 1147-F3
VIA HOLGURA
3900 SD 92130 1188-B6
VIA HONDITA
2200 ESCN 92027 1110-C5
VIA HONDONADA
15000 SD 92129 1169-H7
VIA HUELVA
13700 SD 92129 1189-F4
VIA INCA
4700 SDCo 92028 1048-H1
VIA INSPIRAR
1600 SDCo 92069 1128-C4
VIA IPANEMA
2900 CRLB 92009 1147-H3
VIA ISABEL
11600 SDCo 92019 1271-J4
VIA ISIDRO
1300 OCN 92056 1087-B4
VIA JACQUELINA
11600 SDCo 92019 1271-J4
VIA JAZMIN
- SCLE 92672 1023-B2
VIA JUANITA
800 SMCS 92069 1128-C1
2700 CRLB 92008 1106-H3
VIA JUDY
2600 CRLB 92008 1106-C6
VIA JULITA
300 ENCT 92024 1147-C6
VIA KENORA
9600 SDCo 91977 1271-C6
VIA KINO
8100 SD 92122 1228-E4
VIA LA CANTERA
10000 SD 92129 1189-F5
VIA LA CRESTA
800 SDCo 92021 1252-H2
VIA LACTEA
13800 SD 92129 1189-E3
VIA LA CUESTA
600 CHV 91913 1311-B4
1100 SDCo 92029 1149-H2
VIA LADERA
700 SDCo 92029 1149-H1
1700 SMCS 92069 1108-B7
VIA LADERA RD
1400 SDCo 92028 999-B6
VIA LADETA
2000 SD 92037 1247-H2
VIA LA GARDENIA
12600 PWY 92064 1170-C6
VIA LA GITANO
15300 PWY 92064 1170-C6
VIA LAGO AZUL
16500 SDCo 92067 1168-F6
VIA LA IZQUIERDA
15400 SDCo 92064 1191-B5
VIA LA JOLLA
4400 OCN 92057 1087-B1
VIA LA MANCHA
1500 SDCo 91901 1234-F6
VIA LA MIRADA
12600 SDCo 92082 1070-B4
VIA LAMPARA
2200 SDCo 91978 1271-G7
2300 SDCo 91978 1291-G1
VIA LA ORILLA
2300 SDCo 92028 1028-B7
VIA LA PALOMA
500 CHV 91910 1311-A4
VIA LA PAZ
100 SMCS 92069 1109-C7
100 SMCS 92069 1129-C1
VIA LAPIZ
4900 SD 92122 1228-F5
VIA LA PLAZA
1600 SDCo 92069 1128-C4
VIA LA RANCHITA
1200 SMCS 92069 1109-C7
VIA LARGA VISTA
- SDCo 92003 1048-C7
- SDCo 92003 1068-C1
VIA LARGO
3600 OCN 92056 1107-G4
VIA LAS BRISAS
100 SMCS 92069 1108-H3
VIA LAS CUMBRES
1000 SD 92111 1268-H2
VIA LA SENDA
14900 SOLB 92014 1167-J7
14900 SOLB 92014 1187-J1
VIA LAS FALDAS
3200 SDCo 91935 1272-D7
VIA LAS LENAS
- SD 92129 1189-B5
VIA LAS MAYAS
10800 SD 92129 1189-H2
VIA LAS PALMAS
1900 NATC 91950 1310-B2
1900 SDCo 91950 1310-B2
VIA LAS POSADAS
10700 SD 92129 1189-G2
VIA LAS RAMBLAS
4400 SD 92122 1228-D3
VIA LAS ROSAS
2800 OCN 92054 1106-G2
3000 OCN 92056 1106-G2
VIA LAS TONADAS
1800 SD 92173 1350-E3
VIA LAS VILLAS
3700 OCN 92056 1107-F4
VIA LATINA
12800 SD 92014 1207-H1
VIA LAURA
2000 SDCo 91935 (1314-F1 See Page 1294)
VIA LA VENTA
400 SMCS 92069 1108-D5
VIA LECHUSA
4600 SDCo 92067 1167-J5
VIA LESLIE
9800 SNTE 92071 1231-D3
VIA LIBERTAD
2900 CRLB 92008 1106-H3
VIA LIDO
1700 SMCS 92069 1108-B7
VIA LIMA
1400 SDCo 92028 1027-J3
VIA LINDA
900 SDCo 92029 1129-H7
VIA LINDA DEL SUR
300 ENCT 92024 1147-C5
VIA LINDA VISTA
10700 SDCo 91978 1271-F5
VIA LISA
14000 PWY 92064 1190-G4
VIA LLANO
11100 SD 92129 1169-H7
VIA LOBO
1700 SDCo 92069 1128-F4
VIA LOMA
2600 SDCo 92028 1048-D2
VIA LOMA DR
17500 PWY 92064 1170-D1
VIA LOMA VISTA
1100 ELCJ 92019 1252-B3
2900 SDCo 92029 1149-H2
VIA LOMITA
1000 ESCN 92027 1110-B6
VIA LOPEZ CT
24900 SDCo 92065 1173-G3
VIA LOS ARCOS
300 SMCS 92069 1109-C7
VIA LOS FAROLITOS
16800 SDCo 92067 1168-G6
VIA LOS NARCISOS
10800 SD 92129 1189-G2
VIA LOS NOPALES
- SDCo 92067 1168-D6
VIA LOS PADRES
4000 OCN 92057 1086-H2
VIA LOS SANTOS
2300 CRLB 92008 1106-G3
VIA LUCIA
2200 SD 92037 1247-J2
VIA LUISENO
3100 SDCo 91901 1254-D1
VIA LUJOSA
3600 ESCN 92025 1150-D3
VIA LUNA
- CHV 91910 1311-A7
- SDCo 92067 1148-J6
VIA MADEIRA
- ESCN 92029 1129-F4
VIA MADERA CIR W
16100 SDCo 92091 1168-C7
VIA MADONNA
11200 SNTE 92071 1231-G5
VIA MADRID
5100 OCN 92057 1066-J4
5100 OCN 92057 1067-A4
VIA MADRINA ST
1500 SD 92111 1268-H2
VIA MAGIA
2800 CRLB 92008 1106-H3
VIA MAJELLA
2400 SDCo 92065 1172-C4
VIA MALAGA
400 ENCT 92024 1147-F6
VIA MALAGUENA
5100 OCN 92057 1067-A4
VIA MALLORCA
8000 SD 92037 1228-A4
VIA MANDRIL
3400 SDCo 91902 1310-G2
VIA MANOS
5000 OCN 92057 1067-C7
VIA MAR AZUL
- CHV 91910 1311-A6
VIA MARBELLA
3100 SDCo 91978 1292-B1
3100 SDCo 91978 1272-B7
VIA MARBRISA
1000 ENCT 92024 1147-E6
VIA MARCALA
14000 SD 92130 1188-D3
VIA MARCHENA
15600 SD 92128 1170-B5
VIA MAR DE BALLENAS
- SD 92130 1208-B3
VIA MAR DE DELFINAS
4100 SD 92130 1208-B3
VIA MARGARITA
31200 SDCo 92003 1068-E2
VIA MARGUERITA
1400 OCN 92056 1087-C3
VIA MARIA
100 SMCS 92069 1109-C7
400 OCN 92057 1086-H1
6300 SD 92037 1247-E2
VIA MARIA ELENA
30000 SDCo 92003 1068-C2
VIA MARIANA
- CHV 91910 1311-A6
VIA MARIN
3200 SD 92037 1228-A5
VIA MARINERO
6800 CRLB 92009 1128-A5
VIA MARIPOSA
3000 CRLB 92009 1128-A5
6800 SDCo 92003 1068-E2
VIA MARIPOSA CT
31200 SDCo 92003 1068-E2
VIA MARIPOSA NORTE
6800 SDCo 92003 1068-F2
VIA MARIPOSA SUR
6900 SDCo 92003 1068-E2
VIA MARK
13300 PWY 92064 1190-G4
VIA MARMOL
10000 SDCo 92026 1109-E1
VIA MARTA
4900 CRLB 92008 1107-A7
VIA MAR VALLE
2100 SD 92014 1187-G7
VIA MASADA
2600 CRLB 92008 1106-H4
VIA MATARO
- ESCN 92029 1129-E4
VIA MAVIS
9900 SNTE 92071 1231-D4
VIA MAXIMO
- CRLB 92009 1127-J4
- CRLB 92009 1128-A4
VIA MEDALLA
4500 SD 92122 1228-D3
VIA MEDANOS
11700 SD 92128 1170-A5
VIA MEDIA
2200 SD 92037 1247-J2
VIA MERANO
2500 SD 92014 1207-H1
VIA MERCADO
3600 SDCo 91941 1271-G5
VIA MERDE
2700 CRLB 92008 1106-C6
VIA MERIDA
11000 SDCo 91941 1271-G5
VIA METATES
300 OCN 92057 1067-B7
VIA MICA
10700 SDCo 91978 1271-F6
VIA MILANO
12100 SD 92128 1190-B1
VIA MIL CUMBRES
900 SOLB 92075 1167-H6
VIA MILPAS
2500 SDCo 92028 998-B6
VIA MINDANAO
5100 OCN 92057 1066-J4
5100 OCN 92057 1067-A4
VIA MIRADOR
- CRLB 92009 1147-J3
VIA MIRALESTE
1000 CHV 91910 1311-A7
VIA MOLENA
1000 ENCT 92024 1147-F6
VIA MOLINERO
15200 PWY 92064 1170-G7
VIA MONADA
1100 CHV 91910 1311-B7
VIA MONALEX
14200 SDCo 92067 1168-G2
VIA MONCLOVA
4300 SD 92122 1228-E4
VIA MONSERATE
1500 SDCo 92028 1047-J5
1600 SDCo 92028 1048-B5
VIA MONTALVO
400 ENCT 92024 1147-F6
VIA MONTANETA
3100 ESCN 92029 1150-A2
VIA MONTANOSA
300 ENCT 92024 1147-F6
VIA MONTE ALEGRE
400 SDCo 92003 1067-F1
VIA MONTECITO
1100 ENCT 92024 1147-F6
VIA MONTE CLARO
12600 PWY 92064 1170-C6
VIA MONTELLANO
5700 SDCo 92003 1067-H2
VIA MONTEREY
16200 SDCo 92091 1168-D6
VIA MONTORO
1100 ENCT 92024 1147-F6
VIA MONZON
9800 SD 92129 1189-F3
VIA MORELLA
100 ENCT 92024 1147-F6
VIA MOURA
12800 SD 92128 1150-D7
VIA MUNERA
2200 SD 92037 1247-J1
VIAN RD
13600 PWY 92064 1190-F2
VIA NACIONAL
400 SD 92173 1350-G5
VIA NANCITA
300 ENCT 92024 1147-C6
VIA NAPOLI
1500 SDCo 92028 997-H4
VIA NARANJA
2500 CRLB 92008 1106-H3
VIA NARANJAL
6200 SDCo 92067 1148-D6
VIA NASCA
12700 SD 92128 1150-D6
VIA NAVAJO
1200 SDCo 92069 1128-B4
VIANDA CT
6800 CRLB 92009 1127-G6
VIANE WY
4800 SD 92110 1268-F1
VIA NESTORE
12800 SD 92014 1207-H1
VIA NICOLE
11600 SDCo 92019 1271-J4
VIA NIEVE
12700 SD 92130 1188-B6
VIA NINA
2100 SD 92037 1247-J2
9900 SNTE 92071 1231-D4
VIA NOMENTANA
- CHV 91910 1310-A4
VIA NORTE
1100 SDCo 92029 1149-H2
VIA OAK GROVE LN
27900 SDCo 92066 410-A8
VIA OCIOSO
1600 SDCo 92069 1128-C3
VIA OESTE DR
2600 SDCo 92028 1028-E7
VIA OPUNTIA
- CRLB 92009 1147-G2
VIA ORANGE WY
2700 SDCo 91978 1271-F7
VIA ORDAZ
10900 SD 92129 1189-H2
VIA ORILLIA
- CRLB 92009 1148-A4
VIA ORO VERDE
200 SDCo 92028 1027-G4
VIA OSTIONES
7000 CRLB 92009 1127-G6
VIA OSTRA
6500 CRLB 92009 1127-J4
VIA OSUNA
3800 SDCo 92091 1168-C7
VIA OTANO
1500 OCN 92056 1087-B4
VIA PACIFICA
16200 SDCo 92091 1168-D7
VIA PADILLA
7000 CRLB 92009 1127-G6
VIA PAJARO
2800 CRLB 92008 1106-H3
VIA PALABRA
4500 SD 92124 1250-A2
VIA PALACIO
200 ENCT 92024 1147-F6
VIA PALMA
3700 SDCo 91941 1271-G5
VIA PALOMA
1500 SDCo 92026 1109-E7
11600 SDCo 92019 1272-A4
VIA PALOMAR
700 SMCS 92069 1108-B7
700 SMCS 92069 1128-C1
VIA PALO VERDE LAGO
- SDCo 91901 1254-F2
VIA PAMELA
18900 SDCo 91935 (1314-F2 See Page 1294)
VIA PANACEA
- SD 92129 1189-B5
VIA PANORAMA
40500 SDCo 92028 997-J3
40500 SDCo 92028 998-A3
VIA PAPEETE
3000 SD 92154 1330-D7
VIA PAPEL
4900 SD 92122 1228-G6
VIA PARADISO
3700 SDCo 92084 1088-F7
VIA PARANZA
6500 CRLB 92009 1127-J4
VIA PARMA
11000 SD 92129 1189-H3
VIA PASAR
9800 SD 92126 1209-E5
VIA PASATIEMPO
3800 SDCo 92091 1168-C7
VIA PASEAR
4300 SD 92122 1228-D3
VIA PATO
15900 SDCo 92067 1168-A5
VIA PATRICIO
10800 SDCo 92082 1049-F3
VIA PATRON
- CRLB 92009 1127-J4
VIA PAUMA
5200 OCN 92057 1067-C7
VIA PAVON
- SMCS 92069 1108-F4
VIA PEDRERA
2200 SD 92037 1247-J1
VIA PEDRO
1500 VSTA 92084 1088-B5
VIA PELICANO
200 OCN 92057 1086-J3
2300 CRLB 92009 1127-G6
VIA PENASCO
16400 SDCo 92065 1171-H3
VIA PENOLES
15400 SD 92128 1170-A6
VIA PEPITA
2900 CRLB 92009 1147-H4
VIA PEQUINITO
10800 SD 92129 1189-G2
VIA PEREZA
9500 SD 92129 1189-E4
VIA PERLITA
3300 SMCS 92069 1108-D6
VIA PESCADO
3200 CRLB 92008 1106-H4
VIA PICANTE
3500 SDCo 91941 1271-G5
VIA PIEDRA
28800 SDCo 92082 1070-C7
28800 SDCo 92082 1090-C1
VIA PISA
2500 SD 92014 1207-H1
VIA PLATILLO
2300 CRLB 92009 1127-G7
VIA PLATO
2700 CRLB 92008 1106-H3
VIA PLAYA DE CORTES
11300 SD 92124 1230-A7
VIA PLAYA LOS SANTOS
5000 SD 92124 1230-A7
VIA PLAZA
- VSTA 92083 1107-C2
VIA POCO
2500 ENCT 92007 1167-F4
VIA PORTOFINO
1200 SDCo 92069 1128-F4
VIA PORTOLA
700 SMCS 92069 1108-C7
700 SMCS 92069 1128-C1
5100 OCN 92057 1067-B7
VIA PORTOVECCHIO
1200 SDCo 92069 1128-B3
VIA POSADA
2800 SD 92037 1227-J5
2900 SD 92037 1228-A5
VIA POSADA DEL NORTE
6000 SDCo 92067 1168-G4
VIA PRADO
1000 SDCo 92028 1027-J4
VIA PRAVIA
2200 SD 92037 1247-J1
VIA PRECIPICIO
4400 SD 92122 1228-D3
VIA PREMIO
3100 CRLB 92008 1106-H3
VIA PRIMERO
1800 OCN 92056 1087-C5
VIA PRIVADA
1100 SDCo 92029 1149-H3
VIA PROMESA
11400 SD 92124 1250-A2
VIA PUERTA
- CRLB 92009 1127-J3
VIA PUERTA DEL SOL
5400 SDCo 92003 1047-H7
5400 SDCo 92003 1067-G1
30000 OCN 92003 1067-G4
30000 OCN 92057 1067-G4
VIA QUINCELEAGUAS
39100 SDCo 92028 999-D3
VIA QUINTO
1800 OCN 92056 1087-C5
VIAR AV
7200 SD 92120 1250-C5
VIA RAFAEL
1200 SDCo 92069 1128-B4
VIA RAMON
1200 SDCo 92029 1149-G2
VIA RANCHEROS
2500 SDCo 92028 1048-C1
2600 SDCo 92028 1028-B7
VIA RANCHEROS WY
2600 SDCo 92028 1048-C1
VIA RANCHITOS
39900 SDCo 92028 997-H3
VIA RANCHO
200 SCLE 92672 1023-B1
VIA RANCHO LN
10100 SDCo 92029 1129-F7
10100 SDCo 92029 1149-F1
VIA RANCHO PKWY
- SD 92027 1130-G7
100 ESCN 92029 1150-A2
100 ESCN 92025 1150-C2
200 ESCN 92029 1149-G1
500 SDCo 92029 1149-G1
1900 SDCo 92029 1129-E7
2900 SD 92025 1130-G7
2900 SD 92025 1150-F1
2900 SDCo 92025 1130-G7
5500 SDCo 92025 1150-F1
14400 SDCo 92027 1130-G7
VIA RANCHO RD
4000 OCN 92057 1086-J4
4300 OCN 92057 1087-A4
VIA RANCHO CIELO
8300 SDCo 92067 1149-B5
VIA RANCHO DEL LAGO
100 SDCo 92003 1067-G2
VIA RANCHO DOS NINOS
2100 SDCo 92065 1172-E3
VIA RANCHO PACIFICA
900 SDCo 92084 1088-G7
VIA RANCHO SAN DIEGO
11300 SDCo 92019 1272-A5
VIA REALZAR
4400 SD 92122 1228-D3
VIA REATA
- VSTA 92083 1107-H2
VIA RECANTO
17400 SDCo 92067 1168-B2
VIA REGLA
6000 SD 92122 1228-G6
VIA REPOSO
3800 SDCo 92091 1168-C7
VIA RIALTO
2300 SD 92037 1227-H6
VIA RIBERA
3200 ESCN 92029 1150-A2
VIA RICARDO
2800 CRLB 92008 1106-H3
VIA RIMINI
13700 SD 92129 1189-H3
VIA RIO
400 OCN 92057 1086-H1
VIA RISA
1500 SDCo 92069 1128-C4
VIA RITA
9800 SNTE 92071 1231-D3
VIA ROBERTO
2700 CRLB 92008 1106-C6
VIA ROBLAR CT
2900 SDCo 92019 1272-D6
VIA ROBLES
2100 OCN 92054 1106-G1
VIA ROJO
2500 CRLB 92008 1106-H3
VIA ROMAYA
3800 NATC 91950 1310-E3
VIA ROMAZA
3000 CRLB 92009 1147-H3
VIA RONDA
1400 SMCS 92069 1109-D7
VIA ROSA
3900 SMCS 92069 1128-C1
VIA ROSARITA
3000 CRLB 92008 1106-H3
VIA ROSE MARIE LN
900 SDCo 92028 1027-H4
VIA ROSWITHA
18200 SDCo 92067 1148-D6
VIA ROTA
18000 SD 92128 1150-D7
VIA SABINAS
3000 CRLB 92008 1106-C6
VIA SALARIA
300 CHV 91910 1310-A4
VIA SALERNO
- SMCS 92069 1129-F1
1400 SDCo 92026 1129-F1
VIA SALVADOR
15600 SDCo 92082 1071-A7
VIA SAN ALBERTO
4100 SDCo 92028 1048-H4
VIA SAN ARRONO
4100 SDCo 92028 1048-H4
VIA SAN ARTURO
4100 SDCo 92028 1048-H4
VIA SAN BLAS
10700 SD 92126 1209-D3
VIA SAN CLEMENTE
7900 CRLB 92009 1147-J3
VIA SAN JACINTO
1200 SDCo 92069 1128-B4
VIA SAN JUAN
4100 SDCo 92028 1048-H4
VIA SAN LORENO
12100 SD 92128 1190-B2
VIA SAN MANZANIA
4100 SDCo 92028 1048-H4
VIA SAN MARCO
10800 SD 92129 1189-H3
VIA SAN ROSARITO
4000 SDCo 92028 1048-G4
VIA SAN SABA
8000 SD 92122 1228-E4
VIA SANSAL
15300 PWY 92064 1170-C6
VIA SANTA BEATRICE
4000 SDCo 92028 1048-G4
VIA SANTA CALIFORNIA
4000 SDCo 92028 1048-G4
VIA SANTA CRUZ
600 VSTA 92083 1107-E1
VIA SANTA DOLORES
4000 SDCo 92028 1048-H4
VIA SANTA FELICE
4000 SDCo 92028 1048-H4
VIA SANTALINA
500 SMCS 92069 1108-D4
VIA SANTA PAULO
600 VSTA 92083 1107-E1
VIA SAN THOMAS
4100 SDCo 92028 1048-H4
VIA SANTIAGO
600 VSTA 92083 1107-E1
3000 CRLB 92009 1127-J5
VIA SARASAN
200 ENCT 92024 1147-F6
VIA SAUCE VEREDA
30000 SDCo 92082 1070-A5
VIA SAVOY
400 ENCT 92024 1147-F6
VIA SCOTT
1900 ESCN 92026 1109-F6
1900 SDCo 92026 1109-F6
VIA SEFTON
11700 SDCo 92019 1271-J4
VIA SEGOVIA
1900 SD 92037 1247-H1
VIA SEGUNDO
2300 SD 92173 1350-F4
VIA SELMA
11900 SDCo 92019 1271-J4
VIA SENDERO
1200 SDCo 92029 1149-G2
VIA SENDERO VISTA
1200 SDCo 92029 1149-G2
VIA SEPULVEDA
4400 SD 92122 1228-E4
VIA SERENA
4300 SDCo 92003 1067-H2
13600 PWY 92064 1170-E5
VIA SERENIDAD
- SDCo 92065 1171-F1
VIA SERRA
300 OCN 92057 1086-H2
4700 SDCo 92028 1048-G2
VIA SERRANO
12100 SDCo 92019 1272-A4
VIA SEVILLE
400 SMCS 92069 1108-C7
400 SMCS 92069 1128-C1
5100 OCN 92056 1107-F4
VIA SHAWNTY
19600 SDCo 91935 (1314-H2 See Page 1294)
VIA SIENA
2300 SD 92037 1227-H6
VIA SILVA
3600 OCN 92056 1107-G4
VIA SIMPATIA
- CRLB 92009 1127-J3
VIA SIMPATICO
16100 SDCo 92091 1168-C7
VIA SINALDA
2000 SD 92037 1247-H2
VIA SINSONTE
1800 SDCo 92027 1130-F3
VIA SINUOSO
1000 CHV 91910 1311-A7
VIA SISTINA
300 CHV 91910 1310-A4
VIA SOBRADO
12800 SD 92128 1150-C7
VIA SOBRETTE
3000 CRLB 92008 1106-H3
VIA SOLANA
2900 SDCo 92029 1149-G2
VIA SOLARO
100 ENCT 92024 1147-F6
VIA SOL ARRIBA
3400 SDCo 92025 1150-E2
VIA SOLEDAD
800 VSTA 92084 1087-J3
VIA SOMBRA
3100 CRLB 92008 1106-H3
VIA SOMBRAS
12700 PWY 92064 1170-C6
VIA SONOMA
8300 SD 92037 1228-B4
VIA SONORA
2100 OCN 92054 1106-G1
VIA SOPLADOR
300 SDCo 92028 1027-J3
VIA SORPRESA
4300 SD 92124 1249-J2
VIA STEPHEN
13300 PWY 92064 1190-G4
VIA SUBRIA
2200 SDCo 92084 1088-D1
VIA SUENA
13000 SDCo 92082 1070-C7
VIA SUSPIRO
2800 SD 92173 1350-D2
VIA TABARA
2200 SD 92037 1247-J1
VIA TALA
4700 SDCo 92028 1048-G2
VIA TALAVERA
5200 SD 92130 1188-D3
VIA TAPIA
100 SDCo 91977 1291-B5
VIA TAQUITA
200 SDCo 92065 1152-J5
VIA TARIFA
18000 SD 92128 1150-D7
VIA TAVIRA
200 ENCT 92024 1147-F6
VIA TAVITO
11600 SD 92128 1170-A6
VIA TAZON
16900 SD 92127 1169-J2
VIA TECA
7800 CRLB 92009 1147-H2
VIA TEMPRANO
11000 SD 92124 1250-A2
VIA TERAMO
700 SDCo 92026 1129-F2
VIA TERCERO
2300 SD 92173 1350-E4
4200 OCN 92056 1087-C5
VIA TERCETO
12700 SD 92130 1188-B6
VIA TERECINA
- CHV 91910 1311-A6
VIA TERESA
1100 SMCS 92069 1109-C7
VIA TERRASSA
1300 ENCT 92024 1147-F7
VIA TESORO
2200 SDCo 91901 1254-C2
VIA THERESA
11200 SNTE 92071 1231-G5
VIA TIEMPO
2000 ENCT 92007 1167-F3
N VIA TIERRA
200 ENCT 92024 1147-E6
VIA TIMOTEO
10800 SDCo 91978 1271-G5
VIA TIZON
5200 OCN 92057 1067-C7
VIA TOMAS
10700 SD 92129 1189-H3
VIA TONALA
3200 CRLB 92008 1106-C6
VIA TONGA
3100 SD 92154 1330-E7

STREET
Block City ZIP Pg-Grid

VIA TONGA CT
800 SD 92154 1330-D7
VIA TOPACIO
2800 CRLB 92008 1106-H3
VIA TORE
200 SDCo 92083 1108-A3
VIA TORINA
2500 SD 92014 1207-H1
VIA TORTOLA
2200 SDCo 91978 1271-G7
2200 SDCo 91978 1291-G1
VIA TOSCANA
- CHV 91910 1311-A6
VIA TRANQUILO
3900 SD 92122 1228-C4
VIA TRATO
- CRLB 92009 1127-J3
VIA TRES VISTA
13600 SD 92129 1189-E3
VIA TRIESTE
1100 CHV 91911 1330-F2
VIA TRUENO
2000 SDCo 91901 1254-B2
VIA TULIPAN
2700 CRLB 92008 1106-H3
VIA ULTIMO
400 ENCT 92024 1147-F6
VIA UNIDOS
1000 SDCo 92028 1027-H4
VIA URNER WY
8000 SDCo 92003 1068-H1
8100 SDCo 92003 1048-J7
VIA VALARTA
5100 SD 92124 1230-A7
5200 SD 92124 1250-A1
VIA VALENCIA
30200 SDCo 92082 1070-G5
VIA VALENTE
1400 SDCo 92029 1149-G2
VIA VALESCO
3100 ESCN 92029 1150-A2
VIA VALLE VERDE
3700 SDCo 92091 1168-C7
VIA VALLE VISTA
1100 SDCo 92029 1149-H3
VIA VALVERDE
6800 SD 92037 1247-G1
VIA VASTAGO
1000 VSTA 92083 1087-E6
VIA VELASQUEZ
7000 CRLB 92009 1127-G6
VIA VENETO
- CHV 91910 1310-A4
2000 ESCN 92027 1110-C7
VIA VENTADA
3500 SDCo 92029 1149-H3
VIA VENUSTO
1400 OCN 92056 1087-C3
VIA VERA
2600 CRLB 92008 1106-C6
32000 SDCo 92003 1048-E7
VIA VERA CRUZ
100 SMCS 92069 1108-E7
100 SMCS 92069 1128-E1
VIA VERANO
6800 CRLB 92009 1128-A5
VIA VERDE
- CHV 91910 1311-A6
2200 SDCo 92019 1252-D5
VIA VIAJERA
16000 SDCo 92091 1168-C7
VIA VIDA NUEVA
1300 SDCo 92026 1109-E6
VIA VIEJAS
2600 SDCo 91901 1254-C1
VIA VIEJAS OESTE
2500 SDCo 91901 1254-B2
VIA VIEJO
13600 SD 92130 1188-A4
VIA VIENTO
3800 SDCo 92028 1028-F7
VIA VIENTO SUAVE
1200 SDCo 92069 1128-F4
VIA VIESTA
2400 SD 92037 1227-H6
VIA VILLEGAS
2300 CRLB 92009 1127-G7
VIA VILLENA
200 ENCT 92024 1147-F6
VIA VISO
28000 SDCo 92082 1091-C3
VIA VISTA
1200 SDCo 92028 1028-C4
VIA VISTA CANADA
6500 SDCo 92067 1168-F6
VIA VISTA DEL RIO
3000 SDCo 92084 1067-H7
VIA VISTA GRANDE
19600 SDCo 92065 1151-G2
VIA VISTA MEJOR
31400 SDCo 92082 1070-A2
VIA VISTA ORIENTE
6000 SDCo 92067 1168-D3
VIA VONNIE
2400 SDCo 92028 1048-C2
VIA VUELTA
3700 SDCo 92091 1168-C7
VIA WAKEFIELD
9900 SNTE 92071 1231-D4
VIA YUHA
5100 OCN 92057 1067-C7
VIA ZAMORA
3200 ESCN 92029 1150-A2
VIA ZANCAS
1000 SDCo 92028 998-B7
1000 SDCo 92028 1028-B1
VIA ZAPADOR
8700 SNTE 92071 1231-C7
VIA ZAPATA
11900 SDCo 92019 1271-J4
11900 SDCo 92019 1272-A4
VIA ZARA
1100 SDCo 92028 1028-E4
VIA ZARA CT
3300 SDCo 92028 1028-D4
VIA ZURITA
5900 SD 92037 1247-H2
VICENTE MEADOW DR
15500 SDCo 92065 1173-A5
VICENTE VIEW DR
12700 SDCo 92040 1212-B3
VICEROY DR
18100 SD 92128 1150-B7
VICKERS RD
2400 SDCo 92028 997-A1
VICKERS ST
7700 SD 92111 1249-B1
VICKI PL
500 ESCN 92026 1109-J7
500 ESCN 92026 1129-J1
VICKIE DR
5100 SD 92109 1247-J4
VICKSBURG DR
1400 ELCJ 92021 1252-A3
VICTOR AV
1000 ELCJ 92021 1251-G3
1100 SDCo 92021 1251-G3
VICTORIA AV
2700 CRLB 92008 1106-J4
2700 CRLB 92008 1107-A4
VICTORIA CIR
2300 SDCo 91901 1234-B5
VICTORIA CT
7500 SD 92114 1290-G2
VICTORIA DR
- ELCJ 92021 1251-H5
E VICTORIA DR
3100 SDCo 91901 1234-D5
N VICTORIA DR
2700 SDCo 91901 1234-C4
W VICTORIA DR
1900 SDCo 91901 1234-B5
VICTORIA GN
1400 ESCN 92025 1150-E3
VICTORIA LN
3000 SDCo 91901 1234-D6
4200 SDCo 92028 998-F7
4200 SDCo 92028 1028-G1
VICTORIA PL
400 VSTA 92084 1087-H4
2800 SDCo 91901 1234-C5
VICTORIA WY
- OCN 92057 1086-H3
- SMCS 92069 1108-J3
- SMCS 92069 1109-A3
30800 SDCo 92026 1069-C2
VICTORIA BAY CT
5600 SD 92105 1290-B1
VICTORIA ESTATES LN
14400 PWY 92064 1190-E1
VICTORIA HEIGHTS PL
3500 SDCo 91901 1234-C5
VICTORIA KNOLLS CT
500 SDCo 91901 1234-C4
VICTORIA KNOLLS DR
500 SDCo 91901 1234-C4
VICTORIA MEADOWS DR
2300 SDCo 91901 1234-B5
VICTORIA PARK TER
1800 SDCo 91901 1233-J5
1900 SDCo 91901 1234-A5
VICTORY DR
1900 SDCo 92084 1108-D3
VICTORY RD
8400 LMSA 91941 1270-J2
VIDAS CIR
1100 SDCo 92026 1109-E7
VIEJAS BLVD
24600 SDCo 91916 1236-A3
VIEJAS RD
- SDCo 91901 1234-J2
- SDCo 91901 1235-A2
VIEJAS CREEK LN
4000 SDCo 91901 1234-F7
VIEJAS CREEK TR
1400 SDCo 91901 1234-F7
VIEJAS GRADE
- SDCo 91901 1235-A2
10300 SDCo 91916 1235-G1
VIEJAS GRADE RD
- SDCo 91901 1234-H4
- SDCo 91901 1235-A3
23100 SDCo 91916 1235-A3
23300 SDCo 91916 1236-A3
VIEJAS VIEW LN
1300 SDCo 91901 1235-A5
VIEJAS VIEW PL
2800 SDCo 91901 1234-C7
VIEJO CASTILLA WY
7500 CRLB 92009 1147-G1
VIENNA ST
3400 SD 92104 1289-F1
VIENTO FUERTE WY
9300 SDCo 91941 1271-B4
VIENTO VALLE
20700 SDCo 92025 1130-F7
VIETTA TER
11600 SD 92126 1208-J1
VIEW PL
4200 SD 92115 1270-C4
VIEW ST
1700 ESCN 92027 1130-C1
2200 OCN 92054 1106-E1
E VIEW ST
100 SDCo 92028 1027-F2
W VIEW ST
100 SDCo 92028 1027-F2
VIEW WY
1600 ELCJ 92020 1251-C5
VIEWCREST CT
10000 SDCo 91977 1271-E6
VIEWCREST DR
7100 SD 92114 1290-F2
VIEW CREST GN
2100 ESCN 92026 1109-C4
VIEWMONT DR
1100 SDCo 92027 1130-C4
VIEWPOINT CT
6300 SD 92139 1290-E7
6300 SD 92139 1310-E1
VIEWPOINT DR
700 SMCS 92069 1128-B2
6200 SD 92139 1310-E1
VIEWPOINT WY
3400 OCN 92056 1106-H1
VIEW POINTE AV
1300 ESCN 92027 1110-A7
VIEW POINTE RW
6300 SD 92128 1170-A5
VIEWRIDGE AV
4300 SD 92123 1249-E2
VIEWRIDGE CT
5200 SD 92123 1249-E1
VIEWRIDGE PL
2300 ESCN 92026 1109-F4
VIEWRIDGE WY
5000 OCN 92056 1107-E3
VIEWSIDE LN
9600 SDCo 92021 1233-C3
VIEW VERDE
3700 SDCo 91902 1310-J2
VIGILANT WY
4800 CRLB 92008 1106-H7
VIGILANTE RD
12400 SDCo 92040 1211-H4
VIGO DR
6600 LMSA 91941 1270-E4
6600 SD 92115 1270-E4
VIKING LN
900 SMCS 92069 1109-A5
VIKING PL
1100 ESCN 92027 1130-E2
VIKING WY
800 SMCS 92069 1109-A5
1800 SD 92037 1227-G6
VIKING GROVE LN
15600 SDCo 92082 1071-A6
VILETTA DR
900 SDCo 92027 1130-C4
VILLA AV
- ImCo 92243 6499-H5
- ELCN 92243 6499-E5
- ELCN 92243 6500-A4
- ImCo 92243 6500-A4
VILLA LN
- ImCo 92243 6500-B4
1600 ELCN 92243 6499-F5
VILLA TER
3400 SD 92104 1269-D6
VILLA ADOLEE
3000 SDCo 91978 1271-F7
VILLA BLANCA CT
400 ENCT 92024 1147-D7
VILLA BONITA
10500 SDCo 91978 1271-F6
VILLA CARDIFF DR
1400 ENCT 92007 1167-E2
VILLA COLINA
3100 SDCo 91978 1271-F6
VILLA CREST DR
1500 ELCJ 92021 1252-B2
VILLA DEL DIOS GN
1800 ESCN 92029 1129-F6
VILLA ESPANA
3100 SDCo 91978 1271-F6
VILLA FLORES
2100 ESCN 92029 1129-E6
VILLAGE CIR
- SDCo 91901 1234-A6
2000 CRLB 92008 1106-E6
VILLAGE DR
400 CHV 91911 1330-C3
400 CRLB 92008 1106-E6
VILLAGE PL
1700 SD 92101 1269-C7
2500 SD 92101 1289-C1
VILLAGE RD
100 ESCN 92026 1109-G4
VILLAGE RUN N
200 ENCT 92024 1147-G6
VILLAGE WY
2400 OCN 92054 1086-D7
VILLAGE CENTER DR
400 ENCT 92024 1147-H5
VILLAGE GLEN DR
9000 SD 92123 1249-D4
VILLAGE GREEN RD
100 ENCT 92024 1147-H6
VILLAGE PARK WY
1700 ENCT 92024 1147-H7
VILLAGE PINE DR
2800 SD 92173 1350-D2
VILLAGE PINE WY
1500 SD 92173 1350-C2
VILLAGE RIDGE RD
11300 SD 92131 1189-J7
VILLAGE SQUARE DR
100 ENCT 92024 1147-G7
VILLAGE VIEW PL
500 SDCo 92028 1027-G3
VILLAGE VIEW RD
1200 ENCT 92024 1147-H4
VILLAGE WOOD RD
1900 ENCT 92024 1147-H7
VILLA GLEN LN
1300 ELCJ 92021 1252-A3
VILLA HERMOSA CT
100 SOLB 92075 1167-D6
VILLA LA JOLLA DR
8500 SD 92037 1228-A4
9000 SD 92093 1228-A4
9000 SD 92161 1228-A4
VILLA MONTE
13200 SDCo 92040 1232-C2
VILLAMOURA DR
17700 PWY 92064 1170-E1
VILLAMOURA WY
13600 PWY 92064 1170-F1
VILLANITAS RD
2100 ENCT 92024 1147-J6
VILLA NORTE
3100 SD 92037 1228-A3
VILLANOVA AV
3500 SD 92122 1228-D5
VILLARICA WY
5700 SD 92124 1229-J7
VILLAS CT
4600 CHV 91902 1310-H3
VILLAS DR
4500 CHV 91902 1310-H3
5400 SDCo 92003 1068-B1
VILLA SIERRA LN
15500 SDCo 92082 1070-J4
15500 SDCo 92082 1071-A4
VILLA SIERRA RD
15100 SDCo 92082 1070-J3
15500 SDCo 92082 1071-A5
VILLA SONOMA
2100 ESCN 92029 1129-F6
VILLA TEMPRA DR
1300 CHV 91911 1330-D3
VILLA VERDE RD
1900 ESCN 92029 1129-G7
VILLA VIEW LN
1300 ELCJ 92021 1252-A2
VILLA ZAPATA
2300 SDCo 91901 1253-J2
VINARUZ PL
16900 SD 92128 1170-C3
VINCA WY
1300 SD 92114 1290-C5
VINCENTE WY
400 SD 92037 1247-F2
VINCETTA CT
5400 LMSA 91942 1270-H1
VINCETTA DR
8100 LMSA 91942 1270-H1
VINE
12500 SD 92130 1188-G7
VINE CIR
1900 ELCN 92243 6499-F7
2000 VSTA 92084 1088-C5
VINE DR
29300 SDCo 91906 (1297-E5
See Page 1296)
VINE LN
9700 SDCo 92029 1149-D3
VINE ST
100 SDCo 92028 1027-F2
400 ELCN 92243 6499-E7
500 OCN 92054 1106-C1
600 ESCN 92025 1129-H4
1400 SD 92103 1268-H7
1700 SD 92101 1268-H7
9600 SDCo 92040 1232-B2
S VINE ST
100 SDCo 92028 1027-F3
VINEWOOD DR
3500 SDCo 92036 1156-E2
VINEWOOD ST
100 ESCN 92029 1129-E3
S VINEWOOD ST
200 ESCN 92029 1129-E3
VINEYARD AV
300 ESCN 92029 1129-D2
1300 VSTA 92083 1107-H3
VINEYARD LN
17700 PWY 92064 1170-E1
VINEYARD RD
300 SMCS 92069 1108-J6
700 SMCS 92069 1109-A5
VINEYARD WY
- SDCo 91901 1234-A6
VINLEY PL
5700 SD 92120 1250-D7
VINTAGE DR
14600 SD 92129 1189-C1
VINTAGE PL
2100 ESCN 92027 1110-B4
VINTAGE POINT DR
800 SMCS 92078 1129-A3
VINTER WY
13200 PWY 92064 1170-E2
VINYARD ST
4500 OCN 92057 1066-H7
VIOLA ST
1200 SD 92110 1268-E2
VIOLET CT
800 CRLB 92009 1127-A6
VIOLET DR
13600 PWY 92064 1190-F3
VIOLET GN
3800 ESCN 92025 1150-C3
VIOLET RDG
3200 ENCT 92024 1148-C5
VIOLET ST
2500 SD 92105 1269-H7
2500 SD 92105 1289-H1
3800 LMSA 91941 1270-F5
VIPER WY
- VSTA 92083 1108-B6
10500 SD 92121 1208-H4
VIREO CT
6600 CRLB 92009 1127-B5
VIREO ST
1700 SDCo 92069 1128-A4
VIRGINIA AV
- SD 92173 1350-H5
4500 SD 92115 1270-D3
VIRGINIA CT
2100 ELCJ 92020 1251-B5
VIRGINIA DR
2600 NATC 91950 1310-A3
VIRGINIA LN
900 ESCN 92027 1110-C6
1600 ImCo 92243 6559-H3
VIRGINIA PL
700 SMCS 92069 1108-C7
VIRGINIA WY
1000 SD 92037 1227-F6
VIRGINIAN LN
9200 SDCo 91941 1271-B1
VIRGIN ISLANDS RD
6800 SDCo 92003 1068-E2
VIRGO PL
11000 SD 92126 1209-C2
E VIRGO RD
3200 SD 92105 1270-B6
W VIRGO RD
3100 SD 92105 1270-B6
VISALIA CT
1200 CHV 91913 1331-B1
VISALIA RW
1700 CORD 92118 1288-J7
2000 CORD 92118 1289-A7
VISCAYA WY
3200 OCN 92056 1106-J1
VISION DR
4300 SD 92121 1228-D1
VISPERA PL
6500 CRLB 92009 1127-G5
VISTA AV
300 ESCN 92026 1109-H5
400 SDCo 92026 1109-H5
3100 LMGR 91945 1270-F6
3600 LMSA 91941 1270-F5
VISTA DR
- SD 92102 1289-G4
- SDCo 92036 1136-D7
- SDCo 91910 1310-D6
8000 LMSA 91941 1270-H3
9200 SDCo 91977 1271-B6
VISTA LN
3200 SD 92173 1350-E3
4700 SD 92116 1269-H3
VISTA PL
400 CHV 91910 1310-D6
900 CORD 92118 1308-J1
4900 SD 92116 1269-D3
VISTA ST
4500 SD 92116 1269-H3
VISTA TER
10900 SDCo 91941 1271-G4
VISTA WY
- ESCN 92026 1109-G7
- CHV 91910 1310-C4
100 SDCo 92021 1252-H4
100 OCN 92054 1106-F2
800 CHV 91911 1330-D1
1700 ELCJ 92019 1252-C7
1700 SDCo 92019 1252-C7
2700 SDCo 91950 1310-B3
3000 OCN 92056 1106-H2
3600 OCN 92056 1107-B2
4200 SDCo 91941 1271-E3
E VISTA WY Rt#-S13
100 VSTA 92084 1087-J5
1100 VSTA 92084 1088-A2
2100 SDCo 92084 1088-A2
2600 SDCo 92084 1067-J6
2600 SDCo 92084 1068-A7
S VISTA WY
2200 CRLB 92054 1106-G2
2200 OCN 92054 1106-G2
W VISTA WY
100 VSTA 92083 1107-C2
100 VSTA 92083 1087-F7
1300 OCN 92056 1107-C2
2100 OCN 92054 1106-F2
W VISTA WY Rt#-S13
300 VSTA 92083 1087-G7
VISTA ABIERTA
300 SDCo 92019 1252-E4
VISTA ACEDERA
2800 CRLB 92009 1147-G3
VISTA ALEGRIA
300 OCN 92057 1086-H4
VISTA ALETA
9400 SDCo 92082 1069-C7
VISTA ARROYO
300 SDCo 92028 1027-H3
4900 SDCo 91941 1271-D2
VISTA AZUL
3800 SCLE 92672 1023-B1
VISTA BELLA
500 OCN 92057 1086-G4
VISTA BLANCA
3800 SCLE 92672 1023-B1
VISTA BONITA
1100 VSTA 92083 1107-J1
3100 CRLB 92009 1127-H7
VISTA BONITA LN
4100 ESCN 92025 1150-E3
VISTA CALAVERAS
4000 OCN 92056 1107-C3
VISTA CAMINO
10200 SDCo 92040 1231-J2
VISTA CAMPANA N
3600 OCN 92057 1086-G4
VISTA CAMPANA S
500 OCN 92057 1086-G5
VISTA CANELA
7900 CRLB 92009 1147-G2
VISTA CANON CT
- SD 92130 1188-J3
VISTA CANYON CIR
- SDCo 92084 1088-F7
VISTA CAPITAN DR
1200 ELCJ 92020 1251-C3
VISTA CAPRI
4100 OCN 92057 1086-J4
4100 OCN 92057 1087-A4
VISTA CATALINA
15600 SDCo 92082 1071-A4
VISTA CHAPARRAL
- CRLB 92009 1147-F3
VISTA CIELO DR
12800 SDCo 91978 1272-C7
VISTA CIELO LN
3200 SDCo 91978 1272-C7
VISTA CLARIDAD
1400 SD 92037 1247-H3
VISTA COLINA DR
1200 SMCS 92069 1128-E3
VISTA CORONA
- SDCo 92028 1048-B3
VISTA CORONADO DR
4200 SDCo 91910 1310-E5
VISTA COYOTE
- SDCo 92040 1231-J2
VISTA DE BONITA
CANADA
4000 SDCo 91941 1271-H4
VISTA DE CHAPARROS
DR
3000 SDCo 91935 1273-B7
3000 SDCo 91935 1293-A1
VISTA DE GOLF
16000 SDCo 92091 1168-C7
VISTA DE LA BAHIA
3600 SD 92117 1248-E5
VISTA DE LA CANADA
3600 ESCN 92029 1150-A4
VISTA DE LA CRESTA
3300 SDCo 92029 1149-G2
VISTA DE LA CRUZ
10100 SDCo 91941 1271-E2
VISTA DEL AGUA WY
10600 SD 92121 1208-E4
VISTA DE LA MESA
6000 SD 92037 1247-F3
VISTA DE LA MONTANA
1900 SDCo 92019 1253-B5
VISTA DE LA ORILLA
3500 SD 92117 1248-E5
VISTA DE LA PATRIA
4500 SDCo 92014 1187-J1
4500 SDCo 92014 1188-A1
VISTA DE LA PLAYA
300 SD 92037 1247-E1
VISTA DE LA ROSA
2900 SDCo 91935 1292-F1
VISTA DE LA TIERRA
4300 SOLB 92014 1187-J1
4400 SDCo 92014 1187-J1
4600 SDCo 92014 1188-A1
4600 SDCo 92014 1168-A7
VISTA DEL CAJON PL
8400 SDCo 92021 1252-A1
8400 SDCo 92040 1232-A7
8400 SDCo 92040 1252-A1
VISTA DEL CAJON RD
12100 SDCo 92040 1232-A7
12100 SDCo 92040 1252-A1
12100 SDCo 92021 1252-A1
VISTA DEL CANON
1200 SOLB 92014 1187-H1
VISTA DEL CAPITAN
10200 SDCo 92040 1232-C2
VISTA DEL CERRO DR
10300 SNTE 92071 1231-E7
VISTA DEL CIELO
- SDCo 91905 (1319-H4
See Page 1298)
VISTA DEL
CONQUISTADOR
2600 SDCo 91935 1293-B4
VISTA DEL CORONADOS
2100 SDCo 92021 1252-H4
VISTA DEL DIOS
5200 SD 92130 1188-D2
VISTA DEL ESCUELA
200 ELCJ 92019 1252-E4
VISTA DEL ESTERO
3000 SD 92154 1350-A5
3000 SD 92154 1349-J6
VISTA DEL INDIO
200 SDCo 92028 1028-A3
VISTA DEL LAGO DR
1500 SDCo 92028 997-J6
VISTA DEL MAR
1600 SDCo 92003 1068-C5
1600 SDCo 92084 1068-C5
7300 SD 92037 1247-E1
VISTA DEL MAR AV
6500 SD 92037 1247-E1
VISTA DEL MAR CT
- CHV 91910 1310-B4
VISTA DEL MONTE DR
900 SDCo 92020 1251-J7
VISTA DEL MONTE WY
900 SDCo 92020 1251-J7
VISTA DEL NORTE
1900 SDCo 92028 1048-A2
VISTA DEL OCEANO
100 SCLE 92672 1023-B1
14800 SDCo 92014 1187-J1
VISTA DE LOMAS
30600 SDCo 92003 1068-B3
VISTA DEL ORO
2700 CRLB 92009 1127-H5
3300 OCN 92056 1086-J7
VISTA DEL ORO WY
8700 SDCo 91977 1291-A1
VISTA DE LOS PINOS
13700 SDCo 91935 1292-G2
VISTA DEL OTERO
- SDCo 92065 1151-H2
VISTA DEL PACIFICO
4300 SDCo 92028 1028-F5
VISTA DEL PIEDRA
2700 SDCo 91935 1293-A4
VISTA DEL RANCHO
400 CHV 91910 1310-D6
400 SDCo 91910 1310-D6
VISTA DEL REY DR
300 ENCT 92024 1147-C7
VISTA DEL RIO
2900 SDCo 92028 998-C4
VISTA DEL RIO WY
4200 OCN 92057 1086-J3
VISTA DEL SAGE
13000 SDCo 92082 1050-D5
VISTA DEL SEMBRADO
2700 SDCo 92025 1130-F7
2700 SDCo 92025 1150-F1
VISTA DEL SOL
9600 SDCo 91977 1271-C4
VISTA DEL SUR
10700 SDCo 91978 1271-G6
VISTA DEL VALLE
BLVD
1200 SDCo 92019 1272-B1
1500 ELCJ 92019 1252-B7
1500 SDCo 92019 1252-B7
VISTA DEL VERDE
8400 SDCo 92021 1232-E7
VISTA DE MATAMO
3200 SDCo 92019 1272-G1
VISTA DE MONTEMAR
1500 SDCo 92021 1252-E3
VISTA DE ORO
1000 SDCo 92029 1149-H3
VISTA DE PALOMAR
2600 SDCo 92028 1048-C1
VISTA DE PAUMA
14900 SDCo 92082 1050-G5
VISTA DIEGO RD
3100 SDCo 91935 1292-G1
3200 SDCo 91935 1272-G7
VISTA ENSUENO
700 SDCo 91901 1233-G7
VISTA ENTRADA
300 OCN 92057 1086-H4
9100 SDCo 92040 1232-G5
VISTA ESPERANZA LN
- SDCo 91901 1255-E5
VISTA FLUME
- ESCN 92026 1109-G3
- SDCo 92026 1109-G3
VISTA GLEN LN
100 VSTA 92084 1087-J6
VISTA GRANDE
3100 CRLB 92009 1127-H7
VISTA GRANDE CT
1800 SDCo 92019 1272-C2
VISTA GRANDE DR
1600 SDCo 92084 1088-A1
1600 VSTA 92084 1088-A1
3700 SD 92115 1270-E5
VISTA GRANDE GN
200 ESCN 92025 1130-A6
VISTA GRANDE PL
2000 VSTA 92084 1088-A2
VISTA GRANDE RD
700 SDCo 92019 1252-D6
1100 SDCo 92019 1272-C1
VISTA GRANDE TER
2100 SDCo 92084 1088-B1
VISTA GRANDE WY
700 OCN 92057 1086-J3
1900 SDCo 92019 1272-C2
VISTA GUYABA
7900 CRLB 92009 1147-H3
VISTA HERMOSA WY
2000 SDCo 92019 1272-C2
VISTA HIGUERA
7800 CRLB 92009 1147-J3
VISTA HILL AV
7800 SD 92123 1249-B6
VISTA HILLS DR
14200 SDCo 92040 1232-F4
VISTA HILLS PL
9500 SDCo 92040 1232-F4
VISTA HORIZON ST
200 SD 92113 1289-H5
VISTA JAMUL
13800 SDCo 91935 1293-D2
VISTA JUANITA CT
2600 LMGR 91945 1270-D7
VISTA LA CUESTA CT
10000 SD 92131 1209-J4
VISTA LA CUESTA DR
11200 SD 92131 1209-J4
VISTA LADERO
13200 SDCo 92040 1232-C5
VISTA LAGO PL
10500 SD 92131 1209-G4
VISTA LAGO TER
2400 SDCo 92029 1129-F7
2400 ESCN 92029 1129-F7
VISTA LAGUNA RD
- SDCo 92028 1048-B3
VISTA LA NISA
- CRLB 92009 1147-F2
VISTA LA QUEBRADA
14700 SDCo 91935 1293-C2
VISTA LOMA CIR
3300 OCN 92056 1107-B1
VISTA LOMAS DR
17900 PWY 92064 1150-E7
VISTA MADERA LN
1000 SDCo 92019 1252-E7
VISTA MADERA WY
2400 SDCo 92019 1252-E7
VISTA MAR
3100 CRLB 92009 1127-H7
VISTA MARAZUL
300 OCN 92057 1086-H4
VISTA MARGUERITE
- SDCo 92021 1251-J1
VISTA MARIANA
2700 CRLB 92009 1127-G7
VISTA MEADOWS WY
100 SMCS 92069 1108-D5
VISTA MERRIAM
100 SDCo 92069 1088-J7
VISTA MINE RD
- ImCo - 411-K11
- ImCo - 431-K1
VISTA MIRANDA
500 CHV 91910 1311-A5
VISTA MONTANA WY
200 OCN 92054 1086-E6
VISTA MONTANOSO
10000 SDCo 92026 1089-E2
VISTA NACION DR
4400 SDCo 91910 1310-E5
VISTA NORTE
14300 SDCo 92025 1130-G6
VISTA NUEZ
7900 CRLB 92009 1147-H3
VISTA OAK PL
- CHV 91910 1310-J7
VISTA OCEANA
3600 OCN 92057 1086-F5
VISTA OLAS
7000 CRLB 92009 1127-G6
VISTA PACIFIC DR
2600 OCN 92056 1087-E5
VISTA PACIFICA
3200 SDCo 92084 1088-F6
VISTA PALMA
7900 CRLB 92009 1147-G2
VISTA PANORAMA
14300 SDCo 92040 1232-G5
VISTA PANORAMA WY
4200 OCN 92057 1086-J3
VISTA PARQUE
10000 SDCo 92040 1232-C3
VISTA PARQUE CT
13200 SDCo 92040 1232-D3
VISTA POINT CIR
- SDCo 92084 1088-G7
VISTA POINTE
3700 SDCo 91902 1310-E3
VISTA PONIENTE DR
13700 PWY 92064 1170-F6
VISTA RAMONA RD
22600 SDCo 92065 1153-C7
23400 SDCo 92065 1173-D1
VISTA RANCHO
17600 SDCo 92067 1168-G1
VISTA RANCHO CT
7300 SDCo 92067 1168-H1
VISTA REAL DR
14100 SDCo 92082 1050-F6
VISTA REY
3600 OCN 92057 1086-F4
VISTA RICA
3100 CRLB 92009 1127-H7
VISTA RICARDO
13800 SDCo 92021 1232-E6
VISTA RIM PL
- SDCo 92084 1088-F6
VISTA ROBLES
3100 SDCo 92019 1272-G1
VISTA ROCOSA
3300 ESCN 92029 1149-J3
VISTA RODEO DR
2200 SDCo 92019 1252-E7
VISTA ROYAL
2300 SDCo 92084 1108-D1
VISTA SAGE LN
13400 SDCo 91935 1292-F2
VISTA SAGE PL
13900 SDCo 91935 1292-F2
VISTA SAN BENITO
- SD 92154 1331-A7
VISTA SAN CARLOS
- SD 92154 1331-B7
VISTA SAN
FRANCISQUITO
- SD 92154 1331-B7
VISTA SAN GUADALUPE
- SD 92154 1331-B7
VISTA SAN IGNACIO
- SD 92154 1331-B7
VISTA SAN ISIDRO
- SD 92154 1331-B7
VISTA SAN JAVIER
- SD 92154 1331-A7
VISTA SAN JOSE
- SD 92154 1331-A6
VISTA SAN JUANICO
- SD 92154 1331-A7
VISTA SAN LUCAS
- CHV 91911 1331-A6
- SD 92154 1331-A6
VISTA SAN MATIAS
- SD 92154 1331-B7
VISTA SAN MIGUEL
3900 SDCo 91902 1310-G4
VISTA SAN PABLO
- SD 92154 1331-B7
VISTA SAN PEDRO
MARTIR
- SD 92154 1331-B7
VISTA SAN RAFAEL
- SD 92154 1331-A7
VISTA SAN RUFO
- SD 92154 1331-B7
VISTA SAN SIMEON
- SD 92154 1331-A7
VISTA SANTA
CATARINA
- SD 92154 1331-B7
VISTA SANTA CLARA
- SD 92154 1331-B7
VISTA SANTA INES
- SD 92154 1331-B7
VISTA SANTA
MARGARITA
- CHV 91911 1331-A6
- SD 92154 1331-A6
VISTA SANTA RITA
- SD 92154 1331-A6
VISTA SANTA ROSALIA
- SD 92154 1331-B7

STREET
Block City ZIP Pg-Grid

VISTA SANTO DOMINGO
- SD 92154 1331-B7
VISTA SANTO TOMAS
- SD 92154 1331-B7
VISTA SECUNDA
9500 SD 92129 1189-E3
VISTA SERENA
12000 SDCo 92040 1232-A1
VISTA SIERRA DR
1000 SDCo 92019 1252-D7
1000 SDCo 92019 1272-E1
VISTA SORRENTO PKWY
- SD 92130 1208-A3
10500 SD 92121 1208-C6
VISTA SUMMIT DR
16700 SDCo 92065 1171-D2
VISTA TERCERA
9500 SD 92129 1189-E4
VISTA TERRAZA CT
12100 SDCo 92082 1070-A6
VISTA VALLE CT
10200 SD 92131 1209-G4
VISTA VALLE DR
10500 SD 92131 1209-H4
VISTA VALLE CAMINO
1000 SDCo 92028 1028-F4
VISTA VALLE VERDE
2200 SDCo 92028 1048-B2
VISTA VALLEY DR
28700 SDCo 92084 1088-E1
28800 SDCo 92084 1068-D7
VISTA VALLEY LN
2200 SDCo 92084 1088-E1
VISTA VALLEY RIM PL
2000 SDCo 92019 1252-D3
VISTA VERDE
700 SMCS 92069 1109-B5
VISTA VERDE DR
1500 ESCN 92027 1110-A5
1500 SD 92037 1247-G1
VISTA VERDE WY
1300 ESCN 92027 1110-B5
VISTA VEREDA
1500 SDCo 92019 1272-C1
VISTA VICENTE CT
24000 SDCo 92065 1173-E4
VISTA VICENTE DR
15400 SDCo 92065 1173-E4
VISTA VICENTE WY
22800 SDCo 92065 1173-C4
VISTA VIEJAS RD
9600 SDCo 91901 1234-A2
VISTA VIEW CT
13200 PWY 92064 1190-F4
VISTA VIEW DR
13100 PWY 92064 1190-F4
VISTA VILLAGE DR
100 VSTA 92083 1087-G6
VISTA VILLAGE DR Rt#-S13
100 VSTA 92084 1087-H6
100 VSTA 92083 1087-H6
VISTA WAY VILLAGE DR
3400 OCN 92056 1106-B4
VISTOSA PL
2600 CRLB 92009 1147-G2
VITA RD
4800 SDCo 91941 1271-F2
VIVA CT
800 SOLB 92075 1187-G1
VIVALDI ST
- ENCT 92007 1167-D2
VIVARACHO CT
4300 SD 92124 1249-J1
VIVARACHO WY
10900 SD 92124 1249-J1
11000 SD 92124 1250-A2
VIVERA DR
5000 SDCo 91941 1271-D2
VIVIAN ST
4000 SD 92115 1270-D4
VIVIENDA CIR
3300 CRLB 92009 1147-J1
VIXEN DR
1300 SDCo 92065 1172-F2
VIZCAINO CT
- SDCo 92026 1109-E5
VLADIC LN
1600 SDCo 92027 1130-C4
VOGE ST
10100 SD 92124 1249-G4
VOGEL RD
1100 ImCo 92243 431-A7
VOIGT DR
3000 SD 92093 1228-A1
3600 SD 92037 1228-B1
VOIGT LN
2900 SD 92093 1227-J1
2900 SD 92093 1228-A1
VOISIN CT
11900 SD 92128 1150-A7
VOLANS ST
11300 SD 92126 1209-C1
VOLCAN RD
- SDCo 92055 1085-J3
- SDCo 92055 1086-A3
200 SDCo 92036 409-L10
200 SDCo 92036 1136-A2
VOLCAN MOUNTAIN RANCH RD
- SDCo 92036 409-K10
- SDCo 92036 1136-A1
VOLCANO CREEK RD
1900 CHV 91913 1311-E6
VOLCAN VIEW DR
1200 SDCo 92036 1136-C6
VOLCAN VIEW WY
3500 SDCo 92066 409-L9
3500 SDCo 92066 410-A9
VOLCLAY DR
7200 SD 92119 1250-F3
VOLMER PEAK CT
1100 CHV 91913 1311-C7
VOLNEY LN
300 ENCT 92024 1147-H7
VOLNEY RD
300 ENCT 92024 1147-H7
VOLTA CT
7100 SD 92111 1268-J2
7200 SD 92111 1269-A1
VOLTAIRE ST
3000 SD 92106 1268-B7
3600 SD 92107 1268-A6
4800 SD 92107 1267-J5
VOLUNTARY RD
1800 VSTA 92084 1087-J3
VOMAC RD
9400 SNTE 92071 1231-B4

VOORHES LN
17400 SDCo 92065 1171-J2
VORTEX PL
4000 ESCN 92025 1150-D4
VOUGHT ST
- CORD 92135 1288-E4
VOYAGER CIR
3400 SD 92130 1187-J6
VOYAGER CT
3500 OCN 92054 1086-F6
VUE DE VILLE CT
1300 SD 92109 1247-J4
VUE DU BAY CT
1400 SD 92109 1247-J4
VUELTA CT
2100 CRLB 92009 1147-F2
N VULCAN AV
100 ENCT 92024 1147-A2
S VULCAN AV
100 ENCT 92024 1147-C7
900 ENCT 92024 1167-C1
1100 ENCT 92007 1167-C1
VULCAN PL
1100 ESCN 92027 1130-E1
VULCAN ST
1300 SDCo 92021 1251-F1

W

WABASH AV
3700 SD 92104 1269-F5
WABASH BLVD
1500 SD 92113 1289-F6
1600 SD 92136 1289-F6
WABASH ST
600 ESCN 92027 1110-B7
WABASKA CT
2100 SD 92107 1268-B7
WABASKA DR
3800 SD 92107 1268-B7
WACHE DR
3000 SDCo 91978 1292-A1
WACO ST
- SD 92111 1248-F5
3300 SD 92117 1248-F5
WADDELL CIR
10200 SD 92124 1249-G2
WADE DR
500 SMCS 92069 1128-C1
WADE ST
8500 SD 92114 1290-H2
WADE WY
12300 SDCo 92021 1252-A1
WAGNER AV
9300 SD 92123 1249-E4
WAGNER DR
1100 ELCJ 92020 1251-D4
WAGNER PL
3600 SD 92123 1249-E4
WAGON GN
1300 ESCN 92027 1130-B2
WAGON RD
3100 SDCo 92004 (1078-H7 See Page 1058)
WAGON TR
100 SDCo 92028 1027-J2
WAGON TONGUE CT
- SDCo 91901 1254-F3
WAGON WHEEL CT
2400 SDCo 91978 1271-G7
WAGON WHEEL DR
1500 OCN 92057 1067-F6
9300 SNTE 92071 1231-E5
10800 SDCo 91978 1271-G7
WAGONWHEEL WY
300 CHV 91902 1310-H4
WAHL RD
500 ImCo 92243 431-A7
WAHL ST
8600 SNTE 92071 1230-F7
WAHUPA RANCH RD
2900 SDCo 92029 1149-J2
WAILEA WY
2200 SD 92154 1330-D7
WAIMEA DR
700 SDCo 92019 1252-C4
WAITE DR
- LMGR 91945 1270-G5
6700 SD 92115 1270-E5
6900 LMSA 91941 1270-E5
7400 LMGR 91941 1270-G5
WAKARUSA ST
8900 LMSA 91942 1251-A7
WAKE AV
200 ELCN 92243 6559-F2
500 ELCN 92243 6560-B2
WAKE RD
- CORD 92118 1309-C5
WAKE ST
5500 LMSA 91942 1270-H1
WAKEFIELD CT
700 ELCJ 92020 1251-B4
WALBOLLEN ST
1300 SDCo 91977 1290-J1
1600 LMGR 91945 1290-J1
WALDEN CT
10300 SNTE 92071 1231-A3
WALDGROVE PL
9900 SD 92131 1209-H5
WALDO CT
10500 SNTE 92071 1231-E5
WALDORF WY
11100 SD 92131 1209-J2
WALDRON CT
10200 SD 92124 1249-G4
WALDRON WY
10200 SD 92124 1249-G4
WALES DR
2000 ENCT 92007 1167-F4
WALES PL
2300 ENCT 92007 1167-F4
WALINCA WY
2500 SDCo 92084 1088-D5
WALKDEN LN
8700 SD 92119 1250-J4
8700 SD 92119 1251-A4
WALKER CT
9000 SD 92123 1249-D6
WALKER DR
2800 SD 92123 1249-D6
WALKER LN
- SDCo 92672 1023-E2
WALKER RD
- ImCo 92227 410-L11
- ImCo 92227 411-A11
WALKER RD Rt#-S30
- ImCo 92227 411-A11
WALKER WY
- ImCo - 431-L2

WALKER WY
100 VSTA 92083 1087-G6
WALKING FERN CV
11200 SD 92131 1209-J1
WALKING H DR
700 SDCo 92004 (1078-J5 See Page 1058)
700 SDCo 92004 (1079-A5 See Page 1058)
WALKING PATH PL
13000 SD 92130 1187-J5
WALKING STICK CT
2500 CHV 91915 1311-H6
WALL PL
100 SDCo 92021 1252-H4
WALL RD
400 ImCo 92243 6499-E2
WALL ST
1000 SD 92037 1227-F6
WALLABY CT
11200 SD 92128 1189-J4
WALLACE CT
900 SD 92113 1289-G5
WALLACE DR
3400 SDCo 91902 1310-G1
WALLACE LN
100 VSTA 92083 1108-A1
WALLACE ST
4000 SD 92110 1268-F5
WALLINGFORD CT
7500 SD 92126 1208-J4
WALLINGFORD RD
10600 SD 92126 1208-J4
WALLSEY DR
6800 SD 92119 1250-J3
6900 SD 92119 1251-A4
WALLY WY
- ELCJ 92021 1252-C2
WALMAR LN
2300 SD 92109 1248-B4
WALNUT AV
100 CRLB 92008 1106-E6
300 SD 92103 1269-A6
600 SD 92103 1268-H6
1100 CHV 91911 1330-A4
1900 SD 92101 1268-H6
W WALNUT AV
300 SD 92103 1269-A6
WALNUT CT
2600 OCN 92056 1087-E5
WALNUT DR
- CHV 91911 1330-F5
WALNUT GN
200 ESCN 92027 1110-E6
WALNUT LN
2000 SDCo 92084 1108-C2
WALNUT RD
11700 SDCo 92040 1231-J7
WALNUT ST
1100 SDCo 92065 1152-E6
WALNUT CREEK DR
1300 ENCT 92024 1167-F1
WALNUTDALE ST
10200 SD 92131 1210-C4
WALNUT GROVE AV
1100 CHV 91913 1311-E6
WALNUT HILLS DR
100 SMCS 92078 1129-A1
WALNUT TREE LN
1200 SDCo 92021 1251-G1
WALNUTVIEW DR
1300 ENCT 92024 1147-F7
WALPEN DR
1100 SD 92154 1350-A1
WALSALL RD
600 SDCo 92019 1252-D6
WALSH ST
200 OCN 92054 1086-D6
WALSH WY
5100 SD 92115 1270-A1
WALSING DR
700 SMCS 92069 1129-E1
WALTER AV
4900 SD 92120 1250-A6
WALTER WY
200 ELCJ 92021 1251-J5
WALTERS CAMP RD
- ImCo - 412-A6
WALTHAM AV
13200 PWY 92064 1190-H4
WALTON PL
3000 SD 92116 1269-E4
WALTON ST
1500 OCN 92054 1086-B5
WALTON WY
700 SDCo 92083 1107-D2
2300 ESCN 92027 1110-C6
WALTON HEATH RW
15500 SD 92128 1170-B5
WALZ CT
11500 SD 92126 1209-B1
WANDA CT
600 ESCN 92026 1109-J7
600 ESCN 92026 1129-J1
6000 SD 92120 1249-J7
WANDA DR
8700 SNTE 92071 1231-E7
WANDA WY
13900 SDCo 91935 1292-H2
WANDERING RD
800 VSTA 92083 1087-F7
800 VSTA 92083 1107-F1
1400 ENCT 92024 1147-G5
WANDERMERE CT
6600 SD 92120 1250-E5
WANDERMERE DR
6300 SD 92120 1250-D6
6700 SD 92119 1250-D6
WANEK RD
2400 ESCN 92027 1110-D6
WANESTA DR
13000 PWY 92064 1190-D4
WANNACUT PL
11500 SD 92131 1209-J1
WAPLES CT
10000 SD 92121 1208-G5
WAPLES ST
9400 SD 92121 1208-G5
WARBLER CT
1600 CRLB 92009 1127-D6
WARBLER WY
5500 SD 92037 1247-G4
WAR BONNET ST
13000 SD 92129 1189-C5
WARD LN
10000 SDCo 91941 1271-D1
WARD PL
1300 ESCN 92026 1109-J5

WARD RD
100 NATC 92136 1309-F1
100 SD 92136 1309-F1
3100 SD 92136 1289-E7
3700 SD 92116 1269-G3
3800 SD 92108 1269-G1
WARDLOW AV
2600 SD 92154 1350-C3
WARDLOW CT
1900 SD 92154 1350-C3
WARE CT
8900 SD 92121 1208-J7
WARE RD
- ImCo 92249 431-C7
WARFIELD WY
600 SDCo 92019 1253-C2
WARHEAD RD
- SD 92106 1288-A5
WAR HORSE ST
12700 SD 92129 1189-C5
WARING CT
3200 OCN 92056 1107-B1
WARING RD
3200 OCN 92056 1107-B1
5500 SD 92115 1269-J1
5500 SD 92115 1270-A1
5500 SD 92120 1270-A1
5500 SD 92120 1250-B6
WARMLANDS AV
800 VSTA 92084 1088-B3
1900 SDCo 92084 1088-B3
E WARMLANDS AV
2200 SDCo 92084 1088-A2
2200 VSTA 92084 1088-A2
WARMWELL DR
8600 SD 92119 1250-J3
WARMWOOD AV
8200 SD 91977 1290-H5
8200 SDCo 91977 1290-H5
WARNER ST
100 OCN 92054 1086-F3
3600 SD 92106 1287-J3
3600 SD 92106 1288-A3
WARNERS DR
900 SDCo 92004 (1079-A6 See Page 1058)
WARNERS RD
24100 SDCo 92065 1173-E3
32100 SDCo 92086 409-K7
WARNOCK DR
1300 SDCo 92065 1172-F3
WARPAINT DR
700 SDCo 92065 1152-F7
WARPAINT PL
1700 ESCN 92029 1129-G5
WARREN PL
5900 LMSA 91942 1250-H7
WARRINGTON ST
1600 SD 92107 1288-A1
2300 SD 92107 1268-B6
WARWICK AV
500 ENCT 92007 1167-D2
WARWICK CIR
4500 OCN 92056 1107-E2
WARWOOD CT
2100 SDCo 92019 1272-B4
WASATCH PL
900 SMCS 92069 1109-B5
WASHINGTON AV
300 OCN 92054 1106-B1
2000 ESCN 92027 1110-C7
8600 LMSA 91941 1271-A2
E WASHINGTON AV
100 ELCJ 92020 1251-G6
700 ELCJ 92019 1251-G6
700 ELCJ 92019 1252-A6
1200 ESCN 92027 1130-A1
1500 ESCN 92027 1110-D5
E WASHINGTON AV Rt#-78
100 ESCN 92025 1129-J2
400 ESCN 92025 1130-A1
W WASHINGTON AV
- ESCN 92029 1129-F2
- ESCN 92025 1129-G2
900 ELCJ 92020 1251-E6
WASHINGTON CIR
2900 SDCo 92029 1129-C6
WASHINGTON PL
1000 SD 92103 1268-H5
WASHINGTON ST
100 VSTA 92084 1087-H6
200 SDCo 92065 1152-G1
800 SD 92103 1269-A5
1700 LMGR 91945 1290-H1
1700 SDCo 91977 1290-H1
2200 LMGR 91945 1270-H7
2500 SDCo 92036 1136-A7
2700 CRLB 92008 1106-D5
21800 SDCo 92070 1135-B3
WASHINGTON ST Rt#-79
2200 SDCo 92036 1136-B7
W WASHINGTON ST
200 SD 92103 1269-A5
300 SD 92103 1268-H6
1500 SD 92110 1268-H6
1600 SD 92101 1268-H6
2200 SD 92140 1268-H6
WASHINGTON HEIGHTS PL
1000 SDCo 92019 1251-H6
WASHINGTON HEIGHTS RD
700 ELCJ 92019 1251-J6
700 SDCo 92019 1251-J6
WASHINGTONIA DR
200 SMCS 92078 1129-A4
WATER ST
- SD 92140 1268-F6
900 SD 92101 1289-B5
1800 SD 92113 1289-B5
5500 ELCJ 92020 1251-C7
5500 LMSA 91942 1251-C7
WATER WY
3600 OCN 92056 1107-C3
WATERBURY
2000 CHV 91913 1311-E4
WATERBURY CT
1300 SMCS 92069 1128-B3
WATERBURY WY
2600 CRLB 92008 1106-J3
WATERCOURSE DR
6800 CRLB 92009 1126-J5
WATERCREST CT
3300 SDCo 91902 1311-A1
WATERCREST DR
5600 SDCo 91902 1311-A1
WATERFALL PL
6200 SD 92120 1249-J7

WATERFORD DR
3300 OCN 92056 1086-J7
WATERHILL RD
11700 SDCo 92040 1231-H4
WATERHOUSE GN
800 ESCN 92026 1109-J7
WATERIDGE CIR
10300 SD 92121 1208-D6
WATERIDGE VISTA DR
10600 SD 92121 1208-D6
WATERLOO AV
600 ELCJ 92019 1252-B7
WATERMAN AV
- ImCo 92243 6499-F3
200 ELCN 92243 6499-F4
1400 ELCN 92243 6559-F1
WATERMAN CT
900 ELCN 92243 6499-F5
6700 SD 92111 1248-J7
WATERSIDE DR
2100 CHV 91913 1311-E4
WATERTON RD
10800 SD 92131 1209-H1
WATERTOWN LN
600 CHV 91913 1311-E3
WATER VIEW CT
8200 SDCo 91977 1290-J6
WATER VIEW LN
600 SDCo 91977 1290-J5
WATERVILLE RD
7800 SD 92154 1351-F2
WATERVILLE LAKE RD
1000 CHV 91915 1311-G5
WATERWOOD CT
2200 CHV 91915 1311-F7
WATKINS CT
11000 SD 92131 1209-H1
WATSON PL
8900 SNTE 92071 1251-A1
WATSON WY
1600 SDCo 92083 1108-A3
1800 VSTA 92083 1108-A4
7200 LMSA 91941 1270-F2
WATSONIA ST
10300 SD 92121 1208-C7
WATT RD
24100 SDCo 92065 1173-E3
WATT WY
16100 SDCo 92065 1173-E3
WATTLE DR
7000 SD 92139 1290-G7
WATWOOD RD
1100 LMGR 91945 1290-F2
1100 SD 92114 1290-F2
WAVE CT
6000 SD 92139 1290-D7
WAVE CREST CT
4000 SD 92109 1247-H7
WAVERLY AV
5300 SD 92037 1247-F2
WAVERLY CT
3400 SDCo 91935 1272-E6
WAVERLY PL
300 ESCN 92025 1129-J2
WAVERLY RD
4600 OCN 92056 1107-E3
WAVERLY DOWNS LN
12100 SD 92128 1170-B7
WAVERLY DOWNS WY
14800 SD 92128 1170-A7
14800 SD 92128 1190-B1
WAWONA DR
3500 SD 92106 1288-B1
3500 SD 92106 1268-B7
3700 SD 92107 1268-B7
WAXFLOWER LN
400 SDCo 92028 1027-J3
WAXIE WY
9300 SD 92123 1229-E7
WAXWING DR
1100 VSTA 92083 1087-F4
WAXWING LN
1200 CHV 91911 1330-G2
WAYFARER DR
9600 LMSA 91942 1251-C5
WAYLAND GROVE CT
13700 PWY 92064 1190-F3
WAYNE AV
500 ELCJ 92021 1251-J4
900 CHV 91913 1311-C5
WAYNE LN
3100 SD 92117 1248-C3
WAYNECREST LN
10000 SNTE 92071 1231-D3
WAYNES WY
900 SDCo 92065 1152-C5
WAYSIDE AV
1000 ELCJ 92021 1251-G3
W D HALL DR
100 ELCJ 92020 1251-G5
WEATHERBY AV
2100 ESCN 92027 1110-C7
WEATHERHILL CT
10600 SD 92131 1209-H2
WEATHERHILL WY
11400 SD 92131 1209-G1
WEATHERLY RD
1500 CRLB 92009 1127-C4
WEATHERS PL
6400 SD 92121 1208-G5
WEATHERSTONE CT
- SD 92130 1208-E2
WEATHERVANE AV
2000 ESCN 92027 1130-D1
WEATHER VANE DR
600 SDCo 92004 (1078-J4 See Page 1058)
700 SDCo 92004 (1079-A4 See Page 1058)
WEATHERVANE PL
1700 ESCN 92027 1130-C1
WEATHERWOOD PL
11600 SD 92131 1210-A2
WEATHERWOOD TER
11000 SD 92131 1210-A2
WEAVER RD
400 ImCo 92227 431-B3
WEAVER ST
1200 SD 92114 1290-C2
WEAVERVILLE ST
1300 CHV 91913 1331-B1
WEAVING LN
17800 SD 92127 1169-H1
WEBB RD
- SD 92106 1288-A5
1700 SD 92101 1289-C2
2600 ImCo 92250 431-E4
WEBER CT
9300 SDCo 91977 1271-B6

WEBSTER AV
2800 SD 92113 1289-E4
WEDGEMERE CT
2700 ESCN 92027 1110-E7
WEDGEMERE RD
1800 ELCJ 92020 1251-C5
WEDGEWOOD AV
2500 ESCN 92027 1130-E1
WEDGEWOOD DR
100 SD 92114 1290-H4
2000 OCN 92056 1086-J7
WEED RD
500 ImCo 92231 431-B7
WEEKEND VILLA RD
1500 SDCo 92065 1152-D2
WEEPING WILLOW RD
3600 OCN 92054 1086-F1
WEEPING WILLOW WY
2100 SDCo 92028 1027-H6
WEERS ST
1300 ELCJ 92020 1251-D4
WEISER AV
7500 SD 92111 1249-A6
WEISS WY
2100 SDCo 92026 1109-H4
WEISSER WY
400 CHV 91911 1330-C3
WEITZEL ST
200 OCN 92054 1086-A7
200 OCN 92054 1106-B1
WELCH PL
- CHV 91911 1331-A3
WELCH RD
1800 SD 92101 1289-C2
WELCOME VW
28900 SDCo 92026 1089-C3
WELCOME WY
15900 SDCo 92065 1173-J4
WELD BLVD
1700 ELCJ 92020 1251-B1
WELDON WY
2500 SDCo 92028 1028-B7
WELK HIGHLAND CT
- SDCo 92026 1069-C7
WELK HIGHLAND DR
28500 SDCo 92026 1089-C1
29300 SDCo 92026 1069-C7
WELK HIGHLAND LN
29500 SDCo 92026 1069-B7
29500 SDCo 92082 1069-B7
WELK VIEW CT
- SDCo 92026 1089-C1
WELK VIEW DR
8800 SDCo 92026 1089-A1
9000 SDCo 92026 1069-B7
WELLBOURN ST
3700 SD 92103 1268-H6
WELLER ST
6800 SD 92122 1228-F4
WELLES ST
3100 SD 92136 1289-E7
WELLESLEY ST
5200 LMSA 91942 1270-G1
WELLESLEY ST E
5400 LMSA 91942 1270-G1
WELLESLEY ST W
5400 LMSA 91942 1270-G1
WELLESLY AV
3300 SD 92122 1228-D5
WELLESLY CT
6300 SD 92122 1228-D5
WELLESLY PL
6500 SD 92122 1228-D5
WELLING WY
100 SD 92114 1290-F4
WELLINGTON LN
1900 VSTA 92083 1108-A4
WELLINGTON ST
2800 SD 92111 1249-A6
WELLINGTON WY
7400 SD 92111 1249-A5
WELLINGTON HILL DR
13100 SDCo 92040 1232-C7
WELLPOTT PL
900 VSTA 92084 1087-H4
WELLS AV
100 ELCJ 92020 1251-F5
WELLS ST
1900 SD 92107 1268-B7
WELLS FARGO TR
700 SDCo 92036 1138-B5
WELLSONA CT
- SD 92131 1209-F1
WELLSTON PT
4600 SD 92130 1188-B4
WELLWORTH PT
5000 SD 92130 1188-D4
WELMER PL
3200 SD 92122 1228-C4
WELMER ST
6600 SD 92122 1228-D4
WELSH RD
10900 SD 92126 1209-D3
WELTON LN
12800 PWY 92064 1190-G5
WELTON ST
400 CHV 91911 1330-B3
WELTY ST
2200 SDCo 92028 998-J5
WEMBLEY ST
7200 SD 92120 1250-A5
WENATCHEE AV
8000 SDCo 92021 1251-G1
8200 SDCo 92021 1231-G7
WENDELA ST
5200 OCN 92056 1087-E2
WENDELL ST
4600 SD 92105 1289-J1
WENDI CT
3800 SDCo 92028 1048-B4
WENDI ST
5600 LMSA 91942 1250-H7
5600 LMSA 91942 1270-H1
WENDY LN
1100 ESCN 92026 1109-J7
WENRICH DR
5900 SD 92120 1250-C6
WENRICH PL
5900 SD 92120 1250-C6
WENSLEY AV
- ELCN 92243 6500-A7
400 ELCN 92243 6499-E7
WENTWORTH CIR
900 VSTA 92083 1108-E2
WENTWORTH CT
3000 SDCo 91935 1272-D5
WENTWORTH DR
3300 SDCo 91935 1272-E5

WENTWORTH PL
- SMCS 92069 1108-J4
WENTWORTH WY
3300 SDCo 91935 1272-D5
WERNER ST
7100 SD 92122 1228-F4
WERNES ST
2000 SDCo 92065 1152-D7
WERRIS CREEK LN
14800 SD 92128 1170-B7
14800 SD 92128 1190-B4
WESCOTT CT
8700 SD 92129 1189-C1
WESLEY DR E
5000 SD 92109 1248-B4
WESLEY DR W
5000 SD 92109 1248-B4
WESLEY PL
6600 SD 92120 1270-D1
WESLEY WY
300 DLMR 92014 1187-G6
1600 VSTA 92083 1107-G4
WESLEYAN PL
4000 SD 92116 1269-G2
WESLEY DRIVE CIR
2300 SD 92109 1248-B3
WESMEAD ST
5800 SD 92114 1290-C5
WESSEX ST
18500 SD 92128 1150-B5
WEST AV
1600 NATC 91950 1309-H2
WEST DR
300 SDCo 92021 1252-H3
1800 VSTA 92083 1107-C1
WEST LN
400 SDCo 92021 1252-H3
1500 SDCo 92014 1187-J1
WEST ST
200 OCN 92054 1106-B2
200 SD 92113 1289-J5
3200 LMGR 91945 1270-F6
3600 LMSA 91941 1270-G5
WEST BLUFF CT
- ENCT 92024 1147-E6
WEST BLUFF DR
900 ENCT 92024 1147-E6
WEST BOUNDRY TKTR
500 SDCo 91901 1234-D2
WESTBOURNE ST
200 SD 92037 1247-E1
WESTBRIDGE GN
3000 ESCN 92029 1150-A2
WESTBROOK AV
7300 SD 92139 1290-H7
WESTBURY AV
7900 SD 92126 1209-A2
WESTBURY RD
3100 SDCo 92084 1088-E7
WESTBY ST
400 CHV 91911 1330-B2
WESTCHESTER AV
10300 SD 92126 1209-E5
WEST CLIFF CT
1800 CRLB 92008 1106-H6
WESTCLIFF DR
700 SMCS 92069 1128-F2
WESTCLIFF PL
3200 SD 92106 1268-C7
WESTDALE CT
100 ELCJ 92020 1251-C5
WESTER AV Rt#-86
300 BRW 92227 431-B2
WESTERLY CT
4700 OCN 92056 1087-D4
WESTERN ST
3900 SD 92110 1268-C4
WESTERN GAILES RW
11200 SD 92128 1189-J3
WESTERN SPRINGS RD
3400 ENCT 92024 1148-C4
WESTERN TRAILS DR
7900 SDCo 92021 1252-A1
WESTERRA CT
4300 SD 92121 1228-C1
WESTGATE PL
3800 SD 92105 1289-G1
WESTHAVEN DR
3700 CRLB 92008 1106-H5
WESTHILL LN
9300 SDCo 92040 1231-H5
WESTHILL RD
8900 SDCo 92040 1231-H5
WESTHILL TER
11500 SDCo 92040 1231-H6
11500 SNTE 92071 1231-H6
WEST HILLS PKWY
8700 SD 92071 1230-H7
8700 SD 92124 1230-H7
8700 SNTE 92071 1230-H7
WESTHILL VISTA
11600 SDCo 92040 1231-H5
WESTINGHOUSE ST
1700 SD 92111 1268-J1
2100 SD 92111 1248-J7
E WESTINGHOUSE ST
1700 SD 92111 1268-J1
WESTKNOLL DR
5300 SD 92109 1247-J4
5300 SD 92037 1247-J4
WESTKNOLL LN
5300 SD 92037 1247-J3
5300 SD 92109 1247-J3
WESTLAKE DR
200 SMCS 92069 1108-G7
WESTLAKE ST
500 ENCT 92024 1147-D7
WESTLAND AV
2200 SD 92104 1289-F1
WESTLEIGH PL
6900 SD 92126 1208-H4
WESTLING CT
16900 PWY 92064 1170-F3
WESTMARK WY
13200 PWY 92064 1190-F4
WESTMINSTER DR
200 ENCT 92007 1167-D2
WESTMINSTER PL
1300 ESCN 92027 1130-D2
WESTMINSTER TER
4900 SD 92116 1269-G2
WESTMONT CT
400 CHV 91902 1311-A4
WESTMONT DR
3100 SDCo 92028 1048-D1
WESTMORE CIR
10900 SD 92126 1209-B3
WESTMORE CT
10900 SD 92126 1209-B3

STREET
Block City ZIP Pg-Grid

WESTMORE LN
10900 SD 92126 1209-B3
WESTMORE PL
1400 OCN 92056 1087-E3
10900 SD 92126 1209-B3
WESTMORE RD
7900 SD 92126 1209-B3
WESTMORELAND RD
2000 ImCo 92251 430-L5
WESTMORLAND ST
1500 CHV 91913 1331-C1
1500 CHV 91913 1311-F7
WESTON CIR
300 VSTA 92083 1087-G3
WESTON RD
4600 SDCo 91941 1271-E3
WESTON ST
2300 SD 92114 1270-E7
WESTONHILL DR
10100 SD 92126 1209-C2
WESTOVER PL
4900 SD 92102 1290-A1
5100 SD 92105 1290-A1
WEST POINT AV
7200 LMSA 91941 1270-F3
WEST POINT DR
1800 CRLB 92008 1106-H6
WESTPORT DR
4400 OCN 92054 1066-G7
4400 OCN 92057 1066-G7
WESTPORT RD
1200 SMCS 92069 1128-B3
WESTPORT ST
2200 SD 92139 1310-D1
3900 SD 92139 1290-D7
WESTRIDGE DR
4500 OCN 92056 1087-D5
WESTRIDGE LN
2100 SDCo 92084 1088-A2
WESTRIDGE PL
11600 SDCo 92040 1231-H5
WESTSIDE RD
- ImCo 92243 430-L6
WEST SIDE RD
- SDCo 92065 1154-F4
- SDCo 92065 1174-D2
WESTVALE RD
9000 SD 92129 1189-C2
WESTVIEW CT
600 CHV 91910 1310-G5
1900 SDCo 92028 1028-A6
WESTVIEW DR
400 CHV 91910 1310-F5
4500 LMSA 91941 1270-H3
WESTVIEW PKWY
10600 SD 92126 1209-E1
WESTVIEW PL
600 CHV 91910 1310-G5
7000 LMGR 91945 1270-F6
WESTVIEW RD
1800 SDCo 92028 1028-A6
15000 PWY 92064 1171-B6
WEST VILLAGE DR
1300 SDCo 92019 1252-F7
1300 SDCo 92019 1272-F1
WESTWARD CT
- SD 92131 1209-F2
WESTWARD HO CIR
1800 SDCo 92021 1252-C3
WESTWAY DR
8400 SD 92037 1227-H4
WESTWIND DR
100 ELCJ 92020 1251-B5
200 ELCN 92243 6559-G1
WESTWOOD CIR
10600 SD 92126 1209-D3
WESTWOOD DR
2000 CRLB 92008 1106-G4
WESTWOOD PL
1400 ESCN 92026 1109-E5
1400 OCN 92056 1087-E3
WESTWOOD RD
2000 VSTA 92083 1107-C1
2100 OCN 92056 1107-C1
WESTWOOD ST
2300 SD 92139 1310-C1
WETHERLY ST
7900 LMSA 91941 1270-H4
WETHERSFIELD RD
9200 SNTE 92071 1230-J6
WEXFORD ST
10500 SD 92131 1189-G7
WEYMOUTH WY
5100 OCN 92057 1066-J4
5100 OCN 92057 1067-A3
WHALE WATCH WY
8400 SD 92037 1227-H4
WHALEY AV
1700 SD 92104 1289-F1
WHALEY RD
- SD 92102 1289-G4
WHALEY ST
100 OCN 92054 1106-D2
WHARTON RD
- SD 92140 1268-E6
9400 SNTE 92071 1231-B5
WHARTON ST
- SDCo 92055 1067-A1
WHEAT ST
3200 SD 92117 1248-D3
WHEATLAND ST
- CHV 91913 1331-B1
WHEATLANDS AV
10700 SNTE 92071 1231-F5
WHEATLANDS CT
9400 SNTE 92071 1231-F5
WHEATLANDS RD
9300 SNTE 92071 1231-F5
WHEATLEY ST
6900 SD 92111 1248-J6
7100 SD 92111 1249-A6
WHEATON ST
5300 LMSA 91942 1270-G1
WHEATSTALK LN
5900 SDCo 91902 1311-B1
WHEATSTONE ST
2700 SD 92111 1248-G6
WHEELER RD
- ImCo 92251 431-A4
- ImCo 92259 430-K3
WHEELER ST
1300 SDCo 91901 1234-B6
WHEELHOUSE DR
4800 SD 92154 1330-J6
WHEEL HUB PL
300 SDCo 92004 1058-G6
WHEELING LN
3100 SDCo 91902 1310-H1

WHELAN DR
7800 SD 92119 1250-H4
WHELAN LAKE RD
3500 OCN 92054 1066-F7
3500 OCN 92054 1086-F1
WHELLOCK WY
9400 SD 92129 1189-E4
WHIGHAM PL
1600 SDCo 92019 1252-B4
WHIMBREL CT
1000 CRLB 92009 1127-B7
WHINCHAT ST
1900 SD 92123 1269-A1
WHIP DR
200 SDCo 92004 (1078-F1 See Page 1058)
WHIPPLE AV
7000 SD 92122 1228-G4
WHIPPLE WY
4900 SD 92122 1228-F4
WHIPPLETREE LN
10800 SDCo 91978 1271-G7
WHIPPOORWILL LN
4800 SDCo 91902 1310-H1
WHIPPORWILL GN
300 ESCN 92026 1109-H5
WHIPTAIL CT
12100 SDCo 92040 1212-C4
WHIRLWIND LN
16800 SDCo 92065 1171-J2
WHIRLYBIRD WY
5800 SDCo 91902 1311-B1
WHISPERING TR
9600 SDCo 91901 1234-A3
WHISPERING BROOK DR
300 VSTA 92083 1087-G3
WHISPERING HEIGHTS LN
- SD 92121 1208-G3
WHISPERING HIGHLANDS DR
1100 ESCN 92027 1130-E1
WHISPERING HIGHLANDS PL
1200 ESCN 92027 1130-F2
WHISPERING HILLS LN
- SD 92130 1208-D2
WHISPERING LEAVES LN
9300 SNTE 92071 1230-H6
WHISPERING MEADOWS LN
13700 SDCo 91935 1292-G3
WHISPERING OAKS DR
16300 SDCo 92065 1171-G3
WHISPERING OAKS LN
16800 SDCo 92065 1171-G3
WHISPERING PALM DR
1500 OCN 92056 1087-E2
WHISPERING PALMS LP
2500 CHV 91915 1311-H5
WHISPERING PINES DR
1500 SDCo 92036 1136-C5
WHISPERING TRAILS DR
700 CHV 91914 1311-G3
WHISPERING TREE LN
12400 PWY 92064 1190-C5
WHISPERING WATER DR
1100 SMCS 92078 1129-B2
WHISPERING WILLOW DR
300 SNTE 92071 1231-C5
WHISPERING WOODS CT
4600 SD 92130 1188-C5
WHISPER TRACE RD
- SDCo 92084 1068-C5
WHISPER WIND DR
500 ENCT 92024 1147-J7
WHISPER WIND LN
2100 ENCT 92024 1147-J6
WHISPER WIND RD
- SDCo 92084 1068-D5
WHISTLER RD
- SD 92106 1287-J5
WHITAKER AV
- CHV 91911 1330-H2
WHITE PL
9500 LMSA 91942 1251-B6
WHITE RD
2900 SD 92106 1288-A7
2900 SD 92106 1308-A1
WHITE ALDER CT
- SD 92127 1169-C2
WHITE BIRCH DR
400 CHV 91902 1311-B3
1800 VSTA 92083 1107-G5
10400 SD 92131 1209-J3
WHITE BUTTE DR
14900 PWY 92064 1190-J4
WHITECAP DR
6700 CRLB 92009 1126-J6
WHITE CAP LN
- OCN 92054 1085-H6
WHITE CHRISTMAS CT
- SDCo 92127 1168-J2
WHITECLIFF DR
2500 SD 92037 1227-H2
WHITE EMERALD DR
5100 SD 92130 1188-D4
WHITEFIELD PL
7700 SD 92037 1227-G6
WHITEFISH LN
3700 OCN 92054 1086-G2
WHITE FOX RUN
100 SDCo 92028 1028-B2
WHITE GOOSE RD
2400 SDCo 91906 (1297-G6 See Page 1296)
WHITEHALL CIR
10900 SD 92126 1209-A3
WHITEHALL RD
1700 ENCT 92024 1147-A2
10800 SD 92126 1209-A4
WHITEHAVEN WY
4900 SD 92110 1268-F1
WHITE HAWK RD
3200 ESCN 92027 1110-F7
3300 ESCN 92027 1130-F1
WHITEHEAD PL
8100 LMSA 91942 1250-H7
WHITEHILLS RD
9900 SDCo 92040 1232-C3
WHITEHORN
9700 SDCo 92021 1233-B3
WHITE HORSE CT
1500 CHV 91902 1311-B3
WHITE HORSE LN
200 SDCo 92028 1047-F3

WHITE LILAC RD
4200 SDCo 92028 998-G7
4200 SDCo 92028 1028-G1
WHITE OAK CT
1900 SMCS 92069 1128-B2
5200 OCN 92056 1087-E2
WHITE OAK DR
1800 SDCo 91901 1254-A1
WHITE OAK PL
2500 ESCN 92027 1110-D6
WHITE OAK WY
12400 PWY 92064 1190-C5
WHITE OWL DR
2500 ENCT 92024 1148-A7
WHITE PINE LN
10000 SNTE 92071 1231-D2
WHITE PINE WY
4400 OCN 92057 1086-J2
WHITEPORT LN
8800 SD 92119 1251-A4
WHITE ROCK STATION RD
13200 PWY 92064 1170-F2
WHITE SAGE LN
3600 SD 92105 1289-G2
WHITE SAGE PT
- SDCo 91906 (1318-B6 See Page 1298)
WHITESAGE RD
500 SMCS 92078 1128-G2
WHITESAIL ST
6700 CRLB 92009 1127-A5
WHITESANDS CT
3700 CRLB 92008 1107-B3
WHITE SANDS DR
- SMCS 92069 1128-A2
WHITE STAR LN
14200 SDCo 92082 1070-F2
WHITESTONE RD
1300 SDCo 91977 1291-E2
WHITE VALE LN
15400 PWY 92064 1170-J6
WHITEWATER DR
13200 PWY 92064 1190-J4
WHITEWATER ST
7000 CRLB 92009 1126-J6
WHITE WING DR
2300 SDCo 91935 1294-E6
WHITEWING PL
1200 CHV 91913 1331-A1
WHITEWOOD PL
200 ENCT 92024 1147-J6
WHITE WOOD CANYON
13600 PWY 92064 1170-F1
WHITEY DR
1700 CRLB 92008 1106-G7
WHITING CT
700 SD 92109 1247-H7
WHITING WOODS DR
1500 SDCo 92026 1109-D1
WHITMAN ST
2200 SD 92103 1268-G5
2800 SD 92110 1268-F4
WHITMORE RD
1200 ImCo 92283 432-D4
WHITMORE ST
400 SD 92102 1289-G3
WHITNEY CT
6900 SD 92111 1248-J6
WHITNEY ST
- CHV 91910 1310-C7
600 CHV 91910 1330-A1
2700 SD 92111 1248-J6
E WHITNEY ST
- CHV 91910 1310-D6
WHITNEY WY
- ELCN 92243 6559-F2
WHITSETT DR
1100 ELCJ 92020 1251-B3
WHITTAKER LN
12200 SDCo 92040 1232-A5
WHITTIER ST
3000 SD 92106 1268-C7
4100 SD 92107 1268-B6
WICHITA AV
600 ELCJ 92019 1252-B6
WICKER PL
1300 ESCN 92027 1110-A6
WICKERBAY CV
12300 SD 92128 1190-A6
WICKHAM WY
2800 CRLB 92008 1106-F3
WICKLEY PL
4600 OCN 92056 1107-E3
WICOPEE PL
3300 SD 92117 1248-D3
WIDDECKE LN
- SDCo 92672 1023-D2
WIDE OAK RD
1700 SDCo 91935 (1315-A3 See Page 1294)
WIDE VALLEY LN
11400 SD 92131 1209-J4
WIDGEON LN
900 CHV 91911 1330-C2
WIDGEON RD
29800 SDCo 91906 (1297-F5 See Page 1296)
WIEBER AV
1800 SD 92101 1289-C2
WIEGAND ST
1000 ENCT 92024 1148-B4
WIEGAND WY
1100 ENCT 92024 1147-F6
WIEGHORST WY
11500 SDCo 92019 1271-J4
WIENERT RD
- ImCo 92251 431-A4
WIEST RD
- ImCo 92233 411-C9
3800 ImCo 92227 431-D3
WIGEON PL
6800 CRLB 92009 1127-D6
WIGGINS WY
900 ELCJ 92020 1251-E7
WIGHT WY
1800 SDCo 92021 1252-A1
WIGHTMAN ST
2400 SD 92104 1269-C5
3600 SD 92105 1269-H5
4700 SD 92105 1270-A5
WIGWAM CT
8800 SNTE 92071 1230-J5
WIKIUP RD
16200 SDCo 92065 1173-E2
WILAJOBI WY
- SDCo 92040 1191-F6
WILBEE CT
2800 SD 92123 1249-D6

WILBER AV
2300 SD 92109 1248-B4
WILBUR AV
700 SD 92109 1247-H5
1900 SD 92109 1248-A4
WILCOX ST
300 OCN 92054 1086-E5
3500 SD 92106 1288-A3
3600 SD 92106 1287-J3
WILD ACRES RD
1500 SDCo 92084 1068-G5
WILDALIER ST
- CHV 91911 1330-H2
WILD BLOSSOM TER
5300 SD 92121 1208-E4
WILDBROOK PL
1900 CHV 91913 1311-E4
WILD CANARY LN
1100 ENCT 92024 1147-J5
WILDCAT CANYON RD
1000 SDCo 92040 1212-F1
1000 SDCo 92040 1192-H6
1100 SDCo 92040 (1193-B3 See Page 1192)
11600 SDCo 92040 1232-C1
15000 SDCo 92065 1173-A6
15000 SDCo 92065 (1193-B3 See Page 1192)
15000 SDCo 92040 1173-A6
WILD COLT PL
14700 SDCo 91935 1273-A5
WILDER WY
- SDCo 92040 1231-H5
WILDERNESS RD
16500 PWY 92064 1170-F3
WILDERNESS WY
- ELCJ 92021 1251-J5
WILDERTHORN LN
8000 SDCo 92021 1251-J1
WILDFLOWER DR
3000 ENCT 92024 1148-C5
WILDFLOWER LN
3500 SDCo 92028 1028-E5
WILD FLOWER LN
13100 PWY 92064 1170-D4
WILDFLOWER PL
600 ESCN 92026 1109-F4
WILD FLOWER WY
8000 SD 92120 1250-D3
WILDFLOWER VALLEY DR
- ENCT 92024 1148-C5
WILD GRAPE DR
9800 SD 92131 1209-G5
WILDGROVE RD
14500 PWY 92064 1170-H5
WILD HOLLY LN
15900 PWY 92064 1170-E5
WILDHORSE LN
500 SMCS 92069 1108-C6
WILD HORSE TR
10500 SNTE 92071 1231-E5
WILD HORSE CREEK
18500 PWY 92064 1150-H6
WILD IRIS PL
1200 CHV 91913 1331-A1
WILD IRIS RD
2300 SDCo 91901 1234-A5
WILDLIFE RD
10000 SD 92131 1210-A4
WILD LILAC CIR
- SMCS 92078 1128-G2
WILD LILAC TR
1800 SDCo 92036 1136-D5
WILDMEADOW PL
1700 ENCT 92024 1147-G4
WILD MUSTANG PL
14700 SDCo 91935 1273-A6
WILD OAK LN
- ESCN 92027 1130-H2
WILD OAK RD
900 CHV 91910 1310-J7
28900 SDCo 92066 1237-C5
WILD OATS LN
3600 SDCo 91902 1311-B1
WILDROSE GN
3800 ESCN 92025 1150-C3
WILDROSE LN
9300 SD 92126 1209-E3
WILD ROSE RD
900 SDCo 92036 1156-D5
WILDROSE TER
6900 CRLB 92009 1127-B6
WILD STALLION PL
14700 SDCo 91935 1273-A6
WILD WEST PL
14400 SDCo 91935 1272-J5
WILDWIND DR
2800 SDCo 92019 1272-B6
WILDWOOD CT
1100 CHV 91913 1331-B1
WILDWOOD DR
600 SDCo 92036 1156-E1
4900 OCN 92057 1087-C1
WILDWOOD LN
- SDCo 91901 1254-F7
WILDWOOD RD
1700 SD 92107 1288-A1
3800 SD 92107 1268-A7
WILDWOOD GLEN LN
- SDCo 91901 1235-F4
- SDCo 91901 1236-A5
WILER DR
800 CHV 91910 1310-G7
WIL EV DR
400 SMCS 92069 1108-J6
WILFRED ST
900 ELCJ 92021 1251-H2
WILGEN RD
21400 SDCo 92029 1129-B5
WILHITE LN
29600 SDCo 92082 1070-G5
WILKERSON CT
7800 SD 92111 1249-A3
WILKES RD
11100 SDCo 92082 1069-G5
28300 SDCo 92026 1089-H2
28400 SDCo 92082 1089-H1
WILKIE WY
100 SDCo 92021 1252-J3
WILKINS RD
- ImCo 92283 432-D5
8200 ImCo 92257 411-C7
WILKINSON DR
200 SMCS 92078 1129-A1
WILKINSON RD
200 ImCo 92233 411-B9
WILLA WY
7900 SD 92119 1250-H4

WILLAMAN DR
- SDCo 92084 1068-D5
WILLAMETTE AV
3900 SD 92117 1248-E2
WILLAPA CV
11400 SD 92131 1209-J1
WILLARD ST
3200 SD 92122 1228-C5
WILLET CIR
- CRLB 92009 1127-D7
WILLET ST
500 ELCJ 92020 1251-G4
WILLIAM AV
1300 CHV 91911 1330-C4
WILLIAMS AV
4900 LMSA 91941 1270-G2
WILLIAMS CT
8700 SNTE 92071 1230-J3
WILLIAMS LN
1800 OCN 92054 1106-F1
WILLIAMS RD
- ImCo 92227 411-D11
- SDCo 91905 430-C7
- SDCo 91905 (1299-G2 See Page 1298)
400 ImCo 92233 411-C11
WILLIAMS TER
- SDCo 92024 1148-D3
WILLIAMS WY
- SD 92145 1229-B2
WILLIAMSBURG LN
4700 LMSA 91941 1270-G3
WILLIAMS RANCH RD
2700 SDCo 92070 1135-E7
WILLIAMSTON ST
800 VSTA 92084 1087-J5
WILLIAM TELL ST
21800 SDCo 92070 1135-B2
WILLIE JAMES JONES AV
300 SD 92102 1290-A5
300 SD 92113 1290-A5
S WILLIE JAMES JONES AV
1100 SD 92113 1290-A5
WILLIS CT
400 ELCJ 92020 1251-C5
WILLIS RD
1900 ELCJ 92020 1251-C5
WILLITS RD
2200 SDCo 91901 1253-G2
WILLMAN WY
5200 SDCo 92028 1047-G7
5200 SDCo 92028 1067-G1
WILLOUGHBY RD
- ImCo 92231 431-B7
- ImCo 92243 431-B7
WILLOW AV
2100 OCN 92054 1086-C5
8900 SNTE 92071 1231-D6
WILLOW CT
10800 SDCo 92127 1169-G3
WILLOW DR
- SDCo 92040 1232-D6
400 SMCS 92069 1108-H5
1900 ELCN 92243 6559-H1
WILLOW GN
700 ESCN 92025 1130-C7
WILLOW LN
- SDCo 92026 1089-B3
1900 SD 92106 1288-C1
9700 SDCo 92029 1149-D4
25700 SDCo 92026 1109-E2
WILLOW PL
6400 CRLB 92009 1127-B4
WILLOW RD
200 SD 92173 1350-G4
12400 SDCo 92040 1232-A1
14200 SDCo 92040 1212-J6
WILLOW ST
100 CHV 91902 1310-F3
100 SDCo 91902 1310-F3
1100 SD 92106 1288-B1
2000 SD 92106 1268-C7
WILLOW TER
8600 SNTE 92071 1231-C7
WILLOW WY
- ELCJ 92019 1251-J6
1800 VSTA 92083 1107-G5
WILLOW BEND DR
1500 SDCo 92019 1272-F1
WILLOW BEND PL
2600 SDCo 92019 1272-F1
WILLOWBROOK CT
800 CHV 91913 1311-E4
1900 ELCJ 92019 1252-C4
WILLOWBROOK DR
1900 OCN 92056 1087-F2
WILLOWBROOK ST
2100 ESCN 92029 1129-E7
2100 SDCo 92029 1129-E7
WILLOWBROOK WY
100 SNTE 92071 1231-B5
WILLOW CREEK CIR
2200 CHV 91915 1311-F5
WILLOW CREEK DR
- VSTA 92084 1088-B3
WILLOWCREEK LN
- SDCo 92028 998-A7
WILLOW CREEK PL
- ESCN 92027 1130-H2
WILLOW CREEK RD
9800 SD 92131 1209-F5
WILLOWCREST WY
400 CHV 91910 1310-F7
WILLOW GLEN DR
800 SDCo 92019 1252-F7
1300 SDCo 92019 1272-D3
WILLOW GLEN RD
1500 SDCo 92028 998-B5
WILLOWGREEN CT
1400 ENCT 92024 1147-G4
WILLOWGROVE AV
8900 SNTE 92071 1231-B6
WILLOWGROVE CIR
9000 SNTE 92071 1231-B6
WILLOWGROVE CT
9000 SNTE 92071 1231-B6
WILLOW GROVE PL
- ESCN 92027 1110-F6
WILLOWGROVE PL
9000 SNTE 92071 1231-C6
WILLOWHAVEN RD
1600 ENCT 92024 1147-G4
WILLOW MEADOW PL
- ESCN 92027 1110-F6
WILLOWMERE LN
5500 SD 92130 1208-E1

WILLOW OAK DR
- SDCo 92065 1172-D5
WILLOWOOD LN
2000 ENCT 92024 1147-H6
WILLOW POND RD
100 SNTE 92071 1231-B5
WILLOW RANCH RD
14000 PWY 92064 1170-G6
WILLOW RANCH TR
15400 PWY 92064 1170-G6
WILLOW RD EXT
14200 SDCo 92040 1232-E1
14300 SDCo 92040 1212-F7
WILLOW RIDGE DR
1900 VSTA 92083 1107-G5
WILLOW RUN RD
13500 PWY 92064 1170-F3
WILLOWS RD
4000 SDCo 91901 1234-F6
5100 SDCo 91901 1235-A5
WILLOWS WY
3800 NATC 91950 1310-D3
WILLOWSIDE LN
3800 SDCo 91977 1271-B4
WILLOWSIDE TER
1200 SDCo 91901 1234-G5
WILLOWSPRING CT
2100 ENCT 92024 1147-J6
WILLOWSPRING DR N
200 ENCT 92024 1147-G5
WILLOWSPRING DR S
500 ENCT 92024 1147-G7
WILLOWSPRING PL
2100 ENCT 92024 1147-J6
WILLOW TREE CT
3400 OCN 92054 1086-E2
WILLOW TREE LN
- ESCN 92027 1110-F6
800 SDCo 92028 1027-H3
WILLOWVIEW CT
1400 ENCT 92024 1167-F1
WILLOW VIEW LN
31000 SDCo 92082 1070-E2
WILLOWWOOD DR
11200 SD 92127 1169-J5
WILLOW WOOD GN
1700 ESCN 92026 1109-D2
WILLS CREEK RD
11300 SD 92131 1210-A2
11300 SD 92131 1209-J1
WILLSON RD
1000 SDCo 92019 1253-D3
WILL VALLEY RD
- SDCo 92060 409-H7
WILMA PL
1500 ESCN 92025 1130-B4
WILMA ST
2700 SDCo 91950 1310-C3
WILMINGTON AV
12100 SDCo 92082 1070-A7
12100 SDCo 92082 1090-A1
WILMINGTON RD
11800 SD 92128 1190-A2
WILSEY WY
12100 PWY 92064 1190-B2
WILSHIRE AV
3600 CRLB 92008 1107-A4
WILSHIRE DR
5300 SD 92116 1269-F2
WILSHIRE RD
200 OCN 92057 1067-C4
1400 OCN 92028 1067-D2
6500 OCN 92028 1047-D7
WILSHIRE TER
3500 SD 92104 1269-C6
WILSON AV
700 ELCJ 92020 1251-E7
1200 NATC 91950 1309-G2
1400 ESCN 92027 1110-B7
3500 SD 92104 1269-F6
4400 SD 92116 1269-F4
WILSON PL
1300 ESCN 92027 1110-C6
WILSON RD
- ImCo 92283 432-D5
1300 SDCo 92065 1153-A7
1500 SDCo 92065 1173-A1
WILSON ST
300 ELCN 92243 6499-G6
2500 CRLB 92008 1106-F3
5100 LMSA 91941 1271-A1
WILSTONE AV
1700 ENCT 92024 1147-A2
WILT RD
1400 SDCo 92028 1028-E5
2600 SDCo 92028 1048-F1
WILTON RD
1800 ENCT 92024 1147-A2
WILTS PL
5100 SD 92117 1248-G1
WILTSIE WY
4800 SD 92124 1249-G2
WILVINN DR
8000 SNTE 92071 1251-B1
WIMBELTON LN
28400 SDCo 92026 1089-D3
WIMBERLY SQ
13000 SD 92128 1189-H5
WINAMAR AV
200 SD 92037 1247-E2
WINAMAR PL
2000 ESCN 92029 1129-G7
WINANS CV
7900 SD 92126 1209-A1
WINCHECK RD
10500 SD 92131 1209-G1
WINCHESTER CT
1200 VSTA 92083 1087-E6
WINCHESTER DR
- ELCJ 92021 1251-H5
WINCHESTER ST
2000 OCN 92054 1086-C7
5500 SD 92139 1310-C2
WINCHESTER WY
9900 SDCo 92040 1232-D3
WIND PL
4000 ESCN 92025 1150-D4
WINDBREAK CT
3300 SD 92130 1187-J5
WINDBREAK RD
13100 SD 92130 1187-J5
WINDBROOK WY
- SD 92131 1209-G2
WIND CREEK RD
- SDCo 91901 1253-J3
- SDCo 91901 1254-A3
WINDCREST DR
800 CRLB 92009 1126-J5

WINDCREST LN
11500 SD 92128 1189-J2
11500 SD 92128 1190-A2
WIND DRIFT DR
900 CRLB 92009 1126-J4
WINDEMERE CT
700 SD 92109 1247-H7
WINDEMERE DR
- SMCS 92078 1128-C6
WINDER ST
1600 SD 92103 1268-H6
WINDERMERE ST
10300 SDCo 92026 1109-F2
WINDERMERE POINT WY
700 OCN 92054 1066-E6
WINDFALL TR
700 SDCo 92036 1138-B6
4600 OCN 92056 1087-D3
WINDFLOWER DR
6400 CRLB 92009 1127-A4
WIND FLOWER WY
300 OCN 92057 1086-J2
WINDFLOWER WY
900 SD 92106 1288-A2
WINDHAM CT
8900 SDCo 91977 1271-A7
WINDING WY
700 ENCT 92024 1147-G5
WINDING CREEK DR
6600 SD 92119 1250-D3
WINDING OAK DR
1000 CHV 91910 1310-J7
1000 CHV 91910 1330-J1
WINDING RIDGE DR
11000 SD 92131 1209-G2
WINDJAMMER CIR
300 CHV 91910 1310-F6
WINDJAMMER WY
4800 CRLB 92008 1106-H7
WINDMILL RD
1300 ELCJ 92019 1251-J7
1300 SDCo 92019 1251-J7
WINDMILL ST
5100 OCN 92056 1087-D2
WINDMILL RANCH RD
600 ENCT 92024 1148-A6
31400 SDCo 92026 1069-E2
WINDMILL VIEW RD
1900 ELCJ 92020 1251-B2
WINDOM PEAK WY
11900 SD 92131 1190-A7
WINDPIPER RD
16200 PWY 92064 1170-G3
WINDRIDGE CIR
900 SMCS 92078 1128-F2
WINDRIDGE DR
1300 SDCo 92020 1251-J7
1400 ELCJ 92020 1252-A7
1400 SDCo 92020 1252-A7
WINDRIFT WY
3500 OCN 92056 1107-G4
WIND RIVER RD
1700 SDCo 92019 1272-B4
WINDROSE CIR
200 CRLB 92009 1127-A7
WINDROSE CT
15800 SD 92127 1169-H5
WINDROSE WY
400 CHV 91910 1310-F5
15800 SD 92127 1169-H5
W WINDS RDG
1600 SDCo 91901 1234-B6
WINDSOCK ST
8400 SD 92154 1351-G1
WIND SOCK WY
- CRLB 92009 1126-J7
WINDSONG LN
1200 SDCo 92026 1109-D1
1300 SDCo 92026 1089-C7
1300 SDCo 92069 1089-C7
WINDSONG RD
7500 SD 92126 1209-A3
WINDSOR CIR
600 CHV 91910 1310-E6
WINDSOR CT
700 VSTA 92084 1087-J6
2700 CRLB 92008 1107-A5
WINDSOR DR
5000 SD 92109 1247-J4
7900 LMSA 91941 1270-H3
WINDSOR PL
700 ESCN 92029 1129-F4
WINDSOR RD
1200 ENCT 92007 1167-E2
3500 OCN 92056 1107-F3
WINDSOR CREEK CT
900 ENCT 92007 1167-E2
WIND STAR WY
- CRLB 92009 1127-A4
WINDSWEPT TER
3600 SD 92130 1188-A4
WINDVANE LN
- CRLB 92009 1126-J6
WINDWARD DR
800 SDCo 92036 1156-E1
WINDWARD LN
800 CRLB 92009 1126-J5
WINDWARD ST
6700 SD 92114 1290-F5
WINDWARD WY
- OCN 92054 1085-J7
400 OCN 92054 1086-A7
WINDWARD RIDGE WY
6500 SD 92121 1208-G3
WINDWOOD WY
2800 SDCo 92019 1272-C6
WINDY LN
300 VSTA 92083 1087-F6
3000 SDCo 91902 1310-D4
WINDY WY
100 SMCS 92069 1108-H5
500 CHV 91914 1311-E3
WINDY BLUFF LN
10700 SD 92121 1208-E4
WINDY HEIGHTS WY
12600 SD 92130 1188-D6
WINDY HILL TER
900 ENCT 92024 1167-E1
WINDY MOUNTAIN LN
13200 SDCo 92082 1050-C7
WINDYRIDGE GN
300 ESCN 92026 1109-G6
WINDY RIDGE RD
7500 SD 92126 1208-J1
7500 SD 92126 1209-A1
WINDY RIDGE WY
11500 SD 92126 1209-A2
WINDY SUMMIT PL
11400 SD 92127 1169-J5

WINEN WY SAN DIEGO CO. STREET INDEX ZILLIOX LN 6630

Thomas Bros. Maps®
COPYRIGHT 2001

STREET
Block City ZIP Pg-Grid

WINEN WY
9000 SD 92123 1249-D6
WINERIDGE PL
800 ESCN 92029 1129-E3
WINEWOOD ST
200 SD 92114 1290-F3
WINFIELD AV
6000 LMSA 91942 1251-A6
WING AV
1800 SDCo 92020 1251-F1
WING ST
2900 SD 92110 1268-D5
WINGATE
4600 OCN 92056 1107-E3
WINGED FOOT GN
2100 ESCN 92026 1109-D4
WING FLIGHT CT
7800 SD 92119 1250-G4
WINGFOOT PL
1700 SDCo 92019 1272-B5
WING SPAN DR
7700 SD 92119 1250-G4
WINLAND HILLS DR
14500 SD 92067 1188-E1
14500 SDCo 92067 1188-E1
WINLOW ST
3100 SD 92105 1270-B6
WINNEBAGO AV
4600 SD 92117 1248-F1
WINNERS CIR
1000 SDCo 92065 1172-H1
5700 SDCo 91902 1311-B2
WINNETKA DR
3000 SDCo 91902 1310-G1
WINNETT ST
1400 SD 92114 1290-D1
WINNEWOOD PL
- SDCo 92028 1048-B3
WINN RANCH RD
- SDCo 92036 1156-G7
WINONA AV
3700 SD 92105 1270-A5
4100 SD 92115 1270-A2
6200 SD 92120 1250-A6
WINONA CT
5100 OCN 92057 1087-C1
WINROW RD
1800 SDCo 92021 1252-C3
WINSHIP LN
2300 SD 92101 1288-G1
WINSLOW RD
300 ImCo 92257 411-B6
3500 OCN 92056 1107-E2
3500 SDCo 92083 1107-E2
WINSOME DR
1500 ESCN 92029 1149-G1
WINSOME PL
300 ENCT 92024 1147-H6
2200 ESCN 92029 1129-G7
2200 ESCN 92029 1149-G1
WINSOME WY
2000 ENCT 92024 1147-H6
WINSTANLEY WY
13300 SD 92130 1188-C4
WINSTON DR
700 SD 92114 1290-A3
WINTER LN
1300 SDCo 92021 1252-A1
WINTER RD
2400 OCN 92056 1087-D6
WINTER CREEK LN
14600 SDCo 92082 1070-G2
WINTERCREEK PL
100 SNTE 92071 1231-B5
WINTERCREST DR
12000 SDCo 92040 1231-J4
12000 SDCo 92040 1232-A4
WINTER GARDENS BLVD
1300 SDCo 92021 1251-J1
5400 SDCo 92040 1251-J1
8300 SDCo 92040 1231-J3
9100 SDCo 92040 1232-A4
WINTER GARDENS DR
12000 SDCo 92040 1251-J1
12000 SDCo 92040 1231-J7
12000 SDCo 92040 1232-A7
12300 SDCo 92021 1232-A7
WINTERGREEN DR
2700 CRLB 92008 1106-G3
12100 SDCo 92040 1232-A4
WINTERGREEN GN
1700 ESCN 92026 1109-G6
WINTER GREEN LN
2400 SDCo 92028 1028-B6
WINTERGREEN PL
400 SMCS 92069 1109-B7
WINTERHAVEN CT
2300 SDCo 92028 1028-C7
WINTERHAVEN LN
2300 SDCo 92028 1028-B7
WINTER HAVEN RD
1100 SDCo 92028 1027-G7
WINTERHAVEN RD
1300 SDCo 92028 1027-J7
1600 SDCo 92028 1028-A7
W WINTER HAVEN RD
700 SDCo 92028 1027-G7
WINTERHAWK LN
100 ENCT 92024 1148-A7
100 ENCT 92024 1167-J1
100 ENCT 92024 1168-A1
WINTER HUNT LN
5300 SD 92130 1208-D2
WINTERS CT
300 SMCS 92069 1108-J7
WINTERS HILL
3000 SDCo 92084 1088-E7
WINTERSWEET ST
1900 SD 92154 1350-D3
WINTERWARM RD
1600 SDCo 92028 1047-J1
1600 SDCo 92028 1048-A1
1800 SDCo 92028 1028-A7
WINTERWOOD LN
7500 SD 92126 1209-A4
WINTHROP AV
2800 CRLB 92008 1107-A4
WINTHROP ST
5100 SD 92117 1228-H7
WIRE MOUNTAIN RD
- SDCo 92055 1085-H4
- SDCo 92055 1086-A4
WIRT RD
1200 ImCo 92233 411-D10
WISCONSIN AV
- OCN 92054 1106-B2
300 ELCJ 92020 1251-B5
700 SDCo 92028 1027-F3
6900 LMSA 91942 1270-E1

S WISCONSIN AV
100 SDCo 92028 1027-F2
WISE ST
- CHV 91911 1330-J2
1000 CHV 91911 1331-A2
WISECARVER LN
3100 SDCo 91935 1274-C6
WISECARVER TKTR
3100 SDCo 91935 1274-C7
WISHBONE WY
3000 ENCT 92024 1148-B3
WISKON WY
32000 SDCo 92061 1051-B6
WISTER DR
9100 SDCo 91941 1271-B1
9200 LMSA 91941 1271-B1
WISTERIA
15300 SDCo 92021 1233-B3
WISTERIA AV
13900 PWY 92064 1190-F3
WISTERIA CT
1900 SDCo 92019 1272-D3
WISTERIA DR
300 SMCS 92078 1128-G2
3300 SD 92106 1268-D6
5100 OCN 92056 1107-F4
WISTERIA GN
1600 ESCN 92026 1109-D6
WISTERIA ST
500 CHV 91911 1330-H3
WISTERIA WY
7100 CRLB 92009 1127-B6
WISTFUL VISTA
7900 SNTE 92071 1230-H7
WITCH CREEK
MOUNTAIN RD
27500 SDCo 92065 1154-C1
WITHAM RD
100 ENCT 92024 1147-F7
WITHERBY ST
100 OCN 92054 1106-B3
3600 SD 92140 1268-F6
3600 SD 92110 1268-G5
3900 SD 92103 1268-G5
WITHERSPOON WY
200 ELCJ 92020 1251-B5
WITT PL
12400 PWY 92064 1190-C3
WITT RD
12200 PWY 92064 1190-B2
WITTMAN WY
3100 SD 92173 1350-F4
WIXOM RD
- ImCo 92243 430-L6
- ImCo 92243 431-A6
WIZARD WY
16000 SDCo 92082 1071-B5
WODEN ST
700 NATC 92136 1309-F1
1800 SD 92113 1289-G7
2300 SD 92136 1289-G7
WOHLFORD ST
5200 OCN 92056 1087-D1
WOLAHI RD
- SDCo 92036 1176-C5
WOLBERT PL
200 SD 92113 1289-F4
WOLFF CT
5800 LMSA 91942 1251-C7
WOLFORD DR
400 SDCo 91977 1290-J4
WOLF POINT CT
600 OCN 92057 1067-C7
WOLFSTAR CT
6100 SD 92122 1228-G5
WOLVERINE TER
- CRLB 92008 1107-D7
WOLVERINE WY
1700 VSTA 92084 1088-B5
WOLVISTON WY
1700 SD 92154 1349-J2
1700 SD 92154 1350-A2
WOMACK LN
400 SDCo 92028 1027-F3
WOMBLE RD
2600 SD 92133 1288-D1
2700 SD 92133 1268-D7
WOMSI LN
15400 SDCo 92061 1050-J5
WOMSI RD
32400 SDCo 92061 1050-J5
WONDER LN
8000 SDCo 92021 1252-A1
WONDERFUL VIEW RD
9400 SDCo 92040 1232-E5
WONDER VIEW DR
2000 SDCo 92084 1088-B2
WONJU CIR
- SDCo 92055 409-A7
WOOD DR
700 ENCT 92024 1147-C3
WOOD LN
15600 SDCo 92082 1071-A3
WOOD ST
4900 LMSA 91941 1271-A2
WOODACRE DR
2300 OCN 92056 1106-H1
WOODBINE PL
1700 OCN 92054 1106-D2
WOODBINE WY
7500 SD 92114 1290-G4
WOODBRIDGE RD
1700 ESCN 92026 1109-D5
WOODBROOK LN
1700 SDCo 92028 1027-G5
WOODBURN ST
1700 ELCJ 92021 1251-H2
WOODBURY CT
2900 CRLB 92008 1107-B4
WOODBURY PL
2100 ESCN 92026 1109-G5
WOODCHUCK PT
10400 SD 92131 1209-J4
WOODCRAFT WY
- SD 92131 1209-H2
WOODCREEK PL
13200 PWY 92064 1190-E2
WOODCREEK RD
900 SDCo 92028 1027-H3
14100 PWY 92064 1190-E2
WOODCREST DR
200 SDCo 92028 1027-F3
WOODCREST ST
1400 CHV 91910 1311-C6
WOODDALE RW
6000 SD 92037 1248-A1
WOODED HILL RD
- SDCo 91948 430-B5

WOODED VISTA LN
12000 SD 92128 1190-A7
WOOD ENERGY RD
200 SDCo 92065 1152-B7
200 SDCo 92065 1172-B1
WOODFORD DR
2900 SD 92037 1227-J6
2900 SD 92037 1228-A6
WOODFORDS PL
1300 CHV 91913 1331-C1
WOODGATE PL
13700 PWY 92064 1190-F5
WOODGLEN PL
2100 ESCN 92026 1109-G5
WOODGLEN TER
1400 CHV 91902 1311-A2
WOODGLEN WY
1900 ELCJ 92020 1251-C3
WOODGLEN VISTA DR
9900 SNTE 92071 1231-C3
WOODGROVE DR
900 ENCT 92007 1167-E2
WOODHAVEN DR
1000 SDCo 91977 1290-J3
1200 OCN 92056 1087-C2
WOODHILL ST
1400 ELCJ 92019 1252-A6
WOODHOLLOW LN
14100 PWY 92064 1190-E2
WOODHOUSE AV
500 CHV 91910 1310-F6
WOODHUE LN
14600 PWY 92064 1190-E1
WOODLAKE DR
900 ENCT 92007 1167-E2
WOODLAND CT
1300 SMCS 92069 1109-C6
4100 LMSA 91941 1271-B4
WOODLAND DR
100 SDCo 92083 1108-B2
100 VSTA 92083 1108-B2
4100 LMSA 91941 1271-B4
WOODLAND GN
1900 ESCN 92027 1110-B5
WOODLAND LN
300 SDCo 92021 1252-J4
WOODLAND PKWY
- SMCS 92078 1129-B1
100 SMCS 92069 1109-B7
100 SMCS 92078 1109-B7
1000 ESCN 92026 1109-B7
1400 SDCo 92069 1109-B7
14000 PWY 92064 1170-G4
WOODLAND RD
2500 SDCo 92036 1136-C7
WOODLAND WY
2500 OCN 92054 1106-F2
3400 CRLB 92008 1106-F5
WOODLAND HEIGHTS GN
1900 ESCN 92026 1109-B3
3100 SDCo 92026 1109-B3
WOODLAND HILLS DR
300 SDCo 92029 1149-J1
400 SDCo 92029 1150-A1
WOODLANDS LN
8500 SD 92037 1228-B4
WOODLANDS GLENN
6900 LMSA 91941 1270-E5
WOODLAND VALLEY GN
2000 ESCN 92026 1109-C4
WOODLAND VISTA DR
9600 SDCo 92040 1232-D3
WOODLARK CT
1500 CHV 91911 1330-F5
WOODLARK LN
- CHV 91911 1330-F5
1700 SDCo 92028 1027-G5
WOODLAWN AV
- CHV 91910 1309-J5
400 CHV 91910 1310-A7
400 CHV 91910 1330-A1
800 CHV 91911 1330-A3
WOODLAWN DR
800 SDCo 92036 1156-D1
9000 SD 92126 1209-D4
WOODLEY PL
800 ENCT 92024 1147-D4
WOODMAN ST
200 SD 92114 1290-F6
1300 SD 92139 1290-F6
1300 SD 92139 1310-G1
1300 SDCo 92139 1310-G1
N WOODMAN ST
300 SD 92114 1290-E4
WOODMEADOW LN
300 SDCo 92065 1153-B5
WOODMONT PL
13100 PWY 92064 1190-D2
WOODMONT ST
13100 PWY 92064 1190-D2
WOODMOSS CT
2000 ENCT 92024 1147-H5
WOODPARK DR
9900 SNTE 92071 1231-E3
WOODPARK WY
200 OCN 92054 1086-F3
WOODPECKER WY
7900 SNTE 92071 1230-H7
WOODPINE DR
1500 SDCo 92019 1272-B4
WOODRAIL DR
1100 VSTA 92083 1087-G4
WOODRIDGE CIR
2800 CRLB 92008 1106-F3
WOODRIDGE LN
- SDCo 92086 409-H6
WOODRIDGE WY
7300 SD 92114 1290-G6
WOOD ROCK LN
15900 SDCo 92065 1172-A4
WOODROSE AV
10000 SNTE 92071 1231-D3
WOODROW AV
700 SD 92114 1290-F3
1400 LMGR 91945 1290-F3
WOODRUFF WY
9300 SNTE 92071 1231-A5
WOODRUN PL
1600 SDCo 92019 1272-B4
WOODRUSH CT
11200 SD 92128 1189-J2
WOODRUSH LN
11200 SD 92128 1189-J2
WOODS DR
500 SMCS 92069 1109-C6
WOODSHADOW LN
100 ENCT 92024 1147-H7

WOODSHAWN DR
7100 SD 92114 1290-F5
WOODS HILL LN
18300 SDCo 92065 1153-C7
WOODSIDE AV
10500 SNTE 92071 1231-F5
11400 SDCo 92040 1231-H4
12100 SDCo 92040 1232-A4
WOODSIDE AV N
10800 SNTE 92071 1231-F5
11000 SDCo 92040 1231-F5
11000 SDCo 92071 1231-F5
WOODSIDE CT
- CHV 91914 1311-F3
WOODSIDE DR
1900 ELCN 92243 6559-H1
WOODSIDE LN
800 ENCT 92024 1147-J5
WOODSIDE PL
600 ESCN 92026 1109-F4
WOODSIDE WY
1000 SOLB 92014 1187-G1
WOODSON CT
18900 SDCo 92065 1172-A2
N WOODSON CT
17200 SDCo 92065 1171-F3
N WOODSON DR
16400 SDCo 92065 1171-F3
S WOODSON DR
15900 SDCo 92065 1171-E3
WOODSON CREST RD
16100 SDCo 92065 1171-B3
WOODSON RIDGE RD
16100 SDCo 92065 1171-B3
WOODSON VIEW LN
17100 SDCo 92065 1171-E3
WOODSON VIEW RD
16300 PWY 92064 1170-F4
WOODSPRING DR
800 CHV 91913 1311-E4
WOODSTOCK PL
13700 SDCo 92082 1090-E6
WOODSTOCK ST
4500 CRLB 92008 1107-B5
WOODSTORK LN
100 SDCo 92028 1027-F6
WOODSTREAM PT
10800 SD 92131 1210-A2
WOODS VALLEY CT
27100 SDCo 92082 1090-E5
WOODS VALLEY RD
13800 SDCo 92082 1090-F5
15200 SDCo 92082 1091-A5
WOODTHRUSH LN
100 SDCo 92028 1027-F5
WOODVALE DR
3800 CRLB 92008 1106-H5
8400 SNTE 92071 1230-J7
WOOD VALLEY TR
16000 SDCo 91935 1273-G5
WOODVIEW CT
1300 OCN 92056 1087-D3
WOODVIEW DR
1200 OCN 92056 1087-C2
WOODVIEW PL
9500 SD 92123 1249-E4
WOODVILLE AV
1300 CHV 91913 1331-D1
WOODWARD AV
200 ESCN 92025 1129-H2
500 ELCN 92243 6499-F5
WOODWARD RD
- SD 92106 1287-J5
WOODWARD ST
500 SMCS 92069 1108-J5
600 SMCS 92069 1109-A4
WOODWAY CT
200 SD 92114 1290-G5
WOODWAYNE DR
10300 SNTE 92071 1231-D3
WOODWIND DR
2100 ENCT 92024 1147-J7
WOODWIND RD
2700 CRLB 92008 1106-F3
WOODWORTH WY
- SD 92133 1268-D7
WOODY LN
13000 PWY 92064 1190-G5
WOODYARD AV
5000 LMSA 91941 1270-G2
WOODY HILLS DR
1500 SDCo 92019 1272-B1
WOOSTER DR
3800 OCN 92056 1087-B6
WORCESTER GN
3800 ESCN 92027 1110-D7
WORCHESTER PL
6900 SD 92126 1208-H4
WORDEN ST
2100 SD 92107 1268-B6
2400 SD 92110 1268-C5
2800 SD 92106 1268-C5
WORKS PL
4700 SD 92116 1269-E3
WORLD TRADE DR
12000 SD 92128 1190-A1
12100 SD 92128 1170-A7
WORMWOOD CT
3700 SDCo 92028 1048-C3
WORMWOOD RD
700 ImCo 92243 431-A7
WORSCH DR
12100 SD 92130 1188-B7
WORSCH WY
4100 SD 92130 1188-B7
WORTHING AV
10800 SD 92126 1209-B3
WORTHINGTON RD
- SDCo 91905 (1320-A3 See Page 1300)
WORTHINGTON RD Rt#-S28
- ImCo 92251 431-A4
- ImCo 92243 431-A4
500 IMP 92251 431-A4
1000 ImCo 92250 431-A4
1900 ImCo 92251 430-L4
WORTHINGTON ST
100 SDCo 91977 1290-J3
800 SD 92114 1290-J3
S WORTHINGTON ST
100 SDCo 91977 1290-J5
100 SDCo 91902 1290-J5
WOTAN DR
1000 ENCT 92024 1167-F1
WRANGLER CT
900 CHV 91902 1310-H4
WRANGLERS DR
300 SDCo 92004 1058-G6

WRELTON DR
600 SD 92037 1247-G5
600 SD 92109 1247-G5
WREN GN
1100 ESCN 92026 1109-E5
WREN ST
1100 SD 92114 1290-D2
7700 SNTE 92071 1230-G7
WREN WY
900 SMCS 92069 1128-E2
WREN BLUFF DR
- SDCo 92127 1169-E4
WREN HAVEN WY
- SDCo 92127 1169-G4
WRIGHT AV
- CORD 92135 1288-G3
WRIGHT PL
1900 CRLB 92008 1127-B3
WRIGHT RD
- ImCo 92250 431-D4
WRIGHT ST
3400 SD 92140 1268-G6
3500 SD 92110 1268-G6
WRIGHT CANYON RD
- SDCo 92040 (1193-E4 See Page 1192)
WRIGHTWOOD RD
31600 SDCo 92003 1068-D1
31800 SDCo 92003 1048-D7
WUESTE RD
1700 CHV 91915 (1312-A5 See Page 1293)
1800 CHV 91915 1332-A1
2200 SD 91915 1332-A1
WULFF ST
800 SMCS 92069 1109-B5
WUNDERLIN AV
6000 SD 92114 1290-C3
WYANDOTTE AV
2700 SD 92117 1228-B7
2700 SD 92117 1248-B1
WYATT PL
1500 ELCJ 92020 1251-D4
WYCLIFFE ST
10000 SNTE 92071 1231-D2
WYCONDA LN
4800 SD 92113 1290-A6
WYCONDA WY
1300 SD 92113 1290-A6
WYE ST
14600 SD 92129 1189-H1
WYEPORT RD
15400 SDCo 92065 1172-A5
WYETH RD
13700 SDCo 92021 1232-E5
WYKES ST
400 CHV 91911 1330-B3
WYMAN WY
9600 SDCo 91977 1271-C7
WYNDEMERE CT
- SDCo 92026 1109-G1
WYNDEMERE LN
- SDCo 92026 1109-G1
WYNDHAVEN DR
13300 SD 92130 1188-A4
13600 SD 92130 1187-J4
WYNELAND RD
15600 SDCo 92025 1151-B3
WYNELL LN
3000 LMGR 91945 1270-J6
WYNGATE PT
13300 SD 92130 1188-C4
WYNN ST
1200 OCN 92054 1086-A5
WYNOLA RD
3700 SDCo 92036 1136-A3
3800 SDCo 92066 1135-G5
WYNOLA ST
100 SDCo 92065 1172-D1
WYNWOOD CT
- ESCN 92027 1130-J3
WYOMING AV
6900 LMSA 91942 1270-E1
WYSTONE DR
1300 SD 92113 1290-A6

X

XANA WY
6700 CRLB 92009 1127-J4
6700 CRLB 92009 1128-A5
XAVIER AV
800 CHV 91913 1311-C5
XENOPHON ST
3000 SD 92106 1268-C7
3800 SD 92107 1268-B6

Y

YACON CIR
200 VSTA 92083 1087-E7
YACON ST
200 VSTA 92083 1087-E7
YAH WY
3600 SDCo 91902 1310-J1
YALE AV
4000 LMSA 91941 1270-F4
YALE DR
3700 OCN 92056 1107-A2
YALE ST
1600 CHV 91913 1311-C5
YAMA ST
2100 SD 92113 1289-G7
YANKEE CT
2100 ESCN 92029 1129-E6
YANKEE POINT WY
800 OCN 92054 1066-E6
YANKTON DR
12900 PWY 92064 1190-D4
YAQUI DR
14000 SDCo 92036 1176-E5
YAQUI RD
1400 SDCo 92004 1058-G5
YAQUI PASS RD
3400 SDCo 92004 (1079-F6 See Page 1058)
3700 SDCo 92004 (1099-F1 See Page 1098)
YAQUI PASS RD Rt#-S3
3700 SDCo 92004 (1099-E6 See Page 1098)
3700 SDCo 92004 (1118-J5 See Page 1098)
3700 SDCo 92004 (1119-A4 See Page 1098)
5600 SDCo 92036 (1118-J5 See Page 1098)

YAQUI WELLS RD
- SDCo 92004 (1118-E5 See Page 1098)
- SDCo 92036 (1118-E5 See Page 1098)
YARMOUTH CT
700 SD 92109 1247-H7
YARROW DR
6100 CRLB 92009 1127-D3
YAZOO ST
14400 SD 92129 1189-H2
YBARRA RD
3300 SDCo 91978 1271-F6
YEARLING CT
5700 SDCo 91902 1311-B2
YEATS CT
- OCN 92057 1067-A4
YELLOW BRICK RD
28900 SDCo 92082 1071-B3
YELLOW PINE CT
- SDCo 92026 1089-B2
YELLOWSTONE PL
9700 SNTE 92071 1231-E4
YELLOWTAIL WY
2000 SD 92139 1290-D7
YELLOWTHROAT RD
13800 PWY 92064 1170-F5
YERBA LN
3500 CHV 91902 1310-G3
YERBA ANITA DR
5200 SD 92115 1270-A1
5400 SD 92115 1269-J1
YERBA ANITA WY
4900 SD 92115 1270-A2
YERBA BUENA DR
3200 SDCo 92028 1028-D1
YERBA SANTA DR
4400 SD 92115 1269-J1
4700 SD 92115 1270-A2
YERBA SANTA RD
23900 SDCo 91963 (1315-J5 See Page 1294)
23900 SDCo 91963 (1316-A5 See Page 1296)
YERBA VALLEY RD
12400 SDCo 92040 1212-D4
YERBA VALLEY WY
12400 SDCo 92040 1212-D3
YERBA VERDE DR
1100 ELCJ 92020 1251-D3
YERMO CT
16500 SDCo 92127 1169-F4
YESTERYEAR LN
2500 SDCo 92028 1028-B2
YETTFORD RD
1700 VSTA 92083 1108-A3
1800 SDCo 92083 1108-A3
YEW LN
9600 SDCo 92029 1149-D4
YMCA WY
100 SD 92102 1289-B4
YNEZ PL
1300 CORD 92118 1288-J7
1400 CORD 92118 1308-J1
YNEZ PTH
3800 SDCo 92004 (1099-E1 See Page 1098)
YOCUM RD
- ImCo 92233 411-C10
YODEL LN
1900 SD 92154 1350-A1
YOKOHAMA CT
5800 SD 92120 1250-E7
YOKUM CT
100 SDCo 92028 1027-E2
YOLANDA AV
9400 SD 92123 1249-F6
YOLANDA PL
2400 SD 92123 1249-F6
YOLO CT
8300 SD 92129 1189-B6
YONGE ST
3000 SD 92106 1268-C7
4000 SD 92107 1268-B6
YORBA CT
1300 CHV 91910 1311-B6
YORBA LINDA CT
24200 SDCo 92065 1173-E2
YORK AV
1200 ESCN 92027 1110-A7
13800 PWY 92064 1190-E2
YORK CT
700 SD 92109 1247-H7
YORK DR
1100 VSTA 92084 1108-B1
1200 SDCo 92084 1108-B2
YORK PL
1500 ESCN 92027 1110-B7
YORK RD
2700 CRLB 92008 1106-J4
YORK RD Rt#-S24
1400 ImCo 92283 432-D4
YORKSHIRE AV
5600 LMSA 91942 1250-J7
YORKTOWN DR
10200 SD 92124 1249-G5
YORKTOWN ST
1500 IMPB 91932 1349-J2
YORK VIEW CIR
1700 SDCo 92084 1108-C2
YOSEMITE ST
3400 SD 92109 1268-A1
3600 SD 92109 1248-A7
4300 CRLB 92008 1106-J5
YOST CIR
5200 SD 92109 1247-J4
YOST DR
1400 SD 92109 1247-J4
YOST PL
5200 SD 92109 1247-J4
YOUNG RD
- ImCo 92233 411-C10
YOUNG ST
1300 ELCJ 92020 1251-D4
YOUNGSTOWN WY
9200 SD 92121 1208-F7
YOURELL AV
1200 CRLB 92008 1106-E3
YOURMAN RD
- ImCo 92243 6560-F3
1000 ImCo 92249 6560-F6
YSABEL CREEK RD
15800 SD 92025 1131-B7
15800 SD 92025 1151-B1
YSIDRO DR
24300 SDCo 92065 1173-E1
YUBA DR
700 CHV 91902 1311-D5
700 CHV 91913 1311-D5

YUCATAN WY
1600 SDCo 92028 1027-F5
YUCCA AV
3300 SD 92117 1248-D3
YUCCA DR
200 ELCN 92243 6559-F1
2500 SDCo 91906 (1297-E5 See Page 1296)
3200 SDCo 92036 1156-E1
YUCCA RD
400 SDCo 92028 1028-D1
1700 OCN 92054 1106-F1
YUCCA ST
14000 SDCo 91935 1272-H7
14000 SDCo 91935 1292-H1
YUCCA TER
900 SDCo 92028 1028-D3
YUCCA TR
10400 SDCo 92026 1089-F2
YUCCA WY
3500 SDCo 92028 1028-D2
YUCCA HILL RD
2200 SDCo 91901 1253-J1
YUCCA RIDGE LN
700 SDCo 92069 1109-B2
YUKI LN
4300 CRLB 92008 1106-G7
YUKON ST
14500 SD 92129 1189-H1
YUMA AV
4700 OCN 92057 1087-B1
4800 OCN 92057 1067-B7
YUMA GN
1000 ESCN 92026 1109-F6
YUMA RD
34600 SDCo 92036 1176-D4
YUMA ST
5700 SD 92110 1268-G3
YVETTE WY
3700 CRLB 92008 1106-G6
YVONNE ST
2800 OCN 92056 1087-C7

Z

Z ST
3500 SD 92113 1289-F6
25800 SDCo 92026 1109-E1
ZABEL CT
8800 SDCo 91977 1271-A5
ZABYN ST
2200 OCN 92054 1106-E1
ZACHARY GN
1500 ESCN 92027 1110-B5
ZADA LN
200 VSTA 92084 1088-A6
ZAGALA CT
11000 SD 92124 1250-A2
ZAMORA WY
4600 OCN 92056 1107-F4
7200 CRLB 92009 1127-F7
ZANE CT
6700 SD 92111 1248-J6
ZANJA PL
24700 SDCo 92065 1173-G2
ZANZIBAR CT
700 SD 92109 1247-H7
ZANZIBAR RD
- ELCJ 92021 1251-J5
ZAPATA AV
10000 SD 92126 1209-B2
ZAPO ST
1700 DLMR 92014 1187-F4
ZAPPONE RD
- ImCo - 411-J11
ZARINA LN
400 ENCT 92024 1147-G5
ZARINA LAKE DR
- SDCo 91905 (1320-A4 See Page 1300)
ZARZA CTE
1100 CHV 91910 1311-A7
ZEALAND WY
8100 LMGR 91945 1270-H7
ZEBRINA PL
6900 CRLB 92009 1127-E6
ZED ST
3900 SD 92117 1248-E4
ZEIGLER CT
15700 SDCo 92065 1173-J4
ZEIJL LN
8500 SDCo 92040 1232-A7
ZEILIN ST
- SDCo 92055 1067-A1
ZEISS ST
1400 OCN 92054 1086-B5
ZELDA AV
4600 LMSA 91941 1270-F3
ZELLER ST
1700 SD 92114 1290-E1
ZEMBER CT
200 VSTA 92083 1108-A2
ZEMCO DR
7500 LMGR 91945 1290-G2
ZEMKE AV
13700 SD 92129 1189-D3
ZENA DR
6400 SD 92115 1270-D5
ZENAKO CT
6000 SD 92122 1228-E6
ZENAKO ST
3900 SD 92122 1228-E6
ZENCARO AV
8800 SD 92123 1249-C6
ZENITH LN
4200 OCN 92056 1107-C2
ZENITH ST
100 CHV 91911 1330-C5
ZENOS RD
1200 ImCo 92250 431-D5
ZENOS WY
4800 OCN 92056 1107-F6
ZEPHYR AV
1500 ELCJ 92021 1252-B2
ZERMATT LN
3600 SDCo 92025 1150-D2
ZEST CT
500 SD 92139 1290-G6
ZEST ST
500 SD 92139 1290-G6
ZETA ST
8200 LMSA 91942 1250-J7
ZEZERE DR
400 OCN 92057 1086-J4
ZIGA DR
28800 SDCo 92082 1071-A7
ZILLIOX LN
500 SMCS 92069 1108-J6

SAN DIEGO CO. INDEX

STREET
Block City ZIP Pg-Grid
ZIMMER CV
5000 SD 92130 1188-D5
ZINFANDEL TER
500 CHV 91913 1311-D4
ZINNIA CT
4300 SD 92154 1330-G7
6800 CRLB 92009 1127-A5
ZION AV
4400 SD 92120 1249-J6
4800 SD 92120 1250-A6
ZION CT
300 SDCo 92065 1153-A7
ZIRBEL CT
11900 SD 92131 1210-B1
ZIRBEL WY
- SD 92131 1210-B1
ZIRCON PL
- CRLB 92009 1127-H5
ZIRCON ST
5500 SD 92114 1290-B2
ZLATIBOR RANCH RD
600 ESCN 92025 1130-C5
1900 SDCo 92025 1130-C5
ZLATIBOR RANCH TER
600 SDCo 92025 1130-C5
ZODIAC ST
6700 CRLB 92009 1127-G5
ZOE ST
3800 SD 92117 1248-E5
ZOLA GN
1800 ESCN 92026 1109-F6
ZOLA ST
3000 SD 92106 1268-C6
ZOLDER CT
2000 SDCo 92019 1272-C4
ZOLDERO RD
11400 SDCo 91941 1271-H4
11400 SDCo 92020 1271-H4
ZONA GALE RD
900 ENCT 92024 1147-F6
ZOO DR
2900 SD 92101 1269-C7
3000 SD 92103 1269-C7
ZOO PL
1800 SD 92101 1269-C7
2000 SD 92101 1289-C1
ZOO RD
- SD 92027 1130-J6
ZORA ST
6000 LMSA 91942 1250-G6
ZORITA CT
11200 SD 92124 1250-A2
ZORO WY
1600 SD 92154 1349-J2
ZUBARON LN
7000 CRLB 92009 1127-G7
ZULU WY
2600 SD 92139 1310-F1
ZUMAQUE ST
6900 SDCo 92067 1168-G3
ZUMBROTA RD
3200 SDCo 91901 1234-D4
ZUNI DR
400 DLMR 92014 1187-F4
ZUNI TR
1600 SDCo 92004 (1099-E1
See Page 1098)
ZURICH DR
1100 SD 92154 1350-A1
ZUTANO LN
1500 SDCo 92028 998-B6

#

1ST AV
- CHV 91910 1310-C4
300 SD 92101 1289-A1
600 ImCo 92283 432-C5
600 CHV 91910 1330-D1
700 CHV 91911 1330-E3
2400 SD 92103 1289-A1
2600 SD 92103 1269-A5
1ST LN
1400 SD 92154 1350-D2
1ST PL
800 SDCo 92029 1149-E2
1ST ST
- CORD 92135 1288-F4
- SDCo 92004 (1121-G2
See Page 1100)
- NATC 91950 1289-H7
- SDCo 92059 1029-J4
100 SDCo 92065 1152-J6
200 ELCN 92243 6499-J6
300 CORD 92118 1288-J5
800 ELCN 92243 6559-J1
1000 ELCJ 92021 1251-H2
1000 SDCo 92021 1251-H2
1100 ENCT 92024 1167-C1
1200 SDCo 92036 1136-B7
1400 CORD 92118 1289-A5
1400 OCN 92054 1086-B7
2100 NATC 91950 1290-A6
3800 SMCS 92069 1128-C1
5100 SDCo 92028 998-J4
9000 SNTE 92071 1231-E6
10600 SDCo 91978 1271-F7
10600 SDCo 91978 1291-F1
N 1ST ST
500 ELCJ 92021 1251-H4
800 SDCo 92021 1251-H4
S 1ST ST
100 ELCJ 92019 1251-H6
100 ELCJ 92020 1251-H6
2ND AV
- CHV 91910 1310-B5
300 SD 92101 1289-A1
600 CHV 91910 1330-C1
700 CHV 91911 1330-D3
2500 SD 92103 1289-A1
2600 SD 92103 1269-A7
E 2ND AV
400 ESCN 92025 1129-J2
400 ESCN 92025 1130-A2
E 2ND AV Rt#-S6
100 ESCN 92025 1129-J3
N 2ND AV
- CHV 91910 1310-B4
3000 NATC 91950 1310-B3
3200 CHV 91950 1310-B3
W 2ND AV
500 ESCN 92025 1129-H3
W 2ND AV Rt#-S6
200 ESCN 92025 1129-J3
2ND LN
1400 SD 92154 1350-D2
2ND PL
19800 SDCo 92029 1149-E2

STREET
Block City ZIP Pg-Grid
2ND ST
- CORD 92135 1288-F4
- ImCo 92249 6560-B7
- SD 92106 1308-A1
- SDCo 92004 (1121-G2
See Page 1100)
- SDCo 92055 1066-B2
- NATC 91950 1289-H7
- SDCo 92059 1029-J4
100 ENCT 92024 1147-B6
200 SDCo 92065 1152-H5
200 ELCN 92243 6499-J6
300 CORD 92118 1288-J5
700 IMPB 91932 1329-F7
800 ENCT 92024 1167-C1
900 IMPB 91932 1349-F1
1400 CORD 92118 1289-A6
1600 ELCN 92243 6559-J1
1800 SDCo 92036 1136-B7
2000 NATC 91950 1290-B6
4900 SDCo 92028 998-H4
10400 SNTE 92071 1231-E3
10700 SDCo 91978 1291-F1
10700 SDCo 91978 1271-F7
10800 SDCo 92040 1231-E3
N 2ND ST
700 ELCJ 92021 1251-J3
1500 SDCo 92021 1251-J3
N 2ND ST Rt#-54
300 ELCJ 92021 1251-J5
S 2ND ST
- ELCN 92243 6559-J2
200 ELCJ 92019 1251-J6
800 SDCo 92019 1251-J7
W 2ND ST
- NATC 91950 1289-H7
- NATC 91950 1309-G1
3RD AV
- CHV 91910 1310-A4
300 SD 92101 1289-A1
800 CHV 91910 1330-C1
1000 CHV 91911 1330-C1
2500 SD 92103 1289-A1
2600 SD 92103 1269-A4
E 3RD AV
100 ESCN 92025 1129-J3
500 ESCN 92025 1130-A2
W 3RD AV
100 ESCN 92025 1129-J3
3RD LN
1400 SD 92154 1350-D2
3RD PL
19400 SDCo 92029 1149-E2
3RD ST
- CORD 92135 1288-F4
- SD 92106 1308-A1
- SDCo 92004 (1121-G2
See Page 1100)
100 ENCT 92024 1147-B6
200 SDCo 92065 1152-H5
200 SDCo 92055 1066-B2
300 SDCo 92036 1136-B7
300 CORD 92118 1289-A6
400 NATC 91950 1289-H7
500 ELCN 92243 6499-J5
500 IMPB 91932 1329-F7
700 ELCJ 92021 1252-A4
800 ENCT 92024 1167-B1
800 CORD 92118 1288-J6
900 IMPB 91932 1349-F1
1700 ELCN 92243 6559-J1
2000 NATC 91950 1290-A7
4500 LMSA 91941 1270-J3
10700 SDCo 91978 1291-F1
10700 SDCo 91978 1271-F7
3RD ST Rt#-S16
- SDCo 92059 1029-H4
3RD ST Rt#-282
300 CORD 92118 1288-H5
E 3RD ST
- NATC 91950 1309-H1
200 NATC 91950 1289-H7
N 3RD ST
100 ELCJ 92019 1252-A5
600 ELCJ 92021 1252-A5
S 3RD ST
100 ELCJ 92019 1252-A5
W 3RD ST
- NATC 91950 1309-G1
4S RANCH PKWY
- SDCo 92127 1169-E3
4TH AV
- CHV 91910 1310-A5
200 SD 92101 1289-A2
600 CHV 91910 1330-B1
800 CHV 91911 1330-C2
2600 SD 92103 1269-A5
2600 SD 92103 1289-A2
E 4TH AV
100 ESCN 92025 1129-J3
300 ESCN 92025 1130-A2
N 4TH AV
- CHV 91910 1310-A4
2200 NATC 91910 1310-A4
W 4TH AV
100 ESCN 92025 1129-J3
4TH LN
1300 SD 92154 1350-C2
4TH PL
19300 SDCo 92029 1149-E2
4TH ST
- CORD 92135 1288-F5
- SDCo 92055 1066-C1
100 ENCT 92024 1147-B6
100 DLMR 92014 1187-F6
200 ELCJ 92019 1252-B4
200 SDCo 92065 1152-H5
500 IMPB 91932 1329-F7
500 NATC 91950 1289-J7
600 SDCo 92019 1252-B4
800 ENCT 92024 1167-B1
900 ELCN 92243 6499-H5
900 IMPB 91932 1349-F1
1500 NATC 91950 1290-A7
1900 SDCo 92036 1136-B7
3100 SD 92114 1290-A7
4400 LMSA 91941 1270-J3
8900 SNTE 92071 1231-E6
10700 SDCo 91978 1291-F1
4TH ST Rt#-S32
200 HOLT 92250 431-E5
4TH ST Rt#-75
300 CORD 92118 1288-H5
4TH ST Rt#-86
400 ELCN 92243 6499-H6
1700 ELCN 92243 6559-J1
4TH ST Rt#-282
300 CORD 92118 1288-H5

STREET
Block City ZIP Pg-Grid
E 4TH ST
- NATC 91950 1309-H1
500 NATC 91950 1289-H7
W 4TH ST
- NATC 91950 1309-G1
200 NATC 92136 1309-F1
5TH AV
- CHV 91910 1310-A5
100 SD 92101 1289-A2
500 CHV 91910 1330-B1
800 CHV 91911 1330-C3
2600 SD 92103 1269-A5
2600 SD 92103 1289-A2
E 5TH AV
200 ESCN 92025 1129-J3
300 ESCN 92025 1130-A3
N 5TH AV
- CHV 91910 1310-A5
W 5TH AV
800 ESCN 92025 1129-J3
5TH PL
9700 SDCo 92029 1149-D3
5TH ST
- SDCo 92055 1066-C1
- SDCo 92059 1029-H4
100 SDCo 92065 1152-H5
100 ENCT 92024 1147-B6
200 SDCo 92036 1136-B7
300 CORD 92118 1288-H6
400 ELCN 92243 6499-H5
500 IMPB 91932 1329-F6
800 NATC 91950 1289-J7
1100 ELCN 92243 6559-H1
1100 IMPB 91932 1349-F2
1300 SDCo 92055 1085-H5
1300 NATC 91950 1290-C6
2300 ENCT 92024 1167-J1
2600 ENCT 92024 1168-A1
4900 SDCo 92028 998-H5
5300 SDCo 92028 999-A5
10700 SDCo 91978 1291-F1
5TH ST Rt#-115
100 HOLT 92250 431-E5
E 5TH ST
- NATC 91950 1309-H1
3100 NATC 91950 1289-J7
N 5TH ST
100 SDCo 92065 1152-H5
W 5TH ST
- NATC 91950 1309-H1
6TH AV
300 SD 92101 1289-B2
2600 SD 92103 1269-A5
2600 SD 92103 1289-B2
E 6TH AV
100 ESCN 92025 1129-J3
200 ESCN 92025 1130-A3
W 6TH AV
100 ESCN 92025 1129-J3
6TH PL
19400 SDCo 92029 1149-D3
6TH ST
- SDCo 92036 1136-B7
- SDCo 92055 1066-C1
- NATC 91950 1309-H1
- ImCo 92249 6560-B7
100 DLMR 92014 1187-F6
100 SDCo 92055 1085-H4
100 SDCo 92065 1152-H5
100 CORD 92118 1288-H6
200 SDCo 92059 1029-H4
200 ELCN 92243 6499-H4
1000 NATC 91950 1289-J7
1100 ELCN 92243 6559-H1
1300 NATC 91950 1290-A7
2200 SDCo 91978 1271-F7
2200 SDCo 91978 1291-F1
7TH AV
100 SD 92101 1289-B2
3500 SD 92103 1269-A6
E 7TH AV
100 ESCN 92025 1129-J3
100 ESCN 92025 1130-A3
W 7TH AV
100 ESCN 92025 1129-J3
7TH PL
12400 SDCo 92029 1149-D3
7TH ST
- ImCo 92281 411-A11
- SDCo 92055 1066-C1
- WEST 92281 411-A11
- ImCo 92249 6560-B7
100 CHV 91911 1330-C5
100 SDCo 92055 1085-H4
100 SDCo 92065 1152-H6
100 DLMR 92014 1187-F6
300 CORD 92118 1288-H6
300 IMPB 91932 1329-G7
300 ELCN 92243 6499-H4
900 IMPB 91932 1349-G1
1100 ELCN 92243 6559-H1
1400 SMCS 92069 1108-C7
1500 NATC 91950 1289-J7
1500 NATC 91950 1290-C6
2200 ENCT 92024 1147-J7
2300 SDCo 91978 1291-F1
2300 ENCT 92024 1148-A7
3000 VSTA 92083 1108-C7
E 7TH ST
- NATC 91950 1309-H1
N 7TH ST
100 SDCo 92065 1152-G5
W 7TH ST
- NATC 91950 1309-H1
800 NATC 92136 1309-G2
8TH AV
- SD 92101 1289-B2
3600 SD 92103 1269-B5
E 8TH AV
300 ESCN 92025 1130-A3
S 8TH AV
- SD 92101 1289-B4
W 8TH AV
100 ESCN 92025 1129-H4
8TH PL
1200 SDCo 92029 1149-D4
8TH ST
- SDCo 92055 1066-D1
100 SDCo 92055 1085-H4
100 CORD 92118 1288-H6
100 DLMR 92014 1187-F6
100 SDCo 92065 1152-G6
400 SD 92014 1187-F6
500 ELCN 92243 6499-G3
600 IMPB 91932 1329-G7
900 IMPB 91932 1349-G1
1000 OCN 92054 1086-A6
1000 ELCN 92243 6559-G1
1400 ImCo 92243 6559-G1

STREET
Block City ZIP Pg-Grid
8TH ST
1500 SMCS 92069 1108-D7
1500 NATC 91950 1290-B7
1500 NATC 91950 1310-A1
1700 ImCo 92243 6499-G3
2000 SDCo 92028 998-J5
2200 SDCo 91978 1291-F1
2400 ENCT 92024 1147-J7
2400 ENCT 92024 1148-A7
5400 SDCo 92028 999-A5
E 8TH ST
- NATC 91950 1309-H1
1400 NATC 91950 1310-A1
1900 NATC 91950 1290-C7
N 8TH ST
100 SDCo 92065 1152-G5
W 8TH ST
- NATC 91950 1309-G1
100 NATC 92136 1309-G1
2100 ENCT 92024 1147-J7
9TH AV
- SD 92101 1289-B2
3900 SD 92103 1269-B4
E 9TH AV
100 ESCN 92025 1129-J4
100 ESCN 92025 1130-A3
W 9TH AV
200 ESCN 92025 1129-J4
1200 ESCN 92029 1129-F4
9TH ST
- SDCo 92055 1066-D1
100 SDCo 92055 1085-G4
100 DLMR 92014 1187-F5
100 SDCo 92065 1152-G6
300 CORD 92118 1288-G6
500 IMPB 91932 1329-G7
900 IMPB 91932 1349-G1
1000 ELCN 92243 6499-G6
1500 SMCS 92069 1108-C7
1600 NATC 91950 1310-A1
1800 ELCN 92243 6559-G1
2100 NATC 91950 1290-A7
2200 ENCT 92024 1147-J6
2200 SDCo 91978 1291-F1
2400 ENCT 92024 1148-A6
12300 PWY 92064 1190-C4
E 9TH ST
- NATC 91950 1309-H1
1300 NATC 91950 1310-A1
N 9TH ST
100 SDCo 92065 1152-G5
W 9TH ST
- NATC 91950 1309-H1
600 NATC 92136 1309-G2
10TH AV
1000 SD 92101 1289-B2
3700 SD 92103 1269-B5
E 10TH AV
100 ESCN 92025 1130-A4
W 10TH AV
100 ESCN 92025 1129-J4
100 ESCN 92025 1130-A4
10TH ST
100 DLMR 92014 1187-F5
200 CORD 92118 1288-G7
300 ELCN 92243 6499-G5
300 SDCo 92065 1152-G6
400 IMPB 91932 1329-H7
900 SDCo 92055 1066-D1
900 IMPB 91932 1349-H1
1000 ELCN 92243 6559-G1
1300 SDCo 92055 1085-H4
1600 NATC 91950 1310-A1
2100 NATC 91950 1290-B7
2200 SDCo 91978 1291-F1
11600 SD 92127 1169-J2
W 10TH ST
1200 NATC 91950 1309-F2
11TH AV
- SD 92101 1289-B3
E 11TH AV
300 ESCN 92025 1130-A4
W 11TH AV
400 ESCN 92025 1129-J4
900 ESCN 92025 1130-A4
1400 ESCN 92029 1129-F5
11TH ST
- ELCN 92243 6499-G6
- SDCo 92055 409-A7
- SDCo 92055 1066-E1
100 SDCo 92055 1085-H4
100 DLMR 92014 1187-F5
100 SDCo 92065 1152-G6
500 IMPB 91932 1329-H7
900 IMPB 91932 1349-H1
1700 ELCN 92243 6559-G1
1700 NATC 91950 1310-A1
2200 ENCT 92024 1147-J6
2300 ENCT 92024 1148-A6
2800 NATC 91950 1290-B7
E 11TH ST
- NATC 91950 1309-H1
N 11TH ST
100 SDCo 92065 1152-G6
W 11TH ST
- NATC 91950 1309-G2
12TH AV
- SD 92101 1289-B4
W 12TH AV
500 ESCN 92025 1129-J5
12TH PL
20200 SDCo 92029 1149-E2
12TH ST
100 SDCo 92055 1085-G3
100 SDCo 92065 1152-F6
100 DLMR 92014 1187-F5
200 ELCN 92243 6499-G4
500 IMPB 91932 1329-H7
900 IMPB 91932 1349-H1
1100 ELCN 92243 6559-G1
1600 NATC 91950 1310-A1
2200 ENCT 92024 1147-J5
2200 ENCT 92024 1148-A5
E 12TH ST
- NATC 91950 1309-J1
W 12TH ST
- NATC 91950 1309-G2
E 13TH AV
200 ESCN 92025 1130-A4
W 13TH AV
500 ESCN 92025 1129-J4
800 ESCN 92025 1130-A4
13TH ST
- SD 92101 1289-B4
100 SDCo 92055 1085-G3
100 DLMR 92014 1187-F5
100 SDCo 92065 1152-F6
400 IMPB 91932 1329-H7
800 NATC 91950 1309-J1

STREET
Block City ZIP Pg-Grid
13TH ST
900 IMPB 91932 1349-H1
2100 ENCT 92024 1147-J5
2200 ENCT 92024 1148-A5
2200 NATC 91950 1310-B1
N 13TH ST
100 SDCo 92065 1152-F6
S 13TH ST
100 SD 92101 1289-B4
W 14TH PL
900 ESCN 92025 1129-J5
14TH ST
- NATC 91950 1309-H2
- SD 92101 1289-B4
- SD 92101 1289-B4
100 SDCo 92055 1085-G3
100 ESCN 92025 1130-A4
100 SDCo 92065 1152-F6
200 ELCN 92243 6499-G6
300 DLMR 92014 1187-F5
800 SD 92154 1329-J7
900 SD 92154 1349-J2
1100 ELCN 92243 6559-G1
1100 IMPB 91932 1349-J2
1100 SD 91932 1349-J2
1300 NATC 91950 1310-A1
2100 ENCT 92024 1147-J5
2100 ENCT 92024 1148-A5
E 14TH ST
500 NATC 91950 1309-J2
N 14TH ST
100 SDCo 92065 1152-F6
W 14TH ST
700 NATC 91950 1309-G2
E 15TH AV
100 ESCN 92025 1130-A4
W 15TH AV
400 ESCN 92025 1129-J5
500 ESCN 92025 1130-A4
15TH ST
- SD 92113 1289-C4
100 DLMR 92014 1187-F5
300 SD 92101 1289-C4
800 SD 92154 1329-J7
900 SD 92154 1349-J2
1100 IMPB 91932 1349-J2
1100 IMPB 92154 1349-J2
1100 SD 91932 1349-J2
1400 NATC 91950 1310-A1
1500 SDCo 92055 1047-A5
E 15TH ST
- NATC 91950 1309-H2
W 15TH ST
- NATC 91950 1309-H2
W 16TH AV
700 ESCN 92025 1129-J5
16TH ST
100 SDCo 92065 1152-F7
300 SD 92113 1289-C4
400 SD 92101 1289-C2
600 SDCo 92055 1047-A5
600 SD 92154 1329-J7
900 SD 92154 1349-J1
1600 NATC 91950 1310-B1
3000 SD 92139 1310-B1
E 16TH ST
- NATC 91950 1309-H2
1100 NATC 91950 1310-A2
S 16TH ST
1000 SD 92113 1289-C4
W 16TH ST
- NATC 91950 1309-G2
17TH AV
300 ESCN 92025 1130-B5
700 SDCo 92025 1130-C4
900 SDCo 92027 1130-C4
1200 SD 92101 1289-C2
17TH ST
100 DLMR 92014 1187-F4
100 NATC 91950 1309-H2
200 SD 92113 1289-C4
300 SD 92101 1289-C4
900 ELCN 92243 6499-F4
1000 NATC 91950 1310-B1
2700 SD 92139 1310-B1
S 17TH ST
100 SD 92113 1289-C4
18TH AV
500 ESCN 92025 1130-A5
18TH ST
100 DLMR 92014 1187-F4
600 SD 92154 1330-A7
900 ELCN 92243 6499-F4
900 SD 92154 1350-A1
1100 ELCN 92243 6559-F1
1100 NATC 91950 1310-C1
2800 SD 92139 1310-C1
E 18TH ST
- NATC 91950 1309-J2
1000 NATC 91950 1310-A2
W 18TH ST
- NATC 91950 1309-G3
19TH ST
- SD 92113 1289-C4
100 DLMR 92014 1187-F4
100 SD 92102 1289-C3
200 SD 92154 1330-A6
300 NATC 91950 1309-G3
800 ELCN 92243 6499-E5
900 SD 92154 1350-A1
1000 ELCN 92243 6559-F1
1000 SD 92101 1289-C3
2400 NATC 91950 1310-B1
2900 SD 92139 1310-C1
E 19TH ST
600 NATC 91950 1309-J2
S 19TH ST
100 SD 92113 1289-C4
20TH ST
- SD 92113 1289-C4
100 DLMR 92014 1187-F4
100 SD 92102 1289-C3
1000 NATC 91950 1310-B1
3100 SD 92139 1310-B1
E 20TH ST
- NATC 91950 1309-J2
1000 NATC 91950 1310-A2
S 20TH ST
100 SD 92113 1289-C4
W 20TH ST
400 NATC 91950 1309-G3
21ST ST
- SD 92113 1289-C4
100 DLMR 92014 1187-F4
100 ELCN 92243 6499-E6
100 SD 92102 1289-C3
E 21ST ST
100 NATC 91950 1309-J2
900 NATC 91950 1310-A2

STREET
Block City ZIP Pg-Grid
S 21ST ST
100 SD 92113 1289-C4
W 21ST ST
400 NATC 91950 1309-H3
22ND ST
- SD 92113 1289-C4
100 DLMR 92014 1187-F4
100 ELCN 92243 6499-E6
300 SD 92102 1289-C3
900 NATC 91950 1310-A2
1500 ELCN 92243 6559-E1
E 22ND ST
- NATC 91950 1309-J3
900 NATC 91950 1310-A2
S 22ND ST
1000 SD 92113 1289-C4
W 22ND ST
- NATC 91950 1309-G3
23RD ST
100 DLMR 92014 1187-F3
100 ELCN 92243 6499-E6
800 SD 92102 1289-C3
900 NATC 91950 1310-A2
1600 ELCN 92243 6559-E1
E 23RD ST
800 NATC 91950 1309-J3
1000 NATC 91950 1310-A3
W 23RD ST
700 NATC 91950 1309-G3
24TH ST
- SD 92113 1289-D4
100 DLMR 92014 1187-F3
100 SD 92102 1289-D3
700 SD 92154 1330-B7
900 NATC 91950 1310-A2
1500 ELCN 92243 6559-E1
1900 SDCo 91950 1310-B2
E 24TH ST
- NATC 91950 1309-J3
800 NATC 91950 1310-A3
W 24TH ST
1500 NATC 91950 1309-G4
25TH ST
- NATC 91950 1309-H3
- SD 92113 1289-D4
100 DLMR 92014 1187-F3
100 SD 92102 1289-D4
1100 SD 92154 1350-B1
1300 SD 92101 1289-D4
26TH ST
100 DLMR 92014 1187-F3
600 SD 92102 1289-D3
900 NATC 91950 1310-A3
2200 SD 92113 1289-D4
E 26TH ST
- NATC 91950 1309-J3
S 26TH ST
900 SD 92113 1289-D6
W 26TH ST
- NATC 91950 1309-H3
26TH STREET RD
100 SD 92101 1289-D2
27TH ST
100 CHV 91911 1330-C5
100 DLMR 92014 1187-F3
100 NATC 91950 1309-J3
200 SD 92113 1289-D4
200 SD 92102 1289-D3
800 SD 92154 1330-C7
900 SD 92154 1350-C2
S 27TH ST
800 SD 92113 1289-D6
28TH ST
- SD 92113 1289-D3
100 SD 92102 1289-D2
200 DLMR 92014 1187-F3
800 NATC 91950 1310-A3
2000 SD 92101 1289-D2
2600 SD 92104 1269-D6
2600 SD 92101 1269-D7
E 28TH ST
- NATC 91950 1309-J3
700 NATC 91950 1310-A3
S 28TH ST
100 SD 92113 1289-E5
1200 SD 92136 1289-E5
W 28TH ST
- NATC 91950 1309-G4
29TH ST
- SD 92113 1289-E3
100 DLMR 92014 1187-F3
100 SD 92102 1289-E2
200 NATC 91950 1309-J4
1000 NATC 91950 1310-A3
2000 SD 92104 1289-E2
2700 SD 92104 1269-E6
S 29TH ST
100 SD 92113 1289-E5
30TH PL
600 SD 92102 1289-E3
30TH ST
- SD 92113 1289-E3
100 SD 92102 1289-E2
600 NATC 91950 1310-A3
1100 SD 92154 1350-D1
1200 CHV 91950 1310-A3
2000 SD 92104 1289-E2
2500 SD 92104 1269-E5
4400 SD 92116 1269-E5
E 30TH ST
- NATC 91950 1309-J4
600 NATC 91950 1310-A3
S 30TH ST
500 SD 92113 1289-E5
1300 SD 92136 1289-E6
W 30TH ST
- NATC 91950 1309-H4
31ST ST
- NATC 91950 1309-J4
- SD 92113 1289-E4
100 SD 92102 1289-E2
2000 SD 92104 1289-E2
3000 SD 92104 1269-E6
S 31ST ST
100 SD 92113 1289-E5
32ND ST
- SD 92113 1289-F3
- SD 92102 1289-E2
200 CHV 91950 1309-J4
400 NATC 91950 1309-G5
400 NATC 91950 1310-C3
2000 SD 92104 1289-E2
2300 SDCo 91950 1310-C3
2500 SD 92104 1269-E6
4400 SD 92116 1269-E3
S 32ND ST
100 SD 92113 1289-F5
1400 SD 92136 1289-F6

STREET
Block City ZIP Pg-Grid
33RD PL
4300 SD 92104 1269-F4
4400 SD 92116 1269-F4
33RD ST
- NATC 91950 1309-J4
- SD 92102 1289-F1
- SD 92113 1289-F4
2600 SD 92104 1289-F4
2700 SD 92104 1289-F1
4400 SD 92116 1269-F4
S 33RD ST
- SD 92113 1289-F5
34TH ST
300 SD 92102 1289-F3
2400 SD 92104 1289-F4
2400 SD 92104 1289-F1
4100 SD 92116 1269-F4
35TH PL
4500 SD 92116 1269-F4
35TH ST
- NATC 91950 1309-J5
- SD 92113 1289-F5
3600 SD 92104 1269-F4
4300 SD 92116 1269-F2
N 35TH ST
- SD 92102 1289-F3
36TH ST
100 SD 92113 1289-G5
300 SD 92102 1289-G4
3500 SD 92104 1269-F4
4400 SD 92116 1269-F4
N 36TH ST
100 SD 92102 1289-F4
37TH ST
200 SD 92113 1289-G5
3400 SD 92105 1269-G6
4200 SD 92104 1269-G4
4400 SD 92116 1269-G4
38TH ST
200 SD 92113 1289-G6
3000 SD 92105 1269-G4
4400 SD 92116 1269-G3
N 38TH ST
1000 SD 92102 1289-G3
1300 SD 92105 1289-G2
39TH ST
700 SD 92113 1289-G5
2800 SD 92105 1269-G4
3800 SD 92116 1269-G3
N 39TH ST
800 SD 92102 1289-G3
1500 SD 92105 1289-G1
40TH ST
200 SD 92113 1289-H5
2500 SD 92105 1269-G5
4500 SD 92116 1269-G4
N 40TH ST
600 SD 92102 1289-G3
1500 SD 92105 1289-G2
41ST ST
700 SD 92113 1289-H6
3100 SD 92105 1269-G4
4400 SD 92116 1269-G4
N 41ST ST
300 SD 92102 1289-H3
42ND ST
600 SD 92113 1289-H5
3400 SD 92105 1269-H4
4400 SD 92116 1269-H3
N 42ND ST
800 SD 92102 1289-H3
1600 SD 92105 1289-H2
43RD ST
- SD 92102 1289-H6
- SDCo 92102 1289-H6
900 SD 92113 1289-H6
1700 NATC 91950 1289-H6
3100 SD 92105 1269-H6
N 43RD ST
300 SD 92102 1289-H4
44TH ST
100 SD 92102 1289-H3
100 SDCo 92102 1289-J4
2400 SD 92105 1289-H1
2500 SD 92105 1269-H5
4100 SD 92115 1269-H4
S 44TH ST
700 SD 92113 1289-H5
45TH ST
200 SD 92113 1289-J5
3000 SD 92105 1269-J5
4100 SD 92115 1269-H4
N 45TH ST
400 SD 92102 1289-J3
46TH ST
200 SD 92113 1289-J5
900 SD 92102 1289-J3
2500 SD 92105 1269-J5
4200 SD 92115 1269-J4
N 46TH ST
400 SD 92102 1289-J4
47TH ST
300 SD 92102 1289-J3
1200 SD 92105 1289-J5
2800 SD 92105 1269-J5
4200 SD 92115 1269-J4
N 47TH ST
- NATC 91950 1289-J6
S 47TH ST
100 SD 92113 1289-J5
200 NATC 91950 1289-J5
300 SD 91950 1289-J5
48TH ST
600 SD 92102 1289-J1
1200 SD 92113 1290-A6
4000 SD 92113 1289-J5
4000 SD 92105 1269-J5
4200 SD 92115 1269-J4
6000 SD 92120 1249-J7
49TH ST
100 SD 92102 1290-A2
1600 SD 92102 1289-J2
3800 SD 92105 1270-A5
4100 SD 92115 1270-A3
6300 SD 92120 1250-A6
S 49TH ST
1000 SD 92113 1290-A5
50TH ST
100 SD 92102 1290-A1
1300 SD 92113 1290-A6
1300 NATC 91950 1290-A6
3600 SD 92105 1270-A5
4100 SD 92115 1270-A4
5000 SD 92120 1250-A5
51ST ST
500 SD 92114 1290-A3
2600 SD 92105 1270-A6
4200 SD 92115 1270-A3
6500 SD 92120 1250-A5

STREET Block City ZIP Pg-Grid

52ND PL
5200 SD 92105 1270-A5
52ND ST
2100 SD 92105 1290-A1
2400 SD 92105 1270-A5
4100 SD 92115 1270-A5
53RD ST
200 SD 92114 1290-B4
2800 SD 92105 1270-B7
4300 SD 92115 1270-A4
54TH PL
4100 SD 92105 1270-B4
4200 SD 92115 1270-B4
54TH ST
400 SD 92114 1290-B3
1800 SD 92105 1290-A1
2400 SD 92105 1270-B5
4200 SD 92115 1270-A2
55TH PL
5000 SD 92115 1270-B2
55TH ST
2100 SD 92105 1290-B1
2100 SD 92114 1290-B4
2400 SD 92105 1270-B6
4500 SD 92115 1270-B1
5100 SD 92182 1270-B1
56TH PL
5500 SD 92114 1290-B3
56TH ST
600 SD 92114 1290-B3
2300 SD 92105 1270-B7
4300 SD 92115 1270-B4
57TH ST
900 SD 92114 1290-B2
58TH PL
5700 SD 92115 1270-B4
58TH ST
100 SD 92114 1290-C5
3800 SD 92105 1270-B6
3800 SD 92115 1270-B4
59TH ST
300 SD 92114 1290-C3
4400 SD 92115 1270-C3
S 59TH ST
400 SD 92114 1290-C5
60TH ST
500 SD 92114 1290-C2
3200 SD 92115 1270-C3
61ST ST
100 SD 92114 1290-C4
N 61ST ST
100 SD 92114 1290-C3
62ND ST
500 SD 92114 1290-D3
4500 SD 92115 1270-C3
63RD ST
300 SD 92114 1290-D3
4500 SD 92115 1270-C2
64TH ST
500 SD 92114 1290-D3
4900 SD 92115 1270-D2
65TH ST
100 SD 92114 1290-D5
N 65TH ST
200 SD 92114 1290-D3
66TH ST
200 SD 92114 1290-E3
S 66TH ST
500 SD 92114 1290-E5
67TH ST
600 SD 92114 1290-E3
4500 SD 92115 1270-E2
68TH ST
200 SD 92114 1290-E3
4200 LMSA 91941 1270-E3
4200 SD 92115 1270-E2
69TH PL
4800 SD 92115 1270-E2
69TH ST
100 SD 92114 1290-E2
1300 LMGR 91945 1290-E2
2300 LMGR 91945 1270-E7
3600 SD 92115 1270-E2
70TH ST
4200 LMSA 91941 1270-E4
4800 SD 92115 1270-E4
5000 LMSA 92115 1228-E1
5100 SD 91941 1270-E4
71ST ST
600 SD 92114 1290-F3
4300 LMSA 91941 1270-F3
4800 SD 92115 1270-F2
72ND ST
4900 SD 92115 1270-F2
73RD ST
4500 LMSA 91941 1270-F3
4800 SD 92115 1270-F3
NW 191ST PL
9600 SNTE 92071 1231-A4
NW 204TH ST
1400 SD 92037 1227-G7
I-5 SAN DIEGO FRWY
- CHV - 1309-H4
- CHV - 1329-J1
- CHV - 1330-A3
- CRLB - 1106-F6
- CRLB - 1126-G2
- CRLB - 1127-A6
- CRLB - 1147-A1
- ENCT - 1147-C5
- ENCT - 1167-D2
- NATC - 1289-C2
- NATC - 1309-G1
- OCN - 1085-G2
- OCN - 1086-A6
- OCN - 1106-C1
- SCLE - 1023-E3
- SD - 1187-H2
- SD - 1207-J1
- SD - 1208-A3
- SD - 1228-B4
- SD - 1248-B2
- SD - 1268-E3
- SD - 1288-J1
- SD - 1289-C2
- SD - 1330-A6
- SD - 1350-D3
- SDCo - 408-H5
- SDCo - 1023-E3
- SDCo - 1085-G2
- SOLB - 1167-D2
- SOLB - 1187-H2
I-8 Bus BUSINESS ROUTE
2000 ELCJ - 1252-C1
9700 SDCo - 1252-C1
13000 SDCo - 1232-E6
I-8 FRWY
- ELCJ - 1251-F4

I-8 FRWY
- ELCJ - 1252-B3
- ELCJ - 1271-C1
- ELCN - 6559-J2
- ELCN - 6560-C1
- ImCo - 430-K6
- ImCo - 431-D6
- ImCo - 432-A5
- ImCo - 6559-F2
- ImCo - 6560-J1
- LMSA - 1251-B7
- LMSA - 1270-E1
- LMSA - 1271-C1
- SD - 1269-H1
- SD - 1270-A1
- SDCo - 430-A6
- SDCo - 1232-J4
- SDCo - 1233-E3
- SDCo - 1234-A5
- SDCo - 1235-F5
- SDCo - 1236-A7
- SDCo - 1236-H7
- SDCo - 1237-A7
- SDCo - 1252-B3
- SDCo - (1299-C1 See Page 1298)
- SDCo - 1300-A2
- SDCo - (1301-A6 See Page 1300)
- SDCo - (1321-F1 See Page 1300)
I-8 MISSION VALLEY FRWY
- SD - 1268-F4
- SD - 1269-B3
I-8 OCEAN BEACH FRWY
- SD - 1268-B5
I-15 AVOCADO HWY
- ESCN - 1109-E3
- ESCN - 1129-F1
- RivC - 998-H3
- RivC - 999-A2
- SDCo - 1028-G4
- SDCo - 1048-H4
- SDCo - 1068-J4
- SDCo - 1088-J1
- SDCo - 1089-B4
- SDCo - 1109-E3
- SDCo - 1129-F1
I-15 ESCONDIDO FRWY
- ESCN - 1109-E3
- ESCN - 1129-H5
- ESCN - 1150-A1
- RivC - 998-H5
- SD - 1150-A1
- SD - 1169-J6
- SD - 1170-A3
- SD - 1189-F6
- SD - 1209-F4
- SD - 1229-F5
- SD - 1249-F3
- SD - 1269-G2
- SDCo - 998-H5
- SDCo - 1028-G4
- SDCo - 1048-J4
- SDCo - 1068-J3
- SDCo - 1088-J1
- SDCo - 1089-A2
- SDCo - 1109-E3
- SDCo - 1129-H5
- SDCo - 1130-A7
- SDCo - 1150-A1
- SDCo - 1209-F4
I-15 TEMECULA VALLEY FRWY
- RivC - 998-J2
- RivC - 999-A1
I-805 JACOB DEKEMA FRWY
- CHV - 1310-B3
- CHV - 1330-G2
- NATC - 1289-H1
- NATC - 1290-A7
- NATC - 1310-B3
- SD - 1208-C6
- SD - 1228-E1
- SD - 1248-J1
- SD - 1249-A3
- SD - 1269-C1
- SD - 1289-H1
- SD - 1330-G2
- SDCo - 1310-B3
Rt#-S1 BUCKMAN SPRINGS RD
1300 SDCo 91906 (1318-A4 See Page 1298)
1300 SDCo 91906 (1317-H1 See Page 1296)
2100 SDCo 91906 (1297-G1 See Page 1296)
2600 SDCo 91906 430-A7
2600 SDCo 92066 430-A7
Rt#-S1 OLD HIGHWAY 80
29800 SDCo 92066 430-A6
Rt#-S1 SUNRISE HWY
6800 SDCo 92066 430-A6
6800 SDCo 92066 1237-G3
6800 SDCo 91948 1237-G3
9500 SDCo 91948 430-B5
10500 SDCo 91948 1218-A1
12200 SDCo 91948 (1217-J1 See Page 1216)
12300 SDCo 91948 (1197-F4 See Page 1176)
14100 SDCo 92036 1176-G2
14300 SDCo 92036 (1177-B6 See Page 1176)
14700 SDCo 92036 (1197-F4 See Page 1176)
Rt#-S2 GREAT STHN OVLD STG RT
- SDCo 92036 410-A11
- SDCo 92036 430-B2
- SDCo 92036 1138-A5
- SDCo 92036 (1158-C7 See Page 1138)
14900 SDCo 92036 430-B2
Rt#-S2 IMPERIAL HWY
- SDCo 92259 430-G6
Rt#-S2 SAN FELIPE RD
21300 SDCo 92036 410-A10
22300 SDCo 92086 410-A10
25600 SDCo 92086 409-K9
29000 SDCo 92070 409-K9

Rt#-S2 SWEENEY PASS RD
- SDCo 92036 430-E4
- SDCo 92259 430-E4
Rt#-S3 BORREGO SPRINGS RD
2500 SDCo 92004 (1078-J3 See Page 1058)
3500 SDCo 92004 (1079-A7 See Page 1058)
3500 SDCo 92004 (1099-A1 See Page 1098)
Rt#-S3 YAQUI PASS RD
3700 SDCo 92004 (1099-E6 See Page 1098)
3700 SDCo 92004 (1118-J5 See Page 1098)
3700 SDCo 92004 (1119-A4 See Page 1098)
5600 SDCo 92036 (1118-J5 See Page 1098)
Rt#-S4 POWAY RD
11600 PWY 92064 1190-H2
11600 SD 92128 1190-B5
12000 SD 92128 1189-G6
15500 PWY 92064 1191-A1
Rt#-S5 ESPOLA RD
14100 PWY 92064 1190-G1
14800 PWY 92064 1170-D3
16900 SD 92128 1170-D3
Rt#-S5 POMERADO RD
- SD 92127 1150-B5
16900 SD 92128 1170-C3
17700 SD 92128 1150-B5
Rt#-S5 RANCHO BERNARDO RD
12500 SD 92128 1170-D3
Rt#-S6 E 2ND AV
100 ESCN 92025 1129-J3
Rt#-S6 W 2ND AV
200 ESCN 92025 1129-J3
Rt#-S6 CANFIELD RD
3400 SDCo 92060 409-G6
Rt#-S6 DEL DIOS HWY
500 SDCo 92029 1149-D2
500 SDCo 92067 1149-D6
1100 ESCN 92029 1129-F6
9800 ESCN 92029 1149-D2
9900 SDCo 92029 1129-F6
Rt#-S6 EL ESCONDIDO DEL DIOS
6900 SDCo 92067 1168-F1
7600 SDCo 92067 1149-A7
7800 SDCo 92067 1148-J7
Rt#-S6 S GRADE RD
31600 SDCo 92060 409-G7
31600 SDCo 92082 409-G7
31600 SDCo 92061 409-G7
Rt#-S6 W GRAND AV
800 ESCN 92025 1129-G3
Rt#-S6 HIGHWAY TO THE STARS
3400 SDCo 92060 409-G6
Rt#-S6 PASEO DELICIAS
6200 SDCo 92067 1168-F2
Rt#-S6 N VALLEY BLVD
100 ESCN 92025 1129-J2
Rt#-S6 S VALLEY BLVD
100 ESCN 92025 1129-J2
Rt#-S6 VALLEY PKWY
900 ESCN 92025 1129-F4
1100 ESCN 92029 1129-F4
Rt#-S6 E VALLEY PKWY
100 ESCN 92025 1129-J2
500 ESCN 92025 1130-A2
1100 ESCN 92027 1130-A2
1800 ESCN 92027 1110-E5
Rt#-S6 W VALLEY PKWY
200 ESCN 92025 1129-H3
Rt#-S6 VALLEY CENTER RD
24700 ESCN 92027 1110-F4
24800 SDCo 92027 1090-E4
24800 SDCo 92027 1110-F4
24800 SDCo 92082 1090-E1
30300 SDCo 92082 1091-A2
31700 SDCo 92082 1071-E1
33600 SDCo 92061 1051-D7
33600 SDCo 92061 1071-E1
Rt#-S6 VIA DE LA VALLE
100 DLMR 92014 1187-G2
600 SD 92014 1187-J2
3200 SD 92014 1188-B1
4000 SDCo 92014 1188-B1
14900 SD 92067 1188-B1
14900 SDCo 92091 1188-B1
15000 SDCo 92067 1168-E3
15000 SDCo 92091 1168-D6
15100 SD 92075 1187-G2
Rt#-7 HIGHWAY
- ImCo 92231 431-E7
Rt#-S7 E GRADE RD
21500 SDCo 92060 409-H7
23500 SDCo 92070 409-H7
Rt#-S8 LINEA DEL CIELO
4800 SDCo 92014 1168-A6
4900 SDCo 92067 1168-C4
Rt#-S8 LOMAS SANTA FE DR
100 SOLB 92075 1167-F7
1500 SDCo 92014 1167-F7
1500 SOLB 92014 1167-F7
1600 SDCo 92014 1168-A6
Rt#-S8 PASEO DELICIAS
6100 SDCo 92067 1168-E2
Rt#-S9 ENCINITAS BLVD
- ENCT 92024 1147-C6
1900 ENCT 92024 1167-J1
Rt#-S9 LA BAJADA
17400 SDCo 92067 1168-A2
17600 SDCo 92067 1167-J2
Rt#-S9 LA GRANADA
4800 SDCo 92067 1168-A3
Rt#-S9 LOS MORROS
17200 SDCo 92067 1168-A2
Rt#-S9 RANCHO SANTA FE RD
100 ENCT 92024 1167-J1
100 SDCo 92067 1167-J1

Rt#-S9 RANCHO SANTA FE RD
2600 SDCo 92067 1168-A1
Rt#-S10 OLIVENHAIN RD
1600 ENCT 92024 1147-F4
1600 CRLB 92009 1147-F4
Rt#-S10 RANCHO SANTA FE RD
2300 CRLB 92009 1128-A7
2300 CRLB 92069 1128-A7
2300 CRLB 92078 1128-A7
2900 CRLB 92009 1147-H3
7200 CRLB 92009 1148-A1
Rt#-S10 N RANCHO SANTA FE RD
100 SMCS 92069 1108-D6
Rt#-S10 S RANCHO SANTA FE RD
100 SMCS 92069 1108-D7
400 SMCS 92069 1128-A3
2100 CRLB 92009 1128-A3
2100 CRLB 92069 1128-A3
Rt#-S11 EL CAMINO REAL
1000 CRLB 92024 1147-E1
1000 ENCT 92024 1147-E1
1000 CRLB 92009 1147-E1
1200 CRLB 92009 1127-E4
1600 CRLB 92008 1127-D1
1800 CRLB 92008 1107-A6
2100 CRLB 92008 1106-H4
2300 OCN 92056 1106-H4
2300 OCN 92054 1106-H4
2400 CRLB 92054 1106-H4
Rt#-S11 N EL CAMINO REAL
100 ENCT 92024 1147-F4
1000 CRLB 92009 1147-F4
1000 CRLB 92024 1147-F4
1000 ENCT 92009 1147-F4
Rt#-S12 DEER SPRINGS RD
100 SMCS 92069 1108-J1
500 SDCo 92069 1088-J7
500 SDCo 92069 1089-A7
500 SDCo 92069 1108-J1
500 SDCo 92069 1109-A1
1000 SDCo 92026 1089-A7
Rt#-S12 PALOMAR AIRPORT RD
- CRLB 92008 1126-H3
- CRLB 92009 1126-H3
1200 CRLB 92009 1127-F2
1200 CRLB 92010 1127-F2
3100 CRLB 92008 1128-A2
3100 SMCS 92069 1128-A2
3100 CRLB 92009 1128-A2
Rt#-S12 W SAN MARCOS BLVD
200 SMCS 92069 1108-H7
300 SMCS 92069 1128-A2
Rt#-S12 N TWIN OAKS VALLEY RD
200 SMCS 92069 1108-H5
Rt#-S13 N MAIN AV
100 SDCo 92028 1027-F2
Rt#-S13 S MAIN AV
100 SDCo 92028 1027-F3
Rt#-S13 E MISSION RD
100 SDCo 92028 1027-H1
2000 SDCo 92028 1028-A1
2500 SDCo 92028 998-B7
Rt#-S13 S MISSION RD
1100 SDCo 92028 1027-G6
2600 SDCo 92028 1047-H1
4900 SDCo 92028 1048-A7
5000 SDCo 92003 1048-A7
Rt#-S13 E VISTA WY
100 VSTA 92084 1087-J5
1100 VSTA 92084 1088-A2
2100 SDCo 92084 1088-A2
2600 SDCo 92084 1067-J6
2600 SDCo 92084 1068-A7
Rt#-S13 W VISTA WY
300 VSTA 92083 1087-G7
Rt#-S13 VISTA VILLAGE DR
100 VSTA 92084 1087-H6
100 VSTA 92083 1087-H6
Rt#-S14 W MISSION AV
300 ESCN 92025 1129-G2
1200 ESCN 92029 1129-G2
Rt#-S14 E MISSION RD
100 SMCS 92069 1108-J7
500 SMCS 92069 1109-B7
1000 SMCS 92069 1129-C1
1400 SMCS 92078 1129-C1
Rt#-S14 W MISSION RD
1000 SMCS 92069 1108-F7
1300 ESCN 92029 1129-E2
2000 SMCS 92078 1129-E2
Rt#-S14 N SANTA FE AV
300 VSTA 92083 1087-G2
300 VSTA 92084 1087-G2
800 OCN 92057 1067-C7
800 OCN 92056 1087-D1
800 OCN 92057 1087-D1
2200 SDCo 92083 1087-G2
2200 SDCo 92084 1087-G2
2200 OCN 92084 1087-G2
2200 VSTA 92056 1087-G2
Rt#-S14 S SANTA FE AV
100 VSTA 92083 1087-H7
100 VSTA 92084 1087-H7
1000 VSTA 92084 1088-A7
1000 VSTA 92084 1108-B2
1000 VSTA 92083 1108-B2
1400 SDCo 92084 1108-B2
1400 SDCo 92083 1108-B2
2600 SMCS 92069 1108-C4
Rt#-15 ESCONDIDO FRWY
- SD - 1269-G6
- SD - 1289-F2
Rt#-S15 E FALLBROOK ST
100 SDCo 92028 1027-G3
Rt#-S15 RECHE RD
1500 SDCo 92028 1027-J4
1700 SDCo 92028 1028-A4

Rt#-S15 S STAGE COACH LN
400 SDCo 92028 1027-J4
Rt#-S16 3RD ST
- SDCo 92059 1029-H4
Rt#-S16 PALA RD
47000 RivC 92592 999-G1
47800 SDCo 92028 999-G1
Rt#-S16 PALA TEMECULA RD
37100 SDCo 92028 999-G3
38600 SDCo 92059 999-G3
41800 SDCo 92059 1029-G2
Rt#-S17 BONITA RD
- CHV 91910 1310-D5
2800 SDCo 91910 1310-E4
3000 SDCo 91902 1310-J1
3600 CHV 91902 1310-H3
Rt#-S17 E ST
- CHV 91910 1310-B5
200 CHV 91910 1309-J6
Rt#-S17 JAMACHA BLVD
8700 SDCo 91977 1291-E2
10600 SDCo 91978 1271-F7
10600 SDCo 91978 1291-E2
Rt#-S17 SWEETWATER RD
5300 SDCo 91902 1290-J6
5300 SDCo 91902 1310-H1
5600 SDCo 91902 1291-A7
Rt#-S21 CAMINO DEL MAR
400 DLMR 92014 1187-F4
Rt#-S21 S CAMINO DEL MAR
100 DLMR 92014 1187-G7
Rt#-S21 CARLSBAD BLVD
200 CRLB 92009 1126-H6
2200 CRLB 92008 1106-D4
3900 CRLB 92008 1126-F1
7100 CRLB 92009 1146-J1
7300 CRLB 92024 1147-A2
7300 ENCT 92024 1147-A2
7400 CRLB 92024 1146-J1
Rt#-S21 N COAST HWY
1000 OCN 92054 1086-A7
1200 OCN 92054 1085-J6
1400 SDCo 92055 1085-J6
Rt#-S21 S COAST HWY
100 OCN 92054 1086-A7
100 OCN 92054 1106-B2
2000 CRLB 92008 1106-B2
Rt#-S21 N COAST HWY 101
100 ENCT 92024 1147-A2
Rt#-S21 S COAST HWY 101
300 ENCT 92024 1147-C7
800 ENCT 92024 1167-D3
900 ENCT 92007 1167-D3
Rt#-S21 GENESEE AV
10400 SD 92037 1208-A7
10400 SD 92121 1208-A7
10400 SD 92093 1208-A7
10700 SD 92121 1207-J7
Rt#-S21 N HWY 101
100 SOLB 92075 1167-E7
Rt#-S21 S HWY 101
100 SOLB 92075 1167-E7
100 SOLB 92075 1187-F1
200 DLMR 92014 1187-F1
200 DLMR 92075 1187-F1
1700 ENCT 92007 1167-E7
Rt#-S21 N TORREY PINES RD
10300 SD 92121 1207-G2
10500 SD 92037 1207-G2
12100 SD 92014 1207-G2
12600 SD 92014 1187-G7
12800 DLMR 92014 1187-G7
Rt#-S22 BORREGO SALTON SEAWAY
- ImCo 92004 410-F7
- ImCo 92259 410-F7
- ImCo 92274 410-F7
- SDCo 92004 410-D7
- SDCo 92004 (1059-J4 See Page 1058)
Rt#-S22 CHRISTMAS CIR
600 SDCo 92004 (1078-H2 See Page 1058)
Rt#-S22 MONTEZUMA VALLEY RD
31300 SDCo 92066 410-A9
33400 SDCo 92066 409-L9
33900 SDCo 92066 1098-A2
34400 SDCo 92004 (1078-D7 See Page 1058)
34400 SDCo 92066 (1078-D7 See Page 1058)
35500 SDCo 92086 409-L9
Rt#-S22 PALM CANYON DR
200 SDCo 92004 (1078-F2 See Page 1058)
700 SDCo 92004 (1079-D2 See Page 1058)
Rt#-S22 PEG LEG RD
1300 SDCo 92004 (1059-J5 See Page 1058)
1300 SDCo 92004 (1079-J1 See Page 1058)
Rt#-S24 BARD RD
1100 ImCo 92283 432-D5
Rt#-S24 COLBY RD
- ImCo 92283 432-D4
Rt#-S24 IMPERIAL DAM RD
1900 ImCo 92283 432-E4
Rt#-S24 IMPERIAL RD
- ImCo 92283 432-E4
Rt#-S24 MERRING RD
800 ImCo 92283 432-E4
Rt#-S24 PICACHO RD
300 ImCo 92283 432-D5
Rt#-S24 ROSS RD
1400 ImCo 92283 432-D5
Rt#-S24 YORK RD
1400 ImCo 92283 432-D4
Rt#-S26 BOARTS RD
400 ImCo 92281 411-B11
400 ImCo 92281 431-B1
Rt#-S26 KALIN RD
- ImCo 92281 411-B11
Rt#-S26 MILLER AV
- ImCo 92281 431-A1

Rt#-S26 MILLER AV
- WEST 92281 431-A1
Rt#-S26 RUTHERFORD RD
- ImCo 92227 411-D11
- ImCo 92281 411-C11
900 ImCo 92233 411-C11
Rt#-S27 KEYSTONE RD
- ImCo 92227 431-C3
- ImCo 92251 431-C3
Rt#-S27 MCCONNELL RD
- ImCo 92227 431-C3
- ImCo 92251 431-C3
Rt#-S28 BARIONI ST
100 IMP 92251 431-B4
Rt#-S28 WORTHINGTON RD
- ImCo 92251 431-A4
- ImCo 92243 431-A4
500 IMP 92251 431-A4
1000 ImCo 92250 431-A4
1900 ImCo 92251 430-L4
Rt#-S29 DREW RD
- ImCo 92273 431-A7
400 ImCo 92231 431-A7
400 ImCo 92243 431-A7
Rt#-S30 BROCKMAN RD
500 ImCo 92231 431-A7
600 ImCo 92243 431-A7
Rt#-S30 EDDINS RD
- ImCo 92233 411-A10
Rt#-S30 FORRESTER RD
- ImCo 92227 411-A11
- WEST 92281 411-A11
1100 ImCo 92243 6559-A3
1800 ImCo 92243 431-A4
2200 ImCo 92251 431-A4
3900 ImCo 92227 431-A4
3900 ImCo 92259 431-A4
5000 ImCo 92281 431-A4
5200 WEST 92281 431-A4
5300 ImCo 92281 411-A11
Rt#-S30 GENTRY RD
5800 ImCo 92227 411-A11
5800 ImCo 92233 411-A11
Rt#-S30 MAIN ST
300 CLPT 92233 411-C10
Rt#-S30 MCCABE RD
- ImCo 92243 6559-A5
1100 ImCo 92243 431-A6
Rt#-S30 WALKER RD
- ImCo 92227 411-A11
Rt#-S31 DOGWOOD RD
- ImCo 92243 431-B3
- ImCo 92249 431-C7
- ImCo 92251 6500-A2
200 BRW 92227 431-B3
400 ImCo 92231 431-C7
1300 ImCo 92243 6560-B5
1300 ImCo 92249 6560-B5
1600 ELCN 92243 6560-B2
1700 ELCN 92243 6500-A5
2100 ImCo 92243 6500-A2
2800 ImCo 92251 431-B3
3600 ImCo 92227 431-B3
Rt#-S32 4TH ST
200 HOLT 92250 431-E5
Rt#-S32 BUTTERS RD
4300 ImCo 92227 431-E1
5300 ImCo 92227 411-E11
Rt#-S32 GONDER RD
- ImCo 92227 431-E2
Rt#-S32 HOLT AV
400 HOLT 92250 431-E5
1500 ImCo 92250 431-E5
Rt#-S32 HOLT RD
2300 ImCo 92250 431-E3
3900 ImCo 92227 431-E3
Rt#-S32 ORCHARD RD
- HOLT 92250 431-E5
1600 ImCo 92250 431-E5
Rt#-S33 BONESTEELE RD
700 ImCo 92250 431-F7
Rt#-S33 GONDER RD
- ImCo 92227 431-E2
Rt#-S33 GREEN RD
4200 ImCo 92227 431-E2
Rt#-S33 HIGHLINE RD
- ImCo 92227 431-E4
2200 ImCo 92250 431-E4
Rt#-S33 KAVANAUGH RD
- ImCo 92250 431-E5
Rt#-S33 KUMBERG MESA RD
- ImCo 92250 431-F7
Rt#-S33 MILLER RD
1000 ImCo 92250 431-F6
Rt#-S34 OGILBY RD
- ImCo - 411-K11
- ImCo - 431-L1
- ImCo - 432-A3
Rt#-52 FRWY
- SD - 1228-H6
- SD - 1229-D6
- SD - 1230-C4
- SD - 1231-A7
- SNTE - 1230-H6
- SNTE - 1231-A7
Rt#-52 SOLEDAD FRWY
- SD - 1228-B7
- SD - 1248-A1
Rt#-54 N 2ND ST
300 ELCJ 92021 1251-J5
Rt#-54 FRWY
- CHV - 1309-J4
- CHV - 1310-B3
- NATC - 1309-J4
- NATC - 1310-B4
- SDCo - 1290-H7
- SDCo - 1291-A4
- SDCo - 1310-C3
- NATC - 1310-E3
Rt#-54 JAMACHA RD
100 ELCJ 92019 1251-J5
100 ELCJ 92019 1252-A6
1000 SDCo 92019 1252-A6
1100 ELCJ 92019 1272-A5
1100 SDCo 92019 1272-A5
1100 SDCo 92020 1272-A5
2700 SDCo 92019 1271-J6
Rt#-54 SOUTH BAY PKWY
5600 SDCo 91902 1290-J6
5600 SDCo 91977 1290-J5
5600 SDCo 91977 1291-A4

Rt#-56 TED WILLIAMS FRWY
- SD - 1188-E5
- SD - 1189-A4
- SD - 1207-J2
- SD - 1208-A1
Rt#-67 HIGHWAY
10200 SDCo 92040 1232-A1
11200 SDCo 92040 1212-A7
11300 SDCo 92040 1211-G1
13000 SDCo 92040 1191-D3
13800 SDCo 92071 1191-E5
13900 SDCo 92064 1191-D3
14400 PWY 92064 1191-D1
15000 PWY 92064 1171-E5
15400 SDCo 92065 1171-F3
17600 SDCo 92065 1172-A3
Rt#-67 JULIAN RD
2500 SDCo 92065 1172-B3
Rt#-67 MAIN ST
900 SDCo 92065 1152-E7
1900 SDCo 92065 1172-D1
Rt#-67 SAN VICENTE FRWY
- ELCJ - 1251-F2
- SDCo - 1231-H4
- SDCo - 1232-A3
- SDCo - 1251-F2
- SNTE - 1231-F7
- SNTE - 1251-F2
Rt#-75 4TH ST
300 CORD 92118 1288-H5
Rt#-75 HIGHWAY
- CORD 92113 1289-B7
1500 CORD 92118 1288-J6
1500 CORD 92118 1289-A6
1900 SD 92113 1289-C5
Rt#-75 ORANGE AV
100 CORD 92118 1288-H7
1300 CORD 92118 1308-J1
Rt#-75 PALM AV
900 IMPB 91932 1329-G7
1300 SD 92154 1329-G7
1300 IMPB 92154 1329-G7
1700 SD 92154 1330-A7
Rt#-75 SILVER STRAND BLVD
500 CORD 91932 1329-D2
500 IMPB 91932 1329-D2
1700 CORD 92118 1308-J1
1900 CORD 92118 1309-A3
1900 CORD 92155 1309-A3
2100 CORD 92118 1329-D2
Rt#-76 HIGHWAY
300 OCN 92057 1086-J2
3400 OCN 92054 1086-J2
4700 OCN 92057 1087-A1
14800 SDCo 92061 1051-H5
19900 SDCo 92061 409-G7
20400 SDCo 92060 409-G7
20400 SDCo 92082 409-G7
23500 SDCo 92070 409-H8
23500 SDCo 92061 409-G8
Rt#-76 MISSION AV
3400 OCN 92054 1086-H2
3800 OCN 92057 1086-H2
4500 OCN 92057 1087-A1
4900 OCN 92057 1067-F6
5300 OCN 92056 1067-D7
5600 SDCo 92084 1067-H5
5600 SDCo 92003 1067-H6
Rt#-76 MISSION RD
5900 SDCo 92003 1067-H3
5900 SDCo 92084 1067-H3
31200 SDCo 92003 1068-A1
31800 SDCo 92003 1048-A7
Rt#-76 PALA RD
2200 SDCo 92003 1048-H2
2200 SDCo 92028 1048-H2
5600 SDCo 92059 409-E6
5600 SDCo 92061 409-E6
7500 SDCo 92059 1029-F4
8500 SDCo 92028 1029-C7
8600 SDCo 92028 1049-A1
16800 SDCo 92061 1051-B5
16800 SDCo 92082 1051-B5
33100 SDCo 92061 1050-H1
Rt#-76 SAN LUIS REY MSN EXWY
800 OCN 92054 1085-J6
800 OCN 92054 1086-A5
Rt#-78 N ASH ST
400 ESCN 92027 1130-A1
400 ESCN 92025 1130-A1
Rt#-78 S ASH ST
100 ESCN 92025 1130-A1
100 ESCN 92027 1130-A1
Rt#-78 BANNER RD
1200 SDCo 92036 1136-B5
36100 SDCo 92036 1156-H1
Rt#-78 N BROADWAY
600 ESCN 92025 1129-H2
800 ESCN 92026 1129-H2
Rt#-78 FRWY
- ESCN - 1129-E2
- OCN - 1106-G2
- OCN - 1107-A2
- SDCo - 1108-B4
- SDCo - 1129-F2
- SMCS - 1108-C5
- SMCS - 1109-A7
- SMCS - 1128-F1
- SMCS - 1129-B1
- VSTA - 1087-G7
- VSTA - 1107-E1
- VSTA - 1108-A2
Rt#-78 HAVERFORD RD
1200 SDCo 92065 1152-F3
Rt#-78 HIGHWAY
- ImCo - 411-L7
- ImCo - 412-A3
- ImCo - 431-J1
- ImCo 92227 410-K10
- ImCo 92227 430-L1
- ImCo 92227 431-A1
- ImCo 92259 410-J10
- ImCo 92259 430-L1
- ImCo 92281 431-A1
- SDCo 92004 410-F10
- SDCo 92036 1138-C1
- WEST 92281 431-A1
1700 SDCo 92004 (1118-J5 See Page 1098)
1700 SDCo 92004 (1119-D5 See Page 1098)
1700 SDCo 92036 (1118-J5 See Page 1098)
3000 SDCo 92004 (1120-J1 See Page 1100)

SAN DIEGO CO. INDEX

SAN DIEGO CO. INDEX

Rt#-78 HIGHWAY

Block	City	ZIP	Pg-Grid
4400	SDCo	92004	(1121-A1
	See Page 1100)		
35600	SDCo	92036	410-A11
35800	SDCo	92036	1136-J7
35800	SDCo	92036	1156-H1

Rt#-78 JULIAN RD

Block	City	ZIP	Pg-Grid
100	SDCo	92065	1152-J4
300	SDCo	92065	1153-J1
1700	SDCo	92065	409-J11
2000	SDCo	92065	1154-D2
18600	SDCo	92070	409-J11
18600	SDCo	92070	1135-B3

Rt#-78 MAIN ST

Block	City	ZIP	Pg-Grid
100	BRW	92227	431-C2
200	BRW	92227	431-C2
200	SDCo	92065	1152-G6

Rt#-78 MERL RD

Block	City	ZIP	Pg-Grid
-	ImCo	92281	431-A1
-	WEST	92281	431-A1

Rt#-78 PINE ST

Block	City	ZIP	Pg-Grid
100	SDCo	92065	1152-G3

Rt#-78 S PINE ST

Block	City	ZIP	Pg-Grid
100	SDCo	92065	1152-G6

Rt#-78 SAN PASQUAL VALLEY RD

Block	City	ZIP	Pg-Grid
100	ESCN	92027	1130-B2
100	ESCN	92025	1130-B2
800	SDCo	92025	1130-B2
800	SDCo	92027	1130-B2
1400	SDCo	92065	1152-C1
2100	SD	92065	409-G11
2100	SD	92027	409-G11
2100	SDCo	92065	409-G11
2100	SD	92027	409-G11
2400	SD	92027	1130-G6
3500	SD	92025	1131-A6
3500	SD	92065	1131-F6
3500	SD	92027	1131-A6
16100	SDCo	92027	1131-F6
16100	SDCo	92025	1131-F6

Rt#-78 E WASHINGTON AV

Block	City	ZIP	Pg-Grid
100	ESCN	92025	1129-J2
400	ESCN	92025	1130-A1

Rt#-79 CUYAMACA HWY

Block	City	ZIP	Pg-Grid
3400	SDCo	92036	1136-B7
3700	SDCo	92036	1156-D1
8200	SDCo	91916	1236-C4
8500	SDCo	92036	1176-F4
9600	SDCo	91916	1216-E3
12500	SDCo	91916	(1196-F4
	See Page 1176)		
13900	SDCo	92036	(1196-F4
	See Page 1176)		

Rt#-79 HIGHWAY

Block	City	ZIP	Pg-Grid
21900	SDCo	92070	409-K8
21900	SDCo	92070	1135-B1
23400	SDCo	92086	409-G5

Rt#-79 JAPATUL VALLEY RD

Block	City	ZIP	Pg-Grid
8100	SDCo	91901	1236-A6
8100	SDCo	91916	1236-A6
23400	SDCo	91901	1235-J6

Rt#-79 JULIAN RD

Block	City	ZIP	Pg-Grid
2200	SDCo	92036	1136-A7
2800	SDCo	92066	1135-D3
2800	SDCo	92070	1135-D3

Rt#-79 MAIN ST

Block	City	ZIP	Pg-Grid
1800	SDCo	92036	1136-B7

Rt#-79 WASHINGTON ST

Block	City	ZIP	Pg-Grid
2200	SDCo	92036	1136-B7

Rt#-S80 ADAMS AV

Block	City	ZIP	Pg-Grid
600	ELCN	92243	6499-E6
600	ImCo	92243	6499-E6

Rt#-S80 EVAN HEWES HWY

Block	City	ZIP	Pg-Grid
-	ImCo	92250	431-A5
200	ImCo	92243	6500-F5
600	ImCo	92243	6499-B6
900	ELCN	92243	6500-C6
900	ImCo	92243	431-A5
1700	ImCo	92273	431-A5
1800	ImCo	92273	430-J6
1900	ImCo	92251	430-J6
2800	ImCo	92259	430-J6

Rt#-S80 MAIN ST

Block	City	ZIP	Pg-Grid
100	ELCN	92243	6499-J6
100	ELCN	92243	6500-A6

Rt#-86 4TH ST

Block	City	ZIP	Pg-Grid
400	ELCN	92243	6499-H6
1700	ELCN	92243	6559-J1

Rt#-86 ADAMS AV

Block	City	ZIP	Pg-Grid
400	ELCN	92243	6499-F6

Rt#-86 HEBER RD

Block	City	ZIP	Pg-Grid
-	ImCo	92243	431-C7
-	ImCo	92249	431-C7
-	ImCo	92249	6560-D7

Rt#-86 HIGHWAY

Block	City	ZIP	Pg-Grid
-	BRW	92227	431-B2
-	ImCo	92227	431-B2
-	ImCo	92243	431-B7
-	ImCo	92249	6560-F7
-	ImCo	92251	431-B3
-	ImCo	92259	410-H7
-	ImCo	92274	410-F4
-	IMP	92243	6499-F2
-	IMP	92251	431-B4
-	IMP	92251	6499-F1
1300	ImCo	92243	6559-J3
1500	ELCN	92243	6559-J2

Rt#-86 N IMPERIAL AV

Block	City	ZIP	Pg-Grid
600	ELCN	92243	6499-F3
1800	ImCo	92243	6499-F3
1800	IMP	92243	6499-F3

Rt#-86 WESTER AV

Block	City	ZIP	Pg-Grid
300	BRW	92227	431-B2

Rt#-94 CAMPO RD

Block	City	ZIP	Pg-Grid
11100	SDCo	91978	1272-A7
11100	SDCo	91978	1271-G5
11100	SDCo	91941	1271-G5
11100	SDCo	92019	1271-J6
12100	SDCo	91978	1292-C1
12700	SDCo	91935	1272-D7
13100	SDCo	91935	1292-F1
14100	SDCo	91935	1293-B6
14700	SDCo	91935	(1313-F2
	See Page 1293)		
16000	SDCo	91917	(1313-F2
	See Page 1293)		
21100	SDCo	91917	(1314-B5
	See Page 1294)		
22000	SDCo	91917	429-J10
22600	SDCo	91980	429-K10

Rt#-94 FRWY

Block	City	ZIP	Pg-Grid
-	LMGR	-	1270-J5
-	LMSA	-	1270-J4
-	LMSA	-	1271-A4
-	SDCo	-	1270-J4
-	SDCo	-	1271-A4

Rt#-94 HIGHWAY

Block	City	ZIP	Pg-Grid
-	SDCo	91906	430-B10
-	SDCo	91963	429-L10
-	SDCo	91963	430-A10
-	SDCo	91980	429-K10
28500	SDCo	91906	(1318-J2
	See Page 1298)		
32100	SDCo	91906	(1319-G1
	See Page 1298)		
36700	SDCo	91906	(1299-H7
	See Page 1298)		
37100	SDCo	91905	(1299-J6
	See Page 1298)		
37700	SDCo	91905	1300-C6

Rt#-94 NW INNIS ARDEN WY

Block	City	ZIP	Pg-Grid
36700	SDCo	91906	(1299-G7
	See Page 1298)		
36700	SDCo	91906	(1319-G1
	See Page 1298)		
37100	SDCo	91905	(1299-G7
	See Page 1298)		
37700	SDCo	91905	1300-A6

Rt#-94 MARTIN L KING JR FRWY

Block	City	ZIP	Pg-Grid
-	LMGR	91941	1270-D7
-	LMGR	91945	1270-D7
-	LMGR	92115	1270-D7
-	SD	91945	1270-D7
-	SD	91945	1290-A2
-	SD	92101	1289-F3
-	SD	92102	1289-F3
-	SD	92102	1290-A2
-	SD	92105	1289-F3
-	SD	92105	1290-A2
-	SD	92114	1290-A2
-	SD	92115	1290-A2
-	SD	92115	1270-D7
-	SD	92115	1290-A2

Rt#-94 OLD HWY 80

Block	City	ZIP	Pg-Grid
36800	SDCo	91905	1300-C6

Rt#-94 RIBBONWOOD RD

Block	City	ZIP	Pg-Grid
2400	SDCo	91905	1300-D5

Rt#-98 HIGHWAY

Block	City	ZIP	Pg-Grid
-	CALX	92231	431-C7
-	ImCo	-	431-H6
-	ImCo	92249	431-D7
-	ImCo	92250	431-F7
-	ImCo	92259	430-G7
-	ImCo	92259	431-A8
900	ImCo	92231	431-E7

Rt#-111 FRWY

Block	City	ZIP	Pg-Grid
-	ImCo	-	6500-E1

Rt#-111 HIGHWAY

Block	City	ZIP	Pg-Grid
-	BRW	92227	431-C1
-	CALX	92231	431-C7
-	CLPT	92233	411-C10
-	ImCo	-	410-J4
-	ImCo	92227	411-C11
-	ImCo	92227	431-C1
-	ImCo	92231	431-C7
-	ImCo	92233	411-B8
-	ImCo	92243	6500-E7
-	ImCo	92243	6560-E1
-	ImCo	92249	431-C7
-	ImCo	92249	6560-F4
-	ImCo	92251	431-C3
-	ImCo	92257	410-L5
-	ImCo	92257	411-A5
-	ImCo	92259	410-K5

Rt#-115 5TH ST

Block	City	ZIP	Pg-Grid
100	HOLT	92250	431-E5

Rt#-115 EVAN HEWES HWY

Block	City	ZIP	Pg-Grid
400	HOLT	92250	431-E5
1500	ImCo	92250	431-D5

Rt#-115 HIGHWAY

Block	City	ZIP	Pg-Grid
-	HOLT	92250	431-E5
-	ImCo	92227	411-D11
-	ImCo	92227	431-D1
-	ImCo	92233	411-C10
2900	ImCo	92250	431-D3

Rt#-115 MAIN ST

Block	City	ZIP	Pg-Grid
-	ImCo	92233	411-C10
500	CLPT	92233	411-C10

Rt#-125 FRWY

Block	City	ZIP	Pg-Grid
-	CHV		1311-E3
-	CHV		1331-F1
-	ELCJ		1251-A2
-	LMGR		1270-J5
-	LMGR		1290-J1
-	LMSA		1251-A5
-	LMSA		1270-J5
-	LMSA		1271-A1
-	SD		1251-A6
-	SD		1331-G6
-	SD		1351-H1
-	SDCo		1270-J4
-	SDCo		1271-A4
-	SDCo		1290-J1
-	SDCo		1291-A3
-	SDCo		1311-D1
-	SDCo		1331-G6
-	SDCo		1351-H1
-	SNTE		1231-A7
-	SNTE		1251-A1

Rt#-163 CABRILLO FRWY

Block	City	ZIP	Pg-Grid
-	SD	-	1229-D6
-	SD	-	1249-B4
-	SD	-	1269-A1
-	SD	-	1289-B1

Rt#-163 FRWY

Block	City	ZIP	Pg-Grid
-	SD	-	1249-A6

Rt#-186 HIGHWAY

Block	City	ZIP	Pg-Grid
-	ImCo		432-B6

Rt#-188 TECATE RD

Block	City	ZIP	Pg-Grid
400	SDCo	91980	429-K10

Rt#-209 CABRILLO MEMORIAL DR

Block	City	ZIP	Pg-Grid
-	SD	92106	1288-A6
-	SD	92106	1308-A1
1800	SD	92106	1287-J5

Rt#-209 CAMINO DEL RIO W

Block	City	ZIP	Pg-Grid
3600	SD	92110	1268-E5

Rt#-209 CANON ST

Block	City	ZIP	Pg-Grid
900	SD	92106	1287-J3
3000	SD	92106	1288-A1

Rt#-209 CATALINA BLVD

Block	City	ZIP	Pg-Grid
200	SD	92106	1287-J4

Rt#-209 ROSECRANS ST

Block	City	ZIP	Pg-Grid
1200	SD	92106	1288-B2
1700	SD	92133	1288-B2
2100	SD	92133	1268-D7
2100	SD	92106	1268-D7
3000	SD	92110	1268-D7

Rt#-241 FOOTHILL TRANS CORR

Block	City	ZIP	Pg-Grid
-	SDCo	92672	1023-C2

Rt#-274 BALBOA AV

Block	City	ZIP	Pg-Grid
2900	SD	92109	1248-F4
3000	SD	92117	1248-F4
4200	SD	92111	1248-F4
7000	SD	92117	1249-B2
7000	SD	92111	1249-B2
8100	SD	92123	1249-B2

Rt#-274 GARNET AV

Block	City	ZIP	Pg-Grid
2800	SD	92109	1248-C5

Rt#-282 3RD ST

Block	City	ZIP	Pg-Grid
300	CORD	92118	1288-H5

Rt#-282 4TH ST

Block	City	ZIP	Pg-Grid
300	CORD	92118	1288-H5

Rt#-282 ALAMEDA BLVD

Block	City	ZIP	Pg-Grid
300	CORD	92135	1288-G6
300	CORD	92118	1288-G6

Rt#-282 POMONA AV

Block	City	ZIP	Pg-Grid
1200	CORD	92118	1288-J6

Rt#-905 FRWY

Block	City	ZIP	Pg-Grid
-	SD	-	1350-G2
-	SD	-	1351-A2

Rt#-905 HIGHWAY

Block	City	ZIP	Pg-Grid
1400	SD	92154	1351-J2
2100	SD	92154	1352-A3

Rt#-905 OTAY MESA RD E

Block	City	ZIP	Pg-Grid
5100	SD	92154	1351-A2
8800	SDCo	92154	1351-F2

AIRPORTS

FEATURE NAME	Address City, ZIP Code	PAGE-GRID
BLACKINTON AIRSTRIP	AIRFLIGHT DR, SDCo, 92082	1069 - G5
BORREGO VALLEY (SEE PAGE 1058)	1820 PALM CANYON DR, SDCo, 92004	1079 - G1
BRAWLEY MUNICIPAL	948 KEN BEMIS DR, BRW, 92227	431 - C1
BROWN FIELD MUNICIPAL	1424 CONTINENTAL ST, SD, 92154	1351 - D1
CALEXICO	801 W 2ND ST, CALX, 92231	431 - C8
FALLBROOK COMM AIRPARK	2141 S MISSION RD, SDCo, 92028	1027 - F6
GILLESPIE FIELD	1960 JOE CROSSON DR, ELCJ, 92020	1251 - D1
IMPERIAL COUNTY	1099 AIRPORT RD, IMP, 92251	6499 - E1
JACUMBA (SEE PAGE 1300)	JACUMBA OLD HWY, SDCo, 91934	1321 - J6
LAKE WOHLFORD RESORT AIRSTRIP	LAKE WOHLFORD RD, SDCo, 92027	1110 - H2
LYALL ROBERTS AIRSTRIP	HWY 76 & COLE GRADE RD, SDCo, 92061	1050 - J3
MCCLELLAN PALOMAR	2198 PALOMAR AIRPORT RD, CRLB, 92008	1127 - E2
MONTGOMERY FIELD	3750 JOHN J MONTGOMERY DR, SD, 92123	1249 - C3
OCEANSIDE MUNICIPAL	480 AIRPORT RD, OCN, 92054	1086 - D4
RAMONA	2450 MONTECITO RD, SDCo, 92065	1152 - B6
SAN DIEGO INTL	3707 N HARBOR DR, SD, 92101	1288 - G1

BEACHES, HARBORS & WATER REC

FEATURE NAME	Address City, ZIP Code	PAGE-GRID
CARDIFF ST BCH	SOUTH COAST HWY 101, ENCT, 92007	1167 - D5
CARLSBAD ST BCH	CARLSBAD BLVD, CRLB, 92008	1106 - D6
CHILDRENS POOL BEACH	COAST BLVD & JENNER ST, SD, 92037	1227 - E6
CORONADO MUNICIPAL BEACH	OCEAN BLVD & MARINA AV, CORD, 92118	1288 - G7
CUYAMACA RESERVOIR	CUYAMACA HWY & SUNRISE HWY, SDCo, 92036	1176 - G4
DEL MAR CITY BEACH	17TH ST, DLMR, 92014	1187 - E4
DEL MAR SHORES BEACH PK	180 DEL MAR SHORES TER, SOLB, 92075	1187 - E2
DOG BEACH	W POINT LOMA BL & VOLTAIRE ST, SD, 92109	1267 - J5
ECOLOGICAL RESERVE	LA JOLLA BAY, SD, 92037	1227 - F5
EL CAPITAN RESERVIOR	EL MONTE RD E, SDCo, 92040	1213 - H6
LA JOLLA SHORES BEACH	LA VEREDA, SD, 92037	1227 - G4
LA JOLLA STRAND PK	NEPTUNE PL & PALOMAR AV, SD, 92037	1247 - E2
LAKE HODGES	ROUTE S6, SD, 92029	1149 - E3
LAKE JENNINGS	JENNINGS PK RD & AMERICAN WY, SDCo, 92040	1232 - E3
LEUCADIA ST BCH	NEPTUNE AV & JUPITER ST, ENCT, 92024	1147 - A4
MARINE STREET BEACH	MARINE ST, SD, 92037	1247 - E1
MISSION BEACH PK	OCEAN FRONT WK & VENTURA PL, SD, 92109	1267 - H1
MOONLIGHT ST BCH	4TH ST & B ST, ENCT, 92024	1147 - B7
MORENA RESERVOIR (SEE PAGE 1296)	OAK DR & BUCKMAN SPRINGS RD, SDCo, 91906	1297 - D3
NEWBREAK BEACH	LOMALAND DR, SD, 92107	1287 - H3
NORTH SEASCAPE SURF BEACH PK	501 S SIERRA AV, SOLB, 92075	1187 - E1
OCEAN BEACH PK	5121 SARATOGA AV, SD, 92107	1267 - H5
OCEANSIDE CITY BEACH	OCEANSIDE BLVD & PACIFIC ST, OCN, 92054	1106 - A2
OTAY RESERVOIR (SEE PAGE 1293)	WUESTE RD, SDCo, 91915	1312 - B7
PACIFIC BEACH PK	OCEAN BLVD & GRAND AV, SD, 92109	1247 - G6
PESCADERO BEACH	PESCADERO AV & CABLE ST, SD, 92107	1267 - H7
SAN CLEMENTE ST BCH	AVD DEL PRESIDENTE, SCLE, 92672	1023 - A1
SAN DIEGO LA JOLLA UNDERWATER PK	LA JOLLA COVE, SD, 92037	1227 - E4
SAN ELIJO ST BCH	S COAST HWY 101 & CHESTERFIELD, ENCT, 92007	1167 - C2
SAN ONOFRE ST BCH	OLD HWY 101, SDCo, 92055	1023 - E4
SAN VICENTE RESERVOIR	MORENO AV, SDCo, 92065	1212 - A2
SHELL BEACH	COAST BLVD & GIRARD AV, SD, 92037	1227 - E6
SHORELINE PK BEACH	SHELTER ISLAND DR, SD, 92106	1288 - C3
SILVER STRAND ST BCH	SILVER STRAND BLVD, CORD, 92118	1309 - C7
SOUTH BEACH	AVD DEL SOL, CORD, 92118	1308 - H1
SOUTH CARLSBAD ST BCH	7201 CARLSBAD BLVD, CRLB, 92024	1146 - J1
SOUTH CASA BEACH	COAST BLVD, SD, 92037	1227 - E6
SWAMIS BEACH	3RD ST & W K ST, ENCT, 92024	1167 - B1
TORREY PINES CITY BEACH	TORREY PINES SCENIC DR, SD, 92037	1207 - G7
TORREY PINES ST BCH	12000 N TORREY PINES RD, SD, 92037	1207 - G6
TOURMALINE SURFING PK	CHELSEA ST & CRYSTAL DR, SD, 92037	1247 - G5
WHISPERING SANDS BEACH	COAST BLVD, SD, 92037	1227 - E7
WINDANSEA BEACH	NEPTUNE PL & FERN GN, SD, 92037	1247 - E1
WIPEOUT BEACH	COAST BLVD, SD, 92037	1227 - E6

BUILDINGS

FEATURE NAME	Address City, ZIP Code	PAGE-GRID
FOR DOWNTOWN BUILDINGS SEE PAGE viii		-
1 AMERICA PLAZA	600 W BROADWAY, SD, 92101	1288 - J3
BOTANICAL BLDG	OLD GLOBE WY, SD, 92101	1289 - C1
CABOT, CABOT & FORBES BLDG	COLUMBIA ST & C ST, SD, 92101	1289 - A3
CASA DEL PRADO	1800 EL PRADO, SD, 92101	1289 - C1
CENTERSIDE BLDG	CAMINO DEL RIO N, SD, 92108	1269 - E2
CLAIREMONT TOWER	BALBOA AV & MOUNT EVEREST BLVD, SD, 92117	1248 - G3
EMERALD PLAZA	402 W BROADWAY, SD, 92101	1289 - A3
FIRST NATL BANK BLDG	401 A ST W, SD, 92101	1289 - A3
GENERAL ATOMICS FACILITY	3550 GENERAL ATOMICS CT, SD, 92121	1208 - A6
HALL OF NATIONS	PAN AMERICAN RD W, SD, 92101	1289 - B1
HOUSE OF HOSPITALITY	1549 EL PRADO, SD, 92101	1289 - C1
JOHN BURNHAM BLDG	1420 INDIA ST, SD, 92101	1288 - J2
KIMMEL, SIDNEY CANCER CTR	3099 SCIENCE PARK RD, SD, 92121	1207 - J6
KOLL BLDG	501 W BROADWAY, SD, 92101	1288 - J3
LA JOLLA CANCER RESEARCH FND	N TORREY PINES RD, SD, 92121	1207 - J6
LA JOLLA GATEWAY	9191 TOWNE CENTRE DR, SD, 92122	1228 - D2
MORMON TEMPLE	7474 CHARMANT DR, SD, 92122	1228 - B3
NEUROSCIENCES INSTITUTE, THE	10640 JOHN JAY HOPKINS DR, SD, 92121	1207 - J7
PERLMAN AMBULATORY CARE CTR	9300 CAMPUS POINT DR, SD, 92037	1228 - B2
PUB SERVICE BLDG	1ST ST & B AV, CORD, 92118	1288 - J5
SALK INSTITUTE	10010 N TORREY PINES RD, SD, 92037	1227 - H1
SAN DIEGO CRUISE SHIP TERMINAL	B ST PIER, SD, 92101	1288 - H3
SAN DIEGO TECH CTR	SCRANTON RD, SD, 92121	1208 - E6
SCRIPPS CORP PLAZA	10650 TREENA ST, SD, 92131	1209 - F4
SCRIPPS RESEARCH INSTITUTE	10550 N TORREY PINES RD, SD, 92037	1207 - J6
SEMPRA BLDG	101 ASH ST, SD, 92101	1289 - A2
SHILEY EYE CTR	9165 CAMPUS POINT DR, SD, 92037	1228 - B2
SOUTH COUNTY ANIMAL SHELTER	5821 SWEETWATER RD, SDCo, 91902	1290 - J6
UNION BANK OF CALIFORNIA BLDG	530 B ST, SD, 92101	1289 - A3
UNITED NATIONS BLDG	PAN AMERICAN RD W, SD, 92101	1289 - B1
WESTMINSTER MANOR	ELM ST & 3RD AV, SD, 92101	1289 - A2

BUILDINGS - GOVERNMENTAL

FEATURE NAME	Address City, ZIP Code	PAGE-GRID
ADMIN BLDG FOR VEHICULAR INSPECTION	ENRICO FERMI DR & MARCONI DR, SDCo, 92154	1352 - B3
COUNTY ADMIN CTR	1600 PACIFIC HWY, SD, 92101	1288 - H2
COUNTY BLDG	S GRAPE ST & E VALLEY PKWY, ESCN, 92025	1130 - A2
COUNTY OPERATIONS CTR	5555 OVERLAND AV, SD, 92123	1229 - D7
DEPARTMENT OF PUB WORKS	5555 OVERLAND AV, SD, 92123	1229 - E7
DESCANSO DETENTION FACILITY	7878 CAMPBELL RANCH RD, SDCo, 91901	1235 - H6
EAST MESA DETENTION FACILITY	446 ALTA RD, SDCo, 92154	1332 - C5
EDUCATION CTR	NORMAL ST & TYLER AV, SD, 92103	1269 - C4
EL CAJON MUNICIPAL COURT	250 E MAIN ST, ELCJ, 92020	1251 - G5
FEDERAL COURTHOUSE	940 FRONT ST, SD, 92101	1289 - A3
FEDERAL JAIL	808 UNION ST, SD, 92101	1289 - A3
FEDERAL OFFICE BLDG	880 FRONT ST, SD, 92101	1289 - A3
GEORGE F BAILEY DETENTION FACILITY	446 ALTA RD, SDCo, 92154	1332 - B6
IMPERIAL COUNTY COURT HOUSE	939 MAIN ST, ELCN, 92243	6499 - G6
JUVENILE HALL	2851 MEADOW LARK DR, SD, 92123	1249 - B6
RAMONA BRANCH MUNICIPAL COURT	1428 MONTECITO RD, SDCo, 92065	1152 - F6
RJ DONOVAN CORRECTIONAL FACILITY	DONOVAN STATE PRISON RD, SDCo, 92154	1332 - A6
SAN DIEGO CITY ADMIN BLDG	202 C ST, SD, 92101	1289 - A3
SAN DIEGO CITY JAIL	446 ALTA RD, SDCo, 92154	1332 - B5
SAN DIEGO CITY OPERATIONS BLDG	1222 1ST AV, SD, 92101	1289 - A3
SAN DIEGO COUNTY COURT HOUSE	220 W BROADWAY, SD, 92101	1289 - A3
SAN DIEGO CO OFFICE OF EDUCATION	6401 LINDA VISTA RD, SD, 92111	1268 - H2
SAN DIEGO MUNICIPAL COURT	1409 4TH AV, SD, 92101	1289 - A2
SAN DIEGO MUNICIPAL COURTS	325 S MELROSE DR, VSTA, 92083	1107 - F1
SAN DIEGO UNIFIED PORT DIST	3165 PACIFIC HWY, SD, 92101	1268 - H7
SELLERS US POSTAL CTR	11251 RANCHO CARMEL DR, SD, 92128	1190 - A1
SOUTHBAY MUNICIPAL COURT	500 3RD AV, CHV, 91910	1310 - B7
STATE HIGHWAY BLDG	JUAN ST & WALLACE ST, SD, 92110	1268 - F4
STATE OFFICE BLDG	1350 FRONT ST, SD, 92101	1289 - A2
UNITED STATES CUSTOMS	I-5 AT US BORDER, SD, 92173	1350 - H5
UNITED STATES FEDERAL COURTS	321 S WATERMAN AV, ELCN, 92243	6499 - F6
US CUSTOMS	HIGHWAY 905, SD, 92154	1352 - A4
WOMENS DETENTION FACILITY LAS COLINAS	9000 COTTONWOOD AV, SNTE, 92071	1231 - D6

CEMETERIES

FEATURE NAME	Address City, ZIP Code	PAGE-GRID
ALL SAINTS CEM	200 PEYRI DR, OCN, 92057	1086 - H2
ALPINE CEM	2495 VICTORIA DR, SDCo, 91901	1234 - B5
CYPRESS VIEW MAUSOLEUM	3953 IMPERIAL AV, SD, 92113	1289 - G4
DEARBORN MEM PK	14361 TIERRA BONITA RD, PWY, 92064	1190 - G2
EL CAJON CEM	2080 DEHESA RD, SDCo, 92019	1252 - C6
EL CAMINO MEM PK CEM	6500 CARROLL CANYON RD, SD, 92121	1208 - H6
ETERNAL HILLS CEM	1999 EL CAMINO REAL, OCN, 92054	1086 - G7
EVERGREEN CEM	MARKET ST, SD, 92102	1289 - G4
FORT ROSECRANS NATL CEM	CABRILLO MEMORIAL DR, SD, 92106	1288 - A7
GLEN ABBEY MEM PK CEM	3838 BONITA RD, SDCo, 91902	1310 - F4
GREENWOOD CEM	IMPERIAL AV & INLAND FRWY, SDCo, 92102	1289 - H4
HOLY CROSS CEM	4470 HILLTOP DR, SD, 92102	1289 - J2
HOME OF PEACE CEM	IMPERIAL AV & 38TH ST, SD, 92102	1289 - G4
JULIAN CEM	FARMER RD & A ST, SDCo, 92036	1136 - A7
LA VISTA CEM	3191 ORANGE ST, SDCo, 91950	1310 - C3
MASONIC CEM	1010 HILLCREST LN, SDCo, 92028	1027 - G1
MEMORY GARDENS CEM	532 ASH ST, SDCo, 92065	1152 - H4
MOUNT HOPE CEM	3751 MARKET ST, SD, 92102	1289 - G4
OAK HILL MEM PK	2640 GLEN RIDGE RD, ESCN, 92027	1130 - F1
OCEANVIEW MEM PK CEM	GODFREY ST & S COAST HWY, OCN, 92054	1106 - B2
SAN MARCOS CEM	1021 MULBERRY DR, SMCS, 92069	1109 - A4
SINGING HILLS MEM PK	2800 DEHESA RD, SDCo, 92019	1252 - F6
VALLEY CTR CEM	28953 MILLER RD, SDCo, 92082	1070 - E7

CHAMBERS OF COMMERCE

FEATURE NAME	Address City, ZIP Code	PAGE-GRID
ALPINE	2157 ALPINE BLVD, SDCo, 91901	1234 - B6
BORREGO SPRINGS (SEE PAGE 1058)	622 PALM CANYON DR, SDCo, 92004	1078 - J2
CARDIFF BY THE SEA	2051 SAN ELIJO AV, ENCT, 92007	1167 - D3
CARLSBAD	5620 PAS DL NORTE, CRLB, 92008	1126 - H3
CARLSBAD CONV & VISITORS BUREAU	400 CARLSBAD VILLAGE DR, CRLB, 92008	1106 - E5
CHULA VISTA	233 4TH AV, CHV, 91910	1310 - B6
CORONADO	1224 10TH ST, CORD, 92118	1288 - H7
EAST COUNTY REGL	201 S MAGNOLIA AV, ELCJ, 92020	1251 - F5
EL CENTRO	1095 4TH ST, ELCN, 92243	6499 - J7
ENCINITAS	138 ENCINITAS BLVD, ENCT, 92024	1147 - C6
ESCONDIDO	720 N BROADWAY, ESCN, 92025	1129 - H1
FALLBROOK	233 E MISSION RD, SDCo, 92028	1027 - F2
GREATER DEL MAR	1104 CM DEL MAR, DLMR, 92014	1187 - F5
GREATER SAN DIEGO	402 W BROADWAY, SD, 92101	1289 - A3
I-15 DIAMOND GATEWAY	12778 RANCHO PENSAQUITOS BLVD, SD, 92129	1189 - G5
IMPERIAL BEACH	600 PALM AV, IMPB, 91932	1329 - G7
INTL VISITORS INFORMATION CTR	1ST AV & F ST, SD, 92101	1289 - A3
JULIAN	2129 MAIN ST, SDCo, 92036	1136 - B7
LAKESIDE	12418 PARKSIDE ST, SDCo, 92040	1232 - B3
LEMON GROVE	3443 MAIN ST, LMGR, 91945	1270 - G6
NATL CITY	711 A AV, NATC, 91950	1309 - H1
OCEANSIDE CC & TOURISM CTR	928 N COAST HWY, OCN, 92054	1085 - J6
OTAY MESA	9163 SIEMPRE VIVA RD, SD, 92154	1352 - A3
POWAY	13172 POWAY RD, PWY, 92064	1190 - E4
RAMONA	960 MAIN ST, SDCo, 92065	1152 - G6
RANCHO BERNARDO	11650 IBERIA PL, SD, 92128	1170 - A3
SAN DIEGO NORTH COUNTY VISITORS-BUREAU	360 N ESCONDIDO BLVD, ESCN, 92025	1129 - H2
SAN DIEGO VISITORS AND CONV CTR	401 B ST, SD, 92101	1289 - A3
SAN MARCOS	939 GRAND AV, SMCS, 92069	1108 - F7
SANTEE	10315 MISSION GORGE RD, SNTE, 92071	1231 - E6
SAN YSIDRO INTERNATL FOREST	663 E SAN YSIDRO BLVD, SD, 92173	1350 - H5
SOLANA BEACH	210 W PLAZA ST, SOLB, 92075	1167 - E7
SPRING VALLEY	3322 SWEETWATER SPRINGS BLVD, SDCo, 91977	1271 - E6
VISITORS INFORMATION CTR	E MISSION BAY DR & CLAIREMONT, SD, 92109	1248 - D7
VISTA	201 E WASHINGTON ST, VSTA, 92084	1087 - H6

CITY HALLS

FEATURE NAME	Address City, ZIP Code	PAGE-GRID
CARLSBAD	1200 CARLSBAD VILLAGE DR, CRLB, 92008	1106 - F5
CHULA VISTA	276 4TH AV, CHV, 91910	1310 - A6
CORONADO	1825 STRAND WY, CORD, 92118	1308 - J1
DEL MAR	1050 CM DEL MAR, DLMR, 92014	1187 - F5
EL CAJON	200 E MAIN ST, ELCJ, 92020	1251 - F5
EL CENTRO	1275 MAIN ST, ELCN, 92243	6499 - G6
ENCINITAS	505 S VULCAN AV, ENCT, 92024	1147 - C7
ESCONDIDO	201 N BROADWAY, ESCN, 92025	1129 - J2
IMPERIAL BEACH	825 IMPERIAL BEACH BLVD, IMPB, 91932	1349 - G1
JULIAN	2129 MAIN ST, SDCo, 92036	1136 - B7
LA MESA	8130 ALLISON AV, LMSA, 91941	1270 - H2
LEMON GROVE	3232 MAIN ST, LMGR, 91945	1270 - G6
NATL CITY	1243 NATIONAL CITY BLVD, NATC, 91950	1309 - H2
OCEANSIDE	300 N COAST HWY, OCN, 92054	1086 - A7
POWAY	13325 CIVIC CENTER DR, PWY, 92064	1190 - E5

FEATURE NAME	Address City, ZIP Code	PAGE-GRID
SAN DIEGO	202 C ST, SD, 92101	1289 - A3
SAN MARCOS	1 CIVIC CENTER DR, SMCS, 92069	1108 - J7
SANTEE	10601 AVD DE MAGNOLIA AV, SNTE, 92071	1231 - E2
SOLANA BEACH	635 SOUTH COAST HWY 101, SOLB, 92075	1187 - E1
VISTA	600 EUCALYPTUS AV, VSTA, 92084	1087 - J6

COLLEGES & UNIVERSITIES

FEATURE NAME	Address City, ZIP Code	PAGE-GRID
BAPTIST COLLEGE	ULRIC ST & EASTMAN ST, SD, 92111	1248 - J7
CALIFORNIA STATE UNIV SAN MARCOS	333 S TWIN OAKS VALLEY RD, SMCS, 92096	1128 - J2
CHRISTIAN HERITAGE COLLEGE	2100 GREENFIELD DR, ELCJ, 92019	1252 - D4
CUYAMACA COLLEGE	900 RANCHO SAN DIEGO PKWY, SDCo, 92019	1271 - J5
FASHION INST OF DESIGN & MERCHANDISING	1010 2ND AV, SD, 92101	1289 - A3
GROSSMONT COLLEGE	8800 GROSSMONT COLLEGE DR, ELCJ, 92020	1251 - A2
IMPERIAL VALLEY COLLEGE	380 E ATEN RD, ImCo, 92243	6500 - E1
MIRACOSTA COLLEGE	1 BARNARD DR, OCN, 92056	1107 - A1
MIRA COSTA COMM COLLEGE SAN ELIJO	3333 MANCHESTER AV, ENCT, 92007	1167 - F3
NATL UNIV	4141 CM DL RIO S, SD, 92116	1269 - G1
NATL UNIV NORTH CO CAMPUS	2022 UNIVERSITY DR, VSTA, 92083	1108 - B3
PALOMAR COLLEGE	1140 W MISSION RD, SMCS, 92069	1108 - F5
PALOMAR COMM COLLEGE	1951 E VALLEY PKWY, ESCN, 92027	1110 - C7
POINT LOMA NAZARENE UNIV	3900 LOMALAND DR, SD, 92106	1287 - J3
SAN DIEGO CITY COLLEGE	1313 12TH AV, SD, 92101	1289 - B2
SAN DIEGO MESA COLLEGE	7250 MESA COLLEGE DR, SD, 92111	1248 - J4
SAN DIEGO MIRAMAR COLLEGE	10440 BLACK MOUNTAIN RD, SD, 92126	1209 - E4
SAN DIEGO STATE UNIV	5500 CAMPANILE DR, SD, 92182	1270 - B1
SCRIPPS INSTITUTION OF OCEANOGRAPHY	8602 LA JOLLA SHORES DR, SD, 92037	1227 - H4
SOUTHWESTERN COLLEGE	900 OTAY LAKES RD, CHV, 91910	1311 - C6
UNITED STATES INTL UNIV	10455 POMERADO RD, SD, 92131	1209 - J5
UCSD	9500 GILMAN DR, SD, 92093	1228 - B1
UCSD-ELEANOR ROOSEVELT COLLEGE	UC SAN DIEGO CAMPUS, SD, 92093	1228 - A2
UCSD-JOHN MUIR COLLEGE	UC SAN DIEGO CAMPUS, SD, 92093	1227 - J2
UCSD-REVELLE COLLEGE	UC SAN DIEGO CAMPUS, SD, 92093	1227 - J2
UCSD SCHOOL OF MEDICINE	UC SAN DIEGO CAMPUS, SD, 92093	1228 - A2
UCSD-THURGOOD MARSHALL COLLEGE	UC SAN DIEGO CAMPUS, SD, 92093	1227 - J1
UCSD-WARREN COLLEGE	UC SAN DIEGO CAMPUS, SD, 92093	1228 - A1
UNIV OF SAN DIEGO	5998 ALCALA PARK, SD, 92110	1268 - G2
WEST COAST UNIV	9682 VIA EXCELENCIA, SD, 92126	1209 - E5
WESTMINSTER THEOLOGICAL SEMINARY	1725 BEAR VALLEY PKWY, ESCN, 92027	1130 - D3

DEPARTMENT OF MOTOR VEHICLES

FEATURE NAME	Address City, ZIP Code	PAGE-GRID
CHULA VISTA	30 N GLOVER AV, CHV, 91910	1310 - A5
EL CAJON	1450 GRAVES AV, SDCo, 92021	1251 - F2
EL CENTRO	233 N IMPERIAL AV, ELCN, 92243	6499 - F6
ESCONDIDO	725 N ESCONDIDO BLVD, ESCN, 92025	1129 - H2
OCEANSIDE	4005 PLAZA DR, OCN, 92056	1107 - C2
POWAY	13301 POWAY RD, PWY, 92064	1190 - E4
SAN DIEGO	3960 NORMAL ST, SD, 92103	1269 - C5
SAN DIEGO CLAIREMONT	4375 DERRICK DR, SD, 92117	1248 - G2
SAN YSIDRO	3702 DEL SOL BLVD, SD, 92154	1350 - E1

ENTERTAINMENT & SPORTS

FEATURE NAME	Address City, ZIP Code	PAGE-GRID
BELMONT PK	3146 MISSION BLVD, SD, 92109	1267 - J3
CAJON SPEEDWAY	1875 JOE CROSSON DR, ELCJ, 92020	1251 - E2
CARLSBAD RACEWAY	6600 PALOMAR AIRPORT RD, CRLB, 92008	1127 - J2
COX ARENA	5500 CANYON CREST DR, SD, 92182	1270 - B1
DEL MAR FAIRGROUNDS	2260 JIMMY DURANTE BLVD, DLMR, 92014	1187 - F2
DEL MAR RACE TRACK	2260 JIMMY DURANTE BLVD, DLMR, 92014	1187 - G2
KNOTTS SOAK CITY USA	2052 ENTERTAINMENT CIR, CHV, 91911	1331 - A6
LEGOLAND FAMILY PK	1 LEGO DR, CRLB, 92008	1126 - J2
QUALCOMM STADIUM	9449 FRIARS RD, SD, 92108	1249 - F7
SAN DIEGO CONV CTR	111 W HARBOR DR, SD, 92101	1289 - A4
SAN DIEGO SPORTS ARENA	3500 SPORTS ARENA BLVD, SD, 92110	1268 - D4
SAN DIEGO VELODROME	2221 MORLEY FIELD DR, SD, 92101	1269 - D7
SAN LUIS REY DOWNS	VIA CASITAS, SDCo, 92003	1068 - C1
SEA WORLD	500 SEA WORLD DR, SD, 92109	1268 - B3

GOLF COURSES

FEATURE NAME	Address City, ZIP Code	PAGE-GRID
ADMIRAL BAKER GC	ADMIRAL BAKER RD & FRIARS RD, SD, 92124	1249 - H6
AVIARA GC	7447 BATIQUITOS DR, CRLB, 92009	1127 - C6
BALBOA PK MUNICIPAL GC	2600 GOLF COURSE DR, SD, 92101	1289 - D1
BERNARDO HEIGHTS CC	16066 BERNARDO HEIGHTS PKWY, SD, 92128	1170 - A5
BONITA GC	5540 SWEETWATER RD, SDCo, 91902	1291 - A7
BORREGO SPRINGS RESORT & CC- (SEE PAGE 1058)	1112 TILTING T DR, SDCo, 92004	1079 - B4
BRIDGES CLUB, THE	18550 SEVEN BRIDGES RD, SDCo, 92067	1148 - F5
BROKEN SPOKE CC	225 WAKE AV, ELCN, 92243	6559 - J2
CARLTON OAKS CC	9200 INWOOD DR, SD, 92071	1230 - J6
CARMEL HGHLND DBLTREE GOLF & TENNIS	14455 PENASQUITOS DR, SD, 92129	1189 - J1
CARMEL MTN RANCH CC	14050 CARMEL RIDGE RD, SD, 92128	1190 - A2
CASTLE CREEK CC	8797 CIRCLE R DR, SDCo, 92026	1069 - B6
CENTER CITY GC	2323 GREENBRIER DR, OCN, 92054	1086 - C7
CHULA VISTA MUNICIPAL GC	4475 BONITA RD, CHV, 91902	1310 - G3
COLINA PK GC	4085 52ND ST, SD, 92105	1270 - A5
CORONADO GC	2000 VISALIA RW, CORD, 92118	1289 - A7
COTTONWOOD AT RANCHO SAN DIEGO GC	3121 WILLOW GLEN DR, SDCo, 92019	1272 - C5
DE ANZA CC	509 CATARINA DR, SDCo, 92004	1058 - G4
DEL MAR CC	6001 COUNTRY CLUB RD, SDCo, 92067	1188 - E2
EAGLE CREST GC	2492 OLD RANCH RD, ESCN, 92027	1130 - H2
EASTLAKE CC	2375 CLUBHOUSE DR, CHV, 91915	1311 - G6
EL CAMINO CC	3202 VISTA WY, OCN, 92056	1106 - H2
EMERALD ISLE GC	660 EL CAMINO REAL, OCN, 92057	1086 - F5
ENCINITAS RANCH GC	1275 QUAIL GARDENS DR, ENCT, 92024	1147 - E3
ESCONDIDO CC	1800 COUNTRY CLUB LN, ESCN, 92026	1109 - D4
FAIRBANKS RANCH CC	15150 SAN DIEGUITO RD, SD, 92067	1188 - C1
FALLBROOK GC	2757 GIRD RD, SDCo, 92028	1048 - E1
LA COSTA RESORT & SPA	2100 COSTA DEL MAR RD, CRLB, 92009	1147 - F1
LA JOLLA CC	7301 HIGH AV, SD, 92037	1247 - F1
LAKE SAN MARCOS CC	1750 SAN PABLO DR, SDCo, 92069	1128 - D2
LAKE SAN MARCOS EXECUTIVE GC	1556 CM DL ARROYO, SDCo, 92069	1128 - B3
LAWRENCE WELK RESORT GC	8860 LAWRENCE WELK DR, SDCo, 92026	1089 - A2
LOMAS SANTA FE CC	1505 LOMAS SANTA FE DR, SOLB, 92075	1167 - H6
LOMAS SANTA FE EXECUTIVE GC	1580 SUN VALLEY RD, SOLB, 92075	1167 - H5
MARINE MEM GC	GOLF COURSE RD, SDCo, 92055	1066 - F5
MEADOW LAKE CC	10333 MEADOW GLEN WY E, SDCo, 92026	1089 - F4
MEADOWS DEL MAR GC	5300 MEADOWS DEL MAR, SD, 92130	1188 - F7
MIRAMAR MEM GC	MIRAMAR WY & MIRAMAR RD, SD, 92126	1229 - B1
MISSION BAY GC	2702 N MISSION BAY DR, SD, 92109	1248 - C5
MISSION TRAILS GC	7380 GOLFCREST PL, SD, 92119	1250 - G5
MORGAN RUN RESORT AND CLUB	5690 CANCHA DE GOLF, SDCo, 92091	1168 - D7
MOUNT WOODSON CC	16422 N WOODSON DR, SDCo, 92065	1171 - E3
NATL CITY GC	1439 SWEETWATER RD, NATC, 91950	1310 - A2
NAVAL STA GC	WABASH BL & NORMAN SCOTT RD, SD, 92136	1289 - F6
OAKS NORTH GC	12602 OAKS NORTH DR, SD, 92128	1170 - C1
OCEAN HILLS CC	4701 LEISURE VILLAGE WY, OCN, 92056	1107 - E5
OCEANSIDE MUNICIPAL GC	825 DOUGLAS DR, OCN, 92057	1066 - H6
PALA MESA RESORT	2001 OLD HWY 395, SDCo, 92028	1028 - G5
PAUMA VALLEY CC	HWY 76 & PAUMA VALLEY DR, SDCo, 92061	1051 - A5
PRESIDIO HILLS GC	4136 WALLACE ST, SD, 92110	1268 - F4
RAMS HILL CC (SEE PAGE 1098)	1881 RAMS HILL RD, SDCo, 92004	1099 - G4
RANCHO BERNARDO INN GC	17550 BERNARDO OAKS DR, SD, 92128	1170 - A2
RANCHO CARLSBAD GC	5200 EL CAMINO REAL, CRLB, 92008	1107 - C6
RANCHO MONSERATE CC	4650 DULIN RD, SDCo, 92028	1048 - H4
RANCHO SANTA FE GC	5827 VIA D LA CUMBRE, SDCo, 92067	1168 - C2
RANCHO SANTA FE FARMS GC	8500 SAINT ANDREWS RD, SDCo, 92067	1168 - G7
RIVERWALK GC	1150 FASHION VALLEY RD, SD, 92108	1268 - H3
ROADRUNNER GOLF & CC (SEE PAGE 1058)	1010 PALM CANYON DR, SDCo, 92004	1079 - B1
SAIL HO GC	10 SELLERS PZ, SD, 92133	1268 - D6
SAN DIEGO CC	88 L ST, CHV, 91911	1330 - D2
SAN LUIS REY DOWNS CC	31474 GOLF CLUB DR, SDCo, 92003	1068 - A1
SAN VICENTE GC	24157 SAN VICENTE RD, SDCo, 92065	1173 - E4
SEA N AIR GC	CORONADO AV, CORD, 92135	1288 - G6
SHADOWRIDGE CC	1980 GATEWAY DR, VSTA, 92083	1107 - J4
SINGING HILLS CC	3007 DEHESA RD, SDCo, 92019	1252 - F6
SKYLINE RANCH CC	18218 PARADISE MOUNTAIN RD, SDCo, 92082	1091 - F4
SPINDRIFT GC	2000 SPINDRIFT DR, SD, 92037	1227 - G5
STEELE CANYON GC	3199 STONEFIELD DR, SDCo, 91935	1272 - E4
STONERIDGE CC	17166 STONERIDGE COUNTRY CLUB, PWY, 92064	1170 - E2
SUN VALLEY FAIRWAYS	5080 MEMORIAL DR, LMSA, 91941	1270 - J2
TECOLOTE CANYON GC	2755 SNEAD AV, SD, 92111	1248 - G6
TORREY PINES MUNICIPAL GC	11480 N TORREY PINES RD, SD, 92037	1207 - H5
TWIN OAKS GC	1425 N TWIN OAKS VALLEY RD, SMCS, 92069	1108 - J4
VINEYARD AT ESCONDIDO GC, THE	925 SAN PASQUAL RD, ESCN, 92025	1150 - C2
VISTA VALLEY CC	29354 VISTA VALLEY DR, SDCo, 92084	1068 - D7
WILLOWBROOK CC	11905 RIVERSIDE DR, SDCo, 92040	1231 - J3

HOSPITALS

FEATURE NAME	Address City, ZIP Code	PAGE-GRID
ALVARADO HOSP MED CTR	6655 ALVARADO RD, SD, 92120	1270 - D1
CHILDRENS HOSP & HEALTH CTR	3020 CHILDRENS WY, SD, 92123	1249 - B5
EL CENTRO REGL MED CTR	1415 ROSS AV, ELCN, 92243	6559 - G1
FALLBROOK HOSP DIST	624 E ELDER ST, SDCo, 92028	1027 - G3
GROSSMONT HOSP	5555 GROSSMONT CENTER DR, LMSA, 91942	1251 - A7
GROSSMONT HOSP ANNEX	WAKARUSA ST, LMSA, 91942	1251 - A7
KAISER FOUNDATION HOSP	4647 ZION AV, SD, 92120	1249 - J6
MISSION BAY HOSP	3030 BUNKER HILL ST, SD, 92109	1248 - C5
NAVAL MED CTR	34800 BOB WILSON DR, SD, 92134	1289 - C2
PALOMAR MED CTR	555 E VALLEY PKWY, ESCN, 92025	1130 - A2
PARADISE VALLEY HOSP	2400 E 4TH ST, NATC, 91950	1290 - B7
POMERADO HOSP	15615 POMERADO RD, PWY, 92064	1170 - C6
SCRIPPS GREEN HOSP	10666 N TORREY PINES RD, SD, 92037	1207 - J6
SCRIPPS MEM HOSP CHULA VISTA	435 H ST, CHV, 91910	1310 - B7
SCRIPPS MEM HOSP ENCINITAS	354 SANTA FE DR, ENCT, 92024	1167 - D1
SCRIPPS MEM HOSP LA JOLLA	9888 GENESEE AV, SD, 92037	1228 - B1
SCRIPPS MERCY HOSP	4077 5TH AV, SD, 92103	1269 - A5
SHARP CABRILLO HOSP	3475 KENYON ST, SD, 92110	1268 - D6
SHARP CHULA VISTA MED CTR	751 MEDICAL CENTER CT, CHV, 91911	1330 - J2
SHARP CORONADO HOSP	250 PROSPECT PL, CORD, 92118	1289 - A6
SHARP MEM HOSP	7901 FROST ST, SD, 92123	1249 - B5
TRI-CITY MED CTR	4002 VISTA WY, OCN, 92056	1107 - B1
UCSD MED CTR HILLCREST	200 W ARBOR DR, SD, 92103	1269 - A5
UCSD MED CENTER-THORNTON HOSP	9300 CAMPUS POINT DR, SD, 92037	1228 - B2
VENCOR HOSP SAN DIEGO	1940 EL CAJON BLVD, SD, 92104	1269 - C4
VETERANS AFFAIRS MED CTR	3350 LA JOLLA VILLAGE DR, SD, 92161	1228 - A2
VILLAVIEW COMM HOSP	5550 UNIVERSITY AV, SD, 92105	1270 - B5

HOTELS

FEATURE NAME	Address City, ZIP Code	PAGE-GRID
ALL SEASONS INNS	699 E ST, CHV, 91910	1309 - J6
AMERICANA INN & SUITES	815 W SAN YSIDRO BLVD, SD, 92173	1350 - E3
BAHIA RESORT HOTEL	998 W MISSION BAY DR, SD, 92109	1267 - J2
BAY CLUB HOTEL	2131 SHELTER ISLAND DR, SD, 92106	1288 - C3
BEST WESTERN BAYSIDE INN	555 W ASH ST, SD, 92101	1289 - A2
BEST WESTERN BEACH TERRACE INN	2775 OCEAN ST, CRLB, 92008	1106 - D5
BEST WESTERN BEACH VIEW LODGE	3180 CARLSBAD BLVD, CRLB, 92008	1106 - E6
BEST WESTERN BLUE SEA LODGE	707 PACIFIC BEACH DR, SD, 92109	1247 - H7
BEST WESTERN CAVALIER MOTOR HOTEL	710 E ST, CHV, 91910	1309 - J6
BEST WESTERN CONTINENTAL INN	650 N MOLLISON AV, ELCJ, 92021	1251 - G4
BEST WESTERN COURTESY INN	1355 E MAIN ST, ELCJ, 92019	1251 - J5
BEST WESTERN ESCONDIDO	1700 SEVEN OAKES RD, ESCN, 92026	1109 - F6
BEST WESTERN FRANCISCAN INN	1635 S MISSION RD, SDCo, 92028	1027 - F5
BEST WESTERN HACIENDA	4041 HARNEY ST, SD, 92110	1268 - F5
BEST WESTERN HANALEI HOTEL	2270 HOTEL CIR N, SD, 92108	1268 - G4
BEST WESTERN INN BY THE SEA	7830 FAY AV, SD, 92037	1227 - E6
BEST WESTERN ISLND PALMS HOTEL & MARINA	2051 SHELTER ISLAND DR, SD, 92106	1288 - B4
BEST WESTERN MARTYS VALLEY INN	3240 E MISSION AV, OCN, 92054	1086 - E5
BEST WESTERN MIRAMAR	9310 KEARNY MESA RD, SD, 92126	1209 - F6
BEST WESTERN OCEANSIDE INN	1680 OCEANSIDE BLVD, OCN, 92054	1106 - C1
BEST WESTERN POSADA INN	5005 N HARBOR DR, SD, 92106	1288 - C2
BEST WESTERN SEVEN SEAS	411 S HOTEL CIR, SD, 92108	1268 - J4
BEST WESTERN STRATFORD INN	710 CM DEL MAR, DLMR, 92014	1187 - G6
BEST WESTERN SUITES CORONADO	275 ORANGE AV, CORD, 92118	1288 - J6
CATAMARAN RESORT HOTEL	3999 MISSION BLVD, SD, 92109	1247 - H7
CLARION CARRIAGE HOUSE DEL MAR	720 CM DEL MAR, DLMR, 92014	1187 - G6
CLARION HOTEL BAY VIEW	660 K ST, SD, 92101	1289 - A4
COMFORT INN & SUITES-ZOO/SEA WORLD	2485 HOTEL CIRCLE PL, SD, 92108	1268 - G4
COMFORT INN AT OLD TOWN	1955 SAN DIEGO AV, SD, 92110	1268 - G6
COMFORT INN LA MESA	8000 PARKWAY DR, LMSA, 91942	1270 - G1
COMFORT SUITES MISSION VALLEY	631 CM DL RIO S, SD, 92108	1269 - A4
COUNTRY INN CARDIFF-BY-THE-SEA	1661 VILLA CARDIFF DR, ENCT, 92007	1167 - E2
COURTYARD BY MARRIOTT	717 SOUTH COAST HWY 101, SOLB, 92075	1187 - E1
COURTYARD BY MARRIOTT	9650 SCRANTON RD, SD, 92121	1208 - E7
COURTYARD DOWNTOWN	530 BROADWAY, SD, 92101	1289 - A3
DANA INN & MARINA	1710 W MISSION BAY DR, SD, 92109	1268 - A3

SAN DIEGO CO.

INDEX

COPYRIGHT 2001 Thomas Bros Maps ®

FEATURE NAME	Address City, ZIP Code	PAGE-GRID
DAYS INN HOTEL CIRCLE	543 HOTEL CIR S, SD, 92108	1268 - J4
DAYS INN LA MESA	1250 EL CAJON BLVD, ELCJ, 92020	1251 - D7
DAYS INN MISSION BAY	2575 CLAIREMONT DR, SD, 92110	1248 - E7
DAYS INN SUITES SEA WORLD	3350 ROSECRANS ST, SD, 92110	1268 - E6
DOUBLETREE CARMEL HIGHLANDS RESORT	14455 PENASQUITOS DR, SD, 92129	1189 - H1
DOUBLETREE CLUB HOTEL	11611 BERNARDO PLAZA CT, SD, 92128	1170 - A3
DOUBLETREE HOTEL	7450 HAZARD CENTER DR, SD, 92108	1269 - A2
DOUBLETREE HOTEL DEL MAR	11915 EL CAMINO REAL, SD, 92130	1208 - A1
EMBASSY SUITES	4550 LA JOLLA VILLAGE DR, SD, 92121	1228 - D2
EMBASSY SUITES SAN DIEGO BAY	601 PACIFIC HWY, SD, 92101	1288 - J4
EMPRESS HOTEL OF LA JOLLA, THE	7766 FAY AV, SD, 92037	1227 - E7
FOUR POINTS HOTEL SAN DIEGO	8110 AERO DR, SD, 92123	1249 - B4
FOUR SEASONS RESORT AVIARA	1500 FOUR SEASONS PT, CRLB, 92009	1127 - C6
GOOD NITE INN SEA WORLD	3880 GREENWOOD ST, SD, 92110	1268 - E5
GOOD NITE INN SOUTH BAY	225 BAY BLVD W, CHV, 91910	1309 - J7
GROSVENOR INN	3145 SPORTS ARENA BLVD, SD, 92110	1268 - E5
HALF MOON INN & SUITES	2303 SHELTER ISLAND DR, SD, 92106	1288 - C3
HAMPTON INN	11920 EL CAMINO REAL, SD, 92130	1207 - J1
HAMPTON INN	5434 KEARNY MESA RD, SD, 92111	1229 - C7
HAMPTON INN -	3888 GREENWOOD ST, SD, 92110	1268 - E5
HANDLERY HOTEL & RESORT	950 HOTEL CIR N, SD, 92108	1268 - H4
HILTON LA JOLLA TORREY PINES	10950 N TORREY PINES RD, SD, 92037	1207 - J5
HILTON SAN DIEGO	1775 E MISSION BAY DR, SD, 92109	1268 - D1
HILTON SAN DIEGO/DEL MAR	15575 JIMMY DURANTE BLVD, SD, 92014	1187 - G2
HOLIDAY INN CARLSBAD BY THE SEA	850 PALOMAR AIRPORT RD, CRLB, 92008	1126 - H3
HOLIDAY INN EXPRESS	3950 JUPITER ST, SD, 92110	1268 - C5
HOLIDAY INN HARBOR VIEW	1617 1ST AV, SD, 92101	1289 - A2
HOLIDAY INN HOTEL & SUITES - OLD TOWN	2435 JEFFERSON ST, SD, 92110	1268 - F5
HOLIDAY INN MISSION BAY/SEA WORLD	3737 SPORTS ARENA BLVD, SD, 92110	1268 - D5
HOLIDAY INN MISSION VALLEY	3805 MURPHY CANYON RD, SD, 92123	1249 - F4
HOLIDAY INN ON THE BAY	1355 N HARBOR DR, SD, 92101	1288 - J2
HOLIDAY INN RANCHO BERNARDO	17065 W BERNARDO DR, SD, 92127	1169 - J1
HOLIDAY INN SAN DIEGO BAYSIDE	4875 N HARBOR DR, SD, 92101	1288 - C2
HOLIDAY INN SELECT HOTEL CIRCLE	595 HOTEL CIR S, SD, 92108	1268 - J4
HOLIDAY INN SELECT MIRAMAR	9335 KEARNY MESA RD, SD, 92126	1209 - E6
HOLIDAY INN SOUTH BAY	700 NATIONAL CITY BLVD, NATC, 91950	1309 - H1
HORTON GRAND HOTEL	311 ISLAND AV, SD, 92101	1289 - A4
HOTEL CIRCLE INN & SUITES	2201 HOTEL CIR S, SD, 92108	1268 - G4
HOTEL DEL CORONADO	1500 ORANGE AV, CORD, 92118	1308 - H1
HOWARD JOHNSON HOTEL HARBOR VIEW	1430 7TH AV, SD, 92101	1289 - B2
HUMPHREYS HALF MOON INN	2303 SHELTER ISLAND DR, SD, 92106	1288 - C3
HYATT ISLANDIA	1441 QUIVIRA RD, SD, 92109	1268 - A3
HYATT REGENCY HOTEL	1 MARKET PL, SD, 92101	1289 - A4
HYATT REGENCY LA JOLLA	3777 LA JOLLA VILLAGE DR, SD, 92122	1228 - B3
INNS OF AMERICA	751 RAINTREE DR, CRLB, 92009	1126 - J6
KINGS INN	1333 HOTEL CIR S, SD, 92108	1268 - J4
LA CASA DEL ZORRO DESERT RESORT- (SEE PAGE 1098)	BORREGO SPRINGS & YAQUI PASS, SDCo, 92004	1099 - F1
LA COSTA RESORT & SPA	2100 COSTA DEL MAR RD, CRLB, 92009	1147 - E1
LA JOLLA COVE SUITES	1155 COAST BLVD, SD, 92037	1227 - F6
LA QUINTA INN	10185 PAS MONTRIL, SD, 92129	1189 - G5
LA QUINTA INN	150 BONITA RD, CHV, 91910	1310 - D5
LA QUINTA INN	630 SYCAMORE AV, VSTA, 92083	1108 - B4
L AUBERGE DEL MAR RESORT & SPA	1540 CM DEL MAR, DLMR, 92014	1187 - F4
LA VALENCIA HOTEL	1132 PROSPECT ST, SD, 92037	1227 - F6
LOEWS CORONADO BAY RESORT	4000 CORONADO BAY RD, CORD, 92118	1309 - E7
MARRIOTT DOWNTOWN	701 A ST, SD, 92101	1289 - B2
MARRIOTT MISSION VALLEY	8757 RIO SAN DIEGO DR, SD, 92108	1269 - D2
MARRIOTT RESIDENCE INN LA JOLLA	8901 GILMAN DR, SD, 92037	1228 - A3
MARRIOTT RESIDENCE INN SORRENTO MESA	5995 PACIFIC MESA CT, SD, 92121	1208 - F5
MARRIOTT RESORT CORONADO ISLAND	2000 2ND ST, CORD, 92118	1289 - A6
MARRIOTT SAN DIEGO MARINA	333 W HARBOR DR, SD, 92101	1289 - A4
PALA MESA RESORT	2001 OLD HWY 395, SDCo, 92028	1028 - H6
QUAILS INN	1025 LA BONITA DR, SDCo, 92069	1128 - C3
QUALITY INN & SUITES	760 MACADAMIA DR, CRLB, 92009	1126 - J5
QUALITY INN	2901 NIMITZ BLVD, SD, 92106	1288 - C1
QUALITY SUITES	9880 MIRA MESA BLVD, SD, 92131	1209 - F3
RADISSON HARBOR VIEW	1646 FRONT ST, SD, 92101	1289 - A2
RADISSON HOTEL LA JOLLA	3299 HOLIDAY CT, SD, 92037	1228 - A3
RADISSON HOTEL - SAN DIEGO	1433 CM DL RIO S, SD, 92116	1269 - B3
RADISSON INN	801 NATIONAL CITY BLVD, NATC, 91950	1309 - H1
RADISSON INN ENCINITAS	85 ENCINITAS BLVD, ENCT, 92024	1147 - C6
RADISSON RANCHO BERNARDO	11520 W BERNARDO CT, SD, 92127	1169 - J3
RAMADA INN	1455 OCOTILLO DR, ELCN, 92243	6559 - G1
RAMADA INN NORTH	5550 KEARNY MESA RD, SD, 92111	1229 - C7
RAMADA INN - OLD TOWN	3900 OLD TOWN AV, SD, 92110	1268 - F5
RAMADA INN SOUTH	91 BONITA RD, CHV, 91910	1310 - D5
RAMADA LIMITED SUITES	12979 RANCHO PENASQUITOS BLVD, SD, 92129	1189 - F5
RAMADA LIMITED SUITES MISSION VALLEY	641 CM DL RIO S, SD, 92108	1269 - A3
RAMADA PLAZA HOTEL CIRCLE	2151 HOTEL CIR S, SD, 92108	1268 - H4
RAMS HILL RESORT (SEE PAGE 1098)	4343 YAQUI PASS RD, SDCo, 92004	1099 - F3
RANCHO BERNARDO INN	17550 BERNARDO OAKS DR, SD, 92128	1170 - B1
REGENCY PLAZA HOTEL	1515 HOTEL CIR S, SD, 92108	1268 - H4
RESIDENCE INN	11002 RANCHO CARMEL DR, SD, 92128	1189 - J1
RESIDENCE INN	5400 KEARNY MESA RD, SD, 92111	1229 - C7
SAN DIEGO HOTEL	339 W BROADWAY, SD, 92101	1289 - A3
SAN DIEGO MARRIOTT LA JOLLA	4240 LA JOLLA VILLAGE DR, SD, 92037	1228 - C2
SAN DIEGO MISSION VALLEY HILTON	901 CM DL RIO S, SD, 92108	1269 - B3
SAN DIEGO PARADISE POINT RESORT	1404 W VACATION RD, SD, 92109	1268 - A2
SEA LODGE	8110 CM DL ORO, SD, 92037	1227 - G5
SHELTER POINT HOTEL	1551 SHELTER ISLAND DR, SD, 92106	1288 - B4
SHERATON SD HOTEL & MARINA EAST	1380 HARBOR ISLAND DR, SD, 92101	1288 - F1
SHERATON SD HOTEL & MARINA WEST	1590 HARBOR ISLAND DR, SD, 92101	1288 - E2
SINGING HILLS LODGE	3007 DEHESA RD, SDCo, 92019	1252 - F6
TAMARACK BEACH RESORT	3200 CARLSBAD BLVD, CRLB, 92008	1106 - E6
TOWN & COUNTRY HOTEL	500 HOTEL CIR N, SD, 92108	1268 - J3
TRAVELODGE HARBOR ISLAND	1960 HARBOR ISLAND DR, SD, 92101	1288 - E2
US GRANT HOTEL	326 BROADWAY, SD, 92101	1289 - A3
VACATION INN	2015 COTTONWOOD CIR, ELCN, 92243	6559 - F1
WELK RESORT CTR	8860 LAWRENCE WELK DR, SDCo, 92026	1089 - B2
WESTGATE HOTEL	1055 2ND AV, SD, 92101	1289 - A3
WESTIN HOTEL HORTON PLAZA	910 BROADWAY CIR, SD, 92101	1289 - A3
WYNDHAM EMERALD PLAZA HOTEL	400 W BROADWAY, SD, 92101	1289 - A3
WYNDHAM GARDEN HOTEL	5975 LUSK BLVD, SD, 92121	1208 - F6

LIBRARIES

FEATURE NAME	Address City, ZIP Code	PAGE-GRID
ALPINE BRANCH	2130 ARNOLD WY, SDCo, 91901	1234 - B6
BALBOA BRANCH	4255 MT ABERNATHY AV, SD, 92117	1248 - H2
BECKWOURTH BRANCH	721 SAN PASQUAL ST, SD, 92113	1289 - H5
BENJAMIN BRANCH	5188 ZION AV, SD, 92120	1250 - A6
BONITA-SUNNYSIDE BRANCH	5047 CENTRAL AV, SDCo, 91902	1310 - J2
BORREGO SPRINGS BRANCH- (SEE PAGE 1058)	652 PALM CANYON DR, SDCo, 92004	1078 - J2
CAMPO-MORENA VILLAGE BRANCH- (SEE PAGE 1298)	31466 HWY 94, SDCo, 91906	1318 - A5
CARDIFF BY THE SEA BRANCH	2027 SAN ELIJO AV, ENCT, 92007	1167 - D3
CARLSBAD CITY	1775 DOVE LN, CRLB, 92009	1127 - E5
CARLSBAD-GEORGINA COLE	1250 CARLSBAD VILLAGE DR, CRLB, 92008	1106 - F4
CARMEL MTN RANCH BRANCH	12095 WORLD TRADE DR, SD, 92128	1190 - A1
CARMEL VALLEY BRANCH	3919 TOWNSGATE DR, SD, 92130	1188 - A5
CASA DE ORO BRANCH	9628 CAMPO RD, SDCo, 91977	1271 - C5
CHULA VISTA CIVIC CTR	365 F ST, CHV, 91910	1310 - B6
CITY HEIGHTS WEINGART BRANCH	3795 FAIRMOUNT AV, SD, 92105	1269 - H5
CLAIREMONT BRANCH	2920 BURGENER BLVD, SD, 92110	1248 - F6
COLLEGE HEIGHTS BRANCH	4710 COLLEGE AV, SD, 92115	1270 - C3
CORONADO PUB	640 ORANGE AV, CORD, 92118	1288 - J6
CREST BRANCH	105 JUANITA LN, SDCo, 92021	1252 - H4
DEL MAR BRANCH	1309 CM DEL MAR, DLMR, 92014	1187 - F5
DESCANSO BRANCH	9545 RIVER DR, SDCo, 91916	1236 - A2
EASTLAKE	1120 EASTLAKE PKWY, CHV, 91915	1311 - F6
EL CAJON BRANCH	201 E DOUGLAS AV, ELCJ, 92020	1251 - F5
EL CENTRO BRANCH	375 S 1ST ST, ELCN, 92243	6499 - J6
EL CENTRO PUB	539 STATE ST, ELCN, 92243	6499 - H6
ENCINITAS BRANCH	540 CORNISH DR, ENCT, 92024	1147 - C7
ESCONDIDO EAST VALLEY BRANCH	2245 E VALLEY PKWY, ESCN, 92027	1110 - D7
ESCONDIDO PIONEER ROOM	247 S KALMIA ST, ESCN, 92025	1129 - J3
ESCONDIDO PUB	239 S KALMIA ST, ESCN, 92025	1129 - J3
FALLBROOK BRANCH	124 S MISSION RD, SDCo, 92028	1027 - F2
FLETCHER HILLS BRANCH	576 GARFIELD AV, ELCJ, 92020	1251 - B4
GEISEL	UC SAN DIEGO CAMPUS, SD, 92093	1228 - A1
IMPERIAL BEACH BRANCH	810 IMPERIAL BEACH BLVD, IMPB, 91932	1349 - G1
JACUMBA BRANCH (SEE PAGE 1300)	44605 OLD HWY 80, SDCo, 91934	1321 - G5
JULIAN BRANCH	2133 4TH ST, SDCo, 92036	1136 - B7
KENSINGTON-NORMAL HEIGHTS BRANCH	4121 ADAMS AV, SD, 92116	1269 - G3
LA JOLLA RIFORD BRANCH	7555 DRAPER AV, SD, 92037	1227 - E7
LAKESIDE BRANCH	9839 VINE ST, SDCo, 92040	1232 - B3
LA MESA BRANCH	8055 UNIVERSITY AV, LMSA, 91941	1270 - H2
LEMON GROVE BRANCH	8073 BROADWAY, LMGR, 91945	1270 - H6
LINCOLN ACRES BRANCH	2725 GRANGER AV, SDCo, 91950	1310 - C2
LINDA VISTA BRANCH	2160 ULRIC ST, SD, 92111	1268 - J1
LOGAN HEIGHTS BRANCH	811 S 28TH ST, SD, 92113	1289 - E5
MALCOLM X-VALENCIA PK BRANCH	5148 MARKET ST, SD, 92114	1290 - A3
MIRA MESA BRANCH	8405 NEW SALEM ST, SD, 92126	1209 - C3
MISSION BRANCH	3861 MISSION AV, OCN, 92054	1086 - F3
MISSION HILLS BRANCH	925 W WASHINGTON ST, SD, 92103	1268 - J5
NATL CITY PUB	200 E 12TH ST, NATC, 91950	1309 - H2
NORTH CLAIREMONT BRANCH	4616 CLAIREMONT DR, SD, 92117	1248 - E2
NORTH PK BRANCH	3795 31ST ST, SD, 92104	1269 - E5
OAK PK BRANCH	2802 54TH ST, SD, 92105	1270 - B7
OCEAN BEACH BRANCH	4801 SANTA MONICA AV, SD, 92107	1267 - J6
OCEANSIDE PUB	330 N COAST HWY, OCN, 92054	1086 - A7
OTAY MESA BRANCH	3003 CORONADO AV, SD, 92154	1350 - D1
PACIFIC BEACH TAYLOR BRANCH	4275 CASS ST, SD, 92109	1247 - J6
PARADISE HILLS BRANCH	5922 RANCHO HILLS DR, SD, 92139	1310 - D1
PINE VALLEY BRANCH	28804 OLD HWY 80, SDCo, 92066	1237 - B7
POINT LOMA BRANCH	2130 POINSETTIA DR, SD, 92107	1268 - B7
POWAY BRANCH	13137 POWAY RD, PWY, 92064	1190 - E4
RAMONA BRANCH	1406 MONTECITO RD, SDCo, 92065	1152 - F6
RANCHO BERNARDO BRANCH	17110 BERNARDO CENTER DR, SD, 92128	1170 - A2
RANCHO PENASQUITOS BRANCH	13330 SALMON RIVER RD, SD, 92129	1189 - E4
RANCHO SANTA FE BRANCH	17040 AVD DE ACACIAS, SDCo, 92067	1168 - D3
SAN CARLOS BRANCH	7265 JACKSON DR, SD, 92119	1250 - F5
SAN DIEGO CENTRAL	820 E ST, SD, 92101	1289 - B3
SAN MARCOS BRANCH	2 CIVIC CENTER DR, SMCS, 92069	1108 - J7
SANTEE BRANCH	9225 CARLTON HILLS BLVD, SNTE, 92071	1231 - B5
SAN YSIDRO BRANCH	101 W SAN YSIDRO BLVD, SD, 92173	1350 - G4
SCRIPPS INSTITUTE	8602 LA JOLLA SHORES DR, SD, 92093	1227 - H3
SCRIPPS RANCH BRANCH	10301 SCRIPPS LAKE DR, SD, 92131	1209 - G4
SERRA MESA BRANCH	3440 SANDROCK RD, SD, 92123	1249 - C4
SKYLINE HILLS BRANCH	480 S MEADOWBROOK DR, SD, 92114	1290 - H5
SOLANA BEACH BRANCH	981 LOMAS SANTA FE DR, SOLB, 92075	1167 - G7
SOUTH CHULA VISTA	389 ORANGE AV, CHV, 91911	1330 - D4
SPRING VALLEY BRANCH	1043 ELKELTON BLVD, SDCo, 91977	1290 - J3
TIERRASANTA BRANCH	4985 LA CUENTA DR, SD, 92124	1249 - H2
UNIV COMM BRANCH	4155 GOVERNOR DR, SD, 92122	1228 - E5
UNIV HEIGHTS BRANCH	4193 PARK BLVD, SD, 92103	1269 - C5
VALLEY CTR BRANCH	29115 VALLEY CENTER RD, SDCo, 92082	1090 - F1
VISTA BRANCH	700 EUCALYPTUS AV, VSTA, 92084	1087 - J6

MILITARY INSTALLATIONS

FEATURE NAME	Address City, ZIP Code	PAGE-GRID
ARMORY	4TH ST & PALM AV, NATC, 91950	1290 - A7
CARRIZO IMPACT AREA	OFF IMPERIAL HWY, ImCo, 92259	430 - G4
CHOCOLATE MTN NAVAL RES AERIAL-GUNNERY	THE BRADSHAW TR, ImCo	411 - F4
EL CENTRO NAVAL AUXILIARY AIR STA	HAVENS RD, ImCo, 92243	431 - A5
FLEET & INDUSTRIAL SUPPLY CTR	937 N HARBOR DR, SD, 92101	1288 - J3
FLEET ANTI-SUB WARFARE	32444 ECHO LN, SD, 92133	1288 - C2
FORT ROSECRANS MILITARY RESV	POINT LOMA, SD, 92106	1287 - J6
IMPERIAL BEACH NAVAL AUX LANDING	TOWER RD, IMPB, 91932	1349 - G2
LA POSTA MICROWAVE STA	LA POSTA RD, SDCo, 91906	1298 - D7
NATL GUARD ARMORY	ARMSTRONG ST & MESA COLLEGE DR, SD, 92111	1249 - A5
NAVAL MED CTR	34800 BOB WILSON DR, SD, 92134	1289 - C1
NORTH ISLAND NAVAL AIR STA	MCCAIN BLVD & ALAMEDA BLVD, CORD, 92135	1288 - D5
SALTON SEA MILITARY RESV	ImCo, 92259	410 - J7
U S COAST GUARD STA	HUMPHREYS RD, SD, 92106	1308 - A3
U S COAST GUARD STA	N HARBOR DR, SD, 92101	1288 - H1
USMC AIR STA MIRAMAR	I-15 FRWY & MIRAMAR WY, SD, 92145	1229 - E4
USMC BASE CAMP JOSEPH H PENDLETON	SAN DIEGO FRWY & BASILONE RD, SDCo, 92055	1023 - H3
USMC RECRUIT DEPOT	BARNETT AV & PACIFIC HWY, SD, 92140	1268 - F6
U S NAVAL AIR FACILITY	WHEELER RD, ImCo, 92259	430 - K4
U S NAVAL AMPHIBIOUS BASE	SILVER STRAND BLVD, CORD, 92118	1309 - C4
U S NAVAL RADIO STA	SILVER STRAND BLVD, CORD, 91932	1329 - E5

FEATURE NAME Address City, ZIP Code	PAGE-GRID
U S NAVAL RESV HARBOR DR, SD, 92136	1289 - F7
U S NAVAL RESV HIGHWAY 78, ImCo	431 - G2
U S NAVAL RESV ImCo	411 - E11
US NAVAL RESV OFF IMPERIAL HWY, ImCo, 92259	430 - H2
U S NAVAL RESV POINT LOMA, SD, 92106	1287 - J5
U S NAVAL RESV POINT LOMA, SD, 92106	1288 - A5
US NAVAL WEAPONS STA FALLBROOK FALLBROOK RD, SDCo, 92055	1027 - C2

MUSEUMS

FEATURE NAME Address City, ZIP Code	PAGE-GRID
AEROSPACE MUS & HALL OF FAME 2001 PAN AMERICAN PZ, SD, 92101	1289 - B2
ANTIQUE GAS & STEAM ENGINE MUS 2040 N SANTA FE AV, VSTA, 92083	1087 - F2
BONITA HIST MUS 4035 BONITA RD, CHV, 91902	1310 - G3
CALIFORNIA SURF MUS 308 N PACIFIC ST, OCN, 92054	1106 - A1
CENTRO CULTURAL DE LA RAZA 2004 PARK BLVD, SD, 92101	1289 - C1
CHILDRENS MUS OF SAN DIEGO 200 ISLAND AV, SD, 92101	1289 - A4
CHULA VISTA HERITAGE MUS 360 3RD AV, CHV, 91910	1310 - B6
CHULA VISTA NATURE CTR 1000 GUNPOWDER POINT DR, CHV, 91910	1309 - H6
FIREHOUSE MUS 1572 COLUMBIA ST, SD, 92101	1288 - J2
HERITAGE OF THE AMERICAS MUS 2952 JAMACHA RD, SDCo, 92019	1271 - J5
HERITAGE PK VILLAGE MUS 220 PEYRIE DR, OCN, 92057	1086 - G2
HERITAGE WALK MUS 321 N BROADWAY, ESCN, 92025	1129 - H2
HOUSE OF PACIFIC RELAT INTNL CTR PAN AMERICAN RD W, SD, 92101	1289 - B1
JAPANESE FRIENDSHIP GARDEN 2215 PAN AMERICAN RD, SD, 92101	1289 - C1
JULIAN PIONEER MUS 2811 WASHINGTON ST, SDCo, 92036	1136 - A7
LA MESA DEPOT MUS 4695 NEBO DR, LMSA, 91941	1270 - H3
MARINE CORPS RECRUIT DEPOT COMMAND-MUS 1600 HENDERSON AV, SD, 92140	1268 - E6
MARITIME MUS 1492 N HARBOR DR, SD, 92101	1288 - J2
MINGEI INTL MUS 1439 EL PRADO, SD, 92101	1289 - B1
MUS OF CONTEMPORARY ART SAN DIEGO 1001 KETTNER BLVD, SD, 92101	1288 - J3
MUS OF MAN 1350 EL PRADO, SD, 92101	1289 - B1
MUS OF SAN DIEGO HIST 1649 EL PRADO, SD, 92101	1289 - C1
NATURAL HIST MUS 1870 EL PRADO, SD, 92101	1289 - C1
OCEANSIDE MUS OF ART 704 PIER VIEW WY, OCN, 92054	1086 - A7
SAN DIEGO AUTOMOTIVE MUS 2080 PAN AMERICAN PZ, SD, 92101	1289 - B1
SAN DIEGO MODEL RAILROAD MUS 1649 EL PRADO, SD, 92101	1289 - C1
SAN DIEGO MUS OF ART 1450 EL PRADO, SD, 92101	1289 - B1
SAN DIEGO MUS OF CONTEMPORARY ART 700 PROSPECT ST, SD, 92037	1227 - E6
SAN DIEGO RAILROAD MUSUEM-(SEE PAGE 1298) 31123 HWY 94, SDCo, 91906	1318 - A7
SAN DIEGUITO HERITAGE MUS 162 RANCHO SANTA FE RD, ENCT, 92024	1167 - J1
SAN MARCOS HIST SOCIETY 270 W SAN MARCOS BLVD, SMCS, 92069	1108 - H7
SERRA MUS 2727 PRESIDIO DR, SD, 92103	1268 - F4
SPRING VALLEY HIST MUS 9065 MEMORY LN, SDCo, 91977	1271 - B5
TIMKEN MUS OF ART 1500 EL PRADO, SD, 92101	1289 - C1
WORLD WAR II FLYING MUS 1850 JOE CROSSON DR, ELCJ, 92020	1251 - E1

OPEN SPACE PRESERVES

FEATURE NAME Address City, ZIP Code	PAGE-GRID
AGUA TIBIA WILDERNESS AREA SDCo, 92060	409 - E5
BEAR, MARIAN MEM NATURAL PK REGENTS RD, SD, 92117	1228 - D7
BLACK MTN PK BLACK MOUNTAIN RD, SD, 92129	1169 - F7
BLUE SKY CANYON ECOLOGICAL RESERVE ESPOLA RD & GREEN VALLEY TKTR, PWY, 92064	1170 - J3
BONSALL PRESERVE S MISSION RD, SDCo, 92003	1048 - A7
CHULA VISTA WILDLIFE RESERVE SAN DIEGO BAY, CHV, 91910	1329 - H3
CIBOLA NATL WILDLIFE REFUGE HIGHWAY 78, ImCo	412 - B5
CREST CANYON OPEN SPACE PK DEL MAR HTS RD & DURANGO DR, SD, 92014	1187 - G4
DALEY RANCH LA HONDA DR, ESCN, 92026	1090 - B6
DINWIDDIE PRESERVE S STAGE COACH LN & BROOKE RD, SDCo, 92028	1027 - J6
EL CAPITAN COUNTY OPEN SPACE PRESERVE WILDCAT CANYON RD, SDCo, 92040	1213 - B2
HELLHOLE CANYON CO O S PRESERVE KIAVO DR & SANTEE LN, SDCo, 92082	1091 - J3
IMPERIAL NATL WILDLIFE REFUGE FISHERS LANDING, ImCo	412 - D11
IMPERIAL WATERFOWL MGMT AREA HIGHWAY 111 & DOWDEN RD, ImCo, 92233	411 - B10
IMPERIAL WATERFOWL MGMT AREA SCHRIMPF RD & DAVIS RD, ImCo, 92233	411 - B8
JACUMBA NAT COOP LND & WLDLFE MGMT-AREA (SEE PAGE 1300) SDCo, 91934	1301 - J3
LA JOLLA NATURAL PK COUNTRY CLUB DR, SD, 92037	1227 - G6
LARWIN PK CARLSBAD VILLAGE DR, CRLB, 92008	1106 - H3
LOS JILGUEROS PRESERVE S MISSION RD & PEPPER TREE LN, SDCo, 92028	1027 - G5
LOS PENASQUITOS CANYON PRESERVE 12020 BLACK MOUNTAIN RD, SD, 92130	1208 - E2
MISSION TRAILS REGL PK 7300 FATHER JUNIPERO SERRA TR, SD, 92124	1230 - C6
MOUNT GOWER COUNTY O S PRESERVE GUNN STAGE RD, SDCo, 92065	1173 - H1
NORTHERN WILDLIFE PRESERVE PACIFIC BEACH DR & NOYES ST, SD, 92109	1248 - B6
OAK OASIS COUNTY OPEN SPACE PRESERVE 12620 WILDCAT CANYON RD, SDCo, 92040	1212 - D2
OPEN SPACE LAUREL ST & N HARBOR DR, SD, 92101	1288 - H1
OTAY COUNTY OPEN SPACE PRESERVE WUESTE RD, SDCo, 91915	1332 - B3
OVERLOOK PK HIGH BLUFF DR, SD, 92130	1187 - J4
ROSE CANYON OPEN SPACE GENESEE AV, SD, 92122	1228 - A6
SALTON SEA NATL WILDLIFE REFUGE SEVERE RD & SINCLAIR RD, ImCo, 92259	410 - L10
SAN ELIJO LAGOON CO PK & ECOLOGIC RES MANCHESTER AV OFF S D FRWY, ENCT, 92067	1167 - G5
SAN MATEO CANYON WILDERNESS ORTEGA HWY, SDCo, 92055	408 - L4
SANTA MARGARITA ECOLOGICAL RESERVE RED MOUNTAIN TKTR, RivC, 92590	998 - D1
SCRIPPS, JAMES BLUFF PRESERVE CM DL MAR, DLMR, 92014	1187 - E2
SEAL ROCK RESERVE COAST BLVD, SD, 92037	1227 - E6
SILVERWOOD WILDLIFE SANCTUARY BARONA RD, SDCo, 92040	1212 - G2
SOLEDAD NATURAL PK ARDATH RD & I-5, SD, 92037	1227 - J7
SOUTH BAY CO BIO STUDY AREA SILVER STRAND BLVD, CORD, 91932	1329 - F4
SWEETWATER MARSH NATL WLDLFE REFUGE 1000 GUNPOWDER POINT DR, CHV, 91910	1309 - G5
SYCAMORE CANYON CO OPEN SPACE-PRESERVE 13920 HIGHWAY 67, SDCo, 92071	1191 - C7
TECOLOTE CANYON NATURAL PK TECOLOTE CANYON, SD, 92111	1248 - F4
TIJUANA RIV NATL ESTUARINE SANCTUARY SUNSET AV, SD, 92154	1349 - H4
TIJUANA SLOUGH NATL WILDLIFE REFUGE 301 CASPIAN WY, IMPB, 91932	1349 - F2
TORREY HIGHLANDS PK LANSDALE DR & DEL MAR HEIGHTS, SD, 92130	1188 - B4
TORREY PINES STATE RESERVE N TORREY PINES RD, SD, 92014	1207 - H1
VOLCAN MTN WILDERNESS PRESERVE VOLCAN RD, SDCo, 92036	1136 - D2
WISTER WATERFOWL MANAGEMENT AREA HIGHWAY 111 & POWELL RD, ImCo, 92257	411 - A6

PARK & RIDE

FEATURE NAME Address City, ZIP Code	PAGE-GRID
PARK & RIDE 195 S TREMONT ST, OCN, 92054	1106 - A1
PARK & RIDE 47TH ST & CASTANA ST, SD, 92102	1289 - J4
PARK & RIDE 62ND ST & AKINS AV, SD, 92114	1290 - D3
PARK & RIDE AMAYA DR & AMAYA CT, LMSA, 91942	1251 - B7
PARK & RIDE FLETCHER PKY & GROSSMONT CTR D, LMSA, 91942	1250 - J7
PARK & RIDE HOLLISTER ST & PALM AV, SD, 92154	1330 - B7
PARK & RIDE INTERSTATE 5 & E ST, CHV, 91910	1309 - J6
PARK & RIDE IRIS AV & 30TH ST, SD, 92154	1350 - D2
PARK & RIDE MASSACHUSETTS AV, LMGR, 91945	1290 - F1
PARK & RIDE N EUCLID AV & MARKET ST, SD, 92102	1290 - A3
PARK & RIDE PALOMAR ST & INDUSTRIAL BLVD, CHV, 91911	1330 - B4
PARK & RIDE SPRING ST, LMSA, 91941	1270 - J4
PARK & RIDE W 8TH ST & HARBOR DR, NATC, 92136	1309 - G1
PARK & RIDE WILSON AV & MILES-OF-CARS WY, NATC, 91950	1309 - H3
PARK & RIDE W SEAWARD AV, SD, 92173	1350 - F3
PARK & RIDE W VALLEY PKWY & N QUINCE ST, ESCN, 92025	1129 - H3
PARK & RIDE LOT 1 3642 AGUA DULCE BLVD, SDCo, 91977	1271 - E5
PARK & RIDE LOT 2 11575 WOODSIDE AV, SDCo, 92040	1231 - H4
PARK & RIDE LOT 3 1785 ESCONDIDO BLVD, ESCN, 92025	1130 - A5
PARK & RIDE LOT 4 CARMEL MTN RD & FREEPORT RD, SD, 92129	1189 - F4
PARK & RIDE LOT 5 1667 MAXSON ST, OCN, 92054	1086 - B7
PARK & RIDE LOT 6 I-15 & MIRA MESA BLVD, SD, 92126	1209 - E3
PARK & RIDE LOT 7 12791 SORRENTO VALLEY RD, SD, 92121	1207 - J2
PARK & RIDE LOT 8 7675 HIGH ST, LMSA, 91941	1270 - G5
PARK & RIDE LOT 9 2300 SWEETWATER RD, SDCo, 91950	1310 - C3
PARK & RIDE LOT 10 12522 MAPLEVIEW ST, SDCo, 92040	1232 - B3
PARK & RIDE LOT 11 871 N BROADWAY, ESCN, 92025	1129 - H1
PARK & RIDE LOT 12 2885 LEMON GROVE AV, LMGR, 91945	1270 - G6
PARK & RIDE LOT 13 7100 ALVARADO RD, LMSA, 91941	1270 - F2
PARK & RIDE LOT 16 12668 SABRE SPRINGS PKWY, SD, 92128	1189 - H6
PARK & RIDE LOT 17 4300 TAYLOR ST, SD, 92110	1268 - G4
PARK & RIDE LOT 18 TED WILLIAMS PKWY & SABRE SPGS, SD, 92128	1189 - J3
PARK & RIDE LOT 19 PALA RD & OLD HWY 395, SDCo, 92028	1048 - H2
PARK & RIDE LOT 20 5196 GOVERNOR RD, SD, 92122	1228 - G4
PARK & RIDE LOT 21 501 SEAVIEW PL, VSTA, 92083	1107 - H1
PARK & RIDE LOT 22 8725 MURRAY DR, LMSA, 91942	1271 - A1
PARK & RIDE LOT 23 1470 E MADISON AV, ELCJ, 92019	1252 - A4
PARK & RIDE LOT 24 I-805 & VISTA SORRENTO PKWY, SD, 92121	1208 - D7
PARK & RIDE LOT 25 1441 E WASHINGTON AV, ELCJ, 92019	1252 - A6
PARK & RIDE LOT 26 CARMEL MTN RD & RANCHO CARMEL, SD, 92128	1189 - J1
PARK & RIDE LOT 29 7838 JAPATUL VALLEY RD, SDCo, 91901	1235 - J6
PARK & RIDE LOTS 30 & 38 1699 SEVEN OAKES RD, ESCN, 92026	1109 - F6
PARK & RIDE LOT 31 10155 RANCHO CARMEL DR, SD, 92128	1189 - J3
PARK & RIDE LOT 32 710 LA COSTA AV, CRLB, 92024	1147 - B1
PARK & RIDE LOT 33 INTERSTATE 15 & DEER SPGS RD, SDCo, 92026	1089 - C6
PARK & RIDE LOT 34 INTERSTATE 15 & MTN MEADOW RD, SDCo, 92026	1089 - D6
PARK & RIDE LOT 35 INTERSTATE 15 & GOPHER CANYON, SDCo, 92026	1068 - J6
PARK & RIDE LOT 37 3601 AVOCADO BLVD, SDCo, 91941	1271 - F5
PARK & RIDE LOT 39 3700 HAYNER DR, OCN, 92056	1107 - B2
PARK & RIDE LOT 40 8627 JAMACHA BLVD, SDCo, 91977	1291 - A4
PARK & RIDE LOT 41 13702 CM CANADA, SDCo, 92021	1252 - D1
PARK & RIDE LOT 42 9001 BLOSSOM VALLEY RD, SDCo, 92021	1232 - F5
PARK & RIDE LOT 43 8002 GILMAN DR, SD, 92037	1228 - A6
PARK & RIDE LOT 44 1928 MORENO ST, OCN, 92054	1106 - D3
PARK & RIDE LOT 45 COLLEGE BLVD & VISTA WY, OCN, 92056	1107 - B2
PARK & RIDE LOT 46 4980 SWEETGRASS LN, SDCo, 92003	1048 - A6
PARK & RIDE LOT 47 1600 VILLA CARDIFF DR, ENCT, 92007	1167 - E2
PARK & RIDE LOT 48 13734 TWIN PEAKS RD, PWY, 92064	1190 - F1
PARK & RIDE LOT 49 7850 NAVAJO RD, SD, 92119	1250 - H4
PARK & RIDE LOT 50 610 PAS DL REY, CHV, 91910	1330 - H1
PARK & RIDE LOT 51 12862 RANCHO PENASQUITOS BLVD, SD, 92129	1189 - F5
PARK & RIDE LOT 52 14350 COMMUNITY RD, PWY, 92064	1190 - E2
PARK & RIDE LOT 53 10060 CARMEL MOUNTAIN RD, SD, 92129	1189 - F4
PARK & RIDE LOT 54 VIA RANCHO PKWY & DEL LAGO BL, ESCN, 92029	1150 - A2
PARK & RIDE LOT 56 BUENA VISTA WY & EAST H ST, CHV, 91910	1311 - B5
PARK & RIDE LOT 57 10330 CARMEL MOUNTAIN RD, SD, 92129	1189 - G3
PARK & RIDE LOT 58 10440 BLACK MOUNTAIN RD, SD, 92126	1209 - E4
PARK & RIDE LOT 59 5230 BANCROFT DR, LMSA, 91941	1271 - B1
PARK & RIDE LOT 60 5480 BANCROFT DR, LMSA, 91941	1271 - B1
PARK & RIDE LOT 61 9307 MURRAY DR, LMSA, 91942	1251 - B7
PARK & RIDE LOT 62 170 CL MAGDALENA, ENCT, 92024	1147 - C7
PARK & RIDE LOT 63 1855 MAIN ST, SDCo, 92065	1152 - E7
PARK & RIDE LOT 64 2245 E VALLEY PKWY, ESCN, 92027	1110 - D7
PARK & RIDE LOT 65 RCHO BERNARDO RD & I-15, SD, 92127	1169 - J2
PARK & RIDE LOT 66 CENTRE CITY PKWY & DECATUR WY, ESCN, 92026	1129 - G1
PARK & RIDE LOT 67 MISSION GORGE RD & W HILLS PKW, SNTE, 92071	1230 - H7
PARK & RIDE LOT 69 855 E BARNHAM RD, SMCS, 92078	1129 - B1
PARK & RIDE LOT 70 MISSION GORGE RD & BIG ROCK RD, SNTE, 92071	1230 - H7
PARK & RIDE LOT 71 SWSWEETWATER SPNGS BL & AUSTIN, SDCo, 91977	1271 - E7
PARK & RIDE LOT 72 N MAGNOLIA AV & ALEXANDER WY, SNTE, 92071	1231 - F7
PARK & RIDE LOT 73 MISSION AV & FRONTIER DR, OCN, 92054	1086 - F4
PARK & RIDE LOT 74 COLLEGE GROVE DR, SD, 92115	1270 - D6

PARKS & RECREATION

FEATURE NAME	PAGE-GRID
ADAMS AVENUE PK, SD	1269 - F3
ADAMS PK, ELCN	6499 - H6
ADOBE BLUFFS PK, SD	1189 - C2
ADOBE RIDGE MINI PK, PWY	1190 - C1
AGUA CALIENTE COUNTY PK, SDCo	430 - C3
AGUILAR PK, ELCN	6499 - F4
ALAMOSA PK, OCN	1087 - C1
ALLEN, DENNIS V PK, SD	1289 - G3
ALLIED GARDENS COMM PK, SD	1250 - A5
ANZA-BORREGO DESERT STATE PK, SDCo-(SEE PAGE 1058)	1078 - E2
ARBOLITOS SPORT FIELDS, PWY	1190 - C1
ASHLEY FALLS PK, SD	1188 - D5
AUGUSTA PK, CHV	1311 - G5
AZALEA PK, SD	1269 - G7
AZTEC PK, LMSA	1270 - H1
BALBOA PK, SD	1269 - D7
BALDERAMA PK, OCN	1086 - B6
BANCROFT COUNTY PK, SDCo	1271 - B5
BANDEL, L C PK, CORD	1288 - G7
BAY BOULEVARD PK, CHV	1309 - J7
BAYSIDE PK, CHV	1329 - H1
BAY TERRACES COMM PK, SD	1290 - G7
BAYVIEW PK, CORD	1288 - H5
BENDIXEN, BETTE PK, PWY	1190 - B6
BERRY PK, SD	1350 - A2
BERRY STREET PK, LMGR	1270 - F7
BIG ROCK PK, SNTE	1250 - H1
BILL BECK PK, ELCJ	1251 - D4
BIRD ROCK PK, SD	1247 - G4
BONITA LONG CANYON PK, CHV	1311 - C3
BONITAS HACIENDAS MINI-PARK, CHV	1311 - B5
BOONE PK, SD	1290 - G5
BORDER FIELD STATE PK, IMPB	1349 - G6
BOSTONIA PK, ELCJ	1251 - J3
BRADLEY PK, SMCS	1128 - D1
BREEZE HILL PK, VSTA	1107 - F1
BRENGLE TERRACE PK, VSTA	1088 - A5
BRIERCREST PK, LMSA	1251 - A7
BRIERLY FIELD, CRLB	1106 - E6
BROWN, MAXTON PK, CRLB	1106 - D4
BUCCANEER BEACH PK, OCN	1106 - B3
BUCKLIN PK, ELCN	6559 - G1
BUENA VISTA PK, VSTA	1107 - H6
CABRILLO HEIGHTS PK, SD	1249 - B4
CACTUS COUNTY PK, SDCo	1232 - C2
CADENCIA PK, CRLB	1127 - J7
CADMAN COMM PK, SD	1248 - C3
CAJON VALLEY PK, ELCJ	1251 - G5
CALAVERA PK, CRLB	1107 - A4
CALUMET PK, SD	1247 - F4
CANNON PK, CRLB	1126 - F2
CANYONSIDE COMM PK, SD	1189 - D7
CAPISTRANO PK, OCN	1086 - A5
CARDIFF PK, ENCT	1167 - D3
CARDIFF SPORTS PK, ENCT	1167 - F2
CARMEL CREEK PK, SD	1188 - B5
CARMEL DEL MAR PK, SD	1188 - B7
CARMEL GROVE PK, SD	1188 - A7
CARMEL MISSION PK, SD	1188 - B6
CARMEL MTN RANCH COMM PK, SD	1189 - H3
CARMEL VALLEY COMM PK, SD	1188 - A6
CARRASCO, JOSEPH PK, OCN	1086 - D7

PARKS & RECREATION — SAN DIEGO CO. POINTS OF INTEREST — PARKS & RECREATION 6638

SAN DIEGO CO.
INDEX

FEATURE NAME Address City, ZIP Code	PAGE-GRID
CARRILLO, LEO PK, CRLB	1127 - J4
CARSON, KIT PK, ESCN	1150 - B2
CEDAR LANE PK, VSTA	1087 - G6
CENTENNIAL PK, CORD	1288 - J5
CERRO DE LAS POSAS PK, SMCS	1108 - E5
CHASE FIELD, CRLB	1106 - F6
CHICANO PK, SD	1289 - C5
CHOLLAS COMM PK, SD	1270 - C7
CHULA VISTA BAYFRONT PK, CHV	1329 - H2
CHULA VISTA COMM PK, CHV	1311 - F5
CITY HEIGHTS COMM PK, SD	1269 - H5
CITY PK, ELCN	6499 - H6
CITY PK, SD	1289 - A3
CIVIC CTR PK, VSTA	1087 - J6
CLAIREMONT COMM PK, SD	1248 - E5
CLAY PK, SD	1270 - D3
CLEATOR COMM PK, SD	1268 - B6
CLEVELAND NATL FOREST, SDCo	1218 - C3
CLIFFRIDGE PK, SD	1227 - J5
COAST BLVD PK, SD	1227 - E7
COBBLESTONE PK, CHV	1311 - E3
COLINA DEL SOL COMM PK, SD	1270 - A5
COLLIER COUNTY PK, SDCo	1152 - H6
COLLIER PK, LMSA	1270 - J3
COLLIER PK WEST, SD	1268 - A6
CORONADO CAYS PK, CORD	1329 - D2
COTTONWOOD 3 COUNTY PK, SDCo	1272 - B5
COTTONWOOD PK, CHV	1311 - D7
CRONAN PK, CORD	1288 - J7
CROSBY STREET PK, SD	1289 - C6
CUVIER PK (THE WEDDING BOWL), SD	1227 - E7
CUYAMACA PK, ELCJ	1251 - E7
CUYAMACA RANCHO STATE PK, SDCo- (SEE PAGE 1176)	1196 - F2
CYPRESS CANYON PK, SD	1210 - B1
DAILARD PK, SD	1250 - D4
DAMON LANE COUNTY PK, SDCo	1271 - H3
DAN DUSSAULT PK, SDCo	1027 - E3
DEL MAR TRAILS PK, SD	1188 - C7
DEPUTY LONNIE G BREWER COUNTY PK, SDCo	1271 - G4
DISCOVERY PK, CHV	1311 - A5
DIXON LAKE REC AREA, ESCN	1110 - D4
DOLPHIN BEACH CLUB, CHV	1311 - H6
DOS PICOS COUNTY PK, SDCo	1171 - H5
DOYLE COMM PK, SD	1228 - C3
DUNES PK, IMPB	1329 - E7
DUSTY RHODES PK, SD	1268 - A5
EAST CLAIREMONT ATHLETIC AREA, SD	1248 - G5
EASTLAKE BEACH CLUB, CHV	1311 - E4
EASTLAKE III PK, CHV	1332 - A2
ECKE, PAUL SPORTS PK, ENCT	1147 - C6
ELFIN FOREST RECREATIONAL RESERVE, SDCo	1149 - B2
ELLEN BROWNING SCRIPPS PK, SD	1227 - E6
EL MONTE COUNTY PK, SDCo	1213 - A6
ELMWOOD PK, ESCN	1130 - A1
EL NORTE PK, ESCN	1110 - A6
EL TOYON PK, NATC	1290 - A7
EMBARCADERO MARINA PK, SD	1288 - J4
EMERALD HILLS PK, SD	1290 - B2
ENCANTO COMM PK, SD	1290 - D2
ESTRELLA COUNTY PK, SDCo	1271 - D4
EUCALYPTUS COUNTY PK, SDCo	1271 - B3
EUCALYPTUS PK, CHV	1310 - A5
EXPLORER PK, CHV	1310 - H6
FALLBROOK PK, SDCo	1027 - H3
FANUEL STREET PK, SD	1247 - J7
FELICITA COUNTY PK, SDCo	1149 - H1
FIRE MTN PK, OCN	1106 - F1
FIRESIDE PK, OCN	1086 - E3
FIRE STA PK, ELCJ	1251 - C4
FLETCHER COVE BEACH PK, SOLB	1167 - E7
FLETCHER HILLS PK, ELCJ	1251 - B5
FLINN SPRINGS COUNTY PK, SDCo	1232 - J5
FRAZIER FIELD, ELCN	6499 - H5
FRIENDSHIP PK, CHV	1310 - B6
FUERTE PK, CRLB	1127 - H6
GARDEN ROAD PK, PWY	1190 - J4
GERSHWIN PK, SD	1248 - D1
GLEN PK, ENCT	1167 - D4
GLORIETTA BAY PK, CORD	1309 - A1
GOLDEN HILL COMM CTR, SD	1289 - D2
GOMEZ PK, ELCN	6500 - A7
GOMPERS PK, SD	1290 - A3
GOODAN RANCH COUNTY PK, SDCo	1191 - C7
GOODLAND ACRES COUNTY PK, SDCo	1271 - A6
GRAND CARIBE SHORELINE PK, CORD	1329 - E1
GRANT HILL PK, SD	1289 - D4
GRANTVILLE PK, SD	1249 - J7
GRAPE DAY PK, ESCN	1129 - J2
GREG ROGERS PK, CHV	1330 - H2
GUAJOME REGL PK, OCN	1087 - F2
HALECREST PK, CHV	1310 - F6
HARBOR ISLAND DR PK, SD	1288 - F2
HARRIS, ADA PK, ENCT	1167 - E2
HARRY GRIFFEN PK, LMSA	1251 - C7
HEISE, WILLIAM COUNTY PK, SDCo	1156 - D5
HELEN BOUGHER PK, SMCS	1109 - C5
HENDERSON, WILLIE SPORTS COMPLEX, SD	1289 - J6
HERITAGE PK, OCN	1086 - H2
HERITAGE PK, CHV	1331 - C1
HERITAGE PK, SD	1268 - G5
HERMOSA TERRACE PK, SD	1247 - E2
HIGHLAND RANCH PK, SD	1190 - A1
HIGHWOOD PK, LMSA	1270 - H4
HILLEARY PK, PWY	1190 - E4
HILLSIDE PK, ELCJ	1251 - C4
HILLTOP COMM PK, SD	1189 - E2
HILLTOP PK, CHV	1330 - D1
HOLIDAY PK, CRLB	1106 - F5
HOLLYWOOD PK, SD	1289 - H1
HOSP GROVE PK, CRLB	1106 - E3
HOURGLASS FIELD COMM PK, SD	1209 - E4
HOWARD LANE PK, SD	1350 - D2
H STREET VIEWPOINT PK, ENCT	1147 - B7
IMPERIAL SAND DUNES REC AREA, ImCo	431 - J3
INAJA MEM PK, SDCo	1135 - C4
INDEPENDENCE PK, CHV	1311 - B6
I STREET VIEWPOINT PK, ENCT	1167 - B1
IVEY RANCH PK, OCN	1086 - H3
JACKSON PK, LMSA	1250 - H7
JACUMBA COMM PK, SDCo- (SEE PAGE 1300)	1321 - H6
JERABEK PK, SD	1210 - A4
JESMOND DENE PK, ESCN	1109 - G3
JOHN F KENNEDY PK, ELCJ	1252 - B5
J STREET VIEWPOINT PK, ENCT	1167 - B1
JUDSON, C S PK, ELCJ	1251 - F5
KEARNY MESA COMM PK, SD	1248 - J5
KEILLER PK, SD	1290 - F3
KELLOGG PK, SD	1227 - G5
KELLY STREET PK, SD	1268 - H1
KENNEDY, JOHN F PK, SD	1290 - A5
KENSINGTON MINI PK, SD	1269 - H3
KIMBALL PK, NATC	1309 - H2
KING, MARTIN L JR MEM COMM PK, SD	1290 - D5
KING, MARTIN LUTHER JR PK, OCN	1086 - J4
KING, MARTIN LUTHER JR PROMENADE, SD	1289 - A4
KNOB HILL PK, SMCS	1109 - D7
KUNKEL PK, LMGR	1270 - H5
LA COLONIA PK, SOLB	1187 - G1

FEATURE NAME Address City, ZIP Code	PAGE-GRID
LA COSTA CANYON PK, CRLB	1147 - H1
LAGUNA RIVIERA PK, CRLB	1106 - J7
LA JOLLA ATHLETIC AREA, SD	1227 - J3
LA JOLLA COMM PK, SD	1227 - E7
LA JOLLA HERMOSA PK, SD	1247 - F3
LAKE JENNINGS COUNTY PK, SDCo	1232 - E3
LAKE MORENA COUNTY PK, SDCo- (SEE PAGE 1296)	1297 - D5
LAKE MURRAY COMM PK, SD	1250 - E6
LAKE PK, OCN	1107 - F3
LAKE POWAY REC AREA, PWY	1170 - H4
LAKEVIEW PK, SMCS	1128 - F3
LAKE VIEW PK, SD	1209 - J3
LAMAR COUNTY PK, SDCo	1271 - A6
LA MESITA PK, LMSA	1251 - A6
LANDES, JOHN PK, OCN	1087 - C7
LANE, FRANK PK, SDCo	1136 - A6
LAS PALMAS PK, NATC	1310 - B2
LAUDERBACH PK, CHV	1330 - C3
LEMON GROVE PK, LMGR	1270 - H7
LEUCADIA ROADSIDE PK, ENCT	1147 - A4
LEVANTE PK, CRLB	1147 - H2
LIBBY LAKE PK, OCN	1066 - J7
LINCOLN ACRES COUNTY PK, SDCo	1310 - C2
LINDA VISTA COMM PK, SD	1248 - J6
LINDBERGH PK, SD	1249 - A3
LINDO LAKE COUNTY PK, SDCo	1232 - B3
LIONS CLUB PK, OCN	1106 - C3
LITTLE OAKS PK, ENCT	1148 - B5
LIVE OAK COUNTY PK, SDCo	1028 - C5
LOMA VERDE PK, CHV	1330 - F4
LOMITA PK, SD	1290 - H3
LOPEZ RIDGE PK, SD	1208 - H3
LOS NINOS PK, CHV	1330 - F4
LOTUS PK, ELCN	6499 - E6
LOWER OTAY COUNTY PK, SDCo	1332 - B3
MACARTHUR PK, LMSA	1270 - J2
MACDOWELL PK, SD	1228 - H7
MACPHERSON, MILDRED PK, ENCT	1167 - C1
MADDOX PK, SD	1209 - A5
MAGEE PK, CRLB	1106 - D5
MARCY PK, SD	1228 - B6
MARINA VIEW PK, CHV	1329 - J2
MARISOL PK, CHV	1310 - H5
MARLADO HIGHLANDS PK, OCN	1086 - E2
MARSHALL PK, OCN	1106 - C2
MARTIN, JESS PK, SDCo	1156 - C1
MASON WILDLIFE COUNTY PK, SDCo- (SEE PAGE 1296)	1316 - G7
MAST PK, SNTE	1231 - B5
MATHEWSON PK, CORD	1288 - J7
MCGEE PK, ELCN	6500 - A6
MCLEOD, ROD PK, ESCN	1109 - G6
MEM COMM PK, SD	1289 - E5
MEM PK, CHV	1310 - B6
MESA VERDE PK, SD	1209 - B5
MESA VIKING PK, SD	1209 - C2
MINI PK, CHV	1311 - E4
MIRA MESA COMM PK, SD	1209 - C3
MISSION BAY ATHLETIC AREA, SD	1248 - C5
MISSION BAY PK, SD	1248 - D7
MISSION HEIGHTS PK, SD	1268 - J2
MISSION HILLS PK, SD	1268 - H5
MISSION TRAILS REGL PK, SD	1250 - E6
MONTCLAIR PK, SD	1269 - F7
MONTEREY HEIGHTS PK, LMGR	1290 - G1
MONTEZUMA PK, SD	1270 - D2
MONTGOMERY WALLER COMM PK, SD	1330 - D7
MOUNT ACADIA PK, SD	1248 - H4
MTN VIEW PK, SD	1289 - H5
MTN VIEW PK, ESCN	1130 - E1
MOUNT ETNA PK, SD	1248 - F2
MOUNT HELIX COUNTY PK, SDCo	1271 - D2
MULLEN, LEO SPORTS PK, ENCT	1147 - F4
MURRAY RIDGE PK, SD	1249 - C7
NANCY JANE COUNTY PK, SDCo	1252 - H3
NESTOR PK, SD	1350 - B1
NOBEL ATHLETIC AREA, SD	1228 - E3
NORMAN PK, CHV	1310 - B6
NORTH CLAIREMONT COMM PK, SD	1248 - F1
NORTHMONT PK, LMSA	1251 - B6
NORTH PK COMM PARK, SD	1269 - D5
NORTH RIVER ROAD PK, OCN	1067 - B6
OAKCREST PK, ENCT	1147 - F7
OAK CREST PK, CHV	1311 - C7
OAK PK, SD	1270 - A7
OAK RIPARIAN PK, OCN	1107 - E3
OCEAN BCH ATHLETIC AREA (ROBB FIELD), SD	1268 - A5
OCEAN BEACH COMM PK, SD	1267 - J6
OCOTILLO WELLS VEHICULAR REC AREA, SDCo- (SEE PAGE 1100)	1121 - H1
OLD IRONSIDES COUNTY PK, SDCo	1253 - D1
OLD POWAY PK, PWY	1190 - F2
OLD TROLLEY BARN PK, SD	1269 - C3
OLIVE GROVE COMM PK, SD	1248 - J2
ORANGE AVENUE FIELDS, CHV	1330 - F4
ORCHARD PK, CHV	1331 - B1
ORPHEUS PK, ENCT	1147 - B5
OTAY PK, CHV	1330 - E5
OTAY VALLEY REGL PK, SD	1330 - G6
PACIFIC BEACH COMM PK, SD	1247 - J5
PACIFIC STREET LINEAR PK, OCN	1106 - A1
PALISADES PK, OCN	1086 - J7
PALISADES PK (LAW ST PARK), SD	1247 - G5
PALM PK, CORD	1288 - H5
PALM RIDGE PK, SD	1330 - G7
PALOMAR PK, CHV	1330 - G3
PALOMAR MTN STATE PK, SDCo	1051 - J1
PALOMARES PK, SDCo	1027 - H6
PANTOJA PK, SD	1289 - A3
PARADISE HILLS COMM PK, SD	1290 - E6
PK DE LA CRUZ, SD	1269 - G6
PK LAND, CHV	1311 - A6
PKSIDE PARK, SD	1310 - E2
PASEO DEL REY PK, CHV	1310 - H7
PENASQUITOS CREEK PK, SD	1189 - A7
PENN ATHLETIC AREA, SD	1310 - F1
PEPPER PK, NATC	1309 - G5
PICACHO STATE REC AREA, ImCo	412 - C11
PICNIC GROUNDS, SDCo	1218 - G7
PINE VALLEY COUNTY PK, SDCo	1237 - B6
PITTMAN, DEBBIE PK, ELCN	6499 - E7
PLUMOSA PK, SD	1268 - C6
POINSETTIA PK, CRLB	1127 - A4
POINT LOMA COMM PK, SD	1288 - A2
PORTER PK, LMSA	1270 - J2
PORTWOOD PIER PLAZA, IMPB	1349 - E1
POTRERO COUNTY PK, SDCo- (SEE PAGE 1296)	1316 - E7
POWAY COMM PK, PWY	1190 - D5
POWAY SPORTS PK, PWY	1190 - E6
POWERHOUSE PK, DLMR	1187 - F4
PRESIDIO COMM PK, SD	1268 - F4
PRINCESS DEL CERRO PK, SD	1250 - C6
RAINBOW PK, SDCo	998 - J5
RAINTREE PK, VSTA	1087 - H5
RAMONA COMM PK, SDCo	1152 - H4
RANCHO BERNARDO COMM PK, SD	1150 - A6
RANCHO DEL ORO COMM PK, OCN	1087 - B3
RANCHO DEL REY PK, CHV	1311 - B6

FEATURE NAME Address City, ZIP Code	PAGE-GRID
RANCHO MISSION CANYON PK, SD	1250 - C4
REAMA PK, IMPB	1349 - E1
RECREATION PK, OCN	1086 - B7
REINSTRA BALL FIELDS, CHV	1330 - F4
RENETTE PK, ELCJ	1251 - E7
RIDGEWOOD PK, SD	1189 - F6
RIVER VIEW PK, SDCo	1231 - J5
ROADRUNNER PK, SD	1249 - H3
ROBERT ADAMS COMM PK, SDCo	1070 - F7
ROHR PK, CHV	1310 - G3
ROLANDO PK, LMSA	1270 - E4
ROLLING HILLS PK, SD	1169 - H7
ROLLING HILLS PK, CHV	1311 - F3
ROSE TEMPLE MEM PK, IMPB	1329 - H7
ROTARY PK, OCN	1106 - A1
ROTARY PK, CORD	1288 - H7
ROTARY PK, CRLB	1106 - E5
SABRE SPRINGS PK, SD	1189 - H5
SALTON SEA STATE REC AREA, ImCo	410 - K5
SAN CARLOS COMM PK, SD	1250 - H5
SANDBURG PK, SD	1209 - B2
SAN DIEGO GAS & ELECTRIC PK, CHV	1330 - F4
SAN DIEGUITO COUNTY PK, SDCo	1168 - A6
SAN ONOFRE ST BCH, SDCo	1023 - C2
SANTA CLARA POINT COMM PK, SD	1267 - J1
SANTEE LAKES REGL PK, SNTE	1231 - A1
SAN YSIDRO ATHLETIC AREA, SD	1350 - F5
SAN YSIDRO COMM ACTIVITY CTR, SD	1350 - F2
SAN YSIDRO COMM PK, SD	1350 - G4
SCOBEE PK, CHV	1311 - F4
SCOTT VALLEY PK, ENCT	1147 - F4
SCRIPPS RANCH COMM PK, SD	1210 - A1
SDG&E PK, CORD	1288 - J5
SEAGROVE PK, DLMR	1187 - F5
SEPULVEDA PK, OCN	1087 - A7
SERRA MESA COMM PK, SD	1249 - D4
SESSIONS, KATE O MEM PK, SD	1248 - A4
SHADOW HILL PK, SNTE	1231 - G6
SHADOWRIDGE PK, VSTA	1108 - A4
SHOREBIRD PK, CHV	1311 - E4
SHORELINE PK, CORD	1288 - H5
SHORELINE PK, SD	1288 - B4
SILVERSET PK, PWY	1190 - D1
SILVERWING PK, SD	1350 - E1
SKYLINE COMM PK, SD	1290 - H4
SKYVIEW PK, SD	1290 - F4
SOLANA HIGHLANDS PK, SD	1187 - J5
SOUTH BAY COMM PK, SD	1350 - A1
SOUTH CREEK NEIGHBORHOOD PK, SD	1190 - A6
SOUTHCREST COMM PK, SD	1289 - H6
SOUTH LANE PK, SDCo	1252 - H4
SOUTH OCEANSIDE PK, OCN	1106 - D3
SPANISH LANDING PK, SD	1288 - E1
SPORTS PK, IMPB	1349 - F1
SPRECKELS PK, CORD	1288 - J6
SPRING CANYON PK, SD	1189 - H7
SPRING CREEK PK, OCN	1067 - E7
SPRING VALLEY COUNTY PK, SDCo	1291 - A4
STAGECOACH PK, CRLB	1147 - J2
STANDLEY COMM PK, SD	1228 - D6
STARKEY PK, SD	1247 - F2
STARK FIELD PK, ELCN	6499 - J7
STAR PK, CORD	1288 - H7
STARRIDGE PK, PWY	1190 - D3
STEELE CANYON COUNTY PK, SDCo	1272 - C6
STELZER, LOUIS A COUNTY PK, SDCo	1232 - D1
SUNBOW PK, CHV	1330 - H1
SUNFLOWER PK, ELCN	6499 - E6
SUNNYSLOPE PK, SD	1330 - B7
SUNRIDGE PK, CHV	1310 - J7
SUNSET CLIFFS PK, SD	1287 - H1
SUNSET PK, LMSA	1250 - F7
SUNSET PK, CORD	1288 - G7
SUNSHINE PK, LMSA	1270 - E3
SUN VISTA PK, ENCT	1147 - J5
SURF AND TURF RECREATION PK, SD	1187 - H2
SWAMIS PK, ENCT	1167 - B1
SWARTHOUT PK, ELCN	6499 - H5
SWEETWATER COUNTY PK, SDCo	1291 - A6
SWEETWATER HEIGHTS PK, NATC	1310 - D3
SWEETWATER LANE COUNTY PK, SDCo	1291 - A2
TECOLOTE COMM PK, SD	1268 - F2
TERALTA NEIGHBORHOOD PK, SD	1269 - G5
TERRA NOVA PK, CHV	1310 - F5
THIBODO PK, VSTA	1108 - A3
TIDE BEACH PK, SOLB	1167 - E6
TIDELANDS PK, CORD	1289 - A6
TIERRASANTA COMM PK, SD	1249 - J1
TIFFANY PK, CHV	1311 - D5
TIJUANA RIVER VALLEY REGL PK, SD	1350 - A4
TODD, BUDDY PK, OCN	1086 - E6
TORREY HILLS NEIGHBORHOOD PK, SD	1208 - B3
TORREY PINES CITY PK, SD	1207 - H7
TOWNSITE PK, VSTA	1087 - H5
TRIANGLE PK, CORD	1288 - H6
TUTTLE PK, ELCJ	1251 - F7
TUXEDO PK, SD	1250 - E3
TWIN TRAILS PK, SD	1189 - C4
TYSON STREET PK, OCN	1106 - A1
UCSD PK, SD	1228 - A1
UNIV GARDENS PK, SD	1228 - F5
UNIV VILLAGE PK, SD	1228 - F4
VALLECITO COUNTY PK, SDCo	430 - C2
VALLE LINDO PK, CHV	1330 - H4
VALLE VERDE PK, PWY	1170 - D3
VAN ZANTEN PK, ELCJ	1252 - A3
VETERANS PK, IMPB	1349 - G1
VETTER PK, CORD	1288 - J7
VIA DEL PARQUE PK, SDCo	1271 - F7
VIEWPOINT PK, ENCT	1147 - C7
VIEWS WEST PK, SD	1189 - F5
VILLA LA JOLLA PK, SD	1228 - A5
VILLA MONTSERATE PK, SD	1229 - G7
VILLA NORTE PK, SD	1229 - J7
VISTA LA MESA PK, LMSA	1270 - E5
VISTA TERRACE PK, SD	1350 - F2
VOYAGER PK, CHV	1311 - B7
WALKER-WANGENHEIM PK, SD	1209 - E4
WALNUT GROVE PK, SMCS	1108 - J1
WASHINGTON PK, ESCN	1130 - B1
WAVE WATER PK, VSTA	1087 - G6
WEISS, MANDELL EASTGATE CITY PK, SD	1228 - C2
WELLS PK, ELCJ	1251 - H4
WESTERN HILLS PK, SD	1248 - F7
WEST HILLS PK, SNTE	1230 - H5
WESTSIDE PK, ESCN	1129 - H4
WESTVIEW PK, SD	1209 - E2
WIDEMAN MEM PK, SD	1290 - E3
WILDERNESS GARDENS COUNTY PK, SDCo	409 - E6
WILDWOOD PK, VSTA	1087 - J6
WILLIAMSON, BUB PK, VSTA	1087 - D7
WINDRIVER COUNTY PK, SDCo	1272 - C4
WINDWOOD PK, SD	1188 - B6
WINTERWOOD COMM PK, SD	1209 - A4
WIRO PK, ENCT	1147 - J6
WOODGLEN VISTA PK, SNTE	1231 - D2
WOODHAVEN COUNTY PK, SDCo	1272 - C3
WOODLAND PK, SMCS	1109 - C6

PERFORMING ARTS

FEATURE NAME	Address City, ZIP Code	PAGE-GRID
CALIFORNIA CTR FOR THE ARTS	340 N ESCONDIDO BLVD, ESCN, 92025	1129 - H2
CASA DEL PRADO THEATRE	EL PRADO, SD, 92101	1289 - C1
COORS AMPHITHEATER	2050 ENTERTAINMENT CIR, CHV, 91911	1331 - B6
COPLEY SYMPHONY HALL	750 B ST, SD, 92101	1289 - B2
EAST COUNTY PERF ARTS CTR	210 E MAIN ST, ELCJ, 92020	1251 - F5
FLEET, REUBEN H SPACE THEATER & SCI-CTR	1875 EL PRADO, SD, 92101	1289 - C1
MOONLIGHT AMPITHEATER	1200 VALE TERRACE DR, VSTA, 92084	1088 - A5
OLD GLOBE THEATRE	OLD GLOBE WY, SD, 92101	1289 - B1
OPEN AIR THEATER	5402 COLLEGE AV, SD, 92182	1270 - C1
PALISADES BLDG	PAN AMERICAN RD W, SD, 92101	1289 - B1
POWAY PERF ARTS CTR	15498 ESPOLA RD, PWY, 92064	1170 - G6
SIMON EDISON CTR FOR PERF ARTS	OLD GLOBE WY, SD, 92101	1289 - B1
SPRECKELS ORGAN PAVILION	PAN AMERICAN RD E, SD, 92101	1289 - B1
SPRECKELS THEATRE	121 BROADWAY, SD, 92101	1289 - A3
STARLIGHT BOWL	PAN AMERICAN PZ, SD, 92101	1289 - B1
WEISS CTR	MANDELL WEISS LN, SD, 92093	1227 - J3

POINTS OF INTEREST

FEATURE NAME	Address City, ZIP Code	PAGE-GRID
ANZA-BORREGO VISITORS CTR- (SEE PAGE 1058)	200 PALM CANYON DR, SDCo, 92004	1078 - E2
ARCO TRNING CTR (US OLYMPC TRNING-CTR)	1750 WUESTE RD, CHV, 91915	1311 - J7
BALLAST POINT LIGHTHOUSE	GUIJAROS RD, SD, 92106	1288 - B7
BIRCH AQUARIUM AT SCRIPPS	2300 EXPEDITION WY, SD, 92093	1227 - H4
KGTV CHANNEL 10	4600 AIR WY, SD, 92105	1289 - J2
MISSION BAY YACHT CLUB	1215 EL CARMEL PL, SD, 92109	1267 - J2
MISSION BEACH PLUNGE	3115 OCEAN FRONT WK, SD, 92109	1267 - H3
OPERATIONAL LIGHTHOUSE	CABRILLO RD, SD, 92106	1308 - A3
PALOMAR OBSERVATORY	COUNTY HIGHWAY S6 & PALOMAR DI, SDCo, 92060	409 - G6
PRINCE OF PEACE ABBEY BENEDCTNE-MNASTRY	605 BENET HILL RD, OCN, 92054	1086 - B4
QUAIL BOTANICAL GARDENS	230 QUAIL GARDENS DR, ENCT, 92024	1147 - D6
SAN DIEGO WILD ANIMAL PK	15500 SAN PASQUAL VALLEY RD, SD, 92027	1131 - A5
SAN DIEGO ZOO	2920 ZOO DR, SD, 92101	1269 - B7
SAN ONOFRE NUCLEAR POWER PLANT	OLD HWY 101, SDCo, 92055	1023 - G5
SPANISH VILLAGE ART CTR	1770 VILLAGE PL, SD, 92101	1269 - C7
TIJUANA ESTUARY NATURAL PRES VIS CTR	301 CASPIAN WY, IMPB, 91932	1349 - F1
TORREY PINES GLIDERPORT	2800 TORREY PINES SCENIC DR, SD, 92037	1207 - H7

POINTS OF INTEREST - HISTORIC

FEATURE NAME	Address City, ZIP Code	PAGE-GRID
BALBOA PK CLUB	PAN AMERICAN RD W, SD, 92101	1289 - B1
CABRILLO NATL MONUMENT	END OF CABRILLO MEMORIAL DR, SD, 92106	1308 - A2
CAROUSEL	PARK BLVD & ZOO PL, SD, 92101	1269 - C7
CASA DE BALBOA BLDG	1649 EL PRADO, SD, 92101	1289 - C1
EAGLE AND HIGH PEAK MINES	OLD MINERS TR, SDCo, 92036	1136 - B6
GASLAMP QUARTER	J ST & 5TH AV, SD, 92101	1289 - A4
HIST FEDERAL BLDG	PAN AMERICAN PZ, SD, 92101	1289 - B1
HIST LIGHTHOUSE	HUMPHREYS RD, SD, 92106	1308 - A2
LOS COCHES MONUMENT	13472 BUSINESS ROUTE I-8, SDCo, 92040	1232 - D6
MISSION SAN ANTONIO DE PALA	PALA MISSION RD, SDCo, 92059	1029 - J4
MISSION SAN DIEGO DE ALCALA	10818 SAN DIEGO MISSION RD, SD, 92108	1249 - G7
MISSION SAN LUIS REY DE FRANCIA	4050 MISSION AV, OCN, 92057	1086 - H2
OLD MISSION DAM HIST SITE	FATHER JUNIPERO SERRA TR, SD, 92124	1230 - F6
OLD TOWN SAN DIEGO STATE HIST PK	TWIGGS ST & JUAN ST, SD, 92110	1268 - F5
PAUMA MISSION	PAUMA RESERVATION RD, SDCo, 92061	1051 - A1
RANCHO BUENA VISTA ADOBE	640 ALTA VISTA DR N, VSTA, 92084	1087 - J6
RANCHO GUAJOME ADOBE	2210 N SANTA FE AV, VSTA, 92083	1087 - G2
SAN PASQUAL BATTLEFIELD STATE HIST	SAN PASQUAL VALLEY RD, SD, 92027	1131 - B7
SANTA YSABEL INDIAN MISSION	HWY 79, SDCo, 92070	1135 - B2
SERRA CROSS	PRESIDIO DR, SD, 92110	1268 - F4
VETERANS WAR MEM	BALBOA PARK, SD, 92101	1269 - C7
WHALEY HOUSE	2482 SAN DIEGO AV, SD, 92110	1268 - F5

SCHOOLS - PRIVATE ELEMENTARY

FEATURE NAME	Address City, ZIP Code	PAGE-GRID
ALL HALLOWS ACADEMY	2390 NAUTILUS ST, SD, 92037	1247 - H1
ALL SAINTS EPISCOPAL	3674 7TH AV, SD, 92103	1269 - B6
BETH ISRAEL DAY JEWISH	2512 3RD AV, SD, 92101	1289 - A1
BLESSED SACRAMENT	4551 56TH ST, SD, 92115	1270 - B3
BOSTONIA CHRISTIAN	211 3RD ST, ELCJ, 92019	1252 - A6
CALVARY CHAPEL OF LA MESA CHRISTIAN	7525 EL CAJON BLVD, LMSA, 91941	1270 - G2
CALVARY CHRISTIAN	885 E VISTA WY, VSTA, 92084	1087 - J5
CALVARY CHRISTIAN	6866 LINDA VISTA RD, SD, 92111	1268 - J1
CALVIN CHRISTIAN OF ESCONDIDO	1868 N BROADWAY, ESCN, 92026	1109 - H5
CARLTON HILLS CHRISTIAN	9735 HALBERNS BLVD, SNTE, 92071	1231 - B4
CHABAD DAY	4905 CATOCTIN DR, SD, 92115	1270 - D2
CHILDRENS CREATIVE & PERF ARTS ACA	4431 MT HERBERT AV, SD, 92117	1248 - F2
CHILDRENS MONTESSORI	2950 S BEAR VALLEY PKWY, ESCN, 92025	1150 - C1
CHRISTIAN	6747 AMHERST ST, SD, 92115	1270 - E2
CHRIST LUTHERAN	7929 LA MESA BLVD, LMSA, 91941	1270 - H2
CHRIST THE CORNERSTONE	9028 WESTMORE RD, SD, 92126	1209 - D3
CHULA VISTA CHRISTIAN	960 5TH ST, CHV, 91911	1330 - B2
CITYTREE PRESBYTERIAN	320 DATE ST, SD, 92101	1289 - A2
COLEMAN PREP	7380 PARKWAY DR, LMSA, 91942	1270 - F1
CORNERSTONE CHRISTIAN	13617 MIDLAND RD, PWY, 92064	1190 - F3
COVENANT CHRISTIAN	505 E NAPLES ST, CHV, 91911	1330 - G1
DEL MAR PINES	3883 QUARTER MILE DR, SD, 92130	1188 - A5
DIEGUENO COUNTRY	14963 CIRCO DIEGUENO, SDCo, 92067	1168 - F7
ESCONDIDO ADVENTIST ACADEMY	1233 W 9TH AV, ESCN, 92029	1129 - G5
ESCONDIDO CHRISTIAN	923 IDAHO AV, SDCo, 92025	1130 - B3
EVANS	6510 LA JOLLA SCENIC DR S, SD, 92037	1247 - J1
FAIRBANKS COUNTRY DAY	6233 EL APAJO, SDCo, 92067	1168 - E6
FAITH COMM	2285 MURRAY RIDGE RD, SD, 92123	1249 - C7
FAITH LUTHERAN	700 E BOBIER DR, VSTA, 92084	1087 - J4
GILLISPIE	7380 GIRARD AV, SD, 92037	1227 - F7
GOOD SHEPHERD	8180 GOLD COAST DR, SD, 92126	1209 - B5
GRACE LUTHERAN	3967 PARK BLVD, SD, 92103	1269 - C5
GRACE LUTHERAN	643 W 13TH AV, ESCN, 92025	1129 - J5
HEARTLAND CHRISTIAN HOME CTR	3327 KENORA DR, SDCo, 91977	1271 - C6
HOLY FAMILY	1945 COOLIDGE ST, SD, 92111	1268 - J1
HOLY SPIRIT	2755 55TH ST, SD, 92105	1270 - B7
HOLY TRINITY	509 BALLARD ST, ELCJ, 92019	1251 - J6
HORIZON CHRISTIAN	4520 POCAHONTAS AV, SD, 92117	1248 - D2
LA JOLLA COUNTRY DAY	9490 GENESEE AV, SD, 92037	1228 - C1
LA MESA CHRISTIAN	9407 JERICHO RD, LMSA, 91942	1251 - B6
LIGHT AND LIFE CHRISTIAN	120 N ASH ST, ESCN, 92027	1130 - B2
MARANATHA CHRISTIAN	12855 BLACK MOUNTAIN RD, SD, 92129	1189 - D5
MARIS, STELLA ACADEMY	7654 HERSCHEL AV, SD, 92037	1227 - F7
MERIDIAN CHRISTIAN	2100 GREENFIELD DR, ELCJ, 92019	1252 - D4
MIDWAY BAPTIST	2460 PALM AV, SD, 92154	1330 - B7
MISSION BAY MONTESSORI ACADEMY	2640 SODERBLOM AV, SD, 92122	1228 - B6
MISSION SAN ANTONIO DE PALA	PALA MISSION RD, SDCo, 92059	1029 - J4
MONTESSORI, MARIA HOUSE	4544 POCAHONTAS AV, SD, 92117	1248 - D2
MOUNT ERIE CHRISTIAN-BAPTIST ACADEMY	504 S 47TH ST, SD, 92113	1289 - J5
NATIVITY	6309 EL APAHO RD, SDCo, 92067	1168 - E6
NAZARETH	10728 SAN DIEGO MISSION RD, SD, 92108	1249 - H7
NORTH COAST CHRISTIAN	1106 WHALEY ST, OCN, 92054	1106 - C2
OLD MISSION MONTESSORI	4070 MISSION AV, OCN, 92057	1086 - H2
OUR LADY	650 24TH ST, SD, 92102	1289 - C3
OUR LADY OF GRACE	2766 NAVAJO RD, ELCJ, 92020	1251 - A4
OUR LADY OF MOUNT CARMEL	4141 BEYER RD, SD, 92173	1350 - F3
OUR LADY OF THE SACRED HEART	4106 42ND ST, SD, 92105	1269 - H5
OUR LADY PERPETUAL HELP	9825 PINO DR, SDCo, 92040	1232 - C3
PARKER, FRANCIS W	4201 RANDOLPH ST, SD, 92103	1268 - H5
PILGRIM LUTHERAN	497 E ST, CHV, 91910	1310 - A6
REFORMATION LUTHERAN	4670 MT ABERNATHY AV, SD, 92117	1248 - J1
RHOADES FOR THE GIFTED	2210 ENCINITAS BLVD, ENCT, 92024	1167 - J1
SACRED HEART ACADEMY	4895 SARATOGA AV, SD, 92107	1267 - J6
SACRED HEART	706 C AV, CORD, 92118	1288 - J7
SAINT CHARLES BORROMEO ACADEMY	2808 CADIZ ST, SD, 92110	1268 - E6
SAINT CHARLES	929 18TH ST, SD, 92154	1350 - A1
SAINT COLUMBA	3327 GLENCOLUM DR, SD, 92123	1249 - D5
SAINT DIDACUS	4630 34TH ST, SD, 92116	1269 - F3
SAINT FRANCIS	525 W VISTA WY, VSTA, 92083	1087 - G7
SAINT JAMES ACADEMY	623 S NARDO AV, SOLB, 92075	1187 - F1
SAINT JOHN OF THE CROSS	8175 LEMON GROVE WY, LMGR, 91945	1270 - H5
SAINT JOHNS	1001 ENCINITAS BLVD, ENCT, 92024	1147 - E7
SAINT JOHNS EPISCOPAL	760 1ST AV, CHV, 91910	1330 - D1
SAINT JUDE ACADEMY	1228 38TH ST, SD, 92113	1289 - G6
SAINT KIERAN	1465 CAMILLO CT, ELCJ, 92021	1252 - A3
SAINT LUKES LUTHERAN CHRISTIAN DAY	5150 WILLSON ST, LMSA, 91941	1271 - A1
SAINT MARTIN ACADEMY	7708 EL CAJON BLVD, LMSA, 91941	1270 - G2
SAINT MARYS CATHOLIC	700 S WATERMAN AV, ELCN, 92243	6499 - F7
SAINT MARYS	130 E 13TH AV, ESCN, 92025	1130 - A4
SAINT MARY, STAR OF THE SEA	515 WISCONSIN AV, OCN, 92054	1106 - B1
SAINT MICHAEL	15542 POMERADO RD, PWY, 92064	1170 - C6
SAINT MICHAEL	2637 HOMEDALE ST, SD, 92139	1310 - E1
SAINT PATRICK	3583 30TH ST, SD, 92104	1269 - E6
SAINT PATRICK	3820 PIO PICO DR, CRLB, 92008	1106 - F6
SAINT PAULS LUTHERAN	1376 FELSPAR ST, SD, 92109	1247 - J6
SAINT PETERS CATHOLIC	450 S STAGE COACH LN, SDCo, 92028	1027 - J3
SAINT PIUS X	37 E EMERSON ST, CHV, 91911	1330 - E2
SAINT RITAS	5165 IMPERIAL AV, SD, 92114	1290 - A4
SAINT ROSE OF LIMA	473 3RD AV, CHV, 91910	1310 - B7
SAINT THERESE ACADEMY	6046 CM RICO, SD, 92120	1250 - C6
SAINT VINCENT DE PAUL	4061 IBIS ST, SD, 92103	1268 - J5
SAN DIEGO ACADEMY	2700 E 4TH ST, NATC, 91950	1290 - B7
SAN DIEGO HEBREW DAY	3630 AFTON RD, SD, 92123	1249 - C4
SAN DIEGO JEWISH ACADEMY	8660 GILMAN DR, SD, 92037	1228 - A4
SAN PASQUAL ACADEMY	17701 SAN PASQUAL VALLEY RD, SDCo, 92025	1131 - F7
SANTA FE CHRISTIAN COMM	838 ACADEMY DR, SOLB, 92075	1167 - G7
SANTA SOPHIA ACADEMY	9806 SAN JUAN ST, SDCo, 91977	1271 - D5
SCHOOL OF THE MADELEINE	1875 ILLION ST, SD, 92110	1268 - F1
SOUTHPORT CHRISTIAN ACADEMY	142 E 16TH ST, NATC, 91950	1309 - H2
SOUTHWESTERN CHRISTIAN	482 L ST, CHV, 91911	1330 - B2
TIERRASANTA CHRISTIAN	10725 ESMERALDAS DR, SD, 92124	1249 - H1
TRI-CITY CHRISTIAN	302 N EMERALD DR, VSTA, 92083	1087 - C7
TRINITY CHRISTIAN	3902 KENWOOD DR, SDCo, 91941	1271 - A5
VALLEY CHRISTIAN	1350 DISCOVERY ST, SMCS, 92069	1128 - D2
VISTA CHRISTIAN	290 N MELROSE DR, VSTA, 92083	1087 - F6
WALDORF OF SAN DIEGO	3547 ALTADENA AV, SD, 92105	1270 - A6
WARREN WALKER	4605 POINT LOMA AV, SD, 92107	1287 - J1

SCHOOLS - PRIVATE HIGH

FEATURE NAME	Address City, ZIP Code	PAGE-GRID
ACADEMY OF OUR LADY OF PEACE	4860 OREGON ST, SD, 92116	1269 - D3
ARMY & NAVY ACADEMY	2605 CARLSBAD BLVD, CRLB, 92008	1106 - D5
BISHOPS EPIS	7607 LA JOLLA BLVD, SD, 92037	1227 - E7
CALVARY CHRISTIAN	885 E VISTA WY, VSTA, 92084	1087 - J5
CALVIN CHRISTIAN	2000 N BROADWAY, ESCN, 92026	1109 - H5
CHRISTIAN	2100 GREENFIELD DR, ELCJ, 92019	1252 - D4
COLEMAN PREP	7380 PARKWAY DR, LMSA, 91942	1270 - F1
COVENANT CHRISTIAN	505 E NAPLES ST, CHV, 91911	1330 - G1
ESCONDIDO ADVENTIST ACADEMY	1233 W 9TH AV, ESCN, 92029	1129 - G5
FAIRBANKS COUNTRY DAY	6233 EL APAJO, SDCo, 92067	1168 - D6
HORIZON CHRISTIAN	5331 MT ALIFAN DR, SD, 92111	1248 - G3
LA JOLLA COUNTRY DAY	9490 GENESEE AV, SD, 92037	1228 - C2
MARIAN	1002 18TH ST, SD, 92154	1350 - A1
MIDWAY BAPTIST	2460 PALM AV, SD, 92154	1330 - B7
NORTH COAST CHRISTIAN	1106 WHALEY ST, OCN, 92054	1106 - C2
PARKER, FRANCIS W	6501 LINDA VISTA RD, SD, 92111	1268 - H2
SAINT AUGUSTINE	3266 NUTMEG ST, SD, 92104	1269 - F7
SAN DIEGO ACADEMY	2700 E 4TH ST, NATC, 91950	1290 - B7
SAN PASQUAL ACADEMY	17701 SAN PASQUAL VALLEY RD, SDCo, 92025	1131 - G7
SANTA FE CHRISTIAN COMM	838 ACADEMY DR, SOLB, 92075	1167 - G7
SOUTHPORT CHRISTIAN ACADEMY	142 E 16TH ST, NATC, 91950	1309 - H2
TRI-CITY CHRISTIAN	302 N EMERALD DR, VSTA, 92083	1087 - C7
UNIV OF SAN DIEGO	5961 LINDA VISTA RD, SD, 92110	1268 - G2

SCHOOLS - PRIVATE JUNIOR HIGH

FEATURE NAME	Address City, ZIP Code	PAGE-GRID
ARMY & NAVY ACADEMY	2605 CARLSBAD BLVD, CRLB, 92008	1106 - D5

SCHOOLS - PUBLIC ELEMENTARY

FEATURE NAME	Address City, ZIP Code	PAGE-GRID
ADAMS, JOHN	4672 35TH ST, SD, 92116	1269 - F3
ADOBE BLUFFS	8707 ADOBE BLUFFS DR, SD, 92129	1189 - C2
ALAMOSA PK	5130 ALAMOSA PARK DR, OCN, 92057	1087 - C1
ALCOTT, LOUISA M	4680 HIDALGO AV, SD, 92117	1248 - C1
ALLEN-ANN DALY	4300 ALLEN SCHOOL RD, CHV, 91902	1310 - G4
ALPINE	1850 ALPINE BLVD, SDCo, 91901	1234 - A5
ANGIER, WILL	8450 HURLBUT ST, SD, 92123	1249 - C4
ANZA	1005 S ANZA ST, ELCJ, 92020	1251 - H7
ARROYO VISTA	2491 SCHOOL HOUSE RD, CHV, 91915	1311 - H6
ASHLEY FALLS	13030 ASHLEY FALLS DR, SD, 92130	1188 - D5
AUDUBON, JOHN J	8111 SAN VICENTE ST, SD, 92114	1290 - H3

SAN DIEGO CO.

INDEX

SAN DIEGO CO.

INDEX

FEATURE NAME Address City, ZIP Code	PAGE-GRID
TROLLEY STA - EL CAJON FRONT ST & W PALM AV, ELCJ, 92020	1251 - E6
TROLLEY STA - ENCANTO/62ND ST IMPERIAL AV & 62ND ST, SD, 92114	1290 - D3
TROLLEY STA - EUCLID AV N EUCLID AV & MARKET ST, SD, 92102	1290 - A3
TROLLEY STA - FASHION VALLEY FRIARS RD & FASHION VALLEY RD, SD, 92108	1268 - J3
TROLLEY STA - GASLAMP/CONV CNTR HARBOR DR & L ST, SD, 92101	1289 - B4
TROLLEY STA - GROSSMONT CTR GROSSMONT CENTER DR, LMSA, 91942	1251 - A7
TROLLEY STA-H ST H ST & SAN DIEGO FRWY, CHV, 91910	1309 - J7
TROLLEY STA - HARBORSIDE 28TH ST & HARBOR DR, SD, 92136	1289 - E6
TROLLEY STA - HAZARD CTR HAZARD CENTER DR & FRAZEE RD, SD, 92108	1269 - A2
TROLLEY STA- IMPERIAL & 12TH TRANS IMPERIAL AV & 12TH AV, SD, 92101	1289 - B4
TROLLEY STA LA MESA BLVD LA MESA BLVD & NEBO DR, LMSA, 91941	1270 - H3
TROLLEY STA LEMON GROVE DEPOT BROADWAY & MAIN ST, LMGR, 91945	1270 - G6
TROLLEY STA - MARKET & 12TH MARKET ST & 12TH AV, SD, 92101	1289 - B3
TROLLEY STA - MASSACHUSETTS AV LEMON GROVE AV & MASSACHUSETTS, LMGR, 91945	1290 - F1
TROLLEY STA - MIDDLETOWN PALM ST & KETTNER BLVD, SD, 92101	1268 - J7
TROLLEY STA - MISSION SAN DIEGO RANCHO MISSION RD & WARD RD, SD, 92108	1269 - G1
TROLLEY STA - MISSION VALLEY CTR MISSION VALLEY CENTER, SD, 92108	1269 - B2
TROLLEY STA - MORENA / LINDA VISTA NAPA ST & FRIARS RD, SD, 92110	1268 - F3
TROLLEY STA - PACIFIC FLEET 32ND ST & HARBOR DR, SD, 92136	1289 - F7
TROLLEY STA- PALM AV HOLLISTER ST & PALM AV, SD, 92154	1330 - B7
TROLLEY STA- PALOMAR ST PALOMAR ST & INDUSTRIAL BLVD, CHV, 91911	1330 - B4
TROLLEY STA - QUALCOMM STADIUM QUALCOMM STADIUM, SD, 92108	1269 - F1
TROLLEY STA - RIO VISTA STADIUM WY & RIO SAN DIEGO DR, SD, 92108	1269 - C2
TROLLEY STA - SANTA FE DEPOT KETTNER BLVD & C ST, SD, 92101	1288 - J3
TROLLEY STA - SANTEE TOWN CTR MISSION GORGE RD & CUYAMACA ST, SNTE, 92071	1231 - D6
TROLLEY STA - SEAPORT VILLAGE HARBOR DR & MARKET ST, SD, 92101	1288 - J3
TROLLEY STA SPRING STREET SPRING ST, LMSA, 91941	1270 - J4
TROLLEY STA - WASHINGTON ST I-5 & WASHINGTON ST, SD, 92110	1268 - G6
TROLLEY STA - WELD BLVD N MARSHALL AV & CUYAMACA ST, ELCJ, 92020	1251 - D1

WINERIES

FEATURE NAME Address City, ZIP Code	PAGE-GRID
BERNARDO 13330 PAS DL VERANO N, PWY, 92064	1170 - D1
DEER PK ESCONDIDO 29013 CHAMPAGNE BLVD, SDCo, 92026	1089 - A1
FERRARA 1120 W 15TH AV, ESCN, 92025	1129 - H5
MENGHINI 1150 JULIAN ORCHARDS DR, SDCo, 92036	1136 - A3
ORFILA VINEYARDS 13455 SAN PASQUAL RD, SD, 92025	1150 - D2
SCHWAESDALL 17677 RANCHO DE ORO RD, SDCo, 92065	1171 - J4
VAN DER VORT ESTATES 300 ENTERPRISE ST, SMCS, 92078	1128 - J1
WITCH CREEK 2000 MAIN ST, SDCo, 92036	1136 - B7
WITCH CREEK 2906 CARLSBAD BLVD, CRLB, 92008	1106 - D5

PRODUCT INFORMATION LIST

THOMAS GUIDES®
INCLUDING ZIP CODES AND BOUNDARIES

CALIFORNIA

Alameda County
Alameda / Contra Costa Counties
Alameda / Santa Clara Counties
Contra Costa County
Fresno / Madera Counties (NEW)
Kern County (NEW)
Kings / Tulare Counties (NEW)
Los Angeles County
★ Los Angeles / Orange Counties
★ Los Angeles / Ventura Counties
Marin County
Napa / Sonoma Counties
Orange County
Orange / Los Angeles Counties
Riverside County
Riverside / Orange Counties
Riverside / San Diego Counties
Sacramento County (Coverage includes portions of Placer & El Dorado Counties)
★ Sacramento / Solano Counties
San Bernardino County
San Bernardino / Riverside Counties
★ San Diego County (Coverage includes portions of Imperial County)
San Diego / Orange Counties
San Francisco County
San Francisco / San Mateo Counties
San Joaquin County (NEW)
San Mateo County
Santa Barbara and San Luis Obispo Counties
★ Santa Barbara and San Luis Obispo / Ventura Counties
Santa Clara County
Santa Clara / San Mateo Counties
Solano County (Coverage includes portions of Napa and Yolo Counties)
Stanislaus / Merced Counties (NEW)
Ventura County

NEVADA - WASHINGTON

★ Clark County, NV (Coverage includes Las Vegas, North Las Vegas, Henderson, Boulder City, Mesquite and Laughlin)
King County, WA
King / Pierce Counties, WA
King / Snohomish Counties, WA
Pierce County, WA
Snohomish County, WA

WASHINGTON, D.C. & VICINITY

Anne Arundel County, MD
Frederick County, MD
Fredericksburg Area, Virginia (NEW) (Coverage includes City of Fredericksburg, Stafford, Spotsylvania, King George, Caroline Counties and Portions of Westmoreland, Louisa and Hanover Counties)
Howard County, MD
Loudoun County, VA
Montgomery County, MD
Northern Virginia & the Beltway
Prince George's County, MD
Prince William County, VA
Western Maryland and Eastern Panhandle of West Virginia (NEW) (Coverage includes Garrett, Allegany and Washington Counties in Maryland, and Morgan, Berkeley and Jefferson Counties in West Virginia)

ROAD ATLAS & DRIVER'S GUIDES

California Road Atlas & Driver's Guide
Pacific Northwest Road Atlas & Driver's Guide (Coverage includes Southwestern British Columbia and Western Idaho)

★ Also available as Thomas Guide & Thomas Guide DigitalEdition™ Combo Packs

METROPOLITAN THOMAS GUIDES®

ARIZONA

Metropolitan Phoenix Area, AZ (NEW)
Metropolitan Tucson Area, AZ (NEW)

CALIFORNIA

★ Metropolitan Bay Area (Coverage includes Metropolitan Areas of Alameda, Contra Costa, Marin, San Francisco, San Mateo, and Santa Clara Counties)
★ Metropolitan Inland Empire (Coverage includes Metropolitan areas of San Bernardino, Riverside, Eastern Los Angeles, and Northeastern Orange Counties)
Metropolitan Monterey Bay (Coverage includes Monterey, Santa Cruz and San Benito Counties)

OREGON

★ Portland Metro Area (Coverage includes Clackamas, Columbia, Multnomah, Washington & Yamhill Counties and Greater Vancouver Area)

WASHINGTON

★ Metropolitan Puget Sound (Coverage includes Metropolitan Areas of King, Pierce, and Snohomish Counties)

METROPOLITAN BALTIMORE & METROPOLITAN WASHINGTON, D.C.

★ Metropolitan Baltimore, MD (Coverage includes Baltimore, Carroll, Harford, Howard and Anne Arundel Counties)
★ Metropolitan Washington, DC (Coverage includes Montgomery and Prince George's Counties, MD, and Northern Virginia)

THOMAS GUIDE DIGITALEDITION™

ToolBox (NEW) - A companion to any Thomas Guide DigitalEdition™. It allows you to customize your maps with a full set of drawing tools, address locator, or GPS interface, and query tools, and e-mail the maps to others.

CALIFORNIA

State of California (NEW) (Includes both the Thomas Guide DigitalEdition™ with detailed maps for the entire state of California, and the Thomas Guide DigitalEdition™ ToolBox)

SOUTHERN CALIFORNIA

Los Angeles / Orange Counties
Los Angeles / Ventura Counties
Metropolitan Inland Empire (Coverage includes all of San Bernardino and Riverside, Eastern Los Angeles and Northeastern Orange Counties)
San Diego County (Coverage includes Imperial County)
Santa Barbara / Ventura Counties

NORTHERN CALIFORNIA

Bay Area (Coverage includes Alameda, Contra Costa, Marin, San Francisco, San Mateo, and Santa Clara Counties)
Sacramento / Solano Counties (Coverage includes Placer, El Dorado, Napa and Yolo Counties)

ARIZONA

Phoenix / Tucson (NEW)

OREGON - WASHINGTON

Portland Metro Area, OR (Coverage includes Clackamas, Columbia, Multnomah, Washington, and Yamhill Counties, and the Greater Vancouver Area)
Metropolitan Puget Sound, WA (Coverage includes all of King, Pierce, and Snohomish Counties)

NEVADA

Clark County (Coverage includes the City of Las Vegas)

THOMAS GUIDE & DIGITALEDITION™ COMBO PACKS

Our Thomas Guide and DigitalEdition™ sold together in one convenient package. Call for more information.

EXPRESS MAPS & EXPRESS WALL MAPS™

Affordable, high quality custom maps designed to your specifications. You select the coverage, choose black & white or full-color, optional ZIP & Census overlays. Lamination & mounting additional. Call for more information.

For more information, or to order, please contact Customer Service at 1-800-899-6277 or e-mail us at cust_serv@thomas.com or visit our web site at www.thomas.com
Our Secure On-line Store is Now Open!

Information subject to change without notice